D1268689

Advance praise for the newest edition of

The Source: A Guidebook to American Genealogy

With the new edition, The Source *remains the essential reference work in American genealogy. It continues to serve as a basic text for beginners and an encyclopedic research tool for experts.*

Jack Simpson
Curator of Local and Family History
The Newberry Library

The third edition of The Source *reflects the dynamic development of genealogical research in the past decade. The distinguished editors have provided an updated arrangement with expanded topics and additional content. The final product is even more user-friendly than earlier editions. Topics have been expanded upon by a virtual who's who of family history experts. This standard reference work should be on every researcher's "must-have" list. This is a resource that is essential to novice and experienced researchers alike.*

Ruth A. Carr, Chief Librarian
Irma and Paul Milstein Division of United States
History, Local History and Genealogy
The New York Public Library

Winner of the prestigious ALA Best Reference Award when it was first published in 1984, the "best" has gotten even better. Some chapters have been combined, new chapters have been added—the one thing that hasn't changed is the emphasis on helping researchers understand the records. The Source *is a true guidebook. Its detailed explanations and numerous illustrations provide researchers from novice to experienced with the information they need in order to locate and use the wealth of records available to today's family historian.*

Barbara Vines Little, CG
President, National Genealogical Society

This tome should be on the shelves of every public library and, especially, every library serving genealogists. . . . More than ever, The Source *is a most worthy research companion for every twenty-first-century genealogist.*

From the "Foreword" of the third edition
Curt B. Witcher, MLS, FUGA, FIGS
Manager, Historical Genealogy Department
Allen County Public Library

This third edition of The Source: A Guidebook to American Genealogy *remains the foremost instructive guide to research sources, tools, and techniques. Greatly expanded, it is designed to encourage researchers to enhance their knowledge and methodology. This invaluable work is essential for any genealogical course, whether for beginners or professionals, undergraduates, grad students, or retired seniors. There is no finer reference tool for genealogists!*

The basics covered in The Source *provide a solid foundation for anyone interested in genealogy or history. Numerous experts describe records in careful detail with graphic examples. Four new chapters address and update carefully selected subjects: technology, reference works and guides, colonial English, and colonial Spanish. Several authorities in their respective fields address immigrant and ethnic research. Chapters detailing standard resources such as census, church, land, tax, court, military, and other topics include new data and, unquestionably, provide the most up-to-date information available in one volume. A list of repositories adds updated references, and bibliographies for each chapter enhance this volume's value for every researcher.*

The Source *will be the reference work of the year for librarians and a bible for novice and professional genealogists alike.*

Wendy Bebout Elliott, Ph.D., FUGA
Professor of History,
California State University, Fullerton
President, Federation of Genealogical Societies

The role of The Source *is to take much of the complexity out of [the family history] process. It is both a handbook and a guide to the primary sources of genealogy; an extraordinary resource of genealogical knowledge, without peer in the fields of family history and genealogy. . . .*

Each time you open its covers, The Source *provides you with a seminar taught by the foremost genealogists in America. . . .*

The Source *is more essential to accurate genealogical research today than it was when the revised edition appeared in 1997. . . . It is a one-volume library of genealogical research knowledge.*

From the "Introduction" of the third edition
Raymond Sanford Wright, III, Ph.D., AG, FUGA
Director, Family History Library

THE SOURCE

REF
CS
49
S65
2006

Library & Media Ctr.
Carroll Community College
1601 Washington Rd.
Westminster, MD 21157

THIRD EDITION

THE SOURCE

A Guidebook to American Genealogy

Edited by Loretto Dennis Szucs
& Sandra Hargreaves Luebking

Ancestry®

Library of Congress Cataloging-in-Publication Data

The source : a guidebook to American genealogy / edited by Loretto Dennis Szucs and Sandra Hargreaves Luebking.—3rd rev. ed.

p. cm.

Includes bibliographical references and index.

ISBN 1-59331-277-6 (hardcover : alk. paper)

1. United States—Genealogy—Archival resources. 2. Untied States—Genealogy—Handbooks, manuals, etc. I. Szucs, Loretto Dennis. II. Luebking, Sandra Hargreaves.

CS49.S65 2006
929'.1072073—dc22

2006005027

Copyright © 2006
Ancestry, a division of MyFamily.com, Inc.
360 West 4800 North
Provo, UT 84604
All rights reserved.

No part of this publication may be reproduced in any form without written permission of the publisher, except by a reviewer, who may quote brief passages for a review.

All brand and product names are trademarks or registered trademarks of their respective companies.

Published 1984. Revised Edition 1997. Third Edition 2006.

10 9 8 7 6 5 4 3 2

Printed in the United States of America.

Dedication

For those who came before me and inspired me;
And for those who continue to support me and to add so much joy to my life:
My husband, Bob;
Julie, Mark, Madelon;
Diana, John, Ryan, Jaclyn, Jessica;
Tricia, John, Lauren, Nolan, Claire;
Laura, Dan, Caroline, Anna, and Kathryn.

Loretto (Lou) Szucs

Dedicated to my family: past, present, and future.
And with love and gratitude to
Jeff, Kevin, Laura, and Kyleen.

Sandra Luebking

Table of Contents

People and Place

Appendixes

Foreword

CURT B. WITCHER, MLS, FUGA, FIGS

The waning days of the twentieth century combined with the dawning moments of this new millennium to produce a series of changes and advances that touched virtually every person's life. Indeed, discoveries in all fields of endeavor touched the face of humanity in often remarkable and sometimes frightening ways. And a number of those significant discoveries impacted the genealogical field as well.

The field of genetics gave us a completely mapped human genome. Surname associations across the world initiated DNA studies as individual researchers began to explore ways this new knowledge could be deployed to solve problems and resolve discrepancies. The medical field reminded us that, increasingly, keys to understanding what our future health will be rest in the knowledge of our respective families' health history. The computer science, mathematics, and technology fields forged paths to more and better data storage, transfer mechanisms, and search protocols. Computer programs and search algorithms can mine immense and dynamic information and image databases, with such work being nearly transparent to both the novice and sophisticated user. Only a few brief years ago, what we take for granted today would have been classed science fiction rather than science fact.

In the midst of all this change, and the new waves of changes arriving at an exponentially increasing pace, we know several constants remain—constants that are as firm and solid as the foundation of any well-built structure. First among these constants is our belief in the true wholesomeness and tremendous worthiness of genealogical research. Investigating and exploring one's family history is an activity that enlightens, intrigues, entices, entertains, provides context, and often gives our lives a sense of purpose. Teachers find it to be an exciting and engaging way to teach history to young students. Counselors and youth advocates know that engaging in family history can restore a troubled person's sense of worth and identity. Appreciating one's past often opens doors to a nearly boundless future. Elder-care specialists know it is a way of keeping the veterans of life connected with both their families and reality.

Another equally significant constant is the continuing, even increasing, need for worthy research-methodology texts—texts that showcase and explain records as well as instruct researchers in best practices. As large information aggregators and data warehouses publish millions of new pages of historical and genealogical records on the Internet each week, the need to provide meaningful instruction to researchers on how to develop a reasonable research hypothesis, as well as how to collect and evaluate relevant data to support or refute such a hypothesis, has never been greater. Information overload, conflicting data sets, and failed attempts to find precise, specialized sources are but a few issues facing contemporary genealogists.

The Source: A Guidebook to American Genealogy exists because of the idealism of this first constant and in response to the call of the second. The careful research, skillful editing, and dedicated work of the two editors and their team of contributors has resulted in a substantive and profound edition of this keystone work. In the pages of *The Source,* one will find significant record groups meaningfully discussed with their research import for genealogists and family historians highlighted. In addition, the treatment of sources for ethnic research, the many appendixes, and the robust bibliographies and source lists serve as additional reading materials and research possibilities for the beginner and pathways to new sources and hidden treasures for more experienced researchers.

Richly illustrated with hundreds of tables, illustrations, and document examples, *The Source* is easy to read yet replete with details such that anyone, regardless of research experience, can find tremendous benefit from its use. This tome should be on the shelves of every public library and, especially, every library serving genealogists. In addition, anyone even casually contemplating genealogical pursuits needs this reference work right next to family papers, research notes, and the computer to be truly successful. More than ever, *The Source* is a most worthy research companion for every twenty-first-century genealogist.

Curt B. Witcher
Historical Genealogy Department Manager
Allen County Public Library
Former president, Federation of Genealogical Societies and the National Genealogical Society
Founding president, Indiana Genealogical Society
Fellow, Utah Genealogical Association

Preface

**LORETTO DENNIS SZUCS, FUGA,
and SANDRA HARGREAVES LUEBKING, FUGA**

This is a wonderful time to have an interest in family history! The richness and diversity of genealogically significant American records is extraordinary and the research opportunities are unlimited. The exploration of one's ancestry is an exciting experience: every family has its own unique story and every one of those stories is more accessible than ever.

Information is power. Yet to piece together a family history, we have to know which records will yield needed information, where to find them, how to use them effectively, how to analyze their contents, and how to preserve our findings so that they will be known and enjoyed by future generations. The goal of this book is to guide researchers in the selection, location, and use of information. To do this, thirty-one expert researchers have come together to share their knowledge and experience with you, the family historian enthusiast.

When Ancestry published the first edition of *The Source: A Guidebook of American Genealogy* in 1984, it quickly became a standard reference in the field of genealogy and family history. That same year, it received the coveted "Best Reference" award from the American Library Association. The 1997 edition, built upon the foundations laid down by its predecessor, sold more than 100,000 copies. A poll of librarians placed *The Source*, sometimes referred to as "the genealogist's bible," at the top of the "Top 10 Genealogy Books" for the wealth of information it offers to beginning and experienced genealogists ("Top 10 Genealogy Books," *Family Chronicle* 3, no. 3 (January/February 1999): 27–28).

Technology has significantly changed the way we do research since the last edition of *The Source* was published. However, the need for a good understanding of records and the fundamental steps for tracing and saving family history remains very much the same.

Although this third edition of *The Source* reflects the same general format as the last, several important changes have been made.

Four completely new chapters have been added. Chapter 2, "Computers and Technology," responds to the growing influence of computers on genealogy while chapter 3, "General

References and Guides," discusses a broad range of resources, from databases and indexes to dictionaries. Chapters 15, "Colonial English Research," and 16, "Colonial Spanish Borderland Research," shed light on records and methods for researching early American roots. In addition, the chapters on "Business, Institution, and Organization Records" (4), "Church Records" (6), and "African-American Research" (14), have been entirely rewritten. Other chapters have been thoroughly updated, in several cases adding the expertise of new authors. Information that was found in the "Twentieth Century" chapter of previous editions has now been folded into chapters where inclusion is most appropriate.

The rapidly changing ways in which information now becomes available means researchers need accurate, updated help in order to succeed. Researchers also require a deep level of comprehension to understand and utilize the sources and methods most likely to produce results. With this in mind, every effort has been made to keep *The Source* relevant to the demands of research in the twenty-first century.

We are confident that the transition from the second edition to this third edition will be smooth and well-received. The changes are significant, but each will greatly increase the book's value to the genealogy community. We hope you agree, and we invite you to send your opinions to books@ancestry.com.

Acknowledgments

To achieve the ambitious goals of this 3rd edition of *The Source*, we depended on the scholarship and experience of many individuals. Because no single individual can be an expert in every aspect of the multifaceted field of genealogy and family history research, we relied upon thirty-one experts who contributed specialized and current information. This volume is built upon the knowledge of the contributing authors (page xv); we are indebted to them all.

We gratefully acknowledge the support of several people at MyFamily.com. From the inception of this project, we have had unwavering encouragement from David Moon, chairman of the board, and Andre Brummer, chief development officer. Without their enthusiasm for the project, we could not have started or continued this tremendous undertaking. We are also indebted to Tim Sullivan, president and chief executive officer, and Michael Sherrod, vice president of Community, Content, and Publishing for their commitment to this reference book that has become the most authoritative guide in the field of genealogy and family history. In her role as director of publishing, Jennifer Utley's experience and wisdom in guiding this project have been priceless and very much appreciated.

We are especially grateful to Matthew Wright. As project manager for this enormous and always challenging project, his skills and patience were truly remarkable. Working with the Editorial Team—Matthew Rayback, Anastasia Sutherland Tyler, Tana Pedersen Lord—has been a joy. Each of one of them has contributed countless hours and an unsurpassed degree of professionalism. We were also extremely fortunate to have the exceptional talents of Robert Davis in designing this work. Thanks also to Mark Vermeulen for his production help.

Every chapter was independently peer reviewed. We have relied greatly upon our many colleagues who offered critiques and suggestions, and we wish to thank them all collectively. Certain individuals who helped to evaluate the material in this volume and to look after critical details deserve special gratitude. They include: Kellene Ricks Adams, Lisa Arnold, Carolyn Baird, Janet Bernice, Jeanie Croasmun, Julie Duncan, Brian Edwards, Joe Everett, Matthew Gibbons, Miri Gifford, Myra Vanderpool Gormley, Joel Graham, Alyssa Hickman Grove, Halicue Gambrell Hanna, Valerie Holladay, Rachel Kilbourne, Echo King, Kurt Laird, David Lee, Adele Marcum, Chad Milliner, Jennifer Browning Payne, Laura Prescott, Gerhard Ruf, Benjamin Spratling, Richard Stauffer, Megan Vandre, and Spencer Woolley. We continue to appreciate the work of Matt Grove, who as senior editor of Ancestry for the last edition of *The Source* provided a sound model for rebuilding this work.

Introduction

RAYMOND SANFORD WRIGHT, III, Ph.D., AG, FUGA

What is the value of this book to you? Why should every genealogist and family historian have a copy? This new edition of *The Source: A Guidebook to American Genealogy* simplifies your search for ancestors. It is fundamental for researchers who use the Internet and just as critical for those who do not.

The Role of *The Source*

In theory, family history research is not complicated. It is a search of records for facts about ancestors' lives. The problem is deciding which records contain the information needed to fill in blanks in a family's history. Add to that the complexity of tracing the current whereabouts of the historical records you want and the importance of accurately evaluating the meaning of their contents, and suddenly the search for your family's history is no longer simple. The role of *The Source* is to take much of the complexity out of this process. It is both a handbook and a guide to the primary sources of genealogy; an extraordinary resource of genealogical knowledge, without peer in the fields of family history and genealogy.

Each time you open its covers, *The Source* provides you with a seminar taught by the foremost genealogists in America. Years of professional experience in research, teaching, and writing have gone into their respective chapters. Begin by reading the first three chapters as they will teach you—or remind you of—essential principles in the search for your family's history. "The Foundations of Family History Research" chapter focuses on the how-to part of the process, and "Computers and Technology" demonstrates how to manage the data you gather as well as find facts about your family on the Web. "General References and Guides" explains the intricacies of the most often consulted references in the field of family history.

From there, move to the chapters that focus on specific record types. Begin with the topics you will use early in your research: business, institution, and organization; census; church; directories; newspapers; and vitals—records of birth, marriage, death, and burial. As you read, refer to the appendixes for information on the genealogical and historical societies and family associations that support and assist your searches. The appendixes also identify the state and national facilities that preserve and make available the records we use, and discuss the Family History Library with its unparalleled collection of genealogically-rich materials that are accessible throughout the country.

Next, if your ancestry is one of the highlighted ethnic groups, read the appropriate chapter. Your ancestors may have come to America from Latin America, or the search for family origins may take you to Native American tribal records. The Jewish contribution to the patchwork quilt we call America also has early origins. African American roots can take you back to the colonial era of American history.

If your ancestors resided within a large city, explore the chapter on urban research. It points out the substantial differences in locating records in highly populated areas and identifies the special tools and finding aids developed to ease this process.

As your skills and understanding progress, study the court, land, and military chapters. Although these are among the most complex of the records we rely upon, the information within these pages will explain their use and how to locate and interpret them. All three chapters provide many illustrations and tables to assist your understanding.

After you have traced your family in this country to the time of its arrival, peruse the chapter on immigration for guidance in consulting ships passenger lists and naturalization records. Should your ancestry go back to pre-Revolutionary times, one of the colonial records chapters will prove essential to continuing the study: that of English or Spanish Borderland research. The appendix on hereditary and lineage societies will suggest resources that you may not have considered.

Genealogy is a dynamic discipline. Newly discovered records as well as more sophisticated approaches to solving longstanding research problems demanded a new edition of *The Source.* At the same time, the tremendous increase in original and abstracted records being placed online creates additional emphasis on the quality of research. This requires conscientious researchers to master and manage detailed knowledge about records that *The Source* expounds upon. Eight years of experience using the revised edition led to changes that editors and authors are certain will make this third edition both easier to use and more applicable to twenty-first-century research.

The Source is more essential to accurate genealogical research today than it was when the revised edition appeared in 1997. To remain informed about newly accessible records *The Source* plays an invaluable role: (1) Every chapter in *The Source* will help you determine the best search terms to use to find records or databases. (2) This volume will expose you to records that will allow you to extend your pedigree back in time to its American beginnings. (3) *The Source* will help you judge the accuracy of the information you find. (4) *The Source* will provide a depth and accuracy of understanding to enable you to correctly evaluate what you find.

Summary

Make no mistake, *The Source* is far more than a guide to searching the Web. It is a one-volume library of genealogical research knowledge. The subtitle describes what this work really provides: *A Guidebook to American Genealogy.* Discover the records created by institutions and government agencies in ancestral hometowns, townships, counties, parishes, and states, and you will find the lives of your relatives chronicled in these documents. *The Source* is your guide on this voyage of discovery.

Contributors

Loretto Dennis ("Lou") Szucs, FUGA, holds a degree in history, and has been involved in genealogical research, teaching, lecturing, and publishing for more than thirty years. Previously employed by the National Archives, she is currently executive editor and vice president of community relations for MyFamily.com, Inc.. She has served on many archives and genealogical boards, and was founding secretary of the Federation of Genealogical Societies. Currently, she serves as a director on the Board of the Federation of Genealogical Societies.

She has edited newsletters and quarterly journals for several genealogical societies, including the Federation of Genealogical Societies' *FORUM*. She authored *They Became Americans: Finding Naturalization Records and Ethnic Origins; Chicago and Cook County Sources: A Genealogical and Historical Guide; Ellis Island: Tracing Your Family History Through America's Gateway*; *The Archives: A Guide to the National Archives Field Branches* (with Sandra Luebking), *and Finding Answers in U.S. Census Records* (with Matthew Wright).

Since 1980, Lou has lectured at numerous genealogy workshops and national conferences. She has presented at the American Library Association conference and has been interviewed for the *Ancestors* series, *ABC News, CNN news*, and most recently on ABC television show, *The View.* In 1995, she was awarded the designation of fellow of the Utah Genealogical Association and has received numerous other awards.

Sandra Hargreaves Luebking, FUGA, holds a BA in anthropology from the University of Illinois at Chicago and has completed graduate course work in history and communications at University of Illinois at Springfield.

Since 1979, Sandra has taught at Samford University's Institute of Genealogy and Historical Research (IGHR), at Birmingham, Alabama. In 1990, she became course I coordinator for IGHR. From 1994 to 2005, Sandra was intermediate studies coordinator for the Genealogical Institute of Mid-America, Springfield, Illinois.

Sandra has conducted research projects for the Smithsonian Institution and for an international clientele. She is a past trustee for the Association of Professional Genealogists and has been a volunteer research assistant at the National Archives–Great Lakes Region.

Sandra is editor of *FORUM*, the national magazine of the Federation of Genealogical Societies. With Loretto D. Szucs, she is the co-editor of two award-winning books. She also contributed chapters to *Professional Genealogy* (2001), Elizabeth Shown Mills, editor, and *Printed Sources* (1998), Kory L. Meyerink, editor.

Honors include: David S. Vogels Jr. Award (Federation of Genealogical Societies, 1992); Outstanding IGHR Alumni (Samford University, 1995); Fellow of the Utah Genealogical Association (1996); Willard Heiss Memorial Lecturer (Indiana Historical Society, 1999); and Richard Slatten Lecture Series presenter (Friends of the Virginia State Archives, 2003).

Suzanne Russo Adams, AG, specializes in Italian research. She is a Brigham Young University (BYU) graduate with degrees in sociology and family history/genealogy. She is pursuing an MA in European history from BYU. Suzanne currently works as the professional services desk manager for Ancestry.com, part of MyFamily.com, Inc. In her more than six years with Ancestry.com, she has worked in both electronic production and content acquisition. She currently serves on the Association of Professional Genealogists Board, on the Utah Genealogical Association Board, and as renewal secretary for the International Commission for the Accreditation of Professional Genealogists.

Robert Charles Anderson, MA, FASG, was born at Bellows Falls, Vermont, and graduated from Harvard University, the California Institute of Technology, and the University of Massachusetts Amherst, at the last of which he received an MA in history. He is a fellow and former president of the American Society of Genealogists and is co-editor of *The American Genealogist*. As director of the Great Migration Study Project, he edits the *Great Migration Newsletter* and is the principal author of *The Great Migration Begins: Immigrants to New England: 1620–1633* (3 volumes, 1995), *The Great Migration: Immigrants to New England, 1634–1635* (3 volumes to date), and *The Pilgrim Migration: Immigrants to Plymouth Colony, 1620–1633* (2004). Robert resides in Derry, New Hampshire.

Mary McCampbell Bell, CG, first became a certified genealogist in 1979. She specializes in southern research and especially Colonial Virginia. She authored chapter 16, "Transcripts and Abstracts," and co-authored chapter 24, "Lineage Papers," in *Professional Genealogy: A Manual for Researchers, Writers, Editors, Lecturers, and Librarians* (Baltimore: Genealogical Publishing Co., 2001). Her articles and record abstracts appeared in *The Virginia Genealogist, National Genealogical Society Quarterly, Genealogical Computing,* and the *South Carolina Magazine of Ancestral Research.* Mary served as president of the National Capital Area Chapter of the Association of Professional Genealogists; trustee and secretary of the Board for the Certification of Genealogists (BCG); governor-at-large, Virginia Genealogical Society; charter member of the Genealogical Speaker's Guild; council member and secretary of the National Genealogical Society (NGS); and program co-chair of the 1988 NGS conference. She received the NGS Award of Merit in 1988; is a lecturer at the National Institute on Genealogical Research (National Archives), Washington, D.C., at annual conferences of both NGS and the Federation of Genealogical Societies; and at Samford University's Institute of Genealogical and Historical Research. She is also coordinator for course 10, "For Lands Sake! Deeper Analysis and Platting," in which students plat difficult problems to be placed on twentieth-century USGS topographic maps. Mary currently serves as a trustee of the Education Fund of BCG. She developed the first "Abstracting for Success" workshop for the Education Fund.

Lloyd deWitt Bockstruck, AB cum laude in biology, MA in early modern European history, MS in library science, has been with the Dallas, Texas, Public Library since 1973. Previously he had been a research assistant in the Graduate School of Library Science at the University of Illinois, secondary teacher and librarian at the Mombasa, Kenya, Baptist High School, and a teaching assistant in the Department of History at Southern Illinois University. He has been on the faculty of the Institute of Genealogical and Historical Research, Samford University, since 1974 and was the first recipient of its outstanding alumni award. He is the author of *Virginia's Colonial Soldiers, Genealogical Research in Texas, Revolutionary War Bounty Land Grants Awarded by State Governments, Naval Pensioners of the United States, 1800–1851,* and *Denizations and Naturalizations in the British Colonies in North America, 1607–1775.* Lloyd received the Award of Merit from the National Genealogical Society in 1982 and was named a fellow of the society in 1993. In 1999 he was awarded the first Filby Prize for Genealogical Librarianship. In 2003 he received the Lifetime Achievement Award from the Northeast Texas Library System. In 2005 the National Society of the Daughters of Founders and Patriots of America presented Lloyd with their highest award, and the Sons of the American Revolution presented him with the Gold Good Citizenship Medal. Lloyd's weekly newspaper column, "Family Tree," appears in *The Dallas Morning News.*

Tony Burroughs teaches at Chicago State University. He was the genealogist featured in *The Real Family of Jesus* (Discovery Channel), and was interviewed on *CBS Sunday Morning*, *CBS News, ABC World News Tonight, BET Nightly News*, and seven episodes of *Ancestors* (PBS). Tony has been quoted in the *New York Times, Wall Street Journal, People Magazine, Time Magazine,* the *Christian Science Monitor, Ebony,* and *Jet Magazine*. His *Black Roots: A Beginners Guide to Tracing the African American Family Tree* (Simon & Schuster) was number one on *Essence Magazine's Best Seller List*. Tony authored "How to Create a Family Tree" in *The Experts Guide to 100 Things Everyone Should Know How to Do* (Random House) and was a co-author of the *African American Genealogical Sourcebook* (Gale Research). He lectures throughout the United States and Canada, delivering more than sixty lectures at national conferences, including seven keynotes. His Soundex research led to correcting a forty-year omission by the National Archives. Former board positions include the Association of Professional Genealogists, the New England Historic Genealogical Society, the Federation of Genealogical Societies, and GENTECH. He is a former president of the Afro-American Genealogical and Historical Society of Chicago. Tony received the Distinguished Service Award from the National Genealogical Society and is a fellow of the Utah Genealogical Association.

Johni Cerny, BS, FUGA, founder and former president of Lineages, Inc., currently owns Johni Cerny, Inc. She received a BS in 1969 from Brigham Young University (BYU) with majors in social work and genealogical research. She was awarded an AA in genealogical research technology from BYU in 1968. Honored by the Utah Genealogical Society, she was made a fellow in 1968. With Arlene Eakle, she edited the first edition of *The Source: A Guidebook of American Genealogy* (1984), and authored many of its chapters. With Wendy Elliott she edited and authored *The Library: A Guide to the LDS Family History Library* (1986). She served as the lead genealogist for the PBS series *African American Lives* (2006). Johni specializes in tracing the origins and ancestry of German immigrants to the United States and African American ancestry, and she compiles the German Emigration Index, a database of German immigrants to the United States whose origins have been documented. She has been engaged in genealogical research for more than thirty-five years; in a professional capacity, since 1979.

Donn Devine, CG, a genealogical consultant from Wilmington, Delaware, is also an attorney for the city and archivist of the Catholic Diocese of Wilmington. He has been a trustee of the Board for Certification of Genealogists since 1992, also serving as the board's pro-bono legal counsel. Donn chairs the National Genealogical Society's (NGS) Standards Committee and, from 1994 to 2002, served on the NGS board. A regular columnist in *Ancestry* magazine, he has been published in major research journals and most recently has been working on use of DNA evidence in genealogical research. A former president of the Delaware Genealogical Society, Donn was founding editor of its journal.

Arlene Eakle, Ph.D., is president and founder of The Genealogical Institute, Inc. Arlene is a professional genealogist with more than thirty years experience in research as a consultant, a seminar presenter, and author. She is an expert in tracing Southern ancestors including those of Native American background. She is also skilled in tracing ancestors from the British Isles, Switzerland, and parts of Germany. She has addressed more than five hundred workshops and seminars in the United States, Canada, and Europe and is the author of more than ninety books, newsletters, scholarly articles, and family histories.

Ann Carter Fleming, CG, CGL, is an author, lecturer, researcher, and volunteer. Ann is the author of *The Organized Family Historian: How to File, Manage, and Protect Your Genealogical Research and Heirlooms* (Nashville: Rutledge Hill Press, 2004) and co-author of *Research in Missouri*, NGS Research in the States Series (Arlington: NGS, 1999), and several family histories. She is past-president of the National Genealogical Society and on the board of St. Louis Genealogical Society.

Kay Haviland Freilich, CG, CGL, is a trustee and immediate past president of Board for Certification of Genealogists (BCG), researcher, author, lecturer, and volunteer who specializes in colonial Pennsylvania and Quaker research. She is the author of the National Genealogical Society (NGS) publication *Research in Pennsylvania* and co-author of three published family histories. Her articles have appeared in *NGS Quarterly*, *NGS NewsMagazine*, the Federation of Genealogical Societies' (FGS) *FORUM*, *Pennsylvania Genealogical Magazine*, and *OnBoard*, the BCG newsletter. Kay serves as verifying genealogist for lineage societies and is a former FGS director and secretary. A frequent speaker at local and national conferences, she was program chair for NGS 1997 in Valley Forge and assistant program chair for FGS 2001 in Davenport, Iowa. For the Genealogical Society of Pennsylvania, she is a counselor at the "Summer Camp for Genealogists" programs and has served on the publications and program committees.

James L. Hansen, FASG, has been since 1974 the reference librarian and genealogical specialist at the Library of the Wisconsin Historical Society, where he assists several thousand researchers a year in their genealogical and historical research. He has taught beginning and advanced genealogical research courses over Wisconsin's Educational Telephone Network. Among his publications are articles on a variety of genealogical topics, a bibliography of territorial Wisconsin newspapers, and a guide to the library in which he works. He is a nationally known speaker, having lectured on genealogical topics around Wisconsin and at numerous conferences (national, state and local) in the United States and Canada. He was the 1994-1995 president of the Association of Professional Genealogists, and in 1995 was named a fellow of the American Society of Genealogists. In 2002 he was awarded the Filby Prize for Genealogical Librarianship at the NGS conference in Milwaukee.

Birdie Monk Holsclaw, CG, is a genealogical researcher, writer, lecturer, and editor. She was the winner of the 2003 National Genealogical Society (NGS) Family History Writing Contest and the 2004 *NGS Quarterly* Award for Excellence. A former indexer of the *NGS Quarterly,* she has served as a board member or committee chair for the Association of Professional Genealogists and the Federation of Genealogical Societies and was a member of GENTECH's data model group. Her major research project is compiling family histories of early deaf and blind children in Colorado pioneer families.

Linda Caldwell McCleary, MLS, hails from Indianapolis, Indiana, but now resides in Arizona. She graduated from Ball State University in Munice, Indiana, with both a BS and a MLS. She has recently retired from the Arizona State Library as a public library development consultant. Previously, Linda held the position of Arizona State Genealogy Librarian for fifteen years. She holds a Certificate in Genealogical Research (Professional) from Brigham Young University. She is currently a director on the Federation of Genealogical Societies Board, a member of the FGS/NGS Records Preservation and Access Committee, charter member of the Arizona Council of Professional Genealogists, past president of the Arizona Genealogical Advisory Board, and a member of the Arizona Historical Society. She has been awarded the Federation of Genealogical Societies' Distinguished Service Award and the National Genealogical Society Distinguished Service Award. She has been engaged in genealogical research for more than twenty-five years.

Kory L. Meyerink, MLS, AG, FUGA, is the editor and primary author of the American Library Association award winning *Printed Sources: A Guide to Published Genealogical Records*. A professional researcher in Salt Lake City, he is a vice-president at ProGenealogists, Inc., where he guides research, writing, and development of Internet genealogy tools. Named a Fellow of the Utah Genealogical Association (UGA) in 2002 for his significant contributions to genealogy, Kory has been accredited since 1980 (Germany, Midwest, Mid-Atlantic, and New England states). He joined the Family History Library as a reference consultant in 1986, later serving as an instructional developer and the library's publications coordinator. Later, as part of the management team at Ancestry.com he managed electronic publications and acquisitions. Past president of the UGA and founding director of the Salt Lake Institute of Genealogy, he has also served as trustee and executive secretary of the Association of Professional Genealogists and on conference committees of the Federation of Genealogical Societies. Kory has written extensively in magazines and journals and is a contributing editor for *Heritage Quest Magazine*. A popular lecturer at national, state, and regional conferences, he also teaches for Brigham Young University and Salt Lake Community College and is the German course creator and director at the National Institute of Genealogical Studies at the University of Toronto.

Gary Mokotoff is an author, lecturer, and leader of Jewish genealogy. He is the first person to receive the Lifetime Achievement Award of the International Association of Jewish Genealogical Societies (IAJGS). He is the author of a number of books including the award-winning *Where Once We Walked*, a gazetteer that provides information about 22,000 towns in central and eastern Europe where Jews lived before the Holocaust, *How to Document Victims and Locate Survivors of the Holocaust*, and *Getting Started in Jewish Genealogy*. He is co-editor of the book *Avotaynu Guide to Jewish Genealogy*. Gary is also known for his application of computers to genealogy. Among his accomplishments is co-authorship of the Daitch-Mokotoff soundex system; the JewishGen Family Finder, a database of ancestral towns and surnames being researched by some 50,000 Jewish genealogists throughout the world; Family Tree of the Jewish people; and the Consolidated Jewish Surname Index. He is publisher of *Avotaynu*, the magazine of Jewish genealogy, and a past president of IAJGS. He is on the Board of Directors of the Federation of Genealogical Societies and the Association of Professional Genealogists.

George J. Nixon is a native of Grants Pass, Oregon. He has been a professional genealogist and resident of Salt Lake City since 1976. He has a degree in history from the University of California, Los Angeles. He specializes in Native American research and also in U.S. and Canadian research.

Gordon L. Remington, FUGA, FASG, a native of Rochester, New York, currently resides in Salt Lake City, where he has maintained a genealogical practice since 1980. He holds a degree in history from the University of Utah. He has been a member of and served in a number of offices in the Association of Professional Genealogists since 1979. He has also been a member of the Utah Genealogical Association (UGA) since 1984 and was the editor of UGA's *Genealogical Journal*. He has published more than forty articles in national and regional genealogical periodicals. He has also lectured on genealogy internationally, nationally, and regionally. In 1992 Gordon was named a fellow of the UGA, and, in 1999, he was elected a fellow of the American Society of Genealogists. He has been a contributing author to all three editions of *The Source: A Guidebook of American Genealogy* (Ancestry, 1984, 1997, 2006) and to *The Library: A Guide to the LDS Family History Library* (1988). In 2002 he published *New York State Probate Records: A Genealogist's Guide to Testate and Intestate Records* and *New York State Towns, Villages, and Cities: A Guide to Genealogical Sources* under the auspices of the New England Historic Genealogical Society.

Christine Rose, CG, CGL, FASG, is a fellow of the American Society of Genealogists, an honor bestowed by peers, based on quantity and quality of publications, and limited to fifty people at any one time. Other honors include the prestigious Donald Lines Jacobus award for two of her genealogy books. As a lecturer she is widely known at national and regional conferences and has for many years been a faculty member of the Samford University Institute of Genealogy and Historical Research. She has authored several guidebooks including *Courthouse Research for Family Historians*, *Nicknames Past & Present*, *Genealogical Proof Standard*, and *Family Associations: Organization and Management*. She also co-authored *The Complete Idiot's Guide to Genealogy*. Christine is an associate of the Board for Certification of Genealogists, former vice-president of the Association of Professional Genealogists, former vice-president of the Federation of Genealogical Societies (FGS), charter member of the Genealogical Speaker's Guild, and is a "Family Association" columnist for the FGS *FORUM*. Her articles have appeared in the *National Genealogical Society Quarterly*, *Ancestry* Magazine, the *American Genealogist*, the *New England Register*, the *New York Record*, and the *Virginia Genealogist*. Her specialities include onsite research throughout the United States, military records, and land records.

George R. Ryskamp, JD, AG, formerly a practicing attorney in Riverside, California, now holds the position of associate professor of History at Brigham Young University, teaching Latin American and southern European family history and the use of American legal documents and concepts in family history. Author of books and numerous articles and a former commissioner and vice chairman for the International Commission for the Accreditation of Professional Genealogists, he currently serves as director of the Center for Family History and Genealogy at Brigham Young University, also directing its flagship Immigrant Ancestor Project. He is a fellow of the Utah Genealogical Association, a Miembro Académico of the Academia Americana de Genealogía, and a corresponding member of the Academia Real Matritense de Genealogía y Heráldica. A former member of the Advisory Council of the New England Historic Genealogical Society and current director of the Basque Family Heritage Project under the University of Nevada at Reno's Center for Basque Studies, he lectures all over the United States and the world. George and his wife, Peggy, are the parents of four children and grandparents to a growing number of grandchildren.

During his thirty-five-year career with the U.S. National Archives and Records Administration (NARA), **John M. Scroggins** created and later directed the regional archives program, managed microfilming operations and audio-visual and cartographic records, and worked on the requirements for several automated systems. After retiring from NARA, he worked briefly for Ancestry.com as director of electronic records. He received the Federation of Genealogical Societies Award of Merit for his efforts to bring the federal government's historical and genealogical records to the people and to build and strengthen archival outreach programs. John holds a BA in history from Jamestown College and an MA in public administration from The American University and is a member of the Academy of Certified Archivists and several genealogical societies.

Juliana Smith edited the *Ancestry Daily News* beginning in 1998 and continues to edit the successor to that newsletter, the *Ancestry Weekly Journal* and its weblog counterpart. She is the author of *The Ancestry Family Historian's Address Book* and has written for *Ancestry* Magazine and *Genealogical Computing.* She is the former editor of the Chicago Genealogical Society's newsletter and has had a life-long interest in family history.

Marian L. Smith is the senior historian at U.S. Citizenship and Immigration Services, Department of Homeland Security (formerly the Immigration and Naturalization Service). She regularly lectures at national and international genealogy conferences on the history and uses of immigration and naturalization records. Marian's articles appear in the National Archives journal *Prologue*, the Federation of Genealogical Societies *FORUM* and other publications. Her research focus primarily involves official immigration agency records held in the National Archives in downtown Washington, D.C.

Megan Smolenyak Smolenyak, author of *Trace Your Roots with DNA: Using Genetic Tests to Explore Your Family Tree; They Came to America: Finding Your Immigrant Ancestor; Honoring Our Ancestors: Inspiring Stories of the Quest for Our Roots;* and *In Search of Our Ancestors: 101 Inspiring Stories of Serendipity and Connection in Rediscovering Our Family History,* has been a genealogist for more than thirty years. Lead researcher for PBS's *Ancestors* and *They Came to America*, Megan is also a consultant with the U.S. Army's Repatriation project to trace families of servicemen who were killed in Korea, WWII, and Vietnam. Recipient of International Society of Family History Writers and Editors awards in 2003 and 2004, she has appeared on the *Today Show, Fox & Friends, Ancestors, NPR,* and other television and radio shows and has spoken at NGS, GENTECH, and numerous other genealogical, historical, military, and ethnic conferences. Her articles have appeared in *Ancestry* Magazine, *Ancestry Daily News, Family Chronicle, Family Tree Magazine, Genealogical Computing, Heritage Quest, NGS NewsMagazine, Everton's Family History Magazine,* and *Association of Professional Genealogists Quarterly*. Megan supports a variety of genealogical initiatives through her Honoring Our Ancestors Grants Program and can be reached at <www.honoringourancestors.com> and <www.genetealogy.com>.

Noted genealogist **David Thackery** passed away on 17 July 1998 at the age of forty-five after suffering a heart attack while jogging near his home in Hyde Park, Illinois. A native of Urbana, Ohio, David had a life-long passion for history and research. He earned a bachelor's degree from Wittenberg University in Springfield, Ohio, and two master's degrees from the University of Chicago in library science and divinity. He joined Chicago's Newberry Library in 1982 and was made head of the research facility's local and family history department in 1983. As head of the department, David dramatically expanded the library's services and collections in the area of family history. In 1988 and 1989, he used a $62,000 grant to buy microfilm from the National Archives to enhance the library's collection of African American family history sources. In his position as curator of local and family history at the Newberry Library, David spent his last years developing one of the nation's foremost genealogy collections. David was a prolific writer and bibliographer, contributing articles to major genealogical publications and compiling some of the best bibliographic sources available for African American researchers.

Elizabeth Crabtree Wells is Special Collection Librarian and University Archivist at Samford University, Birmingham, Alabama. She received her BA from Judson College, MA in history from Auburn University and MLS from the University of Alabama. The Collection at Samford is a repo-sitory of the Alabama Baptist Historical Collection, houses manuscripts and rarities primarily of Alabama, and serves as the Howard College/Samford University Archives. Elizabeth works with churches and community, historical, and genealogical organizations in promoting the preservation and utilization of Alabama's historical records and provides instruction to the university community and others upon request regarding research tools and methodology. She is a lecturer for the Institute of Genealogy and Historical Research and a speaker at National Genealogical Society conferences and state and regional genealogical and historical organizations. Her publications include: *Daughters of the Dream: History of Judson College* with Frances Hamilton; "Genealogy Section," *Magazines for Libraries*; and state advisor (Alabama), *Best Books for Academic Libraries.* Elizabeth is president of the Alabama Genealogical Society, past president of the Society of Alabama Archivists and treasurer of the Alabama Baptist Historical Society. She has served as Trustee of the Southern Baptist Historical Commission, and is an Executive Board member of the Alabama Historical Association.

Curt B. Witcher, MA, FUGA, FIGS, is the manager of the Historical Genealogy Department of the Allen County Public Library in Fort Wayne, Indiana. He is chair of the American Library Association's (ALA) Genealogy and Local History Discussion Group and participates in other genealogical and historical committees of that organization. Curt is a former president of both the Federation of Genealogical Societies and the National Genealogical Society and is the founding president of the Indiana Genealogical Society. He is co-editor of the 1987 through 2005 editions of the *Periodical Source Index*. In 2000 he authored, *African American Genealogy: A Bibliography and Guide to Sources*. Curt was a research consultant for the PBS series *Ancestors* and, since 2003, is on the Genealogy Publications Committee of the Indiana Historical Society (IHS). He served for eight years as the National Volunteer Data Input Coordinator for the Civil War Soldiers System. Curt was distinguished in 1995 as a fellow of the Utah Genealogical Association and received the FGS Rabbi Malcolm H. Stern Humanitarian Award in 1997 and the David Vogels Award in 1999. He was the 2002 ALA-RUSA History Section Genealogical Publishing Company Award winner and in 2003 was honored by the IHS as the Willard Heiss Memorial Lecturer.

Matthew Wright graduated cum laude with a BA in journalism from Brigham Young University. He has participated in family history research, both his own and for others, for more than fifteen years. For the past ten years he has worked in magazine and book publishing, the last seven with an emphasis in family history. He is publications manager for Ancestry Publishing, part of MyFamily.com, Inc., and managing editor of the *Association of Professional Genealogists Quarterly*. He co-authored *Finding Answers in U.S. Census Records* with Loretto D. Szucs. Matthew lives in Provo, Utah, with his wife and three children.

Raymond S. Wright III, Ph.D., AG, FUGA, has a BA in German and an MA and a Ph.D. in European history (University of Utah). He currently serves as Director, Family History Library in Salt Lake City, Utah (2004–present). His past experience includes professor of family history at Brigham Young University (1990–2004), director, BYU Center for Family History and Genealogy <http://familyhistory.byu.edu> (2000–2003) and the Center's Immigrant Ancestors Database project <http://immigrants.byu.edu> (1997–2003), Family History Library operations manager (1979–1990), and European field operations manager (1972–1979). His publications include articles on immigration/emigration topics, family history sources and research methods in professional journals, popular magazines, Internet websites, and three books: *The Genealogists Handbook* (Chicago: American Library Association, 1995); a revised edition of *Meyers Orts- und Verkehrslexikon des Deutschen Reichs* (Baltimore: Genealogical Publishing Co., 2000); and *Ancestors in German Archives*. (Baltimore: Genealogical Publishing Co., 2004). Raymond's research interests include documenting emigrants in sources in their home countries and documenting the immigrant experience in destination countries.

Stephen C. Young was born and raised in London, Ontario, Canada, and now lives in Salt Lake City with his wife, Michelle, and five children. He earned a BA from Brigham Young University in family and local history (1985) and an MA in American history (emphasis in public history) at Bowling Green State University in Ohio (1990). An employee of the Family and Church History Department of The Church of Jesus Christ of Latter-day Saints since 1988, Stephen has enjoyed several assignments during this time in Family History Library administration and a special four-year appointment (1992–1996) in England supervising the British 1881 Census Project. His genealogical research accreditation in English Canadian research has been active with ICAPGen since 1989, and he specializes in English, Loyalist, and Ontario research and history.

1

The Foundations of Family History Research

SANDRA HARGREAVES LUEBKING, FUGA, and LORETTO DENNIS SZUCS, FUGA

There has never been a better time to be a family historian. Recent surveys have found that genealogy ranks as the second most popular hobby in the United States. These surveys conclude that approximately 73 percent of Americans report having an interest in learning more about their family history.[1] And there are as many goals for family historians as there are individuals doing it. Some researchers are trying to find living relatives, and some are creating multimedia presentations to share at the next family reunion. Some want to publish a family history to pass on to future generations while others are studying their family's health history. Some are doing research for clients while others are simply adding names to their new software program. At the same time, most family historians are interested in discovering their family story and preserving it for future generations. All these pursuits make up the exciting adventure that is family history.[2]

This recent surge of interest, coupled with new technology, has changed the face of genealogy. Though there will always be a need to visit brick-and-mortar repositories and to search out original records, computers and the Internet have brought a convenient, inexpensive, and speedy aid to family history.

With heightened interest in the subject, family historians have dramatically increased the number of requests for help and research materials at libraries and archives around the world, a fact that hasn't escaped notice of mass media publications and television broadcasts. Scarcely a day goes by that a genealogy or family history story doesn't make the news. Because of the demand for information and services, commercial and government entities as well as genealogical groups and individuals are producing a constant stream of historical records. The good news for family historians of all interest levels is that new sources and research opportunities are becoming available every day.

Chapter Contents

Taking all of these new developments into account, this chapter is about foundations—acquiring information about the past, evaluating what you learn, and recording and summarizing for the future—and is intended to acquaint you with the practices and procedures that successful genealogists follow. By using these guidelines you will have the tools you need to put together quality family history information and to avoid common, and sometimes costly, errors. This chapter discusses six foundations of family history:

1. Focus on your personal knowledge of your family by beginning with what you know and by identifying and cataloging items often found in the home.

2. Collaborate with others to grow your family tree by interviewing all persons who have information about the family and by using the genealogical community to expand your research.
3. Understand the technological developments in family history research, including the Internet, DNA testing, and computer programs, and how they are changing and simplifying the way family history is researched.
4. Organize and evaluate the information you obtain to avoid research duplication (and enable future generations to know your ancestors—and you).
5. Position your ancestors in place and time by analyzing historical maps and written histories and other records.
6. Know how etiquette, ethics, and certain laws can impact your family history research.

Whether you are a family history novice or a seasoned researcher, the recent technological advances, vast variety and availability of records and information, and online resources make reviewing these family history foundations a helpful exercise. Soon you will embark on one of the most remarkable and compelling journeys of your life: the reconstruction and preservation of your own family's history.

Start with Yourself

Family history research begins with the present: family historians consider what they know about the family from first-hand experience or from the traditions and stories passed down to them. This beginning also includes identifying and cataloging items—heirlooms, documents, or other tangible items—often found in the home. Together, these research paths provide a foundation that should be returned to often for additional clues.

Begin with What You Know

Genealogy how-to guides and courses advise beginners to start with themselves and move backward in time. But this step-by-step approach is good advice for seasoned family historians as well. Those who have done a good amount of research will find an occasional review of traditions, names, or other information useful. Details that seemed inconsequential early in their investigation assume great importance when combined with the more recent research. For newcomers, the process of beginning with ones' self and acquiring the documents that firmly link them to their parents before researching grandparents or earlier generations, will provide a strong foundation that will focus the research and keep it accurate.

Some family historians tend to overlook their family's collateral lines (those lines that do not include direct ancestors). Going back to what you know about collateral lines could help you break down research blocks in direct family lines. Another suggestion is to continue to record the weddings, births, deaths, and other milestones of the current generations. Never become so focused on the deceased that the living are neglected.

It is important to make a tangible record of this knowledge on paper, disk, or audio or video tape. Keeping this information only "in your head" could likely result in forgotten or misremembered events, dates, and relationships. Make this record as detailed as possible. Although the facts may appear too recent to be of interest, your knowledge will soon be history to younger family members. As you record the information, begin with the present generation: yourself and any siblings you may have.

Home Sources

Once you have organized the information you know, you should conduct a survey of home sources: artifacts and documents still in the possession of family and friends. Home sources can include military medals, photographs (figure 1-1), the family Bible, a grandparent's baptismal certificate, or the patent to your great-great-grandparents' homestead. Any of these items could hold clues about your family history. First steps involve discovering these clues, organizing them into a coherent pattern, and then following as they lead you into public records that add to the detail—or perhaps alter the assumptions. Is the medal from the Civil War service of an ancestor? Does a newspaper clipping describe the accidental death of a granduncle's first wife? Did your maternal line immigrate in 1878, as tradition states, and your paternal line in 1778, as grandmother was fond of saying?

Funeral prayer cards, resumes, even articles of clothing can be home sources. The criterion is not an object's monetary worth or research potential. Instead, its value may be purely intrinsic. An object might symbolize a previous owner you've come to know through narratives and research; or an artifact might bring another place or time to life. A musical instrument made by a great-great grandfather who was both a carpenter and a professional musician; a chair with an intricate needlework design on the seat cover stitched by a great-grandmother; and a set of fine china with the family initial hand painted by a great-aunt who worked for Marshall Field's in Chicago: all home sources that connect us to generations past.

Home sources offer three significant opportunities to a family historian. First, the very fact of their survival can tell much about the caretaker—the person or persons who found them to be worthy of saving. Second, they can be genuine sources of evidence: the will preserved for generations that names all of a great-grandfather's children (even the illegitimate ones) or the record of an infant's baptism. Third, a home source can be a key that unlocks the approach to an official record, such as a vital record, a cemetery record, or a court case, to name a few possibilities.

Two faded newspaper clippings offered important clues in one research project. The clippings, pasted in a scrapbook,

Figure 1-1. The apparel of this young family helps to date this photograph to the late nineteenth century. From the Franklin family collection; reproduced by Sunny Nash.

were reports of deaths. One was determined to be the obituary of a merchant who died while visiting family members in the European village of his birth. The translated information provided countless avenues of research. The name of the deceased, his residence, occupation, and date of death led to local historical writings, business and employment sources, a death certificate, and cemetery plot plans. The name and denomination of the minister who conducted the memorial service also proved useful. The listing of other family members, siblings, his widow, and children was especially helpful.

The other clipping contained significantly less detail but its value soon became apparent. This brief death notice included the sentence "Cincinnati papers, please copy." Cincinnati proved to be the home of many family members of the deceased, a woman without close relatives at her place of death, where the original notice was published.

Your research goal for home sources is to organize and catalogue these links to the past and, if you are reasonably skilled or very fortunate, to identify them in time and place. While few clues may be offered, knowledge of dating techniques for a particular object may provide a breakthrough.

Types of Home Sources

Home sources come in many shapes, sizes, and textures. A home source can be a wedding band etched with a date of marriage; a quilt with the name of the quilter and the date of completion stitched on it; the account book of a nineteenth-century female entrepreneur who supported a young family as a dressmaker for the wealthy; a drop-leaf desk with a secret compartment containing an unrecorded deed; or century-old letters chronicling the Civil War from the perspective of a young soldier from Mississippi.

Discussed in the following paragraphs are some of the sources most likely to be found among your possessions.

Photographs. Perhaps the most durable of home sources are pictorial items that depict people as they were: photographs that capture the essence of a lifetime in a second, outlasting the people portrayed. Sometimes family history research results from the need to identify the people in a particularly captivating photograph or to learn what secrets their lives held.

The studio photograph in figure 1-2 of a mother and her triplets was the key to a series of important discoveries about the family. The name and city of the studio in which it was taken was imprinted. Someone had added the words, "Mrs. A. T. Guthridge & triplet daughters 1878." This knowledge led to a census record (1880) and, ultimately, public and private records for the children and their older siblings. Eventually a living descendant was located who was able to provide some memories and home sources about the family.

Dating studio photographs is easier if something is known about the photographer or the establishment, such as the years the business was in the city. Stephen E. Massengill's *Photographers in North Carolina* is one of several references giving biographical information on individual photographers and the city and date range in which they conducted business. *Ohio Photographers, 1839–1900,* by Diane Vanskiver Gagel, is another good example. Publications focused on other locations may be found through Internet searches.

When a photograph does not contain a studio name or year, books such as Karen Frisch-Ripley's *Unlocking the Secrets in Old Photographs* or Joe Nickell's *Camera Clues: A Handbook for Photographic Investigation* may help to date a photograph and place it in a specific location. This in turn can help to identify the persons featured. The dating of a picture begins by deciphering the photographic process that was used. A brief summary follows:

The photographic process dates from 1839, when artist, chemist, and physicist Louis Daguerre invented the daguerreotype process. It utilized a silver-plated copper plate and was used in America almost exclusively until the late 1850s. A pocket-size case, as shown by figure 1-3, sometimes ornately decorated and with a hinged cover, protected the plate. Joan Severa's *My Likeness Taken: Daguerreian Portraits in America, 1840–1860* depicts many of these images.

The ambrotype (a photograph on glass) achieved popularity from about 1855 into the 1860s. Also mounted in a case, the glass that held the negative was backed with dark paint, cloth, or paper. Often confused with the ambrotype is the tintype, or ferrotype, invented in 1856. The tintype is a plate of sheet iron upon which the image appears. The tintype, as shown in figure 1-4, was more durable and less expensive than the ambrotype. Tintypes could be placed in cases or even be covered with glass, but more often they were not mounted. Tintypes continued being made into the early 1900s, mostly in rural areas.

Carte-de-visite photographs were often displayed in albums on parlor tables after 1860. These paper photographs measured approximately 2½ by 4¼ inches and were produced in great quantity through about 1890. From about 1870 until 1910, the larger cabinet-size photograph won favor among portrait sitters.

Modern gelatin dry plates, first manufactured in the United States in 1871, replaced the wet collodion emulsion used since 1864. But widespread use of photography did not occur until the development of a machine that continuously coated photographic paper with emulsion to create roll film, in 1884. In 1888, George Eastman marketed the first portable roll-film camera—the No. 1 Kodak. This camera brought everyday photography into the hands of the public. Within decades it seemed everyone had

Figure 1-2.
"Mrs. A. T. Guthridge & triplet daughters 1878" noted on the back of this studio photograph helped locate Alonzo and Cornelia Guthridge in the 1880 U.S. Federal Census of Macon County, Illinois, with three-year-olds Lorena, Tellena, and Cressida. Courtesy of Sandra Luebking.

Figure 1-3.
A piece of tape on the cover of this dauerreotype's case identifies the photo as "Uncle Joe Beuret (Melanie's Brother)." From the collection of Charles Banet, Fort Wayne, Indiana.

a camera, and improvements on home cameras mushroomed (figure 1-5). In 1891, the first fixed color photos appeared, and by 1914, Kodak was producing panchromatic film which allowed for full color spectrum pictures. Since 1930, color photography advances include improved dyes and high-speed films with low graininess. In 1948 the first Polaroid camera and film were marketed. And by 2006, the general public had moved to digital cameras, recording in both still shots and motion video.

Once the general period of origin of a photograph has been established, other indicators offer more precise dating. Much of nineteenth-century American upper-class society, in dress and habit, patterned itself after that of Queen Victoria. In *Queen Victoria's Family,* Charlotte Zeepvat allows a researcher to compare studio backdrops and props, such as period playthings and furniture used for the royal family with those in an unidentified photograph.

An examination of clothing and hairstyles over decades might also help to demystify a photograph in your possession. Joan Severa's *Dressed for the Photographer* shows Americans, rich and poor, black and white, rural and urban, and how they chose to dress for the photographer. Richard Corson's *Fashions in Hair: The First 5000 Years* illustrates how men's moustaches, sideburns, and beards changed over time as did hairstyles for both genders. Contrast the differences in the four-generational photograph (figure 1-6) where fifty-three-year-old Joseph A. Curtis has a moustache, eighty-two-year-old William H. Curtis has a moustache merging into a full beard that includes sideburns, while twenty-five-year-old Jay Curtis is clean-shaven.

Picture Postcards. Some photographs are picture postcards. The reverse of the Curtis photograph is inscribed with the word "Postcard" and has designated places for the stamp, name and address of the recipient, and correspondence. Photos with family

Figure 1-4. Glued to a page of a scrapbook that belonged to Margaret Howley Dyer, this tintype of unnamed individuals was taken at Coney Island, Brooklyn, New York. Judging by the apparent ages of Raymond and Margaret Dyer *(center of top row and center of middle row, respectively)*, the tintype was made about 1898. Courtesy of Loretto Szucs.

portraits were usually privately printed for distribution to family and friends. Picture postcards can also depict places where your family once lived, including the European village from which the family emigrated, the ships ancestors might have sailed upon, or events conceivably witnessed by past generations. The messages written on postcards can add to your knowledge about the family while providing important insights into the lives of your ancestors.

Postcards were introduced into the United States from Austria in the 1870s. Before World War I, holiday greeting postcards were a popular choice for Christmas, Halloween, and Valentine's Day messages. Topical postcards encompass advertisements or announcements of special events, such as the cards introduced by the 1893 World's Columbian Exposition. Topical cards were also used to depict disasters (such as fires), to provide entertainment, and to promote political figures. View cards are realistic portraits of actual places, people, or objects, tourist attractions and landscapes being the most favored subjects.

Postcards can be dated through their inscriptions, stamps, or styles. Those marked "Private Mailing Card" are likely to have been printed between 1898 and 1902 or, if printed in Europe, between 1899 and 1918. From 1901 to 1907, cards were labeled "Postcard" or "Post Card." Only after 1907 did postal regulations permit correspondence on the back of the card. This information helped date the Curtis postcard photo to after 1907 because the back was split down the middle with space for a note on the left side.

The use of stamps as a dating method is explained at <www.playle.com/realphoto>. Among the clues are: penny postcards were manufactured after 1898, when postal regulations established the penny postcard rate, while cards requiring two cents of postage date from 1873 to 1898.

Popular styles included cards with white borders (1915 to 1930), linen surfaces (1930 to the late 1940s, although some companies continued with this up to 1960) and today's glossy pictures (called chromes) which began in the late 1940s. More style details may be found at <www.ajmorris.com/roots/photo/postcard/style.htm>.

Postmarks and the notes written on the postcard can be obvious dating sources. The postmark on a postcard portrait taken at Coney Island, figure 1-7 dates the photograph to 1908. The inscription on the back provides the names of those pictured.

One of the largest online collections of searchable postcards is from the Detroit Publishing Company Collection, one of America's largest publishers of postcards and photographic views during the early decades of the twentieth century. The collection is spread between at least three repositories. More than 28,000 images of areas east of the Mississippi River are available in the Prints and Photographs Online Collection of the Library of Congress (see <www.loc.gov/rr/print/coll/202_detr.html> for an index and a history of this company and links to related holders). The Colorado Historical Society (Denver) has approximately 13,000 images from the Detroit Publishing Company representing views west of the Mississippi. The Henry Ford Museum and Greenfield Village has approximately 18,000 vintage photographs and 9,500 postcards. Postcards can also be found online at a variety of sites, including the Florida Postcard Collection <www.library.miami.edu/archives/cards/intro.html>, the University of Delaware Library Postcard Collection at <www.lib.udel.edu/digital/dpc/aboutcollection.htm> and the

Figure 1-5. As with many families who did not frequent studios, these children were not photographed until the widespread use of Kodak roll-film cameras. *Left to right:* Vivian, Wilson, Mason, and Milton Hargreaves, c. 1919. Courtesy of Sandra Luebking.

New York State Library collection at <www.nysl.nysed.gov/msscfa/qc16510.htm>.

A collection housed in one museum but with far-ranging potential for researchers is that amassed by Curt Teich, a German immigrant. Teich spent the 1890s photographing cities in the United States. He printed his pictures as postcards at his business establishment in Chicago. The Teich Company became the largest postcard printer of its kind in the world, producing cards for more than seventy-five years. The business archives of more than 350,000 postcards and the original production files are now housed at the Curt Teich Postcard Archives in Lake County Discovery Museum in Wauconda, Illinois, near Chicago. More than 30,000 images are catalogued and available for searching online at <www.teicharchives.org>. Perhaps one of these cards will reveal something about the neighborhood in which your family lived.

Family Bibles. The written record endures in many forms. Letters and personal accounts of events or eras are highly valued for the information they contain—but it is the family Bible that most often becomes the object of diligent searching.

Should you be fortunate enough to possess a family Bible, the following techniques might help you to evaluate its usefulness as a source of information. First, note the date of its publication. Match the publication date against the span of events written upon the page for family history. If the handwritten entries predate the publication, it is a clear indication that they were recorded not as they occurred but at a later date. Next, examine the handwriting used for each entry. Is it all in the same script, indicating that they were written by the same person? Are the entries in the same ink, suggesting that all were made at one sitting? Is there an inscription?

Check each page of a Bible or inherited book for notations or enclosures. Some owners recorded the dates of events, such as memorial services, weddings, and christenings, in the margin adjacent to the Bible text used for the occasion. Others stored small papers between the Bible pages: prayer cards, obituaries from newspapers, meaningful scraps of church bulletins, and even handwritten notes. Such a note enclosed in one Bible contained, in German script, the full name and birth date of each child born to the finder's great-grandparents.

The Library of Virginia holds more than six thousand family Bible records and registers that reflect Virginia connections. The Library has been diligent in adding to this collection, which is housed in Richmond. An online index with links to scanned images is at <www.lva.lib.va.us/whatwehave>.

Diaries and Journals. Diaries and journals are valued highly by family historians. It is easy enough to verify the accuracy of news and events: weather, surroundings, world and local happenings the diarist might have chosen to record. The accuracy and completeness of such entries can, in part, indicate the care with which other, more family-oriented, news was recorded.

Figure 1-6. A depiction of four generations shows how hair styles differed between ages, from clean-shaven to beard and sideburns. The Curtis men with seven-month-old Clyde Curtis, ca. 1913. Courtesy of Sandra Luebking.

Official Documents Held by Family Members. Did family members save copies of documents created by public rather than private entities? Birth, marriage, and death certificates, naturalization papers, military discharges, and legal papers from court actions are among the official records families may choose to retain. Valuable in themselves, such documents become priceless when the original documents have been lost through fire or neglect or are otherwise unavailable to you.

What do the records tell you? Are the names recognizable? Is there evidence of where the original record might be or perhaps the name of the county or church that created the record? Such tips can be springboards to finding other information. A will might be only one of dozens of documents pertaining to an estate that are on file at a county courthouse.

Of course, it is possible that your home copy of a document may never have been in a courthouse. People sometimes found it inconvenient or too expensive to officially record certain events. An early deed or mortgage, an original will, or the marriage certificate of a penniless couple might be the only record of a particular event. Such semi-official records should be stored in a safe place that will slow or prevent their deterioration (see "Preservation of Home Sources," in this chapter).

Privately held documents should be evaluated without bias and with some understanding of their history. Be especially careful to avoid reaching unfounded conclusions about their value. For example, take care with land patents (documents that transferred property from the federal government to private citizens). Patents dated before 2 March 1833 were signed by the president of the United States; after that date, designated officials signed on the president's behalf.

Samplers. For more than two centuries, the making of samplers was part of a young American woman's education. Introduced in the seventeenth century by settlers from England and northern Europe, samplers soon acquired distinctively American characteristics. Authority Mary Jaene Edmonds has determined that samplers were created in American classrooms

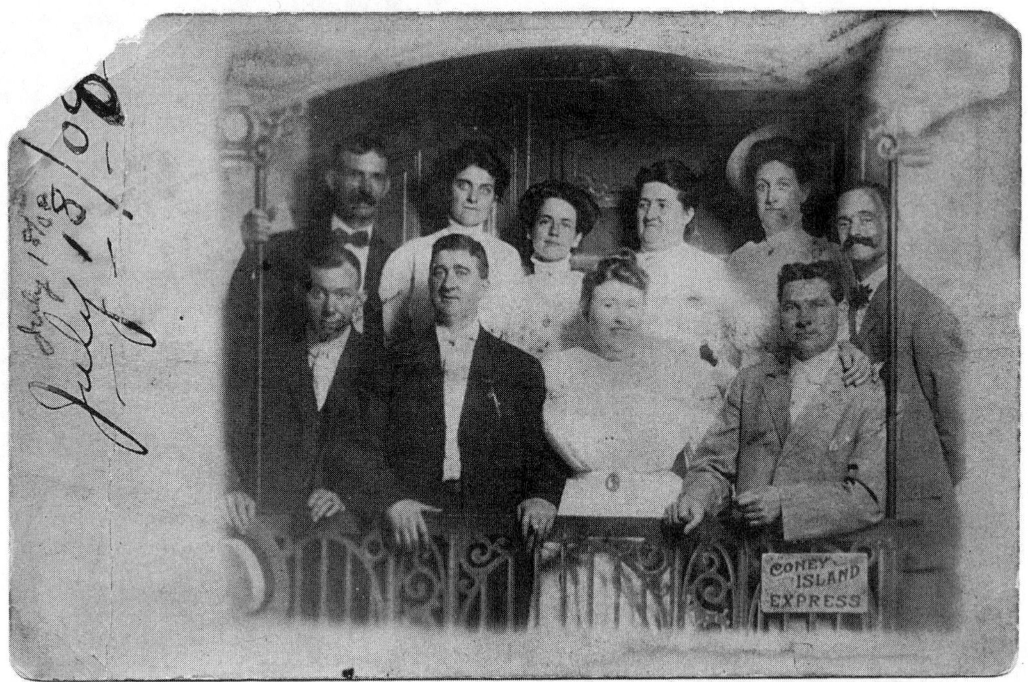

Figure 1-7. 1908 Coney Island postcard. Postal regulations after 1907 permitted correspondence on the back of each card. From the collection of Margaret Pyburn.

This photograph of the village of Paricutin (Mexico) can be dated by the size of the volcano in the background, and by the fact that the volcano was active only from 1943 until 1952. From the collection of Margaret Pyburn.

according to the instructions of teachers. Edmonds has connected numerous samplers back to the influence of private schoolmistresses, whose teachings can be seen in the selection of patterns and the methods of execution. Her studies could lead a family historian to place the making of an heirloom sampler in a particular time and period. Genealogical information was a favored topic of sampler makers, such as young Louisa H. Plympton (born 1812, Middlesex County, Massachusetts). She used the tree of life design to stitch the names and birth dates of six Plympton children (born 1806–1828) on six pieces of fruit hanging on the branches of a tree whose roots show their parents' names and marriage date (October 2, 1805).[3]

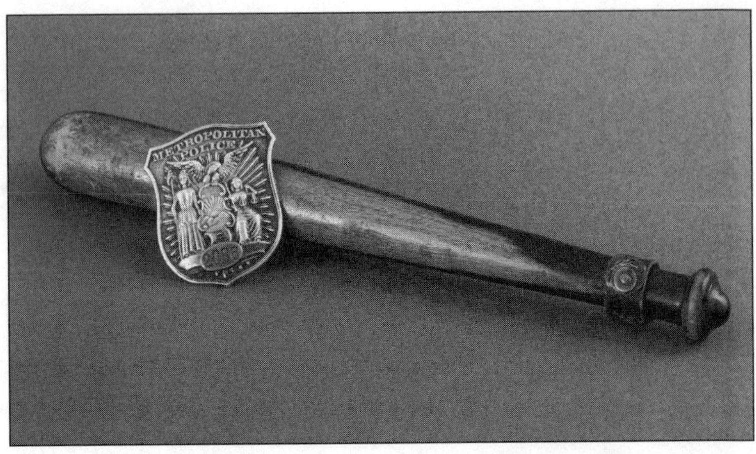

Figure 1-8. Artifacts such as a policeman's night stick and badge that were handed down in the family were helpful in determining the occupation of an ancestor with a common name. Knowing the occupation of the policeman made it possible to identify him in city directories, newspaper stories, and census records. Courtesy of Loretto Szucs.

Other Artifacts. Not all home sources contain as much obvious family information as does the sampler described previously, yet even the most unlikely of trinkets can be revealing by providing identifiers that direct or define a search.

One researcher discovered a police badge (figure 1-8) among her family's home possessions. There was little on it to connect the original owner to a particular police department or time period, yet it opened doors otherwise closed. This object provided an indicator, in this case to an occupation, which distinguished the ancestor from the many other urban dwellers of the same name. Knowledge of the police connection enabled the researcher to track its owner through several years of city directories, providing a given name for the family member, an approximate year of death, and the year of arrival in the city. With these facts, the researcher was able to venture into records of immigration, death, and probate, a difficult task in an urban area.

Jewelry is often a valued family heirloom and can provide genealogical clues as well. A date or a name inscribed on a locket suggest who the owner may have been. If a piece of jewelry has monetary value, it may be fairly easy to date. A book that may help in dating late-nineteenth-century jewelry and perhaps identify a place or manufacturer of origin is Ann Mitchell Pitman's *Inside the Jewelry Box*. Maureen DeLorme's *Mourning Art and Jewelry* gives the history of the memorial art forms. Many color photos depict portrait miniatures, paintings and sculpture, and hair-work memorials, including jewelry that contained locks of hair of the departed.

The dating of antiques, such as furniture or other collectibles, is more complicated. Few family historians are experts in this art, and most will benefit from the professional help available from museums and historical societies. Take the object or a photograph of it to a curio shop or antique show where there are knowledgeable and reliable dealers. Seek more than one opinion, but be willing to pay for such consultations.

"Home" Sources Outside the Home

Not every family is fortunate enough to possess a collection of home sources. For those who have scarcely a photograph or a piece of heirloom jewelry, the initial steps will include a search for artifacts or manuscripts that may have been moved to other places.

A distant relative, a former neighbor, or a one-time business associate of the family may possess photographs or correspondence exchanged a generation or more ago. Or these persons may have knowledge of more distant holders of such artifacts. A researcher who practices tact, patience, and persistence could discover a treasure trove of memorabilia in another's possession. If so, do not expect instant access to what may be valued materials. Instead, establish yourself as a caring, considerate seeker of information and one who is willing to share what you have acquired.

The Internet has become a quick and wonderful way to find old photographs, documents, and heirlooms. Megan Smolenyak's website <http://honoringourancestors.com/library_orphan.html> points to dozens of articles and related websites that are dedicated to returning "orphan" artifacts to families or individuals who seek them. Family trees and locality and surname message boards on sites such as RootsWeb.com and Ancestry.com can also be surprisingly successful in locating precious mementos that have been lost to family members over the years.

Flea markets, antique dealers, and county fairs in the region from which a family came are all potential places to find materials that, even if not specifically linked to your family, can reveal much about the era and location in which they lived. Explore local and regional archives and museums for evidence of your family's past. When visiting the hometown or city where family members once lived, take time to view photographs or collectibles exhibited by area museums or historical societies. These agencies may hold important manuscript materials that might include Civil War correspondence, business records of companies that employed relatives, or the private papers of former neighbors who were prominent in the community. The Clearwater Historical Museum in Orofino, Idaho, holds more than 4,500 historical photographs and artifacts from the Clearwater River drainage region, east and west from the Montana border to the Clearwater River and Snake Rivers at Lewiston, north and south of Shoshone County into parts of Idaho. The collection includes Nez Perce Indian history and artifacts, the history and tools of gold mining and the logging industry, and the antique guns, fine china, and turn of the century medicinal and barber tools brought into the area by early settlers. Pictures of some of their exhibits are online at <www.clearwatermuseum.org>.

There are a number of good finding aids to locate collections of family papers that have left the family's possession and found their way into a repository, perhaps in a distant city. Such collections might include diaries, correspondence, or legal documents acquired by earlier generations, or significant photograph collections that are annotated. *The National Union Catalog of Manuscript Collections*, described in chapter 3, "General References and Guides," can help to locate manuscripts by the name of a family or individual.

Organizing Home Sources

Once you have acquired some information about an object's origin or the date of its creation, prepare a written record of it. Photograph each precious item and arrange the pictures in an archival photo album. Leave space to record all that is known about the object, including professional or personal opinions of value, origin, and age.

A home sources album is good for insurance purposes as well as for preserving background information. It provides a photographic record for the identification of possessions and can help to manage an otherwise overwhelming collection of artifacts or written materials. The amount of organizing and the system you employ will depend on how many home sources you have. Small collections can be grouped by type: artifacts, wearables, or photographs. If you have a Bible, two diaries, several letters, and a journal, the category might be "communication or written." Larger collections of a single category can be subdivided chronologically.

Regardless of the type or amount of material you possess or the system you adopt, managing possessions by organizing and cataloging them makes good sense. One benefit is that you can effectively use the information without excessive handling of the objects. Substituting photographs of home sources (especially those most often referred to for research purposes) allows you to place the originals in a safe location.

After the collection is divided into categories, the inventory begins. Design a simple inventory form that has headings for inventory date, person or persons conducting the inventory, category of home source, and its ultimate destination. List each item, provide a description, note its condition, context (where it was found or is usually kept), any genealogically relevant information it contains, and whatever is known or surmised about its origin.

Computer database programs provide an excellent way to organize such information. A carefully designed database will allow you to print a list of holdings in a variety of ways: by type of object, by date or origin, by name of original possessor, or by present or future caretaker, for example. Enhance the database by adding similar information on all family holdings—even those that some family members may refuse to share or exchange. Suggestions for cataloging appear in Ann Carter Fleming's *The Organized Family Historian* and Rhonda R. McClure's *Digitizing Your Family History*.

Family members who cannot bear to part with objects may permit photographs and/or written summaries to be made. They are more likely to do so if, in exchange, they receive similar information from other holders of home sources.

Preservation of Home Sources

The condition of some items may require an attempt at restoration. If you are not familiar with the techniques necessary to restore or preserve antiques or manuscript material, two options are available. First, you can study a manual on restoration and determine if you are capable of restoring the artifact to your satisfaction. Two useful publications are *Caring for Your Family Treasures*, by Jane Long and Richard Long, and the briefer leaflet *Caring for Family Treasures*.

If time or skill limitations prohibit a do-it-yourself project, a second option is to call upon professionals. Contact area museums or historical societies to obtain the names of qualified persons. Talk to neighbors or antique dealers who have had experience with persons who restore or prepare items for preservation.

Important and irreplaceable photographs or picture postcards can be duplicated, often inexpensively. Artifacts, jewelry, clothing, and samplers can be photographed. Correspondence, Bible pages, diaries, and journals not durable enough to be photocopied can be transcribed (in script or type). Every care should be taken to ensure that the original is duplicated or described carefully in a permanent record.

One of the best methods of preservation is sharing. Provide other family members with items from your collection that may be of emotional value but are not critical to your genealogical record. Any item that can be reproduced in some fashion should also be shared. Not only does your benevolence lessen the risk of a major catastrophe destroying all family treasures, your kindness may encourage others to share with you.

Finally, when these most precious of objects need care beyond what you can provide, consider donating them to family members for safekeeping, or to historical societies, museums, or other places equipped to preserve and protect such items. Whatever you decide, contact the recipient in advance to be sure the person or organization is willing to accept the collection and to determine in what form or condition it would be most welcome. Plan wisely. Leaving a collection of fragile glassware to a library that specializes in printed matter may not be the wisest donation decision.

Collaborate to Grow Your Tree

Many family historians tend to think of genealogy as an individual hobby. Some genealogists lament that no one else in the family cares about the family's history. Usually, that is not the case. Family historians can, and should, interview all persons who have information about the family. The memories and other information obtained through interviews are invaluable in creating a family tree and building a foundation from which to start traditional research. In addition, the genealogical community has numerous avenues that can help you to expand your research. From message boards, to genealogy classes, to genealogical societies, the resources part of this network will prove to anyone that family history is a collaborative pursuit.

Interviews

Your research next moves to conversations and interviews with family members, friends, former neighbors, and perhaps people familiar with the history of a specific area. Their knowledge will supplement your own memories and provide a degree of perspective. Now is the time to capture the precious recollections of the oldest folks. Do not risk losing their important contributions.

Conducting Interviews

Your recollections, and those of others, are unique and vital to your family's story. As these memories undergo the rigors of examination, selection, evaluation, and recording, they become the foundation upon which additional research will be built.

Learning the date and place of your grandparents' marriage from family conversations could save weeks of frustration and expense in locating the official record of that event. One family's belief that "Great-Grandpa was a twin" was a key element in subsequent record searches in England. Although untrue, this conviction ultimately helped locate a sibling's birth record. Both men were born in the same year, the elder in January and the younger in November. Both fact and fiction have their place in your study, and both can provide important clues for future searches.

Oral interviewing is the primary technique by which memories are collected from family members or family friends and acquaintances. Information obtained in this manner can be extremely useful as long as one acknowledges that "human memory is a fragile historical source; it is subject to lapses, errors, fabrications and distortions."[4]

Good interviews do not just happen. You must prepare well for interviewing others. The American Association for State and Local History Book Series offers instruction in *The Oral History Manual* by Barbara W. Sommer and Mary Kay Quinlan. This guide gives techniques for planning, conducting, and transcribing an interview and includes checklists, reproducible forms, summary sheets, and extensive illustrations.

An important caution for new family historians who do not have interviewing experience is that "an interview is not a dialogue. The purpose of oral history interviews is to learn the *narrator's* story."[5] Other essential considerations include making advance arrangements and letting the narrator know what topics you want to discuss. Compile a list of questions, but let the narrator carry the discussion as long as it does not go too far astray. Watch for signs of fatigue and do not overstay your welcome. It is far better to have a narrator count the hours until you return than the minutes until you leave. If you take notes during the interview, examine them as soon as possible after the meeting. Elaborate on entries that are unclear. Consider topics that were not covered or questions that remain unanswered.

The use of a digital or standard audio recorder (with the permission of the person being interviewed) is most successful if you have practiced with the recording equipment in advance. Be sure to bring spare tapes and batteries to the session. As soon as possible afterwards, transcribe the resulting tapes. An interview at risk due to equipment failures or unintelligible conversation might be reconstructed from your notes and recollections if they are still fresh in your mind.

Video cameras and tape recorders can produce powerful supplements to your written record. Tips on how to use such equipment, as well as interviewing techniques, can be acquired from written guides, such as Rob Huberman and Laura Huberman's *How to Create a Video Family History*. Again, common sense prevails: make the narrator aware of the use of such equipment well in advance, practice with the equipment so that its use will not distract the speaker, and review the results as soon as is practical.

Camcorders move interviews away from the realm of "two chairs and a table." Interview sessions can be more informative when speakers perform routine tasks as they talk. Your grandmother may agree to bake bread without a recipe as she has done for years. A grandfather might demonstrate how he painstakingly sands the rungs on the seventh baby cradle he has made. Use the camera to tour the family home, filming the rooms and the outside environs. Visit the schools attended and parks frequented. Capture the past—even the recent past—as part of your family history worthy of preservation.

Of course, a personal visit may not be practical. You may not know where all your relatives are, especially if your family has been separated by divorce or adoption. To overcome this obstacle, try to gather relevant names and addresses from those with whom you are in contact. And make use of online networking resources (see "Networking" in this chapter) to find family members or others who can assist you with research.

Preserving Interviews

It is important to regularly refresh or make copies of cassettes and videotapes—migrating them to new formats—as they will degrade over time. Complicating things further is the fact that machines to play or read them may become obsolete and hard to find or replace. In a relatively short time, for example, the cumbersome reel-to-reel voice recorders were replaced by cassette players and mini cassette players, and home movie cameras were replaced with video cameras. The list of machines that have become obsolete in just a few short years is long and serves as a warning that popular machines used to read information today may not be available for long. Parts for existing machines will also be hard to find and it will be even more of a challenge to find someone to operate or repair them.

Even when they are stored under the best conditions, tapes have been known to self-destruct within just a couple of years, and some CDs and DVDs have been rendered useless in fewer than five years after they were created. Heat, light, high humidity, and dust are just some of the things that will hasten the deterioration of everything from paper to digital images. Storing records under ideal archival conditions will help to preserve them, but it is still advisable to convert these treasures to new media at least every two years.

Experts recommend creating an inventory of documents, photographs, digital albums, video tapes, cassettes, computer files, and heirlooms that have special meaning. It's one thing to gather and archive your precious personal history items, but another to ensure that they will be available and viewable well into the future. The keywords are migration and flexibility: migrate your digital data from format to format through the years and be flexible. Changes in technology are hard to predict, and it's important to be able to adapt. It pays to update your inventory on a yearly basis to make sure that the medium you have chosen is still valid.

Evaluating Traditions

Tradition is "the handing down of statements, beliefs, legends, customs, etc., from generation to generation, especially by word of mouth or by practice, in other words, a story that has come down to us by tradition."[6] Some cultures, such as African American and Native American, hold tradition in high regard as a way of preserving a past for which few written records survive. Anthropologists have found that when tradition is used to transmit culture and family history, the completeness and accuracy of the spoken word are likely to be carefully maintained by the storyteller.

Discovering information about the parents of an Austrian woman who had married a Native American of the Lakota Sioux tribe depended upon oral interviews with those who recalled the woman through tribal tradition. The details proved surprisingly accurate and led to the discovery of death dates and burial information about the woman's parents. The mother and father had followed their daughter to the Dakota reservation but soon departed. Oral tradition placed their destination as Chicago, and in this city were found the father's estate papers, which indicated that contact had been lost with one daughter—a daughter who resided on an Indian reservation.

Unfortunately, not all traditions contain as much truth as the one described previously. It is not uncommon for less-factual stories to follow a pattern, perhaps of separation, lost wealth, or thwarted opportunity. One common theme is that of the "separated brothers." Usually, in this account, three brothers immigrated and separated soon after their arrival in the United States. While there can be truth in such an account, it occurs so often as to be suspect.

Be skeptical about tales of unclaimed wealth. Southern variations may cite treasure buried to conceal it from Union soldiers during the Civil War. The East Coast version may include a castle and inheritance in Kent, Devon, or Surrey, denied the American immigrant. In the Midwest, lost wealth stories are linked to the Great Chicago Fire of 1871, i.e., the desperate family who watched the hired wagon speed away with their possessions before any family member could board.

Most traditions do contain a core of truth, an element that is surprisingly accurate and useful in research. The difficulty in proving these truths might be because the storyteller has assigned the activities to the wrong generation. More than one researcher has found "blended" generations a challenge to sort: was it Jacob's father or his grandfather who fought in the American Revolution? Or an imagined lack of records might discourage verification. To overcome these problems, a researcher must hone and refine the skills of problem solving. One way to do this is to study articles in which tradition or oral history is verified or disproved. Del E. Jupiter's "Matilda Madrid: One Woman's Tale of Bondage and Freedom" depicts methodology used to detect myth and evaluate evidence given in the 1887 testimony of a former slave woman.[7]

Consider all the stories, even those that seem doubtful. Attempt to substantiate each story through verification by others when possible (ask a second party to repeat the story but do not offer leading questions) or through public documents. Include the traditions in your written record, but carefully identify them as "tradition" and note the sources of the information. These citations will be useful as you analyze information with an eye to proving or disproving parts of it.

Note taking and interview skills and the assessment of memories and traditions are critical first steps in the research process. You will come to appreciate the necessity of preserving these memories and personal attributes of people who could move out of your life at any moment. Public records and archival collections, in all likelihood, will outlast the relatives and acquaintances who have knowledge of the family to share. That is why people, not records, provide one of our first sources of information.

Interviews also provide opportunities to locate and identify home sources. You may find a bounty of home sources including heirlooms, manuscript materials, and personally held copies of public records. Your interview notes should contain an illustration (sketch, photograph, or photocopy) and description of the item, the name of the item's holder, how the item was acquired, and as much explanatory information as can be obtained.

Your personal knowledge and memories, the home sources you locate, and the interviews you conduct are the first steps in family history research. Findings from such seemingly humble origins will thrust you into the larger arena of public records and, perhaps, more detailed facts, but you will return to these beginning steps often—each time with an awareness of the information previously collected.

Network to Expand Your Research

Networking—making contact with others who share similar interests—can speed your research progress. Have a research question? Try networking. At a crossroads and not sure in which direction to turn? Try networking. Need someone to talk to about your successes or frustrations? Again, try networking. Networking can take place online, by correspondence, or in person, and can include society membership, classroom participation, and workshop or national conference attendance.

Online

The Internet has changed the ways family historians communicate. E-mailing is a quick, inexpensive, and effective means to communicate. Technology allows the easy flow of e-mail with attached documents and photographs. It's common to hear stories about an individual who has shared a piece of family history with a distant cousin and then received copies of long-sought documents or photographs in return. A brief and polite e-mail to a potential, newfound, or well-known relative is often the beginning of a wonderful exchange. The chart in figure 1-9 will be useful in determining the relationship between you and the relative. When communicating via e-mail, traditional courtesies should be observed.

A mailing list is simply an e-mail party line: every message that a list subscriber sends to the list is distributed to all other list subscribers. Genealogy-related mailing lists can cover surnames, U.S. counties and states, other countries and regions, ethnic groups, and other topics. Subscribing to a mailing list is one of the best ways of connecting to people who share your interests. Many websites host mailing lists, including RootsWeb.com (with over 29,140 lists), Ancestry.com, and Genealogy.com.

A message board is a computerized version of the old-fashioned bulletin board. There are message boards focusing on surnames, localities, and many other topics. By posting a message to the appropriate message board, you create a record through which other researchers can find you. You'll find message boards on Ancestry.com, RootsWeb.com (with over 132,000 message boards), and Genealogy.com.

Some websites allow you to add "digital sticky notes" to content. On RootsWeb.com, these notes are called "Post-em Notes" and can be added to the Social Security Death Index (SSDI), the WorldConnect Project, or to other databases. Post-ems allow you to attach your e-mail address, a link to another website address, or other information to the records of any individual. On Ancestry.com these notes are called "Comments and Corrections." Use these to add to an individual's record alternate names or other comments about the person, both viewable by other researchers. On the Ellis Island website <www.ellisisland.com>, you can add annotations to individual records. All of these additions to records are viewable by other researchers and could potentially help in your research and connect you with other researchers. Search for your ancestors and leave your calling card attached to their names.

Online family tree databases can help you locate others interested in the surnames you are researching. These resources include the Pedigree Resource File on FamilySearch.org, Ancestry World Tree on Ancestry.com, and WorldConnect on RootsWeb.com. You can initiate contact by e-mail.[8] A number of online services also allow you to locate living individuals who may have family information to share.

Repositories/Libraries

There are many libraries, archives, and societies that have excellent and well-known collections of genealogical research materials. The names and contact information for repositories of importance to family historians are given within the chapters and appendixes of this book. Several of these repositories, particularly the smaller ones, maintain lists of researchers and the local area families they are researching.

The LDS Family History Library (FHL) of The Church of Jesus Christ of Latter-day Saints in Salt Lake City, Utah, is perhaps the most widely known repository of genealogical materials. The FHL has been acquiring and preserving genealogical data since its founding in 1894. The library has collected vital information on hundreds of millions of deceased individuals. This data includes print and microform copies of records from all over the

1	2	3	4	5	6	7	8	9
2	Brother/Sister	Aunt/Uncle or Nephew/Niece	Great Aunt/Uncle or Nephew/Niece	Great, Great Aunt/Uncle or Nephew/Niece	G.G.G Aunt/Uncle or Nephew/Niece	G.G.G G. Aunt/Uncle or Nephew/Niece	G.G.G.G.G. Aunt/Uncle or Nephew/Niece	G.G.G.G.G.G. Aunt/Uncle or Nephew/Niece
3	Aunt/Uncle or Nephew/Niece	FIRST COUSIN	First Cousin Once Removed	First Cousin Twice Removed	First Cousin 3 Times Removed	First Cousin 4 Times Removed	First Cousin 5 Times Removed	First Cousin 6 Times Removed
4	Great Aunt/Uncle or Nephew/Niece	First Cousin Once Removed	SECOND COUSIN	Second Cousin Once Removed	Second Cousin Twice Removed	Second Cousin 3 Times Removed	Second Cousin 4 Times Removed	Second Cousin 5 Times Removed
5	Great, Great Aunt/Uncle or Nephew/Niece	First Cousin Twice Removed	Second Cousin Once Removed	THIRD COUSIN	Third Cousin Once Removed	Third Cousin Twice Removed	Third Cousin 3 Times Removed	Third Cousin 4 Times Removed
6	G.G.G Aunt/Uncle or Nephew/Niece	First Cousin 3 Times Removed	Second Cousin Twice Removed	Third Cousin Once Removed	FOURTH COUSIN	Fourth Cousin Once Removed	Fourth Cousin Twice Removed	Fourth Cousin 3 Times Removed
7	G. G. G. G. Aunt/Uncle or Nephew/Niece	First Cousin 4 Times Removed	Second Cousin 3 Times Removed	Third Cousin Twice Removed	Fourth Cousin Once Removed	FIFTH COUSIN	Fifth Cousin Once Removed	Fifth Cousin Twice Removed
8	G. G. G. G. G. Aunt/Uncle or Nephew/Niece	First Cousin 5 Times Removed	Second Cousin 4 Times Removed	Third Cousin 3 Times Removed	Fourth Cousin Twice Removed	Fifth Cousin Once Removed	SIXTH COUSIN	Sixth Cousin Once Removed
9	G.G.G.G.G.G. Aunt/Uncle or Nephew/Niece	First Cousin 6 Times Removed	Second Cousin 5 Times Removed	Third Cousin 4 Times Removed	Fourth Cousin 3 Times Removed	Fifth Cousin Twice Removed	Sixth Cousin Once Removed	SEVENTH COUSIN

Figure 1-9. Relationship chart for determining family relationships. Do a simple problem first: find the relationship between you and your first cousin's granddaughter who shares a common ancestor (your grandparent). Steps: List the common ancestor in square #1. Put your name in square #3 in the top row. In the far left column, list your first cousin in square #3. List his or her granddaughter in square # 5 in the same column. Find the common square–in this example, First Cousin Twice Removed is the relationship between you and your first cousin's granddaughter. Adapted from the "Cousin-Finder" chart developed by N. Dale Talkington, McKinney, Texas.

world, which are made available at the library in Salt Lake City and at Family History Centers throughout the United States and in many foreign countries. Many of the records described in *The Source* have been microfilmed and a good portion are indexed and accessible by visit to the library or a family history center. A catalog of FHL sources is available online at <www.familysearch.org>. Appendix F provides further information about the Family History Library.

Societies

Family historians are usually willing to share findings and exchange ideas and research experiences. This camaraderie results in a vast system of societies working to preserve and make records available and to promote educational opportunities. Participation in society activities as a member and volunteer allows you to pay back some of what you will reap as the beneficiary of society activities and projects. Societies also provide educational opportunities, including instructional articles published in their periodicals, local skill-building sessions, and one- or two-day seminars featuring nationally-known professionals.

Hundreds of genealogical and historical societies across the country seek to preserve records and provide instruction to family historians. Many groups form at the county level because of the research significance of local area records. Organizations also exist to study a single surname or the descendants of a particular couple (see appendix B, "Family Associations"). Ethnic or religious origins account for many such groups, such as the Polish Genealogical Society of America and P.O.I.N.T.—Pursuing Our Italian Names Together. Other societies bring together researchers with common locales of origin, for example, the Palatines to America and Germans from Russia societies.

Virtually all states have a state genealogical society, a state council, or both. In addition to major projects, a state-level group might coordinate the efforts of local societies within the state. Their publications (newsletters and journals) supplement those produced by local societies. Some state organizations, such as the Ohio Genealogical Society, offer chapter membership throughout the country. Other state organizations operate on a less-structured basis.

At the national level, a number of organizations serve individual genealogists or societies. The Federation of Genealogical Societies (FGS) <www.fgs.org> is an umbrella organization for genealogical and historical societies and research institutes such as libraries and archives. The National Genealogical Society (NGS) <www.ngsgenealogy.org> is comprised of individual researchers. The oldest society in the United States is the New England Historic Genealogical Society (NEHGS) <www.nehgs.org>, which celebrated its sesquicentennial in 1995. Appendix C gives contact information for some state and national societies.

Volunteer Efforts

While most societies undertake valuable indexing and preservation activities and produce periodicals and other publications that benefit the genealogical community, there are also efforts by family historians working independently of societies. The availability of online indexes and databases are often the work of these volunteers, as are some national ventures to provide access to local records. The USGenWeb Project at <www.usgenweb.org> is a volunteer-driven site that publishes historical information and resource material such as cemetery indexes and newspaper abstracts. The sites they maintain often provide important local detail about an area's history, geography, and settlement, along with an overview of record availability and access and research tips. More information on USGenWeb is in chapter 2, "Computers and Technology."

Professional Groups

Family historians interact with professional genealogists in several ways. Professionals write articles and books and present lectures that provide new information and give examples of methodologies to help in difficult research situations. Professionals often lead efforts to protect records in jeopardy and to make them available for wide use. Many (but not all) professionals conduct research on a contract basis for others and can assist a family historian with a quest that seems impossible. The research that professionals do ranges from an entire lineage to small but significant tasks in their field of expertise.

In the United States, there are several groups that serve the interests of professional genealogists and their clients, as well as those of the genealogical community. The Association of Professional Genealogists (PO Box 40393, Denver, CO 80204-0393) is a membership organization that does not administer tests, award credentials, or otherwise endorse individual researchers. The association does offer arbitration in the event a dispute arises between any association member and the general public. The APG website at <www.apgen.org> lists members' names, contact details, and areas of expertise.

The Board for Certification of Genealogists (PO Box 14291, Washington, DC 20044) is a certifying body that is not affiliated with any group. BCG screens applicants through a testing process and successful candidates earn the initials CG (Certified Genealogist). A roster of certified genealogists is at the BCG website <www.bcgcertification.org>.

The International Commission for the Accreditation of Professional Genealogists (ICAPGen) offers independent testing without membership. This program, established in 1964 by the Family History Department of The Church of Jesus Christ of Latter-day Saints, is designed to examine and accredit researchers in specialized geographic areas. Those who successfully complete the program receive the initials AG (Accredited Genealogist). In 2000, the LDS Church transferred its ownership and administration of the program to ICAPGen, PO Box 970204, Orem, UT 84097-0204; <www.icapgen.org>.

The American Society of Genealogists (ASG) was founded in 1940 as an honorary society, limited to fifty lifetime members designated as Fellows (identified by the initials FASG). Election to the ASG is based on a candidate's published genealogical scholarship. A list of Fellows and news of the ASG Scholar Award is at the website <www.fasg.org>.

Education

Continuing education is a hallmark of genealogists, who recognize an ongoing need for skill and knowledge building. After the how-to guides (see Bibliography), local class offerings, regional workshops, national conferences, and week-long institutes loom. Institutes are intensive, multi-track programs oriented toward a variety of interests and skill levels. Institutes that have operated for more than a decade include the Genealogical Institute of Mid-America, Springfield, Illinois <www.rootsweb.com/~ilsgs>; the Institute of Genealogy and Historical Research, Birmingham, Alabama <www.samford.edu/schools/ighr>; the National Institute on Genealogical Research, Washington, D.C. <www.rootsweb.com/~natgenin>; and the Salt Lake Institute of Genealogy, Salt Lake City, Utah <www.infouga.org>.

Education can come via the Internet as well. One online course that has earned awards for excellence is *American*

Genealogy: A Basic Course, offered by the National Genealogical Society, Education Department, 3108 Columbia Pike, Suite 300, Arlington, VA 22204-4304 <www.ngsgenealogy.org>.

National conferences are held annually in different parts of the United States. For nearly four decades, the BYU Family History and Genealogy Conference at Brigham Young University in Provo, Utah, has served the genealogical community. For more information about the BYU conference, contact BYU Conferences and Workshops, 136 Harman Continuing Education Building, Provo, UT 84602 <http://genealogyconferences.byu.edu>.

Two national societies offer annual conferences that draw more than a thousand people to scores of lectures and a large display arena featuring vendors of family history products and services. Contact the National Genealogical Society, Conferences, 3108 Columbia Pike, Suite 300, Arlington, VA 22204-4304 <www.ngsgenealogy.org> or the Federation of Genealogical Societies, Conferences, PO Box 200940, Austin, TX 78720-0940 <www.fgs.org> for details of their upcoming conferences. For a full range of educational events of all kinds, use the Federation's online international calendar at <www.fgs.org>. Ancestry.com also offers online classes on a variety of topics <www.ancestry.com>.

Understand Developments in Technology

New technology has changed the way we conduct research and organize the results of our research and the way we publish information and share it on a global scale. Whether using personal computers or the online networks at libraries, family historians are locating and accessing research materials with a few keystrokes. Thousands of reference works and other items that were previously hidden or inaccessible are now identified and put within reach. Technology and a great surge of interest in the field have expedited the publication of enormous databases of census records, vital records, military records, cemetery records, and the like. In addition, the Internet and DNA testing are allowing some researchers to prove lineage in a way never imagined just twenty years ago. Understanding these advancements will simplify the way you conduct and organize your family history.

Internet

The Internet is changing the landscape of family history research, with more genealogical content being added daily. Still, many of the important records needed to complete family history research are not yet online and may not be digitized for years to come—if ever. A number of free online newsletters including the *Ancestry Weekly Journal, Eastman's Online Genealogy Newsletter*, and *RootsWeb Review* offer regular updates on the availability of records, new products and services, and articles written by experts to help family historians of every level of experience. Almost every chapter in this book includes relevant websites, and chapter 2 provides an in-depth discussion of the latest sources and methods for efficient use of computers and technology.

Family History Software

Computers have saved researchers countless hours that would have been wasted in transcribing original records and organizing materials. A wide variety of computer software that facilitates and enhances genealogical research is available. Genealogical programs, such as *Family Tree Maker, Personal Ancestral File* (PAF), and *The Master Genealogist,* make it possible for you to enter names, dates, places, and relationships for an individual into the computer only once, whereupon the program will automatically recognize the individual and link him or her to the appropriate family and generation.

Because new genealogical software programs regularly come on the market, and those already in use are constantly being upgraded, it would be difficult to detail specific products here. A good way to stay informed of what is happening in this quickly changing arena is to participate in one of the many computer interest groups associated with genealogical societies.

Tools and Electronic Files

Much computer hardware, software, and tools, though not made specifically for family history use, are beneficial for family history projects. Pamela Boyer Porter, in her FORUM column "Digitools" identifies aids such as high-speed Internet access and a wireless network as being timesavers for online searching and retrieval.[9] A thumb (or jump) drive takes up little room in a briefcase yet allows for collecting images from the microfilm-to-digital-image copier at the Family History Library. Other devices include a digital camera to photograph everything from tombstones to documents to living relatives; a PDA (Personal Digital Assistant) to keep a genealogy database; and a scanner to reproduce photographs and other documents. Other items to consider are desktop publishing software which has opened new avenues for disseminating family information through personal letters, newsletters, and books, and sound and video editing software that makes it possible to turn sound clips and video into movies and other family history projects.

Computers offer many ways to store and preserve your family history research and projects. Electronic files can be stored on a computer's hard drive, on CDs and DVDs, or on other storage devices. Photo-editing software enables you to restore old photographs and share them with others. A favorite picture of one family historian's grandparents' wedding day was scanned into a computer. Duplicates of the scanned file were stored on the hard drive and on a CD. Photo-editing software was used to clean the scanned image of defects that appeared on the original picture. The restored image was then sent to family

Genetic Genealogy

Donn Devine, CG, CGI

One of the newest developments in genealogy is the use of DNA (deoxyribonucleic acid) as a source of genealogical information. DNA is the substance within every living cell that carries the code for passing on its exact makeup to new cells, and although DNA is uniquely different for each individual, it is similar in cells of related individuals. As applied to genealogical research, distinctive DNA patterns can be used to determine whether and how closely individuals are related to other individuals whose DNA patterns are known.

Genealogical DNA testing looks at the non-coding portions of the DNA strand (sometimes misleadingly called junk DNA) that have no known function. For the most part, these stretches of DNA remain unchanged from generation to generation. However, chance changes, called mutations or polymorphisms, do occur at infrequent intervals, and it is these changes that let us distinguish different lines of descent and determine how closely people may be related to each other from the closeness of their DNA matches. A DNA sequence that is passed on unchanged from one parent to a child is called a haplotype, and these are the distinctive patterns we use to establish genealogical links.

Two Types of DNA

Y chromosome DNA is found only in males and is the type most frequently used in genealogy because almost all of it passes as a single haplotype from father to son, essentially unchanged except for chance mutations. This type of DNA is used to identify a common male ancestor in all-male genealogical lines.

mtDNA is a haplotype that children inherit only from their mothers and can be used to identify all-female genealogical lines. Two people who share the same mtDNA haplotype have a common female ancestor in their all-female maternal lines. But, because mtDNA mutates much more slowly than Y-DNA, she may be too many generations back to identify or be of genealogical significance.

Genealogical Uses for DNA Tests

Additional Identity Item

For those ancestors at the head of an ancestral line, for whom we may know little more than a name and event date or place, a DNA sample from an appropriate descendant will provide the same pattern present in the ancestor, in the absence of any chance mutation along the way. For many family historians, a test of their own DNA is often their first step, providing a genetic signature for a distant paternal-line or maternal-line ancestor. Matching samples from two descendants through different lines provides assurance that the common ancestor's DNA sequence descended unchanged, with no mutation in either line.

Verifying Probable or Suspected Relationships

Verifying relationships is perhaps the most frequent use being made of DNA, as tests can quickly determine whether any two men descend from a common ancestor through their the all-male surname line or whether any two people of either sex are related through their all-female maternal lines to a common female ancestor. However, the number of generations to the common ancestor, if not known from other sources, can be only estimated. A widely publicized example of this application was the Jefferson-Hemings study. There were no sons from President Thomas Jefferson's marriage, but DNA tests showed that a male-line descendant of his slave Sally Hemings shared the same DNA as descendants in two male lines from the president's Jefferson grandfather, proving that a Jefferson fathered at least one of Hemmings's children.[a]

Sorting Family Lines

People with the same surname frequently come from very different ancestral origins. DNA can show which share a common heritage, can show which are unrelated, and, with enough samples associated with ancestral localities of origin, can point modern descendants to their family's geographic origin. For example, there were four families named Smolenyak living near each other in the tiny Slovak village of Osturma, but DNA tests on male Smolenyak descendants from each of the four families showed they were unrelated through the surname line.[b]

Family Reconstruction

Family and surname associations use DNA to confirm links in lines where records are ambiguous or less than convincing. Associations are also establishing previously unknown links of some members' lines to known founder-ancestors. The Stidham Family Association sought proof that two lines, with problematic record links, truly descended from a seventeenth-century ancestor. DNA provided the assurance, but also revealed that another line, with clear documentary evidence of descent, was not biologically connected to the ancestor.[c]

Future Promise

The rest of our DNA, called *autosomal* DNA, is widely used for forensic identification and for verifying paternity but so far has found only limited use in genealogy because individuals receive DNA from each of their parents, which combines to form the individual's DNA. In each following generation, the genetic code is further diluted as DNA passes to a new generation. Most sections of our autosomal DNA represent small haplotype sequences inherited from a relatively small number of unknown ancestors among the thousands we had tens of generations back. Autosomal DNA is likely to find more uses in genealogy as a result of research now underway to identify inheritance patterns for haplotype segments in the DNA of the recombining chromosomes. The Sorenson Molecular Genealogy Foundation is testing sample donors from all over the world, comparing inherited DNA sequences on all their chromosomes with genealogies submitted by the donors (visit <http://smgf.org> for more information.)

Another worldwide research project, the National Geographic Society's Genographic Project, is also searching for DNA markers that can be matched with geographic areas of ancestral origins.

Other laboratories are working on specific genealogical applications of data from autosomal chromosomes. One test of genealogical significance using autosomal DNA can help estimate deep roots. The results of this test are given in percentages, with rather wide confidence limits, and indicate how much of our genetic heritage comes from ancestral groups that originally lived in Sub-Saharan Africa, Europe (including western Asia and the Mediterranean fringe), East Asia, and the Americas. These tests may suggest avenues of research that might otherwise have been overlooked.

Notes

[a] E. A. Foster, et al., "Jefferson Fathered Slave's Last Child," *Nature* 396 (5 November 1998): 27–28.

[b] Family Tree DNA, "Spotlight: Smolenyak DNA Project," *Facts and Genes* 2 (11 August 2003), downloaded 30 May 2004 from <www.familytreedna.com/facts_genes.asp?act=show&nk=2.7>.

[c] Richard L. Steadham, "The Saga of How Our Project Evolved," with link to "Current Results of the Stidham DNA Study," updated 24 February 2004, downloaded 4 June 2004 from <http://homepages.rootsweb.com/~tstiddem/Pages/dna.html>.

Additional References

Arnason, Gardar, Salvor Nordal, Vilhjalmur Arnason, eds. *Blood and Data: Ethical, Legal and Social Aspects of Human Genetic Databases.* Reykjavik: University of Iceland Press, 2004.

Devine, Donn. "Sorting Relationships among Families with the Same Surname: An Irish American DNA Study." *National Genealogical Society Quarterly* 93 (December 2005): 283–93.

Fitzpatrick, Colleen, and Andrew Yeiser. *DNA & Genealogy.* Hoboken, N.J.: Rice Book Press, 2005.

Foster, E.A., et al. "Jefferson Fathered Slave's Last Child," *Nature* 396 (4 November 1998): 27–28.

Gormly, Myra Vanderpool. *Family Diseases: Are You at Risk?* Baltimore, Md.: Clearfield Press, 2002.

Hart, Anne. *How to Interpret Your DNA Test Results for Family History and Ancestry: Scientists Speak Out on Genealogy Joining Genetics.* San Jose, Calif.: Writers Club Press, 2002. Full text online at <www.elibron.com>.

Hartl, Daniel L., and Elizabeth Jones. *Essential Genetics: A Genomics Perspective.* Boston: Jones and Bartlett, 2006.

Johnson, Kirk. "Utah: The Perfect Genetics Lab: Big Family, Mormon Church Records, and Even 19th Century Polygamy are Proving a Boon to the Study of Genes and Genealogy." *New York Times Upfront* 137, no. 10 (14 February 2005): 18(2). HTML format by Scholastic Inc. <www.findarticles.com/p/articles/mi_go1634>.

Kurzweil, Ray. *The Singularity is Near: When Humans Transcend Biology.* New York: Viking Press, 2005.

Leary, Helen F. M. "Sally Heming's Children: Genealogical Analysis of the Evidence." *National Genealogical Society Quarterly* 89 (September 2001): 165–207.

Mielke, James H., Lyle W. Konigsberg, and John H. Relethford. *Human Biological Variation.* New York: Oxford University Press, 2006.

Shawker, Thomas H. *Unlocking Your Genetic History: A Step-by-Step Guide to Discovering Your Family's Medical and Genetic Heritage* (National Genealogical Society Guide, 6). Nashville, Tenn.: Rutledge Press, 2004.

Smith, Gina. *The Genomics Age: How DNA Technology is Transforming the way we Live and Who We Are.* New York: AMACOM-American Management Association, 2004.

Smolenyak, Megan, and Ann Turner. *Tracing Your Roots with DNA: Using Genetic Tests to Explore Your Family Tree.* Emmaus, Pa.: Rodale Books, 2004.

Websites

Genetic Studies

International Society of Genetic Genealogists (ISOGG) <www.isogg.org>

The Sorenson Molecular Genealogy Foundation <www.smgf.org>

World Families Network, "DNA Surname Project List" <www.dnalist.net>

Commercial DNA Search Firms

African Ancestry, Inc.<www.africanamerican.com>

DNA Fingerprint, Stahnsdorf, Germany <http://dna-fingerprint.com>

DNA Heritage, Dorset, UK <www.dnaheritage.com>

DNA Print Genomics <www.dnaprint.com>

Ethnoancestry <http://ethnoancestry.com>

Family Tree DNA <www.familytreedna.com>

GeneTree <www.genetree.com>

Relative Genetics <www.relativegenetics.com>

Trace Genetics <www.tracegenetics.com>

members via e-mail and the prized original picture was stored in a safe container. In this way, the original image is preserved for future generations while many family members enjoy the picture today. For more information, see George C. Morgan's *How to Do Everything with Your Genealogy* and Rhonda McClure's *Digitizing Your Family History*.

Record Your Findings

The information you acquire, collect, and record needs to be organized into a format that is easily understood by you and by others. Once your information is organized, you (and those after you) can evaluate this information to decide what to look for next (and where to look for it) and to avoid duplication in research. The following sections describe how to make the most of traditional organization methods and how to analyze findings to obtain needed information and to help set goals for additional research.

Organization and Documentation

Memories and observations are vulnerable to the ravages of time and should be preserved as soon as possible. Recording and organizing what you remember and what you learn will do more than document and preserve your findings, it will structure your investigation, enabling you to use your research time more wisely and productively. Good record-keeping practices identify what has been found in research and what has yet to be accomplished. What will a box or notebook full of jumbled research notes and documents mean to the person who may come across it months or years from now?

Family Trees and Research Logs

Most researchers use pedigree charts, family group records, and research logs to keep track of their genealogy. Whether paper based or in software, these charts and logs use similar formats and concepts. Pedigree charts provide an overview of generations or lines of descent (figure 1-10). Pedigree charts are "works in progress" where missing entries show areas in which further research is needed.

To organize what is known about a couple and their children, researchers use family group sheets (figure 1-11). These forms provide spaces to record names, parents, children, spouses, dates and places of events, and other information to help identify members of a particular family. Whereas the pedigree chart is an overview of a family line, the family group record organizes and presents detailed information about a specific family.

The research activity log, also called a calendar, lists sources checked. Annotations can indicate what, if anything, was revealed by the source. The research activity log (figure 1-12) is a diary of all sources checked. Because a single entry is made for each source consulted or document (record) acquired, the log is the single most efficient way to keep track of what has been examined. A well-kept research activity log is also a table of contents to the research notes and documents acquired. The assigning of source numbers to each document makes the log a cross-reference to the entries on the family group record.

While some researchers record all research activity onto one centralized form (the research activity log), others prefer to maintain separate logs of Internet research or of correspondence. Their formats are similar to the research activity log, but these auxiliary records reflect ongoing activity that often requires a

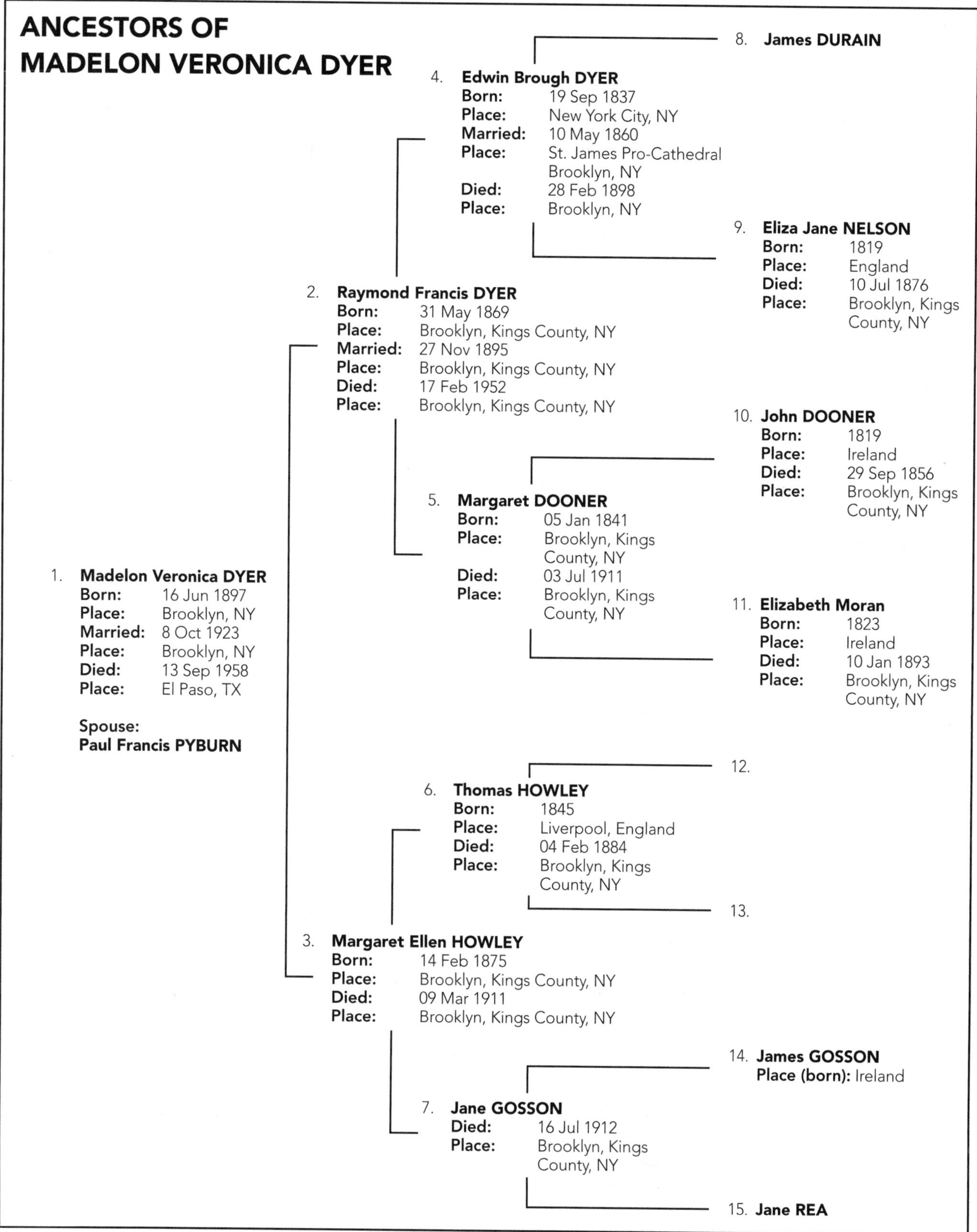

Figure 1-10. This pedigree chart showing the ancestors of Madelon Veronica Dyer depicts her paternal line through her father, Raymond Francis Dyer, by identifying his parents and his grandparents. Her maternal line is shown through her mother, Margaret Ellen Howley, whose parents are listed. Margaret's maternal grandparents, the parents of Jane Gosson, are shown but not the parents of Thomas Howley, indicating they remain unknown.

great deal of follow up. These two additional logs keep URLs, postal addresses, and other contact information in one place.

The website log is a chronological diary of sites visited and information extracted. Log entries can include more detail about randomly or seldom visited sites than for frequently visited sites. For often-used sites, a simple cross-reference could lead to a folder or notebook maintained for that site. For example, each visit to <www.familysearch.org> would be entered on the website log followed by the code for the collection of notes or printouts from that site. Use it to record a succinct evaluation of the quality of the site or data. Notes can indicate the surnames, dates, or locales that were checked on each visit.

A correspondence log is a table of contents to all telephone calls, letters, and e-mails sent and received. Entries are coded to separate note sheets taken for each occasion so that they can be easily retrieved. The correspondence log tells you if you replied to your aunt or if it has really been six months since you sent to New York City for a birth certificate. This log could show amounts of money that were sent to various agencies as well.

Although many family historians use or are switching to computer-based family tree software and logs, understanding how to use and keeping handy the paper-based charts is useful if you find yourself without a computer or if you prefer using paper. Printed forms for research record keeping may be purchased from genealogical societies or vendors or obtained free from the Internet (Ancestry.com provides these charts, which can be downloaded at <www.ancestry.com/trees/charts/ancchart.aspx>).

Source Files

For every source—interviews, photographs, birth certificates, military files, or other—consulted in the research process, there should be a document prepared to which you or others can easily refer to for information. Such a source document could be notes from an interview with your grandmother, transcripts of your great-grandfather's journal found in a repository, a photocopy of a birth certificate, or a digital scan of the front and back of a photograph. If information is the product of speculation (unproven or undocumented), the "document" would be a written summary of the evidence showing the evaluation process. The information found on the source document is entered into family tree software or onto a family group sheet so that you can see it in relation to other facts learned from other sources.

This family tree program or family group sheet entry also states where the source document can easily be found. There are many ways to file your source documents. Some people prefer to file all source documents as paper copies in filing cabinets or binders. Others prefer to keep digital duplicates of word

Family Group Record

Prepared By: Margaret Mary PYBURN — Relationship to Preparer: Granddaughter

Address: 4124 Trowbridge Street El Paso, Texas — Date: 16 Jan 2006 — Ancestral Chart #: 1 — Family Unit #: 3

Husband	Raymond Francis DYER [10]	Occupation(s): Carpenter			Religion: Roman Catholic
	Date—Day, Month, Year	City	County	State or Country	
Born	31 May 1869	Brooklyn	Kings	New York [2]	
Christened					Name of Church
Married	27 Nov 1895	Brooklyn	Kings	New York [3]	Name of Church: Sacred Heart
Died	17 Feb 1952	Brooklyn	Kings	New York [5]	Cause of Death
Buried	20 Feb 1952	Cem/Place: Holy Cross Cemetery	Kings	New York [4]	Date Will Written/Proved: None
Father	"Captain" Edwin Brough DYER [5, 6, 7]	Other Wives			
Mother	Margaret DONER (DOONER) [5, 8]	None			

Wife maiden name	Margaret Ellen HOWLEY	Occupation(s): Housewife			Religion: Roman Catholic
Born	14 Feb 1875	Brooklyn	Kings	New York [5, 9]	
Christened	Unknown	Brooklyn			Name of Church
Died	9 March 1911	Brooklyn	Kings	New York [9]	Cause of Death
Buried	12 March 1911	Cem/Place: Holy Cross Cemetery	Kings	New York [9]	Date Will Written/Proved: None
Father	Thomas HOWLEY [9]	Other Husbands			
Mother	Jane GOSSON (GOSSEN) [9]	None			

✘	Sex M/F	Children Given Names	Birth Day Month Year	Birthplace City	County	St./Ctry.	Date of first marriage/Place / Name of Spouse	Date of Death/Cause / City County State/Country	Computer I.D. #
X	F	1 Madelon Veronica	16 Jun 1897 [1]	Brooklyn	Kings	NY	8 Oct 1923 [11] / Paul Francis PYBURN	13 Sep 1958 [11] / El Paso, El Paso, Texas	--
	M	2 Edwin Brough	18 Aug 1899 [1]	Brooklyn	Kings	NY	Nanette TAYLOR [11]	1 Dec 1926—Brooklyn [11] / Effects of WWI Mustard Gas	
	F	3 Muriel Agnes	3 Jan 1902 [1]	Brooklyn	Kings	NY	27 Nov 1929 [11] / Joseph Raymond	26 Nov 1960 [11] / Brooklyn, Kings, NY	
	F	4 Ethel Marie	16 Oct 1903 [1]	Brooklyn	Kings	NY	15 Jan 1928 [11] / Edwin C. ROSS	29 Jan 1992 [11] / Larkspur, Douglas, CO	
	F	5 Marjorie Ellen	27 Sep 1906 [1]	Brooklyn	Kings	NY	Never married [11]	30 Oct 1945 [11] / Brooklyn, Kings, NY	
		6							

Figure 1-11. This example of a family group sheet uses superscript numbers to identify the source document that provided each particular entry. For example, the birth information for the husband, Raymond Francis Dyer (31 May 1869, Brooklyn, Kings County, New York), is from document #2. A description of this source document appears on the research activity log for Raymond Francis Dyer (see figure 1-12) as source number 2.

Research Activity Log for Raymond Francis Dyer		
Date of Search	**Results and Source Citation**	**Source Number**
22 March 1971	Photograph of children of Raymond and Margaret Dyer. Names and ages of children noted on the reverse side of the photograph dated June 1912, Brooklyn, New York. Photograph in the possession of the researcher, February 2006.	1
5 July 1973	Autobiographical sketch of Raymond Francis Dyer. Brooklyn, New York. Single-page, handwritten autobiographical sketch, dated 31 May 1890. Family papers in the possession of the researcher, February 2006.	2
1 October 1976	Marriage certificate, 27 November 1895, Church of the Sacred Heart, Brooklyn, New York. Certificate provided by church on 1 October 1976.	3
14 August 1977	Undertaker's record. John J. Malone, Undertaker, 2913 Newkirk Avenue, Brooklyn, New York, 29 February 1952. Family papers in the possession of the researcher, February 2006.	4
10 July 1978	Dyer grave marker, Holy Cross Cemetery, Brooklyn, New York.	5
1 August 1978	Death Certificate # 3218 of Captain Edwin Brough Dyer, dated 1 March 1898, Department of Health of the City of Brooklyn, New York.	6
15 September 1978	Obituary for Capt. Dyer. *The Brooklyn Citizen*, 28 February 1898, page 9.	7
11 July 1982	Edwin Dyer probate file #2309-98, 16 March 1898, County Surrogate's Court, Kings County, New York.	8
1 August 1982	Death certificate #5113 of Margaret Howley, dated 9 March 1911. The City of New York Health Department issued Brooklyn, New York, 9 March 1911.	9
3 January 1988	Raymond F. Dyer household, 1900 U.S. census, Kings County, City of Brooklyn, New York, E.D. 414, page 135, line 4, 15 Brooklyn Avenue. National Archives micropublication T623, roll 1062.	10
16 January 1993	List of family birth, marriage and death dates in letter to Margaret M. Pyburn (4124 Trowbridge Street, El Paso, TX 79903) from Muriel Julia Pyburn, (4305 Cambridge Street, El Paso, TX 79903) in a letter dated 16 January 1993, in possession of researcher, February 2006.	11
5 July 1993	Autobiographical sketch of Raymond Francis Dyer, Brooklyn, New York. Single-page, handwritten autobiographical sketch, dated 31 May 1949. Family papers in possession of the researcher, February 2006.	12

Figure 1-12. This page from the research activity log for Raymond Francis Dyer lists sources that have been checked and the resulting documents in chronological order (according to date of discovery). A number is assigned to each source document. When details from a particular document are entered onto a family group sheet, the entry is followed by the appropriate document number (in superscript format).

processing documents, sound and movie clips, and pictures and other digital scans.

An example of how this works is shown by the portrait of the children of Raymond F. Dyer (figure 1-13). This picture held notations on the back indicating the family's location in Brooklyn, New York, and the names of the family members. This information was transferred to a family tree program along with entries from many other sources (for example, census, deed, interviews, newspaper obituary, printed biography, or probate). The photograph, both front and back, was then scanned into a computer, saved as an electronic file on a CD, and printed out to be filed with other source documents for the family or individual. The information in the family tree program included notation to where the scans of the picture could be found.

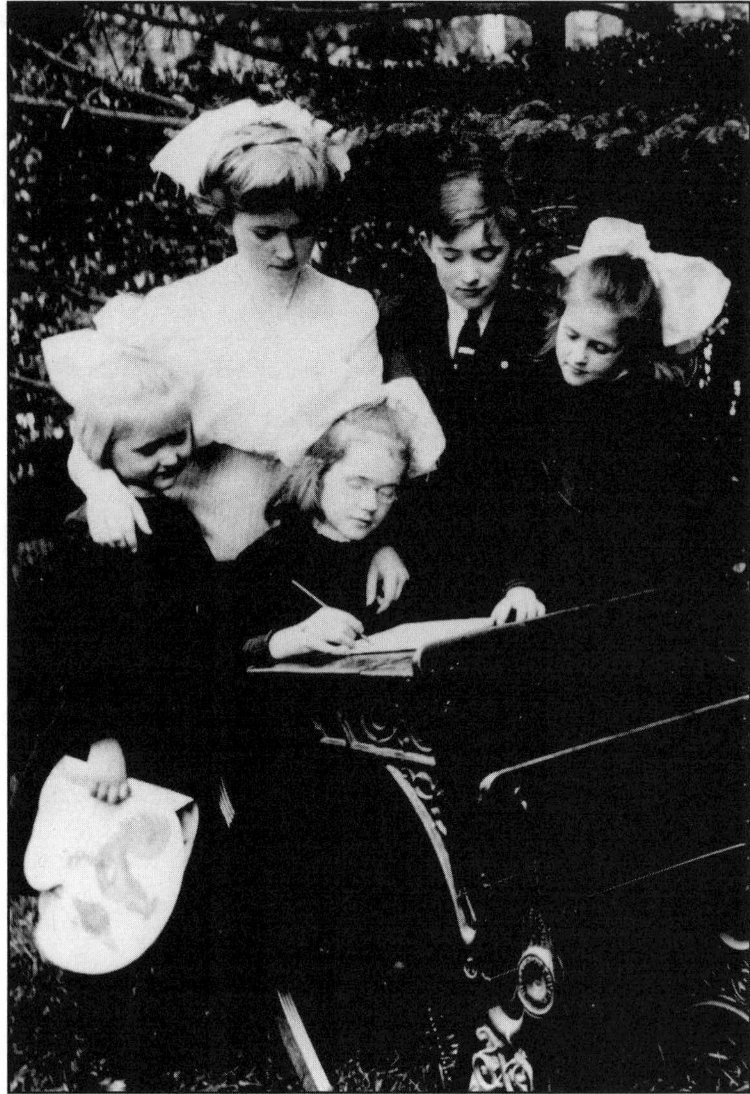

Figure 1-13. Photo taken about 1912 of the children of Raymond F. Dyer. Pictured clockwise (from eldest to youngest) Madelon, Edwin, Ethel, Muriel, and Marjorie. Courtesy of Margaret Pyburn.

The very process of extracting details from a document and entering the information onto a family tree program or family group sheet is an analytical one. By entering information from multiple documents, discrepancies in dates, spellings, or places of origin become obvious. However, care should be taken to ensure that entries are accurate, complete, and legible so that you and others can easily understand them at a later time. Many a research project has been misdirected because of faulty recording of vital information.

No organization system is exclusively correct. A family historian should adopt what is most comfortable and practical. Experts differ widely on how to keep notes and records, so don't be afraid to experiment and modify systems to meet your specific needs. Various methods are explained in "how-to" genealogy guides, available from booksellers and libraries everywhere. Sharon DeBartolo Carmack's *Organize Your Family History Research* describes and illustrates many ways to preserve research information by pen and paper or computer.

Documentation

As described previously, documenting sources for information recorded in your family history files helps you and others verify quickly where information came from and where it can be easily found again if needed. Thus taking time now to document all your sources can save time later. Unfortunately, many family historians have made it a practice to publish or otherwise disseminate research results with incomplete or even without citations of the sources from which their information was derived. Patricia Law Hatcher states, "for every statement of fact—a date, a place, a name, or a relationship—you must provide a citation. A citation states where you found that piece of information."[10]

The specific footnote style is up to author of the family history. *The Source* uses the widely accepted *Chicago Manual of Style*, supplemented on genealogical points by Elizabeth Shown Mills's *Evidence! Citation & Analysis for the Family Historian*. The important point is to indicate sources in an economical yet comprehensive format so that other researchers can judge the quality of the proof and know where to find the cited sources. If the source is "Personal interview, 12 February 2006, with Mable Ann (Alton) Jones, Upper Fairfax, Pierce Co., Washington," say so. If the information is from a will not seen but given in a published abstract of probates, indicate so: "Halifax Co., N.C., wills 3:377, Edward Montford, 3 Nov. 1801, proved Aug. ct. 1802, as cited in Margaret M. Hofmann, *Genealogical Abstracts of Wills 1758 through 1824, Halifax County, North Carolina* (Weldon, N.C.: Roanoke News Co., 1970), p. 121."

Unless you are meeting the requirements of a publisher, it is far more important to be consistent, complete, and efficient than it is to use any given style. If you want to publish a family history in genealogical publications or have it considered by a lineage society or certification group, check their style and make sure your documentation conforms to their requirements.

Numbering Systems

If you decide to compile a family history, or if you run across a compiled or published family history during your research, knowledge of numbering formats is useful. In a numbering system, each individual is assigned a unique identification number that distinguishes him or her from other members in the compilation. A good numbering system allows the user to easily follow lines down through descendants or back toward the original ancestors. Use a system that is recognized by professionals as being adequate. Do not succumb to the temptation to develop your own "personal" numbering system. The best systems are those that are easily understood, well-established, and refined as needed over the years.

Joan Ferris Curran, Madilyn Coen Crane, and John H. Wray's *Numbering Your Genealogy*, elaborates on two systems—the *National Genealogical Society Quarterly* System and the Register System, originated in 1870 by the New England Historic Genealogical Society.

Evaluation and Goal Setting

This volume is replete with potential sources for exploring your family history. Some records will be easily accessed and have a reputation for yielding the kind of biographical information that is essential for building reliable accounts of individuals and families. Most sources, such as census records, will be visited and revisited many times. A good way to become comfortable with sources is to first collect all records, private and public, that pertain to you; then do the same for your parents and grandparents. Confining first-steps research to the twenty-first century provides a good foundation for earlier and often more difficult research. This approach enables you to learn general methods for locating, comparing, and evaluating records and acquire good record-keeping procedures. At the same time, research is being done from the present to the past.

After working with various sources you will be able to rank them according to priority and reliability with more precision. You will soon learn that although records that are accessible and most likely to solve problems should be consulted first, no record should remain undiscovered. A family history is the sum of information from *all* records, and even the hard-to-find or difficult-to-interpret source materials should be consulted.

Research Notes

Two basic record-keeping skills assume great importance in evaluating research. The first is making notes or a transcript. The second is drafting a summary of findings. Clear and accurate recording will help you and others easily understand notes or summaries after the interview, record, or other event has cooled in your mind.

Notes can be informal, such as key points jotted down during an interview of a family member. Keep the entries concise and to the point. If you choose to abbreviate certain words or terms, a key to explain the abbreviations should accompany your notes.

A transcript is a more formal form of note taking. A transcript is a full and complete copy of an original record that may be too fragile to photocopy. Instead, a written or typed copy must be created. Every detail is left intact and there must be no alteration of original wording, intent, or length.

Whether creating notes or a transcript, all opinions or conclusions made by the note taker should be set apart by brackets. This allows the reader to differentiate between original content and the note-taker's commentary. Enter the full date when the note or transcript was made, the site of the note-taking, and the name of the note-taker on each page. Pages should be consecutively numbered. Instructions on note-taking and transcribing (or its condensed versions, the extract or abstract) are in the *BCG Genealogical Standards Manual*, pages 2–8.

Research Summaries

The second skill is to draft regular summaries of your findings. Summaries serve as a report to those who are interested in your work, such as relatives or others searching the same family. Summaries can also encourage in-depth analysis of evidence by providing a new look at material that previously appeared only in chart form. Two ways to summarize findings are narratives and timelines. Both take information from family group sheets and reassemble it into a new format. Whichever style is used, it is critical to link each entry (name, date, place) to the source of information from which it came. This is usually done through references, either using footnotes or endnotes to cite the source.

The most basic summary style is to present the information in narrative form. Novices and experienced researchers alike can benefit from creating short narratives at every stage of their work. A narrative can be as simple as an informal collection of paragraphs about an ancestor or as elaborate as a multi-generational family history suitable for publication. For most researchers, the simple paragraph narrative is the precursor to publication. You need not be an award-winning author to present your findings in this manner. Compose an accurate and concise summary of your research steps and a condensed version of your findings. For added interest, see Patricia Law Hatcher's "Adding Detail to Your Narrative."[11]

The family history timeline, or chronology is another excellent summary tool. This is an outline of events, organized by dates, in the life of a particular person or a span of time in the existence of a family (figure 1-14). A timeline can be an effective research tool. In "The Perspective of Timelines," Laura G. Prescott notes, "Timelines provide us with an orderly, encapsulated view of the past. They are clear and structured ways to help us make connections, solve puzzles, and interpret lives."[12]

The timeline will reveal gaps in research by highlighting omissions of data. For example, the lack of a timeline entry for a man who was living in this country in 1930 needs either an explanation or more census work. It may prove helpful to introduce historical events into the timeline but keep in mind that local events often influenced a subject's life even more than some national events. The opening of the Brooklyn Bridge was a marvel to many but probably did not alter the lives of most non-Brooklyn people. However, as a local event, its influence was significant. A timeline should thus include events of regional significance that may dictate the availability of records (a tornado that destroyed a courthouse, for example).

Consider timelines and narratives to be research status reports that point out inconsistencies, omissions, and potential pursuit opportunities. Regardless of how findings are presented, the resulting summaries should insure that others can reconstruct your research activities. This is achieved by using endnotes or footnotes to give full citations to the source of the information and when and from where the source was acquired. Elizabeth Shown Mills's *Evidence!* gives examples.

Finding Compiled Information

At an early point in our research, it is critical to investigate the possibility that someone may have published a genealogy or has otherwise made available information on your family. How frustrating to spend years researching a family only to learn the entire line was thoroughly researched and well documented in an award-winning family history. It is equally frustrating to spend hundreds of dollars in search of a date of death when the information was posted on a genealogy website long before you even started research and remains there today.

Conduct a general survey to learn what is in print or published online on your ancestor or on the family name. Many libraries have been the recipients of published and manuscript family histories. Begin by checking, online or off, the catalogues of the libraries which serve the areas in which your family lived. Then search the catalogues of the Family History Library of The Church of Jesus Christ of Latter-day Saints (LDS Church) in Salt Lake City, Utah, the Library of Congress in Washington, D.C., and the Allen County Public Library in Fort Wayne, Indiana. These three repositories hold some of the largest collections of family histories.

A number of Internet sites, including Ancestry.com and ProQuest, have published local and family histories online. A project of Brigham Young University is to digitize family histories, many of which are out of print. One easy way to access those that have been digitized is to use the link from the history's title entry in the Family History Catalog at <www.familysearch.org>.

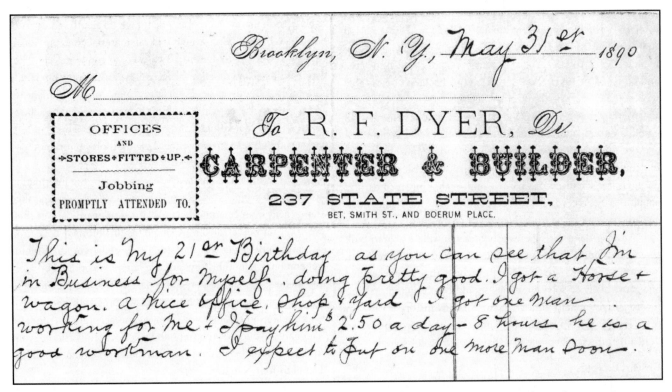

Brooklyn, N. Y., May 31st 1890

M

OFFICES AND STORES FITTED UP. Jobbing PROMPTLY ATTENDED TO.

To R. F. DYER, Dr.

CARPENTER & BUILDER,

237 STATE STREET,

BET. SMITH ST., AND BOERUM PLACE.

This is my 21st Birthday as you can see that I'm in Business for myself. doing pretty good. I got a Horse + wagon. a nice office. shop + yard I got one man working for me + I pay him $2.50 a day - 8 hours he is a good workman. I expect to put on one more man soon.

Excerpt from the personal journal of Raymond F. Dyer, May 31, 1890, on his twenty-first birthday. Courtesy of Loretto Szucs.

Time Line for Raymond Francis DYER

1869, May 31	born 117-119 Tillary Street, Brooklyn, New York [1]
1883, June	graduated from Christian Boys School, St. James Academy, Brooklyn, New York [2]
1883	employed at Artist Engravers Office, 90 Nassau Street, New York, New York [3]
1890	Celebrated 21st birthday, self-employed at 47 State Street, Brooklyn, New York[4]
1895, November 27	Married Margaret Ellen Howley in Brooklyn, New York[5]
1897, June 16	daughter Madelon born at 480 Halsey Street, Brooklyn, New York [6]
1902, December 01	employed by Board of Education, Brooklyn, New York[7]
1936, September 01	retired[8]
1952, February 17	died at 2044 Nostrand Avenue, Brooklyn, New York[9]

[1] Autobiographical sketch of Raymond Francis Dyer. Brooklyn, New York. Single-page, handwritten autobiographical sketch, dated 31 May 1949. Family papers in the possession of the researcher, February 2006.
[2] Ibid.
[3] Ibid.
[4] Autobiographical sketch of Raymond Francis Dyer. Brooklyn, New York. Single-page, handwritten autobiographical sketch, dated 31 May 1890. Family papers in the possession of the researcher, February 2006.
[5] Marriage certificate, 27 November 1895, Church of the Sacred Heart, Brooklyn, New York. Certificate provided by church on 1 October 1976.
[6] Autobiographical sketch of Raymond Francis Dyer. Brooklyn, New York. Single-page, handwritten autobiographical sketch, dated 31 May 1949. Family papers in the possession of the researcher, February 2006.
[7] Ibid.
[8] Letter from Raymond F. Dyer to Madelon Pyburn, dated 1 September 1936. Family papers in the possession of the researcher, February 2006.
[9] Undertaker's record. John J. Malone, Undertaker, 2913 Newkirk Avenue, Brooklyn, New York dated 29 February 1952. Family papers in the possession of the researcher, February 2006.

Figure 1-14. This time line is being prepared from the source documents shown on the research activity log. Endnotes, in proper citation format, indicate which document provided the information. This particular time line does not yet include all references. For example, the 1900 census was checked (figure 1-12, source number 10), but the information has not yet been added to the time line. The time line can also reveal research gaps, such as the opportunity here to search additional censuses.

Use the Periodical Source Index (PERSI) to learn what articles may have appeared in genealogical and historical periodicals since 1847. This major finding aid is available in print, as a CD-ROM, and online (see chapter 3, "General References and Guides" for a detailed explanation of PERSI).

If you are fortunate enough to find collected information on your family or about an individual in your family, the compiler's work and the sources used to compile the work should be checked for accuracy. Always verify information with the original. And if you are sharing data with others, provide the sources from which the information came and, when appropriate, give credit to the original assembler.

Collecting Evidence and Analyzing Data

Experienced genealogists are distinguished by an ability to locate and acquire all available evidence and then interpret the information. All genealogical conclusions should be based on accurately recorded, carefully documented, and well-analyzed records. No possible clue should be ignored, no stone left unturned. This is true even where there is a scarcity of records. Rachal Mills Lennon's words on Southern research are universally applicable:

> The most common cause of stalemates in Southern research is a tendency to conduct *look ups* rather than *investigations*. Pressed for time, researchers seek shortcuts. They typically search for the specific name of the key individual and limit themselves to indexed records. When that basic *look up* fails to yield an answer, many are tempted to *give up*—blaming meager results on 'poor recordkeeping' or 'record destruction.'"[13]

This is a good practice to avoid for all researchers no matter where research is being conducted.

In addition to exhausting every source, analyzing data and assigning people to the correct families requires a combination of common sense, a knowledge of history, and a marshaling of sources. How-to books will give some suggestions, but it is very difficult to explain analytical techniques in a brief discussion. The most comprehensive discussion on the association of evidence and family history research will be found in chapters 14 through 17 of *Professional Genealogy*, edited by Elizabeth Shown Mills. These chapters cover problem analyses and research plans, research procedures, and transcripts and abstracts. Note particularly chapter 17, "Evidence Analysis," by Donn Devine, who is both an attorney and a professional genealogist.

One basic concept is that you seek proof for asserting that any two records apply to the same person. Far too many erroneous pedigrees have used slapdash "name's-the-same" assumptions. Say, for example, that a birth record for a John Smith dated twenty-five years prior to the marriage of another John Smith in Allegheny County, Pennsylvania, was found. Because the bridegroom is known to have been approximately twenty-five years old when he married, can he be correctly assumed to be the John Smith of the birth record? No. He may well be, but without analysis of other records and the family situation, you cannot responsibly make such a conclusion. *The BCG Genealogical Standards Manual*, provides a succinct discussion of the standards of proof, data collection, and evidence evaluation. Although written for the professional, this work will benefit anyone researching family history.

Examples of the analytical process and evaluation of evidence, along with troubleshooting techniques can be found in Marsha H. Rising's *The Family Tree Problem Solver*. Although not for novices, this book introduces sophisticated research strategies that will be more usable as the family historian grows in experience. A helpful presentation on how detailed record analysis can reveal important information and interpretative clues is "Secrets of the Great Migration Study Project: Squeezing More out of the Early New England Records," by Robert C. Anderson.[14]

Discover Your Ancestors in Time and Place

The families, communities, and world in which your ancestors lived influenced their lives, just as you are influenced by the world around you. Understanding the geography associated with an ancestor's life may help you understand some of their decisions and give insights into where to look for additional information on the individual. Likewise, knowing the people, events, history, commerce, and other information about the community in which your ancestors lived can paint a picture that will bring this person to life in a way few records can.

The Geographic Dimension

Genealogical research is assisted by a detailed knowledge of the times and places inhabited by our families. In "Gazetteers: Identifying Research Localities," David Thackery notes that "Genealogy is, among other things, an exercise in geography. Successful research often hinges on identifying the locality in which one's ancestors lived. Once we know the locality, we are in a position to consult the records and histories for the area in an effort to piece together the lives of our forebears."[15]

In one family history project, the ancestor had reportedly moved back and forth between three towns—one in Missouri, one in Kansas, and one in Nebraska. While some researchers would simply pick a state and begin the chase, a seasoned genealogist would start with maps and discover that the three towns lay in adjoining counties where the states came together. In fact, the three towns were within ten miles of each other. Suddenly the problem shifted from a vague project spanning three states and became a neighborhood puzzle that happened to straddle three state lines. No long-distance migrations had occurred.

Gazetteers, maps, and atlases are necessary tools to identify and view these all-important locations. In the previous example, the information from a gazetteer—an index of named places—helped pinpoint the towns on a map. One of the most powerful online digitized versions of a gazetteer is at the U.S. Bureau on Geographic Names website <http://geonames.usgs.gov>. Populated places of all sizes are indexed along with feature and topographic names, such as cemeteries, rivers, and mountains. When a queried place is found, a link to <www.topozone.com> shows the place on a United States Geological Survey (USGS) series map. The search also provides Global Positioning System (GPS) coordinates to make finding a place easy.

Sometimes typing the name of a place into a search engine is adequate to begin a search for a specific location. Always follow up by finding the site on a map. For a broad introduction to types of maps, see Jenny Marie Johnson's *Geographic Information (How to Find It, How to Use It)*. To do United States research, you should at least own an inexpensive atlas such as the Rand McNally annual *Road Atlas*.

The goal for successful research is to locate each place-name on a map contemporary to the time of the event or document being examined, and relate the place to nearby rivers, mountains, valleys, large towns and cities, ports, and adjoining political jurisdictions. The References section provides a number of websites to direct you to online collections of maps. The libraries in your area of research will hold detailed maps of their particular regions and they may provide copies for a small fee. For more about mapping, see chapter 10, "Land Records."

Historical Geography

Most excursions into geography become historical in nature. Discovering historical locations—hamlets that no longer exist, communities that are renamed, or counties whose boundaries have changed—presents another set of challenges. One census might have John Smith born in Mississippi in 1813, while another might say Alabama. In this case, you would need to know that Alabama was created from Mississippi Territory in 1817. A death certificate might list a nonexistent Yellow Bush, Mississippi, but a check of Mississippi place-names might produce Yalobusha County. The problems of shifting political boundaries should be obvious: a householder can appear in various counties or New England towns without ever having moved. The solution in such cases is to find a guide to those changing political boundaries; those containing maps are especially helpful.

Boundaries and Changes

Conducting genealogical research in the United States requires an understanding of county and, in New England (where towns performed governmental activities managed by counties elsewhere), town boundaries. Both usually changed several times before stabilizing. The most current work in print is *Red Book: American State, County, and Town Sources*, edited by Alice Eichholz. *Red Book* shows the year in which each present-day U.S. county was created and gives names of the parent counties (from which the present county was formed). This will suffice for most common research quests and should be consulted every time a new county in a family's history is discovered.

More involved questions should be answered by *Atlas of Historical County Boundaries* edited by John H. Long. Atlases are bound collections of maps that may also include charts and illustrations, tables, and detailed explanations of the maps featured. The types of atlases vary. Some are thematic (pertaining to a specific event, such as the Civil War) as well as location atlases. The *Historical County Boundaries* series takes the theme of county evolution, providing chronologies; separate, detailed maps for each county's different configurations; tables and maps of censuses; and a bibliography. The "Atlas of Historical County Boundaries" project is by the William M. Scholl Center for Family and Community History at the Newberry Library in Chicago, 60 West Walton, Chicago, IL 60610. The ongoing project extends to online interactive maps which depict county formation (up to 1900) from the date entered by the user at <www.newberry.org/ahcbp/ie/index>. By entering, for example, the date of death of your ancestor, you will see the county formation on that exact date. Also evident on these maps is the phenomena whereby a sparsely populated area not officially within a county would fall temporarily under the jurisdiction of an existing county, sometimes for a month or less. This latter phenomena is well-explained in "County Attachments Complicate Search for Local Records" by John Long.[16]

Less expansive guides to the evolution of county boundaries may be ordered from state governments; check their websites. Many titles appear in the bibliography of William Thorndale and William Dollarhide, *Map Guide to the U.S. Federal Censuses, 1790–1920*. The *Map Guide* itself is an excellent reference, showing changes in boundaries for states and territories at ten-year (census) intervals.

Migration and Settlement Patterns

The use of maps is also essential for the study of migration routes. Suppose your ancestor traveled on the Santa Fe Trail from Fort Osage, Missouri, to Clayton, New Mexico, in 1853. What trails were available in that year? Would he have taken the longer mountain or the shorter but dryer desert route? How long would the journey have been? What terrains would be encountered? What campsites would have been used by travelers? These questions could probably be answered by consulting maps held by a repository specializing in the trail. The visual depiction would surely help to recreate your ancestor's journey, regardless of the trail used. But what if your questions were: Were Conestoga wagons the mode of travel? How large were most travel parties? Were Indians a threat in 1853? What did travelers wear? What provisions were packed? What would they eat? And the larger question of when and how was the Santa Fe Trail created?

Obviously, a map is unlikely to answer these kinds of questions. Researchers can supplement map searches with some reading on the history of trails and waterway routes, such as Ray Allen Billington and Martin Ridge's *Westward Expansion* (see "History and Historical Atlases" in the References section). A general background gleaned from such a study can lead to more-specific investigation: this is the historical dimension of genealogy.

The Historical Dimension

Problem solving in family history is easier when you know the historical context in which a situation existed. For instance, some Southern families in the years between the American Revolution and the Civil War tended to wander from one area of newly opened Native American lands to the next. To understand which Native American lands were opened for settlement, you could start with the technical listing by Charles C. Royce, *Indian Cessions in the United States*. From this source you could go on to explore local histories.

A great many examples can be marshaled to prove the importance of understanding history. Suppose an ancestor was a Methodist circuit rider, an occupation about which you might not know much. Initially, this discovery might encourage only simple fact checking. Use of an online reference, such as <www.wikipedia.org>, will provide basic information. But that may provoke a deeper need to know. Two references to historical facts are *The Great American History Finder: The Who, What, Where, When and Why of American History*, by Pam Cornelison and Ted Yanik, and the more comprehensive *The Oxford Companion to United States History*, by Paul S. Boyer, et al.

Somehow, inquiries of a historical nature tend to expand. Could circuit riders be married? How long were they assigned to one circuit? What and how large was a circuit? Where and in what sorts of Methodist records would you look for records about a rider? What is the difference between a circuit rider, a regular Methodist preacher, and a lay exhorter?

Or, even more complicated is the family tradition that says Mary Jones was born a Catholic but was adopted as an eight-year-old by Quakers after the French and Indian War and taken to Pennsylvania. It helps to know that adoption did not exist under colonial law and that the earliest adoption law in the United States seems to have been the 1851 Massachusetts law. Perhaps this "adoption" was really a guardianship. If her parents were Catholic, were there laws suppressing the Catholic Church about 1763, and would there ever have been a Catholic Church register naming Mary? Was it illegal to practice Catholicism in 1763 New York but legal in Pennsylvania?

Such examples could continue endlessly. More than one problem-solving session will be helped by a foray into more detailed references, particularly if the topic is obscure. What reference, devoted to Methodism and circuit riding, is likely to contain the needed detail? Which sources explain anti-Catholic laws in the Mid-Atlantic colonies?

An Internet search is a good place to start. Try typing your research subject into a search engine and then refining your subject entry until you find websites devoted to your topics of interest. The collections of a good local library or a university library (most offer borrowing privileges to non-students for a fee) are also great resources. When possible, use the online access to their catalogues for easier searching. Add subject searches in the catalogues of genealogically-rich repositories, such as Family History Library Catalog (see appendix F, "The LDS Family History Library"). Explore the in-store databases and online catalogues of commercial book dealers (such as <www.amazon.com>, <www.borders.com>, or <www.abebooks.com>). Once specific titles are identified, they may be purchased, ordered through interlibrary loan, or perhaps viewed in their entirety through the magic of electronic books online.

One other observation about how a knowledge of the area and time period helps a researcher place their family—and the documents they created—into historical context. Family historians whose work reaches back to the mid-eighteenth century in Britain or America (quite a stretch for those just starting) will find it necessary to deal with the changing of the calendars from the Julian to the Gregorian in 1752. A good explanation of this and how it affects the interpretation of documents is in Val D. Greenwood's *Researcher's Guide to American Genealogy*.[17] While this is a bit of information you won't need right now, keep it in mind as an example of how each change of locale or era in a research project requires new investigation into its geography and history.

Building a Bibliography

This identification and consulting of titles is called developing a bibliography. If you are fortunate, a bibliography will already have been created. The bibliographic *Harvard Guide to American History*, edited by Frank Freidel, leads the user directly to specific history titles by topics.

An in-depth bibliography requires the addition of articles. Perhaps there is yet no book title on an esoteric topic (hard to believe but possible), or the only reference you can find on a subject includes quotes from an article in a scholarly journal. Locate historical and genealogical articles through PERSI, the Periodical Source Index (see chapter 3, "General References and Guides"). For an index that focuses on historical topics, check Annadel N. Wile, et al., *C.R.I.S.: The Combined Retrospective Index Set to Journals in History, 1838–1974*, for articles on obscure subjects.

Often general works on a specific region will provide much historical data, particularly in an urban area. *The Encyclopedia of Chicago,* by James R. Grossman, et al., devotes several paragraphs to the subject of printing (Chicago was a center for commercial printing in the late nineteenth century). Learning the concentration of print shops was on the near South Side of the city helped locate the residence of the printer Thomas Stone and gave fascinating detail about his occupation. Three titles cited as sources for the encyclopedia article proved even more useful.

If you are concentrating on a particular area and have access to the back issues of historical journals devoted to that area, first seek a cumulative index to the periodical and, if there is none, examine the title pages of each issue to see what was published. Also check the titles in the book review sections.

Although there is usually no one-stop service to build the good bibliography you want, by searching the resources described previously you can develop a bibliography tailored to your research needs. And with such an in-depth knowledge of the world of your ancestors, you stand a much greater chance of solving lineage problems.

Etiquette, Ethics, and Legalities

Family historians who understand how etiquette, ethics, and certain laws affect their family history research are able to move through the research process with less difficultly than those who ignore such considerations. Good etiquette can open closed doors, attention to ethics can help you avoid being duped by false claims or plagiarizing other peoples' work, and being aware of the Freedom of Information Act and the Privacy Act will help you know which records you legally have the right to obtain.

Etiquette

Research etiquette makes good sense no matter where you are researching. Acting in a polite and respectful manner when collecting or presenting family history materials can help maintain easy access to institutions, preserve record availability, and ensure an excellent reputation for all family history researchers. The basic premise is common courtesy—treating others respectfully and complying with the rules and expectations of the repository or other location in which you find yourself. Conduct that seems reasonable while working at your home computer—answering a cell phone and loud or extended conversations—are not appropriate in a library or other repository because they can disturb others.

The staffs of repositories such as libraries, museums, courthouses, archives, or other records centers are usually pleased to answer questions about the use and content of their holdings. However, they seldom have the time to respond to onsite detailed inquiries about a particular family or record. The family historian who prepares well by learning about the local history, geography, and records generated in the research site, will be able to ask intelligent questions without giving a detailed description of their family or their previous research. For suggestions on research etiquette—before, during, and after your visit—in public or private record repositories and libraries, consult James W. Warren and Paula Stuart Warren's *Getting the Most Mileage from Genealogical Research Trips* and Christine Rose's *Courthouse Research.*

Ethics Online and Offline

Although family history research might seem to be a solitary exercise, it is not. Family historians, professional and amateur, are often viewed by the general public and even occasionally by the institutions that serve them, as a collective entity—a group. Because the group is often judged by the actions of a single individual, many genealogical societies, including the National Genealogical Society, publish codes of ethics which they require or encourage their members to sign. Most codes conform to the following guidelines:

General Code of Ethics

To protect the integrity of public records and published materials:

1. I will be courteous and respectful to all record custodians, librarians, archivists, and others who serve the public.
2. I will handle carefully all books or records entrusted to me and return them to the designated place.
3. I will not tear, erase, mark, or remove any document, book, or film, nor will I mutilate, deface, destroy, or otherwise change any part of such document, book, or film.
4. I will present my genealogical findings with honesty and integrity, using permission when necessary and attributing work that is not my own to the proper entity.

Detecting Fraudulent Pedigrees

Although few family historians would knowingly create fraudulent pedigrees, it is important to know that inaccurate or false pedigrees exist so that you do not rely on inaccurate information in your own research. Some researchers, considering their work as "just a hobby" or "just for the family," may have resorted to guess work or to "quick fixes." And just as there have been forgeries in the arts and letters, so there have been forgeries in genealogy. Some researchers may have fallen to the temptation to fabricate a pedigree. Supplying phony noble ancestries for the newly rich has been a profitable business for centuries. An entire issue of the *Genealogical Journal,* "Genealogical Deception," was devoted to case studies in fraud. The editor, Gordon L. Remington, proposed the following guidelines to detect genealogical fraud:[18]

1. Suspicious, inadequate, or no citations.
2. The ancestry provided is "too good to be true."
3. The reasoning doesn't make sense.

Plagiarism

In addition to verifying the veracity of others' pedigrees, you will also want to protect yourself from pitfalls in your own work, including plagiarism and copyright violation. Plagiarism in genealogy is the innocent or intentional use of someone else's words or ideas without giving appropriate credit to that person. Even if an idea, rather than the exact words or text, is used, a source should be cited. If the exact words are used, cite the source and surround the text with quotation marks or, if the quote is more than a few sentences, use the block indent as shown next:

> Don't drag-and-drop too much from the Web into your notes. It's hard to keep straight just who wrote what, and it invites trouble. When you do drag-and-drop some material, it's important to have a consistent system to mark someone else's words and ideas and where they came from. You need to identify the source page, first in your notes and later in your papers.[19]

In summary, employ two rules to avoid plagiarism: (1) always give full credit to the person or source from which the material or text originated; and (2) when quoting another's words, use quotation marks or block indent.

Legalities and Copyright

There are essentially three federal legal issues that concern the family historian: the Freedom of Information Act (FOIA), the Privacy Act, and the Copyright Law. A working knowledge about these legalities is important for family historians because they determine what records may be accessed and the format in which the collected information may be used. While it is not feasible to address all of the legal questions that one might encounter in conducting genealogical research, a few points about each are worth considering.

Freedom of Information Act

The FOIA generally provides that any person has a right, enforceable in court, of access to federal agency records, except certain exempted or excluded records. The FOIA does not affect local or state records; most states have their own laws covering these records. Details about the FOIA are available through the National Archives website at <www.archives.gov/research_room/foia_reading_room/foia_reading_room.html>.

Privacy Act

Understanding privacy rights enables researchers to determine who has access to records. Broadly stated, the purpose of the Privacy Act is to balance the government's need to maintain information about individuals with rights of the individuals to be protected against unwarranted invasions of their privacy stemming from federal agencies' collection, maintenance, use, and disclosure of personal information about them. The Privacy Act of 1974 provides for disclosure of, and personal access to, all federal records containing personal information, regulates their transfer to others, and allows for legal remedies in cases of their misuse under the law.

Current guidelines for FOIA and the Privacy Act are available as *A Citizen's Guide on Using the Freedom of Information Act and the Privacy Act of 1974 to Request Government Records*, located at <www.fas.org/sgp/foia/citizen.html>.

Copyright Law

As you create notes, summaries, or even a published family history, you will need to know what works—or portions of works—are protected under federal law. The law defines how certain photographs and other illustrations, and many intellectual works such as musical or dramatic creations, may not be used without written permission. You will also want to know how the work you seek to publish or otherwise share is protected. For example, facts are not copyrightable. Because much of genealogy is the discovery of facts, much of what you might choose to publish will not be under copyright protection. A researcher can own the arrangement of facts, but this does not mean that because you arranged your family's information in pedigree charts and family group sheets or in a family tree computer program that the items you created are copyrightable. To learn more about the Copyright Law and how it affects your work, visit the U.S. Copyright office at <www.copyright.gov>.

Conclusion

The basic steps presented in this chapter are the foundation upon which to build a good family history research project of any size or depth. These essential methods apply to everyone, regardless of experience. Even professional genealogists began as you will—by applying the guidelines presented at the beginning of this chapter.

What you do next will depend on what kind of information you have found in home sources and family interviews. Every family is unique, but generally the best next step will be to acquire proof (documentation) for family births, marriages, and deaths. Chapter 13, "Vital Records," provides an in-depth study of these records, their accessibility, and how to use them productively.

The need for a geographic and historical context will become apparent as you approach the census records, a good next step. Because census records are essential for locating families and for understanding relationships, their use should be considered early in the research project. As your information base grows, remember that the quality of your research will reflect the care with which you record your findings—so maintain good charts and files.

Use the Internet. While it is not advisable, nor is it even possible, to rely totally on this powerful tool for your research, the billions of records that are online will help to build and expand the history of your family. Chapter 2, "Computers and Technology," provides important tips for using the Internet and genealogy software efficiently and for wisely evaluating information gleaned from the World Wide Web.

Once you understand the basics of building a family history and the acquiring of the fundamental sources of vital and census records, then you are set to dive into other relevant areas of research covered in this volume. Sources described in these first chapters will inevitably point to dozens of other potential records and hours of enjoyable detective work.

It is not surprising that interest in family history is soaring. To discover and understand our family's story is a fascinating journey. To preserve that story is a priceless gift for the generations to come.

Notes

[1] A 2005 poll by Market Strategies, Inc. (MSI), a national research and strategic consulting firm, and MyFamily.com, Inc., determined 73 percent of Americans are interested in discovering their family history. This figure represents a 13 percent increase over a similar Maritz Poll that was conducted in 2000, in which 60 percent of Americans said they were interested in discovering their family history. Visit <www.ancestry.com/learn/library/article.aspx?article=4682> for details.

[2] The common definition of family history is that it is the study of an entire family unit, including collateral as well as direct line descendents. The word genealogy is generally regarded as the more formal investigation of a pedigree as a branch of study, and often describes a research activity that includes only the immediate and direct line of descent. *The Source*, along with most current writers and presenters of the subject, chooses to use the terms interchangeably unless otherwise indicated.

[3] Mary Jaene Edmonds, *Samplers and Samplermakers: An American Schoolgirl Art, 1700–1850* (New York: Rizzoli International, 1991), 64–65.

[4] *History with a Tape Recorder: An Oral History Handbook* (Springfield, Ill.: Oral History Office, Sangamon State University, n.d.), 2.

[5] Ibid., 4.

[6] Definition from <www.answers.com/tradition>.

[7] Del E. Jupiter, "Matilda Madrid: One Woman's Tale of Bondage and Freedom," *National Genealogical Society Quarterly* 91 (March 2003).

[8] Research courtesy encourages that a self-addressed, stamped envelope (commonly referred to as an SASE) accompany genealogical requests in which no payment is enclosed or expected.

[9] Pamela Boyd Porter, "Fourteen Things I Didn't Know I Couldn't Live Without Until I Had Them," *FORUM* 17, no. 4 (Winter 2005): 22–23.

[10] Patricia Law Hatcher, "How Do You Know?" in *Producing a Quality Family History* (Salt Lake City: Ancestry, 1996), 117.

[11] Patricia Law Hatcher, "Adding Detail to Your Narrative," *Ancestry* Magazine 21, no. 4 (July/August 2003).

[12] Laura G. Prescott, "The Perspective of Timelines," *Ancestry* Magazine 22, no. 2 (March/April 2004): 55.

[13] Rachal Mills Lennon, "The Wives of Jonathan Turner: Identification of Women in Pre-Twentieth-Century South Carolina," *National Genealogical Society Quarterly* 92, no. 4 (December 2004): 245–55.

[14] Robert C. Anderson, "Secrets of the Great Migration Study Project: Squeezing More out of the Early New England Records" (paper presented at the 2004 Federation of Genealogical Societies/Texas State Genealogical Society/Austin Genealogical Society conference in Austin, Texas). An audio-tape is available for purchase from <www.willowbendbooks.com>. The syllabus containing handout material is available for purchase from <www.fgs.org>.

[15] David Thackery, "Gazetteers: Identifying Research Localities," *Ancestry* Magazine 12, no. 4 (July/August 1994).

[16] "County Attachments Complicate Search for Local Records" appeared first in *Origins* (newsletter of the Dr. William M. Scholl Center for Family & Community History and the Local & Family History Section at the Newberry Library) 12, no. 2 (Winter 2001): 6–8, and was reprinted in *FORUM* 17, no. 4 (Winter 2005): 11–12.

[17] Val D. Greenwood, *The Researcher's Guide to American Genealogy*, 3rd ed. (Baltimore: Genealogical Publishing Co.), 43–45.

[18] Defined in "Charlemagne or Charlatan: Case Studies in Genealogical Fraud" (paper presented at the 1994 Federation of Genealogical Societies/Virginia Genealogical Society conference in Richmond, Virginia). See also Gordon L. Remington, "A Royal Genealogical Fraud: Prince 'Petros Palaeologos' of the Isle of Wight," *Genealogical Journal* 32, no. 4 (2004): 154–57; and "Gustav Anjou in Cyberspace," *Association of Professional Genealogists Quarterly* 18 (December 2003): 151–55.

[19] Charles Lipson, *Doing Honest Work in College* (Chicago: University of Chicago Press, 2004), 13.

References

Conducting Basic Research and Record Keeping

American Genealogy: A Basic Course. National Genealogical Society. Online at <www.ngsgenealogy.org>. An online study course for various skill levels.

Booth, Wayne C., Joseph M. Williams, Gregory G. Colomb. *The Craft of Research.* 2nd ed. *Chicago Guides to Writing, Editing, and Publishing.* Chicago: University of Chicago Press, 2003.

Carmack, Sharon DeBartolo. *Organize Your Family History Research: Efficient and Effective Ways to Gather and Protect Your Genealogical Research.* Cincinnati: Betterway Books, 1999.

Clifford, Karen. *The Complete Beginner's Guide to Genealogy, the Internet, and Your Genealogy Software Program.* Baltimore: Genealogical Publishing Co., 2002.

Crume, Rick. *Plugging into Your Past.* Cincinnati: Betterway Books, 2004.

Curran, Joan Ferris, Madilyn Coen Crane, John H. Wray. *Numbering Your Genealogy: Basic System, Complex Families, and International Kin (Special Publications of the National Genealogical Society No. 64).* Arlington, Va.: National Genealogical Society, 1999.

Dollarhide, William. *Managing a Genealogical Project.* Updated ed. Baltimore: Genealogical Publishing Co., 2001.

Fleming, Ann Carter. *The Organized Family Historian: How to File, Manage, and Protect Your Genealogical Research and Heirlooms.* Nashville: Rutledge Hill Press, 2004.

Greenwood, Val D. *Researcher's Guide to American Genealogy,* 3rd ed. Baltimore: Genealogical Publishing Co., 2000.

McClure, Rhonda R. *The Genealogist's Computer Companion.* Cincinnati: Betterway Books, 2001.

———. *Digitizing Your Family History.* Cincinnati: Family Tree Books, 2004.

Morgan, George. *How to Do Everything with Your Genealogy.* New York: McGraw-Hill Osborne Media, 2004.

MyFamily.com. *Family History.* CD-ROM (Win). Provo, Utah: MyFamily.com, 2004.

MyFamily.com. *1–2–3 Family Tree: The Fastest Way to Create and Grow Your Family Tree.* Provo, Utah: MyFamily.com, 2003.

Porter, Pamela Boyer, and Amy Johnson Crow. *Online Roots. How to Discover Your Family's History and Heritage with the Power of the Internet.* Nashville: Rutledge Hill Press, 2003.

Prescott, Laura G. "The Perspective of Timelines." *Ancestry* Magazine 22, no. 2 (March/April 2004).

Renick, Barbara. *Genealogy 101: How to Trace Your Family's History and Heritage.* Rutledge Hill Press, 2003.

Wright, Raymond S., III. *The Genealogist's Handbook: Modern Methods for Researching Family History.* Chicago: American Library Association, 1995.

Interviewing and Oral History

American Association for State and Local History. *A Guide to Oral History Interviews.* Technical Leaflet #210. Nashville: American Association for State and Local History, 2000.

Huberman, Rob, and Laura Huberman. *How to Create a Video Family History: The Complete Guide to Interviewing and Taping Your Families Stories & Memories.* Margate, N.J.: ConteQ Communications, 2003.

Kroeber, Karl, ed. *Native American Storytelling: A Reader of Myths & Legends.* Ames, Iowa: Blackwell Publishers, 2004.

Nelson, Hasker. *Listening for Our Past: A Lay Guide to African-American Oral History Interviewing.* United States: Heritage Research Creations, 2000.

Neubauer, Joan R. *From Memories to Manuscript: The Five-Step Method of Writing Your Life Story.* Salt Lake City: Ancestry, 1994.

Neuenschwander, John A. *Oral History and the Law.* 3rd ed., rev. and enlarged. Denton, Tex.: Oral History Association, 2002.

Ritchie, Donald A. *Doing Oral History: A Practical Guide.* 2nd ed. London: Oxford University Press, 2003.

Sommer, Barbara W., and Mary Kay Quinlan. *The Oral History Manual (American Association for State and Local History Book Series).* Walnut Creek, Calif.: AltaMira Press, 2003.

Sturm, Duane, and Pat Sturm. *Video Family History.* Salt Lake City: Ancestry, 1989.

Thompson, Paul. *The Voice of the Past: Oral History.* 3rd ed. London: Oxford University Press, 2000.

Locating and Caring for Home Sources

American Association of State and Local History. *Caring for Family Treasures: Basic How-to from Storage to Donation.* Technical Leaflet #225. Nashville: American Association of State and Local History: 2004.

American Diaries: An Annotated Bibliography of Published American Diaries and Journals. 2 vols. Detroit: Gale Research Co., 1983, 1987.

Hinding, Andrea. *Women's History Sources: A Guide to Archives and Manuscripts Collections in the United States.* New York: R. R. Bowker, 1979.

Lester, Memory Aldridge. *Old Southern Bible Records: Transcriptions of Births, Deaths and Marriages from Family Bibles, Chiefly of the 18th and 19th Centuries*. Reprint, 1990; Baltimore: Clearfield Co., 2002.

Long, Jane S., and Richard W. Long. *Caring for Your Family Treasures*. New York: H. N. Abrams, 2000.

McClure, Rhonda R. *Digitizing Your Family History: Easy Methods for Preserving Your Heirloom Documents, Photos, Home Movies, and More in a Digital Format*. Cincinnati: Family Tree Books, 2004.

Pitman, Ann Mitchell. *Inside the Jewelry Box: A Collectors Guide to Costume Jewelry, Identification, and Values*. Paducah, Ky.: Collector Books, 2004.

Sagraves, Barbara. *A Preservation Guide: Saving the Past and the Present for the Future*. Salt Lake City: Ancestry, 1995.

Smolenyak, Megan. "Website helps return 'orphan' artifacts." Online at <http://honoringourancestors.com/library_orphan.html>.

Taylor, Maureen A. *Preserving Your Family Photographs*. Cincinnati: Betterway Books, 2001.

Weinstein, Robert A., and Larry Booth. *Collection, Use, and Care of Historical Photographs*. Nashville: American Association for State and Local History, 1989.

Dating Home Sources

Corson, Richard. *Fashions in Hair, the First 5000 Years*. 2nd ed. London: Peter Owen Publishers, 2001.

DeLorme, Maureen. *Mourning Art & Jewelry*. Altglen, Pa.: Schiffer Publishing, 2004.

Edmunds, Mary Jaene. *Samplers and Samplermakers: An American Schoolgirl Art 1700–1850*. New York: Rizzoli International Publications, 1991.

Friedman, Daniel. *The Birth and Development of American Postcards: A History, Catalog, and Price Guide to U.S. Pioneer Postcards*. Classic Postcards, 2003.

Frisch-Ripley, Karen. *Unlocking the Secrets in Old Photographs*. Salt Lake City: Ancestry, 1992.

Gagel, Diane Vanskiver. *Ohio Photographers, 1839–1900*. Nevada City, Calif.: Carl Mautz Publishing, 1998.

Massengill, Stephen E. *Photographers in North Carolina: The First Century 1842–1941*. Raleigh: North Carolina Department of Cultural Resources, 2004.

Nickell, Joe. *Camera Clues: A Handbook for Photographic Investigation*. Lexington: University of Kansas Press, 1994.

Pitman, Ann Mitchell. *Inside the Jewelry Box: A Collectors Guide to Costume Jewelry, Identification, and Values*. Paducah, Ky.: Collector Books, 2004.

Severa, Joan. *Dressed for the Photographer: Ordinary Americans and Fashion, 1840–1900*. Ohio: Kent State University Press, 1995.

———. *My Likeness Taken: Daguerreian Portraits in America*. Kent, Ohio: Kent State University Press, 2005.

Zeepyat, Charlotte. *Queen Victoria's Family: A Century of Photographs 1840–1940*. Reprint, Stroud, Gloucestershire, UK: Sutton Publishing, 2003.

Evidence Evaluation and Presentation

Anderson, Robert C. "Secrets of the Great Migration Study Project: Squeezing More out of the Early New England Records." Paper presented at the 2004 Federation of Genealogical Societies conference, Austin, Texas. Audio tape available from <www.willowbendbooks.com>. Syllabus material available from <www.fgs.org>.

Board for Certification of Genealogists. *The BCG Genealogical Standards Manual*. Washington, D.C.: Board for Certification of Genealogists, 2000.

Cerny, Johni, and Arlene H. Eakle. *Ancestry's Guide to Research*. Salt Lake City: Ancestry, 1984.

Croom, Emily Anne. *The Sleuth Book for Genealogists. Strategies for More Successful Family History Research*. Betterway Books, 2000.

Gouldrup, Lawrence. *Writing the Family Narrative*. Salt Lake City: Ancestry, 1992.

Hatcher, Patricia Law. *Producing a Quality Family History*. Salt Lake City: Ancestry, 1996.

———. "Adding Detail to Your Narrative." *Ancestry* Magazine 21, no. 4 (July/August 2003).

Jupiter, Del E. "Matilda Madrid: One Woman's Tale of Bondage and Freedom." *National Genealogical Society Quarterly* 91, no. 1 (March 2003): 41–59.

Leary, Helen F. M. "Finding Truth in a Family Tradition: Sumner Antecedents of Demsey S. Goodman." *National Genealogical Society Quarterly* 81, no. 3 (September 1993).

Lennon, Rachal Mills. "The Wives of Jonathan Turner: Identification of Women in Pre-Twentieth-Century South Carolina." *National Genealogical Society Quarterly* 92, no. 4 (December 2004): 245–55.

Mills, Elizabeth Shown. *Evidence! Citation & Analysis for the Family Historian*. Regional Publishing Co., 2000.

———, ed. *Professional Genealogy: A Manual for Researchers, Writers, Editors, Lecturers and Librarians*. Baltimore: Genealogical Publishing Co., 2001.

Remington, Gordon L. "A Royal Genealogical Fraud: Prince 'Petros Palaeologos' of the Isle of Wight." *Genealogical Journal* 32, no. 4 (2004): 154–57.

Rising, Marsha Hoffman. *The Family Tree Problem Solver: Proven Methods for Scaling the Inevitable Brick Wall.* Cincinnati: Family Tree Books, 2005.

Rubincam, Milton. *Pitfalls in Genealogical Research.* Salt Lake City: Ancestry, 1987.

Law, Medicine, and Genetics

Brooke, Heather. *Your Right to Know: How to Use the Freedom of Information Act and other Access Laws.* Pluto Press, 2005.

Carmack, Sharon DeBartolo. *Carmack's Guide to Copyright & Contracts: A Primer for Genealogists, Writers & Researchers.* Baltimore: Genealogical Publishing Co., 2005.

Charmasson, Henri. *Patents, Copyrights & Trademarks for Dummies.* For Dummies, 2004.

Lipson, Charles. *Doing Honest Work in College: How to Prepare Citations, Avoid Plagiarism, and Achieve Real Academic Success.* Chicago: University of Chicago Press, 2004.

Maida, Pamela, ed. *Freedom of Information Act Guide and Privacy Act Overview.* May 2002 ed. Diane Publishing Co., 2002.

Roderick, Thomas H. "The Y Chromosome in Genealogical Research: From Their Ys a Father Knows His Own Son." *National Genealogical Society Quarterly* 88 (June 2000): 122–43. An introduction to use of Y-DNA.

Savin, Alan. *DNA for Family Historians.* Maidenhead, England: the author, 2000. An excellent thirty-two-page booklet by an author who has organized a family DNA study.

Shawker, Thomas H. *Unlocking Your Genetic History.* Nashville: Rutledge Hill Press, 2004. The first comprehensive work on DNA for genealogists.

County Origins

Eichholz, Alice, ed. *Red Book: American State, County, and Town Sources.* 3rd ed. Provo, Utah: Ancestry, 2004.

Everton, George B., Sr. *The Handy Book for Genealogists.* 10th ed. Logan, Utah: Everton Publishers, 2002.

Kane, Joseph Nathan. *The American Counties: Origins of County Names, Dates of Creation and Population Data, and Published Sources.* 5th ed. Metuchen, N.J.: Scarecrow Press, 2004.

Long, John H., ed. *Atlas of Historical County Boundary Changes.* New York: Charles Scribner's Sons, 1993– . When completed, the series will include forty volumes.

Finding Maps, Atlases, and Place Names

Abate, Frank R., ed. *Omni Gazetteer of the United States of America: Providing Name, Location, and Identification for Nearly 1,500,000 Populated Places and Geographic Features in the Fifty States, the District of Columbia, Puerto Rico, and U.S. Territories.* 11 vols. Detroit: Omnigraphics, 1991.

American Geographical Society Library <www.uwm.edu/Libraries/AGSL/intro.html>, one of North America's foremost geography and map collections, consists of over one million items with a worldwide scope, including more than 500,000 maps and 9,000 atlases.

Arizona State University Libraries <www.asu.edu/lib/hayden/govdocs/maps/geogname.htm> offers links to Place Name Sites in the U.S., by states, and by country.

American Places Dictionary: A Guide to 45,000 Populated Places, Natural Features, and Other Places in the U.S. 4 vols. Detroit: Omnigraphics, 1994.

Bancroft Library of the University of California, Berkeley, <www.lib.berkeley.edu/EART/MapCollections.html> guides users to the vast collection of atlases, maps, and gazetteers at UC and affiliate libraries. A listing of Internet resources in maps and cartography is at the same site.

David Rumsey Collection <www.davidrumsey.com> features over 12,600 high-resolution digital maps from the David Rumsey Map Collection, one of the largest private collections of historic maps in the United States. The collection has thirty-six complete American atlases dating from 1733 to 1885.

Department of the Interior. *Catalog of the United States Geological Survey Library.* 25 vols. Boston: G. K. Hall, 1964. 1st and 2nd supplements. 15 vols. 1972, 1974. Also <http://gos2.geodata.gov/wps/portal/gos> is the Geospatial One Stop guide to finding maps in the divisions of the Department of the Interior (including digitized maps).

Digital Librarian: Maps and Geography <www.digital-librarian.com/maps.html> lists all known sites featuring digitized U.S., Canadian, and worldwide maps and atlases, current and historical.

Gregory, Ian N. *A Place in History: A Guide to Using GIS in Historical Research.* Oxford: Oxbow Books, 2003.

Hargett, Janet L. *List of Selected Maps of States and Territories. Special List Number* 29. Washington, D.C.: National Archives, 1998.

Hayward, John. *A Gazetteer of the United States of America.* Hartford, Conn.: Case, Tiffany, and Co. Online edition NewEnglandAncestors.org <www.newenglandancestors.org>, New England Historic Genealogical Society, 2004.

Johnson, Jenny Marie. *Geographic Information (How to Find It, How to Use It).* Westport, Conn.: Greenwood Press, 2003.

Library of Congress. *The Bibliographic Guide to Maps and Atlases: 2002.* 5 vols. Boston: G. K. Hall, 2003.

Monmonier, Mark. *Mapping It Out: Expository Cartography for the Humanities and Society Sciences (Chicago Guides to Writing, Editing, and Publishing)*. Chicago: University of Chicago Press, 1993.

Newberry Library. *Checklist of Printed Maps of the Middle West to 1900*. Edited by Robert W. Karrow. 13 vols. Boston: G. K. Hall, 1981.

New York Public Library, Research Libraries. *Dictionary Catalog of the Map Division*. 10 vols. Boston: G. K. Hall, 1971.

Rumsey, David, and Edith M. Punt. *Cartographical Extraordinaire: The Historical Map Transformed*. Redlands, Calif.: ESRI Press, 2004.

Thackery, David. "Gazetteers: Identifying Research Localities." *Ancestry* Magazine 12, no. 4 (July/August 1994).

Thiry, Christopher J. J., ed. *Guide to U.S. Map Resource/Map and Geography Round Table (MAGERT) of the American Library Association*. 3rd ed. Lanham, Md.: Scarecrow Press, 2005. A guide to hundreds of map collections and cartographic resources in libraries and repositories throughout the nation.

Thorndale, William, and William Dollarhide. *Map Guide to the U.S. Federal Censuses, 1790–1920*. Reprint, 1987; Baltimore: Genealogical Publishing Co., 2003.

University of Texas at Austin. The Perry-Casteñeda Map Collection at <www.lib.utexas.edu/maps>. This world-renowned collection features several historical maps, urban and other, at the website.

History and Historical Atlases

Billington, Ray Allen, and Martin Ridge. *Westward Expansion: A History of the American Frontier*. 5th ed. New York: Macmillan, 1982.

Boyer, Paul S., et al. *The Oxford Companion to United States History*. London: Oxford University Press, 2001.

Cornelison, Pam, and Ted Yanik. *The Great American History Finder: The Who, What, Where, When and Why of American History*. 2nd updated rev. Boston: Houghton, Mifflin, 2004.

Earle, Jonathan. *The Routledge Atlas of African American History*. Routledge, 2000.

Gilbert, Martin, and Marin Gilbert. *The Routledge Atlas of American History: From First Exploration to the Present Day*. 4th ed. Routledge, 2003.

Grossman, James R., Ann Durkin Keating, and Janice L. Reiff. *The Encyclopedia of Chicago*. Chicago: University of Chicago Press, 2004.

Higgenbotham, Evelyn Brooks, et al. *Harvard Guide to African-American History*. Book and CD-ROM editions. Cambridge, Mass.: Harvard University Press, 2001.

National Geographic Society. *The National Geographic Historical Atlas of the United States*. Washington, D.C.: National Geographic Society, 2004.

Paullin, Charles O., and John K. Wright. *Atlas of the Historical Geography of the United States*. 1932. Reprint, Westport, Conn.: Greenwood Press, 1975.

Royce, Charles C. *Indian Cessions in the United States*. 1900. Reprint, New York: Arno, 1970. Electronic version at <http://memory.loc.gov/ammem> as U.S. Serial Set 4015.

Urdang, Laurence, and Arthur Meier Schlesinger Jr. *The Timetables of American History*. New York: Touchstone, Millennium edition, 2001.

Wile, Annadel N., et al. *C.R.I.S.: The Combined Retrospective Index Set to Journals in History, 1838–1974*. 11 vols. Washington, D.C.: Carrollton Press, 1977.

Wishart, David. *Encyclopedia of the Great Plains*. University of Nebraska Press, 2004.

General Reference

Bentley, Elizabeth. *The Genealogist's Address Book*. Baltimore: Genealogical Publishing Co., 2005.

The Board for Certification of Genealogists. *The BCG Genealogical Standards Manual*. Washington, D.C.: Board for Certification of Genealogists, 2000.

Cerny, Johni, and Wendy Elliott. *The Library: A Guide to the LDS Family History Library*. Salt Lake City: Ancestry, 1988.

Chicago Manual of Style. 15th ed. Chicago: University of Chicago Press, 2003.

Eales, Anne Bruner, and Robert M. Kvasnicka. *Guide to Genealogical Research in the National Archives of the United States*. 3rd ed. Washington, D.C.: National Archives and Records Administration, 2000.

Leary, Helen F. M., ed. *North Carolina Research: Genealogy and Local History*. 2nd ed. Raleigh: North Carolina Genealogical Society, 1996.

Mills, Elizabeth Shown, ed.. *Professional Genealogy*. Baltimore: Genealogical Publishing Co., 2001.

Rose, Christine. *Courthouse Research for Family Historians: Your Guide to Genealogical Treasures*. San Jose, Calif.: CR Publications, 2004.

Szucs, Juliana. *The Ancestry Family Historian's Address Book*. Orem, Utah: Ancestry, 2003.

Warren, James, and Paula Stuart Warren. *Getting the Most Mileage from Genealogical Research Trips*. 3rd ed. St. Paul, Minn.: Warren Research and Publishing, 1998.

Warren, Paula Stuart, and James Warren. *Your Guide to the Family History Library*. Cincinnati: Betterway Books, 2001.

2

Computers and Technology

JULIANA SMITH

Computers have changed the face of family history forever. Once stereotyped as the hobby of old spinster aunts, family history is now a favorite pastime for much of mainstream America. According to the October 2005 comScore report, "More than 11 million American consumers went online during October 2005 to conduct genealogy research."

Today's technology makes it easier to gather and organize information, communicate with other genealogists, publish and share our findings, and preserve our family's history. Information gathered over time, once entered into genealogy software, can be reorganized and reformatted with the click of a mouse. Family databases in electronic format can easily be shared with relatives by e-mail, on websites, or on removable media like CD-ROMs, DVDs, or diskettes.

While visits to places like libraries, archives, courthouses, and cemeteries will still remain a necessary and integral part of genealogical research, much more can now be achieved from the comfort of home. Images of original records, increasingly available online, may eliminate the need to travel to repositories with inconvenient hours of operation to view the records. Growing collections of databases enable genealogists to search huge quantities of data, almost instantaneously, from home computers or at local libraries.

In the past, queries for information on individuals in family trees had to be mailed in to genealogical periodicals, which were in turn mailed to subscribers. Sometimes it would be months between the time they were sent in and when they reached their audience. They were typically browsed quickly and later filed in the trash or stashed in closets. Now these requests can be sent electronically in an instant to targeted audiences of researchers sharing similar research needs. These electronic queries, sent to mailing lists, posted on message boards, or placed on electronic registries are often archived for quick and easy retrieval days, months, and even years later.

The ability to create heirloom charts, restore old photographs, and turn fragile documents into electronic files is now at our fingertips. Saved in electronic formats or printed from desktop publishing tools, our family treasures can now be shared with many family members quickly and inexpensively.

This chapter provides an overview of family history tasks that can be aided by computers and related technologies. It discusses the resources you can find on the World Wide Web, gives tips for searching online databases and websites, and explains how to use the Internet to connect with others through e-mail, mailing lists, and message boards.

Chapter Contents

A section is included on using software to organize and enhance your genealogy. Individual products and tools will not be reviewed, although some may be mentioned as examples. Instead, some guidance will be offered in choosing the products that will best suit your needs. The chapter also addresses important technology issues such as computer security, file backups, and research integrity when using new and ever-changing tools.

Using the Internet for Research

Searchable Databases and Indexes

Among the most spectacular areas of growth over recent years are the offerings of various websites. Databases are also among the most popular of online resources. When the Statue of Liberty–Ellis Island Foundation launched its database of passenger lists <www.ellisisland.org> in April 2001, the site was flooded with 26 million visitors in its first 54 hours of operation. Libraries, government agencies (on local and national levels), genealogical and historical organizations, and commercial entities are seeking ways to better utilize the potential that the Internet offers when it comes to preserving and sharing their collections with a wider audience. As the popularity of these online databases and indexes continues to grow, so do the number of sites that offer them, so it is wise to do periodic reviews of what is available for pertinent areas of interest.

This section will cover some of the types of websites that may hold the resources you seek. Later in this chapter, we will discuss locating databases and indexes in some of the websites mentioned in this section. For a more detailed look at some of the larger databases and indexes that are available online, see chapter 3, "General References and Guides."

Government Websites

Government agencies, such as vital records departments, use the Internet as a way to provide access, and streamline record requests with the ability to order directly from a website or print out an order form. With request procedures, contact information, fees, requirements and restrictions posted on websites, agencies can reduce the time employees spend on answering these types of questions. Many have even taken it a step further by including searchable indexes so that those seeking the records can do the preliminary searching so that staff members can locate the records using the information found in the databases. Some will also accept electronic requests for record copies and payments via credit card or online payment services.

Many state archives offer electronic copies of records, in addition to online versions of catalogs and finding aids for their collections. The Illinois State Archives website <www.sos.state.il.us/departments/archives/archives.html>, for example, includes searchable databases of public domain land tract sales, Illinois servitude and emancipation records, Illinois veterans' records, and statewide marriage and death databases. More localized content can also be found on the site, with county databases for coroner's inquest records, probates, naturalizations, almshouse and poor farm records, birth registers, criminal case files, and more.

The National Archives and Records Administration (NARA) website <www.archives.gov> not only makes available its catalog to the many holdings in Washington, D.C., branches and in its regional facilities, but also includes electronic records on the site. NARA's Access to Archival Databases (AAD) System_<http://archives.gov/aad/index.html> includes databases from the Korean War and World War II, The Japanese-American Internee File, 1942–1946, and the Famine Irish Passenger Record Data File (recording 604,596 persons who arrived in the United States, 1846–1851). Other indexes in the collection that may be useful in adding background information to family trees include indexes to historic photographs, *Index to Civil War Sites*, and the *Work Stoppages Historical File, ca. 1953–ca. 1981.*

In addition to these resources, the Research Room of the NARA website <www.archives.gov/research_room/index.html> offers a number of research guides and a page created specifically for genealogists, as well as links to important information on using NARA facilities (see figure 2-1). This page should be your first stop when planning a research trip to the National Archives in the Washington, D.C., area or in any of the regional branches.

The Church of Jesus Christ of Latter-day Saints

Since 1894, The Church of Jesus Christ of Latter-day Saints (LDS Church) has been collecting records significant to ancestral research. With the release of the FamilySearch site <www.familysearch.org> in May 1999, the LDS Church began bringing some of its collections to the Web. The site launched with the posting of the Family History Library Catalog (FHLC), the International Genealogical Index (IGI), and the Ancestral File. Newer additions include the Pedigree Resource File, the Social Security Death Index (SSDI), Vital Records Index (currently Mexico and Scandinavia), every-name census indexes to the 1880 U.S. Federal Census, the 1881 British Isles Census, and the 1881 Canadian Census, and a database of family history websites.

Ethnic Websites

As immigrants came to the United States, they tended to settle in communities along ethnic lines, and there are many ethnic organizations that are preserving and disseminating some of the records these immigrants created through online access. One example is the Polish Genealogical Society of America (PGSA) <www.pgsa.org>. Its website houses a number of databases, which include, among others, indexes to death notices in Polish language newspapers from Chicago and Baltimore, a marriage index for Polish Catholic parishes in Chicago, Polish Roman Catholic Union of America (PRCUA) Insurance Claim Records, *Poles of Chicago 1837–1937*, and Haller's Army Index (Polish immigrants recruited in America to fight in France for Polish independence during World War I).

Comparable sites exist for many other ethnic backgrounds, including African American, German, Lithuanian, Italian, British, Irish, French, Eastern European.

JewishGen <www.jewishgen.org>, a website created to assist researchers of Jewish descent, includes an online discussion group, reference tools organized by topic and country, community-based information, geographic tools, and a variety of databases. According to the site, "JewishGen's online *Family Tree of the Jewish People* contains data on more than three million people" (see figure 2-2).

Libraries

Just as a research trip to an ancestral hometown should always include a trip to the local library, your online excursions for research in a particular town should also include a trip to the local library's website. Many libraries provide online content, making local collections accessible from anywhere in the world. For example, the Brooklyn (New York) Public Library has made available digitized images of the *Brooklyn Daily Eagle, 1841–1902* on its website <http://eagle.brooklynpubliclibrary.org>.

Even smaller local libraries typically maintain a Web presence and you may find databases of local obituaries, cemetery transcriptions, vital records, church records, directories, or institutional records, depending on the collections they have available. Many libraries also have their catalogs available for searching online. The use of these tools is described later in the "Research Planning" section of this chapter.

Organizations

Genealogical and historical organizations, which have long worked to preserve important records, are also using the Internet to make their collections available on a much larger scale. Some sites require membership to access data collections, while others make information available to members and nonmembers alike. In some cases, requests for more in-depth research can be submitted via online forms or e-mail.

The New England Historic Genealogical Society (NEHGS) website is a good example of what organizations can offer online <www.newenglandancestors.org>. Members of the society have access to this ever-growing online collection of cemetery transcriptions, vital records, biographical compilations, immigration records, periodicals, military records, maps, and more.

Volunteer Projects

A number of online volunteer projects are also making valuable contributions in various areas of family history research.

One of the largest volunteer networks, RootsWeb.com <www.rootsweb.com>, which is supported by MyFamily.com, Inc., has at the time of this publication grown to host in excess of 29,000

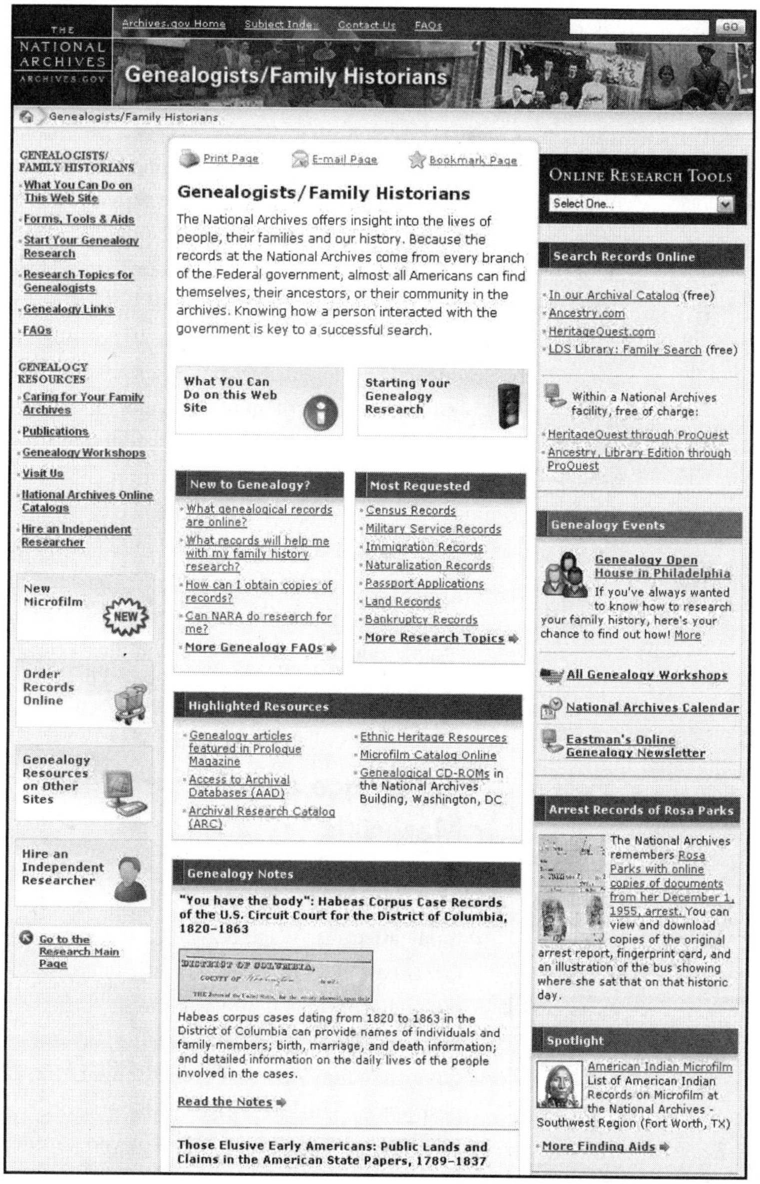

Figure 2-1. The website for the National Archives and Records Administration includes a special section for genealogists <www.archives.gov/genealogy>, which features links to reference materials, forms, access to NARA's catalog, databases, and more.

mailing lists, more than 155,000 message boards, 385 million names in the WorldConnect family trees (which it shares with sister site Ancestry.com), and more than 32,000 free websites for individuals, genealogical organizations, and volunteer projects.

Some volunteer projects, like the USGenWeb <www.usgenweb.org> and WorldGenWeb <www.worldgenweb.org> projects, are organized geographically, containing location-specific reference information and data on country, state, and county levels. Others might address a particular record type, such as the Obituary Daily Times <www.rootsweb.com/~obituary> and the Immigrant Ship Transcribers Guild <www.immigrantships.net>. Databases and helpful information can also be found on the websites of individuals with websites dedicated to family history for a particular area or family.

Commercial Websites

Commercial websites like Ancestry.com <www.ancestry.com> and HeritageQuest <www.heritagequest.com> have made large collections of data available—some free and some available by subscription. HeritageQuest differs from Ancestry.com in that it only sells its subscriptions to libraries, although it also makes many of its images, databases, and indexes available to individual users through the sale of CD-ROMs, DVDs, print publications, and microfilm or microfiche. The largest online collection is available at Ancestry.com, which has databases containing more than 5 billion names. With access to these large data collections, subscribers can do much more research from the comfort of home, at hours convenient to their schedule, freeing up valuable time to search other records that have not yet been made available online.

Among the most popular online resources are user-submitted collections of electronic family trees. Typically hosted by commercial entities online or published on CD-ROM, users submit their electronic family tree databases along with their contact information to large collections in the hopes of connecting with other researchers working on the same lines. While the quality of the trees varies greatly among users, they can be useful in providing clues as to where to look for records that will substantiate the data. In addition to the research benefits, these trees often reunite family branches that have been separated, sometimes for generations, and the sense of kinship that is often born among long-lost cousins can be one of the most rewarding aspects of family history research. More on these collections can be found in the "Communicating and Sharing" section later in this chapter.

The most exciting aspect of online research lies in the growing collections of images of original records that can be accessed online. Because of the inherent cost of this type of endeavor, these collections are usually housed on commercial sites and available only to paying subscribers. All available U.S. Federal Censuses (1790–1930) and some U.K. Censuses are now available online at commercial sites by subscription. These census records and the posting of numerous city directories make it possible for researchers to identify their ancestors through the years and zero in on where to look for records that are not yet online.

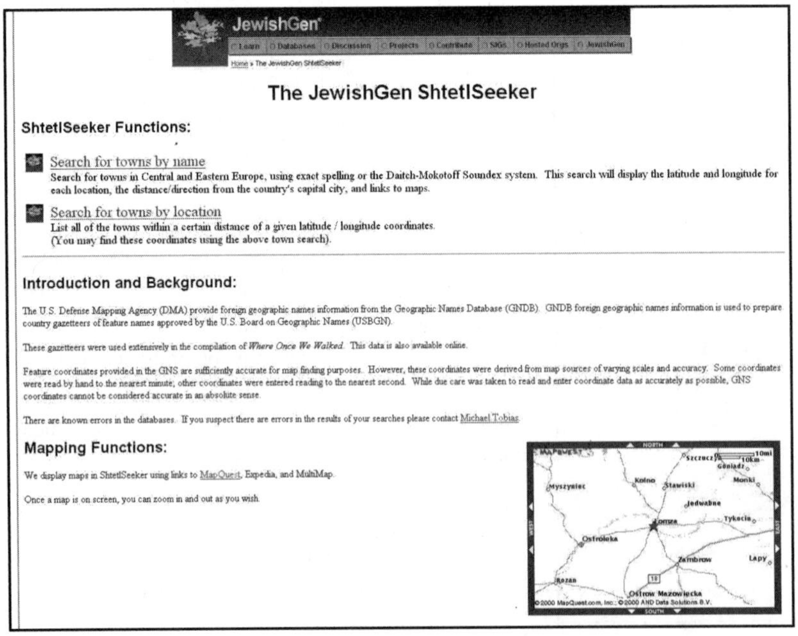

While this has only been a broad overview of the types of databases and indexes that can be found on the World Wide Web, a more complete look at databases and indexes can be found in chapter 3, "General References and Guides."

Figure 2-2. The JewishGen website, created to assist with Jewish genealogical research, also includes tools like the ShtetlSeeker <www.jewishgen.org/ShtetlSeeker>, which is helpful for anyone seeking the location of a town in Central or Eastern Europe.

Reference and Background Materials

Historical events left an imprint on the lives of our ancestors, just as the events of today affect us. Wars, disasters, and economic factors all had an effect and may have caused our ancestors to make decisions that altered the course of their lives. Job and land opportunities; environmental factors like drought, flood, pestilence, and so forth; wars; politics; or religious intolerance may have played a role in an ancestor's decision to move.

Biographies and local histories can add significant details to what we know about an ancestor's world. For years genealogists have compiled indexes to biographies so that family historians could learn more about their ancestors and their ancestor's contemporaries, and now many of those indexes are available online; the American Genealogical Biographical Index and the Biography and Genealogy Master Index, both available at Ancestry.com, are two notable biographical indexes that can be found on the Web. As we learn about the customs and conventions of the era in which our ancestors and their contemporaries lived, we can combine this information with the records we have located to gain a clearer understanding of the choices they made.

Historical information is becoming increasingly easy to find on the Web. The websites of libraries, archives, universities, municipalities, commercial Internet properties, and individuals host a wealth of information that can be useful to family historians.

The Library of Congress's American Memory Project <http://memory.loc.gov>, is an excellent example of what is available, with interviews and narratives from various eras of American history, as well as photographs, sound recordings, and video footage (see figure 2-3). There are also online exhibits offered at the websites of many museums and historical societies that can teach us much about our ancestors' lives in the context of history. The Encyclopedia of Chicago can be found on the website of the Chicago Historical Society <www.chicagohs.org>. Photographs, maps, broadsides and newspapers from Chicago's past can be searched or browsed through this project.

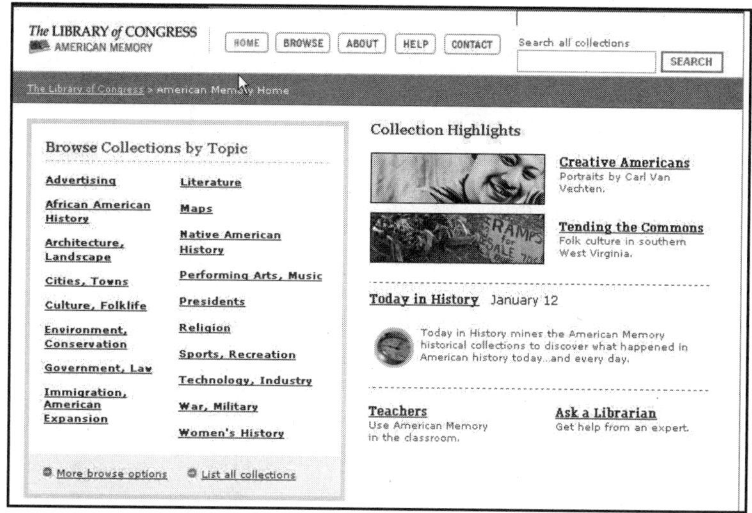

Figure 2-3. On the Library of Congress's American Memory website <http://memory.loc.gov/ammem/index.html>, collections use online photographs and prints, maps, motion pictures, sound recordings, sheet music, manuscripts, books, and other printed materials to help illustrate various time periods, events, and the local history.

Newspapers

Historical newspapers have long been sought as a valuable source of both genealogical data and of historical information for the times and places in which our ancestors lived. For those of us who were not fortunate enough to inherit diaries from our ancestors, historical newspapers can help fill that gap. They can provide details about town gossip; display local reaction to national or global events; give us information on weather, famine, politics, and war; record biases and prejudices of the times; show products our ancestors may have used; and report the prices of goods, services, and living space throughout their recorded history.

The number of historical newspapers available online continues to grow. Libraries like the Brooklyn (New York) Public Library <http://eagle.brooklynpubliclibrary.org> and the Digital Library of Georgia <http://dlg.galileo.usg.edu> are digitizing newspapers, making them searchable and viewable, free through the Web (see figure 2-4). Ancestry.com includes, as part of its subscription service, selected newspapers from the United States, Canada, and the United Kingdom spanning the late-eighteenth century to the present. In addition to projects such as these, which display images of the newspapers, there are also projects where volunteers transcribe items of interest, such as obituaries and sundry clippings.

Local History

Municipality websites often have historical information on the formation and early years of an area; it can be useful to visit the local Chamber of Commerce website as well. The Oregon State Archives hosts a *Historical County Records Guide* for each county in the state <http://arcweb.sos.state.or.us/county/cphome.html>. In addition to records inventories, images, and maps showing boundary changes, county seats, and geography, there are also county histories available.

The Ohio Memory Project <www.ohiomemory.org>, a cooperative effort between the Ohio Historical Society and a number of other historical organizations, libraries, and museums in the state, features a searchable database of more than 25,000 images of photographs, artifacts, archives, manuscripts, natural history specimens, and published materials online.

Even smaller municipalities are seeing the benefits in posting historical information online. Be sure to check for websites on the city and town level, as well as on the county level. Look for a link, or if the site features a search box, search for "history." For more on locating websites, see the section titled "Search Tips: Locating What You Need."

Historic Events

University websites can also be good sources of information. The University of Rochester is compiling a *History of the Erie Canal* online at <www.history.rochester.edu/canal> and the

University of Virginia hosts a comprehensive Civil War project called *The Valley of the Shadow: Two Communities in the American Civil* War <http://valley.vcdh.virginia.edu>. Through records such as correspondence, newspapers, and various others, it chronicles life in two communities, one Northern and one Southern, from 1859 through 1870.

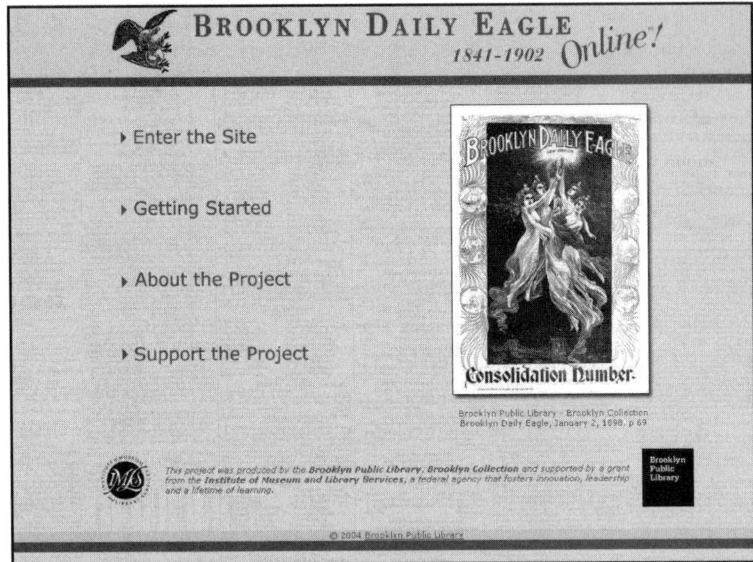

Figure 2-4. The Brooklyn Public Library website <www.brooklynpubliclibrary.org/eagle> is home to an online archive of the *Brooklyn Daily Eagle*, 1841–1902. Images of these historic newspapers can be searched or browsed by date.

Chronological History

In addition to historical exhibits associated with geography, events, and physical components of an area, there are also resources dedicated to various eras. A collaborative effort between the University of Michigan and Cornell University, the *Making of America* (found at <www.hti.umich.edu/m/moagrp> and <http://cdl.library.cornell.edu/moa>) is self-described as "a digital library of primary sources in American social history from the antebellum period through reconstruction" (see figure 2-5).

Military History

Throughout U.S. history, men and women have served in military conflicts. Their service records and the records of their military units can be very helpful to family historians in providing detail and background material. The military aspect of history is among the better-covered, as branches of the military, historians, reenactment groups, veterans organizations and individuals—veterans and civilians alike—seek to preserve the memories of those who have fought for this country.

There are many projects that have been created to make military history records more accessible. These include the *U.S. Civil War Soldiers and Sailors System* <www.itd.nps.gov/cwss>,

Military Links

While some of these facilities, agencies, or organizations may hold some information on individual veterans, many are more focused on historical information regarding military history, units, and conflicts. Please refer to the Web pages for details on the holdings, research, and reference policies before requesting information.

American Battle Monuments Commission
<www.abmc.gov>

Department of Veterans Affairs
<www.va.gov>

United States Marine Corps, History and Museums Division
<http://hqinet001.hqmc.usmc.mil/HD>

National Archives and Records Administration
<www.archives.gov/veterans/military-service-records/get-service-records.html>

Naval Historical Center
<www.history.navy.mil>

U.S. Air Force Historical Research Agency
<www.au.af.mil/au/afhra>

U.S. Army Center of Military History
<www.army.mil/cmh-pg/default.htm>

U.S. Army Institute of Heraldry
<www.tioh.hqda.pentagon.mil>

U.S. Army Military History Institute
<http://carlisle-www.army.mil/usamhi>

U.S. Civil War Center
<www.cwc.lsu.edu>

U.S. Coast Guard Historian's Office (G-CP-4)
<www.uscg.mil/hq/g-cp/history/collect.html>

U.S. Merchant Marine
<www.usmm.org/index.html>

U.S. Military Academy, Museum and Archives
<www.usma.edu/Museum>

a project of the National Parks Service in cooperation with the Genealogical Society of Utah and the Federation of Genealogical Societies. The project indexes and includes basic facts on both Confederate and Union servicemen. Additionally, it includes "histories of regiments in both the Union and Confederate Armies, links to descriptions of 384 significant battles of the war, and other historical information." For some of the government sponsored sites, see the included list of Military Links.

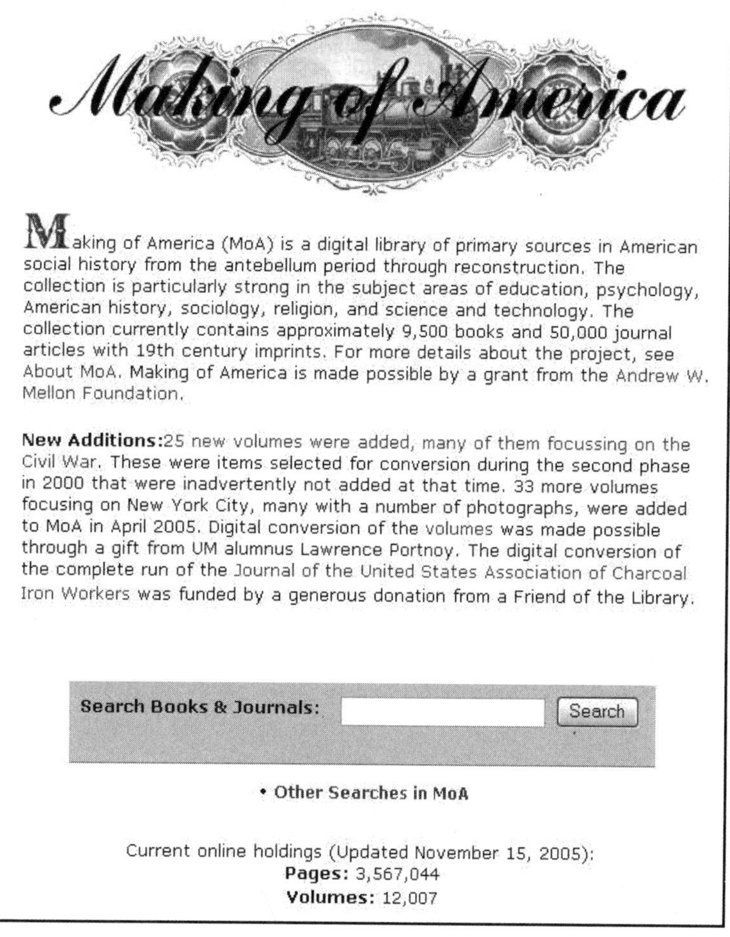

Making of America

Making of America (MoA) is a digital library of primary sources in American social history from the antebellum period through reconstruction. The collection is particularly strong in the subject areas of education, psychology, American history, sociology, religion, and science and technology. The collection currently contains approximately 9,500 books and 50,000 journal articles with 19th century imprints. For more details about the project, see About MoA. Making of America is made possible by a grant from the Andrew W. Mellon Foundation.

New Additions:25 new volumes were added, many of them focussing on the Civil War. These were items selected for conversion during the second phase in 2000 that were inadvertently not added at that time. 33 more volumes focusing on New York City, many with a number of photographs, were added to MoA in April 2005. Digital conversion of the volumes was made possible through a gift from UM alumnus Lawrence Portnoy. The digital conversion of the complete run of the Journal of the United States Association of Charcoal Iron Workers was funded by a generous donation from a Friend of the Library.

Search Books & Journals: Search

• **Other Searches in MoA**

Current online holdings (Updated November 15, 2005):
Pages: 3,567,044
Volumes: 12,007

Figure 2-5. The "Making of America" websites, part of a collaborative online project of the University of Michigan and Cornell University, makes available materials from their respective libraries that document American social history, including books and journals from the nineteenth century. This image is from the University of Michigan site <www.hti.umich.edu/m/moagrp>; the Cornell site is located at <http://cdl.library.cornell.edu/moa>.

Maps

Mapping out boundaries and streets is important for research anywhere, whether it be in a city or in a rural area. Pinpointing where your ancestors lived is critical to locating records. Addresses are often found in directories, vital records, court records, military records, some census enumerations, and naturalization records. For example, by plotting these addresses on a map along with local churches, it is possible to determine where our ancestors worshipped, and where more records might be kept. The addresses can also tell us what civil districts to pursue in checking for locally created records.

In the nineteenth century, many towns sprang up along railroad lines. During this period, railroad routes often determined the routes of travel and migration of our ancestors. The Library of Congress's American Memory Project has, as a part of its larger map collection, a collection of 623 *Railroad Maps, 1828–1900.*

In addition, boundaries often changed over the years and being familiar with these changes can save you time and money that could be wasted looking for records in the wrong jurisdiction. If you were looking for ancestors from the area around Palmerton, Pennsylvania, you would need to know that it fell in Northampton County until 1843, when the county boundaries changed. Since then it has been in Carbon County, Pennsylvania. Similarly, state boundaries may have been redefined and your ancestor may have changed states without even moving.

Many historical and contemporary maps are now available online. One of the largest resources for locating maps is *Odden's Bookmarks: The Fascinating World of Maps and Mapping* <http://oddens.geog.uu.nl/index.html>, which contains links to over 21,500 cartographic sites. The Library of Congress's American Memory Project also contains a large historical map collection.

Sites like Google Maps <www.maps.google.com> and MapQuest <www.mapquest.com> can help pinpoint addresses, but it's important to remember that street names may have changed or been renumbered over the years. For this reason, it's best to use a combination of contemporary and historical maps.

Photographs

Photographs bring an added dimension to family history and while photographs of ancestors may not always be available, it may be possible to locate photographs of the areas in which they lived. Again, the Library of Congress's American Memory Project contains both photographs and images that can give researchers a peek at the world as it looked to their ancestors.

Libraries, historical societies, museums, and local governments are good starting points in your search for historic photos. The San Francisco Public Library maintains a database of 30,000 photographs <http://sfpl4.sfpl.org/librarylocations/sfhistory/sfphoto.htm> that can be viewed by subject (e.g., biography, buildings, businesses, churches, cemeteries, districts, orphanages, schools, and streets), or by the decade from the 1850s through the 1990s.

When using these images, it is important to remember photographs and other materials found on the Web are subject to copyright laws. For more on copyrights, see chapter 1, "The Foundations of Family History Research."

There are a growing number of "orphan" photograph and memorabilia websites now online. These sites rescue lost or abandoned photographs and other mementos from flea markets, garage sales, and online auctions, and post images or descriptions of the item on the site in the hopes of reuniting it with an associated family. These sites include Dead Fred: The Original Online Genealogy Photo Archive <www.deadfred.com> and Ancient Faces <www.ancientfaces.com>. Online auctions such as eBay <www.ebay.com> are also a source of old photographs and postcards.

The Web as a Finding Aid

The Web is also useful in locating other family history artifacts. Family bibles, family histories, and various records in print and on CD-ROMs also often appear on online auction sites. The National Genealogical Society (NGS) website has a searchable index of Bible records that are in its collection <www.ngsgenealogy.org>.

Online bookstores like Amazon.com <www.amazon.com> and Barnes & Noble <www.barnesandnoble.com> make it easy to locate and order reference materials quickly and easily from home. For used, rare, and out of print books, the *Advanced Book Exchange* <www.abebooks.com> provides a searchable database of publications from booksellers around the world.

The Web has also made it easier to look into the collections of distant libraries through their catalogs. Library websites can be located using search engines or through websites such as LibrarySpot <www.libraryspot.com>. Once located, these websites may allow you to order a publication of interest, or copies of certain pages from it, through your local library via an Interlibrary Loan (ILL) request.

The Family History Library (FHL) of the LDS Church has the largest collection of genealogical materials in the world (see appendix F). The catalog of these materials is available online at its site <www.familysearch.org>. Microform publications can be ordered for use at its Family History Centers throughout the world.

Research Planning

Many of the types of resources listed above can be very helpful in planning research. Before traveling to do research, online sources can be referenced to make your trip more productive.

Many libraries and other research facilities now maintain websites that should be visited prior to any trip to learn hours of operation and any usage restrictions. Good examples are the Allen County Public Library in Fort Wayne, Indiana <www.acpl.lib.in.us>, and the FHL in Salt Lake City, which are popular research destinations for genealogists from across the country. Despite the easy access to this information, it is a good idea to follow up with a phone call or an e-mail to ensure that there are no unscheduled closings and that the collections you plan to reference will be available. Sometimes construction, reorganization, or repairs will not be noted on the website.

The website may also have an overview of the collections that are available at that facility. Finding aids and any catalogs that are available on the website, consulted at home, can help you to plan your trip and save valuable research time once you arrive at the facility. It's also a good idea to look around on the Web to make sure that the records you are interested researching onsite are not already available to you online. Should you find that they are, you can focus your trip around records that are not yet available online.

Once materials for a planned trip are located in the catalog, write down or print the complete bibliographic citation. This can save you time locating them in the catalog at the facility. As an added measure, inquire with the staff after arriving at the facility to see if there are any collections that may be useful that are not included in the catalog.

When traveling to do onsite research, government entities also maintain helpful information on their websites detailing policies and what levels of access family historians can expect (see figure 2-1).

The websites of religious administrative offices and archives should be consulted. The website of the Archives of the Evangelical Lutheran Church in America <www.elca.org/archives> is a good example of what is available. A special page is dedicated to "General Information for Family History Researchers" and an online exhibit is described as "a genealogical guide to the congregations, pastors, and records of the numerous Lutheran congregations in Chicago."

Search Tips: Locating What Is Needed

The key to genealogical research has always been in the location of records, and the location of ancestors in those records. When it comes to searching on the Web and in databases, as with traditional research, a little forethought and a good working knowledge of the tools at your disposal can greatly increase your chances of success.

Web Searches

The Web is often compared to a huge library, and using that comparison, the catalogs to the contents of that library are *search engines*. There are many different search engines, and they differ in the way they compile listings, the search functionality they offer, extra features that are available, and the way they rank their results.

Some search engines gather listings by "crawling" or "spidering" websites. These applications are mainly used to create a copy of all the visited pages for later processing that will index the downloaded pages to provide fast searches. Other search engines may create listings from data submitted by users. Meta-search engines will pull results from multiple search engines. Still other search engines may pull their listings using a combination of methods. Because of the variety of search engines, you will want to try your searches with multiple search engines.

Even with all the differences, there are some common strategies that can help you to get the most from whatever search engine you choose.

Use specific terms. If you are searching for a particular research facility, search using the name of the facility, rather than just generic terms (for example, *Allen County Public Library*, rather than just *library*). When searching for a city or town, include the state name as well.

Add a keyword. If a search is yielding too many results, unwanted sites can be excluded by adding a keyword or keywords. For example, if you are searching for genealogy sites related to the surname Dooner, rather than just searching on the surname, you might try searches for: *Dooner genealogy*, *Dooner ancestry*, *Dooner descendant* or, *Dooner family*. Search queries can be refined further by adding a location or date, such as a birth or death date.

Use advanced search functions. Most search engines have advanced search forms that allow users to specify how the terms being sought should appear in results or they may accept Boolean operators ("and," "not," "or," and "near") and search engine math (+ and –). Some search engines support both.

Use "and" or the + sign to specify that results should contain both or all of the terms somewhere on the page. In some cases, the use of these qualifiers is not necessary because the search engine settings may default to only returning results where all terms are included. The popular search engines, Google <www.google.com> and AltaVista <www.altavista.com>, are two such search engines. For example, in Google, searches for *Minnesota naturalizations*, *Minnesota and naturalizations*, or *Minnesota + naturalizations* should all return the same results.

To search for an exact phrase, enclose the phrase in quotation marks (for example, "*Minnesota naturalization records*" will only return searches with the entire phrase listed exactly as it is typed.)

Use "not" and the – sign to exclude a term. For example, if the above search for Minnesota naturalizations was returning too many pages for immigration lawyers, a way to eliminate those hits would be to search for *Minnesota naturalizations not lawyer* or *Minnesota naturalizations – lawyer.*

Use the word "or" to produce results that contain either of the terms. *Minnesota or naturalizations* would produce results containing either Minnesota or naturalizations, but not necessarily both. This can be a particularly useful operator when searching for variations of surnames.

Use the word "near" in searches to limit search results based on how near the search terms are to each other. The value of the proximity (such as "within 10" or "within 25") may vary from one search engine to the next, and some search engines will also allow "followed by" or "adj" (adjacent), which would require that one term immediately follow the other. This can be useful when searching for information about individuals. When searching for information on an ancestor named James Gosson, using the expression *James Gosson* will only produce results if the name appears as the given name followed by the surname. Searching using the keywords *James near Gosson* will also produce results where the website references him as "Gosson, James."

Watch word variations. Think of how words are likely to be used on the site and use them in that form. While most search engines are not case sensitive, they will not recognize variations of words. A search for *Minnesota naturalization* (as in *Minnesota naturalization records*) will return a different set of results than *Minnesota naturalizations*. A search for *Minnesota naturalization OR naturalizations* would cover both sets.

Explore features. In the intensely competitive search engine market, companies are constantly seeking to improve their services by offering expanded features. In addition to advanced search functions, other features include translation software, different types of searches (such as image, news, newsgroups, catalog, audio, or video searches, etc.), parental controls to weed out inappropriate sites, the ability to view cached sites, directories, and more.

Read the help page. Look for the *Help* section to make sure that you are using the correct operators and understand fully the functionality of that particular search engine. Most help pages are clearly written and easy to understand, and by becoming familiar with how they work, your chances of success will greatly increase.

Another good resource for learning about search engines is SearchEngineWatch.com <www.searchenginewatch.com>. This site features tutorials and reviews of various search engines.

Link Directories

Another option to locating information is to turn to websites that feature collections of links relative to a particular topic. Cyndi's List, <www.cyndislist.com>, is the most well-known of these sites related to genealogy (see figure 2-6). The work of genealogist Cyndi Howells, this site housed upwards of 240,000 links as of 2005, classified in more than 150 categories. The site is also searchable. Cyndi's List is a great place to see what kinds of websites are available for a particular topic, and, when used in conjunction with search engines, it can be a big time saver. It is also a great place to turn to for ideas on new avenues to pursue.

Other directories are available with more focused link collections. Vital Records Information <www.vitalrec.com>

provides contact information, fees, and links to U.S. vital records departments. Other directories are available online that, although they weren't created specifically for family historians, can be very useful. FuneralNet <www.funeralnet.com> bills itself as "America's most trusted online obituary, funeral, cremation, and cemetery resource." The National Association of Counties website <www.naco.org> hosts a directory of counties that provides contact information for county courthouses and other helpful county information.

Living People Searches

There are a number of phone and business directories available on the Web. These resources can be very valuable when it comes to locating living family members with whom we have lost contact, or other entities such as funeral homes, cemeteries, churches, schools, libraries, and so on. Popular online phone and address directories include Switchboard.com <www.switchboard.com>, InfoSpace <www.infospace.com>, and Yahoo! People Search <http://people.yahoo.com>.

There are also pay services, such as the MyFamily.com People Finder <http://reunite.myfamily.com>, and U.S. Search <www.ussearch.com>, that charge a fee to search more comprehensive databases for people.

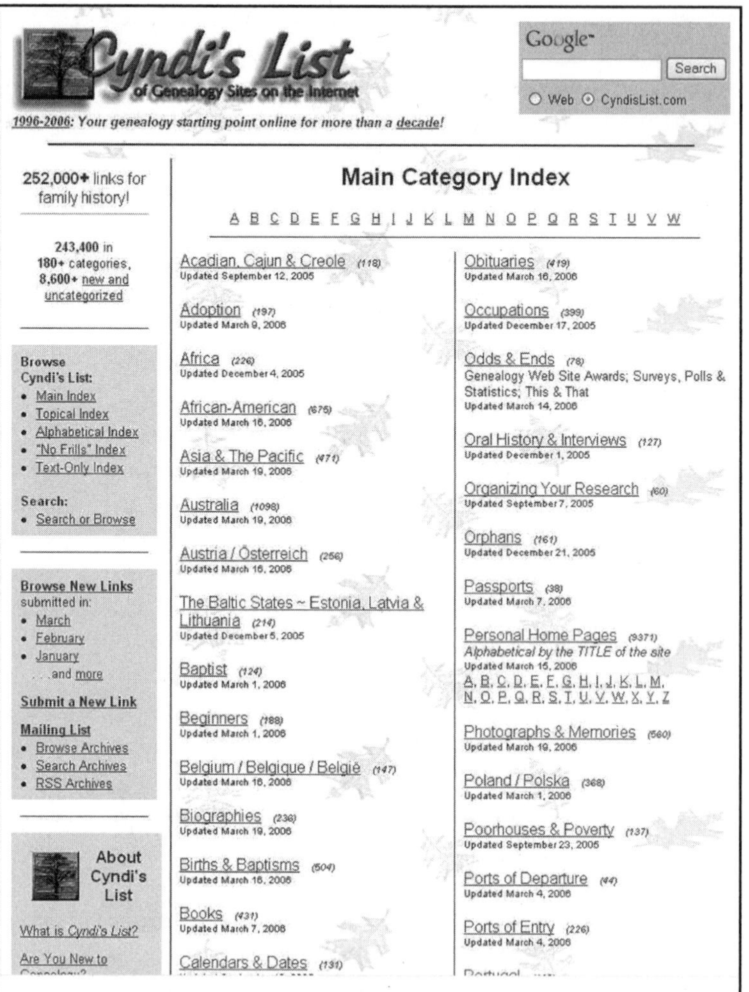

Figure 2-6. Cyndi's List <www.cyndislist.com>, first launched in March of 1996, catalogs over 240,000 genealogically significant websites, cross-referenced by subject and location.

Searching Databases and Indexes

Just as searching the Web requires some knowledge of search engines, when searching online databases and database collections a working knowledge of the search features unique to that particular database is important. Here are some tips for searching individual databases or groups of databases:

Take advantage of advanced search features. In some cases searches will turn up too many results, and in others there may be few or no matches. In either case, keywords and advanced search functions can help. Typically a keyword search is available, but websites frequently feature advanced search functionality tailored to the website's offerings. Separate fields may be available to narrow a search by location, time frame, or record type. When searching for a common name like Smith or Jones, this can mean the difference between spending hours or even days wading through irrelevant hits, or locating an ancestor in minutes or even seconds.

If you receive too many results, you can narrow the search by adding another piece of information. Look at some of the results, noting the fields that are available and the formatting (e.g., abbreviations, spaces, dashes, etc.). If the search interface allows you to specify a keyword, it can be used to help you tailor a more refined search. Some keywords might include a county name, maiden name, Social Security number, dates, military designations and units, or any field for which you have information.

If you don't get any results, try searching for Smith or some other common name to get a feel for what fields are included. Where there are a number of options available in an advanced search, looking at the format of the results and what information is included, you may be able to find some creative ways to search, such as searching for

- a given name (no surname) and the name of the county or town,
- a surname or given name and occupation,
- an address,
- a name and a year, month, or date,
- a name and age, and
- a location and age.

Sometimes less is more. If a search is narrowed too much by the inclusion of too much information, possible matches could be inadvertently excluded. Most databases will only give hits on *exact* matches. A misspelled given name, a date that doesn't quite match up, or a piece of information that is formatted a little differently than the way it is in the database can give false negative results, when in fact, an ancestor is included in the database. For this reason, it's best to start searches wide and, if necessary, narrow results slowly by adding a piece of information at a time.

When specifying a date, try including only the month and year as opposed to the full date. This is particularly helpful when doing advanced searches of databases like the Social Security Death Index (SSDI), as some dates are not included in their entirety.

Relevancy ranked searches. Ancestry.com now offers an alternative search functionality, both on the website and through its genealogical software, *Family Tree Maker*. Using the Ranked Search, the database takes the information you include and returns the most likely matches found in its collections, including those with similar names, dates, or locations. For example, a search for John Smith could give results for Jon Smith and John Smyth. Because this greatly increases the number of hits on any given search, when using the Ranked Search, it is best to include as much information as possible. This will bring the best possible matches to the top of the results.

Try direct searches. When working with large database collections, better results can sometimes be achieved by searching the databases individually. While searches like the global search at Ancestry.com are certainly huge time savers, there are certain advantages of going directly to a database of interest and searching it separately. Check to see if there is a listing of databases sorted by location for a particular collection. By looking at the databases in areas specific to research needs, focus can be directed to those of interest to make searches more effective.

Because these collections may contain a wide variety of databases, including varying degrees of information in different fields, sometimes a "one size fits all" search interface will not be as effective as using one that is created especially for a particular database. Recognizing this, database purveyors may sometimes create more specialized search interfaces for some databases. Databases typically have a search field containing a space for the given name, surname, and a keyword, and some may have more advanced search options that are created especially to cater to that database's contents. For example, a database of passenger arrival records may include a search field for the name of the ship. A search of a collection of databases that include passenger arrivals, census records, military records, and so forth, will likely not have this feature.

Conversely, if an individual database of interest does not have the advanced search functionality needed, try using any advanced search features that are available in searching the larger collection as a whole.

Experiment and use informational help pages. Since every database and every search is unique, it is a good idea to familiarize yourself with the databases you use. As mentioned previously, note the fields available and the format of those fields, as well as the order in which the results are displayed, all of which can help you to find your way around obstacles.

In addition, look for *Help* or *FAQ* (Frequently Asked Questions) pages. These pages can contain important information about a database's functionality and flexibility.

Read the description. It is important to read any descriptions, prefaces, and introductions to the records you are searching. What is the source of the information? What were the criteria for inclusion in the record set or database? What years and areas does it cover? How complete is it? Knowing the answers to these questions can help to determine whether or not your ancestor really should be included in the database.

Given names. If a given name can be specified in a search, be sure to also look for variations, misspellings, or abbreviations of that name. Sometimes only an initial or abbreviation is used, such as "Chas." for Charles or "Thos." for Thomas. Also look for variations and different spellings—Eliza, Beth, Liz, Liza, for Elizabeth; Alex for Alexander; Jim for James; Jon for John. You may find that some websites have added programs that will match common equivalent names and include them in search results, but this isn't always the case. In addition, when searching for an immigrant ancestor, try looking for the name in his or her native language.

Soundex searches or sound it out. Some databases allow Soundex searches. The Soundex is an indexing and filing system based on how words sound rather than how they are spelled. A detailed description of this system and how names are coded is included in chapter 5, "Census Records." Using Soundex functionality, a search for the surname *Poland* would turn up all surnames that share the Soundex Code P453 (e.g., *Poland, Polend, Polant*). When doing Soundex searches, it's important to keep in mind the name variants that you also want to search and make sure they share that code. Using the *Poland* example above, a Soundex search would not turn up *Polan, Polen,* or *Polin,* which would be coded P450. Despite these drawbacks, well thought out searches using the Soundex feature may help you to get positive results, despite misspellings.

For other databases, you may want to say the name aloud, perhaps with an accent, and imagine how someone unfamiliar with the name might spell it based on that sound.

Proximity searches. Where available, a proximity specification allows you to indicate how many words can come in between the criteria you enter. This is particularly valuable when you are searching for surnames that are also given names, such as *William Dennis*. With the proximity search set at the default of *adjacent*, this feature should eliminate false hits that show *William Jones, John Smith,* and *Dennis Johnson* by only showing hits where *William* and *Dennis* are next to each other. Unfortunately, you will still have to deal with entries for *William Dennis Johnson*.

There are also instances where you will want to widen the search. A search in an obituary database may show a listing similar to the one below:

> *Services for Agnes Huggins will be held at . . . Survivors include three sons, James, Ronald, and Joseph.*

In this example, a search with a wider proximity setting, or no proximity at all, will also show this entry to someone who was searching for James Huggins, since both names appear in the entry.

Data range. Some websites may allow narrowing a search to a particular time frame. If you are searching for a common name, try entering your ancestor's estimated life span in these fields. This can greatly reduce the number of hits, ruling out unwanted matches from the wrong time period.

Search for indexing, typographic, and/or OCR mistakes. When investigating the source of a database, it's also important to check these same descriptive materials to determine how a database was created. Depending on the method used, it is possible to predict the type of mistakes that might have been made. With databases created using Optical Character Recognition (OCR) technology, where a document is read electronically and reproduced using specialized scanners and software, similar-looking letters may be misidentified. If the index or database was created by humans, errors found may again be misidentified letters, or simple typographic mistakes.

With records produced using OCR, similar-looking letters and even smudges or spots on the document can confuse the "computer's eye" and subsequently cause misreadings of the text, leading a researcher to missed and incorrect results. However, this technology is improving and while still not perfect, in some cases, it can be more accurate than manual transcriptions, as long as the print is clear and the record is relatively clean of spots and smudges.

For manually created records, with the handwriting that indexers often face, as well as faded print or poor-quality microfilms, it can be difficult even for those familiar with a name to pick it out. Given these challenges, it's not surprising that we run across an occasional misspelling. Some often-confused letters include the following:

- L and S
- T and F
- J, G, and Y
- I and J
- K and R
- O and Q
- P and R
- U and W

Vowels are also frequently misinterpreted, both as other vowels and as some similar-looking consonants. Switching similar-looking letters or vowels in the surnames you are researching can often solve this problem.

In many cases, there may be a problem with the index because of a simple typographical error. Try typing your ancestor's name very fast several times. Is there a common mistake you make? If so, try searching for that. Transposals often occur when one hand gets ahead of the other, such as "hte" instead of "the." Look at the name you are searching for instances where one letter typed by one hand is followed by a letter typed by the other hand. Try reversing these letters. To find other possible keying errors, take a look at your keyboard and try switching some letters in the name for the letters around it on the keyboard.

Wildcard searches can also be helpful. At Ancestry.com, for example, the wildcard must be preceded by the first three letters of the name (for example, "All*"). This will turn up any misspellings that fall after the first three letters.

Trouble with titles. Titles can cause problems when searching for ancestors. A search of one 1850 census index using the given name "Mr." turned up 5,470 hits. In addition, there are 1,238 people who listed the title "Dr." as their given name.

In the same index, a search for "sister" produced 332 matches. While many nuns included their last names, there are a number of them that only included a religious name as their surname ("Marlena, Sister"). These ladies would never be found in a surname search.

If you think your ancestor may have used a title, consider it when performing searches. This typically will not be a problem if the given name is listed in addition to the title and you search for the given name and surname, as the search will still typically pick up the given name as a keyword in that field.

Separated names. Sometimes an unusual space between letters in a name on a record may cause an indexer or transcriber to separate the name in the index. For example, one index to the 1930 census lists a "De Loris Witt." The extended space between the "De" and "loris" in "Deloris" caused the indexer to separate the two (see figure 2-7).

The same principle should be kept in mind with surnames that might be interpreted as two words, such as "DeWitt" or "De Witt." A search for "oconnor" and "o'connor" both turned up 38,871 hits in the 1930 census. A search for "o connor" (including a space) turned up an additional 1,052 hits. In that same census, a search for "mc donald" (with the space) returned 46,798 hits, while a search for "mcdonald" (without the space) returned 58,516.

In addition, sometimes names that you would typically think of as always having a space are indexed without the space. For example, there are 3,725 St. Clairs but only 3,540 Stclairs in the 1930 U.S. census index at Ancestry.com. The omission or insertion of that space can mean the difference between a successful search and an unsuccessful one.

Occasionally spaces can cause problems at the beginning or end of a name, or in a field where text has been removed. If criteria is entered in a field to search and then removed, it is best to remove it by using the delete key or the backspace key. If the search interprets that space as a character, it will only give you results with a space in that field, which may lead to poor results.

CDs and DVDs

Many of the databases that are found on the Web, and some that are not, are available on CD-ROM or DVD. There are several things to think about when deciding whether to purchase data on this type of medium:

- Is the product compatible with the computer that will be used to read it?
- Are the contents of the product clearly listed and will the scope of the data meet research needs?
- Is the data available online, possibly on a free website or through a collection you have access to through a subscription?
- Are there product reviews available for this product or can you consult others who have had experience with it?

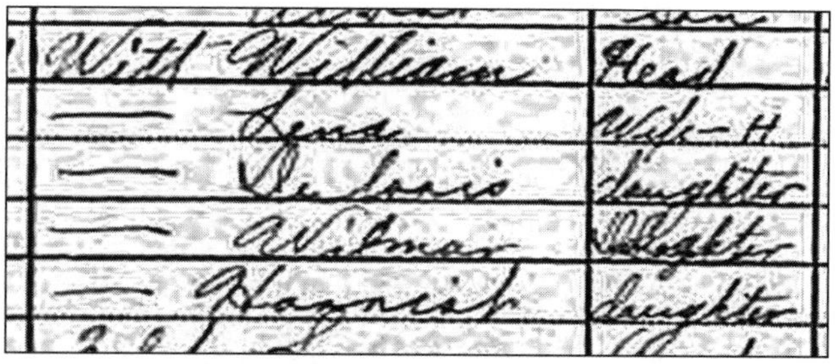

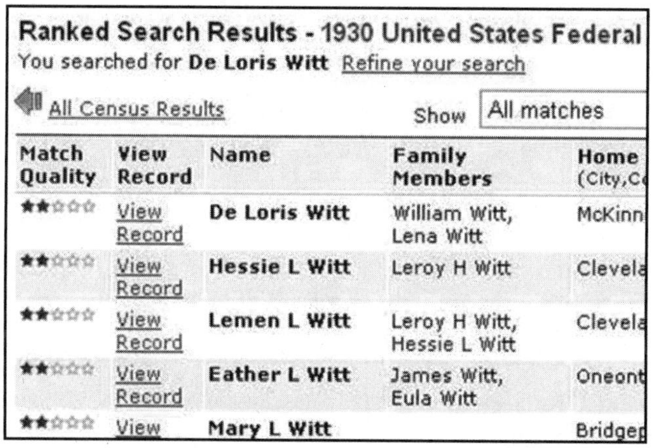

Ranked Search Results - 1930 United States Federal
You searched for **De Loris Witt** Refine your search
All Census Results Show All matches

Match Quality	View Record	Name	Family Members	Home (City,C
★★☆☆☆	View Record	De Loris Witt	William Witt, Lena Witt	McKinn
★★☆☆☆	View Record	Hessie L Witt	Leroy H Witt	Clevel
★★☆☆☆	View Record	Lemen L Witt	Leroy H Witt, Hessie L Witt	Clevel
★★☆☆☆	View Record	Eather L Witt	James Witt, Eula Witt	Oneont
★★☆☆☆	View	Mary L Witt		Bridge

Figure 2-7. One index to the 1930 U.S. Federal census lists a "De Loris Witt." The extended space between the "De" and "loris" in "Deloris" caused the indexer to separate the name in the index.

Citing Electronic Sources

With the huge quantities of information that family historians collect, citing the sources of that information has always been important. With the explosion of information that has been put at our fingertips with new technology, it has become even more critical. While genealogical software has come a long way in this area in recent years, there is still some room for improvement and the citation ability should be of primary importance when choosing a particular brand of software for use.

In addition to changing addresses (which will be discussed in further detail in the next section), there is also the fact that much of the data we receive has several layers of sources. It is not uncommon for a database to be three (or sometimes even more) generations removed from the original record.

While it would be impossible to address all of the forms and styles for citation of electronic sources here, this chapter will address what information should be included, as well as indicate references to resources, both online and offline, where more detailed information can be found. For data found online or on CD-ROM, the following information, where available, should be listed as follows:

- Author—Sometimes this will be an individual, while in other cases it might also be a company or organization
- Complete database, website, or publication title
- E-mail address and any other available contact information for webmaster
- Volumes (if applicable) included in the database
- Original source information (what records or publication was this database drawn from), which should include the following:
  —Author (with address and contact information for individuals if available)
  —Source title
  —Source publisher
  —Date of original publication
- If the source of the original publication is a repository like the National Archives and Records Administration (NARA), a state archive, or the FHL, the internal publication number should also be included. This would include the following
  —NARA Record Group (RG) number
  —NARA Microform Publication number, roll and page
  —State archive series or other record publication number
  —FHL Call number
  —FHL Microform number
- Image or page number where applicable
- Database Uniform Resource Locator (URL) (i.e., the website address)

- Date accessed
- For information received via e-mail
  - — Message originator
  - — Subject
  - — E-mail address
  - — Other contact information where available.
  - — Sent to or through (i.e., to author, or through "Smith RootsWeb mailing list," etc.)
  - — Message date

Listed below are additional resources for more information on electronic source citations:

Gibaldi, Joseph. MLA *Handbook for Writers of Research Papers*. 5th ed. New York: Modern Language Association of America, 1999.

Grossman, John. *The Chicago Manual of Style: The Essential Guide for Writers, Editors, and Publishers*. 15th ed. Chicago: University of Chicago Press. 2003.

Library of Congress, American Memory Project. *The Learning Page: How to Cite Electronic Sources*. Online at <http://memory.loc.gov/ammem/ndlpedu/start/cite/index.html>.

Mills, Elizabeth Shown. *Evidence! Citation & Analysis for the Family Historian*. Baltimore: Genealogical Publishing Co., 1997.

The Regents of the University of Michigan. *The Internet Public Library: FARQs, Citing Electronic Resources*. Online at <www.ipl.org/div/farq/netciteFARQ.html>.

Outdated Internet Addresses

Locating Outdated URLs

One of the biggest challenges of citing electronic sources is the transient nature of Web addresses. Websites often need to restructure or switch to a different website host. When this happens, the URL may need to change. If information from a database is only cited with that address, it may be difficult to locate again for verification or for further research. In some cases

NGS Standards for Use of Technology

Mindful that computers are tools, genealogists take full responsibility for their work, and therefore they

- learn the capabilities and limits of their equipment and software, and use them only when they are the most appropriate tools for a purpose.
- do not accept uncritically the ability of software to format, number, import, modify, check, chart, or report their data, and therefore carefully evaluate any resulting product.
- treat compiled information from online sources or digital databases in the same way as other published sources—useful primarily as a guide to locating original records, but not as evidence for a conclusion or assertion.
- accept digital images or enhancements of an original record as a satisfactory substitute for the original only when there is reasonable assurance that the image accurately reproduces the unaltered original.
- cite sources for data obtained online or from digital media with the same care that is appropriate for sources on paper and other traditional media, and enter data into a digital database only when its source can remain associated with it.
- always cite the sources for information or data posted online or sent to others, naming the author of a digital file as its immediate source, while crediting original sources cited within the file.
- preserve the integrity of their own databases by evaluating the reliability of downloaded data before incorporating it into their own files.
- provide, whenever they alter data received in digital form, a description of the change that will accompany the altered data whenever it is shared with others.
- actively oppose the proliferation of error, rumor, and fraud by personally verifying or correcting information, or noting it as unverified, before passing it on to others.
- treat people online as courteously and civilly as they would treat them face-to-face, not separated by networks and anonymity.
- accept that technology has not changed the principles of genealogical research, only some of the procedures.

©2000, 2001, 2002 by National Genealogical Society. Permission is granted to copy or publish this material provided it is reproduced in its entirety, including this notice.

the database may be removed indefinitely or permanently from the Web, making it completely unavailable.

Google has a *cache* feature and by searching for a website that has disappeared, it may be possible to access the cached version of the website after it has been removed.

If the information was cited properly, it still may be possible to locate either the website at its new URL, or the original source of the information in a physical environment. If the data is still available online, using a search engine to search for the exact website title or the website author's name may turn up its new location. If it is no longer available online, methods covered earlier in this chapter ("The Web as a Finding Aid") may be useful in locating the original records.

Locating Outdated E-mail Addresses

With mailing lists and message boards allowing users to interact and exchange information, there is also the problem of changing e-mail addresses. It's not uncommon for an individual to change e-mail addresses, sometimes several times over the course of a year. Internet Service Providers (ISPs) may be taken over by a different company, customers switch because of service problems, or they may have been using a work e-mail address as their contact information and have subsequently switched jobs. Whatever the reason, these changes can render e-mail citations useless, unless more contact information, such as a street address, is provided.

A number of the resources listed in the section on "People Searches" may be helpful in locating a phone number and many also offer e-mail directories. In addition, there are registries available like the one at *FreshAddress* <www.freshaddress.com> that may be useful (see figure 2-8). Many ISPs and other services also maintain voluntary e-mail directories, although some might only be available to others who use that particular service. The trouble with these is that they are typically voluntary, and if the person being sought never took the time to register his current address or a change of address, it won't be available.

Another option would be to enter the person's name into a search engine and see if it appears anywhere. If it is a common name, try adding *genealogy* or some other keyword, such as a surname interest that you share. You may locate a more recent e-mail address in this manner, perhaps on a message board or query website.

Analyzing and Assessing the Quality of Online Information

Regardless of the advances made by technology, there is still a margin of error that needs to be dealt with when using records found on the Web. Just as you would analyze any record you found in a library, courthouse, or archive, the quality and accuracy of resources found on the Web should be similarly analyzed.

In making an assessment, consider the source. If the information came from an individual's database, whether in an online collection or on a website, are sources included and in good form? If there are no sources cited, or if the citations that are included only lead to someone else's work, it should serve as a warning that the researcher may not be as diligent as he or she should have been, and the data may be suspect.

If the information comes from a larger organization or corporate entity, what is their reputation for quality? Are descriptive materials comprehensive, listing detailed information about the scope of the data? Are original sources for the data provided? What kind of reviews in reputable publications has the product or collection received? Genealogical periodicals are a good source of information on large electronic collections—both non-profit and commercial.

In assessing electronic images, again, consider the source. If the source is an organization or company whose reputation depends on providing quality genealogical products, there really isn't a reason to suspect that images have been manipulated to skew the facts. In fact, it would likely be more beneficial to that entity to provide an unadulterated quality product. However, if the image were the only evidence linking an individual to royalty or some kind of celebrity, it would be a good idea to also consult the original as a precautionary measure. Most of the time, there will not be a problem, but the verification could save time and money down the road.

Figure 2-8. Registries like FreshAddress.com can help you to locate current e-mail addresses when posted addresses have changed.

Organization

Genealogical Software

Computers are an invaluable tool for storing and disseminating the large amount of information that family historians collect during the course of their research. Genealogical software programs help organize this data in one convenient location. This information can then, at the click of a mouse, be formatted in a number of ways, printed on various forms, exported to other formats, and used to plan further research.

Not long ago, the decision of which genealogical software to use was limited to a few programs. With the booming popularity of family history, and advances in related technology fields, there are now many commercial products available, as well as some shareware and freeware. Freeware, as the name implies, is software that is available free from the developer. Shareware is copyrighted software that is available in some form to be downloaded free, but conditionally. The product may only be free for a trial period, or some features or additional support may be unavailable until the product is paid for. Because of the costs associated with developing a product, most of the major software packages are commercial offerings.

Choosing the Right Software

There are a number of considerations in choosing software. The primary requirement is that the software be compatible with your computer, operating system, and any other electronic tools you plan on using with it. If you are running on an older operating system, or have limited or outdated hardware resources, your choices will be more limited and you may not be able to install some newer programs.

While most software is competitive when it comes to the most basic functions, some products may perform better than others in certain areas. Your individual preferences, work habits, and the goals you have in mind for your family history project will dictate which product best suits your needs. Some brands of software have added features, or have even been created entirely to address research characteristics unique to a particular ethnic or religious background. For members of the LDS Church, some software includes fields for LDS ordinance information, and some even allow for electronic submission of files. *Personal Ancestral File* (PAF) is one such program and is distributed free from the LDS Church <www.familysearch.org>. *DoroTree* <www.dorotree.com> has features unique to Jewish research.

There are a number of ways that you can find information on the products that are available. The website of the software purveyor is a good place to begin. In addition to listing any hardware and system requirements, a description of the product and the features it includes, you may find helpful tips, FAQs, awards the product has won, and links to reviews. Some sites offer free demos or "tours" of the product with screen shots and a walk through the software's capabilities.

If you belong to a genealogical society, a mailing list, or just know other genealogists, ask what software others are using, what they have used in the past, and what their experience has been with various products. In addition, there are mailing lists and user groups associated with some products, where users share tips and any problems they have encountered. By joining the list for a short time or reading any archives of previous posts, you can learn about the experiences of others who use the product.

The periodicals of genealogical societies often include product reviews and there are a number of educational opportunities available on the Web. (These will all be discussed later in this chapter in the section titled "Instructional Material for Technology.")

The National Genealogical Society's *Newsmagazine* regularly runs software reviews by genealogist Bill Mumford. He has created a *Genealogical Software Report Card*, which is available online <www.mumford.ca/reportcard>. The *Report Card* assigns weighted points to various software programs based on the number of features available, and their importance and exclusivity, which allows users to see how one brand compares with another in each of twelve categories.

Keeping your personal preferences in mind, the aforementioned resources can help you to make an informed decision on the best software to suit your needs. The following section of the chapter will discuss some of the features that can help you to organize, record, share, analyze, and in some cases, research your family history.

Recording and Reporting

Genealogical software gives users the ability to centralize their information, making research easier and more effective. All of the names, dates, family groups, sources, notes, photographs, plans, and logs are brought together electronically. Scanned images of original records can even be attached to the electronic record of the people to whom they pertain. While this won't eliminate the need to keep the original paper documents, the physical location of those documents can be noted for easy access when needed, and wear and tear from handling will be greatly reduced.

Once information has been entered into the software, it can be presented in a variety of ways, allowing for greater analysis of information. Traditional charts like ancestral charts (also called pedigree charts), family group sheets, and ahnentafels, which formerly had to be handwritten on forms, can be produced quickly and easily. Descendancy charts, which had to be hand drawn (owing to the fact that descending families come in different sizes), can now be automatically created and again, printed quickly and easily. Kinship charts showing the relationship of one person to another, or to all other family members are easily available as well.

Hourglass charts can be created with ancestors listed above an individual and descendants listed below, and standard pedigree charts can now be reformatted both as fan charts or in a vertical style.

All good software programs include a way to cite records and sources. As noted in the previous section on citing electronic sources, citations are critical. Master source and repository lists available in many programs make it easier to cite records that are referred to over and over during the course of research. Programs with good source citation capabilities can make us better researchers, with fields prompting us to enter all the relevant information, which might otherwise be overlooked or forgotten.

There are often sections for notes, which can hold research observations, time lines, and information that doesn't quite fit into the traditional fields. Some software includes special fields for medical information, such as illnesses and causes of death.

Programs usually permit the selection of information that can be included on the forms, allowing the user to print different forms for different purposes (such as pedigrees with names and vital dates for taking along on research trips and for sharing, pedigrees with only names for a quick relationship reference, pedigree charts with causes of death for family health histories to be shared with your physician, etc.).

Notes and citations can also be included in some reports, allowing for a printable, in-depth report on individuals and families. Having this much information available in easily digested formats can make analysis of data easier and more effective. In some cases, the software may warn users when certain inconsistencies are spotted, such as individuals living to be over 120 years old (or possibly some other age, depending on the software), or a death date before a marriage date, and so on.

Some programs also facilitate the creation of heirloom quality charts, with attractive backgrounds, fonts, and formats that are suitable for framing. For family trees too large for home printing, there are also services available that will print oversized charts and even frame them for home decoration.

Sharing

Genealogical software also facilitates new ways of sharing our family history research with others that share an interest in our family lines. Because everyone has their own preference for a particular brand of software, a way is needed for these different brands to communicate with one another. The Family History Department of the LDS Church developed version 1.0 of the Genealogical Data Communications specification (or GEDCOM as it is commonly referred to) in 1985. GEDCOM sets a standard format for the information found in family history databases so that it can be exchanged between individuals, regardless of the type of software used. Information is entered into the genealogical software program and then key elements can be exported into a GEDCOM file, which can then be imported by other software and converted to its own proprietary format to be read.

Software also allows for the merging of new information into family history databases. New information, new individuals, or, if desired, entire branches of a family tree can be merged into an existing file, creating a new and expanded database. Several warnings should be heeded, though, before merging files:

- A backup of the original database should be created before attempting to merge new information. This way if something goes awry in the process the original information can be restored.
- Check and see how your software handles merges, and read instructions carefully either in the software manual or through the Help files. Some programs will perform this function better than others. Look for articles on the subject, or talk to someone using the same software who has performed similar merges.
- Check the accuracy of the information that is being imported against original sources to make sure you aren't importing erroneous information.

In this age of electronic information, privacy is a big concern. When sharing family history files, make sure that sensitive information on living individuals is either removed entirely or hidden, with sensitive fields reflecting that the individual is still living. Again, Help files or software manuals should show how to go about this task.

More information on this aspect of genealogical software can be found in the section on "Communication and Sharing."

Planning and Keeping Track

Planning and keeping track of researched records are critical and ongoing phases of family history research. Realizing this, many companies now include tools that address these needs.

To-do lists record those tasks that need to be done. These can also be called *Research Journals, Research Tasks,* or other similar names. In some cases, the to-do list is combined with, or also serves as a *Research Log*, helping users to track sources that have already been referenced.

Some software allows the linking of tasks with individuals and with repositories, and can be sorted as such. When a trip to a repository is planned, the tasks need only be printed for that repository, for easy reference. Tasks listed by individual can be referenced during the course of research for a quick check of what has been done and what remains to be done.

Several brands of genealogical software allow for the recording of expenses in the logs as well, which can be particularly helpful for professional researchers.

Publishing

A growing number of software programs also include tools for creating publications, such as scrapbooks, family history or ancestor books, and photo albums. Some will take the names and dates that have been entered into the family file and insert them into a text report on that individual that might read something like this:

> *John Smith was born on 14 June 1841 in Brooklyn, Kings County, New York. He married Sylvia Spoon on 15 February 1862, St. Mary Star of the Sea Church, Brooklyn, Kings County, New York. John died on 19 March 1898 in Brooklyn, Kings County, NY. He is buried in Holy Cross Cemetery, Brooklyn, Kings Co., NY.*

This outline can be exported to a word processing format or as an Adobe PDF. Once exported to a word processing format, the information can be enhanced with information that the program is unable to include in this pre-packaged format.

Some software also allows for the export of maps showing family locations, charts, photographs, images, and other reports to be included in the publication. Indexes and title pages can be created, but again, the quality of the information should be checked carefully.

Some software even allows for multimedia files to be added to family files. Images of documents, photographs, and even video can be attached to individuals. Some programs allow for the creation of scrapbooks which can be played online or saved to a CD-ROM or DVD.

Many programs also provide tools for the automatic generation of Web pages using family history information. Since many Internet Service Providers (ISPs) offer free Web space with their service, this is an appealing aspect to many family historians. GEDCOM files can also be easily uploaded to user-submitted lineage collections, like the Ancestry World Tree <www.ancestry.com/awt>, and One Great Family <www.onegreatfamily.com>. When publishing family history information online, genealogists should adhere to National Genealogical Society's Web publishing guidelines. (See *NGS Guidelines for Publishing Web Pages on the Internet* on the facing page.)

Other Features

Most programs offer access to extended support functions and/or user groups, which include message boards, mailing lists, newsletters, and online chat forums. Some bundle other services to extend basic functionality.

For example, *Family Tree Maker* (FTM) <www.familytreemaker.com> can be purchased packaged with subscriptions to online data collections at Ancestry.com. Using a built-in search function, FTM automatically scans through online data collections at Ancestry.com and notifies you when it finds a hit for an ancestor. When a matching record is found you can download the information directly to your file.

Charting all records and information for an ancestor or ancestral family chronologically in a time line can offer a clear, concise look at life events. In fact, the time line of an ancestor can form the framework for a biographical sketch that can be later used in compiling a family history. Technology has made this task much easier because of the ease with which we can insert and manipulate entries. There are any number of ways that you can construct a time line, and there are even programs that will help you to do so. *Legacy* genealogical software <www.legacyfamilytree.com> will chart your ancestors' lifespan, and *Genelines* <www.progenysoftware.com/genelines.html>, (available as stand-alone software or as an add-on to *Legacy*) will help plot your ancestor's life against historical events, in a variety of charts.

The Master Genealogist <www.whollygenes.com> creates a time line automatically as you enter in the records you have found in your research and the Individual Detail Report lists events (or "tags" as they are referred to in the program) chronologically.

In addition to time lines, most software programs feature calendar utilities that can calculate ages or dates of events, even for dates that fell in the transition from the Julian calendar to the Gregorian calendar. Software also allows for date estimations. Appropriate abbreviations can be found in the Help files or in the user's manual.

Once you have chosen your software, and begun entering your information, it is possible to pick up clues and facts that may have been overlooked or forgotten. Things that did not make sense scattered on various records, index cards, or scraps of paper, may suddenly come together to form a clearer picture of an individual or family.

Tips for Using Genealogical Software

- If a manual is available, it is recommended that you read it before using the software. If no user's guide is available, the Help functions and any software tours should be explored thoroughly. Although most programs are very user-friendly, some functions may be overlooked or misused by new users, causing problems in reports and publications that are generated.
- Set up a system for entering new information. If it can't be entered as you go along, create a file or "inbox" for items that need to be added. Your software won't be as useful to you if the database isn't kept current.
- Researchers sometimes keep genealogical information on more than one computer. Maintaining the most current database in each place is a challenge. Choose one location, possibly a desktop computer, as the primary database and only enter new information into that database. When

NGS Guidelines for Publishing Web Pages on the Internet

Appreciating that publishing information through Internet websites and Web pages shares many similarities with print publishing, considerate family historians

- apply a title identifying both the entire website and the particular group of related pages, similar to a book-and-chapter designation, placing it both at the top of each Web browser window using the <TITLE> HTML tag, and in the body of the document, on the opening home or title page and on any index pages.
- explain the purposes and objectives of their websites, placing the explanation near the top of the title page or including a link from that page to a special page about the reason for the site.
- display a footer at the bottom of each Web page which contains the website title, page title, author's name, author's contact information, date of last revision, and a copyright statement.
- provide complete contact information, including at a minimum a name and e-mail address, and preferably some means for long-term contact, like a postal address.
- assist visitors by providing on each page navigational links that lead visitors to other important pages on the website, or return them to the home page.
- adhere to the NGS "Standards for Sharing Information with Others" regarding copyright, attribution, privacy, and the sharing of sensitive information.
- include unambiguous source citations for the research data provided on the site, and if not complete descriptions, offering full citations upon request.
- label photographic and scanned images within the graphic itself, with fuller explanation if required in text adjacent to the graphic.
- identify transcribed, extracted, or abstracted data as such, and provide appropriate source citations.
- include identifying dates and locations when providing information about specific surnames or individuals.
- respect the rights of others who do not wish information about themselves to be published, referenced, or linked on a website.
- provide website access to all potential visitors by avoiding enhanced technical capabilities that may not be available to all users, remembering that not all computers are created equal.
- avoid using features that distract from the productive use of the website, like ones that reduce legibility, strain the eyes, dazzle the vision, or otherwise detract from the visitor's ability to easily read, study, comprehend or print the online publication.
- maintain their online publications at frequent intervals, changing the content to keep the information current, the links valid, and the website in good working order.
- preserve and archive for future researchers their online publications and communications that have lasting value, using both electronic and paper duplication.

©2000, 2001 by National Genealogical Society. Permission is granted to copy or publish this material provided it is reproduced in its entirety, including this notice.

new information is located on a road trip, rather than entering the data into your PDA or laptop computer's software, note it in a word processor or spreadsheet, and then enter the information on the main computer. Before each research trip, update the files in the portable devices for easy reference on the road. This eliminates the risk of having several different databases with varying amounts of information.

- Record sources immediately. Again, with the wealth of information now available, as well as the transient nature of websites, it is critical to document where each piece of information was located.
- Since computers can crash and data can be lost, it is important to make backup copies of your database, storing one in a location outside your home in case of a natural disaster, fire, or flood. For more on this see the section on "Security" towards the end of this chapter.
- Customize report-printing preferences to print the date on all printed reports, so that when referencing these paper copies, it will be possible to determine how current that particular report is.
- Don't rely too heavily on large imports of data. While it takes longer to enter information manually, it may be worth the time. Often, scattered pieces of information

from various sources suddenly come together to prove or disprove names, dates, and relationships as they are entered into the database.

Additional Software Products

There are a number of more specialized software products on the market that can help family historians. *Clooz* <www.clooz.com> is a software program designed to help family historians manage the huge number of records they acquire as they search for their ancestors. Clues collected over the years can be filed neatly in templates and organized into reports.

Another program, *GeneWeaver* <www.geneweaveronline.com> allows for better medical history reporting, creating printed individual health histories, medical genograms, medical pedigree charts showing dates, ages, and causes of death, blank questionnaires, a bibliography of references to medical and genetic health publications, and a checklist of family health history information resources.

There are also products geared toward specific record types. Because maps are such a critical tool for family historians, there are software packages devoted to mapping locations. *DeedMapper* (available from Direct Line Software <http://users.rcn.com/deeds/index.shtml>) gives family historians the ability to plot landownership maps described in deeds grants, surveys, and claims. The website for another popular map program, *Animap* (from Gold Bug software <www.goldbug.com/AniMap.html>), says it features "2,300 maps to show the changing county boundaries for each of the 48 adjacent United States for every year since colonial times." Users can insert markers at locations significant to their ancestry, and the SiteFinder feature contains the locations for 799,000 place names, some of which no longer exist.

There are also programs that can help you write a family history. Similar to the publishing features included in some genealogical software, *Personal Historian* <www.personalhistorian.com> uses events, dates, and notes from genealogical software, text from word processing documents, and photographs, along with information entered into the program, to create a family history. It also comes with a library of "time lines, historical events, cultural fads, and memory triggers" to add interesting elements. As with other software publishing tools, verify the final product for accuracy.

The Association for Gravestone Studies <www.gravestonestudies.org> sells software created for recording gravestone information. There are additional programs, created by companies and individuals, to help you create time lines, plan family reunions, organize photographs, generate alternate spellings for names, and much more.

Related Software and Online Products

Software programs created for purposes other than family history can also be useful. In addition to tasks such as writing letters of correspondence and histories, word processors can also be used to create your own chronology and have the advantage that they allow for the flexibility needed to include as much or as little information needed.

Step 1:

Gather all the records available for a specific family group or individual ancestor and assemble them by date.

Step 2:

Create an entry for each record, including pertinent information from the record and the source description. (Abstracts, extracts, or in some cases, transcriptions of the record can also be included if desired.)

Some typical record entries might look like these:

17 March 1850
Catherine Kelly's death
TOBIN, Catharine; d Mar 17, 1850; bur Mar 19; age 26;
d of consumption; res: 44 N. Water St.
(Website: Known burials at St. Patrick's Cemetery, Rochester, NY, by Richard T. Halsey, August 2001.)

3 June 1880
1880 US Census, Brooklyn, Kings Co., NY
Kelly, Elizabeth, White, Female, 54, boarder
(Hotel Branting, Madison Ave/58th St.), Single, NY, IRE, IRE
(Source Information: NARA film T9-895, E.D. 584, Page 31, SD 1, 466C. At Ancestry.com: Image 31 of 33. Copy of image at C:\Genealogy\Kelly\Elizabeth\1880 Census.jpeg)

1 April 1883
Kelly, Elizabeth died
(Death notice, and death ctf.)
[Transcriptions edited]

Also, from The Sisters of Charity of New York, 1809–1959, Vol. III by Sister Marie de Lourdes Walsh (New York City: Fordham University Press) Chapter 11, pages 225–226:
". . . Meanwhile the home had been incorporated in 1870 under the legal title of St. Joseph's Home for the Aged, with the following Board of Managers:
Mother Mary Jerome Ely
Sister Mary Regina Lawless
Sister Ann Borromeo Obermeyer
Sister Mary Francis Wallace
Sister Maria Dodge
Sister Francis Borgia Taylor

Miss Elizabeth Kelly
Mrs. Daniel Devlin
. . . Miss Kelly continued on the Board until her death in 1883 . . .")

1888–1890
Brooklyn Directory listing
James Kelly, 155 Huntington, Brooklyn, NY, 1889–1890
(Lain's Directory —Ancestry.com database)

Step 3:

Go back through the records and analyze them, looking for more dates that can be filled in. Some examples include the following:

1814–1815
Kelly, James—born
(Estimated from 1880 U.S. Census data)

6 Jun 1819
Kelly, Jane—born
(Death ctf. 10 January 1882 she was 62 years, 7 months, 4 days)

ca. 1821
Kelly family immigrates from Ireland
(Estimated from birth dates and places of James and Catherine found on U.S. Census entries for James and Catherine's daughter Ann Eliza. Also from James Kelly death certificate in 1896—been in country for 75 years = 1821.)

1821 or before
Kelly, Mary A.—born
(1880 Census—daughter Kate's enumeration lists mother born Ireland)

ca. 1823–24
Kelly, Catherine—born
(Estimated from data on Known burials at St. Patrick's Cemetery, Rochester, NY—See 1850)

1866
James Kelly moves to Brooklyn (per death ctf. in 1896—living in city 30 years)

Formatting, sizing, and color-coding can help to make dates stand out, sources easy to pick out, and delineation between individuals simple. It is helpful to also include sources. As entries are added, there may be conflicting information. Having the sources included makes it easier to find where these problems arise, and thus weigh the evidence. In addition, knowing what records have already been found is helpful in planning future research.

To keep the chronology current, make a habit of updating the time line whenever new data is added to your genealogical software program.

Relational Databases and Spreadsheets

Spreadsheets and databases can also be helpful tools for family historians trying to sort out the records of their ancestors, particularly when tracking families over the years through censuses and directories. They are best used in records with consistent formatting; where information can be entered and sorted by consistent fields.

Database search results presented in tabular format can be copied or imported into a spreadsheet and can be customized for further sorting. For example, if you were searching for a common surname in a large city, using various records that include addresses it would be possible to sort throughout by name, address, and year to note patterns and movement.

Relational databases can contain several sets of records, called tables, which can be linked together through common fields. For example, you could catalog all your books, photographs, documents, heirlooms, and so forth, with each catalog in a separate table, but with each entry noting the ancestor or family to which it pertains. This data could then be sorted and you can create reports of all the items you have collected for a particular person or family. Microsoft *Access* is a commonly used program and there are reference books like *Microsoft Office Access 2003 for Dummies* that can help you learn to use the program.[1]

Other uses include making charts that calculate ages throughout the years, inventories of located records, and research logs.

Downloadable Forms

Government agencies and other institutions have found it expeditious to make downloadable records or information request forms available on the Web. Not only does this save these agencies in terms of paper and other associated costs, it benefits researchers as well, in terms of saving time and sometimes postage.

There are also a number of websites that offer free utility forms to genealogists. Many commercial sites, like Ancestry.com and Genealogy.com offer free downloadable charts and forms, such as blank pedigree charts and family group sheets, blank census forms for recording information found on U.S. federal censuses, research and correspondence logs, forms for extractions and abstractions, source summaries, and form request letters (some in various languages).

Computer Organization

Your family history will eventually creep in to most areas of your computer. You will have word processing files, image files,

GEDCOM files, e-mails, lists of favorite websites, and possibly audio and video files. Organizing them for easy retrieval can be a challenge.

Most of the computer files we work with are organized using a series of folders. As the number of files increases, so does the number of folders. If you are not careful, the number of files and folders can get to a point where it is hard to find anything. For this reason, it's a good idea to come up with a standard filing system that can be used across the board, so it will be easier to locate the materials you need.

As family historians, we tend to file information by name, record type, and/or geographically, or a combination thereof. This tendency can be reflected in an electronic filing scheme similar to the one outlined below and illustrated in figure 2-9.

My Family History

- Surnames
  - —Individual folders for surnames filed alphabetically.
    - —Folders for each individual and one for information on the family as a whole.
      - —Documents, photographs, time lines, etc. that reference individuals filed under the appropriate individual or family.
- Ancestral Geographic Locations
  - —Individual folders for countries, states, and/or counties filed alphabetically.
    - —Information or documents pertaining to this geographic location, such as where to find vital records, what census records are available, websites of local societies, maps, etc.

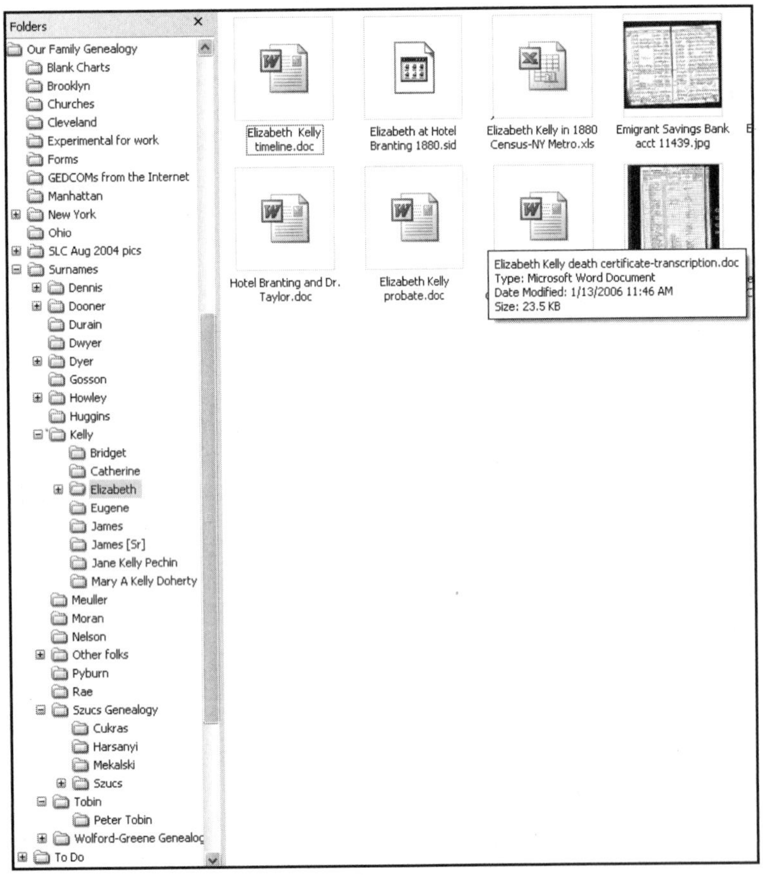

Contact Information

E-mail clients (computer programs used to read and send e-mail) are constantly expanding their capabilities for use in the business world. Many of these capabilities can be modified to suit the business of family historians.

As connections are made with other family historians sharing surname interests, it can be difficult to keep track of who is researching what surname. Try using the contact list in your e-mail client. For each family history contact, include a list of surname and family interests in the notes section. When a piece of information is found for a particular surname, use the *Find* or *Search* function to locate a list of all the contacts that are researching that surname.

Another solution is to set up a mailing distribution lists for each surname. Then when there is information to share or a question to be asked, simply address the message to that distribution list.

Figure 2-9. An electronic filing scheme for computer files, organized by surname and geographical location.

Communication and Sharing

User-Submitted Family Tree Collections

Among the most popular resources made available on the Web are collections of user-submitted family tree files. These collections are typically created as users upload their family data in the form of GEDCOM files. If you do not currently have a file in electronic format, many sites will also let you build your file online by entering your family information into forms.

There are, however, drawbacks to these collections. The quality of the information is often poor, and in many cases the sources for the information are not cited. Each fact should be verified before being incorporated into your family tree.

Adding to the problem is the ease with which individuals can graft entire branches onto their files. Huge files can be downloaded quickly and easily, and merged into existing databases. Because so many researchers do not take the time to seek out records to corroborate the information that they are importing, the spread of bad information can become viral.

Despite these obstacles, there *is* good information in these collections and many researchers have connected with long-lost cousins because of them. Providing that solid research methodology is employed, the clues in these collections can be very helpful and they are tools that should not be overlooked.

Mailing Lists and Message Boards

Queries and communication between genealogists was formerly limited to postings in society periodicals or magazines that often took months to reach their audience, which consisted of other subscribers, fellow society members, or individuals who took the time to seek out copies held in libraries.

Today's technology provides a way for genealogists to post queries, seek advice, and share information easily in real time in the form of mailing lists and message boards. All of this information can be saved in archives, to be searched days, weeks, months, and even years later, and the potential audience for these mailing lists, message boards, and their respective archives is global.

What Are They?

While mailing lists and message boards are similar in purpose, the difference lies in the way the information is distributed. With mailing lists, a copy of every message posted is sent to all of the list's subscribers. In addition, most lists have an online archive where past messages can also be searched. RootsWeb.com hosts nearly 30,000 mailing lists <http://lists.rootsweb.com>.

Message boards are online forums where each message is posted to the board. Users can choose to receive notifications when items are posted to boards of interest. Message boards are also searchable. The largest collection of message boards is available through Ancestry.com and RootsWeb.com <http://boards.ancestry.com> (the same boards can be accessed through either site.) Another popular service is GenForum, which is hosted at Genealogy.com <http://genforum.genealogy.com>. Cyndi's List has an extensive list of forums <www.cyndislist.com/queries.htm>.

There are boards and lists for surnames, geographic locations, and for various other topics, and the content of each

NGS Guidelines for Sharing

Conscious of the fact that sharing information or data with others, whether through speech, documents, or electronic media, is essential to family history research and that it needs continuing support and encouragement, responsible family historians consistently—

- respect the restrictions on sharing information that arise from the rights of another as an author, originator or compiler; as a living private person; or as a party to a mutual agreement.
- observe meticulously the legal rights of copyright owners, copying or distributing any part of their works only with their permission, or to the limited extent specifically allowed under the law's "fair use" exceptions.
- identify the sources for all ideas, information, and data from others, and the form in which they were received, recognizing that the unattributed use of another's intellectual work is plagiarism.
- respect the authorship rights of senders of letters, electronic mail, and data files, forwarding or disseminating them further only with the sender's permission.
- inform people who provide information about their families as to the ways it may be used, observing any conditions they impose and respecting any reservations they may express regarding the use of particular items.
- require some evidence of consent before assuming that living people are agreeable to further sharing of information about themselves.
- convey personal identifying information about living people—like age, home address, occupation, or activities—only in ways that those concerned have expressly agreed to.
- recognize that legal rights of privacy may limit the extent to which information from publicly available sources may be further used, disseminated, or published.
- communicate no information to others that is known to be false, or without making reasonable efforts to determine its truth, particularly information that may be derogatory.
- are sensitive to the hurt that revelations of criminal, immoral, bizarre, or irresponsible behavior may bring to family members.

©2000 by National Genealogical Society. Permission is granted to copy or publish this material provided it is reproduced in its entirety, including this notice.

will vary in accordance with its purpose and the rules set by the administrator. Many of the posts are queries—messages from people seeking to contact others who may have shared ancestors, information on a particular line, or tips on how to go about a certain type of research.

More and more of these forums are also being used to archive transcriptions from records, newspapers, and other sources, and these archives are often indexed by search engines, increasing the exposure of posts. We all have tidbits on people who share our ancestors' surnames, but who we are not quite sure are related. By posting these tidbits to the list or board, you may be able to connect with a descendant of the person or people in the record. Information provided by others reading your post may even help you to either make a connection or rule them out as possible relatives. Even if you don't make any connections, using a message board or mailing list is a great way to help other researchers, learn new strategies, and share methodology.

Before You Post

Before posting anything, it is important to read the welcome message (sent when you sign up for mailing lists), or message board guidelines where available (typically found in a "Links and Announcements" section of the message board). You'll especially want to look for a description of the focus of the list, and what constitutes an acceptable posting and what topics are not appropriate. While a list may focus on a particular country, it may only be for data and queries, and it may not be for the cultural aspects. Others may welcome recipes, traditions, and history. It all depends on the administrator's preferences and this information is helpful to you in deciding whether or not that forum is right for your needs.

Familiarize yourself with what is available and then decide where you will most likely find the answers you seek. There are boards for specific surnames, geographic locations, and specialty topics, such as "Naturalization Records," "Mexican Revolution," "Emigration Patterns," "Icelanders in Dakota," or "Cherokee Nation," to name a few.

Another important aspect that should be investigated is where your replies to a mailing list go. Some lists send responses only to the sender and to send a reply, you need to select "Reply to All." Others may have it set so that all replies go to the entire list. Be careful to note where your replies go. This type of information will also be included in the "welcome message."

Posting Effectively

To get the most from these forums, it is important to craft your message so that it will catch the attention of anyone who has information. Many mailing lists offer digest versions, where each message is attached and only the subject line is visible. In addition, many people simply don't have enough time in the day to read every message that comes through the mailing lists they subscribe to. Most people set up a filter to automatically move them from their inbox into folders that can be browsed when time allows. For busy mailing lists, which can generate hundreds of messages every day, this keeps inboxes from being cluttered and headlines can be scanned for items of interest. (For more on organizing with folders, see the previous section on "Computer Organization.")

For this reason, a good subject line is critical. A subject line of "genealogy" or "searching for ancestors" for a posting to a genealogical mailing list is stating the obvious and won't have the desired effect. In addition, a post to the Kelly surname list should have a more specific subject line than *Kelly ancestors*. Presumably everyone on the list is looking for Kelly ancestors. A good subject line will tell which Kelly, when he or she lived (approximately at least) and where. The following is a good example:

Kelly, James, ca. 1813–1896, IRE>NYC>Brooklyn

Particulars can be filled in later in the body of the message. Your message should contain pertinent information but not the entire family history—just enough to help whoever is reading it to identify the person you are looking for. A brief message that is to the point, but that carries enough information to let people identify the individual should they have any related information is best. Most people don't want to take the time to read a long, drawn-out query. The first paragraph should contain the "who, what, where, and when" of your request. Details can be filled in after you have gotten the attention of your targeted audience.

More tips for effective posting include the following:

- Include only *one request* in your post. Too many requests may decrease your chances for a response. Other inquiries can be better targeted if they are posted separately.
- Include a brief summary of places you have already checked for the information. This way you won't waste other people's time, and your own, as you receive and sort through half a dozen replies telling you to follow leads you have already followed.
- Capitalize SURNAMES so that they are easy to pick out of the post and subject lines. (You should not capitalize an entire message as it makes it more difficult to read and is the online equivalent of shouting.)
- Be careful with abbreviations in your query. Remember that many forums have members from all parts of the world who may not be familiar with the same abbreviations that we use. Spell words out whenever possible. This will eliminate the possibility of misinterpretation.
- Familiarize yourself with online resources so that you don't post unnecessary requests. If you are looking for a geographic location, try some of the online maps that are available to locate an ancestor's town.
- When posting to a mailing list, check your e-mail settings. Make sure to only send plain text to mailing lists.

Others may not have the capability to read HTML-coded messages and you want your message to be readable by as many people as possible.

- Do not send a query as an attachment. Many viruses are transmitted as attachments and as a result, most people wisely refrain from opening attachments on e-mail from people they don't know.
- Sign your post with your name and e-mail address. Some e-mail readers don't show the address that an e-mail is received from and a recipient with the information you are looking for can't respond to you if they don't have your e-mail address. In addition, when the message appears in the archives, your contact information should be easy to pick out.
- Reread your post carefully before you send it. Check for typos. Did you include all the necessary information? (Remember the four W's: Who, What, Where, When) Are all of your facts correct? Have you signed it properly?
- Be careful of what information you post online, particularly when referring to living persons. Be sure to respect people's privacy and keep yourself and your family safe from those who might use information found online for fraudulent purposes.
- If you find information worth sharing, post it to the appropriate list and share the source of the information so that others may benefit from your finds. As you help others, they will be more eager to help you in return.
- Always be polite on the lists and refrain from flaming (angry or insulting messages). No one wants to help someone who is constantly complaining or is mean to others.
- Keep a log of your e-mail messages so you know what requests you have already put out and when.

By using common sense and following simple guidelines, you can benefit greatly from genealogical forums. They are a great place to make friends, find relatives, and retrieve information.

Archives

With the large number of e-mails that many people have to go through, it can be difficult to monitor every e-mail that comes through mailing lists, particularly when one belongs to a number of them, or even just one very busy list. Deleting large numbers of messages can make a person feel that he or she has not adequately scanned everything that has gone through the inbox. When this happens, it can be beneficial to search the mailing list or message board archive to see if anyone has posted anything of interest for your area or surnames of interest. This is also a helpful option if you are looking for an answer to a question that has probably been asked before.

Mailing list archives. To search mailing list archives at RootsWeb.com, go to the mailing list main page <http://lists.rootsweb.com> and locate the list that you are interested in. With the subscription information, there should be a link to any archives that are available. Lists are typically archived by year so if this is your first foray into the archives, you'll want to do searches for each year so that you don't miss anything.

Message boards. Ancestry.com message boards can be searched from the message board main page <http://boards.ancestry.com> using the basic search box. You have a choice of searching for a particular surname board, or searching all the boards for a particular name or term. In addition, by clicking on the "Advanced Search" link in that same line, you can refine your search. For example, search for the surname in the appropriate field and include a location in the space for "Find Messages Containing." This yields hits on any list where that surname and location appear. A Soundex option is also available. GenForum allows you to search for a particular board, but doesn't support the ability to search all of the message boards for a term, nor does it have an advanced search.

Other Considerations

As with other secondary sources, information found on message boards and mailing lists needs to be backed up with evidence, but the connections you make through these forums can provide clues that aren't available anywhere else. Family Bibles, records, photographs, and heirlooms may have traveled down other lines and it is only by connecting with these distant cousins that you may learn of the existence of such artifacts.

In addition, transcriptions posted to message boards and mailing lists make these resources more valuable all the time. After searching for years for my great-grandmother's death date, we were able to locate it after someone posted a transcription of some Brooklyn obituaries from an old newspaper to a mailing list.

Publishing

The goal of family historians is often to publish their family history findings in some form. In some cases that form is electronic. With increased availability of Web space many genealogists are choosing it as the venue on which to publish their family histories. Content and quality varies on these sites, with some individuals only posting undocumented family trees, poorly and hastily thrown together, while others include well-documented findings, with creative text, photos, maps, and other images woven together to create an electronic heirloom.

As described in the section titled "Communication and Sharing," many family historians are also posting their findings by adding their family tree to one of several user-submitted collections of trees. Regardless of the format in which family history information is put on the Web, those who publish their information must recognize that the information will likely be downloaded by others who will possibly not give proper attribution, despite the fact that they may be in violation of copyright laws.

There are alternatives for those who would like to publish their findings in a more private manner. MyFamily.com offers private websites by subscription where family historians can post family trees, electronic images and photographs, family recipes, stories, and news (see figure 2-10). Only those who have been invited by the site administrator can view the content and the administrator can manage the input of site members by designating them as either "guest" (member can see content but not make additions) or "user" (member can view and add to content).

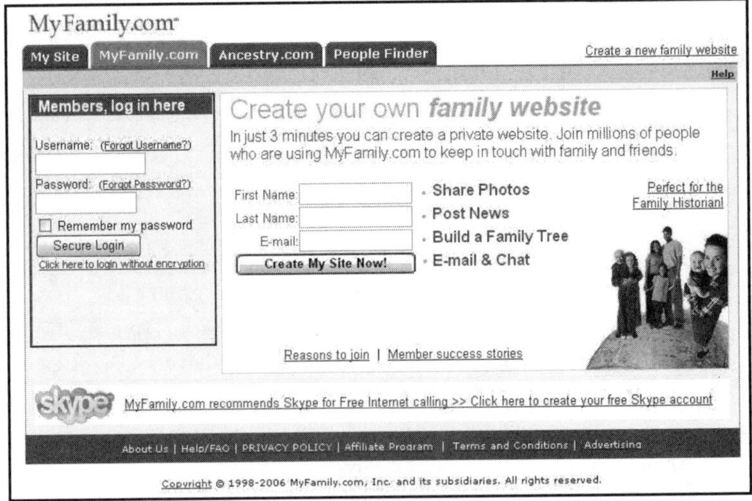

Figure 2-10. MyFamily.com offers private websites by subscription where family historians can post family trees, electronic images and photographs, family recipes, stories, and news.

Education

Family history is an unending learning process. As each generation takes us back, possibly to new geographic locations, we find the need to learn about a new era in history, what record types were available for that time and place, and new techniques to address these changes in venue. Fortunately, in this new so-called "Information Age," the know-how we need can be as close as our home computer.

Major websites of all kinds now offer helpful tutorials and articles aimed at helping family historians find their way around the resources they have to offer. This includes some library and governmental websites, commercial sites, the websites of genealogical and historical organizations, and the websites of individuals. With the wide variety of offerings, even the greenest of newbies can learn necessary skills.

Digital Newsletters

There are a growing number of digital newsletters available from commercial websites, volunteers, and individuals who like to share their experience. Among the early newsletters, Dick Eastman's first newsletter <www.eogn.com> appeared in January 1996 and went out to about 100 people, most of whom were members of CompuServe's Genealogy Forum. The newsletter now has a standard edition and a plus edition, which goes to subscribers who pay a minimal subscription fee.

Ancestry.com launched its first newsletter, the *Hometown Daily News*, in 1997. It evolved into the *Ancestry Daily News* and continues to evolve with new technology, including how-to articles and tips, information on the company's latest offerings and news from the genealogical community.

The premier issue of *RootsWeb Review* was published on 17 June 1998. This weekly e-zine provides news about RootsWeb.com, its new databases, mailing lists, homepages, and websites. It also includes stories and research tips from its readers around the globe.

There are a number of other genealogical newsletters, including the National Genealogical Society's *UpFront*, Avotaynu's *Nu? What's Nu?* (Jewish Genealogy), New England Historic Genealogical Society's *NEHGS eNews* (full text of most articles are only available to NEHGS members), and the genealogy newsletter of About.com <http://genealogy.about.com>. A good way to browse through a list of the newsletters that are currently available is through *Cyndi's List: Magazines, Journals, Columns and Newsletters* <www.cyndislist.com/magazine.htm>.

These tools give readers an enjoyable and easy way to learn a little at a time on a daily or weekly basis, and in most cases, there is no cost associated for the user.

Magazines and Periodicals

Magazines and periodicals have long offered genealogical advice and tutorials, and as research methods have evolved using new technologies, so have these publications. Both commercial offerings and periodicals from non-profit organizations now offer helpful information on the latest technologies and tools.

Ancestry Magazine regularly features articles about using current technology and the latest Internet resources. Back issues of the magazine can be found in the online library at Ancestry.com <www.ancestry.com/learn> (see figure 2-11), along with columns and tips from Ancestry.com newsletters.

Family Chronicle <www.familychronicle.com> also regularly includes Internet-related articles and maintains an online archive of back issues. The *Family Tree Magazine* website also features portions of articles from its magazine, as well as a large number of blank research forms for download.

Blogs

More recently, genealogy "blogs," or "web logs" are being launched online. Similar to newsletters, blogs typically contain

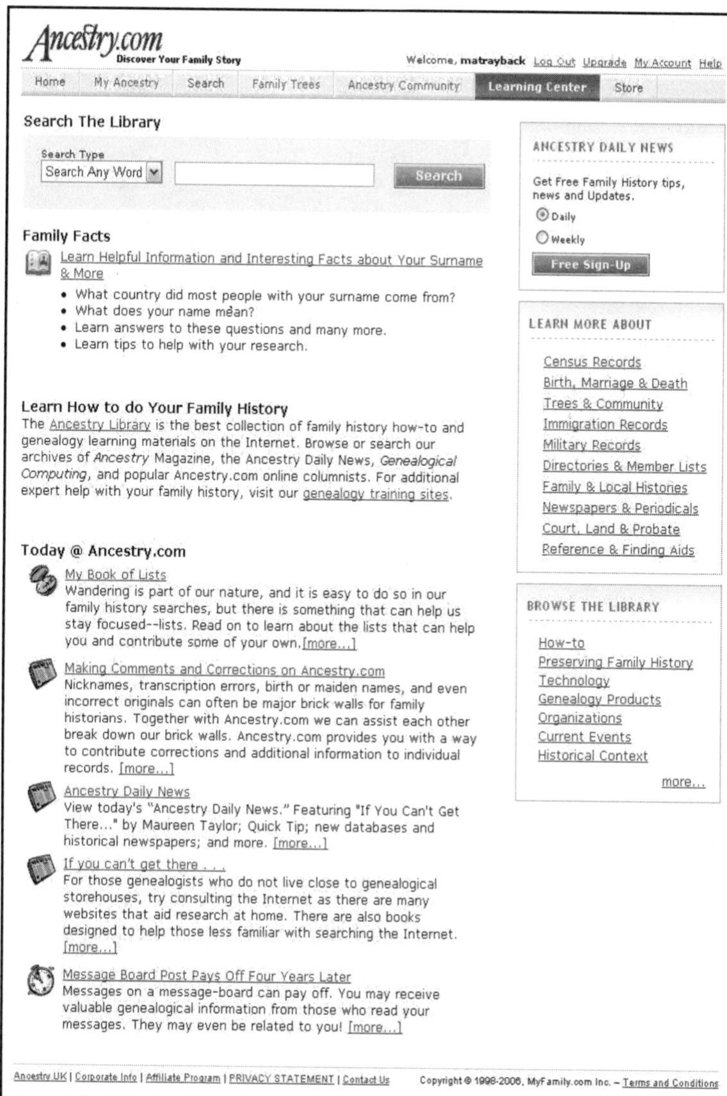

Figure 2-11. The Ancestry.com Library hosts over 10,000 items, including magazine and newsletter articles and tips submitted by users.

helpful news and information, presented in a diary-like format. The author, or "blogger," posts items he or she finds interesting, often inserting commentary, with the most recent posts appearing at the top of the page. Some blogs allow for replies to be posted by readers, while others are restricted to posts by the author or a group of authorized contributors. The headlines or snippets from blogs are sometimes available in formats (RSS or Atom XML format) that can be fed to news aggregators that will collect and display feeds from your favorite blogs.

Online Chats

Internet chats provide a way for participants to communicate in real time with others who share an interest. There are a number of genealogical chat forums available, some through various websites, and some through Internet Relay Chat (IRC) channels. Depending on the venue, sometimes users will need to download an IRC client, or chat program.

Typically an expert is called in to discuss a particular topic and a moderator helps steer the conversation through the chosen topic. Participants type in their questions and the guest expert answers them electronically. Through these chats, users get to interact with professionals and learn in a kind of virtual classroom.

To find out about genealogy chats that are available, see *Cyndi's List: Chat & IRC* <www.cyndislist.com/chat.htm>.

Online Lessons, Distance Education, and Online Classes

The interaction allowed by websites, e-mail, and chats have also given birth to a whole new way to take classes. There are a number of lessons and educational opportunities that can be found on the Web, including some that offer college credits. Many universities also offer independent study courses and some now offer genealogy classes. Brigham Young University has several covering a range of genealogical topics <http://ce.byu.edu/is/site/catalog>.

The National Genealogical Society also offer an eighteen-month home study class called *American Genealogy: A Basic Course*, as well as several online courses, which include *Introduction to Genealogy*, *Federal Population Census Schedules*, and *Special Federal Census Schedules*.

Many of the educational opportunities available require tuition, which varies in range from around thirty dollars to several hundred dollars. There are also some free options, including online lessons at Genealogy.com <www.genealogy.com/university.html>.

Reference Materials for Sale

While there are plenty of educational opportunities available online, there are some topics that require the more in-depth coverage afforded in reference books. With many genealogical vendors online, it is possible to shop from home, with descriptions and sometimes excerpts of publications online. The ability to surf from store to store also allows customers to compare prices and get the best price on products.

Security Issues

Fraud

When purchasing family history products, be sure to do your homework. Choose only reputable companies to do business with. When solicited by marketers of a product or when considering spending large sums of money, it is a good idea to check out the company or organization at the Better Business Bureau (BBB) website <www.bbb.org>. Not only can you search the Bureau's database to determine what kind of record the company has and what kind of complaints have been filed, but there is also helpful information on other ways to prevent identity theft.

Similarly, when hiring researchers, check their credentials thoroughly. The Association of Professional Genealogists (APG) <www.apgen.org> maintains a directory on their website of professionals within their organization. Researchers can be searched for by record type and by the geographic locations where their specialties lie. Members of the APG must agree to uphold the organization's strict code of ethics, and APG will mediate disputes between its members and their clients.

Viruses and Hackers

It is an unfortunate truth that there are a number of dangers inherent when you research using the Internet. Hackers and virus writers, while mostly intent on mischief, also have the potential to invade your computer, steal personal information like Social Security numbers, credit card numbers, and online banking information, and possibly destroy some or all of your data. Systems with broadband Internet connections are particularly vulnerable, since they remain connected to the Internet whenever the computer is in use. Using some form of security to protect your computer should be a priority.

There are a number of reputable products currently available, the most noted among which are produced by Symantec (Norton Security and Anti-Virus Products) <www.symantec.com> and McAfee <www.mcafee.com>.

In addition, just installing a product in some cases may not be enough. With new viruses and avenues of attack being discovered each day, updates to the programs are needed to keep up with the new dangers. With both of the aforementioned services, purchases come with a one-year update package, where updates are automatically sought and installed periodically.

In addition to a multitude of viruses circulating in cyberspace, there are also a lot of hoaxes, with many relating to computer security. But with some hoaxes passing themselves off as updates from reputable companies, it is important to be certain. Both McAfee and Symantec maintain searchable encyclopedias that contain the latest information on both viruses and hoaxes. There are also sites like Snopes.com <www.snopes.com> and the Urban Legends Archive <www.urbanlegends.com>, both of which contain helpful information.

As genealogists, we are taught to verify the accuracy of everything. That is sound advice when it comes to the Internet.

Backups

Despite our best intentions, the possibility always exists of damaging viruses, computer crashes, fires, floods, and other natural disasters. To protect family history and other electronic files, it's important to perform backups regularly. That way, if the unexpected does happen, we haven't lost everything.

What to Back Up

Since most software comes with CDs and can be reinstalled, it is really only necessary to back-up the data portions of files. Family history files that should be backed up include the following:

- GEDCOM files
- Any time lines or spreadsheets you've created
- Scanned images of documents and photographs
- Any family history publications and other related word processing documents you have
- Your e-mail data file and archive
- Contact information for work, friends, and family
- Any audio and video files
- List of favorite websites

How you locate some of these files will depend on what kind of computer you have and what operating system you use, but the Help files should be able guide you to the correct file.

How to Back Up

How you back up your data will depend on the technology you have access to. Because 3.5" diskettes only hold 1.44 megabytes of data, it would likely take quite a few of them to back up everything you need to. For this reason, it is recommended that you invest in a CD- or DVD-writer, a Zip drive, some kind of Flash media, or a removable drive. Many of these options are relatively inexpensive and many computers now come with CD- or DVD-writers as standard components. A trip to your local office supply or computer store can get you up to speed with the most current options available.

Some other suggestions concerning backups include the following:

- Keep a log of your backups and schedule reminders on a calendar to make sure you keep them current.
- Make sure you keep your backups on current technology. If your backup was on a 5 1/4" floppy diskette, would you be able to restore your data today?
- Test your backup. You don't want to find out after a problem strikes that your backup files are unusable.
- Store one or more copies offsite. If some sort of disaster were to hit your home, you would still be able to retrieve the information from the offsite location. Some places to consider might be a family member's house, or a safety deposit box.
- Load a GEDCOM online. A copy of your latest GEDCOM on a password-protected site, like those offered by RootsWeb.com, is backed up offsite and is

accessible from any home computer with an Internet connection.

- Backup to paper. Should something happen to you, the pile of disks in your desk may not be as likely to survive as the album of documents and family trees you have worked so hard to preserve. Printed using archival paper and ink, and preserved with archival quality sheet protectors, your printed family history will last for years to come.

Other Protective Measures

- Your computer is vulnerable to sudden changes in its power supply. Surge protectors and an Uninterruptible Power Supply (UPS) can help you to protect your equipment from unexpected power surges.
- Surge protectors won't protect your computer from a direct lightning strike. In severe storms unplug your computer from its power source and disconnect any phone or cable lines.
- There are fire resistant safes that can help preserve paper and some electronic media for varying periods. Check Underwriters Laboratories (UL) listings on products to see what kind of media they will protect, and how long they will protect them from fire.

Other Gadgets and Helpful Technology

Digital Cameras, Scanners, and Image Editing Software

When digital cameras first hit the market, they were expensive and not in most researchers' budgets. As they have grown in popularity, and as the technology has matured, they have come down drastically in price. Family historians use them as tools for photographing fragile documents, cemeteries and tombstones, pictures that can't be removed from frames, and even microfilm images.

While cameras are no stranger to the genealogist, digital cameras have a distinct advantage in that you can immediately view the photograph you've just taken and know whether or not you got the shot you wanted. This can be very important when taking photographs in a cemetery far from your home, for which visits may be a rare and expensive occurrence.

When a digital camera is not available, traditional photographs can be digitized later using scanners. Scanners have also come down immensely in price, and there are models that are portable enough to take with you in a briefcase to your local courthouse or archive.

Once an image is digital, it can be enhanced for better readability, and defects like cracks and spots on photographs can be removed, using one of many image editing software packages that are currently on the market. Most digital and digitizing equipment comes with software, but alternate programs are available for purchase.

When altering an image, you should always keep a copy of the original. This serves both as a backup, should something go awry in the editing process, and as proof that the changes made were merely cosmetic, should any of your alterations come under scrutiny.

Personal Digital Assistants (PDAs)

Personal digital assistants, or PDAs, are also increasingly popular with family historians. With several software programs available for use with PDAs, genealogists can now take their entire family history file with them in their purse or coat pocket. PDAs are also great for taking notes and making research to-do lists.

Global Positioning Systems (GPS)

Global Positioning Systems (GPS) can pinpoint your position to within fifty feet. These tools can be particularly helpful in recording the location of graves, unmarked old cemeteries, ancestral homes, and other geographical features of significance to family historians. Some genealogical software programs have features that allow you to record the latitude and longitude of significant locations, thus preserving the information for future family historians.

In addition, when traveling or researching in an unfamiliar location, possibly in a foreign country, a GPS system can help get you where you need to go safely.

Removable and Portable Drives

Portable "hard drives" are increasingly useful. Because of the increased capacity that these drives allow, they come in handy when copying files from a desktop computer to a laptop for a research trip, or for backing up files.

With some available in keychain sizes, many of your computer files can come along with you in your pocket when visiting family or some location with a computer.

Continuing Education

This chapter has provided a broad overview of the many ways computers and technology have impacted the work of family historians and genealogists. Because technology never stops evolving, it is necessary to stay current with the latest advancements. A good way to do this is to look for articles in newsletters like the Ancestry.com newsletters <www.ancestry.com/learn>, *RootsWeb Review* <http://newsletters.rootsweb.com/>, *Eastman's Online Genealogy Newsletter* <http://eogn.com>, and in publications like *Ancestry* Magazine (available at newsstands or by subscription at <www.ancestry.com>. Such resources will keep you abreast of developments in the field and will show how new technologies can improve your ability to research.

Notes

[1] Alan Simpson, Margaret Levine Young, and Alison Barrows, *Microsoft Office Access 2003 for Dummies* (Indianapolis, Ind.: Wiley Publishing, 2003).

Glossary

blog Short for Web log, a blog is a Web page that serves as a publicly accessible personal journal for an individual.

bookmark To save the address (URL) of a Web page so that you can easily re-visit the page at a later time.

broadband A type of data transmission in which a single medium (wire) can carry several channels at once.

browser A software application used to locate and display Web pages.

cache A special high-speed storage mechanism.

cyberspace A metaphor for describing the non-physical terrain created by computer systems. Online systems, for example, create a cyberspace within which people can communicate with one another.

dial-up access Connecting a device to a network via a modem and a public telephone network. Because dial-up access uses normal telephone lines, the quality of the connection is not always good and data rates are limited.

e-mail Short for electronic mail, the transmission of messages over communications networks .

e-mail address Name that identifies an electronic post office box on a network where e-mail can be sent; for example, jonsmith@gmail.com.

e-zine Short for electronic magazine. Some e-zines are simply electronic versions of existing print magazines, whereas others exist only in their digital format.

flame An e-mail or newsgroup message in which the writer attacks another participant.

freeware Copyrighted software given away for free by the author.

FTP (File Transfer Protocol) The protocol for exchanging files over the Internet.

hacker A slang term for a computer enthusiast, i.e., a person who enjoys learning programming languages and computer systems and can often be considered an expert on the subject(s).

help Online documentation. Many programs come with the instruction manual, or a portion of the manual, integrated into the program.

homepage The main page of a website. Typically, the homepage serves as an index or table of contents to other documents stored at the site.

inbox A storage device where e-mail is placed.

Internet A global network connecting millions of computers.

Internet Service Provider or ISP A company that provides access to the Internet.

mailing list A list of e-mail addresses identified by a single name. When an e-mail message is sent to the mailing list name, it is automatically forwarded to all the addresses in the list.

message board An online discussion group.

modem Short for modulator-demodulator. A modem is a device or program that enables a computer to transmit data over, for example, telephone or cable lines.

PDF Short for Portable Document Format, a file format developed by Adobe Systems. PDF captures formatting information making it possible to send formatted documents and have them appear on the recipient's monitor or printer as they were intended.

post To publish a message in an online forum, newsgroup, or message board.

search engine A program that searches documents for specified keywords and returns a list of the documents where the keywords were found.

shareware Software distributed on the basis of an honor system. Most shareware is delivered free of charge, but the author usually requests that you pay a small fee if you like the program and use it regularly.

URL The global address of documents and other resources on the World Wide Web such as <www.google.com>.

virus A program or piece of code that is loaded onto your computer without your knowledge and runs against your wishes.

Web page A document on the World Wide Web; every Web page is identified by a unique URL.

website A site (location) on the World Wide Web.

World Wide Web, the Web, or WWW A system of Internet servers that support specially formatted documents.

Source: Webopedia at <www.webopedia.com>

3

General References and Guides

KORY L. MEYERINK, MLS, AG, FUGA

A genealogist researching a family history or pedigree faces mountains of records that may contain some reference to the family or ancestor of interest. This chapter focuses on the major finding aids that enable genealogical researchers to tap these vast resources faster and more efficiently. The finding aids covered in this chapter include *databases,* which are compiled collections of genealogical information; *indexes,* which identify where in a record or set of records information can be found about an individual; catalogs, which help determine where records are; *bibliographies* that identify records; and *directories* of organizations and other researchers. A growing number of these finding aids are now accessible electronically, and that availability will also be discussed.

Databases and indexes, especially in the last decade, have become essential tools in genealogical research. In fact, with the ongoing information explosion and the increased availability of earlier records, databases and indexes are the best tools with which genealogists can search large collections of records successfully. Indeed, the explosion of published sources in the past two decades, with the attendant increase of indexes and other finding aids, means that this chapter can only be an overview of the key kinds of finding aids, with the introduction of some specific examples. For more detailed information on the materials introduced here, as well as an extensive discussion of published versions of most kinds of genealogical records, see the Ancestry companion volume, *Printed Sources: A Guide to Published Genealogical Records*. As appropriate, this chapter will refer to various chapters of that reference book where a more complete discussion, with additional finding aids, is found.

Chapter Contents

Databases and Indexes

A database is any collection of information that is organized for rapid search and easy retrieval. Usually the term refers to computerized (electronic) records, but it can also refer to manual (non-electronic) records. In the past, large databases were published on microfilm and microfiche (manual records), but the recent increase of electronic publishing has led to ever-larger databases being compiled and published. Today, most databases are being posted on the Internet. Others are published on removable media, like compact discs. Many electronic databases are published in both formats. Databases are of great interest to genealogists because they are easily-used sources of information.

Most databases are compiled from other records, and in such situations, the database is considered a derivative, not an original, source. Thus, the information found in such databases must be used with caution. The data provided should be verified against the original records that provided the information because, when databases are created, errors are often introduced during the data entry process. Also, it is an unwise practice for genealogical conclusions to rest on any single reference, be it derivative (such as a database) or even an original. Good research requires the collection, comparison, and careful evaluation of all information available from multiple sources.

A growing number of databases contain new information, originally compiled on computers (such as the Social Security Death Index). Others are derived from older, original records, such as some census databases. A number of the major databases available for genealogical research are discussed in this chapter.

Some manual databases have existed for several decades, since even before the term "database" became popular. Manual databases are often unique and accessible at only one location—usually at the institutions where they were created—although some have been published, usually on microfilm. The more recent development of automated (computerized) databases allows access from more than one location. Access options primarily include the Internet and CD-ROM.

While databases include actual genealogical data, indexes generally give very little genealogical information; rather, indexes are primarily finding aids—they refer the user to other sources of information about a subject. Most family historians seek references to their ancestors in indexes as well as in databases. Indexes are crucial to successful research because they free the researcher to navigate through the information in many sources much more efficiently. While many indexes are topical—that is, they indicate where particular topics are treated—the following discussion focuses on nominal (name) indexes.

Some genealogical indexes have broad application; others have very limited uses. Generally, indexes cover two different categories of records: compiled sources (which usually contain secondary information, such as family or local histories, genealogies written by others, journal articles, and family group sheets) and original sources (which generally provide primary information, such as military rolls, immigration lists, census records, and so on).

Indexes that list individuals may include either the given names of each subject (personal name indexes) or the last name only, with page references for each occurrence of that name (surname indexes). They can be comprehensive (indexing every occurrence of a name in the source) or selective (indexing only major occurrences of the name). In selective indexes, the name of the head of the family may be the only name indexed, although the whole family is described by name in the record entry itself. There may be locality, topical, or major-entry indexes as well.

Indexes compiled by government clerks for wills, deeds, and court cases are personal-name "subject" indexes; they refer only to the principals in each transaction. Witnesses, jurors, clerks, and others mentioned in the documents are rarely indexed. In government records particularly—though not exclusively—indexes may not be strictly alphabetical. For example, all of the A entries may be grouped together but may not be alphabetized—Abbott may come after Arnold. In some indexes, names are arranged by the first letter of the given name, the first three letters of the surname, or the first and third letters of either name; some are alphabetized by the given name irrespective of the first letter of the surname. Others, like the Soundex indexes, are arranged so that names pronounced alike are indexed together.

The original indexes found in most compiled histories generally include topical or surname entries only. Comprehensive, every-name indexes are sometimes compiled later for genealogical use. These supplements may be bound into the original record, written, typed, or printed in a separate volume, or added to the pages of a reprint edition. As you search a record, whether it is compiled or original, check carefully for multiple indexes. You may find them at the end, in the middle, or, conveniently, at the front of the record. Indexes may be indicated in the table of contents as well.

No index is perfectly accurate or complete. Whether prepared manually or by computer, indexes contain errors of omission, incompleteness, and typography. The key to using any index is to understand who created it and why. Successful researchers spend as much time getting to know the index as they do using the index itself. The preface or introduction to the index, "how-to" books and articles, other researchers, and experimenting with the index itself can reveal much about its usefulness.

An index is only as accurate as the source itself. If a family history has errors, those errors will be indexed. Misspelled words, garbled names, and incorrect page references will be indexed as well. It is not the indexer's place to correct errors—even when they are obvious—although some add prefaces or footnotes to warn users. If a record is in a foreign language or has been damaged, names may be undecipherable or illegible. Even a skilled indexer, dealing with unfamiliar names, may misinterpret spellings, placing a name in an entirely different part of the index than it belongs. Cross references for spelling variants and for multiple entries may be omitted due to space, time, or financial considerations.

Indexers select entries according to their own criteria. The best ones describe their selection processes for the reader's benefit. For example, Schneider and Snyder may be indexed together or separately in a surname index. If the index is topical, who chose the topics? Are public officials indexed together, individually by name, or by separate government agencies? Entries in a family history index may be divided into descendants, spouses who married into the family, ancestors of the central couple, and places where the family lived—each in a separate index. Check them all.

Women may have been omitted from an index. If you're looking for Mary Loomis and the index lists only John, Joseph, Michael, and Stephen Loomis, check those entries; the indexer may have included only Mary's brothers and father. Children and grandparents may have been treated similarly.

Any name can be spelled some other way. The Cole family of New York sometimes appears as Kool due to Dutch influence or Kohl due to German influence, yet many families with this name stem from the New England Coles. In strictly alphabetical indexes, such spelling variants must be checked to get all of the data. Be especially watchful for variations with a vowel as the initial letter. Even simple names, such as Ott, can appear as Ot, Otte, Utt, or Autt. Thompson is often spelled without the letter *p*, giving it a different Soundex code in the census and other government indexes.

Both given names and family names may have been translated from other forms. Jacob is the Latin and German form of James. The Slavic Vojtech becomes Adelbert or Albert in English. Polly and Mary are interchangeable, as are Sarah and Sally. The Huguenot Le Counte becomes the Dutch de Graff; and de la Maiste becomes Delamater. Some Germans translated their surnames into English: Zimmerman becomes Carpenter and Schwartz becomes Black. Be wary when you are dealing with the first and second American generations.

When searching indexes, look for less-common names first. For example, for a Mary Loomis-John Smith marriage, check Loomis first because it is less common. If searching a Loomis family history, however, reverse the process: check for John Smith married to Mary Loomis. This method is faster and usually more effective.

The growing popularity of genealogy and the increasing number of genealogical publications means that more and more indexes are being created and published each year. Additional indexes are mentioned throughout this book. The purpose of all of these indexes generally remains the same: to help researchers find individuals faster and to locate important information more easily.

An excellent article on the use of printed indexes is Donald Lines Jacobus's "Tricks in Using Indexed Genealogical Books." In it, Jacobus covers some of these rules in greater detail. Keep in mind that indexes are tools—not sources. For more information on the nature of genealogical indexes, and how to use them more effectively, see Kip Sperry's "Published Indexes," chapter 6 in *Printed Sources*.

Databases and indexes are often confused. In fact, many databases are referred to as indexes, even though they include more information than is traditionally associated with indexes. How do databases differ from indexes? A database is more than an index *if it includes significant information about its subjects.* Typically, an index includes only enough information to 1) identify a subject and 2) reference another source where the researcher can get further information on the subject. While databases usually refer to source information, they may also include some, if not all, of the known information about their subjects. The distinction may seem minor, but it is important to understand from a research perspective. A database may contain sufficient information for a researcher's needs, while an index usually only points to the information—the researcher must still retrieve it from some other source. Access to that source may not be easy and entails another step in the research process. Therefore, databases are usually preferred by researchers.

Types of Databases and Indexes

Biography Indexes

At least 12 million Americans have been the subject of a biographical sketch in collective biography volumes. While many of these sketches are in local histories, more than 5 million appear in books with a nationwide scope, including biographical dictionaries and encyclopedias such as *Who's Who in America* and *Men and Women of Science*. Not only do biographical sketches provide information about the subject's birth, marriage, death, and family, they also usually provide biographical information seldom available in other sources. This may include occupations, political and religious affiliations, military service, educational achievements, lifetime accomplishments, and much more.

Fortunately, locating such sketches has become much easier in the past two decades. To determine if someone has published a brief biography about an ancestor or relative, you must use biographical sources. They are best accessed by a growing number of indexes, many of which are introduced in this chapter. For more information on the following indexes, and many more, as well as the kinds of records they index and how to evaluate them, see chapter 18, "Biographies," in *Printed Sources*.

Census Indexes

After more than three decades of work by hundreds of individuals and dozens of organizations in the genealogical field, statewide census indexes now exist for all extant federal censuses taken from 1790 through 1930. These indexes exist in many forms, including book, microfilm, microfiche, CD-ROM, and Internet databases (see figure 2-1). Furthermore, for most indexes, more than one index exists, permitting researchers to overcome the inherent problems with census indexes. The following discussion can only provide an overview of the nature, use, and cautions when using census indexes. For more information on census indexes, how to evaluate them, and how to overcome their limitations, see chapter 9, "Censuses and Tax Lists," in *Printed Sources*. Observe caution when using census indexes. For example, the indexers may not have been well-trained in early American handwriting; most census indexes have been made from microfilm copies, and the writing may have been faded or difficult to read. Most indexes for the 1850 and later censuses contain only the heads of households and persons in the households with different surnames. Often, two or more indexes exist for the same census; if possible, use them all. However, do not depend on the index alone. If an ancestor was known to have lived in a county when a census was taken but does not appear in the index, search the entire township or county. In larger cities for the post-1850 period, city directories may be helpful as a type of index; see chapter 8, "Directories," and chapter 5, "Census Records," for a thorough discussion of census records.

Electronic Family Trees

One of the most significant types of genealogical databases spawned by the arrival of personal computers in genealogy is the growing collection of electronic family trees. Often these computer files are wrongly called GEDCOM (which stands for Genealogical Data Communications) files, after the file format that allows sharing of genealogical data between software programs. Regardless of their designation, with more than one billion names circulating in such files, all readily searchable, in part or in full, via the Internet, they deserve the attention of all serious family historians. A solid understanding of these increasingly important tools includes knowing the nature and type of such trees, as well as how to search and evaluate them.

Electronic Family Trees are computerized databases of family history information compiled by individual genealogists that represent the core findings of the genealogist's research. Today, virtually every genealogist uses one or more computer programs to file, store, and manage the information they find about their family during their research. These "database management programs," such as Family Tree Maker (FTM), Legacy, The Master Genealogist (TMG), Personal Ancestral File (PAF), Ancestral Quest, and Roots Magic are discussed in chapter 2, "Computers and Technology." It is the publicly distributed output of these programs that is of current interest.

The hallmarks of an electronic family tree include the following elements of the database which are used to manage the data:

- It describes an individual in terms of genealogical identifiers—names with at least some key dates and places (including birth, marriage, and death).
- It links those individuals to other individuals in the database by birth or marriage.
- The database uses standard data fields to permit consistency in searching and presentation (it is not just electronic text).
- It may be published on the Internet and/or on CD-ROM or other electronic media.
- It identifies the name and contact information for the submitter.
- It can usually be shared (downloaded) using the GEDCOM format.

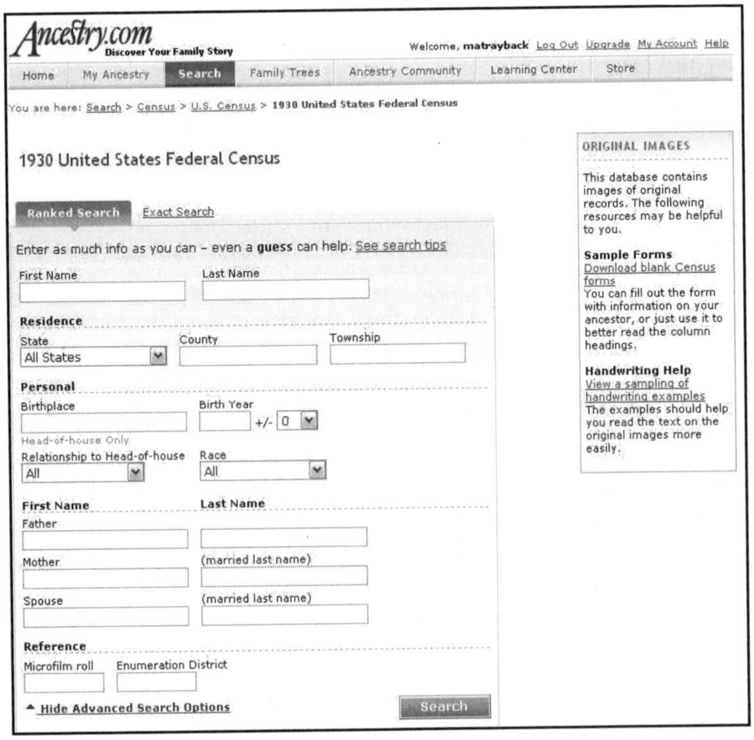

Figure 2-1. U.S. federal census records are fully searchable on various websites, such as Ancestry.com.

Some electronic family trees also include the following elements (at the discretion of the submitter):

- Source citations
- Notes made by the compiler

These individual electronic family tree databases reside on the creator's computer, or may be published on a personal website, copied to a CD-ROM, or contributed to any of a number of large online collections.

Types of Collections. There are two major types of electronic family tree collections: merged and unmerged. In a merged database, all new information submitted by an individual is merged with the existing information, resulting in a list with no duplicate entries. While, in theory, it keeps the database organized, it opens the door to wrong information being merged into the database to exist alongside or, in some cases, to the exclusion of correct information.

To alleviate this concern, most collections of electronic family trees today consist of unmerged databases. Thousands of individual researchers submit their own, self-researched, electronic family tree to a collection. There it resides side-by-side with the contributions of other researchers. Often the same person is included on several family trees. It is then left up to each researcher to evaluate the various entries for the same person and decide which (if any) is correct. Of course, a relative may appear ten, twenty, or even thirty or more times in the same database, if many different people have included him or her in their contribution. For early American ancestors, this is not uncommon.

Searching. While anyone can post their own genealogical database to their personal Web page, the vast majority are published at one (or more) of a number of websites that specifically collect electronic family trees. These sites have each developed a separate name for their collection, along with a search engine that generally allows powerful searches, beyond just first and last names.

Searching electronic family trees can be challenging. The problem with searching such collections is matching the researcher's knowledge to the information in the database. If the submitter only included the individual's name, then including a birth date on the search form will not locate the submitted entry. If the data file reports that John Jones was born "about 1870" then a search for John Jones born 1873 will not identify him in the database.

When searching such collections, the usual rule of thumb is to provide less information, rather than more. If the collection returns too many "hits" or matches, then refine the search with more detail. Depending on the search engine, it is usually better to add a child or parent to the search, rather than a place or date. While other researchers may have input a slightly different place or date, the name of a close relative is more likely to be the same.

However, even this often does not work. If the searcher uses the individual's child as a close relative, but the database has the individual as the most recent generation, listing no children, and linked only to parents, such a search request will not find the person being sought. Therefore, try a number of different searches, including different information each time. This may mean other versions of the name, alternate birth or death dates, or places. Try broadening the place. Using "Montana" for the place may be more successful than the more specific "Hamilton, Ravalli, Montana."

The great benefit of electronic family trees, of course, is that the researcher can gain some key clues about entire new branches for his or her own family tree. Often a previous researcher has had access to information and sources another researcher has no knowledge of, or has not yet taken the time to find.

Conversely, one of the great limitations of most electronic family trees is the failure of the submitter to include source citations, or even notes indicating where the information came from. Without such information, it is very difficult to verify the data.

Evaluation. Evaluating the information in electronic family trees is made more difficult by the typical lack of source citation or notes in most such trees. Therefore, it is crucial to examine the new information and compare it to known information. Due to the rampant copying of family trees, it *is not* satisfactory to simply determine the number of similar (or identical) entries for the persons in question.

The first step in evaluating the information found is to understand how it was probably gathered. The most common sources for the information in electronic family trees include the following:

- Personal knowledge of some family member who provided it to the compiler by way of letter, e-mail, phone call, or other means
- Other electronic family trees published previously
- Published genealogies or family history books
- Journal articles about the family
- Published lineages, such as descent from a Revolutionary War patriot
- Previous research findings by an earlier member of the family

Following are a few guidelines to use when evaluating information in electronic family trees:

First, examine the individual's record for any source citations or notes, and read them carefully. Make sure they pertain to the individual, and not just to the family tree in general, or a different family in the tree. For example, if the 1850 census is cited, but the person was born in 1856, that source does not pertain to that person, although it may well pertain to the parents.

Second, precise dates (day, month, year) and places (town, county, country) suggest there was some credible source behind that data, even if it is not cited. Most researchers don't just make up the data. Determine what sources could have existed for that place, time period, and ethnic group from which the information may have been obtained. For example, since Ohio did not keep any kind of birth records before 1867, an exact birth date and place in 1842 in Ohio usually suggests either a church record, cemetery inscription, death record, or some family record (such as a Bible).

Third, examine the whole tree where the individual appears. Are sources given for some persons? Are there several generations with minimal information, such as just names, with no places or dates (or vague places and dates)? Are there just one or two children in many families? These are clues regarding how carefully (or sloppily) the tree was compiled.

Fourth, seek original records (censuses, death certificates, probate files, and so forth) for the persons of interest which can provide some substantiation of the facts given in the file. You may never find a corroborating document for every fact stated in such databases. True facts sometimes come from sources no longer extant or accessible. Careful research will permit you to judge the validity of the information as a whole.

Ethnic Societies

Societies devoted to researching particular ethnic groups can provide information from data submitted by their members. Two examples of databases that pertain to specific ethnic groups are P.O.I.N.T. (Pursuing Our Italian Names Together <www.point-pointers.net/>), and the Jewish Genealogical People Finder <www.avotaynu.com>.

As with local societies, ethnic societies generally have an Internet presence, and are readily found through general search engines. The "Directories" section later in this chapter identifies additional means of identifying and locating such societies.

Genealogy Indexes

Before conducting extensive research, find out if a genealogy (or family history) for the surname of interest has already been published. Such a find can be of great value, allowing you to build on previous research instead of redoing the same work. Tens of thousands of such works have been published. Many trace the descendants of one person through several generations; others trace the ancestors of a couple. Various combinations also exist but, generally, such books are based on one surname. The use of indexes, catalogs, and bibliographies, many of which are introduced in this chapter, are the critical tools for determining if someone has compiled a history or genealogy that includes your family.

Immigration Indexes

The topic of immigration to the United States is also discussed in chapter 9, "Immigration Records." Immigration records are generally available in two forms: printed lists taken from manuscripts or compilations and unpublished manuscript lists. A mammoth, ongoing work seeking to index all printed immigration records is P. William Filby's *Passenger and Immigration Lists Index*. This work contains more than five million personal names filed alphabetically and includes age (if given), destination, and source citations for approximately 4,000 printed immigration lists. Supplements add approximately 150,000 names every year. Supplements are cumulated every five years. This index has been published on CD-ROM by Family Tree Maker (Genealogy.com) and is available as part of the immigration database at Ancestry.com. Of course, as with all on-going indexes, the CD-ROM is less and less complete as new entries are added to the index, necessitating updates every few years. Two excellent articles by P. William Filby in the *Genealogical Journal* explain this project: "Published Passenger Lists" (1979) and "Published Passenger Lists" (1983). Several other projects and indexes are mentioned in the latter article.

Of the more than 20 million people who came to the United States in the nineteenth century, most are now included in published (book or especially electronic) immigration lists. Many arrival lists compiled by ports of entry survived and have been microfilmed by the National Archives. Indexes exist for arrivals at the following ports for the years indicated:

Baltimore: 1820–74, 1852–97, 1853–66
Boston: 1848–91
Mobile, Alabama: 1820–62
New Bedford, Massachusetts: 1823–74
New Orleans: 1820–50 and 1853–99
New York City: 1820–46 and 1897–1902
Philadelphia: 1800–1906, 1820–74

These indexes are available at the National Archives and its regional branches and at the Family History Library, as well as larger genealogical libraries. Most of these lists are now also indexed on the Internet. Also see *Genealogical Research in the National Archives*, and Loretto Dennis Szucs's and Sandra Hargreaves Luebking's *The Archives: A Guide to the National Archives Field Branches*.

Indexes to Original Records

Most indexes to original records exist on a state, county, or other local level. As such, they are beyond the scope of this chapter. Since *The Source* primarily deals with the original records of genealogy (compiled records are discussed in *Printed Sources*), a fuller discussion of various indexes to original records will be part of the other chapters of this work. However, some indexes, or types of indexes, pertain to research in an entire country, and deserve brief mention here.

Vital Records. The major databases for vital records are discussed throughout this chapter (see International Genealogical Index, Vital Records Index, and U.S. Social Security Death Index). However, since indexes to vital records differ from the databases, some important aspects of those indexes should be mentioned here. As indicated, databases include most of the significant information about an event, for example, the exact date and place of a birth or death, and the parent's names. Many indexes provide much less information. Sometimes only the name of the subject and the year of the event are given, along with a reference number. In large indexes, this may make it difficult to determine which entry pertains to the person a researcher is seeking.

Large indexes may also make it difficult to recognize the subject of the search, if the name was recorded with a much different spelling. The "wrong" spelling of the name may be many pages away from the spelling being searched. Electronic indexes (on the Internet or CD-ROM), may not permit easy searching for variant spellings. Therefore, where possible, search indexes at the smallest locality possible, such as the county for vital records, or the specific church or cemetery. This will help eliminate "noise," or false positives, in the search.

Each state should have an index to the births, marriages, and deaths they have recorded since they required registration at the statewide level. However, those indexes have at least two drawbacks. First, they generally will not include such vital records as were recorded at the local (usually county) level prior to state requirements. Second, many of those indexes are not readily searchable by genealogists. Rather, the researcher must submit a request, with payment, to have whatever index exists searched by a government employee. This does not allow the researcher to carefully search the index for themselves, so it is not known how thoroughly the index was searched.

While privacy rights continue to keep some records closed, and sometimes close records that were previously public, some states have made efforts to provide publicly available indexes of their vital records. Most commonly this is done with death records, although some statewide marriage and birth records exist. Usually birth or marriage indexes are only public long after the events occurred, and the participants are likely to be deceased.

In conjunction with the Social Security Death Index (see the section later in this chapter), the growing number of statewide death indexes provides increasing coverage for twentieth century deaths (and some from earlier dates). Most of the states have made indexes to some or all of their death records available. Most are posted on the Internet, while others are available only on microfilm. Often the Internet indexes are simply another edition of an earlier microfilm index.

Local History Indexes

Many printed genealogies and biographies are buried in the thousands of local histories that have been published throughout the United States in the last century and a half. Once found, they can produce added insight on a particular ancestor—a father's name or place of origin, for example—or add several generations to a lineage. Most local histories are not yet available on the Internet, and must be accessed at the libraries where the books are housed. The proper use of available indexes can greatly assist in identifying and finding these sources, as well as learning if an ancestor may be discussed within its pages.

For more information on the following indexes, and many more, as well as the kinds of records they index and how to evaluate them, see chapter 17, "County and Local Histories," in *Printed Sources*. Those that are generally nationwide in scope are described in the Specific Databases and Indexes section that follows.

Statewide Indexes. A relatively recent development is the creation of statewide indexes to local histories. Many every-name indexes have been published for individual local histories; now works are appearing that include many histories in one alphabetical index. These are personal-name indexes to those for whom a sketch or important information is available. They are not every-name indexes to all the books included. When using these indexes, check every sketch in an area of interest (county, city) for all people having the surname of interest. In this way the ancestor may be found, even if not the subject of a sketch. Statewide biographical sketch indexes are available (usually published as books, but sometimes existing only as card files) for Alabama, Alaska, Arkansas, California, Colorado, Connecticut, Delaware, Florida, Hawaii, Idaho, Illinois, Indiana, Iowa, Kansas, Kentucky, Louisiana, Maine, Maryland, Massachusetts, Michigan, Minnesota, Mississippi, Montana, Nevada, New Hampshire, New Jersey, New York, North Dakota, Ohio, Oregon, Pennsylvania, Rhode Island, South Carolina, South Dakota, Tennessee, Texas, Utah, Virginia, Washington, West Virginia, Wisconsin, and Wyoming. A complete discussion of both published and manuscript indexes, including bibliographic citations, is in chapter 16, "County and Local Histories," of *Printed Sources*.

Local Societies

Many county historical and genealogical societies maintain files of their members' interests. Such files usually include families from the locality served by the society. The information in them reflects the findings of society members as they have researched families of their areas. Since the societies' focus is on serving their members, they are usually quite helpful in connecting inquiries to members with the same family or surname. Most have websites that reflect their area of coverage, and many have posted databases and indexes to local collections.

Locating genealogical societies has become easier in recent years. Searching for them by name in an Internet search engine will usually locate their site. If the name is unknown, or uncertain, use generic terms in the search engine, such as the name of the county or city and the words genealogical and society. The Federation of Genealogical Societies (FGS) is an umbrella organization to which many (but not all) genealogical societies belong. The FGS website <www.fgs.org> includes links to the home pages of their member societies.

Military Indexes

Almost every United States genealogist has one or more ancestors who served in the military, thus creating great interest in military records. In fact, many lineage societies have been formed around service in a particular war. A few select military indexes are mentioned in the Specific Databases and Indexes section that follows.

Many books have been compiled on those who served in other U.S. wars, as described in chapter 11, "Military Records" in this book. Also see the discussion of lineage societies in appendix D, "Hereditary and Lineage Organizations."

Online Academic Research Sources

Many libraries have integrated computer technology, CD-ROM databases, and online searching into their reference services. Library personnel can obtain information from hundreds of subscription databases, including *America, History and Life, Historical Abstracts, Comprehensive Dissertation Abstracts, Encyclopedia of Associations, National Newspaper Abstracts, Standard and Poor's News Service, Social Science Citation Index, ERIC (Educational Resources Information Center)*, and many others.

Typically these databases and indexes have been developed over the last thirty to forty years by major corporations who provide the information, for a fee, to libraries (and sometimes, independent researchers). One such corporation is ProQuest, which vends its genealogical sources under the name Heritage Quest Online. Another is Gale Research Co., which provides libraries with online subscription access to biographies and other genealogically useful material.

However, some indexes and databases, such as those listed above, have genealogical value but are not part of typical genealogical packages from these library vendors. Generally their genealogical value is limited to certain situations and circumstances, but the diligent researcher should be aware of them. Such subscriptions are popular at academic and many major public libraries. Depending on the subscription arrangements, library patrons can access some of these research tools from their homes via the Internet. Others can only be used onsite at the library.

Such research tools require little time to search. They can provide bibliographies of books and articles of interest, including locations of specific reference materials that can be borrowed through interlibrary loan. As an example, one search required just seconds to search 9,000 periodicals covering a ten-year period, yielding thirty-two entries of specific interest. It would have taken at least four months to physically search those periodicals, even with the best of indexes.

Most of these databases are now being distributed on the Internet, although CD-ROM versions are also offered for many. They are available at local research libraries. Usually there is no charge for the researcher to use them because the library pays an annual subscription fee as part of their operating budget. Sources of interest to the genealogist now on CD-ROM (and also available online) include *Biography Index, America, History and Life, Biography and Genealogy Master Index, Congressional Masterfile*, and others.

Many experienced genealogists conduct research in academic libraries. Although large and organized for academic studies, these facilities have the funds to purchase some of the most important research tools available—many of them discussed throughout this book. Almost every academic library has a website where you can explore the potentials for research before signing up. It may be necessary to pay a fee to become a "Friend of the Library" or an Associate in order to gain borrowing privileges and a library card.

Query Files and Online Forums

A useful but often overlooked form of index is the query file. A query is a kind of "want ad" that is published in genealogical periodicals. Individual researchers write brief descriptions of the family they are seeking in the hopes of locating others who know more about the family. The query is a popular approach in genealogy for learning if others are researching a particular family. Almost every genealogical society or periodical maintains or prints a query file for its members or subscribers. In addition, some periodicals exist specifically to publish queries. In a very real sense, queries are indexes to ongoing research. The query seldom contains significant genealogical material, but it does, like other indexes, refer to a source for more information. If a researcher is not a member of the society or does not subscribe to the periodical, there is usually a small fee to place a query. The files or publications, however, are usually available for research at no cost. Over time, the addresses associated with queries often become out of date as researchers move. However, the society that maintains the file may have the researcher's present address.

Periodical Indexes

For more than 150 years, genealogists and genealogical societies have been printing periodicals (serials, journals, or magazines) that include a large variety of original sources, abstracts, transcripts, how-to articles, and compiled family histories. Periodicals spawn periodical indexes, which, even though not every-name indexes, are very helpful. Some of the indexes mentioned above include some genealogical periodicals, but the following focus exclusively on periodicals. For more information on the following indexes, and others, as well as the kinds of records they index and how to evaluate them, see chapter 19, "Genealogical Periodicals," in *Printed Sources*.

Vital Records Databases

Vital records are the building blocks of genealogy. With these records of births, marriages, and deaths, and the locations of those events, the family historian builds a family tree. Hence, they are among the most popular of records. Therefore, some of the most significant databases used in genealogy deal with vital records. Although the term "Vital Records" in the United States tends to refer to government-created records of births, deaths, or marriages, this chapter uses the broader definition, understood in Europe and elsewhere, as any collection of births, marriages, and/or deaths. The chief difference is that under such a definition, information from church registers and some other sources is also considered vital records.

Specific Databases and Indexes

The following list of specific databases and indexes is organized alphabetically. Some groups of small, related databases or indexes are grouped together by subject.

American Biographical Index

One important index to biographical information in local histories is the *American Biographical Index* (*ABI*). Part one is an index of approximately 300,000 biographies from more than 600 volumes for local and national leaders in the United States and Canada. The six-volume index identifies every subject, including dates of birth and death and occupation. The 368 sources used for this collection were published between 1702 and 1956, but fully ninety-two percent of the titles were published before 1920; fifty-five percent of them were published before 1900. Relatively few were published in the early years of this range. In fact, half of the indexed titles were published between 1880 and 1909. Virtually all of the subjects were born in the nineteenth century. A second part, of comparable size, primarily covers more recent persons.

The selection of sources in *ABI* is quite broad, geographically and by scope. The set complements the *Biography and Genealogy Master Index* (*BGMI*), described later in this section, very well because many state and regional sources were used, thus identifying thousands of obscure persons of only local importance. Approximately two-thirds of the sources in *ABI* are not indexed in the *BGMI*. Even fewer are indexed in the *Library of Congress Index to Local History Biographies* (described later in this chapter). It appears that less than ten percent of the individuals included have more than one entry. Therefore, approximately 275,000 distinct individuals are cited in part one alone. The geographic coverage is also very broad. Virtually every state is represented by at least one title, several by two or more.

The index is actually a tool to access the same company's *American Biographical Archives*, which is a microfiche collection of the indexed biographical sketches. Many major research libraries have the microfiche collection, but the index fully references the original publication, so access to the microfiche is not needed. The same company has also created biographical archives and indexes for many areas of the world. The index to the entire collection is termed *World Biographical Index* <www.saur-wbi.de/>.

American Genealogical-Biographical Index (AGBI) (Rider's Index)

The largest and most comprehensive index to published, book-length family histories is Fremont Rider's *American Genealogical-Biographical Index* (*AGBI*). This work is also known as *Rider's Index*. It contains references to more than 4 million individuals, primarily in family histories.

The *AGBI* is an extensive personal-name index that excludes only persons mentioned incidentally or those unrelated to the subjects being indexed, such as witnesses and authors. The primary emphasis is on family genealogies published before 1950, but other valuable genealogical collections are included, such as the *Boston Transcript* (a genealogical column with a wide circulation), the complete United States 1790 census, and published revolutionary war records from most of the colonies.

Each entry contains the subject's complete name, year and state of birth (if known), abbreviated biographical data, and the book and page citation. Every volume contains an explanation of the index. Full bibliographical citations for the sources indexed are in volumes 1, 10, 34, and 54; a supplement is in volume 70. More than 850 sources are indexed. Printed volumes of this index are available at major genealogical libraries, as well as public and university libraries with large genealogy collections. The index is available online at Ancestry.com, and was also published on CD-ROM by Ancestry in 1999.

Ancestral File

Ancestral File, part of FamilySearch.org (sponsored by The Church of Jesus Christ of Latter-day Saints (LDS)), is a lineage-linked database that contains significant genealogical information on more than 35 million persons. First released in 1989, *Ancestral File* offered genealogists a way to share their findings about their ancestors with others. The initial data in the file came from nearly 200,000 family group records submitted by LDS church members. Most of these records were microfilmed; the submission code is listed with the submitter's name, helping the user determine the sources of the information. Millions of subsequent entries have been contributed by thousands of genealogists from throughout the world, both members of the LDS church and others.

Ancestral File was an attempt to create a merged file, which would constantly improve as researchers corrected previously submitted, incorrect information. However, the ease of the correct and merge functions, along with the lack of genealogical experience of many users led to many records being linked to incorrect relatives, and accurate data being replaced by outdated, less accurate information. By 2001, the sponsors decided not to accept any more additions or corrections to *Ancestral File*, making it a closed file. Much of the data is still quite good and it provides, like any other collection of electronic family trees, clues for researchers to verify in other records.

Ancestry World Tree

Part of Ancestry.com, the *Ancestry World Tree* collection of family trees, with about 400 million names, is the largest such collection on the Internet (see figure 2-2). Over 300,000 separate databases mean that the same person may appear several times, often with different information. It also includes the names from the RootsWeb WorldConnect Project, where this same data can be accessed. Both sites have excellent search engines.

The files were all contributed by Ancestry.com subscribers and visitors. There is no cost to submit a file, or to search and download the information. The quality of the information will vary from database to database. Some include sources, but most do not. A few do not permit downloading of the submitted GEDCOM file.

Pedigree Archives

MyTrees/KindredKonnections <www.MyTrees.com> claims to include more than 150 million names in their *Pedigree Archives* collection of electronic trees. Using the index to the collection is free, but viewing or downloading the actual trees requires a subscription. However, researchers can earn limited free access by submitting a new electronic family tree, or participating in the various record extraction projects that the company operates.

Biography and Genealogy Master Index (BGMI)

At least 3,000 nationwide collective biography volumes exist and have been indexed by Mirana C. Herbert and Barbara McNeil in the *Biography and Genealogy Master Index (BGMI)*. It is an ongoing indexing project; a five-volume index first appeared in 1980. Supplemental volumes have been issued every year, with accumulations occurring every fifth year (1985, 1990, 1995, 2000, and 2005). Each cumulative set and supplementary volume contain one alphabetical sequence. The index gives the name ofthe subject of the biographical sketch, years of birth and death (if known), and an abbreviation for the source of the sketch. It is an invaluable tool for locating more than 13 million references to notable people. It concentrates heavily on the twentieth and late nineteenth centuries and includes many living people, making it valuable for locating distant cousins. However, significant numbers of early Americans are also included. The *BGMI* is also available online in many academic and large public libraries, and at Ancestry.com.

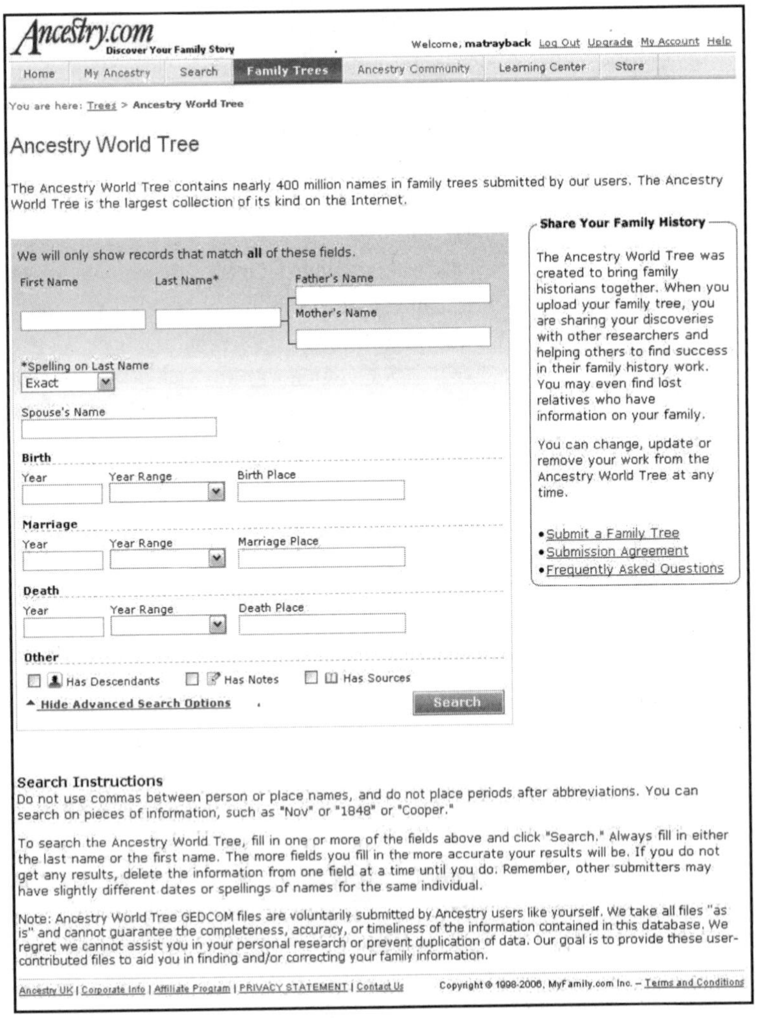

Census Indexes

The 1790 census is included in the *American Genealogical-Biographical Index* discussed earlier. Also, *Century of Population Growth 1790–1900* includes a table of names from the 1790 census, grouped by similar spellings, showing in which states each name appears; it thus serves as a quasi-index for 1790. Some Family History Centers still have the 1984 microfiche of the census indexes from Accelerated Indexing Systems (AIS). This includes all U.S. federal census indexes for 1850 and earlier, but few for later years. The AIS index is divided into nine searches. Searches one through four cover the entire United States for, respectively, 1607 to 1819, 1820 to 1829, 1830 to 1839, and 1840 to 1849 (a few state and colonial lists are also indexed). Search 7a covers the 1850 census into one alphabet.

Two competing, commercial companies have posted census indexes on their subscription Internet sites with powerful search engines. Searches can be nationwide, or can be restricted to a state or county. Some permit Soundex searches, while others permit searches by age or birthplace of the person indexed. Each company, Ancestry.com and Heritage Quest Online, has also posted images of each census at their site. Because of the ever-evolving nature of Internet resources, a specific summary here of their differences would quickly be out of date.

It should be noted, however, that competition has produced improvements in census indexes. Both companies have also produced their census indexes on CD-ROM.

The Church of Jesus Christ of Latter-day Saints, sponsor of the Family History Library, has also completed its long-term project to transcribe the significant information from the 1880 U.S., and 1881 British and Canadian census records. These abstracts include the name of every person in the census, with their age, birthplace, occupation, and family relationships. The powerful search engine allows researchers to search almost any field at almost any geographic level. All of this information is available at FamilySearch.org.

Ancestry.com
Discover Your Family Story
Welcome, matrayback Log Out Upgrade My Account Help
Home | My Ancestry | Search | Family Trees | Ancestry Community | Learning Center | Store
You are here: Trees > Ancestry World Tree

Ancestry World Tree

The Ancestry World Tree contains nearly 400 million names in family trees submitted by our users. The Ancestry World Tree is the largest collection of its kind on the Internet.

We will only show records that match **all** of these fields.
First Name | Last Name* | Father's Name | Mother's Name
*Spelling on Last Name: Exact
Spouse's Name
Birth: Year | Year Range | Birth Place
Marriage: Year | Year Range | Marriage Place
Death: Year | Year Range | Death Place
Other: Has Descendants | Has Notes | Has Sources
Hide Advanced Search Options | Search

Share Your Family History
The Ancestry World Tree was created to bring family historians together. When you upload your family tree, you are sharing your discoveries with other researchers and helping others to find success in their family history work. You may even find lost relatives who have information on your family.
You can change, update or remove your work from the Ancestry World Tree at any time.
• Submit a Family Tree
• Submission Agreement
• Frequently Asked Questions

Search Instructions
Do not use commas between person or place names, and do not place periods after abbreviations. You can search on pieces of information, such as "Nov" or "1848" or "Cooper."

To search the Ancestry World Tree, fill in one or more of the fields above and click "Search." Always fill in either the last name or the first name. The more fields you fill in the more accurate your results will be. If you do not get any results, delete the information from one field at a time until you do. Remember, other submitters may have slightly different dates or spellings of names for the same individual.

Note: Ancestry World Tree GEDCOM files are voluntarily submitted by Ancestry users like yourself. We take all files "as is" and cannot guarantee the completeness, accuracy, or timeliness of the information contained in this database. We regret we cannot assist you in your personal research or prevent duplication of data. Our goal is to provide these user-contributed files to aid you in finding and/or correcting your family information.

Ancestry UK | Corporate Info | Affiliate Program | PRIVACY STATEMENT | Contact Us   Copyright © 1998-2006, MyFamily.com Inc. – Terms and Conditions

Figure 2-2. Members of Ancestry.com can use the Ancestry World Tree to share their family tree and possibly discover others searching along the same lines.

Since censuses remain one of the most popular genealogical sources on the Internet, continued improvements to indexes can be expected.

Civil War Indexes

Statewide indexes exist for those who served from specific states in the Civil War (both Union and Confederate), but the major indexes are in the National Archives or genealogical libraries that have purchased microfilm copies. The three-by-five-inch card index to Civil War pension applications is the largest single index for this war: *General Index to Pension Files 1861–1934* is available at many major genealogical libraries.[1] It covers only those who served the Union cause, or former Confederate soldiers who changed sides. Most of these cards have been indexed by Ancestry.com, where researchers can search the electronic index, and then view an image of the cards for more information, such as pension file numbers. Other indexes to Civil War soldiers are also available at Ancestry.com.

Compiled service records have also been indexed for every known soldier—not only those who applied for pensions. However, they are arranged by state. A consolidated, nationwide index of service in the also Civil War exists. Called the Civil War Soldier's System, it contains the names taken from 5.2 million General Index cards. Sponsored by the National Parks Service, and aided by the Genealogical Society of Utah, the Federation of Genealogical Societies (FGS), and other organizations, the project can be searched at the National Parks Service website.

Family Group Records Collection

The Family Group Records Collection is a manual, lineage-linked database. It is a microfilm collection of family group sheets submitted by members of the LDS church from 1924 to 1978. The almost 10 million family group sheets represent approximately 40 million people, living and deceased. Many of these names also appear in the IGI or in the Ancestral File. The collection is divided into sections.

The Patron Section. The patron section includes 2 million sheets submitted from 1962 to 1978 for people born *since* about 1850 (the last four or five generations). It includes many duplicate family sheets submitted by different genealogists who descended from the same families. Comparing all of the different versions will reveal names and addresses of potential cousins who share the same ancestors; references to family Bibles, letters, and diaries in the possession of living family members and personal accounts written by family members now deceased; clues to family naming patterns, spelling variants of surnames, migrational routes, and places of residence for family members; and exact dates of birth and death known only by the families. Variations of family traditions can also be discerned in these sheets. Most of the sheets in the patron section pertain to the immediate ancestry of American LDS families.

The Main Section. The main section includes approximately 8 million sheets, most of them for deceased persons born before 1870. These sheets were submitted between 1942 and 1969. While documentation was called for on the sheets, the documentation cited is often limited. Often, "family records" was indicated if the information was based on personal records or knowledge. Sheets based on research usually rely on printed family and local histories and parish registers. Some of these family group sheets are the products of professional research by the former Research Department of the Family History Library.

Asterisks (*) mark cross references to show if other group sheets exist (or once existed) for a person as a member of another family. For example, an asterisk on a parent's name might indicate that a sheet showing him or her as a child is or was available. This feature makes the Family Group Records Collection a manual, lineage-linked database.

Though these family group sheets were submitted by members of the LDS church, they document families from which any researcher may have descended. The names and addresses of those who submitted the sheets are also recorded on them, though this contact information is likely to be outdated.

Both sections file the group sheets in strict alphabetical order by the name of the husband of each family, and chronologically by date where there are two or more sheets showing husbands with the same names. There is limited duplication between the two sections. The original group sheets for both sections are available on microfilm at the Family History Library and its Family History Centers. Microfilm numbers are listed in the Family History Library Catalog under the title "Family Group Records Collection."

The Family Groups Record Collection is an alphabetized, compiled source, making it a manual database—not an index. The information in it is only as accurate as the care used in compiling the records. Some family group sheets are known to have errors, especially those for colonial American lines going into England and Europe. Sources are usually given at the bottom of group sheets; however, a careful analysis of the data will show that not all entries came from the sources listed.

Family Tree Maker User Pages

The most popular genealogy software of the 1980s and 1990s was *Family Tree Maker* and the company invited their software users to establish free personal genealogy websites, called "user pages" at the company site. Many responded by posting their own *Family Tree Maker* data on such sites. Access to the various sites is free for both researchers and the software users. However, it is not possible to download the electronic trees into a software program. Researchers can contact the users to request a GEDCOM copy of the file.

The best way to search these pages, now at Genealogy.com, is to use the company's "Internet Family Finder" to search for a name. This makes the search routine somewhat basic, and does not allow significant advanced searching functions. This program has not been promoted much in past years, so most of the files seem fairly static, with few new files being established. It is difficult to determine the current size of this collection of trees. Earlier statements claimed at least 12 million names, and at least 150,000 files.

Genealogical Periodical Annual Index (GPAI)

Since 1962, the *Genealogical Periodical Annual Index (GPAI)* has been a boon to genealogists. Several editors have accepted the task of producing it over the years. This index is in virtually every genealogy library. It is not cumulative from year to year, so each year must be searched separately. It is not an every-name index and includes a personal name only when the individual is the subject of an article. Book reviews and other articles, such as those concerning research methodology, are also indexed. Approximately 300, or roughly one-half, of the genealogical periodicals currently available—specifically, those periodicals that are provided to the indexers at no charge—are indexed. While most major periodicals are included, many small, local periodicals are not. The most recent edition covers periodicals published in 2001.

Genealogical Research Directory

An annual query book published since 1981, each issue of the *Genealogical Research Directory* contains approximately 100,000 new entries from all over the world. Edited by Keith A. Johnson and Malcolm R. Sainty, this source is available at most major genealogical libraries, although most of the purchasers are individual researchers. Any researcher may pay a small fee to list the individuals being sought. (Purchase of the book is not required for a listing.) Its worldwide scope makes it especially useful for finding researchers in other countries who are interested in the same family. Back issues usually remain in print for from three to five years. Similar books exist specifically for England, Germany, and for some other countries.

GeneaNet

An eclectic, private and free website, the GeneaNet site claims to have access to over 80 million entries, most of which appear to be electronic family trees (see figure 2-3). Most of the indexed material is apparently not housed at the site, meaning that it helps provide access to material scattered throughout the Internet.

GenServ

One of the oldest collections of electronic family trees on the Internet, *GenServ* focuses on attracting many "mom and pop databases" which allows them to claim they have information not found elsewhere on the Web. They do charge a fee, primarily to cover the cost of the server. A smaller, low-budget operation, the search engine is adequate to access the approximately 30 million names on the site.

Global Tree

A relative newcomer to the collections of electronic family trees is GenCircles <www.gencircles.com/>, a collection begun in 2000. Their *Global Tree* includes millions of names submitted by users, at no cost. The search engine is fairly robust and includes unique matching software that finds persons in other databases who are apparently the same as the current query.

Greenlaw Index

An index similar to the *Old Surname Index* (described later in this chapter) is *The Greenlaw Index of the New England Historic Genealogical Society*, compiled by William Prescott Greenlaw. Greenlaw was the librarian of the New England Historic Genealogical Society from 1894 to 1929. The citations refer only to works carrying a family through three or more generations in books published from 1900 to 1940. The more than 35,000 entries are arranged alphabetically by surname and given names on three-by-five-inch cards reproduced in two large volumes. The citations also include the ancestor, residence, time period, and source. This index is similar in size and scope to the *Munsell Index*.

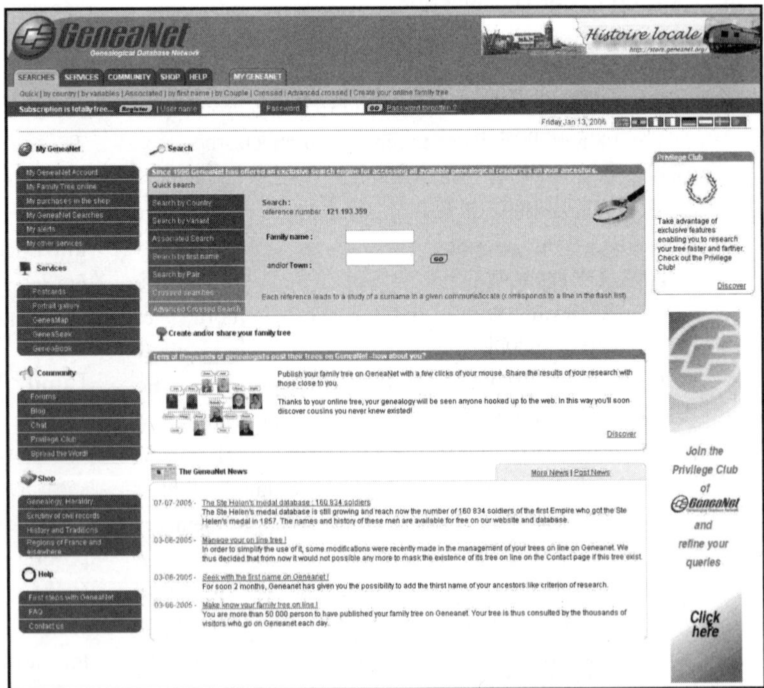

Figure 2-3. GeneaNet provides its users with a number of community tools, as well as a collection of family trees to search <http://geneanet.com>.

Immigration Indexes

Since 1983, the Center for Immigration Research at the Balch Institute for Ethnic Studies in Philadelphia has been publishing transcripts of nineteenth century passenger lists by ethnic group. Groups include Irish, German, Italians and Russians. Each volume has its own complete every-name index. A master index to these transcripts is indirectly available through Genealogy.com as part of their Immigration subscription. Most of these volumes have been published on CD-ROM as well, permitting indexed searches through that medium as well. In addition, others have extracted and published the data from the earliest years of these arrival records and, as of 2006, all extant passenger lists through 1850 (and some later) are available on CD-ROM, with their attendant indexes. For more information on the publication of immigration records, and their indexes, see chapter 14, "Immigration Sources," in *Printed Sources*.

Another 20 million or more names of immigrants are indexed through the database of Ellis Island arrivals. Covering arrivals at the New York port of arrival from 1892 into the 1920s, these abstracts of the passenger lists can be searched by any of several versions of the immigrant's name. The search can be further restricted by timeframe, even down to the name of a specific ship. The original passenger manifests were difficult for the volunteer extractors to read, and many of the foreign names were difficult to read, so creative search techniques and spelling variations will improve the researcher's chances of finding the right family. Available at <www.EllisIslandRecords.org>, the electronic database is also linked to images of the actual arrival lists. Ancestry.com also has indexes of passenger lists for several ports, including New York, from 1851 to 1891.

Index to Genealogical Periodicals (Jacobus' Index)

One of the foremost modern genealogists, Donald Lines Jacobus, saw the need to access the information hidden in periodicals. He published three volumes (1932 to 1953) as a partial index to major genealogical periodicals. A 1983 edition combines the seven separate indexes of the three original volumes into two: name and place. The index includes approximately 20,000 references to people, places, and records appearing in periodicals from 1870 to 1952, by surname, given name, and locality. However, Jacobus did not index periodicals that had their own comprehensive indexes, and he only indexed articles by their main subjects; therefore, his work is not an every-name index (for example, the family record of the Wilsons of Newport is indexed as: Wilson; Family Record, Newport). No individuals are specified. Jacobus' introductions in each volume are invaluable for understanding the scope of the index.

Individual Periodical Indexes

The publishers of many long-lived genealogical periodicals have created, or permitted others to create, comprehensive, cumulative indexes for their own magazines. While most publish annual indexes, those with cumulative indexes are more helpful to the genealogist. Some of these indexes were created as part of a project to publish back issues of the journal on CD-ROM, or even the Internet. A partial list of such periodicals and the volumes covered in each cumulative index follows. Because many indexes are being digitized and placed on the Internet, it's a good idea to visit the Web pages of the organizations to check the status of publications.

The American Genealogist, vols. 1–60 (subject index).

Daughters of the American Revolution Magazine, vols. 1–84, then every five years to vol. 104 ("Genealogy Index").

Detroit Society for Genealogical Research Magazine, vols. 1–10, then every five years to vol. 30.

Genealogical Journal, vols. 1–16 (subject index).

Mayflower Descendant, vols. 1–34 ("Index of Persons").

National Genealogical Society Quarterly, vols. 1–50 (topical indexes).

New England Historical and Genealogical Register Index of Persons, vols. 1–50, 51–148. The Society has published a CD-ROM version of their journal, through 1994, with consolidated index.

New Jersey Genealogical Magazine, vols. 1–30, 31–40, 41–50.

New York Genealogical and Biographical Record, vols. 1–110. An every-name index was published on CD-ROM in 2003.

Notes and Queries Relating to Pennsylvania, 7 vols. 1st–4th series. See Eva D. Schory's *Every Name Index to Egle's Notes and Queries*.

South Carolina Historical and Genealogical Magazine, vols. 1–40, 41–71.

Virginia Genealogist, vols. 1–20.

International Genealogical Index (IGI)

The *International Genealogical Index (IGI)*, begun in 1970 by the LDS church, is an international personal-name database (though it is called an index) of birth, christening, and marriage information about persons now deceased. As of 2006, this database included more than 400 million entries.

Although it is one of the most used sources, the *IGI* is often misunderstood, or its advantages not fully utilized. Almost every one knows that the *IGI* is a mammoth database of births and marriages, that it covers dozens of countries, and that it is available online at FamilySearch.org and at thousands of Family History Centers.

In its most simple definition, the IGI is, indeed, a worldwide database of birth and marriage information.

Always maintained as a computerized file of genealogical information (indeed, its original name was the *Computer File Index*), the database was first published on microfiche. As such, it was distributed to the hundreds of Family History Centers supported by the LDS church, and was available for purchase, and therefore found in some genealogical libraries. With the launch of FamilySearch.org in May 1999, the *IGI* was the major database at that site, making it readily available for individuals around the world.

On the Internet, the divisions of the *IGI* can be searched collectively or individually. Searchers fill out portions of a "family tree" with as much information as they desire. The results list returns entries matching only what was queried.

Therefore, as with most databases, include just enough information on the search screen to provide a list of matches which is not overwhelming, but also will not overlook possible matches. Typically this is just the person's first and last name. For common names, include the year of birth or marriage.

Recently, improvements to the online *IGI* increased the amount of information displayed for many entries, including siblings in some situations. While these changes improve its use, they do not significantly change the nature of the database. Now that updates are happening almost daily, there will be more names to search, making the *IGI* a tool of growing importance.

The Origins of Names in the *IGI*. Where did all the names in the *IGI* come from? Primarily the names come from two sources: individual submissions by researchers and extracts from original records. It is estimated that perhaps a little more than half of the names came from extracts of original records. It is precisely these extracts from parish and other records that are of particular interest to the family historian.

The *IGI* was not designed originally as a genealogical research tool. Therefore, it does not provide some of the features researchers have come to expect from such tools. For example, it does not claim to have included every name in the sources it derives data from. It also does not always fully identify the sources, or the contributors, of the information it contains.

While it is important to know, where possible, the source of the data in the *IGI*, the information is still useful, even without knowing the source. The data is, at least, a statement about a person's birth or marriage, in a specific place. Usually that place is a town or parish. As such, these statements are subject to genealogical verification, using standard research techniques.

The key to understanding the source of an *IGI* entry is the batch number, or film number, provided with most entries. Batch numbers which are all digits (such as 7324512), as well as those beginning with an A-, F- or T- were submitted by researchers, typically members of the LDS Church. Entries beginning with most other letters, commonly C- or M-, come from various extraction (indexing) programs. When you encounter an extraction batch number, you know that the information was taken directly from an original record (discussed in the next section).

Film numbers are also available for most entries in the *IGI*, and the source of that entry is on that microfilm. However, without understanding the batch number, finding an entry on that film may be difficult. For extraction projects, the batch may only be a portion of the records on the film. Within that portion, the records are often chronological. For patron submissions, the batch number often acts as a kind of page number to identify where on the film the entry is found. Submissions after the early 1990s primarily come from patron submissions, and the film only includes a computer printout of the information in the *IGI*. No source or submitter's name is provided.

A few of the entries are not birth or marriage records. Virtually all of these are patron-submitted entries, and may come from a variety of sources, including census records, wills, cemeteries, death records, and similar sources. If an age is provided in the record, the entry is described as a birth, although it was not based on an actual record of birth or baptism. Where there is no indication of a birth year, the death date is used, and, although flagged as such, the database treats that date like a birth date for indexing purposes.

Extraction (Indexing) Programs. From the early 1960s to the early 1990s, the LDS Church added millions of names to the *IGI* that were taken from a series of "extraction" programs administered by the Church. Begun originally by paid staff, the program focused first on extracting birth and marriage information from English parish registers. Soon, Scottish parishes, and various U.S. records were added to the program.

In the early 1970s, the processes had been worked out well enough that the Church began using volunteers. They extracted the data and prepared it for data entry in to a mainframe computer. Volunteers were primarily members of the Church. They typically would go to an extraction site housed in a church building (often the same building with the local Family History Center), receive some training, and then work their way through the handwriting of the parishes. Non-English records were soon added, including German, Scandinavian, and Mexican records.

The extracted records were drawn from the collections of the Family History Library; those outside of the United States were primarily church (parish) registers. Thus, entries in the IGI that trace back to extraction batches can be reviewed in the original record on microfilm. In the United States government vital records, as well as church registers, were used where they were available and fit the criteria.

Obviously there are limitations to such a program. The extractors were volunteers and as such, some excelled while others did not. For some, the reading of old handwriting came easily, while others struggled. Of course mistakes were made, but they are relatively rare, perhaps due to the devotion of those who agreed to volunteer.

With the advent of personal computers, the LDS church extraction program became home-based in the late 1980s.

Volunteers received paper printouts of the microfilmed records, and entered the key information into a template on their home computer.

One significant concept is that of "key information." Although called an extraction project, it was never designed to "extract" all of the information from a record. For example, parish register extractions do not include the names of godparents (witnesses or sponsors), or the age or occupation of the parents, even when it is given in the record. Therefore, it is best to think of these as "abstracted" records, and use the *IGI* as a database which points to sources that will have additional information. The information should be sufficient for you to decide if the person(s) you find are of interest to your research.

Munsell Index

Joel Munsell's *Index to American Genealogies* is a surname index to major American genealogical periodical titles, genealogies, and selected local histories. The reprint edition includes the *Supplement, 1900 to 1908.*

New England Marriages to 1700

Torrey's *New England Marriages to 1700* is a manual database that was created by Clarence A. Torrey, an accomplished genealogist. He spent much of his lifetime searching every genealogy of New England families published prior to the 1950s for evidence of marriages that took place before 1700. The result is this list of 74,000 New England adults of the seventeenth century. It probably identifies more than ninety-five percent of the marriages for that place and time. Although appearing as a set of marriage records (or evidences), this database serves to alert the researcher that a published genealogy exists for an ancestor. It includes almost every couple from more than 2,000 published New England genealogies.

Torrey's *New England Marriages* serves as an index to his files; however, the source of the information is not given in the book index. Rather, the researcher must search Torrey's handwritten notes, which are arranged on seven rolls of microfilm alphabetically by the groom's name. The original notes are at the library of the New England Historic Genealogical Society; microfilm copies of Torrey's files are available from that society or the Family History Library. The notes include cryptic, abbreviated references to published genealogies. Torrey made no attempt to evaluate the information in the genealogies; hence, the index, and his notes, may contain conflicting information. The researcher must determine which, if any, of the sources are correct.

After many years of work, Torrey's notes were also transcribed and published with the index on CD-ROM by the society. This makes accessing the sources of his findings even easier. Three supplements to Torrey's index were created by Melinde Lutz Sanborn and published by the Genealogical Publishing Company of Baltimore in 1991, 1995, and 2003.

Old Surname Index

From its early years, the Family History Library, like many genealogical libraries, indexed articles, genealogies, and family histories in periodicals as well as books. By around 1964, however, it was no longer feasible to analyze the articles and chapters in the new books the library was receiving, and this indexing project was ended. The original index cards, now available only on microfilm, were arranged alphabetically by surname. Approximately 100,000 cards were created, most of which apply to early American and English families. Each card includes the surname and sometimes the given name, the source and page number where the article was found, and an old library call number. Use the library catalog where you research to determine if the indicated source is available. Each source is available at the Family History Library, and most should be available through the library's Family History Centers.

OneGreatFamily

An attempt to create a collection of family trees that incorporates the best of both merged files (like *Ancestral File*) and unmerged collections spurred the development of OneGreatFamily. The unique approach has attracted some 70 million names from 200,000 users in this collaborative file. The sophisticated software program compares the researcher's family tree to others which have been submitted by other subscribers. Where it finds possible connections with other users that suggest pedigree additions, it shows them to the researcher, who can then opt to accept those additions to his or her tree or not. It does not change any other family tree, just the researcher's tree. Thus, it has fewer duplicate trees and names than other collections, since it requires interaction with the researcher. Viewing the index is free, but the matching software program requires an annual fee.

OneWorldTree

OneWorldTree is just one of the online family tree offerings from Ancestry.com. Its unique search tool looks through the thousands of user-contributed trees in the Ancestry World Tree collection and RootsWeb WorldConnect project and combines probable matches into one search result that is linked to all sources. OneWorldTree allows users to edit the information they find. The change will affect the researcher's tree, but also acts as a "vote" for what information will be displayed in the community tree. If you do not have an Ancestry.com subscription, you can view search results that include an individual's name and locations for birth, marriage, and death, but you will not be able to see the entire tree.

You can also use OneWorldTree to create your own family tree online. Building the tree is free, but you must be a registered user. As you add individuals to your tree, OneWorldTree will search its databases for other trees that seem to match yours and alert you when it finds them. If you find records in Ancestry.com databases for family members in your tree, you can link these records directly to an individual.

Other Name Indexes

There are several other indexes and lists of indexes that can be a boon to the genealogist. A sampling follows:

Anita Cheek Milner, *Newspaper Indexes*, 3 vols. (Metuchen, N.J.: Scarecrow Press, 1977–82), indicates where newspaper indexes are located and their scope. It is arranged by state and subdivided by city or county. See also Milner's "Newspaper Indexes," *Genealogical Journal*, 8 (Dec. 1979), 185, and chapter 12, "Newspapers," in this book.

Ronald V. Jackson, Jr., *Early American Series* (Salt Lake City: Accelerated Indexing Systems, 1981–84) is a set of personal-name indexes in book form, much like the company's well-known census indexes. These indexes are statewide and typically cover the colonial and early periods. Tax lists, state censuses, and passenger lists are included in the indexes. Unfortunately, the books do not identify the sources of the data very well, so the information can be cryptic and difficult for less experienced researchers to deal with. Many of these books are available at large genealogy libraries. Electronic versions of these indexes are available at Ancestry.com, along with their other census indexes.

Betty M. Jarboe, *Obituaries: A Guide to Sources,* 2nd ed. (Boston: G. K. Hall, 1989), identifies 3,547 published collections and indexes to death notices and cemetery listings throughout the United States and some foreign countries. An appendix identifies obituary card files in eighteen states.

Pedigree Resource File

In a very real sense, the *Pedigree Resource File* is a successor to *Ancestral File* that overcomes the principle problem with that merged file. Operated by the LDS Church and begun in 1998, this collection allows persons to contribute their electronic family trees without fear of them being changed by someone else's merge or "corrections." The trees are preserved on CD-ROM for presumed long-term storage and security. The trees are not posted on the Internet, but a database of the information is online at FamilySearch.org. That index does identify spouse or parents, if they are in the same family tree, but does not display family groups or pedigree charts, as do virtually all other such collections.

Periodical Source Index (PERSI)

The Periodical Source Index (PERSI) is an indexing project of the Historical Genealogy Department at the Allen County Public Library in Fort Wayne, Indiana. This library has long been known as having one of the best genealogical collections in the United States. The first volume of the index appeared in 1987; it covered periodicals published in the calendar year 1986. Subsequent annual volumes were published. The library has also published a sixteen-volume retrospective PERSI covering periodicals published from 1847 through 1985. The last of its four sections was published in 1995.

Like most major indexes, PERSI is not an every-name index. Rather, it is a subject index; only the subjects of the articles are included. Because families and individuals are often the subjects of articles, many of the citations are for given and family names. PERSI also indexes articles dealing with sources in localities, which are the staple of local periodical publishing. Updates to the index are made regularly, and it currently indexes almost one and a half million articles.

The data in PERSI is filed in five separate parts: U.S. Places, Family Records, Canada Places, Foreign Places, and Research Methodology. Each of these parts includes the same information for the index entries:

- The place or surname covered by the article.
- The type of record (except the Surname section), such as a census or a will.
- Title of the article (often a descriptive title, not always the full title of the article).
- Name of the journal, with volume number, issue number, month, and year. The page number of the article is not provided in the index.

PERSI indexes more periodicals than any other genealogical periodical index—mostly covering the United States, but also including many foreign periodicals from Canada, Germany, England, and other countries. Both historical periodicals and genealogical periodicals are included. Most researchers access PERSI through HeritageQuest Online, a subscription service available through many libraries. The PERSI book volumes are available at most major genealogical libraries. The Allen County Public Library has also published a comprehensive *Bibliography of Genealogical and Local History Periodicals With Union List of Major U.S. Collections*. This list serves to more fully identify the titles indexed in PERSI and also identifies which of several significant libraries throughout the United States have copies of the periodical. It also includes citations for hundreds of family and surname periodicals *not* included in the index.

Revolutionary War Index

For each colonial state, there is at least one volume (often more) identifying its citizens who served in the Revolutionary War. Many of those volumes are indexed in the *American Genealogical Biographical Index* discussed previously. Many of those books are also now available online at various websites. There are, however, three nationwide indexes of note: The *Index of Revolutionary War Pension Applications in the National Archives* is an alphabetical index of all those who applied for a pension or who received bounty land based on Revolutionary War service (some *see* references are included). The index thus includes only those soldiers and sailors who lived until pension laws went into effect and widows who could prove their husbands' revolutionary war service—approximately 80,000 names. The index is available in most genealogical libraries. The original pension files are in the National Archives. The Family History Library and many other repositories have microfilm copies.

In 1991 and 1992, Virgil White published *Genealogical Abstracts of Revolutionary War Pension Files* in four volumes, providing indexed abstracts for each of these files.

The Daughters of the American Revolution (DAR) *Patriot Index Centennial Edition* is a list of more than 125,000 people who aided the cause of the American Revolution with one descendant or more who joined the DAR by 1990. In most cases, lineage papers are available showing some documentation for the patriot and family. An updated, combined index is being prepared by the society. The *Index of Rolls of Honor in the Lineage Books* may also help identify a patriot ancestor. See appendix D, "Heredity and Lineage Organizations," for more information on lineage societies.

Statewide Indexes to Genealogical Periodicals

The following indexes provide subject coverage for many periodicals within the state indicated.

The *Connecticut Periodical Index* and a collection of more than 200 periodicals are at The Pequot Library, 720 Pequot Ave., Southport, Conn. 06490.

Bell, Carol Willsey. *Ohio Genealogical Periodical Index: A County Guide.* 4th ed. Youngstown, Ohio: C. W. Bell, 1983.

Buckway, G. Eileen. *Index to Texas Periodicals.* Salt Lake City: Family History Library, 1987.

Finnell, Arthur Louis. *Minnesota Genealogical Periodical Index.* Marshall, Minn.: Finnell Richter and Assoc., 1980.

Grover, Robert L. *Missouri Genealogical Periodical Index: A County Guide, 1960–1982.* Independence: Missouri Territory Pioneers, 1983.

Quigley, Maud. *Index to Family Names in Genealogical Periodicals.* Grand Rapids, Mich.: Western Michigan Genealogical Society, 1981.

———. *Index to Michigan Research Found in Genealogical Periodicals.* Grand Rapids, Mich.: Western Michigan Genealogical Society, 1979.

Swem, Earl Gregg. *Virginia Historical Index.* 2 vols. in 4, 1934–36. Reprint. Gloucester, Mass.: Peter Smith, 1965.

Trapp, Glenda K., and Michael L. Cook. *Kentucky Genealogical Index.* Evansville, Ind.: Cook Publications, 1985.

University of Arizona Library. *The Arizona Index: A Subject Index to Periodicals About the State.* 2 microfilms. Boston: G. K. Hall, 1978.

U.S. *Social Security Death Index*

The federal government is one of the largest creators of records in the United States. Several government agencies have information about persons who have lived in the United States. One of the most important collections of information is kept by the Social Security Administration. Charged with providing Social Security benefits to all eligible citizens, the agency has had to keep track of millions of Americans. While their records of living persons are protected by rights of privacy, records of deceased persons are available. The Social Security Administration has developed a computer database with minimal information about individuals in its files, and the records of deceased individuals in that computerized file have been released as the *Social Security Death Index.* Several commercial and nonprofit organizations have made these records available online or on CD-ROM.

The *Social Security Death Index* includes information about more than 70 million people who lived in the United States and had a social security number. Virtually all of the persons in the database died after 1961. There are very few records for persons who died from 1937 to 1961. Government updates are available every quarter year, but some publishers update their versions less frequently.

The information provided by the Social Security Administration includes the name of the individual, the complete birth date (day, month, and year), the month and year of death, the state where the Social Security number was issued, the state and zip code for the person's last known residence, and where the death benefit was sent (if all of this information was in the file). The person's residence at the time of death may not appear in the file, especially if the person died before receiving any Social Security benefits or died at a place other than the legal place of residence.

Although the data used by different publishers is the same, each presents the data in different ways. Most convert the zip codes into specific places, but some omit the zip code (in favor of the place name) in their output. Others include information about where a death certificate can be obtained. Most publishers allow the information to be printed or downloaded to a diskette in ASCII and/or GEDCOM formats. Many major genealogy Internet sites include versions of this database, and some smaller sites do as well.

Although the *Social Security Death Index* contains some 70 million names, not all post-1962 deaths are listed. Many persons were not eligible for Social Security death benefits, including federal and state government workers (who had a different retirement program), many self-employed persons (including farmers), young persons, and spouses who did not earn incomes. Other persons are not in the index because their deaths were not reported to the Social Security Administration, they died before the records were computerized, or incorrect information was in the files.

As with every database, the *SSDI* is not perfect; yet it is the largest of the databases and indexes available for deceased U.S. residents.

Vital Records Index (VRI)

Although the *IGI* is the largest genealogical database, a similar, smaller, but no less important collection is the *Vital Records Index (VRI)*. Several years ago, the Family History Library stopped adding extracted entries to the IGI, but the extracting continued. Since the year 2000, these records have been released as a series of "resource files" on CD-ROM. Most notable, perhaps, was the 2001 release of the entire 1880 U.S. Federal Census (discussed elsewhere). The *VRI* files are somewhat smaller in the number of entries, and have been released with less fanfare over the past few years, but they are the results of continuing extraction of birth and marriage records. Two *VRI* files, those for Scandinavia and Mexico, are also available on the Internet at FamilySearch.org. Eventually other *VRI* files will be available online as well.

The Western Europe volume of the *VRI* is a good example of the Vital Records Index. It includes twenty-two CD-ROMs with 9.7 million birth (baptismal) entries and 2.4 million marriage entries from nine major continental European countries. Over half of those entries are for German states, including over one million from Wuerttemberg. Other volumes in the VRI series, released to date, include North America, Australia, Scandinavia, and Middle America—Mexico.

The VRI database can search birth (or christening) records either by the name of the individual or by the parents' names. For the individual search, you can include many search details, or just a few. The search template allows you to enter the given and surname, the year of birth (with a range of up to five years on either side), and the locality. The default search seeks phonetic variants of both the given and surname, but you can choose to search only the exact spelling. The locality can be the entire region (such as Germany), the state (such as Wuerttemberg), the district (county), or the town (city). You can even include the father and/or mother's given and/or surname.

Remember, the more details you provide, the smaller the "results list" will be, and it may even exclude the person you are seeking, if the information you entered is not part of the entry.

A researcher can do more with the *VRI* besides a simple search for individuals. The *VRI* discs contain a list of every parish included, and any number of them can be assigned in a "collection" to be searched. Thus a researcher can search just certain parishes, such as those in neighboring areas. The listing includes the years covered, microfilm numbers of the original registers, and even the total number of birth and marriage entries extracted from every parish. This helps in evaluating how complete the extraction was. For some parishes, several thousand entries are in the *VRI*, while others are represented by less than a hundred.

As with any extracted record, researches should be cautious when using the *VRI*. Most extractions in the field of genealogy are done by volunteers. This can be a special problem when dealing with records in foreign languages, as is the case with most of the regions in the *VRI*. Some records are faint, poorly written, or in other ways difficult to read.

The best an extractor can do is to write exactly what is in the record, but sometimes the records have mistakes as well. Extraction projects are rarely complete. Sometimes a collection is published before all the parts have been extracted. This is a particular problem with many Internet databases, most notably cemeteries and some vital record collections. With the *VRI*, some parishes in some countries were extracted years ago and appear in the IGI. Therefore, consider the *VRI*, in that sense, as a supplement to the *IGI*.

World Family Tree

The first really large collection of electronic family trees was created by *Family Tree Maker*. Users of the popular *Family Tree Maker* software were encouraged to send in their databases to the company where they were published on CD-ROMs, each called a volume of the *World Family Tree*. By 2004 there were more than 230 million names in the 168 volumes of the company's CD-ROMs. Users can search the online index for free, but access to the complete data requires either purchasing the CD-ROM, using it at a library or other repository where it can be found, or subscribing to the *World Family Tree* collection on the Internet. The company's "Internet Family Finder" is the search engine which identifies which CD-ROMs have the names of interest.

Other Finding Aids

Library Catalogs

A number of genealogical libraries have published catalogs of their holdings in some form. Such catalogs can serve as bibliographies or indexes to published genealogies and family histories, depending on how thoroughly the genealogies were cataloged by the library. Some catalogs only reference a book according to the one or two family surnames identified in the title of the book. Others, recognizing that every family includes many branches with different surnames, identify additional surnames in the book that are represented by many entries in the index. Such inclusive catalogs can be seen as a partial index to surnames in family histories.

Therefore, catalogs should be one of the first sources consulted when beginning research on a new family or when one has found new information about an earlier generation. Remember that libraries continue to acquire books after their catalogs are published, so published catalogs are out of date as soon as they are printed. In the past, libraries issued supplements to previous publications to inform readers of their new holdings.

One product of the numerous efforts made over the last two decades to automate libraries has been the online availability of library catalogs. Today most genealogical libraries have catalogs on the Internet, making access even easier than in past years, allowing almost anyone with an Internet connection to access them. They include libraries of great interest to genealogists, such as the Allen County Public Library in Fort Wayne, Indiana, and the New York (City) Public Library, as well as many state libraries. The easiest way to locate the online catalog for a library of interest is to search for the library's name, or location, in one of the major Internet search engines. Also include the word "catalog" as part of the search string, and one of the first responses should be a link to the library's website.

While the growth of the Internet has made increasing numbers of such catalogs available to more and more researchers, many libraries have not yet automated their entire collections; in some cases, only portions of a catalog may be accessible through such media. Also, of course, catalogs contain only descriptions of the actual books or sources. A search on Google or most other Internet search engines will lead to an amazing number of previously hard-to-find titles. The use, value, and differences between various genealogical library catalogs is the subject of significant discussion in chapter 16, "Family Histories and Genealogies," *Printed Sources*. Most of the following catalogs in this chapter are described in further depth there, along with several other catalogs. The following discussion focuses on the use of library catalogs to identify family history books. Library catalogs identify tens of thousands of other valuable genealogical sources as well.

Family History Library Catalog

The Family History Library has the largest single collection of genealogical records in the world. Consequently, the *Family History Library Catalog* is the largest bibliography and finding aid for genealogical research. The catalog entries include detailed, analytical descriptions for each source, book, and manuscript in the collection. The main purpose of the catalog is to describe the records fully enough that practical choices for research can be made.

The catalog is available on the Internet and CD-ROM. Both versions include the same catalog entries, and most of the same features. They both permit the same searches for the following topics:

- Author
- Title
- Place (sometimes called locality)
- Surname (for family histories)
- Keyword (any word in the description of the source)
- Subject
- Microfiche or microfilm number
- Book call number

The Internet version of the catalog is updated regularly, but the CD-ROM is generally updated only every few years (see figure 2-4). The CD-ROM version can be purchased for home or institutional use, making research less dependent on an Internet connection or modem speed.

The Family History Library collection includes more than 150,000 separate family histories cataloged according to one or more surnames. Up to 1,000 new titles are added each month. Approximately twenty percent are surname newsletters, manuscript collections, and biographies; the remainder are genealogies or family histories. Furthermore, eighty percent of the titles in the surname section of the catalog pertain to U.S. or Canadian families. Thus, this catalog lists about 100,000 family histories for North American families, making it the most important and comprehensive bibliography of genealogies available. Each family history is listed under an average of five to nine names, yielding more than 600,000 references.

In addition to published family histories, the catalog describes another 200,000 genealogical source books and histories from throughout the world. It also identifies the original records available on two million rolls of microfilm from nations throughout North and South America, Europe, and other locations around the globe.

Genealogical Library Master Catalog

Perhaps the second most valuable library catalog for genealogy is actually a collection of the catalogs from many libraries. The *Genealogical Library Master Catalog* is a CD-ROM publication of the catalog entries from 18 genealogical libraries around the country, including a few major state library catalogs. Compiled by Rick Crume and published on three CD-ROMs by OneLibrary.com (Glyndon, Minnesota), the 1999 edition of the catalog includes more than 100,000 entries on each disc, with each disc listing a different type of record: family histories, local histories, and genealogical sources.

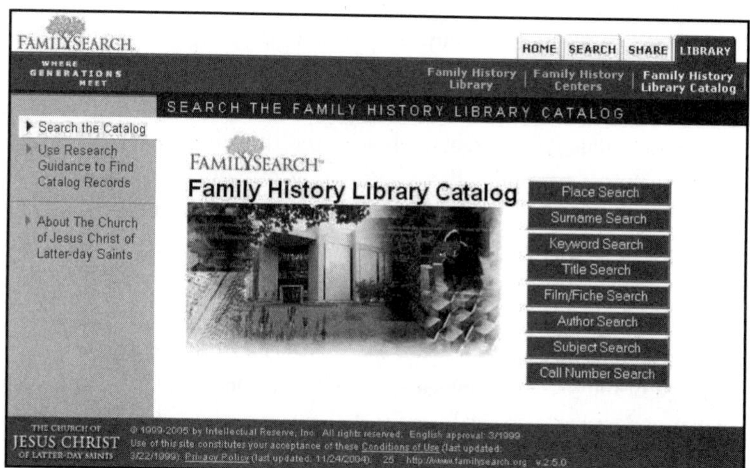

Figure 2-4. The Family History Library can be searched electronically through the FamilySearch website <www.familysearch.org>.

Many of the titles are listed multiple times, as they appear in several of the libraries who contributed to this collection. This allows the researcher to view different catalog entries for such sources, which provides a more complete description of these duplicated sources. An online version of this catalog is available through Ancestry.com.

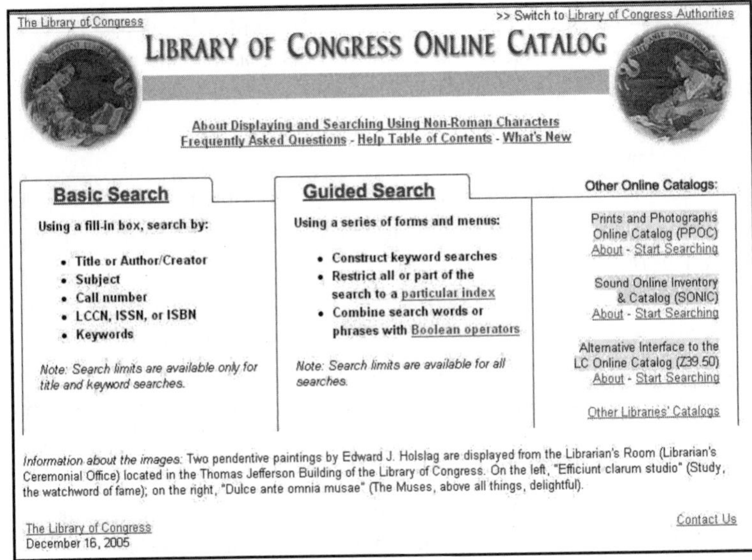

Figure 2-5. The Library of Congress's large collection, which in the past had only been cataloged in occasionally printed volumes, can now be searched via the Internet <http://catalog.loc.gov>.

Library of Congress Catalogs

The Library of Congress has one of the largest collections of genealogies and family histories in the United States. It also has a long history of publishing its genealogical holdings list to benefit researchers seeking to identify sometimes obscure family histories. The 1919 catalog was superseded by Marion J. Kaminkow's *Genealogies in the Library of Congress: A Bibliography*. This catalog can be found in most genealogical and research libraries. It lists the 20,054 genealogies in the library's collection as of 1972. Be sure to check the addenda in each volume, where approximately 700 titles are listed. The Library of Congress has added about 12,000 cross references for surnames mentioned prominently in books about other families.

Arranged alphabetically by surname, the entries contain complete bibliographic citations. *See* and *see also* entries lead the user to genealogies that would usually be overlooked. The books indexed are, of course, available in the Library of Congress, but many can also be found at other major genealogical libraries.

Three supplements have been published to update this catalog. They cover books from 1972 through 1976; between 1977 and 1986; and from 1986 to 1 July 1991. Combined, the supplements list approximately 22,000 recent genealogies.

With the placement of the library's catalog on the Internet, it has not been necessary to issue supplements in paper format (see figure 2-5). Rather, the Library of Congress catalog (found at <www.loc.gov>) is the best place to search for genealogical holdings in the nation's library. However, it is also a good illustration of why online catalogs are not sufficient.

The Library of Congress has been acquiring genealogical sources for almost 200 years, but only since the 1960s have they used a computer to catalog those books. Tens of thousands of genealogical and historical books were cataloged before the days of computers. Many of these sources have not been entered into the computerized catalog. Of those books which had been cataloged in the pre-computer days, only those which had to be re-cataloged (due to being microfilmed, having a new edition, or a change in the original cataloging) would be in the computer catalog, and available on the Web.

Another reason not to rely just on the online catalog is that, contrary to popular opinion, the Library of Congress does not have a copy of every book ever printed in the United States. Especially lacking are genealogies and family histories. Such books are often printed in small quantities and distributed through personal networks. Realizing this, the editors of *Genealogies in the Library of Congress* set out to locate genealogies *not* in the Library of Congress. The result was *A Complement to Genealogies in the Library of Congress*. It is a bibliography of 20,000 genealogies found in one or more of twenty-four major libraries outside of the Library of Congress collection. The format is the same as that of the earlier volume (without cross references). It also indicates in which library the book can be found.

This book includes the more obscure titles and gives their locations. However, it is not comprehensive; several libraries surveyed only portions of their collections. Also, some libraries with major genealogical collections did not participate. The same titles may be in many other libraries as well, so be sure to check the catalog of any local research library. In 2002, the Genealogical Publishing Company reprinted the five print volumes of the Library of Congress genealogical catalogs, along with the *Complement* and made them available to research libraries as a set. This further underscores this collection as one of the most significant finding aids for genealogical research.

National Society Daughters of the American Revolution, Library Catalog

This catalog is another important tool for locating compiled genealogies. While the DAR Library includes mostly major published genealogies, its collection is unique for its holdings of genealogies that were published in very small numbers—sometimes fewer than a dozen copies. Many of its typescript genealogies can be found in no other research library. They are listed in the DAR's *Library Catalog, Volume One: Family Histories and Genealogies*. This catalog, along with a small supplement published in 1984, lists 15,031 titles of family histories and genealogies.

It is arranged alphabetically by the names of the primary families treated. The entries include complete bibliographic citations as well as DAR Library call numbers. In addition to an author index, the catalog has a surname index with approximately 26,000 entries that indicate in which books a surname is prominently mentioned, even if the name is not included in the title of the book. Volume 3 of the catalog, published in 1992, includes references to 4,123 family histories acquired by the library within the previous decade. This library has also made their catalog available online, generally superseding these print catalogs. However, where the print catalogs are available in a research library, they can often be easier to browse when seeking variant spellings for surnames.

New York Public Library—Dictionary Catalog of the Local History and Genealogy Division

The New York Public Library (Fifth Avenue and Forty-second Street, New York, NY 10018) houses an excellent collection of genealogical research material. The eighteen-volume catalog for its genealogical collection, *Dictionary Catalog of the Local History and Genealogy Division*, consists of duplications of the typed and handwritten, alphabetically arranged card catalog. Copies of this catalog are available at most major libraries in the United States. It includes approximately 300,000 references to the 100,000 volumes that were in the collection before 1972. Although most of the books are local histories, approximately 26,000 titles, and perhaps 75,000 references, are genealogies and family histories. The catalog indexes only the major surnames in each book, but it remains very useful. Like most published catalogs, this one has not been added to since publication. However, new acquisitions are identified in the annual *Bibliographic Guide to North American History*, published by G. K. Hall of Boston.

Other Published Library Catalogs

The catalogs discussed here probably identify more than ninety-five percent of the published genealogies and family histories of North American families. All, or most, of these catalogs are available in every major genealogical library, as well as on the Internet. There are, however, several other library catalogs that researchers should be aware of. These should be consulted if you have access to the library described or if more thorough research is needed.

Several library catalogs have been published by the G. K. Hall Company of Boston (in addition to the New York Public Library Catalog described above.) They include those of the Peabody Library (Baltimore), Boston Athenaeum, Los Angeles Public Library, American Antiquarian Society (Worcester, Massachusetts), and others. These can be found in most university and some public libraries.

Library Catalog Networks

Virtually all major public, private, and university libraries have embraced automation and regularly take advantage of the opportunities the computer age provides. These libraries subscribe to one or more computer networks that allow them to locate and catalog books faster by sharing information with other repositories that use the network.

Online Computer Library Center. One of the major networks is the Online Computer Library Center (OCLC). This network is an online catalog of more than 9,000 public, private, and some academic libraries that subscribe to the service. New books are then cataloged only once—by the library that enters the book in OCLC first. Other libraries flag the book as being in their collections and download the description for their catalogs. At libraries that have WorldCat, as the public interface is known, patrons can conduct searches themselves. Librarians also can search OCLC for specific requests. For example, if you know a specific title or an author's name, you can retrieve the full citation and locate the copy nearest to you, which you can then borrow through interlibrary loan.

Research Libraries Network. Several hundred major academic and research libraries belong to the Research Libraries Network (RLIN). While it operates cooperatively, much like OCLC, RLIN offers different search capabilities. In addition to author, title, and subject searches, key words and phrases can be found using sophisticated search techniques. Most major university libraries subscribe to RLIN and will help patrons make searches.

Catalogs of Manuscripts

Thousands of libraries across America have manuscript collections that include genealogies, family histories, and the research notes of professional and amateur genealogists on the many families they have researched. Any unpublished documents—journals, diaries, letters, business records, and church registers, among others—are manuscripts. A genealogy, pedigree chart, or a family history neatly typed or written in almost illegible, abbreviated notes is a manuscript as well. And a printed volume that has handwritten annotations can be a manuscript. In a genealogy or family history, these notes may be corrections to previously printed errors or new information, such as previously missing maiden surnames. In addition to the various library catalog networks, which can also help in locating manuscripts, two important tools are also available.

National Inventory of Documentary Sources (NIDS). Many manuscript collections are too large to be fully described in the brief paragraph that appears in the *National Union Catalog of Manuscript Collections* (discussed elsewhere in this chapter). Most repositories create inventories or finding aids for their large manuscript collections, so researchers can often determine if a manuscript collection has information of value by consulting such finding aids. Unfortunately, most such finding aids have very limited distribution—often only within the library or archive that houses the collection. Recognizing the value of these tools, Chadwyck-Healey, Inc. has begun publishing the finding aids for many research libraries on microfiche. The microfiche is accompanied by an index to the key subjects and persons mentioned in the finding aid. The *National Inventory of Documentary Sources (NIDS)* allows the researcher to get one step closer to the manuscript collection and to learn whether its contents will be of value. While most of these collections have little information of genealogical value, many that do include genealogical information are also described. *NIDS* is available at large research libraries, including government repository libraries. Beginning in 1993, the index to the various inventories was also published on CD-ROM. This valuable research collection is now also available online, as part of *ArchivesUSA* <http://archives.chadwyck.com/> where researchers can access, print, and even download over 3,000 inventories of major manuscript collections.

For more information on locating manuscript collections using these sources, as well as online networks, see, "Finding Manuscript Collections: NUCMC, NIDS, and RLIN," by Mary McCampbell Bell, et al. in *National Genealogical Society Quarterly*.

National Union Catalog of Manuscript Collections. Since 1959, the Library of Congress has solicited detailed descriptions of manuscript collections in public, private, and academic libraries. These indexed and cross-referenced descriptions are published in the *National Union Catalog of Manuscript Collections*. Published annually in printed volumes from 1962 through 1993, and online since 1986, this catalog, often referred to as the *NUCMC*, provides brief descriptions of approximately 120,000 different collections at 2,000 different repositories. While most of these collections are not genealogical, many are biographical, and at least 15,000 of them include genealogical information.

A two-volume cumulative *Index to Personal Names in the National Union Catalog of Manuscript Collections, 1959–1984*, is an alphabetical arrangement of all the "personal and family names appearing in the descriptions of manuscript collections cataloged from 1959 to 1984."[2] Many of the 200,000 names in the index are entries for family information, which is typically genealogical. It is an excellent place to start a search for research notes that someone else may have compiled on a specific family.

Check also for the specific locality where your ancestors lived, the churches and schools they attended, other families they were associated with, and so on. These entries sometimes disclose invaluable sources—the location of a family Bible, diaries, letters, and so forth.

These volumes are especially valuable for records taken to places not associated with your family by relatives or family friends who moved away. For example, the personal papers of Zachariah Johnston, a resident of Rockbridge County, Virginia, were found in Durham, North Carolina. Searches in Rockbridge County disclosed the location of some of his papers in the Virginia Historical Society in Richmond, but failed to disclose that a much larger collection had been deposited in Duke University at Durham, North Carolina, where one of the family members later settled. This collection was cataloged in the NUCMC.

Since the printed NUCMC volumes are typically only found in research libraries, and print copies have not been issued since 1993, the Internet is now the best way to access these descriptions of archive collections. The Library of Congress website includes the catalog entries from 1986 (when they began computerizing the entries) to the present. However, a subscription service called *ArchivesUSA* from Chadwyck-Healey (a ProQuest company) provides the NUCMC entries from the present all the way back to 1959. Look for this subscription service at major research libraries, typically affiliated with a university.

Bibliographies

A bibliography is a list of books, articles, or records. Bibliographies are important tools for researchers because they identify sources of information. Usually published as a book or as part of a book, bibliographies usually have a specific topical focus. They may be arranged by subtopic or be strictly alphabetical. Many are annotated, including brief descriptions of the books cited. Bibliographies are usually created by scholarly researchers seeking to identify important works pertaining to a specific topic or field. Booksellers' catalogs are also a kind of bibliography, although they are usually not as comprehensive as other sources. The value and use of bibliographies in genealogical research cannot be overlooked. They are the subject of significant discussion in chapter 5, "Bibliographies and Catalogs," in *Printed Sources*. Some major bibliographies are described below.

Genealogical and Local History Books in Print

The major source in this field is Marian R. Hoffman's *Genealogical and Local History Books in Print*, covering Family Histories, General Reference and World Resources, and U.S. Sources and Resources (in four volumes).

Major Genealogical Bibliographies

Many librarians, historians, and other bibliographers have created subject bibliographies for genealogical topics over the past three decades. Since library catalogs cannot be expected to identify every book for a specific topic, these bibliographers' efforts produce an important research tool: a well developed bibliography will bring together useful sources from a variety of disciplines, regardless of the age or location. The following important bibliographies should be at most research libraries:

Biographical Books, 1876–1949 and *1950–1980*. New York: Bowker, 1983, 1980. A list of over 25,000 books specifically about individuals. Includes many descent genealogies with significant information about the immigrant ancestor.

Brigham, Clarence Saunders. *History and Bibliography of American Newspapers, 1690–1820*. 2 vols. Worcester, Mass.: American Antiquarian Society, 1947.

Carson, Dina C. *Directory of Genealogical and Historical Publications in the U.S. and Canada*. Niwot, Colo.: Iron Gate Publishing, 1992. Identifies approximately 5,500 family, historical, ethnic, and genealogical journals, newsletters, and magazines by title. An index of publishers to help locate periodicals published by organizations.

Child, Sargent B., and Dorothy P. Holmes. *Checklist of Historical Records Survey Publications*. 1943. Reprint, Baltimore: Genealogical Publishing Co., 1969.

Clegg, Michael Barren. *Bibliography of Genealogical and Local History Periodicals with Union List of Major U.S. Collections*. Ft. Wayne, Ind.: Allen County Public Library Foundation, 1990. Identifies over 4,000 periodicals and their publishers, with a partial list of libraries housing the titles.

Filby, P. William. *A Bibliography of American County Histories*. Baltimore: Genealogical Publishing Co., 1987. Lists 5,000 histories published through 1984, with reference to reprints and new indexes.

———, comp. *American and British Genealogy and Heraldry: A Selected List of Books*. 3rd ed. Boston: New England Historic Genealogical Society, 1983; and *Supplement* (1987). An excellent listing of most books published through mid-1985 that deal with genealogy in the English-speaking world. This bibliography and its supplement list more than 12,800 titles of published genealogical sources. The primary emphasis is on United States sources; however, this bibliography usually excludes county and local histories, family histories, and immigration sources.

———, ed. *Passenger and Immigration Lists Bibliography 1538–1900*. 2nd ed. Detroit: Gale Research Co., 1988. Identifies and describes approximately 2,600 printed sources, including articles, books, and portions of book which name immigrants to North America. These sources are indexed in his *Passenger and Immigration Lists Index*.

Gregory, Winifred. *American Newspapers, 1821–1936*. 1937. Reprint, New York: H. W. Wilson Co., 1967.

Horowitz, Lois. *A Bibliography of Military Name Lists from Pre-1675 to 1900: A Guide to Genealogical Sources*. Metuchen, N.J.: Scarecrow Press, 1990. Arranges over 6,600 published lists by time period and location.

Prucha, Francis Paul. *Handbook for Research in American History: A Guide to Bibliographies and Other Reference Works*. 2nd ed. Rev. Lincoln: University of Nebraska Press, 1994. The best guide to the 1,000 most significant tools for historical research.

Slocum, Robert B., ed. *Biographical Dictionaries and Related Works*. 2nd ed. 2 vols. Detroit: Gale Research Co., 1986. The most comprehensive listing of collective biographies.

UMI Collections and Heritage Quest Online

Since 1979 the *Genealogy and Local History Series*, has been providing a growing collection of genealogical materials on microfiche. Published genealogies are a major part of UMI's Genealogy and Local History collection <www.umi.com/>. Several hundred titles are collected, copied on microfiche, and cataloged every year as sets or "parts" of the collection. These parts are then sold (as separate units) to libraries and archives. Each part is described by a guide that includes complete catalog information with subject, title, and surname indexes. By 2006, at least sixty-four separate parts had been produced, totaling over 27,000 titles, with at least 10,000 genealogies. Many are rare titles, usually published before 1920 and in limited numbers. A number of research libraries subscribe to this collection.

It is precisely these titles which are available as images with every-name indexes through the Internet at Heritage Quest Online <www.heritagequest.com>. However, since it is also possible to purchase these titles as units and individual titles, the list of titles is also online at UMI (another ProQuest company).

UMI also supplies microfilm and photocopies of thousands of out-of-print family histories through their "Books on Demand" service. Even if their extensive catalog of books currently on microfilm does not include a needed source, if you know the title of a book you want and where a copy is located, UMI will obtain permission to copy it (including copyright clearance, if needed) and supply a microfilm or photocopy.

Publishers and Booksellers Catalogs

Other sources for family histories are the catalogs of various publishers that sell new, old (used or rare), and reprinted books, especially family histories. Their surname catalogs (or websites) are arranged similarly to library catalog.

The following publishers may be helpful in locating specific genealogy methodology and family history titles:

Higginson Book Co. <www.higginsonbooks.com>
Picton Press. <www.pictonpress.com/catalog/index.htm>
Willow Bend Books. <www.willowbendbooks.com>

Directories

Directories are important tools for genealogists because they help locate people and organizations that can assist in research. For more information on directories as research tools, see chapter

8, "Directories." Some of the following directories, and many more which are too specific to list here, are now available on the Internet.

Directories of Organizations, Societies, and Institutions

American Library Directory. New York: R. R. Bowker Co., 1908–. This annual (since 1978) directory lists thousands of academic, public, private, and special libraries in the United States and Canada.

Bentley, Elizabeth Petty. *County Courthouse Book*. 2nd ed. Baltimore: Genealogical Publishing Co., 1995. This directory provides addresses, telephone numbers, and county organization dates for more than 3,300 county offices. A list of the records available, search fees, and other information is included for the courthouses that responded to the compiler's survey.

———. *Directory of Family Associations*, 4th ed. Baltimore: Genealogical Publishing Co., 2001. This directory is an A to Z directory that provides addresses, telephone numbers, contact persons, and publications (if any) for more than 5,000 family and surname organizations.

———. *Genealogist's Address Book*, 5th ed. Baltimore: Genealogical Publishing Co., 2005. This directory provides addresses and telephone numbers for thousands of national, state, and local organizations of interest to genealogists. It includes libraries; historical, lineage, and genealogical societies; ethnic and religious organizations; publishers; booksellers; professional organizations; and periodicals. Additional information, such as hours of operation, contact persons, publications, and services is included for those organizations that responded to the compiler's survey.

Smith, Juliana Smith. *The Ancestry Family Historian's Address Book: A Comprehensive List of Local, State, and Federal Agencies and Institutions and Ethnic and Genealogical Organizations*. 2nd ed. Orem, Utah: Ancestry, 2003.

Subject-Specific Directories

Carson, Dina C. *Directory of Genealogical and Historical Societies in the U.S. and Canada* (cited earlier). This directory includes family, historical, ethnic, and genealogical societies in the same listing, arranged by state and thereunder by town. An index provides access by the name of the society.

Directory of Special Libraries and Information Centers. 31st ed. Detroit: Thomson-Gale, 2005. A comprehensive list of more than 21,000 libraries that have special collections and purposes.

Directory of Historical Organizations in the United States and Canada. 15th ed. Nashville: American Association for State and Local History, 2001. A comprehensive list of approximately 14,000 organizations interested in history, including virtually all local and special interest history groups.

Encyclopedia of Associations. Detroit: Gale Research Co., 1987–. This annual directory includes current addresses, functions, and membership requirements of fraternal, ethnic, veteran, hereditary, patriotic, and other associations.

Filby, P. William. *Directory of American Libraries With Genealogy or Local History Collections*. Wilmington, Del.: Scholarly Resources, 1988. Briefly describes the genealogical collections and services of more than 1,500 public and university libraries, state archives, historical societies, and other libraries.

Meyer, Mary K. *Directory of Genealogical Societies in the USA and Canada*. 12th ed. Maryland: the compiler, 1998. This publication identifies almost all genealogical societies and describes their services and publications. It also includes a list of independent genealogical periodicals (periodicals that are not affiliated with a society).

National Historical Publications and Records Commission. *Directory of Archives and Manuscript Repositories in the United States*. 2nd ed. Phoenix: Oryx Press, 1988. This volume identifies hundreds of manuscript collections in a variety of repositories. It includes many references to collections for ethnic and immigrant groups.

Telephone Directories

Local telephone books have always been useful to genealogists—especially for locating living relatives. With the advent of CD-ROM technology, large databases, such as telephone lists, have been collected in a single collection. Publishers of such directories seem to change frequently, but generally local computer stores will have two or three competing products, each offering different search routines and flexibility.

However, most researchers seeking phone numbers of prospective relatives or other researchers turn to any of several Internet sites. Major search engines, such as Google and Yahoo include phone directories as part of their search services. More sophisticated searching, including reverse searches (by phone number), address searches, and other approaches, are usually available at websites specifically designed for phone directory searching. Current sites include Switchboard.com, AnyWho.com, and WhitePages.com (see figure 2-6).

Such databases do not come exclusively from telephone company records. They may be collected from various sources, including mailing lists, voter registrations, driver's licenses, and utility company records. Consequently, some addresses may be out of date.

Directories of Professionals and Other Researchers

Occasionally, researchers want to contact others known to be working on the same family lines or in the same area.

Or, a researcher might want to engage a professional to conduct research on a lineage, topic, or locale. Generally, names of professionals become known from previous publications by them or through the recommendations of others. To find addresses and other information, several directories and indexes of genealogists are available.

The Association of Professional Genealogists publishes an online directory listing its members and, for those who contributed, providing detailed background information. It is searchable by name, geographic specialties, research specialties, related services, and member residence. It is available at the association's website <www.apgen.org>.

The International Commission for the Accreditation of Professional Genealogists (ICAPGen) maintains a list of accredited genealogists who have been tested for ability in specific regions and countries. Updated regularly and listed by area of accreditation, this list is available at <www.icapgen.org>.

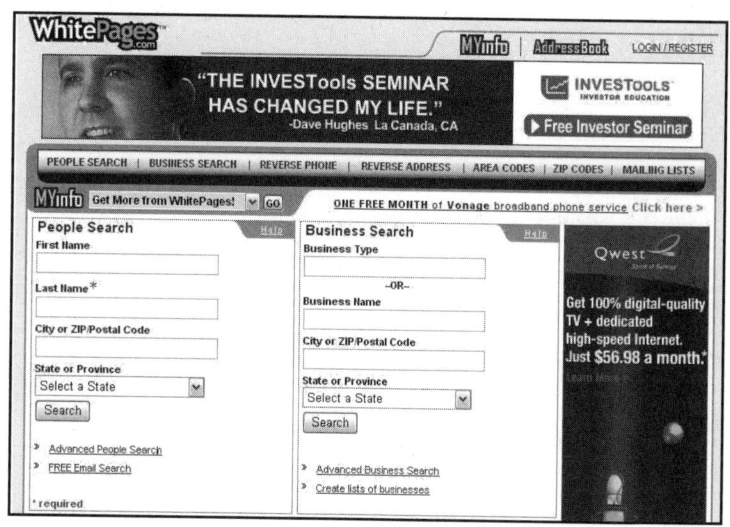

Figure 2-6. Use online phone directories, like WhitePages.com, to find and connect with relatives, friends, and others who might be able to provide research assistance.

The Board for Certification of Genealogists publishes an online list of genealogists and record searchers it has certified for competency. It is searchable by name, state and special interests. It is available through the board's website <www.bcgcertification.org>.

The Genealogical Speakers Guild offers a directory of presenters, their topics, and fees. Listings are available online at <www.genspeakguild.org>.

Who's Who in Genealogy and Heraldry, 2nd ed., edited by P. William Filby and Mary K. Meyer gives much information about 1,100 genealogists chosen for their contributions to the field. Many of them are professional genealogists.

For information on genealogists who may now be deceased there are fewer sources. The best is Frederick A. Virkus's *The Handbook of American Genealogy*. This source includes a list of 2,341 amateur and professional genealogists, with some background information. Volume four (1943) is the most complete, but it omits some names from earlier volumes. It also includes a list of almost 11,000 genealogies in progress with the names of the researchers who were working on them, and a state and county breakdown of genealogists.

Dictionaries

Another important tool for genealogists is dictionaries. Many genealogical records were created in time periods, places, or societies that researchers are not familiar with. Dictionaries are excellent tools to help understand such records. For many, a standard desk or library dictionary is sufficient. Major, unabridged dictionaries available at every library are also useful. Especially note the following specialized dictionaries that are useful for understanding older records:

Black, Henry Campbell. *Black's Law Dictionary*. 8th ed. St. Paul, Minn.: West Publishing Co., 2004. This dictionary defines the terms and phrases of American and English jurisprudence, ancient and modern, and is useful for understanding terms in court records and other legal records.

Evans, Barbara Jean. *A to Zax: A Comprehensive Genealogical Dictionary for Genealogists and Historians*. 3rd ed. Alexandria, Va.: Hearthside Press, 1995. This is an excellent list of terms often encountered by genealogists and their definitions. It also includes a list of nicknames and their usual given names.

Harris, Glen, and Maurine Harris. *Ancestry's Concise Genealogical Dictionary*. Salt Lake City: Ancestry, 1989. This volume defines many out-of-use terms that are often overlooked in many dictionaries, yet frequently found in old documents and sources used by genealogists.

Lederer, Richard. *Colonial American English: A Glossary*. Essex, Conn.: Verbatim Book, 1985. This dictionary explains words found in early American documents that are now archaic, obscure, obsolete, or have different meanings.

Conclusion

Databases, indexes, and other finding aids are perhaps the most important sources genealogists use. They provide access to information that may previously have been difficult, if not impossible, to search. Computer technology makes indexing simultaneously more feasible and more necessary.

How can genealogists learn about new tools and indexes? Involvement with colleagues in professional societies and local genealogy societies is important. So are regular surveys of major genealogical periodicals and those in your area of interest.

Notes

[1] *General Index to Pension Files 1861–1934* (Washington, D.C.: National Archives), microfilm T288, 544 rolls.

[2] *Index to Personal Names in the National Union Catalog of Manuscript Collections, 1959–1984*, ii.

References

American Biographical Index (ABI). New York City: K. G. Saur, 1993.

The American Genealogist. 5th ed. Albany: Joel Munsell's Sons, 1900. Reprint, Detroit: Gale Research Co., 1975.

Bell, Carol Willsey. *Ohio Genealogical Periodical Index: A County Guide*. 4th ed. Youngstown, Ohio: C. W. Bell, 1983.

Bell, Mary McCampbell, et al. "Finding Manuscript Collections: NUCMC, NIDS, and RLIN." *National Genealogical Society Quarterly* 77, no. 3 (September 1989): 208–18.

Bentley, Elizabeth Petty. *County Courthouse Book*. 2nd ed. Baltimore: Genealogical Publishing Co., 1995.

———. *Directory of Family Associations*. 3rd ed. Baltimore: Genealogical Publishing Co. 1996.

Bibliographic Guide to North American History. Boston: G. K. Hall, annual.

Bibliography of Genealogical and Local History Periodicals With Union List of Major U.S. Collections. Fort Wayne, Ind.: Allen County Public Library Foundation, 1990.

Boyer, Carl, III, ed. *Donald Lines Jacobus' Index to Genealogical Periodicals*. Newhall, Calif.: Boyer Publications, 1983.

Brown, Lesley, ed. *The New Shorter Oxford English Dictionary*. 2 vols. Oxford, England: Oxford University Press, 1993.

Buckway, G. Eileen. *Index to Texas Periodicals*. Salt Lake City: Family History Library, 1987.

Carson, Dina C. *Directory of Genealogical and Historical Publications in the US and Canada*. Niwot, Colo.: Iron Gate Publishing, 1992.

Century of Population Growth 1790–1900. 1909. Reprint, Baltimore: Genealogical Publishing Co., 1967.

Chapter, Elizabeth Benton, comp. *Genealogical Guide Master Index of Genealogy in the Daughters of the American Revolution Magazine Volumes 1–84 (1892–1950) with Supplement Volumes 85–89 (1950–55) Combined Edition*. Kansas City, Mo.: National Society of the Daughters of the American Revolution, 1951. Reprint, Baltimore: Genealogical Publishing Co., 1994.

A Complement to Genealogies in the Library of Congress. Baltimore: Magna Carta Books, 1981.

DAR Patriot Index. 3 vols. Baltimore: Genealogical Publishing Co., 2003.

Dictionary Catalog of the Local History and Genealogy Division. Boston: G. K. Hall, 1974.

Directory of Archives and Manuscript Repositories in the United States. 2nd ed. Phoenix: Oryx Press, 1988.

Encyclopedia of Associations. Detroit: Gale Research Co., 1987–.

Evans, Barbara Jean. *A to Zax: A Comprehensive Genealogical Dictionary for Genealogists and Historians*. 3rd ed. Alexandria, Va.: Hearthside Press, 1995.

Filby, P. William. *Directory of American Libraries With Genealogy or Local History Collections*. Wilmington, Del.: Scholarly Resources, 1988.

———. "Published Passenger Lists." *Genealogical Journal* (8 December 1979): 177.

———. "Published Passenger Lists." *Genealogical Journal* (Fall 1983): 112.

———, comp. *American and British Genealogy and Heraldry: A Selected List of Books*. 3rd ed. Boston: New England Historic Genealogical Society, 1983. Supplement, 1987.

———, ed. *Passenger and Immigration Lists Bibliography 1538–1900*. Detroit: Gale Research Co., 1988.

———, ed. *Passenger and Immigration Lists Index*. Detroit, Mich.: Gale Research Co., 1980–.

———, and Mary K. Meyer, eds. *Who's Who in Genealogy and Heraldry*. 2nd ed. Savage, Md.: Who's Who in Genealogy and Heraldry, 1990.

Finnell, Arthur Louis. *Minnesota Genealogical Periodical Index*. Marshall, Minn.: Finnell Richter and Assoc., 1980.

Genealogical Abstracts of Revolutionary War Pension Files. 4 vols. Waynesboro, Tenn.: National Historic Publishing Co., 1991–92.

The *Genealogical Index of the Newberry Library*. 4 vols. Boston: G. K. Hall, 1960.

Genealogical Periodical Annual Index. Bowie, Md.: Heritage Books, 1974–2001.

Genealogical Research in the National Archives. 3rd ed. Washington, D.C.: National Archives and Records Service, 2000. Greenlaw, William Prescott, comp. *The Greenlaw Index of the New England Historic Genealogical Society*. 2 vols. Boston: G. K. Hall, 1979.

Grover, Robert L. *Missouri Genealogical Periodical Index: A County Guide, 1960–1982*. Independence: Missouri Territory Pioneers, 1983.

Herbert, Mirana C., and Barbara McNeil. *Biography and Genealogy Master Index*. Detroit: Gale Research Co., 1980–.

Hoffman, Marian R. *Genealogical and Local History Books in Print*. 3rd ed. Baltimore: Genealogical Publishing Co., 1996–97.

Index to Personal Names in the National Union Catalog of Manuscript Collections, 1959–1984. Alexandria, Va.: Chadwyck-Healey, 1988.

Index of Revolutionary War Pension Applications in the National Archives. National Genealogical Society Special Publication No. 40. Washington, D.C.: National Genealogical Society, 1976.

Index of Rolls of Honor in the Lineage Books. Washington, D.C.: Daughters of the American Revolution, 1916–1940.

Jackson, Ronald V., Jr. *Early American Series*. Salt Lake City: Accelerated Indexing Systems, 1981–84.

Jacobus, Donald Lines. "Tricks in Using Indexed Genealogical Books." *American Genealogist* 30 (April 1954): 85.

———. *Index to Genealogical Periodicals*. Edited by Carl Boyer III. Newhall, Calif.: Boyer Publications, 1983.

Jarboe, Betty M. *Obituaries: A Guide to Sources*. 2nd ed. Boston: G. K. Hall, 1989.

Kaminkow, Marion J. *A Complement to Genealogies in the Library of Congress*. Baltimore: Magna Carta Books, 1981.

———. *Genealogies in the Library of Congress: A Bibliography*. 2 vols. Baltimore: Magna Carta Books, 1972. Supplements 1976–87.

Lederer, Richard. *Colonial American English: A Glossary*. Essex, Conn.: Verbatim Book, 1985.

Library Catalog, Volume One: Family Histories and Genealogies. Washington, D.C.: Daughters of the American Revolution, 1982.

The Library of Congress Index to Biographies in State and Local Histories Baltimore: Magna Carta Book, 1979.

Meyer, Mary K. *Directory of Genealogical Societies in the USA and Canada*. 10th ed. Md.: the compiler, 1994.

Milner, Anita Cheek. *Newspaper Indexes*. 3 vols. Metuchen, N.J.: Scarecrow Press, 1977–82.

Munsell, Joel. *Index to American Genealogies*. 5th ed. 1900. Reprint, Baltimore: Genealogical Publishing Co., 1967.

National Union Catalog of Manuscript Collections. Washington, D.C.: Library of Congress, 1962–present.

Oxford English Dictionary. Oxford, England: Clarendon Press, 1931–86.

Press, Jacques Cattell, ed. *American Library Directory*. New York City: R. R. Bowker, 1908–.

Quigley, Maud. *Index to Family Names in Genealogical Periodicals*. Grand Rapids: Western Michigan Genealogical Society, 1981.

———. *Index to Michigan Research Found in Genealogical Periodicals*. Grand Rapids: Western Michigan Genealogical Society, 1979.

Rider, Fremont, ed. *The American Genealogical-Biographical Index (AGBI)*. Series 2. Middletown, Conn.: Godfry Memorial Library, 1952–2001.

Sanborn, Melinde Lutz. *Supplement to Torrey's New England Marriages Prior to 1700*. Baltimore: Genealogical Publishing Co., 1991.

———. *Second Supplement to Torrey's New England Marriages Prior to 1700*. Baltimore: Genealogical Publishing Co., 1995.

Scanland, Roger. "The Munsell Genealogical Indexes." *Genealogical Journal* 2 (September 1973): 103–8.

Schory, Eva D. *Every Name Index to Egle's Notes and Queries*. Decatur, Ill.: Decatur Genealogical Society, 1981.

Schreiner-Yantis, Netti. *Genealogical and Local History Books in Print*. Springfield, Va.: Genealogical Books in Print, 1976–1992.

Sinclair, Donald Arleigh. *A New Jersey Biographical Index: Covering Some 100,000 Biographies and Associated Portraits in 237 New Jersey Cyclopedias, Histories, Yearbooks, Periodicals, and Other Collective Biographical Sources Published to About 1980*. Baltimore: Genealogical Publishing Co., 1992.

Swem, Earl Gregg. *Virginia Historical Index*. 2 vols. in 4. 1934–36. Reprint, Gloucester, Mass.: Peter Smith, 1965.

Szucs, Loretto Dennis, and Sandra Hargreaves Luebking. *The Archives: A Guide to the National Archives Field Branches*. Salt Lake City: Ancestry, 1988.

Torrey, Clarence A. *New England Marriages Prior to 1700*. Baltimore: Genealogical Publishing Co., 1985.

Trapp, Glenda K., and Michael L. Cook. *Kentucky Genealogical Index*. Evansville, Ind.: Cook Publications, 1985.

University of Arizona Library. *The Arizona Index: A Subject Index to Periodicals About the State*. 2 microfilms. Boston: G. K. Hall, 1978.

Virkus, Frederick A., ed., *The Handbook of American Genealogy*. Vols. 1–4. Chicago: Institute of American Genealogy, 1932–43.

White, Virgil. *Genealogical Abstracts of Revolutionary War Pension Files*. 4 vols. Waynesboro, Tenn.: National Historic Publishing Co., 1991–92.

4

Business, Institution, and Organization Records

KAY HAVILAND FREILICH, CG, CGL, and ANN CARTER FLEMING, CG, CGL

As genealogists and family historians, we seek the basic facts about our ancestors—when and where they were born, married, and died. Another part of our search is to determine the story of their everyday lives. While we begin with the basic census, land, probate, and vital records, we must remember to use every possible source, even those that are more challenging to locate and use. These often-neglected sources—such as business, institutional, and organization records—can help us determine facts and at the same time supply rich contextual information about our ancestors.

With few exceptions, most of our ancestors had some kind of business connection. The ancestor who was a businessman had to keep a record of his transactions, income, and expenses. In later years, corporations maintained the records of all their employees, providing another source of information for researchers. Even the ancestors who followed agricultural occupations may well have purchased their tools from a local merchant or had their wheat processed into flour at the local mill. We may be able to learn the cost of tools or the amount of flour from records kept by that merchant or miller. And because businessmen may have had only one place to record information, we may also find personal and family details in a business record.

Almost from the beginning of American history, individuals have had contact with a wide variety of institutions. They were educated at schools, colleges, and universities. They sought treatment at hospitals and homes for the ill and disabled. When they could not care for themselves, they were housed and fed by orphan asylums and poorhouses. Each institution generated records of its own that can add valuable information to our genealogy.

Chapter Contents

As the country's population grew, our ancestors found it useful to belong to an organization of other individuals who shared occupations, interests, religions, or ethnic backgrounds. Each of these organizations created its own records, which should be considered as a source of genealogical information.

There are three major considerations that apply to accessing the records discussed in this chapter. First, since these are generally private records belonging to the individual or group that created them, there is no requirement that these sources be open for research. The record owner makes that choice. That decision may be influenced by the recent increase in privacy concerns.

Secondly, many of the records exist in manuscript collections in a wide range of repositories, so locating them might be a challenge. Finally, since these records are rarely indexed, research in them will likely require a substantial time commitment.

Researchers who are interested in pursuing business, institutional, and organizational records for their ancestors should first review all known information about that ancestor. Clues about an employer or occupation may appear in an obituary, city directory, or census report. Other clues might come from family mementos and heirlooms. Perhaps a treasured watch was a retirement gift and is engraved with a corporate or organization name. Report cards usually give the name of the school. Diplomas, or even an old football program, will identify the name of an educational facility attended by an ancestor. Using this information, the next step is to pursue the records of those newly identified sources.

While research in this type of record may be challenging and time-consuming, the rewards can be great. Consider these examples:

- A mid-1850s business journal includes the full names and birth dates of three sons born prior to registration of birth records.
- A military hospital entry supplies an exact date of death, leading to a death certificate, funeral home record, obituary, and cemetery record.
- A photograph indicating involvement in the Civilian Conservation Corps leads to a description of an ancestor's corps activity.
- A membership register from a Grand Army of the Republic (GAR) post points to a place and date of death and then to the related information.
- A funeral home record includes the place of burial, leading to information about the previous residence of the deceased and eventually to the identification of an ancestral family.
- A list of schoolchildren links a child to her grandfather who paid for her education.

Business Records

Businesses have employed or served our ancestors at least since the first mill was built to grind grain or saw wood, and a surprising number of employer-employee or buyer-seller records were kept and have survived. The value of business and employment records becomes evident when you consider that many vital events were not recorded by some states until after 1900. Business records are a broad and varied set of records. They include, of course, those records that a business may have kept regarding its customers or employees.

However, researchers must not overlook other records created during a business's existence, even when such records may fall into another genealogical category. These can include local licenses permitting a business to operate (government records), histories of a specific business or an industry, biographical collections of a company's officers or an industry's leaders (in both manuscript and published form), city directories identifying businesses and their owners and employees, and even old photographs naming the photographer. City directories, similar to today's telephone books, included both business information and residential information. Agricultural census records provide information about our ancestors' farming activities, whether for personal or business purposes. In some cases, a business created other records that we also can use in genealogy. Newspapers and mortuary records are the products of businesses, although we seldom label them as business records. While the focus of this section is on the records created by businesses, other records related to the existence of a business or an industry will be noted where especially useful.

Researchers should also not overlook business records of organizations such as churches. Directories, lists of ministers, histories, and ledger books may add valuable pieces to the story of an ancestor. Likewise, researchers should consider the wide scope of businesses when searching for records. While not often thought of as such, sporting activities like horse breeding and baseball leagues are considered businesses and have thus created various records. In Tennessee, breeders received licenses, and those from Knox County are available on microfilm at the LDS Family History Library (1,020,331, item 2) in Salt Lake City and through its network of Family History Centers. The National Farmers Union began in Texas in 1902 as a business to promote legislation to benefit farmers. Statistics kept by organized sporting leagues not only identify an ancestor's occupation, they show the level of talent for that occupation (see figure 4-1).

Throughout America's history, private business concerns have created a huge variety and number of records about themselves and had an equal number of records created about them by others. The information contained in these records can be used in at least three significant ways during genealogical research. (1) On occasion, they provide important genealogical information in the absence of traditional information—as, for instance, a mortuary record where a death or cemetery record cannot be found. (2) More commonly, they provide clues that may lead to other, traditional genealogical records, such as an account book that places the ancestor in a specific location at a certain date. (3) Another important use is to "flesh out" an ancestor's personal history, making him or her "come alive" as an individual.

A common misconception in using business records is our image of rural America as being comprised largely of farmers until the last generation or so. As evidence of this point, it is not well known that by 1880 more than half of the population were engaged in nonfarming occupations.[1] A breakdown by

256 • *The Independent Carolina Baseball League*

BATTING LEADERS
(200 or more at-bats)

Batting average: Eric Tipton, KAN, .375; Bobby Hipps, LEN, .361; Stahle Brown, LEN, .346; Stumpy Culbreth, HCK, .346; Howard Moss, LEN, .341.

Runs: Vince Barton, HCK, 97; Bobby Hipps, LEN, 79; Stahle Brown, LEN, 78; Howard Moss, LEN, 77.

Hits: Howard Moss, LEN, 142; Fletcher Heath, LEN, 135; Glenn "Razz" Miller, KAN, 133; Bobby Hipps, LEN, 122.

Doubles: Fletcher Heath, LEN, 32; Howard Moss, LEN, 31; Stahle Brown, LEN, 29; Pete Susko, HCK, 29.

Triples: Fletcher Heath, LEN, 14; Eric Tipton, KAN, 11; Stahle Brown, LEN, 9; Marvin Watts, KAN, 9.

Home runs: Howard Moss, LEN, 27; Vince Barton, HCK, 26; Marvin Watts, KAN, 13; Eric Tipton, KAN, 12.

Runs batted in: Howard Moss, LEN, 88; Vince Barton, HCK, 82; Eric Tipton, KAN, 76; Marvin Watts, KAN, 70.

INDIVIDUAL PITCHING

Player, club	G	W	L	Pct	IP	R	H	BB	SO
Boutwell, George, LEN	26	17	4	.810	193	85	198	36	93
Hockett, LEN	8	5	2	.714	65	30	74	6	15
Hitchner, Tracey, HCK	24	11	5	.688	162	98	155	98	134
Schesler, Charles, LEN	16	11	5	.688	123	69	165	47	67
Wilson, Morris, CON	13	6	3	.667	72	50	90	24	23
Guise, Witt "Lefty," CON	29	13	7	.650	190	104	199	73	103
White, Jim, KAN	27	13	9	.591	173	103	197	90	147
Swayze, Tom, HCK	25	11	8	.579	159	80	165	61	96
Chitwood, Ken, CON	29	9	7	.563	142	60	144	40	56
Ragland, Frank, LEN	20	5	4	.556	97	54	101	44	29
Willis, CON	19	7	6	.538	125	64	143	36	26
Melton, LEN	20	10	9	.526	143	101	165	76	109
Veach, Al, LEN	24	10	10	.500	168	98	197	50	118
Drefs, Herman, HCK	23	8	8	.500	152	84	162	47	76
Beard, CON	3	1	1	.500	13	11	21	5	4
Terhune, Terry, KAN	23	10	11	.476	154	115	188	40	70
Hart, Tracey, KAN	24	9	10	.474	146	77	173	45	58
Harden, J. W. "Doc," CON/HCK	19	5	6	.455	105	61	119	35	64
Stratton, Earl, HCK	23	7	9	.438	127	99	159	59	40
Roscoe, KAN	17	3	5	.375	94	63	119	31	49
Mills, Dale, HCK	23	5	10	.333	100	93	137	52	54
Daney, Chief, KAN	10	2	4	.333	54	40	76	14	17

PITCHING LEADERS

George Boutwell, LEN, 17–4; Witt Guise, CON, 13–7; Jim White, KAN 13–9; Tracey Hitchner, HCK, 11–5; Charles Schesler, CON, 11–5; Tom Swayze, HCK, 11–8.

Figure 4-1. Records created to document statistics of a sports team put an ancestor in a place and time and show how well he played the sport. From R. G. (Hank) Utley and Scott Verner, *The Independent Carolina Baseball League, 1936–1938: Baseball Outlaws* (Jefferson, N.C.: McFarland and Company, no date).

professions shows that by 1910 agriculture was outnumbered by the combination of manufacturing and trades.[2]

Business and employment records include our ancestors in at least four situations:

- owner of a business
- practitioner of a vocation
- employee of a business
- customer of a business

A researcher must pay attention to all of these situations for each ancestor. Even self-employed ancestors who kept few records and had no employees, such as farmers, can appear as customers of someone else's business. The value of employment records is especially apparent for immigrant ancestors, many of whom settled in large cities, where the nation's largest businesses were also typically located. (See chapter 20, "Urban Research," for information on city research.)

Using business records may not be easy. First, in order to find them you must know your ancestor's location and profession. Even then they can be difficult to find, and those that do exist may be few and far between. Many records no longer exist. Of those that do, some are much more complete than others and may include birthplace, residence (previous and concurrent to employment), relatives and family members, education level, and employment history. Almost none of the records are indexed. Many are stored in locations that make consulting them very difficult, and others have been destroyed or lost through the years. Most business records are private, as were the businesses they chronicle. If the business is still operating, it may not allow access to its records. If the business is defunct, the records will be hard to find. Still, the kind of information and breakthrough possibilities available mean that business records simply should not be overlooked.

Most likely your ancestor did not work for the same employer for the entire length of his or her lifetime. As you search, give priority to the records of the company where he or she worked the longest or to the most recent employer, as recent records are typically more complete. Other suggestions for locating pertinent records are given throughout the chapter.

The following examples illustrate the wide variety of business records kept in local and state collections throughout the United States:

- The University of Wisconsin—Milwaukee has fire and police department records from 1927 to 1963. Some are online at <www.uwm.edu/libraries/arch/safety.htm>.
- The St. Louis Board of Pharmacy has preserved the records of druggists' licenses from 1893 through 1909.
- The Smith-Townsend papers at the Massachusetts Historical Society include the business papers of two generations of Townsend, Massachusetts, businessmen up to 1870.
- The South Carolina Department of Archives and History has the minute book of the Carolina Narrow Gauge Railroad Company from 1872 to 1897.
- The National Archives—Pacific Region in San Bruno, California, has customhouse records for the port of San Francisco.
- The Georgia Department of Archives and History has licenses and bonds for selling liquor from 1850 to 1901.
- The Stevens Family Papers at the New Jersey Historical Society include extensive documentation on the Hoboken Land Improvement Company.

Records Created by the Owners of a Business

Company Records and Histories

For most private businesses, the articles of incorporation, a government document, is usually the first record created by and about the concern. As tax laws became more comprehensive, even family businesses, whether large or small, were incorporated. Articles of incorporation, along with subsequent filings for merger and dissolution, are public records maintained by the government entity located where the incorporation took place, as are notices of board meetings and stock information.

Challenges for the researcher include identifying the correct state and then the office holding the record. Published guides to businesses may be helpful in solving these problems, and a Web search of the company name should also be considered. The secretary of state (or equivalent) in most states maintains two registers: one of current companies, which is often accessible online, and one of defunct or dissolved companies. Each company in the register has a file number. With this number, the researcher may request the corporate case files, which include the original charter, amendments to articles of incorporation, correspondence dealing with name changes and appointments of new directors, statement of dissolution with cause, and court proceedings or claims (if any) against the corporation or its officers. Researchers need to be aware that business may also be incorporated at the federal or local level. Banks are the most common example of a business with a federal charter.

Some incorporation records are available online. One example is Colorado records from 1861 to 1975. Access to these records is available through the archives' business records site <www.colorado.gov/dpa/doit/archives>. The Secretary of State's Office, Commercial Records Unit, maintains the records after 1975.

Businesses must also register their trade names in most states and of course, they must register to collect and pay any necessary state taxes. Based on public information, these registrations also generate a paper trail for the company and for the researcher. (See Colorado Department of Revenue, Taxpayer Service Division <www.businesstax.state.co.us/tradenames/>.) Many state archives hold materials that document the legal history of businesses within their boundaries. They may hold similar records for fraternal organizations, churches, and other nonprofit associations as well.

Frequently corporations maintain their own historical material in a library or archives unit. Along with their own corporate history, the library includes a general history of the industry, and information about parent and related companies in the area. Even if there is no mention of a specific ancestor, the business records will likely tell about his work place, conditions, and work activities. For the most part, these facilities are available by appointment only, if at all.

Local historical societies have accepted many records for research. Often a local history includes a great deal of information about area businesses, information that in turn offers facts about individuals. Company Shops was the name of the town that preceded Burlington, North Carolina, and was established in large part because of the presence of the North Carolina Railroad Company. Among the records that include individual names and are now available in print form are the lists of those who donated funds for the purchase of land on which to build a machine shop. Part of a publication about the town is an appendix that gives the identified birthplaces of 1857 railroad employees (see figure 4-2).

State archives and historical societies house many county business registers. For example, the Utah State Archives in Salt Lake City holds corporate records for businesses in Weber County, Utah, which include an incorporation index, 1871–1959; incorporation records (including articles and bylaws), 1958–65; and affidavits of business firms and partnerships, 1913–63, with indexes. Weber County articles of incorporation before 1958 are in the lieutenant governor's office, which also maintains state incorporation records, although these are located in state offices several miles from the archives.

Account Books

Probably the most common and genealogically useful records are storekeepers' account books. Such volumes of the past were usually handwritten. Over time these were replaced with printed volumes; entries were handwritten. Later volumes were typed. Account books can range in size from small notebooks to bound ledgers, covering such topics as fiduciary accounts, customer or patient visits, and business sales.

The following example is from a printed account book in which the storekeeper identified the individuals involved by family relationships. The *d* means that the goods were delivered to that person; *nr* means "near" or possibly "neighbor."

> Addedle (Adedle, Addle), William, June 38–Dec. 42 nr. Peter Demun of Peack; d John Brady, Andrew Jones, d to Peter Demun, Samuel Alexander, Jerry Rolandt; paid James Alexander note
>
> Adkinson, see Atkinson
>
> Ake, Jacob, Jly 35–Apr 39, son to Jerry, d to Jacob Bodine Jerry, Jly 36–Sep 39, at the Society, Peter Jarvis nr; d to Jacob Bodine
>
> Akeman (Akerman,) John, Jly 42–Jly 43, nr Samuel Alexander
>
> Akerly, Arthur, Apr. 35–May 37; & joint account with Obediah Seward[3]

Another example of the value of these records is from the set of account books of John Avery, a schoolmaster in Huntington, Long Island, from 1763 to 1779, who kept a record for each year he taught the children. Such books could be considered school records, but because most schools were privately run and the teachers paid by the students' families, these are also business records.

Conkling. Capt. Cornelius: Ebenezer Morgan (1767)
Conkling. David: 2 children (1777): Phebe (1778): David (1778–9)
Conkling. Ezekiel: Elizabeth Betsy (1776–8): Philetus (1776–8): Silas (1778)
Conkling. Hubbard: Charlotte (1777): Isaac Wood (1768)
Conkling. Isaac: Timothy (1767): Henry Titus (1766–7)
Conkling. Jeremiah: son (1765): Jacob (1767)
Conkling. John: Phebe (1770–1): Mary (1777): Sarah (1777)
Conkling. Joseph: John (1768)
Conkling. Philip: Patty (1770): Bennet (1776–9): Richard Titus (1765–6)
Conkling. Richard: Titus (1765–67)
Conkling. Richard: Jr; 2 children (1778)
Conkling. Stephen: daughter (betw. 1767)
Conkling. Thomas: Hanah (1778): Lucy (1778): Richard Hults (1777)
Conkling. Thomas. Jr.: son (betw 1763–7): Selah (1767–8): Esther (1767): Zophar (1767)
Conkling. Timothy: Abel (1766. 68): Ezra (1767): Jonathan (1766–8): Timothy (1767)
Conkling. Widow. of West Neck: 2 children (1778)[4]

The Conkling family was a large family in the Huntington area, and it is often difficult for researchers to sort out who belongs to whom.[5] Imagine how illuminating Avery's notations about various Conkling families are, especially since the children are linked to their parents and they can be definitely located in Huntington for the specified years. Although abstracts like these are very useful, other historical (if not genealogical) information may be found in the originals, the locations of which are mentioned in the periodical in which the abstracts appear.

Account and daybooks, in addition to providing some specific information about an ancestor's life away from his home, can also document the ancestor's specific location at that specific time. The record can be especially valuable when that location is temporary or on the frontier., One example is the toll road payments made by those headed to Oregon

APPENDIX B

Employees of the NCRR in 1857 Whose Place of Birth Has Been Identified

ALABAMA:
John Thornton, engineer
J. D. McCauley, Henry Smith, machinists
DELAWARE:
Thomas Fox, machinist
DISTRICT OF COLUMBIA:
Eco Wilkes, railroad agent
KENTUCKY:
D. R. Hislop, engineer
MARYLAND:
Charles Carroll, engineer
Benjamin R. Sergeant, machinist
MASSACHUSETTS:
M. C. Parmenter, engineer
John Scott, James Scott, machinists
MISSISSIPPI:
A. Chilson, engineer
PENNSYLVANIA:
John Cushing, Joseph Fix, machinists
RHODE ISLAND:
Thomas N. Swan, W. C. Swan, engineers
R. W. Swan, machinist
VIRGINIA:
John Binns, engineer
G. W. Fulner, E. G. Marsh, machinists
NORTH CAROLINA:
Wesley Garrett, W. Pollock, Charles C. Davis, engineers
John W. Rippy, John Sharp, William Scott, Calvine Leverness, Calvin Lisemann, Joseph Bird, John Brassington, Griffin Mushaw, William Scott, William Ratler, James Rippy, S. H. Brown, firemen
M. Hoke, Ed King, N. W. West, Will Vestal, M. H. Shepherd, machinists
IRELAND:
Samuel McCutcheon, James R. Murphy, engineers
John Kinney, P. W. Keenan, John Kimery, machinists
SCOTLAND:
Thomas S. Robertson, John Besett, engineers
John Anderson, machinist

Figure 4-2. A local history may well include significant information about ancestors of the area. From Durward T. Stokes, *Company Shops: The Town Built By a Railroad* (Winston Salem, N.C.: John F. Blair, 1981).

in the mid 1800s (see figure 4-3). Wagon train immigrants had to travel over the Barlow Toll Road during the last leg of their trip. Records kept by the toll keeper show the name of the immigrant, his equipment and livestock, the toll due, and the amount paid.[6]

Researchers studying the keeper of the daybook should read every entry in the journal. Paper was not the common commodity it is today, so many businessmen made personal entries in their own daybooks or account books. For those ancestors who did not keep a family Bible, the daybook was the place where family events might be recorded.

Tax Records

The Internal Revenue Act of 1 July 1862 was the first income tax assessed during the Civil War and was intended "to provide Internal Revenue to support the Government and to pay Interest on the Public Debt." Businesses were taxed monthly on their products, with a quarterly tax assessed on some types of income. An annual license was required for many occupations and trades, and an annual tax was charged on all income exceeding $600. The tax was in effect until 1873. While not extant for all locations, researchers should seek any entries for the known businessman of this era. Retained as part of Record Group 58, Internal Revenue Service, at the National Archives and Records Administration, the lists are alphabetically divided by state, division, and district. Microfilm copies are available through the National Archives and its regional offices.

During the war years, William Donovan, residing at 324 New Market, was a coffee merchant in Philadelphia. In September of 1864, he was taxed $279.94 for 27,994 pounds of roasted coffee. As shown in figure 4-4, at the time he still owed $17.50 on a special tax for the previous month. Charles Day of 435 North Second had clothing valued at $1,840, on which he paid a two percent tax, or $37.50.

Small Businesses

During the colonial period, small companies were formed for various specific purposes, most frequently to buy land outside a township or to construct a road or a major new building within a town. These companies would formulate policy, elect officers, collect money, and delegate and supervise the work. They also kept records (usually called minutes), some of which survived and have been published. While the genealogical information in such records may be limited, they do serve to place an ancestor in a place at a particular time, and they attest to the social involvement of an ancestor. In this way, they can lead to additional records for that locality.

If your ancestor owned a small business, there may be a record of the business license in the city or state where he or she did business. The application for a license should include a variety of information, such as the owner's age, birthplace, marital status, and residence, depending on when he applied for the license. Depending on the locality, licenses may be found in the office of the Recorder of Deeds, the Clerk of Court, or another official.

The number of employees of small businesses varies greatly. Employees often number less than twenty and sometimes only two or three, perhaps friends or relatives of the owner. Payroll records may be available; however, personal records may be limited. If the business still exists, contact the present owner for information and records. In some cases, he or she may be a relative of the previous owner and may have been a child when your ancestor worked there.

Corporations

Big businesses employ a large portion of the labor force and typically have kept better employee records for longer periods. Also, these companies are more likely still to be operating, making it easier to locate their records. Before beginning research into a corporation's records, you should do some basic background research: read the company history (if there is one), check periodicals for articles, or request reading suggestions from its public relations office. Many of these companies have substantial archives to house their historical records. Others have deposited their records in local libraries and historical societies. The section "Locating Business Records" in this chapter, describes how to find some of these archives and collections.

Pensions

Today many major corporations have developed pension plans, which require significant information about each employee. Even after the pensioner's death, a widow or child may need to submit documents to prove their relationship to the deceased and therefore their right to continued pension payments or death benefits. While the pension plan is primarily a twentieth-century concept, many of the persons recorded were born in the late nineteenth century, often before birth records were available. The records should include the employee's full name, birth and death information, places of residence, parents and/or spouses, and children's names and birth information. Often, the same corporation employed children or siblings, especially when it was one of the major employers in a locality. Pension records may be available for deceased ancestors. A formal letter should explain and document your relationship to the deceased, and state why you are seeking these records.

Corporate Histories

Many American businesses have official corporate histories. The history of Standard Oil Company took some eighteen years to write, in part because its 35,000 boxes of records took so long to be organized and studied. Some years ago, the Harvard

The following is the only complete recorded list (1848) of "Covered Wagons" coming into Oregon over the "Barlow Road" to Foster's place. It was in an "1845 Counting House Almanac" kept by the toll keeper, and shows date of month, owner, number of wagons, amount due, and how paid. It was among the historical papers of Philip Foster now with the Oregon Historical Society.

Date	Owner	Number	Amount due	How paid
September 3, 1848				
	Daniel Hathaway	1 Wagon	$ 5.00 Due	$5.00 Paid
	Richard Cripe	2 "	10.00 "	9.40 "
	Benjamin Cripe	1 "	5.00 "	5.00 "
	Thomas Gates	2 "	10.00 "	not Paid
	D. S. Baker	1 Buggy	2.50 "	2.50 "
	Rueben Dickens	2 Wagons	10.00 "	not Paid
	W. M. King	2 "	10.00 "	not Paid
	Wm. Bronson	2 "	10.00 "	not Paid
	Leonard Williamson	1 "	5.00 "	5.00 "
	Thomas Burbanks	1 "	5.00 "	4.95 "
	Lovicia Davis, Widow	2 "	10.00 "	4.84 "
	P. C. Cline	2 "	10.00 "	10.00 "
	Orin Kellogg	2 "	10.00 "	left 1 rifle
	James Emery	1 "	5.00 "	5.00 Paid
	John Stipp	3 "	15.00 "	14.00 "
	Jno Patterson	2 "	10.00 "	9.68 "
	Isaac W. Welch	2 "	10.00 "	10.00 "
	Christina Cline	1 "	5.00 "	4.95 "
	John Fraisier	1 "	5.00 "	5.00 "
	Jacob L. Miller	1 "	5.00 "	5.00 "
	J. Miller	3 "	15.00 "	15.00 "
	Robert Houston	2 "	10.00 "	10.00 "
	Christian Miller	2 "	10.00 "	10.00 "
Sept. 4	Reuben Pigg	2 "	10.00 "	10.00 "
	James Robinson	1 "	5.00 "	4.95 "
	James P. Crooks	3 "	15.00 "	15.00 "
	E. B. Wilcocks	3 "	15.00 "	15.00 "
Sept. 5	Chatman Halley	2 "	10.00 "	10.00 "
Sept. 6	Dann Trullinger	2 "	10.00 "	9.95 "
	John Ramsey	2 "	10.00 "	10.00 "
	John Meeker	1 "	5.00 "	5.00 "
	Andrew Bivens	7 cattle		.50 "
	Jesse Bellknap	1 wagon	5.00 "	5.00 "
	Abiatha Newton	2 "	10.00 "	7.50 "
	John W. Starr	1 "	5.00 "	5.00 "
	George Bellknap	1 "	5.00 "	5.00 "
	George W. Bethands	1 "	5.00 "	5.00 "
	John Catlin	2 "	10.00 "	10.00 "
	John Wells	2 "	10.00 "	10.00 "
	John Lindsey	1½ "	7.50 "	7.50 "
	Buel Griffen	1½ "	7.50 "	5.00 "
	Andrew Hagey	2 "	10.00 "	9.00 "
	Wm. Armpriest	1½ "	7.50 "	7.50 "
	M. Hagey	1 "	5.00 "	5.00 "
	J. A. DeShaver	1 "	5.00 "	5.00 "
	John Miller	1 "	5.00 "	5.00 "
	Benjamin B. Jackson	1 "	5.00 "	4.84 "
Sept. 7	David Presley	3 "	15.00 "	12.00 "
	Benjamin Cleaver	5 "	25.00 "	20.00 "
	Sanford Stephens	1 "	5.00 "	4.00 "

Figure 4-3. Business records such as this one from E. L. (Roy) Meyers, *Foster-Pettygrove Store Lists, Barlow Toll Road, 1846–1919: The Story of Two Men from Fort Deposit. They Called It Jack-Knife: History of Eagle Creek Community and School District Number 17* (Portland, Ore.: Genealogical Forum of Portland, 1972) are invaluable in placing ancestors in a specific location, especially one on the frontier.

University Graduate School of Business History began to chronicle individual American business histories. Some of the titles in their series cover the histories of Parker Brothers, Intuit, Macy's, N. W. Ayer & Son, Massachusetts Hospital Insurance Company, and Reed and Barton (see the school's website <http: harvardbusinessonline.hbsp.harvard.edu>). Histories published by corporations themselves frequently include personal information about company leaders; some, such as the Alan Wood Steel history in figure 4-5, also include information about other employees.

Other businesses have some historical information on their websites. General Electric Company supplies the name and address of its corporate library, which is called the Hall of Electrical History <www.ge.com/en/company/companyinfo/at_a_glance/history_story.htm>. A simple Web search by corporate name is usually sufficient to find the company's site.

For other histories, consult the following publications:

Business History, published quarterly by the Harvard Graduate School of Business History. Includes reviews and announcements of historical studies of American businesses.

Cochran, Thomas. *Railroad Leaders, 1845–1890: The Business Mind in Action.* Cambridge: Harvard University Press, 1953. Based on 100,000 letters from sixty-one railroad officials.

Daniells, Lorna M. *Studies in Enterprise.* Boston: Little, Brown, 1957. Includes a list of business histories.

Larson, Henrietta. *Guide to Business History.* Cambridge: Harvard University Press, 1948. Bibliography of histories and printed sources.

Defunct Businesses

Many of our ancestors worked for companies no longer in existence. Some seemingly defunct companies have not actually disappeared but continue in business under a different name and/or ownership, knowledge that is needed to pursue available records. For example, Victor Talking Machine became Radio Corporation of America, also known as RCA. Records of the old company may be transferred to another firm—often the one that bought out the defunct company. In a small city, try contacting present businesses in the same line of work for information about an ancestral company. Remember as well to check corporate histories to see if the defunct company has been purchased by or merged with another company.

The defunct business may have belonged to a trade association or some other group of businesses in the same trade or locality. These organizations may have information on the company in question and may know where their records are. *Business Organizations and Agencies Directory*, edited by Anthony T. Kruzas and Robert C. Thomas, provides addresses of trade, business, and commercial organizations; stock exchanges; labor unions; chambers of commerce; and many other groups.[7] Better Business Bureaus, as well as federal and state government agencies, are also included. Also helpful is David M. Brownstone's and Gordon Carruth's *Where to Find Business Information*, a source that can help locate associations.[8]

Information about old companies may appear in articles in various business magazines. One of the best ways to search this source is the *Business Periodicals Index*, which began in 1958 and is readily available in public libraries. Articles are listed under the industry or company name. The format is similar to the *Reader's Guide to Periodical Literature.*

(No. 97.)

[This Form is for the copy of the Alphabetical List retained by the Assessor, and is like Form 23 without the columns used only by Collectors.]
Assessors must be particular to fill all blanks in this form, as far as practicable, and to number all articles and occupations upon which taxes are assessed to correspond with the entry in the Abstract.

ALPHABETICAL LIST of Persons in Division No: 12, of Collection District No. 1 of the State of Pennsylvania, liable to a tax under the Excise laws of the United States, and the amount thereof, as assessed by Assistant Assessor, and by John W Frazier, Assessor, returned to the Collector of said District for the Month of September, 1864.

No. of Line	Name	Location and Post Office Address	Article or Occupation	No. in Abstract	Quantity or Valuation	Rate of Tax	Amount of Tax upon particular articles	Total	No. of Line
1			Amount brought forward					$12470.85	1
2	Diedrich Henry	127 Holmes	Machinery	✓	48	5%		2 40	2
3	De Paet, Gustav	409 North Second	Bitters & Syrups	✓	900	"		45 00	3
4	Day, Charles	435 " "	Clothing	✓	1860	2%		37 20	4
5	Deimer John & Sons	149 Margaretta	Morocco, &c	✓	2126	5%		106 30	5
6	Dainty James	431 St. John's	"	✓	1064	"		53 20	6
7	Dinov and Wm	326 New Market	Roasted Coffee		lbs 27,994	01c	279.94		7
8	" "	" " Aug 1st	Special Tax		$100		67 50	347 44	8
9	Deimer John & Sons	149 Margaretta	Due on Aug Return		1834	5%		91 70	9
10									10

Figure 4-4. Businessmen were taxed on their inventory when the first federal income tax was established in 1862. Internal Revenue Assessment List for Pennsylvania, Division 12, Collection District 1, September 1864, NARA microfilm M787.

him and knew him well. He was a most forceful and able manager, dominated every situation, given to plain speaking, but bore no malice.

In his intercourse with the mill men he was governed by a spirit of fairness and justice, never minced words and the men admired his courage, and after the "hurt was over" did not feel unkindly towards him.

When I told Edward J. Caine, who had been our furnace builder for 25 years, of Mr. Wood's death, he said: "Well, I have had very many plain talks with 'the boss,' but I liked to work for him, as you always knew just where you stood with him and whether your work was satisfactory."

He was a most excellent example of the fast disappearing "Iron Master."

James Colen, a "roller," entered the army, and was wounded in the ankle at Gettysburg and taken to the hospital in Baltimore. Mr. Alan Wood, Jr., hearing of his being wounded in Baltimore, wrote to his cousins, Mrs. Charles Coates and Mrs. Tyson, to look him up, which they did, and James Colen often referred to the good care which they gave him. He always had trouble with his ankle and gave up rolling, and for many years stocked in the West Flue Mill, and was always one of the best and most loyal men in the mill. He retired about 1903, took a trip to Europe, and died February 19th, 1917.

Joseph Colen was also a sheet and flue roller and also worked at many different jobs in the mill, the last one being scrap packing. He retired May, 1913, on a pension, and died August 26th, 1915.

When a boy at Delaware Iron Works, and swimming in the mill pond, Mr. Howard Wood in playfulness pushed Joseph Colen in the water. Being unable to swim he was rescued with difficulty. In many ways this was fortunate for "Joe," as in after life many shortcomings were overlooked on this account.

Frederick Wood was a bar iron roller and an old employee. He was one of the men who broke the strike in 1876.

After he gave up rolling he was watchman for a number of years, was finally pensioned, and died at the age of 83 years on September 23rd, 1917.

John Campbell came to work at Schuylkill Iron Works soon after it was built, and for many years was roller on the West Flue Mill, and after giving up this job was stocker on the East Flue and No. 4 Flue Mills. He died May 10th, 1908. He was secretary of the Schuylkill Relief Association and a very reliable man.

It was one of his boasts that he had rolled plates heated by three generations of the Beaver family. The first of the family was Henry Beaver, who was a heater soon after the mill was built, and after he retired was janitor of the Presbyterian Church in Conshohocken. He was a tall, venerable-looking man with a long white beard, and looked the patriarch.

66

Figure 4-5. Employee information in a corporate history is common, but the amount of personal information in this Alan Wood Steel publication is unusual. Frank H. Taylor, *History of the Alan Wood Iron and Steel Company, 1792–1920* (N.p.: privately printed, 1920).

If you know where a business was located, you can then write to the local chamber of commerce or state archives for information on what became of the business and its records. The secretary of state should have incorporation records for each state specifying the years a company was in business or if the name was changed. A local town or county historical society may also have knowledge of a business's demise. As mentioned earlier, local cities or counties may have business licenses for unincorporated businesses within their boundaries. Their records may indicate when a business folded and if the owner started a new and similar business.

Information about defunct businesses and record repositories can often be found in local historical societies. These societies are usually quite knowledgeable about the history of their areas, and they may be able to help determine what happened to a local business. Most societies have a website with their current contact information. The *Directory of Historical Organizations in the United States and Canada* also has information on most societies.[9]

Bankruptcy

Not all businesses are successful, of course. Some end up in bankruptcy, a process that creates further records about the business and its owners. For the most part, bankruptcy is governed by federal laws. Records are therefore found in the papers of federal district courts. Historical records are frequently transferred to the appropriate regional archives while more current records are held at the district court involved. For more information, consult chapter 7, "Court Records."

Records Created by the Practitioner of an Occupation

Trades and Professions

Between 1780 and 1870, many of our ancestors became ministers, lawyers, doctors, or other professionals. Another large group became craftsmen. These occupations generated valuable records such as histories and directories in specific areas (see chapter 8, "Directories"). Compiled from several sources, they usually contain secondary information prepared by historians.

Clergy

Most denominations have established an archival facility to maintain their materials, including ministerial records, which may contain valuable genealogical information. Some denominations publish directories of their ministers. Old editions of directories or historical directories, such as the following example, can provide important biographical and genealogical information about an ancestor who was an ordained clergyman or notable church layman.

> Brinkman, Benjamin F., b Graafschap, Mich, May 3, 1863. WTS, 1906. Ord United Presby. Pas Second, Englewood, Chicago, Ill 1906–10; Second, Pella, Ia 1911–17; fin agt Central 1917–20; pas Calvary Cleveland, 1920–21. d Cleveland, Mar 5, 1921.

Breck, John Randlett, b Newbury, Vt, jun, 1831, s of Jacob R. AB, Rutgers C, 1859; NBTS, 1862. Lic Cl Passic, 1862; ord Cl Paramus, 1862. Pas West New Hempstead, N.Y. 1862–65; Spring Valley, N.Y. 1865–69; tchr 1869–71. d Marysville, Tenn Aug 7, 1872.

Brocklos, Albert. Received Presby 1911; pas Ave B, NYC 1911–13; dismissed Meth Ch 1914.

Brodhead, Jacob, b Marbletown, N.Y., May 14, 1782, s of Charles W. AB. Union C, 1801; NBTS 1804; ord Cl Poughkeepsie, 1804. Pas Rhinebeck Flats, N.Y. 1804–09; Collegiate, NYC 1809–13; Crown St, Philadelphia, Pa 1813–26; Broome St, NYC 1826–37; Flatbush, Ulster Co, N.Y. 1837–41; Central, Brooklyn. N.Y. 1841–46. Pres Gen Syn, 1816–17 and 1825–26. d Springfield, Mass Jun 6, 1855.[10]

Researchers can locate the denomination headquarters on the Internet or by using the current edition of the annual *The Yearbook of American and Canadian Churches*.[11] (See chapter 6, "Church Records.") This publication may also help determine the current name of a church, which has merged with another. The yearbook also includes lists of "Depositories of Church History Material and Sources," arranged by denomination, with an appended "Standard Guides to Church Archives."

Lawyers and Judges

Legal professionals have long occupied prominent positions in American society. This profession established the bar as a means of determining each person's qualifications and then required civil registration for those who passed the bar examination. Each state has a state licensing process and a list of currently licensed attorneys available on the state's website.

A valuable source for information about lawyers is the *Martindale-Hubbell Law Directory*, an annual publication that lists nearly every practicing lawyer in the country.[12] First published in the 1860s, most public libraries have recent editions while many law libraries retain the earliest copies. This source gives some biographical information, as well as residence and affiliation with a law firm. Their website <www.martindale.com> includes the capability of searching for current attorneys by name, location, and law school.

In most states and many large cities and counties, books have been written on "The Bench and Bar of . . ." These books contain biographical information on those practicing law in a locality at the time of and prior to publication. *Martin's Bench and Bar of Philadelphia*, for example, includes references to most attorneys who ever practiced in Philadelphia and many colonial lawyers who worked anywhere in Pennsylvania.[13] It also includes an alphabetical list of all those admitted to practice in the courts of Philadelphia, both city and county, and death dates and ages at death for those no longer living at the time of publication (figure 4-6).

Doctors

Similar directories and biographical sketch books exist in many areas for doctors and surgeons (see the References section). Since these professionals, too, were often registered by the government, certificates or licenses should be sought in city, county, and state archives. The Pennsylvania State Archives, for example, has medical licenses from 1894 and dental licenses from 1897.

The American Medical Association has been gathering information on the personal and professional backgrounds of licensed medical practitioners since the late 1800s. The archival collection includes information on more than 350,000 doctors who practiced in the United States from as early as 1804 through 1969, although records prior to 1907 are incomplete. The microfilmed cards are available at the Family History Library and through local family history centers. Figure 4-7 shows the entry for William James from the AMA records. The National

The Philadelphia Bar.

Being a List of the names of gentlemen who have been admitted to practice, as Attorneys-at-law in the County Courts of the City and County of Philadelphia, from 1682 to 1883, with the dates of their admission.

Abbreviations—A-age at death. ADM.-for admitted to practice. ATTY-GEN.-Attorney General. B-for born. B. G. or BRIG. GEN.-for Brigadier General. C. J-Chief Justice. Co-for county. COL. OF VOLS.-Colonel of volunteers, 1861-65. COL.-before christian name, colonel of militia. C. P.-for Common Pleas C. R.-Colonial Records. D-for died. D. C-for District Court. DIRECT'RY-for Philadelphia Directory. IN. PRAC.-for in practice J.-Judge. J. C. P.-Judge of the Common Pleas. J. O. C.-Associate Judge of the Orphans Court. M. C.-for Member of Congress. M. G.-Major General. PA.-for Pennsylvania. P. V.-Pennsylvania Volunteers, 1861-65. PA. MAG-Pennsylvania Magazine. P. J.-President Judge. Q. M. G.-for Quarter-Master-General. S. C.-for Supreme Court of Pennsylvania U. S.-for United States. U. S. C. C.-for United States Circuit Court. U. S. S. C.-for United States Supreme Court. * Name from Sheriff's Deed Book B, which is the date of admission in the Supreme Court, which I have used where an earlier date could not be found.

Abbett, Benjamin Franklin,		Jan. 25, 1868
Edwin L.,		Dec. 5, 1864
Leonidas,		Feb. 5, 1857
Abbey, William Burling,		Nov. 4, 1876
Abbott, Montelius,	*d. May 18, 1877, a. 38*	June 21, 1862
William Holloway,		July 13, 1844
Abrams (Rev.) Joseph,	*d. Mch 30, 1881, a. 69*	Nov. 2, 1839
Joseph Addison,		Nov. 30, 1878
Ackley, John Edward,		Dec. 13, 1879
Ackworth, Edmund,[1]	*Chester Co. Records*	Feb. 23, 1741
John,	*d. Dec. 14, 1744*	Before 1744
Adams, Frederick Mayhew,		Jan. 22, 1847
George Bethune,		Mch 2, 1878
John Bell,	*d. Jan. 4, 1874*	Mch 13, 1855
John,		Nov. 1, 1879
John Quincy,		May 3, 1856
Josiah Robert,		Dec. 5, 1874
Robert, Jr.,		Apl 27, 1872
Thomas Boylston,[2]	*Judge, d. 1832, a. 60*	Dec. 7, 1793
William C.,		Sep. 28, 1872

Figure 4-6. From John Hill Martin, *Martin's Bench and Bar of Philadelphia* (Philadelphia: Rees Welsh and Co., 1883), 243.

Genealogical Society <www.ngsgenealogy.org> maintains the original cards, and copies are available by request for a fee. The *Directory of Deceased American Physicians, 1804–1929* lists almost 150,000 deceased doctors in the two-volume set.[14]

Nurses and other medical personnel are also subject to licensing procedures and are listed on each state website. Lists of all licensed professionals are available by state and county within the state, usually through the state board of medical examiners (or its equivalent) website. Links to all the state boards are found at <www.click-411.com>. A Web search should reveal the list for your state of interest. Also, the National Council of State Boards of Nursing <www.ncsbn.org> provides links to information on each state.

The American Medical Association <www.ama-assn.org/aps/amahg.htm> maintains a list of every physician in the country, which is available on its website. Databases for medical personnel, past and present, are available in some locations. An alphabetical list of Baltimore medical care personnel from 1752 to 1919 is available at <www.mdhistoryonline.net/mdmedicine/cfm/index.cfm>. This list includes dentists, druggists, nurses, and physicians. Another example is in book format, *Hospitals and Medical Doctors in Pittsburg County, Oklahoma,* by J. Boyd Collard.[15]

To search for a physician or doctor in city directories, try the online entries. Go into <www.ancestry.com> and type in the keyword "doctor" or "physician." The list of people with those occupations will appear. This is a quick way to locate all the doctors in that particular directory.

Professional Licenses

Most states require a license for a variety of professions. As part of its Web information, Wisconsin identifies all occupations that require a license at <drl.wi.gov/index.htm>. Among these, in addition to attorneys and medical personnel, are architects, boxers, and funeral directors.

One state, Colorado, has an online searchable database of all licensing boards. This makes it possible to search for information about a living individual by license number, name, and type of license at <www.dora.state.co.us/pls/real/ARMS_Search.Set_Up>. A typical entry includes the city of residence, license number and type, license status (active or inactive), along with the dates for first issuance, last renewal, and expiration. Another field shows if any complaints have been filed against the individual.

Records for teachers date back to the days of the one-room schoolhouse. Teacher certificates include the name of the teacher, date of certification, grade taught, town of residence, and hometown. An index to teacher certificates granted for Rio Grande County, Colorado, for the years 1874–1893 is online at <www.colorado.gov/dpa/doit/archives/schools/teachcerts/teachcerts_top.html>.

Artisans

Artisans, writers, and skilled tradesmen are also the subject of biographical sketches in collective biographies. The following example of a silversmith in Staunton, Virginia, is from a book-length study of local professions.

> C. E. EVARD & BROTHER opened a "New Jewellery and Watch Establishment" in Staunton in June 1849. There were two persons in the silversmith and jewelry business in this vicinity who might have been the principle in this firm. Charles Eugene Evard of Winchester and Charles Edward Evard of Leesburg. This was undoubtedly the Leesburg jeweler, for the same illustration was used in the advertising in Staunton and Leesburg. The name of the brother is unknown. This firm advertised clocks, watches, and jewelry repaired, and warranted at its shop, one door above M. Cushing's Confectionery Store. On July 9, following, the firm had just received from their manufactory a large supply of "silver Table and Tea Spoons, also Dessert and Salt Spoons, Sugar Tongs, Butter Knives, all superior articles and manufactured especially to order. . . . The public generally are informed that the subscribers will sell all kinds of jewellery and spoons much lower than the Baltimore prices." How long this firm continued in business here is not definitely known, but on March 1, 1850, C. E. Evard announced to the public of Leesburg that he had returned to and permanently located himself in Leesburg; so that the firm did business in Staunton not longer than nine months."[16]

Similar books are available for many of the early states. See the References section for other occupational histories.

Other Records

An ancestor need not be prominent to be included in a business record. Many people were recorded by cities because of their occupations. An 1863 register of prostitutes compiled by the Guardians of the Poor in Philadelphia is remarkable for its detail. It includes information about these women's ages, length of time in the city, literacy, marital status, number of children, how long and why they were involved in the profession, other trades they held, parents' occupations, and when, why, and from where they emigrated. Parents' or siblings' names were also recorded. Despite the uniqueness of this particular record, it illustrates the eclectic nature of such records. If a local government was interested in a particular occupation, there are likely to be records among the archives of that government.

A wide range of information is available on other occupations as well that we might not expect to find documented. For example, the Pennsylvania State Archives houses applications for teaching certificates from 1866, a Register of Pilots' Homes and Securities for 1783 to 1876, Philadelphia licenses for peddlers and hawkers from 1820 to 1838, and tavern licenses applied for and granted from 1750 to 1855.[17]

Records Created about Employees

Among our ancestors may exist an old family story telling of an ancestor who was killed "working on the railroads" or who was killed "in a mine accident." Depending on the date of the injury or death, records relating to such accidents may be available. For example, the state of Colorado required mining companies to report accidents (see the following example). The resulting information is now available online <www.denver.lib.co.us/research/genealogy/fatalities.html> and contains a wealth of personal information:

> Buzz, Herman. Death Date: 1919 JAN 4
> Nationality: Austrian. Occupation: Machineman. Yrs Mine Exp:

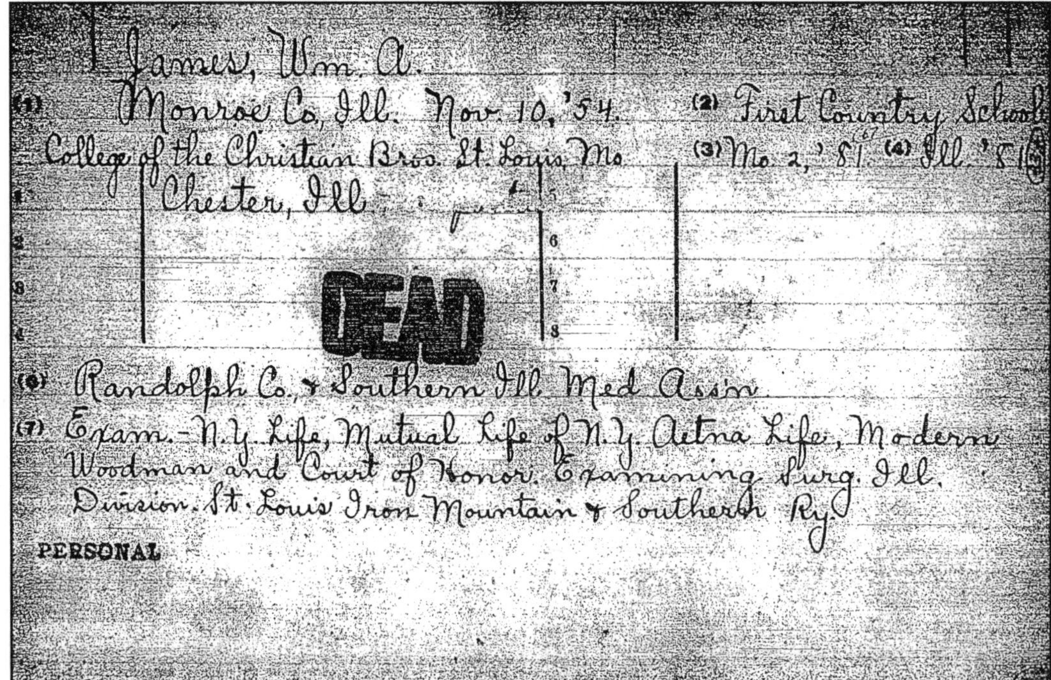

James, Wm. A.
(1) Monroe Co, Ill. Nov. 10, '54. (2) First Country School
College of the Christian Bros. St. Louis, Mo (3) Mo 2, '81 (4) Ill. '81
Chester, Ill.

DEAD

(6) Randolph Co., & Southern Ill. Med Ass'n
(7) Exam.-N.Y. Life, Mutual Life of N.Y. Aetna Life, Modern Woodman and Court of Honor. Examining Surg. Ill. Division. St. Louis Iron Mountain & Southern Ry
PERSONAL

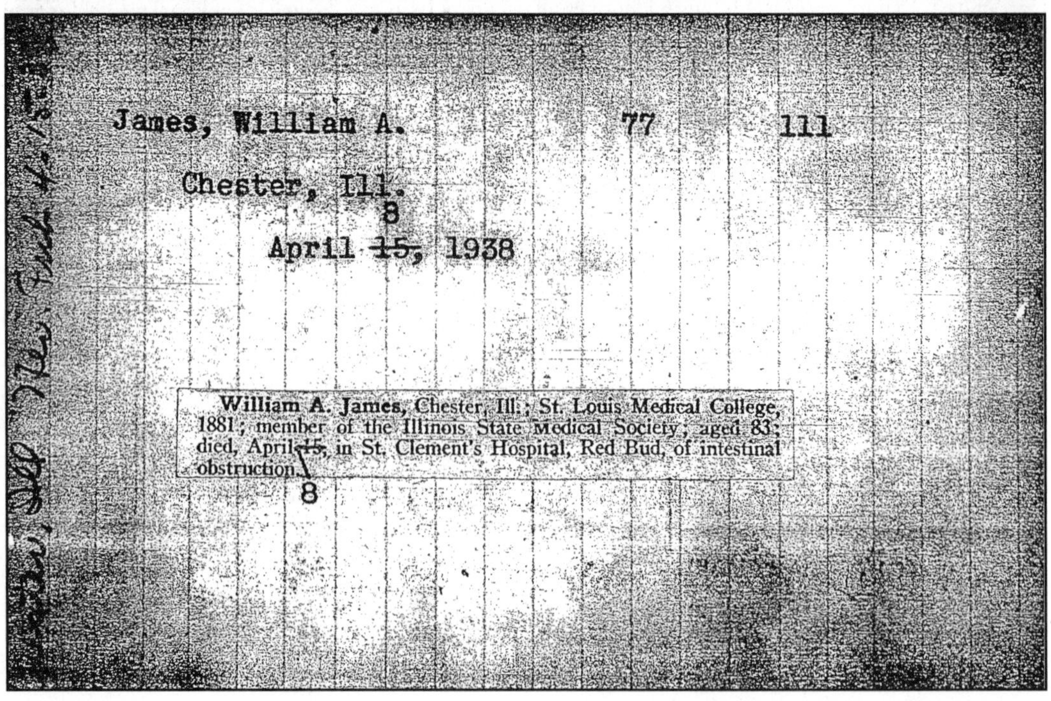

James, William A. 77 111
Chester, Ill.
8
April ~~15,~~ 1938

William A. James, Chester, Ill.; St. Louis Medical College, 1881; member of the Illinois State Medical Society; aged 83; died, April ~~15~~ 8, in St. Clement's Hospital, Red Bud, of intestinal obstruction.

Figure 4-7. Two-page file on William A. James, M.D., of Monroe County, Illinois, from the American Medical Association.

Age at death: 30. Marital Status: M. Surviving children: 3. County: ELP

Company name: D. W. Corley. Name of Mine: Klondyke.

Cause of death/comments: fall of rock.

In many cases, one record may refer indirectly to other potential records. For example, an obituary might mention a union affiliation or church attended. Any tidbit such as these can lead to records created about our ancestors as employees.

Apprentice and Indenture Records

To *indenture* is to bind one person to another for a given period of time in payment for some service. To *apprentice* is to indenture for a certain time for the express purpose of learning an art or trade. The most common type of indenture was probably that used to pay for passage to America. A number of convicts from England indentured themselves as servants for a number of years to pay for their transportation to the southern states where they settled. The Old World system of indenturing apprentices to learn a trade was one of the first imports to America. In colonial days, most apprentices were boys in their teens, often younger than fourteen. The agreement, called an indenture, was signed by the master as well as the parent or guardian of the child.[18] The trades were often family businesses, and many fathers formally took their sons as apprentices. Two examples are Paul Revere, who learned the silversmith trade from his father, and Benjamin Franklin, who was indentured as a printer to his brother James.

Apprentices were usually bound until they were twenty-one, so the length of the indenture specified in the document gives an excellent indication of a child's age. If a boy was bound to his master for twelve years and five months, for example, he was probably about eight and a half years old when the indenture was signed.

In New England, it was not uncommon, especially among poorer families, for children under the age of ten to be bound out. The following 1676 indenture illustrates the kinds of genealogical and historical information available in such records:

> This Indenture witnesseth that I, Nathan Knight, sometime of Black Point, with the consent of my father-in-law [more likely stepfather], Harry Brooken and Elend, his wife, have put myself apprentice to Samuel Whidden, of Portsmouth, in the county of Portsmouth, mason, and bound after the manner of an apprentice with him, to serve and abide the full space and term of twelve years and five months, thence next following, to be full, complete and ended; during which time the said apprentice his said master faithfully shall serve, his lawful secrets shall keep, and commands shall gladly do, damage unto his said master he shall not do, nor see to done of others, but to the best of his power shall give timely notice thereof to his said master. Fornication he shall not commit, nor contract matrimony within the said time. The goods of his said master, he shall not spend or lend. He shall not play cards, or dice, or any other unlawful game, whereby his said master may have damage in his own goods, or others, taverns, he shall not haunt, nor from his master's business absent himself by day or night, but in all things shall behave himself as a faithful apprentice ought to do. And the said master his said apprentice shall teach and instruct, or cause to be taught and instructed in the art and mystery as mason; finding unto his said apprentice during the said time meat, drink, washing, lodging, and apparel, fitting an apprentice, teaching him to read, and allowing him three months towards the latter end of his time to go to school to write, and also double the apparel at the end of said time. As witness our hands and seals, interchangeably put to two instruments of the same purpose, November the twenty-fifth, one thousand six hundred and seventy-six.[19]

From the mid-1700s onward, it was not unusual to find both girls and boys apprenticed when their family circumstances took a downward turn. Children were "bound out" to help earn money for a family, or simply so the family would not have to support them. Sometimes one parent was deceased. Since the trades were not opened to girls, they were most often apprenticed to learn "housewifry."

An example from the Philadelphia Mayor's Office, Records of Indentures, shows several different types of indentures and the kinds of information included in each:

- Mary Stamper was to learn "Housewifry." Her mother's full name is given. Since the term of service was seven years, she was probably almost fourteen years old.
- Mary Barrett was apparently indentured to pay for passage to America, as her service lasted only one year, beginning with her arrival in America. The reference to the mayor of Cork in her indenture is a strong clue about her former residence in Ireland, a necessary fact to know before seeking Mary among Irish records.
- Jacob Grubb was apparently transferred from the apprenticeship of one cordwainer (shoemaker) to another.
- Mary Barbara Leichtin was bound for five years to pay a debt of twenty-one pounds, nine shillings, the cost of her passage from Rotterdam.

If your ancestor was a tradesman, locating information about his apprentices could provide a wealth of information. Some apprenticeship records are available. For example, Kathy Ritter's *Apprentices of Connecticut, 1637–1900*, and Harold B.

Gill, Jr.'s *Apprentices of Virginia, 1623–1800*, contain extracts of records long lost in archives and historical collections that identify apprentices and masters.[20] Indentures can also provide clues about the home or business where the person was to serve. Sometimes the original certificates of indenture still exist as well.

Not all indentures were formal government documents. Some were private arrangements between two families in a neighborhood. While an indenture may have been written, it was never filed with a government agency. Others were arrangements made by a church for one of its members. The Society of Friends oversaw the welfare of its members and made arrangements for their care when needed. The Bradford Monthly Meeting records from 1762 indicate that the children of John Freeman are now under indenture to Robert Thorton and that Freeman himself ought to have some clothing provided for him.[21]

Research on William Plaskett of Trenton, New Jersey, led to the New Jersey Archives, which has extracts of newspaper articles published between 1704 and 1780 relative to New Jersey citizens regardless of where the paper was printed. As an example, an item extracted from the 17 September 1747 *Pennsylvania Gazette* (printed in Philadelphia) indicated that Plaskett had a bound servant named "Sarah Davis, about 27 years of age, middle stature, somewhat freckled, [who] has a small scar in her forehead, and is slow of speech." A Welshwoman, she had run away on 11 September wearing "a calico gown, a black fur hat, shagged on the upper side, with a patch on the crown, and an ozenbrigs apron."[22] This clue turned research to indenture records, which revealed that Plaskett also had another indentured servant: "Abigail Edwards (a servant from Ireland in the ship *Pomona*) . . . four years from Sept. 18th 1746, consideration 13L: customary dues."[23] The fact that William Plaskett had at least two servants during the same year, 1746–47, indicates his financial and social standing, important biographical information collected from business records.

Labor Unions

As American business grew, so did the desire of employees for better working conditions; thus labor unions were created. Because the purpose of labor unions is the improvement of employment conditions, accurate membership records are vital. Many unions have preserved volumes of records, which may contain information relevant to genealogical research. One person's description of the potential treasures vividly suggests the possibilities: "The ITU (International Typographical Union) Headquarters Basement is comprised of a labyrinth of corridors. Each corridor is replete with shelves, filing cabinets, boxes, etc. I would imagine an archivist would be delirious with joy to be [loosed] in this musty atmosphere."[24] This description came from an excellent 1960 survey conducted by the Society of American Archivists' Committee on Labor Records. The survey was sent to 265 organizations, of which 118—forty-five percent—responded, which represents about half of the labor organizations in the country. Unfortunately, some major unions, such as the United Automobile Workers, International Ladies Garment Workers, United Mine Workers, Teamsters, and most railroad and building trade unions, did not reply.

The survey (published as "Labor Union Records in the United States," by Paul Lewinson and Morris Rieger in *American Archivist*) answers several questions about the unions covered and suggests what records the nonresponding unions might have.[25] Although the original survey did not ask about membership records, many of the responses referred to this information.

When researching this source, a knowledge of the union will obviously be helpful, as well as some information about the local (or chapter of the union) to which an ancestor belonged. However, when a family lacks more specific information, the ancestor's union can often be deduced by occupation. An ancestor's residence or employer's name may be sufficient for a helpful union secretary to determine the relevant local for members working in that area, who may even know the history of the union at that company.

If an ancestor was active in one of the twentieth-century trade or labor unions, the Archives of Labor at Wayne State University in Detroit, Michigan, may have information about him or her. The Archives of Labor holds the records of many rank-and-file leaders and officers who participated in the two principal collecting areas of that archive: labor history (predominately twentieth century), with special emphasis on industrial unionism, and urban history, especially twentieth-century reform groups. The holdings include records of the American Federation of State, County, and Municipal Employees; American Federation of Teachers Newspaper Guild; Union of Farm Workers; Industrial Workers of the World; and Congress of Industrial Organizations (CIO) prior to its merger with the American Federation of Labor (AFL). (See Warner Pflug's *A Guide to the Archives of Labor History and Urban Affairs* for details.)[26] While some records are available at local archives, most will be at union or local headquarters.

Railroad Employees

The special status of railroading in America has been recognized in several ways. Railroad workers of the twentieth century received special Social Security numbers and their own pension plans until 1964. Numbers that began with 700–729 were assigned only to railroad employees. More than two million people worked for the railroad companies at their peak around 1920. Furthermore, many railroad company records are easily located. The types of records, as described in two articles in the *National Genealogical Society Quarterly*, include employment applications and files, history cards, and surgeon's certificates.[27]

Magazines and websites supply information about railroad employees and the history of the business. The *Erie Railroad*

Magazine published photos of employees. Those names are indexed and available at <http://freepages.genealogy.rootsweb.com/~sponholz/miscphoto1.html>. The same website provides a list of engineers, accident reports, depot photos, clerical association officers, and other rosters. Another website <www.rootsweb.com/~neresour/OLLibrary/Blue_Book/1920/pages/bb200169.htm> provides the average salary range for various employee positions that worked for the railroads between 1924 and 1931.

A *Biographical Directory of Railway Officials of America* was issued periodically during the nineteenth century.[28] The California State Railroad Museum Library has editions published in 1885, 1887, 1896, 1906, 1913, and 1922. It lacks the 1893 and 1901 editions. The title was published from 1885 to 1922. The same library also has some fifty drawers of employment cards for the Southern Pacific Railroad dating back to 1903.

To determine which railroads merged with another major service, consult *Moody's Transportation Manual* (known as *Mergent Transportation Manual* since 2001), issued annually by Moody's Investors Service, Inc.[29] Current and back issues are available at most public and research libraries. Various Internet sites also provide the history of the railroads and their mergers.

An ancestor who received a pension from certain railroad lines should be on record at the Railroad Retirement Board, 844 North Rush Street, Chicago, Illinois 60611-2092. The board is very helpful in answering requests for information if you can provide the employee's name, position, the railroad for which he worked, and place and dates of employment. There is a nonrefundable fee for a search, regardless of the results. The board has posted some background information online at <www.rrb.gov/mep/genealogy.asp>.

Accessibility and retention of railroad personnel records varies from company to company. Museums and historical societies often house records of local or regional railroads, as do the following examples.

- California State Railroad Museum Library, 111 I Street, Sacramento, California 95814 <www.csrmf.org> maintains employment records for the Southern Pacific Railroad. Employee cards, 1900 to 1930, are available at the Family History Library.
- Chicago Historical Society, North Ave. and Clark Street, Chicago, Illinois 60614 <www.chicagohs.org> has records for the Brotherhood of Sleeping Car Porters.
- Minnesota State Historical Society, 690 Cedar Street, St. Paul, Minnesota 55101 <www.mnhs.org> holds records of the Burlington Northern, Northern Pacific, and Great Northern railroad companies.
- San Diego Historical Society, 1649 El Prado, San Diego, California 92101 <www.sandiegohistory.org> has records for the San Diego and Arizona Railroad Company.

U.S. Government Civilian Personnel

The United States government has long employed civilians along with military personnel. The personnel records for former civilian employees are housed at the U.S. Civilian Personnel Records Center:

National Archives and Records Administration (NARA)
National Personnel Records Center
Civilian Personnel Records
111 Winnebago Street
St. Louis, Missouri 63118
<www.archives.gov/facilities/mo/st_louis/civilian_personnel_records>

These records are only accessible by mail to the former employee or next-of-kin. Personnel files retained by the federal government for employees and civil service personnel, from 1860 to 1951, have surpassed sixty million. Some files require invoking the Freedom of Information Act for access. See Claire Prechtel-Kluskens's "Documenting the Career of Federal Employees" for a concise explanation of the difficult yet potentially fruitful task of searching government personnel records.[30] The records include the date and place of employment, wages, job description, and retirement information. Additional records pertaining to this employee may also be held at another location. Check with the branch of government that employed the civilian.

The personnel file of one civilian government employee is typical of the information available. The individual began working for the U.S. Army at Fort Leavenworth. He later transferred to St. Louis, then Wyoming, Atlanta, and finally Philadelphia, where he retired. From 1876 to 1921, he worked as a clerk at various job levels. His wages and responsibilities increased during World War I, then decreased after the war, with the amounts and duties all set forth. With the locality information, his family can be traced at the various places of residence that might otherwise not be known. Some of his children followed him with every move, while others married and stayed in one of his intermediate stops. Without the valuable information found in the personnel record, any family history would be incomplete.

Social Security Records

For the genealogist, one of the largest and most valuable set of employee records are those of the Social Security Administration. When it was passed as a type of national pension fund in 1935, the Social Security Act created one the largest groups of employment records in the world as well as abundant research opportunities for today's genealogists. Some of our ancestors registered for Social Security immediately; others waited until Medicare took effect in 1966. Either way, their application is one of the most useful records available for twentieth-century ancestors.

The Social Security Administration has issued approximately 330 million numbers since 1936. Since 1988, any child older than two years of age had to have a Social Security number to be claimed as a dependent on an income tax form; today numbers for a newborn infant are requested at the time of birth. Most workers who have been employed since the system was implemented have a number. There are, however, a few exceptions. Until recently, individuals who have never worked, self-employed individuals (including farmers), some people with separate retirement plans, and government employees did not need numbers. For example, many wives who did not work outside the home did not need numbers. Nevertheless, the potential findings make a search for an ancestor's Social Security number worthwhile.

The earliest benefits were paid to individuals who were born as early as 1850 and lived until 1936, including naturalized citizens. The information on a person's specific birthplace may not be recorded anywhere else, just as there may not be any other document that proves parentage. This is especially true for people naturalized before 1906, when detailed birth information was not required for naturalization. The Social Security number itself provides a clue to the ancestor's life. The first three digits of the number indicate the state of residence where the application was made.

In order to enroll in the system, the applicant completed an "Application for Social Security Number" form, also known as an SS-5 form. This form has changed over time, but it usually required the applicant to provide his or her full name (including maiden name), complete birth date and place, parents' complete names, his or her own and employer's address when the application was made, and the date completed. Adult applicants were required to sign the form.

Not all applicants for a Social Security number were young people just beginning their careers. One woman, Mary Haviland, applied for her Social Security number when she was seventy-two years old, the age that other people are retiring. She identified her parents as Paschall Seeds and Ann Agusta Sharpnack and indicated that she was born on 13 December 1878 in Salem, Columbiana County, Ohio. At the time of the application, she was employed by the library board of Warrenton, Missouri, and was living in that town. (See figure 4-8.)

The Social Security Administration has microfilmed the application forms and computerized some of the information on the forms. After review of the microfilm, the forms were destroyed (by agreement with the archivist of the United States) because of the sheer volume of the original records.

Any requests made to the Social Security Administration should include the person's Social Security number. In many instances, the number appears on the death certificate. It may also appear on such family records as insurance policies, identification cards, and employment papers. Some local government records, such as voter lists, tax rolls, and driver's licenses, may also include the Social Security number. Private companies, such as funeral homes and credit reporting agencies, often have the number as well.

The easiest way to locate a Social Security number for individuals who died after 1964 is the Social Security Death Index (SSDI). The index includes name, number, date of birth and death, residence at time of application, and location where death benefits were paid. Understanding the locality information is especially important. Until recent laws required numbers for young children, most people did not apply for a Social Security number until they joined the work force or until they were eligible for benefits. Quite often their location at the time of application was not their birthplace. Likewise, the location where benefits were paid is not necessarily the place of death, as is the case when the deceased did not live in the same area as their beneficiary.

The SSDI is available online at several different genealogy sites, including Ancestry.com, FamilySearch.org, Genealogy.com,

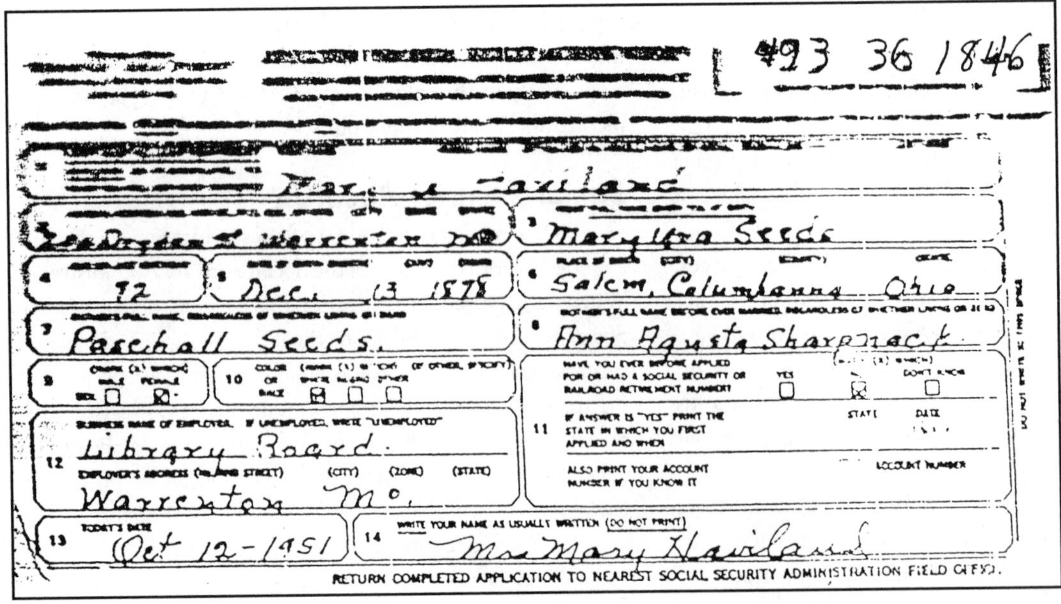

493 36 1846

4 72 — Dec. 13 1878 — Salem, Columbiana Ohio

7 Paschall Seeds — 8 Ann Agusta Sharpnack

HAVE YOU EVER BEFORE APPLIED FOR OR HAD A SOCIAL SECURITY OR RAILROAD RETIREMENT NUMBER — YES — DON'T KNOW

11 IF ANSWER IS "YES" PRINT THE STATE IN WHICH YOU FIRST APPLIED AND WHEN — STATE — DATE

BUSINESS NAME OF EMPLOYER. IF UNEMPLOYED, WRITE "UNEMPLOYED" — Library Board

12 EMPLOYER'S ADDRESS (NUMBER AND STREET) (CITY) (ZONE) (STATE) — Warrenton Mo.

ALSO PRINT YOUR ACCOUNT NUMBER IF YOU KNOW IT — ACCOUNT NUMBER

13 TODAY'S DATE — Oct 12-1951

14 WRITE YOUR NAME AS USUALLY WRITTEN (DO NOT PRINT) — Mrs Mary Haviland

RETURN COMPLETED APPLICATION TO NEAREST SOCIAL SECURITY ADMINISTRATION FIELD OFFICE.

Figure 4-8. Mary Haviland was already seventy-two years old when she completed her application for Society Security.

New England Ancestors, and RootsWeb.com. While each includes the same data, search criteria differ. If the desired record is not found at one site, a researcher should try the others. A search for Mary Haviland on the various sites produced anywhere from twenty-two to thirty-three records. Links to these sites, with background information on Social Security records and SSDI, can be found online at Cyndi's List <www.cyndislist.com/socsec.htm>.

Records Created by Customers of a Business

Insurance Records

A variety of insurance records is available for research and will provide valuable personal information. At the same time, genealogists should be aware that privacy concerns might mean some of the more recent records are closed to research.

Life Insurance

Prior to 1843, a few attempts were made to develop life insurance programs (only one, the Presbyterian Ministers Fund, established in 1758, continues to function). However, as more Americans left the relative security of the farm, the demand for life insurance, along with other kinds of insurance, notably fire and marine insurance, increased.

The growth of cities led directly to the establishment of life insurance companies.[31] Sixteen major life insurance companies formed between 1843 and 1852 survived until at least 1942. By 1875 an additional nineteen companies were founded.

The nature of life insurance makes such records very interesting for a genealogist. Early insurance contracts were brief and loosely worded, but they did contain some data about their clients. Even then, policyholders had to provide information about their lifestyle, health, age, residence, and beneficiaries, who were usually relatives. By 1865, medical information on diseases or health conditions was included, and in 1889, Mutual Life began attaching a medical examination to the policy.[32]

Due to the nature of life insurance, records are maintained for at least the life of the insured. About 1925, life insurance companies developed a formal file retention policy, with each company setting its own guidelines. Some general provisions follow:

- Applications, which were the basis for the insurance contract, are kept while the policy is in force. Applications not approved are destroyed after ten years, and the application of a deceased policyholder is destroyed after twenty years.
- The abstract, or history, cards are retained permanently. These cards contain a summary history of each account.

Other records kept permanently include account or renewal cards (records of premium payments), accumulated dividend cards, canceled checks and bank statements, cash books, directors' minutes and committee records, ledgers, payrolls, and real estate records. Because older records are the most likely to be discarded, it is wise to search relevant records as soon as possible.

The application is most useful for genealogical purposes because it contains the most personal information. Some companies keep original applications permanently or microfilm them. Even if the application is discarded, other records may be helpful in providing relevant information about residence, health, age, and so forth.

> In 1910, one company realized it had lost contact with a considerable number of policyholders or their beneficiaries to whom large sums of money were due. It undertook systematic, often lengthy, searches to find those heirs. Their files are consequently very valuable to the family historian who finds an ancestor or relative in them.[33] Several examples of how to use life insurance records to help reconstruct families can be found in Duane Galles's "Using Life Insurance Policies in Genealogical Research."[34]

The most common way of learning which company insured your ancestor is to contact living family members. Old insurance certificates or personal account books among family papers may also provide this information. Even a cancelled check or a checkbook register may lead to the name of an insurance company. Although these may be among the most difficult records to pursue, they are also among the most helpful.

An example of records that continue to be accessible to researchers are the Denver War Risk Insurance Applicants, 1916–1919. Active duty servicemen entering World War I were entitled to war insurance that provided them with compensation for disabilities or death. Beneficiaries named included wives, mother, or "wife and child." Premiums were deducted from pay during the active period of the war. After the war, serviceman could convert the policies to permanent life insurance policies. An index to Colorado records appears at <www.colorado.gov/dpa/doit/archives/military/war_risk_insurance>.

In 1887, a mutual benefit society in Detroit sold life insurance to Polish Roman Catholic immigrants. Early claims were entered in ledger books and provide limited genealogical information. The records from 1912 to 1938 (later records are not available) are more helpful, and usually include a death certificate and a membership application. Researchers may find the place of birth in Poland and information on other family members. An online index of the insured is available <www.pgsa.org/directory.htm>. Scanned images of the original records may be ordered from the

Polish Genealogical Society of America at PGSA – PRCUA, 984 North Milwaukee Avenue, Chicago, IL 60622-4101.

Abstracts of Union Pacific Railroad life insurance records are available at the Family History Center in Las Vegas, Nevada, and have been microfilmed for access through the Family History Library. Information may include Social Security number, sex, race, occupation, birth date, birthplace, addresses, names of parents, marriage date, death date, cause of death, place of burial, and spouse's name.

Insurance Maps

In order to calculate the risk of the loss of a building, insurance companies prepared maps of the neighborhood. These maps include detailed information about construction materials, number of floors, types of businesses in the area, and size of buildings. They provide an inventory of every home in urban areas of America. The largest creator of fire insurance maps was the Sanborn Company.

The Sanborn Company prepared maps for 12,000 cities from 1867 to the 1950s, providing details on each neighborhood. The Library of Congress houses over 700,000 sheets. Local libraries and societies have collections of the maps for their area. The maps are also available online at public and university libraries that subscribe to this resource. Sanborn is now owned by Environmental Data Resources, Inc., and digital images can be accessed on a subscription basis through <http://sanborn.umi.com>.

With these maps, genealogists can create a more detailed picture of their ancestor's home and neighborhood.

Property Insurance

For more than two centuries, individuals have insured their buildings—whether business or residential. Just as today, the policy holder's objective was to protect himself against financial loss in case a building was destroyed and the insurance company wanted to know the extent of its risk. Rates were determined by building materials, use, and contents. Buildings constructed of wood had higher risk levels than those of brick. Some companies would insure a factory or a livery stable only by special contract. Surveys of a property made before a policy was issued will probably provide the most detailed description available of a business or home. The policy application and history place an ancestor in a specific place at a specific time.

The Library of Virginia holds more than two hundred volumes of individual applications to the Mutual Assurance Society that date from 1796 to 1966; details of the materials and some images are available at the library's website <www.lva.lib.va.us>. Applications give details about the owner and business, and include a sketch of the building, whether it was a plantation home or a modest cottage. The Historical Society of Pennsylvania holds four sets of insurance surveys in its collection. The 1812 survey of Rachel Myers' two-story brick home at 32 Christian Street in Philadelphia describes cornices, closets, mantles, and pediments of the main home and a back building that housed the kitchen "as customary." A final note dated 28 September 1911 notes "this building remains as per survey."[35]

Freedmen Bank Records

Among the most useful sources for tracing African Americans for the period immediately after the Civil War are the records from the various branches of the Freedman's Savings and Trust Company. Chartered by Congress in 1865 to benefit former slaves, branches of this bank were established throughout the South and in some northern states. The branches kept registers of depositors with some personal and family information. While the information varied from branch to branch, it often included name, age, birthplace, residence, and names of former masters and of parents, spouse, children, and siblings. These registers through 1874 have been microfilmed by the National Archives on twenty-seven rolls of microfilm (series M816). A forty-two-volume index is available on five rolls of microfilm (series M817) or on CD-ROM. (See chapter 14, "African American Research.")

Funeral Home Records

The final business record for many ancestors was recorded by the local mortician or funeral director. The information in these records often goes beyond date and place of burial, providing details not found elsewhere. In the case of an Irish mining family in upstate New York, the mortuary records of two sons' burials in 1939 and 1942 provided the most important clues to their origins.

The death certificate, the sexton's burial record, or the obituary, if not all three, identifies the mortician or funeral home. To locate a particular mortuary or any mortuary in a particular town, consult *The Yellow Book of Funeral Directors* or the *National Directory of Morticians*. Either of these directories should be available from a local funeral director or library. This information is also available online at <www.funeral-dir.com/default.htm>. If you are searching for a funeral home by city or county, use a variety of spellings. If the city is St. Louis, look under "St. Louis," "St Louis," or "Saint Louis." Canadian funeral homes are available at <www.generations.on.ca/funeral.htm>. Locations such as Los Angeles, Philadelphia, and St. Louis need to be checked as both county and city names in catalog entries.

If the mortuary has closed, research may reveal the current owner of the records. Often a larger firm buys out a small business and transfers the records to the new owner. Unless someone inquires, those records may just sit in storage unopened. If the new owner does not want the old records, a family member may place them in storage, donate the records to a historical society, or discard the records.

Records of mortuaries and funeral homes that are no longer in operation or that have changed proprietorship can often be found in the custody of the town or county clerk, the local public library or historical society, or even university collections with a local focus. Check the *National Union Catalog of Manuscript Collections* (see chapter 3, "General References and Guides," for morticians' records deposited locally). Likewise, older records for operating funeral homes may be found at the same places. The Historical Society of Pennsylvania has records for the Oliver Bair Funeral Home from 1891. Those through 1920 have been microfilmed; the later ones are the original files. The same society also has records from other establishments, which can be identified by searching the online catalog at <www.hsp.org>. Typical of the information is the following, which is available for Karl R. Peters:

> Residence: 421 Woodbine Avenue, Narberth, Pennsylvania
> Date of death: 1 August 1924
> Birthdate and place, age: 9 April 1880, Germany, 44
> Occupation: Mech. Eng.
> Father, mother: [blank, except to note mother was from Germany]
> Place of Burial: Hazardville, Connecticut[36]

The example in figure 4-9 provides a glimpse into the life of Henry Baumeister. It states his birth date, death date, and the city in Illinois for both events. Family and friends information includes the name of his parents and where they were born, and living siblings, nieces and nephews, plus the name of the pallbearers. This record provides the cause of death, plus underlying conditions and employment history. The name of the cemetery and a plot diagram is included. Armed with this much information, a genealogist should find it easy to uncover other data on Mr. Baumeister.

A copy of the obituary is included in some funeral home records. If the obituary is not included, there is probably a reference to the name of the newspaper(s) contacted. You expect the name of the local paper(s); however, be sure to notice if it lists an out-of-town newspaper and determine why. Most likely, a close relative lived in that town or the deceased had previously lived at that location. Be sure to follow up on this type of information.

When you contact a funeral home, state your relationship to the deceased. The business may be less likely to release the records of a next-door neighbor than those of a parent or grandparent. The best time to obtain copies of these records is if you happen to be a current customer. If possible, try to remember to ask for copies of the records of previous family members when paying the bill for a current funeral. This is generally easier to remember to do if the deceased is a cousin, aunt, or uncle rather than your spouse, child, or parent.

The amount of genealogical information recorded in the early years of record keeping may be limited compared to the amount of information compiled later; however, the early records tend to list the name of the deceased, death date, place of death, cause of death, and name of the informant. Occasionally, the age, residence, occupation, birthplace, and next of kin of the deceased are included.

Modern morticians' records are more complete. The mortician gathers information needed to compile both the death certificate and obituary notice. These records are generally not available to the public, although they are available to the next of kin of the deceased.

The mortician's record should be analyzed carefully for both the information it contains and the research it suggests, such as the following:

1. Occupation. If the occupation of the deceased was unusual or governed by a labor union, investigate employment or union records, respectively.
2. Service in the armed forces. Request military service records if the ancestor was a veteran. If the mortician applied for veteran's burial benefits on behalf of the family, the branch of service will be in the record. Department of Defense Form 214, "Record of Discharge," must accompany the application for burial benefits, and a photocopy may be in the mortician's files. The branch of service may also be identified in the obituary notice.
3. Name and address of the informant. You may be able to contact the informant, or if he or she is deceased, an heir of either the informant or the deceased may own or reside in the residence listed.
4. Hospital, nursing home, or institution where the death occurred. These establishments maintain excellent records. Each institution differs on how long they will retain these records.
5. Cemetery or crematory. If the deceased was buried in a family cemetery plot, cemetery records and tombstone inscriptions will provide information about other family members buried in that plot. Figure 4-10 is a form from the cemetery file, obtained after reviewing the obituary of George F. Myers.
6. Marriage. Follow up on the marriage record to obtain details about the spouse of the deceased.
7. Religious affiliation. The name and location of the church attended by the deceased may be recorded. Church records may offer extensive information about the parents, grandparents, brothers, sisters, and children of the deceased.
8. Fraternal organizations. If the deceased was a member of the Masons, Order of the Elks, Knights of Columbus, or a similar organization, any of these records may provide biographical information.

9. Survivors. The list of survivors usually includes city of residence for family members as well as the names of married daughters, which provide excellent clues to other avenues of research in previously unknown locations.
10. Names of pallbearers. Most likely those serving in this position had some connection to the deceased.
11. Names of parents. These names can then be used to identify siblings of the deceased.

Monument Records

Monument companies keep very good records, often in the form of a card file for each tombstone etched. The name of the purchaser, the deceased, and perhaps an obituary are among their records. Some companies maintain an obituary file as a tool for future sales. They may maintain a file of all obituaries from their local newspapers or only those for burials in their area.

Locating Business Records

Once you know the name of your ancestor's business or place of employment (both former and present if still in operation), several finding aids are available in most public and research libraries to locate business records.

Interestingly enough, the survival of historical business records may turn out to be more likely for records created before 1900 than since. These early records were kept in bound volumes; some had subject or name indexes. Customer orders were kept in order books and invoices in invoice books. Correspondence was copied into letter books and accounts were entered, transaction by transaction, into ledger books. The pre-1890 system was based on double-entry bookkeeping. After 1890, index cards were popular because that data could be easily sorted and arranged. Carbon copies came into use around 1900, and loose-leaf binders, folders, and envelope-like jackets for storage were in use by the 1920s.[37]

Figure 4-9. Funeral Home record of Henry Baumeister, 1957.

IN ACCOUNT WITH: MRS. ANNA WOLF, 717 Post Place, City

KURRUS UNDERTAKING CO.

NAME: Henry Ernst Baumeister	MILITARY OR NAVAL SERVICE? No
RESIDENCE: 717 Post Place, City	HOW LONG IN U. S.? Lifetime
SOC. SEC. NO. / PHONE	HOW LONG IN CITY WHERE DEATH OCCURRED? 65 years
SINGLE, MARRIED, WIDOWED, DIVORCED: Single / HUSBAND OF (OR) WIFE OF	PHYSICIAN (LAST): Dr. C. C. Kane, Coroner
PLACE OF DEATH: Christian Welfare Hospital	CAUSE OF DEATH: Acute Coronary Thrombosis, shock from fracture right femur, arteriosclerosis, Cancer of prostate
DATE OF DEATH: August 29, 1957 DST HOUR 10:30 A M.	CHURCH - MINISTER: Rev. Rayburn Dunbar
DATE OF BIRTH: January 11, 1880	ORGANIZATIONS: Honary member of E. St. Louis Rotary Club
AGE: 77 YRS. 7 MOS. 18 DAYS HRS. OR MIN.	Active in Civic Affairs
PLACE OF BIRTH: Summerfield, Illinois	Served on E. St. Louis City Council 2 years
OCCUPATION: Commercial Agent Illinois Central R. R.	Started as a messenger in 1897 in local
YRS. ENGAGED: 53 years DATE LAST WORKED 1950	freight office.
FATHER — NAME: Ernst Baumeister AGE	DATE OF FUNERAL: Sunday, Sept. 1, 1957 1:30 P.M.
BIRTHPLACE: Germany	CEMETERY: St. Clair Memorial Park
RESIDENCE: Deceased	LOT OWNER'S NAME
	LOT NO.
MOTHER — MAIDEN NAME: Margaret Junger AGE	DATE OF SHIPMENT
BIRTHPLACE: Germany	FROM
RESIDENCE: Deceased	TO
	VIA

CHILDREN	BROTHERS	SISTERS
Nephews and nieces: Philip J. Wolf - Greenwich, Conn; Howard M. Wolf - St. Louis; Louis Baumeister - Belleville; Mrs. Elmer (Margaret) Lill, Belleville	L. E. Baumeister, 15 Granvue Drive, Belleville, Ill	Mrs. Anna Wolf, 717 Post Place, Up 3-7632

Lots: 1 Ernst; 2 Margaret; 3 Emily; 4 Henry E.; XXXXXXXX XXX; 5; 6; 7; 8; 9; 10

Removed ring and gave to Mrs. Wolf (9-17-57)

Pallbearers:
Wm. Popkess, 32 Lindorf Drive
Gene Iberg, 202 Julia Avenue
E. H. Forsing, 5147 Eichelberger, St. Louis
J. L. Burke, 3910 Connecticut St. Louis, Mo
C. M. Roos, 18 Granvue Drive
W. L. Baughman, 1341 N. 31st Street

Heavenly Melody
Rock of Ages
Old Rugged Cross

CEMETERY COPY

THE [C]ATHOLIC CEMETERIES A[S]SOCIATIONS
OF THE DIOCESE OF PITT[SBUR]GH
718 HAZELWOOD AVE., PITTSBU[RG]H 17, PA.

03177

DIVISION 2

ACCOUNT NAME Myers George DATE 6-26- 19

ADDRESS 1437 Page St. CITY Oak Pa

☑ INTERMENT DATE OF DEATH 6-25- 19

☐ REMOVAL AGE 43

☐ RECEIVING VAULT PLACE OF DEATH 1437 Page St.

NAME OF DECEASED Myers George ADDRESS same

BURIAL DATE 6-29- 19 3 TIME 9 a.m. CHURCH St. Gabriel PRIEST PERMIT ☑ UNDERTAKER Cieslak M. H.

DEED IN NAME OF Meyers Mrs. Bridget RELATIONSHIP TO DECEASED grandmother ☐ NON-CATHOLIC ☑ CATHOLIC BURIAL

1. ☐ SINGLE GRAVE SEC. ROW NO. ☐ POOR GROUND ☐ D. P. A.
2. ☐ LOT SEC. E LOT 153 GRAVES
3. ☑ OPEN GRAVE # 4 ☑ O. D. ☐ E. D. O. T. ☐ ☑ ADULT ☐ CHILD 30
4. ☑ LOWERING DEVICE AND GREENS 30
5. ☐ TENT
6. TYPE VAULT ☐ OURS ☐ OTHERS — COMPANY P. V. cave proof SIZE 6
7. ☐ DISINTERMENT OF ORIGINAL INT. MADE 19 TYPE VAULT

FROM SEC. LOT GR. TO SEC. LOT GR. ☐ O. D. ☐ E. D.

8. REASON TO RECEIVING VAULT TIME ALLOWED

SECTION	LOT NO	MONTH	YEAR	DAY	PRICE	FOLIO NUMBER
E	153					

NAME

Bridget Meyers

STREET TOWN STATE

GRAVE	BURIED	DATE	GRAVE	BURIED	DATE
1	Martin Meyers 3-20-1900 Bridget Myers 1-7-10				
2	Anna M. Meyers 1-27-36 George Meyers 5-4-51				
3	John & Ella Kane 3-20-1900				
4	Andrew Cain 12-14-03 Patrick Cain 2-17-13 removed to 602 M #2, 10-29-13				
5	George Myers -29-53				
6					

Figure 4-10. Form from a cemetery file of the Catholic Cemeteries Association of the diocese of Pittsburgh.

The success or failure of your search may depend on your correspondence with the company. Remember when contacting companies that, while they may be consumer-conscious, genealogy is not their business. In your initial letter, explain that you have an interest in the company's history because of a family connection and would like to know if information such as that found in personnel and employment records is available. Remember, these are generally private records, and company policy may restrict access to them.

Many companies prefer to control the searches of their archives themselves, allowing access only to trained staff or volunteers. For example, the Pullman Car Works established search arrangements with the South Suburban Genealogical and Historical Society for its massive file of personnel records. Only society members who belong to the "Pullman Committee" may search records for the more than 200,000 individuals in the collection.[38]

Almost every manuscript collection has some kind of guide to indicate its contents, and many have online catalogs to search. If the Genealogical Society of Utah microfilmed the collection, a copy is available in the *Family History Library Catalog* under the locality with which the record is concerned and is available at the Family History Library or on loan through its Family History Centers. Indentures for Spotsylvania County, Virginia, are found under that county in the catalog.

In New York City, the minutes of the Civil Court Quarter Sessions contain petitions of release from apprentices whose masters have moved from the town. Indenture records of passengers to America are usually in the city where the ship landed—such port cities as Philadelphia, Baltimore, and New York.

Genealogical and historical societies are publishing colonial business records, either as books or as articles in periodicals. Either the Genealogical Periodical Annual Index (GPAI) or Periodical Source Index (PERSI) will help with a literature search for that area. See chapter 3, "General References and Guides," for more details.

For ancestors about whom little is known other than a very general occupational description from a census record or city directory, it may be necessary to consult other sources to identify possible business connections before trying to locate business records. A variety of dictionaries and directories, as discussed next, may be helpful in this regard.

Biographical Dictionaries

Collections of biographies can be very helpful to researchers since they determine the business activities of an ancestor who would not be the subject of an individual book. Some collections are based on a specific occupation, such as the legal directories mentioned previously. For Pennsylvania ancestors with political activities, the recent *Lawmaking and Legislators: A Biographical Dictionary* includes sketches of members of the Pennsylvania state government.[39]

Men of many occupations were included in biographical dictionaries as were people who achieved some prominence in a vocation. In *Biographical Sketches of Knox County (Ohio) Writers*, Mary Q. Elliott included a brief sketch of James Blair, a local farmer who wrote poems that were occasionally published in local newspapers.[40] The sketch indicated that Blair originally came from Blairs Valley, Washington County, Maryland. Subsequent research in Blairs Valley extended the line two more generations.

A variety of specialized sources are available, such as the *Biographical Directory of Railway Officials of America*, published since 1885.[41]

Robert B. Slocum's *Biographical Dictionaries and Related Works* lists dozens of books about authors and others distinguished by their vocations.[42] Indeed, Slocum's entire second volume is a list of vocational collective biographies.

Some directories profile major figures in American history. Many of these individuals were prominent businessmen. Major national collective biographies include the *Dictionary of American Biography* (first published in 1922), the *National Cyclopedia of American Biography*, and a wide variety of "who's who" publications. The *Cyclopedia* began in 1898 by the James T. White Company of New York to give biographical coverage to business leaders, especially young men from the west, with information supplied by the subjects themselves.

Most of these nationwide dictionaries are indexed in *Biography and Genealogy Master Index*, discussed in chapter 3, "General References and Guides." It is easy to check and is available in most research libraries.

With the conclusion of the Civil War and the reunification of the country, American business began to grow rapidly. As businesses grew, so did the amount of records they kept. Only two to six ancestors may have been in the labor force around the year 1900, but odds are that half of them were either working for someone else (hence employed) or in business for themselves (thus creating their own business records). By 1880, farming involved only fifty percent of the work force, and even farming activities were more regularly documented.

Photographs in family records, even unidentified ones, often show owners and employees of local shops and mercantile businesses standing in front of the company sign.

Most residential directories (both city and rural) include the employer's name for each listing. It does not matter if the ancestor lived in a small town or a large city, as directories exist for most areas. The following extract from the 1922 directory of Missoula, Montana, then considered a small town, shows the kind of information you can expect to find.

> Sterriet George H. lab Missoula White P S Co. h rear 601 Phillips

Stetson Harry E, mail carrier R F D 2
Stevens Clare, appr G A Meisinger, r 1529 De Foe
Stevens Harry H, driver, h 208 S 3rd W
Stevens John M, carmn N O Ry, r 117 N 2n W
Stevens Lyman W brkmn N P Ry, r 117 N 2n W
Stevens Russell, student, r 405 S 1st W
Stevenson Derrick, moved to Boxeman, Mont
Stewart C Donald, clk C M & St P Ry, h 246 Edith
Stewart Dee, chauf H L Haines, r 314 W Railroad
Stewart Fleming K, surveyor Forest Service, r Grand Hotel
Stewart Jas A, firemn N P Ry, h 402 W Cedar
Stewart Leighton, formn N P Ry, h 1520 S 7th W
Stewart R D, clk, h Orchard Homes R F D 1
Stewart Thomas, car opr, h Orchard Homes R F D 4
Stewart Wm m, mgr Traffic Service Vureau, h Rattlesnake
Sticht Bert, lab Anton Vogt & Sons, h East Missoula
Sticht Glenn, lab Anton Vogt & Sons, h East Missoula[43]

Note that both the occupation and employer are given. The Northern Pacific Railroad (NPR) appears to have been a major employer. Bert and Glenn Sticht are laborers for Anton Vogt and Sons. This valuable information was previously not known to Sticht family historians.

Local history sources can also identify business firms with which a relative was associated. Centennial histories or local scrapbooks published in special sections of the newspaper or issued separately for distribution at local celebrations often carry lists of historical businesses.

Business Directories

The best method of finding records of existing businesses is to contact the business directly. Although locating addresses for the thousands of smaller companies may require some sleuthing, contact information for the largest companies are found in many sources. One excellent layman's guide to four hundred of the largest U.S. companies is Milton Meskowitz's *Everybody's Business: A Field Guide to the 400 Leading Companies in America.*[44] This book profiles each company in everyday terms, avoiding business jargon and technical language. Among information of interest to a genealogist would be the year of founding, the company's history, the number of employees, and most importantly, whom to contact at the home office for general information. Other books useful for locating company contact information are in the References section.

The complicated world of modern business often makes it difficult to determine whether a company is independent or a subsidiary of a larger corporation. Dun and Bradstreet's annual *America's Corporate Families* helps to clarify the confusion.[45] This directory includes the "family tree" of 11,000 U.S. parent corporations and their 60,000 subsidiaries, indicating which companies own which others. It lists the mergers, acquisitions, name changes, divisions, subsidiaries, and affiliates of most major American corporations.

Once you know the company you are looking for, you still need to know where the office is located. The annual *Ward's Business Directory of U.S. Private and Public Companies* is considered by many to be the best directory in its field and is useful for both large and small companies.[46] In it, each company is listed alphabetically, geographically, by industry, and by amount of sales. Current business address and telephone numbers are provided. The *Ward's Business Directory* may be available through one of your public library subscription databases.

Several other sources list business firms from the past or supply the clues needed to determine the name of a historical business and its dates of operation. Using these records is complicated; so much so that the process has been called the "dragnet" strategy by William G. Roy in "Collecting Data on American Business Officials in the Late Nineteenth and Early Twentieth Century."[47] These materials are available in public and research libraries.

In addition to Dun and Bradstreet's *Directory of Corporate Affiliations* and *Million Dollar Directory*, the *Robert D. Fisher Manual of Valuable and Worthless Securities* lists businesses reorganized, liquidated, or dissolved.[48] Both directories are published annually and are available in the business/economic section of most public and university libraries.

Other directories include Poor's *Manual of Railroads* and Moody's *Manuals* with separate volumes for railroads, municipal governments, banks and finance, and public utilities. Published annually since 1900 by Moody's Investors Service, Inc., a division of Dun and Bradstreet, these directories omit some of the most important companies, such as Carnegie Steel and Standard Oil. They are also less likely to cover decentralized industries, such as books, shoes and boots, and the lumber industry.

Trade Association Directories

Members of most vocations have banded together to exchange information, learn from each other, assess competition, and provide referrals. Generally, these groups have taken the form of trade associations, most of which publish regular directories of their members. Farley's *Reference Directory of Booksellers, Stationers, and Printers in the U.S. and Canada,* published since 1886, and the *Pocket Directory of Shoe Manufacturers*, published by the *Boot and Shoe Reporter* since 1907, are examples of trade directories—although they are now, like most older directories, superseded by different directories and titles. The National Electric Light Association (1923), the National Retail Dry Goods Association (1934), and the National Fire Protection Association (1935) are some of the trade associations that publish directories of members with their specific affiliations. Current trade association directories are listed in the annual *Directories in Print*.[49]

Several references provide information on associations. *Encyclopedia of Associations*, published biannually by Gale Research Company, includes precise addresses, telephone numbers, titles, and frequency of bulletins and newsletters published, library information services offered, employment exchanges, and many other facts and figures for trade associations, many of which have a continuous history from the mid-nineteenth century to the present. Information about more than 12 million current businesses is available at <www.referenceusa.com>. This Internet-based reference service may be available through your local library.

Trade Journals

Periodicals and news sheets have been published for the shipping and maritime industry, for agriculture, and for many other trades since the mid-nineteenth century. Books about an industry may include a discussion of periodicals devoted to the industry. For example, a list of agricultural journals is in Albert L. Demaree's *The American Agricultural Press, 1819–1860*.[50] Periodical sources are traditional materials to consult when checking for historical businesses of any size, and they are as close as your nearest research library. However, if local libraries do not have the volumes you want, check collections in libraries of those cities and towns where the industry was most common. For example, try Pittsburgh for the steel industry, San Francisco or Seattle for the Pacific shipping trade, and Atlanta and Savannah for the turpentine industry.

Manuscript Collections

In 1959, the Library of Congress began a catalog of manuscripts housed throughout the country. Known as the National Union Catalog of Manuscript Collections (NUCMC), it is issued yearly with information on more than two thousand newly cataloged manuscript collections each year.

Through the 1993 catalog (the last catalog to be published), approximately 72,300 collections located in 1,406 repositories had been identified. These annual print catalogs are indexed, and comprehensive cumulative indexes cover 1959 to 1962, 1963 to 1966, 1967 to 1969, and every four or five years thereafter. After 1993, an electronic database was used in lieu of more print editions. This database continues to incorporate current catalog additions and has been made retroactive to 1985. This database can be accessed at <http://lcweb.loc.gov/coll/nucmc/>, along with a list of frequently asked questions. A list of repositories that currently participate in NUCMC is available at <http://lcweb.loc.gov/coll/nucmc/nucmcrepos.html>.

A wealth of information on defunct and current business and employment records can be found in these indexes. For example, Joseph Stulb of Philadelphia worked for Schrack and Company, a nineteenth-century paint firm. The NUCMC index lists the following:

> STULB, Joseph Jr. 72–121
> SCHRACK (C.) and Company, Philadelphia, Pa 72–121

This citation means that they both appear in the collection cataloged 72–121, which was the 121st collection cataloged in 1972. The Schrack entry reads as follows:

> MS 72-121
> Schrack (C) and company, Philadelphia, Pa. Records, 1808–1938. ca. 200,000 items.
> In Eleutherian Mills Historical Library (Greenville, Del.) (various accessions)
>
> Correspondence, accounts, bills and receipts, stock books, formula books (1844–1912), orders, shipping records, banking records, and other business records of a paint, varnish, and color manufacturing firm. Persons represented include Christian Schrack (ca. 1790–1854.), founder of the firm, who began business as a carriage builder; his partner, Joseph Stulb (d. 1898); Stulb's sons, Edwin H Stulb (1850–1920) and Joseph Stulb Jr.; his grandsons, Joseph Reichert Stulb (b.1883) and Edwin H. Stulb, Jr.; and Townsend Willits.
>
> In part, described in A guide to the Manuscripts in the Eleutherian Mills Historical Library, by John B. Riggs (1970) p. 970–971.
>
> Gift 1966 and purchases, 1965–68.[51]

This collection is a wonderful find—approximately two hundred thousand items pertaining to Schrack and Company, Joseph Stulb, his sons, and his grandsons. The entry indicates that the collection is not in Philadelphia or even in Pennsylvania, but rather in a historical library in Delaware. It is worth noting that NUCMC also includes the manuscript collections of several labor unions.

A special cumulative index to the printed NUCMC volumes will speed the finding of business-related collections. This is the three-volume companion publication, *Corporate Names Index, 1959–1984*. This work brings together the names of corporate entities that appeared in the NUCMC for the years indicated. As indicated in the Schrack and Company example, NUCMC helps to identify collections that are "out of place" rather than in the repositories where they might be expected to be found. This index and the NUCMC series are described more fully in chapter 3, "General References and Guides."

Obviously, not all manuscript collections have been cataloged in NUCMC. Thousands of specific archives also exist that may be affiliated with the company you are researching. The *Directory of Archives and Manuscript Repositories in the United States*, published by the National Historical Publications and Records Commission, describes the manuscript holdings of 4,225 repositories and identifies 335 additional institutions.[52] Arranged geographically, the directory also includes a list of repositories by type, including corporate archives, local historical societies, organizational archives, state and university archives, and thirteen other types of repositories. However, even this list is not complete. The directory itself estimates that between six thousand and eleven thousand such repositories exist in the country, any number of which may contain business records. The Repositories of Primary Sources <www.uidaho.edu/special-collections/Other.Repositories.html> provides 5,250 websites that describe manuscripts and archival collections.

Historical Society Holdings

Numerous business records have been deposited in historical societies across the country. Most societies publish an annual report, a quarterly journal, archive inventories, and/or guides to their principal collections in which each set of records is described with dates, names of owners, types of records deposited, restrictions on use (if any), and size of collection. Sample entries from *Manuscripts of the Historical Society of Pennsylvania* follow. The collection includes both company and personal business records.

> 1009. PHILADELPHIA CENTRE SQUARE WATERWORKS. 1801–6. 1 Vol. Presented by the Jenkintown Trust Co., 1936. List of first Subscribers.
>
> 1019. PHILADELPHIA INSURANCE COMPANY. 1814–45. 1 vol. Presented by Mrs. Howard W. Page, 1934. Minutes, accounts, names of officers, and records of general transactions.
>
> 1025. PHILADELPHIA SUGAR REFINING COMPANY RECORDS. 1812. 1 vol. Presented by A.C. Kline, 1863. Articles of association, list of stockholders, constitution, bylaws, and other data.
>
> 108. PERSONAL and PROFESSIONAL RECORDS. 1676–1904. Approximately 500 vols.
>
> John Q. A. McConkey, canal boat owner and shipper (Delaware and Raritan Canal), invoice book, 1877–79, 1 vol.
>
> Mary Ann, John Q.A., and James McConkey, canal boat transportation, boat book, 1847–80. 1 vol.
>
> William McCorkle, advertising and periodical dealer, ledger 1804–87, 1 vol.
>
> James McCurrah and Company, shipping agents, accounts current, 1790–96. 1 vol.: letter book, 1794–1800. 1 vol.
>
> George Mead, shipper and general merchant, receipt book, 1784–88, 1 vol.
>
> David Meredith, Philadelphia merchant, memorandum, and account book, 1813–17, 1 vol.
>
> Jonathan Meredith, Philadelphia tanner, hide accounts, waste, leather, sales, bark, ledger, day, and blotter books, 1784–1800, 34 vols.[53]

Subject Collections

The most comprehensive coverage of unique library collections is *Subject Collections: A Guide to Special Book Collections and Subject Emphasis,* edited by Lee Ash.[54] It is especially valuable for special manuscript collections in public libraries, which are not described in other publications. Sample entries under *Business* are as follows:

> Atlanta Public Library, Ivan Allen, Jr. Dept. of Science.
> Industry & Government. Richard L. Tubesing, Head.
> 10 Pryor Street Atlanta, GA 30303
> Vols. (15,000) Cat. Microfilms
> Budget ($75,000)
>
> Notes: This collection incl. on microform annual reports and Securities Exchange Commission 10-k reports for some 11,000 companies from 1976 to date; current and retrospective stock quotations, stock reports, corporate and industry records and directories and supporting loose-leaf services; information file on Atlanta's largest 10,000 companies from 1976 to date, with annual updates; and current plat maps for the five county Metro-Atlanta area. Atlanta and Georgia business history sections are being developed. Most material in this collection is non-circulating. Telephone ready reference service is provided.
>
> Pomona Public Library, Special Collections
> David Streeter, Libn.
> 625 S. Garey Avenue
> Mailing Add.: P.O. Box 2271
> Pomona, CA 91766
> Uncat. Mss.
>
> Notes: 165 linear feet of Pomona Valley business records incl. 16 water companies and 28 citrus companies; diaries; clubs and organizations; Laura Ingalls Wilder.

Bibliographies

Special bibliographies also carry references to business archives. An annotated list of more than four hundred articles and books on business archives is in Karen M. Benedict's *A Select Bibliography on Business Archives and Records Management.*[55] An example of a bibliography that includes reference to business archives is *Oral History Collection*, edited and compiled by Alan M. Meckler and Ruth McMullin.[56] In it, oral history programs are listed by company, project, or person. Some sample entries follow:

> WEYERHAEUSER, C.D. with C.S. Martin, Weyerhaeuser Timber Company (98 pages, permission required) *Columbia University NY.*
>
> WEYERHAEUSER, CHARLES A. Discussed in Columbia University interview with William L. Maxwell.
>
> WEYERHAEUSER, FREDERICK KING (1895–___) Industrialist. Weyerhaeuser Timber Company (1956, 167 pages, permission required) Columbia University NY.
>
> WEYERHAEUSER, JOHN PHILIP, JR. (1899-1956) Weyerhaeuser Timber Company (41 pages, permission required) Columbia University NY. Discussed in Columbia University interview with Albert B. Curtis.
>
> WEYERHAEUSER TIMBER COMPANY Participants and pages: Volume I: A.E. Aitchison, 85; John Aram, 98; David H. Bartlett, 59; Jack Bishop, 32; Ralph Boyd, 26; Hugh B. Campbell 32; Norton Clapp, 32; R.V. Clute, 65; T.S. Durment, 45; O.D. Fisher, 73; A.N. Frederickson, 71; John H. Hauberg, 126; E.F. Heacox, C.S. Martin and C.D. Weyerhaeuser, 98; F.W. Hewitt, 66; Robert W. Hunt, 85; C.H. Ingram, 12; R.E. Irwin, 40; S.P. Johns, Jr., 46; Don Lawerence, 66; George S. Long, Jr., 46 R.R. Macartney, 44; Charles J. McGough, 66 William L. Maxwell, 112; Howard Morgan, 54; C.R. Musser, 27; Leonard H. Nygaard, 49; Harold H. Ogle, 47; Arthur Priaulx and James F. Stevens, 75; Al Raught, 54; Otto C. Schoenwerk, 40; A. O. Sheldon, 41; H.C. Shelworth, 77; Frand Tarr, 17; G. Harris Thomas, 63; David S. Troy, 36; Roy Voshmik,16; John A. Wahl, 18; Frederick K. Weyerhaeuser, 167; J. Philip Weyerhaeuser, 41; Maxwell W. Williamson, 38. Volume II; Earl R. Bullock, 32; Albert B. Curtis, 103; Wells Gilbert, 26; Roy Huffman, 68; W.K. McNair, 33; Leslie Mallory, 13 S.G. and C.D. Moon, 32; Jack Morgan, 43; J.J. O'Connell, 77; R.E. Saberson, 81; Hugo Schlenck, 113; Gaylord M. Upington and Lafayette Stephens, 75 (1956, 2981 pages, permission required) Columbia University NY.

American Archivist

Each issue of the *American Archivist*, published quarterly by the Society of American Archivists since 1936, contains reviews of new archival guides and "News and Notes" describing the transfer of business records to local archives. To keep track of new collections made available for research, genealogists must review every issue of the *American Archivist*. Copies are available at public and research libraries.

Institutional Records

An entire volume could—and should—be written about institutional records, possibly the most neglected genealogical sources currently available to researchers. Facilities that have cared for individuals through the years have created a multitude of records useful for genealogical research. Some of the institutions discussed in this section are private while others are public in nature and are funded by some level of government. In many cases, involvement with an institution was not entirely a matter of choice: children were placed in orphanages by adults, and convicts were sent to prison after a court decision. Some institutions could also be described as businesses; their placement in this section is a matter of choice. Whatever the ancestor's background, thorough genealogists will try to locate records of any institution known or suspected of having an ancestral connection.

Almshouse/House of Refuge/Poorhouse

Almshouses were established over one thousand years ago, and since that time most societies have made provisions of some type to care for the citizens who could not care for themselves. Depending on the time period, the location, and the type of care provided, the facility might be known as an almshouse, a house of refuge, a poorhouse, or a poor farm. More often than not, they are government funded and operated, frequently on the county level.

Our ancestors may have resided in of one these facilities for any number of reasons. In some cases, their stay was brief; in others, it may have lasted for a number or years or even for most of their lives. Many times they had no family in the area to take over their care. One group of residents was the elderly, who because of illness or the effects of aging simply could not care for themselves any more. Another group was those who suffered from a debilitating illness or handicap that prevented them from working. Still another was children whose parents could not care for them.

Just as the type of support offered varies with the individual institution, so do the records vary. Most of them include the name of the occupant, sex, age, race, and dates of admission and discharge. The record may include health information and date of death if the resident died at the facility. More detailed records might also add marital status, names and birthplaces of parents, personal habits, and amount of education. Typical of the records are those of Shelby County, Illinois. Published abstracts show name, age, sex, state or country of birth, and date of admission (see figure 4-11). The original *Almshouse Register for Shelby County, Illinois* also shows occupation before admission, marital status, birthplace of parents, ability to read or write, health, habits, property brought to the almshouse, authority for admission, and cause of pauperism.[57]

The current location of the records will of course vary. Many remain in the custody of the county, either in the courthouse or an archives facility. Others are found in the offices of the institution that replaced the almshouse. If the county nursing home of today occupies the site of the former county poor farm, the farm's records may well be at the nursing home. Still other records may have been retained by the last director and are now in the hands of descendants. Some records have been microfilmed by the Family History Library and can be located by searching for available county records. Others are identified and located by searching the county's own Web pages or a genealogy list for the county.

A wide variety of records are available online. Some examples follow:

1. Pauper information is available in census records as displayed in this Page County, Iowa, example <www.censusdiggins.com/page_county_iowa_almshouse.html>.
2. Mercer County, Illinois, almshouse records, 1858–1948, at the Illinois Secretary of State website <www.sos.state.il.us/departments/archives/mercer.html#poor>.
3. Morgan County, Colorado, old age pensions, 1933–36, at <www.colorado.gov/dpa/doit/archives/oap/morgan.html>.
4. Warren County, New York, poorhouse records at <www.co.warren.ny.us/records>.

51. George Forsythe	38	M	Md	Nov 9 1875
52. Mary E. Bland	25	F	Il	Jan 8 1876
53. Nancy J. Powel	20	F	Il	Jan 8 1876
54. William E. Powel	5	M	Il	Jan 13 1876
55. John Ryan	65	M	Ire	Jan 29 1876
56. Leon Smith	42	M	Ger	Feb 3 1876
57. Margaret Griffith	55	F	Il	Feb 3 1876
58. Pheba Griffith	43	F	Il	Feb 3 1876
59. Ewing Griffith	13	M	Il	Feb 3 1876
60. Charles Griffith	8	M	Il	Feb 8 1876
61. Daniel McCoy	22	M	Ky	Feb 11 1876
62. William Riley	50	M	Ire	Feb 25 1876
63. William McCabe	38	M	Ire	Feb 25 1876
64. Sarah Sample	31	F	Oh	Feb 25 1876
65. Benjamin Myers	40	M	Il	Feb 25 1876
66. George Myers	8	M	Il	Feb 25 1876
67. Oscar Reynolds	6	M	Il	Feb 25 1876
68. Edward Reynolds	6	M	Il	Mar 3 1876
69. L. Reynolds	5	M	Il	Apr 8 1876
70. James Everet	3	M	Il	Apr 8 1876
71. George Forsythe	?	M	Md	Apr 8 1876
72. Alva Jones	25	F	Mo	Apr 8 1876
73. Charles Purkey	26	M	Il	Apr 10 1876
74. Nolan Purkey	6	M	Il	Apr 19 1876
75. Margaret Jones	4	F	Il	May 11 1876
76. Mary Fleming	1	F	Il	May 11 1876
77. Mary A. Smith	10	F	Il	May 11 1876
78. Peter Smith	3	M	Il	May 11 1876
79. Lovina Martin	21	F	Il	May 11 1876
80. Mary Wilburn	28	F	Il	May 11 1876
81. John Wilburn	3	M	Il	May 11 1876
82. Nevil Davis	38	M	Ky	May 12 1876
83. Sarah Davis	37	F	Il	May 12 1876
84. Nancy Davis	14	F	Il	May 12 1876
85. George Davis	1	M	Il	May 12 1876
86. Raleigh Spurgin	69	M	Ky	May 23 1876
87. Isable Davis	8	F	Il	May 12 1876

Figure 4-11. Several apparent family groups are among the people admitted to the almshouse in these abstracted records prepared by Phyllis Hapner and Judy Graven, *Almshouse Register for Shelby County, Illinois* (N.p.: typescript, 1985). Additional information found in the original volume at the County Clerk's office includes birthplace, age, sex, color, and birthplace of parents.

A typical entry from the Warren County records shows that Homer Jackson was a seventy-year-old black male, a widower, who was admitted to the almshouse in 1880 and died in 1882. Homer stated his father and mother were slaves in Arkansas before they bought their freedom.

Civilian Conservation Corps

"There is hereby established the Civilian Conservation Corps, hereinafter called the Corps, for the purpose of providing employment, as well as vocational training, for youthful citizens of the United States who are unemployed and in need of employment, and to a limited extent as hereinafter set out, for war veterans and Indians, through the performance of development of the natural resources of the United States, its territorial and insular possessions: PROVIDED, That at least ten hours each week may be devoted to general education and vocation training: . . ."[58]

The Civilian Conservation Corps, or CCC, was one of several programs designed to help the country recover from the economic depression that followed the 1929 stock market crash. The CCC started in 1933 and was open to young men age seventeen to twenty-one years of age. Over 4,500 CCC camps were established throughout the United States, employing more than a half million men. Corpsman are credited for planting three billion trees, building bridges, tending to soil conservation, and many other well-needed tasks. Men were sent to camps, often far from home, where they were assigned jobs and lodging. They were expected to send $25 of the $30 monthly salary home to their family.

Corpsmen restored historical structures, developed state parks, established and maintained tree nurseries, built dams, developed wildlife streams and trails, improved beaches, and stocked waterways with fish. They built drinking fountains, fences, lodges, lookout towers, museums, and wildlife shelters.

The CCC came to an end when the attack on Pearl Harbor brought the United States into World War II. Funding was then directed to the war efforts. Many of the same young men went on to serve in the war.

More than likely the genealogist consulting CCC records has already found some clue that indicates participation in the program. Clues can include an original enrollment card, information from an obituary, photographs, or a family tradition. It might be necessary to research several camps before discovering the sought-after ancestor.

A variety of records survive from the camps:

- Enrollment Cards, which supply the name and address of the enrollee, their designated allottee's name and address, date service began, camp assignment, discharge date, and reason for discharge.
- Applications and discharge notifications, which may contain related correspondence.
- Narrative reports.
- Discharge certificates (see figure 4-12).
- Manuals and handbooks documenting enrollment policies, rules, and procedures.
- Correspondence, including letters to and from enrollees about camp experiences.
- Rosters indicating those enrolled at a given camp on a given date.
- Station lists, arranged by type of camp, which include camp locations and project information.
- Photographs documenting both projects and camp life.

Original CCC camp records are available at the Civilian Records Textual Archives at the National Archives in College Park, Maryland. A list of states and campsites within each state can be found on the website for the National Association of Civilian Conservation Corps Alumni (NACCCA) <www.cccalumni.org>. The national headquarters for the NACCCA is located at Jefferson Barracks in St. Louis, Missouri. Formed in 1977, it currently has more than sixty chapters nationwide.

Camp personnel files are available by written request only at the NARA Civilian Personnel Records Center. Further information is available at the NACCCA headquarters and museum at

National Association of Civilian Conservation Corps Alumni (NACCCA)
16 Hancock
P.O. Box 16429
St. Louis, MO 63125-0429

This museum houses many artifacts donated by former CCC alumni and their families, such as camp rosters, copies of enlistment and discharge papers, and camp photos, identified by the company number, which document the camp life. The museum also has handbooks, manuals, menus, and other assorted original documents from the camps as well as original copies of the *Happy Days* weekly newspaper, which are also on microfilm. Alumni and descendants may contact the museum for further information and copies of available documents for a nominal fee.

The company number and name are the key factors to unlock the museum resources. If that information is unknown, write to the National Archives Civilian Personnel Record Center to obtain a copy of the discharge paper for your ancestor. Request all documents that are in the personnel file, not just the discharge paper. This file should include a record of service, a payment record, medical documents, and an enlistment document. An application form and instructions are available at <www.nara.gov>.

Honorable Discharge
from the
Civilian Conservation Corps

EMERGENCY CONSERVATION WORK · 1933 · CCC

TO ALL WHOM IT MAY CONCERN:

This is to Certify That* Larry D. Dallas CC6-281079 a member of the CIVILIAN CONSERVATION CORPS, who was enrolled October 20, 1939 (Date) at 2604th Co. CCC Galesburg, Illinois, is hereby HONORABLY DISCHARGED therefrom, by reason of** EXPIRATION OF TERM OF ENROLLMENT FOR CONVENIENCE OF U. S.

Said Larry D. Dallas was born in [illegible] in the State of Illinois When enrolled he was [illegible] years of age and by occupation a Laborer He had Brown eyes, Brown hair, fair complexion, and was [illegible] feet [illegible] inches in height. His color was WHITE

Given under my hand at 1660th Co. CCC [illegible], Illinois, this thirtieth day of September, one thousand nine hundred and [illegible]

Daniel R. [illegible] (Name) (Title)

* Insert name, as "John J. Doe."
** Give reason for discharge.

C. C. C. Form No. 2
April 5, 1937

Figure 4-12. A discharge certificate like this one from the Civilian Conservation Corps may lead to other useful genealogical information.

Coroner or Medical Examiner

A coroner or medical examiner is contacted when an unnatural or unattended death occurs.

This includes disasters, homicides, suicides, and accidents. When so many individuals perished after the *Titanic* sank, the recovered bodies were taken to Halifax, Nova Scotia, where the local medical examiner prepared a report on each victim. John Jacob Astor was one person whose body was found (see figure 4-13).

If a death certificate is available, look at the signature of the medical official. Was it the doctor, coroner, or the medical examiner? If it was either of the last two, other records may be available for research.

The coroner is a position that was brought to this country from England in the 1600s. The county sheriff worked with the coroner, and often the same person held both offices. The coroner may be appointed or elected to the county position. County court records may indicate that your ancestor was paid to be the coroner or served on the jury that made the official finding based on his evidence. Coroners' records are available in most counties. Some records date back to the 1700s, while others are just a few years old. Unfortunately, this type of record has not been retained in all locations. Some counties have only a ledger book others have the complete file.

During the 1970s, the coroner in large cities was replaced by a medical examiner. The medical examiner must be an M.D., while the coroner may or may not be. A rural community probably has a county coroner who is also the local funeral home director, sheriff, or area physician. The official change from a coroner to that of a medical examiner eventually leads to a change in record access. While records created by a coroner are open to the public, medical examiner's records are only available to the next of kin.

Coroner records (and perhaps some early medical examiner records) may be maintained at the morgue, local historical society, or state archives. Some have been microfilmed, while others are in the original packets. To locate a record in the Family History Library Catalog, search by location, then look under Vital Records or Court Records. Other libraries and archives catalog these records in a similar manner.

The Genealogical Society of Utah has microfilmed some of the early coroner records of metropolitan cities. Figure 4-14 is the first page of a five-page entry from the Coroner's Evidence Book of Philadelphia County, Pennsylvania, recording Isadore Raimonda's fatal stabbing of Dominic Raimonda in 1876. It does not contain extensive genealogical information, stating specifically only the deceased's name, age,

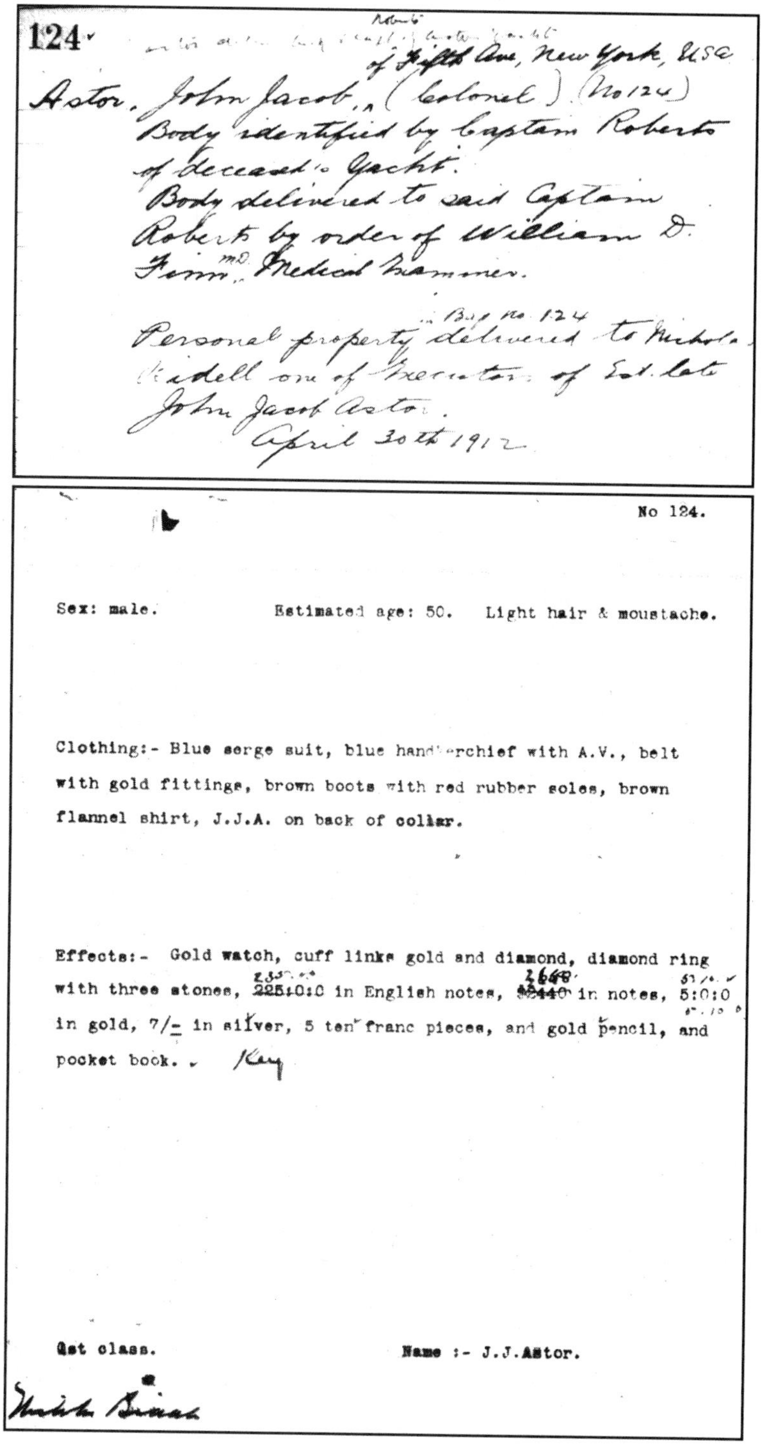

124

Astor, John Jacob, of Fifth Ave, New York, USA (Colonel) (No 124)
Body identified by Captain Roberts of deceased's Yacht.
Body delivered to said Captain Roberts by order of William D. Fenn, M.D. Medical Examiner.

Personal property Bag no. 124 delivered to Nicholas Ridell one of Executors of Est. late John Jacob Astor.
April 30th 1912

No 124.

Sex: male. Estimated age: 50. Light hair & moustache.

Clothing:- Blue serge suit, blue handkerchief with A.V., belt with gold fittings, brown boots with red rubber soles, brown flannel shirt, J.J.A. on back of collar.

Effects:- Gold watch, cuff links gold and diamond, diamond ring with three stones, 225:0:0 in English notes, 2440 in notes, 5:0:0 in gold, 7/- in silver, 5 ten franc pieces, and gold pencil, and pocket book.

1st class. Name :- J.J.Astor.

Figure 4-13. Pages from the coroner file of John Jacob Astor. The top image reads, "Astor, John Jacob, <of Fifth Ave, New York, USA> (Colonel) (No 124) Body identified by Captain Roberts of deceased's Yacht. Body delivered to said Captain Roberts by order of William D. Fenn, <M.D.> Medical Examiner. Personal property <in Bag no. 124> delivered to Nicholas Ridell one of Exectutors of Est. late John Jacob Astor. April 30th 1912." The second pages show the coroners report of the clothing and effects on Astor's person. Notice the handwritten changes, possible made by Nicholas Ridell, who received Astor's body and whose signature is at the bottom of the sheet.

height, and date and cause of death, the hospital to which the deceased was taken, and the name of the attending physician. The jury's verdict is given; Isadore Raimonda was convicted of manslaughter, suggesting a search of prison records.

The records of the coroner or medical examiner (if open) should be examined even when a government-issued death certificate is available. These records, particularly those dated after 1960, will usually contain more detailed information about the death and sometimes about the deceased, leading to clues for additional research; the information found in figure 4-14 suggests several possibilities:

1. Names of the deceased and the defendant. Although not specifically stated, the record implies that Isadore and Dominic were cousins. Approach any further research with this possibility in mind.
2. Translator. The police officer interviewed the wounded Dominic with a translator, so the dying man may have been a recent immigrant. Naturalization records may show if either Dominic or Isadore had petitioned for or received citizenship.
3. Hospital. Check hospital records that still exist for more information.
4. Verdict. The record concludes with the report that Isadore was convicted of manslaughter and sentenced, a notation made later after the appropriate court has dealt with the case. Prison records may contain additional biographical facts about Isadore Raimonda.
5. The coroner also issues death certificates. This document generally provides the deceased's name, age, sex, place of birth, race, occupation, marital status, place of death, date of death, and cause of death.

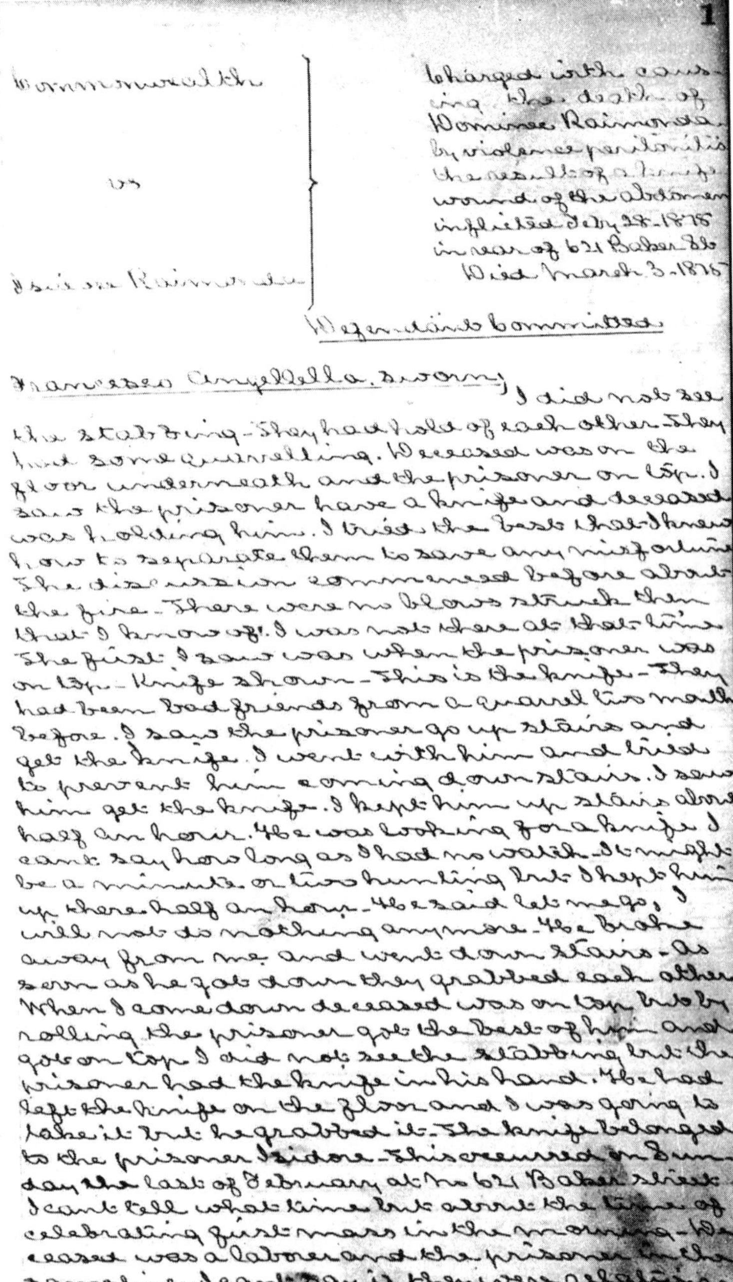

1

Commonwealth vs Isidore Raimonda

Charged with causing the death of Dominic Raimonda by violence peritonitis the result of a knife wound of the abdomen inflicted Feby 28-1875 in rear of 621 Baker St. Died March 3-1875

Defendant Committed

Francesco Angelella, sworn; I did not see the stabbing—They had hold of each other—They had some quarrelling. Deceased was on the floor underneath and the prisoner on top. I saw the prisoner have a knife and deceased was holding him. I tried the best that I knew how to separate them to save any misfortune. The discussion commenced before about the fire—There were no blows struck then that I know of. I was not there at that time. The first I saw was when the prisoner was on top—Knife shown—This is the knife—They had been bad friends from a quarrel two months before. I saw the prisoner go up stairs and get the knife. I went with him and tried to prevent him coming down stairs. I saw him get the knife. I kept him up stairs about half an hour. He was looking for a knife. I can't say how long as I had no watch. It might be a minute or two hunting but I kept him up there half an hour. He said let me go, I will not do nothing anymore. He broke away from me and went down stairs. As soon as he got down they grabbed each other. When I come down deceased was on top but by rolling the prisoner got the best of him and got on top. I did not see the stabbing but the prisoner had the knife in his hand. He had left the knife on the floor and I was going to take it but he grabbed it. The knife belonged to the prisoner Isidore. This occurred on Sunday the last of February at No 621 Baker street. I can't tell what time but about the time of celebrating first mass in the morning. Deceased was a laborer and the prisoner in the same line. I can't say if they were relati[illegible]

Figure 4-14. From the *Commonwealth vs. Isadore Raimonda,* Coroner's Evidence Book, Philadelphia County, Pennsylvania, p. 1. FHL microfilm 965,369, item 1.

In contrast to the very full record on the fatal Raimonda quarrel is an entry in the Coroner's Evidence Book of the New York City coroner in 1862 (figure 4-15).

Usually the records are on file at the office of the coroner or medical examiner. Early records may have been transferred to the city or county clerk's office, the local historical society, or a state archive. The coroner's office will probably know where the old records are located. Some offices will not release the records without proof of relationship to the deceased and a statement indicating how the information in the record will be used. Family history is usually considered a valid reason. Unless the witnesses at an inquest perjured themselves, the testimony should be factual, eliminating erroneous information about the deceased.

Hospital Records

Hospital and physicians' medical records are excellent sources of genealogical information. However, as confidential documents, they are difficult to obtain and are usually available only to the infirmed or the administrator of his or her estate. Like

Received Oct 2, 1862 from Coroner Rainey the inquisition on view of the body of Joseph P. Thompson Dist. Atty's office
I. Ovanderpool

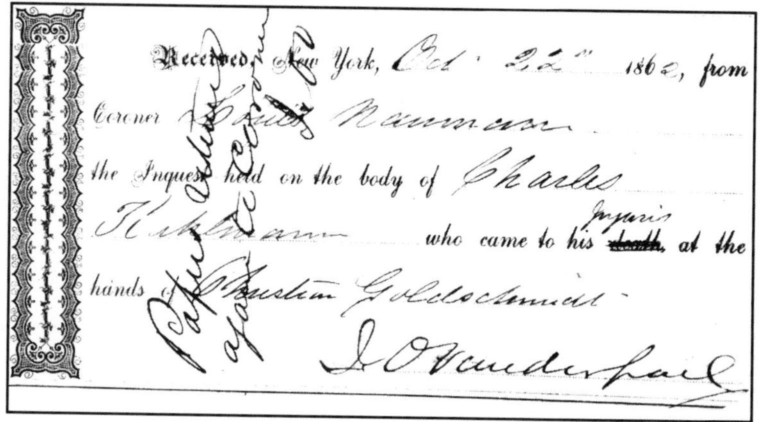

Received New York, Oct. 22nd 1862, from Coroner Naumann the Inquest held on the body of Charles Kiklman who came to his ~~death~~ injuries at the hands of Gustav Goldschmidt
I. Ovanderpool

Figure 4-15. Inquest reports on Joseph P. Thompson, 2 October 1862, and Charles Kikleman [?], 22 October 1862, Coroner's Office Inquests to Deaths, New York City, 1862–64. FHL microfilm 514,332.

the more traditional businesses, hospitals have opened, closed, merged, been taken over, and changed names. As a result, knowledge of the history of the hospital may be needed to locate available records.

Some hospital records from the nineteenth century have been released and microfilmed by the Genealogical Society of Utah, including the early records of the St. Louis City Hospital, which are fairly representative of the content in most records of this period. Figure 4-16 is a page from the St. Louis City Hospital register, 1860.

Normally, early hospital registers will indicate the patient's name, age, birthplace, date of admission, illness or disease, and date of discharge or death, although some records are less informative. In addition to registers, hospitals maintained early death records such as those compiled by the Almshouse Hospital in Philadelphia in 1893 (figure 4-17). The information on death records varies from hospital to hospital, but usually you can expect to find the deceased's name, death date, and cause of death.

The federal government maintains a wide range of hospitals, ranging from those for veterans to those for the insane. Because they are government institutions, records from these hospitals may be more readily available in original, film, or print versions.

The National Home for Disabled Volunteer Soldiers, Northwestern Branch, in Milwaukee, was created to care for the casualties of the Civil War. The buildings are now the oldest continuously inhabited structures in the entire Veterans Administration system. The first admission book was found in a dusty corner; the entries have been abstracted and published. Typical entries include date of application and of military service, military unit, disability, age, marital status, and name of next of kin.[59]

The Archives of the New York Weill Cornell Medical Center (formerly known as the New York Hospital-Cornell Medical Center) is the repository for the official records of medical institutions in New York City ranging from The Cornell University Medical College and the Society of the Lying-In Hospital of the City of New York to the American Women's Medical Association and New York Infant Asylum. Records date as early as 1771 (The Society of the New York Hospital) and as late as 1947 for the New York Nursery and Child's Hospital. Those of the academic units—the medical college, graduate school of medical sciences for example—continue until the present.

The Medical Directory of the City of New York (1899 edition) offered the following description of Nursery and Child's Hospital, which in 1934 was absorbed into the New York Hospital-Cornell Medical Center:

> (1854). 51st Street and Lexington ave. Maintain and care for destitute children under four years of age, and boards the children of wet nurses. Children are received to board at $10 per month. Women of good character, free from contagious diseases, are also admitted to the lying-in department on the payment of $25 or agreeing to remain three months after confinement to nurse two infants. Has a country branch at Staten Island for older children. Apply daily at the hospital from 11 A.M. to 2 P.M. Applications for confinement are best made in person.

In addition to medical records, the archives holds materials on medical education and treatment, photographs, prints, oral histories, and antique medical instruments. Occupying the entire 25th floor of the Hospital, the archives is open for research by appointment. Hours and details of the collection may be found at the website <www.med.cornell.edu/archives>.

WPA Records

The WPA, or Works Progress Administration, was another of the federal programs designed to help the country survive the depression of the 1930s. While some workers built bridges and paved roads, others worked on the Historical Records Survey, creating a wide variety of records that are beneficial to genealogists. They range from the Soundex cards, which are a staple of all census research to cemetery inscriptions and oral interviews that are still invaluable even though they may be of interest only to researchers of a particular area.

A collection at the University of Louisville in Kentucky documents medical history in that state. Of special value and interest is the material gathered during interviews with medical providers and their families. The term medical provider included physicians, dentists, nurses, folk remedy practitioners, and even quacks, producing files that detail rural and urban medicine and health practices in mid-twentieth century Kentucky. The collection is available on microfilm at the Kornhauser Health Sciences Library at the university.

One example of records is the WPA Employment Case Files, 1935–1942, with an index available at <www.colorado.gov/dpa/doit/archives/wpa/laplata.html>.

School Records

The records of schools, colleges, and universities in the United States have gradually developed into valuable sources of genealogical information. School records provide a more personal glimpse of our ancestors than many other types of records. They are available from the 1700s until current day and include everything from elementary education through college, professional school, military academy, or special education training. Any of these facilities may have records that provide information about your ancestor. Among the types of school records available are report cards, class photos, class lists, administrator's records, and rosters of teachers. As with most other records in the United States, school records became more comprehensive after the turn of the twentieth century.

Primary and Secondary Schools

A review of historic school records will quickly show the changes in education over the years. Children from rural farm areas may have attended school only during the winter or nongrowing time. Some schools moved their more advanced students up a grade or even two; today such students are more often offered enrichment courses.

Most commonly found are school board minutes (figure 4-18). While board minutes deal primarily with administrative and financial matters involved in operating the school, they may include such potentially valuable information as the names of administrators and teachers, and reference to other records that might be useful. For instance, these 1873 minutes from McDuffey County, Georgia, refer to a school census. Does that census still exist in the files of the county school district or the county clerk?

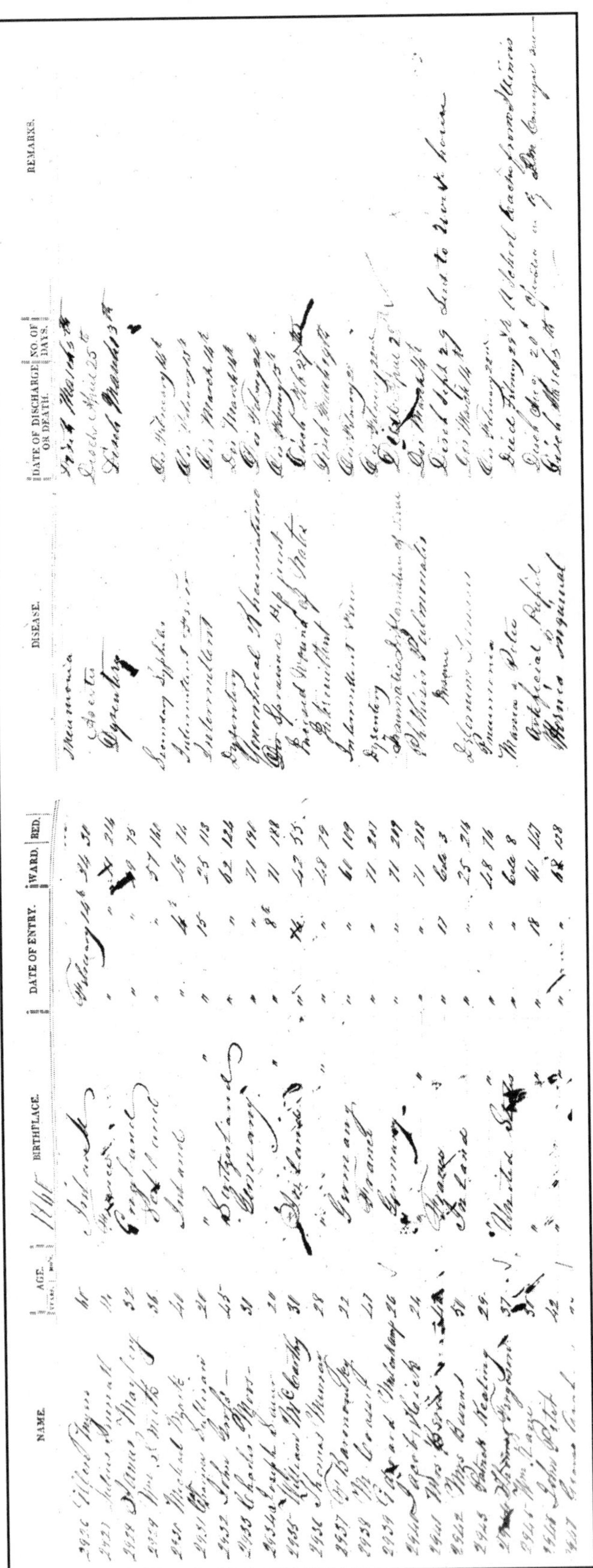

Figure 4-16. From the register of St. Louis Hospital, 1860. FHL microfilm 980,610.

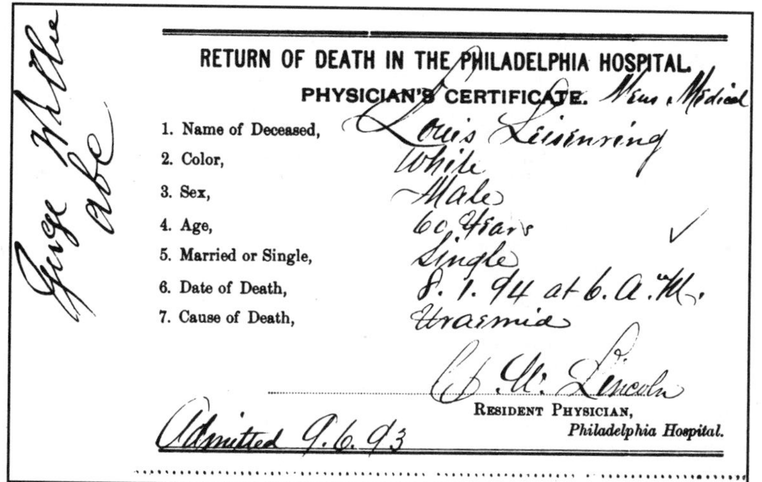

RETURN OF DEATH IN THE PHILADELPHIA HOSPITAL.

PHYSICIAN'S CERTIFICATE. New Medical

1. Name of Deceased, Louis Liesenning
2. Color, White
3. Sex, Male
4. Age, 60 Years
5. Married or Single, Single
6. Date of Death, 8. 1. 94 at 6. A. M.
7. Cause of Death, Uraemia

C. W. Lincoln
RESIDENT PHYSICIAN,
Philadelphia Hospital.

Admitted 9. 6. 93

Figure 4-17. Death certificate of Louis Liesenning, 1 August 1894, Almshouse Hospital, Bureau of Charities, Philadelphia County, Pennsylvania, p. 1. FHL 975,748, item 1.

Teachers' salaries were set by the number of students in attendance rather than by the number of school days taught.

In many cases, school records are held at the state's archives. While a large percentage of the records deal with the business of running a school or school district, records involving individuals are also available. For example, the Wisconsin State Archives holds teachers' contracts from Brown Deer, Granville, and River Hills among other towns. Records of Durham Hill School include teachers' registers with dates, names, ages, and attendance of students.

One good starting point when searching for school records is the Family History Library catalog using the topic "schools" in a known location. Another is a Web search that focuses on the place of residence, the known name of a school, or the catalogs of the state or local archives or historical societies. Researchers should remember to check sources at the local public library, where they might find newspaper articles about school activities and a collection of yearbooks from the local public schools. The county clerk or the current school board may be able to tell a researcher what records still exist and where they are housed.

Many colleges, universities, prep schools, and boarding schools have directories, while listings of local primary schools are more difficult to locate and usually pertain only to a specific area. County histories often mention the early county schools and sometimes list students of a particular graduating year. Local or state historical societies may also have information about an area's early schools. Internet sources may lead you to useful records. The website called *Southern California Yearbooks* <http://4dw.net/socal> has posted images from many high school and college yearbooks from throughout the twentieth century online.

Modern school records are protected by privacy laws, but family members are sometimes able to obtain the information or photocopies of the documents in the files. Because state, local, and school policies govern the availability of school records, you should write to the local school of interest to determine what procedure to follow.

Report Cards

Among family heirlooms and papers, a researcher might find an old report card. From this, the researcher can determine an approximate age, based on the grade level indicated on the report card, as well as learn what subjects the ancestor studied—and how well the student did in his studies. In addition, the school may also have maintained a record book of all grades issued.

Student Lists

Student lists come in a variety of forms. Teachers might have kept a list of their pupils that includes courses studied and grades achieved. A school census might include the student's age as well as a birthplace. See for example, the Custer County, Colorado, Pupil Register for District #3, 1891–96 at <www.colorado.gov/dpa/doit/archives/online.htm#school>.

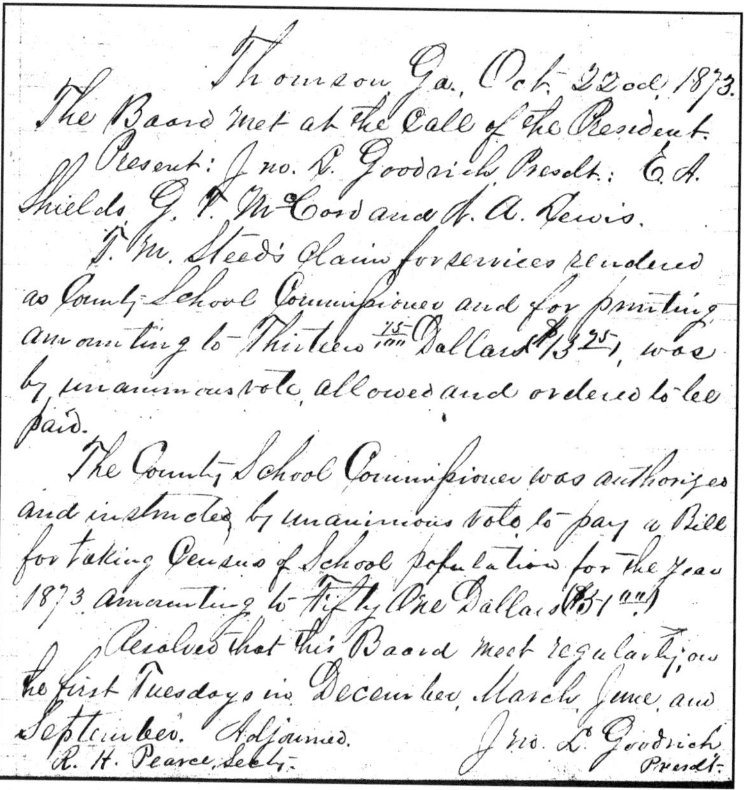

Thomson Ga. Oct. 22nd 1873.

The Board met at the call of the President. Present: Jno. L. Goodrich Presdt.: E. A. Shields, G. F. McCord and A. A. Lewis.

T. M. Steed's Claim for services rendered as County School Commissioner and for printing amounting to Thirteen 75/100 Dollars $13.25, was by unanimous vote, allowed and ordered to be paid.

The County School Commissioner was authorized and instructed by unanimous vote to pay a Bill for taking Census of School population for the year 1873 amounting to Fifty One Dollars ($51 00/100)

Resolved that this Board meet regularly on the first Tuesdays in December, March, June, and September. Adjourned.

Jno. L. Goodrich Presdt.
R. H. Pearce, Secty.

Figure 4-18. School board minutes, 22 October 1873, McDuffy County, Georgia, 1872–1960, p. 25. FHL microfilm 220,521, part 1.

Many metropolitan and rural schools received funds from the local government to cover the cost of educating poor children. Records of children receiving an education at government expense can be found in court records, school board minutes, or town meeting records. The information—name, age, and sex of the child—is typical of all early school records.

Ethnic Schools

Schools devoted to educating a particular ethnic group can also supply a great deal of information about ancestors. Again, it may take some time to locate the records, but many are available.

Schools maintained by the Bureau of Indian Affairs are excellent sources of information and reflect the type of information found in modern school records. These records, maintained by the federal government, have been microfilmed. Records of the Juneau Indian Agency in Alaska are housed at the National Archives—Alaska Region at Anchorage, and were microfilmed by the Genealogical Society of Utah in 1969. The Office of Indian Affairs also compiled school censuses of Indian children taken at the town and county levels throughout the United States at one time or another but without any predictable format or consistency. (See chapter 5, "Census Records," for further information about school censuses.)

Swallow, Antoine	23	Sioux	Male
Swallow, Benjamin	17	"	"
Swamp, Peter	15	Mohawik	"
Sweetcorn, Asa	26	Sioux	"
Sweetmedicine, Henry	21	Cheyenne	"
Swimmer, Thomas	22	Sioux	"
Tahamont, Robert	20	Abanaki	"
Tallchief, Frank	17	Seneca	"
Tallchief, Wesley	20	"	"
Tarbell, Lewis Roy	21	Mohawk	"
Tarbell, Joseph	21	"	"
Tarbell, Mitchell	16	"	"
Tarbell, Thomas	18	"	"
Tarbell, Thomas Hill	19	"	"
Taylor, Clifford	22	Pawnee	"
Tellskie, Jesse	20	Cherokee	"
Tewa, Ponaqua	41	Hopi	"
Tewane, Edward	42	"	"
Tewani, Louis	25	"	"
Tewatly, Cain	23	Cherokee	"
Thomas, David	22	Nez Perce	"
Thomas, Peter	24	Klamath	"
Thomas, Samuel	16	Omaha	"
Thompson, Charles	18	Navajo	"
Thompson, John	19	Winnebago	"
Thompson, Joseph	22	Onondaga	"
Thompson, Louis	20	Navajo	"
Thompson, Newton,	18	Cherokee	"
Thompson, Norman	23	Pomo	"
Thompson, Robert	19	Seneca	"
Thorpe, James	24	Sac & Fox	"

Figure 4-19. The federal government took a census of students at the Carlisle Indian School in 1911 that lists boys and girls separately and gives the tribal membership of each student. FHL microfilm 573,863.

Carlisle Indian Industrial School in Pennsylvania was the first off-reservation government boarding school for Native American children and operated from 1879 to 1918. One of its most famous students was Jim Thorpe, who appears on the 1911 student school census (see figure 4-19). Many original records from the school are at the Cumberland County Historical Society in Carlisle. Microfilmed records include a 1911 census available through the Family History Library, and original records are part of Record Group 75, File 1327 at the National Archives.

Until schools were desegregated in 1954, most districts in the southern states ran separate schools for black and white students. The scholastic census records for these years usually have individual lists for black and white students. Many are microfilmed. Researchers need to be aware that in at least one case, different colors of paper were used for different races (a difference that may not be apparent on a microfilmed copy unless they are so labeled) and the record itself may not indicate the race.

One of the best-known black schools is Tuskegee Institute, founded by Booker T. Washington. Some of the many records pertaining to this institution are online, including the 1915 Class Roster with updated biographical information at <www.afrigeneas.com/library/schoolrosters/tuskegee1915.html>.

Colleges and Universities

The institutions of higher education offer many useful records, and in fact, colleges and universities are excellent sources of genealogical information compared to early primary school records. Records document admission, registration, course of study, and graduation. Additionally, many alumni associations and school archivists have compiled biographies and histories of former students. Many schools have preserved applications for admission containing valuable family information.

Yearbooks document the attendance of an individual at a given time and provide some biographical information; these are usually on file with alumni associations and in college and university libraries. Alumni directories offer subsequent addresses and work history; many also include such personal information as names of spouse and children. If the student had to write a thesis as part of his course work, a copy likely resides in the library. A large number of colleges and universities participate in the NUCMC, thus helping to identify which sources they might hold.

The 1890 Biographical Register of West Point graduates includes Civil War generals from both sides. Not surprisingly, information about Confederate officers is sparse or nonexistent after they resigned from the Union Army. In contrast, entries of

530..(Born Ky.)....**JEFFERSON DAVIS**......(Ap'd Mis.)..23

Military History. — Cadet at the Military Academy, Sep. 1, 1824, to July 1, 1828, when he was graduated and promoted in the Army to

BVT. SECOND LIEUT. OF INFANTRY, JULY 1, 1828.

SECOND LIEUT., 1ST INFANTRY, JULY 1, 1828.

Served: on frontier duty at Ft. Crawford, Wis., 1829, — Ft. Winnebago, Wis., 1829–31, — Yellow River (superintending Sawmill), 1831, — Ft. Crawford, Wis., 1831, — Dubuque Mines, Io., 1831–32, — Rock Island, Ill., 1832, — Jefferson Barracks, Mo., 1832, — and Ft. Crawford, Wis., 1832–33; as Adjutant, 1st Dragoons, at Regimental headquarters,

(FIRST LIEUT., 1ST DRAGOONS, MAR. 4, 1833)

Aug. 30, 1833, to Feb. 5, 1834; on frontier duty at Ft. Gibson, I. T., 1834, — Expedition to Tow-e-ash Villages, 1834, — and Ft. Gibson, I. T., 1834; and on leave of absence, 1834–35.

RESIGNED, JUNE 30, 1835.

Civil History. — Presidential Elector of the State of Mississippi, 1844. Member of the U. S. House of Representatives from Mississippi, 1845–46. Planter, Warren County, Mis., 1835–46.

Military History. — Served in the War with Mexico, 1846–47, as COLONEL, 1ST REG. MISSISSIPPI VOLUNTEERS (RIFLES), JULY 18, 1846, being engaged in the Battle of Monterey, Sep. 21–23, 1846, and as Member of Commission for arranging the terms of capitulation of the place, — and Battle of Buena Vista, Feb. 22–23, 1847, where he was severely wounded.

DISBANDED, JULY 12, 1847.

Re-appointed in the United States Army with the rank of

BRIG.-GENERAL, U. S. ARMY, MAY 17, 1847: DECLINED.

Civil History. — Member of the U. S. Senate from Mississippi, 1847–51, and Chairman of the Senate Committee on Military Affairs, 1849–51. Secretary of War of the United States, Mar. 8, 1853, to Mar. 4, 1857. Member of the U. S. Senate from Mississippi, and Chairman of the Senate Committee on Military Affairs, Mar. 4, 1857, to Jan. 14, 1861. President of the Commission created by Act of June 1, 1860, to examine into the Organization, System of Discipline, and Course of Instruction at the U. S. Military Academy, July 18 to Dec. 13, 1860.

Joined in the Rebellion of 1861–66 against the United States.

Civil History. — President of Life Insurance Company, Memphis, Ten., 1878. Farmer, Beauvoir, Mis., 1879–89. Author of "Rise and Fall of the Confederate Government," 1881.

DIED, DEC. 6, 1889, AT NEW ORLEANS, LA.: AGED 82.

1187..(Born O.)....**ULYSSES S. GRANT**......(Ap'd O.)..21

Military History. — Cadet at the Military Academy, July 1, 1839, to July 1, 1843, when he was graduated and promoted in the Army to

BVT. SECOND LIEUT., 4TH INFANTRY, JULY 1, 1843.

Served: in garrison at Jefferson Barracks, Mo., 1843–44; on frontier duty at Natchitoches, La. (Camp Salubrity), 1844–45; in Military Occu-

(SECOND LIEUT., 4TH INFANTRY, SEP. 30, 1845)

pation of Texas, 1845–46; in the War with Mexico, 1846–48, being engaged in the Battle of Palo Alto, May 8, 1846, — Battle of Resaca-de-la-Palma, May 9, 1846, — Battle of Monterey, Sep. 21–23, 1846, — Siege of Vera Cruz, Mar. 9–29, 1847, — Battle of Cerro Gordo, Apr. 17–18, 1847, — Capture of San Antonio, Aug. 20, 1847, — Battle of Churubusco, Aug. 20, 1847, — Battle of Molino del Rey, Sep. 8, 1847, — Storming

(BVT. FIRST LIEUT., SEP. 8, 1847, FOR GALLANT AND MERITORIOUS CONDUCT IN THE BATTLE OF MOLINO DEL REY, MEX.)

of Chapultepec, Sep. 13, 1847, — Assault and Capture of the City of

(BVT. CAPT., SEP. 13, 1847, FOR GALLANT CONDUCT AT CHAPULTEPEC, MEX.)

Mexico, Sep. 13–14, 1847, — and as Quartermaster, 4th Infantry, Apr. 1, 1847, to July 23, 1848; in garrison at Sackett's Harbor, N. Y., 1848–49,

(FIRST LIEUT., 4TH INFANTRY, SEP. 16, 1847)

as Quartermaster, 4th Infantry, Sep. 11, 1849, to Sep. 30, 1853; in garrison at Detroit, Mich., 1849–50, 1850–51, — Sackett's Harbor, N. Y., 1851–52, — Ft. Columbus, N. Y., 1852, — and at Benicia, Cal., 1852; and on frontier duty at Columbia Barracks, Or., 1852–53, — Ft. Vancouver,

(CAPTAIN, 4TH INFANTRY, AUG. 5, 1853)

Or., 1853, — and Ft. Humboldt, Cal., 1854.

RESIGNED, JULY 31, 1854.

Civil History. — Farmer, near St. Louis, Mo., 1854–59. Real Estate Agent, St. Louis, Mo., 1859–60. Merchant, Galena, Ill., 1860–61.

Military History. — Served during the Rebellion of the Seceding States, 1861–66: in command of a Company of Illinois Volunteers, Apr.–May, 1861; assisting in Organizing and Mustering Volunteers into service, May to June 17, 1861; on march to Quincy, Ill., and in guarding

(COLONEL, 21ST ILLINOIS VOLUNTEERS, JUNE 17, 1861)

the Hannibal and St. Joseph Railroad, Mo., June 17 to Aug. 7, 1861; in

(BRIG.-GENERAL, U. S. VOLUNTEERS, MAY 17, 1861)

command of Ironton, Mo., Aug. 7–17, 1861, — of Jefferson City, Mo., Aug. 17–29, 1861, — and of the District of Southwestern Missouri, headquarters Cape Girardeau, Mo., subsequently extended to embrace Southern Illinois and Western Kentucky, headquarters Cairo, Ill., Sep. 1, 1861, to Feb. 17, 1862, being engaged in the Seizure of Paducah, Ky., at the mouth of Tennessee River, Sep. 6, 1861, — Expedition to and Combat of Belmont, Mo., Nov. 7, 1861, — and armed Reconnoissances into Western Kentucky, making demonstrations upon the Rebel defenses at Columbus, Ky., and Ft. Henry, Ten., Jan. 10–22, 1862; in the Tennessee Campaign (in command), Feb. to Apr., 1862, being engaged in Operations against Ft. Henry, Feb. 2–6, 1862, — Investment and Capture of Ft. Donelson, with 14,623 prisoners and much material of war, Feb. 13–16,

(MAJ.-GENERAL, U. S. VOLUNTEERS, FEB. 16, 1862, TO JULY 4, 1863)

1862, — and Battle of Shiloh, Apr. 6–7, 1862; in command of the District of West Tennessee, Mar. 5 to Oct. 16, 1862; in the Mississippi Campaign (second in command), Apr. to Oct., 1862, being engaged in the Advance upon, and Siege of Corinth, Apr. 10 to May 30, 1862, in immediate command of the Right Wing and Reserve of Major-General Halleck's Army, — and subsequently to July 18, 1862, directed the operations resulting in the Battles of Corinth, Oct. 3–4, and of the Hatchie, Oct. 5, 1862, and commanded in person at the Battle of Iuka, Sep. 19, 1862; in command of the Department of the Tennessee, Oct. 16, 1862, to Oct. 16,

171

Figure 4-20. The amount of information included in a collegiate directory may vary depending on the career path of the graduate, as shown in these entries from George W. Cullum, *The Biographic Register of the Officers and Graduates of the U.S. Military Academy from Its Establishment, in 1802, to 1890, With the Early History of the United States Military Academy* (New York: Houghton, Mifflin, 1881). The sketch of Jefferson Davis includes only brief information about the post–Civil War years while that of Ulysses S. Grant continues for two full pages.

some of the Union leaders cover several pages, providing detailed information about military assignments throughout a career and often an extensive biography (see figure 4-20).

If you know or suspect that an ancestor was a student at England's Cambridge University, you will definitely want to search the alumni database at <www.ancestry.com/search/rectype/directories/cambridge/main.htm>. *Alumni Cantabrigieness* was compiled by J. A. Venn, a former president of Queen's College and offers information from the university's earliest records of about 1261 through 1900. Many of those students later immigrated to America. Each entry offers biographical information including birth date and place, parents' names, siblings' names, occupation, and notable accomplishments.

Private Schools

Some of the best early primary school records were kept by private preparatory and boarding schools whose students were from the region's wealthy families. References to children's parents, residence, curriculum, and activities, as well as individual and class photographs, can more often be found in these school records. Some private schools are operated by religious institutions, and these records may appear with the church records.

Orphanage Records

Orphanages, which date from the seventeenth century in England, were originally workhouses, poorhouses, and asylums.

Modern orphanages hardly resemble those depicted by Charles Dickens, but their purpose is the same: to shelter orphaned and abandoned children. Such institutions have existed in the United States for at least two centuries. They have been operated by civil authorities, religious groups, and private benefactors. The types of records kept vary and are often difficult to locate. For background about orphanages in America, see "The Rise and Demise of the American Orphanage" by Dale Keiger at <www.jhu.edu/~jhumag/496web/orphange.html>.

Orphanages were especially active during the period between the Civil War and the Great Depression, when they cared for more of America's dependent children than any other means. The great majority of these children were more correctly "half orphans" who had lost one parent but still had one living parent. There was a tremendous variation in how the orphanages functioned and in the level of care and education the orphans received.[60]

During the early history of the United States, town and county officials appointed or elected overseers of the poor to deal with paupers and orphaned children. Local courts usually appointed guardians to care for orphans who might be heirs to property. When relatives or local residents were unwilling or unable to care for the child, he or she, if old enough, was bound out to learn a trade. If the child was too young, he or she was sent to an institution, usually maintained on a local level. County court records or probate records may give the date the child was apprenticed, to whom, and the trade to be learned. These are often indexed under "orphans," "apprentices," or "paupers" in court indexes and dockets. For example, the Overseer of the Poor in Ohio County, Indiana, made the following report and financial accounting in May 1827.

> May Term 1827
>
> And now at this time comes Alexander Dale Overseer of the Poor in and for Harrison Township in Ohio County and exhibits an account of Monies by him Received of Wilkerson McCarty Administrator of the Estate of Samuel McCarty Deceased, which the said Administrator States is the sum which was coming to Nancy Smith (Now a pauper of said Harrison Township) as one of the Heirs at Law of the said Decedent amounting to twenty-two Dollars and Ninety Cents #22.90. Out of which Sum of $22.90 it appears he (Dale) has paid to Eleazur Carver the Sum of Sixteen Dollars and Ninety Three 3/4 cents for keeping said pauper the Last half of the Year ending on the first Monday of May 1827 it being the full of the balance due said Carver for keeping the said pauper the year aforesaid. Leaving in the hands of the said Alexander Dale Overseer as aforesaid the Sum of Five Dollars and Ninety Seven Cents.
>
> Aside he (Dale) also exhibits an account against the County for Services by him rendered as Overseer afsd as follows to wit:
>
> To Tending court one day with Carver $1.00
> To Binding out a poor boy to the Cabinet making business 1.00
> To Advertising and letting out Nancy Smith pauper aforesd for 1827 2.00
> For making report of Sale to Clerk 1.00
> For going to Carver's to see pauper and settling with him for keeping pauper one year, the half of his pay 1.00
>
> Amounting in the whole to the sum of $6.00
>
> Which account of Six Dollars is allowed by the Board for the Services aforesaid. And the said Overseer agrees to retain and keep in his hands the aforesaid Five Dollars & Ninety Seven Cents in full satisfaction of the aforesaid Charge against the County to Six Dollars which is approved by the Board.[61]

Orphanages maintained by state and local governments were funded agencies that may have maintained better records than private and church agencies. Their files usually include the child's name, age or date of birth, birthplace, date of admission, names of parents, birthplaces of parents, name and residence of nearest kin, date of discharge, to whom indentured and when, whether the child was orphaned or abandoned, and any remarks. These records are available at orphanages that are still in operation. Otherwise, the records of a state-operated establishment may be with the state archivist or the state's Department of Social and Welfare Services. Write to both offices to insure that you have identified and obtained all existing records. Records of closed orphanages operated below the state level may be deposited with the town, city, or county clerk, the local agency responsible for currently operating orphanages, or a local historical society or research library. Some records may be in the possession of the families of institution officials.

Orphanages operated by religious groups and private benefactors also kept records useful for researchers. The Vine Street Orphan's [*sic*] Home of Chattanooga, Tennessee, operated by the Women's Christian Association of Chattanooga, maintained excellent records, including a diary of the home, lists of subscribers, names and ages of children there, matrons' reports, secretaries' reports, minutes of the Women's Christian Association meetings, and managers' books and journals between 1879 and 1903. Figure 4-21 is a page from the matron's report dated 30 May 1887. It notes which children were placed with families ("Laura Henry taken from the Home by Mrs. DeGrummond May 10th") and also their retrieval ("Martha Bennett taken from Dr. Hall May 16th on account of ill useage [*sic*] by them").

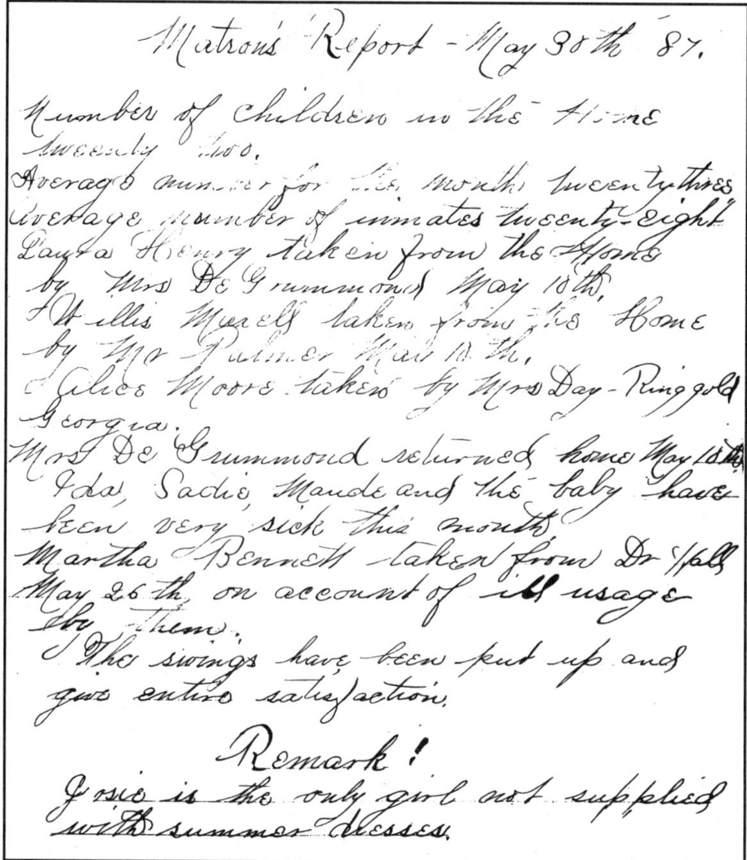

Matron's Report - May 30th 87.

Number of children in the Home twenty two.
Average number for the month twenty three
Average number of inmates twenty-eight
Laura Henry taken from the Home by Mrs De Grummond May 10th,
Willis Murell taken from the Home by Mr Palmer May 11th,
Alice Moore taken by Mrs Day - Ringgold Georgia.
Mrs De Grummond returned home May 18th
Ida, Sadie, Maude and the baby have been very sick this month
Martha Bennett taken from Dr Hall May 26th, on account of ill usage by them.
The swings have been put up and give entire satisfaction.

Remark!
Josie is the only girl not supplied with summer dresses.

Figure 4-21. Matron's report, Vine Street Orphan's Home, Chattanooga, Tennessee, 30 May 1887. FHL microfilm 987,757.

The Applications for Children record book provides more information on placement. Sometime between her admission in May 1887 and an entry dated December 1888, Laura Henry's grandmother asked for custody, but "investigation showed her to be unworthy." Another child, Frankie Tipton, was adopted by the F. McCullum family of Wilmington, Ohio, in December 1888.

The minutes of board meetings also contain valuable information. The August 1887 minutes report that Jennie Davis, who had left two children with the home for two or three years, had remarried a man named Holmes, and that they had had a child of their own. She "intends applying for them," and her husband "prefers [*sic*] a request for the two children. He represents himself as their father. Decided to let them have the one in the Home," but the second, in "a good home with Mrs. Frank George . . . would be left there at least for the present." The managers' books contain administrative information about employee salaries, statistics, health and financial reports, and other information unrelated to a specific orphan.

A much briefer and more formal record, the 1876 Register of the Jewish Foster Home and Orphan Asylum in Philadelphia (see figure 4-22), gives the child's name, age, admission date, birthplace, names and birthplaces of parents, closest kin and address, date of discharge, indenturing, and trade. This register does not explain the circumstances surrounding the child's placement in the home, but many records do.

The early records of nongovernment-operated orphanages that are no longer in existence may be difficult to locate. If the orphanage is or was operated by a religious group, the records may be at its headquarters. The Catholic church, which operated the largest number of nongovernmental orphanages in metropolitan cities, usually maintains diocesan archives. State and local historical societies may have some early orphanage records; university libraries are anxious to get them, and many are in the possession of families of institution officials. Check the NUCMC under the name of the institution, names of officials, and localities where orphanages existed.

Problems with using orphanage records include damage, lack of legibility and availability, and difficulty in determining their location. Court records of placement can sometimes be substituted for incomplete or nonexistent orphanage records. But access to officially-recorded adoption records varies widely from one jurisdiction to another. In Ohio, adoptions after 1 January 1964 are confidential and the records are sealed. Access to records of earlier adoptions in the state is only permitted to adopting parents, the adopted person, and lineal descendants. In contrast, both Alaska and Kansas maintain open adoption records.

The information found in orphanage records can be critically important to the family historian. The Vine Street matron's report of 30 May 1887 notes that Alice Moore was "taken by Mrs. Day, Ringold, Georgia." Unless family records reflect her transfer to the Day household in Georgia, the researcher might spend endless hours searching for records in Chattanooga, Tennessee, since that is where the Vine Street Orphans Home is located. Furthermore, if her name was changed to Day, it might be impossible to trace her parents without the orphanage link to the name Moore.

Orphan Trains

"They put us all on a big platform in some big building while people came from all around the countryside to pick out those of us they wished to take home. I was four years old, and my sister was only two . . ." [62]

The Orphan Trains moved children out of New York City, traveling to the midwest and beyond. Some children had a wonderful life with their new family, while others were not so fortunate. Some children disappeared into the countryside; others became prominent citizens, politicians, and family members. The Orphan Trains were a project conceived by the Rev. Charles Loring Brace of the New York Children's Aid Society with the goal of moving the homeless and helpless children from the streets of the city and finding them homes in more rural areas of the midwest and west (see figure 4-23). Ironically, the Children's Aid Society did not itself operate any orphanages during the placing-out period (see <www.orphantrainriders.com/Menu.html>). Before long, other charitable organizations in New York and Boston had joined the program, and by the end of the 1800s, charities in Ohio, Indiana, and Illinois adopted the program and sent children to states farther west. Between 1853 and 1929, some two hundred thousand children rode the trains.

Records of the transfers may be found at the city asylums that participated in the project or in the deed books of the courthouses of the counties that received the children. Deed books were commonly used to record the adoptions of children (usually males under the age of ten and young females) or the apprenticeships (usually males ten and over). But, do not overlook justice of the peace dockets, guardians' records, county order records, and board of supervisors minutes, among other county records.

An indenture dated 15 December 1860 and recorded in Marion County, Illinois, is between the New York Juvenile Asylum and a farmer named Clifton R. Wills. The agreement outlines the duties of Wills, who is accepting ten-year-old Cornelius Shay as an apprentice. Wills is to instruct Shay in "the art of farming" and in "reading, writing, and arithmetic, as least as far as and including Compound Interest." Wills also agreed to "carefully watch over and guard the morals of the said apprentice, and prevent him from frequenting taverns, porterhouses, play-houses, or gaming houses of any kind."

The Orphan Train Heritage Society of America, Inc., P.O. Box 322, Concordia, Kansas 66901 <www.orphantrainriders.com> functions as a national clearinghouse for all information about the program. Recollections of Orphan Train riders have been published in several sources; one example is Johnson's *Orphan Train Riders: Their Own Stories.*[63] Several websites are available to help researchers trace those who might have ridden the trains.

Indiana <www.rootsweb.com/~inhamilt/otrr.htm>
Iowa <http://iagenweb.org/iaorphans/>
Kansas <www.kancoll.org/articles/orphans/ >
Nebraska <www.rootsweb.com/~neadoptn/Orphan.htm>
Michigan <www.program-source.com/orphan_train_project.htm>

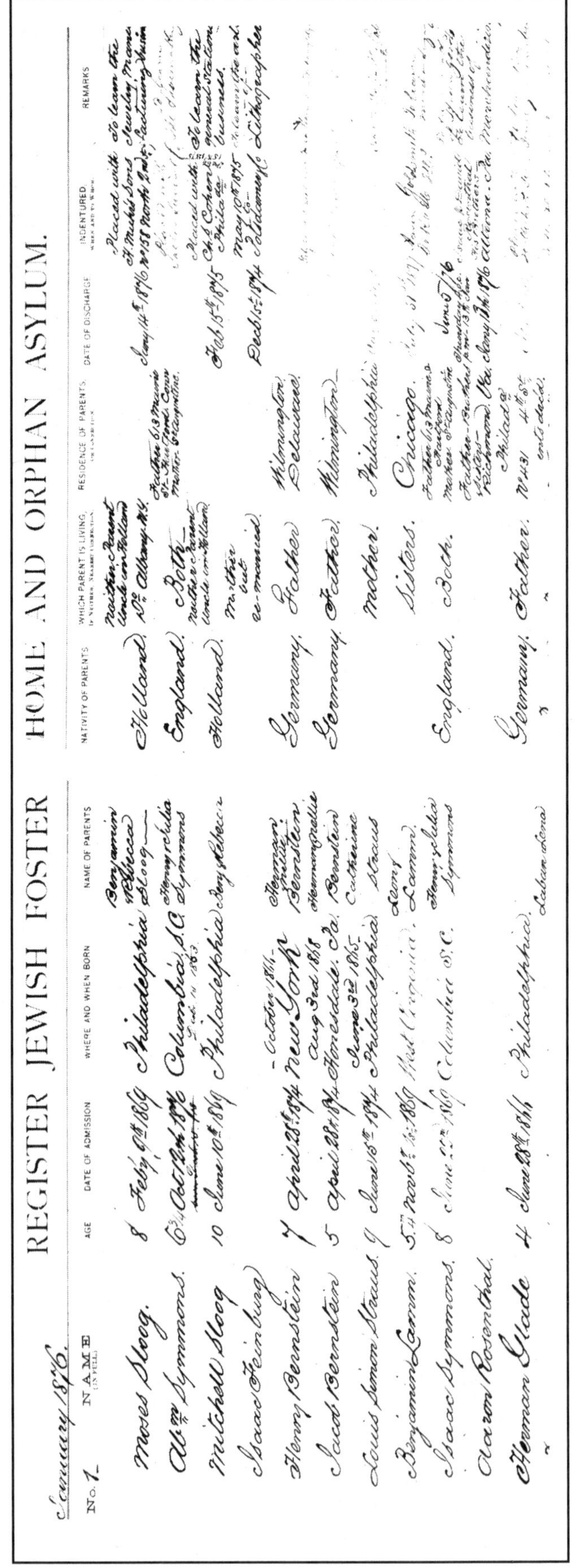

REGISTER JEWISH FOSTER HOME AND ORPHAN ASYLUM.

January 1876. No. 1

NAME (IN FULL)	AGE	DATE OF ADMISSION	WHERE AND WHEN BORN	NAME OF PARENTS	NATIVITY OF PARENTS	WHICH PARENT IS LIVING	RESIDENCE OF PARENTS	DATE OF DISCHARGE	INDENTURED	REMARKS
Moses Sloog	8	Feby 6th 1869	Philadelphia	Benjamin Rebecca Sloog	Holland	neither parent; uncle in Holland	[illegible]	Jany 14th 1876	[illegible]	Placed with [illegible] to learn the [illegible]
Abm Symmons	6 3/4	Oct 22nd 1870	Columbia S.C.	Henry & Julia Symmons	England	Both	[illegible]			
Mitchell Sloog	10	June 10th 1869	Philadelphia	Benj & Rebecca	Holland	Mother but re-married		Feb 15th 1875	[illegible]	[illegible]
Isaac Feinburg								Dec 15th 1874	[illegible]	Lithographer
Henry Bernstein	7	April 28th 1874	New York, October 1866	Herman & Nellie Bernstein	Germany	Father	Wilmington, Delaware			
Jacob Bernstein	5	April 28th 1874	Honesdale, Pa., Aug 3rd 1868	Bernstein	Germany	Father	Wilmington			
Louis Simon Straus	9	June 18th 1874	Philadelphia, June 3rd 1865	Catherine Straus		Mother	Philadelphia			
Benjamin Lamm	5 1/2	Nov 8th 1869	[illegible]	Henry Lamm		Sisters	Chicago	[illegible]	[illegible]	[illegible]
Isaac Symmons	8	June [illegible] 1869	Columbia S.C.	Henry & Julia Symmons	England	Both	[illegible]	June 5/76	[illegible]	[illegible]
Aaron Rosenthal							[illegible]	[illegible]	[illegible]	[illegible]
Herman Glade	4	June 28th 1876	Philadelphia	Leibman & Lena	Germany	Father	No 431 4th St. [illegible]			

Figure 4-22. From the register of the Jewish Foster Home and Orphan Asylum, 1876–1911, Philadelphia, Pennsylvania, January 1876, pp. 1–2. FHL microfilm 1,013,425, item 3.

Missouri <www.umsystem.edu/shs/adoption.html>
Wisconsin <www.rootsweb.com/~wiorphan/>

Other sites offer a history of the program and are valuable to understanding how the trip away from home and all that was familiar affected these children. A good history can be found at <www.kancoll.org/articles/orphans/or_hist.htm> and <www.ancestry.com/library/view/ancmag/701.asp> includes eyewitness accounts.

Contact information for some of the organizations that participated in the Orphan Train follows:

Children's Aid Society
Office of Closed Records
150 East 45th Street
New York, NY 10017

New England Home for Little Wanderers
850 Boylston Street, Suite 201
Chestnut Hill, MA 02167

New York Children's Aid Society
105 East 22nd Street
New York, NY 10021

New York Juvenile Asylum Alumni Affairs Children's Village
Dobbs Ferry, NY 10007

New York Foundling Hospital Records Office
113 Third Avenue
New York, NY 10021

Figure 4-23. A 1902 photograph, taken in New York, of Agnes Wagner with her four brothers before she put them on an Orphan Train for Nebraska. *Standing, left to right:* William, age 14; Agnes, age 26; and Wesley, age 13. *Seated:* Earnest, age 10, and Arthur, age 12. Courtesy of Andre Dominguez.

Prisons and Penitentiary Records

Prisons, as they currently exist, first appeared approximately two hundred years ago. The first modern prison is believed to have been the Walnut Street Jail in Philadelphia, which was established in 1790. It was fashioned after the workhouses of London and other European cities.

Penologists saw a need for more sophisticated correctional institutions and designed what was considered a model prison at Auburn, New York, in 1825. It was followed by Eastern State Penitentiary at Cherry Hill in Philadelphia in 1829. Thousands of prisons, reformatories, correctional institutions, and related penal groups have been established since.

The early criminal judicial system was likely to convict offenders for violations less serious than those of modern offenders. Probation was instituted in the United States at about the same time the prison at Auburn, New York, was established. The purpose of probation was the same then as it is now: to provide supervision for first-time offenders who committed lesser crimes and to avoid imprisoning juveniles.

Information included on prison records is extensive, so researchers may consider themselves lucky to be able to use this group of sources. The records may offer some or all of the following facts about the prisoner's personal and criminal history:

Name	Grade of Education
Age	Habits (alcohol use)
Birth date	Relations (parents living)
Height	Father's place of birth
Weight	Mother's place of birth

Complexion	Conjugal/children
Eye color	Date incarcerated
Hair color	Register number
Nationality	Court where charged
Occupation	Recommitments
Religion	How and when discharged

Jurisdictions

Early prisons were operated, as they are today, by federal, state, local, and military authorities. The correctional institutions of all four jurisdictions are listed in the *Directory: Juvenile and Adult Correctional Departments, Institutions, Agencies and Paroling Authorities*, a publication of the American Correctional Association.[64] This directory includes an organizational description of each institution.

Each jurisdiction has its own prison system. Each state maintains its own correctional facilities, as do most counties. On the federal level, the Federal Bureau of Prisons oversees the institutions that hold those who have committed federal crimes. The most famous of these may be the prison at Alcatraz, which opened as a prison in 1933 and closed in 1963. Alcatraz Prison records, 1934–1963, are online at <www.alcatrazhistory.com/roster.htm>. They show that Alphonse Capone, prisoner number 85, was convicted on income tax laws (figure 4-24). Note 8 explains that he had been transferred from the United States Prison at Atlanta because he was suspected of clandestine correspondence and clandestine transfer of money into the institution. From Alcatraz he was transferred to the Federal Corrections Institution at Terminal Island and then to the United States Prison at Lewisburgh, Pennsylvania.

Current United States penitentiaries, commonly called federal prisons, are located at

Atlanta, Georgia, established 1902
Florence, Colorado, established 1994
Leavenworth, Kansas, established 1906
Lewisburg, Pennsylvania, established 1932
Lompoc, California, established 1959
Marion, Illinois, established 1963
Terre Haute, Indiana, established 1940
White Deer, Pennsylvania, established 1993

An index to prisoners incarcerated in federal facilities since 1982 is available at <www.bop.gov/inmate_locator/index.jsp>. For information on earlier prisoners, write to the following address, with as much information about both the criminal and the crime as possible:

Office of Communications and Archives
Federal Bureau of Prisons
320 First Street, NW
Washington, DC 20534

Types of Records

Unfortunately, there is no complete inventory of the records maintained by each of the early correctional institutions in the United States. The types of records compiled by early Pennsylvania correctional institutions are representative of those found in other states for the same time period and include admission and discharge books, biographical registers, hospital record books, descriptive registers, convict dockets, reception descriptive books, registers of prisoners, death warrants, clemency files, pardon books, and lists of executions.

Admission and Discharge Books contain the name of the inmate, date of admission, race, sex, health, habits (temperance), marital status, immunizations, family diseases, number of convictions, length of sentence, time in county jail, birthplace, occupation, physical and mental health at release, time in prison, and pardon information.

Registers of Prisoners are similar to admission books and list the name of the prisoner, age, race, birthplace, number of convictions, county of residence, court of sentencing, date of sentencing, crime, maximum sentence, and remarks (usually about release). Figure 4-25 is a page from the Register of Prisoners, 1899 to 1901, of the Pennsylvania Industrial Reformatory.

Biographical Registers contain data about the inmate and the inmate's family, which offers valuable facts for genealogical research. The Biographical Register of the Pennsylvania Industrial Reformatory is a good example of the valuable information found in these registers. The information is divided into data about the inmate and data about the inmate's family (see figure 4-26).

Inmate	Family
Name	Insanity
Date of record	Epilepsy
Crime	Dissipation
Maximum sentence	Education
Family	Pecuniary condition
Schools	Occupations
Labor	Pauper or criminal
Religion	Religion
Associations	
Physical stature	
Mental capabilities	
Moral susceptibility	
Health	
Culture	
Addresses of correspondents	

The register in figure 4-26 gives more details than called for by the form. Joseph Larkey's parents are not named in it, but the dates and causes of their deaths are noted. His living relatives were two uncles, Michael and Charles Haggerty of Philadelphia. His grandparents were not identified by name but were listed as deceased. Other records list the names of parents, grandparents, and other relatives in the space for addresses of correspondents. All of this information is, of course, helpful to genealogists.

Prison Hospital Record Books may offer detailed information about the inmate's medical treatment while imprisoned, hospital record books may include a specific date and cause of death. They may contain statistical accounts of the types of illnesses treated and the frequency of treatment.

Descriptive Registers are similar to registers of prisoners, giving the date of entry, name, age, birthplace, occupation, complexion, color of eyes, color of hair, stature, physical marks, sentence, when sentenced, number of convictions, when and how discharged, expiration of sentence, and remarks.

Convict Dockets include some of the information sometimes found in other records, including name of inmate, crime, sentence, when sentenced, court of sentencing, name of prosecutor, date admitted, physical description, when discharged, and how. This list is part of the "A" page from the index to the 1826 Convict Docket of Western Pennsylvania State Penitentiary.

Reception Descriptive Lists of Convicts are an expanded form of early prison registers, and contain detailed information about the prison inmate. The information listed in these records includes the convict's name, age, race, crime, date of reception, date of sentence, county of conviction, occupation before and at the time of arrest, physical description, shoe size, weight, birthplace, education, occupational training, marital status, parental relations at fifteen, drinking habits, relatives in prison, cause of crime, and relative's residence.

Death Warrants consist of the actual warrant and all the supporting documentation of the conviction, and contain information of greater historical than genealogical value. The disposition of appeals for clemency and commutation are often included in the file.

Clemency Files contain requests to the governor for clemency in the sentence of a convict. A narrative in these files explains the circumstances involved in the commission of the crime, the reasons for clemency, and attestations to the character of the convict. The petition was signed by individuals who supported the granting of clemency.

Pardon Books attest to pardons granted to convicts by the state governor and contain little genealogical information. They do include references to the place of conviction and the court of sentencing.

ALCATRAZ The Warden Johnston Years 1933 to 1948

Alcatraz Prisoners
Numbers 51 to 100

#	Inmate Name	Race	Offense	Other
51	Brown, Thurman	B	Robbery, Housebreaking & Assault	Escape Risk Assumed Dead
52	Weston, Herbert	B	Murder (District of Columbia)	Dead
53	Fontaine, Harold	W	Assault with Intent to Kill	(1)
54	Golebrowski, John	W	Sodomy	(2)
55	Moten, Frank	B	Robbery (District of Columbia)	Discharged 1942
56	Brown, Benjamin	B	Murder (District of Columbia)	
57	Simmons, William	W	P.O. Robbery & Assault	
58	Kronz, George	W	Postal Laws: Robbery & Assault	
59	Fondren, Pearl	W	P.O. Robbery, Assault & Conspiracy	
60	Colson, James	W	Assault & Robbing US Mails	
61	Eaton, Ruey	W	Conspiracy, NMVTA, Stealing Govt Property	
62	Beardon, Walter	W	NMVTA	Dead
63	Coleman, Robert	B	Mail Robbery	
64	Waters, Francis	B	Robbery (District of Columbia)	Discharged 1944
65	Marsh, James	W	Robbery of Mail	
66	Messamore, John	W	Assault to Rape & Escape	Army Prisoner Escape Risk (3)
67	Montgomery, Harold	W	Assault on Mail Carrier & Robbery	
68	Watts, J.	W	Assault on Mail Custodian & Robbery	
69	Marques, Armand	W	Arson	Wanted for deportation
70	Fulbright, Floyd	W	NMVTA	Assumed dead
71	Schmidt, Ludwig	W	Robbing US Mail & Assault	Escape Risk Wanted by Immigration for deportation Dead
72	Krug, Charles	W	Sodomy	(4) Released 1936
73	Gogich, Lazar	W	Conspiracy & Counterfeiting	Assumed dead
74	McIntosh, Leo	W	NMVTA	Escape Risk
75	McNeely/McNealy, James	W	P.O. Robbery & Conspiracy	See also 761-AZ Released by Court Order 1940
76	Zuckerman, Louis	W	Sodomy & Assault	Army Prisoner Escape Risk
77	Morland, Thomas	W	Murder (Prisoner at Leavenworth)	
78	Cleaver, Charles	W	Conspiracy & Robbing US Mails	Escape Risk Connections to Chicago Underworld Assumed dead
79	Wareagle, Thomas	I	Kidnapping & NMVTA	(6) Assumed dead
80	Bender, John	I	Stealing Govt Property & Burglary	Army Prisoner (7)
81	Denny, Theodore	I	Assault on Postmaster	
82	Hooker, Stanley	W	NMVTA & Murder (Prisoner at Chillicothe)	
83	Walton, James	W	Robbery & Grand Larceny (District of Columbia)	Escape Risk Dead
84	Thomas, John	W	NMVTA	Dead
85	Capone, Alphonse	W	Income Tax Laws	(8)
86	Carter, William	W	Robbery & Grand Larceny (District of Columbia)	
87	Van Gorder, Hayes	W	Forgery & Using Mails to Defraud	Escape Risk (9) Dead
88	Matchok, Joseph	W	Counterfeiting (Passing)	Escape Risk Discharged 1941 Assumed Dead
89	Buckner, Walter	W	Forging US Obligations	Escape Risk Dead
90	O'Brien, Edward	W	Robbery of Mails & Assault	Discharged 1940 Dead
91	Patterson, Lester	W	Robbery of Mails	
92	Bicks, Frank	W	Murder	(10) Dead
93	Costner, Isaac	W	Robbery of Mails & Assault	Member of Touhey Gang
94	Gempp, William	W	NMVTA & Escape	Escape Risk

Figure 4-24. Entries in the list of Alcatraz Prisoners Numbers 51 to 100 from <www.notfrisco2.com/alcatraz/inmates/data/alist02> include Alphonse Capone (number 85). Note 8 summarizes Capone's prison history in Atlanta, Terminal Island, and Lewisburg, and supplies his date and place of death.

Number	NAME.	AGE	COLOR.	NATIVITY.	No. of Conv.	COUNTY.	COURT.	DATE OF SENTENCE. 1889	CRIME.	MAXIMUM SENTENCE.
1	Moore John G	21	White	Penn^a	1	Huntingdon	Quar. Sessions	Feby 13	Larceny	3 years
2	Schaeffer Frank	19	"	"	1	Dauphin	do	" 18	same	3 "
3	Moran James	17	"	"	1	do	do	" 18	Same	3 "
4	Crawford Marion	17	"	"	1	do	do	" 18	Same	4 "
5	Rafferty Thomas	16	"	"	1	Clearfield	do	" 20	Break'g & Ent'g & Larceny	4 "
6	Keller Chas E	19	"	"	1	Snyder	do	" 26	Larceny	3 "
7	Gassmeyer William	16	"	"	1	Philadelphia	do	March 2	Same	3 "
8	Neibauer Charles	18	"	"	1	do	do	" 2	Same	3 "
9	Carr James	22	"	"	1	do	do	" 2	Burglary	10
10	Humphries George	20	Black	No. Carolina	1	do	do	" 2	Larceny	3 "
11	Flood James	20	White	Penn^a	1	do	do	" 2	Same	3 "
12	Evard Thomas	20	"	"	1	do	do	" 2	Same	3 "
13	Pasquella John		"	Italy	1	do	do	" 2	Assault & Battery to kill	3 "
14	Burns Michael	18	"	Penn^a	1	do	do	" 2	Larceny	3 "
15	Jackson Montgomery	15	Black	"	1	Indiana	do	" 6	Entering dwelling with intent to commit felony	4 "
16	De Ford Chas (alias)	17	White	"	1	Franklin	do	Feby 26	Horse Stealing	10 "
17	Mitchell John	18	"	"	1	Beaver	do	March 8	Casting missiles upon a R.R. car & Assault	3 "
18	Donovan John	19	"	"	1	do	do	" 8		3 "
19	Reed Hiram E	18	"	"	1	Lycoming	do	" 14	Robbery	10 "
20	O'Horron William	17	"	"		Allegheny	do	" 7	Larceny	3 "
21	McKinney James	21	"	Ohio		do	do	" 7	Same	3 "
22	Brooks James	19	"	Penn^a		do	do	" 14	Receiv'g Stolen Goods	3 "
23	Geiger Samuel	18					Oyer & Ter.		[illegible]	10

Figure 4-25. From the Register of Prisoners, 1889–1901, Pennsylvania Industrial Reformary, p. 1. FHL microfilm 1,032,656, item 3.

Lists of Executions include some descriptive information about convicts, including date and time of execution, name, age, weight, and color. In addition, the name of the victim(s) and the arresting sheriff's name will appear.

Military Prisons often have information on POWs who were buried at a cemetery near the hospital or prison camp where they died. The bodies of others were returned to their home area. The cemeteries near Civil War prisons usually have a Union area and another area for the Confederate men. Many national cemeteries have burials from across the country.

The National Archives has microfilmed several sets of records on Civil War prisons that include lists of prisoners, including those at Columbia and Florence, South Carolina; Richmond, Virginia; and Raleigh, North Carolina.[65] Many of the records indicate the company, regiment, and date of death. Names of soldiers held at the Union Army Prison at Alton, Illinois, appear at <www.altonweb.com/history/civilwar/confed/index.html>. Listings include rank, company, state, date and place of capture, date and cause of death, and place of burial.

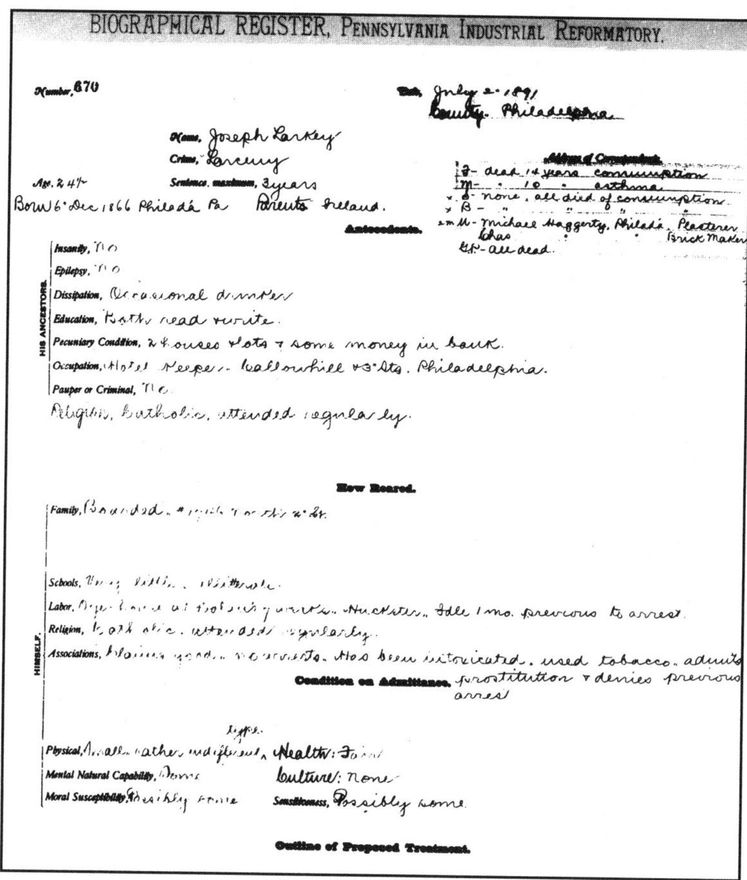

BIOGRAPHICAL REGISTER, PENNSYLVANIA INDUSTRIAL REFORMATORY.

Number, 670 Date, July 2 · 1891 County, Philadelphia

Name, Joseph Larkey
Crime, Larceny
Age, 24½ Sentence, maximum, 3 years
Born 6 Dec 1866 Philada Pa Parents Ireland.

Antecedents.

F - dead 14 years consumption
M - " 10 " asthma
B - none, all died of consumption
S - " "
m U - Michael Haggerty, Philada. Plasterer
Chas " " Brick Maker
G.P. - all dead.

HIS ANCESTORS.
Insanity, no
Epilepsy, no
Dissipation, Occasional drinker
Education, Both read & write.
Pecuniary Condition, 2 houses & lots & some money in bank.
Occupation, Hotel keeper. Callowhill & 3rd Sts. Philadelphia.
Pauper or Criminal, no
Religion, Catholic, attended regularly.

How Reared.

HIMSELF.
Family, Boarded [illegible]
Schools, [illegible]
Labor, [illegible] Huckster. Idle 1 mo. previous to arrest.
Religion, Catholic. attended regularly.
Associations, [illegible] Has been intoxicated. used tobacco. admits

Condition on Admittance. prostitution & denies previous arrest

Physical, Small. rather indifferent. Health: Fair
Mental Natural Capability, None Culture: none
Moral Susceptibility, Possibly some Sensitiveness, Possibly some.

Outline of Proposed Treatment.

Figure 4-26. From the Biographical Register, Pennsylvania Industrial Reformatory, no. 670. FHL microfilm 1,032,655, item 1.

Use of Prison Records

The value of prison records is greater than simply completing the story of an ancestor's life. Most of the time the prison records name other family members and open new research avenues.

For instance, the biographical register shown in figure 4-25 contains at least five leads to follow:

1. Joseph Larkey was born in Philadelphia on 6 December 1866. The 1866 city directory should list all of the Larkey families in that city during the year of his birth, possibly giving clues to parents, grandparents, and other relatives with the same surname.
2. Joseph's father was a hotelkeeper who died fourteen years before his son's incarceration (1877). The city directory of Philadelphia should be searched specifically for a hotelkeeper who is also named Larkey. Later directories should list his widow.
3. Joseph Larkey named Michael and Charles Haggerty as uncles. They are probably maternal uncles, so his mother's family should be sought among the Haggerty families of Philadelphia.
4. Information gained from city directories should lead to a search of the 1870 census for a Larkey family living in Philadelphia, with both parents having been born in Ireland and the head of the household employed as a hotelkeeper.
5. Records of the Catholic church closest to Callowhill and 3rd Street in Philadelphia, where Joseph's father worked, should be examined to see if the family was in the nearest parish.

Researchers should remember that in most cases modern prison records created in the last seventy-two years may fall under the jurisdiction of privacy laws and cannot be released. Family members may obtain the records of deceased convicts and ex-convicts under some circumstances, but you should inquire about those conditions at the prison or correctional agency by letter or telephone.

Availability of Records

Locating prison records requires some searching. Determining the name of the prison from other sources, such as newspaper articles, is very helpful. If you know the place or state of imprisonment, write to the prison itself or to the state department of corrections at the address given in the list previous in this chapter; request photocopies of the records available or their location, if they are no longer maintained by the prison authorities. Requests should list the specific record desired—"the entries from the biographical register, the reception descriptive list, and the clemency file," for example—to insure receiving records of maximum genealogical value.

Determine if the records are currently held by an archival facility, whether public or private. Also determine if the records have been microfilmed and by whom. The records of Pennsylvania prisons, for example, have been microfilmed by the Genealogical Society of Utah, but the actual records are still on file at the prison or at the state archives. Some genealogical societies have indexed extensive records in their county, including prison or jail registers. The printed index may include minimal information, such as name of detainee and the date that he registered at the jail; however, further investigation may reveal the original ledger book or records. One example is Herb Bumgarner's *Jail Register Index, Clackamas County, Oregon, From 1892 to 1925 Except For Years 1903 thru 1906*.

The list of records available on the Internet is large and growing almost daily. Some of the sources follow:

Arkansas State Penitentiary Records, 1918–1920 <http://homepages.rootsweb.com/~xrysta/arpen19181920.htm>

Chicago Police Department Homicide Record Index, 1870–1930, indexes name of deceased, date of death, and sometimes name of another person mentioned in the record. <www.cyberdriveillinois.com/GenealogyMWeb/chrisrch.html>

Colorado corrections records, with an index from 1871 to 1973 <www.colorado.gov/dpa/doit/archives/pen/index.htm>, Colorado state penitentiary and reformatory records <www.colorado.gov/dpa/doit/archives/pen/prison.html>, with biographical information about inmates and their crimes, sentences and paroles or pardons, with mug shots of most inmates.

Jefferson County, Arkansas, Penitentiary Records, 1936–1938 <www.rootsweb.com/~arjeffer/jefferson_county_penitentiary_re.htm>

Missouri State Penitentiary Index and Register of Inmates <www.sos.mo.gov/archives/pubs/archweb/pen.asp>, including prisoner's name, prison number, some background information, crime committed, and date of release.

Pennsylvania Prison Records <www.phmc.state.pa.us/bah/dam/prison.htm>

Utah Index to Criminal Case Files, 1896–1915, plus an index to pardons granted between 1880 and 1920; *Utah Archives Index to Pardons Granted Record Books, 1880–1921* <http://historyresearch.utah.gov/indexes/index.htm>

Wisconsin local and county records of varying periods listed at <www.uwm.edu/Libraries/arch/safety.htm> (Other university libraries or archival facilities have similar records for their area of the country.)

Table 4-1. Ethnic Organizations

Fraternal Benefit Societies, 1940

- Polish National Alliance of the U.S. of N.A., Chicago
- First Catholic Slovak Union, Cleveland
- Croatian Fraternal Union of America, Pittsburgh
- Workmen's Circle, New York City (Jewish)
- Lutheran Brotherhood, Minneapolis (Norwegian)
- Greek Catholic Union of Russian Brotherhoods, Munhall, Pennsylvania
- The Order of Vasa, Chicago (Swedish)
- Workmen's Benefit Fund, Brooklyn (German)
- L'Union St. Jean Baptiste d'Amerique, Woonsocket, Rhode Island
- Slovene National Benefit Society, Chicago
- Western Bohemian Fraternal Association, Cedar Rapids, Iowa
- Verhovay Fraternal Ins. Association, Pittsburgh (Hungarian)
- Ukrainian National Association, New Jersey
- Czecho-Slovak Society of America, Pittsburgh
- Sons of Italy, Philadelphia
- Armenian Democratic Liberal Association, Boston
- Macedonian People's League of USA, Detroit (Bulgarian)

Organizations

Our ancestors belonged to organizations just as we do, and these organizations created records that can tell us more about their lives and interests. Membership records place an individual in a time and place—information that can lead us to other records. Details from membership applications and records often include dates and places that can be very helpful in our genealogical research. The organizations discussed in this section are representative of the types that exist, though in terms of numbers they include only a small percentage of those that have existed over the years.

Fraternal Organizations and Fraternal Benefit Societies

At the beginning of the twentieth century, about eighty-five percent of adult males in the United States belonged to a fraternal organization such as the Masons, Odd Fellows, Knights of Pythias, and Elks. Members in a given society shared a military experience, religion, or occupation. Often the organizations had an ethnic composition, so members shared language, culture, and memories. The social organization was only one benefit to

Table 4.2. Tombstone Initials and Their Meanings

Initials	Meaning
AF&AM	(Masonic)
ALOH	American Legion of Honor
AOH	Ancient Order of Hibernians
AOKMC	Ancient Order of Knights of Mystic Chain
AOUW	Ancient Order of United Workmen
BPOE	Benevolent and Protective Order of Elks
BPOEW	Benevolent and Protective Order of Elks of the World
CK of A	Catholic Knights of America
CSA	Confederate States Army
DAR	Daughters of the American Revolution
FAA	Free and Accepted Americans
F&AM	Free and Accepted Masons
FLT	Friendship, Love, and Truth (Independent Order of Oddfellows)
FOE	Fraternal Order of Eagles
GAR	Grand Army of the Republic
IHSV	Red Cross of Constantine
IOI	Independent Order of Immaculates
IOKP	Independent Order of Knights of Pythias
IOOF	Independent Order of Odd Fellows
IWW	Industrial Workers of the World
KC/K of C	Knights of Columbus
KP	Knights of Pythias
K of STP	Knights of St. Patrick
K of STW	Knights of St. Wenceslas
KKK	Knights of Ku Klux Klan
KSF	Knights of Sherwood Forest
LAOH	Ladies Ancient Order of Hibernians
LOM	Loyal Order of the M.O.O.S.E.
MWA	Modern Woodmen of America
OES	Order of the Eastern Star
SAR	Sons of the American Revolution
SCV	Sons of the Confederate Veterans
UCV	United Confederate Veterans
UDC	United Daughters of the Confederacy
VFW	Veterans of Foreign Wars
WOW	Woodmen of the World

members. Organizations sold, for a relatively low price, insurance that covered sickness, disability, and burial. The organizations also had an obligation to care for the widows and orphaned children of members. The fraternal organizations often published their own newspapers, sponsored classes in Americanization, and supported orphanages, homes for the aged, and social clubs. While there were hundreds such ethnic organizations, the most important ones appear in table 4-1.[66] Descriptions of many fraternal organizations appears in Schmidt's *Fraternal Organizations*.[67]

Membership in fraternal organizations frequently is designated by initials or a symbol on tombstones. Knowing what the initials or the insignia stand for can lead the family historian to additional records for research. A partial list of abbreviations appears in table 4-2. More abbreviations may be found at the ObitCentral <www.obitcentral.com/cemsearch/initials.htm>.

Freemasons

Freemasonry came to the United States from England in 1733, making it one of the earliest fraternal organizations in the country. For more than two centuries, it was an influential institution because of the membership of prominent individuals. Lodge records are generally limited to membership information: date of joining the lodge, rank attained, offices held, and so on. There may be biographical material on some lodge leaders. Members in the Blue Lodge or basic unit are divided into three degrees, with the highest being Master Mason. Membership information is available from existing units. Each state's Grand Masonic Lodge maintains only membership status records but should be contacted first for the name of the probable membership lodge. Contact that lodge for more complete information. The Freemasons website <www.freemasonry.org> is a good place to begin a search for membership organization. Figure 4-27 indicates Fred Harry Carter was a member of the Freemasons.

Modern Woodmen of America

One example of a fraternal benefit society is Modern Woodmen of America. The organization was founded in 1883 by Joseph Cullen Root, who dreamed of a fraternal benefit society that would provide financial security to families from all walks of life. Despite its name, the organization was never limited to those involved in forestry or woodworking, but rather came from a sermon discussing "pioneer woodmen clearing the forest for the benefit of man." Members lived in the less urban areas of the country's north. Members photographed in uniform carried heavy axes and had insignia on their hats, as shown in figure 4-28. One of the most interesting aspects of the Woodmen is the distinctive tombstones found at the graves of members. Likely the design includes a tree stump or the design of one carved on a marker.

Modern Woodmen offers two types of records: the business records of various units, called lodges, and records of benefits paid, which of course are more interesting to genealogists. The first death benefit was issued in 1884 to a Davenport, Iowa, widow, whose husband died from "indiscretion in eating confectionery, ice cream, etc. on the Fourth of July, with the incident excitement and heat." Records from then through 1946 will be searched upon request; details are available at the website <www.modern-woodmen.org./Public/AboutUs/History/>.[69]

Grand Army of the Republic

The Grand Army of the Republic (GAR) was formed to cultivate fraternity, comradeship, and patriotism among Union veterans who had served in the United States on land or sea during the Civil War, 1861–1865. Founded in Illinois in 1866, the organization spread quickly throughout the country. During the late nineteenth century, GAR had considerable influence in state and national politics. Among other things, members promoted the establishment of Memorial Day as a national holiday.

GAR featured a three-tiered organization: posts at the local or precinct level, districts at the county level, and departments at the state level. Meetings had multiple purposes: to promote the organization, to protect and assist disabled soldiers and their families, and to promote appreciation of service to the country through moral, social, and political activity. An example of post records is the Utah register shown in figure 4-29. A list of GAR posts arranged by department may be found in Albert E. Smith, Jr.'s *The Grand Army of the Republic and Kindred Societies: A Guide to Resources in the General Collections of the Library of Congress*, which may be accessed online at <www.loc.gov/rr/main/gar/garhome.html>.[69]

The GAR almost disappeared in the early 1870s, and many state units disbanded. New leadership about 1875 led to new growth, and in 1890, the GAR reached its largest membership of just over 490,000. In 1949, six surviving members permanently closed the organization.[70]

Because membership in the GAR was so widespread, any genealogist with an ancestor who fought in and survived the Civil War should look for membership information on that ancestor.

Survival of the records is good, and many are available in print or on the Web. Some examples follow, and researchers should always check Cyndi's List <www.cyndislist.com.> for additional listings.

Colorado

"Colorado Civil War Grand Army of the Republic Members." Online at <www.denverlibrary.org/research/genealogy/index.html>.

Illinois

Grand Army of the Republic Department of Illinois Transcription of the Death Rolls, 1879–1947. St. Louis: Northcott Publications, 2003. Online at <www.ngpublications.com>.

Kansas

"Index to Necrology Lists in Kansas G.A.R. Encampments, 1884–1942." Online at <www.kshs.org/genealogists/military/gar/garnecrologies.htm>.

Roster of the Members and the Posts, Grand Army of the Republic, Department of Kansas. Topeka: Department of Kansas, 1894.

CARTER, FRED HARRY

ANCIENT AND ACCEPTED SCOTTISH RITE OF FREEMASONRY
SOUTHERN JURISDICTION OF THE UNITED STATES

SEP 12 1945 VALLEY OF ST. LOUIS, SEP 12 1945 19

To the Officers and Members of St. Louis Lodge of Perfection, St. Louis Chapter Rose Croix, Missouri Council Knights Kadosh, Missouri Consistory:

I am a Master Mason in good standing in Cuba Lodge No. 312 under the jurisdiction of the Grand Lodge of Missouri (and late a member ...Degree of the Scottish Rite Bodies in the Valley of ... as shown by Certificate of Good Standing or Dimit attached).

I was born on the 20 day of April 1902 in St. Louis State of Missouri

My residence is Cuba, Missouri. Telephone 68

I have resided in Cuba Missouri. 7 years, 9 months

My business address is Cuba Mo. Telephone 68 or 21

Send mail to P.O. Box 273 Cuba State of Missouri

My occupation is Merchant

(CONTINUED ON OTHER SIDE)

Please Do Not Fold

FEES FOR DEGREES

Lodge,	4° to 14°		$40.00
Chapter,	15° to 18°		30.00
Council,	19° to 30°		30.00
Consistory,	31° to 32°		60.00
		Total,	$160.00

Not less than $40.00 must accompany the petition.

No fee is required for Affiliation, but a brother of the Jurisdiction of any other Supreme Council affiliating with this Consistory must remit $4.00 for Patents of the Thirty-second Degree.

Make check payable to St. Louis Lodge of Perfection No. 1

Mail petition to The Secretary, A.A.S.R. Scottish Rite Cathedral Grand and Lindell Boulevards St. Louis, Mo.

(CONTINUED FROM OTHER SIDE)

My height is 6 feet ... inches; Color of eyes blue Color of hair red

*I have never previously applied for the Scottish Rite Degrees

I now respectfully petition to receive the degrees from the 4th to the 32d. if elected promising always to bear true faith and allegiance to the Supreme Council of the Thirty-third and Last Degree for the Southern Jurisdiction of the United States.

Name of Applicant: Fred Harry Carter

Recommended by: 1. [signature] 2. George A. Seibert

References: 1. C C Coy Cuba, Mo 2. [signature] Cuba, Mo

*If applicant has previously applied for any of the degrees, he will strike out the word "never" and state time, place, and to what Scottish Rite Body application was made.

Please Do Not Fold

Figure 4-27. The Freemasonry card for Fred Harry Carter includes both organization and personal information.

Figure 4-28. Uniformed members of Modern Woodmen of America, a fraternal beneficiary society. Richard Mason Spensley *(left)* belonged to Camp No. 73631, Chicago, Illinois. Photograph c. 1908. Courtesy of Sandra Luebking.

Massachusetts

Sargent, A. Dean, comp. *Grand Army of the Republic: Civil War Veterans, Department of Massachusetts, 1866 to 1947*. Bowie, Md.: Heritage Books, 2002.

Minnesota

Richardson, Antona Hawkins. *Roll of the Dead, 1886–1906: Department of Minnesota, Grand Army of the Republic*. St. Paul: Paduan Press, 2000.

Missouri

Concannon, Marie, and Josiah Parkinson, comps. *Grand Army of the Republic—Missouri Division—Index to Death Rolls, 1882–1940*. Columbia: State Historical Society of Missouri, 1995.

Grand Army of the Republic, Department of Missouri. *Roster of the Department of Missouri, Grand Army of the Republic, and Its Auxiliaries*. Kansas City: Western Veteran, 1895.

Roster of the Department of Missouri, Grand Army of the Republic, 1895. Springfield, Mo.: The Camp, about 1999.

Nebraska

"Nebraska Civil War Veterans." Online at <www.denverlibrary.org/research/genealogy/index.html>.

Oregon

Myers, Jane, comp. *Honor Roll of Oregon Grand Army of the Republic, 1881–1935: Deaths Reported in Oregon of Members of the GAR, Extracted from Proceedings of the Annual Encampments of the Department of Oregon, Grand Army of the Republic*. Cottage Grove, Ore.: Cottage Grove Genealogical Society, about 1980.

Jewish Foundation for Education of Women, 1880 to 1988

Since 1964, the Jewish Foundation for Education of Women has provided nonsectarian scholarship assistance to disadvantaged women seeking to better themselves through higher education. The organization traces its origins to the Louis Down Town Sabbath School, founded in 1880 to help underprivileged children of Jewish immigrants on the Lower East Side. From 1895 to 1932, operating as the Hebrew Technical School for Girls, it offered courses in commercial and industrial arts to young women. Directors closed the school in 1932 and developed a program of scholarship assistance to women. Although the foundation became nonsectarian in 1964, it retained the term "Jewish" in its title as a reminder of its heritage. Manuscript records include correspondence, minutes, annual reports, case files, registers of scholarship recipients, and miscellaneous administrative records.[71]

Notes

[1] *Information Please Almanac, Atlas, and Yearbook*, 35th ed. (New York: Simon and Schuster, 1982), 48.

[2] U.S. Bureau of the Census, "Labor Force and Employment by Industry: 1800–1960," *Historical Statistics of the United States, Colonial Times to 1970*, part 1, series D (Washington, D.C.: Government Printing Office, 1975), 165.

[3] Kenn Stryker-Rodda, "The Janeway Account Books, 1735–1746," *Genealogical Magazine of New Jersey* 33 (January–April 1958): 4.

[4] Kenneth Scott, "Some Huntington, Long Island Residents, 1763–1779," *National Genealogical Society Quarterly* 62 (September 1974): 177.

[5] Conklin Mann, "The Family of Conchelyne, etc. in America," *American Genealogist* 21 (1944–1945): 48–58, 133–47, 210, 215, 246–53; 22 (1945–1946): 111–21, 226–36.

[6] E. L. (Roy) Meyers, comp., *Foster-Pettygrove Store Lists. The Barlow Toll Road 1846–1919: The Story of Two Men from*

Fort Deposit. *They Called It Jack-Knife: History of Eagle Creek Community and School District Number 17* (Portland, Ore.: Genealogical Forum of Oregon, 1991). Originals are part of the Philip Foster Collection at the Oregon Historical Society.

[7] Anthony T. Kruzas and Robert C. Thomas, eds., *Business Organizations and Agencies Directory* (Detroit: Gale Research Co., 1980).

[8] David M. Brownstone and Gordon Carruth, *Where to Find Business Information,* 2nd ed. (New York: John Wiley and Sons, 1982).

[9] *Directory of Historical Organizations in the United States and Canada,* 14th ed. (Nashville: American Association for State and Local History, 1990).

[10] Peter N. Vandenberge, *Historical Directory of the Reformed Church of America, 1625–1965* (New Brunswick, N.J.: Reformed Church in America, 1966), 22.

[11] *The Yearbook of American and Canadian Churches* (Nashville: Abingdon Press), annual.

[12] *Martindale-Hubbell Law Directory* (Martindale, N.J.: Martindale-Hubbell), annual.

[13] *Martins's Bench and Bar of Philadelphia* (Philadelphia: Rees Welsh and Co., 1883).

[14] *Directory of Deceased American Physicians, 1804–1929* (Chicago: American Medical Association, 1993).

[15] J. Boyd Collard, *Hospitals and Medical Doctors in Pittsburg County, Oklahoma* (Lawton, Okla.: the author, 1994).

[16] George Berton Cutten, *The Silversmiths of Virginia from 1694 to 1850* (Richmond: Diete Press, 1952), 172.

[17] Robert H. Dructor, *A Guide to Genealogical Sources at the Pennsylvania State Archives,* 2nd ed. (Harrisburg: Pennsylvania Historical and Museum Commission, 1998), 114, 119, 155, 168.

[18] U.S. Department of Labor, *Apprenticeship Past and Present,* rev. ed. (Washington, D.C.: U.S. Department of Labor, 1964).

[19] Ibid.

[20] Kathy Ritter, *Apprentices of Connecticut, 1637–1900* (Salt Lake City: Ancestry, 1986); Harold B. Gill Jr., *Apprentices of Virginia, 1623–1800* (Salt Lake City: Ancestry, 1989).

[21] Martha Reamy, *Early Church Records of Chester County, Pennsylvania. Vol. 1: Quaker Records of Bradford Monthly Meeting* (Westminster, Md.: Family Line Publications, 1995), 152.

[22] William Nelson, ed., *Documents Relating to Colonial History of New Jersey,* 1st series, vol. 12 (Patterson, N.J.: Press Printing and Publishing Co., 1895), 401.

Figure 4-29. Membership registers like this one from GAR Post #1 in Utah include both military and personal information. FHL microfilm 1,666,083.

COPY OF RECORDS FROM GAR POST # 1 McKean PAGE # 8

NAME & RESIDENCE	BIRTHPLACE	DATE	RANK	ORGANIZATION	REMARKS
131. Butler, Thomas C. SLC	Penna.	ENL. 29 Oct. 1861 DISCH. 30 Aug. 1865	Pvt. do	I. 10th Kan. Inf. do	
132. Gaby, Will D. SLC	Indiana	ENL. 6 Feb. 1862 DISCH. 7 Feb. 1865	Pvt. do	K. 53rd Ohio Inf. do	
133. Lowell, ~~John W.~~ SLC	Vt.	ENL. 6 Aug. 1861 DISCH. 5 Sept. 1865	Pvt. Capt.	G.2nd Arty Ill. Vol or 2nd Ill Inf	
134. Edgerly, Jason H. SLC	New Hampshire	ENL. April 1861 DISCH. 14 April 1865	Pvt. Sgt.	1stUS or Mass H A(B) 12th Mass. H A (G)	
135. Brough, Charles M. SLC	Penn.	ENL. 11 Aug. 1862 DISCH. 21 June 1865	Pvt. Pvt.	H. 15th Penn. Cav. do	Died Nov 16, 1910 In California
136. Gardiner, Frederick	England	ENL. 4 July 1863 DISCH. 7 Aug. 1865	Pvt. Hosp.Stwd	A. 5th L A Inf. do	
137. Pruett, James T.	N.Y.	ENL. 28 Sept. 1861 DISCH. 5 May 1862	 Corp.	H. 52nd Ill Inf do	
138. Bray, William B. SLC	Scotland	ENL. 17 Dec. 1864 DISCH. 24 Oct. 1865	Corp. Corp.	G. 8 Cal. Inf. do	
139. Forshay, Simeon SLC	N.Y.	ENL. Aug. 1862 DISCH. July 1865	Pvt. Corp.	A/ 127th N.Y.Inf. do	Died Aug. 9, 1898
140. Clark, Chas. A. SLC	N.Y.	ENL. 3 Sept. 1864 DISCH 2 June 1865	Pvt. do	6th Minn. Inf. (F) do	
141. Lambert, O.W. (G.O.)?	1BXXX	ENL. 15 Aug. 1861 DISCH 17 Oct. 1865	Pvt. do	56 N.Y.Inf. (E) do	Died Sept 11, 1901 Mt.O
142. Sowles, Hiram B. Silver City, Utah	Albargh, Vt.	ENL. 11 June 1861 DISCH 10 Sept. 1863	1st Sgt. 2nd Lt.	K. 1st Iowa Cav. do	
143. Terdie, Louis SLC	Brussels, Belgium	ENL. 2 Oct. 1861 DISCH 4 Oct. 1864	Pvt. do	A. 3rd Cal. Inf. do	D. July 8, 1889.
144. Hawley, Chas. A. SLC	Cleveland, O.	ENL. 3 June 1862 DISCH 3 June 1865	Bugler do	C. 11th U.S.Inf. do	
145. Mallory, Chas. SLC	New York	ENL. 15 Sept. 1861 DISCH 5 March 1865	Pvt. Com.Sgt	G. 9th Iowa Inf. do	
146. Walton, Geo. W. SLC	N.Y., N.Y.	ENL. 4 Feb. 1861 DISCH 15 Aug. 1865	Pvt. 1st Sgt.	I. 2nd U.S.Arty. C. 3rd Vet.Res.Corps	D. May 4, 1898. Mt.O.
147. Meacham, (Mecham) John W. Tooele	Mercer Co. Pa.	ENL. 12 Aug. 1862 DISCH 13 Nov. 1865	Pvt. do	C. 29th Iowa Inf. do	DD.1888 Bur.Tooele
148. Timmony, E.M.B. Marysvale, Ut.	New Orleans, La.	ENL. 12 May 1861 DISCH 6 April 1865	1st Lt. Capt.	15th U.S.Inf. do	
149. Alves, John SLC	N.Y.	ENL. 25 May 1861 DISCH 24 June 1864	Pvt. do	14 Ill. Inf. do	[illegible]
150. Wallin, Chas. E. SLC	Michigan	ENL. 13 Aug. 1864 DISCH 10 June 1865	Pvt. do	8th Mich. Cav. (B) do	

[23] George W. Neible, "Account of Servants Bound and Assigned Before James Hamilton, Mayor of Philadelphia," *Pennsylvania Magazine of History and Biography* 32 (October 1908): 369.

[24] Paul Lewinson and Morris Rieger, "Labor Union Records in the United States," *American Archivist* 25 (January 1962): 39.

[25] Ibid., 46–57.

[26] Warner Pflug, *A Guide to the Archives of Labor History and Urban Affairs* (Detroit: Wayne State University Press, 1974).

[27] Wendy Elliott, "Railroad Records for Genealogical Research," *National Genealogical Society Quarterly* 75 (December 1987): 271–77. Addendum to the article, *National Genealogical Society Quarterly* 79 (June 1991): 140.

[28] *Biographical Directory of Railway Officials of America* (New York: Simmons-Boardman).

[29] *Moody's Transportation Manual* (New York: Moody's, 2000), issued annually 1963–2000. Since 2001, known as *Mergent Transportation Manual* (New York: Mergent, 2001), issued annually. See <www.mergent.com/publish/product54.asp>.

[30] Claire Prechtel-Kluskens, "Documenting the Career of Federal Employees," *Prologue* 26 (Fall 1994): 180–85.

[31] Shepard B. Clough, *A Century of American Life Insurance: A History of the Mutual Life Company of New York, 1843–1943* (New York: Columbia University Press, 1946), 5.

[32] Ibid., 8.

[33] Harold F. Larkin, "Retention of Life Insurance Records," *American Archivist* 5 (April 1942): 95–98.

[34] Duane Galles, "Using Life Insurance Policies in Genealogical Research," *Genealogical Journal* 20 (1992): 156–71.

[35] Mutual Fire Assurance Policy for 32 Christian Street, Philadelphia.

[36] Records for Karl R. Peters extracted from Oliver Bair Funeral Home, originals at Historical Society of Pennsylvania, Philadelphia.

[37] Oliver Wendell Holmes, "Evaluation and Preservation of Business Archives," *American Archivist* 1 (October 1938): 171–85.

[38] Address all requests to the South Suburban Genealogical and Historical Society, 3000 West 170th Place, Hazel Crest, Illinois 60429-1174 or visit <www.rootsweb.com/~ssghs/pullman.htm#Pullman%20Collection>. A search fee supports the maintenance of the collection.

[39] Craig W. Horle, et al., *Lawmaking and Legislators in Pennsylvania: A Biographical Dictionary,* 2 vols, 1682–1709; 1710–1756 (Philadelphia: University of Pennsylvania Press, 1991, 1997).

[40] Mary Q. Elliott, *Biographical Sketches of Knox County (Ohio) Writers* (Mount Vernon, Ohio: 1937).

[41] T. A. Busbey, *Biographical Directory of Railway Officials of America* (Chicago: Railway Age, 1901). Published biennually since 1885. An online index to individuals connected with St. Louis metropolitan area appearing in biennial years 1887–1985 is at <www.slpl.lib.mo.us/libsrc/railroar.htm>.

[42] Robert B. Slocum, *Biographical Dictionaries and Related Works* (Detroit: Gale Research Co., 1986).

[43] *Missoula City Directory* (Missoula, Mont.: R. L. Polk and Co., 1922), 271. *h* means "house," *r* means "resides at."

[44] Milton Meskowitz, *Everybody's Business: A Field Guide to the 400 Leading Companies in America* (New York: Doubleday/Currency, 1990).

[45] Dun and Bradstreet, *America's Corporate Families* (Parsippany, N.J.: Duns's Marketing Services) annual.

[46] *Ward's Business Directory of U.S. Private and Public Companies* (Petaluma, Calif.: Baldwin H. Ward), annual, available online at <www.galegroup.com/pdf/facts/wards.pdf>.

[47] William G. Roy, "Collecting Data on American Business Officials in the Late Nineteenth and Early Twentieth Century," *Historical Methods* 15 (Fall 1982): 143–51.

[48] *Robert D. Fisher Manual of Valuable and Worthless Securities* (New York: R. D. Fisher), serial.

[49] *Directories in Print* (Detroit: Gale Research Co.), annual.

[50] Albert L. Demaree, *The American Agricultural Press, 1819–1860* (New York: Columbia University Press, 1941), 393–400.

[51] *National Union Catalog of Manuscript Collections* (Washington, D.C.: Library of Congress, 1972), 20.

[52] National Historical Publications and Records Commission, *Directory of Archives and Manuscript Repositories in the United States* (Phoenix: Oryx Press, 1988), available at <www.oryxpress.com>.

[53] *Manuscripts of the Historical Society of Pennsylvania* (Philadelphia: the society, n.d.).

[54] Lee Ash, ed., *Subject Collections: A Guide to Special Book Collections and Subject Emphasis,* 7th ed. (Providence, N.J.: R. R. Bowker Co., 1993).

[55] Karen M. Benedict, *A Select Bibliography on Business Archives and Records Management* (Chicago: Society of American Archivists, 1981).

[56] Alan M. Meckler and Ruth McMullin, comps. and eds., *Oral History Collection* (New York: R. R. Bowker Co., 1975).

[57] Phyllis Hapner and Judy Graven, *Almshouse Register for Shelby County, Illinois* (n.p.: typescript, 1985).

[58] *An Act to Establish A Civilian Conservation Corps, and For Other Purposes, As Amended,* public no. 163, 75th cong., 1st sess. (50 Stat. 319), original act approved 28 June 1937, downloaded from <www.nysccmuseum.com> on 20 October 2003.

[59] Leslie Elizabeth Miljat, *Admission Applications, 1867–1872. National Home for Disabled Volunteer Soldiers, Northwestern Branch, Milwaukee Wisconsin* (Wauwatosa, Wis.: L. E. Miljat, 1991).

[60] Timothy A. Hacsi, *Second Home: Orphan Asylums and Poor Families in America* (Cambridge, Mass: Harvard University Press, 1997), 1–2.

[61] County Commissioners' Minutes, Book B, Ohio County, Indiana, May term, 1827.

[62] Marilyn Irvin Holt, "Orphan Train Genealogy," at <www.ancestry.com/library/view/ancmag/701.asp>.

[63] Mary Ellen Johnson, comp., *Orphan Train Riders: Their Own Stories* (Baltimore: Gateway Press, 1992).

[64] *Directory: Juvenile and Adult Correctional Departments, Institutions, Agencies and Paroling Authorities* (Laurel, Md.: American Correctional Association, 1995).

[65] Lonnie R. Speer, *Portals to Hell: Military Prisons of the Civil War* (Mechanicsburg, Penn.: Stackpole Books, 1997), 385–86.

[66] August E. Bolino, *The Ellis Island Source Book* (Washington, D.C.: Kensington Historical Press, 1985), 119, 121.

[67] Alvin J. Schmidt, *The Greenwood Encyclopedia of American Institutions: Fraternal Institutions* (Westport, Conn.: Greenwood Press, 1980).

[68] Gail Ann Hodges Levis, "My Papa Was a Woodman," *FORUM* 15 (Fall 2003): 1, 21, 22.

[69] Albert E. Smith Jr., *The Grand Army of the Republic and Kindred Societies: A Guide to Resources in the General Collections of the Library of Congress* (Washington, D.C.: Library of Congress, 2001), available online at <www.loc.gov/rr/main/gar/garhome.html>.

[70] "Brief History of the Early GAR," at <http.//pages.prodigy.net/mistergar/pg8hist.htm>.

[71] John D. Stinson, comp., "Guide to the Records of the Jewish Foundation for the Education of Women" (1991), found at New York Public Library website at <www.nypl.org/research/chss/spe/rbk/faids/jewishfound.html>.

References

Business Research and Finding Aids

Ash, Lee. *Subject Collections: A Guide to Special Book Collections and Subject Emphasis.* 7th ed. Providence, N.J.: R. R. Bowker Co., 1993.

Benedict, Karen M. *A Select Bibliography on Business Archives and Records Management*. Chicago: Society of American Archivists, 1981.

Bolino, August E. *The Ellis Island Source Book*. Washington, D.C.: Kensington Historical Press, 1985.

Brownstone, David M., and Gordon Carruth. *Where to Find Business Information*. New York: John Wiley and Sons, 1979.

Cochran, Thomas Childs. *200 Years of American Business*. New York: Basic Books, 1977.

Corporate Names Index, 1959–1984. Alexandria, Va.: Chadwyck-Healey, 1994.

Craumer, Lucille V., ed. *Business Periodicals Index*. New York: H. W. Wilson Co., annual since 1958.

Daniels, Lorna M. *Business Information Sources*. 3rd ed. Berkeley: University of California Press, 1993.

Demaree, Albert L. *The American Agricultural Press, 1819–1860.* New York: Columbia University Press, 1941.

Directory: Juvenile and Adult Correctional Departments, Institutions, Agencies and Paroling Authorities. Laurel, Md.: American Correctional Association, 1995.

Dun and Bradstreet. *America's Corporate Families*. Skokie, Ill.: National Register Publishing Co., annual.

Evans, George H., Jr. *Business Incorporations in the United States, 1800–1943*. Princeton, N.J.: Princeton University Press, 1948.

Historical Statistics of the United States Colonial Times to 1970. Washington, D.C.: U.S. Department of Commerce, 1975.

Holmes, Oliver Wendell. "Evaluation and Preservation of Business Archives." *American Archivist* 1 (October 1938): 171–85.

Larson, Henrietta. *Guide to Business History*. Cambridge, Mass.: Harvard University Press, 1948.

Levis, Gail Ann Hodges. "My Papa Was a Woodman." *FORUM* 15 (Fall 2003).

Manuscripts of the Historical Society of Pennsylvania. Philadelphia: the society, n.d.

Meckler, Alan M., and Ruth McMullin, comps. and eds. *Oral History Collection*. New York: R. R. Bowker Co., 1975.

Meyers, E. L. (Roy), comp. *Foster-Pettygrove Store Lists. The Barlow Toll Road 1846–1919: The Story of Two Men from Fort Deposit. They Called It Jack-Knife: History of Eagle Creek Community and School District Number 17*. Portland: Genealogical Forum of Oregon, 1991.

Miljat, Leslie Elizabeth. *Admission Applications, 1867–1872. National Home for Disabled Volunteer Soldiers, Northwestern Branch, Milwaukee Wisconsin*. Wauwatosa, Wis.: L. E. Miljat, 1991.

Missoula City Directory. Missoula: R. L. Polk and Co., 1922.

Moskowitz, Milton, Michael Katz, and Robert Levering, eds. *Everybody's Business: A Field Guide to the 400 Leading Companies in America*. New York: Doubleday/Currency, 1990.

Robert D. Fisher Manual of Valuable and Worthless Securities. New York: R. D. Fisher, serial.

Roy, William G. "Collecting Data on American Business Officials in the Late Nineteenth and Early Twentieth Century." *Historical Methods* 15 (Fall 1982): 143–51.

Saretsky, Gary D. "North American Business Archives: Results of a Survey." *American Archivist* 40 (October 1977): 413–20.

Schmidt, Alvin J. *The Greenwood Encyclopedia of American Institutions: Fraternal Institutions*. Westport, Conn.: Greenwood Press, 1980.

Slocum, Robert B. *Biographical Dictionaries and Related Works*. 2 vols. Detroit: Gale Research Co., 1986.

Smith, Albert E., Jr. *The Grand Army of the Republic and Kindred Societies: A Guide to Resources in the General Collections of the Library of Congress*. Washington, D.C.: Library of Congress, 2001.

Stryker-Rodda, Kenn. "The Janeway Account Books, 1735–1746." *Genealogical Magazine of New Jersey* 33 (January–April 1958).

U.S. Bureau of the Census. "Labor Force and Employment by Industry: 1800–1960." In *Historical Statistics of the United States, Colonial Times to 1970*. Part 1, series D. Washington, D.C.: Government Printing Office, 1975.

Business Directories

Directories in Print. Detroit: Gale Research Co., annual.

Directory of Business Archives in the United States and Canada. Chicago: Society of American Archivists, 1975.

Directory of Corporate Affiliations. Skokie, Ill.: National Register Publishing Co., annual since 1967.

Dun's Marketing Services. *(Dun's) Million Dollar Directory*. New York: Dun and Bradstreet Corp., annual since 1963.

Fortune Magazine. *Fortune Double 500 Directory*. Trenton, N.J.: Fortune Magazine, annual since 1970.

Hedblaid, Alan, ed. *Directories in Print*. 23rd ed. Detroit: Gale Group, 2003.

Information Please Almanac, Atlas and Yearbook. New York: Simon and Schuster, 1947–, annual.

Kruzas, Anthony T., Kay Gill, and Donald Boyden, eds. *Business Organizations, Agencies, and Publications Directory: Organizations, Agencies, and Institutions*. Detroit: Gale Group, 1986.

Lewingson, Paul and Morris Rieger. "Labor Union Records in the United States." *American Archivist* 25 (January 1962).

Mann, Conklin. "The Family of Conchelyne, etc. in America." *American Genealogist* 21 (1944–1945).

———. "The Family of Conchelyne, etc. in America." *American Genealogist* 22 (1945–1946).

Martindale-Hubble Law Directory. Summit, N.J.: Martindale-Hubble, annual.

National Historical Publications and Records Commission. *Directory of Archives and Manuscript Repositories in the United States*. Phoenix: Uryx Press, 1988.

Neible, George W. "Account of Servants Bound and Assigned Before James Hamilton, Mayor of Philadelphia." *Pennsylvania Magazine of History and Biography* 32 (October 1908).

Nelso, William, ed. *Documents Relating to Colonial History of New Jersey*. 1st series, vol. 12. Patterson, N.J.: Press Printing and Publishing Co., 1895.

Nordland, Rod. *Names and Numbers: A Journalist's Guide to the Most Needed Information Sources and Contacts*. New York: John Wiley and Sons, 1978.

Scott, Kenneth. "Some Huntington, Long Island Residents, 1763–1779." *National Genealogical Society Quarterly* 62 (September 1974).

Spear Dorothea N. *Bibliography of American Directories Through 1860*. Worcestor, Mass.: American Antiquarian Society, 1961.

Standard and Poor's Register of Corporations, Directors and Executives. New York: Standard and Poor's, annual since 1928.

Vandenberge, Peter N. *Historical Directory of the Reformed Church of America, 1625–1965*. New Brunswick, N.J.: Reformed Church in America, 1966.

Ward, Baldwin H., ed. *Ward's Business Directory of U.S. Private and Public Companies*. Petaluma, Calif.: Baldwin H. Ward Publications, annual.

———, ed. *Ward's Directory of 55,000 Largest Corporations*. Petaluma, Calif.: Baldwin H. Ward Publications, annual.

Apprentices

Apprenticeship Past and Present. Rev. ed. Washington, D.C.: U.S. Department of Labor, 1991.

Coldham, Peter Wilson. *Child Apprentices in America, from Christ's Hospital, London, 1617–1778*. Baltimore: Genealogical Publishing Co., 1990.

Cutten, George Berton. *The Silversmiths of Virginia from 1694 to 1850*. Richmond: Diete Press, 1952.

Gill, Harold B., Jr. *Apprentices of Virginia, 1623–1800*. Salt Lake City: Ancestry, 1997.

Herrick, Cheesman A. *White Servitude in Pennsylvania*. 1926. Reprint, New York: Negro University Press, 1969.

Kingsbury, Susan Myra, ed. *The Records of the Virginia Company of London*. 4 vols. Washington, D.C.: U.S. Government Printing Office, 1938.

Miller, Alan N. *Middle Tennessee's Forgotten Children: Apprentices from 1784 to 1902*. Baltimore: Clearfield, 2004.

Pennsylvania German Society. *Record of Indentures of Individuals Bound Out as Apprentices, etc., [in] Philadelphia . . . 1771 to 1773*. Baltimore: Genealogical Publishing Co., 1973.

Ritter, Kathy. *Apprentices of Connecticut, 1637–1900*. Salt Lake City: Ancestry, 1986.

Salinger, Sharon V. *To Serve Well and Faithfully: Labor and Indentured Servants in Pennsylvania*. New York: Cambridge University Press, 1987.

Associations

Encyclopedia of Associations. Detroit: Gale Research Co., biennial.

Coroners' Records

Naanes, Ted, and Loretto Szucs. "Dead Men Do Tell Tales." *Ancestry* Magazine 12, no. 2 (March–April 1994): 6.

Roebuck, Haywood. "North Carolina Colonial Coroners' Inquests, 1738–75." *North Carolina Genealogical Society Journal* 1 (1975): 11–37.

Government

Horle, Craig W., et al. *Lawmaking and Legislators in Pennsylvania: A Biographical Dictionary* 2 vols, 1682–1709; 1710–1756. Philadelphia: University of Pennsylvania Press, 1991, 1997.

Prechtel-Kluskens, Claire. "Documenting the Career of Federal Employees." *Prologue* 26 (Fall 1994): 180–85.

Hospitals and Medical

American College of Surgeons Directory. Chicago: R. R. Donnelley & Sons Co., 1971. Lists open and closed medical and dental schools plus the current list of surgeons.

Clay, Robert Y. "Patients in the Hospital at Williamsburg, 1800–37." *Virginia Genealogist* 24 (1980): 23–28; 90–94.

Collard, J. Boyd. *Hospitals and Medical Doctors in Pittsburg County, Oklahoma*. Lawton, Okla.: the author, 1994.

Directory of Deceased American Physicians, 1804–1929. 2 vols. Chicago: American Medical Association, 1992.

Gilliam, Charles Edgar. "Mount Malado." *Tyler's Quarterly* 20 (1938–39): 138–42, 250. Virginia's earliest hospital.

New York Down-State Medical Center. *History of Long Island College Hospital: Alumni Association Highlights, 1880–1955, and Biographies of Graduates, 1900–1955*. New York: New York Alumni Association, 1961.

Johns, Frank S., and Anne Page. "Chimborazo Hospital and J. B. McCaw, Surgeon in Chief." *Virginia Magazine of History and Biography* 62 (1954): 190–200. An excellent description of revolutionary war hospital records with examples and locations.

Jordan, John W. "Military Hospital at Bethlehem and Lititz during the Revolution." *Pennsylvania Magazine of History and Biography* 20 (1896): 137–57. An undocumented account with patient lists.

Kelner, Joseph. "Examination of Hospital Records." *Case and Comment* 84 (1979): 51–54. Describes access to modern records.

Larrabee, Eric. *The Benevolent and Necessary Institution: New York Hospital, 1771–1971*. Garden City, N.Y.: Doubleday, 1971.

Uppedegraff, Marie. *The Story of Stamford Hospital, 1896–1971*. Stamford, Conn.: Stamford Hospital, 1971.

Williams, William H. "The Industrious Poor and the Founding of the Pennsylvania Hospital." *Pennsylvania Magazine of History and Biography* 97 (1973): 431–43. Established 1751.

Institutions

Clough, Shepard B. *A Century of American Life Insurance: A History of the Mutual Life Insurance Company of New York, 1843–1943*. New York: Columbia University Press, 1946.

Greenwood Encyclopedia of American Institutions. Westport, Conn.: Greenwood Press, 1977–86. Separate volumes deal with labor unions, political parties and government agencies, research institutes and learned societies, farmers organizations, colleges and universities, and foundations.

Larson, David R., ed. *Guide to Manuscripts Collections and Institutional Records in Ohio*. N.p.: Society of Ohio Archivists, 1974.

Preuss, Arthur, *A Dictionary of Secret and Other Societies*, St. Louis: B. Herder Book Co., 1924. Reprint, Gale Research Co., 1966.

Insurance

Clough, Shepard B. *A Century of American Life Insurance: A History of the Mutual Life Company of New York, 1843–1943*. New York: Columbia University Press, 1946.

Galles, Duane. "Using Life Insurance Policies in Genealogical Research." *Genealogical Journal* 20 (1992): 156–71.

Larkin, Harold F. "Retention of Life Insurance Records." *American Archivist* 5 (April 1942): 93–99.

Morticians

The American Blue Book of Funeral Directors. New York: Kates-Boylston Publications, biennial since 1929.

Elder, Charlotte DeVolt. "New Englanders in the Mortuary Records of Savannah, Georgia." *New England Historic and Genealogical Register* 125 (1971): 28–44. Covers 1803–22.

The National Directory of Morticians. Youngstown, Ohio: National Directory of Morticians, 1950–, irregular.

National Yellow Book of Funeral Directors. Youngstown, Ohio: Nomis Publications, annual.

"Undertakers Records." *Maryland Genealogical Bulletin* 20 (1979); 21 (1980).

Organizations

Directory of Historical Societies and Agencies in the United States and Canada. 14th ed. Nashville: American Association for State and Local History, 1990.

Fraternal Directory. San Francisco: Bancroft Co., 1889.

Lewinson, Paul, and Morris Rieger. "Labor Union Records in the United States." *American Archivist* 25 (January 1962): 39–57.

Whalen, William J. *Handbook of Secret Organizations*. Milwaukee: Bruce Publishing Co., 1966.

Wynar, Lubomyr R. *Encyclopedia Directory of Ethnic Organizations in the United States*. Littleton, Colo.: Libraries Unlimited, 1975.

Orphanages and Orphan Train

Allen, Desmond Walls. "Paupers at the Turn of the Century." *Professional Genealogists of Arkansas, Inc. Newsletter* 6, no. 6 (November 1993).

Charlotte County (Florida) Genealogical Society. "Orphan Trains." *Geneagram* 24, no. 1 (June 1991): 44–46.

Coble, Janet. "They Came to Our Town: A Story of Orphan Train Children." *Illinois State Genealogical Society Quarterly* 24, no. 2 (Summer 1992): 102–4.

Fink, Arthur E. "Changing Philosophies and Practices in North Carolina Orphanages." *North Carolina Historical Review* 48 (1971).

Gilbert, Meredith. "Orphan Trains." *Polish Genealogical Society of Texas News* 10, no. 3 (Fall 1993): 26–28.

Greenwood, Peggy Thomson. "City's House of Refuge; Orphanages 1827–1870" and "Orphanages (Part 2) 1870–1900." *St. Louis Genealogical Quarterly* 24, no. 1 (Fall 1990).

Harland, Thomas. "Of Franklin, Whitfield, and the Orphans." *Georgia Historical Quarterly* 29 (1945): 201–16. Bethesda Orphanage in Georgia.

Hasci, Timothy A. *Second Home: Orphan Asylums and Poor Families in America*. Cambridge, Mass: Harvard University Press, 1997.

Illinois State Genealogical Society. *Children of Orphan Trains from NY to IL, and Beyond*. Springfield, Ill.: Illinois State Genealogical Society, 1995.

Johnson, Mary Ellen, comp. *Orphan Train Riders: Their Own Stories*. Baltimore: Gateway Press, 1992.

Jones, Newton B. "The Charleston Orphan House, 1860–1976." *South Carolina Historical Magazine* 62 (1961): 203–14. Organized 1790.

Langsam, Miriam Z. *Children West: A History of the Placing-out System of the New York Children's Aid Society, 1853–1896*. Madison: State Historical Society of Wisconsin, 1964. Describes the records of one of the most important social institutions in New York City.

O'Connor, Stephen. *Orphan Trains: The Story of Charles Loring Brace and the Children He Saved and Failed*. New York: Houghton Mifflin, 2001.

Paul, Ellen, ed. *The Adoption Directory*. 2nd ed. Detroit: Gale Group, 1995.

Pickett, Robert S. *House of Refuge: Origins of Juvenile Reform in New York State, 1815–1857*. Syracuse, N.Y.: Syracuse University Press, 1969. Established 1825.

Rothman, David J. *The Discovery of the Asylum: Social Order and Disorder in the New Republic*. Boston: Little, Brown and Co., 1971.

Speare, Jean E., and Dorothy Paul. *Admission Record Indianapolis Asylum for Friendless Colored Children, 1871–1900*. Indianapolis: Family History and Genealogy Section, Indiana Historical Society, 1978.

Teeters, Negley K. "The Early Days of the Philadelphia House of Refuge." *Pennsylvania History* 27 (1960): 165–87. Established in 1828. Based on minutes of the Board of Inspectors, journals, and daybooks of the house.

Overseers of the Poor and Almshouses

Benton, Josiah Henry. *Warning Out in New England*. 1911. Reprint, Bowie, Md.: Heritage Books, 1992.

"Chautauqua County Home and Infirmary. Poor House for Chautauqua County, New York." *FORUM* 3, no. 4 (Fall 1992). This article identifies journals being abstracted by the Chautauqua County Genealogical Society, P.O. Box 404, Fredonia, NY 14063.

Hapner, Phyllis, and Judy Graven. *Almshouse Register for Shelby County, Illinois*. Typescript. N.p., 1985.

Lainhart, Ann S. "Records of the Poor in Pre-Twentieth-Century New England." *New England Historical and Genealogical Register* 146 (January 1992): 80–85.

———. "Cambridge, Massachusetts, Notifications and Warnings Out (1788 to 1797)." *New England Historical and Genealogical Register* 144 (July 1990): 215.

———. "Weston Cautions, 1757–1803." *New England Historical and Genealogical Register* 144 (July 1990): 215.

Lucas County Infirmary Register, Vol. I, 1855–1882. Book 2, Feb 1868–Mar 1882. Toledo, Ohio: Lucas County Chapter—OGS, 1993. More than 3,500 entries which include births, deaths, indentures, and adoptions of minor children.

McLaird, Lee N. "Haven for Those in Need." *Archival Chronicle* 14, no. 1 (March 1995): 1–2.

Sangamon County Almshouse, Buffalo, Illinois: Inmate Record, Sangamon County Poor Farm. 3 vols. Springfield, Ill.: Sangamon County Genealogical Society, 1993.

Warren, Paula Stuart, and James W. Warren. *Ramsey County Minnesota Relief Records, 1862–1868*. St. Paul: Warren Research and Publishing, 1990.

Prisons

Bumgarner, Herb. *Jail Register Index, Clackamas County, Oregon, From 1892 to 1925 Except For Years 1903 thru 1906*. Clackamas County, Ore.: Clackamas County Family History Society, 1991.

Carleton, Mark T. *Politics and Punishment: The History of the Louisiana State Penal System*. Baton Rouge: Louisiana State University Press, 1971.

Carter, Kent. "The Hanging Judge's Records." *The Record* (newsletter of the National Archives and Records Administration) 1, no. 1 (September 1994).

Kidd, Julie. "Oregon State Penitentiary." *Bulletin of the Genealogical Forum of Oregon, Inc.* 45, no. 2 (December 1995): 75–78. Lists of prisoners extracted from *Report of the Superintendent Oregon State Penitentiary*. Salem, Ore.: W. A. McPherson, State Printer, 1870.

Lewis, Orland F. *The Development of American Prisons and Prison Customs, 1776–1845*. 1922. Reprint, New York: Arno Press, 1962.

New York State Temporary State Committee of Investigation. *County Jails and Penitentiaries in New York State*. Albany, 1966.

Phelps, Richard H. *A History of Newgate [Prison] of Connecticut*. New York: Arno Press, 1969.

Shepard, William. "Records From Old Jail at Cumberland Courthouse, Virginia." *William and Mary Quarterly*, 2nd Series, 12 (1932): 39–40. Records dated 1782 to 1786.

Speer, Lonnie R. *Portals to Hell: Military Prisons of the Civil War*. Mechanicsburg, Penn.: Stackpole Books, 1997.

Teeters, Negley K. "The Early Days of the Eastern State Penitentiary at Philadelphia." *Pennsylvania History* 16 (1949): 261–302.

Railroad

Biographical Directory of the Railway Officials of America. New York: Simmons-Boardman Publishing Co., irregular since 1885. Later editions titled *Who's Who in Railroading in North America*.

Busbey, T. A. *Biographical Directory of Railway Officials of America*. Chicago: Railway Age, 1901.

Cochran, Thomas. *Railroad Leaders, 1845–1890: The Business Mind in Action*. Cambridge, Mass.: Harvard University Press, 1953.

Elliott, Wendy. "Railroad Records for Genealogical Research." *National Genealogical Society Quarterly* 75 (December 1987): 271–77.

Moody's Transportation Manual. New York: Moody's, 2000.

Schools

Ambler, Charles H. "Poor Relief Education, 1818–1847." *West Virginia History* 3 (1941–42): 285–304. Based on school records transferred from the courthouse in Kanawha County to West Virginia University, Morgantown.

Andrews, Edward D. "The County Grammar Schools and Academies of Vermont." *Vermont Historical Society Proceedings* (September 1936): 174ff.

Baird's Manual of American College Fraternities. 20th ed. Menasha, Wis.: Baird's Manual Foundation, 1991.

Finkelstein, Barbara J. "Schooling and Schoolteachers: Selected Bibliography of Autobiographies in the Nineteenth Century." *History of Education Quarterly* 14 (1974): 293–300. An important bibliography.

Fuller, Wayne E. *The Old Country School: The Story of Rural Education in the Middle West*. Chicago: University of Chicago Press, 1982. Includes a description of the records.

Gersman, Elinor M. "A Bibliography for Historians of Education: Historical Perspectives on the Educational Experience in the United States." *History of Education Quarterly* 14 (1974): 279–92.

Hogue, Arthur R. "The Record of an Indian School District, 1837–1844." *Indian Magazine of History* 48 (1952): 185–92.

Index to Georgia Poor-School and Academy Records, 1826–1850. Atlanta: R. J. Taylor Jr. Foundation, 1980. Records include lists of children with names, ages, school attendance, records of parents, and tuition payments.

McMahon, Clara R. P. "A Note on the Free School Idea in Colonial Maryland." *Maryland Historical Magazine* 54 (1959): 149–52.

Morison, Samuel Eliot. *The Founding of Harvard College.* Cambridge, Mass.: Harvard University Press, 1935. Excellent description of the records kept by a university. Alumni registers for many original universities in the United States have been published and will be found in major research libraries.

"Records of Pennsylvania School Children, 1802–1809." *National Genealogical Society Quarterly* 50 (1962): 78. Tax lists included school-age children with their ages.

Sloane, Eric. *The Little Red Schoolhouse: A Sketchbook of Early American Education.* Garden City, N.Y.: Doubleday, 1972.

Staubo, Merete. *History of the Council of School Superintendents, Cities and Villages of the State of New York, 1883–1967.* Ithaca, N.Y.: Cornell University Press, 1971.

Szucs, Loretto Dennis. "Education Records." *Ancestry* Magazine 13, no. 1 (January–February 1995): 20.

Typical Guides to Manuscript Collections

Dructor, Robert M. *A Guide to Genealogical Sources at the Pennsylvania State Archives.* 2nd ed. Harrisburg: Pennsylvania Historical and Museum Commission, 1998.

Guide to the Manuscript Collections of the Historical Society of Pennsylvania. 2nd ed. Philadelphia: Historical Society of Pennsylvania, 1949.

Lovett, Robert W., and Eleanor C. Bishop, comps. *List of Business Manuscripts in Baker Library.* Boston: the library, 1969.

The National Union Catalog of Manuscript Collections. Washington, D.C.: Library of Congress, annual since 1962.

Pflugll, Warner. *A Guide to the Archives of Labor History and Urban Affairs.* Detroit: Wayne State University Press, 1974.

Sample Corporate Histories

Crittenden, Christopher, William S. Powell, and Robert H. Woody, eds. *100 Years 100 Men, 1871–1971: A History of the Edwards & Broughton Company in Raleigh, North Carolina.* Raleigh, N.C.: Edwards and Broughton, n.d.

Ewing, John S., and Nancy P. Norton. *Broadloom and Businessmen: A History of the Bigelow-Sanford Carpet Company, 1825–1953.* Cambridge, Mass.: Harvard University Graduate School of Business History, 1955.

Gibb, George S. *The Whitesmiths of Taunton: A History of Reed and Barton, 1824–1943.* Cambridge, Mass.: Harvard University Graduate School of Business History, 1943.

Hower, Ralph M. *History of Macy's of New York, 1858–1939: Chapters in the History of a Department Store.* Cambridge, Mass.: Harvard University Graduate School of Business History, 1943.

———. *The History of an Advertising Agency: N. W. Ayer & Son at Work, 1869–1949.* Cambridge, Mass.: Harvard University Graduate School of Business History, 1949.

Shinn, Charles Howard. *The Story of the Mine: As Illustrated by the Great Comstock Lode of Nevada.* New York: D. Appleton, 1897.

White, Gerald T. *A History of the Massachusetts Hospital Life Insurance Company.* Cambridge, Mass.: Harvard University Graduate School of Business History, 1955.

Selected Vocational Collective Biographies

Barrett, Walter. *The Old Merchants of New York.* 5 vols. New York: Carleton, 1863–70.

Bell, Charles H. *The Bench and Bar of New Hampshire.* Boston: Houghton, Mifflin, 1894.

The Bench and Bar of Chicago: Biographical Sketches. Chicago: American Biographical Publishing Co., n.d.

Bjerkoe, Ethel Hall. *The Cabinetmakers of America.* Garden City, N.J.: Doubleday, 1957.

Bowers, William S. *Gunsmiths of Pen-Mar-Va, 1790–1840.* Mercersburg, Pa.: Irwinton Publishers, 1979.

Burton, E. Milby. *South Carolina Silversmiths, 1690–1860.* Rutland, Vt.: Tuttle Co., 1968.

Carlisle, Lilian Baker. *Vermont Clock and Watchmakers, Silversmiths, and Jewelers, 1778–1878.* Burlington, Vt.: Stinehour Press, 1970.

Currier, Ernest M. *Marks of Early American Silversmiths.* Watkins Glen, N.Y.: American Life Foundation, 1970.

Cutten, George Barton. *The Silversmiths of North Carolina From 1696 to 1860.* 2nd rev. ed. Raleigh: North Carolina Department of Cultural Resources, 1984.

———. *The Silversmiths of Virginia from 1694 to 1850.* Richmond: Dietz Press, 1952.

De Voe, Shirley Spaulding. *The Tinsmiths of Connecticut.* Middletown, Conn.: Wesleyan University Press for the Connecticut Historical Society, 1968.

Drepperd, Carl William. *American Clocks & Clockmakers.* Boston: C. T. Brandord Co., 1958.

Drost, William E. *Clocks and Watches of New Jersey*. Elizabeth, N.J.: Engineering Publishers, 1966.

Eckhardt, George H. *Pennsylvania Clocks and Clockmakers*. New York: Devin-Adair Co., 1955.

Elliott, Mary Quigley. *Biographical Sketches of Knox County Writers*. Mount Vernon, Ohio: 1937.

Ensko, Stephen Guernsey, and Stephen Guernsey Cook Ensko. *American Silversmiths and Their Marks IV*. Rev. ed. Boston: David R. Godine, 1990.

Foote, Henry Stuart. *The Bench and Bar of the South and Southwest*. St. Louis: Soule, Thomas and Wentworth, 1876.

French, Hollis. *A List of Early American Silversmiths and Their Marks*. 1917. Reprint, New York: Da Capo Press, 1967.

Fried, Frederick. *Artists in Wood: American Carvers of Cigar-store Indians, Show Figures, and Circus Wagons*. New York: C. N. Potter, 1970.

Gardner, Albert Ten Eyck. *Yankee Stonecutters: The First American School of Sculpture, 1800–1850*. New York: Columbia University Press for the Metropolitan Museum of Art, 1945.

Gerstell, Vivian S. *The Silversmiths of Lancaster, Pennsylvania, 1730–1850*. Lancaster, Pa.: Lancaster County Historical Society, 1972.

Gill, Harold B., Jr. *The Gunsmith in Colonial Virginia*. Williamsburg, Va.: Colonial Williamsburg Foundation, 1974.

Heisey, John W. *A Checklist of American Coverlet Weavers*. Williamsburg, Va.: Colonial Williamsburg Foundation, 1978.

Hiatt, Noble W. *The Silversmiths of Kentucky: Together with Some Watchmakers and Jewelers, 1785–1850*. Louisville, Ky.: Standard Print Co., 1954.

Hutslar, Donald A. *Gunsmiths of Ohio 18th and 19th Centuries*. Longrifle Series. York, Pa.: George Shumway, 1973.

Kovel, Ralph M. *A Directory of American Silver, Pewter, and Silver Plate*. New York: Crown Publishers, 1961.

Langdon, John Emerson. *Canadian Silversmiths, 1700–1900*. Toronto: Stinehour Press, 1966.

Lanier, Henry Wysham. *A Century of Banking in New York, 1822–1922*. New York: Gilliss Press, 1922.

Laughlin, Ledlie Irwin. *Pewter in America: Its Makers and Their Marks*. Boston: Houghton, Mifflin, 1940.

Levitt, James H. *For Want of Trade: Shipping and the New Jersey Ports, 1680–1783*. Newark: New Jersey Historical Society, 1981.

Lewis, George E. *The Bench and Bar of Colorado*. Denver: Bench and Bar Publishing Co., 1917.

Lynch, James Daniel. *The Bench and Bar of Texas*. St. Louis: Nixon-Jones Printing Co., 1885.

Martin, John Hill. *Martins Bench and Bar of Philadelphia*. Philadelphia: Rees Welsh and Co., 1883.

Miller, Stephen Francis. *The Bench and Bar of Georgia*. 2 vols. Philadelphia: J. B. Lippincott, 1858.

Palmer, John McAuley. *The Bench and Bar of Illinois*. 2 vols. Chicago: Lewis Publishing Co., 1899.

Parsons, Charles Sumner. *New Hampshire Clocks & Clockmakers*. Exeter, N.H.: Adams Brown Co., 1976.

Proctor, Lucien Brock. *The Bench and Bar of New York*. New York: Diossy, 1870.

Reed, George Irving. *The Bench and Bar of Michigan*. Chicago: Century Publishing and Engraving, 1897.

———. *The Bench and Bar of Ohio*. 2 vols. Chicago: Century Publishing and Engraving, 1897.

Reed, Parker McCobb. *The Bench and Bar of Wisconsin*. Milwaukee: the compiler, 1882.

Rice, Alvin H. *The Shenandoah Pottery*. Berryville, Va.: Virginia Book Co., 1974.

Roberts, Kenneth D. *Planemakers and Other Edge Tool Enterprises in New York State in the Nineteenth Century*. Cooperstown, N.Y.: New York State Historical Association, 1970.

Sams, Conway Whittle. *The Bench and Bar of Maryland*. Chicago: Lewis Publishing Co., 1901.

Shelton, Lawrence P. *California Gunsmiths, 1846–1900*. Fair Oaks, Calif.: Far Far West Publishers, 1977.

Smart, Charles E. *The Makers of Surveying Instruments in America Since 1700*. 2 vols. Troy, N.Y.: Regal Art Press, 1962–67.

Severance, Frank Haywood. *The Holland Land Company and Canal Construction in Western New York*. Buffalo, N.Y.: Buffalo Historical Society, 1910.

The Stoystown and Greensburgh Turnpike Road Company: Minutes, 1815–1826. Southwest Pennsylvania Genealogical Services, 1976.

Wendell, Emory. *Wendell's History of Banking and Banks and Bankers of Michigan*. Detroit: Winn and Hammond, n.d.

5

Census Records

LORETTO DENNIS SZUCS, FUGA, and MATTHEW WRIGHT

When the Founding Fathers of the United States convened the Constitutional Convention in 1787, they had no idea that they would, in the course of their deliberations, create incredible opportunities for generations of American family history researchers. While Article I, Section 2 of the Constitution does not directly mention the preservation of vital personal information for future generations, it does instruct the government to conduct a decennial census in an effort to fairly apportion the number of federal representatives from each state, as well as to decide on the amount of direct taxes to be levied. That effort to take stock of the U.S. population every ten years has produced, as a natural by-product, the greatest source of genealogical information available to U.S. researchers.

Because they contain such important information about individuals, families, and communities, U.S. census records are the most frequently used records created by the federal government. Recognizing their value to researchers, the National Archives began to microfilm federal census records in 1941, and with microfilming came the ability to make duplicate copies, then to digitize them. Because of technological developments, federal census records can now be researched via the Internet from a home computer or at the nearest archives or library.

Beyond the records resulting from the population head counts conducted by the federal government, there are a number of other census records that should not be overlooked by researchers. Agricultural, industry and manufacturing, mortality, slave, and other special census schedules created by the federal government are also worth exploring, as are state and local censuses. Special censuses reveal a great deal about American territories, and some provide hard-to-find details about Native Americans. While the latter vary greatly in content and availability, information not available elsewhere can often be found in them.

Chapter Contents

The Census Is as Vital as Ever

Census records contain the basic documentation for the study of U.S. history, biography, demography, immigration, migration, ethnicity, occupations, economics, social anthropology, medical history, local history, and family history. Social historians, journalists, the media, and government agencies have come to rely on the census as a reliable source for valuable and fascinating pieces of information.

Certain research topics have lent themselves well to the use of the U.S. federal census. Occupational data and property values noted in some census years have been the basis for economic studies, and inquiries regarding Revolutionary War pensioners (1840), Civil War veterans (1890 and 1910), and participants in other expeditions or wars (1930) can aid military research. Reconstruction of historic sites in Philadelphia; an examination of foreign-born farmers, women, and blacks in nineteenth-century Concord, Massachusetts; and regional studies, such as that of Dickinson County, Kansas, have sought support from a combination of records—but notably the census. The 1860 census provided particulars on the domestics in their place of employment, while making possible the reconstitution of their families of origin residing on surrounding farmlands. More recent census records have been used by medical researchers to track families and to study hereditary and communicable disease patterns.

The most popular use of the census, however, is to trace family history. No other source matches the census record's ability to place people in a certain place at a certain time or to provide such a detailed picture of lives and lifestyles at given intervals. The promise of that picture, and of seeing it clearly, keeps researchers going against all odds.

This chapter will provide a brief history of the U.S. federal population censuses from 1790 to 1930, including a section describing the general strengths and limitations of census records. Suggestions in that section will be useful not only for searching federal schedules, but also for searching special and state censuses described later in the chapter. The contents and special features of each federal decennial census are also described in chronological order, followed by a section on related census indexes. Where and how to use census records is discussed in the last part of this chapter. The impact and availability of electronic or digital census resources is discussed throughout.

Historical Background

The actual records of civilization's first population counts have apparently not survived, but there are indications that in early Babylonia, Egypt, and China, inhabitants were counted on a regular basis. There are ancient written accounts of Greek and Romans censuses, but those tallies, too, have been lost over the centuries. On the North American continent, the Spaniards led the way in census-taking, counting heads in 1577 in what was then Mexico.

Since 1790, the U.S. government has taken a nationwide population count every ten years. Though never intended for genealogical purposes, the federal censuses are among the most frequently used records for those looking for links with the past. Unique in scope and often surprisingly detailed, the census population schedules created from 1790 to 1930 are among the most used federally created records. Over the course of two centuries, the United States has changed significantly, and so has the census. From the six basic questions asked in the 1790 census, the scope and categories of information have changed and expanded dramatically.

Article I, Section 2, of the U.S. Constitution required that an enumeration of the people be made within three years after the first meeting of the Congress. In March 1790, after President Washington signed the first census act, Secretary of State Thomas Jefferson sent a copy of the law to each of the seventeen U.S. marshals and instructed them to appoint as many assistants as they needed to take the census.

From 1790 to 1880, census districts were aligned with existing civil divisions. The district marshals were authorized to subdivide each district into reasonable geographical segments to facilitate supervision of the enumeration. Enumeration districts were limited in size to 10,000 individuals by the Census Act of 1850, but final tallies show that the number was usually less than 6,000. In 1880, the Census Office appointed supervisors to further subdivide the districts. In that year, the average population of each of the 28,000 enumeration districts was less than 2,000.[1]

Early censuses were essentially an enumeration of inhabitants, but as the nation grew, so did the need for statistics that would reflect the characteristics of the people and the conditions under which they were living. The logical means for obtaining a clearer picture of the American populace was to solicit more information about individuals. In 1850, the focus of the census was radically broadened. Going far beyond the vague questions previously asked of heads of households, the 1850 census enumerators were instructed to ask various questions about every individual in the household, including their age, sex, color, occupation, and birthplace, along with several other questions. Succeeding enumerations solicited more information; by 1930, census enumerators asked more than thirty questions of every head of household and almost as many questions of everyone else in the residence. As W. S. Rossiter, chief clerk of the Bureau of the Census around the first part of the twentieth century, stated, "The modern census is thus the result of evolution."[2]

The Census Bureau

Although the Constitution called for a census every ten years, there was no special government agency to conduct and

Each decade, enumerators have used different modes of travel to take them from interview to interview. (Source: U.S. Census Bureau, Public Information Office.)

tabulate the results of this massive survey. Until 1840, federal marshals managed the process as best they could. In 1850, the first Census Office was opened in Washington, D.C. However, it was disbanded after the 1850 census and only reestablished in time to take the census and tally the results in 1860, 1870, 1880, 1890, and 1900.

It was not until 1902 that the Bureau of the Census was established as a permanent bureau in the Department of the Interior. In 1903 the bureau was transferred to the Department of Commerce. The Bureau of the Census is responsible for providing statistics about the population and economy of the nation and for collecting, tabulating, and publishing a wide variety of statistical data for government and private users.[3]

Strengths and Limitations of Census Records

Few, if any, records reveal as many details about individuals and families as do the U.S. federal censuses. The population schedules are successive "snapshots" of Americans that depict where and how they were living at particular periods in the past. Census records since 1850 suggest dates and places of birth, relationships, family origins, changes in residence, schooling, occupations, economic and citizenship status, and more.

Once home sources (see chapter 1, "The Foundations of Family History Research") have been exhausted, the census is often the next best starting point for U.S. genealogical research. The availability of statewide indexes for almost every census year makes them logical tools to locate individuals whose precise residence is unknown. While some inaccuracies are to be expected in census records, they still provide some of the most fascinating and useful pieces of personal history to be found in any source. If nothing else, census records are important sources for placing individuals in specific places at specific times. Additionally, information found in the census will often point to other sources critical to completing research, such as court, land, military, immigration, naturalization, and vital records.

The importance of census records does not diminish over time in any given research project. It is always wise to return to these records as discoveries are made in other sources because, as new evidence about individuals is found, some data that seemed unrelated or unimportant in a first look at the census may take on new importance.

When family, vital, or religious records are missing, census records may be the only means of documenting the events of a person's life. Vital registration did not begin until around 1920 in many areas of the United States, and fires, floods, and other disasters have destroyed some official government records. When other documentation is missing, census records are frequently used by individuals who must prove their age or citizenship status (or that of their parents) for Social Security benefits, insurance, passports, and other important reasons.

Problems Created at the Time the Census Was Taken

When evaluating any source, it is always wise to consider how, when, and under what conditions the record was made. By understanding some of the difficulties encountered by enumerators, it becomes easier to understand why some individuals cannot be found in the census schedules or their indexes.

From the first enumeration in 1790 to the most recent in 2000, the government has experienced difficulties in gathering precise information for a number of reasons. At least one of the problems experienced in extracting information from individuals for the first census continues to vex officials today: there were and still are many people who simply do not trust the government's motives. Many citizens have worried that their answers to census questions might be used against them, particularly in regards to taxation, military service, and immigration. Some have simply refused to answer enumerators' questions; others have lied.

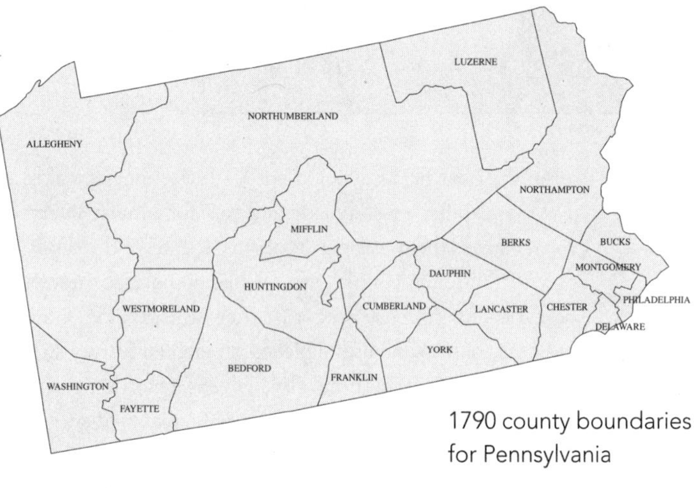

1790 county boundaries for Pennsylvania

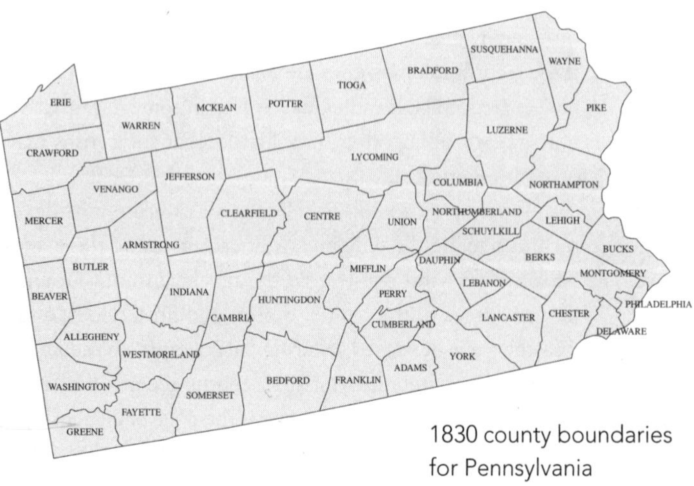

1830 county boundaries for Pennsylvania

Boundaries

In the days before regular mail service, government representatives conducted door-to-door canvasses of their appointed districts. Supervisors subdivided districts using existing local boundaries. The town, township, military district, ward, and precinct most often constituted one or more enumeration districts.[4] Boundaries of towns and other minor civil divisions, and in some cases counties, were ill defined, so enumerators were frequently uncertain whether a family resided in their district or in an adjoining district. For this reason, it is not unusual to find individuals and families listed twice in the census and others missed entirely. Robert C. Anderson, et al., provide excellent examples and an analysis of this rather common problem in "Duplicate Census Enumerations."[5]

Over the years, state, county, township, and city ward boundaries have changed. Any census search can be thrown off by these changes and inconsistencies. For a thorough discussion of boundaries with detailed maps, see William Thorndale's and William Dollarhide's *Map Guide to the U.S. Federal Censuses, 1790–1920*.[6] The introduction to this useful work includes a discussion of duplication in census records.

Historical Perspective

For a better sense of how census takers carried out their duties in a given year, it is useful to imagine the landscape and the modes of travel available in the specific time period. In the earliest census years, travel was obviously more difficult and sometimes very dangerous—conditions that did not improve for decades in the more rural states and territories of the "Wild West."

To complicate the situation further, a large portion of the young nation's population lived in small villages and isolated farms that were dispersed over a large area. It was not uncommon for a census enumerator to make a long trip to a remote farm, only to find no one at home. In these instances, he was left to make a decision—whether to try again on another day, or question farm or household help, neighbors, or even young children. The latter appears to have been an option taken by many. In some situations, enumerators probably found it easier to just guess.

But obtaining answers directly from the head of household or an adult in the house was no guarantee of accuracy either. For a number of reasons, ages are always suspect in census records. Many people tend to be secretive about their age; women may have been particularly sensitive about revealing the truth. One woman tracked in the census taken in New York from 1850 to 1880 claimed to have aged only twelve years in the thirty-year period. According to the 1850 and 1860 censuses of Springfield, Illinois, Mary, wife of Abraham Lincoln, aged only seven years in the ten-year period (figure 5-1). She, or someone reporting for her, claimed that she was twenty-eight in 1850 and only thirty-five in 1860. Dozens of cases have been similarly noted; undoubtedly, some honestly could not remember how old they were. If a person's age was not exactly known, it was frequently rounded off to the closest decade, making ages reported as thirty, forty, fifty, and so on somewhat suspect. Therefore, unless an age reported in the census can be corroborated with another source, it should not be considered totally reliable.

When questions were answered by someone other than the subject of the inquiry, the likelihood of error increased. A husband or wife might not always know the birthplaces of a spouse's parents. A child being quizzed might easily be unsure of the birthplaces of his or her parents. Census schedules do not tell us who answered the enumerator's questions.

An important point to remember is that enumerators simply wrote down the responses given to them. They were not authorized to request any kind of proof, such as birth, marriage, or property ownership records. However, every individual contacted by a government representative was required by law to answer truthfully. Anyone refusing to answer or willfully providing false information was guilty of a misdemeanor and subject to a fine. As early as 1790, offenders were fined twenty dollars, which was split between the marshals' assistants and the government. But relatively few individuals were hauled into court for refusing to answer or for not answering truthfully. It would have been an impossible task for the government to follow through and to investigate everyone's answers.

It was not until 1830 that the census office supplied printed questionnaires or "schedules." The enumerators of the 1790, 1800, 1810, and 1820 censuses returned the results of their canvassing on whatever paper they had. Each also had to post copies of their censuses in two public places in their assigned areas. Presumably, people who could read would see discrepancies or omissions and call them to the attention of officials. Unfortunately few, if any, of these duplicates have survived.

Another factor that comes into play in the accuracy of every census record is the competency of the enumerator who recorded the information. Individuals were not necessarily well-educated or qualified for the job, and anyone who has studied census records knows that good penmanship was not a requirement. Census takers were political appointees who were frequently chosen because they were of the correct political affiliation in a particular time and place, or just knew the right people.

Wages were definitely not an incentive for would-be census takers. In 1790, even the highest pay rate, one dollar for fifty persons, barely covered an enumerator's expenses. In 1920, payment was on a per-capita or per-diem basis—sometimes a combination of the two. An enumerator was paid between one and four cents per person, depending on the urban or rural setting of the district to be counted.

The United States has always been home to a large number of immigrants, and those who did not speak English well presented still another problem for the census taker. Often, enumerators could hardly understand the information given to them by people with foreign accents. Names were frequently misunderstood and misspelled by enumerators, to the extent that many do not even begin with the correct letters, making them hard to find in census schedules and almost impossible to find in indexes. The German name Pfeiffer could easily be heard and committed to paper as Fifer, for example. An Irish census taker in Cleveland recorded the Polish name Menkalski as McKalsky in the 1920 census. Places of birth may have been equally difficult to translate into English.

Whether recording information from a foreign-born or American-born individual, some enumerators took the quickest way to get the job done. Some used initials rather than given names, some used nicknames, and some omitted places of birth, value of real estate, occupations, and other details. In boarding houses, hotels, and clusters of workers' cottages, enumerators could easily overlook entire families.

While enumerators were given basic instructions as early as 1820, it was not until 1850 that the Census Office printed uniform instructions for the enumerators, explaining their responsibilities, procedures, the specifics of completing the schedules, and the intent of each question asked. In 1850, the Census Office also provided enumerators with a large portfolio to accommodate the oversize forms (which measured twelve by eighteen inches), pens, a portable inkstand, ink, and blotting paper. Enumerators were instructed not to fold the pages and not to allow anyone to "meddle with [their] papers." Pages were numbered consecutively as they were completed. Each page was dated on the day it was begun, even if it was not completed until another day. Every page included room for the enumerator's signature, the name of the civil division, the county, the state and, after 1870, the local post office.

According to the 1850 census instructions, the enumerator, on completing the entry for each family, farm, or shop, was to read the information back to the person interrogated so that errors could be corrected immediately. But if an informant was unclear or incorrect in giving information in the first place, this procedure did little to correct errors. A significant portion of the American population could not read or write in the nineteenth century, so if an enumerator misspelled the family surname it could easily have stayed that way, whether or not the enumerator repeated it.

As the enumeration of each sub district was completed, the enumerator was to make two copies, which were to be carefully compared to the original for accuracy. Hand copying, of course, frequently produces mistakes. Experience with the various copies

SCHEDULE I.—Free Inhabitants in Springfield in the County of Sangamon State of Illinois enumerated by me, on the 7th day of November 1850. T. Billoody Ass't Marshal. 120

1	2	3	4	5	6	7	8	9	10	11	12	13	
Dwellings numbered in the order of visitation.	Families numbered in the order of visitation.	The Name of every Person whose usual place of abode on the first day of June, 1850, was in this family.	Age.	Sex.	Color. White, black, or mulatto.	Profession, Occupation, or Trade of each Male Person over 15 years of age.	Value of Real Estate owned.	Place of Birth. Naming the State, Territory, or Country.	Married within the year.	Attended School within the year.	Persons over 20 y'rs of age who cannot read & write.	Whether deaf and dumb, blind, insane, idiotic, pauper, or convict.	
		Abbey Keefner	22	F				Germany					29
		George Eastman	35	M		Trader		Me					30
		Wm. B. Fondy	29	M		Merchant		NY					31
76	28	Abram Lincoln	40	M		Atty at Law		Ky					32
		Mary Lincoln	28	F				"					33
		Robert Lincoln	7	M				Ills					34
		Catharine Gordon	18	F				Ireland					35
77	729	S. B. Opdycke	55	M		Merchant	18000	NJ					36
		Thos Opdycke	14	M				Ills		1			37
		Charlotte Opdycke	15	F				"		1			38
[illegible]	730	William Lowry	70	M		none		Ireland					39
		Eliza Lowry	60	F				Pa					40
													41
													42

SCHEDULE 1.—Free Inhabitants in East Half City of Springfield in the County of Sangamon of Ill enumerated by me, on the 14 day of July 1860. J. H. Chenin Ass't

Post Office Springfield

	1	2	3	4	5	6	7	8	9	10	11	12	13
	Dwelling-houses—numbered in the order of visitation.	Families numbered in the order of visitation.	The name of every person whose usual place of abode on the first day of June, 1860, was in this family.	Age.	Sex.	Color. White, black, or mulatto.	Profession, Occupation, or Trade of each person, male and female, over 15 years of age.	Value of Estate Owned. Value of Real Estate.	Value of Personal Estate.	Place of Birth, Naming the State, Territory, or Country.	Married within the year.	Attended School within the year.	Persons over 20 y'rs of age who cannot read & write.
16	1002	989	Abraham Lincoln	51	m		Lawyer	5,000	12,000	Ky			
17			Mary "	35	f					"			
18			Robt T. "	16	m					Ills		1	
19			Willie W.	9	m					"		1	
20			Thomas "	7	m					"			
21			M. Johnson	18	f		Servant			"			
22			Phillip Dinkell	14	m					"			
23	1003	990	L. J. Snow	38	m				350	Ind			
24			Margaret J. "	38	f					Ills			
25			H. G. "	4	m					"			
26			Frank "	2	m					"			
27	1004	991	Wm. S. Burch	46	m		Clerk	2,000	200	Ky			
28			Mary F.	15	f					Ills			

Figure 5-1. 1850 *(top)* and 1860 *(bottom)* Federal Census entries for the household of Abraham Lincoln, Springfield, Sangamon County, Illinois. The entries appear on pages 120 and 130, respectively.

of the census shows that most copies were not error free. It was cumbersome and tedious to copy names and endless columns of personal information. Most enumerators probably never thought their copies would be read again once the statistical tabulations were completed, so it is easy to believe that many became careless as the job wore on.

As the process was completed, the enumerator was to sign each page of the census, and at the end of each set of copies, to certify that the census had been taken and copied according to instructions. One set was to be filed with the clerk of the county court, and the other two were to be forwarded to the supervisor. As the supervisor received the completed schedules, it was his or her duty to see that every part of the district had been visited and that the copies were in good order. One set was then sent to the state or territory, and the other was forwarded to the U.S. Census Office for statistical analysis. Unfortunately, it is almost impossible to distinguish the original census taken by the enumerator—the one likely to be most accurate—from the copies. While it is usually not possible to know if the original census or a copy was sent, it is relatively easy to recognize the census that was sent to the Census Office. "Researchers can distinguish the latter set from the other two because the Census Office made tabulations directly on the schedules; consequently, the central office copy bears pencil, crayon, and red ink markings on virtually every page."[7]

In 1880, the procedure of making three sets of returns was abandoned. Enumerators forwarded the originals to the Census Office and did not make copies. In an attempt to correct errors, however, the Census Act of 1880 called for "public exhibition of the population returns," and for this purpose it authorized enumerators to make a document listing the name, age, sex, and color of each person enumerated in the district to be filed with the clerk of the county court. If any of these lists have survived, they will be found at the county level.

In most enumerations, census takers were instructed to number each dwelling consecutively in the order of visit, though it was not always clear how these instructions were changed or interpreted from year to year. It should be emphasized that there was no connection between the household numbers (usually the number listed in the first column to the left of the census page) and the locality or address.

Census instructions defined a dwelling as any structure in which a person was living, including a room above a store, a warehouse, a factory, or a wigwam on the outskirts of a settlement. Institutions, such as hospitals, orphanages, poorhouses, garrisons, asylums, and jails, were counted as single-dwelling houses. It was not until the 1880 census that the character and name of the institution were required to be written in the margin. The 1880 census was also the first to include street addresses in cities.

In most years, census instructions stated that all persons temporarily absent on a journey or visit should be counted with the rest of their family in their usual abode. However, children away at school and living near the school or college should be enumerated with that family or institution. "Seafaring men," if they were believed to be still alive, were reported at their homes on land, no matter how long their absence. As such, sailors residing in boarding houses were not to be counted at that location. Expressmen, canalmen, railroad employees, and others engaged in transportation were enumerated with their families, if they returned to their homes at regular intervals.

Census instructions were quite specific as to how enumerators were to map out and proceed through their assigned areas so that no one would be missed. The 1920 instructions, for example, stated

> 68. *Method of canvassing a city block—If your district is in a city or town having a system of house numbers canvass one block or square at a time. Do not go back and forth across the street. Begin each block at one corner, keep to the right, turn the corner, and go in and out of any court, alley, or passageway that may be included in it until the point of starting is reached. Be sure you have gone around and through the entire block before you leave it.*
>
> 69. *The arrows in the following diagram indicate the manner in which a block containing an interior court or place is to be canvassed:*
>
> Department of Commerce, Bureau of the Census, Fourteenth Census of the United States. January 1, 1920: Instructions to Enumerators (Washington, D.C.: Government Printing Office, 1919).

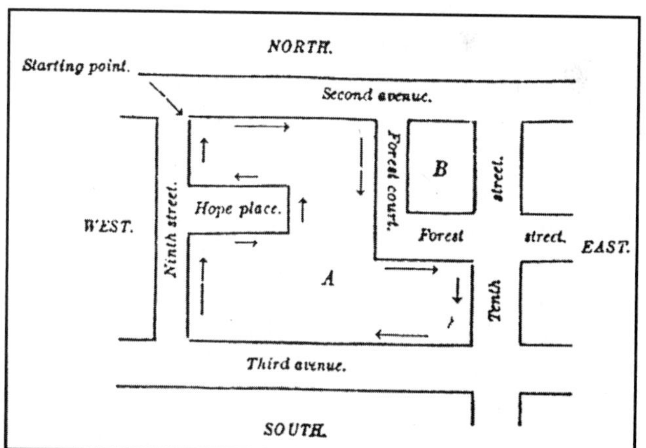

Missing Censuses

According to most authorities, the 1790 census schedules for Delaware, Georgia, Kentucky, New Jersey, Tennessee, and Virginia were burned during the War of 1812. Some records, such as the 1790 records for Virginia, have been reconstructed from state enumerations and tax lists. In later enumerations, city blocks, neighborhoods, townships and sections of townships, and even entire counties are known to be missing from the census schedules, simply because no census was taken in the particular area in a given year or because they were lost before they reached Washington, D.C.

Probably the most noted loss of the federal enumerations is that of the 1890 census. Most of the 1890 schedules were destroyed in a fire in the Commerce Department in 1921. (See description of 1890 census for more info.)

False Census Entries

Another confusing situation in census research can arise when names show up in a district where they do not belong—sometimes more than once. According to Arlene Eakle, Ph.D., "padding the totes," or adjusting the census for political reasons, was not uncommon. "Frontier areas, anxious for statehood, often added bogus names. In 1857, seven counties in Minnesota had wild population totals, complete with fake names on the schedules. Jurisdictions facing increased taxes might also understate their populations to keep overall per capita taxes lower. The 1880 Utah census juggled households to disguise polygamy at a time when federal officials were seeking evidence for the prosecution of those convicted of unlawful cohabitation."[8]

Missing Persons

Bogus entries may have been a frustration in some times and places, but a far greater problem in every census year has been that of undercounting. Whether families or individuals were not counted because they lived in remote areas or because they would not tolerate an enumerator's personal questions, millions have been missed since official government census-taking began. The Census Bureau has acknowledged, for example, "that the 1990 census, which put the U.S. population at 248.7 million, missed an estimated 5 million people—ranging from 1.7 percent of whites to 5.2 percent of Hispanics" (*Chicago Tribune*, Tuesday, 17 March 1992, sec. 2, page 4). While no stone should remain unturned in the search for an individual in the census, the unfortunate truth is that a significant portion of the population has been missed entirely.

Legibility

Probably no other factor causes more frustration for a researcher than finding the general area in which an individual or family should be found in the census and then being unable to read the page or pages of interest. Often, worn and torn pages, faded or smeared ink, and the disintegrating paper of the original census are to blame. Most frequently, however, poor microfilming techniques caused unfocused and blurred sections, overexposed and underexposed pages, and words to be obscured because of tightly bound volumes or mending tape.

Microfilming of federal census records took place in the 1940s, when the technology was in its infancy and techniques had not yet been perfected. Because of the poor quality of the original microfilms, some of the 1850, 1860, and 1870 schedules were microfilmed a second time. The versions can be distinguished because the earlier microfilming included two pages to a frame, while the newer ones have only one census page per frame. Unfortunately, the original census schedules for 1900, 1910, and 1920 were destroyed in 1946 (with the approval of the Archivist of the United States and Congress), and the 1930 originals were destroyed in 1949, so records that are not legible cannot be remicrofilmed.

The quality of microfilms may vary from one copy to another. Generally, the original microfilm is better than later generations of the same. Census microfilms have been duplicated a number of times in order to make the records available to as many researchers as possible. In some cases, the National Archives in Washington, D.C., may have the best copy.

Digitization of microfilmed records offers a second chance to capture these images the right way. A proprietary process used by Ancestry.com, for example, has been used to scan the microfilm in 256 shades of gray (as opposed to black and white) and then to optimize it using software filters. The resultant images are often easier to read than the original.

Handwriting

Poor penmanship, archaic handwriting styles, and symbols are other leading causes of researchers' inability to find or read specific names or information in census records. Many letters can be misinterpreted unless a study is made of the enumerator's handwriting style. For example, uppercase letters L and S are frequently difficult to distinguish. In one district of the 1850 census, the word "lawyer" looks more like "sawyer." Likewise, a birthplace of Missouri might look more like "Mifouri" or "Mipouri" to someone unfamiliar with the long "s" character that took the place of a double "s" in some manuscripts.

Despite the many imperfections of the census, it should again be emphasized that census records are one of the first sources used in almost every genealogical project. They are invaluable for placing an individual in a particular time and place and for connecting the individual to other sources. The foregoing descriptions make it fairly easy to see why census records are not perfect or entirely reliable. But, as noted author Val Greenwood suggests, "no research on an American genealogical problem after the beginning of census is complete until all pertinent census schedules have been searched."[9]

Interpreting Census Information

Professional researchers recommend making photocopies or computer printouts of census pages whenever possible. The

Suggestions for Microfilm Searches by Arlene Eakle Ph.D.

Because most census searches are still made on microfilm, below are some suggestions to make research easier.

1. Become familiar with the surnames in your area so that you can recognize them with only half of their letters distinct. Study a county history, a tax list, or a landowner's atlas.
2. Create a "pony" from the actual entries in the census. How does the writer make a, h, s, p, j, and other letters which could be misinterpreted? Draft an alphabet with uppercase and lowercase letters for comparison. An easy way is to slip a piece of plain paper onto the viewing surface and trace the letters from the page.
3. Use a reader in a darkened room, with a strong light to project the image. Slip a colored piece of paper—pink, yellow, and green are effective—onto the viewing surface.
4. Copy the microfilmed page, enlarging or reducing the image to make it clearer and sharper. Many microfilm copiers have interchangeable lenses.
5. Review the whole schedule so you don't miss important entries that appear out of place. Record all columns for each entry, even if the information seems unimportant, and record all members of the household whether they are familiar or not. In multiple-family dwellings, record all family units living in the building. These families are often related, especially in immigrant settlement areas.
6. Copy the data exactly as it appears in the record. If the given name is abbreviated, copy the abbreviated form. Do not expand it. If the entry is crossed through or changed, copy the entry, the cross-through line, and the changes. Note carefully the last entry on each page. Family units may be split between two pages without a repeat of the surname.
7. Use finding tools and indexes to get into the census quickly, then search the census carefully to get all the data it contains (see the reference list). If all the data is available, it is possible to block out the pedigree for several generations from this source alone. Then, proof can be sought in other records to ensure that names in the pedigree really belong there. If you are researching a common name like Brown or Jones, the censuses can help eliminate those that do not fit, making searches in other sources less time-consuming.

advantages of an actual copy over a transcription are several: it eliminates the danger of transcription mistakes; a copy will include neighbors and provide an overview of the population makeup of the area (except in cases where names are listed in alphabetical order instead of in order of visitation); and a copy makes it easy to go back and reevaluate information as new discoveries are made in the research process.

While information in the census may be quite accurate, at times the order in which data has been entered can be misleading. For example, a head of household recorded in 1820, 1830, or 1840 may not be the oldest person in the house. With only age ranges to distinguish, it is impossible to know who may be a grandparent, a younger brother, or a man with both parents still living at home. Individuals listed in early censuses in any age grouping could be servants, visitors, or boarders not related to the family. Even in 1880 and later, the relationships noted apply to heads of household only. Children listed as sons and daughters of the head of household may be unrelated to the wife.

Census Records and the Role of the National Archives

The National Archives has custody of the federally created census records, including the published 1790 census schedules, negative photostatic copies of the 1800, 1810, 1820, and 1830 census schedules, originals of the 1840, 1850, 1860, and 1870 census schedules, the surviving fragments of the 1890 schedules, and microfilm copies of the 1900, 1910, 1920, and 1930 schedules. Due to their fragile condition, some of the original schedules have been retired and are not available to researchers. The original 1880 census schedules went back to the states and are no longer in the custody of the National Archives. A research book entitled *Guide to Genealogical Research in the National Archives*, 3rd ed. (Washington, D.C.: National Archives and Records Administration, 2001), provides detailed information on federally-created census records from 1790 to 1910. According to the Guide, "Because copies of the census records are now available at the archives field branches, NARA

Suggestions for Online Searches by Juliana Smith

Increasingly, census records can be accessed using electronic media. Below are some tips for searching electronic census indexes.

1. **ADVANCED SEARCH TOOLS.** Most electronic indexes provide users with various options for more effective searching. In cases where you are dealing with common surnames in large cities, it is often helpful to specify more information to narrow down your search. In addition, when an ancestor cannot be located using basic searches, sometimes they can be located by entering different combinations of information, such as first name and township/county/state or other keywords that may be available in the database.
2. **KEYWORDS.** When searching a database, users are typically given the choice of searching by surname, given name, locality, and keyword. If the user begins by using only the surname and state, the resulting matches will likely be too broad. While it is sometimes impossible to include a given name or locality, try narrowing down the search results using keywords. For example, suppose you are searching for an ancestor named John Brown from Mississippi. After putting those details in the search you could also add any other information you know about him in the keyword field, e.g. the township, a country of origin, a language, a date, etc.
3. **SOMETIMES LESS IS MORE.** Keep in mind that databases will only give hits on exact matches. When too much information is included in a search, you run the risk of eliminating a possible hit in cases where names have been abbreviated or misspelled, where variations exist, or when information is missing. (A more detailed article on this topic is available online at: <www.ancestry.com/library/view/columns/compass/1170.asp>.)
4. **GIVEN NAMES.** If you specify a given name, be sure to also look for variations, misspellings, or abbreviations of that name. Sometimes only an initial or abbreviation is used, such as Chas. for Charles or Thos. for Thomas. Also look for variations and different spellings—Eliza, Beth, Liz, Liza, for Elizabeth; Alex for Alexander; Jim for James; Jon for John. If you are looking for an immigrant ancestor, look for his or her name as spelled in the native language.
5. **SOUNDEX SEARCHES.** Many electronic indexes allow for Soundex searches. This may help you to get positive results, despite possible misspellings. For other databases, you may want to say the name aloud. For example, when searching the surname Dwyer data entries are listed as Ware, Toire, Wire, and Weir. Note the phonetic spellings of names and try using different accents.
6. **RESEARCH LOG.** When you are searching for multiple names, and multiple spellings for multiple years, it can be difficult to keep track of where you have searched, when, and for what. Keeping a log of the places you have searched and combination of search terms used, along with results, can save much duplicated effort. With websites that are constantly being updated, bugs worked out, and/or search features enhanced, you may want to go back occasionally to recheck for missing ancestors. Your log can tell you when you last checked a site. The free research calendar at Ancestry.com can be used to record your searches. <www.ancestry.com/save/charts/researchcal.htm>
7. **BEYOND THE INDEX.** While indexes are becoming more and more detailed, there is still more to be found on the original documents. For example, the FamilySearch 1880 U.S. Census and National Index contains the following

name	age
relationship	occupation
sex	birthplace
marital status	father's birthplace
race	mother's birthplace

but you will not find the any of following information that can be found by looking at a copy of the original enumeration:

the family's address
how many families reside in the dwelling
month of birth for children born within the year
whether individuals were married that year
how many months an individual was unemployed
school attendance during the year

whether unable to read if age 10 or older
whether sick or temporarily disabled on the day of enumeration and the reason therefore
whether the individual was blind, deaf-mute, idiotic," insane, or permanently disabled

In addition, as previously discussed, indexes may contain errors, causing you to miss family members that could be found in browsing the enumerations.

8. **USING ONLINE SOURCES TO SAVE TIME DURING LIBRARY AND ARCHIVE VISITS.** With more and more census information becoming available online and on CD-ROM, by performing as many of these searches from the comfort of your home, you can free up valuable research time to search other records and resources when the opportunity arises to visit a facility with a large genealogical collection.

9. **PRINT IT OUT.** Each CD-ROM or website is slightly different, but it is always worth the time and toner to print out a hard copy of pertinent census records for further review. This paper copy can be placed in a binder or folder and accessed when you are not at your computer. The paper copy also helps to ensure that you do not introduce any mistakes into your records while transcribing. A paper copy allows you to compare your new findings with offline information more easily and handwriting or reading errors can be corrected on further review or looking back at the printed form.

no longer searches schedules in response to mail requests. The National Archives will furnish photocopies of census pages only when the researcher can cite the state, county, enumeration district (for 1880, 1900 and 1910), volume number, and exact page on which a family is enumerated." Information about this and other NARA publications is available at the NARA website <www.archives.gov/publications>.

Microfilm Copies

The National Archives has reproduced all of the available federal population census schedules on microfilm. Copies of available 1790 to 1930 censuses for all states and territories can be used in the Microfilm Research Room in the National Archives in Washington, D.C., regional branches of the National Archives, at the Family History Library of The Church of Jesus Christ of Latter-day Saints in Salt Lake City and in its Family History Centers, and at many other private and public libraries. The added options of borrowing census schedules from microfilm-lending companies or purchasing microfilm copies from the National Archives make the census one of the most readily available record sources.

Limitations of Microfilm Copies

As noted earlier, microfilming of the census schedules, indexes, and other heavily used records in the National Archives took place in the 1940s, when the technology was in its infancy. The microfilms of most of the censuses for most years are quite legible. However, there are thousands of census pages from various states and years that cannot be read because of poor focusing or because of too much or too little lighting. Pages of original census schedules were also inadvertently skipped when microfilming took place—some pages may have stuck together when turned, and some may have been missing when the microfilming began. For example, nine pages were missed during the microfilming of the 1820 Virginia schedule. They were subsequently identified and indexed by Gerald M. Petty in "Virginia 1820 Federal Census: Names Not on the Microfilm Copy."[10] In another case, more than 1,000 Illinoisans with names beginning with the letter O were somehow missed when the rest of the 1880 Soundex index was microfilmed. The missing section for the letter O was later transcribed from the original cards by Nancy Gubb Frederick in *1880 Illinois Census Index, Soundex Codes O-200 to O-240*.[11]

Unfortunately, since the 1900, 1910, and 1920 census originals were destroyed, it will be impossible to remicrofilm any illegible pages or pages missed in the original microfilming of schedules for those census years. As mentioned previously, however, advances in scanning technology have provided a way to improve the legibility of some of the damaged pages.

Restrictions on Access to Post-1930 Census Records

To protect the privacy of living individuals, access to population schedules is restricted for seventy-two years after the census is taken, so they are not available to researchers during that time. The Personal Service Branch, Bureau of the Census, P.O. Box 1545, Jeffersonville, IN 47131, will provide, for a fee, official transcripts of census records from 1940 to 2000. Access is restricted to whomever the information is about, their authorized representatives, or, in the case of deceased persons, their heirs or administrators. Use Form BC-600 to request information. Since the Census Day for 1940 was 1 April 1940, this census is scheduled to be released on 1 April 2012.

Federal Population Census Research Procedures

1. How to Find Census Records

All available federal census schedules, from 1790 to 1930, have been microfilmed and are available at the National Archives in Washington, D.C., at the National Archives' regional archives (See appendix G, "The National Archives and Its Regions"), at the LDS Family History Library and Family History Centers throughout North America, at many large libraries, and through microfilm-lending companies. Some state and local agencies may have census schedules only for the state or area served.

In addition to the microfilmed copies of the federal census schedules, digital copies are also increasingly available online and on CD-ROM. These resources can be accessed from personal computers at home or at a library, are generally searchable, and can save researchers a good deal of time and money. Ask your local librarian if your library has access to a U.S. Federal Census collection online or on CD-ROM.

2. Starting Information

It is usually best to begin a census search in the most recently available census records and to work from what is already known about a family. With any luck, birthplaces and other clues found in these more recent records will point to locations of earlier residency.

3. Arrangement of Census Records

The microfilm census schedules are arranged by census year and then alphabetically by name of state; then, with a few exceptions, they are organized alphabetically by name of county. To begin researching microfilmed census records, a researcher must know in which state the subject of interest lived during the census year, and may need to know the county and an exact address if the name is common.

In early census years or in sparsely populated areas, one roll of microfilm may contain all the schedules for one county or several small counties. However, in heavily populated areas, there may be many rolls for a single county. The arrangement of surnames on a page of the schedule is usually in the order in which the enumerator visited the households. To search for a particular name in the microfilm schedules may necessitate scanning every page of a district; however, the increasingly numerous indexes to federal censuses and finding aids have dramatically reduced such tedious work. Finding a particular name in most electronic and digital copies of the schedules is much easier with their built-in global search function.

4. Indexes

The impact of technology on census research is no more evident than in the area of census indexes. While print indexes are still available and useful, digital indexes have become the quickest and easiest way to zero in on ancestors in the federal censuses. See page 185 for an in-depth discussion of Census Indexes and Finding Aids.

5. Catalogs

Five catalogs produced by the National Archives Trust Fund Board are especially helpful in conducting research in federal census records. They are available in print and as searchable

A U.S. Census Geographer works on coverage maps for the 1930 census. (Source: U.S. Census Bureau, Public Information Office.)

publications online through the National Archives <www.archives.gov/publications/microfilm-catalogs.html#census>. They are as follows:

National Archives Trust Fund Board. *The 1790–1890 Federal Population Censuses: Catalog of National Archives Microfilm*. Washington, D.C.: National Archives Trust Fund Board, 1993. This catalog is arranged chronologically, then by state or territory, and then by county. Given for each microfilm publication is the series number and the total number of microfilm rolls in the enumeration. The catalog further identifies each microfilm roll by number and contents.

———. *1900 Federal Population Census: A Catalog of Microfilm Copies of the Schedules*. Washington, D.C., 1978. This catalog lists the 1,854 rolls of microfilm on which the 1900 population census schedules appear. The census schedules are arranged by state or territory and then by county. Numbers for the 7,846 rolls of 1900 Soundex indexes appear in the second half of the book.

———. *The 1910 Federal Population Census: A Catalog of Microfilm Copies of the Schedules*. Washington, D.C., 1982. This catalog lists the 1,784 rolls of microfilm on which the 1910 population census schedules appear. The census schedules are arranged by state or territory and then by county. Numbers for the 4,642 rolls of 1910 Soundex/Miracode indexes appear in the second half of the catalog.

———. *The 1920 Federal Population Census: Catalog of National Archives Microfilm*. Washington, D.C., 1991. This catalog lists the 8,585 rolls of 1920 Soundex indexes in the front portion of the book. The catalog lists 2,076 rolls of 1920 census schedules arranged by state or territory and then by county.

———. *The 1930 Federal Population Census: Catalog of National Archives Microfilm*. Washington, D.C., 2002. Provides roll-by-roll listings of the 1930 census microfilm. Population census schedules are broken down by state, county, and enumeration district, while the beginning and ending codes are provided for each roll of the Soundex. An introduction explains how to use the records, summarizes the instructions to the census enumerators, and tells how to order microfilm copies of schedules, Soundex, and related microfilm.

Researching the Individual Censuses

The information contained in the U.S. Federal Census schedules varies dramatically from the first census in 1790 to the latest available census of 1930. What started in colonial times as a basic headcount evolved into a somewhat lengthy interrogation that yielded tremendous amounts of information useful in genealogical research.

Following is a summary of what to expect in each census schedule, along with research tips. Also, see the chart titled "Comparison of Census Information, 1790–1930" for a summary of questions asked in each census.

1790 Census

The 1790 census began on 2 August 1790. The marshals were expected to finish the census within nine months of the Census Day—by 1 May 1791. Although most of the returns were in long before the deadline, Congress had to extend the count until 1 March 1792. By that time some people probably were counted who had not been born or present in 1790. The official census population count was 3,929,214.

Questions Asked in the 1790 Census

The 1790 census called for the name of the family head; the number of free white males of sixteen years and older; the number of free white males under sixteen; the number of free white females; the number of slaves; the number of other persons; and sometimes the town or district of residence.

The 1790 census instructed the marshals to identify, by age brackets, free white males sixteen years of age or older and those under sixteen. This was designed to determine the country's industrial and military capabilities. Additionally, the first census counted the number of free white females; all other free persons regardless of race or gender; and slaves. A twenty-dollar fine, to be split between the marshals' assistants and the government, would be levied against anyone who refused to answer the enumerator's questions.

Other Significant Facts about the 1790 Census

The Constitution called for a census of all "Persons . . . excluding Indians not taxed" for the purpose of apportioning seats in the House of Representatives and assessing direct federal taxes. The "Indians not taxed" were those not living in the settled areas. In later years, Native Americans everywhere were considered part of the total population, but not all were included in the apportionment figures until 1940.

The government did not provide printed forms, or even paper, until 1830. It was up to each assistant to copy his census return on whatever paper he could find and post it in two public places in his assigned area. Those who saw and could read them were supposed to check for discrepancies or omissions. The highest pay rate, two cents per person, barely covered expenses, especially where settlers were scattered and living in places that were difficult to find or access.

The jurisdictions of the thirteen original states stretched over an area of seventeen present-day states. Census schedules survive for only two-thirds of those states. The surviving schedules were indexed by state and published by the Bureau of

Comparison of Census Information, 1790–1930

Personal Info on Census	1790	1800	1810	1820	1830	1840	1850	1860	1870	1880	1900	1910	1920	1930
Name of family head only	x	x	x	x	x	x								
Headcount by age, gender, …	x	x	x	x	x	x								
Standard census form					x	x	x	x	x	x	x	x	x	x
Names of all individuals							x	x	x	x	x	x	x	x
Age							x	x	x	x	x	x	x	x
Sex							x	x	x	x	x	x	x	x
Color							x	x	x	x	x	x	x	x
Profession or occupation							x	x	x	x	x	x	x	x
Place of birth							x	x	x	x	x	x	x	x
Attended school that year							x	x	x	x	x	x	x	x
Married that year							x	x	x	x	x			
Read or write							x	x	x	x	x	x	x	x
Deaf, blind, insane, idiotic, …							x	x	x	x		x		
Real estate value							x	x	x					
Personal estate value								x	x					
Separate slave schedule							x	x						
Father of foreign birth									x					
Mother of foreign birth									x					
Month of birth											x			
Month of birth that year									x	x				
Male citizen over 21 years									x					
Male over 21 denied vote									x					
Visitation number of dwelling							x	x	x	x	x	x	x	x
Visitation number of family							x	x	x	x	x	x	x	x
Street name in city										x	x	x	x	x
House number in city										x	x	x	x	x
Relationship to family head										x	x	x	x	x
Marital status										x	x	x	x	x
Month of marriage that year									x					
No. of months unemployed										x	x			
Father's birthplace										x	x	x	x	x
Mother's birthplace										x	x	x	x	x
Sickness on census day										x				
Year of birth											x			
No. of years present marriage											x	x		
Mother how many children											x	x		
Number of children living											x	x		
Year of immigration to US											x	x	x	x
No. of years in US											x			
Naturalization status											x	x	x	x
Months attended school											x			

copyright © 2002, MyFamily.com, Inc.

the Census in the early 1900s. The index, *Bureau of the Census, Heads of Families at the First Census of the United States Taken in the Year 1790,* 12 vols. (Washington, D.C.: Government Printing Office, 1908), can be found in most research libraries; it has been reprinted by various publishers over the years. This printed version contains some names not available on the microfilm, including several counties in North Carolina.

Both the original and printed 1790 census schedules are available on microfilm for Connecticut, Maine (then part of Massachusetts), Maryland, Massachusetts, New Hampshire, New York, North Carolina, Pennsylvania, Rhode Island, South Carolina, and Vermont. The schedules for Delaware, Georgia, Kentucky, New Jersey, Tennessee, and Virginia were burned during the War of 1812. (There are substitutes for most of these.) Published and microfilmed 1790 schedules for Virginia were reconstructed from state enumerations and tax lists. (See a list of these schedules on page 271.)

Research Tips for the 1790 Census

Because of the availability of the printed 1790 census schedules, researchers tend to overlook the importance of consulting the original schedules, which are readily available on microfilm. As in most cases, the researcher who relies on printed transcripts may miss important information and clues found only in the original version.

The 1790 census records are useful for identifying localities to search for other types of records for a named individual. The 1790 census will, in most cases, help distinguish the target family from others of the same name; identify immediate neighbors who may be related; identify slaveholders; and spot spelling variations of surnames. Free men "of color" are listed as heads of household by name. Slaves appear in age groupings by name of owner. By combining those age groupings with probate inventories and tax list data, it is sometimes possible to determine names of other family members and the birth order of those individuals.

For a state-by-state listing of census schedules, see *The 1790–1890 Federal Population Censuses: Catalog of National Archives Microfilm.*[12] For boundary changes and identification of missing census schedules, see Thorndale's and Dollarhide's *Map Guide to the U.S. Federal Censuses, 1790–1920.*

1800 Census

The 1800 census began on 4 August 1800. The count was to be completed within nine months. The official census population count was 5,308,483.

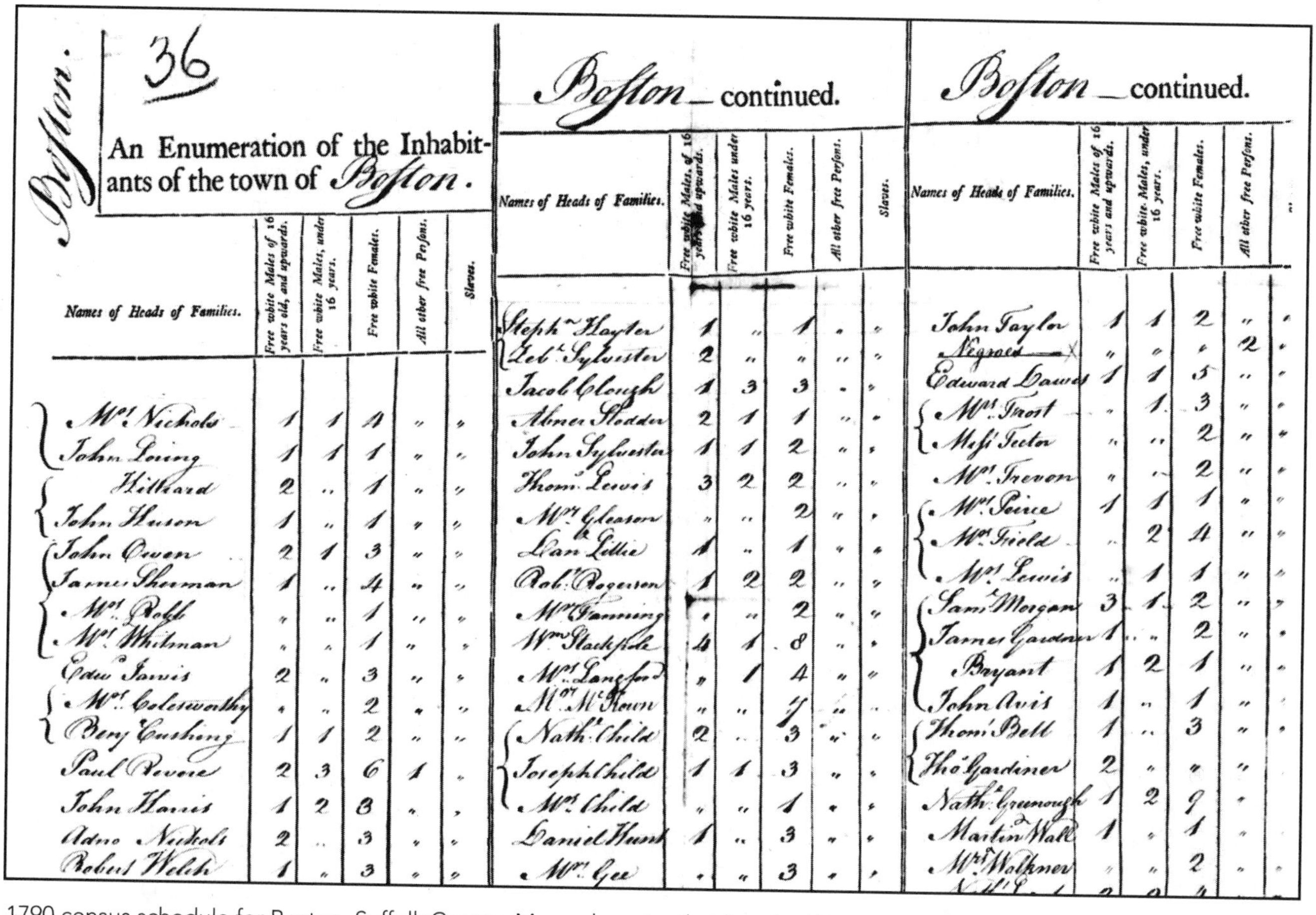

1790 census schedule for Boston, Suffolk County, Massachusetts, that lists Paul Revere.

Questions Asked in the 1800 Census

The census asked the name of the family head; the number of free white males and females in age categories 0 to 10, 10 to 16, 16 to 26, 26 to 45, 45 and older; the number of other free persons except Indians not taxed; the number of slaves; and the town or district and county of residence.

Other Significant Facts about the 1800 Census

Most 1800 census entries are arranged in the order of visitation, but some have been rearranged to appear in alphabetical order by initial letter of the surname.

Research Tips for the 1800 Census

The 1800 census records are useful for identifying localities to search for other types of records for a named individual. The 1800 census will, in most cases, help distinguish the target family from others of the same name; help to determine family size; locate possible relatives with the same name; identify immediate neighbors who may be related; identify slaveholders; and spot spelling variations of surnames. Free men "of color" are listed as heads of household by name. Slaves appear in age groupings by name of owner. By combining those age groupings with probate inventories and tax list data, it is sometimes possible to determine names and birth order of other family members.

For a state-by-state listing of census schedules, see *The 1790–1890 Federal Population Censuses: Catalog of National Archives Microfilm*. For boundary changes and identification of missing census schedules, see Thorndale's and Dollarhide's *Map Guide to the U.S. Federal Censuses, 1790–1920*.

1810 Census

The 1810 census began on 6 August 1810. The count was due within nine months, but the due date was extended by law to ten months. The official census population count was 7,239,881.

Questions Asked in the 1810 Census

The 1810 Census called for the name of the family head; the number of free white males and females in age categories 0 to 10, 10 to 16, 16 to 26, 26 to 45, 45 and older; the number of other free persons except Indians not taxed; the number of slaves; and the town or district and county of residence.

Research Tips for the 1810 Census

The 1810 census records are useful in identifying the locality to be searched for other types of records for a named individual. The 1810 census will, in most cases, help distinguish the target family from others of the same name; help to determine family size; locate possible relatives with the same name; identify immediate neighbors who may be related; identify slaveholders; and spot spelling variations of surnames. Free men "of color" are named as heads of household. Slaves appear in age groupings by name of owner. By combining those age groupings with probate inventories and tax list data, it is sometimes possible to determine names of other family members and the birth order of those individuals. Manufacturing schedules are scattered among the 1810 population schedules.

For a state-by-state listing of census schedules, see *The 1790–1890 Federal Population Censuses: Catalog of National Archives Microfilm*. For boundary changes and identification of missing census schedules, see Thorndale's and Dollarhide's *Map Guide to the U.S. Federal Censuses, 1790–1920*.

1820 Census

The 1820 census began on 7 August 1820. The count was due within six months but was extended by law to allow completion within thirteen months. The official census population count was 9,638,453.

Questions Asked in the 1820 Census

The 1820 census called for the name of the family head; the number of free white males and females in age categories 0 to 10, 10 to 16, 16 to 18 (males only), 16 to 26, 26 to 45, 45 and older; the number of other free persons except Indians not taxed; the number of slaves; and the town or district and county of residence. Additionally, the 1820 census for the first time asked the number of free white males 16 to 18; the number of persons not naturalized; the number engaged in agriculture, commercial, or manufacture; the number of "colored" persons (sometimes in age categories); and the number of other persons except Indians.

Research Tips for the 1820 Census

The 1820 census records are useful for identifying localities to search for other types of records for a named individual. The 1820 census will, in most cases, help distinguish the target family from others of the same name; help to determine family size; locate possible relatives with the same name; identify immediate neighbors who may be related; identify slaveholders; and spot spelling variations of surnames. Free men "of color" are listed as heads of household by name. Slaves appear in age groupings by name of owner. By combining those age groupings with probate inventories and tax list date, it is sometimes possible to determine names of other family members and the birth order of those individuals.

The added questions in the 1820 census break down ages so that it is possible to gauge the age of young men more accurately. However, the redundancy of asking the number of free white males "Between 16 and 18," and "Of 16 and under 26," "Of 26 and under 45," "Of 45 and upwards," is frequently cause for confusion in attempts to calculate the total number of persons in a given household. The column regarding naturalization status may be some indication of length of residency in the United States and the possibility of finding naturalization papers in a local court.

The questions asked regarding number and nature of those involved in agriculture, commercial, or manufacturing enterprises allow researchers to make some distinctions about the occupation of the head and any others in the household who were employed. Some, though admittedly not much, identifying information is available where schedules go beyond stating the number of "colored" persons and provide an age breakdown as well. The 1820 manufacturing schedules are on twenty-nine separate rolls of microfilm.

For a state-by-state listing of census schedules, see *The 1790–1890 Federal Population Censuses: Catalog of National Archives.* For boundary changes and identification of missing census schedules, see Thorndale's and Dollarhide's *Map Guide to the U.S. Federal Censuses, 1790–1920.*

1830 Census

The 1830 census began on 1 June 1830. The enumeration was to be completed within six months but was extended to allow completion within twelve months. The official census population count was 12,860,702.

Questions Asked in the 1830 Census

The 1830 census form called for the name of the head of household; the number of free white males and females in age categories 0 to 5, 5 to 10, 10 to 15, 15 to 20, 20 to 30, 30 to 40, 40 to 50, 50 to 60, 60 to 70, 70 to 80, 80 to 90, 90 to 100, over 100; the number of slaves and free "colored" persons in age categories; there were also categories for deaf, dumb, and blind persons, and aliens; the town or district; and the county of residence.

Other Significant Facts about the 1830 Census

The 1830 census was the first for which the government provided uniform, printed forms to enumerators for the purpose of recording answers to census questions.

Research Tips for the 1830 Census

The 1830 census records are useful for identifying localities to search for other types of records for a named individual. The 1830 census will, in most cases, help distinguish the target family from others of the same name; help to determine family size; locate possible relatives with the same name; identify immediate neighbors who may be related; identify slaveholders; and spot spelling variations of surnames. Free men "of color" are listed as heads of household by name. Slaves appear in age groupings by name of owner. By combining those age groupings with probate inventories and tax list data, it is sometimes possible to determine names of other family members and the birth order of those individuals.

The 1830 census went a step further in breaking down ages, thus allowing more precise knowledge of the household configuration. With the age categories expanded to include those one hundred years and older, it is possible to have a better idea of life spans during that time period. The addition of information regarding those who were deaf, dumb, and blind is an indication that there may be related guardianship or institutional records. The presence of aliens in a household suggests the possibility that those individuals may eventually have been naturalized in a nearby court.

For a state-by-state listing of census schedules, see *The 1790–1890 Federal Population Censuses: Catalog of National Archives Microfilm.* For boundary changes and identification of missing census schedules, see Thorndale's and Dollarhide's *Map Guide to the U.S. Federal Censuses, 1790–1920.*

1840 Census

The 1840 census began on 1 June 1840. The enumeration was to be completed within nine months but was extended to eighteen months. The official census population count was 17,063,353.

Questions Asked in the 1840 Census

The 1840 census form called for the name of the head of household; the number of free white males and females in age categories 0 to 5, 5 to 10, 10 to 15, 15 to 20, 20 to 30, 30 to 40, 40 to 50, 50 to 60, 60 to 70, 70 to 80, 80 to 90, 90 to 100, over 100; the number of slaves and free "colored" persons in age categories; and also had the categories for deaf, dumb, and blind persons and aliens; the town or district; and the county of residence.

Additionally, the 1840 census, asked for the first time the ages of Revolutionary War pensioners and the number of individuals engaged in mining; agriculture; commerce; manufacturing and trade; the navigation of the ocean, canals, lakes, and rivers; learned professions and engineers; the number in school, the number in the family over the age of twenty-one who could not read and write, and the number of insane.

Research Tips for the 1840 Census

The same research strategies used in the previous census apply to the 1840 census. A significant bonus comes from the question regarding revolutionary war pensioners. A search of revolutionary war sources may provide a wealth of genealogical information. A refinement of the occupation categories makes it possible to pursue other occupational sources and easier to distinguish individuals of the same name in the ever-growing population. Reading and writing skills and some indication of the educational level attained add an interesting and more personal dimension to a family history. An indication of the "insane" within a household might point to guardianship or institutional records. For a state-by-state listing of census schedules, see *The 1790–1890 Federal Population Censuses: Catalog of National Archives Microfilm.* For boundary changes and identification of missing census schedules, see Thorndale's and Dollarhide's *Map Guide to the U.S. Federal Censuses, 1790–1920.*

1850 Census

The 1850 census began on 1 June 1850. The enumeration was completed within five months. The official census population count was 23,191,876.

Questions Asked in the 1850 Census

The 1850 census form called for the number of the dwelling house and family in order of visitation; each person's name, age, sex, and color; the territory or country of his or her birth; whether the person attended school or was married within the year; whether the person could read or write if over age twenty; whether the person was deaf-mute, blind, insane, or "idiotic"; whether or not the person was a fugitive from the state; and real estate value of the dwelling house. The census also asked the occupation of males over the age of fifteen.

Separate slave schedules for 1850 asked the name of each slave owner, the number of slaves owned, and the number of slaves manumitted (released from slavery). While the schedules, unfortunately, do not name individual slaves, they asked for age, color, and sex; whether or not the slave was deaf-mute, blind, insane, or idiotic; and whether or not the slave was a fugitive from the state.

Other Significant Facts about the 1850 Census

The 1850 census is frequently referred to as the first modern census because of dramatically improved techniques employed for it and repeated in later years. Printed instructions to the enumerators account for a greater degree of accuracy compared with earlier censuses. The instructions explained the responsibilities of enumerators, census procedures, the manner of completing the schedules, and the intent behind census questions. "In the 1850 census and thereafter, enumerators were required by law to make their count by personal inquiry at every dwelling and with every family, and not otherwise."[13] As enumerations of districts were completed, the enumerator was instructed to make two additional copies: one to be filed with the clerk of the county court and one to be sent to the secretary of the state or territory. The original (or one of the copies) was to be sent to the Census Office for tabulation.

The census showed the names of persons who died after 1 June of the census year and omitted children born after that date. It should be noted that many of the census takers did not get around to their assigned districts until late in 1850; some were as late as October and November.

The enumeration listed every person in the United States except Indians living on government reservations or living on unsettled tracts of land. Indians not in tribal relations, whether of mixed blood or not, who were not living among the white population or on the outskirts of towns, were counted as part of the taxable population. The count was designed to determine the apportioning of representatives among the states.

Research Tips for the 1850 Census

The 1850 schedules included the free and slave population and mortality, agriculture, and industry data. The inclusion of so much personal data for the first time in the 1850 census is an obvious boon to genealogists and social historians. For the first time it is possible to identify families and other groups by name. The inclusion of birthplaces for every individual allow for the plotting of migration routes.

Ages provided in the 1850 census allow researchers to establish dates for searching vital records. While few states officially recorded vital records that early, religious and other records may be pursued with estimated dates of birth gleaned from the census.

The identification of previous residences points to still other record sources to be searched in named localities. The indication of real estate ownership would suggest that land and tax records should be searched. The 1850 census may provide starting information for searching marriage records, probates, and a number of other genealogically important records. Probable family relationships may also be determined through 1850 census records, though it is easy to come to the wrong conclusions. The 1850 census provides valuable insights into occupations and property value. It may also make it possible to spot remarriages and step-relationships and to determine approximate life spans.

For a state-by-state listing of census schedules, see *The 1790–1890 Federal Population Censuses: Catalog of National Archives Microfilm*. For boundary changes and identification of missing census schedules, see Thorndale's and Dollarhide's, *Map Guide to the U.S. Federal Censuses, 1790–1920.*

1860 Census

The 1860 census began on 1 June 1860. The enumeration was completed within five months. The official census population count was 31,443,321.

Questions Asked in the 1860 Census

The census asked for the number of the dwelling house and the family, in order of visitation. For each free person, it asked for his or her name, age, sex, and color; the occupation of persons over age fifteen; the value of real estate; the value of his or her personal estate; the name of the state, territory, or country of his or her birth; whether the person was married during the year; whether the person attended school during the year. It indicated persons over twenty years of age who could not read and write; and whether the person was deaf-mute, blind, insane, an "idiot," a pauper, or a convict.

The information in the slave schedules is the same as those for 1850.

Other Significant Facts about the 1860 Census

The 1860 census was the first to ask the value of personal estates. As enumerations of districts were completed, the enumerator was instructed to make two additional copies: one to be filed with the clerk of the county court and one to be sent to the secretary of the state or territory. The original (or one of the copies) was to be sent to the Census Office for tabulation.

Enumerators were instructed to be as specific as possible concerning the state or territory of each person's birth if in the United States, or the country of birth if foreign born. For example, designations of England, Scotland, Ireland, and Wales and the German states of Prussia, Baden, Bavaria, Württemberg, and Hesse-Darmstadt were preferred to Great Britain and Germany.

Research Tips for the 1860 Census

Research strategies remain the same as those suggested for the 1850 census because the information included in the 1850 and 1860 schedules is essentially the same, except for the addition of the question concerning personal estates. While the added column may be a general indicator of a person's assets, it is doubtful that individuals were likely to disclose true figures, for fear of being taxed accordingly.

For a state-by-state listing of census schedules, see *The 1790–1890 Federal Population Censuses: Catalog of National Archives Microfilm*. For boundary changes and identification of missing census schedules, see Thorndale's and Dollarhide's *Map Guide to the U.S. Federal Censuses, 1790–1920*.

1870 Census

The 1870 census began on 1 June 1870. The enumeration was completed within five months. The official census population count was 38,558,371.

Questions Asked in the 1870 Census

The 1870 census form called for dwelling houses and families to be numbered in order of visitation; and the name of every person whose place of abode on the first day of June 1870 was with the family. The census further asked the age of each

1870 census schedule for Lamar, Barton County, Missouri, that lists famed lawman Wyatt Earp.

individual at his or her last birthday. If a child was one year or less, the age was stated as a fraction of months out of the year, such as 1/12. Additionally, the census asked the sex, color, profession, and occupation or trade of every inhabitant. There were also columns for the disclosure of value of real estate and personal property. The 1870 census asked for the place of birth, specifically the state or territory of the United States, or the country if foreign born (including the province if born in Germany). The schedule provided space to indicate whether or not the father and the mother of the individual was foreign born, and if an individual was born or married within the year, the month in which the event occurred. The census also acknowledged those who had attended school within the year; those who could not read; those who could not write; and the deaf and dumb, blind, insane and the "idiotic" to be identified. Finally, the schedules had space to identify any male citizen of the United States of age twenty-one and older, and any male citizen of the United States age twenty-one and older whose right to vote was denied or abridged on grounds other than rebellion or other crime. (Also see "Non-Population Schedules and Special Censuses," on page 196.)

Other Significant Facts about the 1870 Census

The 1870 census may identify survivors of the Civil War, suggesting they might have military records to be found. Conversely, if an individual does not appear in the 1870 census as expected, it may be a clue that the person was a casualty of the war. In the absence of so many other records from the South for this era, information from the 1870 census can be especially important. A caveat, however, is found in *Map Guide to the U.S. Federal Censuses 1790–1920,* which states, "The 1870 census in the Southern States omits a great many persons."

Research Tips for the 1870 Census

The 1870 census is the first census in which parents of foreign birth are indicated—a real boon in identifying immigrant ancestors. Immigrants who were naturalized and eligible to vote are identified, suggesting follow-up in court and naturalization sources. Indications of a person's color that were intended to be more precise—white (W), black (B), Chinese (C), Indian (I), mulatto (M)—may be helpful in determining individuals' origins. (Also see "Non-Population Schedules and Special Censuses," on page 196.)

For a state-by-state listing of census schedules, see *The 1790–1890 Federal Population Censuses: Catalog of National Archives Microfilm.* For boundary changes and identification of missing census schedules, see Thorndale's and Dollarhide's *Map Guide to the U.S. Federal Censuses, 1790–1920.*

1880 Census

The 1880 census began on 1 June 1880. The enumeration was to be completed within thirty days, or within two weeks for communities with populations of 10,000 or more. The official census population count was 50,189,209.

Questions Asked in the 1880 Census

For each person in every household, the census asked the number of the dwelling house and the family, in order of visitation; the person's name; whether the person was white, black, mulatto, Indian, or Chinese; his or her sex and age, and the month of birth if born within the year; the person's relationship to the head of the household; whether he or she was single, married, widowed, or divorced; whether married within the year; his or her occupation and months unemployed; the name of the state, territory, or country of birth; his or her parents' birthplaces; whether he or she attended school during the year; whether he or she was unable to read if age ten or older; and whether the person was sick or temporarily disabled on the day of enumeration, including the reason therefore. Those who were blind, deaf-mute, "idiotic," insane, or permanently disabled were also indicated as such.

Other Significant Facts about the 1880 Census

In addition to identifying the state, county, and other subdivisions, the 1880 census was the first to provide the name of the street and house number for urban households. The 1880 census was also the first to identify relationship to the head of household; illness or disability at the time the census was taken; marital status; number of months unemployed during the year; and the state or country of birth of every individual's father and mother. Individuals who were born or died after 1 June 1880 were not included in the 1880 census, even though the enumerator may not have questioned the family until well after that date. Indians not taxed are not in regular population schedules. Some may appear in special Indian schedules. (Also see "Non-Population Schedules and Special Censuses," on page 196.)

Research Tips for the 1880 Census

The 1880 census makes it possible to identify the state or country of birth for parents, which is especially important for tracing movements of immigrant ancestors. The census may be used to supplement birth or marriage records for the census year or even to partially replace them where vital records are not recorded elsewhere. The census may also be useful in discovering previously unknown surnames of married daughters, mothers-in-law, cousins, and other relatives living with the family. This is the first census to state relationship to the head of household, but the wife may not be the mother of the children. The 1880 census may also provide clues to genetic symptoms and diseases in earlier generations of a family.

For a state-by-state listing of census schedules, see *The 1790–1890 Federal Population Censuses: Catalog of National Archives Microfilm.* For boundary changes and identification of

1880 census schedule for North Dansville, Livingston County, New York that lists Civil War nurse Clara Barton.

missing census schedules, see Thorndale's and Dollarhide's *Map Guide to the U.S. Federal Censuses, 1790–1920*. Also available are 1885 territorial censuses for Colorado, Florida, Nebraska, Dakota Territory, and New Mexico.

1890 Census

The 1890 census began on 1 June 1890. The enumeration was to be completed within thirty days, or within two weeks for communities with populations of more than 10,000. The official census population count was 62,979,766.

Questions Asked in the 1890 Census

The surviving 1890 schedules provide the address, number of families in the house, number of persons in the house, and number of persons in the family. Individuals are listed by name and the schedules indicate whether or not each person was a soldier, sailor, or marine during the Civil War, and whether Union or Confederate; or whether the person was the widow of a veteran. The census called for each person's relationship to the head of the family; whether he or she was white, black, mulatto, quadroon, octoroon, Chinese, Japanese, or Indian; his or her sex, age, and marital status, and if married, whether he or she was married during the year; if a mother, it asked the number of her children and number living. It also asked for each person's place of birth, and that of his or her father and mother. If and individual was foreign born, the schedules indicate how many years that person had been in the United States at the time of the census, and whether he or she was naturalized or in the process of naturalization. Additionally, it asked for the person's profession, trade, or occupation; the number of months unemployed during the census year; his or her ability to read write, and speak English (if not, his or her language or dialect is listed); whether the person was suffering from acute or chronic disease (if so, it gave the name of disease and the length of time afflicted); whether he or she was defective in mind, sight, hearing, or speech; or whether he or she was crippled, maimed, deformed (with the name of defect), a prisoner, a convict, a homeless child, or a pauper; and whether the home was rented or owned by the head or a member of the family (if so, whether mortgaged). If the head of the family was a farmer, it asked if he or a family member rented or owned the farm, and, if mortgaged, the post office address of the owner.

Other Significant Facts about the 1890 Census

Most of the original 1890 population schedules were destroyed or badly damaged by a fire in the Commerce Department in 1921. Records enumerating only 6,160 individuals—less than one percent of the schedules—survived. Unfortunately, no complete schedules for a state, county, or community survived. Only the following fragments are available:

1. Alabama: Perry County (Perryville Beat No. 11 and Severe Beat No. 8).
2. District of Columbia: Q. Thirteenth, Fourteenth, R.Q. Corcoran, fifteenth, S.R. and Riggs streets, Johnson Avenue, and S Street.
3. Georgia: Muscogee County (Columbus).
4. Illinois: McDonough County, Mound Township.
5. Minnesota: Wright County, Rockford.
6. New Jersey: Hudson County, Jersey City.
7. New York: Westchester County, Eastchester, Suffolk County, Brookhaven Township.
8. North Carolina: Gaston County, South Point Township and River Bend Township; Cleveland County, Township No. 2.
9. Ohio: Hamilton County (Cincinnati) and Clinton County, Wayne Township.
10. South Dakota: Union County, Jefferson Township.
11. Texas: Ellis County, J.P. no. 6, Mountain Peak, and Ovila Precinct; Hood County, Precinct no. 5; Rusk County, Precinct no. 6 and J.P. no. 7; Trinity County, Trinity Town, and Precinct no. 2; Kaufman County, Kaufman.

See the following indexes to these schedules:

- *Index to the Eleventh Census of the United States*. National Archives microfilm M496.
- Nelson, Ken. *1890 Census Index Register*. Salt Lake City: Genealogical Society of Utah, 1984.
- Swenson, Helen Smothers. *Index to 1890 Census of the United States*. Round Rock, Tex.: the author, 1981.

Research Tips for the 1890 Census

Because it is well-known that the 1890 census records were destroyed by fire, few researchers think to check the index to the remaining schedules. (See "Census Indexes and Finding Aids," on page 185.)

Special 1890 schedules enumerating Union veterans and widows of Union veterans of the Civil War are sometimes useful as a substitute for the missing 1890 population schedules. (Also see "Non-Population Schedules and Special Censuses," on page 196.)

For a state-by-state listing of census schedules, see *The 1790–1890 Federal Population Censuses: Catalog of National Archives Microfilm*. For boundary changes and identification of missing census schedules, see Thorndale's and Dollarhide's *Map Guide to the U.S. Federal Censuses, 1790–1920*.

The 1890 Census Substitute

Ancestry.com, the National Archives and Records Administration, and the Allen County Public Library produced an online substitute for the missing census. More than 20 million records were identified for inclusion in the collection, and additions are made regularly as they become available for posting. It includes fragments of the original 1890 census that survived the fire damage, special veterans schedules, several Native American tribe censuses for years surrounding 1890, state censuses (1885 or 1895), city and county directories, alumni directories, and voter registration documents. You can access the census substitute at <www.ancestry.com/search/rectype/census/1890sub/main.htm>.

1900 Census

The 1900 census began on 1 June 1900. The enumeration was to be completed within thirty days, or within two weeks for communities with populations of more than 10,000. The official census population count was 76,212,168.

Questions Asked in the 1900 Census

The 1900 population schedules provide the number of each dwelling house and family, in order of visitation; the name, address, relationship to the head of the household of each person in the

NATIVITY — Place of birth of each person and parents of each person enumerated. If born in the United States, give the *State* or *Territory*; if of foreign birth, give the *Country* only			CITIZENSHIP			OCCUPATION, TRADE, OR PROFESSION of each person TEN YEARS of age and over		EDUCATION				OWNERSHIP OF HOME			
Place of birth of this PERSON	Place of birth of FATHER of this person	Place of birth of MOTHER of this person	Year of immigration to the United States	Number of years in the United States	Naturalization	OCCUPATION	Months not employed	Attended school (in months)	Can read	Can write	Can speak English	Owned or rented	Owned free or mortgaged	Farm or house	Number of farm schedule
13	14	15	16	17	18	19	20	21	22	23	24	25	26	27	28

Standard sections ranging from Nativity to Trade and Education were included in the 1900 Federal Census form. Ownership of home was no longer supplemental. Note column 19; a person had to be only ten years of age to be employed. (Source: U.S. Census Bureau.)

TWELFTH CENSUS OF THE UNITED STATES.

SCHEDULE No. 1.—POPULATION.

State: Kansas
County: Wyandotte
Township or other division of county: X
Name of incorporated city, town, or village, within the above-named division: Kansas City
Enumerated by me on the 6th day of June, 1900, Joseph Teggart, Enumerator.
Supervisor's District No. 2
Enumeration District No. 157
Sheet No. 8
Name of Institution: X
Ward of city: 4
134 A

1900 census schedule from Kansas City, Wyandotte County, Kansas, that lists a young Amelia Earhart.

household; his or her color or race, sex, month and year of birth, age at last birthday, marital status, the number of years married, the total number of children born of the mother, the number of those children living, and places of birth for each individual and the parents of each individual. If the individual was foreign born, the year of immigration and the number of years he or she was in the United States at the time of the census, and his or her citizenship status, if over twenty-one. The schedule also includes each individual's occupation; the number of months he or she was unemployed during the last year; whether the person attended school within the year and if so, the number of months in school; whether the person could read, write, and speak English; whether the home was owned or rented; whether the home was on a farm; and whether the home was mortgaged.

Other Significant Facts about the 1900 Census

The 1900 census is the only available census that provides columns for including the exact month and year of birth of every person enumerated. Previous censuses, and even the 1910, 1920, and 1930 censuses, include only ages. The 1900 census was also the first census to include space to record the number of years couples were married, how long an immigrant had been in the country and whether he or she was naturalized. It was also one of the first censuses to ask whether a home or farm was owned or rented, and whether the owned property was free of mortgage, the number of children born to the mother, and how many were still living. (These same questions were asked on the 1890 census.)

Research Tips for the 1900 Census

Because the Soundex index to the 1900 census is regarded as one of the most inclusive and accurate of the federally created indexes, it is recommended as a good starting point for beginning researchers. Most beginning researchers are able to find some knowledge of family names and residences that will serve as a starting point for searching the 1900 Soundex index. (See "Census Indexes and Finding Aids" on page 185.) The 1900 census is an excellent tool for determining dates and places to search for marriage records, birth records of children, deaths of children, and the marriages of children not listed. It is also a means of verifying family traditions, identifying unknown family members, and linking what is known to other sources, such as earlier censuses, naturalization records (especially declarations of intent to become citizens), school attendance rolls, property holdings, and employment and occupational records. These records can also help to trace and document ethnic origins, and identify overseas and shipboard military service.

Note that some Indian schedules are kept at the end of their corresponding state schedules, instead of the county.

For additional information on the 1900 census, see *1900 Federal Population Census: A Catalog of Microfilm Copies of the Schedules at the National Archives.*[14] For boundary changes and identification of missing census schedules, see Thorndale's and Dollarhide's *Map Guide to the U.S. Federal Censuses, 1790–1920.*

1910 Census

The 1910 census began on 15 April 1910. The enumeration was to be completed within thirty days, or within two weeks for communities with populations of more than 5,000. The official census population count was 92,228,496.

Questions Asked in the 1910 Census

The 1910 census schedules record number of the dwelling house and family, in order of visitation; the street address; each person's name and relationship to the head of household; sex; color or race; age at last birthday; marital status; and length of present marriage. If the person was a mother, it records the

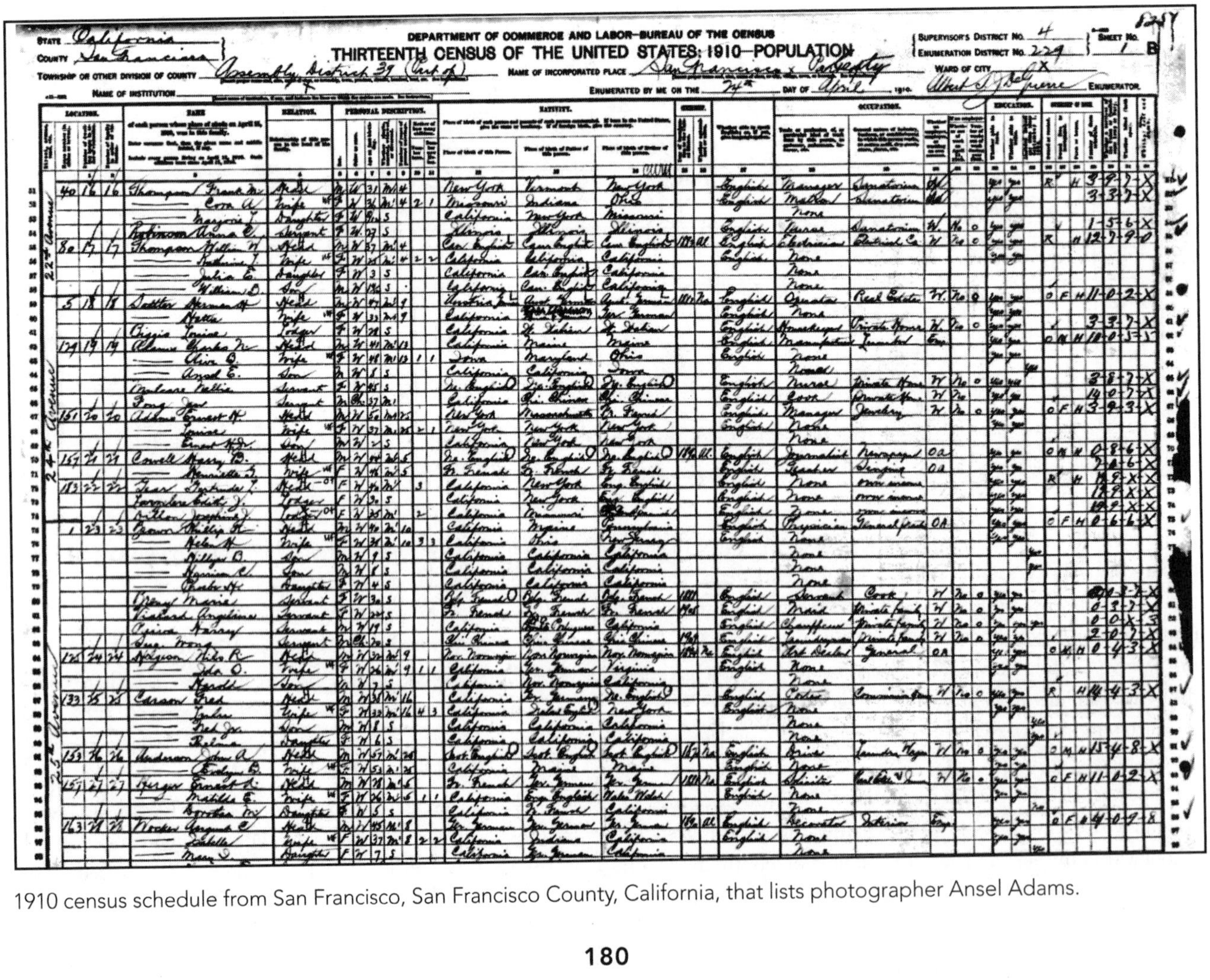
DEPARTMENT OF COMMERCE AND LABOR—BUREAU OF THE CENSUS
THIRTEENTH CENSUS OF THE UNITED STATES: 1910—POPULATION

1910 census schedule from San Francisco, San Francisco County, California, that lists photographer Ansel Adams.

number of her children and number of living children, as well as each person's birthplace and his or her parents' birthplaces. If the individual was foreign-born, it shows the year of immigration and his or her citizenship status; spoken language; occupation; type of employment; and whether he or she was an employer, employee, or was self-employed; the number of weeks he or she was unemployed in 1909, if applicable; and whether he or she was out of work on 15 April 1910. The schedules also show if the individual was able to read and write; if he or she attended daytime school since 1 September 1909; if the home was rented or owned, and if owned, whether it was free or mortgaged, and a house or a farm. Finally, it shows if each person was a veteran of the Union or Confederate army or navy; whether he or she was blind in both eyes; or deaf and dumb. The Indian schedule also recorded the tribe and/or band.

Research Tips for the 1910 Census

The quality of the microfilming of the 1910 census was especially poor when compared to other census schedules. Overexposure in microfilming schedules for Mississippi, for example, rendered hundreds of pages illegible. Additionally, the omission rate in the 1910 Miracode/Soundex appears to be greater than in most other indexes. In many cases, individuals not indexed are present in the census schedules, so it is especially advisable for researchers to continue a search in the actual schedules, even though a name might not show up in an index.

The 1910 census, while not providing as much precise information as the 1900 census (such as exact birth month), does ask years married, and number of children born to the mother, and is a good tool for determining approximate dates and places to search for marriage records, birth and death records of children, and the marriages of children not listed. The 1910 census sometimes makes it possible to verify family traditions, identify unknown family members, and link what is known to other sources, such as earlier censuses, naturalization records (especially declarations of intent to become citizens), school attendance rolls, property holdings, and employment and occupational records. These records will also verify Civil War service, trace and document ethnic origins, and locate military and naval personnel in hospitals, ships, and stations, and those stationed in the Philippines, Alaska, Hawaii, and Puerto Rico.

For additional information on the 1910 census, see *The 1910 Federal Population Census: A Catalog of Microfilm Copies of the Schedules at the National Archives.* For boundary changes and identification of missing census schedules, see Thorndale's and Dollarhide's *Map Guide to the U.S. Federal Censuses, 1790–1920.*

1920 Census

The 1920 census began on 1 January 1920. The enumeration was to be completed within thirty days, or within two weeks for communities with populations of more than 2,500. The official census population count was 106,021,537.

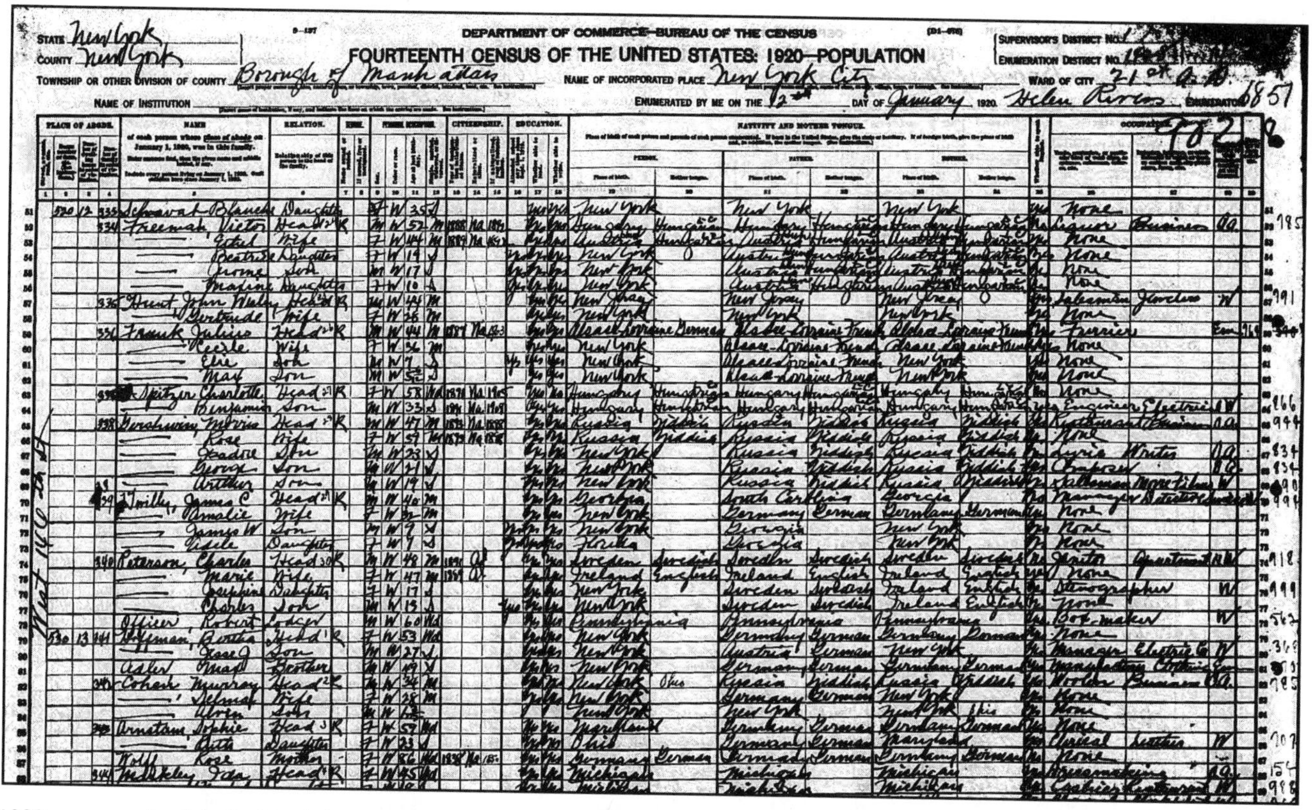

1920 census schedule for Manhattan Borough, New York County, New York, that lists young George and Ira (Isadore) Gershwin.

Questions Asked in the 1920 Census

The 1920 census form called for the name of the street, avenue, road, and such; the house number or farm; the dwelling and family numbers in order of visitation; the name of each person whose place of abode was with the family; the relationship of person enumerated to the head of the family; whether home was owned or rented; if owned, whether free or mortgaged; each individual's sex; color or race; age at last birthday; whether he or she was single, married, widowed, or divorced; the year when he or she emigrated to the United States; whether he or she was naturalized or an alien; if naturalized, the year of naturalization; whether he or she attended school any time since 1 September 1919; whether he or she was able to read or write; the place of each individual's birth; his or her mother tongue; his or her father's place of birth, and mother tongue; his or her mother's place of birth and mother tongue; whether he or she was able to speak English; his or her trade, profession, or particular kind of work done; the industry, business, or establishment in which the person worked, and whether he or she was an employer, salaried or waged a worker, or working on his or her own account. It also includes, if applicable, the number of the corresponding farm schedule.

Other Significant Facts about the 1920 Census

The date of the enumeration appears on the heading of each page of the census schedule. All responses supposedly reflect the individual's status as of 1 January 1920, even if that status had changed between 1 January and the day of enumeration. Children born between 1 January and the day of enumeration were not to be listed, while individuals alive on 1 January but deceased when the enumerator arrived were to be counted.

Unlike the 1910 census, the 1920 census did not have questions regarding unemployment, Union or Confederate military service, number of children, or duration of marriage. It did, however, include four new question columns: one asked the year of naturalization and three inquired about mother tongue. The 1920 census also asked the year of arrival and status of every foreign-born person, and inquired about the year of naturalization for those individuals who had become U.S. citizens. In 1920 the census included, for the first time, Guam, American Samoa, and the Panama Canal Zone.

Also unlike the 1910 census, the 1920 census has a microfilmed index for each state and territory.

Due to boundary modifications in Europe resulting from World War I, some individuals were uncertain about how to identify their national origin. Enumerators were instructed to spell out the name of the city, state, province, or region of respondents who declared that they or their parents had been born in Germany, Austria-Hungary, Russia, or Turkey. Interpretation of the birthplace varied from one enumerator to another. Some failed to identify specific birthplaces within those named countries, and others provided an exact birthplace in countries not designated in the instructions. See *Fourteenth Census of the United States, January 1, 1920: Instructions to Enumerators, produced by the Bureau of the Census.*[16]

There are no separate Indian population schedules in the 1920 census. Inhabitants of reservations were enumerated in the general population schedules.

Enumerators were instructed not to report servicemen in the family enumerations but to treat them as residents of their duty posts. The 1920 census includes schedules and a Soundex index for overseas military and naval forces.

Soundex cards for institutions are found at the end of each state's Soundex index. It is important to note that many institutions, even if enumerated at their street addresses, are found at the end of the enumeration section.

The original 1920 census schedules were destroyed by authorization of the Eighty-third Congress, so it is not possible to consult originals when microfilm copies prove unreadable.

Research Tips for the 1920 Census

The 1920 census is a good tool for determining approximate dates and places to search for marriage records, birth and death records of children, and the marriages of children not listed. The 1920 census sometimes makes it possible to verify family traditions, identify unknown family members, and link what is known to other sources, such as earlier censuses, school attendance rolls, property holdings, and employment and occupational records. In several instances, women, rather than men, have been listed as heads of household in the 1920 Soundex index (figure 5-2); therefore, a search focused on a male name in this index may be unsuccessful.

The 1920 census asked the foreign-born for the year of their arrival in the United States, making it easier to pinpoint the date of passenger arrival records. It also asked the naturalization status of every foreign-born person and inquired about the

COMMERCE—BUREAU OF THE CENSUS [D1—578] SUPER ENUME

THE UNITED STATES: 1920—POPULATION

ME OF INCORPORATED PLACE .... [Insert proper name and, also, name of class, as city, village, town, or borough. See instructions.]

ENUMERATED BY ME ON THE .... DAY OF ...., 1920.

NATIVITY AND MOTHER TONGUE.

Place of birth of each person and parents of each person enumerated. If born in the United States, give the state or territory. If of foreign birth, give the place of birth and, in addition, the mother tongue. (See instructions.)

PERSON.		FATHER.		MOTHER.	
Place of birth.	Mother tongue.	Place of birth.	Mother tongue.	Place of birth.	Mother tongue.
19	20	21	22	23	24

The 1920 census asked the year of naturalization and included a separate column for "Mother Tongue." (Source: U.S. Census Bureau.)

DEPARTMENT OF COMMERCE—BUREAU OF THE CENSUS
FIFTEENTH CENSUS OF THE UNITED STATES: 1930
POPULATION SCHEDULE

State: New Jersey — County: Hudson County — Incorporated place: City of Hoboken — Ward of city: Fifth — Block No. 182 — Enumeration District No. 9-290 — Supervisor's District No. 6th — Sheet No. 9-B — Enumerated by me on April 8th, 1930, Herman J. Horwitz, Enumerator.

1930 Census schedule from Hoboken, Hudson County, New Jersey, that lists a fourteen-year-old Frank Sinatra.

year of naturalization for those individuals who had become U.S. citizens, thus facilitating searches in naturalization records.

Due to the more specific questions asked of immigrants from Germany, Austria-Hungary, Russia, and Turkey regarding their birthplaces and those of their parents, many researchers will be able to discover the exact towns or regions from which their families emigrated. The fact that the 1920 census asked for the mother tongue of each respondent and that of each parent will further help to define the origins of many families.

For additional information regarding the 1920 census, see the following sources:

Green, Kellee. "The Fourteenth Numbering of the People: The 1920 Census." *Prologue* (Summer 1991): 131–45.

National Archives. *The 1920 Federal Population Census: Catalog of National Archives Microfilm.* Washington, D.C.: National Archives Trust Fund Board, 1991.

Shepard, JoAnne (Bureau of the Census). *Age Search Information.* Washington, D.C.: Government Printing Office, 1990.

For boundary changes and identification of missing census schedules, see William Thorndale and William Dollarhide, *Map Guide to the U.S. Federal Census, 1790–1920* (Baltimore: Genealogical Publishing Co., 1987).

1930 Census

The 1930 census was taken on April 1, 1930. The official census population count was 123,202,624.

Questions Asked in the 1930 Census

The 1930 Census form called for the street, avenue, road, and house number; the number of dwelling house and family in order of visitation; the name of each person whose place of abode on April 1, 1930 was with this family; the relationship of this person to the head of the family; whether the home was owned or rented; the value of home, if owned, or monthly rental, if rented; whether the person owned a radio set; whether the family lived on a farm; each person's sex; color or race; age at last birthday; marital condition; and age at first marriage; whether he or she attended school or college any time since Sept. 1, 1929; whether he or she was able to read or write; his or her place of birth, and the place of birth for his or her father and mother; the language spoken at home before coming to the United States; the year of both his or her immigration into the United States and naturalization, if applicable; whether the person was able to speak English; his or her trade, profession, or particular kind of work done, and the industry of business with which he or she was involved, and his or her, class of worker; and whether the person was actually at work the day before the enumerator came. If not, the census includes this person's line number on unemployment schedule, and also asks whether the person was a veteran of the U.S. military or naval force, and if yes, during, what war or expedition. It also includes, if applicable, the number of the corresponding farm schedule (Note: The farm schedules have not survived).

Other Significant Facts about the 1930 Census

A WPA Soundex exists for the 1930 census for the following states only: Alabama, Arkansas, Florida, Georgia, Louisiana, Mississippi, North Carolina, South Carolina, Tennessee, and Virginia. The following counties were Soundexed for Kentucky: Bell, Floyd, Harlan, Kenton, Mehlenberg, Perry, and Pike. The following West Virginia counties were indexed: Fayette, Harrison, Kanawha, Logan, McDowell, Mercer, and Raleigh.

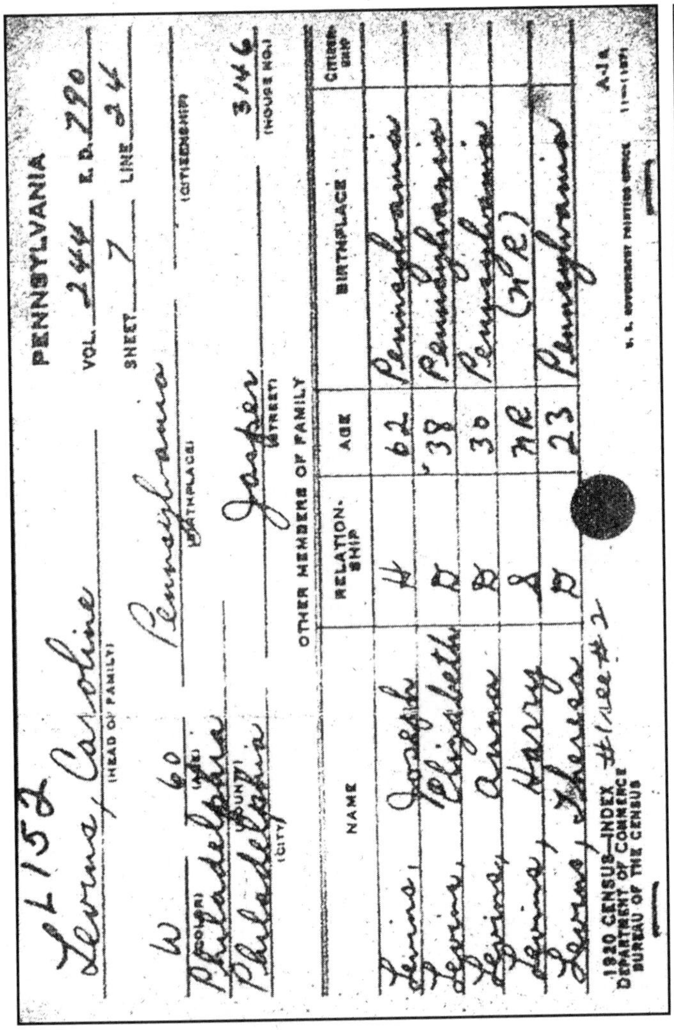

Figure 5-2. 1920 Federal Census schedule *(right)* and Soundex index card *(above)* showing Caroline Levins as head of household, in spite of the fact that her husband, Joseph, is also listed in the schedule.

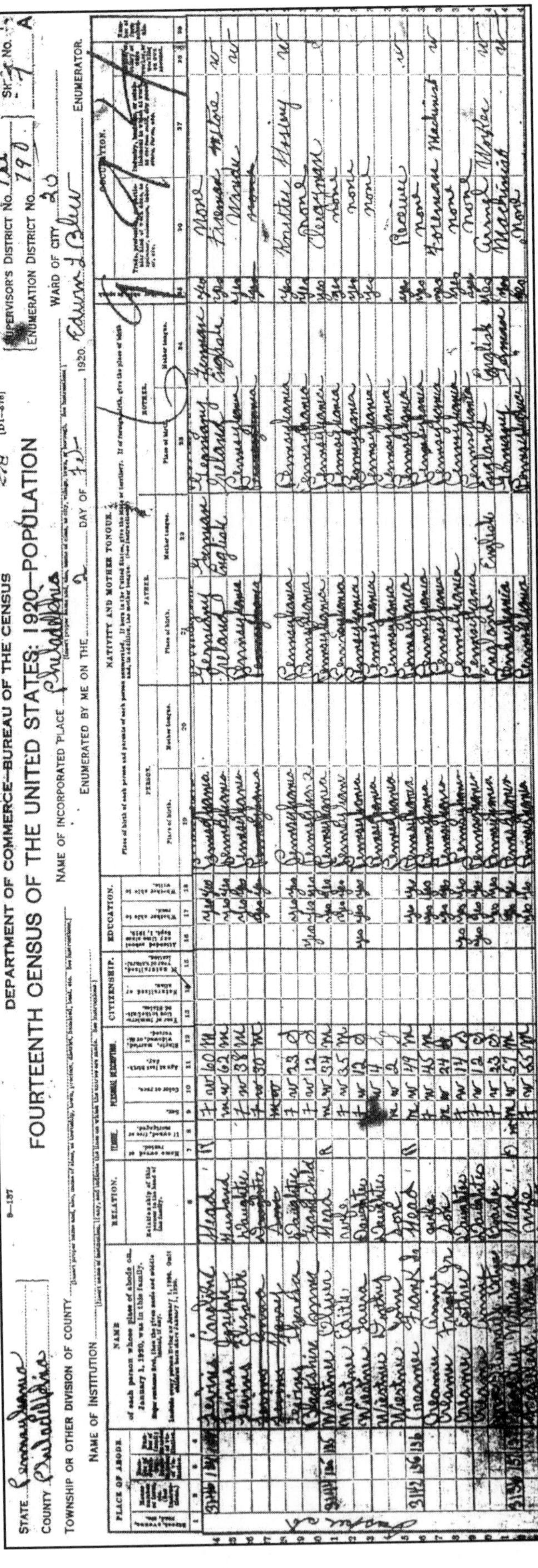

All of the Soundex indexes are in the traditional format, with the exception of Georgia, which is in Miracode. All of the Soundexed states, except for Georgia, list the institutions at the end of the publication. There appear to be no mixed codes for the 1930 census.

Research Tips for the 1930 Census

Since nearly everyone has some knowledge or access to knowledge of family names, relationships, and the family's state of residence in 1930, this census is the widely considered to be the best starting point for research in federal records. Working from known information about the most recent generations, an efficient researcher works backwards in time to discover family relationships and to determine where additional records may be found.

To effectively search the 1930 census, know as much about where the person lived as is possible.

The following finding aids will be available at the National Archives in Washington, D.C. and at NARA's regional records services facilities.

- *Enumeration District Maps for the Fifteenth Census of the United States, 1930.* (National Archives Microfilm Publication M1930), 35 rolls.
- *Index to Selected City Streets and Enumeration Districts, 1930.* (National Archives Microfilm Publication M1931), 11 rolls.
- *Descriptions of Census Enumeration Districts, 1830–1950.* (National Archives Microfilm Publication T1224), rolls 61–90.

For additional information on the 1930 census, see the 1930 census website at <www.nara.gov/genealogy/1930cen.html>.

Note: To complement its collection of 1930 resources, the National Archives has also purchased copies of city directories for 1928–1932. For a complete list of which directories NARA has, see the 1930 website. These are not National Archives publications, but can be purchase from Primary Source Microfilm (an imprint of the Gale Group) <www.galegroup.com/psm/index.htm>.

Census Indexes and Finding Aids

The census is a clear reflection of population growth in the United States. The millions of names and figures added to the census totals over the years have made indexing, particularly of the most populous states, a formidable and expensive task. Recent developments in technology have facilitated indexing and publication, and now a significant and ever-growing number of later statewide and even nationwide census schedules have been indexed. While mistakes and omissions exist in census indexes, it is generally agreed that even an imperfect index can be an invaluable timesaver and is certainly better than no index at all. Improved technology and better editing are making most new compilations more inclusive and more accurate.

Indexes on CD-ROM and Online

Over the past several years, online census indexes have increased in both number and scope. This increase has been driven, largely, by a number of commercial or institutional indexing projects. Ancestry.com, for example, offers a searchable, every-name index of every available U.S. federal census with links to images of the actual census returns. Genealogy.com offers an every-name index to several U.S. federal censuses, including 1790–1820, 1860, 1870, and 1890–1910 on its subscriber site. Another site, Census4All.com, has an every-name index to the 1910 U.S. Federal Census with Vermont, Rhode Island, and New Hampshire presently available. The Census4All indexes can be searched for free, and a list of other members of the household or copies of the actual census schedules desired can be ordered for a fee.

Unlike the 1880 Soundex, which is only a partial index, the LDS Church's FamilySearch 1880 United States Census and National Index is an every-name index, with entries including name, relation to head of household, sex, marital status, race, age, birth place, occupation, and father and mother's birth place. The index is searchable online at FamilySearch and as part of the census collection at Ancestry.com. 1880 Census CD-ROMs are also available for sale at the FamilySearch site <www.familysearch.org>. In addition to its U.S. federal census records, Ancestry.com also offers a large number of state and local census indexes. HeritageQuest's Family Quest Archives CD-ROM collection, <www.heritagequest.com>, contains complete head of household indexes to U.S. Federal Censuses for the 1790, 1800, 1810, and 1870 censuses. Partial indexes are available for 1850, 1900, and 1910.

Fortunately for researchers, libraries with good genealogy collections usually make it a priority to acquire these popular and important indexes, on CD or by subscription on the Internet, as soon as they become available.

In addition to the commercial online census index projects, volunteers from around the country have responded to the need for finding aids by producing, in various formats, indexes to many of the federal censuses. One such volunteer effort, The USGenWeb Census Project can be accessed online at <www.rootsweb.com/~census/states.htm>. Other sites provide links to census data online. These include the following:

Census Links.com <www.censuslinks.com>
Census-Online.com <www.census-online.com>
Cyndi's List—Census <www.cyndislist.com/census.htm>

Census Index Limitations

A common mistake beginners make is to consult an index, find a name, extract the index information, and go no further. Many seem unaware that census indexes are simply finding aids. While there is a certain element of excitement in discovering an ancestor's name in an index, there is greater satisfaction in store for those who view the fuller picture provided in the actual census schedules.

A well-prepared index includes a preface explaining the index parameters (for example, whether it is an every-name index or if only heads of household are included) and identifying specific problems encountered in the process of compiling the index. The wise researcher will read every preface carefully.

In most published census indexes, only the heads of households are listed. If an individual was a child when the census was taken, and if the name of his or her father, mother, or other head of the household in which he or she lived is not known, a long and tedious search may be in store. It may be necessary to look at different census schedules for every entry for a given surname in an index before the correct household is found.

Regardless of the care taken by the creator of an index to make it accurate, no index is perfect. Omissions, misinterpreted names, and misspellings creep into virtually all census indexes. Some indexes are not useful for tracing individuals because information was culled from microfilm that was nearly impossible to read, and sometimes the microfilmed version itself lacks certain information. Examples of the latter are the published federal census indexes from 1790 to 1840. Like the censuses themselves, the indexes are of limited use in finding individuals because only heads of household are listed. Likewise, most post-1840 census indexes include only heads of household and "strays."

Frequently, names are actually included in an index but cannot be found because they are misspelled to the extent that they are unrecognizable. Some surnames have been incorrectly alphabetized when indexers could not decipher even the first letter of a surname. In some handwriting styles, the letter L resembles an S; thus, the handwritten surname Lee might become See in an index. Handwriting styles have caused indexing problems when certain similar-appearing letters have been confused, including T and F; J, G, and Y; I and J; K and R; O and Q; P and R; and U and W.

Page Numbering Problems

Pages of census schedules were originally numbered by the census taker; when the schedules were later arranged and bound, they were often renumbered with a hand stamp. It is common for some volumes to have two or more series of page numbers. A stamped number, when it is present, is usually the page reference used in printed census indexes. It is very important to determine which page number the census indexer was using. Sometimes in an index, for example, the indexer was inconsistent with the page number that he or she used, making it difficult to find names.

History and Quality of Census Indexes

Computer technology has revolutionized the process of indexing census schedules. Computer-generated census indexes are becoming increasingly available in book, microfiche, CD-ROM, and online forms. Despite the advanced technology, however, no index is error-free. Misinterpretations of handwritten census manuscripts and transcription mistakes continue to thwart research, particularly when the first letter of a name is entered into an index incorrectly.

While a number of individuals and genealogical societies have used computers to create census indexes, most such indexes have been created by commercial firms. The oldest of these firms is Accelerated Indexing Systems. Accelerated Indexing produced indexes for every extant state and territory census through 1860, and some for later years, as well as a number of special censuses and census substitutes. These indexes are available online and in CD-ROM format (see page 185).

The schedules for some states and areas have been indexed more than once by different organizations and commercial publishers. But though the year and the locality indexed may be the same, formats and contents can differ dramatically. Names may have been interpreted differently; some publications may include names missed by others; and some may include much more than county, township, and page and microfilm numbers after the names of heads of households. It is wise to check every index when more than one is available for a given time and place.

Misspellings have occurred on several levels. The census enumerator may have misunderstood the name and written it incorrectly. (See table 5-1). Even if the enumerator got it right, the indexer may have misread the enumerator's handwriting or had other difficulties reading the old and fading microfilm. (See table 5-2).

Many indexes, up to and including the 1920 census, cover individual counties only. They can prove especially useful when a name or names cannot be found in a statewide compilation. Because local indexes are frequently compiled by genealogical societies and indexers who tend to be familiar with local name spellings and geographical distinctions, their reliability is sometimes greater than the larger indexes.

Statewide censuses are sometimes interfiled with other sources in single personal name indexes available in state archives. The addresses of state archives and state historical societies are given in the appendixes section.

Indexes from 1790 to 1840

The federal government led the way in publishing census indexes when, in the early 1900s, it published indexed volumes of

Table 5-1. Phonetic Substitutes

a	e,i,o,u,y,ey,eh	m	mm,lm,mb,mn,n
au	ow,ou	mb (as in *comb*)	mm,lm,mn
b	p,v,bb,pp	n	nn,ng,gn (as in *gnat*),kn,m
bb	b,p,pp	ng	n,nk,ch,k,q
c (as in *catch*)	k,g,gh,q,cc,ck	nk	ng,ch,k,q
c (as in *chin*)	ch,cz,s,sh,tch,tsh,z,dg	nn	n
ch	c,k,g,gh,sh,h (as in *Chanukah*), ju (as in San *Juan*)	o	a,e,i,u,aw,ow,eau (as in *beau*)
chr	kr,gr,cr	oey	oy,oe,oi
ck	k,c,g,q	oe	oy,oe,oey
cr	kr,chr,gr	oo	u,ow,ew
cz	c,ch,ts,tz,s,sh,tcr,tsh	ou	u,au,ow,ew.oo
d	dd,t,dt	ow	au,ou.eau (as in *beau*)
dd	d,t,tt	oy	oi,oe,oey
dg (as in *dodge*)	g,j,ch,gg,tj	p	b,pp,ph,bb
ds (as in *bends*)	z,ts	pf	f,pfph,gh,v,lf
dt	d,t,tt	ph	f,gh (as in *laugh*),pf,lf,p
e	a,ee,i,o,u,y,ie,ea	ps (as in *psalm*)	s
ea	e,i,y,ie,ei	q	c,ch,g,k,gh,cc,ck,ng,nk
eau (as in *beau*)	o,aw,ow,au,ou	r	rr,wr,rh
ee	ie,e,i,y,ea,ei	rh	r,rr,wr
ew	u,oo,ou	rr	r,rh,wr
f	v,ph,pf,gh,il (as in *calf*),ff	s	c,sh,tch,z,cz,ss,x
ff	f,ph,gh,v,lf (as in *calf*)	sch (as in *school*)	sh,s,sc,sk,sq
g	c,ch,gg,gh,j,k,q,dg,h (as in *Gila* Monster)	sch (as in *Schwarz*)	s,sh
gg	g,ch,k,q,j	sch (as in *Tisch*)	sh,tsh,tch,ch,cz,ti (as in *nation*),ss
gh (as in *ghost*)	c,ch,g,gg,ch,k,q	sh	s,c,ch,cz,sch,ti (as in *nation*),ss
gh (as in *laugh*)	f,ph,pf,v,lf	sk	sch,sh,s,sc,sq
gn (as in gnat)	n,kn	sq	sc,sk,sch,sh
gr	chr,ke	ss	s,c,ch,ci,sh,sc,z
h	(h is sometimes omitted) ch,wh,w,g (as in *Gila* Monster),ju (as in San *Juan*)	t	d,dd,tt,th
i	a,e,o,u,y,ei,uy,aye	tch	s,sh,c,ch,cz,s,tsh
ie	e,i,y,ee,ea,ei	th	t,tt,d
ih	y,i,ei,ii	ti (as in *nation*)	sh,si,tsh,tch,ch
j	ch,g,dg,gg	tj	j,g,ch,dh,dg,tch,tsch,s
ju (as in San *Juan*)	h,wh,ch	tt	d,dd,t,th,dt
k	c,ch,g,gh,q,nk,cc,ck	ts	tz,cz,z,tzts,cz,z
kn (as in *knot*)	n,gn	u	a,e,i,omou,ew,oo
kr	chr,cr,gr	v	b,f,lf,w
ks	x	w	wh,v,au,ow,h,ju (as in San *Juan*)
l	ll	wh	w,h,ju (as in San *Juan*), oa
lf (as in *calf*)	f,v,ph,pf,gh	wr	r,rh,rr
Ll	l,th	x	s,z,ks,chs
lm (as in *calm*)	m,mm,mb,mn	y	i,e,ij
		z	s,c,sh,sch,x,ds

the extant 1790 census schedules for each state. The individual state volumes have since been privately reprinted and are widely available in libraries with genealogy collections. Some indexes for the years 1790 to 1820 also include the tallies listed for each family. These tallies would be listed as such:

1790

a. free white males age sixteen and older
b. free white males under age sixteen
c. free white females
d. all other free persons
e. slaves

1800–10

a. free white males to age ten (under age ten)
b. free white males to age sixteen (of ten and under sixteen)
c. free white males to age twenty-six (of sixteen and under twenty-six)
d. free white males to age forty-five (of twenty-six and under forty-five)
e. free white males over age forty-five
f. free white females to age ten (under age ten)
g. free white females to age sixteen (of ten and under sixteen)
h. free white females to age twenty-six (of sixteen and under twenty-six)
i. free white females to age forty-five (of twenty-six and under forty-five)
j. free white females over age forty-five
k. other free persons (except Indians not taxed)
l. slaves

1820

a. free white males to age ten (under age ten)
b. free white males to age sixteen (of ten and under sixteen)
c. free white males between ages sixteen and eighteen
d. free white males to age twenty-six (of sixteen and under twenty-six)
e. free white males to age forty-five (of twenty-six and under forty-five)
f. free white males over age forty-five
g. free white females to age ten (under age ten)
h. free white females to age sixteen (of ten and under sixteen)
i. free white females to age twenty-six (of sixteen and under twenty-six)
j. free white females to age forty-five (of twenty-six and under forty-five)
k. free white females over age forty-five
l. slaves
m. free colored persons

Table 5-2: Frequently Misread Letters

A	H,C,O	N	H,W,V,St,Ne
a	o,u,ei,ie,n,w	n	u,a,o,ee,ie,ei,w,m
B	R,P,S	O	C,U,V,D
b	li,le,t,h,l	o	a,u,n,ee,ll,ie,ei,tt
C	G,E,O,Ce	P	R,B,I,J,S,L
c	e,i,o,u	p	ss,g,js,k,f,fs,fa,fi,fr
D	G,S,I,J,T,Ir	Q	Z,D,I,J,G,C
d	u,a,n,ie,ei,ee,ct,o	q	g,y,z,f,ej,ij,j
E	C,G,Ee	R	Pi,B,S,Pe,Pr,Re
e	i,c	r	e,s,i,ei,a
ee	u,n,ll,a,o,ie,ei,w	S	L,I,J,St,Se,F,G,R,T
F	T,S,G,Ti,L	s	r,i,e,c
f	s,j,g,q,t	sc	x
G	S,Q,Z,Ci,L,Se,Is	ss	fs,p,rr,w,m,n
g	y,z,q,f	T	F,S,L,D,Q
H	N,W,He,Sl,St,A,F	t	l,f,lr,i
h	K,li,lc,le	te	k
I	J,L,S,Q,F,T	tt	ll
i	e,c,l	U	V,A,O,N,H
ie	ei,u,ee,n,a,o,w,il	u	ee,a,o,n,ie,ei,ll,w
J	I,L,S,Q,F,T,P	V	N,W,Ir,Jr,B
j	y,g,f,q,z	v	u,n,b,rr,s,r,o,ee,ei,
Jno	Mr,Mo	W	M,N,U,H,St
K	H,R,B,tr,te	w	m,rr,ur,nr,ui,ni,eu,en
k	h,le,lr,te,R,B,H	X	H,Z,N,J
L	S,T,F	x	sc,c,r
l	e,i,t	Y	T,F,Z,Q
ll	tt,ee,u,a,o,ie,ei	y	g,q,j,z,p,ej,ij,if
M	W,H,N,A,Al,Me	Z	G,Q,Y
m	w,rr,ni,in,iv, ev,ai,ui,iu	z	g,q,y,j,p

Indexes from 1850 to 1870

Many statewide indexes for censuses after 1850 include only heads of household and the names of persons in households whose names were different than that of the household head. Obviously, then, a large percentage of the actual population of a state is excluded from such an index. This is especially a problem with common names, and when a child's or woman's name is known but that of the head of household is not.

1880 Soundex

Until recent years, the fastest method for finding names in the 1880 census for most states was to use the Soundex, a partial index that includes only households with children ten years old and under in residence. Compiled by the Work Projects Administration

(WPA), the Soundex index was designed to identify those who would be eligible for Social Security. (An explanation of the Soundex coding system follows this section.)

It is important to remember when using the 1880 Soundex that, while a large portion of the population is not indexed because many families had no children ten years old or under, all individuals and families were supposed to have been included in the original census schedules. Some of the original Soundex index cards survive and have been distributed among various state and local agencies; others have apparently been destroyed. Some of the 1880 cards were lost or misfiled before or when they were microfilmed.

Use the Soundex to determine surname distribution throughout the state. This can be an important clue if you don't know which county to search for a family. You can identify family naming patterns (because each person in the family is listed on the Soundex card, with relationships stated), find orphaned children living with persons of other surnames, and identify grandparents living under the same roof. They are listed in the census schedule, even though they may not be indexed separately. As mentioned, the LDS Church offers an every-name index to the 1880 census in electronic format (see page 185).

1890 Index

A card file to the names on the surviving 1890 schedules is available on two rolls of microfilm titled Index to the Eleventh Census of the United States, 1890 (National Archives microfilm M496). The index is also available in printed form.

Ken Nelson, comp., *1890 Census Index Register* (Salt Lake City: Genealogical Society of Utah, 1984), is an index to the 6,160 names in the surviving fragments of this census. Available on microfilm (1,421,673, item 11), it can also be found in the reference area of the Family History Library (Family History Library book Ref 973 X2n 1890). Also see Helen Smothers Swenson, *Index to 1890 Census of the United States* (cited earlier), and "Veterans Schedules, 1840–1890," on page 197.

1900 Index

The Soundex index to the 1900 census is regarded as one of the most inclusive and accurate of the federally-created indexes. It serves as an efficient key to locating households and individuals in the most genealogically informative census ever taken. Unlike the 1880 census, the 1900 census identifies all heads of household and every adult whose name is different from that of the head of household.

1910 Indexes

The most notable problem with the 1910 census has traditionally been the lack of indexes for most states. Miracode (a slightly modified version of Soundex) and Soundex indexes exist for only twenty-one states: Alabama, Arkansas, California, Florida, Georgia, Illinois, Kansas, Kentucky, Louisiana, Michigan, Mississippi, Missouri, North Carolina, Ohio, Oklahoma, Pennsylvania, South Carolina, Tennessee, Texas, Virginia, and West Virginia. Since Soundex/Miracode indexes are not available for the remaining states, researchers must rely on city directories, county landowners' atlases, enumeration districts, or specially created finding tools (such as the special index to streets and enumeration districts for certain cities), or conduct tedious, page-by-page searches of the census schedules. (For a detailed description, see "Census Indexes and Finding Aids" on page 185.)

Soundex and Miracode indexes were created by the Bureau of the Census for the twenty-one states that lacked a centralized vital statistics bureau at the time the indexes were created. The Miracode system uses the same phonetic code and abbreviations as the Soundex system, but Miracode cards list the visitation numbers assigned by the enumerators, while Soundex cards show the page and line numbers on the appropriate census schedules. With the exception of Louisiana, which uses both, the following states have been indexed using either the Soundex or Miracode systems: Alabama, Arkansas, California, Florida, Georgia, Illinois, Kansas, Kentucky, Michigan, Mississippi, Missouri, North Carolina, Ohio, Oklahoma, Pennsylvania, South Carolina, Tennessee, Texas, Virginia, and West Virginia. Both indexing systems give the surname, first name, state and county of residence, city (if applicable), race, age, and place of birth, as well as the volume number and enumeration district number of the census schedule from which the information was obtained. Some large cities are indexed separately in the 1910 census. Be sure to see separate Soundex listings in the National Archives microfilm catalog for some metropolitan areas in Alabama, Georgia, Louisiana, Pennsylvania, and Tennessee.

The 1910 Census City Street Finding Aid

The Federation of Genealogical Societies (FGS) promoted and coordinated the funding to put to microfilm an important finding aid for the 1910 census. Known as the *Cross-Index to Selected City Streets and Enumeration Districts, 1910 Census*, it was produced in 1984 by the Bureau of the Census to facilitate its work of searching the original schedules for age and other personal data in response to inquiries from individuals and government agencies. This index to city streets and census enumeration districts for thirty-nine cities in the 1910 federal population census is widely available on fifty sheets of microfiche. The index enables users of the population schedules to translate specific street addresses into the appropriate enumeration district number and corresponding volume number of the microfilmed schedules. The city schedules were selected for indexing by the Bureau of the Census based on the frequency of requests for information. The indexes were originally in bound volumes, but they were unbound for microfilming. With the exception of several of the larger cities, the index for each city occupied a single volume. The original arrangement of the indexes has been preserved, with the exception that the boroughs of Manhattan, the Bronx, Richmond (Staten Island), and Brooklyn have been placed under the heading "New York City." There is no index for the borough of Queens.

Entries in the index give for each city a list of city streets and house numbers and show the appropriate enumeration district. The records are arranged alphabetically by name of city and thereunder by street. Named streets, arranged alphabetically, are listed first, followed by numerical streets. Immediately preceding the index portion of each volume is a table listing the enumeration districts covered in the volume, with a cross-reference to the corresponding volume of the original population schedules.

The thirty-nine cities included in the 1910 index follow:

- Akron, Ohio
- Atlanta, Georgia
- Baltimore, Maryland
- Canton, Ohio
- Charlotte, North Carolina
- Chicago, Illinois
- Cleveland, Ohio
- Dayton, Ohio
- Denver, Colorado
- Detroit, Michigan
- District of Columbia
- Elizabeth, New Jersey
- Erie, Pennsylvania
- Fort Wayne, Indiana
- Gary, Indiana
- Grand Rapids, Michigan
- Indianapolis, Indiana
- Kansas City, Kansas
- Long Beach, California
- Los Angeles and Los Angeles County
- Newark, New Jersey
- New York City (excluding Queens)
- Oklahoma City, Oklahoma
- Omaha, Nebraska
- Patterson, New Jersey
- Peoria, Illinois
- Philadelphia, Pennsylvania
- Phoenix, Arizona
- Reading, Pennsylvania
- Richmond, Virginia
- San Antonio, Texas
- San Diego, California
- San Francisco, California
- Seattle, Washington
- South Bend, Indiana
- Tampa, Florida
- Tulsa, Oklahoma
- Wichita, Kansas
- Youngstown, Ohio

The 1910 street index can dramatically reduce the problems and time expenditure involved in searching large cities for which there are thousands of pages of census entries.

1920 Census Soundex

The 2,074 rolls of microfilm for the 1920 census are Soundex indexed on 8,590 rolls of microfilm. The Soundex includes all of the states as well as the then territories of Alaska and Hawaii. The Canal Zone, Puerto Rico, Guam, American Samoa, the Virgin Islands, and military, naval, and various institutions are also indexed.

1930 Census Soundex

The 1930 U.S. Federal Census was released by the National Archives and Records Administration on 1 April 2002. Soundex indexes are available for the states of Alabama, Arkansas, Florida, Georgia, Kentucky (only Bell, Floyd, Harlan, Kenton, Muhlenberg, Perry, and Pike counties), Louisiana, Mississippi, North Carolina, South Carolina, Tennessee, Virginia, and West Virginia (only Fayette, Harrison, Kanawha, Logan, McDowell, Mercer, and Raleigh counties).

To aid in locating entries for other areas, geographic descriptions of census enumeration districts are reproduced in NARA microfilm publication T1224. In addition, NARA has purchased a large number of city directories from a commercial vendor for use in its facilities. More details can be found on NARA's website at <http://1930census.archives.gov>.

Beyond the Index

Experienced researchers know that there is much more to a census search than merely checking an index—whether that index is a book, a microfilmed version of the Soundex, or a computerized database. Unfortunately, too many beginners give up the search if the name sought does not appear in the index; if it does appear, they often seem content with the minimal information found in the index. Those who do not take the time to get the full picture provided by careful study of the actual census schedules usually miss important information and clues to further research. The study should include not only the subject of the search but the general area in which that person lived. To focus on only one name or one family in a given census is to see only a partial picture—somewhat like reading one chapter of a fascinating book.

The Soundex Index System

An index and filing system called the Soundex is the key to finding the names of individuals among the millions listed in the 1880, 1900, 1910, 1920, and, for some states, 1930 federal censuses. The Soundex indexes include heads of households and persons of different surnames in each household.

The Soundex indexes are coded surname (last name) indexes based on the progression of consonants rather than the spelling of the surname. This coding system was developed and implemented by the WPA in the 1930s for the Social Security Administration in response to that agency's need to identify individuals who would be eligible to apply for old-age benefits. Because early birth records are unavailable in a number of states, the 1880 census manuscripts became the most dependable means of verifying dates of birth for people who would qualify—those born in the 1870s. Widespread misspelling caused so many problems in matching names, however, that the Soundex system was adopted. Because locating eligible Social Security beneficiaries was the sole reason for creating the 1880 Soundex, only households with children ten years of age or under were included in that index. All households were included in the Soundex indexes for the 1900, 1910, 1920 and 1930 censuses.

How the Soundex Works

Soundex index entries are arranged on cards, first in Soundex code order and then alphabetically by first name of the head of household. For each person in the house, the Soundex card should show name, race, month and year of birth, age, citizenship status, place of residence by state and county, civil division, and, where appropriate for urban dwellers, the city name, house number, and street name. The cards also list the volume number, enumeration district number, and page and line numbers of the original schedules from which the information was taken.

Coding a Surname

To search for a name it is necessary to first determine its Soundex code. Every Soundex code consists of a letter and three numbers; for example, S655. The letter is always the first letter of the surname. The numbers are assigned according to the following Soundex coding guide:

1 B, P, F, V
2 C, S, K, G, J, Q, X, Z
3 D, T
4 L
5 M, N
6 R

The letters A, E, I, O, U, W, Y, and H are disregarded. Consonants in each surname which sound alike have the same code.

Use of Zero in Coding Surnames

A surname that yields no code numbers, such as Lee, is L000; one yielding only one code number, such as Kuhne, takes two zeros and is coded as K500; and one yielding two code numbers takes just one zero; thus, Ebell is coded as E140. No more than three digits are ever used, so Ebelson would be coded as E142, not E1425.

Names with Prefixes

Because the Soundex does not treat prefixes consistently, surnames beginning with, for example, Van, Vander, Von, De, Di, or Le may be listed with or without the prefix, making it necessary to search for both possibilities. Search for the surname van Devanter, for example, with (V531) and without (D153) the "van-" prefix. Mc- and Mac- are not considered prefixes.

Names with Adjacent Letters Having the Same Equivalent Number

When two or more key letters or equivalents appear together (adjacent) they are coded as one letter with a single number. Thus a double "f" takes a single code (1). This rule is also followed in surnames when the first two letters have the same number equivalent. Pfeiffer, for example, is coded P160. Because "P" is the first letter of the surname, it is used (P---). The next letter, "f", carries the same code (1) as does its equivalent "p" so is disregarded (the "P" takes the place of a 1). The vowels "e" and "i" are disregarded. Next is a double appearance of the letter "f" which is coded as 1 (the second "f" is disregarded). The vowel "e" is disregarded. The letter "r" is represented by 6, and in the absence of additional consonants, the code is rounded off with a zero. Other examples of double-letter names are Lennon (L550), Kelly (K400), Buerck (B620), Lloyd (L300), Schaefer (S160), Szucs (S200), and Orricks (O620). Occasionally the indexers themselves made mistakes in coding names, so it may be useful to try alternate codes based on possible errors. Also be aware that some immigrants with difficult last names may have been Soundexed under their first name; these names would then be listed alphabetically by last name.

Different Names within a Single Code

With this indexing formula, many different surnames may be included within the same Soundex code. For example, the similar-sounding surnames Scherman, Schurman, Sherman, Shireman, and Shurman are indexed together as S655 and will appear in the same group with other surnames, such as Sauerman or Sermon. Names that do not sound alike may also be included within a single code: Sinclair, Singler, Snegolski, Snuckel, Sanislo, San Miguel, Sungaila, and Szmegalski are all coded as S524.

Alphabetical Arrangement of First or Given Names within the Code

As described earlier, multiple surnames appear within most Soundex codes. Within each Soundex code, the individual and family cards are arranged alphabetically by given name.

Marked divider cards separate most Soundex codes. Look also for known nicknames, middle names, or abbreviations of the first name.

Mixed Codes

Divider cards show most code numbers, but not all. For instance, one divider may be numbered 350 and the next one 400. Between the two divided cards there may be names coded 353, 350, 360, 365, and 355, but instead of being in numerical order, they are interfiled alphabetically by given name.

Soundex Reference Guide

For those who are unsure of their Soundex skills, most genealogical software programs and many genealogy websites include a Soundex Calculator. Also, most genealogical libraries have a copy of Bradley W. Steuart's *The Soundex Reference Guide: Soundex Codes to Over 125,000 Surnames.*[17]

Soundex Abbreviations

In addition to the letter-numerical codes, Soundex also uses a number of abbreviations, most of which relate to residents' relationships to the head of the household (see table 5-3). NR (not recorded) is a frequently found abbreviation.

Native Americans, Asians, and Nuns

Names of nuns, Native Americans, and Asians pose special problems. Phonetically spelled Asian and Native American names were either coded as one continuous name or by what seemed to be a surname. For example, the Native American name Shinka-Wa-Sa may have been coded as Shinka (S520) or Sa (S000). Nuns were coded as if "Sister" were the surname, and they appear in each state's Soundex under the code S236, but not necessarily in alphabetical order.

Soundex Research Tips

The Soundex indexes can be especially useful in identifying family units, because all members of the household are listed on the Soundex cards under the name of the head of the household. Often, census searches begin with only a surname and the name of the state in which a person or family lived in a given census year. In such cases, the Soundex can be a means of determining surname distribution throughout the state. A search can often be narrowed to a smaller geographic area within a state. Once the county of origin is determined through census work, whole new paths of research open up. The Soundex can also be used to locate orphaned children living with persons of other surnames

Table 5-3.
Soundex Abbreviations: Relationships to Head of Household

A	Aunt	GM	Grandmother	SF	Stepfather
AdD	Adopted daughter	GNi	Grandniece	SFL	Stepfather-in-law
AdS	Adopted son	GS	Grandson	Si	Sister
At	Attendant	GU	Great-uncle	SiL	Sister-in-law
B	Brother	Hh	Hired hand	SL	Son-in-law
BL	Brother-in-law	I	Inmate	SM	Stepmother
Bo	Boarder	L	Lodger	SML	Stepmother-in-law
C	Cousin	M	Mother	SS	Stepson
D	Daughter	ML	Mother-in-law	SSi	Stepsister
DL	Daughter-in-law	N	Nephew	SSiL	Stepsister-in-law
F	Father	Ni	Niece	SSL	Stepson-in-law
FB	Foster brother	Nu	Nurse	Su	Superintendent
FF	Foster father	O	Officer	U	Uncle
FL	Father-in-law	P	Patient	W	Wife
FM	Foster mother	Pa	Partner (share common abode)	Wa	Warden
FSi	Foster sister	Pr	Prisoner		
GA	Great aunt	Pri	Principal		
GD	Granddaughter	Pu	Pupil	**Citizenship Status**	
GF	Grandfather	R	Roomer	A	Alien
GGF	Great-grandfather	S	Son	NA	Naturalized
GGM	Great-grandmother	SB	Stepbrother	PA	First papers filed
GGGF	Great-great-grandfather	SBL	Stepbrother-in-law	NR	Not recorded
GGGM	Great-great-grandmother	Se	Servant		

and to identify families with grandparents living under the same roof. They are sometimes listed on the Soundex cards, even though they may not be indexed separately.

1900, 1910, 1920, and 1930 Census Enumeration District Descriptions

Because of errors in transcribed names and because of variant spellings of names, a researcher may not be able to locate an entry in the Soundex system for a given head of family or individual living in a specific area. And though a name does not appear in the Soundex, the possibility exists that the individual being sought was indeed enumerated but was somehow missed or incorrectly coded in the indexing process. Those wishing to bypass the 1900, 1910, 1920, or 1930 Soundexes, and to consult the actual schedules for a given town, a minor civil division or geographic area, or a ward of a large city need to know the enumeration district numbers assigned to the particular place.

Arranged alphabetically by state and thereunder by county, the Census Enumeration District Descriptions identify the specific enumeration district numbers assigned within states, counties, and cities. Note that the district boundaries are described in the microfilm series as they were when the censuses were taken and may have changed significantly since then.

Further information on Census Enumeration District Descriptions for the 1900, 1910, 1920, and 1930 censuses is provided in the introduction pages of the following National Archives catalogs:

- *The 1900 Federal Population Census*. National Archives and Records Administration, revised 1996.
- *The 1910 Federal Population Census*. National Archives and Records Administration, revised 2000.
- *The 1920 Federal Population Census*. National Archives and Records Administration, 1998.
- *1930 Federal Population Census*. National Archives and Records Administration, 2002.

Census Locator Maps and Tools for Cities

Even though an ever-growing number of indexes are available to facilitate research in cities and towns, few, if any, indexes are complete. A significant number of city dwellers, though present in the actual census schedules, were missed or misplaced in the indexing process. To remedy the situation, historians, researchers, and librarians have compiled finding aids for a number of metropolitan areas. For example, historian Keith Schlesinger devised a system to locate individuals overlooked by Soundex and other indexing processes. Schlesinger gleaned addresses from city directories, which he found both accurate and accessible, then plotted them on maps of census enumeration districts, which followed the boundaries of voting precincts in most cities. By narrowing the search for a non-indexed individual to one or two enumeration districts, this resource permits the researcher to escape the confinement of the Soundex. The technique is described in Keith Schlesinger's and Peggy Tuck Sinko's "Urban Finding Aid for Manuscript Census Searches."[18]

The staff of the Newberry Library in Chicago has created enumeration district maps for Chicago for the 1880, 1900, and 1910 censuses. Similar maps are available for other cities, and at least one, Mary Lou Craver Mariner's and Patricia Roughan Bellows's *A Research Aid for the Massachusetts 1910 Federal Census*, has been published.[19]

The Family History Library has some unpublished finding aids for some cities that are filed in notebooks with other materials in the census area of the library. The library has also compiled or revised some census finding aids for cities. *Guide to the Use of the United States Census Office 10th Census 1880 New York City* was originally compiled by Barbara Hillman in 1963 for use at the New York Public Library. This unpublished finding aid was revised in 1985 by Raymond G. Matthews. The newer, forty-one-page guide reproduces 1880 Manhattan street maps, and assembly and election districts, and converts ward numbers to corresponding Family History Library census microfilm call numbers. This 1880 finding aid has been published on microfiche.[20]

The U.S. 1910 Federal Census: Unindexed States, A Guide to Finding Census Enumeration Districts for Unindexed Cities, Towns, and Villages is a Family History Library finding aid compiled by G. Eileen Buckway, Marva Blalock, Elizabeth Caruso, Raymond G. Matthews, and Ken Nelson. It is an alphabetical directory, arranged by state, which lists the names of cities and towns not indexed by Soundex or Miracode. It provides the name of the county, enumeration district number, and Family History Library microfilm number for the corresponding 1910 census. For large cities, it gives additional aids, such as call numbers for city directories, street address indexes, enumeration district maps, and others. It is in the reference area at the Family History Library.[21]

Street Indexes to the 1910 Census: Boston, Massachusetts; Des Moines, Iowa; Minneapolis, Minnesota; Queens, New York; Salt Lake City, Utah by Malmberg, Malmberg, Blalock, Atwood, and Payne, is yet another Family History Library finding aid. Produced in 1990, it is a timesaving directory that lists street addresses for the named densely populated areas that were not indexed in 1910. This uncataloged finding aid may be located in reference binder 49b on the second floor of the library or on microfiche.[22]

For researchers having problems locating addresses for the New York Metropolitan area in the state's 1915 census, the Family History Library has made available two important finding aids: *New York City 1915 State Census Street Address Index* is an alphabetical listing of all Manhattan addresses, giving the assembly district, election district, block, and Family History

Using the Soundex—A Case Study

by Suzanne Russo Adams, AG

The first step in searching for an ancestor in the census is to identify the ancestor's name and then list everything you know about him or her, e.g. names, dates, locations. The initial target person should be the head of household for the census year you are searching, since heads of household and people with different last names were usually indexed. A general rule is to search the last census year that is available to you in which your ancestor could have lived, and then to work backward in time.

The following search in the 1920 U.S. Federal Census illustrates the basic steps to finding your ancestors in the census. While this example focuses on a search of the 1920 census at an LDS Family History Center, the same steps will be helpful searches at other libraries.

1. Identify What You Know

For this example, I searched the census for Matteo Russo, my great-grandfather. I already knew that he was born around 1885 in Palermo, Sicily, and that his wife's name is Maria. I also knew that he immigrated to St. Louis, Missouri in the early 1900s and that his children are Phillie Russo, Natale Russo (born about 1915), Tony Russo, Zena Russo, and Dominic Russo.

2. Choose a Census Year

Usually, it is best to start with the most recent census available so you can more easily work backward from the known to the unknown. In this case, however, I decided to search the 1920 U.S. Federal Census.

3. Locate the Soundex Code

The census for the years 1880, 1900, 1920 and parts of 1910 and 1930 have indexes on microfilm known as either Soundex or Miracode. The Soundex system indexes individuals by the sound of their last name. This helps to increase the chance of finding an ancestor if his or her name was misspelled or changed in any way by a census enumerator. Each group of surnames has a code. Use the Soundex system to find the code for your surname of interest. (See page 62) Some libraries have computers or books that aid in finding your surname code. In this example, the surname code for Russo is R200.

4. Locate the Soundex Film

Many LDS Family History Centers and libraries with census film collections have books or binders with the film numbers of both the Soundex and the census. Some libraries have a different numbering system. These film numbers are usually arranged by state and then by Soundex code. Some libraries have labeled their film drawers sufficiently so that you can go to the film drawer and recognize the film that you need by looking for the state (usually arranged in alphabetical order) and then for your Soundex code.

Once I found the film number, I went to the drawer with the 1920 Soundex film and looked first for the state (they should be arranged alphabetically) and then the Soundex code. The box is labeled "U.S. 1920 Soundex, Missouri: R200 John thru R226." There is another film for Missouri that is labeled R200. It contains the index for R163 Williams thru R200 John.

The Soundex system indexes the surname by the sound of the last name and then lists in alphabetical order the first name. Because I was looking for Matteo Russo, I searched the film that began with "R200 John" first.

5. Search for Your Ancestor

After I placed the microfilm on the film reader, I scrolled through it until I found the Soundex code of R200. Once I had found the code, I looked for the first name of the ancestor, then I searched for the surname along with other identifying information such as age, sex, color, birthplace, or name of spouse and children.

I searched the microfilm for a Matteo Russo, white, about forty to forty-five years old, who had the birthplace of Italy or Sicily, and whose wife was Maria, Marie, Mary or any other variation of the name.

As I searched, I passed up the portion of the film that should have contained Matteo Russo. There was no Matteo listed between the Matt and Matthews so I looked for other variations of the name and I looked through all of the first names that began with "M" to see if the first name was misspelled or altered in some way. Could my ancestor have been indexed under a nickname?

As I scrolled through the microfilm, I came to a section that lists several people with the name Mike Russo. One came from Naples, Italy. (I already knew that my ancestor was from Sicily.) Another came from Italy but was too young and not enumerated with a wife named Mary or any of the names of the children that I knew belonged in my ancestral family. I finally came across a forty-year-old Mike Russo, living in St. Louis, Missouri, who was born in Sicily. His wife was listed as Mary and the children were Philipia, Tony, Natale, Dominick, and Vincentia.

I realized this could be my ancestor. According to the information that I already had on the family, it seemed like a good bet. But I continued to scroll through the rest of the "M"s to see if there were other possibilities. A further look didn't yield any results, and based upon several known clues about the family, I was fairly certain that I had found the correct family.

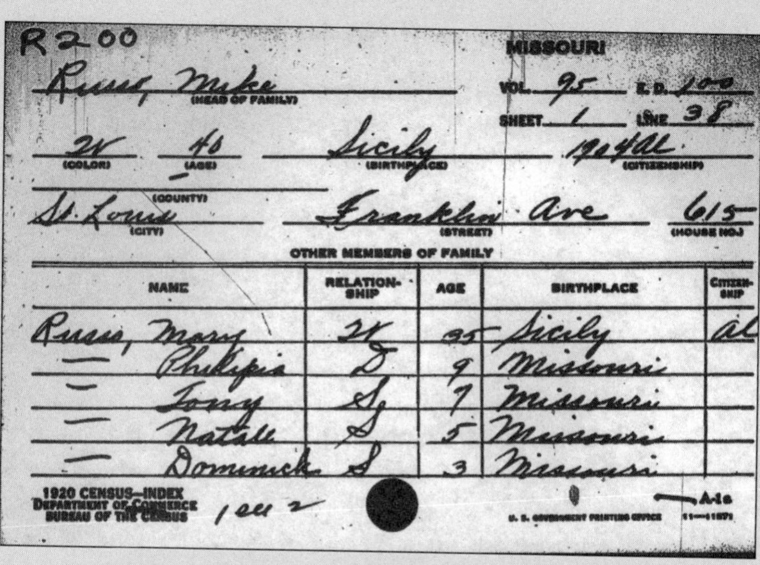
R200 MISSOURI
Russo, Mike (HEAD OF FAMILY) VOL. 95 E.D. 100
SHEET 1 LINE 38
W (COLOR) 40 (AGE) Sicily (BIRTHPLACE) 1904 Al (CITIZENSHIP)
(COUNTY)
St. Louis (CITY) Franklin Ave (STREET) 615 (HOUSE NO.)
OTHER MEMBERS OF FAMILY

NAME	RELATIONSHIP	AGE	BIRTHPLACE	CITIZENSHIP
Russo, Mary	W	35	Sicily	al
— Philipia	D	9	Missouri	
— Tony	S	7	Missouri	
— Natale	S	5	Missouri	
— Dominick	S	3	Missouri	

1920 CENSUS—INDEX
DEPARTMENT OF COMMERCE
BUREAU OF THE CENSUS
U. S. GOVERNMENT PRINTING OFFICE

Once I had located the correct Soundex card, I recorded all the information it contained for use in finding the actual census page. Remember, the Soundex card is not the census, it is merely an index to the census.

In the upper right-hand corner of the Soundex card, I found the information that would lead me to the census page. I recorded the name of my ancestor, the city, county, state, enumeration district, sheet number, and line number. Making a copy of the index card is always a nice addition to a family history. (If you are searching a Miracode index, look for the name of ancestor, state, county, city, volume, enumeration district, and visitation number.)

From the Soundex card, I recorded the following the information:

Mike Russo
St. Louis, St. Louis, Missouri
Enumeration District 100
Sheet 1
Line 38

6. Search the Census

Since I am at a Family History Center, I am ready to go get the film. I went to the census film drawers for the 1920 census and found the film that contains the state, county, city and enumeration district. If I had been searching at another library or archive, I would likely have had to go to a separate index to find the film number. I scrolled through the film until I found the correct county and city, then I looked for the enumeration district and sheet number. (These are generally in the upper right-hand corner of the census page.) When I had located these, I looked for the line number of my ancestor along the right-hand side of the page.

Following the line across the page, I found Mike Russo and his family. I made a copy and recorded the information onto a census extract sheet. Further investigation and interviews with relatives about my Russo relatives revealed that "Mike" was indeed Matteo's nickname. In that light, it makes a lot of sense that I found him listed that way on the census.

Of course, not every census search ends so successfully. Remember to keep looking and not to get discouraged. If you don't find your ancestor in the census he or she should be in, realize that the federal census-taking system has never been perfect. No matter how thoroughly you conduct your search, your family may not even be there.

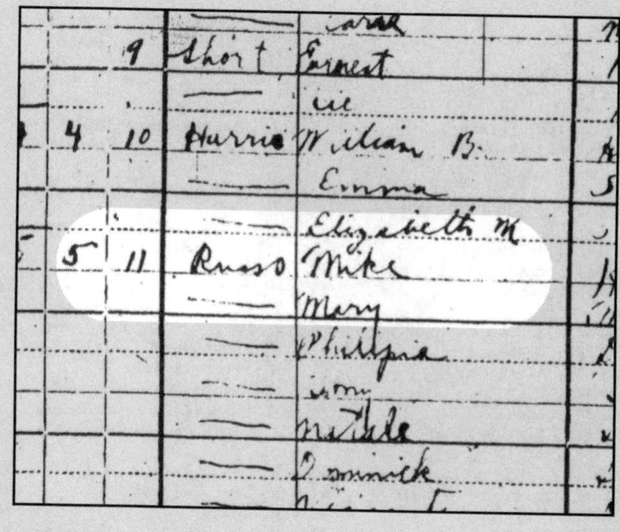

	9	Short	Ernest
4	10	Harris	William B.
		—	Emma
		—	Elizabeth M
5	11	Russo	Mike
		—	Mary
		—	Philipia
		—	Natale
		—	Dominick

Library microfilm numbers. Volume one, *Manhattan*, was compiled by Elaine Justesen and Ann Hughes and edited by Raymond G. Matthews in 1992. Volume two, *Brooklyn*, an equally valuable finding aid, was compiled by Lois Owen and Theodore R. Nelson and edited by Raymond G. Matthews in 1993.[23]

Non-Population Schedules and Special Censuses

In addition to the population schedules, federal, state, and local governments have used the census to gather special information for administrative decisions. These special schedules can be quite useful for family historians.

1885 Census

An act of 3 March 1879 provided that any state could take an interdecennial census with partial reimbursement by the federal government. Colorado, Florida, Nebraska, and the territories of Dakota and New Mexico returned schedules to the secretary of the interior. The schedules are numbered 1, 2, 3, and 5.

- **Schedule No. 1: Inhabitants**—Lists the number of dwellings and families. It also identifies each inhabitant by name, color, sex, age, relationship to head of family, marital status, occupation, place of birth, parents' place of birth, literacy, and kind of sickness or disability, if any.
- **Schedule No. 2: Agriculture**—Gives the name of the farm owner and his tenure, acreage, farm value, expenses, estimated value of farm products, number and kind of livestock, and amount and kind of produce.
- **Schedule No. 3: Products of industry**—Lists the name of the owning corporation or individual, name of business or products, amount of capital invested, number of employees, wages and hours, number of months in operation during the year, value of materials used, value of products, and amount and type of power used.
- **Schedule No. 5: Mortality**—Lists the name, age, sex, color, marital status, place of birth, parents' place of birth, and occupation, and gives the cause of death for every person who died within the twelve months immediately preceding 31 May 1885.

The schedules are interfiled and arranged alphabetically by state and then by county. Schedules for a number of counties are missing. The National Archives has microfilmed the Colorado (M158, eight rolls) and Nebraska (M352, fifty-six rolls) schedules. The originals are in the National Archives.

Research Tips for the 1885 Census

The 1885 census is useful for locating data about individuals who were living on rapidly growing frontiers: Arizona, Colorado, New Mexico, Nebraska, Florida, and North and South Dakota; for locating and documenting newly arrived immigrants from Europe; and for documenting businessmen and farmers—many of them immigrants—who were just getting started in their businesses. The manufacturers schedule (No. 3) for 1885 is the latest one available for research.

Mortality Schedules, 1850–1885

The 1850, 1860, 1870, 1880, and 1885 censuses included inquiries about persons who had died in the twelve months immediately preceding the enumeration. Mortality schedules list deaths from 1 June through 31 May of 1849–50, 1859–60, 1869–70, 1879–80, and 1884–85. They provide nationwide, state-by-state death registers that predate the recording of vital statistics in most states. While deaths are under-reported, the

Name	Age	Sex	Birthplace	Month of Death	Trade	Disease	Days Ill
Benton County, Sauk Rapids District							
AYR [AYER], Frederick	13	M	Minnesota	August		Affect lungs	[not given]
CRAWFORD, Leonard	1	M	Maine	February		Chronic	"
Ramsey County							
GERVAIS, Pierre	8	M	Minnesota	May		Unknown	42
DONNAR, Magdelin	60	F	Canada	April		Fever	15
BOUVAIS, Antoine	80	M	"	January	Farmer	Pulmonary	30
BIBOT, Zoe	25	F	"	April		Cholera	2
BAPTISTE, John	2	M	"	December		Pulmonary	30
PONCIN, Sophie	7	F	Minnesota	July		Cholera	3
RAMSEY, Alex, Jr.	4	M	Pennsylvania	"		Fever	14
FORBES, W. A.	6/12	M	Minnesota	March		Brain inflammation	21
GLASS, Phoebe	8	F	Wisconsin	February		Burned	2
BARBER, Mary Jane	3	F	Iowa	August		Conjestion	3
Albert	2	M	"	"		"	3
LUMLEY, John	23	M	Ohio	July	Stonemason	Cholera	1
GREEN, James	40	M	Pennsylvania	"	Trader	"	1
GLADDEN, Elijah	35	M	Ohio	"	None	"	5
ROBERT, Francis	25	M	Missouri	December	Trader	Consumption	90
GOODHUE, James, Jr.	2	M	Wisconsin	"		Teething	20

Figure 5-3. From Patricia C. Harpole and Mary Nagle, eds., 1850 mortality schedule, *Minnesota Territorial Census* (St. Paul: Minnesota Historical Society, 1972), 100.

mortality schedules remain an invaluable source of information (figure 5-3).

Mortality schedules asked the deceased's name, sex, age, color (white, black, mulatto), whether widowed, his or her place of birth (state, territory, or country), the month in which the death occurred, his or her profession/occupation/trade, disease or cause of death, and the number of days ill. In 1870, a place for parents' birthplaces was added. In 1880, the place where a disease was contracted and how long the deceased person was a citizen or resident of the area were included (fractions indicate a period of time less than a year).

Before the National Archives was established in 1934, the federal government offered the manuscripts of the mortality schedules to the respective states. Those schedules not accepted by the states were given to the National Library of the Daughters of the American Revolution. Copies, indexes, and printed schedules are also available in many libraries (summarized in table 5-4).

The *United States Census Mortality Schedule Register* is an inventory listing microfilm and book numbers for the mortality schedules and indexes at the Family History Library. An appendix lists where the records are found for twelve states whose schedules are not at the library. Originally compiled by Stephen M. Charter and Floyd E. Hebdon in 1990, the thirty-seven-page guide was revised by Raymond G. Matthews in 1992. The second edition includes twelve pages of introduction to this important material. While the reference is not available in book form outside the reference area of the Family History Library, the library has reproduced it on microfiche that can be borrowed through LDS Family History Centers and a few other libraries.[24]

Frequently overlooked by family historians, mortality schedules comprise a particularly interesting group of records. Over the years, many indexes, both in print and electronic have surfaced. Lowell M. Volkel indexed the Illinois mortality schedules for 1850 in *Illinois Mortality Schedule 1850*; for 1860 in *Illinois Mortality Schedule 1860*; and those that survive for 1870 (the 1870 mortality schedules for more than half of the counties in Illinois are missing) in *Illinois Mortality Schedule 1870*.[25] A more recent compilation is James W. Warren, *Minnesota 1900 Census Mortality Schedules*.[26] Ancestry.com offers a search of many of the available mortality schedules as part of its subscription service. As technology makes indexing projects more manageable, we can expect more of these genealogically valuable materials to be indexed.

Research Tips for Mortality Schedules

Mortality schedules are useful for tracing and documenting genetic symptoms and diseases, and for verifying and documenting African American, Chinese, and Native American ancestry. By using these schedules to document death dates and family members, it is possible to follow up with focused searches in obituaries, mortuary records, cemeteries, and probate records. They can also provide clues to migration points and supplement information in population schedules.

Veterans Schedules, 1840–1890

Revolutionary War pensioners were recorded on the reverse (verso) of each page of the 1840 population schedules. Since slaves were also recorded on the verso of the schedules, it is easy to miss pensioner names, especially in parts of the United States where few or no slaves were recorded. Also, many elderly veterans or their widows were living in the households of married daughters or grandchildren who had different surnames or who lived in places not yet associated with the family. By government order, the names of these pensioners were also published in a volume called *A Census of Pensioners for Revolutionary or Military Services*.[27] The names of some men who had received state or Congressional pensions were inadvertently included with the Revolutionary War veterans. The Genealogical Society of Utah indexed the volume in *A General Index to a Census of Pensioners . . . 1840*.[28] These volumes are available in most research libraries. Figure 5-4 is the pensioner's list for Maine.

The National Archives has the surviving schedules of a special 1890 census of Union veterans and widows of veterans. They are on microfilm M123 (118 rolls). The schedules are those for Washington, D.C., approximately half of Kentucky, and Louisiana, Maine, Maryland, Massachusetts, Michigan, Minnesota, Mississippi, Missouri, Montana, Nebraska, Nevada, New Hampshire, New Jersey, New Mexico, New York, North Carolina, North Dakota, Ohio, Oklahoma, Oregon, Pennsylvania, Rhode Island, South Carolina, South Dakota, Tennessee, Texas, Utah, Vermont, Virginia, Washington, West Virginia, Wisconsin, Wyoming, Indian territories, and U.S. ships and navy yards. Schedules for other states were destroyed in the 1921 fire that destroyed the 1890 population schedules. The schedules are arranged by state or territory, thereunder by county, and thereunder by minor subdivisions.

Each entry shows the name of a Union veteran of the Civil War; the name of his widow, if appropriate; his rank, company, regiment, or vessel; dates of his enlistment and discharge, and the length of his service in years, months, and days; his post office address; the nature of any disability; and remarks. In some areas, Confederate veterans were mistakenly listed as well.

Unlike the other census records described in this book, these schedules are part of the Records of the Veterans Administration (Record Group 15). They are discussed in Evangeline Thurber, "The 1890 Census Records of the Veterans of the Union Army," *National Genealogical Society Quarterly* 34 (March 1946): 7–9. Printed indexes are available for some of the 1890 census, and Ancestry.com has indexed all of them as part of its 1890 Census Substitute (see page 178).

Table 5-4: Mortality Schedule Depositories

An asterisk (*) indicates publication. An underline (_) indicates that it has been indexed. For addresses of national and state archives, and the Family History Library, see appendix F.

State	1850	1860	1870	1880	1885	FHL	DAR	NARA Micropublications	State Archives	State Historical Society	Comments
Alabama	•	•	•	•					•		
Arizona	•̲*	•̲*	•̲*	•̲*		•		T655	•		Printed and indexed; State Department of Archives
Arkansas			•*	•*		•	•				
California	•	•	•̲	•			•				DAR has 1870 only
Colorado			•*	•*	•	•	•	T655			
Connecticut	•	•	•	•		•			•		
Delaware	•	•	•	•					•		
Dist. of Col.	•̲	•̲	•̲	•̲*			•	T655			
Florida	•	•	•	•	•			•	•		NARA has 1885 only
Georgia	•*	•	•	•		•	•	T655			
Idaho			•*	•*		•				•	
Illinois	•*	•*	•	•				T1133	•		
Indiana	•̲*	•̲	•̲	•̲			•		•		DAR has Jefferson County only
Iowa	•	•	•	•				T1156		•	
Kansas		•̲*	•̲*	•̲*		•	•	T1130			
Kentucky	•̲*	•̲	•̲	•̲		•	•	M1528			
Louisiana	•̲*	•̲	•̲	•̲		•	•	T655			
Maine	•	•	•	•	•						Originals in Office of Vital Statistics
Maryland	•̲	•	•	•					•		
Massachusetts	•̲	•	•	•			•	T1204			DAR has 1850 only
Michigan	•̲*	•*	•*	•*			•	T1163			
Minnesota	•	•	•			•	•	•		•	NARA has 1870 only
Mississippi	•*	•	•	•					•		
Missouri	•̲	•̲	•	•			•			•	DAR has 1850-60 only
Montana		•	•				•	GR6		•	
Nebraska		•*	•*	•*	•		•	T1128		•	NARA has 1885 only
Nevada		•	•				•			•	DAR has 1870 only
New Hampshire	•	•	•	•		•			•		
New Jersey	•	•	•	•			•	GR21	•		
New Mexico	•	•	•		•					•	NARA has 1885 only
New York	•	•	•	•			•			•	DAR has 1850 and city of Buffalo only
North Carolina	•	•	•	•	•		•	GR1	•		
North Dakota		•	•	•*	•	•			•	•	FHL has 1880 only
Ohio	•*	•		•	•	•		T1159		•	
Oregon	•*	•*	•*	•*					•		
Pennsylvania	•	•	•*	•		•	•	M1838	•		DAR has Mifflin County only
Rhode Island	•	•̲	•̲	•̲			•				
South Dakota		•	•	•	•*	•					FHL has 1880 only; NARA has 1885

Tennessee	•	•		•	•	•	T655			FHL has 1850–60 only
Texas	•*	•*	•	•	•		T1134	•		FHL has 1850–60 only
Utah	•	•	•	•	•		T1134			State copy, LDS Historical Department, Salt Lake City; FHL has 1870 only; originals at Texas State University
Vermont	•*	•*	•	•			GR7	•		NARA has 1870 only
Virginia	•	•	•	•	•		T1132			State library has 1850, 1870–80; DukeUniversity has 1860; FHL has 1870
Washington		•	•	•		•	T1154			
West Virginia	•*	•*	•*	•*	•			•		
Wisconsin	•	•	•	•		•			•	Milwaukee Public Library has 1860–80; DAR has 1850–70
Wyoming			•	•		•				Originals in State Law Library, Cheyenne

1. FHL: LDS Family History Library, Salt Lake City, Utah.
2. DAR: Daughters of the American Revolution, Washington, D.C.
3. NARA: National Archives and Records Administration, Washington, D.C.

Research Tips for Special Veterans Schedules

Veterans schedules can be used to verify military service and to identify the specific military unit in which a person served. A search of the state where an individual lived in 1890 may yield enough identifying information to follow up in service and pension records at the National Archives; it can often trace Civil War veterans to their places of origin. The 1890 veterans schedules have been indexed for every state for which schedules are extant except Pennsylvania.

Slave Schedules, 1850–1860

Slaves were enumerated separately during the 1850 and 1860 censuses, though, unfortunately, most schedules do not provide personal names. In most cases, individuals were not named but were simply numbered and can be distinguished only by age, sex, and color; the names of owners are recorded. Figure 5-5 is a slave schedule for Kentucky. Few of the slave schedules have been indexed. See chapter 14, "African American Research."

Agriculture Schedules, 1840–1910

Agriculture schedules are little known and rarely used by genealogists. They are scattered among the variety of archives in which they were deposited by the National Archives and Records Service. Most are not indexed, and only a few had been microfilmed until recently, when the National Archives asked that copies be returned for historical research. The schedules for 1890 were destroyed by fire, and those for 1900 and 1910 were destroyed by Congressional order. See table 5-5 for the locations of existing schedules.

Research Tips for Agriculture Schedules

Agriculture censuses can be used to fill gaps when land and tax records are missing or incomplete; to distinguish between people with the same names; to document land holdings of ancestors with suitable follow-up in deeds, mortgages, tax rolls, and probate inventories; to verify and document black sharecroppers and white overseers who may not appear in other records; to identify free black men and their property holdings; and to trace migration and economic growth.

Manufacturers Schedules

The first census of manufacturers was taken in 1810. The returns were incomplete, and most of the schedules have been lost, except for the few bound with the population schedules. Surviving 1810 manufacturers schedules are listed in appendix IX of Katherine H. Davidson's and Charlotte M. Ashby's *Preliminary Inventory of the Records of the Bureau of the Census,* Preliminary Inventory 161.[29]

The second census of manufacturers, taken in 1820, tabulated the owner's name, the location of the establishment, the number of employees, the kind and quantity of machinery, capital invested, articles manufactured, annual production, and general remarks on the business and demand for its products. The schedules have been arranged alphabetically by county within each state to make research easier. The originals, deposited in the National Archives (Record Group 29), have been microfilmed with an index on each roll (M279, twenty-seven rolls). The Southeast, New England, Central Plains, and mid-Atlantic regional archives of the National Archives have copies of the series. These indexes have been

CENSUS

OF

PENSIONERS FOR REVOLUTIONARY AND MILITARY SERVICES,

AS

RETURNED UNDER THE ACT FOR TAKING THE SIXTH CENSUS,

IN 1840.

STATE OF MAINE.

Names of pensioners for revolutionary or military services.	Ages.	Names of heads of families with whom pensioners resided June 1, 1840.
YORK COUNTY.		
WATERBOROUGH.		
Noah Ricker	78	Noah Ricker.
Jonathan Knight	77	Simeon C. Knight.
Moses Deshon	76	Moses Deshon.
Abigail Hutchens	87	Abigail Hutchens.
Elizabeth Smith	85	Abner Thing.
Thomas Carpenter	76	Thomas Carpenter.
Sarah McKenney	74	Rufus McKenney.
John Hamilton	75	John Hamilton.
Caleb Lassell	79	Ivory Parcher.
Moses Rhodes	74	Moses Rhodes.
SOUTH BERWICK.		
Mary Chamberlin	90	Josiah W. Seaver.
Lydia Jay	92	Ivory Jay.
Henry Beedle	80	Henry Beedle.
Timothy Berdens	76	John Brooks.
Peliliah Stevens	83	John Welch.
Barsham Allen	76	Barsham Allen.
Charles Sargent	86	Charles Sargent.
Lydia Marr	72	Reuben Bennett.
John Hearl	85	John Hearl.
Peace Peirce	69	Samuel Peirce.
Hannah Peirce	81	Hannah Peirce.
Betsey Nasan	81	Betsey Nasan.
Seammon Chadbourn	85	Seammon Chadbourn.
Benjamin Nealey	58	Benjamin Nealey.
WELLS.		
Aaron Warren	83	Walter Warren.
Samuel M. Jefferd	77	Samuel Jefferd.
Mary Gawen	73	James Goodwin.
Joseph Hilton	85	Joseph Hilton.
Miriam Littiefield	85	Joseph Littlefield, 3d.
Daniel Stuart	87	Joseph Stuart.
William Eaton	85	William Eaton.
Abigail Hobbs	72	James Hobbs.
David Hatch	79	David Hatch.
Joseph Williams	90	Moses Williams.
Benjamin Penny	79	Benjamin Penny.
Joseph Wheelwright	88	Joseph Wheelwright.
SANFORD.		
John Hurton	77	John Hurton.
Hepribeth Jacobs	85	Theodore Jacobs.
Betsey Leavitt	72	Daniel L. Littlefield.
Eunice Goodwin	79	John Lard.
John Quint	79	John Quint.
Samuel Shaw	83	Samuel M. Shaw.
Samuel Shackford	79	Christopher Shackford.
Robert Tripp	76	Robert Tripp.
William Worster	86	Samuel Worster.

Names of pensioners for revolutionary or military services.	Ages.	Names of heads of families with whom pensioners resided June 1, 1840.
YORK COUNTY—Continued.		
SHAPLEIGH.		
Keziah Warren	81	John Pitts.
Jonathan Horn	85	Simon Ross.
Jonathan Ross	91	Gideon Ross.
SACO.		
Stephen Googins	86	Alexander Googins.
John Grace	79	Moses Grace.
Abraham Tyler	77	Abraham Tyler.
PARSONSFIELD.		
Noah Wedgwood	81	Allen Henry.
Levi Chadbourn	82	Levi Chadbourn.
James Brown	83	Edmund Chase.
Jacob Eastman	77	Jacob Eastman.
Josiah Davis	90	Enoch Hale.
Wentworth Lord	84	Wentworth Lord.
William Campnell	80	Nathan Moulton, jr.
George Newbegin	76	George Newbegin.
Thomas Pendexter	68	Thomas Pendexter.
John Stone	82	John Stone.
Thomas Towle	98	Thomas Towle.
Nathan Wiggin	80	Nathan Wiggin.
Jonathan Wingate	82	Lot Wedgwood.
NORTH BERWICK.		
Ichabod Wentworth	52	Ichabod Wentworth.
Absalom Stacpole	88	Absalom Stacpole.
Jacob Allen	82	Jacob Allen.
Simeon Applebee	88	Benjamin Applebee.
Jonathan Hamilton	85	Abraham Henderson.
NEWFIELD.		
Simeon Tibbets	88	Silvester Tibbets.
Ebenezer Colby	81	Ebenezer Colby.
Paul Roberts	78	Nathaniel Roberts.
LYMAN.		
Nathan Raymond	86	Francis Eldreg.
Thomas Murphey	85	Joseph Murphey.
Joshua Gilpatrick	82	Benjamin Goodwin.
Silas Grant	86	Peter Grant.
Jeremiah Roberts	86	Jeremiah Roberts.
Rebecca Ricker	83	George W. Ricker.
Simeon Chadbourn	91	Simeon Chadbourn.
Elizabeth Lord	78	Elizabeth Lord.
John Burbank	88	Reuben Goodwin.
Uriah Hanscomb	59	Felard Davis.
William Clark	88	William Clark.
Amaziah Goodwin	77	James Goodwin.
Isaac Coffin	84	Issaac Coffin.

Figure 5-4. Revolutionary War veterans and military pensioners of Maine, 1840, in *A Census for Revolutionary or Military Services* (1841; reprint, Baltimore: Genealogical Publishing Co., 1954), 1.

compiled and printed as Indexes to *Manufacturers' Census of 1820: An Edited Printing of the Original Indexes and Information*.[30]

No manufacturers schedule was compiled for the 1830 census. The 1840 schedules included only statistical information. Except for a few aggregate tables, nothing remains of these tallies.

From 1850 to 1870, the manufacturers schedule was called the "industry schedule." The purpose was to collect information about manufacturing, mining, fishing, and mercantile, commercial, and trading businesses with an annual gross product of $500 or more. For each census year ending on 1 June, the enumerators recorded the name of the company or the owner; the kind of business; the amount of capital invested; and the quantity and value of materials, labor, machinery, and products. Some of the regional archives of the National Archives have microfilm copies of the schedules for the specific states served by the region.

In 1880, the census reverted to the title "manufacturer's schedule." Special agents recorded industrial information for certain large industries and in cities of more than 8,000 inhabitants. These schedules are not now extant. However, the regular enumerators did continue to collect information on general industry schedules for twelve industries, and these schedules survive for some states. The manufacturer's schedules for later years were destroyed by Congressional order. See table 5-5 for the locations of extant schedules.

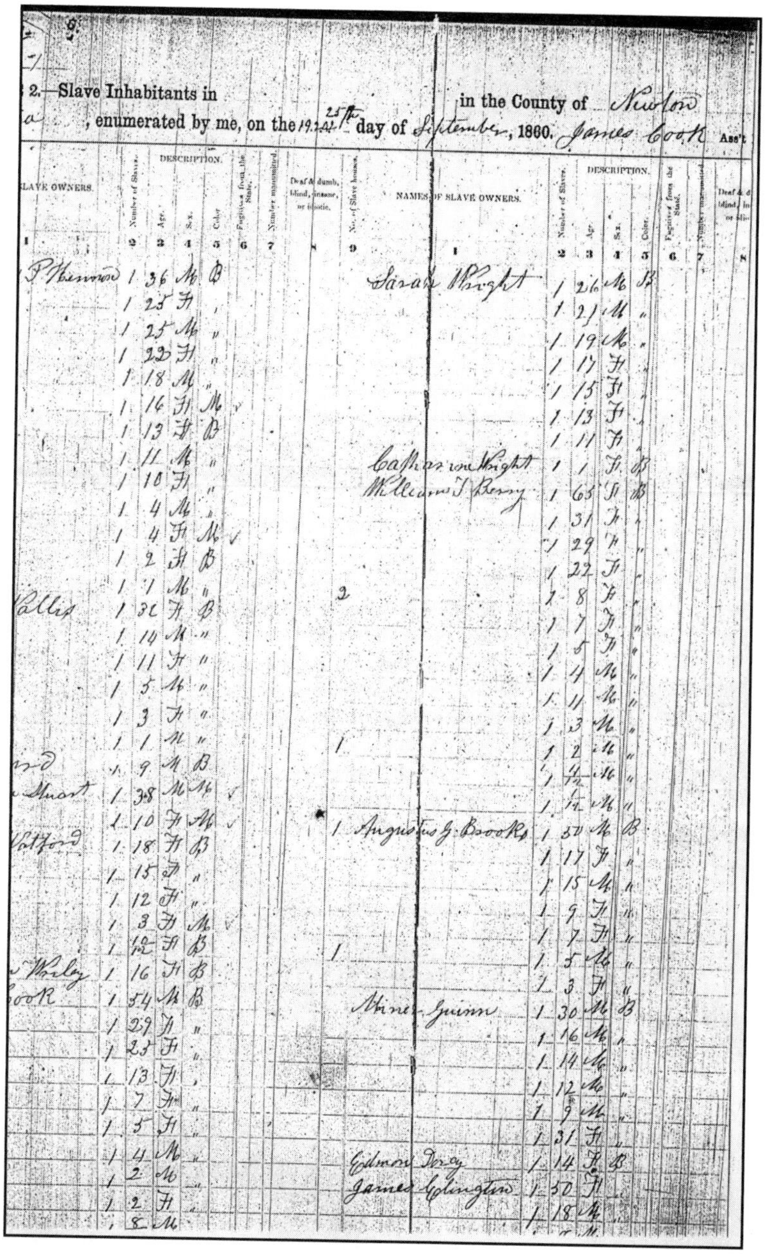

Figure 5-5. A slave schedule from the 1860 census for Newton County, Georgia, listing the name of the slave owner, number of slaves, and each slave's age, sex, and color.

Social Statistics, 1850–1880

Social statistics schedules compiled from 1850 to 1880 contain three items of specific interest for the genealogist: (1) The schedules list cemetery facilities within city boundaries, including maps with cemeteries marked; the names, addresses, and general description of all cemeteries; procedures for interment; cemeteries no longer functioning; and the reasons for their closing. (2) The schedules also list trade societies, lodges, clubs, and other groups, including their addresses, major branches, names of executive officers, and statistics showing members, meetings, and financial worth. The 1880 schedules were printed by the Government Printing Office, and most government document sections of public and university libraries have them. (3) The schedules list churches, including a brief history, a statement of doctrine and policy, and a statistical summary of membership by county. The schedules for 1850 through 1900 are not listed in Davidson and Ashby, *Preliminary Inventory of the Records of the Bureau of the Census*. Those for 1906, 1916, and 1926 are printed; the originals were destroyed by order of Congress. Church records are especially helpful for researching immigrants, and the census of social statistics is a finding tool to locate the records of a specific group. See table 5-5 for the locations of extant schedules.

Special schedules are valuable because they document the lives of businessmen and merchants who may not appear in land records. If population schedules give manufacturing occupations connected with industry, search the manufacturing schedules for more clues. It is also possible to trace the involvement of an individual in a fraternal club, trade society, or other social group.

Table 5-5. Summary of Special Census Schedules, 1850-80

For addresses of national, state, and library archives, and the Family History Library, see appendix F.

State	Schedule	1850	1860	1870	1880	Location/Comments
District of Columbia	Agriculture	•	•	•	•	Duke University, Durham, N.C.
	Social statistics	•	•	•	•	
	Industry		•	•	•	
	Manufacturers				•	
Georgia	Agriculture	•	•	•	•	Duke University
	Social statistics	•	•	•	•	
	Manufacturers	•	•	•	•	
Illinois	Agriculture	•	•	•	•	State Historical Library
	Industry	•	•	•		
	Social statistics	•	•	•	•	
	Manufacturers				•	
Kentucky	Agriculture	•	•	•	•	Duke University
	Industry	•	•	•		
	Social statistics	•	•	•		
	Manufacturers				•	
Louisiana	Agriculture	•	•	•	•	Duke University; copy in state Department of Legislature Reference, Baton Rouge, La.
	Social statistics	•	•	•		
	Manufacturers				•	
Maryland	Agriculture	•	•			Hall of Records; social statistics schedule for Baltimore City/County only survives
	Industry	•	•			
	Social statistics	•				
Massachusetts	Agriculture		•	•		State archives
	Industry		•	•		
	Social statistics		•			
Minnesota	Agriculture		•	•	•	Minnesota Historical Society
	Industry				•	
	Social statistics		•	•		
	Manufacturers		•	•	•	
Mississippi	Agriculture	•	•	•	•	Department of Archives
	Industry	•	•	•		
	Social statistics	•	•	•		
	Manufacturers				•	
Montana	Agriculture			•	•	1870, State Historical Society; 1880 agricultural schedule at Duke University; other schedules at State Historical Society
	Industry			•		
	Social statistics			•		
	Manufacturers				•	
Nebraska	Agriculture		•	•	•	National Archives and Records Administration
	Industry		•	•	•	
	Social statistics		•	•		
	Manufacturers				•	

State	Schedule	1850	1860	1870	1880	Location/Comments
Nevada	Agriculture				•	Duke University
North Carolina	Agriculture	•	•	•	•	Department of Archives
	Industry	•	•	•	•	
	Social statistics	•	•	•		
	Manufacturers				•	
Pennsylvania	Agriculture	•	•	•	•	National Archives and Records Administration
	Industry	•	•	•	•	
	Social statistics	•	•	•	•	
	Manufacturers	•	•	•		
Tennessee	Agriculture	•	•	•	•	Duke University
	Industry	•	•	•		
	Social statistics	•	•	•		
	Manufacturers				•	
Texas	Agriculture	•	•	•	•	State library
	Industry	•	•	•	•	
	Social statistics	•	•	•		
	Manufacturers				•	
Utah	Agriculture	•	•	•	•	Genealogical Society of Utah has a microfilm of the three schedules; originals in LDS Historical Department
	Industry	•	•	•		
	Manufacturers				•	
	Mining			•		
Vermont	Agriculture	•	•	•		Public Records Commission
	Industry	•	•	•		
Virginia	Slave		•			Duke University
	Agriculture		•			
	Industry		•			
	Social statistics		•			
Wisconsin	Agriculture	•	•	•	•	State Historical Society of Wisconsin
	Industry	•	•	•	•	
	Social statistics	•	•	•		
	Manufacturers				•	
Wyoming	Agriculture				•	Duke University

For those states not included in this table, check with the state archive or library first. (When these schedules were disposed of by the National Archives, state archives were given first rights to them.) Then check with the state historical society or state university with historical collections.

State and Local Censuses

Population counts taken by state and local governments, though generally more difficult to find than the federal decennial censuses, can be very useful in family history research. In some cases, state and local census details will supplement information found in the federal counts; in others they may provide the only census information available for a given family or individual.

State Censuses

State censuses were often taken in years between the federal censuses. In some places, local censuses were designed to collect specific data, such as the financial strengths and needs of communities; tallies of school-age children and potential school populations to predict needs for teachers and facilities; censuses of military strength, cavalry horse resources, and grain storage; enumeration for revenue assessment and urban planning; and lists to monitor African Americans moving into northern cities.

As noted by Ann S. Lainhart in her comprehensive study *State Census Records,* tallies taken at the state level take on special importance for researchers attempting to fill in gaps left by missing censuses.[31] For example, state and territorial censuses taken in Colorado, Florida, Iowa, Kansas, Nebraska, New Jersey, New Mexico, New York, North Dakota, and Wisconsin between 1885 and 1895 can partially compensate for the missing 1890 federal census schedules.

Additionally, some remarkably detailed state censuses are available for recent years. The Florida State Archives, for example, has 1935 and 1945 state enumerations. Like most other state schedules, the Florida state manuscripts are not indexed; they are arranged alphabetically by county and then geographically by election precincts. As with research in most state censuses, users must obtain election precinct numbers to expedite a search.

Probably no other state enumeration surpasses the 1925 Iowa state census in terms of genealogical value. In that year, Iowa asked for the names of all its residents and their relationship to the head of that household; the place of their abode (including house number and street in cities and towns); their sex, color or race, age at last birthday, place of birth, and marital status. It also asked if they were foreign born, the year they were naturalized, the number of years they had been in the United States, and the number of years they had been in Iowa; their level of education; the names of their parents (including mother's maiden name), as well as the places of their birth; their parents' age, if living; and place of marriage of parents. There were nine specific questions relating to military service; nine questions regarding occupation; one about church affiliation; and six questions related to real estate, including the amount for which each listed property owner's house was insured.

A useful indication of what the Family History Library has on state and other censuses is "U.S. State and Special Census Register: A Listing of Family History Library Microfilm Numbers." It is an inventory, arranged by state and census year, describing the contents of each census and providing microfilm numbers for most known existing state censuses. The unpublished listing, compiled by G. Eileen Buckway and Fred Adams, was revised in 1992 and is available in the reference area of the Family History Library.[32]

On the facing page is a summary of state census schedules for the years 1623 to 1950 that includes the date, comments on them, and their current locations. (The notation "Ltd." following the census year indicates that only a partial census of the state was completed or is available. A census date is only included for censuses where at least the name of the head of the household is listed. Territory censuses are also included where applicable. Special thanks to Ann S. Lainhart for her assistance in preparing this summary.) The vast wealth of data available in these local enumerations can take several forms.

Local Censuses

Local population schedules usually resemble those of corresponding federal enumerations, but those taken in New York and Boston during the colonial period included details later incorporated in federal censuses. Beginning as early as 1703, some cities required that a census be taken of their population. Although these city and town censuses are not as numerous as the federal population schedules, some may be worth the time it takes to find them.

Census Substitutes

In the absence of official census records, genealogists and historians have shown ingenuity in filling the resulting gaps. An interesting 1776 census was compiled from oaths of allegiance ordered by the colonial government of Maryland. Several of the lists are arranged in family units, with ages given for each person (figure 5-6). The pattern was later used for U.S. federal schedules. In 1778, a second census tallied those who opposed the American Revolution. Included on this second list are Quakers, Mennonites, and others who refused to take oaths, as well as some remaining Tories. Tax lists and city directories also make useful substitutes for missing censuses.

School Censuses

Traditionally, school censuses have been taken to ensure that local facilities and teachers are adequate, and to plan for future appropriations. These schedules count the children of school age. Some lists are in family units with parents' names included. Some only list children and their ages (figure 5-7). School districts or archives of the institutions that created the records are the most likely to have these types of records.

Constable's or Sheriff's Census

The constable's or sheriff's census (also called a police census) actually had little to do with law enforcement, but the

State Census Schedules, 1623 to 1950

Alabama
1818 Ltd., 1820 Ltd., 1821 Ltd., 1823, 1850, 1855, 1866, 1907 Ltd.

Alaska
1878 Ltd., 1879 Ltd., 1881 Ltd., 1885 Ltd., 1890–95 Ltd., 1904 Ltd., 1905 Ltd., 1906–07 Ltd., 1914 Ltd., 1917 Ltd.

Arizona
1866 Ltd., 1867 Ltd., 1869 Ltd., 1872 Ltd., 1874 Ltd., 1876 Ltd., 1880 Ltd., 1882 Ltd.

Arkansas
1823 Ltd., 1829 Ltd., 1865 Ltd., 1911 Ltd.

California
1788 Ltd., 1790 Ltd., 1796 Ltd., 1797–98 Ltd., 1816 Ltd., 1836 Ltd., 1844 Ltd., 1852

Colorado
1861, 1866 Ltd., 1885

Connecticut
No record of an applicable state census has been found.

Delaware
1782 Ltd.

District of Columbia
1803, 1867, 1878

Florida
1825, 1855 Ltd., 1866 Ltd., 1867 Ltd., 1868 Ltd., 1875 Ltd., 1885, 1895, 1935 Ltd., 1945 Ltd.

Georgia
1798 Ltd., 1800 Ltd., 1810 Ltd., 1827 Ltd., 1834 Ltd., 1838 Ltd., 1845 Ltd., 1852 Ltd., 1853 Ltd., 1859, 1865 Ltd., 1879 Ltd.

Hawaii
1878 Ltd., 1890, 1896 Ltd.

Idaho
No record of an applicable state census has been found.

Illinois
1810 Ltd., 1818 Ltd., 1820 Ltd., 1825 Ltd., 1830 Ltd., 1835 Ltd., 1840 Ltd., 1845 Ltd., 1855 Ltd., 1865 Ltd.

Indiana
1807 Ltd., 1853 Ltd., 1857 Ltd., 1871 Ltd., 1877 Ltd., 1883 Ltd., 1889 Ltd., 1901 Ltd., 1913 Ltd., 1919 Ltd., 1931 Ltd.

Iowa
1836 Ltd., 1838 Ltd., 1844 Ltd., 1846 Ltd., 1847 Ltd., 1849 Ltd., 1851 Ltd., 1852 Ltd., 1854 Ltd., 1856, 1885, 1895,1905, 1915, 1925

Kansas
1855 Ltd., 1865, 1875, 1885, 1895, 1905. 1915, 1925

Kentucky
No record of an applicable state census is available.

Louisiana
1853 Ltd., 1858 Ltd.

Maine
1837 Ltd.

Maryland
1776 Ltd., 1778 Ltd.

Massachusetts
1855, 1865

Michigan
1837 Ltd., 1845 Ltd., 1854, 1864, 1874, 1884, 1888 Ltd., 1894, 1904

Minnesota
1849 Ltd., 1853 Ltd., 1855 Ltd., 1857 Ltd., 1865 Ltd., 1875, 1885, 1895, 1905

Mississippi
1801 Ltd., 1805 Ltd., 1808 Ltd., 1810 Ltd., 1816 Ltd., 1818 Ltd., 1820 Ltd., 1822 Ltd., 1823 Ltd., 1824 Ltd., 1825 Ltd., 1830 Ltd., 1833 Ltd., 1837 Ltd., 1840 Ltd., 1841 Ltd., 1845 Ltd., 1850 Ltd., 1853 Ltd., 1860 Ltd., 1866 Ltd.

Missouri
1797 Ltd., 1803 Ltd., 1817 Ltd., 1819 Ltd., 1840 Ltd., 1844 Ltd., 1852 Ltd., 1856 Ltd., 1860 Ltd., 1864 Ltd., 1876 Ltd., 1880 Ltd.

Montana
No record of an applicable state census is available.

Nebraska
1854 Ltd., 1855 Ltd., 1856 Ltd., 1865 Ltd., 1869 Ltd., 1885

Nevada
1862–3 Ltd., 1875

New Hampshire
No record of an applicable state census has been found.

New Jersey
1855 Ltd., 1865 Ltd., 1875 Ltd., 1885, 1895, 1905, 1915

New Mexico
1790 Ltd., 1823 Ltd., 1845 Ltd., 1885 Ltd.

New York
1790 Ltd., 1825 Ltd., 1835, 1845, 1855, 1865, 1875, 1892, 1905, 1915, 1925

North Carolina
1786 Ltd.

North Dakota
1885 Ltd., 1915, 1925

Ohio
No actual state censuses were taken, but there are lists of eligible voters called quadrennial enumerations.

Oklahoma
1890 Ltd., 1907 Ltd.

Oregon
1842 Ltd., 1843 Ltd., 1845 Ltd., 1849 Ltd., 1850 Ltd., 1853 Ltd., 1854 Ltd., 1855 Ltd., 1856 Ltd., 1857 Ltd., 1858 Ltd., 1859 Ltd., 1865 Ltd., 1870 Ltd., 1875, 1885 Ltd., 1895, 1905

Pennsylvania
No record of an applicable state census has been found.

Rhode Island
1774 Ltd., 1777 Ltd., 1782 Ltd., 1865, 1875, 1885, 1905, 1915, 1925, 1935

South Carolina
1825 Ltd., 1839 Ltd., 1869 Ltd., 1875 Ltd.

South Dakota
1885 Ltd., 1895 Ltd., 1905, 1915, 1925, 1935, 1945

Tennessee
1891 Ltd.

Texas
1829–1836

Utah
1852 Index to Bishops Report, 1856 Territorial Census

Vermont
No record of an applicable state census has been found.

Virginia
1782 Ltd., 1783 Ltd., 1784 Ltd., 1785 Ltd., 1786 Ltd.

Washington
1856 Ltd., 1857 Ltd., 1858 Ltd., 1860 Ltd., 1871 Ltd., 1874 Ltd., 1877 Ltd., 1878 Ltd., 1879 Ltd., 1880 Ltd., 1881 Ltd., 1883 Ltd., 1885 Ltd., 1887 Ltd., 1889 Ltd., 1891 Ltd., 1892 Ltd., 1898 Ltd.

West Virginia
No record of an applicable state census has been found.

Wisconsin
1836, 1838 Ltd., 1842, 1846 Ltd., 1847 Ltd., 1855 Ltd., 1865 Ltd., 1875, 1885, 1895, 1905

Wyoming
1875 Ltd., 1878 Ltd.

local constable, often under the eye of the sheriff, was the official most often used to assemble data required for administrative decisions. For example, from 1769 to 1770, the governor of Connecticut required an enumeration of "how many parsons partayn to ech family, and how many boshels of wheat, and of Indian corne, ech famyly hath."

Another sheriff's census was taken by the Committee of Safety and Relief, 16 April 1814, to account for settlers on the Niagara Frontier (western New York) who were "victimized during the War of 1812." Money was raised in Albany by voluntary donation to provide aid for these settlers.

Pennsylvania's tax assessors took septennial (every seven years) censuses from 1763 to 1807, listing taxable inhabitants by township. Occasionally, the list covered males age sixteen to forty-five only, thus making a militia census. Tax assessors were exempt along with teachers, physicians, provincial and state government leaders, militia captains, and others. Their names were not included on the same lists. Exempt status was set by law.

Church/Civil Censuses

In areas where a church was established and supported by the civil government, enumerating the population was often the responsibility of church officials. The most common examples come from New England, but others can be found among church wardens' records in Virginia and South Carolina.

As a more modern example, The Church of Jesus Christ of Latter-day Saints enumerated its members in Pottawatomie, Iowa, as part of the Iowa state census ordered in 1847 for all residents. These church schedules contain the standard information asked for in the Iowa tally, but also include wagons, guns, and the number of family members ill, aged, or infirm, and oxen, cattle, and horses. These data suggest a dual function for the census to comply with the Iowa law and to prepare for transporting a large body of people westward, a project even then under way (figure 5-8). Emigrating companies were enumerated in tens and hundreds before they embarked, the organization under which they traveled to Utah.

Other censuses were taken in Utah in 1852 and 1856. These tallies are valuable because many people did not survive the trek across the Great Plains and the Rockies; comparing the two censuses helps clarify mortality figures. Many of the companies that Brigham Young sent to colonize the Mormon Corridor before 1872 (Rocky Mountain valleys stretching from Mexico to Canada and from Las Vegas to San Bernardino, California) made summaries of individuals, professions, states of health, wagons, cattle, and weapons. Many of these schedules are among the collections of the LDS Church Historical Department.[33] More widely known are the twentieth-century census cards (1914 to 1960), which enumerate all LDS families in organized wards. They are available for research on microfilm at the Genealogical Society of Utah (figure 5-9).

Settlers Census

Still another example is the Holland Land Company Census of 1806 (figure 5-10). The Holland Land Company had great

1776 CENSUS OF SUSQUEHANNAH HUNDRED, HARFORD COUNTY, MD.
Taken by Charles Gilbert

Name	Age
Small, Robert	30
Elizabeth	21
John	9mos.
Beacor, George	15
Hare, Patience	11
Small, John	27
Wilson, Andrew	46
Lidiea	36
James	10
Cathron	8
Benjamin	4
Andrew	2
Hallett, John	25
Prigg, Mary	25
Brown, George	14
Hare, Sarah (Widow)	39
Mary	17
Sarah	6
Daniel	3
Rigdon, Charles	27
Molton, Mathew	15
Sulliven, Nathaniel	13
Donovan William	23
Rachel	19
Anos	6mos.
Durbin, Avariller	25
Delila	2
Judd, Daniel	40
Hanah	39
William	17
Daniel	11
Joshua	9
Rachel	8
Ann	6
Elisabeth	3
James	3mos.
Thomson, Edward	45
Jamine	30
Martha	10
Mallon	6
Mary	3
William	1
Sullavin, James	17

Name	Age
Horton, William	55
Elisabeth	32
William	14
Mary	12
James	10
Sarah	8
Elisabeth	5
Ruth	1
2 negroes	
Cummins, Paul	35
Hannah	27
Samuel	9
James	3
Barns, Joseph	45
Horner, James	29
Mary	28
Elisabeth	7
Thomas	6
Casandrew	4
Mary Gilbert	1
Baker, Jenny Mary	11
2 negroes	
Clarke, Elizabeth	18
Culver, Benjamin	24
1 negro	
Culver, Ann	62
1 negro	
Suillovon, John	27
Margret	18
Coolley, John	21
Rigdon, Sarah	62
Sarah	23
Pritchart, Mary	12
Bedelhall, John	27
5 negroes	
Michael, Belsher	48
Ann	28
John	14
James	13
Bennet	8
Jacob	6
Susannah	4
Daniel	2
William	8mos.

Name	Age
Macantraus, Hugh	24
Feeby	31
Mary	3mos.
Hall, Josias	24
Mecarty, Owing	22
3 negroes	
Choislin, Thomas	41
Young, Thomas	40
Chisholm, Thomas	11
Chisholm, John	7
Hampton, John	85
Ann	84
Mitchel, John	31
Mary	34
Gaberil	19
Elisabeth	6
Rachel	4
Fredrick	1
Purkins, Ritchard	16
Taylor, Ritchard	12
Cortny, Thomas	32
Sarah	27
Jonas	10
John	8
Hollas	6
Semelia	5
Sarah	3
Thomas	2mos.
Brown, James	13
1 negro	
Knight, Jonathan	56
Ellender	46
Holliday, Mary	12
West, Thomas	45
Ann	39
Elisabeth	17
James	14
Thomas	12
Samuel	6
Sarah	6
Mary	3
Isaac	1
Wright, Charles	30

Figure 5-6. 1776 census of Susquehannah Hundred, Barford County, Maryland, from 1776 Census of Maryland (published by B. Sterling Carothers, 14423 Eddington Dr., Chesterfield, MO 63017).

difficulty getting payments from settlers on their lands in central and western New York. Its census assessed the resources of these settlers and, hence, their ability to pay. The 1806 data is especially valuable, as many of these people moved on before the 1810 federal census. For some, it is the only record of their stop in New York City.

Importance of Local Censuses

Local censuses can be useful in discovering the names of children who are listed in pre-1850 census schedules by age groupings only. Similarly, these censuses may be used to determine the number living in a household and compared with birth and death records. They may also verify specific residences of individuals who moved too rapidly to be recorded in other sources; and they may identify neighbors and other community members whose records can provide additional clues for tracing families and individuals back in time. Comparing local census schedules with tax records and other property sources is often one of the best ways to distinguish individuals of the same or similar names.

African American Census Schedules

From about 1830 on, northern cities increasingly felt the need to monitor African Americans who were moving from the South seeking freedom and work. In 1863, in the midst of the Civil War, Ohio called for the number and names of African Americans who had immigrated to Ohio from other states since 1 March 1861, their current township of residence, and their state of origin. Thirteen counties in southeastern Ohio submitted schedules. Hamilton County refused because the numbers were too great and its staff too limited.

Household censuses of Philadelphia's African American population were taken in 1838 and 1856 by the Pennsylvania Abolition Society and in 1847 by the Society of Friends. In addition to the variables listed in the federal census, the records of 11,600 households contain information describing membership in church, beneficial, and temperance societies; income, education level, and school attendance; house, ground, and water rent; how freedom was acquired; and the amount of property brought to Pennsylvania. These superb records constitute the most detailed information we have describing any population group in the mid-nineteenth century; they are being computer-processed as part of an urban-immigrant study of African Americans in Philadelphia conducted by Temple University.

The National Archives has issued a separate list of "Free Black Heads of Families in the First Census of the U.S. 1790" as Special List 34. This compilation by Debra L. Newman is available free of charge upon request from the National Archives. An expanded version for New York is *Free Black Heads of Households in the New York State Federal Census 1790–1830*, compiled by Alice Eichholz and James M. Rose.[34]

NARA has also published *List of Selected African Americans from the 1890 and 1900 Federal Population censuses of Delaware and Related Census Publications "Agriculture in the State of Delaware" (1901) and "Negroes in the United States" (1904)*, which reproduces lists of selected African Americans from the 1890 and 1900 censuses of Delaware as well as other related Bureau of

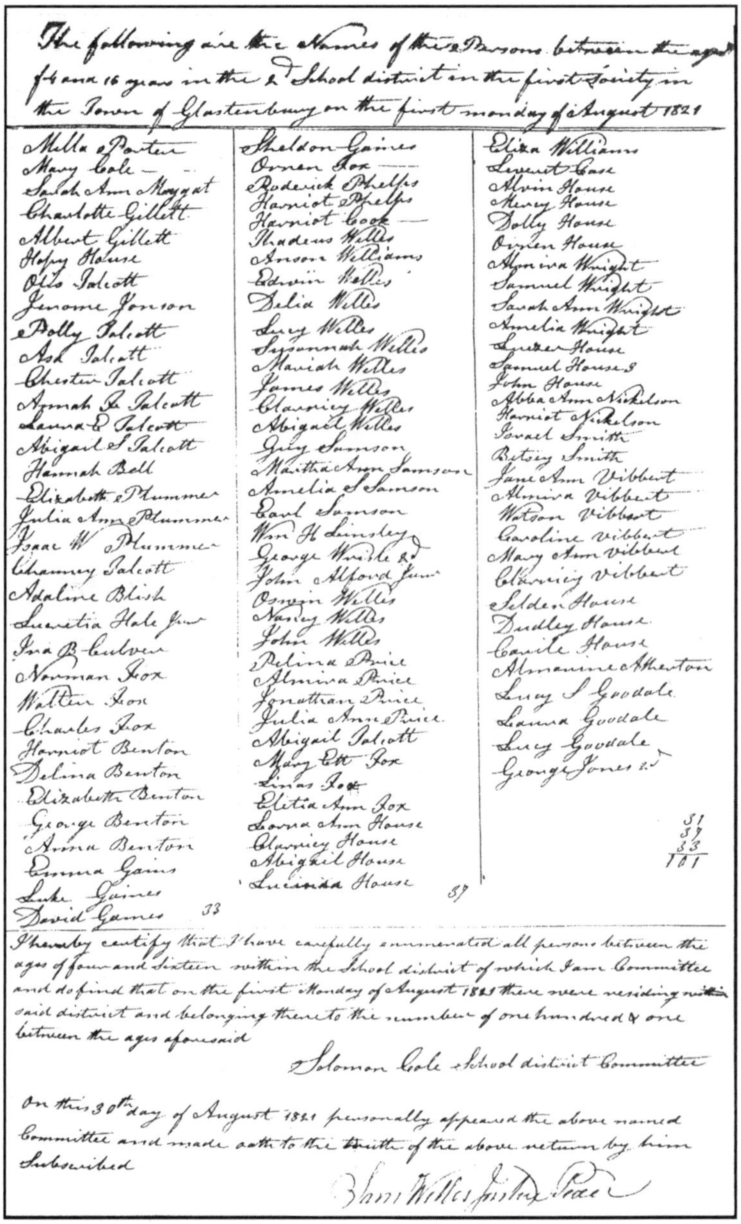
The following are the Names of the Persons between the ages of four and 16 years in the 2d School district in the first Society in the Town of Glastenbury on the first monday of August 1821

Milla Porter	Sheldon Gaines	Eliza Williams
Mary Cole	Ormen Fox	Lunent Case
Sarah Ann Moggat	Roderick Phelps	Alvin House
Charlotte Gillett	Harriot Phelps	Mercy House
Albert Gillett	Harriot Cook	Dolly House
Hopy House	Thadeus Welles	Orrin House
Otis Talcott	Anson Williams	Almira Wright
Jerome Jonson	Edwin Welles	Samuel Wright
Polly Talcott	Delia Welles	Sarah Ann Wright
Asa Talcott	Lucy Welles	Amelia Wright
Chester Talcott	Susannah Welles	Luther House
Aymah Talcott	Mariah Welles	Samuel House 2d
Laura E Talcott	James Welles	John House
Abigail S Talcott	Clarrisy Welles	Abba Ann Nickelson
Hannah Bell	Abigail Welles	Harriot Nickelson
Elizabeth Plummer	Guy Samson	Israel Smith
Julia Ann Plummer	Martha Ann Samson	Betsey Smith
Isaac W Plummer	Amelia S Samson	Jane Ann Vibbert
Chauncy Talcott	Earl Samson	Almira Vibbert
Adaline Blish	Wm H Linsley	Watson Vibbert
Lucretia Hale Jun	George Wardle 2d	Caroline Vibbert
Ira B Culver	John Alford Jun	Mary Ann Vibbert
Norman Fox	Osmin Welles	Clarrisy Vibbert
Walter Fox	Nancy Welles	Selden House
Charles Fox	John Welles	Dudley House
Harriot Benton	Pelina Price	Cavile House
Delina Benton	Almira Price	Almanine Atherton
Elizabeth Benton	Jonathan Price	Lucy S Goodale
George Benton	Julia Ann Price	Laura Goodale
Anna Benton	Abigail Talcott	Lucy Goodale
Emma Gains	Mary Ett Fox	George Jones 2d
Luke Gaines	Linus Fox	
David Gaines	Eletia Ann Fox	
	Laura Ann House	
	Clarrisy House	31
	Abigail House	37
	Lucinda House	33
33	37	101

I hereby certify that I have carefully enumerated all persons between the ages of four and sixteen within the School district of which I am Committee and do find that on the first Monday of August 1821 there were residing within said district and belonging thereto the number of one hundred & one between the ages aforesaid

Solomon Cole School district Committee

On this 30th day of August 1821 personally appeared the above named Committee and made oath to the truth of the above return by him subscribed

John Welles Justice Peace

Figure 5-7. First Monday of August, 1821, School Census, Glastonbury, Connecticut, p 2. The originals are in the Connecticut State Library, Hartford.

Figure 5-8. "Typescript of A Journal of the Emigration Company of Council Point, Pottawatomie Co., Iowa," June 1852, p. 29; GS A979,2/H2be.

1852, June | Emigration Co. Journal p. 29

No	Captain of 1st Ten	No. in Family	Wagons	Oxen	Cows	Mules	Sheep	Horses	men fit for duty	Miscellaneous
1	Thomas Robins	8	2	4	6	"	"	2	1	Dropped from the Capt. ship of disobedience
2	John Tidwell	10	2	7	5	"	8	"	2	
3	Telemachus Rogers	9	2	6	4	"	"	3	1	Appoint Captain in the place of T. Robins.
4	E.Crowel (in pencil)									
5	David Adams	11	1	4	2	"	"	"	1	
6	Richard Lowe	3	1	"	"	"	"	2	1	
7	~~John Trout~~		2							Backed out
8	~~Stephensen M. Trout~~		1							Backed out
9	Henry Howland	7	2	6	2	"	"	2	2	
10	John Heldredge		1	4	6	"	"	"	2	
11	David Ross	8	1	7	2	"	"	"	2	
12	A. D. Boyington	6	1	4	3	"	"	"	1	
	Amount------	62	13	42	30	"	8	9	13	Amount (p. 27)
	Captain of 2nd Ten									
1	John M. King	8	1	4	4	"	2	"	2	
2	James Mathews	3	1	4	4	"	"	"	1	
3	John Gilespie	2	1	2	4	"	"	"	1	
4	Eleazer King Senr	4	1	6	2	"	"	"	1	
5	Eleazer King Junr.	6	1	4	4	"	"	1	1	
6	~~James Henderson~~		1							Backed out
7	Josuha Gillat	6	1	4	2	"	"	"	1	
8	Robert Forester	3	1	3	4	"	"	"	1	
9	George Howley	3	1	5	1	"	"	"	2	
10	Absolam Yates	4	1	4	2	"	"	"	1	
11	John Merry	6	1	2	4	"	"	"	1	
12	Robert McKell	4	1	4	4	"	"	"	2	Amount
	Amount------	49	11	42	35	"	2	1	14	

Figure 5-9. Entry for the John Frank Pincock family from the 1930 census of LDS Church members. FHL microfilm 245,155.

CENSUS OF CHURCH MEMBERS—1930

Sugar WARD — FAMILY NAME Pincock

Fremont STAKE — ADDRESS Sugar, Idaho

DATE TAKEN July 14, 1930 — R. F. D. #1

Name	SEX Male or Female	P. HOOD MEMBER OR CHILD	WHEN BORN Day	Month	Year	WHERE BORN	SOCIAL RELATION	WARD RECORD NUMBER
Father's Name: John Frank	M	S.	15	January	1880	Utah	Married	545-2
Mother's Maiden Name: Susie S. Blackford	F	M	22	January	1881	England	Married	546-2
Children's Names—Oldest First: Joseph B.	M	T.	8	May	1911	Idaho	Single	547-2
Alice	F	M	10	August	1913	Idaho	Single	548-2
Thelma	F	M	4	February	1915	Idaho	Single	549-2
Grace	F	M.	10	April	1917	Idaho	Single	550-2
Ruth	F	M	4	January	1919	Idaho	Single	551-2
Grant	M	M	10	April	1922	Idaho	Single	552-2
Paul	M	C	27	May	1924	Idaho	Single	481-2

CENSUS TAKEN BY Eula Haldram

CHECKED WITH WARD RECORD BY [signature] WARD CLERK

the Census publications <www.archives.gov/genealogy/census/population/1890-delaware.html>.

Reconstructed 1790 Census Schedules

Census schedules are extant for only two-thirds of the thirteen states originally covered in the 1790 Census. Concerned genealogists have reconstructed substitute schedules for the missing states using tax lists and following the pattern set by the Bureau of the Census in *Bureau of the Census Records of State Enumerations, 1782–1785.*[35] These substitutes for 1790 schedules include:

Delaware

deValinger, Leon, Jr. *Reconstructed Census for Delaware.* Washington, D.C.: National Genealogical Society, 1954.

Georgia

Georgia Department of Archives and History. *Some Early Tax Digests of Georgia.* Atlanta: Department of Archives, 1926. Also available are several volumes of printed land lotteries, 1805 to 1820, available in most research libraries, and a pamphlet that describes the state's head-right (land bounty for attracting new settlers) and lottery system, including eligibility qualifications. This pamphlet is available upon request from the Georgia Department of Archives and History. Lotteries include precise qualifications for land ownership for each person drawing land in specific counties created as a result of the land awards. Figure 5-11 shows which years applied to which counties for lotteries.

Kentucky

Heinemann, Charles B. *"First Census" of Kentucky, 1790.* 1940; reprint, Baltimore: Genealogical Publishing Co., 1971.

New Jersey

Norton, James S. *New Jersey in 1793.* Distributed by The Everton Publishers, Box 368, Logan UT 84321. Based on military census lists and ratables.

Stryker-Rodda, Kenn. *Revolutionary Census of New Jersey: An Index, Based on Ratables of the Inhabitants During the Period of the American Revolution.* New Orleans: Polyanthos, 1972.

The Library of the Daughters of the American Revolution, Washington, D.C., has twenty-four microfilm rolls of New Jersey tax lists for 1783 which can also substitute for 1790 data.

Tennessee

Creekmore, Pollyanna. *Early East Tennessee Tax-Payers.* Easley, S.C.: Southern Historical Press, 1980. Originally printed in East Tennessee Historical Society Publications beginning in 1951.

Sistler, Byron, and Barbara Sistler. *Index to Early East Tennessee Tax Lists.* Nashville: Byron Sistler and Associates, 1977.

Virginia

Bureau of the Census Records of State Enumerations, 1782–1785. 1908; reprint, Baltimore: Genealogical Publishing Co., 1970.

Fothergill, Augusta B., and John M. Naugle. *Virginia Tax Payer 1782–1787. Other Than Those Published in the United States Census Bureau.* 1940; reprint, Baltimore: Genealogical Publishing Co., 1971.

Schreiner-Yantis, Nettie, and Virgina Love. *The 1787 Census of Virginia.* Baltimore: Genealogical Publishing Co., 1987.

Because substitutes for the 1790 census have been so useful, numerous reconstructions of other missing schedules are also under way. Tax

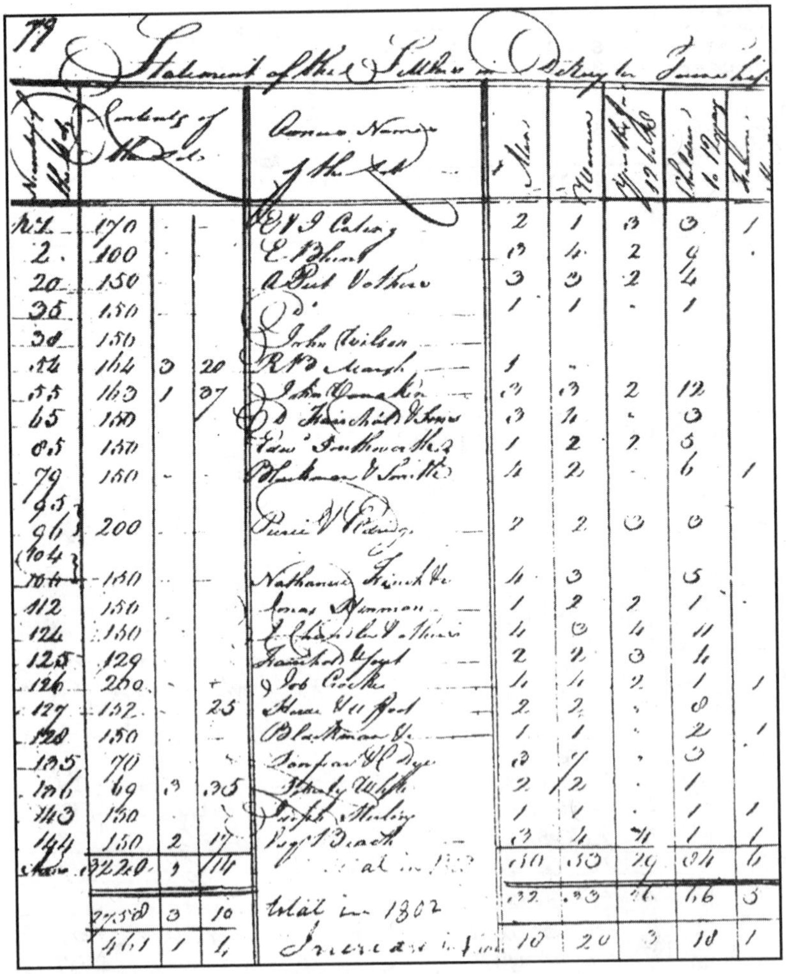

Figure 5-10. Statement of settlers, Holland Land Company census, 1806. The original papers are in the possession of Central New York Park and Recreation Commission; microfilm copies are in Cornell University, Department of Manuscripts and Archives, Ithaca, NY 14853.

African Americans in the Federal Censuses By David T. Thackery

It has been widely noted that African Americans were enumerated as all other U.S. residents from 1870 (the first census year following the Civil War and emancipation) onward. Prior to 1870, however, the situation was far different. Although free African Americans were enumerated by name in 1850 and 1860, slaves were consigned to special, far less informative, schedules in which they were listed anonymously under the names of their owners. The only personal information provided was usually that of age, gender, and racial identity (either black or mulatto). As in the free schedules, there was a column in which certain physical or mental infirmities could be noted. In some instances the census takers noted an occupation, usually carpenter or blacksmith, in this column. Slaves aged 100 years or more were given special treatment; their names were noted, and sometimes a short biographical sketch was included. In at least one instance, that of 1860 Hampshire County, Virginia, the names of all slaves were included on the schedules, but this happy exception may be the only instance when the instructions were not followed.

Sometimes the listings for large slaveholdings appear to take the form of family groupings, but in most cases slaves are listed from eldest to youngest with no apparent effort to portray family structure. In any event, the slave schedules themselves almost never provide conclusive evidence for the presence of a specific slave in the household or plantation of a particular slaveowner. At best, a census slave schedule can provide supporting evidence for a hypothesis derived from other sources. Prior to 1850 there were no special slave schedules for the manuscript census, as slave data was recorded as part of the general population schedules. In these, only the heads of household were enumerated by name.

In the absence of any contradictory information, it might be assumed that a family of freed people enumerated in the 1870 census was living not far from its last owner, whose surname they also bore. There would, of course, be reasons to dispute both assumptions. (Knowledge of the Civil War history of a locality could come into play here; for example, such relative stability would not have existed in a Georgia county that was in the path of Sherman's march to the sea.) Even so, this assumption represents one of the more obvious exploratory lines of research, especially in the absence of any other options. The first step in testing the hypothesis would be to search for slaveowners of the same surname in the 1860 slave schedules of the county in which the African American family resided in 1870.

Starting in 1850, another supplemental schedule, the mortality schedule, listed all deaths within a year before the regular census enumeration. The deaths of blacks and mulattoes, both free and slave, are recorded in them, even though their names have not been included in many of the indexes to these schedules. The deaths of slaves were generally enumerated in four fashions: unnamed (as in the slave schedules), but perhaps with the owner identified; by first name only; by first name and surname; and by first name with the owner noted.

lists, oaths of allegiance, land entities, militia lists, petitions, road records, and other sources, though never as complete as censuses, can go far toward filling the gaps left by lost or destroyed census schedules. Table 5-6 is a checklist of census substitutes.

In order to use substitutes effectively, it is important to know what specific categories of people are included in each source and which ones were left out. Many potential census substitutes are described in detail in various chapters of this book, and some of these substitutes can be found printed with indexes. Still other sources have been stored, and sometimes forgotten, in various state archives, courthouses, and historical agencies.

Censuses of Native Americans

In some years, separate censuses of Native Americans were taken by the federal government and the Bureau of Indian Affairs. While some early Native American populations were tabulated by missionary priests and colonial authorities, specific examples of such tallies have not been located.

The 1860 and 1870 federal censuses noted only Native Americans living in non-Native American households. Native Americans who were not taxed (living on reservations) and members of nomad tribes in unsettled territories were not counted. It is safe to say that those enumerations of Native Americans made before 1880 are incomplete and frequently inaccurate. Additionally, in many instances, Native American origins are not indicated.

1880 Native American Census

In 1880, a special enumeration was taken of Native Americans living near military reservations in the Dakota and Washington territories and the state of California. The census included the name of the tribe, the reservation, the agency, and the nearest post office; the number of people living in the household, with a description of the dwelling; the Native American name with English translation for each family member; the relationship of each person to the head of household; marital and tribal status; and occupation, health, education, land ownership, and source of sustenance. Some enumerators also added customs and lifestyle data.

The *1880 Census of Indians, Not-Taxed* is in four volumes in National Archives Record Group 29. Volumes 1 and 2 cover Fort Simcoe, Washington, and Tulalip, Washington Territory. Volume 3 covers Fort Yates, Dakota Territory, and volume 4 covers California.

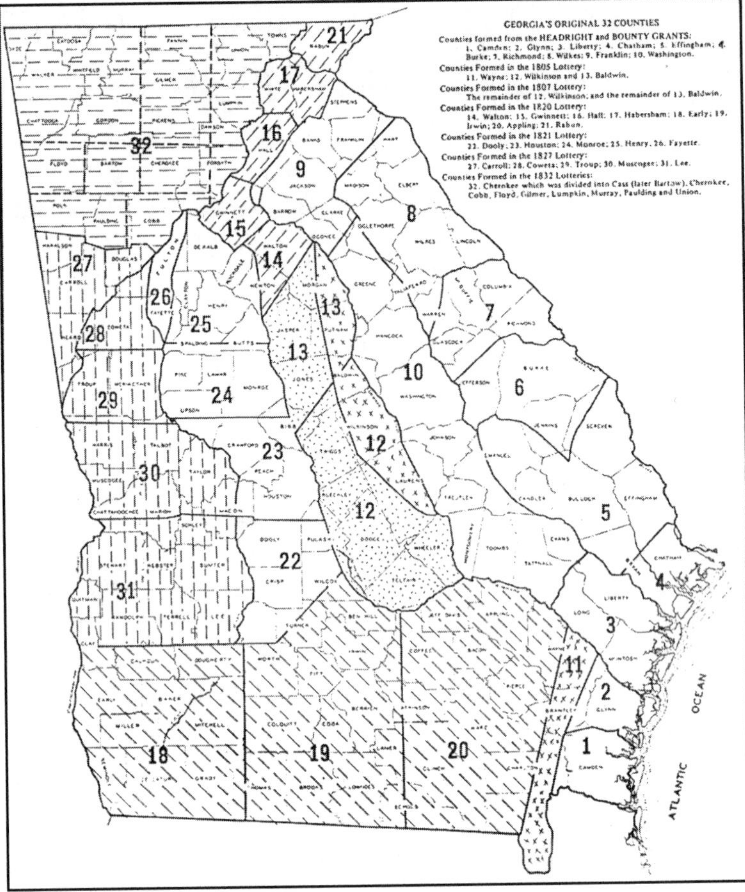

Figure 5-11. From the Rev. Silas Emmett Lucas Jr., *The Creation of Georgia Counties, 1777–1932*; a separately published map, copyright 1982. Used with permission.

1885–1940 Native American Censuses

The 1885 to 1940 Indian census rolls are on National Archives microfilm M-595 (692 rolls). Census enumerations were taken regularly, though not annually, by Indian agents on each reservation from 1885 to 1940. Throughout these rolls are scattered letters written by agents describing why returns were not taken with instructions to enumerators on how to take the census. Vital records are noted in the age column or appended in separate lists.

In 1978, E. Kay Kirkham, Field Operations, Genealogical Society of Utah, updated and corrected the National Archives listing of Native American bands and tribes in these 692 microfilm rolls. He compiled an index for all tribes and bands, with Indian agency, National Archives reel number, and Genealogical Society of Utah call number. Tribes are found under several agencies during the period covered by the census, so it is important to study the history of the tribe before beginning research. Copies of this register are available in the Family History Library's American reference area. Copies can be made on request for use in family history centers to access the lists more easily. There is no master name index to the Native Americans themselves.

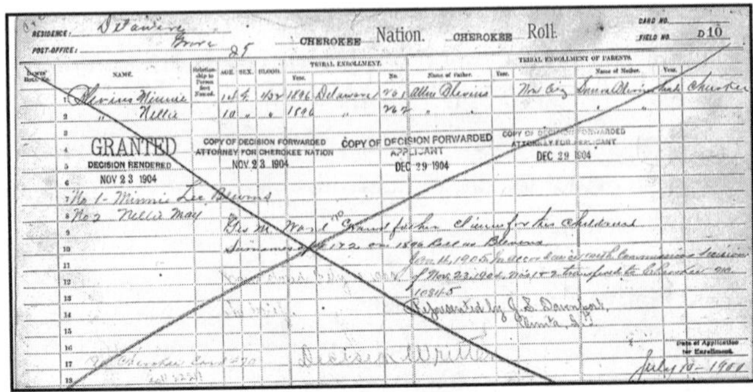

Dawes Commission enrollment card dated 1896.

Three copies of the census were made: one for the federal government in Washington (now transferred to the National Archives); a second for the Superintendent at Indian Affairs (Bureau of Indian Affairs); and a third for the Indian agency. Many Bureau of Indian Affairs copies were destroyed. Some local copies are still in agencies' possession or have been transferred to National Archives regional archives.

1898–1906 Indian Census Cards Index

The Indian Census Cards Index was compiled by the Dawes Commission to verify individual rights to tribal allotments for the Five Civilized Tribes (Cherokee, Chickasaw, Choctaw, Creek, and Seminole). To search this index, send the name of the tribe, name of the individual, approximate date of birth or death, and location to the Director, National Archives—Southwest Region, Box 6216, Fort Worth, TX 76115. Copies of the index are available from the Five Civilized Tribes Center, Bureau of Indian Affairs, Muskogee Agency, Fourth Floor, Federal Building, Muskogee, OK 74401, and through the Family History Library.

Table 5-6. Potential Census Substitutes

Tax Rolls
__ Poll tax
__ Personal property
__ Real estate
__ 1863 income tax
__ 1798 property tax
__ Assessors' lists
__ Faculty lists
__ Rate lists

Land Records
__ Entries plats
__ Plat maps
__ Lotteries
__ Processioning lists
__ Perambulations
__ Ground rents
__ Quitrents
__ Debt books
__ Permits to settle
__ Land grant lists
__ Suspended land grants
__ Headright claims
__ Lists of indentured servants
__ Immigrant land allowances
__ Inquisitions
__ Devises' lists
__ Heir lists

Court Records
__ Oaths of allegiance
__ Registers of papists (Roman Catholics)
__ Lists of attorneys
__ Lists of constables
__ Lists of jurors
__ Jury pay lists
__ Jury attendance lists
__ Commissions of officials
__ Appointments of Justices of the peace
__ Lists of gamekeepers

Road Records
__ Petitions
__ Plats
__ Appointments of road officials

Voters' Records
__ Voters' register
__ Voters' lists
__ Poll books
__ Register of intended voters
__ Register of freemen
__ Lists of freeholders
__ Lists of rejected voters
__ Oaths of office
__ Loyalty oaths
__ Freemen admissions

Militia Records
__ Militia lists
__ Muster rolls
__ Muster-in rolls
__ Muster-out rolls
__ Payrolls
__ Lists of males over age 16
__ Troop returns
__ Enlistments
__ Enrollments
__ Lists of recruits
__ Substitutes
__ Lists of rejected men
__ Wagoners' rolls
__ Casualty lists

Church Records
__ Pew rents
__ Membership lists
__ Rate rolls
__ Collection lists
__ Subscription lists
__ Lists of paupers

School Lists
__ Matriculation lists
__ Attendance lists
__ Examination lists
__ Tuition lists
__ Subscription Lists
__ Pupil lists
__ Teacher lists

Legislative Records
__ Petitions
__ Memorials

Ships' Records
__ Crew lists
__ Register of seamen
__ Seamens' oaths
__ Seamens' certificates
__ Officers' lists
__ Sick rosters
__ Death registers
__ Casualty lists

Miscellaneous Records
__ City directories
__ Register of prisoners
__ Register of slaves
__ Register of free negroes
__ Prisoners of war
__ Manumission lists
__ Register of unmarried persons
__ Orphans' register
__ Lists of physicians
__ Lists of midwives
__ Lists of strangers

In the 1910 census, a special Indian schedule is sometimes found at the end of regular population schedules for some counties. For example, NV 1910 lists tribe, tribe of father, tribe of mother, proportion of Native American blood, and number of times married.

1910–1939 Indian School Census

The Bureau of Indian Affairs took separate Indian school censuses from 1910 to 1939. These include the names of all children between six and eighteen years of age, and their sex, tribe, degree of Native American blood, distance from home to the school, parent or guardian, and attendance during the year. Some schedules are available on microfilm, but most are still in original form in the Federal Records Center for the region where the tribe was located. Unlike other population census records, these often include the mother's surname.

Native American census records can be used to identify relationships, mothers' full names, aliases, ancestral rights, and inheritances. These census records, however, apply only to Native Americans registered with the Bureau of Indian Affairs. Many Native American families never enrolled with the government. These persons are recorded in the regular census schedules, usually without evidence of their Native American ties.

Other miscellaneous records document Native American populations. Supplementary rolls list births, deaths, and sometimes marriages. Deduction rolls give deaths or removals from the jurisdiction. Additional rolls include arrivals and births. Allotment rolls list those entitled to payment and the payments received. For a more detailed description of these and other Native American sources, see chapter 19.

Notes

[1] Carmen R. Delle Donne, *Federal Census Schedules, 1850–80: Primary Sources for Historical Research* (Reference Information Paper 67, 1973) is filled with interesting details on why and how the census was taken, 1850 to 1880.

[2] U.S. Department of Commerce, *Bureau of the Census. A Century of Population Growth from the First Census of the United States to the Twelfth, 1790–1900* (Washington, D.C.: Government Printing Office, 1909; reprint, Baltimore: Genealogical Publishing Co., 1967). This resource includes much information about the 1790 census and a list of common surnames and their distribution in the states.

[3] Szucs, Loretto Dennis, and Sandra Hargreaves Luebking, *The Archives: A Guide to the National Archives Field Branches* (Salt Lake City: Ancestry, 1988).

[4] Delle Donne, *Federal Census Schedules*.

[5] Robert C. Anderson, et al., provide excellent examples and an analysis of this rather common problem in "Duplicate Census Enumerations," *American Genealogist* 62 (April 1987): 97–105; 62 (July 1987): 173–81; 62 (October 1987): 241–44.

[6] William Thorndale and William Dollarhide, *Map Guide to the U.S. Federal Censuses, 1790–1920* (Baltimore: Genealogical Publishing Co., 1987).

[7] Ibid., xxi.

[8] Arlene H. Eakle, "Census Records," in *The Source: A Guidebook of American Genealogy* (Salt Lake City: Ancestry, 1984).

[9] Val D. Greenwood, *The Researcher's Guide to American Genealogy*, 2nd ed. (Baltimore: Genealogical Publishing Co., 1990).

[10] Gerald M. Petty, "Virginia 1820 Federal Census: Names Not on the Microfilm Copy," *Virginia Genealogist* 18 (1974): 136–39.

[11] Nancy Gubb Frederick, *1880 Illinois Census Index, Soundex Codes O-200 to O-240* (Evanston, Ill.: the compiler, 1981).

[12] *The 1790–1890 Federal Population Censuses: Catalog of National Archives Microfilm* (Washington, D.C.: National Archives Trust Fund Board, 1993).

[13] Delle Donne, *Federal Census Schedules*.

[14] *National Archives, 1900 Federal Population Census: A Catalog of Microfilm Copies of the Schedules* (Washington, D.C., 1978).

[15] National Archives, *The 1910 Federal Population Census: A Catalog of Microfilm Copies of the Schedules* (Washington, D.C., 1982).

[16] *Department of Commerce, Bureau of the Census, Fourteenth Census of the United States, January 1, 1920: Instructions to Enumerators* (Washington, D.C.: Government Printing Office, 1919).

[17] Bradley W. Steuart, *The Soundex Reference Guide: Soundex Codes to Over 125,000 Surnames* (Bountiful, Utah: Precision Indexing, 1990).

[18] Keith Schlesinger and Peggy Tuck Sinko, "Urban Finding Aid for Manuscript Census Searches," *National Genealogical Society Quarterly* 69 (September 1981): 171–80.

[19] Mary Lou Craver Mariner and Patricia Roughan Bellows, *A Research Aid for the Massachusetts 1910 Federal Census* (Sudbury, Mass: Computerized Assistance, 1988).

[20] *Guide to the Use of the United States Census Office 10th Census 1880 New York City*, FHL microfiche 6,047,913.

[21] *U.S. 1910 Federal Census: Unindexed States, A Guide to Finding Census Enumeration Districts for Unindexed Cities, Towns, and Villages*, FHL book 973 X2bu 1910, FHL microfiche 6,101,340.

[22] *Street Indexes to the 1910 Census: Boston, Massachusetts; Des Moines, Iowa; Minneapolis, Minnesota; Queens, New York; Salt Lake City, Utah*, FHL microfiche 6,104,151.

[23] Raymond G. Matthews, ed., *New York City 1915 State Census Street Address Index*; Vol. 1, *Manhattan*, FHL book 974.71 X22m v.1., FHL microfiche 6,101,203; Vol. 2, *Brooklyn*, FHL book 974.71 X22m, v.2, FHL microfiche 6,101,620.

[24] *United States Census Mortality Schedule Register*, FHL microfiche 6,101,876.

[25] Lowell M. Volkel, *Illinois Mortality Schedule 1850*, 3 vols. (Indianapolis: Heritage House, 1972); *Illinois Mortality Schedule 1860*, 5 vols. (Indianapolis: Heritage House, 1979); *Illinois Mortality Schedule 1870*, 2 vols. (Indianapolis: Heritage House, 1985).

[26] James W. Warren, *Minnesota 1900 Census Mortality Schedules* (St. Paul, Minn.: Warren Research and Marketing, 1991–92).

[27] *A Census of Pensioners for Revolutionary or Military Services* (1841, various years; reprint, Baltimore: Genealogical Publishing Co., 1996).

[28] Genealogical Society of Utah, *A General Index to a Census of Pensioners . . . 1840* (Baltimore: Genealogical Publishing Co., 1965).

[29] Katherine H. Davidson and Charlotte M. Ashby, comps., *Preliminary Inventory of the Records of the Bureau of the Census, Preliminary Inventory 161* (Washington, D.C.: National Archives and Records Service, 1964).

[30] *Indexes to Manufacturers' Census of 1820: An Edited Printing of the Original Indexes and Information* (Reprint, Knightstown, Ind.: Bookmark, n.d.).

[31] Ann S. Lainhart, *State Census Records* (Baltimore: Genealogical Publishing Co., 1992).

[32] G. Eileen Buckway and Fred Adams, comps., "U.S. State and Special Census Register: A Listing of Family History

Library Microfilm Numbers," FHL book 973 X2be 1992; CCF 594,855.

[33] LDS Church Historical Department, 50 North West Temple, Salt Lake City, UT 84150.

[34] Alice Eichholz and James M. Rose, comps., *Free Black Heads of Households in the New York State Federal Census 1790–1830*, Gale Genealogy and Local History Series, vol. 14 (Detroit: Gale Research Co., 1981).

[35] Bureau of the Census, *Bureau of the Census Records of State Enumerations, 1782–1785* (1908; reprint, Baltimore: Genealogical Publishing Co., 1970).

References

The 1790–1890 Federal Population Censuses: Catalog of National Archives Microfilm. Washington, D.C.: National Archives Trust Fund Board, 1993.

Anderson, Robert C., et al. "Duplicate Census Enumerations." *American Genealogist* 62, no. 2 (April 1987): 97–105; 62, no. 3 (July 1987): 173–81; 62, no. 4 (October 1987): 241–44.

Barrows, Robert G. "The Ninth Federal Census of Indianapolis: A Case Study in Civic Chauvinism." *Indiana Magazine of History* 73, no. 1 (March 1977): 1–16.

Bureau of the Census. *A Century of Population Growth from the First Census of the United States to the Twelfth, 1790–1900.* Washington, D.C.: Government Printing Office, 1909; reprint, Baltimore: Genealogical Publishing Co., 1967.

Bureau of the Census. *Fourteenth Census of the United States, January 1, 1920: Instructions to Enumerators.* Washington, D.C.: Government Printing Office, 1919.

Bureau of the Census. *Heads of Families at the First Census of the United States Taken in the Year 1790.* 12 vols. Washington, D.C.: Government Printing Office, 1908.

Bureau of the Census. *Records of State Enumerations, 1782–1785.* 1908; reprint, Baltimore: Genealogical Publishing Co., 1970.

Burroughs, Tony. *Black Roots: A Beginner's Guide to Tracing The African American Family Tree.* New York City: Fireside, 2001.

Carpenter, Niles. *Immigrants and Their Children 1920: A Study Based on Census Statistics Relative to the Foreign Born and the Native White of Foreign or Mixed Parentage.* Census Monographs VII. Washington, D.C.: Department of Commerce, Bureau of the Census, 1927.

Census Enumeration District Descriptions, 1830–1890 and 1910–1950. National Archives Microfilm Publication T-1224, 146 rolls.

Census Enumeration District Descriptions, 1900. National Archives Microfilm Publication T-1210, 10 rolls.

A Census of Pensioners for Revolutionary or Military Services. 1841, various years. Reprint, Baltimore: Genealogical Publishing Co., 1996.

Conzen, Michael P. "Spatial Data from Nineteenth Century Manuscript Censuses: A Technique for Rural Settlement and Land Use Analysis." *Professional Geographer* 21, no. 5 (September 1969): 337–43. A primer on mapping the enumerator's route.

Creekmore, Pollyanna. *Early East Tennessee Tax-Payers.* Easley, S.C.: Southern Historical Press, 1980.

Davenport, David P. "Duration of Residence in the 1855 Census of New York State." *Historical Methods* 18, no. 1 (Winter 1985): 5–12.

Davidson, Katherine H., and Charlotte M. Ashby, comps. *Preliminary Inventory of the Records of the Bureau of the Census. Preliminary Inventory No. 161.* Washington, D.C.: National Archives and Records Service, 1964.

Delle Donne, Carmen R. *Federal Census Schedules, 1850–80: Primary Sources for Historical Research.* Reference Information Paper 67. 1973.

deValinger, Leon, Jr. *Reconstructed Census for Delaware.* Washington, D.C.: National Genealogical Society, 1954.

Dollarhide, William. *New York: State Censuses & Substitutes.* Bountiful, Utah: Heritage Creations, 2005.

Dubester, Henry J. *State Censuses: An Annotated Bibliography of Censuses of Population Taken After the Year 1790 by States and Territories of the United States.* Washington, D.C.: Bureau of the Census, 1948; reprint, Knightstown, Ind.: Bookmark, 1975.

Eichholz, Alice. *Red Book: American State, County, and Town Sources.* Rev. ed. Provo, Utah: Ancestry, 2004. Chapters appear alphabetically by state. Within each state chapter is a description of available federal, state, special, and local censuses and their respective finding aids.

———, and James M. Rose, comps. *Free Black Heads of Households in the New York State Federal Census 1790–1830.* Gale Genealogy and Local History Series, vol. 14. Detroit: Gale Research Co., 1981.

Fishbein, Meyer H. *The Censuses of Manufacturers, 1810–1890.* Reference Information Paper 50. 1973.

Fothergill, Augusta B., and John M. Naugle. *Virginia Tax Payers 1782–1787. Other Than Those Published in the United States Census Bureau.* 1940; reprint, Baltimore: Genealogical Publishing Co., 1971.

Franklin, W. Neil, comp. *Federal Population and Mortality Census Schedules, 1790–1890 in the National Archives and the States: Outline of a Lecture on Their Availability, Content and Use.* Special List no. 24. Washington, D.C.: National Archives and

Records Service, General Services Administration, 1971. The greater part of this work describes the federal censuses and their availability in 1971. However, a discussion of mortality schedules is still valid. The compiler's bibliography cites some relatively obscure but important finding aids.

Frederick, Nancy Gubb. *1880 Illinois Census Index, Soundex Codes O-200 to O240*. Evanston, Ill.: the compiler, 1981.

A *General Index to a Census of Pensioners . . . 1840*. Baltimore: Genealogical Publishing Co., 1965.

Georgia Department of Archives and History. *Some Early Tax Digests of Georgia*. Atlanta: Department of Archives, 1926.

Giltner, Charlotte L. "Interpreting the 1790 Census." *Detroit Society for Genealogical Research Magazine* 51, no. 3 (Spring 1988): 110, 112.

Green, Kellee. "The Fourteenth Numbering of the People: The 1920 Federal Census." *Prologue* 23, no. 2 (Summer 1991): 131–45.

Greenwood, Val D. *The Researcher's Guide to American Genealogy*. 2nd ed. Baltimore: Genealogical Publishing Co., 1990. Particularly pp. 181–253.

Guide to Genealogical Research in the National Archives. Washington, D.C.: National Archives, 1983. Particularly pp. 9–38.

Heinemann, Charles B. *"First Census" of Kentucky, 1790*. 1940; reprint, Baltimore: Genealogical Publishing Co., 1971.

Hinckley, Kathleen W. *Your Guide to the Federal Census: For Genealogists, Researchers, and Family Historians*. Cincinnati: Betterway Books, 2002.

Hollingsworth, Harry. "History and Availability of United States Census Schedules, 1850–1880." *Genealogical Journal* 7, no. 3 (September 1978): 143–50.

Indexes to Manufacturers' Census of 1820: An Edited Printing of the Original Indexes and Information. Reprint, Knightstown, Ind.: Bookmark, n.d.

Justesen, Elaine, and Ann Hughes, comps. *New York City 1915 State Census Street Address Index*. Edited by Raymond G. Matthews. Vol. 1, Manhattan. Salt Lake City: Family History Library, 1992.

Lainhart, Ann S. *State Census Records*. Baltimore: Genealogical Publishing Co., 1992.

McLeod, Dean L. "Record Source Failure; Some Implications for Analysis." *Genealogical Journal* 7, no. 2 (June 1978): 98–105.

Mariner, Mary Lou Craver, and Patricia Roughan Bellows. *A Research Aid for the Massachusetts 1910 Federal Census*. Sudbury, Mass.: Computerized Assistance, 1988. An index by towns and counties of enumeration districts, wards, and precincts and where to locate them on the microfilm. Enables a researcher to find town by roll, volume, and page number. Includes a large foldout street map of 1910 Boston with the wards indicated, plus county maps for the entire commonwealth.

National Archives and Records Administration. Federal Population and Mortality Schedules, 1790–1910, in the National Archives and the States. Washington, D.C.: National Archives, 1986. Two microfiche.

———. *Guide to Genealogical Research in the National Archives*. 3rd. ed. Washington, D.C.: National Archives and Records Administration, 2001.

National Archives and Records Service. *Cartographic Records of the Bureau of the Census*. Preliminary Inventory no. 103. Washington, D.C., 1958. Includes a concise administrative history of federal census-taking. Following the inventory is a list showing the availability in the National Archives of maps of enumeration districts for each of the censuses, 1880 to 1940. The list is arranged by state, thereunder by county, and thereunder by locality.

———. *Geographic Index to Census Microfilm (Major Subdivisions)*. This is the title of National Archives and Records Service Form NAR T56, bound, processed sets of completed copies of which comprise this finding aid. The forms are arranged alphabetically by state and thereunder alphabetically by county and major city. The forms show, for each subdivision, where applicable, the numbers assigned the rolls of microfilm that reproduce the schedules for that subdivision for each of the decennial censuses, 1800 to 1880. Sets of this finding aid are available for use in the Microfilm Reading Room of the National Archives.

———. *Population Schedules, 1800–1870: Volume Index to Counties and Major Cities*. National Archives and Records Service Lists, no. 8. Washington, D.C., 1969. Each bound volume of schedules in the National Archives bears an identifying number which is shown in this publication. Its arrangement is alphabetical by name of state and thereunder by name of county.

———. Records of the Bureau of the Census. Preliminary Inventory no. 161. Washington, D.C., 1964. Includes an administrative history of census-taking, an outline of preservation problems, and a description of the population schedules (1790 to 1950).

National Archives Trust Fund Board. *Federal Population Censuses, 1790–1890: A Catalog of Microfilm Copies of the Schedules*. Washington, D.C.: National Archives Trust Fund Board, 1979. This catalog is arranged chronologically, thereunder by state or territory, and then by county. Given for each microfilm publication is the series number and the total number of microfilm rolls in the enumeration. The catalog further identifies each microfilm roll by number and contents.

———. *1900 Federal Population Census: A Catalog of Microfilm Copies of the Schedules.* Washington, D.C., 1978. This catalog lists the 1,854 rolls of microfilm on which the 1900 population census schedules appear. The census schedules are arranged by state or territory and then by county. Numbers for the 7,846 rolls of 1900 Soundex appear in the second half of the book.

——. *The 1910 Federal Population Census: A Catalog of Microfilm Copies of the Schedules.* Washington, D.C., 1982. This catalog lists the 1,784 rolls of microfilm on which the 1910 population census schedules appear. The census schedules are arranged by state or territory and then by county. Numbers for the 4,642 rolls of 1910 Soundex/Miracode appear in the second half of the catalog.

———. *The 1920 Federal Population Census: Catalog of National Archives Microfilm.* Washington, D.C., 1991. This catalog lists the 8,585 rolls of 1920 Soundex in the front portion of the book. The catalog lists 2,076 rolls of 1920 census schedules arranged by state or territory and then by county.

Nelson, Ken. *1890 Census Index Register.* Salt Lake City: Genealogical Society of Utah, 1984.

Norton, James S. *New Jersey in 1793.* Distributed by The Everton Publishers, Box 368, Logan UT 84321.

Owen, Lois, and Theodore R. Nelson, comps. *New York City 1915 State Census Street Address Index.* Edited by Raymond G. Matthews. Vol. 2, Brooklyn. Salt Lake City: Family History Library, 1993.

Parker, J. Carlyle. *City, County, Town and Township Index to the 1850 Census Schedules.* Detroit: Gale Research Co., 1979. Designed to identify cities, counties, towns, and townships in every state as they were in 1850, this alphabetically arranged list matches localities with appropriate census microfilm numbers. Its usefulness is not limited to the 1850 census because it can be used as a gazetteer to locate places that no longer exist and places that have been lost due to boundary changes.

Petty, Gerald M. "Virginia 1820 Federal Census: Names Not on the Microfilm Copy." *Virginia Genealogist* 18 (1974): 136–39.

Schedules of the Colorado State Census of 1885. National Archives Microfilm Publication M-158, 8 rolls.

Schedules of the Florida State Census of 1885. National Archives Microfilm Publication M-845, 13 rolls.

Schedules of the Nebraska State Census of 1885. National Archives Microfilm Publication M-352, 56 rolls.

Schedules of the New Mexico Territory Census of 1885. National Archives Microfilm Publication M-846, 6 rolls.

The schedules of the 1885 Dakota Territory census are divided, the appropriate portions being held by the state historical societies of North and South Dakota. In addition to the federally supported 1885 state censuses, other states took censuses without federal support (see the sources listed earlier).

Schlesinger, Keith R. "An 'Urban Finding Aid' for the Federal Census." *Prologue* 13, no. 4 (Winter 1981): 251–62.

———, and Peggy Tuck Sinko. "Urban Finding Aid for Manuscript Census Searches." *National Genealogical Society Quarterly* 69, no. 3 (September 1981): 171–80.

Shepard, JoAnne (Bureau of the Census). *Age Search Information.* Washington, D.C.: Government Printing Office, 1990.

Sistler, Byron, and Barbara Sistler. *Index to Early East Tennessee Tax Lists.* Nashville: Byron Sistler and Associates, 1977.

Stephenson, Charles. "The Methodology of Historical Census Record Linkage: A User's Guide to the Soundex." *Journal of Family History* 5, no. 1 (Spring 1980): 112–15. Reprinted in *Prologue* 12, no. 2 (Fall 1980): 151–53.

Steuart, Bradley W. *The Soundex Reference Guide: Soundex Codes to Over 125,000 Surnames.* Bountiful, Utah: Precision Indexing, 1990.

Straney, Shirley Garton. "1800 Census, Cumberland County; A Contribution." *Genealogical Magazine of New Jersey* 60, no. 1 (January 1985): 27–34.

Street Indexes to the 39 Largest Cities in the 1910 Census. National Archives Microfiche Publication M-1283.

Stryker-Rodda, Kenn. *Revolutionary Census of New Jersey: An Index, Based on Ratables of the Inhabitants During the Period of the American Revolution.* New Orleans: Polyanthos, 1972.

Swenson, Helen Smothers. *Index to 1890 Census of the United States.* Round Rock, Tex.: the author, 1981.

Szucs, Loretto Dennis, and Sandra Hargreaves Luebking. *The Archives: A Guide to the National Archives Field Branches.* Salt Lake City: Ancestry, 1988.

Thorndale, William. "Census Indexes and Spelling Variants." APG [Association of Professional Genealogists] *Newsletter* 4, no. 5 (May 1982): 6–9. Reprinted in Arlene Eakle and Johni Cerny, eds. *The Source: A Guidebook of American Genealogy.* Salt Lake City: Ancestry, 1984, pp. 17–20.

———, and William Dollarhide. *Map Guide to the U.S. Federal Censuses, 1790–1920.* Baltimore: Genealogical Publishing Co., 1987.

Thurber, Evangeline. "The 1890 Census Records of the Veterans of the Union Army." *National Genealogical Society Quarterly* 34 (March 1946): 7–9.

U.S. Bureau of the Census. *200 Years of U.S. Census Taking: Population and Housing Questions, 1790–1990.* Washington, D.C.: Government Printing Office, 1989. Earlier editions had different titles: *Population and Housing Inquiries in U.S. Decennial Censuses, 1790–1970* (1973) and *Twenty Censuses: Population and Housing Questions, 1790–1980* (1979).

U.S. Census Office. *Eighth Census, 1860. Eighth Census, United States—1860.* Act of Congress of Twenty-third May, 1850. Instructions to U.S. Marshals. Instructions to Assistants. Washington, D.C.: G. W. Bowman, 1860. Enumerator's instructions for the 1860 census (omitted from Wright and 200 Years of U.S. Census Taking).

U. S. Congress. Senate. *The History and Growth of the United States Census.* Prepared for the Senate Committee on the Census by Carroll D. Wright. S. doc. 194, 56 cong., I sess., serial 385b. Reprint, 1967. In the appendixes are reproduced the schedules of inquiry of each of the decennial censuses from 1790 to 1890 and the instructions for the taking of each of the decennial censuses from 1820 to 1890.

U.S. Library of Congress. *Census Library Project. State Censuses: An Annotated Bibliography of Censuses of Population Taken After the Year 1790 by States and Territories of the United States.* Prepared by Henry J. Dubester. Washington, D.C.: Government Printing Office, 1948.

———. *Index to the Eleventh Census of the United States, 1890.* National Archives Microfilm Publication M-496, 2 rolls.

———. *Special Schedules of the Eleventh Census (1890) Enumerating Union Veterans and Widows of Union Veterans of the Civil War.* National Archives Microfilm Publication M-123, 118 rolls. The schedules for the states alphabetically from Alabama through Kansas and part of Kentucky were destroyed before the veterans schedules were acquired by the National Archives in 1943. Only the schedules for the states in the latter part of the alphabet are thus available for use. In recent years, state-by-state indexes for the veterans schedules have become available. They must, of course, be used with the same caution as any census indexes.

U.S. National Archives. *Federal Population Censuses, 1790–1890.* Washington, D.C.: National Archives, various dates.

———. *1900 Federal Population Census.* Washington, D.C.: National Archives, 1978.

———. *1910 Federal Population Census.* Washington, D.C.: National Archives, 1982.

———. *1920 Federal Population Census.* Washington, D.C.: National Archives, 1991.

Vallentine, John F. "Effective Use of Census Indexes in Locating People." *Genealogical Journal* 4, no. 2 (June 1975): 51–58.

———. "State and Territories Census Records in the United States." *Genealogical Journal* 2, no. 4 (December 1973): 133–39.

Volkel, Lowell M. *Illinois Mortality Schedule 1850.* 3 vols. Indianapolis: Heritage House, 1972.

———. *Illinois Mortality Schedule 1860.* 5 vols. Indianapolis: Heritage House, 1979.

———. *Illinois Mortality Schedule 1870.* 2 vols. Indianapolis: Heritage House, 1985.

Warren, James W. *Minnesota 1900 Census Mortality Schedules.* St. Paul, Minn.: Warren Research and Marketing, 1991–92.

Warren, Mary Bondurant. "Census Enumerations: How Were They Taken? Do Local Copies Exist?" *Family Puzzlers* no. 475 (November 1976): 1–16.

Wright, Carroll D. *The History and Growth of the United States Census.* Washington, D.C.: Government Printing Office, 1900; reprint, New York: Johnson Reprint, 1966. A basic source for background and details of the census-taking process, 1790 to 1890. There is nothing as detailed for later censuses.

6

Church Records

ELIZABETH CRABTREE WELLS, MA, MLS

Church records are a rich resource for the genealogical and historical researcher. In many parts of the country, church records predate civil records. They therefore document vital events, giving birth, marriage, and death information that might otherwise be lost. Besides providing names and dates, church records may reveal relationships between people and depict a family's status in the community. In addition, entries of a personal nature are not uncommon, and these can offer a glimpse into an ancestor's character or habits.

If church records are so valuable a tool, why do researchers often neglect these records? Perhaps the answer lies in the historical complexity of religious organization, evidenced by a large number of denominations. *The Columbia Encyclopedia* identifies more than two hundred religious denominations under the main heading "Protestantism."[1] Furthermore, the majority of these denominations have undergone many changes—splits or mergers resulting in the formation of various branches or sects—or philosophical differences that, when unresolved, have ended with the demise of a denomination or sect. To further complicate matters, the records created about the members of a denomination may be housed locally, regionally, or nationally. These conditions can make the identifying of an individual church and the locating of its records quite difficult.

Another factor that contributes to the under use of church records is terminology. Churches use a unique vocabulary to describe who they are and what they do. Sometimes the same concept is described with different terms by different denominations. An example may be taken from denominational hierarchy. Baptist churches join together in associations, Lutherans and Presbyterians form synods, Methodists unite in conferences, and Episcopalian and Roman Catholic churches are linked to the diocese. Knowing these differences in terms helps to identify the records to explore.

Even within records, terms can differ. In some congregations, the arrival and removal of members were regularly recorded. While these records can be especially helpful in providing information about a member's old and new communities, and making it possible to track members from one location to another, they are often called by different names and are thus frequently overlooked. The Society of Friends typically called them certificates of removal, Baptists called them letters of admission, some called them letters of transfer, and some called them dismissions. In The Church of Jesus Christ of Latter-day Saints they are certificates of membership.

Chapter Contents

Confusion over terminology also applies when one tries to interpret entries within a particular record. For example, marriage dispensations in the Roman Catholic Church authorize a priest to perform the marriage ceremony despite the presence of conditions that normally forbade this. The religious law that was being circumvented will be identified in the dispensation papers. Two laws are "Disparity of Cult or Worship" and "Affinity." Knowing that "Disparity" forbids marriage of a Catholic to a nonbaptized person and that "Affinity" forbids marrying the third cousin or any near-blood relative of one's deceased husband or wife helps the researcher understand more about the people who were to be wed. It is worth noting that the most frequently requested dispensation was from publication of the banns. Banns were the formal church announcement of an intended marriage, made on a specific number of Sundays prior to the marriage.

Finally, the practice of many ethnic groups to maintain congregational records in their native language can present an obstacle for a researcher who does not read or understand that language. Particularly in the decades following the establishment of a church by an immigrant group, it is possible to find church records in Dutch, German, Polish, Spanish, and so on. Many old Catholic parish registers were written in Latin. With logic and a dual-language dictionary, the record can usually be deciphered. In some cases, the services of a translator may be needed.

Despite these many obstacles and challenges, a search of church records is becoming less formidable with each passing year. Today's technology has merged with years of records preservation by archivists, curators, and researchers to make records more readily available. Improved access and knowing how religion developed in America enables a seeker to more fully utilize this important source.

Church records vary a great deal in content and emphasis according to the basic theology and the social role of each denomination. Studying the background of the "Old Country" churches helps us to better understand the organization of the "New World" churches. One useful distinction is between "state" churches and so-called "free" churches.

State Churches and Free Churches

The "state" churches were those European churches in which every Christian in the state or kingdom was considered a member. Because of doctrinal differences and the concept of the church's place in the political arena, the state church records took on a different degree of importance and significance to the local congregation and to the civil community. The keeping of parish registers in countries with state churches was obligatory. This task usually fell to the pastor or the parish priest.

In contrast to the "state" church, the "free" or "gathered" churches emphatically rejected inclusive and obligatory membership in the church from birth. Rather, only those who had been "born again" in Christ and baptized as an adult could be considered true members of the church. While the records of the state church required noting the birth of a child and his or her baptism, the records of the free church may have only mentioned a birth, perhaps as an occasion for celebration by the congregation; the free church focused instead on the importance of the person's rebirth in Christ and his or her conduct. These details were carefully recorded, while other events of the congregation were noted solely at the discretion of the church clerk.

Theology was not the only factor that determined the types of records to be kept. Sometimes it was the local church clerk or official who would decide what events would be worth recording. In Scandinavia and many German states, the Lutheran church was the established church. The Lutheran pastor was a quasi-public official who was the authorized recorder of births, deaths, and marriages. Similarly, in England, a 1538 Act of Parliament required all ministers of the Church of England to record baptisms, marriages, and burials in their parishes. In 1597, another parliamentary act reinforced the original law, requiring that duplicates of parish records be sent annually to the bishop of the pertinent diocese (thereby creating the valuable bishops' transcripts). Pastors were also official record keepers in Scotland, the Netherlands, Switzerland, and certain German states where Calvinism became the established faith.

In areas of Europe where Roman Catholicism was the established faith, parish priests were the official recorders of baptisms, marriages, and burials. These priests were accountable to more than local parliaments, however. In 1563, the church's Council of Trent issued a decree requiring proof of baptism before marriage. Subsequent decrees reinforced this edict, notably that of Pope Paul V in 1614, which made parish registers obligatory.

Churches in America

This distinction between "state" or "free" church in the Old Country came with the immigrants who ventured to the New World. The churches established by these newcomers reflected the clergy, the doctrine, and the record-keeping practices of the congregations back home.

In most of the American colonies, state churches were established. In New England, the Congregational church generally held sway. To the South (Virginia, Georgia, and South Carolina), the Church of England (Protestant Episcopal) became the established church. There were, however, important exceptions. Maryland, though originally founded as a haven for Roman Catholics, was for a time Anglican. And in New Netherland (now New York), as long as the Dutch were in control, the Dutch Reformed Church (the Reformed Protestant Dutch Church until 1867 and now the Reformed Church in America) was the established church. It was the only Christian denomination that could hold public worship. The Dutch minister married nearly every couple and baptized nearly every child in the city prior to the English takeover in 1664.

Some of these established churches functioned on a colonial or state level until well after the American Revolution. But the variety of immigrant groups, each with their own religious preferences, ultimately defeated most attempts to impose religious uniformity.

Following the American Revolution, traditional record-keeping practices changed to accommodate a more mobile society, intent on westward movement. As families left the established Eastern seaboard, they sometimes left the traditional church as well, adopting a pioneer spirit that included a different religious fervor. Churches along the migration routes still featured the established denominations, but they were decidedly less dominant. Instead, the more open, less restrictive, and less formal evangelical movements prevailed. Baptist, Church of God, Methodist, and Presbyterian took hold and flourished.

Baptism, First Baptist Church, Trussville, Alabama. Held in the Cahaba River, ca. 1910. From the First Baptist Church, Trussville Collection, Special Collection, Samford University Library, Birmingham, Alabama.

Despite their religious preferences, these pioneers did not always have the luxury of their particular clergy. For example, a Methodist in Louisiana could have married in a Congregationalist Church. A Kentucky Episcopalian may have been buried by a circuit-riding Baptist or Presbyterian preacher. If these events were not documented by a civil authority, they may have been noted in the records of the closest local congregation or painstakingly scripted into the diary of an itinerant minister. Your ancestor's records may have been kept but perhaps not in the county, parish, or congregation where you expect to find them.

While there are numerous and widely variant religious groups in the United States, there are at least five types of records that are kept by almost all churches. These are records of (1) baptism and christening, (2) marriage, (3) death and burial, (4) confirmation, and (5) membership. Although the format and emphasis may vary among the denominations, there are some universal characteristics of these record types.

Types of Church Records

Baptism and Christening Records

When an infant was baptized or christened, the pastor recorded the names of the child and parents. A place of residence may appear, particularly if the pastor was serving a circuit rather than a single church or parish. Some records include names of sponsors or godparents, who were often close friends or relatives of the parents.

Figure 6-1 is a transcription of the christening register of Albemarle (Protestant Episcopal) Parish, Surry and Sussex Counties, Virginia, ca. 1739–1741. These entries predate the change from the Julian to the Gregorian calendar in September 1752. Before then, the year began on 25 March. Dates between 1 January and 15 March listed both the current and succeeding year, for example, 5 January 1746/47. Under the present calendar, this date would be 5 January 1747. The transcriber retained the original double-dating system to avoid confusion. In the religious traditions that do not practice infant baptism, baptisms of adults or those who have "achieved the age of accountability" are included in the records. The person's name is listed, with the date and place of the event included. Sometimes, the clerk noting the event may include other information about the person, such as age and place of residence.

Some denominations required newcomers be baptized even though a baptism had been performed in a church of a previous denomination. Even within a single denomination a second baptism may have occurred. Some early New England churches deemed baptism necessary for acceptance of a church member moving from one congregation to another. Hence there may be a record of baptism in both the former and the welcoming church.

For accuracy of research, and because of the possibility of adult baptism, a date of baptism should not be confused with a date of birth. The two are distinct. Months, or even years, can elapse between the two events. This potential interval between events suggests that a search for a baptism should extend well beyond the year of birth. The 8 April 1832 baptism of Samuel Herney (Hanney/Hennich) is easy to find in the church records of the Salem Reformed Church in Holmes County, Ohio, because it occurred within four weeks of his birth date, listed as 15 March 1832. But had the search been for the baptism of any of Samuel's eleven siblings, born 1806 to 1827, the researcher

ALBEMARLE PARISH REGISTER 9

Arthur s. of John Burnham and w. Mary; b. June 14; c. Oct 21, 1740; gdpts. William Willie, Arthur Smith, Jean Bennet.

Anne d. of Benja Adams and w. Agnes; b. Sept 29; c. Dec 4, 1740; gdpts.---.

Agnes and Jane, 2 of 3 d. of John Stigal and w. Winnifred; b. Feb 3; c. Feb 4, 1740/1; gdpts.---

Anne d. of Robert Newman and w. Catharine; b. Jan 11; c. March 15, 1740/41; gdpts. Francis Walker, Mary Bobbit, Amy Bobbit.

Amy d. of Charles Hay and w. Sarah; b. Nov 9; c. 1737; gdpts.---.

Amy d. of Charles Mabry and w. Rebecca; b. Dec 9, 1740; c. March 29, 1741; gdpts. Simon Gale, Amy Freeman, Mary Gillum.

()ne d. of Nathl Hawthorn and w. Susanna; b. April 7, c. June 17, 1739; gdpts. Peter Hawthorn, Frances Hawthorn, Eliza Weaver.

Anne d. of Joseph Clarke and w. Margaret; b. July 11, 1740; c. May 4, 1741; gdpts. William Willie, Eliza Willie, Mary Berry.

()y d. of John Weaver and w. Eliza; b. April 15; c. June 28, 1741; gdpts. John Vincent, Mary Shelton, Bridget Tatum.

()y d. of Thomas Musslewite and w. Sarah; b. Sept 4, 1740; c. June 28, 1741; gdpts. John Stigal, Eliza Tatum, Eleanor Smith.

()my d. of Philip Bailey and w. Mary; b. June 19; c. July 19, 1741; gdpts. Alexr Dickens, Lydda Dickens, Mary Shelton.

Arthur s. of Charles Delahay and w. Eliza; b. July 13; c. Sept 13, 1741; gdpts. Henry Freeman, jr, Francis Hutchins, Sarah Ellis.

Amy d. of Abraham Evans and w. Eliza; b. June 19; c. Sept 13, 1741; gdpts. Joshua Rolland, Hannah Bell, Eliza Rolland.

Abigail d. of Thomas Davis and w. Jean; b. Dec 1, 1740; c. Oct 4, 1741; gdpts. Richard King, Mary (), Mary Emmery.

Anne d. of Stephen Pepper and w. Jean; b. Sept 16; c. Nov 12, 1741; gdpts. Richard Pepper, Simon Murphy, Sarah Alsobrook, Susanna Ellis.

Anne d. of Wm Freeman and w. Eliza; b. Dec 28, 1741; c. Jan 24, 1741/2; gdpts. Wm Moss, Susanna Freeman, Anne Sandefour.

() d. of Robert Sandefour and w. Anne; b. Dec 11, 1741; c. Jan 24, 1741/2; Wm Freeman, Susanna Freeman, Eliza Denton.

Figure 6-1. From Gertrude Richards, trans. and ed., *Register of the Albemarle Parish Surrey and Sussex* [counties, Virginia], *1739–78*, index by Florence M. Leonard (Richmond: National Society Colonial Dames of America in the Commonwealth of Virginia, 1958), 9.

may have met with disappointment. These children are listed on the same page as the 1832 baptism, along with parents Frederich and Catharine. For each, an entry indicates the date of baptism is not known. However, a full date of birth is given for every child and both parents (who were born in 1781 and 1788).

Marriage Records

Most denominations have recorded marriages of their members, but exceptions include the early Puritans, who viewed marriage as a civil contract. Puritan marriages were performed by a civil magistrate and were not recorded in the church register. It is worth noting, however, that even when a denomination does not require marriage registration, the church clerk might consider the event important enough to enter into the conference minutes or some other record. Or, the bride's new name might appear in the membership list. Other evidence of a marriage might be found in a minister's private papers or diary.

In many areas, notably the southern states, church marriage records predate civil marriage records by decades. South Carolina, for example, did not require marriage licenses until 1911 or birth or death record marriages until 1 January 1915. In such situations, the church entry assumes even greater research significance. Brent Holcomb's three volumes, *South Carolina Marriages 1688–1799; South Carolina Marriages 1800–1820;* and *Supplement to South Carolina Marriages* present marriage information from parish registers, Quaker meeting records, and miscellaneous court records.[2]

Church marriage records vary widely in content. Some provide only the names of the bride and groom and the date. Others might list the names of both parents or identify witnesses. Figure 6-2 is a published transcription of records of the First (Congregational) Church in Huntington, Long Island, New York. In this illustration, the pastor included the previous residences of the couple.

Some ministers were more detailed in their record keeping. Entries penned by Reverend Nathaniel Braun of the Hebron Moravian Church in Dauphin (now Lebanon) County, Pennsylvania, exceed most recordings of the era by providing far more information than was normally entered.

> Dec. 27, 1801. William Weitzel (single) youngest son of the long departed Martin Weitzel, farmer, and Anna Maria, born in Fellberger, his wife, and Elizabeth Rudy, youngest daughter of the departed Abraham Rudy, and Catharine, his wife, born Huber, at present wife of George Glosbrenner, by Rev. National Braun. The stepfather, George Glossbrenner, and Sister Braun were witnesses.[3]

Death and Burial Records

Death records found in church documents vary in length and detail. Many contain much more information than just the date of death or burial. Some are useful in locating an immigrant

MARRIAGES.

A record of Marriages Consummated by Me E. P. Ab Anno 1723 Ad Annum &c.

Place of Marriage	Year	Mo.	Day	Names of Parties Married	Places of their abode before Marriage.
Huntington,	1723	Octobr.	31	Epenetus Platt and	
				Sarah Scuddar	Huntington
		Decemr.	18	Jonathan Foster and	
				Elisabeth Chichester	Huntington
	1724	June	1	Daniel Keleg and	Norwalk In Connecticot
				Unice Jarvis	Huntington
			30	Stephen Miller and	Bedford On ye main
				Sarah Warin	Oysterbay
		Decemr.	21	Richard Drage and	
				Mary Coone	Oysterbay.
			22	Samuel Plumbe and	
				Anna Roe	Huntington
	1724/5	Feby.	10	Jonathan Smith and	Stamford in Connectcot
				Temperance Whitman	Huntington.

Figure 6-2. From Moses L. Scudder, comp., *Records of the First Church in Huntington, Long Island, 1723–79* (Huntington, N.Y.: By the compiler, 1899), 61.

ancestor's birthplace, as in the following from St. John's Lutheran Church, Cabarrus County, North Carolina:

1. Buried in Salisbury December 12, 1797 Henriette, daughter of Pastor Storch; born July 3, 1797; died December 11, 1797 of a cold; attained the age of 5 months and 7 days.
2. Buried on January 13, 1798 at Buffalo Creek the son of Peter Guillmann and his wife Barbara, born Nov. 15, 1797; died of convulsions Jan. 12, 1798; and he was not baptized; attained the age of 8 weeks and 1 day.
3. Buried at Coldwater March 12, 1798 Catharine, born Nov. 14, 1734 in the German part of Lorraine. Her father was George Schuffet. She married Michael Klein, who died in 1782. From this marriage there descended 14 children, of whom 7 are still living; moreover, 54 grandchildren and until now 8 great grand children. In the year she married John Schmidt. From this marriage there are no children. The deceased expired March 11, 1798 from a prostration. She attained an age of 63 years and 4 months, less 3 days.
4. Buried at Buffalo Creek April 11, 1798 Mary Catharine, daughter of Michael Ritschi, born Dec. 20, 1797; died April 9, 1798 of convulsions. She attained an age of 3 months and 9 days.
5. Buried at Buffalo Creek May 20, 1798 John, son of John Sassamann and his wife; born August 7, 1797; died from convulsions May 19, 1798; attained an age of 10 months and 8 days.
6. Buried at Rocky River Church July 29, 1798 Jacob, son of Daniel Boger and his wife Elizabeth, born April 26, 1785; died July 27, 1798 of dysentery; attained the age of 13 years, 3 months, and 1 day.
7. Buried at Coldwater Church August 26, 1798 Mary Elizabeth, born August 26, 1724 at Schweigern in Wuertemberg. Her father was Mathias Berringer. She married in 1750 Christian Bernhard; bore 10 children, of whom 5 are still living. She saw 26 grandchildren, of whom 5 are now dead. She died August 24, 1798 of hectic fever and attained an age of 74 years, less 2 days.[4]

These detailed entries provide names, birth and death dates of the person, and burial information. In several cases, the decedent's foreign birth place is identified. The recorder provides names and number of spouses, marriage dates, how many children the individual begat, and the cause of death. Side notes regarding the person's character or "state of grace" enhance the record entry.

Although today few churches permit burials on their premises, this practice was not uncommon in earlier centuries. Immaculate Conception Churchyard Cemetery in Sutter Creek, Amador County, California, completely surrounds the Old Catholic church. Tombstones date from 1858 to 1982; most are from the 1860s, 1870s, and 1880s. Some of the inscriptions provide good detail. The marker for Luga Glavinovich gives the death date "30 Maggio 1874" (30 March), age "all eta di 46 anni" (46 years), and origin "Nativo di Pocie, Isola Brazza, Dalmazia."[5]

Because these burials often pre-date the keeping of official county records, a church burial book may be the only evidence of interment. When tombstones do not remain in church cemeteries, consult church officials to learn if an entry book was maintained for the burials. Such a book, or a recording in another church record, might predate the keeping of official county records, thus being the only evidence of the death and burial.

A related church death record that can provide a wealth of genealogical information is a transcript of the eulogy delivered by a minister at the funeral or memorial service. While eulogies tended to be designated for the wealthy or clergy, they were also given to more common folk, particularly those who were active in the church. Eulogies will carry dates and places and will likely include some family relationships. For example, a eulogy for "Mrs. Martha Robbins, the eldest daughter of Mr. Ahbel and Mrs. Abigail Wright, of Wethersfield [Connecticut]" showed that "she was born in that town, on the 24th of January, 1796" and adds the information that she was the mother of eight and includes dates for two of her children who died young.[6]

Searches for eulogies should begin at the local church and extend to the central depository for the specific denomination. In addition, many college and public libraries, universities, and archives have significant historical or religious collections. Search their catalogues under "funeral sermons," "memorial tributes," and "obituaries" as well as "eulogies." The American Antiquarian Society lists ten thousand eulogies in its online catalog at <www.americanantiquarian.org>.

Confirmation Records

Churches that conduct baptism of infants generally allow for a confirmation. A confirmation brings the confirmand into adult membership in the church. The age at confirmation varies within denominations. It can be as young as seven or restricted to "adults." Most churches confirm between the ages of thirteen and eighteen (see figure 6-3). While most American Protestant denominations that practice confirmation list only the names of those confirmed and the date of the event, some may go beyond. German-American Lutheran and Reformed confirmation registers often include the date and place of baptism. Episcopalian clerks will include baptismal information in the confirmation records and file a report with the bishop. Because confirmation marks the person's entry into full membership in the congregation, most entries include the age. If not, this usually can be determined by knowing the practices of the denomination.

Figure 6-3. Many denominations require baptized persons to confirm their faith before being fully accepted into the church. These young people have just completed the confirmation ceremony marking the end of a year-long program of study under Pastor Zurbrig of the First Evangelical Church of Bensenville, Illinois, 1948. Courtesy of Warren E. Luebking.

Membership Records

Another record category that is common to most faiths is the membership list, often called a membership roll. Each denomination dictates exactly how the record is kept and who is responsible for its maintenance and updating. Some churches have special portions of the church record book reserved only for membership. Others may organize membership by family name, noting each family member and his or her status of affiliation.

Some membership rolls are simple lists. The more creative clerk may have separated the lists by gender, noting changes in a person's name after marriage or adding significant dates (such as departure from the community or burial) after each entry. An entry can also reflect how the person became a member. Entries in the rolls of the First Presbyterian Church of Deerfield, Lenawee County, Michigan, 1853–1890, show that Mrs. Amelia M. Morse was "received into our Church by Certificate from the Congregational Church in Craftsbury, Vermont," while Mrs. Miranda Canfield was received from the first Presbyterian Church in Kendall, Orleans Co., New York.[7]

Membership data, no matter the format, is extremely important. From even the simple gender-separated lists, a researcher may find a family by matching males and females with the same surnames and the date they joined the church. The researcher can then take the names and date and conduct a further search of the church conference record. Such is the case in the records of the Congregational Methodist Church at Harmony (Pine Hill, Alabama). The church membership roll shows A. Holiway, male, October 1879, and Lula Holiway, female, October 1879. Searching conference records for this month and year produces the following record of 4 October 1879:

> The congregation met at the river near Wm. Traylors for the purpose of witnessing the ordinance of baptism and A. Holiway *and his wife* Lula was baptized by M. Prescott after which the church assembled for religious service.[8]

It is worth noting that some church registers, particularly in the mid-nineteenth century, contain two membership lists, one marked "whites" and one labeled "colored." A biographical sketch for Baptist minister Archibald A. Baldwin (1800–1864) includes this paragraph:

> "From 1852 to 1858 he was pastor of the Midlothian African Church, a church organized in 1846, with six white and fifty-four colored members....It is interesting to see the interest felt at this period in the religious welfare of the colored people. Nearly all the churches

of the Middle District Association had colored members. For example in 1855, Powhatan Church had 270 colored members and Red Lane 101."[9]

Other Types of Records

The standard records just described are excellent resources, but there are other church-related materials worthy of examination. These include minutes, financial reports, and publications. All of these can be produced by a church or congregation or at a non-local level, such as a higher governing or related body, or by evangelical and missionary work.

Minutes and Administrative Records

Administration records can include details on the functioning of a denomination (as opposed to an individual church). The seven-volume *Ecclesiastical Records of the State of New York* transcribes selected Dutch Reformed church administrative records and correspondence, providing good information on the denomination and individuals who served in key positions.[10]

The congregational business or church conference minutes offer an in-depth look into matters concerning the local church, such an ancestor's work in the church, an individual's monetary contributions, and matters of discipline. This following example comes from the Pisgah Cumberland Presbyterian Church Records in Gallatin County, Illinois, on 19 June 1842:

> Where as publick [*sic*] fame has declared Sister Magdelane Thompson guilty of some unchristian conduct in getting angry at a neighbour and using unchristian language resolved that J.S. Alexander and Robert S. Donaldson be appointed a committee to convers [*sic*] with said Sister and report to the session next Thirsday [*sic*] night.[11]

The local churches of some denominations also kept detailed records of committee memberships and duties, family registers, and pew rentals. The Reverend Elias Nason, M.A., notes, "It appears that each member of the parish built his own pew in the meeting house, on a spot selected by himself, and that those who paid the heaviest taxes were entitled to the first choice. The names of the most fortunate were thus quaintly recorded by John Steel, the parish clerk":[12]

> Dunstable, October 21st, 1757, An acount [*sic*] of [the] Names of [the] Fifteen Higest [*sic*] Payers which was to Draw [the] Pew Ground as They were voted By [the] Second Parish in Dunstable first of all:
>
> Joseph Fletcher [the] 1st........No 8
> Ebenr Parkhurst [the] 2d........No 9
> Samuel Taylor [the] 3d.........No 13
> Capt. John Cumings [the] 4th .....No 2
> John Steel [the] 5th .....No 15
> Abraham Kendall [the] 6th.....No 7
> Ebenr Proctor [the] 7th.....No 4
> Lt. John Kendall [the] 8th.......No 1
> Ens. John Swallow [the] 9th .....No 3
> Joseph Spaulding [the] 10th ....No 14
> Timothy Read [the] 11th .....No 10
> Ebenr Butterfield [the] 12th ..... No 12
> David Taylor [the] 13th .....No 5
> Josiah Blodgett [the] 14th .....No 6
> Joseph Taylor [the] 15th ....No 11.
> John Steel
> Comtee
> Ebenr Sherwin

Financial or Budget Reports

Financial records reflect a church's decisions about raising and spending funds. The treasurer might record only the total amount given to the general fund. However, the members who contribute monies to a special cause or need are often listed along with the amount they gave.

Financial information may appear in church minutes. The session minutes of the Indiana Presbyterian Church of Knox County, Indiana, include the following notations about monies in 1835: "Feb 22, One dollar returned into treasury by David McCord; one dollar returned in treasury by M. S. Smith. March 23, Archld. Simpson returned .50 by self, M. S. Smith .50; March 24, May Smith returned .50."[13]

If a church extended ongoing financial aid to a needy family, the sums and payouts may appear in the financial accounts. Occasionally, repayments and donations noted are for other than cash and may give research clues. Carpentry work to repair a church roof, for example, may point to the occupation of the giver.

Local Publications

Local churches also publish information. The weekly church bulletin, which might double as the order of the weekly worship service, or a weekly newsletter may list who joined, who was ill, who died, who married, and who was buried. Such publications may also include

- A sermon that names those in need of special prayers.
- A tribute or memorial notice that gives more detail and family information than the secular newspaper obituary.
- Announcements of special publications, such as centennial anniversary booklets about the local church.

Non-Local Records

In addition to records created by the local congregation, there are documents produced at the area or state denominational level. Most denominations have at least two levels of organization above the local parish or church. The first tier above individual churches is generally administrative in nature and governs or oversees many churches in a particular region. Records at this level include minutes of general meetings or conferences and may have only passing reference to specific individuals.

Denominational Records

The highest level of organization may be the national convention (Baptist), conference (Presbyterian), or congress, depending on the denomination. This governing body creates or maintains denominational records that deal with the overall functioning of the denomination and its history. Here will be found records of ministers, officials or laymen in leadership roles, and other significant persons. Records about ministers might include orders of ordinations, listings of pastoral service, and pulpit changes. There will usually be published and manuscript records containing tributes, biographies, and obituaries of clergy and lay leadership. These kinds of records are usually archived at the main centralized facility for that denomination but are sometimes found at university libraries.

Records of Religious Activities

The Religious Press

Most denominations at one time or another have produced newspapers such as the nineteenth-century *Christian Leader*, published in Utica, New York, for the Universalist Church or the *American Friend*, the Quaker-oriented publication.[14] Other denominations were well-represented in ecumenical publications that covered vast areas and represented more than one denomination. The Christian Advocate titles (*Western Christian Advocate, Southern Christian Advocate, Texas Christian Advocate, Canada Christian Advocate*, and so forth) primarily published news about Methodist congregations, but entries for Baptists and Presbyterians appear often.

Researchers who think such literature contains only doctrinal statements and sermons will be pleasantly surprised. A wealth of detail lies within the pages of the religious press, as evidenced by this 1873 entry:

> Rauch: Fell peacefully asleep in Jesus, in Linn Co., Iowa, May 19th, 1873, Father Tobias Rauch, aged 80 years and 25 days . . . was born Vohringen on the Neckar, superior bailiwick Sulz, Wurtemberg. On 19 May 1873, died of old age, in Linn Co., Iowa. He and first wife were Lutherans, she being a widow with three children when they married. She died after a comparatively short duration, after bearing him three children, all living in Cleveland. After marrying a second time, came to America in 1833, settling in Liverpool, Columbiana Co., Ohio. Converted in Summit Co., Ohio. 1865 to Linn Co., Iowa, where joined Ottercreek Congregation. Survived by wife, 12 children, a number of grandchildren and great-grandchildren. Preceded in death by daughter, Sister Steinnage. 12 May 1873 funeral: Rev. W. Kolb preached in German from Luke 2:29, 31; Rev. F. Methfessel preached in English from III Tim. 4:7, 8, chosen by widow.[15]

Because these papers had wide distribution (subscriptions to the *Western Christian Advocate* were commonly sold throughout Illinois, Indiana, Kentucky, Michigan, and Ohio), content was far-ranging. One common practice was to carry a notice to other newspapers to copy the text, i.e., "N.Y. Baptist Register will please copy." This item was intended to disperse the information even more widely and can be a clue to the origin of the subject of the article.

The publishers ran the press as a business, much like the local newspaper. Ministers often sold subscriptions to supplement their retirement funds. Another way editors would subsidize the paper was to use the last page for advertisements, preferably paid for by advertisers in cash. Your ancestor may have advertised a business, written a personal item, campaigned for office, or been fondly remembered in the obituary or another personal entry column. Many of these periodicals were short-lived, but some issues may survive. A chart of some indexes and abstracts for religious newspapers appears in table 6-1.

Circuit Riders

Although circuit riding was not exclusive to the Methodists, it is they who seem most often associated with the topic. Writing of the Indiana frontier, James H. Madison describes these lone figures well. "Alone and on horseback, his saddlebag filled with a Bible, the Methodist *Discipline*, and a hymn book, he traveled hundreds of miles to preach and minister to pioneers scattered over his circuit. Efficiently and effectively he brought the church to the people. Usually possessed of frontier wisdom and practicality rather than a theology degree, the circuit rider was a welcome figure who understood the hardships of pioneer life and the joys of a new cleared field, a fatted hog, or a newborn baby."[16]

The practice of circuit riding endured into the twentieth century in some areas, Baptists and Presbyterians also rode the circuit, along with other denominations. These riders predated "stationed" preachers and the establishment of churches. Although not all were ordained (especially in the early years), most performed the services expected of an ordained minister. They would conduct ceremonies of baptism and marriage and, if their time of arrival permitted, burial. The ceremony might be recorded on a scrap of paper or in a journal maintained by the circuit rider. Whether notice would eventually be recorded at a county courthouse (and if so, which courthouse) depended on many variables, including the record-keeping abilities of the rider, the route he took, and whether monies had been entrusted to him to pay the recording fee at the courthouse. For these and

Table 6-1. Some Nineteenth-Century Religious Newspapers Transcribed or Indexed

Sandra Hargreaves Luebking, FUGA, March 2006

Most religious newspapers reported events for members of other denominations as well as their own. These events occurred in locales all over the country, far beyond the areas supposedly served by the newspaper.

Denomination	Title of Newspaper	Years Indexed and Area of Coverage	Index or Abstract. General Notes
Adventist	*Adventist Review*		Carried obits of only prominent members
African Methodist Episcopal	*The Christian Recorder*	1861–1902	Microfilm C-4526 (11 reels) at Boston University Libraries, School of Theology, <http://library.bu.edu>. An index through 1876 (ongoing) is at Harvard College Library (password needed) <http://hcl.harvard.edu/research/guides/af_am/newspapers>.
Baptist	*Alabama Baptist; South Western Baptist*	1843–current AL + other Southern	*Alabama Baptist,* 1843–present and indexes 1843–1900 and 1957–present at Samford University Library, Birmingham, Alabama.
	Baptist Courier	1869–1900 South Carolina	Samford University Library, Birmingham AL 35209
	Biblical Recorder	North Carolina	1834–1907 at Wake Forest University; 1834–1940 at Samford University Library, Birmingham AL 35209
	Christian Index	1822–79 Georgia	by Mary Overby: *Christian Index Obituaries, 1822–1879,* (Macon: Georgia Baptist Historical Society, Mercer University, 1975); *Christian Index Obituaries 1880–1899* (same publisher, 1982); and *Marriages Published in the Christian Index* (Georgia Baptist Historical Society, 1971). Originals at Georgia Baptist History Depository, Mercer University Main Library; 1822–1940 at Samford University Library, Birmingham AL 35209.
	Florida Bapt. Witness	1885–1940	Samford University Library, Birmingham AL 35209
	Tennessee Baptist	Tennessee	Samford University Library, Birmingham AL 35209
	Texas Baptist	1856–84 Texas	Abstracts by Helen Mason Lu. Also on microfiche from Write Dallas Genealogical Society, P.O. Box 12648, Dallas TX 75225-0648. <www.dallasgenealogy.org>
	Register	1832–34 New York	*American Vital Records from* The New York Register. 1822–34. (American Baptist Soc, 1965)
	Religious Herald	1828–1938 Virginia	*WPA Guide ... Supplement # 1: Index to Obituary Notices, 1828–1938. Same title, Supplement No. 2: Index to Marriage Notices 1828–1838.* Clearfield, 1996. Original issues 1828–date at Samford University Library, Birmingham AL 35209.
	South Carolina Baptist...	1835–65 and 1866–87	*...Working Christian, and Baptist Courier.* Abstracted in. *Marriage and Death Notices from Baptist Newspapers of South Carolina,* by Brent Holcomb, (Reprint Co., 1981). <www.scmar.com>.
	Western Recorder	Kentucky	*Western Records Indexes, 1965*–by Chauncery R. Daley Jr. (Louisville, KY: Southern Baptist Theological Seminary).
Freewill Baptist	*Morning Star* and seven other titles	1811–51 New England, esp. ME and NH	*Death Notices from Freewill Baptist Publications, 1811–1851* by David C. Young and Robert L. Taylor, (Heritage Books, 1985). *Marriage and Divorce Notices from Freewill Baptist Publications 1819–1851.* (Heritage Books, 1994). Includes notices for Quakers, Methodist, etc.
Christian	*Michigan Christian Herald*	1850–59	The *Michigan Christian Herald* Index 1850–1859 (Detroit 1991) is at <www.ancestry.com>. Microfilm at Family History Library. Original issues at Bentley Library, University of Michigan.
Christian Reformed	*The Banner* or *The Banner of Truth*	1866–1983	The Family History Library has microfilmed a scrapbook of clippings, 1866–1983, that was maintained by Ruby Mossel.
Disciples of Christ	*Christian Messenger*	1888–94	Microfilm at Family History Library and at Center for American History Texas Newspaper Collection, Dallas.
Dutch Reformed	*Christian Intelligencer*	1830–77	Abstracts of marriages and deaths published in 17 volumes by New York Genealogical & Biographical Society <www.newyorkfamilyhistory.org>
Episcopal	*Southern Churchman*	1835–1941	*Index to Marriage Notices, 1835–1951.* (Baltimore: Clearfield, reprint 1996).

Denomination	Title of Newspaper	Years Indexed and Area of Coverage	Index or Abstract. General Notes
Evangelical			See United Brethren
German Reformed	*The Messenger*	1830–39	*Genealogical Abstracts from Newspapers of the German Reformed Church 1830–1839* by Barbara Manning. (Heritage Books, 1992); & same title/author 1840–1843. (Heritage Books, 1995).
Jewish	*The St. Louis Jewish Light...*	1947–95	...and *The Jewish Post and Opinion* index in progress for the Saul Brodsky Jewish Community Library, St. Louis, <www.jewishinstlouis.org>
Lutheran	*United Church Herald*	1958–72	Obits index at Luther Theological Seminary, 2375 Como Ave. West, St. Paul, Minn 55108 <www.luthersem.edu>
Mennonite	*Herald of Truth, Gospel Witness...*	1864–current	... and *Gospel Herald, Evangelical Mennonite; Christian Evangelical;* and *Christlicher Bundesbote.* Obituary Index online at the Mennonite Library and Archives: <www.bethelks.edu/services/mla/indexes.html>.
Methodist	*Alabama Christian Advocate*	1881–1929	Indexes and Abstracts to Marriages and Obituaries, 1881–1929 by Franklin S. Moseley. Original index and issues held by Huntingdon College, Montgomery, Alabama; copies at Samford University Library, Birimingham, AL
	Christian Advocate & Journal	Sept 1827–Aug 1831	*Genealogical Gleanings from the Christian Advocate & Journal and Zion's Herald.* Dolores Haller & Marilyn Robinson. Heritage Books, 1989.
	Nashville Christian Advocate, previously the *Nashville and Louisville Christian Advocate*	1846–1910	*Index to Deaths for various years, ca1846–1910,* by Jonathan Kennon Thompson Smith online at <www.tngenweb.org>. *Genealogical Abstract of Marriages and Deaths, 1846–1851* by Annie Sandifer Trickett, (Dallas: 1985). Original issues at Luther L. Gobbel Library, Lambuth University Library, Jackson, TN; <www.lambuth.edu>.
	New Orleans Christian Advocate	Obits 1852–55 and Marriages 1851–60	Obits in *Claiborne Parish Trails Quarterly* 1:63; Marriages & Obits in *The Genie* 1:23 p59.
	New York Christian Advocate	1879, 1880	*Abstract of Vitals* Transcribed at <http://historicalsocietyunitedmethodistchurch.org/genealogy.htm>.
	Southern Christian Advocate	Indexed 1837–78.	*Marriage & Death Notices: Southern Christian Advocate 1837–1867,* 2 vols and *Marriage Notices 1868–1878; Death & Obit Notices 1867–1878* by Brent Holcomb, Box 21766, Columbia, SC 28221; <www.scmar.com/>
	Southern Christian Advocate	1837–1948	Indexes online at <www.wofford.edu/sandorTeszlerLibrary/archives/archivesObituarySearchForm.asp>
	South Carolina Christian Advocate	1948–68	Indexes online at <www.wofford.edu/sandorTeszlerLibrary/archives/archivesObituarySearchForm.asp>
	South Carolina United Methodist Advocate	1968–	Indexes online at <www.wofford.edu/sandorTeszlerLibrary/archives/archivesObituarySearchForm.asp>
	Texas Wesleyan Banner and *Texas Christian Advocate*	1850–54 and 1857–85	Seven volumes of abstracts, including a cumulate index, by Helen Mason Lu, Dallas, Texas. The Dallas Genealogical Society sells these on microfiche. Dallas Genealogical Society, P.O. Box 12648, Dallas TX 75225-0648; <www.dallasgenealogy.org>.
	Western Christian Advocate	Abstracts, 1834–50.	*Abstracts of Obituaries in the Western Christian Advocate, 1834–1850.* Waters, et al., Indiana Historical Society, 315 West Ohio St., Indianapolis IN 46204.
Moravian	*People's Press*	1851–92	*Death Notices from the* People's Press, *Salem, North Carolina.* Robert M. Tompkins, (Forsyth County Genealogical Society, 1997). A secular paper, the *People's Press* carried Moravian news items for Salem, NC, etc.
Presbyterian	*Banner of Peace & Cumberland Presbyterian Advocate*	1843–53 mostly TN, but also NY to CA	Scroggins, Margaret B., compiler. *Banner of Peace & Cumberland Presbyterian Advocate, 1843–1853.* Published by compiler, P.O. Box 473, Poplar Bluff, MO 63901, 1988. This paper was published at Lebanon, TN.
	Charleston Observer	1827–45	*Marriage and Death Notices from the* Charleston Observer *1827–1845.* Brent Holcomb. <www.scmar.com>
	The Christian Magazine...	1843–63	*Associated Reformed Presbyterian Death and Marriage Notices from The Christian Magazine of the South, The Erskine Miscellany, and The Due West Telescope* by Lowry Ware, South Carolina Magazine of Ancestral Research, P.O. Box 21766, Columbia, SC 29221. <www.scmar.com>

Denomination	Title of Newspaper	Years Indexed and Area of Coverage	Index or Abstract. General Notes
	Southwest Presbyterian	several titles, 1846–85.	See various titles by Helen Lu, i.e., *Southwest Presbyterian Newspaper Abstracts, 1869–1850.* Also on microfiche from Dallas Genealogical Society, P.O. Box 12648, Dallas TX 75225-0648; <www.dallasgenealogy.org>.
	Watchman and Observer	1845–55	*Marriage and Death Notices from the* Watchman and Observer *1845–1855.* Brent Holcomb. <www.scmar.com>
Quakers	*American Friend*	1894–1960	Quaker Friends Necrology index at <www.earlham.edu/~libr/quaker>
United Brethren in Christ	*Religious Telescope*	1835–63 obit & misc. item index	<www.rootsweb.com/~usgenweb/oh/rt.htm> to search various of these years.
	Christian Conservator	1885–1954	An obituary index by Huntington University for this title is online at <www.huntington.edu/ubhc/ubhcobit.html>. Also, condensed obituaries from other titles 1836–1894 appear in the Bush-Meeting Dutch (details at the website).
	The United Brethren	1945–94	An obituary index by Huntington University for this title is online at <www.huntington.edu/ubhc/ubhcobit.html>.
	UB	1994–2003	An obituary index by Huntington University for this title is online at <www.huntington.edu/ubhc/ubhcobit.html>.
Universalist	*Christian Leader*	1874–78 New York	Issues at Andover-Harvard Theological Library, Cambridge, MA Monroe County NY entries published *Hear Ye-Hear Ye* 16:1 (Winter 95), Rochester (NY) Genealogical Society

other reasons, it is highly probable that a marriage conducted by a circuit rider, however legal in the eyes of the church, would not appear in the civil records of that county.

The Minutes of the Methodist Conferences Annually Held in America; From 1773 to 1813 lists riders and their admission into the church, the date of ordination, and tenure.[17] There are some obituaries as well, some with excellent genealogical data. An attempt to gather information on circuit riders and on early "settled" pastors (up to 1920) is titled The Circuit Rider Database and is available on RootsWeb.com.[18]

A search for information on services performed by early riders should include the National Union Catalogue of Manuscripts Collection. A search for the subject "Circuit Riders" revealed dozens of manuscripts, including a single volume belonging to Edward Page (1787–1867), a rider who served in Pennsylvania, Delaware, Maryland, and New Jersey. His "Commonplace book, 1825–1876," located at Rutgers University Libraries in New Brunswick, New Jersey, records marriages performed 1825–1838 and 1842–1864.[19]

Missionaries and the Evangelical Movement

If your ancestor was a home or foreign missionary, you may find records, reports, and correspondence that provide excellent information. Because the mission movement was such an integral component of many denominations, the reports of the various mission stations were incorporated as a part of the larger annual denominational report. Not only were names and numbers reported, but often more personal or biographical information was shared about the interests and work of the missionaries. The health of missionaries or their family members may also be discussed. Additionally, news of births, marriages, or deaths in their families or in the communities in which they worked could be included.

These records as well as personal papers of the missionaries may be found in denominational or academic archives and libraries. Southern Baptists, for example, have a repository for resources related to foreign mission work at the International Mission Board (Richmond, Virginia <www.IMB.org>) and for home missions at the North American Mission Board (Atlanta, Georgia <www.namb.net>) and the Southern Baptist Library and Archives (Nashville, Tennessee <www.sbhla.org>). The Congregational Library and Archives in Boston, Massachusetts, has an extensive collection of that denomination's missionary records, which are described at <www.14beacon.org>. Additional depositories are listed in the denomination repository.

Missionaries were generally commissioned by individual denominations, but they were also assigned by other organizations, agencies, and cooperative interdenominational efforts as well. The records created by these organizations may also describe communities, churches and schools, and the people of the area. Preserving this material has resulted in microfilmed collections that open many doors. The following serve only as examples.

Papers of the American Home Missionary Society, 1816–1936 (385 reels and guide): The American Home Missionary Society was formed in 1826 by representatives of the Congregational, Presbyterian, Dutch Reformed, and Associate Reformed churches. This Society was the largest organization of its kind in the United States throughout the nineteenth-century. Following the Civil War, the society sent missionaries south to establish schools for all children, especially the recently freed slaves. Their collected materials detail the work of the society and its missionaries, supplying information about the communities and their people. The original documents are housed at the Amistad Research Center, Dillard University, New Orleans, Louisiana. The website is <www.tulane.edu/~amistad>. The full microfilm collection is also held by the Archives of the Billy Graham Center (see following) and other libraries and archives.

The American Missionary Association Papers, 1841–1878 (73 reels): The American Missionary Association was established in 1846 as an interdenominational missionary society devoted to abolitionist principles. The major support for the association came from Congregationalists, but it was also financially aided by Wesleyan Methodists, Free Presbyterians, and Freewill Baptists. In 1865 the association became the official agency of the Congregational churches for conducting educational work among the freedmen. Gradually, as support from other denominations declined, the association became an exclusively Congregational organization. These materials provide detailed records of schools established and the community reaction. The original records are housed at the Amistad Research Center, Dillard University, New Orleans, Louisiana. <www.tulane.edu/~amistad>.

This Catholic First Communion photograph was taken by Schanz Studio of Fort Wayne, Indiana, n.d. From the collection of Reverend Charles Banet.

The American Sunday School Union Papers: 1817–1915 (170 reels with guide): The American Sunday School Union began in Philadelphia, Pennsylvania, in 1817, as the Sunday and Adult School Union. It adopted its present name in 1824 when it was organized to promote the establishment of Sunday Schools and libraries in developing territories and states. A nondenominational organization, it drew members from the Baptist, Episcopal, Methodist, Presbyterian, Moravian, Dutch Reformed, Congregational, Lutheran, German Reformed, and Friends churches. Reports and correspondence of the Union's missionaries provide insights and information into their daily work, details about the communities (including some hand-drawn maps), and the people with whom they worked. Original papers are held in the Presbyterian Historical Society of Philadelphia (website <www.history.pcusa.org>) and the microfilm collection is in the Archives of the Billy Graham Center (see following).

The Archives of the Billy Graham Center: The Billy Graham Center Archives in Wheaton, Illinois, is an archives of Christian history that is not linked to a particular denomination. The BGC Archives collects records on the activity of evangelism, specifically evangelism that occurs outside of churches. If an ancestor was a missionary, pastor, or Christian worker associated with one of the nondenominational ministries, this is where a search would begin. Resources include papers of and pertaining to the Africa Inland Mission, the China Inland Mission, the Women's Union Missionary Society, the Mission Aviation Fellowship, Short Terms Abroad, the Moody Church, and the Billy Graham Evangelistic Association, among others. Within these collections could be correspondences, diaries, personal files, oral history interviews, or photographs about a particular missionary. In addition to papers of individuals, there are records of organizations involved in evangelism, including files of congresses and of conferences and interviews with those prominent in Christian work. Holdings information and research policies can be found online at <www.wheaton.edu/bgc/archives/archhp1.html>.[20]

Finding Church Records

Identify the Denomination

To find church records, the researcher must identify the denomination of an ancestor and the actual church of affiliation. In some families, this decision poses no problem due to a continuing religious tradition. However, individuals or families at times changed denominations; in such a case, a search is required. Perhaps the family Bible or other papers—baptismal certificates, wedding announcements, organizational certificates, or obituaries—will offer clues. These documents may reveal an organization tied to a specific denomination, a church name, or the identity and title of the person officiating at a religious ceremony or event.

Civil marriage or death records, if they exist, should provide the officiate's name. Determining that this person is clergy can help researchers identify the denomination and perhaps the congregation or local church. In small towns or rural areas, county histories often list ecclesiastical leaders and where they served. In larger cities, city directories usually list clergy and their associated church.

Marriage records are particularly good sources for determining a denomination or a church. Although a direct ancestral pair may have been married by the local justice of the peace, one or more of their siblings may have preferred a religious ceremony. Customarily, a wedding takes place in the bride's church or is performed by her pastor. Therefore, the marriages of the bride's and groom's sisters may be a link to determine which church the family attended.

Civil death records may not provide the name of the minister who conducted the service. However, these records, when thoroughly examined, can assist in the search. For example, the death certificate may note if the decedent was in the hospital; contacting the hospital may lead to information about religious affiliations and thus to a church. Likewise the death certificate usually identifies the funeral home. Funeral home records tend to list the name of the person who officiated at the service, which again may lead to a church.

Finding your ancestor's denominational connection may require taking a few detours in your research path. But this knowledge is useful in targeting a local church that he or she may have attended. A map (contemporary to the time period) of the area in which an ancestor lived can help pinpoint a specific church close to your ancestor's place of residence. In urban areas, where transportation was swift and easy, church selection may have been impacted by more than just proximity. Immigrants often attended churches where their native language was spoken, which might have been more important to them than the denomination itself. For this reason, a search of all nearby churches that held services in the native language of your ancestor may also be helpful.

Locate the Records

Once the denomination has been identified and decisions are made about the name of the most likely church of attendance, the next challenge is to locate the actual records. This quest can be yet another research adventure because early records can reside in many places.

The obvious first place to look for church records is at the church itself. If the church is still in existence and the name has not changed, use a current print telephone directory or search online for contact information.

If a church has merged with another of the same denomination, or changed denominations, the yearbook of the present denomination, such as *Annual of the Alabama Baptist State Convention*, should have the name, address, and current pastor of the new congregations.[21]

Some churches may have simply ceased to exist. Should this be the case, contact another church of the same denomination in the area and inquire about the location of the records. Utilize all available local and denominational information, including personal recollection, to help unravel the mystery. The records may have been retained by the clerk for safekeeping or, if his clerkship continued, merged with those of the new congregation. Follow the church clerk's path and you may find the new church and/or the records.

Correspondence with the church may be conducted via letter, telephone, or e-mail. When inquiring about the records and their availability, ask about the church's policies for research and confine the request to specific dates and people. Be patient. Remember that the church is not in the genealogical business. However, the majority of church personnel will want to assist in locating former members and may search the records for you, as their busy schedules permit. Should this occur, offer to reimburse for copies and time, and consider making a donation to the church, perhaps as a memorial to your ancestor.

Finally, certain denominations require that the records of defunct churches be sent to a central archive. See the section in this chapter that gives denominational contact information, or contact the state organization of the denomination.

Missing Records

If records have disappeared from the church, they may be in private hands. Sometimes the church clerk maintained the records for so many years that they became regarded as personal possessions. Or in the case of a church split, merger, or closing, the records were retained by the clerk for safekeeping. These can be difficult to locate. If possible, visit the area and contact as many relatives and former members of the church as possible.

Once the records are located, the owner may be persuaded to place them in a repository. Such was the case concerning the record book of the United Baptist Church of Christ at Mount

Pisgah, Blount County, Alabama, 1836–1876. The book was sent to a Texas relative following the death of the person who had held it for several years. The Texas family retained the original and transcribed the volume, then donated both the treasured book and the useful transcript to the Alabama Baptist repository.

If the records are known to have been destroyed, perhaps in a fire, the personal records of former pastors may be an effective substitute. Many clergymen recorded events in a diary, along with comments about sermons or church activities. After the minister's death, the diary may have stayed with the family, been sent to a denominational archives, or ended up in an antique store. The daybook of Presbyterian minister John Webster Bailey was found at a flea market by researcher Mary Balderstone. From May 1882 to September 1890, Reverend Bailey served churches in Indiana, New York, and Vermont. He recorded more than nine hundred names of members in his book along with baptisms, confirmations, marriages, deaths, and removals. Many entries are annotated, such as, "Moved to Goshen, Ind.," or "Mrd Walter Hathaway."[22]

To locate missing or substitute records of this type, see the "Finding Aids" section.

Libraries and Archives

In some communities, the local public library is the repository of genealogical materials, including church records. Larger public libraries may have a genealogical reference specialist who can assist you. You can locate libraries through print or online directories or by consulting the *American Library Directory*.[23] In addition to the library, contact the community historical or genealogical society.

The denominational archive seeks to retain records of churches both extant and defunct. While some denominations maintain an independent repository, many denominations select a denominational college or university to serve in this role. The Gardner A. Sage Library of the New Brunswick Theological Seminary (affiliated with Rutgers University) is home to the official archives of the Reformed Church in America <www.rca.org/aboutus/archives/index.html>. The Friends Historical Library, founded in 1871, is located at Swarthmore College, Swarthmore, Pennsylvania <www.swarthmore.edu/Library/friends/index.html>. Their holdings represent the largest collection in the world of Quaker meeting archives, either in the original manuscripts or on microfilm. Denominational institutions of this kind also house the church records and papers of ministers and lay leaders, as well as other related historical materials. The state denominational office can help in locating the archive.

State college and university libraries may also collect church records. The state archives and library is yet another repository to search. In some states, the state historical society has become the official archives for certain denominations; for example, the State Historical Society of Wisconsin <www.wisconsinhistory.org> serves as the repository of the United Church of Christ in that state.

Certain private libraries, not affiliated with a religious denomination, contain a vast amount of genealogical data, including church records. An example is The New York Genealogical and Biographical Society in New York City, which holds (among other important church record collections) the original Vosburgh Collection of New York State Church Records (also available on microfilm from the Family History Library in Salt Lake City). The Library of the National Society, Daughters of the American Revolution, in Washington, D.C. <www.dar.org/library/speccol.cfm> houses Bible records, private papers of ministers and lay persons, and church and denominational histories. And the manuscript department of the New England Historic Genealogical Society has collected family Bible records for over 150 years.[24]

Finding Aids

Many church records have been preserved through microfilm projects at the regional, state, and local levels. The largest ongoing microfilming activity is that of the Genealogical Society of Utah (GSU). GSU is a non-profit entity of The Church of Jesus Christ of Latter-day Saints. Microfilming teams cover the entire United States and work worldwide. The first public notice of newly acquired microfilm that is available for patron use appears in the Family History Library Catalog online at <www.familysearch.org>. Search the catalog by subject or region to locate church records, histories, and related materials.

The International Genealogical Index (IGI) indexes the entries captured on microfilm processed by GSU. Because of its plentiful baptism, confirmation, and marriage records, the IGI is a valuable resource for family historians who seek church records. Researchers who follow the indexed entry back to its source are usually richly rewarded. A reel number for the microfilm of the original records is often given, thus leading to the possibility of additional family information within the records of that church.

The National Union Catalog of Manuscript Collections (NUCMC) can help to locate out-of-place church records—those that are not in a church or a repository designated as the denominational archives. Repositories submit holdings details to the Library of Congress, which maintains the NUCMC database. The names and chief subjects of the collections are then indexed and made accessible through surname, subject, and author searches. Out-of-place reports made since 1985 may be searched online at <www.loc.gov/coll/nucmc>. Earlier reports will be in the printed volumes of the National Union Catalogue of Manuscript Collections. (See chapter 3, "General References and Guides").

The Periodical Source Index, better known as PERSI, is the largest and most widely used subject index covering genealogy and local history periodicals in North America and Canada. There are currently more than 1.7 billion searchable records representing almost six thousand periodicals received by the Allen County Public Library in Ft. Wayne, Indiana, since 1847. This is not a full text index but can locate articles and transcriptions that are primarily about church records. PERSI is available in several formats: print, CD-ROM, and online subscription service.

Early church record abstracts were often published in limited quantities, making them hard to find and quite expensive. The advent of CD-ROMs has removed that limitation. For example, six volumes of *Encyclopedia of American Quaker Genealogy* by William Wade Hinshaw are available on CD-ROM from Genealogical Publishing Company.[25] Another CD-ROM collection is *Pennsylvania German Church Records 1729–1870*.[26] Two newer issues are *Records of the Churches of Boston* and *Plymouth Church Records 1620–1859*.[27] Remember to use these collections with the knowledge that, despite the best efforts of the abstractor or transcriber, mistakes occur and data may be omitted. Therefore, make every effort to locate the original record or a microfilm copy.

A relatively new and growing resource is the USGenWeb Church Records Project. This began in 2000 and now has contributions for many counties. The project relies on contributions by volunteers who transcribe local area church records, church histories, minutes, and other useful information. Their work is placed online and accessed through the main website at <www.rootsweb.com/~usgenweb/churches>. Although individuals' names are not always indexed, a search by state and county name will reveal the title of the record and then display the transcription. Many of the transcribed entries are from the pre-1800 era.

During the period 1938–1942, the Works Progress Administration (later called the Work Projects Administration), or WPA, located and inventoried church records in many states. This was part of the Historical Records Survey (HRS), the most ambitious archival survey ever undertaken in the United States. Although the goal of the HRS was to locate, describe, and publish all church (and other public and some private) records, much remained undone when the project ended in 1942. The extent of completion varies from state to state. For example, in Vermont, only three books were published. Both the published volumes and the far greater amount of unpublished survey material can be used to discover what records were available and where they were located during the time of the HRS survey. Information about the printed volumes and remaining manuscripts is usually available at the appropriate state archives.[28]

Access to Records

If the original records have not been microfilmed or catalogued but are still in the custody of the church, obtaining permission to see the record is required. Religious records are not public records, and the caretaker is not legally obliged to provide information or to allow examination. When requesting data from local church records, state the request in specific terms. Provide names and dates or, at the least, a short time span for a search. Do not expect the pastor or secretary to perform long involved searches.

Churches with large memberships often have websites that give a research policy and an e-mail address. If a request is made by postal mail, it should include a self-addressed, stamped envelope. After any request, be patient and allow adequate time for a response. Be patient; allow time for a response. Often work of this type is done by church volunteers who have many other responsibilities. If the church staff is kind enough to look up and send information, a thank-you note and small donation is in order. If an on-site inspection is possible, an appointment should be scheduled for the church staff's convenience. During your visit, treat the records carefully and acknowledge your appreciation. Consider making a small donation in your ancestor's honor or to be used by the church towards records preservation.

If an on-site visit is not possible, contact the local library or historical society for a list of local researchers who may be willing and able to conduct research in these records. If appropriate, suggest that the records might be loaned to an archive or repository for preservation and then returned to the owner.

Summary

To most effectively locate and use church records, a researcher must consult all available civil and/or private records, talk with residents in the area, and initiate contact with a variety of repositories and organizations that may house the records. Armed with all this information, you are ready to tackle the records themselves. Some general and denominational specific suggestions for success follow.

Church records allow the researcher to view an ancestor and/or community in a particular place and time as no other documents can. These materials provide an added dimension of one's culture and heritage. Contained in the pages of these volumes are the joys and sorrows, disappointments and successes of our people.

Contact Information, Sources, and Commentary on Selected Denominations

The following entries provide information to better direct research. Most entries give repository contact information and a sources to assist the reader in finding and understanding records. The researcher is encouraged to consult the general references at the chapter's end for a more comprehensive listing of titles.

Entries for a few denominations include brief commentary to identify complicated historical changes that need to be considered

Tent revival at Fairmont Baptist Church, Red Level, Alabama, n.d. From Special Collection, Samford University Library, Birmingham, Alabama.

when undertaking research. Those entries with commentary may or may not include repository contact information and other sources.

Most denominations have undergone many changes over the years, and they continue to evolve. The church denominational name your ancestor knew may not exist today. It is recommended that the following references be consulted before research begins:

- The American Yearbook of Churches at <www.electronicchurch.org>
- The Billy Graham Research Center at <www.wheaton.edu/bgc/archives/nowatch.html>

These two sites provide current and more detailed information about denominations and give links to many archives.

Finally, study the history of the area. For example, in slave-holding states prior to the Civil War, records of the local area's established churches should be consulted for entries that will include African Americans.

These notes are neither exhaustive nor inclusive but are presented merely to serve as information to better direct research in some denominations.

Adventist

Contact Information

Adventist Heritage Center
James White Library
Andrews University
Berrien Springs, MI 49104-1400
E-mail address: ahc@andrews.edu

Goddard Library
Gordon-Conwell Theological Seminary
130 Essex Street
South Hamilton, MA 01982
Web address: www.gordonconwell.edu/library/hamilton/index.php

Seventh-Day Adventists General Conference Archives
1501 Old Columbia Pike
Silver Spring, MD 20904-6600

African American Religions

Sources

The Black Church in America. Indianapolis: Lilly Endowment, 1992.

Directory of African American Religious Bodies: A Compendium by the Howard University School of Divinity, edited by Wardell J. Payne. Washington, D.C.: Howard University Press, 1991.

Encyclopedia of African American Religions, edited by Larry G. Murphy, J. Gordon Melton, and Gary L. Ward. New York: Garland Publishers, 1993.

Raboteau, Albert J. *A Fire in the Bones: Reflections on African-American Religious History.* Boston: Beach Hill Press, 1995.

Richardson, Harry V. *Dark Salvation: The Story of Methodism as It Developed Among Blacks in America*. Garden City, N.Y.: Anchor Press, 1976.

Sanders, Cheryl Jeanne. *Saints in Exile: The Holiness-Pentacostal Experience in African-American Religion and Culture*. New York: Oxford University Press, 1999.

African Methodist Episcopal

Commentary

Organized in 1816, the African Methodist Episcopal Church is a United States Methodist Church not affiliated with the United Methodist Church governmentally. It developed from a congregation formed by some Philadelphia-area slaves and former slaves who built Bethel African Methodist Church in that city. In 1799, Richard Allen was ordained minister of the church by Bishop Francis Asbury of the Methodist Episcopal Church. In 1816, Allen was consecrated as bishop of the newly formed Methodist Episcopal Church. After the Civil War, the church grew rapidly in the South. It holds a general conference every four years and has about 1,200,000 members. The website for the Fifth Episcopal District Headquarters in Los Angeles <www.ame-church.org> has links to dozens of other AME church sites.

Baptists

Commentary

There are approximately 134 separate kinds of Baptists, including Southern, United, Regular, Seed Baptist (Indiana), Primitive, Freewill (sometimes Free Will), Seventh Day, Regular, Landmark, and Independent Fundamental. Try to determine the kind of Baptist your ancestor was and narrow your search to a state and county. Baptists have this basic organizational pattern: churches belong to associations (composed of churches from a particular area/county) and to a state convention. Records are usually maintained by the church, but the associational or state offices can be of assistance in locating a church, or information if the church is defunct. Today, many Baptist archives and repositories, regardless of their own particular affiliation, acquire materials from all types of Baptist denominations. Should the repository that is contacted not have the requested church records, it may still be able to assist in a search.

Contact Information

American Baptist

Samuel Colgate Baptist Historical Library of the American Baptist Historical Society
1100 South Goodman Street
Rochester, NY 14620-2532
Web address: http://67.98.94.4/abhs

American Baptist Historical Society
Archives Center
PO Box 851
Valley Forge, PA 19482-0851

Andover Newton Theological School
(including the Backus Historical Society)
210 Herrick Road
Newton Centre, MA 02459
Web address: www.ants.edu/ftlibrary/index.htm

Freewill Baptist

The Edmund S. Muskie Archives and Special Collection Library
Bates College
70 Campus Avenue
Lewiston, ME 04240

Missionary Baptist (Southern)

Southern Baptist Library and Archives
The Southern Baptist Convention Building
901 Commerce Street
Nashville, TN 37203-3630
Web address: www.sbhla.org

Woman's Missionary Union
Hunt Library and Archives
Highway 280 East
100 Missionary Ridge
Birmingham, AL 35242-5235
E-mail address: library@wmu.org

Special Collection Baptist Historical Collection
Furman University Library
3300 Poinsett Highway
Greenville, SC 29613
Web address: http://library.furman.edu

Georgia Baptist History Depository
Jack Tarver Library
Mercer University
1300 Edgewood Drive
Macon, GA 31207
Web address: http://mainlib.mercer.edu

North Carolina Baptist Historical Collection
Z. Smith Reynolds Library
PO Box 7777
Wake Forest University
Winston-Salem, NC 27109-7777
Web address: www.wfu.edu/zsr

Special Collections
Riley-Hickingbotham Library
Ouachita Baptist University
Box 3729
Arkadelphia, AR 71998
Web address: www.obu.edu/library

Baptist Center History Library
Baptist Convention of Maryland-Delaware
10255 Old Columbia Road
Columbia, MD 21046-1716

Mississippi Baptist Historical Collection
Leland Speed Library
101 West College Street
PO Box 127
Clinton, MS 39060
E-mail address: library@mc.edu

Virginia Baptist Historical Society Library
PO Box 34
University of Richmond, VA 23173

Special Collection
Samford University Library
800 Lakeshore Dr.
Birmingham, AL 35229
Web address: http://library.samford.edu/about/special.html

James Boyce Centennial Library
Southern Baptist Theological Seminary
2825 Lexington Road
Louisville, KY 40280
E-mail address: archives@lib.sbts.edu

The Texas Baptist Historical Collection
4144 N. Central Expressway, Suite 110
Dallas, Texas 75204
E-mail address: tbhc@bgct.org

The Roberts Library
Southwestern Baptist Theological Seminary
PO Box 22000
Fort Worth, TX 76122
Web address: www.swbts.edu/libraries/roberts.cfm

Primitive Baptist

The Primitive Baptist Library
416 Main Street
Carthage, IL 62321
E-mail address: bwebb9@juno.com
Web address: www.carthage.lib.il.us/community/churches/primbap/pbl.html

Swedish Baptist

Bethel Theological Seminary Library
3949 Bethel Dr.
St. Paul, MN 55112

Swenson Swedish Research Center
Box 175
Augustana College
639 38th Street
Rock Island, IL 61201-2296
E-mail address: sag@augustana.edu

Seventh Day Baptist

Seventh Day Baptist Library
Seventh Day Baptist Building
Plainfield, NJ 07060

Seventh Day Baptist Historical Society Library
PO Box 1678
Janesville, WI 53547-1678
E-mail address: sdhist@inwave.com

Sources

Brackney, William Henry, ed. *Historical Dictionary of the Baptists*. Lanham, Md.: Scarecrow Press, 1999.

Encyclopedia of Southern Baptists. 4 vols. Nashville: Broadman, 1958–82

Helmbold, F. Wilbur. "Baptist Records for Genealogy and History." *National Genealogical Quarterly* 61 (September 1973): 168–78.

Lasher, George W. *The Ministerial Directory of the Baptist Churches in the United States of America*. Oxford, Ohio: Ministerial Directory Co., [1899].

Leonard, Bill. *Dictionary of Baptists in America*. Downers Grove, Ill.: Intervarsity Press, 1994.

McBeth, Leon. *The Baptist Heritage*. Nashville, Tenn.: Broadman Press, 1987.

McLaughlin, William G. *New England Dissent, 1630–1833: The Baptists and Separation of Church and State*. 2 vols. Cambridge, Mass.: Harvard University Press, 1971.

Menkus, Belden. "The Baptist Sunday School Board and Its Records." *American Archivist* 24, no. 4 (October 1961): 441–44.

Piepkorn, Arthur Carl. "The Primitive Baptists of North America." *Baptist History and Heritage* 7 (January 1972): 33–51.

Starr, Edward Caryl. *A Baptist Bibliography, Being a Register of Printed Material By and About Baptists*. 25 vols. Rochester, N.Y.: American Baptist Historical Society, 1947–76.

Brethren in Christ Church

Contact Information

Brethren in Christ Church Historical Library and Archives
Messiah College
PO Box 3002, 1 College Avenue
Grantham, PA 17027-9795
E-mail address: dsteckbe@messiah.edu

Church of the Brethren

Contact Information

Ashland Theological Library
Roger E. Darling Memorial Library
910 Center Street
Ashland, OH 44805
Web address: www.ashland.edu/seminary/academics-library.html

Brethren Historical Library and Archives
1451 Dundee Ave.
Elgin, IL 60120
E-mail address: kshaffer_gb@brethren.org

Beeghly Library
Juniata College
1815 Moore Street
Huntingdon, PA 16652
E-mail address: library@juniata.edu

German-American Pietist-Anabaptist background

Bethany Theological Seminary
Butterfield and Meyers Rds.
Oak Brook, IL 60521

Church of Christ, Scientist

Contact Information

Archives and Library of the Mother Church
The First Church of Christ, Scientist
Christian Science Plaza
International Headquarters
175 Huntington Avenue
Boston, MA 02115

Longyear Museum
Daycroft Library
1125 Boylston Street (Route 9)
Chestnut Hill, MA 02467
E-mail address: letters@longyear.org

Church of God

Sources

For all bodies under this name, see the current *Yearbook of American and Canadian Churches* <www.electronicchurch.org>

Church of Jesus Christ of Latter-day Saints, The (Mormons; Latter-day Saint Church; LDS)

Commentary

The Church of Jesus Christ of Latter-day Saints, also known as the Mormon Church, was organized by Joseph Smith Jr., in Fayette, New York, on 6 April 1830. As membership grew, so did persecution, causing members to move from New York to Ohio, then to Missouri and Illinois. By the late 1840s, the Mormons were again migrating, this time to what would become Utah. A more detailed history is at <www.mormon.org>. In addition to the expected record-keeping of vital events, the Church took a census every four years from 1914 to 1950 (except for 1945 during World War II). Not all members were included, but for many who were, the entire family is listed along with places and dates of birth. In addition, more than in any other denomination, Latter-day Saints are encouraged to keep journals and personal records. Church members have contributed more than eight million family group records for searching by all who are interested in their family's heritage. Indexes to many of these records will be found online at <www.familysearch.org>. Similar records can also be found on <www.ancestry.com>, including an *LDS Member Name Index, 1830–45*, and the *LDS Biographical Encyclopedia*.

Contact Information

Family History Library
35 North West Temple Street
Salt Lake City, UT 84150-3400
E-mail address: fhl@ldschurch.org

LDS Church Historical Department
Archives/Library
50 East North Temple
Salt Lake City, UT 84150

Brigham Young University
Center for Church History
Provo, UT 84602

Sources

Jensen, Andrew. *LDS Biographical Encyclopedia.* 4 vols. Draper, Utah: Gregg Koffard Books, 2003. Also online at <www.ancestry.com>.

Ludlow, Daniel H., ed. *Encyclopedia of Mormonism.* 5 vols. New York: Macmillan, 1992.

Churches of Christ

Contact Information

Harding Graduate School of Religion Library
1000 Cherry Rd.
Memphis, TN 38117

Congregational

Commentary

As a result of mergers, schisms, and other historical developments, at least three denominations contain Congregational Churches or former Congregational Churches: Congregational Christian Churches (National Association), Unitarian Universalist Association, and the United Church of Christ. Many early Congregational Church records will be found in compilations such as Jay Mack Holbrook, *Massachusetts Vital Records to 1850* (Oxford, Mass.: Holbrook Institute, 1983) series published by The New England Historic Genealogical Society and in other New England town vital record books.

Contact Information

Congregational Library and Archive
14 Beacon Street
Boston, MA 02108

Sources

Taylor, Richard H. *Southern Congregational Churches.* Benton Harbor, Mich.: R. H. Taylor, 1994.

Youngs, J. William T. *The Congregationalists.* New York: Greenwood Press, 1990.

Disciples of Christ

Contact Information

Christian Theological Seminary
1000 W. 42nd Street
Indianapolis, IN 46208
Web address: www.cts.edu

Carl Johann Memorial Library
Culver-Stockton College
#1 College Hill
Canton, MO 63435

The Disciples of Christ Historical Society
1101 Nineteenth Avenue South
Nashville, TN 37212
Web address: www.dishistsoc.org

Lexington Theological Seminary
631 S. Limestone
Lexington, KY 40508
Web address: www.lextheo.edu/library.html

Mary Couts Burnett Library
Texas Christian University
PO Box 198400
Fort Worth, TX 76219

Sources

Garrison, W. E., and A. T. DeGroot. *The Disciples of Christ, a History*. St. Louis: Bethany Press, 1948.

Harrell, David Edwin, Jr. *Quest for a Christian American 1800–1865: A Social History of the Disciples of Christ.* Vol 1. in the series, Religon and American Culture. Tuscaloosa: University of Alabama Press, 2003.

———. *Sources of Division in the Disciples of Christ, 1865–1900.* Vol 2. in the series, Religon and American Culture. Tuscaloosa: University of Alabama Press, 2003.

Episcopal Church U.S.A.—see also Protestant Episcopal

Contact Information

The Archives of the Episcopal Church U.S.A.
Records Administration Office: Episcopal Church Center
815 Second Avenue
New York, NY 10017-4594
E-mail address: Research@episcopalarchives.org

Historical Society of the Episcopal Church
PO Box 2098
Manchaca, Texas 78652-2098

Evangelical Congregational Church

Contact Information

Evangelical Congregational Historical Society
Evangelical School of Theology
121 S. College Street
Meyerstown, PA 17067
E-mail address: theisey@evangelical.edu

Evangelical Covenant Church of America

Contact Information

Evangelical Covenant Church of America
Archives and Special Collections of North Park University
3225 West Foster Avenue
Chicago, IL 60625-4895
E-mail address: archives@northpark.edu

Evangelical Free Church of America

Contact Information

Evangelical Free Church of America
901 East 78th Street
Minneapolis, MN 55420
E-mail address: adminfin@efca.org

Evangelical United Brethren Church—see also Methodist

Sources

Leedy, Roy B. *The Evangelical Church in Ohio Being a History of the Ohio Conference and Merged Conferences of the Evangelical Church in Ohio, Now the Evangelical United Brethren Church, 1816–1951.* Cleveland: Evangelical Press, 1959.

Greek Orthodox

Contact Information

Greek Orthodox Archdiocese of North America
Department of Archives
8 East 79th Street
New York, NY 10021
E-mail address: archives@goarch.org

For other Eastern Orthodox Church archives, see the *Yearbook of American and Canadian Churches* <www.electronicchurch.org>.

Huguenot (French Protestants of the Reformed Church)

Contact Information

The Huguenot Historical Society
18 Broadhead Avenue
New Paltz, NY 12561
E-mail address: library@hhs-newpaltz.org

The Huguenot Society of America
122 East 58th Street
New York, NY 10022
Web address: www.huguenotsocietyofamerica.org

The National Huguenot Society
9033 Lyndale Avenue S. #108
Bloomington, MN 55420-3535
Web address: www.huguenot.netnation.com

Sources

Allen, Cameron. "Records of the Huguenots in the United States, Canada, and the West Indies with Some Mention of Dutch and German Sources." A paper delivered at the World Conference on Records and Genealogical Seminar, 5–8 August 1969, Area F-10, Salt Lake City, sponsored by The Church of Jesus Christ of Latter-day Saints. FHL microfiche 6039362. Much of this material also appears in "Huguenot Migrations" in the American Society of Genealogists, *Genealogical Research: Methods and Sources,* 256–90. Vol. 2. Washington, D.C.: American Society of Genealogists, 1971.

Baird, Charles W. *History of the Huguenot Emigration to America.* 2 vols. reprinted as one. Baltimore: Genealogical Publishing Co., 1998.

Butler, Jon. *Huguenots in America: A Refugee People in New World Society* (Harvard Historical Mongraphs). Harvard University Press, 1984.

Jewish

Contact Information

American Jewish Archives
3101 Clifton Ave.
Cincinnati, OH 45220
Web address: www.americanjewisharchives.org/intro.html

American Jewish Historical Society
10 Thornton Dr.
Waltham, MA 02154
Web address: www.ajhs.org

YIVO Institute for Jewish Research
555 W. 57th Street
New York, NY 10019

Sources

Avotaynu: The International Review of Jewish Genealogy. 1985–. PO Box 900, Teaneck, NJ 07666.

Kurzweil, Arthur, and Elie Wiesel. *From Generation to Generation: How to Trace Your Jewish Genealogy and Family History.* New York: Jossey-Bass, 2004.

Rottenberg, Dan. *Finding Our Fathers: A Guidebook to Jewish Genealogy*. 1977; reprint, Baltimore: Genealogical Publishing Co., 1998. Especially note chapter 6, "Jewish Sources in America."

Stern, Malcolm H. *First American Jewish Families: 600 Genealogies, 1654–1977*. 1978; reprint, Baltimore: Genealogical Publishing Co., 1991.

Lutheran

Commentary

Lutheran church records rank among the best available in terms of research content and preservation. They are invaluable for tracing German or Scandinavian ancestors, even though the numerous synods may appear baffling. Frederick S. Weiser, an authority on German records, has translated, transcribed, and published volumes of primarily Lutheran church records and documents of Lutheran pastors. His publications, both monographs and periodical articles, focus on the Lutheran church records from Maryland, Pennsylvania, and New York.

As a result of a merger in 1988, the majority of American Lutherans now belong to a unified body called the Evangelical Lutheran Church in America (ELCA).

The American Church, formed in 1960, was composed largely of the Evangelical Lutheran Church (Norwegian American), the United Evangelical Lutheran Church (Danish American), and American Lutheran Church (Midwestern German American). The Lutheran Church in America (LCA) was formed in 1962 by the consolidation of the Augustana Evangelical Church (Swedish American), Finnish Evangelical Lutheran Church (Finnish American), American Evangelical Lutheran Church (Danish American), and the United Lutheran Church in America (German American) churches of the eastern and midwestern United States.

Contact Information

The Evangelical Lutheran Church in America
321 Bonnie Lane
Elk Grove, IL 60007
E-mail address: archives@elca.org

The creation of the ELCA also began an archival system featuring regional repositories

ELCA Region 1 Archives (Alaska, Idaho, Montana, Oregon, Washington)
Mortvedt Library
Pacific Lutheran University
Tacoma, WA 98447-0013
Web address: www.plu.edu

ELCA Region 2 Archives (Arizona, California, Colorado, Hawaii, New Mexico, Nevada, Utah, Wyoming)
Pacific Lutheran Theological Seminary
2770 Marin Ave.
Berkeley, CA 94708-1597
Web address: www.plts.edu

ELCA Region 3 Archives (Montana, North Dakota, South Dakota)
2481 Como Ave. W.
St. Paul, MN 55108-1445

ELCA Region 4 Archives (Arkansas, Kansas, Louisiana, Missouri, Nebraska, Oklahoma, Texas)

For Arkansas and Oklahoma:
Arkansas-Oklahoma Synod
4803 S. Lewis Ave.
Tulsa, OK 74105-5199

For Kansas and Missouri:
Bethany College
Wallerstedt Learning Center
421 N. First Street
Lindsborg, Kansas 67456-1897
Web address: www.bethanylb.edu

For Texas and Louisiana:
The Rev. Arnold Moede
205 Coventry
Seguin, TX 78155

For Nebraska:
Ms. Vivian Peterson
1325 N. Platte Ave.
Fremont, NE 68025

ELCA Region 5 Archives (Illinois, Iowa, Wisconsin, upper Michigan)
333 Wartburg Place
Dubuque, IA 52003-7797

ELCA Region 6 Archives (Indiana, Kentucky, lower Michigan, Ohio)
Trinity Lutheran Seminary
2199 E. Main Street
Columbus, OH 43209
Web address: www.trinitylutheranseminary.edu/Library-EducationalResources/HammaLibrary.asp

ELCA Region 7 Archives (New York [except Metropolitan New York City], New Jersey, eastern Pennsylvania, New England, and the non-geographic Slovak-Zion Synod)
Lutheran Archives Center
7301 Germantown Avenue
Philadelphia, PA 19119
E-mail address: mtairyarchives@ltsp.edu

For Metropolitan New York Synod:
Lutheran Church Archives
Hormann Library
Wagner College
Staten Island, NY 10301

ELCA Region 8 Archives (Delaware, Maryland, central and western Pennsylvania, northern Virginia, West Virginia, Washington, D.C.)

For western Pennsylvania, West Virginia, and western Maryland:
Archives
Thiel College
75 College Avenue
Greenville, PA 16125

For central Pennsylvania, Delaware, eastern Maryland, and Washington, D.C.:
A. R. Wentz Library
Lutheran Theological Seminary
Gettysburg, PA 17325

ELCA Region 9 Archives (Alabama, Florida, Georgia, Mississippi, North Carolina, South Carolina, Tennessee, Virginia, and the Caribbean Synod)

For North Carolina:
ELCA North Carolina Synod
1988 Lutheran Synod Drive
Salisbury, NC 28144

For South Carolina:
ELCA South Carolina Synod
PO Box 43
Columbia, SC 29202-0043

For Alabama, Florida, Georgia, Mississippi, Tennessee, and the Caribbean Synod:
ELCA Region 9 Archives
Lutheran Theological Southern Seminary
4201 N. Main Street
Columbia, SC 29203
Web address: www.ltss.edu

For Virginia:
ELCA Virginia Synod
PO Drawer 70
Salem, VA 24153

Sources

Bodensieck, Julius, ed. *The Encyclopedia of the Lutheran Church*. 3 vols. Minneapolis: Augsburg Publishing House, 1965.

Luecker, Erwin L., ed. *Lutheran Cyclopedia*. St. Louis: Concordia, 1975.

Nelson, E. Clifford, ed. *The Lutherans in North America*. Philadelphia: Fortress Press, 2003.

Roebel, A. G. *Palatines, Liberty, and Property: German Lutherans in Colonial British America*. Reprint, Baltimore: John Hopkins University Press, 1998.

Wittman, Elisabeth. "The Evangelical Lutheran Church in America Churchwide Archives." *Illinois Libraries* 74 (November 1992): 467–69.

Lutheran—Finnish American Churches

Contact Information

Finnish American Historical Archives
Finlandia University
601 Quincy Street
Hancock, MI 49930

Lutheran—Missouri Synod

Commentary

The second largest Lutheran denomination is the Missouri Synod. This church is much more theologically conservative than those that merged to form the Evangelical Lutheran Church in America. Largely Midwestern and German in background, it also contains some Slovak and Finnish Lutheran congregations.

Contact Information

Concordia Historical Institute
Department of Archives and History of the Missouri Synod (LCMS)
801 De Mun Avenue
St. Louis, MO 63105
E-mail address: webmaster@chi.lcms.org

Lutheran—Swedish American Churches

Contact Information

The Swenson Center
Box 175
Augustana College
639 38th Street
Rock Island, IL 61201-2296
E-mail address: sag@augustana.edu

Lutheran—Wisconsin Synod (Wisconsin Evangelical Lutheran Synod)

Commentary

This denomination is ultra-conservative in its doctrine. It is German American in background, and the congregations are concentrated in the upper Midwest with a scattering elsewhere.

Contact Information

WELS Archives
Wisconsin Lutheran Seminary
1831 N. Seminary Drive, 65W
Mequon, WI 53092
E-mail address: archives@wls.wels.net

Mennonites

Commentary

Founded in Switzerland in the 1500s after secession from the Zurich state church, the followers of Jacob Ammann broke from the other Mennonites in Switzerland and Alsace in 1693. Most Amish Mennonites immigrated to Pennsylvania in the eighteenth century when others rejoined the main Mennonite group. Mennonites place the Bible as the sole rule of faith and shun worldly ways and modern innovation (education and technology). The sacraments are adult baptism and communion.

Contact Information

Contact Information for Selected Mennonite Historical Libraries and Archives
Web address: www.bethelks.edu/services/mla/guide/guide.html

Mennonite Historical Library
1700 S. Main
Goshen, IN 46526
E-mail address: mhl@goshen.edu
Web address: www.goshen.edu/mhl

Center for Mennonite Brethren Studies
1717 South Chestnut Avenue
Fresno, CA 93702
Web address: http://fresno.edu/dept/library/cmbs

Mennonite Historical Library
Musselman Library
Bluffton College
280 West College Avenue, Ste.1
Bluffton, OH 45817-1196

Mennonite Library and Archives
Bethel College
300 East 27th Street
North Newton, KS 67117-0531
Web address: www.bethelks.edu

Menno Simons Historical Library Hartzler Library
Eastern Mennonite University
1200 Park Road
Harrisonburg, VA 22802-2462
Web address: www.emu.edu/library

Lancaster Mennonite Historical Society
2215 Millstream Rd.
Lancaster, PA 17602
Web address: www.lmhs.org

Sources

The Mennonite Encyclopedia. 5 vols. Scottdale, Pa.: Herald Press, 1990.

Methodist

Commentary

Today's Methodist Church is the descendent of several predecessors. They are (briefly) the following: Methodist Episcopal Church (1784–1939), Methodist Episcopal Church, South (1845–1939), Methodist Protestant Church (1828–1939), Methodist Church (1939–1968), United Brethren in Christ (1800–1946), Evangelical Association (1803–1922), United Evangelical Church (1894–1922), Evangelical Church (1922–1946), Evangelical United Brethren (1946–1968), and United Methodist Church (1968–present). For further details, consult the time line at <www.gcah.org/UMC_timeline.htm>. In addition to church and conference records, the Methodists published state conference newspapers, such as the nineteenth-century *Southern Christian Advocate*. An index to obituaries in the *Southern Christian Advocate (1837–1948, South Carolina Methodist Advocate (1948–1968) and South Carolina United Methodist Advocate (1968–)* is at Wofford College Library Archives (Spartenburg, S.C.) at <www.wofford.edu/sandorTeszlerLibrary/archives/archivesObituarySearchForm.asp>.

The Evangelical United Brethren published some English and some foreign-language newspapers; an index to the obituaries in several of these UB denominational papers is at <www.huntington.edu/ubhc/ubhcobit.html>. An index to the following denominational newspapers may be searched at <www.huntington.edu/ubhc/ubhcobit.html>: *Christian Conservator* (1885–1954) *The United Brethren* (1954–1994); The UB (1994–2003); The Religious Telescope (1834–1849); *Der Christliche Apologete*, 1888–January 1889; *Der Christliche Botschafter*, selections from 1836–1865, *Die Deutsche Telescope* (The German

Telescope), April 1847–April 1850; *Evangelical Messenger*, 1848–1866; *Die Evangelische Zeitschrift* (The Evangelical Journal), January–November 1894; *Der Frohliche Botschafter* (The Joyful Messenger), December 1851–April 1866; and *Die Geschaeftige Martha* (The Busy Martha), July 1841–December 1851.

Contact Information

Archives and Special Collections
Roy O. West Library
DePauw University
Greencastle, IN 46153
Web address: www.archives@depauw.edu

Center for Evangelical United Brethren Studies
United Theological Seminary
1810 Harvard Blvd.
Dayton, OH 45406
Web address: www.utscom@united.edu

Center for Methodist Studies at Bridwell Library
Perkins School of Theology
Southern Methodist University
Dallas, TX 75222
Web address: www.smu.edu/bridwell/html/studies.html

Historical Society of The United Methodist Church
Webaddress: http://historicalsocietyunitedmethodistchurch.org/genealogy.htm

Interdenominational Theological Center Library
671 Beckwith Street S.W.
Atlanta, GA 30314
Web address: www.itc.edu

Manuscript Department
Duke University Library
Duke University
Durham, NC 27706
Web address: www.lib.duke.edu

Marston Memorial Historical Center and Archives
Free Methodist Church
PO Box 535002
Indianapolis, IN 46253-5002
E-mail address: History@fmcna.org

New England Methodist Historical Society Library
Boston University
School of Theology
745 Commonwealth Ave.
Boston, MA 02215

Pitts Theology Library
Emory University
Atlanta, GA 30322
Web address: www.pitts.emory.edu

The Swenson Swedish Center
Box 175
Augustana College
Rock Island, IL 61201

The United Library
2121 Sheridan
Evanston, IL 60201
E-mail address: k-kordesh@garrett.edu

United Methodist Archives Center
General Commission on Archives and History of the United Methodist Church
PO Box 127
Drew University
Madison, NJ 07940
Web address: http://depts.drew.edu/lib/methodist/index.html

Sources

Batsel, John, and Lyda Batsel. *Union List of United Methodist Serials 1773–1973*. General Commission on Archives and History, United Methodist Church with the United Methodist Librarians Fellowship, and Garrett Theological Seminar, 1974.

General Commission on Archives and History of the United Methodist Church. *The Directory.* Madison, N.J.: United Methodist Church, 1981.

Harmon, Nolan B., ed. *The Encyclopedia of World Methodism.* 2 vols. Nashville: United Methodist Publishing House, 1974. Prepared and edited under the supervision of the World Methodist Council and the Commission on Archives and History.

Minutes of the Methodist Conferences Annually Held in America; From 1773 to 1813 Inclusive Volume The First. New York: 1813; reprint, Swainsboro, Ga.: Magnolia Press, 1983.

Richey, Russell E., and Kenneth Rowe, eds. *The Methodist Experience in American: A Sourcebook*. Nashville: Abingdon Press, 2000.

Moravian

Contact Information

Moravian Archives
41 West Locust Street
Bethlehem, PA 18018
E-mail address: morarchbeth@enter.net

Moravian Archives
Box L
Winston-Salem, NC 27108
E-mail address: nblum@mcsp.org

Moravian Historical Society
214 East Center Street
Nazareth, PA 18064
Web address: www.moravianhistoricalsociety.org

Sources

Fries, Adelaide, et al. *Records of the Moravians in North Carolina, 1752–1866*. 11 vols. out of print. Vol. 12, 1856–66, edited by C. Daniel Crews and Lisa D. Bailey. Raleigh: North Carolina Archives, 2002.

Hamilton, J. Taylor, and Kenneth G. Hamilton. *History of the Moravian Church: The renewed Unitas Fratum, 1722–1957*. Bethlehem, Pa.: Interprovincial Board of Christian Education, 1967.

Hamilton, Kenneth G. "The Resources of the Moravian Church Archives." *Pennsylvania History* 27 (1960): 263–72.

Reichel, Levin T. *The Moravians in North Carolina*. Baltimore: Clearfield Co., 2002; reprint of 1857 editon.

Native American Religions

Sources

Carmody, Denise Lardner, and John Tully Carmondy. *Native American Religions*. New York: Paulist Press, 1993.

Collins, John James. *Native American Religions: A Geographical Survey*. Lewiston, N.Y.: Edwin Mellen Press, 1991.

McCoy, Isaac. *History of Baptist Indian Missions*. 1840; reprint, Springfield, Mo.: Particular Baptist Press, 2003.

Shea, John Gilmary. *History of the Catholic Missions among the Indian Tribes of the United States*. New York: Arno Press, 1969.

Nazarene

Contact Information

Nazarene Archives/Church of the Nazarene
6401 The Paseo
Kansas City, MO 64131
E-mail address: archives@nazarene.org

Pentecostal

Contact Information

Holy Spirit Research Center
Oral Roberts University
7777 South Lewis Avenue
Tulsa, OK 74171
E-mail address: hsrc@oru.edu

Flower Pentecostal Heritage Center
Assemblies of God Archives
1445 Boonville Avenue
Springfield, MO 65802
E-mail address: Archives@ag.org

Hal Bernard Dixon, Jr. Pentecostal Research Center
Church of God (Cleveland, Tenn.)
260 11th Street, N.E.
Cleveland, TN 37311
E-mail address: Dixon_research@leeuniversity.edu

International Pentecostal Church Archives and Research Center
PO Box 12609
Oklahoma City, OK 73157
E-mail address: archives@iphc.org

Presbyterian

Commentary

The father of America Presbyterianism was Francis Makemie (1658–1708), of Scotch-Irish descent, who came to the eastern shore of Maryland in 1683 where he began preaching. In 1716 the Synod of Philadelphia was formed. The colonial revival caused a temporary division (1745–58) into Old Side and New Side bodies. Presbyterianism grew rapidly and by the beginning of the Revolution ranked second to Congregationalism as the most numerous religious body in the colonies. The Plan of Union of 1801 provided for cooperation between Presbyterians and Congregationlists on the frontier, and a large number of Congregational churches became Presbyterian. Resulting controversy divided the main body of American Presbyterians into Old School and New School bodies in 1837–38. Division over the Civil War caused the southern bodies to form the Presbyterian Church in the United States; the northern wings merged in 1869–70 as the Presbyterian Church in the U.S.A. The United Presbyterian church was formed in 1858 by the union of two covenanter groups, the Associate Reformed and the Associate. In 1958 the Presbyterian Church in the U.S.A. merged with the United Presbyterian Church as the United Presbyterian Church in the U.S.A. The sacraments are infant baptism and communion. The church is organized as a system of courts in which clergy and lay members participate at local, regional, and national levels. Services are simple with emphasis on the sermon.

Contact Information

Presbyterian Historical Society
Montreat Office
PO Box 849
Montreat, NC 28757
Web address: www.history.pcusa.org

Philadelphia Office
425 Lombard Street
Philadelphia, PA 19147-1516
Web address: www.history.pcusa.org

Presbyterian Historical Center
12330 Conway Road
St. Louis, MO 63141
Telephone: (314) 469-9077
Web address: www.pcanet.org/history/collections.html

McCormick Theological Seminary
McGaw Library
5555 South Woodlawn Avenue
Chicago, IL 60637

Princeton Theological Seminary
Speer Library
Mercer Street and Library Place
PO Box 111
Princeton, NJ 08540

Sources

Beecher, Willis Judson. *Index of Presbyterian ministers containing names of all ministers of the Presbyterian Church in the United States of America.* Philadelphia: Presbyterian Board of Publication, [1883].

Hall, William K. *The Shane Manuscript Collection: A Genealogical Guide to the Kentucky and Ohio Papers.* Galveston, Tex.: Frontier Press, 1990.

Hart, D. G., ed. *Dictionary of the Presbyterian & Reformed Tradition in America.* Downers Grove, Ill.: InterVarsity Press, 1999.

Miller, William B. "Church Records of the United States: Presbyterian." A paper delivered at the World Conference on Records and Genealogical Seminar, 5–8 August 1969, Salt Lake City, sponsored by The Church of Jesus Christ of Latter-day Saints.

Spence, Thomas H., Jr. *The Historical Foundation and Its Treasures.* Montreat, N.C.: Historical Foundation, 1960.

Union Catalog of Presbyterian Manuscripts. Presbyterian Library Association, 1964.

Witherspoon, E. D., comp. *Ministerial Directory of the Presbyterian Church, U.S., 1861–1967.* Doraville, Ga.: Foote and Davis, 1967.

Protestant Episcopal—Episcopal Church, USA

Commentary

The Episcopal Church does not maintain central membership lists. The local church maintains its records, unless it becomes defunct, then the records are transferred to the diocesan archives. To determine whether a particular church is active, contact the archives or use an Episcopal Web resource, such as <http://anglicansonline.org/usa>, which lists by state all ECUSA churches and provides information about the denomination.

For information regarding records of the colonial Church of England in what is now the United States, consult the collection at Lambeth's Palace in London and those of the Society for the Propagation of the Gospel in Foreign Parts. The Society kept extensive records of the colonists requesting parish priests and complaining about the "dissenters" and reports and letters of more than three hundred missionaries. These records have been microfilmed and are available at many archival and academic repositories.

Contact Information

Archives of the Episcopal Church
606 Rathervue Place
PO Box 2247
Austin, TX 78768
E-mail address: Research@episcopalarchives.org

Sources

O'Connor, Daniel. *Three Centuries of Mission: The United Society for the Propagation of the Gospel 1701–2000.* New York: Continuum, 2000.

Painter, Bordon W. *The Anglican Vestry in Colonial America.* New Haven, Conn.: Yale University Press, 1965.

Reformed Church in America or Dutch Reformed

Commentary

This denomination was established in North America in New Amsterdam. The first services were held on Manhattan Island in 1628, and a church was built as early as 1633. Until becoming the Reformed Church in America (RCA) in 1867, this denomination was known as the Reformed Protestant Dutch Church. It was the only Christian denomination permitted to hold public worship in New Amsterdam until the English takeover of 1664. The Dutch minister married nearly every couple and baptized nearly every child in the city prior to that time, conducting these sacraments for all nationalities and races. Manhattan's collegiate Dutch Reformed churches form a corporation within the RCA that owns the original records of the collegiate churches from 1639 (only copies exist of the earliest registers) through 1806, when some churches began to keep their own registers. Transcripts have been published by The New York Genealogical and Biographical Society (NYG&B) in various forms, such as Harry Macy Jr., "Dutch Reformed Records of New York City in the NYG&B

Library," *NYG&B Newsletter* (Spring 1994). It may also be found online at online at The New York Genealogical and Biographical Society, <www.newyorkfamilyhistory.org>. The NYG&B Society has also published Hugh Hastings, *Ecclesiastical Records State of New York, 1901–16* (Albany: J. B. Lyons, state printer, 1901–1916), which features selected transcripts of the church administrative records and correspondence. See also The Holland Society of New York for lists of members, 1649–1829, and other holdings.

Contact Information

General

Holland Society of New York
Manuscript Collection
122 East 58th
New York, NY 10022
E-mail address: hollsc@aol.com

Archives of the Reformed Church in America.
New Brunswick Theological Seminary
21 Seminary Place
New Brunswick, NJ 08901
E-mail address: rgasero@rca.org

Dutch

Christian Reformed

Heritage Hall
The Archives of Calvin College and Theological Seminary
3201 Burton Street, SE
Grand Rapids, MI 49546

German—see United Church of Christ

For other Reformed churches, see the *Yearbook of American and Canadian Churches* <www.electronicchurch.org>

Sources

De Jong, Gerald Francis. *The Dutch Reformed Church in the American Colonies*. Grand Rapids, Mich.: Eerdmans Publishing Co., 1978.

A Guide to Local Church Records in the Archives of the Reformed Church in America. New Brunswick, N.J.: Reformed Church in America Archives. A regularly updated guide; ordering instructions at <www.rca.org>.

The Historical Directory of the Reformed Church in America, 1628–2000. Historical Series of the Reformed Church in America, no. 37. Edited by Russell Gasero. Grand Rapids, Mich.: Eerdmans Publishing Co., 2001.

Roman Catholic

Commentary

The Roman Catholic Church is the largest Christian church in the world. Traditionally Catholic records have been kept at the parish level, so the vast majority of sacramental records (baptism, marriage, communion, confirmation, burial, and other original records) will be found at the church in which the event took place. However, older records and those of closed parishes have often been moved to diocesan archives or occasionally to historical societies or university archives. Locating records of older churches can be challenging. Begin looking for the church at the parish level and then consult local diocesan sources, which can at least provide information on where those records can be found. Links to many helpful sites dealing with historical and record-keeping information can be found at the World Wide Catholic Web Directory at <www.catholic.net/RCC/Indices>. This site also has links to various dioceses and parishes, religious orders, schools, colleges, and universities.

Contact Information

Special Collections Division
Joseph Mark Lauinger Library
Georgetown University
3700 O Street NW
Washington, D.C. 20057-1006
Web address: www.library.georgetown.edu

University of Notre Dame Archives
607 Hesburgh Library
Nortre Dame, IN 46556
E-mail address: Archives.1@nd.edu

American Catholic History Research Center & University
101 Life Cycle Institute
Catholic University of America
Washington, DC 20064

Sources

Baton Rouge Diocese. *Diocese of Baton Rouge Catholic Church Records*. 21 vols., 1707–1898. Baton Rouge: Diocese of Baton Rouge Department of the Archives, 1978–.

Curran, Francis X., S. J. *Catholics in Colonial Law*. Chicago, 1965; reprint, Clark, N.J.: Lawbook Exchange, 2003.

Ellis, John Tracy. *Catholics in Colonial America*. Baltimore: Helicon Press, 1963.

Findlen, George L. "The 1917 Code of Canon Law: A Resource for Understanding Catholic Church Registers." *National Genealogical Society Quarterly* 93 (June 2005): 126–47.

Hebert, Donald J *Southwest Louisiana Records, to 1897*, and *Southern Louisiana Records, to 1895*. 40 vols. Eunice, La.:

Hebert Publications. Translates and transcribes several Louisiana parishes.

Humling, Virginia. *U.S. Catholic Sources: A Diocesan Research Guide.* Salt Lake City: Ancestry, 1995.

Linck, Joseph C. *Fully Instructed and Vehemently Influenced: Catholic Preaching in Anglo-Colonial America.* Philadelphia: St. Josephs University Press, 2002.

McAvoy, Thomas T. "Catholic Archives and Manuscript Collections." *American Archivist* 24 (1961): 409–14.

The Official Catholic Directory. National Register Publishing, 2001.

O'Toole, James M. "Catholic Records: A Genealogical and Historical Resource." *Register* (October 1989): 251–63.

Salvationists—The Salvation Army

Contact Information

The Salvation Army National Headquarters
Archives Center
615 Slaters Lane
PO Box 269
Alexandria, VA 22313

Schwenkfelder

Contact Information

Schwenkfelder Library & Heritage Center
150 Seminary Street
Pennsburg, PA 18073
E-mail address: info@schwenkfelder.com

Shakers—The United Society of Believers in Christ's Second Appearing

Contact Information

Shaker Library
707 Shaker Road
New Gloucester, ME 04260
E-mail address: brooksl@shaker.lib.me.us

Williams College
Archives and Special Collections
55 Sawyer Library Drive
Williamstown, MA 01267
Web address: www.Williams.edu/library/archives

Western Reserve Historical Society
History Library
10825 East Blvd.
Cleveland, OH 44106

Society of Friends (Quaker)

Commentary

The Society of Friends was an important religious group from the seventeenth century onward in North America. They spread throughout New England and into New York, Pennsylvania, New Jersey, the Carolinas, Tennessee, Virginia, Ohio, and Indiana. The Quakers are organized into meetings designated for worship (First Day Meetings), congregational business (Monthly Meetings), meetings that combine a group of congregations from a specific area that come together for worship and business (Quarterly Meetings), and meetings that have jurisdiction over a wide geographical area (Yearly Meetings). Quakers usually chose not to register marriages in civil records prior to the close of the nineteenth century, and most Quakers did not use tombstones until the mid-nineteenth century. These omissions add importance to the consistent and thorough record-keeping found in Quaker meeting records, which record a family's births, deaths, and marriages. Certificates of removal were issued when a Quaker moved from one meeting to another and also appear in the monthly meeting minutes of both the transferring and receiving congregations.

Contact Information

Friends Historical Library of Swarthmore College
500 College Avenue
Swarthmore, PA 19081-1905
Web address: www.swarthmore.edu/library/friends

The Quaker Collection @ Magill Historical Library
Haverford College Library
370 Lancaster Avenue
Haverford, PA 19041
E-mail address: genealog@Haverford.edu

The Quaker Collection @ The Hege Library
Guilford College Library
5800 West Friendly Avenue
Greensboro, NC 27410
Web address: www.guilford.edu/library/fhc

Archives New England Yearly Meeting of the Religious Society of Friends (Quakers)
Rhode Island Historical Society Library
121 Hope Street
Providence, RI 02906

QuakerMeetings.com
A website with information about all the Quaker congregations (Meetings) that have ever existed in the United States.

Sources

Abstracts of the Records of the Society of Friends in Indiana, Part One through Six (1962–1975) with Index. By Willard Heiss. Indiana Historical Society, 1972. Covers Indiana Meetings. Reissued as volume 7 of Hinshaw's *Encyclopedia* series. The Indiana Historical Society did not release the Heiss work for inclusion in the CD.

Berry, Ellen, and David Berry. *Our Quaker Ancestors: Finding Them in Quaker Records.* Baltimore: Genealogical Publishing Co., 2002; reprint of 1987 edition.

Comfort, William W. "Quaker Marriage Certificates." *Friends Historical Bulletin* 40 (1951): 67–80.

Elliot, Errol T. *Quakers in the American Frontier: History of the Westward Migrations, Settlements, and Developments of Friends on the American Continent.* Richmond, Ind.: Friends United Press, 1969.

Heiss, Willard. *Abstracts of Records of the Society of Friends in Indiana.* Volume 7 of the *Encyclopedia of American Quaker Genealogy* by Hinshaw (see following). Vol. 7 published Indianapolis: Indiana Historical Society, 1977. Vols. 1 and 2 revised by Ruth Dorell and Thomas Hamm, 1996–99.

Hinshaw, William Wade, ed. *Encyclopedia of American Quaker Genealogy.* 6 vols. 1936; reprint, Baltimore: Genealogical Publishing Co., 1991–96. Available on CD-ROM from Genealogical Publishing Co., Baltimore. Also available on Ancestry.com.

Index to Encyclopedia of American Quaker Genealogy. CD-ROM. Baltimore: Genealogical Publishing Co., 1999.

Jacobsen, Phebe R. *Quaker Records in Maryland.* Annapolis, Md.: Hall of Records, 1966.

Jones, Rufus M. *The Quakers in the American Colonies.* 1911; reprint, New York: Russell and Russell, 1962.

Unitarian and Universalist

Contact Information

Unitarian Universalist Association
25 Beacon Street
Boston, MA 02108

Curator, Manuscripts and Archives
Harvard University Divinity School
Andover-Harvard Theological Library
45 Francis Avenue
Cambridge, MA 02138-1994

Meadville Theological School of Lombard College
Wiggin Memorial Library
5701 South Woodlawn Avenue
Chicago, IL 60637
E-mail address: rsuszek@meadville.edu

Congregational

Congregational Christian Historical Society
14 Beacon Street
Boston, MA 02420
Web address: www.14beacon.org

Divinity Library and University Library
Yale University
New Haven, CT 06520

Hartford Theological Seminary Library
Hartford, CT 06105

Harvard Divinity School Library
Cambridge, MA 02140

Evangelical and Reformed

Evangelical Synod Archives
Eden Theological Seminary
475 East Lockwood Avenue
St. Louis, MO 63119
Web address: www.eden.edu/Archives/edenarch.html

Evangelical and Reformed Historical Society
Philip Schaff Library
Lancaster Theological Seminary
555 West James Street
Lancaster, PA 17603
E-mail address: erhs@lts.org

The United Church of Christ

Commentary

The heritage and history of the United Church of Christ incorporates several antecedent traditions. The United Church of Christ was founded in 1957, when the Evangelical and Reformed Church united with the Congregational Christian Churches. The Evangelical and Reformed Church was formed in 1934 by the merger of the Reformed Church in the United States (RCUS) and the Evangelical Synod of America. The Congregational Christian Church was formed in the 1800s. The United Church of Christ is organized by congregations, which are represented at a general synod that sets policy.

Contact Information

Archives of the United Church of Christ
700 Prospect Avenue
Cleveland, OH 44115
E-mail address: kellyb@ucc.org

Sources

Clark, Elmer T. *The Small Sects in America*. Rev. ed. New York: DIANE Publishing Co., 1981; revision of 1937 edition.

Hinke, William J. "German Reformed Church Records in Pennsylvania." *National Genealogical Society Quarterly* 37, 2 (June 1949): 33–38.

Rosenberger, Francis C. "German Church Records of the Shenandoah Valley as a Genealogical Source." *Virginia Magazine of History and Biography* 66 (April 1958): 195–200.

Notes

[1] *Columbia Encyclopedia*, 6th ed., s.v. "Protestantism." New York: Columbia University Press, 2001–05.

[2] Brent Holcomb, *South Carolina Marriages 1688–1799* (Baltimore: Genealogical Publishing Co., 1995); Brent Holcomb, *South Carolina Marriages 1800–1820* (Baltimore: Genealogical Publishing Co., 1995); Brent Holcomb, *Supplement to South Carolina Marriages* (Baltimore: Genealogical Publishing Co., 1995).

[3] USGenWeb Project, "Church: Marriages: Hebron Moravian Church, 1751–1811: Dauphin (now Lebanon) Co," <ftp.rootsweb.com/pub/usgenweb/pa/dauphin/church/hebr0001.txt>.

[4] Translation of *Records of St. John's Evengelical Lutheran Church, at Buffalo Creek, Concord, Cabarrus County, North Carolina,* microfilmed by the North Carolina Department of Archives and History, Division of Archives and Manuscripts, Raleigh, North Carolina.

[5] The Island of Brazza is located just off the Dalmation coast in the Adriatic Sea, Croatia. USGenWeb Project, "Immaculate Conception Churchyard Cemetery, Sutter Creek, Amador County, California," <http://ftp.rootsweb.com/pub/usgenweb/ca/amador/cemeteries/immaculate.txt>, trans. Robert Tenuta, Illinois.

[6] Laura Prescott Duffy, "Using Eulogies in Your Research," *Ancestry* Magazine 21 (March/April 2003), this article is also available online at Ancestry.com, <www.ancestry.com/library/print/ancmag/7236.htm>.

[7] *Presbyterian Church of Deerfield, Michigan*, FHL microfilm 955,794.

[8] *Records of the Congregational Methodist Church at Harmony, Pine Hill, Randolph County, Alabama 1870–1897,* microfilm MFC 1474, Samford University Library, Special Collection, Birmingham, Alabama.

[9] George Braxton Taylor, *Virginia Baptist Ministers Third Series* (Lynchburg, Va.: J. P. Bell Co., 1912), 42.

[10] Hugh Hastings, *Ecclesiastical Records of the State of New York* (Albany: J. B. Lyons, state printer, 1901–16), 7.

[11] RootsWeb.com, *Pisgah Cumberland Presbyterian Church, Gallatin County, Illinois*, p. 22, <www.rootsweb.com/~ilgallat/new_chur.htm>.

[12] Elias Nason, *A History of the Town of Dunstable, Massachusetts* (Boston: Alfred Mudge and Son, 1877), 96. Provided by Laura Prescott.

[13] *Minutes of the Session of the Indiana (August 13, 1812–March 6, 1842) and Upper Indiana (06 March 1842–September 7, 1873), Presbyterian Churches Knox County, Indiana,* typed transcript by Mary Aline Polk, Helen Polk, Mary R. Hribal, 1965, p. 20. Copy in the possession of Sandra Luebking, Illinois.

[14] Copies of the *Christian Leader* are at Andover-Harvard Theological Library, Cambridge, Mass.; the *American Friend* is at Earlham College, which has a necrology index at <www.earlham.edu/~libr/quaker>.

[15] *Evangelical-Messenger 3 Jul 1873*, microfilm, United Theological Seminary Center for the Evangelical United Brethren Hertage, Dayton, Ohio, #289.9305, p. 211, transcribed by Anne Dallas Budd, Ashland, Ohio, 2004.

[16] James H. Madison, *The Indiana Way: A State History* (Indianapolis: Indiana University Press, 1986), 101.

[17] *The Minutes of the Methodist Conferences Annually Held in America; From 1773 to 1813 Inclusive Volume The First* (New York: Daniel Hitt and Thomas Ware Publishers, John C. Totten Printer, 1813; reprint ed., Swainsboro, Magnolia Press, 1983).

[18] The Circuit Rider Database, at <www.rootsweb.com/~ohauglai/index1.htm>, contains information on early pastors in pioneer churches.

[19] National Union Catalog of Manuscript Collections, <http://lcweb.loc.gov/coll/nucmc>. Item indexed under author: Edward Page, 1787–1867, input 19880819, current control no. DCLV88-A1126.

[20] Wayne D. Weber, "Genealogical Resources in the Archives of the Billy Graham Center, Parts 1 and 2," *FORUM* 15 (Summer and Fall 2003) 2:1, 20–22; 3:9–12.

[21] *Annual of the Alabama Baptist State Convention*, microfilm MFA 2.1, call number BX6470.1 A4, Samford University Special Collections Library.

[22] Indiana entries appear in "Presbyterian Church, Cambridge City, Indiana. Rev. J. W. Bailey, Pastor," *Hoosier Genealogist* 22, no. 1 (March 1982). New York and Vermont entries are in "The Church Notebook of Rev. J. W. Bailey, Pastor," *New York Genealogical & Biographical Record* 113 (1984): 235–37.

[23] *American Library Directory* (New York: R. R. Bowker). This directory can be found in the reference area of most libraries. In smaller libraries, it might be found in the librarian's office.

[24] *Bible Records from the manuscript collections of the New England Historic Genealogical Society*, CD-ROM #SCD-BR, New England Historic Genealogical Society, 2004.

[25] William Wade Hinshaw, *Encyclopedia of American Quaker Genealogy*, 6 vols. (1969; reprint, Baltimore: Genealogical Publishing Co., 1991–94), also on CD-ROM with full index, same title and publisher. *Abstracts of the Records of the Society of Friends in Indiana, Part One through Six (1962–1975) with Index* by Willard Heiss, which was first published by the Indiana Historical Society in 1972 and covers Indiana Meetings, was reissued as volume 7 of Hinshaw's *Encyclopedia* series. The Indiana Historical Society did not release the Heiss work for inclusion in the CD.

[26] *Pennsylvania German Church Records 1729–1870*, CD-ROM #7130 (Genealogical Publishing Co., n.d).

[27] Robert J. Dunkle and Ann S. Lainhart, transcribers, *Records of the Churches of Boston*, CD-ROM (New England Historic Genealogical Society, 2003); David Thomas Konig, ed., *Plymouth Church Records 1620–1859*, CD-ROM (New England Historic Genealogical Society, 2004).

[28] The WPA church record inventories, for various reasons, may contain incomplete information. For example, one of the New Hampshire inventories shows "no information given" for the early records for the town of Pembroke. In fact, the New Hampshire Historical Society holds the original records.

References

Allison, William H. *Inventory of Unpublished Material for American Religious History in Protestant Church Archives and Their Repositories*. Washington, D.C.: Carnegie Institute, 1910.

American Library Directory. New York: R. R. Bowker. This directory can be found in the reference area of most libraries. In smaller libraries, it might be found in the librarian's office.

Carroll, Bret E. *Routledge Historical Atlas of Religion in America*. New York: Routledge, 2001.

Check List of Historical Records Survey Publication: Bibliography of Research Projects Reports. WPA, 1943; reprint, Baltimore: Genealogical Publishing Co., 1998.

Dunkle, Robert J., and Ann S. Lainhart, transcribers. *Records of the Churches of Boston*. CD-ROM. New England Historic Genealogical Society, 2003.

Gaustad, Edwin Scott, and Philip L. Barlow. *New Historical Atlas of Religion in America*. 3rd ed. New York: Oxford University Press, 2001.

———, and Leigh E. Schmidt. *The Religious History of America: the Heart of the American Story from Colonial Times to Today*. Rev. ed. San Francisco: HarperSanFancisco, 2002.

Greenwood, Val D. *The Researcher's Guide to American Genealogy*. Baltimore: Genealogical Publishing Co., 2000.

Hastings, Hugh. *Ecclesiastical Records of the State of New York*. Albany: J. B. Lyons, state printer, 1901–16.

Hebert, Donald J. *A Guide to Church Records in Louisiana*. Eunice, La.: the author, 1975. See also: <www.acadian-cajun.com/hebpubl.htm>.

Hefner, Loretta L. *The WPA Historical Records Survey: A Guide to the Unpublished Inventories, Indexes, and Transcripts*. Chicago: Society of American Archivists, 1980.

Holcomb, Brent. *South Carolina Marriages 1688–1799*. Baltimore: Genealogical Publishing Co., 1995.

———. *South Carolina Marriages 1800–1820*. Baltimore: Genealogical Publishing Co., 1995.

———. *Supplement to South Carolina Marriages*. Baltimore: Genealogical Publishing Co., 1995.

Holbrook, Jay Mack. *Massachusetts Vital Records to 1850*. Oxford, Mass.: Holbrook Institute, 1983. Series on 30 microfiche.

Konig, David Thomas, ed. *Plymouth Church Records 1620–1859*. CD-ROM. New England Historic Genealogical Society, 2004.

Macy, Harry, Jr. "Dutch Reformed Records of New York City in the NYG&B Library." *NYG&B Newsletter* (Spring 1994). It may also be found online at the New York Genealogical and Biographical Society, <www.newyorkfamilyhistory.org>.

Mead, Frank S., Samuel S. Hill, and Craig D. Atwood. *Handbook of American Denominations*. 11th ed. Nashville: Abingdon Press, 2001.

Melton, J. Gordon. *National Directory of Churches, Synagogues, and Other Houses of Worship*, ed. by John Kroll. Detroit: Gale Research Co., 1994.

Milner, Anita Cheek, comp. *Newspaper Indexes: A Location and Subject Guide for Researchers*. 3 vols. Metuchen, N.J.: Scarecrow Press, 1977, 1979, 1982.

Kirkham, E. Kay. *A Survey of American Church Record: Major and Minor Denominations before 1880–1890*. 4th ed. Logan, Utah: Everton Publishers, 1978.

Newman, William M., and Peter L. Halvorson. *Atlas of American Religion: The Denominational Era, 1776–1990*. Walnut Creek, Calif.: Altamira Press, 2000.

Pennsylvania German Church Records 1729–1870. CD-ROM #7130. Baltimore: Genealogical Publishing Co., n.d.

Pettee, Julia. *List of Churches: Official Forms of the Names for Denominational Bodies With Brief Descriptive and Historical Notes*. Chicago: American Library Association, 1948.

Sweet, William Warren. *Religion on the American Frontier, 1783–1840: A Collection of Source Materials*. New York: Cooper Square Publishers, 1940, 1964. Separate volumes for Baptists, Methodists, Congregationalists, and Presbyterians.

Weber, Wayne D. "Genealogical Research in the Archives of the Billy Graham Center." 2 parts. *FORUM* 15, no. 2; 15, no. 3 (Summer and Fall 2003).

Internet Resources

Use the Internet to search catalogs of libraries and repositories or to find a Web page dedicated to a particular denomination, topic, or person in American religious history. Some sites which aid in this are:

American Council of Churches. *The Yearbook of American and Canadian Churches*. New York: National Council of Churches, 2003. <www.electronicchurch.org>.

American Society of Church History <www.churchhistory.org>.

National Union Catalog of Manuscript Collections (NUCMC). Washington D.C.: Library of Congress, 1959–. Entries submitted before 1986 are in book format. After 1986, online at: <www.loc.gov/coll/nucmc>.

Questia.com at <www.Questia.com> offers full page online text of many religious history books and articles (including many older and hard-to-find titles).

7

Court Records

SANDRA HARGREAVES LUEBKING, FUGA,
LORETTO DENNIS SZUCS, FUGA, and ARLENE H. EAKLE, PH.D.

Court records are the raw essence of American history. From colonial times to the present, legal documents reveal the customs, the attitudes, the social structures, and the struggles of the rich and the famous as well as those of otherwise unnoticed men and women. From the national landmark cases that have changed the way we all live to the smaller court decisions that have shaped the lives of a forgotten few, court records are a rich and under-used source for family, local, and national information. No other collection illustrates our personal or our national history with such depth and detail.

Whether appearing as litigants, witnesses, jurors, appointees to office, petition signatories, or in some other role, surprisingly few people have escaped mention in court records at some time during their lives. During this nation's early years, Americans were expected to attend local court proceedings when they were in session. It was a civic duty, and citizens could be fined if they did not attend. That courthouses and their warehouses continue to run out of storage space is testimony to the fact that Americans frequently turn to the courts to seek justice. The paper trail left behind by these major and trivial legal events can provide incredible clues and insights into the lives and times of our ancestors.

Chapter Contents

Importance of Courts in American Society

America's predominantly English heritage established a tradition of equitable and just court processes in which the people have a right to participate actively.[1] A majority of American colonists were English, and they were accustomed to seeking redress in the courts. With relative freedom from royal supervision in the New World and with court enforcement of religious as well as civil laws, American courts tried many matters that were not subject to court action in other parts of the British empire and that are now considered too minor to warrant criminal action. In many places, until the time of the Civil War, people were criminally prosecuted for such crimes as gossiping, witchcraft, scolding a husband, being publicly disrespectful to a minister, and refusing to attend church services. Indeed, some of these "blue laws," as they were called, are still on the books today, although they are not enforced.

The benefits for the family historian are considerable. It is not unusual for a single case to have involved between seventy-five and one hundred people, all of them being named in the course of court action.[2]

Local courts were units of government as well as judicial bodies. They issued licenses to lawyers, physicians, merchants, peddlers, ordinaries (public inns), midwives, ferry operators, and clergy; regulated apprenticeships; established weights and measures; provided for inspection of goods and services; ordered the destruction of harmful pests and beasts; paid bounties for heads, tails, and skins; oversaw education for orphans and the poor; built housing for paupers and the maimed, sometimes in conjunction with a local church; built roads and bridges and oversaw their maintenance; called local militia units to muster; assessed taxes and collected them.[3]

Most of these administrative functions are now filled by county commissions, city councils, and other administrative agencies established for that purpose, each with its own records.

Courts also served a social function in bringing a region's people together regularly. Court week (every three months) was a festive occasion. On Monday mornings, courthouses buzzed with activity as people argued about the cases on the docket. Deeds were registered, wills probated, taxes paid, county records audited, elections held, and marriages contracted. Sessions were often juggled to avoid planting and harvest time so that most people could attend.

Courts measured, almost precisely, the moral, physical, spiritual, and economic condition of the people within their jurisdictions. A scolding wife, a quarrelsome neighbor, a Sabbath card-player, the owner of cattle wandering beyond their bounds, a dangerous liberal who freed his slaves and gave them land, an alien (non-English before 1776 or non-American after) applying for citizenship, a blind man applying for tax-exempt status—all of these and many, many more "ordinary" citizens appeared in court.

When court records have been destroyed—as when courthouses have burned—lost records have been reconstructed as far as possible so that legal business can continue. In short, it is safe to say that even the most modest individuals before World War I in America will have appeared in court records at least once during their lifetimes.

This chapter will acquaint you with legal terms, teach you how to read court material, tell you where to find the records, and describe what you can expect to find in civil, criminal, divorce, equity, and probate court records.

Preliminary Work

Since the publication of the last edition of *The Source*, a number of Internet sites—especially those created by states and counties—have published helpful guides, inventories, and some personal name indexes to court files. However, relatively few original court file images are currently found online. Because of the incredible volume of material in courts, warehouses, and archives in this country, and because of the cost involved in scanning them all, in most cases, it will still be necessary to visit the courthouse or regional archives personally or to order copies of files by mail. A quick online search for the county in question will likely provide a good overview of what's available in a given area. A particularly helpful source for locating county court records is USGenWeb at <www.usgenweb.com>. For more information on how to search online, see chapter 2, "Computers and Technology," in this book.

Before setting off for the courthouse in the area where ancestors lived, it will be to the researcher's advantage to learn as much as possible about the locale from published sources. Many county boundary lines have changed over the years, and in many cases records have been moved from one place to another. Some records are stored off site, and it will save time, money, and grief if you know where the records are likely to be found. *Red Book: American State, County, and Town Sources*, edited by Alice Eichholz, provides a state-by-state guide for locating court records.[4] Detailed county maps combined with county-by-county listings that include date of formation of each county, parent county (in cases where it is not the original county), year span of records available, and the address for each county facilitate research in every state. Additionally, *Red Book* includes special information about missing records, renamed counties, and other advice critical to research. *Courthouse Research for Family Historians*, by Christine Rose, provides practical advice for preparing for a trip to the courthouse, detailed information on using court indexes, and tips on how to interpret the records once they are found.[5]

When research centers on a particular state or region, it is a good tactic to consult guides specific to the locale. An excellent example is Diane Rapaport's *New England Court Records: A Research Guide for Genealogists and Historians*.[6] Written by a genealogist who is a former trial lawyer, the book explains legal concepts and terms and then identifies locations of New England state and federal court records found at courthouses and archives, in books, and on microfilm and the latest CD and Internet databases.

The Family History Library (FHL) of The Church of Jesus Christ of Latter-day Saints makes available microfilm copies of court records of many counties through its main library in Salt Lake City and through its system of Family History Centers located across the United States and around the world. Consult the Family History Library Catalog to see what may be available for your county of interest online at <www.familysearch.org>. See also appendix F, "The LDS Family History Library," for information about the FHL and its collection.

Federal and Territorial Courts

Consider the possibility of an ancestor having appeared in federal or territorial court. Perhaps an aged veteran, denied compensation by the pension board, appealed the decision before a federal district court. Or your ancestor may be among the thousands of southerners who found it necessary to apply for bankruptcy following the Civil War. Other federal court involvement includes tax evasion, patent infringement, some admiralty cases, the granting of citizenship (see chapter 9, "Immigration and Naturalization Records"), and disputes between citizens who reside in different states. Figure 7-1 is a page from an admiralty case.

Research in federal district and circuit courts (earlier courts that eventually merged with district courts) and territorial courts (those that functioned prior to the establishment of state and federal courts) begins by identifying the residence of the ancestor at the time of trial or hearing. Next, locate the courts that are listed in figures 7-3 and 7-4 on a map (contemporary to the time period being researched). Or, consult a local history of the area for information on the courts of jurisdiction for that era and region. Federal circuit court cases can provide much personal information. In "'You have the body' Habeas Corpus Case Records of the U.S. Circuit Court for the District of Columbia, 1820–1863,"[7] author Chris Naylor notes finding cases relating to both criminal and civil matters, such as apprenticeships, custody disputes, child support, guardianships, domestic abuse, false promises of marriage, and family abandonment. Habeas corpus is a court order from a judge instructing a person who is detaining

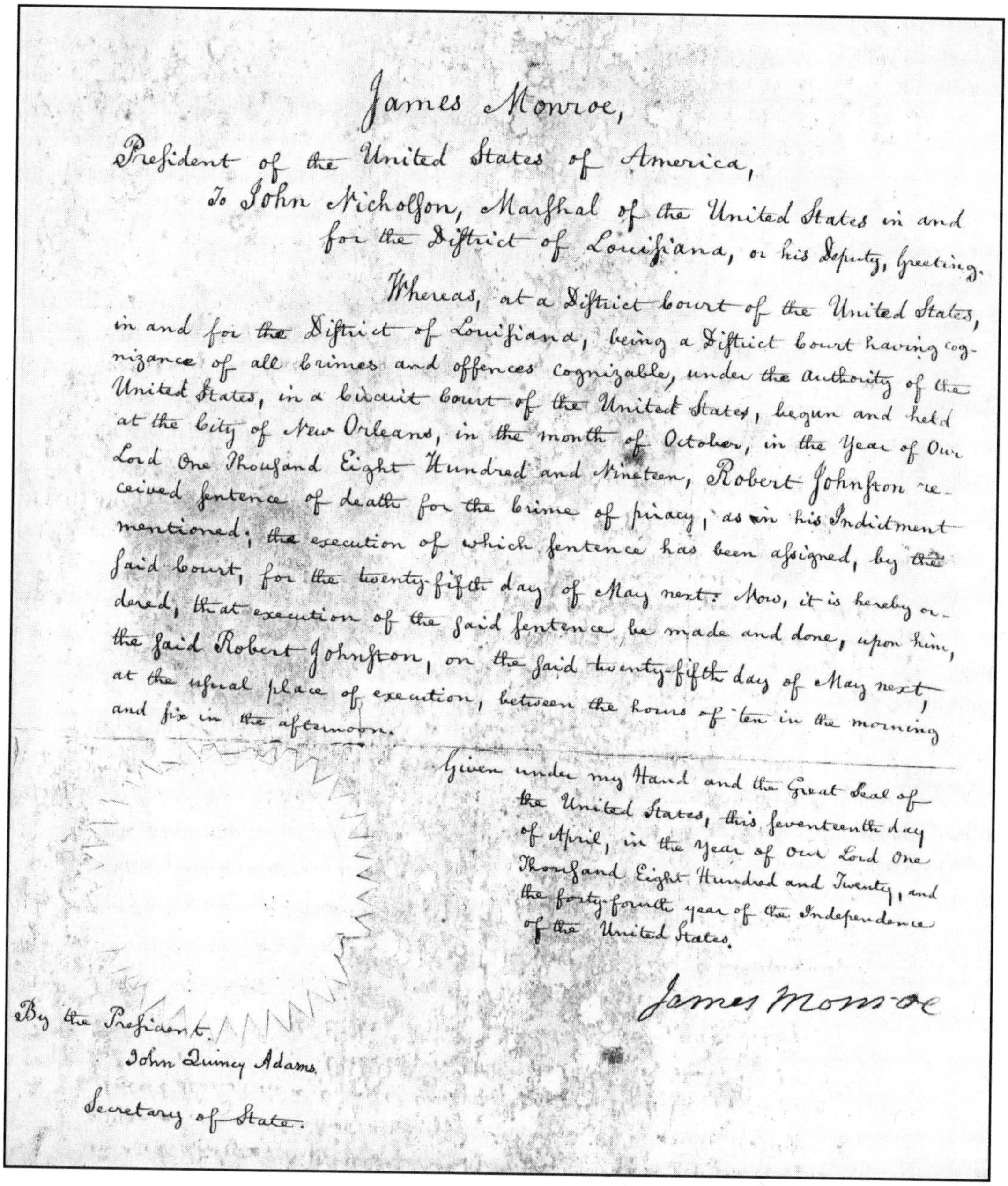

James Monroe,
President of the United States of America,
To John Nicholson, Marshal of the United States in and for the District of Louisiana, or his Deputy, greeting.

Whereas, at a District Court of the United States, in and for the District of Louisiana, being a District Court having cognizance of all Crimes and offences cognizable, under the authority of the United States, in a Circuit Court of the United States, begun and held at the City of New Orleans, in the month of October, in the Year of Our Lord One Thousand Eight Hundred and Nineteen, Robert Johnston received sentence of death for the crime of piracy, as in his Indictment mentioned; the execution of which sentence has been assigned, by the said Court, for the twenty-fifth day of May next: Now, it is hereby ordered, that execution of the said sentence be made and done, upon him, the said Robert Johnston, on the said twenty-fifth day of May next, at the usual place of execution, between the hours of ten in the morning and six in the afternoon.

Given under my Hand and the Great Seal of the United States, this seventeenth day of April, in the year of Our Lord One Thousand Eight Hundred and Twenty, and the forty-fourth year of the Independence of the United States.

James Monroe

By the President.
John Quincy Adams.
Secretary of State.

Figure 7-1.
A page from an 1813 admiralty case in which privateer and freebooter Jean Lafitte, his brother Pierre, and others are charged with aiding and abetting a criminal act "in thus receiving a large quantity of foreign goods which goods had been unlawfully put shore from a certain vessel or vessels laying at Anchor near the Lake of Berataria and which goods were subject to Revenue Duties, the same not having been paid." The original record, which is at the National Archives—Southwest Region (Fort Worth, Texas), is similar to millions of admiralty documents that can be found at the National Archives.

another to bring the detainee before the court for a specific purpose. Although Naylor's article focuses on the U.S. Circuit Court for Washington, D.C., other federal circuit court records will yield similar gold mines of information.

Federal court records comprise the single largest group of records maintained by the National Archives. Court records, in the majority of cases, will be found in manuscript form at the regional archives. Appendix G, "The National Archives and Its Regions," gives contact information for each regional archives and lists the states for which they have collected court records. Each regional archives publishes a holdings list that may be ordered by mail or viewed online at <www.archives.gov/locations>. Archives personnel can help you identify the specific court that would have held jurisdiction over a specific case.

Another aspect to federal court record research is the testimony of persons who appeared before special courts or claims commissions appointed to hear petitions by citizens who have been adversely affected by action (or lack of action) on the part of the federal government. One example is the claims by southerners who had remained loyal to the Union cause during the Civil War and sought compensation for property that was confiscated by Union troops during the war.

Federal court and claims records are fully described in *Guide to Federal Records in the National Archives of the United States*, a three-volume work published in 1995.[8] The text is regularly updated online and is fully searchable at <www.archives.gov/research/guide-fed-records>. For each category of federal holdings, court or other records, an administration history is followed by descriptions of holdings by state. For Alabama court records, for example, the key federal collection titles cover territorial courts, district and circuit courts, and courts of the Confederate States (District Court). A summary of holdings for each collection includes, if available, the microfilm publication number. As an example, in the mid-nineteenth century, a naturalization could occur in any court of record, be it county, state, or federal. If the subject of a search was believed to be naturalized in south Alabama during the Civil War, a search of county and state records would be required, as well as a search of the Confederate States District Court. An online search of *Guide to Federal Records* using the terms "confederate court" and "naturalization" identifies textual records that are available, including those for the Confederate States District Court. Included among those for the southern division of the district of Alabama are "records concerning naturalization, 1861–64," located at the regional archives in Atlanta.[9]

Legal Terms

Laws—the rules of conduct by which society is governed—consist of case law (decisions of the courts based on local custom and common usage, or "common law") and statute law (legislative enactment). The basic law of most states is the common law, inherited from England and based on custom and usage. It is what "seems fair" in a community but is articulated in judicial interpretations, opinions, minutes, and orders. Legislative assemblies enact laws for situations not covered by common law or where serious disagreement exists about what is fair. In certain instances, a statute is designed specifically to change or nullify local custom. For example, where local blue laws required businesses to close on Sundays so employees could attend church, "fairness" was a hardship for Seventh-Day Adventists and Jews because their Sabbaths fall on Saturday. Local authorities, by drafting laws making Sunday closing optional, have changed the custom.

Judicial jurisdiction is the fundamental authority of a court to hear a controversy between parties, to consider the merits of each side, and to render a decision that is binding upon the parties involved.

Original jurisdiction is the authority to commence a case—to hear it for the first time. Civil cases under forty shillings in value were tried first before a justice of the peace in colonial times and today before small claims courts. *Appellate jurisdiction* is the authority to review, upon request, questions of law that arise in the trial of a case. Not all cases can be appealed. The jurisdiction of appeals courts determines the cases acceptable for review. *Exclusive jurisdiction* is the sole authority to try a case. *Concurrent jurisdiction* means that more than one court may try the same case. Litigants choose which court to use. *General jurisdiction* is the authority to try almost any case brought before the court except for a few limitations set by law. *Special jurisdiction* is the authority to handle specific matters—probate, divorce, military, etc. Often these courts also have exclusive jurisdiction to try their cases. *Limited jurisdiction* is the authority of a court to try cases specified by law only or involving less than certain sums of money. Justice of the peace courts are limited courts.

The parties in a legal conflict include the plaintiff, who seeks a remedy under the law and starts legal action against the defendant, who must answer the charge. Either party may be represented by legal counsel or power of attorney.

All cases brought before courts of law are called actions. There are three main types:

1. Legal actions (private parties against private parties) arise over injuries done by one individual to the physical being, the property—real or personal—or the reputation of another. Suit is brought to enforce private rights or to seek compensation for injuries. The parties are often encouraged to settle matters out of court. The most common legal actions are torts—property damage, trespass, libel, assault, negligence, and so on.
2. Criminal actions (state or people versus person) involve the protection of society. These cases can never be settled out of court, although modern plea-bargaining can reduce or eliminate punishment. Criminal offenses include felonies

(murder, robbery, burglary, rape), misdemeanors (petty theft, vagrancy, drunkenness, prostitution, breaking the Sabbath), and in more recent years, less serious matters classified as offenses or violations (overtime parking, unlicensed dogs).

3. Equitable actions are cases determined by "reasonable justice" and "common good" because legal remedies are inadequate or because enforcing the full letter of the law would be unjust. For example, a man borrows money to buy land. He agrees to repay the money with interest by a specific date or forfeit the land. If he is unable to pay, he could be held to the letter of the law and lose all he has invested. The money owed, however, may be less than the value of the land. The court can order the land sold, pay the money owed, and give the man what remains. This is a fairer solution.

Equitable actions usually involve property rights and serve as a substitute for legal actions, in which the remedy is limited to monetary damages, and may be inadequate to remedy the harm. The remedy of the court sitting in equity can be an order of specific performance—to deliver goods promised, to restore animals to their proper owners, to replace equipment damaged, to execute and deliver a deed, or to rewrite a document or report. It could be a mandatory injunction to prevent a certain action. It could also be a bill of account for monies spent in a guardianship. Probate, divorce, and adoption are equity actions.

The basic difference between legal and equitable actions (which today are usually combined under the term "civil actions") and criminal actions is apparent with the question, "Does the offense threaten a well-ordered society?" When a man backs his automobile into his neighbor's car, the neighbor can sue for damages. This is a civil case. However, drunk driving threatens everyone on the same road and thus can be prosecuted as a criminal offense.

In the early stages of American legal development, legal and equitable actions were combined, while a strong distinction was maintained for criminal actions. Few jurisdictions have three separate courts in which each handles a specific action. Most have one judicial body that handles them all, although it may clearly indicate which hat is worn: "The Court of Rhea County sitting in equity" or "The Criminal Court of Rhea County."

The U.S. judicial system is a dual one with national (federal) courts, whose personnel are appointed by the federal government to adjudicate (try) cases under the U.S. Constitution or federal statutory law, and a system of state courts, whose personnel are elected or appointed to try cases under state constitutions, statutory laws, and local custom. Both systems have two types of courts:

1. Trial courts, where cases originate. The jury or, in its absence, the judge, decides what happened and whether, within a given rule of law, the facts constitute guilt or innocence of the accused. Trial courts make up the majority of our system.
2. Appellate courts, to which losing parties can appeal for further consideration of a case. These courts may, but usually do not, call witnesses or have juries. The court accepts the evidence of the previous trial presented in the form of a brief or trial résumé and then reviews points of the law where an error has been made in the earlier trial. Some appellate courts also have original jurisdiction.

Figures 7-2, 7-3, and 7-4 show the relationships between trial and appeals courts. They also introduce the variety of courts that can be found in researching family lines.

Genealogists will encounter many new terms and legal phrases in court records—too many to list here. A standard reference is *Black's Law Dictionary*, available in almost every public library, county law library, and university or college library. Most college bookstores carry the current edition. Many family historians prefer the fourth or an earlier edition, available from used booksellers, for their fuller treatment of obsolete terms found in old records. An excellent online reference is Bouvier's 1856 law dictionary[10] at <www.constitution.org>. Bouvier supplements definitions with information on the treatment under various laws. To understand the nuances and double meanings of words with legal applications, use *Burton's Legal Thesaurus*.[11] *Burton's* includes some five thousand legal terms, definitions of foreign phrases, and a valuable every-word index.

Court Procedures

Court procedures differ slightly from state to state, and more than three centuries have seen the evolution of American court procedures, yet many procedures date from the Middle Ages. On 1 June 1872, federal courts changed their procedural rules to conform to those of the states within which they were located. An overview of civil, criminal, and equity actions will define basic words and illuminate what is happening in court minutes and on the dockets.[12]

Starting the Action (Pleadings) in Civil Cases

Every civil action begins with the issuing of a writ, in modern times usually a writ of summons, a command that notifies the defendant to appear before the court to answer a charge. The clerk, upon request of the plaintiff or an attorney, issues the writ under the court's authority.

The court directs the sheriff or constable to serve the initiating writ on the defendant. In most jurisdictions, the defendant must receive it personally, but in a few, the sheriff can leave it with an adult member of the family or with someone in charge at the place of business. The usual procedure is for the sheriff to produce the original writ, tell the defendant its contents, and provide him or her with a copy. The sheriff will then make out a return, usually on the back of the original writ, stating where, when, and upon whom he has served it, sign it, and return it to the clerk of the court on or before the return day specified in the writ. The writ and the return are filed in the case file or packet as part of the permanent record of the case. In most cases, an action cannot proceed until the writ has actually been served. The notable exception is in divorce actions. The writ may be published in newspapers when the defendant is outside of the court's jurisdiction or when his or her whereabouts are unknown. In some cases, property may be seized by the sheriff to compel an absent defendant to appear.

The next step is the filing of the plaintiff's claim. This pleading may be called a statement of claim, a complaint, or a petition. The purpose of the declaration or petition is to explain clearly the plaintiff's reason for taking action so that the defendant knows the nature of the claim and so that there is "a cause of action sufficient in law" to justify a judgment in favor of the plaintiff. The declaration and notice are filed with the court clerk, and a copy is served on the defendant or his attorney. In some jurisdictions, only the attorneys exchange pleadings, not filing them with the clerk of the court until they have been completed or until a judgment may be entered.

The defendant then counters with an answer or affidavit of defense admitting or denying the various claims contained in the plaintiff's declaration. It may also present new information bearing on the defense. It is filed with the court clerk, and a copy is served upon the plaintiff or his attorney. If the defendant fails to file an answer within the time allowed by law, the plaintiff is entitled upon motion of the court to enter judgment by default for "failure to file and answer." The clerk enters the judgment in

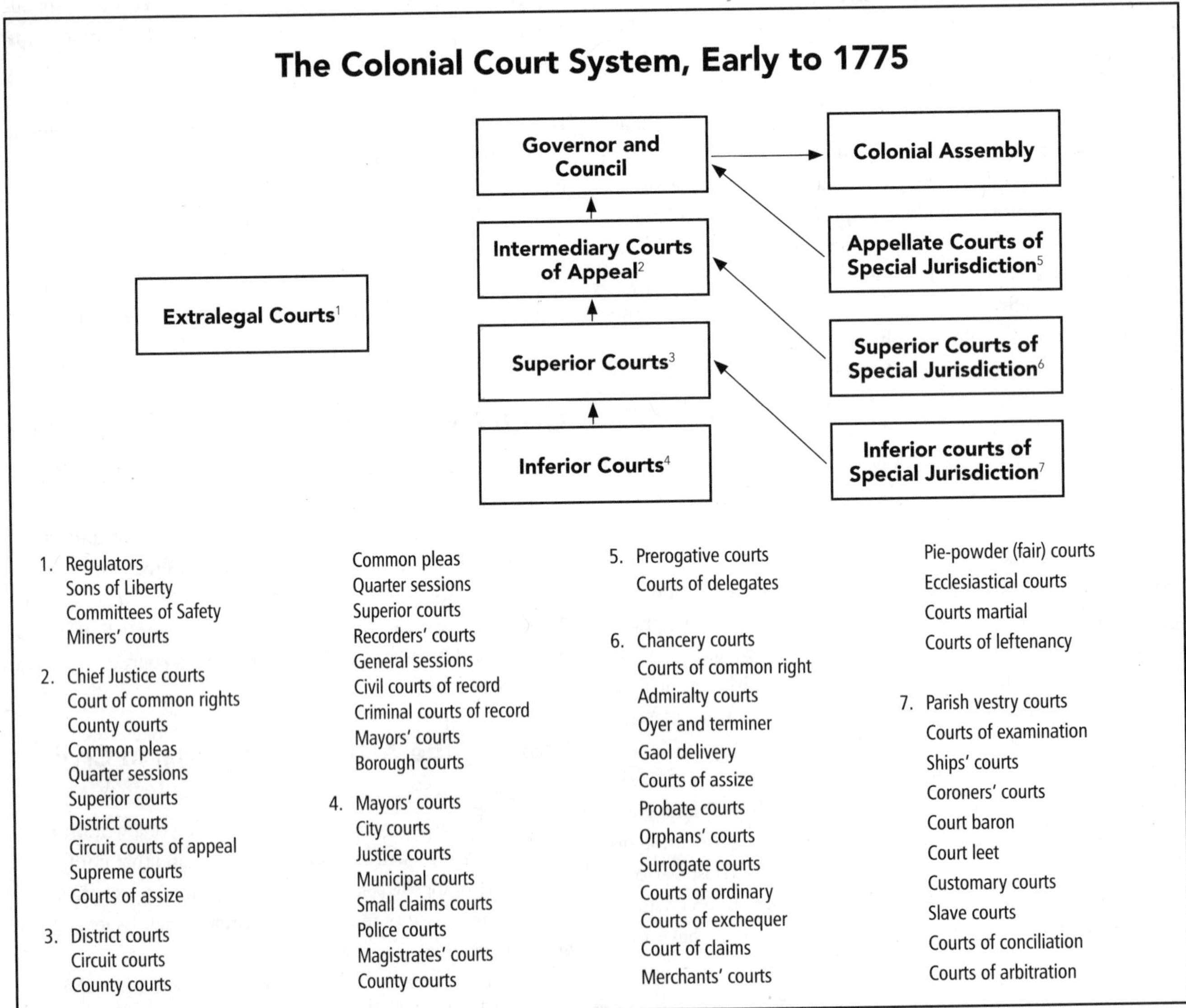

Figure 7-2. The colonial court system, early to 1775.

the court records, and the court provides for the enforcement of the judgment.

When the declaration and answer have been filed, and if the case has not been judged before, then it is "at issue"—ready for trial before a judge and jury. (In many courts, the parties can waive a jury trial and elect to have their case tried before the judge alone.) The case is then scheduled on the court's docket. In earlier times, there could be repeated exchanges of pleas between the plaintiff and the defendant, each exchange with its own name, like reply or replication, rejoinder, sur rejoinder, and rebutter.

Most jurisdictions encourage litigating parties to settle their case out of court to save time and money. When it happens, the clerk usually notes it in the court records. Some jurisdictions require that civil cases under a certain amount be brought before a court of arbitration or conciliation before a trial. At this point, there are certain motions that can be entered to delay (stay) judgment. These motions pertain to points of law (legal technicalities). A record of them and their disposition is also part of the case file.

Starting the Action (Pleadings) in Criminal Cases

When a crime has been committed, the offender must be brought, by some legal process, before a tribunal to hear the complaint and take appropriate action. Before the days of organized law enforcement, in any locality, the citizens of a community were responsible to see that offenses were reported and the alleged offenders physically brought to court (presentment). Presentment could be made by private persons, constables, town watchmen, selectmen of the town, elected town presenters, grand jurors, government officials, paid informers, church wardens, tithing men, or by the court itself. For example, during the seventeenth century, the English tithing system was

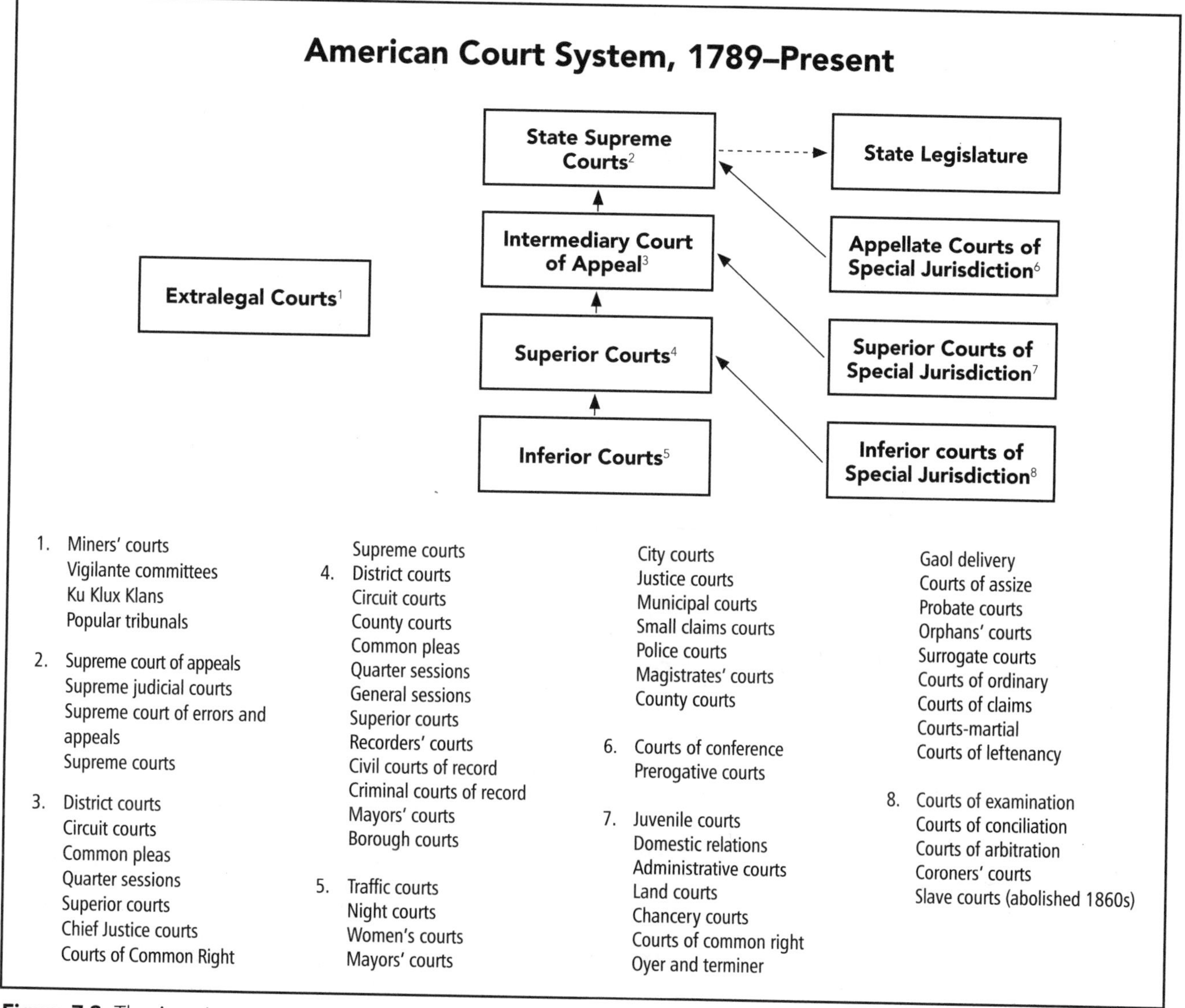

Figure 7-3. The American court system, 1789 to the present.

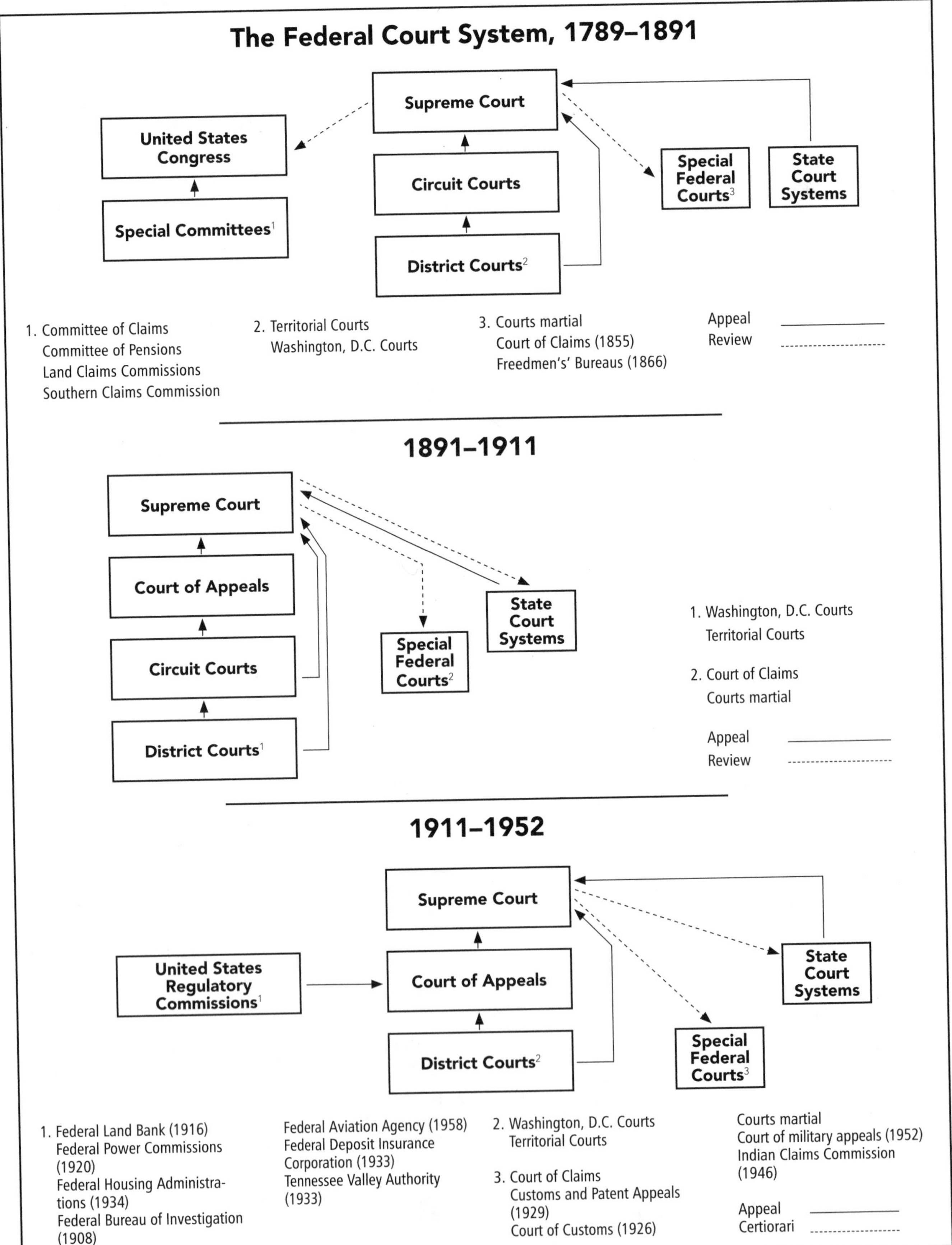

Figure 7-4. The federal court system, 1789 to 1952.

established in some colonies for short periods of time. Every male over age twelve was enrolled in a tithing (usually ten households), and one was appointed tithing man, responsible to inspect the households under his supervision regularly so that "sin and disorder may be prevented and suppressed," to see that everyone attended church on Sunday and kept the day holy, retired at curfew, and did not play cards or engage in other illegal gaming. The tithing man had to report offenders to the court or be fined.

Today, the injured person, or the state acting for society as a whole, enters a complaint. The court orders the offender to be summoned, usually by means of a warrant or writ of capias issued to an authorized officer (the sheriff, marshal, or other police officer). The officer takes the person named in the writ into custody and usually holds him or her in jail. This officer must produce the accused before the court at a specified time for a hearing. If the apprehension was legal, the person will be recommitted to jail or released on bail to await trial. If not, he or she will be released unconditionally.

Bail is the posting of a bond, a written promise to pay a set amount of money if the accused does not appear in court, and a cash deposit, surety bond from an insurance company, or pledge of property may be required to guarantee payment. In default of bail, the accused is committed to jail and kept in custody until the case is disposed of by trial or appeal. Capital crimes may have no provisions for bail.

If the crime is minor, the matter may be disposed of by a summary trial before the magistrate without a jury. For example, if the police arrest a vagrant upon the street without a formal complaint having been made, the magistrate decides both facts and law. The amount of the fine or the type of punishment a magistrate may impose is limited by statute.

In most cases, however, the next step is a preliminary hearing held before a magistrate to determine if the evidence against the accused is sufficient to justify holding him or her for trial. Guilt or innocence is not the issue. Witnesses are often called to testify, and the court, in some jurisdictions, requires the testimony to be written, attested, and signed by the witnesses.

The magistrate must prepare a copy of the hearing and the case, usually within a limited number of days, to send to the court where the trial is to take place. It contains the name of the defendant, the nature of the charge, the names of the prosecutors and witnesses (sometimes their evidence), the information upon which the arrest was made, and the bail bond.

In earlier times in the case of murder, the coroner held an inquest before a jury, which heard evidence and rendered a verdict about the cause of death. The coroner then provided a return to the court based upon this semi-judicial investigation. This report was usually presented at the preliminary hearing and became a part of the court record. In recent years, coroners' records have come under the jurisdiction of the state or county medical examiners and no longer include a determination of guilt set by an inquest jury.

In the next step, the defendant is brought before the court (arraigned), either to plead guilty and be sentenced at once without further trial or to plead not guilty and be bound over for the trial.

Collecting Testimony

At the point when the trial is scheduled, civil and criminal procedures are similar. Witnesses are summoned by subpoena to appear at the trial on behalf of the plaintiff or the defendant. If witnesses must bring documents, the writ describes them. The sheriff, marshal, or constable must serve the subpoena directly on the witness and submit a return to the court. If the witness fails to appear at the time and place specified, a bench warrant is issued on the spot for his or her arrest, and an officer of the court goes out to find the witness.

A representative of the court interviews and takes depositions from witnesses who live outside the jurisdiction of the court or who are ill, maimed, or unable to appear in person. Sometimes the testimony consists of answers to written questions (interrogatories) prepared by the court and forwarded to a local court where the witness resides.

These written statements must be attested, and the witness must sign them. Depositions, and any interrogatories, become part of the permanent record of the court. In early cases, these depositions may be the only written accounts of what the witnesses actually said. They are especially valuable if an out-of-state family member is providing testimony needed to probate an estate or divide a piece of property.

The Trial

Trial procedures may be prescribed by law or by local custom. The jury is selected by drawing names from a list prepared at the beginning of the court term (these lists are recorded in the minutes) or by summoning "twelve good and lawful men, housekeepers" as their names appeared in rotation on the tax rolls. Each party has the right to challenge jurors and dismiss those it feels are "prejudicial to the case." The jury is then to perform its duties impartially, based on the evidence presented. Where jury trial is waived, the judge considers the case. A non-jury trial will usually be shorter, with fewer documents.

Presenting the case includes statements by the plaintiff and the defendant (or their attorneys), testimony from the witnesses and cross-examination, introduction of written depositions, review of documents or other exhibits before the court, summation of the case with a parting speech to the judge and/or jury by each side, and instructions to the jury on the points of law at issue. At this point, the jury or the judge retires to consider the case and arrive at a verdict. The verdict must be unanimous.

Rendering judgment is the judge's responsibility. The judge relies on the verdict of the jury or personal deliberations to arrive at a decision. In early days, verdict and judgment were given the same day. More recently, there may be up to ninety days between the two. The clerk of the court is required by law to record the names of the parties, the judgment, amounts of money recovered (if any), and the time allowed for meeting the judgment. For example, a money award for damages to crops and fences by a stampeding herd of cattle, to be paid within sixty days, will be entered in the court record. A receipt for payment is often filed with the court, and the clerk may paste it at the top or bottom of the page where the judgment is recorded in the case file or packet.

Before 1865, a jail sentence was unusual. Local jails served only to hold the accused for trial. Criminal courts were often called "gaol delivery" because they emptied the jails of prisoners. Instead of "doing time," the convicted person might be whipped, pilloried, submerged in cold water, forced to labor on a public project, or sentenced to pay fines and damages. Capital crimes brought death or banishment.

Imprisonment for debt was common in most jurisdictions during the colonial period and even later. Eventually, the courts determined that incarceration rendered a debtor incapable of working to repay the debts. With this realization, more debtors faced fines than prison. Some records of sentencing for debt (or later bankruptcy, see figure 7-5) include lists of creditors and assets. An excellent history of how the courts dealt with debtors will be found in *Debtor's Dominion: A History of Bankruptcy Law in America.*[13] Consult the reference section under Bankruptcy and Debt for other studies.

Enforcing the Judgment (Execution)

Once a judgment is rendered, the court commands the sheriff, marshal, or constable to carry it out. Some courts ordered imprisonment or labor until the judgment had been met.

In the case of debt, imprisonment was often useless because the person in custody had no way to earn the money. "Judgment-proof" debtors—those certified by the court as unable to pay—could laugh at creditors.

If the judgment debtor owned property, the court issued an order for the sheriff to seize and sell it (known as "attachment") to satisfy the creditor's claims. In some jurisdictions, the property must be taken into custody before judgment is given as security that the creditor can recover if the debtor fails to make payment. A companion action is distraint—property is taken into custody to impel the debtor to come to court. When the person appears in court, the property is returned. Personal property is actually brought to the courthouse, and the officer in charge makes an inventory. In some jurisdictions the creditor must post a bond for the value of the property attached to indemnify the officer against unlawful seizure.

Seizure of real property consists of recording a writ against the title, called a judgment lien, and giving notice to the person in possession that the land has become court property and cannot be disposed of or sold by the owner. Homesteads (dwelling house and a small piece of garden property), pensions, bankrupt property, property in hands of guardians or trustees, cemeteries, tools of trade, and insurance are usually exempt from attachment.

If the debtor fails to make payment, the sheriff takes control of the property and posts it for sale by publicly advertising on placards, in newspapers, by town crier, or by Sunday notice in church. Then the property is auctioned to the highest bidder, and the proceeds go to the creditor for redress, costs, and damages.

Each step generates court records. Brief summaries appear in minutes, orders, and judgments; documents, testimony, and exhibits (plus copies of orders), writs, judgments, and notices will be found in the case packets.

New Trials and Appeals

A litigant, usually the loser but sometimes the winner if he or she received less than petitioned for, can appeal the case within a specified period of time. Each state determines by law which court may hear which appeals. Federal judiciary acts provide similarly on the federal level. Some states have only one appeals court; some allow only specific cases to be appealed; and some place a limit on the amount of damages an appeals court can handle.

When the appellate court issues a writ allowing the case to be heard, the litigants prepare briefs containing the facts of the case, errors committed, and reasons why appeal is sought. After printing became common, briefs were printed in multiple copies for the judges, attorneys, litigants, case files, and news media.

New trials or appeals are granted if the judge erred on the admissibility of evidence, the verdict was contrary to the evidence, the verdict was contrary to the law, the judge erred in the charge to the jury, and/or new evidence becomes available.

When errors occur, the case is tried only on the legal technicalities involved, not on the evidence offered in the trial. The judges consider the matter individually, then collectively, and render their opinions—usually in writing—at a later date.

If the court grants a new trial, the case is sent back to the trial court and the whole case is retried in accordance with rules laid down by the appeals court.

Equity Cases

Common equity cases are probate disputes, estate divisions, divorce proceedings, adoptions, dissolution of partnerships, and other cases involving property rights.

The Bill (Declaration or Petition)

The action begins by filing a bill stating the plaintiff's case and praying the chancellor (judge) for relief. The bill must state

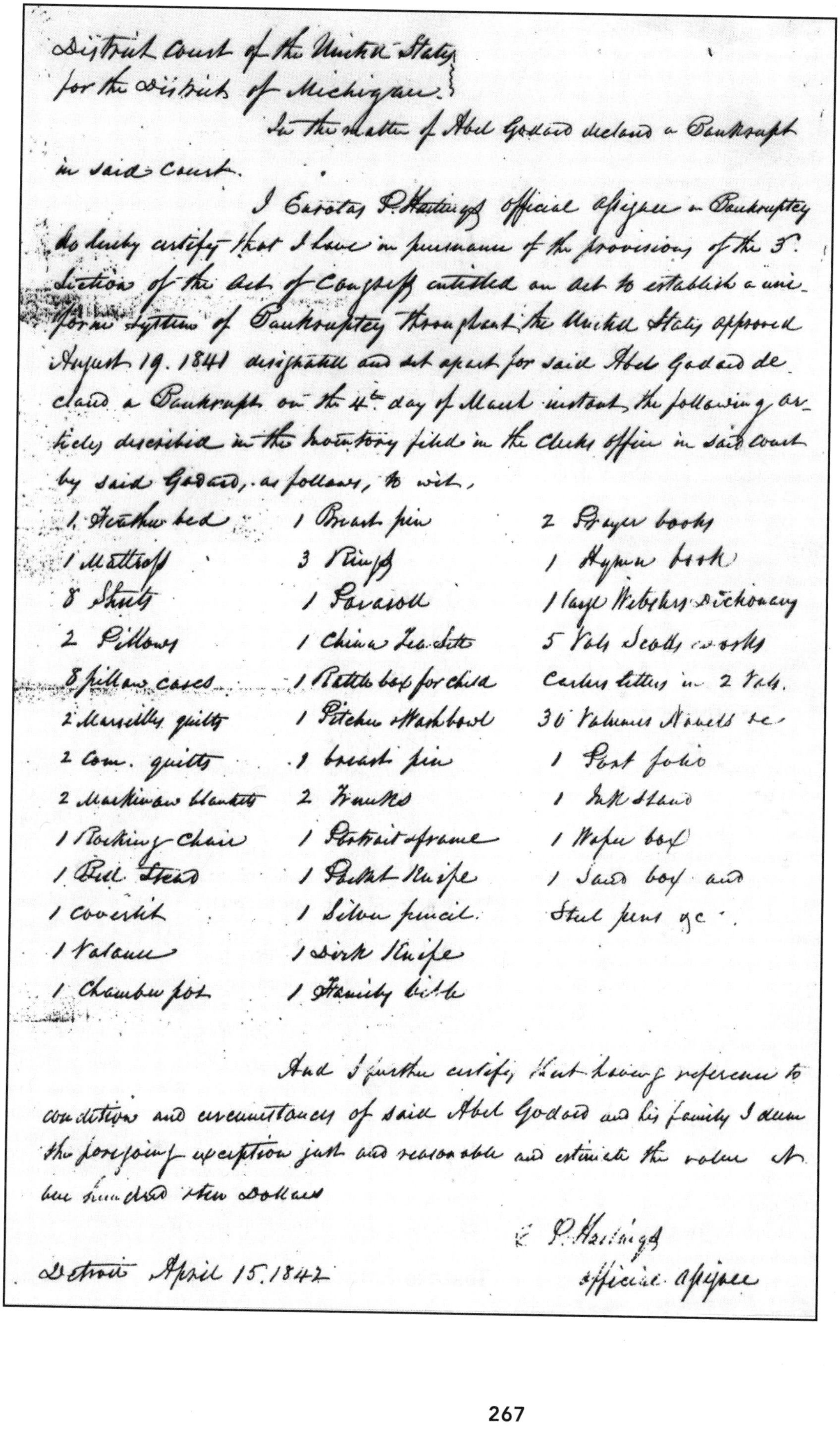

District Court of the United States
for the District of Michigan

In the matter of Abel Godard declared a Bankrupt in said Court.

I Carolus P. Hastings Official Assignee in Bankruptcy do hereby certify that I have in pursuance of the provisions of the 3rd Section of the Act of Congress entitled an Act to establish a uniform System of Bankruptcy throughout the United States approved August 19. 1841 designated and set apart for said Abel Godard declared a Bankrupt on the 4th day of March instant the following articles described in the Inventory filed in the Clerks office in said Court by said Godard, as follows, to wit,

1 Feather bed	1 Breast pin	2 Prayer books
1 Mattress	3 Rings	1 Hymn book
8 Sheets	1 Parasoll	1 large Websters Dictionary
2 Pillows	1 China Tea Sett	5 Vols Scotts works
8 pillow cases	1 Rattle box for child	Carters letters in 2 Vols.
2 Marseilles quilts	1 Pitcher & Wash bowl	30 Volumes Novels &c
2 Com. quilts	1 breast pin	1 Port folio
2 Mackinaw blankets	2 Trunks	1 Ink stand
1 Rocking Chair	1 Portrait & frame	1 Wafer box
1 Bed Stead	1 Pocket Knife	1 Sand box and
1 Coverlet	1 Silver pencil.	Steel pens &c.
1 Valance	1 Dirk Knife	
1 Chamber pot	1 Family bible	

And I further certify, that having reference to condition and circumstances of said Abel Godard and his family I deem the foregoing exception just and reasonable and estimate the value at One hundred & ten Dollars

C. P. Hastings
Official Assignee

Detroit April 15. 1842

Figure 7-5. A bankruptcy filing from the U. S. District of Michigan found at the National Archives—Great Lakes Region. From a glance at the list of assets, one might assume that this individual was well-read and had led a fairly comfortable existence to this point.

every fact entitling the plaintiff to relief. After printing became more common, many courts required these bills to be printed and presented in court as bound volumes.

Filing and Service

The bill is filed with the clerk of the court, and a copy is served on the defendant as prescribed by statute or rules of the court. A proof of service (return) must appear on the back of the record. At this point, the bill may be tested to determine if it is sufficient to entitle the plaintiff to a remedy at equity. This is called a demurrer (meaning to delay or stay).

Answer

The answer, setting up every circumstance the defendant will use, must be filed within the time stated. If there are several defendants, each may file an answer, although one will suffice. If the defendant fails to file or admits all the allegations, judgment by default or decree *pro confesse* (judgment because of confession) will be given. The case ends here.

Hearings and Proof

Equity trials are generally conducted without a jury. The chancellor has the power to decide both questions of fact as a jury and questions of law as a judge. The rules of evidence applicable to suits at law also apply, but the proceedings are more direct. Frequently, in cases without serious dispute over the facts, no oral testimony is introduced. The matter is argued to a conclusion upon the allegations set forth in the bill and answer. If proof is necessary, it is usually brief. There are four common methods of presenting proof:

1. Depositions. Obtained by written questions or through oral examination by counsel, summarized and written. Such depositions are valuable where family members have moved from their birthplaces to unknown places, for their residences are recorded.
2. Reference to special examiners (masters). This is a convenient method where the facts are complicated or where several hearings are necessary. The chancellor commissions a member of the bar to determine the facts of the case and make a report, including testimony and findings on the facts. The chancellor uses the report as a basis for the decree but is not bound to accept the findings of the master.
3. Jury trial. Generally, equity litigants have no right to a jury trial, though the court may submit questions of fact to a jury if it chooses. The chancellor is not bound by the jury's verdict. In some states, however, the right to a jury trial in chancery cases is given by constitution or statute and can be set aside only for reasons that would justify a judge in setting aside a verdict in any law action, as, for instance, where the verdict was contrary to the evidence.
4. Hearings before the court take place when the trial judge permits litigants or their legal representatives to present oral or written arguments.

Decrees

A decree is the judgment or sentence determining the rights of the parties to the suit. A decree is final when it decides the whole case, reserving no further questions for the future judgment of the court. A decree dismissing a bill or ordering specific performances of a contract would be final. It is interlocutory when it reserves any question for future judicial consideration—for instance, ordering the delivery of property to a receiver or granting a temporary injunction.

A decree in equity is generally easier to enforce than a judgment in law. When the chancellor orders a person to execute a deed, perform a contract, account for trust funds, cancel a mortgage, or any of the various things it may order, the person must comply or be subject to fine or imprisonment. Disobedience to the order is contempt of court. All the machinery of the government, including the army, may be used to enforce a decree of equity.

Probate

Probate cases are distinctive enough to be discussed separately from equity proceedings. The records they generate are among the most valuable genealogical materials we have in America. They are also among the most complicated, filled with pitfalls for the unwary.

In *New York State Probate Records: Genealogist's Guide to Testate and Intestate Records*, Gordon Remington says, "To the genealogical purist, the title 'Probate Records' may not be quite accurate, for technically this term refers only to persons leaving wills (Testate) and not those who died without one (Intestate). The word probate, however, has come to mean the general class of records associated with an estate. Even *Black's Law Dictionary* (6th edition) states that 'in current usage this term has been expanded to refer to the legal process wherein the estate of a decedent is administered.'"[14]

The probate process transfers the legal responsibility for payment of taxes, care and custody of dependent family members, liquidation of debts, and transfer of property title to heirs from the deceased to an executor/executrix (where there is a will), to an administrator/administratix (if the person dies intestate—without a will), or to a guardian/conservator if there are heirs under the age of twenty-one years or in cases where a person has become incompetent through disease or disability.

Testate Estates

When a person makes a last will and testament, he or she leaves a *testate* estate. Originally, only personal property (money and movables) could be bequeathed (given posthumously) by will. Not until 1540 did the Statute of Wills first permit land and other real property to be devised (granted posthumously) by will. Some authors have asserted a distinction between a will and a testament, applying one to real property and the other to personal property, but courts have uniformly held the terms to be equivalent. The phrase "last will and testament," like many deliberately redundant legal phrases, combines synonymous Anglo-Saxon and Norman-French terms.

Wills are of three different kinds: (1) Attested wills are prepared in writing and signed by responsible witnesses who certify to the court that the will was written at the instance of the deceased of his or her own free will and choice and that he or she was of sound mind at the time. (2) Holographic wills are handwritten entirely by the person making the will, signed, dated, and not witnessed. If any other person writes on the will, it is invalid. In addition, the will must be found among the individual's important papers. It cannot be filed with an attorney or other third party unless all valuable papers are so filed. In some jurisdictions, this kind of will is not valid. (3) Nuncupative wills are oral, deathbed wills dictated to witnesses who convert them to writing at the earliest possible moment and present them to the court within a specified period of time after the person dies. In some jurisdictions, this kind of will is also invalid.

Intestate Estates

When a person dies without a will, or leaves an invalid will, his or her property becomes an intestate estate. It is divided according to settlement shares determined by law. In most states, if the deceased is a married man, the widow receives a prescribed interest in any real property her husband owned (known as her dower rights) and a prescribed share of his personal property, and the rest is divided equally among the children. If a child is dead, his share is divided among his own legal heirs. An illegitimate child is entitled to inherit from his or her mother. Unless the father has acknowledged his parenthood in writing, duly witnessed and accepted by the court, or unless he later marries the mother, a child born of unmarried parents cannot inherit from the father. Some states allow the father to petition for a legislative act to legitimize his children so they can inherit, and some allow naturalization of deceased persons by special act so their heirs can inherit.

If a person dies without issue, his or her estate passes to the spouse. If there is no spouse, the estate passes to his or her parents and brothers and sisters. In some states, descent of property goes no further than this. In some, lines of descent become quite complicated, with provision even for nephews, second cousins, and others.

In community property jurisdictions (Louisiana, California, Washington, Idaho, etc.), the property that a husband and wife own at the time of marriage and the property that each individually inherits afterward remain separate property; the property that they acquire together during their married life becomes community property in which each has an undivided one-half interest. Upon the death of one spouse, the common estate automatically reverts to the surviving spouse in fee simple—that is, with the right to sell, mortgage, exchange, bequeath, or gift by written document.

Dower and Curtesy

In non-community property states, a woman has a dower right or life-estate, usually in one-third of her husband's real property. This right must be legally recognized in all transactions, including transfers of land. A man has the right of curtesy—a life-estate in any property his wife owned when they married or in any she inherits in her own right during the marriage—providing they had at least one living child who could inherit from them. Otherwise, he has a right to one-third of her property only.[15] Marriage settlements contracted before the time of marriage can change these provisions.

Dower rights in Colonial America were based upon English common law and were practiced in most, if not all, colonies. One of the first states to enact specific provisions for widow's dower land was North Carolina in 1784. Lee Albright and Helen F. M. Leary, in *North Carolina Research: Genealogy and Local History* write:

> The widow, upon her petition, was put into possession of a third of the land her husband had owned at his death, plus enough provision to support her and the minor children for a year. In the personal property division she received the same portion a child did. If slaves were part of her 'child's part' she held them only for her lifetime; at her death they returned to her husband's other heirs. If the deceased had no children, however, a third of the personal estate went to the widow absolutely, even if that third included slaves.[16]

Tennessee, which initially applied North Carolina's law, soon made changes. Beginning in 1813, a widow became entitled to a year's support in provisions and the use of crops from her husband's estate. Eventually, tools, leather, and iron were included, then household goods were added. By 1825, widows received one-half of the personal estate as well as the real estate share. An 1833 refinement gave the widow "1 plow, 1 hoe, 1 set gears for plowing, 1 iron wedge, 1 horse, mule, or yoke of oxen." Throughout this time, the intent of the law was to allow the widow to continue living in the family home. For a full discussion of the dower application process and the documents created, see Gary R. Toms and William R. Gann, *Widows' Dowers of Washington County, Tennessee*,[17] from which this paragraph was adapted. This title is the first known book of compiled dower records and should be examined by all researchers hoping to locate similar documents in Tennessee or elsewhere.

Under recent legislation, however, a woman has the right to renounce her dower claim to her husband's estate. She must acknowledge that full disclosure of the total worth of the estate was made and that she understands what she is renouncing. This protects the estate against undue litigation. A man cannot legally disinherit his wife and leave her destitute, on the public's mercy. In most jurisdictions, welfare help is denied, even in cases of divorce, if the husband is in a position to pay for the wife's upkeep. Some states now designate a share of the intestate spouse's entire estate to the survivor, as an alternative to dower or curtesy, though this applies only to real estate.

Guardianship

A guardian is a responsible individual of legal age appointed or acknowledged by the court to manage the property ownership of those incompetent by reason of youth or mental or physical handicap to handle their own affairs. A guardian may also be called a conservator, a curator, a tutor, or a receiver.

An orphan is a minor whose father is dead or whose deceased mother left separately owned property to her child but excluded the father. In both cases, a guardian is appointed to assume the legal responsibilities of property ownership. In other words, the "orphan" may have a living parent in either case. Such a child may also be called a ward or infant. It is also common for a mother or father to be appointed guardian of his or her own children without implying adoption, formal or otherwise.

The appointment of a guardian for a minor may be a separate court process from probate, handled by a different court. Depending on the jurisdiction, the appointment of a guardian for an adult who is incompetent to handle his or her own affairs may require two separate court processes: the first to declare him or her incompetent, and the second to appoint someone to act in his or her behalf.

Probate Proceedings

Since the procedures followed in both testate and intestate cases are almost identical, both can be considered together. Most states require that probate begin the first term of court following the death of a property owner, between thirty and ninety days after death.

1. Usually, the principal heir petitions the court for authority to begin the probate process. Until recent years these petitions were made verbally and recorded only in the probate minute books. However, some jurisdictions require written petitions bearing the names of all heirs, their residences, and their ages; these are filed with the original estate papers. Such petitions are especially valuable because they may be the only documents that list all the heirs. Figure 7-6 is an example of a petition to commence probate.

In a testate estate, the executor petitions for letters testamentary or authority to probate the will. In an intestate case, the surviving spouse or oldest son normally petitions for letters of administration or authority to administer the estate according to the laws of the jurisdiction.

Petition for Probate of Will and Letters Testamentary In the County Court of Johnson County, Nebraska In re Estate of George Hindenach Deceased.

PETITION

Your petitioner, Hannah Hindenach who is of legal age, shows: That George Hindenach late a resident of Spring Creek Precinct, in Johnson County Nebraska, died at his residence, in Johnson County Nebraska, on or about the 9 day of September A.D. 1895 leaving a last will and testament, executed in due form of law, as your petitioner believes which is now on file in this Court: that the subscribing witnesses to said instrument are T. Appelget of Tecumseh, Nebraska, and T. E. Fairall of Tecumseh, Nebraska; that said Will nominated Hannah Hindenach as executrix thereof, and that Hannah Hindenach is willing to accept the trust as Executrix that said decedent died seized of real estate in said Johnson County of the estimated value of $5000.00; that the said decedent was possessed of personal property in the said State of Nebrasska of the estimated value of $600.00.

Your petitioner further shows that the devisees, legatees, heirs at law in the absence of a will, and other persons interested in said matter are as follows:

Name	Age	Residence		Relationship to Deceased
Hannah Hindenach	45	P.O.	Tecumseh	Widow
George Hindenach Jr.	25	"	"	Son
Lillie Hindenach	22	"	"	Daughter
Bessie Hindenach	17	"	"	"
Ella Hindenach	15	"	"	"
Anna Hindenach	13	"	"	"
Josie Hindenach	11	"	"	"
Charles Hindenach	8	"	"	Son
Mary Hindenach	6	"	"	Daughter
Stella Hindenach	4	"	"	"

Your petitioner therefore prays that a day may be fixed for hearing the proof of the execution of said instrument; that all the persons listed herein may be notified by Publication three weeks prior to said hearing, to show cause if any there be, why said instrument shall not be recorded as the last will and testament of said decedent.

Figure 7-6. Petition to commence probate by Hannah Hindenach, 9 September 1895, Johnson County Court. Typescript of a holograph in Johnson County Courthouse, Tecumseh, Nebraska.

It is the responsibility of the executor or the administrator to look out for the best interest of the estate, the needs of the heirs, and the claims of the creditors.

2. Proving the will is a step that applies only to testate cases. The document is presented to the court. The witnesses to the will appear and attest that they saw the individual sign the will,

that he or she was in sound mental condition and that he or she expressed his or her own free will. The court, after hearing this sworn testimony, will order that the will be recorded. Wills judged invalid are not proved and, hence, are not recorded in the will book but can often be found among the loose or miscellaneous papers of the courthouse or town hall. They will not appear in the index to probate records, and they are rarely microfilmed. You have to ask for these records to be searched at the courthouse. Some jurisdictions now provide for pre-proved wills. At the same time the will is signed by the testator, the witnesses swear in writing before a notary that the testator was of sound mind and acting freely. Wills executed in this manner are accepted for probate without the witnesses appearing personally.

Some jurisdictions require that all heirs of the estate be notified and present at the reading and recording of the will. Anyone who would argue against the admission of the will to probate may make claim then or generally forfeit any future right to contest the will.

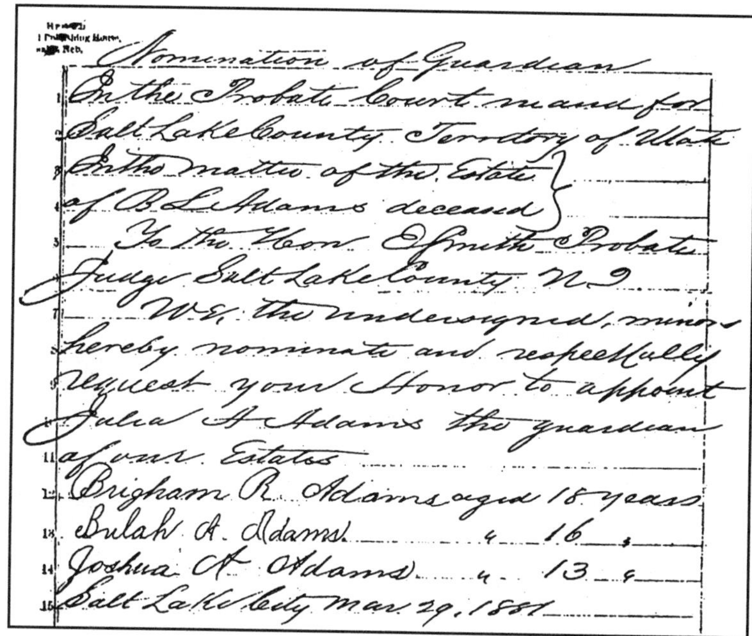

Nomination of Guardian
In the Probate Court in and for
Salt Lake County, Territory of Utah
In the matter of the Estate
of B. L. Adams deceased
To the Hon. E. Smith Probate
Judge Salt Lake County N. 9
We, the undersigned, minors
hereby nominate and respectfully
request your Honor to appoint
Julia A. Adams the guardian
of our Estates
Brigham R. Adams aged 18 years
Bulah A. Adams " 16 "
Joshua A. Adams " 13 "
Salt Lake City Mar. 29, 1881

Figure 7-7. Nomination of guardian petition of Julia A. Adams, 29 March 1881, Salt Lake County, Utah Territory.

3. The executor designated in the decedent's will must be formally approved by the court. In intestate cases, the court appoints the administrator. Each state prescribes the order in which persons are entitled to be appointed, but, in general, this order is maintained: spouse, one of the children, parents, grandparents, brothers or sisters, uncles, aunts, nephews, nieces, great-uncles, great-aunts, first cousins, creditors, anyone legally competent, public administrators, etc.

4. An administrator must post a bond equal to the worth of the assets of the estate to insure his or her faithful performance of duty and to protect the heirs in cases of misconduct. In most states, an executor is not required to file a large bond if the decedent's will exempts him or her from that trust.

Bondsmen were usually relatives or family friends until recently, when bonding companies replaced personal sureties. If the wife is executrix, the bondsmen will usually be her relatives. If a brother or son is executor, they will be chosen from the family of the deceased. Bondsmen can also be heirs to the estate.

5. In most testate and all intestate estates, three disinterested people (often relatives who are not potential heirs) are appointed by the court to inventory and appraise all the property of the estate. They are usually ordered to submit the inventory at the next term of court or within ninety days. This inventory protected the executor or administrator from excessive claims against the estate and protected heirs against fraud or pilfering of their inheritance. The court also used it to set probate fees, as in modern practice. As a result, the values given to each item were close to current market value, although there seems to have been a tendency to keep them low. Thus, the fees levied against the estate were lower.

6. As soon as the inventory is made, publication of the pending probate is published. In early times, notices were tacked on the doors of courthouses, town halls, churches, etc. Later, the court required public posting at the town hall and publication three successive weeks in the major county, town, or district newspaper before probate to give interested parties opportunity to be present to voice disagreement or to present claims against the estate. The law required preservation of those publication notices. Some jurisdictions keep copies of the newspapers in which notices appeared at the county courthouse or town hall, while others clip the notices and preserve them with the case packet. It is thus possible to find missing issues of newspapers at the probate authority.

7. Another step taken before probate begins is assigning an allowance for the dependents from a portion of the estate (usually the amount is determined annually) until the estate is settled and distributed. It may take the form of cash, income-producing property (such as a herd of cattle), or money from the court-authorized sale of certain property. Usually the property so designated is exempt from creditors' claims. At this time, also, the widow's dower right will often be set off to provide for her support.

8. In estates involving minors or incompetent individuals, a guardian is appointed to receive and assume stewardship over their respective shares. Figure 7-7 is a petition of minor children for their mother to be appointed guardian. As with administrators and executors, guardians must post a bond equal to the worth of the orphan's estate. Figure 7-8 is an example of the required bond.

9. To raise funds for the support of the widow and children or to convert perishables to cash, it is frequently necessary to conduct periodic sales of property under the surveillance of the court. First, the administrator/executor or guardian petitions the court for authority to sell, stipulating the items, why the income is needed, and how much is expected to be realized. If the court authorizes the sale, a public auctioneer is appointed and a careful account is kept of what was sold, how much each item brought, and to whom the item went.

10. In some jurisdictions, executors/administrators or guardians must account annually to the court for income received and expenses paid out of the estate, and for what purposes. In others, executors may be required only to account upon request from heirs or creditors. Because these records show heirs who die and women who marry before final settlement, they are extremely valuable for the genealogist.

11. Prior to the final settlement and distribution of the estate among the heirs, additional publication notices are issued to give claimants one last chance to voice their desires.

12. The executor/administrator must make a final accounting of receipts and disbursements of the estate before the remaining property can be divided and the responsibility ended. Figure 7-9 shows a final accounting.

GUARDIAN'S BOND.

Know all Men by these Presents, That Polly Cripe as principal, and Davis Butler & Francis M. Jeffers as Sureties, all of the County of Iowa in the State of Iowa, are held and firmly bound unto said County for the use of Sarah Jane Blackater in the penal sum of Six Hundred Dollars, for the payment of which well and truly to be made. we do jointly and severally bind ourselves, and our lawful representatives. Witness our hands and seals, this third day of June 1865

The condition of the above obligation is such, that if the above named Polly Cripe who has been appointed Guardian of the said Sarah J Blacketer shall faithfully discharge the office and trust of such Guardian according to law, and shall render a fair and just account of such Guardianship from time to time, whenever thereunto required by law and render and pay to said minor all moneys, goods and chattles, title papers and effects, which may come to the hands or possession of such Guardian belonging to such minor when such minor shall be entitled thereto, or to any subsequent Guardian, should such Court so direct, then this obligation to be void, or otherwise to remain in full force and virtue.

Polly her X mark Cripe [SEAL.]
[SEAL.]
Davis his + mark Butler [SEAL.]
Francis M. Jeffers [SEAL.]

ATTEST. H. H. Willits County Judge.

The above bond was approved and filed by me, this 3rd day of June 1865

A. H. Willits

Co. Judge of Iowa County, Iowa

Figure 7-8. Guardian's bond of Polly Cripe, for Sarah Jane Blackater, 3 June 1865, Iowa County, Iowa. Originals are in the Iowa County Courthouse, Marengo, Iowa.

13. When all parties concerned come to an agreement or when all heirs are twenty-one years of age, the property is divided and distributed to those heirs entitled to receive it, the case is closed, and the executor/administrator is released. In many probate jurisdictions, lengthy division documents will be found listing all heirs and their addresses, husbands of female heirs, and second marriages of widows. In some states, these settlement documents are found in the Office of the Land Recorder—Division of Real Estate.

14. As each heir receives his or her portion of the estate, he or she signs a receipt or release to the executor/administrator. These receipts give the name of the heir, the amount and description of property received, the name of the executor/administrator, the names of guardians of minor children, and the name of the deceased. These releases are filed among the original estate papers.

Probate records can provide an intimate glimpse into the lifestyle of an ancestor and specific facts about the family. From wills you can discover how often the men on your pedigree entrusted their assets to a wife, whether all sons inherited equally, how the daughters fared in comparison, whether a man distributed his property to his children before his death, and who was instructed to care for the widow and younger children or for incapacitated or handicapped family members. Servants were sometimes released by will and slaves freed.

What provision was made for the widow? Was firewood delivered to her door? Were living quarters and a cash allowance for needed purchases provided? Did the allowance end on remarriage? What was to happen to her portion of the estate if she remarried?

What are the demographics of your family? Who lived in the household? What was the ratio of adults to children, males to females? Did the men live to see their grandchildren? Did the women outlive the men? How many children reached adulthood before their parents died? What were the sizes of your family units? What standard of living did your family have? Did they read and write? Did a bequest include paintings, a family Bible, fine furniture, a carriage, or musical instruments?

Also revealed in a will is biographical information: title, occupation, religious affiliation, age, place of residence, place of property ownership, associates of the family, and relationship to prominent families in the area.

Did your ancestor bequeath assets to charities, such as schools, hospitals, and churches? Did he make a contribution for the upkeep of roads and bridges? Did she support a political party?

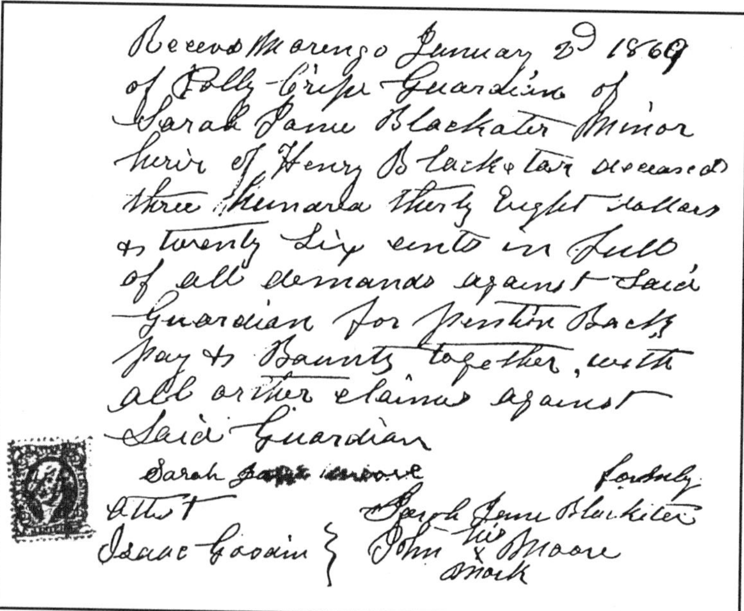

Received Marengo January 2d 1869
of Polly Cripe Guardian of
Sarah Jane Blackater Minor
heir of Henry Blackstar deceased
three hundred thirty Eight dollars
& twenty six cents in full
of all demands against said
Guardian for Pension Back
pay & Bounty together, with
all other claims against
said Guardian

Sarah ~~Jane~~ Moore formerly
Attest Sarah Jane Blackiter
Isaac Goodin } John his x Moore
mark

Figure 7-9. Final account of Polly Cripe, guardian of Sarah Jane Blackater, 3 June 1865. Original is in Iowa County Courthouse, Marengo, Iowa.

A comparison of inventories from one generation of the family to another will show improvements in living conditions—from fireplace cooking to stoves, from enclosed bedsteads to heated bedrooms, from wooden platters to china. Glass in windows, unless bequeathed as heirlooms to a family member, could be sold separately from a house, so panes may be listed in the inventory as well.

Sometimes an item will be missing from an inventory because the owner gave it away before his or her death, because it was sold to cover debts prior to death, or because it is specified in the will and falls in the executor's charge. Some inventories will end with "things unseen or forgotten," a category with an arbitrary dollar value assigned.

An inventory is also useful for distinguishing between persons of the same name by matching inventory contents, such as horses, cattle, and pigs, with tax rolls and agricultural census entries. You can also prove the relationship between a man and his children with property, real or personal, listed in inventories and wills from one generation to the next.

How did your ancestor speak? Indications of local dialect and pronunciation can be found in spelling variants, especially when a will is a holograph. It can also reveal personality, character, and level of formal education.

The probate inventory gives other insights into your family's life and how your family compared to others in the community.[18] If items are listed room by room and the rooms labeled, you know who slept where. A man was often judged by the kind of bed he slept in, so inventories usually listed bed and bedding in considerable detail: bed curtains imply a canopied bed to keep out cold drafts. Featherbeds, sheets, coverlets, blankets, and spreads may also be listed separately.

Table linens may be listed (damask, diaper, flaxen, canvas); cooking utensils and dishes (pewter, wood, china, porcelain, silverplate, brass); lighting (candles, lamps, wicks, lantern glass, and lighter fluids). In poor households, a clock might represent almost a quarter of the estate's total value. Pots and pans may be valued by weight, since that is the way they were bought and sold. Unfamiliar items, such as kimblins, piggins, and eshons (cheese vats and presses), may appear.

The processes of cooking, brewing, baking, dairying, and washing are described in the kinds of utility tubs and bowls used. The presence of smoothing tables or boards and flat irons indicate that clothes were ironed before wearing, and bedding may also have been "smoothed." Sanitary facilities inside the house could consist of chamber pots and close stools, often both. The larder hints at diet—butter, cheese, ham, bacon, hanging beef, salt pork, potatoes. Particular trades or occupations emerge from tools, mercantile inventory, record books, contents of barns, granaries, and crops in the field.

American Probate Law

Despite their usefulness, probate records are filled with traps for the unwary genealogist. The first pitfall is contemporary law. Probate is a function of state authority, with only one federal prohibition: primogeniture, or passing a landed estate automatically to the eldest son, is forbidden; by 1811, all former colonies had revoked it by statute. Because probate is a state function, probate procedures vary from state to state and have changed over time.

In addition to the pitfalls presented by ignorance of legal language and past laws, another problem may arise if a researcher concentrates only on the case files or probate packet. You should not overlook other records leading to probate that appear among the records of other courts. For example, the Court of Common Pleas in Pennsylvania was responsible for hearing evidence of incompetence and determining the status of such individuals.

Appearance Docket, Vol. A, p. 536, Perry County, Pennsylvania, contains the petition of John River, brother-in-law of Peter Arnold of Buffalo Township, to issue a writ of incompetence since Peter Arnold was a habitual drunkard. Peter's heirs are listed as George, Peter, William, and daughter Barbara, wife of George Varns. The court confirmed the petition on 16 March 1824. By 10 November 1827, Peter had reformed and petitioned the court to have his rights restored. The court granted his request and released the guardian.[19]

Table 7-1 is a checklist of documents produced by probate courts.[20] Important supporting legal documents can also be found in these non-probate categories of records:

- Bastardy papers
- Child custody papers
- Aliases
- Unfiled documents
- Manumissions
- Certificates of freedom
- Dower releases
- Marriage settlements
- Foreclosures
- Liens
- Land sold for back taxes
- Congressional petitions
- Annulments
- Orphans' court records
- Claims
- Legitimation of children
- Name changes
- Loose papers
- Inquisitions of lunacy
- Petitions for freedom
- Apprenticeships
- Marriage contracts
- Lis Pendens
- Deeds
- Tax liens
- Legislative papers
- Divorces
- Adoptions
- Appeals
- Attachments of property

Also available at law libraries are the state law codes. To locate a law effective when your ancestor was alive, check the current law code (dower rights, for instance, or age when a minor could make a will). Get the reference to the next earliest code when the law was changed or modified and work backward in time until you find the law as it was.

Although this process seems tedious, it is sometimes necessary and nearly always illuminating. The law determines the specifics in much of the probate process. Court officials do not explain what they are doing or their reasons for acting in a certain way in the records. They expect you to know that already.

The law also determined the ages at which your ancestors could transact legal business. Table 7-2 summarizes the most common ages (and exceptions) in the United States.

When courthouse fires have occurred, these other court documents may have survived if they were filed in other buildings or kept among the personal papers of justices or court officials. Some of these records are used legally in lieu of probate processes. For example, Jacob Hoofman (Hoffman) Sr. died intestate in Fairfield County, Ohio, leaving sixteen children. The probate clerk, when a search was requested, found no will, but a careful search brought an extremely detailed deed to light.

Jacob had distributed his lands to his children before his death but had died before the deed he executed for his son

Table 7-1. A Checklist of Documents Produced by Probate Courts

Court Records
- __ Estate docket
- __ Guardianship docket
- __ Claims docket
- __ Minutes
- __ Orders
- __ Decrees
- __ Judgments
- __ Executions
- __ Appeals
- __ Indexes

Petitions
- __ Letters testamentary
- __ Administration
- __ Guardianship
- __ Appointment or change of guardian
- __ Redress for misuse or waste of property
- __ List of heirs
- __ Renunciation

Wills
- __ Written
- __ Nuncupative
- __ Holographic
- __ Codicils

Bonds
- __ Administrator
- __ Executor
- __ Guardian
- __ Appraiser
- __ Trustee

Inventories
- __ Real estate
- __ Personal property
- __ Guardians
- __ Conservators
- __ Partnership
- __ Minors' estates
- __ Appraisals
- __ Appraisers warrants
- __ Reports

Publications
- __ Advertisements
- __ Announcements
- __ Notice to heirs
- __ Notice of sales
- __ Notice to creditors

Accounts
- __ Administrator
- __ Executor
- __ Guardian
- __ Trustee
- __ Conservator

Divisions
- __ Commission reports
- __ Settlements
- __ Decrees of distribution
- __ Dower rights
- __ Courtesy rights
- __ Awards
- __ Private disbursement
- __ Ledgers
- __ Guardians' final report
- __ Probate decrees
- __ Certificates of devise
- __ Assignments of real estate
- __ Order of distribution
- __ Decree of heirship

Releases
- __ Executor
- __ Administrator
- __ Trustee
- __ Guardian
- __ Heirs
- __ Conservator

Claims
- __ Petitions
- __ Registers
- __ Accounts
- __ Appeals

Miscellaneous
- __ Unrecorded wills
- __ Widows' allowances
- __ Orders to find heirs
- __ Sales documents
- __ Marriage settlements
- __ Waivers
- __ Changes of name
- __ Legitimization
- __ Memoranda
- __ Appeals
- __ Judgments
- __ Estate taxes

Table 7-2. Ages of Legal Action*

Legal Action	Legal Age	Exceptions/Comments
Inherit	From birth	An unborn child can also inherit
Be enumerated in census	From birth	Usually heads of household only until 1850
Attend school	5	Some schools accepted three year olds
Witness documents	14 (male); 12 (female)	The age of discretion under the common law was 14 (males) and 12 (females). Some exceptions are listed below
Testify in court	14 (male); 12 (female)	
Choose guardian	14 (male); 12 (female)	Must be 21 in New York. No choice until age of; then, if guardian appointed by court is unacceptable, can select another subject to court approval
Serve as apprentice	14 (male); 12 (female)	Standard term was to 21 (male), 18 (female), or time of marriage. If apprenticed before age of discretion, bound only to ages 14/12. Must have written deed which allowed for apprentice's content, except for orphans on the public charge
Show land to processioners	14 (male); 12 (female)	Males only; southern states. (Procession means to walk around the boundary lines of local property owners.)
Be punished for crime	14 (male); 12 (female)	Some general exceptions before 1860. Complicated changes in the 20th century
Sign contracts	14 (male); 12 (female)	May be required to confirm contract after arriving at majority
Act as executor	14 (male); 12 (female)	Usually administrator with will annexed so the court had some controls. Age 17 in Massachusetts, Rhode Island, Missouri; age 18 in Mississippi. Bondsman who could act as co-executor required in Vermont
Bequeath personal property by will	14 (male); 12 (female)	Age 18 in Connecticut, Massachusetts, Virginia; age 18 (male) and 16 (female) in New York; age 21 in Vermont. Property may be held in custody of court pending review
Marry	14 (male); 12 (female)	Parental consent required in most states until age 21 (male) and 18 (female). Married child not subject to control of parents, could remarry on death of spouse consent if underage. Age 18 (male) and 14 (female) in Mississippi, Ohio, Indiana; age 18 (male) and 15 (female) in Minnesota; age 17 (male) and 14 (female) in Illinois; age 16 (male) and 14 (female) in Iowa. Marriage is valid without parental consent, but officiator could be fined. Annulment or divorce only way to void the marriage
Be taxed	16	Males only were counted; females appear as "heirs of . . . "
Muster into militia	16	Males only
Procession land	16	Procession means to walk around the boundary lines of local property owners
Take possession of land holdings	16	"In possession of" on tax rolls signifies that the person named is at least 16
Practice trade	18	Some cities licensed tradesmen to practice their profession/occupation at age 18
Release of guardian	21 (male); 18 (female)	
Own land	21	Some states allowed females these rights at age 18
Devise land by will	21	
Be taxed	21	Full poll responsibility unless exempt
Plead or sue in court	21	
Be naturalized	21	After meeting residence requirements
Fill public office	21	Age 25 or older required for some offices
Serve on jury	21	Grand jury, petit jury, coroner's jury
Vote	21	Linked to 21 as age of land ownership, a prerequisite to voting in colonies

*Based in part on Judge Tapping Reeve, *The Law of Baron and Femme, of Parent and Child, Guardian and Ward, Master and Servant, and of the Powers of the Courts of Chancery; With an Essay on the Terms Heir, Heirs, Heirs of the Body,* 3rd ed. (1862; reprint, Clark, New Jersey: Lawbook Exchange, 1998). This is an important legal treatise on family law describing the common law in America and exceptions created by statute law or specific traditions inherited from Spanish or French law codes. The author assumes legal knowledge on the part of the reader, so use *Black's Law*

(Continued)

Dictionary. The original text predates the abolition of slavery and includes a discussion of law relating to slaves and their rights. It also predates much of the legal reform of the late nineteenth century, which substantially changed the laws in several states.

For the modern period, consult Chester G. Vernier, *American Family Laws: Comparative Study of the Forty-Eight American States, Alaska, District of Columbia, and Hawaii to 1 Jan. 1938,* 5 vols. with 1938 Supplement (1931; reprint, Westport, Conn.: Greenwood Press, 1971), a state-by-state study of marriage, parent-child relationships and responsibilities, divorce, and probate in all aspects. These volumes have extensive indexes, making it easy to check specifics. Both works can be found in most law libraries.

Simon could be recorded. The property went into his estate. Jacob had recorded the transaction in his own account book and the court accepted the transaction, requiring only that a quitclaim deed be signed by all sixteen children and their spouses. The document is invaluable, but it was found in the deeds, not the probate records.

Many probate records have been published by societies and individuals. As is true with any extract, some transcripts are complete and others are incomplete or have been misread. "Check the Original! Two Lessons Learned the Hard Way" *(National Genealogical Society Quarterly)* is an instructive two-part commentary on the perils of not checking compiled works against original records.[21] Part 1, "Hardy of South Carolina—A 'Discreet' Omission to Hide an Indiscretion" by John Anderson Brayton, matches a 1969 abstract of the 1769 will of Mathew Hardy of St. John's Parish, Colleton County, South Carolina, against a verbatim transcription of the will. He notes the abstract "omitted the primary heir and left out significant information that changed the entire thrust of the document."[22] Brayton suspects the omissions were to hide a master-slave concubinage hinted at in the will.

In Part 2, "Mallory-Blunt of Virginia—A Miscopied Name Blocks Line," Shana Elizabeth Proffitt gives evidence of an error in a long-accepted compilation by a leading English authority that resulted in a nearly thirty-year mystery. Proffitt's examination of the original files corrects the name: Michael, not Henry Blunt. The amendment of the error "will provide certain Blunt family descendants with a previously unknown connection to the Mallory family of colonial Virginia."[23] As Proffitt notes, "Errors happen amid notetaking, writing, and publishing, and those errors stymie research."[24]

Another problem in probate research is that not all people are referenced in probate records. New England demographic research comparing wills and probate inventories with tax rolls and other inhabitants' lists shows that less than 50 percent of the male population was included among inventories and less than 40 percent left wills. In some areas, the percentage was below 25 percent. Less than 10 percent of the women had either wills or inventories. While some people had little or no property to inventory, a substantial number seem to have deliberately made provision for their estates to pass to their heirs without probate.[25]

Probate records are of uneven value when it comes to establishing specific death dates. Some probate records include the date of death. Some indexes include the date of death, while the probate record does not. Where the death date is not given, the date of the acknowledgment of witnesses is usually the first record made in the probate process, followed by admission of the will to probate. In some jurisdictions, however, the witnesses acknowledged their signatures and certified the mental soundness of the testator at the time the will was drafted—not after the person's death. To avoid these problems, the safest date to use is the date the will was recorded—usually between thirty and ninety days after the death of the testator.

Relationships between legatees and testator were seldom defined. As a consequence, brothers and nephews are mistaken for sons, sisters-in-law and daughters-in-law appear as unmarried daughters, and daughters with unknown married names may be unidentifiable. The legatees sometimes are mentioned by first names only. "In-law" was often a synonym for "step" and adopted kin. Because of these ambiguities, it is wise to corroborate all relationships with other sources.

Probate records can provide valuable leads to those relationships. Nine clues that may help determine relationship have been formulated by eminent genealogist Donald Lines Jacobus[26]:

1. In states that allowed the eldest son a double portion of his father's estate, an estate with seven shares had six heirs, not seven.
2. Daughters unmarried at the time a will was drafted may have been married by the time it was probated. The will and subsequent documents will contain different names. Watch given names carefully and always check all males listed in the final settlement, especially if they are not listed in the will as potential sons-in-law.
3. Statements such as "my daughters Mary and Martha shall have five shillings each with what I have already given them" and "my daughter Grace shall have £30 to make her equal with her sisters" imply that some daughters were married and had already received their portions.
4. Special terminology may reveal relationships: "a femme sole" is an unmarried woman; "coverture" refers to a married woman.
5. Where two executors are named in a will, one is usually the relative of the testator and the other a relative of the spouse. Both sides of the family were represented to safeguard the interests of all parties and to keep peace.

6. Bondsmen are usually relatives who are willing to stand the risks and who have some leverage over the persons they guarantee. If the wife is executrix, the bondsmen will usually be her relatives. Where her maiden surname is unknown, look carefully at the names of the bondsmen.
7. Guardians are usually relatives who have no potential interest in the estate. With some careful calculations, you can decide who these would be and perhaps identify missing surnames.
8. When the court has to determine who inherits, unless extenuating circumstances dictate otherwise, the estate is usually awarded to heirs of the whole blood (related by blood to both sides of the family) rather than an heir of the half blood (related to one side only). In this way, the property is more likely to stay in the family.
9. Second marriages of widows are most frequently documented among probate and guardianship records, as their new husbands assume responsibilities of the estate. This makes probate records especially valuable.

Sometimes, family members are omitted from a will because they are otherwise provided for. A man can settle a jointure on his wife at the beginning of the marriage in lieu of dower rights or subsequent claims against the estate. During colonial times, when the law of primogeniture was in effect, the eldest son was frequently not mentioned in the will, for the real property descended automatically to him. Most American men also owned other lands in fee simple that could be described and left to younger sons.

As daughters married, they were customarily given their portions in cash, land, household furnishings, food, horses, slaves, etc. Sons were given their property when they reached the age of majority or planned to marry. A family account book recorded the property conveyed to each child. If, when the father's estate was later settled, a child contested the settlement, this account showed what each marriage portion was. Thus, children who had received their shares were frequently omitted from the will.

The importance of probate records to the genealogist is recognized by the regional projects, online and in print, that produce indexes. An example of print works are Thornton W. Mitchell, *North Carolina Wills: A Testator Index, 1665–1900*. Carol Willsey Bell, *Ohio Wills and Estates to 1850: An Index*, and Brent Holcomb, *Abstracts of South Carolina Wills* for several counties. These three projects are models for needed work in other areas.[27]

Divorce Actions

Divorce as a court action was introduced to the American colonies by Puritan settlers during the early 1600s. In 1620, Plymouth officials viewed marriage as a civil rather than an ecclesiastical matter. This recognition opened the door to the possibility of civil divorce. At least nine divorces were granted in Plymouth prior to 1691, when Plymouth and Massachusetts Bay were united into a single colony.

Records indicate the first colonial American divorce, however, was granted not in Plymouth but in Massachusetts Bay. In 1639, James Luxford's wife was able to show evidence that James already had a wife. The court seized Luxford's property and fined and punished him.[28]

Divorce was not the tradition in the England the early colonists had left. At the time of the founding of America, an English divorce was rare, expensive, time-consuming, against Anglican law, and frowned upon socially. Lawrence Friedman states, "Henry VIII had gotten a divorce; but ordinary Englishmen had no such privilege. The very wealthy might squeeze a rare private bill of divorce out of Parliament. Between 1800 and 1836 there were, on the average, three of these a year. For the rest, unhappy husbands and wives had to be satisfied with annulment (no easy matter), or divorce from bed and board (*a mensa et thoro*), a form of legal separation. Separated couples had no right to remarry.[29]

A study of the English system that formed the basis of divorce law in all the colonies is Lawrence Stone's three volumes: *Road to Divorce: England, 1530–1987; Uncertain Unions: Marriage in England, 1660–1753*; and *Broken Lives: Separation and Divorce in England, 1660–1857*.[30]

During the American colonial period, the extent and type of divorce differed from colony to colony. In New England, where marriage was considered a civil contract, courts granted civil divorces from early times. Grounds included adultery, abuse, neglect, and desertion by the husband. In other colonies, if divorce was allowed at all, grounds were limited to dissolving a marriage that was within the prohibited degrees of consanguinity or affinity.[31]

In the middle or border colonies—New York, New Jersey, and Pennsylvania—divorces were handled either by the governor and his council or by petition to the Assembly. Adultery or prolonged desertion were the only grounds recognized. New York did grant absolute divorces *(a vinculo matrimonii)* prior to 1675, thereafter only *a mensa et thoro* divorces.[32] Penn's laws of 1682 gave Pennsylvania spouses the right to a "Bill of Divorcement" if their marriage partner was convicted of adultery.

The situation was restrictive in the southern colonies, where most followed the English tradition of no absolute divorce and only rare instances of divorce from bed and board.[33] Here, the Church of England had greater influence, thus few civil divorce laws were in effect until after the American Revolution. Eighteenth-century North Carolina law, for example, did not provide for absolute divorce, and, although legal in the nineteenth century, non-absolute divorce was rare. The few separations that were granted were in the form of orders of the General Court for separate maintenance, often called alimony. Records of these cases will be at the North Carolina State Archives among the Legislative Papers.[34]

In contrast, prior to its becoming a part of the United States in 1803, Louisiana's Superior Council regularly granted divorces of bed and board as shown by surviving French colonial records. These were almost always based on the charge of cruelty.[35]

Following the American Revolution, divorce laws and attitudes towards divorce generally broadened, although regional differences remained strong. Divorce in the South continued to be rare. But in all of the original colonies and most of the other states divorce by legislative petition was allowed. This "legislative" or "private act" divorce required a petitioner's case to be heard before either the territorial or state legislature.

As these petitions increased in number, overburdened legislatures gave the judicial function to the regular courts. Maryland provides an example. By the mid-1830s, the Maryland legislature was granting slightly more than thirty divorces a year. By 1842, the number of divorces sought was so great that primary jurisdiction was transferred to the courts. Nine years later, the Maryland Constitution of 1851 prohibited legislative divorce entirely.[36]

Profound differences have always existed from one state to another. Each state determines when legislative divorce ceases and goes to local courts and then which court will handle divorce cases—superior court, equity court, probate court, or family or domestic court. The procedure basically allows the judge to decide what is just and equitable in each case within the limits set by the law. Because of this lack of uniformity, a researcher must study the development of divorce in each relevant jurisdiction. Studies such as Thomas E. Buckley's *The Great Catastrophe of My Life: Divorce in the Old Dominion*, which examines the 471 surviving divorce petitions to the Virginia legislature for the years 1786 to 1851,[37] is one example of a regional work that would prove useful to Virginia researchers. (See the suggested readings on divorce in the references section at the end of this chapter.)

The divorce rate escalated after the Civil War. In some areas of the Midwest and West, legal tolerance of divorce ranged from slightly permissive to wide open. In Iowa, between 1870 and 1880 the divorce rate jumped from forty-nine to sixty per hundred thousand of population. Factors that may have contributed to this were a liberalizing of religious beliefs, varied ethnic and racial values, and disruptively high rates of migration.[38]

Throughout the latter half of the nineteenth century and well into the twentieth century, only one state defied the rising numbers. The laws of South Carolina, despite an experiment with a divorce clause from 1868 to 1878 (during which time not one divorce was granted), did not allow for an absolute divorce until the 1949 Divorce Act went into effect. Only then was divorce allowed and jurisdiction placed in the Court of Common Pleas.

Divorce Records and Their Location

Divorce records will be found in colonial court records and territorial and state legislatures, as well as in county, state, and territorial courts. Pre-Revolutionary divorces may be found in colonial legislative records. Copies of the private acts for divorce may be recorded in the Colonial Office volumes, available in print in large research libraries. Each volume is individually indexed for all documents abstracted or calendared. Originals are in the Public Record Office, Ruskin Ave., Kew, Richmond, Surrey, TW9 4DU, UK.

Multivolume sets of selected abstracts for most of the original colonies have been printed in archive series at government expense and can be found in most large research libraries throughout the United States. Abstracts should be used as indexes to the originals.

Divorces filed in the years immediately before and following statehood may be in the proceedings of the territory or the state's legislative body. The granting of a divorce was usually recorded as a Private Act in the legislative proceedings. There should also be evidence of the divorce, such as details of settlement, at the county of residence of the plaintiff. Legislative divorces continued to be granted in some areas long after the same powers were granted to the regular courts, so researchers should check the records of assembly and council as well as the court records. Delaware was the last holdout of legislative divorce, which survived in that state until 1897. Legislative divorces will appear in printed volumes that can serve as name indexes to the original files.

Most nineteenth-century and some earlier divorces will be found in county or circuit courts or their counterparts in the county where filing occurred. These will be in civil court records that are usually well indexed. Divorce records may be recorded in volumes with the regular court cases or in separate volumes reserved for divorce cases. The index provides quick identification of a divorce because the plaintiff and defendant will carry the same surname.

Some indexes and abstracts are in print (a few are listed in the reference section), others are online. Various indexes to local civil case files that contain divorce are online, including those for the Utah counties of Cache (1860–87), Davis (1875–86), Salt Lake (1852–87), and Weber (1852–87). These are at <http://historyresearch.utah.gov/indexes/index.html>.

The manner of entry in court books or in a case file or case packet parallels the record-keeping of other civil cases. A case file may provide affidavits, lists of children with their ages, property inventories, and other data. The date and place of marriage, ages or dates of birth of the couple, places of birth, and the grounds for the divorce are usually included. Divorce records may list the names of other family members, since the children may be in the custody of grandparents, uncles, or close family friends.

Some states require a certificate of divorce, with a copy filed at the state bureau of vital statistics. New Hampshire has issued certificates since 1880; other states did not begin this practice until well into the 1930s. Court records are public records, but those issued in the past fifty years might be protected by privacy legislation, and the permission of the divorced party may be required to get the data. Some states do not have certificates on file but can verify dates and refer queries to the court that has the record.

A researcher may find the first indication of a divorce in local newspapers. Early newspapers often carried notices placed by husbands to warn local tradesmen that they would no longer be responsible for debts incurred by their ex-wives. On occasion, wives also placed notices of freedom. This pair of entries, is from in the *Vermont Gazette:*

> January 7, 1796: Whereas my husband, Enoch Darling, has at sundry times used me in an improper and cruel a manner as to destroy my happiness and endanger my life, and whereas he has not provided for me as a husband ought, but expended his time and money unadvisedly, at taverns, to the detriment of myself and his family, I notify the public that I am obligated to leave him and shall henceforth pay no debts of his contracting. Phebe Darling, alias Phebe Adams, Bennington.
>
> January 7, 1796: Phebe, my wife has left my bed and board without just cause or provocation. I will not pay debts of her contracting. Enoch Darling, Bennington.[39]

Newspapers also carried legal notices to inform missing parties and creditors of the pending case. (During the colonial period, notices were posted on the town bulletin board at the courthouse, church, or city hall). If the location of a defendant was known, he would be served with papers by a court official. If the whereabouts were unknown, a notice was published in the newspapers. Such news notices often ran as long as forty weeks. As communications improved, the time was gradually decreased to three to four weeks. Some newspapers, particularly the urban press, would publish lists of divorces granted. (See chapter 12, "Newspapers," for instructions on how to find old newspapers.)

The disposition of property in any divorce case is determined by state statute or by equitable decision of the court. Alimony is the allowance a woman is entitled to receive from her husband during separation and after divorce. The amount is usually set by the court based on the financial circumstances of the husband and the needs of the wife. In rare instances, a husband may be granted alimony from his wife. Alimony can be paid in monthly or annual installments or as a single lump sum, and the obligation usually ends when the spouse remarries. In some jurisdictions, a wife guilty of adultery is denied alimony; in others she receives payment regardless of such circumstances.

In South Carolina, which did not recognize divorce until 1950 (except for a brief period from 1868 to 1878[40]), or states that severely limited the grounds for divorce, courts accepted petitions for alimony to provide for the needs of family members who wished to live apart.

In most jurisdictions, until recently, if the wife was not guilty of adultery, she was entitled to her full dower and one-third of her husband's property at his death, even though a divorce had taken place. Some jurisdictions subtracted from the dower the amount already received in alimony. A husband could claim, by right of curtesy, one-third of the wife's property.

As they do today, courts outlined provisions for children of dissolved marriages at the time the divorce was granted. In the 1832 divorce of Patrick and Susannah Martin in Gibson County, Indiana, the children Jane and Martha went to the father while the mother received "the babe, two beds, two colts, and one cow."[41] The custody of children is usually awarded based upon individual circumstances, although some jurisdictions today permit children above a certain age (eight to fourteen) to choose which parent they wish to live with.

The law may have stipulated that the father must help pay for the upbringing of the children. The amount was determined by the court, based upon the earning ability of the father and the number of children. Few legal remedies were available for cases of non-payment.

Most divorce files prior to the mid-twentieth century are open to researchers. Some modern courts seal all or part of the records of divorce proceedings, and they are available only to the parties.

Divorce Meccas

Certain states (or counties or colonies) gained reputations for easy divorce. Stringent laws in one state led to migration into states and cities where divorces were easier to obtain. Ashtabula County in Ohio, which was readily accessible from New York, Pennsylvania, and Ontario, Canada, granted many divorces to non-Ohio residents. Chicago granted four hundred divorces in 1868 alone. Indiana had no residency requirements until 1859 and Utah Territory not until 1878.

Early Utah quickly gained the reputation of being a divorce "mecca," with its broad grounds for divorce, inexpensive court procedures, and lack of residency requirements. Thus, Christina Anderson, in 1866 Weber County, could obtain an divorce for abuse and maltreatment, grounds that were not allowed in eastern courts.[42] When out-of-state people began arriving to take advantage of this situation, Utah stiffened its residency requirements and lengthened the waiting period.

About 1890, the city of Sioux Falls, South Dakota, became the newest divorce mecca in the United States. As the hub of major railroad lines, the city, on the eastern border, featured easy access for divorce seekers. An abundance of attorneys and courtrooms and a thriving night life perpetuated its image as a "rollicking and extremely lenient divorce colony."[43] The short residency requirement of just ninety days in the county where filed and the practice of notification by publication, not delivery, meant the defendant need not respond in order for a divorce to be granted.

Western states, in particular, gained notoriety for their liberal divorce laws. There the divorce rate rose faster than in northeastern or southern states, even when discounting migratory divorces. Two Census Bureau studies conducted 1867–1887 and 1887–1906, showed that the most common single ground for divorce in the Western states was desertion. A high percent of these were by females who left husbands behind when they headed west, perhaps because leaving was easier and less expensive than petitioning for a divorce. But most divorces due to desertions were filed by males. A wife who refused to join her husband in the West, choosing instead to remain in their former home in the East, was considered a deserter in jurisdictions whose laws stated that a husband's domicile constituted the family domicile.[44]

This extreme rise in numbers was in part responsible for movements in the latter part of the nineteenth century to regularize and control divorce in the entire United States. But it was difficult to change state statutes, and, even when done, enforcement was defective. Divorce would continue as would the debate and controversy.

Types of Court Records

Most courts in America are courts of record—that is, they are required by law to keep a record of their proceedings. Inferior courts, not required by law to keep a record, usually do so for their own convenience. They need to know what they did and when. Before the days of shorthand and court transcript machines, the clerk received complete written depositions, testimony of witnesses, summons, writs, and often attorneys' arguments so he had a complete record of the essential parts of the case. From these and his own notes, the clerk prepared minutes, orders, and judgments.

While practices vary from one court to another and between state and federal courts, the kinds of records summarized in table 7-3 can be found. In addition to the records in table 7-3, the court process produces sheriff and constable files, coroners' inquests, jury and jail records, and attorney lists.

Some states file all cases together in one set of volumes, with one set of case files running chronologically by date and number. Other states use a different set for divorces, equity proceedings, and so on. Probate records are almost always separate.

Although the case file is an invaluable collection of testimony and exhibits that may include photographs, marriage certificates, wills, receipts for the division of property in an estate, writs, and subpoenas, it is created only for matters before the court that involve litigants. The administrative activities of the court, such as the binding out of apprentices, the exemption of the elderly from taxes or military service, appointments of road inspectors or militia officers, and memorials for soldiers killed in war are recorded only in the minutes and orders of the court.

Indexes

Indexes to court records are usually incomplete. Some list only the surnames of the litigants (*Potts v. Abernathy*, 12, 81–3, 289), some approach docket-style entries (*William Potts v. Robert Abernathy*, Case in Common Pleas: Warrant, 12; deposition, 81–83; report, 289) and some index plaintiffs only (William Potts, 12, 81, 82, 83, 289). Since 1900, some courts have prepared typewritten indexes by plaintiff and defendant, with separate subject indexes for the use of bench and bar. Rarely do these official indexes list jurors, witnesses, attorneys, justices, and other parties mentioned. Administrative court actions are not indexed either. While most courts have retained original indexes or microfilmed copies of the originals, almost all courts have moved to or are in the process of moving to computerized indexes to retrieve current case files.

During the 1930s, the Work Projects Administration (WPA) organized several court indexing projects using out-of-work schoolteachers, secretaries, and executives. Projects in West Virginia, Tennessee, Ohio, and other parts of the country have made searching for court records almost painless. A good example of the thoroughness of the WPA index comes from the 1823 to 1829 minute dockets of Rhea County, Tennessee. Col. George Gillespie is not mentioned in the original index, but the WPA index includes sixty-seven entries for him.

Dockets

When a judicial body agrees to hear a case, it is placed on the court docket until trial. Abbreviated entries are made on the dockets for all changes in the status or pending action of the case for each term of court until the case is closed, carried over, or settled out of court, or until judgment is rendered. Thus, any time a case is pending, its current status may be determined by examining the docket. Most cases were on docket for at least three or four terms of court.

Most courts maintain several different dockets: criminal, civil, equity (chancery), miscellaneous (condemnations, lunacy commitments, disqualification of voters, adoptions, divorces, tax foreclosures, insolvency, estates, and so forth), stets (cases removed from the regular docket because they have been inactive for several years), and claims (claims of creditors against estates and property). A court that maintains separate dockets will usually separate its other records into distinct volumes. Some courts maintain only one court docket for all types of

Table 7-3. Types of Court Records and the Forms They Take

Record	Type	Bound Volume	Filed Papers	Loose Papers	Case File
Indexes (alphabetical):	Plaintiff	•			
	Defendant	•			
	Reverse	•			
	Every name	•			
Dockets: calendar or waiting list of pending cases, in the order they will be considered by the court	Civil	•			
	Criminal	•			
	Equity	•			
	Chancery	•			
	Estate	•			
	Orphans'	•			
	Guardian	•			
	Probate	•			
	Name change	•			
	Claims	•			
	Insolvents'	•			
	Bankruptcy	•			
	Divorce	•			
	Adoption	•			
	Lunacy	•			
	Reference	•			
	Execution	•			
	Appearance	•			
	Appeals	•			
	New actions	•			
Minutes: descriptive entries of all actions taking place in the court process	Journals	•			
	Register of actions	•			
	Appeal briefs		•		•
Orders: official record of all orders of the judge(s)	Journals	•			
	Writs		•		•
	Summons		•		•
	Warrants		•		•
	Subpoenae		•		•
	Actions	•			
	Indictments				•
	Presentments				•
	Executions	•			•
	Stays (demurrers)	•			•
	Injunctions				•
	Foreclosures				•
	Attachments				•
	Distraints		•		
	Jury lists				
Judgments: final decisions, punishments, and awards made by the court	Satisfied	•			

Record	Type	Bound Volume	Filed Papers	Loose Papers	Case File
	Short	•			
	Equity	•			
	Decrees	•			
	Fines	•			
	Liens	•			
	Verdicts	•			
	Opinions	•			
	Decisions	•			
	Reports		•		
	Appeals		•		
	Bills of costs		•		
Case files or packets: all original papers placed in the hands of the court during a court case	Civil				•
	Criminal				•
	Equity				•
	Estate				•
	Orphans'				•
	Probate				•
	Chancery				•
	Divorce				•
	Adoption				•
	Claims				•
	Insolvents'				•
	Lunacy				•
	Bankruptcy				•
	Appeals				•
				Bonds	•
				Depositions	•
				Testimony	•
				Declarations	•
				Inventories	•
				Documents	•
				Exhibits	•
				Receipts	•
				Petitions	•
				Affidavits	•
				Pleas	•
				Pleadings	•
				Allegations	•
				Complaints	•
				Inquisitions	•
				Examinations	•
				Promissory notes	•
				Letters	•
				Appraisals	•
				Arbitration reports	•

cases. Sometimes duplicate dockets are prepared for judges, attorneys, or court clerks. Many dockets are indexed by plaintiff, by defendant, or by both; naturally, such indexes vary a great deal in form. Dockets may also be called "minute dockets," combining two records into one.

The value of dockets is in their use as an index. They are not alphabetically arranged, but reading them is faster than having to read every page. For example, if searching for the surname Potts, 1813 to 1845, begin with the dockets for the first term of court in 1813. Searching the dockets through twenty-two terms of court to 1 September 1818 reveals "William Potts v. Robert Abernathy Crd o" (carried over). This notation indicates that a case involving William Potts was placed on the docket but that no judgment had been made. Searching the quarterly dockets reveals that the case appeared on the docket and was carried over in December 1818, March 1819, June 1819, September 1819, December 1819, and March 1820.

From these entries can be found information in both the minutes and the orders for each term of court through March 1820, when the case was closed. At this point, most court clerks place all of the miscellaneous papers pertaining to the case into one file labeled with the term of court in which judgment was rendered, the title of the case, and the case number. This case file is now the point of interest, supplementing the minutes and orders. If the court kept judgment records, they too will be arranged chronologically. Thus, entrance to the minutes, the orders, the judgments, and the case files is gained by using the dockets.

Court Minutes

All actions of the court are briefly recorded by the clerk in the minutes. Though rarely indexed, minutes are valuable. Where dockets and indexes are missing, minutes will identify terms of court where an ancestor's cases appear. Early courts tended to meet every three months for a week or until business was completed. The minute books generally record the term of the court ("June term"), the month and year of meeting, and the place of sitting. In colonial days and on the early western frontier prior to the building of a courthouse, the court could be held in a private home or a business establishment, such as a tavern. The names of the justices present were next recorded. The court's business, as it took place, was then entered in diary form. At the end of the court's term, the clerk's signature would appear, followed by "CC" (Clerk of Court) or another designation. The justices often signed as well, to authenticate the minutes.

Court minutes at the county level will reflect a variety of matters. Minutes will include civil suits, criminal cases (although not if the penalty was death or if cared for by another court) and the settlement of estates. In addition, some or all of the following may appear: the appointments of officeholders, i.e., overseers of the poor, coroners, justices of the peace, jurors, and tax officials; the issuing of business licenses for ferries, mills, and taverns; the consideration of reports and petitions; coroners' inquests; appointment of guardians for those unable to manage their own affairs; apprenticeships; manumission of slaves; stock marks and brands; matters concerning taxes and public buildings; and some land matters. In short, the full range of court activities will fall within the recorded minutes. The minutes may not always be complete enough to include the names of all witnesses and jurors; however, it is far easier to search through unindexed minutes than it is to examine the individual papers filed in each case file for each term of court.

Orders

Orders of the court are recorded by law in most jurisdictions for future reference. Executions are an important kind of order, often rating a separate volume for recording. They are directed to the sheriff, marshal, or constable to enforce, usually include a brief résumé of the court case, and describe the judgment to be carried out.

Many items of court business, especially before 1800, have nothing to do with litigation, for courts were administrative bodies as well as courts of law. The following extracts from court minutes and orders will show you the potential value of these records.

Appointment of Guardians

The following entry, from the Order Book of the Augusta County Court, Virginia, 1750, is the only indication of the fact that James Berry was the guardian and not the father of these orphans:

> Ordered that James Berry be appointed Guardian of John Berry, James Berry, and William Berry orphans of James Berry, dec'd.

This item distinguishes between the three James Berrys.

Memorials

The court may also order a memorial resolution as an expression of the community's respect for the deceased. Here is an 1849 example:

> The death of Chapman Johnson occurred at the residence of John B. Baldwin in Richmond on the 12th of June 1849. The Court expressed respect and admiration for him. A motion to obtain a memorial to such a truly great and good man was made. He had many social and mental virtues and legal abilities, an ardent and unselfish patriotism, and monumental purity as a statesman.
>
> Ordered that the court present to the presses of Staunton and Richmond for publication and a special copy to the family: 14 June 1849.

> Having learned that Chapman Johnson, who was for many years a citizen of their town and acknowledged head of the legal profession, not only here but in the Commonwealth of Virginia, and who departed this life in the city of Richmond on the 12th of June it is due alike to their feelings and the public sentiment of the community that the Augusta County Bar Association gives publically their deep sense of loss, their affectionate regard for his memory, and their sympathy to his estimable family. Mr. Johnson became a resident of the town of Staunton more than 40 years ago. His profound learning as a lawyer and his distinguished eloquence as an orator endeared all to him. More than 20 years ago he removed himself to Richmond, but his removal did not sever the ties which bound him to Augusta County. A portion of each year was spent by him within our borders. In 1829, though of Richmond, he represented Augusta County at the convention to revise the State Convention. Our loss, with yours, is great.
>
> It was further decided that the court would wear the badge of mourning for 30 days.[45]

This entry would be invaluable to a researcher who was unable to locate Chapman's whereabouts or unable to determine when or where he died.

Naturalizations

While the subject of naturalizations is discussed in great detail in chapter 9 "Immigration and Naturalization Records," it is important to note here that often the only references to early naturalizations are the court orders granting citizenship. An 1851 example from the Augusta County, Virginia, Court Order Book announces:

> It is ordered by this court that Samuel Johnston formerly of Ireland who declared his intention to become a citizen of this state some 2 years ago having resided in the United States at least 4 years and in Virginia at least 1 year, be granted United States Citizenship.[46]

Furthermore, swearing-in formalities for a witness or a jury member often require a statement of citizenship status such as, "I, William Patrick, of Trenton, New Jersey, late of Dublin, Ireland, age 42, do declare . . ." This type of brief note, which would not have been discovered using an index, points out the necessity of reading original court records in their entirety for the time period and area of research.

Judgments

In some jurisdictions, when judgment is given by the court and the case is closed, the court clerk is required to make an extensive minute entry with abridgement of the case and its resolution in a special book of judgments. These volumes are popular legal sources for lawyers and members of the bench because of their brevity. Before the days of printed court opinions, these judgments formed the precedents for future legal decisions. Below are some examples taken from the Eastowne (Westchester), New York, Mayor's Court for 1657:

> Eastowne May ye 1: 1657. where as it doth appeare in court that Roger miles Jarmia Akenes and hendrick corneloson waare the caus of kiling wine [swine] to the number of seven yet being a actidentall thing therefore the sentance of the coreut is yt they shall pay thirty shilings to anne quinbe proposinably and cost of coreut which is eighttene shilings and to be performed in ten days
>
> Eastowne may ye 1: 1657. whereas it appears in curuet that Larans Turner is in deted to hendrick Corneloson five pounds Sterling thirteen shilings yet becaus ten of the catel were not keept at winter ther fore the sentense of the couert is that Larans Turner shall pay to hendrick Corneluson five pounds Sterling acording to the complaint and [?] cost of coreut which is seven shiling
>
> mary Corneluson plantiv against gorg wright in an action of slander
>
> Eastowne may ye 1: 1657. it being proved in coreut that gorg wright hath ruyestly betwen mary Corneluson and good wife [illegible word] that was formerly ended therfore the sentens of the cureut is that gorg wright is fined and shall pay to mary Corneluson three gilders and cost of court which is fourtene shilings to be performed in ten days
>
> June ye 12 1657. Richard Ponten plantive in the case of mary corneluson is plantive in atction of batrey against ales martin
>
> September ye 1: 1657. Thomas martine plantive against Josiah Gilbord in a aktion of slander wher as it cannot be proved that Josiah Gilbord hath slanderd Thomas martin therfor for the sentanc of The cureut is that Thomas martin is to pay all cost of cureut which amounts to six shilings and three pense to be pad in 10 days.[47]

Case Files

Case files are among the most valuable of all court records because they contain original copies of evidence, writs, testimony, subpoenas, publications, etc., and thus are usually the most complete. In these files will be found details that are never recorded in the minutes, orders, or judgments. In some jurisdictions, court clerks group all closed case files into one large bundle for each term of court and label it with that term. However, other court clerks assign case numbers to their files and access them through plaintiff-defendant cross-indexes.

Case files may contain one document or hundreds of them. Even before shorthand, most significant testimony was taken down in writing and, if not signed by witnesses, at least attested by the court. Because of the tremendous volume of case files that have been created over the years, the vast majority of them have not been microfilmed or digitized. It is usually necessary to conduct personal research or to send a representative to most courthouses (or the warehouses or archives where case files may be stored) in order to view them.

Witnesses Lists

Most courts reimbursed witnesses, an arrangement that encouraged participation from those who had to travel long distances or leave employment to appear. Witness books and lists show the names of witnesses and the amounts they received in payment. Some lists even include the addresses and ages of the witnesses named. These lists may not have been complete. Nevertheless, they provide another means of identifying ancestral families in the cases where they exist.

Jury Records

There are commonly three types of juries: the grand jury, the petit jury, and the coroner's jury.

The grand jury, or indictment jury, consists of one to twenty-three members and holds a preliminary hearing court to consider the evidence against a person accused of a crime and to determine if the evidence justifies holding the defendant for trial. They can also present those suspected guilty of law violations for punishment based upon their own personal knowledge.[48]

The petit jury, or trial jury, consists of six to twelve persons and acts as an impartial body to hear the evidence of the case and to reach a just decision based upon that evidence. When a coroner's jury was used it consisted of three to twenty-four members and was charged with hearing evidence about deaths under questionable circumstances.

Most courts maintain separate records of jury duty. For each court term, a specific number of names is drawn from a list of all those eligible to serve, prepared from the tax records or voters' lists on file in the county. The jurors' list will show the jurors' names, addresses, occupations, and sometimes ages. Jurors excused or exempt are indicated with the reason for the dismissal. Each person selected is summoned to appear by the court. Coroners' juries are also called by drawing and summons, but they serve only for specific cases.

In most jurisdictions, a jury call is mandatory unless the person has an acceptable excuse for refusing. Originally, the only records kept were the summons and minute entries made by the court clerk. Before long, however, many jurisdictions began to reimburse jurors for travel costs and loss of employment income while on duty and to keep careful records of jury service as a basis for payment. When the court meets in session each day, a roll call of jurors determines who is present.

Many courts require grand juries to keep careful records of their investigations in separate volumes. These records contain the roll call and description of the case under consideration, including testimony of witnesses, reports, and findings of the jury. The actual trial record of a case after indictment contains a summary of the findings of the grand jury, but its own minutes are usually more complete.

In a jury book, you will find each case listed with the names of jurors who served on the case, the court term, the case number, and the number of the juror. Some courts prefer to record petit, grand, and coroner juries separately, while others use the same volume for all three types.

The attendance record gives the names and addresses of the jurors, the days served, the days defaulted, date excused from service, and the kind of jury—petit, grand, or coroner's—on which each juror served. From this attendance record, payment is made for the number of days served.

Not all jurisdictions use or preserve discharge certificates. Each certification shows the name and address of the juror, the date of discharge from jury duty, and sometimes the reason for discharge—death, disability, end of term, etc.

The genealogical value of jury records lies in such information as names, occupations, and addresses. Jury records can also prove that the person named is still alive at that date, that he or she is a citizen of the jurisdiction, that he or she owns property—real estate or its equivalent—in the jurisdiction, and that he or she is of legal age. If a juror dies or moves from the jurisdiction during service, normally the record will note it.

Attorney Records

The attorneys who appear in court on behalf of the plaintiff or defendant are not always lawyers. In fact, several colonies in early years actually banned the practice of law by attorneys-at-law—professional lawyers educated in techniques and procedures of law. Instead, this role was taken by attorneys-in-fact, proxies for the plaintiff or defendant who pleaded the case for someone else before the court.[49] In most colonies, they were literate and experienced individuals, though not technically trained.

As universities were founded and travel and communication with England improved, the number of attorneys-at-law increased while attorneys-in-fact decreased in proportion. By the time of the American Revolution, the colonies had trained lawyers and learned judges, but lay attorneys still acted for many decades.

There are two main types of records concerning attorneys. The first is letters of attorney, or permission for an attorney-in-fact to appear before the court on behalf of a plaintiff or defendant. Such a letter is very similar to the letters testamentary or administrative in a probate case and contains the name of attorney, the party granting proxy, the case involved, and the date when permission is granted.

The second is rolls of attorneys. Most courts maintain separate volumes of attorneys and members of the local bar who are licensed and approved to appear before that particular court. Each roll contains the name of the attorney, the sponsor, and the date of the admission to the bar. Some rolls also contain dates of death, disbarment, removal from the jurisdiction, etc. Some jurisdictions require law students to register as prospective bar members. These registrations contain the name and address of the student, the lawyer under whom the intern will serve, school, sponsors, and the report of the board of law examiners concerning qualifications. Sometimes the date and place of birth, age, and even parents' names are included. To learn more about researching attorneys, see chapter 4, "Business, Institution, and Organization Records."

Sheriff (Marshal, Constable, Chief of Police) Records

In every action filed in the courts of record, a sheriff is called upon to perform some service. The sheriff serves the official writs, summons, and subpoenas and must execute all final judgments of the court. The sheriff is responsible for the preservation of the peace, enforcement of laws, arresting felons and committing them to jail, and executing the mandates, orders, and directions of the court. The sheriff has the power to command every person above fifteen years of age to respond for the protection of the jurisdiction and preservation of the peace in times of emergency or be subject to fine or imprisonment. In so acting, the sheriff represents the sovereignty of the state, and no one in a county is superior to the sheriff.

The counterpart of the sheriff in a large municipality is the chief of police; in the federal court system, the marshal. The constable serves in a like manner within the area served by a magistrate or justice of the peace: he serves as the sheriff in any matter within the jurisdiction of the local magistrate. The constable has the same powers and responsibilities within a more limited sphere of authority.

The records preserved by the sheriff can be conveniently divided into those produced as executive officer of the court and those produced as an instrument of law enforcement.

Records Produced as Court Executive

The sheriff is responsible to serve all writs issued by the court. Original writs are unserved writs. They may be current ones about to be served or old ones for persons whose whereabouts are unknown or whose fees for service have not been paid. Some jurisdictions require that the sheriff preserve a copy of all writs that he served. Some sheriffs maintain a running list of the writs they have received for service. This list contains the type of writ, the date issued, the names and addresses of the parties, the court term, case number, and the date filed.

In some jurisdictions, record of all writs is kept in the same volume. In others, various kinds of writs are recorded in separate volumes—*capias* (arrest warrants), summons, warrants, executions, sales of condemned property, etc.

Most sheriffs also preserve a docket recording all writs served and any resultant sales of property. This docket will give the names of the parties, court, term and case number, title of the action, date filed, attorney named, costs and fees, disposition (judgment and execution) of the case, and the sheriff's signature.

Some sheriffs keep a special volume recording all deeds transferred by sheriff's sale. These show the description of the property, the date and amount of sale, the name and address of the grantee, and the date of the deed.

A lien book is similar, recording all liens on property within their jurisdiction that have resulted from court order. They will show the date of the lien, the parties involved, date of sale notice, location, and description of property.

Because the sheriff is frequently responsible to select as well as summon the jurors for each court term, he will often have a copy of the court's jury records.

Records Produced in Law Enforcement

Many sheriffs maintain a fingerprint and "mug" file; however, such files are of such recent origin that it is rare for the genealogical researcher to encounter them.

In most jurisdictions, the sheriff is responsible for the care and supervision of the local jail and its occupants. Unknown to most researchers, jail records are available as early as 1695 and perhaps earlier. Because the majority of incarcerations in the past were for debt, not crime, many Americans appeared at least once in these records before debt no longer was a cause of imprisonment.[50]

Before the American Revolution, jails were used to detain offenders awaiting trial, debtors, and witnesses. Violators of laws sometimes had to wait as long as a year before being brought to trial, and debtors were held until their property could be condemned and sold to pay the debts. Debtors with no property were released.

Some jurisdictions—Georgia, for example—"farmed out" convicts and debtors for labor and board beginning during the last quarter of the eighteenth century or the first quarter of the nineteenth century.[51] Jail records include journals kept by sheriffs, jail wardens, or deputies. They are similar to daybooks and show the name and sex of every prisoner, the type of sentence and its length, dates of commitment and discharge, and reason for discharge: death, pardon, termination of sentence, etc. (For a more complete treatment of jail records, see chapter 4, "Business, Institution, and Organization Records.")

The register of prisoners contains the prisoner's physical description (hair, eyes, weight, height—later records contain fingerprints and photograph), name and address, age, occupation, date and place of birth, habits and distinguishing characteristics, crime committed, sentence, education, previous prison record, dates of commitment and discharge, name of committing official, etc. This record can also be called the admission record, commitment register, prisoner's docket, or discharge book; it is required by law in most jurisdictions. Some even include the destinations of discharged offenders.

Some jurisdictions have required medical records since the early days of their jails. This register contains the name, physical description, age, sex, mental condition, and a brief medical history of each prisoner requiring medical attention. As part of this history, names and ages of parents, siblings, spouses, and children are often included.

The prisoners' daily record shows the daily roll of prisoners, their names, the date, the number of meals served, the total cost per day for each prisoner, etc. Because the United States had no penitentiaries for several decades for those convicted in federal courts under federal laws, separate records were kept on these prisoners in regular jails so that claims for costs could be submitted to the federal government.

Since 1814, jail keepers have been required to keep separate records of all prisoners of war either awaiting trial or imprisoned after conviction—again, for reimbursement by the government. The contents of these registers are similar to the regular registers, but they also contain information concerning capture and military unit.

Most jurisdictions require that the jail keeper prepare an inventory of prisoners' property taken into custody during their term of imprisonment. The prisoner's name and signature is usually found in these records, along with the list of property.

Some jails preserve a record of all prisoners who are transferred to another jail showing the name, date of commitment, date and place of transfer, reason for transfer, and so forth.

In one family research project, Bridget Nixon proved decidedly elusive. A family tradition held that her alcoholism alienated her family. Her children were housed with relatives, and the husband finally divorced her, then remarried and reunited the children. Finding documents to support the tradition, however, was difficult until a search of jail records revealed her activities in St. Paul, Minnesota, from 1856 to 1860.

Aug 1856 p. 77	Criminal Court City of St. Paul vs Bridget Nixon Disorderly conduct, no return of process
20 Nov 1856 p. 84	Cited Bridget Nixon for drunkenness arrested by officer White W.R. Miller, City Marshall
Nov 1856 p. 90	Police Court of St. Paul United States vs Bridget Nixon Threats of violence Defendant committed in default of recognizance to keep the peace Orlando Simons, City Justice.
May 26 1857	Report of the Chief of Police W.R. Miller submits claims for boarding of prisoners Mrs. Bridget Nixon, intoxication arrested by Officer Powers 25 May
11 June 1957 [*sic*]	Mrs. Nixon arrested for intoxication by Officer Wollers, 26 May
21 July 1857	Bridget Nixon arrested for assault and battery by Officer Morton, 16 July.
7 Dec. 1858 p. 156	Arrests—Mrs. Nixon, intoxication by Officer Morton, 1 Dec.
17 June 1859 p. 39	Report, Chief of Police, W. Crosby Mrs. B. Nixon, disorderly conduct arrested by Officer Miller
20 May 1859	City of St. Paul vs Bridget Nixon Disorderly conduct Defendant fined $10.00 and committed in default of payment
27 June 1859 p. 46	Identical entry [duplicate or repeat of offense not clear][52]

How to Search Court Records

Although some court records have been microfilmed, printed in books, or digitized, the vast majority of them have not. In most cases it is to the researcher's great advantage to visit the courthouse or the archives where the records may be stored and to search the original records personally. As mentioned previously, with the ever-enhancing technological tools available to us today, it is usually possible to at least determine the availability and access policies of a given jurisdiction before ever embarking on a trip to the courthouse. Using a home computer or taking advantage of the nearest public library, begin with an Internet search for the county court most likely to have records for the place and time period needed. Learn the dates of their holdings that are accessible, their research policy for onsite visits, and the address and open hours of the facility.

Regardless of the form in which you view the court record: original, machine copied, or compiled by a group or individual, always include a full citation of the records location and condition so that you or others can locate the source of your findings at a later date.

Searching Original Court Records

Onsite

Begin an onsite search with the index to court cases—civil, criminal, or equity—whichever is pertinent to your search (figure 7-10). Early indexes may depict only the name of the plaintiff. Since around 1840, most courts have both a plaintiff and a defendant (or reverse) index. This index will give the case number or the box in which the case file or packet (also called a case jacket) is stored.

Next, ask the clerk for the case file by the case or box number. You will receive a packet of documents folded or rolled into a bundle and secured with a string or a rubber band. In more complex cases, the case file may be in a large container. This file has the loose documents and copies of the important papers of the case.

Then examine the docket book entries, using the dates for the beginning of the case and the date it was closed by judgment, which you will find on the outside of the case file. Entries are either made numerically by case number or chronologically by date of case. A quick glance will tell you which applies. Examine all the entries for the case to see if there are other references you need to check. For example, the docket book may note: "Exhibits 1-14 in storage vault" or "Companion case, No. 4321."

From the case file, decide whether you will begin with the orders, judgments, or other documents. Wherever you find a reference to another document that does not appear in your file, seek it out. Watch carefully for evidence that the case was appealed to a higher court or that the parties settled by arbitration.

If there is not a suitable index, or no index at all, search a jurisdiction's records page by page and entry by entry. Begin on the first page for the period of time an ancestor lived in the area and work through each page. Copy all entries with pertinent data. Before using a digital camera or a photocopy machine, request the permission of the clerk. There could be rules against either. If facsimile reproduction is not available, take extreme care to transcribe all documents completely and accurately. Words or phrases that cannot be deciphered should be followed with a note to that effect in brackets. If an entry seems incorrect, such as the surname spelled differently within a single document, transcribe each appearance exactly. You can follow one of the entries with a question mark or comment—again, in brackets. Your finished copy should be as faithful a reproduction as would be a camera image or a machine copy.

By Mail or Representative

An alternative to onsite searching is to contact the courthouse or engage someone to visit on your behalf. To search by mail, request a photocopy of the indexes or dockets for the period of time and the surnames you are searching. This is a short, easy request, for which you can expect to pay a fee. When you get your index copies, order the files you wish, giving specific case numbers. It is wise to ask for a cost estimate before the files are copied, although some courts will bill you; then you can send the right amount when you order the files. Some courts will supply estimates over the telephone or by e-mail. Nearly every court or archives has a website with full contact information.

If you have an extensive list of cases to check, hire a local genealogist to search them for you and provide extracts or photocopies of both the recorded copies in bound volumes and the case files, omitting duplicate documents. Do not ask court personnel to make extensive searches for you. They have neither the time nor the interest to do a careful job, and a missed entry

Figure 7-10. Index to equity cases, Cass County, Illinois. Photocopy of original in Cass County Courthouse, Sigourney, Illinois.

Index to Cases--Plaintiff

47730—ILLINOIS OFFICE SUPPLY CO., OTTAWA, ILL.

PLAINTIFF	DEFENDANT	ACTION	Box No.
Davis Jeremiah Ex parte	to sell Real Estate	Petition	1
Duncan Joseph	Samuel Duval, etal	Foreclosure	2
Dowler Jeremiah R.	Geo. B. Thompson	Petition	5
Davis James a	Heirs of Philip Schaeffer	Partition	6
Dummer H. E. adm.	John J. Moseley	Foreclosure	[illegible]
Dutch John	Alfred Dutch	Foreclosure	[illegible]
Davidson R. B.	John T. Goodpasture etal	Petition	[illegible]
Ketrick Jacob H.	Ossian M. Ross	Foreclosure	[illegible]
Decker John etal Gdn.	of Charles [illegible]	Petition to sell Real Estate	[illegible]
Dutch John R.	Joseph T. Dunbar etal	Foreclosure	9
Dummer Henry E.	John B. Thompson	Enforce Mechanics Lien	10
Dutch, Esra J, Gdn.	of Wm. Dutch, etal,	Petition to sell Real Estate	10

can be misleading. A particularly good way to find a good genealogist in the area of interest is to consult *The APG Directory of Professional Genealogists* current edition. The Association of Professional Genealogists (APG) also maintains an online directory of researchers at <www.apgen.org/index.html>.

Searching Copied Court Records

Microfilmed Copies

Many court records have been microfilmed by the Genealogical Society of Utah, including some case files. They are kept in state archives and county offices. Consult the catalog of the Family History Library to determine which microfilms are in their collection. Some states and counties have microfilmed their early records to provide better access for users, without handling fragile volumes. Courthouse or archives staff should be able to provide a list of microfilming that is available only regionally.

When you use microfilm, be sure to read introductions or annotations in the catalog carefully so as to understand what may be missing from the film or problems discovered during the filming process, such as erroneous page numbering by a clerk.

Scanned or Digitized Copies

As with microfilmed versions, digitized copies of records found online or scanned copies in print form are generally considered to be faithful reproductions of the original. Rarely will someone alter the contents of these reproductions although the possibility does exist. Because of the high probability of accuracy, a scanned, digitized, or microfilmed record is considered as acceptable as the original. The limitation is that few of these reproduced versions will include every record pertaining to a particular case. For example, a will might be digitized in its entirety. But the associated papers in the case files, giving names of creditors, payments made by the executor to support a widow and children, and a full listing of the possessions of the deceased may not be digitized. Always expect there to be more records associated with a case and whenever possible, do the onsite research.

Searching Compiled Court Records

Compiled court records are those that have been hand-copied or typed and then produced in manuscript form or published online or as a printed version. Such publishing may be done by an interested researcher acting alone or from a project of an area's genealogical society or the USGenWeb team. An online search by name of county and state followed by "court records" should produce some options to explore that include both online and paper copies. While compiled records have some limitations to consider, their use is both practical and valuable.

Value of Compiled Court Records

While it is best to rely upon original documents for research accuracy, there are many benefits to first viewing a compiled version. One obvious value is availability. Many transcripts were created during the nineteenth century and predate the loss or destruction of the originals. Although the quality varies widely, these transcripts may represent the only existing copies of some of the records.

Another benefit is indexing. Most transcribed works are fully indexed, providing the names of all witnesses, jurors, court personnel, attorneys, and litigants. In addition, they usually give the volume and page number of the original record and sometimes the case number. Thus, the published volumes can serve as an effective and more complete index to the originals.

Finally, a carefully prepared copy can aid in comprehension. The unfamiliar handwriting of a court clerk, the prevalence of legal terms, Latin and French words, unknown abbreviations, and fading ink can make original court records difficult to read. A well-trained, experienced compiler-editor can often make a better transcript than an untrained researcher. Such a copy can be used as a guide to understand the words in the original document and can thus save hours of poring over hard-to-read documents.

As a result of these circumstances, published transcripts can prove invaluable to the researcher who recognizes the limitations of such compilations and uses them wisely. One of the most important aspects to wise use is to understand the format in which the copied material is presented.

A compiler of published court records, online and in print, has at least three format options in which to present the content. These are abstracts, extracts, or verbatim transcriptions. Each format has value and limitations. One key question for the user of a printed or online record is: does the copied version portray a full or an abbreviated version of the original? An explanation of these three options and other data-collection standards will be found in *The BCG Genealogical Standards Manual*. Following is a short explanation of the formats.

Abstracts and Extracts

Extracts and abstracts are abbreviated versions of original documents; no attempt is made to copy the original entirely. Below are examples of extracted entries. The numbers in parentheses refer to the original page numbers.

March 16, 1779

(400) Garrat Wheeler exempted from levy.

(402) Elizabeth, wife of James Thorpe, soldier in the Continental Army, with small children, allowed L25.

(406) Commission for priv. examination of Mille, wife of Charles Cummins, as to deed to Robert Cummins.

(406) Joseph Crouch as Captain, Jacob Warwick and Alexr. Maxwell as First Lieutenants - qualified.

(407) Elizabeth Wilson, soldier's wife, with small children, allowed L20.

(407) Admn. of estate of William Wallace granted widow Jane.
(408) Court appoints John Graham guardian of Joseph Graham, orphan of David Graham.[53]

Note that the format of each extracted entry is similar. The compiler has included certain elements of identification that enable the researcher to recognize an individual or event. An extract is a precise copy of one or more parts or sections of a document.

An abstract usually offers more detail. An abstract summarizes essential points or important details from a document. It shows those key elements in an abbreviated format and omits the boilerplate language. An example of an abstract is:

> Abstract from Records *of the Court of Sessions of Westchester County (New York)*
> Bayley v. Baly
> December 1st 1691/1692 Mary Bayly by Mr. Antill complaint against husband Nathan Baly with warrant to appear on December 17 at Westchester Court.

One can readily see that neither the extract nor the abstract gives the full and complete text of a document. Furthermore, in both cases it is the compiler (extractor or abstractor) who decides what information to present. And the compiler may or may not be a genealogist. Therefore, it is prudent to consult the original record for additional detail as well as for the accuracy of the prepared copy.

Transcriptions

Verbatim transcripts record every word with original punctuation and spelling. The editor will indicate in brackets any additions made by him or her. The following is an example:

> *Records of the Court of Sessions of Westchester County (New York)*: (Westchester Historical Society Publications, Vol. 1)
>
> At a Court of Sessions held at Westchester for Ye County of Westchester by their Maj[es]ties Authority p[r]esent John Pell Justice & Quorum presed[en]t of the Court: John Palmer Justice of ye peace & Quorum & Daniel Strang & William Barnes Esqrs Justices of ye peace Decem[ber] ye 1st: 1691 - absent Joseph Theale Esqr Justice of ye Peace [1692 crossed out: 1691 inserted]
>
> The Court opened
>
> The Grand Jury Called & Appeared (Viz.)

Robert Hustead	John fforgeson
John fferis Senjor	Robt Hustead Junjor
John Mullenax	John Hadden Senjor
Joseph Hunt	Edwd Hadden
John Hunt	John Winter
John Quinby Junjor	Tho. Bedient
John Baly	Samll Palmer
	William Chadderton

> The Court Adjurnes till Thursday morning
>
> Constables Called

Westchester	
Eastchester	x
Rochell	Same
Momoroneck	x
Rye	x
& per younkers	x
Bedford	x all absent but westchester
	Rochell Same

> [Page 2]
>
> Mary Bayly Enters a Compl[ain]t against her husband Nathan baly by Mr. Antill her Atturney by petition
>
> [next is crossed out] the Court hears the Complt and orders that Nathan Baly shall be sent for by a special warr[an]tt & that he appear on ye 17th Instant to Answer ye above said Complt directed to ye Sherrif or his Deputy And if he doth not appeare at the time appointed at westchester Court the matter is deferred for further Examination unto Justice pell & Justice Theale.[54]

Annotated transcripts are verbatim transcriptions with records from other courts, case files, and/or court opinions to reconstruct the whole case. (Rarely, however, are all papers in the case file used.) Each of these formats offers value to the researcher. The potential, however, for copying errors or inadvertent omission of important detail makes it necessary to consult the original version whenever possible.

Once the researcher understands the format chosen by the compiler—and the possibility of omission of detail or associated records—it is time to evaluate the quality of the work. Note the comments of one editor concerning a series of transcriptions:

> In reproducing these old records the manuscript has been faithfully followed, even when this means repeating obvious slips made by the old scribes, such as omissions of words, repetitions of words, or the use of words clearly wrong. The only liberty taken with the original text has been . . . to supply in brackets the missing word or words, where the old paper . . . has left enough letters of the defective word to justify this.[55]

The attention to detail evident in the above quote is a strong indication of a quality transcription.

Finding Compiled Court Records

As suggested earlier, an Internet search either on your home computer or at the nearest public library is the best way to get an overview of what has been published and where the published records can be found and used. Unfortunately, there is no complete bibliography of titles or websites containing compiled records. A search of the online catalog of the regional library would be helpful as would use of <www.oclc.org/worldcat/open/default.htm>. Below are some suggestions about other places to look.

1. Published state archives. Most of the original colonies/states authorized publication of original court records in series called archives. Such compiled volumes as *Pennsylvania Archives* and *Maryland Archives* are examples. Complete sets are available in several large research libraries and some are available online. Consult Benjamin Barnett Spratling III, "Court and Legal Records," in *Printed Sources: A Guide to Published Genealogical Records*, for a state-by-state (and colony) guide to compilations of this nature.[56]
2. Local histories, particularly those published around the turn of the nineteenth century, may contain extracts or transcribed court records. Some are accurately reproduced with careful indexes; some have many errors. Be sure to check for appendixes, special sections of documents, and quotations in the middle of town and family sections. Early histories are becoming more accessible due to digitization, so use sites that feature these publications.
3. Abstracts, extracts, indexes, and complete transcripts of court records can be found in journals, occasional publications, annual volumes, and special series. These can be accessed through a search of the *Periodical Source Index*, referenced in chapter 3, "General References and Guides."
4. William Jeffrey Jr., "Early New England Court Records: A Bibliography of Published Materials," contains a listing of the records published, the dates covered, name of court; title, author, and bibliographic data of printed volume; description and index; brief analysis of editing done and omissions.[57]
5. Evarts B. Green and Richard B. Morris, *A Guide to the Principal Sources for Early American History (1600–1800) in the City of New York*, contains a separate section of printed sources, including court records, found in various record depositories in New York City. They are arranged by subject and thereunder by state and locality.[58]
6. Bradley Chapin, *Criminal Justice in Colonial America, 1606–1660*, is a valuable description of courts and their jurisdictions and specific crimes for which punishment was meted out before 1660 in America.[59] The author includes a list of selected cases and a full bibliography of early sources. Since there are no printed reports, few indexes, and missing volumes for this period, the list is especially valuable. The genealogist who is searching for an American ancestor in this early period will benefit from a careful study of this book.
7. Volumes of court records have been published privately, by societies, archives, universities, and the trade press. For example, Joan W. Peters *Military Records, Patriotic Service, & Public Service Claims from the Fauquier County, Virginia, Court Minute Books, 1759–1784*.[60]

Finding Early Laws

It is useful to know what laws were in effect in a state at the time an ancestor lived there. Hein's *Session Laws of American States and Territories: A Compilation of All States and Territories, 1775–2003*[61] is the most complete coverage of all fifty states, as well as the District of Columbia, Puerto Rico, Guam, and the Virgin Islands. This is the original record of each state's legislative sessions. A companion work for pre-1775 is *Colonial Session Laws*, which is also published by William S. Hein and Company. Copies can be found at most major law libraries. A list of the contents of this publication, which comprises more than 88,000 microfiche, is online at <www.wshein.com/Catalog/Default.aspx> as of January 2006. An earlier, though still useful, collection of microfiche may be more readily available at smaller libraries: *Session Laws of the American States and Territories Prior to 1900*.[62] For laws not cited in full, references to the revisions in each state law code are given, providing a reference to follow the changes backward in time. The years for which printed laws are available are summarized in table 7-4.

Check with state archives and historical societies for publications that provide the early laws of their respective states. One example of many is the printed work by the Historical Bureau of the Indiana Library and Historical Department, *The Laws of Indiana Territory, 1801–1809*. Many early references of this nature are online with searchable text, such as the Archives of Maryland's Legislative Records (1634–2000s) at <http://aomol.net/html/legislative.html> or Alabama legislative records at <www.legislature.state.al.us/misc/history/timeline.html>, or H. P. N. Gammel's *The Laws of Texas, 1822–1897*, which consists of documents covering each congressional and legislative session and including the constitutions and early colonization laws. The first ten volumes of *The Laws of Texas* are available from the University of North Texas Libraries at <http://texinfo.library.unt.edu/lawsoftexas/default.htm>. Some states archives assemble and publish historical laws on a particular subject. "Missouri's Early Slave Laws" (laws from Missouri Territorial to 1850s) are explained at <www.sos.mo.gov/archives/education/aahi/earlyslavelaws/slavelaws.asp>.

Federal session laws are published at the conclusion of each session of Congress as *United States Statutes at Large*. This is

Table 7-4. Printed Laws of the United States (Pre–1900)

State	Colony Special Laws	Territory	State	Miscellaneous
Alabama		1818	1819–99	
Arizona		1864–99		
Arkansas		1818–35	1836–99	
California			1849–99	
Colorado		1861–76	1876–99	Jefferson Territory, 1859–61
Connecticut	1639–73		1776–1899	Special acts, 1837–99
Dakota		1862–89		
Delaware	1704–41		1776–1899	
Florida		1822–45	1845–99	
Georgia	Dates not given		1787–1899	
Idaho		1863–88	1890–99	
Illinois		1809–17	1818–99	
Indiana		1801–51	1816–99	
Iowa		1838–45	1846–98	
Kansas		1855–61	1861–99	
Kentucky			1792–1898	
Louisiana			1812–99	District (under jurisdiction of Indiana Territory), 1804; Territory of Orleans, 1804–11
Maine			1820–99	Resolves, 1820–39; private and special acts, 1820–49
Maryland	Dates not given		1777–1898	
Massachusetts	Dates not given		1777–1899	Resolves, 1776–1838
Michigan		1821–35	1835–99	
Minnesota		1849–57	1857–99	
Mississippi		1799–1816	1817–98	
Missouri		1813–18	1820–99	
Montana		1864–89	1889–99	
Nebraska		1855–67	1866–99	
Nevada		1861–64	1864–99	
New Hampshire	1680–1726		1783–1899	
New Jersey	1703–22		1776–1899	
New Mexico		1846–99		
New York	Dates not given		1777–1899	
North Carolina	1669–1751		1777–1899	
North Dakota			1889–99	
Northwest		1788–1801		
Ohio			1803–98	
Oklahoma		1890–99		
Oregon		1890–99		
Pennsylvania	Dates not given		1776–1899	
Rhode Island	1647–1719		1776–1899	
South Carolina	1692–1734		1776–1899	
South Dakota			1890–99	
Tennessee			1796–1899	Territory of the U.S.A. South of the River Ohio, 1792–95
Texas			1846–99	
Utah		1851–94	1896–99	
Vermont			1778–1898	
Virginia			1776–1899	
Washington		1854–87	1889–99	
West Virginia			1861–99	
Wisconsin		1836–48	1848–99	
Wyoming		1869–90	1890–99	

To find session laws, use items 1 and 2, found at law and large university libraries.

1. John D. Cushing *Session Laws of the American States and Territories Prior to 1900.* Selected reprints by colony or state are available from <www.frontierpress.com>.
2. William S. Hein & Co., Inc. *Session Laws of American States and Territories: A Compilation of All States and Territories, 1775–2003. Update 4: A Complete Checklist.* A companion work for pre-1775 is *Colonial Session Laws* by the same publisher.
3. The Historic State Codes Preservation Project of the Georgetown Law Library is making scanned titles of early state laws available. Their collection contains 960 titles, approximately 50% of the historic state codes identified in print as of 2006. A list of titles scanned and in progress, and purchasing instructions, are at <www.ll.georgetown.edu/states/historic_codes/index.cfm>.

considered the official source for the Public and Private session laws of the United States Congress. Browseable and index-searchable facsimile image files of the *Statutes at Large* from 1789 to 1875 are offered by the American Memory project of the U.S. Library of Congress. The earlier statutes are online at "A Century of Lawmaking for a New Nation" <http://memory.loc.gov/ammem/amlaw/lawhome.html>.

Not only do early sessions laws help in the interpretation of court and other records researchers use, but many of these collections include what are termed private laws, such as a name change or the granting of a divorce that occurs in the early legislature of a state. Tracing the history of a law is not difficult. Most law libraries are open for public use. A call before you go can verify public access, hours of operation, availability of copy machines, and fees (if any).

Selected Proceedings and Courts

Adoption Records

Adoption records usually result from court processes, although there are three methods through which adoption can take place: (1) agreement without judicial proceedings, (2) agreement filed in a court of law and accompanied by court order, and (3) petition filed in a court of law and accompanied by a court order. The first method is not considered legally binding in most states today.

Under Roman civil law, which forms the basis of the legal systems in Louisiana and Texas, adoption was an integral part of family law and was often used to increase prestige and family wealth. Native Americans also practice adoption to varying extents. English common law, upon which the legal systems of most

Table 7-5. Statutes Granting Adoption Jurisdiction

State	Date	Court
Connecticut	1864	Probate
Delaware	1890	Orphans'
Georgia	1855	Superior
Hawaii	1903	Circuit
Illinois	1855	County, circuit
Indiana	1867	County, circuit
Kentucky	1860	Circuit, equity, criminal
Maine	1867	Probate
Maryland	1892	Circuit
Massachusetts	1851	Probate
Missouri	1853	Recorder of Deeds
New Hampshire	1862	Probate
New Jersey	1877	Orphans'
New York	1873	Surrogate
North Carolina	1872	Superior
Ohio	1859	Probate
Oregon	1864	County
Pennsylvania	1855	Common pleas
Rhode Island	1872	Probate, municipal
South Carolina	1882	Common pleas
Tennessee	1852	County, circuit
Texas	1850	
Vermont	1853	Probate
Virginia	1891	Chancery
West Virginia	1882	Circuit

The years given refer to the passage of an adoption law or statute. Prior to these years, adoptions in many areas were formalized by private acts of the legislature or by session laws. See table 7-2 to find pre-1900 session laws. A useful work is U.S. Children's Bureau, *Adoption Laws in the United States: A Summary of the Development of Adoption Legislation and Significant Features of Adoption Statutes, With the Text of Selected Laws. Bureau Publication No. 148.* Emelyn Foster Peck, ed. (Washington, D.C.: Government Printing Office, 1925).

of the states are based, had no provision for adoption until 1926. Even though adoption statutes in America precede this date by nearly a century in some states, the majority did not provide for legal adoption until the latter half of the nineteenth century. Hence, legal adoption of a child by two people who are not the biological parents is a fairly recent action. Table 7-5 indicates when the first statutes granting adoption were passed in the original thirteen states and selected others and the court that was given jurisdiction by the state codes.

Adoptions, even those later recognized by court action, often begin within the family. For this reason, family traditions are important. Learn what family members know, including favorite nieces and grandsons who have been confidants of family members most likely to know the facts.

Next, check the facts in actual documents (see figure 7-11). The documents and traditions in the case of Harry Chester Lee, below, are examples. According to a granddaughter:

> Great-Grandma Bandina Hinkle Lee, as you know, was Grandpa's [Harry Chester Lee's] adopted mother. However . . . his . . . real mother was Aunt Mary [Bell Hinkle] Garwood, Bandena's [*sic*] sister. I know she died [1927] after I was born & indications show Grandpa knew it. It must have been very hard for the poor woman, because she was living in Chicago by that time & she couldn't acknowledge her granddaughter & her first great grandchild. Anyhow the narrative is very interesting.

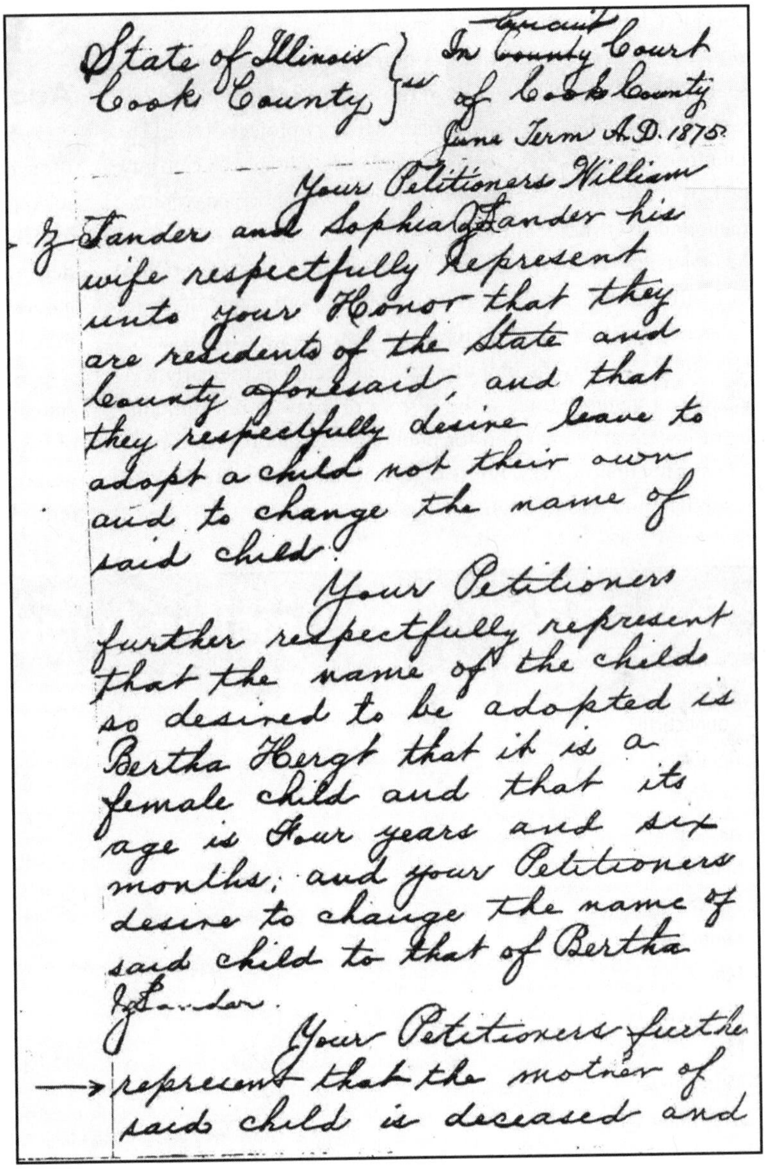

State of Illinois } ss In ~~County~~ Circuit Court
Cook County } of Cook County
June Term A.D. 1875.

Your Petitioners William J. Zander and Sophia J. Zander his wife respectfully represent unto your Honor that they are residents of the State and County aforesaid, and that they respectfully desire leave to adopt a child not their own and to change the name of said child.

Your Petitioners further respectfully represent that the name of the child so desired to be adopted is Bertha Hergt that it is a female child and that its age is Four years and six months; and your Petitioners desire to change the name of said child to that of Bertha J. Zander.

Your Petitioners further represent that the mother of said child is deceased and

Figure 7-11. While adoption records have been sealed off from public view in almost every state, that was not always the case. This court document is that of child Bertha Hergt, adopted by William and Bertha Zander in 1875. Note the initial misspelling of the name that was probably corrected after the document was recorded. This example points to the importance of considering alternative spellings when records are not found where they were expected to be.

This Harry Chester Lee was born 21 June 1883, in a Chicago foundling home under the name of Chester Perry. Bandina Hinkle Lee picked him up from the foundling home at the age of three days, and he lived with her and her husband, Benjamin P. Lee, until they adopted him, at age thirteen. Bandina was Mary Bell's half-sister from Peoria County, Illinois.

A 1974 letter requesting the adoption papers brought the information from the presiding judge of Cook County Circuit Court that "all adoption files in Cook County are impounded."

Attempts to find a documented connection between Harry Chester Lee (Chester Perry) and Mary Bell failed. Cook County birth records yielded no data for Chester Perry. An inquiry to Cook County Court regarding maternity was not answered, and there were no other records on file in Cook County. It is interesting, however, that Harry cared for Mary Bell Garwood in her later years. He was present at her death and provided the information on her death certificate. He also selected and paid for her burial place and funeral marker. Family members concluded that she was Harry's mother.

The Adoption Process

The petition sets out information concerning the child (or sometimes adult requiring custodial care) to be adopted, the biological parents, and the adopting parents. State statutes vary in the amount and type of data required, but generally they contain the name, residence, and age or date of birth of the child; a description of any property the child might possess; the agency or person having present custody of the child; sometimes the sex, race, religion, place of birth, brothers and sisters (if any); names and residences of the parents or guardian; and the adoptive parents' names, residences, ages, religious affiliations, marital status, place and date of marriage, and fitness to adopt. In many states, if the child is illegitimate, the father is not recorded. Massachusetts, Illinois, New York, and Pennsylvania require that no indication of illegitimacy be given.

All parties who have an interest in the proceedings are notified of the date and time of the proceedings. Copies of these notifications are found in the case file. In Vermont, publication of adoption proceedings and proposed name changes had to appear for three successive weeks in the local newspapers before the hearing was held. Then the clerk of the probate court was required to submit annual returns of all such proceedings and name changes to the secretary of state.[63] In this case, duplicate records are available in newspapers and in state archives.

Consent of the biological parents and their sworn and written statements relinquishing their rights to the child must be part of the case file. If the child is in the care of a guardian or institution, the guardian or institution provides consent. Children over a certain age—varying from eight to fourteen—are also required to give formal consent to the adoption.

Only a few states do not require a formal investigation of the adopting parents and the child. In other states, the proposed home, financial status, health, mental condition, occupation, and social standing in the community of the adopting parents are investigated along with the physical and mental condition and heritage of the child. Reports of these investigations become a part of the case file.

The hearing may be closed or open according to the judgment of the court. Evidence, testimony, and the above documents presented at the hearing provide the basis for a judgment and court decree. The decree may be interlocutory (requiring a waiting period of six months to one year before the adoption is final) or final (no waiting period). Usually, as part of the decree, the child's name is changed to that of the adopting parents and the birth certificate is also changed accordingly.

If any party involved disagrees with the adoption, the case file will contain petitions for pending appeals to reconsider, annul, or revoke the decree. The grounds and procedures for such appeals vary considerably from one state to another.

In an attempt to protect both children and adoptive parents, some states have passed laws restricting adoption records. Most states limit access to adoption records only to the parties involved (with court permission). In a few states, the decree is open to the public, but the case files can be examined only with court permission. Some states leave the choice of access up to the court.[64]

Records of adoptions that predate these laws are usually found among the regular records of the courts having adoption or family law jurisdiction, though in many courts, even the index references to adoption cases have been completely marked out so as to make those specific entries illegible. Ask to see the court docket or indexes covering the period of time of the search. Check carefully all surnames relating to your pedigree, for a relative may have adopted the child. Note the number and name of the case and ask the clerk for the case files you wish by number and name only, not by subject. If you want copies and cannot make them yourself, request them by page or document date, not by name of document.

In some courthouses, there is little problem because the records are in files accessible to the public, and coin-operated copy machines are nearby. For sealed records, you will have to follow the rules of access set down by the court or the legislature. In most cases, the individual concerned must request the records in person.

For information on the historical laws and traditions of adoption, see E. Wayne Carp, *Adoption in America: Historical Perspectives*.[65] Carp describes indenture and adoption in nineteenth-century orphanages, while contributing authors present a historical comparison of Catholic and Jewish adoption practices in Chicago, 1833–1933, and a look at the Washington Children's Home Society, 1895–1915.

Rights of Inheritance

The primary purpose behind early adoption laws was to provide a legal heir for the adoptive parent. Hence, in most states adopted children inherit just as though they were "heirs of the body." In some jurisdictions, rights of inheritance are severely restricted. Property that is designated for "heirs of the body" by the testator cannot be inherited by adopted children in Maine, New Jersey, Ohio, Oklahoma, Rhode Island, Vermont, Utah, and West Virginia. Parents cannot inherit from adoptive children in Georgia, Oklahoma, and Tennessee.[66]

Citizenship

Alien children adopted by American parents do not automatically become citizens of the United States; however, the residence requirement is lowered to two years. The proceedings for children are less complicated than for adults.

Admiralty Courts

Before 1697, no special courts of admiralty existed. Maritime matters were handled by existing common law courts sitting with juries. The English government asked these courts to enforce the Trade and Navigation Acts, but jury members, who had themselves been guilty of violating those same laws, were reluctant to convict their fellow citizens. These breaches included failure to enter, clear, and register vessels, neglecting to carry the proper certificate, trading in ships not English-built, navigating without the proper number of seamen, smuggling, and illicit trade. The Boston Tea Party was a revolt against the harshness of these acts.[67]

In 1697, American Courts of Vice-Admiralty were established by the English government in the chief seaports or districts (groups of colonies). They were completely separate from the courts of the colonies in which the seaports were located. The governor served as vice-admiral of the colony but usually appointed someone to be the judge of the court. Prosecutors attempted to bypass sympathetic juries by bringing their cases before the vice-admiralty, where jury trial was prohibited and prosecutors could hope for convictions. Colonial judges, however, were also hesitant about convicting Americans of violating the admiralty laws, particularly smuggling and illegal trade.

In 1763, a vice-admiralty court for all of America was established in Halifax, Nova Scotia, with British officials and judges. It heard its first cases in 1764, but protests from the colonies forced its removal to Boston, with branch courts at Philadelphia and Charleston. This court gradually fell into disuse, although it was not formally abolished.

With the outbreak of the American Revolution and the collapse of the British courts, the Continental Congress suggested that each state provide a court of admiralty or return admiralty jurisdiction to the regular courts. Jury trial was a prominent feature in the courts. The U.S. Constitution later vested admiralty jurisdiction in the federal district courts. See table 7-6 for a state-by-state summary.

Admiralty Jurisdiction

Originally, admiralty courts limited their coverage to the mouths of rivers and the seacoasts of America. Gradually, their jurisdiction was expanded to cover a wide variety of cases. This breadth of action yields some valuable data for genealogists.

Jurisdiction of matters included seamen's wages—the most common cause the courts treated—bottomry (mortgaging a ship as security for payment of a loan), charter parties (contracts between merchants and mariners for merchandise to be carried), partnership (where two or more agree to share and share alike in some venture and one or more refuses to keep his part of the bargain), salvage (retrieving goods from wrecked vessels), claims for injuries to property or persons, contracts for building and furnishing ships, claims for money loaned or advanced, collisions, brutality, neglect of duty, insufficient food, and impressment

Table 7-6. State Admiralty Courts, 1776–89

State	Title of Court[a]	Date Formed	Appeals to Congress Allowed	Jury Trial
Connecticut	County Maritime Courts (Long Island Sound counties)	1776	No	
Delaware	Court of Admiralty	Before 1778	No	
Georgia	Court of Admiralty	1777	No	
Massachusetts	District Admiralty Courts (3)	1775	No	After 1778
Boston		1776	No	
Maryland	Court of Admiralty	1763; renewed 1776	Yes	1776[b]
North Carolina	Court of Admiralty	1777	No	1777
New Hampshire	Court of Admiralty	1776	Yes	
New Jersey	Court of Admiralty	1776 (abolished 1799)	No	
New York	No court established. British-occupied after 1776.			
Pennsylvania	Court of Admiralty for Port of Pennsylvania	1778 (abolished 1780)	After 1780	Before 1780
Rhode Island	Maritime Court	1776	Before 1780	
	Court of Admiralty	1780		
South Carolina	Court of Admiralty	1776	After 1777	1776
Virginia	Court of Commissioners in Admiralty	1775	After 1779, cases between two persons of the state excluded	1776
	Court of Admiralty	1776		

Based upon 131 *U.S. Reports*, Appendix, xx–xxii. Jurisdiction of state admiralty courts transferred to U.S. District Courts in 1789, under the Federal Judiciary Act, 1st Congress, Sess. I, Ch. 20 (Statute 1, 24 September 1789).

(Endnotes)

a Almost all states permitted trail by jury for prize cases.

b Maryland Admiralty cases 1776–1812 are indexed at <www.mdarchives.state.md.us/msa/refserv/genealogy/html/govtdocs.html>; Maryland's records of its Court of Vice Admiralty, 1754–1775, are transcribed at <www.mdarchives.state.md.us/msa/speccol/sc4600/sc4646/html/title.html>.

(being kidnapped and forced to serve against one's will). These courts also had jurisdiction over prizes—enemy vessels and their cargo seized during wartime. Such cases were common in New York and South Carolina. Violations of pine masts were also handled by the admiralty courts—the king reserved all white pines of more than twenty-four inches in diameter and three feet in height for ships' masts for the Royal Navy. Anyone caught cutting them was tried before an admiralty court.

Admiralty courts had civil and criminal jurisdiction over merchants who dealt with mariners, owners of ships, and all persons having any relation to maritime transactions: those who built ships; those who equipped, manned, and supplied them; those who landed, loaded, and unloaded them; those who freighted them; those employed in their service; and those who damaged, injured, or violated their duty to or on public streams, fresh water, ports, rivers, and creeks with the ebbing and flowing of the tides as far as the high-water mark on shores or banks. If your ancestors lived along the shoreline, most of their legal business would have been transacted in admiralty courts, not the local county courts.

Admiralty records have been preserved on both sides of the Atlantic. English records are in the Public Record Office among the records of the Lords of Trade, Board of Trade, and High Courts of Admiralty. Many of them have been calendared or abstracted and printed by order of Parliament. Some English records fell into the hands of American courts during the American Revolution. For example, the records of the Vice-Admiralty Court of New York are at the National Archives—Northeast Region.[68] American records are found among the files of the court that exercised jurisdiction. Records for the state admiralty courts are in the state archives; some extracts have been published.

In addition to the regular court records, such as dockets, minutes, and case files, admiralty courts include such evidence as ships' records and records kept by seamen: ship registers, enrollments, licenses, crew lists, manifests, passenger lists, seamen's contracts, clearance papers, logbooks, private letters, and other correspondence carried by ships and seized as part of its cargoes.

For additional reading on admiralty courts, see the reference section at the end of this chapter.

Appeals Courts

Appeals courts review cases begun initially in other courts upon request of one or more litigants in the case. Some appeals courts also transfer cases from lower courts for review upon crucial points of law. This power is called *certiorari.* Few appeals courts are concerned with questions of fact. That is, no witnesses testify, and no jury determines the facts of the case. The court accepts the evidence of the previous trial and reviews questions of law—points on which alleged errors have been committed by the lower court. An exception is the Maryland Provincial Council, which will hold a full retrial. Usually, however, appeals made on new evidence are sent back to the lower court for retrial.

During the colonial period, most appeals courts also had original jurisdiction in cases involving land title, admiralty, probate, equity, divorce, criminal cases involving life or limb (capital cases), and all civil suits over £20 (increased eventually to £100).

Usually these appeals courts consisted of the royal governor and his council in judicial session, following the model of the Privy Council of the King. Naturally, they were reluctant to surrender such judicial powers. These courts were called by various titles: Court of Assistants (Connecticut), Court of Magistrates (New Haven), Supreme Court (New Hampshire), General Court (Virginia), Court of Appeals (New Jersey and Georgia), and Provincial Court (Maryland).

In some of the colonies, the legislative assembly also handled appeals: Connecticut, Maryland, and Virginia assemblies heard divorce and land title cases until 1683, then these were transferred to the governor and council. Rhode Island and New York assemblies heard equity cases. In contrast, Pennsylvania, Delaware, Rhode Island, and Massachusetts established supreme courts very early with jurisdiction equivalent to that of the English Court of King's Bench, and Delaware specifically vested equity jurisdiction in its Common Pleas Court after 1726.

After the American Revolution, most state constitutions established supreme courts as the highest appellate courts in most states, although, in theory, appeal can be made to the United States Supreme Court.

Appeals courts also issue these standard administrative enforcement writs: *mandamus,* ordering government officials to perform their duties; *certiorari,* ordering the review of a case from a lower trial court; *habeas corpus,* ordering the presentation of the accused before a magistrate for trial; and *quo warranto,* ordering an officeholder to prove by what authority an office is held.

The courts of ultimate appeal during the colonial period were the King in Privy Council and/or Parliament. Such appeals were expensive and time-consuming, involving amounts over £100 to £500 in value and taking almost two years to reach a verdict. As a result, only 265 cases were appealed. Some legislative assemblies restricted appeals to the king, and the Palatines (the Carolinas and Maryland) required the proprietor's permission to appeal.[69]

During the American Revolution, appeals were limited to admiralty and military cases heard by the Continental Congress. The unsettled conditions and costs involved resulted in few appeals until the new government began to function. Then claims and cases were appealed to Congress as well as the Supreme Court.

Some state supreme courts did not assume conventional shape until after the Revolution. For example, Kentucky, at one point in the early eighteenth century, had two courts of appeal to handle an enormous number of land title disputes, and the Texas Supreme Court in the Reconstruction period was so erratic that its rulings are never cited as serious precedents.[70]

Special courts of appeal were created from time to time to meet specific needs. In Virginia, the General Court (governor and council) heard criminal appeals well into the nineteenth century, before they were transferred to the Virginia Supreme Court. In Tennessee, it was impossible to survey land prior to settlement, resulting in overlapping and duplicate claims. The Tennessee Supreme Court of Errors and Appeals tried these land cases until 1834. In North Carolina, the circuit court judges met regularly in a Court of Conference to discuss important cases and points of law. Gradually, it became a regular supreme court. New Jersey's Prerogative Court and Maryland's Court of Delegates handled probate of wills and administration of estates.

Intermediate appeals courts relieved the workload of the state supreme courts, and they are courts of last resort for most cases. County and superior courts, such as Common Pleas and Quarter Sessions for appeals from justice, and municipal courts are examples.

Records of appeals courts are similar to those discussed previously under civil, criminal, and equity cases, with two important exceptions: trial briefs and court opinions.

Trial Briefs

Since appeals courts did not usually hear trials, summaries of evidence and testimony—trial briefs—transmitted the facts of the case. These summaries have survived in most courts, and they are extremely valuable where the original case files no longer exist. Each judge in the court had a copy, with copies for the case file and trial attorneys. The earliest are in manuscript, but surprisingly soon they were printed. Supreme Court briefs were printed and bound from 1832 on.

Finding Appellate Court Opinions

Court opinions are decisions of the judges in each case along with reasoning and references to precedents. The first opinions were given orally and noted briefly in the court minutes or orders. Written opinions were required of all Supreme Court judges by a congressional act of 1834, and they became popular in other appeals courts, for they could be printed, circulated, and cited in similar cases, thus saving a great deal of research and correspondence.

Many appeals court records have been summarized, indexed by plaintiff (some defendant cross-indexes are available), and printed. (See figure 7-12 for courts with printed reports.) More than six thousand volumes representing some 500,000 different cases were in print volumes (called "case reporters"; see table 7-7)

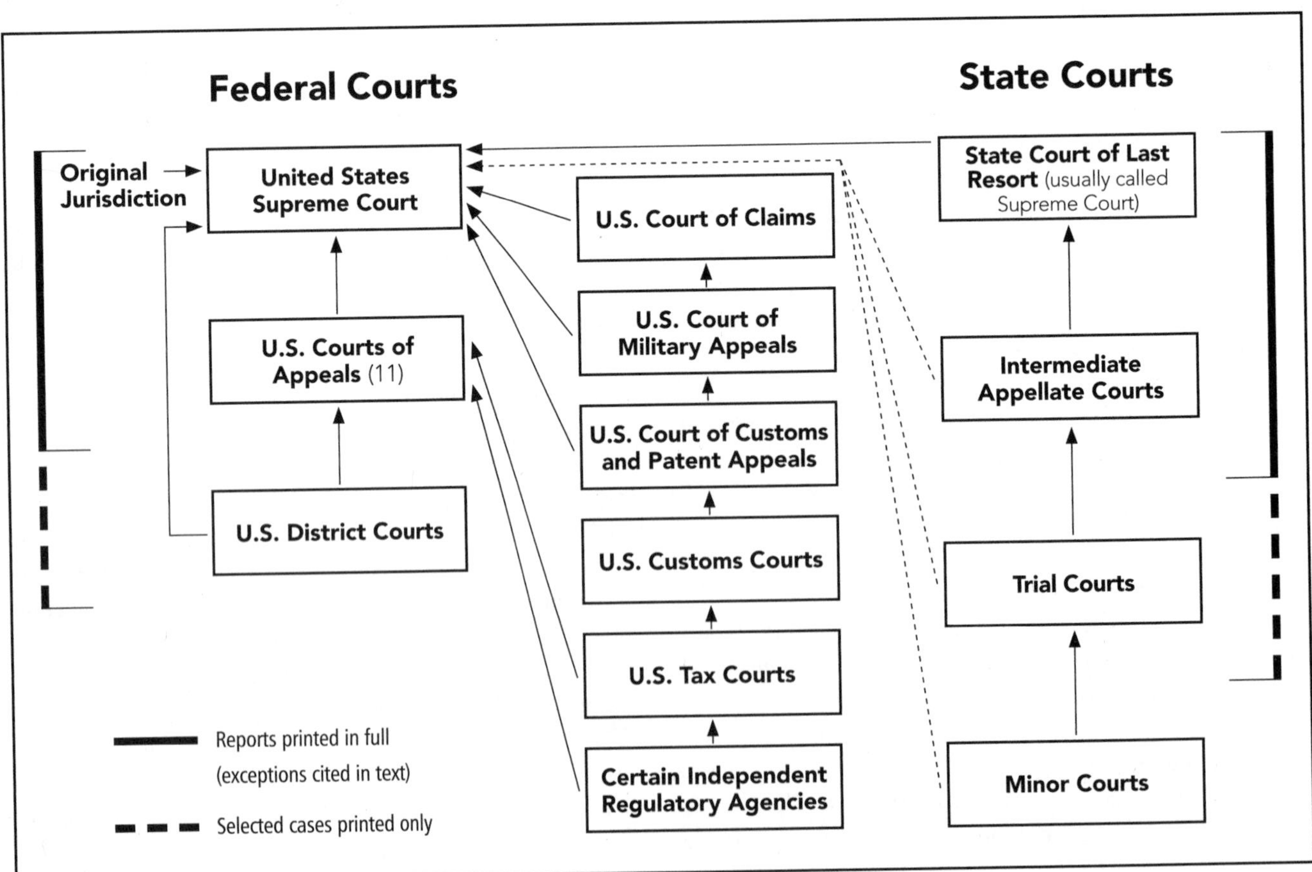

Figure 7-12. Courts for which printed reports are available.

Table 7-7. Summary of U.S. Reports

Number of Volumes	Name of Court Reporter	Years Covered	Report Volume
1–4	Dallas	1790–1800	U.S. Reports 1–4
1–9	Cranch	1801–15	U.S. Reports 5–13
1–12	Wheaton	1816–27	U.S. Reports 14–25
1–16	Peters	1828–45	U.S. Reports 26–41
1–24	Howard	1843–60	U.S. Reports 42–65
1–2	Black	1861–62	U.S. Reports 66–67
1–23	Wallace	1863–74	U.S. Reports 68–90

in legal libraries across the United States by 1896. Many more have appeared since then. Regardless of the publisher of these volumes, these case reporters essentially feature the same basic information about an appeals case:

- *Caption*: the name or names of parties in the case.
- *Docket Number*: the number assigned by the court to track a case through the litigation process (new docket numbers are at each level of the litigation process).
- *Citation*: the citation or reference to the place where the case has been published.
- *Names of Attorneys and Judges*.
- *Opinion*: the decision of the judge.

The large number of persons and actions represented within these pages make case reporters a rich and important source for family historians. Using the reporters (and compiled indexes, called "digests") may at first be challenging, but most law libraries provide printed instructions for their use. In addition, there are excellent easy-to-read guides published online by university law schools for their students. A useful aid is a free tutorial offered by the law library of Georgetown University at <www.ll.georgetown.edu/tutorials/cases/one/index.html>. It is titled "Cases and Digests Research Tutorial" (E. B. Williams Library Tutorials).

Another way to learn about case reporters and their indexes is to read "Court and Legal Records," by Benjamin Barnett Spratling III.[71] A portion of Mr. Spratling's clear and practical advice is summarized as follows:

Case Reporters

Many decisions made by judges of appellate courts are published in case reporters in summary format. Not all appellate court decisions are in reporters, and most of the published opinions are those appealed from trial courts. Case reporters are published for individual states, for regions, for federal cases, and for certain specialized areas within the law, such as bankruptcy. These reporters are found in law libraries; the major law libraries (often connected with universities) have case reporters for all states.

Because reporters are arranged chronologically, the books covering the years of an ancestor's residence in a particular area is one way to check case reporters.

Each case reporter volume is indexed by a "table of cases," usually found at the front of the book. The table of cases can list all plaintiffs and defendants found within the case reporter or, in early years, only the first named plaintiff in each case.

American Digest System

To bypass having to search the indexes of each case reporter volume, the American Digest System is a series of what might be termed "master" or "cumulative indexes." The digests provide reference to cases in several different reporters. The American Digest System is a massive collection with volumes issued periodically to index case reporters for the entire United States. The series consists of many volumes but one of primary interest to genealogists would be *1906 Decennial Edition of the American Digest: A Complete Table of American Cases From 1658 to 1906 vols. 21–25.*[72]

These five volumes index thousands—although not all—appellate court cases in the United States. Only plaintiffs are indexed. There are quirks in the indexing system; Mr. Spratling provides pointers for overcoming them and for interpreting the citation that leads to the correct volume or volumes of the case reporter. If a particular volume is not in a library, the citation will permit the researcher to request the price for a copy of the reported case from the appropriate state law library.

The Federal Digest

The Federal Digest[73] is a series that indexes records of the Supreme Court of the United States, the U.S. Circuit courts of appeals, and the district courts of the United States. These publications will be found at most law libraries and at U.S. Document Depository libraries. Of interest to family historians are:

- Volumes 66, 67, and 68 of *The Federal Digest*. These contain an index (by name of plaintiff of cases from 1754 to 1941.
- *Cases Decided in the Court of Claims of the United States.* This reports cases from 1863 to the present. Volume 89

Table 7-8. Published Reports from Federal Courts

U.S. Appeals Court/Cases	Dates	Titles and Contents of Reports
Supreme Court	1790 to present	*U.S. Reports.* First 90 volumes identified by court reporter; reprint of vols. 1–90 labeled *U.S. Reports* with reporter's name; vols. 91 on titled *U.S. Reports* Cases indexed at University of Houston <www.digitalhistory.uh.edu/supreme_court/supreme_court.cfm>.
U.S. Court of Appeals	1781 to present	*U.S. Reports* 1781–87 printed in 2 Dallas (vol. 2, *U.S. Reports*). See <www.fedcir.gov/>.
U.S. District Courts	1789 to present	Gerogetown Law Library *The Federal Reporter,* selected cases only.
U.S. Court of Claims	1855–63	*Reports of the Court of Claims Submitted to the House of Representatives*
	1863 to present	*Cases Decided in the Court of Claims in the U.S.* Vol. 30 indexes vols. 1–29; vol. 54 indexes vols. 30–54; vol. 62 indexes vols. 55–61
U.S. Court of Military Appeals		*Decisions of the Court of Appeal*
U.S. Court of Customs and Patent Appeals	1930 to present	*Reports of the Court of Customs and Patent Appeals of the U.S.* Each volume has a plaintiff-defendant index
U.S. Court of Customs Appeals	1909–29	Reports published by the Treasury Department under various titles. Indexes in each volume
Prize Cases Appealed to Continental Congress	1776–80	Includes Committee on Appeals cases referred to Court of Appeals. 109 Cases listed 131 *U.S. Reports* 1889), xix–xlix. Each listing gives the title of the case, a brief description, court from which the appeal was made, dates of appeal and consideration, whether referred to committee or court
Prize Cases of Revolutionary War, Committee on Appeals	1776–80	38 cases
Prize Cases of Revolutionary War	1776–80	56 cases from all states except New York, Court of Appeals which had no prize court

Source: Laurence F. Schmeckebier and Roy B. Eastin, *Government Publications and Their Use,* 2nd. rev. ed. (1969; reprint, Ann Arbor, Mich.: University Microfilms International, 1987).

is an index to vols. 1 through 89, which cover 1863 to 1939. *Reports of the Court of Claims Submitted to the House of Representatives* covers an earlier period, from 1853 to 1863, but may be found only in larger libraries.

- *Federal Cases (Circuit and District Courts), 1789–1880,* is a thirty-one-volume set reporting federal cases. Vol. 31 is the index to the first thirty volumes of reports. It is a plaintiff and defendant index.

Table 7-8 is a summary of published reports from federal courts. Microfilm copies of these court records are available for purchase from the National Archives and Records Service, General Services Administration, Washington, DC 20408.[74]

Online Indexes

Since the advent of the twenty-first century, the emphasis is no longer on printed indexes but on websites that are subscriber-based. Although the number of institutions or law firms that subscribe is limited, most major law libraries do have access. Consult the availability at these sites for research in more recent indexes.

There are a number of free sites that offer searching of case decisions, although years and regions may be limited. Some examples of free sites are: Over 610 selected historic cases (as early as 1806), are indexed by parties at Cornell University Law School's Legal Information Institute, <www4.law.cornell.edu/supct/cases/topic.htm>. Supreme Court decisions since 1893 are indexed and fully searchable at FindLaw <www.findlaw.com/casecode/supreme.html>. A database compiled by the U.S. Air Force of Supreme Court decisions 1937–1975 and 1992 forward, is online at <www.access.gpo.gov/su_docs/supcrt/index.html>. Full text of decisions, 1937 to 1975, is at <www.fedworld.gov/supcourt>.

A new project at the USGenWeb provides good possibilities for court records research. Historic court case reports are being transcribed for searching online at <www.rootsweb.com/~archcrtc>. The index and print pages are imaged until each page is transcribed into searchable text. As of 1 February 2006, various years of state supreme or appellate courts are online for five states: Illinois, Maine, Massachusetts, Mississippi, and North Carolina, as well as a U.S. Supreme Court volume that covers from organization to 1827.

Claims Courts

The right—first guaranteed by the English government and incorporated into federal and state constitutions—to petition the government for redress of grievances provides an excellent source of genealogical data because our ancestors used it so freely.

Common grievances were compensation for supplies and provisions supplied in war; for unfair dealings of the government

Table 7-9. Claims Made against the U.S. Government

Table of Claim	Date	Name Index	NARA Record Group	Comments/Description
Claims Barred By Statute of Limitations, Adjusted and Allowed	1810	See comments		Printed in *American State Papers.* Use Phillip W. McMullin, *Grassroots of America* (Provo, Utah: Gendata, 1972) for some claims as volume indexes are unreliable. Online index and text for American State Papers at <http://memory.loc.gov/ammem/amlaw/hlawquery.html>.
Claims of Persons, Circumstances Barred by Limitations	1792	Yes		1,500 revolutionary war soldiers pensioned under an act of 27 March 1792. See Mary G. Ainsworth, "Recently Discovered Records Relating to Revolutionary War Veterans Who Applied for Pensions Under the Act of 1792," *National Genealogical Society Quarterly* 46 (1958): 8–13, 73–78
Private Claims Submitted to Congress	1774 to present		360 233 (House) 46 (Senate)	Published as *Congressional Documents.* Arranged alphabetically to form an easily accessible index, 1789–1891 (House), 1815–1909 (Senate). Fully searchable text online at <http://memory.loc.gov/ammem/amlaw/hlawquery.html>. This site also allows searches by Congressional Session for both House and Senate. Visit <www.archives.gov/> and use the Federal Records Guide at <www.archives.gov/research/guide-fed-records>.
Quartermaster Claims	1839–94	NARA M-film M1999: Index to Quartermaster Claims. 1 roll.	92	Four manuscript vols., claims relating to services, supplies, or transportation furnished to or requisitioned for the army. Supporting documents may have been destroyed. Includes Mexican War claims, 1847–58, and civilian claims (mostly Mexican War teamsters), 1848–60
Fourth of July Claims	1861–70 1871–90	Volume indexes Partial indexes only	92	Sixty-eight vols. (manuscripts with supporting case files); include rejected claims. Volumes arranged by auditors' numbers, related papers filed by register numbers. 29 vols. (manuscripts with supporting case files); arranged by year. Rejected claims arranged by box numbers. Incomplete 2-vol. register to rejected claims. Must prove loyal citizen of loyal state. Valuable, covers country. 36 vols. (manuscripts with supporting correspondence and case files)
Civil War Claims	1861–94	Some volume indexes	92	Transportation, personal services for persons later deceased, horses and mules, extra duty, bounty arrears, property damage, rents, and other matters. Indexes, where they exist, are incomplete.
Transportation Claims	1871–87	Some volume indexes	92	131 registers, including ocean and lake vessels, railroad accounts connected with military operations, ferries
Confederate Horse Claims	1901–14	No	92	Claims for paroled Confederate soldiers whose arms and horses were seized by Union soldiers in violation of the terms of surrender. Files arranged by members from general correspondence of the quartermaster general, 1890–1914
Alabama Claims	1872	Yes	76	List of documents and correspondence in the cases of U.S. and Great Britain indexing the claims for losses to Confederate ships Alabama, Shenandoah, Florida, Tallahassee. Description of cases in Revised List of Claims . . . Known as the Alabama Claims Preliminary Inventory 135, Records Relating to Civil War Claims, United States and Great Britain.
Southern Claims Commission	1871–80	Yes	217	Approved claims
			233	Disallowed claims filed with records of House of Representatives. Gary B. Mills, comp., *Southern Loyalists in the Civil War: A Composite Directory of Case Files Created by the U.. Commissioners of Claims, 1871–1880, Including Those Appealed to the War Claims Committee...* (Reprint, Baltimore: Genealogical Publishing Co., 2004). 22,298 claims were submitted by Southerners who swore they were loyal to the Union; 7,092 were allowed. Includes interrogatories (detailed questionnaires) filled out by all applicants A search path for locating granted and disbarred claims is at <www.slcl.org/branches/hq/sc/scc/steps.htm>. The Tennessee State Library index identifies 3, 929 Tennesseans who submitted claims; see <www.state.in.us/sos/statelib/pubsvs/sccintro>.

Claims of Citizens of Kansas	1858–61	online index to Strickler at <www.territorialkansasonline.org>		Report of General H.J. Strickler, Commissioner for Auditing Claims for Kansas Territory 35th Cong., 2nd Sess., H. Misc. Doc. 43, serial 1017 (1858–59); 36th Cong., 2nd Sess., H. Reports 104, serial 1106. Indexes are incomplete. Claims awarded for property damage by marauding raiders, e.g., Quantrell
Hearings, Committee on War Claims	1910–14	Volume indexes		63rd Cong., 2nd Sess., H. Reports 124. Many available on microfiche
Claims Commissions, United States and Mexico	1839–1938	Yes	76	Include cases of seizure of property, quartering of troops, illegal arrest and maltreatment of prisoners, boundary claims, prize cases submitted by local residents. Several thousand claims were accepted. See Preliminary Inventory 136: Records of United States and Mexican Claims Commission
War Relocation Authority (Japanese Americans)	1941–46	Japanese American Internee Data File and Index at <http://aad.archives.gov/aad/display-partial-records.jsp?>	210	9,000 Japanese-Americans moved out of military zones in California, Oregon, Washington, Arizona, Arkansas, and Hawaii voluntarily. More than 100,000 were forced to evacuate by the War Relocation Authority. See Preliminary Inventory 77: Records of the War Relocation Authority
World War II Exclusion Files	1941–48		153	Relocation of German and Italian aliens, U.S. citizens of German and Italian heritage in military zones. Alphabetically arranged by surname

More detail on these claims records and their locations and finding aids are in Anne Bruner Eales and Robert M. Kvasnicka. *Genealogical Research in the National Archives* (NARA, 2000), pp 307–14. For information on the record groups listed, see Robert B. Matchette, et al., *Guide to Federal Records in the National Archives of the United States* (NARA, 1995); regularly updated web version at <www.archives.gov/research/guide-fed-records>.

and its personnel; for unpaid wages, pensions, or other compensation promised; for lack of protection against local enemies and foreign powers; and for jurisdiction and boundary changes.

Although this discussion is limited to claims against the U.S. government and its courts, equivalent actions and records can be found in state court files and among the records of counties, towns, and cities.

Table 7-9 is a summary of the types of claims made from 1774 through World War II with the agency responsible to deal with them, the record group number, and a brief description of the contents and/or location.

Most claims against the U.S. government before 1855 were presented to Congress and referred to committees on claims of the Senate and the House of Representatives (see "Private Claims and Claims Committees of the U.S. Congress," below). The inability of these committees to examine in detail all the claims submitted, together with the difficulty of getting Congress to appropriate the necessary funds to pay favorable claims, amounted to a denial of justice to many citizens. In addition, the number of claims became too great. A separate Court of Claims, established in 1855, did not solve the problem because it had no authority to render judgment. Its job was to investigate claims and forward all evidence, testimony of witnesses, law briefs of solicitors and claimants, and opinions and recommendations of the court to the Committee of Claims, House of Representatives, for final consideration of those cases recommended favorably. Those reported unfavorably were placed upon the calendar for Congressional consideration. This amounted to having each case tried twice and solved nothing. In 1863, the court was given power to render final judgment in all cases with the right of appeal to the Supreme Court for cases involving more than $3,000. From 1855 to the end of 1881, it heard more than 13,000 cases. By an amendment passed in 1868 to the Act of 1863, the clerk of the court was required to submit an annual return to Congress containing a list of all judgments rendered by the court, the amount of redress granted, the parties involved, and a brief synopsis of the nature of the claim.

The procedures and practices of the Court of Claims are very similar to those followed in regular courts of law except that all testimony and evidence is in writing. Twenty-five printed copies of all briefs must be filed (if the case is under $3,000, the briefs are printed at public expense) with the clerk of the court at least one day prior to the hearing of the case. No court costs are required except those of the claimant's personal attorney. Cases must be presented by legal counsel. There is no jury. Before 1868, all claimants had to prove that they had been loyal citizens of the Union during the Civil War. Since that time, the amnesty oath pardoning Confederates has voided this provision. Table 7-10 is a summary of the court's growing jurisdiction.

The National Archives has published listings of the case files and related records with descriptions of what they contain, how they are filed, and indexes that can be used in Preliminary Inventories 47 and 58 (titles provided in table 7-11). Some of this information is available online at <www.archives.gov>. Therefore, it is not necessary to go into detail concerning these records here. Table 7-11, prepared for the convenience of the

Table 7-10. United States Court of Claims

Jurisdiction	Date Established	Date Abolished	Indexes Located
Investigate, report findings to Congress General jurisdiction, violations of contracts entered into by government agencies, violations of Indian treaties, patent infringements, unlawful imprisonment, over assessment of overpayments of taxes, payment of army, navy, civilian personnel, and unlawful seizure of property.	1855	1863	Cases indexed in *Cases Decided in the Court of Claims of the United States 1855–1863* (Washington: Government Printing Office, 1867). Court of Claims
Try claims, render final judgment.	1863		Court of Claims
Admiralty claims.		1930*	Court of Claims
Equity claims	1870		Court of Claims
Appeals to Supreme Court, plaintiff over $3,000, defendant all cases.	1866**	1925***	Supreme Court records in the National Archives
District of Columbia—jurisdiction cases.	1880	1915†	Court of Claims
Cases originally handled by Congressional committees. The majority were claims for seizure of stores, supplies, and damages resulting from the occupation of Union troops during the Civil War.	1883, 1887		Indexes 1884–1943 on microfilm M2007, U.S. Court of Claims Docket Cards for Congressional Case Files, ca 1884–1943. 5 rolls.
Claims under interdepartmental agencies. Also includes naval bounty claims arising from the Spanish-American War.	1883, 1887		Court of Claims
Claims arising from depredations by French warships and privateers on American commerce, 1793–1801 (French spoliations). Court to investigate and report to Congress. The U.S. abandoned all claims for reparations against France in 1801, but the claimants continued to press for payment. 5,574 claims were filed with the court; all claims were settled with heirs.	1885	1908	Indexes to the files are in RG 205, Records of the Court of Claims Section (Justice). Included is the publication *French Spoliation Awards by the Court of Claims of the United States Under the Act of January 20, 1885* (Washington: U.S. Court of Claims, 1934) which gives the name of each original claimant, vessel, master, and case file number.
Concurrent jurisdiction given to federal district courts under $1,000; to circuit courts $1,000–$10,000.	1887		Pertinent district or circuit courts
Claims for property taken or destroyed by Indians under treaty with the U.S. government, 1814–91 (Indian Depredations). Cases usually involve isolated miners, ranchers, towns, stage coaches, wagon trains, and railroad lines.	1891†† 1915	1920	Same as French cases above. List of claims 49th Cong., 1st Sess., H. Exec. Doc 125, serial 2399
Indian claims. In 1946, Indians were given the right to present claims against the U.S. government like other U.S. citizens.	1946		Court of Claims, 400 cases to 1960

* Since 1930, only foreigners can sue for admiralty claims in this court. Citizens must petition federal admiralty courts.

** The law of 1863 gave right of appeal to the Supreme Court, but the court refused to hear appeals that were reviewable by the Department of the Treasury. Treasury jurisdiction was abolished in 1866.

*** Since 1925, the Supreme Court has had the right to choose the cases it hears.

† A large number of cases arising from long-standing Civil War claims were canceled. The number of cases handled after 1915 was small.

†† From 1796 to 1891, cases heard by Department of the Interior and its predecessors, report made to Congress. Few awards were made before 1891.

Table 7-11. Court of Claims Record Locations

Original Records	Dates Covered	Located
Original indexes, dockets, minutes, judgments books, register of attorneys	1855 to present	Court of Claims
Case files: general jurisdiction	1855–1939	Court of Claims, Record Group 123, National Archives
	1939–46	Federal Records Center, Suitland, Maryland
	1946 to present	Court of Claims
Other	1855–1943	Court of Claims, Record Group 123, National Archives
	1943 to present	Court of Claims
Attorney General records	1855–1945	Court of Claims Section, Department of Justice, Record Group 205, National Archives
	1945 to present	Attorney General Office, Department of Justice
Reports to Congress	1855–63	Committee on Claims, records of House of Representatives, Record Group 233, National Archives
Printed Records	**Dates Covered**	**Located**
Reports to Congress	1855–63	Congressional Documents and Reports, government documents libraries
Court reports	1863	Cases Decided in the Court of Claims of the United States, vols. 1 to present available in most large law libraries. Each volume indexed separately, general indexes vol. 30 (vols. 1–29); vol. 54 (31–54); vol. 62 (55–62)

researcher from these inventories, indicates the kind of records produced, the dates covered, and the locations of the original records themselves. Congressional records—both original and printed—contain pertinent information concerning the Court of Claims and its cases through the annual reports submitted by the court. The procedures outlined earlier for use with claims presented to Congress can be followed to use Court of Claims information.

Even though the court and parts of its jurisdiction were not established until the latter half of the nineteenth century, documents and evidence sometimes date from the Revolutionary War period. In addition, many claims are submitted by and awarded to heirs of the original claimants.

For example, the French Spoliations cases, arising from incidents in the 1790s but continuing for a century, include ledgers, account books, insurance policy registers, notarial records, letter books, day books, executors' accounts of liquidation of estates, ships' registers and logs, lists of crew members who served aboard vessels, and so on. Case files also include certificates of appointments of administrators, executors, legal representatives, powers of attorney, and proof of death. The Court of Claims, in an effort to substantiate the claims submitted, ordered evidence collected from customs and marine records in French ports and archives. Authenticated copies of these French materials, together with English translations, were sent to the State Department, and certified copies were introduced as evidence in the claims cases. Even though these records are copies of copies and thus subject to error, most originals have since been destroyed or lost. Maritime records kept by U.S. Customs officials at ports of entry—registrations, registers, oaths, proofs of ownership, licenses, enrollments—were also included.

Among the case files of the Congressional-jurisdiction records are muster rolls, certificates of death and burial, oaths of allegiance, inventories of property, statements and records of military service, records of courts-martial, and tax lists. The naval bounty claims contain lists of seamen who served on vessels during the Spanish-American War. The U.S. Court of Claims did not handle claims for pensions, although many were submitted to Congress.

Coroners' Records

The coroner's foremost responsibility is to conduct inquests when a death occurring within his or her jurisdiction involves the possibility of foul play, violence, or suicide. The inquest determines if a criminal act has been committed and, if so, the potential guilty party. In some jurisdictions, the inquest is ordered by the court, in some by justices of the peace, and in some by the county attorney. In fact, in jurisdictions where an official coroner is not appointed, the justice of the peace or the county (district) attorney serves in this capacity. More recently, coroners have been replaced by medical examiners—especially in urban areas.

In every county in the nation, by law, accidental deaths, or deaths where the cause is questionable, must be investigated by the county coroner or medical examiner. Because we associate coroners so closely with murders, we may forget that they are likely to be involved in the following types of death: suicide;

accident; sudden death of a person in apparently good health; person unattended by a practicing, licensed physician at death; death involving suspicious or unusual circumstances; criminal abortion; poisoning or adverse reaction to drugs and/or alcohol; disease constituting a threat to public health; disease, injury, or toxic agent resulting from employment; death during medical diagnostic or therapeutic procedures; death in any prison or penal institution; death while involuntarily confined in jail, prison, hospital, or other institution or in police custody; whenever a body is to be cremated, dissected, or buried at sea; any unclaimed body; any dead body brought into a new medico-legal jurisdiction without proper medical certification; and D.O.A. (dead on arrival) at hospital. The results of such investigations may generate reports in the form of a few lines or several reams of paper. Case files are frequently full of personal information and rare glimpses into the personalities under investigation.

As with almost every other kind of record collection used by family historians, the existence and condition of the coroner's records may vary from state to state and from county to county. They may also vary dramatically in content from year to year. As a rule, twentieth-century inquests are more detailed, sometimes running several hundred pages. Inquests for earlier years may consist of only a few lines in a ledger.

The coroner's qualifications and personality frequently determined how and what kinds of records were kept. In most counties in the United States, the coroner is still an elected position—and, according to some, the job may be one of the most powerful in a given county. Some counties have completely done away with coroner's positions, and inquests are now under the jurisdiction of the medical examiner's office.

Cook County, Illinois, for example, moved away from the coroner system in December 1976. At that time, inquest records came under the jurisdiction of the Cook County medical examiner, and the coroner's verdict (or a determination of guilt), previously a part of the procedure, was no longer included in the record. It is probable that a television journalist's exposé on the Cook County coroner's procedures was responsible for significant changes in procedure. Before the story broke, it had been acceptable to pull less-than-qualified individuals off the street to serve on an inquest jury. The $24 per day paid to jurors had special appeal to vagrants in the area. As a part of the exposé, a television camera panning the jurors caught most of them asleep while evidence was being presented, and waking just in time to decide if the death in question was accidental or a suicide.

While inquest records began as early as 1878 in Cook County, it was not until 1911 that individual inquest files included personal details. But even a few lines in a ledger can provide important leads to follow.

An inquest "upon the body of Alexander Goetzinger Murray," dated 19 May 1903 in Cook County, presented the following verdict: "The said A.G. Murray now lying dead at 205 North Pk Ave in said City of Chicago, County of Cook, State of Illinois, came to his death on the 18th day of May A.D. 1903 on the lawn at the NE corner of Washington Boul. and Franklin Ave, Austin, Illinois, from valvular disease of the heart." Names of the jurors were of little help, but the list of witnesses together with their addresses provided some good hints for follow-up research. Interestingly enough, the most important clues came from the "description of property found on the body," in this case, a lodge button that led to an investigation of Masonic records.

In a typical "history of case for statistical purposes," a 1935 Chicago inquest proved to be full of genealogical and general-interest details. The form asked for full name of deceased, address, age, sex, marital status, color, birthplace, how long in United States, how long in city, birthplace of father, birthplace of mother, religion, housing conditions, present occupation, employed by whom, past occupation, wages or salary due, amount of life insurance and to whom it was payable, value of personal and real estate property, level of education, number of dependents, and ten questions regarding the decedent's physical and mental health at the time of death. The last questions ask for cause of accident or catastrophe, the place of death, and the recommendation of the jury.

When Joseph Kustak died, the coroner's jury determined the cause of death to be accidental. He had "bumped a bedroom door against a shut off gas valve, causing an accidental flow of gas." But there were pages of testimony where relatives and acquaintances told the jury what they thought of his state of mind when they had last seen him. The information on the form, combined with witnesses' accounts, provided an unusually vivid portrait of the deceased (see figure 7-13).

While these examples provide a rough overview of what may be found in one city, there are equally fascinating records for just about every other county in the nation.

How does one go about finding coroners' records? First, examine family traditions and records for any potential clues that would point to this collection of records. In some cases, a death certificate will state that a coroner's inquest was held. Anytime there is a suspicious death or a death by any of the aforementioned causes, an investigation may be in order. Newspaper accounts of unusual deaths are often the best way to key in on dates—an important tip, since most coroners' records are not indexed and may be found only by date of the event. Fortunately, some of these records (such as the last two cited here) have been microfilmed and may be available at the LDS Family History Library in Salt Lake City, Utah, and Family History Centers.

In recent years, a number of coroners' and medical examiners' record indexes have become available online through state and local archives and historical agencies. The Illinois State Archives, for example, has posted an index to such records at <www.sos.state.il.us/departments/archives/archives.html>.

Courts-Martial Records

The purpose of military courts is to insure orderly operations and exact obedience. The United States has traditionally maintained a small standing army during times of peace, depending upon local militia or civilian conscripts to supplement these soldiers in times of war.

Local militias and state-authorized troops made up the bulk of American armed forces from colonial times until the Civil War. During the Revolutionary War, the soldiers who formed the Continental Army were drawn from these local units. As a result, records exist both at the federal level for the continental troops and at the colonial/state level.

Before 1689, all military offenses were tried before regular law courts. With the passage of the English Mutiny Act in 1689, courts-martial heard military violations at the county/town and colonial levels.

Every able-bodied man from the ages of sixteen to sixty (except those specifically exempted by law), fully armed at his own expense, was required to serve in the county or town militia. These militia units were required to hold at least four private (local) musters and one or two general (county) musters per year at which they were to drill and to become proficient in the use of arms. At all musters, the captains of the companies were to keep an attendance record on each man and a record of the offenses and delinquencies of attendance and equipment of all men of the respective companies and report the same to the courts-martial. The courts-martial convened once a year in each county after the general muster of the county. In this militia court sat a majority or all of the captains of the county. They reviewed the ages and capabilities of all those on the muster lists, dropped those too old or disabled, inquired into the absences and delinquencies reported, and imposed fines. Militia watches were outlined,

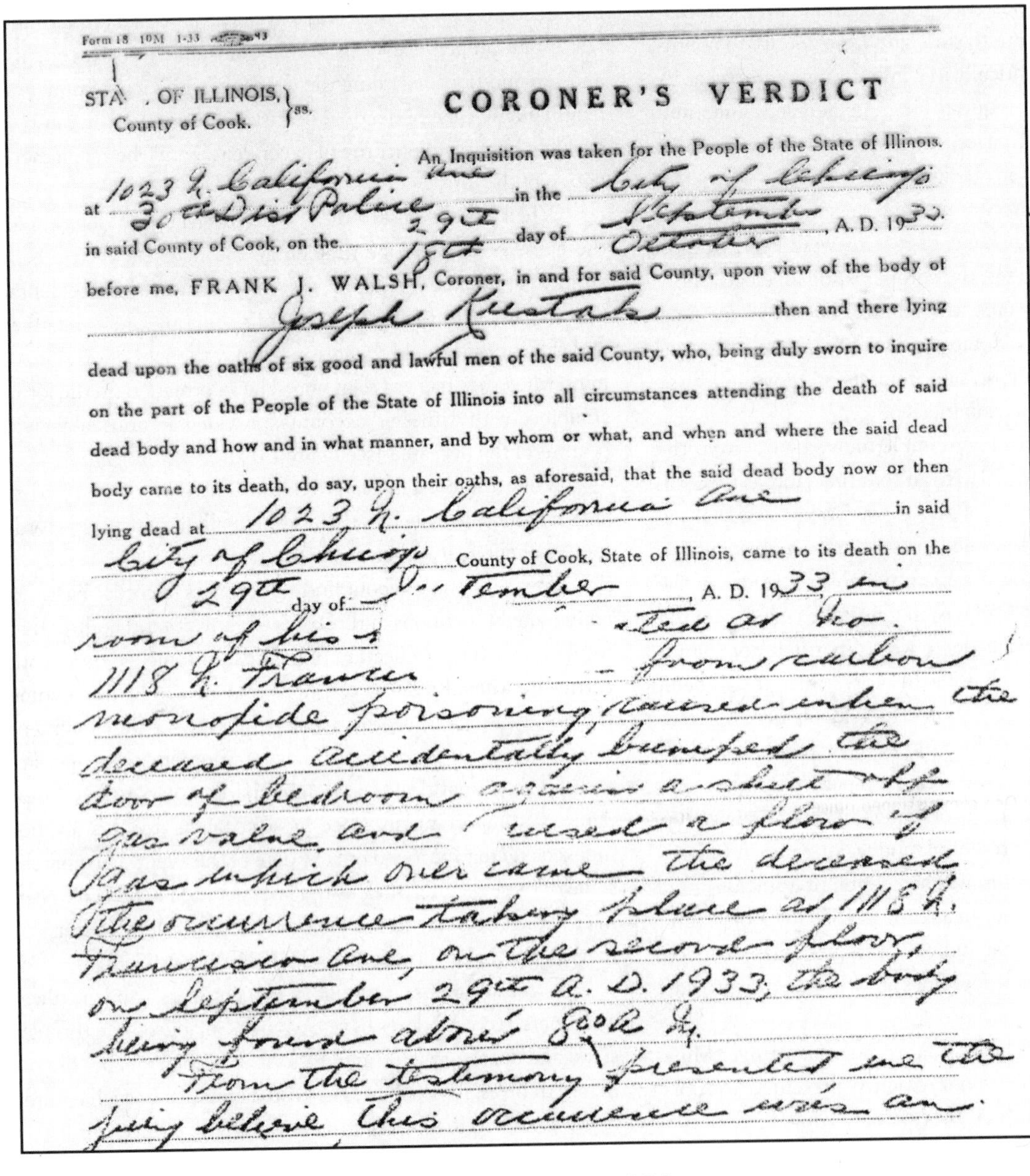

Form 18 10M 1-33

STATE OF ILLINOIS, County of Cook. } ss.

CORONER'S VERDICT

An Inquisition was taken for the People of the State of Illinois, at 1023 N. California Ave 30th Dist Police in the City of Chicago in said County of Cook, on the 29th 18th day of September October, A. D. 1933, before me, FRANK J. WALSH, Coroner, in and for said County, upon view of the body of Joseph Kustak then and there lying dead upon the oaths of six good and lawful men of the said County, who, being duly sworn to inquire on the part of the People of the State of Illinois into all circumstances attending the death of said dead body and how and in what manner, and by whom or what, and when and where the said dead body came to its death, do say, upon their oaths, as aforesaid, that the said dead body now or then lying dead at 1023 N. California Ave in said City of Chicago County of Cook, State of Illinois, came to its death on the 29th day of September, A. D. 1933, in room of his [illegible] at No. 1118 N. Francisco – from carbon monoxide poisoning caused when the deceased accidentally bumped the door of bedroom against a shut off gas valve and released a flow of gas which overcame the deceased. The occurrence taking place at 1118 N. Francisco Ave, on the second floor, on September 29th A. D. 1933; the body being found about 8 o'clock [illegible].

From the testimony presented we the jury believe this occurrence was an

Figure 7-13. The coroner's verdict on the cause of death of Joseph Kustak in 1933.

assigned, and reported on also. In some jurisdictions, the militia captain was also responsible for tax assessment, and tax districts coincided with militia districts.

The professional, standing army of the United States dates from 1789. In times of war, it is supplemented by National Guard and reserve units, state militias, and civilians conscripted directly from the unorganized militia—all males of military age. There are three types of military jurisdiction: military law, or the Code of Military Justice; martial law, or temporary rules enforced by soldiers governing both military and civilian populations; and military governments, or administrative functions exercised by military personnel and organizations over civil populations as a result of war.

The Code of Military Justice outlined by Thomas Jefferson and John Adams in 1776 to govern Washington's volunteers has evolved into the Uniform Code of Military Justice, which was adopted on 31 May 1951 to make all branches of the armed forces subject to the same courts, trial procedures, and appellate review.

The National Guard is subject to this system when under federal control, and states have adopted similar provisions when operating under state authority, in training or local emergencies., Reserve units are subject to military law while on active duty and during annual training camps. All members of the U.S. armed forces are subject to the code at all times. This code is enforced in military courts-martial. Although provided for by the Constitution, these tribunals derive their authority from the executive branch rather than the judicial and thus are completely separate from the regular system. Cases are not reviewable by civil courts, nor can appeal be made to civil courts. Table 7-12 summarizes the types of courts-martial.

Courts-martial exercise exclusive jurisdiction over all persons subject to military law for violation of the military code. Military offenses under the code include insubordination, failure to obey orders, being absent without leave, and disrespect for officers; courts-martial exercise concurrent jurisdiction with civilian law courts over offenses such as murder, theft, rape, and burglary. Under this system, violators may be tried, convicted, and punished twice for the same crime.[75]

Courts-martial files deposited in the National Archives, Judge Advocate General's Office, contain records of the general courts-martial, courts of inquiry, and military commissions for the period 1809 to 1938. Included are documents describing the personnel and organization of the courts, changes and specifications, pleas and arraignments of the defendants, papers and exhibits submitted to the court for consideration, proceedings, findings, and sentences, reports of reviewing authorities, and statements of actions by the secretary of war and the president. Table 7-13 is a summary of these records.

In 1776, when Congress established authority for military courts, no sentence of a general courts-martial could be carried out until confirmed by Congress. This proved to be impractical and was soon modified to apply only to high-ranking officers or death sentences. A little later, the president of the United States had to confirm all convictions of the death penalty in military trials. Noncommissioned soldiers could appeal only to the authority who appointed the military court. Under the National Defense Act of 4 June 1920, a Board of Review was established for review of all general courts-martial cases before punishment could be carried out. In 1952, Congress provided for a Court of Military Appeals through which civilian judges could review all military convictions and appeals from lower tribunals. In its first

Table 7-12. Types of United States Courts-Martial

Court	Membership	Offenses	Punishment
Court of inquiry	Appointed upon request of the accused	Any non-capital or capital offense	Determined by the nature of the offense. If there is sufficient evidence for court martial, records are admissible as evidence in later trial
Summary court-martial*	One commissioned officer	Any non-capital or capital offense	Confinement at hard labor for 1 month, restriction for 2 months, or forfeiture of 1/2 of 1 month's pay
Special court-martial	Three or more commissioned officers	Specific cases of a non-capital nature	Discharge, confinement at hard labor for 6 months, forfeiture of 2/3 of 6 month's pay, reduced rank. Officers punishable only 60 days by confinement and forfeiture
General court-martial	Five or more commissioned officers and 1 law officer**	Any offense, especially subject to capital cases and those punishable by death	Any punishment not forbidden by the Military Code

* Cadets and officers cannot be tried in a summary court-martial.

** The law officer instructs the court on points of proper law

year, it heard 108 suits on appeal and in 50 percent of the cases reversed the decision rendered by the Board of Review.[76]

Martial Law and Military Governments

Martial law consists of rules temporarily applied to civilians under the direction of military officers. Authority for martial law must originate from Congressional grant or presidential power and is enforced by military tribunals. If local units of government are unable to cope with war, insurrection, invasion, or other disruptive forces, Congress or the president can order a military government to replace these local units and supply administrative controls. Examples include federal occupation of Southern territory during the Civil War (martial law) and the Reconstruction government exercised in Southern states following the end of the Civil War, when the South was physically and financially unable to direct its own affairs. The jurisdiction of military forts in Indian Territory of the American West is another important example.[77]

Justice of the Peace Courts

A "JP," or justice of the peace, was a judge of a local court that held limited jurisdiction. Most JPs heard legal action for small claims, tried persons accused of misdemeanors, and conducted preliminary examinations of prisoners. They could perform civil marriages and officially record an indenture between a master an apprentice. In some states, JPs had limited criminal jurisdiction as well: assault and battery, vagabonds, punishing vice and immorality, fining Sabbath breakers, and other misdemeanors punishable by fines. Appeals from justices of the peace were always allowed. In many states, justices kept records of testimony, in almost all states they were required to maintain dockets. In addition to the aforesaid matters, these records may list appointments of constables, overseers of the poor, township assessors, or election judges. Most JP offices were abolished in the mid-twentieth century although some, notably in the eastern states, survive today.

Name Changes

Every state provides for legal name changes. The circumstances, however, vary from state to state, and so do the courts having jurisdiction to authorize name changes.

An early source that includes the American colonies to 1782 is *An Index to Changes of Name Under Authority of Act of Parliament 1760–1901*, compiled by W. P. W. Phillimore and Edward A. Fry.[78] The original introduction includes an essay on the "Law and Practice of Change of Name" by Phillimore, one of the foremost genealogists of his day.

Legislative control of name changes continued until roughly 1850 to 1865 in America. Some state legislatures still have power to legalize names, although it is rare for them to do so. Regular courts with divorce jurisdiction usually have the power to legalize name changes today. Some have separately

Table 7-13. Records of United States Courts-Martial

Records	Dates	Record Group Number	Comments
Records of general courts-martial and courts of inquiry, U.S. Navy	1799–1867	125, NARA m-film M237	Originals cover 1799–1943. Partially name-indexed. Must know approximate date; for some records must know offense as well. Records include name, rank, ship or station, alleged offense, place and date of trial, sentence. May include medical fitness for duty, prison reports, requests to change discharge from dishonorable to honorable. Dossiers include transcript of testimony.
Proceedings of general courts-martial, Marine Corps	1798–1866	27	Arranged chronologically, must know date of court-martial.
Civil War Courts Martial	1861–1865	125	In 1997, author-researcher Thomas P. Lowry began reading the nearly 80,000 court martial files of Union soldiers. Lowry has since published several titles pertaining to these files, i.e., *Curmudgeons, Drunkards, and Outright Fools: Courts-Martial of Civil War Union Colonels.* (Lincoln, Neb.: Bison, 2003). See also, Trevor K. Plante "The Shady Side of the Family Tree: Civil War Union Court-Martial Case Files" Prologue 30:4 (Winter 1998) at <www.archives.gov/publications/prologue/1998/winter>.
Court-martial records, Office of Judge Advocate General (U.S. Army)	1805–1939	153, NARA m-film M1105, Registers of the Records of the Proceedings of the U.S. Army General Courts Martial, 1809–1890. 8 rolls.	Case files for general courts-martial, courts of inquiry, military commissions. Arranged by case number. Name index, 1891–1917. The National Archives is compiling a name index for pre-1891 files. Some files include dates of birth, places of residence, dependents, as well as transcripts of trial. Separate series of files exist for 1805–15 (incomplete) and for 1861–65. Registers showing name, rank, unit, place, and date of court provide a partial index to all series. Files dated before 1812 are incomplete.

indexed volumes in which these are recorded, and some list them in the regular court orders or judgments.

Name changes are especially important where divorce or adoption has occurred. For this reason it is a good idea to search the indexes name by name for all pedigree surnames and for those names that married into your lines. List any entries that appear promising, then check the case files referred to for essential information.

Private Claims and Claims Committees of the U.S. Congress

Between 1789 and 1946, nearly 2500 cubic feet of private claims records were created. This includes more than 500,000 private claims that were brought before Congress between 1789 and 1909 (First through Sixtieth Congresses). Incredibly, petitions and memorials account for over half the total volume of the unpublished records of Congress before 1900. These records contain a wealth of family and local history information and many are easily accessible thanks to online indexes at the American Memory Project website of the Library of Congress, <http://memory.loc.gov>.

In hearing private claims, Congress serves as a court of last resort where persons seeking redress of grievances involving the federal government may petition. The petitioner in most situations has been denied redress by administrative and judicial reviews. The grievance, which may involve towns, states, fraternal organizations, churches, unions, fellowships, as well as individuals, is then brought or referred to Congress. The workload of private claims resulted in the creation of the Committee on Claims (House of Representatives) in 1794 and the Senate Claims Committee in 1816. Eventually these committees were further divided according to the type of appeal: military pensions, Revolutionary claims, war claims, and private land claims being some. A full explanation of the Congressional claims process and instructions for locating the records that were created will be found in Charles E. Schamel, "Untapped Resources: Private Claims and Private Legislation in the Records of the U.S. Congress." See also, Chris Naylor, "Those Elusive Early Americans: Public Lands and Claims in the *American State Papers*."[79]

Southern Claims Commission

As one of the special commissions charged with a specific role, the Southern Claims Commission was established in 1871 to receive, examine, and consider claims submitted by Southern Unionist citizens seeking compensation for supplies that had been confiscated by or furnished to the Union Army. A typical case file contains the petition, a deposition or testimony of the claimant or a witness, the report of the commissioners, and miscellaneous papers. Content often includes family information, as does the file of Nancy Hays of Gibson, Glascock County, Georgia. Her 1872 disallowed claim shows Nancy to be about ninety years old; her first husband, William G. Wilcher, died in 1865. In 1867 she married Hays. One of the witnesses, W. J. Wilcher, knew William G. Wilcher from his earliest recollection. The claims files are on NARA M1407, "Barred and Disallowed Case Files of the Southern Claims Commission, 1871–1880," 4,829 fiche. See chapter 6, "Records of the Claims Committees," *Guide to the Records of the U.S. House of Representatives at the National Archives, 1780–1989* for details of holdings (Record Group 233) online at <www.archives.gov/legislative/guide/house/table-of-contents-short.html>. A step-by-step search path may be printed from the St. Louis County Library website at <www.slcl.org/branches/hq/sc/scc/steps.htm>. A print index is Gary Mills's *Southern Loyalists in the Civil War.* A Tennessee State Library and Archives online index identifies nearly four thousand Tennesseans who petitioned. The index is at <http://tennessee.gov/tsla/history/military/sccintro.htm>.

Re-Recording of Missing Records

If you are unsuccessful in locating court records for an individual in what you think is the right court and time period, it may be worth looking at indexes or files for a later period. For any number of reasons, an individual may have had cause to re-register legal documents such as wills, deeds, or petitions. Court fires, floods, and other courthouse mishaps were often the incentives that took aliens back into court long after they had applied for citizenship. The following is an example of the re-recording of a petition filed in Cook County Court (Chicago), Illinois in 1880—after the Great Chicago Fire of 1871 had destroyed earlier court records:

> In the matter of the application 28389–1180 of Bernard Cahn for restoration of the order of his naturalization as a Citizen of the United States and said matter having come on this day to be heard upon the petition filed herein, and upon proofs, exhibits and evidence heard in open Court and it appearing to the Court there from the Court finds
>
> That on the 1st day of November 1858 said petitioner appeared in this Court and showed to the Court that he had resided within the limits and under the jurisdiction of the United States for and during the full term of five years last preceding said 1st day of November 1858.
>
> That afterwards and on the 9th day of October 1871 the records of this Court including the record of the said order and also the said Certificate of Naturalization issued to said petitioner were totally destroyed by fire without the fault of the petitioner.

Extralegal Courts

In the colonial "back country," as on the frontiers of Texas, Wyoming, and Arizona, outlaw elements of society, both organized and disorganized, lived by plundering established settlements. Law and order were ineffective or nonexistent. Vigilante movements were a citizens' response.

Between 1765 and 1769, for instance, lawlessness reached its height in the Carolinas. Armed outlaw bands and individuals congregated in outlaw communities throughout the "back country." A Ranger-Regulator unit, organized with the approval of the South Carolina governor and Assembly to deal with these outlaw bands, drew up a "plan of regulation" and began acting. People without a fixed residence were apprehended, tried before Regulator courts, and punished—whipped, deported, put to work, or, occasionally, executed. Immoral persons were whipped, and negligent fathers and mothers were returned to their family responsibilities. To prevent interference from colonial officials and judicial personnel who neither understood nor cared about frontier problems, the only processes from Charleston allowed were actions for recovery of debts. The Regulators became the government in this area, deciding all disputes at militia courts on the muster field. On 25 March 1769, the Regulator movement ended peaceably when circuit courts were created to provide local justice. Estimates of the number of men who actually participated range from three thousand to five thousand. Richard Maxwell Brown, in *The South Carolina Regulators*, has made a detailed study of 118 participants.[80] Records of Regulator actions are sparse, consisting of correspondence, diaries, and militia courts-martial minutes. The governor pardoned on 31 October 1771 the seventy-six men officially identified as part of the movement.[81]

In North Carolina, a similar Regulator movement was much more violent. The colonial government flatly refused to consider the grievances of the back country Regulators and called out the state militia. In a short battle with some two thousand Regulators at the Alamance River on 16 May 1771, eighteen men were killed. Fifteen of the movement's leaders were tried for treason, and six were hanged. The governor proclaimed amnesty for those who would take an oath of allegiance, and some six thousand did.[82]

Ethan Allen and his Green Mountain Boys in Vermont and Bacon's Rebellion in Virginia are two more examples of such movements.

The difference between extralegal and illegal is narrow. A legislative act prohibiting group action (mob rule) renders a specific action illegal. The banding of a group of citizens together for mutual protection usually involves appointment of leader(s) and a secretary, keeping a written record of proceedings, and making group decisions (rules) binding upon all regardless of approval. This kind of action is extralegal—outside the law.

Extralegal courts do produce records—a wide variety of "official" or approved documents as well as reports of investigations, newspaper accounts, and correspondence between participants, witnesses, and government officials. For a provocative and fact-filled description of archives relating to extralegal bodies, see Richard Maxwell Brown's "The Archives of Violence," in *American Archivist*.[83]

To provide legislative, executive, and judicial functions when regular government institutions had ceased to function effectively during the Revolutionary War, the colonials used the same system adopted by the Puritans a century earlier when they overthrew and executed Charles I in England.

By 1774, two separate governments functioned in most of the colonies: assemblies and governors under British control, and those created by the revolutionary colonial leadership. These two governments met in immediately successive sessions, frequently with the same membership. When Parliament abolished the regular assemblies, the revolutionary governments assumed complete control. Each colony sent representatives to the Continental Congress; each appointed a provincial assembly, a provincial council, and various district, county, and town governing committees. By the time the war started, each of the colonies had created a functioning system of local and provincial self-government. They operated under a combination of martial and civil law until state constitutions could be ratified and regular government re-established.

Some meetings of freeholders (freemen) had been organized as early as 1766. In Westmoreland County, Virginia, 114 freemen joined for common defense and safety, forming the basis for subsequent citizen action as the revolution approached and selecting patriot representation for their extralegal provincial congress in the 1770s.[84]

Committees of Correspondence (observation) corresponded with members in the colony and with committees in other colonies. They provided political information, creating and consolidating pre-Revolutionary sentiment with frequent meetings. By 1774, every colony but Pennsylvania and North Carolina had Committees of Correspondence.

Committees of Safety were the executive powers that carried out the orders of the Continental Congress and enforced the Articles of Association that all colonies had signed. County-level committees frequently usurped the powers of the regular county courts, some even requiring that every suit brought before a regular court of law had to be authorized by the committee. They also appointed military officials and judicial personnel for certain courts; appointed patrols to control African Americans; exchanged prisoners; fined militia members for refusal to serve; relocated, paroled, or jailed Loyalists (Tories); punished counterfeiters; administered loyalty and test oaths; supervised elections to provincial congresses and the Continental Congress; ordered lists of taxable property and census rolls; censored publications and speech, frequently jailing offenders; passed moratoria on collection of debts or confiscations to be paid to creditors; corresponded and cooperated with other committees; offered bounties and premiums for manufacture of needed items—cotton, wool, lime, steel, etc.; regulated travel; controlled horse racing, billiard playing, and dances; seized vessels and prizes; made lists of inhabitants to submit to Provincial Councils; and inventoried estates of suspected Loyalists.

The local militias were under their direct control. They tried all cases of disobedience and reported to the provincial congresses. Once state constitutions were ratified, the extralegal units were replaced by regular governments.

The original minutes, correspondence, and loose papers of these committees are located, almost without exception, in state archives. Unfortunately, they are almost never used in genealogical research, although they are often the earliest indications of Revolutionary War activity. Their minutes also provide judicial records for the years 1774 to 1782, between the discontinuance of crown courts and the establishment of state courts.

Mining Districts and Their Records

In areas richly endowed with mineral resources—Pennsylvania, West Virginia, Alabama, Georgia, and the entire western United States—are many jurisdictions called mining districts. Like the New England towns, they kept order until county and local governments functioned smoothly. In 1866 there were five hundred districts in California, two hundred in Nevada, one hundred in Arizona, one hundred in Idaho, one hundred in Oregon, fifty in Montana, fifty in New Mexico, and fifty in Colorado. Twelve California counties were called mining counties for their principal industry.[85] Their records will show the recording of deeds, transfers of title, claims, abstracts, surveys, mortgages, probates, and other court processes.

Almost every mining district kept written records of some sort from the beginning, as claims had to be registered, although many did not survive fire, migration, or a thin vein. In other areas, major mining camps became county seats, and their records were the first public records.

Mining district records, though rare, are valuable precisely because of that rarity. Almost invariably they are the only written evidence available for their period. In California, where the population in 1848 was 14,000 and, by the end of 1849, more than 100,000, no government records could hope to be comprehensive.

Miners' Courts

In the absence of legally appointed law enforcement personnel, citizens of mining communities had to provide their own systems of justice. Although the criminal cases confronting these "popular tribunals" have caught the public imagination, the miners' courts or *alcades* dealt much more frequently with civil problems.[86] They fixed the size of claims (which varied greatly from one camp to another), determined the boundaries of districts, and made simple rules governing the working and abandoning of claims and trespassing on the claims of others.

These courts were active only when occasion arose. In smaller camps, guilt and punishment were often determined by the whole assembly of miners; in the larger mining communities, this responsibility was delegated to a jury, and sometimes legal counsel was available. Justice was usually summary.

Compared with the "lynch-law" of cattle ranges, vigilante committees in mining towns represented a more formal administration of justice, more closely paralleling indictment and trial in statutory courts. Justice in Montana and other territorial mining camps was based in part on the examples set in the preceding decade in California, from which many of the Montana miners had come. For further study, see the reference section at the end of this chapter.

Vigilante Societies

Around 1830–1840, some whites in northern cities became alarmed about the flow of African Americans fleeing slavery. Other whites openly encouraged the blacks to come, operating the underground networks and providing new identities, work, and schooling once they arrived. Both types of groups kept records; the Vigilant Committee of Philadelphia is one example.[87]

New Jersey's numerous vigilante groups have been documented in Anthony S. Nicolosi's "The Rise and Fall of the New Jersey Vigilant Societies," in *New Jersey History*, a comprehensive study by location, county, name, place of meeting, date established, earliest meeting, latest meeting, and date dissolved. He also includes mutual protection associations for merchants, and his notes include locations of records.[88]

Many frontier vigilance committees disbanded as soon as a specific emergency ended. Others had a long tenure.[89] An example of a formal vigilance society is one organized in 1851 in San Francisco with a constitution, bylaws, and newspaper publication. The organization grew from two hundred initial signatories, keeping painstaking records, until it was superseded by state-organized court systems in August 1859. It continued to meet as an organization until late in 1859. Between six thousand and eight thousand men were formal members.[90]

Special Courts

The American court system has included separate courts for such specific population groups as Native Americans, who were treated as a foreign power; slaves, who had few civil rights (in some areas, "free persons of color" were legally treated as slaves); Confederates, whose governments abolished federal power in local courts; and citizens of foreign powers, who exercised jurisdiction over American soil at varying times. Only the Native American courts still function.[91]

Indian Courts

Records of Native American–white cases, settled according to treaty provisions, are scattered among state records for New

York, North Carolina, and many of the western states. Sometimes they are clearly identified in archival finding aids, but usually they are filed with treaty papers or among court or commission case files, so the genealogist must read archive inventories carefully. See the chapter reference section. Records of tribal courts usually remain with the tribe.

Native Americans not living on reservations and not enrolled on tribal rolls have assumed American citizenship. Their records will be found in the local courts. Because Native Americans could expect juries to rule in favor of whites, they avoided court processes as much as possible. Jail records and cases brought before justices of the peace may be more common but are also more difficult to locate.

Black Courts

Slaves were usually tried in a separate set of courts presided over by one or two justices of the peace with assistance from local land holders. Free persons "of color," although not slaves, were rarely treated as were whites and sometimes were required to appear before slave courts.

Manumission—setting a slave free—was a court process. A certificate of freedom was issued to each member of the family manumitted and also recorded by the court. Look for a formal marriage ceremony following manumission, since freedom brought with it other rights as well.

Some jurisdictions distinguished between freedmen and free African Americans who had never been slaves or whose freedom had been won very early in their ancestry. Both are usually identified by color in the records and thus are distinguishable from whites of the same name.

The Inferior Court minutes for Jones County, Georgia, contain the petition of a free black for recognition of his freedom. He had been seized as property of a debtor, sold at a sheriff's sale in 1811, and, finally, eight years later, had come to court seeking his freedom again. The same court granted a petition for a guardian for three free black minors to protect their property.[92]

North Carolina records show cases where a man would free his slaves by will at the time of his death. Some even provided them with land or other property. Because emancipation was against the law in North Carolina, the county records rarely disclose such details. Usually, the land was left by will in the hands of an executor who was instructed privately about the wishes of the testator. Among the appeals cases, however, will be details from relatives who felt slighted or neighbors who resented living next to African Americans.

In South Carolina, the Magistrates and Freeholders Court handled all matters under the laws for "the better ordering of slaves" under authority originally granted in 1690 and revised in 1740, 1743, and 1783. This court could inflict any punishment allowed by law. Death sentences were carried out immediately. Before 1783, the proceedings were written and sent to the clerk of the crown in Charleston. Later they were recorded in the district courts. This duplication is important because fires in some South Carolina courthouses destroyed their early records, as occurred in Abbeville County.

The St. Louis Circuit Court Historical Records Project provides a database of Freedom Suits Case Files, 1814–1860 consisting of 292 legal petitions brought by or on behalf of persons of color held in slaver within the St. Louis area. See <www.stlcourtrecords.wustl.edu/about-freedom-suits-series.php>.

Slave courts and proceedings have not been studied in any depth, but the chapter reference section contains several references.

Other Courts

Other powers have exercised jurisdiction on American soil at varying times. Examples are the Confederate courts, 1861 to 1865; the Spanish systems in Florida, the Mississippi River delta area, Texas, and the American Southwest; the French control of the Mississippi River Valley and its tributaries; the Mexican claims and jurisdiction in the Southwest; and the Dutch occupation of New Netherlands. See the reference section at the end of this chapter for an introduction to these systems and their records.

Notes

[1] The word "people" is misleading. At first, it meant all white men, then all men regardless of color eligible to vote, and finally, in 1918, all adults eligible to vote. It did not then, and does not now, mean all persons.

[2] Bradley Chapin, *Criminal Justice in Colonial America, 1606–1660* (Athens: University of Georgia Press, 1983), 99–142.

[3] See Bruce C. Daniels, *Town and County: Essays on the Structure of Local Government in the American Colonies* (Middletown, Conn.: Wesleyan University Press, 1978).

[4] Alice Eichholz, ed., *Red Book: American State, County, and Town Sources*, 3rd ed. (Provo, Utah: Ancestry, 2004).

[5] Christine Rose, *Courthouse Research for Family Historians* (San Jose, Calif.: CR Publications, 2004).

[6] Diane Rapaport, New *England Court Records: A Research Guide for Genealogists and Historians* (Burlington, Mass.: Quill Pen Press, 2006).

[7] Chris Naylor, "'You have the body' Habeas Corpus Case Records of the U.S. Circuit Court for the District of Columbia, 1820–1863," *Prologue* 37, no. 3 (Fall 2005), online at <www.archives.gov/publications/prologue/2005/fall/habeas-corpus.html>.

[8] Robert B. Matchette, et al., *Guide to Federal Records in the National Archives of the United States*, 3 vols. (Washington, D.C.: National Archives and Records Administration, 1995). Updated

and searchable online at <www.archives.gov/research/guide-fed-records>.

[9] Ibid. Found online under Records of District Courts of the United States (Record Group 21) 1685–1993, table of contents, 21.2.9 Records of the Confederate States District Court for the Southern Division of the District of Alabama, textual records (in Atlanta), accessed on 1 February 2006.

[10] John Bouvier, *A Law Dictionary: Revised Sixth Edition, 1856,* online at <www.constitution.org>.

[11] William C. Burton, *Burton's Legal Thesaurus* (New York: Macmillan Library Reference, 1998).

[12] Based on Clarence N. Callender, *American Courts: Their Organization and Procedures* (New York: McGraw-Hill, 1927).

[13] David Skeel, *Debtor's Dominion: A History of Bankruptcy Law in America* (Princeton, N.J.: Princeton University Press, 2001).

[14] Gordon L. Remington, *New York State Probate Records: Genealogist's Guide to Testate and Intestate Records* (Boston: New England Historic Genealogical Society, 2002), vii.

[15] For an authoritative discussion of dower and curtesy, see "The Decline of Dower," in Lawrence M. Friedman, *A History of American Law,* 3rd ed. (New York: Touchstone, 2005), 322–23.

[16] Lee Albright and Helen F. M. Leary, "Designing Research Strategies," in *North Carolina Research: Genealogy and Local History* (Raleigh: North Carolina Genealogical Society, 1996), 36.

[17] Gary R. Toms and William R. Gann, *Widow's Dowers of Washington County, Tennessee 1803–1899* (Milford, Ohio: Little Miami Publishing, 2004).

[18] "Inventories as a Source of Local History: Houses, Farmers, Industries, and Professions," *Amateur Historian* 4 (1958–59): 157–61, 186–95, 227–31, 320–24; B. C. Jones, "Inventories of Goods and Chattels," *Amateur Historian* 2 (1955–56): 76–79.

[19] As cited in Harry A. Focht, "Hidden Genealogical Data in Court Records," *Perry Historians* 8 (1983): 2–3. The record also documents Peter Arnold's second marriage.

[20] From Vincent L. Jones, et al., *Family History for Fun and Profit* (Salt Lake City: Genealogical Institute, 1972). Used with permission.

[21] John Anderson Brayton, Part 1, "Hardy of South Carolina—A 'Discreet' Omission to Hide an Indiscretion," and Shana Elizabeth Proffitt, Part 2, "Mallory-Blunt of Virginia—A Miscopied Name Blocks Line," in Notes and Documents, "Check the Original! Two Lessons Learned the Hard Way," *National Genealogical Society Quarterly* 90, no. 1 (March 2002): 69–73.

[22] Brayton, "Hardy of South Carolina," 69.

[23] Proffitt, "Mallory-Blunt of Virginia," 71.

[24] Ibid., 73.

[25] Kenneth Lockridge, "A Communication," *William and Mary Quarterly* 3rd ser., 25 (1968): 516–17; Daniel Scott Smith, "Underregistration and Bias in Probate Records: An Analysis of Data From Eighteenth Century Hingham, Massachusetts," *William and Mary Quarterly* 3rd ser., 32 (1975): 100–110.

[26] Donald L. Jacobus, "Probate Law and Custom," *American Genealogist* 9 (1932): 4–9.

[27] Thorton W. Mitchell, *Carolina Wills: A Testator Index, 1665–1900,* 4th printing (Baltimore: Clearfield, 2001); Carol Willsey Bell, *Ohio Wills and Estates to 1850: An Index* (Columbia, Ohio: the author, 1981); Brent Holcomb, *Abstracts of South Carolina Wills* (Easley, S.C.: Southern Historical Press, 1977).

[28] Glenda Riley, *Divorce: An American Tradition* (New York: Oxford University Press, 1991), 12.

[29] Lawrence M. Friedman, *History of American Law,* 3rd ed. (New York: Touchstone, 2005), 142.

[30] Lawrence Stone, *Road to Divorce: England, 1530–1987; Uncertain Unions: Marriage in England, 1660–1753;* and *Broken Lives: Separation and Divorce in England, 1660–1857,* 3 vols. (Oxford, England: Oxford University Press, 1990–93).

[31] George Ryskamp, "Common-Law Concepts for the Genealogist: Marriage, Divorce, and Coverture," *National Genealogical Society Quarterly* 83 (September 1995): 165–79.

[32] Ibid., 173.

[33] Friedman, *A History of American Law,* 142.

[34] Raymond A. Winslow Jr., "County Records," in *North Carolina Research: Genealogy & Local History,* ed. Helen F. M. Leary, rev. ed. (Raleigh: North Carolina Genealogical Society, 1996).

[35] Riley, *Divorce,* 30.

[36] James Van Ness, "On Untieing the Knot: The Maryland Legislature and Divorce Petitions," *Maryland Historical Magazine* 67 (1972): 171–75.

[37] Thomas E. Buckley, *The Great Catastrophe of My Life: Divorce in the Old Dominion* (Chapel Hill: University of North Carolina Press, 2002).

[38] Glenda Riley, *The Female Frontier: A Comparative View of Women on the Prairie and the Plains* (Lawrence: University Press of Kansas, 1988), 22.

[39] Marsha Hoffman Rising, *Vermont Newspaper Abstracts 1783–1816* (Boston: New England Historic Genealogical Society, 2001), 115.

[40] Before 1868, a legislative act or the district courts of equity could grant divorce or separate maintenance but did so only rarely. From 1868 to 1878, when divorce could be obtained in

the courts of common pleas only 163 divorces were granted. Divorce was not legalized until 1950. South Carolina State Archives at <www.state.sc.us/scdah/vit.htm#divorce>, accessed 30 January 2006.

[41] Gibson County (Indiana) Circuit Court, civil order book D, August 1829–February 1838, p 113.

[42] The Division of State Archives website at <http://archives.utah.gov/inventories-ac.htm> lists this the *Christina Anderson v. Peter Anderson* divorce in the Weber County (Utah) Probate Court, Civil and Criminal case files (series 1593), entry 117.

[43] Riley, *Divorce*, 99.

[44] Riley, *Divorce*, 68.

[45] Memorial Upon the Death of Chapman Johnson, order book, spring term 1849, Augusta Co., Virginia, transcribed from original in Augusta County Courthouse, Staunton, Virginia.

[46] Order of Naturalization for Samuel Johnston, July Term, 1851, order book, Augusta Co., Virginia, transcript from original in Augusta County Courthouse, Staunton, Virginia.

[47] "Minutes of Court of Sessions, 1657–78," *Westchester County Historical Publications* 2 (1926): 1–39.

[48] An excellent description of how a grand jury functions is Richard D. Younger, "The Grand Jury on the Frontier," *Wisconsin Magazine of History* (Autumn 1956): 3–8 ff. Not consecutive.

[49] See Anton H. Chroust, *The Rise of the Legal Profession in America*, 2 vols. (Norman: University of Oklahoma Press, 1965).

[50] A very interesting, well-documented study of the use of jails and punishment in New York State is Philip Klein, *Prison Methods in New York State* (1920; reprint, Brooklyn: AMS Press, 1976). It traces the development and history of most of the penal institutions in the state. See also Douglas Greenberg, "The Effectiveness of Law Enforcement in Eighteenth Century New York," *American Journal of Legal History* 20 (1976): 173–207.

[51] See Derrell Roberts, "Joseph E. Brown and the Convict Lease System," *Georgia Historical Quarterly* 44 (1960): 399–410.

[52] Police Court Minutes, St. Paul, Minnesota, printed as appendix in Annual Report of City Council, St. Paul, Minnesota, 1856–60. Copies available in rare book vault, St. Paul Public Library, St. Paul, Minnesota.

[53] Lyman Chalkley, *Chronicles of the Scotch-Irish Settlement in Virginia, Extracted From the Original Court Records of Augusta County, 1745–1800*, 3 vols. (1962; reprint, Baltimore: Genealogical Publishing Co., 1965).

[54] "Records of the Court of Sessions of Westchester County (New York)," *Westchester Historical Society Publications* 1 (1924): 33, 44 ff.

[55] "Introduction," in *Archives of Maryland: Proceedings of the Court of Chancery of Maryland, 1669–1679*, vol. 51 (Baltimore: Maryland Historical Society, 1934).

[56] Benjamin Barnett Spratling III, "Court and Legal Records," in *Printed Sources: A Guide to Published Genealogical Records*, ed. Kory L. Meyerink (Salt Lake City: Ancestry, 1998), 438–66.

[57] William Jeffrey Jr., "Early New England Court Records: A Bibliography of Published Materials," *American Journal of Legal History* 1 (1957): 119–47, reprinted from the *Boston Public Library Bulletin*.

[58] Evarts B. Green and Richard B. Morris, *A Guide to the Principal Sources for Early American History (1600–1800) in the City of New York*, 2nd ed. (New York: Columbia University Press, 1967).

[59] Bradley Chapin, *Criminal Justice in Colonial America, 1606–1660* (Athens: University of Georgia Press, 1983).

[60] Joan W. Peters, *Military Records, Patriotic Service, & Public Service Claims from the Fauquier County, Virginia, Court Minute Books, 1759–1784* (Westminster, Md.: Heritage Books, 2004).

[61] William S. Hein and Co., *Session Laws of American States and Territories: A Compilation of All States and Territories, 1775–2003. Update 4 A Complete Checklist* (Buffalo, N.Y.: William S. Hein and Co., 2005), microfiche.

[62] Redgrave Information Resources Corp., *Session Laws of the American States and Territories Prior to 1900* (Westport, Conn.: Redgrave Information Resources Corp., 53 Wilton Road, Westport, CT 06880).

[63] *General Statutes of Vermont (1863)* (Reprint, Wilmington, Del.: Michael Glazier, 1987), 416–17.

[64] See Walter Lee Sheppard, "Confidential and Sealed Records: Their Effect on Genealogical Research," *American Genealogist* 50 (1974): 203–9.

[65] E. Wayne Carp, *Adoption in America: Historical Perspectives* (Ann Arbor: University of Michigan Press, 2002).

[66] Jean J. McVeetney, "Comparative Study of Laws of Adoption of Minors," *Women Lawyers Journal* 47 (1961): 13–21.

[67] See O. M. Dickerson, *The Navigation Acts and the American Revolution* (Philadelphia: Lippincott, 1951).

[68] Some of these records have been edited by Judge Charles M. Hough, *Reports of the Cases in the Vice-Admiralty of the Province of New York* (New Haven: Yale University Press, 1925), but these represent only about 40 percent of the total number. See Loretto Dennis Szucs and Sandra Hargreaves Luebking, *The Archives: A Guide to the National Archives Field Branches* (Salt Lake City: Ancestry, 1988).

[69] See A. M. Schlesinger, "Colonial Appeals to the Privy Council," *Political Science Quarterly* 28 (1913): 279–97; and Joseph Henry

Smith, *Appeals to the Privy Council From the American Plantations* (New York: Columbia University Press, 1950). For Palatine jurisdiction, see Baillard Lapsley, *The County Palatinate of Durham* (Cambridge, Mass.: Harvard University Press, 1900). There was little difference in the powers granted the Palatinate in England and America; the problems arose in enforcing them so far away from the support of the royal government.

[70] Edward H. Hilliard, "When Kentucky Had Two Courts of Appeal," *Filson Club Historical Quarterly* 34 (1960): 228–36; George Shelley, "The Semicolon Court in Texas," *Southwestern Historical Review* 48 (1944–45): 449–68.

[71] Spratling, "Court and Legal Records." This chapter includes a listing of State Appellate Courts, an explanation of the colonial courts and selected published works of each colony and state.

[72] *1906 Decennial Edition of the American Digest: A Complete Table of American Cases From 1658 to 1906, vols. 21–25.* (St. Paul, Minn.: West Publishing, 1907).

[73] *The Federal Digest* series is published by West Publishing, St. Paul, Minnesota.

[74] Revolutionary War Prize Cases, 1776–87 (M213); Appellate Case Files, 1792–1831 (M214); Minutes, 1790–1950 (M215); Dockets, 1797–1950 (M216); Attorney Rolls, 1790–1951 (M217); Index to Appellate Case Files (M408).

[75] See Hubert D. Hoover, "Army Courts-Martial," in *Legal Essays in Honor of O. K. McMurray* (Berkeley: University of California Press, 1935), 165–86.

[76] See Daniel Walker and C. George Niebank, "The Court of Military Appeals: Its History, Organization and Operation," *Vanderbilt Law Review* 6 (1952): 228–40.

[77] John R. Kirkland, "Military Occupation in the South Atlantic States During Reconstruction, 1865–1876" (Ph.D. dissertation, University of North Carolina, 1967); "The Reconstruction Courts of Texas, 1867–1873," *Southwestern Historical Quarterly* 62 (1958): 141; James E. Sefton, *The U.S. Army and Reconstruction, 1865–1877* (Baton Rouge: Louisiana State University Press, 1967).

[78] W. P. W. Phillimore and Edward A. Fry, comps., *An Index to Changes of Name Under Authority of Act of Parliament 1760–1901* (1905; reprint, Baltimore: Genealogical Publishing Co., 1968).

[79] Charles E. Schamel "Untapped Resources: Private Claims and Private Legislation in the Records of the U.S. Congress," *Prologue* 27, no. 1 (Spring 1995); Chris Naylor, "Those Elusive Early Americans: Public Lands and Claims in the *American State Papers* 1789–1837," *Prologue* 37, no. 2 (Summer 2005). Both articles online at <www.archives.gov/publications/prologue>.

[80] Richard Maxwell Brown, *The South Carolina Regulators* (Cambridge, Mass.: Harvard University Press, 1963).

[81] Regulator Pardon of 31 October 1771, in *Miscellaneous Records, South Carolina Department of Archives and History*, vol. PP, (Charleston, n.d.), 45–47, published by government order.

[82] See John S. Bassett, "The Regulators of North Carolina, 1765–1771," *American Historical Association, Annual Report, 1894* (Washington, D.C.: AHA, 1895), 143–212; Elmer Douglas Johnson, "The War of the Regulators: Its Place in History," (master's thesis, University of North Carolina, 1942); and William S. Powell, ed., *The Regulators of North Carolina: A Documentary History, 1759–79* (Raleigh: State Department of Archives and History, 1971).

[83] Richard Maxwell Brown, "The Archives of Violence," *American Archivist* 41 (1978): 431–44.

[84] "Westmoreland Resolutions," *Virginia Historical Register* 2 (1849): 15–18. Originals in Virginia Historical Society, Richmond, Virginia.

[85] *Reports on U.S. Mineral Resources* (Washington, D.C.: Government Printers, 1866), 236.

[86] An *alcade* was a Mexican court after which many miners' courts were patterned and named. See Charles H. Shinn, *Land Laws of Mining Districts* (Baltimore: Johns Hopkins University Studies in History and Political Science, 2nd ser., 1884).

[87] Joseph A. Borome, "The Vigilant Committee of Philadelphia," *Pennsylvania Magazine of History and Biography* 92 (1968): 320–51.

[88] Anthony S. Nicolosi, "The Rise and Fall of the New Jersey Vigilant Societies," *New Jersey History* 68 (1968): 29–53. See also "The Vigilance Committee: Richmond During the War of 1812," *Virginia Magazine of History and Biography* 7 (1900): 225–41, 406–18.

[89] J. W. Caughey, "Their Magesties the Mob: Vigilantes Past and Present," *Pacific Historical Review* 26 (1957): 217–34.

[90] Richard Maxwell Brown, "San Francisco Vigilantes of 1856," in *Reflections of Western Historians*, ed. John Alexander Carroll (Tucson: University of Arizona Press, 1969). See also Williams's *History of the San Francisco Committee of Vigilance of 1851* (1921; reprint, New York: De Capo Press, 1970). The original papers are deposited in the Huntington Library, San Marino, California. For a careful analysis of 2,500 applications for membership, see Richard Maxwell Brown, *Strain of Violence: Historical Studies of American Violence and Vigilantism* (New York: Oxford University Press, 1975).

[91] Jack Kleiner, "United States Law on American Indians," *Case and Comment* (July–August 1971): 3–7, summarizes the legal rights of Native Americans on reservations; the impact of the Civil Rights Act of 1968, which included the Indian Bill of Rights; tribal judicial systems; and the impact of recent legislation.

[92] See Inferior Court Minutes, 13 April 1819, Jones County, Georgia, pp. 61–63, and January term, 1817, p. 97, for examples. Originals in Jones County Courthouse, Georgia.

References

This reference section begins with guides, bibliographies, and sources of general interest on law in the colonies and early states, then continues with specific subject titles. Some attempt has been made to avoid duplicating sources unless they apply to more than one subject area.

General Guides, References, and Inventories

Bentley, Elizabeth P. *County Courthouse Book*. 2nd ed. Baltimore: Genealogical Publishing Co., 1995.

Callender, Clarence N. *American Courts: Their Organization and Procedures*. New York: McGraw Hill, 1927.

Eakle, Arlene. *Family History for Fun and Profit: 30th Anniversary Edition*. Provo, Utah: Genealogical Institute, 2002.

Eichholz, Alice, ed. *Red Book: American State, County, and Town Sources*. 3rd ed. Provo, Utah: Ancestry, 2004.

Flaherty, David H. "A Select Guide to Manuscript Court Records of Colonial New England." *American Journal of Legal History* 9 (1967): 107–26.

Friedman, Lawrence M. *A History of American Law*. 3rd ed. New York: Touchstone, 2005.

Gersack, Dorothy Hill. "Colonial, State, and Federal Court Records: A Survey." *American Archivist* 36 (1973): 33–42.

Greenwood, Val D. *The Researcher's Guide to American Genealogy*. 3rd ed. Baltimore: Genealogical Publishing Co., 2000.

Haskins, George L. "Court Records and History." *William and Mary Quarterly* 3rd ser., 5 (1948): 547–52.

Hasse, Adelaide R. *Materials for a Bibliography of the Public Archives of the Thirteen Original States Covering Colonial Period and State Period to 1789*. 1908; reprint, New York: Argonaut Press, 1966.

Hoffer, Peter Charles. *Law and People in Colonial America*. Baltimore: Johns Hopkins University Press, 1998.

Jeffrey, William, Jr. "Early New England Court Records: A Bibliography of Published Material." *Boston Public Library Quarterly* (1954). As reprinted in *American Journal of Legal History* 1 (1957): 119–47.

Kammen, Michael G. "Colonial Court Records and the Study of Early American History: A Bibliographical Review." *American Historical Review* 70 (1965): 732–39.

Low, Erick Baker. *A Bibliography on the History of the Organization and Jurisdiction of State Courts*. Williamsburg: National Center for State Courts, 1980.

Maduell, Charles R. "Genealogy From Law Books." *New Orleans Genesis* 9 (1972): 42–43. Includes specific examples from state court reports.

Matchette, Robert D. *Guide to Federal Records in the National Archives*. Washington, D.C.: National Archives and Records Administration, 1995. Online version at <www.archives.gov>.

Neagles, James C. *Military Records: A Guide to Genealogical and Historical Research*. Salt Lake City: Ancestry, 1990.

New York State Archives. *List of Pre-1874 Court Records in the State Archives*. Albany: Office of Cultural Education, New York State Education Department, 1984.

Nunis, Doyce B., Jr. "Historical Studies in United States Legal History, 1950–59: A Bibliography of Articles Published in Scholarly Non-Law Journals." *American Journal of Legal History* 7 (1963): 1–27.

Prager, Herta, and William W. Price. "A Bibliography on the History of the Courts of the Thirteen Original States, Maine, Ohio, and Vermont." *American Journal of Legal History* 1 (1957): 336–62; 2 (1958): 35– 52, 148–54.

Pound, Roscoe. *Organization of Courts*. Boston: Little, Brown, 1940; reprint, Westport Conn.: Greenwood Press, 1979.

Rose, Christine. *Courthouse Research for Family Historians*. San Jose, Calif.: CR Publications, 2004.

Rust, Barbara. "The Right to Vote: The Enforcement Acts and Southern Courts." *Prologue* 21, no. 3 (Fall 1989): 231–38.

Ryskamp, George R. "Fundamental Common-Law Concepts for the Genealogist: Marriage, Divorce, and Coverture." *National Genealogical Society Quarterly* 23 (September 1995): 165–79.

Salmon, Marylynn. *Women and the Law of Property in Early America*. Chapel Hill: University of North Carolina Press, 1986.

Schwartz, Bernard, Barbara Wilcie Kern, and R. B. Bernstein, eds. *Thomas Jefferson and* Bolling v. Bolling: *Law and the Legal Profession in Prerevolutionary America*. San Marino, Calif.: Huntington Library Press, 1997.

Sell, Gary L. *Legal Materials on Microform: A Bibliography*. 3rd ed. Provo, Utah: Brigham Young University, 1976.

Spratling, Benjamin Barnett, III. "Court and Legal Records." In *Printed Sources: A Guide to Published Genealogical Records*, edited by Kory L. Meyerink. Salt Lake City: Ancestry, 1998.

———. "Court Records: Far Beyond Probate." *Ancestry Magazine* 14, no. 4 (July–August 1996): 5–8.

Taylor, D. Joshua. "Trial by Community." *Utah Genealogical Society Quarterly* 1, no. 1 (December 2005): 2–8.

Tompkins, Dorothy Campbell. *Court Organization and Administration: A Bibliography*. Berkeley: University of California Press, 1973.

Weinberg, Allen. "Court Records: Orphans Among Archives." *American Archivist* 23 (1960): 167–74.

Admiralty Court Records

Andrews, Charles M. *The Colonial Period of American History: England's Commercial and Colonial Policy*. Vol. 4. New Haven: Yale University Press, 1938. An excellent historical treatment of the courts of admiralty in the colonies.

Dickerson, O. M. *The Navigation Acts and the American Revolution*. Philadelphia: Lippincott, 1951.

Hough, Charles M. *Reports of the Cases in the Vice-Admiralty of the Province of New York*. New Haven: Yale University Press, 1925.

Morris, Robert C. "From Piracy to Censorship: The Admiralty Experience." *Prologue* 21, no. 3 (Fall 1989): 186–95.

Owen, David R., and Michael C. Tolley. *Courts of Admiralty in Colonial America: The Maryland Experience 1634–1776*. Durham, N.C.: Carolina Academic Press, 1995.

Plowman, Robert J. "An Untapped Source: Civil War Prize Case Files 1861–65." *Prologue* 21, no. 3 (Fall 1989).

Towle, Dorothy S. *Records of the Vice-Admiralty Court of Rhode Island: 1716–1752*. Washington, D.C.: American Historical Association Committee on Legal History, 1939. Contains incomplete extracts of cases and a history of admiralty jurisdiction in Rhode Island.

Ubbelohde, Carl. *The Vice-Admiralty Courts and the American Revolution*. Chapel Hill: University of North Carolina Press, 1960. A good description of the courts before 1763 and their influence on the American Revolution.

Adoption Records

Current law on post-1930 adoption has made access to early records more difficult. See chapter 1, "The Foundations of Family History Research," for a discussion of freedom of information laws that may be used to get access.

Carp, E. Wayne. *Adoption in America: Historical Perspectives*. Ann Arbor: University of Michigan Press, 2002.

Leary, Morton L. *The Law of Adoption Simplified*. New York: Oceana Publications, 1948.

Zainaldin, Jamil. "The Emergence of a Modern American Family Law, Child Custody, Adoption and the Courts, 1796–1851." *Northwestern University Law Review* 73 (1979).

Whitmore, William. H. *The Law of Adoption in the United States, and Especially in Massachusetts*. Albany: Joe Munsell, 1876; reprint, Clark, N.J.: Lawbook Exchange, 2003.

Bankruptcy and Debt

Mann, Bruce H. *Republic of Debtors: Bankruptcy in the Age of American Independence*. Cambridge, Mass.: Harvard University Press, 2003.

Skeel, David. *Debtor's Dominion: A History of Bankruptcy Law in America*. Princeton, N.J.: Princeton University Press, 2001.

Owens, James K. "Documenting Regional Business History: The Bankruptcy Acts of 1800 and 1841." *Prologue* 21, no. 3 (Fall 1989): 178–85.

Szucs, Loretto Dennis. "To Whom I Am Indebted: Bankruptcy Records." *Ancestry* Magazine 12, no. 5 (September–October 1994): 26–27.

Thompson, Elizabeth Lee. *The Reconstruction of Southern Debtors: Bankruptcy after the Civil War*. Athens: University of Georgia Press, 2004.

Watkins, Beverly. "To Surrender All His Estate: The 1867 Bankruptcy Act." *Prologue* 21, no. 3 (Fall 1989): 207–14.

Case Studies and Record Use

Ball, Walter V. "Family Records from County Court Order Books." *National Genealogical Society Quarterly* 58 (1970): 3.

Brayton, John Anderson. "Hardy of South Carolina—A Discreet Omission." Part I of "Check the Original! Two Lessons Learned the Hard Way." *National Genealogical Society Quarterly* 90, no. 1 (March 2002): 69–73.

Farnham, Charles W. "Lower Court Cases: A Genealogist's Tool." *National Genealogical Society Quarterly* 49 (1961): 200.

Fernandez, Angela. "Record-Keeping and Other Troublemaking: Thomas Lechford and Law Reform in Colonial Massachusetts." *Law and History Review* 23, no. 2 (Summer 2005): 235–78.

Hendrix, GeLee Corley. "Backtracking Through Burned Counties: Bonds of Louisiana, Mississippi, Georgia, and the Carolinas." *National Genealogical Society Quarterly* 78, no. 2 (June 1990): 98–114.

King, George H. S. "Maiden Names Used After Marriage." *American Genealogist* 47 (1971): 44.

Klein, Fannie J. *Federal and State Court Systems: A Guide*. Cambridge, Mass.: Ballinger Publishers, 1977.

Proffitt, Shana Elizabeth. "Mallory-Blunt of Virginia—A Miscopied Name." Part II of "Check the Original! Two Lessons Learned the Hard Way." *National Genealogical Society Quarterly* 90, no. 1 (March 2002): 69–73.

Randall, Ruth. "An Interracial Suit for Inheritance: Clues to Probable Paternity for a Georgia Freedman, Henry Clay Heard Sherman." *National Genealogical Society Quarterly* 89, no. 2 (June 2001): 85–97.

Rutman, Darrett B., and Anita H. Rutman. "Now-Wives and Sons-in-Law: Parental Death in a Seventeenth Century Virginia County." In *Chesapeake in the Seventeenth Century.* Chapel Hill: University of North Carolina Press, 1979.

Semonche, John E. "Common-Law Marriage in North Carolina: A Study in Legal History." *American Journal of Legal History* 9 (1965): 320–49.

Stevenson, Noel. "Genealogical Research in the Law Library." *American Genealogist* 18 (1941): 100–103. Genealogical applications of printed court reports.

Claims: Courts and Private (see also, Federal)

Eales, Anne Bruner, and Robert M. Kvasnicka. *Guide to Genealogical Research in the National Archives.* Washington, D.C.: General Services Administration, 2000. See chapter 16, "Claims Records."

Luebking, Sandra H. "Southern Claims Commission—Disallowed Claims." *FORUM* 17, no. 2 (Summer 2005): 13–15.

Mills, Gary B. *Southern Loyalists in the Civil War: A Composite Directory of Case Files Created by the U.S. Commissioners of Claims, 1871–1880, Including Those Appealed to the War Claims Committee of the U.S. House of Representatives and the U.S. Court of Claims.* Baltimore: Genealogical Publishing Co., 2004.

Naylor, Chris. "Those Elusive Early Americans: Public Lands and Claims in the American State Papers, 1789–1837." *Prologue* 37, no. 2 (Summer 2005). Online at <www.archives.gov/publications/prologue/2005/summer>. Accessed 5 February 2006).

Schamel, Charles E. "Untapped Resources: Private Claims and Private Legislation in the Records of the U.S. Congress." *Prologue* 27, no. 1 (Spring 1995). Online at <www.archives.gov/publications/prologue/1995/spring/private-claims-2.html>. Accessed 22 March 2006.

Colonial Courts

Billings, Warren M. *A Little Parliament: The Virginia General Assembly in the Seventeenth Century.* Richmond: Library of Virginia, 2004.

Chiroazzi, Michael, and Marguerite Most, eds. *Prestatehood Legal Materials: A Fifty-State Research Guide, Including New York City and the District of Columbia.* Vols. 1 and 2. Binghamton, N.Y.: Haworth Press, 2006.

Chitwood, Oliver Perry. *Justice in Colonial Virginia.* Baltimore: Johns Hopkins Press, 1905; reprint, Clark, N.J.: Law Book Exchange, 2001.

Daniels, Bruce C. *Town and County: Essays on the Structure of Local Government in the American Colonies.* Middletown, Conn.: Wesleyan University Press, 1978.

Fernandez, Angela. "Record-Keeping and Other Troublemaking: Thomas Lechford and Law Reform in Colonial Massachusetts." *Law & History Review* 23, no. 2 (Summer 2005): 235–78.

Greene, Jack P. "The Publication of the Official Records of the Southern Colonies." *William and Mary Quarterly* 3rd ser., 14 (1957): 268–80.

Mirow, M. C. *Latin American Law: A History of Private Law and Institutions in Spanish America.* Austin: University of Texas Press, 2004.

Reinsch, Paul Samuel. *English Common Law in the American Colonies.* Madison: University of Wisconsin, 1899; reprint, Clark, N.J.: Lawbook Exchange, 2005. Online at <www.lawbookexchange.com>.

Surrency, Edwin C. "The Courts in the American Colonies." *American Journal of Legal History* 11 (1969): 253–76, 347–76.

Whitney, Edson L. *Government of the Colony of South Carolina.* Baltimore, 1895; reprint, Baltimore: Johns Hopkins Press, 1973. Chapter 2 describes South Carolina's pre-Revolutionary admiralty courts.

Criminal Courts

Brown, Richard Maxwell. "The Archives of Violence." *American Archivist* 41, no. 4 (1978): 431–44.

Chapin, Bradley. *Criminal Justice in Colonial America, 1606–1660* Athens: University of Georgia Press, 1983. See pages 99–142.

Friedman, Lawrence M. *Crime and Punishment in American History.* New York: BasicBooks, 1993.

Klein, Philip. *Prison Methods in New York State.* New York: Columbia University Press, 1920.

Pound, Roscoe. *Criminal Justice in America.* New Brunswick, N.J.: Transaction Publishers, 1998.

Scott, William B. *Criminal Proceedings in Colonial Virginia: (Records of) fines, examination of criminals, trials of slaves, etc., from March 1710 (1711) to (1754). (Richmond County, Virginia).* Athens: University of Georgia Press, 1984.

Divorce

Bamman, Gale W., and Debbie W. Spero. *Tennessee Divorces, 1797–1858: Taken from 750 Legislative Petitions and Acts.* Thorndike, Mass.: Van Volumes Unlimited, 1990.

Basch, Norma. *Framing American Divorce: From the Revolutionary Generation to the Victorians.* Berkeley: University of California Press, 2001.

Bell, Carol W. *Ohio Divorces: The Early Years, 1794–1947.* Youngstown, Ohio: the author, 1994.

Blattner, Theresa. *Divorces, Separations, and Annulments in Missouri, 1769 to 1850.* Bowie, Md.: Heritage Books, 1992.

Buckley, Thomas E. *The Great Catastrophe of My Life: Divorce in the Old Dominion.* Chapel Hill: University of North Carolina Press, 2002. An examination of the 471 surviving divorce petitions to the Virginia legislature for the years 1786 to 1851.

Cohen, Sheldon S. "The Broken Bond: Divorce in Providence County, 1749–1809." *Rhode Island History* 44 (1985): 67–79.

Cohn, Henry S. "Connecticut's Divorce Mechanism, 1636–1969." *American Journal of Legal History* 14 (1970): 35–54.

Cott, Nancy F. *Public Vows: A History of Marriage and the Nation.* Cambridge, Mass.: Harvard University Press, 2002.

Hartog, Hendrik. *Man and Wife in America: A History.* Cambridge, Mass.: Harvard University Press, 2000.

Index to Divorce Cases of the Thirteenth Judicial Circuit Court of Alabama, 1816–1918. Mobile: University of South Alabama Archives, 1994.

Kitchin, S. B. *A History of Divorce.* London: Chapman and Hall, 1912; reprint, Clark, N.J.: Lawbook Exchange, 2002. Online at <www.lawbookexchange.com>.

Phillips, Roderick. *Untying the Knot: A Short History of Divorce* [Abridged]. Cambridge, England: Cambridge University Press, 1991.

Riley, Glenda. *Divorce: An American Tradition.* Lawrence: University of Nebraska Press, 1997.

Salmon, Marylynn. "Divorce and Separation." In *Women and the Law of Property in Early America.* Chapel Hill: University of North Carolina Press, 1989.

Spratling, Benjamin B. "Court and Legal Records." Chapter 12 in *Printed Sources: A Guide to Published Genealogical Records,* edited by Kory L. Meyerink, 438–466. Salt Lake City: Ancestry, 1998.

Stone, Lawrence. *Road to Divorce: England, 1530–1987; Uncertain Unions: Marriage in England, 1660–1753;* and *Broken Lives: Separation and Divorce in England, 1660–1857.* 3 vols. Oxford, England: Oxford University Press, 1990–93.

Van Ness, James S. "On Untieing the Knot: The Maryland Legislature and Divorce Petitions." *Maryland Historical Magazine* 67 (1972): 171–75.

Winslow, Raymond A., Jr. Part II: "County Records." In *North Carolina Research: Genealogy & Local History,* edited by Helen F. M. Leary. Rev. Ed. Raleigh: North Carolina Genealogical Society, 1996.

Woolsey, Theodore D. *Divorce and Divorce Legislation, Especially in the United States.* 2nd ed. rev. New York: Chas Scribner's Sons, 1882; reprint, Clark, N.J.: Lawbook Exchange, 2001.

Federal, Confederate, and Territorial Courts

Beers, Henry Putsey. *Guide to the Archives of the Government of the Confederate States of America.* 1968.

Blume, William, and Elizabeth Gaspar Brown. *Digests and Lists Pertaining to the Development of Law and Legal Institutions in the Territories of the United States: 1787–1954.* 6 vols. Ann Arbor, Mich.: University Microfilm, 1965–79.

Chiroazzi, Michael, and Marguerite Most, eds. *Prestatehood Legal Materials: A Fifty-State Research Guide, Including New York City and the District of Columbia.* Vols. 1 and 2. Binghamton, N.Y.: Haworth Press, 2006.

Corriston, Mark A. "Discovering Frontier History Through Territorial Court Records." *Prologue* 21, no. 3 (Fall 1989): 222–29.

Klein, Fannie J. *Federal and State Court Systems: A Guide.* Cambridge, Mass.: Ballinger Publishers, 1977.

McReynolds, Michael, comp. *List of Pre-1840 Federal District and Circuit Court Records Located in Federal Record Centers.* Washington, D.C.: Government Printing Office, 1972. Special List, 31.

Szucs, Loretto Dennis, and Sandra Hargreaves Luebking. *The Archives: A Guide to the National Archives Field Branches.* Salt Lake City: Ancestry, 1988.

Ulasek, Henry T., and Marion Johnson. *Records of the United States District Court for the Southern District of New York.* Preliminary Inventory 116. Washington, D.C.: National Archives and Records Service, 1959.

Younger, Richard D. "The Grand Jury on the Frontier." *Wisconsin Magazine of History* (Autumn 1956): 3–8 ff. Not consecutive.

Wilson, Don W. "Federal Court Records in the Regional Archives System." *Prologue* 21, no. 3 (Fall 1989): 176–77.

Indian Court Records

Barr, Charles Butler. *Records of the Choctaw-Chickasaw Citizenship Court Relative to Records of Enrollment of the Five Civilized Tribes, 1898–1907.* Independence, Mo.: C. B. Barr, 1990.

Brown, Loren N. "The Choctaw-Chickasaw Court Citizens." *Chronicles of Oklahoma* 16–4 (1938): 425. Online at

<http://digital.library.okstate.edu/chronicles>. Accessed 05 February 2006.

Compiled Laws of the Cherokee Nation. Tahlequah, Ind. Terr.: National Advocate Press, 1881; reprint, Clark, N.J.: Lawbook Exchange, 1998.

Ford, Jeanette W. "Federal Law Comes to Indian Territory." *Chronicles of Oklahoma* 58, no. 4 (1980–81): 432–39. Online at <http://digital.library.okstate.edu/chronicles>. Accessed 05 February 2006.

Harring, Sidney L., Frederick Hoxie (series editor), Neal Salisbury (series editor). *Crow Dog's Case: American Indian Sovereignty, Trial Law, and United States Law in the Nineteenth Century (Studies in North American Indian History)*. Cambridge, England: Cambridge University Press, 1994. Addresses American Indian Law, the Creek Nation, Alaska, and more.

Hill, Edward E. *Guide to Records in the National Archives of the United States Relating to American Indians.* Washington, D.C.: National Archives and Records Service, 1984. This guide is well-indexed and gives specifics on the courts maintained by Indian agencies. The records themselves are not described in detail.

Indian Claims Commission. Vols. 30–43. Online at <http://digital.library.okstate.edu>. Accessed 05 February 2006.

Knight, Oliver. "Fifty Years of Choctaw Law, 1834–1884." *Chronicles of Oklahoma* 31, no. 1 (1953): 76. Online at <http://digital.library.okstate.edu/chronicles>. Accessed 05 February 2006.

Reid, John. *A Law of Blood: The Primitive Law of the Cherokee Nation.* New York: New York University Press, 1970.

Thompson, William P. "Courts of the Cherokee Nation." *Chronicles of Oklahoma* 2, no. 1 (1924): 63. Online at <http://digital.library.okstate.edu/chronicles>. Accessed 05 February 2006.

Laws, Statutes, Legal Terms

Abrams, Kerry. "Polygamy, Prostitution, and the Federalization of Immigration Law." *Columbia Law Review* 105, no. 3 (April 2005): 642–716. Online at <www.columbialawreview.org>.

Babbitt, Charles J. *Hand-List of Legislative Sessions and Session Laws Statutory Revisions, Compilations, Codes, Etc., and Constitutional Conventions of the United States and its Possessions and of the Several States to May, 1912*. Boston: Trustees of the State Library of Massachusetts, 1912; reprint, Clark, N.J., Lawbook Exchange, 2003.

Black, Henry Campbell. *Black's Law Dictionary: Definitions of Terms and Phrases of American and English Jurisprudence, Ancient and Modern.* 4th ed. St. Paul, Minn.: West Publishing, 1951. Newer editions of *Black's* are published regularly but genealogists seem to prefer the *Fourth Edition*.

Bouvier, John. *A Law Dictionary: Adapted to the Constitution and Laws of the United States of America and of the Several States of the American Union.* Rev. 6th ed. Online at <www.constitution.org>. Gives laws of states as of 1856. There were 18 editions to Bouvier, the last was published in 1914.

Bramwell, B. S. "Frequency of Cousin Marriages." *Genealogists' Magazine* 8 (1939): 305–16.

Burton, William C. *Burton's Legal Thesaurus.* New York: Macmillan Library Reference, 1998.

Chroust, Anton H. *The Rise of the Legal Profession in America.* 2 vols. Norman: University of Oklahoma Press, 1965.

Duhaime's Law Dictionary. Online at <www.duhaime.org/Dictionary>. Current and common legal terms only.

Evans, Barbara Jean. *The New A To Zax: A Comprehensive Genealogical Dictionary for Genealogists and Historians.* 2nd ed. N.p., 1990.

Georgetown Law Library. The Historic State Codes Preserva tion Project. <www.ll.georgetown.edu/states/historic_codes>. Scanning early state codes printed 1840–1930. See website for a full list by state.

Hein, William S., and Co. *Colonial Session Laws.* Microfiche. Buffalo, N.Y.: William S. Hein, 2003.

Hein, William S., and Co. *Session Laws of American States and Territories: A Compilation of All States and Territories, 1775–2003.* Update 4: A Complete Checklist. Microfiche. Buffalo, N.Y.: William S. Hein, 2005.

Myrick, Shelby, Jr. "Legal Terminology in Genealogical Research in the U.S.A." Salt Lake City: World Conference on Records, 1969. Area 1–10. Includes a useful glossary with terms often omitted from modern dictionaries.

RIRC. *Session Laws of the American States and Territories Prior to 1900.* Westport, Conn.: Redgrave Information Resources, 1988.

Weiner, Carol Z. "Is a Spinster an Unmarried Woman?" *American Journal of Legal History* 21 (1977): 27–31.

Mining District Records

Greever, William S. *The Bonanza West: The Story of the Western Rushes, 1848–1900.* Moscow: University of Idaho Press, 1990.

Marshal, Thomas Maitland. "Miners Laws of Colorado." *American Historical Review* 25 (1919–20): 426.

Mucibabich, Darlene. *Life in Western Mining Camps: Social and Legal Aspects, 1848–1872.* Hicksville, N.Y.: Exposition Press, 1977.

Mumrey, Nolee. *Early Mining Laws of Buckskin Joe*. Boulder, Colo.: the author, 1961.

———. *History and Proceedings of Buckskin Joe*. Boulder, Colo.: the author, 1961.

Paul, Rodman W. *Mining Frontiers of the Far West. An expanded edition by Elliott West*. Albuquerque: University of New Mexico Press, 2001.

Shinn, Charles H. *Institutional Beginnings of a Western State*. Johns Hopkins University Studies in History and Political Science, 2nd ser. Vol. 7. Baltimore, 1880. Discusses the lead mines of Iowa.

———. *Mining Camps: A Study in American Frontier Government*. 1884; reprint, Gloucester, Mass.: Peter Smith, 1970. Includes an excellent description of the Spanish/Mexican legal system.

———. *Land Laws of Mining Districts*. Johns Hopkins University Studies in History and Political Science, 2nd ser. Vol. 12. Baltimore, 1884; reprint, Brooklyn, N.Y.: AMS Press, 1989.

Smith, Duane A. *Rocky Mountain Mining Camps: The Urban Frontier*. Niwot: University of Colorado Press, 1992.

Probate and Dower

Albright, Lee, and Helen F. M. Leary. "Designing Research Strategies." Chapter 2 in *North Carolina Research: Genealogy and Local History*, edited by Helen F. M. Leary. 2nd ed. Raleigh: North Carolina Genealogical Society, 1996.

Bernstein, Charles B. "Will and Probate Records in the United States." In *Avotaynu Guide to Jewish Genealogy*, edited by Sallyann Amdur Sack and Gary Mokotoff, 168–74. Bergenfield, N.J.: Avotaynu, 2004.

Devine, Donn. "The Widow's Dower Interest." *Ancestry* Magazine 12, no. 5 (September–October 1994): 20–22.

———. "Probate Records: An Underutilized Source." *Ancestry* Magazine 12, no. 3 (May–June 1994): 14–15.

Dorman, John Frederick. "Colonial Laws of Primogeniture." World Conference on Records, 1969 (Salt Lake City: Genealogical Society of Utah, 1969).

Greenwood, Val D. "Understanding Probate Records and Basic Legal Terminology," "What About Wills?" and "The Intestate." In *The Researcher's Guide to American Genealogy*. Baltimore: Genealogical Publishing Co., 2000.

Haskins, George L. "Curtesy in the United States." *University of Pennsylvania Law Review* 100 (1951): 196–223.

Hill, Ronald A. "Using Records to Understand Ancestral Motives: The Thwarted Will of Christopher Lean of Cornwall." *National Genealogical Society Quarterly* 92, no. 4 (December 2004): 269–84.

Jacobus, Donald Lines. "Probate Law and Custom." *American Genealogist* 9 (1932): 4–9.

Keim, Clarence Ray. "Primogeniture and the Law of Entail in Colonial Virginia." *William and Mary Quarterly* Series 3, 25 (October 1968): 546–86.

Morris, Richard B. *Primogeniture and Entailed Estates in America*. New York: Columbia University, 1927.

Remington, Gordon L. *New York State Probate Records: A Genealogist's Guide to Testate and Intestate Records*. Boston: New England Historic Genealogical Society, 2002.

Shammas, Carole, Marylynn Salmon, and Michael Dahlin. *Inheritance in America from Colonial Times to the Present*. Galveston, Tex.: Frontier Press, 1997.

Southwick, Neal S. "The Coordinate Use of Wills and Deeds." *Journal of Genealogy* 2 (1973): 154–56.

Toms, Gary R., and William R. Gann. *Widow's Dowers of Washington County, Tennessee 1803–1899*. Milford, Ohio: Little Miami Publishing, 2004.

Regional and State Guides

Aiken, John. "New Netherlands Arbitration in the 17th Century." *Arbitration Journal* 29 (1974): 145.

Alaska State Archives. *Record Group Inventory: District and Territorial Court System*. Juneau: Alaska State Archives, Department of Administration, 1987.

Ames, Susie M., ed. *County Court Records of Accomack-Northampton, Virginia 1640–1645*. University Press of Virginia, 1973.

Bailey, Robert E., et al., eds. *A Summary Guide to Local Government Records in the Illinois Regional Archives*. Springfield: Illinois State Archives, Office of the Secretary of State, 1992.

Bakken, Gordon Morris. "The Courts, the Legal Profession, and the Development of Law in Early California." [HTML] *California History* 2003. California Historical Society, San Francisco. Available from <www.amazon.com>, 1 January 2003, as an e-doc.

Barker, Bette Marie, et al., eds. *Guide to Family History Sources in the New Jersey State Archives*. Rev. ed. Trenton, N.J.: Division of Archives and Records Management, New Jersey Department of State, 1992.

Beckstead, Douglas S. *The Judicial System in Utah: Organic Act to the Twentieth Century*. Salt Lake City: Utah State Archives, 1988.

Bell, Carol Willsey. *Ohio Guide to Genealogical Sources*. Baltimore: Genealogical Publishing Co., 1988.

Brown, Richard Maxwell. *The South Carolina Regulators*. Cambridge, Mass.: Harvard University Press, 1963.

Carroll, Mark M. *Homesteads Ungovernable: Families, Sex, Race, and the Law in Frontier Texas, 1823–1860*. Austin: University of Texas Press, 2001.

Chaulkey, Lyman. *Chronicles of the Scotch-Irish Settlement in Virginia, Extracted From the Original Court Records of Augusta County, 1745*. 3 vols. 1912; reprint, Baltimore: Genealogical Publishing Co., 1999.

Dolan, John P., and Lisa Lacher. *Guide to Public Records of Iowa Counties*. Des Moines, Iowa: Connie Wimer, 1986.

Edgerton, Keith. *Montana Justice: Power, Punishment, & the Penitentiary*. Seattle: University of Washington Press, 2004.

Fielder, George. *The Illinois Law Courts in Three Centuries 1673–1973: A Documentary History*. Chicago: Physician's Record Co., 1973.

Ford, Jeanette W. "Federal Law Comes to Indian Territory." *Chronicles of Oklahoma* 58 (1980–81): 432–39.

Gagle, Diane VanSkiver. "Ohio Court Records." *Ohio Genealogical Society News* 36, no. 6 (November/December 2005): 197–98.

Grivas, Theodore. *Military Government in California, 1846–1850, With a Chapter on Their Prior Use in Louisiana, Florida and New Mexico*. Glendale, Calif.: Arthur H. Clarke, 1963.

Guzik, Estelle M., ed. *Genealogical Resources in the New York Metropolitan Area*. New York: Jewish Genealogical Society, 1989.

———. *Genealogical Resources in New York*. New York: Jewish Genealogical Society, 2003.

Hogan, Roseann Reinemuth. *Kentucky Ancestry: A Guide to Genealogical and Historical Research*. Salt Lake City: Ancestry, 1992.

Holcomb, Brent. *Abstracts of South Carolina Wills*. Easly, S.C.: Southern Historical Press, 1977.

Lang, Margaret. *Early Justice in Sonora*. N.p.: Mother Lode Press, 1963.

Leary, Helen F. M., ed. *North Carolina Research: Genealogy and Local History*. 2nd ed. Raleigh: North Carolina Genealogical Society, 1996.

Minnesota Historical Society Library and Archives Division. *Genealogical Resources of the Minnesota Historical Society*. St. Paul: Minnesota Historical Society Press, 1989.

Mitchell, Thornton W. *North Carolina Wills: A Testator Index, 1665–1900. Corrected and Revised Edition in One Volume*. 4th ed. Baltimore: Genealogical Publishing Co., 2001.

Morris, Richard B., ed. *Select Cases of the Mayor's Court of New York City, 1674–1784*. Washington, D.C.: American Historical Association, 1935; reprint, Millwood, N.Y.: Kraus Reprint Co., 1975.

McKnight. "The Spanish Legacy to Texas Law." *American Journal of Legal History* 3 (1959): 222, 229.

Padgett, Patricia Ann. "Legal Status of Women in Colonial Virginia, 1700–1785." MA thesis, College of William and Mary, 1967.

Peters, Joan W. *Military Records, Patriotic Service, and Public Service Claims from the Fauquier County, Virginia, Court Minutes Books, 1759–1784*. Westminster, Md.: Heritage Books, 2004.

Rapaport, Diane. *New England Court Records: A Research Guide for Genealogists and Historians*. Lexington, Mass.: Quill Pen Press, 2006.

Ray, Susanne Smith, et al., comps. *A Preliminary Guide to the Pre-1904 County Records in the Archives Branch*. Richmond: Virginia State Library and Archives, 1987.

Ride, Millard Millburn, ed. *This Was the Life: Excerpts from the Judgment Records of Frederick County, Maryland 1748–1765*. 1979; reprint, Baltimore: Genealogical Publishing Co., 1984.

Robinson, William M., Jr. *Justice in Grey: A History of the Judicial System of the Confederate States of America*. Cambridge, Mass.: Harvard University Press, 1941.

Russell, George Ely. "Court Depositions and Affidavits as Evidence of Age in Maryland, 1637–1657." *Maryland Magazine of Genealogy* 2 (1979): 68–75.

Sanborn, Melinde Lutz. *Ages from Court Records, 1636–1770: Essex, Middlesex, and Suffolk Counties, Massachusetts*. Baltimore: Genealogical Publishing Co., 2003.

Scott, Kenneth, ed. *New York Historical Manuscripts: Minutes of the Mayor's Court of New York, 1674–1675*. Baltimore: Genealogical Publishing Co., 1983.

Snyder, Terri L. *Brabbling Women: Disorderly Speech and the Law in Early Virginia*. Ithaca, N.Y.: Cornell University Press, 2003.

Utley, Robert M. *Lone Star Justice: The First Century of the Texas Rangers*. New York: Berkeley Books, 2003.

Wiener, Frederick B. *Civilians Under Military Justice: British Practice Since 1689, Especially in North America*. Chicago: University of Chicago Press, 1967.

Wolfe, William A., and Janet B. Wolfe. *Names and Abstracts from the Acts of the Legislative Council of the Territory of Florida, 1822–1845*. Tallahassee: Florida State Genealogical Society, 1991.

Wyatt-Brown, Bertram. *Southern Honor: Ethics and Behavior in the Old South*. New York: Oxford University Press, 1982.

Slave Law and Court

Crawford, Paul. "A Footnote on Courts for Trial for Negroes in Pennsylvania." *Journal of Black Studies* 5 (December 1974): 167–74.

Hoffer, Peter Charles. *The Great New York Conspiracy of 1741: Slavery, Crime, and Colonial Law*. Lawrence: University Press of Kansas, 2003.

Klebaner, Benjamin J. "American Manumission Laws and the Responsibility for Supporting Slaves." *Virginia Magazine of History and Biography* 63 (1955): 443–53.

McPherson, Robert G. "Geor.gia Slave Trials, 1837–1849." *American Journal of Legal History* 4 (1960): 257–84; 364–77. Includes cases.

Missouri's Early Slave Laws: A History in Documents. Laws Concerning Slavery in Missouri, Territorial to 1850s. Online at <www.sos.mo.gov/archives/education/aahi/earlyslavelaws/slavelaws.asp>. Description of the *Code Noir* in Colonial Louisiana and the Black Code in the Missouri Territory.

Schafer, Judith Kelleher. *Becoming Free, Remaining Free: Manumission and Enslavement in New Orleans, 1846–1862*. Baton Rouge: Louisiana State University Press, 2003.

Senesè, Donald J. "The Free Negro and the South Carolina Courts, 1790–1860." *South Carolina Historical Magazine* 68 (1967): 140–53, 265.

Steel, Edward M., Jr. "Black Monongalians: A Judicial View of Slavery and the Negro in Monongalia County, 1776–1865." *West Virginia* 34 (1972–73): 331–59.

Tushnet, Mark V. *Slave Law in the American South:* State v Mann *in History and Literature*. Lawrence: University Press of Kansas, 2003.

Special Topics

Bramwell, B. S. "Frequency of Cousin Marriages." *Genealogists' Magazine* 8 (1939): 305–16.

Gordon, Sarah Barringer. *The Mormon Question: Polygamy and Constitutional Conflict in Nineteenth Century America*. Chapel Hill: University of North Carolina, 2002.

Miller, Alan N. *Middle Tennessee's Forgotten Children. Apprentices from 1784 to 1902*. Baltimore: Clearfield, 2004.

———. *East Tennessee's Forgotten Children: Apprentices from 1778 to 1911*. 2000; reprint, Baltimore: Clearfield, 2003.

Naanes, Ted, and Loretto D. Szucs. "Dead Men Do Tell Tales: Coroner's Records." *Ancestry* Magazine 12, no. 2 (March–April 1994): 6–11.

Naylor, Chris. "You have the body" Habeas Corpus Case Records of the U.S. Circuit Court for the District of Columbia, 1820–1863." *Prologue* 37, no. 3 (Fall 2005). Online at <www.archives.gov/publications/prologue/2005/fall/habeas-corpus.html>.

Phillimore, W. P. W., and Edward A. Fry, comps. *An Index to Changes of Name Under Authority of Act of Parliament...1760–1901*. Phillimore, 1905; reprint, Baltimore: Genealogical Publishing Co., 1968.

———. "Terms of Relationship in Colonial Times." *American Genealogist* 55 (1979): 52–54.

Porter, Roy, and David Wright, eds. *The Confinement of the Insane: International Perspectives, 1800–1965*. Cambridge, England: Cambridge University Press, 2003.

Provine, Dorothy. *District of Columbia Indentures of Apprenticeship, 1801–1893*. Lovettsville, Va.: Willow Bend Books, 1998.

Sanborn, Melinde Lutz. *Ages from Court Records, 1636–1700, Essex, Middlesex, and Suffolk Counties, Massachusetts*. Baltimore: Genealogical Publishing Co., 2003.

8
Directories

GORDON L. REMINGTON, FASG, FUGA

DIRECTORY: A book containing one or more alphabetical lists of the inhabitants of any locality, with their addresses and occupations; also a similar compilation dealing with the members of a particular profession, trade, or association, as a Clerical or Medical Directory, etc.[1]

While a directory can often in itself be a source of interesting genealogical and biographical information, its chief value lies in its use as an aid to locating a person in place and time. One type of directory groups people by a common residence. A second groups them by a common association or attribute. In addition, many directories list organizations rather than individuals and are sometimes called registers, catalogs, annuals, yearbooks, or guides. Whatever its title, contents, or method, a directory always lists and locates members of a group. This chapter gives a history of directories, describes the limitations and resources of seven kinds of directories, and provides numerous examples of how to use them.

The *Oxford English Dictionary* cites J. Brown's *The Directory or List of Principal Traders in London* (1732) as the earliest use of the word *directory* as defined at the beginning of this chapter. Lists of inhabitants or associates are extant from at least two hundred years earlier. Dorothea N. Spear, in the introduction to her *Bibliography of American Directories Through 1860*, gives a concise account of the history of directories in the United States:

> Although as early as 1665 in New York a grouping of residents by streets was shown in the Records of the Dutch Magistrates, the first directory-type listing of the inhabitants of an American city of which we have knowledge is a Baltimore broadside. It is entitled *The Following Lists of Families, And Other Persons Residing in the Town of Baltimore, Was Taken in the Year 1752, By a Lady of Respectability*, and is believed to have

Chapter Contents

been printed between 1830 and 1840 by Joseph Townsend (1756–1841) from the original manuscript in the Maryland Historical Society. Next came the two Charleston directory lists of 1782 and 1785 printed in the *South Carolina and Georgia Almanack* for those years, owned by the Charleston Library Society and reprinted in 1951. Philadelphia has the honor of having produced the first separately printed directories in this country, two rivals issued in 1785, the earlier being *MacPherson's Directory for the City and Suburbs of Philadelphia,* first issued on 16 November 1785, and the second, *The Philadelphia Directory,* by Francis White, first issued on 29 November 1785. The John MacPherson edition is to be found in the Philadelphia Free Library and in the Historical Society of Pennsylvania, while the White volume is owned by the Philadelphia libraries and the American Antiquarian Society . . . . New York quickly followed Philadelphia with *The New-York Directory of 1786,* by David Franks, which was frequently reprinted in later years. The New York Historical Society and the New York Public Library own original copies of this directory. Following the lead of the most progressive cities, many others throughout the country began to issue directories in rapid succession . . . The compilation of the early directories was usually a side issue rather than the principal line of the compiler's work. Therefore it is natural to find that some of the authors combined the listing with their duties as letter carriers, postmasters, county constables, school principals, teachers, and brokers. Often the modest compiler's own name and address were not even included in the alphabetical listing. The majority of these publications, however, were issued by newspaper offices. From the mid-nineteenth century we find separate directory publishers such as the well-known firms of George Adams and of Damrell & Moore of Boston, C. S. Williams of Cincinnati, and the John F. Trow and John Doggett Companies of New York, William H. Boyd, who had offices in New York, Philadelphia, and Washington, and many others. Boyd advertised in 1859 that he owned the largest collection of directories in the world and was prepared to publish the directory of any city or state. We know that he issued directories for many of the eastern and midwestern cities. Then came the R. L. Polk Company of New York and Detroit, with numerous branch offices. It presumably became the largest directory publisher and so continues today. The price of directories ranged from twenty-five cents to four dollars by the end of the 1850s, whereas the comprehensive Polk publications of today cost us fifty dollars a copy. It is true that the earliest attempts were quite crude, often with the names sorted only under each letter but not completely alphabetized. In the early volumes there were no house numbers, so the locations given were quite general; sometimes the millers and merchants were located merely "next the bridge" or "opposite the town hall."[2]

Originally, the two basic types of directories (residence and attribute) were more or less combined. The business orientation of the early directories influenced their development and content. Just as the census was designed primarily for congressional apportionment and not for genealogical purposes, the directory is limited as a genealogical source by the intent of its compilers.

The early English directories listed "principal traders" and "gentleman of accompte." It is doubtful that the "Lady of Respectability" who compiled the *List of Families, and Other Persons* in Baltimore, 1752, included in her list those families and "other persons" who weren't "respectable." Although such economic and class distinctions became less apparent later, it was not until the second half of the nineteenth century that directories regularly included common laborers, and even then they usually left out transient residents.

As cities grew in the nineteenth century, directories became more detailed. They included special sections devoted to businesses, organizations, churches, and even steamship lists along with the list of general inhabitants. These special sections eventually evolved into nongeographic directories by the late 1800s. The directories considered in this chapter are:

1. City directories
2. Telephone directories
3. County and regional business directories
4. Professional directories
5. Organizational directories
6. Religious directories
7. Post office and street directories

Finding a directory, the first step in using one, is also the most difficult step, particularly for researchers far from major record centers. Before attempting to locate a directory, you should be aware that the directory you want might not exist. It may be that a directory was never published for a particular place or group in the year of interest or that no copies of a directory known to have existed have survived. The law that requires copyrighted material be deposited in the Library of Congress dates only from 1870. Some directories were originally published for short-term use and were disposed of when they became obsolete. In addition, libraries may gradually dispose of their directory collections due to lack of space or low demand.

Another major consequence of publication for short-term use is low-quality paper. Individual pages may deteriorate badly. A binding can always be replaced, but when segments of the printed page tear off and are swept up at the end of the day by the library custodian, they are gone forever. Microform reproduction has helped to preserve older directories, but in many cases, image reduction and poor exposure make the microfilm or microfiche copies hard to read.

Gale Research Company, of Detroit, Michigan, publishes the most comprehensive guides to existing directories. These are *Directories in Print*; *City and State Directories in Print*; and *International Directories in Print*. These periodic publications, which succeed the *Directory of Directories* first published by Information Enterprises in 1980, are available at most public and university libraries. The current editions will, however, cover only those directories in print as of their own respective dates of publication. Their chief value for genealogical research is to provide current addresses and telephone numbers of publishing companies with directory libraries and the names and addresses of organizations for which directories may have been published in the past.

Locating Directories

City Directories

Surprisingly, access is not a significant problem with city directories. You can find city directories in almost every local library in the country, though larger libraries might have a greater variety. Go first to the public library nearest the place you are researching; if you can't travel there, telephone its reference desk. The reference librarian may be willing to photocopy the pages you need and send them to you or give you the desired information verbally. Reference staffs are quite busy, however, so a letter may be better if you're not in a hurry.

Most libraries, historical societies, and archives at the state level have fairly extensive collections of in-state directories and may also have directories from major out-of-state cities. On the national level, the Library of Congress in Washington, D.C., and the American Antiquarian Society in Worcester, Massachusetts, house major collections of directories. The Family History Library in Salt Lake City, Utah, has a wide variety of city directories, both in book form and on microform. Many of the original city directories that have been microformed have been discarded. Others, because of space consideration, have been relegated to high-density storage and must be retrieved for you. Only directories on microfilm are accessible through the worldwide system of LDS Family History Centers.

If you can't travel to a state or national repository, consider employing a record searcher to search the directories for you. If you have someone do a directory search for you, be sure to specify the parameters. For instance, if you do not want all entries of the surname Smith, ask for those on a certain street, at a certain address, or with particular first names.

If you can't locate the directory you want through any of the previously mentioned places, you may need to write the directory publishing company. The following is information on the two main directory publishing companies in business in the United States today:

Haines & Company, Inc.
8050 Freedom Ave., N.W.
North Canton, OH 44720-6985
Phone: (800) 843-8452
Fax: (330) 494-5862

Hill-Donnelly Information Services
(Hill Donnelly Cross Reference Directories)
10126 Windhorts Rd.
Tampa, FL 33619
Phone: (813) 832-1600
Fax: (813) 832-1694

Gale Research's *City and State Directories in Print* lists the cities that the Haines and Hill-Donnelly directories cover in a special subject index under "Cross-Reference Directories." R. L. Polk directories are also listed under "Cross-Reference Directories" in the subject index but simply as "Polk's City Directories [name of state]." The specific cities Polk publishes are listed under "Polk's City Directories" in each state section, not under the name of the city itself. These companies may have directory libraries for their own publications dating back several years, and R. L. Polk has branch offices in many cities. To find the nearest branch office that may have directories of interest, call the main office listed previously. These companies probably do not have copies of directories published by other, now defunct, companies. Fortunately for researchers, the older directories of many American cities are available in microform through the efforts of Research Publications (now a division of Primary Source Microfilm), which completed the first part of a five-segment project early in 1967 by recording on microfiche city directories through 1860 listed in Spear's bibliography.

SEGMENT I, consisting of 6,292 microfiche, encompassed the pre-1861 collection of directories at the American Antiquarian Society, which contains almost two-thirds of Spear's titles. Almost one hundred libraries contributed one or more additional directories to complete the microfiching of Spear's bibliography. Of Spear's almost 1,600 titles, all but forty-five were microfilmed, a completion rate of better than ninety-seven percent.

SEGMENT II, consisting of 372 reels of microfilm, covers the years 1861 to 1881. To keep the project manageable, it was limited to the fifty largest cities of the period, with some others added for regional representation. Research Publications used the collection of the American Antiquarian Society, created its own bibliography, and arranged for microfilming.

SEGMENT III, consisting of 746 microfilm reels, covers the same cities and uses the same format but extends coverage from 1882 to 1901. The editors note that "during the period included, and running through the years covered by Segment 3, the city directories were printed on very poor paper. Many of the directories are literally falling to pieces. The microfilm collection will insure continued availability and access to this important research source."

Supplements to Segment III are currently being published in units of twenty-five reels each as previously unavailable directories are located. There have been twenty-six units of twenty-five reels added since the completion of Segment III.

SEGMENT IV, consisting of eighty-seven units of fifty reels each, includes directories for fifty-three cities for the years 1902 to 1935. As cities such as New York grew more populous, the frequency with which directories were published diminished, so directory representation may not be complete for every year in this segment. The filming of Segment IV is still in process.

SEGMENT V, consisting of thirty-two units of fifty reels each, covers the years 1936 to 1965, is still in the process of being microfilmed.

These microform reproductions are available for purchase individually or in segments. The Library of Congress has the entire set, while state and local libraries may choose only to purchase directories of interest in their areas. The Family History Library has most of Segment I (those directories that it didn't already have in its collection) and almost all of Segments II, III, and IV in its collection.

You can view a catalog of the microform directories, both those completed and those in process, via the Primary Source Microfilm homepage <www.galegroup.com/psm>.

Two finding aids specifically designed for genealogists seeking information in nineteenth-century directories have been published volume ten of Gale Research's *Genealogy and Local History Series*, Nathan C. Parker, *Personal Name Index to the 1856 City Directories of California*, and in volume thirteen, Elsie L. Sopp, *Personal Name Index to the 1856 City Directories of Iowa*. These indexes can be used in conjunction with the Research Publications microfiche for the pre-1861 period.

Locating City Directories Online

Not surprisingly, a significant number of city directories are available on the Internet. There are two basic formats. Some city directories have been digitized and are viewable in the same way as an original paper or microfilm version. Many more have been transcribed. Transcribed directories could contain transcription errors but are easier to search.

Examples of digitized directories can be found at:

www.Delawarecitydirectory.com
www.Wisconsincitydirectory.com

In the late 1990s, Primary Source Media (now Primary Source Microfilm) announced an ambitious plan called "City Directories Online." By late 1999, it was intended that 300,000 pages of city directories covering the years would be published (imaged) on the Web with full text searching. Access was by subscription on a "pay-for-use" basis. Unfortunately, this project was discontinued as of 31 December 2001, and visitors to that site are now directed to <www.galegroup.com/psm/>.

Many transcribed city directories can be found at Ancestry.com under the subject "Directories and Member Lists." Most of the directories transcribed on Ancestry.com are from the nineteenth and first half of the twentieth centuries and cover a wide range of cities. A special effort was made to transcribe circa 1890 directories as a substitute for the lost 1890 census. The list of transcribed directories on Ancestry.com is continually growing. In a 1999 article in the *Ancestry Daily News*, Brian G. Anderson listed only six directories on the website. By the end of 2005, the site had thousands. The search engine on Ancestry.com allows for the entire directories database to be searched for one name.

Other transcribed city directories can be found under the subject "City Directories" at CyndisList.com. Cyndi's List gives not only links to specific transcribed city directories but also links to sites detailing the location of original city directories in libraries and historical societies, as well as links to articles and general information resources about directories.

Telephone Directories

Telephone directories are classic examples of publications made of low-quality paper for short-term use. Whether obsolete telephone directories are retained by local and state libraries may depend on space considerations and the physical condition of the older directories. The Library of Congress has some telephone directories.

Business Directories

Business directories can be found in most of the repositories mentioned previously. Both the Library of Congress and the Family History Library have such directories, but the collection of the Library of Congress is more comprehensive. A list of the directories in the Library of Congress as of 1931 was printed in Colleen Neal's *Lest We Forget: A Guide to Genealogical Research in the Nation's Capital*. These business directories were often published by the same companies that published city directories, so private directory libraries should also be consulted (see the addresses cited earlier in this chapter).

Law Directories

Every law library should have at least one current law directory. How many—if any—back issues are kept and for how far back depends on the individual library and its storage capabilities. Even if the library has kept old directories, access to them may be limited. Large public libraries often keep back issues for reference. You might also find law directories through local and state bar associations. Again, whether they have back issues may depend on their space limitations. The American Bar Association has not kept past directories since 1981.

The Library of Congress has a complete set of the Martindale-Hubbell Directory from 1931 on. The library has only selected copies of earlier directories, the earliest Hubbell directory being from 1871 and the earliest Martindale-Hubbell directory being from 1885.

The publishing companies themselves maintain libraries, but access is a problem. The best approach is a specific written request. The addresses of the two oldest law list compilers are as follows:

Martindale-Hubbell, Inc.
Reed Reference Publishing
121 Chanlon Rd
New Providence, NJ 07974-1541
Phone: (908) 464-6800
<www.martindale.com>

Campbell's List, Inc.
P.O. Box 428
Maitland, FL 32751
Phone: (800) 249-6934, (407) 644-8298, (407) 644-3376
Fax: 407-740-6494
<www.campbellslist.com>

Both websites contain an online directory of current lawyers.

Medical Directories

Medical school libraries should have the most current edition of the *American Medical Directory* readily available. Your access to back issues may depend on the individual library's policy. For example, the Eccles Health Science Library at the University of Utah School of Medicine in Salt Lake City, Utah, keeps a complete collection of the directory available to the general public. Local and state medical associations may also maintain old directories, including those published on a regional level.

R. L. Polk published a *Medical and Surgical Register of the United States and Canada,* which was in its fifth edition by 1898. You may have a hard time finding early issues of this register; the Library of Congress does not seem to have any.

The Library of Congress maintains a complete collection of the *American Medical Directory.* If you can't get to a large medical library, consider sending a letter to the American Medical Association, which publishes the directory. For a small fee, its library and archive will also provide biographical details available from its database on physicians from 1878 to 1969. Contact

AMA Library and Archives
P.O. Box 109050
Chicago, IL 60610-9050
Phone: (312) 464-5000
Fax: (312) 645-4184

This database, essentially a card index, is now on 237 reels of microfilm at the Family History Library and can be found as "Deceased American Physicians, 1864–1970" under the subject "United States—Occupations."

Civil and Military Service Directories

According to an 1816 act of Congress providing for a biennial register of the civil and military service of the United States, twenty-five copies of the register were to be deposited in the Library of Congress. In 1851, a provision was added that allowed for a copy to be sent to the secretary of state of each state. Presumably, the Library of Congress and state libraries and archives contain copies today.

The Library of Congress has apparently transferred the older registers to the National Archives, but you should check both repositories. State libraries and archives may not have kept the registers from all of the years, so there may be gaps. States in the former Confederacy may not have copies of the registers for 1861 to 1865.

Professional Directories

The Library of Congress and local and state archives will probably have some directories relevant to their areas of interest. If you can find a publisher of pre-twentieth-century professional directories that is still in business today, see if it maintains a directory library. *Directories in Print* can aid in this task. The addresses of the publishers of the two professional directories of special interest to genealogists are as follows:

The American Blue Book of Funeral Directors
Kates-Boylston Publications/UCG
1255 Route 70, Suite 31-S,
Lakewood, NJ 08701
Phone: (800) 500-4585
Fax: (732) 901-8650
www.kates-boylston.com/

American Cemetery Association Membership Directory and Buyer's Guide
(Originally published by American Cemetery Association; the organization changed its name to the International Cemetery and Funeral Association)
1895 Preston White Drive, Suite 220
Reston, VA 20191
Phone: (703) 391-8400; (800) 645-7700
Fax: (703) 391-8416
<www.ICFA.org> (the website has an online directory of members)

Religious Directories

Access is the major problem in locating religious directories. Common designations such as "Baptist" and "Methodist" may comprise several distinct denominations. You will therefore need to research the ancestor's exact religion to find the appropriate directory. Also, the denomination as it existed in the nineteenth century may be defunct or have merged with another group. In such a case, lack of a modern directory showing church locations may limit your access to the original records.

The best way to determine the existence and location of a directory for the denomination of interest is to look for a church archive for the particular denomination. Such archives may have back issues of these directories, as well as information on where to find the records of modern churches. Also, check the seminary or training college libraries for the denomination.

Among public repositories, check the Library of Congress, state and local libraries, and general university libraries (particularly those that were once denominational), but don't stop there. The Library of Congress, for example, has *The Official Catholic Directory* only as early as 1886, although the directory has been published since 1817. In such a case, contact the publisher:

P.J. Kenedy and Sons
Reed Reference Publishing
121 Chanlon Road
New Providence, NJ 07974
Phone: (800) 521-8110

Post Office Directories

Most research libraries should have the Gale Research reprint of *The Street Directory of the Principal Cities of the United States...to April 1908*, available in their reference sections. The Library of Congress and the Family History Library have copies. The Library of Congress should also have other back issues of post office directories.

Comprehensiveness of Directories

When consulting any directory, keep in mind why it was compiled. If an individual was not at home when the city directory agent called, his or her name may not appear for that particular year. Even today, the general population must cooperate to put together a city directory. The agent or compiler usually leaves a notice on the door if the resident is not home, and not everyone will take the time or trouble to respond. The compiler may not follow up if it is too costly. Methods in the nineteenth century may have been considerably more primitive. Business and professional directories may have required a fee for inclusion. If you can't find an ancestor in the alphabetical sequence of a directory, be sure to check the beginning for listings received too late to be included.

City directories, however, seem to lack the most for their subject matter, if only for their scope. In some cities, early directories were published in the same year by competing companies, and they did not always include the same people. If an ancestor is not listed in a directory but should be, check for transpositions of letters —Tohmson instead of Thomson, for example. Names may also be spelled differently. Early New York City directories often contained lists of variant name spellings. Pittsburgh city directories listed the names Meyers, Meyer, Myers, and Myer together until the 1860s. Some early directories grouped names with the same initial letter but did not list them in strict alphabetical sequence. Consider the type style when using early directories, particularly those from the eighteenth century. Don't misread the old double-ess character (ſ) as f.

The date on the title page of a directory is usually that of publication and does not necessarily indicate when the information was compiled. Often, a directory will state that it is for the "year ending" on a particular day. Remember that many city dwellers rented rather than owned their residences and may not have stayed at one address for long; this fact does have an impact on using the directory for census searches (see discussion later in the chapter). While it refers to a non-urban area, the following excerpt from the foreword to the *Alaska Directory and Gazetteer for 1934–1935* helps to explain the difficulties of listing people constantly on the move:

> This Second Biennial Edition of the Alaska Directory and Gazetteer represents a complete new compilation of the residents and business houses of the Territory of Alaska . . . Extreme care has been taken to secure the most complete and accurate information possible but the publishers cannot assume responsibility for any accuracies [*sic*] or omissions. A frontier country, one-fifth the size of the United States, with its approximately 29,000 white population distributed among more than 400 widely scattered towns and settlements, present[s] difficulties which subscribers will appreciate. The shift of population from point to point in the Territory by seasonal occupation and winter vacationing in the States offer further problems of reporting proper locations of many residents. In order to meet these situations, the issuing of supplements from time to time prior to publication of the next directory proper will be continued. Also, all purchasers are entitled to two years reference, inquiry and tracing service.[3]

City Directories

City directories are primarily useful for locating people in a particular place and time. They can tell you generally where an ancestor lived and give an exact location for census years. They are also useful for linkage with sources other than censuses.

There are usually several parts to a city directory. The section of most interest to the genealogist, of course, is the alphabetical listing of names, for it is there that you may find your ancestor. The other parts of a directory are equally important, however, as they will help you utilize the information contained in the alphabetical listings more efficiently. Street directories and ward boundary descriptions will be discussed in detail later in the chapter. There are also sections listing government offices, churches, civic and fraternal organizations, and businesses. These sections may be separated or combined.

Whenever you use a directory, however, it is important to refer to the page showing abbreviations used in the alphabetical section of the directory, usually following the name in each entry. Some abbreviations are quite common, such as *h* for home or *r* indicating residence. There may even be a subtle distinction between *r* for residents who are related to the homeowner and *b* for boarders who are not related.

Some city directories list adult children who lived with their parents but were working or going to school. Look for persons of the same surname residing at the same address. If analyzed and interpreted properly, these annual directories can tell you (by implication) which children belong to which household, when they married and started families of their own, and when they established themselves in business. In cases where a specific occupation is given, you can search records pertinent to that occupation.

There may be a page at the beginning of the alphabetical section that gives changes, additions, and deletions—usually due to removals, but sometimes due to death. Some city directories also give special facts—separate listings for African Americans or places of birth and death, for example, but such notations are usually for one year only and are not the norm.

Beginning in the late-nineteenth century, but more regularly in the twentieth century, city directories have often contained a "reverse" street directory, listing streets alphabetically, then the names of the people residing at each address. This is an important tool for identifying persons of different surnames residing at the same address. Another kind of "reverse" directory—by telephone number—has also become part of modern directories.

Once an ancestor has been found in a city directory, there are several ways the information can be used to gain access to, or link with, such sources as censuses, death and probate records, church records, naturalization records, and land records.

Using Census Records with Directories

The usefulness of city directories for gaining access to census records of urban areas cannot be overstated. Even where census indexes exist, there is always the possibility that the census taker or the indexer erred in the spelling or coding of the surname. In such cases, it is just as difficult to find someone in an indexed urban area as it is in an unindexed urban area, and the methodology for doing so is the same.

Indexes to the decennial federal census currently exist in one form or another for every state for the years 1790 through 1930. For those federal censuses as yet unavailable to the general public (from 1940 on), the census bureau will conduct a search in an urban area only if a precise address for the census year is known.

Most state censuses are as yet unindexed.

The federal census for most urban areas is divided into at least wards. Beginning with the 1880 census, wards are further subdivided into enumeration districts. Some state censuses for urban areas are divided into election districts or other sub-ward designations. For a city directory to be useful in making a census search, you must know the correct ward or enumeration district of a particular address for the census year desired. There are several aids to locating the correct ward or enumeration district.

Street Directories

Street directories vary depending on the publisher of the city directory and the date of publication. At best, they give you the exact ward or wards through which a street runs, as well as cross streets. At worst, they simply list the names of the streets in alphabetical order. Even such a limited listing can be valuable if notations of name changes are included.

If a street runs through several wards, checking the cross street nearest to the street address for an ancestor helps determine the correct ward to search. The 1910 street directory for Rochester, New York (see figure 8-1), shows that Portland Avenue runs through wards 8, 16, 18, and 22. Suppose the ancestor lived at 1100 Portland Avenue. The closest cross street is Pomeroy Street, which lies entirely within Ward 22. Ward 22 is therefore the proper ward to search.

The one problem that you might encounter when using street directories to determine the correct ward is if the street of interest forms the boundary between wards. In such a case, you need to determine which side of the street the address of interest lies on and, depending on whether the address number is even or odd, you should be able to determine in which ward it lies. While the even and odd numbering of streets may now be standardized, it cannot be assumed that there was any consistency in the nineteenth century. You may have to use maps in conjunction with the street directory, however, to make this determination.

Maps

If street directories alone cannot provide the proper ward, or if identification of a specific enumeration district is desired, maps can be utilized to find the appropriate census subdivision. There are basically three kinds of census maps: those created with ward or enumeration district boundaries, those without boundaries, and those with boundaries added after publication.

Maps created with boundaries are the most useful. Many city directories were published with maps showing ward boundaries that can be used in conjunction with the street directories. City maps showing ward boundaries were also created independently of city directories for other reasons—as guides or for insurance purposes, for instance. The Library of Congress has an excellent collection of city maps created from 1840 to 1900 showing ward boundaries. This collection has been acquired by the Family History Library, adding to an already good city map collection. (See chapter 20, "Urban Research," for more information on city maps.)

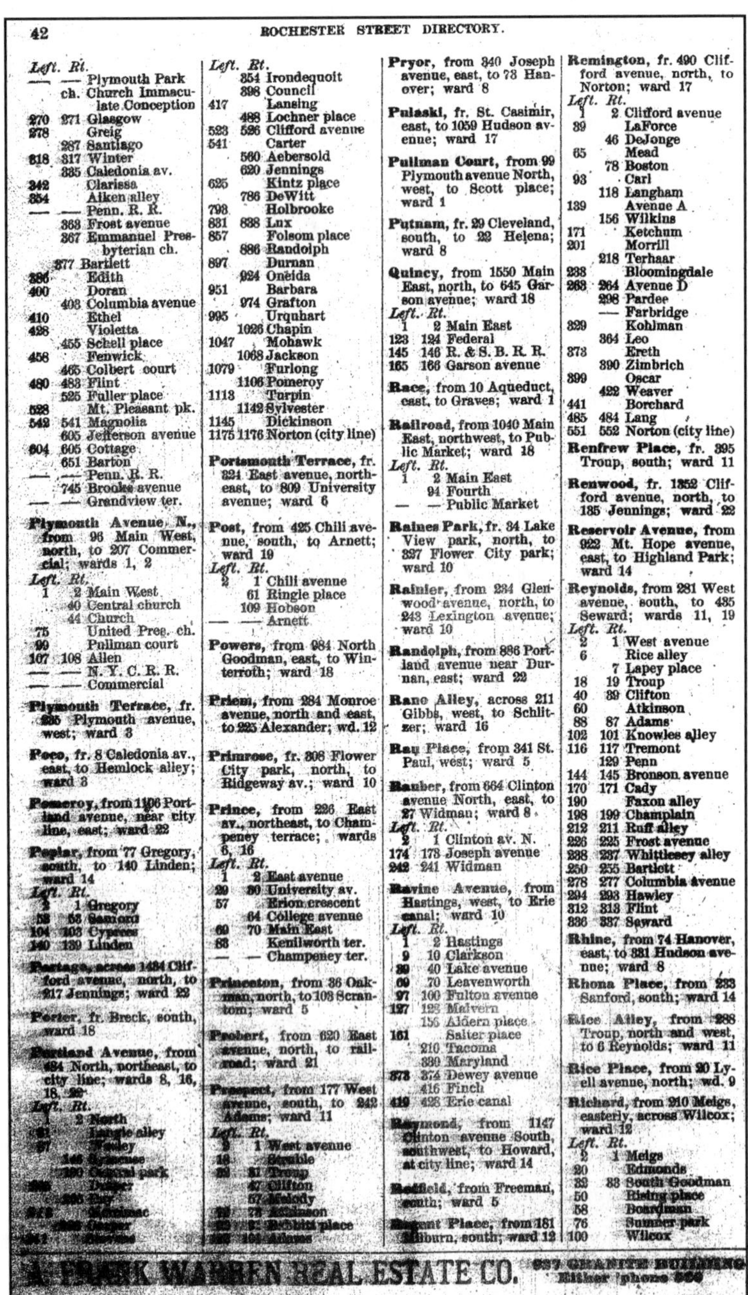

42 ROCHESTER STREET DIRECTORY.

Left. Rt.
— — Plymouth Park
ch. Church Immaculate Conception
270 271 Glasgow
278 Greig
287 Santiago
318 317 Winter
335 Caledonia av.
342 Clarissa
354 Aiken alley
— — Penn. R. R.
363 Frost avenue
367 Emmanuel Presbyterian ch.
377 Bartlett
386 Edith
400 Doran
408 Columbia avenue
410 Ethel
428 Violetta
455 Schell place
458 Fenwick
465 Colbert court
480 483 Flint
525 Fuller place
528 Mt. Pleasant pk.
542 541 Magnolia
605 Jefferson avenue
604 605 Cottage
651 Barton
— — Penn. R. R.
745 Brooks avenue
— — Grandview ter.

Plymouth Avenue N., from 96 Main West, north, to 207 Commercial; wards 1, 2
Left. Rt.
1 2 Main West
40 Central church
44 Church
75 United Pres. ch.
99 Pullman court
107 108 Allen
— — N. Y. C. R. R.
— — Commercial

Plymouth Terrace, fr. 235 Plymouth avenue, west; ward 3

Poco, fr. 8 Caledonia av., east, to Hemlock alley; ward 3

Pomeroy, from 1106 Portland avenue, near city line, east; ward 22

Poplar, from 77 Gregory, south, to 140 Linden; ward 14
Left. Rt.
2 1 Gregory
58 53 Samoru
104 103 Cypress
140 139 Linden

Portage, across 1484 Clifford avenue, north, to 217 Jennings; ward 22

Porter, fr. Breck, south, ward 18

Portland Avenue, from 484 North, northeast, to city line; wards 8, 16, 18, 22
Left. Rt.
1 2 North

Left. Rt.
854 Irondequoit
898 Council
417 Lansing
488 Lochner place
523 526 Clifford avenue
541 Carter
560 Aebersold
620 Jennings
625 Kintz place
786 DeWitt
798 Holbrooke
831 838 Lux
857 Folsom place
886 Randolph
897 Durnan
924 Oneida
951 Barbara
974 Grafton
995 Urquhart
1026 Chapin
1047 Mohawk
1068 Jackson
1079 Furlong
1106 Pomeroy
1113 Turpin
1142 Sylvester
1145 Dickinson
1175 1176 Norton (city line)

Portsmouth Terrace, fr. 824 East avenue, northeast, to 809 University avenue; ward 6

Post, from 425 Chili avenue, south, to Arnett; ward 19
Left. Rt.
2 1 Chili avenue
61 Ringle place
109 Hobson
— — Arnett

Powers, from 984 North Goodman, east, to Winterroth; ward 18

Priem, from 284 Monroe avenue, north and east, to 225 Alexander; wd. 12

Primrose, fr. 308 Flower City park, north, to Ridgeway av.; ward 10

Prince, from 226 East av., northeast, to Champeney terrace; wards 6, 16
Left. Rt.
1 2 East avenue
29 30 University av.
57 Erion crescent
64 College avenue
69 70 Main East
88 Kenilworth ter.
— — Champeney ter.

Princeton, from 36 Oakman, north, to 108 Scranton; ward 5

Probert, from 620 East avenue, north, to railroad; ward 21

Prospect, from 177 West avenue, south, to 242 Adams; ward 11
Left. Rt.
1 West avenue

Pryor, from 340 Joseph avenue, east, to 73 Hanover; ward 8

Pulaski, fr. St. Casimir, east, to 1059 Hudson avenue; ward 17

Pullman Court, from 99 Plymouth avenue North, west, to Scott place; ward 1

Putnam, fr. 29 Cleveland, south, to 22 Helena; ward 8

Quincy, from 1550 Main East, north, to 645 Garson avenue; ward 18
Left. Rt.
1 2 Main East
123 124 Federal
145 146 R. & S. B. R. R.
165 166 Garson avenue

Race, from 10 Aqueduct, east, to Graves; ward 1

Railroad, from 1040 Main East, northwest, to Public Market; ward 18
Left. Rt.
1 2 Main East
94 Fourth
— — Public Market

Raines Park, fr. 34 Lake View park, north, to 327 Flower City park; ward 10

Rainier, from 234 Glenwood avenue, north, to 243 Lexington avenue; ward 10

Randolph, from 886 Portland avenue near Durnan, east; ward 22

Rano Alley, across 211 Gibbs, west, to Schlitzer; ward 16

Ray Place, from 341 St. Paul, west; ward 5

Rauber, from 664 Clinton avenue North, east, to 27 Widman; ward 8
Left. Rt.
2 1 Clinton av. N.
174 173 Joseph avenue
242 241 Widman

Ravine Avenue, from Hastings, west, to Erie canal; ward 10
Left. Rt.
1 2 Hastings
9 10 Clarkson
39 40 Lake avenue
69 70 Leavenworth
97 100 Fulton avenue
127 128 Malvern
156 Aldern place
161 Salter place
210 Tacoma
330 Maryland
373 374 Dewey avenue
416 Finch
419 428 Erie canal

Raymond, from 1147 Clinton avenue South, southwest, to Howard, at city line; ward 14

Redfield, from Freeman, south; ward 5

Regent Place, from 181 Milburn, south; ward 12

Remington, fr. 490 Clifford avenue, north, to Norton; ward 17
Left. Rt.
1 2 Clifford avenue
39 LaForce
46 DeJonge
65 Mead
78 Boston
93 Carl
118 Langham
139 Avenue A
156 Wilkins
171 Ketchum
201 Morrill
218 Terhaar
238 Bloomingdale
268 264 Avenue D
298 Pardee
— Farbridge
329 Kohlman
364 Leo
373 Ereth
390 Zimbrich
399 Oscar
422 Weaver
441 Borchard
485 484 Lang
551 552 Norton (city line)

Renfrew Place, fr. 395 Troup, south; ward 11

Renwood, fr. 1352 Clifford avenue, north, to 185 Jennings; ward 22

Reservoir Avenue, from 922 Mt. Hope avenue, east, to Highland Park; ward 14

Reynolds, from 281 West avenue, south, to 435 Seward; wards 11, 19
Left. Rt.
2 1 West avenue
6 Rice alley
7 Lapey place
18 19 Troup
40 39 Clifton
60 Atkinson
88 87 Adams
102 101 Knowles alley
116 117 Tremont
129 Penn
144 145 Bronson avenue
170 171 Cady
190 Faxon alley
198 199 Champlain
212 211 Ruff alley
226 225 Frost avenue
238 237 Whittlesey alley
250 255 Bartlett
278 277 Columbia avenue
294 293 Hawley
312 313 Flint
336 337 Seward

Rhine, from 74 Hanover, east, to 331 Hudson avenue; ward 8

Rhona Place, from 233 Sanford, south; ward 14

Rice Alley, from 288 Troup, north and west, to 6 Reynolds; ward 11

Rice Place, from 20 Lyell avenue, north; wd. 9

Richard, from 210 Meigs, easterly, across Wilcox; ward 12
Left. Rt.
2 1 Meigs
20 Edmonds
32 33 South Goodman
50 Rising place
58 Boardman
76 Sumner park
100 Wilcox

A. FRANK WARREN REAL ESTATE CO. 337 GRANITE BUILDING Either 'phone 360

Figure 8-1. From a 1910 street directory for Rochester, New York.

There are also maps with census enumeration district boundaries for the 1880, 1900, 1910, and 1920 censuses. These maps are available at the Washington National Records Service, 4205 Suitland Rd., Suitland, Maryland, or they can be ordered from the Cartographic and Architectural Branch (NNSC), National Archives, Washington, D.C. 20408. The Family History Library has microfiche copies of these maps for forty-seven major cities in 1910. The appropriate call numbers can be found in the Family History Library's *1910 Census Register.*[4]

Maps without boundaries help if you can find a description of the ward or enumeration district boundaries. Sometimes there will be a description of ward boundaries in the city directory itself, even if there is no map and the street directory does not contain ward designations. In this case, you can draw the ward boundaries on a map, but be sure to use a map that was published near the date of the directory.

Enumeration district descriptions exist for 1880, 1900, 1910, and 1920. These descriptions indicate the boundaries of each district. They constitute National Archives Microfilm Publication T1224 and are available at the main and regional archives of the National Archives as well as the Family History Library.

Drawing ward and enumeration district boundaries on a map can be a time-consuming process, but it is sometimes necessary in cases where such maps do not exist or are inaccessible to a researcher intent on locating an ancestor in the census.

Maps with boundaries added after publication are time-savers, but take care that such maps have been drawn correctly, or you will have to search a long time to find the right entries. The Newberry Library in Chicago has constructed a 1900 atlas for the city of Chicago from the enumeration district maps. This atlas is especially valuable for finding alleys, courts, and other short streets. The Family History Library is adding ward and enumeration district boundaries to maps already in its collection. Another general source of city maps is E. Kay Kirkham's *A Handy Guide to Record Searching in the Larger Cities of the United States*. The maps included street indexes, so Kirkham's is a useful compilation. Take care, however, as this book does not cover all of the major cities for which such maps are available, nor do the maps always cover every census year. In addition, most of the maps are taken from atlases dated 1855, 1866, and 1878; the ward boundaries may not correspond to those existing in the closest census years.

Some detailed maps are becoming available on the Internet. For example, regardless of census indexes, Chicago has always been difficult to search, because of the size of the population and the large number of immigrants whose names might be misspelled. In such a case, using city directories to find a street address requires a good map showing ward and/or enumeration district boundaries. The website *A Look at Cook* <www.alookatcook.com> contains many useful maps for the federal censuses from 1870 to 1930, as well as for locating World War I draft registration boards.

Street Indexes

The 1910 census was originally not indexed for many of the major urban areas of the country. Microfiche street indexes compiled by the Census Bureau for thirty-nine major cities were distributed to all National Archives branches under the auspices of the NARA (National Archives and Records Administration) Gift Fund of the Federation of Genealogical Societies. The Family History Library also has this microfiche collection and has added indexes for five more cities. The street indexes generally break each street down by address number and indicate the enumeration district in which the number can be found.

Even with the advent of the indexed 1910 census online, there are going to be instances where the indexers couldn't read a name or it was misspelled by the census enumerator. In such a case it is necessary to resort to the "old fashioned" way of finding a census entry via a street address and finding aid such as a street index or map. City directories are indispensable tools in obtaining the requisite street address in order to conduct such a search.

The New York City Municipal Archives has specialized street indexes for the 1905, 1915, and 1925 state censuses of New York City (Manhattan and the Bronx). The Family History Library has these indexes and has also compiled its own street index for the 1915 state census of Manhattan. Other libraries and societies may have compiled street indexes for their particular urban areas or may have purchased the microfiche mentioned previously.

Special Finding Aids

Many local libraries and societies have created their own aids to finding the correct ward or enumeration district for a particular address. The Family History Library has created an enumeration district index for all states for which there are no 1910 Soundex or Miracode indexes. (See chapter 5, "Census Records.") Other examples of privately compiled finding aids are Mary Lou Craver Mariner's and Patricia Roughan Bellows's *A Research Aid for the Massachusetts 1910 Federal Census*, and Barbara Hillman's *Guide to the Use of the United States. Census Office, 10th Census, 1880, New York City*. Mariner and Bellows list the 1910 census enumeration districts for wards of various Massachusetts cities, and Hillman actually uses contemporary assembly and election district maps, and aligns them to the proper enumeration district for the 1880 census of New York City. In both cases, you must have a street address for your ancestor in order to locate him or her; this information can be obtained from the city directory corresponding to the census year.

It would be impossible to list all of the specialized guides available for particular cities and particular censuses. The best rule of thumb before searching the census of an urban area is to call the local library or genealogical society for the city or browse the Internet to determine if a street index or finding aid does exist.

Methodology

The basic methodology for locating an ancestor in the census using city directories is to find the street address of that ancestor in a directory for the year of or close to the date of the census. Keep in mind that an ancestor might have moved between the date of the census and the compilation of the directory for the same year, so it is always a good idea to check the directories for either side of a census year in order to be certain of all possible addresses. If a member of the family in question was born, married, or died in the census year and vital records were kept by the city in that year, then the address that appears on the vital record may be a more accurate locator. Once an address is found, the next step is to determine the ward or enumeration district in which that address was located. It should be possible to do this using the finding aids mentioned previously. Once the proper ward or enumeration district is determined, it is a matter of reading the district page by page until the family is found.

Prior to 1880, few cities were divided below the ward level in the census. New York and Philadelphia were among those that were. Fortunately, there are two enumerations for the 1870 census for these cities, the second of which lists the exact street address for each family. If an ancestor can be located in the second enumeration (which often contains a minimal amount of information, as it was basically a recount), then a corresponding entry can be found in the first enumeration using not only the ward number but the subdistrict designation. For more information, see chapter 5, "Census Records," and chapter 20, "Urban Research."

Beginning in 1880, the name of the street is usually listed in the margin of the census page, and the house number is listed along with the visitation numbers (dwelling and family). When a ward and enumeration district have been located for a post-1880 census using one of the finding aids mentioned previously, the family can usually be found by looking for the street name, then house number.

The following examples illustrate two different ways to find an ancestor in the 1910 census for two unindexed cities: Rochester, New York, and Baltimore, Maryland.

The 1910 city directory for Rochester, New York, showed that Harvey F. Remington had a home at 7 Reservoir Avenue (see figure 8-2). The street directory for Rochester showed that Reservoir Avenue was contained entirely in the 14th Ward (see figure 8-1). The index to enumeration districts for the 1910 census showed that the 14th Ward of Rochester consisted of enumeration districts 138 through 144. A 1910 enumeration district map does exist for Rochester, but it was unavailable for consultation at the time the search was made. Fortunately, the 1910 city directory for Rochester had a map showing ward boundaries (see figure 8-3). Using the enumeration district descriptions, it was determined that Reservoir Avenue lay in the 141st Enumeration District (see figure 8-4). It was then simply a matter of reading that enumeration district—but in this case looking for the street name was useless, as the name of the street was not given in the margin for this particular address. By reading each family entry, the Harvey F. Remington family was found on sheet 11B, line 72.[5]

According to the 1911 city directory of Baltimore, John L. Alcock, a lumber exporter, had a home at 2742 St. Paul Street (see figure 8-5). The street directory in 1911 did not give ward designations; it stated only the streetcar line that served a particular address (see figure 8-6). Fortunately, Baltimore is one of the thirty-nine cities for which a census bureau street index exists.

Reference to the street index showed that even-numbered addresses on St. Paul Street from 2600 to 2800 were in Enumeration District 191 (see figure 8-7). By searching this enumeration district, the John L. Alcock family was found on sheet 9B, line 72.[6]

The 1910 census will likely remain unindexed longer than the pre-1880 censuses. For this reason, existing enumeration district maps and street indexes for the major cities are listed in table 8-1. It should be stressed that similar finding aids exist for the other post-1870 censuses, and they can be utilized in the same manner as illustrated previously when searching the Soundex fails.

Remington Alvah C physician 576 West av
Charles W laborer 438 Exchange bds 2 Johnson [993 do
Clifford E florist 1023 South av house
Edith F cashier 201 Powers bldg bds 192 N Union
Elizabeth Miss bds 175 Rosedale
Eva P Mrs teacher East High School h 44 Quincy
Frederic remd to New York city
Frederick carpenter bds 130 Main W
Frederick B instructor (at Industry) h 409 Linden
Genevieve Miss bds 389 Brown
Harvey F lawyer 911 Wilder bldg h 7 Reservoir av [1Reservoir av
Janet stenographer 23 City Hall house
Louise A widow Edward C house 656 Lake av [Union
Margaret A widow Charles E h 192 N
Stanley D salesman 612 Granite bldg b 580 Averill av
Typewriter Co 44 East av
Walter C (*Barnard, Porter & Viall*) 17 N Water bds 656 Lake av
William B clerk 64 Trust bldg bds 7 Reservoir av
Willis S steward Roch State Hospital house do [der

Figure 8-2. Entry for Harvey F. Remington in the 1910 street directory for Rochester, New York.

Using City Directories to Find World War I Draft Registration Districts

Another use for city directories is as an aid to locating the draft registration district in which an ancestor registered for the 1917–1918 draft. Inasmuch as the draft registration eventually encompassed all men born between 1873 and 1900, it is an extremely useful record to find. Full birth dates are given, and places of birth are given in the 1917 draft, including exact places in Europe for immigrants. Marital status, number of dependents, next of kin, employment information, and physical description are also provided.

Unfortunately, the draft registration cards are not yet fully indexed, and in large cities, you need to know the draft registration board to which your ancestor would have reported in order to find his registration card. Most cities had at least four draft boards, but New York City (189), Chicago (86), and Philadelphia (51) top the list.

Unfortunately, draft registration district maps do not exist for every city. The Family History Library has microfilmed maps of the following areas:

Alabama—Birmingham
California—Los Angeles, San Diego
Colorado—Denver
Connecticut—Bridgeport, Hartford, New Haven
Georgia—Atlanta
Illinois—Chicago
Indiana—Indianapolis
Kansas—Kansas City
Kentucky—Louisville
Louisiana—New Orleans
Maryland—Baltimore
Massachusetts—Boston
Minnesota—Minneapolis, St. Paul
Missouri—Kansas City
New Jersey—Jersey City
New York—Albany and Rensselaer, Buffalo, Bronx, Brooklyn, Manhattan, Queens, Richmond (Staten Island), Rochester, Schenectady, Syracuse
Ohio—Cincinnati, Cleveland, Toledo

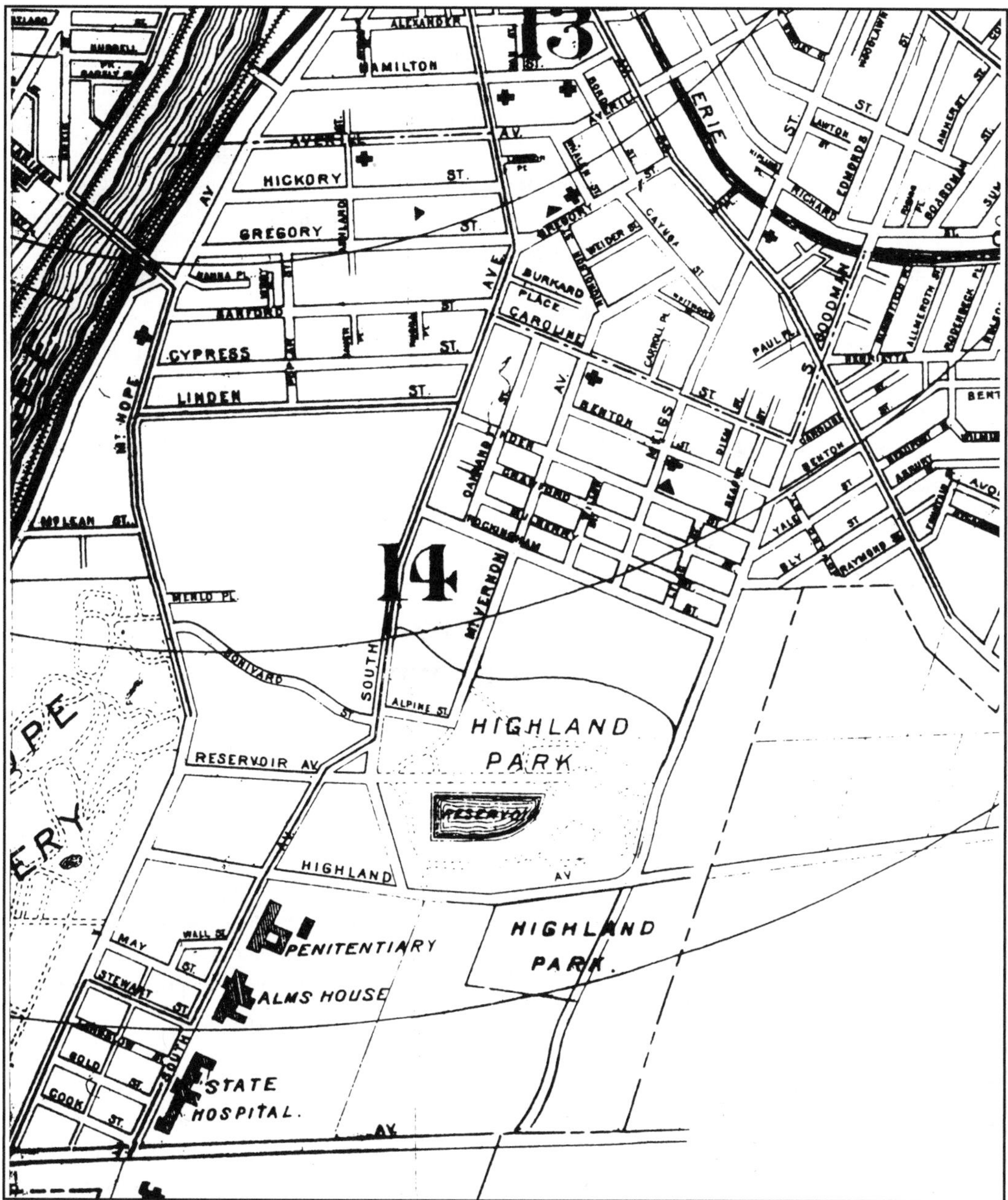

Figure 8-3. Portion of a map of the city of Rochester, New York, 1910, from the street directory.

Pennsylvania—Allegheny, Luzerne, Pittsburgh, Philadelphia, Reading, Scranton, Westmoreland
Rhode Island—Providence
Texas—Dallas
Washington, D.C.
Washington—Seattle
Wisconsin—Milwaukee[7]

The Family History Library Catalog notes that:

Some of these maps are draft board maps showing the boundaries of the draft boards while others are just street and road maps which are helpful to some degree. The maps were filmed in the order as listed. The maps are enclosed in plastic sleeves for protection due to their fragile condition and age.

Many of the maps are discolored or faded from age and this may make them difficult to use.

As an additional finding aid, the Family History Library has published a Register of World War I Selective Service System [boards and their locations] draft registration cards, 1917–1918: For Selective Service addresses for major cities as a noncirculating finding aid, use call number 973 M2wws, microfiche number 6039066.

Noting that the information in the book was taken from the *Second Report of the Provost Marshall General to the Secretary of War*, the book contains draft board addresses for the following cities:

California— Los Angeles, San Francisco
Colorado—Denver
Connecticut—South New Haven
Illinois—Chicago, Cook County
Indiana—Indianapolis
Louisiana—New Orleans
Maryland—Baltimore
Massachusetts—Boston (suburbs Brighton, Dorchester, Hyde Park, Jamaica Plain, Roxbury, West Roxbury)
Michigan—Detroit
Minnesota—Minneapolis, St. Paul
Missouri—Kansas City, St. Louis
New Jersey—Newark, Jersey City
New York—Buffalo, New York City (Bronx, Brooklyn, New York City, Queens, Richmond/Staten Island)
Ohio Cincinnati, Cleveland,
Oregon—Portland
Pennsylvania—Allegheny, Luzerne, Philadelphia, Pittsburgh
Rhode Island—Providence
Washington—Seattle
Wisconsin—Milwaukee

Methodology

In order to find an ancestor in a large city in the World War I draft records, you first need a street address. The most likely source is from a city directory, but street addresses from the 1920 census, marriage records, and birth records of children can also be utilized. Once you find a street address, you can use a map that has draft boards already drawn on it, or you can use a contemporary map to find the nearest draft board. It is important to use a contemporary map as street names may have changed

```
140. Ward 14 (part of) Election district 3
     Bounded by Caroline
                So. Goodman
                Rockingham
                South Ave.

141. Ward 14 (part of) Election district 4
     excluding State Hospital for Insane.
     Bounded by North boundary of Mt.Hope Cemetery
                Mt.Hope Ave.,Bonivard,South Ave.
                Mt.Vernon, Rockingham
                So. Goodman, Highland Ave., City
                  line, Elmwood, Lehigh Valley R.R
                Westfall Road
                Genesee River

142. Ward 14 (part of) Election district 5 (part of)
     Bounded by Averill Ave.extended, Averill Ave.
                South Ave., Hickory, Ashland
                Gregory, Mt.Hope Ave., Clarissa
                Genesee River
```

Figure 8-4. Descriptions of the enumeration districts of the sixteenth supervisor's district of New York. Bureau of the Census, thirteenth census. National Archives microfilm T1224, roll 35; FHL microfilm 1,374,008.

and some streets may no longer exist. You can then look at the draft registration cards for that district and hope to find your ancestor.

For instance, Martin Gross, a laborer, was listed at 107 South 14th Street in Pittsburgh, Pennsylvania, in a 1917 directory.[8] There were 21 draft boards in Pittsburgh.

Reference to the Family History Library's abovementioned finding aid indicates that Draft Board No. 14 was located at 40 South 14th Street. It doesn't take a map to know that these places must be close by, but a map confirmed the addresses were just a few blocks apart. The registration cards of Draft Board 14 revealed that Martin Gross, residing at 107 14th Street, registered on 12 September 1918. He was born 30 April 1873, was native born, worked as an inspector at a steel tube mill and his "nearest relative" was "Mrs. Katherine Gross," presumably his wife.

The same methodology can be used to find individuals in other cities.

Using Death and Probate Records with Directories

When you know that an ancestor died in a large city, you can use his or her presence in a directory to approximate the date of death. This makes voluminous city death and probate records much easier to search. It is often easier, however, to estimate the date of a man's death because, unlike a recently widowed woman, a widower will not be designated as such. Take care with this method: an individual's nonappearance in a directory does not always indicate death. Sometimes a person disappears for a year or so and then mysteriously reappears at the same address. More likely than not, the ancestor was there all the time. Remember how the source was compiled. It is best, therefore, to check directories for several years after an individual's first disappearance to determine if that ancestor died or moved away. Beginning in the twentieth century, however, some directories list a date of death for an individual who had died since the last directory was compiled if that information was provided to the publisher, usually by a related person residing at the same address.

Unless a death date is provided or a man appears in one directory at a particular street address and his widow appears at the same address in the year following, you should not assume that you will find a death or probate record in the year immediately following his disappearance. This is especially true where older individuals (particularly widows) are involved. They may still be alive and living with children. It is also possible that a "widow" was actually a divorcee—particularly in the nineteenth century—and that her husband's death will not be found prior to her appearance as such in the directory. Nevertheless, even a date with which to begin a death or probate search is valuable.

Methodology

James Renwick and Ellen/Helen Gibson were married in Scotland in 1814. They had three known children: Andrew, born 1815; Alexander, born 1818; and Marion, born 1820. Sometime between 1820 and 1833, they immigrated to New York City (Manhattan). We first found James in the *1833–34 New York City Directory* at 406 Washington Street.[9] In the 1850 Manhattan census, Ellen was living alone, presumably as a widow.[10] A search of *Doggett's New York City Directories 1845–46* and *1846–47* revealed the following entries:

1845–46	1846–47
Renwick, Alexander, stonecutter, 400 Washington Renwick, James, boarding 400 Washington[11]	Renwick, Ellen, widow James, boarding, 400 Washington

In 1845–46 there was also a James Renwick, professor, living at another address. We can draw several conclusions from these entries. Additional research showed that Alexander, the son, was a mason by trade. The Alexander Renwick who appears at 400 Washington Street was a stonecutter. Thus, it is probable that the James Renwick also residing at that address is the ancestor. We verified this conclusion with the 1846–47 directory. Although neither Alexander nor James appears, the entry for "Renwick, Ellen, widow James, boarding 400 Washington" indicated that James had died sometime between 1845 and 1846. We knew from previous research that Alexander had moved to Pittsburgh by this time.

Manhattan death registers also exist for this time period. These records are arranged alphabetically by the first letter of each surname for each year. To search the entire 1840–50 decade would have been tedious and time consuming. A search in the 1845 death registers quickly yielded this entry:

5 June 1845
James Renwick, age 59
400 Washington St.
Disease of Heart
Place of burial: Scotch Presbyterian Cemetery
Sexton: C. A. Stewart[12]

As it turned out, this record quickly and efficiently provided the only mention of James Renwick's age at a given date.

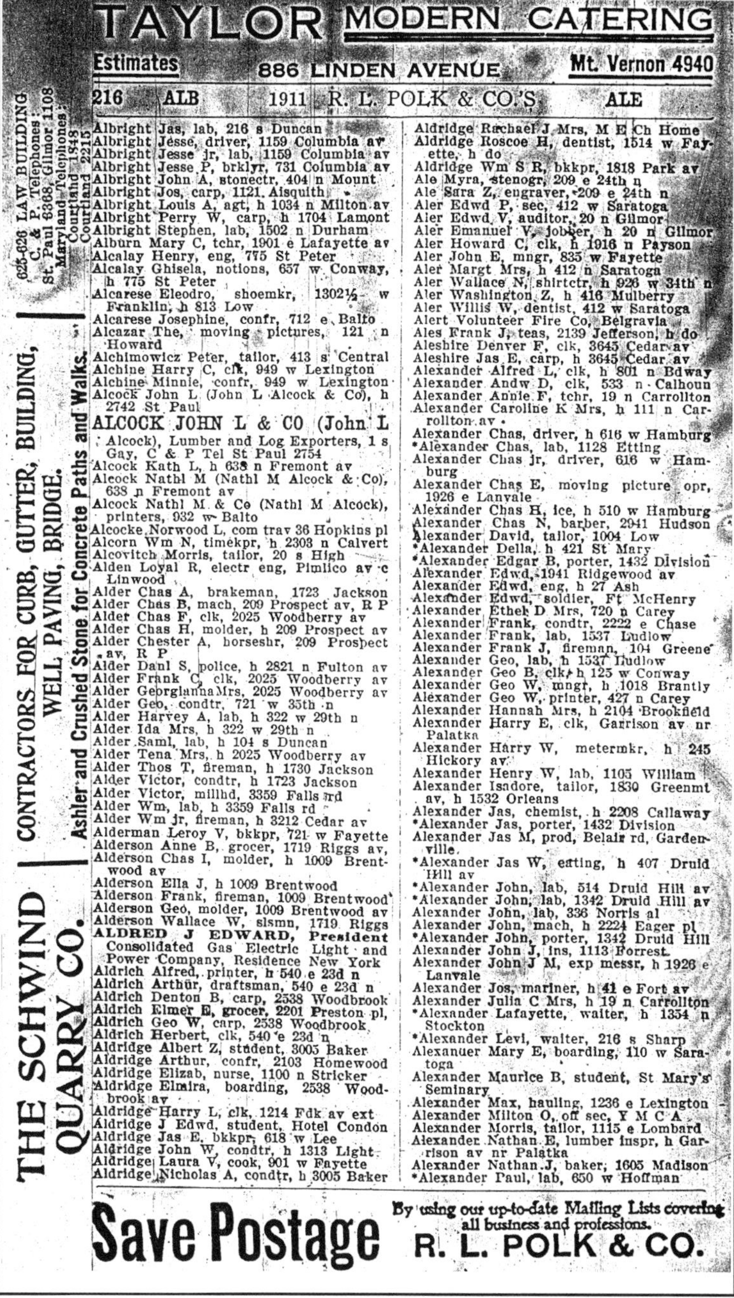

TAYLOR MODERN CATERING
Estimates 886 LINDEN AVENUE Mt. Vernon 4940

216 ALB 1911 R. L. POLK & CO.'S ALE

THE SCHWIND QUARRY CO. | CONTRACTORS FOR CURB, GUTTER, BUILDING, WELL PAVING, BRIDGE. Ashler and Crushed Stone for Concrete Paths and Walks. | 625-628 LAW BUILDING C. & P. Telephones: St. Paul 6368, Gilmor 1108 Maryland Telephones: Courtland 1848 Courtland 2215

Albright Jas, lab, 216 s Duncan
Albright Jesse, driver, 1159 Columbia av
Albright Jesse jr, lab, 1159 Columbia av
Albright Jesse P, brklyr, 731 Columbia av
Albright John A, stonectr, 404 n Mount
Albright Jos, carp, 1121 Aisquith
Albright Louis A, agt, h 1034 n Milton av
Albright Perry W, carp, h 1704 Lamont
Albright Stephen, lab, 1502 n Durham
Alburn Mary C, tchr, 1901 e Lafayette av
Alcalay Henry, eng, 775 St Peter
Alcalay Ghisela, notions, 657 w Conway, h 775 St Peter
Alcarese Eleodro, shoemkr, 1302½ w Franklin, h 813 Low
Alcarese Josephine, confr, 712 e Balto
Alcazar The, moving pictures, 121 n Howard
Alchimowicz Peter, tailor, 413 s Central
Alchine Harry C, clk, 949 w Lexington
Alchine Minnie, confr, 949 w Lexington
Alcock John L (John L Alcock & Co), h 2742 St Paul
ALCOCK JOHN L & CO (John L Alcock), Lumber and Log Exporters, 1 s Gay, C & P Tel St Paul 2754
Alcock Kath L, h 638 n Fremont av
Alcock Nathl M (Nathl M Alcock & Co), 638 n Fremont av
Alcock Nathl M & Co (Nathl M Alcock), printers, 932 w Balto
Alcocke Norwood L, com trav 36 Hopkins pl
Alcorn Wm N, timekpr, h 2303 n Calvert
Alcovitch Morris, tailor, 20 s High
Alden Loyal R, electr eng, Pimlico av c Linwood
Alder Chas A, brakeman, 1723 Jackson
Alder Chas B, mach, 209 Prospect av, R P
Alder Chas F, clk, 2025 Woodberry av
Alder Chas H, molder, h 209 Prospect av
Alder Chester A, horseshr, 209 Prospect av, R P
Alder Danl S, police, h 2821 n Fulton av
Alder Frank C, clk, 2025 Woodberry av
Alder Georgianna Mrs, 2025 Woodberry av
Alder Geo, condtr, 721 w 35th n
Alder Harvey A, lab, h 322 w 29th n
Alder Ida Mrs, h 322 w 29th n
Alder Saml, lab, h 104 s Duncan
Alder Tena Mrs, h 2025 Woodberry av
Alder Thos T, fireman, h 1730 Jackson
Alder Victor, condtr, h 1723 Jackson
Alder Victor, millhd, 3359 Falls rd
Alder Wm, lab, h 3359 Falls rd
Alder Wm jr, fireman, h 3212 Cedar av
Alderman Leroy V, bkkpr, 721 w Fayette
Alderson Anne B, grocer, 1719 Riggs av,
Alderson Chas I, molder, h 1009 Brentwood av
Alderson Ella J, h 1009 Brentwood
Alderson Frank, fireman, 1009 Brentwood
Alderson Geo, molder, 1009 Brentwood av
Alderson Wallace W, slsmn, 1719 Riggs
ALDRED J EDWARD, President Consolidated Gas Electric Light and Power Company, Residence New York
Aldrich Alfred, printer, h 540 e 23d n
Aldrich Arthur, draftsman, 540 e 23d n
Aldrich Denton B, carp, 2538 Woodbrook
Aldrich Elmer E, grocer, 2201 Preston pl,
Aldrich Geo W, carp, 2538 Woodbrook
Aldrich Herbert, clk, 540 e 23d n
Aldridge Albert Z, student, 3005 Baker
Aldridge Arthur, confr, 2103 Homewood
Aldridge Elizab, nurse, 1100 n Stricker
Aldridge Elmira, boarding, 2538 Woodbrook av
Aldridge Harry L, clk, 1214 Fdk av ext
Aldridge J Edwd, student, Hotel Condon
Aldridge Jas E, bkkpr, 618 w Lee
Aldridge John W, condtr, h 1313 Light
Aldridge Laura V, cook, 901 w Fayette
Aldridge Nicholas A, condtr, h 3005 Baker
Aldridge Rachael J Mrs, M E Ch Home
Aldridge Roscoe H, dentist, 1514 w Fayette, h do
Aldridge Wm S R, bkkpr, 1818 Park av
Ale Myra, stenogr, 209 e 24th n
Ale Sara Z, engraver, 209 e 24th n
Aler Edwd P, sec, 412 w Saratoga
Aler Edwd V, auditor, 20 n Gilmor
Aler Emanuel V, jobber, h 20 n Gilmor
Aler Howard C, clk, h 1916 n Payson
Aler John E, mngr, 835 w Fayette
Aler Margt Mrs, h 412 n Saratoga
Aler Wallace N, shirtctr, h 926 w 34th n
Aler Washington Z, h 416 Mulberry
Aler Willis W, dentist, 412 w Saratoga
Alert Volunteer Fire Co, Belgravia
Ales Frank J, teas, 2139 Jefferson, h do
Aleshire Denver F, clk, 3645 Cedar av
Aleshire Jas E, carp, h 3645 Cedar av
Alexander Alfred L, clk, h 801 n Bdway
Alexander Andw D, clk, 533 n Calhoun
Alexander Annie F, tchr, 19 n Carrollton
Alexander Caroline K Mrs, h 111 n Carrollton av
Alexander Chas, driver, h 616 w Hamburg
*Alexander Chas, lab, 1128 Etting
Alexander Chas jr, driver, 616 w Hamburg
Alexander Chas E, moving picture opr, 1926 e Lanvale
Alexander Chas H, ice, h 510 w Hamburg
Alexander Chas N, barber, 2941 Hudson
Alexander David, tailor, 1004 Low
*Alexander Della, h 421 St Mary
*Alexander Edgar B, porter, 1432 Division
Alexander Edwd, 1941 Ridgewood av
Alexander Edwd, eng, h 27 Ash
Alexander Edwd, soldier, Ft McHenry
Alexander Ethel D Mrs, 720 n Carey
Alexander Frank, condtr, 2222 e Chase
Alexander Frank, lab, 1537 Ludlow
Alexander Frank J, fireman, 104 Greene
Alexander Geo, lab, h 1537 Ludlow
Alexander Geo B, clk, h 125 w Conway
Alexander Geo W, mngr, h 1018 Brantly
Alexander Geo W, printer, 427 n Carey
Alexander Hannah Mrs, h 2104 Brookfield
Alexander Harry E, clk, Garrison av nr Palatka
Alexander Harry W, metermkr, h 245 Hickory av
Alexander Henry W, lab, 1105 William
Alexander Isadore, tailor, 1830 Greenmt av, h 1532 Orleans
Alexander Jas, chemist, h 2208 Callaway
*Alexander Jas, porter, 1432 Division
Alexander Jas M, prod, Belair rd, Gardenville
*Alexander Jas W, eating, h 407 Druid Hill av
*Alexander John, lab, 514 Druid Hill av
*Alexander John, lab, 1342 Druid Hill av
Alexander John, lab, 336 Norris al
Alexander John, mach, h 2224 Eager pl
*Alexander John, porter, 1342 Druid Hill
Alexander John J, ins, 1113 Forrest
Alexander John J M, exp messr, h 1926 e Lanvale
Alexander Jos, mariner, h 41 e Fort av
Alexander Julia C Mrs, h 19 n Carrollton
*Alexander Lafayette, waiter, h 1354 n Stockton
*Alexander Levi, waiter, 216 s Sharp
Alexander Mary E, boarding, 110 w Saratoga
Alexander Maurice B, student, St Mary's Seminary
Alexander Max, hauling, 1236 e Lexington
Alexander Milton O, off sec, Y M C A
Alexander Morris, tailor, 1115 e Lombard
Alexander Nathan E, lumber inspr, h Garrison av nr Palatka
Alexander Nathan J, baker, 1605 Madison
*Alexander Paul, lab, 650 w Hoffman

Save Postage By using our up-to-date Mailing Lists covering all business and professions. R. L. POLK & CO.

Figure 8-5. From R. L. Polk and Co. 1911 city directory for Baltimore, Maryland.

Using Church Records with Directories

You can use city directories to gain access to church records. In most major cities, civil marriage records have existed longer than in rural areas. In Philadelphia, for example, civil marriages have been recorded since 1860, while, in the rest of Pennsylvania, the normal starting date is 1885. Similarly, Pittsburgh records begin in 1875. Since there was little governmental apparatus to record marriages effectively, it was up to the clergyman who performed the service to return the information to the city authorities. In states where marriages were recorded at the county level, large cities benefited from this registration by being included on that level.

Whatever the circumstances under which marriages were recorded, the information given is very similar: the names of the bride and groom, the license date, the marriage date, sometimes names of witnesses, and almost always the name of the clergyman or magistrate who performed the marriage.

Methodology

According to Philadelphia's 1900 census, Christian and Sophia Hochwald had been married for thirty-eight years.[13] Christian had lived in Philadelphia before this date, so a check in the marriage registers might determine Sophia Hochwald's maiden name. The microfilm copy of the Board of Health marriage registers for 1862 was extremely faded but was clear enough to find a possible marriage entry on 3 May 1862.[14] Reverend G. Wiehle performed the marriage, and his address was 531 St. John Street. The Philadelphia city directories showed that this man was the pastor of the Salem German Reformed Church on St. John Street.[15] Now a check in church records can be made for this couple's marriage, membership, and children's baptisms. See the sections on telephone and religious directories for information on how to locate such records.

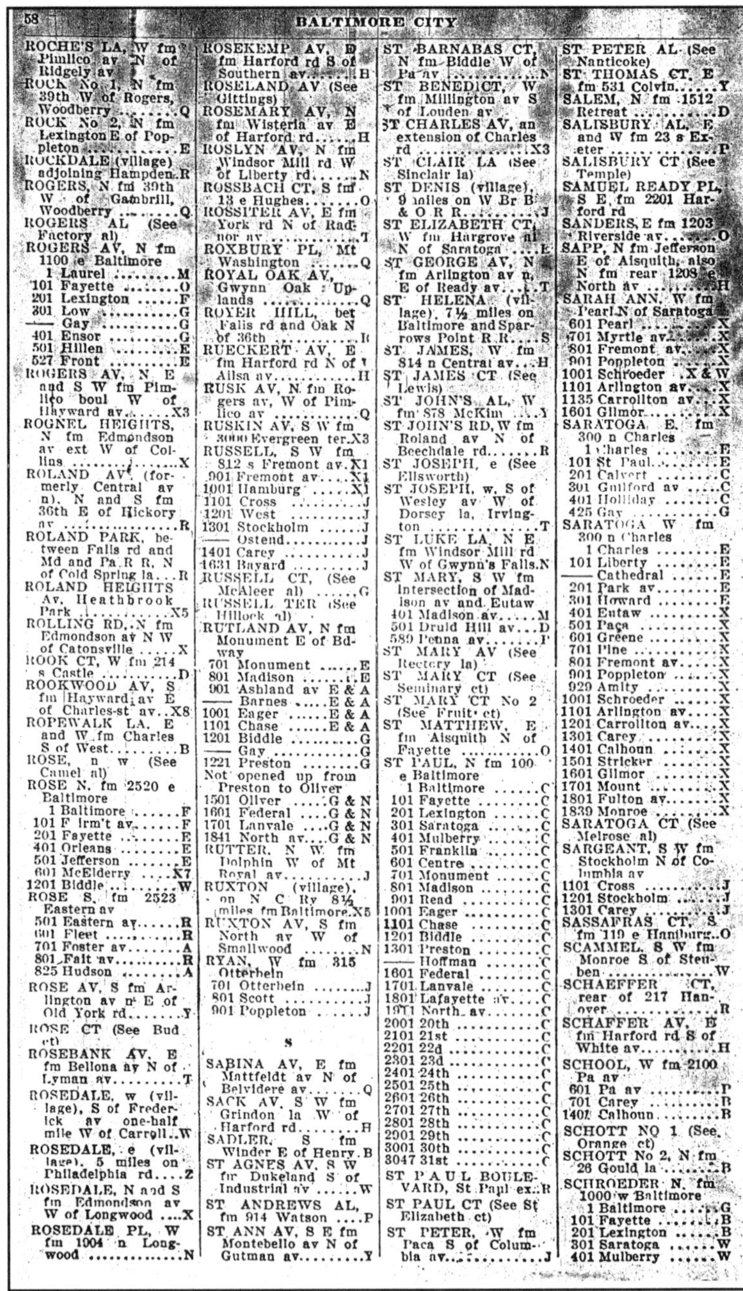

58 BALTIMORE CITY

ROCHE'S LA, W fm Pimlico av N of Ridgely av
ROCK No 1, N fm 39th W of Rogers, Woodberry ....Q
ROCK No 2, N fm Lexington E of Poppleton ....E
ROCKDALE (village) adjoining Hampden..R
ROGERS, N fm 39th W of Gambrill, Woodberry ....Q
ROGERS AL (See Factory al)
ROGERS AV, N fm 1100 e Baltimore
1 Laurel ....M
101 Fayette ....O
201 Lexington ......F
301 Low ....G
—— Gay ....G
401 Ensor ....G
501 Hillen ....E
527 Front ....E
ROGERS AV, N E and S W fm Pimlico boul W of Hayward av.......X3
ROGNEL HEIGHTS, N fm Edmondson av ext W of Collins X
ROLAND AV (formerly Central av n), N and S fm 36th E of Hickory av ....R
ROLAND PARK, between Falls rd and Md and Pa R R, N of Cold Spring la...R
ROLAND HEIGHTS Av, Heathbrook Park X5
ROLLING RD, N fm Edmondson av N W of Catonsville X
ROOK CT, W fm 214 s Castle ....D
ROOKWOOD AV, S fm Hayward av E of Charles-st av..X8
ROPEWALK LA, E and W fm Charles S of West..........B
ROSE, n w (See Camel al)
ROSE N, fm 2520 e Baltimore
1 Baltimore ......F
101 Firm't av.......F
201 Fayette ....E
401 Orleans ....E
501 Jefferson ......E
601 McElderry X7
1201 Biddle ....W
ROSE S, fm 2523 Eastern av
501 Eastern av......R
601 Fleet ....R
701 Foster av.......A
801 Fait av.........R
825 Hudson ....A
ROSE AV, S fm Arlington av n E of Old York rd.......Y
ROSE CT (See Bud ct)
ROSEBANK AV, E fm Bellona av N of Lyman av.........T
ROSEDALE, w (village), S of Frederick av one-half mile W of Carroll..W
ROSEDALE, e (village), 5 miles on Philadelphia rd....Z
ROSEDALE, N and S fm Edmondson av W of Longwood X
ROSEDALE PL, W fm 1004 n Longwood ....N
ROSEKEMP AV, E fm Harford rd S of Southern av.......H
ROSELAND AV (See Gittings)
ROSEMARY AV, N fm Wisteria av E of Harford rd......H
ROSLYN AV, N fm Windsor Mill rd W of Liberty rd......N
ROSSBACH CT, S fm 13 e Hughes.......O
ROSSITER AV, E fm York rd N of Radnor av ....T
ROXBURY PL, Mt Washington ....Q
ROYAL OAK AV, Gwynn Oak Uplands ....Q
ROYER HILL, bet Falls rd and Oak N of 36th ....R
RUECKERT AV, E fm Harford rd N of Ailsa av............H
RUSK AV, N fm Rogers av, W of Pimlico av ....Q
RUSKIN AV, S W fm 3000 Evergreen ter.X3
RUSSELL, S W fm 812 s Fremont av.X1
901 Fremont av....X1
1001 Hamburg X1
1101 Cross ....J
1201 West ....J
1301 Stockholm ......J
—— Ostend...........J
1401 Carey ....J
1631 Bayard ....J
RUSSELL CT, (See McAleer al) ......G
RUSSELL TER (See Hillock al)
RUTLAND AV, N fm Monument E of Bdway
701 Monument ......E
801 Madison ....E
901 Ashland av E & A
—— Barnes .....E & A
1001 Eager ......E & A
1101 Chase ......E & A
1201 Biddle ....G
—— Gay ....G
1221 Preston ....G
Not opened up from Preston to Oliver
1501 Oliver .....G & N
1601 Federal ....G & N
1701 Lanvale ....G & N
1841 North av....G & N
RUTTER, N W fm Dolphin W of Mt Royal av...........J
RUXTON (village), on N C Ry 8½ miles fm Baltimore..X5
RUXTON AV, S fm North av W of Smallwood ....N
RYAN, W fm 315 Otterbein
701 Otterbein ....J
801 Scott ....J
901 Poppleton ......J

S

SABINA AV, E fm Mattfeldt av N of Belvidere av.......Q
SACK AV, S W fm Grindon la W of Harford rd.........H
SADLER, S fm Winder E of Henry.B
ST AGNES AV, S W fm Dukeland S of Industrial av ......W
ST ANDREWS AL, fm 914 Watson ....P
ST ANN AV, S E fm Montebello av N of Gutman av.........Y
ST BARNABAS CT, N fm Biddle W of Pa av ....N
ST BENEDICT, W fm Millington av S of Louden av
ST CHARLES AV, an extension of Charles rd X3
ST CLAIR LA (See Sinclair la)
ST DENIS (village), 9 miles on W Br B & O R R...........J
ST ELIZABETH CT, W fm Hargrove al N of Saratoga ....E
ST GEORGE AV, N fm Arlington av n, E of Ready av....T
ST HELENA (village), 7½ miles on Baltimore and Sparrows Point R R....S
ST JAMES, W fm 814 n Central av...H
ST JAMES CT (See Lewis)
ST JOHN'S AL, W fm 878 McKim ....Y
ST JOHN'S RD, W fm Roland av N of Beechdale rd.......R
ST JOSEPH, e (See Ellsworth)
ST JOSEPH, w, S of Wesley av W of Dorsey la, Irvington ....T
ST LUKE LA, N E fm Windsor Mill rd W of Gwynn's Falls.N
ST MARY, S W fm intersection of Madison av and Eutaw
401 Madison av.....M
501 Druid Hill av...D
589 Penna av.......P
ST MARY AV (See Rectory la)
ST MARY CT (See Seminary ct)
ST MARY CT No 2 (See Fruit ct)
ST MATTHEW, E fm Aisquith N of Fayette ....O
ST PAUL, N fm 100 e Baltimore
1 Baltimore C
101 Fayette C
201 Lexington C
301 Saratoga C
401 Mulberry C
501 Franklin C
601 Centre C
701 Monument C
801 Madison C
901 Read C
1001 Eager C
1101 Chase C
1201 Biddle C
1301 Preston C
—— Hoffman C
1601 Federal C
1701 Lanvale C
1801 Lafayette av....C
1911 North av.......C
2001 20th C
2101 21st C
2201 22d C
2301 23d C
2401 24th C
2501 25th C
2601 26th C
2701 27th C
2801 28th C
2901 29th C
3001 30th C
3047 31st C
ST PAUL BOULEVARD, St Paul ex..R
ST PAUL CT (See St Elizabeth ct)
ST PETER, W fm Paca S of Columbia av..............J
ST PETER AL (See Nanticoke)
ST THOMAS CT, E fm 531 Colvin......Y
SALEM, N fm 1512 Retreat ....D
SALISBURY AL, E and W fm 23 s Exeter ....P
SALISBURY CT (See Temple)
SAMUEL READY PL, S E fm 2201 Harford rd
SANDERS, E fm 1203 Riverside av........O
SAPP, N fm Jefferson E of Aisquith, also N fm rear 1208 e North av ....H
SARAH ANN, W fm Pearl N of Saratoga
601 Pearl X
701 Myrtle av.......X
801 Fremont av......X
901 Poppleton X
1001 Schroeder ..X & W
1101 Arlington av....X
1135 Carrollton av...X
1601 Gilmor..........X
SARATOGA, E, fm 300 n Charles
1 Charles ....E
101 St Paul.........E
201 Calvert C
301 Guilford av C
401 Holliday C
425 Gay ....G
SARATOGA W fm 300 n Charles
1 Charles ....E
101 Liberty ....E
—— Cathedral ......E
201 Park av.........E
301 Howard ....E
401 Eutaw X
501 Paca X
601 Greene X
701 Pine X
801 Fremont av.....X
901 Poppleton X
929 Amity X
1001 Schroeder X
1101 Arlington av....X
1201 Carrollton av...X
1301 Carey X
1401 Calhoun X
1501 Stricker X
1601 Gilmor X
1701 Mount X
1801 Fulton av.......X
1839 Monroe X
SARATOGA CT (See Melrose al)
SARGEANT, S W fm Stockholm N of Columbia av
1101 Cross ....J
1201 Stockholm ......J
1301 Carey ....J
SASSAFRAS CT, S fm 119 e Hamburg..O
SCAMMEL, S W fm Monroe S of Steuben ....W
SCHAEFFER CT, rear of 217 Hanover ....R
SCHAFFER AV, E fm Harford rd S of White av..........H
SCHOOL, W fm 2100 Pa av
601 Pa av ....P
701 Carey ....B
1401 Calhoun.........B
SCHOTT NO 1 (See Orange ct)
SCHOTT No 2, N fm 26 Gould la ....B
SCHROEDER N, fm 1000 w Baltimore
1 Baltimore ......G
101 Fayette ....B
201 Lexington ......B
301 Saratoga ....W
401 Mulberry ....W

Figure 8-6. From R. L. Polk and Co. 1911 city directory for Baltimore.

Using Naturalization and Land Records with Directories

It may seem odd to group naturalization and land records together, but methodologically they are very similar. They both reflect the parameters of residence in an area. If a person owned a home in a city, there should be some record of its purchase when the family moved into the city and its sale when the family changed residences or moved out of the city. Finding the first and last years of residence narrows down the search for these land records, which, in a city like New York or Boston, can be voluminous.

Similarly, finding an immigrant's first year of residence in a city narrows down the naturalization records you'll have to search. In cases where these records are indexed, knowing that one of two naturalized immigrants of the same name lived in the city before the other may differentiate the two.

Methodology

James Renwick appeared in the city directories of New York beginning in 1833. He made his declaration of intention on 3 February 1835.[16] During that time period, declarations were usually filed after three years of residence; the information in James Renwick's case corresponds nicely with his residence in New York City. He may have arrived too late in 1832 to be included in that year's directory.

Renwick is an uncommon name, but this method, for both land and naturalization records, works well when the surname is more common and differentiation using auxiliary sources is necessary.

Telephone Directories

Telephone directories are the descendants of city directories, with the criterion for inclusion simply being subscription to the phone service. Telephone directories are useful as locators in place and time—but primarily for twentieth-century research. However, they won't include such useful information as occupation or the names of spouses and children—unless the subscriber has requested and paid for this information to be included. Moreover, there are always unlisted numbers and persons who do not wish their addresses or given names to be printed even if their phone numbers are. The usefulness of telephone directories in genealogy is, therefore, somewhat limited.

Nevertheless, a book "with no plot, but a cast of thousands" can't be all bad. When used in conjunction with other sources, telephone directories can help to locate living distant relatives or modern successors to nineteenth-century churches and funeral homes.

STREETS	HOUSE NOS.	E. D.
St Joseph West	(outside city)	---
St. Luke Lane	(outside city)	---
St. Mary	---	155;280
St. Mary Avenue	(see Rectory Lane)	---
St. Mary Court	(see Seminary Court)	---
St. Mary Court No. 2	(see Fruit Court)	---
St. Matthew	---	52;51;76
St. Paul	(0-99) odd	47
	(0-99) even	37
	(100-200)	47
	(300-400)	46 ✓
	(500)	159
	(600) odd	160
	(600) even	159
	(700)	160;159
	(800-1000) odd	160
	(800-1000) even	161
	(1100) odd	174
	(1100) even	161
	(1200-1400)	174
	~~(1500-1600)~~	~~175~~
	(1900) odd	178
	(1700) even	179
	(1800)	178
	(1900) odd	180
	(1900) even	181
	(2000-2100)	181
	(2200-2300)	184
	(2400-2500) odd	187
	(2400-2500) even	188
	(2600-2800) odd	192
	(2600-2800) even	191
	(2900) odd	192
	(2900) even	193
	(3000-3200)	193
	(3300-end)	195

Figure 8-7. From a 1910 street index for Baltimore; FHL microfilm 6,331,480, pt. 3.

Methodology

In the early 1990s I was contacted by a man from Australia who was seeking his father—an American sailor who had been stationed there in the closing days of World War II. The client had only his father's name and the name of the ship on which his father had served. Through naval muster rolls available at the National Archives, it was determined that his father had enlisted in a certain Midwestern city. City directories for that city in 1945 and 1946 showed the client's father living with his parents and a brother who was also in the navy, but their names disappeared from the city directories in the 1950s without a clue as to where they had gone. The Social Security Death Index revealed the death of the brother on the West Coast in the early 1970s, and his death certificate indicated that the client's father was then living in New England—but no one of that name listed with a New England address in PhoneDisk USA, a nationwide telephone database on CD was the right man.

While the surname was not as common as Smith, for example, and the given names were relatively uncommon, dozens of entries for the names of the client's father and brother were found in PhoneDisk USA. Nevertheless, letters and self-addressed, stamped envelopes were sent to each of the addresses. Some were returned as undeliverable—the individual had moved or died—and many were returned by the addressees, indicating no knowledge of the persons named in the letter, which had been carefully worded to avoid a negative response if the client's father did not wish to be found.

At last, a response was received from the client's father. He was among those listed in PhoneDisk USA and was living in a Southern state. Without this current nationwide telephone directory, locating the client's father would have been like looking for a needle in a haystack.

PhoneDisk USA and similar CD-ROM telephone directories are becoming obsolete because of the wide availability of online telephone databases. Not all of these databases provide e-mail addresses, and in cases where contacting a long-lost relative may be a sensitive matter (especially in cases of adoption), the old-fashioned letter with a S.A.S.E. may be more advisable.

County and Regional Business Directories

The business directory, as a distinct entity, evolved partly from special sections in city directories and partly from the needs

Table 8-1. Directories on Microform

This table serves two purposes. The first is to list those cities in each state for which Research Publications has microform directories and for which years. Please note that some years within date ranges may not be available and that other years not represented in this table may now be available. Check with your library or archive for the most up-to-date information.

The second purpose is to show compatibility with the 1910 census by showing whether Soundex or Miracode indexes exist for a city or if there is an enumeration district map or street index for a city. Those cities and states that are not included in the Research Publications microform series, but for which 1910 finding aids exist, are bracketed.

State/City	Date/1910 Census Compatibility
Alabama:	Soundex (entire state)
Birmingham	1902–35/Soundex (Alabama Cities)
Greene County	1855/56, 1862–1935
Mobile	1837–1935/Soundex (Alabama Cities)
Montgomery	1880–1935/Soundex (Alabama Cities)
Arizona:	
Phoenix	1903–35/Street Index
Tucson	1902–35
Arkansas:	Miracode (entire state)
Little Rock	1871–1901
Texarkana	1904–34
California:	Miracode (entire state)
Bakersfield	1915–35
Fresno	1926–35
Long Beach	1907–35/Street Index
Los Angeles	1873–1935/Street Index
Marysville	1853–58
Nevada City	1856
Oakland	1869–81, 1902–35
Sacramento	1851–81, 1902–35
San Diego	1903–35/Street Index
San Francisco	1850–1934/Street Index
Stockton	1852–56, 1902–35
Tuolumne Co.	1856
Colorado:	
Colorado Springs	1902–35
Denver	1859–1935/Street Index
Grand Junction	1902–35
Leadville	1882–1903, 1905–11
Connecticut:	
Regional	1849–58
Ansonia	1902–35
Bristol	1902–35
Bridgeport	1855–81, 1902–35/Enumeration District Map
Danbury	1882–1935
Hartford	1799–1935/Enumeration District Map
Meriden	1872–81
Middletown	1868–1931
New Haven	1840–1935/Enumeration District Map
New London	1855–60, 1902–35
Norwich	1846–1935
Stamford	1882–1933
Southington	1882–1935
[Waterbury]	Enumeration District Map
Delaware:	
Regional	1859/60
Wilmington	1814–1935
District of Columbia:	
Washington	1822–1935/Street Index
Florida:	Miracode (entire state)
Jacksonville	1902–35
Miami	1916–35
Orlando	1902–35
Pensacola	1903–34
St. Petersburg	1914–35
Tampa	1903–35/Street Index
Georgia:	Soundex (entire state)
Regional	1850
Atlanta	1859–1935/Soundex (Georgia Cities)/Street Index
Augusta	1841–59/Soundex (Georgia Cities)
Columbus	1859/60, 1906–34
Savannah	1848–1934/Soundex (Georgia Cities)
Hawaii:	AISI Index
Honolulu	1902–36
Idaho:	Idaho G.S. Index
Boise	1901–35
Pocatello	1902–35
Illinois:	Miracode (entire state)
Regional	1847–60
Alton	1858
Belleville	1860, 1901–35
Bureau County	1858/59
Chicago	1839–1929/Street Index

State/City	Date/1910 Census Compatibility
Evanston	1902–35
Galena	1854–59
Joliet	1872–1935
Kane County	1857–60
Moline	1855–59, 1901–35
Peoria	1844–1935/Street Index
Quincy	1855–60
Randolph County	
Rockford	1857–60, 1902–35
Rock Island	1855–59, 1902–35
Springfield	1855–60, 1901–35
Will County	1859/60
Indiana:	
Regional	1858–61
Evansville	1858–1934/Enumeration District Map
Fort Wayne	1858–81, 1902–35/Street Index
Gary	1908–35/Street Index
Indianapolis	1855–1935/Street Index
Jefferson County	1859
Lafayette	1858–59, 1901–35
Lawrenceburg	1859/60
Logansport	1859/60
Madison	1859–60
New Albany	1856–60, 1903–36
Richmond	1857–61, 1901–35
Shelbyville	1860/61
[South Bend]	Street Index
Terre Haute	1858–60/Enumeration District Map
Iowa:	
Regional/State	1846, 1902–23
Burlington	1856–59, 1902–35
Davenport	1853–81
Des Moines	1866–1935/Enumeration District Map/Street Index (FHL)
Dubuque	1856–1929
Henry County	1859/60
Iowa City	1857, 1919–34
Keokuk	1854–60
Muscatine	1856–60
Sioux City	1884–1935
Kansas:	Miracode (entire state)
Atchison	1859–61
Emporia	1902–35
[Kansas City]	Street Index
Leavenwoth	1860–61, 1902–34
Ottawa	1903–33
Topeka	1868–80, 1902–35
[Wichita]	Street Index
Kentucky:	Miracode (entire state)
Regional	1859/60
Covington	1861–87, 1902–32

State/City	Date/1910 Census Compatibility
Lexington	1806–82, 1902–35
Louisville	1832–1935
Louisiana:	Soundex (entire state)
New Orleans	1805–1935/Miracode (Louisiana Cities)
Maine:	
Regional	1849–56
Augusta	1861–82, 1886–89, 1892–98, 1902–35
Bangor	1834–59
Biddeford	1856–57, 1902–34
Portland	1823–1935/Enumeration District Map
Saco	1849, 1902–34 (with Biddeford)
Westbrook	1902–34
Maryland:	
Baltimore	1752/1796–1930/Street Index
Frederick	1859/60
Massachusetts:	
Regional	1849–59
Boston	1789–1935/Enumeration District Map/Street Index (FHL)
Brockton	1874–80, 1882–1935/Enumeration District Map
Brighton	1850
Brookline	1868–81
Cambridge	1847–1931/Enumeration District Map
Charlestown	1831–74
Chelsea	1847–80, 1902–35
Clinton	1856, 1902–35
Dorchester	1850
East Boston	1848–52
Fall River	1853–1935/Enumeration District Map
Fitchburg	1847–60
Gloucester	1860, 1882–1935
Haverhill	1853–61, 1902–35
Holyoke	1882–1935/Enumeration District Map
Lawrence	1847–61/Enumeration District Map
Leominster	1882–1935
Lowell	1832–1935/Enumeration District Map
Lunenburg	1834
Lynn	1832–80, 1902–35/Enumeration District Map
Malden	1868–81
Medford	1849, 1902–30
Milford	1856, 1901–34
New Bedford	1836–82, 1902–34/Enumeration District Map
Newburyport	1849–60, 1902–36
Pittsfield	1859/60
Plymouth	1846–60
Quincy	1868–81
Roxbury	1847–60
Salem	1837–81, 1902–35

State/City	Date/1910 Census Compatibility
Massachusetts (cont.):	
Somerville	1851/Enumeration District Map
South Boston	1852
Southbridge	1854
Springfield	1845–81/Enumeration District Map
Taunton	1850–59, 1902–35
Woburn	1868–77
Worcester	1828–1935/Enumeration District Map
Michigan:	Miracode (entire state)
Regional	1856–60
Ann Arbor	1902–35
Battle Creek	1901–35
Coldwater	1902–23
Detroit	1837–1934/Street Index
Grand Rapids	1856–1935/Street Index
Kalamazoo	1902–35
Petoskey	1903–35
Minnesota:	
Duluth	1881–1935/Enumeration District Map
Minneapolis	1865–1935/Enumeration District Map/ Street Index (FHL)
St. Anthony	1859/60
St. Paul	1856–1935/Enumeration District Map
Mississippi:	Soundex (entire state)
Jackson	1860
Vicksburg	1860
Missouri:	Miracode (entire state)
Regional	1860
Kansas City	1859–1921
St. Joseph	1905–33
St. Louis	1821–1935
Montana:	
Territory	1868–80
Billings	1902–35
Butte	1902–34
Great Falls	1903–35
Livingston	1904–35
Nebraska:	
Hastings	1903–34
Omaha	1866–1935/Street Index
Nevada:	
Territory	1862–81
New Hampshire:	
Regional	1849
Concord	1830–61, 1902–35
Dover	1830–81, 1902–35
Great Falls	1848
Keene	1827–31, 1871–80, 1902–35

State/City	Date/1910 Census Compatibility
Manchester	1844–1935/Enumeration District Map
Nashua	1841–82, 1902–35
New Ipswich	1858
Peterborough	1830
Portsmouth	1817–61, 1903–34
New Jersey:	
Regional	1850/51
Atlantic City	1902–35
[Bayonne]	Enumeration District Map
Camden	1860, 1863–1931/ Enumeration District Map
Elizabeth	1865–1935/Street Index/ Enumeration District Map
Essex County	1859
Hoboken	(with Jersey City Enumeration District Map)
Jersey City	1849–1901/Enumeration District Map
Newark	1835–1935/Street Index/Enumeration District Map
New Brunswick	1855–61
Passaic	Enumeration District Map
Paterson	1855–1935/Street Index/Enumeration District Map
Trenton	1844–81, 1902–35/Enumeration District Map
New Mexico:	
Albuquerque	1905–35
New York:	
Regional	1850–59
Albany	1813–1935/Enumeration District Map
Auburn	1857–60, 1861–81, 1902–35
Binghamton	1857–60, 1909–24
[Bronx]	Street Index (w/Manhattan)
Brooklyn	1822–1934/Street Index
Buffalo	1828–1935/Enumeration District Map
Cortland	1902–35
Elmira	1857–1935
Geneva	1857, 1902–35
Greenpoint	1854
Hudson	1851–57, 1902–35
Ithaca	1882–1901, 1903–35
Kingston	1857–58, 1902–35
Long Island	check phase one
Middletown	1857/58, 1905–35
Morrisania	1853
Newburgh	1856–76, 1902–35
New York City	1786–1934/Street Index (Manhattan)
Ogdensburg	1857
Oswego	1852–59, 1902–35
Poughkeepsie	1843–61, 1902–35
[Queens]	Street Index(FHL)/Enumeration District Map
Rochester	1827–1935/Enumeration District Map
Rome	1857–60, 1903–34

State/City	Date/1910 Census Compatibility
Schenectady	1841–61, 1902–35/Enumeration District Map
[Staten Island]	Street Index
Syracuse	1844–1935/Enumeration District Map
Troy	1829–1935
Utica	1817–1935/Enumeration District Map
Watertown	1840–55
Westchester Co.	1860/61
Williamsburg	1847–54
Yonkers	1859/60, 1902–31/Enumeration District Map
North Carolina:	Miracode (entire state)
Asheville	1902–24
[Charlotte]	Street Index
Greensboro	1903–35
Raleigh	1903–35
North Dakota:	
Fargo	1902–34
Ohio:	Miracode (entire state)
Regional	1853–61
Akron	1859–60/ Street Index
[Canton]	Street Index
Chillicothe	1855–61, 1902–34
Cincinnati	1819–1935/Street Index
Circleville	1859
Cleveland	1837–1935
Columbus	1843–1935
Dayton	1850–1935/Street Index
Delaware	1859–60, 1902–35
Hamilton	1858–59
Mansfield	1858/59, 1902–35
Marietta	1860/61, 1902–35
Mt. Vernon	1858/59
Portsmouth	1858–59, 1908–35
Sandusky	1855–78, 1902–35
Springfield	1852–60, 1902–35
Steubenville	1856/57, 1902–35
Toledo	1858–1935
[Youngstown]	Street Index
Zanesville	1851–61, 1902–36
Oklahoma:	Miracode (entire state)
Enid	1905–35
Oklahoma City	1902–35/Street Index
Tulsa	1909–35/Street Index
Oregon:	
Astoria	1902–34
Portland	1863–1935/Enumeration District Map
Pennsylvania:	Miracode (entire state)
Regional	1844–60
Carnegie	1902–35
Chester	1859/60, 1902–31
Erie	1853–1935/Street Index
Erie County	1859/60
Harrisburg	1839–1935
Lancaster	1843–60, 1903–35
Lancaster Co.	1843–60
Monongahela V.	1859
Norristown	1860/61, 1902–35
Philadelphia	1785–1935/Miracode (City)/ Street Index
Pittsburgh	1813–1935
Reading	1806/56–1935/Street Index
Scranton	1861–1935
Wilkes–Barre	1882–1919
Williamsport	1866–1934
West Chester	1857
Rhode Island:	
Regional	1849
East Providence	1902–35
Newport	1856–58
Pawtucket	1857/58, 1867–81, 1886, 1880–35/ Enumeration District Map
Providence	1824–1935/Enumeration District Map
Westerly	1884–86, 1888–90, 1892, 1894, 1896, 1898 1900–35
South Carolina:	Soundex (entire state)
Camden	1816/24
Charleston	1782–1935
Columbia	1859–60, 1903–35
South Dakota:	
Sioux Falls	1902–35
Tennessee:	Soundex (entire state)
Regional	1860/61
Chattanooga	1871–81, 1902–35/Soundex (Tennessee Cities)
Clarksville	1859/60
Knoxville	1869–1935/Soundex (Tennessee Cities)
Memphis	1849–1935/Soundex (Tennessee Cities)
Nashville	1853–1935/Soundex (Tennessee Cities)
Texas:	Soundex (entire state)
Amarillo	1903–35
Austin	1857, 1903–35
Beaumont	1903–35
Dallas	1875–1935
Fort Worth	1877–79, 1902–36
Galveston	1856–1935
Houston	1882–1935
San Antonio	1877–1935/Street Index
Waco	1882–1934
Utah:	
Logan	1904–35
Ogden	1882–1935

State/City	Date/1910 Census Compatibility
Utah (cont.):	
Salt Lake City	1867–1935/Enumeration District Map/ Street Index (FHL)
Vermont:	
Regional	1849–60
Barre	1902–35
Brattleboro	1902–35
Burlington	1865–1935
Virginia:	Soundex (entire state)
Regional	1852
Norfolk	1801/51–1935
Petersburg	1859, 1902–35
Richmond	1819–1935/Street Index
Wythe County	1857
Washington:	
Bellingham	1902–35
Everett	1902–35
Seattle	1872–1935/Street Index
[Spokane]	Enumeration District Map
[Tacoma]	Enumeration District Map
West Virginia:	Soundex (entire state)
Clarksburg	1905–35
Wheeling	1839–1934

State/City	Date/1910 Census Compatibility
Wisconsin:	
Regional	1857–59
Appleton	1882–1901, 1904–34
Beloit	1858
Fond du Lac	1857–57, 1903–34
Green Bay	1903–29
Janesville	1858–60
Kenosha	1858, 1903–35
Madison	1851–81, 1903–35
Milwaukee	1847–1935/Enumeration District Map
Mineral Point	1849
Oshkosh	1857, 1861–81, 1903–28
Racine	1850–59, 1902–35
Rock County	1857–58
Watertown	1902–35
Waukesha	1858
Whitewater	1858
Wyoming:	
Laramie	1908–35
Regional:	
The East	1846
Mississippi	1844
New England	1849–60
The South	1854
The West	1837
Western Reserve	1852

of people in sparsely populated rural areas to communicate their services to one another. Because the rural economy often centered on the county seat, these early business directories were usually organized by county or region. In addition to the names of farmers and businessmen, they contained advertisements of goods and services; although they were primarily business oriented, they also served as general directories in those rural areas. Much like a modern almanac, they often included other useful information.

A regional (multicounty, state, or market area) business directory combines a city directory's specialized business sections with a county directory's wide geographic market coverage. As communications developed, nineteenth-century manufacturers, farmers, and those with service-oriented businesses found that directories covering more than their own county were quite useful and even necessary. These regional business directories varied in comprehensiveness. The earlier ones, often called advertising directories, mentioned only those businesses that could afford to be included. By the late 1800s, however, statewide business directories listed nearly every place and a variety of businesses, from farms to pharmacies. County directories can also be found in nineteenth- and early-twentieth-century county histories and atlases.

Information obtained from county or regional business directories helps locate people in place and time. County business directories that include farmers, like city directories, narrow census searches to specific townships. This is especially useful when an ancestor married someone from another township in the same county and the marriage record doesn't state which township. Some county business directories also contain dates and places of birth, dates of marriage, length of residence in the town, names of children, and other biographical details on their subjects as well as names.

You can use regional business directories in the same way. A region can be defined as an entire state or a geographic area, such as a valley or a coast. If you know which state an ancestor lived in but not the exact place, regional directories can help, although they are less likely to give such extensive biographical information, and their coverage may be limited.

How to Use County and Regional Business Directories

The Gazetteer and Business Directory of Monroe County, New York for 1869–1870 is a typical county business directory. On the page displayed in figure 8-8, the residents of the rural town of Henrietta are listed alphabetically. The information following each name, when properly interpreted, is very enlightening. For example, the entry for Alvy Remington indicates that his post office was in West Henrietta; thus, it was the closest settlement as well. His land was in lot 10, range 6, according to the survey of the land company that originally owned the land. By occupation he was a farmer and owned ninety-five acres. If he had leased his land, this also would have been indicated.

There are three other Remingtons in Henrietta in this directory: George T., Seth W., and William T. Without knowing anything about the family, one could conclude that there is some relationship between Alvy, Seth, and William on the basis of the lot and range information. In fact, William and Seth were Alvah (the correct spelling) Remington's sons. William had fifty-seven acres, the directory tells us, while Seth had only one. A bit of family history provides a gloss on the directory information. Thomas Remington, Alvah's father, originally purchased lot 10, range 6, in the 1820s from a consortium of Dutch land speculators. Alvah bought out his brothers and sisters then distributed the land among his own children. The fact that Seth had only one acre in 1870 helps explain the relationship between father and son: when Alvah died in 1888, he left nothing to Seth's children because Seth had been unable to pay back a debt to his father before he had died in 1885.

Quirk, Mathew, (Brighton,) lot 11, R. 6, farmer 72.
Raas, Frederick, (West Henrietta,) lot 25, R. 5, farmer 23.
Raynor, Leonard, (West Henrietta,) lot 12, R. 6, farmer leases 90.
REEVE, JOHN, (Henrietta,)(*with Thomas,*) lot 22, R. 1, farmer 340.
Reeve, Thomas, (Henrietta,) (*with John,*) lot 22, R. 1, farmer 340.
Reeves, George, (West Brighton,) lot 1, R. 3, farmer 1½.
Remington, Alvy, (West Henrietta,) lot 10, R. 6, farmer 95.
Remington, George T., (Henrietta,) lot 22, R. 2, farmer 11.
Remington, Seth W., (West Henrietta,) lot 10, R. 6, farmer 1.
Remington, William T., (West Henrietta,) lot 10, R. 6, farmer 57.
Renner, John, (West Brighton,) lot 3, R. 5, farmer 21.
Richardson, David H., (Henrietta,) lot 10, R. 3, farmer 180.
Roberts, George M. C., (Henrietta,) lot 11, R. 3, farmer leases 116.
Sherman, Oliver B., (West Henrietta,) lot 25, R. 4, farmer 100.
Shilling, Frederick, (West Henrietta,) lot 23, R. 6, farmer 35.
Sholts, Henry, (West Brighton,) lot 4, R. 5, farmer 68.
Short, Andrew, (Henrietta,) lot 15, R. 3, farmer 34.
Sibbey, Elisha, (Henrietta,) lot 16, R. 1, farmer 99.
SIBLEY, ELISHA, (North Rush,) lot 18, Scott Tract, farmer 106.
SIMMONS, EDWARD, (Henrietta,) lot 16, R. 3.
Sipperly, John, (Henrietta,) lot 19, R. 2, farmer 50.
Skilton, William, (Henrietta,) lot 17, R. 1, farmer 30.
Slade, Hannah Mrs., (Henrietta,) lot 15, farmer 50.
Slow, Jacob, (West Henrietta,) lot 22, R. 5, wagon maker.
Smith, Charles J., (West Henrietta,) lot 31, R. 4, farmer 80.
Smith, David, (Henrietta,) lot 2, R. 2, retired farmer 80.

Figure 8-8. From Hamilton Child, *The Gazetteer and Business Directory of Monroe County, New York for 1869–1870* (Rochester, N.Y.: Erastus Darrow, 1870), 195.

One of the earliest regional directories is *The American Advertising Directory: Manufacturers and Dealers in American Goods for the Year 1831*. Most of the listings are in the Northeast manufacturing area, but places as far (in 1831) from the East Coast as Nashville, Tennessee, had at least one listing. This contrasts starkly with the *New Mexico Business Directory* for 1907–8, which mentions every city, town, and village in New Mexico as well as El Paso, Texas, and Denver, Colorado. The town of Central had 450 inhabitants, but only fifteen entries were given:

> CENTRAL
>
> Postoffice and important town in Grant county, 9 miles east of Silver City, the most convenient railroad point. Mining, stockraising, farming and fruitgrowing the principal industries. Population 450.
>
> Bayard Smelting & Mining Co, W D Murray mgr.
> Crowley J, postmaster, justice peace, drugs.
> GOULD BROS, general merchandise.
> Hamilton A, mines and mining
> Helde Mrs. G W, millinery and dressmaker.
> Link B T, fruitgrower and dairy.
> McMillen Geo, mines and mining.
> MURRAY BROS, general merchandise.
> MONTGOMERY & DALRYMPLE, meat market.
> Reed Mrs W, restaurant.
> Rendall L G, notary public.
> Rodgers Clark, fruitgrower.
> Stephens Chas, fruitgrower.
> SWEENEY W H, general merchandise.
> Wiley J A, saloon.[17]

Note that the postmaster was also the justice of the peace and pharmacist for the town. The directory does not list the men who worked on the fruit farms and in the mines. This 1912 directory is, however, more detailed and for a smaller region than the 1831 directory cited previously.

Special Problems

Business directories are limited in that the editor selected which businesses to include, sometimes based on subscription. If your ancestor was a businessman but was not mentioned, it doesn't mean that he wasn't there.

Another problem with regional directories is availability. These directories seem to have been published much less regularly than the yearly city directories, making them harder to find.

Professional Directories

The late nineteenth-century business directory, as might be expected, coincided with a proliferation of specialized professions. As *Directories in Print* confirms, the number of professional directories at present is astounding. Refer to that work for information on twentieth-century professional directories. In this section we will consider only law, medicine, civil and military service, and a category called miscellaneous. We will consider each of these professions separately due to the different circumstances under which each directory was published.

Law

The description of law directories in the original *Directory of Directories* is representative of the history of professional directories and the criteria by which they are compiled:

> Background: 'Law Lists' refers to a group of directories which provide varying amounts of information about lawyers, and which were formerly certified by a committee of the American Bar Association as being ethically appropriate sources in which lawyers could make known their availability for consultation. As a result of the United States Supreme Court decision in 1977 governing advertising by lawyers and subsequent actions by the ABA, the Standing Committee on Law Lists no longer certifies law lists, state or national, as being in compliance with any rules or standard. (In response to requests for guidance from some states the committee prepared proposed guidelines for state regulation of law lists which were submitted to committees of the ABA and reported to the ABA house of delegates in August 1979.) About sixty law lists were formerly certified by the committee and described in the 'Directory Information Service.' These listings, revised as needed, are continued in this volume. The law list which has operated longest under a single title is 'Campbell's List,' established in 1879. 'Martindale-Hubbell Law Directory,' resulted from a merger of 'Martindale's American Law Directory,' founded in 1868, and 'Hubbell's Legal Directory,' founded in 1870; it is currently the largest of the law lists and among the most highly regarded. Covers: Martindale-Hubbell, a national list, and the state and regional directories published by the Legal Directories Publishing Company, Inc., are the only comprehensive law lists which include every attorney nationally or in an area. There are no law lists which attempt to include every attorney in a special field. In fact, the essence of the appeal of law lists is exclusivity: all lists charge fees for inclusion (usually based on the population of the area where a given attorney practices, and ranging to $600 or more), except [that] comprehensive lists include a minimum listing without a fee; many lists operate on the basis of 'exclusive representation,' i.e., they list only one firm in a given locality. A few, such as the 'Rand McNally List of Bank-Recommended Attorneys,' operate on the basis of recommendations or sponsorships. Some lists use rating systems, and firms listed are coded for ability, diligence, and so forth., as evaluated by peers. Entries include: Even within a single law list, entries may run from a brief name-and-address notation to one or two pages or more, depending upon the size of the firm and how much it is willing to spend for its listing. In a typical full entry, a firm name, address, and phone will be given along with names and backgrounds of partners and names of typical clients; associates may also be listed. Many lists include uniformly less data. Arrangement: The most frequent use of a law list is in finding a lawyer in a location where the user has no contacts. Therefore, nearly all law lists are geographical in arrangement. Indexes: Alphabetical indexes by personal name may or may not be provided. Price: Part of the service provided by law list publishers is the free distribution of their lists to lawyers listed and to others who can be assumed to be users of the services of lawyers listed. There is no ethical restriction on the sale of law lists, but it was the experience of the DOD staff in compiling law list material that many publishers are not anxious to give laypersons information about their publications to promote commercial sales; whether this lack of cooperation resulted from a desire to enhance the exclusive image of their lists or for other reasons is not clear.[18]

Law directories are generally arranged by state and are frequently not indexed. In the past, law directories could generally be found on the local and state level. In areas where such regional directories are not available prior to the advent of the national directories in the 1870s, you can usually find lawyers in general business directories. Most law directories today are national-level directories, but there are some on the state and local levels, particularly in large metropolitan areas.

Law directories locate an individual in place and time for the purposes of gaining access to, or linking with, other sources, including other directories. Other significant data may include the law school graduated from, or in cases where law was read, the state in which the lawyer was first admitted to the bar. You may also find other biographical information that helps you trace an individual lawyer's career and suggests other records to search.

Medicine

The *American Medical Directory*, published under the auspices of the American Medical Association, has existed only since 1906. Unlike law directories, it is published intermittently, so a complete collection may not cover every year since 1906. The directory is arranged by state, and the later editions also contain alphabetical listings. Before 1906, medical directories were published by private companies or by local and state medical associations. Some city directories contained separate lists for doctors, and doctors were listed in general business directories as well.

The *American Medical Directory* presently contains the following information: name, address, year licensed, medical school, type of practice, primary and secondary specialties, and board certifications. Some of the earlier editions also contain year of birth and year graduated from medical school.

Medical directories help you locate a person in place and time and provide links with other sources.

Civil and Military Service

In 1816, Congress passed a bill providing for the biennial publication of a register "containing correct lists of all the officers and agents, civil, military, and naval, in the service of the United States." This list contained the individual's name and office, pay, place of birth, and place of residence. The resolution further provided that the registers should be current as of 30 September the year preceding the publication date. Thus, the civil register for 1864 would reflect information collected in 1863. In 1851, the state from which the person was appointed was added.[19]

Although the main register of government civil servants contained the names of military and naval officers, separate registers for these two services were also eventually published. These registers are considerably more detailed than the general register. They contain the date of enlistment or entry into the service and the date the most recent rank was achieved. In addition, the state of birth and state from which an officer was appointed are invaluable as links to other sources when military service records are not readily available.

These army and navy registers include officers only. Army and navy registers accounted for regular (career) service only. Therefore, an ancestor known to have been an officer in the Civil War may not be listed if he was part of the volunteer army. Directories of army and navy officers might also be found in directories for graduates of the appropriate service academies.

The general register is arranged alphabetically. The army register is arranged by regiment, with a name index and a list of where each regiment was stationed in the year of publication. The navy register is arranged by ship rather than regiment and includes the location of each ship. The Marine Corps is listed in the navy register.

The government of the United States has probably generated more paper than any single organization in the history of this country. If an ancestor worked for the government, there should be a record of it somewhere. These registers can connect you with those records when information more specific than "he worked for the government" or "he was an army officer" is unavailable.

Miscellaneous Professions

Early directories exist for a number of professions. R. L. Polk published the following directories before 1920:

Dental Register of the United States
Architects' and Builders' Directory of the United States
Marine Directory of the Great Lakes
Ohio Architects' and Builders' Directory
Pennsylvania Architects' and Builders' Directory
Western New York Architects and Builders' Directory

The Library of Congress has these early professional directories: *The Dentist Register* (1879); *Banker's Almanac and Year Book* (1844); *Rand McNally Banker's Blue Book* (1872); and *Polk's World Bank Directory* (1895). Perhaps the best way to find out whether an early professional directory exists is to find that profession in the *Directory of Directories* and contact the publisher.

One directory that has been published only since 1932 is nevertheless relevant to earlier genealogical research: *The American Blue Book of Funeral Directors,* published every two years. Any professional directory locates an ancestor in time and place, but the funeral director's blue book lets you trace a funeral home to the present day and, if it has gone out of business, perhaps determine the successor and thus where the records might be. A funeral home in business in 1932 may have existed for fifty years. In a given community, its records could almost substitute for death registers.

Similarly, the *American Cemetery Association Membership Directory and Buyer's Guide* can help in locating cemeteries where your ancestors might be buried, especially if the name or ownership of the cemetery has changed.

How to Use Professional Directories

Following are two hypothetical examples relevant to our use of various professional directories:

The ancestor in question is known to have been a doctor in the greater New York City area about 1910, but whether in Manhattan, Brooklyn, Queens, the Bronx, Staten Island, Long Island, Westchester County, Connecticut, or New Jersey is unknown. The *American Medical Directory* for 1909 had an alphabetical listing, and Lucy Criddle Jones was easily located in its New York City section (see figure 8-9).

This listing indicates that Lucy Criddle Jones was born in 1872, that she graduated from Syracuse University Medical School in 1898, and that in 1909 she lived at 212 East 53rd Street. (Office addresses are indicated separately from home addresses.) From this information, positive identification can be made using Manhattan city directories and, subsequently, the census. In addition, medical school records can be consulted.

Robert Nelson Eagle was known to have been a lieutenant in the U.S. Army before the Civil War, and family lore held that he had served with Robert E. Lee. Eagle was listed in the army register for 1860 (see figure 8-10) as serving with the Second Regiment of Cavalry, of which Robert E. Lee was lieutenant colonel. Eagle had entered the service as a first lieutenant on 3 March 1855. He was born in New York but appointed from Texas. Since the register also gave the location of the Second

Regiment in 1860, the census for that year as well as military records could be consulted.

Organizational Directories

Like professional directories, organizational directories are highly specialized and suited to the needs of a particular organization. Two examples of such directories are university alumni directories and fraternity directories. If your ancestor belonged to some other organization, you can consult *Directories in Print* to see if a directory for that organization currently exists and, if so, contact the organization and determine if it has any earlier directories.

These sorts of directories, however, may not be published annually and so may not appear in *Directories in Print*. You may even have to consult the *Encyclopedia of Associations* (published annually by Gale Research) to find a specific directory for the particular organization in which you are interested. In some cases, an organizational directory does not tell you the names of its members but may provide the addresses of various branches to which you can write. This would be helpful in cases where an ancestor belonged to an organization in the 1800s that is no longer active and for which you must locate records. The kind of information given in an organizational directory can range from a mere address to dates of transfer or membership, or even of birth and death.

JONES, CATESBY ⊕—Md.1,'93; 7 E. 32d St.; 9-1, 4-5.
JONES, CHAS. NOALE DIXON ⊕—N.Y.1,'83; 601 W. 179th St.; 8-10, 6-7; Or.
JONES, DAVID H. (b 1874) ⊕—N.Y.5,'97; 213 W. 101st St.; 12-1, 4-7:30.
Jones, Henry Woodward (b 1847)—Mich.7,'74; 301 W. 107th St.
Jones, Horace Loomis—Pa.2,'81; 126 W. 127th St.; 7-9, 6-8.
JONES, ISRAEL C. ⊕—O.9,'71; Home for Incurables, Fordham; until 10.
Jones, Leonard W.—Ont.5,'02; office, Manhattan Eye and Ear Hospital.
JONES, LUCY CRIDDLE (b 1872) ⊕—N.Y.15,'98; 212 E. 53d St.; 12-1:30, 6-7.
Jones, Robt. Mortimer—H—N.Y.9,'06; 136 Madison Ave.; 11-1, 5-6; ALR.
Jones, Roland D.—Pa.1,'81; 56 E. 59th St.; 9-1.
JONES, S. BEACH—N.Y.1,'72; Park Ave. and 62d St.; 12-1; N.
Jones, Walter Hastings—H—N.Y.9,'86; The Ansonia, 73d St. and Broadway; 9-10, 1-2, 5-6.
Jones, Wm. Fredk.—Vt.2,'33; 323 W. 19th St.; 8-9, 1-2, 6-8.
JONES, WM. J., Jr.—N.Y.20,'99; 233 W. 118th St.; 5-7.

Figure 8-9. From *American Medical Directory, 1909*, 3rd ed. (Chicago: American Medical Association Press, 1909), 799.

How to Use Organizational Directories

Here is a hypothetical example of the joint use of two organizational directories. A modern descendant of the Weed family discovers an old fraternity pin in the attic bearing the Greek letters Alpha Delta Phi. On the back of the pin, the initials H.A.W. are inscribed. Some time ago, this family had moved to the West Coast from New York and had lost all touch with the family in the East. In fact, Grandpa Weed had been reluctant to talk about his ancestors beyond the information that "they came from New York."

Seizing upon this artifact as a potential key to the Weed family mysteries, the modern Weed tries to locate information on H.A.W. His best approach would be to find some list of past fraternity members, but there was none listed in *Directories in Print* at the local library. There was, however, a listing for *Baird's Manual of American College Fraternities.* Upon calling the publisher (the local library did not have this source), the modern Weed encounters a typical problem for genealogists: the publisher would rather sell him the book than provide, free of charge, the address of the Alpha Delta Phi Fraternity Alumni Association. Fortunately, Weed's library had the *Encyclopedia of Associations* and provides him—free of charge—with the information he desired. After Weed sends a request for information, the alumni association sends him a copy of the following page from the 1966 *Catalogue of the Alpha Delta Phi,* the listing for the chapter at Columbia University:

1836
Hillyer, Giles Mumford
Hobart, John Henry
Jay, John
McVickar, Henry
Ward, Henry, Jr.
Waters, George Gilfert
Weed, Harvey Augustus

1837
Aldis, Charles
Blatchford, Samuel
Chittenden, Nathaniel William
Fessenden, Henry Partridge
Galsey, Anthony
Leggett, William Henry
MacMullen, John
Tucker, John Ireland
Vanderbilt, John, Jr.
Whitlock, Samuel H.[20]

A letter accompanying the page indicates that this is the only Weed with the initials H.A. in the general index to the catalogue, which also lists him as deceased.

This information led Weed to examine the *Columbia University Alumni Register,* which reveals that, not only did

Harvey Augustus Weed graduate in 1836, he went on to receive a higher degree in 1839.

> Weed, Edgar Theodore MD 1881, 39 W 87 NYC
>
> Weed, Edwin Dunning AB 1894, 2218 E 1 Duluth Minn, Clergy
>
> Weed, Eleanor Hill (see Sharp, Elearnor Weed)
>
> Weed, Ethel Georgine AM 1906, Maplewood NJ
>
> Weed, G B ent 1834 P&S, decd.
>
> Weed, Harvey Augustus AB 1836, AM 1839 C, d. 1872
>
> Weed, John Went 1819 P&S, decd.
>
> Weed, John Waring LLB 1868, d. Nov 7, 1915
>
> Weed, Lowry Albert AB 1916 (cl 1914). Internat'l Composition Co 25 Broadway NYC[21]

10 SECOND REGIMENT OF CAVALRY.

NAME.	Rank in the Reg't.	Army.		Original entry into service.		Born in.	
Colonel.							
Albert S. Johnston,	3 Mar. 55	B. G. bvt.	18 Nov. 57	(*d*) Bvt. 2 lt. 2 inf.	1 July, 26	Ky.	T
Lieutenant Colonel.							
Robert E. Lee,	3 Mar. 55	Col. bvt.	13 Sept. 47	Bvt. 2 lt. eng.	1 July, 29	Va.	V
Majors.							
William J. Hardee,	3 Mar. 55	L. C. bvt. Comm't cadets, M. A. with loc. rank of L. C.	20 Aug. 47	2 lt. 2 drag.	1 July, 38	Ga.	G
George H. Thomas,	12 May, 55	Bvt.	23 Feb. 47	2 lt. 3 art.	1 July, 40	Va.	Vi
Captains.							
Earl Van Dorn,	3 Mar. 55	M. bvt.	20 Aug. 47	Bvt. 2 lt. 7 inf.	1 July, 42	Miss.	M
Edmund K. Smith,	3 Mar.	Bvt.	20 Aug.	Bvt. 2 lt. 5 inf.	1 July, 45	Fla.	Fl
James Oakes,	3 Mar.	Bvt.	8 Sept.	Bvt. 2 lt. 2 drag.	1 July, 46	Pa.	Pa
Innis N. Palmer,	3 Mar.	Bvt.	13 Sept.	Bvt. 2 lt. m. rifles,	1 July,	N. Y.	N.
George Stoneman,	3 Mar.			Bvt. 2 lt. 1 drag.	1 July,	N. Y.	N.
William R. Bradfute,*	3 Mar.			Capt.	3 Mar. 55	Tenn.	Te
Albert G. Brackett,*	3 Mar.			Capt.	3 Mar.	N. Y.	In
Charles J. Whiting,	3 Mar.			(*e*) Bvt. 2 lt. 2 art.	1 July, 35	Mass.	Ct
Nathan G. Evans,	1 May, 56			Bvt. 2 lt. 1 drag.	1 July, 48	S. C.	S.
Richard W. Johnson,	1 Dec.			Bvt. 2 lt. 6 inf.	1 July, 49	Ky.	K
First Lieutenants.							
Joseph H. McArthur,	3 Mar. 55			Bvt. 2 lt. 2 inf.	1 July, 49	Mo.	M
Charles W. Field,	3 Mar.			Bvt. 2 lt. 2 drag.	1 July,	Ky.	K
Kenner Garrard,	3 Mar.			Bvt. 2 lt. 4 art.	1 July, 51	Ky.	Oi
Walter H. Jenifer,*	3 Mar.			(*f*) 1 lt. 3 drag.	9 Apr. 47	Md.	M
William B. Royall,*	3 Mar.			1 lt.	3 Mar. 55	Va.	M
William P. Chambliss,*	3 Mar.			1 lt.	3 Mar.	Va.	Te
Robert Nelson Eagle,*	3 Mar.			1 lt.	3 Mar.	N. Y.	Te
John T. Shaaff,	1 May, 56			Bvt. 2 lt. 6 inf.	1 July, 51	D. C.	D.
George B. Cosby,	1 May,			Bvt. 2 lt. m. rifles,	1 July, 52	Ky.	K
William W. Lowe,	1 Dec.	Adjt.	31 May, 58	Bvt. 2 lt. 2 drag.	1 July, 53	Ind.	Io
John B. Hood,	18 Aug. 58			Bvt. 2 lt. 4 inf.	1 July,	Ky.	K

Figure 8-10. From *Adjutant General's Office, Official Army Register for 1860* (Washington, D.C.: Government Press, 1860), 16.

The register also indicates that Harvey Augustus Weed died in 1872. Without knowing his exact date of birth, the modern Weed estimates, based on the date of Harvey's first degree, that Harvey was in his late forties when he died. Grandpa Weed had been born in 1870; perhaps this was the reason he knew little of his past. With the information from the *Alumni Register*, the modern Weed checks Columbia University's records, which allow him to extend the line by linking them with other sources.

Special Problems

Locating organizational directories is the major problem. Since many of them are published after the fact—that is, they are really books that contain membership lists since the organization's inception—more recent copies may be just as valuable as earlier copies. Some directories, however, may prune earlier membership lists. Check the organization itself and the Library of Congress first, then go to major university and public libraries in the area where the school is located.

Religious Directories

Religious directories began as books containing directions for the order of public or private worship. As time passed, some denominational directories began to include lists of clergy and/or churches. Eventually the listings outweighed the direction, and these books became directories in the modern sense. Some denominational directories have dropped all statements of creed, such as *The Official Catholic Directory*, first published in 1817. Religious directories may also be called registers, annuals, and yearbooks. The information they include differs from denomination to denomination, the minimum amount being the name and address of the church and its pastor.

The information contained in religious directories is significant in two ways. If an ancestor was a clergyman, such directories can guide you to his places of service. This is especially true in the case of itinerant ministers; religious directories narrow down these ministers' assigned working areas. Also, as with funeral and cemetery directories, religious directories may suggest where to find the contemporary records of the church where the ancestor worshipped.

How to Use Religious Directories

Suppose the ancestor was a Baptist in Rochester, New York, in the first half of the nineteenth century. *The American Baptist Register* for 1852 shows four Baptist churches in Rochester, the two earliest having been established in 1818 and 1834.[22] We know the ancestor lived in Rochester before 1834, so he probably belonged to the First Baptist Church. A check of Baptist churches in modern Rochester shows that the First Baptist Church still exists. We write to its pastor, requesting a check in early records for mention of our ancestor.

In another hypothetical example, the ancestor was a Baptist minister named Henry Smith who lived somewhere in New York around 1850. A check of all Baptist associations in New York revealed only one Henry Smith, who preached at Hastings, Westchester County (see figure 8-11). With this information we don't need to check all of the Henry Smiths in the 1850 census index of New York; we can zero in on the relevant one.

New York Association.

CHURCHES.	CONST.	COUNTIES.	PASTORS.	BAPT.	MEMBERS
First Church, N. Y.,	1762	New York,	S. H. Cone, D. D.,	15	557
First Church, Staten Island,	1785	Richmond,	Samuel White,	2	177
Middletown,	1792	Rockland,	J. W. Griffiths,		56
Abyssinian, N. Y.,	1808	New York,	J. T. Raymond,	8	373
North Beriah, N. Y.,	1809	New York,	J. S. Backus,	26	235
Ebenezer, N. Y.,	1825	New York,	G. L. Marsh,	2	98
Greenport, L. I.,	1832	Suffolk,	C. J. Hopkins,		151
Zion, N. Y.,	1832	New York,	Thomas Henson,		378
Newburgh,	1833	Orange,	James Scott,	5	103
Sixteenth St., N. Y.,	1833	New York,	J. W. Taggart,	54	714
Berean, N. Y.,	1838	New York,	J. R. Stone,	20	420
Sag Harbor, L. I.,	1844	Suffolk,	E. W. Bliss,	9	137
Welsh, N. Y.,	1833	New York,	Thomas H. Davies,		167
Monticello,	1836	Sullivan,	———		49
Piermont, First,	1839	Rockland,	———	1	48
Bethesda, N. Y.,	1841	New York,	N. B. Baldwin,	16	130
Middletown, First,	1842	Orange,	S. S. Barrett,	4	62
Hempstead,	1842	Rockland,	E. J. Williams,		21
Cold Spring, L. I.,	1842	Suffolk,	W. B. Harris,		40
Bloomingdale, N. Y.,	1843	New York,	S. Wilkins.	3	130
Parksville,		Sullivan,	Wm. W. Murphy,		67
First Mariner's,	1843	New York,	J. R. Steward,	11	122
Providence, N. Y.,	1845	New York,	———	1	66
Newtown, L. I.,		Queens,	———		15
Central, Brooklyn,	1847	Kings,	J. W. Sarles,	11	172
West, Staten Island,	1848	Richmond,	William Pike,	5	31
Olive Branch, N. Y.,	1849	New York,	———	19	183
Oyster Bay, L. I.,	1724	Suffolk	Marmaduke Earle,		39
East Marion, L. I.,	1847	Kings,	Erastus Denison,	4	35
Hastings, First,	1850	West Chester,	Henry F. Smith,	9	28
Shiloh, Newburg,	1848	Orange,	Elisha Hawkins,	14	27
			Total,	239	4582

Figure 8-11. From J. Lansing Burrows, ed., *American Baptist Register for 1852* (Philadelphia: American Baptist Publication Society, 1853), 237.

Post Office and Street Directories

Post office and street directories were originally published by the government to help deliver the mail correctly before the advent of zip codes. Post office directories list all active post offices in the year of publication. For instance, *The Street Directory of the Principal Cities of the United States . . . to April 1908* contains the names of streets and the cities with streets by those names. This was necessary in cases where the sender listed only a street address, with no city and no return address. The directory was published mainly for the use of the Division of Dead Letters and should not be confused with the street directories discussed with city directories.

How to Use Post Office and Street Directories

You can use both of these types of directories with old family letters. If you have a letter that bears only the name of a town and state and the town cannot be found in any modern gazetteer, it may no longer exist, or the name may have been changed. A post office directory from the right period gives you the location. If the letter bears only an address on Religious Street and the date of 13 January 1908, the original envelope having been lost, the street directory can help. A 1908 directory shows:

Reliance Place
  Flushing, N.Y.
  (Elmhurst)

Relic Alley
  Pittsburg, Pa.

Relief
  Oil City, Pa., 1-20

Relief Alley
  Allegheny, Pa.
  Pittsburg, Pa.

Relief Ave.
  Poplar Bluff, Mo., 200-600

Religious
  New Orleans, La., 1400-1999

Rellis
  Saginaw, Mich., 200

Relyea Place
  New Rochelle, N.Y., 1-20

Rembert
  Memphis, Tenn., N.
    61-662 S.[23]

Thus, in 1908, Religious Street existed only in New Orleans. If, however, the name is Relief, you would have more cities to consider. This method can be used with any stray street address, including photographers' addresses on the backs of old photographs.

Notes

[1] *The Oxford English Dictionary* (Oxford: Clarendon Press, 1961), 393.

[2] Dorothea N. Spear, *Bibliography of American Directories Through 1860* (Worcester, Mass.: American Antiquarian Society, 1961), 5–10.

[3] *Alaska Directory and Gazetteer 1934–1935* (Seattle: Alaska Directory Co., 1935), foreword.

[4] The Family History Library's *1910 Census Register* is not available online, but the same information leading to enumeration district maps can be found in the Family History Library Catalog online under the "[name of the city]—Census-1910" or "[name of the city]—Maps".

[5] 1910 U.S. Census, Rochester, Monroe County, New York, vol. 145, E.D. 141, sheet llB, line 72, NARA Microfilm Publications T624, Roll 991. Available on FHL microfilm 1,375,004.

[6] 1910 U.S. Census, Baltimore, Baltimore County, Maryland, vol. 24, E.D. 191, sheet 9B, line 72, NARA Microfilm Publications T624, Roll 556. Available on FHL microfilm 1,374,569.

[7] FHL microfilm 1,498,803.

[8] 1918 Polk's Pittsburgh City Directory (R. L. Polk and Co.), 1201.

[9] *Doggett's New York Directory 1833–1834* (New York: John Doggett Jr., 1834), 505.

[10] 1850 U.S. Census, New York City, New York County, New York, ward 5, folio 125, dwelling 937, family 1837, NARA microfilm M432, roll 537.

[11] *Doggett's New York City Directories 1845–46* and *1846–47* (New York: John Doggett Jr.), 302, 326.

[12] Entry for James Renwick, 5 June 1845, Manhattan Death Register, vol. 14, 1844–45. Available on FHL microfilm 447,550.

[13] 1900 U.S. Census, Philadelphia, Philadelphia County, Pennsylvania, vol. 167, E.D. 412, sheet 7, line 24, NARA microfilm T623, roll 1461. Available on FHL microfilm 1,241,461.

[14] Marriage Record of Christian [Hochwald?] and [illegible], 3 May 1862, Philadelphia Board of Health Marriage Registers, 1860–1863, 193. Available on FHL microfilm 978,997.

[15] *McElroy's Philadelphia City Directory 1862* (Philadelphia: E. C. and J. Biddle, 1862), 862.

[16] Declaration of Intention of James Renwick to Become a Naturalized Citizen of the United States, New York Co., N.Y., Naturalization Records Court of Common-Pleas, Bundle 26, no. 69, 3 November 1840. Available on FHL microfilm 901,057.

[17] *New Mexico Business Directory . . . 1907–1908* (Denver: Gazetteer Publishing Co., 1907), 217.

[18] James M. Ethridge, ed., *The Directory of Directories* (Detroit: Information Enterprises, 1908), 245, reprinted by permission.

[19] Adjutant General's Office, *Register of Officers and Agents, Civil, Military and Naval in the Service of the United States 30 Sept. 1863* (Washington, D.C.: Government Printing Office, 1864), notes.

[20] Executive Council of the Alpha Delta Phi, *Catalogue of the Alpha Delta Phi, 1832–1866* (New York: Alpha Delta Phi, 1966), 101.

[21] The Committee on [the] General Catalogue, *Columbia University Alumni Register, 1754–1931* (New York: Columbia University Press, 1932), 931.

[22] J. Lansing Burrows, ed., *American Baptist Register for 1852* (Philadelphia: American Baptist Publication Society, 1853), 236.

[23] *Street Directory of the Principal Cities of the United States Embracing Letter-Carrier Offices Established to April 30, 1908* (Washington, D.C.: Postmaster General, 1908), 637.

References

1918 Polk's Pittsburgh City Directory. R. L. Polk and Co., 1918.

Adjutant General's Office. *Register of Officers and Agents, Civil, Military and Naval in the Service of the United States 30 Sept. 1863.* Washington, D.C.: Government Printing Office, 1864.

Andersson, Brian G. "City Directories." *Ancestry Daily News* (11 January 1999).

Alaska Directory and Gazetteer 1934–1935. Seattle: Alaska Directory Co., 1935.

Burrows, J. Lansing, ed. *American Baptist Register for 1852.* Philadelphia: American Baptist Publication Society, 1853.

Burton, Robert E. "City Directories in the United States, 1784–1820: A Bibliography with Historical Notes." MS thesis, University of Michigan, 1956. Gives locations of directories.

Catalog of City, County, and State Directories Published in North America. New York: North American Directory Publishers, 1967. May help to identify and locate directories no longer in print.

City and State Directories in Print, 1990–1991. 1st ed. Detroit: Gale Research Co., 1989.

City Directories of the United States Pre 1860 Through 1901: Guide to the Microfilm Collection. Woodbridge, Conn.: Research Publications, 1983.

Committee on the General Catalogue. *Columbia University Alumni Register, 1754–1931.* New York: Columbia University Press, 1932.

Davis, Marjorie V. *Guide to American Business Directories.* Washington, D.C.: Public Affairs Press, 1948. May help to identify and locate directories no longer in print.

Directories in Print, 1992. 9th ed. Detroit: Gale Research Co., 1991.

"Directories in the Library of Congress." *American Genealogist* 13 (1937): 46–53; 27 (1951): 142.

Doggett's New York Directory 1833–1834. New York: John Doggett Jr., 1834.

Doggett's New York City Directories 1845–46. New York: John Doggett Jr., 1846.

Ethridge, James M., ed. *The Directory of Directories.* Detroit: Information Enterprises, 1908. Reprinted by permission.

Executive Council of the Alpha Delta Phi. *Catalogue of the Alpha Delta Phi, 1832–1866.* New York: Alpha Delta Phi, 1966.

Hillman, Barbara. *Guide to the Use of the United States. Census Office. 10th Census 1880 New York City.* New York: New York Public Library, 1963.

Hinckley, Kathleen W. "Skillbuilding: Analyzing City Directories." *OnBoard–Newsletter of the BCG* 2, no. 2 (May 1968).

Hofstetter, Eleanore O., and Harold C. Livesay. "Pre-Civil War Directories Sources in American History." *RQ* 8 (1968): 174–76.

International Directories in Print, 1989–90. 1st ed. Detroit: Gale Research Co., 1988.

Kirkham, E. Kay. *A Handy Guide to Record Searching in the Larger Cities of the United States.* Logan, Utah: Everton Publishers, 1974.

Klein, Bernard. *Guide to American Directories.* 5th ed. Englewood Cliffs, N.J.: Prentice-Hall, 1962.

Knights, Peter R. "The Plain People of Boston." *Scientific American* (November 1981). Includes a perceptive appendix on directories.

Mariner, Mary Lou Craver, and Patricia Roughan Bellows. *A Research Aid for the Massachusetts 1910 Federal Census.* Sudbury, Mass.: Computerized Assistance, 1988.

McElroy's Philadelphia City Directory 1862. Philadelphia: E. C. and J. Biddle, 1862.

Morgan, George G. "City vs. Telephone Directories." *Ancestry Daily News* (15 June 2001).

Moriarty, John H. "Directory Information Materials for New York City Residents, 1626–1786: A Bibliographic Study." *Bulletin New York Public Library* (October 1942).

Neal, Colleen. *Lest We Forget: A Guide to Genealogical Research in the Nation's Capital.* Annandale, Va., 1982.

New Mexico Business Directory . . . 1907–1908. Denver: Gazetteer Publishing Co., 1907.

Parker, Nathan C. *Personal Name Index to the 1856 City Directories of California.* Genealogy and Local History Series, vol. 10. Detroit: Gale Research Co., 1980.

Second Report of the Provost Marshall General to the Secretary of War. Washington, D.C.: Government Printing Office, 1919.

Smith, Juliana. "Fun with City Directories." *Ancestry Daily News* (25 September 2000).

———. "Using Directories." *Ancestry Daily News* (20 March 2000).

Sopp, Elsie L. *Personal Name Index to the 1856 City Directories of Iowa.* Genealogy and Local History Series, vol. 13. Detroit: Gale Research Co., 1980.

Spear, Dorothea N. *Bibliography of American Directories Through 1860.* Worcester, Mass.: American Antiquarian Society, 1961.

Street Directory of the Principal Cities of the United States . . . to April 1908. 5th ed. 1908. Reprint, Detroit: Gale Research Co., 1973.

Street Directory of the Principal Cities of the United States Embracing Letter-Carrier Offices Established to April 30, 1908. Washington, D.C.: Postmaster General, 1908.

9

Immigration Records

LORETTO DENNIS SZUCS, FUGA, KORY L. MEYERINK, MLS, AG, FUGA, and MARIAN SMITH

We are all descended from immigrants. Whether they came to America in prehistoric times via the Bering Strait or later on ships or airplanes, at some point in history, every person's ancestors came from somewhere else. And almost everyone has a strong desire to know why, when, and from where their ancestors emigrated. Most of us begin with the simple goal of finding "Old Country" origins. Yet the quest usually does not end when that discovery is made. Once we begin tracking ancestors back in time and across continents, we are often drawn so deeply into the story that it's difficult to stop searching. There are always a few more relationships to be proved and details to be learned. And when finally discovered, the ancestor's homeland takes on a fascination of its own. We find ourselves intrigued with histories and cultures, wanting to know as much as possible about "our people." Scarcely any phase of family history research is as fascinating as tracking immigrant origins—and scarcely any phase is as challenging.

Knowing the immigrant's birthplace or last place of residence before emigrating is essential to finding more information in the native land. Yet, unless the ancestors arrived relatively recently in the United States, family origins may have been forgotten. Because most foreign records are kept at the town level, discovering the name of a native town, county, or parish is an important goal. Without that information, it is impossible to know where to conduct research in the country of origin.

Chapter Contents

Every American hoping to link generations and reach back in time will ultimately be faced with immigration questions. The twofold purpose of this chapter is to facilitate the search for immigrant origins by (1) identifying the principles of immigration research, and (2) describing a vast body of American sources that document immigration.

The sources described in this chapter focus on the original records most likely to provide key immigration information about ancestors and other relatives who came to North America, specifically the United States. Many such sources have been indexed, abstracted, or transcribed into books, and in recent years, onto CD-ROMs and Web pages. The growing body of published immigration sources is the subject of an extensive chapter, "Immigration Sources," in *Printed Sources: A Guide to Published Genealogical Records*, edited by Kory L. Meyerink.[1]

Principles of Immigration Research

There is no "universal" record source that can be counted upon to provide the name of an immigrant's ancestral home. Rather, there are dozens of records that may, depending on the time period and ethnic nature of the family, provide the necessary information. For this reason, it is important to follow certain principles when researching an immigrant ancestor. These principles include

- identifying the immigrant clearly,
- learning the historical background,
- using the right research approaches,
- searching American records thoroughly first, and
- knowing the process of immigration.

Identifying the Immigrant

The ability to trace individuals and families successfully is greatly enhanced if researchers begin by making every effort to learn everything possible about the immigrant or family using U.S. record sources. An immediate concern should be to learn the full name of the immigrant and the names of as many other family members as possible. It is sometimes necessary to trace the lives of all the immigrant's children in order to obtain the critical clues that will tell exactly where the immigrant was born.

Biographical Information

To clearly identify an immigrant in records of the country from which the person came, you must know:

The full name. Given names and surnames (last names) are necessary. It is useful to learn all of the immigrant's given names, such as Johann Wilhelm Karl Hummel. Some individuals went by a second name, a confirmation name, or a nickname. Not only will learning the full name help to identify a person in the records of the country of origin; sometimes the name alone, or part of the name, can be a clue to the immigrant's original country or region.

A date. A birth date is preferable, but a date of marriage, a record of a religious event, military release, or other such information may substitute for a birth date, as long as the event took place in the native country. A complete date (day, month, and year) should be sought, but it is sometimes possible to identify an individual with only the year of an event.

A place of origin. Eventually, you must determine the specific place (town or parish) where the immigrant was born or lived before coming to the United States. This is the focus of immigrant origin research for most researchers. Sometimes it is possible to learn the specific town from records in the native country, but you should try to determine it from American records.

A relative. Family relationships—especially parentage—are important. The more you know about a family as a whole, the easier it is to correctly identify the immigrant in records of his or her native country. If it is not possible to discover the father's name, seek the mother's name or the name of a spouse, brother, sister, or other close relative (uncle, aunt) as a substitute. Not only will this information help identify the person in native records, but you may be able to learn more about a brother's or son's place of origin than about the ancestor who is the subject of your search. Many of the sources discussed in this chapter might name the native towns of some family members, yet not include your immediate ancestor.

While some records might not indicate specifically where the person came from, they might provide clues that will lead to others until you find a record that finally shows the town of origin. If at all possible, learn the following about the immigrant:

Family stories, traditions, and heirlooms. Surprising clues may survive in family traditions, letters, diaries, journals, religious records, postcards, photographs, scrapbooks, and mementos that have been saved over the years. Linked with a basic knowledge of the immigrant's homeland—including the leading industry of the native district, common occupations, names of nearby towns, rivers, mountains, and other features of the area—a family story, a tradition, or an heirloom could provide the breakthrough that will identify the exact immigrant origins.

Friends and neighbors. Many immigrants traveled together or settled among friends from their native land. When a particular immigrant cannot be located, track neighbors and associates. When you find their places of origin, see if your ancestor is nearby. In Duke University Library in Durham, North Carolina, is an account book among the personal papers of Zachariah Johnston. It includes money loaned to family members and close associates from the time the Johnston family left Ireland, to their initial settlement near Bethlehem, Pennsylvania, to their stop in Augusta County, Virginia, to their residence in Lexington, Virginia, just south of the Augusta County line. The same names appear and reappear. The whole group left Ireland in 1709 and stayed together at least until Zachariah died in 1800. They are recorded, along with their specific townland in Ireland, in that little account book. These families intermarried more than ten times during that century. For other examples of this approach, read Hank Z. Jones Jr.'s "Finding the Ancestral Home of a Palatine Forefather: The Case of Martin Zerbe," in *Pennsylvania Genealogical Magazine*; and "The Braun and Loesch Families: Neighbors in Germany and America," in *Quarterly of the Pennsylvania German Society*.[2]

Religion. Records created by religious organizations comprise a likely source of information in the country of origin. By learning the immigrant's religion, you can further identify him or her, limit your searches to records most likely to include the immigrant, and gain clues to more specific geographical origins. For example, a Protestant German ancestor was more likely to have come from northern Germany than from a southern area. Often, entire religious colonies traveled together and are documented in religious literature. Knowing, for example, that an immigrant Englishman was a Quaker can significantly change your research approach. (See chapter 6, "Church Records.")

Ethnicity. The natural security of living among people who speak the same language and have the same cultural or religious background is the bonding force that has traditionally kept ethnic communities together. Immigrants, particularly those who did not speak English, tended to settle in enclaves within cities and to cluster in specific regions of the United States. It was common for immigrants arriving in large numbers as a result of difficulties in their home countries to settle together on this side of the ocean, and then to migrate *en masse* within the United States. Many immigrants felt a need to transplant and preserve, as much as possible, their culture and lifestyle as it existed in their native lands. Immigrant groups frequently founded their own churches, schools, banks, boarding houses, and other institutions. They also had their own academic, athletic, charitable, fraternal, occupational, and social organizations. Volumes have been written about virtually every ethnic group. Ethnic presses generated newspapers and histories that focused on specific communities. Many ethnic publications survive that could be invaluable for those who want to learn more about the lives and times of their immigrant ancestors. Biographical sketches of Mrs. Isabella Atlanta Anderson and Jonas Anton Anderson, published in Algot E. Strand's *A History of the Norwegians of Illinois* (figure 9-1), are typical of those found in ethnic publications.[3] In most cases, birthplace, names of parents, spouse, and children, details of the family or individual's arrival in the United States, and other interesting information will surface in these historical sources. To learn what motives your ancestor may have had in coming to the United States, which groups came in what time period, where large concentrations of national groups typically settled, and other important information about settlement patterns, consult one or more of the works that focus on the specific ethnic group.

Name changes. Sometimes immigrants chose to change their names. A surname change was the result of a conscious choice to become Americanized, but usually it simply evolved during years of life in a new culture that used a language foreign to the immigrant. Name changes are therefore most common among foreign-speaking immigrants. Many individuals went to court to register and make a name change official, while others never bothered with the formalities. If a name change is suspected, a look at court records might be well worth the effort. Some preliminary reading can be interesting and will almost always enhance the potential for success in the long run. (Several useful titles are identified in the chapter reference section.)

Where to Look for Immigration Information

There are advantages to beginning a search with at least some knowledge about the immigrant's voyage. Certain tactics used to learn the place of origin require knowing as much as possible about when and where the immigrant arrived in America, and from where in the native country he or she came. Try to calculate the date of immigration as closely as possible. Knowing the name of the ship that brought the individual or family to the United States is desirable, but it is not entirely impossible to discover that specific information at some later point in the project. Because so many passenger lists have been digitized in recent years, searches of online immigration databases or CDs are logical starting points. It should be noted, however, that names of individuals may have been missed or deciphered incorrectly in indexes. Searching passenger lists, page by page, may be the only way to find someone if a specific time frame of arrival is known. (See the "Immigration Records" section later in this chapter.)

Date of immigration. If the approximate date of immigration can be determined, it is usually possible to locate passenger lists and records of ethnic or religious groups. Census records are particularly useful for learning this information. The 1900, 1910, 1920, and 1930 U.S. Federal Censuses usually provide the approximate year of arrival, though census information is not entirely reliable. Children's birthplaces in the 1850 through 1880 censuses can also help determine the year of arrival.

Once the date of immigration has been established, it is easier to determine the location of other important records, including naturalization papers. A date of immigration may also suggest when the immigrant was granted a release from military service in the native country.

Place of departure. If American records document the port or city the immigrant left, a number of records from the country of departure may indicate the name of the hometown. These include emigration lists (departure lists), indexes, newspapers, church records, and other records at the port of departure. From these, it may be possible to learn the date of immigration as well as the ship's name, which may be necessary to locate your ancestor in U.S. arrival records.

Port or city of arrival. Immigrants often stayed in the city of arrival for months or years before moving on. If you learn where your ancestor arrived in America, it may be possible to find applications for naturalization, church records, and government vital records, including marriage, death, and birth records. Any of these are likely to provide more clues about the ancestral home.

Name of the ship. The name of an immigrant's ship is more than an interesting biographical footnote. It may be necessary to find passenger lists, place of departure and arrival, and the names of other immigrants in the group. Sometimes the name of the ship that brought an immigrant ancestor to America will be remembered and handed down as the only clue to native origins.

Reason for immigrating. Biographical and family sources often imply why the immigrant came to America. In some cases, knowing why a person immigrated can help in locating ethnic or

His father died in Norway in 1860. His mother is still living in Eidegaarden, Vestre Aker, Norway.

Mr. Anderson's machine shop, which will be referred to in another part of this history, is at 147 Fulton street. The family resides at 470 Austin avenue.

MRS. ISABELLA ATLANTA ANDERSON

Divides the distinction of having been born on the Atlantic Ocean with the renowned "Sloop

Mrs. Isabella Anderson.

Girl," Mrs. Atwater, mentioned in the first part of this volume. This fact also explains her somewhat unusual middle name, Atlanta.

Mrs. Anderson was born on board the Norwegian steamer "Norge," May 21, 1861, while her parents were on their way to America. Her father is Mr. K. B. Olson, a well known manufacturing tailor, of this city, and her mother's maiden name was Miss Susan Stene.

Mrs. Anderson received her education in the Chicago public schools and was confirmed in the first Norwegian Lutheran church on the North side by Rev. Mikkelsen.

When twenty years of age she was joined in holy wedlock to Mr. Hans Ludvig Anderson, May 24, 1881. Her husband hailed from Fossen, Norway, and became a very prominent business man in Chicago, being engaged in the wholesale booth and shoe business, at his death, which occurred Feb. 4, 1903, leaving his family amply provided for.

This marital union was blessed with three children; one son and two daughters: Cyrus A., born March 4, 1884; Irene Harriet, Febr. 3, 1888, and Grace Susette, Febr. 17, 1892.

Mrs. Anderson's mother departed this life on July 19, 1906, but her father is still living and active in business.

Mrs. Anderson has never cared much about social clubs or distinctions, her inclinations having been more toward the duties of a good housewife and mother. When it came to charitable work, she has, however, been very much interested. She was one of the first two lady members on the board of directors of the Norwegian Old People's Home Society, on which she has served for a number of years. She has also been interested in the Norwegian Lutheran Children's Home Society and other charitable work among her countrymen.

With her family Mrs. Anderson attends the Wicker Park English Lutheran Church and resides in her own home at 98 Fowler street.

JONAS ANTON ANDERSON.

The manufacturer of cameras and photographic specialties at 65 E. Indiana street, Chicago, was born Nov. 28, 1840, to Peter and Margrette Anderson, of Christiania, Norway. The parents came to America, with the subject of our sketch, in 1852, locating in Detroit, Mich., where they landed in July. Jonas had attended school in Norway and for some time went to school in Detroit, but at the age of 14 he was apprenticed to learn the carpenter trade. After five years in Detroit he came to Chicago, in 1857. Here he continued to work at his trade until 1862, when he engaged in the building business on his own account. In 1869 he started the making of cameras and other

Figure 9-1. Biographical sketches such as these, from Algot E. Strand, *A History of the Norwegians of Illinois* (Chicago: J. Anderson, 1905), often provide immigration information that is not available elsewhere.

religious group records, the date of immigration, or the places of departure and arrival.

Immigrant's original country or region. Sometimes knowing the country or region a person left is enough to begin a search in the records of that area, and those records may suggest the place of departure.

Historical Background

Since 1607, some 57 million immigrants have come to America from other lands. Approximately 10 million passed through on their way to some other place or returned to their original homelands, leaving a net gain of more than 47 million people:

1607–1790:	900,000
1790–1819:	250,000
1820–1860:	5,000,000
1861–1880:	5,100,000
1881–1920:	23,400,000
1921–1960:	8,200,000
1961–1990:	14,000,000

Additional immigration statistics can be found at <http://factfinder.census.gov>.

In 1907, immigration peaked at 1,285,349.[4] (See figures 9-2 and 9-3.)

Between 1607 and 1790, early European immigration was mostly from Britain (England, Scotland, Ulster Ireland, Southern Ireland, Wales) and Germany. However, the largest number of immigrants were the forced immigrants from Africa, who accounted for approximately 40 percent of the colonial immigrants to the future United States. Based on a careful review of current demographic studies by immigration historians, the approximate distribution of immigrants before 1790 was as follows (see figure 9-4):[5]

Africa	360,000
England	230,000
Ulster	135,000
Germany	103,000
Scotland	48,500
Ireland	8,000
Netherlands	6,000
Wales	4,000
France	3,000
Jews	2,000
Sweden/Finland	500

Before 1790, North America's Anglo population was confined to the area east of the Appalachian Mountains, with only a scattering of Americans over the line along the frontiers. However, as the numbers of immigrants continued to climb, the frontiers had to be constantly pushed back, eventually bringing the immigrants to the Rocky Mountains and northern plains states. During the last two hundred years of immigration to the United States, the numbers of immigrants have risen and fallen in response to conditions in America as well as abroad.

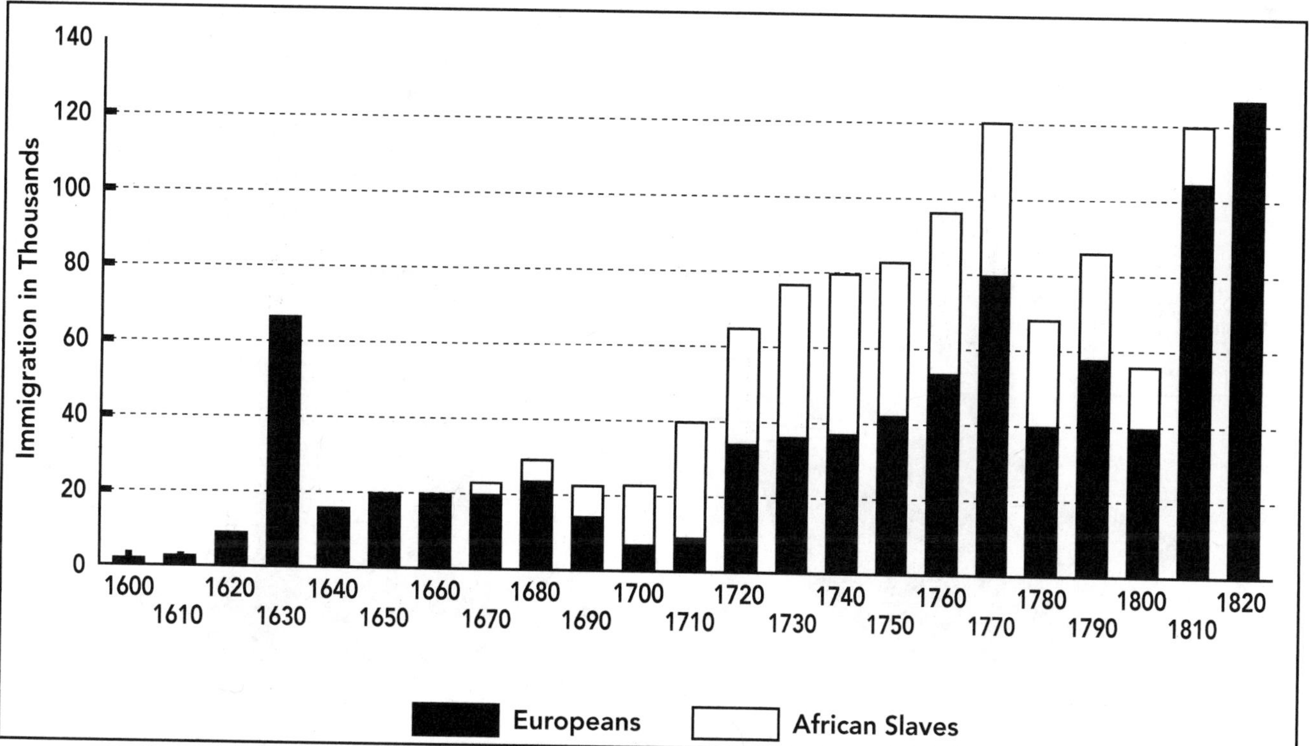

Figure 9-2. Pre-1820 Immigration to the United States.

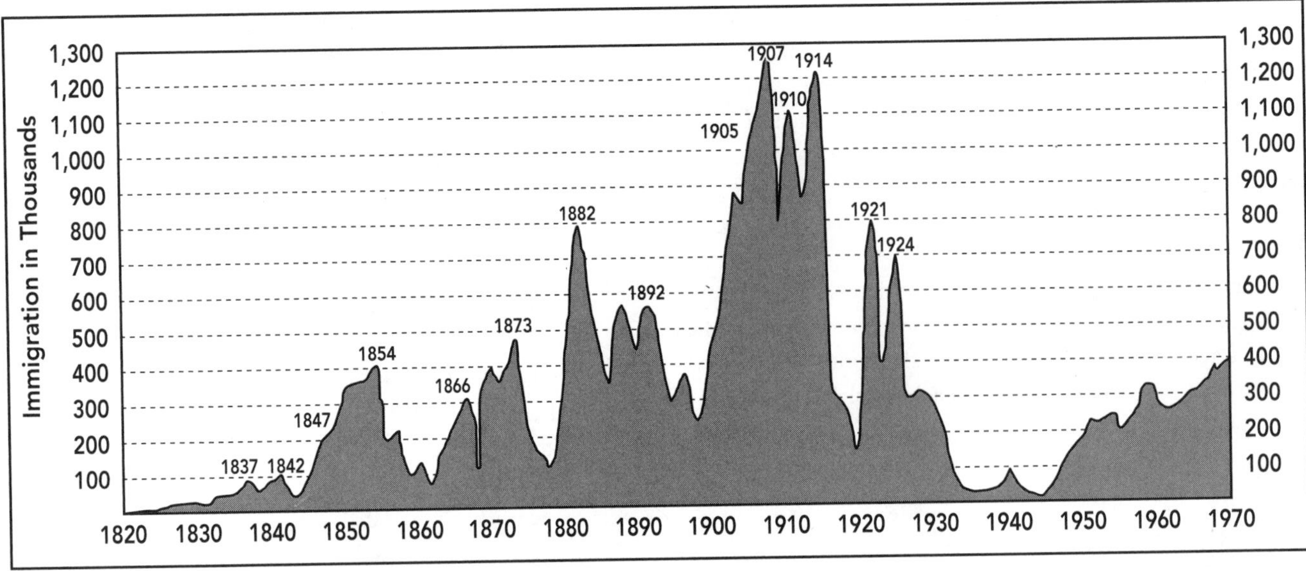

Figure 9-3. Immigration to the United States from 1820 to 1970.

The ethnicity of immigrants also changed considerably over time (table 9-1). Between 1820 and 1855, Ireland contributed the largest single group of immigrants. Germany, especially Prussia, contributed 20 percent of the immigrants during those years. A smattering from other parts of Europe and an introduction of people from China and Mexico rounded out the population.[6]

Before 1885, most European immigrants originated north of the Alps and west of the Elbe River. After 1885, the so-called New Immigration came from southern and eastern Europe, with the largest number of immigrants from Italy and Russia (mostly Jews). These immigrants concentrated in urban centers where jobs were available and where synagogues, churches, neighbors, and immigrant aid societies cushioned the immigrant experience. Most of these families were too poor to buy land when they arrived in America, and many heads of family had skilled and semi-skilled occupations.[7]

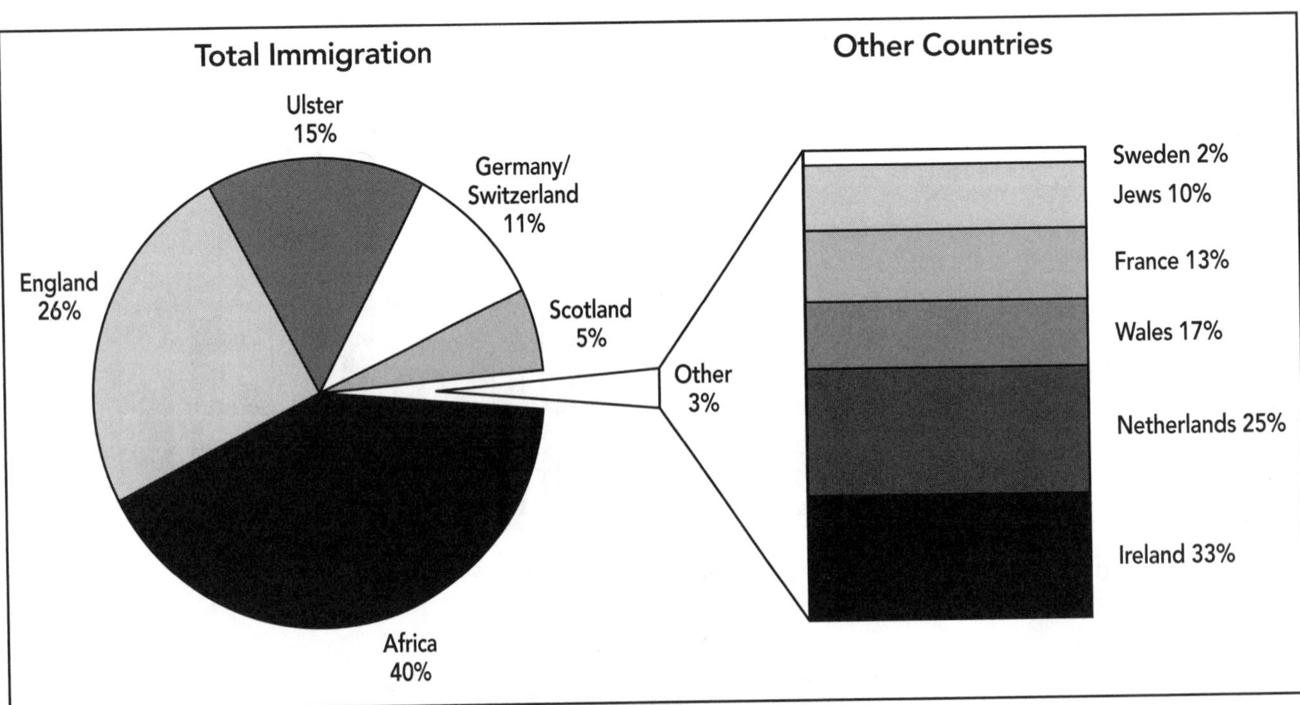

Figure 9-4. Total immigration to the United States to 1790.

Table 9-1. Top U.S. Ancestry Groups in 1790 and 2000

1790 U.S. Ancestry***
(Based on Evaluated 1790 Census Figures)

Ancestry Group	Number (1790 Estimate)	Percentage of Total
English	1,900,000	47.5
African	750,000	19.0
Scotch-Irish	320,000	8.0
German	280,000	7.0
Irish	200,000	5.0
Scottish	160,000	4.0
Welsh	120,000	3.0
Dutch	100,000	2.5
French	80,000	2.0
Native American	50,000	1.0
Spanish	20,000	0.5
Swedish and other	20,000	0.5
Total U.S. population	**4,000,000**	**100**

*** Meyerink based this table largely on the analysis of 1790 census data by Thomas L. Purvis in "The European Ancestry of the United States Population, 1790," *William & Mary Quarterly,* 3rd series, 41 (1): 85–. There has been much discussion about the ethnic stock of colonial America as various scholars have tried to use the 1790 census to arrive at precise figures. This cannot be done precisely, as the method depends on assigning *every 1790 head of household to one, and only one, ancestry* based on the presumed origin of the surname. American ancestry, even in 1790, was not always from only one race or nation. At that time many Americans already had five to seven generations in America, including ancestors from different countries.

Purvis and others have been criticized for their methodology in determining these figures (e.g., Akenson, same issue, p. 102–), but this is the best estimate available and is defended by Purvis (in the same issue). While not specifically accurate, the numbers are surely close. However, Purvis and earlier studies focused only on the white population in 1790. Meyerink has rounded Purvis's figures to the nearest percent (to account for the lack of precision), then adjusted them (to the nearest half-percent) to include the non-white (i.e., African and limited [eastern] Native American) population. The actual census count (including African Americans) for the area enumerated was 3,929,625, but did not include the Northwest Territory and areas under French or Spanish control (upwards of 50,000 people), nor most Indian tribes. Hence the rounded figure of 4 million.

Earlier studies attempting to discern America's colonial "ethnic stock" include: American Council of Learned Societies, "Report of the Committee on Linguistic and National Stocks in the Population of the United States," *Annual Report of the American Historical Association, 1931,* vol. 1 (Washington, D.C.: 1932), as well as *A Century of Population Growth, 1790–1900* (Washington, D.C.: Government Printing Office, 1909).

2000 U.S. Ancestry
(groups with more than two million)

Ancestry	2000 count	Percent
German	42,885,162	15.2
African American	36,419,434	12.9
Irish	30,594,130	10.9
English	24,515,138	8.7
Mexican	20,640,711	7.3
Italian	15,723,555	5.6
Franco-American*	10,846,018	3.9
Hispanic*	10,017,244	3.6
Polish	8,977,444	3.2
Scottish	4,890,581	1.7
Dutch	4,542,494	1.6
Norwegian	4,477,725	1.6
Scotch-Irish	4,319,232	1.5
American Indian	4,119,301	1.5
Swedish	3,998,310	1.4
Puerto Rican	3,406,178	1.2
Russian	2,652,214	0.9
Chinese	2,432,585	0.9
TOTAL U.S. POP	**281,421,906**	**N/A**

From: U.S. Census Bureau, Census 2000, table DP-1 and DP-2
*Franco-American comprises French (except Basque), French Canadian, and Acadian/Cajun. Hispanic does not include those specifically claiming Mexican, Puerto Rican, or other country specific ancestry.

In 1910, Russian immigrants comprised 20 percent of the foreign population of New York State and 25 percent of New York City; immigrants from Austria and Hungary comprised 12 percent and 14 percent, respectively; and Italians comprised 17 percent of the foreign population in New York, 18 percent in the city. By 1910, one-fourth of the foreign-born population of New York City had arrived within the previous five years; they spoke a variety of languages, practiced a variety of religious customs, and demanded a wide range of food.[8]

By the time of the 2000 census, immigrants had come to the United States from virtually every country on the earth. That census revealed that English ancestry no longer prevailed. German was the leading ancestry, followed by African American; Irish was third, followed by English. The others comprising the top ten were Hispanic, Italian, French, Polish, American Indian, and Dutch. Table 9-1 identifies each ancestry group with more than 1 million claimants in 2000.

The Value of History

Millions of immigrants from all over the world have brought unique customs and great diversity to the United States. And while certain principles of research may be applied to almost any country, there comes a time in every investigation when something of the specific history and the customs of the place from which our ancestors emigrated must be understood. Immigrants' experiences were not isolated. Groups were forced to leave by religious oppression, famine, agricultural and industrial revolution, the threat of conscription, and war. Other groups were lured by the American dream—the idea of commoners being able to own their own land.

From the documented and well-studied experiences and patterns of a national group, we can begin to understand the motives and individual histories of our own ancestors as they molded their destinies by leaving behind all that they had known. With an understanding of the customs and regulations of the time in which our ancestors traveled, we can know what kinds of records may have been created. Some of these record sources are unique to particular groups and might be the sole means of discovering the specific origins of ancestors.

America's immigration history is two-sided. To search records successfully, it is most helpful to study the newcomer both as emigrant (leaving the old country) and immigrant (coming to America). A brief outline of almost any nation's history can be gleaned from a standard encyclopedia, but the deeper the understanding you have of a specific group of people, the more likely you are to find clues to continue a search and to understand the personalities of individuals. For example, how might an ancestor's life have been radically changed by the pogroms in Russia? Nicholas V. Riasanovsky addresses that and a number of other issues that a diligent researcher should know about the country in *A History of Russia*.[9] Riasanovsky describes and illustrates the cultural, economic, geographical, and social aspects of "Russia before the Russians," "Appanage Russia," "Muscovite Russia," "Imperial Russia," and "Soviet Russia."

If you want to know more about living conditions and concerns of your British grandparents from 1830 to 1902, for example, a book like G. M. Young's *Victorian England: Portrait of an Age* will provide an unusual degree of detail.[10] Histories of this sort abound, and they provide not only the necessary background information for the researcher, but they also enhance appreciation of the lives of ancestors who lived in times very different from our own.

Besides learning something of the history of an ancestor's national group, it is beneficial for the family historian to understand what occurred after an immigrant arrived in the United States. Were entrance records kept on this side of the ocean? Where might an immigrant have chosen to live immediately after his or her arrival? Where did others of the same nationality settle, and what kinds of documents survive from ethnic communities? Was the immigrant likely to have been naturalized? If so, where and when?

Researchers will find a rich storehouse of printed material to expedite their immigration research. Consider such important immigration sources as Roger Daniels's *Coming to America: A History of Immigration and Ethnicity in American Life*, Philip Taylor's *The Distant Magnet: European Emigration to the U.S.A.*, and Oscar Handlin's *Immigration as a Factor in American History*, which cover the emigration experience and its broadest implications; or the histories of particular groups, such as James G. Leyburn's *The Scotch-Irish: A Social History*, Rowland Tappan Berthoff's *British Immigrants in Industrial America, 1790–1950*, Andrzej Brozek's *Polonia Amerykaska: The American Polonia*, Albert Camarillo's *Chicanos in a Changing Society: From Mexican Pueblo to American Barrios in Santa Barbara and Southern California, 1848–1930*, and Jay P. Dolan's *The Immigrant Church: New York's Irish and German Catholics*.[11]

History journals and dissertations often provide even more detailed discussions of why people emigrated, when and how they traveled, what they did when they got to the United States, and what kinds of records will divulge their individual names and personal facts. Not only do writings such as Oliver MacDonagh's "The Irish Famine Emigration to the United States," in *Perspectives in American History*, Robert Swierenga's "Dutch Immigrant Demography, 1820–1880," in *Journal of Family History*, or Paula Kaye Benkart's "Religion, Family, and Community Among Hungarians Migrating to American Cities, 1880–1930," provide critical insights in themselves, but they will usually point to original and often obscure records used by the authors to prove their theses.[12]

Ethnic and Religious Groups

It would be impossible to cite all of the sources valuable for immigration research, but the determined researcher will find an abundance of published material on specific ethnic and religious groups available in or through public, university, and private libraries. Because every national and religious group of people can be considered an ethnic group, "ethnic" is an important subject heading to consider when searching any library catalog.

Probably one of the most definitive and useful background sources for all ethnic groups is Stephen Thernstrom's *Harvard Encyclopedia of American Ethnic Groups*.[13] This reference work, found in most large libraries, includes the basic information about the multitude of people who make up the population of the United States. It is a succinct, authoritative treatment of the origins and histories of 106 ethnic groups; it includes twenty-nine thematic essays, eighty-seven maps, and a critical bibliography for each section. Among the many important points made by the *Encyclopedia* is the fact that few ethnic groups are evenly distributed throughout all regions of the United States. There is a definite tendency for ethnic groups to concentrate in some areas and to avoid others. Though somewhat dated, the depth and scope of the work and the many specialized bibliographies make the *Encyclopedia* a very useful source for ethnic research.

If religion was a catalyst that sent many an immigrant from his or her homeland, it was also the glue that bound ethnic communities together in the new country. The immigrant church and synagogue were extensions of Old World traditions and provided forms of assistance that were often an integral part of immigrants' lives. Records kept by religious institutions can be among the most useful in tracing immigrant origins. It is not uncommon for immigrant church registers to note the foreign birthplaces of those baptized, married, confirmed, transferring in or out of a church, or buried. Native towns or parishes are sometimes listed for sponsors or witnesses of religious events as well. The records of religious organizations, such as schools, orders, newspapers, orphanages, hospitals, old people's homes, and fraternal organizations are other potential sources for biographical information that may be otherwise hard to find for an immigrant. Methods and sources for finding immigrant church records are discussed in chapter 6, "Church Records," and Jewish records are discussed in chapter 18, "Jewish American Research."

Research Approaches

Using U.S. Sources First

To find an immigrant's origins, it may be necessary to comb through every piece of information and every record an immigrant and his or her contemporary relatives left in America. Clues may come from compiled genealogies and pedigrees; census records; land records; court documents; employment records; fraternal organizations; insurance companies; religious records; vital records; military records; federal and state sources; or immigration files. The most common mistake is to begin a search in foreign sources before exhausting American records. You are most likely to find the immigrant's birthplace or last foreign residence in American records: search them thoroughly before getting into sources created in the country of origin.

Family and Home Sources

In some cases, the *only* evidence of a family's origins will be found in personal possessions. For more information, see chapter 1, "The Foundations of Family History Research."

Organizing and Evaluating Material for Clues

A particularly useful way to organize information and clues is to keep a summary of the people the immigrant came in contact with—potential relatives (father-in-law, spouses of children, brothers-in-law) and traveling companions. After you have tracked the individual through life, make a summary of contact points: sponsors and godparents for children, witnesses for deeds and wills, fellow soldiers or officers in military units, neighbors who settled near each other, business partners, surnames of those marrying into the family, and those who worshipped in the same religion, or were buried in the same cemetery lot.

Previous Research

After reviewing home and family sources, look for research that has been completed by others. Begin with large collections of compiled records before original records, because they are usually easy to search and often provide important clues. Electronic family trees and databases often include helpful information about immigrants. See chapter 3, "General References and Guides." You may find that someone else has already identified the immigrant's place of origin. Even if you do not find the place of origin, you will probably uncover important clues that will lead to this information. As you work through these records, seek information for both the immigrant ancestor and other members of the family.

Local Resources

Libraries, archives, and societies in the area where an immigrant settled may have collected previous research about local people. For example, local genealogies, biographies, town or county histories, and genealogical and historical periodicals may furnish place-of-origin information. Seek compiled works done at the town, county, state, or provincial level. Also look for local genealogical or historical societies that may publish periodicals or have research registration programs that could provide valuable information.

Among local records, first seek records related to the immigrant's death. These include church records, vital records, obituaries, cemetery records, and probate records. These may give the immigrant's date and place of birth, or the names of parents and other relatives or friends. They can also provide important clues about religion, naturalization, length of residence, arrival, and property in the old country.

After death records, seek out the records of other vital events, such as the immigrant's marriage and births of children. Vital record entries for marriages and births were kept by both church and civil authorities. Other local original records include a wide variety of record types. Use census records, city directories, court records, and land and property records to establish where an immigrant settled, his or her occupation, neighbors, and other information.

Voter registrations are not available for every city or county in the United States, but when they are, they can be valuable sources of immigration information. Typically the registrations (usually in list form) are kept at the county level and provide the full name, address, birth date, birthplace, and, for naturalized citizens, the naturalization court and date (figure 9-5). Many

Major Settlements, Immigration, and Naturalization: A Chronology, 1562–2004

1562: French Huguenots established a colony on Parris Island near Beaufort, South Carolina, but abandoned it within two years.

1565: The earliest Hispanic settlers within the area of the United States settled Saint Augustine, Florida, in 1565.

1598: Hispanics settled in New Mexico.

1607: Jamestown, Virginia, was founded by English colonists.

1614: The first major Dutch settlement was founded near Albany, New York.

1619: The first black slaves arrived at Jamestown.

1620: The Mayflower, carrying Pilgrims, arrived in Massachusetts.

1623: New Netherland (Hudson River Valley) was settled as a trading post by the Dutch West India Company.

1629–40: The Puritans migrated to New England.

1634: Lord Baltimore founded Maryland as a refuge for English Catholics.

1642: The outbreak of civil war in England brought a decrease in Puritan migration.

1648: The treaty ending the Thirty Years' War stipulated that only the Catholic, Lutheran, and Reformed religions would be tolerated in Germany henceforth. Religious intolerance motivated large numbers of Germans belonging to small sects, such as Baptist Brethren (Dunkers), to leave for America.

1649: Passage of Maryland Toleration Act opened the door to any professing trinitarian Christianity.

1654: North America's first Jewish immigrants fled Portuguese persecution in Brazil, arriving at New Amsterdam.

1660: Acting on mercantilist doctrine that the wealth of a country depends on the number of its inhabitants, Charles II officially discouraged emigration from England.

1670: English courtiers settled the Carolinas.

1681: Quakers founded Pennsylvania based on William Penn's "holy experiment" in universal philanthropy and brotherhood.

1683: The first German settlers (Mennonites) arrived in Pennsylvania.

1685: Huguenots fleeing religious intolerance in France and the Revocation of the Edict of Nantes by Louis XIV settled in South Carolina.

1697: The slave trade monopoly of the Royal African Company ended and the slave trade expanded rapidly, especially among New Englanders.

1707: A new era of Scottish migration began as a result of the Act of Union between England and Scotland. Scots settled in colonial seaports. Lowland artisans and laborers left Glasgow to become indentured servants in tobacco colonies and New York.

1709: In the wake of devastation caused by wars of Louis XIV, German Palatines settled in the Hudson Valley and Pennsylvania.

1717: The English Parliament legalized transportation to American colonies as punishment; contractors began regular shipments from jails, mostly to Virginia and Maryland.

1718: Discontent with the land system: absentee landlords, high rents, and short leases in the homeland motivated large numbers of Scotch-Irish to emigrate. Most settled first in New England, then in Maryland and Pennsylvania.

1730: Germans and Scotch Irish from Pennsylvania colonized Virginia valley and the Carolina back country.

1732: James Oglethorpe settled Georgia as a buffer against Spanish and French attack, as a producer of raw silk, and as a haven for imprisoned debtors.

1740: The English Parliament enacted the Naturalization Act, which conferred British citizenship on alien colonial immigrants in an attempt to encourage Jewish immigration.

1745: Scottish rebels were transported to America after a Jacobite attempt to put Stuarts back on the throne failed.

1755: French Acadians were expelled from Nova Scotia on suspicion of disloyalty. The survivors settled in Louisiana.

1771–73: Severe crop failure and depression in the Ulster linen trade brought a new influx of Scotch-Irish to the American colonies.

1775: The outbreak of hostilities in American colonies caused the British government to suspend emigration.

1783: The revolutionary war ended with the Treaty of Paris. Immigration to America resumed, with especially large numbers of Scotch-Irish.

1789: The outbreak of the French Revolution prompted the emigration of aristocrats and royalist sympathizers.

1790: The first federal activity in an area previously under the control of the individual colonies: An act of 26 March 1790 attempted to establish a uniform rule for naturalization by setting the residence requirement at two years. Children of naturalized citizens were considered to be citizens (1 Stat. 103).

1791: After a slave revolt in Santo Domingo, 10,000 to 20,000 French exiles took refuge in the United States, principally in towns on the Atlantic seaboard.

1793: As a result of the French Revolution, Girondists and Jacobins threatened by guillotine fled to the United States.

1795: Provisions of a naturalization act of 29 January 1795 included the following: free white persons of good moral character; five-year residency with one year in state; declaration of intention had to be filed three years prior to filing of the petition.(1 Stat. 414).

1798: An unsuccessful Irish rebellion sent rebels to the United States. Distressed artisans, yeoman farmers, and agricultural laborers affected by bad harvests and low prices joined the rebels in emigrating.

U.S. Alien and Sedition Acts gave the president powers to seize and expel resident aliens suspected of engaging in subversive activities.

Naturalization requirements were changed to require fourteen years' residency; the declaration of intention was to be filed five years before citizenship (1 Stat. 566).

Aliens considered to be dangerous to the peace and safety of the United States were to be removed; registration officials were required to send their reports to the courts. (1 Stat. 570).

1802: Residency requirements of the 1795 act were reasserted; children of naturalized citizens were considered to be citizens (2 Stat. 153).

1803: War between England and France resumed. As a result, transatlantic trade was interrupted and emigration from continental Europe became practically impossible.

Irish emigration was curtailed by the British Passenger Act, which limited the numbers to be carried by emigrant ships.

1804: The widows and children of aliens who died prior to filing final papers were granted citizenship.

1807: Congress prohibited the importing of black slaves into the country. Individual states previously prohibited importation of slaves: Delaware in 1776; Virginia, 1778; Maryland, 1783; South Carolina, 1787; North Carolina, 1794; Georgia, 1798. South Carolina reopened importation of slaves in 1803.

1812: The War of 1812 between Britain and the United States brought immigration to a halt.

1814: The War of 1812 ended with the Treaty of Ghent.

1815: The first great wave of immigration to the United States brings 5 million immigrants between 1815 and 1860.

1818: Liverpool became the most-used port of departure for Irish and British immigrants, as well as considerable numbers of Germans and other Europeans as the Black Ball Line of sailing packets began regular Liverpool-New York service.

1819: The first significant federal legislation relating to immigration: passenger lists to be given to the collector of customs; reporting of immigration to the United States on a regular basis; specific sustenance rules for passengers of ships leaving U.S. ports for Europe (3 Stat. 489).

1820: The U.S. population was at 9,638,453. One hundred and fifty-one thousand new immigrants arrived in 1820 alone.

The government of Prussia attempted to halt emigration by making it a crime to urge anyone to emigrate.

1824: Alien minors could be naturalized upon reaching twenty-one years of age if they had lived in the United States for five years, and the residency period between filing a declaration and a petition (final papers) was shortened to two years (4 Stat. 69).

1825: Great Britain officially recognized the view that England was overpopulated and repealed laws prohibiting emigration.

The first group of Norwegian immigrants arrives from their overpopulated homeland.

1830: Public land in Illinois was allotted by Congress to Polish revolutionary refugees.

1837: Financial panic. Nativists claimed that immigration lowered wage levels, contributed to the decline of the apprenticeship system, and generally depressed the condition of labor.

1840: The Cunard Line began passenger transportation between Europe and the United States, opening the steamship era.

1845: The Native American party, precursor of the nativist, anti-immigrant Know-Nothing party, was founded.

1846: Crop failures in Europe. Mortgage foreclosures sent tens of thousands of dispossessed to United States.

1846–47: Irish of all classes emigrated to the United States as a result of the potato famine.

1848: Failure of German revolution resulted in the emigration of political refugees to America.

1855: Castle Garden immigration receiving station opened in New York City to accommodate mass immigration.

Alien women married to U.S. citizens became U.S. citizens by marriage. (10 Stat. 604). The law was repealed in 1922.

1856: The Know-Nothing movement was defeated in the presidential election. An Albany convention to promote Irish rural colonization in the United States was strongly opposed by Eastern bishops and thus unsuccessful.

1860: New York became "the largest Irish city in the world." Of its 805,651 residents, 203,760 were Irish-born.

1861–65: The Civil War caused a significant drop in the number of foreigners entering the United States. Large numbers of immigrants serve on both sides during the Civil War.

1862: Aliens who received honorable discharges from the U.S. Army were not required to file declarations prior to filing petitions for naturalization (12 Stat. 597).

The Homestead Act encouraged naturalization by granting citizens title to 160 acres, provided that the land was tilled for five years.

1864: Congress centralized control of immigration with a commissioner under the secretary of state. In an attempt to meet the labor crisis caused by the Civil War, Congress legalized the importation of contract laborers.

1875: The first direct federal regulation of immigration was established by prohibiting entry of prostitutes and convicts. Residency permits were required of Asians (18 Stat. 477).

1880: The U.S. population was 50,155,783. More than 5.2 million immigrants entered the country between 1880 and 1890.

1882: The Chinese exclusion law was established, curbing Chinese immigration. A general immigration law of the same year excluded persons convicted of political offenses, "lunatics," "idiots," and persons likely to become public charges. A head tax of fifty cents was placed on each immigrant.

A sharp rise in Jewish emigration to the United States was prompted by the outbreak of anti-Semitism in Russia.

1883: In an effort to alleviate a labor shortage caused by the freeing of slaves, the Southern Immigration Association was founded to promote immigration to the South.

1885: Contract laborers were denied admission to United States by the Foran Act. However, skilled laborers, artists, actors, lecturers, and domestic servants were not barred. Individuals in the United States were not to be prevented from assisting the immigration of relatives and personal friends.

1886: The Statue of Liberty was dedicated.

1888: The first act since 1798 providing for the expulsion of aliens became law.

1890: New York had the distinction of being home to as many Germans as Hamburg, Germany.

1891: The Bureau of Immigration was established under the Treasury Department to federally administer all immigration laws (except the Chinese Exclusion Act). Congress added health qualifications to immigration restrictions. Classes of persons denied the right to immigrate to the United States included the insane, paupers, persons with contagious diseases, persons convicted of felonies or misdemeanors of moral turpitude, and polygamists (26 Stat. 1084).

Pogroms in Russia caused large numbers of Jews to immigrate to the United States.

1892: Ellis Island replaced Castle Garden as the reception center for immigrants.

Immigration of Chinese to the United States was prohibited for ten years; Chinese illegally in the United States could be removed (27 Stat. 25).

1893: Chinese legally in the United States were required to apply to collectors of internal revenue for certificates of residence or be removed (28 Stat. 7).

Immigration Act of 1893 created Boards of Special Inquiry to examine excluded immigrants at ports of entry, and provided for appeals of the Board decisions.

1894: The Immigration Restriction League was organized to lead the restrictionist movement for the next twenty-five years. The league emphasized the distinction between "old" (northern and western European) and "new" (southern and eastern European) immigrants.

Aliens who received honorable discharges from the U.S. Navy and U.S. Marine Corps were not required to file declarations prior to filing petitions for naturalization (28 Stat. 124).

1894–96: To escape Moslem massacres, Armenian Christians began emigrating to the United States.

1897: President Cleveland vetoed literacy tests for immigrants.

1900: The U.S. Population at 75,994,575. More than 3,687,000 immigrants were admitted in the previous ten years.

1903: Extensive codification of existing immigration law. Added to the exclusion list were polygamists and political radicals (anarchists or persons believing in the overthrow by force or violence of the government of the United States or any government, or in the assassination of public officials—a result of President McKinley's assassination by an anarchist).

1905: As a protest against the influx of Asian laborers, the Japanese and Korean Exclusion League was formed by organized labor.

1906: The Bureau of Immigration and Naturalization was established. The purpose of the act of 29 June 1906 (32 Stat. 596) was to provide for a uniform rule for the naturalization of aliens throughout the United States. The law, effective 27 September 1906, was designed to provide "dignity, uniformity, and regularity" to the naturalization procedure. It established procedural safeguards and called for specific and uniform information regarding applicants and recipients of citizenship status. Rule Nine of the code required that all blank forms and records be obtained from and controlled by the Bureau of Immigration, "Those alone being official forms. No other forms shall be used." Knowledge of English became a basic requirement for citizenship.

1907: Between 1907 and 1922, U.S. law (34 Stat.1228) dictated that American citizen women who married alien husbands lost their U.S. citizenship and could not regain their citizenship until their husband naturalized. While it was the exception rather than the rule, some women, especially single adults , found it necessary or desirable to become naturalized citizens themselves.

An increased head tax on immigrants was enacted. People with physical or mental defects or tuberculosis and children unaccompanied by parents were added to the exclusion list. Japanese immigration was restricted.

1907–8: A Japanese government agreement to deny passports to laborers going directly from Japan to the United States failed to satisfy West Coast exclusionists.

1910: The Mexican Revolution sent thousands to the United States seeking employment.

1913: The Alien Land Law passed by California effectively barred Japanese, as "aliens ineligible for citizenship," from owning agricultural land in the state.

1914–18: World War I halted a period of mass migration to the United States.

1917: To the exclusion list were added illiterates, persons of "psychopathic inferiority," men and women entering for immoral purposes, alcoholics, stowaways, and vagrants.

The Jones Act made Puerto Ricans U.S. citizens and eligible for the draft.

1919: Anti-foreign prejudice was transferred from German Americans to alien revolutionaries and radicals in the Big Red Scare. Thousands of aliens were seized in the Palmer raids, and hundreds were deported.

1921: The first quantitative immigration law set temporary annual quotas according to nationality. The emergency immigration quotas heavily favored natives of northern and western Europe and all but closed the door to southern and eastern Europeans. An immediate drop in immigration followed.

1922: The Cable Act of 1922 made women's citizenship independent of marriage, so she no longer gained citizenship by marriage. Hence the provision to ease naturalization for women married to citizens. Alien wives of U.S. citizens were allowed to file for citizenship after one year of residency (42 Stat. 1022).

1923: A strong anti-immigrant movement spearheaded by the Ku Klux Klan reached peak strength.

1924: The National Origins Act, the first permanent immigration quota law, established a discriminatory quota system, non-quota status, and a consular control system.

The Border Patrol was established (49 Stat. 153).

1929: The stock market crash and economic crisis prompted demands for further immigration reductions and as a result, the Hoover administration ordered rigorous enforcement of a prohibition against the admission of persons liable to be public charges.

1930: The U.S. population was 123,203,000. Only 528,000 new immigrants arrived in the previous decade, the lowest number since the 1830s.

1933: As Hitler's anti-Semitic campaign began, Jewish refugees from Nazi Germany emigrated.

1934: Filipino immigration was restricted to an annual quota of fifty by the Philippine Independence Act.

1936: American women who had lost their citizenship because they married aliens were allowed to regain citizenship by taking oaths of allegiance to the United States (49 Stat. 1917).

1939: World War II began.

1940: The Alien Registration Act, also known as the Smith Act, called for registration and fingerprinting of all aliens age 14 and older within or entering the U.S (54 Stat. 1137). Approximately 5.5 million aliens were registered.

1941: Immigrant groups supported the united war effort as the United States entered World War II.

1942: Japanese Americans were evacuated from their homes and moved to detention camps.

Through the Bracero Program, Mexican laborers were strongly encouraged to come to the United States to ease the shortage of farm workers brought on by World War II.

1943: Legislation provided for the importation of agricultural workers from North, South, and Central America, Canada, and the Caribbean—the basis of the "Bracero Program."

The Chinese exclusion laws were repealed.

1945: Thousands of Puerto Ricans emigrated to escape poverty. Many settled in New York.

1946: The War Brides Act facilitated the immigration of foreign-born wives, fiancé(e)s, husbands, and children of U.S. armed forces personnel.

1948: The Displaced Persons Act, the first U.S. policy for admitting persons fleeing persecution, allowed 400,000 refugees to enter the United States during a four-year period.

1950: The Internal Security Act increased grounds for exclusion and deportation of subversives were enacted. All aliens were required to report their addresses annually.

1952: The Immigration and Naturalization Act brought into one comprehensive statute the multiple laws which governed immigration and naturalization to date: reaffirmed the national origins quota system; limited immigration from the Eastern Hemisphere while leaving the Western Hemisphere unrestricted; established preferences for skilled workers and relatives of U.S. citizens and permanent resident aliens; tightened security and screening standards and procedures; and lowered the age requirement for naturalization to eighteen years (66 Stat. 163).

The McCarren-Walter Immigration and Naturalization Act extended token immigration quotas to Asian countries.

1953–56: The Refugee Relief Act admitted more than 200,000 refugees beyond existing quotas.

Visas were granted to some 5,000 Hungarians after the 1956 revolt. President Eisenhower invited 30,000 more to come on a parole basis.

1954: Ellis Island closed.

1957: Special legislation admitted Hungarian refugees.

1959: Castro's successful revolution in Cuba began the emigration of refugees.

1960: The United States paroled Cuban refugees.

1962: The United States granted special permission for the admission of refugees from Hong Kong.

1965: Congress amended the immigration law (effective 1968): The National Origins Quota System was abolished, but the principle of numerical restriction by establishing 170,000 hemispheric and 20,000 per-country ceilings and a seven-category preference system (favoring close relatives of U.S. citizens and permanent resident aliens, those with needed occupational skills, and refugees) for the Eastern Hemisphere and a separate 120,000 ceiling for the Western Hemisphere was maintained (79 Stat. 911).

The Cuban refugee airlift program admitted Cubans to the United States under special quotas for the next eight years.

1970: The Immigration Act of 1965 was amended by President Nixon, further liberalizing admission to the United States.

1972: Congress passed the Ethnic Heritage Studies Bill, encouraging bilingual education and programs pertaining to ethnic culture.

1976: The 20,000-per-country immigration ceilings and the system of preference system for Western Hemisphere countries was applied, and separate hemispheric ceilings were maintained.

1978: The separate ceilings for Eastern and Western Hemisphere immigration were combined into one worldwide limit of 290,000.

1979: Congress appropriated more than $334 million for the rescue and resettlement of Vietnamese "boat people."

1980: The Refugee Act removed refugees as a preference category and established clear criteria and procedures for their admission, reducing the worldwide ceiling for immigrants from 290,000 to 270,000.

The so-called "Freedom Flotilla" of Cuban refugees came to the United States.

1986: Comprehensive immigration legislation legalized aliens who had resided in the United States in an unlawful status since 1 January 1982; established sanctions prohibiting employers from hiring, recruiting, or referring for a fee aliens known to be unauthorized to work in the United States; created a new classification of temporary agricultural worker and provided for the legalization of certain such workers; and established a visa waiver pilot program allowing the admission of certain non-immigrants without visas.

Separate legislation (Marriage Fraud Amendment) stipulated that aliens deriving their immigrant status based on a marriage of less than two years apply within ninety days after their second-year anniversary to remove conditional status.

1989: Allowed for the adjustment from temporary to permanent status of certain non-immigrants who were employed in the United States as registered nurses for at least three years and met established certification standards.

1990: Comprehensive immigration legislation increased total immigration; created separate admission categories for family-sponsored, employment-based, and diversity immigrants; revised all grounds for exclusion and deportation; authorized the attorney general to grant temporary protected status revised and established new non-immigrant admission categories; revised naturalization authority and requirements; and revised enforcement activities. Perhaps most important for genealogical purposes, the 1990 law transferred the exclusive jurisdiction to naturalize aliens from the Federal and State courts to the Attorney General. As a result, after 1992 (and after two centuries), courts no longer naturalized nor did they create or keep naturalization records.

1991: The Armed Forces Immigration Adjustment Act granted special immigrant status to certain types of aliens who had honorably served in the Armed Forces of the United States for at least twelve years.

1992: The Soviet Scientists Immigration Act permitted permanent resident status to a maximum of 750 scientists, excluding spouses and children, from the independent states of the former Soviet Union and the Baltic states.

1993: The North American Free-Trade Agreement Implementation Act allowed temporary entry on a reciprocal basis between the United States, Canada, and Mexico. It also established procedures for the temporary entry into the United States of Canadian and Mexican citizen professional business persons to render services for remuneration.

1994: The Violent Crime Control and Law Enforcement Act authorized establishment of a criminal alien tracking center, revised deportation procedures for certain criminal aliens who are not permanent residents, provided for expeditious deportation for denied asylum applicants, provided for improved border management through an increase in resources, and strengthened penalties for passport and visa offenses.

1996: Measures were established to control U.S. borders, protect legal workers through worksite enforcement, and remove criminal and other deportable aliens. As a result, many improvements were made in border control including an increase in border personnel, equipment, and technology.

1999: An amendment of the Immigration and Nationality Act was made to provide that an adopted alien less than eighteen years old may be considered a child under such act if adopted with or after a sibling who is a child under such Act.

2000: A modification was made of the provisions governing acquisition of citizenship by children born outside of the United States.

Naturalization became easier for immigrants who served with special guerrilla units or irregular forces in Laos.

A child born outside the United States automatically becomes a citizen of the United States when certain conditions are fulfilled, such as when at least one parent of the child is a citizen of the United States, whether by birth or naturalization, or when the child is under the age of eighteen years old.

A waiver was provided of the oath of renunciation and allegiance for naturalization of aliens having certain disabilities.

2002: Unmarried sons and daughters of certain Vietnamese refugees are extended eligibility for refugee status.

2003: An additional five-year extension was granted to the Special Immigrant Religious Worker Program.

On March 1, 2003, services formerly provided by the Immigration and Naturalization Service (INS) transitioned into the Department of Homeland Security (DHS) under U.S. Citizenship & Immigration Services (USCIS).

2004: An amendment of the Immigration and Nationality Act aimed to improve the process for verifying an individual's eligibility for employment.

* Donald J. Bogue, *The Population of the United States: Historical Trends and Future Projections* (New York: The Free Press, a Division of Macmillan, Inc., 1985); Mary Kupies Cayton, Elliott J. Gorn, and Peter W. Williams, eds., *Encyclopedia of American Social History,* 3 vols. (New York: Scribner, 1993); *INS Fact Book: Summary of Recent Immigration Data* (U.S. Department of Justice, Immigration and Naturalization Service Statistics Division, July 1993); Stephanie Bernardo Johns, *The Ethnic Almanac* (Garden City, N.Y.: Doubleday, 1981); John F. Kennedy, *A Nation of Immigrants* (New York: Harper and Row, 1964); George Thomas Kurian, *Datapedia of the United States 1790–2000: America Year by Year* (Lanham, Md.: Bernan Press, 1994).

Smith, Marian L. "An Overview of INS History" *Originally published in A Historical Guide to the U.S. Government,* ed. George T. Kurian. New York: Oxford University Press, 1998. Reprinted with permission. <http://uscis.gov/graphics/aboutus/history/articles/OVIEW.htm>

lists will note the number of years the voter was a resident of the state and county.

Immigration Sources

After the previously-mentioned sources have been investigated, a search of immigration records is in order. Citizenship (naturalization) papers, oaths of allegiance, alien registrations, passenger lists, passport applications, and immigrant aid society records fall into this category. Some records, though created for other purposes, will provide evidence of citizenship status. If the immigrant served in the U.S. military, there may be special naturalization papers connected with that service. Local and federal courts usually record military naturalizations in separate ledgers, and these may be indexed with other naturalizations in that jurisdiction. Some religious denominations kept separate lists of immigrant families as they arrived, reporting on their arrival, place of origin, and where they settled.

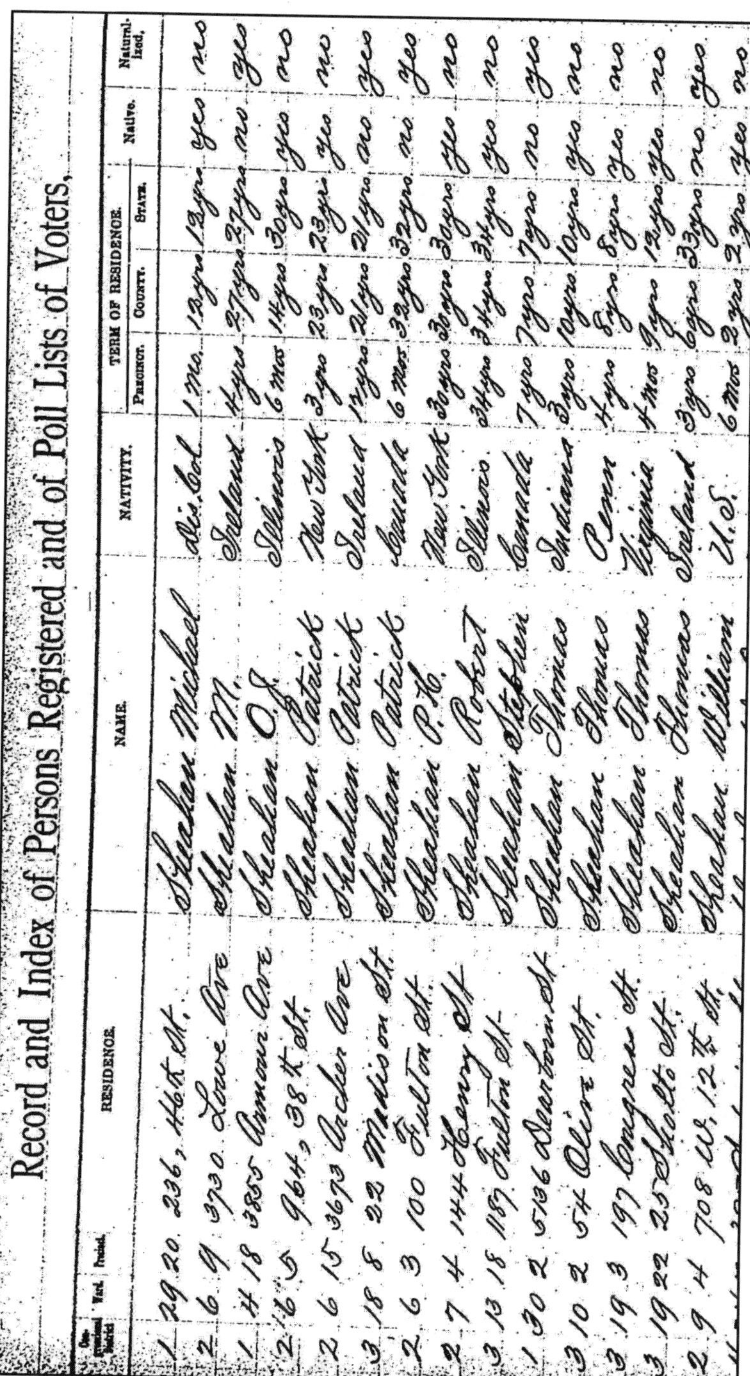

Record and Index of Persons Registered and of Poll Lists of Voters,

Cong. District	Ward	Precinct	Residence	Name	Nativity	Term of Residence: Precinct	County	State	Native	Naturalized
1	29	20	236, 46th St.	Sheahan Michael	Dis. Col.	1 mo.	12 yrs	12 yrs	yes	no
2	6	9	3730 Lowe Ave	Sheahan M.	Ireland	4 yrs	27 yrs	27 yrs	no	yes
1	4	18	3855 Armour Ave	Sheahan O.J.	Illinois	6 mos	14 yrs	30 yrs	yes	no
2	16	5	964, 38th St.	Sheahan Patrick	New York	3 yrs	23 yrs	23 yrs	yes	no
2	6	15	3673 Archer Ave	Sheahan Patrick	Ireland	14 yrs	21 yrs	21 yrs	no	yes
3	18	8	22 Madison St.	Sheahan Patrick	Canada	6 mos	32 yrs	32 yrs	no	yes
2	6	3	100 Fulton St.	Sheahan P.H.	New York	30 yrs	30 yrs	30 yrs	yes	no
2	7	4	1447 Henry St	Sheahan Robert	Illinois	34 yrs	34 yrs	34 yrs	yes	no
3	13	18	187 Fulton St.	Sheahan Stephen	Canada	7 yrs	7 yrs	7 yrs	no	yes
1	30	2	5136 Dearborn St	Sheahan Thomas	Indiana	8 yrs	10 yrs	10 yrs	yes	no
3	10	2	54 Olive St.	Sheahan Thomas	Penn	4 yrs	8 yrs	8 yrs	yes	no
3	19	3	197 Congress St.	Sheahan Thomas	Virginia	4 mos	9 yrs	12 yrs	yes	no
3	19	22	25 Sholto St.	Sheahan Thomas	Ireland	3 yrs	6 yrs	33 yrs	no	yes
2	9	4	708 W. 12th St.	Sheahan William	U.S.	6 mos	2 yrs	2 yrs	yes	no

Figure 9-5. Page from an 1892 poll list of Chicago voters that was found in the Cook County, Illinois, County Recorder's Office. The records have since been microfilmed and are available through the Illinois State Archives and through several microfilm rental libraries.

Passenger arrival lists for most available ports and time periods are indexed and are available in card files, books, or on CDs. More recently images of passenger lists have been linked to indexes and posted online, so approximate dates may be sufficient to begin a search. Lists of ship arrivals may be useful in determining possible arrival dates if an approximate arrival date or a ship name is known. Note, however, that a ship may have arrived in North America several times in a year. Details of immigration records are further discussed later in this chapter.

While none of the records mentioned should be overlooked, most American immigration and naturalization records before 1906 fail to name the town where the immigrant was born or lived in the old country. A passenger list for the ship *Rhine* (figure 9-6) is typical of passenger lists created before the late 1880s in that it includes only the country of origin for each passenger, rather than naming a city or town.

The Immigration Process

In their eagerness to find the town or city that was home to their ancestors, researchers frequently spend too much time and energy looking in the wrong places—or in the right places but in the wrong sequence. For example, as novices, many are tempted to begin immigrant research with a search of passenger lists. This is a natural instinct since most researchers have a strong desire to find detailed documentation of the ship on which their ancestors came to America. Such a passage, after all, is a seminal event in the history of any family. From a passenger list, we hope to learn exactly where an immigrant ancestor came from, how old he or she was at the time, what occupation he or she claimed, the ports of departure and arrival, and anything possible about the journey. But getting answers to these questions depends on when and where an

(B.) PASSENGERS' LIST.

District of New York, Port of New York.

I, J. B. Jordan Master of the Ship Rhine do solemnly, sincerely and truly swear that the following List or Manifest, subscribed by me, and now delivered by me to the Collector of the Customs of the Collection District of New York, is a full and perfect list of all the passengers taken on board of the said Ship Rhine at London from which port said Ship Rhine has now arrived; and that on said list is truly designated the age, the sex, and the occupation of each of said passengers, the part of the vessel occupied by each during the passage, the country to which each belongs, and also the country of which it is intended by each to become an inhabitant; and that said List or Manifest truly sets forth the number of said passengers who have died on said voyage, and the names and ages of those who died.

So help me God.

Sworn to this Aug. 9 1873 before me [signature] J B Jordan

List or Manifest of all the Passengers taken on board the Ship Rhine whereof J B Jordan is Master, from London burthen 1064 tons.

Names	Age: Years	Age: Months	Sex	Occupation	The country to which they severally belong	The country in which they intend to become inhabitants	Died on the voyage	Part of the vessel occupied by each passenger during the voyage
Selly Seelig	46		Male	Taylor	Germany	United States		Steerage
Henriette Seelig	44		Female	Wife	"	"		
Oskar Do.	15		Male	Spinster	"	"		
Johanna do	18		Female	Spinster	"	"		
Thomas Hayes	40		Male	Labourer	England			
Thomas Do.	17		"	Do	"			
George do	11		"	Child	"			
Louise do	9		Female	"	"			
Elizabeth do	7		"	"	"			
Wm. H. do	5		Male	"				
Alfred Pennett	28		"	Gardener	"	"		
Fredrick Murrock	23		"	Mechanic	"	"		
Emily Do.	24		Female	Wife	"	"		
George Hinkley	21		Male	Brick Maker	"	"		
William Ruscoe	33		"	Labourer	"	"		
Elizabeth Do.	33		Female	Wife	"	"		
Elizabeth do	10		"	Child	"			
Emma do	8		"	"	"			
Helen do	7		"	"	"	"		
William do	5		Male	"	"	"		
Robert do	3		"	"		"		
Rosetta do	1		Female	"		"		
William Dunham	38		Male	Carpenter	"	"		
Lucy Do.	10		"	Child	"	"		
Wm. Thom do	6		"		"	13-8 "		
Jane Blankine	25		Female	Wife	United States	"		
Jean Bastendorf	24		Male	Carpenter	Germany	3-2 "		
Michael Hayes	24		"	Labourer	United States	"		
Elizabeth B. Jordan	44		Female	Wife	United States	"		1st Cabin
Rose Belle do	10		"	Child	"	"		"
Joseph do	8		Male	"	"	"		"
Frank do		5	"	"	"	3-3 "		"

26

16-10

Cabin 2-2

Figure 9-6. Passenger lists created before the late 1800s, such as this one for the ship *Rhine*, which sailed from London to the port of New York on 9 August 1873, rarely indicate a precise birthplace. Found on Ancestry.com.

ancestor arrived in the United States. Until the 1880s, a typical passenger list gave only the name, age, sex, occupation, country of origin, and destination of the passenger. The native town was seldom named.

Is the port of the ancestor's arrival known with certainty? Are passenger arrival lists indexed for the port of entry and for the right time period? If there is an index for the port, will the person of interest appear in the index, or can he or she be identified in the long list of frequently misspelled names? If the surname is a common one, how will the person be distinguished from others? While many individuals traveled in groups, making them easier to find, a larger number came to the United States on their own. Unless you are fairly certain of the date and port of arrival, or unless you can quickly and surely identify the immigrant by name, age, occupation, or traveling companions, it may be better to postpone a passenger list search until other sources have been investigated.

Immigration Patterns

Success in finding an immigrant's origins is often dependent on understanding group immigration patterns. Some immigrants came directly to the United States from their places of birth. Many, however, came via other countries where they may have stayed for months, years, or even generations. Some French Huguenots stayed for extended periods in Germany, Switzerland, Holland, England, or some other place before coming to America. The Palatines who immigrated in 1709 to New York came via England and Ireland. English, Irish, French, and several other nationalities may have made Canada their home before coming to the United States. Some Germans went to Russia, Lithuania, or Brazil before establishing residency in America. Australia, the Carribean, and South America were stopping places for many groups before they came here. The researcher who is unaware of these possibilities may miss births, marriages, or records of deaths of parents or spouses in the temporary residences.

Another overlooked fact is that immigrants did not always stay in the United States. Many came as adventurers or looking for temporary jobs that would enable them to return to their homelands with their savings. Some immigrant groups traveled back and forth across the ocean as work opportunities presented themselves. Some researchers have documented two or more generations settling in this country, and then have been puzzled by the sudden disappearance of one or more of the family members. In some cases the fathers or both parents, and in other cases the children, became disenchanted with the American lifestyle and returned to the home country permanently. When a family or individual being tracked in American records suddenly disappears, it is easy to assume that there was a death or a move within the U.S. In these less-than-common circumstances, it sometimes pays to look back into the records of the country of origin.

Tickets

The purchase of tickets and travel accommodations was usually done through an emigration agent. Early agents were appointed by church or emigrant groups to secure the best price and to insure that fellow travelers were not cheated. These agents, some of whom were pastors or church clerks, traveled with the group to their destination. Later agents worked for shipping lines to fill steerage compartments so the trip was profitable for the company. They were licensed by local authorities and paid on commission or percentage, some by the length of the journey and some by the total cost of the ticket and provisions. For a more detailed description of how these agents operated, see R. J. Dickson's *Ulster Emigration to Colonial America, 1718–1775*, Norman McDonald's *Canada: Immigration and Colonization, 1841–1903*; and Clifford Neal Smith's and Anna P. Smith's *American Genealogical Resources in German Archives*.[14]

Indentures

During the Colonial Era, emigrants too poor to pay their own way could agree to sell themselves into service for the cost of their passage. Those who contracted through an emigrant agent before they left their country of origin were referred to as indentured servants. They carried a copy of the contract with them, knowing in advance how much time they owed. These contracts would be sold to employers in the New World. Those who did not negotiate contracts before they left redeemed the cost of their passage and provisions by selling themselves to the highest bidder once they arrived in America. They were called redemptioners. English emigrants were most often indentured with articles signed before a magistrate; Germans usually redeemed their passages at auction. Richard B. Morris's *Government and Labor in Early America* is the classic work on the subject.[15] Other studies examine servitude in individual colonies—for example, Warren B. Smith's *White Servitude in Colonial South Carolina*.[16] A list of these local studies is included in Barbara Bigham's "Colonists in Bondage: Indentured Servants in America," *Early American Life*.[17] Finding indentures can be difficult, but a few are beginning to appear in print. An excellent example is Farley Grubb's *German Immigrant Servant Contracts, Registered at the Port of Philadelphia, 1817–1831*.[18]

The Journey

Conditions on the immigrants' voyage changed and improved over time, especially with the advent of steamships in the mid-1800s which considerably shortened the journey. Also, as early as the 1810s, some foreign governments established rules and regulations regarding the number of immigrants a ship could carry, based on its size. Because much of the interest in the nature of the voyage pertains to colonial immigrants, the following descriptions will provide a general picture.

Emigrants traveling from German principalities to Pennsylvania faced a long, three-part journey. The first stage was the trip down the Rhine to Rotterdam or Amsterdam. Wrote one 1750 voyager:

> This journey lasts from the beginning of May to the end of October, fully half a year, amid such hardships as no one is able to describe adequately with their misery. The cause is because the Rhine boats from Heilbronn to Holland have to pass by twenty-six custom houses, at all of which the ships are examined, which is done when it suits the convenience of the custom-house officials. In the meantime the ships with the people are detained long, so that the passengers have to spend much money. The trip down the Rhine lasts therefore four, five, and even six weeks. When the ships come to Holland, they are detained there likewise five to six weeks. Because things are very dear there, the poor people have to spend nearly all they have during that time.[19]

The second stage was from Rotterdam to the English port of Cowes on the Isle of Wight, then the principal port for immigrant traffic, although ships also stopped at Dover, Plymouth, London, and other ports. Here was another delay while ships awaited customs clearance, provisioning, and favorable winds. This phase took fourteen to twenty-one days.

The final stage of the journey was the seven-to-twelve week ocean crossing, later shortened by steam to fewer than fourteen days. The passengers were densely packed into the steerage decks below the ship's waterline. Shipping companies, to increase profits and cut expenses, often filled the cargo spaces with people too, rather than carry adequate food and water. By the mid-nineteenth century, government authorities required minimum rations of food and water from the ships' provisions; but earlier travelers risked disease, storm, and a high mortality rate. For a detailed description of the ocean voyage, see Philip Taylor's *The Distant Magnet: European Emigration to the U.S.A.*[20]

The process of arrival in the new country generated another series of records. The Reverend Henry M. Muehlenberg described the arrival process in a report to his superiors in Halle, Germany, in 1769:

> After much delay one ship after another arrives in the harbor of Philadelphia, when the rough and severe winter is before the door. One or more merchants receive the lists of the freights and the agreement which the emigrants have signed with their own hand in Holland, together with the bills for their travel down the Rhine and the advances of the "newlanders" for provisions, which they received on the ships on account. Formerly the freight for a single person was six to ten louis d'ors, but now it amounts to fourteen to seventeen louis d'ors [one louis d'ors equalled about $4.50]. Before the ship is allowed to cast anchor at the harbor front, the passengers are all examined, according to the law in force, by a physician, as to whether any contagious disease exists among them. Then the arrivals are led in procession to the City Hall and there they must render the oath of allegiance to the king of Great Britain. After that they are brought back to the ship. Then announcements are printed in the newspapers, stating how many of the new arrivals are to be sold. Those who have money are released. Whoever has well-to-do friends seeks a loan from them to pay the passage, but there are only a few who succeed. The ship becomes the market-place. The buyers make their choice among the arrivals and bargain with them for a certain number of years and days. They then take them to the merchant, pay their passage and their other debts and receive from the government authorities a written document, which makes the newcomers their property for a definite period.[21]

Many aspects of the immigrant experience were traumatic—selling all earthly possessions, traveling for weeks to reach a new land, watching loved ones sicken and die far from the rest of the family. Many immigrants cushioned the shock by living, at least temporarily, with family and friends who had already immigrated. When searching census records, it is sometimes helpful to record the names of all boarders listed in a multiple-family dwelling, because they are often related to the head of house even if the surname is different. As the family head of house acquired work and earned some income, the family moved into its own residence, often rented, sometimes owned.

American Sources for Documenting Immigrants

Family Histories

Published genealogies and family histories comprise one of the most significant compiled sources. These genealogies, generally compiled by family members, may include biographies, pictures, maps, time lines, and heraldry; some include documentation, others do not. Often these genealogies go back to the original immigrant with information concerning ethnic and geographical beginnings. They generally tend to show all that was known about the family at the time it was written. Technological advances of the past few years have facilitated research, publication, and the distribution of thousands of genealogies and family histories. In some cases, nearby or distant relatives have completed well-documented genealogies, and their work can spare you hours of work and frustration. It may be that someone else has identified your immigrant ancestor's place of origin in a published work. Keep in mind, however, that it always pays to double-check the accuracy of any such research.

Two useful finding aids for locating published genealogies are the Family History Library surname catalog, which identifies approximately 60,000 North American genealogies; and the catalogs of the Library of Congress. Among them is Marion J. Kaminkow's *Genealogies in the Library of Congress: A Bibliography* and *Genealogies Cataloged by the Library of Congress Since 1986*.[22] Most archives, historical societies, and genealogical societies have special collections and indexes of genealogies of value to immigrant origin researchers. Search as many library catalogs and indexes as possible. Collections vary from one library to another, and the ever-growing number of published family histories increases the potential for finding information on one or more of your immigrant ancestors as time goes by. Ancestry.com is continually adding family histories to its site at <www.ancestry.com>, and Brigham Young University's Family History Archive is building on its collection at <www.lib.byu.edu/fhc>.

Electronic Family Trees

Since the 1980s, family historians have been creating personal genealogical computer databases based on the results of their research findings. They have, in turn, contributed their personal "electronic family trees" to a growing number of collections available on CD-ROM and/or the Internet, where others can search for clues to their own research. The most popular and largest electronic family trees are OneWorldTree at Ancestry.com, WorldConnect at RootsWeb.com, Pedigree Resource File and Ancestral File at FamilySearch <www.familysearch.org>, and World Family Tree at Genealogy.com. Factoring in the many duplications, these collections still provide varying detail about scores of millions of people. Among those entries will be hundreds of thousands of immigrants. Many entries for immigrants simply identify that they were born in a different country, but some include specific statements about an immigrant's hometown. While most such databases lack adequate source citations, such specific statements are usually readily proved in church records or other sources in the ancestral country.

International Genealogical Index

This well-known index is actually a database of births and deaths, listing hundreds of millions of names by country or state. It serves as a partial index to church births and marriages, and is one of the most helpful tools for finding specific individuals or localizing where surnames were most common.

Early in your research check the International Genealogical Index (IGI) at the Family History Library, one of its family history centers, or at one of selected libraries across the United States. It is the largest genealogical database in the world. It indexes and abstracts births and marriages in civil and church records with some other records for some countries. The index is easy to check because it is available on the Internet, on microfiche, or on CD-ROM and combines spelling variants in one alphabetized sequence. Most countries can be searched by county, or by searching the entire country. For more information on the IGI, see chapter 3, "General References and Guides."

Local Histories and Biographies

Published histories of towns, counties, or regions in which an ancestor lived are often the key to identifying the national and ethnic origin of an immigrant. Histories of a locality's churches, schools, or businesses may also mention the immigrant. If an ancestor is included with the area's founding families or was a prominent citizen, a local history may include an account of his or her life.

Despite their tendency to focus on society's most prominent citizens, state and local histories, biographies, and biographical encyclopedias can be useful for tracking down some immigrants' origins. State, county and local histories were especially popular during the late nineteenth century and the first twenty or thirty years of the twentieth century. Many were produced on a subscription basis and biographical sketches of the subscribers formed a substantial part of each history. Centennial publications of various institutions, organizations, churches, cities, and towns were frequently financed and formatted in a similar manner. If the subject of the biographical sketch was an immigrant, the exact birthplace might have been noted in such a source. If an immigrant or his parents did not make it into the pages of a biographical work, there is always a chance that the accomplishments of a sibling, or one or more descendants, will appear somewhere in print.

Local histories often mention less prominent immigrants as well. Common folk become especially important if they were among an area's original settlers. Immigrants often considered it a mark of success to be included in the typical local histories of the nineteenth century, even if they had to pay to be included. If an immigrant was willing to spend the necessary money, the publisher would include him, no matter how obscure he was. Often, the names of immigrants are included in lists of early settlers as members of a founding church, as original town settlers, landholders, and school teachers, or in cemetery and sexton records. Bibliographies of local histories and biographical sources are available for most countries, states, and provinces where immigrants settled.

Histories are also available for many ethnic and religious groups. Examples include Martin Ulvestad's *Nordmændene i Amerika* [Norwegians in America], and Rose Rosicky's *A History of Czechs (Bohemians) in Nebraska*.[23]

Some of the best sources of information about a given group or individual originate in the ethnic community itself. Immigrant groups clung together to sustain their memories, culture, and communication with the old country. Every ethnic organization in the United States has played a role in preserving and perpetuating group identity and national pride. Hundreds of ethnic organizations have flourished and published periodicals, newspapers, and historical and biographical albums—frequently in their native tongue. Histories produced by ethnic presses may focus on the national, state, or local level. A typical volume reviews the history of the group from its earliest involvement in American history, extols the group's contributions to the development of the United States, and pays tribute to members of the ethnic group who had become prominent for one reason or another. Biographical sketches in these volumes tend to describe group members in only the most glowing terms, but frequently the degree of detail is very useful. Many a genealogical breakthrough can be attributed to an ethnic biographical sketch. *Chicago und sein Deutschthum* is one such example.[24] Among the volume's biographical sketches are many that give a specific date and place of birth of the subject as well as date of immigration, former places of residence, arrival date in the country and the city, educational and occupational history, and names of parents, spouse, and children. The reader must be proficient in German, however, because this Chicago source is printed in that language.

Histories also exist for most religious groups, such as Henry R. Holsinger's *History of the Dunkers and the Brethren Church*.[25] Histories of larger ethnic and religious groups, such as Germans or Episcopalians, can also provide valuable background information about migration and settlement patterns.

In addition to local and group histories, biographical sketches are often found in local and national collective biographical works. These were very common in the last half of the nineteenth century. Many other biographical records have been published and can be located in local libraries. An excellent bibliography listing more than 16,000 national and international collective biographies from around the world is Robert C. Slocum's *Biographical Dictionaries and Related Works*.[26]

Mirana C. Herbert's and Barbara McNeil's *Biography and Genealogy Master Index*, is one of several published biographical references described in chapter 3, "General References and Guides."[27] This index includes more than eight million references to three million individuals profiled in approximately 1,500 histories, blue books, and "who's who" compilations. Like any other index, it is not all inclusive, but it will tease the imagination and point to other potential sources. This index gives the name of the subject of the biographical sketch, birth and death years, and cites the source for the sketch. By following through to cited sources, it is sometimes possible to find the foreign origins of a family.

Local histories and biographies are among the most popular of sources for locating information about nineteenth century immigrants, regardless of ethnic group or social status, particularly for those who settled in rural areas. For more information on the bibliographies and indexes to these sources, see Kory L. Meyerink's chapters, "County and Local Histories" and "Biographies" in *Printed Sources: A Guide to Published Genealogical Records*. *Biography and Genealogy Master Index* as well as a large number of other local histories and biographical sources are available by subscription at Ancestry.com.

Census Records

Census records from as early as 1850 indicate birthplaces for individuals and possible dates of immigration. Later census records provide more specific information on individuals as well as their parents. U.S. federal census records are widely available on microfilm in many large libraries, archives, and through online subscription services such as Ancestry.com. (See chapter 5, "Census Records.")

While U.S. census records rarely indicate the exact birthplace of an individual, significant immigration facts can be gleaned from the federal enumerations, especially in later years. From 1850 to 1870, every person's country or state of birth was shown. Censuses from 1880 to 1930 asked for birthplaces of both parents as well. Because the country of birth was asked for on the census, responses such as Hannover, Baden, or Cassel invariably refer to the German state, not the city of the same name.

With the federal census indexed for all years that are available to the public, the census is a logical starting point for determining family origins. Judging from ages and birthplaces, it is usually possible to estimate the date of arrival in the United States, even in earlier enumerations. Beginning with the 1900 census, more detailed immigration information was required. The 1920 census asked for specific birthplaces (state, province, or city) of foreigners who had been born in a country whose boundaries had been changed in World War I (the German, Austrian, Russian, and Ottoman empires). Approximately half of the enumerators complied with this requirement. Other clues in the 1920 census, such as mother tongue, may provide additional insights.

Even if you are unable to find your own ancestor's country of origin in census records, the discovery of another relative's origins or those of others of the same surname may prove helpful. With the availability of census indexes, it may prove useful to survey the occurrence of a given surname in a statewide index. Frequently individuals of the same family settled in close proximity. Concentrations of an unusual surname will provide a starting place to search for additional information.

State censuses can also be useful in tracking family origins. In addition to the standard questions asked by federal censuses, the 1925 Iowa State Census, for example, asked for the names of parents, mother's maiden name, nativity of parents, place of parent's marriage, military service, occupation and religion.

It should be remembered that, while census records are extremely useful in immigration research, the information provided in them is not entirely reliable. An individual might not have remembered his or her age exactly. Sometimes, foreigners fearing problems with a strange new government did not answer questions honestly, especially those that related to citizenship status. Some immigrants could not remember accurately the date of their arrival in the United States or the date of their naturalization. When they did, however, and when the date was recorded correctly, this information will facilitate naturalization and passenger list searches.

Societies

Many historical, lineage, genealogical, fraternal, and ethnic societies may have records concerning immigrants. Such societies often collect records, such as family and local histories, oral histories, church records, newspapers, cemetery collections, passenger lists, manuscripts, organization membership applications, early settler indexes, military records, directories, and other records that may help with your search. Genealogical and historical societies are organized for almost every geographic locality. Historical societies for most ethnic and religious groups also exist—for example, the American Historical Society of Germans from Russia. Also search for pioneer or old settler societies. Contact these various kinds of societies to learn about their services and hours. They are usually very cooperative and can help locate good local researchers. Genealogical and historical societies should be approached early in most searches.

Publications of genealogical and historical societies are especially rich and unique sources of local information. Especially useful are those groups such as Polish Genealogical Society of America <www.pgsa.org>; The Irish Ancestral Research Association <www.tiara.ie>; and other ethnic organizations that specialize in helping family researchers in with more specific immigration questions. Some genealogical societies, libraries, and archives maintain surname registries that have proved useful in linking individuals with similar research interests. These organizations tend to focus on the ethnic groups prominent in their respective areas, and this will be reflected in their publications. Newsletters and quarterlies published by societies can be especially rich sources of information on immigrant groups. *The Ancestry Family Historian's Address Book,* by Juliana Szucs Smith, is a comprehensive list of local, state, and federal agencies and institutions, and ethnic and genealogical organizations.[28] Most such societies now have Internet sites and can be readily found through careful use of such Internet search engines as Google. Even if you don't know the name of a society, enter keywords, such as the name of the county or ethnic group, and words such as "historical" or "genealogical" and "society" into the search engine. Likely the society you are seeking will be one of the first few hits. Internet message boards such as those at RootsWeb.com and Ancestry.com are also popular places where researchers can exchange helpful information on specific ethnic groups and immigration themes. See chapter 2, "Computers and Technology," for effective ways to search for genealogical and historical societies.

Historical Societies

Small and large, historical societies across the nation have collected and preserved pieces of local history that may not be found elsewhere. Historical organizations are traditional storehouses for manuscripts, letters, journals, news clippings, biographical and obituary files, old photographs and yearbooks, local business and institutional histories, memorial and cemetery records, and artifacts. Old settler and pioneer information found in historical societies will often point to Old World origins.

In Pennsylvania, for example, several county historical societies have "family reports" with information previously collected and filed by family name. Some societies will send photocopies of the materials they have on hand for a fee. When requesting information, write or call ahead to be sure of the particular society's research policy. Some of these files are also available on microfilm at the Family History Library and its family history centers throughout the United States.

Immigrant Societies

The records of societies an immigrant may have joined during his or her life may be hard to locate. Arriving foreigners often received financial and other assistance from immigrant aid societies that helped them settle in their new home. An immigrant may have sent money back to his or her family or brought relatives from the old country through an immigrant aid society. These societies were usually associated with ethnic, religious, or community organizations. The most famous is the Hebrew Immigrant Aid Society. Ask local and ethnic historical societies for addresses of immigrant aid societies that operated in their area.

Immigrant aid societies sprang up to supply information on lodgings, work opportunities, and local resources; to provide credit references and sometimes cash or food where needed; to advise and caution immigrants against the unscrupulous; to collect and forward mail; to coordinate group insurance and benefits for living family members; and to aid in burial of loved ones and with legal transactions unfamiliar to new immigrants. These societies kept some invaluable records. See G. A. Dobbert's "An On-Line System for Processing Loosely Structured Records," in *Historical Methods*, for the use of 1,700 obituaries clipped by the German Immigrant Society of Cincinnati, Ohio; and John Guertler and Adele Newburger's *Records of Baltimore's Private Organizations: A Guide to Archival Resources* for ethnic and immigrant societies in the city of Baltimore.[29] The YWCA operated institutes for women to help them adjust, learn English, and care adequately for their families. See Nicholas V. Montalto's *The International Institute Movement: A Guide to Records of Immigrant Society Agencies in the United States* for a state-by-state listing of aid societies for women immigrants.[30] Erna Risch's important work, "Immigrant Aid Societies Before 1820," in *Pennsylvania History*, discusses societies for Germans, Scots, Irish, and others throughout the

American colonies.[31] Also useful is Bradford Luckingham's "Benevolence in Emergent San Francisco: A Note on Immigrant Life in the Urban Far West," in *Southern California Quarterly*, which describes societies for French, Germans, Catholics, Protestants, seamen, ladies, Hebrews, and others.[32]

Records of former immigrant aid societies continue to come to light. A recent example is the records of a New York savings bank founded by Irish immigrants in 1850. Data in the records included immigrants' places of birth in Ireland, names of family members, and ship arrival information. The earliest records have recently been abstracted by Kevin J. Rich as *Irish Immigrants of the Emigrant Industrial Savings Bank, 1850–1853*.[33] The Emigrant Bank records have also been scanned and indexed and they are available at Ancestry.com.

Fraternal Organizations

After the immigrant settled, he or she may have sought the company of people with similar interests and joined an ethnic or fraternal organization like the Veterans of Foreign Wars, a Jewish Landsmanschaft, the Grange, a Masonic lodge, Knights of Columbus, and so forth. Although they may be difficult to locate, ethnic and fraternal society records sometimes provide crucial immigration information. A book that helps locate some of these societies is the *Encyclopedia of Associations: Regional, State, and Local Organizations*.[34]

Public libraries normally have guides to help locate these organizations. Particularly useful for locating societies dealing with immigrants is Lubomyr R. Wynar's *Encyclopedic Directory of Ethnic Organizations in the United States*.[35]

Periodicals

Genealogical, lineage society, religious, and historical periodicals are most helpful when you know the area in which an immigrant settled, and his or her ethnic group. Genealogical and historical societies usually publish periodicals about the people in the geographic area or ethnic group they cover. Family organizations often publish newsletters with immigrant information.

Periodicals often reprint a wide variety of material, including abstracts from original sources that discuss immigrants. Periodicals may include the following:

- Passenger list abstracts
- Naturalization list abstracts
- Sketches about early pioneers
- Ethnic group background information
- Genealogical sketches
- Pedigrees and *ahnentafels*

Periodicals published by genealogical societies are good places to publish queries asking for information about immigrant ancestors. There are sometimes fees for this service (especially for nonmembers). Also check indexes for previous queries and answers. Genealogical and historical societies in the United States have been churning out publications for more than 150 years. One of the quickest and most efficient ways to locate articles that relate to an ethnic group is to consult one of the periodical source indexes discussed in chapter 2, "Computers and Technology." One of the largest compilations is the *Periodical Source Index (PERSI)*, a comprehensive place, subject, and surname index to current genealogical and local history periodicals.[36] The Foreign Places section of *PERSI*, for example, can be particularly helpful in immigration research; it is arranged first by country, then by record type. European locations may contain current smaller political subdivisions; for example, Great Britain may include materials of a regional nature; Germany includes entries for German provinces, as well as pre-unification East and West Germany, Prussia, and so forth; and U.S.S.R. includes articles pertaining to the Ukraine, Latvia, Lithuania, and other countries once part of the Soviet Union. *PERSI* is available online at Ancestry.com and HeritageQuestOnline.com and on CD-ROM from Ancestry.com.

Library and Archive Collections

Libraries and archives in the area where an immigrant settled may have collected previous research about local people. For example, local genealogy collections, vertical files, scrapbooks, school records, newspapers, obituaries, and histories of organizations, towns, and counties are sources that may reveal an immigrant's origins.

A growing number of organizations are devoted exclusively to collecting and preserving materials for specific immigrant or ethnic groups. An example of a repository dedicated to a particular ethnic group is the Swenson Swedish Immigration Center (Augustana College, 639 38th Street, Rock Island, IL 61201-2296) <www.augustana.edu>. See listings for other single-nationality collections listed under the appropriate ethnic groups listed at the end of this chapter.

Look for catalogs, inventories, guides, or periodicals that describe the holdings of archives and libraries, then study these guides before visiting the repository. An example of a helpful guide is Suzanna Moody and Joel Wurl's *The Immigration History Research Center: A Guide to Collections*.[37] The Immigration History Research Center <www1.umn.edu/ihrc> was founded at the University of Minnesota (311 Anderson Library, 222-21st Avenue South, Minneapolis, MN 55455) in 1965 to encourage study of the role of immigration and ethnicity in shaping the society and culture of the United States and to collect the records of twenty-four American ethnic groups originating from eastern, central, and southern Europe and the Near East. Working closely with ethnic communities, the Research Center has preserved and made available for research priceless documents of immigrant America, including personal papers, newspapers, books, periodicals, and the records of churches and cultural, fraternal, and political organizations. Ethnic collections include those for Albanians, Armenians, Bulgarians, Byelorussians, Carpatho-Ruthenians, Croatians, Czechs, Estonians, Finns, Greeks, Hungarians, Italians, Jews (Eastern European), Latvians, Lithuanians, Macedonians, Poles, Romanians, Russians, Serbs, Slovaks, Slovenes, and Ukrainians, and people from the Near East.

Foreign Collections in American Libraries and Archives

The Family History Library has several thousand reels of microfilmed emigration registers available to all genealogists. The library also has microfilm copies of original records pertaining to the Jews in Poland; they are available at Hebrew University in Jerusalem as well. These records are written in Polish, and their accessibility in Poland today is limited. However, in the United States they are available to anyone within driving distance of an LDS Family History Center.

Vital Records

The amount of information provided in vital records varies from county to county and from year to year. As a rule, vital records are limited in their usefulness as clues to immigrant origins, but it is always worth seeking out every vital record available for every member of the family if immigrant origins are being sought. In most instances, birth, marriage, and death records provide only the country of birth and not the hoped-for native town.

When using vital records, first seek records related to the immigrant's death. These may give the immigrant's birthplace and date, or the names of parents, relatives, or friends. They can also provide important clues regarding religion, naturalization, length of residence, arrival, and property in the old country.

After death records, seek out the records of other vital events, such as the immigrant's marriage and his or her children's births. Generally, records of later periods contain more information than earlier ones. While indication of birthplace is rare, it does sometimes appear. This illustrates the importance of locating every possible record, even when the likelihood of immigration information is slight.

As in every other aspect of genealogical research, the records of siblings, aunts and uncles, and even distant relatives can be very important. For example, members of an Irish family tracing their ancestry documented events and activities of their father's, grandfathers', and great-grandfathers' lives back to the immigrant's arrival in the United States in 1836. To their great disappointment, other than the census and death records noting Ireland as the birthplace, nothing in any of the records provided clues to specific origins. At the suggestion of a professional researcher, the family began to collect information on all the other children of the immigrant. Fortunately, on the death certificate of the eighth of the immigrant's twelve children, more specific information appeared. The father's birthplace was listed as Wexford, and the mother's as Queenstown. Had the research not been extended to include the great uncles and aunts, it is doubtful that the project could have progressed.

For a complete discussion of vital records, see chapter 13, "Vital Records."

Ecclesiastical Records

For the new immigrant, a local religious congregation could alleviate "culture shock." The church or synagogue was a haven that offered services in a familiar tongue, and its officials and members were often known to the immigrant. The formality of christening a child born en route or solemnizing a marriage begun as a shipboard romance provided a ritual sanction for the move. In some denominations, letters of recommendation for church membership were surrendered shortly after arrival. Loose documents kept by individual immigrants have seldom survived, but some religious denominations kept records of recommendations and removals.

Whenever possible, study immigrant church registers; patterns sometimes emerge that will point to the foreign home for an entire group. For example, while searching for a certain immigrant in Catholic Church records in a small Indiana town, a genealogist searched baptism and marriage entries in several ledgers. The native towns were noted in the church registers for many of those receiving the sacraments, as well as for the witnesses and sponsors. Unfortunately, there was no such notation identifying the birthplace of the subject of interest. The astute genealogist did not give up there, however. Knowing that sponsors and witnesses are frequently close relatives and friends, he noted the names of all the towns mentioned in the registers during the time the family resided in the parish. Next, he took a detailed map of the area near a recognizable city mentioned in the church register. Some towns were not on the map, but most were located, though their names had been misspelled in the registers. This study revealed that a large number of towns cited were within a thirty-mile radius of the central city on the detailed map. Once the Indiana genealogist focused on a specific area in Germany, another genealogist specializing in German research was able to find emigration records for the family of interest. In recent years, dedicated researchers have indexed a number of church records of various denominations. Some have been published by small presses; others remain in the card catalogs of various historical archives. Joseph M. Silinonte's published volume of *Bishop Loughlin's Dispensations, Diocese of Brooklyn 1859–1866* is an excellent example of a book that has provided extraordinary clues to foreign origins.[38] In this case, information in the dispensations granted by the Diocese of Brooklyn, New York, for such things as the marriage of a Catholic to a non-Catholic included the birthplaces of the bride and groom, many of whom were immigrants.

Cemeteries

Surviving cemetery and mortuary records are important sources for immigrant research. Sometimes the only recording of an original name or the exact birthplace is on a tombstone. For example, one family historian had reached a "dead end" in researching the Doner name in New York. After many tries at locating cemetery records, it was discovered that the original cemetery deed had been recorded under the name Dooner. Once alerted to the original spelling, the researcher was able to determine when family members changed the name spelling, and to continue researching the correct spelling in older records.

Often, children and other relatives of immigrants honored the memory of their deceased ancestors by noting the person's birthplace on his or her tombstone. Ethnic cemeteries, ethnic sections of larger cemeteries, and family burial plots of immigrants can be veritable gold mines for determining ethnic origins. Whenever possible, visit cemeteries personally to inspect and photograph monuments.

Funeral Homes

For immigrants, especially those living in cities or ethnic clusters, it was most common to conduct business with those who came from the same or similar backgrounds. The undertaker with Irish origins would best understand the needs and wants of his fellow countrymen when it came time for a wake and burial; likewise, a Jewish undertaker was best qualified to handle religious burial rituals for members of the Jewish community. Over the years, the undertaking establishments begun by immigrants have frequently changed in one way or another or have disappeared completely. Whether changes came about because of a shift in ethnic makeup of a neighborhood, the transfer of the business to another generation, or the complete shutdown of the undertaking company, it is frequently difficult to discover what has become of mortuary or undertaker's records. Contacting currently operating cemeteries and funeral homes of the same ethnic or religious background may be the best method of tracking down the records of older mortuaries. Genealogical and historical societies, especially those with an ethnic focus, are also good sources of information because a typical goal for that kind of an organization is to preserve and publish information with historical and genealogical value.

Newspapers

Newspapers provide a variety of immigration information. Search both the local newspapers where the immigrant settled and the ethnic newspapers in the immigrant's language or for the cultural group. In addition to obituaries (described later in the chapter), newspapers from the immigrant's lifetime may also give the following kinds of information to help find an immigrant's place of origin:

- Lists of passengers or new arrivals
- Immigrants treated in a local hospital
- Lists of immigrants who came as indentured servants or apprentices
- Missing relative or friend queries
- Marriage announcements
- Notices of probates of estates

Many of the immigrants had relatives and friends who had already come to America and frequently tried to locate them with newspaper advertisements. About ten German-language newspapers served German immigrants in or near Philadelphia by 1776. In addition, there were the English-language papers. Examples of extracts of inquiries and advertisements include Anita L. Eyster's "Notices by German and Swiss Settlers Seeking Information of Members of their Families, Kindred, and Friends Inserted Between 1742–1761" in *Pennsylvania Berichte* and 1762–1779 in the *Pennsylvania Staatsbote*," in *Pennsylvania German Folklore Society*; and Edward Hocker's *Genealogical Data Relating to the German Settlers of Pennsylvania and Adjacent Territory. From Advertisements in German Newspapers Published in Philadelphia and Germantown, 1743–1800.*[39]

Many Irish who settled in Boston used the newspapers to seek friends and relatives who arrived earlier. Often, their queries indicated where in Ireland the person they were seeking came from. Abstracts of thousands of notices from 1831 to 1930 have been gathered in Ruth-Ann Harris and Donald M. Jacobs's *The Search for Missing Friends: Irish Immigrant Advertisements Placed in the* Boston Pilot.[40]

Immigrants often had to redeem the cost of their passage by indenture. Announcements of new arrivals to be sold into indentureship were printed in newspapers, with dates of auction. After the negotiations were over, the results were also printed in newspapers.

Newspapers, now increasingly available online, carry more than indentures or letters and announcements seeking relatives. They also publish probate processes originating in Europe and obituaries of family members who died in Europe. Be sure to research both the original papers, often available on microfilm through interlibrary loan, and the abstracts published in the local newspaper. Indeed, immigrants can appear in newspapers for a variety of reasons, as this excerpt shows:

> Philadelphia, September 17. 1747.
>
> Run away, on the 11th of this instant September, at night, from William Plaskett, of Trenton, a Welsh servant woman, named Sarah Davis, about 27 years of age, middle stature, somewhat freckled, has a small scar in her forehead, and is slow of speech: Had on when she went away, a callicoe [*sic*] gown, a black fur hat, shagged on the under side, with a patch on the crown, and an ozenbrigs apron. Whoever takes up

and secures said servant woman, so as her master may have her again, shall have Twenty Shillings reward, and reasonable charges, paid by William Plaskett.[41]

Ethnic newspapers can be particularly helpful. According to Lubomyr R. and Anna T. Wynar, "The major function of the ethnic press lies in its role as the principal agent by which the identity, cohesiveness, and structure of an ethnic community are preserved and perpetuated."[42] Unusual or special events in the lives of working-class immigrants that were routinely unnoticed by major daily newspapers often warranted lengthy articles in ethnic and religious newspapers. Birth, marriage, anniversary, and death notices and articles in ethnic newspapers can be invaluable sources for discovering immigrant origins. Even mention of an individual's running for public office, a promotion, or a trip to visit family in the native country may provide personal details that will not be found elsewhere.

An increasing number of historic newspapers are now appearing online, making it easier to find references to immigrants. Major collections are available through the two major genealogical subscription sites, <www.ancestry.com> and <www.proquest.com>. Many others are identified on newspaper-specific sites, such as <www.newspaperarchive.com>. In addition, local collections are growing in many states, often as part of a state library consortium.

Obituaries

Obituaries are excellent sources for biographical information about immigrants. In addition to the name and death date of the immigrant, surviving family members, church affiliation, spouses, parents, occupations, burial places, and, most importantly, the native town in the old country may be noted. For many an immigrant, an obituary may have been the only "biographical sketch" ever written for him or her.

For example, research on Carl Schultz, a Mecklenburg immigrant to Wisconsin, was stymied because of his common name and the lack of good biographical information. His obituary, while not providing the town of origin, gave the year of immigration. This information then made it possible to identify him in the Hamburg passenger lists, which indicated his native town.

Obituaries were usually published in local and church newspapers. Some also appear in church, professional, company, and school periodicals. Although brief death notices appeared in the earliest newspapers, traditional obituaries are most common after the mid-1800s.

Obituary collections are appearing on the Web even faster than many of the newspapers from which they were taken. Many websites now exist which either collect obituaries, or point to obituary collections on the Internet. Several such sites are noted in chapter 3, "General References and Guides."

City Directories

City directories are among the best sources for tracking an immigrant through the years (see chapter 8, "Directories," and chapter 20, "Urban Research"). Immigrants have typically settled in cities in the United States, especially in Eastern Seaboard cities, until they could find better opportunities in rural areas. City directories generally provide the names, occupations, and addresses of working adults in any given household, and are an important means of tracking individuals from year to year. While directories of residents may date back to a city's earliest days, no directory is all-inclusive. Unfortunately, foreigners, especially those who did not speak English, were those most frequently excluded or overlooked as city directories were compiled. Some groups, such as the Poles in Chicago, independently published city or community directories in their own language to compensate. Ethnic and local historical societies have frequently microfilmed or reprinted these special directories.

While city directories seldom, if ever, name the town or even country the immigrant came from, they can provide other important information. From a directory you may learn, within a year or two, when the immigrant arrived. Carefully tracking the addresses of others with the same surname may reveal unknown siblings or children. City directories can also help you determine which church of the family's preferred denomination was nearest the family residence.

Immigration Records

Passenger Lists

Passenger arrival lists are among the most-used sources for documenting our ancestors' immigration. Unfortunately, however, lists were not kept for every ship, some lists have been lost, and some are not indexed. The content of passenger lists has also changed significantly over the years. Passenger lists created before the 1880s rarely indicate the immigrant's town of origin. In earlier years of record-keeping, lists typically showed only the immigrant's name, age, and country of origin or the ship's last port of call. The formats of lists in the 1880s gradually evolved to include more detailed information, including the place of origin.

The vast majority of immigration records are the passenger arrival lists kept by the U.S. federal government (after 1820) or by other authorities (cities, states, port officials, and shipping lines).

While most passenger lists have been indexed for U.S. ports, a few lists remain unindexed. However, this is changing as Ancestry.com and other online services are transcribing and posting arrival lists at a fast pace. As with all indexes and transcripts, there are errors—especially errors of omission or misreading. In addition to the problem of simply missing names in transcription, individuals who departed from a country illegally may not have been recorded at all. Children who emigrated with their parents were not usually included before 1820. Even if you find the name you are looking for in the index, in many cases it will be impossible to identify that person with a great degree of certainty. Illegible handwriting on passenger lists, combined with misspelled names, incorrect ages, and only a vague name of the country or region of origin, give passenger lists the distinction of being the most difficult-to-use immigration sources. What's more, you may not know if the immigrant traveled alone or with other family members or friends. In other words, how will you know if John Miller, age twenty-three, laborer, is the right one if there are several others of the same name and similar description? Very often, one or more of the family would travel to America, get a feel for the new land, establish residency, and then send for other family members. Sometimes parents left their children with relatives at home until they were able to bring them over. Sometimes the father was the solitary pioneer, sending for the family after establishing himself in America. Often, young, unmarried adults set out alone to find a new life in a new world.

As with other government documents, passenger lists were not intended to be genealogical documents, but rather were a means of monitoring immigrant arrivals. There were, historically, up to seven different ways in which lists of passengers may have been created. These include lists made and filed with (1) the port of embarkation, (2) ports of call along the route, (3) the port of arrival, (4) newspapers at the port of departure, (5) newspapers at cities of arrival, (6) a copy kept with or as part of the ship's manifest, and (7) notations of passengers in the ship's log. In addition, some travelers recorded the names of their fellow passengers in diaries, journals, and letters home. If the group was chartered by a government agency, a specific church, or an emigrant aid society, a list may have been kept with the official archives of the project. If the ship was quarantined for disease, a copy of the list was attached to medical reports. Germans arriving in Pennsylvania from 1727 to 1808 were required to take an oath of allegiance and an oath of abjuration when they landed in Philadelphia. All able-bodied males age sixteen or older were taken immediately before a magistrate when they arrived.

Some of these passenger lists are official lists that were required by law; others were private recordings. For family historians, the fact that multiple copies were *sometimes* made improves the chances that at least one survived for most immigrants. The main problem is in finding the lists.

Official U.S. government passenger lists are available from 1820 through the 1950s for most of the ports in the United States with customs houses. Those available in the National Archives on microfilm are tabulated in *Immigration and Passenger Arrivals: A Select Catalog of National Archives Microfilms*.[43] They are divided into customs passenger lists (original lists, copies, or State Department abstracts) and immigration passenger lists (original lists) with pertinent indexes. Microfilm publication numbers are given where appropriate. A list of *Immigration and Passenger Lists 1800 to 1859* that have been filmed is available online at <www.archives.gov/genealogy/immigration/passenger-arrival.html#film>. Copies are also available for searching at the Family History Library and its Family History Centers located throughout the United States. Selected passenger lists are available at some public libraries. The Allen County Public Library in Fort Wayne, Indiana, for example, has a large collection of passenger list microfilms. Online access to digitized passenger lists is detailed later in this chapter, under the heading of "Improved Access to Passenger Lists."

Passenger records are not always available for all ports during all time periods. For example, no official records exist until those of the late nineteenth century for persons entering the United States through Canada or Mexico (see "Border Crossings" later in this chapter). There are a few passenger lists for San Francisco, but the official lists for that port were destroyed by fire in 1851 and 1940. Reconstructed lists are among the many lists indexed in P. William Filby's with Mary K. Meyer's *Passenger and Immigration Lists Index*.[44]

In addition to the passenger lists kept by the state and federal governments, there are some city lists. The *Baltimore City Passenger Lists, 1833 to 1866*, have a Soundex index. The originals are in the Baltimore City archive, and the Family History Library has microfilm copies that can be used at LDS Family History Centers.

For pre-1820 official lists, researchers must rely on surviving ship cargo manifests. Many colonial and U.S. ports kept copies of manifests filed as a requirement of clearance. Extant manifests have been scattered among archives, museums, and other historical agencies, but most surviving lists have been published and are indexed in *Passenger and Immigration Lists Index*.

The amount of information included for each passenger varies from one list to another. Some lists give the names of ship and passengers, country of origin, and port of arrival only. Others also include sex, age, occupation, and place of residence when ticket was purchased. On some lists, the passengers are grouped into family units, on some they are listed by tickets, on some they are arranged in alphabetical order, and on others they are arranged in the order which the passengers boarded the ship. The name of the ship's master and dates of departure and arrival will be found on some.

Passenger lists created after 1820 are usually separate documents if the ship was a passenger liner. If the ship was a cargo vessel that also carried passengers, the names were listed on the ship's manifest with the master, crew, and cargo. Before 1820, most immigrants were not declared as passengers, and many were landed in harbors where customs houses had not been established.

Masters who landed passengers without permission, however, could be forced to return them or give security to customs officials by bond to cover costs of removal for illegal entry. Some ports required the payment of a head tax and issued certificates or permits to land. When the federal government

Figure 9-7. Sample from P. William Filby, *Passenger and Immigration Lists*. Reproduced from a promotional brochure issued by Gale Research Co., 1982.

Special Feature: "See" references guides users to family entries

Specific source containing arrival record (and possible additional information). No need for endless and perhaps fruitless searches through many different books, magazines, and manuscripts.

Name of passenger

Port of arrival

Date of arrival

Accompanying dependants or relatives

Ages

PASSENGER AND IMMIGRATION LISTS INDEX — **Botterfas**

Bostrom, O 40; New York, N.Y., 1845 ***6411*** *p64*
Bostwick, Arthur n.a.; Connecticut, 1620–1650 ***275*** *p14*
Bostwick, E R n.a.; San Francisco, Cal., 1850 ***7156*** *p132*
Bostwick, J S n.a.; San Francisco, Cal., 1850 ***7156*** *p132*
Bostwick, V M n.a.; San Francisco, Cal., 1852 ***7156*** *p88*
Bostwick, William n.a.; New York (State), 1775 ***4930*** *p118*
Bostworth, W n.a.; San Francisco, Cal., 1850 ***7156*** *p143*
Bosur, Abraham n.a.; North Carolina, 1701 ***2334*** *p29*
Bosveld, Joan Hend n.a.; Philadelphia, Pa., 1738 ***9041*** *p237*
Bosveld, Johan Joost n.a.; Philadelphia, Pa., 1738 ***9041*** *p237*
Boswall, Thomas n.a.; Virginia, 1637 ***702*** *p31*
Boswell, Ann n.a.; America, 1745 ***1223*** *p17*
Boswell, Ann n.a.; America, 1745 ***1223*** *p40*
Boswell, Ann n.a.; America, 1748 ***1222*** *p29*
Boswell, Ann n.a.; Virginia, 1655 ***2772*** *p39*
Boswell, Anthony n.a.; Barbados, 1679 ***1223*** *p17*
Boswell, Benj n.a.; Philadelphia, Pa., 1775 ***1632*** *p235*
Boswell, Benjamin 15; Philadelphia, Pa., 1775 ***2128*** *p143*
Boswell, Benjamin 15; Philadelphia, Pa., 1775 ***9151*** *p366*
Boswell, Bush n.a.; America, 1740 ***702*** *p34*
Boswell, Bush n.a.; No port mentioned 1740 ***9151*** *p473*
Boswell, Charles, Jr. n.a.; America, 1740 ***702*** *p34*
Boswell, Charles, Jr. n.a.; No port mentioned 1740 ***9151*** *p473*
Boswell, Charles, Sr. n.a.; America, 1740 ***702*** *p34*
Boswell, Charles, Sr. n.a.; No port mentioned 1740 ***9151*** *p473*
Boswell, Edw n.a.; Georgia, n.d. ***1322*** *p65*
Boswell, Edward n.a.; Virginia, 1726 ***1222*** *p29*
Boswell, Eliza n.a.; Virginia, 1650 ***2772*** *p39*
Boswell, Hannah n.a.; America, 1740 ***702*** *p34*
Boswell, Hannah n.a.; No port mentioned 1740 *p473*
Boswell, Isaac n.a.; New England, 1620–1650 2
Boswell, Isaac n.a.; New England, 1620–1650 2
Boswell, Jo 17; St. Christopher, 1635 ***3283*** *p81*
Boswell, Jo 17; St. Christopher, 1635 ***9151*** *p66*
Boswell, John n.a.; Maryland, 1720 ***1222*** *p29*
Boswell, John n.a.; Maryland, 1726 ***1222*** *p29*
Boswell, John n.a.; Massachusetts, 1630 ***281*** *p60*
Boswell, John n.a.; Salem, Mass., 1630 ***263*** *p67*
Boswell, John n.a.; Virginia, 1652 ***2772*** *p39*
Boswell, John 21; Maryland, 1683 ***9590*** *p243*
Boswell, Leticia n.a.; America, 1740 ***702*** *p34*
Boswell, Letitia n.a.; No port mentioned 1740 ***9151*** *p473*
Boswell, Mary n.a.; America, 1751 ***1223*** *p162*
Boswell, Mary n.a.; Maryland, 1726 ***1222*** *p29*
Boswell, Morch n.a.; Virginia, 1655 ***2772*** *p39*
Boswell, Samll n.a.; Virginia, 1650 ***2772*** *p39*
Boswell, Samuel n.a.; America, 1773 ***1223*** *p17*
Boswell, Samuell 23; Virginia, 1635 ***3283*** *p115*
Boswell, Samvel 23; Virginia, 1635 ***9151*** *p94*
Boswell, Tho n.a.; Virginia, 1655 ***2772*** *p39*
Boswell, W n.a.; San Francisco, Cal., 1850 ***7156*** *p17*
Boswell, William n.a.; Maryland, 1720 ***1222*** *p29*
Boswell, William n.a.; Pennsylvania, 1682 ***2979*** *p636*
Boswetn, Mr. n.a.; Boston, Mass., 1763 ***9750*** *p24*
Boswick, Venetia n.a.; Nevis, 1654–1663 ***943*** *p83*
Bosworth, Cap n.a.; Boston, Mass., 1767 ***9750*** *p70*
Bosworth, B M 30; Baltimore, Md., 1820 ***9258*** *p88*
Bosworth, Benjamin n.a.; Hingham, Mass., 1620–1650 ***275*** *p174*
Bosworth, Daniel n.a.; Massachusetts, 1620–1650 ***275*** *p94*
Bosworth, Heny n.a.; Boston, Mass., 1765 ***9750*** *p46*
Bosworth, J D n.a.; San Francisco, Cal., 1852 ***7156*** *p79*
Bosworth, John n.a.; Virginia, 1739 ***1222*** *p29*
Bosworth, Wm 45; New Orleans, La., 1820 ***7460*** *p52*
Bosworth, Zaccheus n.a.; Massachusetts, 1630 ***281*** *p61*
Bosworth, Zaccheus n.a.; Salem, Mass., 1630 ***263*** *p67*
Bosworth, Zacheus n.a.; Boston, Mass., 1620–1650 ***275***

Botel, Francois 17; Louisiana, 1719 ***3418*** *p200*
Botello, Francesca Ojeda n.a. *SEE* Botello, Lazaro
Botello, Josef n.a. *SEE* Botello, Lazaro
Botello, Lazaro n.a.; New Orleans, La., 1779 ***9436*** *p68*
Wife: Francesca Ojeda n.a.
Son: Josef n.a.
Boter, Thomas n.a.; Germantown, Pa., 1683–1710 ***7820*** *p431*
Boter, Thomas n.a.; Germantown, Pa., 1710 ***3313*** *p412*
Botermer, Jacob n.a.; Philadelphia, Pa., 1844 ***9291*** *p181*
Boteshway, Wenzel n.a.; Philadelphia, Pa., 1754 ***9041*** *p648*
Botge, August n.a.; Philadelphia, Pa., 1873 ***9291*** *p181*
Both, Anna Maria n.a.; Texas, 1846 ***2484*** *p83*
Both, J Chr 19; Texas, 1849 ***2504*** *p57*
Both, Johann Martin n.a.; Philadelphia, Pa., 1752 ***9041*** *p497*
Both, Peter n.a.; Philadelphia, Pa., 1743 ***9041*** *p339*
Both, William n.a.; Philadelphia, Pa., 1868 ***9291*** *p181*
Bothacker, Christoph n.a.; Philadelphia, Pa., 1752 ***7820*** *p281*
Botham, J n.a.; San Francisco, Cal., 1852 ***7156*** *p88*
Bothe, Aug n.a. *SEE* Bothe, Carl August
Bothe, Carl n.a. *SEE* Bothe, Carl August
Bothe, Carl August n.a.; Texas, 1845 ***2484*** *p83*
Wife: Sophie Schraeder n.a.
Child: Carl n.a.
Child: Aug n.a.
Child: Marie n.a.
Child: Ludwig n.a.
Bothe, E n.a.; Texas, 1854 ***2504*** *p57*
With family
Bothe, Ludwig n.a. *SEE* Bothe, Carl August
Bothe, Marie n.a. *SEE* Bothe, Carl August
Bothe, Sophie Schraeder n.a. *SEE* Bothe, Carl August
Bothel, Hein n.a.; Texas, 1846 ***2484*** *p83*
Botheley, Joseph 22; Maryland, 1774 ***2128*** *p23*

Bothe, Carl August n.a.; Texas, 1845 *2484* *p83*
***Wife:* Sophie Schraeder n.a.**
***Child:* Carl n.a.**
***Child:* Aug n.a.**
***Child:* Marie n.a.**
***Child:* Ludwig n.a.**

p519
Bothmann, Heinrich n.a.; America, 1778 ***8640*** *p8*
Bothmann, Heinrich n.a.; America, 1854 ***8590*** *p6*
With wife & 2 children
Bothmer, August 23; Texas, 1847 ***2504*** *p57*
Bothmer, Hein Wilh Anton n.a.; Texas, 1845 ***2484*** *p83*
With wife & 2 children
Bothner, Gottfried n.a.; Philadelphia, Pa., 1840 ***9291*** *p181*
Bothner, Ludwick 32; Philadelphia, Pa., 1737 ***9041*** *p169*
Bothner, Ludwig n.a.; Philadelphia, Pa., 1737 ***7820*** *p105*
Bothner, Ludwig n.a.; Philadelphia, Pa., 1737 ***9041*** *p170*
Bothner, Ludwig n.a.; Philadelphia, Pa., 1737 ***9041*** *p172*
Bothoroyd, James n.a.; Philadelphia, Pa., 1871 ***9291*** *p181*
Boths, Henrich Julius n.a.; Philadelphia, Pa., 1753 ***7820*** *p301*
Bothus, A n.a.; San Francisco, Cal., 1852 ***7156*** *p71*
Bothwall, James n.a.; Philadelphia, Pa., 1828 ***9291*** *p181*
Bothwell, Alexander n.a.; Wilmington, Del., 1790 ***2046***
Bothwell, David n.a.; Georgia, 1789 ***5243*** *p62*
Bothwell, David n.a.; No port mentioned 1789 ***702*** *p16*
Bothwell, James n.a.; Philadelphia, Pa., 1828 ***9291*** *p181*
Bothwell, Jno n.a.; Philadelphia, Pa., 1852 ***9291*** *p181*
Bothwell, John n.a.; America, 1805 ***3450*** *p23*
Bothwell, John n.a.; America, 1805 ***702*** *p114*
Bothwell, Joseph n.a.; Philadelphia, Pa., 1866 ***9291*** *p181*
Bothwick, Alexander n.a.; Philadelphia, Pa., 1866 ***9291***

Botsen, P 1; New York, N.Y., 1846 ***4880*** *p644*
Botsen, Theod 30; New York, N.Y., 1846 ***4880*** *p644*
Botsford, John n.a.; America, 1753 ***702*** *p34*
Botsford, John n.a.; America, 1753 ***9151*** *p473*
Bott, Andreas n.a.; Philadelphia, Pa., 1785 ***9042*** *p7*
Bott, Anna Catha n.a.; Philadelphia, Pa., 1785 ***9042*** *p7*
Bott, Anna Maria n.a.; Philadelphia, Pa., 1785 ***9042*** *p7*
Bott, Barbara n.a.; Philadelphia, Pa., 1785 ***9042*** *p7*
Bott, Bartle Hendrick n.a.; Philadelphia, Pa., 1754 ***9041*** *p668*
Bott, Carl n.a.; Philadelphia, Pa., 1865 ***9291*** *p181*
Bott, Casper n.a.; Philadelphia, Pa., 1785 ***9042*** *p7*
Bott, Christian n.a.; Philadelphia, Pa., 1848 ***9291*** *p181*
Bott, Edward n.a.; Philadelphia, Pa., 1854 ***9291*** *p181*
Bott, Elioner n.a.; Barbados, 1663–1679 ***943*** *p125*
Bott, Emrich n.a.; Maryland, 1765 ***9916*** *p58*
Bott, George n.a.; Philadelphia, Pa., 1754 ***9041*** *p643*
Bott, Hans Emrich 42; Philadelphia, Pa., 1743 ***9041*** *p336*
Bott, Hans Philip n.a.; Philadelphia, Pa., 1767 ***7820*** *p380*
Bott, Henrick n.a.; Philadelphia, Pa., 1732 ***9041*** *p74*
Bott, Hermanus n.a.; Philadelphia, Pa., 1743 ***9041*** *p337*
Bott, Hermanus n.a.; Philadelphia, Pa., 1743 ***9041*** *p338*
Bott, Hermanus 46; Philadelphia, Pa., 1743 ***9041*** *p335*
Bott, Isaac n.a.; New England, 1675 ***9151*** *p468*
Bott, James n.a.; Philadelphia, Pa., 1812 ***9291*** *p181*
Bott, Joh Balthasar n.a.; Philadelphia, Pa., 1732 ***7820*** *p76*
Bott, Johan Balser n.a.; Philadelphia, Pa., 1732 ***9041*** *p71*
Bott, Johan Balthasar n.a.; Philadelphia, Pa., 1732 ***9041*** *p77*
Bott, Johan Balzar n.a.; Philadelphia, Pa., 1732 ***6665*** *p485*
Bott, Johan Henrich n.a.; Philadelphia, Pa., 1748 ***7820*** *p184*
Bott, Johann Balthasar n.a.; Philadelphia, Pa., 1732 ***9041*** *p76*
Bott, Johann Emrich n.a.; Philadelphia, Pa., 1743 ***7820*** *p160*
Bott, Johann Emrich n.a.; Philadelphia, Pa., 1743 ***9041*** *p337*
Bott, Johann Emrich n.a.; Philadelphia, Pa., 1743 ***9041*** *p339*
Bott, Johann Hennrich n.a.; Philadelphia, Pa., 1748 ***9041*** *p375*
Bott, Johann Henrich n.a.; Philadelphia, Pa., 1748 ***9041*** *p374*
Bott, Johann Jonas n.a.; Philadelphia, Pa., 1748 ***9041*** *p374*
Bott, Johann Jonas n.a.; Philadelphia, Pa., 1748 ***9041*** *p375*
Bott, Johannes n.a.; Philadelphia, Pa., 1743 ***7820*** *p159*
Bott, Johannes n.a.; Philadelphia, Pa., 1754 ***7820*** *p330*
Bott, Johannes n.a.; Philadelphia, Pa., 1754 ***9041*** *p616*
Bott, Johannes n.a.; Philadelphia, Pa., 1754 ***9041*** *p618*
Bott, John n.a.; Philadelphia, Pa., 1785 ***9042*** *p7*
Bott, John n.a.; Philadelphia, Pa., 1854 ***9291*** *p181*
Bott, John n.a.; Philadelphia, Pa., 1871 ***9291*** *p181*
Bott, Jon n.a.; Virginia, 1653 ***2772*** *p39*
Bott, Joseph n.a.; Philadelphia, Pa., 1858 ***9291*** *p181*
Bott, Joseph n.a.; Philadelphia, Pa., 1870 ***9291*** *p181*
Bott, Mary n.a.; Philadelphia, Pa., 1785 ***9042*** *p7*
Bott, Peter 35; Philadelphia, Pa., 1743 ***9041*** *p335*
Bott, Sigmund n.a.; Philadelphia, Pa., 1868 ***9291*** *p181*
Bott, Thomas n.a.; Philadelphia, Pa., 1858 ***9291*** *p181*
Bott, Ursilla n.a.; Philadelphia, Pa., 1732 ***9041*** *p73*
Bott, Wendel n.a.; Maryland, 1763 ***9916*** *p46*
Bott, William n.a.; Philadelphia, Pa., 1845 ***9291*** *p181*
Bottam, John n.a.; Virginia, 1623 ***1272*** *p45*
Bottam, John n.a.; Virginia, 1623 ***3283*** *p179*
Bottcher, Auguste 30; Texas, 1848 ***2504*** *p57*
Bottcher, John G n.a.; Philadelphia, Pa., 1856 ***9291*** *p181*
Bottcher, Susanne Marie n.a.; America, 1854 ***8590*** *p5*
Botte, Friedke n.a.; Texas, 1846 ***2484*** *p87*
Botte, Friedr n.a.; Texas, 1845 ***2484*** *p83*
Botte, Wilhelm n.a.; Texas, 1846 ***2484*** *p83*

began to regulate immigration in 1820, each ship was required by law to submit an official list of passengers carried. Masters who failed to comply could be fined and denied port clearance.

Federal control brought about the creation of two types of passenger arrival records: customs passenger lists (1820 to 1891); and immigration passenger lists (1891 to 1957). A thorough discussion of the nature and history of U.S. passenger lists is Michael Tepper's *American Passenger Arrival Records*.[45] A succinct guide to using those lists and the available indexes is John P. Colletta's *They Came in Ships: A Guide to Finding Your Immigrant Ancestor's Arrival Record*.[46]

Published Lists and Indexes

One of the most significant developments in genealogy was the compilation of indexes to some of the previously published immigration lists. An early project was the *Passenger and Immigration Lists Index* (cited previously), which contains more than 4.2 million entries for immigrants from the British Isles and Europe (see figure 9-7). In this source, all names in each list are indexed: where maiden names are found, the women are indexed under both their married and maiden names; if a man has two or more given names, he is listed under each of his given names in the source. By contrast, Ralph B. Strassburger and William John Hinke's *Pennsylvania German Pioneers: A Publication of Original Lists of Arrivals in the Port of Philadelphia from 1727 to 1808*, include Johannes Andreas Hoffman from three different lists.[47] All three lists, however, are indexed under Johannes Andreas only. Thus, if you were looking for Andreas Hoffman, you would find only two entries in the index, when there are actually three. In Filby's *Passenger and Immigration Lists Index*, however, he is indexed under both Johannes and Andreas, thus making him retrievable from the Strassburger and Hinke compilation as well.

In Filby's index, each immigrant is identified by name (spelled as it appeared in the source), age (if given), place of arrival, year of arrival, source code, and page number. All persons traveling together are listed with the head of the household as a group and cross-referenced to all family members who immigrated together. *Passenger and Immigration Lists Index* covers only lists that have been printed. It does not include entries from the original passenger arrival records. The index is also available on CD-ROM and in the immigration collection subscription at <www.ancestry.com>.

An important aid to the series is *Passenger and Immigration Lists Bibliography, 1538–1900*, compiled by P. William Filby.[48] Each source listed is cited in full with a descriptive annotation of contents, coverage, and related immigration lists (see figure 9-8). For the sources that have been reprinted, the facts of publication for the reprint are given. All the sources identified in the 1988 bibliography have now been indexed.

Of the original 262 lists described in Lancour's bibliography, 30 percent are emigrant lists recorded at the port of embarkation, 8 percent are passenger lists recorded at the port of arrival, 4 percent are ships' lists, and approximately 15 percent are compiled works on settlers in specific localities drawn from church records, convict and pauper lists, naturalizations, customs lists, legal papers and petitions, county histories, oaths of allegiance, and other records.

Colonial Lists

Before 1820, the American colonies made virtually no effort to require lists of immigrants arriving in what is now the United States. Indeed, prior to the Revolutionary War (1775 to 1783) there

Index **Passenger and Immigration Lists Bibliography • First Supplement** **Page 98**

Johannes,
Bremen to Baltimore, 1834 0258
Emden, Germany, to Charleston, 1857 9664
John, England to Barbados, 1677 1252
John Bertram, Hamburg to N.Y., 1864 .. **1133.18, .38, .54**
John and Dorothy, England to New England, 1637-1639 3540
John and Sarah, England to New England, 1651-1652

Katzka, Russia; possibly Kratzka **3394**
Kearny County, Kans., nat'zations, 1909-1937 ...... **3755**
Kedar, Liverpool to Halifax, 1864 6213
Kell, Germans from, n.d. 5463
Kendall County, Ill., Norwegians to, 1835-1837 2574
Kent, British from,
1634-1637, to New England 0378
1655-1775, bonded passengers **1217.4**

Page 25 **Passenger and Immigration Lists Bibliography • First Supplement**

2919
HARVEY, D.C. *Holland's Description of Cape Breton Island, and Other Documents.* (Public Archives of Nova Scotia, pub. 2). Halifax: Public Archives of Nova Scotia, 1935, pp. 147-168.

A census of Cape Breton Island in 1818 (see Appendix B) lists inhabitants of various areas, with specific locality, age, time on the Island, country of origin, country of parents, trade, marital status, children. Identifies 1,022 ho... of arrival.

2965
HAYNES, EMMA ... German Refugees ... from Minsk on Dec... ican Historical So... (Spring 1982), pp. 55-66.

Almost 900 Volg... names of relatives ... of 1921. Many ca... determine which ...

2973.2
HAYNES, EMM... Lists." In *Clues,* ...

Germans from Ru... years 1876-1899... ages and occupati...

2974.1
HAYNES, EMM... Lists." In *Clues,* ...

Mostly Germans f... Baltimore or Halif...

2974.4
HAYNES, EMMA SCHWABENLAND ... Lists." In *Clues,* 1982, pt. 2, pp. 23-28.

About 700 passengers, mostly Germans from R... Data includes age, occupation, and often destina... York).

2518 **Passenger and Immigration Lists Bibliography • First**

2518
GEUE, ETHEL HANDER. "Ship *Canapus.* Departed Bremen: Arrived Galveston, December 19, 1848." In *The Roadrunner,* vol. 7:4 (Aug. 1981), p. 6.

Names 30 persons, with ages and places of origin and destination. Extracted from Geue, *New Homes in a New Land . . . 1847-1861* (item no. 2504 in main volume of this bibliography) and previously taken from microfilm in state archives, Austin, Texas.

2525.15
GIBBS, ANN. "Earliest Ripley County [Indiana] Naturalizations, 1818-1843." In *The Hoosier Genealogist,* vol. 22:3 (Sept. 1982), pp. 63-67.

About 100 persons, each name with age, place of origin, date of immigration, and date of naturalization or of first papers.

2525.40
GIBBS, ANN. "Switzerland County [Indiana] Naturalizations, Oct. 1825- Apr. 1829." In *The Hoosier Genealogist,* vol. 22:2 (June 1982), pp. 42-44.

About 80 persons, mostly from Switzerland and the British Isles. Indicates date of intention to become a citizen; identifies name of court and country of origin.

Gray Line, vol. 1:2 ...
Refers to 19th-century ... variations in the spelli... occupation, nationalit...

2763.20
GREAT REGISTER ... *tration of the Domic... Santa Clara . . . 1884*
Lists 8,496 names wit... local residence, date ... registration.

2763.25 — 2763.33
"THE GREAT REG... [California]." In *Ash...*
2763.25
---Vol. 11:4 (Oct. 1974) ... precincts).
2763.26
---Vol. 12:2 (Apr. 197... pp. 134-135. (Belmont...
2763.27
---Vol. 13:1 (Jan. 197... Butler precincts); vol. ... Mountain, Bryant, Ca...

Figure 9-8. Samples from P. William Filby, *Passenger and Immigration Lists Bibliography, 1538–1900* (Detroit: Gale Research Co., 1981).

was no federal government to make such a request. Therefore, control of immigration was left to the original colonies. Inasmuch as they were British colonies, and nearly 80 percent of the white immigrants before 1790 came from British countries, there was no need to record these arrivals. According to Michael Tepper, "Even for ships carrying the original colonists—the so-called first comers, first purchasers, first planters, etc.—there are few actual lists of passengers, certainly few that are undisputed."[49]

In light of this situation, it is fortunate that any colonial immigrants were recorded at all. In fact, a large majority of immigrant families have been documented, but, as Tepper points out when discussing the original settlers, they "are largely recorded—where they are recorded at all—in ancillary records and documents."[50] Use of such "ancillary records," including lists of departure from British countries, is a great boon to colonial immigration studies. They allow identification of at least some members of an immigrant's family (usually the head) for upwards of 70 to 80 percent of the colonial white immigrants. The vast majority of these records have been published over the past few decades, with the happy result that virtually all of them are indexed in Filby's *Passenger and Immigration Lists Index*.

Because of the great interest in, and availability of, the colonial Pennsylvania lists, some discussion is warranted here. Beginning in 1727, Pennsylvania required that non-British immigrants (essentially Germans) be identified. Three lists were compiled for these Pennsylvania German immigrants: (1) the captain's lists made on board the ship by the ship's mate from the manifest; (2) lists of oaths of allegiance to the king of Great Britain that were signed by all male immigrants over age sixteen who were well enough to march in procession to a magistrate (these two lists were submitted to the Pennsylvania government on large, loose sheets of paper and not all of them have survived); and (3) lists of signers of the oath of fidelity and abjuration. The oath was a renunciation of claims to the throne of England by "pretenders" and a denial of the right of the pope to outlaw a Protestant monarch. Those males of age sixteen and upwards who were well enough to walk to the courthouse also signed these renunciations in a series of bound ledger volumes that have survived intact. The editors of *Pennsylvania German Pioneers*, Strassburger and Hinke, calculated that only two out of five passengers are recorded on the signed lists.

The original order of the names on the lists is important. The first signatures are often those of the leaders, for the Palatines (immigrants from the Rhine River Valley of Germany—the Palatinate) came in groups. The names themselves are significant, for they may represent a whole church group or a group of related families. For these reasons, copy the whole passenger list where the ancestor appears and study the names carefully. The lists serve as a check to identify the correct ancestor in church registers, census lists, news announcements, and other records. The spelling of names on the captains' lists is often inaccurate and different from the way the names appear on the other two.

The signatures are significant as well. The original printed volumes of *Pennsylvania German Pioneers* in which these lists appear contain the printed versions of all three lists, with the second volume reproducing in facsimile the original signatures as they appear on the third list. When the Genealogical Publishing Company reprinted the set, it did not reproduce the volume of signatures. However, a 1992 reprint by Picton Press of Camden, Maine, includes the signature volume as well.

U.S. Customs Passenger Lists (1820–ca. 1891)

Custom Passenger Lists or Customs Manifests were filed by the shipmasters with the collector of customs in each port. In accordance with the law, the list provided the name of the ship and her master, port of embarkation, date and port of arrival, and the name, age, sex, occupation, and nationality of each passenger. The original lists were prepared in duplicate on board ship and signed by the master of the vessel (under oath) and the customs authority. One copy was filed with the collector of customs; the other copy was returned to the master to be kept with the ships' papers. On the list, the master was also required to record births and deaths during the voyage. Under a British/American law of 1855, copies of the passenger lists for British ships were also given to the British consuls in the American port. Because there were no forms regulating size or appearance of the passenger lists from 1820 to about 1891, passenger list formats varied widely.

Original lists are extant for Baltimore, Boston, New Orleans, New York, and Philadelphia as well as some minor Atlantic, Gulf Coast, and Great Lakes ports. All lists surviving in U.S. customs houses at those ports were transferred and shipped in the mid-1930s to the National Archives in Washington, D.C. There, archivists filled gaps in the record using available substitutes from records of the State Department. Copies or abstracts of the original lists were made by the collectors of customs and sent quarterly to the secretary of state. In them, the information was usually abbreviated, and copying errors were undoubtedly made. Transcriptions were also made for 1819 to 1832 lists from the copies sent to the Department of State. They are arranged by name of district or port, name of vessel, and name of passenger. The transcripts are third-generation copies and, as such, contain many errors.

Customs officials were also responsible to see that each ship entering and leaving port was licensed and registered. They also recorded ships' manifests listing crew, passengers, and cargo; ships' logs with statements on the conditions of the passengers, and births, marriages, and deaths at sea; payroll accounts with signatures for seamen; ships' accounts for provisions advanced to emigrants; and miscellaneous documents that related to the ship itself. These documents, sometimes called shipping records, sometimes referred to as customs records, can be found either in the possession of the shipping company, the customs house, or in local and federal archives.

New York City—Castle Garden and Ellis Island (1855–1892)

New York City was the port of entry for by far the largest number of immigrants. Of the 5,400,000 people who arrived between 1820 and 1860, more than two-thirds entered at New York. By the 1850s, New York was receiving more than three-quarters of the national total of immigrants, and by the 1890s more than four-fifths.[51]

In 1855, Castle Garden, an old fort on the lower tip of Manhattan, was designated as an immigrant station by the State of New York. When a new federal law excluding paupers and others was passed in 1882, New York continued to operate Castle Garden under contract to the U.S. government. But by 1890 its facilities had long since proved to be inadequate for the ever-increasing number of immigrant arrivals. After a government survey of potential locations, federal authorities chose Ellis Island as the site to establish an entirely new United States immigration station. Several Manhattan sites were rejected because earlier immigrants had been ruthlessly exploited as they left Castle Garden. On the island, immigrants could be screened, protected, and filtered more slowly into the new culture. The Ellis Island Immigration Center was officially dedicated on New Year's Day in 1892.

Information on passengers who arrived at the Port of New York is available online at Ancestry.com <www.ancestry.com> and from the passenger lists microfilm published by the National Archives. Microfilm indexes for the New York City port are available only for the years 1820 to 1846; 1897 to 1902; 1902 to 1943; and 1944 to 1948.

Ancestry.com has digitized and indexed passenger lists for the Port of New York, 1851 to 1891, and the Statue of Liberty–Ellis Island Foundation has made available an automated database index to New York arrivals 1892 to 1924. (See "The Ellis Island Database: Maximizing Your Results" on page 394. Both Ancestry.com <www.ancestry.com> and Ellis Island <www.ellisisland.org> have linked pictures of some of the ships to the passenger lists so that researchers can get a better idea of the conditions under which ancestors traveled. Some images are also available from the Library of Congress (figure 9-9).

Immigration Passenger Lists (1891–1957)

As the result of an act of 1891, immigrants arriving in the United States were to be recorded by federal immigration officials; the resulting lists date from 1891 for most ports. The National Archives has published these lists on microfilm and a great number of them have been made available online. See the NARA website <www.archives.gov/genealogy/immigration> for an up-to-date list of what is available. The records contain the following information: name of master, name of vessel, ports of arrival and embarkation, date of arrival, and, for each passenger,

Figure 9-9. "The magnificent steamships Egypt and Spain: Of the national steamship line, between New York and Liverpool." Published by Currier and Ives, New York, c1879. Courtesy of Library of Congress Prints and Photographs Division.

name, place of birth, last legal residence, age, occupation, sex, and remarks (figure 9-10).

Passenger lists dating from 1883 to 1891 for the port of Philadelphia, which one would expect to find among the customs lists, are included with the immigration list records. Records concerning immigrant detentions and board of special inquiry hearings at Philadelphia from the 1870s to ca. 1909 can be found in the National Archives Mid-Atlantic Region in Philadelphia (Record Group 85).

With the introduction of standard federal forms in 1893, passenger list information was changed to include the following: name of shipmaster, name of vessel, ports of arrival and embarkation, date of arrival, and the following information for each passenger: full name; age; sex; marital status; occupation; nationality; last residence; final destination; whether in the United States before and, if so, when and where; whether going to join a relative and, if so, the relative's name, address, and relationship to the passenger. Other revisions of the format included race (1903); personal description and birthplace (1906); and name and address of the nearest relative in the immigrant's home country (1907). It should be noted that these lists include not only names of immigrants but also of visitors and Americans returning from abroad. At the same time, lists of first and second class cabin passengers did not always survive. Passenger lists are arranged by port and thereunder chronologically.

Border Crossings

The National Archives of the United States has several collections of arrival indexes and manifests for persons crossing the border between the United States and Canada. Most of these are listed as records of the St. Albans District, but they are not limited to those who actually came through St. Albans. Rather, the district encompassed most of the U.S.-Canadian border. The records begin in 1895 and cover arrivals as late as 1954. The microfilmed collections, most of which are also available through the Family History Library and its centers, include:

St. Albans District Manifest Records of Aliens Arriving from Foreign Contiguous Territory. These 1,169 rolls of microfilm include Soundex cards that abstract the original manifests and give detailed information pertaining to border crossings. All crossings (from Maine to Washington) are included between 1895 and 1917. Beginning in 1917, the records are limited to border crossings east of the Montana-North Dakota state border. After 1927, the records are limited to crossings in the New York-Vermont region. However, this includes major eastern Canadian seaports where U.S. officials processed ship passengers bound for the United States.

Soundex Index to Canadian Border Entries Through the St. Albans, Vermont District, 1895–1924. These four hundred rolls of microfilm include Soundex cards that abstract the original manifests and give detailed information pertaining to border crossings. All crossings (from Maine to Washington) are included between 1895 and 1917. Beginning in 1917, the records are limited to border crossings east of the Montana-North Dakota state border. From 1895 to 1927 the Soundex cards correspond to a passenger list record. After 1927, the records are limited to crossings in the New York-Vermont region, and comprise the entire record (i.e., there is no corresponding passenger list). However, this includes major eastern Canadian seaports where U.S. officials processed ship passengers bound for the United States.

Soundex Index to Entries into the St. Albans, Vermont District Through Canadian Pacific and Atlantic Ports, 1924–1952. The ninety-eight rolls of index cards in this set pertain to border crossings mainly in the New York-Vermont area.

Manifests of Passengers Arriving in the St. Albans, Vermont District Through Canadian Pacific and Atlantic Ports, 1895–1954. These 640 rolls contain the passenger lists of ship arrivals at Canadian ports of entry and passenger lists of arrivals at U.S.-Canada land border ports of entry. Indexed by the previously-mentioned Soundex cards, the lists are arranged by year, month, then port of arrival (a different arrangement than applies to lists at U.S. seaports). Arrivals at Canadian Atlantic ports are included for all years, but ship arrivals at Canadian Pacific ports are included only for earlier years (to 1917 or 1927).

Manifests of Passengers Arriving in the St. Albans, Vermont District Through Canadian Pacific Ports, 1929–1949. These twenty-five rolls of microfilm contain the passenger lists of ship arrivals at Canadian ports of entry and passenger lists of arrivals at U.S.-Canada land border ports of entry. There is no published index.

St. Albans District Manifest Records of Aliens Arriving from Foreign Contiguous Territory, 1895–1924. These six rolls of microfilm are of card indexes of arrivals at small ports in Vermont. Each port is arranged alphabetically. This is especially useful for identifying Canadians who settled in New England.

Detroit District Manifest Records of Aliens Arriving from Foreign Contiguous Territory. This collection includes 117 rolls of microfilm of the original card manifests, arranged alphabetically, for persons entering the United States through Detroit, and some other Michigan ports from 1906 to 1954. Many of the cards refer to passenger and crew lists found on an additional twenty-three rolls of microfilmed passenger and alien crew lists of vessels arriving at Detroit, 1946 to 1957.

Recently, the National Archives has begun microfilming border crossings for later years in western Canada and for arrivals across the Mexican border. Information on these records is sketchy but will undoubtedly be described in genealogical periodicals as the records become available.

Improved Access to Passenger Lists

Over the past few years, abstracts of many customs lists naming millions of passengers have been made available. Some have been published in the traditional method, in printed volumes, while others have appeared on CD-ROM. Some have had the benefit of publication in both mediums. Now they are also on the Web, as part of a subscription site.

Since the early 1990s, major genealogical publishers have been issuing abstracts of the arrival lists for various U.S. ports. Each published list, while appearing in various formats, almost always gives the name, age, origin and destination of each passenger. Also included is the ship name as well as the dates and ports of departure and arrival.

The Genealogical Publishing Company (GPC) of Baltimore, Maryland <www.genealogical.com>, has primarily published information port by port from the earliest years of the available lists. Generally its lists are in one alphabetical sequence for the time period covered, with the ship name, port, and arrival date as elements in the tabular presentation of the data.

Scholarly Resources (SR) in Wilmington, Delaware <www.gale.com/psm>, has printed multiple-volume sets, covering arrivals of specific ethnic groups, usually regardless of the port of arrival. Produced in conjunction with the Balch Institute Center for Immigration Research, their format was to produce each ship's list as a transcript of passengers, in the order of the lists, although limited to those who fit the ethnic scope of the publication. A key limitations to the Balch Institute work is that it includes only the five major ports and does not include the State Department transcripts for any port. Thus, their published transcripts are not always identical to the information on the microfilms of the passenger lists.

Book Publication. Publishers have gradually made almost all of the pre-1850 lists available in various formats, and sometimes from different compilers (transcribers). For most ports, these publications appear to have included virtually all of the counted arrivals, as documented by William J. Bromwell in *History of Immigration to the United States*.[52] Thus these publications seem to document

- all passengers on all the extant lists,
- U.S. residents returning from abroad,
- that very few lists were lost, and
- more arrivals than previously shown in the statistics for some ports.

A few observations about these publications are in order. First are the passenger lists published in book form (see table). For the books published by GPC, there appear to be more names in the books than actual counted passenger arrivals (according to Bromwell). For example, the book listing New York arrivals in the 1820s includes over 85,000 names, yet Bromwell's numbers suggest just under 83,000 persons arrived through New York in that decade. The two numbers for the 1830 to 1832 New York arrivals differ by an even greater amount (just over 5,000). The Baltimore, Maryland, and Charleston, South Carolina, lists also seem to show more arrivals than originally reported to Congress (and summarized by Bromwell). These differences likely are due to indexing techniques.

Passenger Lists Published in Book Form

Publisher	Port/ Ethnic Group	Years	Names in book(s)	Total arrivals
GPC (rpt)	All ports	1820	10,241	10,311
GPC	New York City	1820–1829	85,454	82,970
GPC	New York City	1830–1832	65,000	59,731
GPC	Philadelphia	1800–1819	40,000	unknown
GPC	Baltimore	1820–1834	50,000	41,845
GPC	Charleston, S.C.	1820–1829	6,200	4,066
GPC	Providence, R.I.	1798–1808; 1820–1874	abt. 4,000	unknown
SR	Germans, 2 vols	1840–1845	abt. 97,000	136,406
SR	Germans, 9 vols	1850–1855	abt. 700,000*	744,843
GPC	Irish (NYC only)	1846–1851	651,931	unknown

* Includes many non-Germans

However, the ethnic-oriented publications are a different case. These titles rely on the transcribing done by the Balch Institute, whose criteria were not always fully inclusive of every immigrant of a particular ethnic group.

Exact numbers of ethnic arrivals are also difficult to come by. Irish-born immigrants were not fully separated in the original lists. Those from Northern Ireland were grouped with English, Welsh, and Scots as "Great Britain and Ireland." It is believed that about a million persons left Ireland during the famine, yet the published list of "Famine Immigrants" documents only about two-thirds of that number.

The post-1850 German coverage is discussed later in this chapter, while the 1840 to 1845 publication, with only about 71 percent of the German arrivals, requires more explanation. Since only the original lists were transferred to the Balch Institute, and only for the five major ports, the missing Germans for this time period may be in the arrival lists of smaller ports, or in missing originals from the major ports. Of the five major ports, both Baltimore and New Orleans have many gaps in their original records, and were also favored by many German arrivals.

Therefore, these artificially low numbers (in the German collections) should not suggest missing lists, but rather incomplete transcribing. Diligent researchers will turn to the various microfilmed card indexes for the ports of interest, or to the electronic publications discussed later in this chapter.

Electronic Publications. Of course, the sheer numbers of arrivals documented in these passenger lists suggests that traditional book volumes would be an expensive and cumbersome way to publish such data. Therefore, publishers have turned to electronic publication for large amounts of information. Most such publications are issued either on disc or the Internet; many are now appearing in both formats However, there are important differences between these formats for researchers seeking a specific passenger.

With a database on disc, the user can usually call up a portion of the list (usually alphabetical), and then browse for the surname(s) of interest. This can be a very useful way to locate names whose spelling the researcher cannot predict. While current immigration collections on disc do not use advanced search techniques, the ability to browse the name list is an advantage over most Web searches. Some websites offer only exact name matches. Others also offer a Soundex search, but even that approach does not bring all variants of a surname together. For example, the names Thompson and Thomson are coded differently under the Soundex indexing system.

Unfortunately, the issues are not as clear for the more recent databases of ethnic group arrivals. First, exact numbers of arrivals are not readily available for post-1855 arrival. Further, different definitions of ethnic groups are used between the original lists and the published abstracts. The Customs Passenger Lists generally used the column showing the country of birth. However, many Germans were born in France and Hungarians in Austria, to name just two examples. Database developers often used a different definition for selecting names to include in a database. The problems relating to the Irish "Famine Immigrants" lists have been noted previously.

Another key example is the series of *Germans to America*, whose first five years (1850 to 1855) included only the passenger lists for ships on which at least 80 percent of the passengers were shown to have German surnames. Interestingly, all of the passengers (including non-Germans) were transcribed into those volumes. Later volumes changed the criteria, ostensibly including all persons who described themselves as Germans, regardless of the percentage on the ship's list, but no others. This then raises the question about Germans who claimed to have been born in France, or some other country.

CD-ROM Port of Arrival Collections

As published by Genealogy.com

CD#	Port	Years	Names on CD	Total arrivals*
256	Boston	1821–1850	161,000	199,223
273	New York City	1820–1850	1.6 million	1,650,675
359	Philadelphia	1800–1850	abt. 140,000*	136,353
259	Baltimore	1820–May 1852	89,000	155,924+
260	Baltimore	1851–1872	138,000	unknown
358	New Orleans	1820–1850	273,000	278,246
N/A	Total 5 ports	1820–1850	2,263,000	2,411,832

* For the 1820–1850 time period
+ To the end of 1851

CD-ROM Ethnic Group Collections

As published by Genealogy.com

CD#	Ethnic Group	Years	Names on CD
355	Germans	1850–1874	2 million
356	Germans	1875–1888	1.5 million
357	Irish (Boston, NYC)	1846–1865	1.5 million
264	Irish	1846–1851 (Boston) 1866–1886 (NYC)	1.5 million
362	Irish/British (& others)	1866–1873	200,000
353	Italians	1880–1893	413,000
360	Russians/Jewish	1850–1896	430,000

Despite the lack of information about the total number of immigrants within these time periods for any particular ethnic group, it is still clear that millions of immigrants are now easier to find through these CD-ROM and Internet collections than they have been in the past. Indeed, all of these electronic "ethnic" collections include passengers arriving in New York during the previously unindexed years of 1846–1897, along with other years and other ports. Of course, not all of the customs lists have been abstracted. However, of the "nearly twenty million persons" on these early passenger lists, slightly over half are now in electronic form.

Finding an immigrant in the electronic (abstracted) customs lists can still be a challenge since spelling of names was not consistent, and the search engines (on the Web or the

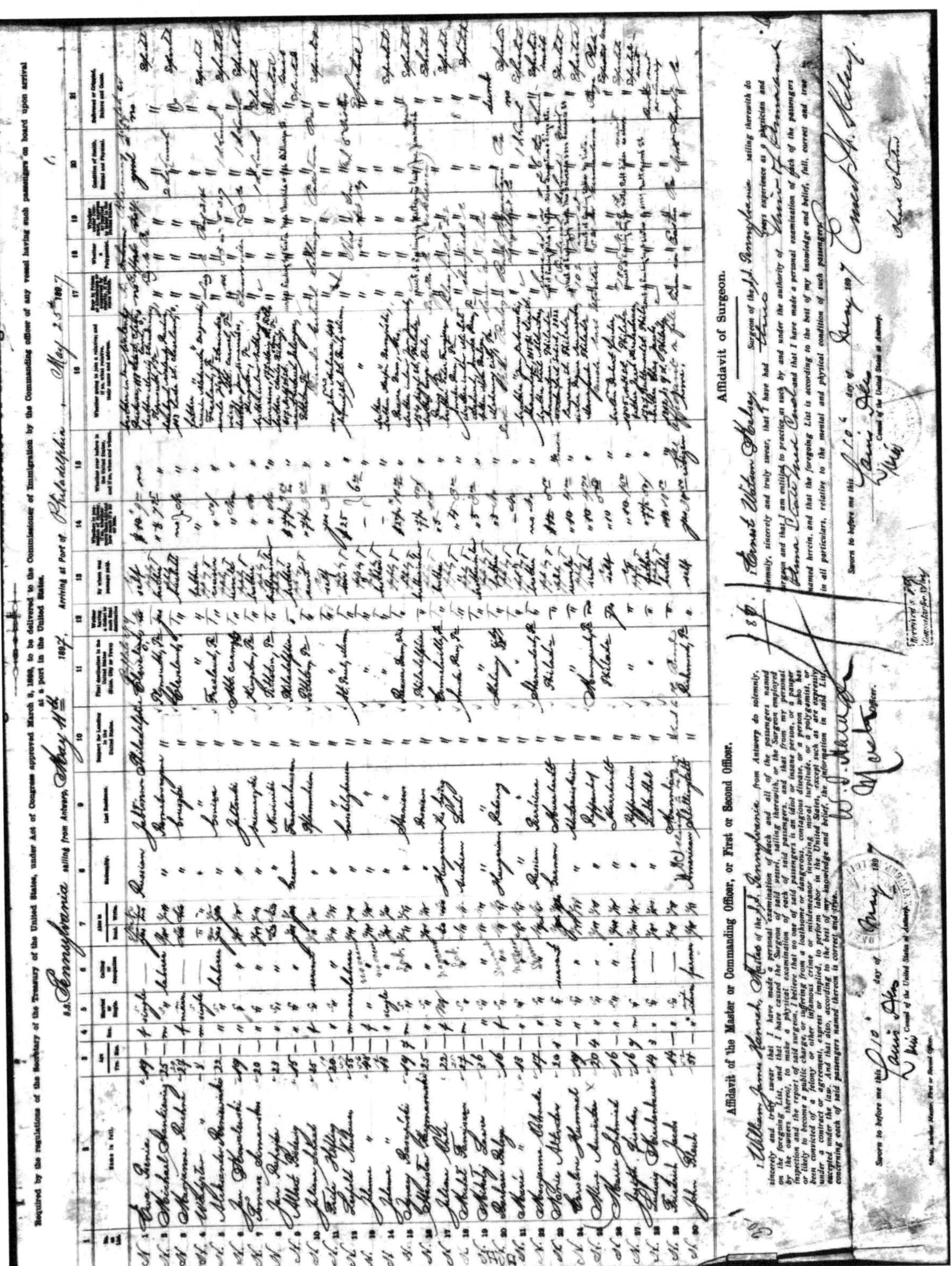

Figure 9-10. Passenger list of the *S.S. Pennsylvania* that sailed 11 May 1897 from Antwerp and arrived at the Port of Philadelphia on 25 May 1897. Found on Ancestry.com.

CD-ROMs) are not always as useful as they could be. However, at least for the early years, there appears to be very little loss of the actual lists. Therefore, if your immigrant ancestor falls into any of the following groups, it would be wise to check these electronic collections, even if earlier research has failed to identify the immigrant:

- Arrived by 1850 (especially at the five major ports)
- Arrived at Baltimore by 1872
- Was a "German" arriving between 1850 and 1888
- Was an Irish arrival between 1846 and 1886
- Was an Italian arriving between 1880 and 1893
- Came from the Russian Empire (especially Jews) between 1850 and 1896

In order to maximize your chance of finding an immigrant, try searching both the appropriate discs and the Internet. Also use a wide variety of spellings, and watch for a broad time period. Further, if you are aware of several immigrants in the same family, search for all of them. A recent search for a child with the given name of Bernhard almost missed the family, because the child was transcribed as Reinhard. It was only because of several other identification factors that he was recognized. His Civil War pension had identified his age, port of arrival, approximate year of arrival, and his mother's given name. Add to that his uncommon surname and his residence in the same rural county with two older men who also fit this immigration family (older half-brothers), and the identification was complete. The fact that some immigrants traveled back to their homeland and will be found on passenger lists more than once and with different traveling companions can further confuse a search.

CDs. Genealogy.com, now part of MyFamily.com, Inc., has produced many lists on CD-ROM which are now also available through its Internet site, <www.genealogy.com> and at Ancestry.com <www.ancestry.com>. Genealogy.com publications include transcripts created for all of the five major ports, through at least 1850, as well as electronic editions of the multi-volume ethnic publications created by the Balch Institute.

Passenger Lists Online. Because of its scope and functionality, the American Family Immigration History Center Ellis Island database naturally attracts a lot of attention (see "The Ellis Island Database: Maximizing Your Results" on page 394), but it is not the only immigration-oriented database on the Internet. The following are a few of the more notable ones that may facilitate your research. Thanks to Megan Smolenyak who provided text for this section

The Ancestry.com Immigration Collection—Additions to the Ancestry.com Immigration Collection are ongoing. However, at this writing, there are a number of significant databases within the collection that are worthy of mention. Complete database descriptions are available at Ancestry.com, but the following list provides some basic information about each. Because they are rather unique, some titles in the collection might otherwise be overlooked. They include:

—American Emigrant Ministers, 1690–1811. This volume contains a list of ministers and other clergy who applied for and received funds from the English crown to compensate for passage to the Americas. Included in the geography are the areas of the West Indies, the entire United States, and Canada. This record includes the emigrant's name, date of departure, destination, and other interesting facts.

—New York Emigrant Savings Bank, 1850–1883. The Emigrant Savings Bank was established in 1850 by members of the Irish Emigrant Society. The bank ended up serving thousands of Irish immigrants who fled to America following the infamous Potato Famine. The bank kept many volumes of records including an Index Book; a Test Book; a Transfer, Signature, and Test Book; and a Deposit-Account Ledger. This database is an index to these records providing the given name and surname of the depositor, their account number, account date, and year and place of birth, if given. In addition, each indexed individual is linked to the image on which they appear where more information may be available. While the majority of the emigrants found in this collection will be Irish, you may occasionally find emigrants of other nationalities as well.

—The Great Migration Begins includes more than one thousand sketches, each dedicated to a single immigrant or an immigrant family, arriving in New England between 1620 and 1633. Each sketch contains information on the immigrant's migration dates and patterns, on various biographical matters (including occupation, church membership, education, offices, and land holding), and on genealogical details (birth, death, marriages, children, and other associations by blood or marriage), along with detailed comments and discussion, and bibliographic information on the family.

—Sons of the Utah Pioneers Card Index, 1847–50. This database is an index of people who came to Utah between 1847 and 1850. Information found within this database includes the pioneer's name, birth date, birthplace, death date, death place, and name of the company he or she traveled with.

Passenger Lists

In most cases, the passenger list indexes on Ancestry.com are linked to the actual passenger list images.

—Atlantic and Gulf Coasts and Ports on the Great Lakes, 1820–63. This database, contains names on passenger lists from Alexandria, Virginia (1820–65); Annapolis, Maryland (1849); Bangor, Maine (1848); Barnstable, Massachusetts (1820–26); Bath, Maine (1825–67); Beaufort, North Carolina (1865); Belfast, Maine (1820–51); Bridgeport, Connecticut (1870); Bridgeton, New Jersey (1825–28);

Bristol and Warren, Rhode Island (1820–71); and Cape May, New Jersey (1828).

—Baltimore Passenger Lists, 1820–1948. This database is an index to the passenger lists of ships arriving from foreign ports at the port of Baltimore, Maryland from 1820–1948.

—Boston Passenger Lists, 1820–1948. This database is an index to the passenger lists of ships arriving from foreign ports at the port of Boston, Massachusetts from 1820–1943.

—Florida Passenger Lists. This database is an index to passenger lists of ships arriving from foreign ports at various Florida ports. The index includes Pensacola (citizens: Jun. 1924 – Aug. 1948, aliens: Mar. 1946 – Nov. 1948) (also includes passenger lists of ships departing from Pensacola for Aug. 1926 – Mar. 1948); Panama City (citizens: 1933–1936, aliens: 1927–1939).

—Galveston Passenger Lists, 1896–1948. This database is an index to the passenger lists of ships arriving from foreign ports at the port of Galveston, Texas and the sub-ports of Houston, Brownsville, Port Arthur, Sabine, and Texas City.

—New Orleans Passenger Lists. This data set contains alphabetical listings of approximately 273,000 individuals who arrived at New Orleans from foreign ports between 1820 and 1850.

—New York Passenger Lists. This database is an index to the passenger lists of ships arriving from foreign ports at the port of New York from 1851–1891 and 1935–1938.

—Philadelphia Passenger Lists, 1800–1945. This database is an index to the passenger lists of ships arriving from foreign ports at the port of Philadelphia, Pennsylvania from 1800–1945.

—Passenger Lists of Vessels Arriving at San Francisco, 1893–1953. This database is an index to the passenger lists of ships arriving from foreign ports at the port of San Francisco. When completed this index will cover the years 1893–1953.

Lists of Specific Ethnic Groups

—Dutch Immigrants to America, 1820–1880. This database contains information on over 56,000 Dutch immigrants who came to America between 1820 and 1880. The information was extracted from the National Archives passenger lists of ships arriving at various Atlantic and Gulf ports. The list includes vessels disembarking at Baltimore, Boston, New Orleans, New York, Philadelphia and other smaller ports. The passenger lists used in this compilation includes approximately 100,000 separate ship manifests.

—Chinese Exclusion Case Files. These indexes include "Chinese Exclusion" case files among the immigration investigation files created in Hawaii, San Francisco, under the Chinese Exclusion Acts passed by Congress between 1882 and 1930, and repealed in 1943.

—Immigrants in Pennsylvania from 1727 to 1776. This is a collection of upwards of thirty thousand names of German, Swiss, Dutch, French and other immigrants in Pennsylvania.

—Immigration of Irish Quakers to Pennsylvania, 1682–1750.

—The German immigration into Pennsylvania through the port of Philadelphia, 1700 to 1775.

—Scandinavian Immigrants in New York 1630–1674: With Appendices on Scandinavians in Mexico and South America, 1532–1640 Scandinavians in Canada, 1619–1620 Some Scandinavians in New York in the Eighteenth Century German Immigrants in New York, 1630–1674.

Emigration Lists

—Baden, Germany Emigration Lists 1866–1911. This index, compiled by the Badischen Generallandesarchive Karlsruhe and microfilmed by the Genealogical Society of Utah, contains the names of over 28,000 persons who left Baden between 1866 and 1911.

—Brandenburg Emigration Lists. This database is a collection of government records regarding persons emigrating from the province in the 19th century. Each record provides the emigrant's name, age, occupation, residence, destination, and year of emigration. Part of an ongoing project, the database now contains the names of more than 36,800 persons.

—Pennsylvania German Pioneers. This database contains the original lists of German pioneers who arrived at the port of Philadelphia from the years 1727 to 1808.

—Lists of Swiss Emigrants in the Eighteenth Century to the American Colonies. This database represents the history of Swiss emigration to the Americas in the eighteenth century. Originally located in the State Archives of Zurich, it contains the ship lists of emigrants to the American colonies from Switzerland, in particular to the Carolinas and Pennsylvania. Each list contains, where possible, the names of family members who departed, their birth date, baptism date, the town or province of departure, the date of departure, the name of the ship, and their destination. This is an invaluable research tool for anyone with Swiss ancestors who emigrated to America between 1700 and 1800.

—The Wuerttemberg Emigration Index. This database includes thousands of German and Prussian immigrants to the United States that made application to emigrate at Wuerttemberg, Germany. This collection, filmed at Ludwigsburg, contains the names of approximately 60,000 persons who made application to leave Germany from the late eighteenth century to 1900. The information supplied on each person includes: name, date and place of birth, residence at time of application and application date, and microfilm number.

Naturalization Lists

—Names Of Foreigners Who Took The Oath Of Allegiance To The Province And State Of Pennsylvania, 1727–1775, With The Foreign Arrivals, 1786–1808.

—New York Count Index to Declaration of Intent for Naturalization, 1907–1924.

—*New York Petitions for Naturalization* from National Archives and Records Administration, Northeast Region. *Soundex Index to Petitions for Naturalization filed in Federal, State, and Local Courts located in New York City, 1792–1906.*

—Pennsylvania Naturalizations, 1740–1773.

—Philadelphia, 1789–1880 Naturalization Records.

—Utah Declarations of Intentions, 1878–1895

Hamburg Emigration Records—An index of emigration records for Hamburg, a point of departure for millions of our European ancestors, can be searched online <www.ltyr.hamburg.de>. These records, which are also available on microfilm through the Family History Library (see page 418), cover the period 1850 to 1934. When the Hamburg State Archive made the decision to index the records, they opted to start with 1890 and work forward in time. As of this writing, the 1890 to 1910 time frame has been completed. If your ancestors came a little later or earlier, check the site periodically to see if the years that interest you have been incorporated.

While searching the database is free, you will be charged to access all the details pertaining to a specific record—and that data will appear in text format, not as a digitized image. Fortunately, you will usually be provided enough information (such as year of departure, country of origin, year of birth, and so forth.) to determine whether it's the person you're seeking, and batch pricing is available (check the site for current prices) if you have multiple searches to do.

Canadian Immigration Records—When the United States tightened its immigration policies after WWI, many Ellis Island-era immigrants were unable to bring their family members to America. Consequently, many of their relatives immigrated to Canada. So pronounced was this pattern, in fact, that current day Americans of Southern and Eastern European origin almost certainly have some Canadian cousins, whether they know of them or not.

For this reason, the National Archives of Canada's database of 1925 to 1935 arrivals <www.collectionscanada.ca/02/020118_e.html> is a valuable resource, not only for Canadians seeking their immigrant ancestors, but for many of us from other countries. This database conveniently picks up just about where the Ellis Island database trails off, so if you can't find the place of origin for your grandfather who came to Ohio, perhaps his brother's Canadian record will have the information you seek.

While digitized images of the records are not available online, basic details are and you can place an order by mail or fax to obtain a copy for a nominal fee. Processing usually takes six to eight weeks, so you might want to consider hiring a local researcher if you're in a hurry.

Immigrant Ships Transcribers Guild—This tremendous, all-volunteer effort to upload searchable transcriptions of passenger lists to the Internet <http://immigrantships.net> now includes more than 5,000 ships listed by ship's name, port of departure, port of arrival, captain's name and surnames. To date, more than half a million immigrants are included.

Sources for Keeping up With Online Passenger Lists—Joe Beine provides an excellent selection of links <http://home.att.net/~wee-monster/onlinelists.html> to online transcriptions of passenger records and indexes. Entries toward the top of the page are organized by port of arrival. Scroll toward the end of the page to find links listed by foreign origin, such as Portuguese, Norwegian, Dutch, Italian, Irish, Icelandic, German, Finnish, English, and Danish.

Cyndi's List <www.cyndislist.com> has links and references to information on most nationalities, including Armenian, French, Jamaican, Estonian, Australian, Chinese, and Welsh. There are also sections titled "Ships and Passenger Lists" and "Immigration and Naturalization."

When Passenger Lists Are Not Indexed

As noted in the very detailed description of passenger lists in *Guide to Genealogical Research in the National Archives*, the lists were "written by many different hands over many years and conditions of their preservation before they were placed in the National Archives were not ideal."[53] Many lists are difficult to read; some brittle pages have broken away, and smeared ink has blurred words beyond recognition. Unless an immigrant's name can be found in an index, or unless the exact date and port of arrival are known, searching through voluminous and hard-to-read passenger lists can be exhausting and futile work.

For the Port of New York, there are some potentially helpful finding aids. On twenty-seven rolls of National Archives microfilm is *Registers of Vessels Arriving at the Port of New York from Foreign Ports, 1789–1919*.[54] The volumes, most of which identify ships by name, country of origin, type of rig, date of entry, master's name, and last port of embarkation, are arranged in chronological order of arrival. If a researcher can eliminate some vessels because of port of embarkation or date, the search may be more manageable. More readily available to most is Bradley W. Steuart's *Passenger Ships Arriving in New York Harbor (1820–1850)*.[55] The latter covers unindexed peak immigration years. A volume that has been in use for years is *The Morton Allan Directory of European Passenger Steamship Arrivals*.[56] The *Morton Allan Directory* includes information on vessels arriving at New York (1890 to 1930) and at Baltimore, Boston, and Philadelphia (1904 to 1926).

The Ellis Island Database: Maximizing Your Results

By Megan Smolenyak Smolenyak

Recent years have been a boon for genealogists in many arenas, but none more so than online immigrant databases. One of the most conspicuous examples is the collection of digitized passenger arrival records available for searching at the American Family Immigration History Center (AFIHC) website <www.ellisisland.org>. And while this resource can greatly speed your search, locating immigrant ancestors in it can still be challenging for a variety of reasons. Learning a few useful tactics can maximize the chances of finally finding the details of an elusive great-grandfather's arrival in North America. Some of the strategies discussed here can also be applied to other online databases.

The Database

If you're one of the more than 100 million Americans with one or more ancestors who came through Ellis Island, the 1 April 2001 launch of the Ellis Island database, with its more than 22 million indexed passenger and crew entries between 1892 and 1924, was a thrill. Thanks to a massive, all-volunteer effort, these records were transcribed, linked to digital images of ships' manifests, and uploaded to the Internet. In addition to providing easy access to these records, this database also includes the first-ever indexing of 1892 to 1897 New York arrivals.

Many researchers quickly found ancestors simply by entering names at the site, but others faced additional obstacles. Perhaps the name they were seeking was very common, making it difficult to tell which individual was the correct ancestor. Or maybe the surnames were unusual and complex, so that entries could be hidden behind creative spellings. Still others might have found the text version of the information linked to the wrong manifest or a "no image available" message. Fortunately, there are ways to address all of these situations.

Ellis Island: Basic Search

According to family tradition, Patrick Nelligan came to the United States from Ireland as an infant in the 19-teens. To find his record, go to <www.ellisisland.org> and enter his name in the fields provided. This brings up the *Matching Passenger Records* page, which indicates that just one such individual was found in the database:

Name of Passenger: **Patrick Nelligan**
Residence: **Abbeyfeale, Irelalnd [*sic*]**
Arrived: **1913**
Age on Arrival: **0**

Note: Newcomers to the site will need to register to gain access (although there are no fees). On subsequent visits simply enter your user name and password at the beginning of each search session.

Since the information meshes with expectations, click on the passenger's name to be taken to the *Passenger Record,* which furnishes several additional details:

Ethnicity: **British, Irish**
Date of Arrival: **October 3, 1913**
Age on Arrival: **4 months**
Gender: **male**
Marital Status: **Single**
Ship of Travel: **Adriatic**
Port of Departure: **Queenstown, Cork, Munster, Ireland**

From here, there are several options including *Add to Your Ellis Island File, View Original Ship Manifest,* or *View Ship.* Selecting *View Original Ship Manifest* will lead you to the *Original Ship Manifest* page that may lead to additional details.

On this page is a miniature version of the scanned manifest image. To take a closer look, click on the small magnifying glass to the right of the image. A separate page with the image will open, but it is the second half of the two-page record. Maneuver to the first page of the manifest by using *previous* or *next* on the *Original Ship Manifest* page. In this case, it's necessary to click *next* to go to the first page, even though you would intuitively expect to find it by clicking *previous.* Since some rolls of microfilm were scanned in backwards, this is a fairly frequent occurrence, so it's helpful to get in the habit of trying both *previous* and *next.*

Once you've opened the first page, speed the search by noting the line number listed at the top of the image. This particular image says that Patrick will be on line 13, and using the scroll bar, he is quickly found. A glance at the page says that—not surprisingly—four-month-old Patrick was not traveling alone. With him were his mother, Catherine, and sisters, Josephine and Margaret. In addition to their ages and last residence of Abbeyfeale, there is information that the closest relative they've left behind is Patrick's grandfather, Patrick Collins, and that they're traveling to join his father, Martin Nelligan, who's apparently residing in Ansonia, Connecticut. A quick peek at the last column will also reveal the interesting tidbit that Patrick's sisters were born in Ansonia, while he was born in Abbeyfeale. To obtain a copy of this genealogically-packed document, either order a copy from AFIHC via the website (see the site for current prices) or note the source information and make a copy from microfilm at your closest National Archives branch, Family History Center (FHC), or other major repository.

Ellis Island: Tactics

The preceding example was very clear-cut, but not all searches are quite this easy. Because of certain nuances of the database, employing specific tactics will improve the odds of obtaining the best possible results, regardless of your circumstances. The following suggestions are especially helpful in sniffing out evasive immigrant ancestors or all possible variations of a surname.

Alternate Spellings

If there aren't any exact matches, try *Alternate Spellings*. When you enter a surname and there are no matches, the site automatically leads to a group of thirty likely phonetic and handwriting variations, which can be viewed one at a time as if each variation was searched initially. Many users fail to make the best use of this feature because they are too quick to dismiss alternatives they couldn't fathom, but it is worth experimenting with as many alternate spellings as you can possibly imagine. The results are ranked by likeliness, so most of the hidden matches are found early in this process, but thoroughness occasionally pays off. The spelling alternatives generated are well thought out (taking into account letters that can be easily confused, Southern and Eastern European spelling quirks, and other factors) and that they only include names that are definitely in the database.

Name & Gender Edit

When you get even a single match to the name requested, you will be taken to a page entitled *Matching Passenger Records* and shown exact matches only. However, near the top of the page, there are options to view *Close Matches Only, Alternate Spellings Only, Sounds Like Only*, or *All Records*.

A bit of clarification of terms is warranted here. *Close Matches* would be more easily understood as "names starting with the same letters." Searching for Szmolen, for example, will bring up names such as Szmolenszky under this category. For this reason, if a surname is frequently misspelled, try typing just the first few letters and selecting *Close Matches* to see what versions might surface. *Alternate Spellings*, by contrast, are variations of the surname found within the database, so a search for Szmolen would bring up Szmolan and Szmalen here (the system presents the two alternatives it determines to be the best fit). Clicking *All Records* will give exact matches, close matches and alternate spellings, so routinely selecting this option will bring up more candidates for consideration.

If you would like a more complete list of alternative spellings—thirty instead of just the top two—click on the *Name & Gender* edit button after reaching the *Matching Passenger Records* page. Here, select any two at a time to be included in your search. By momentarily detouring to this list of thirty, you can refine or expand the search by choosing any pair of alternatives or systematically working through the entire list with fifteen pairs. This will ultimately uncover more of the people you are seeking.

First or Given Names

For the first name, experiment with all four options. The natural tendency is to enter the entire first name of the immigrant, and if he had a straightforward name such as John, this may well work. But maybe the John you are seeking entered the country as Jan, Johan or Jean. To find such people, you could enter just "J" to get a list of all immigrants with that surname whose first names start with this letter. This tactic will result in extra names to sift through but ensures that you'll get all appropriate candidates. As with the surname field, using the leading letters works with the first name (for example, Ja to find Jan and Janos), but only if you have entered a complete last name. Finally, if you want to find all the people with a given surname, a fourth option is to leave the first name field blank.

Ellis Island: Overlooked Features

Two features of the AFIHC website are under-utilized and worthy of mention. Once we reach the *Passenger Record* summary for an ancestor, most of us immediately view the original ship manifest and ignore the other two choices: *Add to Your Ellis Island File* and *View Ship*. Clicking the first option saves the search for future reference so you can easily access it without having to repeat the search process. The *View Ship* option displays an image (and gives the option to purchase a copy, if desired) of the ship your ancestor arrived on, making it a little easier to truly appreciate the journey that brought him or her to New York.

Steve Morse's Tools

The Ellis Island database is an amazing resource with great depth of content and customized functionality, such as the *Alternate Spellings* feature just covered. But even so, many researchers were still unable to unearth their ancestors in the database when it first appeared. Steve Morse had this experience when seeking his wife's relatives and decided to do something about it.

Since the advent of the Ellis Island database, Morse has introduced a series of powerful search forms that he makes available for free at <www.stevemorse.org>. While AFIHC's database allows you to focus your search by specifying criteria (for example, gender, age, and so forth.), you must do so sequentially. Morse's tools enable you to delineate multiple criteria all at once. They also handle unexpected spellings—of both names and places—exceptionally well, and make it possible to locate most missing manifest images. The following list shows Morse's assorted search options, but we'll focus primarily on his white, blue, gray, and missing manifests forms. The site includes an excellent set of Frequently Asked Questions (FAQs) to help you understand every nuance, and you may wish to explore them even if you're the type who typically skips FAQs.

Steve Morse Search Options for Ellis Island

Overview: Which Ellis Island Search Form to use

White Form: Generic form for searching the Ellis Island Database in One Step

Blue Form: Searching the Ellis Island Database in One Step for Jewish Passengers

Gray Form: Short Form for Searching the Ellis Island Database in One Step

Missing Manifests: Find Manifests missing from the Ellis Island Database in One Step

Ship Pictures: Obtaining Pictures of Ellis Island Passenger Ships in One Step

Ship Lists: Searching for Ships in the Ellis Island Microfilms in One Step

Morton Allan Directory: Searching for Ships in the Morton Allan Directory in One Step

While it's a personal decision whether to start the majority of your searches at the Ellis Island or Steve Morse site, if any of the following apply to you, you'll probably have quicker success with particular Morse forms, as shown in table A.

Table A: Which Morse Forms to Use for Selected Search Scenarios

If . . .	. . . use this form.
• you know some details of the immigration • you need to narrow the field	white
• the name and/or town of origin are prone to misspelling • you want to find people from a particular village	gray
• you're researching Jewish passengers	blue
• the ship's manifest is missing or mislinked	missing manifests, ship lists

Morse White Form

Sometimes we know a few details about an immigrant arrival. Many of us grew up with stories of Grandma coming here when she was sixteen years old on a ship called the *S.S. Amerika*. Or we may be dealing with a situation where the name of the immigrant is so common that we need a means to narrow the list of candidates. In either case, the white form provides maximum searching flexibility because it includes all of the following fields: first name or initial, last name (with *starts with, is exactly*, and *sounds like* options), gender, year of arrival (range), age at arrival (range), ship name, and town name.

Figure A shows the example of Leslie Towne Hope, better known as Bob Hope. If you enter "Leslie Hope" at the Ellis Island site, you will not find his arrival, but because of his fame, it is easy to find additional details that make it possible to locate his entry using the white form. A quick search of the Internet reveals that he came to the U.S. in 1908 on the *S.S. Philadelphia*. Combining these details with the name Leslie and last names starting with "H" pops up two-year-old Leslie Hape from Bristol, England.

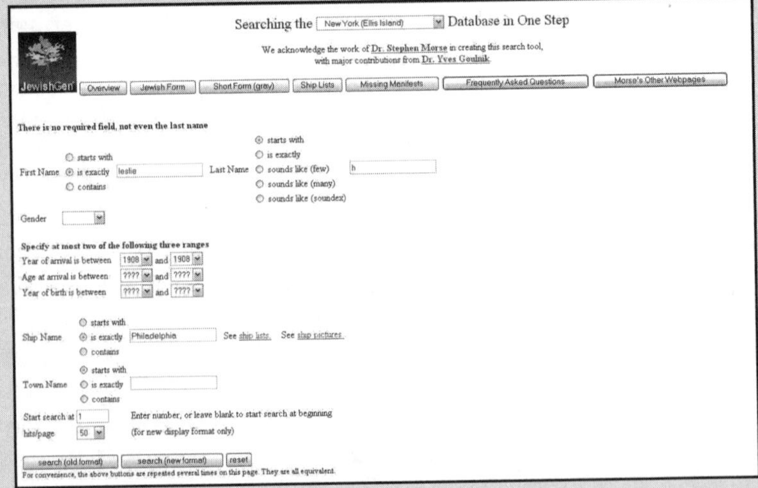

Searching the New York (Ellis Island) Database in One Step

We acknowledge the work of Dr. Stephen Morse in creating this search tool, with major contributions from Dr. Yves Goulnik.

JewishGen | Overview | Jewish Form | Short Form (gray) | Ship Lists | Missing Manifests | Frequently Asked Questions | Morse's Other Webpages

There is no required field, not even the last name

First Name: ○ starts with ◉ is exactly ○ contains — leslie

Last Name: ◉ starts with ○ is exactly ○ sounds like (few) ○ sounds like (many) ○ sounds like (soundex) — h

Gender

Specify at most two of the following three ranges

Year of arrival is between 1908 and 1908

Age at arrival is between ???? and ????

Year of birth is between ???? and ????

Ship Name: ○ starts with ◉ is exactly ○ contains — Philadelphia — See ship lists. See ship pictures.

Town Name: ◉ starts with ○ is exactly ○ contains

Start search at 1 — Enter number, or leave blank to start search at beginning

hits/page 50 — (for new display format only)

search (old format) | search (new format) | reset

For convenience, the above buttons are repeated several times on this page. They are all equivalent.

Figure A. Using Morse's White form to locate Bob Hope's arrival.

Similarly, you could use this same search flexibility to separate Italian Marinos from Cuban ones, identify the Johnsens who left from Stockholm as opposed to other ports, find the Robinsons who came during the 1892 to 1897 unindexed void, or locate Schmidts of draft age.

Morse Gray Form

During Ellis Island's peak, the majority of passengers were of Southern or Eastern European origin, meaning that many had names that were long, complicated, or strange-sounding to American ears. And while—contrary to popular myth—every effort was made to correctly record immigrants' names (and to transcribe them letter for letter when the database was created in the 1990s), a lot of variation inevitably crept in. For example, the twenty-one Smolenyaks who came through Ellis Island can be found in the database under fifteen spellings, including Szuwlyenak, Szmslenak, Szmolmak, Smolina and C...oleniak.

Due to all this creative spelling, descendants of such passengers frequently find it difficult to identify their ancestors. One alternative is to seek all passengers hailing from a particular place (if you're fortunate enough to have this information) since the gray form offers search-by-town capability. But because the hometowns of our ancestors were just as prone to misspelling as their names, this tactic won't always work.

Fortunately, Morse's gray form (see figure B) makes it possible to find virtually all names and towns masked by unexpected spellings. Using it, both last names and town names can be searched with *starts with or is, sounds like,* and *contains* options (first names can also be searched by all but the *sounds like* option). So if you're searching for an ancestor named Motyczka who came from Barwinek, Poland, you could search for the following:

Last name starts with: Moty and *Town name starts with:* Bar
or
Last name sounds like: Motyczka and *Town name starts with:* B
or
Last name contains: otyczka
or
Town name sounds like: Barwinek
or
Last name starts with: Mot and *Town name contains:* winek

The possible combinations are endless and experimenting with them will reveal many more people than you would imagine. In general, the *sounds like* option (a version of Soundex searching) casts the widest net and is the best choice if you want to be as comprehensive as possible and don't mind wading through a long list. But if such a search yields too many hits, you may want to use the other options to reduce the number of candidates.

Morse Blue Form

Morse's blue form (see figure C) is designed specifically for finding Jewish passengers. It defaults

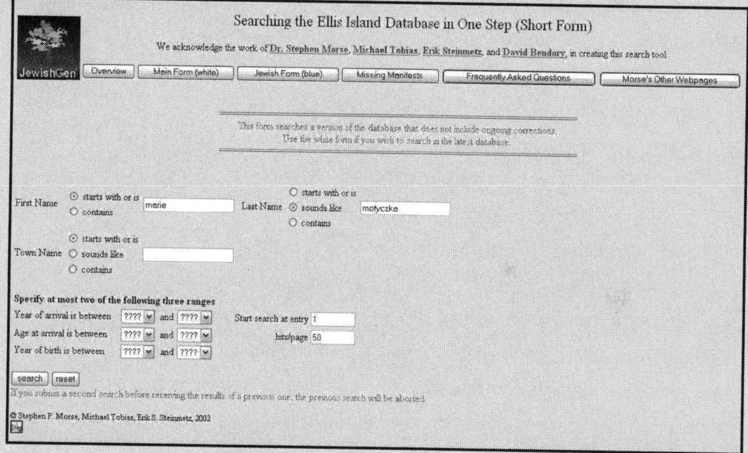

Searching the Ellis Island Database in One Step (Short Form)

We acknowledge the work of Dr. Stephen Morse, Michael Tobias, Erik Steinmetz, and David Bendory, in creating this search tool

JewishGen | Overview | Main Form (white) | Jewish Form (blue) | Missing Manifests | Frequently Asked Questions | Morse's Other Webpages

This form searches a version of the database that does not include ongoing corrections. Use the white form if you wish to search in the latest database.

First Name: starts with or is / contains — marie
Last Name: starts with or is / sounds like / contains — motyczka
Town Name: starts with or is / sounds like / contains

Specify at most two of the following three ranges
Year of arrival is between ???? and ????
Age at arrival is between ???? and ????
Year of birth is between ???? and ????
Start search at entry 1
hits/page 50

search | reset

If you submit a second search before receiving the results of a previous one, the previous search will be aborted.

© Stephen P. Morse, Michael Tobias, Erik S. Steinmetz, 2002

Figure B. Morse's Gray form for searching on name and place spelling variations.

Figure C. Morse's Blue form for searching for Jewish passengers.

to sifting through those who were identified as being of the "Hebrew" race in the Ellis Island database, but allows the user to select other ethnicities (for example, Russian, Polish, and so forth) for inclusion. This form provides true search-by-town and Soundex capabilities and many flexible search parameters. In addition to the options available through the gray form, for instance, the researcher can also enter a *first name of companion,* a useful feature for those whose ancestors traveled as a family. If the passenger you seek was Jewish, the blue form should be your default.

Morse Missing Manifests Form

Although it happens less frequently than before, you may occasionally find an ancestor listed, only to discover that no image of the manifest is available or that the manifest that appears is for the wrong ship or date. In rare cases, some images were accidentally not scanned into the Ellis Island database (if so, you can write to <dberrors@ellisisland.org> to have the error logged and eventually corrected), but the good news is that it is possible to find most images in spite of incorrect or broken links. This is because the text information is in a separate database from the images themselves, and you can usually use the information contained in the text version to lead you to the correct image.

Since manifest searching is slightly more complicated than the other Morse forms, the best way to demonstrate is through an actual example. A researcher who wanted to look at the record for Janos Valyo, who arrived (according to the *Passenger Record* page) on 1 February 1892 on the *Pennland,* was taken instead to the *Rhynland* manifest. If you replicate this search, you'll find the line number (173, from the text database) just above the incorrect image appearing in the *Original Ship Manifest* view.

Armed with the arrival date, ship's name and line number, you can then go to Morse's Missing Manifest form and start by entering the date—1 February 1892—and hitting *display image.* This will take you to the opening page of NARA microfilm roll 581, which covers the period from 2 January to 8 February 1892, in 806 frames.

Since you know that you're looking for an arrival on February 1—roughly four weeks into the five weeks covered by this roll—you can estimate and jump forward through about 80 percent of the 806 pages by entering *645* (.8 x 806) in the frame field. Doing so will lead you to an arrival for February 2, so it's clear you've gone too far. Experimenting with frame numbers, you can back-pedal until you hit frame 608, the opening page for the *Pennland.* Then using the +1 frame button, you can look for Janos Valyo on line 173, which you'll find on frame 613. Once you find the desired image, be sure to note the microfilm and frame numbers so you'll be easily able to find it again using this same form.

Ellis Island: Final Tips

If you've used the appropriate Morse tools and every tactic you can think of and still can't find your elusive prey, you might want to try

- **maiden names**—Italian women in particular were apt to travel under their maiden names, a habit that could even lead to gender confusion (for example, Maria Domenica DeNicco is listed as Domenico DeMicco, a twenty-seven-year-old male).
- **both farm and patronymic names**—Those of Scandinavian origin should try this, even if all the other documents pertaining to their ancestor use just one of the names (for example, Nels Elvik is recorded as Nels Hanson).
- **reversing first and last names**—This tip pertains to people of all ethnicities (for example, Hungarian Gabor Nagy appears as Nagy Gobor; British citizen Halvard Lie appears as Lie Halward).
- **others your ancestor may have traveled with**—If you know or suspect that several family members came together, try names other than that of your direct ancestor, especially if any had simpler or more unusual first names (for example, when unable to find Margaret Marton, a search for her son Anton revealed the family).

Naturalization Records

Naturalization is the legal procedure by which an alien becomes a citizen of a state or country. Every nation has different sets of rules that determine citizenship. While citizenship documents are sought by family historians, both for their sentimental and for their informational value, probably no other records are more difficult to fully understand or locate. Complex and ever-changing naturalization laws and interpretations of laws have resulted in the dissemination of a great deal of incorrect information in this area of research. Unfortunately, many inaccuracies have found their way into genealogical publications. Sometimes, naturalization documentation cannot be found simply because an immigrant was not naturalized. Historically, the number of non-naturalized aliens in the United States has been significant. Tabulations of the 1890 through 1930 censuses indicate that 25.7 percent of the foreign-born population was not naturalized or had filed only declarations of intention. As John Newman points out in *American Naturalization Processes and Procedures, 1790–1985*, "Many aliens lived their lives as positive contributors to their community and new nation without formally acquiring citizenship."[57] He further notes that the constitutions of some states allowed aliens who had filed only declarations of intention to vote, and, except for certain periods when full citizenship was required, to own land. Another important point made by Newman is the fact that many individuals believed themselves to be citizens by derivation from parent or spouse.

Naturalization during the American Colonial Period

The naturalization process in what is now the United States has been an important issue since the seventeenth century. American colonists, subject to the British Crown, considered themselves only "inhabitants" of the colonies, and therefore assumed protection of the laws of Great Britain. According to the practice in England, aliens could acquire citizenship either by letters of denization or by naturalization through an act of Parliament. Denization, though not requiring an oath of loyalty, allowed the transfer of properties and real estate to heirs. Aliens wishing to qualify for public office, to vote, to own a ship, and, in most cases, to own land, had to become naturalized British citizens. Only through parliamentary action could an alien obtain full citizenship status. Finding it necessary to attract immigrants, the American colonies made citizenship and land available. Most of the citizenship records surviving from the American colonial period consist only of lists of oaths of allegiance signed by individuals as they disembarked from the immigrant ships.[58]

In 1740, Parliament enacted new laws that allowed the colonies to naturalize aliens without having to obtain a special act in London. These laws failed to end disputes over the jurisdiction and authority of colonial governments that overrode English law with their own acts. In 1773, the crown disallowed naturalization acts from Pennsylvania and New Jersey, and through an order-in-council instructed colonial governors to cease assenting to such statutes. The strict policy prompted the charge in the Declaration of Independence that George III had endeavored to limit the population growth of the United States by "obstructing the laws for the naturalization of foreigners."

The Continental Congress had resolved on 6 June 1776 "that all persons abiding within any of the United Colonies and deriving protection from the laws of the same owe allegiance to the said laws, and are members of such colony."[59] No oath was required from members of the Continental Congress or from soldiers enlisting in the American army. Those enlisting during the revolution were sworn to be true to the United States of America and to serve them honestly and faithfully. Congress later required an oath for all officers in Continental service and for all holding civil office from Congress. For a detailed discussion of the naturalization process during the Revolutionary Period, see Frank George Franklin's *The Legislative History of Naturalization in the United States*.[60]

Passed by Congress on 26 March 1790, the first naturalization act (1 Stat. 103) provided that any free white persons who had resided for at least two years in the United States might be admitted to citizenship on application to any common law court in any state where they had resided for at least one year. Citizenship was granted to those who satisfied the court that they were of good character and who took an oath of allegiance to the Constitution. Their children under age twenty-one also became citizens.

On 29 January 1795, Congress repealed the 1790 act and passed a more stringent law (1 Stat. 414) which provided that free white aliens might be admitted to citizenship under certain conditions. It required applicants to declare in court their intention to become citizens of the United States and to renounce any allegiance to a foreign prince, potentate, state, or sovereignty three years before admission as citizens. It increased the period of residence required for citizenship from two to five years. The act also required one year's residence in the state in which the court was held and to which application was made. Aliens who had "borne any hereditary title, or been of any of the orders of nobility" were required to renounce that status. These actions could be taken before the supreme, superior, district, or circuit court of any state or of the territories, or before a circuit or district court of the United States. As with the 1790 act, citizenship was automatically granted to the minor children of those naturalized.

From 1798 to 1800, during the undeclared war with France, Federalist leaders pushed through Congress four alien and sedition acts curbing freedom of speech and of the press, and curtailing the rights of foreigners in the United States. One of the statutes, approved 18 June 1798 (1 Stat. 566), required the filing of a declaration of intention at least five years before admission to citizenship, and residence of fourteen years in the

United States and five years in the state or territory where the court was held. Condemned for its severity, the law was replaced with a new naturalization law (2 Stat. 153) reasserting the basic provisions of the 1795 act. The act of 1802 specified that free white aliens might be admitted to citizenship provided they: (1) declared their intention to become citizens before a competent state, territorial, or federal court at least three years before admission to citizenship, (2) took an oath of allegiance to the United States, (3) had resided at least five years in the United States and at least one year within the state or territory where the court was held, (4) renounced allegiance to any foreign prince, potentate, state, or sovereignty, and (5) satisfied the court that they were of good moral character and attached to the principles of the Constitution. While generally poor sources for biographical detail, some naturalization documents survive as evidence of citizenship status.

The 1802 legislation was the last major act affecting the basic nature of naturalization until 1906. Revisions during this period simply altered or clarified details of evidence and certification.

With the ratification of the Fourteenth Amendment to the Constitution on 28 July 1868, "all persons born or naturalized in the United States and subject to the jurisdiction thereof are citizens of the United States and the state in which they reside."

New States and Territories

As the United States acquired territory by treaty or purchase, it also acquired jurisdiction over people living on that land at the time. Acquisitions included Louisiana in 1803, Florida—including Mississippi and Alabama—in 1819, and Alaska in 1867. By joint resolution of Congress, Texas residents were granted citizenship in 1845. By acts of Congress, citizenship was conferred upon residents of Hawaii in 1900, of Puerto Rico in 1917, and of the Virgin Islands in 1927. The names of individuals given citizenship by legislative act were often omitted, and the group may be referred to as a whole.

The United States has always agreed to validate property titles of persons who become citizens because they lived on newly acquired territories. To validate the title, however, a private land claim had to be filed, and these claims can be very valuable. The current land owner must document claim to the title, and if the grant was originally given to a father or grandfather, the claimant had also to prove descent. Some such files contain four to seven generations of genealogical proof through family Bible pages, original land transactions, genealogy charts, and affidavits and testimony of neighbors and relatives. See the *Guide to Genealogical Research in the National Archives* (cited earlier).

Significant Changes in 1906

By the beginning of the twentieth century, investigations into the naturalization process revealed a troubling lack of uniformity among the courts and a scandalous degree of naturalization fraud. Progressive reformers and the public became concerned, and as a result a new Bureau of Immigration and Naturalization was created under the act of 29 June 1906 (32 Stat. 596 sec. 3). The 1906 Act provided the first uniform rule for the naturalization of aliens throughout the United States. After September 1906, naturalization forms could be obtained exclusively from the Bureau of Immigration and Naturalization. The new forms were expanded to include each applicant's age, occupation, personal description, date and place of birth, citizenship, present and last foreign addresses, ports of embarkation and entry, name of vessel or other means of conveyance, and date of arrival in the United States; also included were spouse's and children's full names with their respective dates and places of birth, and residence at the date of the document. The declaration of intention of actor Errol Flynn (figure 9-11) was filed in the Common Pleas Court of Bergen County, New Jersey, on a standard federal form in 1939. Typical of many would-be U.S. citizens, Fermi began the naturalization process in a court near the place where he arrived in the United States and finalized the procedure in another county and state where he took up permanent residency. In this case, the final papers were taken out in Chicago. Fermi's declaration of intention is filed together with his petition at the National Archives—Great Lakes Region in Chicago, where citizenship documentation is also available for his wife, Laura.

Women and Children

An act of 10 February 1855 granted citizenship to alien wives of citizens if they "might lawfully be naturalized under the existing laws" (10 Stat. 604). Prior to 1922, women and children automatically became derivative U.S. citizens when the husband or father naturalized, or upon the woman's marriage to the citizen husband. Conversely, between 1907 and 1922 U.S. law dictated that American citizen women who married alien husbands lost their U.S. citizenship, and could not regain citizenship until the husband naturalized. While it was definitely the exception rather than the rule, some women, especially single adults, found it necessary or desirable to become naturalized citizens themselves (figure 9-12).

An act of 22 September 1922 (42 Stat. 1021) had significant effects on the status of women. By this act a woman could no longer become a citizen by virtue of her marriage to a citizen, but, if eligible, might be naturalized by compliance with the naturalization laws; no declaration of intention was required if she was already married to a citizen husband. A woman could still lose citizenship by marriage after 1922, specifically if her husband was racially barred from naturalization (section 3), nor could the woman be naturalized while married to a racially ineligible husband (section 5). An act of 3 March 1931 repealed the provisions regarding the husband's race, and thereafter women no longer lost citizenship by any marriage, and all wives of aliens who lost citizenship by marriage prior to 1922 no longer had to naturalize to regain their U.S. citizenship. Rather, they could take an oath of allegiance before a court in the United States and, upon taking the oath, be repatriated. Courts usually filed the women's applications and oaths separately, but they may occasionally be found among the court's naturalization records. Figure 9-13 is an example of the thousands of oath of allegiance documents created in the courts after 1936 to document the repatriation of women who lost citizenship by marriage prior to 1922. Under the 1936 act, women living abroad who previously lost citizenship could repatriate by taking the oath of allegiance before a consular officer at a U.S. embassy. Documentation of oaths taken abroad, as well as duplicates of those taken in any court within the U.S., are duplicated in the records of the Immigration and Naturalization Service. Requests for the federal copies must be made under the Freedom of Information Act and sent to Washington, D.C.

Military Service

Aliens who served in the U.S. military and received honorable discharge were given special consideration. An act of 17 July 1862 (12 Stat. 597) stated that:

> Any alien, of the age of twenty-one years and upwards, who has enlisted, or may enlist in the armies of the United States, either the regular or the volunteer forces, and has been, or may be hereafter, honorably discharged, shall be admitted to become a citizen of the United States, upon his petition, without any previous declaration of intention to become such; and he shall not be required to prove more than one year's residence.

Designed to encourage aliens to enlist for the Civil War, similar legislation applied to later wars as well. Many individuals have misunderstood this law and reported it to mean that those serving in the military gained automatic citizenship. It should be emphasized that this was not the case. With the length of residency shortened and the declaration of intention waived, the process was expedited. Instead of naturalization "first papers," some courts may have filed military discharges for some individuals. Frequently, military naturalization papers (or "soldier naturalization" papers) were filed independently, making it necessary to consult a separate military index. Military naturalization records were, however, included in the WPA-created indexes described later in this section. It should be noted that, when the WPA indexes were microfilmed, the reverse sides of normally blank cards were sometimes missed. An index card for William C. Wilson (figure 9-14) illustrates the importance of a thorough search.

An act of 26 July 1894 (28 Stat. 124) extended naturalization privileges to those who had "served five consecutive years in the United States Navy or one enlistment in the United States Marine Corps" so long as they had received an "honorable discharge."

Another modification regarding the naturalization of soldiers, sailors, and veterans came about because of World War I. An act of 9 May 1918 (40 Stat. 542) consolidated military naturalization laws and stated that: "Any alien serving in the military or naval service of the United States during the time this country is engaged in the present war may file his petition for naturalization without making the preliminary declaration of intention and without proof of the required five years residence within the United States." The act provided for immediate naturalization of alien soldiers, waiving the required declaration of intention or first paper, certificate of arrival, and proof of residence. Members of the armed forces were naturalized at military posts and nearby courts instead of at their legal residences. A comprehensive index to World War I soldier naturalizations (except those at Camp Devins, Massachusetts) can be found at the National Archives, Washington, D.C., in Record Group 85, entry 29.

African Americans, Native Americans, and Asians

A law approved on 14 July 1870 opened the naturalization process to persons of African nativity or descent (16 Stat. 256). In the early years, members of some American Indian tribes were admitted to citizenship through treaty provisions and under special statutes. Prior to 1924, the most important law relating to Indian citizenship was the Allotment Act of 8 February 1887 (24 Stat. 387). This statute conferred citizenship on (1) every Indian born in the United States to whom allotments were made by this act or any law or treaty and (2) every Indian born in the United States who had voluntarily taken up within its limits a residence that was "separate and apart from any tribe of Indians" and had "adopted the habits of civilized life." By an act of 9 August 1888, every Native American woman who was a member of a tribe and married to a U.S. citizen was declared to be a citizen (25 Stat. 392). The act of 2 June 1924 provided that all Indians born in the United States were to be citizens (43 Stat. 253).

At the same time, Native Americans born outside the United States, in Canada, Mexico, the Caribbean, or other Americas, remained barred from naturalization on racial grounds until 1940. Asians were also barred from citizenship due to race. Chinese gained the right to naturalization in 1943, East Indians and Filipinos in 1946, and all others in 1952 when the racial requirement disappeared from U.S. immigration law.

Recent Government Changes

The Bureau of Immigration and Naturalization later became the Immigration and Naturalization Service (INS) and operated under that name, controlling and managing the process and records of naturalization, until 2002. With the creation of the Department of Homeland Security, and mounting concerns regarding the efficiency of the INS in identifying aliens, Congress mandated radical changes. The INS was dismantled and many of their functions became the responsibility of the new U.S. Citizenship and Immigration Services (USCIS) division of the Department of Homeland Security. These changes have little effect on researchers seeking historical documentation of a relative's naturalization. Such records as were created by the INS are now under the jurisdiction of the USCIS <http://uscis.gov/graphics>.

Genealogical Information in Naturalization Documents

A great number of alien residents never became naturalized, for various reasons; therefore, citizenship documentation for these individuals is nonexistent. Also, some individuals did not decide to become naturalized citizens until they had been residents of this country for many years. Extreme examples have been found—some men and women did not become citizens for seventy or eighty years after immigration—but most people began naturalization proceedings within five years of their arrival in the United States.

A most important fact to remember is that the format and content of naturalization records varied dramatically from county to county, from state to state, and from year to year *prior to 1906* when the Bureau of Immigration and Naturalization was established. After September 1906, when the new law went into effect, uniform naturalization forms were required by all courts involved in naturalization.

Before 1906, state, county, and other courts printed various naturalization forms and certificate formats. Some courts, following directions of the 14 April 1802 Act (2 Stat. 153), were careful to record the name, birthplace, age, nation and allegiance, country from which emigrated, and the intended place of settlement of each registering alien. For example, the declaration of intention for Homer Hayes (figure 9-15) provides the kind of detail sought by all family historians but rarely found in naturalization documents created before 1906. Unfortunately, the great majority of the pre-1906 records do not reflect the directions of the 1802 Act. A typical naturalization record for this time period will provide only the name and location of the naturalizing court, the name of the person seeking naturalization, a statement renouncing allegiance and fidelity to any foreign prince, potentate, state or sovereignty (naming country of origin), and the date of the event (declaration of intention, petition, or final certificate). If the individual being naturalized could write, a signature on citizenship documents may be worth all the effort of the search. An examination of a large number of these records suggests that many immigrants could not write; thus, their marks may be the only confirmation of their desire to become American citizens. Another disappointing fact is that many naturalization documents were copied onto forms in ledger books by county clerks. Often, the clerk's handwriting is mistakenly accepted as the petitioner's signature. Scanning other naturalization entries in a particular volume will usually make it possible to determine whether or not the signature is that of the clerk or the petitioner. Many of the earlier records contain little information that is of genealogical value, but significant exceptions in some states and counties make it advisable to conduct a thorough search of all potential naturalization documentation for the person or persons of interest. Figure 9-16, from a court in Carroll County, Maryland, is representative of the variety of forms used by local courts before 1906. Usually, very little biographical information is offered in these early records.

Becoming a Citizen: The Process and the Records

The first Naturalization Act provided that an alien who wished to become a citizen could apply to "any common law court of record, in any of the states wherein he shall have resided for the term of one year at least."

Aliens interested in becoming citizens of the United States generally took the following steps:

Declaration of Intention (First Papers). Usually, the declaration of intention was the first step in the naturalization process. First papers were normally completed soon after arrival in the United States, depending on the laws in effect at the time. (See the "Major Settlements, Immigration, and Naturalization: A Chronology" section.) Certain groups, such as women and children, were exempt in early years. After 1862, those who were honorably discharged from U.S. military service were excused from this initial procedure. Until 1906, the content of forms for declarations of intention varied dramatically from county to county and court to court. A large percentage of the first papers created before 1906 contain very little biographical information. Declarations of intention produced after 26 September 1906 generally contain the following information: name, address, occupation, birthplace, nationality, country from which emigrated, birth date or age, personal description, date of intention, marital status, last foreign residence, port of entry, name of ship, date of entry, and date of document. Declarations of intention, affidavits, petitions, and oaths of allegiance were generally filed together in the court in which the final steps to citizenship were taken. Affidavits and final oaths were not always recorded on separate forms, depending on the court and the year. When they do exist as individual papers, they are usually filed with the final papers, as in the case of Patrick McNamara, who was naturalized in the United States Court in Cuyahoga County (Cleveland), Ohio. See figures 9-17, 9-18, 9-19, and 9-20.

Petition (Second or Final Papers). Naturalization petitions were formal applications submitted to the court by individuals who had met the residency requirements and who had declared their intention to become citizens. As with the declarations of intention, informational content varied dramatically from court to court. Most petitions created before 1906 offer very little in terms of personal information. After 1906, the following information might be found: name, address, occupation, date emigrated, birthplace, country from which emigrated, birth date or age, time in the United States, date of intention, name and age of spouse, names of children, ages of children, last foreign residence, port and mode of entry, name of ship, date of entry, names of witnesses, date of document, address of spouse, and photograph (after 1929).

Certificate of Naturalization. Most pre-1906 certificates contain only the name of the individual and the name of the court and the date of issue. Certificates were issued to the naturalized citizens upon completion of all citizenship requirements. As in the cases of the declarations of intention and the petitions, the amount of information provided on the certificate may vary greatly from court to court and from year to year. In some cases, the certificate will provide the name; address; birthplace or nationality; country from which emigrated; birth date or age; personal description; marital status; name of spouse; names, ages, and addresses of children; date of document, and photograph (after 1929).

Naturalization Certificate Stubs. Generally, the court did not retain copies of certificates issued to new citizens, but certificates were usually issued from bound volumes. Typical volumes were designed in a check book fashion, with the certificate to the right side of the page, and a stub to the left to be kept as a permanent record of the person to whom the certificate was issued. These "naturalization stub books," as they are sometimes called, vary in content from court to court and from year to year, but they sometimes contain useful genealogical information. Some court officials regarded stub books as a duplication of records that occupied needed space and ordered them destroyed. If certificate stubs have survived, they may be found in the creating courts, archives, and historical agencies. See, for example, figure 9-21, a page from a stub book for the U.S. District Court, Northern District of Ohio, for Julius August Behnke. It shows his age, when and where he declared his intention to become a citizen, names, ages, and places of residences of his wife and children, and the date of issue of the certificate of naturalization.

Certificates of Arrival. Aliens who arrived in the United States after 29 June 1906 were subject to an additional naturalization requirement under the 1906 naturalization law. Before they could be naturalized, federal naturalization officials (INS) had to prove the applicant's lawful admission as an immigrant by verifying their official immigration record, usually a ship passenger list. Once the immigration record was located, arrival information was certified on a form called a certificate of arrival. The title of the document has frequently led to misunderstanding, causing some to state that certificates of arrival were issued to immigrants upon their arrival in the United States. In fact, the certificates of arrival were not issued until the immigrant applied for naturalization, some five or more years after entry. The certificate of arrival was then forwarded to the court where the immigrant had applied for citizenship and served as proof of the immigrant's eligibility to naturalize. Most clerks of court then filed the certificates among the court's naturalization records, but certificates of arrival were not always preserved by all courts.

Where to Search for Naturalization Documents

Prior to 1906 an alien could be naturalized in any court of record, and the court record is the only record of a naturalization. In most cases it is best to begin a search for naturalization documents in courts in the county where the immigrant is known to have resided. It is not uncommon to discover that immigrants, anxious to become citizens, began the citizenship process by taking out first papers in the county in which they first arrived in this country. One may have started the process somewhere on the Eastern Seaboard, for example, and then completed the requirements in the county or state when final residency was established in the Midwest. It is also not uncommon to find an immigrant who filed multiple declarations of intention in various courts as he moved around the country.

In addition to county and federal courts, there may have been city or municipal courts, marine courts, criminal courts, police courts, or other courts having authority to naturalize in the area where the immigrant lived. Often it was a matter of the alien simply choosing to travel to the most conveniently located court—and the courthouse in an adjoining county might have been more convenient than the courthouse in the county of residence.

While all naturalization records are supposed to be permanent records and kept indefinitely by the courts, major and minor situations have caused records to be lost, destroyed, or moved from their creating agencies. Floods, fires, carelessness, politics, and other acts of humans and nature have destroyed some records and made others inaccessible. Over the years some long-forgotten naturalization records have been rediscovered in warehouses, attics, and basements. Still other collections have been carefully maintained by museums, libraries, and historical and genealogical societies. State archives and historical agencies typically strive to preserve and catalog these historical records. If a record is not immediately found at the county level, an investigation of any such records kept at the state level may be in order.

Some courts will have master naturalization indexes, but many will have separately indexed volumes of naturalization records that will need to be examined book by book. Frequently, the naturalizations of military personnel and the so-called "minor naturalizations" (a strange term, given that no one under age twenty-one could be legally naturalized by a court) are in separate volumes and may be easily overlooked. It is not unheard of to find naturalization records intermingled with other court records; some have even been found among land records. An excellent source for locating courts and naturalization records is Alice Eichholz's *Red Book: American State, County, and Town Sources*.[61]

Millions of naturalization records from counties all over the United States have been microfilmed by the Genealogical Society of Utah and are available at the LDS Family History Library in Salt Lake City. Copies or the microfilm may be borrowed through LDS family history centers. In some cases, it may be more convenient to access naturalization indexes and files through the Family History Library if the records have been microfilmed.

Naturalization Indexes

Although most courts had previously indexed their naturalization records, the 1906 naturalization law required them to do so. Most of the federal court naturalization indexes can be found at the National Archives regional facilities, and many of them are published on microfilm.

During the 1930s and 1940s, a number of states participated in projects sponsored by the U.S. Immigration and Naturalization Service and carried out by the Work Projects Administration (WPA), to locate, photograph, and/or index naturalization records predating 27 September 1906. Though proposed as a nationwide project, funding was secured only for INS districts in New England, New York, and Chicago. As a result, there are several indexes to naturalizations in all courts in these districts.

There are several enormous naturalization indexes that should be consulted initially if the alien of interest lived in one of the areas covered by these compilations. One of the largest is *Index to Naturalization Petitions of the United States District Court for the Eastern District of New York 1865–1957,* described in a pamphlet of the same title.[62] The records which have been microfilmed consist of approximately 650,000 three-by-five-inch cards that index bound and unbound naturalization petitions. The cards are arranged in three groups covering the periods July 1865 to September 1906, October 1906 to November 1925, and November 1925 to December 1957. The cards within each group are arranged alphabetically by the name of the person naturalized.

Index cards for the first group include the name of the naturalized individual, the date of naturalization, and the volume and record number of the naturalization petition. These cards may also contain such information as the address, occupation, birth date or age, former nationality, and port and date of arrival of the person naturalized, and the name of the witness to the naturalization.

The cards for the second and third groups show the name and the petition and certificate numbers of the person naturalized and generally include the address, age, and date of admission to citizenship.

The petitions to which these microfilmed index cards relate are in the National Archives—Northeast Region. They have not yet been microfilmed.

Petitions for the period from July 1865 to September 1906 are arranged in bound volumes. The information on each petition varies. Petitions dated 1 July 1865 to 5 July 1895 indicate the city of residence, former nationality of petitioner, name of witness, dates of petition, and admission to citizenship. Petitions dated from 5 July 1895 through 26 September 1906 may also contain information on the petitioner's occupation, date and place of birth, and port and date of arrival in the United States; the name, address, and occupation of the witness; and the signature of the alien.

Petitions filed after September 1906 are unbound and are arranged numerically by petition number. They usually indicate the occupation, place of embarkation, and date and port of arrival of the petitioner; name of the vessel or other means of conveyance into the United States; the court in which the alien's declaration of intention was filed and filing date; marital status; name and place of residence of each of the applicant's children; date of the beginning of the alien's continuous U.S. residence; length of residence in the United States; names, occupations, and addresses of witnesses; and signatures of alien and witnesses.

A caveat in the descriptive pamphlet states the following:

> The index reproduced on this microfilm publication refers only to those aliens who sought naturalization in the U.S. District Court for the Eastern District of New York, located in Kings County, New York. An alien, however, could become a naturalized citizen through any court of record, making it possible for those living in any of the five counties that make up the eastern district to seek naturalization through the city or county courts in the counties in this district. This index, therefore, does not contain the names of all individuals naturalized in the counties of Kings, Queens, Richmond, Suffolk, and Nassau. The clerks of these county courts will, as a rule, have custody of the naturalization records of aliens who became citizens in their courts.

The National Archives—Great Lakes Region in Chicago has in its custody the Soundex index to more than 1.5 million naturalization petitions from northern Illinois, northwestern Indiana, southern and eastern Wisconsin, and eastern Iowa. The microfilmed records are described in *Soundex Index to Naturalization Petitions for the United States District and Circuit Courts, Northern District of Illinois, and Immigration and Naturalization Service District 9, 1840–1950*.[63] The index consists of 162 cubic feet of three- by five-inch cards arranged in Russell-Soundex order and thereafter alphabetically by given name. The index includes civil and military petitions.

TRIPLICATE
(To be given to declarant)

No. ......

UNITED STATES OF AMERICA

DECLARATION OF INTENTION
(Invalid for all purposes seven years after the date hereof)

ss: In the ...... Court
of ...... at ......

I, ERROL LESLIE FLYNN
(Full true name, without abbreviation, and any other name which has been used, must appear here)
now residing at 601 No. Linden Drive, Beverly Hills, California
(Number and street) (City or town) (County) (State)
occupation Actor-author, aged 29 years, do declare on oath that my personal description is:
Sex Male, color White, complexion Fair, color of eyes Grey
color of hair Brown, height 6 feet 2 inches; weight 186 pounds; visible distinctive marks None
race Irish; nationality British
I was born in Hobart, Australia on June 20, 1909
(City or town) (Country) (Month) (Day) (Year)
I am married. The name of my wife XXXXXX and is Liliane Marie Madeleine
we were married on May 5, 1935, at Yuma, Ariz.; she XXX was
(Month) (Day) (Year) (City or town) (State or country)
born at Blaye, France, on July 10, 1908, entered the United States
(City or town) (State or country) (Month) (Day) (Year)
at New York, N. Y., on Aug. 28, 1930, for permanent residence therein, and now
(City or town) (State) (Month) (Day) (Year)
resides at with me. I have no children, and the name, date and place of birth,
(City or town) (State or country)
and place of residence of each of said children are as follows: ......

I have not heretofore made a declaration of intention: Number ......, on ......
at ......
(City or town) (State) (Name of court) (Date)
my last foreign residence was Mexicali, Mexico
(City or town) (Country)
I emigrated to the United States of America from Mexicali, Mexico
(City or town) (Country)
my lawful entry for permanent residence in the United States was at Calexico, Calif.
(City or town) (State)
under the name of Errol Leslie Flynn, on May 9, 1936
(Month) (Day) (Year)
on XXXXXXX foot
(If other than by vessel, state manner of arrival)

I will, before being admitted to citizenship, renounce forever all allegiance and fidelity to any foreign prince, potentate, state, or sovereignty, and particularly, by name, to the prince, potentate, state, or sovereignty of which I may be at the time of admission a citizen or subject; I am not an anarchist; I am not a polygamist nor a believer in the practice of polygamy; and it is my intention in good faith to become a citizen of the United States of America and to reside permanently therein; and I certify that the photograph affixed to the duplicate and triplicate hereof is a likeness of me.

I swear (affirm) that the statements I have made and the intentions I have expressed in this declaration of intention subscribed by me are true to the best of my knowledge and belief: So help me God.

Errol Leslie Flynn
(Original signature of declarant without abbreviation, also alias, if used)

Errol Leslie Flynn

Subscribed and sworn to before me in the form of oath shown above in the office of the Clerk of said Court, at Los Angeles, California this 20th day of December, anno Domini, 19 38. Certification 33-61783 from the Commissioner of Immigration and Naturalization showing the lawful entry of the declarant for permanent residence on the date stated above, has been received by me. The photograph affixed to the duplicate and triplicate hereof is a likeness of the declarant.

[SEAL]

R. S. Zimmerman, Clerk U. S. District Court
Clerk of Southern District of California Court.
By ...... Deputy Clerk.

Form 2202—L—A
U. S. DEPARTMENT OF LABOR
IMMIGRATION AND NATURALIZATION SERVICE

14—2023
U. S. GOVERNMENT PRINTING OFFICE

Figure 9-11. In 1938, Errol Leslie Flynn declared his intention to become a citizen of the United States in Beverly Hills, California. Information on Flynn's declaration of intention is typical of that found on naturalization documents of the era.

While the Soundex index includes references to naturalizations that took place in Illinois, Indiana, Wisconsin, and Iowa, a great portion of the records cited in the index are not physically located at the National Archives. Naturalization records in the custody of the National Archives—Great Lakes Region, with one exception, consist of records for persons naturalized in certain federal (not county or state) courts. The one exception is copies (not originals) of county naturalization records for 1871 through 1906 for Chicago/Cook County, Illinois. A sampling of the Soundex index described previously (figure 9-22) illustrates the standard format used for the cards and the kind of information about the individual that may or may not be included. Besides the name of the naturalized citizen, it is especially important to note the name of the court in which the naturalization took place and the petition number (when it is included on the card) when following through with a search for the actual naturalization documents. Normally, all biographical information recorded in the original document was copied to the Soundex card. If the spaces on the card for date of birth, birthplace, date and place of arrival in the United States, and so forth, are blank, it is likely that the original naturalization documents did not include that information.

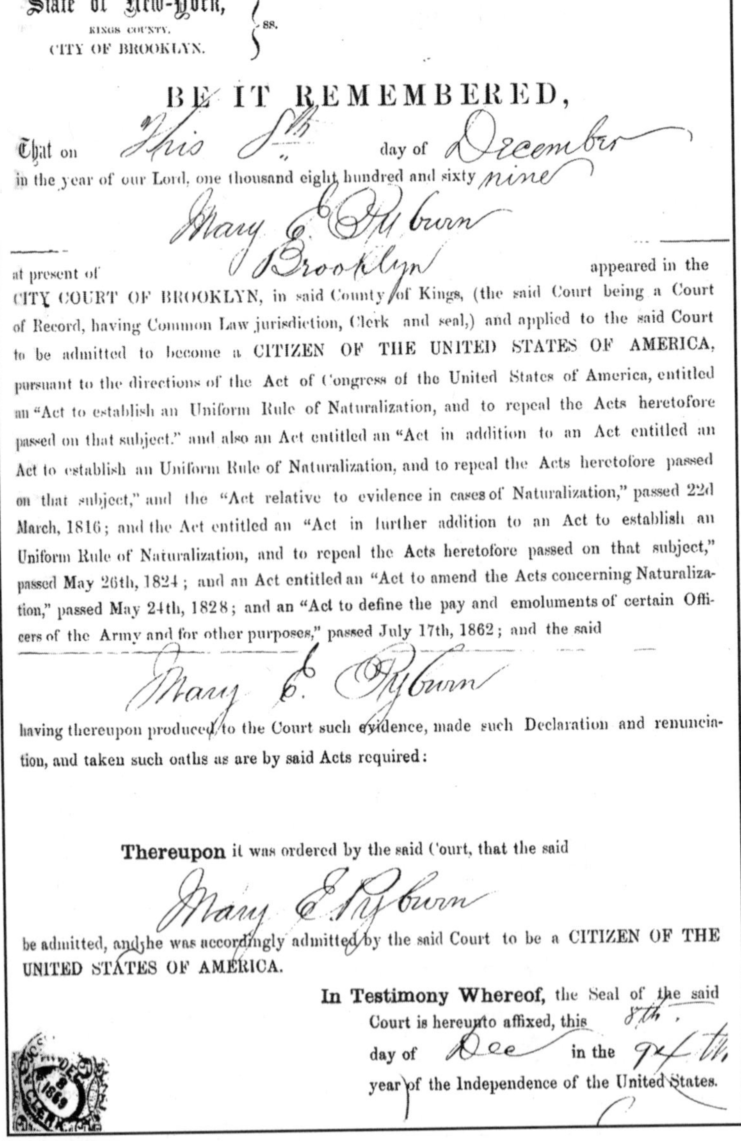

State of New-York, KINGS COUNTY, CITY OF BROOKLYN. } ss.

BE IT REMEMBERED,

That on This 8th day of December in the year of our Lord, one thousand eight hundred and sixty nine

Mary E. Pyburn

at present of Brooklyn appeared in the CITY COURT OF BROOKLYN, in said County of Kings, (the said Court being a Court of Record, having Common Law jurisdiction, Clerk and seal,) and applied to the said Court to be admitted to become a CITIZEN OF THE UNITED STATES OF AMERICA, pursuant to the directions of the Act of Congress of the United States of America, entitled an "Act to establish an Uniform Rule of Naturalization, and to repeal the Acts heretofore passed on that subject." and also an Act entitled an "Act in addition to an Act entitled an Act to establish an Uniform Rule of Naturalization, and to repeal the Acts heretofore passed on that subject," and the "Act relative to evidence in cases of Naturalization," passed 22d March, 1816; and the Act entitled an "Act in further addition to an Act to establish an Uniform Rule of Naturalization, and to repeal the Acts heretofore passed on that subject," passed May 26th, 1824; and an Act entitled an "Act to amend the Acts concerning Naturalization," passed May 24th, 1828; and an "Act to define the pay and emoluments of certain Officers of the Army and for other purposes," passed July 17th, 1862; and the said

Mary E. Pyburn

having thereupon produced to the Court such evidence, made such Declaration and renunciation, and taken such oaths as are by said Acts required:

Thereupon it was ordered by the said Court, that the said

Mary E Pyburn

be admitted, and she was accordingly admitted by the said Court to be a CITIZEN OF THE UNITED STATES OF AMERICA.

In Testimony Whereof, the Seal of the said Court is hereunto affixed, this 8th day of Dec in the 94th year of the Independence of the United States.

Figure 9-12. Before 1922, the vast majority of alien women derived citizenship from their husbands or fathers who were already U.S. citizens. However, the example of Mary E. Pyburn, naturalized in a Brooklyn, New York, court in 1869, points to the possibility of exceptions to the rule. Indexes to naturalizations should be searched for all family names.

While there is no comprehensive index to other naturalizations in its custody, the National Archives—Great Lakes Region also has naturalization documents for other federal courts in Illinois, Indiana, Michigan, Minnesota, Ohio, and Wisconsin for certain years.

The National Archives—New England Region has original copies of naturalization records of the federal courts for the six New England states. Individuals were also naturalized in state, county, and local courts. The branch has copies (dexographs—white-on-black photographs) of such court records between 1790 and 1906 for Maine, Massachusetts, Rhode Island, Vermont, and New Hampshire. For Connecticut there are originals of some state, county, and local naturalizations for the years 1790 to 1974. An index to naturalization documents filed in courts in Connecticut, Maine, Massachusetts, New Hampshire, and Rhode Island is also at the National Archives—New England Region. The index contains some cards for New York and Vermont as well, but the records to which they refer are not among the photocopies at that regional archive. The New England WPA index consists of three- by five-inch cards arranged by name of petitioner and by the Soundex system. The index refers to the name and location of the court that granted citizenship and to the volume and page number of the naturalization record.

For a listing of naturalization records and indexes available for research in the regions of the National Archives, see Loretto Dennis Szucs and Sandra Hargreaves Luebking's *The Archives: A Guide to the National Archives Field Branches*.[64]

Federal Copies of Post-1906 Naturalization and Citizenship Records

An important feature of the 1906 naturalization law required that for all naturalizations performed on or after 17 September 1906, all records were to be prepared in duplicate, with one copy forwarded to the Immigration and Naturalization Service (INS)

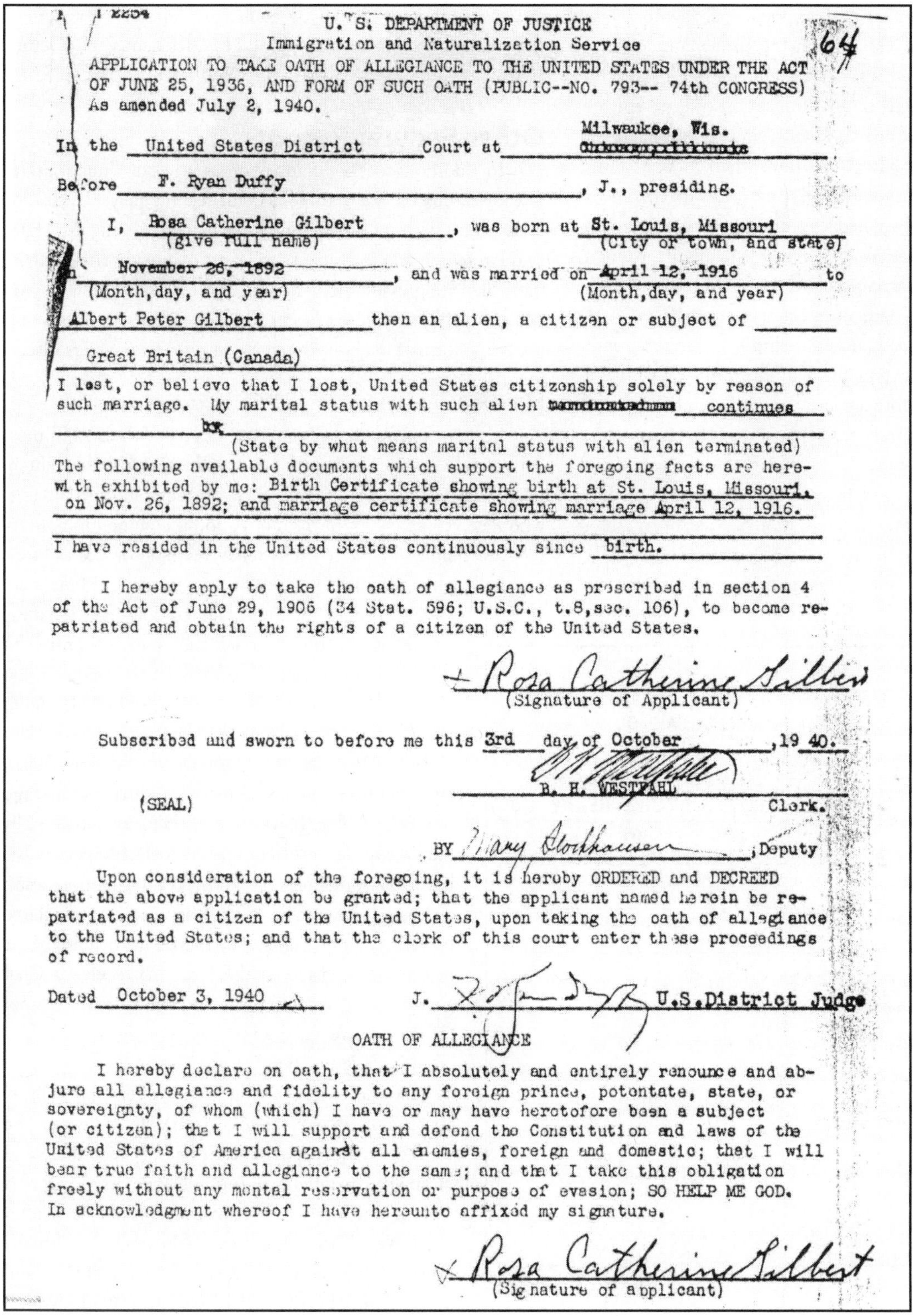

U. S. DEPARTMENT OF JUSTICE
Immigration and Naturalization Service
APPLICATION TO TAKE OATH OF ALLEGIANCE TO THE UNITED STATES UNDER THE ACT OF JUNE 25, 1936, AND FORM OF SUCH OATH (PUBLIC--NO. 793-- 74th CONGRESS) As amended July 2, 1940.

In the United States District Court at Milwaukee, Wis.

Before F. Ryan Duffy, J., presiding.

I, Rosa Catherine Gilbert (give full name), was born at St. Louis, Missouri (City or town, and state) November 26, 1892 (Month, day, and year), and was married on April 12, 1916 (Month, day, and year) to Albert Peter Gilbert then an alien, a citizen or subject of Great Britain (Canada)

I lost, or believe that I lost, United States citizenship solely by reason of such marriage. My marital status with such alien continues (State by what means marital status with alien terminated)

The following available documents which support the foregoing facts are herewith exhibited by me: Birth Certificate showing birth at St. Louis, Missouri, on Nov. 26, 1892; and marriage certificate showing marriage April 12, 1916.

I have resided in the United States continuously since birth.

I hereby apply to take the oath of allegiance as prescribed in section 4 of the Act of June 29, 1906 (34 Stat. 596; U.S.C., t.8, sec. 106), to become repatriated and obtain the rights of a citizen of the United States.

Rosa Catherine Gilbert
(Signature of Applicant)

Subscribed and sworn to before me this 3rd day of October, 1940.

(SEAL)

B. H. WESTFAHL
Clerk.

BY Mary Stockhausen, Deputy

Upon consideration of the foregoing, it is hereby ORDERED and DECREED that the above application be granted; that the applicant named herein be repatriated as a citizen of the United States, upon taking the oath of allegiance to the United States; and that the clerk of this court enter these proceedings of record.

Dated October 3, 1940 J. U.S. District Judge

OATH OF ALLEGIANCE

I hereby declare on oath, that I absolutely and entirely renounce and abjure all allegiance and fidelity to any foreign prince, potentate, state, or sovereignty, of whom (which) I have or may have heretofore been a subject (or citizen); that I will support and defend the Constitution and laws of the United States of America against all enemies, foreign and domestic; that I will bear true faith and allegiance to the same; and that I take this obligation freely without any mental reservation or purpose of evasion; SO HELP ME GOD. In acknowledgment whereof I have hereunto affixed my signature.

Rosa Catherine Gilbert
(Signature of applicant)

Figure 9-13. Thousands of U.S.-born women lost their American citizenship when they married foreigners. This record for Rosa Catherine Gilbet, first filed in U.S. District Court in Milwaukee, is now at the National Archives—Great Lakes Region. Similar documents survive in courts across the country, and many are preserved in various regional archives of the National Archives.

in Washington, D.C. The INS thus compiled a master set of all naturalization papers from that date until March 31, 1956, all arranged by naturalization certificate number. INS copies naturalization records are referred to a "Certificate Files," or "C-Files." It is important to note that INS C-Files dated 1906 to 1929 (and in some cases dated 1929 to 1956) may contain documents not filed with court records. All C-Files contain a duplicate copy of the actual naturalization certificate. As a result researchers who locate a post-1906 naturalization among court records should consider requesting the INS copy as well.

Beginning in the 1920s, the INS also created C-Files in citizenship (as opposed to naturalization) cases. Files containing applications, correspondence, and a duplicate certificate, relate to persons who acquired U.S. citizenship in a manner other than naturalization by a court. These include children who derived citizenship through the naturalization of a parent, or by birth abroad to a U.S. citizen parent, and who applied for a certificate of citizenship after 1929 (and when 21 years old). There are also C-Files for women who derived citizenship by marriage before 1922 and applied for a certificate of citizenship after 1940. A separate series of C-Files documents women who lost citizenship by marriage before 1922 and resumed U.S. citizenship by taking an oath of allegiance after 1936. Note that women who resumed their citizenship by taking the oath could do so before a court in the United States or before a U.S. Consul abroad. If before a court, a record should be found among court naturalization records. If before a U.S. Consul, the only record is the INS C-File.

The U.S. Citizenship and Immigration Services (USCIS), formerly the Immigration and Naturalization Service, maintains a duplicate file of naturalizations that took place after 27 September 1906. All requests for copies of post-1906 naturalization or citizenship records should be mailed to: Director, Freedom of Information/Privacy Act (FOIA), 111 Massachusetts Avenue, N.W., 2nd Floor, ULLICO Building, Washington, D.C., 20529.

Other Federal Records

In addition to the many records in the United States already discussed, some other federal records may identify the immigrant's place of origin. These records are usually used later in the research process because the records already discussed are more likely to provide the name of the native town. However, on occasion, military records, Social Security records, or others may provide information about the immigrant found nowhere else.

Military Records

Military records are among the most important and most extensive U.S. records of genealogical value. Because the military needed to fully identify the soldiers who fought and the veterans who received pensions, birth information is common in military records. Immigrants were often ready recruits for the military, especially when they had few relatives in America. Many were willing to fight for their adopted country, including, paradoxically, those who left their native countries to avoid military service. As with most other genealogical records, the more recent records include more information. Indeed, records of Revolutionary War service seldom identify the birthplace of the soldier, let alone his home in the native country. By the time of the Civil War, however, enlistment records usually indicated at least the country where an immigrant was born, and sometimes the town. Although immigration decreased during the Civil War, a surprisingly large number of immigrants who arrived in the early years of the war enlisted in the army. To receive a Civil War pension, veterans did not have to require proof of birth; however, the birthplace of the veteran was often included on pension application forms.

By the end of the nineteenth century, military enlistment records almost invariably indicated the town of birth. Any significant military record created during the twentieth century will aid most researchers seeking the native towns of immigrants born after 1875. World War I draft records documented virtually every adult male between the ages of eighteen and forty-five in the years 1918 to 1920. World War II draft records have recently become available for some states, and they are found in some regions of the National Archives. They would include virtually any immigrant born between 1875 and 1900, whether they had been naturalized or not. For more information on these and other military records, see chapter 11, "Military Records."

W-425

Family name	Given name or names
WILSON.	WILLIAM C.

Address "O"

Certificate no. (or vol. and page)	Title and location of court
V.C.P. 64. SOLDIER.	(CAMBRIDGE, ILL) CIRCUIT COURT, HENRY CO.

Country of birth or allegiance	When born (or age)
NORWAY.	"O"

Date and port of arrival in U.S.	Date of naturalization
1854-14Yrs in U.S.	FEBRUARY-4-1868

Names and addresses of witnesses
J.S.SHAWALTER. "O"
PHILLIP EMMERT. "O" (OVER)

U.S. Department of Labor, Immigration and Naturalization Service. Form No. 1-IP.

ADDITIONAL INFORMATION IN COURT RECORD

Certificate canceled (date and court)

Why canceled

Expatriated Deceased

Other facts of record WILLIAM C. WILSON-ENLISTED IN THE U.S. ARMY, IN Co.H.13th REG'T ILL'S VOL.

DISCHARGED-MAY-15-1866.

Figure 9-14. Both sides of a WPA-created index card, which indicates the military service of William C. Wilson. The original card is from The Soundex Index to Naturalization Service District 9, 1840–1950, at the National Archives—Great Lakes Region, Chicago.

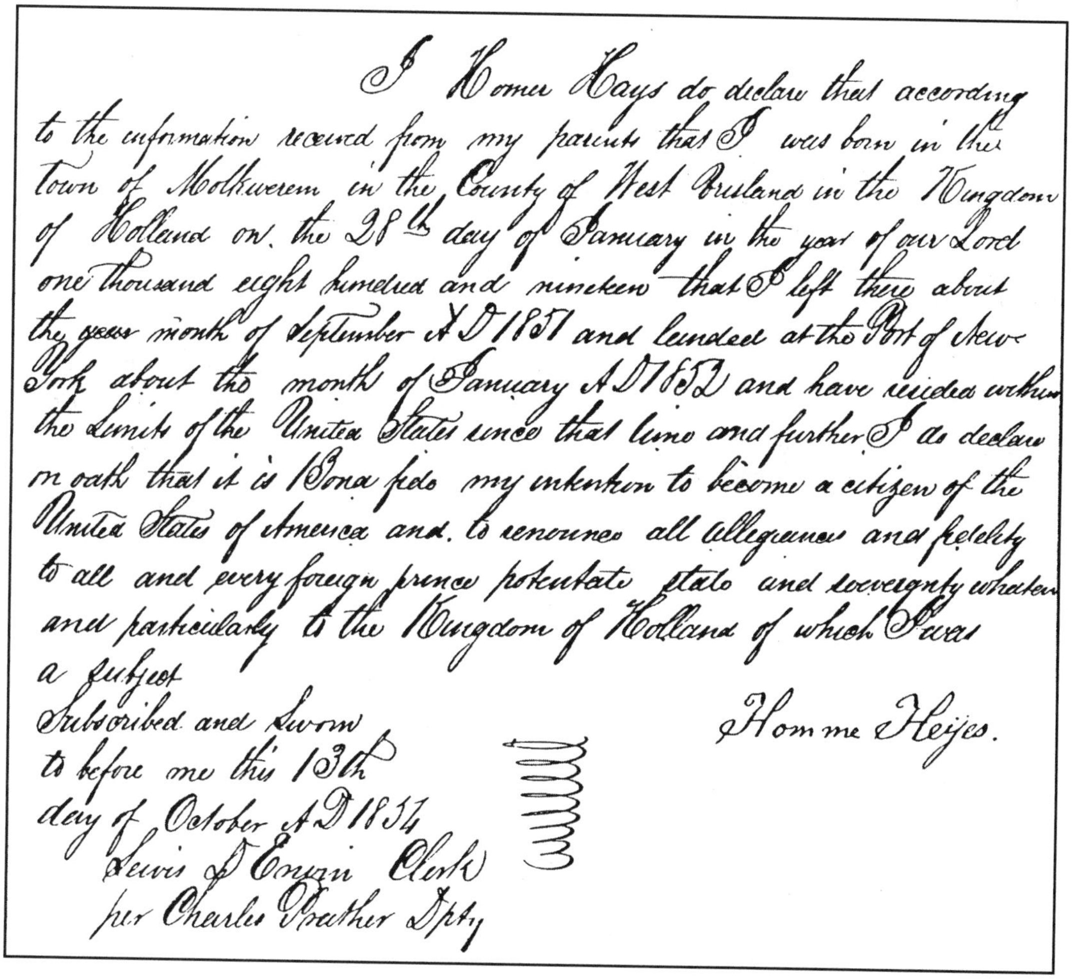

I Homer Hays do declare that according to the information received from my parents that I was born in the town of Molkwerem in the County of West Vriesland in the Kingdom of Holland on the 28th day of January in the year of our Lord one thousand eight hundred and nineteen that I left there about the year month of September A D 1851 and landed at the Port of New York about the month of January A D 1852 and have resided within the Limits of the United States since that time and further I do declare on oath that it is Bona fide my intention to become a citizen of the United States of America and to renounce all allegiance and fidelity to all and every foreign prince potentate state and sovereignty whatever and particularly to the Kingdom of Holland of which I was a subject

Subscribed and Sworn
to before me this 13th
day of October A D 1854
Lewis J Erwin Clerk
per Charles Prather Dpty

Homme Heijes.

Figure 9-15. This naturalization document was evidently penned by a clerk who spelled the subject's name "Homer Hayes." Note that the subject (who probably signed the document himself), spelled his own name "Homme Heijes." The disparity in the spelling of both the first name and the surname on the same paper clearly illustrates one reason that it is often impossible to locate individuals in indexes. Courtesy of the Illinois State Archives.

Social Security Records

Beginning in the 1930s, the federal government made Social Security benefits available for an increasingly large number of U.S. citizens. To apply for these benefits, the individual had to file an application for a Social Security number. This application, called an SS no. 5 form, required a specific statement about the person's date and place (town) of birth. By the 1940s, many citizens had obtained Social Security numbers. They could include virtually any immigrant born in the last third of the nineteenth century. These records are discussed in greater detail in chapter 13, "Vital Records."

Homestead Records

Homestead records can also offer valuable clues. Much of the great prairie lands of the United States and Canada were settled by immigrants. Immigrants were required to have at least filed a declaration of intent to be naturalized before applying for homestead land, and the application often called for specific birth information. Indeed, the immigrant ancestor may have had any number of dealings with the federal government, even including federal court cases. Any such records will be important in documenting the immigrant's life and, if the records date from after the Civil War (1865), they very likely will provide significant information about the immigrant's foreign origins. See chapter 10, "Land Records" for more information.

Alien Registration

The term "Alien Registration" has appeared at various times in U.S. history and may relate to a variety of different records found in federal, state, or local records. The principal sets of records referred to by the term "Alien Registration" are as follows:

Court registration 1802 to 1828. Registration of aliens with a local court of record was required from 1802 to 1828. (Customs officers in Salem and Beverly, Massachusetts, recorded passenger lists with aliens clearly marked, 1798–1800. These records are in the National Archives.) Enforcing this law during the War of 1812 has given us some valuable data for persons immigrating after 1800. Many of these are indexed in the *Passenger and Immigration Lists Index* (cited earlier). Adherence to the law varied from court to court. Some ignored the requirement, while others took detailed information from the alien and incorporated the data in a declaration of intention to become a U.S. citizen.

Registry Files, 1929 to 1944. The Registry Act of 2 March 1929 allowed for the registration, or legalization, of immigrants who arrived prior to 1924 but for whom no immigration record could be found (see figure 9-23). Most immigrants who applied for Registry did so because they wanted to naturalize, and were unable to do so as long as the government could not verify their arrival from an official immigration record. Researchers often find evidence of Registry activity on index cards for Canadian or Mexican Border arrivals, which in Registry cases usually have the word "Registry" stamped or appearing on the card. Researchers searching seaport arrival records may find a card bearing the notation "C.R." followed by a number. The number refers to a Certificate of Registry or Certificate or Lawful Entry, suggesting the existence of a Registry file. Note that the CR-number is not the file number, and should not be included in any request. Registry Files remain with the Immigration and Naturalization Service (now in the Department of Homeland Security) and are available only via a Freedom of Information Act request.

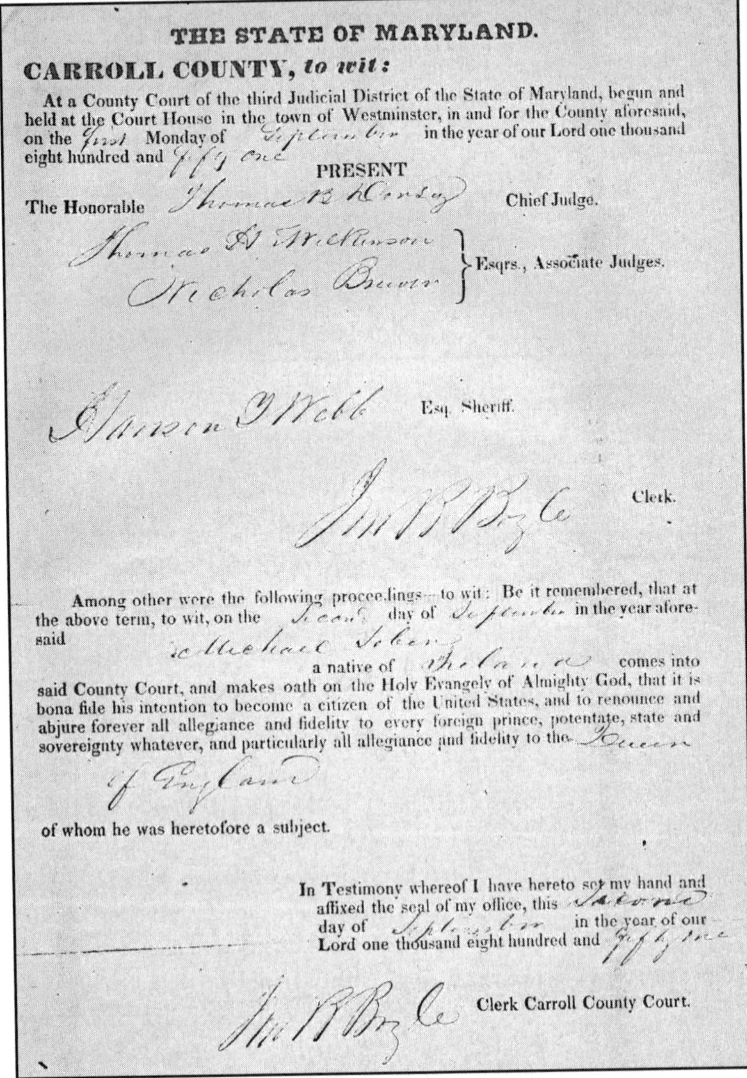

THE STATE OF MARYLAND.

CARROLL COUNTY, *to wit:*

At a County Court of the third Judicial District of the State of Maryland, begun and held at the Court House in the town of Westminster, in and for the County aforesaid, on the first Monday of September in the year of our Lord one thousand eight hundred and fifty one

PRESENT

The Honorable [illegible] Chief Judge.

Thomas H. Wilkinson
Nicholas Brewer } Esqrs., Associate Judges.

[illegible] Esq. Sheriff.

[illegible] Clerk.

Among other were the following proceedings—to wit: Be it remembered, that at the above term, to wit, on the Second day of September in the year aforesaid Michael Tobin a native of Ireland comes into said County Court, and makes oath on the Holy Evangely of Almighty God, that it is bona fide his intention to become a citizen of the United States, and to renounce and abjure forever all allegiance and fidelity to every foreign prince, potentate, state and sovereignty whatever, and particularly all allegiance and fidelity to the Queen of England of whom he was heretofore a subject.

In Testimony whereof I have hereto set my hand and affixed the seal of my office, this Second day of September in the year of our Lord one thousand eight hundred and fifty one

[illegible] Clerk Carroll County Court.

Figure 9-16. 1851 declaration of Michael Tobin from Carroll County, Maryland.

Alien Registration, 1940–1944. Under the Alien Registration Act of 1940, also known as the Smith Act, all aliens in the United States aged fourteen and older were required to register with the Immigration and Naturalization Service and be fingerprinted. With registration each alien was issued a unique Alien Registration number and an Alien Registration Receipt card (figure 9-24) to be carried on his or her person. Immigrants who later naturalized gave their card back to the government, but if an immigrant remained an alien after 1941 the card could be preserved among home sources. From 1950 to 1979, registered aliens were required to report their address to INS every January in the Annual Alien Address Report Program. INS kept only the last address on file, and that survives only if the INS maintained an A-file on the immigrant.

State alien registrations. At times various states took it upon themselves to register all aliens within their jurisdiction. The most well-known state alien registration was conducted by the state of Michigan in the early 1930s.

Enemy Alien Registration

When the United States is at war, the country classifies all citizens of the country with which it is at war as "enemy aliens." It is important to note that an enemy alien registration applied only to those aliens who were 1) living within the United States, 2) were citizens of a country against which the United States had declared war, and 3) had not become naturalized U.S. citizens.

This practice dates to at least the country's first war with a foreign power, the War of 1812. Over 10,000 names listed by state, with dates of arrival, are published in Kenneth Scott's *British Aliens in the United States During the War of 1812*.[65] While early lists may not always provide exact towns of origin, they will help establish when an immigrant arrived in the country.

The first large-scale effort to register enemy aliens within the U.S. was conducted by the Department of Justice during World War I. Germans, Italians, and citizens of other Axis powers registered at their local post office. The multi-page form was completed in triplicate. One copy went to the Justice Department in Washington, D.C. Another copy went to the state capitol of the state where the enemy alien registered. The third copy went to the local county or municipal law enforcement officer, usually a county sheriff or city chief of police. In the 1920s, Congress granted authority to destroy the World War I enemy alien records, and a very small number survive today.

United States of America.

PROBATE COURT OF CUYAHOGA COUNTY, OHIO.

BE IT REMEMBERED, that on the 21 day of Oct in the year of our Lord one thousand eight hundred and eighty-seven Patrick McNamara an alien and native of Ireland personally appeared before me, DANIEL R. TILDEN, Judge of the Probate Court of Cuyahoga County, Ohio, and declared on his solemn oath that he first arrived in the United States in the month of April A. D. 1887, and that it is his bona fide intention to become a CITIZEN OF THE UNITED STATES, and to renounce forever all allegiance and fidelity to every Foreign Prince, Potentate, State or Sovereignty whatsoever, and particularly Victoria Queen of whom he is a subject, and subscribed his name to said declaration, which remains of record in my office.

FIRST PAPER.

In Testimony Whereof, I have hereunto subscribed my name officially, and affixed the seal of said Court, at the City of Cleveland, this 21st day of Oct A. D., 1887

Daniel R. Tilden Probate Judge.

By T. F. McConnell Clerk.

Figure 9-17. First paper (declaration of intention) of Patrick McNamara, Cuyahoga County (Cleveland), Ohio.

The enemy alien registration documents for the State of Kansas can be found at the National Archives Central Plains Region in Kansas City, Missouri.

The Justice Department also required enemy aliens to register during World War II. Registration began in February 1942 and continued through the spring. Once registered, enemy aliens received a small pink identification card, or booklet, containing biographical information and a photograph. The identification cards are often found among family papers. If the immigrant naturalized during or after World War II, the enemy alien identification card may be found inside their INS file. Enemy aliens interned during World War II may have an additional file among Department of Justice files at the National Archives in College Park, Maryland.

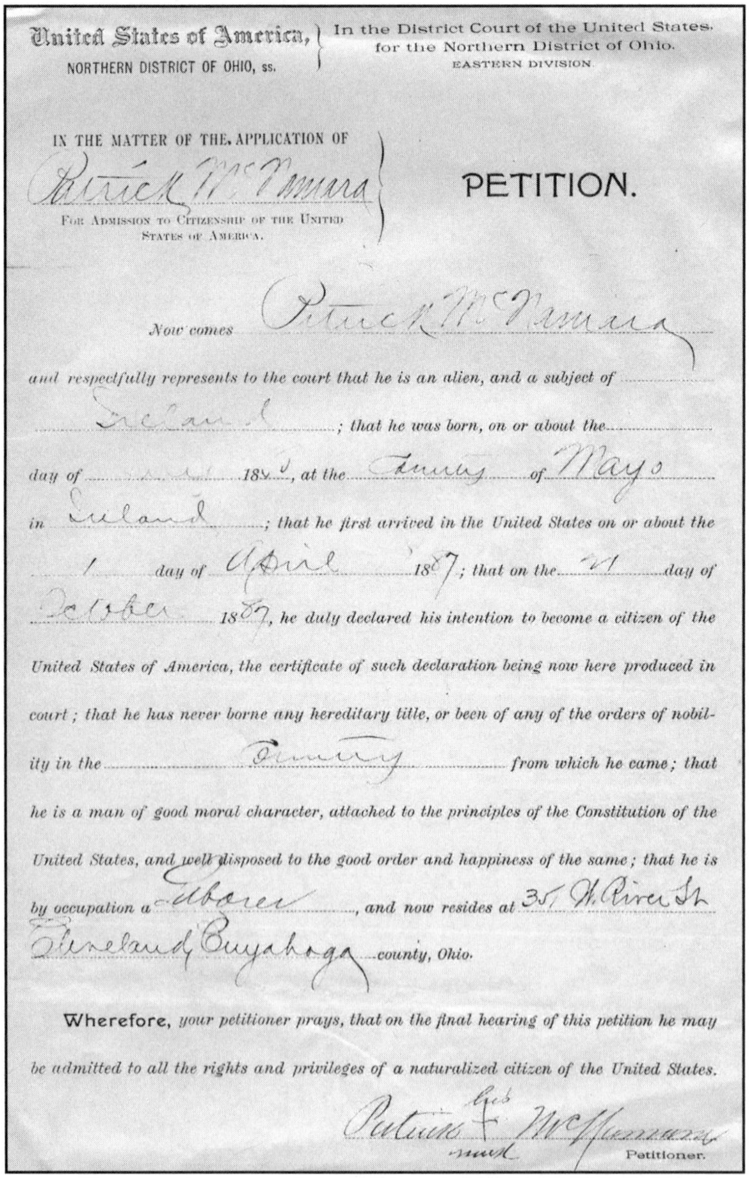

United States of America, NORTHERN DISTRICT OF OHIO, ss. } In the District Court of the United States for the Northern District of Ohio. EASTERN DIVISION

IN THE MATTER OF THE APPLICATION OF Patrick McNamara FOR ADMISSION TO CITIZENSHIP OF THE UNITED STATES OF AMERICA.

PETITION.

Now comes Patrick McNamara *and respectfully represents to the court that he is an alien, and a subject of* Ireland*; that he was born, on or about the* ... *day of* ... 184..., *at the* County *of* Mayo *in* Ireland*; that he first arrived in the United States on or about the* 1 *day of* April 1887*; that on the* 21 *day of* October 1887*, he duly declared his intention to become a citizen of the United States of America, the certificate of such declaration being now here produced in court; that he has never borne any hereditary title, or been of any of the orders of nobility in the* Country *from which he came; that he is a man of good moral character, attached to the principles of the Constitution of the United States, and well disposed to the good order and happiness of the same; that he is by occupation a* laborer*, and now resides at* 35 W. River St Cleveland Cuyahoga *county, Ohio.*

Wherefore, *your petitioner prays, that on the final hearing of this petition he may be admitted to all the rights and privileges of a naturalized citizen of the United States.*

Patrick his mark McNamara
Petitioner.

Figure 9-18. Petition of Patrick McNamara, Cuyahoga County (Cleveland), Ohio.

Immigrant Records after 1 July 1924

The United States changed its practice for documenting the arrival and admission of immigrants beginning 1 July 1924. Immigrants admitted for permanent residence on or after that date should have a visa on file with INS. After 1928 all immigrants admitted with a visa were issued an Immigrant Identification Card which, if found among family papers, suggests the existence of a visa file. In addition to standard information also found on the passenger list, visa documents include a photo, information about the immigrant's spouse, children, and parents, and residence for five years prior to emigration. Additionally, most visas have certified vital records attached, the documents having been submitted with their visa application. Visas remain in the custody of the Department of Homeland Security (INS) and are subject to the Freedom of Information Act (see figure 9-25).

Passports

Some immigrants returned to visit family and relatives in the native country. Often, they applied for U.S. passports. These records will usually indicate their birthplace or the destination for the visit, which is likely near the native town.

More than 2,150 microfilms of U.S. passport records from the National Archives and Department of State have been released for research. These records from the U.S. Passport Office are travel documents "attesting to the citizenship and identity of the bearer." People of all walks of life used passports. The first extant passport given to an individual is dated July 1796. Passports generally became more popular in the late 1840s, but until the outbreak of World War I in 1914, American citizens were generally permitted to travel abroad without passports. Naturally, the requirement to carry a passport caused a significant increase in the numbers issued. By 1930, the U.S. government had issued more than 2.5 million passports.

To receive a U.S. passport, a person had to submit some proof of U.S. citizenship. This was usually in the form of a letter, affidavits of witnesses, and certificates from clerks or notaries. By 1888 there were separate application forms for native citizens, naturalized citizens, and derivative citizens. Passport applications often include information regarding an applicant's family status, date and place of birth, residence, naturalization (if foreign-born), and other biographical information. Twentieth-century applications often include marriage and family information as well as dates, places, and names of ships used for travel.

The microfilmed passport records, registers, and indexes are available from the earliest dates to about 1925. They are arranged in several sets; each passport application series is arranged chronologically. A number is assigned to most applications. For some years there are registers but no actual applications. You must use the registers and indexes to determine an application's date (and number, where applicable) in order to locate a particular application. Microfilm copies are available from the LDS Family History Library and through its family history centers. Applications for 1925 and later are in the custody of the Passport Office, Department of State, 1425 K St. N.W., Washington, D.C. 20520.

Seamen's Protection Certificates

Similar in purpose to passports, and equally applicable to immigrants and native citizens, were the Seamen's Protection Certificates, available as early as 1796 due to a Congressional act. Each district collector of customs was required to keep a register of seamen who chose to apply for a protection certificate, which would testify to his U.S. citizenship. Although most seamen were not naturalized citizens, those who were should have recorded their hometown when applying for this protection. The applications and registers were acquired by the U.S. Customs Department, and are now housed in the National Archives, or their regional archives, as part of Record Group 36. Of even greater value, due to the ease of searching, is a collection of abstracts of these certificates, indexed by two card indexes (one covering New York City, and the second including most other ports). Available for about seventy ports, the abstracts cover various dates, from as early as 1812 to the 1860s. Not yet microfilmed, these abstracts and their indexes, are available only at NARA.

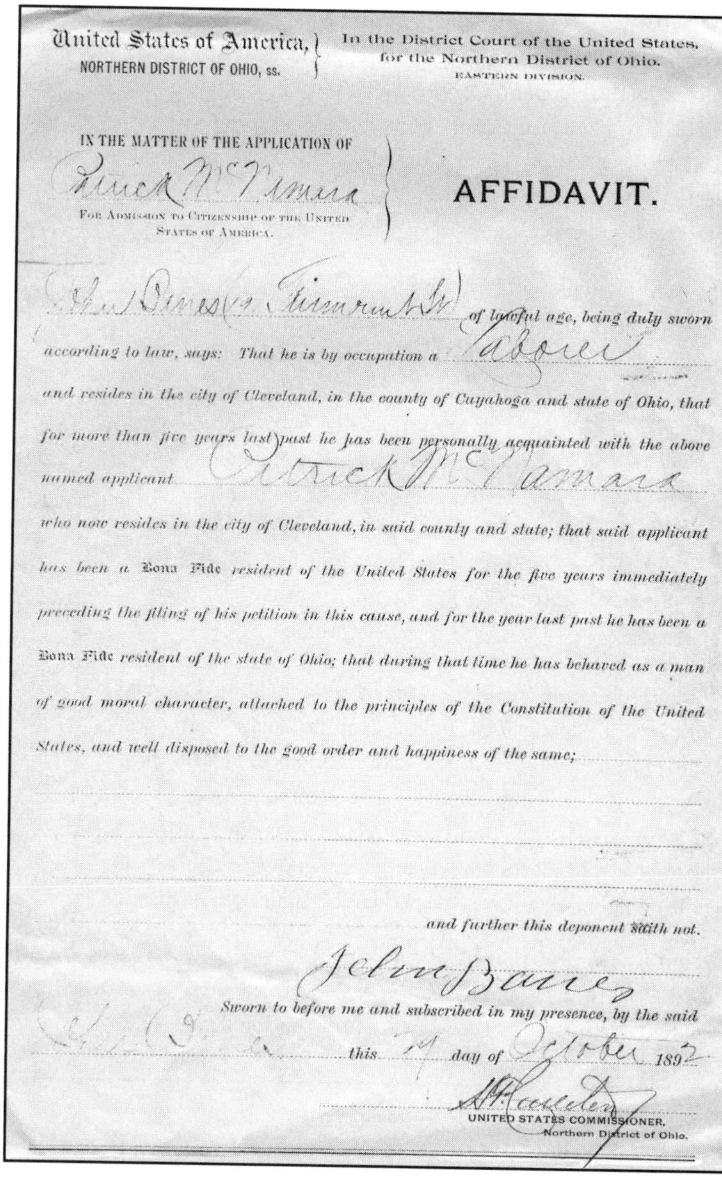

United States of America, NORTHERN DISTRICT OF OHIO, ss. | In the District Court of the United States, for the Northern District of Ohio. EASTERN DIVISION.

IN THE MATTER OF THE APPLICATION OF Patrick McNamara For Admission to Citizenship of the United States of America.

AFFIDAVIT.

John Barnes of lawful age, being duly sworn according to law, says: That he is by occupation a Laborer and resides in the city of Cleveland, in the county of Cuyahoga and state of Ohio, that for more than five years last past he has been personally acquainted with the above named applicant Patrick McNamara who now resides in the city of Cleveland, in said county and state; that said applicant has been a Bona Fide resident of the United States for the five years immediately preceding the filing of his petition in this cause, and for the year last past he has been a Bona Fide resident of the state of Ohio; that during that time he has behaved as a man of good moral character, attached to the principles of the Constitution of the United States, and well disposed to the good order and happiness of the same;

and further this deponent saith not.

John Barnes

Sworn to before me and subscribed in my presence, by the said this 29 day of October 1892

UNITED STATES COMMISSIONER, Northern District of Ohio.

Figure 9-19. Affidavit of a witness on behalf of Patrick McNamara, Cuyahoga County (Cleveland), Ohio.

Foreign Sources and Strategies

If, after carefully searching American sources, a reference to the town from which the immigrant left is still undiscovered, it is sometimes possible to use foreign sources to determine immigrant origins. When searching records in the country of origin, the general process is to search nationwide records first. Next, search other records that will narrow the possible locations until the right one is found. The foundation for such a search lies in the information located in American records. The following sections will facilitate systematic searches of records in the country of origin. As new information is gathered, consider which tactic to apply next.

Name etymologies can help identify the region a name comes from, its meaning, and common spelling variations. For less-common surnames these books often provide clues to localize the surname. Regard such sources with caution because they may not be comprehensive in the sources surveyed, and a name's presence in one location does not preclude it from appearing elsewhere, especially for occupational or descriptive names. Surname etymologies exist for most major countries that emigrants left. For example, an etymology for German surnames is Hans Bahlow's *Deutsches Namenlexikon*.[66]

Nationwide Records

Some countries in Europe have kept significant records at a nationwide level. Also, many countries have many fully indexed compiled records where the emigrant may appear. Where these records are available and indexed, they are excellent tools that may identify the emigrant. Countries that have been influenced by British law have some excellent national-level records, more and more of which are being indexed. Published genealogical collections in Germany, France, the Netherlands, Belgium, Switzerland, and other countries may also be helpful.

Published Genealogy Compendia

In many countries, books are published which collect genealogies (lineages) of hundreds or thousands of families. Usually the families come from the same geographic region or social rank. The higher classes tend to be better represented in most compendia and they often mention emigrants. They are often published as periodicals. Indexes are published only occasionally for many of these compendia. An outstanding series with approximately two hundred volumes for Germany is the *Deutsches Geschlechterbuch*.[67]

Indexes and Bibliographies

Many countries have bibliographies of published family histories with alphabetical indexes to the major surnames included in the books and articles cited. Periodical indexes may also help locate emigrant families. The comprehensiveness of these sources varies by country. The genealogies cited in these bibliographies or indexes often mention emigrants. The chapter reference section identifies some of the most significant of these.

Foreign Researchers and Collections

It is often possible to find a person researching your immigrant's surname in the very country the immigrant left. You can place queries in local genealogical periodicals or ask local genealogical societies in the foreign country for a list of researchers. A particularly useful publication for immigrant research is Keith A. Johnson and Malcolm R. Sainty's *Genealogical Research Directory*, an annual volume identifying researchers and the families they are working on.[68] Each annual edition includes thousands of new listings from many countries throughout the world. There are many private researchers in Europe who keep a file of emigrants, often culled from newspaper announcements and government records.

The next step is to search the records that may have been created when he or she left the native country. Records of departure are generally easy to access and almost always identify the place where the emigrant left. However, not all such records have been preserved, and others are not indexed or available on microfilm. Furthermore, some emigration was illegal. In such cases, there will be few, if any, records of departure.

The country of departure is generally not hard to discover from other sources; the district is more difficult to determine. For this reason, learn as much as possible about the emigrant, including the state or area of residence and the port of departure. Immigration sources, such as passenger arrival lists, usually identify the port of departure (see figure 9-26).

When a family or an individual decided to emigrate, there were several steps they followed—some to comply with the law, some to prepare for their journey, and some based on local custom or tradition. Each step generated records. Many countries required the emigrant to receive permission to leave. If the emigrant obeyed this law (approximately

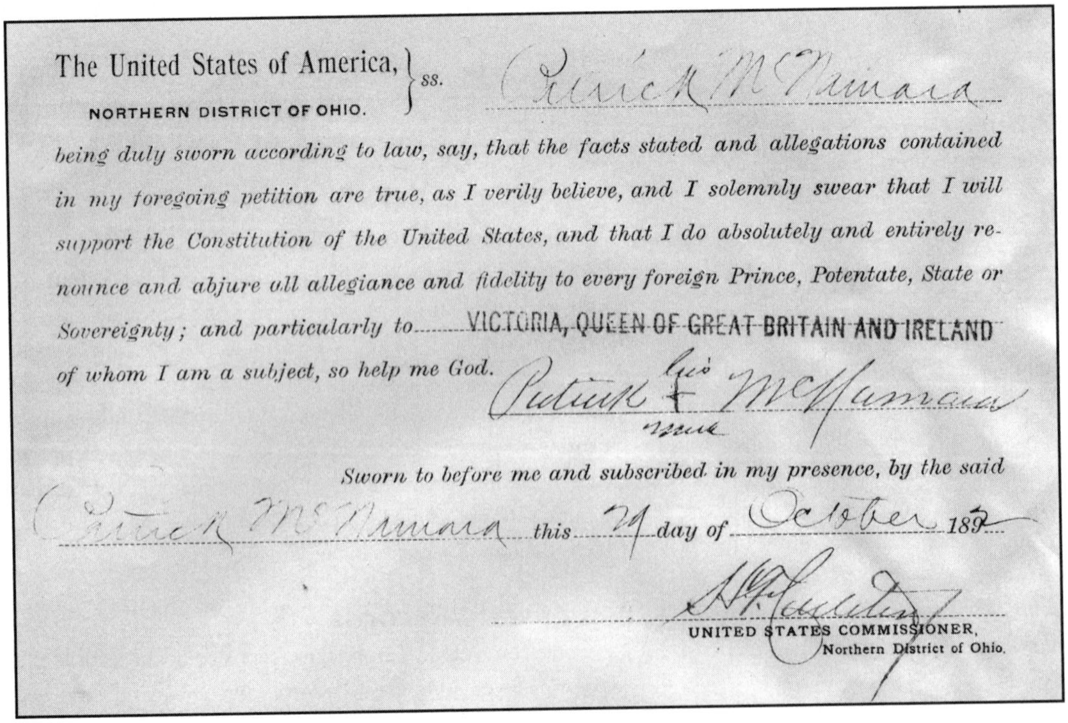

The United States of America, } ss. Patrick McNamara
NORTHERN DISTRICT OF OHIO.

being duly sworn according to law, say, that the facts stated and allegations contained in my foregoing petition are true, as I verily believe, and I solemnly swear that I will support the Constitution of the United States, and that I do absolutely and entirely renounce and abjure all allegiance and fidelity to every foreign Prince, Potentate, State or Sovereignty; and particularly to VICTORIA, QUEEN OF GREAT BRITAIN AND IRELAND *of whom I am a subject, so help me God.* Patrick his + mark McNamara

Sworn to before me and subscribed in my presence, by the said Patrick McNamara *this* 24 *day of* October 189

UNITED STATES COMMISSIONER,
Northern District of Ohio.

Figure 9-20. Final oath of Patrick McNamara, Cuyahoga County (Cleveland), Ohio.

one-third emigrated without permission), there may be an application to leave or a passport. Emigrants also had to book passage and board a vessel for the new country. Each of these steps potentially saw the creation of a new record. Records of departure in the country of origin are called emigration records. Most of them give the name, age, close relatives or traveling companions, and usually the last place of residence (sometimes the birthplace) of the emigrant.

Departure records are generally kept under the jurisdiction of the port city (such as passenger departure lists) or by the state or national government where the emigrant lived, such as permissions to emigrate. To use such lists, you should know the emigrant's state or region of residence, and/or the port of departure. Sometimes knowing only the country of origin allows access to these records. You also need to know when the emigrant left that country or port. These sources may be difficult to use; however, a growing number are indexed. The archives in some countries and provinces, in order to better document emigration, have prepared indexes of emigrants from particular regions. In other cases, private authors have compiled or indexed specific emigration records. The following discussion describes many of these records.

The emigration/immigration process generated a wealth of records, both personal and administrative, to keep track of who emigrated, where they were going, the status of their personal affairs at the time they left, and their ability to care for their own needs on arrival. Some have been indexed and abstracted by government order or by genealogists who need faster access. Many more are available on microfilm through the National Archives and its regional archives system and through the Family History Library and its family history centers.

Some important projects to publish emigration lists are ongoing. For example: In the first half of the twentieth century, Germans accounted for 20 percent of this new growth of the immigrant population in the United States. Close to 1 million of these Germans made applications to emigrate at Wuerttemberg. To date, Trudy Schenk and Ruth Froelke have transcribed handwritten lists and indexed the names of 131,000 individuals who emigrated from Wuerttemberg from 1750 to 1900 in *The Wuerttemberg Emigration Index*.[69]

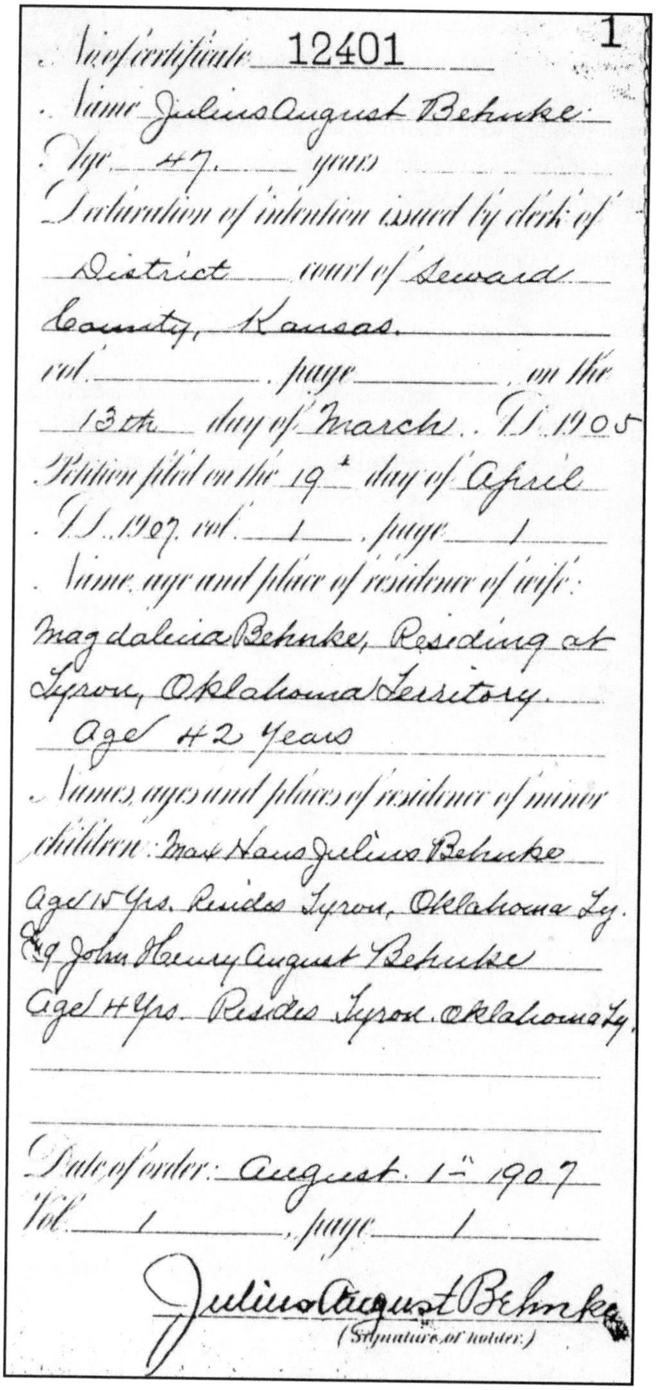

No. of certificate 12401 1
Name Julius August Behnke
Age 47 years
Declaration of intention issued by clerk of District court of Seward County, Kansas.
vol. ____, page ____, on the 13th day of March A.D. 1905
Petition filed on the 19th day of April A.D. 1907 vol. 1, page 1
Name, age and place of residence of wife: Magdalena Behnke, Residing at Tyrone, Oklahoma Territory. Age 42 Years
Names, ages and places of residence of minor children: Max Hans Julius Behnke Age 15 Yrs. Resides Tyrone, Oklahoma Ty. & John Henry August Behnke Age 4 Yrs. Resides Tyrone, Oklahoma Ty.
Date of order: August 1st 1907
Vol. 1, page 1
Julius August Behnke
(Signature of holder.)

Figure 9-21. From a stub book for naturalization certificates. This one was issued to Julius August Behnke in the U.S. Court, Northern District of Ohio, Cleveland. The original stub book is now preserved at the National Archives—Great Lake Region in Chicago.

Letters of Manumission

If the head of the house was tied to the soil on which he lived by medieval serf-lord commitments, the first step was to obtain a letter of manumission. This document freed him, usually with payment of a fee, from these obligations.

Sale of Property

If the head of the house owned property, he would advertise it for sale or dispose of it among family members who stayed behind. Some emigrants left their property in the care of relatives or friends and returned to sell it after they were sure they could make a success of their move to America. These documents are duly recorded with the proper authorities, often with direct statements of intent to emigrate or precise locations in the New World.

Letters of Recommendation

Letters of recommendation from local church authorities stating that the emigrant was a member of the congregation in good standing were often obtained by would-be emigrants. With these documents in hand, the emigrant could approach local authorities for permission to leave.

Permit to Emigrate

The permit to emigrate certified that the emigrant's bills were paid, affairs in the community were settled, and that he or she was free to leave. The passport allowed the emigrant to cross country, provincial, and district boundaries. In some countries, the permit to emigrate and the passport were combined in a single exit visa issued by district or provincial authorities. These identification papers were carried on the person of the emigrant, and copies may still be in the family's possession.

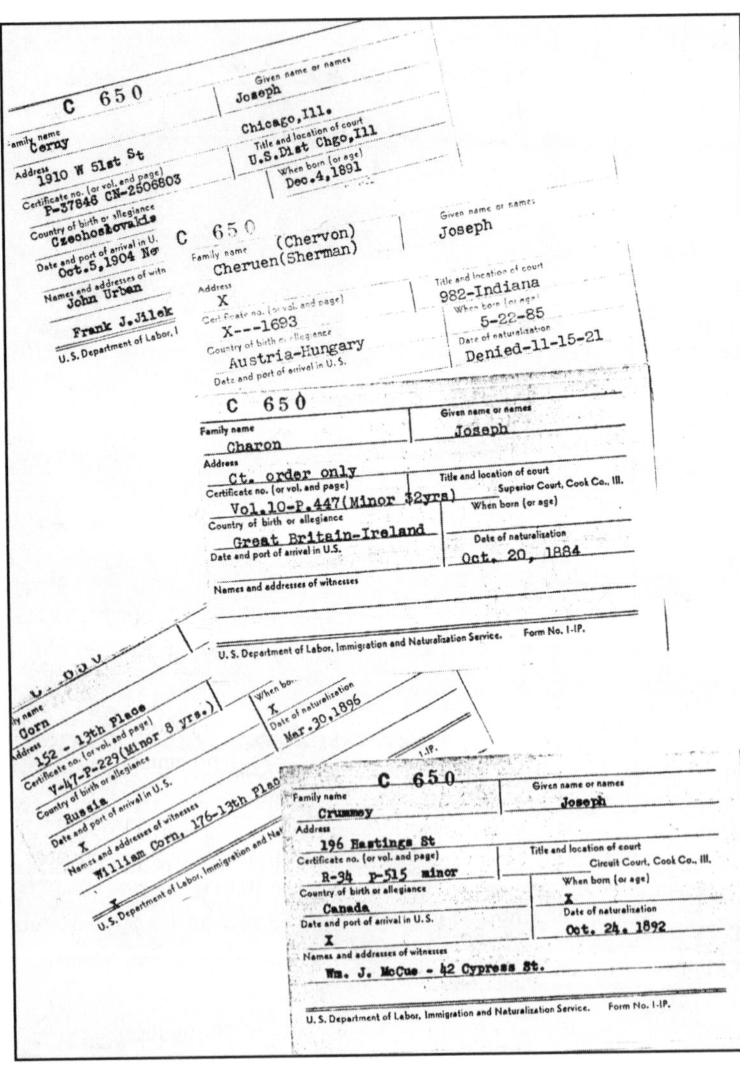

C 650
Family name: Cerny
Given name or names: Joseph
Address: 1910 W 51st St
Chicago, Ill.
Title and location of court: U.S.Dist Chgo,Ill
Certificate no. (or vol. and page): P-37846 CN-2506803
When born (or age): Dec.4,1891
Country of birth or allegiance: Czechoslovakia
Date and port of arrival in U.S.: Oct.5,1904 NY
Names and addresses of witnesses: John Urban, Frank J. Jilek
U.S. Department of Labor

C 650
Family name: (Chervon) Cheruen(Sherman)
Given name or names: Joseph
Address: X
Title and location of court: 982-Indiana
Certificate no. (or vol. and page): X---1693
When born (or age): 5-22-85
Country of birth or allegiance: Austria-Hungary
Date of naturalization: Denied-11-15-21
Date and port of arrival in U.S.

C 650
Family name: Charon
Given name or names: Joseph
Address: Ct. order only
Certificate no. (or vol. and page): Vol.10-P.447(Minor 2yrs)
Title and location of court: Superior Court, Cook Co., Ill.
When born (or age)
Country of birth or allegiance: Great Britain-Ireland
Date of naturalization: Oct. 20, 1884
Date and port of arrival in U.S.
Names and addresses of witnesses
U.S. Department of Labor, Immigration and Naturalization Service. Form No. 1-IP.

Family name: Corn
Address: 152 - 13th Place
Certificate no. (or vol. and page): V-47-P-229(Minor 8 yrs.)
When born: X
Date of naturalization: Mar.30,1896
Country of birth or allegiance: Russia
Date and port of arrival in U.S.: X
Names and addresses of witnesses: William Corn, 176-13th Place
X
U.S. Department of Labor, Immigration and Nat

C 650
Family name: Crummey
Given name or names: Joseph
Address: 196 Hastings St
Certificate no. (or vol. and page): R-34 P-515 minor
Title and location of court: Circuit Court, Cook Co., Ill.
When born (or age): X
Country of birth or allegiance: Canada
Date of naturalization: Oct. 24, 1892
Date and port of arrival in U.S.: X
Names and addresses of witnesses: Wm. J. McCue - 42 Cypress St.
U.S. Department of Labor, Immigration and Naturalization Service. Form No. 1-IP.

Figure 9-22. A sampling of cards from the WPA-created Soundex Index to Naturalization Petitions for the United States District and Circuit Courts, Northern District of Illinois and Immigration and Naturalization District 9, 1840–1950.

Shipping Company Records

An invaluable tool for English research is P. Mathias and A. W. H. Pearsall's *Shipping: A Survey of Historical Records*.[70] The survey is in two parts: (1) shipping companies and their record holdings and (2) shipping records in county and other record offices. There is an index of named ships, an index of persons and firms, an index of places and principal trades, and there are separate entries for dozens of shipping firms. Often, passenger lists retained by these shipping companies can be substituted for official lists missing for English ports. Where lists exist in United States or European ports, they can be compared for details. Included among the collections are pictures of ships sailing of each line.

Emigration Permission

While the largest collections of emigration records pertain to passenger departure lists, many other lists of emigrants await the diligent researcher. Often overlooked by North American researchers are the foreign records that document the permission many emigrants were often required to receive before leaving their home country. Of course, legal requirements did not mean that every emigrant requested, or received, such permission. Many left as "clandestine" emigrants and so do not appear in such records. A growing number of such records are now available either as microfilms of original documents, published abstracts or indexes, or as databases on CD-ROM or the Internet.

Shortly before the Revolutionary War broke out, England required permission to move to the colonies. These records, identifying over 6,000 people with their specific town of origin, were transcribed in Peter W. Coldham's *Emigrants from England to the American Colonies, 1773–1776*.[71]

During the 1700s, the Swiss cantons of Bern and Basel kept regular records of people requesting permission to emigrate. At the same time, authorities in the canton of Zurich requested local authorities (chiefly the church ministers) to identify those who had and were leaving from their parishes. Abstracts from these records, identifying about 5,000 emigrants, were published by Albert Bernhardt Faust and Gaius Marcus Brumbaugh as *Lists of Swiss Emigrants in the Eighteenth Century to the American Colonies*.[72]

Several German publications include abstracts from similar emigration records housed in state archives. One excellent example is Inge Auerbach's *Auswanderer aus Hessen-Kassel, 1840–1850*.[73] Most of this volume is an alphabetical list of persons named in the emigration documents, but it serves to abstract those records as it provides the emigrant's name, age, town of residence, destination, year of departure, and other

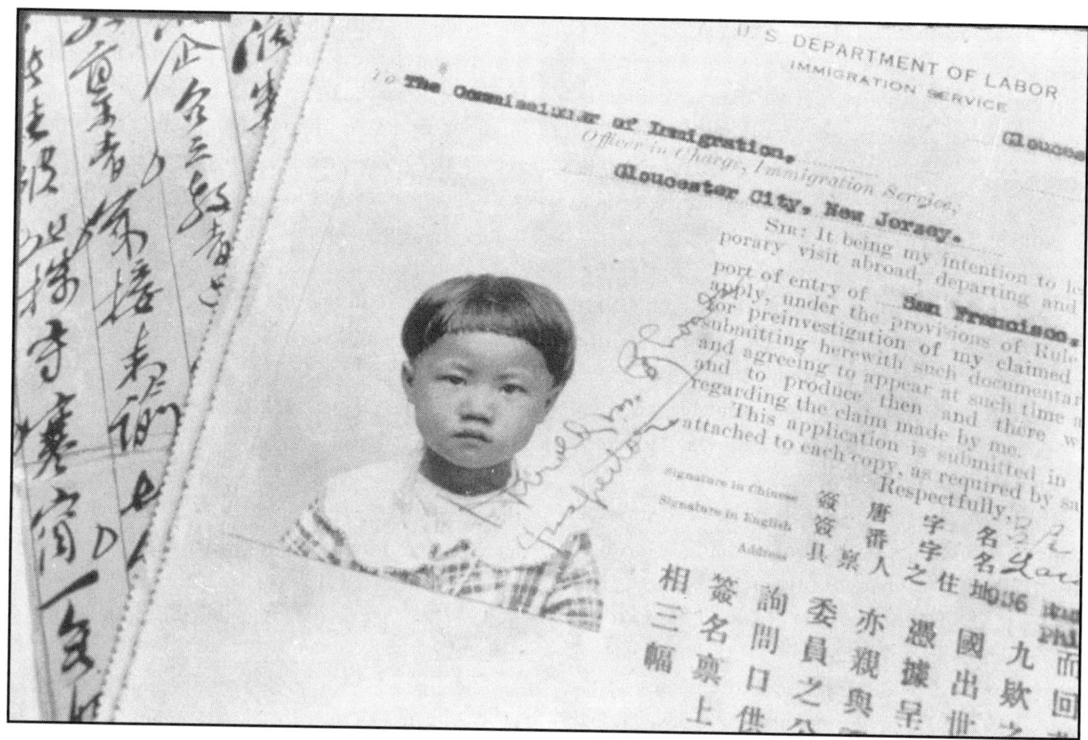

Figure 9-23. Certificate of residence from the Chinese Exclusion files. In accordance with the Chinese exclusion laws (1882–1943), which were passed to restrict Chinese immigration to the United States, the Immigration and Naturalization Service barred Chinese from entering the United States between 1882 and 1924; the laws were designed especially to exclude laborers. Chinese residents of the United States who wished to visit China had to make formal application to the INS and establish their identity and occupation (students and merchants were exceptions to excluded occupations) to ensure they would be able to reenter the United States.

information for about 10,000 emigrants. Similar published sources exist for many other German states or regions.

As valuable as microfilm collections of the original records, are, they are very difficult for English-speaking researchers to use, since they are often complex documents with inadequate (if any) indexes. For this reason, abstracts of such records are extremely valuable, such as Trudy Schenk's and Ruth Froelke's index of 131,000 emigrants from 1750 to 1900 in *The Wuerttemberg Emigration Index*.[74] This index is now also available online at Ancestry.com where it joins other databases available only online, such as Marion Wolfert's *Brandenburg, Prussia Emigration Records*. This is an ongoing project identifying over 36,000 emigrants from one key Prussian province during the 1800s.

Less prominent websites also house significant emigration sources, particularly sites based in our ancestral countries. *The Baden and Wuerttemberg Emigration* website <www.auswanderer-bw.de/auswanderer> available in English and German, is extremely useful, since it identifies more than 300,000 emigrants.

Port of Departure Lists

Some ports made lists of passengers as they departed. These included such information as age, occupation, and last place of residence or birthplace, which can be of particular value in determining an ancestor's place of origin. While some of these records have not been preserved, many others are now on microfilm. Where available, these are excellent sources for determining the emigrant's origin. Many of the existing departure lists are available at the Family History Library and other research libraries that specialize in emigration records. Of particular interest are the records of the Scandinavian ports and those of Hamburg. Unfortunately, the records of Europeans who emigrated through other ports, such as Bremen, LeHavre, Amsterdam, Rotterdam, and Antwerp, have either been destroyed or lost. There are also published transcripts and indexes for some ports and countries. Significant published departure lists for Europe and Great Britain are noted in the chapter reference section.

Hamburg Passenger Lists

The Hamburg passenger lists comprise the most significant collection of port of departure lists for immigration research. They contain the names of millions of Europeans who emigrated through Hamburg between 1850 and 1934 (except 1915 through 1919). Nearly one-third of the people who emigrated from central and eastern Europe during this time are included on these lists. If your ancestors emigrated from these areas, the Hamburg passenger lists could provide important information about them, including their native towns. Extensive indexes make these records easier to use than most other passenger lists and emigration records. These lists and indexes are on 486 rolls of microfilm at the Family History Library. Some of these same materials are available online for a fee (see page 393.)

The Hamburg passenger lists are made up of two sections: the direct lists, which include passengers who left Hamburg and sailed directly to their destination without stopping at other European ports, and the indirect lists, which identify passengers who stopped at other European ports before sailing to their final destination. About 20 percent of the immigrants leaving Europe took indirect routes.

Most of the Hamburg passenger lists have been indexed. The only ones not indexed are those from 1850 to 1854, which are arranged alphabetically. There are two sets of indexes: the *Fifteen-Year Index to the Direct Hamburg Passenger Lists, 1856–1871*, and the regular indexes.

The fifteen-year card index arranges all the names on the direct lists from 1856 to 1871 in one alphabetical index. Though it is convenient to use, this index is not complete. After checking the index, you may still need to use the regular index for the same time period. The regular indexes are more complete, but they are more difficult to use.

The regular indexes, for both the direct passenger lists and the indirect list, are divided into segments that cover one year or part of a year. The direct indexes begin with 1854 lists and end with 1934 lists. The indirect indexes begin in 1854 and end in 1910. To use the index, you must find the year the emigrant departed and the initial letter of the ancestor's surname. Names are arranged by the first letter of the surname only, so you may need to search the entire section to find the person you are looking for. Sometimes the index pages for one letter were continued on blank pages under another letter. Usually a notation will refer you to the proper letter for the continuation. An index entry contains the name of the ship, the departure date, the passenger's name, the ship's captain, the destination port, and the page on the actual passenger lists with this information.

For more information on the Hamburg Passenger Lists and how to use them, see *The Hamburg Passenger Lists*.[75]

Localizing the Surname

When departure records are not available, or if the state or region of residence is not known, it may be possible to narrow the search by determining the general region or area where the family came from or where the surname is most common. After the surname has been localized, there may be local emigration indexes or other sources available that cover only specific regions or localities.

Records exist at all levels of jurisdiction. Some emigration and even vital records are kept on a national, regional, provincial, county, or local level. The more closely a residence is determined, the more levels of records you can search.

Directories

To localize a specific, uncommon surname, it is often useful to check city and telephone directories. Computerized telephone directories are available for Germany and the Netherlands on CD-ROM and in France through Minitel computer services. Expect similar sources to become available for other major countries within the next few years. With such tools, you can

DESCRIPTION OF REGISTRANT.
(To be filled in by registration officer.)

Age 83 years 2 months. Mouth wide
Height 5 ft. 2" Chin short, thick
Weight 130 Hair gray
Forehead normal Complexion fair
Eyes gray Face broad
Nose large
Distinctive marks
Name Mrs. Rosena Schultz,
Address Paola, Kas., RR #9.
c7—1123

Figure 9-24. An alien registration card from the National Archives—Central Plains Region.

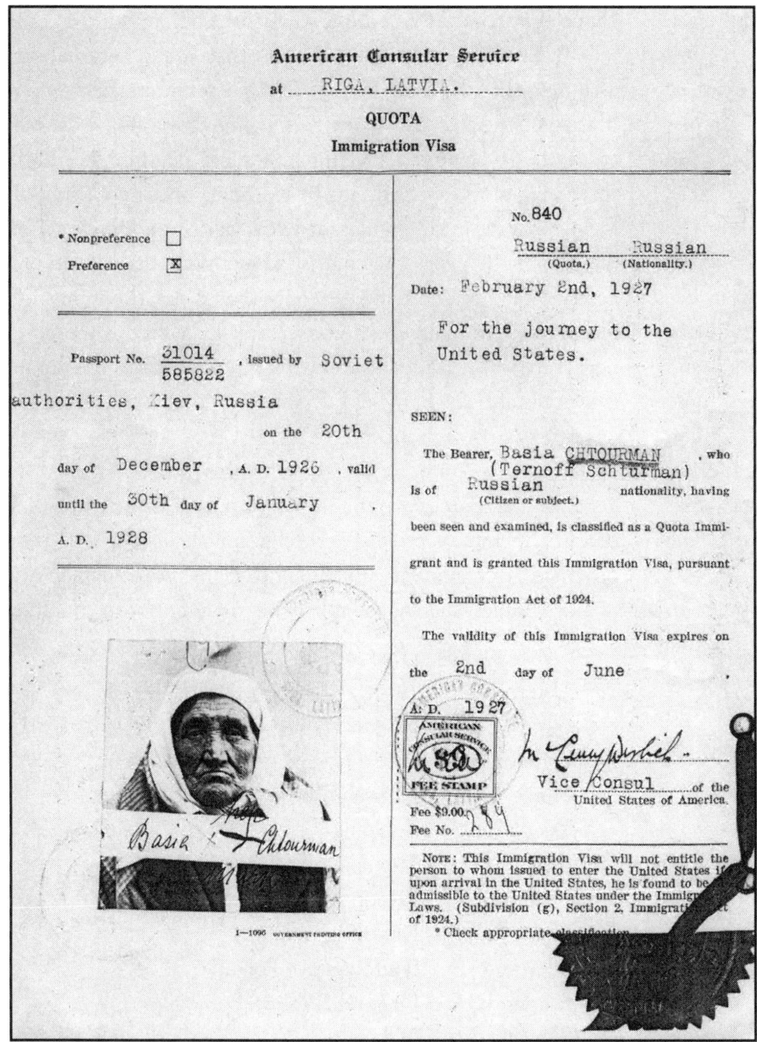

American Consular Service
at RIGA, LATVIA.
QUOTA
Immigration Visa

No. 840

* Nonpreference ☐
Preference ☒

Russian Russian
(Quota.) (Nationality.)

Date: February 2nd, 1927

For the journey to the United States.

Passport No. 31014 585822, issued by Soviet authorities, Kiev, Russia on the 20th day of December, A. D. 1926, valid until the 30th day of January A. D. 1928

SEEN:

The Bearer, Basia CHTOURMAN (Ternoff Schturman), who is of Russian (Citizen or subject.) nationality, having been seen and examined, is classified as a Quota Immigrant and is granted this Immigration Visa, pursuant to the Immigration Act of 1924.

The validity of this Immigration Visa expires on the 2nd day of June A. D. 1927

Vice Consul of the United States of America.

Fee $9.00
Fee No. 289

AMERICAN CONSULAR SERVICE
FEE STAMP

Basia Chtourman

NOTE: This Immigration Visa will not entitle the person to whom issued to enter the United States if upon arrival in the United States, he is found to be inadmissible to the United States under the Immigration Laws. (Subdivision (g), Section 2, Immigration Act of 1924.)

* Check appropriate classification.

Figure 9-25. Front of the visa packet issued to Basia Chtourman, who was born in 1850 in Ustingrad, Russia. She left Kiev in 1936 to join her son in Buffalo, New York. Tragically, she never reached her destination; she became ill and died in Halifax, Nova Scotia. Her visa, however, remains on file with the INS.

search for a name for the entire country. While this approach locates currently living persons with the surname, you may find relatives of the emigrant or other persons interested in your research. Often, families with the same surname (if it is not a common surname) know the area where the family originated.

Several research libraries have good collections of city directories of the nineteenth century from major cities of several countries. These directories may identify the emigrant, if he or she lived in a city. They also serve to indicate how common the surname was in the region where the city was located. To use older directories to localize a surname, search all available city directories for the country where the immigrant was born. Note the number of occurrences of the surname compared to the total names (or pages) in the directory. You will usually find that uncommon surnames are more strongly represented in one or two cities. This indicates the region where the name was most common.

Reading the Place Name

The final principle to consider when tracking an immigrant's origin is the necessity of reading the place name after it is correctly located. There is nothing more frustrating to an immigration researcher than finding the long-sought place name and then learning that such a town does not exist in the native country.

Some sources are more likely to give an accurate place of origin than others. When a place name is found in the records, use gazetteers and other reference tools to evaluate the information. After information about an immigrant's place of origin is discovered, you will need to interpret the findings. To accurately read the place name you have found, you need to understand foreign spellings and then evaluate if you have found the place name.

Place Name Changes

Many places have been known by more than one name historically. Place names have changed when other countries occupied weaker countries. Bratislava in Slovenia was known as Pressburg under German rule. Some changes were for political reasons; Kitchener, Ontario, was Berlin before World War I. Other changes have evolved over time. Oxfordshire, England, is still sometimes referred to as Oxon, its old name, while Hants is the common abbreviation for the English county of Hampshire. Examples of similar name changes include the following:

Christiania	Oslo
Hindenburg	Zabrze
Königsberg	Kaliningrad
Tilsit	Sovetsk
Chemnitz	Karl-Marx-Stadt
Lemburg	L'vov, now L'wow
Schneidemühl	Pia

Spelling

Foreign place names have often been misspelled in American records because the clerks who wrote it did not know the foreign spelling. And often the spelling was not standardized in the foreign location itself, so many variations may exist. Such errors in spelling can sometimes make it very difficult to interpret the correct locality. Spelling errors can be of several types:

Phonetic spelling. Some letters have a different sound in other languages. For example, in many languages *J* is pronounced like the English *I* or *Y*; *J* in French is pronounced like *Zi* in English.

In Polish, *X* is often used for the *ks* sound. The Swedish *å* is often written in English as *o*.

Misreading. Handwritten or gothic printed letters can be misinterpreted either by you or by a previous reader. Example: The German handwritten letter *W* can be confused with M and the letter *K* often looks like *R*. The German *ss* is written like the Greek letter beta (*β*) and is often misread as a capital B. Also, the German practice of capitalizing all nouns may make many words appear to be proper place names.

Special characters. Many languages use special symbols, often called diacritics, that indicate changes in sound, and sometimes alphabetical order of the letters. Sometimes these characters are eliminated in the new language. The German umlaut (¨) may be translated as the letter *e* following another vowel; therefore, the German *ü* often (but not always) becomes the English *ue*. The Czech *š* may have become *sh* or *sch*. The Dutch *ij* is usually translated as *y*.

English versions. The proper spelling of a town name in English may be quite different than the spelling in the native language. In such cases, you may find the native spelling of a town but not recognize it because it is not the spelling used in English. This is usually only a problem with larger cities that are well known in North America, such as the following:

Antwerp	Anvers or Antwerpen
Geneva	Genève, Genf, or Ginevra
Ratisbone	Regensburg
Brunswick	Braunschweig
Cassel	Kassel
Prague	Praha
Posnania	Posen or Poznan
Gothenburg	Göteborg
Prussia	Borussua (Latin)
Cologne	Köln
Vienna	Wien
Nuremberg	Nürnberg
Venice	Venezia
The Hague	s'Gravenhage

Multiple Places with the Same Name

Once you have found an actual town name, it may still be difficult to identify the town. Often there was more than one town in a country with the same or similar names. For example, there are ninety-six places named Newton or New Town in Great Britain and at least ten towns (and dozens of hamlets) named Lindenberg in Germany. Scotland has four Kildonans. While the city of Hoorn is well known in the Netherlands, there are also six villages and hamlets with that name, while another town and two hamlets are named Horn. This is why it is so important to know more about the area the immigrant came from, such as the name of the state, province, or county. It is also helpful to know of nearby cities.

Place Names that Are Not Towns of Origin

By far the most common mistake that researchers make is in assuming that the place name they have found in their research is that of the very town where the immigrant lived. In many cases, they have found a legitimate foreign location, but it is not the immigrant's home. It may be the name of the country, state, or region where the immigrant lived, but the researcher is not familiar enough with the country to identify it as such. In other cases, it may be the name of a city that is not the immigrant's home since, in many cases, the nearest large city or the port of departure was recorded as the home. In other cases the name of the city is also the name of the state or province. Here are some examples of these problems.

Country, state, regional, and provincial names. Many genealogical sources about immigrants only give the name of the country, region, or province. Foreign names of states, counties, provinces, or regions are unfamiliar to many researchers. Beware of place names, such as the following, that are not town names:

Deutschland	Germany
Österreich	Austria
Bayern	Bavaria
Franconia	Franken
Norge	Norway
Cechy	Bohemia
Eire	Republic of Ireland
Piedmont	Region in northwestern Italy
Fyn	Danish island
Silesia	Southwestern Poland
Burgundy	Region in eastern France
Schwaben	Old German Duchy in southern Germany
Valencia	Region in eastern Spain
Wessex	Southern counties in England
Erz	Mountain range on German-Czech border
Holland	Two provinces in the Netherlands
Siebenburgen	Transylvania region in Romania

City and county share the same name. Many states or provinces have a major or capitol city with the same name as the state. If you find the names Baden, Hannover, Kassel, Luxembourg, Bern, Utrecht, Derby, or similar names in censuses or some other records, they likely apply to the county or state with that name and not the specific cities of those names. The name of the city Darmstadt often applied to the entire portion of Hesse that was ruled from the city of Darmstadt. Even the name Lüneburg in Germany can apply to the city or to the extensive region around the city. In fact, in many countries, districts are named after the chief city. Often the immigrant came from the district of that name, not the city.

Nearby large city. If you find the name of a large or well-known city, the ancestor is probably not from the city itself, but rather from some smaller, lesser-known place nearby. While some immigrants were from large cities, most were from rural areas. In fact, the same forces also encouraged many persons to migrate to the larger cities, where jobs were more plentiful. Because most people in North America were unfamiliar with small localities, immigrants often referred to their homes by the name of some significant, well-known city nearby. Thus, while many immigrants claimed to have come from London or Berlin, in reality the person was usually from a smaller town near London or Berlin. In some cases, the immigrant came from a place much further away and there seems to be no valid reason for citing the big city. One "Berlin" emigrant was finally found in Cottbus, some eighty miles away. It is also possible that the immigrant traveled through the big city or lived there for a short period before leaving the old country.

Figure 9-26. Major European ports of departure.

If the records say that the immigrant came from a large city, look for clues that he or she actually came from a small town. A person who indicated to have been from a large city would not likely have had an occupation associated with small-town life, such as farming or fishing. Family traditions regarding trips to the market or traveling several miles to church are also clues that the immigrant came from a small town.

Port cities. Sometimes the place name found is really the port where the immigrant left the old country. However, the chances that he actually lived in the port city are slim. The major and many minor port cities for emigrants included Amsterdam, Antwerp, Bremen, Copenhagen, Cork, Danzig, Genoa, Gothenberg, Hamburg, Hull, Le Havre, Liverpool, Londonderry, Marseilles, Naples, Odessa, Oslo, Queenstown, Rotterdam, Southampton, Stockholm, Trieste, and others. Of course, such a city could be an important clue because departure records exist for some cities, and local police records in others may document the immigrant.

Notes

[1] Kory L. Meyerink, ed., *Printed Sources: A Guide to Published Genealogical Records* (Salt Lake City: Ancestry, 1998).

[2] Henry (Hank) Z Jones Jr., "Finding the Ancestral Home of a Palatine Forefather: The Case of Martin Zerbe," *Pennsylvania Genealogical Magazine* 29 (1975): 129–32; "The Braun and Loesch Families: Neighbors in Germany and America," *Der Reggeboge* 10 (April 1976): 11–13.

[3] Algot E. Strand, *A History of the Norwegians of Illinois* (Chicago: J. Anderson Publishing, 1905).

[4] *An Immigrant Nation: United States Regulation of Immigration, 1798–1991* (Washington, D.C.: U.S. Department of Justice, 1991), 34.

[5] These numbers are based on a careful reading of the works of major American immigration historians, including Bernard Bailyn, *Voyagers to the West* (New York, Knopf, 1986); David Cressy, *Coming Over: Migration and Communication between England and New England in the Seventeenth Century* (New York: Cambridge University Press, 1987); Roger Daniels, *Coming to America* (New York: Harper Collins, 1990); Marcus Lee Hansen, *The Atlantic Migration, 1607–1860* (New York: Harper and Row, 1940); and Maldwyn Allen Jones, *American Immigration* (Chicago: University of Chicago Press, 1960).

[6] John F. Vallentine, "Tracing the Immigrant Ancestor," *Genealogical Journal* 3 (1974): 5.

[7] Peter Roberts, *The New Immigration: A Study of the Industrial and Social Life of East Europeans in America* (Reprint, New York: Arno Press, 1970).

[8] Philip Taylor, *The Distant Magnet: European Emigration to the U.S.A.* (New York: Harper and Row, 1971).

[9] Nicholas V. Riasanovsky, *A History of Russia*, 2nd ed. (New York: Oxford University Press, 1969).

[10] G. M. Young, *Victorian England: Portrait of an Age* (New York: Oxford University Press, 1964).

[11] Roger Daniels, *Coming to America: A History of Immigration and Ethnicity in American Life* (New York: Harper Collins, 1990); Taylor, *Distant Magnet*; Oscar Handlin, *Immigration as a Factor in American History* (Englewood Cliffs, N.J.: Prentice Hall, 1959); James G. Leyburn, *The Scotch-Irish: A Social History* (Chapel Hill: University of North Carolina Press, 1962); Rowland Tappan Berthoff, *British Immigrants in Industrial America, 1790–1950* (Cambridge, Mass.: Harvard University Press, 1953; reprint, New York: Russell and Russell, 1968); Andrzej Brozek, *Polonia Amerykaska: The American Polonia* (Warsaw, Poland: Interpress Publications, 1980); Albert Camarillo, *Chicanos in a Changing Society: From Mexican Pueblo to American Barrios in Santa Barbara and Southern California, 1848–1930* (Cambridge, Mass.: Harvard University Press, 1979); Jay P. Dolan, *The Immigrant Church: New York's Irish and German Catholics* (Baltimore: Johns Hopkins University Press, 1975).

[12] Oliver MacDonagh, "The Irish Famine Emigration to the United States," *Perspectives in American History* 10 (1976): 357–446; Robert Swierenga, "Dutch Immigrant Demography, 1820–1880," *Journal of Family History* 5 (Winter 1980): 390–405; Paula Kaye Benkart, "Religion, Family, and Community Among Hungarians Migrating to American Cities, 1880–1930" (Ph.D. dissertation, Johns Hopkins University, 1975).

[13] Stephen Thernstrom, *Harvard Encyclopedia of American Ethnic Groups* (Cambridge, Mass.: Belknap Press of Harvard University Press, 1980).

[14] R. J. Dickson, *Ulster Emigration to Colonial America, 1718–1775* (London: Routledge and Kegan Paul, 1966); Norman McDonald, *Canada: Immigration and Colonization, 1841–1903* (Toronto: Macmillan of Canada, 1976); Clifford Neal Smith and Anna P. Smith, *American Genealogical Resources in German Archives* (New York: R. R. Bowker, 1977).

[15] Richard B. Morris, *Government and Labor in Early America* (New York: Harper and Row, 1965).

[16] Warren B. Smith, *White Servitude in Colonial South Carolina* (Danielsville, Ga.: Heritage Papers, 1972).

[17] Barbara Bigham, "Colonists in Bondage: Indentured Servants in America," *Early American Life* 10 (1979): 30–33, 83–84.

[18] Farley Grubb, *German Immigrant Servant Contracts, Registered at the Port of Philadelphia, 1817–1831* (Baltimore: Genealogical Publishing Co., 1994).

[19] Gottlieb Mittelberger, "Journey to Pennsylvania in the Year 1750," trans. Carl T. Eben, in Strassburger with Hinke, *Pennsylvania German Pioneers* 1:xxxiii.

[20] Taylor, *Distant Magnet*.

[21] Ibid., xxxvii.

[22] Marion J. Kaminkow, ed., *Genealogies in the Library of Congress: A Bibliography*, 2 vols. and 2 supplements (Baltimore: Magna Carta Book Co., 1972, 1977, 1987, 2001); *Genealogies Cataloged by the Library of Congress Since 1986* (Washington, D.C.: Library of Congress Cataloging Distribution Services Center, 1991).

[23] Martin Ulvestad, *Nordmændene i Amerika* [Norwegians in America], 2 vols. (Minneapolis: History Book Company's Forlag, 1907–10); Rose Rosicky, *A History of Czechs (Bohemians) in Nebraska* (Omaha: Czech Historical Society of Nebraska, 1929).

[24] *Chicago und sein Deutschthum* (Chicago: German Press Club, 1902).

[25] Henry R. Holsinger, *History of the Dunkers and the Brethren Church* (North Manchester, Ind.: L. W. Shultz, 1962).

[26] Robert C. Slocum, *Biographical Dictionaries and Related Works*, 2 vols., 2nd ed. (Detroit: Gale Research, 1986).

[27] Mirana C. Herbert and Barbara McNeil, *Biography & Genealogy Master Index* (Detroit: Gale Research, 1980–).

[28] Juliana Szucs Smith, *The Ancestry Family Historian's Address Book* (Orem, Utah: Ancestry, 2003).

[29] G. A. Dobbert, "An On-Line System for Processing Loosely Structured Records," *Historical Methods* 15 (Winter 1982): 16–22; John Guertler and Adele Newburger, *Records of Baltimore's Private Organizations: A Guide to Archival Resources* (New York: Garland Press, 1981).

[30] Nicholas V. Montalto, *The International Institute Movement: A Guide to Records of Immigrant Society Agencies in the United States* (St. Paul: Immigration History Research Center, 1978).

[31] Erna Risch, "Immigrant Aid Societies Before 1820," *Pennsylvania History* 3 (January 1936): 15–32.

[32] Bradford Luckingham, "Benevolence in Emergent San Francisco: A Note on Immigrant Life in the Urban Far West," *Southern California Quarterly* 55 (1973): 431–44.

[33] Kevin J. Rich, *Irish Immigrants of the Emigrant Industrial Savings Bank, 1850–1853* (Massapequa, N.Y.: Broadway-Manhattan Co., 2001).

[34] *Encyclopedia of Associations: Regional, State, and Local Organizations*, 29th ed., annual (Detroit: Gale Research Co., 2002).

[35] Lubomyr R. Wynar, *Encyclopedic Directory of Ethnic Organizations in the United States* (Littleton, Colo.: Libraries Unlimited, 1975).

[36] *Periodical Source Index (PERSI)* (Allen County Public Library Genealogy Department, 1987–; annual volumes published since 1986).

[37] Suzanna Moody and Joel Wurl, eds., *The Immigration History Research Center: A Guide to Collections* (New York: Greenwood Press, 1991–).

[38] Joseph M. Silinonte, *Bishop Loughlin's Dispensations, Diocese of Brooklyn 1859–1866* (The author, 1996).

[39] Anita L. Eyster, "Notices by German and Swiss Settlers Seeking Information of Members of their Families, Kindred, and Friends Inserted Between 1742–1761 in *Pennsylvania Berichte* and 1762–1779 in the *Pennsylvania Staatsbote*," *Pennsylvania German Folklore Society* 3 (1938): 32–41; Edward Hocker, *Genealogical Data Relating to the German Settlers of Pennsylvania and Adjacent Territory. From Advertisements in German Newspapers Published in Philadelphia and Germantown, 1743–1800* (Baltimore: Genealogical Publishing Co., 1981).

[40] Ruth-Ann Harris and Donald M. Jacobs, *The Search for Missing Friends: Irish Immigrant Advertisements Placed in the* Boston Pilot, 18 vols. (Boston: New England Historic Genealogical Society, 1989–97), also available at <www.newenglandancestors.org>and on CD.

[41] William Nelson, ed., *Documents Relating to Colonial History of New Jersey*, 1st series, vol. 12 (Patterson, N.J.: Press Printing and Publishing Co., 1895), 401–2.

[42] Lubomyr R. and Anna T. Wynar, *Encyclopedic Directory of Ethnic Newspapers and Periodicals in the United States*, 2nd ed. (Littleton, Colo.: Libraries Unlimited, 1976), 3.

[43] *Immigration and Passenger Arrivals: A Select Catalog of National Archives Microfilms*, rev. ed. (Washington, D.C.: National Archives Trust Fund, 1991).

[44] P. William Filby with Mary K. Meyer, *Passenger and Immigration Lists Index* (Detroit: Gale Research Co., 1981–).

[45] Michael Tepper, *American Passenger Arrival Records* (Baltimore: Genealogical Publishing Co., updated and enlarged in 1993).

[46] John P. Colletta, *They Came in Ships: A Guide to Finding Your Immigrant Ancestor's Arrival Record*, rev. 3rd ed. (Salt Lake City: Ancestry, 2002).

[47] Ralph B. Strassburger and William John Hinke, *Pennsylvania German Pioneers: A Publication of Original Lists of Arrivals in the Port of Philadelphia from 1727 to 1808* (Norristown, Pa.: Pennsylvania German Society, 1934).

[48] P. William Filby, comp., *Passenger and Immigration Lists Bibliography, 1538–1900*, 2nd ed. (Detroit: Gale Research Co., 1988). This bibliography updates Harold Lancour's original *Bibliography of Passenger Lists* (New York: New York Public Library, 1937), which was revised and enlarged by Richard Wolfe (New York: New York Public Library, 1963).

[49] Tepper, *American Passenger Arrival Records*, 16.

[50] Ibid.

[51] Maldwyn A. Jones, *Destination America* (New York: Holt, Rinehart, and Winston, 1976), 78.

[52] William J. Bromwell, *History of Immigration to the United States* (New York: Redfield, 1856).

[53] *Guide to Genealogical Research in the National Archives*, rev. ed. (Washington D.C.: National Archives Trust Fund board, 1991), 41.

[54] *Registers of Vessels Arriving at the Port of New York from Foreign Ports, 1789–1919*, NARA microfilm M1066.

[55] Bradley W. Steuart, *Passenger Ships Arriving in New York Harbor (1820–1850)* (Bountiful, Utah: Precision Indexing, 1991).

[56] *The Morton Allan Directory of European Passenger Steamship Arrivals* (Immigrant Information Bureau, 1931).

[57] John J. Newman, *American Naturalization Processes and Procedures, 1790–1985* (Indianapolis: Indiana Historical Society, 1985).

[58] Linda R. Green, "Citizenship and Naturalization in Colonial America from Pre-Revolutionary Times to the United States Constitution," *Illinois State Genealogical Society Quarterly* 14 (Fall 1992): 152–58.

[59] *Journals of Congress*, II, 16 January 1777.

[60] Frank George Franklin, *The Legislative History of Naturalization in the United States* (New York: Arno Press and the New York Times, 1969).

[61] Alice Eichholz, ed., *Red Book: American State, County and Town Sources*, 3rd. ed. (Provo, Utah: Ancestry, 2004).

[62] *Index to Naturalization Petitions of the United States District Court for the Eastern District of New York 1865–1957* (National Archives Trust Fund Board, 1991).

[63] *Soundex Index to Naturalization Petitions for the United States District and Circuit Courts, Northern District of Illinois, and Immigration and Naturalization Service District 9, 1840–1950* (National Archives Trust Fund Board, 1991).

[64] Loretto Dennis Szucs and Sandra Hargreaves Luebking, *The Archives: A Guide to the National Archives Field Branches* (Salt Lake City: Ancestry, 1988).

[65] Kenneth Scott, *British Aliens in the United States During the War of 1812* (Baltimore: Genealogical Publishing Co., 1979).

[66] Hans Bahlow, *Deutsches Namenlexikon* (Munich, Germany: Verlagsbuchhandlung, 1972).

[67] *Deutsches Geschlechterbuch* (Limburg an der Lahn, Germany: C. A. Starke, 1889–).

[68] Keith A. Johnson and Malcolm R. Sainty, *Genealogical Research Directory* (Washington, D.C.: Johnson and Sainty, 1985–).

[69] Trudy Schenk and Ruth Froelke, *The Wuerttemberg Emigration Index*, 8 vols. (Salt Lake City: Ancestry, 1986–2002).

[70] P. Mathias and A. W. H. Pearsall, *Shipping: A Survey of Historical Records* (Newton Abbot, England: David and Charles, 1980).

[71] Peter W. Coldham, *Emigrants from England to the American Colonies, 1773–1776* (Baltimore: Genealogical Publishing Co., 1988).

[72] Albert Bernhardt Faust and Gaius Marcus Brumbaugh, *Lists of Swiss Emigrants in the Eighteenth Century to the American Colonies* (Washington, D.C.: National Genealogical Society, 1920–25).

[73] Inge Auerbach, *Auswanderer aus Hessen-Kassel, 1840–1850*, vol. 2, Veroeffentlichungen der Archivschule Marburg, Institut fuer Archivwissenschaft, no. 12 (Marburg, Germany: Institut fuer Archivwissenschaft, 1988).

[74] Schenk and Froelke, *Wuerttemberg Emigration Index*.

[75] *The Hamburg Passenger Lists* (Salt Lake City: Genealogical Society of Utah, 1984).

References

Once the national origins of an individual have been discovered, there is a great and ever-increasing assortment of background materials worth pursuing. A public library is a logical place to begin research. Most collections will include a basic history for any given ethnic group. Through computer networking, libraries can track down even the most obscure materials that will facilitate the search and add to the enjoyment of any research project. Many large public libraries and university and college libraries have special ethnic collections, as do some private libraries. The overwhelming amount of information currently available on ethnic groups and immigration in general makes it impossible to outline all of it in this chapter.

Immigration Background Sources

The following lists attempt to identify the most broadly available or useful histories, bibliographies, and immigrant lists. For a more complete discussion and a list of such sources, see the chapters on "Ethnic Sources" and "Immigration Sources" in *Printed Sources: A Guide to Published Genealogical Records*, edited by Kory L. Meyerink (Salt Lake City: Ancestry, 1998).

Adamic, Louis. *From Many Lands.* New York: Harper and Bros., 1940.

Agueros, Jack, et al., eds. *The Immigrant Experience.* New York: Dial Press, 1971.

Allen, James Paul, and Eugene James Turner. *We the People: An Atlas of America's Diversity.* New York: McMillan, 1988.

Appel, John J. *The New Immigration.* New York: Pitman Publishers, 1971.

———. *Immigrant Historical Societies in the USA.* New York: Arno Press, 1980.

Archdeacon, Thomas J. *Becoming American: An Ethnic History.* New York: Free Press, 1983.

Auerbach, Frank L. *Immigration Laws of the United States.* Indianapolis: Bobbs-Merrill, 1961.

Bahr, Howard M., and Bruce A. Chadwick, eds. *American Ethnicity.* Lexington, Mass.: Heath, 1979.

Barton, Josef J. *Peasants and Strangers.* Cambridge, Mass.: Harvard University Press, 1975.

Benton, Barbara. *Ellis Island: A Pictorial History.* New York: Facts on File, 1985.

Bernard, Richard. *The Melting Pot and the Altar.* Minneapolis: University of Minnesota Press, 1980.

Bernardo, Stephanie. *The Ethnic Almanac.* Garden City, N.Y.: Dolphin Books, Doubleday, 1981.

Bigham, Barbara. "Colonists in Bondage: Indentured Servants in America." *Early American Life* 10 (1979): 30–33, 83–84.

Bodnar, John. *The Transplanted: A History of Immigrants in Urban America.* Bloomington: Indiana University Press, 1987.

Bogue, Donald J. *The Population of the United States: Historical Trends and Future Projections.* New York: Macmillan, 1985.

Bolino, August C. *The Ellis Island Source Book.* Washington, D.C.: Kensington Historical Press, 1985. In addition to a history of Ellis Island, this volume provides an exhaustive immigration bibliography.

Boorstin, Daniel J. *The Americans: The Democratic Experience.* New York: Random House, 1973.

Brye, David L. *European Immigration and Ethnicity in the United States and Canada: A Historical Bibliography.* Santa Barbara, Calif.: ABC-Clio Information Services, 1982.

Buenker, John D., Nicholas C. Burckel, and Rudolph J. Vecoli. *Immigration and Ethnicity: A Guide to Information Sources.* Detroit: Gale Research Co., 1977.

Carpenter, Niles. *Immigrants and Their Children 1920: A Study Based on Census Statistics Relative to the Foreign Born and the Native White of Foreign or Mixed Parentage.* Census Monographs VII. Washington, D.C.: Department of Commerce, Bureau of the Census, 1927.

Cayton, Mary Kupies, Elliott J. Gorn, and Peter W. Williams, eds. *Encyclopedia of American Social History.* 3 vols. New York: Scribner, 1993.

The Church of Jesus Christ of Latter-day Saints. *Research Outline: Tracing Immigrant Origins.* Salt Lake City: The Church of Jesus Christ of Latter-day Saints, Family History Library, 1992.

Coldham, Peter W. *Emigrants in Chains: A Social History of Forced Emigration to the Americas of Felons, Destitute Children, Political and Religious Non-conformists, Vagabonds, Beggars and Other Undesirables, 1607–1776.* Baltimore: Genealogical Publishing Co., 1992.

Cole, Donald B. *Immigration City: Lawrence, Massachusetts, 1845–1921.* Chapel Hill: University of North Carolina Press, 1963.

Coleman, Terry. *Going to America.* New York: Pantheon Books, 1972.

Commager, Henry Steele, ed. *Immigration and American History.* Minneapolis: University of Minnesota Press, 1961.

Cordasco, Francesco, ed. *A Bibliography of American Immigration History.* Fairfield, N.J.: Augustus M. Kelly Publishers, 1978.

———. *The Immigrant Woman in North America: An Annotated Bibliography of Selected References.* Metuchen, N.J.: Scarecrow Press, 1985.

———. *The New American Immigration: Evolving Patterns of Legal and Illegal Emigration: A Bibliography of Selected References.* New York: Garland, 1987.

Daniels, Roger. *Coming to America: A History of Immigration and Ethnicity in American Life.* New York: Harper Collins, 1990.

Dashefsky, Arnold, ed. *Ethnic Identity in Society.* Chicago: Rand McNally, 1976.

Dinnerstein, Leonard, and David M. Reimers. *Ethnic Americans: A History of Immigration.* New York: Harper and Row, 1987.

Directory of Historical Organizations in the United States and Canada. Nashville, Tenn.: American Association for State and Local History, 1994. This biennial lists addresses, telephone numbers, and other important information for state historical societies and agencies as well as those for local and specialized collections.

Eichholz, Alice, ed. *Red Book: American State, County, and Town Sources.* 3rd ed. Provo, Utah: Ancestry, 2004.

Eldridge, Grant J., ed. *Encyclopedia of Associations: Regional, State, and Local Organizations.* 4th ed. 5 vols. Detroit: Gale Research Co., 1994.

Erickson, Charlotte, ed. *Emigration from Europe, 1815–1914: Select Documents.* London: Adam and Charles Black, 1976.

Ethnographic Bibliography of North America. 4th ed. 5 vols. Behavior Science Bibliographies. New Haven, Conn.: Human Relations Area Files, 1975. Supplement (3 vols.) added in 1990.

Fermi, Laura. *Illustrious Immigrants: The Intellectual Migration from Europe, 1930–1941.* Chicago: University of Chicago Press, 1968.

Fleming, Thomas J. *The Golden Door.* New York: W. W. Horton, 1970.

Glazer, Nathan, and Daniel P. Moynihan, eds. *Ethnicity: Theory and Experience.* Cambridge, Mass.: Harvard University Press, 1975.

Greeley, Andrew M., and Gregory Baum, eds. *Ethnicity.* New York: Seabury Press, 1977.

Guide to Genealogical Research in the National Archives. Rev. ed. Washington D.C.: National Archives Trust Fund board, 1991.

Handlin, Oscar. *The Uprooted: The Epic Story of the Great Migrations That Made the American People.* New York: Grosset and Dunlap, 1951.

———. *The American People in the Twentieth Century.* Cambridge, Mass.: Harvard University Press, 1954.

———. *Immigration as a Factor in American History.* Englewood Cliffs, N.J.: Prentice Hall, 1959.

Hansen, Marcus L. *The Atlantic Migration, 1607–1860.* New York: Harper, 1961.

Harkness, George E. *The Church and the Immigrant.* New York: Doran, 1921.

Heaps, Willard A. *The Story of Ellis Island.* New York: Seabury Press, 1967.

Heaton, Elizabeth Putnam. *Steerage.* New York: L. Heaton, 1919.

Herbert, Mirana C., and Barbara McNeil. *Biography Genealogy Master Index.* Detroit: Gale Research Co., 1980–.

History of the Immigration and Naturalization Service. Washington, D.C.: Government Printing Office, 1980.

Hodges, Patrick, and Flavia Hodges. *A Dictionary of Surnames.* New York: Oxford University Press, 1988.

Hoglund, A. William. *Immigrants and Their Children in the United States: A Bibliography of Doctoral Dissertations, 1885–1982.* New York: Garland, 1986.

Holli, Melvin G., and Peter d'A. Jones, eds. *The Ethnic Frontier.* Grand Rapids, Mich.: Eerdmans Publishers, 1977.

Hutchinson, E. P. *Legislative History of American Immigration Policy, 1798–1965.* Philadelphia: University of Philadelphia Press, 1981.

Immigration and Naturalization Service. *Foreign Versions, Variations, and Diminutives of English Names, Foreign Equivalents of United States Military and Civilian Titles.* Washington, D.C.: Government Printing Office, 1970.

———. *An Immigrant Nation: United States Regulation of Immigration, 1798–1991.* U.S. Department of Justice, Washington, D.C.: Government Printing Office, 1991.

Johns, Stephanie Bernardo. *The Ethnic Almanac.* Garden City, N.Y.: Doubleday, 1981.

Jones, Maldwyn. *American Immigration.* New York: Holt, Rinehart. and Winston, 1960.

———. *Destination America.* New York: Holt, Rinehart, and Winston, 1976.

Kennedy, John F. *A Nation of Immigrants.* New York: Harper and Row, 1964.

Kettner, James H. *The Development of American Citizenship, 1607–1870.* Chapel Hill: University of North Carolina Press, 1978.

Kraut, Alan M. *The Huddled Masses: The Immigrant in American Society, 1880–1921.* Arlington Heights, Ill.: Harlan Davidson, 1982.

Kurian, George Thomas. *Datapedia of the United States 1790–2000: America Year by Year.* Lanham, Md.: Bernan Press, 1994.

Lieberson, Stanley. *Ethnic Patterns in American Cities.* New York: Free Press, 1963.

Lind, Marilyn. *Immigration, Migration and Settlement in the United States: A Genealogical Guidebook.* Cloquet, Minn.: Linden Tree, 1985.

Luckingham, Bradford. "Benevolence in Emergent San Francisco: A Note on Immigrant Life in the Urban Far West." *Southern California Quarterly* 55 (1973): 431–44.

Makower, Joel, ed. *The American History Source Book.* New York: Prentice Hall, 1987.

Marden, Charles F., and Gladys Meyer. *Minorities in American Society.* 4th ed. New York: D. Van Nostrand, 1973.

Meyerink, Kory L. "Immigration Sources." In *Printed Sources: A Guide to Published Genealogical Records*, edited by Kory L. Meyerink. Salt Lake City: Ancestry, 1998.

Miller, Sally M. *Ethnic Press in the United States: A Historical Analysis and Handbook.* New York: Greenwood Press, 1987.

Miller, Wayne Charles. *A Handbook of American Minorities.* New York: New York University Press, 1976.

———, et al. *A Comprehensive Bibliography for the Study of American Minorities.* New York: New York University Press, 1976.

Montalto, Nicholas V. *The International Institute Movement: A Guide to Records of Immigrant Society Agencies in the United States.* St. Paul: Immigration History Research Center, 1978.

Moody, Suzanna, and Joel Wurl, eds. *The Immigration History Research Center: A Guide to Collections.* New York: Greenwood Press, 1991.

Moreno, Barry. *Encyclopedia of Ellis Island.* Westport, Conn.: Greenwood Press, 2004.

Morrison, Joan, and Charlotte Fox Zabusky. *American Mosaic: The Immigrant Experience in the Words of Those Who Lived It.* 2nd ed. Pittsburg: University of Pittsburg Press, 1993.

National Historical Publications and Records Commission. *Directory of Archives and Manuscript Repositories in the United States.* 3rd ed. Phoenix: Oryx Press, 1990.

Neagles, James C. "Immigrant Ancestors." In *The Library of Congress: A Guide to Genealogical and Historical Research.* Salt Lake City: Ancestry, 1990.

Novotny, Ann. *Strangers at the Door.* Riverside, Conn.: Chatham Press, 1971.

Nugent, Walter. *Crossings: The Great Transatlantic Migrations, 1870–1914.* Bloomington: Indiana University Press, 1992.

Periodical Source Index (PERSI). Fort Wayne, Ind.: Allen County Public Library Genealogy Department, 1987–.

Pfeiffer, Laura Szucs. *Hidden Sources: Family History in Unlikely Places.* Orem, Utah: Ancestry, 2000.

Powell, Sumner Chilton. *Puritan Village: The Formation of a New England Town.* Garden City, N.Y.: Doubleday, 1965.

Reimers, David M. *Still the Golden Door: The Third World Comes to America.* New York: Columbia University Press, 1985.

———. *The Immigrant Experience.* New York: Chelsea House Publishers, 1989.

Risch, Erna. "Immigrant Aid Societies Before 1820." *Pennsylvania History* 3 (January 1936): 15–32.

Rosen, Philip. *The Neglected Dimension: Ethnicity in American Life.* South Bend, Ind.: Notre Dame Press, 1980.

Scott, Franklin D. *The Peopling of America: Perspectives on Immigration.* Washington, D.C.: American Historical Society Association, 1972.

Silinonte, Joseph M. *Bishop Loughlin's Dispensations, Diocese of Brooklyn, 1859–1866.* Brooklyn, N.Y.: the author, 1996.

Slocum, Robert C. *Biographical Dictionaries and Related Works.* 2 vols. 2nd ed. Detroit: Gale Research Co., 1986.

Smith, Jessie C., ed. *Ethnic Genealogy: A Research Guide.* Westport, Conn.: Greenwood Press, 1983.

Smith, Warren B. *White Servitude in Colonial South Carolina.* Danielsville, Ga.: Heritage Papers, 1972.

Sowell, Thomas. *Ethnic America: A History.* New York: Basic Books, 1981.

Szucs, Loretto Dennis. "Ethnic Sources." In *Printed Sources: A Guide to Published Genealogical Records,* edited by Kory L. Meyerink. Salt Lake City: Ancestry, 1998.

———. *They Became Americans.* Salt Lake City: Ancestry, 1998.

———, and Sandra Hargreaves Luebking. *The Archives: A Guide to the National Archives Field Branches.* Salt Lake City: Ancestry, 1988.

Taylor, Philip. *The Distant Magnet: European Emigration to the U.S.A.* New York: Harper and Row, 1971.

Thernstrom, Stephan. *Harvard Encyclopedia of American Ethnic Groups.* Cambridge, Mass.: Belknap Press of Harvard University Press, 1980.

Tift, Wilton, and Thomas Dunne. *Ellis Island.* New York: W. W. Norton, 1971.

Vecoli, Rudolph J., and Suzanne M. Sinke, eds. *A Century of European Migrations, 1830–1930.* Chicago: University of Illinois Press, 1991.

Wasserman, Paul, and Alice E. Kennington. *Ethnic Information Sources of the United States: A Guide to Organizations, Agencies, Foundations, Institutions, Media, Commercial and Trade Bodies, Government Programs, Research Institutes, Libraries and Museums, Religious Organizations, Banking Firms, Festivals and Fairs, Travel and Tourist Offices, Airlines and Ship lines, Bookdealers and Publishers' Representatives, and Books, Pamphlets, and Audiovisuals on Specific Ethnic Groups.* 2nd ed. 2 vols. Detroit: Gale Research Co., 1983.

Wittke, Carl F. *We Who Built America: The Saga of the Immigrant.* Cleveland: Western Reserve University Press, 1964.

Wynar, Lubomyr R. *Encyclopedic Directory of Ethnic Organizations in the United States.* Littleton, Colo.: Libraries Unlimited, 1976.

———, and Anna T. Wynar. *The Encyclopedic Directory of Ethnic Newspapers and Periodicals in the United States.* Littleton, Colo.: Libraries Unlimited, 1976.

Yans-McLaughlin, Virginia, and Marjorie Lightman. *Ellis Island and the Peopling of America: The Official Guide.* New York: New York Press, 1997.

Published Passenger and Emigration Lists and Sources for Locating Ships

Anuta, Michael J. *Ships of Our Ancestors.* 2nd ed. Baltimore: Genealogical Publishing Co., 1993.

Baca, Leo. *Czech Immigration Passenger Lists.* 4 vols. Richardson, Tex.: the compiler, 1983–91.

Boyer, Carl, III. *Ship Passenger Lists.* 4 vols. Newhall, Calif.: 1977–80.

Burgert, Annette K. *Eighteenth-Century Emigrants From German-Speaking Lands to North America.* Breinigsville, Pa.: Pennsylvania German Society, 1983–.

Cassady, Michael. *New York Passenger Arrivals, 1849–1868.* Papillion, Nebr.: Nimmo, 1983.

Coldham, Peter Wilson. *The Complete Book of Bonded Passengers to America.* 9 vols. Baltimore: Genealogical Publishing Co., 1983–85.

Colletta, John P. *They Came in Ships: A Guide to Finding Your Immigrant Ancestor's Arrival Record.* Rev. 3rd ed. Orem, Utah: Ancestry, 2002.

Cutler, Carl C. *Queens of the Western Ocean: The Story of America's Mail and Passenger Sailing Lines.* Annapolis, Md.: U.S. Naval Institute, 1961.

Ferguson, Laraine K. "Hamburg, Germany, Gateway to Ancestral Home." *German Genealogical Digest* 2, no. 1 (first quarter 1986): 10–14.

Filby, P. William. *Passenger and Immigration Lists Bibliography, 1538–1900: Being a Guide to Published Lists of Arrivals in the United States and Canada.* 2nd ed. Detroit: Gale Research Co., 1988.

———, and Mary K. Meyer, eds. *Passenger and Immigration Lists Index: A Guide to Published Arrival Records of More Than 1,775,000 Passengers Who Came to the New World Between the Sixteenth, Seventeenth, and Eighteenth Centuries.* Detroit: Gale Research Co., 1981. Supplements 1982–.

———, and Mary K. Meyer, eds. *Passenger and Immigration Lists of Arrivals in the United States and Canada in the Seventeenth, Eighteenth and Nineteenth Centuries.* 3 vols. Detroit: Gale Research Co., 1981. Supplements 1982–.

Filby, P. William, Mary K. Meyer, and Dorothy M. Lower. *Passenger and Immigration Lists Index.* Detroit: Gale Research Co., 1981– (including supplements).

Glazier, Ira A., and Michael Tepper, eds. *The Famine Immigrants: Lists of Irish Immigrants Arriving at U.S. Ports 1850–1855.* 7 vols. Baltimore: Genealogical Publishing Co., 1983–87.

———. *Italians to America: Lists of Passengers Arriving at U.S. Ports, 1880–1899.* 2 vols. to date. Wilmington, Del.: Scholarly Resources, 1992–.

———, and P. William Filby, eds. *Germans to America: Lists of Passengers Arriving at U.S. Ports, 1850–1855.* 28 vols. to date. Wilmington, Del.: Scholarly Resources, 1988–.

Guillet, Edwin C. *The Great Migration: The Atlantic Crossing by Sailing Ship Since 1770.* Rev. ed. Toronto: University Press, 1963.

Hall, Charles M. *Antwerp Emigration Index.* Salt Lake City: Heritage International, 1986.

Haury, David A., ed. *Index to Mennonite Immigrants on U.S. Passenger Lists, 1872–1904.* North Newton, Kans.: Mennonite Library and Archives, 1986.

Immigration Information Bureau. *Morton Allen Directory of European Passenger Steamship Arrivals.* 1931; reprint, Baltimore: Genealogical Publishing Co., 1993.

Jones, Hank Z, Jr. *More Palatine Families: Some Immigrants to the Middle Colonies, 1717–1776, and Their European Origins.* San Diego: the author, 1991.

Kludas, Arnold. *Great Passenger Ships of the World.* Translated by Charles Hodges. 6 vols. Cambridge, England: Patrick Stephens, 1975–86.

Lancour, Harold. *Bibliography of Passenger Lists.* New York: New York Public Library, 1937.

Mathias, P., and A. W. H. Pearsall. *Shipping: A Survey of Historical Records.* Newton Abbot, England: David and Charles, 1980.

McManus, J. *Comal County, Texas, and New Braunfels, Texas German Immigrant Ships, 1845–1846.* St. Louis: F. T. Ingmire, 1985.

Mitchell, Brian, comp. *Irish Passenger Lists 1847–1871.* Baltimore: Genealogical Publishing Co., 1988.

The Morton Allan Directory of European Passenger Steamship Arrivals. Immigrant Information Bureau, 1931.

National Archives Trust Fund Board. *Immigrant and Passenger Arrivals: A Select Catalog of National Archives Publications.* Revised. Washington, D.C., 1992.

Olsson, Nils William. *Swedish Passenger Arrivals in New York, 1820–1850.* Chicago: Swedish Pioneer Historical Society, 1967.

Owen, Robert Edward, ed. *Luxemburgers in the New World.* 2 vols. Esch-sur-Alzette, Luxembourg: Editions Reliures Schortgen, 1987.

"Passenger Arrivals at Salem and Beverly, Massachusetts, 1798–1800." *New England Historical Genealogical Register* 106 (1952): 203–9.

Potter, Constance. "St. Albans Passenger Arrival Records." *Prologue* 22 (Spring 1990): 90–93.

Prins, Edward. *Dutch and German Ships.* Holland, Mich.: the compiler, 1972.

Rasmussen, Louis J. *San Francisco Ship Passenger Lists.* 4 vols. Baltimore: Genealogical Publishing Co., 1978.

Reider, Milton P., and Norma Gaudet Rieder, eds. *New Orleans Ship Lists.* 2 vols. Metairie, La., 1966–68.

Rockett, Charles Whitlock. *Some Shipboard Passengers of Captain John Rockett (1828–1841).* Mission Viejo, Calif.: the compiler, 1983.

Schenk, Trudy, Ruth Froelke, and Inge Bork. *The Wuerttemberg Emigration Index.* 8 vols. Salt Lake City: Ancestry, 1988–2002.

Schrader-Muggenthaler, Cornelia. *Alsace Emigration Book*. 2 vols. Apollo, Pa.: Closson Press, 1989–91.

———. *Baden Emigration Book*. Apollo, Pa.: Closson Press, 1992.

Ships Passenger Lists, Port of Galveston, Texas, 1846–1871. Easley, S.C.: Southern Historical Press, 1984.

Smith, Clifford Neal. *Reconstructed Passenger Lists for 1850: Hamburg to Australia, Brazil, Canada, Chile, and the United States*. 4 vols. McNeal, Ariz.: Westland Publications, 1980.

Smith, Eugene W. *Passenger Ships of the World, Past and Present*. Boston: George H. Dean, 1978.

Steuart, Bradley W. *Passenger Ships Arriving in New York Harbor (1820–1850)*. Bountiful, Utah: Precision Indexing, 1991.

Strassburger, Ralph Beaver, comp., and William John Hinke, ed. *Pennsylvania German Pioneers: A Publication of the Original Lists of Arrivals in the Port of Philadelphia from 1727 to 1808*. 3 vols. Norristown, Pa.: Pennsylvania German Society, 1934.

Sweiringa, Robert P., comp. *Dutch Immigrants in U.S. Ship Passenger Manifests, 1820–1880: An Alphabetical Listing by Household Heads and Independent Persons*. 2 vols. Wilmington, Del.: Scholarly Resources, 1983.

Tepper, Michael, ed. *Emigrants to Pennsylvania, 1641–1819: A Consolidation of Ship Passenger Lists from Pennsylvania Magazine of History and Biography*. Baltimore: Genealogical Publishing Co., 1978.

———. *Immigrants to the Middle Colonies*. Baltimore: Genealogical Publishing Co., 1978.

———. *New World Immigrants: A Consolidation of Ship Passenger Lists from Periodical Literature*. 2 vols. Baltimore: Genealogical Publishing Co., 1988.

———. *Passenger Arrivals at the Port of Baltimore, 1820–1834, From Customs Passenger Lists*. Baltimore: Genealogical Publishing Co., 1982.

———. *Passenger Arrivals at the Port of Philadelphia, 1800–1819: The Philadelphia Baggage Lists*. Baltimore: Genealogical Publishing Co., 1986.

———. *American Passenger Arrival Records: A Guide to the Records of Immigrants Arriving at American Ports by Sail and Steam*. 2nd ed. Baltimore: Genealogical Publishing Co., 1993.

Wolfe, Richard. *Bibliography of Passenger Lists*. New York: New York Public Library, 1963.

Yoder, Don, ed. *Pennsylvania German Immigrants, 1709–1786: Lists Consolidated from Yearbooks of the Pennsylvania German Folklore Society*. 1984; reprint, Baltimore: Genealogical Publishing Co., 1989.

Zimmerman, Gary J., and Marion Wolfert. *German Immigrants: Lists of Passengers Bound From Bremen to New York*. 3 vols. Baltimore: Genealogical Publishing Co., 1988.

Naturalization

Bockstruck, Lloyd deWitt. *Denizations and Naturalizations in the British Colonies in America, 1607–1775*. Baltimore: Genealogical Publishing Co., 2005.

Filby, P. William. *Philadelphia Naturalization Records*. Detroit: Gale Research Co., 1982.

Green, Linda R. "Citizenship and Naturalization in Colonial America from Pre-Revolutionary Times to the United States Constitution." *Illinois State Genealogical Society Quarterly* 24 (Fall 1992): 152–58.

Franklin, Frank George. *The Legislative History of Naturalization in the United States*. New York: Arno Press and the New York Times, 1969.

Holcomb, Brent H. *South Carolina Naturalizations, 1783–1850*. Baltimore: Genealogical Publishing Co., 1985.

Journals of Congress, II, 16 January 1777.

National Archives Trust Fund Board. *Index to Naturalization Petitions of the United States District Court for the Eastern District of New York, 1865–1957*. Washington, D.C.: National Archives and Records Administration, 1991.

Newman, John J. *American Naturalization Records, 1790–1990: What They Are and How to Use Them*. 2nd ed. Bountiful, Utah: Heritage Quest, 1998.

Schaefer, Christina K. *Guide to Naturalization Records of the United States*. Baltimore: Genealogical Publishing Co., 1997.

Scott, Kenneth. *Early New York Naturalizations, 1790–1840*. Baltimore: Genealogical Publishing Co., 1981.

Soundex Index to Naturalization Petitions for the United States District and Circuit Courts, Northern District of Illinois, and Immigration and Naturalization Service District 9, 1840–1950. National Archives Trust Fund Board, 1991.

Szucs, Loretto Dennis. *They Became Americans*. Salt Lake City: Ancestry, 1998.

———, and Sandra Hargreaves Luebking. *The Archives: A Guide to the National Archives Field Branches*. Salt Lake City: Ancestry, 1988.

Wolfe, Richard J. "The Colonial Naturalization Act of 1740; With a List of Persons Naturalized in New York Colony, 1740–1769." *New York Genealogical and Biographical Record* 94 (1963): 132–47.

Wyand, Jeffrey A., and Florence L. Wyand. *Colonial Maryland Naturalizations*. Baltimore: Genealogical Publishing Co., 1986.

10

Land Records

SANDRA HARGREAVES LUEBKING, FUGA

Chapter Contents

Land records provide two types of important evidence for the genealogist. First, they often state kinship ties, especially when a group of heirs jointly sells some inherited land. Second, they place individuals in a specific time and place, allowing the researcher to sort people and families into neighborhoods and closely related groups. By locating people with reference to creeks and other natural features, the deeds, land grants, and land tax lists help distinguish one John Anderson, son of Mark, from another John Anderson in the same county. Prior to the Civil War, most free adult males owned land; so if the land records of an area have survived but do not mention your ancestor, you should reevaluate the assumption that he or she lived in the area.

Most beginning genealogists underestimate the importance of using land records to pin persons to specific locales. Donald Lines Jacobus, considered the founder of scientific New England genealogy, wrote of Connecticut, "The most important town records, genealogically, are the land records."[1] In the South, which has far fewer vital records than New England, the land records are even more crucial to genealogical success.

This chapter on land is divided into two major parts. The first describes deeds, survey systems, military bounty land, private land claims, and taxes, and offers some information on real property law. The second half is a synopsis of each state's land grant records, along with historical notes and bibliographic references. Observe especially the distinction between "state-land states" (where the state or colony made the land grants) and "public-domain states" (where the federal government made the grants). The first part of the chapter explains these two systems; the state-by-state synopsis indicates which system was used in each state.

Many of the land records mentioned in this chapter have been microfilmed. The Genealogical Society of Utah (a nonprofit entity of The Church of Jesus Christ of Latter-day Saints in Salt Lake City) includes state land grants and county and some city deeds among its routinely microfilmed records. Consult its catalog at <www.familysearch.org>. However, despite the society's vast number of land records on microfilm, you should not regard its catalog as a complete inventory of what survives.

Other microfilmed records belong to libraries and archives that have made available their manuscript collections of private land company papers and other records. The millions of federal land patents have been digitized and are available from the Bureau of Land Management, by mail or at its website <www.glorecords.blm.gov/>, described later in this chapter's public land section and state-by-state synopsis.

Deeds

Deeds form the bulk and backbone of American land records. They are fairly uniform in format and content, can normally be located in routinely predictable jurisdictions (usually the county), and generally present few difficulties. As one of the most important components of civil law (as opposed to criminal law), deeds contain a fair measure of legal terms. Val Greenwood, with the advantage of a law degree, has discussed some basic legal concepts about land in his *Researcher's Guide to American Genealogy*.[2] Patricia Law Hatcher's *Locating Your Roots: Discover Your Ancestors Using Land Records* has a comprehensive glossary of terms.[3] *Black's Law Dictionary* will assist with legal definitions.[4] A detailed description of deed contents is in Raymond A. Winslow, Jr.'s "Land Records" in *North Carolina Research: Genealogy and Local History*.[5] Following is an overview of deeds and other records found in deed books. Some remarks on more technical aspects are given below in the section on the "Use of Land Records."

The term "deed" can be used broadly to mean a legal document of transfer, bargain, or contract, or narrowly for a warranty deed by which the seller warrants (guarantees) the title to the land being sold. Deed books contain many types of title conveyances and contracts: deeds in fee simple (a term meaning "absolute" ownership); mortgages transferring property rights as security for a debt; dower releases waiving a wife's rights; quitclaim deeds releasing whatever title or right is held (whether valid or not); deeds of gift transferring land without a reciprocal consideration except perhaps "love and affection"; powers of attorney appointing legal agents; marriage property settlements between spouses either before or after the marriage; bills of sale transferring property that is usually not land; and various forms of contracts such as leases, partnerships, indenture papers, adoptions, and other performance bonds. These last five were not ordinarily recorded, though probate bonds were common in probate volumes. Deed books from before the Civil War, especially in colonial years, were more miscellaneous in their contents, even including animal brands, occasional wills, slave manumissions, apprentice papers, petitions, depositions, tax lists, and whatever else the clerk decided to preserve on a convenient page.

European settlers and their governments brought to the colonies the principle that before land could be privately owned the government had to pass title into private hands. Thus, for any tract of land there should be a first-title deed, which is normally called a grant or patent. Usually the authorities sought from the local Indian tribes a cession of Indian title, though this concept of owning land was foreign to the Indian view of communal occupancy. Once the Indian title was terminated to the satisfaction of the whites, the government could grant title for a tract to an individual, corporation, or, in the case of federal grants, even to a state. All subsequent transfers of a tract are by deed or analogous conveyance, or by inheritance.

In the United States, responsibility for guaranteeing legal title rests with the buyer and seller. Today, property transfers usually require a professional title searcher or lawyer, who attempts to verify a valid, unencumbered title transfer by tracing the chain of title back to the first-title grant. The government limits itself to the role of a referee—supplying the rules, recording the results, and adjudicating disputes brought to court. To simplify such title searches, title abstract and insurance companies have arisen to make professional searches and sell insurance against defective titles. Such companies have compiled indexes to title transfers in their local areas. If a genealogist can afford the high expense, such a title company could compile an ancestor's local land records. Also, there are cases where the local deed office holdings have been destroyed recently, but abstracts survive in the private title company records.

An important fact follows from the American system of deed registrations: records are usually sought by the name of the buyer or seller rather than the tract name or number. This means that a break in the chain of recorded owners can complicate a genealogist's understanding of why, in the absence of a deed, John Smith now owns land that Mary Smith owned ten years ago. The land could have passed from mother to son by will with proof only in the probate records, or it could have passed by intestate probate and not have been recorded at all. It could also be that the two persons are unrelated and that Mary sold the land to Paul Williams, who then sold it to John Smith, neither of the deeds being recorded, perhaps to save the cost of the clerk's fees. Or perhaps the deed from Mary Smith to John Smith was by sheriff's sale and indexed under the sheriff's name as seller. Such a sheriff's sale for delinquent taxes raises the point that tax foreclosures affecting the land would be in court records, while a bankruptcy suit might be processed in another county entirely.

A registry system called Torrens attempts to resolve some of these problems. Named for Robert Richard Torrens, the South Australian legislator who developed it in the late 1850s, Torrens ideally records in one place under the title of the tract all former owners and all rights, interests, and liens to which the property is subject. Having established the registry as mandatory and complete, the government can then issue guaranteed certificates of title to a new owner. While available in some states or urban areas, Torrens has not operated in the United States as intended and a researcher is unlikely to encounter it unless he or she is searching in an urban area.

Urban Searches

Although deeds and other land documents of big cities resemble their small-town counterparts, the excessively high number of daily property transactions in highly populated areas made traditional indexing (by names of seller/grantor and buyer/grantee) impractical. Instead, some urban areas in public land states used the legal description as the finding aid and the tract book as the ledger. Following is a simplification of the process using a deed as an example.

1. A deed (property conveyance) submitted to city or county officials for recording was copied (entered) into a deed book. A file (conveyance) number was assigned, usually chronologically according to when the deed was entered. Depending on the work load of the clerks, this could be long after the deed was brought into the office.
2. A clerk entered the date of recording, the names of the parties (abbreviated, such as Taylor to Roberts), and a notation as to the type of transaction (WD, warranty deed; QC, quit claim deed; TD, deed of trust; and so forth) into the tract book. The conveyance number was also entered, providing a cross-reference to the recorded deed.

Some cities, such as Chicago, where city deeds are intermingled with those of the county, added an interim step to the process by substituting a second set of numbers for the conveyance number in the tract book entry. This second set of numbers codes the volume and page number of the recorded deed to make locating the recorded deed easier. Regardless of whether a conveyance number or a finding number is used, the research begins with the tract book.

Cook County has more than 1,000 tract books dating back to the Great Fire of 1871. Unless the researcher is fortunate enough to have a legal description (from a court document, family papers, land ownership map, or a patent), an address must be learned from a city directory, tax list, or other source. Addresses tend to be less permanent than legal descriptions, thus allowances must be made for street and numbering changes over time. Translating an 1855 address into a present-day address requires its own series of research steps. Once a current address is identified, the parcel's legal description may be obtained from the city or county tax office. The legal description will lead to the tract book where the appropriate entries and numbers are copied, and that in turn leads to the recorded deed.

Instead of thumbing though a deed book, however, the urban researcher will probably find the deed on microform. Cities were eager to adopt new technology to aid the workflow, hence the early use of computers to maintain name indexes makes more recent searches easier. However, these indexes seldom include deeds recorded prior to the date computerization began. In the unlikely situation where the name index does go back to early years, the careful researcher will still examine the appropriate tract book, seeking the single-line entry for each legal activity that affected the property. This can include court matters (such as bankruptcy, divorce, lawsuits, or probate), liens, mortgages, judgments, tax sales, deeds of transfer, and so forth.

Other urban property search peculiarities are described in specialized research guides, such as Ann Lainhart's *A Researcher's Guide to Boston*; Loretto Dennis Szucs's *Chicago and Cook County: A Historical & Genealogical Guide*; Connie S. Terheiden's and Kenny R. Burck's *Guide to Genealogical Resources in Cincinnati and Hamilton County, Ohio*; Estelle Guzik's *Genealogical Resources in the New York Metropolitan Area*; and Ted Steele's *A Guide to Genealogical Research in St. Louis*.[6] Also valuable are articles, such as Leslie Corn's "New York City Research Guide, Part One: Vital Records, Property Records, and Estate Records"; Kay Haviland Freilich's "Genealogical Research in Pennsylvania," with suggestions for Philadelphia; and Jane Gardner Aprill's "New Orleans: Jewels in the Crown."[7] Urban area websites can prove useful: <http://digital.library.pitt.edu/pittsburgh> features many land ownership maps of Pittsburgh.

Only a handful of hardy transcribers have confronted the demands of big city property abstracting or indexing. Notably, William R. Graven, whose Cincinnati titles include *Index to Selected Hamilton County, Ohio Recorder's Books, 1801–1820* and, with Eileen Mullen, *Hamilton County, Ohio, Index of Early Deed Books, 1804–1806 and 1814–1817*.[8]

Deed Indexes

The variety of records in deed books requires the user to develop certain search skills. Because few researchers have the time to read, page by page, the forty, fifty, or one hundred volumes of deeds in an average county or independent city, the user usually turns to the index. Seller indexes are also called direct or grantor indexes; buyer indexes are indirect, reverse, or grantee indexes. Some counties have indexes that only alphabetize the sellers, which forces a researcher to read all index entries from A to Z to check the buyers (for example, the buyers would be listed next to the sellers, but only the sellers are alphabetized). Before relying on a deed index, it is wise to make an informal sampling of the contents of the deed volumes to see if they contain records significantly different from deeds and if these different sorts of records are indexed along with the deeds. For example, some deed volumes have been found to contain wills. These wills were not indexed in either the deed or the probate indexes.

While cumulative deed indexes may be in alphabetical order ("alpha" order), running indexes are not, because names are continually being added. Some running indexes merely group surnames under their first letter (initial order), so all *A* surnames are together (unalphabetized), all *B* surnames together, and so forth, with special pages for Mc and O'. Occasionally, a clerk ignored the patronymic prefix and indexed MacDonald, for example, with *D* surnames and O'Carroll under C. Other indexing variations are explained in Christine Rose's *Courthouse Research for Family Historians*.[9]

Other problems with indexes are sins of omission—creating only a grantor index, mistakenly omitting a name, or ignoring non-deed items. This last problem is fairly common, especially in alphabetized master-deed indexes compiling all the deed volumes of the last one hundred or two hundred years. Whether the indexer will consider the barrel brand of Thomas Forehall, cooper, worth indexing is doubtful, especially because it was recorded 150 years ago and can serve no contemporary purpose. The researcher must always choose between trusting the index or checking the book (or needed years) page by page. Deeds with more than one buyer or seller may be indexed under the first's name only, another reason to take the time to read page by page if the problem warrants it. There is also the occasional deed that provides information on a surname different from either the seller or buyer. On 7 May 1763, William and Betty Eskridge of Northumberland County, Virginia, sold land to Thomas Williams and, in passing, the deed gave a beautiful account of the Neale family, former owners of the land.[10]

Deed Abstracting

Once you've found an actual entry in the deed volume, either by using the index or by page-by-page scanning, you should have a fairly standard format for abstracting entries. It is wise to train yourself to *first* write down the source (or, if you have photocopied the entry, to immediately write the source on the photocopy). The source includes the archive, library, or website where you found the record as well as the record type, volume and page, or document number and date. Below are three examples.

Maryland State Archives—Charles Co., Md., deeds 10:231 (microfilm)

King Co., Wa., courthouse, county auditor's office, deeds 27:13

Draper Papers (State Historical Society of Wisconsin, Madison), 6BB35 (microfilm 889,101 Family History Library, Salt Lake City)

Bureau of Land Management: General Land Office Records, online <www.glorecords.blm.gov/>, Sparta Land Office, Patent Document #3766, issued 15 August 1837 (viewed 12 February 2006)

Printed notekeeping forms help some people remember to copy such sources. Be sure also to include your name and the date when you found the record.

Abstracting is a necessary skill to acquire, since many early deed books are too fragile to photocopy. Instructions are given in Helen Leary's "Abstracting" in *North Carolina Research: Genealogy and Local History*.[11] Below is an example of an abstracted deed.

Barnwell Dist, SC, deeds vol. H, 1814–15, p. 318, 27 Oct 1813: Samuel Sprawls, Barnwell Dist, to John Ashley, residence not given, $20, 46 acres on branch of Tinkers Creek, adj Mary Collins and said John Ashley

signed: Samuel Sprawls
wit: Edmond Brown, J.C. Starpkins (also Starkin)
recorded 21 Nov 1814

Some users forget that the deed book is a copy of an original paper and that, therefore, the deed book signatures are usually in the clerk's handwriting—they are not holographs. Some jurisdictions, however, did require a signature on the copy they retained, so watch for them. Likewise, the seal—in wax and later in paper—beside the seller's signature was real on the original; but, in the deed book, the clerk drew a stylized circle surrounding the word "seal." The use of personal wax seals has long been out of fashion; but in the colonies, men were expected to have or borrow some sort of sealing device, which usually supplemented the illiterate's mark. Even English peasants as early as the thirteenth century were required by law to seal their signatures; in fact, there was a time when the seal was the official attestation and the person's mark was auxiliary. By the late seventeenth century, the seal was merely a traditional ornament.[12] Consequently, heraldic devices on colonial seals probably do not prove a signer had a coat or arms. In fact, George Washington had a seal with a device different from the family coat of arms, a fairly typical situation.

Seals and signatures are, however, minor problems compared to late recording. Since running indexes show names in chronological order, a 1735 deed recorded in 1802 is so out of place that the researcher may not carry the search far enough to spot it. Actual examples include a deed dated 31 March 1800 and recorded 21 March 1896 in Montgomery County, Georgia, with another in the same place dated 30 December 1791 and recorded 110 years later on 30 July 1901.[13] In the same general category are deeds rerecorded after a courthouse or town hall burned. Also be alert to indexes that show only the recording date, because behind the 1827 date could be an 1818 deed. If the ancestor died in 1823, the researcher might mistakenly conclude from the index that an 1827 deed could not be the ancestor's.

State-Land States

Deeds normally locate the land tract by some legal description with a survey. The thirty states where the federal government granted land each use the federal township and range system and include a special subcategory called private land claims. Before discussing them, however, this chapter will describe the remaining twenty states, called state-land states, which granted their own lands and have various surveying systems.

The twenty state-land states are the thirteen original states from New Hampshire to Georgia, plus Maine, Vermont, West Virginia, Kentucky, Tennessee, Texas, and Hawaii. For the last two, consult the "Summary of State Land Records" at the end of this chapter. The remaining eighteen can be divided between the six New England states, which used the New England town system, the transitional state of New York, and the remaining states from Pennsylvania and New Jersey southward, which used the Southern system of metes and bounds.

Southern Land Grants

The "tomahawk" grant is part of American folklore. The buckskin-clad squatter cut blazes on a perimeter of trees that surrounded his newly picked tract of wilderness, and then off he went to a land office to get a deed. He entered his claim (the petition) and got official authorization (a warrant) to have the tract surveyed to produce a legal description (the plat) so that the government could grant title to that piece of land (the first-title deed, usually called a grant or patent).

In the absence of a surveyed grid of meridians, baselines, townships, and ranges by which the land can be legally described, the description must use local features, usually called "metes and bounds," which requires the "measuring" and "naming" of boundary features. The distances in patents and deeds were usually in poles, rods, or perches, all sixteen and a half feet.

Here is part of a simple description: "Starting at the ash tree in the split rock, then 139 poles to where the spring branch enters Crooked Creek, then up said creek its meanders to a three-notch oak, then. . . ." A surveyed compass course read: "Starting at the ash tree in the split rock, then North 41 degrees East 139 poles to where the spring branch enters Crooked Creek, then up said creek its meanders South 14 poles, South 3 degrees West 25 poles, South 9 degrees East 13 poles to a three-notch oak. . . ."

Strictly speaking, because they used compass bearings, nearly all southern tracts were not in metes and bounds. A more correct term is the "indiscriminate" survey, meaning that the survey was not part of any larger survey grid. This chapter, however, will employ the common composite term of "indiscriminate metes and bounds." Since the natural or man-made features of the description tended to disappear over the years, the property owner, in the company of local officials, neighbors, and sometimes a surveyor, might retrace the property bounds and mark again from memory or from a new survey those points that were disappearing or lost. This walking and remarking of the bounds was called "processioning."[14]

Unlike in New England, lands in the Southern system were usually allotted directly to individuals. In New York, a transition zone, large grants were often made to wealthy individuals who subdivided and sold the grants in small parcels. In Pennsylvania, New Jersey, and the colonies to the south, the allotted lands were usually farm-size tracts that went directly to individuals. There were some very large grants in the southern colonies, especially Virginia. Two of the largest were 92,000 acres to Benjamin Borden and 118,000 acres to William Beverley, both in 1739 in the upper Shenandoah Valley, and both part of the total 539,000 acres granted by 1740 to eight individuals or partnerships.[15]

Land offices handled the paperwork of petitioning and obtaining the individual grants. It is extraordinary that in the colonies from Pennsylvania to Georgia and their offspring of West Virginia, Kentucky, and Tennessee, no land offices were destroyed in a major fire. In the Civil War, the state capitals of Virginia and South Carolina were burned, yet the land office records survived. Nearly every one of the early states south of Pennsylvania still has a land office either as a distinct section of the state archive or as a division of an active state office.

The authority granting colonial lands was not always the government. There were three variations: (1) The English monarch controlled the government and granted the land through the governor. Examples are New York after 1689, South Carolina after 1729, and Georgia after 1754. (2) The monarch controlled the government but gave a private citizen or citizens (proprietors) the right to grant the land; examples are the Northern Neck Proprietary of Lord Fairfax in Virginia and the Granville District of Earl Granville in North Carolina. Or (3) the English monarch allowed a private citizen or citizens to control the government and grant the land, as in Pennsylvania under the Penns and in Georgia under the trustees, 1733 to 1754. Where the proprietors were distinct from government, there will be land office records distinct from government records, as in New Jersey, Virginia, and North Carolina, though these records may later have been added to the government archives, as in Virginia and North Carolina but not New Jersey. (See the state-by-state summary at the end of this chapter.)

There were several ways to acquire first title to lands, but usually the four steps of petition, warrant, survey/plat, and grant/patent were followed. (*Patent* and *grant* sometimes have different meanings.[16] In this chapter, however, they are used interchangeably to mean the first-title deed.)

The *petition* is a request to take up land. The petitioner may have gone before the appropriate officials—the colony's council or the land office clerk—and presented a satisfactory reason for getting land, such as paying the purchase price, being promised land for military service, bringing an immigrant into the colony and thus becoming eligible for the headright land bounty (especially used in the South), or being able to produce a government order for a specified amount of land.

The *warrant* certifies the right to a specific acreage and authorizes an official surveyor to survey it, assuming no prior and conflicting claims.

The *plat*, sometimes called a *survey*, is the surveyor's drawing of the legal description so that the land is identifiable—his certification that everything is in order so far as the warrant, approved acreage, and legal description are concerned.

The *patent/grant* is the government's or proprietor's passing of title to the patentee/grantee. This is the first-title deed and the true beginning of private ownership of the land.

The government or proprietor usually entered a copy of the patent in a bound volume as a permanent, official record. The plats were sometimes recorded in volumes, and the surveyor's loose copy was sometimes also kept. The North Carolina Land Office, for example, has many loose surveys. Some land offices kept permanent warrant records; some did not. The petition was rarely recorded because the warrant was the formal statement of an authorized petition, though petitioner information is occasionally found in council minutes—especially for colonial headrights.

Bringing oneself or another person to the colonies entitled the importer to a "headright" of land at specific historical periods. Virginia granted fifty acres per importation, but sailors abused it by claiming fifty acres every time they sailed to Virginia, then sold their claims. In the case of indentured servants, the fifty acres went to the person who paid the servant's passage. These headrights could be bought and sold, so the person claiming two hundred acres for importing four persons was not necessarily the person who actually paid the passage costs. Thus, if Mark Randle claimed 450 acres for transporting nine persons, including Mary Randle, it is possible Mark merely bought headrights to nine persons and never saw or knew Mary. It is also possible that Mary paid her own passage and sold her headright rather than claim the land. Furthermore, the nine persons need not have come on the same ship nor arrived in the same year.[17] New England did not have this system of headrights as a rule, though granting free land to town settlers was a form of reward for immigration. The Northern proprietors rarely gave headrights—the Calverts did for a time—because they sold land for a profit. The Crown tried at times to make the colonies grant lands to indentured servants at the end of their service, but this was uncommon. Despite these caveats, the headright lists are valuable as the major or only immigration record for most colonial immigrants from the British Isles to the South.

The patent and related documents rarely give kinship information, so their great value is in locating the grantee in a specific time and place. See "Creating a Plat" on page 438.

Survey Systems and Terms By Mary McCampbell Bell, CG, CGL

It is important to set the scene in the early colonial period. According to Sarah S. Hughes in her classic work, *Surveyors and Statesmen,*[1] the immigrants came from England where the fields were nicely marked off with hedges or fences. Virginia was open territory filled with creeks, marshes, and ridges, and it was not easy to transfer specified acreage and rectangular dimensions to this terrain. And until the land was surveyed, it could not belong to an individual. The indiscriminate surveys were the result of a land policy where the individual was allowed to select land prior to any official surveying. This practice allowed the best land to be taken up first, thus explaining the patenting of irregular shapes. People re-patented their original acreage to add adjacent land (the "overage" or "plush" is the newly patented land). In the patent margins, there is usually a notation that indicates "new" land, "old" land (previously owned land), and "escheated" (land reverted to the Crown, usually due to lack of heirs) and "lapsed" land (land not seated within the three-year limit).

The early surveys, crude in comparison to the twentieth century, used a rudimentary technology, primarily the thirty-two-point compass, from 1635 until the 360 degree compass card became accepted in the 1670s. Even into the 1700s, patents and deeds in the Tidewater counties often used a combination of both compasses. The thirty-two-point compass card, also called the Mariner's Compass Rose, measured angles down to a quarter point, whereas before surveyors could only measure right angles. It used the names of the wind directions, such as North or North by East. Dividing each ninety-degree quadrant into eight parts gives eight 11-degree, 15-minute sections. The compass using magnetic North was marked by 360 degrees and divided into 90 degree segments instead of 32 points. If the call was "N by E" then it translated into "N11¼°E". This method of describing calls became the standard practice by the 1690s. (When platting, simply round the fractions off to the half or whole degree when using a ruler with a scale of tenths). The directions are shown thus:

32 Point Compass	Actual Degree	Degree on land compass or protractor
N	360°	0°
N by E	11.25°	11° 15′
N NE	22.5°	22° 30′
NE by N	33.75°	33° 45′
NE	45°	45°
NE by E	56.25°	56° 15′
E NE	67.5°	67° 30′
E by N	78.75°	78° 45′

32 Point Compass	Actual Degree	Degree on land compass or protractor
E	90°	0°
E by S	101.25°	78° 45′
E SE	112.5°	67° 30′
SE by E	123.75°	56° 15′
SE	135°	45°
SE by S	146.25°	33° 45′
SSE	157.5°	22° 30′
S by E	168.75°	11° 15′

New England Towns

While the Southern and New England land systems shared most of the same terminology, they differed fundamentally in that New England grants usually went to a group of men called town proprietors. Upon receipt of a block of land, these town proprietors surveyed parts of their large tract, apportioned out village home sites and field strips for themselves and others, and oversaw the subsequent disbursements of "divisions" of land until all the grant had passed into private ownership except for the town commons and local government lots. Thus, whereas the Southern grants to individuals created a rural landscape of scattered farms with very few towns, the New England grants created a society of villages.

The origin of the New England town extends back to the first settlers of Plymouth and Massachusetts Bay, where the Pilgrims and Puritans strove to establish a congregation-community uniting church and civil government into God's commonwealth. As new lands were needed to feed the growing population, groups of prospective settlers would petition a colony's government for land to establish a new town, praying to be constituted the official proprietors to distribute the land within the town. The town was a geographical unit extending beyond the village to some agreed boundaries with the neighboring towns. The early towns were irregularly shaped; the later ones tended to run six miles by six miles in size. Thus, the town bounds had to be established so that a formal grant could be issued to the proprietors. The religious fervor of Puritanism later declined, but the town form of the congregation-community survived and was carried throughout most of New England and even into eastern New York and northeastern New Jersey. There was, however, a pressing tendency for people to move out of the village to be nearer their fields, which led to the buying and exchanging of land parcels to consolidate property into farms.

The classic analysis of the origins of the New England town is Sumner Chilton Powell's *Puritan Village: The Formation of a New England Town*, a book with valuable English local sources on

32 Point Compass	Actual Degree	Degree on land compass or protractor
S	180°	0°
S by W	191.25°	11° 15′
S SW	202.5°	22° 30′
SW by S	213.75°	33° 45′
SW	225°	45°
SW by W	236.25°	56° 15′
W SW	247.5°	67° 30′
W by S	258.75°	78° 45′

32 Point Compass	Actual Degree	Degree on land compass or protractor
W	270°	0°
W by N	281.25°	78° 45′
W NW	292.5°	67° 30′
NW by W	303.75°	56° 15′
NW	315°	45°
NW by N	326.25°	33° 45′
N NW	337.5°	22° 30′
N by W	348.75°	11° 15′

Early surveys were often grossly inaccurate. An error of one link, or about eight inches, in three to five chains was considered normal.[2] According to Hughes, the 320-pole formula was widely used to survey along the shorelines. Two sides of a roughly rectangular survey (parallelogram) would extend into the woods approximately one mile or 320 poles (one pole equals 16.5 feet) and the sides parallel to the water measured a distance in poles half the total number of acres specified in the patent. The early surveys tended to measure in whole poles, and fractions were rarely used. Whenever the term "and thus into the woods" is used in an early patent, it indicates the 320-pole formula was used and the measurement is one mile. Since copying mistakes were common, it is wise to copy the full land descriptions. An illustration of this is the survey and plat made by George Washington on 30 March 1752 for Daniel Osborne of Frederick County, Virginia. The last call of the survey clearly states "N 65° W 100 poles," yet when it was platted, it was obvious the call should have been N 65° E 100 poles.[3]

Notes

[1] Sarah S. Hughes, *Surveyors and Statesmen: Land Measuring in Colonial Virginia* (Richmond, Va.: The Virginia Surveyors Foundation, Ltd. and the Virginia Association of Surveyors, 1979), Hughes quotes the English surveyor, John Love, who wrote in his work, *Geodaesia: or the Art of Surveying and Measuring of Land Made Easie* (London, 1688), about the problem of transferring a specified acreage and rectangular dimensions to a terrain cut through with creeks, marshes, and ridges." [p. 1] Hughes makes the point that since people were allowed to select their own land, it did not have to be contiguous to settled land nor be any regular shape. The irregular shapes show that people wanted to have the best land they could acquire within their patent bounds. (pp 4–5).

[2] "Changing Chains," at <www.surveyhistory.org/changing_chains.htm/>. Article reprinted from 1986 *Reflections*, a publication of First American Title Insurance Company. Printed in *Backsights* magazine published by Surveyors Historical Society. Viewed online 29 April 2004).

[3] George Washington, Land Survey for Daniel Osborne, Frederick County, Virginia, 30 March, 1752, Lilly Library, Manuscript Collections, University of Indiana, at <www.indiana.edu/~liblilly/history/history5.html>.

the origins of English immigrants.[19] The literature is accessible through David Grayson Allen's *In English Ways: The Movement of Societies and the Transferral of English Local Law and Custom to Massachusetts Bay in the Seventeenth Century*.[20] For colonial land history in New England, see Edward T. Price's "Dividing the Land: Early American Beginnings of Our Private Property Mosaic," and Roy Hidemichi Akagi's *The Town Proprietors of the New England Colonies: A Study of Their Development, Organization, Activities and Controversies, 1620–1770*.[21]

The New England town system has several implications for genealogists, starting with the need to determine which records are on the county level and which are on the town level. Early Massachusetts Bay towns recorded their own deeds until counties were created in 1643. Early towns on eastern Long Island also recorded their own deeds until the Duke of York's New York proprietary required registration in Suffolk County. Connecticut, Rhode Island, and Vermont recorded and still record deeds on the town level. Aside from deeds, the researcher should also check for early proprietor minutes on the town level. More generally, New England research requires that towns be treated as mini-counties. Thus, while counties are not as important as in the South, there are three levels of jurisdiction in New England—state, county, and town.

Features of Town Land Distribution

Some of the technical aspects of the New England land system have been well summarized by genealogist David Stoddard:

> A. *Commoners and Non-Commoners* . . . The term[s] "commoner" and "proprietor" are synonymous. "Proprietor" simply replaces "commoner" as the proper legal term.
>
> Commoners were originally those to whom the General Court [the legislature] had made a grant of land in common for settlement, very often without giving them entire control. They formed a quasi-corporation. The right of a commoner might be conveyed in a land

Creating a Plat

By Mary McCampbell Bell, CG

In order to plat a tract, one must understand the terminology:

- Metes are the angles of the property—in other words, they tell us how many degrees we must turn in a certain direction, such as North 69° West.
- Bounds are the boundary lines of the property. They tell us how far we must walk along that North 69° West angle before we either stop or turn in another direction. They are usually measured in poles/rods/perches, which all mean the same thing. Each pole/rod/perch contains 16½ feet.
- Courses, better known as "calls," are the compass directions from the beginning point on a boundary line to the end point of the same line (for example, N69°W to where the next call N39°W begins). They are the combined metes and bounds (for example, N69°W 160 poles).
- In order to find the correct beginning direction on our plat, we must have a constant marker that can always be found. This is our "anchor." Surveyors use a compass that shows magnetic north, and this is what we use as our "anchor" on our plat. The direction of north is always where we begin. Before placing a plat on a map, we need a geographic anchor on the map such as a road or creek. One of the best anchors are old fence lines. Many date from the original patent.

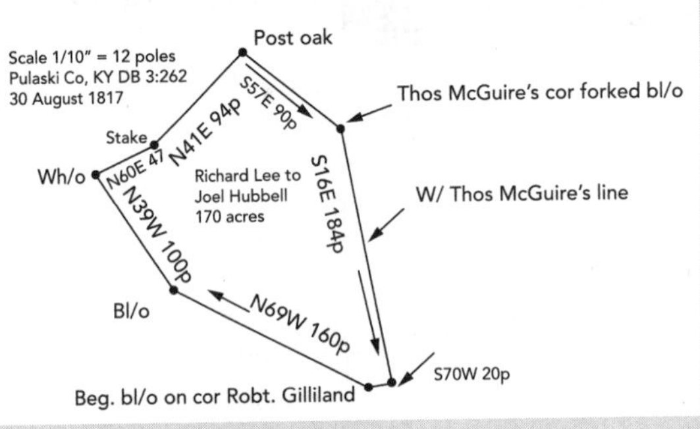

Platting Guidelines

- Before beginning to plat, read through the deed or patent and identify all the metes and bounds and descriptive matter.
- Underline the calls/courses (combination of corners, lines, and directions) and put a number by each one: (1) Beg. at bl/o on Robt Gilliland's corner and running with his line N69°W 160 poles.

a. The "corner/point" is where one starts or changes direction: "Beginning at" or "thence N390W."

b. The "line" or boundary tells us about the neighbors, waterways, and so forth: "With Thomas McGuire's line."

c. The "directions" are the number of compass degrees and number of poles/perches: "N69°W 160 poles."

- Using graph paper, always draw an arrow on the paper pointing towards north before you begin!
- Write down the scale! USGS 7.5 maps 1/10" = 12 poles (remember fractions can be rounded up or down).
- Always mark your beginning point on the plat such as "Beg. at..." followed by an arrow to indicate the direction.
- Always write the calls (such as N69°W 160p) inside the plat and the descriptive matter along a line outside the plat (such as "along Thomas McGuire's line" or the "post oak").

Measurements

1 mile = 80 chains = 320 poles, rods, or perches = 5,280 feet

1 chain = 4 poles, rods, or perches = 66 feet= 100 links

1 pole, rod, or perch = 25 links = 16½ feet.

1 link = 7.92 inches

Platting can be done with a protractor, a circular 360° compass, or a land measure compass divided into the four quadrants of 90° each. Graph paper is used to keep the plat on course. A ruler with the tenth scale is invaluable and is used by surveyors and engineers. The USGS Topographic maps are used for platting because the large scale allows us to see individual houses, barns, cemeteries, roads, and contour lines. They use the scale of 1:24,000. This means that 1 inch on the ruler equals 24,000 feet on the ground. 1/10th of an inch on the ruler equals 12 poles. There are 120 poles to the inch.

transaction or inherited and one who thus became entitled to a right was not necessarily entitled to vote in the town meetings when township privileges had been conferred upon the inhabitants. On the other hand, because a man was entitled to a vote in the town did not entitle him to a voice in the control of the common lands. . . . The land community and the political community were distinct and separate bodies.

The town could enter into transactions with the proprietors; and they in turn could make grants to the town. In plantations where the inhabitants were all commoners, the two bodies acted as one and there would be no "proprietors' records" kept. For instance, Groton, Mass., was settled in 1655, yet there are no proprietors' records until 1713.

As the population of the towns increased, it became necessary to protect the commoners' rights. Hampton, now in New Hampshire, is a good example: (1) 1641—Persons who were not freemen present at town meetings; (2) 1662—Voted "that no man be considered an inhabitant, or act in town affairs but he that hath one share at least of commonage, according to the first division"; (3) 1700—Voted that no one should vote unless a freeholder and none to vote to dispose of lands, unless he is a commoner. In towns such as these, the serious researcher will generally find separate proprietors' records either in a separate book or as the initial part of the first town book. . . .

Two ways existed for the satisfying of claims by non-commoners: (1) Increase the number of commoners; (2) Grant lands to newcomers without accompanying the rights to commonage, either to an individual by name or to all of a given class, such as Barnstable granting 4 acres to every widow.

B. *Division of Common Lands* . . . The valuation of a man's estate, made from the tax-list, was the principal basis of division (Haverhill, Ipswich, Dedham, Hartford, many Connecticut River towns, settlements along Long Island Sound).

C. *Restrictions Upon Alienation* . . . Great care was taken to preserve the original character of the community and to control its membership. A Connecticut law of 1659 declared no inhabitants shall make sale of house and lands until put forth to the town for approval; an item in Guilford, Connecticut, Town Book refers to no one being able to sell OR purchase unless by consent of the community; Watertown, Massachusetts, in 1638 had a provision "against selling town lots to forrainers."

D. *Common Field* . . . The proportions of land cultivated in common varied greatly throughout New England; largely based on necessity. Connecticut and Massachusetts laws gave authority to townsmen or selectmen, or, when there were none, to the major part of the freemen.

Common fields were found in most towns. They were formed: (1) Due to lack of means to fence separately; (2) Due to difficulty of fencing (land along the Connecticut River); (3) Due to convenience. Fences were maintained by each owner according to his share of land enclosed.

E. *Home Lots, Acre Rights, Pitches* . . . Home/house lots differed in size in different New England towns, and quite often in the same town; (1) Barnstable, 6 to 12 acres; (2) Haverhill, 5 to 22 acres; (3) Groton, 10 to 20 acres. They were often proportioned as to the "quality and estate" of the possessor. . . .

Acre rights or lots indicate the share owned by any one person in the common lands. It is entirely different from home/house lots. Value varied greatly. In Billerica a ten-acre lot or right in common land was equivalent to 113 acres of upland or twelve acres of meadow. In Groton there were sixty-acre rights; twenty-acre rights, and so forth. with 755 rights in all. A sixty-acre right would have entitled the owner one complete partition to 3242 acres of common land. Pitches are rights drawn in a division that entitled the drawer to lay out a lot of land in the commons wherever he might choose.[22]

Public-Domain States

The U.S. government has sold or given away more than 1 billion acres of land (not including Alaska). In the process it granted more than 5 million patents kept in 9,386 bound volumes in the Springfield, Virginia, office of the Bureau of Land Management (BLM). An even greater mass of records in the National Archives represents the paperwork granting those patents. Searching for the record of a particular land grant from the federal government requires contacting both the BLM and the National Archives. To know what to request means understanding something of how the federal government processed the paperwork.

Federal Land Grants

From 1776, when Congress promised land to German auxiliaries (sometimes incorrectly known as "Hessians"), and for a quarter of a century afterward, the U. S. Government experimented, mostly in Ohio, to find a workable public land policy. By 1803, when Ohio became a state, the major characteristics of the federal land system had been set:

1. The federal government, not the state, would dispose of the western lands, which the original states had ceded,

Georgia in 1802 being the last to surrender its western claims.

2. Before any grants were made, the Indian title had to be removed and the land surveyed in rectangular townships of six-mile squares. Some partial townships would exist due to the curvature of the earth.
3. The disposal of the vacant land would be handled through land offices located near settlers.
4. War service (at least prior to the Civil War) usually brought the veterans a right to free land.
5. Legally registered entry claims and military bounty land could usually be sold before a patent was obtained (homesteads could not).
6. Valid land titles obtained from previous French, Spanish, and British governments would be honored.

By 1880, Congress had passed more than 3,500 laws dealing with public lands. In summary, the federal government granted lands in seven broad categories:

Disposed Public Domain	Approximate Acreage
1. Sales and miscellaneous	300,000,000
2. Homesteads	285,000,000
3. Grants to states	225,000,000
4. Military bounty	73,000,000
5. Private land claims	22,000,000
6. Railroad grants	91,000,000
7. Timber culture, etc.	35,000,000
Total disposed	1,031,000,000
Remaining federal lands	411,000,000
State-owned lands	462,000,000
Total U.S. acreage	1,904,000,000[23]

Thus, the disposed public domain was more than 1 billion acres. It included all states west of the Mississippi except Texas and Hawaii, all states north of the Ohio River west of Pennsylvania, and the four Gulf states of Louisiana, Mississippi, Alabama, and Florida.

Much of the public domain was transferred to private or state title, though not so smoothly as a description of the system might suggest. Engineering Indian cessions was often slow and deceitful; white settlers lived for years on Indian land without any legal claims to the land they cleared and farmed; land speculators amassed doubtful legal claims which they petitioned Congress to make good; private land claims under foreign title were proven with fake documents and perjury; dry lands were purchased at cut-rate "swamp" prices; timber lands and cattle ranges were "homesteaded" by frontmen acting for timber and cattle companies; and mineral lands, such as the iron deposits of the Mesabi Range in Minnesota, were acquired through bogus entrymen. When the government allowed squatters first claim on lands (preemption rights), the neighbors bearing witness for each other might testify to earlier arrival dates than were true. In short, confusion and fraud were common. Just because the land-entry paperwork adheres to formula does not mean it presents the truth.

Clearly, good genealogy may require an understanding of frontier history. A good place to begin is in *Western Expansion, A History of the American Frontier* by Ray Allen Billington and Martin Ridge.[24] It is a masterful summary of American frontier history with an extensive bibliography. Other recommended histories of public lands:

Donaldson, Thomas. *The Public Domain: Its History with Statistics*. New York: Johnson Reprint Corp., 1970 reprint of 1884 GPO original. House Misc. Doc. 45 pt. 4, 47th Cong., 2nd Sess.

Gates, Paul W. *History of Public Land Law Development*. Reprint. Arno Press, 1979. Robbins, Roy Marvin. *Our Landed Heritage: The Public Domain, 1776–1970*. 2nd ed. Lincoln: University of Nebraska Press, 1976.

Rohrbough, Malcolm J. *The Land Office Business: The Settlement and Administration of American Public Lands, 1789–1837*. Belmont, Calif.: Wadsworth Publishing Co., 1990.

Treat, Payson Jackson. *The National Land System, 1785–1820*. New York: E. B. Treat, 1910; reprint, William S. Hein & Co., 2003.

An older, though still useful work, is Lawrence B. Lee's "American Public Land History: A Review Essay."[25] A more general work is *Public Land Bibliography*, published by the Bureau of Land Management.[26] To go deeper into the literature, access to the library catalogs of two major government agencies is online. The National Agricultural Library search database is at <http://agricola.nal.usda.gov/> and collections at the United States Geological Survey Library may be searched at <http://library.usgs.gov/>. In 1879, Congress created the U.S. Public Land Commission to take stock of past and future land policies. In addition to its general report and Donaldson's 1,500-page history (cited above), the commission also compiled 1,300 pages of U.S. land laws in *Laws of the United States of a Local or Temporary Character and Exhibiting the Entire Legislation of Congress Upon Which the Public Land Titles in Each State and Territory Have Depended*, published by the U.S. Public Land Commission.[27]

In short, the subject of United States land law history is voluminous. In summary: Public domain lands were first sold by auction in New York City in 1787 and in Pittsburgh in 1796 but not successfully. Then, on-the-spot local land offices were created, the earliest in Ohio in 1800—the first of 362 land districts to span the continent. Newly opened lands were offered at auction, then at a set minimum price—$2 an acre from 1796 to 1820. Credit was allowed on ever-easier terms, and the minimum tract size was reduced from 640 to 320 acres. Overextension of credit and the resulting panic of 1819 caused the elimination of long-term credit in favor of eighty-acre minimums at $1.25 an acre. Congress passed many relief acts for those who still owed money under the abolished credit system, and it also gave general preemption rights in 1841.

From the 1820s, Congress became increasingly generous in giving away lands to finance military wagon roads (from 1823), canals (1827), river improvement (1828), swamp reclamation (1849), railroads (1850), colleges (1862), and desert reclamation (1894). In 1832, minimum purchases dropped to forty acres, and from 1842 to 1853, land was donated to early settlers in Florida, Oregon/Washington, and New Mexico/Arizona. The famous 1862 Homestead Act gave a settler 160 acres (eighty within railroad grant areas) for living on the land for five years and improving it. The donation and homestead acts required the claimant to show U.S. citizenship or an already-filed declaration of intent to become a citizen, valuable information for a genealogist. Later laws increased homestead acreage in arid areas, including the Desert Land Act of 1877 for 640 acres in a dozen Western states; the Kincaid Act of 1904 for 640 acres in western Nebraska; the Enlarged Homestead Act of 1909 for 320 acres in seven Mountain West states; and the Stock-Raising Homestead Act of 1916 for 640 acres. The Homestead Act was in effect until 1986 (the 1976 repeal granted a ten-year extension on claims in Alaska). America's last homesteader was a Vietnam veteran and native Californian named Kenneth Deardorff. In 1974 he filed a homestead claim on 80 acres of land in southwestern Alaska. He fulfilled all requirements in 1979 and received a patent in May 1988.[28] General cash sales and preemption rights had been stopped in 1891, though some sales and much leasing of federal mineral and grazing lands continue to the present.

As always, the researcher should understand the paperwork flow. After the Indian title was extinguished and private land claims, if any, were adjudicated and surveyed, the surveyor-general's office established a principal meridian and baseline, then surveyed at six-mile intervals to create townships of thirty-six sections, each a mile square. The manner of describing these resulting squares is the legal description, illustrated in figures 10-1 and 10-2. Because many states have more than one principal meridian, the meridians are part of the legal description—for example, NW 1/4 of SE 1/4, Sec. 9, T13S, R11E, 6th P.M. The standard descriptive text on the surveying system, *The GlO Survey Primer (circa 1921)*, is online at <www.glorecords.blm.gov/Visitors/PLSS>. A brief but well-done work in print is *Ohio Lands: A Short History*.[29]

Once the land was surveyed and could be legally described, a local land office was opened, the auction was held, and land was available at the minimum price to claimants/entrymen who paid a credit installment (before 1820) or a down payment on a cash purchase. In addition to cash, applicants could obtain land through a variety of congressional acts which allowed for preemption (the opportunity for "squatters" to purchase land they had occupied and improved); donation (various acts granting certain land to qualifying settlers in states such as Arkansas, Florida, Oregon, and Washington); homestead, mineral, timber culture, and desert land (land given to qualified persons who could demonstrate compliance to the conditions of a particular act); and bounty warrants or scrip. Each land office was run jointly by two officials: a registrar, who recorded entries and kept track of which tracts were claimed or still open, and a receiver, who handled the money. These officials kept daily journals and account ledgers and sent periodic summaries to the national headquarters—first the Treasury Department and, from 1812, the newly created General Land Office (GLO). The local land office kept a separate file for each entry and two indexes by area: (1) the tract book, which was a written description of each entry on sheets arranged by township and range and (2) a township plat, which was a map of entries for each township showing patented tracts.

Once the entryman had fulfilled the requirements of purchase or homesteading, the local officials sent the case file (the entryman's paperwork and the final certificate of entitlement to a patent) to GLO headquarters in Washington, D.C., which confirmed that all paperwork was in order and issued a patent (first-title deed) transferring the land from the government to the private individual (or to the states, railroads, canal companies, and so forth). The GLO headquarters recorded chronologically a copy of the patent in a bound volume by state and district and stored the land-entry case file. After 30 June 1908, patents were recorded chronologically in one continuous, national series regardless of state. This series is indexed for all patentees. The new owner may then have had the patent recorded in the county deed book, or the state may have had an agreement with the GLO that the appropriate county and state authorities would be automatically informed of all patents, because the new lands were often exempt from property taxes for a set term, such as five years.

Homestead case files tend to be richer in genealogical information than the cash, credit, and bounty-warrant files. A homestead final certificate file usually includes the homestead application, certificate of publication of intention to complete the claim, final proof of homesteading (testimony from the claimant and his or her witnesses), and a final document authorizing issuance of a patent (see figure 10-3). A certified copy of the naturalization papers, if needed for the application, may be present. The final proof documents give the claimant's name, age, and post office address, describe the tract and the house, date the establishment of residence, give the number and relationship of the members of the family, and note citizenship, crops, acres under cultivation, and testimony of witnesses. For illustrations of some of these documents and a good overview of homestead records, see E. Wade Hone's *Land and Property Research in the United States*.[30]

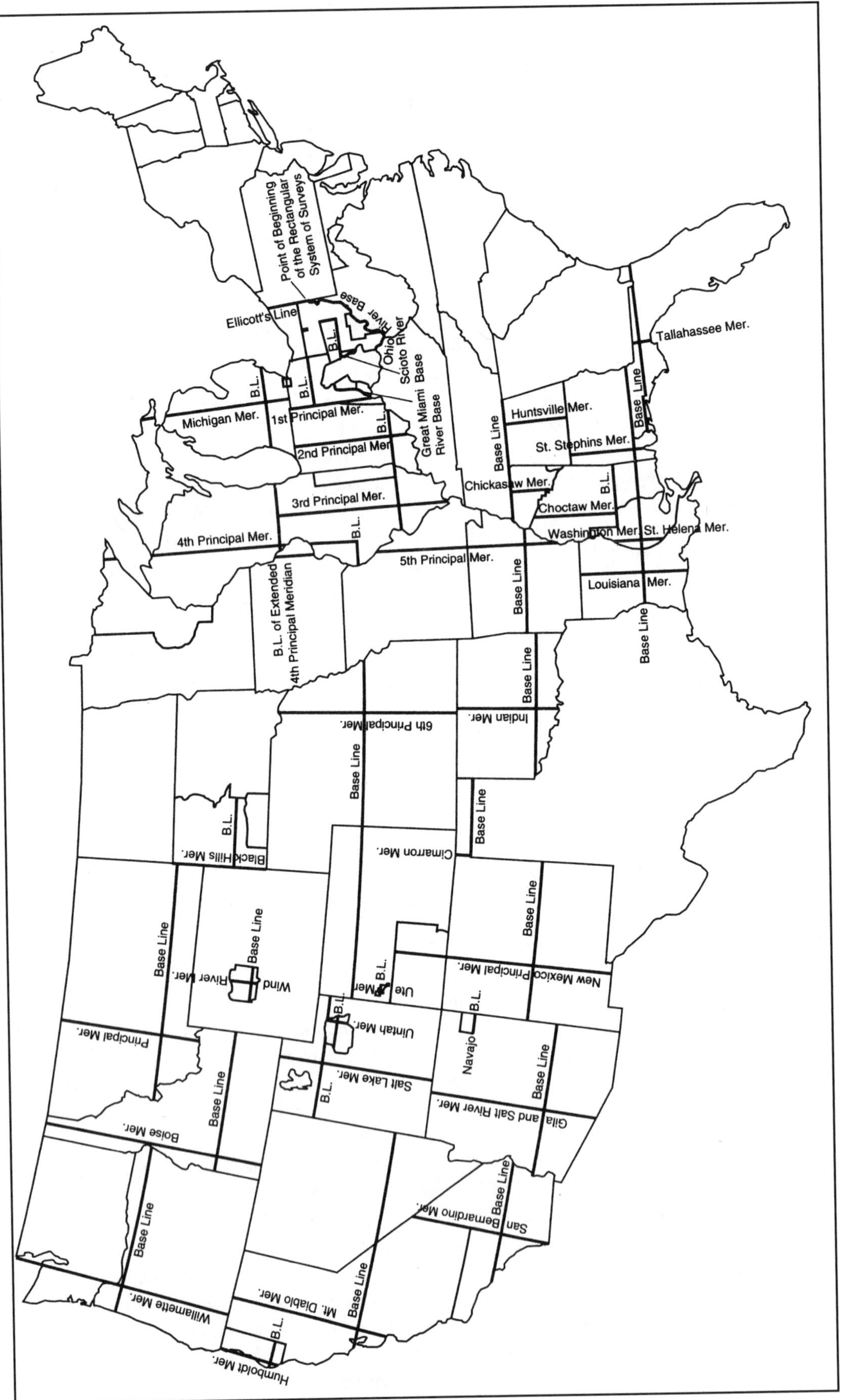

Figure 10-1. The principal meridians and baselines used to survey in the public land states. The points of intersection are "initial points." See figure 12-3. From E. Wade Hone, *Land and Property Research in the United States* (Salt Lake City: Ancestry, 1997 p 104).

Not all claims—homestead and otherwise—were brought to patent. If the entryman did not obtain title by the deadline for the final charges or complete the homestead residency of five years, then the entry claim was canceled and stored, now available from the National Archives and Records Administration, Washington, DC 20408. However, some went to state and regional federal archives. For the genealogist, these canceled case files, traceable through the tract books (see following), are valuable records of an ancestor's life and sometimes give clues about why the claim was never completed. The number of canceled entries is large:

	Entries	Patents	Percent Canceled
Homestead Act	1,968,264	783,053	60.2
Timber Act	290,300	67,382	76.8
Desert Land Act	87,247	23,984	72.5

More than 1,185,000 homestead entries were never patented but should have files containing some of the same information as patented case files, plus a date and reason for the cancellation.

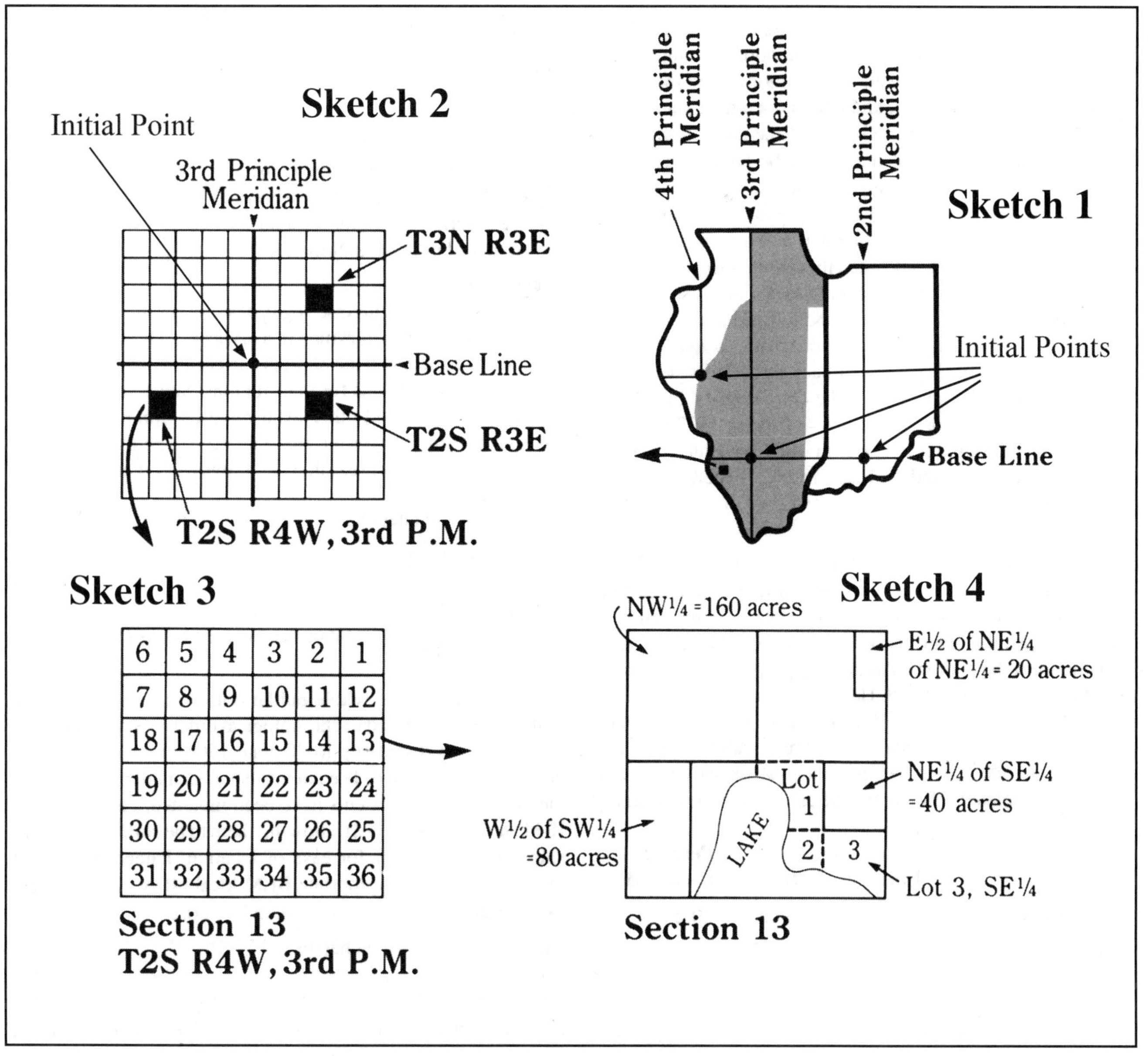

Figure 10-2. Most legal descriptions of a parcel of land include the principal meridian, such as "3rd p.m.," shown in sketch 1, top right. From the initial point, ranges are numbered as "east" or "west" of the principal meridian and townships are numbered as "north" or "south" of the baseline (see sketch 2, top left). Each township has 36 sections (sketch 3, lower left) and each section is further reduced (sketch 4, lower right) to describe and locate the parcel.

Bureau of Land Management (BLM)

In 1946, the GLO and the Grazing Service were consolidated into the Bureau of Land Management (BLM), which today holds many GLO records or is the agency title under which the National Archives and its regional branches store GLO records—Record Group 49. The BLM is divided into eastern and western states. Its working records—the tract books, plats, and patents—for all the eastern states are at the Eastern States Office, 7450 Boston Blvd., Springfield, VA 22153. The eastern states comprise all public-domain states east of the Mississippi River and all states on the river's west bank (Louisiana to Minnesota). Most western states have their own offices; however, Washington's is with the Portland, Oregon, office, and the Great Plains states are under adjoining states farther west. The local land offices and GLO headquarters made duplicate tract and plat books, so the researcher often has a choice of several repositories for microfilm or original records (see the summary at the end of this chapter).

Each step of the process from survey to patent has left records potentially helpful to genealogists:

Survey Plats and Field Notes

Government surveys were made prior to the allocation of public land. Surveyors began in Ohio and moved west as each territory or area was opened for settlement. Survey plats are drawings of boundaries. Survey field notes describe land formations and conditions. Plats and notes may include specific, crude drawings of homes and outbuildings on the property and in some instances give the names of settlers living in the area surveyed. The cadastral survey field notes and township plats for twenty-five of the thirty public domain states surveyed under the rectangular system of surveys are located in the Eastern States Office of the BLM (Ohio, Indiana, Illinois, Iowa, and Missouri are located in the National Archives).[31] The plats have been microfilmed and are usually deposited in the same locations as the tract books. Similar records may be in the state's land office (most common), the state archive, or the appropriate regional federal archive (see "Summary of Land Records by State," at the end of this chapter). Some states have made their plats and field notes available as scanned images for online viewing. The federal township plats for Illinois have been scanned and are available for viewing at <http://landplats.ilsos.net/Flash/FTP_Illinois.html>. Wisconsin's field notes are searchable by legal description at <http://libtext.library.wisc.edu/SurveyNotes/Use.html>.

Tract Books

Tract books record the names of the land entryman (and in some areas, subsequent buyers), a description of the land and the number of acres, the type and date of entry, and the patent number. Tract books are arranged by legal description, i.e., geographical location. The tract books may reveal the names of claimants and patentees who, for whatever reason, do not appear in the Bureau of Land Management's online index, explained below.[32] To expedite a search, determine the land office or the county where land was patented (see "Obtaining a Legal Description," which follows). These books have been microfilmed, and the appropriate eastern (Eastern States Office) or western states offices have sets for their regions. The Family History Library in Salt Lake City and some state archives, regional archives, and other local research libraries also have tract books on microfilm.

Patents

Patents transfer land ownership from the U.S. government to a private party. Patents are the first records in a chain of title to a piece of property (see figure 10-4). The originals or duplicates for the whole public domain are in the Eastern States Office of the BLM. The patent documents result primarily from cash entries, homestead and military bounty land warrants. Each patent document has a primary identification number in the upper left-hand corner, the name of the patentee, the land office that handled the transaction, a full legal description of the property, and a signature and date reflecting the president of the United States of America in office at the time of purchase (only a very few early patents or certificates issued to the patentee and found among family memorabilia, were actually signed by a president).

Finding Patents

General Land Office - Automated Records System (GLO-ARS)

As March 2006, more than 4.2 million documents from before 1 July, 1908, mostly cash and homestead patents issued by the United States, can be viewed online at the Bureau of Land Management's excellent website <www.glorecords.blm.gov>. Federal patents dating from the late 1780s to 1 July 1908 have been scanned and indexed for the eastern states of Alabama, Arkansas, Florida, Illinois, Indiana, Louisiana, Michigan, Minnesota, Mississippi, Missouri, Ohio, and Wisconsin. The cash and homestead entries for Iowa (1820–1908) should be completed in 2006.

For the western states, most of the pre-July 1908 data is already in the database. As the data is verified against the land patent certificate for accuracy, the image is connected to the index entry. Automation of the remainder of the records in BLM possession, notably the serial patents (1 July, 1908 and later) continues. Serial patents are filed numerically instead of by state, thus covering the eastern and the western public land states. Project completion of the remaining two million records is expected by 2010. More information on the GLO-ARS is available from 7450 Boston Blvd., Springfield, VA 22153; telephone (703) 440-1600; or at <www.glorecords.blm.gov>. Users should read introductory materials carefully to take advantage of the full range of search methods.

Figure 10-3. The 1897 affidavit of Virgil W. [Wyatt] Earp (right) states he has met the military service requirement to homestead under the Soldiers' and Sailors' Homestead Act of June 8, 1872. This act allowed honorably discharged soldiers and sailors with at least 90 days of service to apply up to four years of their service towards the settlement requirement (five years) of the Homestead Act of 1862.

HOMESTEAD PROOF—TESTIMONY OF CLAIMANT.

Virgil W. Earp, being called as a witness in his own behalf in support of homestead entry, No. 1449, for SW¼ SE¼ - Sec. 17 - and N½ NE¼ & SE¼ NE¼ Sec. 20, 12 N. R. 4 W., testifies as follows:

Ques. 1.—What is your name, age, and post-office address?

Ans. Virgil W. Earp - 57 years old Kirkland Az.

Ques. 2.—Are you a *native-born* citizen of the United States, and if so, in what State or Territory were you born?*

Ans. I am Born in State Kentucky

Ques. 3.—Are you the identical person who made homestead entry, No. 1449, at the Prescott, Arizona land office on the 5 day of Jany, 1898, and what is the true description of the land now claimed by you?

Ans. I am. SW¼ SE¼ - Sec. 17 and N½ NE¼ and SE¼ NE¼ - Sec. 20 - 12 N. R. 4 W.

Ques. 4.—When was your house built on the land and when did you establish actual residence therein? (Describe said house and other improvements which you have placed on the land, giving total value thereof.)

Ans. January - 1 - 1898 - Established actual residence then. House - 12x18 - Adobe. House frame 14x20 - 2 rooms - Stable - Well - Corral - about 2 acres under wire fence - Value - about $200.

Ques. 5.—Of whom does your family consist; and have you and your family resided continuously on the land since first establishing residence thereon? (If unmarried, state the fact.)

Ans. Myself and wife. Yes.

Ques. 6.—For what period or periods have you been absent from the homestead since making settlement, and for what purpose; and if temporarily absent, did your family reside upon and cultivate the land during such absence?

Ans. I was absent once for 30 days to see a sick relation. My wife resided on the homestead

Ques. 7.—How much of the land have you cultivated each season, and for how many seasons have you raised crops thereon?

Ans. From 2 to 3 acres. One season. Land most valuable for grazing

Ques. 8.—Is your present claim within the limits of an incorporated town or selected site of a city or town, or used in any way for trade and business?

Ans. No Sir.

Ques. 9.—What is the character of the land? Is it timber, mountainous, prairie, grazing, or ordinary agricultural land? State its kind and quality, and for what purpose it is most valuable.

Ans. Grazing Land, Adobe Poor Quality. Most valuable for grazing

Ques. 10.—Are there any indications of coal, salines, or minerals of any kind on the land? (If so, describe what they are, and state whether the land is more valuable for agricultural than for mineral purposes.)

Ans. Nothing of the kind

Ques. 11.—Have you ever made any other homestead entry? (If so, describe the same.)

Ans. No Sir.

Ques. 12.—Have you sold, conveyed, or mortgaged any portion of the land; and if so, to whom and for what purpose?

Ans. No Sir.

Ques. 13.—Have you any personal property of any kind elsewhere than on this claim? (If so, describe the same, and state where the same is kept.)

Ans. Horses and cattle running on the range

Ques. 14.—Describe by legal subdivisions, or by number, kind of entry, and office where made, any other entry or filing (not mineral), made by you since August 30, 1890.

Ans. Never made any

(Sign plainly with full christian name.) Virgil W Earp

*(In case the party is of foreign birth a certified transcript from the court records of his declaration of intention to become a citizen, or of his naturalization, or a copy thereof, certified by the officer taking this proof, must be filed with the case. Evidence of *naturalization* is only required in final (*five-year*) homestead cases.)

Land-Entry Case Files

The finding of a patent suggests there is an associated case file. Case files (except for some canceled files never sent to GLO headquarters) are held at the Old Military and Civil Records, National Archives and Records Administration. The contents of these files depend in part on how the land was patented: as cash, credit, military bounty land, preemption (a type of cash file), donation, homestead, or mineral, timber culture, or desert land. Case files that document cash or credit purchases may have the receipt(s) for payment. A file created for a purchase under the Homestead Act of 1862 may include the entryman's declaration of intent or final naturalization papers, supporting documents and witness testimonies, bounty-land warrants (if used in lieu of cash) or preemption documents (if used for homestead in lieu of cash), and declarations of intent or final naturalization papers (which may have been submitted to satisfy homestead requirements). The files are arranged by the act which provided for the type of patenting, the state and land district from which the property was purchased, and thereunder numerically. The patent (see "Finding Patents," above), or tract book (see "Obtaining a Legal Description," following) will provide the land district, document number, and date of purchase. This information, and the patent number, must accompany the request for the case file. The files may be ordered online or by mail from the National Archives, Washington, DC 20408; e-mail <inquire@nara.gov>; or order online from <www.archives.gov/research_room>. Instructions are on the GLO-ARS website.

Unindexed Patents: Legal Description

The legal description is the key to locating an unindexed patent. There are three ways to find the legal description. (1) Search the tract books. See appendix A, "Tract Book and Township Plat Map Guide to Federal Land States" in Hone's *Land and Property Research.*[33] (2) Locate the patent recorded in a deed book (the grantor will be the U.S. government) or a reference to the tract in a subsequent deed. (3) Calculate the legal description from a historical atlas. These historical atlases are often called plat books because they featured land ownership plat maps. Some good discussion concerning these atlases is in Richard W. Stephenson's *Land Ownership Maps*, and in the *List of Geographical Atlases in the Library of Congress* published by the Library of Congress.[34] A number of maps have been reproduced on microfiche from the Library of Congress. Libraries which hold the microfiche set generally catalogue it as LC G&M Land Ownership Maps (1983). Historical atlases—and subscription county histories, for that matter—were a Midwestern phenomenon, which makes especially valuable the Newberry Library, *Checklist of Printed Maps of the Middle West to 1900*, which lists pre-1900 plat maps and plat books for the states of Illinois, Indiana, Iowa, Kansas, Michigan, Minnesota, Missouri, Nebraska, North Dakota, Ohio, South Dakota, and Wisconsin.[35]

The Homestead Act of 1862

The Homestead Act of 1862 (12 Stat. 392, effective January 1, 1873) provided for the taking up of one quarter section (160 acres) or a less quantity of unappropriated public lands by a person meeting the following provisions:

- Any person who is the head of a family, or who has arrived at the age of twenty-one years (did not have to be twenty-one if served not less than fourteen days in the Army or Navy of the United States (sections 1, 6).
- Is a citizen of the United States or have filed his declaration of intention to become such (section 1).
- Who has never borne arms against the United States Government or given aid and comfort to its enemies (amended January 1, 1867 to allow Confederate veterans to homestead).
- Land is for the purpose of actual settlement and cultivation (section 2).
- May enter (record with the land office registrar) the land upon payment of $10 (section 2).
- No land or lands acquired under the provisions of this act shall in any event become liable to the satisfaction of any debt or debts contracted prior to the issuing of the patent (section 4).

The patent was to be issued only after five years of entry (or within two years thereafter) and the applicant had to prove settlement or cultivation (no periods of absence more than six months). Provisions were made in case of the death of the homesteader (see section 2). Source: Appendix to the Congressional Globe, 37th Congress, 2nd Session Laws of the United States, page 352 (May 20, 1862), Chap. LXXV. An Act to secure Homesteads to Actual Settlers on the Public Domain; at <http://memory. loc.gov/cgi-bin/ampage?collId=llcg&filename=061/llcg061.db&recNum=913>. See figure 10-3.

Figure 10-4. Daniel Kinard's 1849 patent is an example of a typical cash-entry sale. Patents give the patentee's residence, the legal description of the parcel(s), the certificate number (needed to order the case file) and the date of purchase.

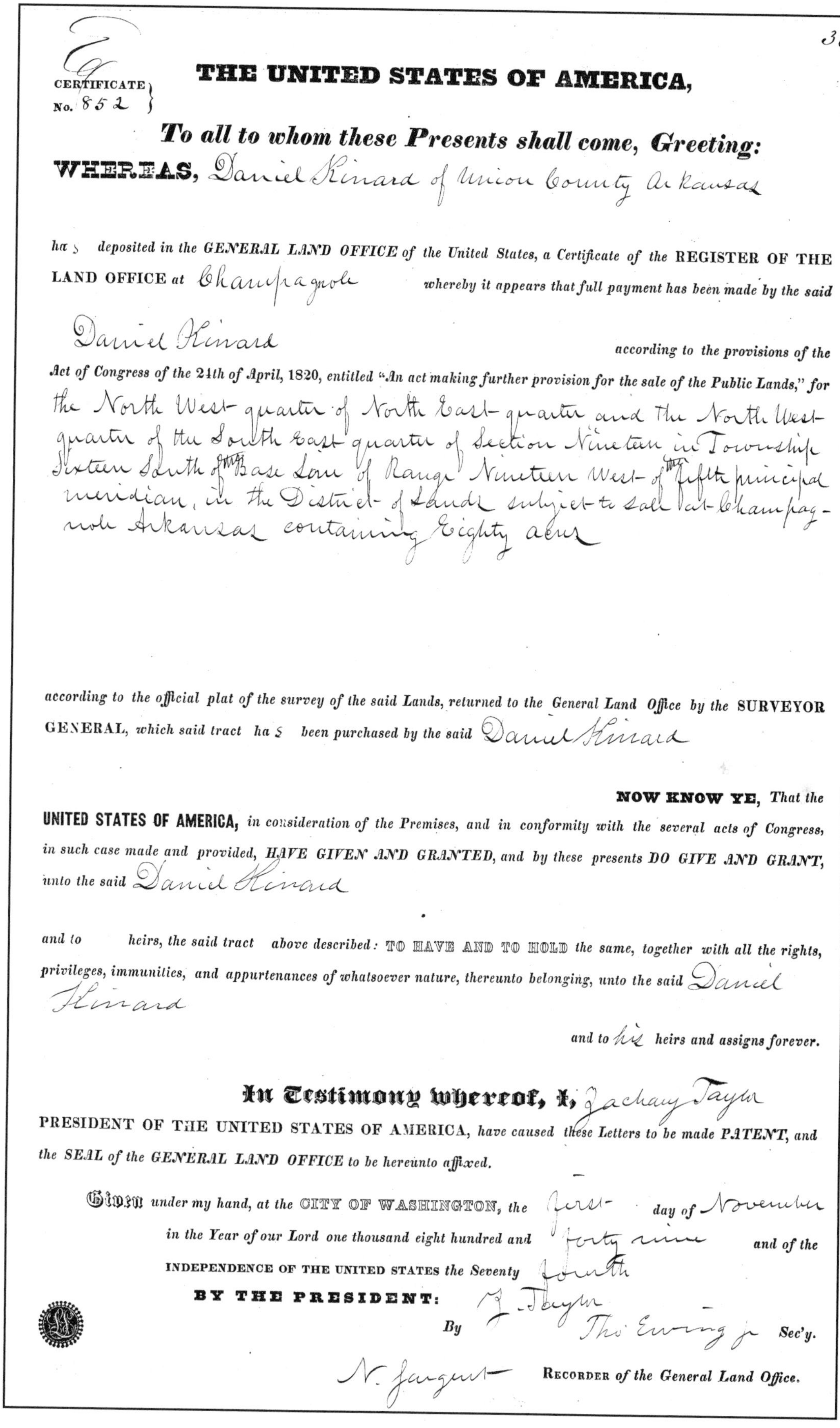

30

CERTIFICATE No. 852

THE UNITED STATES OF AMERICA,

To all to whom these Presents shall come, Greeting:

WHEREAS, Daniel Kinard of Union County Arkansas

has deposited in the GENERAL LAND OFFICE of the United States, a Certificate of the REGISTER OF THE LAND OFFICE at Champagnole whereby it appears that full payment has been made by the said Daniel Kinard according to the provisions of the Act of Congress of the 24th of April, 1820, entitled "An act making further provision for the sale of the Public Lands," for the North West quarter of North East quarter and the North West quarter of the South East quarter of Section Nineteen in Township Sixteen South of the Base Line of Range Nineteen West of the fifth principal meridian, in the District of Lands subject to sale at Champagnole Arkansas containing Eighty acres

according to the official plat of the survey of the said Lands, returned to the General Land Office by the SURVEYOR GENERAL, which said tract has been purchased by the said Daniel Kinard

NOW KNOW YE, That the UNITED STATES OF AMERICA, in consideration of the Premises, and in conformity with the several acts of Congress, in such case made and provided, HAVE GIVEN AND GRANTED, and by these presents DO GIVE AND GRANT, unto the said Daniel Kinard

and to heirs, the said tract above described: TO HAVE AND TO HOLD the same, together with all the rights, privileges, immunities, and appurtenances of whatsoever nature, thereunto belonging, unto the said Daniel Kinard

and to his heirs and assigns forever.

In Testimony whereof, I, Zachary Taylor PRESIDENT OF THE UNITED STATES OF AMERICA, have caused these Letters to be made PATENT, and the SEAL of the GENERAL LAND OFFICE to be hereunto affixed.

Given under my hand, at the CITY OF WASHINGTON, the first day of November in the Year of our Lord one thousand eight hundred and forty nine and of the INDEPENDENCE OF THE UNITED STATES the Seventy fourth

BY THE PRESIDENT: Z. Taylor

By Tho. Ewing jr Sec'y.

N. Sargent RECORDER of the General Land Office.

In 2005, Arphax Publishing Co. of Norman, Oklahoma <www.arphax.com> began producing county maps listing original patentees and their year of purchase. These "patent maps" are produced in two editions, Homesteads and Deluxe. The latter adds a road and a geographical feature map for each Congressional township. Indexes to names of patentees makes these an extremely useful tool for researchers (see figure 10-5).

Indian Reservations and Allotments

From 1830 to 1934, the government dissolved many Indian reservations by first allotting each Indian a tract of land, then selling the remainder. The records of such allotments are voluminous, and many have been microfilmed as Bureau of Indian Affairs agency records (Record Group 75). For instance, the records of the Winnebago Agency, Nebraska, are in the National Archives–Central Plains Region in Kansas City, Missouri, and include land sales, 1902–10; Santee acknowledgments of allotments, 1885; lists of Ponca and Santee tribe members never receiving allotments, 1936–41, and so forth.

In 1855, Congress extended military bounty land laws to Indians, entitling veterans from the Revolutionary War and the Indian Wars of 1818 and 1836 to warrants that could be exchanged for public lands. A few earlier acts had specified bounty lands for Indians, but this act marked the first time land was made available on a large scale. Finding applications is explained in Mary Francis Morrow's "Indian Bounty Land Applications."[36]

The National Archives has maps pertaining to American Indians, mostly in the western United States, circa 1800–1944. A substantial number of these maps show the names of individuals within the boundaries of the lands granted or allotted to them. Considerable place name information also appears on these maps. A card index provides access to these maps by state, thereunder by tribe or reservation.[37]

Preemption Rights

The problem of settlers claiming land before surveyors arrived was a very pressing one that Congress attempted to solve by preemption rights. Despite passing many different preemption acts before 1840, Congress did not seem to address the issue to the satisfaction of settlers before the 1841 act.[38] Claims clubs, which were private associations sworn to enforce their members' claims when local land was offered for sale or homesteading, sprang up in various areas and were especially numerous and active in Iowa and Minnesota and the adjoining states to the west. Often armed and intimidating, members would attend land

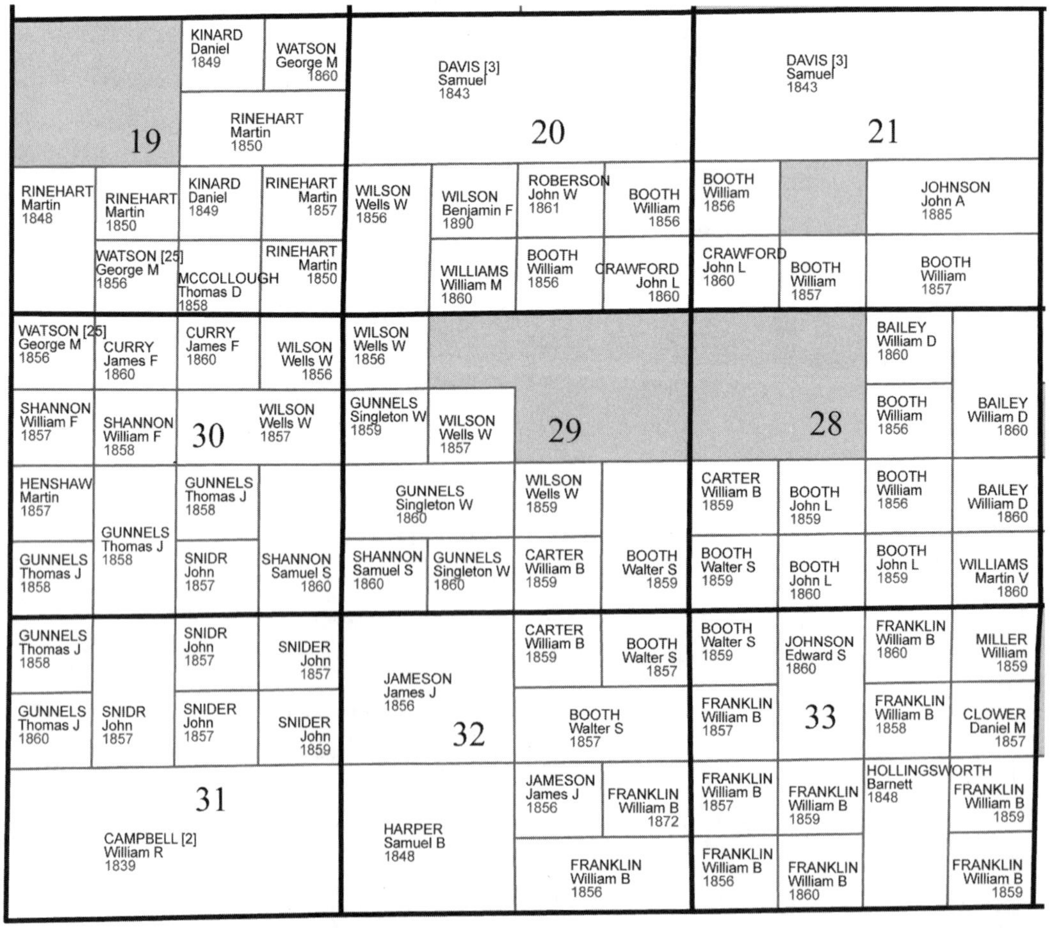

Figure 10-5. This map of T16S R9W in what is now Columbia County, Arkansas (established 1852 from Union County) shows Daniel Kinard's two parcels in section 19. Because the map gives names and purchase dates for all federal patents, Kinard's "neighborhood" can be reconstructed for various years. Township map from *Family Maps of Columbia County, Arkansas, Deluxe Edition* (Norman, Okla.: Arphax Publishing Co., 2005). Used with permission.

office auctions as a group to convince non-members not to enter lands the members claimed. Such clubs were often quite formal in organization and kept records, some of which have survived and may be at an area historical society. A record book (1864–65) of the Prickly Pear Valley Club for the Protection of Claims or Ranches is at the Library and Archives Department of the Montana Historical Society in Helena. It gives resolutions and a register of claims.

At its best, preemption offered only first rights of purchase. Preemption records, which are housed at the National Archives, are not indexed. They will appear in land entry case files, but finding them requires a legal description or the name of the individual who ultimately received the federal land patent. Either piece of information may be obtained by searching the original entries in the appropriate tract book, then using the information (legal description or name) to search the GLO-ARS database and then order the land entry case file.

Titles to State Lands

The land offices of public domain states will not be described here. These states received title to large acreage from the federal government and in turn sold or leased it to individuals. These records are in state land offices and archives. If you suspect that your ancestor had land dealings with a state, you can write either the state archive or the state secretary of state's office to determine the location of the records. In many states, they are still held by the equivalent of a state land commissioner or by a state land board (as in Colorado).

Private Land Claims

There was a special type of federal land grant called the private land claim, wherein the American government recognized as valid certain land grants made by the earlier French, Spanish, and British governments in areas acquired by the United States after the American Revolution. These areas were the Old Northwest north of the Ohio River, the Gulf states from Florida to Louisiana, the tier of states on the west bank of the Mississippi, and the Spanish Southwest from New Mexico to California, but not including Texas.

Sometimes the foreign legal titles were quite old and meticulously documented; often they were vague claims without clear bounds. Near villages it was common to find communal fields divided into long, individually owned arable strips surrounded by a communally maintained fence. Also characteristic, though not universal, were the "long lots"—narrow, adjoining tracts, each a few hundred feet wide, along a road or river and each running far back into the woods or prairie, sometimes a mile or more. The French and Spanish authorities also made larger grants, such as the square leagues common in Texas and the rancheros in California. Barring the usual losses, the Spanish and French administrations usually kept adequate records, and land titles were recorded and preserved.

The Texas General Land Office today has a series of sixty-nine volumes of Spanish and Mexican records. (See chapter 17, "Hispanic Research," for a discussion of Hispanic records.) The Spanish land system is discussed in detail for Texas, New Mexico (with Colorado), Arizona, and California in Henry Putney Beers's *Spanish & Mexican Records of the American Southwest: A Bibliographical Guide to Archive and Manuscript Sources*.[39]

When the U.S. government assumed control of areas containing Spanish and French grants, it had to create private land claims commissions to separate the authentic and legal titles from the fraudulent and dubious. (It is said that nine hundred Kaskaskia, Illinois, claims were perjured.)[40] In addition to land claims commissions, standing committees were appointed in the House of Representatives and the Senate of the United States. Prior to the Civil War, the records focus most heavily on attempts by individuals to confirm land titles in what are now the states of Louisiana, Missouri, Mississippi, Arkansas, Illinois, Michigan, and Iowa—areas that were formerly French and/or Spanish—and Florida, which included lands under either Spanish or British grants. After the Civil War, the committees were occupied with claims concerning former Mexican lands from the New Mexico Territory (present states of New Mexico and Arizona) to California.[41] By international law, the new government was obliged to recognize the valid property titles of the previous regime. Validation was not an easy, nor a quick, process. Pursuit of claims by petitioners sometimes lasted decades. Richard W. Meade, his wife and his descendants, labored for over 100 years to obtain satisfaction of his 1803 claim against Spain which had been assumed by the United States under a treaty. Members of the Meade family submitted claims in every Congress between the 16th and the 52nd (1819–93) except for the 17th and 38th, and they continued to pursue settlement until at least 1911.[42]

The private land claims ruled valid by the claims commissions of the U.S. state and federal courts are first-title deeds surveyed outside the regular federal system of townships and ranges. For example, on figure 10-6, a survey of Vincennes, Indiana, the federal survey lines stop at the irregular lots and tracts of the private land claims of the old French outpost called Vincennes Common. Even today, the legal titles run back to the confirmed first-title patents of the Vincennes private claims validated by the governor of the Northwest Territory, as directed by a Congressional resolution of 1788. The legal description of this land is not in terms of sections, townships, and ranges, but in terms of the lot numbers the governor assigned to the validated and surveyed private land claims at Vincennes. The general system of private land claims, however, did not always run smoothly. Some perfectly good pre American titles were not presented to claims commissions, engendering litigation much later.

"Private land claims" can also refer to the claims directly presented to Congress for private relief. These papers could be in different archives, depending on the administrative route taken. Claims to 1837 are recorded in *The American State Papers, Class VIII, Public Lands* and *The American State Papers, Class IX, Claims* and are indexed in Phillip W. McMullin's *Grassroots of America*.[43] The National Archives has congressional records, case files, and plat maps of private claims. According to the *Guide to Genealogical Research in the National Archives*,

> Originals of the congressional committee reports to Congress on private land claims are among the Records of the U.S. Senate, Record Group 46, and the Records of the U.S. House of Representatives, Record Group 233. They are filed by session of Congress, thereunder by name of committee, and thereunder chronologically.
>
> Committee reports on individual land claims considered from 1826 to 1876 by the two congressional committees on private land claims are collected and published in *Reports of the Committees on Private Land Claims of the Senate and House of Representatives*, 2 vols. (45th Cong., 3d sess. Misc. Doc. 81, serial 1836). Each volume is indexed by name of claimant or subject, but many names were omitted. Also available is an "Index to Reports of Committee on Private Land Claims, House of Representatives" on pages 5–20 of *House Index to Committee Reports* by T.H. McKee (Y1.3:C73/2). The Congressional Serial Set provides digested summaries and alphabetical lists of private claims presented to the U.S. Congress from the 1st to the 60th Congress (1789–1909).[44]

Online Access to Private Land Claim Documentation

Ancestry.com offers at least two databases of private land claims: U.S. House of Representative Private Claims, Vol. 1 and Land Claims in Mississippi Territory, 1789–1834. The latter comes from the American State Papers.

The Law Library of Congress at <http://memory.loc.gov/ammem/amlaw/lawhome.html> offers full-text search and page

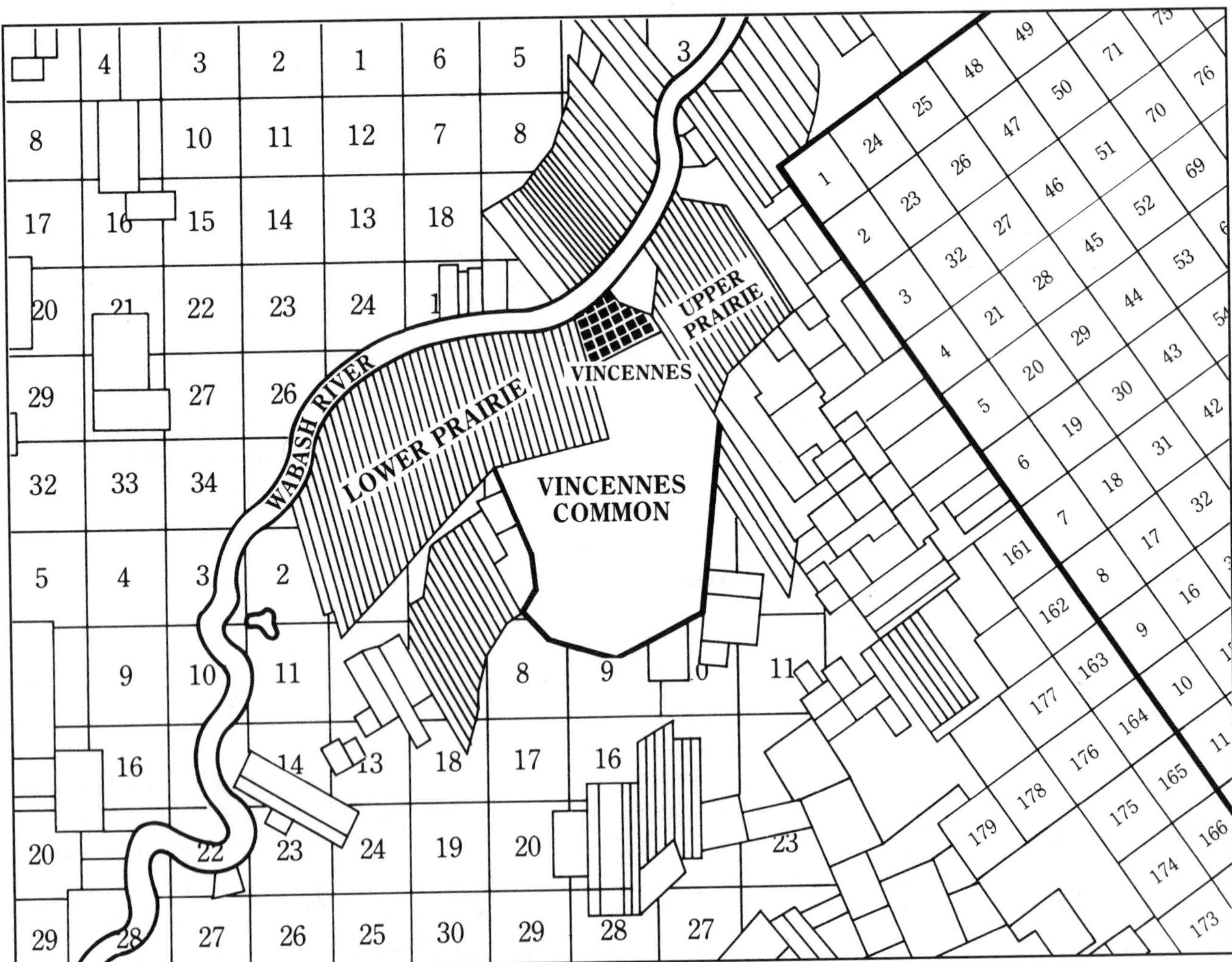

Figure 10-6. Private land claims, reflecting early French grants, surveyed within the federal township and range system in Vincennes, Indiana. Leonard Lux, *The Vincennes Donation Lands* (Indianapolis: Indiana Historical Society, 1949), map in pocket.

images of the U.S. Serial Set, House Journal, Senate Journal, and the American State Papers. A surname and given name search can be done either as separate titles or collectively to locate all references to a claim.[45] It is necessary to read all the entries for full detail. For example, references in the House Journal to the petition of John Potter of North Carolina appear sporadically from 9 April 1806 through 15 March 1810, when the petition is shown as denied.[46] Yet only the American State Papers explain that Potter seeks permission to locate land on a warrant issued by the British government in 1755.[47] The warrant, obtained from Lord Dunmore, governor of the then-colony of Virginia, was for 3,000 acres and was granted to Robert Munford, who served as chaplain in the War of 1755. Munford assigned the warrant to John Potter who, in 1780, located in the western part of Virginia (now Kentucky). Unfortunately, Potter, "by mistake or accident," failed to return the survey to the proper office, and lost the land. In 1790 he relocated but afterwards discovered the land was covered by other claims. Subsequently, Kentucky refused to locate the warrant, as did Virginia. Potter sought to use the warrant in the Virginia Military Tract of Ohio. His claim denial was explained, "it is inconceivable to the commission how the United States should become liable to satisfy a claim originating . . . of the King of Great Britain."[48]

Private land claims are also found in various court records, because disapproved claims could be taken to court. In fact, Congress, in abolishing particular claims commissions, routinely authorized the holders of unsettled claims to prosecute their cases through the courts. Case files concerning land grants originally made by Spanish and Mexican authorities in California between 1769 and 1846 have been reproduced on microfilm as *Private Land Grant Cases in the Circuit Court of the Northern District of California, 1852–1910*.[49] The microfilm includes maps. For further reading, see Paul W. Gates's *History of Public Land Law Development*, and his "Private Land Claims in the South," in the *Journal of Southern History*; Louis Pelzer's "The Private Land Claims of the Old Northwest Territory" in *Iowa Journal of History and Politics*; T. P. Martin's "The Confirmation of French and Spanish Land Titles in the Louisiana Purchase"; Lemont K. Richardson's "Private Land Claims in Missouri" in *Missouri Historical Review*; E. Wade Hone's "Private Land Claims" and "Congressional Collections" chapters in *Land and Property Research*; and "Spanish and Mexican Land Grants in the Southwest: A Symposium," edited by Clark S. Knowlton.[50]

Military Bounty Land

The granting of military bounty land in the United States to encourage enlistments or reward previous service began in colonial times, but its legislative heyday was from 1788 to 1855, though claims were still being received by the federal government in the 1960s. Genealogists find bounty-land records especially attractive because they serve the dual role of locating persons in time and place and of proving military service. Applications sometimes contain a wealth of information, especially when heirs claimed lands.

Colonial legislatures gave land for military service, such as for the Narragansett campaign of King Philip's War, 1675 to 1676, but these were mostly private acts passed to reward meritorious service to the colony. In 1701, Virginia passed an act promising two hundred acres free of quitrents for twenty years to those who would make armed settlements on the Indian frontier. The Crown's proclamation of 1763 ordered the colonies to give bounty land for service in the French and Indian War to "reduced" (indigent) officers and to British Army privates mustered out in the colonies who intended to remain there. This did not include militia units. In 1776, Congress promised so-called "Hessian deserters" fifty acres but had few takers. Also in 1776, Congress promised bounty land to soldiers of the Continental line, with privates and noncommissioned officers to get one hundred acres, captains three hundred acres, and other ranks various amounts. States that likewise promised or afterward gave bounty lands were Massachusetts (with Maine), New York, Pennsylvania, Maryland, Virginia, the Carolinas, and Georgia.[51] Lloyd D. Bockstruck's *Revolutionary War Bounty Land Grants Awarded by State Governments* is a master index to approximately 35,000 persons named in the grants from these nine states.[52] The states that did not give Revolutionary War bounty lands were New Hampshire, Rhode Island, Connecticut, New Jersey, and Delaware.

North Carolina was the most generous, giving 640 acres (a square mile) to a private in the Continental line. The tract was in Tennessee; no bounty land warrants were located within the present-day boundaries of North Carolina. Maryland gave the smallest amount, fifty acres to a private, but that state had very little western land to give. Figure 10-7 and table 10-1 shows the locations of the Revolutionary War and War of 1812 military reserves. Massachusetts grants were in what became Maine but were in no specific reserve. Privates who got a one hundred-acre warrant from the federal government for revolutionary service were not eligible for a Massachusetts state grant. Soldiers of the Continental line from other states could take both the federal and their state land bounties. (See the "Summary of Land Records by State" at the end of this chapter for brief references to bounty-land records. For Massachusetts, see Maine.) Paul Gates's *History of Public Land Law Development*, discusses aspects of various state grants. Gates states, without elaborating, that Connecticut gave bounty land; but this seems to refer to the "Fire Lands" in Ohio granted to Connecticut residents burned out in the revolution rather than to grants to soldiers.[53] Virginia is discussed below because its bounty-land records are widely scattered.

Congress was slow to redeem its promise of land for its soldiers. In 1788, it directed that bounty-land warrants be issued to those applying. But the U.S. Military District in Ohio, the only federal lands where federal revolutionary warrants could be used until 1830, did not open until 1796—a full fifteen years after victory at Yorktown. By then, the Ohio Company and John Cleves Symmes in 1787 and 1788 had purchased millions of Ohio acres on credit from Congress and were permitted to pay one-seventh of the price in federal bounty-land warrants. Therefore, land offices of the two speculations accepted some federal warrants, the earliest locales where they could be used. The Ohio Company Purchase records are at Marietta College (<www.marietta.edu/~library>). The private Symmes papers were mostly destroyed in a fire. Congress also created three military reserves for veterans of the War of 1812, but there were no federal reserves after these three, which were in Illinois, Arkansas, and Missouri. Warrants usable in the Virginia and U.S. military districts in Ohio were made redeemable by scrip acts in 1830 and 1832, respectively, in any GLO land offices in Ohio, Indiana, and Illinois. In 1842, all federal bounty-land warrants were made good for purchases at any GLO land office.

The 1788 act also stipulated that the warrants were assignable, meaning the soldier could sell his warrant and not wait to take the land. This created an instant market in bounty warrants and allowed land speculators to accumulate large quantities of warrants and land. Paul Gates shows that fewer than one soldier (or his heirs) in ten got land by using his warrant under any federal bounty-land act. Instead, most soldiers sold their rights, using the back of the warrant to assign it to the buyer, who might in turn assign the warrant to another buyer. Sometimes the assignment left the buyer's name blank, to be filled in by the last purchaser. The warrant certificates issued to Mexican War veterans were folios, with the insides and back unprinted so they could be used for assignments.

The warrant market was big business, especially when warrants were no longer restricted to military reserve lands (this happened under an act in 1842). Major brokerage firms dealt extensively in warrants, buying in the eastern states and selling to western land brokers and settlers. Financial newspapers in the boom years of the 1850s frequently carried price quotations. The government set a price ceiling from 1820 by charging a flat $1.25 per acre for most of its lands. The average market price peaked at about $1.20 an acre in 1854–55 for 160-acre warrants, just before the market was flooded by the act of 1855.[57] More warrants were used in Iowa than in any other state, and it is estimated that half of Iowa was purchased with bounty-land warrants.

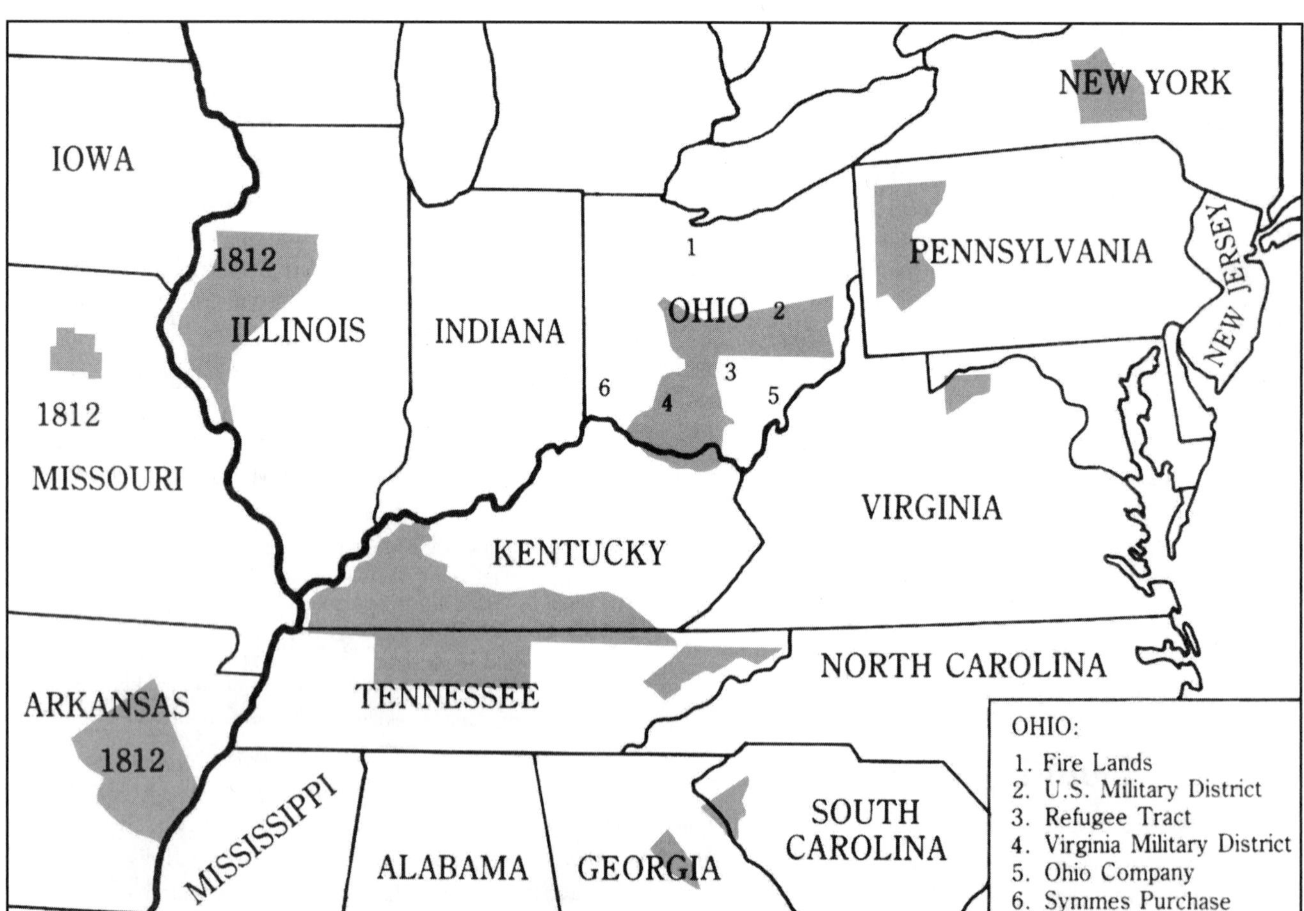

Figure 10-7. Federal and state military land reserves for veterans of the Revolutionary War and the War of 1812.

The federal government gave no bounty land for service after 1855, but Union veterans of the Civil War received special homestead rights in 1870, when an amendment to the 1862 Homestead Act gave them the right to claim 160 acres within railroad grant areas (other homesteaders got only 80). Another amendment in 1872 gave Union veterans the right to deduct the length of their war service from the five-year residency needed to prove a homestead.

To get a federal bounty-land warrant it was necessary, under any act from 1788 to 1855, for the soldier or heirs to apply. The warrant applications may be ordered from the National Archives, either online at <https://eservices.archives.gov/orderonline/>, or by mail using NATF form 85. The details necessary to order an application will be found in various indexes, cited in the following section under the appropriate war. This information is necessary because the applications are arranged by the year of the act of Congress that authorized them, the certificate or warrant number, and the number of acres granted for warrants under the acts of 1847 to 1855. If the name of a warrantee does not appear in one of the indexes cited, the National Archives will, for a fee, search for the land warrant. Instructions are available at the website cited in this paragraph.

To obtain land, the federal warrant had to be surrendered, usually to a federal land office, in exchange for a patent. The patents, like any other GLO patents, are indexed in the GLO-ARS by name of patentee. (If the warrant was assigned, the name of the patentee will be different than the name of the veteran to whom the warrant was originally issued. A search of warrantees for whom federal land was patented is also available at the GLO-ARS.) The surrendered warrants are in land-entry case files of the patentees. They may be ordered from the National Archives, either online at or by mail to National Archives and Records Administration, Attn: NWCTB, 700 Pennsylvania Avenue, NW, Washington, DC 20408, using NATF form 84. The case file categories are briefly described in Harry P. Yoshpe's and Philip P. Brower's *Preliminary Inventory of the Land-Entry Papers of the General Land Office*.[55]

The following summary, with added explanatory remarks, of the various warrant acts is from Inventory No. 22, and Kenneth Hawkins, "Research in the Land Entry Files of the General Land Office (Record Group 49), General Leaflet Number 67, 1995, revised and updated at <www.archives.gov/publications/general_information_leaflets>. The number of warrants issued gives the researcher an idea of how many soldiers, or heirs of soldiers, applied under each act. Reference citations are to the respective acts of Congress. (Citation 2 *Stat.* 236 means volume 2 of *U.S. Statutes at Large*, p. 236. M804 means National Archives microfilm publication M804.) References for a search of each war's bounty-land applications is added.

1. Revolutionary War Warrants in the U.S. Military District in Ohio

Date	Act	Warrant Numbers
9 July 1788	Continental Congress Journals 34: 307	1–14220
16 March 1803	2 Stat. 236	1–272
15 April 1806	2 Stat. 378	273–2500

Table 10-1. Federal and State Bounty-Land Acreage, Revolutionary War

Rank	U.S.	Georgia	Maryland	Massachusetts	New York		North Carolina	Pennsylvania	South Carolina	Virginia
Major General	1,100	—	50	100	5,500	—	25,000+	2,000	100	15,000
Brigadier General	850	1,955	50	100	4,250	—	12,000	1,500	100	10,000
Colonel	500	1,150	50	100	2,500	2,000	7,200	1,000	100	6,667
Lieutenant Colonel	450	1,035	50	100	2,250	2,000	5,760	800	100	6,000
Major	400	920	50	100	2,000	2,000	4,800	600	100	5,333
Captain	300	575–690	50	100	1,500	1,500	3,840	500	100	4,000
Lieutenant	200	460	50	100	1,000	1,000	2,560	400	100	2,666
Ensign	150	460	50	100	1,000	1,000	2,560	300	100	2,666
Noncommissioned Officers	100	345	50	100	500	500	1,000	250	100	200–400
Private	100	230–287½	50	100	500	500	640	200	100	100–300

Initially, these assignable warrants were redeemable only for land in the U.S. Military District in Ohio, other than as previously mentioned in the private tracts of Judge Symmes and the Ohio Company. Privates and non-commissioned officers of the Continental line from any state received 100 acres, ensigns 150, lieutenants 200, captains 300, majors 400, lieutenant colonels 450, colonels 500, brigadier generals 850, and major colonels 1,100. The initial minimum grants in the district were for quarter townships of the five-mile dimensions—i.e., five miles to a side or 16,000 acres, thereby requiring warrantees to band together through an agent to reach 4,000 acres or sell out to get some value from their warrants. By 1800, lots as small as one hundred acres were available. In 1832, entries in the district were ended, and those still holding warrants were allowed to trade them for scrip negotiable at GLO land offices in Ohio, Indiana, and Illinois. From 1842, such scrip was accepted at any GLO land office.

Many warrant application files for the 1788 act were destroyed by fires in 1800 and 1814. Where the warrantee's name is known, a substitute card was made with the note "no papers." These cards and the surviving application files are interfiled with the surviving Revolutionary War pension files, all microfilmed on M804, Revolutionary War Pension and Bounty-Land Warrant Application Files, in 2,670 rolls. This series is indexed for pensions and warrantees in National Genealogical Society, *Index of Revolutionary War Pension Applications in the National Archives* and in Virgil D. White's *Genealogical Abstracts of Revolutionary War Pension Files*, and online at <www.heritagequest.com>.[56] Both indexes and M804 cover "selected records" only. One note: White's last volume indexes names appearing in other individual's pensions. This could be next-of-kin or a person providing an affidavit supporting the applicant's statements.

To aid soldiers who had not met the deadline of the 1788 act, Congress passed a time extension in 1803 that was amended in 1806. The warrants of these acts are numbered in one sequence. Nearly all surrendered warrants, from numbers 1–6912 of the 1788 act, were destroyed. Surviving surrendered warrants of the 1788, 1803, and 1806 acts are filed in land-entry case files and are on *U.S. Revolutionary War Bounty Land Warrants Used in the U.S. Military District of Ohio and Related Papers (Acts of 1788, 1803, 1806)*, in sixteen rolls.[57] Since patents were rarely placed in the case files, the U.S. Military District land-entry case files usually contain only the surrendered warrant. The files were microfilmed sequentially, and missing warrants were either lost, misplaced, or never surrendered for land. The few surrendered for scrip under the 1832 and later acts are in that series, but they are cross-referenced on M829. On roll 1 of M829 are two ledgers indexed in Smith's *Federal Land Series*, vol. 2, once used to record the issuance of warrants. Roll 1 of M829 also has indexes to the ledgers done and/or microfilmed by the National Archives. The pamphlet accompanying M829 describes these records and is available upon request from the National Archives.

2. War of 1812 Warrants in U.S. Military Districts in Illinois, Arkansas, and Missouri

Date	Act	Warrant Numbers
24 Dec. 1811 11 Jan. 1812 6 May 1812 27 July 1842	2 Stat. 669 2 Stat. 672 2 Stat. 729 5 Stat. 497	1–28085 for 160 acres
10 Dec. 1814	3 Stat. 147	1–1101 for 320 acres

The acts of 1811 and 1812 promised 160 acres to privates and non-commissioned officers who enlisted in regiments raised by Congress and who served for five years, unless discharged sooner or killed. To encourage longer enlistments, the 1814 act doubled the acreage for those who enlisted after 10 December 1814. Officers were given no bounty lands until the acts of 1850 to 1855. The warrants were not legally assignable except by inheritance, and the GLO retained the warrant certificates, issuing the veteran a certificate of notification. These warrants were redeemable only in military reserves in Illinois, Arkansas, and Missouri until the act of 1842 made them redeemable at any GLO land office. The warrants became legally assignable in 1852.

The earliest bounty land warrants for service in the War of 1812, issued at the time of the war, are partially reproduced and indexed on M845, War of 1812 Military Bounty Land Warrants 1815–1858, in fourteen rolls. This microfilm also contains warrants for War of 1812 service qualified for under the Act of 1842. Patentees in the Arkansas and Missouri reserves are indexed on roll 1, as are Illinois patentees with surnames beginning with C and D. A CD-ROM index to the film is *War of 1812 Military Bounty Land Warrants 1815–1858* by April Leigh Helm and Matthew L. Helm, et al.[58] A published index to these records is Virgil D. White's *Index to War of 1812 Pension (and Bounty-Land Warrant) Files*.[59] Because War of 1812 warrants were not legally assignable until 1852, the patent indexes in the GLO-ARS should serve as indexes to original warrantees, though Gates shows that the land speculators got large parts of the reserves, presumably by having the patents processed in the names of the warrantees. This means many veterans patented land they probably never saw. The pamphlet accompanying M848 describes these records and is available upon request from the National Archives. Aside from these microfilmed warrants, there may also be unmicrofilmed warrant application files and land-entry case files in Record Group 15, and scrip files from 1830 are in Record Group 49.

3. Applications for Bounty-Land Scrip

Date	Act	Warrant Numbers
30 May 1830 13 July 1832	4 Stat. 422 4 Stat. 578	1–1994
2 March 1833	4 Stat. 665	1–225
3 March 1835	4 Stat. 770	1–970
31 Aug. 1852	10 Stat. 143	1–1689

A shortage of land available for patenting in the U.S. military districts prompted Congress to issue scrip that could be exchanged for unused warrants. At first good only in GLO land offices in Ohio, Indiana, and Illinois, the scrip, printed in acreage denominations, was eventually unrestricted by acts of 1833 and 1842. A good discussion of military bounty-land scrip and warrants, including those for the Canadian Refugees (1798–1801) and Canadian Volunteers (1815), is in Hone's *Land and Property Research in the United States*.

4. Mexican War Bounty-Land Warrants

Date	Act	Warrant Numbers
11 Feb. 1847	9 Stat. 125	#1–7585 for 40 acres 1–80689 for 160 acres

Congress, in the Mexican War, authorized ten regiments and offered privates and non-commissioned officers (but not officers) 160 acres for serving one year or more and 40 acres for serving less than a year. Alternately, the veteran could apply for $100 or $25 in scrip at six percent interest, acceptable for any payment due to the U.S. government. (This dollar scrip was different from the acreage scrip mentioned in entry number 3 above.) There were no military districts created for Mexican War bounty land, the warrants being redeemable at any GLO land office. They were assignable. As usual, few warrantees, or heirs of warrantees, actually patented land using their warrants. The surrendered warrants are in the land-entry case files of the patentees. The best finding aid to Mexican War warrantees is Index to Mexican War Pension Files, 1887–1926 (T-317), which gives filing information for bounty land warrants granted under the act of 1847.

5. The Acts of 1850–55

Date	Act	Warrant Numbers
28 Sept. 1850	9 Stat. 521	1–103978 for 40 acres 1–57718 for 80 acres 1–27450 for 160 acres 1–9070 for 40 acres
22 March 1852	10 Stat. 3	1–1699 for 80 acres 1–1223 for 160 acres 1–4 for 10 acres 1–542 for 40 acres 1–359 for 60 acres
3 March 1855	10 Stat. 701	2–49491 for 100 acres 1–6 for 100 acres 1–97096 for 120 acres 1–115783 for 160 acres

The acts of 1850 to 1855 were not to encourage enlistments but to reward former service. The act of 1850 extended bounty land to officers and enlisted men who had not previously received land and who had served in any war since 1790, including the Indian wars. Nine months' service brought 160 acres, four months' service 80 acres, and one month's service 40 acres. Since there was initial confusion over whether the act made warrants assignable, the GLO commissioner later ruled that it did not. The act of 1852 explicitly made them assignable and extended the 1850 act to militiamen who served after 1812.

The 1855 act extended bounty-land privileges even further by making 160 acres the minimum entitlement and reducing service to fourteen days or even less. Those who traveled 1,200 miles in service were eligible even if they served less time. A veteran or his heirs who had previously received fewer than 160 acres could apply for the balance. Eligibility was extended to chaplains, wagon masters, militia rangers, and volunteers of certain campaigns such as Kings Mountain, the Nickojack Campaign in Tennessee, and the Cook County volunteers in the Black Hawk War. An act of 14 May 1856 extended the 1855 benefits to naval veterans and any Revolutionary War service.

Figures from Inventory No. 22 (omitting scrip because it redeemed already-issued warrants) show that the warrant totals issued by these categories of acts are:

War	Total Warrants
Revolutionary War	16,720
War of 1812	29,186
Mexican War	88,274
Acts of 1850 to 1855	464,419
Total	598,599

Considering that 77.6 percent of these bounty-land warrants are in the miscellaneous categories of the 1850 to 1855 acts and that each warrant should have an application file with the veteran's documentation of service or affidavits from next of kin documenting their relationship to him, locating the 1850–1855 warrant applications is important to genealogists. The first search is of the GLO-ARS, to determine if a patent was granted to the veteran or his heirs and if that patent is indexed. If the veteran's name or name of next of kin does not appear, consult the microfilmed and published indexes shown above for each war. At the GLO-ARS website, <www.glorecords.blm.gov/>, are search paths for ordering warrant applications using the information provided by a successful search. If the name does appear in an index, and the researcher is fairly certain of bounty-land eligibility, engage the services of the National Archives for a fee-based search. Provide as much definite information as is possible.

Fraudulent Applications

A special problem is fraudulent warrant applications, especially where heirs claimed a soldier's rights. Mrs. Ellen Reed and her two children received bounty-land warrant no. 61,656 in 1849 for the Mexican War service of Richard Reed, private, Company D, First U.S. Artillery Regiment. Two months later, Richard's mother applied as his next of kin and showed that, on his supposed marriage day in Mississippi, he was fishing on the Kennebec in Maine. Ellen's warrant was canceled and a new one issued to the mother.[60] This problem of potential fraud is large enough to be a major contaminant. Gates notes 59,190 warrants for which caveats against delivery had been filed by 1856, thus suspecting further action on patenting.[61] Why waste research time worrying about such obscure points? Experienced researchers know that solutions often come from unpredictable quarters.

For example, bounty-land eligibility for service in the War of 1812 was first limited to able-bodied enlisted men age eighteen to forty-five. Mrs. Abigail O'Flyng's husband and three sons had served. Two sons had been killed, yet none of the four was eligible for bounty land. Her husband had been over forty-five, one son was under eighteen, and the two dead sons had been promoted to officers just before they died. The 1816 Act for the Relief of Patrick and Abigail O'Flyng and of Edmund O'Flyng, ended the age restrictions and allowed enlisted men promoted to officers to receive land. Also, by private act of Congress, her husband received 480 acres, the youngest son 160 acres, and the heirs of the dead sons their half pay for five years.[62] (See figure 10-8). Such a case tests a genealogist's expertise. Does he or she understand the scope and intent of the record group searched? Nearly all government records—federal, state, and local—are created as a result of statutes that should be read. Have unlikely records, such as private acts of Congress, been searched? Has the researcher screened other records many years later in which some legal actions resurface?

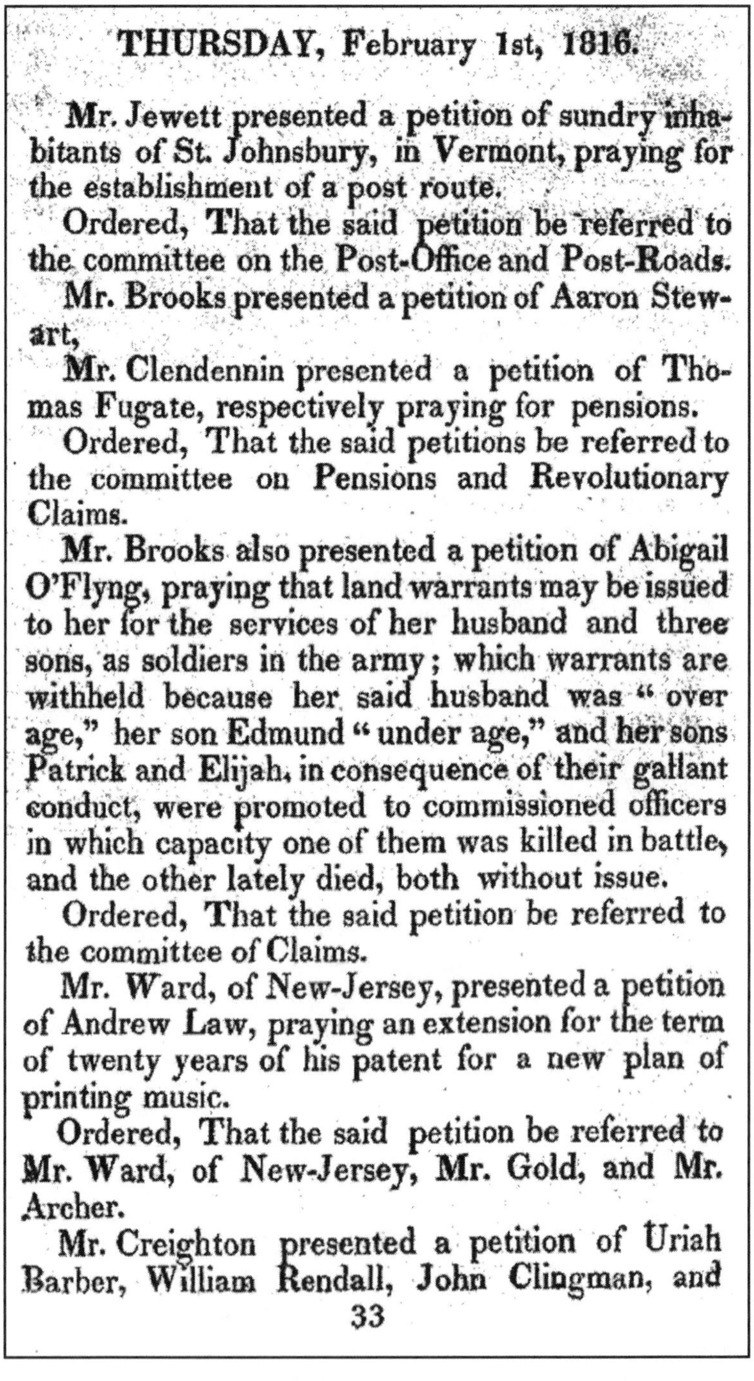

This last question is not rhetorical. Col. Robert Porterfield was killed in the revolution. His son Robert received from Congress a warrant for "about 6,000 acres." But the land was in Kentucky, where title disputes dominated land sales. The Porterfield land was lost in a court battle due to superior conflicting claims. In 1860, Congress authorized scrip for Robert's heirs, to whom 153 warrants for forty acres each were issued. In 1900, twenty-one of these warrants were still outstanding and unlocated for land given on Revolutionary War service.[63]

THURSDAY, February 1st, 1816.

Mr. Jewett presented a petition of sundry inhabitants of St. Johnsbury, in Vermont, praying for the establishment of a post route.

Ordered, That the said petition be referred to the committee on the Post-Office and Post-Roads.

Mr. Brooks presented a petition of Aaron Stewart,

Mr. Clendennin presented a petition of Thomas Fugate, respectively praying for pensions.

Ordered, That the said petitions be referred to the committee on Pensions and Revolutionary Claims.

Mr. Brooks also presented a petition of Abigail O'Flyng, praying that land warrants may be issued to her for the services of her husband and three sons, as soldiers in the army; which warrants are withheld because her said husband was "over age," her son Edmund "under age," and her sons Patrick and Elijah, in consequence of their gallant conduct, were promoted to commissioned officers in which capacity one of them was killed in battle, and the other lately died, both without issue.

Ordered, That the said petition be referred to the committee of Claims.

Mr. Ward, of New-Jersey, presented a petition of Andrew Law, praying an extension for the term of twenty years of his patent for a new plan of printing music.

Ordered, That the said petition be referred to Mr. Ward, of New-Jersey, Mr. Gold, and Mr. Archer.

Mr. Creighton presented a petition of Uriah Barber, William Rendall, John Clingman, and

33

Figure 10-8. The petition of Abigail O'Flyng, presented to the House of Representatives by Mr. Brooks, gives family information. From House Journal, Thursday, 1 February 1816, page 257, online at <http://memory.loc.gov/amlaw/lawhome.html>.

For background on bounty lands, see the National Archives's *Guide to Genealogical Research in the National Archives*; Paul Gates's "Military Bounty Land Policies," in *History of the Public Land Law Development*; Hone's *Land and Property Research in the United States*; and James W. Oberly's *Sixty Million Acres: American Veterans and the Public Lands Before the Civil War*.[64]

Virginia Military District

An extraordinary flood of Revolutionary War bounty-land warrants poured from Richmond, partly because Virginia had the largest state population and partly because it granted warrants not only to its Continental line but to its state line as well. The distinction rests on who paid the soldiers—Congress or Virginia.

The first military reserve was created south of Green River in Kentucky and subsequently expanded west of the Tennessee. There were no bounty lands within present-day Virginia or West Virginia. In 1784, Virginia ceded its claim to the area north of the Ohio River, reserving the 4 million acres between the Scioto and Little Miami Rivers for redemption of its bounty-land warrants. This Virginia Military District in Ohio was federal land for which first-title land grants were reserved solely for the Virginia warrants of veterans of the Continental line. A series of ever more liberal acts broadened where warrants could be used and by whom until, in 1852, Congress agreed that all Virginia Revolutionary War warrants could be exchanged for scrip accepted at any GLO land office. Large numbers of these assignable warrants were sold; an estimated one-quarter of the Virginia Military District was acquired by twenty-five men.[65]

The paperwork flow was: (1) warrant application to Richmond; (2) warrant issued to warrantee; (3) selection of desired land in Kentucky or Ohio reserves and survey by official surveyor; (4) paperwork for Kentucky lands to the Virginia Land Office or, from 1792, the Kentucky Land Office, or the federal capital for Ohio lands; and (5) patent for Kentucky land sent to patentee or federal patent sent to Richmond for relay to Ohio patentee.[66]

Thus, there should be four major repositories today for Virginia bounty-land records. There are, however, seven. The land offices of Virginia, Kentucky, and Ohio are described in the state summaries at the end of this chapter. The microfilmed federal patents are in the BLM Eastern States Office in Springfield, Virginia. The surrendered warrants are in Record Group 49 at the Textural Reference Branch in Washington, D.C. The sixth major collection is the Illinois Historical Survey Collection in the University of Illinois Library, Urbana-Champaign, which has the papers of Richard Clough Anderson, surveyor of the Virginia Military District in Ohio. Clifford Neal Smith has brought this collection to the attention of a wide audience by his indexes in the *Federal Land Series*, especially vol. 4, which is devoted to the district. He estimated that "about 64 percent of Virginia's obligations to its veterans were satisfied by the land grants in the Virginia Military District of Ohio."[67] The seventh major collection is the Anderson-Latham Collection at the Library of Virginia. Allen Latham, son-in-law of Richard C. Anderson, in business with B. G. Leonard, handled claims of the soldiers and their heirs. This collection contains papers of Anderson and Latham and is described online at <www.lva.lib.va.us/findaid/23634.htm>.[68]

Loyalist Lands

The confiscation of Loyalist lands in the revolution—what might be called "negative bounty land"—is a subject that deserves both extended research and a bibliographical source essay. Below is a brief discussion.

The British government made a commendable effort to compensate Loyalist losses, and Loyalists had to list their lost property to claim that compensation. One of the best sources is Alexander Fraser, ed., *United Empire Loyalists Enquiry into the Losses and Services in Consequence of Their Loyalty. Evidence in Canadian Claims*.[69] From this excellent source book comes the example of John Fowler. The claim (p. 293) of Fowler, formerly of Stockbridge, Massachusetts, indicates he was a native of Guilford, Connecticut, lived in Stockbridge, fled to New York during the war and hired a farm on Long Island, was carried a prisoner to Stamford, Connecticut, and ultimately settled in Kingston, Ontario. "Produces deed dated 19th July, 1770, whereby Mark Hopkins in considn. of £30 lawful Conveys to Claimt. forty acres in Stockbridge. Says he purchased 35 acres adjoining, from his Br., in 1770 for about £25," and so on. "Produces a letter from his Father in Law saying that his Personal Property had been sold to the amount of £100 Lawful." Aside from separating the various John Fowlers, this record helps fill a page in the Fowler family genealogy.

Such claims name only a small percentage of Loyalists. Two New Jersey studies revealed that of 275 known Loyalists of Bergen County, only twenty-nine claims could be found, while for the approximately 1,200 estates confiscated in New Jersey, there exist only 239 Loyalist claims.[70]

The official files of Loyalist claims are in the Public Record Office in London, partly summarized in Peter Wilson Coldham's *American Loyalist Claims: Abstracted from the Public Record Office, Audit Series 13, Bundles 1–35 and 37*.[71] The manuscript sources are identified in Gregory Palmer's *A Bibliography of Loyalist Source Material in the United States, Canada, and Great Britain*, a helpful book but one intended for experts.[72] A useful reference is "American Revolution: Overseas Records Information 52" at the British National Archives website, <www.catalogue.nationalarchives.gov.uk/RdLeaflet.asp?>. Section 6 of this leaflet is titled "American Loyalist Claims." There is no comprehensive bibliography to literature on the confiscation of Loyalist estates. (One land record of potential help in identifying children is the land given in Canada and Nova Scotia to Loyalists under royal instructions of 1783, which promised one hundred acres to heads of Loyalist families and fifty acres each to their children and to single men. See Marion Gilroy's *Loyalists and Land Settlement in Nova Scotia*.)[73]

Taxes

Things taxed have included carriages and watches, windows and whiskey, land and slaves. Taxes on documents and tea helped start a war. Arkansas Territory's sudden tax on bounty lands in the 1820s was enacted and due before the news had time to reach out-of-state owners, permitting the quick seizure and sale of "delinquent" lands. As this variety suggests, name lists of such taxes must be used with a cautious understanding of who should be on the list and who should not.

Colonial and antebellum counties and towns usually taxed free adult males a set, uniform amount called the poll (head, capitation) tax, which became due when a young man reached age twenty-one (sixteen or eighteen in some areas) and ceased to be due when a man reached some age, such as fifty or sixty. Searching a series of such annual tax lists can locate sons coming of age. Sometimes the law made a father liable for a head tax for sons sixteen to twenty so that sons first moved through the yearly tax lists as unnamed tallies under their father's name. The great failing of the system is that it seldom works for women, who were usually not subject to such a poll tax but who might own and be taxed for land. North Carolina illustrates the variability of the poll tax ages. In colonial years, it set the white male poll at ages sixteen and upward, changed it to twenty-one and upward from the revolution, exempted men over fifty from 1801, made it twenty-one to forty-four beginning in 1835, and from 1868 laid the poll tax on males between twenty-one and fifty.[74] The wary researcher must be aware of these shifting limits.

However, for all their limitations, poll tax lists can be combined with property tax lists as a substitute census. To identify clearly who owed what, clerks sometimes added useful descriptors. For example, the 1799 list for Warren County, Kentucky, has John Taylor Slick, John Taylor Cooksland, John Taylor gambler, John Taylor one eye, and John Taylor hatter.[75] The first two mean "on Salt Lick Creek" and "on land owned by Cook." A long series of such county tax lists can be crucial to identifying men with common names and showing when men entered and left the county, though lists often omit a man for a year or two when he is obviously still living on the same land. This means researchers should read at least eight years before and after a man first appears and disappears.

Names are often listed in initial order, meaning all surnames beginning with A are grouped together—but not alphabetically (see figure 10-9). Apparently, clerks received tax lists from various justices of the peace, constables, or militia captains and copied from each list first all the A surnames, then all the B surnames, and so forth. While some of the neighborhood proximities are lost, initial name order lists are easy to search for one surname. Researchers should always check the end of the county list, where the clerk would often add the names of the late, delinquent, and insolvent.

Other typical omissions are children, slaves and indentured servants (except as unnamed but taxed property), landless men over the poll tax age, paupers, ministers, justices of the peace, militia officers, tax assessors, and men granted exemption for whatever reason. An Indiana statute of 1826 exempted "all

1814 Tax Digest

Names of People			Quality of Land			Granted to	Joining of	County	Waters	Slaves	Town Lots	Carriages	Stock in Trade	Lawyer	Doctor	Studs	Mulattoes	Dollars	Cents	
			1st	2nd	3rd															
Clarke County, Georgia			1814 Tax Digest				Capt Johnston's District		[GMD 217-Georgia Factory District]											
[6]	Roberson	David																	31	1/4
[6]	Richardson	John																	31	1/4
[6]	Roberson	Jane *widow*		200	200	Aplin	Lane	Clarke	Oconee	5								2	31	1/4
[6]	Ramey	Absalom		287.5		Gorum	Cox	Clarke	Cedar C	3								2	18	3/4
	Do				90		Moore	Clarke	Cedar C											
	Do				78		Strong	Clarke	Oconee											
[6]	Ramey	Daniel								15								5	00	
[6]	Ramey	Edmond																	31	1/4
[6]	Smith	John *sadler*			97	Briant	Marble	Clarke	Oconee										43	
[6]	Steward	Alfred			150	Aplin	Cocke	Clarke	Oconee										50	
[6]	Strong	Wm Senr		237	476	Ashworth	Strong	Clarke	Big C	33								12	53	
	Do				569	Gardner	Haynes	Clarke	Oconee											
[6]	Stidmond	James			50	Hinson	Randolph	Clarke	Oconee										37	1/2
[6]	Smith	John L.																	31	1/4

Figure 10-9. This 1814 tax digest (transcript) shows widow Jane Roberson is taxed on 200 acres of second rate land and 200 acres of third rate land originally granted to [Mr.] Aplin and joining [Mr.] Lane's property in Clarke County, Georgia, near the Oconee waterway. She is also taxed on five slaves. From: *Clarke County Georgia Tax Digest 1811-1820*. Transcribed by Mary Hoit Abbe, et al. (Athens, Ga.: Clarke-Oconee Genealogical Society, 2005:134). Used with permission.

persons who had served in the land or naval service of the United States, during the Revolutionary War, from the payment of a poll tax, and a tax upon personal property" if the veteran gave an affidavit to a justice of the peace.[76] There are also, inevitably, those who were overlooked.

Original lists as received by the clerk survive for 1771 Bute County, North Carolina, and have been compared to the final county-wide copy.[77] On the left are nine adjoining entries of a local list compared with the poll entries on the right of the final county list (in initial order of the original):

Local List	County List With Polls	
Joshua Taylor	not listed	
John Linch Jr.	John Lynch Jr.	1
John Faulcon, Henry Brown	John Falcon	2
John Baxter, John Weedon, Sharp Balthrop (& 1 sl.)	John Baxter	4
Rossen Allen, Drury Allen	Rossen Allan	2
Geo. Elliott Sr., Wm Stevenson (& 7 sl.)	George Elliott	9
James Elliott, Thos. Rosser	James Elliott	2
Richd. Towns	Richard Town	1
David Towns, sons David & John	David Towns	3

Obviously, the final county list has significantly fewer names. It is surprising that so many of the hidden surnames differ from that of the head of the household.

Several reconstituted state "censuses" have been compiled from county tax lists, such as the substitute for 1790 Kentucky and 1840 Texas "censuses." They can be great time-savers in localizing a man's state residence, but calling these reconstitutions "censuses" runs counter to the need of researchers to understand the nature of their sources. The 1790 federal census attempted to record everyone under some head of household. The 1790 Kentucky tax lists did not. Thus, the 1790 reconstituted Kentucky census cannot completely replace the lost 1790 Kentucky census schedules. This does not diminish the usefulness of the tax records.[78]

One great advantage of the county tax lists is that many states also received and stored copies. Thus, when the records of Buckingham County, Virginia, were destroyed by fire, its main surviving records became the yearly tax lists in Richmond.

Quitrent

The quitrent was a land tax typical of colonies from New York south; New Englanders took pride in being free of this remnant of feudal dues. In English manorial society the land obligations due the manor, such as plowing and haying the lord's land, were commuted to an annual money payment. Upon payment, the obligations were "quit" for the year. Land patents in New York and colonies to the south stipulated a yearly quitrent that went either to the Crown, as in Virginia south of the Rappahannock River, or to the proprietor, as in Virginia in the Northern Neck. The revolution generally saw the abolishing of quitrents.

Broken runs of annual quitrent books survive, along with the related rent rolls, though no colony has complete yearly series. Locating surviving quitrents is not simple, especially because many were the private property of proprietors and thus were lost during and after the revolution. Significant numbers of landowners successfully avoided the lists, and there was great resistance to paying quitrents in general, especially for lands held for speculation and not farmed. Producing even approximately complete lists was often administratively impossible. One massive effort was made in Virginia in 1704; it provides a good but incomplete survey of surnames south of the Rappahannock River, the area north of the river being in the Northern Neck and its quitrents due not to Virginia but to the proprietary. The standard, though dated, general study is Beverley W. Bond, Jr.'s *The Quit-Rent System in the American Colonies*.[79]

Federal Direct Taxes

There have been three federal direct tax series that produced name lists, all to raise money for armies. In 1798, the French war scare led to a direct tax on real property and slaves (1 *Stat.* 580 and 597), which produced extensive name lists, though how complete and far down the economic scale is not clear. One local historian praises the comprehensiveness of this tax on dwelling houses: "In common with other towns, the Federal Direct Tax on Rehoboth [Massachusetts] lists the names of the owners and tenants of every dwelling house in the town, data which are found in no other record. . . . This 1798 dwelling house list, together with the census for 1800 . . . enables us to reconstruct a far more complete record for Rehoboth at the end of the eighteenth century than is possible in any other period of that century."[80]

Unfortunately, the 1798 direct tax has survived only in fragments. (A janitor of the Boston Customs House used sections of the Massachusetts/Maine lists to fire his stoves.)[81] No lists have been found for Kentucky, New Jersey, North Carolina, South Carolina, or Virginia/West Virginia. Most surviving lists have been microfilmed, though not in a single series. The locations of known manuscripts, many very incomplete, follow. (The addresses of state historical societies are in appendix E, "Historical Societies"):

- Connecticut: Connecticut Historical Society
- Delaware: Historical Society of Delaware
- Georgia (part of Burke County): Georgia State Archives
- Maine, Massachusetts, New Hampshire: New England Historic Genealogical Society
- Maryland and District of Columbia: Maryland Historical Society; Maryland State Archives
- New York (vicinity of Clinton and Franklin counties): Vermont Historical Society

Pennsylvania: National Archives (717 volumes filmed as M372)
Rhode Island: Rhode Island Historical Society
Tennessee: Tennessee State Library
Vermont: Vermont Historical Society

To raise money for the War of 1812, the federal government again resorted to a direct tax from 1814 to 1816. Even fewer lists survive. The Connecticut Historical Society holds lists for 1814 to 1816 "for many towns," and Hancock County, Maine, survives for 1815. The 1813 law directed that $3 million be collected and apportioned among the states by population. The state governments were allowed to pay the federal treasury the amount levied on their citizens (less fifteen percent for saving the cost of collection) and in 1814 seven states did so, with four states doing the same in 1815 and 1816.[82] Perhaps this explains why few lists are extant—few were made.

The greatest number of federal direct tax lists, called assessment lists, are those from the Civil War to as late as 1917, when the government levied income taxes, property taxes, and license fees. These taxes were directed more to wealth rather than the broader earlier taxes and therefore capture a smaller proportion of the adult male population; however, they do provide specific information on propertied individuals. The records are in Record Group 58, Records of the Internal Revenue Service. The National Archives has microfilmed the assessment lists for most states, focusing primarily on lists of 1862 to 1866. These microfilms are listed in table 24 of *Guide to Genealogical Research in the National Archives*, which also identifies those manuscript assessment lists found only in the regional offices of the National Archives.[83]

As the Confederate states were conquered, the direct taxes were extended to them. Since many Southerners were unable to pay, the government sold much Southern land for taxes. In using the National Archives microfilms of Civil War direct taxes, note that each state has a different microfilm publication number—M754 for Alabama, M756 for California, M764 for Illinois, and so forth—and therefore a separate pamphlet explaining each state's lists. These pamphlets are available from the National Archives upon request. (New York and New Jersey were microfilmed together as M603.)

Influences of English Law

With some exceptions, American land law still reflects its English origins. The important exceptions are the French civil law in Louisiana, Spanish law in the Southwest, and Polynesian communal-use concepts in Hawaii. English property law, which means both land conveyance and inheritance law, was extremely complex and plagued by a nearly crushing mass of technicalities. This was especially true in the seventeenth and eighteenth centuries, when the United States was founded. The colonies lacked the judges, lawyers, law schools, and elaborate court system to implement English property law in all its complexity, but most of the basic concepts crossed the Atlantic and exist in the land records genealogists use.

One major distinction is between *real* and *personal* property, which arose in Norman England to distinguish between property the courts could restore to a dispossessed owner and property for which the courts would grant compensation for losses. The distinction is conveniently—if only roughly—between land (and its "fixtures") and movables. Because leases were deemed personal property and because deed registries record mostly real property, leases were normally not recorded. Hence, for reasons of early English law, tracing Americans who rented rather than bought farms can be very frustrating because their leases probably do not appear in the land records.

Another English concept is between *freehold* and *copyhold*, the first being for lands held in England by free men and the latter by *villeins* (i.e., peasants bound legally to the manor). The villein succeeded to the lands of his father upon payment of customary dues (fines), whereupon the record of such holdings was copied into the manor court roll—hence the name copyhold. In the American colonies, such copyhold was never successfully established because feudal and manorial structures did not exist in the colonies. The few instances where provincial proprietors tried to establish them, such as in Maryland and the Carolinas, were short-lived experiments in the face of all the unoccupied land surrounding these artificial manors. Thus, the American genealogist encounters freehold law that developed in contrast to a concept—copyhold—not normally found in American records. The one important remnant of feudalism that did gain a partial foothold in the colonies from New York to Georgia was the quitrent, a sum owed by a freeholder to his feudal superior. (See "Quitrent" in the section called "Taxes.")

A third aspect of property law in England was the doctrine of estates, which assumed that all land in England was owned only by the Crown and thus any subject held merely an "estate" in that land. Such holdings (tenures) could be with right to will or deed the land to another (fee simple), with right to a life interest that ended at the tenant's death (life estate), or with right for the land to pass inalienably to one's direct descendants so long as any existed (fee tail). The last—"to X and the heirs of his body"—might be land entailed without a sex restriction or it might be entailed only to male heirs (tail male) or, rarely, only to female heirs (tail female).

Out of these various historical concepts from the feudal-manorial world as they survived in English common law came legal records that genealogists encounter and need to understand. Not only did copyhold fail to flourish in the colonies, the idea that the Crown "really" owned all the land also failed. Therefore, American law was centuries ahead of English law in developing the legal sense of fee simple as an absolute (allodial) ownership. "Absolute" in this sense is restricted by eminent domain, taxation, zoning, and the public interest. Public interest, as an example, might restrict a private citizen from damming a fishing stream that ran through his land.

Two remnants of English law encountered in colonial records, mostly south of New England, are *livery of seizin* and the *lease and release*. Livery of seizin was a very old method of transferring land tenure by actually handing pieces of the property to the new owner. It means to take delivery of possession. Here is how lawyer William Blackstone described it:

> Livery in *deed* is thus performed. The feoffor [seller], lessor, or his attorney, together with the feofee [buyer], lessee, or his attorney . . . come to the land, or to the house; and there, in the presence of witnesses, declare the contents of the feoffment or lease, on which livery is to be made. And then the feoffor, if it be of hand, doth deliver to the feofee, all other persons being out of the ground, a clod or turf, or a twig or bough there growing, with words to this effect. 'I deliver these to you in the name of seizin of all the lands and tenements contained in this deed.'[84]

Whether Americans performed all these steps is conjectural. Certainly such deeds were occasionally used in the colonial period in both New England and the South. In 1714, in Westmoreland County, Virginia, Arthur Harris "made Livery and Seizin of the Lands and Appurtinances within mentioned by delivering Turff and Twigg and the Ring of the Door of the Chief Mansion House on the Lands."[85] These odd phrases were formula; nothing individual should be read into them.

Though livery of seizin was uncommon, the system of lease and release—two parts—flourished in Southern colonies in the 1700s. The intent of this document in seventeenth-century England was to avoid the legal fee of having deeds recorded publicly. Under Henry VIII, the Statutes of Uses dictated that the person having the use of any land had the obligations of that land as well, such as taxes, feudal dues, and so forth If land was leased, then by the Statute of Uses the only interest remaining to the lessor was the reversion of the land at the end of the lease's term. If that reversion was then released to the lessee, the land was sold without a bargain and sale, thus circumventing the law requiring public registration and fee. Here again, the form is formula and not a lease at all. The genealogist should read both documents because the lease often omits the wife's name because her husband could lease property without her consent. Also, the two serve as duplicate copies for such easily miscopied information as intricate metes and bounds descriptions and difficult-to-read proper names.

English property law (land law and inheritance) prior to the Victorian reforms was extraordinarily complex, dependent on technicalities, and steeped in a vocabulary now long obsolete. The manner in which land was inherited contains many subtle clues that nearly all researchers will pass by in ignorance. It is unfortunate that legal history studies in America are both rare and usually inadequate and that genealogists have few convenient compilations of American property law that are aimed toward the non-lawyer. Three important exceptions are Carole Shammas, Marylynn Salmon's and Michel Dahlin's *Inheritance in America From Colonial Times to the Present*; Marylynn Salmon's *Women and the Law of Property in Early America*; and "An American Law of Property" and "The Land: And Other Property" in Lawrence M. Friedman's *A History of American Law*.[86]

Property was divided into the real (mostly land) and the personal (usually movables). In seventeenth- and eighteenth-century England, in intestate cases where no legal will existed, the personal property, but not land, was probated through the ecclesiastical courts with equal distribution to all children, while land was given under the common law to the heir-at-law. These differing courts for personal and real property account for why, at least in the colonial South, land is rarely mentioned in estate inventories: in England, such inventories were generally made by the ecclesiastical probate courts only, which did not usually probate land.

Primogeniture developed elaborate rules for identifying the heir-at-law in the absence of children. If there were children, the heir-at-law was the eldest son (or, if dead, his heir-at-law). In the absence of a son, the daughters jointly inherited as heirs-at-law. After 1540, the testator (maker of the will) could bequeath land, but lands not mentioned in the will were treated as intestate and went to the heir-at-law. The major exception was entailed lands, meaning lands bequeathed by an ancestor to a person and that person's lineal descendants. The legal entailing phrase was "to X and the heirs of his or her body lawfully begotten." (The phrase "to his heirs and assigns forever" is not an entail.) Such land entailed to X could not be bequeathed by will so long as it remained entailed, because entailed lands went to the heir-at-law. Widows had a right to a life interest in one-third of their husband's lands, to be surrendered if they remarried. An excellent case study is Margaret Hickerson Emery's "The Adeustone-Rogers Families of Virginia: Tracing a Colonial Lineage through Entailment and Naming Patterns," in the *National Genealogical Society Quarterly*.[87]

The genealogist interested in colonial lineages should note how the land was inherited and how the personal property was disposed, if the inheritance existed in a time and colony governed by primogeniture and entail. If something strange seems to be happening, try to determine the local inheritance laws governing that time and place. Entailed lands and dower rights were protected from the debts owed by the estate, which may also give clues. (Figure 10-10 is a release of dower example. More information on dower is in chapter 9, "Court Records.")

A summary of "Inheritance Laws Circa 1720 in the American Colonies" appears as table 1.1 in *Inheritance in America from Colonial Times to the Present* by Shammas, et al.[88] But there is no simple summary for each colony showing which laws were in effect for which years for real/personal property or for other years for testate/intestate probates. John Frederick Dorman's "Colonial Law of Primogeniture" is helpful.[89] Richard B. Morris's "Colonial Law Governing the Distribution and Alienation of Land," in *Studies in the History of American Law with Special Reference to the Seventeenth and Eighteenth Centuries*, asserts that colonial practice was varied, uncertain, and debatable even to the colonial judges.[90]

Two English laws worth knowing are the 1670 Statute of Distribution (22 & 23 Charles II c. 10 as amended 1 James II c. 17) and the 1677 Statute of Frauds (29 Charles II c. 3). (An English statute is cited by chapter number of the acts passed by the Parliament sitting in a regnal year of the sovereign. Thus, the 1677 act is chapter 3, 29th regnal year of Charles II.) The 1670 statute dictated that personal property (not real property) was distributed like this:

1. To children where no widow survived: whole property was divided equally among the children; a lone child received all.
2. To children and widow: two-thirds to the children or their heirs and one-third to the widow.
3. To widow where no children survived: one-half to widow and one-half to the father of the deceased if alive or, failing him, to the mother or the brothers and sisters.
4. When no widow and children survived, property went to the father if alive or, failing him, to the mother or the brothers and sisters.

The Statute of Frauds provided that personal property could no longer be disposed by oral testament and that executors/

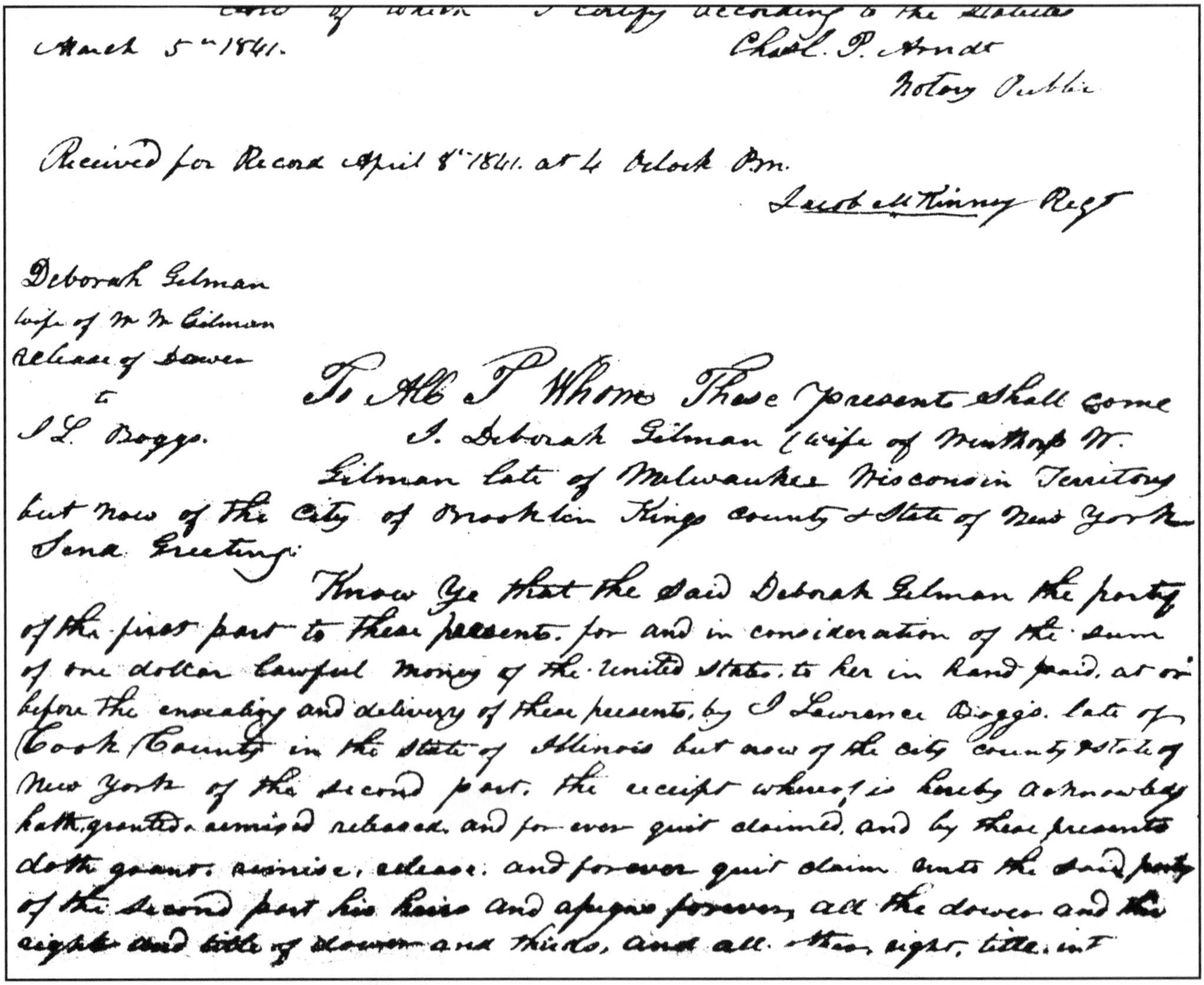

and of which I certify according to the statutes
March 5th 1841. Chas. P. Arndt
Notary Public

Received for Record April 8th 1841. at 4 O'clock P.m.
Jacob McKinney Regr

Deborah Gilman
wife of W. W. Gilman
Release of Dower
to
J. L. Boggs.

To All To Whom These presents Shall Come
I, Deborah Gilman (wife of Winthrop W. Gilman late of Milwaukee Wisconsin Territory but now of the City of Brooklin Kings County & State of New York Send Greeting:
Know Ye that the said Deborah Gilman the party of the first part to these presents, for and in consideration of the sum of one dollar lawful money of the United States, to her in hand paid, at or before the ensealing and delivery of these presents, by J. Lawrence Boggs. late of Cook County in the State of Illinois but now of the city county & state of New York of the second part, the receipt whereof is hereby acknowledged hath granted, remised released, and for ever quit claimed, and by these presents doth grant, remise, release, and forever quit claim unto the said party of the second part his heirs and assigns forever, all the dower and the right and title of dower and thirds, and all other right, title, int

Figure 10-10. This dower release gives more than one place of residence for the parties involved. For details on dower, see chapter 7, "Court Records." *Source:* Gilman to Boggs, Brown Co., Wisc., deed vol. M, 1841–50, p. 31, recorded 20 April 1841.

administrators must distribute such property as stipulated by will. Personal property not disposed by will was treated as intestate.

Although there are many local exceptions, English law was in force in the colonies to some degree where more specific colonial statutes did not exist, but the colonies could and did enact differing laws if "not repugnant" to English law and custom. The New England colonies, Pennsylvania, and Delaware granted equal divisions of land and movables in intestates with a double share to the eldest son. (The eldest daughter, in the absence of brothers, had no like double portion.) If the land could not be conveniently divided, it could go to the inheriting son provided he justly compensated the other heirs. Rhode Island seems to have used primogeniture until 1770 (except from 1718 to 1728). Maryland abolished primogeniture in 1715, substituting equal division. The remaining colonies (New York, New Jersey, Virginia, the Carolinas, and Georgia), all royal, retained primogeniture until the American Revolution: . Georgia, in its earliest years, experimented with entailing lands by patent to male heirs, but it was an unpopular system.

If the heir-at-law automatically inherited entailed and intestate lands, then the eldest son need not be mentioned in his father's will. For example, in 1713, a John Taylor of Julian Creek, Norfolk County, Virginia, made a deed stating that the will of his brother Richard (Richard was alive) did not leave seventy-five acres to Richard's eldest son and in fact did not name this eldest son at all. Since the land had come to Richard from their father, John feared that if the land were not specifically transferred to the eldest son, he himself or his heirs would inherit this tract because John was the eldest son and primogeniture was the law in Virginia. Therefore, John, in his deed, gave seventy-five acres belonging to Richard to Richard's eldest son, Richard, Jr. Richard, Sr.'s will survives and indeed does not mention the seventy-five acres or his eldest son.[91]

No English law required a testator, in disinheriting a child, to name him or her or to leave such a disinherited child the proverbial one shilling. As an unfortunate result, many wills ignore some children, leaving the genealogist in doubt as to whether the omission means the person was disinherited, dead, or not a child of the testator. Other records must be used to establish such points.

However, good genealogy is a conjunction of many types of records that together reinforce a pedigree and simultaneously test it. Land records are an essential strand in that web of proof but are only one part. For example, the problem was to identify which of several Isaac Lindseys in Maury County, Tennessee, married in 1808 and died in Navarro County, Texas, in 1852.[92] An 1810 will by John Lindsey named a son, Isaac, who was a good chronological fit for the Texan, but this John had no deeds in Maury. Because Maury was opened to white settlement by an 1805 Indian cession and because the Lindsey family was certainly there by 1807, this absence of deeds or patents from the state of Tennessee was puzzling until local history provided an

Software for Mapping

Compiled by Birdie Monk Holsclaw, CG

It is strongly recommended that the researcher gain a basic understanding of manual mapping techniques before attempting to use mapping software. New software is always being developed, so watch for announcements and reviews in genealogical journals and newsletters.

Deed-Chek 7.0 (Windows). Emerald Data, Inc., 2440 Sandy Plains Road, Building #7, Marietta, Ga. 30066. <www.deedchek.com>. Draws single deeds with ability to add housepad and landscaping detail; can handle curves.

DeedMapper 3.0 (Windows). Direct Line Software, 71 Neshobe Road, Newton, Mass. 02468. <http://users.rcn.com/deeds/>. Compiles and prints single or multiple "metes and bounds" maps. For a small additional charge, computer "topographic" map overlays are available, showing streams, roads, railroads, and public land sections.

Deed Plotter + for Windows 1.0 (Windows). Greenbrier Graphics, LLC, 438 Lockbridge Road, Meadow Bridge, W. Va. 25976. <www.greenbriergraphics.com/>. Compiles and prints single or multiple maps; allows rotation and curves. Handles "metes and bounds" as well as "rectangular" surveys. Can generate maps directly from legal descriptions in word processing programs.

LANDcalc 1.17 (Macintosh, Mac OS X Classic mode). COMPUneering Inc., 113 McCabe Crescent, Thornhill, Ontario L4J 2S6 CANADA. <www.compuneering.com/landcalc.php>. Comprehensive map drawing program for surveyors; very technical. Compiles single or multiple tracts on screen or printer; many labeling options. Price determined by number of data points (thirty or three hundred). More features available in LANDesign.

Muncy's Plat Pronto 1.6 (Windows). B. W. Muncy, Inc., P.O. Box 11663, Lexington, Ky. 40577-1663. <www.bwmuncy.com>. Draws single plats; user can insert bitmap pictures into the plat.

explanation. In 1783, North Carolina had allowed the purchase of Tennessee lands still held by Indians. The Maury County area had been claimed in 5,000-acre tracts by wealthy North Carolinians, but only in 1805 and 1806 could whites actually settle there. The Lindseys had arrived to legally "new" lands that had actually been long owned.

The deeds, court minutes, tax lists, marriages, and other usual records sorted out four groups of Lindseys—a justice of the peace who lived in the eastern part of the county, a late-coming family who settled in the southwestern corner, two brothers who owned land but never settled in the county, and the group to whom the Texan apparently belonged.

In the absence of deeds, the Texan's family was localized by three steps: (1) the 1809 court minutes contained an oath about a lease from Long heirs to John Lindsey; (2) various road overseer appointments placed the targeted Lindseys on Little Bigby Creek in the center of the county; and (3) the 5,000-acre tract of the Long family, purchased in 1783, was plotted, locating it on Duck River, which runs through the center of Maury County, and overlying Little Bigby Creek. Thus, the Long acres included Little Bigby Creek. Clearly, John Lindsey had leased his Little Bigby land from the Longs, not purchased it.

The rest of the proof included tracing the family back through Georgia into South Carolina. John had a brother who died, leaving three small sons who had come to Maury with their uncle John. One of these sons was named Isaac, while a second son had a son of his own named Isaac, neither being the Isaac who had married in 1808 and gone to Texas. Thus, the Texan was the one named in the 1810 will. By reading many volumes page by page, by plotting land grants, by following clues through several states, and through the fortunate survival of records, it was possible to see these Lindseys in Maury in the years 1805 to 1830, to sort out the different families, and to single out individuals. Land records underlie the whole proof, though alone they could never have untangled the lineage.

Several contributors have greatly enhanced the contents of this chapter. William Thorndale, whose text and arrangement in the first edition of *The Source* continues to be the core strength of the chapter; Mary McCampbell Bell, CLS, CGL, who provided the overview of early surveying in Virginia, designed the "Creating a Plat" figure, and revised the State Summary for Virginia; Birdie Monk Holsclaw, CG, who submitted the Mapping Software section; and Christine Rose who reviewed the Military Bounty Land section.

Summary of Land Records by State

This summary locates the first-title grants or patents for each state. Because all states except Connecticut, Rhode Island, and Vermont have recorded deeds and mortgages in the county and independent city, the deeds are assumed to be there unless otherwise stated. In short, the deeds should be easy to find, assuming they have not been destroyed. A general and current source for deed repository sites and addresses is Alice Eichholz, editor, *Red Book: American State, County, and Town Sources, 3rd edition* (Provo, Utah: Ancestry, 2004). By contrast, the location of the original land grants and patents can vary widely from state to state, hence this summary. The state summary references provided here to early district land office holdings will be greatly enhanced by a reading of "Records of the Bureau of Land Management (Record Group 49) 1685–1993," part of the regularly updated Web version of Robert B. Matchette et al., *Guide to Federal Records in the National Archives of the United States* (1995 print) at <www.archives.gov/research_room>. Keys to using this summary are as follows:

1) For the thirty states identified as public land states:

"Hone" refers to E. Wade Hone, *Land and Property Research in the United States* (Salt Lake City: Ancestry, 1997).

"GLO-ARS" directs the reader to the online General Land Office Automated Records System at <www.glorecords.blm.gov>. This site includes links to state-held materials, unique indexes, and special projects, such as the GenWeb Project on Land Records. NOTE: The CD-ROMs published for some states as part of the GLO-ARS project contain excellent introductory material, some unique to that state and some more general.

"BLM-ESO" refers to the Bureau of Land Management's Eastern States Office, located at 7450 Boston Blvd., Springfield, VA 22153. When appropriate, the address and website for the appropriate BLM office for a Western state is given.

"Inventory No. 22" refers to Harry P. Yoshpe and Philip P. Brower, *Preliminary Inventory of the Land-Entry Papers of the General Land Office*. (1949; reprint, San Jose, Calif.: Rose Family Association, 1996).

"NARA" refers to the National Archives and Records Administration and is followed by the name of the regional archives. The location of and contact information for each regional archive is at <www.archives.gov/facilities/>.

"NA-DC" signifies the National Archives and Records Administration offices in Washington, D.C. When used in connection with private land claims, please note the following:

"Private Land Claims" are the case files of claims concerning the initial ownership of land and are in the National Archives in Washington, D.C. The claims may be indexed in one or more of these publications.

(a) **"ASP"** *American State Papers, Public Lands 1789–1837 and Claims*, 9 vols. (1832–61; reprint, Greenville, S.C.: Southern Historical Press, 1994). These volumes are available for full-text search at <www.memory.loc.gov/ammem/amlaw/lawhome.html>. Philip W. McMullin, *Grassroots of America* (Reprint. Greenville: Southern Historical Press, 1994) is an essential name index to the print and the online editions. The cases which appear in the *American State Papers* involve disputes or appeals over private land titles heard by land commissioners prior to 1837.

(b) *Reports of the Committees on Private Land Claims of the Senate and House of Representatives,* 2 vols. (45th Cong., 3rd sess., Misc. Doc 81, serial 1836). These volumes collect committee reports on individual land claims considered from 1826–76 by the two congressional committees on private land claims. Each volume is indexed by name of claimant or subject, but many names were omitted (see text under "Private Land Claims").

(c) The *Congressional Serial Set* provides digested summaries and alphabetical lists of private claims presented to the United States Congress from the 1st to the 60th Congress (1789–1909). These claims appear in an alphabetical list that may facilitate the locating of original entries or documents. An index to the Congressional Serial Set is at <http://memory.loc.gov/ammem/amlaw/lwss.html>.

Addresses and websites of state land offices (where relevant) are provided. Contact information for state historical societies and state archives will be found in appendix E, "Historical Societies," and appendix H, "State Archives."

2) For the states identified as state land states:

"Bockstruck" refers to Lloyd deWitt Bockstruck, *Revolutionary War Bounty Land Grants Awarded by State Governments* (Baltimore: Genealogical Publishing Co., 1996). Page numbers are given for the introductory notes about the process and requirements determined by each state.

The titles and websites cited for each state are obviously only a small number of what is available. There are countless other references that will prove useful. This summary attempts to provide record locations as of 2005. Remember that generalizations have exceptions and that records are sometimes transferred. Always inquire to verify locations before beginning research.

Alabama

Public-domain state with two principal meridians (established 1805 and 1807) and fifteen GLO land districts. The first opened at St. Stephens in 1806, and the last closed at Montgomery in 1927 (see Hone, 270–80). NARA's Southeast Region in Atlanta, Georgia, holds local office registers, tract books, and correspondence, 1805–54, for Cahaba, Huntsville, Mobile, and St. Stephens district land offices. Similar records for the other local offices are at the NA-DC. The BLM-ESO has the original patents, tract books, cadastral survey field notes, and township plats. Alabama's federal patents are indexed and scanned in the GLO-ARS; a CD-ROM version of the index may be ordered online. NA-DC has the land-entry case files as described in Inventory No. 22, and a card index to Alabama federal patentees to 30 June 1908 (excluding private land claims). Case files for private land claims are at NA-DC. Some are indexed in Fern Ainsworth, *Private Land Claims: Alabama, Arkansas, and Florida* (Natchitoches, La.: the author, 1978). State and some county copies of ledgers, tract books, plats, and correspondence are at the Alabama Department of Archives and History, 624 Washington Avenue, Montgomery, Alabama 36130-0100; <www.archives.state.al.us>. See "Old Land Records of Madison County, Alabama," *Family Puzzlers* no. 622 (20 September 1979): 2–3. Marilyn Davis Barefield has abstracted GLO district records, using mostly state duplicates rather than GLO originals. In addition to *Old Cahaba Land Office Records & Military Warrants, 1817–1853* (Greenville, S.C.: Southern University Press, 1986), she has published, in eight volumes, the land office records and military warrants for Demopolis; Huntsville; Mardisville, Lebanon, and Centre; Montgomery; Sparta and Elba; Tuskaloosa; and St. Stephens. Many private land claims were processed through the St. Stephens office, and this volume contains entries from the *American State Papers*. Pre-1813 records for Alabama south of thirty-one degrees should be in Tallahassee in the West Florida archive. Also see James F. Doster, "Land Titles and Public Land Sales in Early Alabama," *Alabama Review* 16 (1963): 108–24; and David Lightner, "Private Land Claims in Alabama," ibid., 20 (1967): 187–204.

Alaska

Public-domain state with five principal meridians (three established from 1905 to 1911 and two in 1956). Alaska was under the jurisdiction of the Russian American Company until 1867; the company's papers (1802–67) are microfilmed on M11, seventy-seven rolls. Trade, not settlement, was the company's goal, and the NARS pamphlet accompanying the microfilm collection does not mention any land title collection. An act of 1884 first authorizing a civilian governor expressly excluded general U.S. land law from Alaska except for mines and mining claims. The earliest of three GLO land districts opened at Sitka in 1885 (see Hone, 281). NARA's Pacific Alaska Region in Anchorage, Alaska, holds records of the Alaska state office and the Anchorage, Circle City, Fairbanks, Juneau, Nukalo, Rampart, Sitka, and St. Michael district land offices. These records include local office registers, tract books, and correspondence, 1885–1977, and rejected, canceled, and relinquished serial application case files, 1908–69. Serial patents are being indexed and scanned for GLO-ARS. Obtain patents from the BLM Alaska State Office, 222 W. 7th Ave., #13, Anchorage, AK 99513-5076; <www.ak.blm.gov>. Inventory No. 22 lists exactly fifty-six cash entries and 133 homestead patents for all of Alaska. NA-DC has the land-entry case files as described in Inventory No. 22, and a card index to Alaska patentees to 30 June 1908 (excluding private land claims). The Alaska State Archives and Records

Management in Juneau has descriptions and maps of mining claims. Seek deeds at the office of the district recorder in the judicial districts (Alaska's equivalent to counties).

Arizona

Public-domain state with two principal meridians (established 1865 and 1869). The earliest of Arizona's three GLO land districts opened in Prescott in 1870 (see Hone, 282–84). NARA's Pacific Region in Laguna Niguel, California, holds records of the Arizona state office and the Florence, Phoenix, Prescott, and Tucson district land offices. These include registers, tract books, and correspondence, 1870–1970; serial patent case files, 1970; and rejected, canceled, and relinquished serial application case files, 1908–55. Serial patents are being indexed and scanned for GLO-ARS. Order patents from the BLM Arizona State Office, P.O. Box 16563, Phoenix, AZ 85004-2203 (222 N. Central Ave.); <www.az.blm.gov/azso.htm>. This office also holds original tract books, cadastral survey field notes, and township plats (all of which are duplicated and at BLM-ESO). NA-DC has the land-entry case files as described in Inventory No. 22, and a card index to Arizona patentees to 30 June 1908 (excluding private land claims). Arizona was part of the Mexican Cession of 1848; case files for private land claims are at NA-DC or contact the BLM New Mexico State Office, P.O. Box 27115, Santa Fe, NM 87502-0115 (1474 Rodeo Road). See *The Court of Private Land Claims for the Adjudication of Spanish and Mexican Land Titles in Colorado, New Mexico, Arizona, Nevada, Utah, and Wyoming* (on microfilm).

Arkansas

Public-domain state with one principal meridian (established 1815). There were eight GLO land districts, beginning and ending with Little Rock, 1821 to 1933 (see Hone, 285–95). NARA's Southwest Region in Fort Worth, Texas, holds local office registers, tract books, and correspondence, 1857–61 and 1877–79 for Champagnolle, Clarksville, Dardanelle, and Little Rock district land offices. Other local office records are in the Arkansas State Land Office, Room 109, State Capitol, Little Rock, AR 72201. The BLM-ESO has the original patents, tract books, and township plats. Arkansas's federal patents are indexed and scanned in the GLO-ARS; a CD-ROM version may be ordered online. The NA-DC has the land-entry case files as described in Inventory No. 22. Case files for private land claims are at NA-DC. Some are indexed in Fern Ainsworth, *Private Land Claims: Alabama, Arkansas, and Florida* (Natchitoches, La.: the author, 1978). After the Louisiana Purchase in 1803, settlers overran Indian lands in what would become Arkansas. Some of this land was returned to the Indians by the federal government, including the counties of Lovely and Miller, now part of Oklahoma. Abstracts of the depositions of expelled settlers are included in Melinda Blanchard Crawford and Don L. Crawford, *The Settlers of Lovely County and Miller County, Arkansas Territory, 1820–1830* (Rockport, Maine: Picton Press, 2002). Arkansas held one of the War of 1812's military reserves. The warrants and an index are available on NARS microfilm M848, *War of 1812 Military Bounty Warrants, 1815–1858*, fourteen rolls. A circa 1860 listing of patentees in the reserve is Katheren Christensen, *Arkansas Military Bounty Grants (War of 1812)* (Hot Springs, Ark.: Arkansas Ancestors, 1971). Desmond W. Allen has published *Arkansas Land Patents Through 1908* (Conway, Ark.: Arkansas Research, 1990), a fifty-seven volume series with information taken from the GLO-ARS. Allen has transcribed and indexed Arkansas donation lands (1871–1955) and swamp lands (1855–2001). These entries are for federal lands that were given to and disposed by the state of Arkansas. They are published as regional county volumes with a separate volume for the school lands (1853–1997) of Section 16.

California

Public-domain state with three principal meridians (established 1851 to 1853). The first of ten GLO land districts opened at Los Angeles and Benicia in 1853 (see Hone, 296–304). NARA's Pacific Region (San Francisco) at San Bruno has local office registers, tract books, and correspondence, 1858–1981; serial patent case files, 1963–74; and rejected, canceled, and relinquished serial application case files, 1908–74 for district offices except for the Los Angeles area. NARA's Pacific Region at Laguna Niguel holds similar local district records for Bakersfield, Los Angeles, and Riverside. The BLM-ESO has original patent documents, tract books, cadastral field notes, and township plats. The BLM California State Office, 2800 Cottage Way, Suite W-1834, Sacramento, CA 95825-1886, has copies of pre-1908 patents and tract books and township plats. Serial patents are being indexed and scanned for GLO-ARS. The NA-DC has the land-entry case files as described in Inventory No. 22, and the GLO headquarters has originals of the tract books and township plats. The California State Archives has two collections of Spanish and Mexican land grant records from the Office of the U.S. Surveyor General for California. An index to Spanish and Mexican land grant maps, 1855–1875 is at <www.ss.ca.gov/archives/archives_e.htm>; or see J. N. Bowman, "Index to the Spanish-Mexican Private Land Grant Records and Cases of California" (microfilmed typescript at Bancroft Library, Berkeley, 1958). NA-DC has microfilmed federal California court records regarding private land claims, 1852–1910 (NARA microfilms T1207, T1214, T1215, and T1216). Case files for private land claims are at NA-DC.

Because the government could not control the hordes of 1849 miners, it pretended they did not exist, and there are no GLO records of 1849 gold rush claims. See Joseph Ellison, "The Mineral Land Question in California, 1848–1866," *Southwestern Historical Quarterly* 30 (1926): 34–55; William Wilcox Robinson,

Land in California, the Story of Mission Lands, Ranchos, Squatters, Mining Claims, Railroad Grants, Land Scrip [and] Homesteads (Berkeley: University of California Press, 1948; reprint, University of California Press, 1979); Rose H. Avina, *Spanish and Mexican Land Grants in California* (New York: Arno Press, 1976); Paul W. Gates, *Land and Law in California: Essays on Land Policies* 49 (Ames: Iowa State Press, 1992), and David Vaught, "A Tale of Three Land Grants on the Northern California Borderlands," *Agricultural History* (Spring 2004).

Colorado

Public-domain state with three principal meridians (established 1855 and 1880). The earliest of thirteen GLO land districts opened at Golden City in 1863 (see Hone, 305–317). NARA's Rocky Mountain Region in Denver holds GLO local office records for the more than seventy land districts formerly covering Colorado, New Mexico, Montana, the Dakotas, and Utah. Serial patents are being indexed and scanned for GLO-ARS. Obtain patents from the BLM Colorado State Office, 2850 Youngfield St., Lakewood, CO 80215-7076, which also has copies of the tract books and township plats. The NA-DC has the land-entry case files as described in Inventory No. 22, and the GLO headquarters originals of the tract books and township plats. Case files for private land claims are at NA-DC. See LeRoy R. Hafen, "Mexican Land Grants in Colorado," *Colorado Magazine* 4 (1927): 82–93; George L. Anderson, "The Canon City or Arkansas Valley Claim Club, 1860–1862," ibid. 16 (1939): 201–10; "The Middle Park Claim Club, 1861," ibid. 10 (1933): 189–93; and a series of articles collectively titled "Spanish Land Grants in New Mexico and Colorado," *Journal of the West* 19 (July 1980): 1–99. Also see Joseph O. Van Hook, "Mexican Land Grants in the Arkansas Valley," *Southwestern Historical Quarterly* 40 (1936–37): 58–75. Between 1999 and 2004, *Boulder Genealogical Society Quarterly* published the names of first purchasers of original land tracts in Boulder County.

Connecticut

State-land state surveyed in variations of the New England town. First settled 1634 to 1635 in the Connecticut River Valley, its river towns formed a united government in 1639 without a charter from England. The New Haven colony was founded in 1638 and absorbed into Connecticut under the royal charter of 1662, which authorized a corporate colony (one that chooses its own governor). Connecticut was thus always free to grant its own lands, which it did through the General Court (assembly or legislature), usually to town proprietors but sometimes to individuals by grant or sale. The records are at the state archive in the Connecticut State Library; many of the colonial land records have been microfilmed. Volume 14 of *Collections of The Connecticut Historical Society* (Hartford, Conn.: The Society, 1912) includes all the Hartford land records from 1639 to the 1680s. An index is the *General Index of the Land Records of the Town of Hartford, 1639–1879* (Hartford: Connecticut Historical Society, 1873–83); this *General Index* has been placed online (2003) at the website of The New England Historic and Genealogical Society, <www.newenglandancestors.org>, for use by members. The Connecticut State Library also has such pertinent papers as the Robert C. Winthrop Collection, 1631 to 1794, and the William F. J. Boardman Collection, 1661 to 1835, both of which include land papers. Conveyances are recorded in the towns, not the counties. Proprietor records are rich in land records. See Nelson P. Mead, "Land System of the Connecticut Towns," *Political Science Quarterly* 21 (1906): 59–76 and Dorothy Deming, *The Settlement of the Connecticut Towns* (New Haven, Conn.: Tercentenary Commission, 1933). See Bockstruck, ix, regarding military bounty land awarded by Connecticut.

Delaware

State-land state surveyed in indiscriminate metes and bounds. Delaware is unique among the thirteen colonies in not having some colonial jurisdiction within its bounds that granted first titles to its lands. See Edward F. Heite, ed., *Delaware's Fugitive Records: An Inventory of the Official Land Grant Records Relating to the Present State of Delaware* (Dover: Delaware Division of Historical and Cultural Affairs, 1980). The successive absorption of New Sweden into the Dutch colony of New Netherlands and then into the English proprietary of James, Duke of York, means the early Delaware grants were made in New York. In 1682, the Duke of York conveyed his claims in present-day Delaware to William Penn, whose Pennsylvania proprietary granted Delaware's lands until the revolution. In 1770, the Delaware legislature ordered the New York grants transcribed, since published as *Original Titles in Delaware Commonly Known as the Duke of York Records 1646–1679* (Wilmington: Delaware General Assembly, 1903), abstracted in the *Maryland and Delaware Genealogist*, vols. 5–15, 18 (1964–74, 1977). See also B. Fernow, *Documents Relating to the History of the Dutch and Swedish Settlements on the Delaware River* (Albany, N.Y.: Argus, 1877). Warrants and surveys from the Penn proprietary, 1682 to 1776, are in the Delaware Hall of Records in Dover, as are tax records of the levy courts. The proprietary quitrents are at the Historical Society of Pennsylvania in Philadelphia. Forty-five Maryland grants are listed in Percy G. Skirven, "Durham County: Lord Baltimore's Attempt at Settlement of His Lands on the Delaware Bay, 1670–1685," *Maryland Historical Magazine* 25 (1930): 157–67. Also see A. R. Dunlop, "Dutch and Swedish Land Records Relating to Delaware . . . ," *Delaware History* 6 (1954–55): 25–51. The most recent deeds are in the three Delaware counties. Most early deeds were transferred from the counties to the Delaware Public Archives. Ten volumes of *Kent County, Delaware, Land Records,* have been published covering 1680–1775, the first eight by Mary Marshall Brewer, the last two by Irma Harper. Deeds for New Castle County, 1673–1765, are published in seven volumes by Carol Bryant and Carol J. Garrett. The deeds of Sussex County, 1681–1805, with some gaps, were compiled by various authors between 1990 and 2002.

District of Columbia

The Federal District of the United States, originally a ten-mile square taken from Maryland and Virginia, was created by acts of 1790 and 1791. Originally, the District included the town and county of Alexandria, Virginia, and the city of Georgetown, Maryland. The area ceded by Virginia was retroceded in 1846, and in 1878 Georgetown was annexed, giving the city its present limits and making the city of Washington coextensive with the District of Columbia. Until 1879, the area within the District but outside both Georgetown and Washington City was known as Washington County.

The land records include deed books, 1792–1869, and other typical legal documents, such as bills of sales, mortgages, and manumissions of slaves. Although the earliest deeds (1792–1869) are at NA-DC, indexes to all the records are maintained at the Office of the District of Columbia Recorder of Deeds. Both records and indexes have been microfilmed (deeds 1792–1886 and general index 1792–1919) and are available at the Family History Library in 694 rolls. Land transactions prior to 1792 are found among the records for Maryland or Virginia. See Bessie Wilmarth Gahn, *Original Patentees of Land at Washington Prior to 1700* (1836; reprint, Baltimore: Clearfield, 1998) for the earliest landowners.

Through the years, when Alexandria County was within the District of Columbia, it recorded its own deeds, as did the city of Alexandria. See John Frederick Dorman, "A Guide to the Counties of Virginia: Alexandria County (Arlington County)," *Virginia Genealogist* 3 (1959): 126–27.

Florida

Public-domain state with one principal meridian (established 1824). Of the five GLO land districts, the earliest opened at Tallahassee in 1825; the last closed at Gainesville in 1933 (see Hone, 318–22). NARA's Southeast Region in Atlanta, Georgia., holds local records of the Gainesville district land office, including local office lists and correspondence, 1879 and 1932–33. The BLM-GLO has the original patents, tract books, and township plats. Florida's federal patents are indexed and scanned in the GLO-ARS; a CD-ROM version of the index may be ordered online. NA-DC has the land-entry case files and a card index to Florida patentees to 30 June 1908 (excluding private land claims). Case files for private land claims are at NA-DC, as are Florida donation entry files (ca. 1842) under the Florida Armed Occupation Act of 1842, which granted 160 acres to settlers able to bear arms.

In 1821, Spain surrendered to the United States present-day Florida, including British/Spanish East Florida and, west of the Apalachicola River, the portion of British/Spanish West Florida that remained after the United States had seized western West Florida in 1810. Parts of the surviving British/Spanish provincial archives formerly at Saint Augustine and Pensacola are now in the State Library and Archives of Florida in Tallahassee. Several congressional land commissions and many courts grappled with private land claims. Records used as evidence in reviewing Spanish grant claims, dating 1763 (or earlier) through 1821, are digitized at <www.floridamemory.com/Collections/SpanishLandGrants>. The East Florida private land claims (1824–28) are on microfilm (seventeen rolls), as are East Florida Spanish land grant archives (1764–1844) (eight rolls). The Historical Records Survey published five volumes on *Spanish Land Grants in Florida* (Tallahassee, 1940–41), which are reported to contain British grants and private land claims as well.

Early tax rolls are held by the counties but the Florida State Archives has some dating between 1829 and 1881. Most have been microfilmed. See also George C. Whatley and Sylvia Cook, "The East Florida Land Commission: A Study in Frustration," *Florida Historical Quarterly* 50 (1971): 39–52; Charles L. Mowat, "The Land Policy in British East Florida," *Agricultural History* 14 (1940): 75–77; and S.W. Martin, "The Public Domain in Territorial Florida," *Journal of Southern History* 10 (1944): 174–87.

Georgia

State-land state surveyed partly in indiscriminate metes and bounds and partly in lottery lots. The state archives in Atlanta holds the grants, surveys, and related papers for Georgia from the colony's founding. Its major records and indexes are microfilmed. Indexes of land holdings include an admirable work by Marion R. Hemperley, *Georgia Surveyor General Department: A History and Inventory of Georgia's Land Office* (Atlanta: State Printing Office, 1982). A sampling of other titles issued by the department include Marion R. Hemperley and Pat Bryant, *English Crown Grants, 1755–1775*, 9 vols. (1972–74); Pat Bryant, *Entry of Claims for Georgia Landholders, 1733–1775* (1975); and Alex M. Hitz, *Authentic List of All Land Lottery Grants Made to Veterans of the Revolutionary War by the State of Georgia (1820, 1827, 1832)* (1955).

The three major means of granting land in Georgia were headrights (usually two hundred acres for heads of households plus fifty acres for each family member and slave), Revolutionary War bounty warrants (for citizens purportedly loyal to the revolutionary government), and lotteries. The headrights are listed in *Index to the Headright and Bounty Grants of Georgia, 1756–1909* (1970; reprint, Greenville, S.C.: Southern Historical Press, 1992). The revolutionary war bounty warrant files are very incomplete and quite confusing. Bockstruck labels Georgia's system as the most complex of all the governments, but pages x–xiv explain the process and comments on works intended as "complete" lists.

The lotteries began with an act of 1803 and disposed of public lands in ceded Indian territories in 1805, 1807, 1820, 1821, 1827, and 1832. Eligibility required Georgia residency with extra draws for special categories, such as revolutionary war service. See Robert Scott Davis, Jr., *Research in Georgia* (1981; reprint, Greenville, S.C.: Southern Historical Press, 1991), or go online to <www.sos.state.ga.us/archives> for a summary of qualifications for each lottery. The statewide lists for all lotteries are in print and online (see above website) but may give only winning draws—except for the 1805 list, which shows all persons eligible under the enabling act of 1803. Its year's residency requirement from May 1802 makes it a good substitute for the missing 1800 Georgia federal census. There are some county eligibility lists in manuscript for later lotteries, and these might identify additional Revolutionary War veterans. See also Robert S. Davis, Jr., and Silas Emmett Lucas, Jr., *The Georgia Land Lottery Papers, 1805–1914: Genealogical Data from the Loose Papers Filed in the Georgia Surveyor General Office Concerning the Lots Won in the State Land Lotteries and the People Who Won Them* (1979; reprint, Greenville, S.C.: Southern Historical Press, 1987). Prior to 1777, Georgia conveyances were recorded only in Savannah and survive mostly in the state archives. See *A Preliminary Guide to Eighteenth-Century Records Held by the Georgia Department of Archives and History* (Atlanta: Georgia Department of Archives and History, 1976). The R. J. Taylor, Jr., Foundation of Atlanta has published indexes to several of these colonial records and plans to publish more. The State Tax Commission lists for 1787 to 1899 have been microfilmed. For essential background on headright grants, subsequent laws, Indian treaties, land reserves, boundaries, maps, county surveys, surveyors' field notes, frauds, and land transfers in Georgia see Farris W. Cadle, *Georgia Land Surveying: History and Law* (Athens: University of Georgia Press, 1991), or the excerpts provided at the website noted above.

Hawaii

State-land state unique in the Union for the Polynesian origins of its land titles. Hawaiian lands have never been part of the federal public domain. Prior to European settlement, the idea of absolute fee-simple land title did not exist. Instead, there was a hierarchy of right of use descending from the king through chiefs and subchiefs to commoners. The royal family or high chiefs gave Europeans and Americans similar rights of use, which the foreigners interpreted as absolute ownership. In 1848, a Royal Land Commission sought to resolve the confusion and allocate permanent ownership by confirming royal patents or allocating land to the government, which then awarded grants. Records of original titles by the land commission are in the state archive, while the grants by purchase are at the Land Management Section of the Department of Land and Natural Resources, 1151 Punchbowl St., Honolulu, HI 96813; <www.hawaii.gov/dlnr/bc/bc>. This site offers a search of land transfers from 1976 forward, by document number or name of grantee or grantor. The major parts of both collections have been microfilmed. Deeds for all of the islands (1844–1900) with an index (1845–1917) have been microfilmed in 108 reels. See titles by Jon J. Chinen, *Original Land Titles in Hawaii* (the author, 1961); *The Great Mahele: Hawaii's Land Division of 1848* (Honolulu: University of Hawaii Press, 1994); and *They Cried for Help: The Hawaiian Land Revolution of the 1840s and 1850s* (Xlibris Corporation, 2002). See also, Thomas Marshall Spaulding, *Crown Lands of Hawaii* (Honolulu: University of Hawaii, 1923) and Robert H. Horwitz, *Public Land Policy in Hawaii: An Historical Analysis* (Honolulu: University of Hawaii, 1969).

Idaho

Public-domain state with one principal meridian (established 1867). Of the five GLO land districts, the earliest offices opened in Boise City and Lewistown in 1866. (See Hone, 323–25). The township plats and the records for the Office of Surveyor General of Idaho, 1913–50 are at NARA-Pacific Alaska Region in Seattle. This region also holds microfiche of the records for the Lewiston Land Office (1874–1908) and local office registers, tract books, and correspondence, 1866–1973, and rejected, canceled, and relinquished serial application case files, 1908–66, for the other GLO district offices. Serial patents are being indexed and scanned for GLO-ARS. Order patents from the BLM Idaho State Office, 1387 S. Vinnell Way, Boise, ID 83709; <www.id.blm.gov>. This office also has copies of the tract books and township plats. The NA-DC has the land-entry case files as described in Inventory No. 22 and also the GLO headquarters originals of the tracts books and township plats.

Illinois

Public-domain state with three principal meridians (established 1805 and 1815). Of the ten GLO land districts, the earliest opened at Kaskaskia in 1809 and the last closed at Springfield in 1876. Some land in pre-1821 east-central Illinois was sold through the Vincennes land district (see Hone, 326–34). NARA's Great Lakes Region in Chicago holds some local office registers, tract books, and correspondence from all the Illinois land districts, including Vincennes. Other records of these offices are in the Illinois State Archives, which has indexed *Illinois Public Domain Land Tract Sales* at <www.cyberdriveillinois.com/departments/archives/archives.html>. This same site offers access to the 3,457 digitized federal township plats of Illinois (also available on CD-ROM). The BLM-ESO has original patents and tract books. Illinois's federal patents are indexed and scanned in the GLO-ARS. NA-DC has the land-entry case files as described in Inventory No. 22, and the cadastral survey field notes and township plats. Case files for private land claims are at NA-DC.

See ASP or Fern Ainsworth, *Private Land Claims: Illinois, Indiana, Michigan and Wisconsin*. (Natchitoches, La.: the author, 1980). One of the War of 1812 military reserves for bounty-land warrants was in west-central Illinois; some records are at the state archives. NARA M848, *War of 1812 Military Bounty Land Warrants, 1815–1858*, misses some Illinois entries so use House Doc. 262, 26th Congress, 1st sess., 1840, reprinted with an index as Lowell M. Volkel, *War of 1812 Bounty Lands in Illinois* (Thomson, Ill.: Heritage House, 1977) to identify patentees in the military tract. See also, *War of 1812 Military Bounty Land Warrants, 1815–1858*, compiled and indexed by April Leigh Helm, Matthew L. Helm, et al., CD-ROM produced by FamilyToolbox.net Inc., 2003. See Paul W. Gates, "The Disposal of the Public Domain in Illinois, 1848–1856," *Journal of Economics and Business History* 3 (1931): 216–40; James E. Wright, *The Galena Lead District: Federal Policy and Practice, 1824–1847* (Madison: State Historical Society of Wisconsin, 1966); and Carl J. Ekberg, *French Roots in the Illinois Country: the Mississippi Frontier in Colonial Times* (University of Illinois Press, 2000). The early French grants are found in the Raymond H. Hammes Collection, microfilmed by GSU and titled "Colonial and Territorial Research Collection of Illinois." For maps, see Arlyn Kay Sherwood, *Illinois State Library's Complete Holding of Illinois County Land Ownership Maps and Atlases (Illinois Libraries)*, (Springfield: Illinois State Library, 1984).

Indiana

Public-domain state with two principal meridians (established 1799 and 1805). Of the six GLO land districts, the earliest opened at Vincennes in 1807; the last closed at Indianapolis in 1876 (see Hone, 335–45). The Cincinnati district land office issued several thousand patents for lands in southeastern Indiana within "the Gore." This was a roughly triangular-shaped area bounded by the Ohio-Indiana border, the Greenville Treaty line, and the Ohio River. NARA's Great Lakes Region in Chicago has some local office registers, tract books, and correspondence from these district offices. Other district office records were transferred to the auditor of state but are now in the state archive. Databases for some are at <www.in.gov/icpr/archives/databases>. The BLM-ESO has the original patents and tract books, cadastral survey field notes, and township plats. Indiana's federal patents are indexed and scanned in the GLO-ARS. Those sold through Cincinnati are scanned and indexed as Ohio records. NA-DC has the land-entry case files as described in Inventory No. 22, the cadastral field notes, and township plats. The land entries for the Cincinnati land district (1801–40) and Vincennes land district (1807–77) are indexed in Margaret R. Waters, *Indiana Land Entries*, 2 vols. (1948; reprint, Baltimore: Genealogical Publishing Co., 2004).

Vincennes was settled by 1733 and experienced a large influx of Americans after the revolution—a white enclave within Indian lands. Information on the earliest inhabitants is in Clifford Neil Smith's *French and British Land Grants in the Port Vincennes (Indiana) District, 1750–1784* (1996; reprint, Baltimore: Genealogical Publishing Co., 2004). For private land claims, see Fern Ainsworth, *Private Land Claims: Illinois, Indiana, Michigan and Wisconsin*. (Natchitoches, La.: the author, 1980). See also Malcolm J. Rohrbough, "The Land Office Business in Indiana, 1800–1840," in *This Land of Ours: The Acquisition and Disposition of the Public Domain* (Indianapolis: Indiana Historical Society, 1978), 39–59 and Stephen Frederick Strausberg, "The Administration and Sale of Public Land in Indiana 1800–1860" (Ph.D. dissertation, Cornell University, 1970).

Iowa

Public-domain state with one principal meridian (established 1815 in Arkansas). Iowa had nine land districts, the earliest opening in 1838 in Burlington and Dubuque, the last closing at Des Moines in 1910 (see Hone, 346–53). NARA's Central Plains Region in Kansas City, Missouri., holds local registers, tract books, and correspondence, 1836–1909 for the districts. The BLM-ESO has original patents and tract books. Iowa's federal patents are the last of the Eastern States to be indexed and scanned in the GLO-ARS. NA-DC has the land-entry case files as described in Inventory No. 22, the cadastral field notes, and township plats.

More than 20,000 settlers were in Iowa prior to the first land sales and thus had no legal title to their claims. To prevent speculators and latecomers from buying such improved lands at land office auctions, the settlers and speculators formed claims clubs to rig the auctions on grounds of first settlement. See Allan G. Bogue, "The Iowa Claims Clubs: Symbols and Substance," *Mississippi Valley Historical Review* 45 (1958): 231–35; Benjamin F. Shambaugh, ed., *Constitution and Records of the Claim Association of Johnson County, Iowa* (Iowa City: University of Iowa Press, 1894; Roscoe L. Lokken, *Iowa Public Land Disposal* (Iowa City: State Historical Society of Iowa, 1942); Robert P. Swierenga, *Pioneers and Profits: Land Speculation on the Iowa Frontier* (Ames: Iowa University Press, 1968); and "The Iowa Land Records Collection: Periscope to the Past" online at <www.lib.uiowa.edu/spec-coll/Bai/swierenga.htm>.

Kansas

Public-domain state with one principal meridian (established 1855). Of the eleven GLO land districts, the first opened at Lecompton in 1856, and the last closed at Topeka in 1925 (see Hone, 354–66). NARA's Central Plains Region in Kansas City, Mo., holds local office registers, tract books, and correspondence, 1854–1919. The Kansas State Historical Society <www.kshs.org/genealgists/land> has tract books on microfilm and a finding aid, *Kansas Tract Books*, on the Kansas reference shelf. Obtain patents from the BLM New Mexico State Office, P.O. Box 27115, 1474 Rodeo Rd., Santa Fe, NM 87502-0115, <www.nm.blm.gov>, which also has copies of the tract books and township plats for Kansas. Serial patents are being indexed and scanned for GLO-ARS. NA-DC has the land-entry case files as described in Inventory No. 22 and the GLO headquarters original tract books and township plats. Significant portions of Kansas fell within railroad land grants, the land offices of the Santa Fe and the Rock Island railroads being especially important. The Kansas State Historical Society Center for Historical Research, 6425 Southwest Sixth Ave., Topeka, Kansas 66615-1099, <www.kshs.org>, holds some of these papers. Many early settlers were homesteaders. Homestead land-entry case files are at NA-DC; some homestead application information is at NA-Central Plains Region. Case files for land purchases made under the Timber Culture Act of 1873 (western half of the state) are at NA-DC. See Samford A. Mosk, "Land Tenure Problems in the Santa Fe Railroad Grant Area" and George L. Anderson, "The Administration of Federal Land Laws in Western Kansas, 1880–1890: A Factor in Adjustment to a New Environment," in *Public Land Policies: Management and Disposal* (Ayer Co. Publishers, 1979); Paul W. Gates, *Fifty Million Acres: Conflicts over Kansas Land Policy, 1854–1890* (Reprint, University of Oklahoma Press, 1979); and Lawrence Bacon, *Kansas and the Homestead Act, 1862–1905* (Arno Press, 1979).

Kentucky

State-land state surveyed in indiscriminate metes and bounds east of the Tennessee River and in townships and ranges west of it. The Kentucky Land Office Division, Capitol Building, Frankfort, Kentucky 40601-3493 <http://sos.ky.gov/land/>, is an active department of the Office of Secretary of State and still issues an occasional new grant because the land-grant process, though rarely used, is still in effect in Kentucky for vacant, ungranted lands. Warrants, surveys, patents, and other records are in the land office, indexed and microfilmed, and open to public research; many indexes are online at the previously listed website. In 1792, Virginia sent to Kentucky its loose land papers relevant to Kentucky along with copies of its Virginia grants to Kentucky lands.

The separate categories of Kentucky grants are:

1. Virginia Grants, 1782–92. Sixteen volumes of 10,000 warrants issued by Virginia, including service in the French and Indian War, and transcribed in Richmond in the 1790s by order of the Kentucky legislature. See Joan E. Brookes-Smith, *Master Index: Virginia Surveys and Grants, 1774–1791* (Frankfort: Kentucky Historical Society, 1976).
2. Old Kentucky Grants, 1793–1856. Twenty volumes of military, seminary, academic, treasury warrant, and preemption grants made by Kentucky. See Kentucky Historical Society, *Index for Old Kentucky Surveys and Grants and Tellico Surveys & Grants Microfilmed by Kentucky Historical Society* (Frankfort: Kentucky Historical Society, 1975).
3. Grants South of Green River, 1797–1866. Eighteen volumes of non-military headrights of two hundred acres in the military reserve. These grants were first given as a relief for squatters.
4. Kentucky Land Warrants, 1816–73. Forty-three volumes covering lands east of the Tennessee River purchased from the state.
5. Tellico Grants, 1803–53. Two volumes describing 572 grants in the small Cherokee cession of 1805 in eastern Kentucky. See the *Index* listed in no. 2 above.
6. County Court Orders, 1835–2000. Largest series with over 70,000 warrants sold by each county court east of the Tennessee River for any vacant lands within its bounds. Online search at <http://sos.ky.gov/land/nonmilitary/patentseries/courtorders>.
7. Grants west of the Tennessee River, 1822–58. Eleven volumes surveyed in townships and ranges.
8. Grants South of Walker's Line, 1825–1923. Loose papers from Kentucky's right to grant lands in Tennessee north of 36 degrees 30 minutes, the intended state line. Walker ran the (present) line too far north. Researchers should also check the Tennessee land records for these grants. See James W. Sames III, *Four Steps West: A Documentary Concerning the First Dividing Line in America . . . Virginia, North Carolina, Kentucky, Tennessee* (1971; reprint, Versailles, Ky.: the author, 1994).
9. Warrants for Headrights, 1827–49. One volume containing fifty-five grants that probably belong in one of the other collections but became separated.

These and some other early land records are indexed in Willard Rouse Jillson, *The Kentucky Land Grants: A Systematic Index to All of the Land Grants Recorded in the State Land Office at Frankfort, Kentucky, 1782–1924*, Filson Club Publication No. 33 (1925; reprint, 2 vols. Baltimore: Genealogical Publishing Co., 1994) and his *Old Kentucky Entries and Deeds: A Complete Index to All of the Earliest Land Entries, Military Warrants, Deeds and Wills of the Commonwealth of Kentucky* (1926; reprint, Baltimore: Genealogical Publishing Co., 1999). These categories of land records have been summarized here because Kentucky suffered more than any other state from land-title litigation, because of the convergence of three unfortunate circumstances: liberal land-granting by Virginia in an area distant from its supervision; Kentucky's settlement during the turmoil of the revolution and its Indian wars, which meant that claims were frequently abandoned; and a tendency toward do-it-yourself rather than professional surveying. The resulting litigation produced a bonanza of depositions about first settlers, though such records are scattered in various courthouses and manuscript collections. An important collection is the microfilmed Kentucky Court of Appeals deed books, 1780 to 1909, in thirteen reels, and Michael

L. Cook and Bettie A. Cook, *Kentucky Court of Appeals Deed Books, 4 vols.* (Evansville, Ind.: Cook Publications, 1987). A Virginia Land Court sat at several Kentucky forts in 1780 to hear claims involving land north of Green River. Its transcripts appear in "Certificate Book of the Virginia Land Commission, 1779–80," *Register of the Kentucky State Historical Society* 21 (1923): 3–323. There were never any private land claims in Kentucky. The county tax lists, 1782 to ca. 1825, have been microfilmed and some are indexed, such as James F. Sutherland, *Early Kentucky Householders, 1787–1811* (1986; reprint, Clearfield, 2002) and *Early Kentucky Landholders, 1787–1811* (1986; reprint, Baltimore: Genealogical Publishing Co., 2000).

See Kandie Adkinson, "The Kentucky Land Grant System" *Saddlebag Notes Technical Leaflet*, from *The Circuit Rider*, publication of the Historical Confederation of Kentucky 13:3 (May/June 1990), online at <www.sos.state.ky.gov/land/reference/resources.htm>; Philip Fall Taylor, *A Calendar of the Warrants for Land in Kentucky, Granted for Service in the French and Indian War* (1917; reprint, Baltimore: Genealogical Publishing Co., 2004); Samuel M. Wilson, *Catalogue of Revolutionary Soldiers and Sailors of the Commonwealth of Virginia to Whom Land Bounty Warrants Were Granted* (1913; reprint, Baltimore: Genealogical Publishing Co., 2002); and George Mark Harding, "The Uncertainly of Early Kentucky Land Titles," *Genealogy* no. 64 (October 1981): 1–4.

Louisiana

Public-domain state with two principal meridians (established 1807 and 1819). Of the five GLO land districts, the first opened at Opelouses in 1805, and the last closed at Baton Rouge in 1927 (see Hone, 367–71). NARA's Southwest Region in Fort Worth, Texas, holds records of the Baton Rouge, Greensburg, and Monroe district land offices. These include local office registers, tract books, and correspondence, 1832–1907. The papers of the other offices are in the Louisiana State Land Office, Box 44124, Baton Rouge, LA 70804. The BLM-ESO has original patent documents, tract books, cadastral field notes, and township plats. Louisiana's federal patents are indexed and scanned in the GLO-ARS; a CD-ROM version of the index may be ordered online. NA-DC has the land-entry case files as described in Inventory No. 22 and a card index to Louisiana patentees to 30 June 1908 (excluding private land claims). For private land claims, see ASP. Some of the materials in *American State Papers, Public Lands* were reorganized along geographical lines in Charles R. Maduell, *Federal Land Grants in the Territory of Orleans; the Delta Parishes* (New Orleans: Polyanthos, 1975).

The French and Spanish governments of Louisiana left many pre-1804 papers, but the land-grant papers seem to have suffered more losses than other categories of records. The Spanish Louisiana Cabildo judicial records (1769–1804) at the Louisiana Historical Center in New Orleans are on microfilm and are rich in land transactions. Because a fairly fluent knowledge of French and Spanish is required to read handwritten records, these pre American records are beyond the average genealogist's reach. However, the Historical Records Survey transcribed in nineteen volumes the records from the District of Baton Rouge in Spanish West Florida, and these are indexed in Stanley Clisby Arthur, *Index to the Archives of Spanish West Florida, 1782–1810* (New Orleans: Polyanthos, 1975). See also NARS microfilm T1116 in seven rolls for the HRS typescripts of the Archives of the Spanish Government of West Florida, 1789 to 1816. The Historical Records Survey issued a *Survey of Federal Archives in Louisiana: Land Claims and Other Documents* (Baton Rouge: Historical Records Survey, 1940). Seek deeds in the notarial records or deed books of the parishes, Louisiana's equivalent of counties. See also Harry Lewis Coles, Jr., *History of the Administration of Federal Land Policies and Land Tenure in Louisiana, 1803–1860* (Ayer Co. Publishers, 1979); Frances P. Burns, "The Spanish Land Laws of Louisiana," *Louisiana Historical Quarterly* 11 (1928): 557–81; Elizabeth Gaspar Brown, "Legal Systems in Conflict: Orleans Territory 1804–1812," *American Journal of Legal History* 1 (1957): 35–75; Glenn R. Conrad, *Land Records of the Attakapas District*, vol. 1, *The Attakapas Domesday Book: Land Grants, Claims, and Confirmations in the Attakapas District, 1764–1826* (Lafayette, La.: Center for Louisiana Studies, 1990); and Ory G. Poret, "History of Land Titles in the State of Louisiana" at <www.state.la.us/slo/default.htm>.

Maine

State-land state surveyed in coastal areas in the usual New England towns and into townships in the backwoods areas. In the 1620s and 1630s, a number of vaguely defined large tracts were granted that overlapped each other and snarled later land titles. Then Massachusetts exploited the English Civil War to assert claims to Maine during 1652 to 1674, which further confused titles, as did the abandonment of nearly all Maine settlements during the Indian wars beginning in the 1670s.

Here is a drastic simplification of history: The Kennebec River was a dividing line, the area west and south being in the Ferdinando Gorges proprietary (granted 1622 and 1639) that was purchased by Massachusetts in 1677, while the area east and north of the Kennebec to the Saint Croix River was granted to James, Duke of York, in 1664. Reverting to the crown upon his overthrow, this eastern area was granted to Massachusetts in 1691 with reservation to the Crown of rights to grant first titles. Thus, until the American Revolution, Massachusetts granted Maine lands west of the Kennebec as proprietor, while it granted lands east of the river only with Crown confirmation. Also scattered along the coast were those large and small overlapping early grants, which land developers/speculators purchased and resurrected by many lawsuits. A fifteen-mile strip on each side of the Kennebec itself was an outstanding example, as described in Gordon E.

Kershaw, *The Kennebec Proprietors, 1749–1775* (Portland: Maine Historical Society, 1975). In 1783, Massachusetts created the Committee for the Sale of Eastern [Maine, for instance] Lands. The Maine State Archives considers these records to be the beginning of the Maine Land Office that is now a division of the archive in Augusta. The enabling act for Maine's 1820 statehood reserved half its public lands for disposal by Massachusetts, these lands being surveyed into blocks intermixed with Maine's half. In 1853, Maine bought Massachusetts' remaining Maine lands. The state archive in Augusta has essentially the records since the revolution, including microfilms of Massachusetts land sales. See Glendon J. Buscher Jr., *A Brief History of the Land Court* (1998; revised March 22, 2004), which references the Torrens System of Land Registration, and *The Nature and Evolution of Title* (March 4, 2003). Both may be viewed online at <www.mass.gov/courts/courtsandjudges/courts/landcourt>.

Massachusetts and Maine issued Revolutionary War bounty land grants but no specific reservation was established. See Bockstruck, xiv–xv and xvi. Revolutionary War veteran land grants are microfilmed in thirteen reels. York County was created in 1640 and was Maine's only functioning county until 1760. Its deeds (1642–1737) were published as *York Deeds*, 18 vols. (Portland, Maine: John T. Hull, et al., 1887–1910) and have been microfilmed up to 1850. The counties of Aroostook and Oxford each have two deed-registration districts. See also James Sullivan, *History of Land Titles in Massachusetts* (Boston: I. Thomas and E.T. Andrews, 1801); *Note by the Commissioner on the Sources of Land Titles in Maine* in *Revised Statutes of Maine, 1883*; Frederick S. Allis, ed., *William Bingham's Maine Lands, 1790–1820* (Boston: Colonial Society of Massachusetts, 1954), vols. 36–37 in *Collections, Colonial Society of Massachusetts*; and the microfilm publication of papers of Bingham's estate agent, John Black, in Lawrence Donald Bridgham, "Maine Public Lands 1781–1795: Claims, Trespassers, and Sales" (Ph.D. dissertation, Boston University, 1959).

Maryland

State-land state surveyed in indiscriminate metes and bounds except for lots in the military tract in the extreme western end of the state. The Calverts, Lords Baltimore, were proprietors of the colony from its founding in 1634 until the American Revolution. Their political control passed into other hands from 1654 to 1660 and 1692 to 1715, but their land-granting rights did not. In 1641, a surveyor-general was appointed, in 1680 a specific land office was established, and in 1684 a land council was created to oversee disposal of land. At about the same time, the previous headright system was replaced by cash sales of proprietary lands. The names of those persons transported and claimed for headright grants are indexed online at the state archive <www.mdarchives.state.md.us/msa/refserv/genealogy/html/land.html>. Entries are from Gust Skordas, *The Early Settlers of Maryland, an Index to Names of Immigrants Compiled from Records of Land Patents, 1633–1680* (reprint, Baltimore: Genealogical Publishing Co., 2002) and Carson Gibb's *Supplement to The Early Settlers of Maryland*. See also Peter Wilson Coldham's *Settlers of Maryland 1679–1783 Consolidated Edition* (Baltimore: Genealogical Publishing Co., 2002). The archive holds the land office papers, all microfilmed, including the warrants and patents from 1634. See the online descriptions for details. The state archives has extensive indexes to all its land records, including the tract names of the Maryland properties; see *Maryland State Archives Guide to Government Records* at the above website. Colonial deeds were recorded at the county courts but have been collected at the state archives and microfilmed. There were also conveyances in the Provincial and the General Court of the Western Shore, all likewise at the indexes and archives. For all, indexes and or inventories may be online or in print or card format. The proprietary patents stipulated a quitrent, which was payable to the proprietor, not the government. See Beverley W. Bond, "The Quitrent System in Maryland," *Maryland Historical Magazine* 5 (1910): 350–65. The manuscript rent rolls listing the tracts within each county and the debt books listing individuals and their lands are scattered, and many have been lost, but there are significant collections in the archives and in the Calvert Papers of the Maryland Historical Society in Baltimore. See Morris L. Radoff, et al., *The County Courthouses and Records of Maryland, Part Two: The Records* (Annapolis, Md.: Hall of Records Commission, 1963). See also Clarence P. Gould, *The Land System in Maryland, 1720–1765* (1913; reprint, Ayer Co. Publishing, 1979); Paul H. Giddens, "Land Policies and Administration in Colonial Maryland, 1753–1769," *Maryland Historical Magazine* 28 (1933): 142–71; and Canville D. Benson, "Notes on the Preparation of Conveyances by Laymen in the Colony of Maryland," ibid., 60 (1965): 428–38. Maryland surveyed fifty-acre lots in its western panhandle and granted them as military bounty lands to Revolutionary War veterans; see Bockstruck, xv–xvi. A list of recipients also appears in J. Thomas Scharf, *History of Western Maryland* (1882; reprint, Baltimore: Genealogical Publishing Co., 2003).

Massachusetts

State-land state surveyed in irregular New England town bounds in the east and in more regular town rectangles in the west. Massachusetts pioneered the New England system of towns with its grants by the legislature (General Court) to groups of settlers (town proprietors) who, in turn, oversaw land distributions within their town areas. Often, the General Court had likely frontier areas surveyed into convenient town-size tracts—six-mile squares were common—and offered publicly to potential proprietors for settlement. The proprietors' system is described in John Frederick Martin, *Profits in the Wilderness: Entrepreneurship and the Founding of New England Towns in the Seventeenth Century* (Chapel Hill, N.C.: University of North

Carolina Press, 1991) and in *Great Migration Newsletter,* available at <www.newenglandancestors.org>.

The Massachusetts Bay colonial records of such grants are in Nathaniel B. Shurtleff, ed., *Records of the Governor and Company of the Massachusetts Bay in New England,* 5 vols. (Boston: W. White, 1853–54). Plymouth colonial records are in Shurtleff, *Records of the Colony of Plymouth in New England,* 12 vols. (Boston: W. White, 1855–61); vol. 12 is deeds (1620–51). The deeds for Massachusetts Bay were recorded in town records until the creation of counties around 1643, although land transactions continued to be recorded in some towns after this date. Plymouth colony was joined by charter with Massachusetts Bay in late 1691. In 1685, it had been divided into three counties that recorded conveyances. Several Massachusetts counties were later divided into deed-registration districts: Berkshire into three districts in 1788, Bristol into two in 1837, Middlesex into two districts in 1854, Essex into two in 1869, and Worcester into two in 1884, each with its own courthouse. The Salem registry of Essex County, aside from its own deeds, also has those of old Norfolk County (1637–1714) and Ipswich (including Newbury and later Rowley) town deeds (1640–94). These and deeds from the important county of Suffolk (Boston) are on microfilm at the Family History Library (Suffolk is 1629 through 1885, along with indexes 1639–1920).

It should be obvious from these brief facts that you must allow for variations in where, when, and what local land records survive. Town proprietor records also often survive, and some have been published. Property valuations and taxes for 1760 to 1771 and 1780 to 1811 have been microfilmed in four and nineteen rolls respectively. See also James Sullivan, *The History of Land Titles in Massachusetts* (Boston: I. Thomas and E.T. Andrews, 1801) and Robert Charles Anderson, ed., *Great Migration Newsletter* (cited above), for examples of the land acquisition process in individual towns. Massachusetts, in 1801, granted Revolutionary War bounty land in that part of Massachusetts in the District of Maine; see Bockstruck, xvi.

Michigan

Public-domain state with one principal meridian (established 1819). Michigan was under British jurisdiction until 1796, when the American government assumed control of Detroit. The five-to-eight-mile Toledo Strip on the Michigan-Ohio border, now in Ohio, was under Michigan jurisdiction until 1835; see Gordon Mitchell, "Ohio–Michigan Boundary War," parts I & II, *Professional Surveying* 24:6 (June 2004) and 24:7 (July 2004). The earliest GLO land office opened in 1804 in Detroit, and the last closed in Marquette in 1925 (see Hone, 372–84). The BLM turned over a set of the tract books and township plats to the Bentley Historical Library of the University of Michigan, 1150 Beal Ave., Ann Arbor, MI 48109 <www.umich.edu/~bhl>. There are microfilms at some other Michigan libraries. The BLM-ESO has original patents, tract books, cadastral survey field notes, and township maps. Michigan's federal patents are indexed and scanned in the GLO-ARS; a CD-ROM version of the index may be ordered online. NA-DC has the land-entry case files as described in Inventory No. 22. Case files for private land claims are at NA-DC; they are combined with those of Wisconsin. Per Hone, some Michigan claims were still being litigated in the early 1900s. Some claims are indexed in Fern Ainsworth, *Private Land Claims: Illinois, Indiana, Michigan and Wisconsin* (Natchitoches, La.: the author, 1980). See Joyce Kirkwood, *First Land Owners of Marquette County, Michigan, from U.S. Tract Records* (Michigan Genealogical Council, 1991) as one of several titles by various authors and publishers that list first purchasers or reprint information from atlases and plats. See also D. Jones, "The Survey and Sale of the Public Land in Michigan, 1815–1862" (M.A. thesis, Cornell University, 1952).

Minnesota

Public-domain state with two principal meridians (established 1831 and, far south in Arkansas, 1815). Of the dozen GLO land districts, the earliest opened in 1848 at Falls Saint Croix River, Wisconsin, and moved to Stillwater, Minnesota, in 1849; the last closed at Cass Lake in 1933 (see Hone, 385–400). Before 1908, records of Alexandria, Minneapolis, Red Wing, Root River, St. Cloud, Stillwater, and Winona had been transferred to Duluth. When Duluth and Crookston districts were closed in 1925, the first copy of the records was transferred to the Minnesota Historical Society, as were the Cass Lake district records in 1933. There are no records for Ojibway. NARA's Great Lakes Region in Chicago holds some local office records of the Benson, Forest City, Greenleaf, Litchfield, and Minneapolis district land offices, 1844–82. The BLM-ESO has original patents, tract books, cadastral survey field notes, and township plats. Minnesota's federal patents are indexed and scanned in the GLO-ARS; a CD-ROM version of the index may be ordered online. NA-DC has the land-entry case files as described in Inventory No. 22. Tract books are available at the State Archives, which is a part of the Minnesota Historical Society, and the records are housed at the Minnesota History Center in St. Paul, home of the Minnesota Historical Society; <www.mnhs.org>. See Matthias N. Orfield, *Federal Land Grants to the States with Special Reference to Minnesota,* University of Minnesota Studies in the Social Sciences (Minneapolis: the author, 1915); C. J. Ritchey, "Claim Associations and Frontier Democracy in Early Minnesota," *Minnesota History* 9 (1928): 85–95; C. E. Worth, "The Operation of the Land Laws in the Minnesota Iron District," *Mississippi Valley Historical Review* 13 (1927): 483–98; and Gregory Kinney and Lydia Lucas, *Guide to the Records of Minnesota's Public Lands* (St. Paul: Minnesota Historical Society, Division of Archives and Manuscripts, 1985).

Mississippi

Public-domain state with five principal meridians (established 1803 to 1833). Of the eight GLO land districts between 1806 and 1925, the earliest opened in Washington in 1807, and the last closed in Jackson in 1925 (see Hone, 401–09). NARA's Southeast Region in Atlant, holds local office registers, tract books, and correspondence, 1807–1917, from these district offices. Territorial land and court records (1798–1817) at the state archives have been microfilmed in five rolls. The BLM-ESO has original patents, tract books, cadastral survey field notes, and township plats. Mississippi's federal patents are indexed in the GLO-ARS; a CD-ROM version of the index may be ordered online. NA-DC has the land-entry case files as described in Inventory No. 22. For private land claims, numerous along the Gulf and the Mississippi River, see ASP. Some are indexed in Fern Ainsworth, *Private Land Claims: Mississippi and Missouri* (Natchitoches, La.: the author, n.d.). Some early land transfers, mortgages, deeds of the British and Spanish periods, and abstracts of land titles submitted when claims were filed, are in May Wilson McBee, *The Natchez Court Records, 1767–1805: Abstracts of Early Records* (reprint, Baltimore: Genealogical Publishing Co., 2003). The records of the Mississippi Land Office, a state agency, are now in the Mississippi Department of Archives and History, including some early records for the southern part of the state. It should be remembered that the area south of thirty-one degrees was part of Spanish West Florida until 1810–11; thus, West Florida archives are partly in the state archive at Tallahassee and partly in Seville, Spain. See Richard S. Lackey, "Credit Land Sales, 1811–1815: Mississippi Entries East of the Pearl" (M.A. thesis, University of Southern Mississippi, 1975) and Robert V. Haynes, "The Disposal of Lands in Mississippi Territory," *Journal of Mississippi History* 24 (1962): 226–52.

Missouri

Public-domain state with one principal meridian (established 1815). The earliest of the eight GLO land districts opened at Saint Louis in 1818, and the last closed in Springfield in 1922 (see Hone, 410–22). Their records are at the Missouri State Archives, <www.sos.mo.gov/archves>. The BLM-ESO has original patents and tract books. Missouri's federal patents are indexed and scanned in the GLO-ARS. NA-DC has the land-entry case files as described in Inventory No. 22, cadastral survey field notes, and township plats. The opening of the first land office was delayed by extensive private land claims requiring adjudication, then delayed again by the New Madrid earthquakes of 1811–12. See *Minutes of the First and Second Board of Commissioners, Missouri 1805–1812 and 1832–1835* (1981; reprint, St. Louis: St. Louis Genealogical Society, 1998). Congress in 1815 granted scrip for up to 640 acres to sufferers in such "injured lands" with claims to be processed prior to opening the federal lands to public sales. These claims and others are listed in the several titles by Mountain Press of Signal Mountain, Georgia, at <www.mountainpress.com>. Case files for private land claims are at NA-DC. See *Missouri Land Claims* (1835; reprint, New Orleans: Polyanthos, 1976) and Walter Lowrie, *Early Settlers of Missouri as Taken from Land Claims in the Missouri Territory* (1834; reprint, Easley, S.C.: Southern Historical Press, 1986). By 1793, Spanish Upper Louisiana had five administrative districts, from north to south: Saint Charles, Saint Louis (the provincial capital), Sainte Genevieve, Cape Girardeau, and New Madrid (which included Arkansas). These districts became the new American counties.

In 1795, a Spanish surveyor-general was appointed for Upper Louisiana. The *Recorder of Land Titles, 1805–1872* (includes the Spanish concessions); the *Livres Terriens* land books of the French inhabitants of St. Louis; *United States Land Sales, 1818–1904*; and *Individual Private Claims, 1818–1852*, are at the Missouri State Archives. These archives also contain a manuscript collection titled *French and Spanish Land Grants, 1790–1803*. One of the War of 1812 bounty-land reserves was in Missouri, for which an index and other records are available on NARS microfilm M848, *War of 1812 Military Bounty Land Warrants, 1815–1858*, in fourteen rolls. See also, the same title, compiled and indexed by April Leigh Helm, Matthew L. Helm, et al., CD-ROM produced by FamilyToolbox.net Inc., 2003. See Paul W. Gates, *History of Public Land Law Development* (W. H. Gaunt and Sons, 1987).

Montana

Public-domain state with one principal meridian (established 1867). The earliest of the nine GLO land districts opened at Helena in 1867 (see Hone, 423–28). NARA's Rocky Mountain Region in Denver holds local office registers, tract books, and correspondence, 1867–69; serial patent case files, 1963–68; and rejected, canceled, and relinquished serial application case files, 1908–55. BLM-ESO has duplicate original survey plats and field notes. Serial patents are being indexed and scanned for GLO-ARS. Order patents from the BLM Montana State Office, P.O. Box 36800, 5001 Southgate Drive, Billings, Montana 59107-6800; <www.mt.blm.gov>; it also has copies of the tract books and township plats. NA-DC has the land-entry case files as described in Inventory No. 22. The Montana Historical Society, in cooperation with the Homestead National Monument of America, is collecting oral history from those who homesteaded between about 1910 and 1930; <www.his.state.mt.us/research/library/Homestead_survey.asp>. See William S. Peters and Maxine C. Johnson, *Public Lands in Montana; Their History and Current Significance*, Regional Study no. 10 (Missoula, Mont.: Bureau of Business and Economic Research, 1959).

Nebraska

Public-domain state with one principal meridian (established 1855). Of the thirteen GLO land districts, the earliest opened in

1855 in Omaha, the last closed at Alliance in 1933 (see Hone, 429–33). NARA's Central Plains Region in Kansas City, Mo., holds some district office records; others are in the Nebraska State Historical Society <www.nebraskahistory.org>. The society has microfilmed all the tract books in fifty-three rolls and indexed applications filed in selected counties in the western part of Nebraska. The society also has the Burlington Railroad Land Records, which are indexed by name of purchaser. Obtain patents from the BLM Wyoming State Office, P.O. Box 1828, 5353 Yellowstone Ave., Cheyenne, WY 82003, which also has copies of the tract books and township plats. Serial patents are being indexed and scanned for GLO-ARS. NA-DC has the land-entry case files as described in Inventory No. 22. The Kinkaid Act of 1904 was a special homestead law that applied only to the western and central portions of Nebraska. This act allowed for a 640-acre homestead (as opposed to 160 acres), the size that was needed for productive agriculture and ranching in the relatively arid Sand Hills and high plains regions of Nebraska. The land grant to the Union Pacific Railroad totaled a tenth of Nebraska, but its land office records were mostly destroyed in a fire. See Barry B. Combs, "The Union Pacific Railroad and the Early Settlement of Nebraska, 1868–1880," *Nebraska History* 50 (1969): 1–26. See "U.S. Government Land Laws in Nebraska, 1854–1904," at the Nebraska State Historical Society website and Homer Socolofsky, "Land Disposal in Nebraska, 1854–1906: The Homestead Story," in Paul Wallace Gates, ed., *Public Land Policies: Management and Disposal* (Ayer Co. Publishers, 1979).

Nevada

Public-domain state with one principal meridian (established 1851 in California). Nevada had four GLO land districts; the first opened in 1864 at Carson City (see Hone, 434–36). NARA's Pacific Regions in San Francisco and Laguna Niguel, Ca., hold local office registers, tract books, and correspondence, 1862–1977, and rejected, canceled, and relinquished serial application case files, 1908–74. Obtain patents from the BLM Nevada State Office, Box 12000, 1340 Harvard Way, Reno, NV 89520-0006, <www.nv.blm.gov>, which also has copies of the tract books and perhaps some township plats. Serial patents are being indexed and scanned for GLO-ARS. NA-DC has the land-entry case files as described in Inventory No. 22 and the GLO headquarters original tract books and township plats. It also has a card index to Nevada patentees to 30 June 1908. See *The Court of Private Land Claims for the Adjudication of Spanish and Mexican Land Titles in Colorado, New Mexico, Arizona, Nevada, Utah, and Wyoming* (on microfilm) and John M. Townley, "Management of Nevada's State Lands, 1864–1900," *Journal of the West* 17 (1978): 62–73.

New Hampshire

State-land state surveyed in irregular New England town bounds along the coast and in fairly rectangular towns farther west and north. In the 1620s, John Mason was granted the land between the Merrimack and Piscataqua rivers, but he and his heirs failed to establish a successful proprietary colony. Beginning around 1641–42, Massachusetts claimed jurisdiction over the area, which fell within old Norfolk County, Massachusetts. The land records for old Norfolk are now at Salem in Essex County, Massachusetts. In 1679, New Hampshire escaped from Massachusetts control and became a royal province, while the Masonian assignees received qualified right to grant subject to local court decisions.

Prior to 1741, Massachusetts also claimed the Merrimack Valley and established several towns there until New Hampshire's authority was confirmed by royal decree in 1741. New Hampshire then began granting land west of the Connecticut River in what is now Vermont—the Hampshire Grants—but never prevailed against the competing New York claims. The New Hampshire Division of Archives and Records Management has the major early land records and has published *New Hampshire Provincial and State Papers,* 40 vols. Available on microfilm and CD-ROM, this collection is accessible through "Index to State Papers of New Hampshire" at <www.sos.nh.gov/archives/>. Records on the town charters are in vols. 24–25 (1894–95), the town grants in vols. 27–28 (1895), the Masonian patent papers in vol. 29 (1896), and the Hampshire Grants in Vermont in vol. 26 (1895). Deeds from 1679 were recorded at the provincial capital until about 1771. These are at the Division of Archives and Records Management and have been microfilmed. The New England Historic Genealogical Society and the Family History Library have growing collections of microfilmed deed and other land records from New Hampshire.

The first counties were created in 1769 and took over the recording of conveyances. See Jonathan Smith, "Town Patents Under Belcher," *Massachusetts Historical Society Proceedings* 45 (1911–12): 197–210; John F. Looney, "Benning Wentworth's Land Grant Policy: A Reappraisal," *Historical New Hampshire* 23 (1968): 3–13; and Maurice H. Robinson, *A History of Taxation in New Hampshire* (New York: 1903).

New Jersey

State-land state (though the state never owned the land) surveyed in indiscriminate metes and bounds, plus some New England towns south of Staten Island. Compared to the other colonies, New Jersey had complex political and land-granting jurisdictions. After the fall of New Sweden and then New Netherlands, the area was granted to James, Duke of York, who re-granted it to two proprietors. After several more transfers and agreements, a 1686 West Jersey existed with its capital at Burlington while a corresponding East Jersey was governed from Perth Amboy. The dividing line between the two was poorly surveyed and caused conflicting land grants. In 1702, the proprietors surrendered governance to the Crown but retained the right to grant vacant lands. From 1702 to 1738, New York and the reunified New Jersey had the same royal governor. In the late 1740s, land riots in East Jersey opposed the titles of the proprietors.

New Jersey is unique among the thirteen colonies in that its proprietors retained their rights after the revolution to grant lands and receive escheated land. They still retain these rights. Proprietary shares pass down the generations by inheritance and purchase like any other property. Consequently, proprietary land records (warrants, surveys, and patents) remain at the proprietary offices in Burlington and Perth Amboy. The major series have been microfilmed. Since colonial deeds had also been recorded at the two Jersey capitals, the New Jersey legislature in 1795 ordered them all transferred to Trenton. They are now in the state archives and have been microfilmed in separate series. Deeds after 1785 should be in the counties. The early Jersey deeds are published in William Nelson, *Patents and Deeds and Other Early Records of New Jersey, 1664–1703* (1899; reprint, Baltimore: Genealogical Publishing Co., 2000). Microfilm of deeds recorded to 1900, and mortgages to about 1850, for most New Jersey counties are at the New Jersey State Archives. Some are in print, i.e., Clyde W. Downing, *Sussex County New Jersey Deed Abstracts, (1785–1804)*, 6 vols to date (Kent, Wash.: the author, 1999–).

Kenn Stryker-Rodda has noted three special problems concerning early New Jersey property conveyances: (1) only an estimated twenty-five percent of the colonial deeds were recorded; (2) Jerseymen tended to record deeds when they needed to mortgage property, hence monied people are less likely to appear in the land records than the impecunious; and (3) the Alexander papers at the New York Historical Society include surveys, deeds, and correspondence useful for East Jersey research, and the Penn and Logan papers in Philadelphia are needed for land research in West Jersey. See John E. Pomfret, *The New Jersey Proprietors and Their Lands, 1664–1776* (Princeton, N.J.: D. Van Nostrand, 1964); Brendon McConville, *These Daring Disturbers of the Public Peace: The Struggle for Property and Power in Early New Jersey* (University of Pennsylvania Press, 2003); Crestview Lawyers Service, *Colonial Conveyances: Provinces of East & West New Jersey*, 2 vols. (Summit, N.J.: Crestview Lawyers Service, 1974); Charles H. Winfield, *History of the Land Titles in Hudson County, N.J., 1609–1871* (New York: Wynkoop & Hallenbeck, 1872), 1–25; and James C. Connolly, "Quit Rents in Colonial New Jersey," *Union County Historical Society Proceedings* 1 (1923): 3–12.

New Mexico

Public-domain state with one principal meridian (established 1855). The first of New Mexico's four GLO land districts opened at Santa Fe in 1858 (see Hone, 437–39). Two NARA regions, Rocky Mountain Region in Denver and Southwest Region in Fort Worth, Texas, hold the GLO/BLM records of the New Mexico state office and the Clayton, Folsom, Fort Sumner, La Mesilla, Las Cruces, Roswell, Santa Fe, and Tucumcari district land offices. Housed at the New Mexico State Records Center and Archives, 404 Montezuma, Santa Fe, NM 87505, <www.nmcpr.state.nm.us>, are Spanish and Mexican land grants and related records, 1685–1846, and case files of the Court of Private Land Claims in New Mexico, 1892–1912. There is an online index, 1685–1912, to these at <www.nmcpr.state.nm.us/archives/land_grants.htm>. Order patents from the BLM New Mexico State Office, P.O. Box 27115, 1474 Rodeo Rd., Santa Fe, NM 87502-1449, <www.nm.blm.gov/>, which also has copies of the tract books and township plats. Serial patents are being indexed and scanned for GLO-ARS. NA-DC has the land-entry case files as described in Inventory No. 22 and the GLO headquarters original tract books and township plats. NA-DC's Inventory No. 22, 55–56, lists only 344 New Mexico donation patents under the 1854 Donation Act (see also Hone, 156). New Mexico private land grants are still being adjudicated, see (2001) U.S. General Accounting Office, "Treaty of Guadalupe Hidalgo: Definition and List of Community Land Grants in New Mexico: Report to Congressional Requesters," downloadable in English and Spanish at <www.loc.gov/rr/hispanic/ghtreaty>. The large secondary literature is conveniently listed in Annabelle M. Oczon, "Land Grants in New Mexico: A Selective Bibliography," *New Mexico Historical Review* 57 (1982): 81–87. See "Researching New Mexico Land Grants" at the New Mexico Commission of Public Records, State Records Center and Archives, <www.nmcpr.state.nm.us/archives/land_grants.htm>.

New York

State-land state surveyed in several systems: indiscriminate metes and bounds, large manors with tenant farms, New England towns on eastern Long Island and along the Connecticut border, and large tracts in central and western New York often surveyed in townships, ranges, and lots. Very large grants were always a common feature of New York land policy, the government officials finding it convenient (and lucrative both for fees and sharing the spoils) to have entrepreneurs do the subdividing and selling or leasing in farm-size parcels. Maps locating these major tracts have been printed often. One source is J.R. Bien, *Atlas of the State of New York* (New York: J. Bien & Co., 1895).

Several mammoth tracts in the western part of the state came into the hands of Phelps-Gorham, Robert Morris, and the Holland Land Company. The original papers of the Holland Land Company are in Amsterdam, The Netherlands, but they are available in the United States on microfilm. The Holland Land Company Project at the Reed Library, State University of New York, College of Fredonia, Fredonia, New York 14063 has identified other holdings in the United States concerned with the Holland Land Company and is collecting microfilmed copies. See O(rasmus) Turner, *Pioneer History of the Holland Purchase of*

Western New York (reprint, Bowie, Md.: Heritage Books, 1991). William Wyckoff, *The Developer's Frontier: The Making of the Western New York Landscape* (New Haven, Conn.: Yale University Press, 1988) looks at the Holland Land Company as a developer. Karen E. Livsey, *Western New York Land Transactions, 1804–1824* (Baltimore: Genealogical Publishing Co., 1991) and *Western Land Transactions, 1825–1835* (Baltimore: Clearfield Co., 1996), help to locate settlers and their land and index the microfilmed records of the Holland Land Company.

The private papers of the large Hudson River manors may be necessary to complete a genealogy, since tenants who leased but did not buy land may never appear in the county conveyance records. See Berthold Fernow, *Documents Relating to the History and Settlement of the Towns Along the Hudson and Mohawk Rivers (With the Exception of Albany) from 1630 to 1682* (Albany, N.Y.: Weed, Parsons, 1881). The background history is excellently summarized in Sung Bok Kim, *Landlord and Tenant in Colonial New York: Manorial Society, 1664–1775* (Chapel Hill: University of North Carolina Press, 1978) and Henry B. Hoff, "Manors in New York," *The New York Genealogical and Biographical Newsletter* 10 (1999): 55–58, 11 (2000): 13–17. In 1650, the Dutch government of New Netherlands recognized Connecticut's title to Long Island east of Oyster Bay, though Long Island was soon reunited with New York under the Duke of York's proprietary (1664–89). See Berthold Fernow, *Documents Relating to the History of the Early Colonial Settlements Principally on Long Island* (Albany, N.Y.: Weed, Parsons, 1883). Deeds in these early New England towns were recorded in the town, not the county, prior to the successful extension of Suffolk County jurisdiction. This is also sometimes true of the debatable land east of the Hudson adjoining Connecticut and Massachusetts, where New Englanders settled on lands claimed by New York. (See the Vermont entry for lands granted in what is now that state by New York.)

The major land records—patents, deeds, and land grant applications—of the colonial and state government are in the state archives at <www.archives.nysed.gov>. They are listed in New York State Archives, *Public Records Relating to Land in New York State* (Albany: New York State Archives, 1979). They are on microfilm. Land grant applications, abstracted and indexed, are partly available in New York Secretary of State, *Calendar of N.Y. Colonial Manuscripts, Indorsed Land Papers, in the Office of the Secretary of State of New York, 1643–1803* (Albany, N.Y.: Weed, Parsons, 1864; reprint, Harrison, New York: Harbor Hill Books, 1987). In 1784, the Board of Commissioners of the Land Office was established to dispose of the state's remaining public lands.

New York allotted its Revolutionary War soldiers bounty land, giving privates five hundred acres (see Bockstruck, xvii). The military reserve in the Finger Lakes region was surveyed into six hundred-acre lots so that veterans could take their one hundred-acre federal bounty alongside their state bounty in lieu of one hundred acres in Ohio. Most veterans sold their claims and never settled in the military tract. The surveyed land in this reserve was distributed by lottery drawing; hence, the title of the state's published list of recipients: New York Legislature, *The Balloting Book, and Other Documents Relating to Military Bounty Lands in the State of New York, New York Legislature* (Albany, N.Y.: Packard & Van Benthuysen, 1825). See Robert S. Rose, "The Military Tract of Central N.Y." (M.A. thesis, Syracuse University, 1935). An earlier military tract was established northeast of the Adirondacks, but very few accepted this poor land. For background on New York's varied land tenure and law, see Robert L. Fowler, *History of the Law of Real Property in New York* (New York: Baker, Voorhis, 1895); S. G. Nissinson, "The Development of a Land Registration System in New York," *New York History* 20 (1939): 16–21; Armand LaPotin, "The Minisink Grant: Partnerships, Patents, and Processing Fees in Eighteenth Century New York," ibid. 56 (1976): 28–50; Charles W. Spencer, "The Land System of Colonial New York," *New York State Historical Association Proceedings* 16 (1917): 150–64; Arthur E. Sutherland, "The Tenancy on the New York Manor," *Cornell Law Quarterly* 41 (1956): 620–39; and H. Gresham Toole, "The Dutch Land System of New Netherlands," *Marshall Review* 2 (1938): 31–39.

North Carolina

State-land state surveyed in indiscriminate metes and bounds. By charter in 1663 (amended 1665), eight proprietors received a grant of all lands between 29 degrees and 36 degrees 30 minutes, the latter being the present North Carolina-Virginia line. In 1729, George II bought seven of the eight shares and made the Carolina proprietary a royal colony (actually three colonies—the two Carolinas and, in 1732, Georgia). The eighth share belonged to Lord Carteret, later Earl Granville, whose one-eighth part was laid off using the already surveyed Virginia line. Thus the northern half of present-day North Carolina composed the Granville District, where Earl Granville had the right to grant lands and collect quitrents, though not to govern. The boundary of the Granville District was the present southern line of the counties of Rowan-Davidson-Randolph projected east to the ocean. This Granville line was not even partially surveyed until the 1740s, when a land office was opened, only to be closed permanently about 1763. See Margaret M. Hofmann's five-volume *The Granville District of North Carolina 1748–1763 Abstracts of Land Grants* (Weldon, N.C.: 1988–1995). George Stevenson's introduction in vol. 1 provides important information relating to the Granville District.

The Granville grants, as well as the grants from the early proprietary, the royal colony, and the state government, are in the North Carolina State Archives <www.ah.dcr.state.nc.us>. There are both card and online indexes. An excellent description of these records and the early land distribution process is in

Margaret M. Hofmann, "Land Grants," in *North Carolina Research: Genealogy and Local History*, edited by Helen F.M. Leary (Raleigh: North Carolina Genealogical Society, 1996), 313–28. Hofmann has abstracted grants from the proprietary period in *Province of North Carolina, 1663–1729, Abstracts of Land Patents* (Weldon, N.C.: Roanoke News, 1979); the crown colony era in *Colony of North Carolina 1735–64: Abstracts of Land Patents Volume 1* and *Colony of North Carolina 1765–75: Abstracts of Land Patents Volume 2* (1982–84); and the state period in *North Carolina Abstract of State Grants* (Ann Arbor, Mich.: Print-Tech, 1998).

Headrights were offered throughout the colonial period, though the requirements and acreage varied. For such stipulations, see the introduction to Caroline B. Whitley, *North Carolina Headrights: A List of Names, 1663–1774* (Raleigh: Historical Publications Section, Division of Archives and History, North Carolina Department of Cultural Resources, 2001).

Deeds were recorded in the counties, though irregularly in the earliest years. North Carolina's military bounty-land act was the most generous of the states in granting 640 acres (in Tennessee) to a private in the Continental line. Researchers should read George Stevenson's description of the state's bounty-land records as given in Leary's *North Carolina Genealogy* (cited previously), 384–90 and Bockstruck, xvii–xx. Also see Weynette Parks Haun, *Old Albermarle County North Carolina Book of Land Warrants and Surveys, 1681–1706* (Durham, N.C., Haun, 1984) and her titles of abstracts of various county deeds, such as *Chowan County, North Carolina Deed Books* (Durham, N.C.: Haun, 1998). See titles by Albert Bruce Pruitt or Elizabeth "Pat" Shaw Bailey for abstracts or indexes to other land records (county and earlier). See also, George Henry Swathers, *The History of Land Titles in Western North Carolina* (1938; reprint, Arno Press, 1979); Dan Lacy, "Records in the Offices of Registers of Deeds in N.C.," *North Carolina Historical Review* 14 (1937): 213–29; Jacquelyn H. Wolf, "Patents and Tithables in Proprietary North Carolina, 1663–1729," ibid. 56 (1979): 263–77; and Marvin L. Michael Kay, "The Payment of Provincial and Local Taxes in North Carolina, 1748–1771," *William and Mary Quarterly*, 3rd series, 26 (1960): 218–40.

North Dakota

Public-domain state with one principal meridian (established 1815 in Arkansas, North Dakota being surveyed much later). The earliest of North Dakota's seven GLO land districts opened at Pembina in 1870 (see Hone, 440–47). The bulk of their records are in the State Historical Society of North Dakota <www.state.nd.us/hist>. NARA's Rocky Mountain Region in Denver holds local office registers, tract books, and correspondence, 1864–1950, and rejected, canceled, and relinquished serial application case files, 1908–50, of the Bismark, Creelsburg, Devils Lake, Dickinson, Fargo, Grand Forks, Minot, and Williston district land offices. Obtain patents from the BLM Montana State Office, P.O. Box 36800, 5001 Southgate, Billings, Montana 59107-6800, <www.mt.blm.gov>, which also has copies of the tract books and township plats for North Dakota. Serial patents are being indexed and scanned for GLO-ARS. NA-DC has the land-entry case files as described in Inventory No. 22 and the GLO headquarters original tract books and township plats. See N. Thomas, "Distribution of the Public Domain in Dakota Territory" (M.A. thesis, University of South Dakota, 1944).

Ohio

Public-domain state with a complicated surveying history. Aside from the Virginia Military District's indiscriminate metes and bounds, Ohio has a dozen different township-and-range surveys, the major principal meridians being established from 1785 to 1819. A map (2003 issue), "Original Land Subdivisions of Ohio," at <www.dnr.state.oh.us/geosurvey>, shows the variety of Ohio surveys, including some that used five-mile square townships. Researchers should be alert to four different boundary jurisdictions in early Ohio:

1. The actual surveys with their meridians and baselines (or lack of same in the Virginia Military District). See C. E. Sherman, *Original Ohio Land Subdivisions*, 4 vols. (1949; reprint, Columbus: Ohio Department of Natural Resources, 1982). Vol. 3 recounts the history of the various surveys and gives detailed maps showing the numbering of townships. This book is a must for early Ohio research.
2. The various tracts as they opened for settlement, such as the Seven Ranges, the U.S. Military District, the Congress Lands east of Scioto River, and the Congress Lands west of Miami River. A map of these tracts is frequently reproduced in Ohio how-to books, such as Kip Sperry, *Genealogical Research in Ohio* (Baltimore: Genealogical Publishing Co., Inc., 2003).
3. The land office districts, such as Symmes's private land office at Cincinnati, the GLO's Chillicothe land office (1801–76), and the Virginia Military District's land office, also at Chillicothe. For GLO districts, see Inventory No. 22, 57–59, and Hone, 448–60.
4. The counties with their registries of deeds. See Randolph Chandler Downs, *Evolution of Ohio County Boundaries* (1927; reprint, Columbus: Ohio Historical Society, 1970).

The state auditor of Ohio is in charge of the State Land Office <www.auditor.state.oh.us>. The *Official Ohio Lands Book* by Dr. George W. Knepper may be downloaded from <www.auditor.state.oh.us/StudentResources/OhioLands/ohio_lands.pdf>. The office also has an index to all Ohio patentees except the Symmes Purchase and the Connecticut Western Reserve, both of which were issued as single patents. Most Symmes land papers apparently burned. The location of the Connecticut Land Company papers is not known. There are land papers for the Western Reserve, both in the Western Reserve Historical Society, Cleveland, and in the Connecticut State Library, Hartford.

Settlers in the Western Reserve sometimes dealt through the Susquehannah Land Company and the Phelps-Gorham Land Company. See Julian P. Boyd and Robert J. Taylor, *The Susquehannah Company Papers*, 11 vols. (1930; reprint, Ithaca, N.Y.: Cornell University Press, 1962–71). The original papers in the Connecticut State Archives, titled "Susquehannah Settlers, 1755–1796" and "Western Lands, 1783–1789," include many references to the Fire Lands and the Connecticut Land Company. The papers and an every-name index are microfilmed. The Phelps-Gorham papers in the New York State Archives in Albany also include numerous references to Ohio lands, such as "Vol. 145. Book of Conveyances of Lands in Ohio, 1795–1808."

A major listing of early Ohio entrymen and patentees is Clifford Neal Smith, *Federal Land Series* (1972–1986; reprint, Baltimore: Genealogical Publishing Co., 2004). Included are pre-1835 grants in the U.S. Military District of Ohio; state grants made within the Virginia Military District of Ohio; and U.S. patents (mostly Ohio) 1788–1814. Smith's introductions should be read by any genealogist working in early Ohio records.

The earliest of Ohio's nine GLO land districts opened in 1800 in Marietta and Steubenville; the last closed at Chillicothe in 1876. The records of these land offices are divided between the State Archives in the Ohio Historical Center, which has original land survey field notes, land survey plats, tract and entry books, and index cards related to federal lands and Virginia Military District lands; and the Ohio Historical Society, which holds surveys and first transfers of land. Research inquiries will be answered by the OHS Archives/Library of the Ohio Historical Society. The BLM Eastern States Office has original patents, tract books, and a five-volume index to Ohio patents, ca. 1800 to 1820. Ohio's federal patents are indexed and scanned in the GLO-ARS; a CD-ROM version of the index may be ordered online. The NA-DC has the land-entry case files as described in Inventory No. 22, cadastral survey field notes, and township plats. The two major military reserves in Ohio for Revolutionary War veterans—the Virginia Military District and the U.S. Military District—were discussed earlier in this chapter under "Bounty Lands." Also see William Thomas Hutchinson, *Military Bounty Lands of the American Revolution in Ohio: The Management of Public Lands in the United States*" (1927; reprint, Ayer Publishing Co., 1979).

The Connecticut Western Reserve was not a military reserve, nor did Connecticut grant its soldiers bounty land. Several categories of sufferers in the American Revolution were granted lands in Ohio. The inhabitants of Connecticut towns burned by British/Loyalist raiders received compensation in the Fire Lands of the Western Reserve, also called the Sufferers' Lands. Pro-independence refugees from Canada and Nova Scotia received land in the Refugee Tract. See Smith's *Federal Land Series*, vol. 1, sources F and G, for sufferers and refugees. Tax records for 1800 to 1838 at the Ohio Historical Society are microfilmed.

See William E. Peters, *Ohio Lands and Their Subdivision*, third edition (Ayer Co. Publishers, 1979). Peters' seventeen-volume typescript, "Code of Land Titles in Ohio. A Compilation from Official Records of All Charters, Indian Treaties, Grants..." (1935), is microfilmed and available at several major Ohio research libraries. See also Mayburt Stephenson Riegel, *Early Ohioans' Residences from the Land Grant Records* (Mansfield: Ohio Genealogical Society, 1976). Family Tree Maker's Family Archives CD-ROM (2004), "Ohio Land and Tax Records," lists about 60,000 persons who bought land in southwestern, southeastern, east, and east-central Ohio from 1800 to 1840 (from the series by Ellen T. Berry and David A. Berry); the 1,000 associates of The Ohio Company, 1788–92 (from Albion M. Dyer, *First Ownership of Ohio Lands*, [1911]); and about 50,000 names from Esther Powell, *Early Ohio Tax Records*, listing Ohio residents, about 1820–25, and including the 1801 tax list of the Virginia Military District.

Oklahoma

Public-domain state with two principal meridians (established 1870 and 1881). Of the eleven GLO land districts, the earliest opened at Guthrie and Kingfisher in 1889, and the last closed at Guthrie in 1927 (see Hone, 461–63). The records of these local offices are at the State Archives and Records Management <www.odl.state.ok.us/oar/land-records>. While it never had a unified territorial government, eastern Oklahoma was called the Indian Territory after an 1830 act of Congress. It continued until 1907; the major tribes each having their organized governments, complete with tribal capitals. Only in 1889 was present-day Oklahoma opened to the federal land-disposal process operated by the GLO. What made Oklahoma settlements spectacularly different were the formal land rushes with their opening-day stampedes to stake claims to already surveyed quarter sections. Those who illegally jumped the gun were called "sooners." The last major land tract was distributed by lottery rather than land rush. Order patents from the BLM New Mexico State Office, P.O. Box 27115, 1474 Rodeo Rd., Santa Fe, NM 87502-0115, which also has copies of the tract books and township plats for Oklahoma. Serial patents are being indexed and scanned for GLO-ARS. NA-DC has the entry-land case files as described in Inventory No. 22 and the GLO headquarters original tract books and township plats.

Before Indian lands were opened for white settlement, each tribal member received an individual land allotment. While there is no one repository for the Indian allotment records, the researcher should check NARA—Central Plains Region in

Kansas City, Missouri, and the Southwest Region in Fort Worth, Texas, and also the National Archives microfilm publications. The Indian Archives Division of the Oklahoma Historical Society, Oklahoma City, holds the records of many tribes. See "Oklahoma Land Records in the OHS Research Library" at the Oklahoma Historical Society website, <www.ok-history.mus.ok.us>; *Guide to Genealogical Research in the National Archives* (Washington, D.C.: National Archives and Records Service, 2001), 216–224] and Anna Billie Clevenger, *Surname Index to Federal Land Track Books of Oklahoma Territory,* 22 volumes, Southwest Oklahoma Genealogical Society, <www.sirinet.net/~lgarris/swogs/pub.html>; and Joseph F. Rarick, J.S.D., Alfred E. Murrah, and David Ross Boyd, "A Guide to Rarick's Oklahoma Indian Law Titles" at <www.thorpe.ou.edu/treatises/guideidx.html>.

Oregon

Public-domain state with one principal meridian (established 1851). Of the six GLO land districts, the earliest opened in Oregon City in 1855 (see Hone, 464–66). The district office records are at NARA's Pacific Alaska Region in Seattle. Order patents from the BLM Oregon State Office, P.O. Box 2965, 333 SW 1st Ave., Portland, OR 97208-2965, <www.or.blm.gov>, which also has copies of the tract books and township plats. This office has an index *by location* to the master title plats, use plats, supplemental plats, historical indexes, and cadastral survey plats. Serial patents are being indexed and scanned for GLO-ARS. NA-DC has the land-entry case files as described in Inventory No. 22 and the GLO headquarters original tract books and township plats. The Donations Land Claim Act of 1850 and the Homestead Act of 1862 distributed much of the arable land. Oregon's earliest white and mixed-blood settlers were entitled to free federal land under the Donation Act of 1850. An index and abstracts are on NARA microfilm M145, *Abstracts of Oregon Donation Land Claims, 1852–1903,* in six rolls, which serves as an index to the case files reproduced in NARS microfilm M815, *Oregon and Washington Donation Land Files, 1851–1903,* in 108 rolls. Because of a law forbidding their reproduction, the naturalization certificates in M815 case files were not microfilmed. The law was changed in the 1970s, so naturalization records referred to in these files can now be obtained from NA-DC. Donation case files are valuable because they should contain a statement of the date and place of birth of the entryman. See Genealogical Forum of Portland, Ore., <www.gfo.org>, for a list of publications of the provisional land claims (1845–49) and the donation land claims (5 vols). See also Jerry A. O'Callaghan, "The Disposition of the Public Domain in Oregon" (Ph.D. dissertation, Stanford University, 1952).

Pennsylvania

State-land state surveyed mostly in indiscriminate metes and bounds, though the donation and depreciation lands north of Pittsburgh were surveyed in rectangular, numbered lots. William Penn, as proprietor, established a land office in 1682 that became the Division of Land Records until a merger in 1981. The land records will be found at the Pennsylvania State Archives, 350 North Street, Harrisburg, PA 17120-0090, <www.phmc.state.pa.us/bah/dam>, including such major land series as applications for warrants, original warrants, original surveys, patents, and military grants—all microfilmed in many hundreds of reels and widely available. Included are warrant and patent receipts (1781–1809), mortgages and valuations (1773–93), and colonial quitrent books and rent rolls. There are also smaller but no less valuable collections, such as depositions (1683–1881), caveats (1699–1890), title papers (1784–1852), and so forth, which have also been microfilmed. Donna Bingham Munger's landmark publication, *Pennsylvania Land Records, A History and Guide for Research* (Wilmington, Del.: Scholarly Resources, 1991) is required reading on the subject.

The Penn proprietary was very businesslike in disposing of its lands at a fixed price (no headrights) as supervised by an appointed surveyor and a commission/board of property, which helps explain its wealth of records. The archive is constructing tract maps for each county and has completed these "warrantee township maps" for most of the counties. They are available for purchase. A valuable feature of many Pennsylvania grants is the tract names—at least for earlier tracts—such as "Lithuania" or Levi Andrew Levi's "Uncircumcision." Such names may give ethnic and religious clues. To the records mentioned above should be added the first nine volumes of Pennsylvania grant records, discovered in the Philadelphia City Hall in 1952 and now indexed in Allen Weinberg and Thomas E. Slattery, *Warrants and Surveys of the Province of Pennsylvania Including the Three Lower Counties, 1759* (Philadelphia: Philadelphia Department of Records, 1965). See John E. Pomfret, "The First Purchasers of Pennsylvania, 1681–1700," *Pennsylvania Magazine of History and Biography* 80 (1956): 137–63.

The *Pennsylvania Archives*, 3rd series (138 volumes), includes land grants, i.e., William Henry Egle, *Warrantees of Land in the Several Counties of the State of Pennsylvania, 1730–1898,* vols. 24–26 (Harrisburg, Pa.: State Printer, 1898–1899), vols. 24–26. and tax lists. The *Pennsylvania Archives*, 2nd series, vol. 19 (1893) contains minutes of the Board of Property, 1687–1732, and has been reprinted as William Henry Egle, *Early Pennsylvania Land Records* (reprint, 2000; also available on Family Archive CD 7512 by Genealogical Publishing Co.). See Christine Crawford-Oppenheimer, *Lost in Pennsylvania? Try the Published Pennsylvania Archives* (Philadelphia: Genealogical Society of Pennsylvania, 1999) and Mary Dunn, *Index to Pennsylvania's Colonial Records Series* (1991; reprint, Genealogical Publishing Co., 1996), which indexes the first sixteen volumes.

The lands north of Pittsburgh reserved for the Pennsylvania continental line were called the Donation Lands (see Bockstruck, xx–xxi). Certificates were also issued to Pennsylvania troops entitling them to cheap lands in compensation for the ravages of inflation on their pay; these were called Depreciation Lands. The records are in the Division of Land Records, though most soldiers sold their rights rather than settle on the lands. See William Henry Egle, *Virginia Claims to Land in Western Pennsylvania Published with an Account of the Donation Lands of Pennsylvania* (1896; reprint, Baltimore: Genealogical Publishing Co., 2003), excerpted from the *Pennsylvania Archives*. Pennsylvania had several major boundary controversies with its neighbors, and various colonies gave grants of their neighbors' lands. From about 1753 to 1782, Connecticut claimed and settled the upper Delaware River Valley (the Delaware Company papers are mostly lost) and the Wyoming Valley along the Susquehanna River. Its records are published in Julian P. Boyd and Robert J. Taylor, *The Susquehannah Company Papers*, 11 vols. (Wilkes-Barre, Pa.: Wyoming Historical and Geological Society, and Ithaca, N.Y.: Cornell University Press, 1930–71). The Pennsylvania Surveyor General's Office papers on Connecticut patents in seventeen townships in Luzerne County, 1785 to 1810, have been microfilmed in twenty-five reels. Also on microfilm are the *Susquehannah Settlers, 1755–96* and *Western Lands, 1783–89*. An every-name index makes these papers valuable for genealogical research, especially because many men died before their claims were satisfied, necessitating mention of heirs as well as other property details.

In southwestern Pennsylvania around the time of the revolution were three active Virginia counties. See Raymond M. Bell, "Virginia Land Grants in Pennsylvania," *Virginia Genealogist* 7 (1963): 78–83, 103–7, 152–62, and 11 (1967): 126–27, and John F. Vallentine, "Research in Virginia's District of West Augusta," *Genealogical Journal* 4 (1975): 141–47. See also W. R. Shepherd, "The Land System of Provincial Pennsylvania," *American Historical Association Annual Report* (1895): 117–25. For early settlers living along Pennsylvania's southeastern border, be alert for possible Maryland land records. See James T. Lemon, *The Best Poor Man's Country: Early Southeastern Pennsylvania* (Johns Hopkins University Press, 2002) for information on settlement and the role of cultural backgrounds in land use; and Kay Haviland Freilich, "Genealogical Research in Pennsylvania" *National Genealogical Society Quarterly* 90 (March 2002): 7–36, for a current description of land records locations.

The Holland Land Company also had lands in Pennsylvania and operated a land office in Philadelphia. Its records, mostly in Dutch, have been microfilmed by the Genealogical Society of Utah on 202 rolls; film 1,421,412, item 2, provides an inventory.

Rhode Island

State-land state surveyed in New England towns. These towns, in the colonial period, were particularly strong relative to the colony's central government. Deeds were recorded by the towns, not the counties, although the colonial government for some time also recorded some conveyances. These transactions have been preserved in a four-volume collection, "Rhode Island Land Evidence," which is located at the Rhode Island State Archives, 337 Westminster St., Providence, RI 02903; <www.state.ri.us>. The earliest of the four volumes is abstracted in Dorothy Worthington, *Rhode Island Land Evidences, Vol. 1, 1648–1696, Abstracts* (1921; reprint, Baltimore: Genealogical Publishing Co., 1970). This was the only volume to be published, although abstracts of volumes 2, 3, and 4 have been printed in *Rhode Island Roots*, the periodical of the Rhode Island Genealogical Society. The four land evidence volumes are the major land records held by the state archives, though it has a few other records with land information. Information on town grants can be found in John R. Bartlett, *Records of the Colony of Rhode Island and Providence Plantations in New England*, 10 vols. (Providence: Rhode Island General Assembly, 1857–65); and Charles Wyman Hopkins, *The Home Lots of the Earliest Settlers of the Providence Plantations. With Notes and Plats* (1886; reprint, Boston: Genealogical Publishing Co., 2004). A list of towns, holdings, and contact information is in Alice Eichholz, *Red Book: American State, County and Town Sources*, rev. ed. (Salt Lake City: Ancestry, 2004).

South Carolina

State-land state surveyed in indiscriminate metes and bounds. A proprietary colony from 1670 to 1719 and a royal colony from 1719 to 1775, South Carolina's gradual separation from North Carolina was recognized by parliament in 1729 and confirmed by the partial running of their dividing line in 1735. Subsequent segments were later run ever farther west, and many settlers unexpectedly found themselves inhabitants of the neighboring colony. Each colony made some grants in the other's territory. South Carolina had headright grants, which are sometimes in council journals from the 1749 to 1773 period. See Brent H. Holcomb, *North Carolina Land Grants in South Carolina* (1980; reprint, Baltimore: Genealogical Publishing Co., 1999) and A.S. Salley, Jr., *Warrants for Land in South Carolina, 1672–1711*, rev. ed. (Columbia: University of South Carolina Press, 1973).

The colonial and state surveys/plats and grants are in the state archives and have been microfilmed. There are separate series with indexes for the proprietary, royal, and state periods. Land office business was suspended all through the 1720s, South Carolina having expelled the proprietary government in 1719. The situation was resolved when George II bought out the proprietors in 1729. In 1731, a more regularized processing of land titles was implemented, with the proprietary titles and claims to be registered as "memorials." In 1744, this memorializing of land titles was required of all titles granted from 1731, a system that helped the government identify quitrent obligations. Five manuscript volumes of quitrents exist for the 1733 to 1774 period. See Alan D. Watson, "The Quit Rent System in Royal South Carolina," *William and Mary Quarterly*, 3rd series, 33 (1976): 182–211.

South Carolina land records created before the revolution may refer to the counties of Colleton, Craven, Berkeley, and Granville; these were nonfunctioning but useful as geographical locators. Deeds and mortgages were recorded only at Charleston until 1769–72, and until 1785, such records from local courthouses continued to be sent to and stored in Charleston. Pre-1719 records are at the South Carolina Department of Archives and History, 8301 Parklane Road, Columbia, South Carolina 29223 <www.state.sc.us/scdah>. The collection includes plats and grants, virtually complete, from 1731; nearly complete records of grants and conveyances, 1671–1730; memorials of land titles, 1732–75; and microfilm of deeds available to 1920. There is an online index at <www.archivesindex.sc.gov> to plats for state land grants, 1784–1868. Printed references include Charles H. Lesser, *South Carolina Begins: The Records of a Proprietary Colony, 1663–1721* (Columbia: South Carolina Department of Archives and History, 1995); Silas Emmett Lucas, Jr., *An Index to Deeds of the Province and State of South Carolina 1719–1785 and Charleston District 1785–1800* (Easley, S.C.: Southern Historical Press, 1977); and Clara A. Langley, *South Carolina Deed Abstracts, 1719–1772*, 4 vols. (Spartanburg, S.C.: 1983). From 1785 to 1799, there were first seven and then nine "old" districts, where conveyances were stored. About 1799, these large districts were abolished and conveyances were recorded and stored at twenty-four small "new" districts. (These districts have been called counties since 1868.) See Michael E. Stauffer, *County Formation in South Carolina* (Columbia: South Carolina Department of Archives and History, 1994). The need, until about 1769–72, to go to Charleston to record conveyances, the turmoil of the revolution from 1775 to 1783, and the loss of many "old" district records means South Carolina deeds created before 1800 are very incomplete. The original tracts in the up-country vicinity of the Broad, Tyger, and Enoree rivers have been platted and published as Union County Historical Foundation, *Land Grant Maps* (Union, S.C.: A Press, 1976). South Carolina passed a bounty-land act and established a small military reserve. See Bockstruck, xxi–xxii. A unique land source is the state's Reconstruction attempt to buy land for black freedmen. Some records exist showing whites selling to the project and blacks buying. See Carol K. Rothrock, *The Promised Land; The History of the South Carolina Land Commission, 1869–1890* (Columbia: University of South Carolina Press, 1969). See also "Granting of Land in Colonial South Carolina," *South Carolina Historical Magazine* 77 (1976): 208–12; Robert K. Ackerman, *South Carolina Colonial Land Policies* (Columbia: University of South Carolina Press, 1977); David A. Means, "The Recording of Land Titles in South Carolina . . . ," *South Carolina Law Quarterly* 10 (1957–58): 346–419; Marion C. Chandler and Earl W. Wade, *The South Carolina Archives: A Temporary Summary Guide*, 2nd ed. (Columbia: South Carolina Department of Archives and History, 1976), 5, 8–9, 41; and Robert L. Meriwether, *The Expansion of South Carolina 1729–1765* (Kingsport, Tenn.: Southern Publishers, 1940).

South Dakota

Public-domain state with three principal meridians (established 1855 and 1878, and in Arkansas in 1815). Of South Dakota's eight GLO land districts, the earliest opened in Vermillion in 1861; in 1909 the Mitchell office moved to Gregory (see Hone 464–77). The records of these offices are in NARA's Rocky Mountain Region in Denver. Order patents from the BLM Montana State Office, P.O. Box 36800, 5001 Southgate Drive, Billings, Montana 59107-6800 <www.mt.blm.gov>, which also has copies of tract books and township plats for South Dakota. Serial patents are being indexed and scanned for GLO-ARS. NA-DC has the land-entry case files as described in Inventory No. 22 and the GLO headquarters original tract books and township plats. See Charles L. Green, *The Administration of the Public Domain in South Dakota* (Pierre, S.D.: Hipple Printing, 1939) and N. Thomas, "Distribution of the Public Domain in Dakota Territory" (M.A. thesis, University of South Dakota, 1944).

Tennessee

State-land state surveyed in indiscriminate metes and bounds, except the lands west of the lower Tennessee River, which were surveyed in five-mile-square townships. In 1777, North Carolina annexed its western reserve (now the state of Tennessee), established Washington County, and opened a land office there to issue purchase-warrants for lands ceded by the Indians. That office was closed in 1781. In 1783, North Carolina set aside a military reservation in what is today upper middle Tennessee, out of which bounty lands were to be issued as payment to its Revolutionary War soldiers. In its "land-grab act" of 1783, North Carolina opened for entry its entire western reserve outside the military and Cherokee reservations. At a price of £10 for every one hundred acres, nearly 4 million acres were entered, mostly by speculators, and to a large extent for lands not yet relinquished by the Indians. In that same year North Carolina enacted laws permitting military warrants to be satisfied outside the reservation, and some 8 million acres of Tennessee lands eventually were taken up in this fashion, again largely by speculators who had bought up the soldiers' warrants. See Shirley Hollis Rice, *The Hidden Revolutionary War Land Grants in the Tennessee Military Reservation* (reprint. Lawrenceburg, Tenn.: Family Tree Press, 1992).

In 1789, North Carolina ceded its western reserve to the U.S. government but continued to issue grants for lands in the area during the years of federal control (1790–1796). Disputes involving North Carolina, Tennessee, and the United

States prevented Tennessee from opening offices for the sale of public lands for more than a decade after statehood. In terms reached in the Compact of 1806, the United States set aside a Congressional Reservation lying mostly west of the lower Tennessee River, on lands still claimed by the Chickasaw. The United States withheld settlement from that area and disallowed the satisfying of outstanding North Carolina warrants and entries there. Tennessee was permitted to open land offices for the sale of its own lands outside the Congressional Reservation but was required to continue honoring outstanding North Carolina warrants in those areas.

Beginning in 1806, Tennessee enacted laws that addressed and defined the rights of those who had squatted on vacant and unappropriated lands. Occupant grants sought to encourage immigration and recognize the rights of actual settlers by granting small amounts of land based on residence and improvements made to the property. The remainder of the grants issued by the state of Tennessee, representing the bulk of the total, were based on general land sales. These purchase grants eventually sold for as little as 1 cent per acre. The lands of west Tennessee were opened in 1818, when the Chickasaw surrendered their rights. This district was laid out on a grid system; preferential rights were given to occupants, and offices were opened for land sales. Once again, however, Tennessee was required to satisfy outstanding North Carolina warrants and entries.

The Cherokees had relinquished their rights to the lands of Tennessee in piecemeal fashion, giving up the lands along the southern boundary in 1805 and 1806. The remainder of their lands, the Cherokee Reservation, was ceded in treaties dated 1819 and 1835; the resulting Hiwassee and Ocoee districts were laid out under the GLO land system. Because this area had been exempt from military warrants and from entries under the 1783 act, it was the only section unencumbered by North Carolina claims that had caused so much confusion in the rest of the state.

Grants issued by Tennessee, as well as those North Carolina grants issued for Tennessee lands, are on microfilm along with a card file that indexes and summarizes them. Surviving warrants, entries, and surveys are available on microfilm at the Tennessee State Library and Archives, <www.state.tn.us/sos/statelib>, as Record Group 50. For further discussion of Tennessee's land history and laws, see Irene M. Griffey, *Earliest Tennessee Land Records & Earliest Tennessee Land History* (2000; reprint, Baltimore: Clearfield Co., 2003); Billie R. McNamara, *Tennessee Land: Its Early History and Laws* (Knoxville, Tenn.: 1997); Timothy R. and Helen C. Marsh, *First Land Grants of Sumner County, TN 1786–1833* (Greenville, SC: Southern Historical Press, 2003); Daniel Dovenbarger, "Land Registration in Middle Tennessee" (M.A. thesis, Vanderbilt University, 1981); and Thomas B. Jones, "The Public Lands of Tennessee," *Tennessee Historical Quarterly* 27 (1): 13–36 (Spring 1968).

Texas

State-land state surveyed in often rectangular metes and bounds with some large tracts subdivided into numbered blocks often a mile square. Many rivers have parallel long lots running back from the water. The first Spanish settlements in Texas were at Nacogdoches in 1716 and San Antonio in 1718; over the next 120 years, approximately 26 million acres were granted by the Spanish and Mexican governments. Entrepreneurs such as Stephen Austin, Sterling Robertson, Martin de Leon, and Benjamin Milam contracted with the Mexican government to bring settlers into Texas. In return, they received large grants and established their own land offices. The Texas Constitution of 1836 validated all Spanish and Mexican land grants provided they conformed to the laws in effect at their issuance, though title disputes were heard by the state courts. Also in 1836, the Texas legislature created the Texas General Land Office, which still manages 22 million acres, including lucrative gas and oil lands. When Texas entered the Union in 1845, it retained its right to sole disposal of its public domain.

Since 1836, the Texas General Land Office has overseen the transfer of most of the public land into private ownership. Its archives, along with the county deeds, are the major Texas land source for researchers and can be found at the Texas General Land Office, Archives and Records Division, Research Room 500, 1700 N. Congress Ave., Austin, TX 78701-1495. The collections may be summarized as follows (excluding its important Spanish archives of the pre-Republic period and numerous issuances of scrip):

Bounty grants for service in the Army of the Republic of Texas were awarded at the rate of 320 acres per three months of service.

Donation grants of 640 acres were given for special service during the Texas Revolution. Men who fought at a battle, such as the Siege of Bexar, or San Jacinto, or the heirs of those who fell at the Alamo or Goliad, were eligible.

Headrights were given to those who settled in the Republic of Texas prior to 1 January 1842. Four classes of grants were awarded in the years 1836, 1837, 1842, and 1849. The amount of land depended upon whether the settler was married or single. The first class (those who arrived prior to 2 March 1836) awarded to married men one league (4,423.4 acres) and one labor (177.1 acres); to single men one-third of a league (1,476.1 acres).

Preemption grants (homestead or settler's claims) went to individuals who actually resided on a tract of no more than 320 acres for at least three consecutive years from 22 January 1845. Under an act of 1854, preemptors could locate no more than 160 acres. Under an act of 1870, married men could locate no more than 160 acres and single men no more than 80 acres. The last preemption was approved in 1899.

School lands were sold to individuals under an act of 1874, and the proceeds went into the common school fund.

The above and other holdings are detailed in the publication "History of Texas Public Lands," available at the Texas General Land Office website <www.glo.state.tx.us/archives/archives.html>. The database contains a listing of all original land grants that have been issued an abstract number by the Texas General Land Office. *Abstracts of Original Land Titles: Volumes and Supplements*, once offered in eight volumes, is available on CD-ROM. There are county maps showing the original surveys for each county and indexes by county to all grant records. Two major indexes to early grants are *Guide to Spanish and Mexican Land Grants in Texas* (Austin: Texas General Land Office, 1988), which revised the 1974 *Index* by Virginia H. Taylor and considers Trans-Nueces grants; and compiler Galen D. Gresser, *Catalogue of the Spanish Collection*, 2 vols. (Austin: Texas General Land Office, 2003). There are also published indexes to some of the other grant series. In 1855, the Texas Adjutant-General's office was destroyed along with its bounty warrants, donation records, and muster rolls, which necessitated creating a Court of Claims (1856–1860) whose records are in the land office. NARA's Southwest Region in Fort Worth reports no GLO or private land claims records. See Reuben McKitrick, *The Public Land System of Texas, 1823–1910* (1918; reprint, Arno Press, 1979).

Utah

Public-domain state with two principal meridians (established 1855 and 1875). The earliest of Utah's GLO land districts opened in 1868 at Salt Lake City (see Hone, 478–480). NARA's Rocky Mountain Region in Denver, Colorado, holds GLO records of the Utah state office and the Cedar City, Moab, Richfield, Salt Lake City, and Vernal district land offices, such as registers, tract books, and correspondence, 1869–1970. Order patents from the BLM Utah State Office, 324 South State St., Suite 400, Salt Lake City, UT 84111-2303, which also has copies of tract books and township plats. Serial patents are being indexed and scanned for GLO-ARS. NA-DC has the land-entry case files as described in Inventory No. 22 and the GLO headquarters original tract books and township plats. It also has a card index to all Utah patentees to 30 June 1908. Case files for private land claims are at NA-DC.

When the first Mormons settled in Utah in 1847, their church allotted lands and encouraged communal irrigation systems and living in villages rather than on farms. While these practices worked well in semi-arid Utah, they did not conform to the federal policy of having people live on 160-acre homesteads. Thus, when the first GLO land office opened in 1869 it was often necessary to have entrymen—usually LDS Church officials—take out homestead patents and then redeem them piecemeal to actual owners. These transactions are recorded in county deed books. See Lawrence L. Linford, "Establishing and Maintaining Land Ownership in Utah Prior to 1869," *Utah Historical Quarterly* 42 (1974): 126–43 and Lawrence B. Lee, "Homesteading in Zion," ibid., 28 (1960): 28–38.

Vermont

State-land state surveyed in fairly rectangular New England towns. Although New Hampshire, New York, and Massachusetts all made grants in present-day Vermont, many of the settlers were from Connecticut, having migrated up the Connecticut River Valley. Any standard history of colonial Vermont will explain the New Hampshire-New York dispute of 1749 over control of Vermont, and the latter's simple solution of declaring itself independent of any jurisdiction during the 1776 to 1791 period. A brief account is in William H. Dumont, "The New York-Vermont Land Dispute, 1749–1791," *New York Genealogical and Biographical Record* 100 (1969): 91–95. The standard discussion is Matt Bushnell Jones, *Vermont in the Making* (Cambridge: Harvard University Press, 1939). Check also the Phelps-Gorham Collection at the New York State Archives, Albany, for documents relating to the Gore, a narrow strip of land along the New York-Connecticut-Vermont border.

The state's official land records are mostly in the Archives Division, Office of the Secretary of State, 26 Terrace St., Montpelier, Vermont 05600-1103 <www.vermont-archives.org>. The Vermont secretary of state's *State Papers of Vermont* has published several volumes on land records: vol. 2, Franklin H. Dewart, *Charters Granted by the State of Vermont* (1922); and vols. 5–7, Mary Greene Nye, *Petitions for Grants of Land 1778–1811* (1939); *Sequestration, Confiscation and Sale of [Loyalist] Estates* (1941); and *New York Land Patents 1688–1786 Covering Land Now Included in the State of Vermont (Not Including Military Patents)* (1947). Vol. 2 listed above has been indexed in Jay Mack Holbrook, *Vermont's First Settlers* (Oxford, Mass.: Holbrook Research Institute, 1976). Also see Holbrook, *Vermont Land Grantees 1749–1803* (Oxford, Mass.: Holbrook Research Institute, 1986), which identifies the first 15,000 land grants by New Hampshire (58 percent are in present-day Vermont), and Herbert W. Denio, "Massachusetts Land Grants in Vermont," *Publications of the Colonial Society of Massachusetts* 24 (1920–22): 35–59. Vermont deeds are recorded in the towns, surviving records being microfilmed at least to 1850. Also see Florence May Woodward, *The Town Proprietors in Vermont* (New York: Columbia University Press, 1936), 2.

Virginia

State-land state surveyed in indiscriminate metes and bounds. Virginia settlement began under a private stock company called the Virginia Company of London. The Crown revoked the company's charter in 1624. Only near the end of this period did the company begin granting land for private ownership, and there are a few references in surviving records to patents in the 1619 to 1624 period.

There were several types of "rights" that people used in order to obtain fifty acres of patented land (1) "personal right" for bringing themselves into the colony; (2) "transportation rights" for paying another person's passage to Virginia. Each person coming into the colony supposedly got fifty acres, but usually it was the person who paid their passage who received the land; (3) "military rights" to persons willing to settle in hostile territory (these were seldom used); (4) "headrights" to people brought into the colony. Headrights could be saved and exchanged in later years for a larger piece of land. Or, *headright claims* could be sold to someone else. In the latter case, the original recipient's name appears in the headright list as the basis for the claim of the other person. Since these headright lists were notoriously fraudulent and were sold and re-sold and sometimes completely fabricated, it is difficult to determine if the name belongs to an actual person. A law passed in 1725 abolished the headrights, and after that, land was purchased directly from the Crown with a (5) treasury right. A warrant redeemable in land was purchased from the land office and this became the primary method of obtaining land. The warrants and surveys for the colonial land patents were destroyed on an annual basis. See Richard Slatten, "Interpreting Headrights in Colonial-Virginia Patents: Uses and Abuses," *National Genealogical Society Quarterly* 75 (September 1987): 169–79; James W. Petty, "Seventeenth-Century Virginia County Court Headright Certificates, *The Virginia Genealogist* 45 (2001): 3–22, 112–22; and Petty's "William Gany and Thomas Savage's Headright," *Magazine of Virginia Genealogy* 42 (2004): 91–96.

Virginia's land office records in the royal period (1624–1776) and for statehood are in the Library of Virginia in Richmond. Some patents may have been omitted since the patent books were created from the county clerk's list of patents. These have been microfilmed with indexes. The holdings are described in Minor T. Weisiger, "Virginia Land Office" (Research Notes no. 20), issued 2002, <www.lva.lib.va.us/whatwehave/land>. The same site has indexes to Virginia Land Office patents (pre-revolutionary) and grants (post-revolutionary), and the Northern Neck grants and surveys. A survey of these holdings is Daphne S. Gentry, *Virginia Land Office Inventory 3rd ed.*, revised by John S. Salmon (reprint; Richmond, Va.: 1988). The first fourteen patent books (1623–1732) are abstracted in three volumes by Nell Marion Nugent, *Cavaliers and Pioneers* (1934; reprint, Virginia State Library and Archives, 1992). Later patent books (1732–82) are included in the five-volume continuation of this series by Dennis Hudgins, *Cavaliers and Pioneers: Abstracts of Virginia Land Patents and Grants* (Richmond: Virginia Genealogical Society, 1994–2005). The excellent introductions in these volumes offer the most complete explanations of Virginia land records.

The Northern Neck Proprietary of the Fairfax family, between the Potomac and Rappahannock rivers, was granting lands after 1690. Its patent books and surveys are also in the Library of Virginia and have been microfilmed and also scanned and indexed online (see following). An online database at the Library of Virginia is titled "Virginia Land Office Patents and Grants/Northern Neck Grants and Surveys." The index includes images for the pre-1779 land patents; Land Office grants after 1779; Northern Neck grants (1692–1862); and recorded Northern Neck surveys (1786–1874). The unrecorded Northern Neck surveys prior to 1782 are on microfilm.

Virginia had entail until 1776 and primogeniture until 1786. A special complication with Virginia entail was the absence of a way to terminate (dock) the entail except by an act of the legislature for estates worth more than £200. Dower for wives and courtesy rights for husbands are other important legal concepts relating to land ownership that the researcher must understand.

Tax records are important sources for researching Virginia land. The only extant quitrent records (1704) are in the Public Records Office in England, but have been published several times. The most reliable readings of this 1704 list are in Louis des Cognets Jr., *English Duplicates of Lost Virginia Records* (Princeton, N.J.: the author, 1958): 123–232; and Thomas J. Wertenbaker, *The Planters of Colonial Virginia* (New York: Russell & Russell, 1959): 183–247. The 1704 rolls only cover the area south of the Rappahannock, because the Northern Neck quitrents belonged to the Fairfax Proprietary. Mrs. G. Dice, "Lord Fairfax Rent Rolls," *National Genealogical Society Quarterly* 39 (1951): 113–18. Extensive land tax lists from 1782 to the present are in the Library of Virginia, and most created before 1850 have been microfilmed and are available on interlibrary loan. See Conley L. Edwards III, *Using Land Tax Records in the Archives,* Research Notes no. 1 (Richmond: Virginia State Library and Archives, 1999).

There are other Virginia records with some relation to land that deserve mention. A microfiche publication by Ransome B. True, *Biographical Dictionary of Early Virginia, 1607–1660* (Jamestown: The Association for the Preservation of Virginia Antiquities, 1982), lists in its 1982 edition approximately 120,000 entries for more than 33,000 persons and includes deeds (though few of Nugent's patents). The bounty-land warrants by Virginia for the French and Indian War, Dunmore's War, and especially the American Revolution are numerous (see Bockstruck, xxii–xxiv). In the 1770s and 1780s, Virginia had several active counties in what is now southwestern Pennsylvania. See John F. Vallentine, "Research in Virginia's District of West Augusta," *Genealogical Journal* 4 (1975): 141–47; Raymond M. Bell, "Virginia Land Grants in Pennsylvania," *Virginia Genealogist* 7 (1963): 78–83, 103–7, 152–62; ibid., 11 (1967): 126–27.

Virginia has a significant number of independent cities that keep their own conveyances; some have records from colonial times. Alice Eichholz, *Red Book: American State, County and Town Sources,* rev. ed. (Salt Lake City: Ancestry, 2004), lists Virginia's independent cities. The "Burned Record Counties Database" online at the Library of Virginia contains a growing collection of local court records, principally deeds and probate records, generally used as exhibits in a court case. Because these items are generally from a locality other than that in which the case occurred, the copy may be the only extant copy of the document.

The secondary literature on Virginia land is extensive. For instance, see Fairfax Harrison, *Virginia Land Grants, a Study of Conveyancing in Relation to Colonial Politics* (1925; reprint, Willow Bend Books, 1998); W. Stitt Robinson, *Mother Earth: Land Grants in Virginia, 1607–1699* (Williamsburg, Va.: n.p., 1957); William H. Seiler, "Land Processioning in Colonial Virginia," *William and Mary Quarterly*, 3rd series, 6 (1949): 416–36; Robert Young Clay, *Virginia Genealogical Resources* (Detroit: Detroit Society for Genealogical Research, 1980): 11–12, 19–26; Gertrude E. Gray, *Virginia Northern Neck Land Grants 1694–1742*. 3 vols. (Baltimore: Genealogical Publishing Co., 1988); and Peggy Shomo Joyner, *Abstracts of Virginia's Northern Neck Warrants & Surveys: Orange and Augusta Counties 1730–1754*, 4 vols. (Portsmouth, Va.: the author, 1985). Additionally, Carol McGinnis, *Virginia Genealogy: Sources and Resources* (reprint. Baltimore: Genealogical Publishing Co., 1998), includes a chapter on land and court records; and two CD-ROMs, *Virginia Colonial Records* and *Virginia Vital Records* (Baltimore: Genealogical Publishing Co.) include early land and tax records. The latter contains virtually every article dealing with early Virginia lands and taxes published in *The Virginia Magazine of History and Biography*, the *William and Mary Quarterly*, and *Tyler's Quarterly*. Also, Patricia Law Hatcher, *Locating Your Roots: Discover Your Ancestors Using Land Records* (Cincinatti: Betterway Books, 2003); Roger G. Ward, *1815 Directory of Virginia Landowners & Gazetteer*. 6 vols. (Athens, Ga.: Iberian Publishing Co., 1997–2000); Barbara Vines Little, "Virginians and Their Land," *Virginia Genealogical Society Newsletter*, 25:2 (April 1999), reprint The LEE Genealogy "Info Hub" at <http://members.tripod.com/~LeeHouse/little.htm>; Edgar MacDonald, "Defective Surveys 1761–1799," *Magazine of Virginia Genealogy* 30 (1992): 318–323 and "Copies of Grants Not Called For" *Magazine of Virginia Genealogy* 30 (1992): 131–136; Edward T. Price, *Dividing the Land: Early American Beginnings of Our Private Property Mosaic* (Chicago: The University of Chicago Press, 1995); Richard Slatten, "Caveated Land Surveys," *Magazine of Virginia Genealogy*, 28 (1990), 159–164, 281–6; Vol. 29, (1991): 72–6; "Caveated Surveys Settled in the General Court." *Magazine of Virginia Genealogy* 28 (1990): 17–26; and "Lodged Land Surveys: A Series," *Magazine of Virginia Genealogy*. 26 (1988): 179–94, 273–83; 27 (1989): 44–51, 114–19, 206–15, 282–89; 28 (1990): 37–47.

Washington

Public-domain state with one principal meridian (established 1851). Of Washington's seven GLO land districts, the earliest opened in 1854 in Olympia, and the last closed in Seattle in 1927 (see Hone, 481–483). The records of these are at NARA's Alaska Northwest Region in Seattle. Order patents from the BLM Oregon State Office, P.O. Box 2965, 333 SW 1st Ave., Portland, Oregon 97208-2965 <www.or.blm.gov>, which also has copies of the tract books and township plats. This office has an index *by location* to the master title plats, use plats, supplemental plats, historical indexes, and cadastral survey plats. Serial patents are being indexed and scanned for GLO-ARS. NA-DC has the land-entry case files as described in Inventory No. 22 and the GLO headquarters original tract books and township plats. Washington's earliest white and mixed-blood settlers were entitled to free federal land under the Donation Act of 1850. An index and abstracts are on NARA microfilm M203, *Abstracts of Washington Donation Land Claims, 1855–1902*, in one roll, which serves as an index to the case files reproduced on NARS microfilm M815, *Oregon and Washington Donation Land Files, 1851–1903*, in 108 rolls. Donation case files are valuable because they typically contain a statement of the date and place of birth of the entryman. Because of a law forbidding their reproduction, the naturalization certificates in the M815 case files were not microfilmed. They can now be obtained from the National Archives. See Frederick Jay Yonce, "Public Land Disposal in Washington" (Ph.D. dissertation, University of Washington, 1966) and Roy Otto Hoover, "The Public Land Policy of Washington State: The Initial Period, 1889–1912" (Ph.D. dissertation, Washington State University, 1967).

West Virginia

State-land state surveyed in indiscriminate metes and bounds. Since West Virginia was part of Virginia until 1863, its first-title grants prior to the Civil War were made by Virginia. The colonial grants are in separate series for the Virginia royal government and for the Northern Neck Proprietary. They include significant portions of present West Virginia. (For the Northern Neck boundary, see the Virginia entry, above.) West Virginia land records are at the State Auditor, Capitol Building 1, Room W-100, Charleston, West Virginia 25305, <www.wvauditor.com>, along with extensive grant records, 1754 to 1864 and 1748 to 1912, also microfilmed. Pursuant to a 1951 act of the legislature, the state auditor attempted to collect and index all identifiable grantees: Edgar B. Sims, *Sims Index to Land Grants in West Virginia*, Mary F. Tessiatore, ed. (1952; reprint, Baltimore: Genealogical Publishing Co., 2003). Also see Edgar B. Sims, *Making a State: Formation of West Virginia, Including Maps, Illustrations, Plats, Grants. . . .* (Charleston, WV: State Auditor, 1956). The Virginia royal/commonwealth and Northern Neck grants are in the Library of Virginia (see Virginia, above, for database and microfilm information), as are West Virginia Land Tax Lists, 1782–1900, on microfilm.

Researchers doing colonial and antebellum genealogy in West Virginia must remember that they are actually working with Virginia records. Thus, the bounty-land laws for the French and Indian War, Dunmore's War, and the revolution apply to West Virginia. Likewise, the extension of Virginia counties into southwestern Pennsylvania in the 1770s and 1780s has ramifications for early West Virginia migrations—parts of those counties included West Virginia. The *Virginia Genealogist* and other Virginia genealogical and historical journals have much on early West Virginia lands. See Carol McGinnis, *West Virginia Genealogy: Sources and Research* (1988; reprint, Baltimore: Genealogical Publishing Co., 1998).

Wisconsin

Public-domain state with one principal meridian (established 1831). Of the nine GLO land districts, the earliest opened in 1834 at Mineral Point; the last closed in 1925 at Wausau (see Hone, 484–93). The local records of these districts are at the Wisconsin Board of Commissioners of Public Lands (BCPL), 125 S. Webster, Room 200, Madison, Wisconsin 53703. The mailing address is P.O. Box 8943, Madison, Wisconsin 53703. These include the field notes, which may be searched at <http://bcpl.state.wi.us>, and the plat maps, which have been scanned to CD-ROM, one per county. This site has background information on public land distribution in Wisconsin and the records created. The BCPL also holds copies of the documents ("state patents") used to transfer about 10 million acres of land sold or transferred by the Wisconsin state government to private parties. These may be searched by legal description. NARA's Great Lakes Region in Chicago holds GLO records of the Wassau district land office, 1888 and 1905. The BLM-ESO has original patents, tract books, cadastral survey field notes, and township plats. Wisconsin's federal patents are indexed and scanned in the GLO-ARS; a CD-ROM version of the index is available. The NA-DC has the land-entry case files as described in Inventory No. 22. Case files for Private Land Claims are at NA-DC. Some are indexed in Fern Ainsworth, *Private Land Claims: Illinois, Indiana, Michigan, and Wisconsin* (Natchitoches, La.: the author, 1980). See Paul W. Gates, "Frontier Land Business in Wisconsin," *Wisconsin Magazine of History* 52 (1962): 306–27. For locating maps and atlases see Betsy J. Parks, *A Guide to Land Ownership Maps and County Atlases of Wisconsin, 1836–1950* (Madison, Wisc.: State Historical Society of Wisconsin, 1986).

Wyoming

Public-domain state with two principal meridians (established 1855 and 1875). Of Wyoming's six GLO land districts, the earliest opened in Cheyenne in 1870 (see Hone, 494–497). The records of these offices are mostly in NARA's Rocky Mountain Region in Denver; the Wyoming state archive, <http://wyoarchives.state.wy.us> has records for entries not brought to patent and county maps online that show range and township. Obtain patents from the BLM Wyoming State Office, Box 1828, 5353 Yellowstone Ave., Cheyenne, WY 82003, <www.wy.blm.gov>, which also has copies of the tract books and township plats. Serial patents are being indexed and scanned for GLO-ARS. NA-DC has the land-entry case files as described in Inventory No. 22 and the GLO headquarters original tract books and township plats. See *The Court of Private Land Claims for the Adjudication of Spanish and Mexican Land Titles in Colorado, New Mexico, Arizona, Nevada, Utah, and Wyoming* (FHL US/CAN Film 1016975–1016996). See also George Watson, *The Struggle of the Cattleman, Sheepman, and Settler for Control of Lands in Wyoming, 1867–1910 (Management of Public Lands in the United States)* (Arno Press, 1979).

Notes

1 Donald Lines Jacobus, "Connecticut," in *Genealogical Research Methods and Sources*, ed. Milton Rubincam and Kenn Stryker-Rodda, vol. 1 (Washington, D.C.: American Society of Genealogists, 1960–71), 129.

2 Val Greenwood, *Researcher's Guide to American Genealogy*, 3rd ed. (2000; reprint, Baltimore: Genealogical Publishing Co., 2003).

3 Patricia Law Hatcher, *Locating Your Roots: Discover Your Ancestors Using Land Records* (Cincinnati: Betterway Books, 2003), 188–203.

4 The most recent version is Bryan A. Garner, ed., *Black's Law Dictionary*, 8th ed. (West Group, 2004), although all editions are useful for historical terms.

5 Raymond A. Winslow Jr., "Land Records," in *North Carolina Research: Genealogy and Local History*, 2nd ed. (Raleigh: North Carolina Genealogical Society, 1996), 209–20.

6 Ann Lainhart, *A Researcher's Guide to Boston* (Boston: New England Historic Genealogical Society, 2003); Loretto Dennis Szucs, *Chicago and Cook County: A Historical & Genealogical Guide* (Salt Lake City: Ancestry, 1996); Connie S. Terheiden and Kenny R. Burck, *Guide to Genealogical Resources in Cincinnati and Hamilton County, Ohio* (Milford, Ohio: Little Miami Publishing, 2003); Estelle Guzic, *Genealogical Resources in the New York Metropolitan Area* (New York: Jewish Genealogical Society, 2003); and Ted Steele, *A Guide to Genealogical Research in St. Louis* (University City, Mo.: the author, n.d.).

7 Leslie Corn, "New York City Research Guide, Part One: Vital Records, Property Records, and Estate Records," New England Historic Genealogical Society, <http://newenglandancestors.org/articles/research>; Kay Haviland Freilich, "Genealogical Research in Pennsylvania," *National Genealogical Society Quarterly* 90 (March 2002): 7–36; and Jane Gardner Aprill, "New Orleans: Jewels in the Crown," *FORUM* 13 (Fall 2001).

8 William R. Graven, *Index to Selected Hamilton County, Ohio Recorder's Books, 1801–1820* (Milford, Ohio: Little Miami Publishing, 2000); William R. Graven and Eileen Mullen,

Hamilton County, Ohio, Index of Early Deed Books, 1804–1806 and 1814–1817 (Milford, Ohio: Little Miami Publishing, 2004).

[9] Christine Rose, *Courthouse Research for Family Historians* (San Jose, Calif.: CR Publications, 2004), 16–23, 30–35.

[10] Indenture from William Eskridge and wife Betty to Thomas Williams, 7 May 1763, Northumberland County, Virginia, deed book 6, pp. 220–22, FHL microfilm 032,675.

[11] Helen F. M. Leary, "Abstracting," in *North Carolina Research*, 106–16.

[12] J. Harvey Bloom, "Seals," *Genealogists' Magazine* 13 (1959): 111.

[13] Indenture from Dempsey Wood Sr. to Hardy Wood, 31 March 1800 (recorded 21 March 1896), Montgomery County, Georgia, deed book 2W, 404–05, FHL microfilm 218,775; Indenture from Glasingham Haney Sr. to Dempsy [*sic*] Wood, 30 Dec. 1791 (recorded 30 July 1901), Montgomery County, Georgia, deed book 2U, 5–6, FHL microfilm 218,779.

[14] Winslow, "Land Records," 227–28.

[15] Robert D. Mitchell, *Commercialism and Frontier: Perspectives on the Early Shenandoah Valley* (Charlottesville: University Press of Virginia, 1977), 31–33.

[16] Margaret M. Hofmann, writing in chapter 31, "Land Grants," in *North Carolina Research Genealogy*: "The terms land grant and land patent often are used interchangeably to denote the document transferring ownership of vacant land from a granting authority to a private person. The technical term for the document, however, is patent and the government action, a grant of patent" (313).

[17] Headrights are well-discussed in James W. Petty, "Seventeenth Century Virginia County Court Headright Certificates," *Virginia Genealogist* 45 (2001): 3–22, 112–22; and James W. Petty, "William Gany and Thomas Savage's Headright," *Magazine of Virginia Genealogy* 42, no. 2 (May 2004): 91–96.

[18] Royal Grant to Ezekiel Backler, 11 August 1774 (recorded 15 March 1773), South Carolina royal grants, book 32, 49; FHL microfilm 022,596.

[19] Sumner Chilton Powell, *Puritan Village: The Formation of a New England Town* (1963; reprint, Middletown, Conn.: Wesleyan University Press, 1970).

[20] David Grayson Allen, *In English Ways: The Movement of Societies and the Transferral of English Local Law and Custom to Massachusetts Bay in the Seventeenth Century* (Chapel Hill: University of North Carolina Press, 1981).

[21] Edward T. Price, "Dividing the Land: Early American Beginnings of Our Private Property Mosaic," geography research paper no. 238 (Chicago: University of Chicago Press, 1995); James W. Petty and Roy Hidemichi Akagi, *The Town Proprietors of the New England Colonies: A Study of Their Development, Organization, Activities and Controversies, 1620–1770* (1924; reprint, Philadelphia: Press of the University of Pennsylvania, 1963).

[22] David F. Stoddard, "Land System of the New England Colonial Colonies," *Connecticut Nutmegger* 11 (1979): 556–64. Capitalization standardized.

[23] *Brief Notes on the Public Domain* (Bureau of Land Management, 1957), 21.

[24] Ray Allen Billington and Martin Ridge, *Western Expansion, A History of the American Frontier*, 6th ed. (University of New Mexico Press, 2001).

[25] Lawrence B. Lee, "American Public Land History: A Review Essay," *Agricultural History* 55 (1981): 284–99.

[26] Bureau of Land Management, *Public Land Bibliography* (Washington, D.C.: Bureau of Land Management, 1962).

[27] U.S. Public Land Commission, *Laws of the United States of a Local or Temporary Character and Exhibiting the Entire Legislation of Congress Upon Which the Public Land Titles in Each State and Territory Have Depended* (1881; reprint, Arno Press, 1979), House exec. doc. no. 47, pts. 2–3, 46th cong., 3rd sess., serial no. 1976.

[28] "Found: America's Last Homesteader!" Homestead National Monument of America, <www.nps.gov/home/homesteader.html>.

[29] *Ohio Lands: A Short History*, 8th ed. (Columbus: Auditor of State, 1997).

[30] E. Wade Hone, *Land and Property Research in the United States* (Salt Lake City: Ancestry, 1997), 140–46.

[31] "General Land Office," <www.glorecords.blm.gov/Visitors/GLO.asp>.

[32] Kenneth Hawkins: "Since GLO-ARS covers only patented entries, it does not serve as an index to the many thousands of cancelled or relinquished land case files for eastern public-land states. To obtain file information on eastern states cancelled entries, researchers must consult the General Land Office tract books." General Information Leaflet Number 67, "Research in the Land Entry Files of the General Land Office (Record Group 49)," 1997, <www.archives.gov/publications/general_information-leaflets/67.html>.

[33] Hone, *Land and Property Research in the United States*, 213–67.

[34] Richard W. Stephenson, *Land Ownership Maps* (Washington, D.C.: Library of Congress, 1967); Library of Congress, *List of Geographical Atlases in the Library of Congress*, 8 vols. (Washington, D.C.: Library of Congress, 1909–74).

[35] Newberry Library, *Checklist of Printed Maps of the Middle West to 1900*, 11 vols. (Boston: G. K. Hall, 1980).

[36] Clifford Neal Smith, *Federal Land Series*, 4 vols., 1972–86 (Reprint, Baltimore: Genealogical Publishing Co., 2004).

[37] Mary Francis Morrow, "Indian Bounty Land Applications," *Prologue* 25 (Fall 1993), available on the National Archives and Records Administration website, <www.archives.gov/publications/prologue/1993/fall/indian-bounty-land-applications.html>.

[38] See table 25, "Checklist of National Archives Publications Relating to Cartographic Records," in Anne Bruner Eale and Robert M. Kvasnicka, *Guide to Genealogical Research in the National Archives of the United States*, 3rd ed., p. 348. An excellent summary of Native American land records is chapter 13, "Native American Land Records," in Hone, *Land and Property Records*, 201–12. See also, chapter 19, "Native American Research" in this book.

[39] The 1841 Preemption Act allowed anyone who was the head of a family (including widows) or over twenty-one, and who was a U.S. citizen or had declared intention to become one, to stake a claim on any tract up to 160 acres and then buy it from the government for $1.25 per acre. (Some lands were not open to preemption.) See Hone, *Land and Property Research in the United States*, 137–40.

[40] Henry Putney Beers, *Spanish & Mexican Records of the American Southwest: A Bibliographical Guide to Archive and Manuscript Sources* (1979; reprint, Louisiana State University Press, 1989), 44–60, 141–56, 247–68, 328–39.

[41] Payson Jackson Treat, *The National Land System, 1785–1820* (1910; reprint, William S. Hein and Co., 2003), 215.

[42] "Records of the Committee on Claims and Other Claims Committees, 1816–1946," chapter 6, *Guide to the Records of the U.S. Senate at the National Archives (Record Group 46)*, item 6.14 and 6.15, <www.archives.gov/legislative/guide/senate/chapter-06.html>.

[43] "Records of the Claims Committees," Chapter 6, *Guide to the Records of the U.S. House of Representatives at the National Archives, 1789–1989* (Record Group 233), item 6.7, at <www.archives.gov/legislative/guide/house/chapter-06.html>.

[44] There are two editions of the *American State Papers*. McMullin's work indexes the Gales and Seaton edition, but not the Duff Green edition, which is consequently not cited here. U.S. Congress, *The American State Papers, Class VIII, Public Lands* and *The American State Papers, Class IX, Claims* (Washington, D.C.: Gales and Seaton, 1832–61; reprint, Greenville, S.C.: Southern Historical Press, 1993); Phillip W. McMullin, *Grassroots of America* (1972; reprint, Greenville, S.C.: Southern Historical Press, 1993).

[45] *Guide to Genealogical Research in the National Archives*, 3rd ed. (Washington, D.C.: National Archives Trust Fund Board, 2001), 298.

[46] The most comprehensive index of private land claims in the *American State Papers* is McMullin, *Grassroots of America*.

[47] House Journal, <http://memory.loc.gov/cgi-bin/ampage>, image 283.

[48] *American State Papers*, land claims 2:84, <http://memory.loc.gov/ammem/amlaw/lawhome.html>.

[49] *Private Land Grant Cases in the Circuit Court of the Northern District of California, 1852–1910*, NARA microfilm T1207.

[50] Paul W. Gates, *History of Public Land Law Development* (Washington, D.C.: Public Land Law Review Commission, 1968), 87–119; Paul W. Gates, "Private Land Claims in the South," *Journal of Southern History* 22 (1956): 183–204; Louis Pelzer, "The Private Land Claims of the Old Northwest Territory," *Iowa Journal of History and Politics* 12 (1914): 363–93; T. P. Martin, "The Confirmation of French and Spanish Land Titles in the Louisiana Purchase" (M.A. thesis, University of California, Berkeley, 1914); Lemont K. Richardson, "Private Land Claims in Missouri," *Missouri Historical Review* 50 (1955–56): 132–44, 271–86, 387–99; Hone, "Private Land Claims," 131–36, and "Congressional Collections," 156–58; Clark S. Knowlton, ed., "Spanish and Mexican Land Grants in the Southwest: A Symposium," *Social Science Journal* 13 (October 1976): 1–63.

[51] See Ancestry.com database, "Land Grants to Georgia's Revolutionary War Widows," <www.ancestry.com>.

[52] Lloyd D. Bockstruck, *Revolutionary War Bounty Land Grants Awarded by State Governments* (Baltimore: Genealogical Publishing Co., 1996).

[53] Paul Gates, *History of Public Land Law Development* (Washington, D.C.: Public Land Law Review Commission, 1968), 251–57.

[54] Ibid., 278.

[55] Harry P. Yoshpe and Philip P. Brower, *Preliminary Inventory of the Land-Entry Papers of the General Land Office* (1949; reprint, San Jose, Calif.: Rose Family Association), 7–9, known as Inventory No. 22.

[56] *National Genealogical Society, Index of Revolutionary War Pension Applications* (Washington, D.C.: National Genealogical Society, 1976); Virgil D. White, *Genealogical Abstracts of Revolutionary War Pension Files* (Waynesboro, Tenn.: National Historical Publishing Co., 1993).

[57] *U.S. Revolutionary War Bounty Land Warrants Used in the U.S. Military District of Ohio and Related Papers (Acts of 1788, 1803, 1806)*, NARA microfilm M829.

[58] April Leigh Helm and Matthew L. Helm, et al., *War of 1812 Military Bounty Land Warrants 1815–1858* (Champaign, Ill.: FamilyToolbox.net, 2004).

[59] Virgil D. White, *Index to War of 1812 Pension (and Bounty-Land Warrant) Files* (Waynesboro, Tenn.: National Historical Publishing Co., 1989).

[60] James W. Oberly, "Military Bounty Land Warrants of the Mexican War," *Prologue* 14 (1982): 28.

[61] Gates, *History of Public Land Law Development*, 279.

[62] Testimony from <http://memory.loc.gov/ammem/amlaw/lawhome.html>, a site maintained by the Law Library of Congress. In just one month, February 1816, the petition of Abigail O'Flyng was read in the House of Representatives (*U.S. House Journal*, 1816, 14th cong., 1st sess., 1 February 1816, vol. 10, 257), and bounty land was granted "for extraordinary military services." (*U.S. House Journal*, 1816, 14th cong, 1st sess., #302) Family and service information is recorded in the act's quick passage through congress. Correspondence, O'Flying descendant Ms. Margaret Behnke, February 2000.

[63] Treat, *The National Land System*, 340.

[64] National Archives, *Guide to Genealogical Research in the National Archives* (Washington, D.C.: National Archives and Records Service, 1982), 133–39; Paul Gates, "Military Bounty Land Policies," in *History of the Public Land Law Development* (Washington, D.C.: Public Land Law Review Commission, 1968), 249–84; James W. Oberly, *Sixty Million Acres: American Veterans and the Public Lands Before the Civil War* (Kent, Ohio: Kent State University Press, 1990).

[65] Gates, *History of Public Land Law Development*, 256.

[66] Ibid., 255.

[67] Clifford Neal Smith, *Federal Land Series*, vol. 4, pt. 1 (1982). Also see Clifford Neal Smith, "Virginia Land Grants in Kentucky and Ohio, 1784–1799," *National Genealogical Society Quarterly* 61 (1973): 16–27; John Salmon, "Revolutionary War Records in the Archives & Records Division of the Virginia State Library," *Genealogy* no. 70 (July 1982): 2–10; Gaius Marcus Brumbaugh, *Revolutionary War Records . . . Virginia Army and Navy Forces With Bounty Land Warrants for Virginia Military Scrip; From Federal and State Archives* (Washington, D.C., 1936); Willard Rouse Jillson, *Old Kentucky Entries and Deeds: A Complete Index to All of the Earliest Land Entries, Military Warrants, Deeds and Wills of the Commonwealth of Kentucky*, Filson Club publication no. 34 (1926; reprint; Baltimore: Genealogical Publishing Co., 1999); Margie G. Brown, *Genealogical Abstracts Revolutionary War Veterans Scrip Act 1852* (Decorah, Iowa: Anundsen Publishing Co., 1990); William Lindsay Hopkins, *Virginia Revolutionary War Land Grant Claims 1783–1850 (Rejected)* (Richmond, Va: the author, 1988).

[68] Anderson-Latham Collection, 1777–1881, accession 23634, personal papers collection, Library of Virginia, Richmond, Va., 117 surveys.

[69] Alexander Fraser, ed., *United Empire Loyalists Enquiry into the Losses and Services in Consequence of Their Loyalty. Evidence in Canadian Claims*, 2 vols. (1905; reprint, Genealogical Publishing Co., 1994). Second Report of the Bureau of Archives for the Province of Ontario.

[70] Kenn Stryker-Rodda, "Limit of 18th Century Sources in New York and New Jersey," *Families* 11 (1972): 121.

[71] Peter Wilson Coldham, *American Loyalist Claims: Abstracted from the Public Record Office, Audit Series 13, Bundles 1–35 & 37* (Washington, D.C.: National Genealogical Society, 1980).

[72] Gregory Palmer, ed., *A Bibliography of Loyalist Source Material in the United States, Canada, and Great Britain* (Westport and London: Meckler Publishing and the American Antiquarian Society, 1982).

[73] Marion Gilroy, *Loyalists and Land Settlement in Nova Scotia* (1937; reprint, Baltimore: Genealogical Publishing Co., 2002).

[74] Raymond A. Winslow Jr., "Tax and Fiscal Records," in Helen F. M. Leary, *North Carolina Research: Genealogy and Local History*, rev. ed. (Raleigh: North Carolina Genealogical Society, 1996), 231–32.

[75] Poll Tax List, 1799, Warren County, Kentucky, tax lists 1799, 5–6, 14, 17; FHL microfilm 008,255.

[76] *Laws of the State of Indiana . . . Tenth Session* (Indianapolis: Douglas and Maguire, printers, 1826), 68.

[77] "Bute Co., N.C.: 1771 Tax List," *North Carolinian* 7 (1961): 899–907; "Franklin-Warren-Vance Cos. Area Father-Son Relationships in 1771," *North Carolinian* 11 (1965): 1,499–515.

[78] A noteworthy assemblage of various tax lists is Early Kentucky Tax Records from *The Register of the Kentucky Historical Society* (1984; reprint, Baltimore: Genealogical Publishing Co., 2004).

[79] Beverley W. Bond Jr., *The Quit-Rent System in the American Colonies* (New Haven, Conn.: Yale University Press, 1919).

[80] Richard LeBaron Bowen, *Early Rehoboth: Documented Historical Studies of Families and Events in this Plymouth Colony Township*, vol. 4 (Rehoboth, Mass.: the author, 1950), 143–45.

[81] Edward W. Hanson and Homer Vincent Rutherford, "Genealogical Research in Massachusetts: A Survey and Bibliographical Guide," *New England Historical and Genealogical Register* 13 (1981): 177.

[82] Dall W. Forsythe, *Taxation and Political Change in the Young Nation, 1781–1833* (New York City: Columbia University Press, 1977), 59.

[83] *Guide to Genealogical Research in the National Archives*, 335.

[84] William Blackstone, *Commentaries on the Laws of England* (Oxford: Clarendon Press, 1766), book 2, 315.

[85] Deed of feoffment from Arthur Harris to James Heaburn, 26 March 1744 (recorded 5 April 1744), Westmoreland County,

Virginia, deeds and wills, book 9, 347–48; FHL micrfilm 034,272.

[86] Carole Shammas, Marylynn Salmon, and Michel Dahlin, *Inheritance in America From Colonial Times to the Present* (New Brunswick: Rutgers University Press, 1987); Marylynn Salmon, *Women and the Law of Property in Early America* (Chapel Hill: University of North Carolina Press, 1986); Lawrence M. Friedman, *A History of American Law,* rev. ed. (New York: Simon and Schuster, 1985).

[87] Margaret Hickerson Emery, "The Adeustone-Rogers Families of Virginia: Tracing a Colonial Lineage through Entailment and Naming Patterns," *National Genealogical Society Quarterly* 77, no. 2 (June 1989): 89–106.

[88] Shammas, Salmon, and Dahlin, *Inheritance in America,* 32–33.

[89] John Frederick Dorman, "Colonial Law of Primogeniture," 1–12, *World Conference of Records* (Salt Lake City: Genealogical Society of Utah, 1969).

[90] Richard B. Morris, "Colonial Law Governing the Distribution and Alienation of Land," in *Studies in the History of American Law with Special Reference to the Seventeenth and Eighteenth Centuries* (New York: Columbia University Press, 1930), 69–125.

[91] Deed of Release from John Tyler the Aged to Richard Taylor, 17 July 1713 (date of recording unknown), Chesapeake City, successor to Norfolk Co., Virginia, deed book 9, pp. 261–62; FHL microfilm 032,829; Will of Richard Taylor, 26 Sept. 1729, proved 19 February 1730/1 (never officially recorded), Chesapeake City, Virginia, unrecorded wills book 1722–26, p. 22.

[92] William Thorndale, "The Lindseys of Maury County, Tennessee," typescript, located in FHL (Salt Lake City, n.d.).

References

General Reference

Allen, David Grayson. *In English Ways: The Movement of Societies and the Transferral of English Local Law and Custom to Massachusetts Bay in the Seventeenth Century*. Chapel Hill: University of North Carolina Press, 1981.

Anderson-Latham Collection, 1777–1881. Accession 23634. Personal Papers Collection, The Library of Virginia, Richmond, Va. 117 surveys.

Aprill, Jane Gardner. "New Orleans: Jewels in the Crown." *FORUM* 13 (Fall 2001).

Blackstone, William. *Commentaries on the Laws of England, Book 2*. Oxford: Clarendon Press, 1766.

Bowen, Richard LeBaron. *Early Rehoboth: Documented Historical Studies of Families and Events in this Plymouth Colony Township*. Vol. 4. Rehoboth, Mass.: the author, 1950.

Brown, Margie G. *Genealogical Abstracts Revolutionary War Veterans Scrip Act 1852*. Decorah, Iowa: Anundsen Publishing Co., 1990.

Bureau of Land Management. *Brief Notes on the Public Domain*. Washington, D.C.: Bureau of Land Management, 1957.

———. *Public Land Bibliography*. Washington, D.C.: Bureau of Land Management, 1962.

"Bute Co., N.C.: 1771 Tax List." *North Carolinian* 7 (1961): 899–907.

Corn, Leslie. "New York City Research Guide, Part One: Vital Records, Property Records, and Estate Records." New England Historic Genealogical Society. <http://newenglandancestors.org/articles/research>.

Dorman, John Frederick. "Colonial Law of Primogeniture." I–12, World Conference of Records. Salt Lake City: Genealogical Society of Utah, 1969.

Eales, Anne Bruner, and Robert M. Kvasnicka. *Guide to Genealogical Research in the National Archives*. 3rd ed. Washington, D.C.: National Archives and Records Service, 2001.

Early Kentucky Tax Records from The Register of the Kentucky Historical Society. 1984; reprint Baltimore: Genealogical Publishing Co., 2004.

Eichholz, Alice, ed. *Red Book: American State, County, and Town Sources*. Provo, Utah: Ancestry, 2004.

Forsythe, Dall W. *Taxation and Political Change in the Young Nation, 1781–1833*. New York City: Columbia University Press, 1977.

"Franklin-Warren-Vance Cos. Area Father-Son Relationships in 1771." *North Carolinian* 11 (1965): 1,499–515.

Freilich, Kay Haviland. "Genealogical Research in Pennsylvania." *National Genealogical Society Quarterly* 90 (March 2002): 7–36.

Friedman, Lawrence M. *A History of American Law.* 3rd ed. New York: Touchstone, 2005.

Garner, Bryan A., ed. *Black's Law Dictionary.* 8th ed. West Information Publishing Group, 2004.

Gates, Paul W. *History of Public Land Law Development*, pp. 87–119. Washington, D.C.: Public Land Law Review Commission, 1968.

———. "Private Land Claims in the South." *Journal of Southern History* 22 (1956): 183–204.

Gilroy, Marion. *Loyalists and Land Settlement in Nova Scotia*. 1937; reprint, Genealogical Publishing Co., 2002.

Graven, William R. *Index to Selected Hamilton County, Ohio Recorder's Books, 1801–1820*. Milford, Ohio: Little Miami Publishing, 2000.

Greenwood, Val D. *Researcher's Guide to American Genealogy*. 3rd ed. 2000; reprint, Baltimore: Genealogical Publishing Co., 2003.

Guzic, Estelle. *Genealogical Resources in the New York Metropolitan Area*. New York: Jewish Genealogical Society, 2003.

Hanson, Edward W., and Homer Vincent Rutherford. "Genealogical Research in Massachusetts: A Survey and Bibliographical Guide." *New England Historical and Genealogical Register* 13 (1981): 177.

Hatcher, Patricia Law. *Locating Your Roots: Discover Your Ancestors Using Land Records*. Cincinnati: Betterway Books, 2003.

Hone, E. Wade. *Land and Property Research in the United States*. Salt Lake City: Ancestry, 1997.

Hopkins, William Lindsay. *Virginia Revolutionary War Land Grant Claims 1783–1850 (Rejected)*. Richmond, Va.: the author, 1988.

Jacobus, Donald Lines. "Connecticut." *Genealogical Research Methods and Sources*. Edited by Milton Rubincam and Kenn Stryker-Rodda. Vol. 1. Washington, D.C.: American Society of Genealogists, 1960–71.

Jillson, Willard Rouse. *Old Kentucky Entries and Deeds: A Complete Index to All of the Earliest Land Entries, Military Warrants, Deeds and Wills of the Commonwealth of Kentucky*. Filson Club publication no. 34. 1926; reprint; Baltimore: Genealogical Publishing Co., 1999.

Knepper, George W. *Official Ohio Lands Book*. At <www.auditor.state.oh.us/StudentResources/OhioLands/ohio_lands.pdf>.

Knowlton, Clark S., ed. "Spanish and Mexican Land Grants in the Southwest: A Symposium." *Social Science Journal* 13 (October 1976): 1–63.

Laws of the State of Indiana . . . Tenth Session. Indianapolis: Douglas and Maguire, printers, 1826.

Lee, Lawrence B. "American Public Land History: A Review Essay." *Agricultural History* 55 (1981): 284–99.

Martin, T. P. "The Confirmation of French and Spanish Land Titles in the Louisiana Purchase." MA thesis, University of California, Berkeley, 1914.

Mitchell, Robert D. *Commercialism and Frontier: Perspectives on the Early Shenandoah Valley*. Charlottesville: University Press of Virginia.

Morrow, Mary Francis. "Indian Bounty Land Applications." *Prologue* 25 (Fall 1993).

Mullen, Eileen. *Hamilton County, Ohio, Index of Early Deed Books, 1804–1806 and 1814–1817*. Milford, Ohio: Little Miami Publishing, 2004.

Palmer, Gregory Palmer. *A Bibliography of Loyalist Source Material in the United States, Canada, and Great Britain*. Westport and London: Meckler Publishing and the American Antiquarian Society, 1982.

Pelzer, Louis. "The Private Land Claims of the Old Northwest Territory." *Iowa Journal of History and Politics* 12 (1914): 363–93.

Richardson, Lemont K. "Private Land Claims in Missouri." *Missouri Historical Review* 50 (1955–56): 132–44, 271–86, 387–99.

Rose, Christine. *Courthouse Research for Family Historians: Your Guide to Genealogical Treasures*. San Jose, Calif.: CR Publications, 2004.

Rubincam, Milton, and Kenn Stryker-Rodda, eds. *Genealogical Research Methods and Sources*. Vol. 1. Washington, D.C.: American Society of Genealogists, 1960–71.

Salmon, John. "Revolutionary War Records in the Archives & Records Division of the Virginia State Library." *Genealogy* 70 (July 1982): 2–10.

Salmon, Marylynn. *Women and the Law of Property in Early America*. Chapel Hill: University of North Carolina Press, 1989.

Shammas, Carole, Marylynn Salmon, and Michel Dahlin. *Inheritance in America from Colonial Times to the Present*. New Brunswick: Rutgers University Press, 1987.

Smith Clifford Neal. "Virginia Land Grants in Kentucky and Ohio, 1784–1799." *National Genealogical Society Quarterly* 61 (1973).

Szucs, Loretto D., and Sandra H. Luebking. *The Archives: A Guide to the National Archives Field Branches*. Salt Lake City: Ancestry, 1988.

Thorndale, William. "The Lindseys of Maury County, Tennessee." Typescript. At Family History Library.

Winslow Jr., Raymond A. "Tax and Fiscal Records." In Helen F. M. Leary, *North Carolina Research: Genealogy and Local History*. Rev. ed. Raleigh: North Carolina Genealogical Society, 1996.

Claims

Beers, Henry Putney. *Spanish & Mexican Records of the American Southwest: A Bibliographical Guide to Archive and Manuscript Sources*. 1979; reprint, Louisiana State University Press, 1989.

Coldham, Peter Wilson. *American Loyalist Claims: Abstracted from the Public Record Office, Audit Series 13, Bundles 1–35 & 37*. Washington D.C.: National Genealogical Society, 1980.

Fraser, Alexander, ed. *United Empire Loyalists Inquiry into the Losses of Services in Consequence of Their Loyalty. Evidence in the Canadian Claims*. 2 vols. Toronto: King's Printer, 1905.

Gates, Paul W. "Private Land Claims in the South." *Journal of Southern History* 22 (1956): 183–204.

Lainhart, Ann. A *Researcher's Guide to Boston* (Boston: New England Historic Genealogical Society, 2003).

Martin, T. P. "The Confirmation of French and Spanish Land Titles in the Louisiana Purchase." MA thesis, University of California, Berkeley, 1914.

McKee, T. H. "Index to Reports of Committee on Private Land Claims, House of Representatives." *House Index to Committee Reports* (Y1.3:C73/2): 5–20.

McMullin, Phillip W. *Grassroots of America*. 1972; reprint, Greenville, S.C.: Southern Historical Press, 1993.

Montaya, Maria. *Translating Property: The Maxwell Land Grant and the Conflict over Land in the American West, 1840–1900*. Berkeley: University of California Press, 2003.

Naylor, Chris. "Those Elusive Early Americans: Public Lands and Claims in the American State papers, 1789–1837." *Prologue* 37, no. 2 (Summer 2005). At <www.archives.gov/publications/prologue/2005/summer/state-papers.html>.

Pelzer, Louis. "The Private Land Claims of the Old Northwest Territory." *Iowa Journal of History and Politics* 12 (1914): 363–93.

Reports of the Committees on Private Land Claims of the Senate and House of Representatives. 2 vols. 45th cong., 3rd sess., misc. doc. 81, serial 1836.

Smith, Clifford Neal. *French and British Land Grants in the Post Vincennes (Indiana) District, 1750–1784. Four Parts in One. Originally Published as Monographs 1–4, Selections from* "The American State Papers." 1996; reprint, Baltimore: Clearfield Press, 2004.

Steele, Ted. A *Guide to Genealogical Research in St. Louis*. University City, Mo.: the author, n.d.

Szucs, Loretto Dennis. *Chicago and Cook County: A Historical & Genealogical Guide*. Salt Lake City: Ancestry, 1996.

Terheiden, Connie S., and Kenny R. Burck. *Guide to Genealogical Resources in Cincinnati and Hamilton County, Ohio*. Milford, Ohio: Little Miami Publishing, 2003.

Colonial Land

Akagi, Roy Hidemichi. *The Town Proprietors of the New England Colonies: A Study of Their Development, Organization, Activities and Controversies, 1620–1770*. 1924; reprint, Peter Smith Publishers, 1963.

Allen, David Grayson. *In English Ways: The Movement of Societies and the Transferral of English Local Law and Custom to Massachusetts Bay in the Seventeenth Century*. Chapel Hill: University of North Carolina Press, 1981.

Cronin, William. *Changes in the Land: Indians, Colonists, and the Ecology of New England*. New York: Hill and Wang Publishers, 2003.

Ely, James W., Jr. *Property Rights in the Colonial Era and Early Republic (Property Rights in American History: From the Colonial Era to the Present)*. Garland Publishing, 1997.

Emery, Margaret Hickerson. "The Adeustone-Rogers Families of Virginia: Tracing a Colonial Lineage Through Entailment and Naming Patterns." *National Genealogical Society Quarterly* 77, no. 2 (June 1989): 89–106.

Hofmann, Margaret M. Writing in "Land Grants." Chapter 31 in *North Carolina Research Genealogy and Local History*, edited by Helen F. M. Leary. 2nd ed. Raleigh: North Carolina Genealogical Society, 1996.

Leary, Helen F. M. "Abstracting." In *North Carolina Research Genealogy and Local History*, edited by Helen F. M. Leary. 2nd ed. Raleigh: North Carolina Genealogical Society, 1996.

Leary, Helen F. M. *North Carolina Research: Genealogy and Local History*, edited by Helen F. M. Leary. 2nd ed. Raleigh: North Carolina Genealogical Society, 1996.

Morris, Richard B. "Colonial Law Governing the Distribution and Alienation of Land." *Studies in the History of American Law with Special Reference to the Seventeenth and Eighteenth Centuries*. New York: Columbia University Press, 1930.

Petty, James W. "Seventeenth Century Virginia County Court Headright Certificates." *Virginia Genealogist* 45 (2001): 3–22, 112–22.

———. "William Gany and Thomas Savage's Headright." *Magazine of Virginia Genealogy* 42, no. 2 (May 2004): 91–96.

Powell, Sumner Chilton. *Puritan Village: The Formation of a New England Town*. Middletown, Conn.: Wesleyan University Press, 1970.

Price, Edward T. *Dividing the Land: Early American Beginnings of Our Private Property Mosaic. University of Chicago Geography Research Paper No. 238*. Chicago: University of Chicago Press, 1995.

Stoddard, David F. "Land System of the New England Colonial Colonies." *Connecticut Nutmegger* 11 (1979): 556–64.

Sturtz, Linda L. *Within Her Power: Propertied Women in Colonial Virginia (New World in the Atlantic World Series)*. New York: Routledge, 2002.

Winslow, Raymond A., Jr. "Land Records." In *North Carolina Research Genealogy and Local History*, edited by Helen F. M. Leary, 209–20. 2nd ed. Raleigh: North Carolina Genealogical Society, 1996.

Maps & Mapping

Arphax Publishing Co. Norman, Okla. <www.arphax.com>. Producers of patent maps in Deluxe and Homestead editions.

Fox, Michael J. "The Map Collection." *Genealogical Research: An Introduction to the Resources of the State Historical Society of Wisconsin*. Madison: State Historical Society of Wisconsin, 1979. Update edition, 1986.

Library of Congress. *List of Geographical Atlases in the Library of Congress*. 8 vols. Washington, D.C.: Library of Congress, 1909–74.

The Newberry Library. *Checklist of Printed Maps of the Middle West to 1900*. 11 vols. Boston: G. K. Hall, 1980.

Stephenson, Richard W. *Land Ownership Maps*. Washington, D.C.: Library of Congress, 1967.

Wilford, John Noble. *The Mapmakers*. Rev. ed. Alfred A. Knopf, 2000.

Military Bounty Land

Bockstruck, Lloyd D. *Revolutionary War Bounty Land Grants Awarded by State Governments*. Baltimore: Genealogical Publishing Co., 1996.

Brumbaugh, Gaius Marcus. *Revolutionary War Records . . . Virginia Army and Navy Forces with Bounty Land Warrants for Virginia Military Scrip; from Federal and State Archives*. Washington, D.C., 1936.

Helm, April Leigh, et al., comps. *War of 1812 Military Bounty Land Warrants 1815–1858*. CD-ROM. Champaign, Ill.: FamilyToolbox.net, 2003.

Lutz, Paul V. "Land Grants for Service in the Revolution." *New York Historical Society Quarterly* 48 (1964): 221–35.

National Genealogical Society. *Index of Revolutionary War Pension Applications in the National Archives*. Washington, D.C.: National Genealogical Society, 1976.

Oberly, James W. "Military Bounty Land Warrants of the Mexican War." *Prologue* 14 (1982): 25–34.

———. *Sixty Million Acres: American Veterans and the Public Lands Before the Civil War*. Kent, Ohio: Kent State University Press, 1990.

Prechtel-Kluskens, Claire. "The Robert Archibald-Elizabeth McCormick Marriage and Other Details About the Archibald-McCormick-Johnson Families of Virginia, Ohio, and Indiana in a Bounty-Land Warrant Application." *National Genealogical Society Quarterly* 92 (September 2004): 221–27.

Smith, Clifford Neal. *Federal Land Series: A Calendar of Archival Materials on the Land Patents Issued by the United States Government, with Subject, Tract, and Name Indexes. Vol 2: 1799–1835. Federal Bounty-Land Warrants of the American Revolution*; and *Vol 4, Parts 1 & 2, Grants in the Virginia Military District of Ohio*. 1972–86; reprint, Baltimore: Genealogical Publishing Co., 2004.

Vivian, Jean H. "Military Land Bounties During the Revolutionary and Confederation Periods." *Maryland Historical Magazine* 61 (1966): 231–56.

White, Virgil D. *Genealogical Abstracts of Revolutionary War Pension Files*. National Historical Publishing, 1993.

———. *Index to War of 1812 Pension Files*. National Historical Publishing Co., 1989.

Public Land

Billington, Ray Allen, and Martin Ridge. *Western Expansion, a History of the American Frontier*. 6th ed. University of New Mexico Press, 2001.

Donaldson, Thomas. *The Public Domain: Its History with Statistics*. House misc. doc. 45 pt. 4, 47th cong., 2nd sess. 1884; reprint, New York: Johnson Reprint, 1970.

Gates, Paul W. *History of Public Land Law Development*. Washington D.C.: Public Land Law Review Commission, 1968.

———. *Fifty Million Acres. (The Management of Public Lands in the U.S. Series)*. Ayer Company Publishers, 1979.

———. Allan G. Bogue, et al. *The Jeffersonian Dream: Studies in the History of American Land Policy and Development*. University of New Mexico Press, 1996.

Igler, David. *Industrial Cowboys: Miller and Lux and the Transformation of the Far West 1850–1920*. Berkeley: University of California Press, 2001.

Merrill, Karen R. *Public Lands and Political Meaning: Ranchers, the Government, and the Property Between Them*. Berkeley: University of California Press, 2002.

Pincetl, Stephanie S. *Transforming California: A Political History of Land Use and Development*. Johns Hopkins University Press, 2003.

Riley, Glenda. *Taking Land, Breaking Land: Women Colonizing the American West and Kenya, 1840–1940*. University of New Mexico Press, 2003.

Robbins, Roy Marvin. *Our Landed Heritage: The Public Domain, 1776–1970*. 2nd ed. Lincoln: University of Nebraska Press, 1976.

Rohrbough, Malcolm J. *The Land Office Business: The Settlement and Administration of American Public Lands, 1789–1837*. Belmont, Calif.: Wadsworth Publishing Co., 1990.

Smith, Clifford Neal. *Federal Land Series: A Calendar of Archival Materials on the Land Patents Issued by the United States*

Government, with Subject, Tract, and Name Indexes. 4 vols. 1972–86; reprint, Baltimore: Genealogical Publishing Co., 2004.

Treat, Payson Jackson. *The National Land System, 1785–1820*. 1910; reprint, William S. Hein and Co., 2003.

U.S. Public Land Commission. *Laws of the United States of a Local or Temporary Character and Exhibiting the Entire Legislation of Congress Upon Which the Public Land Titles in Each State and Territory Have Depended*. House exec. doc. no. 47, pts. 2–3, 46th cong., 3rd sess., serial no. 1976. 1881; reprint, Arno Press, 1979.

Yoshpe, Harry P., and Philip P. Brower. *Preliminary Inventory of the Land-Entry Papers of the General Land Office*. Preliminary Inventory 22. 1949; reprint, San Jose, Calif.: Rose Family Association, 1996.

Surveying

Bedini, Silvio A. *With Compass and Chain: Early American Surveyors and Their Instruments*. Professional Surveyors Publishing Co., 2001.

Bureau of Land Management. *Manual of Instructions for the Survey of the Public Lands of the United States*. Technical Bulletin 6. Washington, D.C.: Department of the Interior, 1973.

Department of the Interior. *Catalog of the United States Geological Survey Library*. 24 vols. plus a first supplement of 11 vols. and a second of 4. Boston: G. K. Hall, 1964, 1972–74.

Hughes, Sara S. *Surveyors and Statesmen: Land Measuring in Colonial Virginia*. Richmond, Va.: Virginia Surveyors Foundation and The Virginia Association of Surveyors, 1979.

Linklater, Andro. *Measuring America: How the United States Was Shaped by the Greatest Land Sale in History*. Reissued ed. Plume Books, 2003.

Taxation

Bond, Beverley W., Jr. *The Quit-Rent System in the American Colonies*. New Haven, Conn.: Yale University Press, 1919.

Carroll, Cornelius. *The Beginner's Guide to Using Tax Lists*. 1996; reprint, Baltimore: Genealogical Publishing Co., 2004.

Ely, Richard T. *Taxation in American States and Cities*. Thomas Y. Crowell and Co., 1888.

Perkins, Edwin J. *The Economy of Colonial America*. 2nd ed. Columbia University Press, 1988.

Internet Resources

Claims

Knetsch, Joe. "Private Land Claims: Sources of the Problems." *Professional Surveyor* 24, no. 9 (September 2004). <http://www.profsurv.com/newpsm/archive.php>.

U.S. Congress. *The American State Papers, Class VIII, Public Lands* and *the American State Papers, Class IX, Claims*. Washington, D.C.: Gales and Seaton, 1832–61; reprint, Greenville, S.C.: Southern Historical Press, 1993. <www.memory.loc.gov/ammem/amlaw/lawhome.html>.

Military Bounty Land

Butler, Stuart L. "Genealogical Records of the War of 1812." *Prologue* 23, no. 4 (Winter 1991). <www.archives.gov/publications/prologue>.

National Archives. *Guide to Federal Records in the National Archives of the United States*. 3 vols. Washington, D.C.: National Archives, 1996. <www.archives.gov/records_of_congress/senate_guide>.

Public Land

Hawkins, Kenneth, comp. "Research in the Land Entry Files of the General Land Office (Record Group 49)." *General Information Leaflet Number 67*. Washington, D.C.: National Archives, 1997. <www.archives.gov/publications/general_information_leaflets>.

Potter, Constance. "De Smet, Dakota Territory, Little Town in the National Archives." *Prologue* 35, no. 4 (Winter 2003). <www.archives.gov/publications/prologue>.

Surveying

Knetsch, Joe. "Meandering: View of Instructions." *Professional Surveyor* 24, no. 2 (February 2004). <http://www.profsurv.com/newpsm/archive.php>.

San Francisco Estuary Institute. "Map Interpretation III. Projections and Survey Systems." <www.sfei.org/ecoatlas/GIS/MaInterpretation/ProjectionsSurveySystems.html>.

Virginia Surveyors Foundation. Sells many manuals and guides that are otherwise difficult to find (i.e., Lowell Stewart's *Public Land Surveys: History, Instructions, Methods*. Ames: University of Iowa Press, 1935.) <www.surveyhistory.org>

Taxation

Rabushka, Alvin. "The Colonial Roots of American Taxation, 1607–1700." *Policy Review*, no. 14 (2002). <www.policyreview.org/AUG02/rabushka_print.html>.

Rosen, Harvey S. "Taxation." Microsoft Encarta Online Encyclopedia 2004. <http://encarta.msn.com/encyclopedia_761573037/Taxation.html>

11
Military Records

LLOYD deWITT BOCKSTRUCK, MA, MS
and SANDRA HARGREAVES LUEBKING, FUGA

Military endeavors span the history of America. From King Phillip's War in 1675–76 to the Gulf Wars of the twenty-first century, every generation of our ancestors who have lived in this country have been involved in or affected by conflict. Participation ranged from 125,000 in the Philippine Insurrection to an estimated five million in the Civil War. Many others who did not serve created draft registration records. Involvement was not limited to white native-born males but included the newly-arrived foreign born of all ethnic groups as well as minorities, American Indians, blacks, and in certain instances, women. The abundance and variety of records generated by military service, the distribution of veterans' benefits, and the interaction with civilians provide a template of rich personal detail about service personnel, their families, and often, the general citizenry.

The first indication of an ancestor's involvement with the military may come from family stories or from personal papers that have been retained (see figure 11-1). If there is no information of this type, or if the reference is so general that it lacks the specifics needed for further research, there are still avenues to explore to determine if there was a history of military service. Particularly for the twentieth and twenty-first centuries, records associated with an individual's death (death certificates, obituaries, funeral or memorial programs, and cemetery records and grave markers) will provide the evidence needed to conduct a search of military records. This chapter also presents ways to locate service, pension, and other types of military records when details such as rank or regiment are yet to be determined.

Chapter Contents

The uses and value of military records in genealogical research for ancestors who were veterans are obvious, but military records can also be important to researchers whose direct ancestors were not soldiers in any war. Collateral relatives of an ancestor, such as siblings or cousins, may have served in a war, and their service or pension records could assist in finding information on the family of the primary interest. Due to the amount of genealogical information contained in some military pension files, they should never be overlooked during the research process. Those records not containing specific genealogical information are of historic value and should be included in any overall research design. The wars considered in this chapter are grouped as follows:

Colonial wars

King Philip's War...1675–76
King William's War...1689–97

Queen Anne's War 1702–13
King George's War 1744–48
French and Indian War 1754–63

Revolutionary War and frontier conflicts 1775–1811

Post-revolutionary wars to 1848
War of 1812 1812–15
Indian Wars 1815–58
Mexican War 1846–48

Civil War 1861–65

Spanish-American War 1898

Philippine Insurrection 1899–1902

Modern wars
World War I 1917–18
World War II 1941–45
Korean War 1950–53
Vietnam War 1965–73
Gulf Wars & Conflicts (Desert Storm, etc.) 1990–

At least some remnant exists of records for every war that the colonies and states were involved in; but, as with other records maintained in the United States during the first centuries of its existence, there is little uniformity of content or style in those records. The information that follows organizes sources and finding aids by war or conflict. Entries are divided into two principal categories: service records and records of veterans' benefits. This is followed by some categories of miscellaneous records that supply genealogical information.

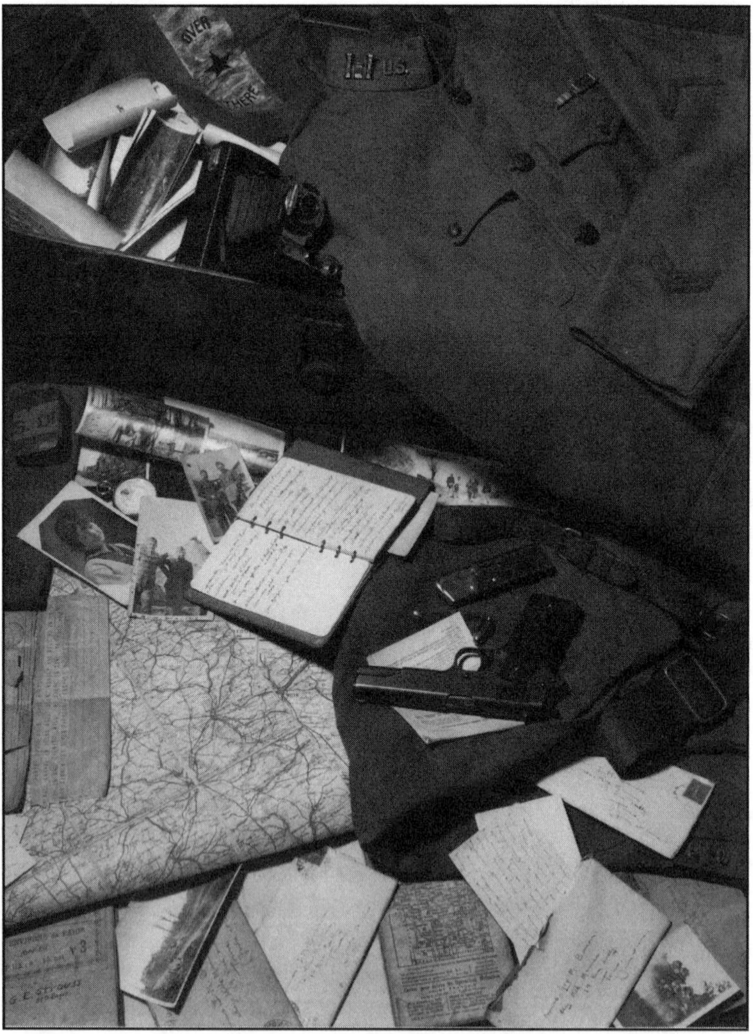

Figure 11-1. Mementos from the footlocker of Captain Godfrey Eric Strauss (55th Engineers), arranged for a photography project by his grandson. These and other items contained within the locker provided a wealth of detail about Captain Strauss's military activities in the First World War. Courtesy of Christopher Eric Strauss, photographed by Kenneth Stevens Strauss, 28 March 1979.

Colonial Wars (1607–1774)

Service records of soldiers in the colonial wars will be found in the collections of state and local agencies rather than those of the federal government. Colonial service records, if available, have more historical than genealogical information and usually provide only the name of the soldier and the colonial unit in which he served. They consist primarily of rosters, rolls, and lists that survived the wars and several repository fires. Most of these rosters and rolls have been published and can be found in genealogical and historical libraries throughout the nation (see the chapter reference list).

Despite the scanty genealogical information these records provide, you should not ignore them. They may be sparse, but few records in general exist for this time period that can help you locate an ancestor. The presence of a soldier in a particular unit may be a valuable clue to his place of residence as well as useful in identifying his family in other records of the same location, even though there may be problems in distinguishing between two or more soldiers with the same name.

Early (Pre–World War I) United States Military Records in General

The greatest volume of original military records is held by the National Archives and Records Administration (NARA). Many pre–World War I records can be searched in person at the National Archives. Microfilm copies of significant pre–World War 1 collections and indexes have been microfilmed and many libraries have copies. The library with the largest collection of microfilmed U.S. military records is the Family History Library of The Church of Jesus Christ of Latter-day Saints. Genealogists who have access to the microfilmed records can search them more efficiently by following the tables presented in this chapter. To effectively use the collection of the Family History Library in Salt Lake City or one of its Family History Centers, check the current "U.S. Military Records Research Outline" which may be ordered or printed from <www.familysearch.org>. This provides a cross-reference from the NARA microfilm number to the call number assigned by the Family History Library.

The scope of content and the complexity of arrangement of the military records most often consulted by researchers is fully explained in Anne Bruner Eales and Robert M. Kvasnicka, *Guide to Genealogical Research in the National Archives of the United States.*[1] Six chapters of this essential *Guide* are devoted to military records.

Genealogists most often seek information from three general types of records that are available from NARA: (1) military service records; (2) pension claims files; and (3) bounty-land warrant applications (granted only for service in the Mexican and earlier wars). Once a pre–World War I record (or records) is identified in an index, a photocopy request should be sent to the National Archives and Records Administration. Requests may be made online at the National Archives website, <www.archives.gov>, or by mail using NATF Form 86 for service records and NATF Form 85 for pension or bounty-land files. A search of these records cannot be completed without the full name of the veteran, his branch of service, the state from which he served, and the war in which he served. Expect an eight-week processing time before you receive the records. Details for ordering and printable forms are on the website.

In addition to original federal records, there are large collections of military records that document state military activity by service personnel. An example of these are the World War II bonuses that some states paid to veterans. Many of the records held at the state level are being indexed and digitized and placed online by state government repositories. Local and county-wide projects by volunteers and major databases by commercial enterprises have also contributed to the wealth of online resources. Because the list of important websites grows daily, only a few are listed at the end of this chapter.

Much information appears in manuscript and print form as well. Take full advantage of the excellent histories of military wars and conflicts, the personal written accounts of those who witnessed action, and published lists, such as the many Revolutionary War roster lists and other service records that may be found in historical and genealogical periodicals. For a list of titles of rosters for early wars, consult the chapter reference list.

Service Records

Revolutionary War and Frontier Conflicts (1775–1811)

Some of the original service records of the Revolutionary War were destroyed by fire, but those that have survived are on file at the National Archives, compiled primarily from rosters and rolls of soldiers serving in the Continental Army, state lines, and militia units, with additions from correspondence and filed reports of military officers. These service records contain much more genealogical information than colonial records: name, rank, and military organization of the soldier. Included in some records are the name of the state from which the soldier served; the date that his name appears on one or more of the rolls; sometimes the date or dates of his enlistment, or the date of his appointment; and, rarely, the date of his separation from the service. His physical description, date and place of birth, residence at the time of enlistment, and other personal details are also included in some categories. For example, in the size roll for Captain Aaron Ogden's Company, 1st Regiment of New Jersey, we find these men:

> WILLIAM JONES, private, 22, 5'4"; brown [eyes], fair [hair]; taylor [tailor]; b. & res. Woodbridge, Essex Co., enl. 15 June '77.
>
> WILLIAM McMULLIN, private, 36, 5'8 1/2"; black, fair; laborer; b. Glenarm, Embrim, Ireland; res. Mendham, Morris Co.; enl. 16 Feb. '78; deserted at Morris Hutts, 18 Apr. '82, retaken 28 June '82, 100 lashes.[2]

Revolutionary War service records are indexed, and microfilm and print versions of this index are widely distributed. The service records themselves can be searched at the National Archives or on microfilm at many libraries with strong genealogy collections. See table 11-1 for film numbers and titles.

Loyalists and German Auxiliary Troops

Many American colonists retained their allegiance to the British crown. Known as Loyalists, they probably comprised about one-third of the colonial population. In some areas they may have been in the majority. Some of them simply refused to support the revolutionary cause. Others took up arms against it. With the defeat of the British, many fled to other points of the Empire, notably to what was called Canada West (Ontario) and the Canadian Maritime Provinces.

The British forces were also augmented by a large contingent of German auxiliaries imported to America to help suppress the rebellion. Inaccurately labeled mercenaries or

Table 11-1. List of Microfilmed Military Service and Other Records, 1775–1811*

Record or Index	NARA Microfilm Number	Comments/Access
Compiled Service Records of Soldiers Who Served in the American Army During the Revolutionary War	M881	At least one jacket envelope for each soldier containing card abstracts of entries relating to that soldier from original records.
General Index to Compiled Military Service Records of Revolutionary War Soldiers	M860	Considered the most comprehensive name index to compiled service records, this lists soldiers who served in the American army during the Revolutionary War. The index also contains entries for several small series of Revolutionary War compiled service records of sailors, members of army staff departments, and other persons associated with the American army and navy. Each card of the index gives the name and unit of a soldier or civilian and sometimes rank, profession, or office.
Index to Compiled Service Records of Volunteer Soldiers Who Served . . . from North Carolina	M257	
Index to Compiled Service Records of Volunteer Soldiers Who Served . . . in Connecticut Organizations	M920	
Index to Compiled Service Records of Volunteer Soldiers Who Served . . . in Georgia Organizations	M1051	A name index listing the name and unit of each soldier or civilian employee and sometimes rank, profession, or office.
Card Indexes for Delaware, Maryland, Massachusetts, New Hampshire, New Jersey, New York, Pennsylvania, Rhode Island, South Carolina, Vermont, and Virginia	NA	Available only at NARA; not microfilmed.
Compiled Service Records of American Naval Personnel and Members of Departments of Quartermaster General and Commissary General of Military Stores Who Served During the Revolutionary War	M880	
Index to Compiled Service Records of Revolutionary War Naval Records, T516, 1 roll.		
Revolutionary War Rolls, List of Jackets, 1775–83	M246	Shows militia rolls, payrolls, supply lists for each regiment. These are the volumes in which the men will be listed. Most of the men will appear in more than one list, so check them all. Use M860 index, above, first.
Numbered Record Books Concerning Military Operations and Service Pay, Settlements of Accounts, Supplies, War Department Collection of Revolutionary War Records.	M853	
Miscellaneous Numbered Records (The Manuscript File) War Department Collection of Revolutionary War Records	M859	Original records, approximately 35,000 items. Includes civilians in war service: paymasters, wagons, judges, chaplains, medical officers, teamsters, and others.
Special Index to Numbered Records in the War Department Collection of Revolutionary War Records, 1775–83	M847	Indexes all or some of the names in M859 and M853.
Compiled Service Records of Volunteer Soldiers Who Served From 1784–1811	M905	Service records of soldiers who served in the various Indian campaigns, insurrections, and disturbances that occurred in the post-revolutionary period. Arranged by U.S. organization, alphabetically by state or territorial organizations, thereunder by military unit, then alphabetically by surname of soldier.
Index to Compiled Service Records of Volunteer Soldiers Who Served From 1784–1811	M694	Indexes M905.
War Department Collection of Post-Revolutionary War Manuscripts, 1784–1811	M904	Includes muster rolls.
Every-Name Card Index at NARA Only	NA	Index not on microfilm; search only at NARA.

Record or Index	NARA Microfilm Number	Comments/Access
Central Treasury Records of the Continental and Confederation Government Relating to Military Affairs, 1775–89	M1015	Includes military pay and muster rolls which can be used as evidence of service. Also included are company and account books of officers.
Papers of the Continental Congress, 1774–89	M247	Includes muster rolls, payrolls, wagoneer lists, claims for pay by revolutionary war soldiers and officers, many of whom did not live long enough to file for pension.
Miscellaneous Papers of the Continental Congress, 1774–89	M332	Records that are not a part of the numbered sequence of Continental Congress papers reproduced in M247, including despatches and letters, reports of committees, bonds, receipts, deeds of cession of western lands, credentials of delegates to the Congress, and broadsides issued by the Congress.
John P. Butler, comp., *Index to Papers of the Continental Congress,* 5 vols. (Washington, D.C.: NARS, 1978)	NA	Published work; not on microfilm. A comprehensive personal name and major subject index to documents of the Continental Congress.

* Although only the NARA microfilm number is provided for each record or index listed, microfilm sets of many of these records are available at the Family History Library and at other libraries with strong genealogy collections.

Sources:
Microfilm Resources for Research. (Washington, D.C.: National Archives and Records Administration, 2000).
Guide to Genealogical Research in the National Archives (Washington, D.C.: National Archives and Records Administration, 2000).
Arlene Eakle and Johni Cerny, eds., *The Source: A Guidebook of American Genealogy,* 1st ed. (Salt Lake City: Ancestry, 1984).

Hessians, these troops originated not only from Hessen Kassel and Hessen Hanau, but also from Braunschweig, Ansbach-Bayreuth, Waldeck, and Anhalt-Zerbst. Perhaps as many as 7,000 of the nearly 32,000 German auxiliary troops remained in North America.

There are many printed works of genealogical value pertaining to Loyalists and German auxiliary troops in the American Revolution. Consult the relevant bibliographies at the end of this chapter.

Post-Revolutionary Wars (1812–48)

There are federal service records for the War of 1812, the Indian Wars, and the Mexican War. The information included, like that in the service records of soldiers in the colonial wars and the Revolutionary War, has been indexed and microfilmed (see table 11-2).

The majority of the War of 1812 compiled service records are arranged by state or territory, thereunder by unit. If a unit's designation did not include the name of a state or territory, such as the U.S. Volunteers, U.S. Rangers, Captain Bookers Company, U.S. Volunteers (Virginia), it will appear separately. Likewise, during the Mexican War, special units came from the Indian nations, the Mormons (Mormon Battalion), and from New Mexico (Santa Fe Battalion of the Missouri Mounted Volunteers). Each unit will have compiled its own records.

Some rosters of men who served from a particular state have been placed online by sate agencies. For example, the Ohio Historical Society offers "War of 1812 Roster of Ohio Soldiers" at <www.ohiohistory.org>.

Civil War (1861–65)

The first step in finding service records for a Union or Confederate volunteer soldier who served in the Civil War is The Civil War Soldiers and Sailors System (CWSS) at <www.civilwar.nps.gov/cwss>.[3] The CWSS is a database that identifies whether the serviceman was Union or Confederate, his state of muster, his unit and its function (cavalry, infantry, etc.), his regiment, and his rank. Clicking on the link to the veteran's regiment provides a history, including muster in and muster out dates, the various other units to which the particular regiment was attached, and the regiment's service history, including major battles. Also included is information on more than 1,200 Civil War soldiers and sailors who received the Congressional Medal of Honor; prisoner records of Union prisoners at Andersonville and Confederate prisoners at Fort McHenry; the location of every identified Civil War soldier buried in the cemeteries operated by the National Park Service; and details about the 10,500 battles and skirmishes fought during the War.[4]

Eventually, the names of all Union and Confederate Naval personnel will be included in the CWSS. The first phase was to enter the names of approximately 18,000 African American sailors from various historical navy documents. Information for each name includes at least some of the following: place of birth, age, complexion, occupation, height, place, date, and term of enlistment and rating. A chronological list of places or vessels and dates served, if shown on muster rolls, also appears.

Union Service Records

The Union soldier entries for the Civil War Soldiers and Sailors System (CWSS) are from microfilmed *Indexes to the*

Table 11-2. Service Records Indexes, 1812–1848

Title	NARA Microfilm Number	Comments
Index to Compiled Records of Volunteer Soldiers Who Served During the War of 1812	M602, 234 rolls	There are also microfilm records for Mississippi (M678, 22 rolls), Louisiana (M229, 3 rolls), North Carolina (M250, 5 rolls), and South Carolina (M652, 7 rolls).
Index to Compiled Service Records of Volunteer Soldiers Who Served During the Indian Wars and Disturbances, 1815–58 (encompasses all of the indexes listed in the "comments" column)	M629, 12 rolls	

Also Available

State	Disturbance and Date	Microfilm Publication	Number of Rolls
Alabama	Creek War, 1836–37 Cherokee removal, 1838 Florida War, 1836–38	M244, index M243, index M245, index	2 1 1
Florida	Florida War, 1836–56	M1086, service records	63
Georgia	Cherokee disturbances and removal, 1836–38	M907, index	1
Louisiana	Florida War, 1836–38 War of 1837–38	M239, index M241, index	1 1
Michigan	Patriot War, 1838–39	M630, index	1
New York	Patriot War, 1838	M631, index	1
North Carolina	Cherokee disturbances and removal, 1836–38	M256, index	1
Tennessee	Cherokee disturbances and removal, 1836–38	M908, index	2

Title	NARA Microfilm Number	Comments
Index to Compiled Records of Volunteer Soldiers Who Served During the Mexican War, 1846–48	M626, 41 rolls	Service records are available for Mississippi (M863, 9 rolls), Pennsylvania (M1028, 13 rolls), Tennessee (M638, 15 rolls), Texas (M278, 19 rolls), Mormon Battalion (M351, 3 rolls).

Table 11-3. Microfilmed Indexes and Compiled Service Records for Union Army Volunteers

State	Microfilm Publication: Index	Microfilm Publication: Compiled Military Service Records
Alabama	M263, 1 roll	M276, 10 rolls
Arizona Territory	M532, 1 roll	
Arkansas	M383, 4 rolls	M399, 60 rolls
California	M533, 7 rolls	
Colorado Territory	M534, 3 rolls	
Connecticut	M535, 17 rolls	
Dakota Territory	M536, 1 roll	M1960. 3 rolls
Delaware	M537, 4 rolls	M1961, 117 rolls
District of Columbia	M538, 3 rolls	
Florida	M264, 1 roll	M400, 11 rolls
Georgia	M385, 1 roll	M403, 1 roll
Idaho Territory (see Washington Territory)		

State	Microfilm Publication	
	Index	Compiled Military Service Records
Indiana	M540, 86 rolls	
Iowa	M541, 29 rolls	
Kansas	M542, 10 rolls	
Kentucky	M386, 30 rolls	M397, 515 rolls
Louisiana	M387, 4 rolls	M396, 50 rolls
Maine	M543, 23 rolls	
Maryland	M388, 13 rolls	M384, 238 rolls
Massachusetts	M544, 44 rolls	
Michigan	M545, 48 rolls	
Minnesota	M546, 10 rolls	
Mississippi	M389, 1 roll	M404, 4 rolls
Missouri	M390, 51 rolls	M405, 854 rolls
Montana (see Washington Territory)		
Nebraska Territory	M547, 2 rolls	M1787, 43 rolls
Nevada	M548, 1 roll	M1789, 16 rolls
New Hampshire	M549, 13 rolls	
New Jersey	M550, 26 rolls	
New Mexico Territory	M242, 4 rolls	M427, 46 rolls
New York	M551, 159 rolls	
North Carolina	M391, 2 rolls	M401, 25 rolls
Ohio	M552, 122 rolls	
Oklahoma (Indian Territory) (see Arkansas, Colorado Territory, Kansas, Missouri, New Mexico, and Texas)		
Oregon	M553, 1 roll	M1816, 34 rolls
Pennsylvania	M554, 136 rolls	
Rhode Island	M555, 7 rolls	
South Carolina	None	
Tennessee	M392, 16 rolls	M395, 220 rolls
Texas	M393, 2 rolls	M402, 13 rolls
Utah Territory	M556, 1 roll	M692, 1 roll
Vermont	M557, 14 rolls	
Virginia	M394, 1 roll	M398, 7 rolls
Washington Territory	M558, 1 roll	
West Virginia	M507, 13 rolls	M508, 261 rolls
Wisconsin	M559, 33 rolls	
Wyoming (see Washington Territory)		
Volunteer U.S. Colored Troops	M589, 98 rolls	
Cavalry Regiments (All)		M1817, 107 rolls
Artillery Regiments (All)		M1818, 299 rolls
1st Infantry Regiments		M1819, 18 rolls
2nd thru 7th Infantry Regimentsb		M1820, 116 rolls
8th thru 13th, including the 11th (new) Infantry Regiments		M1821, 102 rolls
54th Massachusetts Colored Infantry		M1898, 20 rolls
55th Massachusetts Colored Infantry		M1801, 16 rolls
Union Volunteers Not Raised by States or Territories (Except Veterans Reserve Corp and U.S. Colored Troops).	M1290, 36 rolls	
U.S. Volunteers (former Confederate soldiers, 1st and 6th Regiments only)		M1017, 65 rolls
Veteran Reserve Corps	M636, 44 rolls	

Sources:
<www.archives.gov/research/alic/reference/military/civil-war-service-records-pamphlets.html> as of 10 February 2006.
Guide to Genealogical Research in the National Archives (Washington, D.C.: National Archives and Records Service, 2000):140.
i. Online index to microfilmed indexes is at <www.civilwar.nps.gov>.
ii. Includes the 3d Tennessee Volunteers (African descent), 6th Louisiana Infantry (African descent), and 7th Louisiana Infantry (African descent).

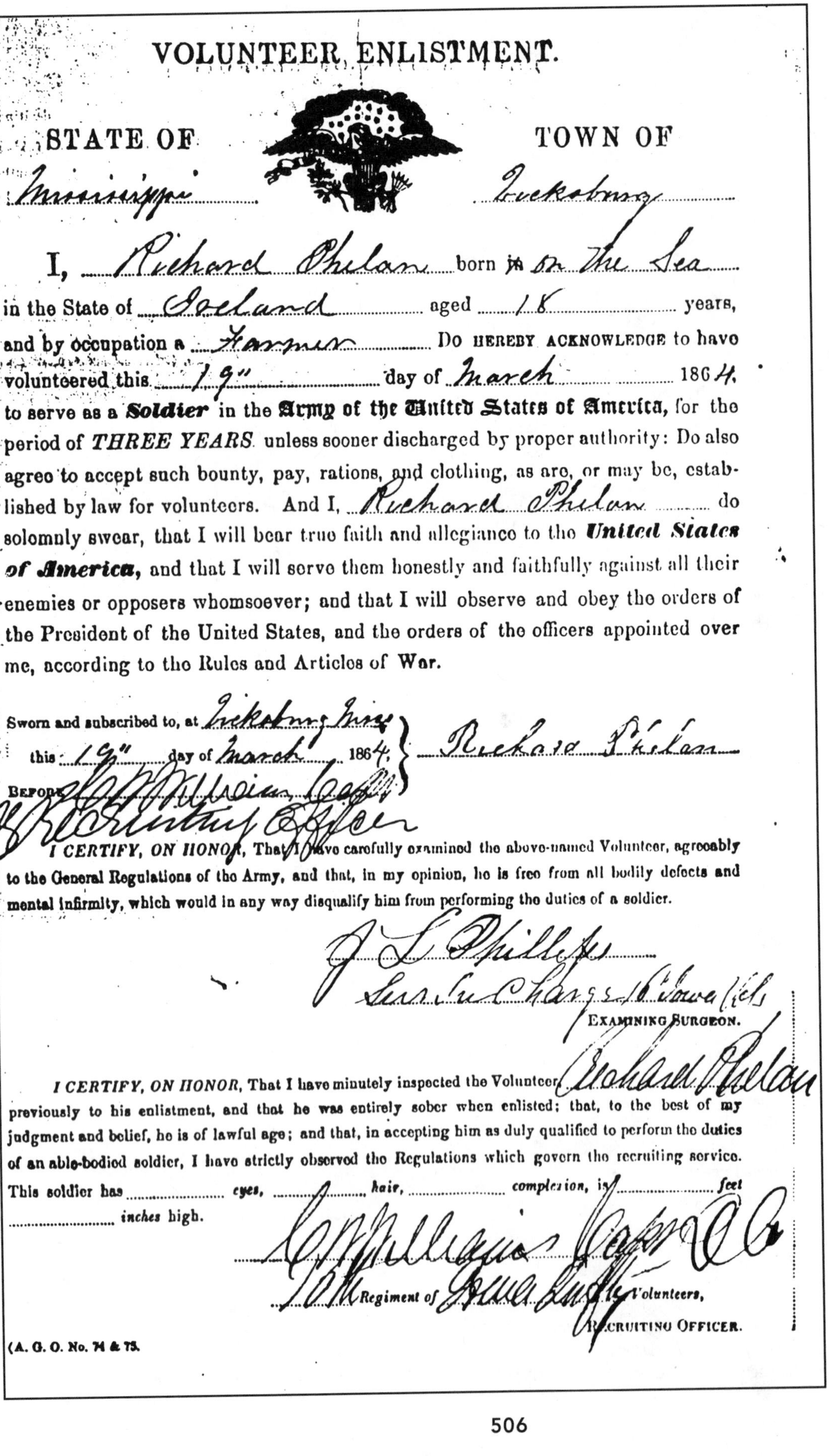

VOLUNTEER ENLISTMENT.

STATE OF Mississippi TOWN OF Vicksburg

I, Richard Phelan born in on the Sea in the State of Ireland aged 18 years, and by occupation a Farmer Do HEREBY ACKNOWLEDGE to have volunteered this 19" day of March 1864, to serve as a **Soldier** in the **Army of the United States of America,** for the period of *THREE YEARS* unless sooner discharged by proper authority: Do also agree to accept such bounty, pay, rations, and clothing, as are, or may be, established by law for volunteers. And I, Richard Phelan do solemnly swear, that I will bear true faith and allegiance to the ***United States of America,*** and that I will serve them honestly and faithfully against all their enemies or opposers whomsoever; and that I will observe and obey the orders of the President of the United States, and the orders of the officers appointed over me, according to the Rules and Articles of War.

Sworn and subscribed to, at Vicksburg Miss this 19" day of March 1864, } Richard Phelan

BEFORE C. M. Williams Capt Recruiting Officer

I CERTIFY, ON HONOR, That I have carefully examined the above-named Volunteer, agreeably to the General Regulations of the Army, and that, in my opinion, he is free from all bodily defects and mental infirmity, which would in any way disqualify him from performing the duties of a soldier.

J. L. Phillips
Surg. in Charge 16 Iowa Vols
EXAMINING SURGEON.

I CERTIFY, ON HONOR, That I have minutely inspected the Volunteer, Richard Phelan previously to his enlistment, and that he was entirely sober when enlisted; that, to the best of my judgment and belief, he is of lawful age; and that, in accepting him as duly qualified to perform the duties of an able-bodied soldier, I have strictly observed the Regulations which govern the recruiting service. This soldier has .... *eyes,* .... *hair,* .... *complexion,* is .... *feet* .... *inches* high.

C. M. Williams Capt Co
16th *Regiment of* Iowa Infy *Volunteers,*
RECRUITING OFFICER.

(A. G. O. No. 74 & 75.

Figure 11-2. The compiled military service records of a soldier can be as useful to a researcher as the pension records. When Richard Phelan provided the information for this Volunteer Enlistment paper, he gave his place of birth as "on the Sea" in the State of Ireland. (Note: Phelan had first enlisted in March 1862 in Davenport, Iowa, and reenlisted in 1864 at Vicksburg, Mississippi.)

Compiled Service Records of Volunteer Union Soldiers that are listed under "Index" in table 11-3. Finding a soldier in the CWSS index at <www.civilwar.nps.gov/cwss> will provide enough information to order the service records from the National Archives. Use NATF Form 86, or order online at <www.archives.gov>.

The service records contain enlistment papers (see figure 11-2), muster rolls, prisoner-of-war papers, death reports, and others. Enlistment papers often contain a description of the soldier and the place where he enlisted.

The compiled service records have only been microfilmed for a fraction of the states and territories. A list appears in table 11-4. Note that some of the titles pertain to southern states, such as Alabama and Arkansas. Although these states belonged to the Confederacy, the service records in this collection are for the men who volunteered for the Union Army. With the exception of South Carolina, every state, including those in the Confederacy, raised Union volunteer units.

If the name you are looking for does not appear in the CWSS database, consult *The Roster of Union Soldiers, 1861–1865*, edited by Janet B. Hewett.[5] This is the printed version of the Union state, territorial, U.S. Colored Troops, and regular army indexes, but it does not index the Veterans Reserve Corps.

Union Draft Records, 1863–65. The U.S. government enacted a draft in March 1863, creating a pool of men age twenty to forty-five who were subject to conscription. Assuming they were physically fit, the law affected white citizens as well as most aliens who had declared their intention to naturalize. The draft records include consolidated lists and descriptive rolls which give a man's name; place of residence; age as of 1 July 1863; occupation; marital status; state, territory, or country of birth; and the military organization (if a volunteer) of which he was a member. Occasionally a personal description or place of birth appears on the descriptive rolls. The records are among the collection of the Records of the Provost Marshal General's Bureau (RG110) and have not been microfilmed. They are filed by state and thereunder by congressional district. To determine the number of the congressional district for the county in which a man lived, consult Kenneth C. Martis's *The Historical Atlas of United States Congressional Districts 1789–1983*.[6]

Case files of drafted aliens concern only aliens who were drafted and released from 1861 to 1864. The files may include

Table 11-4. Microfilmed Indexes and Compiled Service Records for Confederate Army Volunteers

State	Microfilm Publication	
	Index	Compiled Military Service Records
Alabama	M374, 49 rolls	M311, 508 rolls
Arizona Territory	M375, 1 roll	M318, 1 roll
Arkansas	M376, 26 rolls	M317, 256 rolls
Florida	M225, 9 rolls	M251, 104 rolls
Georgia	M226, 67 rolls	M266, 607 rolls
Kentucky	M377, 14 rolls	M319, 136 rolls
Louisiana	M378, 31 rolls	M320, 414 rolls
Maryland	M379, 2 rolls	M321, 22 rolls
Mississippi	M232, 45 rolls	M269, 427 rolls
Missouri	M380, 16 rolls	M322, 193 rolls
North Carolina	M230, 43 rolls	M270, 580 rolls
South Carolina	M381, 35 rolls	M267, 392 rolls
Tennessee	M231, 48 rolls	M268, 359 rolls
Texas	M227, 41 rolls	M323, 445 rolls
Virginia	M382, 62 rolls	M324, 1,075 rolls
Consolidated Index[1]	M818, 26 rolls	M258, 123 rolls
General and Staff Officers	M818, 26 rolls	M331, 275 rolls

Also see "Former Confederates Who Served in the Union Army," part of National Archives microfilm publication M1290 (36 rolls), titled *Index to Compiled Service Records of Volunteer Soldiers Who Served in Union Organizations Not Raised by States or Territories*; and *Compiled Service Records of Former Confederate Soldiers Who Served in the First Through Sixth U.S. Volunteer Infantry Regiments, 1864-1866*, National Archives Microfilm Publication M1017 (65 rolls).

Source: *Guide to Genealogical Research in the National Archives* (Washington, D.C.: National Archives and Records Administration, 2000), 145.

1. The index (M818) and compiled service records (M258) are to Confederates who served in military organizations raised directly or otherwise formed by the Confederate government or who served in some capacity other than belonging to a unit at or below the regimental level.

name, district from which drafted, country of citizenship, age, length of time in United States, and a physical description. The files are in alphabetical order by surname in the collection of the Department of State and are available only at the National Archives.[7]

Exemption Lists. Names of men who were ineligible to be drafted may be found in area newspapers of the period. These tended to be published by county. The names are grouped by reason for exemption, including age, physical or mental disability, paid commutation (in certain years a draft-eligible male could pay a prescribed sum in lieu of serving), sending an acceptable substitute, or having other persons totally dependent, such as a widowed mother or motherless children under twelve years of age.

Confederate Service Records

When Richmond was evacuated by the Confederate government in April 1865, the centralized military personnel records of the Confederate Army were taken to Charlotte, North Carolina, by the Confederate Adjutant and Inspector General, Samuel Cooper. When the Confederate civil authorities left Charlotte after agreeing to an armistice between the armies in North Carolina, President Jefferson Davis instructed Cooper to turn the records over, if necessary, to "the enemy, as essential to the history of the struggle." When General Joseph E. Johnston learned, after the armistice, that the records were at Charlotte, he turned them over to the Union Commander in North Carolina, saying, "As they will furnish valuable materials for history, I am anxious for their preservation, and doubt not that you are too."

The Confederate records surrendered or captured at the end of the war and taken to Washington, D.C., have been augmented by other records collected or copied in later years. In 1903, the War Department began to compile a service record for each soldier by copying the entries pertaining to him in these records. The result is an immense file of "compiled service records," from which inquiries about Confederate soldiers are answered. Because of the efforts made over many years to incorporate all available information into this file, it is by far the most complete and accurate source of information about Confederate soldiers. This collection, held by the National Archives, is identified as the compiled military service records of Confederate officers, noncommissioned officers, and enlisted men.

The compiled military service record of a Confederate soldier consists of one or more card abstracts and usually one or more original documents. Each card abstract entry comes from such original records as Confederate muster rolls, returns, descriptive rolls, and Union prison and parole records. If the original record of a soldier's service was complete, the card abstracts may serve to trace his service from beginning to end, but they normally do little more than account for where he was at a given time. The compiled military service record may provide the following information of genealogical interest: age, place of enlistment, places served, place of discharge or death, and often, physical description.

To access the above described service records, locate the soldier's entry in the CWSS at <www.civilwar.nps.gov/cwss>. The reference will provide the state from which the veteran served, his rank, and the regiment. This information may then be used to view the microfilmed records (see table 11-3) or to order the records from the National Archives. To order the records, use NATF Form 86, or order online at <www.archives.gov>. The Confederate soldier entries in the CWSS were drawn from the *Consolidated Index to Compiled Service Records of Confederate Soldiers*.[8] Copies of these 553 rolls are available at the National Archives and at the Family History Library as well as major repositories. Table 11-3 provides a state-by-state summary of the microfilm.

If no record can be located in the CWSS, there is another set of Confederate records: those which were never identified as pertaining to a specific soldier or were not used in compiling the service records when the government ceased that project. The *Unfiled Papers and Slips Belonging to Confederate Compiled Service Records* are contained on 442 rolls in alphabetical order.[9]

A comprehensive printed source is *The Roster of Confederate Soldiers, 1861–1865*, edited by Janet B. Hewett.[10] See also Hewett's *Supplement to the Official Records*.[11]

Confederate Deaths as Prisoners of War

Approximately 28,000 Confederate soldiers, sailors, and citizens died as prisoners in the North. While federal legislation from 1867 to 1873 provided for the reburial of Union soldiers in national cemeteries and for durable headstones, this early legislation made no specific provision for Confederate dead. Their graves were sometimes given thin headstones with a grave number and the soldier's name. Other Confederate graves were marked with wooden headboards that disintegrated, although the names were often preserved in cemetery burial registers.

Finally, in 1912, a typescript register of Confederate soldiers and sailors buried in federal cemeteries was compiled in accordance with a 1906 statute, to provide for marking the graves of Confederate soldiers and sailors who died in Union prisons. The register has been microfilmed as *Register of Confederate Soldiers, Sailors, and Citizens Who Died in Federal Prisons and Military Hospitals in the North, 1861–1865* and is now part of Record Group 92.[12] Record Group 92 also includes some records of the Office of the Commissioner for Marking the Graves of Confederate Dead not reproduced on the microfilm: the commissioner's incoming and outgoing correspondence and other burial registers, lists, and correspondence pertaining to particular cemeteries.

The War Department Collection of Confederate Records, Record Group 109, includes registers of deaths in *Selected*

Records of the War Department Relating to Confederate Prisoners of War 1861–1865.[13] Particularly useful is a two-volume series of registers of prisoner deaths compiled by the Office of the Commissary General of Prisoners (rolls five and six). The volumes are alphabetically arranged by name of deceased and show the name; rank; regiment; company; place and date of capture; place, date, and cause of death; and number and locality of grave for each individual. The information in these registers may be used to supplement the information on the *Register of Confederate Soldiers, Sailors, and Citizens Who Died in Federal Prisons and Military Hospitals in the North, 1861–1865*, but burial information is frequently unavailable or obsolete.[14] Rolls ten through twelve are a five-volume series of registers of prisoner deaths compiled by the Surgeon General's Office and arranged by the states in which the deceased served. They contain most of the information described previously.

State Confederate Records

The War Department Collection of Confederate Records is not complete, even though great efforts were made to assemble all official information. A soldier may have served in a state militia unit that was never mustered into the service of the Confederate government. Records of service in such units, if extant, may be in the state archive or in the custody of the state adjutant general. Since the federal government of the United States did not pay benefits to Confederates, pensions and other state benefits are recorded only in state records (see Confederate Pension Records, following).

The Family History Library has the largest collection of microfilmed state Confederate records. The call numbers for ordering the microfilms through family history centers are most easily located in the catalogue.

Military Academy and Court Records

Two additional categories of Civil War–era records require mention: military academy records and Reconstruction court records. Many Confederate officers received their early training in Southern military academies. Others attended West Point and had to choose which side to support. For information on military academy records, consult Bvt. Major-General George W. Cullum's *Biographical Register, Officers and Graduates of the U.S. Military Academy, West Point, New York*; Stanley P. Tozeski's *Preliminary Inventory of the Records of the U.S. Military Academy*; and Jon L. Wakelyn's *Biographical Dictionary of the Confederacy*.[15]

Court records created during Reconstruction may also reveal personal information about those who served the Confederacy. The confiscation of land by the Reconstruction government led to lengthy and bitter court battles. And some of those who were prosperous businessmen or farmers before the Civil War found it necessary to file bankruptcy during the Reconstruction period. Although these records are seldom used by family historians, they can yield numerous details about Southern soldiers even though they are not technically military records. Bankruptcies and other court records are discussed in chapter 7, "Court Records."

Modern Wars, 1898 to the Present

Service records for soldiers serving in the armed forces after the Civil War are not as readily available as for earlier conflicts because of lack of microfilming or, for World Wars I and II and later, privacy restrictions.

Spanish-American War and Philippine Insurrection

Most of the volunteers who fought in the Spanish-American War were from the states of Illinois, New York, Ohio, and Pennsylvania. One well-known regiment, however, was made up of volunteers throughout the country: the Rough Riders, men of the First United States Volunteer Cavalry Regiment who served in Cuba under Lieutenant Colonel Theodore Roosevelt.[16] The compiled service records for 1,235 Rough Riders may be viewed online at the NARA website, <www.archives.gov>. An index and instructions for its use accompanies the records. Indexes to the compiled military service records for the rest of the volunteers in the 16,000 man army are listed in table 11-5.

The outbreak of hostilities in the Philippine Islands in February 1899 required volunteer forces to reinforce regular U.S. Army units and replace Spanish-American troops still serving there. These volunteer units raised for the Philippine insurrection bore "U.S. Volunteer" designations and not state designations. Therefore, volunteers who served in the Philippines in a regiment bearing a state designation will be found in the Spanish-American compiled service records, while those who served in regiments designated as "U.S. Volunteer" will appear in the Philippine Insurrection compiled service records. The Philippine Insurrection is the last conflict in which the War Department compiled military service records for volunteers.[17]

The indexes to both collections are shown in table 11-5. There are no privacy restrictions on these records. NATF Form 86 should be used to order service records.

World War I to Present

Records for military personnel who served within the last seventy-five years are restricted to the veteran, requesters with release authorization signed by the veteran or, if the veteran is deceased, the next of kin. Many of the federal records in this category are housed at the National Personnel Records Center (NPRC).[18] Records protected by privacy laws cannot be copied or viewed by the public, but some information contained in the records can be provided. Also, records can become available at a later date, as happened on June 11, 2005, when the Archival Programs Division at the NPRC opened the following holdings:

- Navy enlisted personnel files for individuals who were separated from the navy between 1885 and September 8, 1939.

- Marine Corps enlisted personnel files for individuals who served between 1906 and 1939.
- A selection of approximately one hundred and fifty records of prominent individuals (persons of exceptional prominence) who have been deceased ten years or more. NPRC will add to this initial transfer on a regular basis.

Written requests for the above listed records will be processed on Standard Form 180, the same as for other military records from the NPRC. The form and information about requests may be seen at <www.vetrecs.archives.gov>.

Documents issued to the veteran at time of discharge (or to his or her next of kin, in case of death) usually contain important genealogical information. The NPRC encourages contacting the veteran or next of kin to get this information, or to get written authorization from the veteran or the next-of-kin of a deceased veteran. However, under the Freedom of Information Act (amended 1974), NPRC will release some information without the veteran's authorization, such as an individual's dates of service, branch of service, military education, decorations and awards (eligibility), present and past duty assignments (including geographical location), To determine what other details are available and to learn the process for obtaining the information, check the Freedom of Information Act and the Privacy Act at <www.archives.gov/st-louis/military-personnel/foia-info.html>.

On 12 July 1973, a fire at NPRC in St. Louis destroyed approximately 16–18 million records from Official Military Personnel Files. Eighty percent of the army records for personnel discharged November 1, 1912 to January 1, 1960, and seventy-five percent of the air force records for personnel discharged September 25, 1947 to January 1, 1964 (having names alphabetically after Hubbard, James E.), were destroyed. When NPRC receives a request for service and separation verification, they reconstruct a file using alternative sources of documents from state and federal agencies, particularly the Department of Veteran Affairs. There are no plans at this time to reconstruct the records of deceased personnel where no benefits are owed.[19]

World Wars I and II Draft Registration

Certain draft records were not in the fire. World War I draft registration cards for approximately 24 million men have been microfilmed and are available for searching. The cards give the full name of the registrant, date and place of birth, race, citizenship status, occupation and employer, personal description, marital status, and the name and address of the nearest relative (see figure 11-3). They are filmed as *World War I Selective Service System Draft Registration Cards* by state, county or city, draft board, and registrant except for Connecticut, Massachusetts, and Rhode Island which are arranged by divisions and counties.[20] The World War I draft records have also been indexed and digitized and may be searched and viewed at <www.ancestry.com>.

Table 11-5. Microfilmed and Online Indexes to Service Records and Pensions, 1898–1902

Title	Microfilm Publication	Comments
General Index to Compiled Service Records of Volunteer Soldiers Who Served During the War with Spain, 1898–1901[1]	M871 (126 rolls)	This general comprehensive index identifies the compiled service records of volunteer soldiers regardless of their military units. Each index card gives name, rank, and unit in which the soldier served.
Rough Riders Index to Carded Records		Online at <www.archives.gov/research/arc/topics>
Index to Compiled Records of Volunteer Soldiers Who Served During the Philippine Insurrection	M872 (24 rolls)	Numerous miscellaneous records are included. Files can include news clippings and printed reports as well as original documents. The personnel file for one veteran injured at Kutubic Bay, Philippines, exceeds two hundred pages.
Index to Compiled Service Records of Volunteer Soldiers Who Served During the War With Spain in Organizations from the State of Louisiana	M240 (1 roll)	
Index to Compiled Service Records of Volunteer Soldiers Who Served During the War with Spain in Organizations from the State of North Carolina	M413 (2 rolls)	
General Index to Pension Files, 1861–1934	T288 (544 rolls)	Index cards are arranged alphabetically by surname of veteran and show the name of the veteran; name and class of dependent, if any; service data; application number or file number; and, for an approved claim, certificate number or file number and state from which the claim was filed.

1. The only microfilm publication of compiled military service records for the Spanish-American War is M1087, *Compiled Service Records of Volunteers Who Served in the Florida Infantry During the War with Spain.* 13 rolls.

A special category of World War II draft registration cards exists for males born between 18 April 1877 and 16 February 1897. These cards are identified as being from the "Fourth Registration." The cards give the name of the registrant, his residence, address, telephone number, age, place and date of birth, and the name and contact information of a person who would always know his whereabouts. The cards are arranged alphabetically by state, thereunder alphabetically by name of registrant. Original records for some states are available for viewing at National Archives regions: NARA's Northeast Region in New York City holds cards for New York City, the state of New Jersey, and Puerto Rico, and NARA's Great Lakes Region in Chicago has cards for men who lived in Illinois, Indiana, Michigan, Ohio, and Wisconsin. Nine hundred and ninety-eight registration cards for Ohio men have been digitized and are available for viewing at <www.archives.gov/research/arc>.

Figure 11-3. Giovanni Tenuta, 1887–1954. Courtesy of Robert M. Tenuta. *Below:* The selective service registration card, dated 5 June 1917, for Italian-born Giovanni Tentuta. Found on Ancestry.com, World War I Draft Registration Cards, 1917–18, roll 1,674,740, image 74, card # 133, viewed 12 February 2006.

World War II Army Enlistment Records

This series of computerized data files contains records of approximately 9 million men and women who enlisted in the U.S. Army between 1938 and 1946, including the Women's Army Auxiliary Corps and the Enlisted Reserve Corps. The series does not include records for army officers, members of other military services, or enlistments from other time periods. In general, the records contain the serial number, name, state and place of residence, place and date of enlistment, grade, place and year of birth, civilian occupation, and marital status. The Electronic Army Serial Number Merged File at <http://aad.archives.gov/aad> is not complete but covers a majority of the army enlistments. Other World War II electronic records are being added to this site on a regular basis.

Regular U.S. Army Enlistments

If a search of the relevant index or indexes does not reveal a service record for an individual, remember that there was another capacity other than that of volunteer or draftee. The veteran could have served in the regular U.S. Army. The registers of enlistments for the period 1798 to 1914, except those for hospital stewards, quartermaster sergeants, and ordnance sergeants, have been microfilmed as *Registers of Enlistments in the U.S. Army, 1798–1914.*[21] Prior to 1821, the records of officers are included as well. The records are arranged in subcategories of time blocks.

Form 1 2513 REGISTRATION CARD

1 Name in full: Giovanni Tenuta (Given name) (Family name) 30

2 Home address: 977 Oakwood Ave Kenosha Wisc (No.) (Street) (City) (State)

3 Date of birth: Feb 20 1887 (Month) (Day) (Year)

4 Are you (1) a natural-born citizen, (2) a naturalized citizen, (3) an alien, (4) or have you declared your intention (specify which)? Dec. – First papers

5 Where were you born? Morano Principo Italy (Town) (State) (Nation)

6 If not a citizen, of what country are you a citizen or subject? Italy

7 What is your present trade, occupation, or office? Laborer

8 By whom employed? Simmons Mfg Co. Where employed? 19 Kenosha Wisc

9 Have you a father, mother, wife, child under 12, or a sister or brother under 12, solely dependent on you for support (specify which)? 1 child

10 Married or single (which)? Married Race (specify which)? Caucasian

11 What military service have you had? Rank —; branch army; years 4; Nation or State Italy

12 Do you claim exemption from draft (specify grounds)? yes Support of parents

I affirm that I have verified above answers and that they are true.

Giovanni Tenuta (Signature or mark)

48 2 6 A

REGISTRAR'S REPORT

1 Tall, medium, or short (specify which)? Short Slender, medium, or stout (which)? Slim

2 Color of eyes? Brown Color of hair? Black Bald? No

3 Has person lost arm, leg, hand, foot, or both eyes, or is he otherwise disabled (specify)? —

I certify that my answers are true, that the person registered has read his own answers, that I have witnessed his signature, and that all of his answers of which I have knowledge are true, except as follows:

Chas. F. Boylan (Signature of registrar)

Precinct 5

City or County Kenosha

State Wisconsin 6/5/17 (Date of registration)

Records of Veterans' Benefits

Although bounties, paid in money and land, were sometimes provided as an enlistment incentive, the provision of benefits, especially the granting of pensions, was not widespread until after the Revolutionary War. Early fighters in Indian skirmishes and local riots submitted claims for supplies, equipment, and time spent to both legislative assemblies and county courts. Claims of this nature are discussed at greater length in chapter 7, "Court Records."

Pension Records (1774–1811)

The first congressional legislation authorizing the payment of pensions for Revolutionary War service was dated 26 August 1776, but the government did not begin paying pension allowances until 28 July 1789; applications for pensions were made to the federal government from that date. Many of the early applications were destroyed by fire in 1800 and 1814. A partial record of the earlier pensioners is included among reports to Congress in 1792, 1794, and 1795.

Although applications for pensions were made to the U.S. government, they were initiated in the courts of the counties and towns in which the veterans lived. Note that a Pension Board refusal often led the claimant to seek relief from Congress directly. (See Chapter 7, American Court Records for details.)

The pension records for the Revolutionary War and later wars can contain much of genealogical value: affidavits made by the veteran and his neighbors or associates to support his claim, summaries of his service, the military organization in which he served, the dates of his service, his date and place of birth, names of heirs, relationship to others who served with him, his movements after the war, and information from family Bible records. Sometimes the Bible pages, torn out of the book, are enclosed as evidence.

For example, the Revolutionary War pension file of Reuben Johnson was filed in Anderson District, South Carolina, on 19 November 1832. The file is too long to reproduce in its entirety but is illustrative even in summary. Reuben Johnson filed a sworn statement with the justice of the peace of Anderson District to apply for a pension for his Revolutionary War services as a member of the Fourth Regiment of the North Carolina Line. He enlisted with Richard Phillips in 1776 at Surry County, North Carolina, and served for two and one-half years in the command of Captain Joseph Philips. On his statement he also named the marches in which he took part. After reenlisting, he was present at the siege of Charleston, where he was taken prisoner by the British.

While his affidavit does not indicate his birth date or place of birth, many applications do contain that information, as well as the veteran's residences after the war.

Reuben's wife applied for a widow's pension after her husband's death. This document contains information of greater importance. Nancy Johnson's affidavit of 29 March 1843 states that she was the widow of Reuben Johnson, that they were married 20 November 1788, and that her husband died 26 January 1833. Her sister Margaret Burroughs made a sworn statement that her sister was Nancy Johnson, nee Greenlee, who had married Reuben Johnson in North Carolina many years before. Margaret was six years old when Nancy and Reuben were married and did not know the exact date of their marriage, but she knew Reuben and Nancy had moved to South Carolina with her father, Peter Greenlee, and that the two families lived on the same plantation. Peter died about forty years before her testimony. Her mother died 1 December 1842.

Reuben Johnson's file also contained a copy of his marriage record from Wilkes County, North Carolina. The documents in Reuben Johnson's file permit the researcher to outline his movements from the time of his enlistment to his death and document two generations of ancestry.[22]

All of the contents of all of the application files are reproduced on microfilm in *Revolutionary War Pension and Bounty-Land Warrant Applications Files*.[23] Each roll begins with an introduction that gives the eligibility requirements of the various resolutions and acts of Congress from 1776 to 1878 that established pensions for Revolutionary War service.

A second microfilm publication, *Selected Records from Revolutionary War Pension and Bounty-Land Warrant Applications Files*, has far fewer rolls because it reproduces all records from files containing up to ten pages but only significant genealogical documents from larger files.[24] Copies of both microfilm reproductions are on file at libraries throughout the country, including the Family History Library and its Family History Centers.

A digitized version of the *Selected Records* microfilm publication (M805) may be searched by the name of the applicant at the website of Heritage Quest <www.heritagequest.com>. However, as explained, a file of ten reproduced pages could actually contain more, making it prudent to subsequently search in the more complete M804, *Revolutionary War Pension and Bounty-Land Warrant Applications Files*. The application number gleaned from either microfilm collection may be used to order the full file from the National Archives using NATF Form 85, or online ordering at <www.archives.gov>.

A four-volume set by Virgil D. White will prove useful in locating information from these files: *Genealogical Abstracts of Revolutionary War Pension Files*.[25] Also helpful are the compilations by Murtie J. Clark, including *The Pension Lists of 1792–95; with Other Revolutionary War Pension Records* (Baltimore: Genealogical Publishing Co., 1991. Reissued 1996) and the National Genealogical Society's Special Publication No. 40, *Index of Revolutionary War Pension Applications in the National Archives* (Washington, D.C.: NGS, 1976). This last publication will identify certain applications that were rejected.

Rejection of Revolutionary War pension applications did not necessarily mean that the applicant made a dishonest claim. Hundreds of applicants simply could not provide the necessary proof of service to be awarded a pension. The majority of applications were filed when Congress granted permission to all veterans in 1832. Discharges had often been lost or, in many cases, never issued. Comrades-in-arms who could have attested to service were often deceased or had moved away.

The Act of 1832, mentioned earlier, required pension applications to include the birthplace, age, and residence of the applicant, and more. Applications may also include mention of a soldier substituting for another relative who was drafted into service. Once all of the applications pertaining to a veteran were received, including those of the widows and other claimants, they were combined into one file.

Bounty-Land Records

Bounty-land warrants were authorized by Congress in 1776 as a substitute for the wages it was unable to pay its soldiers. If the soldier was deceased, his heirs took claim to the land after the war. The number of acres granted was based upon the soldier's rank and ranged from 100 to 1,100 acres. More information on laws and acreage can be found in chapter 10, "Land Records." This method of decreasing military costs worked so well that bounty-land warrants continued to be issued for post–Revolutionary War service. Congress eventually authorized bounty-land warrants to be issued for military service performed prior to 1855.

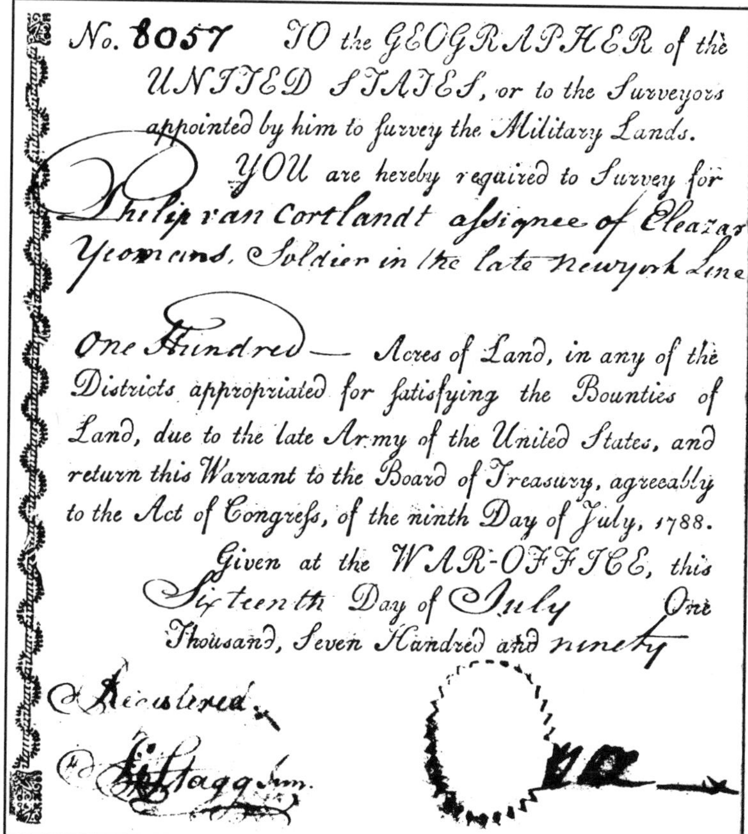

No. 8057 TO the GEOGRAPHER of the UNITED STATES, or to the Surveyors appointed by him to survey the Military Lands.

YOU are hereby required to Survey for Philip van Cortlandt assignee of Eleazar Yeomans, Soldier in the late New york Line

One Hundred — Acres of Land, in any of the Districts appropriated for satisfying the Bounties of Land, due to the late Army of the United States, and return this Warrant to the Board of Treasury, agreeably to the Act of Congress, of the ninth Day of July, 1788.

Given at the WAR-OFFICE, this Sixteenth Day of July One Thousand, Seven Hundred and ninety

Registered

Figure 11-4. Bounty-land warrant 8057, 15 July 1790, for Philip van Cortlandt, assignee of Eleazar Yeomans. National Archives. FHL microfilm 1,025,145.

The number of applicants for bounty lands far exceeded the number of persons applying for pensions, but the bounty-land warrant application file is basically the same as that of the pension application file. The application provides the veteran's name, age, residence, the military organization in which he served, and the term of his service. If his widow or other heirs made claim, their names, ages, and places of residence are given. Not all veterans actually farmed the land granted to them. Many assigned their warrants to others for a fee. Figure 11-4 shows bounty-land warrant 8057, which designates Philip van Cortlandt, the assignee of Eleazar Yeomans, a soldier in the New York line. Yeoman's claim for one hundred acres was authorized by an act of Congress on 9 July 1788 and assigned to van Cortlandt on 16 July 1790.

Not all bounty-land applications were approved. The claimant had to prove his service in the war in exactly the same manner that a pensioner had to prove his service. Again, a rejected claim did not necessarily indicate that the claimant's service was never rendered, only that the claimant was not able to provide sufficient proof.

An estimated 450,000 bounty-land claims are on file in the National Archives. Some early claims were destroyed by the fires previously mentioned, but those remaining are available from the National Archives upon request using NATF Form 85. In addition to land grants made by the federal government for Revolutionary War service, Connecticut, Georgia, Maryland, Massachusetts, New York, North Carolina, Pennsylvania, South Carolina, and Virginia chose to reward their soldiers with bounty land. Lloyd DeWitt Bockstruck has indexed the bounty-land records from these nine states in *Revolutionary War Bounty Land Grants Awarded by State Governments*.[26]

Pension Records (1789–1861)

Pension records exist for the period between the end of the Revolutionary War and the beginning of the Civil War, primarily dealing with the War of 1812, the Indian Wars, and the Mexican War. All of the indexes to these pension records have been published. These records are classified in three groups as the Old War Series Pension Records. These records pertain to pension applicants who were disabled or killed while serving in any war after the close of the Revolutionary War and before the start of the Civil War (except for the War of 1812 pensions included in the regular War of 1812 pension application files). A few files relating to naval service of men who were killed or disabled during the Civil War are included.[27] The original applications are located at the National Archives and can be requested in the same manner as all of the records discussed earlier using NATF Form 85. These pension applications have been indexed; the microfilmed indexes are available at NARA regions, the Family History Library, and some other libraries. Indexes for Revolutionary War pension applications and the index for Civil War Union pension applications are increasingly available online.

The USGenWeb Archives has embarked on a project to provide transcriptions of pension-related materials for all wars prior to 1900. The project, named the USGenWeb Pension Project, will accept transcripts, extracts, and abstracts of pensions and pension-related material. Submissions are placed in the USGenWeb Archives directory of the state and county of principal residence of the pensioner. An early submission to the project is the application for Mexican War veteran James M. Phelan, filed in Clay County, Arkansas, under the act if January 29, 1887. The Survivors Brief states that Phelan served in Hacker's Company, the 20th Illinois Volunteer Infantry Regiment, as a private. He enlisted 25 June 1846 and was discharged 18 June 1847. Phelan was born 8 October 1824. The General Affidavit shows he is a resident of Piggott in Clay County, Arkansas, and owns 103 ½ acres of land in Union County, Illinois, three miles north of Dongola, with a value of about $25. His income is derived from renting the farm for "about $67 per year after taxes and other expenses" and the $8 per month pension he already receives.[25] Details about the USGenWeb Pension Project are provided at <www.rootsweb.com/~usgenweb/pensions>.

War of 1812 Pensions

Pension application files for veterans of the War of 1812 include applications of veterans still living after 1871, when Congress authorized pensions to veterans who did not later support the Confederate States of America. Applications for death, disability, and regular service from widows and other claimants are included in the same collection. A second act of Congress in 1878 authorized pensions for veterans who saw as few as fourteen days of active duty. Virgil D. White's two-volume *Index to War of 1812 Pension Files* indexes applicants eligible for pensions or bounty lands under these two acts.[29]

These pension files give the veteran's name, age, and place of residence. If he was married, the marriage date and the maiden name of his wife are stated. The unit in which he served, the date and place of enlistment, and the date and place of discharge are also given. The widow's pension file will provide her name, age, place of residence, their pertinent marriage information, the date and place of the veteran's death, his enlistment date and place, and the date and place of his final discharge. The pension files are available from the National Archives, but the microfilmed indexes are available in various libraries throughout the United States.

Indian Wars Pensions

There were several Indian Wars between 1817 and 1858. The files of claims submitted for pensions are alphabetically indexed by name in T318, *Index to Indian Wars Pension Files, 1892–1926*. A printed index is *Index to Indian Wars Pension Files, 1892–1926* transcribed by Virgil D. White.[30] In addition to the usual types of records found in pension applications, the Indian wars records contain a family questionnaire and, for the veteran, a personal history questionnaire. The family questionnaire shows the maiden name of the wife; date and place of the marriage of the couple and the name of the person who performed the ceremony; name of a former wife, if any, and date and place of her death or divorce; and names and dates of birth of living children.

The pension files are located at the National Archives. For pension application files concerning men who were disabled or killed in Indian wars and in whose behalf no service claims were made, see the records in the Old Wars series (discussed earlier). For pension applications relating to persons who served in an Indian campaign during the War of 1812, Mexican War, or Civil War, see the pension indexes relating to claims based on service in that war (following).

Mexican War Pensions

Pension application files from the Mexican War were authorized by Congress in 1887, permitting veterans and their widows to file claims with the government. New restrictions specified a minimum of sixty days of service, a minimum age at application of sixty-two, or the requirement of being disabled or dependent.

These files contain basically the same information required in other pension applications, but also required the maiden name of the wife, the names of former wives, death or divorce information about previous wives, and the names and birth dates of living children. Pension applications were accepted between 1887 and 1926. They are indexed by name, and the index has been microfilmed as *Index to Mexican War Pension Applications, 1887–1926*.[31] Copies of the files can be obtained from the National Archives. Published versions of the index to Mexican War pensions include *An Index to Mexican War Pension Applications* transcribed by Barbara Schull Wolfe; *Index to Mexican War Pension Files* by Virgil D. White; and Navena Hembree Troxel's thirteen volume *Mexican War Index to Pension Files, 1886–1926*.[32] Each of these indexes has its own unique attributes.

Civil War and Later Pension Records (1861–1934)

The Civil War and later series of pension applications files relate chiefly to army, navy, and marine service performed between 1861 and 1916. The records of service in Confederate forces are not included in this file.

Federal pensions were granted to veterans of the Spanish-American War of 1898, the Philippine Insurrection of 1899 to 1902, and other conflicts of the era. Pensions based upon such service are included in the same index for Union Civil War veterans: *General Index to Pension Files, 1861–1934.*[33] This index is also available as an online database at <www.ancestry.com>, titled "Civil War Pension Index: General Index to Pension Files, 1861–1934."

If a Civil War veteran's widow, minor children, or parents applied for pension after the veteran's death, their applications will be indexed by the name of the veteran. Microfilm copies of the General Index to Pension Files 1861–1934 are available at the National Archives, their regions, the Family History Library, and many libraries with large genealogy collections.

Civil War pension application files are the best of the early military documents compiled and contain valuable genealogical information. These files do not all contain the same amount of information, but one can expect to find at least some of the following information: the name of the veteran, the military or naval unit in which he served, the date and place of his enlistment, his birth date and place, the date and place of his marriage, the names and birth dates of his children, the maiden name of his wife, information about subsequent marriages, the date and place of his discharge, physical disabilities connected with service-related injuries, and his residences since his discharge. There will also be general affidavits of individuals who could attest to his disabilities and copies of the findings of examining physicians at the time of his injury and during subsequent periodic physicals.

Each pension applicant was required to complete a Declaration for an Original Invalid Pension. The full pension file may also contain applications by widows or other dependents after the death of the veteran. James W. Reddish, a resident of Hancock County, Kentucky, sought his pension on 2 February 1891. His application is based on service in the Kentucky Infantry Volunteers. It gives his physical description and describes injuries to his right foot and the dislocation of an elbow, and the contracting of measles in the hospital which resulted in the loss of sight of his left eye.

After James's death, his widow, Matilda Raddish [*sic*] filed a Declaration for a Widow's Pension. She gives James's death date as 19 February 1894. She noted that she was married on 5 January 1885 at Owensboro, Kentucky, and that both she and James were widowed at the time of their marriage. The dates of death for each of the former spouses is provided. She gives her maiden name as Matilda Sweat. She had one minor child, Alonzo Reddish, born in March 1884.

The brother of James W. Reddish was Markus L. Reddish, who also served in the Civil War. A Declaration for Dependent Pension of a Mother or Father was submitted by Polly Ann Right, their mother. She stated that Markus had died of measles while in the service at Corinth, Mississippi, on 6 July 1862. She had married his father 2 October 1836 at Daviess County, Kentucky. After her husband died 1 March 1863 at Ohio County, Kentucky, she married Amos Right, who had in turn died 5 July 1880.

Polly Ann Right had four sons in the Union Army at one time, and her husband was killed by Confederate troops as he worked on their farm. This unusual family situation is fully explained in the collected Civil War pension files of the entire family. This family's files are representative of the majority of the records on file.

Pensioners also completed periodic requests for additional information. The file of Solomon Winne, Kingston, New York, shows documentation of the maiden name of his wife, the date of their marriage, and the names and birth dates of their living children. Because she died a few months before her husband, his pension file included a copy of her death certificate. The document provides the exact date of her death, her age at the time of her death, the names and birthplaces of her parents, and where she was buried.

Winne's file also included an unusual document. His daughter, Mary H. Swarthout of Kingston, New York, filed an application to be reimbursed for expenses related to his last illness. He died 20 July 1909 at the Old Soldier's Home in Bath, New York, owing $75 for his board at the time of his death. He owned no real estate, personal property, or money.

Another document in the pension file is the termination of the pension. If the cause was death—the most common reason—the death date is usually listed.

One of the most valuable contributions that a pension file from any era can make in genealogical research is listing the veteran's residences after discharge The World War I pension file of Giovanni Tenuta shows residences in Wisconsin and Italy (see figure 11-5). Westward expansion sent many families leapfrogging states between censuses in the post–Civil War years. Tracing the exact movements of individuals and families during that period is difficult at best and sometimes impossible without the assistance of the "road maps" provided in these pension files.

Confederate Pensions

Because the Confederacy was dissolved after the war, no central governmental agency provided pensions for service or disability of Confederate soldiers. Some of the former Confederate states, including Alabama, Arkansas, Florida, Georgia, Kentucky, Louisiana, Mississippi, North Carolina, Oklahoma, South Carolina, Tennessee, Texas, and Virginia, authorized pensions to veterans and their widows. Each state had its own regulations which applicants had to meet. In each case, however, the pension could be paid only if the applicant continued to reside within the borders of the state. If he or she moved elsewhere, the applicant had to qualify under the regulations of the new jurisdiction. State repositories may provide online searches of collections relating to pensions and other assistance that was given to veterans who resided in their states (regardless of their state of enlistment). The Library of Virginia website at <www.lva.lib.va.us/whatwehave/mil> offers several databases of state-created Confederate files. "Confederate Pension Rolls, Veterans and Widows," consists of pension applications and amended applications filed by resident Virginia Confederate veterans and their widows, and "Confederate Disability Applications and Receipts" are applications to the Board of Commissioners on Artificial Limbs from injured soldiers. Other online indexes are in the list of websites that appears at the end of this chapter.

Figures 11-6 and 11-7 illustrate pages from the the Soldier's Application for Confederate Pension from the State of Texas. The record lists the veteran's name, date and place of enlistment, residence, date and place of birth, injuries resulting from military service, marital status, the number and ages of his children, the age of his wife, the number of years he resided in Texas, and his occupation. There is no standard format for pension applications for the Confederacy, but the Texas application is representative of most of the others. Figure 11-8 is a Widow's Application for Confederate Pension.

Miscellaneous Records

Burial Records

The National Archives does not have a record of every soldier who died in service or as a veteran. It does have registers and lists of burials at national cemeteries and post cemeteries of military installations in the United States, Cuba, the Philippines, Puerto Rico, and China. In most cases, if a soldier was buried in a private cemetery, no record of the burial will be kept by the Federal Government. For searching non-federal burials, see chapter 13, "Vital Records."

The early burial registers primarily record burials of active-duty soldiers except in the case of frontier army posts, where family members and civilian dependents were also buried in the post cemeteries. Learning where a soldier or veteran is buried is the first step to finding a record of the burial. There are two major indexes to assist in the search. The first is a master index to the burial locations of veterans and their dependents who have been buried in the cemeteries under federal jurisdiction. This index is available at the website of the National Cemetery Administration, and is found at <http://gravelocator.cem.va.gov>. It includes entries for burial locations of veterans and their dependents in national cemeteries, state veterans cemeteries, and various other Department of the Interior and military cemeteries. The second index is at the website of the American Battle Monuments Commission (ABMC) <www.abmc.gov>. This site offers searches of names of those killed or missing in action. For World War II, the site notes, "We only have the records of those casualties that are buried in our cemeteries or are placed on the Walls of the Missing—a total of 176,399 records. There were 405,399 American casualties in World War II." The ABMC index includes air force casualties.

One associated collection of burial records that is not part of the two indexes is the group of applications for headstones to be placed at the graves of soldiers and veterans. These range in date from 1879 to 1924. The information in the applications includes the name and address of the headstone applicant, name of the veteran, rank, years of service, place and date of burial, and sometimes the date and cause of death. Most of these applications are filed by state, then by county, then by cemetery. Applications for headstones for soldiers, sailors, and marines buried outside the United States between 1911 and 1924 are arranged by country of burial. Soldiers buried in the cemeteries of the National Home for Disabled Volunteer Soldiers for whom headstone applications were made are arranged by the name of the home.

A card file indexing applications for headstones for 1870 to 1903 has been compiled and includes the serviceman's name, military organization, date and place of death, name and location of the cemetery, and date of the application. These cards are arranged alphabetically by the surname of the soldier and include Confederate and post–Civil War veterans' applications. This card file index is available as *Card Records of Headstones Provided for Deceased Union Civil War Veterans, ca. 1879–ca. 1903.*[34]

The names of 228,639 Union soldiers who were buried in more than 300 national cemeteries during the Civil War are published in *Roll of Honor: Names of Soldiers Who Died in Defense of the American Union, Interred in the National Cemeteries, Numbers I–XIX.*[35] Originally published by the Quartermaster General's Office in 1868, the entries are arranged by name of cemetery and thereunder alphabetically by name of soldier. The date of death is shown. An alphabetical list of soldiers and a comprehensive, state-by-state index to burial sites is Martha and William Remy's *Index to the Roll of Honor.*[36] Lists from the national *Roll of Honor* often appear on state agency or county organization websites. The archives or historical libraries of many states have published their own roll of honor for the Civil War and other conflicts or significant battles fought within the borders of the state. These regional rolls of honor record service personnel whose burial was within state lines, regardless of where the enlistment occurred.

Do not overlook the online and published records maintained by lineage societies and service organizations. Notable are the *Sons of the American Revolution Patriot Index CD, Edition III* which includes tombstone photographs for over 800 people and 732,000 records; and the "Necrology of the Grand Army of the

Figure 11-5. After serving in the U.S. Army in World War I, Giovanni Tenuta (figure 11-3) made his home in Kenosha, Wisconsin. In 1937, he moved back with his family to Marano Principato, province of Cosenza, region of Calabria, Italy. Communication regarding Tenuta's disability pension went between Washington, D.C., and Italy. These pages are part of case file #06-148-140 obtained from the Department of Veteran Affairs, Chicago, Illinois. Courtesy of Robert M. Tenuta.

TRANSLATION

TENUTA

In Re: TENUTA, Giovanni
C 6 148 140

TOWN OF MARANO PRINCIPATO

CERTIFICATE OF DEATH

The undersigned Registrar, having consulted the Registers of Vital Statistics

CERTIFIES

that Giovanni Tenuta, 67 years old, Italian citizen, residing in Marano Principato, born in Marano Principato, son of the late Filippo and of the late Gelsomina Savaglio, by civil status, widower,by employment farm laborer.

Died in this Town on the 22nd day of the month of December 1954, as it appears from the Register of Death Records for the Year 1954, Part I, Series A, Document No. 19.

The present is issued on plain paper for charity use.

From the Municipal Hall, January 17, 1955.

The Registrar of Vital Statistics

(signed illegible)

(Sealed)

7/24/46

Veterans administration

Washinton

Gentlemen

this is Giovanni Tenuta

#. 2825681 P.V.T Co C 318th Infantry 80th Division

I am in able to work because I am Marich Reumatism and I am 60 year of age

I was born in 1887 on february 20th

please if you can help me I would appreciate very much and you can sent it to me here in

Marano principato
Cosenza, Italy.

Inclosed find Doctor Certificat

JUL 3 1946

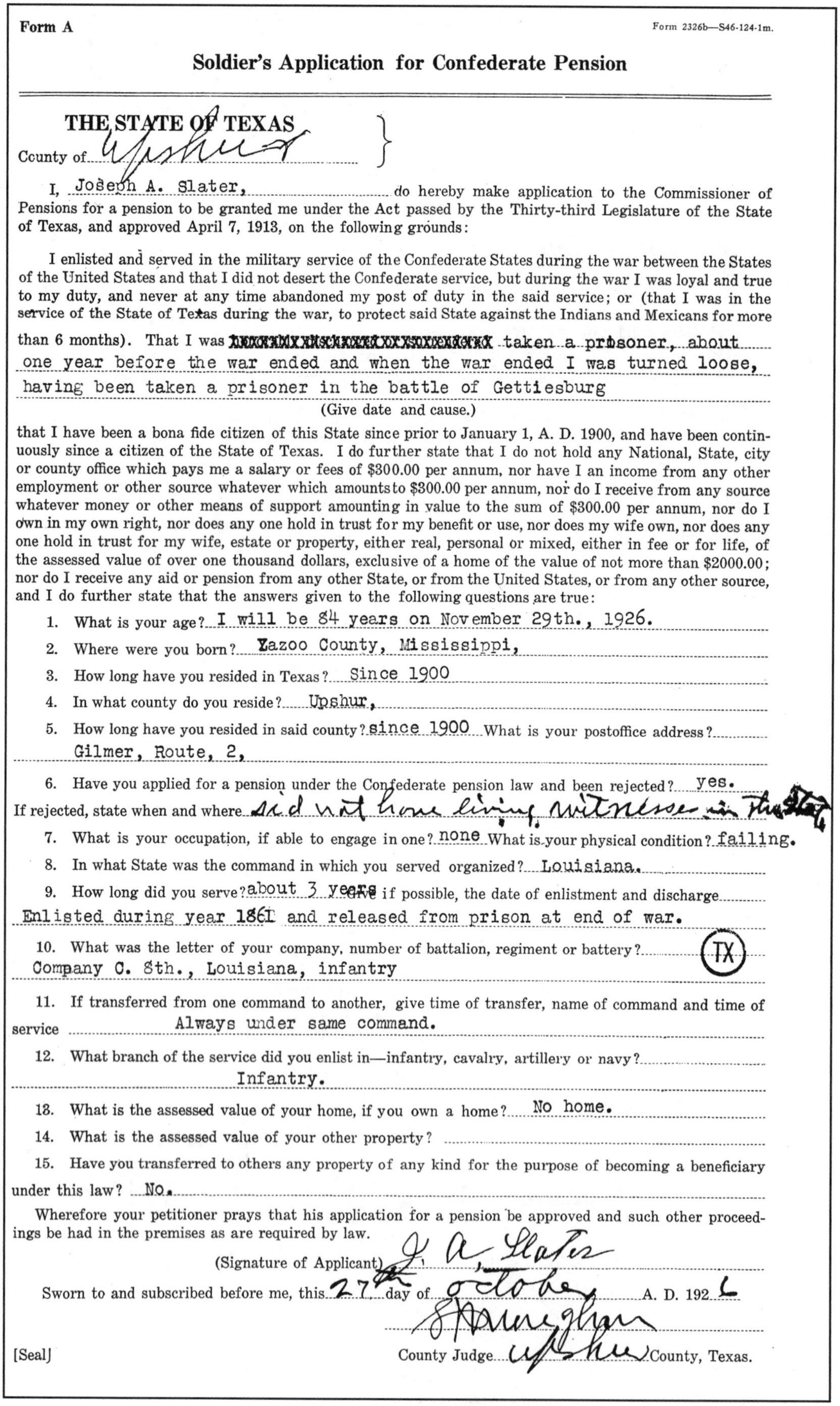

Form A

Form 2326b—S46-124-1m.

Soldier's Application for Confederate Pension

THE STATE OF TEXAS }
County of Upshur }

I, Joseph A. Slater, do hereby make application to the Commissioner of Pensions for a pension to be granted me under the Act passed by the Thirty-third Legislature of the State of Texas, and approved April 7, 1913, on the following grounds:

I enlisted and served in the military service of the Confederate States during the war between the States of the United States and that I did not desert the Confederate service, but during the war I was loyal and true to my duty, and never at any time abandoned my post of duty in the said service; or (that I was in the service of the State of Texas during the war, to protect said State against the Indians and Mexicans for more than 6 months). That I was ~~xxxxxxxxxxxxxxxxxxxxxxxxx~~ taken a prisoner, about one year before the war ended and when the war ended I was turned loose, having been taken a prisoner in the battle of Gettiesburg

(Give date and cause.)

that I have been a bona fide citizen of this State since prior to January 1, A. D. 1900, and have been continuously since a citizen of the State of Texas. I do further state that I do not hold any National, State, city or county office which pays me a salary or fees of $300.00 per annum, nor have I an income from any other employment or other source whatever which amounts to $300.00 per annum, nor do I receive from any source whatever money or other means of support amounting in value to the sum of $300.00 per annum, nor do I own in my own right, nor does any one hold in trust for my benefit or use, nor does my wife own, nor does any one hold in trust for my wife, estate or property, either real, personal or mixed, either in fee or for life, of the assessed value of over one thousand dollars, exclusive of a home of the value of not more than $2000.00; nor do I receive any aid or pension from any other State, or from the United States, or from any other source, and I do further state that the answers given to the following questions are true:

1. What is your age? I will be 84 years on November 29th., 1926.
2. Where were you born? Yazoo County, Mississippi,
3. How long have you resided in Texas? Since 1900
4. In what county do you reside? Upshur,
5. How long have you resided in said county? since 1900 What is your postoffice address? Gilmer, Route, 2,
6. Have you applied for a pension under the Confederate pension law and been rejected? yes.
   If rejected, state when and where did not have living witnesses in the State
7. What is your occupation, if able to engage in one? none What is your physical condition? failing.
8. In what State was the command in which you served organized? Louisiana.
9. How long did you serve? about 3 years if possible, the date of enlistment and discharge Enlisted during year 1861 and released from prison at end of war.
10. What was the letter of your company, number of battalion, regiment or battery? (TX) Company C. 8th., Louisiana, infantry
11. If transferred from one command to another, give time of transfer, name of command and time of service Always under same command.
12. What branch of the service did you enlist in—infantry, cavalry, artillery or navy? Infantry.
13. What is the assessed value of your home, if you own a home? No home.
14. What is the assessed value of your other property?
15. Have you transferred to others any property of any kind for the purpose of becoming a beneficiary under this law? No.

Wherefore your petitioner prays that his application for a pension be approved and such other proceedings be had in the premises as are required by law.

(Signature of Applicant) J. A. Slater

Sworn to and subscribed before me, this 27th day of October A. D. 1926

S. Harrington

[Seal] County Judge Upshur County, Texas.

Figure 11-6. Joseph A. Slater served in the Confederate Army, Louisiana infantry, during the Civil War. His 1926 pension application was made to the State of Texas because he was then a Texas resident. His pension was twenty-five dollars per month, payable quarterly. File 42550, reproduced from the holdings of the Texas State Archives.

Republic" index at the Kansas State Historical Society website <www.kshs.org/genealogists/military/gar/garnecrologies>.[37] The latter identifies more than 13,000 individuals for whom a notice of death was published in the encampment proceedings of the GAR, Department of Kansas. For more information about the resources of military-related organizations, see appendixes D, "Hereditary and Lineage Organizations," and B, "Family Associations."

There are card file records of World War I–era soldiers who died overseas between 1917 and 1922. These files consist mainly of grave registrations, records of American names in European chapels, and records of American soldiers who were buried in Russia. They are arranged alphabetically by surname of the soldier or name of the cemetery. The collection of grave registrations includes the name of the soldier, military organization, date of death, a statement that he was killed in action, name and address of the nearest relative or guardian, and name of the chapel. The record of American names in European chapels includes the name of the soldier, military organization, date of death, statement that the soldier was killed in action, name and address of the nearest relative or guardian, and name of the chapel. These records are all on file in Record Group 92, Records of the Quartermaster General, in the National Archives.

The National Archives website <www.archives.gov> provides two databases: "U.S. Military Personnel Who Died from Hostile Action (Including Missing and Captured) in the Korean War 1950–1957" and "U.S. Military Personnel Who Died (Including Missing and Captured or Declared Dead) as a result of the Vietnam Conflict, 1957–1997." Names in both databases are alphabetically listed and information includes military rank or grade, branch of service, home of record, date and category of casualty. The Vietnam index adds place of death and date of birth.

Names of U.S. and Coalition Casualties during the War in Iraq are posted regularly, with photographs when available, at a War in Iraq section of CNN online. The site may be searched by name at <http://edition.cnn.com/SPECIALS/2003/iraq/forces/casualties>.

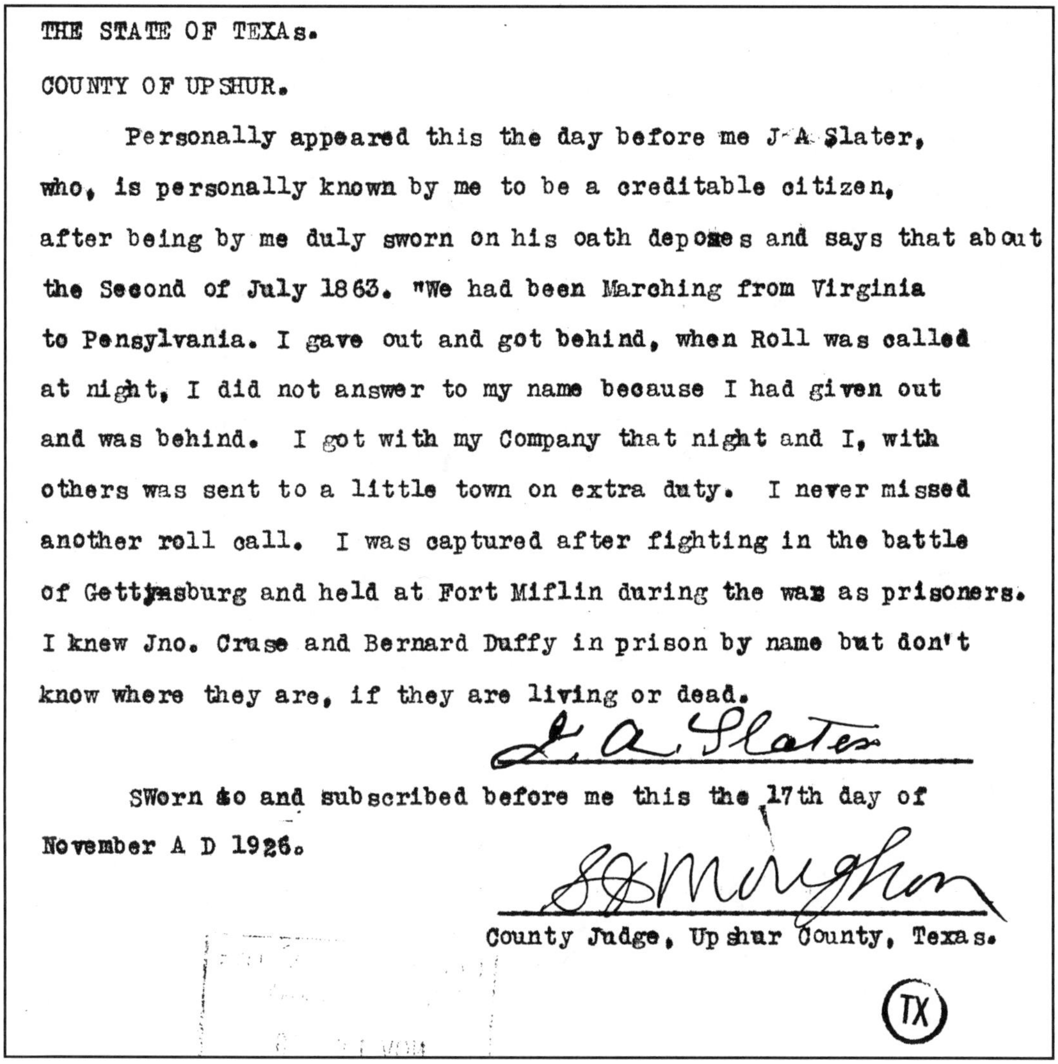

THE STATE OF TEXAs.

COUNTY OF UPSHUR.

Personally appeared this the day before me J A Slater, who, is personally known by me to be a creditable citizen, after being by me duly sworn on his oath deposes and says that about the Second of July 1863. "We had been Marching from Virginia to Pensylvania. I gave out and got behind, when Roll was called at night, I did not answer to my name because I had given out and was behind. I got with my Company that night and I, with others was sent to a little town on extra duty. I never missed another roll call. I was captured after fighting in the battle of Gettysburg and held at Fort Miflin during the war as prisoners. I knew Jno. Cruse and Bernard Duffy in prison by name but don't know where they are, if they are living or dead.

J. A. Slater

SWorn to and subscribed before me this the 17th day of November A D 1926.

S. J. Morghen

County Judge, Upshur County, Texas.

(TX)

Figure 11-7. In answer to a query, Confederate veteran Joseph A. Slater explains why he missed roll call. Slater's two-dozen page file includes his handwritten letters. File 42550, reproduced from the holdings of the Texas State Archives.

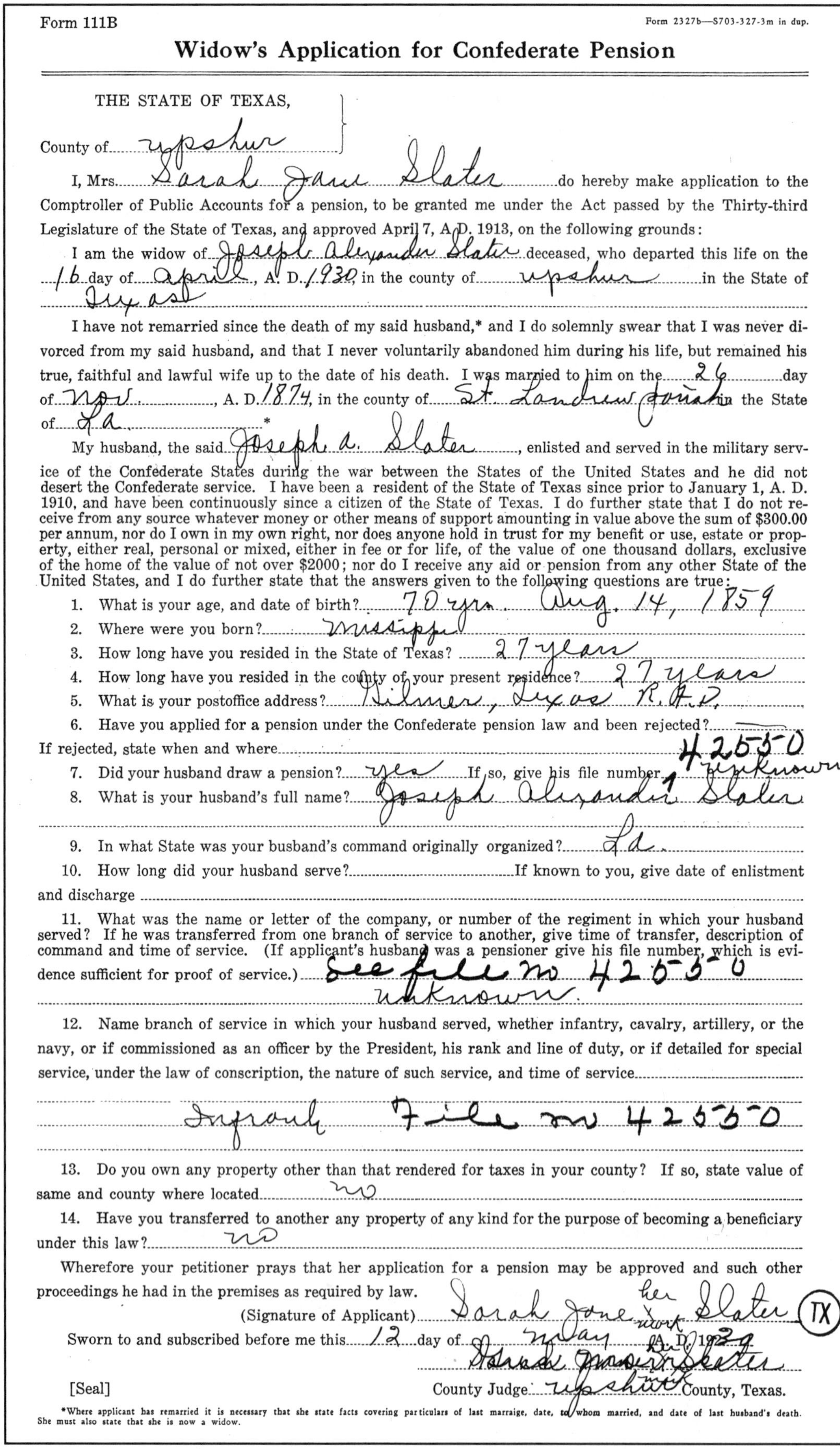

Form 111B

Form 2327b—S703-327-3m in dup.

Widow's Application for Confederate Pension

THE STATE OF TEXAS,

County of upshur

I, Mrs. Sarah Jane Slater do hereby make application to the Comptroller of Public Accounts for a pension, to be granted me under the Act passed by the Thirty-third Legislature of the State of Texas, and approved April 7, A. D. 1913, on the following grounds:

I am the widow of Joseph Alexander Slater deceased, who departed this life on the 16 day of april, A. D. 1930, in the county of upshur in the State of Texas

I have not remarried since the death of my said husband,* and I do solemnly swear that I was never divorced from my said husband, and that I never voluntarily abandoned him during his life, but remained his true, faithful and lawful wife up to the date of his death. I was married to him on the 26 day of Nov., A. D. 1874, in the county of St. Landrew Parish in the State of La.*

My husband, the said Joseph A. Slater, enlisted and served in the military service of the Confederate States during the war between the States of the United States and he did not desert the Confederate service. I have been a resident of the State of Texas since prior to January 1, A. D. 1910, and have been continuously since a citizen of the State of Texas. I do further state that I do not receive from any source whatever money or other means of support amounting in value above the sum of $300.00 per annum, nor do I own in my own right, nor does anyone hold in trust for my benefit or use, estate or property, either real, personal or mixed, either in fee or for life, of the value of one thousand dollars, exclusive of the home of the value of not over $2000; nor do I receive any aid or pension from any other State of the United States, and I do further state that the answers given to the following questions are true:

1. What is your age, and date of birth? 70 yrs. Aug. 14, 1859
2. Where were you born? Mississippi
3. How long have you resided in the State of Texas? 27 years
4. How long have you resided in the county of your present residence? 27 years
5. What is your postoffice address? Gilmer, Texas R.F.D.
6. Have you applied for a pension under the Confederate pension law and been rejected? —

   If rejected, state when and where
7. Did your husband draw a pension? yes If so, give his file number. 42550 unknown
8. What is your husband's full name? Joseph Alexander Slater
9. In what State was your husband's command originally organized? La.
10. How long did your husband serve? If known to you, give date of enlistment and discharge
11. What was the name or letter of the company, or number of the regiment in which your husband served? If he was transferred from one branch of service to another, give time of transfer, description of command and time of service. (If applicant's husband was a pensioner give his file number, which is evidence sufficient for proof of service.) See file No 42550 unknown.
12. Name branch of service in which your husband served, whether infantry, cavalry, artillery, or the navy, or if commissioned as an officer by the President, his rank and line of duty, or if detailed for special service, under the law of conscription, the nature of such service, and time of service

    Infranty File no 42550
13. Do you own any property other than that rendered for taxes in your county? If so, state value of same and county where located no
14. Have you transferred to another any property of any kind for the purpose of becoming a beneficiary under this law? no

Wherefore your petitioner prays that her application for a pension may be approved and such other proceedings he had in the premises as required by law.

(Signature of Applicant) Sarah Jane her mark Slater

Sworn to and subscribed before me this 12 day of May A. D. 1929

Sarah Jane her mark Slater

[Seal] County Judge upshur County, Texas.

*Where applicant has remarried it is necessary that she state facts covering particulars of last marriage, date, to whom married, and date of last husband's death. She must also state that she is now a widow.

Figure 11-8. After the death of her husband in 1930, Sarah Jane Slater filed a Widow's Application for Confederate Pension, which gives the date and place of her marriage to Joseph A. Slater. File 46512, reproduced from the holdings of the Texas State Archives.

Censuses and Listings (Federal)

For a discussion of censuses, see chapter 5, "Census Records." Federal census information involving military service was taken in 1840, 1890, 1910, and 1930. At the time of the 1840 federal population census, enumerators were asked to list all living pensioners of the Revolutionary War or other military service. These names and the accompanying information have been published in *A Census of Pensioners for Revolutionary or Military Services; with Their Names, Ages, and Places of Residence, as Returned by the Marshals of the Several Judicial Districts Under the Act for Taking the Sixth Census*.[38] This census may be searched online at major indexing and databases sites. The 1840 census provides the veteran's name, age, and residence.

The schedules for the 1890 census of pensioners for the states of (in alphabetical order) Alabama through Kansas and approximately half of those for Kentucky are missing. The remaining schedules for the latter half of Kentucky through Wyoming (including Washington, D.C.) have been microfilmed as *Special Schedules of the Eleventh Census (1890) Enumerating Union Veterans and Widows of Union Veterans of the Civil War* and are available for online searching at major indexing and databases sites.[39] This special 1890 census provides the veteran's name; rank; company, regiment, or vessel; dates of enlistment and discharge; length of service in years, months, and days; aliases; post office address of the institution in which living at the time of the enumeration; and disabilities incurred in service.

Enumerators were instructed to include information on those who had served in the army, navy, or Marine Corps of the United States in the war of the rebellion, and who were survivors at the time of the 1890 census, or the widows of soldiers, sailors, or marines. Contrary to these instructions, many census takers added entries for veterans who served in the Confederacy forces, or the widows of Confederate veterans.

The 1910 and 1930 federal population censuses have a category devoted to military personnel. The 1910 census indicates whether an individual was a "survivor" of the Union Army, Union Navy, Confederate Army, or Confederate Navy. The question was to be asked of all males over the age of 50 who were born in the United States or all foreign born males who immigrated to this country before 1865. The 1930 census also listed veterans. Enumerators were directed to exclude persons who served only during peacetime. The war or expedition was to be entered by an abbreviation: World War, "WW"; Spanish-American War, "Sp"; Civil War, "Civ"; Philippine Insurrection, "Phil"; Boxer rebellion, "Box"; or Mexican Expedition, "Mex."[40] These more recent censuses are less likely to be in print but online searches and microfilm are available.

The U. S. Pension Office was directed by Congress to prepare a list of Pensioners on the Roll as of January 1, 1883. The pensioners were primarily Union veterans from the Civil War and survivors of the War of 1812 but also included veterans of other service. If a family member was receiving pension a based on a deceased veteran's service, their name was shown. The information recorded included the pension certificate file number, the name and location of the recipient, the monthly amount received, the effective date of the pension and reason for the benefit. The listings of several states are online at <www.arealdomain.com/pensioners1883.html>.

Censuses (State)

Special state censuses of pensioners were taken in Alabama in 1907 and in Arkansas in 1911. In addition, some general state censuses taken between 1865 and 1905 included questions about military service. Some of these general censuses indicate only if a person had served in the military. Others, such as Wisconsin's 1885, 1895, and 1905, lists "Soldiers and Sailors of the Late War" giving name, rank, company, regiment, state from which served, and post office address. A listing by state of schedules which included military service queries is in Ann Lainhart's *State Census Records*.[41]

Discharge Records

Each county in the United States was required to record the honorable discharge of soldiers and sailors who served in World War I and World War II. Some discharges for the Civil War and Philippine Insurrection are also on record, as well as some dishonorable and medical discharges.

The records are kept in local courthouses and usually consist of typed or handwritten transcripts of the original documents given to the soldier. Some of these discharge records from county collections have been microfilmed by the Genealogical Society of Utah, but most have not.

The records may contain the individual's name, race, rank, serial number, reason for discharge, birthplace, age at time of enlistment, occupation, and a personal description. His or her service record, sometimes included with the discharge record, gives the length of service, prior service, marital status, arms and horsemanship qualifications, advancement, battles, decorations, honors, leaves of absence, physical condition, and character evaluation.

Prisoner of War Records

The National Archives has records relating to British and American prisoners of war for 1812 to 1815, including miscellaneous correspondence and lists of prisoners sent from the Treasury Department to the Adjutant General's Office and from the Navy Department to the Adjutant General's Office. Some of these records have been microfilmed by the National Archives as *Records Relating to War of 1812 Prisoners of War*[42]. These are indexed in *Index to War of 1812 Prisoners of War*.[43] The National Archives website <www.archives.gov> offers searches of lists of prisoners for three eras: World War II (service personnel held in Japanese internment camps), the Korean War, and the Vietnam War. A database titled "Andersonville Prisoners of War" at <www.ancestry.com> indexes a collection of records compiled by the National Park Service of inmates between 1863 and 1865. For additional information of Confederate prisoners during the Civil War, see "Confederate Deaths as Prisoners of War" following the "Civil War Service Records—Confederates" section in this chapter.

Questionnaires (State)

An index to biographies of Civil War veterans who were living in Tennessee in 1922 is at the Tennessee State Library and Archives website <www.state.tn.us/tsla/history/military/civilwar.htm>. These records are filled with valuable information, including the veteran's name, residence, age, place of birth, occupation, the unit he served in during the war, his parents' names and birthplaces, the names of his paternal grandparents, and their residence. The residence of the veteran's father and all facts known about parents, grandparents, and great-grandparents (including when the family came to America, property owned by the veteran and his parents, education, and the general quality of the veteran's life) are included in these sketches.

The "World War I History Commission Questionnaires" is a fully-searchable database to information on over 14,900 Virginia veterans who responded to a 1928 survey by the Virginia War History Commission. Each record is linked to digitized images of each page of the questionnaire, as well as any accompanying material such as photographs. Detailed information about personal background, including names of parents and their places of birth, names of the veteran's wife and children, the veteran's war record, and often one or two photographs are in the files. Separate two-page questionnaires prepared for nurses are in the databases. The database is at the Library of Virginia, <www.lva.lib.va.us/whatwehave/mil>.

State Militia Records and Private Collections

Military records, which may be referred to as militia records, were also created and preserved by state and local jurisdictions. Their contents are much like those described earlier. These militia records, however, are often the first to be disposed of because local militias no longer exist. They will be found scattered through state archives, historical societies and museums, military forts (both those still active and museums for those discontinued), and among the papers in the county clerk's office. These records may sometimes be located using state and local record inventories.

Private collections of military records also exist, often housed in a records repository some distance from the location where they were created or refer to. Check the *National Union Catalog of Manuscripts Collections of the Library of Congress (NUCMC)* (see chapter 3, "General References and Guides").

Veterans Homes

Records pertaining to the national (federal) veterans homes are dated 1866–1938 and are part of Records of the Veterans Administration (Record Group 15) and Records of the U.S. Soldiers' Home (Record Group 231). Honorably discharged officers, sailors, soldiers, or marines who served in regular, volunteer, or other forces of the United States (or in the organized militia or in the National Guard called into federal service) were eligible if they were disabled by disease or wounds, without adequate means of support, and incapable of earning a living. These records are available on microfilm as *Historical Registers of National Homes for Disabled Volunteer Soldiers, 1866–1938*.[44] All or part of the microfilm collection is at the National Archives regional facilities and the Family History Library. Below is a list of the National Homes for Disabled Volunteer Soldiers (now known as Veterans Administration Centers) and the dates of their creation:

Eastern Branch, Togus, Maine: 1866
Central Branch, Dayton, Ohio: 1867
Northwestern Branch, Wood, Wisconsin: 1867
Southern Branch, Kecoughtan, Virginia: 1870
Western Branch, Leavenworth, Kansas: 1885
Pacific Branch, Sawtelle, California: 1888
Marion Branch, Marion, Indiana: 1888
Roseburg Branch, Roseburg, Oregon: 1894
Danville Branch, Danville, Illinois: 1898
Mountain Branch, Johnson City, Tennessee: 1903
Battle Mountain Sanitarium, Hot Springs, South Dakota: 1907
Bath Branch, Bath, New York: 1894
Saint Petersburg Home, Saint Petersburg, Florida: 1930
Biloxi Home, Biloxi, Mississippi: 1930
Tuskegee Home, Tuskegee, Alabama: 1933

The case files for the veterans who resided in some of these homes have been indexed at the NARA website, <www.archives.gov>. Databases include "Sawtelle Disabled Veteran's Home, Los Angeles Case Files, 1880–1933" and "Records of the Veterans Administration in the National Archives, Kansas City, Mo—Leavenworth Soldiers Home, Leavenworth, Kansas, Sample Case Files of Veterans" (Record Group 15).

A far greater number of veterans homes are managed by state or county governments. These homes are administrated by a state agency that is often part of a larger veterans benefits and care program. The state government website should have contact information under the subject "veterans." Many of these homes are members of the National Association of State Veterans Homes. The NASVH maintains a website, <www.nasvh.com>, which lists state veterans homes, their date of establishment, a photograph, contact information, and a link to their website. Rosters or admittance records of state homes may be associated with applications for state pensions, as is "Missouri Confederate Pensions and Home Applications," a microfilm of records from the veterans home at Higginsville. The originals are held by the Missouri State Archives; the microfilm is at the St. Louis County (Missouri) Library. An index to 485 veterans who resided at the Tennessee Confederate Soldiers Home located east of Nashville, and photographs of their tombstones, is online at <www.tennessee-scv.org>, the website of the Col. Randal W. McGavock, Camp #1713 of the Tennessee Division, Sons of Confederate Veterans.

Women in the Military

Women have participated in or been associated with military service throughout the history of this country. They have served the Armed Forces as cooks, hospital matrons, laundresses, seamstresses, and nurses. In smaller numbers, they have been spies, endured combat, military prisons and hospitals, and have been battlefield casualties. One of several titles that documents the combat role of women is De Anne Blanton and Lauren M. Cook's *They Fought Like Demons: Women Soldiers in the Civil War*.[45]

Among the records about women and the military are applications for War Department appointments or employment. These are filed in the Records of the Office of the Secretary of War (Record Group 107). Entries found in Registers and Lists of Appointments and Employees, 1863–1913 may show the employee's name, state from which appointed, date of appointment, position and office, and remarks about salary, promotions, discharges, or death. Another series of records is in the Records of the Office of the Surgeon General (Record Group 112). This holds service information about hospital attendants, matrons, and nurses. These and other series are meticulously described in Charlotte Palmer Seeley's *American Women and the U.S. Armed Forces: A Guide to the Records of Military Agencies in the National Archives Relating to American Women*.[46]

World War I Gold Star Mothers

Between 1930 and 1933, trips to Europe for eligible mothers and widows of U.S. soldiers who had died overseas during World War I were paid for by the United States government. The trips were provided so that these women, Gold Star Pilgrims, could see the graves of their sons and husbands. The records that describe the trips and the death and internment of the soldiers are among the Burial Files and Grave Registration records in the Records of the Office of the Quartermaster General (Record Group 92).[47] The files can include letters of application by the women and related correspondence and details of the trip. A database indexed by name of woman is at <www.ancestry.com> titled, "U.S. World War I Mother's Pilgrimage, 1930." Each record gives the name of the widow or mother, city and state of residence, and relationship to the deceased. The decedent's name, rank, unit, and cemetery is also provided. Nearly eleven thousand mothers and widows, including approximately six thousand women who made the trip, are listed.

Additional Sources

There are three goals that will help the genealogist to discover information about a military ancestor: (1) acquire a view of historical context; (2) identify the original records that require searching; and (3) examine secondary sources, such as compilations of material not easily found elsewhere.

Hundreds of volumes pertain to the military history of the United States and to the service and pension/bounty-land programs that were in effect prior to the modern wars. These provide the setting and the conditions, legal and social, which your military ancestor would have experienced; hence, the historical context.

Records may be identified in two highly recommended sources: James C. Neagles's *U.S. Military Records: A Guide to Federal and State Sources, Colonial America to the Present* and Anne Bruner Eales's and Robert M. Kvasnicka's *Guide to Genealogical Research in the National Archives of the United States*.[48] Both describe in detail the specific records that hold primary evidence of military involvement. Also useful, although less detailed, are Trevor K. Plante's "An Overview of Records at the National Archives Relating to Military Service," and *U.S. Military Records* in the Research Outline series published online by the Family History Library at <http://www.familysearch.org>. The essential website for finding information on federal records and finding aids is <www.archives.org>, the website of the National Archives and Records Administration.

The final goal, to examine secondary sources, is accomplished by exploring transcripts, indexes, and compilations that bring together a variety of information. These may be published as online databases or in print, CD, or microform editions. While there is no known comprehensive bibliography to compiled sources, a partial list of printed materials and websites is provided at the end of this chapter.

Notes

[1] Anne Bruner Eales and Robert M. Kvasnicka, *Guide to Genealogical Research in the National Archives of the United States* (Washington, D.C.: National Archives and Records Administration, 2000).

[2] Old Loan Records, "Central Treasury Records of the Continental and Confederation Governments Relating to Military Affairs, 1775–1789," book 75, 1782, NARA microfilm M1015, roll 4.

[3] The Civil War Soldiers and Sailors database is a joint project of the National Archives, the National Park Service, the Federation

of Genealogical Societies, and the Genealogical Society of Utah.

[4] Curt B. Witcher, "The Civil War Soldiers and Sailors System: Complete and Reborn," *FORUM* 16 (Winter 2004): 31–32.

[5] Janet B. Hewett, ed., *The Roster of Union Soldiers, 1861–1865*, 33 vols. (Wilmington, N.C.: Broadfoot Publishing Co., 1997–2000).

[6] Kenneth C. Martis, *The Historical Atlas of United States Congressional Districts 1789–1983* (New York: Free Press, 1982).

[7] These records are described in detail in Eales and Kavasnicka, *Guide to Genealogical Research in the National Archives of the United States* (Washington, D.C.: National Archives and Records Administration, 2000), 144.

[8] *Consolidated Index to Compiled Service Records of Confederate Soldiers*, NARA microfilm M253.

[9] *Unfiled Papers and Slips Belonging to Confederate Compiled Service Records*, NARA microfilm M347.

[10] Janet B. Hewett, ed., *The Roster of Confederate Soldiers, 1861–1865*, 16 vols. (Wilmington, Del.: Broadfoot Publishing, 1995–96).

[11] Janet B. Hewett, *Supplement to the Official Records* (Wilmington, Del.: Broadfoot Publishing, 1997–98).

[12] *Register of Confederate Soldiers, Sailors, and Citizens Who Died in Federal Prisons and Military Hospitals in the North, 1861–1865*, NARA microfilm M918.

[13] *Selected Records of the War Department Relating to Confederate Prisoners of War 1861–1865*, NARA microfilm M598.

[14] *Register of Confederate Soldiers, Sailors, and Citizens Who Died in Federal Prisons and Military Hospitals in the North, 1861–1865*, NARA microfilm M918.

[15] George W. Cullum, *Biographical Register, Officers and Graduates of the U.S. Military Academy, West Point, New York*, 3rd ed. (Boston: Houghton-Mifflin, 1891); Stanley P. Tozeski, *Preliminary Inventory of the Records of the U.S. Military Academy* (Washington, D.C.: National Archives and Records Service, 1976); and Jon L. Wakelyn. *Biographical Dictionary of the Confederacy* (Westport, Conn.: Greenwood Press, 1977).

[16] See Mitchell Yockelson, "'I Am Entitled to the Medal of Honor and I Want It' Theodore Roosevelt and His Quest for Glory," *Prologue* 30 (Spring 1998), reprinted at <www.archives.gov/publications/prologue>.

[17] Trevor K. Plante, "Researching Service in the U.S. Army During the Philippines Insurrection," *Prologue* 32 (Summer 2000), reprinted at <www.archives.gov/publications/prologue>.

[18] The National Personnel Records Center is located at 9700 Page Ave., St. Louis, MO 63132-5100.

[19] For more information on how to reconstruct information lost in this fire, visit the U.S. National Archives and Records Administration website at <www.archives.gov/st-louis>.

[20] *World War I Selective Service System Draft Registration Cards*, NARA microfilm M1509.

[21] *Registers of Enlistments in the U.S. Army, 1798–1914*, NARA microfilm M233.

[22] Pension Application #W10156 for Reuben Johnson and Nancy Johnson, service from North Carolina. *Revolutionary War Pension and Bounty-Land Warrant Applications Files*, NARA Microfilm M804, roll 475, image 548–57.

[23] *Revolutionary War Pension and Bounty-Land Warrant Applications Files*, NARA microfilm M804.

[24] *Selected Records From Revolutionary War Pension and Bounty-Land Warrant Applications Files*, NARA microfilm M805.

[25] Virgil D. White, *Genealogical Abstracts of Revolutionary War Pension Files* (Waynesboro, Tenn.: National Historical Publishing Co., 1990–92).

[26] Lloyd deWitt Bockstruck, *Revolutionary War Bounty Land Grants Awarded by State Governments* (Baltimore: Genealogical Publishing Co., 1996).

[27] Anne Bruner Eales and Robert M. Kvasnicka, *Guide to Genealogical Research in the National Archives of the United States* (Washington, D.C.: National Archives and Records Administration, 2000), 174.

[28] Mexican War Survivors Brief and General Affidavit for James M. Phelan, Clay County, Arkansas, dated 02 June 1894, <ftp://ftp.rootsweb.com/pub/usgenweb/ar/clay/military/mexwar/pensions/phelanj.txt>.

[29] Virgil D. White, *Index to War of 1812 Pension Files* (Waynesboro, Tenn.: National Historical Publishing Co., 1989).

[30] Virgil D. White, transcriber, *Index to Indian Wars Pension Files, 1892–1926* (Waynesboro, Tenn.: National Historical Publishing Co., 1987).

[31] *Index to Mexican War Pension Applications, 1887–1926*, NARA microfilm T317.

[32] Barbara Schull Wolfe, transcriber, *An Index to Mexican War Pension Applications* (Indianapolis: Heritage House, 1985); Virgil D. White, *Index to Mexican War Pension Files* (Waynesville, Tenn.: National Historical Publishing, 1989); Navena Hembree Troxel, *Mexican War Index to Pension Files, 1886–1926* (Gore, Okla.: VT Publications, 1983–95).

[33] *General Index to Pension Files, 1861–1934*, NARA microfilm T288.

[34] *Card Records of Headstones Provided for Deceased Union Civil War Veterans, ca. 1879–ca. 1903*, NARA microfilm M1814.

[35] *Roll of Honor: Names of Soldiers Who Died in Defense of the American Union, Interred in the National Cemeteries, Numbers I–XIX* (Baltimore: Genealogical Publishing Co., 1994).

[36] Martha and William Remy, comps., *Index to the Roll of Honor* (Baltimore: Genealogical Publishing Co., 1995).

[37] *Sons of the American Revolution Patriot Index CD, Edition III*, CD-ROM (Progeny Publishing, 2002).

[38] *A Census of Pensioners for Revolutionary or Military Services; With Their Names, Ages, and Places of Residence, as Returned by the Marshals of the Several Judicial Districts Under the Act for Taking the Sixth Census* (Washington, D.C.: Baltimore: Genealogical Books in Print, 1996).

[39] *Special Schedules of the Eleventh Census (1890) Enumerating Union Veterans and Widows of Union Veterans of the Civil War*, NARA microfilm M123.

[40] Questions asked by the enumerators appear in *Twenty Censuses: Population and Housing Questions, 1790–1980* (Washington, D.C.: Bureau of the Census, 1979; facsimile reprint, Orting, Wash.: Heritage Quest, 2000).

[41] Ann Lainhart, *State Census Records* (Baltimore: Genealogical Publishing Co., 1992; reprint, 2004).

[42] *Records Relating to War of 1812 Prisoners of War*, NARA microfilm M2019.

[43] *Index to War of 1812 Prisoners of War*, NARA microfilm M1747.

[44] *Historical Registers of National Homes for Disabled Volunteer Soldiers, 1866–1938*, NARA microfilm M1749.

[45] De Anne Blanton and Lauren M. Cook, *They Fought Like Demons: Women Soldiers in the Civil War* (Baton Rouge: Louisiana University Press, 2002).

[46] Charlotte Palmer Seeley, *American Women and the U.S. Armed Forces: A Guide to the Records of Military Agencies in the National Archives Relating to American Women*, rev. Virginia C. Purdy and Robert Gruber (Washington, D.C.: National Archives and Records Administration, 2002).

[47] Constance Potter, "World War I Gold Star Mothers Pilgrimages," *Prologue* Part I, 31 (Spring 1999); Part II 31 (Summer 1999). Reprinted at <www.archives.gov/publications/prologue>.

[48] James C. Neagles, *U.S. Military Records: A Guide to Federal and State Sources, Colonial America to the Present* (Salt Lake City: Ancestry, 1994); Anne Bruner Eales and Robert M. Kvasnicka, *Guide to Genealogical Research in the National Archives of the United States* (Washington, D.C.: National Archives and Records Administration, 2000).

References

The following lists standard published sources in both paper and microform formats. Most of these titles have been published, microfilmed or digitized; however, some exist only in manuscript form. To find ways to access these works, consult the Web pages of the respective state archives, access the catalog of the Family History Library in Salt Lake City, or use a search engine to locate specific titles or online versions.

Sources Covering Various States and Time Periods

Ashton, Sharron S. *Marriages and Deaths, 1838–1840: Army and Navy Chronicle*. Norman, Okla.: S. S. Ashton, 1997.

———. *Marriages, Deaths, and Miscellany, 1833–1837: Military and Naval Magazine of the United States and Army and Navy Chronicle*. Norman, Okla.: S. S. Ashton, 1997.

Blewett, Daniel K. *American Military History: A Guide to Reference and Information Sources*. Reference Sources in the Social Sciences Series. Westport, Conn.: Libraries Unlimited, 1995. 2nd ed., forthcoming.

Bockstruck, Lloyd deWitt. *Naval Pensioners of the United States, 1800–1851*. Baltimore: Genealogical Publishing Co., 2002.

Callahan, Edward W. *List of Officers of the Navy of the United States and of the Marine Corps from 1775 to 1900*. Gaithersburg, Md.: Olde Soldier Books, 1988.

Carroll, John M., and Byron Price. *Roll Call on the Little Big Horn, 28 June 1876*. Ft. Collins, Colo.: Old Army Press, 1974.

Cullum, George W. *Biographical Register, Officers and Graduates of the U.S. Military Academy, West Point, New York*. 3rd ed. 9 vols. Boston: Houghton-Mifflin, 1891.

Deputy, Marilyn, and Pat Barben. *Register of Federal United States Military Records, A Guide to Manuscript Sources at the Genealogical Library Salt Lake City and the National Archives in Washington, D.C.* 3 vols. Bowie, Md.: Heritage Books, 1986.

Eales, Anne Bruner, and Robert M. Kvasnicka. *Guide to Genealogical Research in the National Archives*. 3rd ed. Washington, D.C.: National Archives Trust Fund Board, 2000.

Heitman, Francis B. *Historical Register and Dictionary of the United States Army, from Its Organization September 29, 1789, to March 2, 1903*. 2 vols. 1965. Reprint, Baltimore: Genealogical Publishing Co., 1994. Indexed online at <www.ancestry.com>.

Horowitz, Lois. *A Bibliography of Military Name Lists from Pre-1675 to 1900: A Guide to Genealogical Sources*. Metuchen, N.J.: Scarecrow Press, 1990.

Johnson, Richard S., and Debra Johnson Knox. *How to Locate Anyone Who Is or Has Been in the Military: Armed Forces Locater Guide*. Military Information Enterprises, 1999.

Lainhart, Ann. *State Census Records*. Baltimore: Genealogical Publishing Co., 1992. Reprint, 2004.

List of Pensioners on the Roll January 1, 1883 Giving the Name of Each Pensioner, the Cause for Which Pensioned, the Post Office Address, the Rate of Pension per Month, and the Date of Original Allowance as Called for by Senate Resolution of December 8, 1882. 5 vols. Baltimore: Genealogical Publishing Co., 1970.

Martis, Kenneth C. *The Historical Atlas of United States Congressional Districts 1789–1983*. New York: Free Press, 1982.

Moebs, Thomas. *Black Soldiers, Black Sailors, Black Ink: Research Guide on African Americans in the U.S. Military History 1526–1900*. Chesapeake Bay, Va.: Moebs Publishing Co., 1994.

Neagles, James C. *U.S. Military Records: A Guide to Federal and State Sources, Colonial America to the Present*. Salt Lake City: Ancestry, 1994.

Powell, William H. *List of Officers of the Army of the United States from 1779 to 1900 Embracing a Register of All Appointments by the President of the United States in the Volunteer Service During the Civil War and of Volunteer Officers in the Service of the United States June 1, 1900*. Detroit: Gale Research Co., 1967.

Schubert, Irene, and Frank N. Schubert. *On the Trail of the Buffalo Soldier II: New and Revised Biographies of African Americans in the U.S. Army, 1866–1917*. Lanham, Md.: Scarecrow Press, 2004.

Seeley, Charlotte Palmer. *American Women and the U.S. Armed Forces: A Guide to the Records of Military Agencies in the National Archives Relating to American Women*, revised by Virginia C. Purdy and Robert Gruber. Washington, D.C.: National Archives and Records Service, 2002.

Tozeski, Stanley P. *Preliminary Inventory of the Records of the U.S. Military Academy*. Washington, D.C.: National Archives and Records Service, 1976.

Twenty Censuses: Population and Housing Questions, 1790–1980. Washington, D.C.: Bureau of the Census, 1979. Facsimile reprint, Orting, Wash.: Heritage Quest, 2000.

United States Army, Quartermaster General's Office. *Burial Registers for Military Posts, Camps, and Stations, 1768–1921*. Microfilm, M2014, 1 roll. Washington, D.C.: National Archives Microfilm Publication.

U.S. Veterans Administration. *Abstracts of Service Records of Naval Officers ("Records of Officers") 1798–1893*. Microfilm, M330, 19 rolls. Washington, D.C.: National Archives Microfilm Publications.

———. *List of Navy Veterans for Whom There Are Navy Widows' and Other Dependents' Disapproved Pension Files ("Navy Widows' originals"), 1861–1910*. Microfiche, M1391, 15 microfiche. Washington, D.C.: National Archives Microfiche Publications, 1985.

———. *Registers of Enlistments in the United States Army, 1789–1914*. Microfilm, M233, 80 rolls. Washington, D.C.: National Archives Microfilm Publications, 1963.

White, Virgil D. *Index to Old Wars Pension Files 1815–1926*. 2 vols. Waynesboro, Tenn.: National Historical Publishing Co., 1987. Revised edition published in 1993.

———. *Index to U.S. Military Pension Applications of Remarried Widows for Service Between 1812 and 1911*. Waynesboro, Tenn.: National Historical Publishing Co., 1999.

Sources, by State, That Cover Various Time Periods

Arizona

Akey, Elizabeth J. *Military Burials in Arizona*. Tucson, Ariz.: Arizona Genealogical Society, 1987.

Arkansas

Payne, Dorothy E. *Arkansas Pensioners 1818–1900, Records of Some Arkansas Residents Who Applied to the Federal Government for Benefits Arising from Service in Federal Military Organizations (Revolutionary War, War of 1812, Indian and Mexican Wars)*. Easley, S.C.: Southern Historical Press, 1985.

Georgia

Payne, Dorothy E. *Georgia Pensioners (American Revolution, War of 1812, Mexican War)*. 2 vols. McLean, Va.: Sunbelt Publishing Co., 1985–86.

North Carolina

Kearney, Timothy. *Abstracts of Letters of Resignations of Militia Officers in North Carolina 1779–1840*. Raleigh, N.C.: Waleworth, n.d.

Colonial Wars, 1607–1774

Various States

Baker, Mary Ellen. *Bibliography of Lists of New England Soldiers*. Boston: New England Historic Genealogical Society, 1977.

Bodge, George Madison. *Soldiers in King Philip's War*. 3rd ed. Baltimore: Genealogical Publishing Co., 1976.

Clark, Murtie June. *Colonial Soldiers of the South 1732–1774*. 1983. Reprint, Baltimore: Genealogical Publishing Co., 1999.

Coleman, Emma Lewis. *New England Captives Carried to Canada Between 1677 and 1760 During the French and Indian Wars.* 2 vols. Bowie, Md.: Heritage Books, 1989.

Dobson, David. *The French and Indian War from Scottish Sources.* Baltimore: Clearfield Co., 2003.

———. *Scottish Soldiers in Colonial America: Part One and Part Two.* Baltimore: Clearfield Co., 1977.

Ford, Worthington C. *British Officers Serving in America, 1754–1774.* Boston: Press of D. Clapp and Son, 1894.

Lucier, Armand Francis. *French and Indian War Notices Abstracted from Colonial Newspapers.* 5 vols. Bowie, Md.: Heritage Books, 1999.

———. *Pontiac's Conspiracy & Other Indian Affairs: Notices Abstracted from Colonial Newspapers, 1763–1765.* Bowie, Md.: Heritage Books, 2000.

Connecticut

Andrews, Frank DeWette. *Connecticut Soldiers in the French and Indian War.* Vineland, N.J.: the compiler, 1923.

Buckingham, Thomas. *Roll and Journal of Connecticut Men in Queen Anne's War.* New Haven: Acorn Club of Connecticut, 1916.

Jacobus, Donald Lines. *List of Officials Civil, Military, and Ecclesiastical of Connecticut Colony from March 1635 Through 11 October 1677 and of New Haven Colony Throughout Its Separate Existence Also Soldiers in the Pequot War Who Then or Subsequently Resided Within the Present Bounds of Connecticut.* Baltimore: Clearfield Co., 1989.

Judd, Sylvester. *Connecticut Archives: Selected Papers of Colonial Wars.* Microfilm, 7 rolls.

Rolls of Connecticut Men in the French and Indian Wars, 1755–1762. 2 vols. Hartford: Connecticut Historical Society, 1903–05.

Shepard, James. *Connecticut Soldiers in the Pequot War of 1637, with Proof of Service, a Brief Record for Identification and References to Various Publications in Which Further Data May Be Found.* Meriden, Conn: Journal Publishing Co., 1913.

Delaware

Delaware Archives. Vol. 1, "Military." Wilmington, Del.: Mercantile Printing Co., 1911.

Peden, Henry C. *Colonial Delaware Soldiers and Sailors, 1638–1776.* Westminster, Md.: Family Line Publications, 1995.

Maryland

Peden, Henry C. *Colonial Maryland Soldiers and Sailors, 1634–1734.* Westminster, Md.: Willow Bend Books, 2001.

Massachusetts

Burrage, Henry S. *Maine at Louisburg in 1745.* Augusta, Maine: Burleigh and Flint, 1910.

Donahue, Mary E. *Massachusetts Officers and Soldiers, 1702–1722: Queen Anne's War to Dummer's War.* Boston: New England Historic Genealogical Society, 1980.

Doreski, Carole. *Massachusetts Officers and Soldiers in the Seventeenth Century Conflicts.* Boston: New England Historic Genealogical Society, 1982.

Goss, K. Davis, and David Zarowin. *Massachusetts Officers and Soldiers in the French and Indian Wars 1755–1756.* Boston: New England Historic Genealogical Society, 1985.

MacKay, Robert E. *Massachusetts Soldiers in the French and Indian Wars 1744–1755.* Boston: New England Historic Genealogical Society, 1978.

Peirce, Ebenezer W. *Peirce's Colonial Lists, Civil, Military and Professional Lists of Plymouth and Rhode Island Colonies . . . 1621–1700.* Baltimore: Genealogical Publishing Co., 1968.

Roberts, Oliver A. *History of the Military Company of Massachusetts Now Called the Ancient and Honorable Artillery Company of Massachusetts 1637–1888.* 4 vols. Boston: Alfred Mudge and Son, 1895–1901.

Stachiw, Myron O. *Massachusetts Officers and Soldiers 1723–1743: Dummer's War to the War of Jenkins' Ear.* Boston: New England Historic Genealogical Society, 1979.

Voye, Nancy S. *Massachusetts Officers in the French and Indian Wars, 1748–1763.* Boston: New England Historic Genealogical Society, 1975.

Watkins, William K. *Soldiers in the Expedition to Canada in 1690 and Grantees of the Canada Townships.* Boston: the author, 1898.

New Hampshire

Indian and French Wars Revolutionary Papers. Microfilm, 2 rolls.

Hammond, Isaac W. *Rolls of the Soldiers in the Revolutionary War, 1775, to May, 1777.* Vol. 14 of Provincial and State Papers of New Hampshire. Concord, N.H.: Parsons B. Cogswell, 1885. The rolls of various Indian and French wars not published in Adjutant General's report in 1866 appear on pp. 1–30.

Potter, Chandler E. *The Military History of the State of New Hampshire 1623–1861.* Part 1. Baltimore: Genealogical Publishing Co., 1972.

Roll of New Hampshire Men at Louisburg, Cape Breton, 1745. Concord, N.H.: E. N. Pearson, 1896.

New Jersey

Military Officers Recorded in the Office of the Secretary of State, Trenton, New Jersey; Colonial Wars, 1668–1774. Microfilm, 1 roll.

New Jersey Records: French and Indian War 1755–1764. Microfilm, 1 roll.

New Jersey Wars: Index to Colonial Period, 1665–1774. Microfilm, 1 roll.

New York

Meyers, Carol. *Early Military Records of New York 1689–1738.* Sangus, Calif.: RAM Publishers, 1967.

Muster Rolls of New York Provincial Troops 1755–1764. Bowie, Md.: Heritage Books, 1990.

New York Colonial Muster Rolls, 1654–1775: Report of the State Historian of the State of New York. Baltimore: Genealogical Publishing Co., 2000.

North Carolina

Howell, Frances G. *North Carolina Military Collection.* Goldsboro, N.C.: F. G. Howell, 1997.

Pennsylvania

Bradshaw, Audrey E. *Pennsylvania Soldiers in the Provincial Service 1746–1759.* The author, 1985.

Officers and Soldiers in the Service of the Province of Pennsylvania, 1744–1764. Pennsylvania Archives, 2nd Series, vol. 2, 417–528. Harrisburg, Pa.: Harrisburg Publishing Co., 1906.

Officers and Soldiers in the Service of the Province of Pennsylvania, 1744–1765. Pennsylvania Archives, 5th Series, vol. 1, 1–368. Harrisburg, Pa.: Harrisburg Publishing Co., 1906.

Rhode Island

Chain, Howard M. *Rhode Island in the Colonial Wars: A List of Rhode Island Soldiers & Sailors in King George's War, 1740–1748; and a List of Rhode Island Soldiers and Sailors in the Old French & Indian War, 1755–1762.* Baltimore: Genealogical Publishing Co., 1994.

———. *Rhode Island Privateers in King George's War, 1739–1748.* Providence: Rhode Island Historical Society, 1926.

Collins, Clarkson A. *A Muster Rolls of Newport County Troops Sent Toward Albany in 1757.* Providence: Roger Williams Press, 1961.

Niles, Samuel. *Rhode Island's Victory at Louisburg in 1745.* East Greenwich, R.I.: Society of Colonial Wars in the State of Rhode Island and Providence Plantations, 1986.

South Carolina

Andrea, Leonardo. *South Carolina Colonial Soldiers and Patriots.* Columbia, S.C.: R. L. Bryan Co., 1952.

Draine, Tony, and John Skinner. *South Carolina Soldiers and Indian Traders, 1725–1730.* Columbia, S.C.: Congaree Publications, 1986.

Warren, Mary Bondurant. *South Carolina Newspapers: The South Carolina Gazette, 1760.* Danielsville, Ga.: Heritage Papers, 1988. Rosters of French and Indian War veterans appear on pp. 75–92.

Virginia

Bockstruck, Lloyd deWitt. *Virginia's Colonial Soldiers.* Baltimore: Genealogical Publishing Co., 1988.

Crozier, William A. *Virginia Colonial Militia, 1651–1776.* Baltimore: Genealogical Publishing Co., 1973.

Eckenrode, Hamilton J. *List of the Colonial Soldiers of Virginia.* Baltimore: Genealogical Publishing Co., 1980.

Lewis, Virgil A. *History of the Battle of Point Pleasant Fought Between White Men and Indians at the Mouth of the Great Kanawha River (Now Point Pleasant, West Virginia) Monday, October 10th, 1774, The Chief Event of Lord Dunmore's War.* Harrisonburg, Va.: C. J. Carrier Co., 1974.

———. *The Soldiery of West Virginia in the French and Indian War; Lord Dunmore's War; the Revolution; the Later Indian Wars; the Whiskey Insurrection; the Second War with England; the War with Mexico. And Addenda Relating to West Virginians in the Civil War. The Whole Compiled from Authentic Sources.* Baltimore: Genealogical Publishing Co., 1972.

Lord Dunmore's War: Pittsburgh Rolls, Romney Rolls, Romney and Winchester Public Service Claims, West August Public Service Claims. Microfilm, 1 roll.

Poffenbarger, Livia Simpson. *Battle of Point Pleasant, First Battle of the American Revolution, October 10, 1774.* 4th ed. Pt. Pleasant, W.Va.: Mattox Printing Service, 1976.

Smyth, Cecil B. *Dunmore's War 1774: A Concise Narrative of the 1774 Campaign of the Virginia Frontiersmen Against the Indian Tribes of the Ohio Valley.* Midlothian, Va.: C. B. Smyth, 1995.

Taylor, Philip F. *A Calendar of the Warrants for Land in Kentucky Granted for Service in the French and Indian War.* Baltimore: Genealogical Publishing Co., 1975.

Thwaites, Reuben Gold, and Louis Phelps Kellogg. *Documentary History of Dunmore's War 1774.* Harrisonburg, W.Va.: C. J. Carrier Co., 1974.

New France and New Spain

Baca, Evelyn Lujan. "Spanish Enlistment papers 1770–1816: Filiaciones Espanol." *New Mexico Genealogist* 37 (1998): 9–18.

Barron, Bill. *The Vaudreuil Papers: A Calendar and Index of All the Personal and Private Papers of Pierre de Rigaud de Vaudreuil, Royal Governor of the French Province of Louisiana, 1743–1753.* New Orleans: Polyanthos, 1975.

Deville, Winston. *French Troops in the Mississippi Valley and on the Gulf Coast, 1745.* Ville Platte, La.,1986.

———. *Louisiana Colonials: Soldiers and Vagabonds*. Mobile, Ala.: W. DeVille, 1963.

———. *Louisiana Recruits 1752–1758. Ship Lists of Troops from the Independent [sic] Companies of the French Colony of Louisiana.* Cottonport, La.: Polyanthos, 1973.

———. *Louisiana Troops 1720–1770.* Fort Worth, Tex.: American Reference Publishers, 1965.

Kinnaird, Lawrence. *Spain in the Mississippi Valley, 1765–1794.* Washington, D.C.: Government Printing Office, 1949.

Madeull, Charles R. *The Census Tables for the French Colony of Louisiana from 1699 through 1722.* Baltimore: Clearfield Co., 1983.

McDermott, John F. *The Spanish in the Mississippi Valley, 1762–1804.* Urbana: University of Illinois Press, 1974.

Mills, Elizabeth. *Natchitoches Colonials: Military Rolls, and Tax Lists, 1722–1803.* Chicago: Adams Press, 1981.

Olmsted, Virginia L. "Spanish Enlistment Papers of New Mexico, 1732–1800." *National Genealogical Society Quarterly* 77 (1979) 229–36, 294–301; 78 (1980) 51–60, 121–22.

Robichaux, Albert J. *Louisiana Census and Militia Lists, 1770–1789.* 2 vols. Harvey, La., 1973–74.

Sanders, Mary E. *Records of Attakapas District, Louisiana.* 3 vols. Lafayette, La., 1962–74.

Revolutionary War

Various States

African American and American Indian Patriots of the Revolutionary War. Washington, D.C.: National Society Daughters of the American Revolution, 2001.

Benson, Adolph B. *Sweden and the American Revolution.* Baltimore: Clearfield Co., 1926.

Bockstruck, Lloyd DeWitt. *Revolutionary War Bounty Land Grants Awarded by State Governments*. Baltimore: Genealogical Publishing Co., 1996.

A Census of Pensioners for Revolutionary or Military Services; With Their Names, Ages, and Places of Residence, as Returned by the Marshals of the Several Judicial Districts Under the Act for Taking the Sixth Census. Washington, D.C., 1841, 1956. Reprint, Baltimore: Genealogical Books in Print, 1996.

Claghorn, Charles E. *Naval Officers of the American Revolution, a Concise Biographical Dictionary.* Metuchen, N.J.: Scarecrow Press, 1988.

———. *Women Patriots of the American Revolution: A Biographical Dictionary.* Metuchen, N.J.: Scarecrow Press, 1991.

Clark, Murtie June. *Index to U.S. Invalid Pension Records, 1801–1815.* 1991. Reprint, Baltimore: Genealogical Publishing Co., 2000.

———. *The Pension Lists of 1792–1795, with Other Revolutionary War Pension Records.* Baltimore: Genealogical Publishing Co., 1991. Reissued 1996.

———. *The Pension Roll of 1835.* 4 vols. Baltimore: Genealogical Publishing Co., 1992.

A General Index to a Census of Pensioners for Military Service, 1840. Genealogical Society of The Church of Jesus Christ of Latter-day Saints. Baltimore: Genealogical Publishing Co., 1965.

Dandridge, Danske B. *American Prisoners of the Revolution.* Baltimore: Genealogical Publishing Co., 1967.

Duncan, Louis C. *Medical Men in the American Revolution, 1775–1783.* Carlisle Barracks, Pa.: Medical Field Service School, 1931.

Gephart, Ronald M. *Revolutionary America 1763–1789, a Bibliography.* 2 vols. Washington, D.C.: Library of Congress, 1984.

Godfrey, Carlos E. *The Commander-in-Chief's Guard: Revolutionary War.* Baltimore: Genealogical Publishing Co., 1972.

Greene, Robert Ewell. *Black Courage 1775–1783, Documentation of Black Participation in the American Revolution.* Washington, D.C.: National Society Daughters of the American Revolution, 1984.

Harper, Josephine L. *Guide to Draper Manuscripts*. Madison, Wis.: State Historical Society of Wisconsin, 1983.

Hatcher, Patricia Law. *Abstract of Graves of Revolutionary Patriots.* 4 vols. Dallas: Pioneer Heritage Press, 1987–88.

Heitman, Francis B. *Historical Register of Officers of the Continental Army During the War of the Revolution, April 1775 to December 1783.* Baltimore: Genealogical Publishing Co., 1967. Indexed online at <www.ancestry.com>.

Is That Service Right? Washington, D.C.: National Society Daughters of the American Revolution, 1986.

Kaminkow, Marion J., and Jack Kaminkow. *Mariners of the American Revolution.* Baltimore: Magna Carta Book Co., 1967.

Les Combattants Francais de la Guere Americaine 1778–1783. Baltimore: Genealogical Publishing Co., 1969.

Letter from the Secretary of War, Communicating a Transcript of the Pension List of the United States. . . . [June 1, 1813]. Washington, D.C.: A and G Way, 1813.

Letter from the Secretary of War, Transmitting a Report of the Names, Ranks, and Line of Every Person Placed on the Pension List in Pursuance of the Act of the 18th March 1818, &c. Baltimore: Southern Book Co., 1959.

McLane, Curren R. *American Chaplains of the Revolution.* Louisville, Ky.: National Society Sons of the American Revolution, 1991.

National Genealogical Society. *Index of Revolutionary War Pension Applications in the National Archives.* Bicentennial edition, rev. and enl. Washington, D.C.: National Genealogical Society, 1976.

Neagles, James C. *Summer Soldiers: A Survey and Index of Revolutionary War Courts-Martial.* Salt Lake City: Ancestry, 1986. Online database at <www.ancestry.com>.

Newman, Debra L. *List of Black Servicemen Compiled from the War Department Collection of Revolutionary War Records.* Washington, D.C.: National Archives, 1974.

O'Brien, Michael J. *A Hidden Phase of American History, Ireland's Struggle for Liberty.* Baltimore: Genealogical Publishing Co., 1973.

Pensioners of Revolutionary War Struck off the Roll with an Added Index to States. Baltimore: Clearfield Co., 1989.

Pension List of 1820. Baltimore: Genealogical Publishing Co., 1991.

Peterson, Clarence S. *Known Military Dead During the American Revolutionary War 1775–1783.* Baltimore, 1959.

Pierce, John. *Pierce's Register, Register of the Certificates Issued by John Pierce, Esquire, Paymaster General and Commissioner of Army Accounts for the United States to Officers and Soldiers of the Continental Army Under Act of July 4, 1783.* Baltimore: Genealogical Publishing Co., 1969.

Rejected or Suspended Applications for Revolutionary War Pensions with an Added Index to States. Baltimore: Genealogical Publishing Co., 1969.

Resolutions, Laws, and Ordinances Relating to the Pay, Half-pay, Commutation of Half-Pay, Bounty Lands and Other Promises Made by Congress. Baltimore: Genealogical Publishing Co., 1998.

Saffell, William T. R. *Records of the Revolutionary War.* 3rd ed. Baltimore: Genealogical Publishing Co., 1969.

Schweitzer, George K. *Revolutionary War Genealogy.* Knoxville, Tenn., 1982.

Smith, Clifford Neal. *Federal Land Series, a Calendar of Archival Material on the Land Patents Issued by the United States Government, with Subject, Tract and Name Indexes.* 4 vols. in 5. Chicago: American Library Association, 1972–86.

Sons of the American Revolution Patriot Index CD, Edition III. CD-ROM. Progeny Publishing, 2002.

U.S. House of Representatives. *Digested Summary and Alphabetical Index of Private Claims Which Have Been Presented to the House of Representatives from the First to the 31st Congress, Exhibiting the Action of Congress on Each Claim.* 3 vols. Baltimore: Genealogical Publishing Co., 1970.

White, J. Todd, and Charles H. Lesser. *Fighters for Independence: A Guide to Sources for Biographical Information on Soldiers of the American Revolution.* Chicago: University of Chicago Press, 1977.

White, Virgil D. *Genealogical Abstracts of Revolutionary War Pension Files.* 4 vols. Waynesboro, Tenn.: National Historical Publishing Co., 1990–. A cumulative index completes the set.

———. *Index to Revolutionary Service Records.* 4 vols. Waynesboro, Tenn.: National Historical Publishing Co., 1995.

Alabama

Pierce, Alycon. *Selected Final Pension Payment Vouchers, 1818–1864. Alabama: Decatur, Huntsville, Mobile, Tuscaloosa.* Lovettsville, Va.: Willow Bend Books, 1997.

Arizona

Hough, Granville W. *Spain's Arizona Patriots in Its 1779–1783 War with England During the American Revolution.* Laguna Hills, Calif.: the author, 1999.

California

Hough, Granville W. *Spain's California Patriots in Its 1779–1782 War with England During the American Revolution.* 2 vols. Laguna Hills, Calif.: the author, 1998–1999.

Canada

DeMarce, Virginia E. *Canadian Participants in the American Revolution: An Index.* Arlington, Va.: V. DeMarce, 1980.

Connecticut

Abstracts from Meetings Held to Determine Procedure of Connecticut Towns in the Revolutionary War, 1774–1784. Microfilm, 4 rolls.

Boyle, Joseph L. *Fire Cake and Water: The Connecticut Infantry at the Valley Forge Encampment.* Baltimore: Clearfield, 1999.

Connecticut Archives: Revolutionary War (Selected Papers), Series 1–3, 1763–1820. Microfilm, 60 rolls.

Connecticut Revolutionary Pensioners. Baltimore: Genealogical Publishing Co., 1982.

Jacobus, Donald Lines. *Revolutionary War Records of Fairfield, Connecticut.* 1932. Reprint, Baltimore: Genealogical Publishing Co., 2004.

List and Returns of Connecticut Men in the Revolution, 1775–1783. Hartford: Connecticut Historical Society, 1909.

Minority Military Service Connecticut 1775–1783. Washington, D.C.: National Society Daughters of the American Revolution, 1988.

Revolutionary War Orderly Books of Regiments and Companies of the Continental Army. Microfilm, 8 rolls.

Rolls and Lists of Connecticut Men in the Revolution, 1775–1783. Hartford: Connecticut Historical Society, 1901.

White, David O. *Connecticut's Black Soldiers, 1775–1783.* Pequot, Conn., 1973.

Delaware

Delaware Archives. Vols. 1–3. Wilmington, Del.: Mercantile Printing Co., 1911–19.

Gooch, Eleanor B. "Delaware Signers of the Oaths of Allegiance." *National Historical Magazine* 75 (September–December 1941); 76 (January 1942).

Peden, Henry C. *Revolutionary Patriots of Delaware, 1775–1783: Genealogical and Historical Information on the Men and Women of Delaware Who Served the American Cause During the War with Great Britain, 1775–1783.* Westminster, Md.: Family Line Publications, 1995.

United States Treasurer Department, Accounting Offices. *Final Revolutionary War Pension Payment Vouchers Delaware.* Microfilm, M2079, 1 roll. Washington, D.C.: National Archives Microfilm Publication.

Whiteley, William G. *The Revolutionary Soldiers of Delaware.* Wilmington: Historical Society of Delaware, 1896.

District of Columbia

Pierce, Alycon T. *Selected Final Pension Payment Vouchers, 1818–1864: District of Columbia.* Leesburg, Va.: Willow Bend Books, 1998.

Georgia

Arnold, H. Ross. *Georgia Revolutionary Soldiers & Sailors, Patriots, & Pioneers.* 2 vols. Decatur, Ga.: Georgia Society Sons of the American Revolution, 2001.

Candler, Allen D. *Revolutionary Records of the State of Georgia.* 3 vols. Atlanta: Franklin-Turner Company, 1908.

Davis, Robert Scott. *Georgia Citizens and Soldiers of the American Revolution.* Easley, S.C.: Southern Historical Press, 1979.

———. *Georgians in the Revolution at Kettle Creek (Wilkes Co.) and Burke County.* Easley, S.C.: Southern Historical Press, 1986.

Hemperley, Marion. *Military Certificates of Georgia 1776–1780 on File in the Surveyor General Department.* Atlanta: State Printing Office, 1983.

Houston, Martha L. *600 Revolutionary Soldiers and Widows of Revolutionary Soldiers Living in Georgia in 1827–28.* Ann Arbor, Mich.: Edwards Brothers, 1946.

Knight, Lucian L. *Georgia's Roster of the Revolution.* Baltimore: Genealogical Publishing Co., 1967.

McCall, Ettie. *Roster of Revolutionary Soldiers in Georgia.* 3 vols. Baltimore: Genealogical Publishing Co., 1968.

O'Kelley, Nicole M., and Mary B. Warren. *Georgia Revolutionary Bounty Land Records, 1783–1785.* Athens, Ga.: Heritage Papers, 1992.

United States Treasurer Department, Accounting Offices. *Final Revolutionary War Payment Vouchers: Georgia.* Microfilm, M1746, 6 rolls. Washington, D.C.: National Archives Microfilm Publication.

Warren, Mary Bondurant. *Revolutionary Memoirs and Muster Rolls.* Athens, Ga.: Heritage Papers, 1994.

Indiana

English, William Hayden. *Conquest of the Country Northwest of the River Ohio, 1778–1782, and Life of Gen. George Rogers Clark Volumes I and II.* New York: Arno Press, 1971. The bounty-land recipients in Clark Co., Indiana, as well as muster and pay rolls, appear on pp. 1034–1122.

List of Non-commissioned Officers and Soldiers of the Virginia Line on Continental Establishment Whose Names Appear on the Army Register and Who Have Not Received Bounty Land. Indianapolis: Ye Olde Genealogy Shoppe, n.d.

Kentucky

Calendar of the George Rogers Clark Papers of the Draper Collection of Manuscripts. Utica, Ky.: McDowell Publications, 1985.

Carstens, Kenneth C. *The Calendar and Quartermaster Books of General George Rogers Clark's Fort Jefferson, Kentucky, 1780–1781.* Bowie, Md.: Heritage Books, 2000.

———. *The Personnel of George Rogers Clark's Fort Jefferson and the Civilian Community of Clarksville, Kentucky 1780–1781.* Bowie, Md.: Heritage Books, 1999.

Harding, Margery H. *George Rogers Clark and His Men: Military Records, 1778–1784.* Frankfort, Ky.: Kentucky Historical Society, 1981.

Seineke, Katherine W. *The George Rogers Clark Adventure in the Illinois and Selected Documents of the American Revolution at the Frontier Posts.* New Orleans: Polyanthos, 1981.

Quisenberry, Anderson C. *Revolutionary Soldiers in Kentucky: Containing a Roll of the Officers of Virginia Line Who Received Land Bounties; a Roll of the Revolutionary Pensioners in Kentucky; a List of the Illinois Regiment Who Served Under George Rogers Clark in the Northwest Campaign.* Baltimore: Genealogical Publishing Co., 1974.

Louisiana

DeVille, Winston. *Louisiana Soldiers in the American Revolution.* Ville Platte, La.: Smith Books, 1991.

Hough, Granville W. *Spain's Louisiana Patriots in Its 1779–1783 War with England During the American Revolution.* Midway City, Calif.: SHHAR Press, 2000.

Pierce, Alycon T. *Selected Final Pension Payment Vouchers, 1818–1864. Louisiana: New Orleans.* Athens, Ga.: Iberian Publishing, 1996.

Maine

Fisher, Carleton E. *Soldiers, Sailors, and Patriots of the Revolutionary War: Maine.* Louisville, Ky.: National Society Sons of the American Revolution, 1982.

Flagg, Charles A. *An Alphabetical Index of Revolutionary Pensioners Living in Maine.* Baltimore: Genealogical Publishing Co., 1967.

House, Charles J. *Names of Soldiers of the American Revolution Who Applied for State Bounty under Resolves of March 17, 1835; March 24, 1836; and March 20, 1836 as Appears of Record in the Land Office.* Baltimore: Genealogical Publishing Co., 1967.

Maine Old Cemetery Association. *Revolutionary War Soldiers Index.* Microfiche, 13.

Maryland

Brumbaugh, Gaius M. *Maryland Records: Colonial, Revolutionary, County and Church from Original Sources.* 2 vols. Baltimore: Genealogical Publishing Co., 1985.

———, and Margaret R. Hodges. *Revolutionary Records of Maryland.* 1924. Reprint, Baltimore: Genealogical Publishing Co., 2003.

Calendar of Maryland State Papers: The Red Books; the Brown Books; the Executive Miscellanea. Annapolis, Md.: Hall of Records, 1950–55.

Carothers, Bettie S. *Maryland Oaths of Fidelity.* 2 vols. The author, n.d.

———. *Maryland Soldiers Entitled to Lands Westward of Fort Cumberland.* The author, 1973.

Clements, S. Eugene. *Maryland Militia in the Revolutionary War.* Silver Spring, Md.: Family Line Publications, 1987.

Journal and Correspondence of the Council of Safety, 1775–1777. Archives of Maryland, vols. XI, XVI, and XXI. Baltimore: Maryland Historical Society, 1892–1901.

Journal and Correspondence of the State Council, 1777–1789. Archives of Maryland, vols. XLIII, XLV, XLVII, and XLVIII. Baltimore: Maryland Historical Society, 1924–31.

Meyer, Mary K. "Revolutionary War Soldiers Granted Pensions by the State of Maryland." *Bulletin of the Maryland Genealogical Society* 4 (November 1963); 7 (February 1966).

———. *Westward of Fort Cumberland: Military Lots Set Off for Maryland's Revolutionary Soldiers with an Appended List of Revolutionary Soldiers Granted Pensions by the State of Maryland.* Finksberg, Md.: Pipe Creek Publications, 1993.

Muster Rolls and Other Records of Service of Maryland Troops in the American Revolution, 1775–1783. Archives of Maryland, vol. 18. Baltimore: Genealogical Publishing Co., 1972.

Newman, Harry W. *Maryland Revolutionary Records.* Washington, D.C.: the compiler, 1938.

Papenfuse, Edward C. *An Inventory of Maryland State Papers.* Vol. 1. *The Era of the American Revolution, 1775–1783.* Annapolis, Md.: Hall of Records Commission, 1977.

Peden, Henry C. *Maryland Public Service Records, 1775–1783: A Compendium of Men and Women of Maryland Who Rendered Aid in Support of the American Cause Against Great Britain During the Revolutionary War.* Westminster, Md.: Willow Bend Books, 2002.

———. *Revolutionary Patriots of Anne Arundel County, Maryland.* Westminster, Md.: Family Line Publications, 1992.

———. *Revolutionary Patriots of Baltimore Town and Baltimore County, Maryland 1775–1783.* Silver Spring, Md.: Family Line Publications, 1988.

———. *Revolutionary Patriots of Calvert and St. Mary's Counties, Maryland 1775–1783.* Westminster, Md.: Family Line Publications, 1996.

———. *Revolutionary Patriots of Caroline County, Maryland 1775–1783.* Westminster, Md.: Family Line Publications, 1997.

———. *Revolutionary Patriots of Cecil County, Maryland 1775–1783.* Westminster, Md.: Family Line Publications, 1991.

———. *Revolutionary Patriots of Charles County, Maryland 1775–1783.* Westminster, Md.: Family Line Publications, 1997.

———. *Revolutionary Patriots of Dorchester County, Maryland 1775–1783.* Westminster, Md.: Family Line Publications, 1998.

———. *Revolutionary Patriots of Frederick County, Maryland 1775–1783.* Westminster, Md.: Family Line Publications, 1995.

———. *Revolutionary Patriots of Kent and Queen Anne's Counties, Maryland 1775–1783.* Westminster, Md.: Family Line Publications, 1995.

———. *Revolutionary Patriots of Prince George's County, Maryland 1775–1783.* Westminster, Md.: Family Line Publications, 1997.

———. *Revolutionary Patriots of Talbot County, Maryland 1775–1783.* Westminster, Md.: Family Line Publications, 1998.

———. *Revolutionary Patriots of Washington County, Maryland 1775–1783.* Westminster, Md.: Family Line Publications, 1998.

———. *Revolutionary Patriots of Worcester & Somerset County, Maryland 1775–1783.* Westminster, Md.: Willow Bend Books, 1999.

———. *Revolutionary Patriots of Maryland, 1775–1783: A Supplement. Second Supplement.* Westminster, Md.: Willow Bend Books, 2000–02.

Pierce, Alycon T. *Selected Final Pension Payment Vouchers, 1818–1864. Maryland: Baltimore.* Lovettsville, Md.: Willow Bend Books, 1997.

Powell, Judy. *Maryland Revolutionary War Records, 1727–1851.* Roanoke, Tex.: J. Powell, 1993.

Scharf, John S. *History of Western Maryland.* Philadelphia: Louis H. Everts, 1882. Bounty-land recipients appear in vol. 1, pp. 146–61.

Stewart, Rieman. *A History of the Maryland Line in the Revolutionary War, 1775–1783.* Society of the Cincinnati of Maryland, 1969.

Massachusetts

Allen, Gardner Weld. *Massachusetts Privateers of the American Revolution.* Cambridge, Mass.: Harvard University Press, 1927.

Draper, Belle. *Honor Roll of Massachusetts Patriots Heretofore Unknown, Being a List of Men and Women Who Loaned Money to the Federal Government During the Years 1777–1779.* Boston, 1899.

Hambrick-Stowe, Charles E., and Donna D. Smerlas. *Massachusetts Militia Companies and Officers in the Lexington Alarm.* Boston: New England Historic Genealogical Society, 1976.

Massachusetts Soldiers and Sailors of the Revolutionary War. 16 vols. Boston: Wright and Potter Printing Co., 1896–1908. There is a seventeen-roll microfilm supplement: *Massachusetts Archives Revolutionary War Index Appendix.*

Minority Military Service: Massachusetts, 1775–1783. Washington, D.C.: National Society Daughters of the American Revolution, 1989.

Muster/Payrolls and Various Papers (1763–1808) of the Revolutionary War. Microfilm, 44 rolls.

U.S. War Department. *Personnel Returns of the 6th Massachusetts Battalion, 1779–1780, and Returns and Accounts of the Military Store of the 8th and 9th Massachusetts Regiment, 1779–1782.* Microfilm, M913, 1 roll. Washington, D.C.: National Archives Microfilm Publication.

Mexico

Hough, Granville W. *Spain's Patriots of Northwestern New Spain from South of the U.S. Border in Its 1779–1783 War with England During the American Revolution.* Midway City, Calif.: SHHAR Press, 2001.

Mississippi

Pierce, Alycon T. *Selected Final Pension Payment Vouchers, 1818–1864. Mississippi: Natchez & Jackson.* Athens, Ga.: Iberian Publishing Co., 1997.

New Hampshire

Batchellor, Albert Sullivan. *Miscellaneous Revolutionary Documents of New Hampshire.* Manchester, N.H.: John B. Clark, 1910.

Bouton, Nathaniel. *State Papers, Documents and Records Relating to the State of New Hampshire.* Vol. 8. New York: AMS Press, 1973.

Gilmore, George C. *Roll of New Hampshire Soldiers at the Battle of Bennington, August 16, 1777.* Baltimore: Clearfield Co., 1995.

Hammond, Isaac Weare. *Rolls of the Soldiers of the Revolutionary War.* 4 vols. Concord, N.H.: Parsons B. Cogswell, 1885–89.

Mevers, Frank C. *Composite Index to Volumes XIV-XVII (Revolutionary Rolls) of the New Hampshire State Papers.* Bowie, Md.: Heritage Books, 1993.

New Jersey

Campbell, James W. S. *Roster Officers of the New Jersey Continental Line in the Revolutionary War Who Were Eligible to Membership in the Society of the Cincinnati.* Bowie, Md.: Heritage Books, 1987.

Damages by the British in New Jersey, 1776–1782 [and] Damages by the Americans in New Jersey, 1776–1782. Microfilm, 2 rolls.

Indexes to Revolutionary War Manuscripts. Microfilm, 9 rolls.

Pierce, Alycon T. *Selected Final Pension Payment Vouchers, 1818–1864. New Jersey: Trenton.* 2 vols. Westminster, Md.: Willow Bend Books, 2000.

Revolutionary War Manuscripts, New Jersey, Numbers 1–10811. Microfilm, 30 rolls.

Revolutionary War Slips, Single Citations of the New Jersey Department of Defense Materials. Microfilm, 120 rolls.

Stratford, Dorothy A. *Certificates and Receipts of Revolutionary New Jersey.* Lambertville, N.J.: Hunterdon House, 1996.

Stryker, William S. *Extracts from American Newspapers: Documents Relating to the Revolutionary History of the State of New Jersey.* New Jersey Archives, 2nd Series, vols. 1–4.

———. *Official Roster of the Officers and Men of New Jersey in the Revolutionary War.* Baltimore: Genealogical Publishing Co., 1967.

Index of Official Roster of the Officers and Men of New Jersey in the Revolutionary War. Newark, N.J.: Works Progress Administration, 1941.

New York

Balloting Book and Other Documents Relating to Military Bounty Lands in the State of New York. Ovid, N.Y.: W. E. Morrison, 1983.

Fernow, Berthold. *New York in the Revolution.* Cottonport, La.: Polyanthos, 1972.

Knight, Erastus C. *New York in the Revolution as Colony and State: Supplement.* Albany, N.Y.: Oliver A. Quayle, 1901.

Mather, Frederic G. *Refugees of 1776 from Long Island to Connecticut.* Albany, N.Y.: J. B. Lyon Co., 1913.

Muster and Pay Rolls of the War of the Revolution, 1775–83. Collections of the New York Historical Society, vols. 47 and 48. New York: the society, 1916.

Roberts, James A. *New York in the Revolution as Colony and State.* 2nd ed. Albany, N.Y.: Brandow Printing Co., 1898.

North Carolina

Bailey, James D. *Commanders at Kings Mountain.* Greenville, S.C.: A Press, 1980.

Caruthers, Eli. *Revolutionary Incidents and Sketches of Characters, Chiefly in the "Old North State."* Greensboro, N.C.: Guilford County Genealogical Society, 1985.

Draper, Lyman. *King's Mountain and Its Heroes, History of the Battle of Kings Mountain October 7th 1780, and the Events Which Led to It.* Baltimore: Genealogical Publishing Co., 1978.

Haun, Weynette P. *North Carolina Revolutionary Army Accountants, Secretary of State Treasurer's and Comptroller's Papers.* 3 vols. to date. Durham, N.C.: the compiler, 1988–.

Index to Revolutionary Army Accounts, 1776–1792. Microfiche, 6.

Military Land Warrant Book 1783–1841. Microfilm, 1 roll.

Moss, Bobby Gilmer. *Roster of the Patriots in the Battle of Moores Creek Bridge.* Blacksburg, S.C.: Scotia-Hibernia Press, 1992.

North Carolina Revolutionary Army Accounts, 1776–1792. Microfilm, 10 rolls.

North Carolina Revolutionary War Pay Vouchers. Microfilm, 73 rolls.

North Carolina Revolutionary Military Papers. Microfilm, 2 rolls.

North Carolina Revolutionary War State Pensions to Invalids and Widows, 1784–1808. Microfilm, 3 rolls.

Pruitt, Albert B. *Tennessee Land Entries Military Bounty Land, Martin Armstrong's Office.* 8 vols. Whitakers, N.C.: A. B. Pruitt, 1996.

———. *Glasgow Land Fraud Papers: 1783–1800 North Carolina Revolutionary Bounty Land in Tennessee.* 2 vols. N.p.: A. B. Pruitt, 1988.

Roster of Soldiers from North Carolina in the American Revolution with an Appendix Containing a Collection of Miscellaneous Records. Baltimore: Genealogical Publishing Co., 1967.

Schenck, David. *North Carolina, 1780–81: Being a History of the Invasion of the Carolinas by the British Army.* Bowie, Md.: Heritage Books, 2000.

Snow, Carol. *Volunteer Revolutionary Soldiers from North Carolina.* Toast, N.C.: C and L Historical Publications, 1993.

White, Emmett R. *Revolutionary War Soldiers of Western North Carolina.* 2 vols. Easley, S.C.: Southern Historical Press, 1984–1998.

White, Katherine. *The King's Mountain Men: The Story of the Battle with Sketches of the American Soldiers Who Took Part.* Baltimore: Genealogical Publishing Co., 1970.

Ohio

Jackson, Ronald Vern. *Ohio Military Land Warrants, 1789–1801.* North Salt Lake, Utah: Accelerated Indexing Systems International, 1988.

Smith, Clifford Neal. *Grants in the Virginia Military District of Ohio.* Vol. 4 of Federal Land Series. Chicago: American Library Association, 1982–86.

U.S. Veterans Administration. *U.S. Revolutionary War Bounty Land Warrants Used in the U.S. Military District of Ohio and of Related Papers (Acts of 1788, 1803, and 1806).* Microfilm, M829, 16 rolls. Washington, D.C.: National Archives Microfilm Publications.

Pennsylvania

American Revolutionary War Card File. Microfilm, 54 rolls.

Baumann, Roland M. *Guide to the Microfilm of the Miscellaneous Manuscripts of the Revolutionary War Era, 1771–1791 (Manuscript Record Group 275) in the Pennsylvania State Archives, 1 roll.* Harrisburg, Pa.: Pennsylvania Historical and Museum Commission, 1978.

Carousso, Dorothy H. *How to Search for Your Revolutionary Patriot in Pennsylvania.* Philadelphia: Genealogical Society of Pennsylvania, 1975.

Cope, Harry E. *List of Soldiers and Widows of Soldiers Granted Revolutionary War Pensions by the Commonwealth of Pennsylvania.* Greeneburg, Pa.: Daughters of the American Revolution, 1976.

Egle, William H. *Journals and Diaries of the War of the Revolution with List of Officers and Soldiers, 1775–1783.* Pennsylvania Archives, 2nd Series, vol. 15. Harrisburg, Pa.: Secretary of the Commonwealth, 1892.

———. *Muster Rolls of the Navy and Line, Militia and Rangers, 1775–1783.* Pennsylvania Archives, 3rd Series, vol. 23. Harrisburg, Pa.: Secretary of the Commonwealth, 1898.

———. *Pennsylvania in the War of the Revolution, Associated Battalions and Militia, 1775–1783.* Pennsylvania Archives, 2nd Series, vols. 13–14. Harrisburg, Pa.: Clarence M. Busch, 1890–92.

———. *Pennsylvania Women in the American Revolution.* New Orleans: Polyanthos, 1972.

———. *Rolls of Soldiers of the Revolution Pennsylvania Line Found in the Department of the State, Washington, D.C.* Pennsylvania Archives, 2nd Series, vol. 15, 371–560. Harrisburg, Pa.: E. K. Meyers, 1890.

———. *Soldiers of the Pennsylvania Line Entitled to Donation Lands.* Pennsylvania Archives, 3rd Series, vol. 3, 607–57. Harrisburg, Pa.: Harrisburg Publishing Co., 1896.

Gunning, Kathryn McPherson. *Selected Pension Payment Vouchers 1818–1864. Pennsylvania: Philadelphia & Pittsburgh.* 2 vols. Westminster, Md.: Willow Bend Books, 2000.

Linn, John B., and William Egle. *List of Officers and Men of the Pennsylvania Navy, 1775–1781.* Pennsylvania Archives, 2nd Series, vol. 1, 243–434. Harrisburg, Pa.: Clarence M. Busch, 1896.

———. *List of "Soldiers of the Revolution Who Received Pay for Their Services," Taken from Manuscript Record, Having Neither Date nor Title, but Under "Rangers on the Frontiers, 1778–83."* Pennsylvania Archives, 5th Series, vol. 4, 597–777. Harrisburg, Pa.: Harrisburg Publishing Co., 1906.

———. *List of Soldiers Who Served as Rangers on the Frontier, 1778–83.* Pennsylvania Archives, 3rd Series, vol. 23, 193–356. Harrisburg, Pa.: William Stanley Ray, 1898.

———, and William H. Egle. *Pennsylvania in the War of the Revolution, Battalions and Line, 1775–1783.* Pennsylvania Archives, 2nd Series, vols. 10–11. Harrisburg, Pa.: Secretary of the Commonwealth, 1895–96.

Miscellaneous Manuscripts of the Revolutionary War Era, 1771–1791. Microfilm, 1 roll.

Montgomery, Thomas L. *Muster Rolls of the Pennsylvania Navy, 1776–79.* Pennsylvania Archives, 5th Series, vol. 1, 415–609. Harrisburg, Pa.: Harrisburg Publishing Co., 1906.

Muster Rolls and Papers Relative to the Associators and Militia of the Counties. Pennsylvania Archives, 5th Series, vols. 5–8; 6th Series, vols. 1–2. Harrisburg, Pa.: Harrisburg Publishing Co., 1906.

Pennsylvania Historical and Museum Commission. *Guide to the Microfilm of the Records of Pennsylvania Revolutionary Governments 1775–1790.* Harrisburg, Pa.: Pennsylvania Historical and Museum Commission, 1978.

Records of Pennsylvania's Revolutionary Governments, 1775–1790. Microfilm, 54 rolls.

Richards, Henry M. M. *The Pennsylvania-Germans in the Revolutionary War, 1775–1783.* Baltimore: Genealogical Publishing Co., 1978.

Soldiers Who Received Depreciation Pay as per Cancelled Certificates on File in the Division of Public Records Pennsylvania State Library. Pennsylvania Archives, 5th Series, vol. 4, 105–83. Harrisburg, Pa.: Harrisburg Publishing Co., 1906.

Trussell, John B. B. *The Pennsylvania Line: Regimental Organization and Operations, 1776–1783.* Harrisburg, Pa.: Pennsylvania Historical and Museum Commission, 1977.

Whipkey, Harry E. *Guide to the Microfilm of the Records of Pennsylvania's Revolutionary Government, 1775–1790: (Record Group 27) in the Pennsylvania State Archives: 54 Rolls: A Microfilm Project.* Harrisburg, Pa.: Pennsylvania Historical and Museum Commission, 1978, c. 1979.

Rhode Island

Card Index to Military and Naval Records, 1776–1780. Microfilm, 19 rolls.

Cowell, Benjamin. *Spirit of '76 in Rhode Island with Cowell's "Spirit of '76": An Analytical and Explanatory Index by James N. Arnold.* Baltimore: Genealogical Publishing Co., 1973.

Gunning, Kathryn Mcp. *Selected Final Pension Payment Vouchers, 1818–1864: Rhode Island.* Westminster, Md.: Willow Bend Books, 1999.

Minority Military Service: Rhode Island, 1775–1783. Washington, D.C.: National Society Daughters of the American Revolution, 1988.

Rhode Island Revolutionary Names Index, 1776–1780. Microfilm, 22 rolls.

Smith, Joseph J. *Civil and Military List of Rhode Island, 1647–1800.* Providence, R.I.: Preston and Rounds Co., 1901.

South Carolina

Accounts Audited of Claims Growing out of the Revolution in South Carolina. Microfilm, 165 rolls.

Andrews, John L. *South Carolina Revolutionary War Indents: A Schedule.* Columbia, S.C.: SCMAR, 2001.

Annuitants Paid at Charleston 1828–1857; Annuitants Paid at Columbia, 1790–1857. Microfilm, 1 roll.

Bailey, J. D. *Some Heroes of the American Revolution.* Easley, S.C.: Southern Historical Press, 1976.

Bodie, William W. *Marion's Men: A List of Twenty-five Hundred.* Charleston, S.C.: Heisser, 1938.

Draine, Tony, and Edd Bannister. *Guide to South Carolina Pensions and Annuities, 1783–1869.* Columbia, S.C.: Draban Publications, 1991.

———, and John Skinner. *Revolutionary War Bounty Land Grants in South Carolina.* Columbia, S.C.: Congaree Publications, 1986.

Ervin, Sara. *South Carolinians in the Revolution.* Baltimore: Genealogical Publishing Co., 1965.

Gilmer, Georgia, and Elmer Parker. *American Revolution Roster of Fort Sullivan, 1776–1780.* Moultrie, S.C.: Fort Sullivan Chapter, Daughters of the American Revolution, 1980.

Helsley, Alexia J. *South Carolinians in the War for American Independence.* Columbia, S.C.: South Carolina Dept. of Archives and History, 2000.

Lewis, James A. *Neptune's Militia: The Frigate South Carolina During the American Revolution.* Kent, Ohio: Kent State University Press, 1999.

McCardy, Edward. *The History of South Carolina in the Revolution, 1775–1780.* New York: Russell and Russell, 1969.

Moss, Bobby B. *The Patriots at the Cowpens.* Greenville, S.C.: A Press, 1985.

———. *The Patriots at King's Mountain.* Blacksburg, S.C.: Scotia-Hibernia Press, 1990.

———. *Roster of South Carolina Patriots in the American Revolution.* Baltimore: Genealogical Publishing Co., 1983.

Pierce, Alycon T. *Selected Final Pension Payment Vouchers, 1818–1864. South Carolina: Charleston.* Athens, Ga.: Iberian Publishing Co., 1996.

Revill, Janie. *Copy of the Original Index Book Showing the Revolutionary Claims Filed in South Carolina Between August 20, 1783 and August 31, 1786.* Baltimore: Genealogical Publishing Co., 1969.

Salley, Alexander S. *Audited Accounts of Revolutionary Claims Against South Carolina.* 3 vols. Columbia, S.C.: State Company, 1935–43.

———. *Journal of the Commissioners of the Navy of South Carolina October 8, 1776–March 1, 1779, July 22, 1779–March 23, 1780.* 2 vols. Columbia, S.C.: State Company, 1912–13.

———. *South Carolina Provincial Troops Named in Papers of the First Council of Safety of the Revolutionary Party in South Carolina, June–November, 1775.* Baltimore: Genealogical Publishing Co., 1977.

Stub Entries to Indents Issued in Payment of Claims Against South Carolina, Growing out of the Revolution. 12 vols. Columbia, S.C.: State Company, 1919–57.

Tennessee

Bates, Lucy W. *Roster of Soldiers and Patriots of the American Revolution Buried in Tennessee.* Rev. ed. Brentwood: Tennessee Society, Daughters of the American Revolution, 1979.

Texas

Hough, Granville W. *Spain's Texas Patriots in Its 1778–1783 War with England During the American Revolution.* Midway City, Calif.: SHHAR Press, 2000.

Thonhoff, Robert H. *The Texas Connection with the American Revolution.* Burnett, Tex.: Eakin Press, 1981.

Vermont

American Revolution Records. Microfilm, 4 rolls.

Crocket, Walter H. *Soldiers of the Revolutionary War Buried in Vermont.* Baltimore: Genealogical Publishing Co., 1973.

Fisher, Carleton Edward, and Sue Gray Fisher. *Soldiers, Sailors, and Patriots of the Revolutionary War—Vermont.* Camden, Maine: Picton Press, 1992.

Goodrich, John E. *Rolls of the Soldiers in the Revolutionary War, 1775 to 1783.* Rutland, Vt.: Tuttle Co., 1904.

Virginia

Abercrombie, Janice L., and Richard Slatten. *Virginia Revolutionary Publick Claims.* 3 vols. Athens, Ga.: Iberian Publishing Co., 1992.

Brown, Margie G. *Genealogical Abstracts Revolutionary War Veterans, Script Act 1852.* Decorah, Iowa: Anundsen Publishing Co., 1990.

Brumbaugh, Gaius M. *Revolutionary War Records.* Baltimore: Genealogical Publishing Co., 1967.

Burgess, Louis A. *Virginia Soldiers of 1776.* 3 vols. Spartanburg, S.C.: Reprint Co., 1973.

Calendar of Virginia State Papers and Other Manuscripts. Vols. 1–3. New York: Kraus Reprint Corp., 1968.

Church, Randolph W. *Virginia Legislative Petitions, Bibliography, Calendar, and Abstracts from Original Sources, 6 May 1776–21 June 1782.* Richmond: Virginia State Library, 1984.

Dorman, John Frederick. *Virginia Revolutionary Pension Applications.* 51 vols. to date. Cumulative Index, v. 1–50, 4 vols.

Eckenrode, Hamilton J. *Virginia Soldiers of the American Revolution.* 2 vols. Richmond: Virginia State Library and Archives, 1989.

George Rogers Clark Papers. Microfilm, 13 rolls.

Gwathmey, John H. *Historical Register of Virginians in the Revolution: Soldiers, Sailors, Marines 1775–1783.* Baltimore: Genealogical Publishing Co., 1987.

Hopkins, William L. *Virginia Revolutionary War Land Grant Claims 1783–1850 (Rejected).* Richmond, Va., 1988.

Jackson, Luther P. *Virginia Negro Soldiers and Seamen in the Revolutionary War.* Norfolk, Va.: Guide Quality Press, 1944.

McAllister, Joseph T. *Virginia Militia in the Revolutionary War.* Bowie, Md.: Heritage Books, 1989.

Minnis, M. Lee. *The First Virginia Regiment of Foot 1775–1783.* Lovettsville, Va.: Willow Bend Books, 1998.

Nottingham, Stratton. *Soldiers and Sailors of the Eastern Shore of Maryland.* Westminster, Md.: Family Line Publications, 1995.

Pierce, Alycon T. *Selected Final Pension Payment Vouchers 1818–1864. Virginia: Richmond & Wheeling.* 2 vols. Athens, Ga.: Iberian Publishing Co., 1996.

Sanchez-Saavedra, E. M. *A Guide to Virginia Military Organizations in the American Revolution 1774–1787.* Richmond: Virginia State Library, 1978.

Special Report: Preservation of Revolutionary War Veteran Gravesites in Virginia; Report of the Joint Legislative Audit and Review Commission to the Governor and General Assembly of Virginia. Richmond: Commonwealth of Virginia, 2001.

Stewart, Robert A. *History of Virginia's Navy of the Revolution.* Richmond, Va.: Mitchell and Hotchkiss, 1933.

U.S. Veterans Administration. *Virginia Half-Pay and Other Related Revolutionary War Pension Application Files.* Microfilm, M910, 18 rolls. Washington, D.C.: National Archives Microfilm Publications.

Van Schreeven, William J. *Revolutionary Virginia, the Road to Independence.* 7 vols. in 8. University Press of Virginia, 1973–83.

Virginia Revolutionary War Bounty Warrants. Microfilm, 29 rolls.

Virginia Revolutionary War Public Service Claims. Microfilm, 6 rolls.

Virginia Revolutionary War Public Service Claims: Culpeper County Classes. Microfilm, 1 rolls.

Virginia Revolutionary War Rejected Claims for Bounty Land. Microfilm, 15 rolls.

Virginia Revolutionary War State Pension Applications. Microfilm, 15 rolls.

Virginia Revolutionary War State Pensions. Richmond: Virginia Genealogical Society, 1980.

Wardell, Patrick G. *Virginia/West Virginia Genealogical Data from Revolutionary War Pension and Bounty Land Warrant Records.* 6 vols. Bowie, Md.: Heritage Books, 1988–98.

Wilson, Howard M. *Great Valley Patriots: Western Virginia in the Struggle for Liberty, A Bicentennial Project.* Verona, Va.: McClure Press, 1976.

Wilson, Richard Eugene. *Index to the George Rogers Clark Papers: The Illinois Regiment; Based on the Microfilmed George Rogers Clark Papers at the Virginia State Library and Archives.* Microfiche, 2. Chicago: Society of the Colonial Wars in the State of Illinois and the Sons of the Revolution in the State of Illinois, 1998.

Wilson, Samuel M. *Catalogue of Revolutionary Soldiers and Sailors of the Commonwealth of Virginia to Whom Bounty Warrants Were Granted by Virginia for Military Service in the War of Independence.* 1913. Reprint, Baltimore: Genealogical Publishing Co., 2002.

West Indies

Hough, Granville W. *Spanish, French, Dutch, and American Patriots of the West Indies During the American Revolution.* Midway City, Calif.: SHHAR Press, 2001.

West Virginia

Johnston, Ross B. *West Virginians in the American Revolution.* Parkersburg, 1939–47. Reprint, Baltimore: Genealogical Publishing Co., 2002.

Reddy, Anne W. *West Virginia Revolutionary Ancestors Whose Services Were Non-Military.* 1930. Reprint, Baltimore: Genealogical Publishing Co., 2003.

Loyalists in the Revolutionary War

Antliff, W. Bruce. *Loyalists Settlements 1783–1789: New Evidence of Canadian Loyalist Claims.* Ontario: Ministry of Citizenship and Culture, 1985.

Brown, Wallace. *The Good Americans: The Loyalists in the American Revolution.* New York: William Morrow and Co., 1969.

Bunnell, Paul L. *The New Loyalist Index.* Bowie, Md.: Heritage Books, 1989.

———. *Research Guide to Loyalist Ancestors: A Directory to Archives Manuscripts and Published Sources.* Bowie, Md.: Heritage Books, 1990.

The Centennial of the Settlement of Upper Canada by the United Empire Loyalists, 1784–1884. Boston: Gregg Press, 1972.

Clark, Murtie J. *Loyalists in the Southern Campaign of the Revolutionary War.* 3 vols. 1981. Reprint, Baltimore: Genealogical Publishing Co., 1999–2003.

Coldham, Peter Wilson. *American Loyalist Claims.* Washington, D.C.: National Genealogical Society, 1980.

———. *American Migrations 1765–1799: The Lives, the Times, and Families of Colonial Americans Who Remained Loyal to the British Crown Before, During, and After the Revolutionary War, as Related in Their Own Words and Through Their Correspondence.* Baltimore: Genealogical Publishing Co., 2000.

Demond, Robert O. *The Loyalists in North Carolina During the Revolution.* Hampden, Conn.: Archer Books, 1964.

Dubeau, Sharon. *New Brunswick Loyalists: A Bicentennial Tribute.* Lambertville, N.J.: Generation Press, 1983.

Dwyer, Clifford S. *Index to Series I of American Loyalists Claims.* DeFuniak Springs, Fla.: RAM Publishing, 1985.

———. *Index to Series II of American Loyalists Claims.* DeFuniak Springs, Fla: RAM Publishing, 1985.

East, Robert A. *Connecticut's Loyalists.* Chester, Conn.: Pequot Press, 1974.

Fitzgerald, E. Keith. *Loyalist Lists, Over 2000 Loyalist Names and Families from the Haldimand Papers.* Ontario Genealogical Society, 1984.

Gilroy, Marion, comp. *Loyalists and Land Settlement in Nova Scotia.* Baltimore: Genealogical Publishing Co., 1980.

Great Britain Exchequer and Audit Department. *American Loyalists Claims: Series I and II.* Microfilm, 189 rolls.

Hammond, Otis Grant. *Tories of New Hampshire in the War of the Revolution.* Boston: Gregg Press, 1972.

Hancock, Harold B. *The Loyalists of Revolutionary Delaware.* University of Delaware Press, 1977.

Hodges, Graham R. *The Black Loyalist Directory: African Americans in Exile After the American Revolution.* New York: Garland Pub. in association with the New England Historic Genealogical Society, 1996.

Jones, E. Alfred. *The Loyalists of Massachusetts, Their Memorials, Petitions and Claims.* London: Saint Catherine Press, 1930.

———. *The Loyalists of New Jersey, Their Memorials, Petitions, Claims, Etc., from English Records.* Newark: New Jersey Historical Society, 1927.

Kelby, William. *Orderly Book of the Three Battalions of Loyalists Commanded by Brigadier-General Oliver de Lancey, 1776–1778.* Baltimore: Genealogical Publishing Co., 1972.

Lambert, Robert S. *South Carolina Loyalists in the American Revolution.* Columbia: University of South Carolina Press, 1987.

Livinston, Mildred R. *Upper Canada Sons and Daughters of United Empire Loyalists.* Kingston, Ontario: Brown and Martin, 1981.

Maas, David E. *Divided Hearts: Massachusetts Loyalists 1765–1790. A Biographical Directory.* Boston: New England Historic Genealogical Society, 1980.

Montgomery, Thomas L. *Forfeited Estates Inventories and Sales, Pennsylvania Archives.* 6th Series, vols. 12–13. Harrisburg, Pa.: Harrisburg Publishing Co., 1907.

Moss, Bobby Gilmer. *Roster of the Loyalists at the Battle of Moores Creek Bridge.* Blacksburg, S.C.: Scotia-Hibernia Press, 1992.

———. *Roster of the Loyalists in the Battle of King's Mountain.* Blacksburg, S.C.: Scotia-Hibernia Press, 1998.

New, M. Christopher. *Maryland Loyalists in the American Revolution.* Centerville, Md.: Tidewater, Publishers, 1996.

Palmer, Gregory. *A Bibliography of Loyalist Source Material in the United States, Canada, and Great Britain.* Westport, Conn.: Meckler Publishing Co., 1982.

Paltsits, Victor Hugo. *Minutes of the Commissioners for Detecting and Defeating Conspiracies in the State of New York.* Albany County Sessions 1778–1781. 3 vols. in 2. Boston: Gregg Press, 1972.

Peck, Epaphroditus. *The Loyalists of Connecticut.* New Haven, Conn.: Yale University Press, 1934.

Peterson, Jean, and Lynn Murphy. *The Loyalist Guide to Nova Scotian Loyalists and Their Documents.* Halifax: Nova Scotia Public Archives, 1983.

Pruitt, Albert Bruce. *Abstracts of Sales of Confiscated Loyalist Land and Property in North Carolina.* The author, 1989.

Reid, William D. *The Loyalists in Ontario: The Sons and Daughters of the American Loyalists of Upper Canada.* 1973. Reprint, Baltimore: Genealogical Publishing Co., 1994.

Rush, John E. *Carleton's Loyalist Index: A Select Index to the Names of the Loyalists and Their Associates Contained in the British Headquarters Papers, New York City, 1774–1783 (The Carleton Papers).*

Ryerson, Adolphus E. *The Loyalists of America: Their Times from 1620–1816.* 2 vols. Toronto: William Briggs, 1880.

Sabine, Lorenzo. *Biographical Sketches of Loyalists of the American Revolution.* 2 vols. Port Washington, N.Y.: Kennikat Press, 1966.

Siebert, Wilbur H. *Loyalists in East Florida, 1774–1785.* 2 vols. Boston: Gregg Press, 1972.

———. *The Loyalists of West Florida and the Natchez District.* N.p., 1916. Reprinted from the *Mississippi Valley Historical Review* 2 (March 1916).

Smith, Clifford Neal. *Notes on Hession Soldiers who Remained in Canada and the United States after the American Revolution, 1775–1784.* Westland Publications, 1992.

Thomas, William H. B. *Remarkable High Tories: Supporters of King and Parliament in Revolutionary Massachusetts.* Bowie, Md.: Heritage Books, 2001.

Stark, James H. *The Loyalists of Massachusetts and the Other Side of the American Revolution.* Boston: W. B. Clarke Co., 1910.

Tyler, John W. *Connecticut Loyalists: An Analysis of Loyalist Land Confiscations in Greenwich, Stamford, and Norfolk.* New Orleans: Polyanthos, 1977.

Van Tyne, Claude H. *The Loyalists in the American Revolution.* Bowie, Md.: Heritage Books, 1989.

Wallace, W. Stewart. *United Empire Loyalists. A Chronicle of the Great Migration.* Boston: Gregg, 1972.

Wright, Esther C. *Loyalists of New Brunswick.* Hantsport, Nova Scotia: the author, 1981.

Yoshpe, Harry B. *The Disposition of Loyalist Estates in the Southern District of New York.* New York: AMS Press, 1967.

German Auxiliary Troops in the Revolutionary War

Burgoyne, Bruce E. *The Waldeck Soldiers of the American Revolution.* Bowie, Md.: Heritage Books, 1991.

DeMarce, Virginia E. *Mercenary Troops from Anhalt-Zerbst, Germany Who Served with the British Forces During the American Revolution.* McNeal, Ariz.: Westland Publications, 1984.

———. *The Settlement of Former German Auxiliary Troops in Canada After the American Revolution.* Supplement. Sparta, Wis.: Joy Reisinger, 1984.

Dickore, Marie P. *Hessian Soldiers in the American Revolution, Records of Their Marriages and Baptisms of Their Children in America Performed by the Rev. G.C. Coster, 1776–1783, Chaplain of Two Hessian Regiments.* Cincinnati, Ohio: C. J. Krehbiel Co., 1959.

Dulfer, Kurt. *Hessische Truppen im Amerikanischen Unabhängigkeitskrieg (Hetrina).* 6 vols. Marburg, Germany: Institut für Arachivwissenschaft, 1972–90.

Eelking, Max von. *The German Allied Troops in the North American War of Independence, 1776–1783.* Genealogical Publishing Co., 1969.

Journal of the Johannes Schwalm Historical Association 1 (1981).

Kelly, Arthur C. M. *Hessian Troops in the American Revolution: Extracts from the Hetrina.* 6 vols. Rhinebeck, N.Y.: Kinship, 1991–95.

Lowell, Edward J. *The Hessians and Other Auxiliaries of Great Britain in the Revolutionary War.* Williamstown, Mass.: Corner House, 1970.

Merz, Johannes Helmut. *The Hessians of Nova Scotia.* Hamilton, Ontario: German Canadian Historical Book Pub., 1997.

———. *The Hessians of Upper Canada.* Hamilton, Ontario: German Canadian Historical Book Pub., 1997.

———. *Register of German Military Men Who Remained in Canada After the American Revolution.* Hamilton, Ontario: German Canadian Historical Book Pub., 1997.

Miles, Lion G. *Guide to Hessian Documents of the American Revolution, 1777–1783: Transcripts and Translations from the Lindgerwood Collection at Morristown National Historical Park, Morristown, New Jersey.* Boston: G. K. Hall, 1989.

———. *Hessians of Lewis Miller.* Millville, Pa.: Precision Printers, 1983.

Reuter, Claus. *Brunswick Troops in North America 1776–1783: Index of All Soldiers Who Remained in North America.* Bowie, Md.: Heritage Books, 1999.

Rosengarten, Joseph G. *German Allied Troops in the American Revolution: J.R. [sic] Rosengarten's Survey of German Archives and Sources.* Bowie, Md.: Heritage Books, 1993.

Smith, Clifford Neal. *Annotated Hessian Chaplaincy Record of the American Revolution, 1776–1784: Christenings, Marriages, Deaths.* McNeal, Ariz.: Westland Publications, 1999.

———. *British and German Deserters, Discharges, and Prisoners of War Who May Have Remained in Canada and the United States, 1774–1783.* McNeal, Ariz.: Westland Publications, 1988.

———. *Brunswick Deserter Immigrants of the American Revolution.* Thomson, Ill.: Heritage House, 1973.

———. *Deserters and Disbanded Soldiers from British, German, and Loyalist Military Units in the South, 1782.* McNeal, Ariz.: Westland Publications, 1991.

———. *Mercenaries from Ansbach and Bayreuth, Germans Who Remained in America After the American Revolution.* Thomson, Ill.: Heritage House, 1974.

———. *Mercenaries from Hessen-Hanau Who Remained in Canada and the United States After the American Revolution.* DeKalb, Ill.: Westland Publications, 1976.

———. *Muster Rolls and Prisoner-of-War Lists in American Archival Collections Pertaining to the German Mercenary Troops Who Served with British Forces During the American Revolution.* DeKalb, Ill.: Westland Publications, 1976.

———. *Notes on Hessian Soldiers Who Remained in Canada and the United States After the American Revolution, 1775–1784.* McNeal, Ariz.: Westland Publications, 1992.

———. *Some German-American Participants in the American Revolution.* McNeal, Ariz.: Westland Publications, 1990.

Städtler, Erhardt. *Die Anebach-Bayreuther Truppen im Americanischen Unabhängigkeitskrieg, 1777–1783.* Nürnberg, Germany: Gesellachaft für Familienforschung in Franken, 1956.

Wilhelmy, Jean-Pierre. *Les Mercenaires Allemand in Quebec du XVIIIe Siecle et Leur Apport a la Population.* Beloeil, Quebec: Maison des Mots, 1984.

Frontier Clashes, 1784–1811

Various States

Clark, Murtie June. *American Militia in the Frontier Wars, 1790–1796.* 1990. Reprint, Baltimore: Genealogical Publishing Co., 2003.

Dent, David L. *Foreign Origins, Comprising an Enumeration of Men of Foreign Birth Enlisted in the United States Army from 1798 to 1815; Together with the Dates & Places of Enlistment and Ages of the Men; the Whole Conveniently Arranged by State Alphabetically; and Identifying in the Case of Each Man with No Exception the Town or City of Birth Abroad; to Which Is Appended a Complete Index of All Names Included in the Work.* Arlington, Va.: C. M. Kent, 1981.

White, Virgil D. *Index to Volunteer Soldiers, 1784–1811.* Waynesboro, Tenn.: National Historical Publishing Co., 1987.

Georgia

Smith, Gordon Burns. *History of the Georgia Militia, 1783–1861.* 4 vols. Milledgeville, Ga.: Boyd Publishing, 2000–01.

Indiana

Muster Rolls and Payrolls of Militia and Regular Army Organizations in the Battle of Tippecanoe, November 1811. Microfilm, T1085, 1 roll. Washington, D.C.: National Archives Microfilm Publications.

Kentucky

Clift, Garrett Glenn. *The "Corn Stalk" Militia of Kentucky, 1792–1811; A Brief Statutory History of the Militia and Records of Commissions of Officers in the Organization from the Beginning of Statehood to the Commencement of War of 1812.* Frankfort, Ky.: Kentucky Historical Society, 1957.

North Carolina

Kearney, Timothy. *Abstracts of Letters of Resignations of Militia Officers in North Carolina 1779–1840.* Raleigh, N.C.: Walsworth Publishing Co., 1992.

Pennsylvania

Montgomery, Thomas Lynch. *Militia Rolls 1783–1790.* Pennsylvania Archives, 6th Series, vol. 3.

———. *Muster and Pay Rolls, Pennsylvania Militia, 1790–1800.* Pennsylvania Archives, 6th Series, vol. 5.

Western Expedition (Whiskey Rebellion) Accounts. 1794–1804. Microfilm, 2 rolls.

Virginia

Butler, Stuart L. *Virginia Soldiers in the United States Army, 1800–1815.* Athens, Ga.: Iberian Publishing Co., 1986.

War of 1812

Various States

Carr, Deborah E. W. *Index to Certified Copy of List of American Prisoners of War, 1812–1815, as Recorded in General Entry Book Ottawa, Canada.* N.p., 1924.

Fredericksen, John C. *Free Trade and Sailor's Rights: A Bibliography of the War of 1812.* Westport, Conn.: Greenwood Press, 1985.

Peterson, Clarence Stewart. *Known Military Dead During the War of 1812.* Baltimore, 1955.

Scott, Kenneth. *British Aliens in the United States During the War of 1812.* Baltimore: Genealogical Publishing Co., 1979.

U.S. Department of State. *"War of 1812 Papers" of the Department of State 1789–1815.* M588, 4 rolls. Washington, D.C.: National Archives Microfilm Publication.

U.S. Veterans Administration. *Compiled Military Service Records of Maj. Uriah Blue's Detachment of Chickasaw Indians in the War of 1812.* M1829, 1 roll. Washington, D.C.: National Archives Microfilm Publication.

———. *Compiled Service Records of Maj. McIntosh's Company of Creek Indians in the War of 1812.* M1830, 1 roll. Washington, D.C.: National Archives Microfilm Publication.

———. *War of 1812 Military Bounty Land Warrants 1815–1858.* M848, 14 rolls. Washington, D.C.: National Archives Microfilm Publication.

White, Virgil D. *Index to War of 1812 Pension Files, 1815–1926.* 3 vols. Waynesboro, Tenn.: National Historical Publishing Co., 1989.

Arkansas

Christensen, Katheren. *Arkansas Military Bounty Grants (War of 1812).* Hot Springs, Ark.: Arkansas Ancestors, 1971.

Connecticut

Johnston, Henry Phelps. *Record of Service of Connecticut Men in the I. War of the Revolution; II. War of 1812; III. Mexican War.* Hartford, Conn.: Case, Lockwood and Brainard, 1889.

Delaware

Delaware Archives Military Records. Vols. 4 and 5. Wilmington, Del.: Star Publishing Co., 1916.

Georgia

Georgia Military Affairs. Vol. 3, 1801–13; Vol. 4, 1814–19.

Kratovil, Judy Swaim. *Index to War of 1812 Service Records for Volunteer Soldiers from Georgia.* Atlanta, Ga.: the compiler, 1986.

Illinois

Elliott, Isaac H. *Record of the Services of Illinois Soldiers in the Black Hawk War, 1831–32, and in the Mexican War, 1846–8 . . . With an Appendix Giving a Record of the Services of the Illinois Militia, Rangers and Riflemen, in Protecting the Frontier from the Ravages of the Indians from 1810 to 1813.* Springfield, Ill.: H. W. Rokker, 1882.

War of 1812 Bounty Lands in Illinois. Thomas, Ill.: Heritage House, 1977.

Indiana

Franklin, Charles M. *Indiana War of 1812 Soldiers Militia.* Indianapolis: Ye Olde Genealogie Shoppe, 1984.

Kentucky

Clift, G. Glenn. *Remember the Raisin! Kentucky and Kentuckians in the Battles and Massacre at Frenchtown, Michigan Territory in the War of 1812.* Frankfort: Kentucky Historical Society, 1961.

Kentucky Soldiers in the War of 1812. Baltimore: Genealogical Publishing Co., 1969.

Quisenberry, Anderson C. *Kentucky in the War of 1812.* Baltimore: Genealogical Publishing Co., 1969.

Louisiana

Casey, Powell A. *Louisiana in War of 1812.* Baton Rouge: 1963.

De Grummond, Jane Lucas. *The Baratarians and the Battle of New Orleans.* Baton Rouge: Louisiana State University Press, 1961.

Louisiana 1812 Pension Applications. Microfilm, 9 rolls.

Morazan, Donald R. *Biographical Sketches of the Veterans of the Battalions of Orleans, 1814–1815.* Legacy Publishing Co., 1979.

Pierson, Marion J. B. *Louisiana Soldiers in the War of 1812.* Baton Rouge: Louisiana Genealogical and Historical Society, 1963.

———. *Louisiana Soldiers in the War of 1812.* Baltimore: Clearfield Co., 1999.

Maryland

Huntsberry, Thomas V., and Joanne M. Huntsberry. *Maryland War of 1812 Privateers.* Baltimore: J. Mart, 1983.

———. *North Point War of 1812.* N.p., 1985.

———. *Western Maryland/Pennsylvania Virginia Militia in Defense of Maryland, 1805 to 1815.* Baltimore, 1983.

Marine, William M. *The British Invasion of Maryland, 1812–1815.* Hatboro, Pa.: Tradition Press, 1965.

Wright, F. Edward. *Maryland Militia War of 1812.* 8 vols. Silver Spring, Md.: Family Line, 1979–92.

Massachusetts

Barker, J. *Records of the Massachusetts Volunteer Militia Called Out by the Governor of Massachusetts to Suppress a Threatened Invasion During the War of 1812–14.* Boston: Wright and Potter Printing Co., 1913.

Michigan

Miller, Alice D. *Soldiers of the War of 1812 Who Died in Michigan.* Ithaca, Mich.: the author, 1962.

Mississippi

Rowland, Mrs. Dunbar. *Mississippi Territory in the War of 1812.* Publications of the Mississippi Historical Society, vol. 4. Jackson: Mississippi Historical Society, 1921.

U.S. Veterans Administration. *Compiled Service Records of Volunteer Soldiers Who Served During the War of 1812 in Organizations from the Territory of Mississippi.* Microfilm, M678, 22 rolls. Washington, D.C.: National Archives Microfilm Publications.

Missouri

Dunaway, Maxine. *Missouri Military Land Warrants, War of 1812.* Springfield, Mo.: the author, 1985.

Military Land Warrants in Missouri, 1819. Denver: Stagecoach Library for Genealogical Research, 1988.

Williams, Betty Hariky. *Soldiers of the War of 1812 with a Missouri Connection.* 2 vols. Independence, Mo.: Two Trails Pub., 2002.

New Hampshire

Potter, Charles E. *Military History of the State of New Hampshire, 1623–1861.* Baltimore: Genealogical Publishing Co., 1972.

New Jersey

Records of Officers and Men of New Jersey in Wars 1791–1815. Trenton, N.J.: State Gazette Publishing Co., 1909.

New York

Index of Awards on Claims of the Soldiers of the War of 1812, New York Adjutant General's Office. Baltimore: Genealogical Publishing Co., 1969.

North Carolina

Muster Rolls of the Soldiers of the War of 1812 Detached from the Militia of North Carolina in 1812 and 1814. Baltimore: Genealogical Publishing Co., 1976.

Ohio

Garner, Grace. *Index to Roster of Ohio Soldiers, War of 1812.* Spokane: Eastern Washington Genealogical Society, 1974.

Miller, Phyllis B. *Index to the Grave Records of Servicemen of the War of 1812, State of Ohio.* Brookville, Ohio: Dillon's Printery, 1988.

Roster of Ohio Soldiers in the War of 1812. Columbus, Ohio: Edward T. Miller Co., 1916.

Pennsylvania

Baker, Harrison S. *Index to the Muster Rolls of the Pennsylvania Volunteers in the War of 1812–1814.* Pomeroy, Ohio: Society of the War of 1812 in the State of Ohio, 1997.

Muster Rolls of the Pennsylvania Volunteers in the War of 1812–1814. Reprinted from *Pennsylvania Archives,* 2nd Series, vol. 12. Baltimore: Genealogical Publishing Co., 1967.

Pennsylvania War of 1812 Pensions, 1866–1896. Microfilm, 27 rolls.

Rhode Island

Smith, Joseph J. *Civil and Military List of Rhode Island, 1800–1850.* Providence, R.I.: Preston and Rounds Co., 1901.

South Carolina

Service Records: War of 1812 Records of the First, Second, and Third Regiment. 5 microfiche. South Carolina Historical Society.

Tennessee

1814 Court Martial of Tennessee Militiamen. Signal Mountain, Tenn.: Institute of Historical Research, 1993.

McCown, Mary Harden, and Inez E. Burns. *Soldiers of the War of 1812 Buried in Tennessee.* Johnson City, Tenn.: Overmountain Press, 1977.

Moore, Mrs. John Trotwood. *Record of Commissions of Officers in the Tennessee Militia, 1796–1811.* Baltimore: Genealogical Publishing Co., 1977.

Sistler, Byron, and Samuel Sistler. *Tennesseans in the War of 1812.* Nashville: Byron Sistler and Associates, 1992.

Texas

Fay, Mary Smith. *War of 1812 Veterans in Texas.* New Orleans: Polyanthos, 1979.

Vermont

Roster of Soldiers in the War of 1812–14. St. Albans, Vt.: Messenger Press, 1933.

War of 1812, 1812–1814, 1849–1851. Microfilm, 4 rolls.

Virginia

Butler, Stuart Lee. *A Guide to the Virginia Militia Units in the War of 1812.* Athens, Ga.: Iberian Publishing Co., 1988.

———. *Virginia Soldiers in the United States Army, 1800–1815.* Athens, Ga.: Iberian Publishing Co., 1986.

Virginia Auditor of Public Accounts. *Virginia Militia in the War of 1812 from Rolls in the Auditor's Office at Richmond.* 2 vols. Baltimore: Genealogical Publishing Co., 2001.

Indian Wars, 1815–1858, & Post 1865

Various States

Carroll, John M. *Roll Call on the Little Big Horn, 28 June 1876.* Fort Collins, Colo.: Old Army Press, 1974.

Hays, Tony. *The Cherokee Wars.* Chattanooga, Tenn.: Kitchen Table Press, 1987.

Michno, Gregory F. *Encyclopedia of Indian Wars: Western Battles and Skirmishes, 1850–1890.* Missoula: Mountain Press Publishing, 2003.

O'Neal, Bill. *Fighting Men of the Indian Wars: A Biographical Encyclopedia of the Mountain Men, Soldiers, Cowboys, and Pioneers Who Took Up Arms During America's Westward Expansion.* Stillwater, Okla: Barbed Wire Press, 1991.

United States Court of Claims. *Index of Indian Depredation Claims.* Washington, D.C.: Government Printing Office, n.d.

———. *Supplementary Index of Indian Depredation Claims: Nos. 7701 to 10841 Including Changes Made in Earlier Cases, November 1896.* Washington, D.C.: Government Printing Office, 1896.

U.S. Veterans Administration. *Compiled Service Records of Michigan and Illinois Volunteers Who Served During the Winnebago Indian Disturbances, 1827.* Microfilm, M1505, 3 rolls. Washington, D.C.: National Archives Microfilm Publications.

White, Virgil D. *Index to Indian Wars Pension Files, 1892–1926.* Waynesboro, Tenn.: National Historical Publishing Co., 1987.

———. *Index to Volunteer Soldiers in Indian Wars and Disturbances, 1815–1858.* 2 vols. Waynesboro, Tenn.: National Historical Publishing Co., 1994.

Alabama

Alabama Volunteers Cherokee Disturbances and Removal, 1836–1839. Cullman, Ala.: Gregath Co., 1982.

Horn, Robert C. *Creek Indian War Index to Records of Volunteer Soldiers from Alabama.* Dadeville, Ala.: Genealogical Society of East Alabama, 1983.

———. *Index to Compiled Service Records for Alabama Soldiers in the Florida Indian War, 1836–1838.* Auburn, Ala.: Genealogical Society of East Alabama, 1987.

Watson, Larry S. *Creek Soldier Casualty Lists: Seminole War 1836.* Laguna Hills, Calif.: Histree, 1987.

Arkansas

Morgan, James Logan. *Arkansas Volunteers of 1836–37: History and Roster of the First and Second Regiments of Arkansas Mounted Gunmen, 1837–1837, and a Roster of Captain Jesse Bean's Company of Mounted Rangers.* Newport, Ark.: Morgan Books, 1984.

California

California State Militia Index to the Muster Rolls of 1851 to 1866. Microfiche, 23.

Florida

Soldiers of Florida in the Seminole Indian, Civil and Spanish-American Wars. Macclenny, Fla.: R. J. Ferry, 1983.

U.S. Veterans Administration. *Compiled Service Records of Volunteer Soldiers Who Served in Organizations from the State of Florida During the Florida Indian Wars, 1835–1858.* Microfilm, M1086, 63 rolls. Washington, D.C.: National Archives Microfilm Publication.

Georgia

Thaxton, Donna A. *Georgia Indian Depredation Claims.* Americus, Ga.: Thaxton Co., 1988.

United States War Department. *Claims for Georgia Militia Campaigns Against Frontier Indians, 1792–1827.* Microfilm, M1745, 5 rolls. Washington, D.C.: National Archives Microfilm Publications.

Illinois

Illinois Volunteers in the Mormon War: The Disturbances in Hancock County, 1844–1846. Palmer, Ill.: Genie Logic Enterprises, 1997.

Whitney, Ellen M. *The Black Hawk War, 1831–1832.* Collections of the Illinois State Historical Library, vols. 25–27. Springfield: Illinois State Historical Library, 1970–78.

Indiana

Loftus, Carrie. *Indiana Militia in the Black Hawk War.* The author, n.d.

Maine

Aroostock War. Historical Sketch and Roster of Commissioned Officers and Enlisted Men Called into Service for the Protection of the Northeastern Frontier of Maine. From February to May 1839. Baltimore: Clearfield Co., 1989.

Michigan

Barnett, Le Roy. *Michigan's Early Military Forces.* Detroit: Wayne State University Press, 2003.

Oregon

Victor, Frances F. *The Early Indian Wars of Oregon.* Salem, Ore.: F. C. Baker, State Printer, 1894.

Tennessee

Douthat, James L. *1837 Tennessee Volunteers: Muster Rolls for Various Counties.* Signal Mountain, Tenn.: Institute of Historic Research, 1993.

Index, Tennesseans in the Seminole War (Florida War) 1818 and 1836. Microfilm, 1 roll.

Military Records, 1813–1836. Microfilm, 1 roll.

Officers of the Cherokee War, 1836–1846, Muster Rolls and Index to Tennesseans. Cherokee Removal, 1836. Microfilm, 2 rolls.

Tennessee Military Elections, 1796–1862. Microfilm, 22 rolls.

Sprague, John T. *The Origin, Progress, and Conclusion of the Florida Wars.* Gainesville, Fla.: University Press, 1964.

Volunteer Soldiers in the Cherokee War, 1836–1839.

Texas

Brown, John Henry. *Indian Wars and Pioneers of Texas.* Austin, Tex.: State House Press, 1988.

Defenders of the Republic of Texas: Texas Army Muster Rolls, Receipt Rolls, and Other Rolls, 1836–1841. Austin, Tex.: Laurel House Press, 1989.

Devereaux, Linda E. *The Texas Navy: Fighters for Freedom for the Republic of Texas Who Are Among the Unsung Heroes of Days of Yesterday.* Nacogdoches, Tex.: Ericson Books, 1983.

Dixon, Sam H. *The Heroes of San Jacinto.* Houston: Anson Jones Press, 1932.

Ingmire, Frances Terry. *The Texas Frontiersman, 1839–1860: Minute Men, Militia, Home Guard, Indian Fighter.* St. Louis, Mo.: F. T. Ingmire, 1982.

———. *The Texas Ranger Service Records, 1830–1846.* St. Louis, Mo.: Ingmire Publications, 1982.

———. *Texas Ranger Service Records, 1847–1900.* 6 vols. St. Louis, Mo.: F. T. Ingmire, 1982.

Miller, Thomas Lloyd. *Bounty and Donation Land Grants of Texas 1835–1888.* Austin: University of Texas Press, 1976.

Muster Rolls of the Texas Revolution. Austin: DRT, 1986.

Republic of Texas Pension Application Abstracts. Austin: Austin Genealogical Society, 1987.

Stephens, Robert W. *Texas Ranger Indian War Pensions.* Quannah, Tex.: Nortex Press, 1975.

White, Gifford E. *They Also Served: Texas Service Records from Headright Certificates.* Nacogdoches, Tex.: Ericson Books, 1991.

Wilbarger, J. W. *Indian Depredations in Texas.* Austin: Eakin Press, 1985.

Washington

Washington Territorial Volunteers' Papers: Indian War Muster Rolls 1855–1856. Olympia, Wash.: Office of the Secretary of State, Division of Archives and Records Management, 1990.

Mexican War, 1846–1848

Various States

Breithaupt, Richard H. *Aztec Club of 1847: Military Society of the Mexican War Sesquicentennial History 1847–1997.* Universal City, Calif.: Walika Publishing Co., 1998.

Ericson, Joe E. *From the Rio Grande to the Halls of Montezuma: Mexican War Miscellany.* Nacogdoches, Tex.: J. Ericson, 1996.

Peterson, Clarence S. *Known Military Dead During the Mexican War, 1846–48.* Baltimore: Genealogical Publishing Co., 1957.

Troxel, Navena Hembree. *Mexican War Index to Pension Files, 1886–1926.* Gore, Okla.: VT Publications, 1983–1995.

White, Virgil D. *Index to Mexican War Pension Files.* Waynesboro, Tenn.: National Historical Publishing Co., 1989.

Wilcox, Cadmus M. *A Complete Roster of Mexican War Officers, 1846–1848: Both Army and Navy, with Alphabetical Index.* Richardson, Tex.: Descendants of Mexican War Veterans, 1994.

Wolfe, Barbara Schull. *An Index to Mexican War Pension Applications.* Indianapolis: Heritage House, 1985.

Alabama

Butler, Steven R. *Alabama Volunteers in the Mexican War: A History and Annotated Roster.* Richardson, Tex.: Descendants of Mexican War Veterans, 1996.

Arkansas

Allen, Desmond Walls. *Arkansas' Mexican War Soldiers.* Conway, Ark.: Arkansas Research, 1988.

Connecticut

Johnston, Henry Phelps. *Record of Service of Connecticut Men in the I. War of the Revolution II. War of 1812 III. Mexican War.* Hartford, Conn.: Case, Lockwood and Brainard, 1889.

Florida

Soldiers of Florida in the Seminole Indian, Civil and Spanish-American Wars. Macclenny, Fla.: R. J. Ferry, 1983.

Illinois

Elliott, Isaac H. *Record of the Services of Illinois Soldiers in the Black Hawk War, 1831–32, and in the Mexican War, 1846–8.* Springfield, Ill.: H. W. Rokker, 1882.

Indiana

Perry, Oran. *Indiana in the Mexican War.* Indianapolis: William B. Burford, 1908.

Kentucky

Report of the Adjutant General of the State of Kentucky: Mexican War Veterans. Frankfort, Ky.: John D. Woods, 1889.

Maryland

Wells, Charles J. *Maryland and District of Columbia Volunteers in the Mexican War.* Family Line, 1991.

Michigan

Barnett, Le Roy. *Michigan's Early Military Forces.* Detroit: Wayne State University Press, 2003.

Joint Documents of the Senate and House of Representatives at the Annual Session of 1848. Joint Document No. 7, pp. 31–43.

Welch, Richard. *Michigan in the Mexican War, First Regiment of Michigan Volunteers.* Durand, Mich., 1967.

Mississippi

U.S. Veterans Administration. *Compiled Service Records of Volunteer Soldiers Who Served in Organizations from the State of Mississippi.* Microfilm, M863, 9 rolls. Washington, D.C.: National Archives Microfilm Publication.

New Hampshire

Potter, Charles E. *The Military History of the State of New Hampshire, 1623–1861.* Baltimore: Genealogical Publishing Co., 1972.

New Jersey

Records of Officers and Men of New Jersey in the War with Mexico, 1846–1848.

North Carolina

Ransom, McBride. "The North Carolina Volunteers in the War with Mexico, 1846–1848." *North Carolina Genealogical Society Journal* 26 (2000): 131–76.

Ohio

Reprint Edition of the Official Roster of the Soldiers of the State of Ohio in the War with Mexico, 1846–1848. Ohio Genealogical Society, 1991.

Pennsylvania

Segraves, Antoinette J. "A Guide to Pennsylvania Soldiers in the Mexican War." *Pennsylvania Genealogical Magazine* 36 (1989–90): 55–57, 176–91, 274–84; 37 (1991–92): 22–38, 117–36, 203–18, 335–52.

U.S. Veterans Administration. *Compiled Service Records of Volunteer Soldiers Who Served in Organizations from the State of Pennsylvania.* Microfilm, M1028, 13 rolls. Washington, D.C.: National Archives Microfilm Publications.

Rhode Island

Smith, Joseph J. *Civil and Military List of Rhode Island, 1800–1850.* Providence, R.I.: Preston and Rounds Co., 1901.

South Carolina

Meyer, Jack. *An Annotated Roster of the Palmetto Regiment of South Carolina in the Mexican War, 1846–1848.* Winnsboro, S.C.: Greenbrier Press, 1994.

Tennessee

Brock, Reid, Thomas Brock, and Tony Hays. *Volunteers: Tennesseans in the War with Mexico.* 2 vols. Kitchen Table Press, 1986.

U.S. Veterans Administration. *Compiled Service Records of Volunteer Soldiers Who Served in Organizations from the State of Tennessee.* Microfilm, M278, 19 rolls. Washington, D.C.: National Archives Microfilm Publications.

Texas

Spurlin, Charles D. *Texas Veterans in the Mexican War, Muster Rolls of Texas Military Units.* The compiler, 1984.

U.S. Veterans Administration. *Compiled Service Records of Volunteer Soldiers Who Served in Organizations from the State of Texas.* Microfilm, M278, 13 rolls. Washington, D.C.: National Archives Microfilm Publications.

Utah

Tyler, Daniel. *A Concise History of the Mormon Battalion in the Mexican War 1846–1848.* Glorietta, N.Mex.: Rio Grande Press, 1969.

U.S. Veterans Administration. *Compiled Service Records of Volunteer Soldiers Who Served During the Mexican War in Mormon Organizations.* Microfilm, M351, 1 roll. Washington, D.C.: National Archives Microfilm Publications.

U.S. Selected Pension Application Files for Members of the Mormon Battalion, Mexican War, 1846–1848. Microfilm, T1196, 21 rolls. Washington, D.C.: National Archives Microfilm Publication.

Virginia

Johnston, William P. *Off to War: The Virginia Volunteers in the War with Mexico.* Westminster, Md.: Willow Bend Books, 2002.

Civil War, 1861–1865

Various States

Bobo, James E. *The Confederate States of America Roll of Honor Source Book for Genealogists and Historians.* Memphis: Tennessee Genealogical Society, 2003.

Blanton, De Anne, and Lauren M. Cook, *They Fought Like Demons: Women Soldiers in the Civil War.* Baton Rouge: Louisiana University Press, 2002.

Brewer, Willis. *Alabama: Her History, Resources, War Records and Public Men from 1540 to 1872.* Spartanburg, S.C.: Reprint Co., 1975.

Cullum, George W. *Biographical Register, Officers and Graduates of the U.S. Military Academy, West Point, New York.* 3rd ed. Boston: Houghton-Mifflin, 1891.

Faith in the Fight: Civil War Chaplains. Mechanicsburg, Pa.: Stackpole Books, 2003.

Groene, Bertram Hawthorne. *Tracing Your Civil War Ancestors.* Rev. ed. Winston-Salem, N.C.: John F. Blair Publisher, 1980.

Hewett, Janet B., ed., *The Roster of Confederate Soldiers, 1861–1865.* 16 vols. Wilmington, N.C.: Broadfoot Publishing, 1995–96.

———. *The Roster of Union Soldiers, 1861–1865.* 33 vols. Wilmington, N.C.: Broadfoot Publishing, 1997–2000.

———. *Supplement to the Official Records.* Wilmington, N.C.: Broadfoot Publishing, 1997–98.

Ingmire, Frances Terry. *Confederate P.O.W.'s: Soldiers and Sailors Who Died in Federal Prisons and Military Hospitals in the North.* Nacogdoches, Tex.: Ericson Books, 1984.

Mills, Gary B. *Civil War Claims in the South: An Index of Civil War Damage Claims Filed Before the Southern Claims Commission, 1871–1880.* Laguna Hills, Calif.: Aegean Park Press, 1990.

———. *Southern Loyalists in the Civil War: The Southern Claims Commission: A Composite Directory of Case Files, 1871–1880.* Baltimore: Genealogical Publishing Co., 1994.

Neagles, James C. *Confederate Research Sources: A Guide to Archive Collections.* Salt Lake City: Ancestry, 1986.

Official Army Register of the Volunteer Force of the United States Army for the Years 1861, '62, '63, '64, '65. 9 vols. Gaithersburg, Md.: Ron R. Van Sickle Military Books, 1987.

Pardons by the President: Final Report of the Names of Persons Who Lived in Alabama, Virginia, West Virginia, or Georgia, Were Engaged in Rebellion and Pardoned by the President, Andrew Johnson. Bowie, Md.: Heritage Books, 1986.

Roll of Honor: Names of Soldiers Who Died in Defense of the American Union, Interred in the National Cemeteries, Numbers I–XIX. Quartermaster General's Office, 1868. Reprint, Baltimore: Genealogical Publishing Co., 1994.

Index to the Roll of Honor. Compiled by William and Martha Remy. Baltimore: Genealogical Publishing Co., 1995.

Schweitzer, George K. *Civil War Genealogy.* Knoxville, Tenn., 1981.

Segars, Joe H. *In Search of Confederate Ancestors. The Guide.* Murfreesboro, Tenn.: Southern Heritage Press, 1993.

Special Presidential Pardons for Confederate Soldiers Requesting Pardon from President Andrew Johnson. 2 vols. Signal Mountain, Tenn.: Mountain Press, 1999.

Wakelyn, Jon L. *Biographical Dictionary of the Confederacy.* Westport, Conn.: Greenwood Press, 1977.

Witcher, Curt B. "The Civil War Soldiers and Sailors System: Complete and Reborn." *FORUM* 16 (Winter 2004): 31–32.

Alabama

Alabama 1987 Census of Confederate Veterans. Microfilm, 4 rolls.

Alabama Pension Commission. *Confederate Pension Applications.* Microfilm, 276 rolls.

———. *Applications for Relief by Maimed Confederate Soldiers.* Microfilm, 2 rolls.

Brewer, Willis. *Alabama: Her History, Resources, War Records, and Public Men from 1540 to 1872.* Spartanburg, S.C.: Reprint Co., 1975.

Harris, Sherry. *1862 Alabama Salt Lists.* Granada Hills, Calif.: Harris Press, 1993.

Master Index to 1907 Census of Alabama Confederate Soldiers Indexed and Compiled from Alabama State Archives Microfilm. Cullman, Ala.: Gregath Pub. Co., 1990–1993.

Arkansas

Allen, Desmond Walls. *Arkansas's Damned Yankees: An Index to Union Soldiers in Arkansas Regiments.* Conway, Ark.: Arkansas Research, 1987.

———. *Arkansas Union Soldiers Pension Applications Index.* Conway, Ark.: Rapid Rabbit Copy Co., 1987.

———. *Index to Arkansas Confederate Pension Applications.* Conway, Ark.: Arkansas Research, 1991.

———. *Index to Arkansas Confederate Soldiers.* 3 vols. Conway, Ark.: Arkansas Research, 1990.

Arkansas State Auditor. *Arkansas Confederate Pension Records.* Microfilm, 121 rolls.

———. *Miscellaneous Arkansas Confederate Pension Records.* Microfilm, 2 rolls.

Ingmire, Frances Terry. *Arkansas Confederate Veterans and Widows Pension Applications.* St. Louis, 1985.

McLane, Bobbie J., and Capitola Glazner. *Arkansas 1911 Census of Confederate Veterans.* 4 vols. N.p., 1977–88.

Pickett, Connie. *Old Soldiers Home: Arkansas Confederate Soldiers and Widows.* St. Louis: Frances T. Ingmire, 1985.

California

Orton, Richard H. *Records of California Men in the War of the Rebellion, 1861 to 1867.* Detroit: Gale Research Co., 1979.

Parker, J. Carlyle. *A Personal Name Index to Orton's Records of California Men in the War of the Rebellion, 1861 to 1867.* Detroit: Gale Research Co., 1978.

Colorado

Biennial Reports of the Adjutant General, 1861. Denver, 1866.

Colorado Territory Civil War Volunteer Records: A Comprehensive Index to the Twelve Volumes of Military Clothing Books Found in the Colorado State Archive Containing the Historical Background of the Volunteers of Colorado Territory During the Civil War Period, 1861–1865. Littleton, Colo.: Columbine Genealogical and Historical Society, 1994.

Connecticut

Smith, Stephen R. *Record of Service of Connecticut Men in the Army and Navy of the United States During the War of the Rebellion.* Hartford, Conn.: Case, Lockwood and Brainard Co., 1889.

Dakota

Dakota Militia in the War of 1862. 58th Congress, 2nd Session, Senate Document No. 241. Washington, D.C., 1904.

Delaware

Scharf, John Thomas. *History of Delaware, 1609–1888.* Appendix, "Roster of Delaware Volunteers in the War of the Rebellion," vol. 1, i–xxxiii. Port Washington, N.Y.: Kennikat Press, 1972.

Florida

Florida Comptroller's Office. *Pension Claims of Confederate Veterans and Their Widows.* Microfilm, 169 rolls.

Hartman, David W. *Biographical Rosters of Florida's Confederate Pension Supplements.* Cumming, Ga.: T. O. Brooke, 1999.

Soldiers of Florida in the Seminole Indian, Civil, and Spanish-American Wars. Macclenny, Fla.: R. J. Ferry, 1983.

White, Virgil D. *Register of Florida CSA Pension Applications.* Waynesboro, Tenn.: National Historical Publishing Co., 1989.

Georgia

Brightwell, Juanita S., Eunice S. Lee, and Elsie C. Fulghum. *Roster of the Confederate Soldiers of Georgia 1861–1865, Index.* Spartanburg, S.C.: Reprint Co., 1982.

Brooke, Ted O., and Linda Geiger. *Index to Georgia Confederate Pension Supplements.* Cumming, Ga.: T. O. Brooke. 1999.

Cornell, Nancy J. *The 1864 Census for Re-organizing the Georgia Militia.* Baltimore: Genealogical Publishing Co., 2000.

Georgia Confederate Pension Applications. Microfilm, 634 rolls.

Harris, Sherry. *1862 Georgia Salt Lists.* Harris Press, 1993.

Henderson, Lillian. *Roster of the Confederate Soldiers of Georgia 1861–1865.* 6 vols. Hapeville, Ga.: Longino and Porter, 1959–64.

Jones, Patricia K. *Pensions and Relief for Confederate Veterans and Widows of Georgia.* Ozark, Mo.: Dogwood Printing, 2002.

Smedlund, William S. *Camp Fires of Georgia Troops, 1861–1865.* Kennesaw Mountain Press, 1994.

White, Virgil D. *Index to Georgia Civil War Confederate Files.* Waynesboro, Tenn.: National Historical Publishing Co., 1996.

Illinois

Illinois Military Census 1861–1862: List of all Males 18 to 45 Arranged by County. Microfilm, 21 rolls.

Pratt, Marion D. *Illinois Men in the Union Navy During the Civil War.*

Reece, J. N. *Report of the Adjutant General of the State of Illinois.* 8 vols. Springfield, Ill.: Phillips Brothers, 1900–02.

Volkel, Lowell. *Illinois Soldiers and Sailors Home at Quincy, Admission of Mexican War and Civil War Veterans.* 2 vols. Thomson, Ill.: Heritage House, 1975–80.

Indiana

Terrell, William H. H. *Report of the Adjutant General of the State of Indiana.* 8 vols. Indianapolis: Alexander H. Conner, 1865–69.

Trapp, Glenda K. *Index to the Report of the Adjutant General of the State of Indiana First Volume, an Every Name Index to Volumes I, II, and III. Second Volume, an Every Name Index to Volume IV.* 2 vols. Evansville, Ind.: Trapp Publishing Service, 1986–87.

Iowa

Alexander, William L. *List of Ex-Soldiers, Sailors, and Marines Living in Iowa.* Des Moines, Iowa, 1886.

Baker, N. B. *Report of the Adjutant General and Acting Quartermaster General of the State of Iowa, January 1, 1865, to January 1, 1866.* Des Moines, Iowa, 1866.

Thrift, William H. *Roster and Record of Iowa Soldiers in the War of the Rebellion Together with Historical Sketches of Volunteer Organizations, 1861–1866.* 6 vols. Des Moines, Iowa: Emory H. English, 1908–11.

Kansas

Noble, P. S. *Report of the Adjutant General of the State of Kansas . . . 1861–1865.* 2 vols. Topeka: Kansas State Printing Co., 1896.

Kentucky

Kentucky Confederate Pension Board. *Civil War Pension Applications.* Microfilm, 50 rolls.

Lynn, Stephen D. *Confederate Pensioners of Kentucky: Pension Applications of the Veterans & Widows, 1912–1946.* Baltimore: Gateway Press, 2000.

Report of the Adjutant General of the State of Kentucky [Union]. 2 vols. Utica, Ky.: McDowell Publications, 1984–88.

Report of the Adjutant General of the State of Kentucky. Confederate Kentucky Volunteers War 1861–65. Hartford, Ky.: McDowell Publications, 1979–80.

Simpson, Alicia. *Index of Confederate Pension Applications, Commonwealth of Kentucky*. Frankfort, Ky.: Division of Archives and Records Management, 1978.

Louisiana

Booth, Andrew B. *Records of Louisiana Confederate Soldiers and Louisiana Confederate Commands*. 3 vols. Spartanburg, S.C.: Reprint Co., 1982.

Burns, Loretta E. *Louisiana 1911 Census: Confederate Veterans or Widows*. Pasadena, Tex.: C and L Printing, 1995.

Burt, W. G. *Annual Report of the Adjutant General of the State of Louisiana for the Year Ending December 31st, 1899*. New Orleans: State Papers, 1890.

"Confederate Pension Records [Index]." *Louisiana Genealogical Register* XXXVII (1990): 170–87, 238–57, 332–56; XXXVIII (1991): 83–92, 141–52, 277–86, 370–81; XXXIX (1992): 70–79, 135–44, 294–303, 383–92; XL (1993): 79–91, 169–79, 286–95, 362–72; XLI (1994): 58–67, 139–48, 244–52, 268–375; XLII (1995): 79–87, 283–90, 381–83, 474–79; XLIII (1996): 82–87, 182–85; 280–85, 379–86; XLIV (1997): 49–47, 171–80, 269–80, 391–95; XLV (1998): 87–93, 175–84, 243–46, 344–50; XLVI (1999): 31–45, 172–86, 275–92, 366–76; XLVII (2000): 76–86.

Jenks, Houston C. *An Index to the Census of 1911 of Confederate Veterans or Their Widows Pursuant to Act 71 of 1906*. Baton Rouge: F and M Enterprises, 1993.

Louisiana Board of Pension Commissioners. *Confederate Pensions*. Microfilm, 152 rolls.

Maine

Annual Report, 1861–66. Supplement: Alphabetical Index of Maine Volunteers, Etc., Mustered into the Service of the United States During the War of 1861. Augusta, Maine: Stevens and Sayward, 1867.

Hodson, John L. *Annual Report of the Adjutant General of the State of Maine, for the Year Ending December 31, 1863*. Augusta, Maine, 1863.

———. *Returns of Desertions, Discharges, and Deaths in Maine Regiments*. Augusta, Maine, 1864.

Maryland

Goldeborough, W. M. *Maryland Line in the Confederate Army, 1861–1865*. Gaithersburg, Md.: Butternut Press, 1983.

Hartzler, Daniel D. *Marylanders in the Confederacy*. Silver Spring, Md.: Family Line Publications, 1986.

Huntsberry, Thomas V. *Maryland in the Civil War*. 2 vols. Baltimore: J. Mart Publishers, 1985.

Newman, Harry Wright. *Maryland and the Confederacy: An Objective Narrative of Maryland's Participation in the War Between the States, 1861–1865; with Annotations of Important Personalities and Vital Events of the War*. Annapolis, Md.: Newman, 1976.

Reamy, Martha, and Bill Reamy. *History and Roster of Maryland Volunteers Wars of 1861–5 Index*. Westminster, Md.: Family Line Publications, 1990.

Toomey, Daniel Carroll. *Index to the Roster of the Maryland Volunteers, 1861–1865*. Harmans, Md.: Toomey Press, 1986.

Williams, L. Allison, J. H. Jarret, and George W. F. Vernon. *History and Roster of Maryland Volunteers, War of 1861–5*. Silver Spring, Md.: Family Line Publications, 1987.

Massachusetts

Massachusetts Soldiers, Sailors, and Marines in the Civil War. 8 vols. Norwood, Mass.: Norwood Press, 1931–15. Vol. 9, *Index to Army Records*, pertains to vols. 1–6 and part of 7. Boston: Wright and Potter Printing Co., 1937.

Record of the Massachusetts Volunteers, 1861–65. Boston, 1868–70.

Michigan

Alphabetical General Index to Public Library Sets of 85,271 Names of Michigan Soldiers and Sailors Individual Records. Lansing, Mich.: Wynkoop, Hallenbeck Crawford Co., 1915.

Record of Service of Michigan Volunteers in the Civil War, 1861–1865. 46 vols. Kalamazoo, Mich.: Ihling Brothers and Everand, 1905.

Robertson, John. *Annual Report of the Adjutant General of the State of Michigan for the Year 1864*. Lansing, Mich., 1865.

———. *Annual Report of the Adjutant General of the State of Michigan for the Years 1865–66*. Lansing, Mich., 1866.

———. *Michigan in the War*. Rev. ed. Lansing, Mich., 1882.

United States Civil War Soldiers Living in Michigan in 1894. St. Johns, Wash.: Genealogists of Clinton County Historical Society, 1988.

Minnesota

Minnesota in the Civil and Indian Wars, 1861–1865. 2 vols. St. Paul, Minn.: Pioneer Press Co., 1890.

Warming, Irene B. *Minnesotans in the Civil and Indian Wars: An Index to the Rosters in Minnesota in the Civil and Indian Wars, 1861–1865*. St. Paul, Minn.: Minnesota Historical Society, 1936.

Mississippi

Howell, H. Grady. *For Dixie Land I'll Take My Stand! A Muster Listing of All Known Mississippi Confederate Soldiers, Sailors and Marines.* 4 vols. Madison, Miss.: Chickasaw Bayou Press, 1998.

Mississippi Auditor's Office. *Confederate Soldiers and Sailors & Widows Pension Applications.* Microfilm, 94 rolls.

Rietti, J. C. *Military Annals of Mississippi. Military Organizations Which Entered the Service of the Confederate States of America from the State of Mississippi.* Spartanburg, S.C.: Reprint Co., 1976.

Rowland, Dunbar. *Military History of Mississippi 1803–98, Taken from the Official and Statistical Register of the State of Mississippi, 1908.* Pp. 420–556. Spartanburg, S.C.: Reprint Co., 1988.

Wiltshire, Betty Couch. *Mississippi Confederate Grave Registrations.* 2 vols. Bowie, Md.: Heritage Books, 1991.

———. *Mississippi Confederate Pension Applications.* Carrollton, Miss.: Pioneer Publishing Co., 1994.

Missouri

Confederate Roll of Honor: Missouri. Warrensburg, Mo.: West Central Missouri Genealogical Society and Library, 1989.

Fox, Peggy B. *Missouri Confederate Pensions and Confederate Home Applications Index.* Hillsboro, Tex.: Hill College Press, 1996.

Missouri Adjutant General. *Confederate Pension Applications and Soldiers' Home Admission Applications.* Microfilm, 27 rolls.

Simpson, Samuel P. *Annual Report of the Adjutant General of Missouri.* Jefferson City, Mo.: Emory S. Foster, 1866.

Nebraska

Allen, John C. *Roster of Soldiers, Sailors, and Marines of the War of 1812, the Mexican War, and the War of the Rebellion Residing in Nebraska, June 1, 1893.* Lincoln, Nebr.: Jacob North and Co., 1893.

Dudley, E. S. *Roster of Nebraska Volunteers From 1861 to 1869.* Hastings, Nebr.: 1888.

History of the State of Nebraska. Vol. 1, pp. 227–318. Evansville, Ind.: Unigraphics, 1975.

Patrick, John R. *Report of the Adjutant General of the State of Nebraska.* Des Moines, Iowa, 1871.

Piper, J. A. *Roster of Soldiers, Sailors, and Marines of the War of 1812, the Mexican War, and the War of the Rebellion Residing in Nebraska, June 1, 1895.* York, Nebr.: Nebraska Newspaper Union, 1895.

Pool, Charles H. *Roster of Veterans of the Mexican, Civil, and Spanish-American Wars Residing in Nebraska, 1915.* Lincoln: Nebraska Secretary of State, 1915.

Nevada

Cradlebaugh, J. *Annual Report of the Adjutant General for 1865.* Carson City, Nev.: John Church, 1866.

Laughton, C. E. *Roster of Volunteers.* Biennial Report of the Adjutant-General, pp. 29–55. N.p., 1884.

Nevada Adjutant General. *Nevada Territory and State Civil War Muster Rolls and Index.* Microfilm, 2 rolls.

New Hampshire

Ayling, Augustus D. *Revised Register of the Soldiers and Sailors of New Hampshire in the War of the Rebellion, 1861–66.* Concord, N.H.: Ira C. Evans, 1895.

New Jersey

Stryker, William S. *Record of Officers and Men of New Jersey in the Civil War, 1861–1865.* 2 vols. Trenton, N.J.: John L. Murphy, 1876.

New York

Phisterer, Frederick. *New York in the War of the Rebellion, 1861 to 1865.* 3rd ed. 6 vols. Albany, N.Y.: J. B. Lyon Co., 1912.

A Record of the Commissioned and Non-Commissioned Officers and Privates of the Regiments Organized in the State of New York. 4 vols. Albany, N.Y., 1864–68.

Registers of New York Regiments in the War of the Rebellion. 46 vols. Albany, N.Y., 1894–1906.

North Carolina

Bradley, Stephen E. *North Carolina Confederate Home Guard Examinations, 1863–1864.* Keysville, Va.: S. E. Bradley, 1993.

———. *North Carolina Confederate Militia Officers Roster as Contained in the Adjutant-General's Officers Roster.* Wilmington, N.C.: Broadfoot Publishing Co., 1992.

Clark, Walter. *Histories of the Several Regiments and Battalions from North Carolina in the Great War, 1861–65.* 5 vols. Wilmington, N.C.: Broadfoot Publishing Co., 1991.

Cook, Gerald W. *The Last Tarheel Militia 1861–1865: The History of the North Carolina Militia and Home Guard in the Civil War, and Index to Over 1,100 Militia Officers.* Winston-Salem, N.C.: G. W. Cook, 1987.

Manarin, Louis H. *North Carolina Troops 1861–1865, a Roster.* 12 vols. to date. Raleigh, N.C.: State Department of Archives and History, 1968–.

Moore, John W. *Roster of North Carolina Troops in the War Between the States During the Years 1861, 1862, 1863, 1864, and 1865.* 4 vols. Raleigh, N.C.: Ashe and Gatling, 1882.

North Carolina State Auditor. *Applications for Confederate Soldiers' and Widows' Pensions.* Microfilm, 105 rolls.

Wegner, Ansley Herring. *Phantom Pain. North Carolina's Artificial-Limbs Program for Confederate Veterans. Including an Index to Records in the North Carolina State Archives Related to Artificial Limbs for Confederate Veterans*. Raleigh, N.C.: Office of Archives and History, North Carolina Department of Cultural Resources, 2004.

Ohio

Alphabetical Index to Official Roster of the Soldiers of the State of Ohio in the War of the Rebellion. Works Progress Administration, 1938.

Official Roster of the Soldiers of the State of Ohio in the War of the Rebellion, 1861–1866. 12 vols. Akron, Ohio: Werner Co., 1893–95.

Petty, Gerald M. *Index of the Ohio Squirrel Hunters Roster*. Columbus, Ohio: Petty's Press, 1984.

Oklahoma

Chase, Marybelle W. *Indian Home Guards Civil War Service Records*. Tulsa, Okla.: M. W. Chase, 1993.

———. *Index to Civil War Service Records—Watie's Cherokee Regiments*. Tulsa, Okla.: M. W. Chase, 1989.

Index to Applications for Pension from the State of Oklahoma Submitted by Confederate Soldiers, Sailors, and Their Widows. Oklahoma City: Oklahoma Genealogical Society, 1969.

Oklahoma Board of Pension Commissioners. *Confederate Pension Applications for Soldiers and Sailors*. Microfilm, 22 rolls.

Oklahoma Confederate Pension Applications Submitted by Confederate Soldiers, Sailors, and Their Widows. Oklahoma City: Oklahoma Genealogical Society, 1969.

Oregon

Reed, C. A. *Report of the Adjutant General of the State of Oregon for the Years 1865–6*. Salem, Ore.: H. L. Pittock, 1866.

Pennsylvania

Alphabetical Card File, Pennsylvania Soldiers, 1861–1866 (Based on Bates' History of Pennsylvania Volunteers). Microfilm, 80 rolls.

Alphabetical Index of Civil War Soldiers. Microfilm, 80 rolls.

Bates, Samuel P. *History of Pennsylvania Volunteers 1861–5*. 5 vols. Harrisburg, Pa.: State Printer, 1869–71.

Russell, A. L. *Annual Report of the Adjutant General of Pennsylvania, 1863*. N.p., 1864.

Rhode Island

Dyer, Elisha. *Annual Report of the Adjutant General of the State of Rhode Island and Providence Plantations for the Year 1865*. Providence, R.I.: E. Freeman and Sons, 1893–95.

South Carolina

Broken Fortunes: South Carolina Soldiers, Sailors, and Citizens Who Died in the Service of Their Country and State in the War for Southern Independence, 1861–1865. Charleston: South Carolina Department of Archives and History, 1992.

Crawley, Patrick. *Artificial Limbs for Confederate Soldiers*. Columbia: South Carolina Department of Archives and History, 1992.

Helsley, Alexia J. *South Carolina's African American Confederate Pensioners, 1923–1925*. Columbia: South Carolina Department of Archives and History, 1998.

Recollections and Reminiscences, 1861–1865 Through World War I. 12 vols. to date. South Carolina Division, United Daughters of the Confederacy, 1990–.

Rivers, William J. *Roll of the Dead: South Carolina Troops, Confederate States Service*. Columbia: South Carolina Department of Archives and History, 1995.

Salley, A. S. *South Carolina Troops in Confederate Service*. 3 vols. Columbia, S.C.: R. L. Bryan Co., 1913.

South Carolina Confederate Pension Applications, 1919–1925. Microfilm, 34 rolls.

South Dakota

Dakota Militia in the War of 1862. 58th Congress, 2nd Session, Senate Document No. 241. Washington, D.C., 1904.

Tennessee

Dyer, Gustavus W. *Tennessee Civil War Veterans Questionnaires*. 5 vols. Easley, S.C.: Southern Historical Press, 1985.

Index to Tennessee Confederate Pension Applications. Nashville: Tennessee State Library and Archives, 1964.

Sistler, Samuel. *Index to Tennessee Confederate Pension Applications*. Nashville: B. Sistler, 1995.

Tennessee Board of Pension Examiners. *Tennessee Confederate Soldiers and Widows Pension Applications*. Microfilm, 181 rolls.

Tennessee's Confederate Widows and Their Families. Cleveland, Tenn.: Cleveland Public Library, 1992.

Tennesseans in the Civil War: A Military History of Confederate and Union Units with Available Rosters of Personnel. 2 vols. Nashville: University of Tennessee Press, 1985.

Wiefering, Edna. *Tennessee Confederate Widows and Their Families: Abstracts of 11,190 Confederate Widows Pension Applications*. Cleveland, Tenn.: Cleveland Public Library Staff and Volunteers, 1992.

Texas

Davis, Kathryn Hooper, and Linda Ericson Devereaux, and Carolyn Reeves Ericson. *Texas Confederate Home Roster—with Added Data from Confederate Home Ledgers.* Nacogdoches, Tex.: Ericson Books, 2003.

Ingmire, Frances T. *Confederate Officers of Texas.* Signal Mountain, Tenn.: Mountain Press, 1983.

Johnson, Sidney S. *Texans Who Wore the Gray.* Tyler, Tex., 1907.

Kight, L. L. *Their Last Full Measure: Texas Confederate Casualty Lists 1861–1865.* 3 vols. Arlington, Tex.: G. T. T. Publishing, 1997.

Kinney, John M. *Index to Applications for Texas Confederate Pensions.* Rev. ed. Austin: Archives Division Texas State Library, 1977.

Mearse, Linda. *Confederate Indigent Families Lists of Texas, 1863–1865.* San Marcos, Tex.: L. Mearse, 1995.

Miller, Thomas L. *Texas Confederate Script Grantees C.S.A.* N.p., 1985.

Texas Comptroller's Office. *Confederate Pensions: Applications Approved and Rejected.* Microfilm, 700 rolls.

Thompson, Jerry. *Mexican Texans in the Union Army.* El Paso: Texas Western Press, 1986.

Twelfth Annual Meeting of the United Confederate Veterans Dallas, Texas April 12–25, 1902. Dallas: Dallas Genealogical Society, 1979.

White, Virgil D. *Index to Texas CSA Pension Files.* Waynesboro, Tenn.: National Historical Publishing Co., 1989.

Wright, Jody F., ed. *Czechs in Gray—and Blue, Too!* San Antonio: J. F. Wright, 1998.

Yeary, Mamie. *Reminiscences of the Boys in Gray, 1861–1865.* Dayton, Ohio: Morningside, 1986.

Vermont

Benedict, George. G. *Vermont in the Civil War.* 2 vols. Salem, Mass.: Higginson Book Co., 1995.

Peck, Theodore S. *Revised Roster of Vermont Volunteers and Lists of Vermonters Who Served in the Army and Navy of the United States During the War of the Rebellion, 1861–66.* Montpelier, Vt.: Press of the Watchman Publishing Co., 1892.

Virginia

Applications for Relief of Needy Widows. Microfilm, 28 rolls.

Calendar of Virginia State Papers and Other Manuscripts. Vol. 11. New York: Kraus Reprint Co., 1968.

Krick, Robert E. L. *Staff Officers in Gray: A Biographical Register of the Staff Officers in the Army of Northern Virginia.* University of North Carolina Press, 2003.

Nuckels, Ashley K. *Commonwealth of Virginia Civil War Pensioners.* A. K. Nuckels, 2003.

Virginia Office of the Comptroller. *Civil War Pensioners' Applications.* Microfilm, 219 rolls.

Virginia Regimental Histories Series. 83 vols. to date. Lynchburg, Tenn.: H. E. Howard, 1982–. The series deals with each Virginia unit and each Virginia soldier. Each volume contains a unit history and an annotated muster roll of every man who served in that unit.

West Virginia

Annual Report of the Adjutant General for the Year Ending December 31, 1864. Wheeling, W.Va.: John F. M'Dermot, 1865.

Annual Report of the Adjutant General for the Year Ending December 31, 1865. Wheeling, W. Va.: John Frew, 1866.

Lang, Theodore F. *Loyal West Virginia from 1861 to 1865.* Baltimore: Deutsch Publishing Co., 1895.

Wisconsin

Chapman, Chandler P. *Roster of Wisconsin Volunteers, War of the Rebellion, 1861–65.* Madison, Wis., 1886.

Wisconsin Volunteers, War of the Rebellion, 1861–1865. Arranged Alphabetically. Madison, Wis.: Democrat Printing Co., 1914.

Spanish American War and Philippine Insurrection, 1898–1902

Various States

Coston, William Hilary. *The Spanish American War Volunteer.* Freeport, N.Y.: Books for Libraries Press, 1971. A discussion of African American volunteers.

Plante, Trevor K. "Researching Service in the U.S. Army During the Philippines Insurrection." *Prologue* 32 (Summer 2000). Reprinted at <www.archives.gov/publications/prologue>.

Roster of Women Nurses Enlisted for Spanish-American War by DAR Hospital Corps.

Yockelson, Mitchell. "'I Am Entitled to the Medal of Honor and I Want It' Theodore Roosevelt and His Quest for Glory." *Prologue* 30 (Spring 1998). Reprinted at <www.archives.gov/publications/prologue>.

Arizona

Herner, Charles. *Arizona Rough Riders.* Appendix 3, "Muster-In Roll," pp. 234–44. Tucson: University of Arizona Press, 1970.

Arkansas

Allen, Desmond Walls. *Arkansas Spanish-American War Soldiers.* Conway, Ark.: Arkansas Research, 1988.

California

California Volunteers in the Spanish-American War of 1898. Sacramento, 1899.

Connecticut

Connecticut Volunteers Who Served in the Spanish-American War, 1898–1899. Hartford: Connecticut Adjutant General's Office, 1899.

Florida

Soldiers of Florida in the Seminole Indian, Civil and Spanish-American Wars. Macclenny, Fla.: R. J. Ferry, 1983.

United States Record and Pension Office. *Compiled Service Records of Volunteer Soldiers Who Served in the Florida Infantry During the War with Spain.* Microfilm, M1087, 13 rolls. Washington, D.C.: National Archives Microfilm Publication.

Georgia

Thaxton, Carlton J. *Roster of Spanish-American War Soldiers from Georgia.* Americus, Ga.: Thaxton Co., 1984.

Illinois

Roster of Illinois Volunteer in the American-Spanish War, 1898–99. Illinois Adjutant General Report, X. 349–685.

Indiana

Gore, James K. *Record of Indiana Volunteers in the Spanish-American War, 1898–1899.* Indianapolis: Indiana Adjutant General's office, 1900.

Kansas

Fox, S. M. *13th Biennial Report of the Adjutant General of the State of Kansas, 1901–02.* Topeka, Kans.: Adjutant General's Office, 1902.

Kentucky

Report of the Adjutant General of the State of Kentucky: Kentucky Volunteers, War with Spain, 1898–1899. Frankfort, Ky.: Glove Printing Co., 1908.

Louisiana

Wright, Nancy Lowne. *Louisiana Volunteers in the War of 1898.* Wright Shannon Pub., 1989.

Maryland

Riley, Hugh Ridgely. *Roster of the Soldiers and Sailors Who Served in Organizations from Maryland During the Spanish-American War.* Silver Spring, Md.: Family Line Publications, 1990.

Minnesota

Eleventh Biennial Report . . . Including Military Operations . . . up to November 30, 1900. St. Paul, Minn.: Minnesota Adjutant General's Department, 1901.

Richardson, Antona H. *Minnesotans in the Spanish-American War and the Philippine Insurrection, April 21, 1898–July 4, 1904.* St. Paul, Minn.: Paduan Press, 1998.

Missouri

Missouri Adjutant General's Office Report for 1897–98. Jefferson City Tribune Printing Co., 1898.

New Jersey

Report of the Adjutant General of New Jersey. Somerville: New Jersey Adjutant General's Office, 1899.

New York

New York in the Spanish-American War, 1898. 3 vols. Albany, N.Y.: J. B. Lyon, 1902.

North Carolina

Cumber, Kimberly A. "Index to Roster of North Carolina Volunteers in the Spanish-American War, 1898–1899." *North Carolina Genealogical Society Journal* 24 (1998): 252–95.

Roster of the North Carolina Volunteers in the Spanish-American War 1898–1899. Raleigh, N.C.: Press of Edwards and Broughton, 1900.

Ohio

Broglin, Jana Sloan. *Index to Official Roster of Ohio Soldiers in the War with Spain, 1898–1899.* Mansfield: Ohio Genealogical Society, n.d.

Hough, Benson W. *The Official Roster of Ohio Soldiers in the War with Spain, 1898–1899.* Columbus, Ohio: Edward T. Miller Co., 1916.

Ohio Adjutant General. *Report of Herbert B. Kingsley, Adjutant General of Ohio from November 15, 1898 to April 30, 1899, Inclusive.*

Oregon

Gantenbein, C. U. *The Official Records of the Oregon Volunteers in the Spanish War and Philippine Insurrection.* 2nd ed. Salem, Ore.: Oregon Adjutant General's Office, 1903.

Pennsylvania

Stewart, Thomas J. *Record of Pennsylvania Volunteers in the Spanish-American War, 1898.* W. S. Ray, State Printer, 1900.

———. *Record of Pennsylvania Volunteers in the Spanish-American War, 1898.* 2nd ed. Harrisburg: Pennsylvania Adjutant General's Office, 1901.

South Dakota

Robinson, Doane. *History of South Dakota.* 2 vols. Chicago: B. F. Brown and Co., 1904, v. 1, 426–62.

Tennessee

Spanish-American War, 1898. Microfilm, 3 rolls.

Utah

Saldana, Richard H. *Index to the Utah Spanish-American War Veterans,* 1898. A.I.S.I. Publishers, 1988.

Vermont

Vermont Adjutant and Inspector General's Office. *Vermont in the Spanish-American War.* Montpelier, Vt.: Capital City Press, 1929.

West Virginia

Biennial Report of the Adjutant General of West Virginia, 1899–1900. Charleston: West Virginia Adjutant General's Office, 1900.

Wyoming

Bartlett, Ichabod S. *History of Wyoming.* 3 vols. Chicago: S. J. Clarke Publishing Co., 1918. Vol. 2, 289–303.

World War I, 1914–1918

Haulsee, William M. *Soldiers of the Great War.* 3 vols. Washington, D.C.: Soldiers Record Publishing Association, 1920.

Lockman, Frank F. *Roster of U.S. Marines, World War I Era, 1917–1918–1919, A-Z.* Yucca Valley, Calif.: FFL Military Personnel Research, 1995–97.

Newman, John J. *Uncle We are Ready: Registering Men, 1917–1918, A Guide to Researching World War I Draft Registration Cards.* North Salt Lake City, Utah: Heritage Quest, 2001.

Schaefer, Christina K. *The Great War: A Guide to the Service Records of All the World's Fighting Men and Volunteers.* Baltimore: Genealogical Publishing Co., 1998.

U.S. Bureau of Naval Personnel. *Officers and Enlisted Men of the United States Navy Who Lost Their Lives During the World War, from April 6, 1917 to November 11, 1918.* Washington, D.C.: Government Printing Office, 1920.

U.S. Selective Service System. *World War I Selective Service System Draft Registration Cards.* Microfilm, M1509, 4,277 rolls. Washington, D.C.: National Archives Microfilm Publication.

U.S. War Department. *Pilgrimage for the Mothers and Widows of Soldiers, Sailors, and Marines of the American Forces Now Interred in the Cemeteries of Europe as Provided by the Act of Congress of March 2, 1929.* Washington, D.C.: Government Printing Office, 1930.

———. *Register of Indians in World War I.* Microfilm, M1871, 1 roll. Washington, D.C.: National Archives Microfilm Publication.

Alabama

Nuckols, Ashley K. *Deaths, American Expeditionary Forces, 1917, 1918, Alabama.* N.p.: A. K. Nuckols, 1995.

World War I Service Records, 1918–1919. Microfilm, 38 rolls.

Arizona

Nuckols, Ashley K. *Deaths, American Expeditionary Forces, 1917, 1918, Arizona.* N.p.: A. K. Nuckols, 1995.

Arkansas

Allen, Desmond Walls. *Index to Arkansas' World War I Soldiers.* 6 vols. Conway, Ark.: Arkansas Research, 2002.

Nuckols, Ashley K. *Deaths, American Expeditionary Forces, 1917, 1918, Arkansas.* N.p.: A. K. Nuckols, 1995.

California

California Adjutant General's Office. *World War I Draft Report: List of California Men Who Enlisted or Were Inducted into the Army, Navy, or Marine Corps.*

Nuckols, Ashley K. *Deaths, American Expeditionary Forces, 1917, 1918, California.* N.p.: A.K. Nuckols, 1995.

Colorado

Roster of Men and Women Who Served in the World War from Colorado, 1917–1918.

Nuckols, Ashley K. *Deaths, American Expeditionary Forces, 1917, 1918, Colorado.* N.p.: A. K. Nuckols, 1995.

Connecticut

Connecticut Adjutant General's Office. *Connecticut Service Records; Men and Women in the Armed Forces of the United States During the World War, 1917–1920.* 3 vols. Hartford, Conn.: Office of the Adjutant General, 1941.

Nuckols, Ashley K. *Deaths, American Expeditionary Forces, 1917, 1918, Connecticut.* N.p.: A. K. Nuckols, 1995.

Delaware and District of Columbia

Nuckols, Ashley K. *Deaths, American Expeditionary Forces, 1917, 1918, Delaware and District of Columbia.* N.p.: A. K. Nuckols, 1995.

Florida

Nuckols, Ashley K. *Deaths, American Expeditionary Forces, 1917, 1918, Florida.* N.p.: A. K. Nuckols, 1995.

World War I Service Cards. Microfilm, 11 rolls.

Georgia

Boss, Bert E. *The Georgia State Memorial Book*. N.p.: American Memorial Pub. Co., 1921.

Nuckols, Ashley K. *Deaths, American Expeditionary Forces, 1917, 1918, Georgia*. N.p.: A. K. Nuckols,1995.

Hawaii

Kuykendall, Ralph S. *Hawaii in the World War*. Honolulu, Hawaii: Historical Commission, 1928.

Idaho

Biennial Report, 1917–18.

Nuckols, Ashley K. *Deaths, American Expeditionary Forces, 1917, 1918, Idaho*. N.p.: A. K. Nuckols, 1995.

Illinois

Fighting Men of Illinois.

Nuckols, Ashley K. *Deaths, American Expeditionary Forces, 1917, 1918, Illiniois*. N.p.: A. K. Nuckols,1995.

Indiana

Gold Star Honor Roll: A Record of Indiana Men and Women Who Died in the Service of the United States and Allied Nations in the World War, 1914–1918.

Nuckols, Ashley K. *Deaths, American Expeditionary Forces, 1917, 1918, Indiana*. N.p.: A. K. Nuckols, 1995.

Iowa

Nuckols, Ashley K. *Deaths, American Expeditionary Forces, 1917, 1918, Iowa*. N.p.: A. K. Nuckols, 1995.

Kansas

Nuckols, Ashley K. *Deaths, American Expeditionary Forces, 1917, 1918, Kansas*. N.p.: A. K. Nuckols, 1995.

Kentucky

Nuckols, Ashley K. *Deaths, American Expeditionary Forces, 1917, 1918, Kentucky*. N.p.: A. K. Nuckols, 1995.

Louisiana

Nuckols, Ashley K. *Deaths, American Expeditionary Forces, 1917, 1918, Louisiana*. N.p.: A. K. Nuckols, 1995.

Maine

Maine Adjutant General. *Roster of Maine in the Military Service of the United States and Allies in the World War 1917–1919*. 2 vols. August, Maine: Published under the Direction of James W. Hanson, the Adjutant General, 1929.

Nuckols, Ashley K. *Deaths, American Expeditionary Forces, 1917, 1918, Maine*. N.p.: A. K. Nuckols, 1995.

Maryland

Maryland in the World War 1917–1919, Military and Naval Service Records. 3 vols. Baltimore: Maryland War Records Commission, 1933.

Nuckols, Ashley K. *Deaths, American Expeditionary Forces, 1917, 1918, Maryland*. N.p.: A. K. Nuckols, 1995.

Massachusetts

Nuckols, Ashley K. *Deaths, American Expeditionary Forces, 1917, 1918, Massachusetts*. N.p.: A. K. Nuckols, 1995.

Michigan

Nuckols, Ashley K. *Deaths, American Expeditionary Forces, 1917, 1918, Michigan*. N.p.: A. K. Nuckols, 1995.

Minnesota

Minnesota in the War with Germany. 2 vols.

Nuckols, Ashley K. *Deaths, American Expeditionary Forces, 1917, 1918, Minnesota*. N.p.: A. K. Nuckols, 1995.

Mississippi

Master Alphabetical Index, World War Veterans, Army. Microfilm, 2 rolls.

Nuckols, Ashley K. *Deaths, American Expeditionary Forces, 1917, 1918, Mississippi*. N.p.: A. K. Nuckols, 1995.

World War I Military Service Cards: United States Army and Marines. Microfilm, 40 rolls.

World War I Military Service Cards: United States Navy. Microfilm, 7 rolls.

Missouri

Nuckols, Ashley K. *Deaths, American Expeditionary Forces, 1917, 1918, Missouri*. N.p.: A. K. Nuckols, 1995.

Raupp, William A. *Report of the Adjutant General of Missouri, January 10, 1921– December 31, 1924*. Jefferson City, Mo.: Hugh Stephens, 1925.

Montana

Nuckols, Ashley K. *Deaths, American Expeditionary Forces, 1917, 1918, Montana*. N.p.: A. K. Nuckols, 1995.

Nebraska

Nuckols, Ashley K. *Deaths, American Expeditionary Forces, 1917, 1918, Nebraska*. N.p.: A. K. Nuckols, 1995.

Roster of Soldiers, Sailors, and Marines Who Served in the War of the Rebellion, Spanish-American War, and World War. Lincoln, Nebr., 1925.

Nevada

Nuckols, Ashley K. *Deaths, American Expeditionary Forces, 1917, 1918, Nevada*. N.p.: A. K. Nuckols, 1995.

Sullivan, Maurice J. *Nevada's Golden Stars: A Memorial Volume Designed as a Gift from the State of Nevada to the Relatives of Those Nevada Heroes Who Died in the World War*. Reno: A. Carlisle, 1924.

New Hampshire

Nuckols, Ashley K. *Deaths, American Expeditionary Forces, 1917, 1918, New Hampshire*. N.p.: A. K. Nuckols, 1995.

New Jersey

Nuckols, Ashley K. *Deaths, American Expeditionary Forces, 1917, 1918, New Jersey*. N.p.: A. K. Nuckols, 1995.

New Mexico

Nuckols, Ashley K. *Deaths, American Expeditionary Forces, 1917, 1918, New Mexico*. N.p.: A. K. Nuckols, 1995.

New York

Nuckols, Ashley K. *Deaths, American Expeditionary Forces, 1917, 1918, New York*. N.p.: A. K. Nuckols, 1995.

Nuckols, Ashley K. *Deaths, American Expeditionary Forces, 1917, 1918, New York State*. N.p.: A. K. Nuckols, 1995.

North Carolina

North Carolina Adjutant General. *Annual Reports 1917–1918*.

Nuckols, Ashley K. *Deaths, American Expeditionary Forces, 1917, 1918, North Carolina*. N.p.: A. K. Nuckols, 1995.

North Dakota

Nuckols, Ashley K. *Deaths, American Expeditionary Forces, 1917, 1918, North Dakota*. N.p.: A. K. Nuckols, 1995.

Roster of Men and Women Who Served in the Army or Naval Service (Including the Marine Corps) of the United States or Its Allies from the State of North Dakota in the World War 1917–18. 4 vols. Bismarck, N.Dak.: Bismarck Tribune Co., 1931.

Ohio

Nuckols, Ashley K. *Deaths, American Expeditionary Forces, 1917, 1918, Ohio*. N.p.: A. K. Nuckols, 1995.

Ohio Adjutant General's Office. *The Official Roster of Ohio Soldiers, Sailors, and Marines in the World War, 1917–1918*. 23 vols. Columbus, Ohio: F. J. Heer Printing Co., 1926–29.

Oklahoma

Hoffmann, Roy. *Oklahoma Honor Roll, World War I, 1917–1918*.

Nuckols, Ashley K. *Deaths, American Expeditionary Forces, 1917, 1918, Oklahoma*. N.p.: A. K. Nuckols, 1995.

Oregon

Nuckols, Ashley K. *Deaths, American Expeditionary Forces, 1917, 1918, Oregon*. N.p.: A. K. Nuckols, 1995.

Pennsylvania

Nuckols, Ashley K. *Deaths, American Expeditionary Forces, 1917, 1918, Pennsylvania*. N.p.: A. K. Nuckols, 1995.

Rhode Island

Nuckols, Ashley K. *Deaths, American Expeditionary Forces, 1917, 1918, Rhode Island*. N.p.: A. K. Nuckols, 1995.

South Carolina

Nuckols, Ashley K. *Deaths, American Expeditionary Forces, 1917, 1918, South Carolina*. N.p.: A. K. Nuckols, 1995.

South Carolina Adjutant General's Office. *The Official Roster of South Carolina, Soldiers, Sailors, and Marines in the World War, 1917–1918*. 2 vols. Columbia: General Assembly, 1929.

South Dakota

Nuckols, Ashley K. *Deaths, American Expeditionary Forces, 1917, 1918, South Dakota*. N.p.: A. K. Nuckols, 1995.

Tennessee

Nuckols, Ashley K. *Deaths, American Expeditionary Forces, 1917, 1918, Tennessee*. N.p.: A. K. Nuckols, 1995.

World War I, Gold Star Records. Microfilm, 7 rolls.

World War I Veterans and Ex-Servicemen's Records, 1910–1920. Microfilm, 10 rolls.

Texas

History of Texas World War Heroes. Dallas: Army and Navy History Co., 1920.

Nuckols, Ashley K. *Deaths, American Expeditionary Forces, 1917, 1918, Texas*. N.p.: A. K. Nuckols, 1995.

Texas Veterans of Czech Ancestry. Austin: Eakin Press, 1999.

Utah

Nuckols, Ashley K. *Deaths, American Expeditionary Forces, 1917, 1918, Utah*. N.p.: A. K. Nuckols, 1995.

Warrum, Noble. *Utah in the World War: The Men Behind the Guns and the Men and Women Behind the Men Behind the Gun*. Salt Lake City: Utah State Council of Defense, 1924.

Vermont

Johnson, Herbert T. *Roster of Vermont Men and Women in the Military and Naval Service of the United States and Allies in the World War, 1917–1919*. Rutland, Vt.: Tuttle, 1927.

Nuckols, Ashley K. *Deaths, American Expeditionary Forces, 1917, 1918, Vermont*. N.p.: A. K. Nuckols, 1995.

Virginia

Nuckols, Ashley K. *Deaths, American Expeditionary Forces, 1917, 1918, Virginia*. n.p.: A.K. Nuckols, 1995.

Washington

Nuckols, Ashley K. *Deaths, American Expeditionary Forces, 1917, 1918, Washington*. N.p.: A. K. Nuckols, 1995.

West Virginia

Nuckols, Ashley K. *Deaths, American Expeditionary Forces, 1917, 1918, West Virginia*. N.p.: A. K. Nuckols, 1995.

Wisconsin

Nuckols, Ashley K. *Deaths, American Expeditionary Forces, 1917, 1918, Wisconsin*. N.p.: A. K. Nuckols, 1995.

Wyoming

Nuckols, Ashley K. *Deaths, American Expeditionary Forces, 1917, 1918, Wyoming*. N.p.: A. K. Nuckols, 1995.

World War II, 1939–1945

Kaufman, Isidor. *American Jews in World War II: The Story of 550,000 Fighters for Freedom*. 2 vols. New York: Dial Press, 1947.

Knox, Debra J. *WW II Military Records: A Family Historian's Guide*. Spartanburg, S.C.: MIE Pub., 2003.

United States Navy Dept. Office of Information. *State Summary of War Casualties*. 50 vols. Washington, D.C.: U.S. Navy, 1946.

Arkansas

United States Selective Service System. *World War II Draft Cards (Fourth Registration) for the State of Arkansas*. Microfilm, 75 rolls.

Delaware

Casey, Lowell A. *Try Us: The Story of the Washington Artillery in World War II: Louisiana Casualty Lists W.W. II*. Baton Rouge: Claitor's Pub. Division, 1971.

United States Selective Service System. *World War II Draft Cards (Fourth Registration) for the State of Delaware*. Microfilm, M1936, 10 rolls. Washington D.C.: National Archives Publications.

Maryland

Maryland in World War II. 4 vols. Baltimore: War Records Division of the Maryland Historical Society, 1950–56.

United States Selective Service System World War II Draft Cards (Fourth Registration) for the State of Maryland. Microfilm, M1937, 66 rolls.

Oregon

Spencer, Leonard. A *Partial List of Military Casualties and MIAs from the State of Oregon During World War II*. Portland: Genealogical Forum of Oregon, 1993.

South Carolina

The Official Roster of South Carolina Serviceman and Servicewomen in World War II, 1941–1946.

Texas

History of the Second World War: A Memorial, a Remembrance, an Appreciation. 5 vols. Dallas: Historical Publishing Co., 1948.

West Virginia

United States Selective Service System. *World War II Draft Cards (Fourth Registration) for the State of West Virginia*. Microfilm, M1939, 56 rolls. Washington, D.C.: National Archives Microfilm Publication.

Korea, Vietnam, Gulf Wars

Bin, Alberto, Richard Hill, and Archer Jones. *Desert Storm: A Forgotten War*. Praeger Publishers, 1998.

Lowry, Richard S. *Gulf War Chronicles: A Military History of the First War With Iraq*. Lincoln, Neb.: iUniverse, 2003.

Joes, Anthony James. *The War for South Viet Nam, 1954–1975*. Rev. ed. Westport, Conn.: Praeger Press, 2001.

Jordan, Kenneth N., Jr. *Forgotten Heroes: 131 Men of the Korean War Awarded the Medal of Honor 1950–1954*. Schiffer Publishing, 1995.

Internet Resources

United States—General

American Merchant Marine at War: Revolution to World War II to Today <www.usmm.org>

Civil War [Compiled] Service Records [Index] <www.ancestry.com>

Civil War Pension Index: General Index to Pension Files, 1861–1934 <www.ancestry.com>

Civil War Soldiers and Sailors System <www.civilwar.nps.gov/cwss>

Medal of Honor Recipients Civil War <www.army.mil/cmh-pg/mobciv.htm>

Nationwide Gravesite Locator
<http://gravelocator.cem.va.gov/j@ee/servlet/NGL_v1>

Revolutionary War Pension and Bounty Land Warrant Application Files <www.heritagequest.com>.

U.S. Military Personnel Who Died (Including Missing and Captured and Declared Dead) as a result of the Vietnam conflict, 1957–1995.
<www.archives.gov/research/vietnam-war/casualty-lists>.

U.S. Military Personnel Who Died From Hostile Action (Including Missing and Captured) in the Korean War, 1950–1957.
<www.archives.gov/research/korean-war/casualty-lists/>

U.S. Naval Deaths, World War I <www.ancestry.com>

The Vietnam Veteran's Memorial
<http://thewall-usa.com/index2.html>

World War I Draft Registration Cards and Index, 1917–1918 (digitized) <www.ancestry.com>

State Resources

Alabama

Alabama Civil War Service Cards File
<www.archives.state.al.us/civilwar/index.cfm>

Arkansas

Arkansas Confederate Home
< http://arkansashistory.arkansas.com/resource_types/military_records/default.asp>

Colorado

Colorado State Archives
<www.colorado.gov/dpa/doit/archives>

1. Colorado Volunteers Transcript of Records Index (Civil War)
2. Colorado Volunteers from the New Mexico Campaign (1862)
3. Colorado Volunteers in the Spanish-American War (1898)
4. Colorado Veterans' Grave Registrations 1862–1949
5. Colorado Civil War Casualties Index

Connecticut

1. Noble Pension Database
<www.cslib.org/noble.asp>
2. World War I Veterans Database
<www.cslib.org/ww1.asp>
3. Fitch's Home for Soldiers
<www.cslib.org/fitch.asp>

Florida

1. Florida Confederate Pension Application Files
<www.floridamemory.com/collections/pensionfiles/>
2. World War I Service Cards
<www.floridamemory.com/collections/WWI>

Idaho

Civil War Veterans in Idaho
<http://idahohistory.net/civilwar.html>

Illinois

Illinois State Archives
<www.sos.state.il.us/departments/archives/archives.html>

1. Database of Illinois War of 1812 Veterans
2. Database of Illinois Winnebago War Veterans
3. Database of Illinois Black Hawk War Veterans
4. Database of Illinois Mexican War Veterans
5. Database of Illinois Civil War Veterans
6. Database of Illinois Civil War Veterans Serving in the U.S. Navy
7. Database of Illinois Civil War Veterans of Missouri Militia
8. Database of Illinois Spanish-American War Veterans
9. Database of 1929 Illinois Roll of Honor
10. Database of Soldiers' and Sailors' Home Residents (1867–1916)

Indiana

Indiana Soldier's and Sailor's Children's Home
<www.in.gov/icpr/archives/databases/issch/intro.html>

Kansas

1. Kansas Adjutant General's Report, 1861–1865
<www.kshs.org/genealogists/military/civil_war_adjgenl.htm>
2. Enlistment Papers of the 19th Kansas Cavalry, 1868–1869
<www.kshs.org./genealogists/military/19thkansasenlistmentpapers.htm>
3. Kansas Adjutant General's Report, 1898–1899
< www.kshs.org/genealogists/military/adjgenlspanam.htm>
4. Necrology of the Grand Army of the Republic, Department of Kansas
<www.kshs.org/genealogists/military/gar/garnecrologies>

Louisiana

Confederate Pension Application Index Database
<www.sec.state.la.us/archives/gen/cpa-index.htm>

Maryland

Maryland State Archives
<www.mdarchives.state.md.us/msa/homepage/html/homepage.html>

1. Muster Rolls and Other Records of Service of Maryland Troops in the American Revolution

2. History and Roster of Maryland Volunteers War of 1861–1865, 2 vols.

3. The Maryland Line in the Confederate Army, 1861–1865

Missouri

Soldiers of the Great War (killed during World War I)
<www.slpl.lib.mo.us/libsrc/soldiers.htm>

St. Louis City and St. Louis County Vietnam Dead
<www.slpl.lib.mo.us/libsrc/vietnam.htm>

World War I Military Service Cards Database
<www.sos.mo.gov/ww1>

New York

New York Civil War Soldier Database
<www.archives.nysed.gov/a/researchroom/rr_mi_civilwar_dbintro>

North Carolina

The MARS index incorporates a number of record groups including the Revolutionary War account books
<www.ncarchives.dcr.state.nc.us>

Oklahoma

Index to Oklahoma's Confederate Pension Records
<www.odl.state.ok.us/oar/archives/collections.htm>

Ohio

War of 1812 Roster of Ohio Soldiers
<www.ohiohistory.org/resource/database/rosters.html>

Pennsylvania

Pennsylvania State Archives
<www.digitalarchives.state.pa.us/>

1. Civil War Veterans' Card File
2. Revolutionary Military Abstract Card File
3. World War I Service Medal Application Cards
4. Spanish-American War Veterans' Card File of United States Volunteers
5. Mexican Border Campaign Veterans' Card File
6. Militia Officers Index Cards, 1775, 1800

South Carolina

Confederate Pension Applications – Digital Images
<www.archivesindex.sc.gov/search/default.asp>

Tennessee

Tennessee State Library
<www.tennessee.gov/tsla/>

1. Tennessee Confederate Pension Applications: Soldiers and Widows
2. Tennessee World War I Veterans
3. Tennessee Civil War Veteran's Questionnaires
4. Tennessee Confederate Physicians
5. Tennessee Confederate Soldiers' Home: Application Index
6. Index to Service Abstracts of Soldiers in Tennessee Volunteer Units in the Spanish American War
7. Index to Tennessee Gold Star Records

Texas

1. Confederate Pension Applications
< www.tsl.state.tx.us/arc/pensions/index.html>

2. Texas Adjutant General Service Records, 1836–1935
< www.tsl.state.tx.us/arc/service/index.html>

3. Mexican War: Palo Alto and Rosaca de la Palma Casualty List
<www.library.ci.corpus.christi.tx.us/mexicanwar/paloalto.htm>

Virginia

Library of Virginia
<www.lva.lib.va.us/whatwehave/mil>

1. Dunmore's War (Virginia Payrolls/Public Service Claims, 1775)
2. Culpeper County Classes, 1781
3. Revolutionary War Bounty Warrants
4. Revolutionary War Land Office Military Certificates
5. Revolutionary War Public Service Claims
6. Revolutionary War Rejected Claims
7. Revolutionary War Virginia State Pensions
8. Index to War of 1812 Pay Rolls and Muster Rolls
9. Confederate Disability Applications and Receipts
10. Confederate Pension Rolls, Veterans and Widows
11. Index to Virginia Confederate Rosters
12. Robert E. Lee Camp Confederate Soldiers' Home Applications for Admission
13. World War I History Commission Questionnaires
14. Virginia Military Dead Database

Wisconsin

Roster of Wisconsin Volunteers, War of the Rebellion, 1861–1865
<www.wisconsinhistory.org/roster>

12

Newspapers

LORETTO DENNIS SZUCS, FUGA, and JAMES L. HANSEN, FASG

The technological advances of recent years have revolutionized the way family historians discover and use records. Nowhere is that more evident than in the area of newspaper research. As a steadily increasing number of large metropolitan dailies and small-town dailies and weeklies become accessible on the Internet, we suddenly have a powerful new tool to discover incredible details about our ancestors' lives—details that are often unavailable elsewhere. Historical newspapers give us the remarkable ability to see history through eyewitness accounts, while contemporary newspapers keep us current with today's domestic and international happenings. With just a few clicks of the mouse, we can view a news item or an obituary from yesterday or from a hundred years ago.

Scanning technology makes it possible for us to see and print accurate reproductions of old newspapers from the convenience of our own homes. Indexes created using optical character recognition (OCR) software allow us to search through hundreds of thousands of pages for names or events in mere seconds. Coverage is uneven at this point, but if one of the digitized newspapers is one you need, it can be invaluable. For anyone who has had to conduct a page-by-page search of unindexed original or microfilmed papers, this development is nothing short of wonderful.

In just a few short years, government agencies and commercial entities have placed millions of pages of our individual and collective history online, enabling us to see the original documents firsthand. In these cases, we are no longer dependent on abstracts or transcripts to fill the gaps in our family stories. Being able to search newspaper databases allows us to discover long-lost relatives who were living in unexpected places and involved in stories we never imagined. Consider the man who disappeared from records in New York in 1850 but was found in a Chicago newspaper database for that same year. Or the woman who disappeared from records in the town where she had resided all of her life, only to be found in a search of a newspaper database of a distant town. An item in the digitized

Chapter Contents

and indexed newspaper led to the story of how the woman had gone to live with her daughter in this town because of declining health, and how she had passed away in a place where no one had thought to look for records.

Essentially every currently published newspaper has a website. While some include only contact and other basic information, others include much more detailed and rich content. An increasing number of current newspapers post most, if not all, of their articles and archives online, either free or for a fee. Many libraries, genealogical and historical societies, commercial companies, and individuals have extracted, compiled, indexed, and digitized items from newspapers and made them available online in various forms.

Many newspaper databases include fully searchable text versions that can be browsed or searched using a computer-generated index. The accuracy of every newspaper index varies according to the quality of the original images. The images for most newspapers can be browsed sequentially, or via links to specific images, which may be obtained through the search results. Over time, the name of a newspaper may have changed and the time span it covered may not always be consistent. Also, the date range of some Internet collections may not represent the complete published set or time period needed. Check the local library or historical society in the area in which your ancestors lived for more information about other available newspapers. When the subject or individual of your search cannot be located through an index, and if a place and date range (death date, etc.) are known, try browsing the full text of a specific newspaper. Such full-text searches should be conducted as frequently as possible because, in addition to the chance to find an ancestor, there is no better way to capture the thinking, the culture, and the very essence of the time and place where your ancestors lived.

How have newspapers become such an important research tool for so many in such a short period of time? And what are the secrets to using them to their fullest potential? It has been said that newspapers are the first rough draft of history. As such they are of great importance to students of history, sociology, law, medical research, economics, marketing, and many other fields. Because newspapers are so heavily used, there has been a significant demand to make newspapers more accessible to the masses. This chapter will focus on the great potential that this ever-growing research tool has to offer, with a special focus on the ways that family historians can best put newspapers to use in their research.

The National Digital Newspaper Program

The National Digital Newspaper Program, launched by the National Endowment for the Humanities (NEH) and the Library of Congress in late 2004, plans to digitize 30 million pages, spanning the years 1836 through 1922. *Stars and Stripes*, a newspaper published by the United States Army from 1918 to 1919, was the first project to go online at the Library of Congress website as a result of the joint effort <www.loc.gov>. Because the fonts used in newspapers prior to 1836 do not lend themselves to OCR technology, those newspapers were not included in the first phase of scanning, and copyright laws set the limit at the other end of the series. Eventually, the Library of Congress site will host an online bibliography of newspapers that will tell where every newspaper (since the first newspaper published in 1690 to the present day) is located—whether online or offline. In a speech to members of the National Press Club in November 2004, NEH Chairman Bruce Cole said, "This digitizing will democratize knowledge by making it available to anyone with an Internet connection. But just as important and revolutionary, it is also going to create something new. The sheer volume of information in newspapers has been an obstacle. Newspapers carry three thousand to seven thousand words on a page. The new technology overcomes that. The page is scanned; it's tagged with name, date, and page number—metadata. The process turns the enormous volume of material into a searchable asset. And this asset will be easy to use" <www.neh.gov/whoweare/speeches/11162004.html>.

Examples of Online Newspapers

Because they understand the importance of newspapers to general and family historians, authors, students, journalists, and those in dozens of other professions; commercial entities like Ancestry.com <www.ancestry.com>, ProQuest <www.ProQuest.com>, and Readex <www.readex.com> have invested heavily in newspaper digitizing projects.

The Historical Newspaper Collection at Ancestry.com, available by subscription, includes pages from newspapers across the United States, UK, Canada, and other countries, dating from 1765 through the present. In addition to fully-searchable images of the *New York Times*, the *Atlanta Constitution*, and other large city publications, the Ancestry.com collection includes a wide variety of small town publications such as the *Adams Centinel* published in Gettysburg, Pennsylvania, from the beginning of the nineteenth century, and the *Ohio Repository* (1815 to 1861 with some gaps), which was published in Canton, Ohio.

The ProQuest Historical Collection, available at many libraries, includes full-text and full-image articles from several major American city newspapers from 1849 to 2001, including the *New York Times*, the *Chicago Tribune*, the *Wall Street Journal*, the *Boston Globe*, and a few others.

For those with an interest in early-American research, Readex, a division of Newsbank, has posted *Early American Newspapers, 1690–1876 Series I* online. Based largely on Clarence Brigham's *History and Bibliography of American Newspapers, 1690–1820*, this collection offers a fully text-searchable database of over one million pages, including cover-to-cover reproductions of historical newspapers such as the *Boston Gazette*, the *Gazette of the United States*, the *New York Evening Post*, and others. This collection is available at some public libraries, through some educational institutions, and to members of the New England Historic Genealogical Society <www.nehgs.org>.

Another good example of a subscription service offering digitized newspapers is NewspaperARCHIVE.com, which, according to its website <www.newspaperarchive.com>, adds a million pages of new content each month. There are also a growing number of pay-per-view newspaper sites that charge a fee for access to articles that can be identified by free online indexes.

State and Local Projects

The Utah Digital Newspapers project, launched in 2002 through a Library Services and Technology Act grant administered by the Utah State Library, is a great example of what individual states are doing to make newspapers accessible to the masses. The digitization process, developed at the University of Utah, is regularly adding searchable images of Utah newspapers printed from 1879 to 1956 <www.lib.utah.edu/digital/unews>.

The *Brooklyn Daily Eagle Online* is a remarkable project, produced by the Brooklyn Public Library (NY), and supported by a grant from the Institute of Museum and Library Services. Pages of the now-defunct *Brooklyn Daily Eagle* can be searched by name, date, or subject for the years 1841 to 1902 <www.brooklynpubliclibrary.org/eagle>. The *Eagle* is important not only because it carried news of what was for a long time the third largest city in the United States, but also because it included news from the rest of the New York Metropolitan area and the world in general. Because of the enormity of the collection, the digitization project has been broken into several phases. Phase I, which covers the period from 26 October 1841 to 31 December 1902, and is currently online, represents only half of the *Eagle's* years of publication.

Newspaper Abstracts, Extracts, and Photographs

A growing number of historical agencies are partnering with libraries to post newspaper archives or portions of newspaper collections online. An example is a *Chicago Daily News* collection of photographs (1902 to 1933) housed at the Chicago Historical Society. The collection is now viewable at the Library of Congress website <http://memory.loc.gov/ammem/ndlpcoop/ichihtml/cdnhome.html>.

In addition to the searchable full-page newspapers that are continuously going online, volunteers regularly post historical newspaper items on local interest sites such as those hosted by RootsWeb.com <www.rootsweb.com>. In many cases, obituaries and other newspaper clippings are the only sources to include birthplaces of the deceased, making them especially important for those seeking the origins of ancestors whose birth took place in a different state or country. The newspaper clipping database at RootsWeb.com <www.rootsweb.com> contains over 400,000 entries. The U.S. GenWeb Project <www.usgenweb.org>, hosted by RootsWeb.com, has been posting obituaries from various newspapers since 2000.

Obituaries

Obituaries from recently published and archived newspapers are available on a growing number of websites. Typing the word "newspapers" or "obituaries" into a search engine will lead to a vast array of old and current biographical information about individuals living in the United States and almost everywhere else on the globe. Typing the word "newspapers" or "obituaries" plus a specific place name will generally lead to a well of fascinating information and new clues for future research. Cyndi's List of Genealogy Sites on the Net <www.cyndislist.com/obits.htm> includes an alphabetically arranged list of hundreds of obituary links. Obituary Central <www.obitcentral.com> is a site with its own archive, searchable from the main page, as well as a state-by-state directory of obituary search engines. An amazing and always growing number of obituaries from current and historical newspapers are being posted daily.

The Obituary Hunter on Ancestry.com includes hundreds of thousands of recent obituaries from hundreds of newspapers. Ancestry.com scours the Internet daily to find new obituaries and extracts the facts into the database. In each case, the source of the information is provided, along with links to the full obituary text. It is a popular site for locating information on a recently deceased family member, ancestors, friends, former classmates, business associates, and celebrities.

The Denver Public Library <http://denverlibrary.org/whg/gene.html> is one of many libraries that have posted local obituaries online. The "Denver Obituary Index" covers various periods between 1939 and 1974, as well as 1990 through 2004. Newspaper sources for the obituary index include the *Denver Post* and the *Rocky Mountain News*.

The Cleveland Public Library <www.cpl.org> index to area obituaries from the early 1800s to the present is a similar project. And Cleveland, like many other urban areas, has benefited from the work of ethnic groups whose members have prepared indexes with a special focus on newspapers. The Cleveland Jewish Genealogy Society has an index of Jewish obituaries from 1902 to 1974: <www.clevelandjgs.org/resources.htm>.

The Value of Newspapers

Newspapers are the day-to-day (or week-to-week) diaries of community events. They are accounts of the lives of famous and ordinary people written as events happened, making them an excellent source for family history. Newspapers usually serve a geographic region, and may also be oriented toward a particular ethnic, cultural, social, or political group. Because newspapers preserve the collected thoughts of many minds, they reflect moral, cultural, educational, and political development more broadly than do the isolated thoughts of an individual's correspondence or diary. Nowhere can a clearer idea be gained of public sentiment than in the American newspaper.

While records of birth, marriage, and death are the most commonly sought and the most consistently helpful, only the genealogist's imagination and resourcefulness limit the newspaper's usefulness in supplying clues about historical events, local news items, probate court and legal notices, real estate transactions, political biographies, announcements, notices of new and terminated partnerships, business advertisements, and notices for settling debts.

List of Genealogical Information that Can Be Found in Newspapers

Abandonment and missing persons announcements
Advertisements—individuals and commercial entities advertised goods and services
Anniversary notices—marked significant milestones in the lives of individuals and historic events and places
Announcements—local and city government, meetings, special events, public service, many named individuals
Arrests—names of arrested individuals, arresting officer, and cause for the arrest
Award notices—for scholastic, sports, and occupational accomplishments, as well as heroic deeds
Auction announcements—sometimes named individuals, slaves, household items, tools, and animals being auctioned
Bankruptcies—legal notices named not only the principal in the case, but sometimes witnesses and relatives
Birth announcements—provided names of newborn and parents in certain papers and certain years
Birthdays—especially milestone birthdays
Biographical sketches—unexpected information about individuals in the community served by the newspaper
Business announcements—openings and closings of businesses, hiring, anniversary stories, tributes to founders
Casualties—listed in fires, accidents, wars, etc.
Celebrations—holidays, birthdays, anniversaries, how they were celebrated by named individuals
Cemetery information—stories about cemeteries, cemetery removals, obituaries that lead to additional cemetery information
Census—stories about census taking and statistical reports
Charitable causes—announcements of events and fundraisers for various organizations and individuals
City council reports—large and small city council proceedings often name individuals
Civil War—battles, and lists of deaths, deserters, draftees, injured, and volunteers (see figures 12-1 and 12-2)
Clubs—lists of people and calendars of events
Committee reports—from social groups and governments
Coroner reports—covered accidents, murders, unidentified bodies, and deaths where no physician was present
Court—notices of cases filed, trials, etc.
Crimes—stories about victims and perpetrators
Cultural—overview of what was going on in certain times and places
Death notices—provided by families, local government, or funeral directors (see figure 12-2)
Deeds—announcements real estate transactions
Divorce—sometimes in list form, sometimes in court proceedings, sometimes a gossip item
Draft notices—especially during the Civil War, sometimes including names of substitutes
Engagement announcements—biographical information found in some small town and large city papers
Engravings—engravings of individuals, buildings, landscapes, advertised wares, etc. used before photography
Entertainment—fiction articles, cartoons, reviews of books, theatre, and movies, etc.
Epidemics—stories about epidemics and lists of individuals who lost their lives
Estate—sales and settlements
Ethnic—news of ethnic groups and leaders
Events—from notices about small social groups (sewing circles, card players) to major public events
Eyewitness accounts—stories of personal and historical events in the words of people who saw what was happening
Firemen—stories about local heroes, rosters of firemen, promotion announcements, photos of individuals and groups
Fires—notices of fires involving homes, businesses, or whole communities
Floods—consequences of floods, sometimes named victims, and eyewitness accounts
Foreclosures—legal notices of foreclosures on real estate, homes, businesses
Foreign language news—often provided ethnic origins of local individuals
Funeral details—sometimes available when a death announcement or obituary is not
Fraternal organizations—events and social notes
Gossip—small-town newspapers often filled pages with the comings and goings and non-essential news items

The New-York Times.

VOL. X....NO. 2906. NEW-YORK, MONDAY, JANUARY 14, 1861. PRICE TWO CENTS.

THE NATIONAL CRISIS.

Important Dispatches from Washington.

LATEST FROM CHARLESTON.

IMPORTANT PROCEEDINGS OF CONGRESS.

Figure 12-1. The headlines of the Monday, 14 January 1861 *New York Times* announce the latest in the "national crisis" that would become the American Civil War.

Graduation—lists of graduates, sometimes includes biographical information and photographs

Heroes—often providing biographical sketches and accounts of heroic actions

Historical events—flashbacks to events that took place in the history of the community

Illness—small town papers typically reported on serious illnesses of citizens

Immigration and migration—notices of arrivals and departures

Indentured servants—notices of legal transactions and runaways

International news—and the effects it had on the community

Land sales—descriptions of the land and names of grantors and grantees

Legal notices—covering a number of case types, sometimes named more than the principals in a case

Letters to the Editor—provided insights into the personalities of individuals

Marriage announcements—sometimes a list of marriages in a given county for a specific time period, sometimes detailed stories (see figure 2-2)

Missing people—notices posted about missing individuals, including physical descriptions and names and addresses of those searching

Military—casualty lists, stories and lists of local servicemen and women

Moved—notices of individuals moving into or out of a town

Music programs—events named participants in church, school, and organizational programs

Naturalizations—lists of recently naturalized American citizens

Neighborhood news—specific information pertaining to a local area, often provided details about residents

Obituaries—sometimes contained biographical information available nowhere else

Other newspapers—notices, particularly in obituaries, for other city newspapers to please copy

Religious events—announcements of special religious events that were landmarks in the lives of individuals or institutions

Reunions—class, family, and organizational reunions with names and out-of-town addresses of attendees

Robberies—reported by local authorities or individuals themselves

Parties—often including guest lists, games played, and food served

Patents—granted for inventions

Personals—often included rich details about just about anything about individuals

Picnics—stories concerning the when, where, and who was involved in a picnic

Photographs—a wide range of possibilities for finding photos of famous and non-famous, buildings, special interest

Plays—local talent named in theatrical performances

Policemen—stories about local heroes, rosters of policemen, promotion announcements, photos of individuals and groups

Politicians—stories and records of achievements and wrongdoings

Prices—the cost of goods and services in a time and place

Probate notices—often listed the principals and others involved in a hearing

Public announcements and advertisements

Real estate—sales of homes and business properties

Religious—news of religious institutions, announcements of new pastors and clergy, new buildings, anniversaries, etc.

Runaway announcements—notices (with names and physical descriptions) of apprentices or slaves who have run away

School boards and school news—minutes, lists of members, events

Shipping—notices and schedules of ships arriving in local ports, sometimes noting names of important passengers

Slaves—notices about sales and runaways, sometimes the story of a slave

Social pages—announce upcoming marriages, parties, fundraisers, social events of all types

Statistics—population, demographics, etc.

Tax—tax rolls and lists of delinquents

Technological advances—stories about first trains, streetlights in towns and cities, radio, air flights, etc,

Testimonials—recognizing and honoring individuals for various deeds

Tornadoes—consequences of tornadoes, sometimes including victims' names and eyewitness accounts

Transcripts—notable speeches and trials

Visitors—stories of out-of-town guests and former residents, especially in small town papers

Wedding stories—sometimes include family history of bride and groom, names of attendants, how they dressed, lists of guests

Youth organizations—announcements about Boy Scouts, Girl Scouts, and other youth activities and awards

Newspapers are especially important for family historians as they are a partial substitute for nonexistent civil records. Obituaries, for example, often fill the gap when a death record

LIST OF VOLUNTEERS

In the service of the General Government, from Indiana county:

CENTRE TOWNSHIP.

Samuel McCutcheon,	A. Rankin McMullen,
G. W. Lowman,	R. B. Stewart,
Samuel Lowman,	Wm. Kunkle,
Thompson Smith,	John Myers,
Watson Smith,	G. C. Cribs,
Thomas Carson,	Washington Hamill,
Samuel Job,	John Flickinger,
Calvin Stevens,	Robert Sherman,
G. W. Johnston,	James EcElhose,

Samuel Hays.—19.

RECAPITULATION.

Armagh borough,	16
Cherryhill township,	59
East Wheatfield township,	41
Green township,	56
Indiana borough,	70
Shelocta borough,	04
Rayne township,	36
South Mahoning township,	36
Washington Township,	36
White township,	38
Conemaugh township,	58
Canoe township,	69
Young Township,	35
Montgomery Township,	58
East Mahoning township,	39
Centre township,	19
Total,	670

There are still 15 districts in the county to hear from, from all of which we hope to receive a report at an early day.

Fort Henry is situate in the east bend of the Tennessee river, five or six miles below the Kentucky line. It was built in August, and was intended, in conjunction with Fort Donelson, right across on the Cumberland river, for the defence of the Cumberland and Tennessee valleys, but was not occupied more than nominally until Columbus was seized by Gen. Polk, in September.

MARRIED,

On the 6th inst, at the residence of the bride's father, by Rev. J. C. Greer, Mr. Westly Stevens and Miss Mary Ann Forowalt, all of Indiana County, Pa.

On the same day, by the same, at the residence of the bride's father, Mr. James Rugh, of Decatur, Illinois, and Miss Mary Truby, of Mechanicsburg, Indiana County, Pa.

On the 6th inst., by J. E. Coulter, Esq., Mr. Jacob Shank, of White township and Miss Margaret Kuntz, of Cherryhill township.

At Joliet, Illinois, on the 16th ult., by Rev. Kidd, Mr. William A. Steel, of St. Louis, (formerly of Blairsville,) to Miss F. Louise, only daughter of Hon. Lorenz P. Sanger.

On the 30th ult., by G. Wiggins, Esq., Mr. Noah Fry, of Cherryhill tp., to Miss Catharine C. Lowe, of Brushvalley tp.

On the 9th, by Rev. Franklin Orr, Mr. Daniel Elgin to Miss Martha Lewis, all of this county.

On the 21st, by the same, Mr. Hugh Lowry to Miss Mary J. Robinson, all of this county.

On the 22d by the same, Mr. W. H. Clawson to Miss S. E. Baker, all of this county.

DIED.

On the 10th ult., of Typhoid fever, Nancy, wife of Mr. John Henderson, of Conemaugh township, aged 55 years.

On the 10th inst., of Diptheria, James Sylvanus Sutton, son of J. E. and M. A. Coulter, aged 5 years and 5 months.

On the 1st inst., of spinal affection, Lucy, wife of Mr. John F. Smith, of Canoe township, in the 40th year of her age.

On the 6th tnst., of Diptheria, a daughter of Mr. Levison, of White township, aged about 2 years.

On the 10th inst., in White township, George Duncan, aged about 65 years.

On the 6th inst., Mrs. Hannah, wife of Thomas B. Allison, Esq., of Marchand, Indiana county, aged about 50 years.

On the 9th inst., in Washington tp., at the residence of Michael W. Kunkle,

Figure 12-2.
The 12 February 1862 issue of the *Indiana Messenger* (Indiana, Pennsylvania) included a list of volunteers, recent marriages, and recent deaths.

is nonexistent or cannot be found. Newspapers are also an important source of marriage information, particularly in those states where marriages were not recorded until the twentieth century. They take on added importance where official public records have been destroyed. All Cook County, Illinois, official records, for example, were destroyed in the Great Chicago Fire of 1871. Newspapers consequently become even more critical in reconstructing the history of the city and tracing the roots of its settlers.

Newspapers are unofficial sources, and as such, they often provide incidental information not recorded elsewhere. Because of their unofficial nature, they are not bound by forms used by official government sources. A newspaper account of a marriage might, for example, indicate that it took place at the home of the bride's parents, perhaps even naming them; it might list the occupation of the groom, or indicate that the ceremony was part of a double wedding in which the bride's sister was also being married. None of these details is likely to appear in the marriage record at the courthouse.

Newspapers are not limited to a particular geographical area and may include reports of births, marriages, and deaths of local citizens, even when they occurred in a neighboring county or another state. Discovering the date and place of an event through a newspaper account can open doors to additional research sources and documentation.

The Evolution of Newspapers

The newspapers we know and take for granted today are the products of some three centuries of development, and are quite different from their colonial predecessors. After a single-issue attempt in 1690, the *Boston News-Letter*, starting in 1704, was the first regularly published newspaper in what is now the United States. Its basic format—four pages, with content concentrating on international news and "literary" matter, with a wealth of advertising and legal notices—remained generally standard for newspapers for the next century and a half. The early newspaper was very much a local product, designed to convey news of the wider world to the citizens of a particular community. Little attention was given to local news, which everyone presumably knew already.

Three nineteenth-century developments changed the newspaper dramatically: the invention of the power printing press, the development of the railroads (which allowed much wider distribution of a paper), and the increasing demand for news, particularly during the Civil War. The major city dailies, with their telegraphic news-gathering, large steam presses, and railroad-based distribution systems, began to dominate the international, national, and state news-reporting functions. As a result, papers in smaller communities had to concentrate on local news if they were to survive and prosper.

What Can Be Found

Most family historians turn to the pages of a newspaper to search for information about births, deaths, and marriages—the vital events in the lives of ancestors—yet, an incredible amount of detail can be found in the stories of their everyday lives. Their "ordinary activities" might individually or collectively provide genealogical detail and clues and insights into their personalities.

The front pages of metropolitan dailies were primarily concerned with international, national, and state affairs. Occasionally, big city papers would also pick up items from distant or rural areas that had news appeal outside their own communities. In contrast, small country or community newspapers were primarily concerned with local people and their immediate surroundings. Genealogically, these small papers are especially valuable.

Vital Statistics

One of the most useful genealogical applications of newspapers is for vital statistics—as substitutes for or supplements to civil or other sources for birth, marriage, and death information. In older newspapers, notices of births, deaths, and marriages appeared almost anywhere in the publication. Because of their brevity they made good filler items—to fill in a few lines at the end of a column or a page. Unless you read every page thoroughly, you may miss a notice. Column headings can be misleading too. An unsuspecting researcher looking for the death notice or obituary of an ancestor who had died in a construction accident might easily miss the article headed "Blown to Eternity" if the search is concentrated on a personal name. A twentieth-century attitude toward newspapers will not be of much help in reading an eighteenth-century publication.

Obituaries

Because there is a wealth of biographical information to be found in obituaries, family historians generally seek them before doing further research in newspapers. For many individuals, the obituary was the only "biographical sketch" ever written (see figure 12-3). In addition to names, dates, and places of birth, marriage, and death, the obituary often identifies relationships of the deceased as child, sibling, parent, grandparent, and so forth, to numerous other individuals. Obituaries may even suggest other documentation of an individual's death. A mention of a hospital in a different county, for instance, might lead you to a previously hard-to-find death certificate. If the obituary records the place of burial or the officiating minister, you'll likely be able to use that information to find church or cemetery records. Likewise, if the newspaper indicates that the death was sudden or unexpected, you might search for a record of a coroner's inquest. Of course, the wealth of detail in an informative obituary may open up many other research avenues.

IN MEMORY OF LOVED PIONEER

Joseph Barborka, who passed away in Iowa City, Iowa, on Thursday morning, December 1, 1921, at the age of 82 years and four months was born in Bohemia on August 2, 1839 and came to America with his wife and six small children: when this family reached Chicago the entire amount of their money was two cents. The industrious father at once found work at his trade, that of watchmaker, and at the end of two years he moved to Iowa City, where he opened a jewelry store, which business he conducted until the year 1900.

Five children survive—Augusta of Iowa City; James Barborka, instructor of music at Point Loma, California; Mrs. Rose Hess of New York City; Joseph Barborka, Jr., a jeweler of Denison, Iowa, and a celebrated harpist; and Mrs. Minnie Struble of Iowa City. Two grandsons are also living— Dr. C. J. Barborka of Rochester, Minn.; and Geoffrey Barborka of Point

JOSEPH BARBORKA

Loma, California. During the months of his last illness he was with his daughters, Augusta and Minnie, and had every care and comfort which these loving children could bestow.

Mr. Barborka was an expert constructor of tower clocks, and among his works that live after him as living monuments of his genius are the tower clocks in the post-office buildings of St. Joseph, Missouri; Louisville, Kentucky; Omaha, Nebraska; and many other cities; also the clocks in St. Mary's church and the City Hall in Iowa City. Another master-work of his is a ring watch with the

Figure 12-3.
The *Iowa City Press Citizen* of Tuesday, 6 December 1921 featured the obituary for and picture of local resident Joseph Barborka.

The amount of information on deaths found in newspapers will not be consistent over the years. Practices also varied in different parts of the country, and individual papers and editors had differing attitudes toward obituaries. Very early obituaries tended to limit the account to one or two lines. A typical early nineteenth-century entry stated the name of the deceased, perhaps an age or estimated age (rarely found in other sources), the date of death, and the last residence; mention of the funeral was sometimes included. Further details of the death may have been given, but rarely were survivors named. The fact that a husband or wife was "left with ten children to mourn the loss" may be the extent of the help provided in such a notice. Parents' names were rarely given except in the case of a child, and even these may merely say: "Baby Mary departed this life to live with the angels."

While older newspapers often disappoint the researcher for their lack of lengthy obituaries, even a few lines like those found in a newspaper clipping dated 14 February 1814 can provide a gold mine of information:

> Died in Licking County, the 6th instant,
> Mrs. Elizabeth Davis consort of Mr. Isaac Davis, aged 26 years. She has left a disconsolate husband and three small children to deplore her loss.

Because official government vital records do not exist prior to the early twentieth century in most places, this newspaper death notice may be the only source for determining the death date of Elizabeth Davis, her age, the name of her husband and that she had three small children. This information may also open the door to possible court, cemetery, land, or other records.

As the nineteenth century progressed, an increasing amount of information was furnished. It is not uncommon to find biographical accounts that include birth dates, marriage dates and places, and children's and grandchildren's names. While the small-town newspaper could find space to print details on the deaths of even common people, this policy was not practical for the metropolitan press. Large dailies printed lengthy obituaries only of the prominent, the powerful, the wealthy—those for whom a fee was paid to laud their lives or whose passing was considered newsworthy. In short, there are no set rules on the amount of information that can be expected. You won't know until you look.

When searching for death information, it's wise to look for all newspapers that may have served the area in which the individual of interest lived. One newspaper may have included more details than another, so it's important not to limit the search to one title or edition. Most cities currently have only one or two daily newspapers, but a century ago that city may have had five or six, any one of which might have carried the death notice of the person of interest. Even comparatively small communities had at least two papers—usually, one Democratic and one Republican. Also, unlike today's papers, which often share a printing plant or even editorial staff, older papers were often fiercely competitive, and each paper had its own strengths of coverage.

If you cannot find an obituary during the dates you would expect to find it, consider a more general search of the newspapers printed around the same time. Searching papers dated before a known death date can help you find news of a serious illness that may have preceded the death. A story of a prominent member of the community falling gravely ill and of family members traveling to be at the bedside often made the headlines in large and small towns. You may find details that you will not find elsewhere, if you begin your search of a weekly paper at least two weeks before the date of death. Also, there may be details published much later than the traditional one to three days after the individual's death. The news of the death may have reached the paper shortly before the printing deadline and a fuller obituary may have followed later.

The circumstances of the death will often determine where information appears within the newspaper itself. Accidental deaths, murders, and suicides were news items and were therefore placed in attention-getting spots, but the deceased might not be accorded a separate obituary. The word *suddenly* is a clue that the death was unnatural and that a coroner's inquest may have been held, even if it was not reported.

When considering possible obituary sources, it is wise to go beyond the community where the individual died and to check the place or places where the individual previously lived. Many people spent their later years with children and died far from where they had lived most of their adult lives. But, if they still had connections with the hometown, there is a good chance that an obituary will appear there, perhaps a more detailed one than will be found in the place of death, where that person was just a new or temporary resident. However, the opposite may also be true, depending on the policies of the individual papers or whether it was a slow news week in a particular community. When the deceased had previously lived elsewhere or had significant links to another city, it was common to see an obituary or death notice requesting that another city newspaper "please copy," thus providing a lead to earlier residences and perhaps a place to search for additional relatives or information.

The *Atlanta Constitution* of 16 January 1875 carried the notice that Col. Charles T. Goode had passed away and it provides leads to his previous residences:

> The telegraphic wires yesterday flashed sad news when it conveyed the intelligence of the death, at Americus, Georgia, of Col. Charles T. Goode, the silver-tongued orator, as he was justly termed by all who knew him. Of the nature of the disease that snatched him away in the prime of his manhood, we are not advised. Col. Charles T. Goode was the son of Thomas W. Goode of Upson County. He was born in Upson County about 1834 or 1835, and resided there a short time previous to the war. He married a daughter of Gen. Eli Warren of Houston County then moved to that county.

Death and Funeral Notices

In addition to obituaries, other sources of information for a person who is deceased include death or funeral notices (see figure 12-4), burial permit lists, and death lists. They may not include the wealth of useful detail that obituaries do, but they can provide important documentation of deaths.

Death or funeral notices were paid announcements. Unlike the obituary, the notice usually stated only the name of the decedent, when and where the death occurred, and, occasionally, the name of a survivor. An example might be: "Dyer, Harry, 26th inst., funeral from St. James at 1 pm, thence by carriage to Greenwood Cemetery." Even this simple statement can provide needed clues to continue research in church, cemetery, court, and other records. Many ancestors will not be found in paid announcements because survivors either did not deem them necessary or couldn't afford them. In hard economic times, such as the Great Depression, there were noticeably fewer paid announcements.

Official lists of the dead are commonly found in newspapers. This kind of list gives the meager information supplied to the newspaper from city or county records and was included

REST IN PEACE.

The Remains of Winthrop Farley Are Entombed.

The funeral services over the remains of Winthrop Farley were held in the Fourth ward meeting house yesterday at 3 p. m., Bishop E. Stratford presiding.

The remains were taken from Undertaker Larkin's establishment to the residence, where the immediate relatives joined and proceeded to the church.

Owing to the decomposed condition of the remains they were not taken from the hearse and the services were brief.

The congregation on being called to order by Bishop Stratford, sang "How Firm a Foundation. Prayer was offered by Elder Welsh and the audience sang that soul-inspiring hymn, "O, My Father, Thou that Dwellest In that High and Glorious Place."

Elder Francis A. Brown spoke for a few moments. He spoke consolingly to the relatives present, giving them assurances that though now they were separated from his loved face, they would see him again if they would comply with the laws of God. He had known the deceased for thirty-six years, and the acquaintance had always been of a pleasant character. He did not feel to mourn, for the departed brother had, with Saint Paul, "fought the good fight" and finished his work on earth. If those whom he had left behind would follow his example and emulate his virtues they would be in the path that leadeth to eternal life.

D. H. Peery endorsed the remarks. His knowledge of the deceased enabled him to say he was a true and honorable man. All he desired was that when he himself died those who had known him through life would be able to say of him as much as he could say of Elder Farley. Through his noble character and the lesson of life he has left the sting of death was removed.

Bishop J. C. Dalton of Manassa gave a brief account of the death of Elder Farley, really the first information the family had of the cause of his sudden demise. He was followed by Joseph Parry and Bishop Stratford, who testified to the integrity, honesty and worth of the deceased.

The services closed by singing "'Mid Scenes of confusion," and benediction by Bishop T. J. Stevens.

A large number of carriages and people followed the remains to the Ogden cemetery, where they were interred, Counselor Gwilliam dedicating the grave.

Winthrop Farley had lived in Ogden since 1890. He has been prominent in early days in building up this lovely city, patiently enduring the hardships necessary to lay the foundation of Ogden. He greatly aided in building the Weber canal and was for many years one of the directors of the canal company. The canal and water right is now a piece of property that in the near future will be worth hundreds of thousands of dollars, and has already served its purpose in building up hundreds of homes.

In a church capacity he has long been prominent. He was ordained a high priest in 1851 and was for a number of years counselor to Bishop Stratford until his departure.

May he rest in peace and may his family one day be brought together in a reunion that knows no parting.

Asa Farley heard of his father's death at Soda Springs and took the first train. Ed. Farley, who had not been here for several years, heard of it in Montana and hastened down. Other relatives came hurriedly from other parts of the surrounding states and attended the funeral.

The pall bearers were six sons of the deceased, Asa, Edward, David, Lafayette, Lorenzo and Joseph.

Figure 12-4.
On 29 January 1890, Ogden, Utah's the *Standard* featured a description of local resident Winthrop Farley's funeral services.

as a free service to the readers. Other printed lists that provide needed death dates or places include lists of war dead, disaster victims, and deceased members of fraternal organizations. Names of policemen and firemen who died within the year were often published periodically. Sometimes all of the area deaths were noted simultaneously at the end of the year, or as part of the summary of the previous year in a January issue.

Newspapers can also explain why certain death or other vital records cannot be found. The following article from the *Brooklyn Daily Union Argus* (12 February 1878) calls attention to a problem that was all too common in municipalities in every part of the country:

> Death Certificates
>
> The untidy bundles of death certificates which have hitherto made an unsightly appearance on the shelves of the record room of the Health Department have been by years in volume, and now appear in the form of a library reference—but not for general reference, as the Board yet holds to the fallacy that public documents do not belong to the public.

Cemetery Information

Frequently, it is difficult to track cemeteries that have been moved, or to guess where someone may have been buried. Area newspapers may be especially useful in finding answers. Consider the article from the *New York Daily Times* of 29 March 1854 that explains where the poor of the New York City area were buried.

> NEW POTTER'S FIELD.
>
> A proposition is before the Board of Governors for the purchase of additional lands on Ward's Island for the purposes of a City Cemetery, or Potter's Field. It is time that the remains of paupers were interred in some quarter better fitted for their last resting-place than the one now used on Randall's Island. A more disgusting spectacle can scarcely be conceived than the trenches filled with coffins, loosely covered with earth and subject to trespass, which now receive the bodies of the City's poor. The old Potter's Field was a disgrace to the City, years ago; and continual use has made it much worse. The dictates of propriety point to the obvious requirement of a new location.

Marriages

Marriage items, like other vital records in newspapers, varied considerably, both over time and from one newspaper to another. The listings range from brief announcements or lists of licenses to full, detailed accounts of the wedding ceremony itself, occasionally including even a list of wedding gifts.

Marriage license notices appear frequently in both city and rural newspapers. Often, these were posted weekly and in many instances noted the age of the bride and groom, as well as their places of residence. The *Central Illinois Gazette* of West Urbana ran this fairly typical notice on 12 May 1858:

> The following marriage licenses have been issued since our last report:
> P. Haynes to Temps Green,
> J.R. Thomas to M.J. Stacy,
> W.I. Traywick to Willella Gray,
> J.Y. Pearce to Cora Pearce
> COLORED
> Charley Weathers to Van King

The best sources for engagement and marriage information are local papers (see figure 12-5). Generally only the socially and politically elite were newsworthy enough to get coverage in metropolitan dailies. Because couples getting married frequently traveled to the place of marriage—perhaps they eloped or went to the bride's hometown, or went to another state where there was no waiting period—newspaper accounts can frequently provide the clues leading to an otherwise elusive record. And that account might appear in a paper wherever the bride or groom was known.

Stories of marriages that may otherwise be lost to the ages are sometimes found in newspaper accounts. The following example from the *Brooklyn Daily Standard Union* of 13 April 1906 included this:

> MARRIAGE FOLLOWS CHANCE MEETING OF PLAYMATES
>
> A romance which began in Bukranis, Austria, several years ago, resulted, to-day, in the marriage, in the Third District Municipal Court, by Justice Rosenthal, of Jacob Canderer, 23 years old, and Miss Tillie Fried, 22 years old. The husband, who is a jeweler, at 294 Grand street, came to this country five years ago. A year later Miss Fried, who had been playmates in the old country, came to the United States with her parents, who live at 36 Belmont avenue. One day this week Miss Fried happened to go into Canderer's store to look at some jewelry. They had not heard from each other since he left Europe. It didn't take them long, however, to renew the acquaintance that had been broken off, and when the jeweler proposed marriage he was quickly accepted. As Justice Rosenthal is a friend of the bride, it was decided to have him perform the ceremony.

As with death information, there's always a chance that a marriage may have been registered in an unexpected town or county. The clipping from the *Arkansas Gazette* of Little Rock, Arkansas, dated 8 January 1916 leads one to wonder. At which end of the railroad line was the following marriage registered?

> With the train going the maximum speed allowed by the condition of the track, last night B.B. Rice and Miss Dee Ellington stood up between the seats, faced the preacher, steadied themselves as the car jolted and swerved, and plighting their troth were made man and wife. Rev. S. L. Halloway, pastor of the Baptist church here, performed the ceremony.

When brides and grooms ran across restrictive marriage laws in their home county, they frequently found a place with more liberal legislation. Waukegan, Illinois, was just one of the places where Chicago couples went for a quick wedding. An article in the *Waukegan Daily Sun* (31 December 1925) stated that "Waukegan, as a marriage ground, more than held its own through 1925, showing an increase of approximately 434 marriages, which is healthy to say the least." The article noted that a change in the Michigan law, demanding a five-day notice that was also in effect in Wisconsin, had "boomed" the local marriage business. The newspaper article indicated that "scores of Chicago couples who once went to Michigan to get wedded now choose between Crown Point, Indiana and Waukegan."

Births

Birth announcements, though less common in newspapers, could be found in certain places and in various time periods. Sometimes they appeared in a society column and sometimes in the most unexpected places. Generally, birth announcements did not include details, and sometimes even the names of the parents or the baby were overlooked. Some newspapers, especially in the twentieth century, included hospital lists of babies born, including the names of the parents and their respective addresses. Small town newspapers were likely to provide fascinating tidbits of information about people in the community. Under the headline, "Little Locals," the 12 July 1889 *Carroll County Democrat* (Huntington, Tennessee) provides dozens of one-line items under the headline, including a birth announcement:

> Mrs. R. H. Caldwell is reported sick this week.
> These are lovely nights. It is not raining.
> Nath Peoples killed two white cranes this week.
> Hogs are dying in this section of the county with what is called red mange.
> Mrs. Will Collins presented her husband with a fine girl last Monday evening.
> George Woodard, who lives near Bennet's mill, has a chicken without wings!

Divorce

While not always written with such detail, the following 1884 article from the *Champaign County Herald* (Illinois), stories and court recordings of divorces often appeared in big city and small-town papers.

> Mary Smith says she was married to John on May 10, 1881 and that he beat and abused her generally in a manner that indicated that he did not love her as in days of yore. He has willfully absented himself for more than two years and for these reasons she submits to the court whether she ought not to be made a free woman so that she can try it over again.

The *Ohio Repository* of Canton, Ohio, published on 4 April 1849, presented surprising information for those who think divorces didn't happen in earlier times. "Divorces crowd, in formidable array, the business files of all our State Legislatures, bearing ample testimony to the fact that ill assorted marriages are a principle of American life. At the late session of the Kentucky Legislature one hundred and ninety-six divorces were granted."

Wedding Anniversaries

Wedding anniversaries celebrating twenty-five, fifty, or more years of marriage were of special interest in local papers (see figure 12-5). For example, the golden wedding of Mr. and Mrs. Joseph V. Parkinson merited two full columns on the front page, including a complete review of their fifty years together, in the *Rensselaer Semi-Weekly Republican*, Jasper County, Indiana, in 1901. Another anniversary notice that appeared in the pages of the *Cleveland Plain Dealer* of 27 February 1935 provided wonderful details of the 68th wedding anniversary of Civil War Veteran Nicholas Weidenkopf. Complete with a photo of the anniversary couple, the detailed article stated that "Nicholas Weidenkopf, president of the board of the Soldiers' and Sailor's Commission and his wife, Kate, today were receiving congratulations on the 68th anniversary of their marriage." The newspaper account stated that Mr. Weidenkopf, who was ninety-two, and his wife, who was eighty-eight, were observing the event quietly at their residence at 1223 Summit avenue in Lakewood, and that during the day, Mr. Weidenkopf put in the usual amount of time working at his office. Besides being active in the veterans' organizations, the article mentions other social groups in which the ninety-two-year-old held memberships. Weidenkopt was quoted as saying, "I'm the only living member of the First Ohio Light Artillery. We were on our way to battle twelve days after Fort Sumpter was fired on, and took part in the first land battle of the war."

While rich details of special events like these can be extremely helpful in understanding the lives of our ancestors, unless it is well indexed, it may be necessary to conduct a page by page search of the newspaper of interest.

Abandonment and Missing People Notices

Pre-dating the "personals" pages of a later era, the *Ohio Repository* of 7 May 1835 posted a notice that Lydia Cogan anxiously awaited word about her missing husband. It was not uncommon to find physical descriptions of missing individuals such as this in early papers. This newspaper account provides details about Jacob, Lydia, and Imerand that would not be found elsewhere.

> CAUTION: On the 21st inst. My husband, Jacob Cogan, left me with eight children and absconded with another woman. He is about 45 years old, has dark hair, heavy eyebrows, black beard, a scar on his forehead over the right eye, a lump on the right arm and one on his leg. He had on a blue cloth coat and pantaloons of the same, one of his little fingers is cut off. The woman he went off with is named Imerand Shaner, aged about 25 years, has sandy hair, freckled face, and letters marked on her arm. She was born in Germany. This notice is given to caution the public of the character of this pair. Any information as to the place of their location will be thankfully received in order that they may be brought to justice. Lydia Cogan, Sandyville, Tuscarawas County, Ohio. April 25, 1835.

Local News

Hometown newspapers are often the only place where the lives of so many are so closely detailed. In the years before international and national news filled big city papers, even they had room to tell about the local heroes, creditor's claim to an estate, stories of local businesses, visitors in town, a duel, a stolen watch, a broken leg, and other surprising stories about our ancestors (figure 12-6). There simply isn't a better place to see what was going on in the lives of individuals and families than in old newspapers. The following examples represent the kinds of items that can be found in local papers.

It was customary for individuals setting up business in a new community to announce the fact in the local paper. In the 1760s, the *South Carolina Gazette* was filled with such notices. Robert Catherwood, "surgeon to the hospitals and garrisons in East Florida" (16 February 1767), opened a practice with an announcement, and a Mrs. Grant proposed "to practice midwifery having studied that art regularly and practiced it afterwards at Edinburgh: Certificates of which she can produce from the Gentlemen whose lectures she attended, and likewise from the professors of Anatomy and Practice of Physick in that city. . . ." (29 December 1768).

A few interesting examples culled from the *Newport Mercury* (26 August 1809) provide insights into the bustling Rhode Island city. Typical of newspapers of its time, the front page notified readers about items of local interest, including a meeting called by Ephraim Bowen, Grand Master of the Rhode Island Grand Lodge of Masons. Although the meeting announcement doesn't provide many biographical details, it does place Bowen in a place and time and links him with an organization where other records may be available.

Most of the *Mercury* was devoted to national and international news. A lengthy article described the French Code of Conscription. The news that all Frenchmen between the age of twenty and twenty-five complete were subject to conscription had implications not only for the French, but for Americans as well.

While the majority of the stories in the Newport paper do not relate to a specific family or individual, they do provide an overview of what was going on in that particular time and place. They also give us a pretty good idea of what was important to

HARRY L. VAIL IS DEAD AT 76

Former Newspaperman and Public Official Was Ardent Republican

Harry L. Vail, former newspaperman, county clerk, county commissioner and attorney, died today in his home at 8319 Carnegie avenue following a short illness. He was 76.

Mr. Vail

Mr. Vail was the father of Herman L. Vail, member of the law firm of Spring, Sayre & Vail. Funeral plans were to be announced later in the day.

Born in Cleveland, the son of Judge Isaac C. Vail, Mr. Vail was educated in Cleveland public schools and graduated from Ohio Wesleyan University in 1879.

He started his newspaper career as reporter for the old Cleveland Voice. He became city editor of the paper. He also was a member of the staff of the Cleveland Herald.

While he was following the newspaper profession he began the study of law in the office of Judge Stevenson Burke. Later he was admitted to the Ohio bar.

He served two terms as county clerk, from 1894 to 1900, and two terms as county commissioner, from 1908 to 1912. It was during his commissionership that High Level Bridge was built.

An ardent Republican, he was associated in politics with Mark Hanna, Myron T. Herrick, President McKinley, Theodore Burton and other notable Republicans.

was a 32d degree Mason, member of Tyrian Lodge No. 370. Surviving are his widow, Sarah; his son, and a sister, Mrs. Iza Fowler of Delaware, O.

"SECRET SEVEN" PLAN RECEPTION

Chamber Mystery Group Will

Civil War Vet and Wife Mark 68th Anniversary of Wedding

Mr. and Mrs. Nicholas Weidenkopf

NICHOLAS WEIDENKOPF, president of the board of the Soldiers' and Sailors' Commission, and his wife, Kate, today were receiving congratulations on the 68th anniversary of their marriage.

Mr. Weidenkopf is 92. His wife is 88. They were observing the event quietly at their residence, 1223 Summit avenue, Lakewood. During the day Mr. Weidenkopf put in the usual amount of time working at his office.

Besides being active in the veterans' organizations, Mr. Weidenkopf is president of the Commercial Travelers' Association and served as fire commissioner from 1861 to 1865. They have one son, Burton R. Weidenkopf, former city surveyor.

"I am the only living member of the First Ohio Light Artillery," he confided. "We were on our way to battle 12 days after Ft. Sumpter was fired on and we took part in the Battle of Philipi, the first land battle of the war."

STATE CUTS PRICES ON LIQUOR BRANDS

Reductions Range From 10 to 50 Cents at Stores

Press State Service

COLUMBUS, Feb. 27—New prices for 12 brands of liquor sold in state stores will be in effect Monday. Prices of 10 brands were reduced and two were increased.

GERMANY PREPARES TO NAZIFY THE SAAR

Rapid Introduction of New Laws Planned by Cabinet

By United Press

BERLIN, Feb. 27—The cabinet last night approved a series of decrees for swift and thorough Nazification of the Saar basin, when it is taken over by the Reich on Saturday.

The government approved all agreements with France relative to purchase of the rich Saar mines and on the Saar territory's debts. In all

Figure 12-5. The sixty-eighth wedding anniversary of two local residents receives attention in the 27 February 1935 edition of the *Cleveland Plain Dealer.*

THE ATLANTA CONSTITUTION

VOL. XLIV.—No. 302. ATLANTA, GA., FRIDAY MORNING, APRIL 12, 1912.—EIGHTEEN PAGES. PRICE: FIVE CENTS.

TRYING TO CHEAT GALLOWS JEFFERSON TAKES MORPHINE

Columbus Man, Doomed to Be Hanged Today, Thought to Be Dying.

HE SWALLOWED POISON SOON AFTER MIDNIGHT

At 2:30 This Morning Physicians Were Working With Him, But Had Almost Given Up Hope—Jefferson Took the Poison in the Presence of the Sheriff.

WILSON MANAGER SAYS HE'LL BOLT IF CLARK IS NAMED

McCombs Declares He Would Work for Republican Against the Democratic Nominee.

WOULD WOODROW WILSON FOLLOW HIS MANAGER?

By John Corrigan, Jr.

WHO IS THE PRETTIEST YOUNG WOMAN IN ATLANTA? PAGE OF CONTESTANTS IN CONSTITUTION SUNDAY

HOWELL MILL ROAD RESIDENTS PRAY FOR A STREET CAR LINE

HE GOES INTO BEYOND

GEN. FRED D. GRANT

GEN. FRED GRANT YIELDS HIS SWORD AT DEATH'S CALL

Son of Famous Civil War Soldier Passes With Shocking Suddenness in New York Hotel.

HIS PRESENCE IN CITY NOT GENERALLY KNOWN

In an Hour After Mrs. Grant Hysterically Telephoned for a Physician, Gen. Grant Was Dead—Heart Failure Given as the Cause of His Death.

"Get Physician Quick."

COLONEL WALTERS TO FURTHER WORK OF HIS DEAD SON

Before Vast Throng He Consecrates Life to Ridding Albany of Vice.

SAYS DEATH OF SOLICITOR WAS DUE TO AN ACCIDENT

GEORGIA PRESS FOR UNDERWOOD

Asserted 85 Per Cent of Weeklies Are for Alabamian.

Underwood Managers Assert That Number of Those Which Have Expressed an Opinion Are for Underwood.

Figure 12-6. This issue of the *Atlanta Constitution* from Friday, 12 April 1912, features a number of articles of local interest, including an announcement about the upcoming Atlanta beauty contest.

readers at that time. Newspapers are great for providing snapshots of the world our ancestors knew.

Though obituaries and other biographical details that family historians hope to find were usually absent in newspapers of that era, the 1809 *Newport Mercury* did provide a few useful details. For example, a notice was given to the creditors of the estate of Sarah Mumford, late of Newport. Readers were allowed to "exhibit their claims" to her unsolvent estate in the newspaper for a period of six months. The notice posted by Henry Mumford, executor, on 7 August 1809 might lead to court and other records surrounding her death, as well as any other records of financial problems of the deceased.

Even a business notice can be enlightening for those who want to know more about an ancestor. The following announcement appeared on the back page of the same Newport newspaper: "Albert V. Gardiner informs his friends and the public that he has removed his store of goods to 102 Thames Street, lately occupied by Sally M. Smith & Co. where he has constantly on hand and for sale a large and valuable assortment of English, India, French, Dutch, Scotch and American manufactured goods. Including an elegant assortment of ladies hats and bonnets. Every article for mourning is constantly at hand." This article tells us something about Albert V. Gardiner and his interests as well as giving us a closer look at a small Newport business and the merchandise available in those days.

The *Atlanta Constitution* of 16 January 1875 includes a typical mix of information that could be found in a big city paper of that era. The headlines provide the reader with a sense of the general population's viewpoint, and what citizens were going through just ten years after the close of the Civil War. Quite predictably, there was a great deal of grumbling and irreverence concerning the federal government of the United States. The fact that the people of Atlanta were still struggling was evident in the unusually large number of bankruptcy and other legal notices in that issue.

There were also notices of meetings of Confederate soldiers, and the obituaries of two former Confederate heroes.

Other items of note in the Atlanta paper were the shipping news (listing arrivals of ships), a railroad schedule, and even lists of guests who were staying at the Atlanta hotels that week. It provided the names of the guests and their home residences—most of which were southern cities, but there were some visitors from New York and other northern spots.

There were several articles complaining about the deplorable condition of the streets and the mud that Atlanta citizens and wagons had to pull themselves through to get from one place to another.

As with other old newspapers, ads in the Atlanta paper make for fascinating reading in themselves. Under the subheading of "Drugs, Oils, etc.," the newspaper advised the people that opium could be bought for $11 a pound, bicarbonate of soda $7 a pound, and Epson salts was priced at $6 a pound.

In another ad, Dr. S. B. Collins announced his painless opium antidote, noting the destructive nature of this popular drug.

The weekly editions of community newspapers give a personal glimpse of people found nowhere else. Country papers would allow plenty of space for a column prepared by a local resident to tell of recent births, upcoming or recent marriages, illnesses, visitors to the community, former residents vacationing with relatives in their old home, and news of a more personal nature. A common example of the kind of clues to be found is one which reads, "Miss Marjorie Dyer of our town is visiting her cousin Miss Margaret Howley in Fort Wayne." This example gives another location of family members and possibly a surname previously unknown. These columns also note anniversaries, parties, reunions, and achievements such as a promotion or a school award. Newcomers to a community often received the attention of the columnist, and former residents were naturally included.

The "local brevities" sections in some newspapers are quick updates on residents of the community and they can be rich sources of unique information not found elsewhere. Three notices in the *Brooklyn Union Argus* of 13 June 1879 are good examples of what can be found.

> A gold watch valued at $200 stolen on the 4th instant from the residence of Mrs. Mary Richardson, 41 Pierrepont Street, was yesterday recovered by Detective Lowery from a pawnshop in the Bowery.
>
> Edward Lamb, twenty-eight years of age, of 172 High Street, had a leg broken yesterday by the scales of the ice cart he was driving falling on him.
>
> Michael Gallagher seventeen years of age, of 189 John Street, lost a finger yesterday by the machinery in the tin factory corner of York and Adams Street.

School News

School news might include awards won and detailed coverage of a graduation, complete with a class picture or even individual photographs of the graduates. School board minutes, lists of teachers and pupils, and other school events are also frequently recorded. An example of a social event for which the guest list was printed appeared in the 12 May 1858 issue of the *Central Illinois Gazette*. The article described the costumes worn by named guests at a masquerade party held at Mr. R. H. Carter's. The names of the invited puts them in West Urbana, Illinois, and it gives us an idea of how people entertained themselves in 1858.

Local news columns are one of the most important sources for data on women and children—two groups of people who rarely appear in other records in their own right. Local columns also provide clues leading to other records. If you find that your great-grandmother belonged to a Methodist charitable organization or a sewing circle sponsored by a church, it is a clear indication of church membership. If the religious affiliation was previously unknown, the researcher has a valuable lead.

Biographical Sketches

Newspapers carry biographical sketches in a variety of guises—birthday announcements, testimonials, feature articles, and other items. Sometimes these items are indexed; sometimes they can only be found by searching page by page.

Membership lists, printed minutes, and summaries of events for fraternal organizations, benevolent associations, lists of retirees, political groups, musicians, firemen, and policemen are common. You will sometimes be able to find group photographs.

Proud of their local heroes, newspapers often recounted the accomplishments of community citizens.

A good example can be found in the *Brooklyn Standard Union* of 30 September 1931. This clipping is an example of the work done by volunteers who posted it to the Brooklyn Information page at <http://bklyn-genealogy-info.com>:

> Police Forget Roll-Call But Save Baby Girl's Life
> Work Over Child for 90 Minutes in Greenpoint Station House
>
> A frantic fight to save the life of Anna Gillinos, eleven months, lying still from convulsions on a table in the reserve room of the Greenpoint station house, ended successfully after 90 minutes work early today. The child's whimpering cry came after four policeman had worked for an hour and a half over her limp body, using every known means of artificial respiration.
>
> As she stirred Lieutenant John Shattuck turned to the men around him, and said, "That is the most welcome cry in this station house since it was built."
>
> His associates, who had dropped everything else to stand watch over the child, said nothing, but there faces were stained with tears, for (?) since the child's mother, Mrs. Anna Gillinos of 2357 23rd street, Astoria, had rushed into the station house at 7 o'clock, crying, "My baby's dead, my baby's dead." They had even forgotten the 8 o'clock roll call and the daily turn out of men to help her. A few seconds after she had arrived Ambulance Surgeon Regan of Greenpoint Hospital was on hand to help.

Legal Notices

The requirement that some judicial actions (in cases including more persons than the principals) cannot be concluded without public notice carries side benefits for the

THE GETTYSBURG GAZETTE.

GETTYSBURG :—(PENNSYLVANIA)—PRINTED BY WILLIAM B. UNDERWOOD AND MATTHIAS E. BARTGIS.

Nº. 30] FRIDAY, AUGUST 12, 1803. [Vol. I.

The GETTYSBURG GAZETTE is printed every Friday morning and forwarded to fubfcribers as directed, at Two DOLLARS per annum ; one Dollar to be paid at the time of fubfcribing, and the other, at the expiration of fix months.

Advertifements will be thankfully received, and inferted four times at one Dollar per fquare, and twenty Cents for every fubfequent infertion.

Naturalization.

THOSE who are Friends to our prefent government, who have emigrated from a land of oppreffion, and wifh to be naturalized, at our next court, (the 22d inft.) may call on the fubfcriber, who will prepare the neceffary papers, make application to the Court, &c. and not charge one cent for his trouble.

J. T. HAIGHT.

Auguft 4th.

SHERIFF's SALE.

BY Virtue of fundry writs of Venditioni Exponas, to me directed, Will be EXPOSED to

Public Sale,

on Wednefday the 24th day of Auguft enfuing, at the Court houfe in Gettyfburg,

A certain LOT of GROUND, in Greenfield, known in the plan of faid town, by No. 25. adjoining York & Centre ftreets, in the town aforefaid.

ALSO,

Two certain LOTS of GROUND lying and being in Gettyfburg, known by the numbers 181 and 182, adjoining lots of James Gettys, and Frederick Rimmel, now Doctor Samuel Huey. Seized and taken in execution, as the property of Peter Spyker, and to be fold by

GEORGE LASHELLS.

From the BOSTON CHRONICLE.

THE EXAMINER. No. IV.

TEXT. "A Democracy is fcarcely tolerable at any period of national hiftory. Its omens are always finifter, and its powers are unpropitious.—It is on its trial here ; and the iffue will be civil War, Defolation, and Anarchy. No wife man, but difcerns its imperfections ; no good man, but fhudders at its miferies ; no honeft man, but proclaims its fraud ; and no brave man, but draws his fword againft its force. The inftitution of a fcheme of Polity fo radically contemptible and vicious, is a memorable example of what the Villainy of fome men can devife, the Folly of others receive, and both eftablifh, in defpite of reafon, reflection, and fenfation." [P. Folio, & Brad. Paper.]

We choofe to repeat the above Paragraph, as it is the cloven foot of Federalifm. Here are fentiments which portray, in forcible characters, the views and defigns of a Faction, who claim the exclufive appellation of Friends to Order and Supporters of good Principles. They pretend to reprobate Democracy ; and yet appeal to the People, for the purpofe of drawing the fword, to oppofe the Government now in operation. This is Federal Democracy, in oppofition to Republican Democracy.

The fword is to become the Arbiter of our national Rights ; the Citizens are to affemble in hoftile array : Inftead of the pen, to defcribe the legitimate limits of our civil Polity, the fword is to make the indelible mark where our Privileges begin, and where our Rights end. This is Federal Order, which every brave man, wife man, and good man is to approbate, and fubftantiate. He who does not fubfcribe to it, is to have his throat cut, or become an Outcaft of Society, and be contemned as a man who is void of reafon and reflection ; is to ftand "as a monument of the Villainy of what fome men could devife and adopt." would be decided. Then might we adopt the language of Mr. Otis, that "the doors of the Temple of Juftice would be burft open, and the building filled with a Banditti ;" and that "the wreck of the Conftitution was floating on every wave." Then would Religion bow down its head like a bullrufh, the facred Temple of the Supreme Being be demolifhed, the Minifters of the Gofpel be driven from their refpective habitations ; "Innovation," Deifm, and Atheifm progreffing with rapid ftrides through the Land ; and every veftige of Morality and Decency obliterated. Then might we exclaim, "How is the City become defolate, that was full of People !" while every focial connection, which cements Society and harmonizes the human mind, would be diffolved ! The fword of civil War would be as portentous to the deftiny of America, as the flaming fword which threatened our firft Parents in the garden of Eden. Then would Governeur Morris exultingly fay, "We, the Senate, are affembled to fave the People from their worft Enemies, to fave them from themfelves !" What a glorious fulfilment of his Prophecy !

Not that I am difpofed to treat this fubject with levity ; but I fhould wifh to know the Author of the Paragraph who is defirous to draw his fword. Pray, Sir, where do you refide, and what is your prefent employment ? Have you lately loft an Election ; and do you think to get reftored amidft the general fquabble ? As you are fo zealous in the caufe, pleafe to favor the Public with your Name ; let us know the Auxiliaries engaged in this defperate enterprize ; let us have the roll of "brave men" embattled to ftab every one who is willing to fupport the Syftem of Government now in operation. Erect your ftandard, beat your drums, open your rendezvous, and march your drawn-fword Veterans through the ftreets of Bofton ; parade them in Stateftreet ; and, if you pleafe, command your Banditti to mount their Cockades, as the infignia of "good Principles and fteady Habits." Summon the "Wife Men of the Eaft," the our Country from difgrace and ruin ; and we heard that 15,000 men were on the march for New-Orleans. Every Federalift on the Exchange was extolling their Bravery and Patriotifm. Nothing was then faid about Democracy ; though fuch a procedure would have been in direct oppofition to all the Principles which thofe perfons pretend to advocate. They want a few men "in a hole," on fome occafions, to govern ; and, at other times, the People, in the utmoft extent of Democracy, are to take the reins of Government : That is, when it will anfwer their purpofes that a Junto fhould rule, then they are for an Ariftocratic Branch ; but, if we are fo happy as to have a Prefident and a Legiflature to counteract their defigns, they are for the People in a body to execute their projects. The Fact is, their objects are, War and an Alliance with England ; and every meafure which promotes this grand ultimatum, is the ne plus ultra with them.

When we talk of War, it is proper to know who are to be the Warriors, who are to be the fighting Men. We have a number of negociating Warriors, fpeculating Warriors, and bank Warriors ; but where are we to find the war-worn Warriors ? The fpeculating Warriors anticipate the rife and fall of Stocks ; their lift of Killed and Wounded, compofe Sellers and Buyers. An army of Stock-jobbers always hang in the rear of a fighting Army. The lofs of 20,000 men in a battle, gives the negociating troops an immenfe advantage ; they gain a victory of per centum. Every broken limb and wounded Soldier is calculated into dollars and cents, and the toto is from 15 to 30 per cent, clear profit. The groans of the hofpitable are hofannas to the Stock Exchange ; and, before a Speculator prefumes to buy or fell, he looks over the lift of Killed and Wounded of the combatting Armies : He fmiles if he has bought a Bear ; and frowns if he has fold a Bull. There never was a tear fhed by them over an unfortunate Soldier.

We have another kind of Warriors, emphatically ftyled tea-table Warri-

The Gettysburg Gazette of Friday, 12 August 1803, announces a sheriff's sale, gives information on naturalization, and features an article from the *Boston Chronicle*.

genealogist. Legislatures either provided for and supported an official county or community publication, or they designated existing newspapers for these purposes. Examples of listed actions include land sales for payment of taxes, administration in probate, proving of wills, heirship determination and the settlement of estates, pending divorce proceedings, sales of properties of insolvent estates, and more. When court records are not available for any reason, these public notices can help fill the gap. Or, a legal notice spotted in a newspaper search might direct the researcher to otherwise unknown court records. The chance spotting in a newspaper of a court docket might be the only clue leading to a divorce case that solves a perplexing genealogical problem. The growing number of digitized and indexed newspapers online makes findings like this increasingly common.

In larger cities, this function was often covered by a special kind of professional newspaper, devoted entirely to publishing legal notices. For example, the *Chicago Daily Law Bulletin*, which began publication in 1854, has calendars, reports, and public notices from every court for Chicago and Cook County. For the genealogist, these entries can be the key to locating original case files and other court records.

Actually, any legal record could be printed in a newspaper, wherever local authorities were required to make public a specific set of facts or where they felt it to be in the public interest to do so.

Patents Granted

Patents for inventions were occasionally mentioned in local papers. Learning that an ancestor was an inventor may come as a surprise to some researchers, and this sort of information was not easily located before the days of the Internet. A list of local residents who were granted patents was located on a search of the Brooklyn Page <http://bklyn-genealogy-info.com>. The original list was published in the *Union Argus* of 5 June 1879:

> The following named residents of this city are reported by Mr. A.V. Brieson for having patents issued to them:
>
> J.B. Fuller—electric candle
>
> S.H. Miller—shade supporting attachment
>
> J.I. Healey—Vehicle Wheel Hub
>
> W. Nagle—device for stretching the toes of boots and shoes

Public Announcements and Advertisements

Paid advertisements, common from the beginning of newspaper publication, chronicle the products, housing, transportation, dress, and reading habits of our ancestors. Particularly relevant for the genealogist are advertisements about insolvent debtors, forced land sales, educational opportunities, and professional services.

Early newspapers frequently carried touching advertisements from worried relatives who had lost contact with loved ones. These ads often provided the missing individual's personal description, clothing description, last known whereabouts, and the destination, if known, of a lost traveler. For example, the *Pensylvanusche Berichte* of Philadelphia, on 22 June 1759, ran the following notice in German. This translation comes from Hocker's *Genealogical Data Relating to the German Settlement*.

> Nicholas Emrich, Allemangel, Albany Township, Berks County, inquires for his two sons, and one daughter. The older son, Valentin, is married; the other son Friedrich, is single.

These notices were particularly common in papers that were directed to a particular immigrant group. For example, the New England Historic Genealogical Society has issued several volumes of *The Search for Missing Friends; Irish Immigrant Advertisements Placed in the Boston Pilot*, covering the period from 1831 to 1876 and an expanded CD version covering the years 1831 to 1920. In a similar project, the New York Genealogical and Biographical Society published *Voices of the Irish Immigrant: Information Wanted Ads in the Truth Teller, New York City, 1825–1844* in 2005. Transcribed and indexed from New York City's first Catholic newspaper by Diane Haberstroh and Laura DeGrazia, the *Truth Teller* ads mention names of several thousand immigrants living all over North America and nearly 1,000 places of origin in Ireland.[1]

The following is an example from the *Boston Pilot* of 9 February 1867 and excerpted in *The Search for Missing Friends*:

> Information Wanted: Of Mrs. Mary O'Connor (maiden name Mary Shanahan) and her sister Catherine Shanahan, who came to this country about seventeen years ago; when last heard from about 9 yrs ago, was living in New Orleans, LA. Any information of them will be thankfully received by their sister, Margaret Shanahan, who came to this country in May 1866 and is anxious to hear from them. Address Margaret Shanahan, Holyoke, MASS.—New Orleans papers please copy." An advertisement of 16 February 1867 adds that the sisters were "natives of the parish of O'Dorney, county Kerry."

Common, too, were notices that horses and other property had been lost or stolen, claims against estates, and even announcements by irate husbands like this one in 1776:

> Whereas the Wife of Joseph Cartwright having eloped from him sundry times, he requests all persons not to trust her, as he will not pay any debts she may contract.
>
> Joseph Cartwright

One wife defended herself vigorously in the *Boston Evening Post* in 1762:

> I find in your last Monday's Papers that my husband informed the Publick That I have eloped—and that I run him into Debt, and has given a Caution not to Trust me on his Account. Although I am very sensible that neither he or I are of much Importance to the Publick, for he has no Estate to entitle me to any Credit on his account; yet I desire you to be so kind to me, as to let the Publick know That I never run him in Debt in my Life, nor never eloped, unless it was to Day Labour, to support me and the Children, which I am of necessity Obliged to do; and shall be ever glad to do my Duty to him, and wish he would for the future behave to me in such a Manner that I may do it with more Ease than heretofore.
>
> Her
>
> Mary X. Wellington
>
> Mark

In some cases, stories like that of Mary Wellington may lead to court records, but even when they do not, news items of this nature can shine a light on the circumstances under which our ancestors lived.

Historical Perspectives in Newspapers

Whether or not you have an interest in genealogy, old newspapers are a fascinating source for reading about life as it was in another time and place. Headlines easily lure us into every part of a newspaper page, making it very hard to stay focused on research goals.

Most newspapers, large and small, included news from other places, especially as it related to the interests of the local population. An interesting example is from the *Adams Sentinel* (Gettysburg, Pennsylvania), published 13 September 1826.

> EDUCATION IN IRELAND AND NEW ENGLAND
>
> According to the population returns of Ireland for 1821, there were 820,757 children between the age of five and ten; and between the ages of five and fifteen, 1,748,663. According to the education returns, there are 569,073 children receiving the advantages of instruction. If we suppose the scholars to be confined to the ages between five and ten, there must be, therefore, 351,684 children totally deprived of its benefits; or, if we suppose the pupils to be confined to the ages between five and fifteen, there must be 1,179,590, or more than two thirds of the whole number. In Massachusetts, according to the recent returns, there is only one in two thousand of the adult population who cannot read, and in Connecticut the proportion is nearly if not quite as favorable.

Another interesting example comes from the *Ohio Repository* (Canton, Ohio) 4 April 1849. Although the article does not name individuals, it alerted readers of a potential problem with forged land warrants—a problem that carries forward for those now researching the same historical warrants for genealogical purposes.

> FORGED LAND WARRANTS.—The Philadelphia American says that the number of forged bounty land warrants now in existence, it is asserted by one who has some acquaintance with them, is extremely great, and there is need of caution by those who purchase them.

Almost every newspaper contained articles boasting of the very latest in technological advances. A sample from the 18 July 1853 edition of the *Adams Sentinel* (Gettysburg, Pennsylvania) included this item.

> On Friday last, at 4 1/2, p.m., Samuel Lawrence, Esq., was in Boston, having left Lasalle, Illinois, at three o'clock, Wednesday, p.m., preceding. He came by way of Chicago, looked in upon Cleveland, called at Buffalo, was sped over the plain by the 'lightning express' train to Albany, and whisked over the Western and Worcester Railroads to Boston! Once, and within the memory of the middle-aged man of this day, Buffalo was considered quite 'out west.'—Chicago, but yesterday, was a 'far-off-land.' Now, a merchant shakes hands and bids good-bye to his customers 180 miles west of that, and in two days and one hour and a half—greets his friends in Boston! It is in fact only eleven hundred and fifty miles!

Even very early newspapers contained fascinating information about groups and individuals. Published within a quarter of an inch of each other, three brief items from the *Ohio Repository* of 18 June 1819 contain clues for the family historian. The three sentences show emigration patterns that may help determine future search strategies.

> On the 21st ult, a caravan consisting of 11 covered wagons, 2 coaches, a number of single horses, and about 120 persons, under captains Blackman and Allen, crossed Powles Hook Ferry, on their way to the state of Illinois.
>
> In one week there arrived at St. Andrews, Maine, two vessels, with 600 passengers from Ireland.
>
> Upwards of 200 passengers lately arrived at Quebec, from England; and 320 arrived at St. Johns, N.F. from England and Ireland.

Newspapers in later years often provided personal details about locals who were visiting or had moved to another place. After the San Francisco earthquake, a headline in the *Brooklyn Daily Standard Union* of 22 April 1906 noted: "William Gray's Family is Safe—Receives Telegram From His Son, Who Is in the Stricken City. Has 27 Relatives There."

Not all useful newspaper information was published immediately after an event. Historical features, columns, and articles that describe events of the same date ten, twenty, or fifty years previous can all provide useful information. Frequently, papers published special historical issues to commemorate both community milestones and notable anniversaries of the paper itself. These special issues frequently contain a wealth of historical information gathered from many sources. For some communities, they are the only published history.

Just as useful may be the regular historical column published over several years by a dedicated local historian. These columns, which often range widely, frequently contain biographical and historical information recorded nowhere else. Sometimes local libraries or historical societies, recognizing the importance of such a series, will have clipped the columns and organized

IF YOU WANT TO BE VALUED, MAKE YOURSELF SCARCE---German

Let's try to cheer with smiles and song
The sorry lives of men
With whom we meet, for it won't be long
Till our paths must part again.
—Nixon Waterman.

The Weekly Sentinel

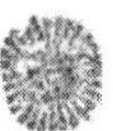

No cheating or bargaining will ever get a single thing out of Nature's "establishment" at half price. To we want to be strong?—we must work. To be hungry?—we must starve. To be wise?—we must look and think. Ruskin.

ESTABLISHED 1833. WEDNESDAY FORT WAYNE'S GREATEST NEWSPAPER APRIL 17, 1912. VOL. IXXX No. 26.

MORE THAN 1,300 LOSE LIFE WHEN GREAT LINER TITANIC ON MAIDEN TRIP STRIKES ICEBERG IN MID-ATLANTIC AND SINKS TO SEA'S BOTTOM

RESCUE STEAMER IS SLOWLY CREEPING IN

Save for 868 Picked Up by Carpathian, All Aboard Magnificent Steamer Went Down to Watery Grave.

MEN OF GREAT PROMINENCE MISSING

Hope for Details of Disaster Centers in Rescue Steamer Due in New York on Thursday Night.

New York, April 17.—In faintest touch with the wireless station at Sable Island, the Cunard liner, Carpathia, with 868 survivors of the sunken Titanic on board, was creeping down the coast early this morning, making the best time for this port that foggy conditions along the Atlantic shore line would permit.

These 868, picked up from the lifeboats of the Titanic at 2 o'clock Monday morning, four hours after that greatest of liners had collided with an iceberg off the banks of Newfoundland and gone down, are believed to represent all the survivors of the 2,180 passengers and crew of the Titanic. The latest estimates are that 1,312 persons perished in this most frightful disaster in marine history.

FINAL HOPE IS DISPELLED.

Hope clung desperately yesterday to the belief that the steamers Virginian and Parisian, of the Allan line, may have picked up survivors in addition to those on board the Carpathia, but this was practically dispelled at 11 o'clock, when the Sable Island wireless station reported that the Parisian had no survivors on board, and when the officers of the Allan line in Montreal issued a statement that the captain of the Virginian had sent them a wireless message saying he had "arrived at the scene of disaster too late to be of service."

Both the Virginian and the Parisian, therefore, appear to hold out no hope of further reducing the extent of the calamity. The Virginian has proceeded on her way for Europe.

REACHES NEW YORK THURSDAY NIGHT.

The Carpathia, having on board the only survivors accounted for, is coming in slowly to New York. All hope for details of the tragedy and its effects are centered on this ship. She will be in wireless communication with Sable Island tonight with Nantucket on Thursday and she will reach New York some time Thursday night.

London, Paris and New York are grief stricken and overwhelmed by the news of the disaster. Tearful crowds of relatives and friends of passengers on board the Titanic thronged the steamship offices in all three cities, waiting hour after hour for news that more often than not, when it does come, means bereavement and sorrow. People in Paris and London went to bed last night in the belief that all the passengers on board the Titanic had been saved; this morning brought them the appalling truth.

Of the survivors on board the Carpathia by far the larger number are women and children.

MEN OF PROMINENCE MISSING.

Many men of great prominence on two continents are among the missing. No word has been received of Col. John Jacob Astor; his wife, however, has been saved. Alfred G. Vanderbilt was not on board the Titanic as at first reported; he is in London.

Isidor Straus, the New York millionaire merchant and philanthropist, who was on board, has not been reported among the survivors.

New York, April 16.—The news that the Titanic had sunk came in a brief wireless dispatch to Cape Race, N. F., shortly after 7 o'clock last night from the White Star liner Olympic, which reported that the Titanic had foundered at about 2:25 Monday morning in latitude 41:16 north and longitude 50:14 west. The message added that the steamship Carpathia, then on her way to Naples, had reached the scene of the wreck at daybreak and found only boats and wreckage and that all the Titanic's boats were accounted for and "about 675 souls saved, crew and passengers, latter nearly all women and children."

This news was confirmed shortly afterward by officials of the White Star line here, who announced that the Olympic had sent them a wireless dispatch that the Titanic had sunk.

Grave Fears for Rest.

... wireless dispatch received early today at Boston, which was relayed by the Olympic from the Carpathia, stated that the Carpathia had 866 of the Titanic's passengers on board, mostly women and children, concluding with the words: "Grave fears are felt for the safety of the balance of the passengers and the crew."

The wireless dispatch from Cape Race, N. F., telling of the sinking also gave the information that the steamship Californian was remaining and searching the vicinity of the disaster. That the Virginian may have some of the ship wrecked passengers of the Titanic on board was indicated in a telegram received here from St. Johns at 2:15 this morning, which stated that she would bring to St. Johns such survivors as she "may rescue." Inasmuch as the Virginian was bound for Liverpool she would hardly return to the New Foundland port unless for humanitarian reasons.

The air was biting cold and the chill that rose from the ice floes caused the passengers to hover close together to keep warm. All through the night the life boats bobbed helplessly between the shifting cakes of ice, while the survivors prayed for dawn to come.

Carried Hundreds to Death.

Shortly after 2 o'clock the sinking Titanic made her great dive into the sea, carrying with her hundreds of persons to death.

Daylight came and with it arrived the Cunarder Carpathia which found only the score of life boats filled with crew and passengers floating helplessly about the vicinity where the Titanic had passed under the waves.

The names of 201 first class and 116 second class passengers who had been saved from the Titanic, making a total of 317 names, have already been received. According to the last report from Captain Rostron, of the Carpathia, there are about 800 survivors of the Titanic on board, which would show that 483 persons had been saved whose names had not been sent in by wireless.

During the morning great throngs of people crowded lower Broadway in front of the White Star line offices, and police reserves were called to control the big crowd.

Of the 201 first class passengers thus far accounted for 132 are women, 63 men and six children. Of the 116 second cabin passengers reported surviv-

(Continued on Page 2, column 1.)

Some of Those Who Escaped Death in Titanic Disaster

THE ILL-FATED TITANIC, THE CAPTAIN AND SOME OF ITS NOTABLE PASSENGERS.

Wm. T. Stead (above). Capt. E. S. Smith (below). Mrs. John Jacob Astor. John Jacob Astor. Maj. Archibald Butt, President Taft's Aide.

GLADIEUX'S LEAD WAS BUT 36 VOTES OVER OPPONENT

Race for Sheriff's Place on Ticket Narrowed Down to Slender Margin With Moeller Second.

SCHWIER, BUTT AND BLACK ARE VICTORS

Koenig, Moran and Moellering Named for Representatives by Democrats in County Primary.

LOSS OF LIFE ON THE TITANIC AS SHOWN BY NEAR-BY COMPARISON.

A comprehensive idea of the terrible loss of life in the sinking of the Titanic may be gained from a comparison of figures with the population of nearby Indiana

Official Totals of the Primary Vote.

Judge Circuit Court.

John W. Eggeman..........8,008

A. C. Gladieux..........1,719

Coroner.

Edward H. Kruse..........8,421

Surveyor.

Ralph Guenther..........4,284

Commissioner, First District.

Ramond J. Mourey.......... 834
J. Jacob Lanz.......... 900
William Gernhardt..........1,111
Clayton A. Lindemuth..........1,178

EXPERTS SEEK TO ANALYZE CAUSE

Navigation Experts Discuss Sinking of Magnificent Titanic, Which Was Supposedly Unsinkable.

ICEBERGS SOURCE OF GRAVEST PERIL

PLEAD FOR NEWS ALL THRO' NIGHT

Anxious Vigil to Learn the Fate of Friends and Relatives.

TAFT MAKING INQUIRY

New York, April 16.—All through the night the officers of the White Star line and the newspapers were besieged by scores of persons anxious to learn the fate of relatives or friends on board the Titanic, while a flood of telegrams, cablegrams and telephone messages were received, bringing eager inquiries from different parts of the country.

President Taft sent a number of dispatches to Halifax inquiring about the safety of Major Butt, his military aide, whose name does not appear in the list of survivors.

Wireless operators worked through the night trying to send and pick up calls from the scene of the disaster. The wireless was handicapped in the early morning by a thunderstorm, which finally silenced wireless transmission for a time.

Names Begin to Come.

Gradually the names of the rescued began to come through by wireless by way of Cape Race from the Carpathia, and were posted in the companys offices. There were some who scanned the lists and turned away with faces showing hopes realized, but the many who came were disappointed and grief stricken. A squad of police and an extra force of clerks were called to take care of the inquiries.

Vincent Astor, son of Col. John Jacob Astor, remained up through the night trying to learn the fate of his father. Word came that Mrs. John Jacob Astor, his stepmother, and her maid, were safe aboard the Carpathia.

Members of the Guggenheim and Straus families had representatives at the White Star offices throughout the night in anticipation of some definite word being received concerning Isador Straus and Benjamin Guggenheim, who were among the prominent passengers on the Titanic. These names were not in the survivors' lists received up to 8:30 o'clock. Numerous inquiries were received regarding the fate of Henry B. Harris, the theatrical manager and his wife. The list shows that Mrs. Harris had been saved, but no word came regarding her husband.

Will Arrive Thursday.

Vice President Franklin, of the International Mercantile marine, said today that he had heard that the Cunarder Carpathia would arrive here on Thursday evening and that his information was that there were 675 survivors of the Titanic on board.

Mr. Franklin said that he did not expect to receive any further wireless messages from the Olympic on this side of the Atlantic and that Captain Haddock, of that steamship, would soon be in position to send all his wireless reports to the London office.

(Continued on Page 2, Column 1.)

New York, April 16.—Experts of navigation and ship building today attempted to analyze the causes of the sinking of the supposedly unsinkable Titanic on the basis of the meager information available. Lewis Nixon, the eminent naval architect, is inclined to think the Titanic was either traveling at full speed or perhaps crashed into a berg so tremendous that there was practically no give.

"If the Titanic hit one of those great ice masses," said Mr. Nixon, "it is likely that she struck one that had no more give than a rock. Under these circumstances something had to give way, and as the iceberg did not, the great ship had to crumple up. It is conceivable that an impact of this sort might have buckled her longitudinal plates from end to end, shearing off and starting rivets and opening up the water tight compartments throughout the length of the vessel."

Naval Constructor's View.

Robert Stocker, naval constructor of the Brooklyn navy yard, said:

"In the case of the Titanic I am inclined to think that her sinking was due to the effect of grounding rather than to the impact of collision. Frequently a ship strikes what is known as a "pinnacle rock," ripping open her keel. The iceberg against which the Titanic smashed her bow may have had some such submerged projection which did additional damage to the keel. If the forward bulkheads of the vessel had held after the impact which smashed the bow, it certainly seems that the relative buoyancy of the remaining compartments would have been sufficient to keep the ship afloat. I am compelled to believe that a great many of her compartments must have been punctured or sprung a leak."

Render Ship Helpless.

"Under ordinary circumstances, water-tight compartments will preserve a ship from sinking," said A. L. Hopkins, vice president of the Newport News Ship-building and Dry Dock company, "but smashing into an iceberg could produce shattering effects that would render a ship helpless beyond the protection of any design yet known. In fore and after collisions where the compartments are punctured, the lowering of either end of the ship produces an increased strain on the other compartments."

Granting that only the forward bulkhead of the Titanic had been crumpled by the impact with the iceberg, Mr. Hopkins was inclined to think that the relative buoyancy of the remaining compartments would have been sufficient to save the vessel. Inasmuch as he was not familiar with the relative division of the Titanic compartments he could not estimate how many compartments must have given way under the impact of the collision.

Source of Grave Peril.

Icebergs, such as the one that spelled disaster for the Titanic, are one of three sources of gravest peril to vessels navigating the north Atlantic. The other two are fog and derelicts. The iceberg menace has been greater this spring than in any recent year.

In the past fifty years there have been an even dozen disasters to big liners for which icebergs were responsible. A majority of these occurred off New Foundland and the Grand Banks, in the general vicinity of the Titanic's grave.

The drift ice this spring has been farther south than for years. Vessels arriving here and abroad have reported ice fields extending far down into the southern track, and skippers have told

(Continued on Page 3, Column 5.)

Fort Wayne, Indiana's the *Weekly Sentinel* of Wednesday, 17 April 1912, announces news of the sinking of the *Titanic* and includes pictures of the ship and some of its famous passengers.

DIRECT WIRE SERVICE
UNITED PRESS
The United Press Serves 650 Evening Newspapers — Special Wire to Daily Citizen Office.

Iowa City Daily Citizen.

12 PAGES
PAGES 1 TO 6
PART ONE

26th YEAR—DAILY EXCEPT SUNDAY | IOWA CITY, IOWA, TUESDAY, APRIL 17, 1917 | PRICE TWO CENTS—NUMBER 68

German Torpedo Fires at United States Destroyer

FRANCO-BRITISH OFFENSIVE OVER 170 MILE FRONT ON TODAY

Three Million Allied Soldiers in the Field Against the German Defenders of Cambrai-St. Quentin Line--Italians Plan Offensive.

London April 17—The long awaited Franco British offensive was on today over a front of 170 miles, with 3,000,000 allied soldiers and an unprecented number of cannons driving against the German defenders of the Cambrai-St. Quentin and Soissons-Rheims line.

In stormy weather with high winds and rain the British established themselves two miles from the Cambrai road along an eleven mile front from Fayet to Epehy. Once this road is cut, St. Quentin and Lafere must fall.

Still driving ahead the French today organized the positions they conquered in their first smash yesterday when they captured 10,000 prisoners. Strong counter attacks between Soissons and Rheims were repulsed with heavy loss to the Germans, it was officially stated today.

Laon is another of the important German supply centers now menaced.

Say French Lost Heavily

Berlin, April 17—French troops suffered heavily in unavailing attempts to break the German line yesterday, it was officially announced. More than 2100 French soldiers were captured.

Offensive on Isonzo Front

Rome, April 17—Italy may start an offensive on the Isonzo front to prevent Turkish reinforcements be-
rrrrrraɼgplasarste
ing sent against the Franco-British offensive. Heavy Italian artillery is reported to have caused great loss among the Austrians. A large number have also been taken prisoners.

GERMANY TO MAKE STATEM'T

TO GIVE TERMS ON WHICH PEACE WOULD BE NEGOTIABLE SOON

Christians. April 17—Germany is shortly to issue to neutrals a statement on the terms on which she considers peace negotiable, according to rumors in diplomatic circles today. It is not believed there will be many concessions from the German peace offer last December.

That the German government is behind the offer to obtain a separate peace from Russia is apparent here and American diplomats have been so advised.

ANTI-GERMAN RIOTS REPORTED

Rio De Janeiro, April 17—Widespread anti German riots were reported from Porto Alegre today. Details are lacking.

STRIKE AFFECTS METAL OUTPUT

NO CONFIRMATION OF DISORDER IN BERLIN HAS BEEN OBTINED

Amsterdam, April 17—Germany's general strike is crippling the output of metal and wood and tying up transportation facilities, according to dispatches received here. There was no confirmation of disorder in Berlin. Semi-official dispatches, however, insisted the strike affected very few industries and was without general public support.

Strike Fizzling Out

Berlin, April 17—(censored)—The general strike, fomented by extreme socialists as a protest against the reduction of the bread ration fizzled out. Only a few factories were forced to suspend by the strike. Not a single munition plant was affected, officials declared. Business apparently continues as usual. On

NATIONS SHOULD NOT AGREE TO MAKE SEPARATE PEACE

Washington, April 17—Senator Sherman today introduced a resolution authorizing the United States to agree with the allies that none will conclude a separate peace with Germany and that peace shall only be concluded with joint action of the United States.

TO CONFER WITH WILSON REGARDING CONSCRIPTION BILL

Washington, April 17—In an effort to bring about non-partisan support of the administration's conscription army bill, President Wilson today asked Representative Mann, republican floor leader of the house and Representative Lenroot to confer with him at the White House.

FEAR SUBMARINE ATTACK ON N. Y.

HARBOR BEING GUARDED BY SUBMARINE NETS—DOUBLE SEARCH FOR U-BOATS

New York, April 17.—The greatest city in the world was today menaced by German submarines. The harbor is guarded by submarine nets. Fire Island, which reported the submarine attack on the Smith, is only thirty-five miles from the entrance of New York Bay. If successful in eluding the American patrol ships the submarine might slip into Long Island Sound and bombard towns.

Army aviators at Governor's Island took to the air and searched for the submarine. It is probable that coast cities will be ordered to keep guard after night.

BULGAR - TURKEY BREAK REPORTED

ZURICH DISPATCHES SAY THESE

THE MOTHER OF A BOY

I didn't raise my boy to be
a coward;
I want my boy to go if there
is war.
I want to stand and watch
him proudly marching,
I want to gaze upon him
from the door.
I do not want to lose him
or to keep him,
I only long and long to have
him be
A man whene'er his country
comes to sweep him
Into her surging legions of
the free.

I do not want my boy to be
a craven;
I love him; and I'd hate to
see him go;
And yet I'd rather lose him,
sadly lose him,
Than have him hide in fear
to face the foe.
I've prayed with all the spirit
of a woman
For peace, and that our
struggle might not come;
But if it does I want him
brave and human,
My boy must march away
with flag and drum.

I'd give him, yes, a thousand
times I'd give him,
With all he means to me of
love and joy;
Because I would not love
him if he wasn't
My ideal of a woman's kind
of a boy.
I do not harbor hate or
yearn for vengeance,
I would not crush a violet
with my hand;
But if it comes to fighting,
then I want him
To be a man and struggle
for his land.

I want my boy to go if we
must enter
This mad world conflict raging
in its might;
With all it means to me to
have him leave me,
I'd give him to his country,
help him fight;
For, so I think a mother
does her duty,
And keeps her faith with
honor and with God;
I didn't raise my boy to be
a coward,
I'd rather have him dead
and turned a clod.

—Baltimore Sun.

TRY VOLUNTEER SYSTEM FIRST

HOUSE EXPECTED TO ADOPT PLAN FOR PRESIDENT TO CALL FOR 500,000 MEN

Washington, April 17—It appeared today that the volunteer plan will be given a trial before conscription is put into effect. The proposal likely to be adopted in the house will be for the president to call for 500,000 to 1,000,000 volunteers to be raised within ninety days. If the volunteer system does not work, conscription would be tried. The senate seems to favor conscription from the outset.

Secretary Baker voicing the administration's stand today declared in the house military committee that he would be compelled to reject all compromises but was willing to yield on some minor points as age of conscription but he insisted on the selective conscription plan.

At the republican senate caucus today it was decided the republican senators would stand behind the president's conscription plan.

MYSTERIOUS AEROPLANE SAID TO BE MAKING FLIGHTS

Boston, April 17—Captain Rush, commandant of the navy yard today took official note of the reports that a mysterious aeroplane has been

THOUSANDS TO BE IN PARADE

The following are the speakers who will address the patriotic rally which will be held in this city Wednesda ynight:

Senator O. A. Byington,
Professor Bohumil Shimek
Rev. H. B. Boyd.

Another recruit, William H. Rogers brought the total number of men in Company A Engineers up to eighty-seven this morning and it is expected that following the mammoth rally tomorrow night in this city that the enlistments will be increased by many more.

If weather like that experienced here today, prevails tomorrow night it is expected that practically every person in Iowa City will throng the streets to witness the parade and hear the speakers.

The marchers, will form at 7 o'clock tomorrow night at their respective halls and will march to the armory on East Washington street where the parade will start. The line of march will be as follows:

Line of March

North on Clinton to Iowa avenue, east on Iowa avenue to Dubuque street, south on Dubuque street to Washington, west on Washington to Clinton, south on Clinton to College, east on College to Linn, north on Linn to Washington, west on Washington to the armory where the paraders will disband.

The speaking will follow the parade and the addresses will be delivered from a stand opposite the Liberal Arts building.

The organizations and lodges, labor unions and bands and other societies who will take part follow:

Marshal—Colonel R. P. Howell
Fife and Drum Corps
G. A. R.
Company A Engineers
Iowa Cavalry
Hospital Unit
Homeopathic and S. U. I. hospital nurses
University band
S. U. I. Cadets
Royal Neighbors
Woman's Relief Corps
Sons of Veterans
Moose Lodge Band
Knights of Columbus
Ancient Order of Hibernians
Elks
Iowa Woman's Club
Daughters of Isabella
Moose
Eagels
Woodmen
Odd Fellows
Redmen
Sokols
C. S. P. S.
Knights of Pythias
Woman's Gymnasium Association
Graduate Students (S. U. I.)
Boys Band.
Grammar and High school pupils (public and parochial)
Fire Department.

Any lodges, organizations or societies who are not mentioned above are also urged to march in the parade.

AUTOMOBILES SHOULD KEEP OFF WASHINGTON STREET DURING MARCH

Mayor F. K. Stebbins requests automobiles to stay off Washington street and Clinton street between Washington and Iowa Avenue where the automobile show is being held, during the parade tomorrow night.

DR. STUCKEY TO LEXINGTON, KY.

IOWA UNIVERSITY MAN ELECTED PRESIDENT OF SAYRE COLLEGE

Dr. Lorin Stuckey, professor of economics and sociology in Iowa university has been elected president

ENLISTMENTS IN COMPANY A ENGINEERS

William H. Rogers
J. Otis Brown
Clarence Phipps
Walter Phipps
Gerald L. Schillig
Harry F. Crane
Fred J. Fackler
Charles A. Egglestone
Walter A. Lewis
Harold D. Benda
Fred E. Seitz
Louis A. Douglas
John T. Gertito
Gale O. Files
Gordon J. Dinsmore
Jesse W. Cozine
Earl W. Copsin
Frank G. Kennon
Justin H. Trundy
(re-enlisted)
Fred C. Sturm
Ralph C. Boarts
George Brueckner
Clifford J. Rogers
Ernest Rosencrans
(re-enlisted)
Noble K. Cozine
Edwin T. Royce
Frank C. Blazek
Joseph C. Mencl
Lloyd G. Frederick

ENLISTMENTS IN TROOP "C" FIRST IOWA CAVALRY

Clem J. Shay
Arthur A. Michael
George D. Linn

ALIEN ENEMIES MUST GIVE UP THEIR WEAPONS

Every resident of Iowa City, German born, who is not a naturalized citizen of the United States, must turn over his "firearms, weapons, or component parts thereof" to Marshall Frank Mezik, which may be in his possession, within the next twenty-four hours.

This was the demand issued by the marshal following the receipt of an edict from Washington, D. C., ordering that all unnaturalized enemy aliens be relieved of their dangerous weapons at once. The move is said to be one of the first acts of the government to eliminate possible trouble from pro-Bermans who are not citizens of the country.

Marshal Mezik declares that the ruling will be enforced to the letter and asserts that those who refuse to comply with the edict will suffer the consequences which means severe punishment. Local authorities, it is believed, are in possession of the names of the German residents of the city who are not naturalized and that it will not be difficult to trail those who do not submit to the regulation. Following is he order received by the police chief:

Order From Gregory.

"Under the proclamation of the president, dated April 6, 1917, it is unlawful for alien enemies to have in their possession the following articles:

"Any firearm, weapon or implement of war, or component part thereof, ammunition, Maxim or other silencer, bomb or other expolsive or material used in the manufacture of explosives; anw aircraft or wireless apparatus or any form of signaling device, or any form of cipher code, or any paper, document, or book written or printed in cipher, or in which there may be invisible writing.

"Your co-operation in enforcing this proclamation is earnestly desired and you are requested if possible, to post notices or otherwise notify all alien enemies within your locality to bring to police headquarters and surrender any and all articles which it is unlawful for them to have in their possession. A detailed receipt should be given for

AMERICAN VESSEL ATTACKED BY U-BOAT OFF N. ENGLAND COAST

Washington, April 17.—Germany fired the first shot of the war against America today and it missed.

Reports from Fire Island off New England say that at about 3:30 this morning an enemy submarine was sighted by the destroyer Smith.

The submarine was running submerged and fired a torpedo at the United States warship, missing by only thirty yards. The submarine disappeared. Redoubled search is being made for submarines.

The U-boat which attacked the Smith was reported hovering off Jersey between Atlantic City and Asbury Park and only a short distance from New York City. Whether it has just come from Germany or has been laying off the coast for some time getting its supplies from a hidden base is not known.

M'ADOO ASKS ADVICE OF BANKERS ON BOND ISSUE

Washington, April 17—Secretary McAdoo today called upon the big bankers for suggestions on floating the seven billion dollar bond issue.

McAdoo also conferred with the federal reserve board for their advice. The bond bill is expected to pass the senate by tonight. Senator Stone objected to certain features but said he would vote for the bill. Senator Simmons in an eloquent plea for the bill said that financial aid was about all the United States could extend to the allies at present. "Let's do it without hesitation," he said.

PATENT MEDICINE INEBRIATES MAN

A ma ngiving his name as John Farall, was arrested by Officer Ben Moore this morning at a rooming house on South Dubuque street charged with intoxication. In the man's suit bag the police found two bottles of a patent medicine which is said to contain a large percentage of alcohol.

The police were told that Farall had been in bed for forty-eight hours before he was arrested and had been consuming large quantities of the medicine.

Farall will sober up before he is taken before the mayor.

ELKS ARRANGE TO MARCH IN PARADE

The Elks will meet at 7 o'clock Wednesday night in their club house and will proceed from there to the place where the big patriotic rally parade will be held. The regular meeting of the Elks will be held at 8:30 o'clock that night instead of at 8 o'clock.

WHEAT PRICES DROP SEVERAL POINTS

Chicago, April 17—News that the Canadian government has placed wheat and wheat flour on the free list demoralized the wheat pit here today. May wheat opened at 4 1-2 below yesterday's close. Then it lost another 5 1-2 getting down to $2.26.

MANY URGE MEXICAN ALLIANCE WITH GERMANY

El Paso, April 17—Unofficial reports from Mexico City stated today that the Carranza proposal for neutrality was opposed and that several speakers openly advocated an alliance with Germany against the United States.

AMES STUDENTS READY TO SERVE COUNTRY

Ames, April 17—Every one of the 3500 men and women attending the state college here in a great outdoor meeting this noon indicated their willingness to serve their country against Germany.

The men without exception will take the compulsory drill daily. The

CLINIC DRAWS MANY DOCTORS

MEDICAL COLLEGE IS HOLDING ITS ANNUAL CLINIC TODAY AND TOMORROW

At 2 o'clock this afternoon, 200 doctors and physicians, mostly from Iowa, had registered for the eighth annual clinic of the college of medicine in the University being held today and tomorrow. Dr. J. T. McClintock, head of the committee in charge, declares that everything indicates that this year's meeting will be more successful than any other held. More doctors are expected this afternoon and evening.

The program was opened at 8 o'clock this morning in the surgical amphitheatre of the hospital with a clinic in eye, ear, nose and throat for the general practitioneer, by Dr. L. W. Dean, dean of the college of medicine. President W. A. Jessup welcomed the visitor at 9:30. Between 10 and 12 o'clock Dr. C. P. Howard, professor of theory and practice of medicine, conducted a clinic in internal medicine.

This afternoon at 1 o'clock Dr. Clarence Van Epps, professor of therapeutics, gave a clinic in neurology and Dr. Dean began a clinic for those interested in head specialties. Other clinics this afternoon are being conducted by Dr. J. B. Kessler and Dr. A. H. Beifeld. At 4:30 the clinics will be suspended for all to attend the Iowa Coe baseball game. Tonight after an address by Dr. E. P. Joslin of the Harvard Medical school on "The Management of Diabetic Cases" at 7:30 in liberal arts auditorium, a smoker and entertainment at Company A hall will be given. The Glee club will sing and there will be boxing and wrestling.

Tomorrow the program will change from medicine and clinics will be given as follows:

8 a. m. Clinic in Gynecology and Obstetrics, Dr. W. R. Whiteis, surgical amphitheatre.

10 a. m. Clinic in General Surgery, Dr. C. J. Ronan, surgical amphitheatre.

1 p. m. Clinic in Genito Urinary Surgery, Dr. N. G. Alcock, surgical amphitheatre.

2 p. m. Clinic in Orthopedic Surgery, Dr. Arthur Steindler, surgical amphitheatre.

3 p. m. Radiographic Demonstration, Dr. Bundy Allen, radiographic rooms.

YETTERS TO ASSIST RECRUITING WORK

In line with the other efforts to assist in recruiting Yetters are today giving the entire space in one of their big windows to a military display designed to picture to young men the scenes and sentiments of war time. Large dry goods houses are doing this in many cities over the country with good effect on the public. Yetters are making this contribution to the patriotic sentiment of the hour. No merchandise will be displayed in the window, and it will be devoted entirely to war features.

The Tuesday, 17 April 1917, *Iowa City Daily Citizen* is filled with headlines about the Great War and the United States's imminent entry into the conflict.

them in scrapbooks; sometimes they have been gathered and published in books or pamphlets. When using these columns from a secondary source, it is wise to check the newspaper files to be sure all of the columns were included.

The "ten, twenty, or fifty years ago" columns are also worth reading. In addition to providing reference to otherwise unconsidered events, they sometimes preserve information from newspaper files that may have later been lost. One such item that appeared in the *Brooklyn Daily Standard Union* on 24 June 1906 included a history of the First Reformed Church. The article tells "the remarkable story of the old Dutch landmark in Flatbush, naming many of the people who played prominent roles in its establishment and early years." The article moves on to the churchyard and epitaphs therein, some of which were etched in Old Dutch. As the few newspaper transcriptions were made a hundred years ago, it may be that the stones themselves are no longer legible. The birth and death of a young girl are expressed in Dutch in a way, the paper says "which characterizes that somber grace and tenderness which has forever passed away."

The *Ohio Repository* on 19 May 1852, had a "Looking Back" column that took stories from old timers. Some of these old timers' recollections are priceless. First hand accounts of people who witnessed history are preserved in newspaper stories from the earliest times, and continue to this day in all parts of our country.

Under the heading of "Pioneer History," a lengthy column recalls the fascinating events of a criminal trial that took place under the most primitive conditions. "The first court in Painesville was held in Captain Skinner's barn, in 1801, sometime after it was removed to the opening, now Painsville, where there were but a few houses." The story recounts a number of most unusual circumstances of the trial and how the jurors retired to the woods to agree upon their verdict. Except for the newspaper account, it would be difficult, if not impossible, to understand the judicial process that played out in the earliest years of the country's history.

Military Draft Information

In certain places, during certain wars, some newspapers published military draft information. As more and more newspapers are indexed, digitized, and placed online, the chances of finding these gems are greatly increased. When individuals do not show up in other military sources, newspapers may provide the only way of understanding why. Those who were exempt for disability, were over age, or who furnished substitutes and others can sometimes be tracked through newspaper accounts.

THE SIKESTON HERALD

Volume XXXXI. | Published Thursdays at 119 W. Malone Ave. Sikeston, Mo., by Clint H. Denman | SIKESTON, MISSOURI, THURSDAY, DECEMBER 11, 1941 | Entered as second class matter March 9, 1908 at postoffice in Sikeston, Missouri | Number 50

United States Congress Today Declared War on Germany and Italy

The World This Week

"The United States can accept no result save victory, final and complete," President Roosevelt declared in his first message to the people of the United States following the outbreak of war with Japan. The message was delivered from the White House on Tuesday night. "Powerful and resourceful gangsters have banded together to make war upon the whole human race," President Roosevelt said. "Their challenge has now been flung at the United States. We are now in this war. We are all in it—all the way. Every single man, woman and child is a partner in the most tremendous undertaking of our American history."

* *

Wall Street went through its first air-raid rehearsal Tuesday in confused excitement. By the time the "all clear," sounded, investors had lost hundreds of millions of dollars by semi-hysterical selling.

* *

The Office of Production Management drafted a program this week to suspend for about two weeks the production of passenger automobiles and approximately 30,000 other non-essential products in which rubber is used until a comprehensive plan for the industry can be worked out in the light of threatened cessation of supplies from the Orient.

* *

The Army announced last night that it had ringed the nation with

Holiday Shopping in Sikeston Is Reaching Record Proportions

With Christmas still two weeks off, holiday shopping is far in excess of last year's volume, Sikeston merchants said this week.

Again and again the story was told of heavy buying, as people seem to have money and are spending it for Christmas. A slackening of the buying program may come as the result of the war, some merchants thought, but it is too soon to judge as yet just what effect America's entry into the world-wide struggle will have on local conditions.

One fact is evident, storekeepers said, and that is that people are spending more money on individual items, buying higher-priced and better quality merchandise than they did last year.

The difficulty of securing merchandise will be the one factor that will slow down holiday business, many merchants reported. Again and again, in stores dealing in stockings and in those selling diamonds, the story is told of how hard it is to buy goods from the wholesaler.

Local jewelers report that orders are taken with no guarantee of fullfilment. Jewelry houses are busy with defense orders, making delicate mechanisms for airplanes and time-bombs. Link bracelets and necklaces and dainty wrist watches are having to wait their turn and their place seems to be at the back of the line.

Other merchants also say that they will probably be able to sell four or five times the goods they will be able to get before Christmas.

So, this year, more than ever, it will be a good idea to do Christmas shopping as early as possible. Because there are just eleven more shopping days until Christmas, and it will be a case of first come, first served.

Streets and Stores In Holiday Array

Despite the war and the heavy hearts it is causing, a trip through Sikeston's business district, bedecked with Christmas garlands and brightly lighted in Christmas colors, will bring back that Christmas spirit which has been almost eclipsed with the war news this week.

Never before has Sikeston been so lovely, as fresh evergreens, intertwined with red, green and

Draft Board to Rush Classification

Within 30 or 40 days, all Scott county registrants will be classified, Draft Clerk Wayne Buckhanon said this morning. To date approximately 2300 of the county's 4300 registrants have been classified, and the work is to be speeded up in anticipation of heavier calls after the first of the year.

As long as Class 1-A registrants are available for call, no re-classifying of Scott county men

Red Cross War Fund Requested

Scott county's quota in the $50,000,000 needed by the American Red Cross for war relief work in the Pacific is $5900, according to a telegram received this week by John J. Reiss, chairman of the Scott county chapter of the organization.

Rev. Jos. P. Read, who is bringing to a successful conclusion Sikeston's Roll Call drive for $1100, was named county chairman for the new drive at a brief meeting of the chapter board here yesterday. No definite plans for the new drive have been made, but it is hoped that the Roll Call can be definitely completed Monday to clear the way for the new solicitation.

Norman H. Davis, chairman of the American Red Cross, stated in his telegram to Mr. Reiss:

"Again the American Red Cross is called upon to serve our nation in war. Both nationally and locally we face vast and definite responsibilities for services to our armed forces and for relief to distressed civilians. To provide essental funds, Red Cross is today launching a campaign for a war fund of fifty millions dollars. The President will on Friday issue a proclamation supporting this appeal. Chapters will be allowed to retain fifteen per cent of the funds raised for local war relief expenditures."

The quota for the State of Missouri is $1,667,900. It is hoped that the entire amount can be raised by January 1.

WELCOME WAGON NOT A CIVIC ENTERPRISE

Last week The Herald carried

McMullin Man Killed by Auto

Burl Montgomery, 47-year-old farmer of the McMullin community, was almost instantly killed early Sunday morning when he was struck by an automobile driven by Murl Greenlee, dairy worker of Sikeston, as the former walked along Highway 60 east of the Sikeston Cotton Oil Mill.

At an inquest held by Coroner Clyde Poe, Greenlee was absolved of blame.

Mr. Montgomery was taken at once to the Sikeston General Hospital, where he died within a short time. Funeral services were held and interment was made in the Blodgett cemetery with Welsh service. Mr. Montgomery is survived by his wife. He had for the past several years farmed on the R. D. Mow land near McMullin.

According to the report of members of the State Highway Patrol, Mr. Montgomery walked in front of Greenlee's car and the accident was unavoidable. Both Montgomery and his companion, Jonathon Hensley, also of the McMullin community, were said to be under the influence of liquor.

AIR SCHOOL CLASS IS LEAVING THIS WEEK

Aviation cadets of the Missouri Institute of Aeronautics who have completed their course of training here, will leave this week for further training at the Army basic school in Enid, Okla.

This is the first class of the local school to be sent to Enid.

A new Army Air Corps regulation forbids the publishing of the

Declaration Against Japan Was Made by the Congress Monday

ROOSEVELT IS MOST POWERFUL PRESIDENT

President Roosevelt has the authority today to seize and control any system of transportation, to take possession of radio stations, or to command any factory to place its entire output at the disposal of the United States.

Mr. Roosevelt, by signing the joint congressional resolution declaring this country to be in a state of war with Japan, automatically became the most powerful president in the history of the United States.

Several new war-time powers have been vested in the president since Woodrow Wilson led the United States into war with Germany in 1917.

RULES ISSUED FOR CONDUCT IN AIR RAID

WASHINGTON, D. C.—In event of an air raid—"above all, keep cool!"

That was Rule No. 1 in a set of preliminary instructions issued today by F. H. LaGuardia, director of the Office of Civilian Defense.

Other rules in case of an air raid:

Stay at home. Get off the street.

Put out lights. Stay away from windows.

Don't scream—keep quiet and do not run for shelter—walk!

Don't believe wild rumors; await official notice from local officers.

America's declared enemies were increased to three this morning when the Congress declared war against Germany and Italy, following similar action taken Monday morning against Japan.

Sinking of the 29,000-ton Japanese battleship Haruna by Army bombers off the northern coast of Luzon in the Philippines was announced today by Secretary of War Stimson.

The latest declarations of war, which were regarded as inevitable following the outbreak of war in the Pacific, were unanimous, as both Houses of Congress rushed through resolutions for the signature of President Roosevelt. Miss Jeanette Rankin, representative from Montana, sole objector to the declaration of war against Japan, did not vote against war in this morning's action.

The declaration of war on Japan, placing this country on a full-wartime basis for the first time since 1918, followed a surprise attack by Japan on Pearl Harbor, American stronghold in the Pacific, early Sunday morning with a reported list of 3000 casualties and 1500 fatalities.

News of the attack, which occurred at the very moment envoys from Japan were discussing with Secretary of State Cordell Hull means of preserving amicable rela-

In Sikeston, Missouri, the *Sikeston Herald* of Thursday, 11 December 1941, announces the U.S. declaration of war on Germany and Italy. Along side these major announcements are articles about holiday shopping in Sikeston.

An enormous project of the volunteers of the Brooklyn (New York) Information Page <http://bklyn-genealogy-info.com> is the posting of newspaper items from old Brooklyn newspapers. This group has worked for years to transcribe several of the daily papers there. A posting from the 19 November 1863 issue *Brooklyn Daily Union* that can be found in the archives of that site included a sample of a Civil War clipping. Under the heading of The Draft in the 3rd District, the following decisions by the Board of Enrollment were reported:

> Held for service—Hy. C. Burr, and John ML Stueinger
> Furnished Substitutes—Wm. A. Huggins furnished John J. Riley;
> John Dimons furnished R. Durheim,
> John M.S. Stenrinzer furnished John Fritz
> Exempted by Disability—Thos. Brambick
> Over age—J. Hood, Ed Hackett, Dan Mullen
> Paid $300—E.R. Thomas
> Non-resident—G.F. Cook
> In Naval Service—Henry Foster, Phil Ketten
> Aliens—David Barry of 83 Gold Street; Thomas R. Gagot, 163 North 2nd, Garrett Moote, 91 Gold Street.

How many of us would have ever thought to look in newspapers to find out which of our ancestors were eligible for the draft, and which ones paid $300, or furnished someone else to serve in his place?

Immigration, Migration, and Shipping Information

Newspapers are especially helpful in tracing migrations from one place to another. Indexes and electronic records have become powerful tools for accessing newspapers and other records from around the world. In the personal and local news columns, we can trace trips to see distant relatives, farewell parties for families about to move, and visits back home from those who had moved away. Sometimes letters back home were published in the newspaper, especially those that reported on the destination. Announcements, letters to the editor, and "Marine Intelligence" include such useful entries as lists, and names of ships docking or cleared for departure.

Historical information about policies and attitudes that regulated immigration can often be best understood by reading newspapers of the time period being studied. For example, the common question of what happened to immigrants who were sent to Ward's Island was addressed in the 3 June 1858 edition of the *New York Times* that follows:

> Commissioners of Emigration
>
> The Commissioners paid a visit of inspection, accompanied by several invited guests, to the Institutions on Ward's Island yesterday. The number of immigrants now there is about 1,100, of whom about 700 are in the hospitals. The conduct of the Institution appeared to be exceedingly judicious and the result is shown in the greatly improved appearance of the grounds and the still more marked improvement in the finances of the Board. The old system of maintaining the inmates in idleness, and paying servants to do all the work of the Island, farming, gardening, smoothing the grounds, cooking and even washing and ironing for them, has been discarded and all the inmates who are well are required to work. The result has been an immense economy in the administration of the Institution on the island. The grounds are kept in order, an extensive and very fine sea wall has been built, fifty or sixty acres of land are in excellent cultivation, and this work as well as other building services of the other buildings is done almost wholly by the inmates.

Now, did you ever think to look at Ward's Island in the census if your ancestor is missing in that timeframe?

It may be impossible to learn much about a specific shipping incident or shipwreck, however, a careful search of newspapers in port cities may yield helpful information, or clues for furthering a search. An item published in the *Ohio Repository* (Canton, Ohio), 27 August 1856, provided some sobering statistics under the headline "Perils of the Deep." The article stated: "During the six months ending July 1, 1856, 333 vessels have been reported either lost or damaged, among which were 110 ships, 91 schooners, 60 brigs, 54 barks, and 18 steamers." If family tradition holds that an individual was shipwrecked or involved in any unusual event on the high seas, the best course is to learn everything possible about the incident. Some newspaper accounts will provide whatever details were available from witnesses, if any. Some newspapers even named those who perished in shipwrecks, though these accounts may not be entirely reliable.

Runaway Slaves and Indentured Servants

Early American newspapers are full of announcements from masters about their slaves or servants. Notices offered slaves for sale or hire, listed runaways, reported captures, and sought the return of runaways, indentured servants, and apprentices. Physical descriptions and descriptions of clothing are usually very detailed.

Newspapers are important sources for tracing blacks before the Civil War. Announcements of sales, with complete physical descriptions, can be combined with probate files, slave census schedules, cemetery inscriptions, church records, and other resources to provide as complete a record as possible for a slave or a free black family. For blacks involved in rebellions or accused of local crimes, the news accounts can be combined with court and coroner's records to round out information.

The plea of Samuel Shilling, published in the *Ohio Repository* (Canton, Ohio) 22 March 1827 offered three cents and a thimble reward, stating,

> Ran away from the subscriber, living in Lawrence township, on Saturday night the 10th of March inst. an indented apprentice to the Tailoring Business, named Frederic Shopley, a ruff-tuff bull of a Dutchman, 20 years old; about 5 feet 5 inches high; fair hair and complexion—Had on light clothes and mixed stockings. The public are cautioned against harboring him—Any person taking up and returning him shall have the above reward but no charges.
>
> Samuel Shilling
> March 17, 1827

Reunions

Depending on the newspaper, space allowance within the newspaper, and whether or not events were reported, reunion stories of all sorts appeared in many publications. For some, having his or her name included in a reunion story was the only press they would get in a lifetime. Reunion stories made for popular reading in almost every community. Reports of school, club, and family reunions were most common, and these stories (sometimes accompanied by photos) are good sources for connecting people and fleshing out what is already known about individuals and groups. Occasionally, the story of a reunion of long-separated family members got the attention of the media. An example of a story that has the potential of solving a family history puzzle was published in the *Brooklyn Standard Union*, 22 September 1931:

> Mrs. Richard Policke, 204 Prospect Place, was surprised yesterday when a man and a woman rang her doorbell and the man said:
>
> "Hello, Rose, I'm Fritz. It sure has been a long time."
>
> It developed that Charles F. Feisel, a wealthy California ranch and realty owner, decided after 40 years of toil to take his first vacation. Leaving Hollywood with his wife, he came to Brooklyn to look for his sister. They were separated in 1893 after coming to America from Germany. With the capital of $8, Mr. Feisel started West, reaching Los Angeles in 1895. Mr and Mrs. Feisel are stopping at the Hotel McAlpin.

How to Find Newspapers

A sensible place to begin searching for the newspaper of interest is at a home or library computer. With the help of a search engine such as Google, it is usually possible to locate newspaper titles. There is no doubt that millions of newspaper pages have yet to be digitized, but the number of areas already covered is amazing. In addition to fully searchable page images, indexes and abstracts to newspapers are constantly being added by libraries, genealogical and historical societies, government agencies, commercial entities, and individuals. Ease of access and use of online newspapers makes them an obvious source of first resort. Plugging the term "newspapers" and the place of publication into a search engine is likely to turn up a variety of possibilities to investigate.

As individuals, genealogical societies, and local and state archives are continuing to digitize newspapers, it's a good idea to periodically check various websites in order to see what progress is being made in the area of your interest. Cyndi's List <www.cyndislist.com> includes a great number of newspaper sources, and RootsWeb.com <www.rootsweb.com> hosts thousands of geographically arranged pages, many of which include indexes to various newspaper sources.

Whether using the Internet or not, one of the first steps in the process is to identify papers that served the area of interest and that have hopefully survived. The same basic reference tools that help us in using periodicals guide the intelligent use of newspapers. The three most needed tools are bibliographies (What was published?), inventories of library and depository holdings (Where is it?), and indexes (How do I find what I want in it?).

Locating local newspapers of the past can be a little more challenging, but certainly not impossible. A visit to the website of the library or archives of the state in which an ancestor lived is a good starting point when using the Internet. Many states have inventoried newspapers, and the titles and publication dates are usually alphabetically arranged by county on the sites.

Early-American Newspapers

Researchers interested in early newspapers have been particularly well served. Papers published between 1690 and 1820 are thoroughly described in Brigham's *History and Bibliography of American Newspapers, 1690–1820*. The Readex Corporation, in conjunction with the American Antiquarian Society, has for many years sponsored the Early American Newspapers Project to make available in microform all of the newspapers described by Brigham. The project gathers volumes and issues from various holding libraries to make the files as complete as possible, then microfilms them for distribution to libraries. They were originally issued on a proprietary medium called Microprint (similar to a large microcard), that required special readers and copiers, but they are now available on microfilm. The series, which is continuing, will most often be found in larger research libraries. Also, many of the libraries holding files of pre-1820 newspapers have microfilmed those files and made them available to the larger research community. More recently, Readex, a division of Newsbank, posted *Early American Newspapers, 1690–1876* online. Based largely on Brigham's work, this collection offers a fully text-searchable database of over one million pages, including cover-to-cover reproductions of historical newspapers, including the *Boston Gazette*, *Gazette of the United States*, *New-York Evening Post*, and others. This collection is available to members of the New England Historic Genealogical Society <www.nehgs.org> and at some public and university libraries.

County histories can also be a good place to learn what newspapers were published in a county. In them, newspapers are often accorded lengthy treatment, from the earliest in the county until the publication date of the history. If a newspaper is still being published, it might be possible to use an Internet search engine to track it down, as more and more currently published papers have a Web presence. Otherwise, the a*Gale Directory of Publications and Broadcast Media* should provide a location and current title. Newspapers are listed therein by state and community of publication. The predecessor of this directory began publishing in 1869, so older editions in libraries can often identify the titles of newspapers that have since ceased publication.

Union lists—catalogs that describe the holdings of multiple libraries—are also helpful in locating newspaper files: Clarence Brigham, *History and Bibliography of American Newspapers, 1690–1820*; Winifred Gregory, *American Newspapers, 1821–1936: A Union List of Files Available in the United States and Canada*; and the U.S. Library of Congress, *Newspapers in Microform: United States, 1848–1983* are essential. For most states, other union lists exist. Usually arranged by state and community, union lists give information on specific libraries, historical societies, newspaper offices, and private collections where these newspaper files have been located. They also tell the time period covered by each newspaper and its frequency of publication. Reference departments in most public and university libraries will hold the national lists and the union lists necessary for their areas. For specific titles, see the chapter reference section.

When trying to identify the newspapers that covered a particular area, it is important to remember that the coverage area of a particular paper was controlled more by the competition than by any civil boundaries. If there were no newspapers published in a particular community of interest, a nearby town may have been the news center serving the area. The area served might include another county or even a county across a state line. Make a careful study of maps for clues of area coverage. Keep in mind that a particular newspaper may have changed editors or political orientation over the years. Other papers may have appeared and disappeared in an area for short periods of time.

Once the potential newspaper files have been identified, locating files covering the time period needed may be the next challenge. Union lists, because they are outdated, are less helpful in these cases, but they will often identify libraries or repositories where collections reside or resided. When appropriate possibilities have been identified, the first step should be to see if that institution has an online catalog. Virtually every library today has a website and most libraries have some portion of their catalog online. Caution is advised however, as some library catalogs may not include special categories such as newspapers. Sometimes these special categories have separate catalogs, whether online or not. Also, catalogs vary widely in their size, ease of use, and ability to perform various searches. A newspaper bibliography can be complex, and sometimes there is no simple or straightforward way to determine which newspaper will be most helpful, especially in cases where twenty or more newspapers served a metropolitan area. The help of a librarian can be invaluable in tracking down needed papers.

If a paper of interest can be identified and its files located in one or more libraries, consider the possibility of obtaining microfilm reproductions of the paper through interlibrary loan. If it is not available on loan or the paper has not been microfilmed, it may be possible to write to the holding institution and request a search for a specific item, if you know the date and place of the event. Many libraries will undertake a brief search (usually of one paper) if sufficient identifying information can be provided. Be willing to pay any necessary search and copy charges. Search policies vary widely from one library to another and are subject to change. More extensive searching may require a personal visit or the services of a professional researcher. Whenever possible, there is no substitute for a personal search. Only you are likely to recognize the passing mentions of other relatives or family members that make serendipitous finds possible.

United States Newspaper Program

Since the publication of Gregory's *American Newspapers*, which covered the period from 1821 to 1936, historians and librarians have been interested in bringing it up to date and making it more complete. State historical societies, state libraries, university libraries, archives, and many state library consortia have become involved. The result is that nearly every state has had some kind of newspaper identification, cataloging, and microfilming program, and many institutions have published lists of their specific holdings or union lists covering multiple repositories (see the chapter reference section). These projects have always been somewhat limited in scope and haphazard in execution. For some states, the increasingly outdated *American Newspapers* was still the best newspaper identification and location guide.

Far and away the most comprehensive program to update and expand Gregory's bibliography began in 1973. The Organization of

American Historians, with the support of funds from the National Endowment for the Humanities (NEH), began planning for what is now known as the United States Newspaper Program. Iowa was chosen as the pilot state, because it did not then have a statewide newspaper bibliography and because it had an average number of newspapers and repositories. The project, known as the Iowa Pilot Project, was completed in 1979. The outcome of the project was the listing of Iowa newspapers in both an automated catalog and a published list (cited in the chapter reference section), thus demonstrating that a national project was feasible.

In 1981, the Online Computer Library Center (OCLC) in Dublin, Ohio, agreed to accept newspaper records into its database, thereby acting as the computer network for the project. In 1982 and 1983, respectively, the Library of Congress and six national newspaper repositories began to catalog (or re-catalog) their holdings and enter the data into the OCLC database. The holdings of the national repositories, some 35,000 titles from all fifty states, provided the bibliographic foundation for projects by the various states' projects, testing the guides and procedures developed for the national plan.

In the fall of 1982, NEH invited universities, libraries, archives, and historical societies to submit applications for grants covering their own states. In July 1983, the first awards were made, and the United States Newspaper Project was up and running. Altogether, the project has involved all fifty states, the District of Columbia, Puerto Rico, and the U.S. Virgin Islands in planning and/or implementation of projects. In addition, eight national newspaper repositories (plus the Library of Congress) have also participated in the program.

Newspapers cataloged through the project can be identified on OCLC's WorldCat (available online in most libraries), which in 2003 began to include detailed holdings. Every several years, the program also issues the *United States Newspaper Program National Union List* on microfiche, which also provides detailed holdings information. Several states have also published union lists based on project data. Links and contact details for the various state programs can be found on the USNP website: <www.neh.gov/projects/usnp.html>.

The National Digital Newspaper Program, launched by the National Endowment for the Humanities (NEH) and the Library of Congress in late 2004 (discussed at the beginning of this chapter) is just the latest step in making newspapers an even more important tool for tracing family history.

Accessibility of Newspapers

Few researchers are likely to find old newspapers in their original format. Because of the high acid content of newsprint, their considerable bulk, and the difficulties of proper storage, newspapers were seen as natural candidates for extensive microfilming. Commercial firms and newspaper repositories continued to microfilm newspapers until the ease of digitizing made that mode more practical and economically feasible. As a result of microfilming and digitizing projects, newspapers have become one of the most accessible sources available for research. Many libraries and historical societies will loan microfilm at a nominal cost. It is usually unnecessary to contact the original publisher or its successor, because most historical papers are now in public repositories.

Newspapers in College and University Libraries

While the purpose of newspaper collections in university and college libraries is primarily to support the research needs of the university faculty and students, it is sometimes possible for researchers not affiliated with the college to access these collections. It's certainly worth the effort to investigate the holdings of the nearest college or university library if needed publications are not found online, as their collections can be quite extensive. For example, the newspaper collection at the University of Illinois, Urbana-Champaign <www.library.uiuc.edu/administration/collections/tools/developmentstatement/newspapers.htm> began with Illinois newspapers in 1914, and soon expanded to include major United States and foreign dailies. The estimated holdings there now include 73,000 reels of microfilm consisting of 369 general interest domestic titles, 312 general interest foreign titles, 172 subject-oriented titles, and 8,800 microcards representing 13 titles. In addition, the Newspaper Library has current subscriptions to 515 United States and foreign newspapers and more than three thousand volumes of reference guides, bibliographies, histories, and newspaper indexes. The pattern is typical of the collection policies of most libraries in higher learning institutions. The University of Oregon Libraries <http://libweb.uoregon.edu/govdocs/indexing/newspaperhistory.html> includes a history of newspaper publishing in the state and a description of their newspaper indexing project.

Newspapers in Government Libraries Archives and Historical Agencies

As previously mentioned, the Library of Congress <www.loc.gov> is leading the way in efforts to preserve and digitize newspapers, but a number of state and local governments are also heavily involved. The newspaper collection in the Arkansas Historical Commission includes files of about three thousand titles published at some 250 different places in Arkansas, 1819 to the present. In addition to papers featuring state and local news, there are also religious, professional, and special interest publications. The newspaper catalog lists publications by city, county, and title. Although a beginning and ending date is listed for each title, there may be missing issues. Like most other libraries and institutions with collections, the Arkansas History Commission cannot undertake newspaper research, but will copy articles with the proper date and place citation. Their website <www.ark-ives.com/selected_materials/index.php#religion> provides a description of holdings and details for ordering information.

The Nebraska Library Commission maintains an interesting website with a listing (though not complete) of a large number of newspapers that are available online <www.nlc.state.ne.us/nsf/news.html>.

Search Strategies

Once a file of the newspaper from the ancestor's time and location has been located, what information can you find in it? Just look and see. There really is no better way to learn about old newspapers than to spend some time reading them. To fully tap their potential, begin at the front page of the first issue available in the time period of your search and proceed issue by issue, page by page, through the entire publication. Obviously, the size of large metropolitan papers makes it impractical to read all papers, but perusing a few issues can provide a helpful overview of the layout and philosophy of the paper and unexpected clues for further research. In addition to zeroing in specific events such as death or marriage dates, a wider search approach may yield additional information on other family members and the community in general. Bits of useful information that fill in gaps in family and local history can be found in newspapers and nowhere else. When items of interest are found, carefully note them, or print them out or photocopy them if possible. It is important to note the exact newspaper title, date, page number, and even the location on the page for future reference and for documentation purposes. How disappointing it is to find an orphan newspaper clipping that doesn't provide a date or the source of publication.

Indexes and Abstracts

Because newspapers are such voluminous and time-consuming resources, the researcher needs to use whatever shortcuts may be available. As noted previously, a surprising number of newspapers have at least partial indexes available. In addition, many researchers have abstracted items of genealogical interest from newspaper files. Some of these indexes and abstracts have been published and are widely available; others may be available only at a particular repository. Exploring Internet options is usually the most expeditious way to begin a search. Online searching (through Google or another search engine) for genealogical resources in or for a particular locality should always include searches (or keeping an eye out) for newspaper-related finding aids.

Some older tools can still be useful, too. Betty Jarboe, *Obituaries: A Guide to Sources,* is a good state-by-state directory for obituary indexes. Anita Milner, *Newspaper Indexes: A Location and Subject Guide for Researchers,* identifies and locates unpublished indexes and card files. Wherever you are searching, it is worth asking about any available indexes, particularly unpublished ones. They are often not listed (or not easily found) in library catalogs.

The most commonly used newspaper index in book form is the *New York Times Index,* because of the tremendous volume of material it covers and because it is available in so many public, college, and university libraries. Coverage of the *New York Times Index* now extends back to 1851 (with variations in coverage). This index covers published articles by subject matter and indexes names as well. Since most metropolitan newspapers report important events at approximately the same time, the *Times* index serves as an index to other newspapers for the same subjects. For example, the *New York Times Index* identifies major battles of the Civil War and includes some casualty lists. Once the date of a particular battle has been identified, you can check other newspapers for similar lists of local men killed or wounded in the same engagement. The index is especially valuable when the casualty lists were issued weeks or even months after the battle was fought.

There is also a separately published *New York Times Obituaries Index* with 390,000 entries covering 1858 to 1968 and a supplement covering 1969 to 1978. Official death lists and casualty lists are not indexed. References for casualty lists may appear in the *New York Times Index* under subject headings such as "Philippine Insurrection, casualty lists . . ." etc.

The family historian need not search even the annual volumes of the *New York Times Index* for a particular name of interest. The personal names listed in the *New York Times Index* from 1851 to 1999 have been gathered in the *Personal Name Index to the New York Times Index 1851–1974* and its 1975 to 1999 supplement. The *Personal Name Index* includes only those names listed in the *New York Times Index,* not every name mentioned in the individual issues of the *New York Times.* In more recent times, the availability of the entire files of the *New York Times* online has permitted a wider range of searches to the entire files, but the print indexes are still useful.

Numerous major-city daily newspapers have been indexed in recent years, in much the same fashion as the *New York Times.* Most of these indexes are of relatively little use to genealogists because they are intended to index major news, not the "minor" items the genealogist most needs to find. Not even the *New York Times Index,* which normally fills several shelves in a library's reference section, includes every name. Of more genealogical utility are those indexes that were created by genealogists (or local historians) or at least were created to index newspaper items of genealogical interest.

The American Antiquarian Society, of Worcester, Massachusetts, pioneered the indexing of many early newspapers. The society indexed marriages and deaths that appeared in the *Columbian Sentinel* of Boston from 1784 to 1840, a major achievement because this newspaper printed marriage and death notices from all over the country and included 80,000 names. Other indexing projects of the society have been a death index to the *Christian Intelligencer* of the Reformed Dutch Church, 1830 to 1871, an index to marriages and deaths in the *New York Weekly Museum*, 1788 to 1817, and an index of obituary notices of the *Boston Transcript*, 1875 to 1930. Copies of these newspaper indexes have been deposited in the Library of Congress, the New York Public Library, and the New England Historic Genealogical Society.

The *Index of Obituaries of Boston Newspapers 1704–1800* abstracts deaths within Boston (1704 to 1800) and outside of Boston (1704 to 1795). Brent Holcomb, *Marriage and Death Notices from Baptist Newspapers of South Carolina, 1835–1865* has abstracted and indexed the marriages and deaths that were reported in numerous South Carolina newspapers. Kenneth Scott has also compiled vital records and other genealogical information printed in the *New York Post-Boy* and other eighteenth-century New York and Philadelphia papers.

Newspaper indexing projects have long been popular among the hundreds of genealogical societies and libraries serving genealogists across the nation. The Chicago Genealogical Society has published several indexes to births, marriages, and deaths that appeared in several Chicago newspapers from 1833 to 1848. Many of these indexes are known only to the compilers and those who may be familiar with local library collections. Indexes of this sort are sometimes mentioned on societies' or libraries' websites; some have even been made available online.

Many partial newspaper indexes and abstracts have been published in genealogical society newsletters and publications, and can best be approached through the *Periodical Source Index (PERSI)* published by the Allen County Public Library of Fort Wayne, Indiana, and available online.

In the 1930s, the Work Projects Administration (WPA) and related programs compiled, among other projects, numerous newspaper indexes. Some were published, and others remain in manuscript form. They are notable because they tended to cover large time spans. The *General Index to Contents of Savannah Georgia Newspapers*, which covers 1763 to 1830, was issued in twenty-seven volumes. The *Virginia Gazette Index, 1736–1780* was published in 1950 and more than 200 libraries hold it. Both indexes are in the Library of Congress.

All newspaper indexes and abstracts should be used as guides to items in the papers, not substitutes for them. Comprehensive indexes are virtually unknown. Few indexes cover gossip columns, advertisements, announcements, passenger lists, and other equally important items. For these, search page by page. A shortcut of sorts is to check the vital records indexes first to narrow down time periods when the family lived in each area, and then search these periods page by page in the local papers, covering all columns.

Religious Newspapers

The general interest newspaper as we know it is not the only possible source of biographical and genealogical information. Many religious denominations have sponsored newspapers. In addition to religious and doctrinal news and features, these papers often give considerable attention to the activities of the denomination's members—not only the clergy, but also many of its other members. If you know an ancestor's religious affiliation, the effort to find copies of the religious newspaper is often worthwhile because they offer details not found in other sources. A respected member of a religious group will often command more attention within that community than elsewhere.

Newspapers can be particularly important for those denominations that otherwise have rather poor genealogical records, such as the various Methodist and Baptist groups. Also, religious papers were among the first to give significant attention to obituaries. It is not uncommon to find a denominational paper in the 1830s with a full page of obituaries, when the typical secular paper ran two or three brief death notices at best. Sometimes the obituary dwelt more on the religious history of the deceased than the genealogical history, but even then significant clues often appear.

In one case, a search was made of all existing daily papers printed in Chicago at the time of a person's death. Each paper noted his death, age, and last known address. Only a few of the papers provided funeral information. However, the weekly Catholic diocesan newspaper included his town of origin in Europe, the year he immigrated to the United States, the year he arrived in Chicago, the year he became a member of the parish, the date of his marriage, the maiden name of his wife, the names of their children, and those of their children's spouses. The flowery eulogy that one expects to find in a turn-of-the-century publication was also provided, along with the names of the clergy in attendance at the funeral service.

Religious newspapers will most often be found in institutions connected with the denomination—archives, historical societies, seminary or denominational college/university libraries—but don't overlook the more traditional sources, such as state historical libraries and archives or the libraries of public colleges and universities with significant newspaper collections. Also, because the distinction between a denominational newspaper and a denominational journal was often a fine one, a search of periodical bibliographies is often necessary. The vagaries of bibliographical description often place what, by format, are clearly newspapers among the periodicals. For example, the various editions of the *Christian Advocate*, an important Methodist newspaper, are listed in the *Union List of Serials*, not in Gregory's *American Newspapers*.

Because religious papers include only a segment of an area's population, they are spread more thinly than secular papers.

There may well be only a single newspaper for a particular denomination covering an entire state or region, or for smaller denominations, covering the entire United States. Like secular papers, religious papers have come and gone. A particular state in the 1830s may have been covered only by a distant regional paper; by the 1870s it may have had its own publication. While at a slower rate, some religious newspapers are being digitized and posted online. An example is a project of the Cleveland Jewish Genealogy Society <www.clevelandjgs.org/resources.htm> that provides an index of Jewish obituaries, 1902 to 1974.

The University of Notre Dame's Catholic newspaper collection <http://archives.nd.edu/cathnews/cathnote.htm#4> has long been regarded by American Catholic historians as one of the finest in the United States. The formation of the collection dates back to the late nineteenth century, when James F. Edwards (1850 to 1911), one of Notre Dame's first and foremost librarians, obtained extended runs of the *United States Catholic Miscellany*, the *Truth Teller*, the *Catholic Mirror*, and a number of other Catholic newspapers published in the nineteenth century.

A fairly comprehensive list of denominational websites can be found at Hartford Seminary's Institute for religious organizations (under links to denominations) <http://hirr.hartsem.edu/org/faith_denominations_homepages.html>. Visiting the links for the various denominations is a good way to discover what newspaper publications may be available for each.

While more limited in scope, *Religious Newspapers in the Old Northwest to 1861: A History, Bibliography, and Record of Opinion* provides insights that would be helpful to anyone looking for information in that area and time.

Ethnic and Foreign-Language Newspapers

Newspapers have traditionally been a source of pride, a means of bonding, and a way for members of ethnic groups to read news written specifically for and about their own communities. Unfortunately, collections of ethnic and foreign language newspapers have been scattered, and until the advent of the Internet, it has been difficult for the average researcher to find or access many of the collections. A few ethnic bibliographies were helpful, yet few were comprehensive.

James P. Danky, newspaper and periodical librarian at the State Historical Society of Wisconsin in Madison, Wisconsin, led a project to produce a comprehensive guide to newspapers and periodicals of African Americans. *The African-American Newspapers and Periodicals: A National Bibliography and Union List* is a description of more than 6,500 titles and their locations.[2] A follow-up grant has been awarded to the Society from the National Endowment for the Humanities to preserve African American periodicals on microfilm. The Wisconsin Historical Society <www.wisconsinhistory.org/libraryarchives/aanp> has online images of *Freedom's Journal*, the first African American owned and operated newspaper published in the United States (1827 to 1829).

A history of African American newspapers that leads to dozens of these publications can be found at <http://cti.itc.virginia.edu/~aas405a/newspaper.html>.

Immigrants arrived in the United States with their own culture, customs, and language. They were all hungry for news from their homelands, where most had left relatives and friends. The foreign-language press opened a natural channel of communication to bridge the Old World and the new environment.

Where major local newspapers often overlooked or carried one-line death notices of persons who, the person often received detailed notice in his or her ethnic newspaper. If you don't read the language, broad searches in a foreign-language paper may not be possible, but an obituary reads like an obituary in virtually any language. If an item can be located, perhaps by recognizing your ancestor's name, it can usually be copied and translated later, either through the word-by-word dictionary method or through the services of someone who does read the language.

Ethnic organizations are still numerous throughout the United States, and most of them publish their own foreign-language newspapers. Large collections can be found in the Immigration History Research Center at the University of Minnesota <www.ihrc.umn.edu> and at a number of major libraries, archives, and state historical organizations. These centers seek and preserve immigrant materials for all groups.

More specialized collections, concentrating on a particular group, include the Swenson Swedish Immigration Research Center at Augustana College in Rock Island, Illinois <www.augustana.edu/swenson>, and the Czech and Slovak American Genealogical Society of Illinois <www.csagsi.org> and the Polish Genealogical Society of America <www.pgsa.org>.

The Polish Society published *Index to the Obituaries and Death Notices Appearing in the Dziennik Chicagoski,* which is available as a set of four volumes, covering 1900 through 1930. These works have approximately 80,000 names of individuals whose obituaries or death notices were published in the *Dziennik Chicagoski*, Chicago's leading Polish newspaper. If you have any family ties with Chicago, these volumes are a tremendous help in finding relatives and family members in Polonia's largest Polish community.

The Denni Hlasatel Obituary Index is available on CD from the Czech and Slovak American Genealogy Society of Illinois through their CSAGSI Store at <www.csagsi.org>. This index is considered a "must" for those doing research on Czechs in Illinois. (For more details see chapter 9, "Immigration Records.")

Current Newspapers

Current newspapers are especially useful in locating unknown relatives. Distant relatives may still be living in old hometowns though the direct ancestor moved away. Obituaries in current papers may provide biographical details not available elsewhere. Thousands of current newspaper obituaries can be found by typing a name, or the name of a town plus the word newspaper into a search engine such as Google. The Obituary Collection at Ancestry.com <www.ancestry.com> contains recent obituaries culled daily from hundreds of newspapers on the Internet.

Additionally, current newspapers at least occasionally feature historical articles about the community and its people, particularly in conjunction with centennials, sesquicentennials, and so on of either the community or the newspaper. These articles may also provide useful leads for furthering research. The availability of an ever-increasing number of online newspapers has put a wide variety of newspapers at our fingertips.

Conclusion

As with any other genealogical or historical source, a degree of skepticism is needed as we read through the pages of the past. The hurried nature of news-gathering—then, as now—has often led to error. Not everything found in print is accurate. Yet, while the quality of information found in newspapers varies greatly, there's often no other way to glean more personal and personality-revealing details about ancestors and other family members. Sometimes newspapers fill in gaps in family stories, and sometimes they provide vital records where no other proof of birth, marriage, or death exists. They are entertaining and enlightening. They are accounts of the lives of famous and ordinary people written as they happened, making them an excellent source for family history.

Notes

[1] Diane Haberstroh and Laura DeGrazia, *Voices of the Irish Immigrant: Information Wanted Ads in the Truth Teller, New York City, 1825–1844* (New York: New York Genealogical and Biographical Society, 2005).

[2] James P. Danky and Maureen E. Hady, eds., *African-American Newspapers and Periodicals: A National Bibliography* (Cambridge, Mass.: Harvard University Press, 1998).

References

The following lists of works related to newspapers are extensive but by no means exhaustive. The references include research aids, identifying and locating specific newspapers with content descriptions and suggestions on use where appropriate, as well as abstracts of newspaper data.

Not every newspaper has survived the ravages of time and neglect, and not all those that have survived (at least to the present) are available for research. Those identified in the various bibliographies are those that have (in most cases) been stored in research institutions. It is entirely possible that the newspaper file you need is still sitting on a shelf (or attic) in a newspaper office, in a shed of the former editor's grandson, or is uncataloged in the basement of a library, museum, or historical society. Original research to track down those elusive resources may be necessary, but check the available bibliographic resources to be sure it is necessary.

As this chapter is concerned with American newspapers, no reference is made to British or non-U.S. foreign newspapers, American newspapers in England and elsewhere, or English-language newspapers elsewhere in the world.

How-Tos, Analytical Studies

Clark, Thomas D. "The Country Newspaper as a Source of Social History." *Indiana Magazine of History* 48 (1952): 217–32.

Eakle, Arlene H. *Were Your Ancestors Front-Page News?* Salt Lake City: Genealogical Institute, 1974.

Golembiewski, Thomas. *The Study of Obituaries as a Source for Polish Genealogical Research.* Chicago: Polish Genealogical Society, 1983.

Hosman, C. Lloyd. *Newspaper Research.* Indianapolis: Heritage House, 1985.

Lantz, Herman R. "Use of the Local Press in Historical Research." *Mid-America* 38 (1956): 172–79.

Mott, Frank Luther. *American Journalism: A History, 1690–1960.* 3rd ed. New York: Macmillan, 1971.

Park, Robert Ezra. *The Immigrant Press and Its Control.* Westport, Conn.: Greenwood Press, 1970.

Schwarzlose, Richard Allen. *Newspapers, a Reference Guide.* New York: Greenwood Press, 1987.

Sniffen, Irene G. "Newspapers as a Genealogical Resource." *National Genealogical Society Quarterly* 68 (September 1980): 179–87.

Guides to "Current" Newspapers

American Newspaper Directory. New York: George P. Rowell and Co., 1869–1908, annual.

Editor and Publisher. *International Year Book.* New York: Editor and Publisher, 1921–, annual. Issued 1921–1958 as "International Year Book Number" of *Editor and Publisher.*

Gale Directory of Publications and Broadcast Media. Farmington Hills, Mich.: Gale Group, 1880–, annual. As *American*

Newspaper Annual (1880–1909); *American Newspaper Annual and Directory* (1910–29); *N. W. Ayer & Sons Directory of Newspapers and Periodicals* (1930–69); *Ayer Directory, Newspapers, Magazines, and Trade Publications* (1970–71); *Ayer Directory of Publications* (1972–82); *IMS . . . Ayer Directory of Publications* (1983–85); *IMS Directory of Publications* (1986); *Gale Directory of Publications* (1987–89); *Gale Directory of Publications and Broadcast Media* (1990–).

Milner, Anita Cheek. *Newspaper Genealogical Column Directory.* 6th ed. Bowie, Md.: Heritage Books, 1996. Preliminary ed., 1975; 1st ed., 1979; 2nd ed., 1985; 3rd ed., 1987; 4th ed., 1989; 5th ed., 1996.

Working Press of the Nation. Burlington, Iowa: National Research Bureau, 1945–, annual.

National Bibliographies

Barnes, Timothy M. "Loyalist Newspapers of the American Revolution, 1763–1783; Bibliography." *Proceedings of the American Antiquarian Society* 83 (1973): 217–83.

Brigham, Clarence S. *History and Bibliography of American Newspapers, 1690–1820.* 2 vols. Worcester, Mass.: American Antiquarian Society, 1947. Brigham's "Additions and Corrections to History and Bibliography of American Newspapers" appeared in the *Proceedings of the American Antiquarian Society* 72 (1971): 15–62.

Clarke, Avis G. *An Alphabetical Index to the Titles in American Newspapers.* Oxford, Mass., 1958. Clarke is particularly useful when the title of a paper, but not the place of publication, is known.

Gregory, Winifred. *American Newspapers, 1821–1936: A Union List of Files Available in the United States and Canada.* 1937. Reprint, New York: Kraus, 1967.

Hoornstra, Jean, and Trudy Heath. *American Periodicals, 1741–1900: An Index to the Microfilm Collections—American Periodicals 18th Century, American Periodicals, 1800–1850, American Periodicals, 1850–1900, Civil War and Reconstruction.* Ann Arbor, Mich.: University Microfilms International, 1979.

Lathem, Edward Connery. *Chronological Tables of American Newspapers, 1690–1820; Being a Tabular Guide to Holdings of Newspapers Published in America Through the Year 1820.* Worcester, Mass.: American Antiquarian Society, 1972. Companion to Brigham, above.

Union List of Serials in Libraries of the United States and Canada. 3rd ed. 5 vols. New York: H. W. Wilson, 1965. Although it excludes general-interest newspapers covered by Gregory's *American Newspapers*, the *Union List of Serials* does include listings for many religious and special-interest publications that appeared in newspaper format and often contained obituaries and other materials of interest to the genealogical researcher.

U.S. Library of Congress, Catalog Management and Publication Division. *Newspapers in Microform: United States, 1848–1983.* 2 vols. Washington, D.C.: Library of Congress, 1984.

United States Newspaper Program National Union List. 5th ed. Microfiche. Dublin, Ohio: OCLC, 1999.

Religious Newspapers

Allbaugh, Gaylord P. *History and Annotated Bibliography of American Religious Periodicals and Newspapers Established From 1730 Through 1830.* 2 vols. Worcester, Mass.: American Antiquarian Society, 1994.

Ames, Charlotte. *Directory of Roman Catholic Newspapers on Microfilm—United States.* Notre Dame, Ind.: Memorial Library, University of Notre Dame, 1982.

Batsel, John D., and Lyda K. Batsel. *Union List of United Methodist Serials, 1773–1973.* Evanston, Ill.: Garrett Theological Seminary, 1974. Prepared in cooperation with the Commission on Archives and History of the United Methodist Church, United Methodist Librarians' Fellowship and Garrett Theological Seminary.

Flake, Chad S. *A Mormon Bibliography, 1830–1930.* Salt Lake City: University of Utah Press, 1978. *Ten Year Supplement.* Salt Lake City: University of Utah Press, 1989. *Indexes to A Mormon Bibliography and Ten Year Supplement.* Salt Lake City: University of Utah Press, 1992.

Hebrew Union College—Jewish Institute of Religion. American Jewish Periodical Center. *Jewish Newspapers and Periodicals on Microfilm, Available at the American Jewish Periodical Center.* Cincinnati: the center, 1984.

Microfilm Catalog of Baptist Historical Materials. Nashville: Historical Commission, Southern Baptist Convention, 1984. Supplement published in 1989.

Norton, Wesley. *Religious Newspapers in the Old Northwest to 1861: A History, Bibliography, and Record of Opinion.* Athens: Ohio University Press, 1977.

Spencer, Claude E. *Periodicals of the Disciples of Christ and Related Religious Groups.* Canton, Mo.: Disciples of Christ Historical Society, 1943.

Stroupe, Henry S. *The Religious Press in the South Atlantic States, 1802–1865.* Durham, N.C.: Duke University Press, 1956.

Willging, Eugene P., and Herta Hatzfeld. *Catholic Serials of the 19th Century in the United States; a Descriptive Bibliography and Union List.* 1st series, 2 vols.; 2nd series, 15 vols. Washington, D.C.: Catholic University of America Press, 1959–68. The first series, which covered those states with a smaller publication history, first appeared in the *Records of the American Catholic Historical Society of Philadelphia*, September 1954–December 1963.

Ethnic Newspapers

Arndt, Karl J. R., and Mary E. Olson. *The German Language Press of the Americas*. 3rd rev. ed. 3 vols. Munich: K. G. Saur, 1976–1980.

Balys, Jonas. *Lithuanian Periodicals in American Libraries: A Union List*. Washington, D.C.: Library of Congress, 1982.

Danky, James P., and Maureen E. Hady, eds. *African-American Newspapers and Periodicals: A National Bibliography*. Cambridge, Mass.: Harvard University Press, 1998.

Danky, James P., ed. *Native American Periodicals and Newspapers, 1828–1982; Bibliography, Publishing Record, and Holdings*. Westport, Conn.: Greenwood Press, 1984.

Edelman, Hendrik. *The Dutch Language Press in America*. Nieuwkoop, The Netherlands: De Graaf Publishers, 1986.

Ethnic Serials at Selected University of California Libraries: A Union List. Los Angeles: University of California, 1977. A useful source for Asian American, Hispanic, and African American publications.

Haberstroh, Diane, and Laura DeGrazia. *Voices of the Irish Immigrant: Information Wanted Ads in the Truth Teller, New York City, 1825–1844*. New York: New York Genealogical and Biographical Society, 2005.

Henritze, Barbara K. *Bibliographic Checklist of African American Newspapers*. Baltimore: Genealogical Publishing Co., 1995.

Hoerder, Dirk. *The Immigrant Labor Press in North America, 1840s–1970s; an Annotated Bibliography*. New York: Greenwood Press, 1987. Vol. 1: migrants from Northern Europe; Vol. 2: migrants from Eastern and Southeastern Europe; Vol. 3: migrants from Southern and Western Europe.

Hoglund, A. William. *Union List of Finnish Newspapers Published by Finns in the United States and Canada, 1876–1985*. Minneapolis: Finnish-American Newspapers Microfilm Project, 1985.

Hovde, Oivind M., and Martha E. Henzler. *Norwegian American Newspapers in Luther College Library*. Decorah, Iowa: Luther College Press, 1975.

Kestercanek, Nada. *Croatian Newspapers and Calendars in the United States*. Scranton, Pa.: Marywood College, 1952. Reprint, San Francisco: R. and E. Research Associates, 1971.

Marzolf, Marion. *The Danish-Language Press in America*. New York: Arno Press, 1979.

Setterdahl, Lilly. *Swedish American Newspapers: A Guide to the Microfilms Held By the Swenson Swedish Immigration Research Center, Augustana College, Rock Island, Illinois*. Rock Island: Augustana College Library, 1981.

University of Minnesota. Immigration History Research Center. *The Newspaper and Serial Holdings of the Immigration History Research Center, University of Minnesota*. St. Paul: the center, 1984–. Part 1: Ukrainian American periodicals; Part 2: Italian American periodicals; Part 3: Finnish American periodicals, Baltic American periodicals, West Slavic American periodicals, East Slavic American periodicals.

Wepsiec, Jan. *Polish American Serial Publications, 1842–1966; An Annotated Bibliography*. Chicago, 1968.

Wynar, Lubomyr R., and Anna T. Wynar. *Encyclopedic Directory of Ethnic Newspapers and Periodicals in the United States*. 2nd ed. Littleton, Colo.: Libraries Unlimited, 1976. Lists "current" publications.

Zeps, Valdis J. *Lettica in Microform; A Subject Guide*. Madison, Wis.: Association for the Advancement of Baltic Studies, 1982.

Specialty Newspapers

Dornbusch, Charles E. *Stars and Stripes: Check List of the Several Editions*. New York: New York Public Library, 1948. "Reprinted From the *Bulletin* of the New York Public Library of July 1948." Supplement, New York: New York Public Library, 1949. "Reprinted From the *Bulletin* of the New York Public Library of July 1949."

Labor Papers on Microfilm: A Combined List. Madison: State Historical Society of Wisconsin, 1965.

Lutz, Earle. "Soldier Newspapers of the Civil War." *Papers of the Bibliographical Society of America* 46 (1952): 373–86.

Rudeen, Marlys. *The Civilian Conservation Corps Camp Papers: A Guide*. Chicago: Center for Research Libraries, 1991.

The Walter S. and Esther Dougherty Collection of Military Newspapers: A Guide to the Microfilm Edition. Ann Arbor, Mich.: University Microforms International, 1993.

Newspaper Sources by State

For each state, the institution bearing primary responsibility for that state's participation in the U.S. Newspaper Program is identified. For further information and up-to-date contact information and links, check the Program website <www.neh.gov/projects/usnp.html>.

Alabama (Alabama Department of Archives and History)

Ellison, Rhoda C. *History and Bibliography of Alabama Newspapers in the 19th Century*. Birmingham: University of Alabama Press, 1954.

Alaska (Alaska Historical Collections, Alaska State Library)

Alaska Newspapers on Microfilm. 1998. Online at <www.library.state.ak.us/hist/newspaper/about.html>.

Arizona (Arizona State Library)

Arizona Newspapers on Microfilm. Phoenix: Department of Library, Archives and Public Records, 1989.

Arkansas (Special Collections Division, University of Arkansas Libraries)

Arkansas Union List of Newspapers. Fayetteville: University of Arkansas Libraries, 1993.

Historical Records Survey. *Union List of Arkansas Newspapers, 1942. A Partial Inventory of Arkansas Newspaper Files Available in the Offices of Publishers, Libraries, and Private Collections.* Little Rock, Ark.: Historical Records Survey, 1942.

California (Center for Bibliographical Studies and Research, University of California, Riverside)

Leach, Marianne. *Newspaper Holdings of the California State Library.* Sacramento: California State Library Foundation, 1986.

Union List of Newspapers in the Libraries of San Diego and Imperial Counties. 3rd ed. San Diego: Serra Cooperative Library System, 1990.

Union List of Newspapers in Microforms in the California State University and College Libraries. 2nd ed. Fullerton: California State University, Fullerton, 1975.

Colorado (Colorado Historical Society)

Oehlerts, Donald E. *Guide to Colorado Newspapers, 1859–1963.* Denver: Rocky Mountain Bibliographic Center, 1964.

Connecticut (Connecticut State Library)

Gustafson, Don. *A Preliminary Checklist of Connecticut Newspapers, 1755–1975.* 2 vols. Hartford: Connecticut State Library, 1978.

Delaware (University of Delaware Library)

Union List of Newspapers in Delaware. Newark, N.J.: Delaware Newspaper Project, University of Delaware Library, 1990.

District of Columbia (Washingtoniana Division, Martin Luther King Jr. Memorial Library)

Millington, Yale O. "A List of Newspapers Published in the District of Columbia, 1820–1850." *Papers of the Bibliographical Society of America* 19 (1925): 43–65.

Florida (University of Florida, Gainesville)

Georgia (University of Georgia, Athens)

Georgia Newspapers on Microfilm at the UGA Libraries. Athens: University of Georgia Libraries, 1977.

Hawaii (Hamilton Library, University of Hawaii at Manoa)

Hawaii State Archives. *Hawaii Newspapers and Periodicals on Microfilm: A Union List of Holdings in Libraries of Honolulu.* Honolulu: Hawaiiana Section, Hawaii Library Association, 1977.

Hawaii Newspaper Project. *Hawaii Newspapers: A Union List.* Dublin, Ohio: OCLC, 1987.

Idaho (Idaho State Historical Society Library and Archives)

University of Idaho Newspaper Holdings as of July 1, 1975. Moscow: University of Idaho Library, 1975.

Illinois (Illinois Historical Society, University of Illinois at Urbana, Champaign, and Chicago Historical Society)

Bibliography of Foreign Language Newspapers and Periodicals Published in Chicago. Chicago Public Library Omnibus Project, 1942.

Newspapers in the Illinois State Historical Library. Springfield: the library, 1998.

Scott, Franklin W. *Newspapers and Periodicals of Illinois, 1814–1879.* Vol. 6. Rev. and enl. Collections of the ISHS Library. Springfield: Trustees of the Illinois State Historical Society, 1910.

Indiana (Indiana Historical Society and Indiana University, Bloomington)

Miller, John W. *Indiana Newspaper Bibliography: Historical Accounts of All Indiana Newspapers Published From 1804–1980 and Locational Information for All Available Copies, Both Original and Microfilm.* Indianapolis: Indiana Historical Society, 1982.

Iowa (State Historical Society of Iowa, Iowa City)

Iowa Pilot Project of the Organization of American Historians. The Library of Congress, United States Newspaper Project. *A Bibliography of Iowa Newspapers, 1836–1976.* Iowa City: Iowa State Historical Department, 1979.

Iowa Union List of Newspapers. Dublin, Ohio: OCLC, 1994.

Kansas (Kansas State Historical Society)

Anderson, Aileen. *Kansas Newspapers: A Directory of Newspaper Holdings in Kansas.* Topeka: Kansas Library Network Board, 1984.

Haury, David A. *Guide to the Microfilm Collection of the Kansas State Historical Society.* Topeka: Kansas State Historical Society, 1991. Supplement, 1993–.

Kentucky (University of Kentucky Libraries)

Evans, Herndon J. *The Newspaper Press in Kentucky.* Lexington: University of Kentucky, 1975.

Kinkead, Ludie, and T. D. Clark. *Checklist of Kentucky Newspapers Contained in Kentucky Libraries.* Lexington, 1935.

Louisiana (Special Collections, Louisiana State University Libraries)

Historical Records Survey. *Louisiana Newspapers, 1794–1940. List of Louisiana Newspaper Files in Offices of Publishers, Libraries, and Private Collections in Louisiana.* Baton Rouge: Louisiana State Library, 1941.

Louisiana Newspaper Project Printout, April 1990. Baton Rouge: Louisiana Newspaper Project, LSU Libraries, 1990.

McMullen, T. N., ed. *Louisiana Newspapers, 1794–1961; a Union List of Louisiana Newspaper Files Available in Public, College, and University Libraries in Louisiana.* Baton Rouge: Louisiana State University and Agricultural and Mechanical Library, 1965.

Maine (Maine State Archives)

Maryland (Maryland State Archives)

Maryland Newspaper Project. *A Guide to Newspapers and Newspaper Holdings in Maryland.* Baltimore: Maryland State Department of Education, Division of Library Development and Services, 1991.

White, Les, et al. *Newspapers of Maryland: A Guide to the Microfilm Collection of Newspapers at the Maryland State Archives.* Annapolis: Maryland State Archives, 1990.

Massachusetts (Boston Public Library)

Boston Public Library. *A List of Periodicals, Newspapers in Principal Libraries of Boston and Vicinity.* Boston: Trustees of the Library, 1897.

Michigan (Library of Michigan and Clarke Historical Library, Central Michigan University)

Brown, Elizabeth Read. *A Union List of Newspapers Published in Michigan Based on the Principal Newspaper Collections in the State With Notes Concerning Papers Not Located.* Ann Arbor: University of Michigan, Department of Library Science, 1954.

Hathaway, Richard. *Ethnic Newspapers and Periodicals in Michigan: A Checklist.* Ann Arbor: Michigan Archival Association, 1978.

Leasher, Mary. *Newspapers on Microfilm; Holdings of the Clarke Historical Library, September 1987.* Mt. Pleasant: Clarke Historical Library, 1987.

Michigan State Library. *Michigan Newspapers, Preliminary Bibliography, a Partial List of Michigan Newspapers Based Upon a Survey of Public Libraries and Newspaper Offices in the State of Michigan.* Lansing: State Department of Education, 1966.

Michigan Newspapers on Microfilm. 7th ed. Lansing: Michigan State Board of Education, State Library Service, 1985.

Minnesota (Minnesota Historical Society)

Hage, George S. *Newspapers on the Minnesota Frontier, 1849–1860.* St. Paul: Minnesota Historical Society, 1967.

Mississippi (Mississippi Department of Archives and History)

Historical Records Survey. *Mississippi Newspapers, 1805–1904.* Jackson, Miss.: Works Progress Administration, 1942.

Mitchell Memorial Library, Mississippi State University. *Union List of Newspapers.* Mississippiana, vol. 2. Jackson: Mississippi Library Commission, 1971.

Missouri (University Libraries, University of Missouri-Kansas City)

Newspapers in Missouri, a Union List, 1994. 3 vols. Kansas City, Mo.: University Libraries, University of Missouri-Kansas City, 1994.

Taft, William H. *Missouri Newspapers, When and Where, 1803–1963.* Columbia: State Historical Society of Missouri, 1964.

Montana (Montana Historical Society)

Montana Historical Society Newspaper Project. *A Union List of Montana Newspapers in Montana Repositories.* Dublin, Ohio: OCLC, 1986.

Nebraska (University of Nebraska-Lincoln and Nebraska Historical Society)

Diffendal, Anne P. *A Guide to the Newspaper Collection of the State Archives, Nebraska State Historical Society.* Rev. ed. Lincoln: Nebraska State Historical Society, 1977.

Nevada (University of Nevada-Reno)

Lingenfelter, Richard E., and Karen R. Gash. *The Newspapers of Nevada: A History and Bibliography, 1854–1979.* Reno: University of Nevada Press, 1984.

New Hampshire (Dartmouth College and New Hampshire State Library)

New Jersey (Rutgers University and New Jersey Division of Archives and Records Management)

Wright, William C., and Paul A. Stellhorn. *Directory of New Jersey Newspapers, 1765–1970.* Trenton: New Jersey Historical Commission, 1977.

New Mexico (University of New Mexico General Library)

Grove, Pearce S., et al. *New Mexico Newspapers; a Comprehensive Guide to Bibliographical Entries and Locations.* Albuquerque: University of New Mexico Press, 1975.

Stratton, Porter A. *The Territorial Press of New Mexico, 1834–1912.* Albuquerque: University of New Mexico Press, 1969.

New York (New York State Library; on-line catalogs of newspapers in the State Library, and in other repositories at <www.nysl.nysed.gov/nysnp>)

A Bibliography of Newspapers in Two New York State Counties. 2 vols. Fredonia: State University of New York, College at Fredonia, 1975. Installment 1: Chautauqua County; Installment 2: Cattaraugus County.

Chautauqua County Historical Society. *A Guide to Newspapers in Microform in Chautauqua County, New York.* Westfield, N.Y.: the society, 1982. Part 1: guide; Part 2: microfilm index.

Faibisoff, Sylvia G. *Bibliography of Newspapers in Fourteen New York Counties.* Cooperstown: South Central Research Library Council, New York State Library Association, 1978. Covers Allegany, Broome, Cayuga, Chemung, Chenango, Cortland, Delaware, Otsego, Schuyler, Seneca, Steuben, Tioga, Tompkins, and Yates counties.

Mercer, Paul. *Bibliographies and Lists of New York State Newspapers: An Annotated Guide.* Albany: New York State Library, 1981.

Newspapers on Microfilm: A Listing of Newspapers on Microfilm in Allegheny, Chemung, Schuyler, Steuben, and Yates Counties. Corning, N.Y.: Southern Tier Library System, 1981.

Szczygiel, Rosemary. *Union List of Long Island Newspapers.* Stony Brook, N.Y.: Long Island Library Resources Council, 1995.

U.S. Newspapers on Microfilm at the New York State Library. Albany: New York Newspaper Project, 2000.

North Carolina (State Library of North Carolina)

Jones, H. G., and Julius H. Avant. *Union List of North Carolina Newspapers, 1751–1900.* Raleigh: State Department of Archives and History, 1963.

Jones, Roger C. *Guide to North Carolina Newspapers on Microfilm: North Carolina Newspapers Available on Microfilm From the Division of Archives and History.* 6th rev. ed. Raleigh: North Carolina Division of Archives and History, 1984.

North Dakota (State Historical Society of North Dakota)

Kolar, Carol K. *Union List of North Dakota Newspapers, 1864–1976.* Fargo: North Dakota Institute for Regional Studies, 1981.

Ohio (Ohio Historical Society)

Gutgesell, Stephen. *Guide to Ohio Newspapers, 1793–1973: Union Bibliography of Ohio Newspapers Available in Ohio Libraries.* Columbus: Ohio Historical Society, 1976.

Oklahoma (Oklahoma Historical Society)

Foreman, Carolyn T. *Oklahoma Imprints, 1835–1907; a History of Printing in Oklahoma Before Statehood.* Norman: University of Oklahoma Press, 1936.

Stewart, John, and Kenny Franks. *State Records, Manuscripts, and Newspapers at the Oklahoma State Archives and Oklahoma Historical Society.* Oklahoma City: Oklahoma Historical Society, 1975.

Oregon (University of Oregon Libraries)

University of Oregon, Library. *Oregon Newspapers on Microfilm.* Portland: Genealogical Council of Oregon, 1991.

Pennsylvania (State Library of Pennsylvania)

Pennsylvania Historical Survey. *A Checklist of Pennsylvania Newspapers.* Harrisburg: Pennsylvania Historical Commission, 1944. Vol. 1 (all published): Philadelphia County.

Newspapers on Microform, Pattee Library, Pennsylvania State University. New ed. University Park: Pennsylvania State University Library, 1978.

Pennsylvania Newspapers and Selected Out-of-State Newspapers. Harrisburg: State Library of Pennsylvania, 1976.

Rossell, Glenora E. *Pennsylvania Newspapers: A Bibliography and Union List.* 2nd ed. Pittsburgh: Pennsylvania Library Association, 1978.

Puerto Rico (Library System, University of Puerto Rico)

Rhode Island (Rhode Island Historical Society)

Chudacoff, Nancy F. *Providence Newspapers on Microfilm, 1762 to the Present; a Bibliography and Subject Guide.* Providence, 1974.

South Carolina (South Caroliniana Library, University of South Carolina)

Moore, John Hammond. *South Carolina Newspapers.* Columbia: University of South Carolina Press, 1988.

South Dakota (South Dakota State Historical Society)

Checklist of South Dakota Newspapers in the South Dakota Historical Society and the Historical Resource Center at Pierre. Pierre: South Dakota Historical Society, 1976.

Tennessee (University Libraries, University of Tennessee-Knoxville)

John Willard Brister Library. *Newspapers on Microforms*. Memphis: Memphis State University, 1975.

Tennessee State Library and Archives. State Library Division. *Tennessee Newspapers: A Cumulative List of Microfilmed Tennessee Newspapers in the Tennessee State Library*. Nashville: Tennessee State Library, 1978.

Texas (Center for American History, University of Texas)

HARLiC Union List of Newspapers. Houston: Houston Area Research Library Consortium, 1992.

Historical Records Survey. *A Union List of Texas Newspapers, 1831–1939*. San Jacinto, Tex.: Museum of History Association, 1941.

Texas State Library, Austin, Information Services Division. *Newspapers on Microfilm*. Austin: Public Services Department, 1978.

U.S. Virgin Islands (Division of Libraries, Archives and Museums)

Gregg, Kathleen. *Virgin Island Newspapers, 1770–1983*. Charlotte Amalie, St. Thomas: Department of Conservation and Cultural Affairs, 1984.

Utah (University of Utah)

Thatcher, Linda. *Guide to Newspapers Located in the Utah State Historical Society Library*. Salt Lake City: Utah State Historical Society, 1985.

Vermont (University of Vermont Libraries, and Vermont Department of Libraries)

Vermont Newspaper Project Catalog. Available at <http://vtnp.uvm.edu>.

Virginia (Library of Virginia)

Cappon, Lester J. *Virginia Newspapers, 1821–1935: A Bibliography With Historical Introduction and Notes*. New York: Appleton-Century, 1936.

Washington (Washington State Library)

Hamilton, Katryn S. *Newspapers on Microfilm in the Washington State Library*. Olympia: Washington State Library, 1980.

Palmer, Gayle L. *Washington State Union List of Newspapers on Microfilm*. Olympia: Washington State Library, 1991.

West Virginia (West Virginia University Libraries)

West Virginia Newspapers: A Union List by Place of Publication. Dublin, Ohio: OCLC, 1987.

Wisconsin (Wisconsin Historical Society)

Hansen, James L. *Wisconsin Newspapers, 1833–1850: An Analytical Bibliography*. Madison: State Historical Society of Wisconsin, 1979.

Oehlerts, Donald E. *Guide to Wisconsin Newspapers, 1833–1957*. Madison: State Historical Society of Wisconsin, 1958.

Wyoming (University of Wyoming Libraries)

Homsher, Lola. *Guide to Wyoming Newspapers, 1867–1967*. Cheyenne: Wyoming State Library, 1971.

Guides to Indexes and Abstracts

Brayer, Herbert O. "Preliminary Guide to Indexed Newspapers in the United States, 1850–1900." *Mississippi Valley Historical Review* 33 (1946): 237–58.

Jarboe, Betty M. *Obituaries: A Guide to Sources*. 2nd ed. Boston: G. K. Hall, 1989.

Milner, Anita Cheek. *Newspaper Indexes: A Location and Subject Guide for Researchers*. 3 vols. Metuchen, N.J.: Scarecrow Press, 1977–82. Includes unpublished indexes and card indexes.

New England Library Association. Bibliography Committee. *A Guide to Newspaper Indexes in New England*. Holden, Mass.: New England Library Association, 1978.

Periodical Source Index (PERSI). Available on CD-ROM and to Ancestry.com subscribers.

General Indexes and Abstracts

Abajian, James. *Blacks in Selected Newspapers, Censuses and Other Sources: An Index to Names and Subjects*. 3 vols. Boston: G. K. Hall, 1977.

Anastas, Walter, and Maria Woroby. *A Select Index to "Svoboda," Official Publication of the Ukrainian National Association, Inc., a Fraternal Association*. St. Paul, Minn.: Immigration History Research Center, University of Minnesota, 1990–. Vol. 1: 1893–99; Vol. 2: 1900–07.

Falk, Byron A., and Valerie R. Falk. *Personal Name Index to "The New York Times Index" 1851–1974*. 22 vols. Succasunna, N.J.: Roxbury Data Interface, 1976–1983. 1975–1999 Supplement. 8 vols. Sparks, Nev.: Roxbury Data Interface, 2001–2002. Single alphabetical index to millions of personal names buried in the *New York Times* indexes. Poor coverage of ca. 1905-to-1912 period because of weakness of original indexes. An excellent source for identifying an individual's "fifteen minutes of fame."

Haller, Dolores, and Marilyn Robinson. *Gleanings From the* Christian Advocate and Journal *and* Zion's Herald, *September 1827–August 1831*. Bowie, Md.: Heritage Books, 1987.

Hayward, Elizabeth. *American Vital Records From the* Baptist Register, *1824–1829, and the* New York Baptist Register, *1829–1834.* Mt. Airy, Md.: Pipe Creek, 1991.

Holloway, Lizabeth M., et al. *Medical Obituaries: American Physicians' Biographical Notices in Selected Medical Journals Before 1907.* New York: Garland Publishing Co., 1981.

Index of Obituaries of Boston Newspapers 1704–1800. 3 vols. Boston: G. K. Hall, 1968.

Manning, Barbara. *Genealogical Abstracts From Newspapers of the German Reformed Church.* Bowie, Md.: Heritage Books. 1830–1839 (1992); 1840–1843 (1995).

Martin, George A. *Marriage and Death Notices From the* National Intelligencer, *Washington, D.C., 1800–1850.* 3 reels of microfilm. Washington, D.C.: National Genealogical Society, 1976.

Mennonite Archives. "MennObits." Indexed obituaries from the *Herald of Truth*, 1864–1908; *Gospel Witness*, 1905–1908; and *Gospel Herald*, 1908–1998. Available online at <www.goshen.edu/mcarchives/MennObits>.

New York Times. *Index.* 1851–present. Published annually since 1913. 1851–1912 covered by indexes originally printed for use by *New York Times* staff, as well as newly prepared indexes.

New York Times Obituaries Index, 1858–1968. New York: New York Times, 1970. Supplement, 1969–78. New York: New York Times, 1980. Contains more than 390,000 listings compiled from the *New York Times Index.* Alphabetically arranged list of names giving year of death and reference to the obituary in the *New York Times.*

Unrau, Ruth. *Index to Obituaries in the* Mennonite Weekly Review, *1924–1990.* North Newton, Kan.: Bethel College, 1991.

Ware, Lowry. *Associated Reformed Presbyterian Death and Marriage Notices From the* Christian Magazine of the South, *the* Erskine Miscellany, *and the* Due West Telescope, *1843–1863.* Columbia: South Carolina Magazine of Ancestral Research, 1993.

Waters, Margaret, Dorothy Riker, and Doris Leistner. *Abstracts of Obituaries in the* Western Christian Advocate, *1834–1850.* Indianapolis: Indiana Historical Society, 1988.

Young, David C., and Robert L. Taylor. *Death Notices From Freewill Baptist Publications, 1811–1851.* Bowie, Md.: Heritage Books, 1985.

Indexes and Abstracts by State

The listings for the states are only a sample of those available. Some states have had very few indexes and abstracts published, others could have their lists extended almost indefinitely. Many more are held in typescript, printout, or microform at a limited number of research institutions. Check also at websites for local libraries and genealogical societies in the area of interest.

Alabama

Foley, Helen S. *Marriage and Death Notices From Alabama Newspapers and Family Records, 1819–1890.* Easley, S.C.: Southern Historical Press, 1981.

———. *Obituaries From Barbour County, Alabama, Newspapers, 1890–1905.* Easley, S.C.: Southern Historical Press, 1981.

Gandrud, Pauline Jones. *Marriage, Death, and Legal Notices From Early Alabama Newspapers, 1819–1893.* Easley, S.C.: Southern Historical Press, 1981.

Wellden, Eulalia Yancey. *Death Notices From Limestone County, Alabama, Newspapers, 1828–1891.* N.p., 1986.

Alaska

DeArmond, Robert N. *Subject Index to* The Alaskan, *1885–1907, a Sitka Newspaper.* Juneau: Alaska Division of State Libraries, 1974.

Hales, David A. *An Index to the Early History of Alaska as Reported in the 1903–1907 Fairbanks Newspapers:* Fairbanks News, *September 1903–May 1905;* Fairbanks Evening News, *May 1905–June 1907.* Fairbanks: Elmer E. Rasmuson Library, University of Alaska, 1980.

Stallings, Mike. *Index to the* Seward Gateway, *a Newspaper, 1904–1910.* Seward, Alaska: Seward Community Library, 1983.

Arizona

Underhill, Lonnie E. *Index to the Tombstone, Arizona,* Daily Nugget. Tucson: Roan Horse Press, 1984.

Arkansas

Martin, James Logan. *Arkansas Newspaper Index, 1819–1845.* Newport, Ark.: Morgan Books, 1981.

California

Alaworth, Mary Dean. *Gleanings From Alta California: Marriages and Deaths Reported in the First Newspaper Published in California, 1846 Through 1850.* Rancho Cordova, Calif.: Dean Publications, 1980.

———. *More Gleanings From Alta California: Vital Records Published in California's First Newspaper, Year—1851.* Rancho Cordova, Calif.: Dean Publications, 1982.

Gold Rush Days: Vital Statistics Copies From Early Newspapers of Stockton, California. 6 vols. Stockton, Calif.: San Joaquin Genealogical Society, 1958–1989. Covers 1850–66.

Purdy, Tim I. *Index to Birth and Death Notices of the Lassen Advocate Newspaper of Susanville, California, 1868–1899.* Susanville, Calif.: Lahontan Images, 1986.

Colorado

Denver Public Library. "Denver Obituary Index." Covers 1939–40, 1942–43, 1960–74, 1990–2000. Available online at <www.denver.lib.co.us>.

Griffin, Walter R., and Jay L. Rasmussen. "A Comprehensive Guide to the Location of Published and Unpublished Newspaper Indexes in Colorado Repositories." *Colorado Magazine* 49 (Fall 1972): 326–39.

Connecticut

Gingras, Raymond. *Quelques francos au Connecticut: Notes, Références, et Index des Nécrologies Parties dans des Journeaux de 1963 à 1975.* Quebec: the author, 1976.

Ireland, Norma Olin, and Winifred Irving. *Index to* Hartford Times *"Genealogical Gleanings," 1912–1916.* Fallbrook, Calif.: Ireland Indexing Service, 1974.

Scott, Kenneth, and Roseanne Conway. *Genealogical Data From Colonial New Haven Newspapers.* Baltimore: Genealogical Publishing Co., 1979.

Delaware

Delaware Genealogical Abstracts from Newspapers. Wilmington, Del.: Delaware Genealogical Society, 1995–2000. Vol. 1: deaths from the *Delaware Gazette*, 1854–59, 1861–64; Vol. 2: marriages from the *Delaware Gazette*, 1854–59, 1861–64; Vol. 3: marriages and deaths, 1729–1853; Vol. 4: marriages and deaths from the *Delaware Gazette*, 1865–74; Vol. 5: marriages and deaths from the *Delaware Gazette*, 1875–79.

Wright, F. Edward. *Delaware Newspaper Abstracts.* Silver Spring, Md.: Family Line Publications, 1984. Vol. 1: 1786–95.

District of Columbia

Pippenger, Wesley E. *The* Georgetown Courier *Marriage and Death Notices, 1865–1876.* Westminster, Md.: Willow Bend Books, 1998.

Georgia

Colket, Meredith B., Jr. "Indexes to Savannah, Georgia, Newspapers." *National Genealogical Society Quarterly* 69 (September 1981): 181–83.

Hartz, Fred R., and Emily K. Hartz. *Genealogical Abstracts From the* "Georgia Journal" *(Milledgeville) Newspaper.* Vidalia, Ga: Gwendolyn Press, 1990–. Vol. 1: 1809–18; Vol. 2: 1819–23; Vol. 3: 1824–28; Vol. 4: 1829–35; Vol. 5: 1836–40.

Huxford, Folks. *Genealogical Material From Legal Notices in Early Georgia Newspapers.* Easley, S.C.: Southern Historical Press, 1989.

LeMaster, Elizabeth T. *Abstracts of Georgia Death Notices From the* Southern Recorder, *1830–1855.* Orange, Calif.: Orange County Genealogical Society, 1971.

———. *Abstracts of Georgia Marriage Notices From the* Southern Recorder, *1830–1855.* Orange, Calif.: Orange County Genealogical Society, 1971.

Warren, Mary Bondurant. *Marriages and Deaths, Abstracted From Extant Georgia Newspapers.* 2 vols. Danielsville, Ga.: Heritage Papers, 1968–1972. Vol. 1: 1763–1820; Vol. 2: 1820–30.

Hawaii

McKinzie, Edith Kowelohea. *Hawaiian Genealogies: Extracted From Hawaiian Language Newspapers.* 2 vols. Laie, Hawaii.: Institute for Polynesian Studies, 1983–85.

Illinois

Chicago Genealogical Society. *Vital Records From Chicago Newspapers.* 7 vols. Chicago: Chicago Genealogical Society, 1971–80. Covers 1833–48.

Helge, Jan, and Paula Malak. *The Greater Roseland Area of Chicago; Newspaper Extracts, 1882–1894.* South Holland, Ill.: South Suburban Genealogical and Historical Society, 1992.

Koss, David. "Chicago Obituaries in Der Christliche Botschafter, 1844–1871." *Chicago Genealogist* 11 (Summer 1979): 5–11.

Indiana

Beeson, Cecil. *Newspaper Items From the* Hartford City Telegram, *Hartford City, Indiana.* Fort Wayne, Ind.: Public Library, 1972.

Capt. Jacob Warrick Chapter, NSDAR. *Warrick County, Indiana Newspapers, Standard and Enquirer of Boonesville.* Owensboro, Ky.: McDowell Publications, 1981.

Cox, Carroll O., and Gloria M. Cox. *New Harmony, Indiana, Newspaper Gleanings, 1825–1844.* Owensboro, Ky.: McDowell Publications, 1980.

Fort Wayne and Allen County Public Library. *Index to Obituary Records as Found in the* "Journal Gazette," *Fort Wayne, Indiana.* Fort Wayne, Ind.: the library, 1973–76. Vol. 1: 1900–18; Vol. 2: 1938–49; Vol. 3: 1971–75.

Smith, W. W. *Newspaper Abstracts of Owensville and Gibson County, Indiana, 1872–1915, Being a Reprint of the Information Contained in the Several Editions of a True Record.* Evansville, Ind.: Tri-State Genealogical Society, 1978.

Wilke, Katherine. *Newspaper Gleanings, Union City, Randolph County.* Union City: the author, 1969. Vol. 1: 1873–83.

Iowa

Newspaper Abstracts. 4 vols. Jamaica, Iowa: Guthrie County Genealogical Society, 1984. Vol. 1: *Panora Weekly Umpire,*

Panora, Iowa, January–December 1888; Vol. 2: *The Guthrian,* 1903–1904; Vol. 3: *Umpire-Vedette,* Panora, Iowa, January–December 1889; Vol. 4: *Vedette,* Panora, Iowa, January–December 1891.

Kansas

Branigar, Tom. *Birth and Death Notices From Early Chapman Newspapers, 1884–1901.* Abilene, Kans.: Dickinson County Historical Society, 1981.

Herrick, James L. *Death Notices as Listed in* Neosho Valley/Hartford Times, *and Burials in Hartford Cemetery, Lyon County, Kansas (Tombstone Inscriptions and Sexton's Records): Supplemented With Information From the* Hartford Call. Topeka, Kans.: Topeka Genealogical Society, 1978.

Pantle, Alberta. "Death Notices From Kansas Territorial Newspapers, 1854–1861." *Kansas Historical Quarterly* 18 (1950): 302–23.

Kentucky

Clift, G. Glenn. *Kentucky Obituaries, 1787–1854.* Baltimore: Genealogical Publishing Co., 1984. Reprinted from a series originally published in the *Register of the Kentucky Historical Society.*

Green, Karen Mauer. *The Kentucky Gazette, 1787–1800: Genealogical and Historical Abstracts.* Galveston, Tex.: Frontier Press, 1983.

———. *The Kentucky Gazette, 1800–1820: Genealogical and Historical Abstracts.* Galveston, Tex.: Frontier Press, 1985.

Nagle, Eric C. *Vital Records from Newspapers of Paris, Kentucky, 1813–1870.* Dayton, Ohio: Ford and Nagle, 1999.

Louisiana

Assumption Pioneer Newspaper: Deaths, weddings, births, 1850–1912. Houma, La: Terrebonne Genealogical Society, 2002. "As published in *Terrebonne Life Lines.*"

Chauvin, Philip, Jr. *Houma Newspaper Deaths, 1855–1981.* Houma, La.: Terrebonne Genealogical Society, 1988.

Mayers, Brenda LaGroue, and Gloria Lambert Kerns. *Death Notices From Louisiana Newspapers.* 6 vols. Baker, La.: Folk Finders, 1984–85. Vol. 1: 1811–19; Vol. 2: 1822–1914; Vol. 3: 1833–1917; Vol. 4: 1847–93; Vol. 5: 1824–87; Vol. 6: 1836–77.

Maine

Labonte, Youville. *Necrologies of Franco-Americans Taken From Maine's Newspapers.* Auburn, Maine: the author, 1977. Vol. 1: 1966–76.

Young, David. *Index of Selected Obituaries:* Kennebec Journal, *1825–1354,* Oxford Observer, *1826–1828,* Oxford Democrat, *1833–1855.* Farmington, Maine: Mantor, Library, University of Maine at Farmington, 1977.

———, and Elizabeth Keene Young. *Vital Records From Maine Newspapers, 1785–1820.* 2 vols. Bowie, Md.: Heritage Books, 1993.

Maryland

Arps, Walter E., Jr. *Before the Fire, Genealogical Gleanings From the* Cambridge *(MD)* Chronicle, *1830–1855.* Lutherville, Md.: Bettie Carothers, 1978.

Barnes, Bobert. *Gleanings From Maryland Newspapers, 1727–1795.* 3 vols. Lutherville, Md.: Bettie Carothers, 1975–76.

———. *Marriages and Deaths From Baltimore Newspapers, 1796–1816.* Baltimore: Genealogical Publishing Co., 1978.

———. *Marriages and Deaths From the Maryland Gazette, 1727–1839.* Baltimore: Genealogical Publishing Co., 1973.

Green, Karen Mauer. *The* Maryland Gazette, *1727–1761; Genealogical and Historical Abstracts.* Galveston, Tex.: Frontier Press, 1989.

Hollowak, Thomas L. *Index of Marriages and Deaths in the (Baltimore)* Sun, *1837–1850.* Baltimore: Genealogical Publishing Co., 1978.

———. *Index to Marriages and Deaths in the (Baltimore)* Sun, *1851–1860.* Baltimore: Genealogical Publishing Co., 1978.

———. *Indices of the Obituaries in the* Jednosc-Polonia. Chicago: Polish Genealogical Society, 1983. The most important Polish newspaper in Baltimore.

———. *Baltimore's Polish Language Newspapers: Historical and Genealogical Abstracts, 1891–1925.* Baltimore: Historyk Press, 1992.

Wright, F. Edward. *Marriages and Deaths of the Lower Delmarva, 1835–1840: From Newspapers of Dorchester, Somerset and Worcester Counties, Maryland.* Silver Spring, Md.: Family Line Publications, 1987.

———. *Newspaper Abstracts of Cecil and Harford Counties, 1822–1830.* Silver Spring, Md.: Family Line Publications, 1984.

———. *Western Maryland Newspaper Abstracts, 1786–1810.* 3 vols. Silver Spring, Md.: Family Line Publications, 1985–87.

———, and I. Harper. *Maryland Eastern Shore Newspaper Abstracts.* 8 vols. 1790–1834. Silver Spring, Md.: Family Line Publications, 1981–87.

Massachusetts

American Antiquarian Society. *Index of Marriages in the* Massachusetts Centinel *and the* Columbian Sentinel, *1784–1840.* 4 vols. Boston: G. K. Hall, 1961.

Codman, Ogden. *Index of Obituaries in Boston Newspapers, 1704–1800.* 3 vols. Boston: G. K. Hall, 1968. The index is in two parts: deaths within Boston, 1704–1800; deaths outside Boston, 1704–95.

Harris, Ruth-Ann M., and Donald Jacobs. *The Search for Missing Friends; Irish Immigrant Advertisements Placed in the* Boston Pilot. Boston: New England Historic Genealogical Society, 1989–1999. Vol. 1: 1831–50; Vol. 2: 1851–53; Vol. 3: 1854–56; Vol. 4: 1857–60; Vol. 5: 1861–65; Vol. 6: 1866–70; Vol. 7: 1871–76. Expanded CD-ROM version (2002) covers 1831–1920.

Historical Records Survey. *Index to Local News in the* Hampshire Gazette, *1786–1937.* 3 vols. Boston: Historical Records Survey, 1937.

Rosen, David. *Boston Jewish Advocate Wedding Announcements Database* and *Boston Jewish Advocate Obituary Database*. Both cover 1905–2002. Available online at <www.jewishgen.org/databases>.

Michigan

Cowles, Jane A., et al. *Condensed Transcripts of Obituaries in the Region of Southeast Isabella County, Michigan and Surrounding Area.* Owensboro, Ky.: McDowell Publications, 1980.

DeZeeuw, Donald J. *Death and Marriage Items Abstracted From the* Lansing State Republican, *1861–1871, and Some Divorces and Name Changes Noted in the Michigan Territorial and State Laws.* Lansing: Mid-Michigan Genealogical Society.

Minnesota

Anoka County Newspapers: Marriage Records, 1863–1870; Death Records, 1863–1870. Anoka, Minn.: Anoka County Genealogical Society, 198[?].

The White Bear Press*—A Genealogical Index, January 1, 1911 to 27 August 31, 1988.* White Bear Lake, Minn.: White Bear Lake Genealogical Society, 1988.

Mississippi

Mississippi Genealogical Society. *Newspaper Notices of Mississippians, 1820–1860.* Jackson: Mississippi Historical Society, 1960. Reprinted from *Journal of Mississippi History* vols. 18–21 (1956–59).

Wiltshire, Betty Couch. *Marriages and Deaths From Mississippi Newspapers.* 4 vols. Bowie, Md.: Heritage Books, 1987–89. Vol. 1: 1837–63; Vol. 2: 1801–50; Vol. 3, 1813–50; Vol. 4, 1850–61.

Missouri

Jackson, Vivian Poe, and Wanda Poe Fitzpatrick. *Genealogical Gleanings From Cape Girardeau, Mo. Newspapers.* 2 vols. 1849–62. Cape Girardeau, Mo.: the authors, ca. 1988.

McManus, Thelma S. *Ripley County (Missouri) Records: Obituaries, 1874–1910.* Doniphan: the author, 1979.

Rising, Marsha Hoffman. *Genealogical Data From Southwest Missouri Newspapers, 1850–1860.* Springfield, Mo.: the author, 1985.

———. *Genealogical Data From Southwest Missouri Newspapers, 1860–1870.* Springfield, Mo.: the author, 1987.

———. *The* Springfield Advertiser, *Greene County, Missouri, 1844–1850.* Springfield, Mo.: the author, 1984.

St. Louis Public Library. "St. Louis Obituary Index." Covers 1880–1921, 1943–45, 1992–2002. Available online at <www.slpl.lib.mo.us/libsrc/obit.htm>.

Stanley, Lois, and Maryhelen Wilson. "Death and Estate Notices, *Missouri Gazette,* 1808–1822." *National Genealogical Society Quarterly* 65 (September 1977): 226–33; 67 (September 1979): 193–201.

Stanley, Lois, George F. Wilson, and Maryhelen Wilson. *Death Records From Missouri Newspapers: The Civil War Years, Jan. 1861–Dec. 1865.* St. Louis: the authors, 1983.

Nebraska

Heil, Leila R. *Genealogical Abstracts From the* Tecumseh Chieftan, *Johnson County, Nebraska, Official Newspaper, 1873–1900.* N.p., 1970.

New Hampshire

Evans, Helen F. *Index of References to American Women in Colonial Newspapers Through 1800.* Bedford, N.H.: the bibliographer, 1979–87. Vol. 1: New Hampshire, 1756–70; Vol. 2: New Hampshire, 1771–85.

Hammond, Otis G. *Death and Marriage Notices From the* New Hampshire Gazette, *1765–1800.* Lambertville, N.J.: Hunterdon House, 1970.

New Jersey

Lupp, Robert E. *New Jersey Obituaries Index, 1974–1983.* Trenton, N.J.: Division of State Library, New Jersey State Department of Education, 1983.

Nelson, William. "Extracts From American Newspapers Relating to New Jersey, 1704–1775." *New Jersey Archives,* series 1, vols. 11–12, 19–20, 24–29, 31.

Wilson, Thomas B. *Notices From New Jersey Newspapers, 1781–1790.* Lambertville, N.J.: Hunterdon House, 1988.

New York

Gottesman, Rita S. *The Arts and Crafts in New York: Advertisements and News Items From New York City Newspapers.* 3 vols. New York: New York Historical Society, 1938–49. Reprinted from the society's *Collections,* 1936, 1948, 1949. Vol. 1: 1726–76; Vol. 2: 1777–99; Vol. 3: 1800–04.

Hoff, Henry B. "Marriage and Death Notices in New York City Newspapers." *NYG&B Newsletter* 2 (1991): 3–5. A listing of available indexes and abstracts, both published and manuscript.

Hoff, Henry B. "Marriage and Death Notices in Long Island Newspapers." *NYG&B Newsletter* 2 (1991): 20–21. A listing of available indexes and abstracts, both published and manuscript.

Losee, John, and Clara Losee. *Death Notices, Dutchess and Columbia County, New York, 1859–1918, From Red Hook Newspapers.* Rhinebeck, N.Y.: Kinship, 1991.

New York Daily Tribune *Index, 1875–1906.* 31 vols. New York: Tribune Association, 1876–1907.

Scott, Kenneth. *Genealogical Data From Colonial New York Newspapers: A Consolidation of Articles From the New York Genealogical and Biographical Record.* Baltimore: Genealogical Publishing Co., 1977.

———. *Genealogical Abstracts From the* American Weekly, *1719–1746.* Baltimore: Genealogical Publishing Co., 1974.

———. *Genealogical Data From the* New York Post Boy, *1743–1773.* Washington, D.C.: National Genealogical Society, 1973.

———. *Rivington's New York Newspaper: Excerpts From a Loyalist Press, 1773–1783.* New York: New York Historical Society, 1973.

Smith, Mrs. Edwin P. *Deaths, Births, and Marriages From Newspapers Published in Hamilton, Madison County, N.Y., 1818–1886.* 1958. Reprint, Mt. Airy, Md.: Pipe Creek Pub., 1991.

North Carolina

Broughton, Carrie L. *Marriage and Death Notices From* "Raleigh Register" *and* "North Carolina State Gazette," *1799–1825.* 1945. Reprint, Baltimore: Genealogical Publishing Co., 1975.

———. *Marriage and Death Notices in* "Raleigh Register" *and* "North Carolina State Gazette," *1826–1845.* 1947. Reprint, Baltimore: Genealogical Publishing Co., 1968.

———. *Marriage and Death Notices in the* "Raleigh Register" *and* "North Carolina State Gazette," *1846–1867.* 1949–50. Reprint, Baltimore: Genealogical Publishing Co., 1975.

Topkins, Robert M. *Marriage and Death Notices From Extant Asheville Newspapers, 1830–1870: An Index.* Raleigh: North Carolina Genealogical Society, 1977.

———. *Marriage and Death Notices From the* "Western Carolinian" *(Salisbury, N.C.) 1820–1842: An Indexed Abstract.* 1975. Reprint, Spartanburg, S.C.: Reprint Co., 1982.

Ohio

Cleveland Public Library. *Cleveland Necrology File.* Covers the *Cleveland Plain Dealer*, 1850–1975, and other scattered papers. Available online at <www.cpl.org/Index.asp>.

Green, Karen Mauer. *Pioneer Ohio Newspapers, 1793–1810: Genealogical and Historical Abstracts.* Galveston, Tex.: Frontier Press, 1986.

———. *Pioneer Ohio Newspapers, 1802–1818: Genealogical and Historical Abstracts.* Galveston, Tex.: Frontier Press, 1988.

Herbert, Jeffrey G. *Index of Death Notices and Marriage Notices Appearing in the* Cincinnati Daily Gazette, *1827–1881.* Bowie, Md.: Heritage Books, 1993.

Wilke, Katherine. *Newspaper Death Records, Darke County, Ohio.* 4 vols. Union City, Ind., 1968. Vol. 1: 1850–80; Vol. 2: 1880–85; Vol. 3: 1886–91; Vol. 4: 1892–98.

Oklahoma

Bogle, Dixie. *Cherokee Nation Births and Deaths, 1884–1901.* Venita: Northeast Oklahoma Genealogical Society, 1980.

———, and Dorthy Nix. *Cherokee Nation Marriages, 1884–1901.* Venita, Okla.: Abraham Coryell Chapter, DAR, 1980.

Mauldin, Dorothy Tincup. *Cherokee Advocate Newspaper Abstracts.* Tulsa: Oklahoma Yesterday Pubs., 1991–. Vol. 1: 1845–77; Vol. 2: 1877–80; Vol. 3: 1880–83; Vol. 4: 1883–93.

Parker, Doris Whitehall. *Footprints on the Osage Reservation.* 2 vols. Pawhuska, Okla.: the author, 1984. Covers 1894–1907.

Vanpool, Fern P. *Obituaries and Death Notices Printed in* Miami Daily News-Record, *Miami, Oklahoma.* Genealogical Records Committee, Oklahoma Society, DAR, n.d.

Pennsylvania

Hawbaker, Gary T. *Runaways, Rascals and Rogues; Abstracts From Lancaster County, Pennsylvania Newspapers.* Hershey, Pa.: the author, 1987. Vol. 1: "Lancaster Journal," 1794–1810.

Heilman, Robert A. *Deaths Reported in* "Der Libanon Demokrat," *a German-Language Newspaper Published at Lebanon, Pennsylvania, 1832–1864.* Bowie, Md.: Heritage Books, 1990.

Hocker, Edward W. *Genealogical Data Relating to the German Settlers of Pennsylvania and Adjacent Territory: From Advertisements in German Newspapers Published in Germantown, 1743–1800.* Baltimore: Genealogical Publishing Co., 1980.

Meier, Judith A. H. *Elopements and Other Miscreant Deeds of Women, as Advertized in the Pennsylvania Gazette, 1730–1789.* Norristown, Pa.: J. A. H. Maier, 1986.

Rentmeister, Jean R. *Marriage and Death Notices Extracted From the Genius of Liberty and Fayette Advertiser of Uniontown, Pa., 1805–1854.* Apollo, Pa.: Closson Press, 1981.

Scott, Kenneth. *Abstracts From Ben Franklin's* Pennsylvania Gazette, *1728–1748*. Baltimore: Genealogical Publishing Co., 1975.

———, and Janet R. Clarke. *Abstracts From the* Pennsylvania Gazette, *1748–1755*. Baltimore: Genealogical Publishing Co., 1977.

———. *Genealogical Abstracts From the* American Weekly Mercury, *1719–1746*. Baltimore: Genealogical Publishing Co., 1974.

———. *Genealogical Data From the* Pennsylvania Chronicle, *1767–1774*. Washington, D.C.: National Genealogical Society, 1980.

Rhode Island

Taylor, Maureen A. *Runaways, Deserters, and Notorious Villains from Rhode Island Newspapers*. Camden, Me.: Picton Press, 1994–2001. Vol. 1: *The Providence Gazette*, 1762–1800; Vol. 2: Additional from the *Providence Gazette* and all other Rhode Island Newspapers, 1732–1800.

South Carolina

Elliott, Colleen M. *Marriage and Death Notices From the* Keowee Courier, *1849–1883*. Easley, S.C.: Southern Historical Press, 1979.

Holcomb, Brent H. *Marriage and Death Notices From Baptist Newspapers of South Carolina, 1835–1865*. Spartanburg, S.C.: Reprint Co., 1981.

———. *Marriage and Death Notices From Camden, South Carolina Newspapers, 1816–1865*. Easley, S.C.: Southern Historical Press, 1978.

———. *Marriage and Death Notices From the Up-country of South Carolina: As Taken From Greenville Newspapers, 1826–1863*. Columbia, S.C.: South Carolina Magazine of Ancestral Research, 1983.

———. *Marriage and Death Notices From Columbia, South Carolina Newspapers, 1792–1839*. Easley, S.C.: Southern Historical Press, 1982.

———. *Marriage and Death Notices From the* "Pendleton *(South Carolina)* Messenger," *1807–1851*. 1977. Reprint, Easley, S.C.: Southern Historical Press, 1979.

———. *Marriage and Death Notices From the* "Lutheran Observer," *1831–1861; Southern Lutheran, 1861–1865*. Easley, S.C.: Southern Historical Press, 1979.

———. *Marriage and Death Notices From the* "Southern Christian Advocate." Easley, S.C.: Southern Historical Press, 1979–1980. Vol. 1: 1837–60; Vol. 2: 1861–67.

———. *Marriage and Death Notices From Upper South Carolina Newspapers, 1843–1865*. Easley, S.C.: Southern Historical Press, 1977.

Revill, Janie. *Marriage and Death Notices Abstracted From Newspapers Published in Camden, South Carolina, 1822–1842*. Columbia, S.C., 1936.

Salley, Alexander S. *Marriage Notices in* "Charleston Courier," *1803–1808*. 1919. Reprint, Baltimore: Genealogical Publishing Co., 1976.

———. *Marriage Notices in the* "South Carolina" *and* "American General Gazette," *1766–1781;* "The Royal Gazette," *1781–1782*. 1914. Reprint, Baltimore: Genealogical Publishing Co., 1976.

Wilkinson, Tom C. *Early Anderson County, South Carolina Newspapers Marriages and Obituaries, 1841–1882*. Easley, S.C.: Southern Historical Press, 1978.

Wilson, Teresa E., and Janice L. Grimes. *Marriage and Death Notices From the* Southern Patriot. Easley, S.C.: Southern Historical Press, 1982–86. Vol. 1: 1815–30; Vol. 2: 1831–48.

South Dakota

Ferris, Edna M. *Jones County in Memory*. Pierre, S.D.: the author, 1989. Collection of obituaries and memorials from newspapers and funeral homes.

Johnson, Linda. *Newspaper Extracts From Java, South Dakota, 1903–1918*. Seattle: the author, 1991.

Tennessee

Baker, Russell P. *Marriages and Obituaries From the* "Tennessee Baptist," *1844–1862*. Easley, S.C.: Southern Historical Press, 1879.

Eddlemon, Sherida K. *Genealogical Abstracts From Tennessee Newspapers, 1791–1808*. Bowie, Md.: Heritage Books, 1988.

———. *Genealogical Abstracts From Tennessee Newspapers, 1803–1812*. Bowie, Md.: Heritage Books, 1989.

———. *Genealogical Abstracts From Tennessee Newspapers, 1821–1828*. Bowie, Md.: Heritage Books, 1991.

Garrett, Jill K. *Obituaries From Tennessee Newspapers, 1851–1899*. Easley, S.C.: Southern Historical Press, 1980.

Lucas, Silas Emmett, Jr. *Marriages From Early Tennessee Newspapers, 1794–1851*. Easley, S.C.: Southern Historical Press, 1978.

———. *Obituaries From Early Tennessee Newspapers, 1794–1851*. Easley, S.C.: Southern Historical Press, 1978.

Scoggins, Margaret B. Banner of Peace *and* Cumberland Presbyterian Advocate; *Abstracts of Marriage, Death, and other Notices, 1843–1853*. Poplar Bluff, Mo.: the author, 1988.

Texas

Cawthon, Juanita Davis. *Marriage and Death Notices, Marion County, Texas and Environs, 1853–1927.* Shreveport, La.: the author, 1980.

El Paso Genealogical Society. *Births, Deaths, and Marriages From El Paso Newspapers Through 1885 for Arizona, Texas, New Mexico, Oklahoma and Indian Territory.* Easley, S.C.: Southern Historical Press, 1982.

Lu, Helen Mason. *Texas Methodist Newspaper Abstracts, 17 April 1850–17 Sept. 1881.* 4 vols. Dallas: the author, 1987.

Swenson, Helen S. *Early Texas News, 1831–1848; Abstracts From Early Texas Newspapers.* St. Louis: F. T. Ingmire, 1984.

Utah

Historical and Genealogical Register of Indexes to Corinne, Utah Newspapers, 1869–1875. Brigham City, Utah: Golden Spike Chapter, Utah Genealogical Association, 1975.

Vermont

Rising, Marsha Hoffman. *Vermont Newspaper Abstracts, 1783–1816.* Boston: New England Historic Genealogical Society, 2001.

Virginia

Cappon, Lester J., and Stella F. Duff. Virginia Gazette *Index.* 2 vols. (1736–1780). Williamsburg: Institute of Early American Culture, 1950.

Headley, Robert K. *Genealogical Abstracts From 18th-Century Virginia Newspapers.* Baltimore: Genealogical Publishing Co., 1987.

Hodge, Robert Allen. *Death Notices,* Virginia Herald, *Fredericksburg, Virginia, 1788–1836.* Fredericksburg, Va.: the author, 1981.

McIlwaine, H. R. *Index to Obituary Notices,* "Richmond Enquirer," *May 9, 1824–1829;* "Richmond Whig," *1824–1838.* 1923. Reprint, Baltimore: Genealogical Publishing Co., 1979.

Obituary Notices From the Alexandria Gazette, *1784–1915.* Compiled by the staff of Lloyd House, Alexandria Library. Bowie, Md.: Heritage Books, 1987.

Washington

McNeill, Ruby Simonson. *Lewis County, Washington, Newspaper Abstracts.* 5 vols. Spokane: the author, 1978. Vol. 1: 1884–86; Vol. 2: 1887–89; Vol. 3: 1890–93; Vol. 4: 1894–96; Vol. 5: 1897–99.

Townsend, Homer. *Obituaries From the* Skamania County Pioneer *Newspaper, Skamania County, Washington, 1900–1929.* Goldendale, Wash.: the author, 1985.

West Virginia

Hassig, Carol. *Wetzel County, WV, Obituary Book, 1870–1940.* 2 vols. New Martinsville, W.V.: Wetzel County Genealogical Society, 1981–92.

Hodge, Robert Allen. *An Index for the* Martinsburg Gazette, *Martinsburg (West) Virginia.* Fredericksburg, Va.: the author, 1973–74. Vol. 1: 1810–15; Vol. 2: 1823–33; Vol. 3: 1834–39; Vol. 4: 1839–48; Vol. 5: 1851–55.

Wisconsin

Albertz, Sally P. *Fond du Lac Comonwealth Newspaper: Genealogical Items Extracted From Newspapers Dated January 1863 Through December 1870.* Fond du Lac, Wisc.: the author, 1988.

Gee, Patricia, and Wilma Foley. *Marriages and Deaths in the* "Depere News," *1871–1883.* Dearborn, Mich.: the authors, 1976.

———. *Deaths in the* "Green Bay Advocate," *1870–1880.* Dearborn, Mich: the authors, 1976.

———. *Marriages in the* "Green Bay Advocate," *1870–1880.* Dearborn, Mich.: the authors, 1976.

Noonan, Barry C. *Index to Green Bay Newspapers, 1833–1840.* Monroe, Wis.: Wisconsin State Genealogical Society, 1987.

Obituary Index, 1939–1971, the New North, Rhinelander Daily News; *Obituary Index, 1972–1975,* Rhinelander Daily News. 2 microfilm reels. N.p., 1983.

Stevens Point Area Obituary Index. Covers 1872–the present. Available online at <http://library.uwsp.edu/depts/archives/obits/osearch.htm>.

13
Vital Records

JOHNI CERNY, BS, FUGA

Vital records, as their name suggests, are connected with central life events: birth, marriage, and death. These records are prime sources of genealogical information, but, unfortunately, official vital records (those maintained by county and state governments), are available only for relatively recent time periods. Marriage records, the oldest of the vital records, will be considered first. The more recent records of birth and death will follow. The chapter concludes with a discussion of records related to the burial of an individual and suggestions for cemetery searches.

Chapter Contents

Marriage Records

The registering of marriages in the United States is a quasi-religious, quasi-legal social function (see figure 13-1) that has been influenced by religious belief, custom, and English law since the earliest colonial settlements. The effective researcher needs a complete understanding of the jurisdictions responsible for maintaining these records, the types of records kept by each jurisdiction, the periods in which various types of records were maintained, the circumstances peculiar to each colony and state that created the necessity for registering marriages, and the factors that produced changes in these registrations.

Complicating matters is the fact that the United States, unlike England and some European countries, does not have a national registration program. Instead, marriage registration is the responsibility of the individual states. Furthermore, marriage registration was never uniformly implemented among the states. Prior to state registration requirements, towns in New England and counties in the remainder of the nation were the primary jurisdictions charged with maintaining marriage records. Thus, records can ordinarily be found dating from when a town or county was created. Some states, however, such as Pennsylvania and South Carolina, have not required subordinate jurisdictions to keep marriage records until more recent times.

Jurisdictions

Marriage records in the United States have been, and in some cases still are, kept by churches, ministers, justices of the peace, state boards of health, colonial governors, military personnel, and local (county and town) governments.

State Boards of Health/Bureaus of Vital Statistics

The most important recordkeeping agencies for marriages in the United States today are the state boards of health or bureaus of vital statistics (or their equivalents). Even though these agencies are primarily state bodies, large cities usually have their own registries. However, few states had them until after 1850. Vermont (1770) and Washington, D.C. (1811) were the first to form them; Colorado (1968) was the last. Even when the requirement existed, the laws were seldom enforced; consequently, many genealogists are reluctant to spend the time necessary to search for marriage records on file with these agencies for early periods. However, residents of heavily populated cities often are not mentioned in local histories or biographical publications. Quite often they can be found only in major record sources. Thus, it is imperative to search for whatever records may exist. The Vital Records Information website <www.vitalrec.com> gives dates of registration and the cost or procedure for ordering vital records from each state. Similar information is available from The National Center for Health Statistics which publishes *Where to Write for Vital Records—Births, Deaths, Marriages, and Divorces* at <www.cdc.gov/nchs/howto/w2w/w2welcom.htm>. This publication may be downloaded and saved on your personal computer.

Figure 13-1. A bridal portrait taken in Fort Wayne, Indiana, year unknown. From the collection of Reverend Charles Banet.

Colonial Governors

Many of the earliest marriage records were kept by the offices of colonial governors. While not numerous, many of these records are still in existence, usually in state archives. Some of these records are in print or available on CD-ROM. Many have been indexed online, such as "North Carolina Marriage Records Index 1741–2000" available at <www.ancestry.com>.

Military Personnel

Colonial, state, and federal military officers and ships' officers (military and civilian) often performed marriages and recorded them in ships' logs, daybooks, and private journals. Those records can be found among military records maintained by the federal government and in historical societies, libraries, and museums.

Town and County Governments

Town clerks in New England and county clerks elsewhere have been responsible for registering most marriages in the United States. Marriage records were kept in New England beginning in the 1600s and in the South beginning in the 1700s. Clerks issued documents granting permission for a couple to marry, and then they received notification that the ceremony had taken place from the ministers and justices of the peace in the towns or counties.

There is little uniformity in the marriage record-keeping practices among the states. Researchers should thus become familiar with the laws and customs of each area and time period to be researched. Most jurisdictions maintained more than one form of document, and the information required on different documents often varied. For example, Kentucky marriage registers usually include the names of the bride and groom, the date and place of the marriage, and the officiating authority. The marriage license, issued as a separate record for the same couple, could also include residence, age, place of birth, names of parents, and occupation.

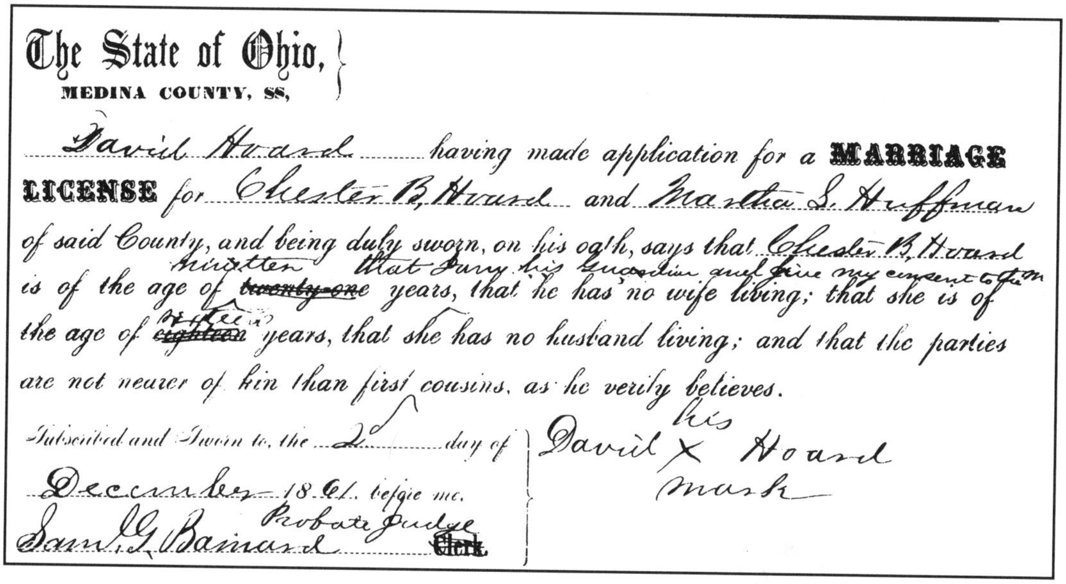

The State of Ohio, }
MEDINA COUNTY, SS, }

David Hoard having made application for a MARRIAGE LICENSE for Chester B. Hoard and Martha S. Huffman of said County, and being duly sworn, on his oath, says that Chester B. Hoard is of the age of ~~twenty-one~~ nineteen years, that I am his guardian and give my consent to them that he has no wife living; that she is of the age of ~~eighteen~~ [illegible] years, that she has no husband living; and that the parties are not nearer of kin than first cousins, as he verily believes.

Subscribed and Sworn to, the 2d day of December 1861, before me.
Sam'l G. Barnard ~~Clerk~~ Probate Judge

David his X mark Hoard

Figure 13-2. David Hoard's application for a marriage license for Chester B. Hoard and Martha S. Huffman, Medina County, Ohio, 2 December 1861, book 1. p. 29. FHL microfilm 55,536, pt. 3.

Churches

Churches were among the earliest keepers of marriage records. By 1640, Virginia and Massachusetts had passed laws requiring ministers to provide records of the marriages they performed to civil officials in the county or parish. Records of marriages in areas that did not require periodic reporting remained with the minister or the church.

Many churches, especially in the frontier areas, did not keep extensive records, and many records have been lost or destroyed. New England churches, Quaker Monthly Meetings, and the German churches kept and have preserved the most complete records. (See chapter 6, "Church Records.")

Justices of the Peace

Most states have authorized the election or appointment of justices of the peace who can perform marriages. Like ministers, justices have also been required to submit records of the marriages they performed to civil authorities. Justices also maintained their own registers, often in the personal account books in which they recorded the fees paid. These sometimes contain marriage and other genealogical information not forwarded to the civil authorities and should not be overlooked by the researcher, even when civil records are available. Justices' registers can be found in the care of county clerks, local historical societies, libraries, and descendants of the justices themselves. Several are on microfilm at the Family History Library of The Church of Jesus Christ of Latter-day Saints (LDS Church), and some have been published by local genealogical societies.

Types of Marriage Records

Consent Affidavits

The minimum legal age for marriage varies from one place to another. While some jurisdictions have required consent regardless of age, most demanded consent affidavits from a parent or legal guardian only for those under the minimum age—usually twenty-one for males, eighteen for females. Sometimes a parent or guardian appeared with the underage person and gave verbal permission. The record will show that the parent was present and was known to the clerk but may not record the name. A detailed, printed consent form was part of the marriage license in a few localities.

The father of the underage person usually gave consent, especially in the South. When a mother has given consent, the father was likely deceased. When both parents were deceased, the legal guardian granted permission to marry. If the guardian is related to the person getting married, their relationship may be stated.

Figure 13-2 is an application for a marriage license by David Hoard for Chester B. Hoard and Martha S. Huffman in Medina County, Ohio. In it, David Hoard states that he is Chester B. Hoard's guardian and gives his consent to the marriage.

Consent documents are found in town and county jurisdictions throughout the United States, but they are more numerous in the South and former frontier regions, where early marriages were encouraged.

Declarations of Intent

Declarations of intent to marry have been required in one form or another in all colonies and states from colonial times. The practice may have been abandoned in a particular place for a period of time, only to be reinstated later. There are many types of declarations of intent, both written and oral.

Banns

The publishing of banns was a church custom during the colonial and later periods. Banns were usually read in church on three consecutive Sundays (sometimes during public meetings); in some areas they were posted in public places as well. Their purpose was to give local residents the opportunity to state their objections to a marriage. Delaware and Ohio considered the publication of banns equivalent to a license to about 1898. The following is a sample of what might be included in a published banns:

> I publishe [*sic*] the Banns of Marriage between Robert Preston of New Haven and Priscilla Fuller of Milford. If any known cause or just impediment why these two persons should not be joined together in Holy Matrimony, ye are to declare it. This is the 1st time asking.
>
> **Daniel Stout, Reverend.**

Intentions

These records were similar to banns but were filed with the town or county clerk. Intentions include the names and places of residence of the prospective bride and groom and the date the intention was filed. Unlike banns, intentions were not generally read aloud but were posted in public places for a prescribed period of time. As with banns, intentions were to give others the opportunity to voice objections to the union. Many intentions filed in New England have been published in book form or are online. Notably, New England Historic Genealogical Society offers both indexes and records for various years and places in Massachusetts at its website <www.newenglandancestors.org/research/Database/MASS_BMD>.

Bonds

Marriage bonds were not required by all colonies or states but have been common in the South. Bonds were posted prior to the issuing of the required marriage license in some states and were the sole documents required in others. Bonds were posted by the groom alone or with a second person, usually the father or the brother of the bride, to defray the costs of litigation in the event the marriage was nullified.

Bonds were posted in the jurisdiction where the marriage was to take place, often in the bride's home county. These bonds, the only marriage records maintained in some jurisdictions, were usually annotated with the marriage date after the ceremony. It was rare for a marriage not to take place within a few days of the posting of the bond, even though many bonds do not bear the annotation. Although the missing information could mean that the marriage did not take place, more often it reflects poor record keeping or failure of the justice or minister to report the marriage to local officials.

Marriage bonds were required in North Carolina from 1741 to 1868. The bonds have since been placed in the custody of the North Carolina State Archives. The Archives has compiled two master name indexes, one to brides and one to grooms. The index is available at the Archives.

Figure 13-3 is an example of a bond typically found in the South.

Contracts

Marriage contracts are relatively uncommon. They were usually drawn up when one or both parties was wealthy or might inherit a substantial estate, and wished to protect the inheritance rights of heirs.

Marriage contracts have also been used in second marriages. Property left to a widow by her first husband could be protected with a marriage contract. Such documents guarantee the distribution of property to the children of the first husband. Without such a contract, the property inherited at the death of the first husband became the property of the second husband at the time of marriage. He could dispose of that property as he desired, without provision for his stepchildren. Marriage contracts are recorded among marriage records or are filed with court records or deeds.

Marriage contracts were widely used in Louisiana during the colonial period. Under civil law, the French and Spanish used formal marriage contracts to protect their property, regardless of their social position or wealth. These documents are of unequaled value in genealogical research because they list extended family relationships and often the place of origin of the immigrant ancestor. The following contract between Charles de Lavergne and Marie Joseph Carriere illustrates the superb detail of the documents.

> **June 16, 1739**
>
> CHARLES de LAVERGNE, Lieutenant on half-pay, of this Province of Louisiana, son of Mr. PIERRE de LAVERGNE, Counsellor at Chatelet of Parish, and of Dame ELIZABETH BILLET his father and mother, a native of parish, Parish of St. Eustache
>
> with
>
> Demoiselle MARIE JOSEPH CARRIERE, minor daughter of the deceased Sieur ANDRE CARRIERE and of Dame MARGUERITTE HARLUT her father and mother, a native of Mobile, Bishopric of Quebec. The named Dame MARGUERITTE HARLUT now wife of Sieur LOUIS TIXERRANT being present.
>
> Consenting for the minor being Sieur JOSEPH CARRIERE her uncle and tutor.
>
> Consenting on the part of the named Sieur de LAVERGNE, Mr. de BIENVILLE, Chevalier of the Royal and Military order of St. Louis, Governor of this Province, of Louisiana, Mr. de SALMON, Commissioner of the Marines of this Province and Madame his wife, Mr. DIRON DARTAGUETTE, Chevalier of the Royal and Military Order of St. Louis, Commandant at Mobile, Mr. BELLUGA Captain

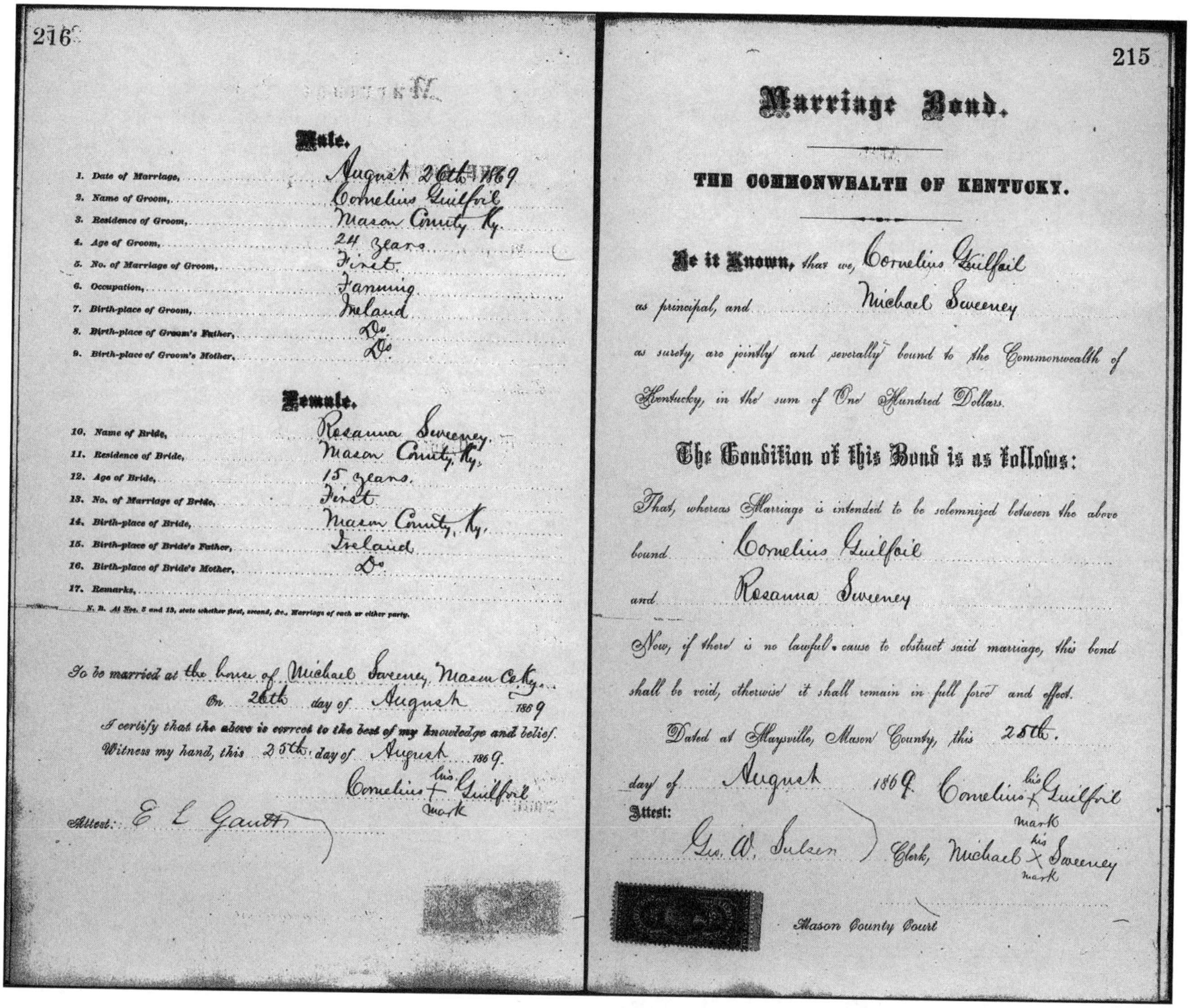
216

Male.

1. Date of Marriage, August 26th 1869
2. Name of Groom, Cornelius Guilfoil
3. Residence of Groom, Mason County Ky
4. Age of Groom, 24 years
5. No. of Marriage of Groom, First
6. Occupation, Farming
7. Birth-place of Groom, Ireland
8. Birth-place of Groom's Father, Do
9. Birth-place of Groom's Mother, Do

Female.

10. Name of Bride, Rosanna Sweeney
11. Residence of Bride, Mason County Ky
12. Age of Bride, 15 years
13. No. of Marriage of Bride, First
14. Birth-place of Bride, Mason County Ky
15. Birth-place of Bride's Father, Ireland
16. Birth-place of Bride's Mother, Do
17. Remarks,

N. B. At Nos. 5 and 13, state whether first, second, &c., Marriage of each or either party.

To be married at the house of Michael Sweeney, Mason Co Ky
On 26th day of August 1869
I certify that the above is correct to the best of my knowledge and belief.
Witness my hand, this 25th day of August 1869.
Cornelius his X mark Guilfoil
Attest: E L Gantt

215

Marriage Bond.

THE COMMONWEALTH OF KENTUCKY.

Be it Known, that we, Cornelius Guilfoil as principal, and Michael Sweeney as surety, are jointly and severally bound to the Commonwealth of Kentucky, in the sum of One Hundred Dollars.

The Condition of this Bond is as follows:

That, whereas Marriage is intended to be solemnized between the above bound Cornelius Guilfoil and Rosanna Sweeney

Now, if there is no lawful cause to obstruct said marriage, this bond shall be void, otherwise it shall remain in full force and effect.

Dated at Maysville, Mason County, this 25th day of August 1869. Cornelius his X mark Guilfoil

Attest: Geo. W. Sulser Clerk, Michael his X mark Sweeney

Mason County Court

Figure 13-3. Marriage bond for Cornelius Guilfoil and Rosanna Sweeny, great-grandparents of actor George Clooney, Mason County, Kentucky, 25 August 1869, Marriage records, 1789–1978. FHL microfilm 1,534,055.

of the King's vessel, Mr. DeVILLER FRANSSURE, Lieutenant of the King's vessel, presently of this Colony, his friends and friends of his deceased parents.

And for the named Demoiselle MARIE JOSEPH CARRIERE, Sieur and Dame TIXERRANT her step-father and her mother, Sieur JOSEPH CARRIERE her uncle and tutor, Sieur JACQUES CARRIERE also her uncle, Dame FRANCOISE JALOT widow CARRIERE, Aunt of Demoiselle MARIE MARGUERITTE CARRIERE, her sister, Sieur LOUIS TIXERRANT her brother, Mr. and Madame de LIVAUDAIS her cousin, Mr. the Chevalier de LOWBOY, of the Royal and Military Order of St. Louis, Captain of the Infantry of the Marines, Mr. D'AUTHERIVE, Chevalier of the Royal and Military Order of St. Louis, Mr. de BELISLE, Mr. BOBE DESCLOSEAUX, comptroller of the Marines, Mr. DUBREUIL VILLARS, contractor for the King's fortifications in this colony.

This marriage to be solemnized in the Holy Roman Apostolic Catholic Church.

This document collated and entered in the minutes of the Royal Notary, at New Orleans on the 17 of June of 1768. /s/ Garic, Notary.[1]

Marriage Licenses

Marriage licenses are the most common marriage records in the United States. They are issued by the appropriate authority prior to the marriage ceremony, and they have come to replace the posting of banns and intentions. Marriage licenses, which grant permission for a marriage to be performed, are returned to civil authorities after the ceremony.

Applications for marriage licenses have been required in some jurisdictions in addition to or in place of bonds. Applications are often filled out by both the bride and groom and typically contain a large amount of genealogical information. They may list the full names of the bride and groom, their residences, races, ages, dates and places of birth, previous marriages, occupations, and their parents' names, places of birth (state or country), and occupations. Recent laws require health certificates attesting to the absence of diseases that could be passed on to children.

For most locations, marriage license applications can be found for periods beginning after the Civil War. Indiana, Wisconsin, and Utah counties maintained them earlier. The application form does not include the marriage date.

Marriage licenses exist in varying forms. Figure 13-4, a certified copy of a marriage license issued in the county in Illinois where the marriage took place, is much like licenses from most towns or counties. A standard form generally asks for the names of the bride and groom, their residence at the time of application, the date the marriage was performed, the date the license was issued, the place of the marriage, and the name of the person performing the marriage ceremony.

A license from Spencer County, Kentucky (figure 13-5), illustrates the style of license used during earlier periods in the South. Note that the return after the ceremony is annotated at the bottom of the license in the minister's handwriting.

Certified copies of marriage records are certified to be correct, but there is a possibility of error in any typescript. It is best to request photocopies when you write a town or county clerk.

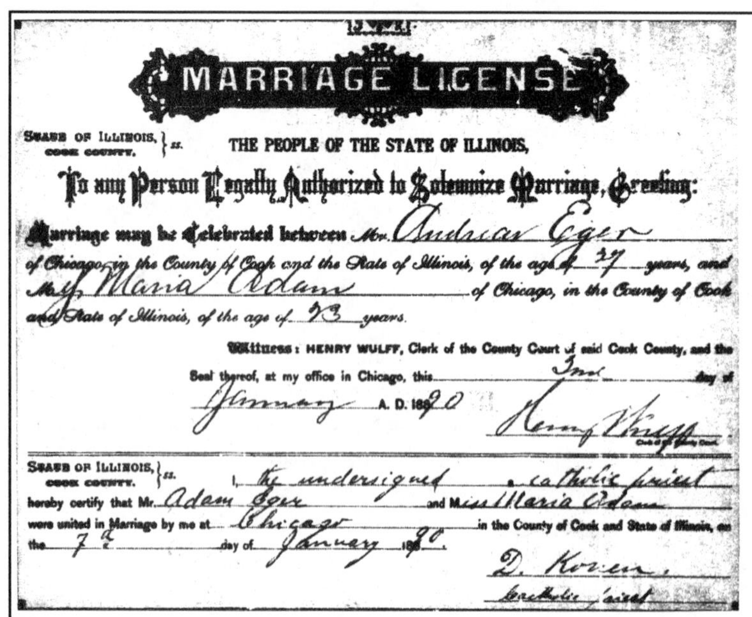

MARRIAGE LICENSE

State of Illinois, Cook County, } ss. THE PEOPLE OF THE STATE OF ILLINOIS,

To any Person Legally Authorized to Solemnize Marriage, Greeting:

Marriage may be Celebrated between Mr. Andreas Eger of Chicago, in the County of Cook and the State of Illinois, of the age of 27 years, and Miss Maria Adam of Chicago, in the County of Cook and State of Illinois, of the age of 23 years.

Witness: HENRY WULFF, Clerk of the County Court of said Cook County, and the Seal thereof, at my office in Chicago, this 2nd day of January A. D. 1890

Henry Wulff

State of Illinois, Cook County, } ss. I, the undersigned, a catholic priest hereby certify that Mr. Adam Eger and Miss Maria Adam were united in Marriage by me at Chicago in the County of Cook and State of Illinois, on the 7th day of January 1890.

D. Koren,
Catholic priest

Figure 13-4. A certified copy of a marriage license issued in the Illinois county where the marriage took place. It is much like licenses from most towns or counties.

Marriage Certificates

Marriage certificates are given to the couple after the ceremony is completed and are thus usually found among family records. There are exceptions, however. Figure 13-6 is from a volume of marriage certificates on file in Medina County, Ohio. These certificates, however, are similar to marriage licenses issued in other places. The bride and groom usually receive a marriage certificate for their family records containing similar historical information, signatures of witnesses, and so on.

Marriage Registers and Returns

Colonial and state governments have required that marriages performed within their jurisdictions be reported to civil authorities. The town or county clerk then compiles marriage registers, though these registers are rarely complete. Those who officiated at marriages in rural areas were often reluctant to travel the distances required to comply with the law. Sometimes, also, ministers' records were lost or destroyed before the marriages were properly reported. Itinerant preachers, who crossed jurisdictional boundaries, rarely registered marriages at all. Couples sometimes obtained a license, filed a bond, or made applications in one jurisdiction and then married in another, but ministers filed returns only in their own counties. Still, marriage returns are the only documents that provide evidence that the marriage actually took place.

Marriage registers differ from one jurisdiction to another. Some required only the names of the couple and the date of the marriage. Registers are normally arranged in chronological order by year, though there can be overlap in registers that were infrequently updated. The Spencer County, Kentucky, marriage register shown in figure 13-7 provides the date of marriage, names of the parties, name of the person who performed the marriage, the place of marriage, the names of witnesses, and the certificate number.

Some registers exist in the absence of licenses. This is true for registers in Virginia and West Virginia after 1853, which provide the marriage date, minister, names of the parties, their ages, places of birth, residences, parents, and occupations. Many of these registers have been transcribed.

Most marriage registers are compiled from written returns submitted by ministers and justices. The lists are copied into the register by a clerk and are thus subject to transcription errors. Figure 13-8 is from the returns register of Daviess County, Kentucky.

Not all marriage returns were entered into a register. Some were simply noted on the license or bond; others were written on scraps of paper filed loosely in the clerk's office, either in alphabetical

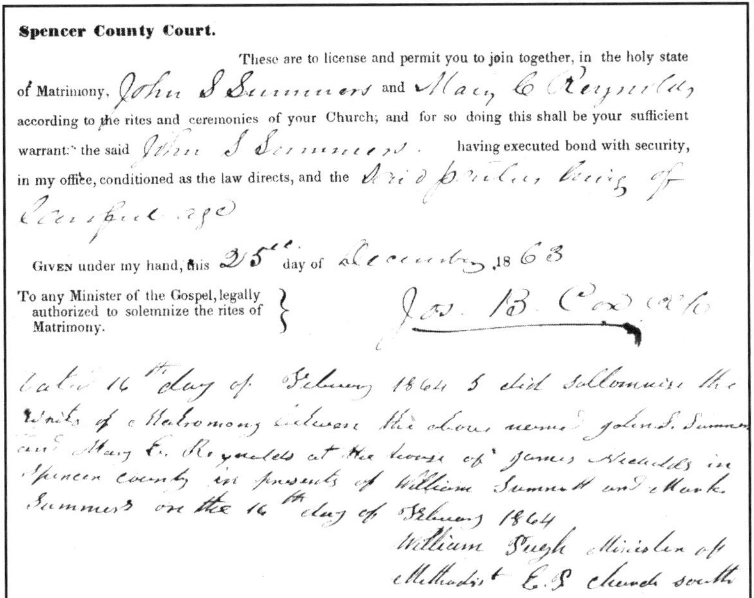
Spencer County Court.

These are to license and permit you to join together, in the holy state of Matrimony, John S Summers and Mary C Reynolds according to the rites and ceremonies of your Church; and for so doing this shall be your sufficient warrant: the said John S Summers having executed bond with security, in my office, conditioned as the law directs, and the [illegible]

GIVEN under my hand, this 25th day of December 1863

To any Minister of the Gospel, legally authorized to solemnize the rites of Matrimony.

Jos. B. Cox

[illegible] 16th day of February 1864 I did solemnize the rites of Matrimony between the above named John S. Summers and Mary C. Reynolds at the house of James Reynolds in Spencer county in presents of William Summers and Mark Summers on the 16th day of February 1864

William Pugh Minister of Methodist E. C. church south

Figure 13-5. Marriage license of John S. Summers and Mary C. Reynolds, Spencer County, Kentucky, 25 December 1863, Marriage Book B, p. 22. FHL microfilm 482,642, certificate 412.

order or by the first letter of the groom's surname. Most loose returns have been microfilmed for easier use.

Locating Marriage Records

Marriage records were issued and maintained by town and county jurisdictions before state registration was established. Marriage records are usually indexed by the surname of the groom, but a few jurisdictions have compiled cross-indexes to the maiden name of the bride. Some states are collecting these early marriage records from the local jurisdictions—but because no comprehensive list of these repositories exists, you must write to the town or county first. Addresses, including zip codes, for every county and town clerk are in the current edition of *Red Book: American State, County, and Town Sources*.[2]

Online Availability

Marriage indexes (and some digitized images) are online for many counties and at least one state has combined county indexes into a statewide index. The Illinois Statewide Marriage Index contains Illinois county marriage records dated 1763–1900 and can be searched at <www.sos.state.il.us/GenealogyMWeb/marrsrch.html>.

Table 13-1 includes a list of statewide marriage indexes online. Hundreds of websites feature collections of county marriage records; currently the USGenWeb Project houses most of them at Rootsweb.com. Search the Web routinely for new statewide and county databases.

Table 13-2 lists marriage (along with some birth and death) records that have been compiled and published on CD-ROM. The table includes remarks on the content and extent of coverage.

A project of FamilySearch.org and FamilySearch Indexing to digitize the microfilmed vital records held in the Granite Mountain Records Vault began in the United States with the records of the state of Georgia. The project will eventually include vital records from the entire collection. The first major record sets to be published on FamilySearch.org will include vital records from North and South America, areas of the Pacific, and the British Isles.

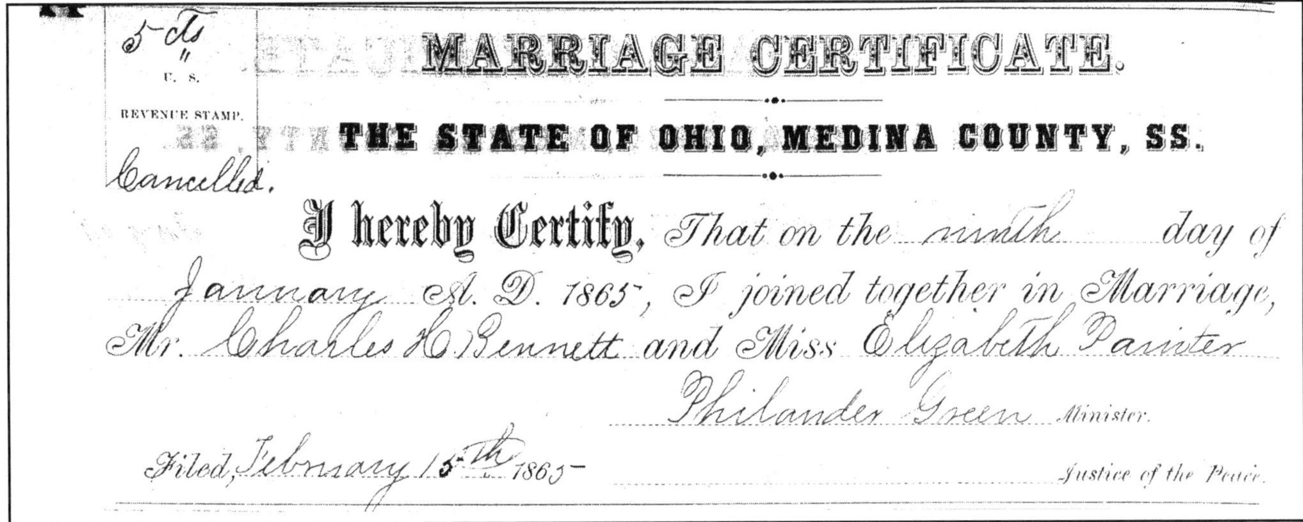
5 cts U. S. REVENUE STAMP. Cancelled.

MARRIAGE CERTIFICATE.

THE STATE OF OHIO, MEDINA COUNTY, SS.

I hereby Certify, That on the ninth day of January A. D. 1865, I joined together in Marriage, Mr. Charles H Bennett and Miss Elizabeth Painter

Philander Green Minister.

Filed, February 15th 1865 Justice of the Peace.

Figure 13-6. Marriage certificate of Charles H. Bennett and Elizabeth Painter, Medina County, Ohio, 15 February 1865, Book 2, p. 14. FHL microfilm 55,537, pt. 3.

Genealogical Society of Utah

The Family History Library in Salt Lake City, Utah, houses millions of sources, including microfilmed records from most of the United States. The collection is available in its entirety in Salt Lake City, but copies of the microfilms can be obtained through Family History Centers located throughout the United States (see appendix vii, "The LDS Family History Library," for locations). This collection includes thousands of original marriage registers and collections of bonds, consents, licenses, and applications. Many names and dates have been extracted from the microfilmed collection and placed in the International Genealogical Index which may be accessed at the Library, its centers, or online at <www.familysearch.org>. There are also lists of statewide marriage indexes and records available through the Family History Library. These are shown in table 13-3.

The Library has, in book or manuscript form, marriage entries that have been transcribed by the Daughters of the American Revolution (DAR) or Work Projects Administration (WPA). The transcripts often have cross-indexes to brides, annotations from ministers' journals and account books, newspaper announcements, and even the personal knowledge of the compiler. For these and other transcripts, it is always wise to check the original records when they are available.

Writing for Marriage Records

Researchers who cannot use the Family History Library's collection or online sources, can write to town or county record custodians. For a fee, clerks will search the local records and send a copy of the information requested.

Because of recently passed privacy laws, state boards of vital records and bureaus of vital statistics may require you to file a form stating your relationship to the bride and groom and the purpose of the request, but they will usually provide records for family history purposes.

Marriage records can be obtained from numerous sources within a county. Most counties registered marriages in marriage registers, but some filings may be found in court records and deed books. Common law marriages, if referred to at all, would be found in court records, which are rarely indexed (unlike deed books) and require substantial research time. However, they should not be overlooked.

Family Records

Family records, such as family Bibles, journals, diaries, and personal histories, often include marriage documents or references to marriages. Certificates, contracts, and divorce records can also be found in personal collections. Some family records have been donated to local historical societies, libraries, universities, or state archives. Manuscripts of unpublished family histories contain valuable genealogical information and are also found in these kinds of libraries, all of which usually have guides to their manuscript collections.

Printed Records

The number of printed volumes of marriage records grows daily as genealogy enthusiasts continue to make contributions to the field. These volumes are available through libraries, historical and genealogical societies, booksellers, publishers, and

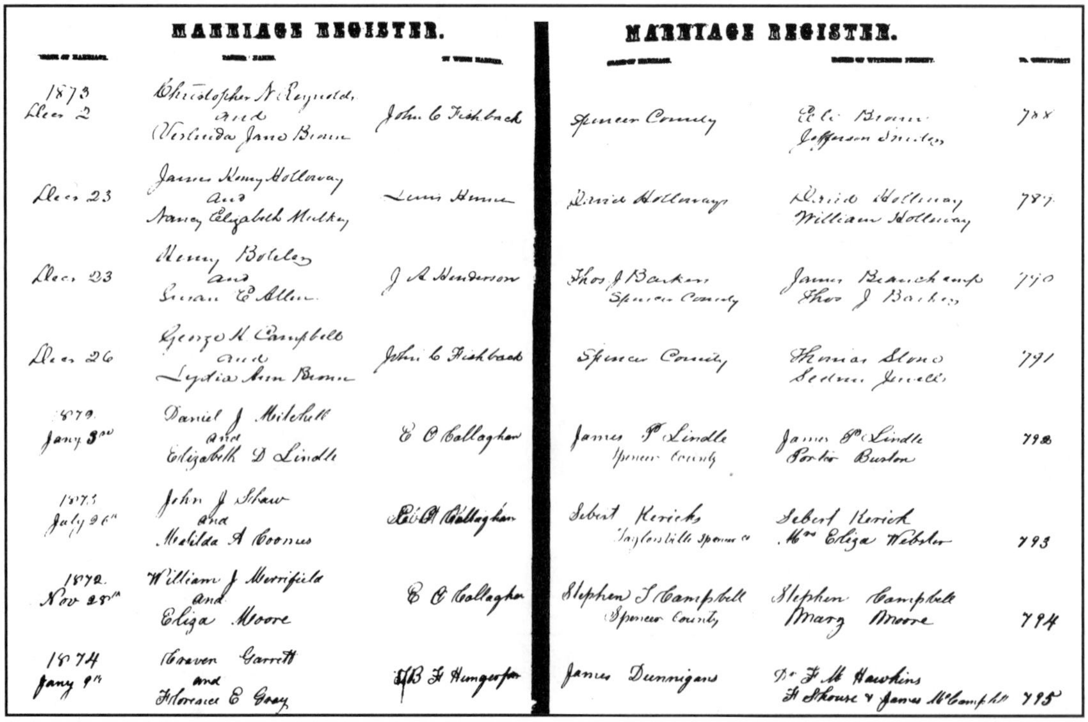

MARRIAGE REGISTER. MARRIAGE REGISTER.

1873 Dec 2	Christopher N. Reynolds and Verlinda Jane Brown	John C Fishback	Spencer County	E. C. Brown, Jefferson Snider	788
Dec 23	James Henry Holloway and Nancy Elizabeth Mulkey	Lewis Hume	David Holloway	David Holloway, William Holloway	789
Dec 23	Henry Boteler and Susan E Allen	J A Henderson	Thos J Barker, Spencer County	James Beauchamp, Thos J Barker	790
Dec 26	George K Campbell and Lydia Ann Brown	John C Fishback	Spencer County	Thomas Slone, Sedron Jewell	791
1874 Jany 8th	Daniel J Mitchell and Elizabeth D Lindle	E O Callaghan	James P Lindle, Spencer County	James P Lindle, Porter Burton	792
1873 July 26th	John J Shaw and Matilda A Coomes	Rev E O Callaghan	Sebert Kericks, Taylorsville Spencer Co	Sebert Kerick, Mrs Eliza Webster	793
1872 Nov 28th	William J Merrifield and Eliza Moore	E O Callaghan	Stephen T Campbell, Spencer County	Stephen Campbell, Mary Moore	794
1874 Jany 9th	Craven Garrett and Florence E Gray	S B Hungerford	James Dunnigan	Dr F M Hawkins, H Shouse & James McCampbell	795

Figure 13-7. From the Spencer County, Kentucky, marriage register, 10 April to 31 July 1862. FHL microfilm 482,494.

Date	Parties Names	Return of marriage
1817 May 15th	John B Blackwell to Nancy Hollins	A Certificate of the marriage of the parties was returned to me and duly acknowledged as follows "This may Certify I joined together John B Blackwell and Nancy Hollins in the holy state of matrimony this 29 of May 1817 Daniel T Pinkston Minister. Test William R Griffith clerk D County
July 8th	James Hollins to Rachel Taylor	This may Certify That I joined together James Hollins and Rachel Taylor in holy Wedlock this 10th day of July 1817 Daniel T Pinkston Minister. Acknowledged before me William R Griffith clk
Same	William McFarland to Frances Field	not found
July 10th	David Hamilton To Elizabeth Crabtree	I Job Hobbs minister do Certify that I celebrated marriage rites agreeable to a License handed one between Hamilton and Elizabeth Crabtree on the 17th day of July 1817 Job Hobbs. Return. ackn. before me this 8th Jany 1818 William R Griffith clk
July 21st	James Bartlett to Una Lay	This is to Certify that I joined together the within named James Bartlett and Una Lay in the holy state of matrimony this 14th of Augt 1817 Daniel T Pinkston minister. True Copy of the return made on the License to me Test William R Griffith clerk
August 1st	William Sisk to Ann Brown	A Certificate of the marriage of the parties was returned to my office by the minister as follows "This is to Certify that I sollemnized the rites of Matrimony between William Sisk and Ann Brown according to the within License I say by me solemnized August 3rd 1817 Thomas Downs minister of the Gospel" Test William R Griffith Clerk DC

Figure 13-8. Daviess County, Kentucky, marriage returns. FHL microfilm 582,231.

Table 13-1. Searchable Marriage Record Databases Online as of March 2006

State	Database Title	Address	Fee	Comments
Alabama	Alabama Marriages, 1807–1920	www.ancestry.com/search/rectype/inddbs/4192a.htm	Yes	Two databases include 150,000 records.
Arkansas	Arkansas Marriages to 1850	www.ancestry.com/search/rectype/inddbs/2082a.htm	Yes	Includes 18,000 records; incomplete
	Arkansas Marriages, 1820–1992	http://ancestry.com/search/db.aspx?dbid=7841	Yes	Incomplete. See database description for list of counties.
	Arkansas Marriages, 1779–1992	http://ancestry.com/search/db.aspx?dbid=7845	Yes	Incomplete See database description for list of counties.
California	California Marriage Index, 1949–86	www.vitalsearch-ca.com/gen/ca/_vitals/camarrin.htm	Yes	
Colorado	Colorado Marriage Search, 1975–Present	www.sctc.state.co.us/marriages/divorces.aspx	No	Colorado State Department of Health and Environment website.
	Colorado Marriages, 1859–1900	http://ancestry.com/search/db.aspx?dbid=4364	Yes	Incomplete. See database description for list of counties.
	Colorado Marriages, 1968–Present	www.sctc.state.co.us/marriages/default.aspx	No	
Connecticut	Connecticut Marriages to 1800	www.ancestry.com/search/db.aspx?dbid=1044	Yes	From church records.
	Connecticut Marriage Index, 1959–2001	www.ancestry.com/search/rectype/inddbs/7158.htm	Yes	
Delaware	Delaware Marriages, 1645–1944	http://ancestry.com/search/db.aspx?dbid=7863	Yes	See database description for places and dates.
Florida	Florida Marriages, 1822–50	http://ancestry.com/search/db.aspx?dbid=4019	Yes	See database description for content.
	Florida Marriages, 1851–75	www.ancestry.com/search/db.aspx?dbid=5323	Yes	Lists 7,000 marriages.
Georgia	Georgia Marriages to 1850	www.ancestry.com/search/rectype/inddbs/2085a.htm	Yes	More than 87,000 marriages.
	Georgia Marriage Records, 1851–1900	www.ancestry.com/search/rectype/vital/gamarr/main.htm	Yes	90,000 marriages.
	Georgia Marriage Records, 1699–1944	http://ancestry.com/search/db.aspx?dbid=7839	Yes	See database description for places and dates.
Illinois	Illinois State Marriage Index, 1763–1900	www.cyberdriveillinois.com/GenealogyMWeb/marrsrch.html	No	Ongoing project.
	Illinois Marriages, 1790–1860	www.ancestry.com/search/db.aspx?dbid=7851	Yes	
	Illinois Marriages to 1850	www.ancestry.com/search/rectype/inddbs/2086a.htm	Yes	155,000 names.
	Illinois Marriage Records, 1851–1900	www.ancestry.com/search/db.aspx?dbid=7857	Yes	Incomplete; ongoing.
Indiana	Indiana Marriages to 1850	www.ancestry.com/search/rectype/inddbs/2087a.htm	Yes	Nearly 200,000 names.
	Indiana Marriages, 1800–1941	www.ancestry.com/search/rectype/inddbs/5059a.htm	Yes	
Iowa	Iowa Marriages to 1850	www.ancestry.com/search/db.aspx?dbid=2088	Yes	10,500 records.
	Iowa Marriages, 1851–1900	www.ancestry.com/search/db.aspx?dbid=4460	Yes	Incomplete.
Kansas	Kansas Marriage Index, 1854–73	www.ancestry.com/search/db.aspx?dbid=3444	Yes	22,000 marriages.
Kentucky	Kentucky Marriages, 1802–50	www.ancestry.com/search/rectype/inddbs/2089a.htm	Yes	145,000 names.
	Kentucky Marriages, 1851–1900	www.ancestry.com/search/rectype/inddbs/4428a.htm	Yes	Incomplete.
	Kentucky Marriage Records, 1973–2002	www.vitalsearch-ca.com/gen/ky/_vitals/kymaygen.htm	No	
	Kentucky Marriage Records, 1973–99	http://ancestry.com/search/db.aspx?dbid=8787	Yes	Statewide.
Louisiana	Louisiana Marriages to 1850	www.ancestry.com/search/rectype/inddbs/2090a.htm	Yes	29,000 names.
	Louisiana Marriage Records, 1851–1900	www.ancestry.com/search/db.aspx?dbid=5228	Yes	Incomplete.
	Louisiana Marriages, 1718–1925	http://ancestry.com/search/db.aspx?dbid=7837	Yes	See database description for places and dates.
Maine	Maine Marriages to 1875	www.ancestry.com/search/db.aspx?dbid=5266	Yes	Incomplete.
	Maine Marriages, 1892–1996	www.ancestry.com/search/db.aspx?dbid=6904	Yes	
	Maine Marriage Index, 1892–1966, 1976–96	www.state.me.us/sos/arc/geneology	No	

State	Database Title	Address	Fee	Comments
Maryland	Maryland Marriages, 1655–1850	http://ancestry.com/search/db.aspx?dbid=7846	Yes	See database description for places and dates.
	Maryland Marriages, 1667–1899	http://ancestry.com/search/db.aspx?dbid=4729	Yes	See database description for places and dates.
Massachusetts	Massachusetts Marriages to 1800	www.ancestry.com/search/db.aspx?dbid=2091	Yes	29,000 names.
Michigan	Michigan Marriages to 1850	www.ancestry.com/search/rectype/inddbs/2092a.htm	Yes	13,000 names.
	Michigan Marriage Records, 1851–75	www.ancestry.com/search/db.aspx?dbid=5299	Yes	
Minnesota	Minnesota Marriage Index, 1997–2001	http://ancestry.com/search/db.aspx?dbid=8721	Yes	Statewide.
Mississippi	Mississippi Marriages to 1825	www.ancestry.com/search/db.aspx?dbid=2093	Yes	8,500 names.
	Mississippi Marriages 1826–1900	www.ancestry.com/search/db.aspx?dbid=4585	Yes	See database description for places and dates.
	Mississippi Marriages, 1776–1935	http://ancestry.com/search/db.aspx?dbid=7842	Yes	See database description for places and dates.
Missouri	Missouri Marriages to 1850	www.ancestry.com/search/rectype/inddbs/2094a.htm	Yes	125,000 names.
	Missouri Marriages, 1851–1900	www.ancestry.com/search/rectype/inddbs/4474a.htm	Yes	Incomplete.
	Missouri Marriages, 1766–1983	http://ancestry.com/search/db.aspx?dbid=7843	Yes	See database description for places and dates.
Nebraska	Nebraska Marriages, 1856–98	http://ancestry.com/search/db.aspx?dbid=7871	Yes	See database description for places and dates.
New Jersey	New Jersey Marriages, 1665–1800	www.ancestry.com/search/db.aspx?dbid=2095	Yes	45,000 names.
New York	New York Marriages to 1784	www.ancestry.com/search/db.aspx?dbid=3177	Yes	Incomplete.
New York City	New York City Marriage Records Index, 1908–36	www.italiangen.org/NYCMarriage.stm	No	Separate indexes for brides and grooms.
North Carolina	North Carolina Marriage Bonds, 1741–1868	http://ancestry.com/search/db.aspx?dbid=4802	Yes	See database for description of places and dates.
	North Carolina Marriage Collection, 1741–2000	http://content.ancestry.com/iexec/?dbid=8909	Yes	See database description for places and dates.
Ohio	Ohio Marriages, 1803–1900	www.ancestry.com/search/rectype/inddbs/5194a.htm	Yes	Incomplete. See database description for places and dates.
Oregon	Oregon Marriages, 1906–20	http://ancestry.com/search/db.aspx?dbid=5193	Yes	400,000 records.
South Carolina	South Carolina Marriages, 1641–1965	http://ancestry.com/search/db.aspx?dbid=7840	Yes	A collection of marriages from various sources.
South Dakota	South Dakota Marriages, 1905–49	http://ancestry.com/search/db.aspx?dbid=8561	Yes	Statewide.
Tennessee	Tennessee Marriages to 1825	www.ancestry.com/search/rectype/inddbs/2099a.htm	Yes	45,000 names.
	Tennessee Marriages, 1851–1900	www.ancestry.com/search/rectype/inddbs/4125a.htm	Yes	Incomplete.
Texas	Texas Marriages, 1967–2002	www.vitalsearch-ca.com/gen/tx/tx_/txmarrim-go.htm	Yes	
	Texas Marriages to 1850	www.ancestry.com/search/rectype/inddbs/3000a.htm	Yes	17,000 names.
	Texas Marriages, 1851–1900	www.ancestry.com/search/rectype/inddbs/4325a.htm	Yes	Incomplete.
Virginia	Index to Marriage Records	http://lvaimage.lib.va.us/collections/MG.html	No	Card File, 1700s–1800s
	Virginia Marriages to 1800	www.ancestry.com/search/rectype/inddbs/3002a.htm	Yes	85,000 names.
	Virginia Marriages, 1740–1850	www.ancestry.com/search/rectype/inddbs/3723a.htm	Yes	300,000 names.
	Virginia Marriages, 1851–1929	www.ancestry.com/search/db.aspx?dbid=4498	Yes	Incomplete.
	Virginia Marriages, 1851–1929	www.ancestry.com/search/db.aspx?dbid=3976	Yes	Six counties, and Richmond.
Washington	Washington Marriages, 1802–1902	http://ancestry.com/search/db.aspx?dbid=7874	Yes	See database description for places and dates.
Washington, D.C.	Washington, D.C. Marriages to 1825	www.ancestry.com/search/rectype/inddbs/2084a.htm	Yes	9,000 names.
West Virginia	West Virginia Marriages, 1863–1900	www.ancestry.com/search/db.aspx?dbid=4484	Yes	
	West Virginia Marriages, 1784–1969	www.wvculture.org/vrr/va_mcsearch.aspx	No	Ongoing project. Check site often for updates.
Wisconsin	Wisconsin Marriages, Pre-1907	www.ancestry.com/search/rectype/inddbs/4997a.htm	Yes	920,000 names
	Wisconsin Marriages, 1973–97	http://ancestry.com/search/db.aspx?dbid=8744	Yes	Statewide.

Table 13-2. Birth, Marriage and Death Records Published on CD-ROM as of March 2006

Title	Remarks	Publisher
Alabama Marriages, 1800–1900	Does not contain records from every county.	Genealogy.com
Alabama Vital Records, Alabama Deaths, 1908–1959	Covers all Alabama counties; 1,363,539 records.	Ancestry.com
Alabama Vital Records, Alabama Marriages, 1808–1920	Collections covers 54 of 67 counties; 163,000 records.	Ancestry.com
Alabama, South Carolina, and Georgia Marriage Index, 1641–1944	Collection does not contain every marriage that took place in these locations between 1641 and 1944.	Genealogy.com
Arkansas Marriage Index, 1779–1992	Does not contain records from every county; date span varies from county to county.	Genealogy.com
Arkansas Marriage Index, 1850–1900	Does not contain records from every county; date span varies from county to county.	Genealogy.com
Arkansas Vital Records, Marriages	Five separate databases; 277,000 brides and grooms.	Ancestry.com
Arkansas, Mississippi, Missouri, and Texas Marriage Index, 1766–1981	Collection does not contain every marriage that took place in these locations between 1766 and 1981.	Genealogy.com
Arizona, Colorado, Nebraska, New Mexico, Oregon, and Washington Marriage Index, 1727–1900	Collection does not contain every marriage that took place in these locations between 1727 and 1900.	Genealogy.com
California Birth Index, 1905–1995	Complete index.	Holosupplies.com
Connecticut Marriages, 1635–1860	Does not contain records from every county; date span varies from county to county.	Genealogy.com
District of Columbia, Delaware, Maryland, and Virginia Marriage Index, 1740–1920	Collection does not contain every marriage that took place in these locations between 1740 and 1920.	Genealogy.com
Georgia Vital Records, Marriages 1775–1900	Covers 72 counties.	Ancestry.com
Illinois, Indiana, Kentucky, Ohio, and Tennessee Marriage Index, 1720–1926	Collection does not contain every marriage that took place in these locations between 1720 and 1926.	Genealogy.com
Illinois Marriage Index, 1851–1900	Does not contain records from every county.	Genealogy.com
Illinois Vital Records, Marriages 1791–1900	Covers 78 counties; 271,000 records.	Ancestry.com
Indiana Marriage Index, 1850–1920	Does not contain records from every county.	Genealogy.com
Indiana Vital Records, Birth Index, 1850–1920	Lists 1,530,485 birth records from 68 counties inventoried by the Works Progress Administration.	Heritage Quest
Indiana Vital Records, Death Index, 1800–1941	Lists 867,134 deaths from 67 counties inventoried by the Works Progress Administration.	Heritage Quest
Indiana Vital Records Marriage Index, 1850–1920	Contains records from 68 counties inventoried by the Works Progress Administration.	Heritage Quest
Indiana Vital Records, Selected Counties	220,000 records from 84 counties.	Ancestry.com
Iowa Vital Records, Marriages 1835–1900	Covers 52 counties; 164,020 records.	Ancestry.com
Kentucky Vital Records, Marriages, 1780–1920	212,000 records from 75 of 120 counties.	Ancestry.com
Kentucky Vital Records, Deaths, 1911–1993	Statewide coverage; over 2.5 million records.	Ancestry.com
Louisiana Marriage Index, 1718–1925	Lists 570,000 individuals; Does not contain records from every county.	Genealogy.com
Maine Marriage Index, 1743–1891	Lists 230,000 individuals; Does not contain records from every county.	Genealogy.com
Maryland Marriage Index, 1655–1850	Lists 258,000 individuals; Does not contain records from every county.	Genealogy.com
Maryland, North Carolina, and Virginia Marriage Index, 1624–1915	Collection does not contain every marriage that took place in these locations between 1624 and 1915.	Genealogy.com
Massachusetts Probate, Town, and Vital Records, 1600s–1900s	Lists 160,000 individuals; Does not contain records from every Massachusetts town; record span varies by location.	Genealogy.com
Massachusetts Vital Records, 1690–1890	More than 1,000,000 records from 14 counties.	Ancestry.com
Mayflower Vital Records, Deeds, and Wills, 1600s –1900s	A major resource for descendants of Mayflower families.	Genealogy.com
Michigan Vital Records, Deaths, 1971–1996	Statewide coverage; over 2,000,000 records.	Ancestry.com
Michigan and Wisconsin Marriage Index, 1830–1900	Lists 161,000 individuals; Does not contain every marriage that took place in these locations between 1830 and 1900.	Genealogy.com

Title	Remarks	Publisher
Mississippi & Florida Marriage Index, 1800–1900	Lists 191,000 individuals; Does not contain every marriage that took place in these locations between 1800–1900.	Genealogy.com
Missouri Vital Records, Deaths from Selected Counties and Years	140,000 records from 87 counties.	Ancestry.com
Missouri Vital Records, Marriages, 1767–1900	115,000 records from 90 counties.	Ancestry.com
Missouri Vital Records Suite	Contains 140,000 death records and 115,000 marriage records. Website lists counties covered in this collection.	Ancestry.com
New York Marriage Index #2, 1740s–1880s	Does not contain records from every county; date span varies by county.	Genealogy.com
North Carolina Marriage Index, 1850–1900	Lists 126,000 individuals; Does not contain records for every county.	Genealogy.com
Ohio Marriage Index, 1789–1850	Lists 607,000 individuals, excluding Fulton and Monroe counties.	Genealogy.com
Ohio Vital Records #1, 1790s – 1870s	Lists 93,000 individuals; Does not contain records for every county.	Genealogy.com
Ohio Vital Records #2, 1750s–1880s	Lists 70,000 individuals from 76 of 88 counties.	Genealogy.com
Ohio Vital Records, Marriages Selected Counties	302,430 records from 14 counties.	Ancestry.com
Oregon Vital Records, Deaths 1903–1998	Statewide, 1.4 million records.	Ancestry.com
Pennsylvania Vital Records, 1700s –1800s	Lists 87,000 individuals published originally in the Pennsylvania Magazine of History and Biography and the Pennsylvania Genealogical Magazine.	Genealogy.com
Rhode Island Vital Records, 1636–1930	Over 900,000 birth, marriage and death records.	Ancestry.com
Selected Areas of New York Marriage Index, 1639–1916	Lists 216,000 individuals; collection does not contain every marriage that took place in New York during those years.	Genealogy.com
South Carolina: Records and Reference	Excellent collection of marriages and deaths abstracted from South Carolina newspapers and other printed sources.	Ancestry.com
Southeastern Pennsylvania Birth Index, 1690–1800	Lists 476,000 individuals found in the registers of 213 churches, meetings, and pastoral records. Contents originally published in the 13 volume set, Pennsylvania Births.	Genealogy.com
Tennessee Marriage Records, 1787–1866	Lists 278,000 individuals who married in 18 counties in Middle Tennessee; originally compiled by Edithe Whitley. Dates vary by county.	Genealogy.com
Tennessee Vital Records, Marriages from Selected Counties and Years	168,272 records form 36 counties.	Ancestry.com
Texas Marriage Index, 1850–1900	Lists 272,000 individuals; does not contain records from every county; date span varies by county.	Genealogy.com
Texas Vital Records, Deaths, 1964–1998	Over 3.9 million records statewide.	Ancestry.com
Texas Vital Records, Marriages, 1824–1900	147,900 names from 90 counties.	Ancestry.com
United States Marriage Index, 1691–1850	Lists 1,169,074 names; dates vary by state (Alabama, Arkansas, California, Georgia, Illinois, Indiana, Iowa, Kentucky, Louisiana, Michigan, Minnesota, Mississippi, Missouri, North Carolina, Oregon, Tennessee, Texas, Virginia, and Washington, D.C.	Genealogy.com
U.S. and International Marriage Records, 1340–1980	Lists 1,383,00 individuals from all fifty United States and thirty-two different countries; compiled by Bill Yates. Very incomplete.	Genealogy.com
Virginia Vital Records, Marriages, 1670–1929	852,000 names from 80 of 94 counties.	Ancestry.com
Virginia Vital Records, Births, 1656–1896	Contains 53 databases, 317 records from 21 counties.	Ancestry.com
Virginia Vital Records, Deaths, 1660–1896	73,000 records from Chesterfield, Clarke, Culpeper, Floyd, Prince Edward, Prince William, Rockingham, and Washington counties.	Ancestry.com
Virginia Vital Records Suite Virginia Vital Records: Births 1656–1896 Virginia Vital Records: Marriages 1670–1929 Virginia Vital Records: Deaths, 1660–1896	Births: 317,000 records from a variety of sources. Marriages: 426,000 records from 80 of 94 counties. Deaths: 73,000 records from 10 counties.	Ancestry.com
Virginia Vital Records #1, 1600s–1800s	Indexed images from these publications: Virginia Vital Records, Virginia Marriage Records, Virginia Will Records, Virginia Land Records, Virginia Military Records, Virginia Tax Records Database of records from Virginia Magazine of History and Biography; William and Mary College Quarterly; and Tyler's Quarterly.	Genealogy.com

Table 13-3. Statewide Marriage Indexes and Records from the Family History Library's Vital Records Collection as of March 2006

State	Marriage Index	Marriage Records	Comments
Alabama	1936–1959	1936–1992	Indexed by year
Arkansas	By county	By county	See FHL catalog for county of interest.
California	1960–1985		
Los Angeles County		1850–1905	Applications.
	1856–1950	1856–1944	Applications, Licenses, Certificates
	1851–1920	1851–1924	Certificates
		1894–1905	Birth Cards
San Diego		1850–1866	Includes mission records
San Francisco	1913–1915	1913–1915	Licenses for city and county
	1913–1915	1913–1915	Affidavits for licenses for city and county
	1904–1906	1860–1973	Re-recorded marriages
Colorado	1900–1939; 1975–1992		Card Index; no index 1940–1974; no corresponding records.
Connecticut	By town	By town	Large collection of indexes and records.
Delaware	1680–1934		Card Index
		1861–1861	Bonds
		1889–1894	Licenses
District of Columbia	1811–1870	1870–1929; 1933–1950	
Florida	1927–1969	By county	Indexed by year
		1928–1950	Licenses and certificates
Georgia	1964–1992		No corresponding records.
	By county	By county	Large collection of 19th- and 20th-century indexes and records. See catalog for individual counties.
Hawaii	1826–1910		Hawaii, Maui, Kauai, Molokai
	1884–1896 Grooms, A–Z	1884–1896	Hawaii, Molokai, Oahu, Kauai
	1884–1894 Brides, A–O		
	1909–1949	1909–1925	
Idaho	By county	By county	See FHL catalog for individual counties; years vary.
Illinois	By county	By county	See FHL catalog for individual counties; years vary widely according to county.
Cook County	1871–1916	1871–1920	From 1894, marriage licenses for the city of Chicago maintained separately. Within each sequence of 100 numbers, Cook County licenses come first, followed by licenses from Chicago.
Indiana	By county	By county	See catalog for individual counties; years vary widely according to county.
Iowa	By county	By county	See FHL catalog for county of interest.
Kansas	By county	By county	See catalog for individual counties; years vary widely according to county.
Kentucky	1973–1995		Grooms and brides indexes; no corresponding records.
		1874–1875	Marriage returns by county.
Louisiana	By county	By county	See FHL catalog for county of interest.
Orleans Parish		1807–1815	
		1870–1942	Indexes to ledgers guide users to license and certificate number.
Maine	Pre-1892		
	1895–1953		Bride's Index only.
	1892–1907		
	1908–1922		
Massachusetts	1841–1905	1844–1895	
	1906–1910	1906–1910	
Michigan	By county	By county	See FHL catalog for county of interest.
Minnesota	By county	By county	See FHL catalog for county of interest.

State	Marriage Index	Marriage Records	Comments
Mississippi	By county	By county	See FHL catalog for county of interest.
Missouri	By county	By county	See FHL catalog for county of interest.
Montana	By county	By county	See FHL catalog for county of interest.
Nebraska	By county	By county	Dates covered vary by county. See catalog for individual counties.
Nevada	1968–1991		Index only; no corresponding records.
	By county	By county	See FHL catalog for county of interest.
New Hampshire	1640–1900		
	1938–1947	1938–1947	
		1677–1937	Corrections and additions to records only.
New Jersey		1711–1878	Arranged by first letter of surname.
		1727–1878	Bonds by first letter of surname, then by date.
	1848–1864	1848–1900	Indexes by county.
New York			
New York City	1784–1910		Indexes only; no records.
	1839–1887		Few marriages for 1829–1847; no records between January 1875 to August 1876.
	1881–1965		Index to births in all six Boroughs of New York.
	1898–1937	1897–1938	Grooms index only; Bronx Borough
	1866–1937	1866–1937	Manhattan Borough
	1897–1937	1897–1932	Grooms and Brides Card Index, Richmond Borough
North Carolina	By county	By county	Large collection of 19th and 20th century indexes and records. See catalog for individual counties.
Ohio		By county By county	See FHL catalog for county of interest.
Oklahoma			
Indian Territory		Dates Vary	Marriages of White settlers and Native Americans in various districts within Indian Territory. Microfilm copies of records from the Oklahoma Historical Society.
Oregon	1906–1924		Index only; no corresponding records.
	By county	By county	Large collection of 19th- and 20th-century indexes and records. See catalog for individual counties.
Pennsylvania			FHL collection of county vital records generally covers only the years 1894–1906 and varies according to county.
Allegheny County	1885–1925	1885–1905; 1937–1950	
Pittsburgh	1875–1885	1875–1909	Ministers' returns of marriages.
Dauphin County		1885–1950	Includes Harrisburg; each volume indexed separately.
Philadelphia County			
Philadelphia City	1885–1916	1885–1915	Affidavit of Applicants for Marriage License
		1860–1885	
		1857–1938	Marriages performed by the mayors of Philadelphia.
		1880–1908	Magistrate's Court No. 9 only.
Rhode Island	1853–1900	1853–1900	Micro–reproduction of computer printout at the Rhode Island Department of Health.
Tennessee	1837–1937	1919–1974	Not all records forward to the state; check country records for records not found in this collection.
	By county	By county	Large collection of 19th- and 20th-century indexes and records. See catalog for individual counties.
Texas		1966–2000	CD-ROM collection.
Utah	By county	By county	Record coverage dates approximately 1885–1966. See FHL catalog for county of interest.
Vermont		1909–1954	Marriages arranged alphabetically.
Virginia		1853–1935	Arranged by county.
West Virginia	By county	By county	See FHL catalog for county of interest.
Wisconsin	By county	By county	Marriages through 1907 with indexes. See catalog for individual counties.

private distributors. They vary in usefulness. Some collections improve upon a poor original record by adding details about a couple and their families. However, the quality of such a volume always depends on the skill of the transcriber in reading illegible handwriting and damaged records. Because a transcribed copy rarely includes all the information contained in the original record, you should also look at the original entry whenever possible.

The following is an example of the alphabetized and printed marriage records kept by two brothers who were justices of the peace in Washington County, Pennsylvania: Squires Isaac and Joseph F. Mayes. They married more than 3,000 couples, most of whom eloped to the Mayes' border town from West Virginia and Ohio because Pennsylvania did not require a marriage license.

DEGARMO, MARTHA
to John Stiger
both of Triadelphia,
Ohio Co., WV
14 January 1871
DEGARMO, MARTHA E.
to Eli Johnston
both of Ohio Co., WV
17 June 1882

—

DELANEY, JONATHAN
of Wheeling, Ohio Co., WV
to Rosabella Faulkner
of Belton, Marshall Co., WV
5 November 1865
DELANY, William C.
to Mary Virginia Crow
both of Wheeling, Ohio Co., (W)VA
24 August 1862[3]

Genealogical periodicals published by state and county genealogical societies also include marriage records. You can find large collections of these periodicals in many local libraries, or you can receive your own copies of such publications by joining the societies.

Newspapers have printed marriage announcements and engagements for decades. These articles often contain such information as the names of the parents of the bride and groom, place of residence after the marriage, and names of those in attendance at the wedding.

Special Problems Encountered When Using Marriage Records

An estimated thirty percent of the marriage records in this country are incomplete. Many marriage returns were never submitted to civil authorities, and countless others have been lost. Hamilton County, Ohio, which recorded marriages for Cincinnati, is an interesting example. Many records were lost in a courthouse fire. Years later the WPA copied those that survived, combining applications, licenses, and returns and then indexing them. Local genealogists reconstructed some from ministers' daybooks, original certificates, and newspaper accounts. The DAR also collected marriage records from family and local sources. Because each of these collections came from different sources, the researcher must check them all; even so, some marriages will not have been recorded. Careful checking of all versions becomes important upon considering that Cincinnati, like many American cities, was a "Gretna Green" (a no-questions-asked marriage locale in Scotland) for couples from up and down the Ohio River and from a wide circle of counties in Indiana and Kentucky, as well as Ohio. Therefore, if there is no record in the nearby county where a couple may have lived, chances are good that the entry may be found among the Cincinnati marriage records, even though they are incomplete.

Marriage records are often inaccurate. Brides and grooms have sometimes deliberately provided falsified information. To reduce their workloads, clerks often entered the date of the marriage at the time the license was issued instead of waiting for the return. Thus, marriage information should be compared with other facts known about an individual. Additional research may be necessary to resolve discrepancies.

Spelling variants are also a problem in marriage records. Many clerks did not ask couples how their names were spelled but wrote them based on their pronunciation instead. All possible spellings of a surname should be checked before assuming that a couple is not in a given record.

Many marriage records are virtually illegible due to faded entries, damaged ledger books, poor handwriting, and poorly microfilmed originals. Published marriage records can assist in clarifying unreadable entries. If poor microfilming is the problem, contact the county or town and request a photocopy or certified copy of the original. Sometimes more than one type of marriage record can be obtained.

If a marriage record is not on file for an ancestor, other records can reveal an approximate date of marriage. The 1900 and 1910 U.S. Federal Censuses list the number of years a couple had been married. The 1930 U.S. Federal Census shows marital condition and age at first marriage. The marriage date may be calculated from any or all these entries. The 1910 Civil War pension application files contain marriage information. If a veteran's widow filed for a pension, she had to produce proof of the marriage by obtaining an affidavit from the appropriate minister or civil authorities, supplying a copy of the marriage certificate, or sending sworn statements from persons who could testify to the marriage date and place.

Births and Deaths in Public Records

Many British and European countries began keeping birth and death records nationally in the nineteenth century. Before then, churches maintained registers of christenings and burials, and colonial settlers in America brought British laws and customs with them. Thus, churches were initially the sole keepers of vital records; ministers in many colonies were required by law to report christenings and burials to civil authorities. In some areas, consequently, these events are recorded in both civil and church records. Eventually, some colonies, primarily those in New England, passed laws requiring local town or county clerks to maintain records of births and deaths. Massachusetts had the most comprehensive laws pertaining to birth and death registration, and many of its early records have been published.

During the nineteenth century, England and other European countries instituted national registration systems, primarily to compile medical statistics as information on epidemic diseases. The United States did not implement the practice until much later. The majority of the states did not require registration until the first quarter of the twentieth century, and then the responsibility for registering births and deaths was left to the individual states rather than the federal government, accounting for different starting dates and differences in the data called for. The earliest cities to require civil registration were New Orleans (1790), Boston (1848), Philadelphia (1860), Pittsburgh (1870), and Baltimore (1875). Fourteen states also initiated registration before 1880:

Delaware:	1860	New Jersey:	1878
Florida:	1865	New York:	1880
Hawaii:	1850	Rhode Island:	1853
Iowa:	1880	Vermont:	1770
Massachusetts:	1841	Virginia:	1853
Michigan:	1867	Wisconsin:	1876
New Hampshire:	1840	Washington, D.C.:	1871

The National Center for Health Statistics publishes *Where to Write for Vital Records—Births, Deaths, Marriages, and Divorces* online at <www.cdc.gov/nchs/howto/w2w/w2welcom.htm>. It lists, for each state, the dates on which the records began, the types of records kept, the cost of certified copies, and the address of the records custodian in each state. The fees listed in it are subject to frequent increase. It takes six to eight weeks on average for state offices to respond to requests; however, some states may take up to six months. Many states will expedite orders and have contracted with VitalChek (<www.vitalchek.com>) to offer that service. Expect to pay extra fees and express postage costs for this service.

Even in areas with early registration laws, enforcement was haphazard, particularly in rural and frontier areas. West Virginia is a good example of the incompleteness of early vital records. The initial law requiring registration was passed by the Virginia legislature to become effective in 1853, when West Virginia was still part of Virginia. The exact extent of citizen compliance is difficult to estimate, but professional genealogists know that many births and deaths were not registered. Property owners were more likely to register the birth of a slave than the birth of their own children because registering a slave was a protection of personal property rights. Sometimes a couple registered one or more children but not all. Undoubtedly the difficulty of traveling long distances over rough terrain contributed to the lack of compliance.

Even when early vital records are incomplete, you should examine them. Of course, you are not limited to vital records alone for birth and death information. A natural beginning for research is a survey of available family records. Family Bibles, family record books, journals, diaries, and letters often note births and deaths of family members. (For a discussion of some sources of birth information found in an average family, see chapter 1, "The Foundations of Family History Research.")

During the period when civil authorities did not require vital records, births and deaths were regularly recorded in the family Bible among literate, religious families. These entries often supply the only complete birth and death dates for individuals who were born or died before the twentieth century, although other forms of family records sometimes contain mention of births and deaths as they occurred. Various groups of the Daughters of the American Revolution (DAR) have compiled many volumes of family Bible records, frequently including evaluations of the accuracy and authenticity of the records. The DAR collections are available at the DAR Library in Washington, D.C., and in libraries of state and local DAR groups throughout the United States (see appendix D, "Hereditary and Lineage Organizations"). The Genealogical Society of Utah has microfilmed the DAR main collection and many state publications; they are available through the Family History Centers of the Family History Library.

Other government and legal documents also contain birth and death information: New England town records, coroners' reports, probate records, land records, mortality schedules, and military records, among others. These sources, including family records, are discussed in other chapters, so mention of them in this chapter will be limited.

A coroner's report is issued when an inquest is held to investigate unusual or unknown circumstances related to a death. When the inquest is complete, the report includes the causes of death, the autopsy findings, where held, testimony about the circumstances existing at the time of the death, and the findings of the coroner's jury. Coroner's reports are public records available for use by researchers, and they may be requested from the state, county, or city coroner's office. Not all deaths of unknown or suspicious nature result in a coroner's inquest; but when there is evidence that an ancestor died in an unusual manner or was murdered, coroners' records should be examined. There are medical examiners (as coroners are more frequently called today) at city, county, and state levels, and their records may be found at all three levels. (See chapter 4, "Business, Institution, and Employment Records.")

Probate records can also contain birth and death information. In them, the exact date of death may be listed for the individual whose estate is in probate; the names and dates of birth of his or her minor heirs may also be found in the record. These records are usually found in the probate court or the court having probate jurisdiction in a town or county. They are also public records and are available to the genealogist upon request to the probate clerk. (See chapter 7, "Court Records.")

Court minutes seem to be a "catch-all" for miscellaneous items recorded to give them public credibility. For example, John Wills, clerk of the Council for West Jersey, an administrative court, entered a complete list of his brothers and sisters followed by his own children at the end of his minute book, vol. 3 (18 April 1712 to 6 February 1721/22), just before the index. Thus, the clerk made his family vital records a matter of public record.

Occasionally, land and property records contain birth and death information. Sometimes the death date of a person leaving property to heirs appears in a deed executed after his or her death. Birth information is sometimes included in applications for public lands or homesteads filed with the federal government. (See chapter 10, "Land and Tax Records.")

Mortality schedules were included as part of the decennial (every ten years) census enumerations between 1850 and 1900. These schedules give the name, age, sex, color, occupation, birthplace, month and year of death, cause of death, number of days ill, the attending physician, and other details for persons who died within the year prior to the taking of the census. The 1890 and 1900 mortality schedules were destroyed. To locate those still in existence, see chapter 5, "Census Records." The Genealogical Society of Utah has microfilmed a large number of mortality schedules. They are available at the Family History Library and through its Family History Centers. Use an online search engine to find searchable databases of these mortality schedules.

Military pension files also contain valuable birth and death records. The date and place of birth of the veteran, the dates of birth of his children, and the date and place of birth of the veteran's widow (if she received a pension) are included in the file in some cases. (See chapter 11, "Military Records.")

Birth and death records are also found in church records, such as parish registers, which list christenings, burials, births, and deaths. Some churches took special church census enumerations that are of use to the researcher. Some ministers and evangelists kept vital records for their members in personal journals and diaries, and some churches have established historical societies or departments to collect and maintain official church membership records. The headquarters of the affiliate churches ordinarily maintain the records, but some may be found in local church offices. Inquire at a local church about the existence and location of the records of interest. (See chapter 6, "Church Records.") Personal records of ministers and other church officials can be found by consulting the *National Union Catalog of Manuscript Collections (NUCMC)*. (See chapter 3, "General References and Guides," for more information on indexes.)

As the twenty-first century progresses, insurance and business records will play an increasingly important role in establishing genealogical facts. An excellent example of such records is Connie Bell's and Vernell Walker's *Union Pacific Railroad Life Insurance Claims Data*.[4] These alphabetically arranged records contain vital records and other documents supporting insurance claims. The compilers attempted to abstract all information of genealogical importance. Some of the details include name of the deceased, Social Security number, sex, race, occupation, date and place of birth, address, date of marriage, date and cause of death, place of burial, parents' names, and spouse's name. This collection is available on microfilm through the Family History Library.

Other insurance companies and businesses have compiled similar records, but researchers are just beginning to locate and abstract them. Check repository catalogs periodically and inquire at national and local genealogical societies about "works in progress" to determine if a source of interest is in the making. (See also chapter 4, "Research in Business, Institution, and Organization Records".)

Military records are discussed at length in chapter 11, but note particularly that vital records information appears in such filings as World War I Selective Service Registration, benefits applications, such as those for pensions of admittance to veteran's home.

Fewer vital records exist for the period prior to 1900, so researchers must search more obscure records on the chance of finding the details needed to identify people and document relationships. An example that is an excellent source for pre-1900 vital information is the *Gentleman's Magazine,* a periodical published in Great Britain that contained information about people from the United States, Jamaica, Antigua, Barbados, and the West Indies. The periodical published columns listing births, marriages, and deaths of British citizens at home and abroad. See David Dobson's *American Vital Records from the* Gentleman's Magazine, *1731–1868*.[5]

Private sources, such as newspapers, morticians' records, hospital and doctors' records, business and employment records, and local published histories also contain birth and death information. Some of these records are also discussed in detail in other chapters.

Contents of Birth Records

Early birth records gave little information beyond the name of the child, date and place of birth, and parents' names. Some localities listed only the name of the father—particularly in early New England town and church records, as the following example from the town records of Simsbury, Connecticut, shows (an 'ſ' appears where appropriate).

SIMSBURY RECORDS. 119

James the first Son of James Tullar was Born the firſt Day of January A : D : 1737/8

Eli Tullar Son of James Tullar was Born the: 14th Day of february A : D 1740/41:

[226] Jerusha the Daughter of Return Holcomb was Born aprill the : 3 : anno : Dom : 1734 :

Stephen the Sone of Return Holcomb was born September the : 23 : A : D : 1736 :

Timothy Case the Son of Richard Case was born the 2nd Day of February A : D 1759.

Lucy the Daughter of Gillet Adams was born feb : 14th A : D : 1731/2 :

Anne Granger the Daughter of George Granger was born July the : 19th : 1732 :

Rhoda the Daughter of George Grainger was born Aprill : 26th A : D : 1735 :

Simsbury Connecticut Birth, Marriage and Deaths (Hartford: Albert C. Bates, 1898), 119.

Early birth records are distressingly sparse, with a heavy concentration found in New England only. In the colonial period, church records that can serve as birth records were kept in Pennsylvania, New York, New Jersey, and Virginia, with Virginia trailing far behind the others. Quaker records for all of the states mentioned previously are far superior to most others, providing the exact dates of birth and death for members of that faith. They have been well preserved; many are included in William Wade Hinshaw's *Encyclopedia of American Quaker Genealogy*, available in most genealogical libraries in the United States.[6] These volumes cover the monthly meeting records of the Carolinas, Tennessee, New Jersey, New York, North Carolina, Ohio, Pennsylvania, and Virginia. Willard Heiss has expanded coverage with a seventh volume for Indiana, but it is not on the CD-ROM. Heiss' printed volume was published by the Indiana Historical Society in 1972.[7]

By the mid-nineteenth century, birth records in the United States began to include more detailed information. For example, beginning in 1853, some Virginia and West Virginia county birth registers included the mother's maiden name instead of her married name—obviously helpful information in identifying the maternal ancestry of a child.

Early birth records can be obtained from town or county clerks in the area in which an ancestor was born. These records, too early to fall under the jurisdiction of recent privacy laws, are public records. However, when writing for a birth or death record, state your relationship to the ancestor of interest in case the clerk requires it. Your inquiry should indicate the specific record desired; give the ancestor's full name and as much identifying information as possible (especially if the ancestor has a common surname). Providing the exact date of birth, if known, or an estimated five-year birth period, will help clerks find the right record. The average fee for birth or death records at the county level is seven dollars; send that amount with your request. If additional funds are required, the clerk will either request the balance in advance or send the material and ask you to forward the balance. Most jurisdictions will search their records for a five-year period, but few will search further unless specifically requested to do so.

The Genealogical Society of Utah has microfilmed birth records of thousands of towns and counties throughout the United States, concentrating heavily upon the states east of the Mississippi River. These microfilms are available at the Family History Library and upon request through its Family History Centers.

The printed vital records of New England towns are also available at the Family History Library; those that have been microfilmed can be borrowed through the Family History Centers. Many state and local historical society libraries have copies, and many of the larger metropolitan city libraries with genealogical collections, such as the New York Public Library and the Los Angeles Public Library, also have copies of the printed records. The town records of Massachusetts have been published on CD-ROM as well by the Genealogical Publishing Company. The Holbrook Research Institute has microfiche copies for the vital records in Massachusetts towns that were never printed; a price list is available on request (see Archive Publishing at <www.archivepublishing.com>).

Even though births were not widely recorded during the early years of America's existence, those records that do exist may provide the only source of exact birth data for your ancestors. They should always be searched.

Modern birth records (post-1910) are maintained by the states. They are extremely valuable, but many researchers, learning birth information from home sources, fail to obtain birth certificates. This reluctance is most unfortunate and can result in an inaccurate or incomplete family genealogy. Modern birth records contain much more information than earlier records. Although birth certificates vary from state to state, most of them share much information in common.

Figure 13-9 is a birth certificate that is fairly representative of those compiled in most states. It contains the following information about the child and its parents:

Child

Name
Birthplace
Date of birth
Sex
Hospital
Time of birth

Father

Name
Race
Birthplace
Age
Occupation

Mother

Name
Race
Birthplace
Age
Occupation
Residence
Term of residence in the community
Term of pregnancy
Marital status
Number of other living children
Number of other deceased children
Number of children born dead

Most modern birth records are protected by the privacy laws passed by the federal government during recent years. However, some states have allowed microfilming of births after masking entries for illegitimate and stillborn births.

Despite such gaps, these records are obviously useful. Most states require a request form to be completed before they will issue a copy or abstract of a birth certificate. Such a form will often request more information than you have, but you should fill it out as completely as possible, estimating dates and places as accurately as you can. Some states will search more than a five-year period, while others limit the search to a single, approximate year of birth. If the record cannot be found in the year listed, a few states refund the fee; most do not. Each request should state your relationship to the individual and the purpose for which you will use the data. Family history and genealogical research purposes are acceptable reasons in most states.

A rarely used form of birth record is the delayed birth certificate. When Social Security benefits were instituted in 1937, individuals claiming benefits had to document their births even if their states of residence had not required birth registration at the time of their births. The 1880 and 1900 U.S. Federal Census enumerations were partially or fully indexed to help provide this documentation. Another method was to file evidence as part of an application for a delayed birth certificate.

The individual applying had to submit a petition to the county court stating his or her name, address, date and place of birth; father's name, race, and place of birth; and evidence to support the facts presented. The evidence could be in the form of a baptismal certificate, Bible record, school record, affidavit from

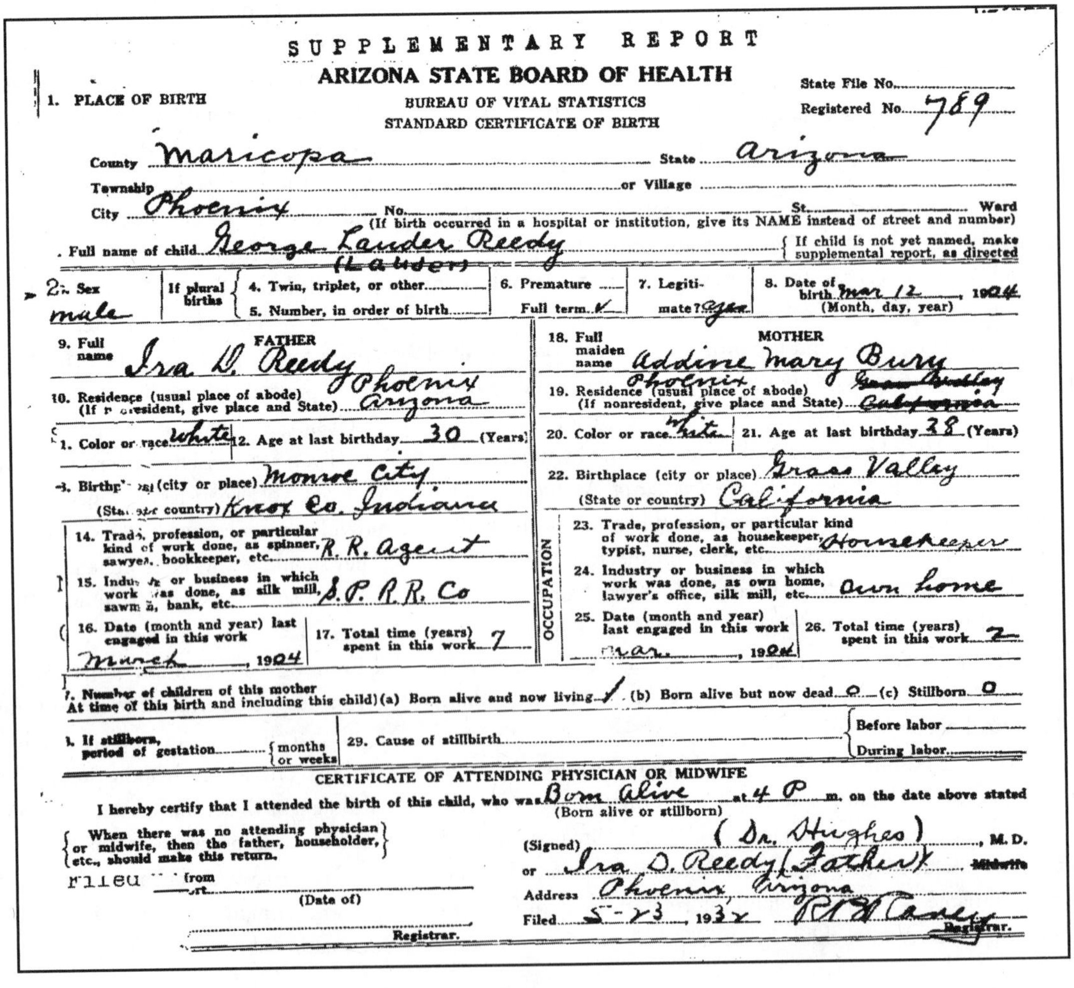

Figure 13-9. An Arizona birth certificate for George Lander Reedy.

SUPPLEMENTARY REPORT
ARIZONA STATE BOARD OF HEALTH
BUREAU OF VITAL STATISTICS
STANDARD CERTIFICATE OF BIRTH

1. PLACE OF BIRTH — State File No. ______ Registered No. 789

County Maricopa State Arizona
Township ______ or Village ______
City Phoenix No. ______ St. ______ Ward
(If birth occurred in a hospital or institution, give its NAME instead of street and number)

Full name of child George Lander Reedy (Lauder) { If child is not yet named, make supplemental report, as directed

2. Sex male | 3. If plural births | 4. Twin, triplet, or other ______ 5. Number, in order of birth ______ | 6. Premature ______ Full term ✓ | 7. Legitimate? yes | 8. Date of birth Mar 12, 1904 (Month, day, year)

FATHER

9. Full name Ira D. Reedy
10. Residence (usual place of abode) (If nonresident, give place and State) Phoenix Arizona
11. Color or race white 12. Age at last birthday 30 (Years)
13. Birthplace (city or place) Monroe City (State or country) Knox Co. Indiana
14. Trade, profession, or particular kind of work done, as spinner, sawyer, bookkeeper, etc. R. R. Agent
15. Industry or business in which work was done, as silk mill, saw mill, bank, etc. S. P. R.R. Co
16. Date (month and year) last engaged in this work March, 1904
17. Total time (years) spent in this work 7

MOTHER

18. Full maiden name Addine Mary Bury
19. Residence (usual place of abode) (If nonresident, give place and State) Phoenix ~~Grass Valley California~~
20. Color or race White 21. Age at last birthday 28 (Years)
22. Birthplace (city or place) Grass Valley (State or country) California
23. Trade, profession, or particular kind of work done, as housekeeper, typist, nurse, clerk, etc. Housekeeper
24. Industry or business in which work was done, as own home, lawyer's office, silk mill, etc. own home
25. Date (month and year) last engaged in this work Mar., 1904
26. Total time (years) spent in this work 2

27. Number of children of this mother At time of this birth and including this child) (a) Born alive and now living 1 (b) Born alive but now dead 0 (c) Stillborn 0

28. If stillborn, period of gestation ______ months or weeks | 29. Cause of stillbirth ______ | Before labor ______ During labor ______

CERTIFICATE OF ATTENDING PHYSICIAN OR MIDWIFE

I hereby certify that I attended the birth of this child, who was Born alive at 4 P m. on the date above stated (Born alive or stillborn)

When there was no attending physician or midwife, then the father, householder, etc., should make this return.

(Signed) (Dr. Hughes) M. D.
or Ira D. Reedy (Father) Midwife
Address Phoenix, Arizona
Filed 5-23, 1932 R H Casey Registrar.

Filed ______ (from ______) (Date of) ______ Registrar.

the attending physician or midwife, application for an insurance policy, birth certificate of a child, copy of an application for a Social Security account number, or an affidavit from a person having definite knowledge of the facts.

Delayed birth certificates list vital information abstracted from the supporting evidence. Most states have delayed birth records, some of which are indexed and easily usable. Some delayed birth records have been filed for individuals born as early as 1840. These records are usually filed in the county where the individual applied—not in the county of birth. Though relatively uncommon, these records provide information about individuals and their parents for periods when vital records were not widely kept. The records and testimony used as supporting evidence for the document can lead you to other information sources and also show which relatives were living at the time the certificate was applied for.

Families in transition when children were born present a research problem. Often, families moving when a child was born waited just long enough for the mother to recover and then moved to an adjoining town or state, where the infant's birth was recorded. In such cases, if you move back in time from the known to the unknown, you will know where the birth was recorded when you may know nothing of where the birth occurred—so check the obvious; find out if the birth was recorded after the fact. The resulting document will give you the actual place of birth, and you can then make searches there also.

Contents of Death Records

Early death records in the United States provide little more than the name of the deceased, the date of death, and the place of death. Burial records contain basically the same information. Occasionally the record will list the name of the deceased's spouse. These early records appear in town, county, and church records, most extensively in New England, where they were kept as late as 1900.

Death records of the nineteenth century are more detailed in many jurisdictions. They often include the name of the deceased, date, place, and cause of death, age at the time of death, place of birth, parents' names, occupation, name of spouse, name of the person giving the information, and the informant's relationship to the deceased. Race is listed in some records. Some southern states also note if the deceased was a slave.

Modern death records (post-1910), though comparatively recent, are steadily increasing in value. People are living longer, and death records often provide information about birth as well as death.

Modern death certificates have not been standardized throughout the United States, but, like birth certificates, most of them contain the same types of information. Figure 13-10, a death certificate from Oklahoma, is representative of most contemporary death certificates. It includes the deceased's name, sex, race, date of death, age at the time of death, place of death, date of birth, place of birth, marital status, name of spouse, Social Security number, occupation, residence, father's name, mother's name, cause of death, and place of burial. Records from other states generally provide the birthplace of the deceased's parents. The Social Security number is not always included, but, when it is, it can be invaluable because other records (subject to right-of-privacy laws) may be accessible if you have the Social Security number.

As any experienced researcher knows, death records are only as accurate as the knowledge of the person who provided the information. Many informants are unaware of the name of parents or are unsure about dates and places of birth. Always try to find additional information about parents and dates and places of birth whenever possible.

In response to a request, some states will supply a photocopy of the certificate filed at the time of death, while some make a transcript of the basic information on a preprinted form, certifying it as a true copy. A photocopy is preferable. Not only does it eliminate the danger of errors in transcription; it will also include more data. The clues of cemetery, undertaker, informant, residence at time of death, and other details that take you from the death certificate to other records are found only on the original.

The following is an example. When genealogist Harry L. Carle first requested the death certificate of his grandfather Harry Chester Lee, he requested a certification of death abstracted from the death register (figure 13-11).

Harry received this certification with a request for payment. He sent a check and a request for the original certificate, explaining what information he was looking for. Note that it did not need to be certified ("sealed"). The court clerk's reply provided the name of the physician, L.E. Hedgecock, and the undertaker, Ray A. Fox. The clerk also suggested writing the Department of Vital Statistics in Des Moines and provided the address.

When Harry pursued his request to the Des Moines office, he received a photocopy of the original certificate filed with the state (figure 13-12). It was obviously worth the extra correspondence to get this certificate. From it, Harry discovered that Harry Lee had lived in Hampton only six years before his death; that his wife, Sylvia Smith Lee, the informant, was fifty-six years old; that Harry had been born in Chicago; and that he had been a stage worker. It also gave his parents' names and places of birth, the date and place of burial, the attending physicians' names, and the fact that Harry Lee had suffered from heart disease for about five years before it proved fatal.

Death records are valuable corroborating evidence for family traditions handed down generation after generation without verification. They also help distinguish between two or more people with the same name. For example, one prominent Texas

ATTENDING PHYSICIAN
CERTIFICATE OF DEATH
STATE OF OKLAHOMA · DEPARTMENT OF HEALTH

LOCAL REGISTRAR'S FILE NO. 138 — STATE FILE NO. 011047

DECEASED NAME (First, Middle, Last): 1. Charles Henry West
DATE OF DEATH (Month, Day, Year): 2. May 22, 1978
SEX: 3. Male
RACE: 4. White
AGE Last Birthday (Years): 5a. 91
UNDER 1 YEAR (Mos, Days): 5b.
UNDER 1 DAY (Hours, Min): 5c.
DATE OF BIRTH (Month, Day, Year): 6. Febr. 27, 1887
COUNTY OF DEATH: Rogers
CITY, TOWN, OR LOCATION OF DEATH: 7b. Claremore
INSIDE CITY LIMITS: 7c. XX Yes / No
HOSPITAL OR OTHER INSTITUTION: 7d. Claremore Health Center
STATE OF BIRTH (If not in U.S.A., Name Country): 8.
CITIZEN OF WHAT COUNTRY: 9. USA
Married / Never Married / Widowed / Divorced: 10. Widowed XX
SURVIVING SPOUSE (If wife, give maiden name): 11.
SOCIAL SECURITY NUMBER: 12. 440-20-1707
USUAL OCCUPATION (Give kind of work done during most of working life, even if retired): 13a. Building Contractor
KIND OF BUSINESS OR INDUSTRY: 13b. Home Builder
RESIDENCE – STATE: 14a. Oklahoma
COUNTY: 14b. Rogers
CITY, TOWN, OR LOCATION: 14c. Claremore
INSIDE CITY LIMITS: 14d. Yes XX / No
STREET AND NUMBER: 14e. 600 S. Choctaw
FATHER – NAME (First, Middle, Last): 15. William Andrew West
MOTHER – MAIDEN NAME (First, Middle, Last): 16. Laura Stewart
INFORMANT – NAME: 17a.
MAILING ADDRESS (Street or R.F.D. No., City or Town, State, Zip): 17b.

MEDICAL CERTIFICATION

PART I. DEATH WAS CAUSED BY (Enter only one cause per line for (a), (b), and (c))
18 CAUSE OF DEATH — IMMEDIATE CAUSE
Condition if any, which gave rise to immediate cause(s), stating the underlying cause last
(a) Myocardial Infraction Acute
DUE TO OR AS A CONSEQUENCE OF
(b)
DUE TO OR AS A CONSEQUENCE OF
(c)
Approximate Interval Between onset and Death

PART II. OTHER SIGNIFICANT CONDITIONS (Conditions contributing to death but not related to cause given in part I (a))
AUTOPSY: 19a. Yes / No
IF YES Were findings considered in determining cause of death: 19b. Yes / No

Notice to attending physician: Do not sign this certificate unless you are the physician who attended the deceased for a natural illness—unrelated to injury or poisoning—to which the patient has apparently succumbed, provided that death did not occur while deceased was in penal incarceration or during a therapeutic procedure in which death was not reasonably medically expected. For enumeration of deaths subject to investigation and certification by Medical Examiner, refer to O.S. Title 63, Sec. 938, or contact office of Chief Medical Examiner in Oklahoma City.

CERTIFICATION – PHYSICIAN: 20a. I attended the deceased from 3-15-78 to 5-22-78
And last saw him/her alive on: 20b. 5-22-78
I did/did not view body after death: 20c. did
DEATH OCCURRED AT: 20d. 17:30 M at the place, on the date stated, and to the best of my knowledge, due to the cause(s) stated
CERTIFIER – NAME (Type or Print): 21a. M. E. Gordon, M. D.
SIGNATURE OF CERTIFIER / Degree: 21b. [signature]
DATE SIGNED (Month, Day, Year): 21c. 5-23-78
MAILING ADDRESS – CERTIFIER: 21d. P. O. Box 669, Claremore, Oklahoma 74017
THE DECEDENT was pronounced dead on: 22a. 5-22-78
AT: 22b. 17:30 M
BURIAL, CREMATION, REMOVAL (Specify): 23a. Burial
DATE: 23b. May 25, 1978
CEMETERY OR CREMATORY – NAME: 23c. Welch Cemetery
LOCATION (Crematory or Cemetery) City: 23d. Welch, Oklahoma
FUNERAL HOME NAME AND ADDRESS: Claremore Funeral Home, Inc.
FUNERAL DIRECTOR: 24b. George F. Raper
LOCAL REGISTRAR SIGNATURE: 25a. [signature]
DATE RECD. BY LOCAL REG.: 25b. 5-24-78
DATE RECEIVED BY STATE REGISTRAR: 26. MAY 25 1978

State Department of Health
State of Oklahoma
OKLAHOMA CITY, OKLAHOMA 73152

ROGER C. PIRRONG
STATE REGISTRAR OF VITAL STATISTICS

CERTIFIED COPY MUST HAVE EMBOSSED SEAL

I hereby certify the foregoing to be a true and correct copy, original of which is on file in this office. In testimony whereof, I have hereunto subscribed my name and caused the official seal to be affixed, at Oklahoma City, Oklahoma, this date.

JAN. 24, 1980

Figure 13-10. Certificate of death of Charles Henry West, Oklahoma, 22 May 1978, file number 01147.

STATE OF IOWA,

COUNTY REGISTRAR
Vital Statistics

County of Franklin

CERTIFICATION OF DEATH

NAME OF DECEASED Harry Chester Lee Sex Male

Date of Death November 10, 1940. Place of Death Hampton, Iowa

Date of Birth or Age of Deceased 57 years Date Filed November 1940

Cause of Death Coronary heart disease

I HEREBY CERTIFY that the above information was taken from the Record of Death on file in this office in accordance with the law of Iowa requiring filing of vital records. Recorded in Book 4 Page "L".

Date March 12, 1975. Helen O'Dea
County Registrar and Clerk of District Court

[SEAL] By Carole Dohlman
Deputy Clerk

Figure 13-11. Certificate of death of Harry Chester Lee, 10 November 1940, Franklin, Iowa. In possession of Harry L. Carle, 8035 186th S.W. Edmonds, WA 98020. This and subsequent documents are used with permission.

family gave me its personal files and family sources to produce a family history. Their records included a maternal ancestor named Nettie Green, who was married to Robert Michael. Public records produced a Nettie Green who was also married to a Robert Michael. Thinking they were the same Nettie Green, I extended that family line back two hundred years to the immigrant ancestor. The paternal ancestors were less accommodating; in the process of identifying them, I requested the death certificate of Nettie's husband. It clearly stated that he had married Nettie Bunting. Furthermore, Albert Robert Michael had always used his middle name. His descendants did not even know that he had a different given name. The marriage records supported the death record; Nettie Bunting was indeed the ancestor, and we bade farewell to two hundred years of the Green family.

Death records, both early and modern, can help you identify others related to the decedent. The information provided in the records is usually given to the authorities by a close relative. If the relative is a married daughter, the record will state her married name. Aunts, uncles, in-laws, cousins, and other relatives are listed as informants on death records. Each new name is a clue to the identity of other ancestors that should be pursued.

The death record informant may not have been the person who provided vital statistics to the funeral director or to the cemetery sexton. The death certificate names both the funeral home and the place of burial, so check both the mortician's records and the sexton's records to confirm the information on the death record and to look for additional information not included in the death certificate. Once you know the exact date of death, you can more easily look for an obituary notice in a local newspaper. Obituaries usually at least summarize the deceased's life, sometimes including other towns of residence. They may also list all of the living heirs, as well as the names of parents, brothers, and sisters. Tracking backward with these clues, you can look for other members of the family and additional historical information.

In short, you should routinely request birth and death records for ancestors who were born or who died during the period for which records are available in a particular locale. They are rich in genealogical information and may serve to clarify discrepancies in family records.

Problems with Birth and Death Records

The use of vital records is not without its difficulties. The problem of an informant not knowing dates and places of birth when providing death information has already been mentioned. Many record collections are incomplete, necessitating additional searches in other records to fill the gaps.

Legibility is also a problem in many handwritten records. It is sometimes worthwhile to ask for help from someone skilled in reading various types of handwriting when a certificate or register entry is not easily decipherable.

A third problem is that early records may contain a variety of surname spellings—none of them spellings currently used by branches of the family. Early record clerks, like early census enumerators, often spelled people's names as they heard them pronounced. When looking for birth or death records from earlier periods, consider all possible spelling variations, especially phonetic spellings, before concluding that no record exists. This is especially important for urban areas, where more than one person having the same name is the rule rather than the exception.

A related problem is that records were often indexed many years after they were compiled. The person doing the indexing had to interpret the handwriting in the record just as the researcher must, and his or her skills may not have been well developed. The obvious errors in indexes are a *T* read as an *F*, a *P* as an *R*, and an *L* as an *S*. Take these possibilities into consideration, too, as you try to determine all the possible spellings of a surname.

Some researchers stop searching if they cannot find an ancestor's name in an index. But some indexes have an error rate in excess of twenty-five percent, meaning that more than twenty-five percent of the individuals in the indexed records were not included in the index. If you know the approximate date of a birth or death, settle down to a page-by-page search before concluding that your ancestor is not in the records.

Legally restricted access represents an important limitation of modern vital records. Different states regulate who can access vital records and under what circumstances. Some new laws attempt to reduce the assumption of a false identity for fraudulent purposes (for example, assuming the identity of a deceased person to obtain credit cards to be used for defrauding merchants). Other laws protect the privacy of people still living. Regardless of the reasons behind such laws, you should research

I HEREBY CERTIFY THAT THIS IS A TRUE AND CORRECT COPY MADE OF THE ORIGINAL CERTIFICATE ON FILE IN THIS OFFICE IN ACCORDANCE WITH THE LAW OF IOWA REQUIRING FILING OF VITAL RECORDS. THIS RECORD IS NOT VALID IF THIS PHOTOCOPY HAS BEEN ALTERED OR IF IT DOES NOT BEAR THE RAISED SEAL OF THE DEPARTMENT OF HEALTH.

Norman L. Pawlewski
NORMAN L. PAWLEWSKI
STATE REGISTRAR

Carson E. Whitlow
CARSON E. WHITLOW, CHIEF
DIVISION OF RECORDS & STATISTICS DATE APR 15 75

DEPARTMENT OF COMMERCE
Bureau of the Census

IOWA STATE DEPARTMENT OF HEALTH
Division of Vital Statistics
Certificate of Death

State Office No. 35-6-135

1. PLACE OF DEATH: (a) County Franklin Township Washington (b) City or Town Hampton (c) Hospital or Institution: Name and Street Address (d) Length of stay in Hospital or Inst. In this community 6 years

2. USUAL RESIDENCE (HOME) OF DECEASED: (a) State Iowa (b) County Franklin (c) City or town Hampton (d) Street No. (e) If foreign born, how long in U. S. A.? 3 (b) IF VETERAN, NAME WAR

3. (a) FULL NAME Harry Chester Lee
3. (c) Social Security Account Number 475-23-3422

4. Sex Male 5. Color or Race White 6. (a) Single, married, widowed or divorced married
6. (b) Name of husband or wife Sylvia Smith 6. (c) If alive, give age 56 years
7. Birth date of deceased June 21, 1883
8. Age Years 57 Months 4 Days 19
9. Birthplace Chicago, Ill
10. Usual Occupation Stage Worker
11. Industry or business
12. Name (Father) Benjamin Lee
13. Birthplace Peoria, Ill
14. Name (Mother) B Hinkle
15. Birthplace Glee ford, Ill
16. (a) Informant's own signature Mrs Sylvia C Lee (b) Address Hampton, Iowa
17. (a) Burial (b) Date thereof Nov. 13. 40 (c) Place of burial or cremation Hampton Cemetery Location Hampton, Iowa
18. (a) Signature [signature] (b) Address Hampton, Ia (c) License No. 2026
19. Signature W T Wells District 359 Date received Nov 13 1940 Filed No. 43 Cx. DEC 14 40

MEDICAL CERTIFICATION
20. DATE OF DEATH Nov. 10, 1940
21. I CERTIFY that death occurred on the date above stated; that I attended deceased from 11/10 1940 to 11/10 1940, and that I saw h.. alive on 4/10 1940
Immediate cause of death Coronary Heart Disease Duration 5 yrs?
Due to Hypertension &
Due to arteriosclerosis.
22. If death was due to external causes, fill in the following:
23. (a) Signature L. E. Hedgecock M.D. (b) Address Hampton, Iowa (c) Date signed 11/13/40

Figure 13-12. Certificate of death of Harry Chester Lee, 15 April 1975, state of Iowa. Certified copy owned by Harry L. Carle.

the access-restriction laws that exist in the states where you will be conducting research. (See the discussion of right-of-privacy laws in chapter 1, "The Foundations of Family History Research.")

Finding Aids for Birth and Death Records

There are numerous aids for locating vital records. Most towns and counties have indexes to birth and death records. Even if the indexes are not complete, they can often facilitate research. Many local historical and genealogical societies have published birth and death records in their periodicals, newsletters, and journals; they should be examined whenever available. A few collections of birth and death records have been published in CD-ROM format. These appear in table 13-2 along with many marriage records collections. Finally, family members may be able to send photocopies of birth and death records in their possession. It is worth a letter, telephone call, or e-mail to inquire.

Always check for duplicate copies at county, city, town, and state levels. Many counties kept vital records before the states did. After state registration began, counties and cities continued to maintain registers of vital events. If one set of records is lost or incomplete, you can check the other.

The Family History Library has a significant collection of microfilmed birth and death records and indexes. Table 13-4 is a state-by-state list of available birth indexes and records. Table 13-5 lists death indexes and records. This collection is expanded regularly, so consult the Family History Library Catalog <www.familysearch.org/Eng/Library/FHLC/frameset_fhlc.asp> for the most current entries. The number of searchable online databases of statewide birth and death indexes keeps growing. Table 13-6 provides a list of databases and where to access them. Use your search engine to check regularly for newly published databases.

The Social Security Death Index (SSDI) provides birth date, death date, last known residence, and where the last payment was sent for persons who received benefits from the Social Security Administration. Approximately 98 percent of the people listed died after 1962; the earliest died in 1937. Those who held Social Security numbers but did not receive benefits or whose death was not reported to the administration, will not be listed. This index will help you pinpoint the date an ancestor died or at least narrow it to a month and year, making it easier to obtain the right death certificate from a county or state record office. The SSDI can be searched online at Ancestry.com for a fee and at other websites for free; however, the search engine on Ancestry.com produces the best results when you have very limited information.

The Social Security Administration has a microfilmed copy of every individual's Social Security application (Form SS-5), as well as claim files. These documents contain information not given in the index, including: Full name at birth, mailing address, age at last birthday, date of birth, place of birth, father's full name, mother's full name, sex, race, employer's name and address, and date signed. Copies of Form SS-5 (figure 13-13) can be obtained from the Social Security Administration at a cost of $27.00 each (in 2004). If you find an entry using the Ancestry.com SSDI search, click on "Get Copy of Original Application" to generate a letter to the Social Security Administration.

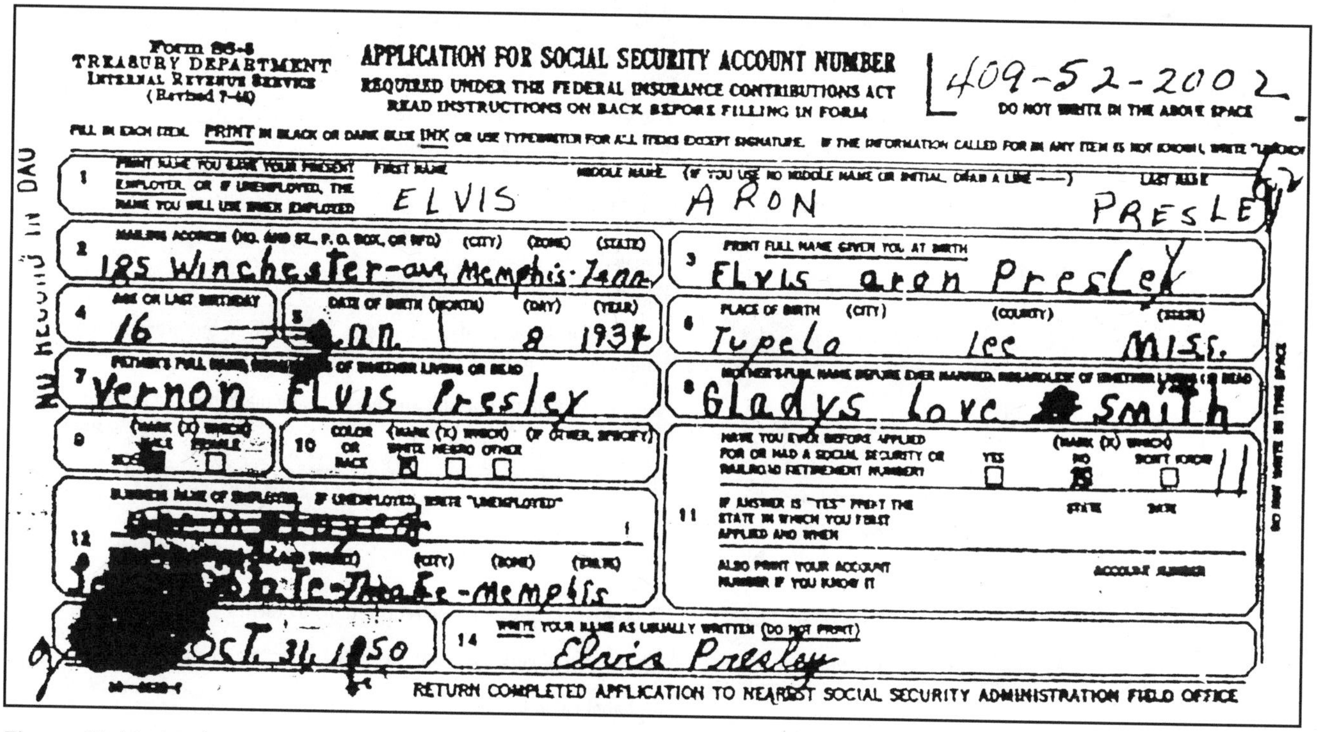

Form SS-5
TREASURY DEPARTMENT
INTERNAL REVENUE SERVICE

APPLICATION FOR SOCIAL SECURITY ACCOUNT NUMBER
REQUIRED UNDER THE FEDERAL INSURANCE CONTRIBUTIONS ACT
READ INSTRUCTIONS ON BACK BEFORE FILLING IN FORM

409-52-2002
DO NOT WRITE IN THE ABOVE SPACE

1. ELVIS ARON PRESLEY
2. 185 Winchester-ave Memphis-Tenn
3. Elvis aron Presley
4. 16
5. Jan. 8 1934
6. Tupelo Lee Miss.
7. Vernon Elvis Presley
8. Gladys Love Smith
13. Oct. 31, 1950
14. Elvis Presley

RETURN COMPLETED APPLICATION TO NEAREST SOCIAL SECURITY ADMINISTRATION FIELD OFFICE

Figure 13-13. Application for Social Security Account Number (also called a SS-5 form) for Elvis Aron Presley.

Table 13-4. Statewide Birth Indexes and Records from the Family History Library's Vital Records Collection as of March 2006

State	Birth Indexes	Birth Records	Comments
Alabama	1917–1919	1908–1959	
Arizona		1855–1926	Certificates arranged by county and then chronologically by date recorded. Records for 1925 not included.
California	1905–1995		Alphabetical by surname index on CD-ROM.
Alameda County		1873–1901	Includes indexes.
	1875–1971		Delayed births only.
Oakland		1870–1904	Card index included.
Los Angeles County	1866–1920		
	1866–1968		Index to delayed certificates only.
	1884–1932	1884–1932	
		1905–1923	Certificates filmed by year and then certificate number. Use 1884–1932 index to obtain date and certificate number.
	1943–1964	1943–1964	Delayed certificates of birth only.
Los Angeles City	1879–1905		Corresponding records not available at the FHL.
		1943–1964	
San Diego County	1870–1910	1870–1905	
	1943–1975		Index only; no corresponding records at the FHL.
Delaware		1861–1913	Quarterly returns arranged alphabetically or chronologically.
		Pre-1913–1923	Records incomplete prior to 1913.
District of Columbia		1874–1897	Includes index to certificate numbers.
Hawaii	1896–1909	1896–1903	
		1904–1909	
	1909–1949	1909–1925	
	1859–1938	1859–1903	Delayed birth registrations only.
		1904–1925	Delayed birth registrations only.
Illinois	1916–1938	1916–1945	Excluding Chicago.
		1842, 1849–1872	
Chicago		1878–1922	Use Cook County Birth Index, 1871–1916.
		1871–1915	Birth registers compiled by Cook County.
Cook County	1871–1916		
		1878–1894	Births outside the city of Chicago.
		1916–1922	
	1871–1948		Delayed birth indexes only.
		1916–1918	Delayed and corrected birth records.
Iowa	By County	By County	Collection includes certificates, returns, and delayed birth registrations; dates vary according to county. See FHL catalog for county records.
Kentucky	1911–1995		One index by name of child; another index by maiden name of mother.
	1911–1954		
Maine	1892–1922		No corresponding records at FHL.
Massachusetts	1841–1905	1841–1895	
		1901–1905	Birth registers by county.
	1906–1910		
		1753–1900	Delayed and corrected birth registrations by town.
Michigan	By County	By County	Dates covered vary by county. See FHL catalog for county records.
New Hampshire	Early-1900		Alphabetical index.
New Jersey		1848–1900	

State	Birth Indexes	Birth Records	Comments
New York			
New York City	1830–1865	1847–1873	Manhattan Borough.
	1866–1897	1866–1897	Card index; Manhattan birth certificates.
	1888–1965		
		1898–1909	Manhattan, Queens, Richmond Boroughs
North Carolina		1913–1922	Certificates.
Ohio	1908–1911		
Oregon		1842–1900	Delayed birth filings.
Pennsylvania			
Philadelphia		1829–1882	Birth authentications filed 1867–1891.
		1860–1915	Returns filed by physician, midwife
		1860–1903	Birth registers.
		1872–1915; 1967–1981	Birth correction cards.
Pittsburgh		1870–1905	
Rhode Island	1853–1900	1853–1900	
	1846–1898	1846–1898	Delayed births.
Tennessee		1908–1912	Annual enumeration of births.
Texas	1903–1953		
		1926–1995	Collection on CD-ROM.
Vermont	1871–1908	1871–1908	Alphabetical card index.
		1909–1954	Alphabetical card file.
Virginia	1853–1950	1853–1941	
Washington	1900–1980		Index to delayed birth records.
	1907–1954	1907–1948	Includes delayed birth certificates, 1850–1960.
West Virginia		1853–1860	Arranged by county.
		1852–1930	Also includes delayed registrations.
Wisconsin	1852–1907		Births in this index may be found in county records.
		1937–1942	Delayed birth records.

Table 13-5. Statewide Death Indexes and Records from the Family History Library's Vital Records Collection as of March 2006

State	Death Indexes	Death Records	Comments
Alabama	1908–1959	1908–1974	
Arizona		1870–1951	Certificates arranged by county and then chronologically. Records for 1950 not included.
Arkansas	1914–1923; 1934–1946; 1914–1948		Corresponding records not available at FHL.
California	1905–1988; 1940–1990		Original certificates on file with the State Registrar of Vital Statistics. A copy of each certificate on file with County Recorder at place of death.
Alameda County		1859–1903	Includes indexes and mortuary records for 1873–1891.
Oakland		1870–1904	Card index included.
Los Angeles County	1884–1932	1884–1932	
		1908–1945	Certificates in numerical order; some out of order; some certificates missing.
	1873–1920	1877–1905	
San Diego County	1851–1905	1876–1905	Volume B not available for filming; includes Coroner's Reports.
San Francisco County		1865–1904	Indexes filmed with some volumes; some missing years.
Delaware		1855–1910	Quarterly returns arranged alphabetically or chronologically.
		1910–1955	Records incomplete prior to 1913.
District of Columbia	1855–1965	1855–1965	
		1888–1933	Records for persons who died outside the District of Columbia and were returned for burial.
Florida	1877–1969		Florida Combined Death Index.
		1877–1969	Arranged in order of certificate number; search index previously for certificate number.
Georgia	1919–1999		Corresponding records not available at FHL.
Hawaii	1896–1909	1896–1903	
	1909–1949	1909–1925	
		1861–1892	Reports of burials in the Kingdom of Hawaii.
Idaho	1911–1950		Index on CD-ROM from the Idaho Department of Health and Welfare.
	1911–1932	1911–1937	
Illinois	1916–1938	1916–1945	
		1946–1947	Includes stillbirths; no index.
Chicago	1871–1933		
		1878–1915	Read card catalog notes for instructions on how to access these death certificates.
	1916–1938	1916–1922	
	1916–1938	1916–1945	
		1877–1930	Homicides only.
Cook County	1871–1916		
		1878–1909; 1916–1922	
		1872–1911	Coroner's inquest records.
		1879–1904	Death certificates issued by the Coroner.
Iowa	By County	By County	Dates covered vary according to county. See FHL catalog for county records.
Kentucky	1911–1995		
		1886–1910	
		1911–1955	
Louisiana		1905–1929	Certificates.
Maine	1892–1922		No corresponding records at FHL.
Massachusetts	1841–1971	1841–1899	
		1901–1905	Death registers by county.
		1753–1900	Delayed and corrected death registrations by town.

State	Death Indexes	Death Records	Comments
Michigan	By County	By County	Dates covered vary by county. See FHL catalog for county records.
Minnesota		1900–1955	Records arranged by county in chronological order.
Missouri	By County	By County	Dates covered limited and vary by county. See FHL catalog for county records.
New Hampshire	Early-1900		Alphabetical index.
		1901–1937	Certificates.
New Jersey		1848–1900	
New Mexico	1889–1940	1889–1942 1927–1945	
New York			
New York City		1795–1865	Alphabetical within year and month.
	1868–1890	1866–1919	Index cards; Manhattan death certificates.
		1920–1949	Manhattan certificates.
		1823–1898; 1868–1918	Coroner's inquisitions.
		1829–1887	Richmond County
North Carolina	1906–1974 1968–1994	1906–1994	Stillbirths, 1914–1953; Fetal deaths, 1960–1974.
Ohio	1908–1944		
	1908–1911	1908–1944	
		1941–1964	Veteran's grave reports.
Oregon	1903–2000		Check county listings for death certificates.
Pennsylvania	By County	By County	Dates covered vary by county.
Philadelphia		1807–1840	Burial records.
		1832–1860	
		1860–1903	
	1904–1915	1904–1915	
Pittsburgh	1851–1857		
		1870–1905	
Rhode Island	1853–1900	1853–1900	
	1901–1920	1901–1950	Includes out-of-town deaths.
South Carolina	1915–1944	1915–1944	
Tennessee		1908–1912	Annual enumeration of deaths.
	1914–1950	1914–1950	
Texas		1800–1976	Records prior to 1903 in alphabetical order.
	1903–1945	1903–1963	
	1943–1973		
		1964–1998	Collection on CD-ROM.
Utah	1899–1905	1904–1951	Chronological order by county and year.
Vermont	1871–1908	1871–1908	Alphabetical card index.
		1909–1954	Alphabetical card file.
Virginia		1853–1912	
Washington	1907–1979	1907–1960	
West Virginia		1853–1860 1917–1973	Arranged by county.
Wisconsin	1862–1907 1959–1997	1862–1907	

Table 13-6. Searchable Birth and Death Index Databases Online as of March 2006

State	Database Title	Address	Fee	Comments
Alabama	Alabama Deaths, 1908–59	www.ancestry.com/search/rectype/inddbs/5188a.htm	Yes	Statewide coverage.
Arizona	Arizona Birth Index, 1887–1928	http://genealogy.az.gov	No	Index links to a PDF image of the original record.
	Arizona Death Index, 1878–1953	http://genealogy.az.gov	No	Index links to a PDF image of the original record.
Arkansas	Arkansas Death Index, 1914–50	http://content.ancestry.com/iexec/?htx=List&dbid=8771&ti=0	Yes	Statewide coverage.
California	California Birth Index, 1905–95	www.ancestry.com/search/rectype/inddbs/5247.htm	Yes	
	California Birth Index, 1905–95	www.vitalsearch-ca.com/gen/ca/_vitals/cabirthm.htm	Yes/ No	Subscription and non-subscription services available.
	California Death Index, 1905–95	www.vitalsearch-ca.com/gen/ca/_vitals/cabirthm.htm	Yes/ No	Subscription and non-subscription services available.
	California Death Index, 1940–97	http://ancestry.com/search/db.aspx?dbid=5180	Yes	Best search engine.
	California Death Index, 1940–97	http://userdb.rootsweb.com/ca/death/search.cgi	No	Good search engine.
Connecticut	Connecticut Marriage Index, 1959–2001	www.ancestry.com/search/rectype/inddbs/7158.htm	Yes	
	Connecticut Death Index, 1949–2001	www.ancestry.com/search/rectype/inddbs/4124a.htm	Yes	
Florida	Florida Death Index, 1936–98	www.ancestry.com/search/db.aspx?dbid=7338	Yes	1936–1960, 1996–1998 each year indexed separately; others grouped.
Georgia	Georgia Deaths, 1919–98	www.ancestry.ca/search/rectype/inddbs/5426a.htm	Yes	
Idaho	Idaho State Death Index, 1911–51	http://abish.byui.edu/specialcollections/fhc/ Death/searchForm.cfm	No	
	Western States Historical Marriage Record Index	http://abish.byui.edu/specialcollections/fhc/gbsearch.htm	No	Includes AZ, CA, CO, ID, NV, OR, WA, WY; currently 280,000 marriages and growing.
	Idaho Death Index, 1911–51	www.ancestry.com/search/rectype/inddbs/6856.htm	Yes	
Illinois	Illinois Death Index, 1916–50	www.sos.state.il.us/departments/archives/idphdeathindex.html	No	
	Illinois Pre-1916 Death Index	www.sos.state.il.us/departments/archives/death.html	No	Periodic updates until records for all counties have been indexed.
	Illinois Statewide Marriage Index, 1763–1900	www.sos.state.il.us/departments/archives/marriage.html	No	
Chicago	Chicago Police Homicides Index, 1870–1930	www.sos.state.il.us/GenealogyMWeb/chrisrch.html	No	
Cook County	Cook County Coroner's Inquest Record Index, 1872–1911	www.cyberdriveillinois.com/departments/archives/cookinqt.html	No	
Indiana	Indiana Death Index, 1882–1920	http://ancestry.com/search/db.aspx?dbid=7834	Yes	Statewide coverage.
Kentucky	Kentucky Death Index, 1911–2000	http://vitals.rootsweb.com/ky/death/search.cgi	No	
	Kentucky Death Index, 1911–2000	www.ancestry.com/search/rectype/inddbs/3077a.htm	Yes	Best search engine with soundex.
Louisiana	Louisiana Statewide Death Index, 1900–1949	www.ancestry.com/search/rectype/inddbs/6697.htm	Yes	
Orleans Parish,	Orleans Parish Birth Index, 1796–1902	www.rootsweb.com/~usgenweb/la/orleans/birth-index.htm	No	Incl. New Orleans.
	Orleans Parish Death Index, 1804–1915	www.rootsweb.com/~usgenweb/la/orleans/death-index.htm	No	Ongoing project, check often.
	New Orleans Death Index, 1837–57 & 1870	http://nutrias.org/~nopl/info/louinfo/deaths/deaths.htm	No	From the Daily Picayune newspaper.

State	Database Title	Address	Fee	Comments
Maine	Maine Death Index, 1960–97	www.ancestry.com/search/rectype/inddbs/6703.htm	Yes	
	Maine Death Index, 1960–97	www.state.me.us/sos/arc/geneology	No	
	Maine Marriage Index, 1892–1966, 1976–96	www.state.me.us/sos/arc/geneology	No	
Maryland	Maryland Death Index, 1898–1951	http://mdvitalrec.net/cfm/index.cfm	No	Maryland State Archives two databases cover these years.
Baltimore County	Baltimore County Death Index, 1875–1972	http://mdvitalrec.net/cfm/index.cfm	No	Maryland State Archives—two databases cover these years.
Massachusetts	Massachusetts Death Index, 1970–2003	http://ancestry.com/search/db.aspx?dbid=7457	Yes	Statewide.
	Town Birth Records Prior to 1850	http://ancestry.com/search/db.aspx?dbid=4094	Yes	See database description for names of towns included in this 90,000 name index.
	Town Death Records Prior to 1850	http://ancestry.com/search/db.aspx?dbid=4080	Yes	See database description for names of towns included in this 95,000 name index.
Boston	Boston Vital Records, 1630–99	http://ancestry.com/search/db.aspx?dbid=1022	Yes	
Michigan	Michigan Death Index, 1867–97	www.mdch.state.mi.us/pha/osr/gendisx/search.htm	No	
	Michigan Deaths, 1971–96	www.ancestry.com/search/rectype/inddbs/3171a.htm	Yes	
Minnesota	Minnesota Birth Certificate Index, 1900–1911	http://people.mnhs.org/bci/	No	Additional years being added periodically.
	Minnesota Deaths, 1908–2002	http://people.mnhs.org/dci/Search.cfm	No	
	Minnesota Death Index, 1908–2002	www.ancestry.com/search/rectype/inddbs/7316.htm	Yes	
Missouri	Missouri Birth & Death Records Database	www.sos.mo.gov/archives/resources/birthdeath/default.asp	No	Pre-1909 records only.
St. Louis	St. Louis City Death Records, 1850–1908	www.ancestry.com/search/rectype/inddbs/5696.htm	Yes	
Montana	Montana Death Index, 1954–2002	www.ancestry.com/search/rectype/inddbs/5437.htm	Yes	
New Mexico	New Mexico Death Index Project, 1899–1940	www.rootsweb.com/~usgenweb/nm/nmdi.htm	No	
New York	New York City Deaths, 1892–1902	www.ancestry.com/search/rectype/inddbs/6492.htm	Yes	Incomplete.
	New York City Death Index, 1891–1936	www.italiangen.org/NYCDEATH.STM	No	
North Carolina	North Carolina Deaths, 1908–96	http://ancestry.com/search/db.aspx?dbid=8908	Yes	Separate database for each year.
Ohio	Ohio Death Certificate Index, 1913–44	www.ohiohistory.org/dindex	No	
	Ohio Death Index, 1958–2002	http://ancestry.com/search/db.aspx?dbid=5763	Yes	
Oregon	Oregon Death Index, 1903–30	www.heritagetrailpress.com/Death_Index/	No	New data added periodically.
	Oregon Death Index, 1903–98	http://ancestry.com/search/db.aspx?dbid=5254	Yes	Statewide.
Rhode Island	Rhode Island Birth Index, 1636–1930	http://ancestry.com/search/db.aspx?dbid=4262	Yes	Statewide.
	Rhode Island Death Index, 1630–1930	http://ancestry.com/search/db.aspx?dbid=4264	Yes	Statewide.
South Carolina	South Carolina Death Index, 1915–49	http://ancestry.com/search/db.aspx?dbid=8741	Yes	Statewide.
South Dakota	South Dakota Birth Records	www.state.sd.us/applications/PH14Over100BirthRec/index.asp	No	Records created 100 years ago and earlier.
	South Dakota Birth Index, 1856–1903	http://ancestry.com/search/db.aspx?dbid=6996	Yes	Statewide.
	South Dakota Death Index, 1905–55	http://ancestry.com/search/db.aspx?dbid=8659	Yes	Statewide.
Tennessee	Index to Tennessee Death Records, 1914–25	www.state.tn.us/sos/statelib/pubsvs/death2.htm	No	
Memphis	Memphis/Shelby Co. Death Index, 1848–1945	http://history.memphislibrary.org	No	

State	Database Title	Address	Fee	Comments
Texas	Texas Death Records, 1964–98 Texas Death Records, 1964–98	http://vitals.rootsweb.com/tx/death/search.cgi www.ancestry.com/search/rectype/inddbs/4876a.htm	No Yes	
Utah	Utah Deaths, 1905–51	www.ancestry.com/search/rectype/inddbs/6967.htm	Yes	
Vermont	Vermont Death Index, 1981–2001	www.ancestry.com/search/rectype/inddbs/3269.htm	Yes	
Virginia	Death Records Indexing Project, 1853–96 Virginia Birth, Marriage, and Death Databases	http://eagle.vsla.edu/drip www.ancestry.com/search/locality/dbpage.htm?t=2&y=0&c=49	Yes Yes	Ongoing project.
Washington	Washington Death Index, 1940–96	www.ancestry.com/search/rectype/inddbs/6716.htm	Yes	
West Virginia	West Virginia Birth Index, 1816–1929 West Virginia Death Index, 1853–1954	www.wvculture.org/vrr/va_bcsearch.aspx www.wvculture.org/vrr/va_dcsearch.aspx	No No	A work-in-progress, check back often for newly added counties. 1917–1954 for most counties; some earlier records for a few counties. Also a work-in-progress.
Wisconsin	Wisconsin Deaths, 1820–1907 Pre-1907 Vital Records	www.ancestry.com/search/rectype/inddbs/4984.htm www.wisconsinhistory.org/vitalrecords/	Yes No	

Cemetery Records

Cemetery records and headstone inscriptions are also sources of birth and death information. The custom of burying the dead in areas set aside for that purpose goes back thousands of years, but the genealogist's interest focuses mainly on historic periods in Jewish and Christian communities. The records of this type most commonly found are church burial registers, sextons' records, cemetery deed and plot registers, burial permit records, grave opening orders, and monument (gravestone) inscriptions.

Such records usually supplement standard sources of genealogical information, but sometimes they represent the only information that can be found pertaining to the birth and death of an ancestor. Using these records effectively requires specific knowledge of their content, availability, and location. The following section, based on Arlene Eakle's *How to Search a Cemetery*, appeared in the first edition of *The Source.*[8] It has since undergone extensive revision by Jeanne Gentry, president of the Oregon Historic Cemeteries Association, and Lynette Strangstad, a consultant on burial ground preservation and author of *A Graveyard Preservation Primer*.[9] Johni Cerny and Sandra Luebking added the new material in this edition and the updated Reference list.

Cemetery Research

Searching in cemeteries compensates for the effort it requires if only for the information cemeteries provide about children under the age of twenty-one. In the twenty-first century, where the death rate for children is fewer than eight per one thousand live births (see figure 13-14), we often fail to realize that the local cemetery may contain the only evidence of some young nineteenth-century lives.

The cemetery is also, sadly enough, sometimes the only place to find real evidence of some women's lives. A woman, hidden in her father's household during her growing years and recorded in pre-1850 censuses as "female 5–10 years of age," who dies before 1850, may be located under her given name for the first time on her headstone.

For example, James Bell, born in 1773, was married three times and lost two wives in childbirth. His first wife, twenty-five-year-old Sarah, died four hours after giving birth to twins, both of whom survived. His second wife, also named Sarah, died at age seventeen, thirty-five days after giving birth to a namesake daughter who also died thirty-one days later. The third wife, Margaret, died at age sixty-eight. Their son James is buried between his parents in the cemetery of the old Stone Church in Fort Defiance, Virginia. The family Bible and the cemetery plot are the only records of the existence of these women.

Even though colonial gravestones are often long-since gone or illegible, the surviving gravestones in a cemetery are important sources of information for immigrants. Sometimes the only recording of the original surname is on a gravestone, overlooked by a genealogist who was unaware that the family name had been Americanized and thus missed the original spelling in the alphabetical list. Had the grave plot itself been checked, the person's juxtaposition to known family members would have drawn attention to the difference in the name. The period of time when the largest number of immigrants arrived—1820 to 1920—coincides with gravestones that have survived.

Types of Cemeteries

The Church Burial Yard

Most churches, until around World War II, were constructed on lots large enough to provide their members with burial grounds. Even churches in large cities had adjacent burial yards.

Some of these still exist; however, as cities grew, church membership increased, and real estate values rose, the need for larger burial facilities developed. Burial grounds were established in the suburbs while the old plots were used as building sites. Sometimes the graves were moved; sometimes they were not.

Public Cemeteries

Most local civil jurisdictions in the United States have some sort of public burial ground. Some are maintained by the counties; however, most of them are village, town, township, or city burial sites. Some national and state jurisdictions maintain burial facilities for veterans and their families.

Family Burial Plots

Family burial grounds are still common in rural areas of the United States. With the enforcement of health codes that require burial permits, the use of licensed morticians, and regulations governing health hazards, such private plots are disappearing. In the nineteenth century or earlier, most rural families had family burial sites; usually the site was on the farm first settled by the family in the area. These cemeteries are the most difficult to locate, but obviously they are most valuable for establishing family identity. Today properties on which those cemeteries are located are often in the hands of unrelated persons. Fences are left in disrepair and gravestones are often overturned, broken, buried, carried away, or otherwise lost. Some, however, are still well preserved and cared for by descendants or local historical societies.

Figure 13-14. Maternal mortality rates were high during 1900 to 1930. At the beginning of the twentieth century, for every thousand live births, six to nine women in the United States died of pregnancy-related complications, and approximately one hundred infants died before age one year. ("Achievements in Public Health, 1900–1999: Healthier Mothers and Babies," in *Morbidity and Mortality Weekly Report* 48, no. 38 (1 October, 1999): 849, at <www.cdc.gov/mmwr/preview/mmwrhtml/mm4838a2.htm>, Centers for Disease Control and Prevention, Department of Health and Human Services). The Bebout family lost four children under thirteen months of age, and the mother, Stella, died in childbirth in 1919 at the age of thirty-six. Surviving children pictured with their father are *(at left)*, Ernest Mayo (born 1910); Claude Alexander (born 1902); and Atha Pearl (born 1905) holding William Woodrow (born 1916). Courtesy of Wendy Bebout Elliott.

Commercial Memorial Parks

Since World War II, with the development of large, highly transient city populations, a new sort of burial institution has come into being: the commercially owned and operated nonsectarian facility.

Types of Records

Written Sources

Entries in burial registers are chronological as the funerals occurred. If the registrar noted which plot the person was buried in, you can sometimes deduce relationships, a valuable clue because gravestones may have been destroyed or never placed on the grave, women's maiden names are often not recorded, and children may not have been mentioned in previous records.

Church Burial Registers. Churches that have affiliated burial grounds usually maintain records of interments in their burial registers. These records sometimes include the names of other family members, as the following register from Killinger's Church shows.

> (62) 1826. Jan. 7, Buried Isaac *Lotch,* son of Johannes & Elisabeth Lotch. b. May 20, 1822; bapt. May 10, 1823, by Rev. Hemping. d. Jan. 6, 1826, cause: Gichtern. age: 3 yrs. 8 most less 4 days.
>
> Jan. 10, Buried Daniel Deiwler, in the David's cong. son of Albrecht & Catharina Deiwler. b. Febr. 16, 1771, in Upper Paxton twp. Dauphin county. bapt. by Rev. Mr. Enderlein. married in 1795 to Anna Maria Fissler. They had 11 children, 5 sons & 6 daughters. d. Jan. 9, 1826, Cause: Hitziges Fieber. age 54 yrs. 10 most 24 days.
>
> Jan. 11, buried in Hoffman's congr. Margaretha *Hoffman,* da. of Johannes & Catharina Herman. b. Nov. 7, 1753 in Heidelberg twp. Berks county. bapt. & confirmed in Lutheran religion. married Apr. 22, 1772, Johann Nicolaus Hoffman. They had 12 children, 6 sons & 6 daughters. 2 daughters preceded her as also her husband, d. Apr. 28, '14; cause of death: Pilger's Fieber. d. Jan 9, 1826, survived by 84 grandchildren & 21 great-grandchildren. Age: 72 yrs, 2 most 2 days.[10]

Finding such registers today presents a problem. Some have been placed in central church archives or church-affiliated university libraries (see chapter 6, "Church Records"); some have descended through the heirs of ministers or clerks along with other personal effects; some are stored in the original meetinghouses. In short, you may have to hunt for them.

Sexton's Records. All municipal cemeteries, many large denominational facilities shared by two or more churches in a community, all commercially operated memorial parks, and a few large family burial grounds have offices or official caretakers where you can expect to find a registry of burials called the sexton's book (figure 13-15). Such records also list the plots available—occupied, owned, or not owned—described in sufficient detail for sale and resale. The sexton's record is thus an accurate record of cemetery deeds and plats.

Cemetery Deeds. The original cemetery deeds, like the deeds to any real estate, are given to the owner of the plat; however, recorded copies are retained by the sexton in separate cemetery deed books. Sales, transfers, and bequests of title to this property are duly recorded also.

Plat Records. In areas before local governments were functioning effectively, graves were dug where convenient with no concept of plots; often, the burial wasn't recorded. With the platting of cemeteries, selling of plots, and registering of deeds, attempts were made to record earlier burials. In many instances, the names and burial dates could be obtained, but the actual location of the grave was lost. Figure 13-16 is a plat record that was reconstructed after burials in the last four decades of the nineteenth century; for that reason, it is incomplete.

Burial Permit Records. Since around 1920, state health departments have regulated burials. Today, very few jurisdictions permit burials except by licensed morticians, who either obtain or determine that someone else has obtained a certified burial permit from the city or county authority. These records constitute another valuable source of burial information.

Grave Opening Orders. Most cemeteries preserve records of all grave openings, whether for burial, postmortem exhumation, or transfer of body. These records are known as grave opening orders and usually begin around the time of state registration of deaths. The order shown in figure 13-17 is for a new grave. We can deduce that Matilda Bennion was an adult because children are buried in graves less than five feet in length. Amy Fowler was probably a relative. A researcher would be able to find the death certificate rapidly because its number is given.

Family Bibles. While family Bible records are more appropriately classified as home sources, they are also a primary source—sometimes the only source—for private burials. Usually, such Bibles are still in family hands; however, it has become increasingly popular for local and regional historical societies and other agencies to acquire the personal effects of original settlers and early families of their areas. The National Archives and the Library of Congress in Washington, D.C., also have collections of Bible records sent as evidence in various claims against the United States government. These pages have been removed from their case files and arranged in alphabetical order. Lists of the Bible records are available upon request.

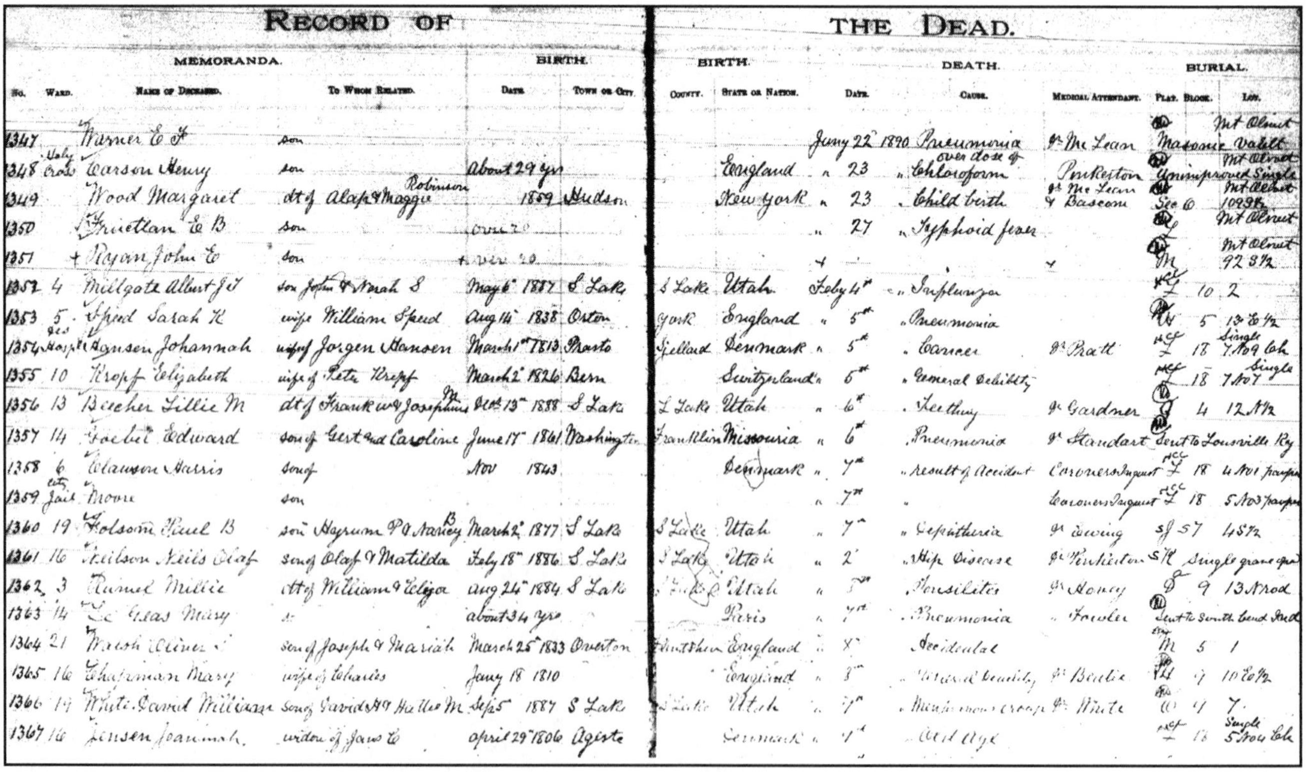
RECORD OF THE DEAD.

No.	Ward	Name of Deceased	To Whom Related	Birth Date	Town or City	County	State or Nation	Death Date	Cause	Medical Attendant	Plat	Block	Lot
1347		Warner E F	son					Jany 22 1890	Pneumonia	Dr McLean			Mt Olivet Masonic Vault
1348	Valy Cross	Carson Henry	son	About 29 yrs			England	23	over dose of Chloroform	Pinkerton			Mt Olivet Unimproved Single
1349		Wood Margaret	dt of Alap & Maggie Robinson	1869	Hudson		New York	23	Child birth	Dr McLean & Bascom	Sec 6		Mt Olivet 10898
1350		Grietlan E B	son	over 20				27	Typhoid fever				Mt Olivet
1351		Ryan John E	son	over 20									Mt Olivet 9238½
1352	4	Millgate Albert J	son of John & Norah S	May 6 1887	S Lake	S Lake	Utah	Feby 4	Influenza			10	2
1353	5	Speed Sarah K	wife William Speed	Aug 14 1838	Orton	York	England	5	Pneumonia			5	13 & 4½
1354		Hansen Johannah	wife of Jorgen Hansen	March 1 1813	Prasto	Sjelland	Denmark	5	Cancer	Dr Pratt		18	7 Row 6 Single lot
1355	10	Kropf Elizabeth	wife of Peter Kropf	March 2 1826	Bern		Switzerland	6	General debility			18	7 Row 7 Single
1356	13	Beecher Lillie M	dt of Frank W & Josephine M	Oct 13 1888	S Lake	S Lake	Utah	6	Teething	Dr Gardner		4	12 N ½
1357	14	Foebel Edward	son of Gert and Caroline	June 17 1861	Washington	Franklin	Missouria	6	Pneumonia	Dr Standart	Sent to Louisville Ky		
1358	6	Clawson Harris	son of	Nov 1843			Denmark	7	Result of accident	Coroners Inquest		18	4 Row 1 pauper
1359	City Jail	Moore	son					7		Coroners Inquest		18	5 Row 3 pauper
1360	19	Folsom Paul B	son Hyrum P & Nancy B	March 2 1877	S Lake	S Lake	Utah	7	Diphtheria	Dr Ewing		57	4 S ½
1361	16	Neilson Neils Olaf	son of Olaf & Matilda	Feby 18 1886	S Lake	S Lake	Utah	2	Hip Disease	Dr Pinkerton			Single grave
1362	3	Rumel Millie	dt of William & Eliza	Aug 24 1884	S Lake	S Lake	Utah	7	Tonsilitis	Dr Honey		9	13 N rod
1363	14	Le Gless Mary		about 34 yrs			Paris	7	Pneumonia	Fowler	Sent to South Bend Ind		
1364	21	Marsh Oliver	son of Joseph & Mariah	March 25 1833	Overton		England	8	Accidental			5	1
1365	16	Chapman Mary	wife of Charles	Jany 18 1810			England	8	General debility	Dr Beattie		9	10 E ½
1366	19	White David William	son of David H & Hattie M	Sept 5 1887	S Lake	S Lake	Utah	7	Membranous croup	Dr White		9	7
1367	16	Jensen Joannah	widow of Jens C	April 29 1806	Agerste		Denmark	7	Old age			1	Single 5 Row 6 lot

Figure 13-15. Sexton's record, Salt Lake City Cemetery, Utah, 1890. FHL microfilm 1,299,170.

Monuments and Memorials

Few experiences in family history offer more intrigue, interest, and even recreation than searching for monuments and their inscriptions. Even when written records are available and seemingly complete, these sources should always be used.

Prominent, influential, and affluent families often present special gifts—stained glass windows, altar pieces, sacramental services, confessionals, ornaments, statues—in the name and memory of their deceased relatives. Plaques or inscriptions give names, dates, and relationships of those involved with such gifts.

Sometimes the family may make contributions in lieu of flowers toward a special trust fund, organization, or project in the memory of a deceased loved one. Records are often maintained of all who contribute, the amount of the contribution, and the date made. Indications of this type of memorial will be found in newspaper accounts, court records, home sources, and the records of the person or institution responsible for the fund or project.

The burial of a loved one in a tomb or raised vault rather than a grave is customary among some ethnic groups and is the practice of some families. These tombs are normally in a special part of the cemetery or in mausoleums created expressly for this purpose. The inscriptions found on the tombs themselves are similar to regular monument inscriptions. The decoration of the tomb is an important part of the memorial. Burial registers may be stored in a special cupboard inside the tomb.

The ashes of the cremated are usually placed in urns and preserved in vaults at the crematory itself, at the cemetery where the other family members are interred, or in the home of a family member. Inscriptions may be etched on a plaque or other label.

Monuments with inscriptions are extremely varied, ranging from wooden crosses rotted into illegibility to long marble slabs with paragraphs of biography inscribed upon them. Dates of birth and death, places of birth and death (especially when far removed from the place of burial), names of parents, names of spouses, occupation, brothers and sisters, and special circumstances of life can be found. Some typical inscriptions follow.

From a cemetery in Manchester, Vermont:

In Memory of Rufus Munson, who Died Sept. 13th, 1797 in the 35th year of his Age & left a Widow & four children of the first two letters of thare names is thus:

C.M: G.M: B.M: P.M:

From Old Burying Ground, Newport, Rhode Island:

Wait daughtr of	**Also William**
William and	their son
Desire Tripp	died March
died April 24	7th 1784 Aged
1780 aged 10	22 mo
mo 10 days	

Also his Wife's Arm
Amputated Feby 20th 1786

CEM 118 LOT NO. 16

WEST TIER	EAST TIER
No. 5 NAME INTERMENT NO. NAME INTERMENT NO.	No. 5 NAME Joe Harrop INTERMENT NO. 1-17-1959 NAME INTERMENT NO.
No. 4 NAME INTERMENT NO. NAME INTERMENT NO.	No. 4 NAME Edwin Broadbent INTERMENT NO. Harrop NAME 3-11-1961 INTERMENT NO.
No. 3 Req NAME Dorothy Edith INTERMENT NO. Webb Mackay NAME 7-8-1963 INTERMENT NO.	No. 3 NAME Anny Harrop Pauline INTERMENT NO. Smith NAME INTERMENT NO.
No. 2 NAME ELIZABETH ANN INTERMENT NO. WEBB NAME INTERMENT NO.	No. 2 NAME ARTHUR R. K. TAYLEY INTERMENT NO. 10-20-1907 NAME INTERMENT NO.
No. 1 CU NAME William J. Webb INTERMENT NO. 12-13-1972. NAME INTERMENT NO.	No. 1 NAME SARRAH ANN HARROP INTERMENT NO. 7-24-1921 NAME INTERMENT NO.

LOT OWNERSHIP RECORD
Heber J. Grant 2642

William J. Webb 5576 5 West 1/2 trans to Melba F Davies #22636	Sarah Ann Harrop 5577

Figure 13-16. A reconstruction from existing records of Block 2, Lot 16, sexton's office, Salt Lake City Cemetery. FHL microfilm 1,299,161.

From a cemetery in Norton, Massachusetts:

In Memory of
Mr Joseph Hill
Who Died
Dec 6, 1826
Aged 66 years
My sledge & Hammer ly reclined
My Bellows too have lost their wind.
My fire's extinct My forge decayed
And [in] the dust my vice is laid;
My iron's spent my coals are gone
My nail are drove My work is done.

From a cemetery in Mottville, Michigan:

Ransom Beardsley
Died Jan 24 1850
Aged 56 yr. 7 mot 21 days
A Vol. in the War of 1812
No Pension!

Genealogists should also be aware of indirect evidence that can be found in monument decorations. Decorations can express occupations, age, sex, interests, cause of death, religious affiliation, membership in ethnic and fraternal organizations, and philosophies of life (figure 13-18).[11] Such details are rarely recorded by transcribers, but sketches and photographs can preserve these symbolic messages.

The date when the stone was placed on the grave is very important. Obviously, one placed two days after the funeral is usually more reliable than one placed fifty years later, although there are exceptions. Gravestones, like cars, have distinctive styles and materials depending upon the year they were made that can provide clues about the time of placement. Figure 13-19 provides some typical examples.

By carefully studying the vintage of the gravestone, the researcher can more accurately determine the validity of its inscription. Modern gravestones with ancient dates indicate replacement of an earlier gravestone or considerable time lapse between death and grave marker.

Most older and some new graves sink, leaving a slightly depressed area outlining the dimensions of the grave. If no age or birth date is given, you can determine which graves are of children and which are of adults by measuring which are more than five feet in length.

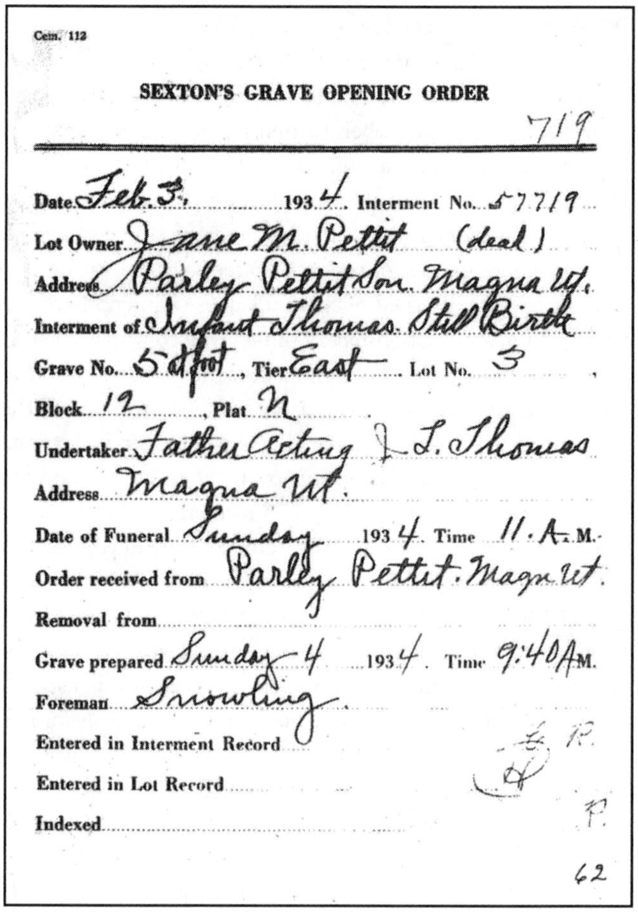

Research Preparation

When you search a cemetery, you should arrive with as many clues as you can: surname variants, people who married into your family, maiden names of women on your pedigree, and dates of settlement and migration into and out of the area. Be sure to check land records and county or town histories to learn precisely when and where the first family member settled in the area, when and from where subsequent members of the family arrived in the area, precise property descriptions for graveyards located on family land or nearby farms, land reserved for burial grounds or conveyed to church or township authorities, bequests in wills to maintain a graveyard, location of families in relationship to churches in the area, church affiliations of family members, and the location of families in relationship to cities and villages in the county.

Check death certificates for the names of all cemeteries in which family members are buried. Usually, family members are buried in clusters. Even where surnames are familiar, consider the probability that persons buried nearby are related to you.

Cem. 112

SEXTON'S GRAVE OPENING ORDER

719

Date Feb. 3, 193 4. Interment No. 57719

Lot Owner Jane M. Pettit (dead)

Address Parley Pettit Son Magna Ut.

Interment of Infant Thomas Still Birth

Grave No. 5 ft, Tier East Lot No. 3

Block 12, Plat N

Undertaker Father Acting J. T. Thomas

Address Magna Ut.

Date of Funeral Sunday 193 4. Time 11 A. M.

Order received from Parley Pettit. Magna Ut.

Removal from

Grave prepared Sunday 4 193 4. Time 9:40 A M.

Foreman Snowling.

Entered in Interment Record

Entered in Lot Record

Indexed

62

Figure 13-17. Sexton's grave opening order for Jane M. Pettit, 3 February 1934, Salt Lake City Cemetery, Utah. FHL microfilm 1,652,983.

Acquire death certificates for all children of the pedigree ancestor you are seeking.

Cemetery Research Projects

Investigate the possibility of cemetery research projects in the area of your ancestry. Some are one-person operations and some are large-scale projects carried out under the supervision of a project director. Some projects index names of those buried in a particular cemetery, township, or county; others build databases of tombstone inscriptions. The results of these efforts may be online at personal, organizational, or commercial websites.

An international project of the Jewish Genealogical Society is JewishGen Online Worldwide Burial Registry (JOWBR). This is a database of names and other identifying information from cemeteries and burial records worldwide, from the earliest records to the present. The master index is at <www.jewishgen.org/databases/cemetery>.

Another ongoing project is the USGenWeb Tombstone Transcription Project <www.rootsweb.com/~cemetery/memor_2.html>. This has a very large collection of cemetery records contributed by vollunteers, as well as an index to nearly 8 million obituaries, which generally tell where interment took place. The Cemetery Transcription Library at <www.Interment.net> currently has 3.5 million records from 7,500 cemeteries around the world and adds new information daily. You can search millions of cemetery records (and find photographs of many tombstones) at Find A Grave <www.findagrave.com>. Both sites encourage users to submit records and have downloadable software available for that purpose. Table 13-7 features some excellent websites related to cemeteries, tombstone inscriptions, and obituaries.

Check printed compilations of cemetery inscriptions. Earning the gratitude of all researchers, county and state genealogical societies, in cooperation with Boy Scout troops, the U.S. Department of Energy, the U.S. Army Corps of Engineers, university and college units, and other interested parties have restored, copied, indexed, and otherwise preserved the information from gravestones. The results are printed in scattered volumes of local proceedings, newsletters, and journals. The inscriptions are copied by people who know local surnames and who may know where persons are buried for whom there are no gravestones. The volume is usually indexed and will have a location map showing where cemeteries are in relation to modern roads.

Cemetery Associations

Consult card indexes to inscriptions of cemetery associations (where they exist) for locations of cemeteries and plots. These indexes can save you hours of searching time and provide evidence of family members unknown to you who may be buried nearby. Some cemetery associations active in the United States today are shown in table 13-8. Most associations publish newsletters and hints on how to copy gravestone data or how to preserve cemeteries, including funding resources and work assignments. Some publish maps showing locations of cemeteries or display the sites on their Web pages, along with cemetery databases and links to cemetery-related sites.

Finding Cemeteries

If the cemetery name is not known, a county-wide search can be conducted. Procure a detailed county or city map with churches and cemeteries marked on it. County road maps are usually available through county or state highway departments,

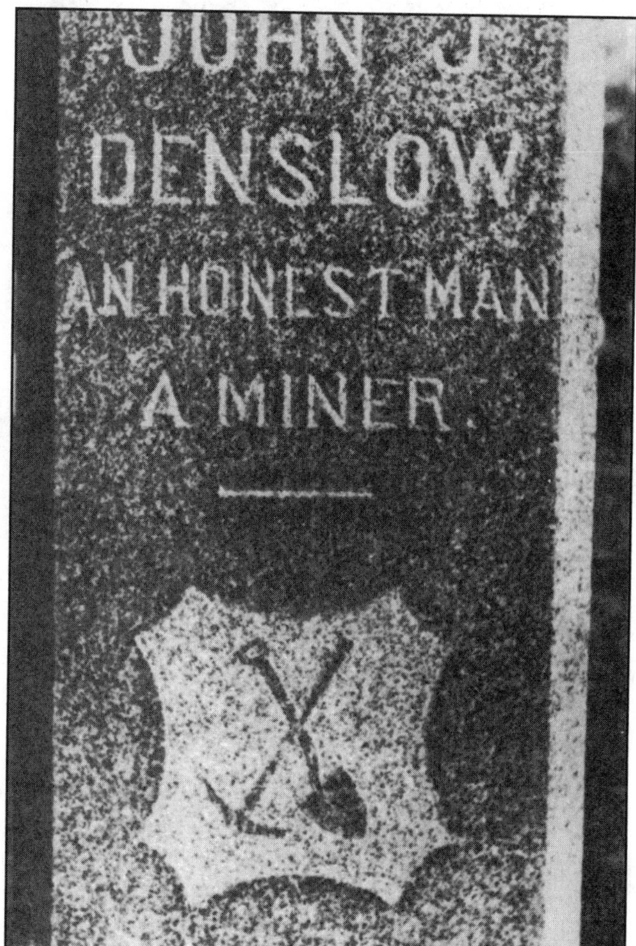

Figure 13-18. Miner's tombstone *(right)*; physician's tombstone *(left)*. Photographs taken in 1975, Mt. Olivet Cemetery, Salt Lake City, Utah.

assessors' offices, or registrars of deeds. In rural areas, it is also helpful to have a U.S. Geological Survey quadrangle map for the area you are researching, because some inactive cemeteries may not be indicated on the current county map. Mark the cemeteries nearest the land holdings or residences of family members directly on your map.

If the name of a cemetery is known, try searching for its location at the U.S. Bureau on Geographic Names website <http://geonames.usgs.gov>. If a cemetery is located, the response will identify the correct USGS 7.5 series map and give the latitude and longitude of the property. A link is offered to <www.topozone.com> where the cemetery will be shown on a USGS series map. Another option is to link to TerraServer for a contemporary aerial photograph of the terrain.

Many cemetery and tombstone inscription projects are including Global Positioning System (GPS) coordinates in their data files. Coordinates are also available from the search at the U.S. Board on Geographical Names described previously. Having the GPS location makes finding the cemetery easy. Graves also may be identified with GPS and adding the coordinates to transcription notes will mark the grave's location despite heavy snow or changes in terrain. For example, Samuel J. Kitterman, 1874–1968, is buried in the Kitterman Cemetery, Wapello County, Iowa. The grave's coordinate is 41° 02' 31" N 92° 20' 34" W.[12]

If these processes seem elaborate, consider that a county may cover more than six hundred square miles. You could spend hours driving and asking local residents, who may know less than you do about the area, without ever locating the cemetery where your ancestors are buried.

When searching for family burial plots, you are dependent upon your own keen observation and the help of local residents once you are within half a mile of the cemetery's location. Since the 1930s, increasingly large acreages left unattended have succumbed to weeds, brambles, and trees. Some of this land is in the federal land bank. Some has been left by owners who now work in industry. It is not uncommon to find a property owner

Figure 13-19. Image A: Tombstone of the child Antonio Morelli, Mt. Carmel Cemetery, Hillside, Illinois. Courtesy of Robert M. Tenuta. Images B, D, and E: Three tombstones from the tombstone photography project for Rock County, Wisconsin. They are among the more than five thousand photos taken by volunteers Lori and Tim Niemuth. Courtesy of the WIGenWeb-Rock County Project at RootsWeb.com <http://freepages.misc.rootsweb.com/~wirockbios/Tombstones>. Image C: Tombstone of Claude H. Kirk, Grove City Cemetery (formerly Grove City Methodist Church burial ground), Christian County, Illinois. Courtesy of Dr. Gary K. Hargis. Image F: Fallen marker for Louisa Santoro and her second husband, Leonardo Romanelli (pictured), Mt. Carmel Cemetery, Hillside, Illinois. Courtesy of Robert M. Tenuta.

Table 13-7. Some Websites Featuring Cemeteries, Tombstone Inscriptions, and Obituaries as of March 2006

Name	Address	Comments
Cemetery Records Online	www.daddezio.com/cemetery/	An online directory of more than 40,800 local and church cemeteries and over 27,000 family cemeteries. Site provides addresses, maps, and links to tombstone transcriptions (when known to exist).
Find a Grave	http://findagrave.com	This site contains 4.5 million names from over 70,000 cemeteries. Contributors can download Microsoft ExcelTemplates to use for submitting records to Find a Grave.
Funeral Net	http://funeralnet.com	Search for cemeteries, funeral homes, and obituaries at this site. Obituaries have been submitted by funeral homes
Interment.Net	http://interment.net	Search over 3.5 million records from more than 7,500 cemeteries. Site offers "How to Record a Cemetery," online submission forms, and instructions for using Microsoft Word, Excel, Access, and text files for submissions.
Obituary Central	http://obituarycentral.com	Search for obituaries and use a number of research tools, including the "Obituary Links Page," links to online obituaries, cemetery inscriptions, and birth, marriage, and death notices, arranged by state and county.
Obituary Daily Times	http://rootsweb.com/~obituary/	Search an index to nearly 8 million obituaries. Read the contributor handbook to understand the format and abbreviations used. Corresponding obituaries have not been published on this site.
Tombstone Transcription Project	http://rootsweb.com/~cemetery	Search the database created by volunteers who have transcribed tombstone inscriptions. Also, volunteer to transcribe a cemetery in your community.
Virtual Cemetery	http://genealogy.com/vcem_welcome.html	An electronic memorial with a collection of tombstone inscriptions and photographs contributed by users.

who is unaware of a burial plot in his or her woods. The best help may come from older residents who have lived in the area for years or young boys who enjoy rabbit and grouse hunting.

Relocated Cemeteries

In areas where land use has changed from agricultural to urban or industrial, few local people actually know where cemeteries have been relocated, but local historical societies have done much to preserve records of them.

When a dam is built, with subsequent flooding of local areas, or a freeway planned or an energy reservation set aside, surveys of local cemeteries are made to determine if any will be disturbed and, if so, where the bodies will be reinterred. These reinterment projects produce generally accurate records of all graves and inscriptions. Efforts are made to identify the occupants of unmarked graves using family records, the memories of local residents, and public documents.

These interments are usually recorded on file cards that are arranged alphabetically within geographic areas. They are open to the public through mail, e-mail, or telephone requests and the information is usually available without charge or for a minimal copying fee. A good example is the Tennessee Valley Authority, with its thousands of maps, cemetery inscriptions, and other valuable materials all along the Tennessee River. Some maps and cemetery inscriptions are available through the TVA Map Store, 1101 Market Street, Chattanooga, TN 37402-2801. A full list of maps is available at their website <www.tva.gov>.

Military facilities sometimes relocate graves as well. Fort McPherson National Cemetery in Maxwell, Nebraska, opened in 1873 to consolidate twenty-two cemeteries in Colorado, Wyoming, South Dakota, Idaho, and Nebraska. By 1947, the project had been completed. The cemetery is carefully plotted and indexed with control markers throughout the grounds; even so, there are 584 "unknown" graves. Copies of these records are in the National Archives, at Fort McPherson in Maxwell, Nebraska, or online at <www.interment.net>.

Churches that were moved during the years of their existence usually have more than one burial ground. For example, the old cemetery of the Augusta Stone Church in Fort Defiance, Augusta County, Virginia, is walled and stands behind a screen of trees. On a hillside within the walls is the grave of Rachel (Crawford) Berry, who was born on 18 April 1812 and died on 23 May 1832, wife of Thornton Berry. One hundred yards away in the Crawford family plot lies her ten-year-old son, James. Across the main highway lies another portion of the cemetery. This adjoins the new Augusta Stone Church. There lies Thornton Berry, who died on 11 December 1882 at age seventy-two, and his second wife, Nancy, who died in April (year illegible) at age eighty-one, and other members of his family. Had the old portion, which is not visible from the road, been overlooked, the graves of Thornton's first wife and son would not have been found.

It was fairly common for congregations to split during controversies and for the dissenting unit to build separate facilities—meetinghouse and cemetery—a few miles away. An example is found in Virginia. New Providence congregation broke with Old Providence over the procedure of singing hymns in meetings in the early nineteenth century. As a result, there are two churches and two cemeteries located only two miles apart. Sometimes the two congregations reunite at a later time and build a third meetinghouse, closing down the previous two. Furthermore, because it is common for members of the same family to have belonged to different churches, you should plan to search all cemeteries in the immediate vicinity of the family home, regardless of religious affiliations.

The procedure to follow in locating graves differs somewhat depending upon the size of the cemetery. The sexton's records, when they exist, should be searched first regardless of the size or type of gravestone. By looking at the names, you can locate females with surnames of interest who are buried under married names in the plots of other relatives who have surnames unknown to you.

Family cemeteries are usually very small and without sexton's records. You should, therefore, read every gravestone to determine which graves are those of ancestral families. For very large public, church, and private cemeteries, consult the various kinds of sexton's records to determine when family members were buried and the exact locations of each one. Then check the master plat or map showing the individual cemetery plats and their smaller subdivisions (sections, blocks, tiers, etc.) to determine the locations of graves for the period of time in which you are interested. Some cemeteries provide smaller map reproductions on which you can mark the gravesites in which you are particularly interested.

Searching in Cemeteries

It is best to explore cemeteries with one or more companions rather than conducting a search alone. Drive through or walk around the cemetery before examining individual gravestones. Absorb some of the atmosphere of the setting. Consider the location, the upkeep

Table 13-8. Select List of Cemetery Associations and Preservation Organizations

Organization	Website Address
Association for Gravestone Studies 278 Main Street, Suite 207 Greenfield, MA 01301	www.gravestonestudies.org
California Historic Cemetery Alliance PO Box 255345 Sacramento, CA 95805-5345	www.califhistcemeteries.org
Chicora Foundation, Inc. PO Box 8664 Columbia, SC 29202-8664	www.chicora.org
Connecticut Gravestone Network 135 Wells Street Manchester, CT 06040-6127	www.ctgravestones.com
State Association for the Preservation of Iowa Cemeteries 21813 170th Street Birmingham, IA 52535-8046	www.rootsweb.com/~iasapc
Kentucky Cemetery Project Kentucky Historical Society 300 W. Broadway Frankfort, KY 40601	http://catalog.kyhistory.org
Save Our Cemeteries, Inc. PO Box 58105 New Orleans, LA 70158-8105	www.saveourcemeteries.org
Coalition to Protect Maryland Burial Sites, Inc. PO Box 1533 Ellicott City, MD 21041-1533	http://rootsweb.com/~mdcpmbs
National Catholic Cemetery Conference 710 N. River Road Des Plaines, IL 60016-1296	www.ntriplec.com
New Hampshire Old Graveyard Association webmaster@nhoga.org	www.rootsweb.com/~nhoga
Ohio Cemetery Preservation Society PO Box 24180 Lyndhurst, OH 44124-0810	www.rootsweb.com/~ohcps
Oregon Historic Cemeteries Association PO Box 14279 Portland, OR 97293-0279	www.oregoncemeteries.org
Saving Graves http://www.savinggraves.org/about/contactform.html	www.savinggraves.org
Cemetery Association of Tennessee PO Box 210242 Nashville, TN 37221-0242	www.tenncemetery.com
Vermont Old Cemetery Association PO Box 132 Townsend, VT 05353	http://sover.net/~hwdbry/voca
Wisconsin Old Cemetery Association PO Box 141 Windsor, WI 53598-0141	

and condition, size, presence of above-ground burials, fenced-off or enclosed sections, plantings, artwork and statuary, presence of the graves of prominent citizens, positioning of gravestones and their relationship to others, and color and material of the stones. These elements provide evidence of ethnic graveyards, the economic base of the community, historical events, lifestyle and outlook of local residents, and other details.

Next, focus on individual gravestones, looking for naming patterns in the plots. A large name stone in the center with smaller stones around it bearing only given names may indicate Swedish origins. If the smaller gravestones have relationships or initials only, it may indicate German origins.

Note the dates of death. Many gravestones with proximate death dates can indicate an epidemic, a weather disaster, a mine accident, or the close of a generation. For example, in the Darling, Minnesota, Swedish cemetery, burials took place starting about 1870. They were the children of the immigrant generation who arrived in Minnesota just before the turn of the century with their parents or were born shortly after their arrival in America.

A Swedish cemetery will have gravestones in gray, sand, pink, and other warm, soft colors. The setting will be uncluttered, with open spaces around the plots and scanty data on the stones. Polish graves have large, heavy black or red gravestones in rows, with precise dates and frequently the original spelling of the surname. Early New England and Virginia origins show up in ornate carvings of winged death heads, weeping willows, and all-seeing eyes on gravestones large enough to include the essential facts and a scriptural verse. These gravestones are liberally interspersed with flat, biographical gravestones giving full details of family relationships. Quaker gravestones were exactly twelve inches high until well into the nineteenth century. Quaker stones with incomplete or missing inscriptions may have been "oversize" monuments that Quaker leaders ordered trimmed to customary size.

Many cemeteries have special sections set aside for specific kinds of burials. The sexton's records for the paupers' section will be found among poor relief or workhouse records; African American, Asians, and Native Americans may be buried in "colored" sections; religious sections may contain Catholics, Jews, or Muslims. Those who died without the sacraments of a church may be found in an unconsecrated section of a religious cemetery. In Masonic sections, burials are in crypts or wall vaults. Watch for other sections as well.

The best time of year to conduct cemetery searches is in the early spring, after winter has killed the weeds and before spring briars and grasses begin growing or snakes come out of hibernation. Snow and winter rain will have removed some of the moss from the faces of the gravestones.

Many cemeteries, especially abandoned ones, harbor snakes, chiggers, poison ivy, thorns, and other natural hazards. Wear protective clothing, including gloves and sturdy shoes. Be alert for animals, uneven ground, and other hazards. A can of Mace or another eye-stinging mist may deter dogs. Again, knowledgeable cemetery searchers advise never going to a cemetery alone.

Reading and Photographing Gravestones

Whether an "expedition" to read cemetery stones is a personal or group project, make every effort to secure permission from the proper authorities in advance. Explain the nature of your work and be specific about how you intend to approach the reading or photography. Become familiar with the proper methods of care for these valuable and irreplaceable artifacts. Be aware that in some states practices deemed detrimental to tombstones are against the law.

The popular stones for markers in years gone by were often soft. Often, old inscriptions are so weathered they can hardly be deciphered. Furthermore, there may be an accumulation of moss or lichen on the gravestones. It is improper to use harsh abrasives or wire brushes to remove such growth because these measures further damage the inscriptions and are of questionable value even to the immediate user. Chalking is not a good practice; it can actually stain porous stone. If a gravestone must be cleaned, preservationists recommend gently brushing away loose material with a natural bristle brush, then wetting the gravestone with clean water. Carefully remove organic growth with a natural bristle brush, using a smaller brush to clean incised areas. Thoroughly rinse the stone with clean water and pat the surface dry with a soft towel.[13]

For details on how to make a documentary photograph (as opposed to an artistically pleasing photograph), some good references are available. In *Digitizing Your Family History*, Rhonda McClure gives suggestions for using the special features of a digital camera to photograph gravestones. The chapter "An Introduction to Digital Photography" is a must-read for those contemplating the purchase of a digital camera. And her advice to those who buy is to become thoroughly familiar with your camera *before* you enter the cemetery.[14]

Online, Steve Paul Johnson's "Recording Cemeteries with Digital Photography" at <www.interment.net/column/records/digital/digital.htm> is instructive. Society leaders planning a cemetery recording project will note the increase in productivity with a camera. By hand this avid recorder could transcribe from 250 to 300 tombstones daily. Using a Palm II (handheld computer) he was able to do 75 to 100 tombstones per hour. After perfecting his technique with a digital camera, he can photograph 100 tombstones in 30 minutes without fatigue.

Photographers who prefer a thirty-five millimeter camera may consult, see Daniel and Jessie Lie Farber's *Making Photographic Records of Gravestones*.[15] The Farbers advise that documentary photographs be made only in brilliant sunlight. The light should fall across the face of the gravestone at an angle of approximately thirty degrees. If necessary, a mirror can be positioned to reflect sunlight across the stone. Never attempt to straighten a leaning or fallen gravestone. Doing so could result in permanent damage to the marker. Instead, tilt the camera to correspond with the lean of the stone. A thirty-five millimeter camera is recommended. For black-and-white photographs, tri-X film shot at a shutter speed of 1/250th of a second produces good results. Using a tripod and light meter can further enhance results.

While photographing produces an exact copy of the gravestone, it may not give you a legible reproduction of the text on the stone. Always copy the inscription in your notes in case the photograph does not turn out. And remember, the best preservation method of all is to share the information with others. Duplicate the results of a cemetery photography session and send copies to other family members. Or place the pictures online, perhaps at the USGenWeb Tombstone Transcription Project site <www.rootsweb.com/~cemetery/memor_2.html>. Search the Internet for collections by others, such as the Farber Gravestone Collection of over 13,500 images documenting the sculpture on more than 9,000 gravestones. Most of these stones date prior to 1800 and are in the Northeastern part of the United States. A website and online image database <www.davidrumsey.com/farber> has been created by David Rumsey Cartography Association with the sponsorship of the American Antiquity Society.

Special Problems Encountered When Recording Gravestone Data

Making Gravestone Rubbings. The practice of making impressions by laying paper or fabric onto a tombstone and rubbing it with chalk or charcoal is viewed as potentially destructive by professional preservationists. The following caution, from cemetery conservation activist and author Lynette Strangstad, is worth repeating: "Gravestone rubbing should be strongly curtailed or eliminated due to potential damage to markers. Irreparable and significant damage has been done by people who thought they were careful and knowledgeable. In addition to the damage caused by pigment residue, most visitors are not able to accurately distinguish between sound gravestones and unstable ones. Because of the potential damage, rubbing is best avoided altogether."[16]

Fallen Markers. Markers frequently fall and are buried under an accumulation of undergrowth and topsoil. When working in poorly kept cemeteries, carry a probe long enough to gently check the ground eight to ten inches deep. Carefully check fence lines and hedgerows. Fallen markers that could not be easily replaced may have been carried to the side and propped against a fence or left on the ground. Though they cannot be readily identified with the appropriate plot, the inscriptions are still valuable. Notify the proper authorities of the locations of fallen markers; do not attempt to replace or repair them yourself.

Duplicate Gravestones. When a new gravestone is prepared for a grave, there is always the possibility that the stonecutter will leave the original stone in place; you may thus find two gravestones for the same person. In very old cemeteries, you may also discover some apparent duplicates that are really a headstone and a footstone. A gravestone for the same person may appear in a family cemetery or plot with a second gravestone in the cemetery where the person is actually buried.

Recording Cemetery Data

The more times you copy an inscription, the greater the chance of error. Therefore, take an ample supply of family group worksheets or research notepaper with you and transcribe the data directly on the worksheet or notepaper.

Most researchers copy only the direct genealogical data: dates and places of birth and death, parents, husband, and wife. Such a practice, however, can cause you to overlook the clues indicated in the selection of epitaphs: church affiliation, survivors, occupations, military service, cause of death, physical description, citizenship, and migration patterns.

Another reason for recording all that you find is the fragility of the site. Once you leave the site, the information may no longer be available to you. Many cemeteries are destroyed through vandalism, development, or other circumstances, and what you record on your visit may soon thereafter prove to be the only information available. Consider the potential needs of those working in related fields—landscape historians, archaeologists, folklorists, and preservationists, as well as future family historians who could benefit from your data. Always reread your notes for accuracy and completeness before leaving the cemetery, comparing them to the gravestones.

One manner of insuring a complete recording of data is to plot the site. Because people are usually buried in family units, drawing a diagram of each plot enables you to analyze graves in their relationships to others: size, location, gravestones, and so on. On the backs of your worksheets, sketch the gravestones as they appear in the plot; number each one, then list the inscription and description of the stone by the same number on the worksheets. Where family units are definite, record them on the same worksheet as a family; but where there is any question, list each one on a separate sheet and refer by number back to the plot you have drawn for the relationship of each individual grave to the entire plot. Figure 13-20 is an example taken from the Lexington Presbyterian Church Cemetery in Lexington, Virginia. The numbers refer to the inscription notes, which made it possible to analyze some family relationships.

Unit 1

1. Margaret McDowell, wife of Robert McDowell, died 14 Feb. 1830, age 70.
2. Robert McDowell, born 10 Mar. 1767, died 2 Aug. 1838. Both stones were identical (despite the difference in the sketch).

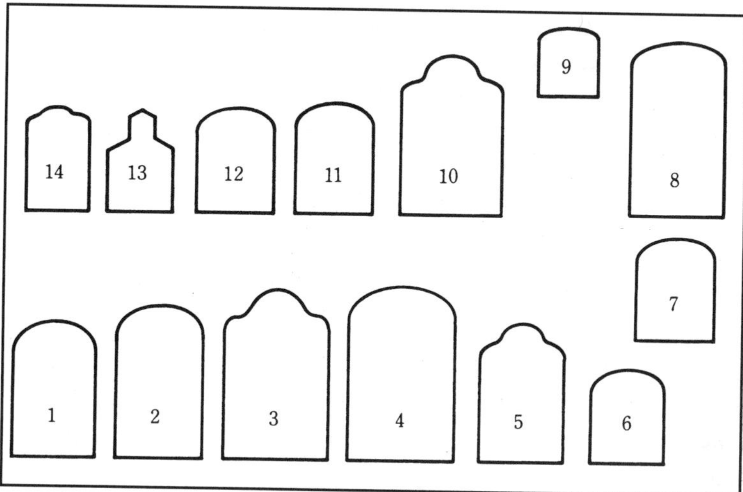

Figure 13-20. Researcher's hand-drawn plot of gravestones showing comparative sizes, shapes, and proximity. All of the markers are of sandstone with legible inscriptions. They were copied from Lexington Presbyterian Church Cemetery, Virginia.

Unit 2

3. Zachariah Johnston, died 7 Jan. 1800, age 57.
4. Ann Johnston, died 25 Aug. 1818, age 77.

Unit 3

5. Sally W. Johnston, wife of Alexander Johnston, born 29 Jan, 1776, died 30 Apr. 1818, age 43.
6. Zechariah G. Johnston, born 18 June 1807, died 28 June 1815, age 6. This inscription was rather hard to read.
7. A.J., no date, child's grave with no other inscription, probably part of the Johnston family and a grandchild of Zachariah and Ann.

Unit 4

8. Ann, daughter of Susan and Thomas Johnston, born 10 Apr. 1803, died 7 oct. 1834.
9. William G. Johnston, son of Susan and Thomas Johnston, born 27 Jan. 1819.
10. Susan, daughter of Susan and Thomas Johnston, died 10 April 1832, age 22.
11. Susan Johnston, wife of Thomas Johnston, died 19 Nov. 1857, age 81.
12. Thomas Johnston, born 10 Jan. 1773, died 27 Dec. 1847.

Individual Burials

13. Elizabeth McDowell, "Our Loving Aunt," born 28 Sept. 1796, died 29 May 1861.
14. Rebecca (Our Sister), wife of William C. Lewis, died 2 April 1857, age 57.

In this plat, family groupings are clear in most cases, and certain hypotheses can be made and tested with evidence from other sources.

Although compiled records cannot fully replace a personal search, historical, genealogical, and patriotic societies have performed a valuable and commendable service in preparing compilations of gravestone inscriptions, especially in view of the annual toll taken on grave markers through neglect, highway construction, suburban development, and reclamation projects. Beware, however, that compiled sources obscure family relationships because the entries are artificially arranged in an alphabetical sequence. The value of such works is dramatically increased when the inscriptions are listed as found in the graveyard, cross-referenced to their specific locations on a map of the cemetery, and indexed by surname on separate pages.

Another weakness of these compilations comes from including only the names, dates of birth and death, and relationships. Indirect evidence and clues are omitted because they are too voluminous. In a printed compilation of gravestones in Tinkling Spring Presbyterian Cemetery in Fisherville, Augusta County, Virginia, the alphabetical sequence reads:

> Cynthia Johnson
> Born 19 Dec 1799
> Died 15 Aug 1887
> Aged 87 years 7 months and 26 days
> Wife of Thomas Johnson
> Thomas Johnson
> died 19 Dec 1865
> Age 75 years, 4 months and 25 days[17]

In the cemetery itself, in a lovely, wrought-iron fenced enclosure, the graves of Cynthia and Thomas lie surrounded by Cynthia's family: her parents, James and Martha Black; and several of her brothers, sisters, and their families. However, nothing in the printed volume connects Cynthia with the Black family.

Preservation of Cemeteries

All researchers need to be concerned about and supportive of the ongoing efforts of cemetery preservation organizations and genealogical and historical societies seeking to bring conservation procedures to the attention of cemetery officials. Individuals and groups interested in familiarizing themselves with this process (which certainly should be done before any cemetery projects are undertaken) would benefit from a study of Lynette Strangstad, *A Graveyard Preservation Primer.* This work was published in cooperation with the Association for Gravestone Studies and is a landmark in the field. Their website at <http://gravestonestudies.org> has a current list of the association's publications.

Funeral Homes and Burial Customs

The records of funeral homes may provide personal information about the deceased, such as full name, age, dates of birth, death, and burial, cause of death, former address and occupation of the deceased and place of death and burial. There may also be notes regarding the funeral services, the name of the person who officiated, and the identity and relationship of whomever made the arrangements. If the body was shipped from or to another city, there may be a copy of the transportation of corpse form that accompanied the remains.

The name of a funeral home may appear in family records or on the death certificate, cemetery office record, or the obituary. A search online by name, city, and state should provide contact information if the business is still in operation or, if the business has closed but the records have been indexed in a database, a website might be given. A search for the J. F. Bell Funeral Home in central Virginia, yielded information on the history of the funeral home, which was established in 1917, and the family that now manages it, descendants of John Ferris Bell (1890–1959). A database to information from the Bell registers is at <www.virginia.edu/woodson/projects/bell>.

Funeral homes are often family owned for two or more generations and records are usually meticulously preserved. Because a funeral home is a privately-owned business, its staff is not obligated to provide information from their registers. Fortunately, most directors will share information in response to a brief and courteous inquiry.

To find records of funeral homes that are no longer operating, see chapter 4, "Business, Institution, and Organization Records."

Funeral and burial customs have varied over the centuries but throughout history, it is location, ethnicity, and religion that determine how the dead will be laid to rest. For example, cremation is required in the faiths of Buddhism and Hinduism yet prohibited for members of the Free Presbyterian Church and the Islamic religion. Many customs, some of which are still followed, date directly from the Victorian period in England, when first upper society and then more commonly-situated folk adopted the fashions and practices of their Queen. Black dress, mourning jewelry, and postmortem photographs or etchings were founded in the nineteenth century. In larger urban areas, mourners' coaches came into being. These were the equivalent of a limousine today; examples may be viewed at <www.hearse.com>.

Many of these objects, including an early hearse, are preserved in the Museum of Funeral Customs in Springfield, Illinois, and some may be viewed on virtual tour at <www.funeralmuseum.org>. An excellent discussion of customs and folkways used by Americans and by certain ethnic and religious groups is featured in Sharon Carmack's *Your Guide to Cemetery Research.*

In the original edition of *The Source,* Arlene Eakle closed this section with words that are still apt. "I confess to a weakness for the emotional impact of searching a graveyard, but the wealth of direct and circumstantial evidence a cemetery can provide would still justify a search on the least sentimental of grounds. Although the extra time, expense, and inconvenience of on-site searches may deter a genealogist, examining these sources with the same care and thoroughness you would bring to library research pays off."

Notes

[1] "Marriage Contract of Charles de La Verge and Marie Joseph Carriere," in *Louisiana Marriage Contracts,* comp. Alice Daly Forsyth and Ghislaine Pleasanton (New Orleans: Polyanthos, 1980), 85.

[2] Alice Eichholz, ed., *Red Book: American State, County, and Town Sources,* 3rd. ed. (Provo, Utah: Ancestry, 2004).

[3] Helen L. Harris, Elizabeth J. Wall, and Betty Treat Petrich, comps., *Marriage Records of Squires Isaac and Joseph F. Mayes* (Pittsburgh: privately published, 1978), 59.

[4] Connie Bell and Vernell Walker, comps., *Union Pacific Railroad Life Insurance Claims Data* (Salt Lake City: microfilmed by the Genealogical Society of Utah, 1990).

[5] David Dobson, comp., *American Vital Records from the Gentleman's Magazine, 1731–1868* (Baltimore: Genealogical Publishing Co., 1987).

[6] William Wade Hinshaw, *Encyclopedia of American Quaker Genealogy,* 6 vols. (1969; reprint, Baltimore: Genealogical Publishing Co., 1991–94); also on CD-ROM with full index, same title and publisher.

[7] Willard Heiss, *Abstracts of the Records of the Society of Friends in Indiana, Part One through Six (1962–1975) with Index* (Indianapolis: Indiana Historical Society, 1972).

[8] Arlene Eakle, *How to Search a Cemetery* (Salt Lake City: Genealogical Institute, 1974).

[9] Lynette Strangstad, *A Graveyard Preservation Primer* (Nashville: American Association for State and Local History, 1988).

[10] St. David's Reformed Church (also known as Killinger Church), Death Register, Dauphin County, Pennsylvania, microfilm copy of typescript at the Family History Library, GSU-020,348, item 7.

[11] A useful list, titled "Gravestone Art, Symbols, Emblems, and Attributes," is in appendix A of Sharon DeBartolo Carmack, *Your Guide to Cemetery Research* (Cincinnati: Betterway Books, 2002) 2150–23.

[12] "The Use of GPS in Locating a Cemetery or Gravesites," at Saving Graves <www.savinggraves.org/education/index.htm>.

[13] More detailed information is at the Oregon Historic Cemeteries Association website at <www.oregoncemeteries.org>. See Jeanne Robinson, "Cleaning Marble Tombstones II."

[14] Rhonda R. McClure, *Digitizing Your Family History* (Cincinnati: Family Tree Books, 2004).

[15] Daniel and Jessie Lie Farber, *Making Photographic Records of Gravestones,* a leaflet published by The Association for Gravestone Studies, 30 Elm St., Worcester, MA 01609 <www.gravestonestudies.org>.

[16] *Preservation of Historic Burial Grounds,* Information Series No. 76, 1993 (Reprint, Washington, D.C.: National Trust for Historic Preservation, 2003).

[17] Howard M. Wilson, *Tinkling Spring: Headwater of Freedom* (Fisherville, Va.: for the congregation, 1954), appendix E.

References

General References

Eichholz, Alice, ed. *Red Book: American State, County, and Town Sources.* 3d. ed. Provo, Utah: Ancestry, 2004.

Heiss, Willard. *Abstracts of the Records of the Society of Friends in Indiana, Part One through Six (1962–1975) with Index.* Indianapolis: Indiana Historical Society, 1972.

Hinshaw, William Wade. *Encyclopedia of American Quaker Genealogy.* 6 vols. 1969; reprint, Baltimore: Genealogical Publishing Co., 1991–94.

McClure, Rhonda R. *Digitizing Your Family History.* Cincinnati: Family Tree Books, 2004.

Marriage, Birth, and Death

Appleton, William S. *Boston Births, Baptisms, Marriages, and Deaths, 1630–1699 and Boston Births, 1700–1800, 1883, 1894.* Reprint, Baltimore: Genealogical Publishing Co., 1994.

Arnold, James N. *Vital Records of Rhode Island, 1636–1850: A Family Register for the People.* 20 vols. Providence, R.I.: Narragansett Historical Publishing, 1891–1912. Index to Arnold's *Rhode Island Vital Records: Rhode Island Cemetery Records.* Microfilm. 11 reels. Salt Lake City: Genealogical Society of Utah, 1950. Contains entries taken from county, church, periodical, military, newspaper, and other sources.

Bartley, Scott Andrew. *Researching American Vital Statistics Records.* Toronto: Heritage Productions, 2001.

Bowman, Fred Q. *10,000 Vital Records of Central New York, 1813–1850.* Reprint, Baltimore: Genealogical Publishing Co., 1999.

———. *10,000 Vital Records of Eastern New York, 1777–1834.* Reprint, Baltimore: Genealogical Publishing Co., 1999.

———. *10,000 Vital Records of Western New York, 1809–1850.* Reprint, Baltimore: Genealogical Publishing Co., 1999.

———. *8,000 More Vital Records of Eastern New York, 1804–1850.* Rhinebeck, N.Y.: Kinship, 1991.

———. *7,000 Hudson-Mowhawk Valley (NY) Vital Records, 1808–1850.* Baltimore: Genealogical Publishing Co., 1997.

California State Register. *California Vital Records Indexes.* Microfiche. Sacramento, Calif.: Office of the State Registrar, 1997. Includes: California Birth Records Index, 1905–97; California Marriage Records Index, 1960–97; California Death Records Index, 1940–97.

Cott, Nancy F. *Public Vows: A History of Marriage and the Nation.* Cambridge, Mass.: Harvard University Press, 2001.

Delaware. Bureau of Vital Statistics. *Index Cards to Delaware Marriages, Baptisms, Births, and Deaths, 1670–1913.* Microfilm. 18 reels. Salt Lake City: Genealogical Society of Utah, 1949. Includes Marriages, 1680 to 1850; Baptisms, 1759–1890; Births, 1759–1890; and Deaths prior to 1888. Index to be used to access vital records of the Delaware Bureau of Vital Statistics.

Dobson, David, comp. *American Vital Records from the* Gentleman's Magazine, *1731–1868.* Baltimore: Genealogical Publishing Co., 1987.

Forsyth, Alice Daly, and Ghislaine Pleasanton, comps. *Louisiana Marriage Contracts.* New Orleans: Polyanthos, 1980.

Goodsell, Willystine. *A History of Marriage and the Family.* Rev. ed. New York: Macmillan, 1934.

Hale, Charles R. *Hale Collection.* 360 reels of microfilm. Salt Lake City: Genealogical Society of Utah, 1949–50. Collection includes cemetery records and newspaper notices from Connecticut; also an index to death and marriage notices by newspaper.

Harris, Helen L., Elizabeth J. Wall, and Betty Treat Petrich, comps. *Marriage Records of Squires Isaac and Joseph F. Mayes.* Pittsburgh: Privately published, 1978.

Hartog, Hendrik. *Man and Wife in America: A History.* Cambridge, Mass.: Harvard University Press, 2002.

Hebert, Donald J. *South Louisiana Records.* 40 vols. Cecilia, La.: the author, 1978–94. Collection covers the following civil parishes (counties): Acadia, Allen, Beauregard, Calcasieu, Cameron, Iberia, Jefferson Davis, Lafayette, St. Landry, St. Martin, St. Mary, Vangeline, and Vermillion.

Howard, George E. *History of Matrimonial Institutions.* 3 vols. Chicago: University of Chicago Press, 1904.

Kemp, Thomas J. *International Vital Records Handbook.* 4th ed. Baltimore: Genealogical Publishing Co., 2002.

Maher, James P. *Index to Marriages and Deaths in the New York Herald*. 3 vols. Baltimore: Genealogical Publishing Co., 1987–2000. Vol. 1: 1835–55; Vol. 2: 1856–63; Vol. 3: 1864–70.

Massachusetts, Secretary of the Commonwealth. *Indexes to Births, Marriages, and Deaths, 1841–1971*. Microfilm. Salt Lake City: Genealogical Society of Utah, 1974–85.

North, S. N. D., comp. Marriage *Laws in the United States, 1887–1906*. Reprint, Conway, Ark.: Arkansas Research, 1994.

Rose, Christine. "Birth, Marriage, and Death." Chap. 10 in *Courthouse Research for Family Historians*. San Jose, Calif.: CR Publications, 2004.

Saxbe, William B., Jr. "Nineteenth-Century Death Records: How Dependable Are They?" *National Genealogical Society Quarterly* 87 (March 1999): 43–54.

Vital Records of [Town], Massachusetts, to the Year 1850. Boston: New England Historic Genealogical Society, 1902–ca. 1920. The official series of published vital records for nearly two hundred towns in Massachusetts; each town printed separately.

White, Lorraine Cook, comp. *The Barbour Collection of Connecticut Town Vital Records*. 55 vols. Baltimore: Genealogical Publishing Co., 1994–2002.

Winslow, Raymond A., Jr. "Marriage, Divorce, and Vital Records." In *North Carolina Research: Genealogy and Local History*, edited by Helen F. M. Leary. 2nd ed. Raleigh: North Carolina Genealogical Society, 1996.

Wisconsin, Bureau of Health Statistics. *Index to Registration of Births, 1852–1907*. 41 microfiche. Madison: Wisconsin State Historical Society, 1979.

———. *Pre-1907 Death Index by Name*. 29 microfiche. Madison: Wisconsin State Historical Society, 1981.

Cemeteries and Gravestones

Beable, W. H. *Epitaphs: Graveyard Humor and Eulogy*. 1925; reprint, Detroit: Singing Tree, 1971.

Bouchard, Betty J. *Our Silent Neighbors: A Study of Gravestones in the Olde Salem Area*. Salem, Mass.: T. B. S. Enterprises, 1991.

Bower, John. *Guardians of the Soul: Angels and Innocents, Mourners and Saints—Indiana's Remarkable Cemetery Sculpture*. Bloomington, Ind.: Studio Indiana, 2004.

Brown, John Gary. *Soul in the Stone: Cemetery Art From America's Heartland*. Lawrence: University Press of Kansas, 1994.

Bunnen, Lucinda, and Virginia Warren Smith. *Scoring in Heaven: Gravestones and Cemetery Art of the American Sunbelt States*. New York: Aperture, 2000.

Burek, Deborah M., ed. *Cemeteries of the United States: A Guide to Contact Information for U.S. Cemeteries and Their Records*. Detroit: Gale Research Co., 1994.

Burns, Stanley B. *Sleeping Beauty II: Grief, Bereavement in Memorial Photography: American and European Traditions*. Pasadena, Calif.: Twelve Trees, 2002.

Carmack, Sharon DeBartolo. *Your Guide to Cemetery Research*. Cincinnati: Betterway Books, 2002.

Eakle, Arlene. *How to Search a Cemetery*. Salt Lake City: Genealogical Institute, 1974.

Farber, Daniel, and Jessie Farber. *Making Photographic Records of Gravestones*. Leaflet available from Association for Gravestone Studies. <www.gravestonestudies.org>.

Florence, Robert. *New Orleans Cemeteries: Life in the Cities of the Dead*. New Orleans: Batture, 1997.

Gillespie, Angus K. "Gravestones and Ostentation: A Study of Five Delaware County Cemeteries." *Pennsylvania Folklife* 19, no. 2 (Winter 1969–70): 34–43.

Grace, Jack and Tom White. *Cincinnati Cemeteries: The Queen City Underground (Images of America)*. Arcadian Publishers, 2004.

Halporn, Roberta. *New York Is a Rubber's Paradise: A Guide to Historical Cemeteries in the Five Boroughs*. Brooklyn, N.Y.: Center for Thanatology Research and Education, 1999.

Helge, Janice. "Managing a Cemetery Project." *FORUM* 13, no. 2 (Summer 2001): 11–14.

Jackson, Kenneth T., and Camilo Jose Vergara. *Silent Cities: The Evolution of the American Cemetery*. New York: Princeton Architectural Press, 1989.

Jalland, Patricia. *Death in the Victorian Family*. New York: Oxford University Press, 1996.

Jeane, D. Gregory. "Southern Gravestones: Sacred Artifacts in the Upland South Folk Graveyard." *Markers IV: The Journal of the Association of Gravestone Studies* (1987): 55–84.

Jones, Constance. *R.I.P.: The Complete Book of Death and Dying*. New York: Harper-Collins, 1997.

Kay, J. H. "Sixty Million Graves: The Virginia Cemetery Extravaganza." *Nation* (19 February 1977): 209–12.

Kiester, Douglas. *Stories in Stone: A Field Guide to Cemetery Symbolism and Iconography*. Layton, Utah: Gibbs Smith, 2004.

Ludwig, Allan I. *Graven Images: New England Stonecarving and Its Symbols, 1650–1815*. Middleton, Conn.: Wesleyan University Press, 1975.

McDonald, Frank E. "Pennsylvania German Tombstone Art of Lebanon County, Pennsylvania." *Pennsylvania Folklife* 25, no. 1 (Autumn 1975).

Meyer, Richard E., ed. *Cemeteries and Gravemarkers: Voices of American Culture*. Ann Arbor: UMI Research Press, 1989.

Mitford, Jessica. *The American Way of Death Revisited.* New York: Alfred A. Knopf, 1998.

Montell, William Lynwood. *Ghosts along the Cumberland: Deathlore in the Kentucky Foothills.* Nashville: American Association for State and Local History, 1971.

Nishiura, Elizabeth. *American Battle Monuments: A Guide to Battlefields and Cemeteries of the United States Armed Forces.* Detroit: Omnigraphics, 1989.

Preservation of Historic Burial Grounds. Information Series no. 76. 1993; reprint, Washington, D.C.: National Trust for Historic Preservation, 2003.

Rees, Nigel. *Epitaphs: A Dictionary of Grave Epigrams and Memorial Eloquence.* New York: Carroll and Graf, 1994.

Roberts, Warren E. "Tools on Tombstones: Some Indian Examples." *Pioneer America* (June 1978): 106–11.

Robinson, David, and Dean R. Koontz. *Beautiful Death: Art of the Cemetery.* New York: Penguin, 1996.

Sloane, David C. *The Last Great Necessity: Cemeteries in American History.* Baltimore: Johns Hopkins University Press, 1995.

Solomon, Jack, and Olivia Solomon. *Gone Home: Southern Folk Gravestone Art.* Montgomery, Ala.: New South Books, 2004.

Spencer, Thomas E. *Where They're Buried: A Directory Containing More Than Twenty-Thousand Names of Notable Persons Buried in American Cemeteries.* 1999; reprint, Baltimore: Clearfield, 2001.

Strangstad, Lynette. *A Graveyard Preservation Primer.* Lanham, Mass.: Rowman and Littlefield, 1995.

———. *Preservation of Historic Burial Grounds (Updated).* Washington, D.C.: National Trust for Historic Preservation, 2003. <www.preservationbooks.org>.

Vlach, John. "Graveyards and Afro American Art." In *Long Journey Home: Folklife in the South.* Chapel Hill, N.C.: Southern Exposure, 1977.

Wilson, Howard M. *Tinkling Spring: Headwater of Freedom.* Fisherville, Va.: for the congregation, 1954.

Woolley, Brian, et al. *Final Destinations: A Travel Guide for Remarkable Cemeteries in Texas, New Mexico, Oklahoma, Arkansas, and Louisiana.* Denton: University of North Texas, 2000.

Worpole, Ken. *Last Landscapes: The Architecture of the Cemetery in the West.* London: Reaktion Books, 2004.

Funerals, Funeral Homes, Morticians, and Miscellaneous

American Blue Book of Funeral Directors. New York: American Funeral Director, published every even-numbered year.

Bell, Connie, and Vernell Walker, comps. *Union Pacific Railroad Life Insurance Claims Data.* Salt Lake City: microfilmed by the Genealogical Society of Utah, 1990.

Coffin, Margaret M. *Death in Early America: The History and Folklore of Customs and Superstitions of Early Medicine, Funerals, Burials, and Mourning.* Nashville: Thomas Nelson, 1976.

Habenstein, Robert W., and William M. Lamers. *The History of American Funeral Directing.* Detroit: Omnigraphics, 1990.

Jerger, Jeanette L. *A Medical Miscellany for Genealogists.* Bowie, Md.: Heritage Books, 1995.

Laderman, Gary. *Rest in Peace: A Cultural History of Death and the Funeral Home in Twentieth Century America.* New York: Oxford University Press, 2003.

Ludwig, Allan I. *Graven Images: New England Stonecarving and Its Symbols, 1650–1815.* Middletown, Conn.: Wesleyan University Press, 1966; reprint, 2000.

McClure, Rhonda R. *Digitizing Your Family History.* Cincinnati: Family Tree Books, 2004.

The Red Book 2004: The National Directory of Morticians. Published by Jack R. Schmidt, National Directory of Morticians, P.O. Box 73, Chagrin Falls, OH 44022. Online at <www.funeral-dir.com>.

Rees, Nigel. *Epitaphs: A Dictionary of Grave Epigrams and Memorial Eloquence.* New York: Carroll and Graf, 1994.

Rogak, Lisa. *Stones and Bones of New England: A Guide to Unusual, Historic, and Otherwise Notable Cemeteries.* Guilford, Conn.: Globe Pequot, 2004.

Scott, Kenneth. "Needlework Samplers and Mourning Pictures as Genealogical Evidence." *National Genealogical Society Quarterly* 67 (September 1979): 167–74.

Yeich, Edwin B. "Die Leich: The Old-Fashioned Country Funeral." *Historical Review of Berks County* (July 1954): 110–11.

14

African American Research

TONY BURROUGHS, FUGA

Contrary to popular belief, many records exist for researching African American genealogy. Some of these records are similar to those of European Americans, but African American sources diverge as American history meanders through prejudice, discrimination, and exclusionism. The 1898 U.S. Supreme Court Case, *Plessy v. Ferguson*, legalized the doctrine of "separate but equal." As segregation flourished, two distinct societies evolved. Parallel organizations and institutions developed and multiplied in both communities. The records of the two populations may compare in type, location, and quantity, but they are catalogued separately. In addition to these records, African American research also yields several kinds of records that are unique.

This chapter examines many of the records available, dealing both with slave and non-slave related records. In cases where the records are the same as European American records, the text will attempt to show researchers how to use these sources to find African Americans most effectively. In other cases, where the records are unique or are similar but have developed separately, the text discusses them in detail. For example, county marriage records exist for both groups, but may be classified as "White" and "Colored" and filed separately. Print publications also illustrate the separation. *Who's Who in America* includes very few African Americans while its counterpart, *Who's Who in Colored America* is *exclusively* African American.[1]

A careful study of African American history provides researchers with a strong foundation for genealogical research. The successful student of African American genealogy will closely examine the history of segregation and the emergence of two different Americas, one white and one black. An understanding of the resulting cultural and societal differences is critical not only to locating records, but also to evaluating their contents. Many of the conditions created by "separate but equal" are pointed out in the following discussion of sources.

Chapter Contents

Oral History and Family Records

African American genealogy begins like all other genealogy: with oral history and family records. Researchers should follow the methods, sources, and examples found in chapter 1, "The Foundations of Family History Research." An example of one type of record that is unique to the African American community, however, is the funeral program.

Attendees at a traditional funeral receive a prayer card after signing the guest register. This is a 2 x 3 inch folded card normally containing the birth and death dates of the deceased, the date and location of the visitation or funeral, a prayer, and, at times, the name and location of the cemetery.

Attendees at a African American funeral are given a funeral program that contains, in addition to information found on a prayer card, a photograph of the deceased and a full obituary. These programs started as folded sheets of white paper and have evolved into elaborate full-color brochures of various textures, with multiple pages and photographs. It appears that these funeral programs began in the 1930s or '40s, possibly because most African Americans were denied the opportunity to publish obituaries in mainstream newspapers. Funeral programs can be found among family memorabilia, and some genealogists are now donating them to libraries. For more information, see Belzora Cheatham's *Funeral Programs/Obituaries of 579 African Americans.*[2]

Research Back to 1870

1870 is a critical date for researchers of African American genealogy. It represents the beginning of an extremely difficult research period: the pre-1870 world of enslaved African Americans. Success in researching in this period actually depends on how thoroughly one has researched records created after 1870. The researcher must use every available post-1870 source to work methodically back in time from the present, to build a strong foundation of evidence before trying to conduct pre-1870 work. Merely using census records, as many novices do, is not enough.

Compiled Sources

After researching oral history, family records, and vital records, researchers should take advantage of compiled sources. Many blacks wrote autobiographies, and many biographies, family histories, and genealogies have been compiled on African American families.

A first step would be to consult *Black Biographical Dictionaries, 1790–1950*. This is a three-volume index of 31,000 biographies contained in 290 rare biographical dictionaries that were published before 1951. The volumes are located in major libraries and can be searched online under the title of *Black Biographies* at Chadwyck Healy, an online database that is not available from home, but may be searched at some libraries.

Another biographical dictionary, *The Dictionary of American Negro Biography*, published in 1982, contains more than 600 biographies of African Americans who died before 1970.[3] Researchers should also consult works such as *Who's Who Among Black Americans, Who's Who Among Afro Americans*, and *Who's Who in Colored America*.[4]

For more recent published biographies, genealogies, and family histories, search the Periodical Source Index (PERSI), which indexes all genealogical journals and newsletters, including African American ones. You may also want to consult the *Journal of the Afro-American Historical and Genealogical Society* directly as well as the ten-year index compiled by Barbara Walker. Researchers should also refer to card catalogues in libraries and colleges in states and communities where their ancestors lived, looking under such subject headings as "Afro Americans Biography," and "Afro Americans Biographical Dictionaries." A thorough discussion of these and other similar sources is covered in Tony Burroughs's *Black Roots: A Beginners Guide to Tracing the African American Family Tree*.[5]

Federal Census Records

African Americans were enumerated by name in federal census population schedules along with other U.S. residents from 1870 to the present. Most researchers will be able to locate African Americans using the same methodology practiced by other genealogists. However, many African Americans are difficult to find in the 1870 census, which is the first census after emancipation. For clues to locating persons in this first post-Civil War federal enumeration, see Tony Burroughs's "Finding African Americans on the 1870 Census," in *Heritage Quest Magazine*.[6]

Prior to 1870, free African Americans were enumerated by name, but enslaved African Americans were listed unnamed, under the names of owners. In 1850 and 1860, slaves were consigned to special, far less informative, slave population schedules, in which the only personal information recorded was age, gender, and racial identity (either black or mulatto). Names were noted on slaves one hundred years old or more; these, however, represent less than 1 percent of the enslaved population. In a few rare instances, the names of all slaves were included on the slave population schedules (see the 1860 censuses of Hampshire County, Virginia and St. Louis, Missouri; and the 1850 census of Bowie County, Texas.)

The slave schedules themselves do not provide conclusive evidence for the presence of a specific slave in the household or plantation of a particular slave owner. Many researchers search a slave schedule for a surname that is the same name as their ancestor's. They then assume the person is the former slave owner and try to match up the ages. This is not a recommended procedure. You must first prove a person is your ancestor and not just someone with the same name.

Furthermore, persons listed as slaves are not clearly identified, and the ages given on schedules are notoriously

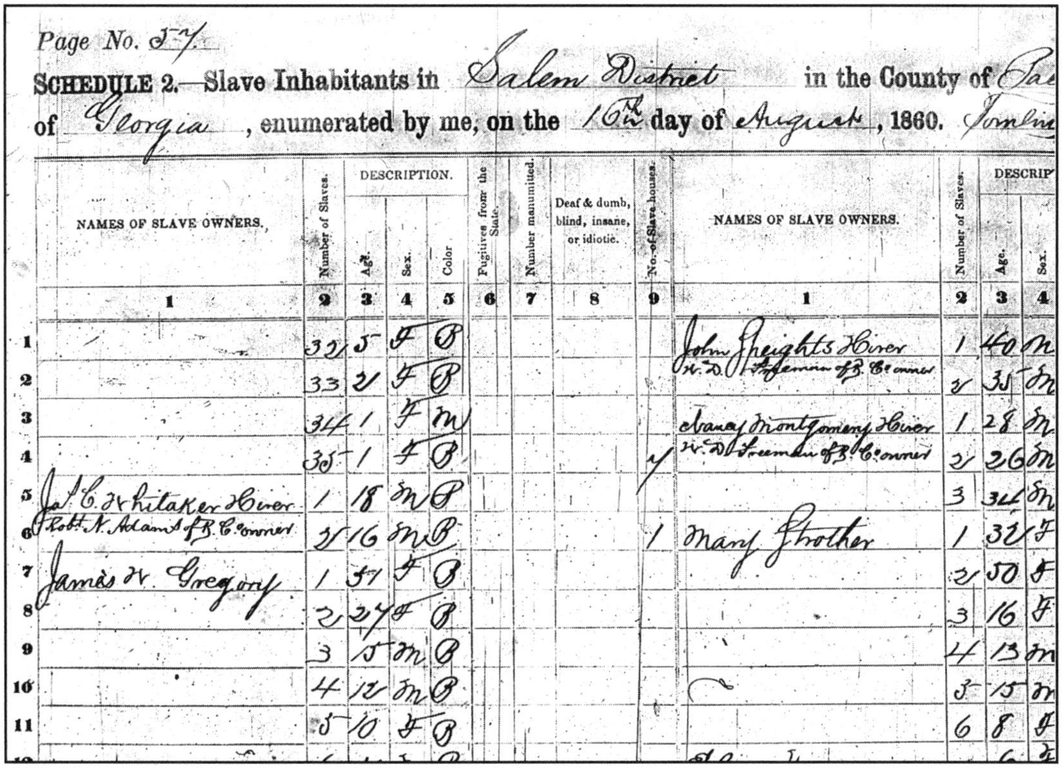

Figure 14-1. 1860 Baldwin County, Georgia Slave Schedule, which lists slave owners as well as persons renting slaves.

inaccurate. Finally, many of the names on slave schedules that are indicated to be slave owners are not in fact owners at all. Census enumerators were instructed to record where slaves were residing, even if they were not living with their legal owners.[7] In some communities, as many as 30 percent of slaves were rented and thus appear in households or groups other than their usual place of residence. (See figure 14-1.)

Prior to 1850 there were no special slave schedules taken during the federal enumerations. Instead, slave data was recorded as part of the general population schedules. In these decades, only the heads of free households were enumerated by name.

Military Records

Blacks have fought in every war this country has waged, from the colonial militia and the American Revolution up to today's Middle Eastern conflicts. Since they often served in higher percentages than their population makeup, military records offer a good source of information to genealogists.

Historically, soldiers were classified as either volunteers or as members of the regular army. For the most part, African Americans served in the volunteer army to fight a war. After the war they returned to civilian life or slavery. Only after the Civil War were blacks allowed to become career soldiers and serve in the peace-time regular army as professional soldiers. There is evidence of some blacks serving in the regular army before the Civil War, but this is rare.

The Regular Army

The first African Americans in the regular army are referred to as Buffalo Soldiers. They were organized in 1866 into the 9th and 10th Cavalry, and the 38th, 39th, 40th, and 41st Infantries; the infantry units were reorganized in 1869 into the 24th and 25th infantries. These soldiers served in most of the states in the West and fought against Native Americans. They also guarded railroads, telegraph lines, and wagon trains.

Blacks served in segregated units until the army was integrated in 1952. They could be enlisted or drafted soldiers until the end of the Vietnam War. At this time the draft ended, so those who have participated in the military since Vietnam, including the current conflicts in the Middle East, have served as career soldiers in the regular army.

In addition to researching soldiers in the regular army, researchers should check for volunteer soldiers (enlisted or drafted) in World Wars I and II, the Spanish American War (1898), the Philippine Insurrection (1899), and earlier conflicts. Search the various branches as well. Blacks served in the Army Air Corps, Navy, Air Force, Marines, State Militia, and the National Guard.

Researching soldiers in the regular army is different than researching volunteers. There are no Compiled Military Service Records (CMSR) for the regular army, but there is a Register of Enlistments, which is similar. Many veterans applied pensions, and they are included in *General Index to Pension Files, 1861–1934*.[8] (This microfilm is often erroneously referred to as the "Civil War Pension Index.")

Refer to chapter 11, "Military Records," for basic sources. The researcher who already knows the regiment can search the *Organization Index to Pension Files of Veterans Who Served Between 1861 and 1900*, which is organized by state, arm of service (infantry, cavalry, artillery), then numerically by regiment.[9] To research blacks in the regular army, consult Irene Shubert's and Frank N. Shubert's *On the Trail of the Buffalo Soldier II: New and Revised Biographies of African Americans in the U.S. Army, 1866–1917*, which has 8,000 biographies.[10] See also, Tony Burroughs's "Researching Buffalo Soldiers for Genealogical and Historical Links," in the *Journal of the Afro-American Historical and Genealogical Society*.[11]

Civil War

Some of the best information for African American genealogy exists in Civil War records. Upwards of 170,000 African Americans served in segregated units called the United States Colored Troops (USCT). The renowned Massachusetts 54th Volunteer Infantry Regiment (that inspired the movie *Glory*, starring Denzel Washington) was the first regiment of African Americans authorized by Congress in 1863, but unofficial regiments from Kansas, South Carolina, and Louisiana were formed earlier. Black regiments from Massachusetts and Connecticut were raised under state sponsorship and retained their state designations.[12] All other regiments had U.S. Colored Troop numerical designations within the infantry, artillery, or cavalry.

Recruits for these regiments came from a variety of circumstances. Some were free blacks who joined regiments raised in the North. Some were slaves from border states that had not seceded. Under these circumstances slave owners "volunteered" services of their slaves in exchange for the bounty that would normally have gone to the recruit. A third group was comprised of those who joined USCT regiments in the South after abandoning their former owners in areas under Union control.

Another group of blacks in the Civil War were those who served in white regiments. It was long thought that blacks were prohibited from serving in white regiments, or that such service was an aberration. Juanita Patience Moss dispelled that myth with her 2004 book, *The Forgotten Black Soldiers in White Regiments During the Civil War*.[13] She uncovered the names of over 1,000 blacks serving in white regiments.

Many veterans applied for pensions and all have military service records. As military service and pension records are covered elsewhere in this volume, they are not discussed in great detail here. Searching for African Americans in the Civil War, however, requires particular care.

First, the units were segregated, so the *Index to Compiled Military Service Records of Volunteer Union Soldiers Who Served with the United States Colored Troops (CMSR)*, should be searched rather than the National Archives indexes microfilmed by state designation as for white soldiers (other than ones listed in Moss' book mentioned previously).[14]

A Company, 532 Engineer Service Battalion, assigned to road building and highway repair in France after the armistice. Acting commander, Captain Godfrey Eric Strauss (55th Engineers), is third from the left, between two YMCA women. Photo taken in May 1919. Courtesy of Christopher Strauss.

Second, the names of former slaves present a special challenge. For a variety of reasons, soldiers served under one name during the service, but often were known by a different name before or after the Civil War. Therefore, searching for a person under the name known in 1870 may or may not locate him on the CMSR.

Third, when oral history says an African American "served" in the Civil War, it may mean that he may have only "worked" in the war effort and was never a member of a military regiment. In these cases, the ancestor might be listed in the Quartermaster General's records (NARA record group 92) as an employee of the military. Among its other duties, the Quartermaster hired civilians to work in procuring and distributing supplies and building fortifications. Or, the person sought may have lived in a contraband camp, where fugitive slaves of secessionist owners sought refuge.

Civil War Pension Records

Because of the problem with names, it is often more successful to begin researching African Americans in the Civil War by searching pension application files, instead of starting with the *Index to Compiled Military Service Records*. If a soldier applied for a pension under one name and served in the war under a different name, both names are noted and indexed on the *General Index to Pension Files*. (See figure 14-2.)

Page 4

Smith. Q . By what name have you been known since you came out of the service? A. Only as Isaac Smith.

Q. Were you known by any other name in service? A. No.

Q. Were you known by any other name before you enlisted?

A. Yes, and my name then was Isaac Veal. I was born in Amit county, Miss., and my father was James Veal and mother was Harriet Veal. I had three brothers, Henry, Cliff and Dunk Veal . Henry and Dunk are dead and Cliff lives at Lecompte in Rapides parish , La. I have a sister Lizzie living at the same place. They never changed their names. I just decided when I left home,to join the service,that I would enlist under the name of Isaac Smith as that was a very common name and I have held to the name ever since. After I came out of the service I thought of taking my old name back but I kept putting it off and never did so,and when I filed my claim some years ago for pension,I thought I would write the Bureau and tell about my right name but some how I never did and just let the matter go . I had no reason for changing my name that I can now give. I belonged,as a slave,to Charles Matthews in Amit county, Miss., and along in 1856, I think it was,I was taken to Lecompte , Rapides parish, La., where I lived until I went in the service. I went from there to New Orleans and joined the army. I had no wife before or while in service . I was never married until soon after I came out of the service and was then married to Polly Peart,and she had never before been married. I got the license at Opelousas St. Landry parish,and our marriage is recorded there in the Court Hose. We were married by Judge Hedspeth - a justice of the peace at the time. I have never been separated from my wife and we are now living here in this home together and there is my wife you see now.

Figure 14-2. Civil War Pension deposition of Isaac Smith/Veal.

Civil War veterans often submitted affidavits for their comrades in support of pension claims. The writing of affidavits was usually a reciprocal affair, and a network of veterans from the same company would write affidavits for one another. Taken as a totality, the pension affidavits can, on occasion, reveal a common background for the applicants. This could be particularly important in researching USCT veterans, as such an approach could uncover veterans from the same locality, or even the same plantation, or contraband camp who enlisted together. Obtaining the pension files of each of the fellow veterans who supplied affidavits for an ancestor's application could reveal important critical detail about the ancestor himself.

As previously noted, slave owners in the border states sometimes collected bounties when their slaves joined USCT regiments. Records for this bounty may be found in the soldier's service record, indicating the name of the former slave owner, hence making the service record far more valuable than is usually the case. The National Archives has special records for these claims.[15]

Compiled Military Service Records

If a veteran's name is located in the pension application files, a service record may be ordered under the name the soldier used during the Civil War. If a pension file is not located, researchers should search the *Index to Compiled Military Service Records*. This index is available on the National Park Service Soldiers and Sailors website at <www.civilwar.nps.gov/cwss>, Ancestry.com, or on microfilm at the National Archives or the Family History Library.[16]

In most instances, especially when dealing with a common name, it will be helpful to consult Frederick Dyer's *Compendium of the War of the Rebellion*, which contains brief histories of all Union regiments, stating where they were organized and where they served. This information will often enable the researcher to identify an ancestor's regiment. For example, if the researcher had an ancestor from Tennessee and it was discovered that three soldiers with his name were on the rolls of three separate regiments, consulting Dyer's might indicate that only one of those regiments was raised in Tennessee. The researcher would then be able to request the correct military service records from the National Archives. The Massachusetts 54th and 55th will be more challenging, however, because they recruited from all the northern states, not just Massachusetts.

Civil War Navy

In researching the Civil War, most genealogists neglect the navy, which has different records and different indexes. The Civil War navy, in contrast to the army, was integrated; approximately 18,000 blacks served in the Civil War navy. David Valuska lists 10,000 in his book, *The African Americans in the Union Navy, 1861–1865*.[17] His number is lower because Valuska identifies only recruits joining at rendezvous stations, which were recruiting ships. Many other slaves walked off plantations and boarded vessels in midstream.

Starting with Valuska's book is a good choice, but all the names of blacks in the navy have been transcribed by Howard University students and are available on the National Park Service's Civil War Soldiers and Sailors website <www.itd.nps.gov/cwss/index.html>. If you have searched the Index to U.S. Colored Troops (Army) and did not find your ancestor, by all means search the navy index at that website. Naval pension applications are included in the "General Index to Pension Files." Because these records are indexed on blue cards, the microfilm is dark and difficult to read.

Confederate Service

Just before the end of the Civil War, the Confederate government adopted a policy to use slave soldiers; however, the policy change came too late for meaningful enactment, and no African Americans actually served as soldiers for the Southern cause. Even so, many slaves served as body servants to their owners or to the owners' sons when they entered Confederate service. Others worked as teamsters or helped build fortifications. After the war some were able to live in retirement homes for Confederate veterans. Civil War service qualified them for pensions paid by the former states of the Confederacy. However, the pensions came so late (the 1920s) that most of the veterans had died.

Records of these pensions may be found in legislative acts (see figure 14-3), at state archives, or in genealogical libraries. The names of blacks with Confederate pensions from South Carolina have been published in Alexia Jones Helsley's *South Carolina's African American Confederate Pensioners, 1923–1925*.[18]

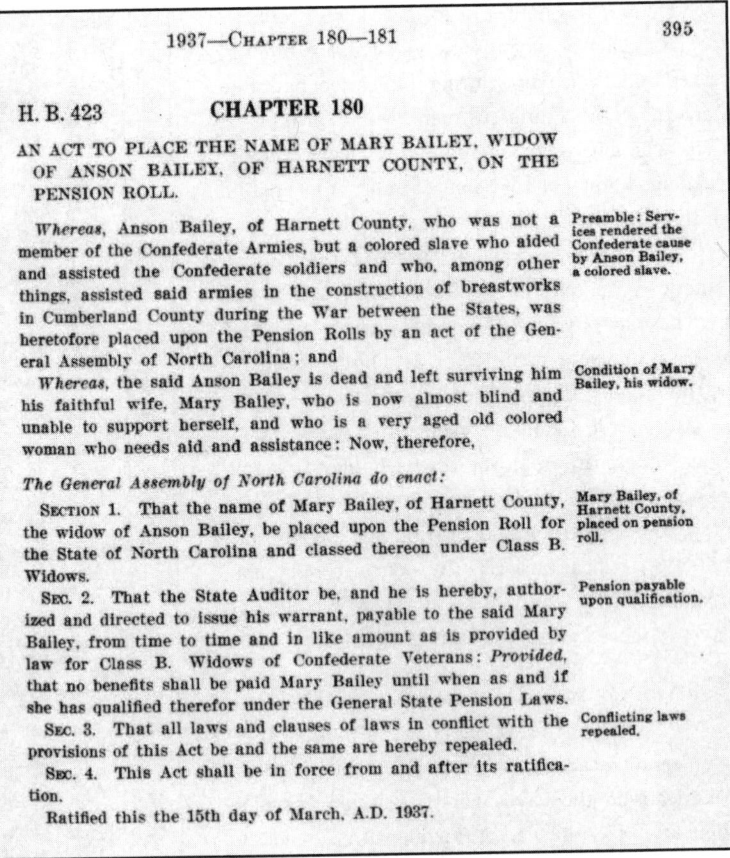

1937—CHAPTER 180—181 395

H. B. 423 CHAPTER 180

AN ACT TO PLACE THE NAME OF MARY BAILEY, WIDOW OF ANSON BAILEY, OF HARNETT COUNTY, ON THE PENSION ROLL.

Whereas, Anson Bailey, of Harnett County, who was not a member of the Confederate Armies, but a colored slave who aided and assisted the Confederate soldiers and who, among other things, assisted said armies in the construction of breastworks in Cumberland County during the War between the States, was heretofore placed upon the Pension Rolls by an act of the General Assembly of North Carolina; and

Preamble: Services rendered the Confederate cause by Anson Bailey, a colored slave.

Whereas, the said Anson Bailey is dead and left surviving him his faithful wife, Mary Bailey, who is now almost blind and unable to support herself, and who is a very aged old colored woman who needs aid and assistance: Now, therefore,

Condition of Mary Bailey, his widow.

The General Assembly of North Carolina do enact:

SECTION 1. That the name of Mary Bailey, of Harnett County, the widow of Anson Bailey, be placed upon the Pension Roll for the State of North Carolina and classed thereon under Class B. Widows.

Mary Bailey, of Harnett County, placed on pension roll.

SEC. 2. That the State Auditor be, and he is hereby, authorized and directed to issue his warrant, payable to the said Mary Bailey, from time to time and in like amount as is provided by law for Class B. Widows of Confederate Veterans: *Provided*, that no benefits shall be paid Mary Bailey until when as and if she has qualified therefor under the General State Pension Laws.

Pension payable upon qualification.

SEC. 3. That all laws and clauses of laws in conflict with the provisions of this Act be and the same are hereby repealed.

Conflicting laws repealed.

SEC. 4. This Act shall be in force from and after its ratification.

Ratified this the 15th day of March, A.D. 1937.

Figure 14-3. Confederate widow's pension for Mary Bailey.

Similar documentation of Confederate service may also be found from the Union side, such as a list of slaves impressed for work on the Nashville and North Western Railroad in October 1863.[19] These records are of particular importance because they supply the name of the slave owner and residence, and a physical description of the slave. Some of the laborers are included on Confederate Slave Payrolls.[20]

Revolutionary War

There are many documented instances of African Americans serving in the American Revolution, despite the fact many of the official records were not extant when the National Archives was established in 1934. Most of the official government records of the Revolutionary War were destroyed by a fire on 8 November 1800; others were lost during the War of 1812.

John E. Ernest's "African-Americans in the American Revolution" documents many instances of blacks filling critical support and active military roles. His essay includes a colony-by-colony summary of the laws and opinions regarding blacks serving. Each colony entry includes the estimated numbers of blacks who served from that colony.

Debra L. Newman compiled *List of Black Servicemen Compiled from the War Department Collection of Revolutionary War Records* and Robert Ewell Greene published two dozen biographies and lists of several hundred other blacks in the Revolutionary War.[21]

In 1984, the Daughters of the American Revolution (DAR) began a massive project to identify all blacks, along with other minorities, (women and Native Americans), who served in the Revolutionary War. The DAR hired James Dent Walker, who had previously supervised a military records section at the National Archives and worked there for over thirty years. In 1988, Walker began original research in a variety of records to identify minorities in the Revolution and published a list of those serving from Rhode Island. Walker left the project after the first publication but the series continued, with compiled lists from each of the original thirteen colonies. The project led to the creation of ten booklets, which were updated and consolidated in 2001 into one larger publication: *African American and American Indian Patriots of the Revolutionary War*.[22]

There were also blacks who fought for the British. Their numbers may have been greater than the number who served the American side. Names of 3,000 blacks (along with their former slave owners) who sided with the British and relocated to Nova Scotia were listed in the *Book of Negroes*, and published in *The Black Loyalist Directory* by Graham Russell Hodges.[23]

The Freedman's Savings and Trust Company (Freedman's Bank)

Serving in the Civil War, many ex-slaves who had labored without wages all their life suddenly had cash in their pockets. In addition to earning a bounty for enlisting in the military, they received $10 a month in pay. Many soldiers sent their money home, but a fair amount was spent on gambling, liquor, and women. Military officers who wanted soldiers to save their money started a military savings bank for the "colored" troops.

General Rufas Saxton, commanding general of the Department of the South, began the Military Savings Bank at Beaufort, South Carolina, in August 1864. In Norfolk, Virginia, General Benjamin Butler undertook a similar enterprise in the fall of 1864. And General Nathaniel Banks established a military savings bank in Louisiana in 1864.[24]

New York businessmen learned of these banks and saw an opportunity. After the Civil War, they applied to the federal government to start a savings bank where soldiers and former slaves could invest their money. On 3 March 1865, the Freedman's Savings and Trust Company, sometimes referred to as the Freedman's Bank, was incorporated by an act of Congress. Accounts from the military savings banks were transferred into the Freedman's Bank.

The first Freedman's Bank was established in Washington, D.C. Later, thirty-six additional branches were opened, mainly in the South, but also in New York, Philadelphia, and St. Louis. Due to mismanagement and fraud, the bank failed in 1874. Its assets were taken over by the federal government and liquidated. Fortunately many of the records were saved and eventually transferred to the National Archives.

Surviving records include signature registers, pass books, questionnaires for lost passbooks, dividend payment schedules, an Index to Deposit Ledgers, voided dividend checks, correspondence, and loan papers and schedules.

The Signature Registers hold the most interest for genealogists (figure 14-4). A Signature Card was completed for each account holder upon opening an account. Many depositors could not read, write, nor sign their names. Because photography was very rare and costly in the 1860s, the means of identification became answers to questions. The bank asked many personal questions of the depositor, about him or her, and about the depositor's family, in the belief that only the depositor was likely to know the answer. The surviving records of this detailed examination have created a gold mine of information for genealogists.

The register format varied among branches and changed over time. The extent to which the forms were filled out also varied. Generally, the questions asked included name; residence; name of spouse, children, parents and siblings; and place of birth. Other genealogical data sometimes included complexion, former residence, occupation, employer, and names of deceased relatives. The early forms asked for name of master and name of mistress. The names of the former slave owners are essential to search enslaved people during the antebellum period.

A seamstress and washerwoman named Nancy Patterson established an account in the Louisville branch on 15 September 1865. In the final "remarks" portion of the signature record, it is noted that she "formerly belonged to Bob Smith, was bot [*sic*] by her mother upon the block in 1854 or 5."[25] No relatives were noted in her record, but in some cases it is not unusual to find three generations chronicled in a single instance.

One typical entry is that for Elias Webb, who held an account in the Vicksburg, Mississippi, branch. His record states that he was born and raised in Anderson District, South Carolina, and was residing in Port Gibson, Mississippi, at the time his account was opened. His father was Moses, his mother Rachel. He had four brothers, listed as Green Webb, Jeremiah Webb, Marcus Webb, and Scipio Lewis. His sisters were listed as Emeline, Mary, and Amanda Webb.[26]

It was not unusual for people to cross a county line to make a deposit in a branch office. Therefore, while the number of cities with branches was limited, those branches served more than just the immediate vicinity. In addition, the bank had agents collecting money from soldiers in the field. The signature records indicate that significant numbers of ex-slaves from at least ten Mississippi counties and three Louisiana parishes opened accounts at the Vicksburg branch.

1216

Record *for* Benjamin [illegible]

Date, and No. of Application, Abram Keller Nov. 29/1866
Name of Master, Abram Keller
Name of Mistress,
Plantation,
Height, and Complexion,
~~Father or Mother?~~ *Married?*
Name of Children, Frank May & Lucy.
Regiment and Company, A. 117th U.S.C.I.
Place of Birth,
Residence, Cynthiana Kentucky
Occupation,

REMARKS,
Children live at Cynthiana Ky

Signature,

1218

Record *for* Lazarus Allen

Date, and No. of Application, Nov. 29. 1866
Name of Master, Dr Cantwell
Name of Mistress,
Plantation,
Height and Complexion,
~~Father or~~ *Mother?* ~~Married?~~ Sarah Ann Johnson
Name of Children,
Regiment and Company, B. 117th U.S.C.I.
Place of Birth,
Residence, Paris. Bourbon Co. Ky.
Occupation,

REMARKS,
Mother lives at Paris. Ky.

Signature,

1217

Record *for* Thomas Armstrong

Date, and No. of Application, Nov. 29. 1866
Name of Master, Wm Mackintosh
Name of Mistress,
Plantation,
Height and Complexion,
~~Father~~ or *Mother?* ~~Married?~~ Gracy Armstrong
Name of Children,
Regiment and Company, B. 117th U.S.C.I.
Place of Birth,
Residence, Cynthiana Kentucky
Occupation, Laborer

REMARKS,
Mother lives at Springfield. O.

Signature,

1219

Record *for* John Mallory

Date, and No. of Application, Nov. 29. 1866
Name of Master, Green B. Mallory
Name of Mistress,
Plantation,
Height and Complexion,
~~Father or Mother?~~ *Married?* Wife Fannie Mallory
Name of Children,
Regiment and Company, B. 117th U.S.C.I.
Place of Birth,
Residence, Georgetown Ky
Occupation, Farmer

REMARKS,
Wife lives at "Rays Fork" P.O. Ky

Signature,

Figure 14-4. Signature Registers from Louisville, Kentucky, Branch of the Freedmen's Bank.

Many of the signature record forms contained space to indicate military regiment and company, providing evidence of Civil War service in the United States Colored Troops. Veterans continued to provide this information for many years after they had mustered out of the service.

There are several ways to access the Signature Registers, which are on microfilm at the National Archives and many genealogical libraries (see figure 14-4).[27] Genealogists have transcribed and indexed records from several branches (see the bibliographies for Alabama, Mississippi, North Carolina, and New Orleans indexes). In addition, prisoners at the Utah State Penitentiary have transcribed all the records, and The Church of Jesus Christ of Latter-day Saints (Mormons) has published the project on a CD-ROM titled *Freedman's Bank Records*.[28]

Like all sources, the CD-ROM has advantages and disadvantages. You can search for names of brothers, sisters, parents, or anyone who is mentioned on the Signature Registers. However, search engine results do not include alternate spellings of surnames. One genealogist who was searching for the surname Harget in New Bern, North Carolina, could not find it on the CD-ROM. However, a check of Bill Reaves's *North Carolina Freedman's Savings and Trust Company Records* revealed that sixteen Hargets opened accounts: eight under Hardgate; six under Hardget; and two under Hardgett.[29] Although these sixteen entries were located on a second check of the CD-ROM, none of these spellings had been suggested for alternate searches.

Therefore a genealogist searching for the surname Harget in New Bern, North Carolina, would have to enter each spelling

The Fraternal Savings Bank & Trust Co. was one of the first African American–owned banks in Memphis, Tennessee. Bank president John Jay Scott is seated at the right. Scott became president in 1910 after managing a highly successful undertaking business in Memphis with his brother, H. W. Wilkerson. Also known as the Scott-Wilkerson Bank, this establishment was not connected with the Freedman's Bank system. Scott had been Chaplain of the Third Alabama Regiment of Spanish American Volunteers and chaplain of A. & M. College at Normal, Alabama. Courtesy of Joan Fletcher.

variation to find the eight Hardgates, six Hardgets, and two Hardgetts.

For a subscription fee, Ancestry.com and Proquest have recently added the Freedman's Bank records to their online databases.

An Index to Deposit Ledgers was the only other record microfilmed. However, it is not an index to the Signature Registers, and the deposit ledgers themselves did not survive. Nevertheless, the index can be proof that an account existed for an ancestor when the Signature Registers did not survive for a branch.

There are a few passbooks that are at the National Archives. Some of the best records yet unfilmed are the questionnaires for lost passbooks. The questionnaires ask for similar information to that which is on the Signature Registers, and can substitute when Signature Registers have not survived. The added bonus is that some questionnaires were completed by descendants of deceased relatives who held accounts. Such a return can pick up additional ancestors and descendants (see figure 14-5).

Also not filmed are dividend payment schedules from 1882 to 1889. These schedules indicate an account's balance and how much was returned after the bank folded. The five payouts returned 62 percent of the depositor's account.

For more details, see Brewer's "Do You Trust That Freedman's Bank?"; Burroughs's "Records Specific to African Americans" in *African American Genealogical Sourcebook*; and Washington's "The Freedman's Savings and Trust Company and African American Genealogical Research."[30]

The Freedmen's Bureau

After the Civil War, 4 million enslaved blacks were released from bondage and subsequently entered the workforce. Millions of refugees returned from the war and destitute whites were jobless. Many were in need of medical care. In 1865 the Freedmen's Bureau was established to transition the nation from war to peacetime and deliver services to these two groups of people. The Bureau was the first major social service agency, enacted as the Bureau of Refugees, Freedmen, and Abandoned Lands. It operated from 1865 to 1868, and was reauthorized from 1868 to 1872 with limited operations.

The bureau's agents delivered medical care, rations, and transportation to destitutes and refugees—primarily white Americans. Its activities among freed people (former slaves) were varied and included drawing up and enforcing labor contracts; registering people and supervising work details; legalizing slave marriages; processing Civil War military claims; establishing schools; conducting trials for complaints, outrages, and murders; managing, leasing, and selling land abandoned by Confederates and sympathizers; and in general, presiding over Reconstruction policy. Some of the bureau's records are rich in genealogical content, and some will reveal the name of the former slave owner.

The records are extremely valuable to white, as well as African American, genealogists. For blacks, the records bridge the gap from 1870 to pre-1865, at times revealing name changes or differences in names. Bureau records are often the main and only link to identify the former slave owner. They may also reveal migration patterns.

For researching whites, Bureau records show refugees who received food, transportation, and medical assistance. Others were farm owners or employed freedmen and were parties to labor contracts. Some taught in Freedmen's Bureau schools or were otherwise employed by the Freedmen's Bureau. And lastly, many whites owned land that was confiscated by the federal government during the Civil War. They had to sign loyalty oaths to get their land back. Some of the land records in the Bureau records are the only evidence of an ancestor owning land.

Administratively, the Bureau was divided into three levels, each with its own set of records. Oliver Otis Howard, the commissioner, had a headquarters office in Washington. The Assistant Commissioners were in charge of individual states, although some had to manage two states in the beginning. Field Offices were established in different cities where agents delivered services. A detailed finding aid for the headquarters records is available, and the aid to the field office records is combined with the aid to the assistant commissioner's records.[31]

Much of the assistant commissioner's records are intra-bureau or intra-government communications, such as statistical reports, that hold little genealogical potential. However, the correspondence and reports of "outrages" (lynchings and other assaults upon African Americans) may be especially valuable. Some of the letters to the commissioner are also very important. Jacqueline A. Lawson has indexed some of them.[32]

Marriages

Of all the assistant commissioners' records, those for Mississippi hold the greatest genealogical potential. Only in Mississippi were local marriage registers included with the state district records. These are from Vicksburg, Davis Bend (just below Vicksburg), Natchez, and Meridian, although there are very few records from the latter. These are among the most informative—and among the most poignant—of any American marriage records. Covering the years 1865 and 1866, these registers record the validation of "slave marriages" that occurred before emancipation. They also document the marriages of men and women who were just beginning life together following the war.[33] Although the names of parents are not provided, the racial identity of the bride and groom and their parents is one of the categories of information included. Their residence is also shown. For the many men who had been Union soldiers, a unit is indicated.

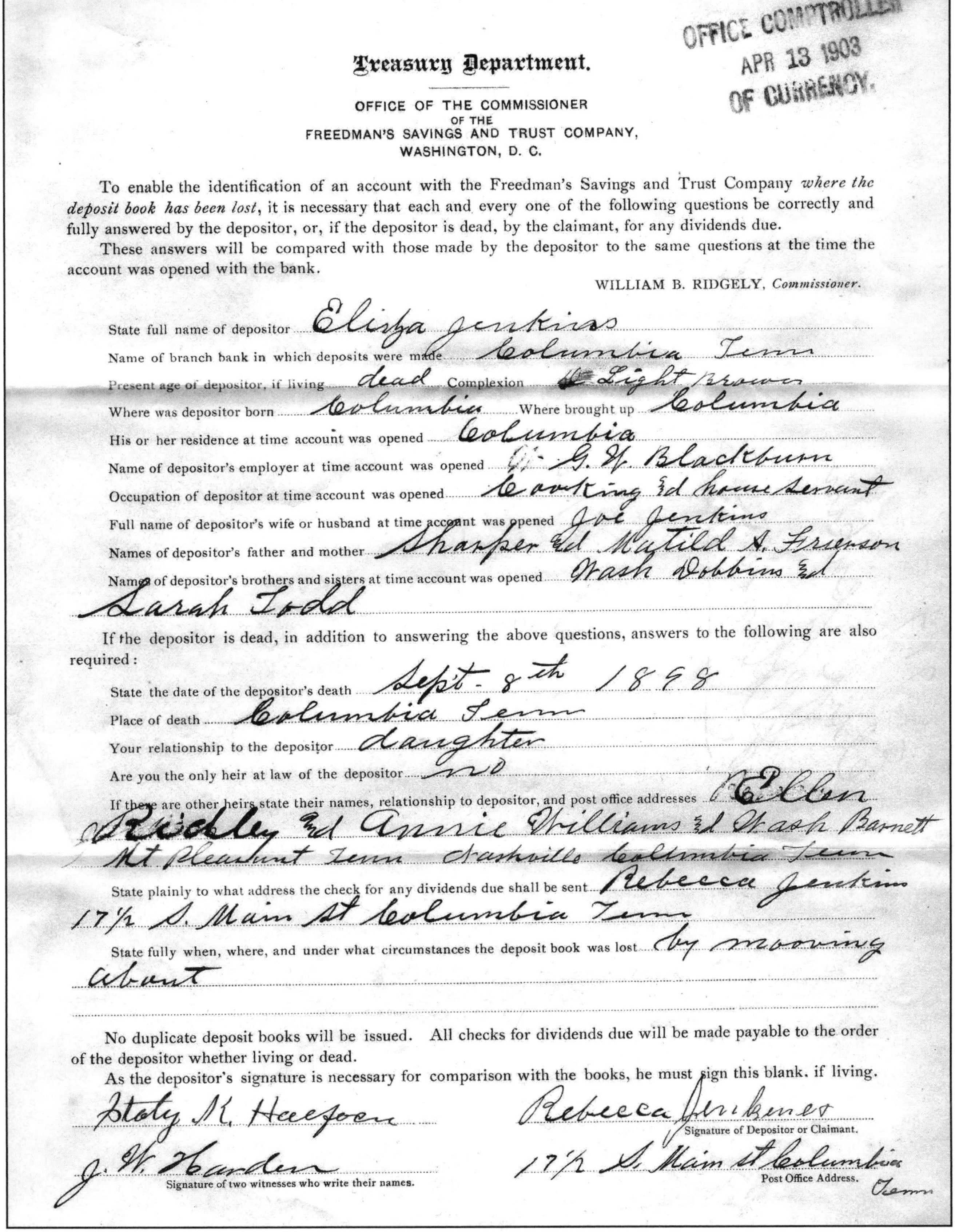

OFFICE COMPTROLLER APR 13 1903 OF CURRENCY.

Treasury Department.

OFFICE OF THE COMMISSIONER
OF THE
FREEDMAN'S SAVINGS AND TRUST COMPANY,
WASHINGTON, D. C.

To enable the identification of an account with the Freedman's Savings and Trust Company *where the deposit book has been lost*, it is necessary that each and every one of the following questions be correctly and fully answered by the depositor, or, if the depositor is dead, by the claimant, for any dividends due.

These answers will be compared with those made by the depositor to the same questions at the time the account was opened with the bank.

WILLIAM B. RIDGELY, *Commissioner.*

State full name of depositor Eliza Jenkins

Name of branch bank in which deposits were made Columbia Tenn

Present age of depositor, if living dead Complexion Light brown

Where was depositor born Columbia Where brought up Columbia

His or her residence at time account was opened Columbia

Name of depositor's employer at time account was opened G. H. Blackburn

Occupation of depositor at time account was opened Cooking and house servant

Full name of depositor's wife or husband at time account was opened Joe Jenkins

Names of depositor's father and mother Sharper and Matild A. Grierson

Names of depositor's brothers and sisters at time account was opened Wash Dobbins and Sarah Todd

If the depositor is dead, in addition to answering the above questions, answers to the following are also required:

State the date of the depositor's death Sept. 8th 1898

Place of death Columbia Tenn

Your relationship to the depositor daughter

Are you the only heir at law of the depositor no

If there are other heirs state their names, relationship to depositor, and post office addresses Ellen Ridley and Annie Williams and Wash Barnett Mt Pleasant Tenn Nashville Columbia Tenn

State plainly to what address the check for any dividends due shall be sent Rebecca Jenkins 17½ S. Main St Columbia Tenn

State fully when, where, and under what circumstances the deposit book was lost by mooving about

No duplicate deposit books will be issued. All checks for dividends due will be made payable to the order of the depositor whether living or dead.

As the depositor's signature is necessary for comparison with the books, he must sign this blank, if living.

Staty K. Haefoen
J. W. Harden
Signature of two witnesses who write their names.

Rebecca Jenkines
Signature of Depositor or Claimant.

17½ S. Main St Columbia Tenn
Post Office Address.

Figure 14-5. Questionnaire filled out by Rebecca Jenkins.

Marriage records from the headquarters have been microfilmed separately, but do not include the marriages from the Mississippi Assistant Commissioner or marriage records from the field offices.[34] They were filmed with the Assistant Commissioner's records.

Labor Contracts

Also important among the Mississippi Assistant Commissioner's records are the labor contracts. Most of these were implemented in 1865, the remainder being drawn up between 1866 and 1868. These agreements were primarily between ex-slaves and plantation owners throughout the state, although not every county is represented.

Given that all members of a freedman's family are usually mentioned by name and that the contracts were sometimes executed with their former owners, the importance of these documents cannot be exaggerated. Many of the laborers are identified by given name and surname, although most are represented only by a first name.

The arrangement on microfilm of this extensive collection of documents will strike the researcher as haphazard, and searching them is problematic. However, the arrangement is chronological, with instances of records for a given county being "clumped" together. A microfiche index to these records was developed by the Mississippi Department of Archives and History. Labor contracts are also found in the assistant commissioner's records for other states, and in some field office records. (See figure 14-6).

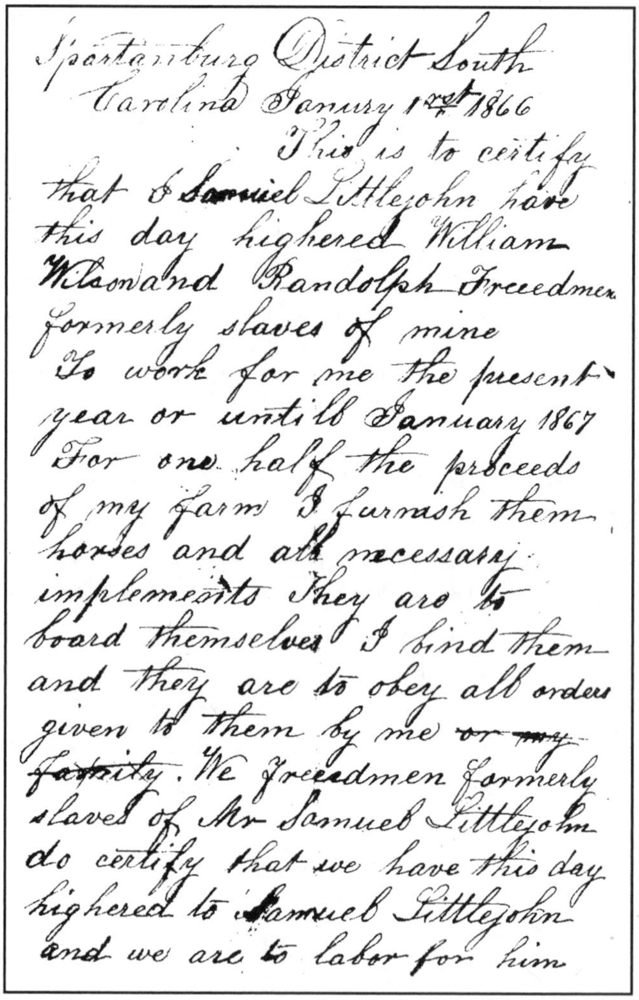

Spartanburg District South
Carolina January 1st 1866
This is to certify
that I Samuel Littlejohn have
this day highered William
Wilson and Randolph Freedmen
formerly slaves of mine
To work for me the present
year or untill January 1867
For one half the proceeds
of my farm I furnish them
horses and all necessary
implements They are to
board themselves I bind them
and they are to obey all orders
given to them by me ~~or my~~
~~family~~. We Freedmen formerly
slaves of Mr Samuel Littlejohn
do certify that we have this day
highered to Samuel Littlejohn
and we are to labor for him

Figure 14-6. 1866, Freedmen's Bureau Labor contract of Samuel Littlejohn.

Transportation

Another useful set of records are those for transportation. Following the Civil War, the Bureau assisted many ex-slaves in their attempts to reunite with family members separated by circumstances of slavery or war. Others seeking jobs or medical attention often needed transportation; many freed people from Virginia and Maryland received transportation out of Washington, D.C. The Bureau also provided transportation to their employees and white refugees. (See figure 14-7).

Field Office Records

The administrative level below assistant commissioner is that of the field offices. Their records are organized by city within each state. As with the state records, the contents of the field office records can vary considerably. The proportion of genealogically useful records is much higher in the field office records than in the records of the assistant commissioners.[35]

In October 2000, Congress passed the Freedmen's Bureau Preservation Act. Since that time the National Archives has been microfilming the entire group of records, alphabetically by state. As the filming for each state is completed, reels are sent to all National Archives regional branches around the United States. The Allen County Public Library has the entire collection, and other libraries with genealogical collections will undoubtedly purchase some, or all, of the microfilm. A Descriptive Pamphlet (DP) accompanies the microfilm for each state, and is essential for item-level descriptions of the records.

Some Bureau records have been transcribed and placed on the Web, but use these with caution.[36] Only a small fraction of the records have been placed on the Web. If transcriptions do not cite a specific National Archives microfilm reel number, or document an original manuscript record at the National Archives in Washington, be leery of the information. There may have been an error or omission in transcription, and the original document should always be checked.

The Bureau and the Bank: Separate Entities

Do not confuse the Freedmen's Bureau with the Freedman's Bank. Some researchers search the Freedman's Bank records

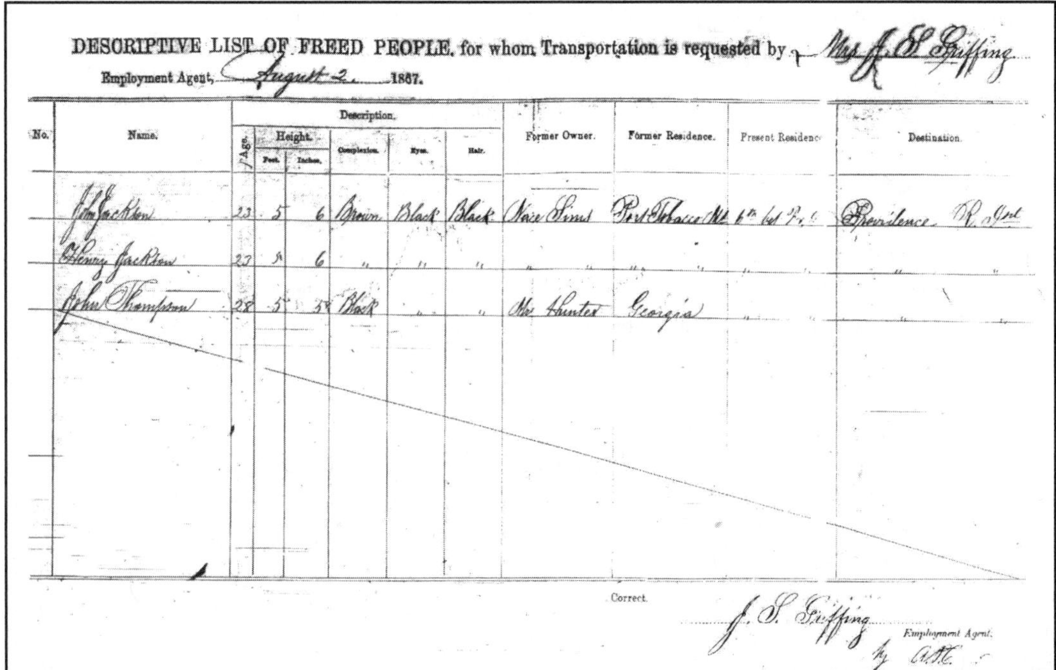

DESCRIPTIVE LIST OF FREED PEOPLE, for whom Transportation is requested by Mrs. J. S. Griffing
Employment Agent, August 2. 1867.

No.	Name.	Age.	Height. Feet.	Height. Inches.	Complexion.	Eyes.	Hair.	Former Owner.	Former Residence.	Present Residence.	Destination.
	John Jackson	23	5	6	Brown	Black	Black	[illegible] Sims	Port Tobacco Md.	[illegible]	Providence R. Isl.
	Henry Jackson	23	5	6	"	"	"	"	"	"	"
	John Thompson	28	5	5	Black	"	"	[illegible] Hunter	Georgia	"	"

Correct. J. S. Griffing, Employment Agent.
by [illegible]

Figure 14-7. 1867 Freedmen's Bureau transportation request.

on CD-ROM and think they have researched the Freedmen's Bureau. They have not.

Congress passed the Freedmen's Bureau Act in 1865 and subsequent legislation to prolong Bureau activities. However, similar to today's unfunded mandates, no financial appropriations accompanied passage of the acts. Since the Bureau was not funded, its services were implemented by the War Department. Records of the Freedmen's Bureau in the National Archives are therefore included with military records.

In contrast, the Freedmen's Savings & Trust Company was a private financial institution with a federal charter. Its operation was not related to the Freedmen's Bureau. Records for the bank are at the National Archives as civilian records.

Military records and civilian records are organized and catalogued separately. Records for the Freedmen's Bureau are in Record Group 105, Bureau of Refugees, Freedmen, and Abandoned Lands. Records for the Freedman's Savings and Trust Company (the Freedman's Bank) are part of Record Group 101, Records of Controller of the Currency. These two completely different groups of records each have their own unique set of inventories, finding aids, and microfilm. See Burroughs, "Records Specific to African Americans" in *African American Genealogical Sourcebook* for more details.[37]

Free Blacks

Unfortunately, most African American genealogists assume that their ancestors were enslaved at the time the Civil War broke out. While this is true for the majority, at least one out of ten African Americans was already free when the first shots were fired on Fort Sumter. The 1860 census records indicate that 200,112 free blacks were living in the North, but another 287,958 free blacks were living in the slave-owning states of the South.

Those who research African Americans must therefore be open to the possibility of encountering an antebellum, free black ancestor. Before searching for slaves, researchers should check for free status by looking on the 1860 census population schedules for free inhabitants. In 1850 and 1860 there are separate free census schedules and slave census schedules.

"Free persons of color," as they were known, were a diverse group of farmers, servants, artisans, and sailors. Many came from families that had been free for several generations, perhaps stemming from the manumission of an ancestor or a liaison between an indentured white woman and a slave. Some were never enslaved, having entered the United States free. Others were runaways who lived in the Northern states. Many were themselves slave owners, particularly elites in Charleston and Louisiana. (See Koger's *Black Slave Owners: Free Black Slave Masters in South Carolina, 1790–1860.*)[38]

Many blacks descended from the slave populations in the Northeast, which existed when slavery was found above the Mason-Dixon Line. Pennsylvania passed a gradual abolition act in 1780, although slavery in the state of New York was not completely abolished until 1827. Approximately ten thousand enslaved blacks were enumerated in New York in the 1820 census. In parts of Ohio and Indiana, the existence of a free black population was due largely to the efforts of North Carolina Quakers who manumitted their slaves when they settled in those states. Many were immediately indentured, thus living in legalized slavery in the north.

In the border states, especially in Maryland, free blacks made up a substantial proportion of the total black population, while in much of the Deep South they were only a tiny minority who occupied a precarious position at best.

Records for Free Persons of Color

In many instances, the records that are of genealogical value for antebellum free blacks are the same as records for whites. For example, the census enumerated all free people, black or white, on the same schedules. Free blacks had to pay taxes and were also listed in city directories.

On the other hand, the United States was a "house divided," and blacks did not legally become citizens until the Fourteenth Amendment was ratified in 1866. This delay in citizenship created many unique records.

Blacks were required in many states to register proof of their free status with the county government. Such documentation could take the form of copies of manumission papers, Free Negro Registers, Certificates of Freedom, or affidavits attesting one's birth to a free woman. Without such proof, free blacks risked abduction and enslavement, even in the North. These registers were also common in the upper South and border states, where they not only provided protection for free blacks but also helped to prevent slaves from passing as free people. The free black registers of Virginia counties have increasingly found their way into print. In one such register is the following noteworthy example:

"I William Moss Clerk of the County Court of Fairfax do hereby certify that the bearer hereof Levi Richardson a light coloured black boy about twenty one years of Age five feet seven Inches high, large nose thin visage . . . a scar on the left side of his head is the son of Sally Richardson a free woman emancipated by Genl. George Washington deceased as appears by an Original Register heretofore granted by the County Court of Fairfax and this day surrendered. Whereupon at the request of the said Levi Richardson I have caused him to be Registered in my office according to law. Given under my hand this 19th day of November 1834."[39]

Similar documentation can also be found in the courthouses of many Midwestern counties. For example, Wright State University microfilmed such records for the counties of Greene, Logan, Miami, and Montgomery in Ohio.[40] More were transcribed by Joan Turpin in *Register of Black, Mulatto and Poor Persons in Four Ohio Counties, 1791–1861*.[41]

The Transition from Slavery to Freedom

At the eve of the Civil War, the vast majority of African Americans were, of course, enslaved. As such, they had no legal rights and could not even claim a legally recognized state of matrimony. Enslaved Africans were considered property. As distasteful as we find it today, this unfortunate fact is the all-encompassing reality that directs the researching of slave genealogy. For this reason, the focus of antebellum research must be on the slave owner, after he (or she) is identified.

Although records generated about blacks after emancipation can be found, genealogically useful records that were contemporary to slavery are usually concerned primarily with the owners of slaves. But learning about the migrations, births, deaths, and marital alliances of the slave-owning family is often the key to achieving success in tracing the lives of their slaves.

Identifying the Last Slave Owner

A common supposition is that emancipated slaves assumed the surnames of their last owners. Were this always true, this critical stage of slave genealogy would be far easier than it is. However, the truth is more complex, which makes research more problematic. Although there are instances when the common assumption holds true, there is ample evidence for slaves maintaining their own surname traditions, regardless of who their owners might have been.[42]

Following emancipation, a slave did not necessarily assume a surname belonging to someone else. Instead, the slave may have used a name legally for the first time which had been in his or her family for several generations. A surname different than that of his last owner could, for example, be that of the owner of a grandparent, so such a name might be a valuable clue for future research.

It is also possible that there were regional naming patterns. For example, a study of a West Virginia county found no instances of ex-slaves with the surnames of their final owners, while studies of Texas and South Carolina freed people indicate approximately a quarter to one third had the surnames of their last owners.[25]

The complex nature of the "surname problem" must be kept in mind as the sources for African American genealogy are considered. If a researcher, without good evidence, assumes the name is the same as the former slave, time might be wasted in the pursuit of the wrong family. The best available evidence is when the former slave reveals the name of his former owner.[43]

There are many sources for identifying the name of the former slave owner. The early Signature Registers of the Freedman's Savings and Trust Company (discussed earlier, and depicted in figures 14-4 and 14-5) sometimes provide evidence of the often confusing and unpredictable reality behind the surnames of ex-slaves. For example, one record from the Vicksburg, Mississippi, branch names the parents of one Jesse Taylor as Robert and Nancy Page. A brother is listed as Simpson Roberts.[44]

Other sources that reveal the name of the last slave owner include records from the Freedmen's Bureau (discussed earlier;

see figures 14-6 and 14-7); Compiled Military Service Records and General Index to Pension Files, 1861–1934 (see figure 14-8, General Affidavit of John Viel/Veal); and ex-slave narratives (see Burroughs's "Records Specific to African Americans" in *African American Genealogical Sourcebook* and Rawick's *The American Slave: A Composite Autobiography*).[45]

Slave owner names may also appear in the records of the Southern Claims Commission. This inquiry board was established by an act of Congress in 1871 to review and make recommendations regarding the claims of Southerners who had remained loyal to the Northern cause and had supplied Union troops with provisions without compensation (see chapter 7, "Court Records"). African Americans (former slaves and free blacks) were among those who either submitted claims or were witnesses who testified on behalf of claimants. The information within these records may link a slave and an owner.[46]

Researching Slavery

To research slave genealogy, it is critical that a researcher understand the history of slavery and of the times and region in which an ancestor lived. To that end, read a general history, such as John Hope Franklin's *From Slavery to Freedom: A History of Negro Americans*.[47] Follow this with a study of a work that centers on the time period and region you are researching, for example, Alan D. Watson *African Americans in Early North Carolina: A Documentary History*.[48] A sampling of titles appears under Historical Sources in the reference section.

One key historical concept is change. The institution of slavery differed by time period, as situations and conditions were constantly changing (see Ira Berlin's *Many Thousands Gone*).[49] Slavery also differed regionally and variations were in part determined by the type of agriculture. Tobacco farms were dominant in Kentucky, Maryland, and Virginia, while sugar ruled in Louisiana. In Alabama, Mississippi, and Texas, cotton was king. Cotton also reigned in up-country Georgia and South Carolina while in low-country Georgia and South Carolina, the main crop was rice.

The size of individual farms or plantations often determined the cultivation methods for these different types of crops. Many researchers assume all slaves lived on plantations. But in 1860 only 53 percent of slaves lived on plantations. The remainder lived on small family farms, where a farmer only owned five to ten slaves, or less. He and his family often worked in fields alongside his slaves. Other farmers were too poor to own slaves and hired (rented) them during planting or harvest season. Other slaves acquired skills such as carpentry, shoe making, and blacksmithing and were often hired out to work for others, or on their own. Professionals and tradesmen, such as doctors, lawyers, and blacksmiths, often hired one or two slaves as helpers or servants. Their income was given to their owner and hired slaves were sometimes able to keep a portion of the income they generated. Hired-out slaves lived lives similar to free blacks.

One way of determining if a slave lived on a plantation, or with a small family farmer or professional, is to locate the slave owner on the census slave schedule. The schedule indicates how many slaves were residing on the owner's property. If the number of slaves owned was greater than twenty-five, it was more likely a plantation.

Plantation Records

Plantations were large commercial operations. They employed twenty-five or more slaves, with the number on some

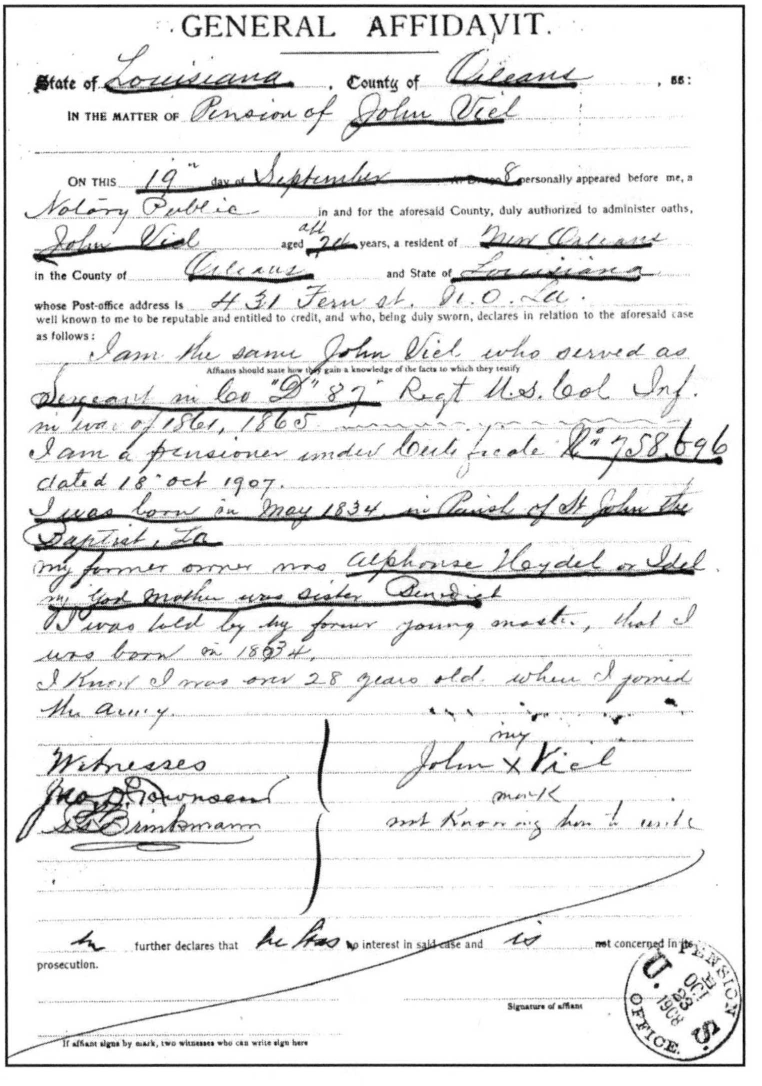

GENERAL AFFIDAVIT.

State of Louisiana, County of Orleans, ss:

IN THE MATTER OF Pension of John Viel

ON THIS 19" day of September A.D. 1908 personally appeared before me, a Notary Public in and for the aforesaid County, duly authorized to administer oaths, John Viel aged 74 years, a resident of New Orleans in the County of Orleans and State of Louisiana whose Post-office address is 431 Fern st. N.O. La. well known to me to be reputable and entitled to credit, and who, being duly sworn, declares in relation to the aforesaid case as follows:

I am the same John Viel who served as Sergeant in Co "D" 87" Regt U.S. Col Inf. in war of 1861, 1865

I am a pensioner under Certificate No 758696 dated 18 oct 1907.

I was born in May 1834 in Parish of St John the Baptist, La

my former owner was Alphonse Haydel or Idel.

my God mother was sister Benedict

I was told by my former young master, that I was born in 1834,

I Knew I was over 28 years old when I joined the army.

Witnesses [illegible] — John his x mark Viel, not knowing how to write

he further declares that he has no interest in said case and is not concerned in its prosecution.

Signature of affiant

If affiant signs by mark, two witnesses who can write sign here

PENSION OCT 23 1908 U.S. OFFICE

Figure 14-8. General affidavit of John Viel/Veal..

climbing into the hundreds. Plantation managers organized the labor using either the task system or the gang system. The task system assigned a quota of work for the day or week to individual slaves. After the quota was reached, the person was free to work for himself or pursue leisure activities. In the gang system, slaves were divided into groups, where everyone worked on the same job with a supervisor, called a "driver," who was often another slave. The drivers were supervised by an "overseer."

Rice tended to be produced by the task system whereas tobacco was usually cultivated with the gang system. In early years, the gang system was used for cotton and sugar but in the late eighteenth and early nineteenth centuries, some planters switched to task system.

The personal papers of a planter will likely contain information on slaves, particularly in cases where the majority of records have survived. Such papers may be in the possession of the family or may have been deposited with a local or state historical society, archives, university, or research library.

As a genre of personal records, so-called "plantation records" are often voluminous and unpredictable. Those parts having genealogical value will make up only a small portion of the whole and may be difficult to pinpoint. Nevertheless, we can gain some sense of the possibilities of these records for slave genealogy if we consider their context.

Plantation records are business records that were usually kept with personal and family papers since the plantation was essentially a family business. This complex and often extensive enterprise could become even more complicated and far-ranging with new holdings being added from dowries and inheritances. Accounts were kept for any number of reasons, whether it was to monitor the price of cotton or to track the yield of a given acreage. Both were considered in the context of the weather conditions from day to day and week to week. Loans and mortgages were a frequent concern as were the affairs of tenants.

Intertwined with these matters was the presence of slave labor on the plantation. Records of slaves may exist in several contexts. Careful records were kept of the distribution of clothes, blankets, or simply lengths of cloth to the slaves; these items were often issued on a regular basis. Field hands were issued tools and implements and presumably held accountable for them.

A plantation owner's "day book" may contain a variety of entries recording observations on the weather, livestock, and crops. It might also note the daily tasks undertaken on the plantation and identify which slaves were dispatched to fix a fence or deepen an irrigation channel. As property, slaves could also be mortgaged or rented; sometimes they were insured, and the owner was normally taxed for each slave he owned, based on their capacity to work. Careful records obviously had to be kept regarding such matters.[50]

A child born of a slave mother became the property of the mother's owner, so it was in the owner's best interest to maintain a record of that birth in the absence of an official vital record. In most cases the slave owner's records may be the only place where slave birth records will be found. Deaths may also be recorded, and could be important to reduce tax liability. Many plantation owners maintained records outlining slave family groups, although, in some instances, one may find only a mother listed with her children. In such cases the identification of a slave father on a large plantation may be difficult. Sometimes the father lived on a neighboring farm.

These manuscript collections may also contain diaries and letters. While the chance that important information concerning slaves would be contained in such items is admittedly slim, it is not impossible. In letters and diaries, often written in faded and difficult-to-read handwriting, the mention of slaves by name may occur infrequently, if at all. And if they are mentioned, their mention will not stand out in any appreciable fashion from the rest of the letter or diary. The whole letter or diary must be read with only a limited expectation of finding any information of genealogical value.

The researcher should also bear in mind that a collection of papers will not necessarily be limited to one person, one generation, or even to a family of the same surname. As the plantation, or parts of it, were sold or transferred or willed to relations and in-laws, the records could also be transferred with the property. Thus, accumulations of plantation records could have a wide familial and geographical scope.

Finding and examining plantation records can be a challenge. Some planters' records have been microfilmed as part of the extensive microfilm series, *Records of Ante-Bellum Southern Plantations from the Revolution through the Civil War* (edited by Kenneth Stampp).[51] This set of 1,500 reels of microfilm is available at many research libraries.

Before 2003 these records were not easy to research, although they are accompanied by very thorough descriptions and reel guides for each series. The reel guides reveal the likelihood of there being any records of interest, as well as their exact location in the microfilm. However, the collection contains no comprehensive list of planters to easily search for a name. The names are listed in the reel guides to each series, but there are fourteen series. The best way to quickly and easily find a planter's name is use a privately published index, such as *A Genealogical Index to the Guides of the Microfilm Edition of Records of Ante-Bellum Southern Plantations from the Revolution Through the Civil War* by Jean L. Cooper.[52]

A Genealogical Index to . . . Records of Ante-Bellum Southern Plantations is a comprehensive index to names of all planters in the collection, across the fourteen series. But even more useful, it indexes information six different ways—alphabetically by surname; surname within each state; by city or county; by state; by name of plantation; and name of plantation within each state.

The six indexes make this an outstanding guide. A listing of plantations by state is extremely hard to come by, let alone one that covers the entire country. Now if you have the name of a plantation, you can determine the owner and location as well. Of course, not all plantation records are microfilmed, but possibly 90 percent have been microfilmed in this Stampp collection.

A Genealogical Index to . . . Records of Ante-Bellum Southern Plantations is very thorough and of high quality. It is an extremely useful guide for doing historical and genealogical research, and is indispensable for doing slave genealogy.

If a planter's records were not microfilmed but have been deposited in a library or historical society (and many have been), there is a good chance that they are listed in the *National Union Catalog of Manuscript Collections (NUCMC)*. The *NUCMC* is a serial reference work that first appeared in 1959 and is published by the Library of Congress. The *NUCMC* contains descriptions of manuscript collections held by hundreds of libraries throughout the country. It became more user friendly with the publication of *Index to Personal Names*, 1959–1984.[53] Some of the *NUCMC* is available online at the Library of Congress website <http://lcweb.loc.gov/coll/nucmc/nucmc.html>.

The researcher of slave genealogy who has focused on a particular slaveholding family should consult the *NUCMC* to see if there are any listings for the papers of members of that family. Such a listing will indicate the repository at which they are held. (See also chapter 3, "General References and Guides.")

Property and Other Records

As stated previously, not all slaves resided on plantations. A single family group or one or two non-related individuals might be found working smaller farms or businesses. In these situations, check local and county records, such as church, newspapers, land and property, court, and vital records, under the name of the slave owner. This process should also be used if the owner is in possession of a large plantation.

Probate Records

As valued assets in an estate, slaves were sometimes mentioned by name when bequeathed to a family member, purchased from someone else, or sold to liquidate the estate. David C. Moore of Duplin County, North Carolina, died in late 1863 or early 1864, leaving to his son Thomas "one half of that portion of my negroes known as Megee Negroes including Martha & her three children excepting those that I purchased from Thomas H. Megee namely Aaron, Mary & three children."[54]

Note that slaves were specifically identified only insofar as the identification served the purposes of the testator. Therefore, slaves may be identified in a will by name and by family—or else grouped anonymously (such as "I will all my slaves to my spouse").

It is sometimes possible to trace a particular slave through two or more wills. The will of Thomas Byrd of Somerset County, Maryland, was probated on 16 March 1757, leaving "a negro girl called Nice" to his daughter Mary Byrd, later wife of Paul Dulany, whose will was probated on 6 March 1773, leaving "one negro woman named Nice" to his son Henry.[55] Interestingly, the reference to Nice in the two wills also provides evidence for relationship between the slave owners.

The location of wills in the slave states has been considerably aided by the indexing of some wills on a statewide basis. Many such indexes have been published.[56] The Genealogical Society of Utah has microfilmed early extant wills for many of the counties in the Southern slave states, while at least one state, North Carolina, has instituted its own microfilming program. Thus, the consultation of these important documents will not necessarily be confined to viewing the originals in a county courthouse, although the researcher should do so whenever possible.

Abstracts or transcriptions of county wills are increasingly finding their way into print. In many of the more recent publications in this genre, references to slaves are retained and special slave indexes are included. However, the researcher of slave genealogy should approach such published will abstracts carefully. If the compiler of such a book has omitted slave data, that fact should be readily apparent after a few minutes of examination. The researcher should then attempt to access microfilm of the records or else plan a genealogical research trip to view the originals.

Unfortunately slave names are not always provided in a will. Their names tend to be listed when there is a small number of slaves in an estate, or the named person was a favored house slave in a large estate. Fortunately the will is only one document in the probate process. Names are more often listed in inventories and appraisals of large estates. Bills of sale may also be found among probate documents if, for example, slaves had to be sold in order to pay an estate's debts.

Deeds and Other Local Records

As with any genealogical research, the quest for African American ancestry requires researchers to become familiar with the records and record-keeping practices of the state and county where their ancestors lived. References to slaves exist in a variety of local record groups. County deed books may contain, in addition to real estate transactions, documentation of slave sales. For example, in Deed Book F-6 of Warren County, Kentucky, one finds certification of a bill of sale, dated 15 July 1813, of $1,500 from Upshaw R. Massey to Jesse Kerby for four slaves: a man named Moses, a woman named Milly, and two boys named Aaron and Robert. Massey and his wife are to "reserve use of said slaves until their own deaths."[57]

But caution should be exercised in interpreting some deed records, particularly deeds in, or of, trust. If a slave is named in a deed of trust, it does not necessarily mean that there was a change in ownership; the slave was probably used as collateral. If the debt for which the slave acted as collateral was eventually discharged, then the slave would remain the property of the original owner.

Court records in the antebellum slave states could document any number of situations involving slaves and their owners, some mundane, others revealing, even tragic. The circuit court records of Estill County, Kentucky, contain the following examples: the record of an inquisition on the body of Stephen, a slave who had died as a result of mistreatment described in great detail by his owner, William P. Noland; a suit by the same William Noland in 1837 against one Joseph Cox over the purchase of "a negro boy named Henry" for $200, in which Noland asserts that the slave had rheumatism and was subject to fits; and testimony in 1846 of a married white woman giving birth to a child fathered by a slave named Mark.[58]

Tax records can also contain references to slaves. In the 1787 "census" of Virginia (actually tax records viewed by genealogists as a "replacement" for the lost 1790 census of that state), slaves are identified by name together with their owners in Mecklenburg and Surry counties.[59] The books of tithables for Norfolk County, Virginia, provide other examples, naming slaves with owners for much of the eighteenth century.[60] Documentation for the buying and selling of slaves can be found in a variety of official sources on the local level. Such evidence is also found in private papers. A pilot project attempting to bring together this information from an array of sources was the Slave Bills of Sale Project of the African-American Family History Association in Atlanta, Georgia. This project transcribed, indexed, and published two volumes of slave bills of sale.[61] The genealogical community can hope that similar efforts will be undertaken throughout the South.

Other Records of Slave Births and Deaths

During the antebellum period, keeping vital records had not yet been mandated by many state governments. For that simple reason, official vital records do not exist for slaves, or for anyone else, in many of the states prior to the Civil War. Yet, as always, there are exceptions. For example, Kentucky enacted legislation in 1852 (repealed in 1862) requiring birth and death registrations in all counties. The birth records were to include children born to slave mothers, indicating date and place of birth, sex, and name of owner. A year later similar legislation was passed in Virginia. It has been noted that slave owners may have been more intent on registering slave births than the births of their own children, a motivation likely arising from the need to protect their property by an act of official registration.[62]

Similar motivations may have spurred the baptism of slaves by their owners. Such baptism records are often just as detailed as those for whites. The majority of such records, at least those which are extant, appear to be from Anglican/Episcopalian churches. Unfortunately, many of these registers have probably been lost, especially those of Virginia.[63] The situation is much better in South Carolina, where the records of a number of Low Country churches survive, many extending well back into the colonial era. These contain extensive slave baptismal records, some including the names of both slave parents as well as owners. The South Carolina Historical Society has microfilmed many of these records and made them available on microfiche.

It has already been noted that the personal papers of slave owners can contain records of slave births and deaths. Consider the possibility of slave births and deaths being noted in the slave owner's Bible, together with those of his own family. To be sure, this was not a typical practice; however, when it did occur it likely reflected a small slaveholding of perhaps one or two slave families who had been in the possession of their owners for several decades.[64]

Runaway Slaves

Slaves sometimes attempted to escape from their owners. Some succeeded; most did not. Runaway slave advertisements, which usually contain physical descriptions and, occasionally, biographical information, can be of interest to the genealogist. However, the identity of an ancestor's owner would have to be known for such an advertisement to be useful. Many advertisements have been transcribed and published, most notably in Lathan A. Windley's *Runaway Slave Advertisements: A Documentary History from the 1730s to 1790*, which covers the states of Virginia, North Carolina, Maryland, South Carolina, and Georgia.[65] Robert K. Headley's *Genealogical Abstracts from the 18th Century Virginia Newspapers*, also contains runaway advertisements.[66]

Advertisements from eighteenth-century Pennsylvania are found in Gary T. Hawbaker's *Runaways, Rascals, and Rogues: Missing Spouses, Servants and Slaves. Abstracts from Lancaster County Pennsylvania Newspapers*, and in Billy G. Smith's and Richard Wojtowicz's *Blacks Who Stole Themselves: Advertisements for Runaways in the Pennsylvania Gazette 1728–1790*.[67] Also of interest is Helen Cox Tregillis's *River Roads to Freedom: Fugitive Slave Notices and Sheriff Notices Found in Illinois Sources*.[68]

Conclusion

Far from the expected dearth of records, African American genealogy presents a wealth of resources. The complications of tracing African Americans are challenging, but can make for interesting and exciting research that is never boring. In the process of studying African American genealogy, researchers will learn much about American history, as well as the plight of African Americans. Non–African Americans will discover new sources to search for their ancestors.

Notes

[1] *Who's Who in Colored America: A Biographical Dictionary of Notable Living Men and Women*, vols. 1–7 (New York: Who's Who in Colored America Corp. and various publishers, 1927–1950).

[2] Belzora Cheatham, *Funeral Programs/Obituaries of 579 African Americans* (n.p.: Belzora Cheatham, 1998), Atlanta, Texas Public Library 920.02 CHE.

[3] Rayford W. Logan and Michael R. Winston, *Dictionary of American Negro Biography* (New York: W. W. Norton, 1982).

[4] *Who's Who Among Black Americans* (Detroit: Gale Research Co. and other publishers, 1975–1995); *Who's Who Among African Americans* (Detroit: Gale Research Co. and other publishers, 1996–present). See note 1 for *Who's Who in Colored America.*

[5] Tony Burroughs, *Black Roots: A Beginners Guide to Tracing the African American Family Tree* (New York: Fireside Division of Simon and Schuster, 2001).

[6] Tony Burroughs, "Finding African Americans on the 1870 Census," *Heritage Quest Magazine* 91 (January/February 2001): 50–56.

[7] Carmen R. Donne, *Federal Census Schedules, 1850–80: Primary Sources of Historical Research, Reference Information Paper No. 67* (Washington, D.C.: National Archives and Records Service, General Services Administration, 1973), 12.

[8] *General Index to Pension Files, 1861–1934*, NARA microfilm T288.

[9] *Organization Index to Pension Files of Veterans Who Served Between 1861 and 1900*, NARA microfilm T289.

[10] Irene Schubert and Frank N. Schubert, *On the Trail of the Buffalo Soldier II: New and Revised Biographies of African-Americans in the U.S. Army, 1866–1917* (Lanham, Md.: Scarecrow Press, 2004).

[11] Tony Burroughs, "Researching Buffalo Soldiers for Genealogical and Historical Links," *Journal of the Afro-American Historical and Genealogical Society* 14 (Summer 1995): 136–51.

[12] The 54th Massachusetts Infantry (Colored), 55th Massachusetts Infantry (Colored), and 5th Massachusetts Colored Cavalry. The 29th Connecticut Volunteer Infantry retained its state designation. The 30th Connecticut Volunteer Infantry became the 31st United States Colored Infantry.

[13] Jaunita Patience Moss, *The Forgotten Black Soldiers in White Regiments During the Civil War* (Westminster, Md.: Willow Bend Books, 2004).

[14] *Index to Compiled Military Service Records of Volunteer Union Soldiers Who Served with the United States Colored Troops*, NARA microfilm M589.

[15] See "Records of Slave Claims Commissions, 1864–1866" and "Registers of Claims, U.S. Colored Troops, 1864–67." Records of the Adjutant General's Office, 1780s–1917 Record Group 94, NARA, Washington, D.C.

[16] *Index to Compiled Military Service Records*, NARA microfilm M589.

[17] David L. Valuska, *The African Americans in the Union Navy, 1861–1865* (New York: Garland Publishing, 1993).

[18] Alexia Jones Helsley, *South Carolina's African American Confederate Pensioners, 1923–1925* (Columbia: South Carolina Department of Archives and History, 1998).

[19] Gale Williams Bamman, "African-Americans Impressed for Service on the Nashville and North Western Railroad, October 1863," *National Genealogical Society Quarterly* 80, no. 3 (September 1992): 204–10. Although this particular record is found in the Tennessee State Library and Archives, Bamman notes that similar records can be found in National Archives Record Groups 92 (Quartermaster General's Office), 94 (Adjutant General's Office), and 109 (Captured Confederate Records).

[20] Slave and other payrolls, 1861–65, War Department Collection of Confederate Records, Record Group 109, NARA, Washington, D.C.

[21] Debra L. Newman, comp., *List of Black Servicemen Compiled from the War Department Collection of Revolutionary War Records*, Special List 36 (Washington, D.C.: National Archives and Records Service, 1974). For Robert Ewell Greene, see especially *Black Courage 1775–1783: Documentation of Black Participation in the American Revolution* (Washington, D.C.: National Society of the Daughters of the American Revolution, 1984).

[22] *African American and American Indian Patriots of the Revolutionary War* (Washington, D.C.: National Society of the Daughters of the American Revolution, 2001).

[23] The "Book of Negroes" was actually a list compiled in 1783 by Sir Guy Carleton, on behalf of the British, of former slaves and free blacks that served with the British or came to the British side during the Revolutionary War and were evacuated to Nova Scotia. The list was compiled to compensate former slave owners who never did receive compensation. Graham Russell Hodges, ed., *The Black Loyalist Directory* (New York: Garland Publishing in Association with the New England Historic Genealogical Society, 1996).

[24] Carl R. Osthaus, *Freedmen, Philanthropy, and Fraud: A History of the Freedman's Savings Bank* (Urbana: University of Illinois Press, 1976), 3.

[25] *Registers of Signatures of Depositors in Branches of the Freedman's Savings and Trust Company, 1865–74*, NARA microfilm, M816, roll 11, Louisville, Kentucky, branch, record no. 1.

[26] Ibid., roll 15, Vicksburg, Mississippi, branch, record no. 1186.

[27] *Registers of Signatures of Depositors in Branches of the Freedman's Savings and Trust Company, 1865–74,* NARA microfilm, M816.

[28] *Freedman's Bank Records,* CD-ROM (Salt Lake City: The Church of Jesus Christ of Latter-day Saints, 2001).

[29] Bill Reaves, *North Carolina Freedman's Savings and Trust Company Records* (Raleigh: North Carolina Genealogical Society, 1992).

[30] Charles Brewer, "Do You Trust That Freedman's Bank?" (presentation at 2003 Federation of Genealogical Societies conference, 3–6 September 2003), tape FGS2003T91; Tony Burroughs, "Records Specific to African Americans—The Freedman's Savings and Trust Company," in *African-American Genealogical Sourcebook,* ed. Paula Byers (Detroit: Gale Research Co., 1995), 57–67; Reginald Washington, "The Freedman's Savings and Trust Company and African American Genealogical Research" *Prologue* 29 (Summer 1997): 170–81.

[31] Elaine Everly and Willna Pacheli, *Preliminary Inventory of the Records of the Field Offices of the Bureau of Refugees, Freedmen, and Abandoned Lands (Record Group 105)* (Washington, D.C.: National Archives and Record Service, 1973).

[32] See Jacqueline A. Lawson, *An Index of African Americans Identified in Selected Records of the Bureau of Refugees, Freedmen, and Abandoned Lands* (Bowie, Md.: Heritage Books, 1995).

[33] For documentation of other slave marriages, see Christopher A. Nordmann, "Jumping Over the Broomstick: Resources for Documenting Slave Marriages," *National Genealogical Society Quarterly* 91 (September 2003): 196–216.

[34] *Marriage Records of the Office of the Commissioner, Washington Headquarters of the Bureau of Refugees, Freedmen, and Abandoned Lands, 1861–1869,* NARA microfilm M1875.

[35] Elaine Everly, *Preliminary Inventory of the Records of the Bureau of Refugees, Freedmen, and Abandoned Lands, Washington Headquarters (Record Group 105)* (Washington, D.C.: National Archives and Record Service, 1973).

[36] Freedmen's Bureau Online at <www.freedmensbureau.com/>.

[37] Burroughs, "Records Specific to African Americans."

[38] Larry Koger, *Black Slave Owners: Free Black Slave Masters in South Carolina, 1790–1860* (Jefferson, N.C.: McFarland and Co., 1985).

[39] Donald Sweig, *Registrations of Free Negroes Commencing September Court 1822 . . .* (Fairfax, Va.: Fairfax County History Commission, 1977), 97.

[40] Stephen Haller and Robert Smith, comps., *Records of Black and Mulatto Persons . . . A printed abstract of these records entitled Register of Blacks in the Miami Valley: A Name Abstract* (1804–1857).

[41] Joan Turpin, *Register of Black, Mulatto and Poor Persons in Four Ohio Counties, 1791–1861* (Bowie, Md.: Heritage Books, 1985).

[42] See Herbert G. Gutman, *The Black Family in Slavery and Freedom, 1750–1925* (New York: Vintage Books, 1976), 230–56.

[43] David T. Thackery, "Crossing the Divide: A Census Study of Slaves Before and After Freedom," *Origins* (newsletter of the Dr. William M. Scholl Center for Family and Community History and the Local and Family History Section at the Newberry Library) 1, no. 2 (March 1989): 1–7.; Gutman, *The Black Family in Slavery and Freedom,* 245.

[44] Vicksburg, Mississippi Branch, account no. 1288, Freedman's Savings and Trust Company Signature Books, NARA microfilm M816.

[45] Burroughs, "Records Specific to African Americans"; George P. Rawick, *The American Slave: A Composite Autobiography* (Westport, Conn.: Greenwood Press, 1972), supplement, series 1, 1977; supplement, series 2, 1979.

[46] See Gary Mills, *Civil War Claims in the South: An Index of Civil War Damage Claims Filed Before the Southern Claims Commission, 1871–1880* (Laguna Hills, Calif.: Aegean Park Press, 1980); and *Southern Loyalists in the Civil War* (1994; Reprint, Baltimore, Md.: Genealogical Publishing Co., 2004). See also Washington, "The Southern Claims Commission: A Source for African American Roots," *Prologue* (Winter 1995): 374–82; and Eales and Kvasnicka, *Guide to Genealogical Research in the National Archives* (Washington, D.C.: National Archives and Records Administration, 2000), 249.

[47] John Hope Franklin, *From Slavery to Freedom: A History of Negro Americans,* 5th ed. (New York: Knopf Co., 1979).

[48] Alan D. Watson, *African Americans in Early North Carolina: A Documentary History* (Raleigh: North Carolina Office of Archives and History, 2005).

[49] Ira Berlin, *Many Thousands Gone: The First Two Centuries of Slavery in North America* (Cambridge, Mass.: Belknap Press of Harvard University Press, 1998).

[50] Insurance policies from the slavery era (pre-1865) were discovered in the archives of several insurance companies, and the California legislature has published the names of slaves who were insured and the slave-owner who purchased the policy. See "Slavery Era Insurance Registry" under "Internet Resources."

[51] Kenneth Stampp, *Records of Ante-Bellum Southern Plantations from the Revolution through the Civil War* (Frederick, Md.: University Publications of America, 1985).

[52] Jean L. Cooper, *A Genealogical Index to the Guides of the Microfilm Edition of Records of Ante-Bellum Southern Plantations from the Revolution Through the Civil War* (Bloomington, Ind.: 1stBooks, 2003).

[53] *Index to Personal Names in the National Union Catalog of Manuscript Collections 1959–1984* (Alexandria, Va.: Chadwyk-Healey, 1988).

[54] The abstract of this will (Duplin County Will Book, vol. 3, entry 85) can be found in Murphy, *Genealogical Abstracts: Duplin County Wills, 1730–1860* (Rose Hill, N.C.: Duplin County, Historical Society, 1982), 120.

[55] Wills, Maryland State Archives, liber 30, folio 351, and liber 39, folio 521, respectively.

[56] Among such published indexes: Austin, *Index to Georgia Wills* (Baltimore: Genealogical Publishing Co., 1985); Mitchell, *North Carolina Wills: A Testator Index, 1665–1900*, rev. ed. (Baltimore: Genealogical Publishing Co., 1992); Sistler, *Index to Tennessee Wills and Administrations, 1779–1861* (Nashville: Sistler, 1990); Torrence, *Virginia Wills and Administrations, 1632–1800: An Index* (Richmond, Va.: National Society of Colonial Dames of America, 1930); and Wiltshire, *Mississippi Index of Wills* (Bowie, Md.: Heritage, 1989).

[57] Abstracted in Murray, *Deed Abstracts of Warren County, Kentucky, 1812–1821* (Dallas: Murray, 1986), 12.

[58] Abstracted by Rogers, *Estill County, Kentucky, Circuit Court Records, 1:3, 7, 2:240* (Irvine, Kent.: the compilers, 1984).

[59] Transcribed in Schreiner-Yantis and Virginia Love, *The 1787 Census of Virginia* (Springfield, Va.: Genealogical Books in Print, 1987).

[60] See Wingo, *Norfolk County, Virginia Tithables 1730–1750* (Norfolk, Va.: the compilers, 1979); and *Norfolk County, Virginia Tithables 1751–1765* (Norfolk, Va.: the compilers, 1981).

[61] *Slave Bills of Sale Project* (Atlanta, Ga.: African-American Family History Association, 1986).

[62] Johni Cerny, "Black Ancestral Research," in *The Source: A Guidebook of American Genealogy*, 1st ed. (Salt Lake City: Ancestry, 1984), 582.

[63] One that has survived and that contains extensive slave birth and baptism listings was transcribed and published in 1897 and was reprinted recently as *The Parish Register of Christ Church, Middlesex County, Va. from 1653 to 1812* (Easley, S.C.: Southern Historical Society, 1988).

[64] For example, see Hugh Buckner Johnston Jr., "Some Bible and Other Family Records," *North Carolina Genealogical Society Journal* 7 (November 1981).

[65] Lathan A. Windley, *Runaway Slave Advertisements: A Documentary History from the 1730s to 1790*, 4 vols. (Westport, Conn.: Greenwood Press, 1983).

[66] Robert K. Headley, *Genealogical Abstracts from the 18th Century Virginia Newspapers* (Baltimore: Genealogical Publishing Co., 1987).

[67] Gary T. Hawbaker, *Runaways, Rascals, and Rogues: Missing Spouses, Servants and Slaves. Abstracts from Lancaster County Pennsylvania Newspapers* (Hershey, Penn.: the author, 1987); Billy G. Smith and Richard Wojtowicz Smith, *Blacks Who Stole Themselves: Advertisements for Runaways in the Pennsylvania Gazette, 1728–1790* (Philadelphia: University of Pennsylvania, 1989).

[68] Helen Cox Tregillis, *River Roads to Freedom: Fugitive Slave Notices and Sheriff Notices Found in Illinois Sources* (Bowie, Md.: Heritage Books, 1988).

References

African American Genealogy

Burroughs, Tony. *Black Roots: A Beginners Guide to Tracing the African American Family Tree*. New York: Fireside Division of Simon and Schuster, 2001.

Byers, Paula, ed. *African-American Genealogical Sourcebook*. Detroit: Gale Research Co., 1995.

Croom, Emily Anne, and Franklin Carter Smith. *Genealogist's Guide to Discovering Your African American Ancestors: How to Find and Record Your Unique Heritage*. Cincinnati: Betterway Publications, 2002.

Linder, Bill. *Black Genealogy: Basic Steps to Research*. Technical Leaflet 135. Nashville: American Association for State and Local History, 1981.

Thackery, David. *Tracking Your African American Ancestors: A Beginner's Guide*. Orem, Utah: Ancestry, 2001.

Witcher, Curt B. *African American Genealogy: A Bibliography and Guide to Sources*. Fort Wayne, Ind.: Round Tower Books, 2000.

Woodtor, Dee Palmer. *Finding a Place Called Home: A Guide to African American Genealogy and Historical Identity*. New York: Random House, 1999.

Biographical Resources

Burkett, Randall K., Nancy Hall Burkett, and Henry Louis Gates Jr., eds. *Black Biographical Dictionaries 1790–1950*. Alexandria, Va.: Chadwyck-Healey, 1991.

———. *Black Biography 1790–1950: A Cumulative Index*. Alexandria, Va.: Chadwyck-Healey, 1991.

Cheatham, Belzora. *Funeral Programs/Obituaries of 579 African Americans*. N.p.: Belzora Cheatham, 1998. Available at Atlanta, Texas Public Library, 920.02 CHE.

Lawson, Sandra K. *Generations Past: A Select List of Sources for Afro-American Genealogical Research*. Washington, D.C.: Library of Congress, 1988. (Update on the Web: Connor,

Paul. *African American Family Histories and Related Works in the Library of Congress*, Research Guide No. 34., Washington 1998 <www.loc.gov/rr/genealogy/bib_guid/aframer>.)

Logan, Rayford W., and Michael R. Winston. *Dictionary of American Negro Biography*. New York: W. W. Norton, 1982.

Who's Who Among African Americans. Detroit: Gale Research Co. and other publishers, 1996–present.

Who's Who Among Black Americans. Detroit: Gale Research Co. and other publishers, 1977–1995.

Who's Who in Colored America: A Biographical Dictionary of Notable Living Men and Women. Vols. 1–7. New York: Who's Who in Colored America Corp. and various publishers, 1927–1950.

Census Records

African American in the 1870 Census. CD-ROM. Salt Lake: Heritage Quest, 2001.

Burroughs, Tony. "Finding African Americans on the 1870 Census." *Heritage Quest Magazine* 91 (January/February 2001): 50–56.

Cheatham, Belzora. "1850 Bowie County Slave Census Schedules, Part 1." *Frontiers Freedmen's Journal* 3, no. 2 (Fall 1994/Winter 1995): 15–36.

———. "1850 Bowie County Slave Census Schedules, Part 2." *Frontiers Freedmen's Journal* 4, no. 1 (Winter/Spring 1996): 5–10.

———. *Slaves and Slave Owners of Bowie County Texas in 1850: 1850 Bowie County Slave Census with information from the 1850 free census*. N.p.: Belzora Cheatham, 1996.

Donne, Carmen R. *Federal Census Schedules, 1850–80: Primary Sources of Historical Research, Reference Information Paper No. 67*. Washington, D.C.: National Archives and Records Service, General Services Administration, 1973.

Free Negro Registers

Sweig, Donald. *Registrations of Free Negroes Commencing September Court 1822*. Fairfax, Va.: Fairfax County History Commission, 1977.

Turpin, Joan. *Register of Black, Mulatto and Poor Persons in Four Ohio Counties, 1791–1861*. Bowie, Md.: Heritage Books, 1985.

Freedman's Bank

Brewer, Charles. "Do You Trust That Freedman's Bank?" Presentation at 2003 Federation of Genealogical Societies conference, 3–6 September 2003, tape FGS2003T91.

Burroughs, Tony. "Records Specific to African Americans—The Freedman's Savings and Trust Company." In *African-American Genealogical Sourcebook*, edited by Paula Byers, 57–67. Detroit: Gale Research Co., 1995.

Freedman's Bank Records. CD-ROM. Salt Lake City: The Church of Jesus Christ of Latter-day Saints, 2001.

Hardy, Linell. *Abstract of Account Information of Freedman's Savings and Trust, New Orleans, Louisiana, 1866–1869*. Bowie, Md.: Heritage Books, 1999.

Holverstott, Lyle J., Maxcy R. Dickson, and J. Eric Maddox, comps. *Preliminary Checklist of Records of the Division of Insolvent National Banks of the Bureau of the Comptroller of the Currency, 1865–1945*. Washington, D.C.: National Archives and Records Service, 1946.

Nesbary, Nettie, et al. *An Index to the Signatures of Deposits of the Mississippi Freedman's Savings and Loan Bank, 1865–1869 for the State of Mississippi: Columbia, Natchez and Vicksburg*. Bowie, Md.: Heritage Books, 1997. Also available as CD-ROM #1263, with images. Heritage Books, 1999.

Osthaus, Carl R. *Freedmen, Philanthropy, and Fraud: A History of the Freedman's Savings Bank*. Urbana: University of Illinois Press, 1976.

Rathbun, Charles. *Names from Huntsville, Alabama, 1865–1869, as Recorded in Registers of Signatures of Depositors in the Huntsville Branch Freedman's Savings and Trust Company, Accounts 1–385*. Littleton, Colo.: Rathbun, 1986.

Reaves, Bill. *North Carolina Freedman's Savings and Trust Company Records*. Raleigh: North Carolina Genealogical Society, 1992.

Washington, Reginald. "The Freedman's Savings and Trust Company and African American Genealogical Research." *Prologue* 29 (Summer 1997): 170–81.

Freedmen's Bureau

Burroughs, Tony. "Records Specific to African Americans—The Freedmen's Bureau." In *African-American Genealogical Sourcebook*, edited by Paula Byers, 68–91. Detroit: Gale Research Co., 1995.

Everly, Elaine. *Preliminary Inventory of the Records of the Bureau of Refugees, Freedmen, and Abandoned Lands, Washington Headquarters (Record Group 105)*. Washington, D.C.: National Archives and Record Service, 1973.

Everly, Elaine, and Willna Pacheli. *Preliminary Inventory of the Records of the Field Offices of the Bureau of Refugees, Freedmen, and Abandoned Lands (Record Group 105)*. Washington, D.C.: National Archives and Record Service, 1973.

Lawson, Jacqueline A. *An Index of African Americans Identified in Selected Records of the Bureau of Refugees, Freedmen, and Abandoned Lands*. Bowie, Md.: Heritage Books, 1995.

Nordmann, Christopher A. "Jumping Over the Broomstick: Resources for Documenting Slave Marriages." *National Genealogical Society Quarterly* 91 (September 2003): 196–216.

Genealogies, Family Histories, and Novels

Haizlip, Shirlee Taylor. *The Sweeter the Juice: A Family Memoir in Black and White*. New York: Simon and Schuster, 1994.

Johnson, Michael P., and James L. Roark. *Black Masters: A Free Family of Color in the Old South*. New York: W. W. Norton, 1984.

Jupiter, Del E. "Agustina and the Kelkers: A Spanish West Florida Line." *National Genealogical Society Quarterly* 80 (December 1992): 265–79.

Jupiter, Del Alexa Egan. *Agustina of Spanish West Florida and Her Descendants: With Related Families of Egan, Kelker, Palmer, and Taylor*. Franklin, N.C.: Genealogy Publishing Service, 1994.

Madden, T. O. *We Were Always Free: The Maddens of Culpepper County, Virginia, a 200-Year Family History*. New York: W. W. Norton, 1992.

Mills, Elizabeth Shown. *Isle of Canes: A Historical Novel*. Provo, Utah: Ancestry, 2004.

Redford, Dorothy Spruill. *Somerset Homecoming: Recovering a Lost Heritage*. New York: Doubleday, 1988.

Ruffin, C. Bernard. "In Search of the Unappreciated Past: The Ruffin-Cornick Family of Virginia." *National Genealogical Society Quarterly* 81 (June 1993): 126–38.

Tademy, Lalita. *Cane River*. New York: Warner Books, 2002.

Taulbert, Clifton. *Once Upon A Time When We Were Colored*. Tulsa, Okla.: Council Oak Books, 1989.

Guides to Black Federal Records

Black Studies: A Select Catalog of National Archives Microfilm Publications. Washington, D.C.: National Archives and Records Administration, 1984.

Eales, Anne Bruner, and Robert M. Kvasnicka, eds. *Guide to Genealogical Research in the National Archives of the United States*. Washington, D.C.: National Archives and Records Administration, 2000.

Washington, Reginald. *Black Family Research: Records of Post-Civil War Federal Agencies at the National Archives*. Reference information paper 180. Washington, D.C.: National Archives and Records Administration, 2003.

Historical Sources

Berlin, Ira. *Many Thousands Gone: The First Two Centuries of Slavery in North America*. Cambridge, Mass.: Belknap Press of Harvard University Press, 1998.

———. *Slaves without Masters: The Free Negro in the Antebellum South*. New York: Oxford University Press, 1976.

Foner, Eric. *Reconstruction: America's Unfinished Revolution, 1863–1877*. New York: Harper and Row, 1988.

Franklin, John Hope, and Alfred A. Moss. *From Slavery to Freedom: A History of Negro Americans*. 8th ed. New York: Knopf Co., 2000.

Gutman, Herbert. *The Black Family in Slavery and Freedom, 1750–1925*. New York: Vintage Books, 1976.

Koger, Larry. *Black Slave Owners: Free Black Slave Masters in South Carolina, 1790–1860*. Jefferson, N.C.: McFarland and Co., 1985.

Litwack, Leon F. *North of Slavery: The Negro in the Free States, 1790–1860*. Chicago: University of Chicago Press, 1961.

Watson, Alan D. *African Americans in Early North Carolina: A Documentary History*. Raleigh: North Carolina Office of Archives and History, 2005.

Journals

Burroughs, Tony. "A Lazy Man's Way to Research." *National Genealogical Society Newsletter* 22 (May/June 1996): 66–67.

Journal of the Afro-American Historical and Genealogical Society Quarterly. Published by the Afro-American Historical and Genealogical Society, P.O. Box 73086, Washington, D.C. 20056-3086. 1980–present.

Periodical Source Index (PERSI). Fort Wayne, Ind.: Allen County Public Library Foundation, 1847–1985 and 1986–present, annual. Indexes genealogical periodicals from 1847 to the present and has surname index. Updates on CD-ROM and the Web at Ancestry.com. Updates are also available on Heritage Quest online.

Walker, Barbara D. *Index to the Journal of the Afro-American Historical and Genealogical Society Quarterly: Issues of 1980–1990*. Bowie, Md.: Heritage Books, 1992.

Military

Bamman, Gale Williams. "African-Americans Impressed for Service on the Nashville and North Western Railroad, October 1863." *National Genealogical Society Quarterly* 80, no. 3 (September 1992): 204–10.

Brewer, Charles C. "African American Sailors and the Unvexing of the Mississippi River." *Prologue* 30 (Winter 1998): 278–86.

Burroughs, Tony. "Researching Buffalo Soldiers for Genealogical and Historical Links." *Journal of the Afro-American Historical and Genealogical Society* 14 (Summer 1995): 136–51.

Dyer, Frederick H. *Compendium of the War of the Rebellion*. Reprint, Dayton, Ohio: Morningside, 1978.

Ernest, John E. "African-Americans in the American Revolution." *FORUM* 16 (Fall 2004): 3, 9–19.

Greene, Robert Ewell, ed. *Black Courage 1775–1783: Documentation of Black Participation in the American Revolution.* Washington, D.C.: National Society of the Daughters of the American Revolution, 1984.

Helsley, Alexia Jones. *South Carolina's African American Confederate Pensioners, 1923–1925.* Columbia: South Carolina Department of Archives and History, 1998.

Hewett, Janet B., ed. *The Roster of Union Soldiers, 1861–1865: United States Colored Troops.* Vols. 4–5. Wilmington, N.C.: Broadfoot Publishing Co., 1997.

Hodges, Graham Russell, ed. *The Black Loyalist Directory.* New York: Garland Publishing in Association with the New England Historic Genealogical Society, 1996.

Matchette, Robert B., et al. "War Department Collection of Revolutionary War Records." In *Guide to Federal Records in the National Archives of the United States*, vol. 1. NARA record group 93. An online version is available at <www.archives.gov/research/guide-fed-records/groups/093.html>.

Moebs, Thomas Truxtun, comp. *Black Soldiers, Black Sailors, Black Ink: Research Guide on African-Americans in U. S. Military History, 1526–1900.* Chesapeake Bay, Va.: Moebs Publishing Co., 1994.

Moss, Jaunita Patience. *The Forgotten Black Soldiers in White Regiments During the Civil War.* Westminster, Md.: Willow Bend Books, 2004.

National Society Daughters of the American Revolution. *Forgotten Patriots: African American and American Indian Patriots in the Revolutionary War.* Washington, D.C.: National Society Daughters of the American Revolution, 2001. Revision forthcoming.

National Society of the Daughters of the American Revolution. *Minority Military Service—Rhode Island 1775–1783.* Washington, D.C.: National Society of the Daughters of the American Revolution, 1988.

Newman, Debra L., comp. *List of Black Servicemen Compiled from the War Department Collection of Revolutionary War Records.* Special List 36. Washington, D.C.: National Archives and Records Service, 1974.

Reidy, Joseph P. "The African-American Sailors' Project: The Hidden History of the Civil War." *Cultural Resource Management* 20, no. 2 (1997): 31–33, 43.

Schubert, Irene, and Frank N. Schubert. *On the Trail of the Buffalo Soldier II: New and Revised Biographies of African-Americans in the U.S. Army, 1866–1917.* Lanham, Md.: Scarecrow Press, 2004.

Valuska, David L. *The African Americans in the Union Navy, 1861–1865.* New York: Garland Publishing, 1993.

Names

Index to Personal Names in the National Union Catalog of Manuscript Collections 1959–1984. Alexandria, Va.: Chadwyk-Healey, 1988.

Thackery, David T. "Crossing the Divide: A Census Study of Slaves Before and After Freedom." *Origins* (newsletter of the Dr. William M. Scholl Center for Family and Community History and the Local and Family History Section at the Newberry Library) 1, no. 2 (March 1989): 1–7.

Runaways

Franklin, John Hope, and Loren Schweninger. *Runaway Slaves: Rebels on the Plantation.* New York: Oxford University Press, 1999.

Hawbaker, Gary T. *Runaways, Rascals, and Rogues: Missing Spouses, Servants and Slaves. Abstracts from Lancaster County Pennsylvania Newspapers.* Hershey, Penn.: the author, 1987.

Headley, Robert K. *Genealogical Abstracts from the 18th Century Virginia Newspapers.* Baltimore: Genealogical Publishing Co., 1987.

Smith, Billy G., and Richard Wojtowicz. *Blacks Who Stole Themselves: Advertisements for Runaways in the Pennsylvania Gazette, 1728–1790.* Philadelphia: University of Pennsylvania, 1989.

Tregillis, Helen Cox. *River Roads to Freedom: Fugitive Slave Notices and Sheriff Notices Found in Illinois Sources.* Bowie, Md.: Heritage Books, 1988.

Windley, Lathan A. *Runaway Slave Advertisements: A Documentary History from the 1730s to 1790.* 4 vols. Westport, Conn.: Greenwood Press, 1983.

Slavery

Austin, Jeannette Holland. *Index to Georgia Wills.* Baltimore: Genealogical Publishing Co., 1985.

Burroughs, Tony. "Records Specific to African Americans—Slave Oral History." In *African-American Genealogical Sourcebook*, edited by Paula Byers, 47–57. Detroit: Gale Research Co., 1995.

Cerny, Johni. "Black Ancestral Research." In *The Source: A Guidebook of American Genealogy*, 1st ed., edited by Arlene Eakle and Johni Cerny. Salt Lake City: Ancestry, 1984.

Cooper, Jean L. *A Genealogical Index to the Guides of the Microfilm Edition of Records of Ante-Bellum Southern Plantations from the Revolution Through the Civil War.* Bloomington, Ind.: First Books, 2003.

Johnston, Hugh Buckner, Jr. "Some Bible and Other Family Records." *North Carolina Genealogical Society Journal* 7 (November 1981).

Miller, Randall M., and John D. Smith, ed. *Dictionary of Afro-American Slavery*. Westport, Conn.: Greenwood Press, 1988; Praeger, 1997.

Mitchell, Thornton W. *North Carolina Wills: A Testator Index 1665–1900*. Rev. Ed. Baltimore: Genealogical Publishing Co., 1992.

Murphy, William L. *Genealogical Abstracts: Duplin County Wills, 1730–1860*. Rose Hill, N.C.: Duplin County, Historical Society, 1982.

Murray, Joyce Martin. *Deed Abstracts of Warren County, Kentucky, 1812–1821*. Dallas: Murray, 1986.

The Parish Register of Christ Church, Middlesex County, Va. from 1653 to 1812. Easley, S.C.: Southern Historical Society, 1988.

Potts, Howard E. *A Comprehensive Name Index to the American Slave*. Westport, Conn.: Greenwood Press, 1997.

Rawick, George P. *The American Slave: A Composite Autobiography*. Westport Conn.: Greenwood Press, 1972. Supplement, Series 1, 1977. Supplement, Series 2, 1979. (See Potts for indexes).

Rogers, Ellen, and Diane, comps. *Estill County, Kentucky, Circuit Court Records, 1:3, 7, 2:240*. Irvine, Kent.: the compilers, 1984.

Schreiner-Yantis, Nettie, and Virginia Love. *The 1787 Census of Virginia*. Springfield, Va.: Genealogical Books in Print, 1987.

Sistler, Byron and Barbara. *Index to Tennessee Wills & Administrations, 1779–1861*. Nashville: Sistler, 1990.

Slave Bills of Sale Project. Atlanta, Ga.: African-American Family History Association, 1986.

Stampp, Kenneth. *Records of Ante-Bellum Southern Plantations from the Revolution through the Civil War*. Frederick, Md.: University Publications of America, 1985.

Torrence, Clayton. *Virginia Wills and Administrations, 1632–1800: An Index*. Richmond, Va.: National Society of Colonial Dames of America, 1930.

Wiltshire, Betty Couch. *Mississippi Index of Wills*. Bowie, Md.: Heritage, 1989.

Wingo, Elizabeth N., and W. Bruce, comps. *Norfolk County, Virginia Tithables 1730–1750*. Norfolk, Va.: the compilers, 1979.

Wingo, Elizabeth N., and W. Bruce, comps. *Norfolk County, Virginia Tithables 1751–1765*. Norfolk, Va.: the compilers, 1981.

Southern Claims Commission

Larson, Sarah. "Records of the Southern Claims Commission." *Prologue* (1980): 207–18.

Mills, Gary B. *Civil War Claims in the South: An Index of Civil War Damage Claims Filed Before the Southern Claims Commission, 1871–1880*. Laguna Hills, Calif.: Aegean Park Press, 1980.

———. *Southern Loyalists in the Civil War*. 1994. Reprint, Baltimore, Md.: Genealogical Publishing Co., 2004.

Washington, Reginald. "The Southern Claims Commission: A Source for African American Roots." *Prologue* (Winter 1995): 374–82.

Internet Resources

General Information

Afrigeneas
www.afrigeneas.com

The African Genealogy Ring
http://x.webring.com/hub?ring=afamgenring

Christine's Genealogy Website for African American Genealogy
www.ccharity.com

Doll's Genealogy Website
www.dollsgen.com

People of Color in the Old South
www.tngenweb.org/tncolor

Cyberpursuits
www.cyberpursuits.com/gen/ethnic-afam.asp

Lest We Forget—African American history and culture, with emphasis on military
www.coax.net/people/lwf

African American Genealogy Web Databases

African American Cemeteries Online—headstone readings
www.prairiebluff.com/aacemetery

Black Biographies—library subscription
http://aabd.chadwyck.com

Freedmens Bureau Online
www.freedmensbureau.com

An Index of African American Obituary and Funeral Notices—Buffalo, New York, 1998
www.geocities.com/nsonigen/bgsad/index.html

Free African Americans of Virginia, North Carolina, South Carolina, Maryland, and Delaware
from Paul Heinegg
www.freeafricanamericans.com

Large Slaveholders of 1860 and African American Surname Matches from 1870
by Tom Blake, 2001–2003
http://freepages.genealogy.rootsweb.com/~ajac

African American Family Histories and Related Works in the Library of Congress, Research Guide No. 34
by Paul Connor, Washington, 1998 (an update of Lawson, Sandra K. *Generations Past: A Select List of Sources for Afro-American Genealogical Research.* Washington, D.C.: Library of Congress, 1988)
www.loc.gov/rr/genealogy/bib_guid/aframer

Louisiana Databases for the Study of Afro-Louisiana History and Genealogy, 1699–1860.
by Gwendolyn Midlow Hall
www.ibiblio.org/laslave

A Partial List of African Americans Lynched in the United States Since 1859; 100 Years of Lynching
by Ralph Ginzburg, Black Classic Press; Lynching in the New South, W. Fitzhugh Brundage, University of Illinois Press
http://ccharity.com/lynchlist.php

Slavery Era Insurance Registry
Insurance policies from the slavery era (pre-1865) were discovered in the archives of several insurance companies and the California legislature has published the names of slaves who were insured and the slave-owner who purchased the policy. The information for about 600 slaves includes county of residence (primarily counties in Kentucky, Mississippi, Missouri, North Carolina, South Carolina, and Virginia) and may include the occupation for which they were insured. In some cases, the age and or death date for the slave is provided. A policy number and the insuring company are cited and copies of policies, ledgers, and documents that discuss slave insurance be examined at the Department of Insurance public viewing rooms and certain libraries.
www.insurance.ca.gov/0100-consumers/0300-public-programs/0200-slavery-era-insur

African American Manuscript Collections

Cornell University—John Henrik Clarke Africana Library
www.library.cornell.edu/africana/index.html

Howard University Moorland-Spingarn Research Center
www.howard.edu/library/moorland-spingarn

Schomburg Center for Research in Black Culture
www.nypl.org/research/sc/sc.html

Articles

Washington, Reginald. "The Freedman's Savings and Trust Company and African American Genealogical Research." *Prologue* 29, no. 2 (Summer 1997).
www.archives.gov/publications/prologue/1997/summer/freedmans-savings-and-trust.html

Burroughs, Tony. "Obituaries for African Americans." *Family Tree Maker On-line*.
www.genealogy.com/genealogy/12_obits.html

WPA Slave Narratives

Born in Slavery: Slave Narratives from the Federal Writers' Project, 1936-1938
Library of Congress—American Memory (Original narratives sent to the Library of Congress, "A Folk History of Slavery." Does not include all WPA narratives in "The American Slave: A Composite Autobiography," edited by George P. Rawick)
http://memory.loc.gov/ammem/snhtml/snhome.html

Sample of WPA slave narratives with photos from the University of Virginia
http://xroads.virginia.edu/~hyper/wpa/wpahome.html

WPA slave narratives
www.ancestry.com

North American Slave Narratives
Beginnings to 1920—narratives (and many biographies) of fugitive and former slaves published in broadsides, pamphlets, or book form in English up to 1920, University of North Carolina, Chapel Hill.
http://metalab.unc.edu/docsouth/neh/neh.html

Miscellaneous African American Websites

Barnetta McGhee White
http://hometown.aol.com/wrendancer

Freedmen and Southern Society Project—sample documents
www.history.umd.edu/Freedmen/fssphome.htm

Tony Burroughs
www.TonyBurroughs.com

15
Colonial English Research

ROBERT CHARLES ANDERSON, MA, FASG

Genealogists who have pushed one or more lines of ancestry back to the time of the Revolutionary War, and who have not previously worked with the records of the seventeenth and eighteenth centuries, will find in this period more variety in the records than they have previously experienced. There are several reasons for this, all of which make the research process highly challenging.

First, the colonists, especially in the seventeenth century, had to solve a problem for which they were not prepared. Planting their settlements in territory previously unoccupied by Europeans, they were unable or unwilling to transfer to the New World the full range of laws and customs of record keeping with which they were familiar. In many colonies, there were not enough men experienced in running the courts and the other similar institutions. The settlers in New England, protesting as they did against many features of the Church of England, would not reproduce the ecclesiastical courts. (In England at the time of migration, probate and many other matters were handled in ecclesiastical rather than civil courts.)

Second, the process of building new institutions had a certain trial-and-error element to it. As a result, almost without exception, the earliest record books, whether generated by town, county, or colony, were an amalgamation of many different types of records entered together in the same volume, sometimes in no particular order. Researchers accustomed to records neatly separated into different books by record type need to be prepared to look for records in unlikely places. At the same time, they also need to be alert to the possibility that records originally entered in one volume will, in modern times, be split out and published in more than one place.

Chapter Contents

Third, the colonists faced a special problem with regard to the transfer of real property. Almost no one in England in the seventeenth century had experience in the original transfer of land from the government to individuals since, with the exception of land recovered from the drained fens, virtually all the land in England had been granted at the time of William the Conqueror (and earlier). Also, most of England was still in the throes of throwing off the old feudal system of land tenure. Consequently, many of the colonists were familiar only with

Proprietors and the Granting of Land

The word *proprietor* may be seen as a description of some part of the landgranting process in each of the thirteen colonies. Despite the widespread application of this term, the meaning is not the same in all of the colonies. In brief, the four New England colonies had a form of proprietary landgranting that was quite distinct from the form used in the seven colonies from Pennsylvania south to Georgia. New York and New Jersey formed a transitional region, which blended the procedures used to the north and south.

In the four New England colonies (New Hampshire, Massachusetts, Rhode Island, and Connecticut), the granting of land took place in two steps. First, the colony legislature granted a substantial plot of undivided land to a group of families that agreed to settle that land within a stated period of time. Second, that group of families chose for themselves the manner in which they subdivided the land, usually based on some combination of wealth and family size. Some towns chose to grant all of their land within a short period of time, while others initially granted only a portion of the land available to them, reserving the remainder for later needs.

This system had also been used in New Haven and Plymouth colonies before their respective mergers with Connecticut and Massachusetts Bay colonies and would also be used in those regions which eventually grew into the states of Vermont and Maine. No quitrents were collected under the New England system. The town was responsible for collecting taxes for the support of the colony, but the assessment of this tax was not based solely on land.

More information on the New England system may be found in Roy Hidemichi Akagi's *The Town Proprietors of the New England Colonies* and John Frederick Martin's *Profits in the Wilderness.*[1]

New York, especially in the English period, had a wider range of landgranting practices than any other colony. In some limited areas, groups of purchasers, mostly from New England, obtained from the colony patents to large portions of land, which they then allocated amongst themselves, just as the New England town proprietors did.[2]

An arrangement unique to New York among the English mainland colonies was the establishment of extensive manors along the Hudson between Manhattan and Albany. These manors were granted to a few individuals at the very top of the social ladder, and these men, in turn, retained ownership of the land and farmed it out to tenants.[3] Because so much of the land in these manors did not change hands in the colonial period, no deeds were generated; this is one of the reasons that research in this area is so difficult.

Finally, New York granted land to individuals by the system of petition, warrant, survey, and patent, as did all the colonies to the south.[4] Thus, New York granted some land in the New England way, some land in the southern way, and other land in a manner of its own.

As noted in the New Jersey section, New Jersey also granted some land in the style of the New England proprietors. The remainder of the land was allocated by the East Jersey and West Jersey Proprietors, again through the sequence of petition, warrant, survey, and patent.[5]

The remainder of the colonies, from Pennsylvania to Georgia, operated one version or another of the system of petition, warrant, survey, and patent by which the first transfer of land was directly from the colony to the individual, without any intermediary, as in the New England way of granting land. A somewhat more detailed explanation of the system of patents may be found in the Virginia section. The proprietors in each of these colonies were a small group of men proceeding under authority of the Crown, except where the grants were made even more directly under aegis of a royal governor.

The precise terminology of the four steps of the landgranting process might differ from jurisdiction to jurisdiction. For example, the first step in the process might be termed *petition, entry,* or *application.* Regardless of the terminology, the process was essentially the same.

Notes

[1] Roy Hidemichi Akagi, *The Town Proprietors of the New England Colonies* (Gloucester, Mass., 1963); John Frederick Martin, *Profits in the Wilderness* (Chapel Hill, N.C., 1991).
[2] Jessica Kross, *The Evolution of an American Town: Newtown, New York, 1642–1775* (Philadelphia, 1983).
[3] Sung Bok Kim, *Landlord and Tenant in Colonial New York: Manorial Society, 1664–1775* (Chapel Hill, N.C., 1978).
[4] E. B. O'Callaghan, comp., *Calendar of N.Y. Colonial Manuscripts: Indorsed Land Papers; in the Office of the Secretary of State of New York, 1643–1803* (Albany, 1864; Harrison, N.Y., 1987).
[5] John E. Pomfret, *The New Jersey Proprietors and Their Lands* (Princeton, N.J., 1964).

manorial landholding, and, with a few notable exceptions, the immigrants to the New World were not interested in replicating this system.

As a result of this concentrated variability, researchers coming to colonial records for the first time will encounter a number of problems they will not have seen while working in the relative regularity of record keeping in the public land states west of the Appalachians or even in the eastern seaboard states after the Revolution. Even more than when researching other times and places, researchers will need to be constantly alert to the different mix of records that must be brought into play in order to solve a genealogical problem. This mix of records will be different for each of the colonies and, within some of the colonies, will be different at different times within the colonial era.

The principal goal in this chapter is to focus on those aspects of colonial record keeping that may be unfamiliar to genealogists already familiar with courthouse research in the newer states. This chapter concentrates on records created before the formation of counties in the colonies and on records maintained in ways and in places not seen in later times. For example, in some instances records that pertain to one colony ended up, for one reason or another, in another colony. This chapter also examines the process by which the colonies moved from an early amorphous mode of record keeping to the more regular and rational system of later years.

For each of the thirteen colonies, this chapter presents three types of information. First, it sets forth a condensed jurisdictional history of the colony, with emphasis on the period prior to establishment of counties, a process that proceeded at a different pace from colony to colony. Second, the section for each colony examines a small selection of records, focusing on one or two record types that were originally recorded in an unusual manner. (There is no attempt to survey all the records available for the colonial period.) Third, each section points out one or two case studies, which are specific articles that demonstrate the way in which these early records may be exploited to solve a difficult genealogical problem. Additionally, where appropriate, the chapter appends to the accounts of some of the colonies information on other colonies that were absorbed by a neighbor colony, and also includes information on portions of colonies that were at least partially settled by 1776 but were later set off as separate states.

In using this chapter, researchers should not limit themselves to the colony that may be of direct interest. Principles of record creation and publication that are described under only one or two colonies may be more widely applicable to other colonies. For example, the description of the system of land distribution found in the Virginia section has relevance for almost all of the colonies outside of New England.

Researching in the colonial period can challenge the researcher in unusual ways, but the rewards may also be great, when the critical clue, or constellation of clues, is found in an unexpected place.

New Hampshire

Jurisdictional History

The first permanent settlement in New Hampshire was made in 1623 at the site of what is now Portsmouth, followed no later than 1628 by the establishment of Dover further up the Piscataqua River. Two more towns, Exeter in 1637 and Hampton in 1638, were established by religious refugees from Massachusetts Bay. These four towns existed as self-governing bodies until they were absorbed by Massachusetts Bay Colony a few years later. For many decades, they formed the bulk of settlement in what became New Hampshire.

When Massachusetts Bay established its first counties in 1643, these four settlements were in Norfolk County (distinct from modern Norfolk County), along with the other settlements between the Merrimack and the Piscataqua, Salisbury and Haverhill. The residents at Dover and Strawbery Bank (Portsmouth), however, did not go along with this scheme, as they had been operating a court of their own from at least 1640. They continued, without surviving evidence of formal concurrence by Massachusetts Bay, as the County of Dover and Portsmouth, also known as the County of Piscataqua.

In 1679 the Crown established the Province of New Hampshire, incorporating the towns of Dover, Portsmouth, Exeter, and Hampton. Old Norfolk County was dissolved, and Salisbury and Haverhill were included in Essex County in Massachusetts. For the next century, the Province of New Hampshire existed as a single jurisdiction, with no governmental entities intervening between the levels of town and province. Then, in 1769, the province was divided into five counties—Cheshire, Grafton, Hillsborough, Rockingham, and Strafford—which began operating as separate entities between that year and 1773.[1]

Records

Once the jurisdictional maneuvering was done in the early 1640s, the towns that form the early core of New Hampshire were served by two county courts. Hampton and Exeter were in (old) Norfolk County, while Dover and Portsmouth were in Piscataqua County.

In Norfolk County, courts were held alternately at Hampton (in the fall) and Salisbury (in the spring). Although Hampton eventually ended up in New Hampshire and Salisbury in Massachusetts, each of these courts covered all the Norfolk County towns. These early Norfolk court records have been published along with the other courts that operated in the area that is now Essex County, Massachusetts.[2] Separate deed registers, referred to as Norfolk Deeds, were maintained for these same towns, and these volumes also contained wills and other probate material. This probate material has been included in the published volumes of Essex County probates, but the deeds have not been published.[3]

The court that sat at Dover and at Portsmouth (Strawbery Banke), known variously as Piscataqua County or Dover and Portsmouth County, entered all its records in a single volume in its earliest years. The book, designated as Volume 1 of the provincial deeds (and a number of succeeding volumes), contains court records, deeds, and probate material. The court records themselves have been extracted and published in the last volume of the provincial and state papers, *New Hampshire Provincial and State Papers*.[4]

Probate records for these first four New Hampshire towns may be found in a number of places. Transcripts of these records have been gathered together in Volume 31 of the *New Hampshire Provincial and State Papers*. Most of the probate documents for the earliest years are taken from the first volume of New Hampshire deeds and from the first volume of Norfolk County deeds. A few additional probate records were recorded in Suffolk County, Massachusetts, which at various times and for various reasons had superior jurisdiction over some estates.

Finally, the recorded deeds for these towns may be found in the same places as the probate and court matter discussed previously. In addition, original land grants and some later transfers between person and person may be found in the town records.

In summary, the published volumes of court and probate records for early New Hampshire have selected their material from several sources, and portions of the original sources have been published in various places.

West of the Merrimack River, the most southerly tier of towns in what is now New Hampshire was part of Massachusetts until the border was adjusted in 1741. Prior to that time, deeds for these towns should be sought in Middlesex, Worcester, or Hampshire County records, as appropriate.

Vermont

In 1791, Vermont was admitted to the Union as the fourteenth state. The area north of Massachusetts and west of the Connecticut River, which became the Republic and then the State of Vermont, was claimed in the colonial period by both New Hampshire and New York, and both made extensive grants of proprietary townships there. Although the Crown eventually ruled in 1764 that this region should be governed by New York, the majority of the early immigrants were New Englanders. Vermont has always been culturally a part of New England.

In the wake of the 1764 ruling, the region fell within the jurisdiction of Albany County, New York. In 1766, Cumberland County was erected for the area between the Green Mountains and the Connecticut River. In 1770 this county was divided, with Gloucester to the north and Cumberland to the south. Finally, in 1772, Charlotte County was set off from Albany County, to include much of northern New York, along with the area that would become northwestern Vermont.

Documents created by New Hampshire relating to the area that would become Vermont have been printed in two volumes of the *New Hampshire Provincial and State Papers*. Volume 10 has a lengthy collection of records on "The Controversy Between New Hampshire, New York, and Vermont...," while Volume 26 is totally devoted to the actual charters of the New Hampshire Grants of townships west of the Connecticut, the earliest of which was issued in 1749.[5]

Case Studies

Steven Edward Sullivan, "The Two Families of Sarah (Libby) (Smith) Dolbear of Hampton and Rye, New Hampshire," *American Genealogist* 73 (1998): 258–71. Sullivan tackles a very difficult problem in spousal identification by using a very wide range of sources, in many different formats. First, he uses many different volumes of the *New Hampshire Provincial and State Papers* for probate, town, and military records. Second, he consults the original documents behind some of these published volumes in the Rockingham County records, which in their earliest years were equivalent to the provincial records. Third, he uses many town records, including vital, land, and tax documents in the original, in microfilm, in typescript, and in published forms. Fourth, he examines many church records, again in many formats.

Janet Ireland Delorey, "John Woodin, Brickmaker, of New Hampshire, Massachusetts, and South Carolina," *American Genealogist* 64 (1989): 65–74, 150–56, 238–45. John Woodin lived, at one time or another, in virtually every town in old Norfolk County, including three of the four towns that formed the core of early New Hampshire. Delorey makes good use of the town, county, and colony records both in Massachusetts Bay and in New Hampshire to follow Woodin throughout his restless career (which ended in South Carolina).

Massachusetts

Jurisdictional History

The first European settlers of Massachusetts Bay Colony were stragglers from elsewhere. Some had resided briefly in the older Plymouth Colony to the south (see the "Plymouth Colony" section on the next page); others had tried to establish settlements to the south of Boston and moved into Massachusetts Bay. The first well-organized settlement was at the site of Salem, where a group of fishermen sat down after a brief residence on Cape Ann.

The Massachusetts Bay Company, recently organized in London, sent out a small flotilla in 1628, which augmented the settlers at Salem. Then, in 1630, a much larger party of nearly a thousand settlers set out under the command of John Winthrop. These settlers landed at Salem and then Charlestown, and soon built new plantations at Boston, Dorchester, Roxbury, and Watertown. Migration to Massachusetts Bay Colony was heavy throughout the 1630s. Many new towns were founded, mostly in the easternmost parts of the colony, but some further to the west, including such towns as Springfield and Northampton on the Connecticut River.

Massachusetts Bay created four counties in 1643: Suffolk, Middlesex, Essex, and Norfolk. The northernmost of these counties, Norfolk County, included the four towns that would eventually form the core of New Hampshire: Portsmouth, Dover, Exeter, and Hampton. (When New Hampshire was established in 1679, Norfolk County was dissolved. The name was used again in 1793, when the southwestern portion of Suffolk County was set off as Norfolk County.)

As the 1640s and 1650s proceeded, Massachusetts Bay also assumed jurisdiction over the communities further east, such as Kittery, York, and Wells. The county of York was established in 1651 to accommodate these settlements. This region remained an integral part of Massachusetts until 1820, with other counties being established there in the interim. Thus, when studying Down East ancestry for the entire colonial period and beyond, genealogists should also resort to Massachusetts colony records in addition to searching the town and county records of Maine.

In 1692, upon the issuance of a new charter after the Glorious Revolution in England, Massachusetts Bay Colony absorbed Plymouth Colony, and the three recently erected counties of that colony became Massachusetts counties.

Plymouth Colony

Plymouth Colony came into existence when the *Mayflower* made landfall off Cape Cod near the end of 1620. The small band of colonists struggled to survive at the town of Plymouth for a number of years. With the arrival of spillover immigrants from Massachusetts Bay Colony in the 1630s, a number of other towns were settled, and the colony began to grow. Over the next few decades, new towns were founded on Cape Cod and to the north and west of the town of Plymouth, toward the borders with Massachusetts Bay to the north and Rhode Island to the west.

For much of the existence of Plymouth Colony, there was a single registry for deeds and probate at Plymouth. In 1685 three counties were erected (Plymouth, Bristol, and Barnstable), which were barely established before Massachusetts Bay Colony absorbed Plymouth Colony in 1692, and these counties became Massachusetts counties.

Most of the records of Plymouth Colony were published in the nineteenth century *Records of the Colony of New Plymouth in New England*, edited by Nathaniel B. Shurtleff and David Pulsifer.[6] The best modern guide to Plymouth Colony history and genealogy is Eugene Aubrey Stratton's *Plymouth Colony: Its History & People, 1620–1691*.[7]

Records

Certainly among the New England colonies, Massachusetts is abnormal in its normality. Unlike Connecticut, Rhode Island, and New Hampshire, Massachusetts very early erected a strong county system. For the most part, deeds and probates are easily located in those jurisdictions, with very few losses over the centuries. The colony records of the Massachusetts Bay General Court, which carried out both legislative and judicial activities, are well-preserved. The minutes of the General Court have been published in *Records of the Governor and Company of the Massachusetts Bay in New England*, 1628–1686, edited by Nathaniel B. Shurtleff.[8]

Even with this regularity, there are some peculiarities of the record-keeping system in this colony that require special attention, most importantly the early transition from town-based to county-based recording of land transfers. Before the creation of the first four counties in 1643, all land records were maintained at the town level. This included both proprietary grants from town to individual and, later, transfers from individual to individual. The General Court required the early towns to submit to the colony the inventories of the landholdings in each town. These inventories survive for a number of communities, including Boston, Watertown, Charlestown, and Cambridge. These documents are sometimes referred to as the "Book of Possessions" for the town.

These town land inventories were sometimes employed also as town deed registers. Towns for which such inventories do not survive also recorded brief entries that may be interpreted as deeds, even for many years after the creation of the counties in 1643. As a rough rule, the more distant the town from the county seat, the more likely that the early deeds for that town were still entered in the town records, even after other towns were using the county deed registry for this purpose. The town of Dedham is a good example. For instance, on 10 February 1650/51, thirty-five brief items of the following form were entered in the first volume of town records: "Elea. Lusher sell to Joh[n] Fraery 2½ acres upland. 2 of swampe together abutting east street east[,] brooke in the swampe west[,] Pet. Woodward south[,] Joh[n] Fraery north."[9] As brief as this entry is, it provides sufficient data to establish this link in the chain of title.

Case Studies

Robert Charles Anderson, "The Daughters of Simon Eire of Watertown and Boston, Mass.," *American Genealogist* 65 (1990): 13–23. Several problems in the Watertown families of Simon Eire and Nicholas Guy are resolved through careful analysis of the grants of large farm lots in Watertown (recorded in the Watertown town records) and analysis of how those lots were disposed of by their original proprietors.

Robert S. Wakefield and Alice H. Dreger, "The Wives and Children of James Cole (circa 1625–1709) of Plymouth Massachusetts," *American Genealogist* 67 (1992): 243–45. The authors sort out a number of difficulties in this family, using court and land records of both Plymouth Colony in the seventeenth century and Plymouth County after its establishment in 1685 and on into the eighteenth century.

Rhode Island

Jurisdictional History

Like Hampton and Exeter among the early New Hampshire towns, all of the earliest Rhode Island towns were settled by religious refugees from Massachusetts. When Roger Williams was banished from Massachusetts late in 1635, he moved south and, in 1636, founded the town of Providence. Two years later, as a direct consequence of the Antinomian Controversy, a large number of families, mostly from Boston and mostly influenced by Anne Hutchinson, removed in early 1638 to the northern end of Aquidneck Island, or Rhode Island, where they founded the town of Portsmouth. Just a year later, a rift at Portsmouth led to the foundation of Newport at the southern end of the island. Finally, in 1643, an assorted group of malcontents began the settlement of Warwick, on the mainland just to the south of Providence.

These four towns formed the core of Rhode Island settlement for some decades. Just a year after the rift that led to the settlement of Newport, the two towns of Newport and Portsmouth settled their differences and began to hold a court jointly for the two towns. Eventually, Providence and Warwick were joined to this body, and court was held jointly among the four towns. This judicial body led to a parallel legislative body.

From time to time, this body split in two with Newport and Portsmouth operating together, separately from Providence and Warwick; however, in each case the four towns soon came back together to operate for legislative and judicial purposes as a single government. In these early years, Rhode Island did not have a charter, so in 1644, Roger Williams traveled to London to acquire such a document. At the Restoration, Williams traveled again to England and received a new charter from Charles II in 1663.

The southern part of the mainland of what is now Rhode Island led a separate existence for several decades. Known variously as the King's Province or Narragansett Country, this region was purchased from the Indians by groups of merchants, mostly from Boston. This region was incorporated in Rhode Island under the terms of the royal charter of 1663 (although this same region had been granted to Connecticut in its charter of 1662).

No counties existed in Rhode Island until 1703, when the colony was divided into Providence and Newport Counties. These jurisdictions initially had virtually no relevance for record keeping, inasmuch as land and probate records were at all times maintained by the towns. The General Court of Trials, which covered the entire colony, did not give way to county courts until 1729.

Records

Rhode Island is, and has always been, the most localized colony or state for record keeping. With minor exceptions, each town or city holds all deeds and all probate materials. For this reason, a large proportion of the surviving records of three of the original four Rhode Island towns have been published. (Most of the early Newport records were accidentally destroyed during the Revolutionary War.)

Providence: *The Early Records of the Town of Providence*, 21 vols. (Providence, 1892–1915).

Portsmouth: *The Early Records of the Town of Portsmouth* (Providence, 1901).

Warwick: *The Early Records of the Town of Warwick* (Providence, 1926); and *More Early Records of the Town of Warwick, Rhode Island: "The Book with Clasps" and "General Records"* (Boston, 2001).

Some of these town records are incorporated in John Russell Bartlett's *Records of the Colony of Rhode Island and Providence Plantations in New England.*[10] This volume also includes early records of the colony court, which combined legislative and judicial functions. For example, Bartlett included sixteen pages of the early records of Portsmouth (after the split in early 1639 that led to the settlement of Newport).[11] Comparison of these transcripts with the above-cited volume devoted to the early records of Portsmouth shows that the same material is presented in the latter on pages one through thirty-four but with far greater fidelity than in the former. The original is badly damaged in this early period. Bartlett took great liberties with the text, inserting text in these bad sections without editorial comment and simply omitting sections that he found difficult to read.

An excellent example of an original manuscript that has been published incompletely and in disjointed parts is "Rhode Island Colony Records 1646–1669."[12] Scattered through this manuscript volume are several sittings of a Court of Quarter Sessions that was held alternately at Portsmouth and Newport. These proceedings have been extracted and published in Howard M. Chapin's *Documentary History of Rhode Island.*[13] But the same manuscript volume also contains sessions of the Court of Trials held from time to time in all the towns of the colony. These have been published in a separate and unrelated pair of volumes *Rhode Island Court Records: Records of the Court of Trials of the Colony of Providence Plantations.*[14]

This court material scattered over three volumes does not, however, exhaust the records in the manuscript volume. As yet, the large number of early Newport deeds also included here, some from as early as 1642, remain unpublished. Given the near-total destruction of early Newport town records, this source, once fully published, will be of great importance for early Rhode Island genealogy.

Case Studies

Bruce C. MacGunnigle, "The Children of Chad Browne of Providence RI: Proved, Disproved, and Unproved," *American Genealogist* 62 (1987): 193–201. This careful study of paternity relies heavily on the wide range of material preserved in the early town records of Providence, including, but not limited to, land and probate records.

William B. Saxbe Jr., "Thomas Walling and His Way with Women: Seventeenth-Century Misconduct as an Aid to Identification," *American Genealogist* 73 (1998): 91–100. Like MacGunnigle, Saxbe also heavily exploits the early Providence town records. However, he also makes good use of the colony court records.

Connecticut

Jurisdictional History

As a direct result of the population pressure in Massachusetts Bay arising from the increase in the migration rate in the mid-1630s, and as a side effect of the narrow doctrinal differences among some of the leading ministers, settlements were begun at three places along the Connecticut River. These three settlements grew into the towns of Hartford, Windsor, and Wethersfield. Even as this demographic movement was taking place, Saybrook, a fortified village, was being built at the mouth of the Connecticut.

Further migration produced new towns along both sides of Long Island Sound (some interspersed with the towns aligned with New Haven Colony, see the following section entitled "New Haven"). In 1645, Pequot was settled further to the east along Long Island Sound on the mainland and was soon renamed New London.

From the earliest days, the towns maintained all land records, including proprietoral grants and deeds from one person to another. At the same time, until the absorption of New Haven Colony, all probates were centrally recorded. In 1666, just four years after the receipt of the royal charter and the incorporation of New Haven Colony, four county courts were established: Hartford, Fairfield, New Haven, and New London. These counties (along with four others created in the eighteenth century) remained the creators of the usual run of civil and criminal court records. Over the decades, however, probate jurisdiction was divided and subdivided, to the point that there were more than a hundred probate districts, many of them containing only one town or city.

Records

The system of probate districts in Connecticut is unlike that in any other colony or state. Neighboring Rhode Island handled probate matters at all times at the town level. Vermont, many of whose earliest settlers came from Connecticut, eventually divided some of its counties into districts for probate purposes, but these districts, once established, did not change in size.

As noted previously, soon after the union of Connecticut and New Haven colonies, four counties were established: Hartford, Fairfield, New Haven, and New London. Throughout the rest of the seventeenth century, the courts of these counties also handled probate matters. In 1719 the legislature began the process of dividing the counties into smaller probate districts, creating Guilford, Windham, and Woodbury districts. From this date forward, the researcher must look in the towns for land records, in the districts for probate records, and in the counties for court records.

By the time of the Revolution, there were twenty probate districts in Connecticut. The last of these erected in colonial times was Westmoreland District, created in May 1775, considered to be derived from Litchfield District. Westmoreland was actually in Pennsylvania, in territory claimed by Connecticut and formally ceded to Pennsylvania in 1782.

The probate records for the Hartford District from 1635 to 1750 have been published by Charles William Manwaring as *Early Connecticut Probate Records*.[15] Since these published records begin in 1635, and Hartford County (and therefore the associated probate district) was not established until 1666, it is clear that the earliest of these documents must have been recorded somewhere besides Hartford County. Manwaring, in fact, took them from a number of sources. Some of the earliest are found in the records of Connecticut Colony.

The bulk of the probate records for the Hartford District down to 1700 were recorded in six volumes. Each volume was a double volume. One side contained the records of the Hartford County court, and the reverse side, with separate pagination, contained the probate records. However, the "court side" also included probate proceedings, such as letters of administration. Thus, in the published version of these records, the proceedings for any given estate might include material from both the "court side" and the "probate side" of the same volume. Furthermore, if the administration of a given estate lingered for some years, some of the documents might have been included in one of the later manuscript volumes but would be entered out of place in the published volume, along with the earlier documents. In addition, when the only surviving version of a given document is in the loose papers, these items are also gathered in the printed version along with the records from the court volumes. The transition to the records of Hartford County, as established in 1666, takes place in the middle of the third of these manuscript court volumes, which covers the years from 1663 to 1677.

New Haven

The towns of New Haven, Milford, and Guilford, close to one another along Long Island Sound, were all organized in 1639 as independent plantations. As the formation of the Confederation of New England loomed imminent in 1643, these three towns, along with Southold on Long Island, joined together as the colony of New Haven. A few other towns on either side of Long Island Sound joined this colony in the years following. Finally, in 1662, when Connecticut Colony finally acquired its own charter, New Haven Colony agreed to merge with Connecticut to form one government.

In addition to the usual range of town records, New Haven Colony held its own courts, the records of which have been published in Charles J. Hoadly's *Records of the Colony and Plantation of New Haven, From 1638 to 1649*, and *Records of the Colony or Jurisdiction of New Haven, from May, 1653, to the Union.*[16] Because there were so few towns in the colony, and because of the preeminence of the town of New Haven itself, these colony records sometimes seem more like New Haven town records.

As with Connecticut Colony, the New Haven towns kept their own land records. An interesting document contains some of the earliest records of this sort for the town of New Haven. Entitled "A Book of All the Lands which Planters at First or by Alienations Since Possess Within New Haven Town," this volume does not reside with the other town records, but is available on microfilm at the New Haven Colony Historical Society. Compiled in 1645 and 1646, the volume recapitulates an earlier list of estates, which in effect lists all the proprietary shares in the town. The clerk who prepared the volume also used it to calculate the annual taxes on this land and to record some of the later sales of this land by the original proprietors or their successors. Thus, this one volume, for a space of about a decade and a half, served three functions: proprietors' record, tax list, and deed register. In about 1659, entries ceased to be made in this record book. Instead, a regular deed register was begun, the tax records were kept separately, and eventually a separate set of proprietors' records was begun.[17]

Case Studies

Gale Ion Harris, "Captain Richard Wright of Twelve-Mile Island and the Burnhams of Podunk: Two Seventeenth-Century Connecticut River Families," ***American Genealogist*** **67 (1992): 32–46.**

Gale Ion Harris, "The Children of Joseph and Mary (Stone) Fitch of Hartford and Windsor, Connecticut," ***American Genealogist*** **68 (1993): 1–10, 95–105.** In each of these articles, Harris combines data from church, court, and medical records with a deep analysis of entire neighborhoods to unravel a number of difficult genealogical networks.

New York

Jurisdictional History

In the early 1620s, the Dutch West India Company built settlements at Manhattan and Albany and claimed for New Amsterdam all the territory from the Connecticut River to the Delaware River. In an attempt to enforce this claim, the Dutch built trading posts on both those rivers. In addition to towns along the Hudson River, they also established settlements on the western most end of Long Island. Most of the early settlements on Long Island, however, were made by New Englanders and were initially part of Connecticut or New Haven colonies.

In 1664 the English conquered the Dutch and took over New Amsterdam. The Dutch briefly conquered the territory again in 1673, but, within a year, New York was back in English hands, where it would stay for the remainder of the colonial period.

In 1683, New York was divided into twelve counties: Albany, Cornwall, Dukes, Dutchess, Kings, New York, Orange, Queens, Richmond, Suffolk, Ulster, and Westchester. Two of these counties, Cornwall and Dukes, were part of the possessions of the Duke of York outside the usual territory of New York. Cornwall covered a part of what would become the state of Maine and was given over to Massachusetts in 1686. Dukes County comprised Martha's Vineyard and Nantucket, which were, in turn, incorporated in Massachusetts in 1692. The remaining ten original New York counties gave rise to the rest of the later New York counties.

Records

The arrangement of probate records in New York is perhaps more complicated than in any other colony. First, during the Dutch period, probate matters might have been handled in a variety of ways. Some were recorded by notaries, such as those preserved by Salomon Lachaire as "New York Historical Manuscripts: Dutch," in *The Register of Solomon Lachaire, Notary Public of New Amsterdam, 1661–1662.*[18] Other probate records are found in the *Minutes of the Orphanmasters of New Amsterdam.*[19] Yet other papers were recorded in the town records of the English towns within New Netherland. (For an overview of records created during the Dutch period, see Charles T. Gehring's "Documentary Sources Relating to New Netherland," in *Colonial Dutch Studies: An Interdisciplinary Approach.*)[20]

Second, in the English period, from 1664 to 1787, and especially after the formation of the original twelve counties, many probate documents were filed centrally, at the province level, as well as at the county level.

Third, abstracts of the wills and administrations in the central, province-wide collection have been published in seventeen volumes of the *Collections of the New-York Historical Society,* issued from 1892 to 1908. The last two volumes in this series contain corrections to the abstracts in the previous volumes; therefore, researchers should always consult the last two volumes in conjunction with the abstracts themselves. These will abstracts should then lead the researcher to the full record in the will registers, or will libers, and in some cases to the original will itself.

Fourth, at the same time, many of these probate cases also were recorded at the county level, with various degrees of survival. Abstracts of many of these have been published as well, on a county-by-county basis.

In 1991, Harry Macy Jr. published a detailed description of the pre-1787 New York probate records. His description includes a table showing the location of originals and copies of the province collection of probate papers, a listing of the records held by the early counties, and a number of recommendations for researching in these records.[21]

Case Studies

Aline L. Garretson, "The Gerritsen-Willemsen Family Record, and The Williamson Family of Gravesend," ***New York Genealogical and Biographical Record*** **133 (2002): 163–76.** The jumping-off point for this article is an extensive family record, covering several generations of the family in the seventeenth and eighteenth centuries and providing information on the migration of the family from the Low Countries to Bermuda to New Amsterdam. The author then uses a wide range of records for New Amsterdam, New York, and New Jersey. These records include town records, deeds and wills, church records, and the published records of the colony government. In particular, in using the printed version of the early wills, Garretson also takes note of later corrections of the earlier printed abstract.

Gale Ion Harris, "The Supposed Children of Thomas Harris of Dutchess County, New York," ***New York Genealogical and Biographical Record*** **133 (2002): 3–18.** Harris examines several Harris families of Dutchess County and neighboring Ulster County, making excellent use of the wills and deeds. Given the recognized difficulty of research in these jurisdictions, Harris also relies on tax lists and Dutch Reformed church records.

New Jersey

Jurisdictional History

Prior to the conquest of New Amsterdam by the English in 1664, the area that was to become New Jersey was a sparsely populated extension of New Amsterdam. Soon after the conquest, the Duke of York granted New Jersey to John Lord Berkeley and Sir John Carteret. In 1676 this region was divided into two proprieties, which were named East Jersey and West Jersey. The proprietors in each of these jurisdictions controlled both the government and the granting of land until 1702, when New Jersey became a royal province. The governor of New York was also the governor of New Jersey, but the proprietors retained control of the land. In 1738, New Jersey became completely independent of New York and, for the remainder of the colonial period, had its own royally appointed governor.

In 1683, East Jersey was divided into four counties: Bergen, Essex, Middlesex, and Monmouth. In the early 1690s, four counties were established in West Jersey: Burlington, Cape May, Gloucester, and Salem. These eight counties were the predecessors of all the remaining New Jersey counties.

Records

Like New York, New Jersey was a region of transition from the town-based proprietary system to the colony-based system. This section focuses on East Jersey to see how this system worked.

Prior to the English takeover in 1664, most of the European population in what would become East Jersey was in the settlement of Bergen, just across the Hudson River from Manhattan. Almost immediately after the grant from the Duke of York to Berkeley and Carteret, township grants were made to settlers who came from various parts of New England. In 1664 the patent for Elizabethtown was issued, and in 1666 this tract of land was subdivided into three parts, thus giving rise to the new towns of Woodbridge and Piscataway. In 1665 the Monmouth Patent was issued, and, within a few years, this area evolved into the towns of Middletown and Shrewsbury. Finally, in 1666 the patent for Newark was granted. Thus, by 1670 most of the settlers in the northeastern part of New Jersey could be found in one of these seven towns, one (Bergen) dating from the period of Dutch settlement, and the other six being formed within five years after the English conquest by men from New England.

These New England-style towns were issued charters by the proprietors. For example, Woodbridge received its charter on 1 June 1669. Among the rights granted was that the "Freeholders or the major part of them are equally to divide the aforesaid tract of upland and meadows among themselves," very much in the way that the proprietors of New England towns operated.[22] However, the patent goes on to require that these town grants made by the freeholders were "to be entered upon record by the Secretary or Recorder General of the province" and "to hold his land by patent from the Lords Proprietors and to pay them . . . rent yearly," which were actions not required in New England. For much land in this part of New Jersey, then, there may well be two distinct records of the original grant: an entry in the town book and a patent issued at the colony level.

The earliest records of the granting of land at the colony level are contained in a series of books that also include a wide variety of other records, including probate matters, Indian deeds, court proceedings, and so on. These volumes were begun before the division of New Jersey into East and West Jersey in 1683. The years 1664 through 1703 have been abstracted into Volume 21 of the *New Jersey Archives* series.[23] This series of records also contains straightforward warranty deeds from person to person, of land earlier granted by the town or colony.

After the division of the region into East and West Jersey in 1683, the focus for landgranting was in the two capitals of Burlington (West Jersey) and Perth Amboy (East Jersey). Although counties were formed very soon after this, the recording of deeds was retained in these two capitals until 1785 (although the recording of mortgages at the county level began in 1766). Thus, for most of the first century of the existence of New Jersey, the researcher must look both in province and town records for information about land transfers. For those generations living in the middle of the eighteenth century, the researcher may need to look in all three jurisdictions: province, county, and town.

Case Studies

Francis James Dallett, "The Inter-Colonial Grimstone Boude and His Family," *Genealogist* 2 (1981): 74–114. This article might have been brought forth as a model for research in several of the colonies. Several members of the family lived at various times in New Jersey, and Dallett has made good use of the published *New Jersey Archives*, especially the wills and the West Jersey Records.

Phyllis J. Miller, "Abraham Garrison of Cumberland County, New Jersey, and Some of His Descendants," *American Genealogist* 74 (1999): 58–71. Miller consults many of the standard court records of Salem and Cumberland counties but also examines Presbyterian church records and New Jersey tax and militia lists in tracing the life of Abraham Garrison and his children.

Pennsylvania

Jurisdictional History

The earliest settlements within the region that became Pennsylvania were made by the Dutch and then, more significantly, the Swedes; however, this period belongs more properly to the history of Delaware. The history of Pennsylvania proper begins with the 1681 charter to William Penn, which was very quickly followed by heavy colonization directed by Penn, with an emphasis on Quaker and German immigrants. Early in the eighteenth century, the Scotch-Irish began to arrive in large numbers, for the most part settling on the western frontier.

Pennsylvania experienced a very brief period of direct royal rule from 1692 to 1694. However, control over both government and land was returned to Penn, and Pennsylvania remained a proprietary colony until the Revolution.

Counties were founded very early, with Bucks, Chester, and Philadelphia being erected in 1682, thus providing the basis for all succeeding counties. Chester replaced and succeeded Upland County, which had been the northernmost of the three lower counties on the Delaware prior to the 1681 charter.

In the 1750s, the colony of Connecticut and the Susquehanna Company, on the basis of a territorial claim of any land to the west of Connecticut along the same parallels, began a number of settlements in northeastern Pennsylvania, in the area of present-day Scranton and Wilkes-Barre. After lengthy disputes, Connecticut relinquished its claims in 1782.

Records

As is the case with most other colonies, a series of colonial and state papers has been published for Pennsylvania, in this instance one of the largest such series, with 138 volumes. In 1997, Christine Crawford-Oppenheimer published a detailed description of and guide to these volumes in *Pennsylvania Genealogical Magazine*.[24] This monograph contains excellent guidance on searching and interpreting the information in these volumes, and also suggests a "plan of attack," a sensible sequence in which to search the volumes. The author includes a bibliography of other publications that also describe this series and related records.

The set of 138 volumes is divided into ten different subseries, the first called *Colonial Records* and the rest designated *Pennsylvania Archives*, First Series through Ninth Series. Records from the colonial period are not limited to the subseries entitled *Colonial Records* but are found throughout the entire set. As one might expect, the *Colonial Records* series contains official documents of the provincial government, mostly the minutes of the Provincial Council.

Almost all of the later series include some material from the period before the Revolution. For example, the Second Series and the Sixth Series include, along with much other material, church records from several different denominations, some as early as the seventeenth century. The Third Series contains some colonial tax records.

Looking more closely at some of the volumes, researchers can see that the eighteenth volume of the Second Series is entitled *Documents Relating to the Connecticut Settlement in the Wyoming Valley*. This volume includes such items as "Minutes of the Susquehanna Company" and "Miscellaneous Papers Relating to the Wyoming Controversy." The nineteenth volume of the same series, originally published in 1893, is entitled *Minutes of the Board of Property of the Province of Pennsylvania* and includes records of land granted by the Pennsylvania government from 1687 to 1732.

Case Studies

Stewart Baldwin, "The English Ancestry of George Pownall of Bucks County, Pennsylvania: With Notes on Thomas Pownall, Governor of Massachusetts Bay and South Carolina," *American Genealogist* 76 (2001): 81–93, 217–26.

This account of a typical Quaker immigrant relies heavily, as one might expect, on Quaker meeting records, both in England and in Pennsylvania. However, there is also frequent use of will books from Pennsylvania counties and from neighboring areas of New Jersey. The interpretation of the records benefits from very careful analysis of Quaker marriage certificates.

David L. Greene, "Christian Gottlieb Dornbläser of Northampton Co., Pa., His Wife Maria Magdalena Frantz, and Their Dornblaser-Dunblazier Descendants," ***American Genealogist*** **65 (1990): 1–12, 74–86, 167–75, 219–27.** This comprehensive account of a Pennsylvania German family relies heavily on church records from several congregations and on probate and deed records from Northampton County and vicinity. Surviving family records also contributed greatly to the finished account of this family.

Delaware

Jurisdictional History

The first permanent settlement within the current borders of Delaware was made in 1638 by the Swedish South Company. The colony was nominally controlled from Sweden but, in fact, received intermittent attention and inadequate resupply from the home country. These immigrants concentrated themselves in the areas now covered by southeastern Pennsylvania; New Castle County, Delaware; and adjoining parts of New Jersey and Maryland.

Peter Stebbins Craig has studied the Swedish (and Finnish) settlers along the Delaware River in great detail, and has compiled his findings in two volumes: *The 1693 Census of the Swedes on the Delaware: Family Histories of the Swedish Lutheran Church Members Residing in Pennsylvania, Delaware, West New Jersey and Cecil County, Maryland, 1683–1693* and *1671 Census of the Delaware.*[25]

In 1655 the Dutch in New Amsterdam, who had built a fort on the Delaware, responded to an attack on that fort by sending an expedition to the Delaware and taking control of the region. The New Amsterdam authorities allowed the Swedish settlers considerable autonomy in their own government but, at the same time, instituted some aspects of their own system, including the offices of *schout* and *schepens.*

When the English conquered New Amsterdam in 1664, control of the Delaware also passed to the English. In parallel with the fate of New York, the settlements on the Delaware briefly returned to Dutch control in 1673 and 1674 but then reverted to the English as one of the provinces of the Duke of York.

In 1682, in anticipation of the arrival of William Penn and the settlers associated with him, the Duke of York transferred the Delaware settlements to William Penn and his associates. The so-called Three Lower Counties were, however reluctantly, an integral part of Pennsylvania until 1704, when they were separated legislatively and obtained their own assembly. Their territory continued under the control of the Penn proprietors until the Revolution. Delaware was the last of the thirteen colonies to achieve its own independent identity but was the first to ratify the Constitution in 1787.

Because the settlements on the Delaware were dependent on New Amsterdam, New York, or Pennsylvania during most of their existence, there are no "colony records" as such. On the other hand, the researcher must be prepared to examine the records of New York, Pennsylvania, Maryland, and New Jersey in resolving many Delaware problems.

Records

Courts certainly operated on the Delaware prior to 1676, under the Swedes, the Dutch, and the English, but very few records of these early bodies have survived. What does exist may be found in records preserved in New Amsterdam and New York: *New York Historical Manuscripts: Dutch, Volumes 18–29, Delaware Papers (Dutch Period) . . . 1648–1664* and *New York Historical Manuscripts: Dutch, Volumes XX–XXI, Delaware Papers (English Period) . . . 1664–1682.*

On 25 September 1676, Governor Edmund Andros of New York promulgated to the Delaware a set of instructions, which had already been in use for more than a decade in New York. The second of these instructions was that "there be three Courts held in the Severall Parts of the River and Bay as formerly to witt. one on New Castell, one above at Upland—Another below att Whorekill."

The most northerly of these three counties, Upland, had the majority of the Swedish settlers. The records of this county have been published for the years from 1676 to 1681 (*The Record of the Court at Upland in Pennsylvania 1676 to 1681 . . .*). In 1681 this upper region of the settlements on the Delaware was chosen for the settlement of William Penn. Upland became Chester, and the later records for this area are found in Chester County.

The records of New Castle County for the same time period have been published as *Records of the Court of New Castle on Delaware 1676–1681*, as have been the records for Sussex County from 1677 to 1710, as *Records of the Courts of Sussex County, Delaware, 1677–1710.*[26]

In 1680 the county structure of Delaware was completed with the erection of St. Jones County, carved out of the northern part of Whorekill County. Later in the same year, the name of Whorekill County was changed to Deale County. In 1683, St. Jones became Kent County and Deale became Sussex County. The Kent County records from 1680 to 1705 were published as Volume 8 of the American Legal Records series.[27]

During the period when New York administered Delaware, the representatives of the Duke of York made grants of land (*Original Land Titles in Delaware Commonly Known as The Duke of York Record . . . From 1646 to 1679*). Those already holding land granted to them under Swedish or Dutch rule were asked to come forward to have their holdings confirmed, and many of these confirmations were recorded in New York.

After 1681 additional new land grants were made by the Penn proprietors of Pennsylvania. The western reaches of Kent and Sussex counties were claimed by Maryland, and records of landholders in these areas may be found in Maryland colony and county records. When this land dispute was eventually settled in favor of Delaware, confirmations of these lands were often entered in the records of the Penn proprietors.

The early court proceedings noted previously included original grants of land, sales of land from one person to another, and probate proceedings. In the early 1680s, very soon after the three "lower counties" came under the Penn government, separate Orphans' Courts were established to handle probate, and registries of deeds were also established.

Case Studies

Col. Charles M. Hansen, "The Paternal Ancestry of Caesar Rodney of Del[aware,] Signer of the Declaration of Independence," ***American Genealogist*** **64 (1989): 97–111.** William Rodney, the grandfather of Caesar Rodney, was born in Bristol, England. He arrived on the Delaware in 1681 as a young man, at the time of the migration of English to that region led by William Penn. William Rodney resided in Kent and Sussex counties until his death in 1708. In documenting this man's life, Col. Hansen relies heavily on the county court records from Kent and Sussex, supplemented by family papers, Philadelphia Quaker marriage records, and some other Pennsylvania colonial records.

Patricia Law Hatcher, "Were the 'Daughters' of Robert Burton of Sussex County, Delaware, Really the Daughters of Comfort (Bagwell) Leatherbury?" ***American Genealogist*** **75 (2000): 250–66.** The families discussed in this article lived for the most part in Sussex County but also spilled over into the Eastern Shore portions of Maryland and Virginia. Through extensive exploitation of the probate and deed records of Sussex County, the author determined that there were two sets of daughters, Burton and Leatherbury, with the same given names.

Maryland

Jurisdictional History

Maryland was settled in 1634, when the *Ark & Dove* was sent out by Lord Baltimore and other members of the Calvert family. In its early years, this region was established as a refuge for Catholics, although other dissenting religions were also attracted to the colony in the seventeenth century. Maryland existed as a family-held proprietary colony until 1689, when control was taken by the Crown. With further political and dynastic changes in England, control of Maryland reverted to the proprietors in 1715, and so it would remain until 1776.

Unlike most of the other colonies, where the county system of government and record keeping came into existence all at once, with several counties formed simultaneously to cover all inhabited parts of the colony, Maryland proceeded to erect one county at a time, the first being St. Mary's in 1637. This was followed by Kent in 1642 (on the Eastern Shore), Anne Arundel in 1650, Calvert in 1654, Charles in 1658, Baltimore in 1659/60, Talbot in 1661/62, and Somerset in 1666. These were all the original counties, and the remaining fifteen counties, along with the city of Baltimore, were later split off from these. Wills were recorded twice, at the colony and the county levels, reducing the impediments to research arising from the loss of county records.

Records

Vast portions of the colonial records of Maryland have been published by the Maryland Historical Society in the series *Archives of Maryland*, now numbering seventy-two volumes, published from 1883 to 1972.[28] These published volumes consist of material extracted from a large number of manuscript volumes of early Maryland records, with the material in any given published volume being selected from several manuscript volumes.

The first volume of *Archives of Maryland* includes in the front matter a detailed inventory of the original volumes from which the published books are drawn, with information on both the original volume (if it survives) and later copies.[29] For example, the first book described is Liber Z, which includes four separate sections, the first covering business relating to the patenting of land and the other three sections containing probate matters. The fourth volume of the *Archives of Maryland*, entitled *Judicial and Testamentary Business of the Provincial Court, 1637–1650*, begins with probate material from the second section of Liber Z, with appropriate marginal notations indicating the page from which the particular extract was taken.[30] The patent records from the first section of Liber Z are not included in the fourth volume of the *Archives of Maryland*.

In the various manuscript copies of these records, Liber Z is gathered in the same volume with Liber A of the original records, which also contains a wide range of record types, including a variety of patent, probate, and court matters. A recently published volume, prepared by V. L. Skinner Jr., presents the material from Libers Z and A, and also from some other early books, in a different format.[31] The abstracts are here presented in a highly condensed format, taken page by page from the original, including the patent material not published in the fourth volume of *Archives of Maryland*.

These examples show that the same material may have been published more than once, in more than one format. They also illustrate that a published volume does not necessarily conform in whole or in part to any one of the manuscript volumes, and vice versa. This feature of the Maryland records, and of the records of several of the other colonies, may require the researcher to consult the original, not just to verify the reading of a particular document but to determine the broader context of that document.

Throughout the colonial period, the granting of land to individuals was, to a greater or lesser extent, in the hands of the Lords Proprietors, members of the Calvert family. During the years when Maryland was a royal colony, from 1689 to 1715, some authority over land policy was relinquished to the royal government but not all. The details of the changes in this authority, and in the officers who administered land policy, may be found in a study by Elizabeth Hartsook, published in 1946, contained in pages 11 through 77 of *Land Office and Prerogative Court Records of Colonial Maryland*.[32] The land was granted in the typical fashion, through warrant, followed by survey, followed by patent.

Case Studies

Donna Valley Russell, "The Boteler Family of Maryland," *American Genealogist* 70 (1995): 9–17. The author corrects a number of errors in previous accounts of this family. She uses a wide range of original colony and county land and probate documents, as well as material from the published *Archives of Maryland*.

Donna Valley Russell, "Robert Burle of Severn River, Anne Arundel County, Maryland," *American Genealogist* 74 (1999): 263–74. In 1649, Robert Burle moved from Virginia to Maryland; he was one of the leaders of a group of Puritans who had been forced to leave the former colony. This article describes the lives of this immigrant, his son, and two grandsons. Given the loss of early Anne Arundel records to fire in 1704, the author relies heavily on the copies of probate records filed with the colony, as well as the colony land patents and rent rolls. The published *Archives of Maryland* are the source for the extensive office-holding of this immigrant, and some early church records are also exploited in the treatment of the third generation.

Virginia

Jurisdictional History

The first settlement in Virginia, at Jamestown, was undertaken in 1607 by the Virginia Company of London. (Thus, like New Amsterdam and Massachusetts Bay Company, Virginia began life as a business operation.) The company was reorganized and rechartered in 1618, but in 1624 the charter was revoked, and Virginia became a royal colony for the remainder of the colonial period.

The county system in Virginia was not created all at once but grew in a series of stages from about 1618 to 1642. The Virginia Company in 1618 ordered the organization of the colony into four jurisdictions known as cities or boroughs. Based on this beginning, various courts were established, which formed the basis for the full-blown counties.[33] By the end of this period, nine counties existed from which all other Virginia counties were descended: Charles City, Elizabeth City, Henrico, Isle of Wight, James City, Northampton, Northumberland, Warwick, and York.

Records

In Virginia, the principal method for transferring land from the colony to individuals for the first century or so of the colony's existence was the headright system, in which land was awarded for each person transported into the colony. A single grant of land might be based on a head of household, the remaining members of the household, and a number of servants, and so might run to many hundreds of acres. (Less important were grants of land based on military service. Later in the history of the colony, rights to acquire land could be purchased.) After the Crown took over Virginia in 1624, these transfers of land were referred to as "crown grants," except for the land distributed after 1649 by the Northern Neck Proprietors, which became known as "proprietary grants." This separate proprietary land office was established by Charles II in that year as part of his political maneuvering in his attempts to regain the throne.

The actual process of making the grant of land was divided into four steps. First, the person or group of persons wishing to exercise a headright or a military right submitted to the land office a petition that stated the number of acres requested and described the location of the land desired. In the case of headright grants, the petition also included the names of the persons upon whom the claim was based. The land office then issued a warrant, authorizing a surveyor to lay out the land. When the survey was completed and returned, the land office then issued a patent, which became the legal basis for ownership of the land.

The massive collection of Virginia land patents, from the years 1623 to 1776, has been abstracted and published in seven volumes, the first three volumes of which were edited by Nell Marion Nugent.[34] Several of these volumes contain extensive and useful introductory essays on the records and the system that created them.

The Northern Neck land office, eventually controlled by the Fairfax family, covered an area in northern Virginia that was eventually divided into nearly two dozen counties in Virginia and West Virginia. The grants made by the Northern Neck propriety have also been published.[35]

In 1987, Richard Slatten published "Interpreting Headrights in Colonial-Virginia Patents: Uses and Abuses," an article that described the granting process in detail and demonstrated techniques for interpreting the patents in the solution of genealogical problems.[36]

This same system, with variations, was used in all colonies other than the four New England colonies (although there were other important landgranting processes in New York and New Jersey). From one colony to another there might be differences in terminology, but the underlying process was much the same. For instance, the initial petition might also be called the "entry" and the survey might be designated the "plat."

Kentucky

Kentucky was admitted to the Union in 1792 as the fifteenth state. When European settlement of the region that would become Kentucky began, the area was under the jurisdiction of Virginia and was first considered to be part of Augusta County. This situation continued until 1772, when Fincastle County was erected, to include all of what became Kentucky. In 1777, Montgomery County was formed, and the Fincastle records came into the possession of that county.

Case Studies

Charles E. Drake, "Drakes of Isle of Wight County, Virginia: Reconstructing an Immigrant Family from Fragile Clues," *National Genealogical Society Quarterly* 79 (1991): 19–32. The author carefully analyzes scattered clues from early deed, probate, and patent books of Isle of Wight County and of the colony of Virginia to estimate the ages of a group of early Drake immigrants to that county and colony. Combining this information with a 1658 passenger list led to the discovery of the English origin of these Drakes. This research was followed up with a study of the early generations of the family, again using a similar range of records.

Margaret R. Amundson, "The Taliaferro-French Connection: Using Deeds to Prove Marriages and Parentage," *National Genealogical Society Quarterly* 83 (1995): 192–98. The author employs a plenitude of deeds and wills from several early Virginia counties, along with a few church records and entries from court order books, to identify the spouses of several members of the French and Taliaferro families of early eighteenth-century Virginia.

North Carolina

Jurisdictional History

As early as the 1650s, some Virginians began to move into the region that became northeastern North Carolina. The colony of Virginia went so far as to make some land grants in this region.

In the 1660s, the Crown made the grant to the Carolina proprietors, for the geographic area that was later divided into North and South Carolina. From 1663 until 1729, the colony was ruled by the proprietors, who granted land under the usual terms. In 1729 seven of the eight proprietors sold their rights to the Crown, and North Carolina became a royal colony. John Carteret, Lord Granville, retained his share of the propriety and continued to grant lands in North Carolina.

The history of the establishment of counties in North Carolina is a tangled affair, from which we extract the essentials. Albemarle County was erected in 1664 and Bath County in 1696. These counties were divided into a number of precincts, which actually functioned as counties. In 1729, Albemarle and Bath were discontinued, and the precincts were then designated as counties, from which all later counties descend.

The counties functioned in the usual fashion for the registry of deeds, but the responsibilities for probate were split between the county and the colony for some time. Until 1760, the originals of all wills were to be sent to the Secretary of State, but many probate documents were retained at the county level. All colonial probate records have been collected in the state archives, and research in those records should be conducted in both the county and colony records.

Records

Colonial, Revolutionary, and early state records of North Carolina were published in twenty-six volumes between 1886 and 1909. The first ten volumes, published in Raleigh between 1886 and 1890, covered the years from 1662 to 1776 and bore the title *The Colonial Records of North Carolina*. Later volumes in the series covered the years from 1776 onward, with the twenty-sixth volume containing a full transcript of the 1790 census for North Carolina. In 1909 a four-volume index to the entire set was published.

More recently, the Carolina Charter Tercentenary Commission and the North Carolina Division of Archives and History have published ten volumes entitled *The Colonial Records of North Carolina [Second Series]* (1963–1999). The first volume in this series has *North Carolina Charters and Constitutions, 1578–1698*, and the last volume presents *The Church of England in North Carolina: Documents, 1699–1741*. Volumes two through six cover *North Carolina Higher-Court Records from 1670 to 1730*, and volumes seven through nine have *Records of the Executive Council from 1664 to 1775*. This section looks more closely at the higher-court records.

The third volume of the second series of *The Colonial Records of North Carolina* has the volume title *North Carolina Higher-Court Records, 1670–1696*.[37] The volume begins with an introductory essay of nearly a hundred pages, including a description of the sources of the documents included in the volume and of the operation of the courts that produced those documents. The records reproduced here are not a connected series of court proceedings but a miscellaneous collection of what has survived from these earliest years. For example, the very earliest documents reproduced are from two very distinct sources: first, loose papers surviving in both official and private collections at the Division of Archives and History and, second, previously published transcripts of court minutes from the early 1670s, the originals of which vanished within the last century.

A complete overview of all colonial record types for North Carolina may be found in Helen F. M. Leary's *North Carolina Research: Genealogy and Local History*.[38]

Tennessee

Tennessee was admitted to the Union in 1796 as the sixteenth state. The region that became Tennessee was part of the area included in the North Carolina charter. European settlement began there in the mid-1760s, pursuant to the conclusion of the French and Indian Wars. The settlers formed an independent governing body called the Watauga Association, which was (re)incorporated into North Carolina just prior to the Revolution. Grants of land in this area were made by North Carolina.

Case Studies

Helen F. M. Leary, "The Two William Boddies of North Carolina: Proof of Relationship and Military Service," *American Genealogist* 66 (1991): 16–29, 106–10, 148–53. This extensive investigation of the ancestry of a William Boddie who died in 1817 reached back to the end of the seventeenth century and began with a detailed study of land records, especially the deed books of Bertie County. The research soon expanded to include land patents, wills, and militia lists. The interpretation of the evidence was assisted by a close examination of the inheritance laws of North Carolina in the middle of the eighteenth century.

Edward L. Strother, "Three John Strothers: But Which One Died in Georgia?" *National Genealogical Society Quarterly* 86 (1998): 189–203. Despite the locality named in the title of this article, the bulk of the argumentation revolves around several Strother families in North Carolina in the latter half of the eighteenth century. The research relies heavily on county deed and probate volumes but also uses tax lists, court proceedings, and military records.

South Carolina

Jurisdictional History

The first permanent settlement within the bounds of what became South Carolina was made at Ashley, under the aegis of the Carolina proprietors. As the colony grew, three proprietary counties were erected in 1682, but these governmental units did not have any record-creating or record-keeping responsibilities.

In 1729 seven of the eight Carolina proprietors sold their rights to the Crown, and South Carolina became a royal colony. In 1769 seven judicial districts were created, and in 1772 the first courts were held outside Charleston. Despite these jurisdictional expansions, all records that might elsewhere be housed at the county level were in South Carolina housed at Charleston.

Records

Despite the existence of counties, judicial districts, and parishes at various times in the colonial period of South Carolina, all South Carolina probate records prior to 1781 were maintained in a single repository in Charleston. Abstracts of colonial wills have been published in various places and are discussed later in this chapter. In 1977, Brent H. Holcomb published an index to inventories for the years 1746 through 1785 called *Probate Records of South Carolina, Volume I: Index to Inventories, 1746–1785*.[39] (This volume does not index the first five volumes of colonial inventories, covering the years from 1736 to 1746.)

In 1960, Caroline T. Moore published three volumes of will abstracts, the first of which was for the years 1670 through 1740.[40] This volume brings together abstracts of documents found in twenty-two different record books of the colony, most of which are titled either "Will Book" or "Miscellaneous Records." The first page of this collection contains three abstracts, taken from three different record books; in each case, these are the only wills represented as coming from these record books. On pages sixteen through eighteen are five abstracts, identified as coming from "Will Book 1671–1727," and these are the only will abstracts from this Will Book. Each is identified as being taken from a transcript made in 1851, with page references (presumably to the original volume) of 2, 3, 73, 187, and 189. Clearly, far more wills were included in these original will volumes than have made their way into this modern compilation.

In 1978, Caroline T. Moore published an additional volume of record abstracts, this time from the records of the secretary of the province.[41] This book contains abstracts of records from six record books, identified by the inclusive dates of the records contained therein, along with some miscellaneous loose papers. The first volume from which abstracts were made, described as "Book 1700–1710," includes abstracts of wills, which were also published in the volume discussed in the previous paragraph, and noted there as having been taken from "Will Book 1687–1710." For example, in both of these sets of abstracts, the first two wills are for John Crosse and his widow Mary Crosse. The abstracts represented as taken from the records of the secretary of the province have more than just the wills abstracted in the earlier volume; there are also many letters of administration, nuncupative wills, and other types of probate records.

Researchers who use these various will abstracts and other probate materials must be wary of the exact source of each document and the nature of the particular copy or version being presented.

Case Studies

GeLee Corley Hendrix, "Going beyond the Database. Interpretation, Amplification, and Development of Evidence: South Carolina's COM Index and Several James Kelleys," *National Genealogical Society Quarterly* 86 (1998): 116–33.

Hendrix explores a modern computerized index to a wide array of colonial South Carolina records. This index provides easy access to, among other sources, the comprehensive collection of colonial South Carolina land grants. The author examines both the value of this index and the pitfalls awaiting those who use the index without taking care to look for errors and omissions in its creation.

John Anderson Brayton, "Hardy of South Carolina—A 'Discreet' Omission to Hide an Indiscretion," ***National Genealogical Society Quarterly*** **90 (2002): 69–71.** The author compares the full text of a colonial will with the modern published abstract, demonstrating the deficiency of the latter.

Georgia

Jurisdictional History

Georgia was founded in 1733, and the Crown granted governance to a group of trustees, headed by James Oglethorpe. This arrangement had some similarities to the system of proprietors of the other southern colonies, and land was granted to individuals by the trustees. The grant to the trustees expired in 1753, and Georgia became a royal colony for the remainder of the colonial period.

Georgia was divided into twelve parishes for some administrative purposes, but these parishes did not generate court, land, or probate records. These functions remained with the colony government. Only with the 1777 constitution were counties established, with eight counties being erected in that year. Thus, there are no county records from the colonial period.

Records

The range of surviving colonial Georgia records is quite limited for several reasons. Georgia existed for less than half a century in the colonial period, retained no records at the county level prior to 1777, and suffered serious record losses beginning during the Revolutionary War. Probate and land records were maintained at Savannah. Robert Scott Davis Jr. has compiled a list of such records as have been published or microfilmed.[42]

In 1904, Allen D. Candler, with the authority of the Georgia legislature, began publishing records from the Public Record Office in England pertaining to Georgia and, by 1916, had brought forth twenty-six volumes. More recently this project has been revived, and six additional volumes have been published, based on the copies obtained by Candler.[43]

As an example of what is contained in this series, the earliest volumes contain the records of the meetings in England of the Trustees for Establishing the Colony of Georgia in America, and of the Common Council of the Trustees. The most recently published volume incorporates "Entry Books of Commissions, Powers, Instructions, Leases, Grants of Land, Etc. by the Trustees" for the years 1732–38.

Case Study

Robert Battle, "Ancestors and Descendants of William Spencer, Immigrant to Georgia in 1742," ***American Genealogist*** **77 (2002): 81–93, 196–207.** Letters published in Volumes 5 and 25 of the *Colonial Records of the State of Georgia* provide the essential clue leading to the discovery of the English origin of this immigrant. The author uses the same set of printed records to support many of his conclusions, including details of the immigrant's office holding and landholding. He also exploits the colonial-era wills. The county records come into play only in the Revolutionary period and later.

Notes

[1] *New Hampshire Provincial and State Papers*, 39:v–xix.

[2] *Records and Files of the Quarterly Courts of Essex County, Massachusetts*, 9 vols. (Salem, 1911–75). In the first volume, see pp. 149–51 and 164–68 for the first surviving records for Hampton and Salisbury Courts.

[3] *The Probate Records of Essex County, Massachusetts*, 3 vols. (Salem, 1916–20).

[4] *New Hampshire Provincial and State Papers*, 40 vols. (Concord, 1867–1943).

[5] *New Hampshire Provincial and State Papers*. "The Controversy Between New Hampshire, New York, and Vermont . . ." is found on pp. 197–500 of volume 10.

[6] Nathaniel B. Shurtleff and David Pulsifer, eds., *Records of the Colony of New Plymouth in New England* (Boston, 1855–61).

[7] Eugene Aubrey Stratton, *Plymouth Colony: Its History & People, 1620–1691* (Salt Lake City, 1986).

[8] Nathaniel B. Shurtleff, ed., *Records of the Governor and Company of the Massachusetts Bay in New England, 1628–1686* (Boston, 1853–54).

[9] Don Gleason Hill, ed., *The Early Records of the Town of Dedham, Massachusetts. 1636–1659. A Complete Transcript* (Dedham, 1892), 171.

[10] John Russell Bartlett, ed., *Records of the Colony of Rhode Island and Providence Plantations in New England*, vol. 1 (Providence, 1856).

[11] Ibid., 70–85.

[12] *Rhode Island Colony Records 1646–1669*, FHL microfilm 947, 963.

[13] Howard M. Chapin, *Documentary History of Rhode Island*, 2 vols. (Providence, 1916, 1919), 2:132–64.

[14] *Rhode Island Court Records: Records of the Court of Trials of the Colony of Providence Plantations*, vol. 1, 1647–62 (Providence,

1920); *Island Court Records: Records of the Court of Trials of the Colony of Providence Plantations*, vol. 2, 1662–70 (Providence, 1922).

[15] Charles William Manwaring, *Early Connecticut Probate Records*, 3 vols. (Hartford, 1902–06).

[16] Charles J. Hoadly, *Records of the Colony and Plantation of New Haven, From 1638 to 1649* (Hartford, 1857); *Records of the Colony or Jurisdiction of New Haven, from May, 1653, to the Union* (Hartford, 1858).

[17] *Great Migration Newsletter* 13 (2004): 3–7, 9–16, 19–21.

[18] Salomon Lachaire, "New York Historical Manuscripts: Dutch," *The Register of Solomon Lachaire, Notary Public of New Amsterdam, 1661–1662* (Baltimore, 1978).

[19] *Minutes of the Orphanmasters of New Amsterdam, 1655–1663* (New York, 1902); *Minutes of the Orphanmasters of New Amsterdam, 1663–1668* (Baltimore, 1976).

[20] Charles T. Gehring, "Documentary Sources Relating to New Netherland," in *Colonial Dutch Studies: An Interdisciplinary Approach*, ed. Eric Nooter and Patricia U. Bonomi (New York, 1988), 33–51.

[21] Harry Macy Jr., "New York Probate Records Before 1787," *NYG&B Newsletter* 2 (1991): 11–15.

[22] Joseph W. Dally, *Woodbridge and Vicinity: The Story of a New Jersey Township* (New Brunswick, N.J., 1873; Lambertville, New Jersey, 1989), 298–302.

[23] William Nelson, ed., *Documents Relating to the Colonial History of the State of New Jersey*, vol. 21, *Calendar of Records in the Office of the Secretary of State. 1664–1703* (Paterson, N.J., 1899; Baltimore, 1976).

[24] Christine Crawford-Oppenheimer, *Pennsylvania Genealogical Magazine* 40 (1997): 101–19; reprinted in 1999 as a separate pamphlet.

[25] Peter Stebbins Craig, *The 1693 Census of the Swedes on the Delaware: Family Histories of the Swedish Lutheran Church Members Residing in Pennsylvania, Delaware, West New Jersey and Cecil County, Maryland, 1683–1693* (Winter Park, Fla., 1993); *1671 Census of the Delaware* (Philadelphia, 1999).

[26] *Records of the Court of New Castle on Delaware 1676–1681* (Lancaster, Pa., 1904); Craig W. Horle, ed., *Records of the Courts of Sussex County, Delaware, 1677–1710*, 2 vols. (Philadelphia, 1991).

[27] Leon deValinger Jr., ed., *Court Records of Kent County, Delaware, 1680–1705* (Washington, D.C., 1959).

[28] *Archives of Maryland*, 72 vols. (Baltimore, 1883–1972). Much of this material is also available online <www.mdarchives.state.md.us/megafile/msa/speccol/sc2900/sc2908/html/index.html>.

[29] Ibid., xiii–liv.

[30] *Archives of Maryland*, vol. 4, *Judicial and Testamentary Business of the Provincial Court, 1637–1650* (Baltimore, 1887).

[31] V. L. Skinner Jr., *Abstracts of the Proprietary Records of the Provincial Court of Maryland, 1637–1658: Patent Record F&B (1640–1658); Patent Record Z&A (1637–1651); Patent Record A&B (1650–1657)* (Westminster, Md., 2002).

[32] Elizabeth Hartsook, *Land Office and Prerogative Court Records of Colonial Maryland*, Publications of the Hall of Records Commission No. 4 (Hall of Records Commission).

[33] Edgar MacDonald, "The Myth of Virginia County Formation in 1634," *National Genealogical Society Quarterly* 92 (2004): 58–63.

[34] Nell Marion Nugent, ed, *Cavaliers and Pioneers: Abstracts of Virginia Land Patents*, 7 vols. (Baltimore, 1963–99).

[35] Nell Marion Nugent, *Supplement, Northern Neck Grants No. 1, 1690–1692* (Richmond, 1980); Gertrude E. Gray, *Virginia Northern Neck Land Grants, 1694–1775*, 2 vols. (Baltimore, 1987, 1988).

[36] Richard Slatten, "Interpreting Headrights in Colonial-Virginia Patents: Uses and Abuses," *National Genealogical Society Quarterly* 75 (1987): 169–79.

[37] Mattie Erma Edwards Parker, ed., *The Colonial Records of North Carolina*, vol. 3, *North Carolina Higher-Court Records, 1670–1696* (Raleigh, 1968).

[38] Helen F. M. Leary, ed., *North Carolina Research: Genealogy and Local History*, 2nd ed. (Raleigh, 1996).

[39] Brent H. Holcomb, *Probate Records of South Carolina, Volume I: Index to Inventories, 1746–1785* (Easley, S.C., 1977).

[40] Caroline T. Moore, *Abstracts of the Wills of the State of South Carolina, Volume 1, 1670–1740* (Columbia, S.C., 1960).

[41] Caroline T. Moore, *Records of the Secretary of the Province of South Carolina, 1692–1721* (Columbia, S.C., 1978).

[42] Robert Scott Davis Jr., *Research in Georgia* (Easley, S.C., 1981), 169–73.

[43] *The Colonial Records of the State of Georgia*, 32 vols. (Atlanta and Athens, Ga.: 1904–89).

References

Archives of Maryland. 72 vols. Baltimore, 1883–1972.

Bartlett, John Russell, ed. *Records of the Colony of Rhode Island and Providence Plantations in New England, 1636–1692*. 10 vols. Providence, 1856–65.

Candler, Allen D., ed. *The Colonial Records of the State of Georgia*. 32 vols. Atlanta and Athens, Ga., 1904–89.

Chapin, Howard M. *Documentary History of Rhode Island*. 2 vols. Providence, 1916, 1919.

The Colonial Records of North Carolina. 10 vols. Raleigh, 1886–90.

The Colonial Records of North Carolina (Second Series). 10 vols. Raleigh, 1963–99.

Craig, Peter Stebbins. *1671 Census of the Delaware*. Philadelphia, 1999.

Crandall, Ralph J., ed. *Genealogical Research in New England*. Baltimore, 1984.

———. *The 1693 Census of the Swedes on the Delaware: Family Histories of the Swedish Lutheran Church Members Residing in Pennsylvania, Delaware, West New Jersey and Cecil County, Maryland, 1683–1693*. Winter Park, Fla., 1993.

Dally, Joseph W. *Woodbridge and Vicinity: The Story of a New Jersey Township*. Lambertville, N.J., 1989.

Davis, Robert Scott, Jr. *Research in Georgia*. Easley, S.C., 1981. See pages 169–73.

deValinger, Leon, Jr., ed. *Court Records of Kent County, Delaware, 1680–1705*. Washington, D.C., 1959.

Gehring, Charles T. "Documentary Sources Relating to New Netherland." In *Colonial Dutch Studies: An Interdisciplinary Approach*, edited by Eric Nooter and Patricia U. Bonomi, 33–51. New York, 1988.

Gray, Gertrude E. *Virginia Northern Neck Land Grants, 1694–1775*. 2 vols. Baltimore, 1987, 1988.

Hartsook, Elizabeth. *Land Office and Prerogative Court Records of Colonial Maryland*. Publications of the Hall of Records Commission No. 4.

Hill, Don Gleason, ed. *The Early Records of the Town of Dedham, Massachusetts. 1636–1659. A Complete Transcript*. Dedham, 1892.

Hoadly, Charles J. *Records of the Colony or Jurisdiction of New Haven, from May, 1653, to the Union*. Hartford, 1858.

———, ed. *Records of the Colony and Plantation of New Haven, 1638–1649, 1653–1664*. 2 vols. New Haven, 1857–58.

Holcomb, Brent H. *Probate Records of South Carolina, Volume I: Index to Inventories, 1746–1785*. Easley, S.C., 1977.

Horle, Craig W., ed. *Records of the Courts of Sussex County, Delaware, 1677–1710*. 2 vols. Philadelphia, 1991.

Kingsbury, Susan Myra, ed. *The Records of the Virginia Company of London*. 4 vols. Washington, D.C., 1906–35.

Lachaire, Salomon. "New York Historical Manuscripts: Dutch." In *The Register of Solomon Lachaire, Notary Public of New Amsterdam, 1661–1662*. Baltimore, 1978.

Leary, Helen F. M., ed. *North Carolina Research: Genealogy and Local History*. 2nd ed. Raleigh, 1996.

MacDonald, Edgar. "The Myth of Virginia County Formation in 1634." *National Genealogical Society Quarterly* 92 (2004): 58–63.

Macy, Harry, Jr. "New York Probate Records Before 1787." *NYG&B Newsletter* 2 (1991): 11–15.

Manwaring, Charles William. *Early Connecticut Probate Records*. 3 vols. Hartford, 1902–06.

Minutes of the Orphanmasters of New Amsterdam, 1655–1663. New York, 1902.

Minutes of the Orphanmasters of New Amsterdam, 1663–1668. Baltimore, 1976.

Moore, Caroline T. *Abstracts of the Wills of the State of South Carolina, Volume 1, 1670–1740*. Columbia, S.C., 1960.

———. *Records of the Secretary of the Province of South Carolina, 1692–1721*. Columbia, S.C., 1978.

Nelson, William, ed. *Documents Relating to the Colonial History of the State of New Jersey*. Vol. 21. *Calendar of Records in the Office of the Secretary of State. 1664–1703*. Paterson, N.J., 1899. Reprint, Baltimore, 1976.

New Hampshire Provincial and State Papers. 40 vols. Concord, 1867–1943.

New York Historical Manuscripts: Dutch, vols. 18–29, Delaware Papers (Dutch Period)...1648–166. Baltimore, 1981.

New York Historical Manuscripts: Dutch, vols. 20–21, Delaware Papers (English Period)...1664–1682. Baltimore, 1977.

Nooter, Eric, and Patricia U. Bonomi, eds. *Colonial Dutch Studies: An Interdisciplinary Approach*. New York, 1988.

Nugent, Nell Marion, ed. *Cavaliers and Pioneers: Abstracts of Virginia Land Patents*. 7 vols. Baltimore, 1963–99.

———. *Supplement, Northern Neck Grants No. 1, 1690–1692*. Richmond, 1980.

Original Land Titles in Delaware Commonly Known as The Duke of York Record . . . . From 1646 to 1679. Wilmington, Del., n.d.

Parker, Mattie Erma Edwards, ed. *The Colonial Records of North Carolina*. Vol. 3. *North Carolina Higher-Court Records, 1670–1696*. Raleigh, 1968.

The Probate Records of Essex County, Massachusetts. 3 vols. Salem, Mass., 1916–20.

The Record of the Court at Upland in Pennsylvania 1676 to 1681. Philadelphia, 1860.

Records and Files of the Quarterly Courts of Essex County, Massachusetts. 9 vols. Salem, Mass., 1911–75.

Records of the Court of New Castle on Delaware 1676–1681. Lancaster, Pa., 1904.

Records of the Colony or Jurisdiction of New Haven, from May, 1653, to the Union. Hartford, 1858.

Rhode Island Court Records: Records of the Court of Trials of the Colony of Providence Plantations. Vol. 1, 1647–62. Providence, 1920.

Rhode Island Court Records: Records of the Court of Trials of the Colony of Providence Plantations. Vol. 2, 1662–70. Providence, 1922.

Shurtleff, Nathaniel B., ed. *Records of the Governor and Company of the Massachusetts Bay in New England, 1628–1686*. 5 vols. in 6. Boston, 1853–54.

Shurtleff, Nathaniel B., and David Pulsifer, eds. *Records of the Colony of New Plymouth in New England*. 12 vols. in 10. Boston, 1855–61.

Slatten, Richard. "Interpreting Headrights in Colonial-Virginia Patents: Uses and Abuses." *National Genealogical Society Quarterly* 75 (1987): 169–79.

Stratton, Eugene Aubrey. *Plymouth Colony: Its History & People, 1620–1691*. Salt Lake City, 1986.

Skinner, V. L., Jr. *Abstracts of the Proprietary Records of the Provincial Court of Maryland, 1637–1658: Patent Record F&B (1640–1658); Patent Record Z&A (1637–1651); Patent Record A&B (1650–1657)*. Westminster, Md., 2002.

Trumbull, J. Hammond. *The Public Records of the Colony of Connecticut, 1636–1776*. 15 vols. Hartford, 1850–90.

Internet Resources

Connecticut Historical Society: www.chs.org

Connecticut State Library: www.cslib.org

Delaware Public Archives: www.state.de.us/sos/dpa

Genealogical Society of Pennsylvania: www.genpa.org/index.html

Georgia Archives: www.sos.state.ga.us/archives

Georgia Historical Society: www.georgiahistory.com

Historical Society of Delaware: www.hsd.org

Historical Society of Pennsylvania: www.hsp.org

Library of Virginia: www.lva.lib.va.us

Maine Historical Society: www.mainehistory.org

Maine State Archives: www.state.me.us/sos/arc

Maryland Historical Society: www.mdhs.org

Maryland State Archives: www.mdarchives.state.md.us/msa/homepage/html/homepage.html

Massachusetts Archives: www.sec.state.ma.us/arc/arcidx.htm

Massachusetts Historical Society: www.masshist.org/welcome

New England Historic Genealogical Society: www.newenglandancestors.org

New Hampshire Division of Archives and Records Management: www.sos.nh.gov/archives

New Hampshire Historical Society: www.nhhistory.org

New Jersey Division of Archives and Records Management: www.njarchives.org

New Jersey Historical Society: www.jerseyhistory.org

New York Genealogical and Biographical Society: www.newyorkfamilyhistory.org

New York State Archives: www.archives.nysed.gov/aindex.shtml

North Carolina Office of Archives and History: www.ah.dcr.state.nc.us

Pennsylvania State Archives: www.phmc.state.pa.us/bah/dam/overview.htm

Rhode Island Historical Society: www.rihs.org

Rhode Island State Archives: www.sec.state.ri.us/archives/index.html

South Carolina Department of Archives and History: www.state.sc.us/scdah

South Carolina Historical Society: www.schistory.org

Virginia Historical Society: www.vahistorical.org

16

Colonial Spanish Borderland Research

GEORGE R. RYSKAMP, JD, AG

In 1793, Gregory White, priest of the Catholic parish in Natchez, Mississippi, wrote the following entry in Spanish in the parish marriage book:

> In the town of Natchez on the 22nd of the month of August of 1793 I Don Gregory White principle (propietario) priest of this parish having read three bans without having resulted in any impediments, wed Policarpio Regillo, legitimate son of Jose and of Maria Rufina residents of Lesuza Province (Corregimiento) of Tholedo and Margarita Thomas, legitimate daughter of Elias Thomas and of Catarina, residents of Virginia, the witnesses were Wendelina Piroth and Israel Lennard and I sign this- Gregorio White.

A Spanish groom, a bride from Virginia, an Irish priest, and two French witnesses—this typifies the Spanish frontier at the greatest extent of Spanish dominion in the last quarter of the eighteenth century. Spain controlled lands from California on the west through Arizona and New Mexico (extending north into Colorado), Texas, Louisiana, the entire Mississippi River Valley (including posts as far north as Illinois), and the Gulf Coast sections of Mississippi and Alabama all the way across Florida to the east coast at Saint Augustine. As Americans schooled in the Frederick Jackson Turner theory of the expansion of the American frontier, many of us fail to recognize the significance of the Spanish presence in large areas that are now part of the territorial United States. Spain not only established the first two successful permanent colonies in the area now comprising the United States (Saint Augustine, Florida, in 1565 and New Mexico in 1598), but by 1800, the Spanish population had reached 26,800 in California, Texas, Arizona, and New Mexico (20,00 in New Mexico alone) and about 48,000 in the Louisiana Territory and the Floridas.[1]

Chapter Contents

This Spanish frontier had established an active and dynamic presence for more than a century before the beginning of the American and French frontiers with which it collided in the eighteenth century. A constant interaction existed among these frontiers, with Britains, Frenchmen, and, ultimately, Americans crossing into, settling among, and interacting with the Spanish administration and people. As a result, many of those early American, British, and French settlers appear in Spanish records along with an extensive number of Spanish subjects. As inveterate record keepers, the Spanish kept extensive and detailed records of governmental administration and daily life. Aided by the common element of the Catholic religion, Spanish records are generally more extensive than their English counterparts during the colonial period, providing an excellent amount of material of interest not only to those who have ancestral lines among the Spanish settlers, but for those with ancestral lines among early American, British, and French settlers within areas under Spanish rule.

This chapter reviews the types and locations of records generated in the Spanish language by the colonial governments of Spain as well as by the Mexican government. It focuses on the southern third of the United States from Florida west through Louisiana to the California coast—all ruled by Spain as part of the colonies of Florida and Louisiana—and the northern frontier of New Spain (the Spanish designation for Mexico). Also covered are the Mexican years from independence in 1821 until the end of the Mexican War in 1849. The chapter is not all-inclusive. Many published materials of local interest may exist that are not mentioned here. A search by geographical areas of interest on the Internet and on WorldCat (the OCLC Library Consortium) at a local university or public library will yield many titles relating to specific places.

If one were creating a library of key reference works, the following would be essential:

Barnes, Thomas C., Thomas H. Naylor, and Charles W. Polzer. *Northern New Spain: A Research Guide.* Tucson: University of Arizona Press, 1981.

Beers, Henry Putney. *Spanish and Mexican Records of the American Southwest.* Tucson: University or Arizona Press, 1979.

———. *French and Spanish Records of Louisiana.* Baton Rouge: Louisiana State University Press, 1989.

Gerhard, Peter. *The North Frontier of New Spain.* Norman: University of Oklahoma Press, 1982.

Platt, Lyman D. "Hispanic-American Records and Research." In *Ethnic Genealogy: A Research Guide*, edited by Jessie Carney Smith, 365–401. Westport, Conn.: Greenwood Press, 1983.

Weber, David J. *The Spanish Frontier in North America.* New Haven, Conn.: Yale University Press, 1992.

———. *The Mexican Frontier, 1821–1846, The American Southwest Under Mexico.* Albuquerque: University of New Mexico Press, 1982.

These volumes cover the entire area of Spanish occupation, with the exception of Florida. They not only provide details concerning types and locations of records, but also a history of the maintenance of the records themselves and the circumstances accompanying their creation.

History of the Spanish Borderlands

A family historian cannot effectively do research without understanding the history of an ancestor's locality and region and how it integrates into the broader spectrum of traditional history. Insight into the history of the Spanish and French presence in what is now the United States is provided by Ray Allen Billington in his foreword to *The Spanish Borderlands Frontier, 1513–1821*, by John Francis Bannon:

> For a generation after 1893 when Frederick Jackson Turner announced his "frontier hypothesis," he and his disciples pictured the population stream that peopled the continent as flowing from east to west, advancing relentlessly from the Atlantic to the Pacific. Its source, they taught, was the British Isles, whence came the Anglo-American pioneers. . . . They were joined at times by other European migrants, the Germans especially, but their cultural language was basically English and the civilization they planted was a British civilization, modified only by environmental forces operating on the frontier. . . .
>
> [I]n stressing this viewpoint, to the exclusion of all others, [Turner] and his followers seriously distorted the truth. Actually four migratory streams contributed to the population of the United States during the era of settlement. The principal flood was, as Turner saw, moving from east to west, and carried with it the Anglo-American culture that laid the foundation on which the nation's civilization rested. But the superstructure built on this foundation was significantly altered as it was joined by lesser population streams during the eighteenth and nineteenth centuries.
>
> One of these originated in Canada and advanced upon the present United States from the northeast; French Canadians, during the seventeenth and eighteenth centuries, occupied much of Michigan and the Illinois country, pushed their posts southward along the Mississippi River to Saint Louis and beyond. . . . A second migratory stream had its source in the Caribbean Islands. From there Spaniards advanced

> upon the mainland from the southeast, establishing themselves in the Floridas, and planting their outposts as far north as the Carolinas and Virginia. The third and most important subsidiary migration began in Mexico. From that Spanish stronghold a northward-moving frontier advanced steadily during the seventeenth and eighteenth centuries, filling the plateaus of northern Mexico, and pushing on into Texas, New Mexico, Arizona and California. By the dawn of the nineteenth century New Spain's mission stations, ranches and presidios swept in a giant arch from eastern Texas to the Bay of San Francisco.[2]

During the last half of the eighteenth century, Spain assumed control of the majority of the land in the modern United States that had been established by the French migratory pattern. In particular, Spain ruled the successful and significant colonies in the Louisiana area, thus extending the area of its control, colonization, and civilization in a giant arch from San Francisco to Saint Augustine.

The history of the Spanish frontier began with the establishment of a colony on the island of Haiti (then known as Hispaniola) by Christopher Columbus on his second voyage. During the first quarter of the sixteenth century, the spread of Spanish dominion was relatively even, going north, west, and south. After first conquering several Caribbean islands, in 1513 Juan Ponce de Leon first explored the North American continent, where he discovered the bay of Saint Augustine in Florida.

The discovery of the Mayans in Yucatan in 1517 and of the Aztec Empire in Mexico in 1519 shifted the attention and direction of Spanish exploration. Beginning with the conquest of the Aztec Empire and the establishment of the colony of New Spain, Spanish attention was diverted west and southwest. Discovery and conquest of Peru, as well as the establishment of trade between Manila and the west coast of New Spain, further diverted Spanish colonization west and southwest. Spain's only contact with the area that became the United States was extensive exploration, but as explorers found no vast and wealthy empires or land and, instead, were frequently met by hostile indigenous peoples, no effort was made to colonize these areas.

By the end of the sixteenth century, Spaniards had effectively explored all of the areas ultimately occupied by Spain within the borders of the United States. Limited Spanish attempts to establish a Florida colony in the second quarter of the sixteenth century failed due to a variety of circumstances. Ultimately, the first colony Spain established in the continental United States was set up at Saint Augustine in 1565, a decision motivated solely by the fact that the French had established, on the Carolina coast, a colony of three hundred people. Within only days after settling the new Spanish colonists at Saint Augustine, Don Pedro Menendez de Aviles, founder of Saint Augustine, moved northward and attacked and destroyed the French colony. In its fight for a portion of Spain's attention and the royal treasury, the colony in Florida became, throughout its life, a stepsister with the primary function of an outpost for defense against the growth of French colonizing efforts and, subsequently, the greater English development.

The most significant development of the North American Spanish frontier was found in New Spain, the area now covering the states of California, Arizona, New Mexico, Texas, and parts of Utah and Colorado. In a matter of a few years, all of central Mexico previously under Aztec domination became part of the colony called New Spain, and within two decades, Nueva Galicia was established to the northwest, still in areas that had been occupied or dominated by the Aztecs. Guadalajara, as the capitol of the province of New Galicia, became a crucial center for the development of all the Spanish borderland area, with many records of genealogical interest either generated by or sent to the provincial governor in Guadalajara, where they can still be found. In 1548, Guadalajara became a bishopric and thus exercised both ecclesiastical and civil authority over the region, which, until the 1770s, covered Texas and the modern Mexican states of Jalisco, Zacatecas, Nuevo Leon, Coahuila, and Tamaulipas.

In that same year, silver was discovered in Zacatecas, with other discoveries following in Guanajuato, Aguascalientes, and further north in Queretaros and San Luis Potosi. Three centuries before the California gold rush, Nueva Galicia experienced North America's first mining boom.

Development in the 1560s pushed north of the Sierra Madre range, and a new province called Nueva Vizcaya was established, including the town of Durango—the northern capital for most of the colonization effort—in 1563. The province of Nueva Vizcaya included the areas now occupied by Arizona and the Mexican states of Chihuahua, Sonora, Sinaloa, and Coahuila. This entire area, as well as the separate political province of New Mexico, was under the ecclesiastical authority of the Bishop of Durango.

For the first time, as they crossed the Sierra Madre range into Nueva Vizcaya, the Spaniards encountered indigenous people not subjugated by the Aztec Empire. Two new concepts in Spanish colonization—the mission and the presidio—came into existence as a result, providing the basis for the Spanish presence and colonization efforts in this borderland area as much as two centuries later. As Spaniards moved north into hostile territories, their first line of colonization became missions established by the Franciscans and, later, Jesuit monks, friars who would preach among the natives as well as teach them trades and the concepts of "civilization." To protect the missions and establish Spanish governmental control, a presidio (Spanish fort) was established.

The mission and the presidio represent the major difference between the Spanish approach to frontier development and colonization and the Anglo-American approach. Spain's colonization came as a result of actions of the central government.

New colonies weren't established without express permission and direction from Spain, or at least from the viceroy in Mexico City. Spain's purpose in colonizing was to establish a new city with an organized government in each new place. Generally, the colonists were accompanied by representatives of two distinct groups: Representatives of the Crown were to make certain that the Royal Treasury received its one-fifth duty on any gold, silver, or other valuables found. Representatives of the Church, usually members of one of the religious orders, would establish a mission. Colonial leaders prepared detailed written reports that were sent back to the viceroy and the Council of the Indies in Spain, and in many cases, no action was taken until a response had been received.

Spain established colonies comprised of organized cities with established patterns of religious and civic life common to Spanish society—a contrast to the approach of Anglo-American and even French exploration, where the first settlers into an area were usually rugged individualists without any direct control or connection with the government in the area they left behind. Most Anglo-Americans were generally not in the habit of reporting back and waiting for instructions before taking action. These Spanish characteristics, of course, are of great value to the historian and, specifically, the family historian today, as they provide extensive detailed records of the various Spanish colonies, their establishment, and their continued operation.

At the end of the 1580s, with the frontier at Durango, a thousand miles south of New Mexico, members of the Royal Court in Spain focused on securing a stronger foothold in the northern frontier. This focus came as a result of the activities of the Englishman Sir Francis Drake, including his attack on Mexican ports in the Pacific during his circumnavigation of the world. At the same time, reports had been brought of the peaceful Pueblo Indians living in agricultural communities and building cities in the area of New Mexico. At the request of Don Juan Oñate, son of a prominent and wealthy New Spain family, the Council of Indies approved a contract that provided Oñate with two hundred fully equipped and supplied men with their own provisions to lead the colonization of New Mexico, initiated in 1598. Continually beset with problems and never considered a success by the wealthy royal standards of other parts of northern New Spain, the New Mexican colony's survival is impressive. While New Mexico had its own governor, many of the elements of civil control were exercised from Durango and Mexico City to the south. Ecclesiastically, New Mexico remained a part of the diocese of Durango from its creation in 1621 until 1850, when the American occupation was completed.

At the end of the seventeenth century, the French, under Pierre de le Moyne, Sieur d'Iberville, established colonies at Biloxi on the Mississippi River and, later, up the river at New Orleans, Natchez, and the Arkansas Post. Concerns with the developing French colonies prompted Spanish expansion into Texas, where, in 1700, San Antonio de Bexar was created to support missions and presidios established in east Texas at the end of the seventeenth century. In 1723, San Antonio became the capital of Texas and the center point for Spanish colonization of Texas.

A second corridor of new Spanish expansion involved the development of the local area along the Gulf Coast and inland, forming the kingdom of Nuevo Santander and state of Nuevo Leon. An extension of this area was that portion of what is now Texas south of the Nueces River. Historically, this area belonged to the Nuevo Santander area and only became a part of Texas following the defeat of Mexico and end of the Mexican War. Even today, much of its culture and society has stronger ties with the Mexican provinces of Tamaulipas and Nuevo Leon than with San Antonio de Bexar.

A third corridor swung up the coast on the western side of the western Sierra Madre range, through the provinces of Nayarit and Sinaloa and into the provinces of Sonora and Baja California. By the beginning of the seventeenth century, the California coastline had been explored, and ships from Manila going to the Mexican port of Acapulco regularly stopped to draw fresh water. Efforts to colonize what is now California didn't come until 1769, with the establishment of San Diego. The initial colonization in California began not from the pressure of a society moving up the coastline but as an attempt to establish connections between northern Sonora and the coast resulting from international pressure by English and Russian explorers.

Beginning in 1763, those pressures took on different dimensions as the French were totally eliminated from North America at the end of the Seven Years War. (Our American portion is called the French and Indian War.) As a result of treaties ending that war, Quebec became a British colony and Louisiana, the Mississippi River Valley, and the Gulf Coast became Spanish colonies. Spanish colonies on the Gulf Coast, including those in both Florida and Louisiana, were governed from the Captaincy General in Cuba, while the rest of Florida became English from 1763 to 1783. Just as the northern provinces of New Spain reported to the viceroy in Nueva España, similarly, reports were sent back to the Captain General of Cuba or, in the earliest time period, to Santo Domingo. The occupation of Louisiana consolidated and even extended the colonization efforts of the French. Interestingly, even the presence of newer French colonists such as the Acadians (French refugees driven out of Nova Scotia by the British) added to the French character of the Spanish colony of Louisiana.

As Spain acquired sovereignty over Louisiana, it lost control of Florida. From 1763 to 1783 Florida was a British colony. Britain returned Florida to Spain at the end of the American Revolution in recognition of Spain's participation on the side of the American colonists. Ultimately, within little more than a generation, those very colonists whom Spain had assisted took over control of both Louisiana and Florida by purchase (under pressure that it would be lost by conquest if the purchase were not accepted). Within two generations Spain lost Texas and within the third, at most, all the Spanish area within what is now the United States.

The discussion above is at best an oversimplified summary of the development of the Spanish and French frontiers. For a family historian, the details about specific localities, settlements, and settlers can be as important as the overall broad picture of that development. A good history, such as *The Spanish Frontier in North America* by David J. Weber, giving a broad historical picture and providing a bibliography of the development of the borderlands areas on the Spanish and French frontiers, would be helpful.

Spanish Colonial Institutions

An understanding of how Spain governed the American colonies will help a researcher better understand the records generated. From the initial financing of the voyage of Columbus by Queen Isabel of Spain, the discovery and colonization of the Americas was a commercial venture. By the time of Columbus's second voyage, the Spanish government was sufficiently concerned about the commercial aspect of his undertaking that treasury (*Hacienda*) representatives were sent to accompany him and a system was set up to govern any future commerce with the colonies. In 1503, the Spanish government established the *Casa de la Contratación de las Indias*, which governed all commercial transactions between Spain and her colonies. This body, established at Seville, remained there until the eighteenth century, when, due to the silting of the Guadalquivir River, the port was no longer accessible and the *Casa de la Contratación* was moved to Cadiz.

In 1519, the *Real y Supremo Consejo de las Indias* (Royal Supreme Council of the Indies) was organized in Madrid to control all governmental affairs and represent the Crown in the American colonies. As colonial government expanded, the various colonies were divided up into *virreinatos* (viceroyalties) and *provincias* (provinces). The *virreinatos* were presided over by a *virrey* (viceroy), who literally represented the king in those colonies. Each *virreinato* also had a legislative/judicial council known as the *audiencia*, which advised the viceroy and had both secondary and original jurisdictions and certain legislative powers. For most of colonial history, the major *virreinatos* were those of Mexico and Peru. They were further divided into *provincias* in which a governor and council held the administrative, legislative, and judicial functions concurrently.

Larger towns or districts were governed by the *alcalde mayor* or *corregidor*. Like the officials discussed earlier, these local officers were appointed by the Crown through the Council of the Indies. Each town also had a governing council called the *cabildo*, composed of a number of councilors as well as local magistrates, law enforcement officers, and royal treasury representatives.

Between 1764 and 1790, the Spanish Crown reorganized colonial government around larger, centralized units called *intendencias*.

All of these colonial divisions were supervised by the *Real Consejo de las Indias* in Madrid, which handled governmental affairs, and by the *Casa de la Contratación de las Indias* in Seville, which handled matters relating to commercial transactions. The latter was, in turn, directly supervised by the *Consejo de las Indias*. Therefore, if a court case arose on a local level, it could be appealed first to the *audiencia;* from there to the *virrey* or directly to the *Consejo de las Indias;* and ultimately to the *Consejo de Castilla* or to the king himself. This procedure applied not only to judicial matters, but to administrative and executive matters as well.

Various overviews of Spanish colonial institutions are found in *Spanish Empire in America* and *Northern New Spain: A Research Guide*.[3]

Ecclesiastical Divisions

The colonies continued the Catholic Church's policy of dividing ecclesiastical affairs into two categories: the organized Church under direction of the local bishop and the religious orders operating under direction of their superiors. In most cases, the frontier missions were organized by members of a religious order, generally Jesuits or Franciscans. Later, as Spanish civilians moved into an area, secular (not of the religious order) parishes were established under the direction of the nearest bishop, with each bishopric and the geographical area over which the bishop served known as a diocese.

Sacramental records can usually be located for the missions and parish churches in the current parish church or diocese to which that parish belongs. Numerous exceptions, of course, exist, where parish records have ended up in diocesan archives, religious order archives, other parishes, state archives, and even private collections, such as that of Yale University or the Huntington Library in California.

Spanish-Language Record Types

As Spain developed her colonies, bringing to them the institutions and activities of the Spanish homeland, basic colonial record types remained similar, if not identical, to those found in Spain itself. Uniformity of government control, as well as uniformity of religion, produced records that, from any colony, or even from Spain, differ only in small details rather than overall concepts necessary for doing research. This means that a beginning family history researcher can utilize materials written for Spain, Mexico, or anywhere else in South or Central America to become familiar with the standard content and format. This also means that even after the colonies' independence, the records in the former colonies tend to be relatively uniform in format and content because of the centralized control exercised by both church and state.

As a help in understanding the content of Spanish language records, the author recommends obtaining a copy of *Finding Your Hispanic Roots* by George R. Ryskamp.[4] Chapters 9 through 15 include sample documents with typed transcriptions in Spanish and translations in English. A survey of record types relating specifically to the Spanish colonial experience can be found on pages 13 through 17 of *Northern Spain: A Research Guide* by Thomas C. Barnes, Thomas H. Naylor, and Charles W. Fultzer. Further developing the ability to utilize particular Spanish records, that same volume contains a discussion of Spanish paleography (older handwriting systems) on pages 18 through 24, as does Chapter 7 of *Finding Your Hispanic Roots*. A helpful aid in learning to read the handwriting in Spanish Catholic Church records is *Spanish Records Extraction*, published by The Church of Jesus Christ of Latter-day Saints in 1981.

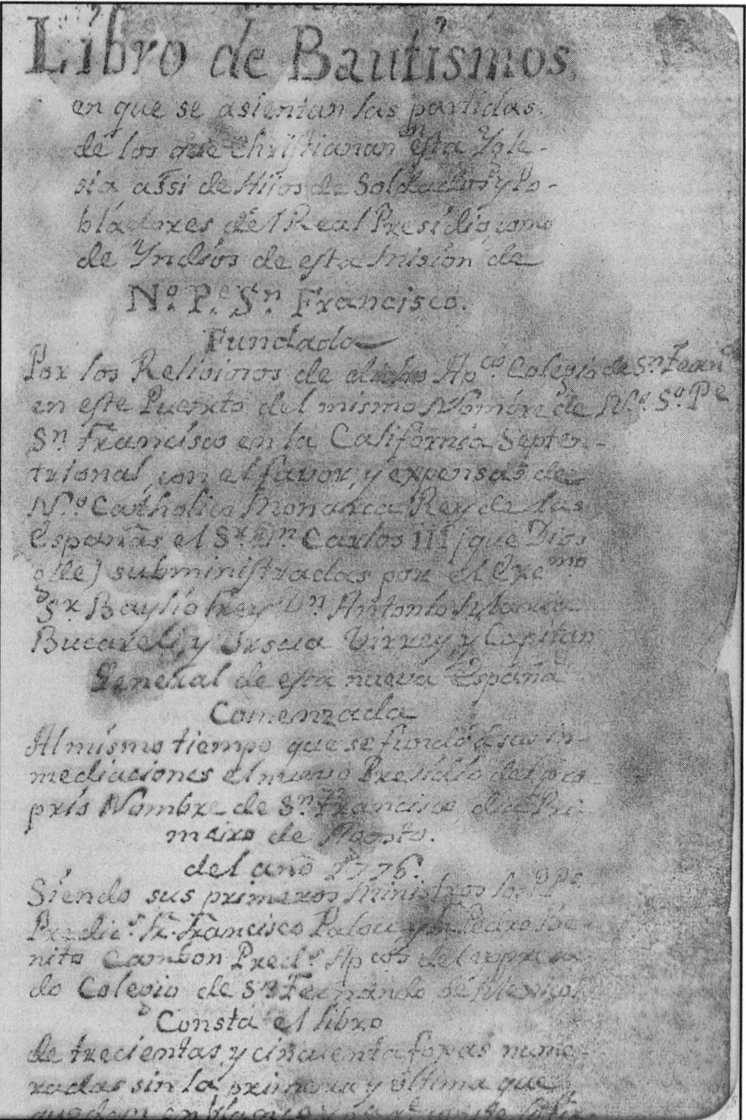
Libro de Bautismos
en que se asientan las partidas
de los que Christianan esta Yglesia assi de Hijos de Soldados y Pobladores del Real Presidio como
de Yndios de esta Mision de
N.º P.e S.n Francisco.
Fundado
Por los Religiosos de dicho Ap.co Colegio de S.n [illegible]
en este Puerto del mismo Nombre de N.º S.º P.e
S.n Francisco en la California Septentrional con el favor, y expensas de
N.ro Catholico Monarca Rey de las
Españas el S.r D.n Carlos III (que Dios le [illegible]) subministrados por el Ex.mo
S.r Baylio Frey D.n Antonio [illegible]
Bucareli y Ursua Virrey y Capitan
General de esta nueva España
Comenzada
Al mismo tiempo que se fundo [illegible] inmediaciones el nuevo Presidio del propio Nombre de S.n Francisco dia Primero de Agosto
del año 1776.
Siendo sus primeros Ministros los P.P.
Predic.s Fr. Francisco Palou y Fr. Pedro Benito Cambon Predic.s Ap.cos del [illegible]
do Colegio de S.n Fernando de Mexico
Consta el libro
de trecientas y cinquenta fojas numeradas sin la primera y ultima que
[illegible]

Figure 16-1. Title page for the first book of baptisms for the San Francisco, California, mission.

Catholic Sacramental Records

Whether generated by monks or friars presiding over missions or by secular priests presiding over organized parish churches, sacramental registers are nearly identical. Parish archives contain nine major categories of records: baptisms, marriages, death or burial records, confirmations, co-fraternity books, account books, censuses, individual documents, and local history materials. The records of the sacraments—the first four categories of baptisms, marriages, deaths, and confirmations—are found in nearly every mission or parish. Generally, they are divided into three separate books or sets of books, with confirmations appearing along with baptisms except in very large parishes. In smaller parishes and in earlier years, all three of the records may have been kept in the same book, although generally within separate sections. Figure 16-1 shows the title page for the first book of baptisms for the San Francisco, California, mission.

Marriage records are especially valuable, as a marriage entry in a Spanish colonial parish usually contains the names and surnames of the bride and groom with an indication of their professions, residences, birthplaces, ages at the time of marriage, parents' names, racial descriptions of the parties, date the marriage was celebrated, name of the parish, and name of the priest performing the marriage. The record also states whether the three canonical admonitions (similar to the English banns) were published or dispensed with. In addition to the above, the marriage certificate records any special difficulties or circumstances surrounding the event. For example, on some occasions there may have been an objection or impediment to the marriage necessitating an apostolic dispensation.

In many cases, marriage records are missing details such as the ages of the bride or groom. Nevertheless, the parents' names are given (although not often in the case of a second marriage) and, frequently, the parents' residence and/or birthplace of the groom. Obviously, this information is particularly valuable as it may be the only clue regarding the town of origin of the male ancestor. The town of origin of the female ancestor in a marriage is usually known, because the vast majority of all marriages are performed in the parish of the woman. The significant value of a marriage entry is illustrated by figure 16-2, a page of marriage entries from the St. Louis Cathedral, New Orleans, Louisiana, during the Spanish period.[5] Note several grooms' birthplaces are shown.

Some parish records will have collections of separate, individual documents, including *testamentos* (wills), *capellanias* (special grants given to the parish in the form of land, money, or other property by its members), *pleitos* (litigation papers), and *expedientes matrimoniales* (marriage petitions containing copies of baptismal records filed by the bride and groom at the time they were requesting marriage).

Frequently, the priest recognized that his sacramental books were documents that would be preserved for centuries and, as a result, made notes about historical moments of particular interest or times and events of national importance. In working through the pages of parish records, watch for these items, such as the date on which the first stone was laid for the building of a new sacristy, visits of important individuals, or tragic events such as fires, floods, or droughts and their impact on the people of the parish. For example, in New Orleans the priest recorded the transfer of the colony to representatives of the Congress of the United States of America in 1803 in his baptismal register. All of these local history materials provide great insight into the lives of one's ancestors and can add significant color and human dimension to the family's history.

PAGE 138

DON MARTIN PALAO, native of Barcelona, Capital of the Principality of Cataluna in Spain, widower of DONA MARTINA PRIETO, son of the Captain of the Army DON MARTIN FERRI PALAO and of DONA ANTONIA PRATS
Married August 20, 1801
DONA ROSALIA ANDRY native this city, widow of DON JOSE VILLABASO the Administrator of the Royal Rents of this Province, daughter of DON LUIS ANDRY and of DONA JUANA LAPIERRE.
Witnesses: Don Antonio Palao and Don Jose Cruzat brother-in-law of the contracting, Dona Juana Lapierre and Don Gilberto Andry, mother and brother of the contracting.

DON ANDRES GONZALES de VILLAMIL native of the Parish of St. Cecilia de Seares, of Castropol, Principality of Asterias in Spain son of DON JUAN GONZALES de VILLAMIL and of DONA JOSEFA LOPEZ de ACEVEDO
Married September 15, 1801
DONA VERONICA CAMBRE native of the Parish of St. John the Baptist, Second German Coast, daughter of DON MIGUEL CAMBRE and of DONA CATARINA JACOBO.
Witnesses: Don Juan Bautista Rolland, Don Juan Bautista Duet and Don Jose Joaquin Velasquez, Dona Babe Cambre sister to the bride.

DON LEONARDO WILTZ native this city son of DON JUAN BAUTISTA WILTZ and of DONA SUSANA LANGLISE
Married October 26, 1801
DONA MARIA PIGUERY native this church parish, daughter of DON ANTONIO JOSE PIGUERY and of DONA MARIA FRANCISCA DASPIT.
Witnesses: Don Andres Chastan, Don Juan Bautista Jourdan, Don Manuel Toledano and Don Juan Bautista Wiltz father of the contracting.

MIGUEL MILLAR native of Santa Cruz de Meche in Galicia, Spain, son of NICOLAS MILLAR and of ANGELA FREYRE
Married November 1, 1801
ANTONIA ABREU native of this city daughter of ANTONIO ABREU and of AGUSTINA DIAS.
Witnesses: Don Fernando and Dona Josefa Moreno and Antonio Munos.

PAGE 139

DON JUAN MARIA CASTAREDE, native of Fleurance in France, son of DON PEDRO CASTAREDE and of DONA JUANA PIS
Married November 3, 1801
DONA HANRRIETA DEGRUYS DUFFOSAR native this city daughter of DON ANTONIO DEGRUYS DUFFOSAR and of DONA HANRRIETA LEISARD.
Witnesses: Don Domingo Meyronne, Don Juan Bautista Labatut and Don Miguel Girodel.

DON JUAN CANON native this city son of DON JUAN CANON and of DONA FELICITE AMELOT
Married November 3, 1801
DONA EULALIA BEAUMONDE, widow of DON LORENZO TRUAVILLE DUVORD, daughter of DON JUAN BEAUMONDE LIVAUDAIS and of DONA AGATA DUFFOSSAT.

91

Figure 16-2. A page of marriage entries from the St. Louis Cathedral, New Orleans, Louisiana, during the Spanish period. Note several grooms' birthplaces are shown.

Censuses (Padrones)

As the reforms of King Charles III extended into the administration of the Spanish colonies, the Council of Indies initiated a series of empire-wide census projects. Previously, some governors in specific colonies and even local officials had censuses prepared, resulting in numerous censuses available for the Spanish colonial areas. *Latin American Census Records* by Lyman D. Platt identifies by specific locality the vast majority of those available.[6]

Spanish censuses are considerably better in detail than their English-language counterparts, normally identifying the head of household by name and surname with occupation and material status and age, and then providing for the household a list of all other members by name, frequently with ages and relationships to the head of household. Some censuses were taken to enumerate specific categories of individuals, such as all resident aliens. Figure 16-3 is a page from the abstract of such a census, that of St. Augustine, Florida, 1786, appearing in *Floridas' First Families: Translated Abstracts of Pre-1821 Spanish Censuses*, by Donna Rachal Mills. For a detailed discussion of the content and use of censuses in Hispanic research, see *Finding Your Hispanic Roots*.

Civil Legal Documents

Notarial Records

As the Spanish colonies moved beyond the initial frontier stage, legal documents were recorded by *escribanos*, or notaries. A summary of the kind of document that would appear in a notary archive indicates a wealth of information for the family historian: wills, adoptions, emancipations, sales of rural and urban land, construction of buildings, proof of purity of blood, nobility records, transfers of titles, dowries, rescue of captives, sales of slaves, marriage contracts, sales of cloth, sales of horses, printing of books, apprenticeship records, contracts with professionals, land titles, executions, inventories of decedents' estates, guardianship estates, mining claims, powers of attorney, and many others.

Lawsuits

Petitions or lawsuits filed as part of the governmental apparatus frequently appear in collections of civil legal documents retained in colonial archives. In some cases, these were lawsuits in the sense that they involved a dispute between two civil parties. In others, they were petitions requesting governmental approval or the granting of privileges, somewhat similar to probate or guardianship petitions in today's courts. Generally, those labeled *petición* were of the type requesting governmental service or approval. A *demanda* was a claim—usually against a third party—relating to a contract or other dispute, the initial document in a litigation action. Similarly, a *diligencia* represents the final order or response of the responsible person to one of the above.

Military Records

Military records of particular interest to the family historian fall into three categories: administrative records of the local presidio or fort; service records (*hojas de servicio*); and censuses (*padrones*).

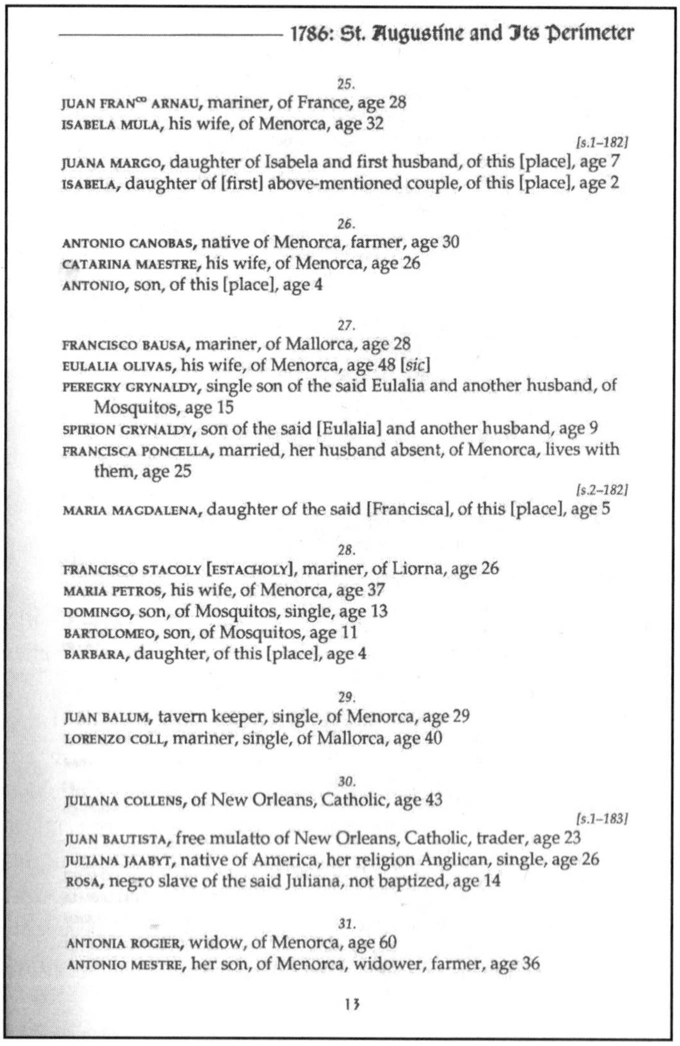

1786: St. Augustine and Its Perimeter

25.

JUAN FRAN^{co} ARNAU, mariner, of France, age 28
ISABELA MULA, his wife, of Menorca, age 32

[s.1–182]

JUANA MARGO, daughter of Isabela and first husband, of this [place], age 7
ISABELA, daughter of [first] above-mentioned couple, of this [place], age 2

26.

ANTONIO CANOBAS, native of Menorca, farmer, age 30
CATARINA MAESTRE, his wife, of Menorca, age 26
ANTONIO, son, of this [place], age 4

27.

FRANCISCO BAUSA, mariner, of Mallorca, age 28
EULALIA OLIVAS, his wife, of Menorca, age 48 [*sic*]
PEREGRY GRYNALDY, single son of the said Eulalia and another husband, of Mosquitos, age 15
SPIRION GRYNALDY, son of the said [Eulalia] and another husband, age 9
FRANCISCA PONCELLA, married, her husband absent, of Menorca, lives with them, age 25

[s.2–182]

MARIA MAGDALENA, daughter of the said [Francisca], of this [place], age 5

28.

FRANCISCO STACOLY [ESTACHOLY], mariner, of Liorna, age 26
MARIA PETROS, his wife, of Menorca, age 37
DOMINGO, son, of Mosquitos, single, age 13
BARTOLOMEO, son, of Mosquitos, age 11
BARBARA, daughter, of this [place], age 4

29.

JUAN BALUM, tavern keeper, single, of Menorca, age 29
LORENZO COLL, mariner, single, of Mallorca, age 40

30.

JULIANA COLLENS, of New Orleans, Catholic, age 43

[s.1–183]

JUAN BAUTISTA, free mulatto of New Orleans, Catholic, trader, age 23
JULIANA JAABYT, native of America, her religion Anglican, single, age 26
ROSA, negro slave of the said Juliana, not baptized, age 14

31.

ANTONIA ROGIER, widow, of Menorca, age 60
ANTONIO MESTRE, her son, of Menorca, widower, farmer, age 36

13

Figure 16-3. A page from the abstract of the census of St. Augustine, Florida, 1786, appearing in *Floridas' First Families: Translated Abstracts of Pre-1821 Spanish Censuses*, by Donna Rachal Mills.

Administrative records are generally reports by military commanders and notices of transfers, purchases of supplies, and other routine activities. It was also necessary during a military campaign to prepare an *auto de guerra* (order of war). *Northern New Spain, a Research Guide* identifies and describes the following sections of an *auto de guerra*:

- A description of an event necessitating military action by the Spaniards, frequently a type of Indian uprising or the decision to establish a Spanish presence in a new area.
- Reports of preliminary actions by individuals or presidio patrols.
- Orders from the governor giving direction as to a military response to be taken. Generally, local initiative was not encouraged, and no action, unless absolutely necessary, would take place until the governor—and, in many cases, the viceroy or even the Council of Indies in Spain—had responded.
- Field diaries of commanders and other documents such as letters or statements from citizens describing the military engagements once troops were placed in action.
- Final assessments by the officials who requested and/or ordered the action to be taken once the campaign was concluded.

Service records (*hojas de servicio*) form a significant part of military records. A service record relates to a specific individual, usually an officer of the rank of sergeant or above, giving his name, rank, place of origin, age, and, in some cases, parents' names. The document will then set forth the time periods in which he served in particular places and/or ranks and give a written summary of his service, highlighting important campaigns and locations where he has served. Figure 16-4 shows the military service record for Felipe Treviño, who served in Havana, Cuba, and Pensacola, Florida.

Census records of military personnel are, in reality, a class of administrative records, generally containing a list of officers and soldiers serving in a presidio at a particular date, with the name and rank of each individual. Many times, however, they include lists of families of the soldiers also residing in the presidio. In such cases, relationships to the individual soldiers as well as ages are frequently given. Figure 16-5 is the initial entry of such a census report for the Mobile Company of San Carlos de Parras, Texas, dated 1 January 1807.[7]

Catholic Church Diocesan Records

The dioceses (bishoprics) of the Catholic Church generated a variety of administrative and canon law documents, as did the colleges, or central headquarters, of the various religious orders. Each college or diocese will have personnel records of the monks or secular priests who served within that jurisdiction, generally providing the birthplace and parentage of the individual cleric. Records such as marriage dispensations, ordinations of priests, censuses of communicants, tithing payment records, and records of bishop's visits may be found in the diocesan archives for the particular diocese to which a parish belonged when the record would have been generated.

Marriage dispensations can prove particularly valuable to the family historian. Under Catholic canon law, a number of impediments to marriage may be dispensed with or forgiven by the bishop, including relationships within the fourth degree of consanguinity (blood relationship) or affinity (relationship by marriage) as well as spiritual relationships such as a godparent. In addition, if an individual came from a residence not within the diocese, a dispensation was required. There are also dispensations that do not relate to marriage records, including a number that may be required for an individual to receive the priesthood. An excellent discussion of those records and detailed analysis of the parts thereof can be found in *Index to the Marriage Investigations of Diocese of Guadalajara, Provinces of Coahuila, Nuevo León, Nuevo Santander, Texas, Volume 1: 1653–1750*, which contains marriage dispensations for the state of Texas and related states in Mexico for the period of 1653–1750.[8] A general discussion of diocesan records is found in Chapter 11 of *Finding Your Hispanic Roots*.

A marriage dispensation record generally outlines the relationship of the individuals involved, in many cases extending backward into the third or fourth generation (to a common great-grandparent), with extensive genealogical data. In those cases where there is a relationship by affinity with a deceased spouse, that spouse will also be identified and the date of death and burial provided. Where the petition is for dispensation because the groom is from outside the diocese, the year and place of birth will be given as well as information concerning the arrival date and even the ship taken to the New World. Although the ultimate dispensation was issued by the bishop and, therefore, these records are contained in the diocesan archives, they are intensely local in nature, generally involving families who have resided in a given locality for several generations. Although somewhat difficult to use because of the length and variety of each document as well as the general lack of indexes to the records, the treasure of information found in a single marriage investigation makes the search well worth it.

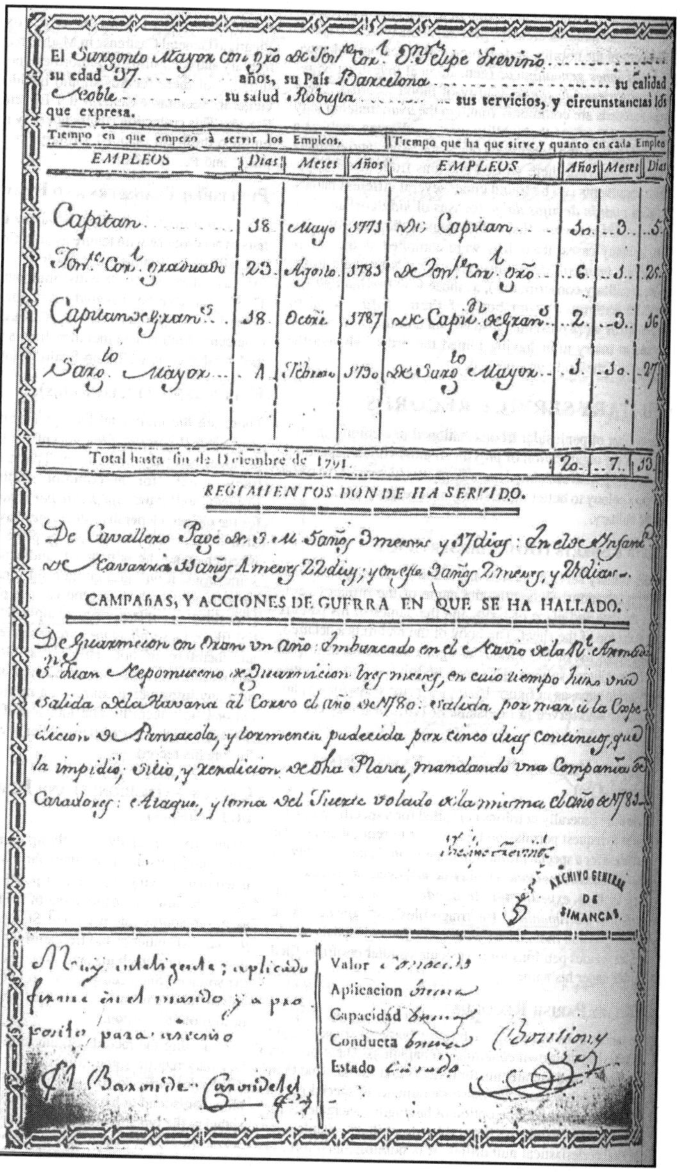

El Sargento Mayor con grado de Ten^te Cor^l D^n Felipe Treviño.......... su edad 37 ..... años, su País Barcelona .... su calidad Noble .... su salud Robusta .... sus servicios, y circunstancias los que expresa.

Tiempo en que empezó à servir los Empleos. | Tiempo que ha que sirve y quanto en cada Empleo

EMPLEOS	Dias	Meses	Años	EMPLEOS	Años	Meses	Dias
Capitan	18	Mayo	1773	de Capitan	10	3	5
Ten^te Cor^l graduado	23	Agosto	1783	de Ten^te Cor^l grado	6	1	25
Capitan de Granad^s	18	Octre.	1787	de Capit^n de Granad^s	2	3	16
Sarg^to Mayor	1	Febrero	1790	de Sarg^to Mayor	1	10	27
Total hasta fin de Diciembre de 1791.					20	7	13

REGIMIENTOS DONDE HA SERVIDO.

De Cavallero Paje de S. M. 5 años 3 meses y 17 dias: In el de Infant^a de Havana 13 años 1 mes y 22 dias; y en esta 3 años 2 meses, y 21 dias.

CAMPAñAS, Y ACCIONES DE GUERRA EN QUE SE HA HALLADO.

De Guarnicion en Oran un año: Embarcado en el Navio de la R^l Armada S^n Juan Nepomuceno de Guarnicion tres meses, en cuio tiempo hizo una salida de la Havana al Corso el año de 1780: salida por mar à la Expedicion de Panzacola, y tormenta padecida por cinco dias continuos que la impidio: sitio, y rendicion de dha Plaza, mandando una Compañia de Cazadores: Ataque, y toma del Fuerte volado de la misma el año de 1781.

ARCHIVO GENERAL DE SIMANCAS

Muy inteligente; aplicado firme en el mando y a proposito para ascenso

Valor conocido
Aplicacion buena
Capacidad buena
Conducta buena
Estado casado

Figure 16-4.
The military service record for Felipe Treviño, who served in Havana, Cuba, and Pensacola, Florida.

Diocesan records are both extensive and available to the public. For example, the archdiocese of Durango, begun in 1606, has an archival collection of 1,120,000 pages—three percent from the 1600s, thirty-two percent from the 1700s, and fifty-nine percent from the 1800s. The entire collection has been microfilmed by the Rio Grande Historical Collections, held at New Mexico State University in Las Cruces. Jack Calligan has published two volumes transcribing New Mexico dispensations in the collection.[9]

Records of the diocese of Guadalajara have been microfilmed by the Genealogical Society of Utah. Marriage dispensations and some other documentation for the decade during which the diocese of Louisiana and Florida was in existence are available on microfilm at the University of Notre Dame. A guide exists for the twelve rolls of microfilm, as well as an index prepared by Elizabeth Gianelloni. Most of the colonial records for the dioceses of Monterrey, Nuevo Leon, and Hermosillo, Sonora, have been lost. The few remaining records from the diocese of Hermosillo, Sonora, have been filmed as part of the University

Census Report of the Mobile Company of San Carlos de Parras, January 1, 1807.
Census of the number of souls in the aforesaid company and their families (sic) on this date, giving their rank.

Rank	Name	M	W	B	G	S	WS	T
Captain	Don Sebastian RODRIGUEZ, 38 yrs. of age, unmarried	1						1
Lieutenant	Vacant							
1st Alferez	Don Jose Antonio AGUILAR, 53 yrs. of age, unmarried	1						1
Chaplain	Don Jose Angel CABAZOS	1						1
Gunsmith	Norato de LUNA, 37 yrs. of age; married to Maria Francisca SOTO, 26 yrs. of age.	1	1					2
Sergeants	Vizente TARIN, 46 yrs. of age; widower.	1						1
	Jose CORONA, 43 yrs. of age; married to Martina URTADO, 41 yrs. one son, 10 yrs. of age, and one daughter, 18 yrs. of age.	1	1	1	1			4
	Martin VALENZUELA, 41 yrs.of age; married to Maria Ysavel VALDES, Spaniard, 28 yrs. of age; three daughters, 12, 3 and 3 yrs. of age, one Spanish woman servant, 29 yrs.	1	1		3		1	6
Drummer	Jose GONZALES, 17 yrs. of age; unmarried.	1						1
Corporals	Rafael SOTO, 41 yrs. of age; unmarried.	1						1
	Jose NAVA, 58 yrs. of age; widower, two daughters, 7 and 4 yrs. old.	1			2			3
	Yldefonso GALVIS, 53 yrs. of age; unmarried.	1						1
	Timoteo NUNEZ, 31 yrs. of age; unmarried.	1						1
	Jose CHACON, 30 yrs. of age; unmarried.	1						1
	Jose ALVARADO, 36 yrs. of age; married to Francisca MARRUJO, coyota, 27 yrs. old; one son 10 yrs. old, one daughter, 9 yrs.	1	1	1	1			4
	Pedro CAMUNEZ, 25 yrs. of age; married to Maria Ygnacia SOTO; mestiza, 16 yrs. old.	1	1					2
Cadets	Don Jose Maria UGARTECHEA, 19 yrs. old; unmarried.	1						1
Soldiers	Jose LOPEZ, 39 yrs. old; married to Martina ADAMS, coyota, 38 yrs; one daughter, 2 yrs. old.	1	1		1			3
	Antonio GARCIA, 39 yrs. of age; widower.	1						1
	Jose PENASLAS (?), 50 yrs. old; unmarried.	1						1
	Juan MORGA, 33 yrs. old; single.	1						1
	Jose TORRES, 35 yrs. old; married to Rafaela RAMIREZ, Indian, 22 yrs. old; two sons, 3 and 2 yrs. old.	1	1	2				4
	Jose LAZARIN, 40 yrs. old; married to Juana Maria RIVAS, coyota, 25 yrs. old; 3 sons, 10, 7 and 6, and 2 daughters, 3 and 1 yr. old.	1	1	3	2			7
	Julian REYES, 38 yrs. of age; married to Micaela RAMIREZ, Spaniard, 28 yrs. old; 1 daughter 6 yrs. old.	1	1		1			3
	Antonio VIELMA, 26 yrs. old, widower.	1						1

1

Figure 16-5. The initial entry of a census report for the Mobile Company of San Carlos de Parras, Texas, dated 1 January 1807.

of Arizona Film Collection #811. The following descriptions identify the geographical areas of the dioceses to which the modern-day states within the United States belonged during their history as part of the Spanish Empire and/or the Mexican Republic.[10]

Arizona

The missions in Arizona were under control of the Jesuits from 1731 to 1767. Following the Jesuit expulsion from the Spanish Empire in 1767 until sometime after 1780, the missions were run by Franciscans from the Franciscan college at Queretaro, Mexico. From 1780 to 1868, the area of Arizona was part of the diocese of Sonora. It should also be noted that during the time period when the area was under the control of missions, the Bishop of Durango made a number of attempts to obtain control of this area. It is possible, therefore, that during the time period 1731 to 1780, there may be Church records concerning Arizona in the diocesan archives of Durango.

California

From the founding of San Diego in 1769 until 1779, California belonged to the diocese of Guadalajara, when it then became part of the diocese of Sonora until 1836. At that time California was divided into two dioceses: San Diego and Los Angeles.

Florida

Both east and west Florida, including what is now the Gulf Coast area of Alabama, belonged to the Santiago de Cuba diocese from 1565 until 1787, when the Havana, Cuba, diocese was created. It remained part of the Havana diocese until 1793 when the diocese of Louisiana and Florida was created. Florida then continued in that diocese until the 1803 transfer of the Louisiana area to the United States. From then until sometime between 1810 and 1821, depending on which part of Florida remained under Spanish dominion, the area belonged to the diocese of Havana, Cuba.

Louisiana

Louisiana was part of the diocese of Quebec, Canada, from 1659 to 1771. With the transfer of Louisiana to Spain, including the entire Mississippi River Valley and the West Florida parishes on the Gulf Coast up to and including parts of modern-day Mississippi, Louisiana became part of the diocese of Santiago de Cuba from 1771 until 1787. As with Florida, Louisiana became part of the creation of the diocese of Havana, Cuba, in 1787 and remained part of that diocese until 1793. From that time until 1803, it formed part of the diocese of Louisiana and Florida. Parts of the Gulf Coast that made up the West Florida parishes and what is now the present-day Gulf Coast area of Mississippi became part of the diocese of Havana, Cuba, in 1803 until takeover by the United States.

New Mexico

From its founding in 1598 until 1620, New Mexico belonged to the diocese of Guadalajara, Mexico. With the creation of the diocese of Durango in 1620, New Mexico became part of that diocese, where it remained until 1850. It should be noted, however, that in many cases the thousand miles of distance between Durango and Sante Fe caused diocesan affairs to be handled at a local level, resulting in a number of records typically found in the diocese, including marriage dispensations, found in the records of the modern diocese of Sante Fe instead. It should also be noted that, in the early years, the missions of New Mexico were under control of the Franciscans.

Texas

From 1703 to 1777, Texas was part of the diocese of Guadalajara, and from that date until 1836, it belonged to the diocese of Linares. Likewise, the portion of Texas south of the Nueces River retained by Mexico until the war with the United States ended in 1848 also belonged to the diocese of Linares. The El Paso area was not originally part of the Spanish province of Texas and Coahuila but formed part of the province of Chihuahua until 1840. It formed part of the diocese of Durango from 1620 until 1846.

Spanish Land Records for the United States

To promote settlement, the Spanish and Mexican governments liberally dispensed land grants. The procedure for obtaining a grant involved applying to the governor, who then sent an order of approval to a local officer to make an examination, survey, and appraisal of the land tract before placing it in the applicant's possession. The notary recorded the receipt of the order and, with the commissioned officer and petitioner, certified the act. A visual inspection, survey, and demarcation of the tract was then made by the local officer, the applicant, appraisers, witnesses, and adjacent landowners. Finally, a written report of the proceedings, in which the applicant was put into possession, was prepared. All of these documents constituted the owner's title, which for Texas, New Mexico, Arizona, and California had to be approved by the viceroy of New Spain at Mexico City.

Land record files, or *expedientes*, were archived locally and sent to Mexico City, New Orleans, or Cuba. During Spanish rule, local officials permitted settlers to occupy land long before the legal requirements had been fulfilled. Surveys were generally not made and title papers not completed, so the *expedientes* remained incomplete. Transfers, exchanges, donations, and partitions of land were made before the local *alcalde* or provincial governor, then recorded in their archives. Because boundaries of the grants were natural landmarks and very vague, and because final title papers were often not issued, controversies would inevitably arise. Disputes over titles to lands, boundaries, and water rights were heard by the same officials, and eventually those documents were filed in the same local archives.

Spanish land grant records contain a variety of documents, including the following:

- Acts of possession
- Boundary proceedings
- Circular letters
- Correspondence
- Decrees
- Decisions and reports of the departmental assembly
- Claims for lands
- Compromises
- Controversies of land
- Confirmations of grants
- Conveyances
- Copartnerships
- Deeds
- Distributions of estates
- Donations of lands
- Dowers
- Exchanges
- Gifts and grants
- Grants of lead mines
- Inventories and partitions of estates
- Lawsuits
- Laws and regulations relating to lands
- Letters
- Mining regulations
- Mining suits
- Mortgages
- Orders for possession
- Orders for the settlement of towns
- Partitions of lands
- Petitions for land
- Petitions for permission to remove
- Powers of attorney
- Proceedings for locations
- Proceedings regarding contested wills
- Proceedings regarding the establishment of towns
- Proceedings regarding the settlement of estates
- Protests against the sale of lands
- Registrations of mines
- Reports
- Revocations of grants
- Titles
- Trespasses
- Wills

Beginning with Louisiana in 1803 and ending with the Gadsden Purchase in 1853, each of the former Spanish colonial areas were transferred to the United States as a result of treaties specifically providing for the legal recognition of titles to land owned by individual Spanish or Mexican citizens and others under Spanish and/or Mexican authority. Similarly, each treaty provided for the handing over of land title documents from Spanish archives to the American authorities. In most cases, such as in New Mexico, the archives were seized by the Americans at the time of conquest and retained *in situ*. In Florida, the withdrawing Spanish officials packed up the materials and shipped them back to Cuba.

In each of the former Spanish colonies, a board of land commissioners was established by the U.S. government for the purpose of evaluating land claims and determining their validity. As each board of commissioners completed its work on a claim, it filed a detailed report of its final determinations.

These procedures were followed in Texas without federal intervention as the determination of land claims was made initially by the Republic of Texas and, subsequently, as all public lands remained in the hands of the state after annexation by the state government of Texas. There, land records acquired by the General Land Office have been classified, indexed, and bound into 175 volumes, covering the years 1720 to 1836.

The two books mentioned previously by Henry Putney Beers will prove helpful in describing the great variety of land documents for all states but Florida. Those interested in Florida land records should consult *Spanish Land Grants in Florida, Volume 1, Unconfirmed Claims: A–C.*[11] Each of the above sources describes existing documentation in land grant files and the process whereby the grant was reviewed and confirmed, as well as the history of the obtaining, retaining, or recapturing of the original Spanish documentation. Each also serves as a starting point for using these claims as they appear in the following:

American State Papers: Documents, Legislative and Executive of the Congress of the United States. 38 vols. Washington: Gales and Seaton, 1832–61.

American State Papers: Public Lands and Claims. 9 vols. Reprint, Greenville, S.C.: Southern Historical Press, 1994.

McMullin, Phillip W., ed. *Grassroots of America, A Computerized Index to the American State Papers: Land Grants and Claims (1789–1837)*. Reprint, Conway, Ark.: Arkansas Research, 1990. Originally published 1972, by Gendex Corporation, Salt Lake City.

The short abstracts in the American State Papers do not adequately describe the potential richness of documentation of a land claim file, which may contain any, and in some fortunate circumstances all, of the following:

1. A petition, generally in Spanish, to the Spanish governor requesting land.
2. The governor's order requesting testimony or information concerning the petitioner.
3. Responsive documentation to the request for testimony, usually identifying family, slaves, ages, and other pertinent information concerning the ability to work the land.
4. A certificate of service indicating the reason for the particular claim, generally showing military or public service by the petitioner.
5. A grant by the governor or the captain general, and a notarial attestation thereof.
6. In those cases where the grant of land was conditional, such as requiring cultivation and/or habitation for a certain time, there may follow a report on the fulfilling of the conditions and a granting of absolute property rights.
7. A verification of the documentation in Spanish by the U.S. government official.
8. A warrant or order of survey.
9. The survey plat.
10. Deeds of sales, gifts, wills, requests, and exchanges showing the subsequent passage of property from the original grant deed to the then current claimant.
11. An application to the U.S. Board of Commissioners for recognition of the claim.
12. The decree of the commissioners or proceedings of the U.S. courts approving or denying the claim.

It should be stressed that the specific documentation, order of presentation of the documents, and the very existence of documents will vary dramatically from one file to another, but the genealogical potential is so rich that it justifies the search.

Locating Colonial Records of Genealogical Value

Describing the location of all of the varied materials available for the Spanish and French colonial periods with an accompanying bibliography of guidebooks, inventories, indexes, and published transcripts is far beyond the scope of this chapter. Rather, descriptions of the archives, libraries, and microfilm collections where a majority of those records may be found, as well as useful Internet sites, appear in this section, followed by specific descriptions of local civil records, census records, and Catholic Church parish records on a state-by-state basis.

Archives in Spain

The archives of Spain are rich in material about the colonial period in the United States. That treasure house has been mined for decades, and excellent guides, indexes, and inventories have been prepared, some to collections in the archives generally, others aimed specifically at the Americas and even at particular regions in the United States. Description of these archives and their collections, including virtual visits, can be found at <www.cultura.mecd.es/archivos/>; computerized access to these collections is available at <www.aer.es>. The following three are the most important, both in quality and quantity of their collections relating to the U.S. Spanish colonial period, but literally hundreds of other libraries and archives in Spain have collections with materials relating to the Americas.[12]

Archivo General de Indias, Seville, Spain, is the primary archive for Spanish colonial documents. Governmental, judicial, commercial, and military records for all of the colonies in the Americas are found here. Local government reports, passenger lists, censuses, and a multitude of other records, often intimately local in nature, are found here. Of particular interest are the *Papeles de Cuba* section, which contains extensive documentation relating to Florida and Louisiana, and the various subsections in the *Gobierno, Justicia,* and *Contratación* sections that relate to New Spain.[13]

Archivo General de Simancas, Valladolid, Spain, is the oldest national archives in Europe. In 1790, all of the sections relating entirely and specifically to the administration of the colonies were sent to Seville to create the *Archivo General de Indias*. There remain, however, many records relating to the Americas that were integrated in collections that covered all of the functions of Spanish government.[14] Notable are those for *Títulos de Indias,*[15] describing appointments to numerous government positions in what is now the United States, and *Hojas de Sevicio Militar en América,* which includes military officers' personnel sheets from posts stretching from Saint Augustine, Florida, to San Francisco, California.[16]

Archivo General de Segovia, Segovia, Spain, as Spain's premier military archive, contains material about military operations in the New World. Of particular interest is the fully indexed section dealing with officers' service files, which includes many who served in military posts in what is now the United States.[17]

Archives in France

Many French archives have material relating to Louisiana and Quebec.[18] Of interest are the Department Archives in port cities such as La Rochelle and those of the navy. By far the largest collections of such materials is found in the:

Le Centre des Archives d'Outre-Mer (CAOM), Aix-en-Provence, France. This is the archive for records of the French overseas ministry and the former French colonies, including Louisiana and Quebec.[19]

Archives in Cuba

Archivo Nacional de Cuba, Havana, Cuba. Although not currently available to U.S. researchers, the national archives of Cuba has many documents relating to Louisiana and Florida.[20]

Archives in Mexico

Archivo General de la Nacion, Mexico City, Mexico. Censuses, correspondence, reports, and diaries concerning political and financial administration, military affairs, ecclesiastical affairs, relations with indigenous peoples, explorations, expeditions, mining, and much more are all found in this collection. Originating as the archives of the viceroy of New Spain, this is the richest collection of Spanish Colonial materials concerning the United States, consisting of 115 record groups containing more than 41,000 volumes.[21]

Those working in the Southwest should be sure to search the excellent index now available online at <www.agn.gob.mx>, especially for the *Californias* and *Provincias Internas* sections.

The Mexican states of Tamaulipas, Nuevo Leon, Coahuila, Sonora, and Baja California all have state archives with material relating to the southwestern United States. Chihuahua and Sonora have notarial archives with relevant materials.[22]

The large and growing set of digital documents and images is at <www.agn.gob.mx/inicio.php?cu=ic&sc=ic>.

Libraries and Archives in the United States

Universities and other libraries and archives in the United States have collected large amounts of materials relating to the Spanish and French colonial periods. Many are copies or transcripts of those found in foreign archives, as well as originals acquired by Anglo-American document collectors in the past. As a researcher moves beyond the basics of parish and census research, the catalogs for these collections should be consulted. In each case, a website is provided to gain more information about these collections, and many offer catalogs, indexes, and even digital documents.

Family History Library, Salt Lake City, Utah. The world's largest collection of microfilms of original documents of genealogical value, the FHL has microfilms of many of the records described elsewhere in this chapter. Anyone researching Spanish colonial records should check to see what is available here, as most can be sent to a local Family History Center for minimal cost. Go to <www.familysearch.org> under Family History Library Catalog, and check for any record source mentioned under "place search" using first the town, then the county, then the state to search for records during the colonial period. If all else fails, try a creative search using keywords.

University of Texas, El Paso, has microfilm holdings relating to the Borderlands area that number over 160 sets, including copies purchased from other microfilming sources such as the University of Texas at Austin, the National Archives, and so forth. For details, go to <www.utep.edu/border>.

University of Texas, Austin has two very large collections containing Borderlands materials: Nettie Lee Benson Latin American Collections (<www.lib.utexas.edu/benson>) and the Center for American History's Research and Collections Division (<www.cah.utexas.edu/divisions/Austin.html>).

University of California, Berkeley. The Bancroft Collection provides original and secondary materials in a variety of formats to support research in the history of the American

West, Mexico, and Central America, with greatest emphasis on California and Mexico from the period of European exploration and settlement onward. For details go to <http://bancroft.berkeley.edu/collections/bancroft.html>.

National Archives, Washington, D.C., has materials concerning those portions of the United States under Spanish or French control during the colonial period.[23] Go to <www.archives.gov/research/tools> for details.

University of Notre Dame, South Bend, Indiana, has manuscripts documenting the history of the Catholic Church in the United States, including correspondence of early missionary bishops, papers of prominent Catholic religious and lay people, and records of significant Catholic organizations, including the originals or microfilms of records for many Catholic colonial parishes and the diocese of Louisiana and Florida. Go to <www.nd.edu/~archives>.

The Documentary Relations of the Southwest (DRSW), Arizona State Museum, University of Arizona, Tucson, Arizona, houses an extensive collection of microfilm relating to the Southwest. Online at <www.statemuseum.arizona.edu/oer/index.shtml>, one can access the *Master Bibliography and Indexes,* which contains over 17,000 records. These records describe an estimated total of 500,000 pages of primary documents dealing with the greater Southwest from 1520 to 1820, which corresponds to the Spanish Colonial era. Documents included cover an extensive geographical area bounded by the 22nd to the 38th parallel of north latitude and by the 92nd to the 123rd meridian of west longitude. This approximates the colonial frontiers of northern New Spain. The documents indexed come from a total of thirty-one archives in Europe and the Americas, including significant materials from the following archives: *Archivo General de Indias* (AGI-Sevilla); *Provincias Internas of Mexico City's Archivo General de la Nación* (AGN-Mexico City); Spanish Archives of New Mexico (Santa Fe, Mexico); Archivo de San Antonio de Béxar (to 1790) (University of Texas, Austin); *Archivo de Hidalgo del Parral* (Parral, Chihuahua); as well as fifteen smaller archives.

Yale University, New Haven, Connecticut. The Latin American Collection of the University Library has the oldest Latin American manuscript collection in the United States, as well as approximately 435,000 printed volumes, plus newspapers and microfilms. Go to <www.yale.edu/las/lcollections.html> for more detail.

Records of Texas

At the time of its independence in 1836, Texas did not include the area south of the Nueces River, then part of the Mexican state of Tamaulipas, or the western area around El Paso, then part of New Mexico. While under Mexican rule, Texas was divided into two provinces: one on the west with its capital in San Antonio and the other in east Texas with its capital in Nacogdoches. Both were part of the larger state of Coahuila-Texas, with its capital in Saltillo, Mexico.

Early settlements in Texas were classified as missions, presidios, or pueblos. The Franciscan Order supervised the missions, military commanders governed the presidios, and each pueblo, a civil settlement developed at or near a mission or presidio, was partially self-governing. Each local government had a *cabildo* or *ayuntamiento* (municipal council) composed of *regiodores* (councilmen) presided over by the *alcalde* (mayor). Generally, there were two *alcalde ordinarios* (municipal judges), the *alguacil mayor* (sheriff), and the *mayordomo de propios* (administrator of public lands). The *mayordomo de propios* also functioned as the *procurado* (attorney). *Escribanos* kept the *cabildo* minutes, served as notaries, prepared legal documents, took depositions, and maintained the local archives. Existing local governmental records for Texas are divided among three archives: the Bexar Archives, the Nacogdoches Archives, and the Laredo Achives.

Bexar Archives

The Bexar Archives contain over 250,000 pages of manuscripts and some 4,000 pages of printed material covering the years 1717 to 1836, reflecting the administration of civil affairs, ecclesiastical matters, exploration, local history, immigration, colonization, and genealogy. The collection of 172 microfilm rolls is prefaced by a general description of the material with a detailed inventory of each roll. Copies of the microfilm are now available at major educational institutions nationwide. Translations done to date are also available on microfilm. Adán Benavides has compiled a comprehensive name guide to the Bexar Archives, based on all substantive documents as they are entered in the microfilm edition.[24]

Nacogdoches Area Archives

The Nacogdoches Archives covers the years 1731 to 1836, with documents arranged in chronological order and classified according to the administrative organization of the Mexican government from 1824 to 1836. Presently located at the Texas State Library, Archives Division, Austin, Texas, the Nacogdoches Archives have been transcribed in eighty-nine volumes, with a card index to the transcriptions. Transcribed copies and other records have been deposited with the University of Texas Archives; the Stephen F. Austin State College Library in Nacogdoches; the North Texas State College Library in Denton; and the Newberry Library in Chicago. Transcriptions of other Nacogdoches records are in custody of the Nacogdoches County clerk.

Seventy-five bound volumes of the Nacogdoches Archives, covering the years 1744 to 1837, prepared by Robert Blake, are kept in the Blake Collection in the Houston Public Library. This collection includes correspondence, diaries, censuses, election returns, bills of sale, a record of foreigners who settled in Nacogdoches from 1827 to 1834, lists of foreigners residing in Nacogdoches, judicial proceedings, marriage contracts, accounting and financial papers, orders, commissions, and other documents. A calendar of the Blake Collection is available at the University of Texas Archives.

Records of the Nacogdoches District Court for the years 1834 to 1862 are in the Stephen F. Austin State College Archive Collection, with copies of court proceedings in the University of Texas Archives. The Texas History Collection of Baylor University has Nacogdoches records from 1770 to about 1900.

Records of the municipality of San Felipe de Austin (where the Texas Provisional government was formed in 1835 and their Declaration of Independence was drafted), covering the years 1810 to 1837, are found at the Belleville County clerk's office. City records of Brazoria, similar in content to those previously described, are in the custody of the county clerk at Angelton.

Laredo Archives

After the Velasco Treaty of 1836 removed all Mexican troops from the region south of the Rio Grande River, the region between the Rio Grande and Nueces Rivers became a no-man's land. When the Mexican War broke out in 1846 after American soldiers occupied Texas, Laredo and all its records became property of the United States. This collection consists of some eight thousand documents, most for the years 1768 to 1868 with a few as early as 1749, including census reports, vital statistics, allotments of land, tax renditions, wills, settlements of estates, and civil and criminal litigations. Transcription of these records was completed in 1941. A partial set of transcriptions, covering only 1755 to 1830 with many gaps, is in the Texas State Archives. The original collection of the Laredo Archives is now in the custody of St. Mary's University Library in San Antonio and is available on sixteen rolls of microfilm covering 1749 to 1872. Access to the original manuscripts is possible with special permission. The Laredo Archives have also been microfilmed for the Southwest Collection at Texas Technological University, Lubbock, Texas, with microfilm copies in many educational institutions. See the St. Mary's University (San Antonio, Texas) Library Catalog online for a complete listing of several indexes of and transcriptions from the collection that have been published in recent years.[25]

Census Records of Texas

Often mixed with the civil records or found in other collections, census records are of particular value to the family historian. The charts on the following pages identify census records for each state together with their location. Some of these censuses list only the head of household, but most list complete families. Military type censuses have generally not been included unless they list all residents.

Spanish Censuses of Texas

Locality	Year(s)	Reference*
General	1774	AGN CA 39:2 20–149
General	1777	BNM
General	1829–36	unknown
General	1840	unknown
Adaes	1739	AGN PI 182:1 1–127
Atacosita	1826	unknown
Barrio Laredo, V.S. Fernando	1809	ROT 2:42–46
General	1790	ROT 1:58–74
Capistrano	1794	ROT 1:165–166
Capistrano	1795	ROT 1:220–221
Cia. Volante of San Carlos de Parras	1807	ROT 2:1–5
El Paso	1692	AGI
El Paso	1784	unknown
Espada	1793	ROT 1:147–149
Espada	1794	ROT 1:164–165
Espada	1796	ROT 1:222–223
Espiritu Santo	1804	ROT 1:385
Galveston	1779	LGR 27:367
Galveston	1783	LGR 27:367
Galveston	1793	LGR 27:367
La Bahía	1790	ROT 1:47–58
La Bahía	1804	ROT 1:381–384
La Bahía	1810	ROT 2:46–64
La Bahía	1811	ROT 2:74–90
La Bahía	1825	UTANLB 1:74–83
Nacogdoches	1792	ROT 1:104–114
Nacogdoches	1792	TSG 13:15–23
Nacogdoches	1793	ROT 1:151–163
Nacogdoches	1794	UTANLB 1:94–104
Nacogdoches	1794	ROT 1:172–180
Nacogdoches	1795	ROT 1:181–193
Nacogdoches	1796	ROT 1:246–257
Nacogdoches	1797	ROT 1:282–294
Nacogdoches	1798	ROT 1:299–310
Nacogdoches	1799	ROT 1:313–327
Nacogdoches	1803	ROT 1:355–371
Nacogdoches	1805	ROT 1:404–418;421–423
Nacogdoches	1806	ROT 1:423–435
Nacogdoches	1809	ROT 2:10–35
Orcoquisac	1807	ROT 2:5–7
**Paso del Norte/Ciudad Juarez	1787–1805	UTEP
**Paso del Norte/Cuidad Juarez	1834	UTEP

Locality	Year(s)	Reference*
**Paso del Norte/Cuidad Juarez	1841–44	UTEP
Purísima Concepción de Acuña	1792	ROT 1:102–104
Purísima Concepción de Acuña	1793	ROT 1:149–150
Purísima Concepción de Acuña	1798	ROT 1:296–297
Purísima Concepción de Acuña	1799	ROT 1:310–311
Purísima Concepción de Acuña	1809	ROT 2:38–39
Real de Barranco, Villa El Paso	1844	unknown
Refugio	1804	ROT 1:386
Rosario	1804	ROT 1:385
San Antonio Valero	1792	ROT 1:93–95
San Antonio Valero	1798	ROT 1:297–299
San Antonio Valero	1804	ROT 1:378–380
San Antonio Valero	1806	ROT 1:435–437
San Antonio Valero	1808	ROT 2:7–8
San Antonio de Béxar	1784	TSL
San Antonio de Béxar	1792	TSL
San Antonio de Béxar	1795	UTANLB 1:5–13;29–36;49–55
San Antonio de Béxar	1803	UTANLB 2:58–66;77–86
San Antonio de Béxar	1803	UTANLB 2:112–117
San Antonio de Béxar	1804	ROT 1:371–377
San Antonio de Béxar	1805	TSL
San Antonio de Valero	1795	ROT 1:215–218
San Antonio de Valero	1796	ROT 1:224–226
San Antonio de Valero	1797	ROT 1:262–265
San Fco. de la Espada	1790	ROT 1:46
San Fco. de la Espada	1792	ROT 1:98–100
San Fco. de la Espada	1795	ROT 1:218–220
San Fco. de la Espada	1797	ROT 1:260–262
San Fco. de la Espada	1803	ROT 1:353–354
San Fco. de la Espada	1804	ROT 1:386–387
San Fernando de Austria	1782	ROT 1:39–44
San Fernando de Austria	1792	ROT 1:75–92
San Fernando de Austria	1793	ROT 1:114–141
San Fernando de Austria	1795	ROT 1:193–215
San Fernando y Presidio de Béxar	1803	ROT 1:327–352
San Fernando y Presidio de San Antonio de Béxar	1797	ROT 1:265–282
San José de Aquallo	1790	ROT 1:44–46
San José de Aquallo	1792	ROT 1:95–98
San José de Aquallo	1793	ROT 1:141–145
San José de Aquallo	1805	ROT 1:419–420
San José de Aquallo	1794	ROT 1:169–172
San José de Aquallo	1797	ROT 1:258–260
San José de Aquallo	1798	ROT 1:294–296
San José de Aquallo	1799	ROT 1:311–313
San Juan Capistrano	1792	ROT 1:101–102
San Juan Capistrano	1793	ROT 1:145–146
San Juan Capistrano	1797	ROT 1:257–258
San Juan Capistrano	1798	ROT 1:294
San Juan Capistrano	1804	ROT 1:377–378
San Juan Capistrano	1809	ROT 2:36–38
San Jose de Palfox	1815	unknown
San Jose de Palfox	1816	unknown
San Marcos de Neve	1809	ROT 2:40–42
Sindic & its ranches	1810	ROT 2:64–73
Terre aux Boeufs	1779	LGR 27:367
Trinidad	1809	ROT 2:8–9
San Antonio Valero	1794	ROT 1:166–169
Valenzuela		LGR 27:367
Ysleta	1790	UTEP
Ysleta (religious census)	1805	UTEP

***AGN CA:** Collections found at the *Archivo General de la Nación* in Mexico City in the section *Californias.*
AGN PI: Collections found at the *Archivo General de la Nación* in Mexico City in the section *Provincias Internas.*
AGI: Archivo General de las Indias.
BNM: The *Biblioteca Nacional de México,* Mexico City.
LGR: The historical manuscripts section of the Loyola University, New Orleans, Louisiana.
ROT: *Residents of Texas,* 1782–1836, a three-volume set containing the Texas census in translated form with an index, published in 1984 by the Institute of Texan Cultures at the University of Texas.
TSG: Texas State Genealogical Society, *Quarterly.*
TSL: Texas State Library (Mexican Collection), Austin.
UTANLB: University Texas, Austin, Nettie Lee Benson.
UTEP: University of Texas at El Paso Library, El Paso.
Six- or seven-digit numbers with no other reference are film numbers from the Family History Library in Salt Lake City. This information was taken primarily from *Latin American Census Records* by Lyman D. Platt, with permission from the author. Where possible, a citation to an archive or library in the United States has been preferred, even though that library may only hold a microfilm copy of the original.

**Paso del Norte is comprised of the villages of Senecú, San Lorenzo, Ysleta, Socorro, and San Elizario.

Catholic Church Records

Catholic missions in Texas and other states had a two-fold purpose: converting the Indians to Christianity and promoting settlement. Missionary efforts by the Franciscans in what is now Texas had begun as early as 1659 with the establishment of the Mission Nuestra Señora de Guadalupe del Paso at El Paso del Norte (Ciudad Juarez, Mexico). By the close of the eighteenth century, the missions had nearly achieved their goals of frontier settlement; by about 1793, records of the numerous missions were placed in the hands of parish churches.

The following chart sets out those parishes and missions of Texas with existing sacramental records from before 1836 and the current location of the originals. Microfilms are available through the FHL and Family History Centers as marked. A more detailed description of these records, the mission histories, and other locations in Texas, New Mexico, Arizona, and California where microfilm and/or photocopies can be consulted is found in Chapter 18 of *Spanish and Mexican Records of the American Southwest*, by Henry Putney Beers.

Texas Parish Records

Name	Modern Location	Record Type∞	Reference*	Format†
Nuestra Señora de los Dolores de los Ais		not extant		
Nuestra Señora de Guadalupe	El Paso (Ciudad Juarez, Mexico)	Ba 1662 Ma 1707 Bu 1663	G G G	FHL FHL FHL
Nuestra Señora de Guadalupe	Nacogdoches	where-abouts unknown		
Nuestra Señora del Refugio	Refugio	Ba 1807–1827 Bu 1807–1825	M M	
^Purisima Concep-cion de Acuna	San Antonio	Ma 1733–1790 Ba 1731–1857 Ma 1731–1823	SF 	 FHL FHL
San Augustin	Laredo	Ma 1764–1796 Ba 1764–1786 Bu 1764–1797 Ba 1788–1860 Ma 1790–1881 Bu 1836–1848 C 1834–1854 Ad 1789–1854	C C C L L L L L	 FHL FHL
**Socorro		Ba 1840–1862 Ma 1845–1857 Bu 1846–1929 Ba 1845–1888 Ma 1867–1926		FHL FHL FHL FHL FHL
**Nuestra Señora de la Purisima Concep-ción de Socorro	Soccoro (El Paso)	Ma 1845–1859 Bu 1846–1863		FHL FHL
**San Antonio de Senecú	El Paso (Senecú, Chihuahua, MX)	Ba 1719–1722 Ba 1772–1825 Ba 1829–1851 Ma 1706–1723 Ma 1772–1851 Bu 1777–1848	G G G G G G	 FHL FHL
^San Antonio de Valero	San Antonio	Ba 1720–1721 Ba 1731–1792 Bu 1720–1721 Ma 1748–1754 Ma 1709–1825 Bu 1709–1782 Bu 1761–1860 Bu 1757	B SF B B SF SF SF B	 FHL FHL
**Our Lady of Mt. Carmel de Ysleta	El Paso	Ba 1772–1940 Ma 1845–1858 Bu 1845–1858		FHL FHL FHL
**San Antonio de Ysleta	El Paso	Ba 1792–1803		FHL
^San Fernando de Bexar	San Antonio	Ba 1731–1858 Ma 1710–1850 Bu 1703–1860 C 1731–1860 Ad 1795–1820	SF SF SF SF SF	FHL FHL FHL FHL FHL
^San Francisco de la Espada	San Antonio	Misc. entries 1818–1822	SF SF	 FHL
^San Francisco Salano	San Antonio	Ba 1703–1708 Ma 1703–1708 Bu 1703–1713	Q SF SF	
^San Jose y San Miguel de Acuna	San Antonio	Ma 1778–1822	SF	
^San Juan Capistrano	San Antonio	Bu 1781–1824	SF	
**‡San Lorenzo del Real	El Paso	Ba 1700–1723 Ba 1777–1847 Ma 1777–1846 Bu 1778–1847 C 1833	G G G G G	 FHL
**‡San Elizario	San Elizario	Ba 1840–1916 Ma 1845–1956 Bu 1846–1956		FHL FHL FHL
San Xavier del Nexera	San Antonio	Ba 1721–1726 Bu 1722	SF SF	

∞**Ad:** Administrative records
Ba: Baptisms
Bu: Burials/deaths
C: Confirmations
Ma: Marriages

(continued)

*B: Bancroft Library, UC Berkeley, California
C: Parish of Camargo, Mexico
G: Nuestra Señora de Guadalupe, Ciudad Juarez, Mexico
L: Parish Church of San Augustin, Laredo
M: Parish Church, Matamoros, Tamaulipas
Q: College of Santa Cruz of Queretaro, Mexico
SF: San Fernando Cathedral

**These parishes are located in the same area just south of present-day El Paso, and there is a considerable amount of overlap between the parish registers. You may find entries in one parish for another of the parishes in the same area. During the colonial era this area was considered part of New Mexico.

†FHL: Filmed by and located in the Family History Library, Salt Lake City, Utah.
Records available on microfilm may cover only some of the years indicated.

‡The parish of San Lorenzo began in 1680 but in 1684 was moved. San Elizario, which began in 1774, was moved in 1789.

^Many of these records have been microfilmed and are available at the FHL under the listing for "Parish Registers, San Fernando Cathedral," but the catalog does not differentiate between parishes.

Records of New Mexico

From its founding in 1598 until American occupation in 1846, New Mexico was a separate political entity extending from the El Paso area in present–day Texas to the area around Durango, Colorado. As such, its records were kept locally at Santa Fe, where they are currently housed in the New Mexico State Records Center, which also has an excellent collection of genealogical materials, both published and manuscript, covering the Spanish and Mexican periods.[26]

The Spanish Archives of New Mexico, 1621–1821, presently held at the Archives Division of New Mexico State Records Center, deals with the administration of the region from the period of Spanish Colonial sovereignty to the establishment of the Mexican government in 1821. Excluded from these archives are official land grant documents and land conveyances in special collections.

The Spanish archives, microfilmed in twenty-two rolls, are calendared chronologically, identified briefly, and can be located by frame number. They include the following:

- Communications and decrees received from the viceroy and commandant-general.
- Copies of communications to the viceroy and commandant-general.
- Reports from local officials and instructions sent to them.
- Censuses.
- Appointments, governors' edicts, minutes, and petitions of the *cabildo* of Santa Fe.
- Military records, including lists of troops, muster rolls, orders, journals of operations, reports of inspections, and service records.
- Judicial records containing litigation proceedings in civil and criminal cases, judgments of the governor and captain general, auxiliary documents (affidavits, petitions, depositions, testimonies, writs, declarations, etc.), and probate records.

The New Mexico State Records Center has forty-two rolls of New Mexican archives microfilm consisting of documents relating to the Mexican government from 1821 to 1846. The Mexican archives have been organized into several record groups according to agency of function, and then subdivided into the following subject matters with documents in each section arranged chronologically: instructions, investigations, journals, judicial proceedings, orders, petitions, reports, and *residencias* (residences of various officials). There are also similar original records relating to New Mexico at the Bancroft Library at the University of California at Berkeley and the Huntington Library in California; these records have been microfilmed and are available at the New Mexico State Record Center. The Hispanic Genealogical Research Center of New Mexico and its journal, *Herencia*, are key points of departure for research in this state.[27]

Unfortunately, the majority of local jurisdiction records of the Territory of New Mexico for the pre-American period have disappeared. Portions of the journal of proceedings of the *Ayuntamiento* of Santa Fe, 1829–36, are in the Zimmerman Library of the University of New Mexico with a typescript in the Bancroft Library. These records are also available on microfilm at the New Mexico State Records Center.

Census Records of New Mexico

The following chart gives the location and availability of census records for New Mexico.

Spanish Censuses of New Mexico

Locality	Year(s)	Reference*
General	1642	MBL 2:21
General	1693	AF 182 #1394
General	1693	AF 181 #1390
General	1705	AF 189 #1447
General	1749–1750	AF 240 #1772; SMC
General	1749–1750	AGN PI 36:10; 501–507
General	1769	AF 254 #1867
General	1777	AF 31 #646
General	1790	SNM, Reel 12; SMC; 581,470
General	1803	AF 266 #1951
General	1823	SMC; MNM, Reel General 1845SMC; MNM; Reel 40

Locality	Year(s)	Reference*
Abiquiu	1790	MBL; SMC
Albuquerque	1802	SMC
Ballecito	1830	ASF; SMC
Cañones	1830	ASF; SMC
Isleta (Corpus Christi de la)	1684	AF 173 #1335
Isleta (Corpus Christi de la)	1815	1,162,467
Jemez	1830	ASF; SMC
Laguna (Sr. S. José)	1801	913,167 item 7
Las Huertas and Bernalitto	1803–1807	ANM 21; 576–583
Pecuries (S. Lorenzo de los)	1707	AF 206 #1556
Pueblo Real	1815	1,162,467
S. José (presidio)**	1684	AF 173 #1336
S. Juan de los Caballeros	1707	AF 206 #1556
San Antonio del Sobina	1827	SMC; MNM, Vol. 80
San Juan	1816	SMC; ASF
San Juan	1816–1817	SMC. ASF
Sandia	1818	SMC; ASF
Santa Clara	1785–1798	SMC
Santa Clara	1818	SMC; ASF
Santa Cruz	1707	AF 206 #1556
Santa Cruz de la Cañada	1822	SMC; ASF
Santa Cruz de la Cañada	1823	SMC; ASF
Santa Fé (presidio)**	1705	AF 189 #1447
Santa Fé (presidio)**	1705	AGN PI 36:6:420–425
Santa Fé (presidio)**	1705	AGN PI 36:7:426–461
Santa Fé (presidio)**	1790	SMC; SNM 21:508–520
Santa Fé (presidio)**	1826	SMC; SNM 6:527–533
Senecu	1815	1,162,467
Socorro	1815	1,162,467

***AF:** *Archivo Franciscano,* Biblioteca Nacional, Mexico City.
AGN PI: Collections found at the *Archivo General de la Nación* in Mexico City for the section *Provincias Internas.*
ASF: Archives of the Archdiocese of Santa Fe, New Mexico.
MBL: Bancroft Library, University of California at Berkeley.
MNM: Mexican Archives of New Mexico.
SNM: Spanish Colonial Archives of New Mexico (on microfilm).
The following are identified only in published form:
SMC: Two books by Virginia Langham Olmsted: *New Mexico Spanish and Mexican Colonial Censuses, 1790, 1823, 1845; and Spanish and Mexican Censuses of New Mexico, 1750 to 1830.*
Six- or seven-digit numbers with no other reference are film numbers from the collection of the LDS Family History Library in Salt Lake City, available through the local Family History Centers.

**Troop Lists

Catholic Church Records of New Mexico

In 1598, Juan de Oñate, accompanied by ten Franciscan missionaries, established missions at a number of Indian pueblos, following the missions with the construction of churches and schools. Although the Franciscan missions in New Mexico began to decline by the second half of the eighteenth century, the amount of historical material generated during this period is significant.

Only a portion of the ecclesiastical records of the Spanish and Mexican periods have survived; these are currently located in the archives of the Archdiocese of Santa Fe. Since there is only limited access to these original records by accredited scholars, the State Records Center, the Henry E. Huntington Library, the Genealogical Society of Utah, and the Archdiocesan Archives have microfilm editions. In addition, a number of these have been extracted and are being indexed and published. Following is a chart of available records, arranged according to mission and church.

Catholic Church Records of New Mexico

Name	Record Type[∞]	Format[†]
*Abiquiu:	Ba 1754–1850 Ma 1756–1826 Bu ?–1777 Bu 1810 C 1736, 1760	FHL, P
*Acoma:	Ba 1725–1777 Ma 1725–1777 Bu 1725–1777	FHL FHL FHL
*Albuquerque: San Felipe	Ba 1703–1736 Ba 1743–1802 Ba 1822–1850 Ma 1726–1855 Bu 1726–1823 Bu 1838–1855 Letters 1745–1810 Letters 1818–1851 Accounts 1818–1861	FHL, MC FHL, MC FHL, MC FHL, MC FHL, MC FHL, MC
*Belen: (See also Tomé)	Index to Ba and Ma Ba 1793–1850 Ma 1826–1884 Bu 1838–1885 Letters 1819–1851	FHL, P FHL FHL FHL
*Bernalillo: Nuestra Señora de los Dolores	Ba 1700–1712 Ma 1700–1712 Bu 1700–1709	FHL FHL FHL
*Cochiti: San Buenaventura	Ba 1736–1827 Ba 1846–1873 Ma 1776–1827 Ma 1846–1873 Bu 1776–1873 Letters 1775–1817 Inventory 1753–1829	FHL, P FHL, P FHL FHL FHL

Name	Record Type∞	Format†
*Galisteo:	Bu 1711–1729	FHL
	Ma 1712–1727	FHL
	Ma 1776–1828	FHL
	Bu 1727–1774	
	Bu 1778–1829	FHL
	Letters 1783–1815	
	Inventory (fragmentary)	
*Isleta: San Augustín	Ba 1726–1776	FHL, P
	Ba 1829–1846	FHL, P
	Ma 1726–1846	FHL, P
	Bu 1726–1776	
	Bu 1829–1842	P
	Letters 1746–1818	
	Letters 1789–1823	
*Jemez:	Ba 1701–1715	FHL
	Ba 1720– 1829	FHL
	Ma 1720–1776	
	Ma 1852–1904	FHL
	Bu (fragmentary)	
	Ma 1701–1776	FHL
	Bu 1701–1776	FHL
*Laguna:	Ba 1720–1776	FHL
	Ma 1700–1711	FHL
	Bu 1715–1719	
	Bu 1726–1776	FHL
	Inventory 1736–1777	
Mansos:	Ma 1691 (fragmentary)	
*Nambe:	Ba 1707–1727	FHL
	Ba 1771–1837	FHL
	Ma 1707–1728	FHL
	Ma 1772–1862	FHL
	Bu 1707–1869	FHL
*Pecos:	Ba 1726–1829	FHL
	Ma 1699–1765	FHL
	Bu 1727–1772	FHL
	Letters 1716–1749	
*Peña Blanca: Nuestra Señora de Guadalupe	Ba 1841–1909	FHL
*Picuris:	Ba 1750–1771	FHL, P
	Ba 1776–1830	FHL, P
	Ba 1835–1850	FHL, P
	Ma 1726–1837	FHL, P
	Bu 1712–1858	
	Inventory 1743–1767 (fragmentary)	
*Pojoaque:	Ba 1779–1839	FHL
	Ma 1744–1853	FHL
	Bu 1779–1852	FHL
*Sandia:	Ba 1771–1846	FHL, P
	Ma 1771–1864	FHL, P
*San Felipe:	Ba 1767–1829	FHL
	Ma 1726–1814	FHL
	Bu 1726–1860	FHL
	Letters 1755–1823	

Name	Record Type∞	Format†
*San Ildefonso:	Ba 1725–1834	FHL
	Ma 1703–1853	FHL, P
	Bu 1840–1855	FHL
	Letters 1824–1852	
	Letters 1817–1834	
*San Juan:	Ba 1726–1837	FHL, P
	Ba 1837–1870	P
	Ma 1726–1776	FHL, P
	Ma 1830–1836	FHL, P
	Ma 1850–1855	FHL
	Bu 1726–1826	FHL
	Bu 1836–1857	FHL
	Letters 1779–1816	
	Letters 1817–1834	
	Inventory 1818–1846	
*San Miguel del Vado:	Ba 1829–1853	FHL, P
	Ma 1829–1878	FHL, P
	Bu 1829–1847	
	Accounts 1842–1855	
	Prenuptial investigations 1829–1834	
	Inventory 1828 (fragmentary)	
*Santa Ana:	Ba 1771–1844	FHL
	Ma 1694–1711	FHL
	Ma 1722–1828	FHL
	Bu 1726–1752	FHL
	Bu 1765–1771	FHL
	Letters 1746–1760	
	Inventory 1712–1753	
*Santa Clara:	Ba 1728–1805	FHL, P
	Ba 1841–1845	FHL
	Ma 1726–1832	FHL, P
	Ma 1844, 1846 (fragmentary)	
	Bu 1712–1713	
	Bu 1714–1719	
	Bu 1723–1724	
	Bu 1800–1801	
	Bu 1726–1843	
	Letters 1815–1832	FHL
	Inventory 1712–1742	
	Census 1818	
*Santa Cruz de la Canada:	Ba 1710–1721	P
	Ba 1731–1767	FHL, P
	Ba 1759–1781 (fragmentary)	
	Ba 1769–1860	
	Ma 1726–1869	FHL, P
	Bu 1726–1789	FHL,
	Bu 1795–1859	FHL
	Letters 1721–1795	FHL
	Letters 1803–1833	
	Letters 1834–1853	
	Misc. incomplete registers, inventories, etc.	
*Santa Fe: San Francisco de Asis (Cathedral)	Ba 1747–1791	FHL, P
	Ba 1796–1848	FHL, P
	Ba 1848–1851	FHL, P
	Ma 1728–1843	FHL
	Ma 1846–1857	
	Bu 1726–1834	FHL
	Bu 1845–1852	FHL

Name	Record Type[∞]	Format[†]
*Santa Fe: San Francisco de Asis (Cathedral) (continued)	Letters 1697–1725 Misc. account books	
*Santa Fe Castrense: (soldiers)	Ba 1798–1833 Ma 1779–1833 Bu 1779–1833	FHL, P FHL FHL
*Santo Domingo: (Also search under Santa Ana)	Ba 1771–1777 Ba 1777–1827 Ba 1829–1846 Ma 1771–1777 Ma 1777–1846 Ma Inf 1835–1845 Ma 1844–1853 Bu 1771–1869	FHL FHL FHL FHL FHL FHL FHL FHL
*Socorro:	Ba 1821–1850 Ma 1821–1853 Bu 1821–1863 Letters 1831–1850	FHL FHL, P FHL
*Taos:	Ba 1701–1850 Ma 1777–1856 Bu 1827–1850	FHL, P FHL FHL
*Tesuque:	Ba 1694–1724 (includes some Ma and Bu, 1694)	
*Tomé:	Ba 1793–1826 Ba 1809–1856 Ba, Ma, Bu 1793–1826 (includes Belen) Ma 1776–1793 Ma 1793–1846 Bu 1809–1855	FHL, P FHL, P FHL FHL FHL
Truches:	C 1845 (fragmentary)	
*Zia:	Ba 1694–1772 Ma 1697–1717 Bu 1709 Bu 1727–1772	FHL FHL FHL
*Zuñi:	Ba 1699–1700 1725–1772 Ma 1697–1776 Bu 1706–1719	 FHL FHL FHL

[∞]**Ad:** Administrative records
Ba: Baptisms
Bu: Burials/deaths
C: Confirmations
Ma: Marriages

[†]**FHL:** Filmed by and located in the Family History Library, Salt Lake City, Utah.
MC: Microfilmed copy exists somewhere other than at the FHL
P: Index, transcription, and/or translation exists
Records may cover only some of the years indicated.

*Microfilmed Archives of Archdiocese only

Records of Arizona

During the Spanish period, the present area of southern Arizona, including a portion of northern Sonora, Mexico, was known as Pimeria Alta. Inhabited by the Pima and Papago Indian tribes, this became the northwestern frontier of New Spain. The southernmost region of Arizona remained under Spanish and Mexican government until the United States purchased it in 1853 for $10 million under the Gadsden Treaty. An Act of Congress on 24 February 1863 created the Territory of Arizona with the boundaries of the modern state as we know it today.

Although space does not allow a detailed listing of the numerous Arizona sources now in Mexican archives, researchers should look for materials in the *Archivo General de la Nación* and *Archivo Histórico de Hacienda, Sección de Temporalidades* in Mexico City; the *Archivo Histórico del Estado de Sonora* in Hermosillo; *Archivo de Estado* in Durango; and the Parral Archives in Chihuahua. Microfilm editions of these records are available in the United States at the University of Alabama; University of Arizona; University of California at Berkeley; Fort Lewis College, Durango, Colorado; Northern Illinois University, DeKalb; University of Minnesota; State University of New York, Stony Brook; State University of New York, Buffalo; Temple University, Philadelphia; University of Texas, Austin; University of Texas, El Paso; Texas Agricultural and Mechanical College, College Station; Texas Christian University, Fort Worth; Tulane University, New Orleans; University of Utah, Salt Lake City; and the Library of Congress.

Census and Catholic Church Records of Arizona

Arizona census and Church records are valuable, though few in number because of the limited number of settlements. Many Arizona settlers, especially those moving into northern Arizona, are not included in any of these.

Spanish Censuses of Arizona

Locality	Year(s)	Reference*
Guevari		AHH
S. Xavier del Bac	1766	AHH
S. Xavier del Bac	1768	SBM
S. Xavier del Bac	1801	AGEM 19; 811:3; ASG, 1986
Tubac	1767	ASG 17:7–12; 1149545; AF 280 #2070
Tubac	1841	AHS 4–2
Tucsón	1766	AHH
Tucsón	1797	JAH 11:18–22
Tucsón	1801	ASG, 1986
Tucsón	1831	ASG 16:5–9, 41–47

Locality	Year(s)	Reference*
Tumacácori	1798	Kiva 19
Tumacácori	1801	ASG, 1986; 811:3
Tumacácori	1841	AHS 4–2

***AF:** Archivo Franciscano, Biblioteca Nacional, Mexico City.
AGEM: Cathedral, Hermosillo, Sonora, México (Arizona microfilm series 422, 40 rolls).
AHH: The *Archivo Histórico de Hacienda*, AGN, Mexico City.
AHS: Arizona Historical Society.
ASG: Arizona State Genealogical Society, *Copper State Bulletin.*
JAH: *Journal of Arizona History.*
Kiva: Alfred F. Whiting, "The Tumacácori Census of 1798" *Kiva* 19, no. 1 (Fall 1953): 1–12.
SBM: The Santa Barbara Mission Archives, California.
Six- or seven-digit numbers with no other reference are film numbers from the collection of the LDS Family History Library in Salt Lake City, available through local Family History Centers.

Catholic Church Records

Catholic Church Records of Arizona

Name**	Modern Location	Type of Record∞	Format†
Guévavi	Los Santos Angeles	Ba 1739–1767 Ma 1739–1767 Bu 1739–1767	MC, P MC, P MC, P
Tubac	San Ignacio	Ma 1814–1824 Bu 1814–1824	MC MC
Tucson	San Augustin	Ba 1793–1849 Ma 1793–1849	MC, P MC, P
Tumacácori	San Jose	Ba 1768–1825 Ma 1768–1825 Bu 1768–1825	MC, P MC, P MC, P
Madelena, Sonora (Contains many persons from Arizona missions)	Santa Maria Magdalena,	Ba 1698–1815 Ba 1698–1824 Ba 1837–1850 Bu 1702–1816 Ma Bu 1702–1825	FHL FHL, P FHL
	San Ignacio	Ba 1720–1812 Ba 1784–1830 Ba 1777–1828 Ba 1801–1822 Ba 1822–1835 Ma 1713–1737 Ma 1797–1840 Ma 1822–1827 Ma Inf 1835,1841–1850, 1846, 1848 (20 de Tucson) Bu 1770–1841 Bu 1697–1788	 FHL FHL FHL FHL FHL FHL FHL FHL

**The archives of the Diocese of Tucson, the original registers of Guevavi and Tumacácori. Those of Tubac and the Sonora Missions are found in the Pinart Collection of the Bancroft Library, University of California at Berkeley. Microfilms of these records are available at the University of Arizona Library, St. Louis University Library, and the Arizona Historical Society. Those of Tucson are on the University of Arizona Film 811, rolls 1 and 11.
∞**Ad:** Administrative records
Ba: Baptisms
Bu: Burials/deaths
C: Confirmations
Ma: Marriages
†**FHL:** Filmed by and located in the Family History Library, Salt Lake City, Utah.
MC: Microfilmed copy exists somewhere other than at the FHL
P: Index, transcription, and/or translation exists
Records may cover only some of the years indicated.

Records of California

California's settlement followed the usual pattern of Spanish colonization—the mission, the presidio, and the pueblo. Under the Franciscan Order's extensive civil authority, a chain of missions bridging lower and upper California was established. Presidios were garrisoned by soldiers, with their commandants having civil and judicial authority within their respective districts located at San Diego, Monterey, Santa Barbara, and San Francisco. California was ceded to the United States under the treaty of Guadalupe Hidalgo in 1848. The territory continued under military government until September of 1850, when it was admitted as a state.

With statehood, local records were transferred to the nine existing counties: San Diego, Los Angeles, Santa Barbara, San Luis Obispo, Monterey, Branciforte, San Francisco, Santa Clara, and Sonoma. Many of these records were later transferred to the surveyor general's office in San Francisco and consequently burned in the 1906 fire.

An extensive collection of Monterey records now held by that county includes criminal proceedings of the Monterey Court, 1807–43; military affairs, 1781–1843; papers from the prefect's office, 1837–49; papers regarding tithes, missions, and religious affairs, 1782–1844; papers connected with Indians, 1833–48; land grants, sales, transfers, suits, and location claims, 1803–49; power of attorney, 1834–49; register of cattle brand, 1835–49; papers on the probate of estates and wills, 1830–48; papers relating claims against the Mexican government, 1841–42, 1846–47; naturalization papers, 1829–42; political affairs, censuses, and elections, 1828–49; *alcalde* and *ayuntamiento* records, 1828–50; official acts of judges, 1842–46; papers regarding ships at sea, 1833–49; index to the Spanish archives; and deeds of grants, 1822–50.

The Bancroft Library at the University of California at Berkeley has transcripts and abstracts of some of these records, while the Huntington Library in California has sixteen volumes on microfilm.

Los Angeles records available from the Huntington Library on microfilm include *alcalde* correspondence, 1823; *ayuntamiento* minutes from 1832; judicial records of civil and criminal cases; records of the Los Angeles prefecture from 1834; register of cattle brands and marks, 1833–52; notarial records; petitions for land; claims for mines; deeds, mortgages, contracts, bankruptcy papers, and wills; inventories of personal and household goods; court-martial papers; censuses; and decrees and proclamations.

The Historical Society of Southern California also has photostats of this collection, and the Los Angeles County Recorder's Office has indexed transcriptions and translations.

The Los Angeles County Law Library has court records from 1839–82, including criminal cases, 1839–50; civil cases, 1839–44; and miscellaneous Spanish records, 1840–50.

The Los Angeles Archives has translations of archives from 1826 to 1845, including a voters' register of 1830 and censuses of 1836 and 1844. Transcripts of these records are in the Bancroft Library with official documents of San Francisco, 1835–57.

Records of San Diego are now in the Records of the Bureau of Land Management (Record Group 49) in the National Archives. Other early records of San Diego are in the Junipero Serra Museum in San Diego, the Bancroft Library, and the San Diego Historical Society Archives.

Records of San Jose are presently in the Santa Clara County Recorder's office. Transcripts of this collection are in the Bancroft Library along with collections of Spanish and Mexican records relating to Santa Cruz, San Luis Obispo, and numerous early settlements.

Provincial records of California were divided between Los Angeles and Monterey until 1846. After much shuffling between various repositories, these records were finally placed in the custody of the Surveyor General in San Francisco but were nearly all destroyed by the fire of 1906. The land records escaped, and some other documents had fortunately been issued as broadsides or pamphlets and were thus preserved in libraries, including laws, decrees, proclamations, instructions, regulations, tables, orders, notices, manifestos, reports, and expositions.

The Bancroft Library has a nearly complete collection of such materials, and a large collection of Mexican documents is also available at the Sutro Library, San Francisco State College.[28]

Census Records of California

As with Arizona, California census records are limited and do not include all towns, missions, or residents.

Spanish Censuses of California

Locality	Year(s)	Reference*
General	1777–79	AGN PI 121:2:277–374
General	1795–96	AGN PI 19:2:63–91
General	1798	AGN CA 49:3:137–188
General	1836	SAC, MBL
Los Angeles	1790	SSC 41:181–182
Los Angeles	1816	SSC 41:228–229
Los Angeles	1816	SSC 43:350–351
Los Angeles	1822	CAL 4:36–39
Los Angeles	1844	SSC 42:360–363
Monterey	1770	AGN CA 76:27
Monterey	1773	AGN CA 66:397–397v
San Diego	1770	AGN CA 76:27
San Diego	1790	SSC 43:107–108
Santa Bárbara	1815	913167 item 1
Santa Bárbara	1840	913167 item 2
Santa Cruz	1845	CAL 4:45–58

***AGN CA:** Collections found at the *Archivo General de la Nación* in Mexico City for the section *Californias.*
AGN PI: Collections found at the *Archivo General de la Nación* in Mexico City for the section *Privincias Internas.*
CAL: *Antepasados*, published by Los Californianos.
MBL: George Hammond, *Guide to Manuscript Collection of the Bancroft Library.*
SAC: Saint Albert's College, Oakland, California.
The following are identified only in published form:
SSC: *Historical Society of Southern California Quarterly.*
Six- or seven-digit numbers with no other reference are film numbers from the collection of the LDS Family History Library in Salt Lake City, available through local Family History Centers.

Catholic Church Records

Catholic Church Records of California

Name	Modern Location	Record Type∞	Reference*	Format†
(Nuestra Señora Reina de los) Los Angeles	Los Angeles	Ba 1826–1864 Ma 1840–1860 Bu 1825–1860	P P P	FHL, P FHL FHL
La Purisima Concepcion	Lompoc	Ba 1788–1850 Bu 1788–1850 Accts 1806–1834	P P P	P P

Name	Modern Location	Record Type∞	Reference*	Format†
San Antonio de Padua	Jolon	Ba 1771–1882 Ma 1773–1872 Bu 1771–1872 C 1778–1872	D–M D–M P/D–M D–M	FHL FHL FHL FHL
Santa Barbara	Santa Barbara	Ba 1786–1858 Ma 1787–1857 Bu 1787–1841 Accts 1791–1843 Accts 1787–1848	S S S S S	FHL, P FHL, P FHL, P
San Buena-ventura	Ventura	Ba 1782–1783 Ma 1782–1893 Bu 1782–1912 C 1833–1860 Ltrs 1806–1842	P P P P D–L	FHL FHL FHL FHL
San Carlos de Borromeo	Carmel	Ba 1770–1896 C 1772–1796 Ma 1772–1908 Bu 1770–1915	D–M D–M D–M D–M	FHL, MC FHL, MC FHL, MC FHL, MC
San Diego de Alcala	San Diego	Ba 1771–1822 Ba 1795–1855 Ma 1783–1938 Bu 1775 1880 C 1789–1904 Accts 1777–1784 Ltrs 1806–1842	P P P P B D–L	FHL, P FHL, P FHL, P FHL, P P
San Fernando Rey	Mission Hills	Ba 1797–1855 Ma 1798–1954 Bu 1798–1852 Ltrs 1806–1846	D–L D–L D–L D–L	P P P
San Francisco de Asis (Dolores)	San Francisco	Ba 1776–1856 Ma 1777–1860 Bu 1776–1856 C 1838–1840 Accts 1805–1828	P P P P D–S	P P P
San Francisco Solano	Sonoma	Ba 1824–1839 Ba 1840–1868 Ma 1840–1908 Ma 1824–1939 Bu 1823–1839 Bu 1840–1878	B P P B B P	P P P
San Gabriel	San Gabriel	Ba 1771–1855 Ma 1774–1855 Bu 1774–1855 C 1771–1851	P P P P	FHL, P FHL, P FHL, P FHL, P
San Jose	San Jose	C 1835–1855 Ba 1797–1859 Ma 1796–1859 Bu 1797–1837 Bu 1837–1859 Ltrs 1807–1844	S D–S D–S D–S S S	 P P P
San Juan Bautista	San Juan Bautista	Ba 1797–1931 Ma 1797–1934 Bu 1797–1934	D–M D–M D–M	FHL, P FHL, P FHL, P
San Juan Capistrano	San Juan Capis-trano	Ba 1777–1853 Ma 1777–1913 Bu 1777–1850	P P P	FHL, P FHL, P FHL, P
San Luis Obispo	San Luis Obispo	Ba 1772–1869 Ma 1772–1902 Bu 1772–1839 C 1778–1906 Ltrs 1806–1816	D–M D–M D–M D–M D–M	FHL, P FHL, P FHL, P FHL, P
San Miguel	San Miguel	Ba 1797–1861 Ma 1797–1861 Bu 1798–1858	D–M D–M D–M	FHL, P FHL, P FHL, P
San Rafael	San Rafael	Ba 1817–1839 Ma 1818–1839 Ma 1840–1875 Bu 1818–1839 Bu 1840– 1854	D–S D–S P D–S P	FHL FHL FHL FHL FHL
Santa Cruz	Santa Cruz	Ba 1791–1857 Ma 1791–1907 Bu 1791–1894 C 1793–1802	D–M D–M D–M D–M	FHL, P FHL, P FHL FHL, P
Santa Ynez	Solvang	Ba 1804–1850 Ma 1804–1850 Bu 1805–1860	P P P	
Soledad (Nuestra Señorade)	Soledad	Ba 1791–1854 Ma 1791–1851 C 1792–1894	D–M D–M D–M	FHL, P FHL FHL

∞**Ad:** Administrative records
Ba: Baptisms
Bu: Burials/deaths
C: Confirmations
Ma: Marriages

***B:** Bancroft Library
D: Diocesan Archives in San Francisco (S), Los Angeles (L), or Monterey (M)
P: In the Mission or Parish Archives
S: Santa Barbara Mission Archive

†**FHL:** Filmed by and located in the Family History Library, Salt Lake City, Utah.
MC: Microfilmed copy exists somewhere other than at the FHL.
P: Index, transcription, and/or translation exists.
Records may cover only some of the years indicated.

Extensive Catholic sacramental registers exist for California, primarily from the system of missions extending from San Diego on the south to Sonoma on the north. The best description of the extant records is found in Rudecinda Lo Buglio's "Survey of Prestatehood Records: A New Look at Spanish and Mexican California Genealogical Records."[29]

Records of Florida

The first European settlement in the United States was at St. Augustine, Florida, in 1565. While various missions were established in other parts of Florida, none of these became permanent, except the mission and military fort at Pensacola in what was known after 1763 as West Florida. At the end of the Seven Years War (French and Indian War) in that same year, Florida was transferred to British control, and Spanish officials and most of the colonists left for Cuba, taking their records with them. After the return of Spanish control in 1783, the colony was largely populated by British colonists and Americans crossing over from the north. In 1810, the Gulf Coast area known as West Florida was declared independent and merged with the American territory of Louisiana. With the Adams-Onis Treaty in 1821, East Florida was sold to the United States.

The majority of records for Florida during its Spanish periods are found in the *Papeles de Cuba* section of the *Archivo General de Indias* in Seville, Spain. Copies of most, if not all, records of interest have been made, and many are published. The following repositories have collections of these materials as well as other records relating to Spanish rule in Florida:

The Florida State Archives, 500 South Bronough Street, Tallahassee, Florida, houses many records relating to the Spanish period, including all the land grant files. Its Web page at <http://dlis.dos.state.fl.us/barm/fsa.html> offers access to an online catalog as well as digitized copies of Spanish land grants.

P. K. Yonge Library of Florida History at the University of Florida in Gainesville offers the best collection of materials covering the Spanish periods in Florida. Its calendars of the John Batterson Stetson Collection, East Florida Papers, and *Papeles Procedentes de Cuba,* developed by the Spanish Florida Borderlands Program, consist of a series of 3 x 5 catalog cards, arranged chronologically within *legajos,* or sections. Efforts are underway to digitize those calendars and place them online. For more detail see <http://web.uflib.ufl.edu/spec/pkyonge/brdrland.html>.

The St. Augustine Foundation Center for Historic Research at Flagler College at St. Augustine, Florida, holds more than 950 reels of primary documents on microfilm from Spanish or Spanish American archives, as well as a large library of secondary materials relating to Spanish Florida. For information about these collections and the computerized database being created from them, go to <www.flagler.edu/about_f/historical.html>.

St. Augustine Historical Society, St. Augustine, Florida, has a research library with more than 8,500 books, documents, manuscripts, and historical papers on Florida history. Go to <www.staugustinehistoricalsociety.org/library.html>.

Library and Archives of the Pensacola Historical Society, Pensacola, Florida, contains manuscripts and reference materials relating to the Spanish period in the West Florida area. See <www.pensacolahistory.org>.

John C. Pace Library, University of West Florida, Pensacola, Florida, houses the Special Collections Department, which preserves, catalogs, and provides reference services to research materials that document the history and development of Pensacola and the West Florida and Gulf Coast regions. For more detail, see <www.lib.uwf.edu/maps/Pace_1.shtml>.

Municipal Archives of the City of Mobile, Alabama, has records from the colonial period relating to the Mobile area and an index to land grant records for the area found in the *Papeles de Cuba*.

Census Records of Florida

Census records provide excellent coverage of the second Spanish period.

Spanish Censuses of Florida

Locality	Year(s)	Reference*
General	1784–1820	GGS
General	1787	FFF
General	1792	AGI, Cuba
General	1812	AGI, Cuba
General	1814	AGI, Cuba
Escambia River	1820	GGS
Pensacola	1784	LGR 27:367
Pensacola	1788	LGR 27:367
Pensacola	1802	LGR 27:368
Pensacola	1805	LGR 27:368
Pensacola	1819	LGR 27:368
Pensacola	1820	LGR 27:368
S. Augustine	1783	1,014,120
S. Augustine	1786	FHQ 18:11–31; FFF; 1,014,120
S. Augustine	1789	AGI, Cuba
S. Augustine (indexed)	1793	1,014,120; FFF
S. Augustine	1805	LGR 27:368
S. Augustine	1812	LGR 27:368
S. Augustine	1813	FFF
S. Augustine (Msqto terr)	1814	1,014,120; FFF
West Florida	1805	LGR 27:368

***AGI, Cuba**: The *Papeles de Cuba* section of the *Archivo General de las Indias* in Seville, Spain.
LGR: Those found in the historical manuscripts section of the Loyola University Library, New Orleans, Louisiana.
The following are identified only in published form:
GGS: *Genealogical Guide to Spanish Pensacola* by William S. Colker.
FHQ: *Florida Historical Quarterly.*
FFF: *Florida's First Families,* Volume I, by Donna Rachal Mills.
Six- or seven-digit numbers with no other reference are film numbers from the collection of the LDS Family History Library in Salt Lake City, available through local Family History Centers.

Catholic Church Records

While a large number of Catholic missions were established at various times during the first Spanish period, only those of St. Augustine and Pensacola had the permanence to maintain parish sacramental records.

Catholic Church Records of Florida

Name	Record Type∞	Reference*	Format†
St. Augustine	Ba 1594–1938 Ma 1594–1924 Bu 1594–1882 C 1594–1923	SAC	FHL, P
Pensacola	C 1793	GGS	

∞**Ad:** Administrative records
Ba: Baptisms
Bu: Burials/deaths
C: Confirmations
Ma: Marriages

***SAC:** St. Augustine Cathedral, Florida.
GGS: *Genealogical Guide to Spanish Pensacola* by William S. Colker.

†**FHL:** Filmed by and located in the Family History Library, Salt Lake City, Utah.
P: Index, transcription, and/or translation exists.
Records may cover only some of the years indicated.

Records of Louisiana

Unlike the areas discussed thus far, Louisiana was initially settled by the French rather than the Spanish, as French explorers and then fur traders came down the St. Lawrence River and into the Great Lakes. French settlement in North America began with Acadia in 1603 and Quebec in 1608. In 1673, Louis Joliet, together with Jesuit priest Jacques Marquette, explored the Great Lakes region and reached the upper Mississippi River from Canada. Colonies were established at Detroit in 1701 and, later on, along the Ohio, Illinois, and upper Mississippi Rivers, including the Arkansas Post in 1686; Fort St. Joseph (Niles, Michigan) in 1697; Fort Miami (Fort Wayne, Indiana) in 1697; Cahokia, Kaskaskia, Prairie du Rocher, and St. Phillippe in Illinois, beginning in 1699; and Fort Michilimakinac (Michigan) in 1715.

In 1682, René Robert Cavellier, Sieur de la Salle, traveled down the Mississippi River to its mouth. While La Salle's attempt at establishing a colony failed, Pierre Le Moyne, Sieur d'Iberville, later traveled from France through the Gulf of Mexico to establish Fort Maurepas at Biloxi in present-day Mississippi. Other French establishments followed: Fort Louis on the Mobile River in 1702; Natchitoches in 1712; Fort Rosalie, now Natchez, Mississippi, in 1716; New Orleans in 1718; and Baton Rouge in 1719. With its capital at New Orleans beginning in 1723, Louisiana became a strong and bustling French colony, covering not only current Louisiana but all the watershed area of the great Mississippi River.

French control of the interior of the American continent was thus assured by the establishment of Louisiana. The colony grew under French control and even more dramatically under Spanish control after 1763. Notable during the latter period were the transfer of the French Acadians to Louisiana after their expulsion by the British in 1763 and the founding of St. Louis, Missouri, in 1764. Extensive records exist for both the French and Spanish periods, including government administrative records, judicial records, notarial records, and city council (*cabildo*) records. The vast majority of these records are currently found in one of the following collections:

Louisiana State Museum Historical Center houses the records of the French Superior Council (1714–69) and the Spanish Judiciary (1769–1803). These criminal and civil court records include many successions with a wealth of genealogical information concerning Louisiana's colonial inhabitants. Also found are many abstracts and translations of colonial documents not housed in the Historical Center, such as the *Dispatches of the Spanish Governors of Louisiana* (1766–96, 27 volumes), which include material generated by Spanish governors, as well as the French *Louisiane Recensements* (1706–41), *Passages* (1718–24), and *Concessions* (1719–24). For more detail, go to <http://specialcollections.tulane.edu/~wc/guidetocollections/louisianaMuseum.html>.

The New Orleans Notarial Archives holds notarial documents from the French and Spanish colonial periods, relevant to all of Louisiana. See <www.notarialarchives.org>.

Special Collections Division of Tulane University in New Orleans houses original manuscripts as well as reference materials related to the Louisiana colonial period, including many family collections. See <www.tulane.edu/~lmiller/ManuscriptsHome.html>.

The Historic New Orleans Collection in New Orleans offers an extensive research library and manuscript material concerning New Orleans in the colonial period, as well as Louisiana materials from the French National Archives, Archives of the Indies of Spain, and the Cuban National Archives. For more detail, go to <www.hnoc.org>.

The *Archives d' Outre Mer* in Aix en Provence, France, and the *Archivo General de Indias* in Seville, Spain, both have major collections of government documents relating to Louisiana. Most have been filmed, transcribed, or indexed, however, and can be consulted in the above-named repositories as well as in a number of university libraries in the United States. Extensive work has been done on microfilming, transcribing, and translating many of the other colonial records of Louisiana. Anyone doing beginning research on families in Louisiana should obtain a copy of Beers' *French and Spanish Records of Louisiana* and read it with great care. Consulting the Internet sites mentioned earlier will provide information on most of the changes that have occurred since the book's printing.

Census Records

Extensive French and Spanish census records are available for Louisiana.

French Censuses of Colonial Louisiana

Locality	Year(s)	Reference*
New Orleans to Ouacha	1724	CTFCL
Dauphin I., Cat I., and Pascagoula	1725	CTFCL
Inhabitants along the Mississippi River	1731	CTFCL
Ft. Maurepas	1699	CTFCL
Mobile (Ft. Louis)	1706	DSGQ; CTFCL
Mobile (Ft. Louis)	1711	CTFCL
Mobile	1721	DSGQ; CTFCL
Natchez (Ft. Rosalie)	1726	FFL
Natchitoches (Ft. St. Jean Baptiste)	1722	CTFCL
New Orleans	1721	CTFCL
New Orleans	1732	CTFCL
New Orleans	1727	CTFCL

***CTFCL:** Charles R. Maduell Jr., *The Census Tables for the French Colony of Louisiana from 1699 Through 1732* (Baltimore: Genealogical Publishing Co., 1972; reprint, Clearfield Co., 2000).

DSGQ: Detroit Society for Genealogical Research Quarterly.

FFL: *First Families of Louisiana.*

Spanish Censuses of Louisiana

Locality	Year(s)	Reference*
Arkansas	1777	AGI, Cuba
Arkansas	1791	AGI, Cuba
Arkansas	1793	LGR 27:367–368
Mississippi	1801	AGI, Cuba
Allemands	1776	AGI, Cuba
Allemands	1784	AGI, Cuba
Allemands	1789	AGI, Cuba
Allemands	1795	AGI, Cuba
Allemands	1799	AGI, Cuba
Acadians	1769	AGI, Cuba
Acadians	1770	AGI, Cuba
Ascensión parish	1770	LGR 27:367–368
Ascensión parish	1777	LGR 27:367–368
Attakapas	1770	AGI, Cuba
Attakapas	1771	AGI, Cuba
Attakapas	1774	AGI, Cuba
Attakapas	1777	LGR 27:367–368
Attakapas	1785	LGR 27:367–368
Attakapas	1795	AGI, Cuba
Attakapas	1799	AGI, Cuba
Attakapas	1803	AGI, Cuba
Avoyelles	1785	AGI, Cuba
Bahía Honda	1783	AGI, Cuba
Baton Rouge	1782	AGI, Cuba
Baton Rouge	1786	AGI, Cuba
Baton Rouge	1787	LGR 27:367–368
Baton Rouge	1795	AGI, Cuba
Baton Rouge	1805	AGI, Cuba
Bayou Teche	1803	LGR 27:367–368
Cabahannocer	1775	AGI, Cuba
Cabahannocer	1776	AGI, Cuba
Cabahannocer	1777	AGI, Cuba
Cabahannocer	1779	AC
Cabahannocer	1789	AGI, Cuba
Cannes Brülées	1795	AGI, Cuba
Cannes Brülées	1799	AGI, Cuba
Chapitoulas	1795	AGI, Cuba
Choctaw islands	1803	LGR 27:367–368
False River	1766	AGI, Cuba
False River	1787	LGR 27:367–368
False River	1790	AGI, Cuba
False River	1795	LGR 27:367–368
False River	1803	LGR 27:367–368
German coast	1784	LGR 27:367–368
German coast	1766	LGR 27:367–368
Iberville	1771	AGI, Cuba
Iberville	1777	LGR 27:367–368
Iberville	1772	LGR 27:367–368
Lafourche	1777	LGR 27:367–368
Lafourche	1788	LGR 27:367–368
Lafourche	1789	LGR 27:367–368
Lafourche	1791	LGR 27:367–368
Lafourche	1798	LGR 27:367–368
Louisiana Regiment	1779	LGR 27:367–368
Manchac	1777	LGR 27:367–368
Manchac	1772	LGR 27:367–368
Manchac	1791	AGI, Cuba
Manchac	1795	AGI, Cuba
Météaire	1796	MVM
Météaire	1799	AGI, Cuba
Mobile	1780	AGI, Cuba
Mobile	1781	AGI, Cuba
Mobile	1784	LGR 27:367–368
Mobile	1786	AGI, Cuba

Locality	Year(s)	Reference*
Mobile	1787	AGI, Cuba
Mobile	1788	LGR 27:367–368
Mobile	1789	AGI, Cuba
Mobile	1795	AGI, Cuba
Mobile	1805	LGR 27:367–368
Mobile (slaves)	1787	LGR 27:367–368
Natchez	1784	LGR 27:367–368
Natchez	1787	LGR 27:367–368
Natchez	1788	LGR 27:367–368
Natchez	1792	LGR 27:367–368
Natchez	1792	899,975
Natchez	1793	AGI, Cuba
Natchez	1794	LGR 27:367–368
Natchitoches	1770	AGI, Cuba
Natchitoches	1774	AGI, Cuba
Natchitoches	1786	AGI, Cuba
Natchitoches	1795	AGI, Cuba
Natchitoches	1787	LGR 27:367–368
New Bourbon	1797	AGI, Cuba
New Feliciana	1793	LGR 27:367–368
New Feliciana	1796	LGR 27:367–368
New Feliciana	1798	AGI, Cuba
New Iberia	1778	LGR 27:367–368
New Iberia	1789	AGI, Cuba
New Madrid	1791	AGI, Cuba
New Madrid	1792	LGR 27:367–368
New Madrid	1793	LGR 27:367–368
New Madrid	1794	LGR 27:367–368
New Madrid	1796	LGR 27:367–368
New Madrid	1797	AGI, Cuba
New Orleans	1767	LGR 27:367–368
New Orleans	1778	LGR 27:367–368
New Orleans (1st q.)	1795	LGR 27:367–368
New Orleans (2nd q.)	1795	LGR 27:367–368
New Orleans (3rd q.)	1796	LGR 27:367–368
New Orleans	1798	AGI, Cuba
New Orleans	1799	AGI, Cuba
Opelousas	1770	AGI, Cuba
Opelousas	1771	AGI, Cuba
Opelousas	1774	MVM
Opelousas	1777	LGR 27:367–368
Opelousas	1785	LGR 27:367–368
Opelousas	1788	LGR 27:367–368
Opelousas	1796	LGR 27:367–368
Ouachita	1790	AGI, Cuba
Pointe du Teiche	1803	AGI, Cuba
Pointe Coupee parish	1766	LGR 27:367–368
Pointe Coupee parish	1776	AGI, Cuba
Pointe Coupee parish	1787	LGR 27:367–368
Pointe Coupee parish	1790	AGI, Cuba
Pointe Coupee parish	1795	LGR 27:367–368
Pointe Coupee parish	1803	LGR 27:367–368
Prairie Aux Mouche	1770	LGR 27:367–368
Rapides	1770	AGI, Cuba
Rapides	1773	AGI, Cuba
Rapides	1789	AGI, Cuba
Rapides	1792	AGI, Cuba
Recruits from Canary I.	1783	LGR 27:367–368
S. Geneviéve	1770	AGI, Cuba
S. Geneviéve	1771	AGI, Cuba
S. Geneviéve	1773	AGI, Cuba
S. Geneviéve	1779	LGR 27:367–368
S. James parish	1769	LGR 27:367–368
S. James parish	1777	LGR 27:367–368
S. James parish	1766	LGR 27:367–368
Tinzas	1785	AGI, Cuba
Tombecbé	1797	AGI, Cuba
Valenzuela	1784	VPL
Valenzuela	1797	LGR 27:367–368

***AC:** *The Acadian Coast in 1779.*

AGI, Cuba: The *Papeles de Cuba* section of the *Archivo General de las Indias* in Seville, Spain.

MVM: Winston De Ville, *Mississippi Valley Melange: A Collection of Notes and Documents for the Genealogy and History of the Province of Louisiana and the Territory of Orlean,* vol. 1 (Ville Platte, La.: Mississippi Valley Melange, 1995).

LGR: Those found in the historical manuscripts section of the Loyola University Library, New Orleans, Louisiana.

VPL: *Valenzuela in the Province of Louisiana,* by Winston de Ville.

Six- or seven-digit numbers with no other reference are film numbers from the collection of the LDS Family History Library in Salt Lake City, available through local Family History Centers.

Catholic Church Records of Louisiana

While the role of the Catholic Church in Louisiana was never as strong as in the Spanish colonies, Catholicism was a strong unifying factor among the French colonists, and its parish records are an important genealogical source.

Catholic Church Records of Louisiana

Church Name	Location	Date of Origin	Record Type∞	Reference*	Format†
St. Joseph	Baton Rouge, LA	1793	Ba 1793–1821 Ma 1793–1840 Bu 1793–1815	DBR DBR DBR	
Fort Maurepas	Biloxi, MI	1699	Bu 1720–1722	ANP	FHL
St. Charles Borromeo	Destrehan, LA	1723	Ba 1739–1755	ADNO	P
Ascension	Donaldsonville, LA	1772	Ba, Ma, Bu 1772–1789 Ba 1785–1823 Ba, Ma, Bu SFPC 1786–1827 Ma 1786–1829 Bu 1785–1841	DBR DBR DBR DBR DBR	
St. John the Baptist	Edgard, LA	1772	Ba 1772–1818 Ma 1772–1818 Bu 1772–1815	ADNO ADNO ADNO	P P P
St. Bernard Merged with St. Gabriel in 1809	Galveztown	1779	See St. Gabriel with whom the records are often mixed		
	Iberville, LA Manchac, LA		See St. Gabriel		
St. Paul the Apostle	Mansura, LA Also includes Avoyelles and Rapides	1797	Ba 1796–1831 Ba SFPC, I 1796–1841 Ma 1806–1830 Bu 1803–1894	ADNO ADNO ADNO ADNO	P P P P
Cathedral of the Immaculate Conception	Mobile , AL AKA Notre Dame du Fort Condé	1703	Ba 1704–1778 Ba 1781–1835 Ba SFPC 1781–1828 Ma 1724–1832 Bu 1726–1828 (gaps)	DM, PAC DM DM DM, PAC DM	FHL, P FHL, P FHL, P FHL, P FHL, P
San Salvador	Natchez, MI	1788	Ba 1789–1804, 1818 Ma 1788–1810 Bu 1788–1798 Bu SFPC 1796–1798	DJ DBR DBR DJ	
Immaculate Conception Formerly St. Francis	Natchitoches, LA	1728	Ba Ma Bu 1729–1791 Ba Ma Bu 1786–1792 Ba 1776–1801 Ba Ma Bu 1801–1822	P P P P	FHL, P FHL FHL FHL
St. Louis (cathedral) (continued)	New Orleans, LA	1719	Ba 1729–1730 Ba 1731–1733 Ba 1744–1815 Ba SFPC 1777–1814 Ma 1720–1730 Ma 1748–1806 Ma 1764–1821 (gaps) Ma SFPC 1777–1830 Bu 1724–1730	ANP ADNO ADNO ADNO ADNO CNO ADNO ADNO ANP	FHL P P P P P P P FHL

Church Name	Location	Date of Origin	Record Type[∞]	Reference*	Format[†]
St. Louis (cathedral)	New Orleans, LA	1719	Bu 1772–1815	ADNO	P
			Bu SFPC 1777–1815 (gaps)	ADNO	P
			C 1789–1841	ADNO	P
St. Landry	Opelousas, LA	1770	Ba , Ma, Bu 1776–1786	ADNO	P
			Ba 1776– 1795	ADNO	FHL, P
			Ba 1796–1827	ADNO	P
			Ba SFPC 1787–1813	ADNO	P
			Ma 1787–1795	ADNO	FHL, P
			Ma 1787–1830	ADNO	P
			Bu 1787–1819	ADNO	P
			C 1777–1795		FHL, P
Assumption	Plattenville, LA	1793	Ba 1793–1815	DBR	
			Ba SFPC 1793–1841	DBR	
			Ma 1793–1817	DBR	
			Bu 1793–1838	DBR	
			Bu SFPC 1793–1838	DBR	
St. Francis of Assisi	Pointe Coupee, LA	1728	Ba, Ma, Bu 1727–1814	ADNO	P
			Ba SFPC 1786–1838	ADNO	P
			Ma SFPC 1786–1841	ADNO	P
			Bu 1785–1841	ADNO	P
St. Bernard	St. Bernard, LA	1785	Ba SFPC 1787–1857	CNO	
			Ba 1801–1851	P (Violet)	
			Bu 1787–1878	P (Violet)	
			Bu SFCP 1787–1887	P (Violet)	
St. James	St. James, LA	1767	Ba , Ma, Bu 1767–1804	ADNO	P
			Ba 1786–1826	ADNO	P
			Ba SFPC 1807–1812	ADNO	P
			Ma 1785–1861	ADNO	P
			Bu 1794–1857	ADNO	P
St. Gabriel	St. Gabriel, LA	1773	Ba , Ma, Bu 1773–1858	DBR	
			Ba 1773–1774	PAC	FHL
Includes records for parishes of Iberville, Manchac, and St. Bernard			Ma 1773–1859	PAC	FHL
			Ba SFPC 1791–1827	DBR	
			Ba , Ma, Bu SFPC 1791–1858	DBR	
			Ba 1773–1831	DBR	
			Ma 1785–1859	DBR	
			Bu 1785–1856	DBR	
St. Martin AKA Attakapas	St. Martinville, LA	1756	Ba, Ma, Bu 1756–1794 gaps	PAC	FHL, P
			Ba, Ma,Bu 1756–1818 gaps	ADNO	P
			Ba, Ma, Bu SFPC 1765–1843	ADNO	P

For detailed descriptions of the registers summarized above, refer to Charles E. Nolan, *A Southern Catholic Heritage, Volume I, Colonial Period 1704–1813* (New Orleans: Archdiocese of New Orleans, 1976.). Indexing of those records found in the Archives of the Archdiocese of New Orleans is found in a multivolume set edited by Earl C. Woods and Charles E. Nolan entitled *Sacramental records of the Roman Catholic Church of the Archdiocese of New Orleans,* vol. 1. 1718–1750; vol. 2. 1751–1771; vol. 3. 1772–1783; vol. 4. 1784–1790; vol. 5. 1791–1795; vol. 6. 1796–1799; vol. 7. 1800–1803; vol. 8. 1804–1806; vol. 9. 1807–1809; vol. 10. 1810–1812; vol. 11. 1813–1815; vol. 12. 1816–1817; vol. 13. 1818–1819; vol. 14. 1820–1821; vol. 15. 1822–1823; vol. 16. 1824–1825; vol. 17 1826–1827; vol. 18. 1828–1829; vol. 19. 1830–1831 (New Orleans: Archdiocese of New Orleans, 1987–99). Records for Southwestern and Southern Louisiana parishes have been indexed in multivolume series by Donald J. Hebert.

[∞]**Ad:** Administrative records
Ba: Baptisms
Bu: Burials/deaths
C: Confirmations
Ma: Marriages
SFPC: Slaves and Free Persons of Color, I for Indians

***ADNO:** Archives of the Archdiocese of New Orleans.
ANP: Archives Nationales, Paris.
CNO: The St. Louis Cathedral Archives in New Orleans.
DBR: The Chancery Archives in Baton Rouge.
DJ: The Chancery Archives in Jackson.
DM: The Chancery Archives in Mobile.
PAC: Public Archives of Canada, Toronto.
P: Records available at the parish indicated.
P (Violet): Records available at the Violet parish.
USWLA: University of Southwestern Louisiana.

[†]**FHL:** Filmed by and located in the Family History Library, Salt Lake City, Utah.
MC: Microfilmed copy exists somewhere other than at the FHL.
P: Index, transcription, and/or translation exists.
Records may cover only some of the years indicated.

Records of the French and Spanish in the Great Lakes and Upper Mississippi

French colonization of the Great Lakes and upper Mississippi area from 1673 to 1720 was discussed in the Louisiana section. While never a major colony, a number of records exist for this region during its French occupation, which ended in 1763 with the transfer of the Great Lakes region to British control and the Mississippi River area to Spain. French records from this area can be found at the Burton Historical Collection in the Detroit Public Library, as well as in archives in Quebec and the *Archives d' Outre Mer* in Aix en Provence, France. Several local libraries in Michigan, Illinois, and Missouri maintain collections of records for this area as well. An excellent overview of research in French Canada, including work in the colonial period in the Great Lakes region before 1763, can be found by reading John P. DuLong's *French-Canadian Genealogical Research.*[30] Also consider visiting DuLong's web page for Acadian and French Canadian genealogy at <http://habitant.org/> and that of the French Canadian Heritage Society of Michigan at <http://fchsm.habitant.org/index.htm>. A comprehensive guide to researching French-Canadian roots is found in *French-Canadian Sources: A Guide for Genealogists*.[31]

Census Records

The following chart identifies the known census records for the Great Lakes and Upper Mississippi regions during the French and Spanish periods and tells where the original census records or microfilm copies can be found. Where possible, a citation to an archive or library in the United States has been preferred, even though that library may only hold a microfilm of the original. In cases where no such copy exists, the foreign archives holding the original copy is identified.

Censuses of the Great Lakes

Locality	Year(s)	Reference*
Illinois	1732	CTFCL
Louisiana	1706	CTFCL
Louisiana	1726	CTFCL
Biloxi	1700	CTFCL
Biloxi	1721	CTFCL
Detroit	1710	ANFP
Detroit and Mission Bois Blanc	1743	ACJ
Detroit	1750	PAC
Detroit	1762	DPL
Detroit	1765	HSP
Detroit	1768	UMI
Detroit	1779	BML
Ft. Saint Joseph	1780	PAC
Detroit	1782	BML; PAC
Arkansas	1794	LGR 27:367–368
Arkansas	1795	LGR 27:367–368
Arkansas	1796	LGR 27:367–368
Arkansas	1798–1799	AGI, Cuba
Illinois	1795	LGR 27:367–368
Illinois	1796	LGR 27:367–368
Petite Cote	1792	PAC
S. Louis	1771–1773	AGI, Cuba
S. Louis	1779	LGR 27:367–368
S. Louis	1795–1796	AGI, Cuba
Wayne County, Michigan	1796	OHS

Information concerning the early Detroit and Michigan censuses was taken from *Michigan Censuses 1710–1830: Under the French, British and Americans*, ed. Donna Russell (Detroit, Mich.: Detroit Society for Genealogical Research, 1982).

***ACJ:** *Archives de la Compagnie de Jésus* in St. Jerôme, Quebec, Canada.
AGI, Cuba: The *Papeles de Cuba* section of the *Archivo General de las Indias* in Seville, Spain.
ANFP: *Archives Nationales de France*, Paris.
BML: Haldimand Papers, British Museum, London.
CTFCL: Charles R. Maduell Jr., *The Census Tables for the French Colony of Louisiana from 1699 Through 1732* (Baltimore: Genealogical Publishing Co., 1972; reprint, Clearfield Co., 2000).
DPL: Burton Historical Manuscript Collection at the Detroit Public Library.
HSP: Historical Society of Pennsylvania, Philadelphia.
LGR: Those found in the historical manuscripts section of the Library at Loyola University, New Orleans, Louisiana.
OHS: Ohio Historical Society.
PAC: Public Archives of Canada at Ottawa, Ontario, Canada.
UMI: Gage Papers, William L Clements Library, University of Michigan.
Six- or seven-digit numbers with no other reference are film numbers from the collection of the LDS Family History Library in Salt Lake City, available through the local Family History Centers.

Catholic Church Records

Catholic Church Records of Colonial Upper Louisiana Territory

Church Name	Modern Location	Date of Origin	Records[∞]	Reference*	Format[†]
Chapel of the Almonry (Ft. de Chartres)	Randolph County, Illinois		Ba 1723–1724 Ma 1723–1724 Bu 1723–1724	MVM	P
St. Anne (Fort de Chartres)	Randolph County, Illinois	1721	Combined Records 1721–1804	BPL; SLCL	FHL/MC/P
Notre Dame de l'Immaculate Conception	Kaskaskia, Illinois	1703	Ba 1695–1799 Ma 1724–1799 Bu 1720–1799 Bu 1723–1724	BPL; SLCL; MVM ANP	FHL/MC/P
La Visitation de St. Phillippe	Arkansas Post, Arkansas		Ba 1761–1764 Ma 1761–1764 Bu 1761–1764		FHL
St. Joseph	Prairie du Rocher, Illinois	1721	Ba 1765– Ma Various years Bu 1772–	BPL; SLCL	FHL/MC
St. Ignace	Machilimakinac		Ma 1695– c. 1821		
Sault Ste. Marie					
St. Mary of the Immaculate Conception (previously St. Antoine)	Monroe, Michigan	1788	Ba 1794– Ma 1794– Bu 1795–	DPL	FHL/MC
St. Anne	Detroit, Michigan	1704	Ba 1704– Ma 1704– Bu 1704–	DPL	FHL/MC/P
Mission de la Revière St. Joseph	Berrien County, Michigan		Combined registers 1720–1773		FHL
Holy Family (Cahokia)	St. Claire, Illinois	1699	Ba 1812– Ma 1850– Bu 1783–1899	BPL; SLCL	MC

[∞]**Ad:** Administrative records
Ba: Baptisms
Bu: Burials/deaths
C: Confirmations
Ma: Marriages

***ANP:** Archives Nationales, Paris.
BPL: The Belleville Public Library, Belleville, Illinois.
DPL: The Detroit Public Library (Burton Collection).
MVM: Winston De Ville, *Mississippi Valley Melange: A Collection of Notes and Documents for the Genealogy and History of the Province of Louisiana and the Territory of Orleans,* vol. 1 (Ville Platte, La., 1995).
SLCL: The St. Louis County Library, St. Louis, Missouri.

[†]**FHL:** Filmed by and located in the Family History Library, Salt Lake City, Utah.
MC: Microfilmed copy exists somewhere other than at the FHL.
P: Index, transcription, and/or translation exists.
Records may cover only some of the years indicated.

Notes

[1] Peter Gerhard, *The North Frontier of New Spain* (Norman: University of Oklahoma Press, 1982), 24–25, online at <http://teaching.arts.usyd.edu.au/history/hsty3080/3rdYr3080/Louisiana/louisiana_after_the_purchase>.

[2] John Francis Bannon, *The Spanish Borderlands Frontier 1513–1821* (Albuquerque: University of New Mexico Press, 1988); Clarence Henry Haring, *The Spanish Empire in American* (New York: Oxford University Press, 1947).

[3] Thomas C. Barnes, *Northern New Spain: A Research Guide* (Tucson: University of Arizona Press, 1981); Clarence Henry Haring, *The Spanish Empire in America* (1940; reprint, Harcourt, 1985.)

[4] George R. Ryskamp, *Finding Your Hispanic Roots* (Baltimore: Genealogical Publishing Co., 1997).

[5] Alice Daly Forsyth, *Louisiana Marriages: A Collection of Marriage Records from the St. Louis Cathedral in New Orleans during the Spanish Regime and the Early American Period: 1784–1806* (New Orleans: Polyanthos, 1977).

[6] Lyman D. Platt, *Latin American Census Records* (Baltimore: Genealogical Publishing Co., 1998).

[7] Taken from page 1 of *Residents of Texas 1782–1836, Volume 2*, by the University of Texas Institute of Texan Cultures.

[8] Raúl J. Guerra Jr., Nadine Vásquez, and Baldomero Vela Jr., *Index to the Marriage Investigations of Diocese of Guadalajara, Provinces of Coahuila, Nuevo Leon, Nuevo Santander, Texas, Volume 1: 1653–1750* (Edinburg, 1989). See also Raúl Guerra Jr., Nadine Vásquez, and Baldomero Vela Jr., *Index to the Marriage Investigations of the Diocese of Guadalajara, Provinces of Coahuila, Nuevo Leon, Nuevo Santander, Texas, 1751–1779, Vol II* (San Antonio, 1997).

[9] Rick Hendricks, ed., and John B. Colligan, comp., *New Mexico Prenuptial Investigations from the Archivos Históricos Del Arzobispado De Durango, 1760–1799* (Las Cruces, N.M., 1997).

[10] Gerhard, *North Frontier of New Spain*, 19–22.

[11] *Historical Records Survey Division of Community Services Program, Work Projects Administration* (Tallahassee, Fla.: State Library Report, 1940).

[12] Direccion General de Archivos y Bibliotecas, *Guía de fuentes Para la historia de Ibero-América conservados en Epsaña*, 2 vols. (Madrid, 1966); José Tudela, *Los Manuscritos de América en las Bibliotecas de España* (Madrid: Ediciones Cultura Hispánica, 1954); Lawrence H. Feldman, *Anglo-Americans in Spanish Archives* (Baltimore: Genealogical Publishing Co., 1991); Lino Gómez Canedo, *Los archivos de la historia de América, periódo colonial española*, 2 vols., Instituto Panamericano de Geograffia e Historia, Comisión de Historia, Publicación Num. 225 (Mexico City: Commisión de Historia, 1961).

[13] Cristobal Bermuda Plata, *El Archivo General de Indias de Sevilla: sede del americanismo* (Madrid, 1951); Charles E. Chapman, *Catalogue of Materials in the Archivo General de las Indias for the History of the Pacific Coast and the American Southwest*, University of California, Publications in History, vol. 8 (Glendale, Calif.: Arthur H. Clark Co., 1927); Charles E. Chapman, *Catalogue of Material in the Archivo General de Indias for the History of the Pacific Coast and the American Southwest*, University of California, *Publications in History*, vol. 8. (Berkeley: University of California Press, 1919); *Indice de documentos de Nueva Espana: existentes en el Archivo de Indias de Sevilla* (México, D.F.: Secretaria de Relaciones Exteriores, 1925–31); Purificación Medina Encina, *Documentos Relativos a la Independencia de Norteamérica Existentes en Archivos Españoles*, Vol. I: *Archivo General de Indias, sección de gobierno, años 1752–1822* (Madrid: Ministerio de Asuntos Exteriores, Dirección General de Relaciones Culturas, 1976).

[14] Angel de la Plaza Bores, *Archivo General de Simancas: Guía del Investigador* (Madrid: Dirección General de Archivos y Bibliotecas, Patronato Nacional de Archivos Históricos, 1962).

[15] Ricardo Magdaleño, *Catálogo XX del Archivo General de Simancas, Títulos de Indias* (Patronato Nacional de Archivos Históricos: Valladolid, 1954).

[16] Archivo de Simancas, *Secretaria de Guerra, Hojas de Servicios de América* (Patronato Nacional de Archivos Históricos: Valladolid, 1958).

[17] *Guía de archivos militares españoles* (Madrid: Ministerio de Defensa, 1995); Federico Heredero Roura and Vincent Cadenas y Vicent, *Archivo General Militar de Segovia: Indice de Expedientes Personales*, 9 vols. (Ediciones Hidalguía: Madrid 1959–63).

[18] Léo Jouniaux, *Généalogie: pratique, métode, recherche* (Paris: Editiones Arthaud, 1991), 95–108; *International Directory of Archives*, 151–152; Joseph Valynseele, *La généalogie: histoire et pratique*, 2nd ed. (Paris: Larousse, 1992), 97–116, *État des inventaires des archives départementales, communales, et hospitalières* (Paris: Archives Nationales, 1984).

[19] Jean Favier, comp., *Les archives nationales: etat général des fonds*, vol. 3, *Marine et outre-mar* (Paris: Archives Nationales, 1978); Valynseele, *La généalogie: histoire et pratique*, 154–65.

[20] Roscoe R. Hill, *Los Archivos Nacionales de la America Latina* (La Habana: Archivo Nacional de Cuba, 1948); Ann Keith Nauman, *A Handbook of Latin American and Caribbean National Arhives, Guía de los archivos nacionales de América Latina y el Caribe* (Detroit: Blaine Ethridge Books, 1983).

[21] *Archivo General de la Nación Guía General* (México, D.F.: Difusión y Publicaciones del Archivio General de la Nación, 1991).

[22] Patricia Rodriguez Ochoa, *Guía general de los archivos estatales y municipales de México* (México, D.F.: Sistema Nacional de Archivos, 1988).

[23] George S. Ulibarri and John P. Harrison, *Guide to Materials on Latin America in the National Archives of the United States* (Washington, D.C.: National Archives and Records Service, General Services Administration, 1974).

[24] Adán Benavides Jr., comp. and ed., *The Béxar Archives, 1717–1836: A Name Guide* (Austin: University of Texas Press, 1989); Chester V. Kielman, *Guide to the Microfilm Edition of the Bexar Archives, 1717–1836*, 3 vols. (Austin: University of Texas Library, 1967–71).

[25] Robert D. Wood, comp., *Indexes to the Laredo Archives*, 2nd ed. (San Antonio: St. Mary's Univeristy Press, 2000).

[26] For detailed information see <www.nmcpr.state.nm.us>.

[27] For more information go to <www.hgrc-nm.org>.

[28] For details on the Sutro Library, a branch of the California State Library, see <www.library.ca.gov>.

[29] Rudecinda Lo Buglio, "Survey of Prestatehood Records: A New Look at Spanish and Mexican California Genealogical Records," *World Conference on Records*, vol. 9 (Salt Lake City: The Church of Jesus Christ of Latter-day Saints), series 714, pp. 8–16, and appendix A.

[30] John P. DuLong, *French-Canadian Genealogical Research* (East Lansing: Michigan State University Press, 1995).

[31] Patricia Keeney Geyh, Joyce Soltis Banachowski, Linda K. Boyea, et al., *French-Canadian Sources: A Guide for Genealogists* (Orem, Utah: Ancestry, 2002).

Internet Resources

California

<www.loscalifornianos.org> Los Californianos

<http://home.earthlink.net/~djmill/index.html> French-Canadian Heritage Society of California links to information involving the Canada-U.S. borderlands and some of the colonial records and history, as well as other groups and organizations that have an interest in this area.

Colonial Louisiana

<www.francogene.com/usa/louisiana.php> A brief overview of the state's history; includes extracts of some early marriages and information and finding aids for early records from the French colonial period.

<www.francogene.com/usa/forts.php> Covers vital records for forts during the French colonial period along the Mississippi River.

<www.francogene.com/usa/illinois.php/> Covers vital records available for forts in French colonial Illinois Territory.

<www.archdiocese-no.org/archives/page4.htm> Genealogy page for the Archidiocese of New Orleans.

<http://globalgenealogy.com/globalgazette/gazrr/gazrr57.htm> Lists extant Acadian church records for Colonial Louisiana and links to early parish registers for the Fortress of Louisbourg, 1713–58, that are online.

<www.archives.nd.edu/guidecon.htm> Online guide to the archives at the University of Notre Dame.

<www.hpl.lib.tx.us/clayton/la002.html> Guide to the records found in *Southwest Louisiana Records* published by Rev. Donald J. Hébert.

<www.vivelacajun.com/Genealogy%20Research/la-books.htm> List of published materials available for research on Colonial Louisiana.

<www.quintinpublications.com/mi.html> Lists publications for records in Michigan beginning in French colonial times.

New Mexico

<www.nmgs.org/Chrchs-records.htm> New Mexico Genealogical Society has posted instructions on where to locate Catholic Church records for New Mexico, as well as links and references to other important sources.

<www.genealogybranches.com/valencia/index.html> An online database that currently contains various records for Belen, New Mexico, for the period 1740–1825.

<www.nmgs.org/Chrchs-citiesA.htm> Catholic records of New Mexico.

<www.hgrc-nm.org/> Hispanic Genealogical Research Center of New Mexico.

Texas

<www.onr.com/user/cat> Catholic Archives of Texas.

Catholic Church

<www.ezresult.com/Society/ReligionandSpirituality/Christianity/Denominations/Catholicism/Dioceses/NorthAmerica/> A listing of links to all the archdioceses in the United States.

Universities and Archives

<http://bancroft.Berkeley.edu> UC Berkeley Bancroft Library.

<www.library.ucla.edu/> UCLA Library.

<www.lib.utexas.edu/> University of Texas, Austin.

<http://library.tulane.edu/> Tulane University Library.

<http://web.uflib.ufl.edu/> University of Florida, Gainesville.

<www.library.yale.edu> Yale Library.

17

Hispanic Research

GEORGE R. RYSKAMP, JD, AG

Few people recognize the extent of Hispanic immigration to the United States. Spanish settlement began in the Caribbean Islands and Mexico more than a century before the English settled Jamestown and Plymouth in 1607 and 1620. The earliest Hispanic settlers within the area of the United States settled Saint Augustine, Florida, on the eastern end of the continent in 1565 and New Mexico, on the western end, in 1598.

The Spanish colonial period represents only the beginning, with immigration continuing to this day as hundreds of thousands of Mexicans, Central Americans, and South Americans, as well as Cubans, Puerto Ricans, and others from the Caribbean, flow into the United States. Many of them ultimately will trace their roots through those American countries to Spain. Others will find that their roots beyond those countries are not Spanish but Native American, French, German, Eastern European, Italian, African, and Portuguese. Just as the United States has been a melting pot, so have been the countries of Central and South America.

Before the end of the colonial period (around 1820), an estimated 12 million Spaniards emigrated primarily to Mexico and Central and South America. The immigration that followed in the next century was even greater. Of a total of 55 million people who emigrated from Europe to the American continents between 1820 and 1920, 22 million went to Latin America—primarily to Argentina, Brazil, Cuba, and Uruguay. Large numbers of them came from Italy, Spain, and Portugal. The flow of immigration did not stop with the Great Depression. From 1946 to 1957, 1.75 million immigrants traveled to Latin America, primarily from Italy and Spain. Spanish immigration was not, of course, entirely to Latin America. Many Spaniards, among them large numbers of Galicians, Basques, and Andalucians, came directly to the United States.

Throughout the years, the descendants of those early immigrants to Latin America have continued to make their way to the United States. Between 1900 and 1930, Mexico alone is

Chapter Contents

estimated to have contributed 2 to 3 million immigrants, half of whom entered the United States illegally. From 1820 to 1906, approximately 20,000 legal immigrants arrived from South America, and from 1907 to 1926, 77,000 more arrived. It is estimated that from 1951 to 1975, 421,000 South Americans came to the United States. These numbers do not include the extensive immigration from Cuba, Puerto Rico, and Central America. In the 1980s, Cubans, Salvadorans, and others fleeing from political oppression and civil war joined with the larger flow of Mexicans and others who came for economic reasons. Recently, an increasing number of Argentines have also come for economic reasons. Immigration authorities often include the Portuguese within the Hispanic population. In addition to extensive migrations from Portugal to the United States, Portuguese immigrants may travel to Brazil and the Azores, and from these last two to the United States.

Unless Hispanic immigrant ancestors came to the United States within living memory, the greatest challenge to the family historian is often identifying the place of origin in the mother country. Fortunately, there are many good records available to Hispanics that can reveal such a place. Nothing is more exciting than a discovery that ancestry leads back to Mexico or bridges the ocean back to Spain. Whether the mother country is Argentina, Cuba, Mexico, Spain, or another Latin American or European country, the types of records to be searched and the process of searching those records remain basically the same. The emphasis of this chapter is on Spanish-language records available in the United States. For a complete understanding of this process, English-language records are briefly discussed where appropriate.

Keys to Success: Basic Research Concepts

Thoroughness

Clues to the place of origin can be challenging to find, especially in records created in the United States. As with any other aspect of family history research, thoroughness is extremely important. Search for all information about the individual, his family and any known friends, and the surname within his specific locality.

Begin with the Known—Move to the Unknown

Many researchers make the time-consuming and frequently unproductive mistake of attempting to locate a link with Spain or Mexico by jumping to the assumed place of origin first. Effective research best begins in the United States, even in the researcher's own home, because the best records for identifying the place of origin in the mother country are found at the immigrant's destination. With one or two exceptions, records that yield information about the place of origin in the mother country—vital records, legal documents, and so forth— will be the same as those used throughout the research process.

Start with a Thorough Preliminary Survey

Once again, following basic rules of good research is important. With each new piece of information—the name of a new family member, a new surname, the port or vessel of arrival, a possible place of origin or at least a former residence—follow the steps of the survey phase. Those steps, as they relate to tracing the Hispanic immigrant, are discussed later.

Learn Specific Emigration, Immigration, and Migration Patterns

Most areas throughout the world have followed basic patterns of immigration, as people moved from one particular region or country to another. An awareness of the patterns unique to the particular time period and area where your ancestors settled can perhaps help identify the region and, in some cases, even the place of origin.

Some migration patterns are generally true for a region over an extended period of time. A good example of this type of pattern is the movement of the Spanish colonial frontier in Mexico into what is now the southwestern United States. Most such migrants to early California came from Baja California, or Sonora, Sinaloa, and Nayarit in Mexico. Migrants moving into Texas were from central Mexico up through the Coahuila area. An understanding of these patterns should be coupled with an awareness that current political units and even the international boundaries may not reflect original patterns of migration and settlement. For example, two regions of Texas have different migration patterns than the central pattern just described. El Paso was traditionally part of the New Mexico area, with a settlement pattern coming up through Chihuahua into the El Paso region and further north into New Mexico. Likewise, the portion of Texas between the Nueces and Rio Grande rivers was, until 1848, politically part of the province of Nuevo Santander. Hence, its migratory patterns relate to the development of that part of northeastern Mexico rather than the development of central Texas.

Similarly, large migration patterns can exist in specific time periods from an origin country into specific countries or regions. Nearly all migrants from the northern Spanish ports of the Basque countries during the last quarter of the nineteenth century were destined for the island of Cuba. Early twentieth century immigration from Galicia centered extensively on the Rio de la Plata area of South America as well as Brazil, where the commonality between the Gallego language and Portuguese assisted the new immigrants. Within the recent past, Italians and southern Germans have also migrated to those same areas.

In addition to broad migration patterns, there have been numerous specific migrations of groups in more limited repetitive patterns. For example, many Spaniards, primarily from the Andalucia and Valencia regions, migrated to Hawaii after being recruited to work on sugar plantations there. They and the next generation of their descendants then migrated primarily to the western United States. Similarly, during the same period a great number of Basques from the Spanish and French Basque regions sought work as sheepherders and farmhands in California, Idaho, and Nevada. Today their descendants can be found throughout this same area, and the largest collection of Basque historical and cultural materials in the United States is housed at the University of Nevada at Reno.

Front and back of a late-nineteenth-century Spanish photo of a brother and sister.

In some cases the research pattern is even more specific: an entire group moved from one area to settle a specific region. Such was the case in the Canary Island migration to found the city of San Antonio in 1730, and also for a series of Canary Island settlements in the Louisiana area between 1766 and 1800. Similarly, and even more specific, a group of colonists was recruited in Guadalajara in 1797 and brought from the port of San Blas to Alta California.

The key for the researcher is to identify immigration patterns to determine whether or not they can point to an immigrant ancestor's place of origin or if they can add insight into the ancestor's life and background. The broad migration patterns discussed previously can be found in general history books of a regional nature. For example, information concerning migration patterns in settling the Spanish Borderlands area of the United States can be found in David J. Weber's *The Spanish Frontier in North America*.[1] Books of a broader nature that deal with immigration are also available. Peter Boyd Bowman's *Indice geobiográfico de más de 56 mil pobladores de la América hispaña* deals with the earliest immigration into the Spanish colonies.[2] Carlos Sixerei Paredes' A *Emigración* is an excellent historical analysis of emigration from Galicia covering the seventeenth to the twentieth centuries.

The References section at the end of this chapter illustrates the kinds of books that can be used as a starting point to identify areas and periods of research. The catalogs of major university collections, many of which are available at local universities or major public libraries through computerized search systems and interlibrary loan, are a logical next source. Items of interest may also be found in local libraries in the area where an immigrant ancestor settled in the United States. In addition, an occasional perusal of the Family History Library Catalog may yield a new acquisition of particular relevance (see chapter 2, General References and Guides). There may also be articles published in major historical and genealogical periodicals that could relate to the immigration patterns for a particular locality or time period.

As these searches are done, the researcher should check each index under migration, emigration, and immigration, as well as the specific localities, in the United States, in the prospective country, and, ideally, in the region of origin. For example, someone whose ancestor is known to have come from Spain to Cuba and from there to the United States might identify a family tradition that the ancestor came from northern Spain in the late 1800s. The individual would then check under Spain, as well as the regional names for the northern Spanish regions: Galicia, Asturia, Santander, and the Basque provinces, as well as Cuba. Such a search would lead the researcher to find books such as those by Juan Carlos de la Madrid Alvarez, *El Viaje de los emigrantes Asturianos a América*, and Maria Pilar Pildain Salazar, *Ir a América: La Emigración Vasca a América (Guipuzcoa 1840–1870)*, both of which provide detailed information concerning migration patterns from these areas in the late 1800s.[3] The first book specifically emphasizes migration to Cuba as the principal migration pattern. The latter book presents a list of immigrants from the Basque province of Guipuzcoa, giving their home parishes taken from passenger lists and other documents from that Spanish province. Once again, the search for the immigrant ancestor is most likely to be rewarded by continued and thorough research, including not only normal genealogical sources but broader historical reference sources.

Using the Clues You Find

As a researcher gains experience with family history, he or she develops an intuitive sense about small details that can connect to other records which may reveal the place of origin of the family. For example, a reference to a Cuban ancestor in a newspaper stating that he served his adopted country in war and in peace might lead a researcher to check military records. Another researcher, finding that an ancestor served in the military prior to 1832 in Puerto Rico or 1820 in Mexico and that the word "Don" appears before the ancestor's name, would then want to search nobility records. Finding the term *doctor* or *bachiller* in a reference to an ancestor, another researcher might ask what university the ancestor possibly attended. In each case, two steps take place: first, the researcher has recognized a small detail or fact in a known record and questioned what that detail could mean; second, the researcher has determined what records might substantiate, expand, or verify that detail in the ancestor's life. The ability to make these creative connections cannot be taught; however, the process of knowing how to analyze people's lives and then asking what type of records may exist can be learned by experience.

General Information

A great uniformity exists in Spanish-language records, because the basic principles of recordkeeping in Spain and the types of records used were transmitted to her colonies during the colonial period—even in areas of the United States once under Spanish or Mexican dominion. For general information on working with records in Latin America and for a discussion of immigration patterns there, as well as for detailed information on specific Latin American countries, consult Lyman D. Platt's *A Genealogical Historical Guide to Latin America*.[4] Several guides to research in Latin America can found at <www.familysearch.org>. Also helpful is George Ryskamp's *Finding Your Hispanic Roots*.[5] This latter book will serve to guide the researcher in using Spanish-language records found in the United States. For work in Spain, consult George Ryskamp's *Tracing Your Hispanic Heritage*.[6] In many cases, the Spanish American researcher will, of course, need to use U.S. records that are neither Spanish nor Mexican in origin.

One of the major challenges genealogists face in any language is learning to use and understand older language forms and handwriting styles. Of great assistance to the beginner is *Spanish Records Extraction*, published by the LDS Church to train record extractors, many of whom speak no Spanish, how to read Spanish-language Catholic parish records.[7] Its workbook approach is an excellent way to learn to read those records. Both of Ryskamp's books also offer help with reading old handwriting. Other more detailed texts are found in the References section.

The ability to read early records develops slowly and can only be obtained through actual experience. Do not try to absorb, in a single reading, all the material written in the old script or unfamiliar Spanish. Instead, have available one or two of the reference works described while attempting to read an early record until an instinctive knowledge of the techniques develops.

You can compensate for any deficiency in formal Spanish instruction by study, patience, and a determination to understand the records. Consulting a good beginning grammar book (and possibly one of the quick introductory Spanish courses), and always having a dictionary at hand will also help to compensate for any deficiency. Do not be discouraged from performing research by a lack of formal training in the Spanish language.

Preliminary Survey

A detailed preliminary survey, particularly for those whose ancestors immigrated during the twentieth century, is extremely important. In many cases—if not most—the immigrant ancestor's place of origin will be found in this phase. As new information about the immigrant ancestor's family, friends, and surname is discovered, the researcher will return to this phase and repeat the third and fourth steps discussed in the following text.

The preliminary survey has a two-fold objective: first, to learn all that one's relatives know about the history of the family; and second, to identify all the research already done on the family. The preliminary survey is accomplished in four steps:

1. Check all home and family sources.
2. Interview other family members.
3. Check online databases for information about family history research done on the family.
4. Check for any printed biographies or histories dealing with the family or its individual members.

Check Home and Family Sources

The beginning researcher is frequently unaware of the wealth of genealogical and family history material in his or her own home. Search in basements, attics, and garages for anything about the family and its early members—at the bottom of that old trunk upstairs may be a letter from a great-grandfather in Spain to his son in Uruguay. You might also find copies of military papers showing that a grandfather fought in the Mexican army during the Mexican Revolution of 1911; or perhaps the long-forgotten birth certificate of one's mother might reveal the name of the small town in Cuba where she was born. Especially significant would be an ancestor's photographs, clothing, or tools, which would give a greater sense of reality to his or her life. After the researcher's own home has been thoroughly searched and all of the various family sources, documents, and personal objects are gathered together in a single place, a similar search in the homes of parents, grandparents, aunts and uncles, and even cousins should offer further source material.

The following list of home and family sources that a person of Hispanic ancestry may encounter will guide the beginning genealogist in searching through his or her home, as well as in asking others to search theirs. Because lifestyles vary from one nation to another, this list includes sources that might be found not only in an Anglo American home but also in the home of a family from Latin America or Spain.

Vital Records

This category includes government or church records of major life events, such as birth or baptism, marriage, and death. While in some cases such certificates were issued at the time of the event, usually copies found in the home are certificates issued by civil or religious authorities years afterward when they were requested to prove the facts surrounding it. For example, in requesting a passport a person may have had to show a certificate of birth to prove his or her citizenship. Once the passport was issued, the certificate of birth was returned to its owners, who might have filed it away among important but frequently forgotten documents. Birth and baptism certificates are most commonly found because a variety of situations require such proof—for example, obtaining a passport or visa, getting married, or requesting Social Security benefits. Likewise, death or marriage records may have been obtained to settle an estate or to make a claim for a pension. If the family has come from one of many Spanish-speaking countries in recent decades or is currently living in one, a copy of the *libro de familia* (family book) may also be found in the home. The *libro de familia* and other vital records are described in chapters 9 and 11 of *Tracing Your Hispanic Heritage* (cited earlier).

Vital records are particularly valuable because they usually identify the specific place from which the ancestor came and give an exact date from which research can be begun in the records of the country of origin. By providing names of parents and usually, in birth or baptismal records, the names of grandparents, a single certificate may give the researcher a small pedigree from which to begin.

Vital records in the adopted country should be read carefully for clues as to another country of origin. For example, one Spanish immigrant came to the United States and later married and had children. His son's birth record indicates that the father was from Barcelona, Spain, and the mother was from Cuba. While this does not clearly identify whether it referred to the city of Barcelona or the province, it at least narrows down the area of the search to locate his place of origin in Spain.

Photographs

Photographs are a particularly important home source. Perhaps more than any single source, photographs make family members seem to come to life. Photographs labeled with names and dates are especially valuable in locating the whereabouts of the ancestor who is pictured. Older photographs frequently have the name of the photographer and the address of the studio, helpful in pinpointing a specific area of ancestral origin.

Photographs can be found in the homes of people of all income and social levels. For example, a local history project of the California State University at Fresno attempting to reconstruct Hispanic local history in the San Joaquin Valley located and identified photographs from the homes of descendants of early migrant farm workers that showed people, places, and details of daily life among Hispanic migrant farm families in the early twentieth century.

Printed Materials

Many families have printed, in limited quantities, a wide variety of formal papers for distribution to friends and relatives. The most common of these are wedding invitations. Death announcements were also widely distributed in the past and can frequently be spotted by their black borders. In Catholic Hispanic countries, baptisms and communions were often announced by formal printed invitations or announcements.

Other printed materials commonly found among the effects of Hispanic ancestors are *relaciones de méritos* (records of merit) and *hojas de servicio* (service sheets). Similar to modern résumés, they were used in search of work or to list the qualifications of an individual to perform an act in a certain capacity; they usually included a variety of interesting biographical material regarding the individual being described. In addition, business or personal calling cards were commonly used at all social levels in Hispanic countries.

Passports, Visas, Work Permits, and Citizenship or Naturalization Papers

These are documents used in the process of leaving the country of birth or citizenship, emigrating to a second country, and attempting to become a citizen of that country. Passports are now issued by national governments, but at one time they were often issued by the civil governors in the provinces of many Hispanic countries, including Spain and Mexico (figure 17-1). Unfortunately for the family historian, the use of passports as a necessary requirement for leaving many countries was not adopted until the twentieth century; before that, a variety of policies and systems governing exit were used. The most popular method involved simply going to a port and embarking on a ship. In most cases, documents proving that a man had already served in the armed forces and had left no debts were the only documents needed to emigrate. In some cases, as with migrant workers coming into the southwestern United States, a work permit issued at the border was necessary to obtain work. Look for such documents preserved among the important papers of the immigrant as they may provide clues to the place of origin in the mother country.

Once in the country of destination, some type of action was necessary to achieve citizenship. In the United States before 1906, this meant first becoming a citizen of one of the states—a process rarely extensive and frequently requiring nothing more than swearing an oath of allegiance to the state. Therefore, from this early period there will probably be fewer citizenship or naturalization documents in existence.

By contrast, the ancestor who immigrated during the twentieth century would most certainly have had some type of

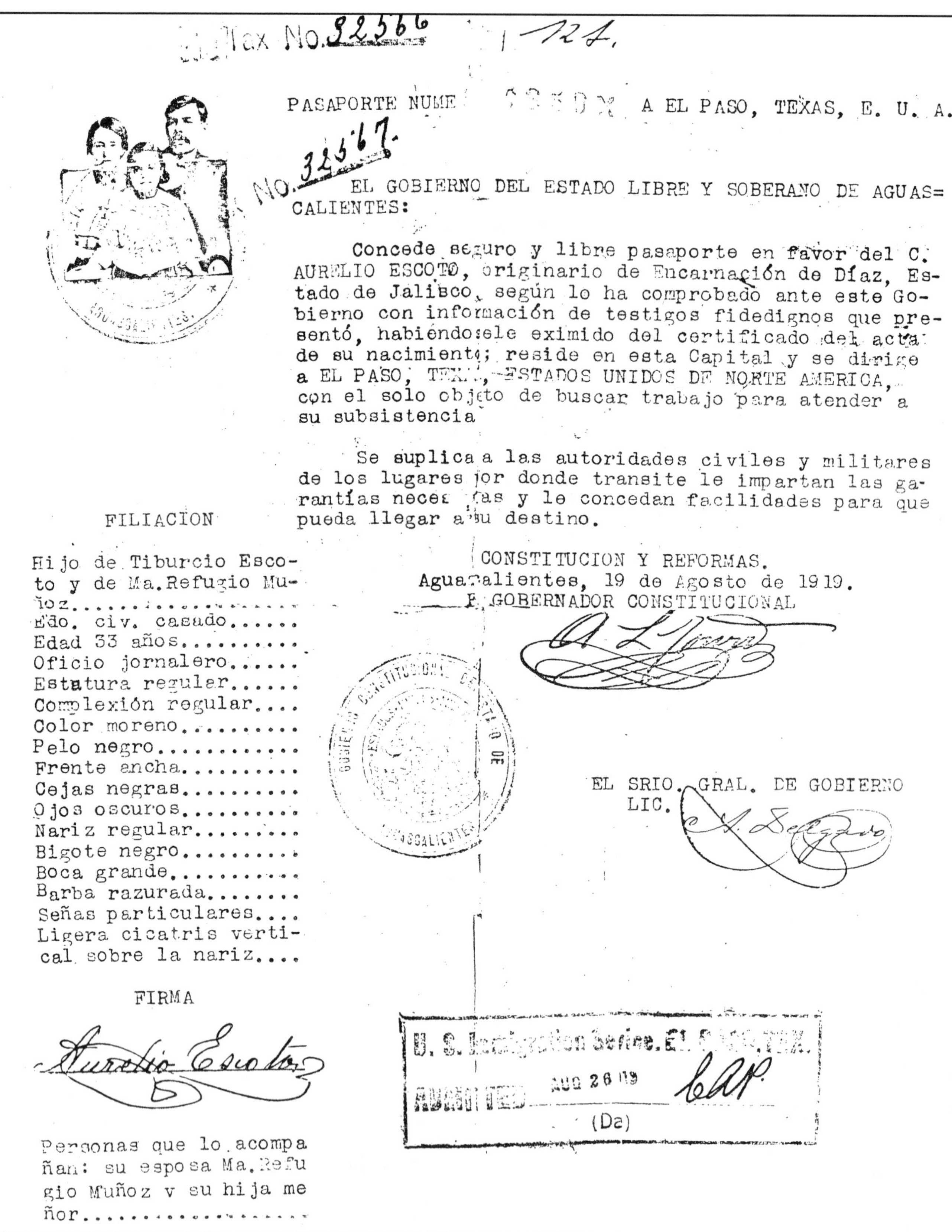
Tax No. 32566 / 124.

PASAPORTE NUME[illegible] A EL PASO, TEXAS, E. U. A.

No. 32567.

EL GOBIERNO DEL ESTADO LIBRE Y SOBERANO DE AGUASCALIENTES:

Concede seguro y libre pasaporte en favor del C. AURELIO ESCOTO, originario de Encarnación de Díaz, Estado de Jalisco, según lo ha comprobado ante este Gobierno con información de testigos fidedignos que presentó, habiéndosele eximido del certificado del acta de su nacimiento; reside en esta Capital y se dirige a EL PASO, TEX., ESTADOS UNIDOS DE NORTE AMERICA, con el solo objeto de buscar trabajo para atender a su subsistencia.

Se suplica a las autoridades civiles y militares de los lugares por donde transite le impartan las garantías necesarias y le concedan facilidades para que pueda llegar a su destino.

CONSTITUCION Y REFORMAS.
Aguascalientes, 19 de Agosto de 1919.
EL GOBERNADOR CONSTITUCIONAL

EL SRIO. GRAL. DE GOBIERNO
LIC. A. Delgado

FILIACION

Hijo de Tiburcio Escoto y de Ma. Refugio Muñoz.................
Edo. civ. casado......
Edad 33 años..........
Oficio jornalero......
Estatura regular......
Complexión regular....
Color moreno..........
Pelo negro............
Frente ancha..........
Cejas negras..........
Ojos oscuros..........
Nariz regular.........
Bigote negro..........
Boca grande...........
Barba razurada........
Señas particulares....
Ligera cicatris vertical sobre la nariz....

FIRMA

Aurelio Escoto

Personas que lo acompañan: su esposa Ma. Refugio Muñoz y su hija menor..................

U. S. Immigration Service, El Paso, Tex.
ADMITTED AUG 26 1919 CAP
(Da)

Figure 17-1. Passport issued by the Mexican state of Aguascalientes in 1919 and found in the California home of this immigrant's descendants.

immigration, residency, or naturalization papers. Immigration documents, if found, will most likely provide certain very important facts, such as the name of the ancestor as recorded when he arrived, the place of origin or port of departure in the home country, and, perhaps, the date of birth and the town and/or province of birth.

Legal Papers

Legal papers encompass a wide variety of records usually relating to financial or property transactions, originally written to establish ownership or transfer ownership of property, both real and personal, or contract rights. Because these were official documents they were usually very carefully preserved, even for several generations beyond the period of actual association with the property or rights. These documents can usually be recognized and distinguished from other kinds of papers by the fact that they will have been written and witnessed by a notary and/or carry an official stamp or seal. Included in this category are *capitulaciones matrimoniales* (marriage contracts), *actos de cesión* (relating to the relinquishment of a particular right or power), *actos de cambio* (relating to a change or transfer), *actos de compra* (relating to the purchase of a property or right), *actos de venta* (relating to the sale of property or right), *actos de donación* (relating to gifts of property or powers or rights), *testamentos* (wills), *cuadernos particionales* (books relating to the division of properties or rights), *contratos de alquileres* (lease or rental contracts), *derechos de sucesión* (succession rights), *inventarios* (inventories, usually relating to some transfer, sale, or division of property or rights), *declaración de herederos* (relating to the rights to certain properties given by the courts to the heirs of an intestate person), and *tutorias* (guardianship papers). In addition, similar papers of a less official nature would be *extractos bancarios* (financial statements or bank extracts) and *polizas de seguros* (insurance policies). For the family historian, these documents can offer much information about the activities, interests, and social position of the ancestral family. They may also provide the only link to the locality from which the family originated.

Letters

Perhaps more than any other category, letters written by members of the family can provide fascinating information for the family historian. Frequently, biographical notes about the activities of a family member, as well as opinions relating to personal, family, local, and national events, will appear in letters. For the genealogist, such letters may be the only link with the mother country. Such was the case for one family that had come to the United States from Uruguay. A great-grandfather remaining in Spain had written a series of letters over a twenty-five-year period to a son in Uruguay. Sixty years later, as the great-granddaughter began the search for her family's origin in Spain, the only clues were those contained in the letters. In addition to naming localities, the letters gave important information about the activities of family members. The last of the letters, written on black-bordered paper by a cousin, related the death of the grandfather who had written all the previous correspondence. The collection of letters became not only a treasure of family history and genealogical information, but a source for the clues needed to locate the family's parish of origin in Spain.

Military Records and Decorations

Since compulsory military conscription has been a regular part of Hispanic life in most countries for at least a century and a half, military documents are frequently among the effects of an ancestor. Such documents usually take the form of papers showing release from military service, as these were often required for an individual to be permitted to emigrate (figure 17-2). The document generally indicates the person's name, the rank attained, the regiment served in and the place of enlistment, in addition to information of a more personal nature such as place of birth, occupation, and age. Besides assisting in locating the place of origin, this information can also be of great value in directing a family historian where to look for additional records relating to military service.

In addition to enlistment and discharge papers, if the ancestor received certain recognitions, such as promotions or decorations for combat service or wounds, such documents will most certainly have been preserved among his effects. These may provide not only research clues but also a particularly exciting view of the person's life, character, and actions.

School and Occupation Records

School and occupation records cover a wide variety of materials relating to the educational and business activities of one's ancestors. Those relating to educational activities might include registration information from a particular school or college (*colegio o universidad),* exam papers, diplomas or titles, awards for particular activities, and records concerning grades (*notas*) or graduation from one level to another.

Occupational records span an even wider range. To cite just a few possibilities, they might include special permits, such as those issued to street vendors, bakers, and many other classes of workers in the cities, or personal business cards or advertisements, such as those sent out by a tailor, or even membership documents for the *gremios* or *sindicatos* (unions, guilds, or syndicates) organized in some larger cities and among some rural farm workers. Of special interest would be work permits issued by immigration authorities.

Newspaper Clippings

Frequently, newspaper clippings have been preserved by family members and friends. In the native country, mention in a local newspaper would most likely be limited to those of the upper class. However, an individual who arrived in the Americas may well have achieved local status, and information relating to

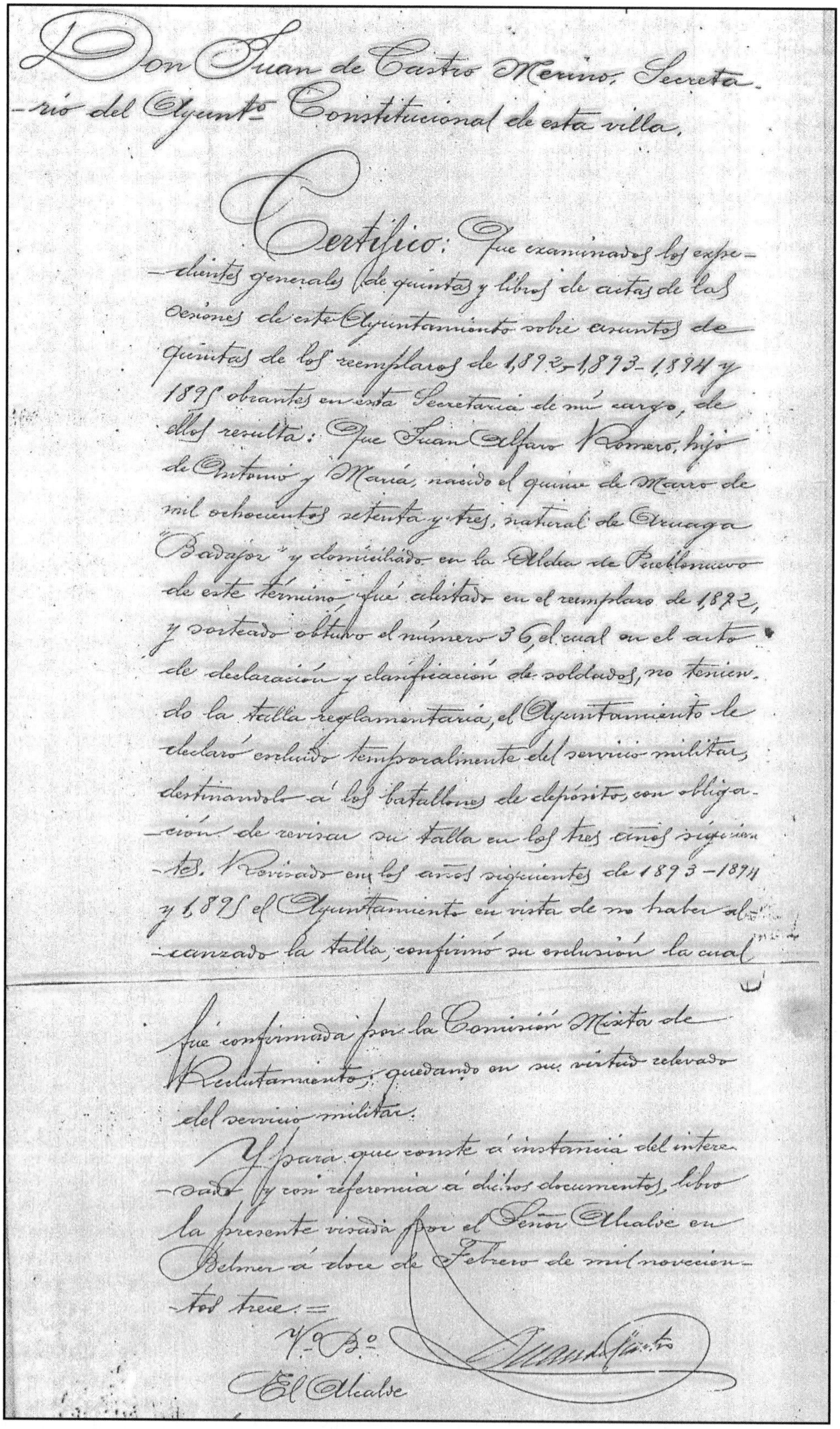

Don Juan de Castro Merino, Secreta-
-rio del Ayunt.to Constitucional de esta villa,

Certifico: Que examinados los expe-
-dientes generales de quintas y libros de actas de las
sesiones de este Ayuntamiento sobre asuntos de
quintas de los reemplazos de 1,892-1,893-1,894 y
1895 obrantes en esta Secretaría de mi cargo, de
ellos resulta: Que Juan Alfaro Romero, hijo
de Antonio y María, nacido el quince de Marzo de
mil ochocientos setenta y tres, natural de Azuaga
"Badajoz" y domiciliado en la Aldea de Pueblonuevo
de este término, fué alistado en el reemplazo de 1,892,
y sorteado obtuvo el número 36, el cual en el acto
de declaración y clasificación de soldados, no tenien-
do la talla reglamentaria, el Ayuntamiento le
declaró excluido temporalmente del servicio militar,
destinandolo á los batallones de depósito, con obliga-
-ción de revisar su talla en los tres años siguien-
-tes. Revisado en los años siguientes de 1893-1894
y 1,895 el Ayuntamiento en vista de no haber al-
-canzado la talla, confirmó su exclusión la cual
fué confirmada por la Comisión Mixta de
Reclutamiento, quedando en su virtud relevado
del servicio militar.

Y para que conste á instancia del intere-
-sado y con referencia á dichos documentos, libro
la presente visada por el Señor Alcalde en
Belmez á doce de Febrero de mil novecien-
-tos trece.=

V.o B.o
El Alcalde

de Castro

Figure 17-2. Certificate of fulfillment of military obligations by standing unsuccessfully for the draft in four consecutive years; issued by the municipal clerk of Belmez, Córdoba, Spain, in 1913 and found in the Massachusetts home of a descendant.

his or her activities and origins may be found in local newspapers (see figure 17-3). Since these articles would have been written based upon information given by persons no longer alive, they may provide a unique source of information relating to the family, its activities, and its origin.

Diaries

Unfortunately, the keeping of a personal diary was not generally characteristic of Hispanic culture. Unlike many nineteenth-century Americans who, at one point or another in their lives, kept some form of personal diary, most Hispanic immigrants did not. Nevertheless, some circumstances may have led an immigrant to keep a diary, such as the influence of Anglo society or a unique position as the founder of an American branch of the family or the designation as unofficial recorder of an event or trip.

National Identity Document or Personal Document (*Documento Nacional de Identidad o Cédula Personal*)

In most Hispanic countries, beginning in the late nineteenth century or early twentieth century, laws were passed relating to the issuance of a personal document (*cédula personal*), which all citizens were required to carry. Locating such a document among the personal effects of an ancestor can be significant, because the point of issuance would probably be the civil register of the district in which the family resided at the time.

Memberships in Private Clubs, Civic or Nobility Organizations, and Political Parties

There appears to be inherent in the Spanish temperament—perhaps in that of everyone—a desire to belong to an organization, particularly elite organizations. A wide variety of organizations have been available to Spaniards at different points in history. Among those available to the noble families were the *ordenes militares* (military orders), *reales maestranzas* (royal riding clubs), and the *cofradias nobles* (noble fraternities). For the past century and a half, following the initial seizure of power by those of more liberal political orientation, other types of organizations

News Notes.

[illegible]

SANTA CLARA, July [illegible].—The funeral of the late Capt. William Smith, who passed away on Wednesday at his residence in Pomeroy avenue, west of Santa Clara, was held this afternoon. The services were conducted at the funeral chapel of Mrs. Emma Hirsch by the Rev. C. A. Mainwaring of the Santa Clara Episcopal church, and the burial was in the Santa Clara cemetery. The following officiated as pallbearers: C. Hills, C. P. Bradbury, R. Thomason and J. Debenham.

Surprise Party.

Miss Fay Springsett was tendered a surprise party by a number of her friends last evening at her home in Jackson street. The evening was pleasantly passed with games, music and dancing and at 12 o'clock a supper was served.

Those present were: Misses Clara Soares, Lydia J. Souza, Minnie L. Noya, Laura B. Martinelli, Dorothy Bakela, Rose E. Farias, Louise Noya, Amelia F. Mello, Minnie M. Mendosa, Mamie C. Madeiros, Olive Martinelli, Lena Munha, L. Cubbini, Viola Smith; Messrs. D. Dias, F. F. Martin, M. G. Dinnie, F. Kiler, Michael Oliveira, Elmer O'Brien, M. Madeiros, Joseph Munha, William Thomas, A. Navarro, J. W. Noya, F. S. Martin, Joseph Azevedo and M. P. Jonquini.

Funeral of J. B. Oliveira.

The funeral of Joseph B. Oliveira, who died very suddenly on Tuesday, was held this morning at 9:30 o'clock from the family residence at 472 Washington street, thence to St. Claire's church, where a requiem mass was celebrated by the Rev. A. V. Raggio. The members of the I. D. E. S. society, of which he was a member, attended the funeral in a body. The burial was in the family plot in the Catholic cemetery. The pallbearers were: F. D. Andrada, A. F. Pedrosa, J. Silva, A. Bettencourt, M. Vierra and A. Cunha.

Figure 17-3. Newspaper obituaries from the *San Jose [California] Mercury Herald.*

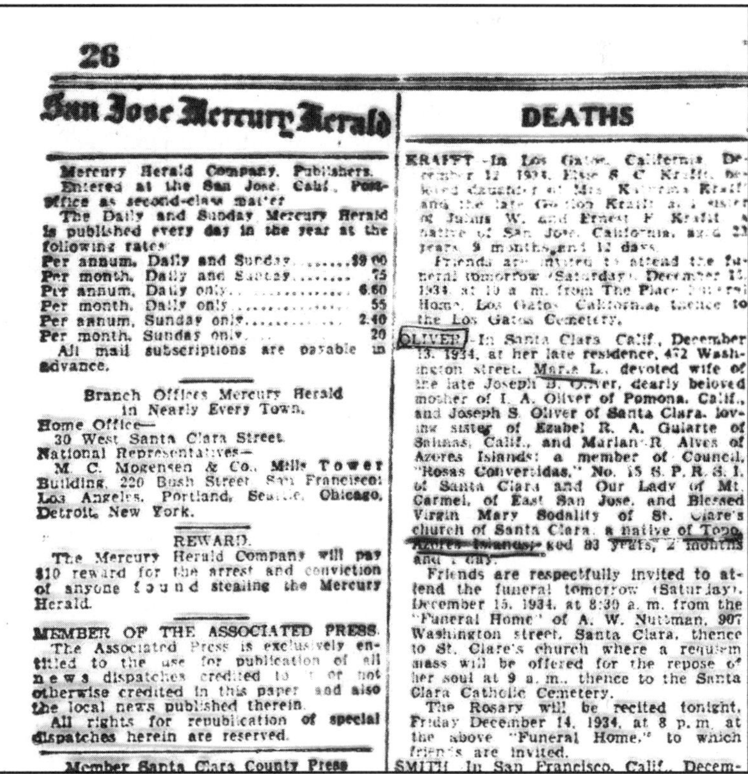

26

San Jose Mercury Herald

Mercury Herald Company, Publishers.
Entered at the San Jose, Calif., Postoffice as second-class matter.
The Daily and Sunday Mercury Herald is published every day in the year at the following rates:

Per annum, Daily and Sunday	$9.00
Per month, Daily and Sunday	.75
Per annum, Daily only	6.60
Per month, Daily only	.55
Per annum, Sunday only	2.40
Per month, Sunday only	.20

All mail subscriptions are payable in advance.

Branch Offices Mercury Herald in Nearly Every Town.
Home Office—
30 West Santa Clara Street.
National Representatives—
M. C. Mogensen & Co., Mills Tower Building, 220 Bush Street, San Francisco; Los Angeles, Portland, Seattle, Chicago, Detroit, New York.

REWARD.
The Mercury Herald Company will pay $10 reward for the arrest and conviction of anyone found stealing the Mercury Herald.

MEMBER OF THE ASSOCIATED PRESS.
The Associated Press is exclusively entitled to the use for publication of all news dispatches credited to it or not otherwise credited in this paper and also the local news published therein.
All rights for republication of special dispatches herein are reserved.

Member Santa Clara County Press

DEATHS

KRAFFT—In Los Gatos, California, December 12, 1934, Elsie S. C. Krafft, beloved daughter of Mrs. K[illegible] Krafft and the late G[illegible] Krafft, and sister of Julius W. and Ernest F. Krafft, a native of San Jose, California, aged 23 years, 9 months and 12 days.
Friends are invited to attend the funeral tomorrow (Saturday), December 15, 1934, at 10 a. m. from The Place Funeral Home, Los Gatos, California, thence to the Los Gatos Cemetery.

OLIVER—In Santa Clara, Calif., December 13, 1934, at her late residence, 472 Washington street, Maria L., devoted wife of the late Joseph B. Oliver, dearly beloved mother of I. A. Oliver of Pomona, Calif., and Joseph S. Oliver of Santa Clara, loving sister of Ezabel R. A. Gularte of Salinas, Calif., and Marian R. Alves of Azores Islands; a member of Council "Rosas Convertidas," No. 15 S. P. R. S. I. of Santa Clara and Our Lady of Mt. Carmel, of East San Jose, and Blessed Virgin Mary Sodality of St. Clare's church of Santa Clara, a native of Topo, Azores Islands, aged 83 years, 2 months and 1 day.
Friends are respectfully invited to attend the funeral tomorrow (Saturday), December 15, 1934, at 8:30 a. m. from the "Funeral Home" of A. W. Nuttman, 907 Washington street, Santa Clara, thence to St. Clare's church where a requiem mass will be offered for the repose of her soul at 9 a. m., thence to the Santa Clara Catholic Cemetery.
The Rosary will be recited tonight, Friday December 14, 1934, at 8 p. m. at the above "Funeral Home," to which friends are invited.

SMITH—In San Francisco, Calif., Decem-

appeared that were less restrictive about membership. Among these were Masonic orders, political parties, and debating clubs (*ateneos*), which appeared in most major cities. In addition, many local parishes had *cofradias* which were open to both nobles and commoners, although frequently on a hereditary basis. Membership, and especially offices held in any of the previously-mentioned organizations, may have been certified by a diploma, certificate, or other type of document which may be found in the collection of family sources within one's home. Such documents can be particularly significant, not only as a glimpse into the active social life of an individual ancestor, but because they can lead to more extensive records kept by the organization. Records of this type are kept in such a wide variety of locations that the only reasonable clue to locating an individual's membership may be in finding some mention of it among home and family sources.

Honorary Distinctions

Honorary distinctions are usually limited to the upper classes in Spain and include such distinctions as honorary doctorates or political awards issued by certification of the universities or cities that made the awards. Military decorations (mentioned previously) could also be included in this category, as well as documents relating to particular literary, artistic, or scientific awards. Also noteworthy, although of a more concrete and less honorary nature, are certificates for the register of industrial and intellectual property, the equivalents of patents or copyrights for literary, scientific, or artistic works.

Biographies or Autobiographies

Biographies are most commonly found for the nobility or for people of political or artistic renown in Hispanic cultures. However, the move to a new country, with its resulting new position in society—as well as the distance from family origins in the mother country—may have prompted a Spanish immigrant, or those around one, to record information about his or her life or the lives of immediate ancestors.

Written Family Histories (Published and Unpublished)

Written family histories are much more common among the nobility of Hispanic countries than in the lower classes. However, as with biographies, immigration to another country may have spurred an individual to record his or her family origins in a family history. Because many of these were of interest only to the family, they will be found in manuscript form rather than published.

Medical Records

Documents in this category will probably be found only for more recent ancestors. Medical record cards, x-rays, medical analyses, and dental and eyeglass prescriptions can all contribute to a knowledge of the ancestor and how he looked. Naturally, such information will most likely be limited to the twentieth century due to the more extensive availability of doctors during this century.

Contact Other Family Members

The second step in a preliminary survey, after a thorough search for home sources, is to check with other family members. The first purpose for this is to make a record of memories and feelings about the family and its ancestors. Older family members such as grandparents, great-aunts and uncles, or cousins from a different branch of the family very likely have memories that have not been passed on. Frequently, memories of other family members add new dimensions to knowledge of the lives and personalities of direct-line ancestors, and also may provide clues for finding the town of origin in the mother country.

The second purpose in making contact with other family members is to ask for their help in searching their homes for the same sources discussed previously. Often, original documents from the immigrant ancestor will have passed through a different branch of the family and may not be in the hands of even immediate cousins.

Contact with other family members can be accomplished in three different ways: questionnaire, letter, or personal visit. The questionnaire is essentially a form letter with a series of questions relating to the family, such as: "Do you remember your grandfather, Juan Garcia? Do you have any idea where he came from in Mexico? Do you have or know someone who has any old documents relating to Juan Garcia? What memories do you have of your parents talking about Juan Garcia? Would you be interested in learning more about Juan Garcia and your other Mexican ancestors?" A space can be left for short answers at the end of each of the questions on the questionnaire.

The questionnaire is the least desirable approach in contacting other family members, since it is the least personal and least likely to get an interested response. This survey approach can best be used to reach a large number of relatives and identify those who have documents or are interested in developing a family history.

A second and better approach is to write a personal letter to each relative. This letter could include many of the same items as the questionnaire. Ideally, the letter would serve as an initial contact that could be followed up by a personal visit with those who show interest.

The most effective form of contacting family members is a personal visit. Through contact with other family members, a researcher can collect a variety of material for use in compiling an interesting and human family history. Some of the most fascinating material will be family tradition gathered through oral interviews. Exercise caution, though, in relying on oral or family tradition, such as descent from royalty or the ancestor who is said to have "accompanied Cortez in the conquest of Mexico." Frequently, the natural desire to improve upon the prestige of the family will cause many such traditions, while based on fact, to become exaggerated with time. While family tradition may help to locate a place of origin in the mother country or pinpoint the original family home or in other ways further the genealogical search, they should be verified by documentation before they are accepted as true.

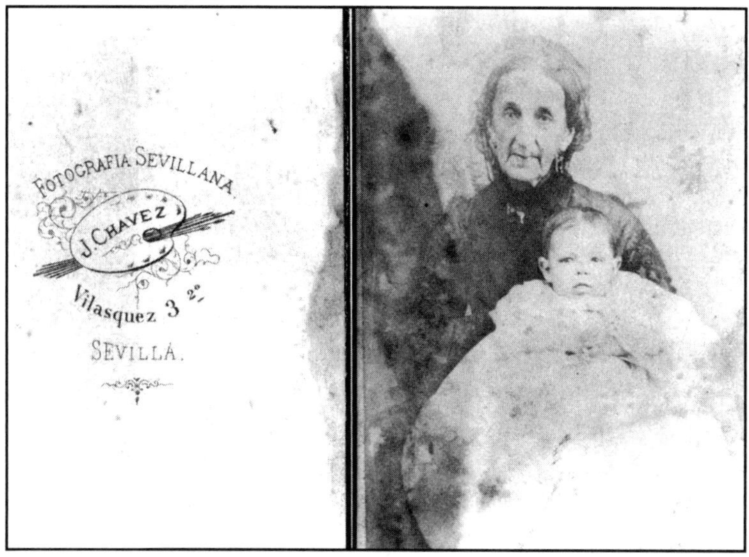

Front and back of late-nineteenth-century Spanish photo showing a detailed photographer's mark on back.

Check Online Genealogical Indexes for Research Previously Done on the Family

After a thorough search of sources available within one's own family has been completed, the researcher should evaluate, as the third step of the preliminary survey, what others have done while tracing family histories and genealogies that could tie in directly with the family. In working with sources outside the family, most family history researchers first check the indexes and records found on the Internet. Several very large collections of records exist, foremost being those gathered and prepared by the LDS Church, which can be found at <www.familysearch.org> and those gathered at <www.ancestry.com>. Of specific interest to the Hispanic researcher at the FamilySearch.org site are the following: the International Genealogical Index, Mexican Vital Records, Pedigree Resource File, and the Ancestral File.

The International Genealogical Index (IGI) is an index of genealogical data for over 1 billion persons gathered from a wide variety of records—though primarily vital records, wills, and censuses—from more than ninety countries. Cross-indexing allows for a variety of pronunciations and name spellings. Entries are generally not linked from one generation to another, nor are there connections between entries for a person's birth and later marriage or appearance as the parent of a child. Significant numbers of persons from Mexico, Guatemala, and Spain appear as a result of a program of extraction of Catholic parish records from those countries, conducted by the LDS Church. The Mexican Vital Records Index is a collection of several million names extracted from parish records that have not yet been placed in the IGI but are available in that separate index, both online and in a CD collection. Similar entries for Spain, France, and Italy are found in a CD collection titled *Western European Vital Records*, available for use in many Family History Centers worldwide.

The Ancestral File and Pedigree Resource File contain millions of names submitted to the LDS Church since 1978 specifically to be included in these computer files. Unlike the IGI, that identifies individual events such as birth and marriage without attempting to link even the events of a single person's life together, these computerized files link families and generations. When a search is made for a specific name in the Ancestral File, all persons in the index by the requested name are then listed on the computer screen. From this point it is possible to request detailed information on any individual listed as well as a family group record and ancestral and/or descendant charts for that person. Once a name is found online in the Pedigree Resource File, the extended information with pedigrees and family group records for the person can be consulted through a series of over 100 CDs found in local Family History Centers or for sale at <www.familysearch.org>.

Unfortunately for the Hispanic researcher, the number of Hispanic references in the Ancestral and Pedigree Resource Files is limited. The primary source for those indexes is submissions made by members of the LDS Church, giving data about their ancestors, although those who are not members of the church are encouraged to submit their genealogical research as well. As a growing number of people submit Hispanic ancestral lines, the significance of these files for the Hispanic researcher will increase.

Numerous other websites should be checked as well. Large commercial sites such as Ancestry.com offer databases similar in format to the Pedigree Resource File. These sites offer many other materials on a subscription-fee basis, although only a small percentage of their offerings is relevant to Hispanic researchers.

The strength of Ancestry.com will be its accumulation of vital and military records, censuses, histories, and other digitized records that will be used to further family history research. Two smaller sites that are relevant to Hispanics are <www.elanillo.com> and <www.ancestros.com.mx>. These sites offer name searches as well as general research information. Other sites can be found by looking at <www.cyndislist.com> under categories such as Spain, Portugal, Hispanic, and Central and South America, as well as Texas, Arizona, New Mexico, and California. A surname search can also be made at <www.google.com.search>. When doing this, use the surname plus words such as "genealogy," "family" or "history" to limit the search to more relevant sites. See chapter 2, "General References and Guides," for more information.

Check for Printed Family Histories and Biographies

The fourth and last step in the preliminary survey is to find out what printed genealogies or biographies are available for the family or family members. This step involves two separate kinds of searches: (1) searching for family surnames and/or family members in biographical dictionaries and genealogical encyclopedias, and (2) searching for monograph histories of one's family or a collateral branch of it. The first of these can easily be accomplished nearly anywhere in the world. A wide variety of biographical and genealogical encyclopedias and dictionaries is available for Spanish surnames. The best starting point is online at <www.saur-wbi.de>. The World Biographical Index found at this site indexes more than fifteen collections of more than 330 biographical works each. A search for a surname or a specific individual on this site will cover more than 4,500 biographical works from all over the world. Two of those collections relate specifically to Spain, Portugal, and Latin America. The first, originally published by Victor Herrero Mediavila and Lolita Rosa Aquayo Hayle, is titled *Indice Biográfico de España, Portugal e Ibero-América.*[8] This index identifies approximately 200,000 historically significant individuals from Roman times to the early twentieth century, compiled from 306 biographical encyclopedias, dictionaries, and collective works covering 700 original volumes published from the seventeenth to the early twentieth century from Spain, Portugal, and Latin America. Those works were copied and the references from all volumes were separated and arranged in alphabetical order. That collection was then microfilmed on 1,070 microfiche and is available through Family History Centers of the LDS Church (microfiche sets 6002170-6002172). A second set, indexed online, is also available through Family History Centers on ninety-eight microfiche (microfiche sets 6131531 through 6131558). Be careful to only ask for the fiche that contains your surname of interest.

The most famous and extensive collection, published by Garcia-Carrafa in Madrid, is the *Enciclopedia Heráldica y Genealógica Hispano Americana.* It was begun in 1920, and the last volume was published in 1963.[9] There are currently eighty-eight volumes covering the letters *AA* through *URR*. The first two volumes of this series contain a study of the science of heraldry, and the remaining volumes contain an alphabetical list of noble and semi-noble families from throughout Spain and her former American colonies. Brief accounts of the history of each family are arranged by surname and trace the family's most notable noble member. Most entries also include illustrations of coats of arms, and frequently there is a limited bibliography that can lead to more extended monographic family histories.

While the nobility of Spain was very widespread, many families will never trace any of their family lines to Spanish nobility. The right to use the coats of arms associated with each of these surnames is limited to those who have direct ancestral ties with a family, and in many cases is limited to the direct male descendants of a family. For this reason, a person of a particular surname should not assume that the family coat of arms listed for that surname belongs to him or her.

Almost every Hispanic country has national and regional dictionaries and encyclopedias that can often be of even greater value to the researcher because they include many families and surnames which are not noble in origin. Some of these, although by no means all, are listed in the References section. Typical of one type of regional book from Spain is *El Solar Catalán, Valenciana y Balear*, which follows the same pattern as the *Enciclopedea heráldica y genealógica Hispano Americana,* referred to previously, but is limited to families (once again primarily noble families) that come from a particular region or country, in this case from Catalonia, Valencia, and the Balearic Islands.[10]

Another type of regional series is typified by Jaime de Querexeta's *Diccionario onamástico y heráldico basco.*[11] This six-volume series lists, in alphabetical order, nearly all the Basque surnames that can be found. While it does not give a family history for most of the names, it does indicate if the name is unique to a particular region and may be useful in helping to locate the particular area that should be searched.

The second type of printed information that should be searched while completing the preliminary survey is articles and books that may have been published about the family, giving its history and usually including a list of living members of the family at the time of publication. Once again, these are found primarily for noble families and for families who have achieved some particular status in Spanish or Hispano American society. Lyman D. Platt's *Latin American Family Histories* is the single best list of these.[12] Others appear as articles in periodicals such as *Hidalguía* (Madrid, Spain) and *The Americas: A Journal of Latin American History*. The LDS Family History Library, as well as many large university and public libraries in the United States and Latin America, have significant numbers of Hispanic family histories in monograph form.

Online library catalogs are numerous. To find a local library of interest, go to <www.google.com> and type your city of interest and the word "library," such as "San Antonio Library." Once you find the library, search its catalog for family histories by typing your surname of interest plus words such as "family history" or "genealogy." The Family History Library in Salt Lake City can be searched online at <www.familysearch.org>. Do your search by surname in its surname section.

In a large university or public library, consult a library consortium such as WorldCat or RLIN. These allow you to search thousands of catalogs in a single search. Again search under your surname plus "family history" and/or "genealogy." Interlibrary loan allows patrons to order many of the books found to be sent to that library for consultation.

In summary, the preliminary survey brings together all the information the researcher and his or her family knows and determines if anyone outside the immediate or known family has done further research on family lines. At this point, organize and evaluate the information from all of these sources to determine objectives and begin doing substantial research in original records to trace the family lines back into the country of origin.

Catholic Church Records

The records of the Roman Catholic Church represent the single best Spanish-language source for finding the family's place of origin. Most important are those found in the local parish. Parish records, which contain a rich collection of materials of interest to the family and local historian, can be divided into two major categories: sacramental records and non-sacramental records. Sacramental records are baptisms, marriages, and confirmations. Non-sacramental records include death or burial records, fraternal order books, account books, censuses, individual documents, and local history materials.

Hispanic Catholic parish records are generally divided between three books or sets of books: one for baptisms, another for marriages, and a third for deaths. Frequently, confirmations are also recorded in the baptismal books, although, during some periods, and especially in larger parishes, a separate book for confirmations may have been maintained. Particularly valuable are marriage records, in which the place of origin is frequently given for the bride and groom and/or their parents.[13] Figures 17-4 through 17-6 show marriage entries from Catholic parish records in Our Lady of Guadalupe, Los Angeles, California, and in Hidalgo del Parral, Chihuahua, Mexico (1759), as well as a printed page of extracts of marriages from the Saint Louis Cathedral, New Orleans, Louisiana (1786), all of which serve to identify the place of origin of the bride and/or the groom in Mexico or Spain. Even in the United States, many Catholic parishes in Spanish-speaking areas continued to maintain parish records in Spanish well into the twentieth century. Always check for these records in their original form; extracts often omit the very details about place of origin that the researcher seeks.

Before a marriage, the standard procedure for the parties involved was to file a marriage petition *(expediente matrimonial, información matrimonial, aplicación matrimonial)* with the parish priest. This petition would contain proof of good standing in the Catholic Church (usually the baptismal certificates of the bride and groom), written permission from the parents if the bride or groom was under twenty-one (though this age varied), and the priest's permission for the marriage to take place. In addition, if the groom was from another parish, there would be a statement by the priest of his parish that the three admonitions had been read or posted there on three consecutive Sundays or holy days. If the father of the bride or groom—whose consent was normally required—was dead, then the death record or date of death of that father would also be included in the marriage petition. In many parishes, such petitions have been conserved and are of particular interest if the groom is from a parish other than the one in which the marriage took place, since the petition may even provide a copy of his baptismal certificate. In American parishes, if the groom came from Spain, statements from witnesses testifying as to his good character and Catholic standing might substitute for the other documents. Often, these witnesses were immigrants like the groom or bride and knew one or both of them in the country of origin.

The marriage petition would also include any special dispensations required from a bishop or the pope for the marriage to take place. In addition to references to *dispensas de consanguinidad,* which were granted to permit marriages between relatives in the fourth degree of blood relationship, marriage entries may offer other interesting information about the bride and groom. If either the bride or the groom lived extensively outside the diocese in which the parish was located, there is usually mention of a special *dispensa,* or note from the bishopric authorizing the marriage. All such information should be noted as the parish research is done because it may provide clues for further research in the diocesan archives. Catholic parish records can be found in microfilmed form by looking in the Family History Library Catalog at <www.familysearch.org> for the ancestral town under "Place Search." Many marriage dispensation records have also been filmed and some even published (see George Ryskamp, *Finding Your Hispanic Roots,* chapter 10).

U.S. Passenger Lists and Border Crossing Records

The best records for identifying the place of origin of the immigrant ancestor, aside from naturalization and citizenship records, are passenger lists. (For a discussion of these, see *They Became Americans* by Loretto Dennis Szucs.)[14] A passenger list is a list of individuals who arrived at or left a port on a ship, generally created by the ship's captain and submitted to the port authorities upon arrival or before sailing. Such lists usually contain at least the name of the head of the family and the number of individuals in the family, but some list all passengers individually, the port of embarkation in Europe, or the destination, and their places of origin. Obviously, if the last is given, a good part of the work of identifying the place of origin is complete. If, for arrival lists, only the port of embarkation is given, it may then be necessary to check records in the place of embarkation, such as port records (where available) or municipal census records for the port city, as the family may have lived there for a period of time before their voyage.

Few passenger lists created before 1820 exist in the United States. However, extensive post-1820 passenger and shipping records have been preserved. Most of these are now on file at the National Archives in Washington, D.C. Those for the ports of Boston, New York, Philadelphia, Baltimore, and New Orleans, for the period 1819 to 1976, are available on microfilm through the LDS Church's Family History Library. Other ports of particular interest for Hispanics are those in Florida, Texas, and California. Chapter 2 of the *Guide to Genealogical Research in the National Archives* contains an excellent discussion of U.S. passenger lists and their availability on a port-by-port basis.[15] *Index of Spanish Citizens Entering the Port of New Orleans Between January, 1840 and December, 1865*, and its companion volume, which covers the period 1819 to 1839, provide an index of all persons with Spanish surnames who passed through the port of New Orleans during this period.[16] Unfortunately, only those from after 1893 give the place of origin. Many of those lists are now available online at <www.ancestry.com>.

Since the border between the United States and Mexico was open until the early part of the twentieth century, with few customs restrictions, few records are available for Mexican border immigration into the southwestern United States during that period. For the period from 1893 to 1953, individual border crossing records created by the Immigration and Naturalization Service are available on microfilm from the National Archives. These are for non-U.S. citizens who were granted legal border-crossing privileges along Mexico's border from California to Texas. For further information, go to <www.archives.gov/genealogy/immigration/border-mexico.html>.

64

Liber Matrimoniorum in Ecclesia

No.	Nomina Contrahentium	Tempus Matrimonii: Annus	Mensis	Dies	Tempus et Ecclesia Baptismi vel locus Nativitatis Sponsi	Parentes Sponsi
1	Sponsi: Rafael Delgado Sponsae: Mª Carmen Galban	1936	July	5	24 october 1914 El Paso Texas. Vide "Liber Bapt." Vol. Pag. No.	Jose Delgado Guadalupe Delgado
2	Sponsi: Rafael Serrato Sponsae: Carmen Fierro				Penjamillo, Michoacan 15 octobre 1914 bapt. 18. Vide "Liber Bapt." Vol. Pag. No.	Jose Serrato Magdalena Zaragoza
3	Sponsi: Sacramento Valdes Sponsae: Daisy Sand DeRome	1936	July	23	Morenci, ariz. nato 1907 - 1 Sept. Vide "Liber Bapt." Vol. Pag. No.	Sacramento Valdez Feliciton Pico
4	Sponsi: Claudio Bernasconi Sponsae: Aloisia Valdez	1936	August	1	Vide "Liber Bapt." Vol. Pag. No.	Claudio Bernasconi Maria Conti
5	Sponsi: José Sachs Sponsae: Celia Ronquillo	1936	August	29	El Paso - Texas - Sacred Heart. El Paso Texas - Sacred Heart Vide "Liber Bapt." Vol. Pag. No.	Antonio Sachs Ramona Garcia de Sachs
6	Sponsi: Timoteo Delgado Sponsae: Isidora Bermudez	1936 1936	August	30	Miami Arizona ~~Ventura Calif~~ Vide "Liber Bapt." Vol. Pag. No.	Timoteo Delgado Maria Campos Delg[illegible]
7	Sponsi: Domingo Zamora Sponsae:	1936			Lerdo Durango	José Zamora

Figure 17-4. Marriage entries from records of the Roman Catholic parish of Our Lady of Guadalupe, Los Angeles, California.

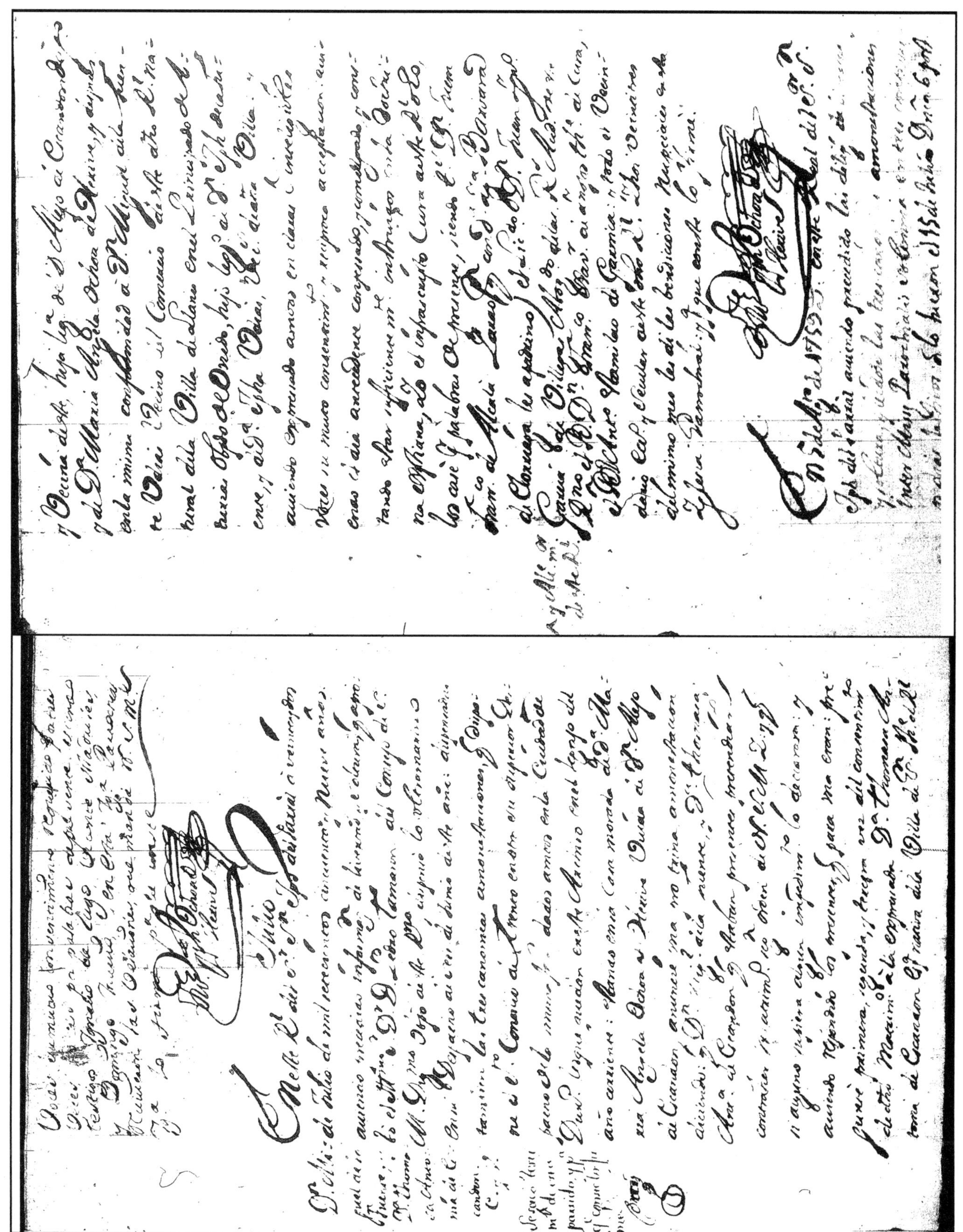

Figure 17-5. Marriage entry, 22 de Julio 1759, Parroquia de San Jose, Hidalgo del Parral, Chihuahua, Mexico. FHL microfilm 162,556.

Major Spanish Colonial Records

Occasionally, searching the records of the American country to which the ancestor immigrated will not yield the place of origin. This is particularly true if the immigrant ancestor arrived during the colonial period (1492–1821), for which there may be no records preserved in America that could indicate the place of origin in Spain. Only when all possible sources in the new country have been exhausted, or a Latin American or U.S. source has provided a clue as to a specific type of record in Spain that should be searched, should a search in Spanish archives begin.

Records relating to Spain's American colonies are of two types: (1) purely local records that were generated for various administrative purposes, and (2) records involving transactions between Spain and her colonies or between private individuals in Spain and others in the colonies. This last category involves a wide variety of transactions: commercial, governmental, travel, and military.

Local records sent to Spain from the American colonies are extremely varied. Some involve explicit details of daily life, as reported by local governors; some include detailed records on particular individuals, such as those compiled by the Inquisition and by the military orders in reviewing the background of a person. Many official government documents were prepared in triplicate, with one copy kept in the local archives, a second copy sent to a viceregal or *audiencia* capital (found today in Latin American national archives), and a third sent to the appropriate governing body in Spain. The most valuable and extensive repository of such local American records in Spain is the *Archivo General de las Indias* in Seville.

Records relating to specific individuals and families residing in the Americas can be found throughout the archives of Spain. When all possible American sources have been exhausted, check potential Spanish archival sources for information to connect ancestors with a specific parish in Spain. In spite of the wide variety of archives that contain such material, the vast majority of documents relating to the Spanish colonies and colonial governments are limited to these three archives:

1. The *Archivo General de las Indias* in Seville, containing records of the *Casa de la Contratación* (Commercial House), *Consejo de Indias* (Council of the Indies), and other entirely colonial administrative entities existing before 1820.
2. The *Archivo Histórico Nacional* in Madrid, containing records for nineteenth-century colonial administration of Cuba, Puerto Rico, and the Philippines.
3. The *Archivo General de Simancas* in the province of Valladolid, containing records of Castilian government before 1800, including many records relating to the Americas found mixed in general administrative sections, such as *Guerra* (War) and *Hacienda* (Treasury).

PAGE 46

PEDRO JOSEF MONTANER native of Palma in Mallorca son of SEBASTIAN MONTANER and of MAGDALENA PERYA
Married February 5, 1786
FELICITE DURIEAU daughter of JUAN BAUTISTA DURIEAU and of CATARINA DAVID.

JUAN BAUTISTA CONET native of ....
Married February 6, 1786
JULIA ORET native of ....(record deteriorated)

PEDRO JOSEF LAMBERT native of the Arkansas Post son of PEDRO LAMBERT and of CATARINA LANDRONY
Married February 7, 1786
CONSTANZA WILS daughter of JUAN BAUTISTA WILS and of SUSANA LANGLISE.

LUIS ANDRAVY native Marseille son of SANTIAGO ANDRAVY and of FRANCISCA LAMBERTE
Married February 9, 1786
JOSEFA OSTEN native of the Imperial States daughter of JUAN LUIS DAUTEN and of MARGARITA BENEVEL, she was married to the deceased Mr. BLAIGNAT.

JOSEF FERNANDES native of Lucena son of ANTONIO FERNANDES and of MARIA NIETO
Married February 19, 1786
MARIA de PRESAS native this Parish daughter of GREGORIO de PRESAS and of MARIA ANTONIA native of Santiago de Meangos, Jurisdiction of Betanses in Galicia.

JUAN BAUTISTA BERNARD native St. Charles Coast of the Germans son of ANDRES BERNARD and of MARGARITA AIDELAMAR
Married February 21, 1786
MARGARITA AIDELMAR native same Parish daughter of ANDRES AIDELEMAR and of MARGARITA ALBERT.

HUGO DANIEL CREPS son of HUGO CREPS and of MARIANA CHOVIN
Married February 21, 1786
LUISA LEFLEAU native of Mobile daughter of JUAN BAUTISTA LEFLEAU and of MARIANA LEFLEAU.

JOSEF de la PENA native of Cadiz, widow of MICAELA PERES, son of ANDRES de la PENA and of MARIA ESTEFANIA BRAVO
Married February 22, 1786
ROSALIA VIERA native of Grand Canaries, widow of JOSEF NAVARRO, daughter of JUAN VIERA and of DOMINGA ROMERO.

JOSEF TRICAUT native of Bordeaux son of JOSEF TRICAUT and of MARIA BARGUERY
Married March 26, 1786
MARIA MARCHAND daughter of PEDRO MARCHAND and of CATARINA BERNARD.
Groom died February 29, 1834
Bride died July 29, 1842

16

Figure 17-6. Page from *Louisiana Marriages: I,* ed. by Alice Daly Forsyth (New Orleans: Polyanthos, 1977), showing marriage extracts from the St. Louis Cathedral of the Roman Catholic Church, New Orleans, Louisiana, 1786.

Extensive guides and inventories exist for each of these archives, in books, handwritten indexes, and online at <www.aer.es>. The last offers actual digital images of many documents in their collections.

Spanish Emigration Records

During the colonial period before 1790, passenger lists were generated by the *Casa de la Contratación* as part of the commercial regulations of the American colonies. Found in the third section of the Archives of the Indies in Seville, the passenger lists can be divided into two categories: (1) *listas* (lists) or *libros de pasajeros* (books of passengers); and (2) *informaciones y licencias* (information and licenses). The former, covering the period from 1509 to 1701, is a series of books recording the names of passengers traveling from Seville to the Indies. (Seville was the only legal port of departure for ships going to the Americas.) The sub-section covering the period from 1534 to 1790 for *informaciones* and *licencias* is a collection of loose copies of petitions requesting special permission or license to travel to the Americas to settle or conduct certain business; in many cases, these were the same individuals who appear in the passenger lists. In nearly all cases, both the passenger lists and the permissions petitions record the name of the emigrant or, in the case of whole families, the name of the head of the family and his place of birth or residence before emigrating to the Americas.

There is some question as to whether even a majority of those actually going to the Americas appear in the passenger lists at Seville. It was, of course, possible to travel by ship to England or France, and from there to go to the colonies on one of the many ships that illegally transported merchandise (contrary to Spain's prohibition of non-Spanish ships in her colonies). It is also likely that many captains were willing, for an appropriate fee, to allow a passenger to embark for the colonies without prior legal approval. Recording was even less complete in the last half of the eighteenth century, following a policy of liberalization, which allowed commerce between the colonies and the ports of Seville, Alicante, Malaga, Cartagena, Barcelona, and La Coruna. After 1792, even more liberal policies allowing trade with any ports in Spain and with many of the non-Spanish ports of Europe and the Americas contributed further to the lack of records. Peter Boyd-Bowman, in the introduction to *Indice biogeográfico de cuarenta mil Pobladores españoles de América en el Siglo XVI*, expresses a belief that passenger lists reflect only about 20 percent of those who actually went to the Americas during at least the first sixty-year period.[17] Others put the number as high as 80 percent. No matter which estimate is correct, there are two important things to remember: (1) the passenger lists at Seville are extremely valuable because, for those names that do appear, they are a key to finding a specific locality of origin in Spain; (2) the immigrant ancestor's non-appearance does not mean that he or she did not emigrate during that time period but is merely an indication that he or she may have been among that percentage of individuals who did not follow the procedures to obtain official approval for immigration to the Americas. (Note that the rich as well as the poor evaded such restrictions for a variety of reasons, including those who came as military personnel, and that failure to follow official procedures is no indication as to the character or financial state of the person involved.)

The staff of the Archives of the Indies at Seville developed an index to the entire section of passenger lists, including both the *listas y libros de pasajeros* and the *informaciones y licencias*. Seven volumes of the *Catálogo de pasajeros a Indias* are now available in printed form, covering the years 1509 to 1599.[18] The entries are arranged by date, with an alphabetical index by surname in the back of the volume. Each entry contains the name of the individual, parents' names (when known), and the residence or place of birth in Spain (figure 17-7). This work is further supplemented by Peter Boyd-Bowman, *Indice geobiográfico de 56 mil pobladores de América*.[19] These two volumes cover the period from 1493 to 1539, which includes nearly all of the 15,000 entries in the first two volumes of the *Catálogo de pasajeros a Indias;* the volumes draw extensively from archives throughout Spain and the Americas to arrive at the 56,000 individuals contained in the index. For the period from 1600 until 1790, the archive's staff compiled a massive card index of the archive's passenger list section that can now be found at <www.aer.es>.

There are no passenger lists available in a single major archive for the nineteenth century, although there are for the period before 1790. During the first years following the end of the colonial period there was little emigration from Spain. However, as the political and social situation stabilized in the former colonies, in Spain the pressure of population increase, agricultural limitations, political unrest, mandatory military service (beginning in 1835), and civil war resulted in increased emigration. By 1840, governors of the coastal provinces in northern Spain and, by 1853, the national government were sufficiently concerned that new regulations controlling emigration were issued. The required documentation, which

4135. CATALINA LEAL, natural de Lebrija, soltera, hija de Francisco Jiménez, veedor de los Reales Alcázares de Sevilla, y de Juana Rodríguez de Hinojosa, a Nueva España, como criada de Rui Díaz de Mendoza.—14 de junio.

5224, N.° 53

4136. ALONSO VALERA, natural de Aracena, soltero, hijo de Juan de Valera y de Elvira López, a Filipinas.—14 de junio.

5224, N.° 54

4137. FRANCISCO DE VEJINES, natural de Los Palacios, hijo de Juan Bueno y de Catalina Jiménez, con su mujer Juana Romera, hija de Sebastián Mateos y de Antona Martín, y su hijo Antón, a Nueva España, en compañía de Antón Vejines.—14 de junio.

5224, N.° 55

4138. PEDRO ALONSO, natural de Trujillo, soltero, hijo de Hernando de Cuevas y de Catalina García, a Nueva España.—14 de junio.

5224, N.° 56

4139. JUAN DE RIVERO, natural de Zamora, hijo de Diego de Rivero y de Antonia Rodríguez, a Nueva España como criado de don Rodrigo de Vivero.—14 de junio.

5224, N.° 57

4140. FRANCISCO RODRIGUEZ, natural de Aldea del Rey, soltero, hijo de Cristóbal Rodríguez y de Constanza Díaz, a Honduras.—14 de junio.

5224, R. 58

4141. ANDRES BARROSO, natural de Santiago de Guatemala, hijo de Andrés Navarro y de Isabel Barroso, a Guatemala de donde vino como paje de Juan Hurtado de Mendoza.—15 de junio.

5224, N.° 59

599

Figure 17-7. Page 616 of vol. 5 of *Catálago de pasajeros a Indias durante los Siglos XVI, XVII, y XVIII*, comp. by Louis Romera Iruela and María del Carmen Galbis Diez (Madrid, Spain: Ministerio de Cultura, 1980), showing extracts from April 1577.

varied from one province to another and over time, included the following:

1. Provincial passport.
2. *Fianza* (bond).
3. Statement from the *alcalde* (local mayor) or corresponding local official as to the person's good conduct and legitimate reasons to travel, and that there are no outstanding obligations, financial or military.
4. *La obligación de paga de reales* (contract for payment of passage).
5. *Licencia de los padres o de esposo* (permission of parents or spouse).
6. *Contrata de embarque* (boarding contract).

The challenge to the researcher is in locating these documents. Provincial passport registers are found in the provincial historical archive of the issuing province (usually the province of embarkation). It is likely that the statement of good conduct, the parents' permission, and possibly the bond will have been prepared and signed before the notary or municipal secretary of the hometown. While these documents may be found among home sources, this information is unfortunately of little value in locating the place of origin.

The boarding contract, passage payment contract, and sometimes the bond may be found in the notarial records of the port city of embarkation. If that port has been identified, a search in its notarial records for the time period might prove helpful. Unfortunately, these documents are not indexed or segregated from other notarial documents, so a personal search among them would be necessary. See chapter 12 of *Tracing Your Hispanic Heritage* for a description of this process.

The *contrata de embarque* is in reality a full passenger list in many cases. Spanish historians' recent interest in these documents has resulted in the identification and indexing of two sets, published in the following books: María Pilar Pildain Salazar's *Ir A América: La emigración Vasca a América* and Juan Carlos de la Madrid Alvarez's *El Viaje de los emigrantes Asturianos a América*.[20] Check the Family History Library Catalog and other library catalogs for similar books.

Although national passports only came into use around 1920 in Spain, passports have been in use for a much longer period in Latin America. In addition, certain Spanish maritime provinces required passports in the nineteenth century, and these are found in the provincial historical archives. Unfortunately, there are no published indexes to these records, and generally there are no internal archive indexes. The Immigrant Ancestors Project of the Center for Family History and Genealogy at Brigham Young University is working on identifying and extracting these emigration records from hundreds of archives in Spain, Italy, France, and Portugal. More about the project and the resulting free searchable index can be found at the project website <http://immigrants.byu.edu>.

Government Service Records

While the exact nature of government service records is as diverse as the government entities themselves, there are three primary types of records of interest to the family historian: *nombramientos* or *empleos; hojas de servicio* and *relacciones de méritos y servicios;* and *pensiones*.

Nombramientos or *Empleos*

Of special interest are those documents relating to the appointment of government officials in the Americas. Because these records deal with specific places in the Americas and also a specific place in Spain, they can be very valuable in linking an immigrant ancestor with a place of origin in the mother country.

The *nombramientos* or *empleos* is an order or decree that names the person to a particular job or promotion. Such documents may provide the name of the person, date and place of birth, parents' names, marital status, and perhaps other personal information. If you are searching in the archives of Spain for government service records, check *Catálogo XX del Archivo General de Simancas, Títulos de Indias*, which indexes records from the *Sección General del Tesoro* (General Treasury Section), from which colonial officials were paid.[21] Although many who held government positions in the colonial period were of the nobility, there were also, in the colonial areas especially, many individuals who were not.

Hojas de Servicio and *Relacciones de Méritos y Servicios*

These were formal documents prepared, and frequently printed, for individuals who were involved in the civil service. In many cases, several copies were filed with the appropriate authorities for use as they saw fit in petitions for promotion or other activities. In some cases, these are listed in published indexes. An example of this is *Indice de Relaciones de Méritos y Servicios Conservadas en la Sección de Consejos* by Ramón Paz, which sets forth the printed *relaciones de méritos* found in the records of the *consejo real* (royal counsel) in the Archivo Histórico Nacional in Madrid.[22]

Pensiones (Pensions)

This last category can be of the greatest interest to the genealogist because of the extensive information that may be provided in proving the relationship of a deceased government worker to the widow, orphans, or other persons who had a right to the pension. A request for a pension is likely to set forth the name of the spouse of the deceased government worker, the names of his or her children, and, frequently, those of his or her parents. It will also very likely set forth the dates and places of his government service. In many cases, it also includes copies of his baptismal or birth certificate, death certificate, marriage certificate, and will. It may also include the same type of records for his spouse and children. Unfortunately, published indexes for these types of records are not extensive, although often the original collections are alphabetically arranged. In exceptional cases where indexes exist, they can be very valuable. An example of this type of index is Antonio Matilla Tascón's *Indice de Expedientes de Funcionarios Públicos, Viudedad y Orfandad, 1763–1872*, which sets forth the pensions granted by the Sección Montepíos (Welfare Section).[23]

Miscellaneous Legal, Court, and Land Records

Never overlook legal documents. It is always possible that the immigrant ancestor may have had to state his place of birth in either court transactions or other documents of a legal nature. Check the indexes to all local court records, and check the grantor and grantee land records indexes. In Hispanic countries, private legal documents were prepared by notaries. Copies are preserved in bound volumes called *protocolos* and can be found in local municipal or provincial or state archives of the country of origin.

Spanish Nobility Records

Spanish nobles were divided into two major categories: titled and untitled. The status of untitled nobility was called *hidalguía. Hidalgo,* or *hijodalgo* (which, literally translated, means "son of something"), is defined in the fundamental thirteenth-century legislation *Siete Partidas* (Partida Segunda, Título XXI) as the nobility that comes to men by lineage. To have the full rights and privileges of an *hidalgo* from that time forward, it was necessary to prove *hidalguía* in a person's lineage running back to at least his or her *bisabuelos* (great-grandparents). Nearly every national archive in Spain has at least one or two sections relating to *hidalgos*. These archives were usually a depository for records that originated from those proving *hidalguía* status as a means of entering a particular institution. The discovery that an ancestor was involved with a particular institution generating nobility records should trigger a search of such records.

Hidalguía records found in local Spanish and some Latin American national archives generally constitute two types: (1) censuses of the nobility and (2) prepared genealogies, known as *informaciones genealógicas* (genealogical investigation reports) or *limpiezas de sangre* (purity-of-blood records). These types of records are commonly found in the *ayuntamiento* (city hall). The censuses of the nobility were used extensively as a means of proving the nobility of one's ancestors, and many proofs of *hidalguía* contain citations from them. These census documents can be found under several different names, including *padrón de hijosdalgo* (census of *hidalgos*) and *lista del estado de los vecinos* (list of the status of the heads of families). In many cases, these lists were compiled as the exceptions to the *impuesto de pechos* (commoner's tax) and to the *quintas* (military conscriptions), as those who had *hidalgo* status were exempted from both of them. *Informaciones genealógicas* were presented also to join a military or civil order and to marry after having joined the order, wherein the *hidalguía* of the bride was proved. Many of these records are found in the two archives of the Reales Chancillerias in Valladalid and Granada. Both collections are indexed in published form and that of Valladalid online <www.aer.es> and that of Granada on a CD-ROM.

Military Service Records

The number of peninsular troops stationed in a colony and the extent of the organization of provincial units varied depending on the time period and the colony. Study the history of the military in a colony to better understand an ancestor's involvement.

Service Sheets (*Hojas de Servicios*)

These military service records are found in all Hispanic military organizations. Generally, the name of the officer or soldier, the date and place of birth, and the names of his parents are at the top of the sheet. The body of the record is a detailed, date-by-date list of the various assignments and ranks of the soldier's military service. This may be brief and occupy only single page, as in figure 17-8, a service sheet for a Spanish officer who served in Louisiana in 1792, or it may contain many pages.

Personal Files or Petitions (*Expedientes Personales*)

These were generally petitions compiled for a specific purpose, such as to request permission to marry or to request and prove worthiness for a special promotion or pension. In many archives, these *expedientes personales* may be arranged in special sections, such as *expedientes de academía* (academy files), *expedientes matrimoniales* (marriage files), or *expedientes de pensión* (pension files), or they may be arranged alphabetically with the various petitions for a particular soldier or officer filed together under his name.

Military Parish Records

The various units of the Spanish army, being overwhelmingly Catholic, had their own *capellanes* (chaplains). These military priests performed sacraments for officers and soldiers and their families, and recorded those sacraments in special parish registers. A soldier had the option of having the sacraments for himself and his family performed by the military chaplain or the local ecclesiastical authorities. It is possible, therefore, to find for a single family within the same generation some baptisms,

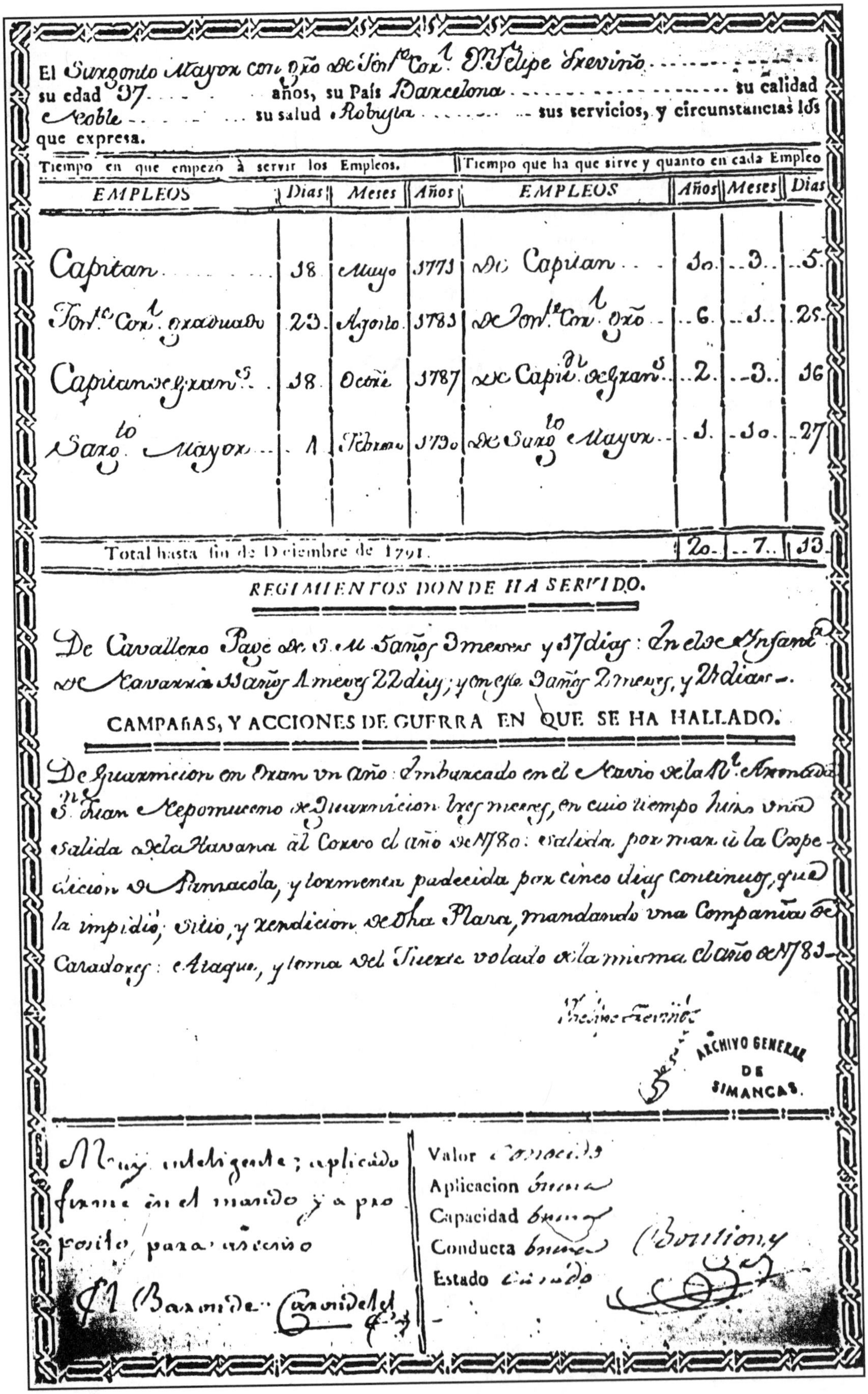

El Sargento Mayor con gdo de Tente Corl Dn Felipe Treviño .... su edad 37 .... años, su País Barcelona .... su calidad Noble ...... su salud Robusta .... sus servicios, y circunstancias los que expresa.

Tiempo en que empezó à servir los Empleos.				Tiempo que ha que sirve y quanto en cada Empleo			
EMPLEOS	Dias	Meses	Años	EMPLEOS	Años	Meses	Dias
Capitan	18	Mayo	1771	De Capitan	10	3	5
Tente Corl graduado	23	Agosto	1783	De Tente Corl gdo	6	1	25
Capitan de Grans	18	Octre	1787	de Capn de Grans	2	3	16
Sargto Mayor	1	Febrero	1790	De Sargto Mayor	1	10	27
Total hasta fin de Diciembre de 1791.					20	7	13

REGIMIENTOS DONDE HA SERVIDO.

De Cavallero Page de S. M. 5 años 3 meses y 17 dias: En el de Infanta de Navarra 11 años 1 meses 22 dias; y en este 3 años 2 meses, y 21 dias.

CAMPAÑAS, Y ACCIONES DE GUERRA EN QUE SE HA HALLADO.

De Guarnicion en Oran un año: Embarcado en el Navio de la Rl Armada S. Juan Nepomuceno de Guarnicion tres meses, en cuio tiempo hizo una salida de la Havana al Corso el año de 1780: salida por mar à la Expedicion de Pensacola, y tormenta padecida por cinco dias continuos, que la impidió; sitio, y rendicion de dha Plaza, mandando una Compañia de Cazadores: Ataque, y toma del Fuerte volado de la misma el año de 178[illegible].

Felipe Treviño

ARCHIVO GENERAL DE SIMANCAS.

Muy inteligente; aplicado firme en el mando y a proposito para ascenso

El Baron de Carondelet

Valor Conocido
Aplicacion buena
Capacidad buena
Conducta buena
Estado casado

Bouligny

Figure 17-8. Military service record of Felipe Treviño, 1792, Louisiana. Archivo de Simancas, Secretaria de Guerra, Hojas de Servico en América, Legajo 7291, VIII, 3, FHL microfilm 1,156,353.

marriages, and last rites performed by local priests and others by military chaplains.

In Spain, access to the military parish records kept by the Vicariato General Castrense in Madrid requires permission from military and ecclesiastical authorities. Inquiries concerning consultation of these records should be addressed to the Vicario General, Secretaria General del Ejército, Alcalá 9, Madrid, España. This collection covers not only records for Spain itself but also those for colonial military units in Cuba, the Philippines, and Puerto Rico. In Mexico, the *presidios* (forts) had their own chaplains; those records are not found in military archives but in local church and civil archives.

Published Transfers and Promotions

It was customary in the Spanish army to maintain promotion lists in accordance with tenure as an officer. In addition, at least annually, the official promotion lists were given in published form as orders, which were distributed throughout the military. These lists have been bound into books and are available in several of the military archives. Generally, they apply to the nineteenth century and include officers serving in the military in the colonies as well as in Spain (figure 17-9).

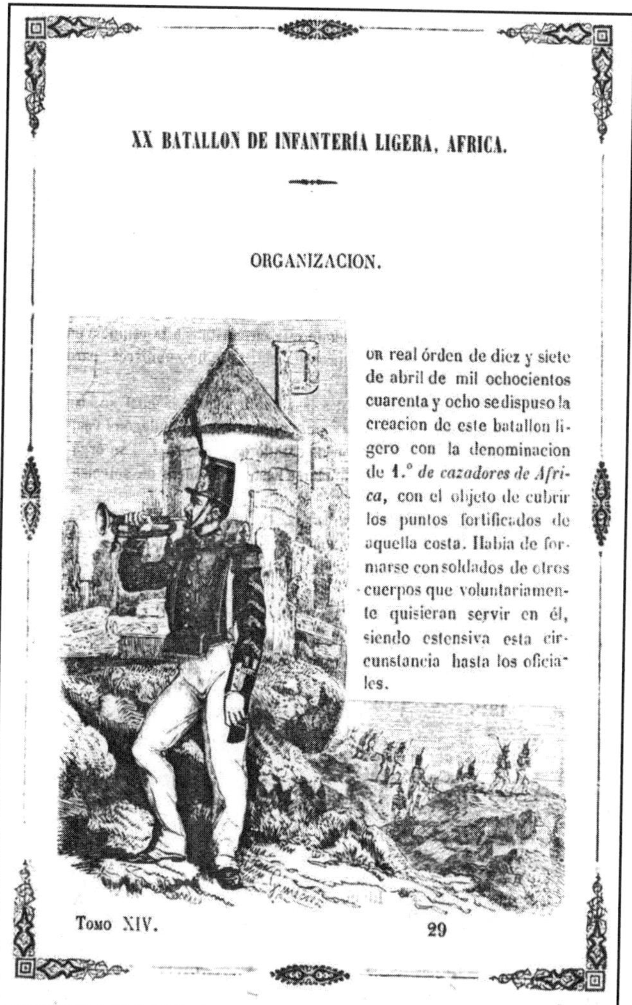

XX BATALLON DE INFANTERÍA LIGERA, AFRICA.

ORGANIZACION.

Con real órden de diez y siete de abril de mil ochocientos cuarenta y ocho se dispuso la creacion de este batallon ligero con la denominacion de 1.° *de cazadores de Africa*, con el objeto de cubrir los puntos fortificados de aquella costa. Habia de formarse con soldados de otros cuerpos que voluntariamente quisieran servir en él, siendo estensiva esta circunstancia hasta los oficiales.

Tomo XIV. 29

Figure 17-9. Title page from a regimental history from the Servicio Histórico Militar in Madrid, Spain.

Enlistments (*Filiaciones*)

These are the individual listings (in some cases on separate sheets called *hojas de filiación*) of the soldiers in the army, as distinguished from the officers. This is the record that is more likely to exist for the common soldier, while the *hoja de servicios* and/or the *expediente personal* is more likely to exist for the officer. Generally, *filiaciones* have the names of the soldier, his parents, his birthplace, place of residence, religion, whether or not he is married, and a physical description. In some cases, these records will also contain information, such as the *hoja de servicio*, which shows the various places where the soldier served. Unfortunately, unless arranged alphabetically as part of the initial filing, these *filiaciones* are much less likely to be indexed and therefore are not easily accessible to the researcher. For this reason, when dealing with a non-officer, it is important to note any information concerning military service found in local or family records. The location of enlistment or the regiment in which a particular soldier served may be the key to finding his record. An excellent collection of those serving during the American Revolutionary period in areas that are now part of the United States has been compiled by Granville Hough.[24]

Censuses (*Padrones*) and Review Lists (*Listas de Revistas*)

Frequently, especially in outlying areas, censuses were taken of military personnel and their families, both officers and enlisted men, serving at particular posts. In addition, it was common to review all the members of a unit in frontier areas, such as in the southwestern United States, where censuses of the *presidios* (frontier posts) frequently included all of the citizens under the responsibility and protection of the unit, as well as the soldiers. Such censuses are found not only in military archives but also in national archives housing government records of the colonial period.

Locating the records of ancestors who served in the military may require some diligence but is well worth the effort. The major difficulty in searching for a military record is that the records tend to have been preserved in archives that correspond to the type of military service. The records of those who served in colonial areas in the Spanish regular army or who served as officers in the provincial or militia units are likely to be found in the archives of Spain. For enlisted personnel in colonial regiments and for national armies after independence, as well as for all military units in some cases, the records will be found in national archives other than those of Spain. In addition, those for militia units may be found in provincial or state municipal archives.

Military census records, reports, promotion lists, and other administrative records were frequently prepared in duplicate or triplicate during the colonial period. One copy was kept locally, a second was sent to the regional *capitania general,* and the last one was sent to colonial administrators in Spain. Although this pattern may make it somewhat difficult to determine with certainty the archives in which the records may be filed, it has nevertheless proved helpful in areas where local archives have been destroyed. Some Latin American military records that were primarily local in nature can be found in Spanish national archives. Excellent examples are the military records of the Spanish American Southwest, which are preserved in the *Archivo General de las Indias* in Seville.

Newspapers

Newspapers have existed for many years in Hispanic countries, even in smaller towns. Many have been microfilmed, and references to them can be located either on microfilm or hard copy in the following:

1. *Newspapers in Microform: Foreign Countries.*
2. Catalog of the Library of Congress.
3. Many university library catalogs (identify these through the Interlibrary Loan Service).
4. Catalogs of the *bibliotecas, hermotecas* (newspaper archives) or *archivos nacionales* of the country and *archivos estatales* of the state or province of interest.

Although obituaries are more common in small-town newspapers in the United States than in Latin American countries, the Hispanic researcher should carefully search all local newspapers in the area where his or her ancestors died for a published obituary.

Census Records

Generally, both in the United States and Latin America, census records have a column to indicate the country of birth. Fortunately, the census records of Spain and Latin America (especially those of the colonial era) sometimes indicate a specific province or parish in the country where the ancestor was born. There are many exceptions, however, particularly in the U.S. federal census records from the Southwest, where frequent and close association with the various Mexican states created an atmosphere in which the census taker would record the name of the Mexican state in response to the census question regarding the state or country in which the person was born. Census records ought to be carefully consulted, therefore, even though they may not ordinarily yield anything more than the country of origin.

Later censuses in many countries, such as the all federal censuses in the United States from 1900 and later, also indicate whether or not the individual was a naturalized citizen, and how long he or she had been in the country. This information indicates the time period in which the person entered the country and whether or not there may be naturalization and citizenship records.

One researcher knew only that his ancestors, Bonifacio Torres and Josefa Rangel, lived in Arizona about the turn of the century. A search for them in the Soundex index for Arizona for the 1900 census resulted in finding the census page reproduced in figure 17-10. From this the researcher learned his ancestors' ages, the year they came to the United States, and that they lived in Florence, Arizona. From the census, the researcher deduced that Josefa Rangel had not been married when she came to this country. He then wrote the Catholic parish church in Florence, asking if there was a marriage record for Bonifacio Torres and Josefa Rangel before 1900. In response, he received a certificate that gave him a marriage date but nothing about their place of origin in Mexico. He then wrote a second letter asking for a verbatim copy of the marriage entry, as he should have done originally. He received a photocopy of the original marriage entry stating that Bonifacio Torres and his family were from Alamos, Sonora, Mexico, and that Josefa Rangel and her family were from Ures, Sonora, Mexico.

Where to Go Next

Once the ancestral hometown has been found in Spain or a country of Latin America, the process has just begun. Records from these countries are among the most complete in the world. Many have been microfilmed and can be located by consulting the Family History Library Catalog online <www.familysearch.org>. Doing a place search for the small town identified as the ancestral hometown should yield Catholic parish records or civil registers or both for that town.

If the town does not appear in the FHL Catalog, then consult a geographical dictionary or ecclesiastical directory to learn more about the place name. That process, as well as how to read and use the various records, is fully described in *Finding Your Hispanic Roots* by George Ryskamp.

Notes

[1] David J. Weber, *The Spanish Frontier in North America* (New Haven: Yale University Press, 1992).

[2] Peter Boyd Bowman, *Indice geobiográfico de más de 56 mil pobladores de la América hispaña* (México, D.F.: Fondo de Cultura Económica, 1985). Volume 1, deals with 1493 to 1519; volume 2, from 1520 to 1539.

[3] Juan Carlos de la Madrid Alvarez, *El Viaje de los emigrantes Asturianos a América* (Gijon, Spain: Biblioteca Histórica Asturiana, 1989); María Pilar Pildain Salazar, *Ir a América:*

7-224.

TWELFTH CENSUS OF THE UNITED STATES. 119 A

SCHEDULE No. 1.—POPULATION.

State: Texas | County: El Paso | Supervisor's District No. 5 | Enumeration District No. 20 | Sheet No. 16

Township or other division of county: Precinct No 1 | Name of Institution: X

Name of incorporated city, town, or village, within the above-named division: El Paso City | Ward of city: 2 (part of)

Enumerated by me on the 14th day of June, 1900, Oscar D Owen, Enumerator.

Line	Street	House No.	Dwelling	Family	Name	Relation	Color	Sex	Month	Year	Age	Marital	Yrs married	Children born	Living	Birthplace	Father's birthplace	Mother's birthplace	Immigr.	Yrs in U.S.	Nat.	Occupation	Months not employed	School (months)	Read	Write	Speak English	Own/Rent	Free/Mortg.	Farm/House	Farm sched.
1		15	354	361	Martinez Francisca	Head	W	F	Oct	1839	60	Wd		2	1	Mexico	Mexico	Mexico	1891	9	Al	Laborer day	0		no	no	no	R		H	
2					Ortega Pedro	Son	W	M	June	1880	19	S				Mexico	Mexico	Mexico	1891	9	Al	Cigar Maker	0		no	yes	no				
3					Williar Ramon	adopt Son	W	M	Aug	1893	6	S				Texas	Mexico	Mexico				At School		9	no	no	no				
4					— Apolonio	adopt Dau	W	F	May	1895	5	S				Texas	Mexico	Mexico							no	no	no				
5		715	357	357	Soto Francisco	Head	W	M	Apr	1841	59	M	21			Mexico	Mexico	Mexico	1891	9	Na	Day laborer	4		no	no	no	R		H	
6					— Felicitas M.	Wife	W	F	June	1851	48	M	21	10	6	Mexico	Mexico	Mexico		Un					no	no	no				
7					— Jesus	Son	W	M	Dec	1884	15	S				Mexico	Mexico	Mexico		Un		day laborer	4		no	no	no				
8					— Dolorez	Dau	W	F	Aug	1889	10	S				Mexico	Mexico	Mexico		Un		At School		6	no	no	no				
9					— Fillippe	Son	W	M	Feb	1892	8	S				Mexico	Mexico	Mexico		Un		At School			no	no	no				
10					— Felicita	Dau	W	F	May	1896	4	S				Mexico	Mexico	Mexico		Un					no	no	no				
11		716	358	358	Moralez Refugio	Head	W	M	Jan	1866	34	M	3			Mexico	Mexico	Mexico	1891	9	Na	Shoe Maker & Rep.	0		yes	yes	no	R		H	
12					— Anastacia	Wife	W	F	Apr	1879	21	M	3	2	1	Mexico	Mexico	Mexico		Un					no	no	no				
13					Madrano Jose	Lodger	W	M	Mar	1880	20	S				Mexico	Mexico	Mexico		Un		Laborer Smelter	0		yes	yes	no				
14		707	359	359	Jaloma Juan	Head	W	M	June	1837	62	M	40			Mexico	Mexico	Mexico	1883	17	Al	Day Laborer	6		no	no	no	O	M	H	
15					— Siverra	Wife	W	F	Feb	1844	56	M	40	15	10	Mexico	Mexico	Mexico		Un					yes	no	no				
16					— Alexander	Son	W	M	Apr	1870	30	Wd				Mexico	Mexico	Mexico	1891	9	Al		8		yes	yes	no				
17					— Juan	Son	W	M	June	1880	19	S				Mexico	Mexico	Mexico		9		Laborer day	6		no	no	no				
18					— Cecilia	Dau	W	F	Aug	1871	28	S				Mexico	Mexico	Mexico		Un		House Servant	0		yes	yes	yes				
19					— Elinda	Dau	W	F	Dec	1873	26	S				Mexico	Mexico	Mexico		Un		House Servant	0		yes	yes	yes				
20					— Ascencia	Dau	W	F	Dec	1875	24	S				Mexico	Mexico	Mexico		Un					yes	yes	yes				
21					— Rebecca	Dau	W	F	Feb	1877	22	S				Mexico	Mexico	Mexico		Un					yes	yes	yes				
22					— Josefa	Dau	W	F	Mar	1880	20	S				Mexico	Mexico	Mexico		Un		House Servant	0		yes	yes	yes				
23					— Anita	Dau	W	F	July	1881	18	S				Mexico	Mexico	Mexico		Un		House Servant	6		yes	yes	yes				
24					— Guadalupe	Gd Dau	W	F	Dec	1883	16	S				Mexico	Mexico	Mexico		Un		House Servant	0		yes	yes	yes				
25					— Francisco	Gd Son	W	M		1887	12	S				Mexico	Mexico	Mexico		Un		At School		9	yes	yes	yes				
26					— Blas	Gd Son	W	M	Feb	1890	10	S				Mexico	Mexico	Mexico		Un		At School		9	no	no	no				
27					— Miguel	Gd Son	W	M		1893	6	S				Texas	Mexico	Mexico							no	no	no				
28					— Flora	Gd Dau	W	F		1896	4	S				Texas	Mexico	Mexico							no	no	no				
29		705	360	360	Chavez Dionicio	Head	W	M	Dec	1867	32	M	2			Mexico	Mexico	Mexico	1891	9	Al	Rock Mason	3		yes	yes	no	O	F	H	
30					— Dionicia C	Wife	W	F	Oct	1869	30	M	2	0	0	Mexico	Mexico	Mexico		Un					yes	no	no				
31					— Fillippa La.	Mother	W	F	May	1851	49	Wd		1	1	Mexico	Mexico	Mexico		Un					yes	no	no				
32		420	361	361	Ernandez Rufino	Head	W	M	Sep	1850	49	Wd				Mexico	Mexico	Mexico	1896	4	Al	Day Laborer track	3		no	no	no	R		H	
33		420			— Felicita	Daughter	W	F	Mar	1882	18	Wd		1	0	Mexico	Mexico	Mexico		Un					no	no	no				
34					Torrez Rita	adopt Daugh	W	F		1897	3	S				Mexico	Mexico	Mexico		Un					no	no	no				
35		419	362	362	Ponce Chas. C	Head	W	M	Oct	1868	31	Wd				Kansas	Virginia	Missouri				Porter RR Train	0		yes	yes	yes	R		H	
36					Contreras Concepcion	Housekeeper	W	F	Oct	1871	28	Wd		1	1	Mexico	Mexico	Mexico		Un		Housekeeper	0		yes	yes	no				
37					— Eliza	Lodger	W	F	Oct	1890	9	S				Mexico	Mexico	Mexico		Un		At School		12	yes	no	no				
38		416	363	363	Barcena Manuel	Head	W	M	May	1874	26	S				New Mexico	Texas	New Mexico				Cigar Maker	0		yes	yes	no	R		H	
39					Bonilla Louisa	Housekeeper	W	F	Jan	1878	22	S				Mexico	Mexico	Mexico		Un		Housekeeper	0		no	yes	no				
40					Bonilla Rouel	Lodger	W	M	Oct	1895	4	S				Texas	New Mex	Mexico							no	no	no				
41					— Ernesto	Lodger	W	M	Feb	1898	2	S				Texas	New Mex	Mexico							no	no	no				
42					— Manuel	Lodger	W	M	May	1900	1/12	S				Texas	New Mex	Mexico							no	no	no				
43		414	364	364	Ruis Leandro	Head	W	M	Feb	1840	60	M	30			Mexico	Mexico	Mexico	1855	45	Na	Day Laborer	6		yes	yes	no	R		H	
44					— Lucia	Wife	W	F	Dec	1840	59	M	30	3	2	Mexico	Mexico	Mexico		Un					no	no	no				
45					— Francisco	Son	W	M	Oct	1871	28	S				Texas	Mexico	Mexico				Day Laborer	6		yes	yes	yes				
46		80	365	365	Chavez Francisco	Head	W	M	Dec	1859	40	M	1			Mexico	Mexico	Mexico	1892	7	Al	House Painter	0		yes	yes	yes	R		H	
47					— Dolorez	Wife	W	F	Mar	1876	24	M	1	0	0	Mexico	Mexico	Mexico		Un					yes	yes	no				
48		81	366	366	Maese Anita	Head	W	F	Oct	1861	38	Wd		9	8	Mexico	Mexico	Mexico		Un					yes	yes	no	R		H	
49					Garcia [illegible]	Dau	W	F	Mar	1878	22	S				Mexico	Mexico	Mexico		Un		Servant			yes	yes	no				
50					— Romulo	Son	W	M	Feb	[illegible]	16	S				[illegible]	[illegible]	[illegible]		Un		[illegible]			[illegible]	[illegible]	[illegible]				

Figure 17-10. 1900 U.S. census schedule, El Paso County, Texas.

La Emigración Vasca a América (Guipuzcoa 1840–1870) (San Sebastián, Spain: Donostia, 1984).

[4] Lyman D. Platt, *A Genealogical Historical Guide to Latin America* (Detroit: Gale Research Co., 1978).

[5] George Ryskamp, *Finding Your Hispanic Roots* (Baltimore: Genealogical Publishing Co., 1997).

[6] George Ryskamp, *Tracing Your Hispanic Heritage* (Riverside, Calif.: Hispanic Family History Research, 1984).

[7] *Spanish Records Extraction* (Salt Lake City: The Church of Jesus Christ of Latter-day Saints, 1981).

[8] Victor Herrero Mediavila and Lolita Rosa Aquayo Hayle, *Indice Biográfico de España, Portugal e Ibero-América*, 4 vols. (New York: K. G. Saur, 1990).

[9] A. Garcia-Carrafa, *Enciclopedia Heráldica y Genealógica Hispano Americana*, 88 vols. (Madrid: AA-URR, 1920–63).

[10] *El Solar Catalán, Valenciana y Balear* (San Sebastián, Spain: Garcia Carrafa, 1967).

[11] Jaime de Querexeta, *Diccionario onamástico y heráldico basco*, 6 vols. (La Gran Enciclopedia Vasca: Bilbao, 1970–75).

[12] Lyman D. Platt, *Latin American Family Histories* (Salt Lake City: Instituto Genealógico Histórico Latinoamericano, 1991).

[13] For a detailed discussion, see George R. Ryskamp, "Catholic Marriage Records as a Source for Immigrant Place of Origin," *Ancestry* Magazine 20 (May/June 2002): 36–41.

[14] Loretto Dennis Szucs, *They Became Americans* (Salt Lake City: Ancestry, 1998).

[15] *Guide to Genealogical Research in the National Archives* (Washington, D.C.: National Archives Trust Fund Board, 1983).

[16] *Index of Spanish Citizens Entering the Port of New Orleans Between January, 1840 and December, 1865* (New Orleans: Charles Mudrell, n.d.).

[17] Peter Boyd-Bowman, *Indice biogeográfico de cuarenta mil Pobladores españoles de América en el Siglo XVI* (Bogotá, Colombia: Instituto Caro y Cuervo, 1964).

[18] Cristóbal Bermúdez Plata, *Catálogo de Pasajeros a Indias. Vol. 1: 1509–1534; vol. 2: 1535–1538; vol. 3: 1539–1559* (Seville, Spain: Imprenta Editorial de la Gavidia, 1940); Luis Romera Iruela y María del Carmen Galbis Diez, *Catálogo de Pasajeros a Indias Siglos XVI, XVII y XVIII, Volumen IV (1560–1566)* (Madrid: Ministerio de Cultura, 1980); María del Carmen Galbis Diez, *Catálogo de Pasajeros a Indias Siglos XVI, XVII y XVIII, Volumen V 1567–1577 (2 tomos)* (Madrid: Ministerio de Cultura, Dirección de Bellas Artes, Archivos y Bibliotecas, 1980); *Catálogo de Pasajeros a Indias Siglos XVI, XVII y XVIII, Volumen VI 1578–1585* (Madrid: Ministerio de Cultura, Dirección de Bellas Artes, y Archivos, 1986); *Catálogo de Pasajeros a Indias Siglos XVI, XVII y XVIII, Volumen VII 1586–1599* (Madrid: Ministerio de Cultura, Dirección de Bellas Artes y Archivos, 1986).

[19] Peter Boyd-Bowman, *Indice geobiográfico de 56 mil pobladores de América*, 2 vols. (México: Fondo de Cultura Económica, 1985).

[20] Mária Pilar Pildain Salazar, *Ir A América: La emigración Vasca a América (Guipuzcoa 1840–1870)*, (San Sebastián, Spain: Donostia, 1984); and Juan Carlos de la Madrid Alvarez, *El Viaje de los emigrantes Asturianos a América* (Gijon, Spain: Biblioteca Histórica Asturiana, 1989).

[21] *Catálogo XX del Archivo General de Simancas, Títulos de Indias* (Valladolid, Spain: Patronato Nacional de Archivos Históricos, 1954).

[22] Ramon Paz, *Indice de Relaciones de Méritos y Servicios Conservadas en la Sección de Consejos* (Madrid, Spain: Cuerpo de Archiveros, 1943).

[23] Antonio Matilla Tascón, *Indice de Expedientes de Funcionarios Públicos, Viudedad y Orfandad, 1763–1872* (Madrid, Spain: Hidalguía, 1962).

[24] Granville Hough and H. C. Hough, *Patriots Series*, 8 vols. (San Antonio, Tex.: Borderlands Press, 1998–2001). For current understanding of their importance, see <www.somosprimos.com/hough/hough.htm> and the Sons of the American Revolution site <www.rsar.org/history/spain.htm>.

References

General

Alarcón, Antonio Menédez. *La Emigración Aturiana a la República Dominicana.* Oviedo, Spain: Consejo de Comunidades Asturianas, 1993.

American Geographical Society. *Index to the Map of Hispanic America.* Washington, D.C.: American Geographical Society, 1945.

Archivo de Simancas. *Secretaria de Guerra, Hojas de Servicios de América.* Valladolid, Spain: Patronato Nacional de Archivos Históricos, 1958.

Atienza, Julio de. *El Diccionario heráldico de appellidos españoles y títulos nobiliarios.* Madrid, Spain: M. Aguilar, 1948.

Basanta de la Riva, Alfredo. *Sala de los Hijosdalgo, Catálogo de todos sus plietos y expedientes y probanzas.* 2d ed. Madrid, Spain: Hidalguía, 1956.

Bermúdez Plata, Cristóbal. *Catálogo de Pasajeros a Indias.* Vol. 1: 1509–34; vol. 2: 1535–38; vol. 3: 1539–59. Seville: Imprenta Editorial de la Gavidia, 1940.

Boyd-Bowman, Peter. *Indice geobiográfico de cuarenta mil Pobladores españoles de América en el Siglo XVI.* Bogotá, Colombia: Instituto Caro y Cuervo, 1964.

———. *Indice geobiográfico de 56 mil pobladores de la América Hispánica.* México, D.F.: Fondo de Cultura Económica, 1985.

———. *Indice biogeográfico de cuarenta mil Pobladores españoles de América en el Siglo XVI.* Bogotá, Colombia: Instituto Cara y Cuervo, 1964.

Bullón Fernández, Ramón. *El Problema de la Emigración y los Crimenos de Ella: Orientaciones más Convenientes Para la Política Económica de España.* Barcelona: Casa Provincial de Caridad, 1914.

Bóveda, Xavier. *Belezas Locais, Bohemia E Aventura Emigrante: Colectánea de Textos Inéditos.* Introductorio, Luis Martul, Carmen Luna, and María Golán. Santiago de Compostela, Spain: Consello da Cultura Galega, 2002.

Cadenas y Vicent, Vicente de. *Archivos militares y civiles en donde se conservan fondos de carácter castrense relacionados con expedientes personales de militares.* Madrid, Spain: Hidalguía, 1975.

Carmagnani, Marcello. *Emigración Mediterránea y América.* Formas y Transformaciones, 1860–1930. Oviedo, Spain: Fundación Archivo de Indianos, 1994.

Carr, Peter E. *Guide to Cuban Genealogical Research: Records and Sources.* Chicago, Ill.: Adams Press, 1991.

Catálogo XX del Archivo General de Simancas, Títulos de Indias. Valladolid, Spain: Patronato Nacional de Archivos Históricos, 1954.

The Church of Jesus Christ of Latter-day Saints. *Resource Papers, Series H. Basic Portuguese Paleography,* 1981.

———. *Spanish Records Extraction.* Salt Lake City: The Church of Jesus Christ of Latter-day Saints, 1981.

———. *French Records Extraction.* Salt Lake City: The Church of Jesus Christ of Latter-day Saints, 1981.

Cruz, António. "Paleografia Portuguesa." In *Ensaio de Manual.* Porto: Universidade Portu Calense, 1987.

Galbis Diez, María del Carmen. *Catálogo de Pasajeros a Indias Siglos XVI, XVII y XVIII, Volumen V 1567–1577 (2 tomos).* Madrid, Spain: Ministerio de Cultura, Dirección de Bellas Artes, Archivos y Bibliotecas, 1980.

———. *Catálogo de Pasajeros a Indias Siglos XVI, XVII y XVIII, Volumen VI 1578 1585.* Madrid, Spain: Ministerio de Cultura, Dirección de Bellas Artes, y Archivos, 1986.

———. *Catálogo de Pasajeros a Indias Siglos XVI, XVII y XVIII, Volumen VII 1586 1599.* Madrid, Spain: Ministerio de Cultura, Dirección de Bellas Artes y Archivos, 1986.

Gallardo, César Yáñez. *Saltar con red: La Temprana Emigración Catalana a América ca. 1830–1870.* Madrid, Spain: Alianza Editorial, 1996.

Gallardo, César Yáñez. *La Emigración Española a América, Siglos XIX y XX.* Dimensión y Características Cuantitativas. Oviedo, Spain: Fundación Archivo de Indianos, 1994.

García Carrafa, A. *Enciclopedia Heráldica y Genealógica Hispano Americana.* 88 vols. AA-URR. Madrid, Spain, 1920–63.

———. *El Solar Catalán, Valenciana y Balear.* San Sebastián: Librería Internacional Churruea, 1967.

Gjerde, Jon. *Major Problems in American Immigration and Ethnic History.* Boston, Mass.: Houghton Mifflin, 1998.

Gonzalez, Juan. *Harvest of Empire: A History of Latinos in America.* New York: Penguin Books, 2000.

Guía de fuentes para la historia de Ibero-América conservadas en España. 2 vols. Madrid, Spain: Dirección General de Archivos y Bibliotecas, 1966.

Guide to Genealogical Research in the National Archives. Washington, D.C.: National Archives Trust Fund Board, 1983.

Heredero Roura, Federico, and Vicente Cadenas y Vicent. *Archivo General Militar de Segovia: Indice de Expedientes Personales.* 9 vols. Madrid, Spain: Ediciones Hidalguía, 1959–63.

Herrero Mediavila, Victor, and Lolita Rosa Aquayo Hayle. *Indice Biográfico de España, Portugal e Ibero-América.* 4 vols. New York: K. G. Saur, 1990.

Humling, Virginia. *U.S. Catholic Sources: A Diocesan Guide.* Orem, Utah: Ancestry, 1995.

Index of Spanish Citizens Entering the Port of New Orleans Between January, 1840 and December, 1865. New Orleans: Charles Mudrell, n.d.

Klein, Herbert. *La Inmigración Española en Brasil.* Oviedo, Spain: Fundación Archivo de Indianos, 1996.

Lohman Villena, Guillermo. *Los americanos en las órdenes militares.* Madrid, Spain, 1947.

Lorey David E. *The U.S.-Mexican Boarder in the Twentieth Century: A History of Economic and Social Transformation.* Wilmington, Del.: Scholarly Resources, 1999.

Madrid Alvarez, Juan Carlos de la. *El Viaje de los emigrantes Asturianos a América.* Gijón, Spain: Biblioteca Histórica Asturiana, 1989.

Matilla Tascón, Antonio. *Indice de Expedientes de Funcionarios Públicos, Viudedad y Orfandad, 1763–1872.* Madrid, Spain: Hidalguía, 1962.

Maduell, Charles R., Jr. *Index of Spanish Citizens Entering the Port of New Orleans Between January, 1840 and December, 1865.* New Orleans, n.d.

———. *Index of Spanish Citizens Entering the Port of New Orleans Between January, 1819 to December, 1839.* New Orleans, n.d.

Magdaleno, Ricardo. *Catálogo XX del Archivo General de Simancas, Títulos de Indias.* Patronato Nacional de Archivos Históricos: Valladolid, 1954.

Millares, Carló Agustín. *Tratado de Paleografía Española* (Texto I). Madrid, Spain: Editorial Espasa-Calpe, S.A., 1983.

———, and José Ignacio Mantecón. *Album de Paleografía Hispanoamericana de los siglos XVI y XVII.* Barcelona: Ediciones El Albir, 1975.

Montes, Mina Ramírez. *Manuscritos Novohispanos.* Ejercicios de Lectura. Universidad Nacional Autonoma de México: México, 1990.

Nava, Julian. *Viva La Raza: Readings on Mexican Americans.* New York: D. Van Nostrand Co., 1973.

Newman, John J. *American Naturalization Records, 1790–1990: What They Are and How to Use Them.* Bountiful, Utah: Heritage Quest, 1995, 1998.

Ocerin, Enrique de. *Indice de los expedientes matrimoniales de militares y marinos que se conservan en el Archivo General Militar, 1761–1959.* Madrid, Spain, 1959.

Paz, Julian. *Catálogo de Manuscritos de las Américas en la Biblioteca Nacional.* Madrid, Spain, 1933.

Paz, Ramon. *Indice de Relaciones de Méritos y Servicios Conservadas en la Sección de Consejos.* Madrid, Spain: Cuerpo de Archiveros, 1943.

Pérez-Prendes, J. M., and Muñoz-Arraco. *El Marco Legal de la Emigración Española en el Constitucionalismo.* Oviedo, Spain: Fundación Archivo de Indianos, 1993.

Pildain Salazar, María Pilar. *Ir a América: La emigración Vasca a América (Guipúzcoa 1840–1870).* San Sebastián, Spain: Donostia, 1984.

Platt, Lyman D. *Latin American Census Records.* Baltimore: Genealogical Publishing Co., 1998.

———. *Hispanic Surnames.* Baltimore, Genealogical Publishing Co., 1996.

———. *Latin American Family Histories.* Salt Lake City: Instituto Genealógico Histórico Latinoamericano, 1991.

———. "The Mexican Military." *In Latin American and Iberian Family and Local History.* Vol. 9 of World Conference on Records. Salt Lake City, 1980.

———. *Una guía genealógico-histórico de latinoamérica.* Salt Lake City: Acoma, 1977.

———. *A Genealogical Historical Guide to Latin America.* Detroit: Gale Research Co., 1978.

Querexeta, Jaime de. *Diccionario onamástico y heráldico basco.* 6 vols. La Gran Enciclopedia Vasca: Bilbao, 1970–75.

Renaud, M. Hyacinthe. *Paléographie Française ou Méthode de Lecture des Manuscrits Français du XIIIe au XVIIe Siègle Inclusivement.* Rochefort: Imprimerie Ch. Thèze, 1860.

Rodríguez Galdo, María Xosé, and Afonso Vázquez-Monxardín. *Patrimonio Cultural Gelgo Na Emigración: Actas Do I Encontro.* Santiago de Compostela, Spain: Consello da Cultura Galega, 1996.

Romera Iruela, Luis y María del Carmen Galbis Diez. *Catálogo de Pasajeros a Indias Siglos XVI, XVII y XVIII, Volumen IV (1560–1566).* Madrid, Spain: Ministerio de Cultura, 1980.

Ruiz, Vicki L. *From Out of the Shadows: Mexican Women in Twentieth-Century America.* New York: Oxford University Press, 1998.

Ryskamp, George R. *Finding Your Hispanic Roots.* Baltimore: Genealogical Publishing Co., 1997.

———. *Spanish Military Records.* Riverside, Calif.: Hispanic Family History Research, 1987.

Sánchez, George J. *Becoming Mexican American: Ethnicity, Culture and Identity in Chicano Los Angeles, 1900–1945.* New York: Oxford University Press, 1993.

Sánchez Alonso, Blanca. *Las Causas de la Emigración Española, 1880–1930.* Madrid, Spain: Alianza Editorial, 1995.

Schaefer, Christina K. *Guide to Naturalization Records of the United States.* Baltimore: Genealogical Publishing Co., 1997.

Shaw, Carlos Martínez. *La Emigración Española a América, 1492–1824.* Oviedo, Spain: Fundación Archivo de Indianos, 1994.

Simón y Morterero, Conrado. *Apuntes de Iniciacion a la Paleografia Española de los siglos XII a XVII.* Hidalguia: Madrid, Spain, 1979.

Sixerei Paredes, Carlos. *A Emigración.* Vigo, Spain: Editorial Galaxia, 1988.

Sowell, Thomas. *Ethnic America: A History. United States of America.* Basic Books, 1981.

Stavans, Ilan. *The Hispanic Condition: Reflections on Culture and Identity in America.* New York: Harper Perennial, 1995.

Sumano, Ma. Elena Bibriesca. *Antologia de Paleografia y Diplomática* (texto I). Universidad Autónoma del Estado de México: México, 1991.

Szucs, Loretto Dennis. *They Became Americans: Finding Naturalization Records and Ethnic Origins.* Salt Lake City: Ancestry, 1998.

Terrero, Angel Riesco. *Diccionario de Abreviaturas Hispanas de los Siglos XIII al XVIII.* Imprime Varona: Salamanca, 1983.

Vigil, James Diego. *From Indians to Chicanos: The Dynamics of Mexican American Culture.* 2d ed. Prospect Heights, Ill.: Waveland Press, 1998.

———. *De América Para a Casa: Correspondencia Familiar de Emigrantes Galegos no Brasil, Venezuela e Uruguai, 1916–1969.* Santiago de Compostela, Spain: Consello da Cultura Galega, 2001.

———. *Estudios Migratorios.* Edited by Xosé Ramón Barreiro Fernández, Pilar Cagiao Vila, Xosé Manoel Núñez Seixas, and Alexandre Vázquez González. Santiago de Compostela, Spain: Consello da Cultura Galega.

———. *Pasado Presente y Futuro de la Emigración Española a Iberoamérica.* Oviedo, Spain: Consejo de Comunidades Asturianas,1993.

———. *Campesinos y Señores en los Siglos XIV y XV: Castilla-La Mancha y América.* Toledo, Spain: Junta de Cominidades de Castilla-La Mancha, n.d.

———. *The U.S.-Mexican Border Environment: A Road Map to a Sustainable 2020.* Edited by Paul Ganster. San Diego, Calif.: San Diego State University Press, 2000.

———. *Between Two Worlds: Mexican Immigrants in the United States.* Edited by David G. Gutiérrez. Wilmington, Del.: Scholarly Resources, 1996.

———. *Immigration Reconsidered: History, Sociology, and Politics.* Edited by Virginia Yans-McLaughlin. New York: Oxford University Press, 1990.

Walsh, Micheline. *Irish Knights and the Spanish Military Orders.* Vol. 1. Dublin, Ireland: Government Publication Sales Office, 1960. Vols. 2 and 3. Dublin: Irish University Press, 1970.

Weber, David J. *The Spanish Frontier in North America.* New Haven: Yale University Press, 1992.

Mexico

García de Miranda, Enriqueta and Falcón de Gyves, Zaida. *Nuevo Atlas Porrúa de la República Mexicana.* México, D.F.: Editorial Porrúa, 1980.

Gerhard, Peter. *A Guide to the Historical Geography of New Spain.* Cambridge, [U.K]: Cambridge University Press, 1972.

———. *The North Frontier of New Spain.* Norman: University of Oklahoma Press, 1982.

———. *The Southeast Frontier of New Spain.* Norman: University of Oklahoma Press, 1993.

Huerta, Herrera, Juan Manuel, and Vicente San Vicente Tello. *Archivo General De la Nación , México, Guía General.* México, D.F.: Archivo General de la Nación, 1990.

Naylor, Thomas H., and Charles W. Polzer. *Northern New Spain: A Research Guide.* Tucson: University of Arizona Press, 1981.

Platt, Lyman D. *Serie de Investigaciones Genealógicas del IGHL.* Salt Lake City: Instituto Genealógico Histórico Latinoamericano, 1991. Vol. 2: *México, Guía General: Divisiones Políticas.* Vol. 3: *México, Guía General: Divisiones Eclesiásticas.* Vol. 4: *México, Guía de Investigaciones Genealógicas.*

Putney-Beers, Henry. *Spanish and Mexican Records of the American Southwest.* Tucson: University of Arizona Press, 1979.

Rodríguez Ochoa, Patricia. *Guía general de los archivos estatales y municipales de México.* México, D.F.: Sistema Nacional de Archivos, 1988.

Ryskamp, George R. *Finding Your Hispanic Roots.* Baltimore: Genealogical Publishing Co., 1997.

Italy and France

The Church of Jesus Christ of Latter-day Saints. *Major Genealogical Record Sources of France.* Series G no. 1. Revised. Salt Lake City, 1976.

Cole, Trafford. *Italian Genealogical Records.* Salt Lake City: Ancestry, 1995.

Colletta, John. *Finding Italian Roots.* Baltimore: Genealogical Publishing Co., 1993.

Jouniaux, Leo. *Genealogia: Pratique. Methode. Recherche.* Paris: Editions Arthaud, 1991.

Pontet, Patrick. *Family History Research in France.* Andover, England, 1997.

Valynseele, Joseph. *La genealogie, histoire et pratique.* Paris: References Larousse, 1992.

Portugal

Anuario católico de Portugal. [Lisboa?]: O Secretariado, 1931.

Archivo Histórico de Portugal. Lisboa: Typographia Lealdade, 1890.

Azevedo, Pedro A. De, and Antonio de Baiao. *O Arquivo da torre do Tombo.* Lisboa, 1905. Serie Fac-Simile, Lisboa. Arquivo Nacional da Torre do Tombo-Livros Horizonte, 1989.

The Church of Jesus Christ of Latter-day Saints. Resource Papers, Series H. *Basic Portuguese Paleography.* Salt Lake City, 1976.

———. *Portuguese Research Outline.* Salt Lake City, 1990.

———. *Word List: Portuguese and Latin.* Salt Lake City, 1995.

Dicionário chorográphico de Portugal, continental e insular. 12 vols. Porto, Portugal: s.n., 1929–49.

Mariz, Jose. *Inventario Colectiveo dos Registos Paroquiais.* Vol. 1: Centro e Sul. Lisboa: Secretaria de Estado Da Cultura, 1993.

———. *Inventario Colectiveo dos Registos Paroquiais.* Vol. 2: Norte. Lisboa: Secretaria de Estado Da Cultura, 1994.

Serrao, Joel. *Roteiro de Fontes da Historia Portuguesa Contemporanea, arquivos de Lisboa: Arquivo Nacional da Torre do Tombo.* 2 vols. Lisboa: Instituto Nacional de Investigacao Cientifica, 1984.

———. Roteiro de Fontes da Historia Portuguesa Contemporanea, arquivos de Lisboa: Arquivos do Etado, Arquivos da C.M. Lisboa: Instituto Nacional de Investigacao Cientifica, 1985.

Spain

Atlas Gráfico de España. 16 vols. Madrid, Spain: Aguilar, 1969.

Bermúdez Plata, Cristóbal. *El Archivo General de Indias de Sevilla, sede del americanismo.* Madrid, Spain, 1951.

Bores, Angel de Plaza. *Archivo General de Simancas.* Guía del Investigador. Madrid, Spain, 1992. 4a. edición.

Crespo Noguera, Carmen. *Archivo Histórico Nacional: Guía.* Madrid, Spain: Ministerio de Cultura, 1989.

Gallo León, Francisco José. *Archivos españoles, Guía del usuario.* Madrid, Spain: Alianza Editorial, 2002.

Guía de Archivos Estatales Españoles. Madrid, Spain: Ministerio de Cultura, 1984.

Guía de Archivos Militares Españoles. Madrid, Spain: Ministerio de Defensa, 1995.

Guía de fuentes para la historia de Ibero-América conservados en España. 2 vols. Madrid, Spain: Dirección General de Archivos y Bibliotecas, 1966.

Guía de los Archivos Estatales Españoles: Guía del Investigador. 2d ed. Madrid, Spain: Ministerio de Cultura Dirección General de Bellas Artes y Archivos Subdirección de Archivos, 1984.

Guía de los Archivos y las Bibliotecas de la Iglesia en España. León: Asociación Española de Archiveros Eclesiásticos, 1985. Vol I: Archivos; Vol II: Bibliotecas.

Madoz, Pascual. *Diccionario geográfico-estadístico-histórico de España y su posesiones de ultramar.* 16 vols. Madrid, Spain: P. Adoz y L. Sagasti, 1845–50. Facsimile edition. Almendralejo, Badajoz: Centro Cultural Santa Ana, 1992–96.

Millares Carlo, Agustín. *Tratado de Paleografia Española.* 3 Vols. Madrid, Spain: Espasa-Calpe, S. A., 1983.

Ministerio de Educación y Ciencia, Dirección General de Archivos y Bibliotecas. *Censo-Guía de Archivos Españoles.* Madrid, Spain, 1962.

Oficina General de Información y Estadística de la Iglesia en España. *Guía de la Iglesia en España.* Madrid, Spain, 1954.

———. *Guía de la Iglesia en España.* Suplementos. Madrid, Spain, 1955, 1956, and 1957.

Ryskamp, George R. *Tracing Your Hispanic Heritage.* Riverside, Calif.: Hispanic Family Research, 1984.

Sánchez Belda, Luis. Archivo Histórico Nacional. Madrid, Spain, 1963.

———. *Guía del Archivo Histórico Nacional.* Madrid, Spain: Dirección General de Archivos y Bibliotecas, 1958.

Periodicals

1. *Hispanic Genealogical Journal* Published by Hispanic Genealogical Society of Houston
   P. O. Box 810561
   Houston TX 77281-0561
   Vol. I (1982)–present

2. *Los Bexareños Newsletter*
   Published by Los Bexareños Genealogical Society
   P. O. Box 1935
   San Antonio, TX 78212
   Vol. I (1984)–present

3. *New Mexico Genealogist. The Journal of the New Mexico Genealogical Society*
   Published by New Mexico Genealogical Society
   P.O. 8283
   Albuquerque, NM 87198-8283
   Vol. I (1961)–present

4. *Noticias para los Californianos*
   Published by Los Californianos, a nonprofit corporation.
   4002 St. James Place
   San Diego, CA 92103-1630
   Vol. (1961)–present

4a. *Antepasados*
   Published by Los Californianos, a nonprofit corporation.
   4002 St. James Place
   San Diego, CA 92103-1630
   Random annual volumes, 8 since 1970(?)

5. *Nuestras Raices*
   Published by The Genealogical Society of Hispanic America
   National Society of Hispanic Genealogy
   P.O. Box 48147
   Denver, CO 80204
   Vol. I (1989)–present

6. *POINTers: Pursuing Our Italian Names Together*
   Published by POINT / POINTers
   Pursuing Our Italian Names Together
   P.O. Box 2977
   Palos Verdes, CA 90274
   Vol. I (1986)–present

7. *Somos Primos*
   Published by Society of Hispanic Historical and Ancestral Research
   SHHAR P.O. Box 490
   Midway City, CA 92655-0490
   Vol. I (1989)–present

8. *Spanish American Genealogist.*
   Issued by The Augusta Society

Harbor City, CA: Hartwell, 1977–present (3 times per year)
Vol. XXIII (1977)–present
Continues *Spanish Genealogical Helper*

9. *Spanish Genealogical Helper*
Issued by The Augusta Society
Hermosa Beach, CA: Hartwell, 1972–1973
Vol. XVII (1974)–Vol. XXII (1976)
Continues *Spanish American Genealogical Helper*
Continued by *Spanish American Genealogist*.

10. *Spanish American Genealogical Helper*
Issued by The Augustan Society
Hermosa Beach, CA: Hartwell
Vol. II (1972)–Vol.III (1973)
Continues *¿Cuestiones?*
Continued by *Spanish Genealogical Helper*

11. *¿Cuestiones?: Spanish American Genealogical Queries*
Issued by The Augusta Society
Hermosa Beach, California: Hartwell,
Vol. I, No. 1 (June 1971)–Vol. 1, No. 10 (June 1972)
Continued by *Spanish American Genealogical Helper*.

12. *The Puerto Rican Connection / La Conexión Puertoriqueña*
Published by The Puerto Rican Connection / La Conexión Puertoriqueña
TPRC, P.O. Box 4152
Mission Viejo, CA 92690-4152

13. *Newsletter (Sociedad Genealogica)*.
Published by La Sociedad Genealógica del Norte de México
Rancho San Javier 109
Nueva Aurora
Guadalupe, Nuevo León
67190 México
Published in Austin, TX
Vol. I (1978)–present

14. *Revista (Cuban Genealogical Society)*.
Published by the Cuban Genealogical Society,
P.O. Box 2650
Salt Lake City, UT 84110-2650
Vol. I (1988)–Vol. VIII (1995)

15. *The Basque Studies Program Newsletter*
Published by the Center for Basque Studies
University of Nevada Press
University of Nevada, Reno
Reno, NV 89557-0076
No. 1 (1968)–present

16. *El Coqui de Ayer: The Puerto Rican Hispanic Genealogical Society Newsletter*
25 Ralph Ave.
Bentwood, NY 11717-2421
Vol. I (1996)–present

17. *The Americas: A Journal of Latin American History.*
Published by The Academy of American Franciscan History
The Catholic University of America
620 Michigan Ave., NE
Washington, D.C. 20064
Vol. 1 (1944)–present

18

Jewish American Research

GARY MOKOTOFF

After the destruction of the First and Second Temples in Jerusalem, Jews were dispersed throughout their known world. This dispersion became known as the Diaspora (Greek for dispersion). Although Jews had the common bond of their religion, they developed separate cultures in different geographic areas.

Chapter Contents

Jews of the Diaspora

Those Jews who migrated to medieval France and Germany became known as Ashkenazic Jews (*ashkenaz* is the Hebrew word for Germany). They subsequently spread south and east to today's Austria, Czech Republic, Slovak Republic, Hungary, and Romania and then eastward to Poland and Russia, dominating the indigenous Jews of these areas and bringing their language, Yiddish, to the entire region. Most Jewish Americans are descended from the Ashkenazic Jews of central and eastern Europe. Those settling in the medieval Iberian Peninsula became known as Sephardic Jews (*sepharad* is the Hebrew word for Spain). Their culture thrived from the twelfth to the fifteenth centuries but came to an abrupt end in Spain with the expulsion of the Jews in 1492. They fled throughout the Mediterranean rim, Holland, and other countries. Almost all Jewish Americans are either Ashkenazic or Sephardic Jews.

Jews who settled in the Middle East in what are now Yemen, Iraq, and Iran are also categorized as Sephardic Jews, though they originally belonged to a separate group known as Oriental Jews. The influence of the Sephardic Jews after their expulsion from Spain dominated the culture of the Oriental Jews. As the Far East was opened to Western civilization in the fourteenth century, Jews traveled eastward to settle in India and China. Probably the best-known Indian Jew today is Zubin Mehta, who has conducted the New York Philharmonic, Israel Philharmonic, and other orchestras. There are no longer Chinese Jews, though they existed into the late-nineteenth century in Kaifeng, China. The Ethiopian Jews comprise another group that developed independently. Their origins are unknown; they claim to be descendants of King Solomon and the Queen of Sheba. Anthropologists state that they are black Africans who converted to Judaism some fifteen hundred years ago. DNA research supports this theory. Most live in Israel today, having been rescued from religious persecution in the 1980s.

Naming Patterns

A cultural factor of interest to genealogists is the way children of Ashkenazic and Sephardic Jews acquire given names. Ashkenazic Jews normally name their children after deceased relatives—usually recently deceased relatives. This rule is often the first clue as to the names of ancestors for whom there is no documentation. For example, if several male children within an extended family born in the same year were given the name Abraham, it usually shows that some common relative with the given name Abraham died shortly before the birth of the children. Two Ashkenazic Jewish genealogists who suspect they might be related will often go through the ritual of comparing given names in their families, looking for a pattern of similar given names.

Jews who follow the Sephardic tradition name their children according to the following pattern: the firstborn son is named after the father's father; the firstborn daughter is named after the mother's mother; second son after the mother's father; and the second daughter after the father's mother.

Origin of Surnames

To this day, Jewish culture has not required hereditary surnames. In the Jewish religion, a person is known by his or her religious given name followed by "son" or "daughter" of the father's given name—for example, Gad son of Jacob or Sarah Malka daughter of Jacob. Consequently, before the nineteenth century, most Ashkenazic Jews did not have hereditary surnames. Through a series of edicts, surnames were forced upon them by Prussia, Russia, and Austria-Hungary—the three major empires of the period—which wanted a unique way of identifying their Jewish citizens. Jews chose occupation names (see figure 18-1) or the names of towns or kept to patronymics. There are some distinguished rabbinic surnames that predate this era of surname acquisition. They include such names as Auerbach, Epstein, Horowitz, Isserles, Lurie, and Rapaport. Most Sephardic surnames had an equally undistinguished origin. They date from the fifteenth century, when Jews were voluntarily or forcibly baptized as Roman Catholics and assumed the surnames of their sponsors. Many Jews who did not convert but had dealings with Christians assumed surnames to disguise their Jewishness. A few Sephardic surnames predate this era, including Abensur, Malka, Sasson, and Shaltiel.

Record Keeping

Historically, Jews have kept notoriously poor records of vital events. This has been because there is no requirement in the religion to keep such records and because such records, if kept accurately, were used as the basis for discrimination by the Christian governments under which the Jews were ruled. The major exception, however, concerns rabbinic dynasties. To be descended from a famous rabbi is considered a mark of honor, and famous rabbis have documented their pedigrees (*yichus* in Hebrew) to show their Jewish "blue blood." There are even alleged ascents of famous rabbis back to King David.

Castes

The Jewish religion has a significant caste system that sometimes helps in tracing ancestry. It is a hereditary, paternal caste passed down from father to sons. There are three castes: Cohanim, Leviim, and Israelites. Members of the highest caste, Cohanim, are the descendants of biblical Aaron. (This has recently been demonstrated through DNA evidence.) Members of this caste were the high priests of the temples when the temples existed. Persons with the surnames Cohen, Kagan, Kogan, Kahn, Kahan, Katz, Kaplan, and Rapoport are invariably Cohanim. Members of the middle caste, Leviim, are descendants of the biblical Levi. They served as the keepers of the temples. Persons with the surnames Levy, Levin, Segal, Landau, Horowitz, and Epstein are invariably Leviim. Most Jews belong to the lowest caste, the Israelites. These hereditary titles can be used as evidence that two men are not related. For example, a man born to the Cohanim caste cannot be related through paternal lines to a man born to the Leviim or Israelite castes. They could be related, however, through maternal lines. It is not possible for modern-day Jews to determine from which of the twelve tribes of Israel they are descended, except the Cohanim and Leviim (those descended from the tribe of Levi).

Jewish Migration to the United States

Jewish migration to the United States is divisible into periods. For each there are sources of information for doing genealogical research.

Dates	*Period*	*Number of Immigrants*
1654–1838	Colonial/federal	Fewer than 15,000
1838–80	German emigration	250,000
1881–1924	Eastern European emigration	2,000,000
1924–44	Pre-Holocaust	100,000
1945–60	Holocaust survivors	250,000
Present	Russian Jews and others	Up to 50,000 per year

Colonial Period (1654–1838)

The first Jews to come to North America arrived in 1654 at the Dutch colony of New Amsterdam (renamed New York

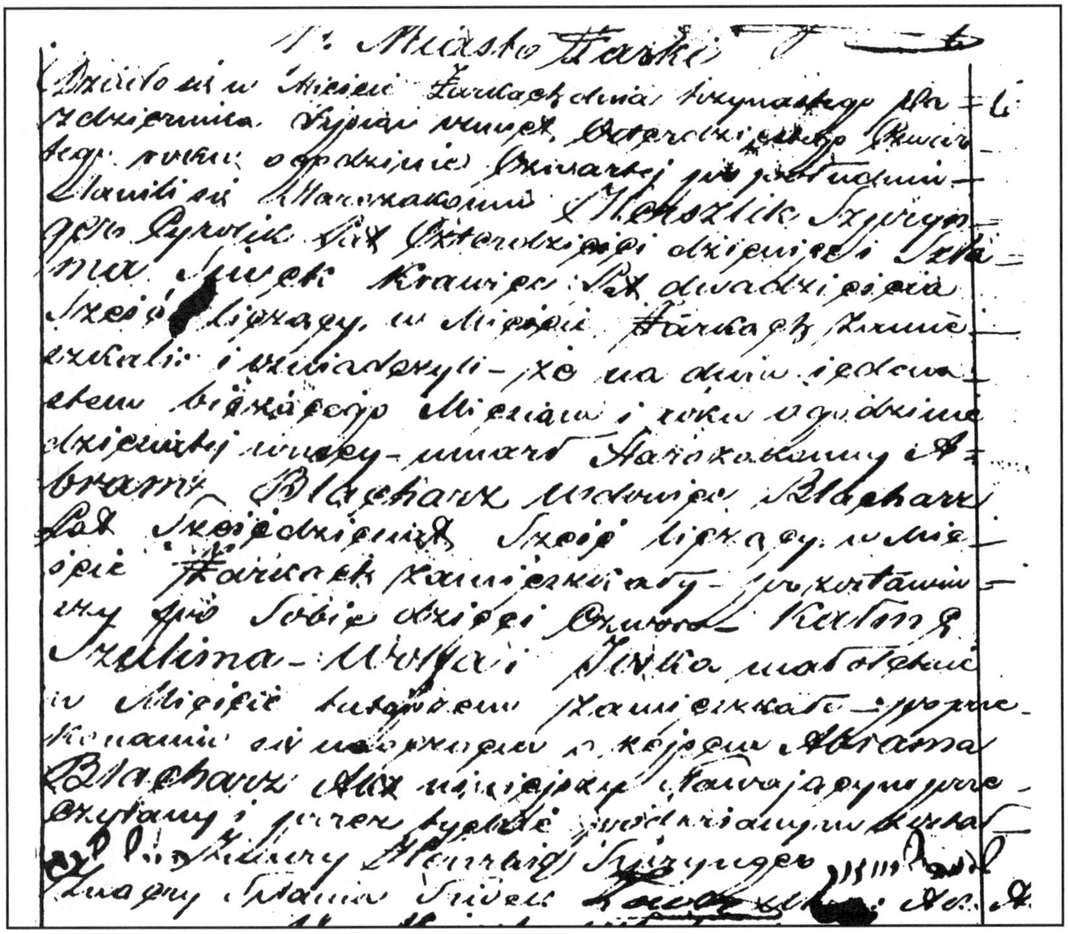

Figure 18-1. The death record of Abram Blacharz, 1844, Zarki, Poland. It indicates that his occupation was that of *blacharz*, Polish for *tinker.*

in 1664). Most were refugees from the Dutch colony of Recife, Brazil, which was conquered by the Portuguese that year. The Jews, fearing persecution from the Portuguese Inquisition, left with plans to go to Holland, the home of many Sephardic Jews who had fled the Spanish Inquisition 150 years earlier. However, they ran out of money and were forced to land at the Dutch colony.

Because Jews in the New World were allowed to practice their religion in a relatively nondiscriminatory environment, record books of American synagogues exist back to colonial times. Besides New York, early Jewish settlements were founded in Savannah, Georgia (1733); Philadelphia (1745); Charleston, South Carolina (1749); Newport, Rhode Island (1763); and Richmond, Virginia (1789).

There are records for this period at the American Jewish Historical Society and the American Jewish Archives, as well as at the synagogue archives themselves.

The definitive genealogical work, now out of print, is *First American Jewish Families* by Rabbi Malcolm H. Stern, FASG.[1] It contains the genealogies (descendants) of every Jewish person known to the author who arrived in the United States before 1838 who remained Jewish for at least one generation. Some fifty thousand persons are identified in it.

German Emigration (1838–80)

Much information about this group can be found using conventional American genealogical resources; little is available through synagogue records. Family historians who have attempted to do German emigration research, Jewish or Christian, know about the paucity of information available for tracing ancestry back to Germany. Ship manifests and citizenship papers provide no clues as to ancestral towns in Germany, so genealogists must dig for information. Family records or death records may hold clues. For example, Jewish immigrants who arrived in the nineteenth century are among the most difficult of Jewish ancestors to document; however, Jewish tombstones of German immigrants have been known to indicate the town of birth (figure 18-2). Check census records as well; census takers sometimes wrote down the town of birth rather than the country of birth on the census record.

Most German Jews left through the ports of Hamburg and Bremen. Emigration lists from Hamburg for the years 1850 to 1934 have survived and are available on microfilm through the Family History Library of The Church of Jesus Christ of Latter-day Saints in Salt Lake City, Utah. Two separate indexes exist, both arranged by year. One, called the direct index, lists ships that sailed directly to the United States. The other, the indirect index, lists ships that stopped at other ports prior to coming across the Atlantic. Virtually no lists from Bremen exist today. They were destroyed in periodic purges. The earliest surviving lists are from 1920. (See chapter 9, "Immigration Records.")

East European Emigration (1881–1924)

In 1881, Czar Alexander II was assassinated, and the Russians blamed it on the Jews. Decades of pogroms against the Jewish population followed. This anti-Semitism, along with deplorable economic conditions, drove millions of Jews from Eastern Europe; 2 million went to the United States. Most Jewish Americans are descended from these persons, and there is a wealth of genealogical information about them.

Passenger Arrival Lists

To learn more about this wave of immigrants (Jewish and others), the U.S. government began documenting them more carefully during the 1890s. Passenger arrival records included age, occupation, nationality, town of last residence, final destination, and other data. Starting in 1906, place of birth was added, and in 1907, name and address of the nearest relative in the immigrant's native country were added. The National Archives in Washington, D.C., has on microfilm the ship manifests and indexes to these lists. Most of these have been digitized and placed on the Internet. The Statue of Liberty-Ellis Island Foundation has records for Ellis Island from 1892–1924 online at <http://ellisisland.org> with an every-name index, but superior access to these images can be found at <http://stevemorse.org>. Records of Castle Garden, predecessor to Ellis Island can be found at <www.castlegarden.org>, as well as on Ancestry.com. Ancestry.com also provides indexes and images of other ports, including Baltimore, Boston, Galveston, Philadelphia, San Francisco, and other ports of less interest to Jewish research. Copies of these microfilms are available through the Family History Library and regional branches of the National Archives. If access to any of these Internet sites or facilities is difficult, you can request copies by writing to the National Archives, Washington, DC 20408.

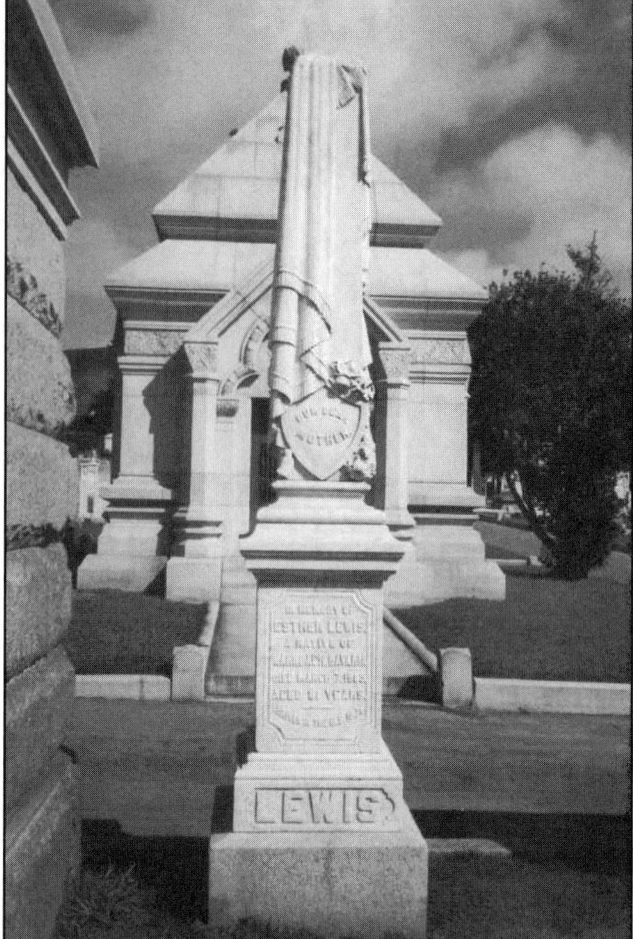

Figure 18-2. This tombstone, located in a San Francisco cemetery, provides invaluable information. Inscribed is the statement, "In memory of Esther Lewis, a native of Wannback, Bavaria, died March 7, 1885, aged 81 years, arrived in U.S. 1828." On the side of the tombstone, inscribed in Hebrew, additional information indicates that she was the daughter of David Sachs. Courtesy of Robert Griffin.

Citizenship Papers

Most Jewish immigrants became citizens of the United States. Even those who decided not to complete the process usually went through the first step by filling out a declaration of intention. The declaration of intention form included a number of questions, such as date of birth, date of marriage, arrival date, name of ship, current address, and, in certain years, name at time of arrival in the United States. Consequently, declarations of intention are valuable resources for Jewish American research. Because the submitter was the actual immigrant, it is not unusual to find more accurate information, such as birth dates, in citizenship papers. The location of these papers depends on which court naturalized the individual. If the certificate of naturalization, thought by many to be the "citizenship papers," is in the family's possession, it will show the county, state, or federal court in which the citizen was naturalized. Contact the court to learn the current location of the records.

Another way to determine the court of naturalization is through voter registration records. Immigrants had to prove their citizenship, and these records often indicate the court where naturalized. Contact the board of elections where the immigrant lived to determine if the records still exist. Otherwise, the long (six months to one year) route must be taken: contact the U.S. Immigration and Naturalization Service, Washington, DC 20530. Some naturalization records have been microfilmed by the Family History Library. For more information on naturalization records, see chapter 9, "Immigration Records."

A Jewish marriage record, called a "ketubah," for Gary Mokotoff and Ruth Lois Auerbach. The Hebrew portion of a ketubah is a two-generation chart in that it includes the Hebrew given names of the fathers of the bride and groom. It will also state whether either father is a Cohen or a Levite (see section on "Castes"). Courtesy of Gary Mokotoff.

KETHUBAH כתובה

Certificate of Marriage

This is to Certify that on the *first* day of the week, the *4th* day of the month of *Tammuz* in the year 57*25*, corresponding to the *4th day* of *July* 19*65* the holy Covenant of Marriage was entered into at *Millburn, New Jersey* between the Bridegroom *Gary Mokotoff* and his Bride *Ruth Lois Auerbach*

The said Bridegroom made the following declaration to his Bride:

"Be thou my wife according to the law of Moses and Israel. I faithfully promise that I will be a true husband unto thee; I will honor and cherish thee; I will work for thee; I will protect and support thee, and will provide all that is necessary for thy sustenance, even as it beseemeth a Jewish husband to do. I also take upon myself all such further obligations for thy maintenance, as are prescribed by our religious statute."

And the said Bride has plighted her troth unto him, in affection and in sincerity, and has thus taken upon herself the fulfillment of all the duties incumbent upon a Jewish wife.

This Covenant of Marriage was duly executed and witnessed this day according to the usage of Israel.

Gary Mokotoff BRIDEGROOM
Ruth Lois Auerbach BRIDE
Rabbi Samuel Jaffe OFFICIANT
Samuel H. Rogers WITNESS
Alan Rosler WITNESS

ב *אחד* בשבת *בארבעה ימים*
לחדש *תמוז* שנת חמשת אלפים ושבע מאות
וחמשה ועשרים לבריאת עולם, למנין שאנו מונין
כאן ___ במדינת אמריקא הצפונית
איך החתן *גדול* ב"ר *יעקב*
אמר לה להדא בתולתא *רחל לאה*
בת ר' ___ הוי לי לאנתו
כדת משה וישראל ואנא אפלח ואוקיר ואיזון ואפרנס
יתיכי ליכי כהלכות גוברין יהודאין דפלחין ומוקרין וזנין
ומפרנסין לנשיהון בקושטא ויהיבנא ליכי מהר בתוליכי
כסף זוזי מאתן דחזי ליכי מדאוריתא ומזוניכי
וכסותיכי וסיפוקיכי ומיעל לותיכי כאורח כל ארעא
וצביאת מרת ___ בתולתא דא
והות ליה לאנתו, ודין נדוניא דהנעלת ליה מבי
אביה בין בכסף בין בזהב ובין בתכשיטין
במאני דלבושא בשמושי דירה ובשמושי דערסא הכל קבל
עליו *גדול ב"ר יעקב* חתן דנן במאה זקוקים
כסף צרוף וצבי *גדול ב"ר יעקב* חתן דנן
והוסיף לה מן דיליה עוד מאה זקוקים כסף צרוף אחרים
כנגדן, סך הכל מאתים זקוקים כסף צרוף וכך אמר
גדול ב"ר יעקב חתן דנן אחריות
שטר כתובתא דא נדוניא דין ותוספתא דא קבלית עלי ועל ירתי
בתראי להתפרע מן כל שפר ארג נכסין וקנינין דאית לי
תחות כל שמיא, דקנאי ודעתיד אנא למקנא,
נכסין דאית להון אחריות ודלית להון אחריות
כלהון יהון אחראין וערבאין לפרוע מנהון שטר
כתובתא דא נדוניא דין ותוספתא דא מנאי ואפילו
מן גלימא דעל כתפאי בחיי ובתר חיי מן יומא דנן ולעלם.
ואחריות שטר כתובתא דא נדוניא דין ותוספתא דא
קבל עליו *גדול ב"ר יעקב* חתן דנן
כחומר כל שטרי כתובות ותוספתות דנהגין בבנות
ישראל העשויין כתקון חכמינו זכרונם לברכה
דלא כאסמכתא ודלא כטופסי דשטרי וקנינא
מן ר' *גדול ב"ר יעקב* חתן דנן
למרת ___ בתולתא דא
על כל מה דכתוב ומפורש לעיל במנא דכשר
למקניא ביה **והכל שריר וקים.**

נאום ___ עד
נאום *אברהם יצחק ב"ר* ___ עד

Designed and Copyright by Samson Press, Baltimore, Md.

Town Societies

Jewish immigrants formed societies based on their towns of origin; these were called *landsmanshaftn* societies. Membership in such a group invariably meant that the person came from the town or a neighboring town. One function of these groups was to buy land in a Jewish cemetery. Even if it cannot be determined that an ancestor was a member of a *landsmanshaftn* society, burial in a plot owned by such a group implies that the ancestor came from that town. (Be aware that the burial societies also sold burial plots to outsiders, so such evidence is not conclusive.) The archives of the YIVO Institute for Jewish Research, 15 W. 16th St., New York, NY 10011, has a large number of records of these societies. The institute has published its holdings in *A Guide to YIVO's Landsmanshaftn Archive*.[2]

Pre-Holocaust Period (1924–44)

Because this period is contemporary, a principal source of information is the individuals themselves or their children. A wealth of twentieth-century documentation on Americans described elsewhere in this book can be used as well.

Holocaust Survivors (1945–60)

Holocaust survivors who were friends and neighbors of victims can often provide valuable information. The *National Registry of Jewish Holocaust Survivors* contains the names of more than one hundred thousand survivors and their families living in the United States and Canada. The book is available in many Holocaust centers and major libraries. A list of institutions can be found at <http://ushmm.org/remembrance/registry>. The organization that created the registry will forward letters to survivors. Write to the American Gathering/Federation of Jewish Holocaust Survivors, 122 W. 30th St., New York, NY 10001.

Holocaust Research

Most Jewish Americans are descended from Ashkenazic Jews who did not have surnames before the nineteenth century. Consequently, it is unusual to trace a Jewish ancestry back more than two hundred years. In fact, most Jewish Americans do not trace their ancestry as much as they document their families; that is, they identify their most ancient ancestor, then trace forward to document all descendants of this ancestor—rarely more than ten generations. Because 50 percent of European Jewry was murdered in the Holocaust (91 percent of Polish Jewry), virtually every Jewish American has relatives who were victims of the Holocaust. (I have documented more than 250 descendants of my great-great-great-grandfather who were murdered—fewer than thirty survivors are known).

Although many Holocaust victims had no surviving immediate family members, there are persons who have remembered them. These remembrances are documented in two of the most important sources of information about Holocaust victims: *yizkor* books and Pages of Testimony.

Yizkor Books

After World War II, the survivors of the Holocaust published books that memorialized the destroyed Jewish communities of Europe. Called *yizkor* books (yizkor means "memorial" or "remembrance" in Hebrew), they commemorate not only the victims but the Jewish communities themselves. To date, more than one thousand towns have been commemorated in this manner.

Although each book was written independently of the others, yizkor books have a typical structure. The first section describes the history of the Jewish community in the town or city from its inception, sometimes hundreds of years ago, to the events of the Holocaust, which invariably culminated in the destruction of all Jewish religious property (synagogues, cemeteries, etc.) and the immediate murder of the Jewish population or their deportation to labor or extermination camps. For the genealogist, this overview section provides much material about Jewish community life in the town.

The next section of a yizkor book is a group of stories that are the personal remembrances of survivors about their families. These usually contain a wealth of information about the particular family. The following section is devoted to families from which there were no survivors. The descriptions are usually brief—one or two paragraphs headed by the names of the father and mother, as well as the names of the children. The final section is a necrology—a list of all the victims from the town.

A searchable index of towns with yizkor books that is updated regularly can be found at <www.jewishgen.org/Yizkor/database.html>. The most complete list of towns in print can be found in *Where Once We Walked—Revised Edition* by Gary Mokotoff and Sallyann Amdur Sack. Any town in this gazetteer that has a code "YB" in its description has a yizkor book. Major yizkor book collections are at the YIVO Institute in New York and the Library of Congress in Washington, D.C. Many public and university libraries with Judaica collections have acquired a good number of these books. A list of them can be found at <www.jewishgen.org/Yizkor/yizlibs.html>. The New York Public Library has placed online the contents of more than eight hundred yizkor books. They can be found at <www.nypl.org/research/chss/jws/yizkorbooks_intro.cfm>.

Pages of Testimony

The major archive and documentation center for the Holocaust is Yad Vashem. Since 1955, Yad Vashem has been attempting to identify, on documents called Pages of Testimony, each of the 6 million Jews who were murdered in the Holocaust. To date, 3 million Holocaust victims have been documented. Yad Vashem has requested persons come forward and submit, on preprinted forms, a host of information about victims, including name; place and year of birth; place, date, and circumstances of death; name of mother, father, and spouse; and, in some cases, name and age of children (see figure 18-3). Each submitter must sign the Page of Testimony and indicate his or her name, address, and relationship to the deceased. Not only do Pages of Testimony provide lineage-linked information about Holocaust victims, they provide a connection to the present through the submitter of the document. If the submitter can be located, he or she can often provide firsthand information about the family. Unfortunately, most Pages of Testimony were written in the late 1950s, more than fifty years ago, and many of the submitters are no longer alive; however, their children can often provide additional information if they can be located. These Pages of Testimony are now online as part of The Central Database of Shoah Victims Names at <www.yadvashem.org>.

Holocaust Centers

Holocaust education centers exist throughout the world. Exhibits depict events during this period, and many have libraries containing literature about the Holocaust. A list of centers that are members of the Association of Holocaust Organizations can be found at <www.ahoinfo.org>.

Sources Independent of Time Period

Jewish Historical Societies

A number of Jewish historical societies in the United States and Canada have documented the history of the Jewish presence in their locales. Many have made this information available in book form. A list of Jewish Historical Societies is located at <www.ajhs.org/academic/other.cfm>.

Jewish Immigrant Aid Societies

For some one hundred years, Jewish immigrants have been assisted by social welfare organizations that helped them settle in the New World. The most comprehensive and oldest is the Hebrew Immigrant Aid Society. The society has case files on each person or family it has helped. The Canadian equivalent is the Jewish Immigrant Aid Society.

רשות הזכרון לשואה ולגבורה, ירושלים

דף-עד

יד ושם

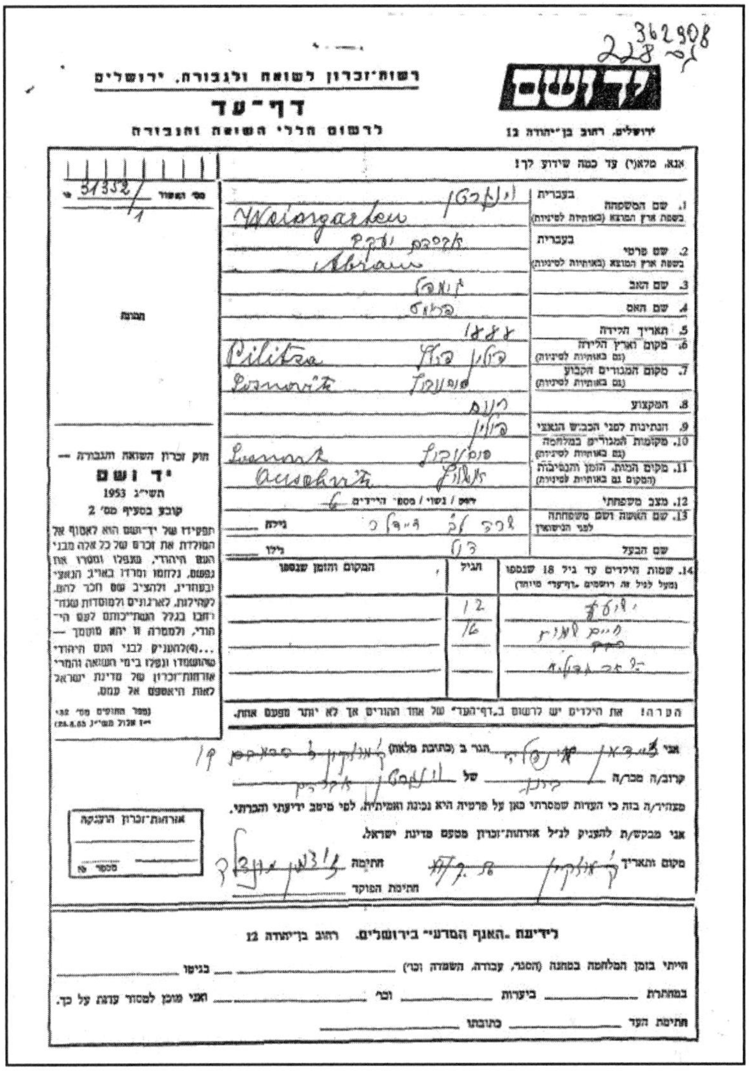

Figure 18-3. A Page of Testimony from Yad Vashem in Jerusalem. This is one for Abram Waingarten. It indicates that he was the son of Gimpel and Frimet, that he was born in 1888 in Pilica, Poland, that he resided in Sosnowiec, and that he died at Auschwitz. Also identified are his wife, Sara Leib Deidler, and two of his six children—Yehoshua, age twelve, and Chaim Schmuel, age sixteen. The person who testified to the named circumstances was Waingarten's daughter, Mindeleh Zeitman, of Kiryat Motkin, Israel.

Getting Records from the Country of Ancestry

The ancestors of most Jewish Americans came to North America less than 150 years ago. This means that research of periods before the twentieth century invariably leads to research in central and eastern Europe. The collapse of Communism has been a blessing for genealogists with roots in this area. In most countries, archives and records offices previously off-limits to inquiries are now open, and capitalist entrepreneurs offer genealogical services. The Family History Library, previously spurned by Eastern Bloc governments, is now microfilming or negotiating to microfilm documents in most countries. Record collections thought destroyed during World War II have been found in other countries or stored in warehouses. Unrestricted travel now is possible in most countries. Information about access to these repositories can be found at the Internet sites for the Jewish genealogical Special Interest Groups (see next page).

Organized Jewish Genealogy

Jewish genealogy is highly organized. There are more than eighty Jewish Genealogical Societies throughout the world. Since 1982 there has been an annual International Conference on Jewish Genealogy that often attracts more than one thousand attendees. There is a strong presence on the Internet, primarily through JewishGen. Special Interest Groups have formed based primarily on country of ancestry. There is a journal of Jewish genealogy: *Avotaynu*.

International Association of Jewish Genealogical Societies. There are some sixty Jewish genealogical societies in the United States and Canada. They are in alliance with societies located in fifteen other countries through an umbrella group: the International Association of Jewish Genealogical Societies (IAJGS) at <www.iajgs.org>. A list of societies is available at the organization's Internet site. Societies hold meetings regularly, usually monthly, with a lecture on some topic of interest to Jewish family historians. More significantly, membership provides an opportunity to share information that will enhance research efforts. In recent years, many societies have begun holding beginners' workshops to encourage other Jewish Americans to trace their ancestry. Most societies publish their own newsletter as well.

International Conference on Jewish Genealogy. An annual conference, sponsored by IAJGS, has been held since 1982 in different locations primarily in North America. The location operates in an approximate ten-year cycle with regular (repeat) sites being Jerusalem, London, Los Angeles, New York, Salt Lake City, Toronto, and Washington, D.C. Information about these conferences can be found at the IAJGS Internet site.

JewishGen. The principal presence of Jewish genealogy on the Internet is JewishGen, <www.jewishgen.org>. More than one thousand volunteers provide assistance in developing and maintaining its databases. Principal components of JewishGen include the following:

- JewishGen Family Finder. A database of ancestral surnames and towns being researched by more than fifty thousand genealogists throughout the world.
- Family Tree of the Jewish People. A database of more than 2 million persons organized in family trees.
- Discussion Group Archives. Messages posted since 1993 to the JewishGen Discussion Group, a daily bulletin board read by more than five thousand subscribers.
- InfoFiles. A comprehensive directory of information resources, organized by both topic and country.
- JewishGen Online Worldwide Burial Registry (JOWBR). Data from Jewish cemeteries.

Betzalel Taratotsky and his son Judel, photographed about 1890 in Volkovysk, Russia. Judel was apprenticed as a bricklayer at age 8, married at age 16, and immigrated to the United States at age 20 in 1904. Courtesy of Judel Taratotsky's grandson, Gary Mokotoff.

Special Interest Groups (SIGs). Because most Jews worldwide do not live in the same country as their ancestors did 150 years ago, Special Interest Groups have evolved within organized Jewish genealogy revolving around country/region of ancestry. These groups' success has been made possible because of the Internet. Members are from all over the world, and they communicate through mailing lists. Each group has its own Internet site that usually includes databases of resources for Jewish genealogy in the area, InfoFiles, and links to other sites. Almost all SIGs are subsidiaries of JewishGen, and links to their homepages can be found at the JewishGen homepage.

Avotaynu: The International Review of Jewish Genealogy. This journal is published quarterly and includes articles from an international group of contributing editors. It includes information on the latest resources available to Jewish genealogists in various parts of the world and includes background articles about the history of Jews in particular areas. Since 1991, Avotaynu, Inc., publisher of the journal, has also produced books of interest to Jewish genealogical researchers. It also publishes the Jewish e-zine of Jewish genealogy *Nu? What's New?* At its website <www.avotaynu.com>, is a Consolidated Jewish Surnames Index database, which contains nearly 700,000 surnames from forty-two databases containing mostly Jewish surnames.

References

Manuals and Source Books

Beider, Alexander. *A Dictionary of Jewish Surnames from the Russian Empire.* Teaneck, N.J.: Avotaynu, 1993. A compilation of fifty thousand Jewish surnames from turn-of-the-century Russia showing etymology, where within the empire the names existed, and variants of names. A ninety-four-page introduction describes the origins and evolution of Jewish surnames in Russia.

———. *A Dictionary of Jewish Surnames from the Kingdom of Poland.* Teaneck, N.J.: Avotaynu, 1996. Comparable to above-named book except coverage is for the area that was the Kingdom of Poland.

———. *A Dictionary of Ashkenazic Given Names: Their Origins, Structure, Pronunciations and Migrations*. Bergenfield, N.J.: Avotaynu, 2002. A comprehensive analysis of fifteen thousand Jewish given names from central and eastern Europe.

———. *A Dictionary of Jewish Surnames from Galicia.* Bergenfield, N.J.: Avotaynu, 2004. Comparable to the other surname books by this author except coverage is for the area that was Galicia.

Faiguenboim, Guilherme, Paulo Valadares, and Anna Rosa Campagnano. *Dictionário Sefardi de Sobrnomes (Dictionary of Sephardic Surnames)*. Rio de Janeiro: Fraiha, 2003. Compilation of 17,000 surnames used by Jews who lived in Spain and Portugal for fifteen centuries before 1492 and then spread throughout the world.

Freedman, Chaim. *Beit Rabannan*. A review of 130 books that are major sources for rabbinical genealogy.

Gorr, Rabbi Shmuel. *Jewish Personal Names: Their Origin, Derivation and Diminutive Forms.* Teaneck, N.J.: Avotaynu, 1992. Some twelve hundred Jewish given names are listed, not in alphabetic order but by root name. Most variants of root names are annotated to show how the name evolved.

A Guide to YIVO's Landsmanshaftn Archive. New York: YIVO Institute for Jewish Research, 1986.

Guzik, Estelle M., ed. *Genealogical Resources in the New York Metropolitan Area.* New York: Jewish Genealogical Society, 1989. A detailed guide to every agency between Albany, New York, and Trenton, New Jersey, that could provide data of use in Jewish genealogical research, including many specific records, hours of operation, public transportation, finding aids, fees, and restrictions.

———. *Genealogical Resources in New York.* New York: Jewish Genealogical Society, 2003. An updated version of the above book but area is limited to New York City and Albany.

Kemp, Thomas. *International Vital Records Handbook.* Baltimore: Genealogical Publishing Co., 2000. Names and addresses of vital records repositories throughout the world.

Krasner-Khait, Barbara. *Discovering Your Jewish Ancestors*. North Salt Lake, Utah: Heritage Quest, 2001. A comprehensive beginners' guide that includes many illustrations and case studies.

Kurzweil, Arthur. *From Generation to Generation: How to Trace Your Jewish Genealogy and Personal History.* New York: HarperCollins, 1994. A very personal approach to each step of the research process.

———, and Miriam Weiner, eds. *The Encyclopedia of Jewish Genealogy.* Vol. 1. *Sources in the United States and Canada.* Northvale, N.J.: Jason Aronson, 1991. A finding aid for sources of Jewish genealogical information.

Malka, Jeffrey S. *Sephardic Genealogy: Discovering Your Sephardic Ancestors and Their World.* Bergenfield, N.J.: Avotaynu, 2003. Definitive guide to tracing Sephardic ancestry.

Menk, Lars. *A Dictionary of German Jewish Surnames*. Bergenfield, N.J.: Avotaynu, 2004. Provides information about more than 13,000 surnames from pre-World War I Germany. Information includes etymology, variants, and when and where the name appeared in Germany.

Mokotoff, Gary. *How to Document Victims and Locate Survivors of the Holocaust*. Teaneck, N.J.: Avotaynu, 1995. A how-to book for locating documentation of individuals caught up in the Holocaust.

———, and Warren Blatt. *Getting Started in Jewish Genealogy*. Bergenfield, N.J.: Avotaynu, 2000. An Internet-oriented primer for Jewish genealogy.

———, and Sallyann Amdur Sack. *Where Once We Walked: A Guide to the Jewish Communities Destroyed in the Holocaust.* Rev. ed. Bergenfield, N.J.: Avotaynu, 2002. A gazetteer of 23,500 central and eastern European localities, arranged alphabetically and indexed phonetically under the Daitch-Mokotoff Soundex System so that various spellings can be readily found.

Pinkassim HaKehillot [Encyclopedae of Towns]. 17 vols. Jerusalem: Yad Vashem, 1984–99. Seventeen volumes with more planned. A detailed history of Jewish communities in many areas of central and eastern Europe; there are five volumes for Poland alone. This series is in Hebrew.

Sack, Sallyann Amdur. *A Guide to Jewish Genealogical Research in Israel.* Rev. ed. Bergenfield, N.J.: Avotaynu, 1995. A detailed guide to the accessibility and holdings of each agency. Appendixes include *yizkor* books and *landsmanshaftn* listed at Yad Vashem Library and a list of towns represented at the 1981 World Gathering of Holocaust Survivors.

———, and Gary Mokotoff. *Avotaynu Guide to Jewish Genealogy*. Bergenfield, N.J.: Avotaynu, 2003. Comprehensive one-hundred-chapter guide to Jewish genealogy written by more than sixty experts in the field.

Wynne, Suzan F. *Finding Your Jewish Roots in Galicia: A Resource Guide*. Bergenfield, N.J.: Avotaynu, 1998. Comprehensive guide to records and other resources in Galicia.

Zubatsky, David S., and Irwin M. Berent. *Sourcebook for Jewish Genealogies and Family Histories*. Teaneck, N.J.: Avotaynu, 1996. A finding aid to published and manuscript genealogies in many Jewish archives and libraries for more than ten thousand surnames.

Collected Genealogies

Freedman, Chaim. *Eliyahu's Branches: The Descendants of the Vilna Gaon and His Family*. Bergenfield, N.J.: Avotaynu, 1997. Identifies more than twenty thousand descendants of this Lithuanian scholar.

Rosenstein, Neil. *The Unbroken Chain: Biographical Sketches and Genealogy of Illustrious Jewish Families From the 15th–20th Century*. 2 vols. Elizabeth, N.J.: The Computer Center for Jewish Genealogy, 1990. An enlarged revision of the 1977 edition. Includes descendants of the Katzenellenbogen family—Hassidic and other rabbis, Mendelssohn, Martin Buber, Karl Marx, Helena Rubinstein. Index of surnames only. Available from the Computer Center for Jewish Genealogy, 654 Westfield Ave., Elizabeth, NJ 07208.

Rosenstein, Neil. *The Lurie Legacy: The House of Davidic Royal Descent*. Bergenfield, N.J.: Avotaynu, 2004. History of this distinguished rabbinic family.

Sackheim, George I. *Scattered Seeds*. 2 vols. Skokie, Ill.: R. Sackheim Publishing. Chronicles thirteen thousand descendants of Rabbi Israel, one of the two martyrs of Rozanoi (Ruzhany), Byelorussia. He was executed after a blood libel of 1659. Indexed. Available from R. Sackheim Publishing Co., 9151 Crawford Ave., Skokie, IL 60076.

Stern, Malcolm H. *First American Jewish Families*. Baltimore: Ottenheimer Publishers, 1991. Reprint of a 1978 edition with an added update section. Contains genealogies of all available Jewish families settled in America prior to 1840, traced where possible to the present. Fifty-thousand-name index. This entire book is online at <www.americanjewisharchives.org/aja/FAJF/intro.html>.

Periodicals

Avotaynu: The International Review of Jewish Genealogy. 1985–, quarterly. Edited by Sallyann Amdur Sack and Gary Mokotoff. (155 N. Washington Ave., Bergenfield, NJ 07621). Articles and data of general Jewish genealogical interest written by an international group of authors. <www.avotaynu.com>

Research Archives and Libraries

American Jewish Archives, 3101 Clifton Ave., Cincinnati, OH 45220 (on the campus of Hebrew Union College). Specializes in data on Jews in the western hemisphere. Contains many genealogies, vital records, biographies, organizational and congregational records, and newspaper indexes. Finding aids: James W. Clasper and M. Carolyn Dellenbach, *Guide to the Holdings of the American Jewish Archives* (Cincinnati: 1979). Also see Zubatsky and Berent, above. <www.americanjewisharchives.org/intro.html>

American Jewish Historical Society, 15 W. 16th St., New York, NY 10011. All areas of American Jewish history, including organizational and institutional records, as well as family documents. <www.ajhs.org>

American Sephardi Federation (ASF), 305 Seventh Ave., New York, NY 10001, is an excellent source for finding Sephardic associations organized by nationality, such as the Turkish-Jewish Society, the Bulgarian-Jewish Association, the Syrian-Jewish Association, or any other oriental or Sephardic Jewish group. The ASF has lists of organizations in the United States and abroad. <www.asfonline.org>

Jewish Immigrant Aid Society, 4600 Bathurst St., Suite 325, Willowdale, Ontario M2R 3V3, Canada. <www.jias.org>

Hebrew Immigrant Aid Society, 333 Seventh Ave., New York, NY 10001. <www.hias.org>

Leo Baeck Institute, 15 W. 16th St., New York, NY 10011. Library and archive of surviving records of Jews from German-speaking lands. <www.lbi.org>

Library of Congress. Jefferson (main) Building, housing the Genealogy and Local History, Independence Ave. between 1st and 2nd St. S.W., Washington, DC. Contains every book submitted for U.S. copyright, city directories, maps, gazetteers, Hebraic Division. Finding aid: James C. Neagles, *The Library of Congress: A Guide to Genealogical and Historical Research* (Salt Lake City: Ancestry, 1990). The Hebraic section is located in the John Adams building. <www.loc.gov>

National Archives and Records Administration, 8th and Pennsylvania Ave. N.W., Washington, DC 20408. The research room has federal censuses 1790 to 1930, passenger arrival records, eighteenth- and nineteenth-century military records, some naturalizations, and land records. Holocaust-related documents from captured German records. Regional branches have microfilmed copies and regional records. Finding aids: *Guide to Genealogical Research in the National Archives*. Rev. ed. Washington, D.C.: National Archives and

Records Administration, 1991; and Szucs, Loretto Dennis, and Sandra Hargreaves Luebking, *The Archives: A Guide to the National Archives Field Branches*. Salt Lake City: Ancestry, 1988. <www.nara.gov>

U.S. Holocaust Memorial Museum, 100 Raoul Wallenberg Place S.W., Washington, DC 20024. Principal repository of Holocaust-related material in the United States. It includes an archives and library. Internet site includes an online catalog to their collection. <www.ushmm.org>

Yad Vashem, P.O. Box 3477, 91034 Jerusalem, Israel. Principal repository of Holocaust-related material in the world. Internet site includes Shoah (Holocaust) Names database. <www.yadvashem.org>

YIVO Institute for Jewish Research, 15 W. 16th St., New York, NY 10011. Library and archive of data from Yiddish-speaking lands. Finding aid: Guzik, *Genealogical Resources in the New York Metropolitan Area* (cited earlier). <www.yivoinstitute.org>

19

Native American Research

CURT B. WITCHER, MLS, FUGA, FIGS, and GEORGE J. NIXON

Introduction

CURT B. WITCHER, MLS, FUGA, FIGS

Chapter Contents

Native American genealogical research is among the most challenging and rewarding of historical research endeavors. Interest in the life patterns, religions, migration, and settlement patterns—indeed, in the entire culture of these earliest inhabitants of the North American continent—remains high. There are numerous fundamental differences between the Native American and the European American cultures, and it is these differences that present the greatest challenge to the genealogist.

In beginning Native American genealogical research, it is important to employ a fundamentally sound research methodology—the same methodology that would be used in compiling any family history. Initially, family sources should be consulted for information about previous generations. These sources include all living relatives, family papers and scrapbooks, daybooks, photograph albums, and diaries (see chapter 1, "The Foundations of Family History Research"). Considering the very strong oral tradition among Native American peoples, special attention should be given to conducting thorough interviews of all relatives.

Sound research methodology mandates that one research from the present into the past, from more recent times to more distant times, building a solid case based on primary and excellent secondary sources. The temptation to begin with the records of a particular tribe and prove the family line forward to a more contemporary ancestor should be avoided. Not only is proving a line from past to present difficult, it does not afford one the opportunity to investigate the widest range of records. Further, it tempts one to make assumptions that are clearly not based on facts and reasonable conclusions drawn from the facts.

Maintaining extensive and accurate records is essential for any genealogical endeavor, but especially so for Native

American research. All places, dates, and other data associated with a potential ancestor should be recorded with appropriate documentation, even if their relevance is unknown or unclear at the time. No piece of data about a potential ancestor is inconsequential.

Adhering to a defined series of research strategies is the most productive way to engage in Native American genealogical research. The researcher must be willing to employ research strategies in a sequence that gathers useful general material first, tribe-specific data second, and, finally, individual (person-specific) data and records. A successful research strategy could be outlined in a manner similar to the following:

1. Thoroughly investigate the areas where ancestral research is being considered for the identities, histories, and cultural attributes of the native peoples.
2. Employ a carefully constructed and consistently applied methodology for locating the greatest number of research documents and data on the tribe of the potential ancestor.
3. Work through all of the materials relating to a particular tribe or nation to obtain the fullest understanding of its peoples and the most complete individual-specific group of records.

This chapter details a number of sources that the Native American genealogical researcher may want to investigate in the process of establishing and documenting a family history.

General Histories and Records

More so than in any other area of genealogical research, knowledge of general history is a crucial factor for the researcher of Native American family history. A good working knowledge of general history will ground one's research in the proper time period, identify a more defined geographic area in which to conduct research, maximize all potential record possibilities, greatly assist in establishing tribal affiliations, and lead to a fuller understanding of the Native American culture. Because Native American naming patterns, kinship terms, and intertribal relations typically were quite different from those experienced by European Americans, it is essential to place one's Native American research in a historical context. Only in the proper historical context, devoid of assumptions and stereotypes, can truly effective Native American genealogical research be conducted.

There are many bibliographies of Native American historical works that should be consulted by the researcher endeavoring to gather general and tribe-specific histories. These bibliographies are useful because they are numerous and rather widely available, and because they greatly assist the researcher in striving to gather a comprehensive collection of documents. Annotated bibliographies compiled by academic institutions and experts in the fields of Native American history, archaeology, culture, etc., often provide a more complete list of sources and easier methods of accessing the specific information. An example of such a work is one by Katherine M. Weist and Susan R. Sharrock, *An Annotated Bibliography of North Plains Ethnohistory*.[1] Besides the descriptive annotations provided in this work, many title entries contain a section entitled "other subjects" in which tribes covered by the particular work are listed, as well as major topics and subjects the author(s) encountered.

Worthwhile bibliographies are near timeless in their research value and should be considered vital aids to anyone conducting consequential Native American genealogical research. In finding and using these publications, more attention should be given to evaluating the authority and expertise of the compiler(s) as well as the comprehensiveness of the listings at the time of publication and much less attention given to the actual date of publication. College and university libraries as well as state libraries and large public libraries typically have many of these research bibliographies, with a surprising number available through interlibrary loan. Researching Native American family history in any state must include investigating the existence of substantial bibliographies in the respective state library.

Establishing tribal affiliation should be a primary objective in the initial stages of Native American research. Determining the tribe of a potential ancestor is essential to continued research because the vast majority of records are grouped, published, and accessed by tribe, clan, or nation. There are several approaches the researcher may need to take in determining tribal affiliation. First, critically evaluate oral traditions and stories preserved and communicated through generations of family members. It is important to remember that recollections of actual events, people, and places tend to fade over time and may be changed or embellished to make individuals appear more favorable than they actually were or to hide less-than-honorable deeds.

Another approach is to engage in a survey of the general histories of a large geographic region or the continent, as well as general histories of the native peoples. Both dated and more recently published histories are useful. These general histories typically provide significant data on village locations and settlement patterns, hunting and gathering areas, and migration patterns. They assist the researcher in beginning to determine the tribe of a potential ancestor. The value of a thorough survey of published histories as well as historical manuscripts such as travel diaries, missionary daybooks, and other ancient writing should not be underestimated.

A remarkable compilation in the realm of general histories that details Native American life at the beginning of the twentieth century in words and photographs is Edward S. Curtis's *The North American Indian, Being a Series of Volumes Picturing and Describing the Indians of the United States and Alaska*.[2] The twenty volumes of descriptive text and photographic plates are complemented by twenty folios of additional photographic images. While some controversy has always surrounded this work, including accusations that Curtis staged many of the photographs, the compilation is still quite significant in both the quantity and detail of information provided. These forty volumes have been reprinted and are available in microform formats. The Library of Congress has also made more than two thousand of these photographic images available on its *American Memory* website, <http://memory.loc.gov/ammem/>.

Some of the classic works of Americana pertaining to early travel and the native peoples provide valuable background data that is essential to exploring all of the record possibilities for Native American research. Henry R. Schoolcraft's *Historical and Statistical Information Respecting the History, Conditions and Prospects of the Indian Tribes of the United States: Collected and Prepared under the Direction of the Bureau of Indian Affairs, per Act of Congress of March 3, 1847*, published in six parts, is an excellent general history covering a variety of topics for numerous tribes including national and tribal histories, antiquities, geography, government, languages, biography, and art.[3] This work has been reprinted several times and is available at many university and large public libraries.

A host of general histories published more recently provide the genealogical researcher with good background data. Eleanor Burke Leacock's and Nancy Oestreich Lurie's *North American Indians in Historical Perspective* is such a work. Its nearly five hundred heavily noted pages detail the history of the major native tribes and clans of North America.[4] Placing the historical past of particular Native American groups into a more general historical context provides a research context more suitable for capitalizing on the record possibilities. General footnote sections, biographical notes, and references all provide the researcher with access to primary and documented secondary source materials. The origins of tribes are traced, with these historical recountings giving the researcher information on the groups of individuals, often called intruders, who interacted with particular tribes. Most general histories can be located in library catalogs under terms such as "Native Americans," "North American Indians," and "Indians of North America." Look for increased use of the most recent term of "First Nations."

A third approach to establishing tribal affiliation is to engage in a thorough study of maps and atlases that place indigenous peoples in particular geographic areas (figure 19-1). These works are often valuable for determining not only the specific tribe of a potential ancestor but also migration and commerce routes, names and sites of villages, and locations of intertribal confrontations. *Atlas of Great Lakes Indian History*, edited by Helen Hornbeck Tanner, is a remarkable example of such a historical atlas.[5] Timelines assist in setting Native American events in context of the encroaching European settlement; narratives complement the detail provided by the numerous maps; and a selected bibliography provides the researcher with hundreds of additional sources of information. That this work is now available as an electronic book testifies to both the significance of this work and the timelessness of its research.

Finally, assistance in determining tribal affiliation can be provided by published local and community histories. Nearly every community has some accounting of its early days, and the compiled histories of cities and towns often contain pages about the earliest inhabitants of the areas. While typically not filled with large amounts of documented data, these works can provide information useful in determining the identity of the native peoples of a specific geographic area. Few county histories made it into print without at least some brief reference to the inhabitants of the area.

Tribe-Specific Data

Once a reasonable hypothesis has established the tribe of a potential ancestor, a host of new sources become available for the researcher to gather information about particular Native Americans. Learning as many specific details about the clan or tribe as possible continues to be of paramount importance, and locating and accessing specific records will increasingly become the focus of research endeavors.

The history of a potential ancestor's tribe is critical to continuing research. It is important to know where and when the tribe existed, the customs of the tribe—especially those customs relating to naming patterns, marriage, and burial practices—and other important life events. Emmet Starr's *History of the Cherokee Indians and Their Legends and Folk Lore* is an extraordinary example of a tribe/nation history containing excellent general data and significant genealogical information.[6] Six chapters of more than 150 pages are devoted to "Old Families and Their Genealogy." Other lists include council members and nearly two hundred pages of biographical sketches. Woven through the entire work is a serious treatment of the customs and legends of the Cherokees. Serious efforts should be made to identify for use several major histories for the tribe or nation being explored.

Though customs varied from one tribe to another, scholars have found that Native Americans generally used two types of names: personal names and honorary names. In some tribes, one or the other of these names was considered sacred. Personal names may have been given or changed at birth, adolescence, the first hunting or war expedition, some notable feat, or the attainment of chieftainship. Tracking and documenting these name changes for any given Native American can be a formidable challenge. To these Native American names, Europeans often added a third, English name. A transitional record is one that indicates both a Native American name and the English name of a potential ancestor. Such records are a great boon to furthering research, but they are somewhat rare.

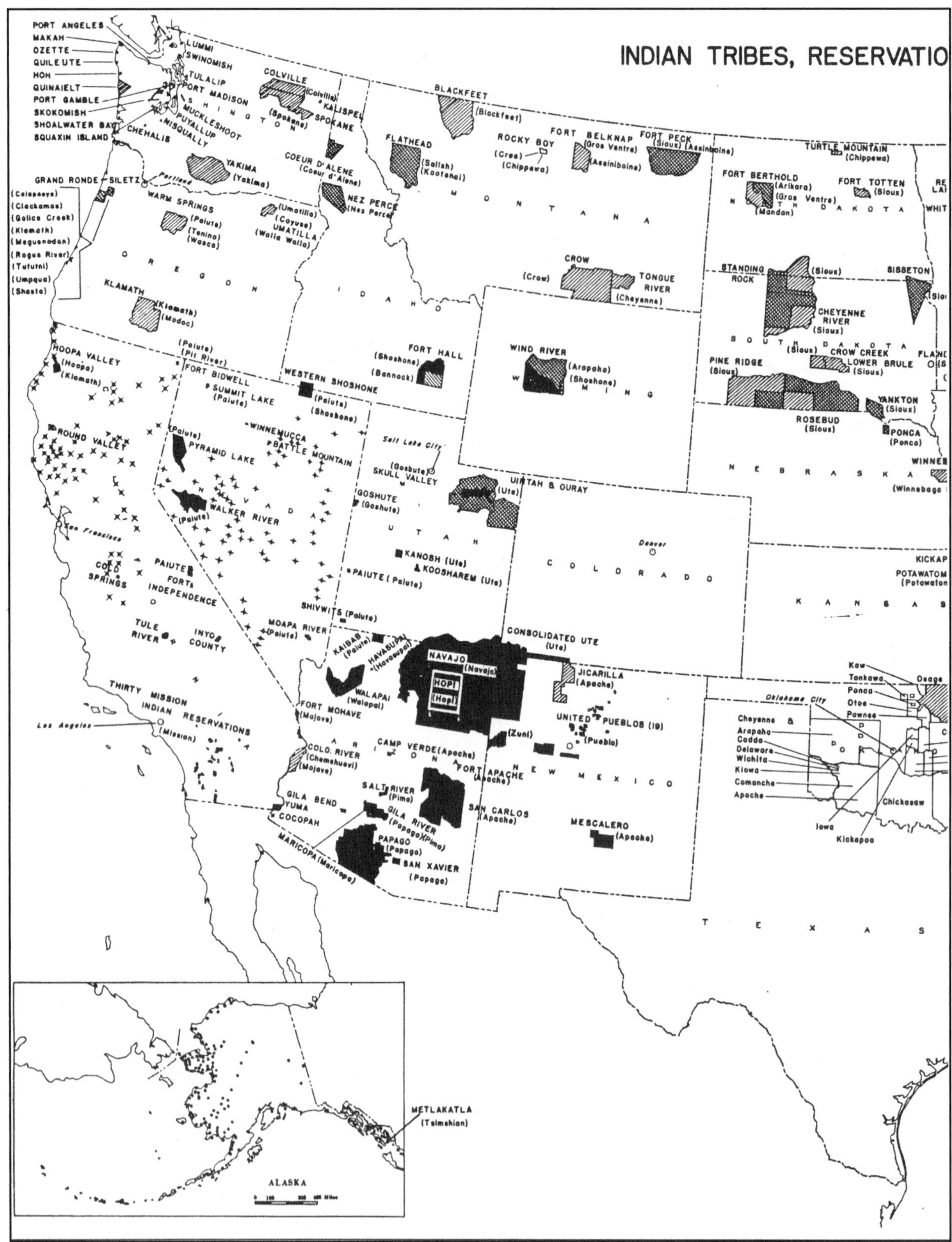

Figure 19-1. Indian tribes, reservations, and settlements in the United States, 1939. From the Bureau of Indian Affairs, RG75, National Archives—Central Plains Region.

NS AND SETTLEMENTS IN THE UNITED STATES
1939
DEPARTMENT OF THE INTERIOR
HAROLD L. ICKES, SECRETARY
OFFICE OF INDIAN AFFAIRS
JOHN COLLIER, COMMISSIONER
FLOYD W. LA ROUCHE
DIRECTOR OF INFORMATION
The principal Indian tribes and many small bands of Indians in the United States are located on reservations, rancherias and other communities, as shown here. In addition there are 29,983 Eskimos and Indians in Alaska.
LEGEND
Reservations allotted in part.
Reservations allotted and open.
Tribal lands.
Colonies in Nevada.
Rancherias in California.
Compiled and drawn by
Sam Attahvich Comanche

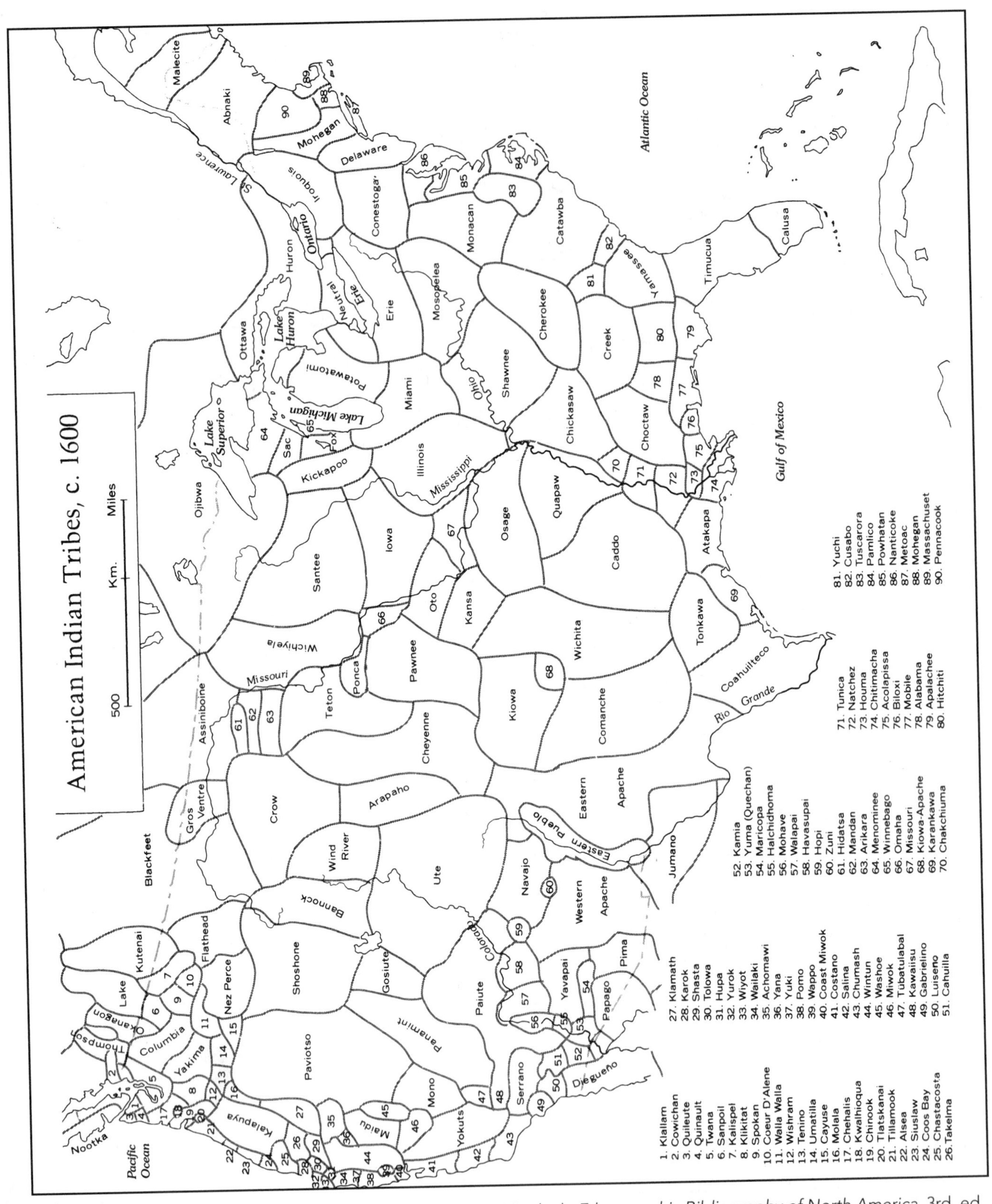

Figure 19-1 (continued). Source: Adapted from George Peter Murdock, *Ethnographic Bibliography of North America*, 3rd. ed. (New Haven, 1960).

Kinship terms have varying meanings among many Native Americans. For example, "father" does not always denote the natural parent. Many tribes are organized matriarchally rather than patriarchally, with lines of descent and property being passed down through the mother's line. The following excerpt is from a classic work of reprinted ethnology reports titled *The North American Indian.*[7] From "An Iroquois Source Book, Volume 1, Political and Social Organization," it indicates how complex such an organization can be for the genealogical researcher, describing some of the laws of descent of the Iroquois league, which was comprised of five nations: Onondaga, Cayuga, Oneida, Mohawk, and Seneca.

> In each of the five nations who composed the original league, there were eight tribes, named as follows: Wolf, Bear, Beaver, and Turtle; Deer, Snipe, Heron, and Hawk. . . . In effect, the Wolf tribe was divided into five parts, and one fifth of it placed in each of the five nations. The remaining tribes were subject to the same division and distribution. . . . The Mohawk of the Turtle tribe recognized the Seneca of the Turtle tribe as a relative, and between them existed the bond of kindred blood. . . . A cross-relationship existed between the several tribes of each nation and the tribes of corresponding name in each of the other nations, which bound them together in the league with indissoluble bonds. . . .
>
> Originally, with reference to marriage, the four tribes first named were not allowed to intermarry; neither were the last four. In their own mode of expressing the idea, each four were brother tribes to each other, and cousins to the other four. . . . At no time in the history of the Iroquois could a man marry a woman of his own tribe, even in another nation. . . . Husband and wife, therefore, were in every case of different tribes. The children were of the tribe of the mother. . . . As all titles, as well as property, descended in the female line, and were hereditary in the tribe, the son could never succeed to his father's title of sachem, nor inherit even his tomahawk. . . .
>
> The mother, her children, and the descendants of her daughters in the female line, would, in perpetuity, be linked with the fortunes of her own tribe; while the father, his brothers and sisters, and the descendants in the female line of his sisters, would be united to another tribe, and held by its affinities.
>
> The next feature of importance in their system of descent was the breaking up of the collateral line. . . . Thus a mother and her sisters stood equally in the relation of mothers to the children of each other; the grandmother and her sisters were equally grandmothers, and so up in the ascending series. . . . Thus the children of two sisters were brothers and sisters to each other; they were all of the same tribe. So also were the children of two brothers, although they might be of different tribes. [2]

Knowledge of the individuals and groups that interacted with Native Americans is important for successful Native American genealogical research because most native peoples had few written records. Indeed, most Native American languages have a written history of only approximately one hundred years, making the researcher dependent almost exclusively upon the records of individuals who interacted directly with the tribes or clans. Understanding the collection-development policies and record-retention schedules of local, state, and national archives, libraries, and societies is vital to successfully locating these primary source accounts and documents. Indeed, understanding the basics of what might be called an *information hierarchy* will greatly assist research endeavors (see figure 19-2).

At the local level, city and county historical societies tend to collect the manuscript or primary source documents as well as very early imprints or first editions, while local public libraries tend to collect published accounts and secondary source materials. Local archives tend to collect official governmental papers as well as those records not kept in the local courthouse, which deal with sale and transfer of property, tax records, and other locally generated documents. State historical societies tend to collect primary source documents that concern multicounty areas of a state or those primary sources that local historical societies do not or cannot maintain in their collections. State libraries typically attempt to collect all consequential secondary source materials for their particular states. Indeed, special state-named collections can be found in many state libraries. In many areas, these special collections are rather comprehensive. Some larger academic libraries contain substantial historical collections and, in very rare cases, even function as the archive for a county. Both primary and secondary source materials at all levels of collection must be consistently consulted to successfully engage in Native American genealogical research.

Combining knowledge of the information hierarchy, of the geographic area historically and contemporarily inhabited by a particular tribe or clan, and of the various individuals and organizations that interacted with specific native peoples will maximize record possibilities. Local and state historical societies and libraries contain many record possibilities that must be explored when collecting Native American data.

Extraordinary record possibilities may also be explored at federal records centers and the National Archives' regional archives. Because the federal government interacted frequently with the Native American tribes and nations during the United States' settlement period, one can expect to find many useful records in repositories that contain federal documents. *Guide to Records in the National Archives of the United States Relating to*

American Indians, compiled by Edward Hill, describes thousands of feet of manuscript collections and many important microform collections.[8] Genealogists can also glean many useful tips from Loretto Dennis Szucs's and Sandra Hargreaves Luebking's *The Archives: A Guide to the National Archives Field Branches*.[9]

The National Archives and Records Administration's (NARA) Southwest Region Archives is particularly rich in Native American records and federal documents relating to native peoples, though useful documents may be found in numerous regional archives as well as at Archives I and Archives II in Washington, D.C., and College Park, Maryland, respectively. NARA's Southwest Region archival holdings cover the states of Arkansas, Louisiana, Oklahoma, and Texas, and contain many documents relating to Cherokees, Chickasaws, Choctaws, Creeks, and Seminoles. The records of the Five Civilized Tribes, as they were called, as well as other Native Americans who were settled in the Indian Territories of Oklahoma, can be found among this region's vast holdings.

Lac du Flambeau Agency, Wisconsin.

Charles Poupart.

Photo

Allotment No.	Age	Degree	Status	Family
360	56	½	Comp.	Wife, Mother, and 8 children.

Main street in Town, about ¾ mile from Agency..7 rooms, 13 windows, 2 doors, cellar. Pump. Outhouse.
Barn, chicken house, cow shed, boathouse.
Team, cow, 25 chickens, 3 ponies.
7 boats.

1866 Husband A very successful guide. Cuts ice and wood in season. Hunts, fishes, traps.
1883 Wife Always busy with large family. Makes moccasins and beadwork.

2 children by first wife and 6 by present wife.
1895 Dau. Marie Poupart Buffalo is married and has own home.
1898 Son Benjamin Poupart is a guide Is now working at fish hatchery.
1904 Son Paul Poupart is a student at Haskell School.
1907 Son Charles A. Poupart attends Public School.
1909 Son Celia Poupart "
1911 Son Louis Poupart "
1912 Dau. Sarah Poupart "
1914 Son William Poupart "

1844 Aged Mother, a widow lives with this family.(78 years)
Charles and Louis are in the Potato Club. Celia raises chickens.

Reimbursable Funds...

Date of Survey.......May 13, 1922.

Figure 19-2. A record of the Charles Poupart family, created by the Lac Du Flambeau Agency, Wisconsin. The original is at the National Archives—Great Lakes Region.

Researchers would be wise to consult NARA's Archival Research Catalog (ARC) at <www.archives.gov/research/arc>. This online catalog lists holdings of NARA's repositories nationwide. While only a percentage of all the documents within the federal archives system are cataloged and listed in ARC, it is nonetheless an excellent access tool that continues to grow in size and utility. On ARC's main Web page, one will find a link to a digital copy of the entire *Guion-Miller Roll Index* as well as Dawes' *Index to the Final Rolls of Citizens and Freedmen of the Five Civilized Tribes in Indian Territory*. Many other Native American records are available on the NARA website as well. One will find an extremely helpful collection of links under the heading of "Indians/Native Americans" in the Archives Library Information Center (ALIC). These link to NARA, the National Park Service, the Library of Congress, universities, and other significant digital research collections.

There are several other fine groups of sources for researchers who are seeking to obtain more tribe-specific information. These include dictionaries, encyclopedias, guides, detailed histories of tribes, federal government documents, and special transcriptions or methodology publications. The more successful researcher of Native American genealogy will pay attention to the finer details of a particular tribe's life and culture—details that may provide valuable clues and additional sources of data.

The Harvard Encyclopedia of American Ethnic Groups devotes more than sixty pages to both a general and tribe-specific treatment of the Native American experience.[10] While it might be considered dated, the information provided in this truly timeless tome is concise and accurate. The maps indicating Native American tribes circa 1600 and the primary locations of 173 Native American groups in 1970 are particularly useful. *The Reference Encyclopedia of the American Indian* contains significant sections devoted to directory data, a bibliography of works accessible by tribe, and biographies of Native Americans.[11] Particularly useful are the lists of reservations, tribal councils, associations, and government agencies.

Important information can be found in many dictionaries and handbooks dealing with the native peoples of North America. Such sources often contain references to other, more detailed works. The three-volume *Dictionary of Indian Tribes of the Americas* contains significant tribe-specific historical details, variant spellings of tribal and clan names, and noteworthy individuals belonging to the Native American group.[12] The various maps are useful, as is the subject and title index. Frederick W. Hodge's *Handbook of American Indians North of Mexico* is a classic work.[13] Organized in a dictionary format, it has long been recognized for providing useful data about various tribes, clans, and nations of Native Americans. In it can be found significant information about Native American tools, well-known individuals, geographic locations, arts and customs, institutions, and languages. Another exemplary classic work is John R. Swanton's *The Indian Tribes of North America*.[14] Its dictionary format makes the more than seven hundred pages of information readily accessible. Both of these later two works have been reprinted numerous times and should be rather widely available.

As oral histories and interviews are used to assist in establishing tribal affiliation, they can also be used to gather more specific details about particular Native American groups, bands, or tribes. Commonly called narratives or firsthand narrative accounts, these materials often represent some of the earliest accounts concerning particular groups of Native Americans. These early accounts were typically by European Americans, such as missionaries, trappers, fur traders, frontier families, and government agents. Firsthand accounts can provide citations to sources that are also narrative or firsthand accounts, well-documented works, or contemporary works that might not be so well-known.

Firsthand accounts can contain the writings of Native Americans as well as those individuals who first interacted with them. A fine example is *American Indian Women: Telling Their Lives*.[15] Also available as an electronic book, this work contains more than fifty pages of notes and bibliography—excellent for leading the researcher to additional sources. An excellent strategy is to always look for both the narratives as well as any notes and references that lead one to still other sources.

Late–twentieth-century firsthand accounts can provide much useful historical and cultural information about particular tribes or groups of Native Americans. These sources are frequently overlooked by researchers who are too focused on individual-specific records. *Wisdomkeepers: Meetings with Native American Spiritual Elders* is a collection of eighteen interviews with Native Americans from thirteen different tribes or confederacies.[16] In this work, the careful reader can learn the native names for particular ancestral homelands, locations and identities of sacred places, important historical details pertaining to little-known and nonfederally recognized tribes, and rough sketches of family narratives, which easily form the core around which family histories can be developed. John Gattuso's *Circle of Nations: Voices and Visions of American Indians* is another richly illustrated collection of contemporary firsthand accounts that provide documentary assistance to the historical researcher interested in a fuller understanding of particular Native American cultures.[17]

Careful researchers should necessarily be concerned about the objectivity of firsthand narrative accounts. It is significant to note through whose eyes the events were being seen. The usefulness of these accounts, though, in providing geographical data and kinship and cultural information, as well as actual names of some Native Americans, cannot be discounted. Larger academic and public libraries, as well as some special libraries, have such works.

Federal government documents are some of the most potentially useful records for obtaining significant data about particular Native American tribes. Two factors contributing to their significance are the frequency of federal government interactions with the native peoples during the settlement of many areas and the large number of documents produced by the Government Printing Office. Additionally, the availability of federal government documents is quite good because there are numerous repositories in most states and many of these documents are available through interlibrary loan.

While federal government documents are plentiful, their use may be challenging for the beginning researcher. The documents have their own classification system, which is designed more for archiving large bodies of material than for accessing those materials. This classification system, commonly known in library circles as the SUDOC system, groups materials by the issuing government agency regardless of subject matter. Native American records may be found filed under "I" for Department of the Interior, "LC" for the Library of Congress, "SI" for Smithsonian Institution, "W" for the Department of War, and "Y" for Congress, etc.

Having access to a good, comprehensive index is important; that one does not exist for the totality of federal government documents is problematic. There are a number of keys, though, to unlocking the rich amounts of information in documents published by the Government Printing Office (see figure 19-3). First, always seek the assistance of a government documents librarian or information professional. For almost every document collection there is at least one person who is expert in its use and committed to assisting others in gaining access to the myriad of data contained in it. Some states and regions even have government document roundtables where information professionals gather on a regular basis to discuss the use and dissemination of data found in federal government documents.

Second, make use of the standard indexes available for accessing government documents, particularly the *Monthly Catalog of United States Government Publications*.[18] The *Monthly Catalog* is the official index to published government documents. Published since 1895, it is the most comprehensive source for document location. Because federal government documents are cataloged by the authoring federal agencies, knowing the possible government agency of publication is helpful in locating documents more quickly. Access to government documents published after 1976 is enhanced by a number of CD-ROM and online versions of the *Monthly Catalog* that are currently available in most larger government document repositories.

GENERAL INDEX.

NUMBER	NAME	STATE	NUMBER	NAME	STATE
27621	Rogers, Theodore	Ark	20981	Rooks, Rosie E.	Ala.
1912	" Thomas J.	I.T.	21926	" Susie	Tenn
9722	" Thomas J.	Ark.	43680	Rookwood, Mary	Mont
26125	" Thomas Jackson	I.T.	8482	Roop, Elisha	Va.
22095	" Thomas M.	Ark.	32674	" G. W.	Va.
251	" Thomas T.	Mo.	5563	" Ida	Va.
1501	" Victoria R.	I.T.	8481	" James A.	W.Va
21620	" Walter Lee	Ga.	32675	" James C.	Va.
9178	" Walter S.	I.T.	8528	" James H.	Va.
16389	" Walter S.	I.T.	3993	" John	N.C.
19248	" Wellington	I.T.	8526	" John H.	Va.
6650	" William	Ga.	3567	" Louisa	Va.
20232	" William C.	I.T.	8527	" Luzilla	Va.
616	" William G.	I.T.	8525	" Mandy	Va.
5859	" William H.	I.T.	5562	" Rebecca	N.C.
26357	" William M.	I.T.	11507	" Wiley W.	Tenn
9725	" William M.	I.T.	34182	" William G.	Va.
24971	" William O.	I.T.	3994	" William R.	Va.
9735	" William P.	I.T.	5564	" William S.	Va.
43800	" William P.	I.T.	38961	Roork, Arminda	Tenn
6743	" William Ridge	I.T.	43760	Rooster, Bettie	I.T.
43800	" William T. Gdn	I.T.	6751	" Lizzie	I.T.
10640	" Wilson	I.T.	2232	Roper, Alexander	N.C.
14062	" Wilson Gdn	I.T.	6549	" Delia	N.C.
1350	Rohr, Lula	I.T.	30894	" E. A.	N.C.
12559	Rohrer, Annie L.	Cal	17495	" Elijah	Tenn
36892	Rolan, Peter	Tex	22624	" Emaline	Tenn
13243	Rolfe, Texie Anna	Okla	33233	" Frances R.	Tenn
1143	Rolin, Henry	Ala	15168	" John Calvin	N.C.
18393	" John	Ala.	22478	" John W.	Tenn
1149	" John	Ala.	2007	" Martha	N.C.
8965	" Walter	I.T.	28732	" Mary J.	Ga.
1147	" William	Ala.	33004	" Myrtle	Ga.
18382	" William Z.	Ala.	34285	" Nancy E.	Ga.
29347	Roling, Mattie J.	Ark.	32853	" Riley	Tenn
38909	Rolins, Fatha	Ind.	39355	" Thomas N.	Ga.
17413	Rolland, Martha J.	I.T.	1028	" William J.	N.C.
32939	" Racheal	Ga.	33391	" William R.	Ga.
9156	Rollen, Annie E.	I.T.	6765	Ropetwister, Anna A.	N.C.
3863	" Elmina	I.T.	21992	" John Gdn	N.C.
21457	" Gordie	Tex.	730	" John	N.C.
8414	Roller, Helen	Mo.	21993	" John	N.C.
3402	Rollin, Alex	Ala.	33551	Ropier, Carroll C.	Ala.
3360	" Cleveland	Ala.	33552	" Oliver C.	Ala.
3419	" Dollie	Ala.	4127	Rose, A. J.	N.C.
3410	" Eliza	Ala.	30564	" Alice	Ida.
6353	" George	Ala.	27882	" Crockett	Wash
3428	" Levada	Ala.	32361	" Easter	Tenn
37150	" Luvida Arlie	I.T.	18223	" Edward	Tenn
3411	" Martha	Ala.	12456	" Edward	W.Va
3404	" Mary	Ala.	26465	" Eli	W.Va
3414	" Mary	Ala.	10247	" Eli	W.Va
1151	" Olie	Ala.	403	" Eliza J.	I.T.
3407	" Richard	Ala.	12452	" Elizabeth	W.Va
3408	" Sallie	Ala.	30100	" Florence	N.C.
3417	" Sam	Ala.	7928	" George	Ark.
3764	Rollings, Dovie	Tenn	25783	" George W.	W.Va
2490	Rolston, Beulah	I.T.	3845	" Ida	Tenn
5380	" James D.	I.T.	25784	" James	W.Va
2491	" John	I.T.	12570	" Jennie	I.T.
25039	" Stella E.	I.T.	18225	" John	Tenn
21395	Romine, Margret C.	Tex.	7591	" John	Ark.
38644	Romines, Malissa	Tenn	39960	" John	W.Va
34977	Ronimous, Charles A.	Mo.	26719	" John C.	W.Va
32112	" Eliza	Mo.	21881	" John T.	Tenn
34976	" William R.	Mo.	18200	" Joshay Gdn	Tenn
37397	Roocks, Francis A.	Ala	18201	" Julia Ann	Tenn
39350	Roody, Minnie	Ga.	24551	" Julia F.	Ark
30655	Rooker, Jossie	I.T.	8257	" Lavicie Emeline	N.C.

Figure 19-3. Index to Applications Submitted for the Eastern Cherokee Roll of 1909 (Guion Miller Roll), 1909–10. Index found online at <http://arcweb.archives.gov>.

There is free online access to the modern version of the *Monthly Catalog* at a site called *GPO Access*, <www.gpoaccess.gov/>. Now called the *Catalog of U.S. Government Publications (CGP)*, this resource is a comprehensive index of more recent publications from all agencies of the United States government. The types of government publications include traditional print, microfiche, electronic resources, audiovisual media, maps, and posters. CGP provides the user with the capability of searching bibliographic records, which describe federal government publications by keyword. At the present time, CGP on the Web is available only from January 1994 to the present. While that recent date is limiting, it is important for researchers to remember that the date (1994) is referring to the publication date of the item, not the date of the subject covered by the particular federal publication. Researchers interested in government information published prior to 1994 should still consult the other print and electronic versions of the *Monthly Catalog* available in depository libraries throughout the country.

Some other standard indexes follow, listed by general time period covered.

A Descriptive Catalogue of the Government Publications of the United States, September 5, 1774–March 4, 1881. Washington, D.C.: Government Printing Office, 1885. Reprints and microform available.

Comprehensive Index of Publications of United States Government, 1881–93. Washington, D.C.: Government Printing Office, 1890. Reprinted in 1953.

United States Government Publications, A Monthly Catalog, 10 vols. Washington, D.C.: Lowdermilk & Company, 1885–94. 10 volumes.

Checklist of United States Public Documents, 1789–1909. Washington, D.C.: Government Printing Office, 1911. Reprints and modified editions available.

Cumulative Subject Index to the Monthly Catalog of United States Government Publications, 1900–1971, 15 vols. Washington, D.C.: Carrollton Press, 1973–75.

It is imperative to consult these indexes when endeavoring to use federal government documents for any type of historical research, most especially for those time periods before 1895. It is also important to note that there are numerous smaller indexes to federal documents that could prove quite beneficial to one's research into tribe-specific data.

Third, continually look for special guides, finding aids, and explanatory publications. As increasing numbers of individuals become aware of the vast amounts of information contained in government documents, new finding aids are developed to complement those that already exist. Documents librarians or local information professionals can assist in locating such guides. A useful contemporary work for the researcher seeking to become more familiar with government documents is the *Introduction to United States Government Information Sources.*[19] This work, also available as an electronic book, will inform you not only how to access federal documents but also of the existence of such specific titles as the *United States Statutes at Large,* which contains the text of Native American treaties from 1778 to 1842 in volume seven.

The richness of materials contained in federal government document collections can scarcely be overemphasized. Histories of tribes; laws relating to allotments, patents, alienation, citizenship, and cessation of tribal relations; reports of various territorial governors dealing with Native Americans; and tribal council resolutions can all be found in government documents. The second volume of Charles J. Kappler's *Indian Affairs: Laws and Treaties* is devoted entirely to eighteenth- and nineteenth-century treaties with Native American tribes.[20] Available as well in reprint, thousands of individual names are included in its more than one thousand pages.

Major microform publishers, such as the University Publications of America division of LexisNexis, make significant document collections pertaining to Native Americans available for research. These collections can include copies of major council meetings, documents from the Office of Indian Affairs, and records of the U.S. Indian Claims Commission. Large public libraries and major universities may include such records in their collections.

Almanacs and ethnic-specific encyclopedias are excellent sources of data for tribe-specific information, lists of primary and secondary source materials, supplemental historical data, and addresses of institutions and organizations that researchers may contact for specific information. *The Native North American Almanac: A Reference Work on Native North Americans in the United States and Canada,* edited by Duane Champagne, is an excellent example of such a work.[21] Among its nearly 1,500 pages are a general bibliography coupled with extensive chapter-specific references and maps indicating locations of tribes and bands. This encyclopedic work covers in some depth nearly every aspect of Native American life. The sections devoted to chronology, research centers and organizations, demography, and major culture areas assist the researcher both in determining tribal affiliation and in gathering substantial quantities of significant works pertaining to a particular tribe or nation. Chapters on law and legislation, languages, religion, and nonreservation populations provide vital tribe- or nation-specific details that enable a researcher to find and access a larger body of records.

Individual-Specific Data

As you continue Native American genealogical research, working from general Native American materials and documents into more tribe-specific accounts and information, focus increasingly on obtaining individual (person-specific) details. As with other stages in the research process, there are a number of records at this level that are useful to genealogists. One example is the applications by individuals who appear on the Eastern Cherokee Roll of 1909, such as that of Will Rogers (figure 19-4). Annual Indian census lists are another example. They became required in 1884. These census records are contained on several hundred rolls of National Archives microfilm. Transitional census records, which indicate both Native American and

English names, are most useful. Be careful in the use of the census materials, however: being listed in the census does not mean that a person was of the particular tribe; there were many mixed-tribe marriages. Only persons on enrollment lists are actually considered tribal members, or enrolled members.

Enrollment records are often called the "official census records" for any given tribe or nation. Typically, they contain the name of the Indian tribe and date of validity, roll number, name (including given name, birth name, and married names), sex, date of death (if applicable), probate number (if applicable), blood degree (degree of Native American blood), names of both parents, and blood degree of parents. If a person or family was denied enrollment, a suit was often filed in court. Significant data may be available in court proceedings of the federal district courts.

Allotment records detail the allotment of land parcels among adult Native Americans who were of at least one-half Native American blood. They are often referred to as "heirship records" because ownership of the land would pass to the allottee's heirs upon death. Will and probate cases carry extra importance for the Native American researcher when they relate to allotted land. Normally, probate material is found in local courthouses. However, when allotted lands on reservation tracts are involved, federal records need to be consulted. Still other property records available for the Native American researcher are land claims. The land-claims system enabled native tribes to file claims against the government for monies owed them for lands taken and not adequately paid for during treaty eras.

Many significant census and enrollment lists are being reprinted in indexed or transcribed form, making the information more widely accessible for today's researchers. *A Complete Roll of All Choctaw Claimants and Their Heirs Existing Under the Treaties Between the United States and the Choctaw Nation* provides a complete alphabetical list, including aliases and English names (where known).[22] Bob Blankenship's series *Cherokee Roots* lists the names from nearly a dozen official lists.[23] These types of publications contribute significantly to the accessibility of Native American historical and genealogical data and should be sought by the family historian.

A number of other works published as monographs contribute substantially to the body of data available to researchers seeking individual-specific records. A more contemporary example, Toni Jollay Prevost's *The Delaware & Shawnee Admitted to Cherokee Citizenship and the Related Wyandotte & Moravian Delaware*, provides many lists, including signers of treaties, property owners, children enrolled in mission schools, and partial citizenship lists.[24] Divided into fourteen sections, it provides many names, dates, and places to assist directly in developing ancestor charts and ancestral proof.

A number of Indian schools were operated as part of the process of attempting to assimilate Native Americans. Records of these schools, which had agricultural, industrial, or missionary focuses, may provide the researcher with plentiful details about a potential ancestor, including such facts as tribal affiliation, degree of Native American blood, names of parents, home address, dates of arrival and departure, attendance records, health cards, and letters to parents and social workers.

An abundance of both tribe-specific and individual-specific records can be found in periodical literature. The historical and

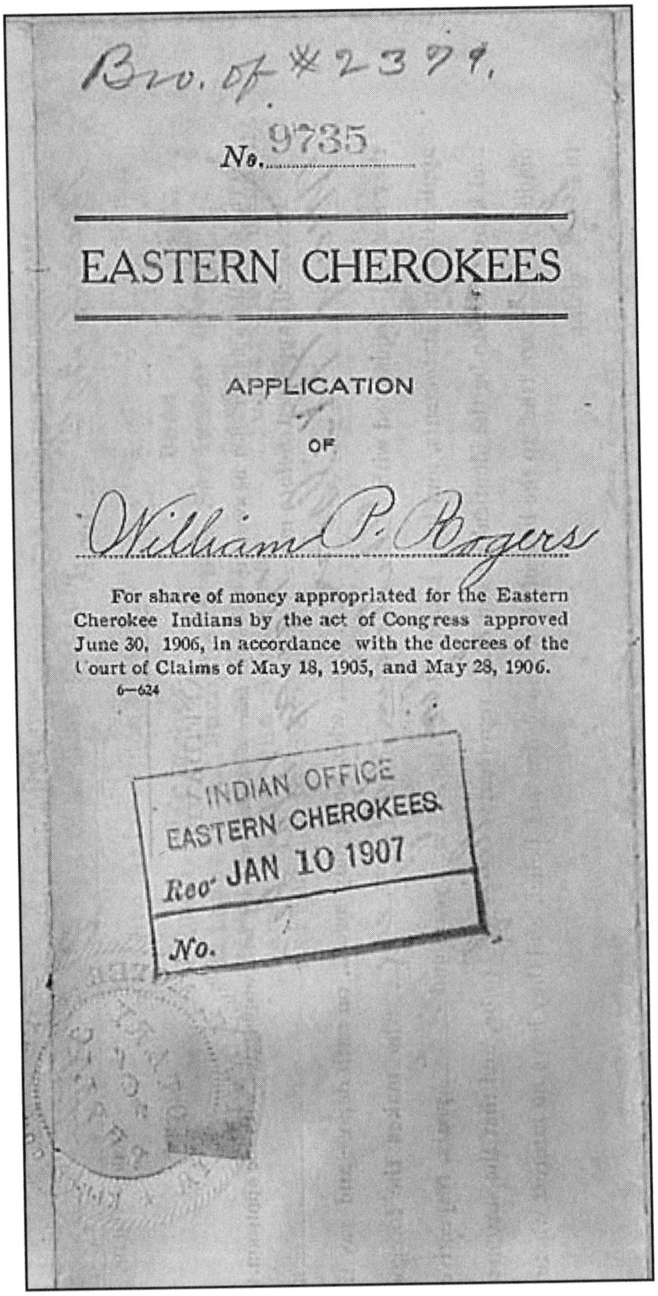

Bro. of #2379.

No. 9735

EASTERN CHEROKEES

APPLICATION

OF

William P. Rogers

For share of money appropriated for the Eastern Cherokee Indians by the act of Congress approved June 30, 1906, in accordance with the decrees of the Court of Claims of May 18, 1905, and May 28, 1906.

6—624

INDIAN OFFICE
EASTERN CHEROKEES
Rec' JAN 10 1907
No.

Figure 19-4. Eastern Cherokee Application #9735 of Will Rogers for a share in money that was appropriated for the Eastern Cherokee Indians by Congress on 30 June 1906. Application file found online at <http://arcweb.archives.gov>.

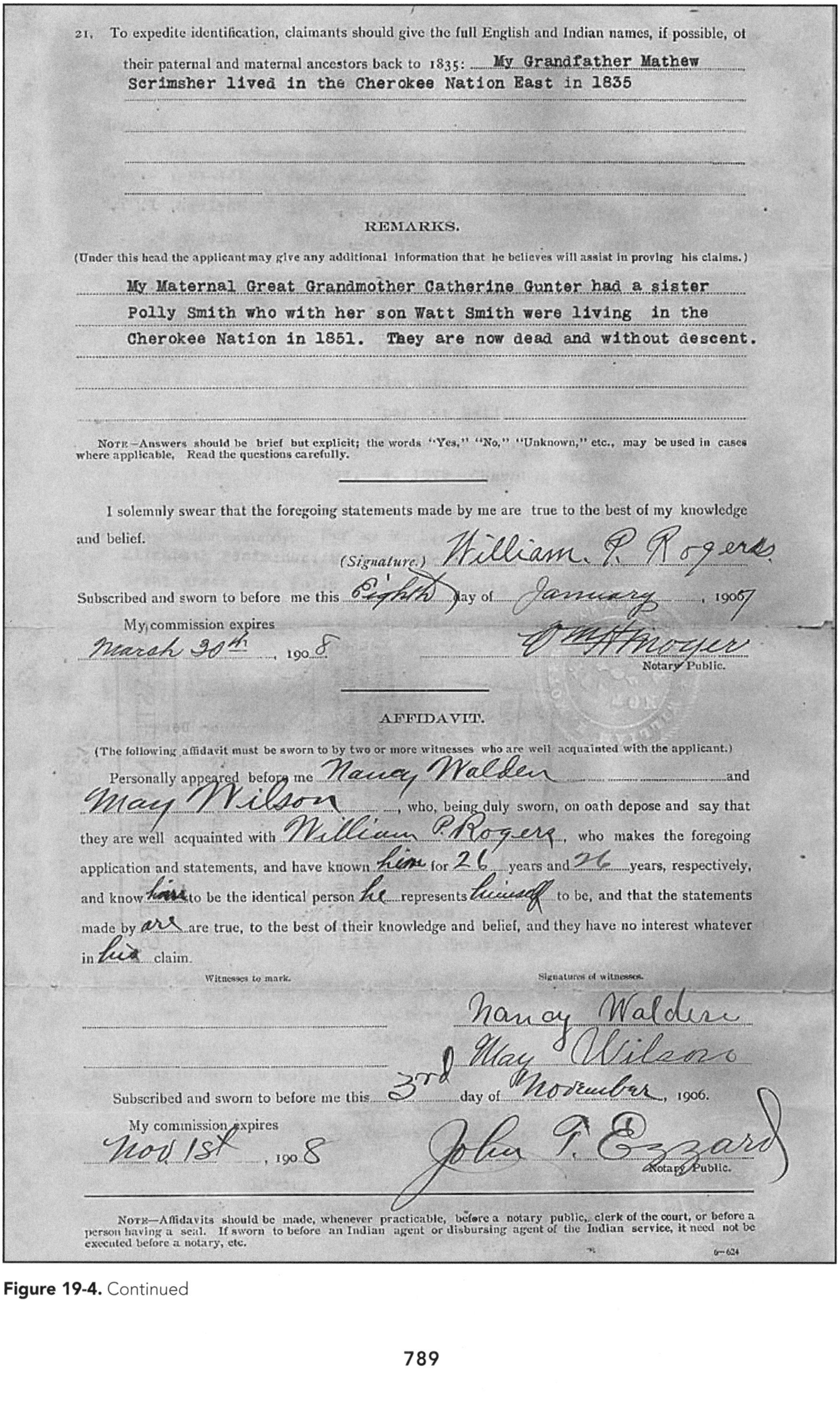

21. To expedite identification, claimants should give the full English and Indian names, if possible, of their paternal and maternal ancestors back to 1835: My Grandfather Mathew Scrimsher lived in the Cherokee Nation East in 1835

REMARKS.

(Under this head the applicant may give any additional information that he believes will assist in proving his claims.)

My Maternal Great Grandmother Catherine Gunter had a sister Polly Smith who with her son Watt Smith were living in the Cherokee Nation in 1851. They are now dead and without descent.

NOTE—Answers should be brief but explicit; the words "Yes," "No," "Unknown," etc., may be used in cases where applicable. Read the questions carefully.

I solemnly swear that the foregoing statements made by me are true to the best of my knowledge and belief.

(Signature.) William P. Rogers

Subscribed and sworn to before me this Eighth day of January, 1907

My commission expires March 30th, 1908

[illegible] Moyer, Notary Public.

AFFIDAVIT.

(The following affidavit must be sworn to by two or more witnesses who are well acquainted with the applicant.)

Personally appeared before me Nancy Walden and May Wilson, who, being duly sworn, on oath depose and say that they are well acquainted with William P. Rogers, who makes the foregoing application and statements, and have known him for 26 years and 26 years, respectively, and know him to be the identical person he represents himself to be, and that the statements made by are are true, to the best of their knowledge and belief, and they have no interest whatever in his claim.

Witnesses to mark.

Signatures of witnesses.

Nancy Walden

May Wilson

Subscribed and sworn to before me this 3rd day of November, 1906.

My commission expires Nov 1st, 1908

John P. Ezzard, Notary Public.

NOTE—Affidavits should be made, whenever practicable, before a notary public, clerk of the court, or before a person having a seal. If sworn to before an Indian agent or disbursing agent of the Indian service, it need not be executed before a notary, etc.

6—624

Figure 19-4. Continued

genealogical periodicals that cover the geographic areas where Native American tribes historically lived, as well as areas of removal and contemporary settlement, should be considered by the serious researcher. Every type of record that can be found in manuscript collections or published in monographs may be available in indexed, abstracted, transcribed, or reprinted form in periodical literature. One of the best subject indexes to these quarterlies and newsletters is the *PERiodical Source Index (PERSI)*, which indexes more than four thousand periodical titles.[25] Another source of access to this material is the *Genealogical Periodical Annual Index (GPAI)*. (See chapter 3, "General Reference and Guides.")[26]

Some of the more notable geographically oriented periodicals include the *Oklahoma Genealogical Society Quarterly*, *Stirpes* (the journal of the Texas State Genealogical Society), and the *Topeka Genealogical Society Quarterly*.[27] These journals contain indexes to and transcriptions of numerous Native American records. They can also provide leads to individuals and institutions that might be contacted for further historical and genealogical data. Other fine periodicals worthy of note cover both general Native American history and tribe- and nation-specific details. *The American Indian Quarterly* provides excellent information about the many sides of Native American life and assists the researcher in the same manner as do general histories; a recently published cumulative index to this quarterly makes accessing this information quite easy.[28] Donna Williams's *Cherokee Family Researcher* and the *Journal of Cherokee Studies* are examples of tribe-specific periodical publications that can provide specific records of genealogical value as well as detailed historical data on particular tribes.[29]

The Bureau of Indian Affairs, its regional offices, and specific tribal offices are rich sources of genealogical information. In fact, they contain the richest collections of individual-specific data for Native Americans. Guides to these collections and offices are available in some major libraries and by contacting the Bureau of Indian Affairs offices in Washington, D.C. Contact the bureau or its organizations directly for both general information and individual-specific requests. Typically, neither the bureau nor tribal offices and archives will engage in genealogical research. Success in interacting with these entities will be determined largely by the specificity of the information request as well as how well that request is contexted with other historical data.

The exploding number of resources available for genealogical researchers on the World Wide Web makes the Internet an invaluable research tool for genealogists exploring Native American family history. The websites of federal agencies, particularly the Library of Congress and the National Archives, as well as tribe-specific websites can provide much information for the researcher looking for individual-specific data as well as information that will lead to sources of individual-specific data. Employing an Internet search engine such as Google and searching for the specific name of the tribe one is investigating often nets the best results. Many sites that provide data about Native Americans have significant links to other related sites. All of these links should be explored to maximize one's potential for identifying sources of new information. If a large number of search results are the outcome of a particular search, using some of the helps and suggestions under an "advanced search" option can be most beneficial.

Employment of sound research methodology, fine attention to detail with complete and accurate recording of all relevant and associated data, and a willingness to search for all possible data from a multiplicity of information sources—these are the keys to successful Native American genealogical research. The following sections provide numerous vital details useful for identifying extant records, becoming familiar with the historical and genealogical data included in those records, and accessing specific materials needed to further research endeavors.

Records Relating to Native American Research in Oklahoma

GEORGE J. NIXON

Interest in Native American genealogy has increased greatly since the 1980s, and access to records of genealogical and historical importance has become easier through microfilming projects undertaken by various federal, state, and privately funded institutions. Because of the interest in Indian tribes of Oklahoma, this section focuses on records available to the genealogist and historian for those tribes (see figure 19-5).

The majority of the records cited in this chapter are available from the Oklahoma Historical Society in Oklahoma City; the Western History Collection at the University of Oklahoma in Norman, Oklahoma; the National Archives—Southwest Region in Fort Worth, Texas; the National Archives in Washington, D.C.; the Family History Library of The Church of Jesus Christ of Latter-day Saints in Salt Lake City; or the American Genealogical Lending Library in Bountiful, Utah.

Indian Removal

During the administration of President Andrew Jackson (1829–1837), the removal of Indians in the East to Indian Territory west of the Mississippi River became an explicit policy. As early as

1803, with the Louisiana Purchase, such removals were officially encouraged, and some Indians did voluntarily move west.

Under Jackson, however, treaties were negotiated that traded tribal lands in the East for land in the unorganized territory west of the Mississippi River. An act of 28 May 1830 (4 Stat. 411) specifically authorized the president to exchange these lands. The actual removals were conducted between 1830 and 1836 by the Office of the Commissary General of Subsistence and were supervised by the military. Some Indians, however, were allowed to move by themselves, and individual Indians who wished to remain in the East could accept a "reservation" of land in fee simple and remain as citizens, giving up all rights of tribal membership. The removal process was largely complete by the late 1840s.

The removal was not without problems, most of which concerned reservations granted to Indians in the East and the compensation to Indians for losses. The three most troublesome treaties were the treaty of 29 December 1835 with the Cherokees, the treaty of 29 September 1830 with the Choctaws, and the treaty of 24 March 1832 with the Creeks.

Numerous treatments of the removal policy are available; among them are Annie H. Abel's *The History of Events Resulting in Indian Consolidation West of the Mississippi* and Grant Foreman's *Indian Removal*.[30]

Cherokee Removal Records

Cherokee removal records include a register of Cherokees who wished to remain in the East, 1817–19; applications for reservations, 1819; Eastern Cherokee census rolls, 1835–84; emigration rolls, 1817–36; and miscellaneous Cherokee removal records, 1820–54.

Four commissions were appointed successively in an attempt to settle different kinds of claims arising from the Cherokee Treaty of 1835.

Records of the First Board of Cherokee Commissioners, 1836–1839

Records of the First Board of Cherokee Commissioners include letters sent, 1835–39; property valuations, 1835–39; changes in assignment of property valuations, 1837–38; reservation claims, 1837–39; reservation claim papers, 1837–39; record of judgments against Cherokee Indians, 1837; decisions on claims of attorneys against the Cherokee Nation, 1837–39; certificate stubs, 1838; and a general abstract of valuations and spoliation allowed and of balances due, 1839.

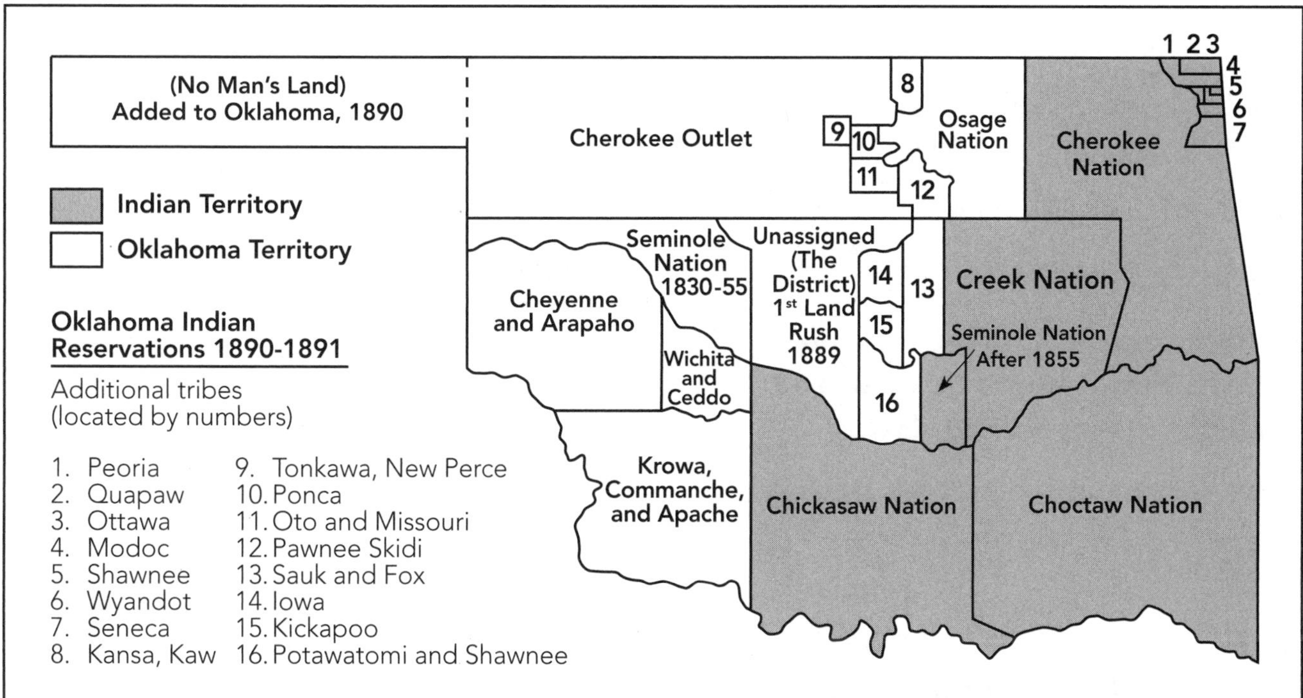

Figure 19-5. Based on Muriel Wright, *A Guide to the Indians of Oklahoma* (Norman: University of Oklahoma Press, 1971), and Josh Morris, et al., *Historical Atlas of Oklahoma* (Norman: University of Oklahoma Press, 1976). The Choctaws arrived west of the Mississippi in 1820; the other four Civilized Tribes soon followed. After the Civil War, other Indian tribes migrated into the nations, settling primarily in western sections and along the Arkansas, Missouri, and Kansas borders. In 1889, the area was divided into Indian Territory (eastern part) and Oklahoma Territory (western part) as a prelude to non-Indian settlement. Specific reservations and allotments were assigned in 1890–91. By 1907, counties were formed throughout Oklahoma and the reservation boundaries disappeared.

Records of the Second and Third Board of Cherokee Commissioners, 1842–1845

Records of the Second and Third Board of Cherokee Commissioners include letters sent, 1842–45; proceedings of the Second Board, 1843; schedule of claims adjudicated by the Second Board, 1843; claim papers of the Second and Third Boards, 1842–45; claims presented in the West, 1845; and register of payments, 1837–45.

Records of the Fourth Board of Cherokee Commissioners, 1846–1847

Records of the Fourth Board of Cherokee Commissioners include letters sent, 1846–47; minutes, 1846–47; claim papers, 1846–47; and register of payments, 1847.

Chickasaw Removal Records

Chickasaw removal records include a census roll of 1831; alphabetical list of Choctaw reserves; census roll of 1846; emigration lists, 1831–57; register of claims for reservations, 1834–36; reports concerning claims for reservations, 1836–41; statements concerning sales of Choctaw orphan lands, 1838–83; statements and schedules, 1831–1906; and miscellaneous Choctaw removals, 1825–58.

Creek Removal Records

Creek removal records include a census roll of 1833; index to Creek reserves (not dated); land location registers, 1834–86; location registers and certificates of contracts, 1834–36; abstracts of Creek contracts, 1836; abstracts of approved contracts for sales of reservations, 1839–1842; reports concerning land of deceased reservees, 1844; miscellaneous records concerning contracts, 1833–57; emigration lists, 1836–38; and miscellaneous Creek removal records, 1827–59.

Apalachicola, Seminole, Kickapoo, Ottawa, Potawatomi, Quapaw, and Wyandot Removal Records

Other removal records include five volumes of miscellaneous muster rolls of 1832 to 1836 that record removals for Apalachicolas and Seminoles, Kickapoos, Ottawas, Potawatomis, Quapaws, and Wyandots.

The Commission to the Five Civilized Tribes (The Dawes Commission)[31]

The Five Civilized Tribes—the Cherokee, Choctaw, Chickasaw, Creek, and Seminole—were so called by the U.S. government because they were more advanced (literate) than many others and had adopted systems of government patterned after those of the United States.

An act approved by Congress on 3 March 1893 (27 Stat. L., 645) provided for the appointment of three commissioners to negotiate with the Five Civilized Tribes for the extinguishment of the tribal title and the allotment of lands in severalty. This commission was generally known as the Dawes Commission for ex-Senator Dawes of Massachusetts, who was appointed chairman. The commission reported directly to the secretary of the interior. In 1895, the number of members was increased to five. At that time, the work of the commission was limited to two fields: a change in the method of land ownership and the abolition of the tribal governments. The commission experienced little success in these endeavors, and on 10 June 1896 (29 Stat. L., 339), the scope of the commission's work was enlarged by an authorization and direction to "hear and determine the application of all persons who may apply to them for citizenship in any of said nations," and the commission was required to file the list of tribal members with the commissioner of Indian Affairs "for use as the final judgment of the duly constituted authorities."

On 28 June 1898 (30 Stat. L., 495), a law generally known as the Curtis Act was approved. The Curtis Act is the basis of all later legislation relating to the affairs of the Five Civilized Tribes. The main features of this act were: (1) the allotment of land in severalty; (2) leasing of tribal lands by the secretary of the interior; (3) the incorporation of cities and towns, the survey of town sites, and the sale of town lots to the lessees at half their appraised value; (4) the prohibition of any payment to tribal governments and provision for making per-capita payments directly to individuals; (5) provision for the payments of all rents and royalties into the Treasury of the United States to the credit of the tribe; and (6) the enlargement of the power of the U.S. courts and the abolition of tribal courts.

Agreements had been made with the Choctaws and Chickasaws on 23 April 1897, with the Creeks on 27 September 1897, and with the Seminoles on 16 December 1897. The Choctaw-Chickasaw and the Creek agreements were embodied in the Curtis Act of 1898. The agreement was confirmed on 24 August 1898, but the Creeks rejected it. The agreement with the Seminoles was ratified by Congress in the act of 1 July 1898 (30 Stat. L., 567).

A new agreement with the Creeks was made on 8 March 1900 and ratified by the act of 1 March 1901. The Cherokees were the last to accept the new conditions, but an act was ratified by the Cherokees on 7 August 1902 and proclaimed by the president on 12 August 1902.

The agreements provided for each member of the Choctaw and Chickasaw nations to receive "land equal in value to 320 acres of the average allottable land," out of which 160 acres were to be designated as a homestead, which was to be inalienable during the life of the allottee but not beyond twenty-one years from the date of the certificate of allotment. Lands not included in the homestead were to be alienable for one-fourth the acreage in one year, one-fourth in three years, and the balance in five years from the date of patent. Each freedman was to be allotted "land equal in value to forty acres of the average allottable land."[32]

The Seminole agreement provided for the division of the land into three classes to be appraised at $5, $2.50, and $1.25 per acre, and for allotments so that each member should have an equal average of 120 acres. Each allottee was required to designate a tract of forty acres, which was "made inalienable and nontaxable as a homestead in perpetuity."[33]

In the Cherokee Nation, the allotments were to be 110 acres of the average allottable land on the basis of the appraisal to be made by the Dawes Commission. Provision was made for a homestead of forty acres, which was to be inalienable and nontaxable during the lifetime of the allottee but not longer than twenty-one years. In the Seminole, Creek, and Cherokee nations, the freedmen (former black slaves of Indian slaveholders) received the same allotments as the Indians by blood.

The closing of the tribal affairs of the Five Civilized Tribes involved, among other tasks, the preparation of a correct tribal roll and division of the land among the members according to the varying provisions of the separate agreements. Applications for enrollment were received from approximately 250,000 people in all parts of the United States, but the final rolls contained the names of approximately 101,000, of whom approximately one-fourth were full blooded.

The enrollment records consist of the application made for enrollment together with all of the records, evidence, and papers filed in connection with the decision of the commissioner.[34]

During the early stages of enrollment, appointments were made by the commission at various places in the different nations at which the Indians and freedmen appeared to apply for enrollment. At that time, the applicants were sworn before a notary public, but their testimony was taken orally and placed upon a card, with the exception of Cherokees. Written testimony was taken in all Cherokee cases. In a great majority of the early enrollments, except Cherokee cases, the only records shown are the statements personally taken from the applicants and placed on the cards, which constitute the enrollment record, together with any other evidence that may have been obtained. In a great many instances, where there was doubt as to the rights of the applicant to enrollment and the applicant could not be identified from the tribal rolls, the written testimony of the applicant was taken and made a part of the record. Additional testimony was also taken at later dates.

After the enrollment of all citizens, by blood or intermarriage, and freedmen, who were clearly identified upon the tribal rolls, was completed, written testimony was taken in all doubtful cases. Written testimony was also taken for all applications made for the identification of Mississippi Choctaws and in practically all other cases as the work neared completion.

The tribal rolls of the various nations came into the possession of the commissioner to the Five Civilized Tribes. They were used for identification and as a basis for enrollment.

When the enrollments were completed, the names of all persons whom the commission had decided were entitled to enrollment were placed on the rolls. These rolls show the name, age, sex, degree of blood, and the number of the census card, generally known as the "enrollment card," on which each citizen was enrolled. A number was placed opposite each name appearing on this roll, beginning at 1 and running consecutively until the final number was completed. This roll was made out in quintuplicate and forwarded to the secretary of the Interior for approval. The secretary returned three copies for the files of the commissioner to the Five Civilized Tribes. The roll thus approved was known as the "approval roll" and was used as the basis for allotments, except in the cases of a large number of Creeks, to whom allotments were made before the approval of their enrollment. These allotments were subsequently confirmed by Congress.

The enrollment records consist of: (1) the census card—the card on which the applicant was listed for enrollment (in the early enrollment, some persons were listed on what is known as a doubtful card, and later on the names appearing on the doubtful cards were transferred to regular census cards); (2) all testimony taken in the matter of the application at various times prior to rendition of the decision granting the application; (3) birth affidavits, affidavits of death, and other evidence and papers filed in connection with the application made for enrollment; and (4) the enrollment as shown on the approved roll.

Many of the records of the Dawes Commission are still in the custody of the Muskogee Area Office of the Bureau of Indian Affairs in Muskogee, Oklahoma. Others have been deposited with the Oklahoma Historical Society in Oklahoma City. The majority of these records have been reproduced on microfilm and are available at the Oklahoma Historical Society; the National Archives records center in Fort Worth, Texas; the University of Oklahoma in Norman, Oklahoma; and the Family History Library in Salt Lake City.[35]

General Records of the Commission to the Five Civilized Tribes

Most of the correspondence received prior to 1901 and copies of letters sent prior to 1906 are in the custody of the Oklahoma Historical Society. This correspondence can also be found in the records of the Indian Division of the Office of the Secretary of the Interior (Record Group 48) and the Bureau of Indian Affairs (Record Group 75).

Index to Letters Received from the Department of Interior, 1907–1914

This index is divided into chronological segments: 1907 to 1908, 1909 to 1910, 1911 to 1912, and 1913 to 1914. Entries are arranged alphabetically by subject and, thereunder, chronologically by the date the letter was written. Information given for each letter includes the date it was written, the file number assigned, and a short summary of the subject.

Register of Letters Received from the Department of Interior ("Special Index"), 1903–1914

Arranged chronologically by date of receipt. Information given for each letter includes the date written, the date received, the name of the sender, the file number assigned, and a short summary of the subject.

Letters Received from the Department of Interior ("Departmental Letters"), 1901–1914

Arranged numerically by file number assigned chronologically by date of receipt within each fiscal year. The letters relate to all phases of the commission's activities, including administration, enrollment, allotment, the leasing and sale of allotted and unallotted land, and the establishment of town sites.

Instructions Received from the Department of Interior, 1900

Carbon copies of letters received from the Department of Interior relating to enrollment and enrollment procedures, the leasing of allotted land, and the removal of non-Indians from allotted land; arranged chronologically by date of receipt and indexed by subject. Many letters transmit opinions of the assistant attorney general on legal issues relating to enrollment and allotment.

Index to Letters Received, 1897–1913

The index is divided into yearly segments. Within each segment, entries are arranged alphabetically by the first two letters of the sender's surname. Information given includes the name of the sender, the date the letter was written, the file number assigned, and a brief summary of the subject.

Registers of Letters Received, 1908–1914

Arranged chronologically by date of receipt. The information given for each letter includes the name and address of the sender, the date the letter was written, the date received, the file number assigned, a brief summary of the subject, and, occasionally, remarks about actions taken.

Registers of Letters Received from the Union Agency, 1906–1909

Arranged chronologically by date of receipt. The information given for each letter includes the date it was written, the date received, the file number assigned, and a brief summary of the subject.

Letters Received ("General Office Letters"), 1900–1914

Original letters and telegrams received from the U.S. Indian inspector for Indian Territory, the Union Agency, other Indian agencies, field offices of the Dawes Commission, including the land offices maintained for each tribe, officials of tribal governments, and the general public. The letters relate to all phases of the commission's activities. Arranged numerically by file number assigned chronologically by date of receipt within each fiscal year.

Letters Received by Commissioner Bixby, 1897–1906

Arranged alphabetically by name of sender until 1901 and thereafter numerically by file number assigned chronologically by date of receipt. The letters relate to the status of applications for enrollment or allotment, the sale and leasing of land, and applications for employment. Many of the books are marked "personal and confidential."

Letters Sent to the Secretary of Interior, 1906–1914

Press copies of letters sent to the secretary of the Interior through the commissioner of Indian affairs. Arranged chronologically by date sent and indexed by subject.

Letters Sent to the Commissioner of Indian Affairs, 1907–1911

Arranged in rough chronological order and indexed by subject.

Letters Sent ("Miscellaneous Letters"), 1895–1914

Press copies of letters sent to the U.S. Indian inspector for Indian Territory, the Union Agency, other Indian agencies, field offices of the Dawes Commission, officials of tribal governments, and the general public. Arranged chronologically by date sent.

Letters Sent by Commissioner Bixby, 1902–1907

Press copies of letters sent by Commissioner Bixby from Washington, D.C., to Commissioner in Charge T.B. Needles in Muskogee and letters sent by Bixby from Muskogee to the secretary of the interior, the commissioner of Indian affairs, and members of Congress. Arranged chronologically by date sent.

Annual Narrative Reports, 1894–1914

Printed copies of the annual reports of the commission's activities submitted to the secretary of the interior. The reports provide detailed information about the activities of the commission. Arranged chronologically by date of report; (no reports for 1897, 1899–1903).

Index to Reference Documents

The index provides the category and file number of each document. The categories used are: A—Cherokee and Delaware; B—Choctaw and Chickasaw; C—Creek; D—Enrollment; E—Leases; F—Reports; and G—Miscellaneous. Arranged alphabetically by subject.

Reference Documents ("Miscellaneous Documents"), 1896–1904

Correspondence, printed congressional documents, copies of agreements with tribal governments, rules and instructions issued by the secretary of the interior or the commission, receipts for rolls and other papers supplied by tribal governments, copies of documents filed in cases heard by the U.S. Supreme Court and other federal courts, and lists of persons admitted to tribal citizenship by U.S. courts. There are also transcripts of hearings in citizenship cases. Arranged in three groups. Within each group, documents are arranged numerically by a file number assigned by the commission.

Records Relating to All Tribes

Index to Enrollment Cards, 1899–1907

Arranged by tribe and then by enrollment category. Entries within each volume are arranged alphabetically by the first two letters of the applicant's surname. Generally, the index provides only the number of the card on which the applicant's name appears, but some volumes also provide the individual's enrollment number. Many of the volumes include the names of persons listed on "doubtful" and "rejected" cards.

Index and Final Rolls, 1914

The index and final rolls are contained in separate volumes. Entries in the index are arranged by tribe, then by enrollment category, and then in roughly alphabetical order by the first two letters of the surname. Entries in the final rolls are arranged by tribe, then by enrollment category, and then numerically by the enrollment number assigned by the Dawes Commission.

Enrollment Cards ("Census Cards"), 1899–1907

These are original fourteen- by seven-inch printed cards annotated with information about persons applying for enrollment. Cards were prepared for each family group and used by enrollment parties traveling throughout Indian Territory to record information about the applicants and actions taken by the commission. The information given for each applicant generally includes name, enrollment number, age, sex, degree of Indian blood, relationship to the head of the family group, references to enrollment on earlier tribal rolls used by the commission to verify eligibility, and parents' names. The cards often include notations about an applicant's birth or death, changes in marital status, references to related enrollment cards, and actions taken by the commission or the secretary of the interior. The cards relating to applicants as freedmen also contain the name of the person who owned the applicant as a slave and the owner of the applicant's parents. These cards have been microfilmed. Arranged by tribe and thereunder by enrollment category. Within each category there are generally three groups: "straight" (persons who were enrolled), "doubtful," and "rejected." Within each group, the cards are arranged numerically by a number assigned by the commission.

Duplicate Enrollment Cards, 1918–1919

Duplicate paper copies of the cards were prepared to reduce the use of the original cards and contain all of the information recorded on the original. There are no copies of Creek-, Seminole-, or Cherokee-by-blood cards. Arranged by tribe, then by enrollment category, and then by type of card (straight, doubtful, or rejected). Within each type, the cards are arranged numerically by a number assigned by the Dawes Commission.

Letters Sent Transmitting Enrollment Schedules, 1901–1907

Press copies of letters sent to the secretary of the interior through the commissioner of Indian affairs transmitting schedules of the names of persons recommended for enrollment and press copies of the schedules. The information given in the schedules includes the person's name, enrollment number, tribal district of residence, and the tribal roll used to verify eligibility. There are occasional remarks about relationships to other persons listed in the schedule. Arranged by tribe and then by enrollment category. Within each volume, the letters are arranged chronologically by date sent.

Enrollment Schedules, 1900–1907

Carbon copies of typed schedules of the names of persons recommended for enrollment. The schedules were submitted to the secretary of the interior in triplicate for approval, and one copy was returned to the commission for reference. The information given for each person includes name, age, sex, degree of Indian blood, and enrollment number. The schedules for the Seminoles also include the band name and a reference to an 1897 Seminole census roll. Arranged by tribal enrollment category. Names within the schedule are arranged numerically by enrollment number.

Report on Enrollment, 1909

A press copy of a report prepared by Joseph W. Howell on the enrollment of the Five Civilized Tribes, which was submitted to the secretary of the interior. The report provides a detailed description of the enrollment procedures, controversial decisions, and difficulties of obtaining records from the tribal governments. There are several appendixes that provide lists of tribal rolls used by the commission.

List of Claimants, 1907

A typed "Departmental List of Persons Who Claim to be Entitled to Enrollment as Citizens and Freedmen of the Five Civilized Tribes Prepared with a View to Remedial Legislation." The list contains the names of 741 persons and includes the tribal affiliation claimed by each and a summary of the facts in each case. Names within the list are arranged alphabetically by surname.

Index to Citizenship Docket

Index to an unidentified citizenship docket that provides only a case number for each claimant under the heading "Nation Number." Arranged alphabetically by the first letter of the claimant's surname.

Records of the Dawes Commission Relating to Cherokee Citizenship

List of Rejected Claimants, 1878–1880

A handwritten copy of a list of persons whose claim to citizenship was rejected by the Cherokee Commission on Citizenship. The only information given for each claimant is the case number and the reason for rejection (by decree, by default, or withdrawn). Arranged chronologically by court term, then by the reason for rejection, and then by case number.

List of Persons Admitted to Citizenship

A printed "List of persons admitted and re-admitted to Cherokee citizenship by the National Council and Commissions on Citizenship in the year 1880, and since that year." The list covers the period from 1880 to 1899 and appears to have been printed for use by the commission. The only information given is the person's name and the date admitted. Arranged (roughly) in alphabetical order by surname.

Cherokee Citizenship Commission Dockets, 1880–1984 and 1887–1889

A record of actions taken by the tribal commission on applications for citizenship. Each docket entry generally includes the applicant's name, age, sex, names of attorneys, the text of the application, a summary of the proceedings held, and the text of the commission's decision. Arranged numerically by case number assigned chronologically by the date the case was opened and indexed by name of applicant.

Record of Births, 1897

A record of children born from 1895 to 1897. The list appears to have been completed in 1897 and contains the child's name, date of birth, and parents' names. Most of the children listed were born in 1897. Arranged by districts of the Cherokee Nation.

Dawes Commission Dockets, 1902

A record of actions taken by the Dawes Commission on applications for citizenship. The information given for each application includes the date filed, the names of the persons covered by the application, the date the attorneys for the Cherokee filed an answer, the commission's decision, the date of appeal to the U.S. court, and the court's decision. Arranged numerically by case number and assigned chronologically by the date the case was opened.

Docket of Cases Appealed, 1896–1899

A record of actions taken by the U.S. Court for the Northern District of Indian Territory on appeals from decisions of the Dawes Commission on applications under the act of 1896. The information given for each case includes the names of the parties and their attorneys, a summary of proceedings and motions filed, and the decision of the court. Arranged numerically by case number assigned chronologically by the date the case was opened. Indexed by name of applicant.

Lists of Applicants, 1902

Typed lists of persons admitted or rejected for citizenship by the U.S. courts for the northern and southern districts of Indian Territory. There are lists for the following actions: applicants admitted by the Dawes Commission and affirmed by the courts, applicants admitted by the court for the Southern District who had been rejected by the commission, applicants denied by the court for the Northern District who had been admitted by the commission, and applicants admitted by the court for the Northern District who had been denied by the commission. The information given for each applicant generally includes the Dawes Commission case number, U.S. court docket number, and Dawes Commission enrollment card number. There are separate lists for admitted and rejected applicants. Within each list, names are arranged alphabetically by surname.

Decisions of the U.S. Court, 1897–1899

Press copies of decisions of Judge William M. Springer of the U.S. Court for the Northern District of Indian Territory on appeals of decisions of the Dawes Commission on applications for enrollment under the act of 1896. The decision of the judge often includes a report on the case prepared by a "special master" appointed by the court. Arranged in roughly chronological order by the date of the decision. Each volume is indexed by the name of the applicant involved in the decision.

Records Relating to Appeals, 1897–1898

Bonds for appeals to the U.S. Supreme Court from decisions of the U.S. Court for the Northern District of Indian Territory, petitions for appeals, and assignments of errors. These records appear to be copies that were filed with the court and subsequently given to the Dawes Commission for reference. Arranged by case number assigned by the date the case was opened.

Lists of Applicants as Freedmen, 1897

Lists of applicants for participation in an award by the U.S. Court of Claims to Cherokee freedmen who had not been included in the roll prepared for payment of the award. The lists include each applicant's name, roll number from the 1880 Cherokee census, roll number from the Wallace roll of Cherokee freedmen, an exhibit number that corresponds to the exhibit number in the Applications for Enrollment as Freedmen, district of residence within the Cherokee Nation, and, occasionally, remarks about other enrollments. These lists were submitted as evidence to the Dawes Commission by the Cherokee National Council in enrollment proceedings. Names within each list are arranged in roughly alphabetical order by applicants' surnames.

Applications for Enrollment as Freedmen, 1897

Notarized applications prepared on printed forms submitted by persons claiming a share of a payment made to Cherokee freedmen in accordance with an award of the U.S. Court of Claims in the case of *Moses Whitmire, Trustee, v. the Cherokee Nation*. The applications and supporting material were submitted by James M. Keys to the commissioner of Indian Affairs between 10 May and 30 June 1897 and may have been a part of the general correspondence of the bureau. It appears that the records were returned to the Dawes Commission for use in enrollment proceedings. The application provides the applicant's name, age, and district of residence in the Cherokee Nation, and the names and ages of other family members. Some letters from claimants and officials of the Cherokee tribal government are included with the application forms. Arranged numerically by exhibit number assigned in roughly chronological order by date of application.

Index to Applications for Enrollment through Intermarriage

A handwritten index to the applications for enrollment through intermarriage. The only information given is the application number. Arranged alphabetically by the first letter of the applicant's surname.

Applications for Enrollment through Intermarriage

Original applications submitted to the Dawes Commission for enrollment, which required any person married to a Cherokee citizen to apply for themselves and their children. The applications or petitions are notarized and provide the name, age, sex, and address of each child, and information in support of the claim to citizenship, such as date of marriage and enrollment on other tribal rolls. In addition to the applications, there are occasionally copies of marriage licenses, statements of witnesses to the marriage, notice of service of a copy of the application on the chief of the Cherokee tribe, and the answer of the tribal government generally rejecting the claim. The Dawes Commission held hearings on the applications at Fort Gibson, but no records of the hearings have been located. Arranged numerically by application number assigned in roughly alphabetical order by the first letter of the applicant's surname.

Dockets to Rejected and Doubtful Applications, 1904–1905

There is one docket for Cherokees by blood and one for freedmen. Within each docket are separate sections for doubtful and rejected applications. Within each section, entries are arranged numerically by case number assigned chronologically by the date the case was opened. Each docket contains an index to names of applicants. This source also contains a record of actions taken on applications classified by the commission as doubtful or rejected. The information for each application includes the names of the applicants and their attorneys, the decision of the commission, the date prepared, the date forwarded to the commissioner of Indian affairs, and the date approved by the secretary of the interior. Many of the doubtful and some of the rejected applications were eventually enrolled, and there are references to enrollment card numbers. The case numbers in these dockets match the application numbers in the applications for enrollment and enrollment card numbers in the enrollment cards (census cards).

Applications for Enrollment, 1898–1907

Original applications for enrollment and supporting evidence submitted to the Dawes Commission. The records include carbon copies of the testimony taken at hearings held by the commission, notices and letters sent to the applicants and the attorneys for both the applicants and the Cherokee tribe, correspondence with the secretary of the interior about the applications, and copies of the commission's decisions. There are applications only for the following categories: doubtful citizens by blood, rejected citizens by blood, doubtful freedmen, rejected freedmen, and newborn freedmen. There are also some memorandum cases, which contain applications rejected under an act of Congress that restricted the commission's jurisdiction. Applications for the bulk of the Cherokee categories are still in the custody of the Bureau of Indian Affairs and have been microfilmed. Arranged by enrollment category and then numerically by application number assigned chronologically by date of application. There are numerous gaps in the applications, and some applications are missing.

Transcripts of Testimony of Applicants, 1910

Carbon copies of transcripts of testimony taken at hearings held by the commission. The majority of the applications relate to children of persons previously enrolled by the commission and persons listed on a roll of "Eastern Cherokees" who were not enrolled. Arranged numerically by application number assigned chronologically by date of application.

Record of Decisions, 1901–1902

A record of actions taken by the commission on applications for enrollment. The information given for each action includes the names of the applicants, names of attorneys for the applicants and the Cherokee tribe, the nature of the decision, and a reference to the enrollment cards. Arranged chronologically by date of decision and indexed by applicant.

Index to the Cherokee Final Rolls

Two indexes to names appearing on the "Final Roll of the Cherokees." One index is contained in a single volume, and the second index is divided into two volumes (*A* through *K* and *L* through *Z*). The only information given in the index is the enrollee's Dawes enrollment number. Arranged alphabetically by the first two letters of the enrollee's surname.

Records Relating to Choctaw and Chickasaw Citizenship

Acts of the Choctaw National Council, 1893–1895

Handwritten copies of "Acts of the General Council Admitting Parties to Citizenship." The text of the acts includes the names of persons and the authority for admission. Arranged chronologically by date of passage.

Lists of Applicants for Choctaw Citizenship, 1902

A typed list of persons who applied for Choctaw citizenship. The information given for each applicant includes the Dawes Commission case number and a reference to the enrollment cards. The list is annotated with an *A* for persons who were admitted and a *D* for persons who were denied. Arranged alphabetically by applicants' surnames.

Lists of Persons Involved in Appeals to U.S. Courts, 1900

Lists of applicants for citizenship whose cases were appealed to the U.S. Court for the Central District of Indian Territory at South McAlester or the Southern District at Ardmore. There are lists for persons admitted by the court, persons admitted by the court who were previously denied by the Dawes Commission, and persons denied by the court who had been previously admitted by the commission. The information given for each person generally includes the Dawes Commission case number, the U.S. court docket number, and references to the Choctaw-Chickasaw Citizenship Court case number. There are also two lists of cases heard by the U.S. Court for the Central District. One is arranged numerically by case number and the other is listed alphabetically by the name of the first person listed in the appeal. Arranged by type of action taken by the court. The names within each list are arranged in rough alphabetical order by surname.

Indexes to Applicants, 1900–1906

Indexes to applications for enrollment under various acts of Congress, including Choctaws applying under the act of 31 May 1900; Choctaw and Chickasaw freedmen testifying at Atoka and Colbert between 4 and 16 June 1900; Choctaw and Chickasaw applicants under the act of 1 July 1902; Choctaw children applying after 25 September 1902; Choctaws also enrolled as Cherokees; Choctaw and Chickasaw applicants listed on rejected and doubtful enrollment cards; and Choctaws and Chickasaws found on earlier rolls who had not applied for enrollment. Each index generally provides only a reference to the enrollment cards. Arranged by type of application. Entries within each index are arranged alphabetically by surname.

Lists of Chickasaw Applicants, 1899–1902

Lists of applicants for enrollment by the Dawes Commission as Chickasaws, persons listed on tribal rolls who had not applied for enrollment, persons admitted by U.S. courts, and persons denied by the Dawes Commission. There are a few copies of marriage certificates and other documents submitted as evidence in enrollment proceedings. Some of the lists are annotated with enrollment numbers. Arranged in rough chronological order by the date compiled.

Lists of Choctaw Applicants, 1899–1902

Lists of applicants or potential applicants for enrollment by the Dawes Commission as Choctaws. There are lists of "Choctaws on the 1896 roll—unenrolled by the Dawes Commission," "Choctaws not having appeared before the Dawes Commission by 28 October 1899," "applicants admitted by the Dawes Commission," and "parties on Choctaw cards who may be on Cherokee Cards." The information given in the lists generally includes the person's name, Dawes Commission enrollment number, and a reference to one of the earlier Choctaw rolls used to determine eligibility for enrollment. Arranged in rough chronological order by the date compiled.

Lists of Pending Applications, 1902–1905

Lists of names of applicants whose applications were pending at the time the lists were compiled. The information given for each applicant includes name, age, sex, and enrollment card number. There are separate lists for Choctaws by blood, Chickasaws by blood, Choctaw freedmen, and Chickasaw freedmen. Within each list, the names are arranged numerically by enrollment card number.

Dockets of Special Enrollment Cases, 1905–1907

There is a separate docket for each type of case. Entries within each docket are arranged numerically by case number assigned chronologically by the date the case was opened. The information given for each case includes the names of all applicants, names of attorneys, a chronological summary of papers filed and proceedings held, the decision of the commission, actions taken by the secretary of the interior, and references to related cases.

Record of Decisions, 1902–1904, 1906–1907

A record of decisions on enrollment applications made by the commission and forwarded to the secretary of the interior for approval. The information given for each decision includes the names of the applicants, enrollment card number, date of decision, action taken by the secretary of the interior, and date of notification to the applicant. There are separate volumes for

Choctaws and Chickasaws. Within each volume, entries are in rough chronological order by date of decision.

Records of the Choctaw-Chickasaw Citizenship Court

Section 31 of an act of Congress of 1 July 1902 (32 Stat. 641) established a Choctaw-Chickasaw Citizenship Court and authorized either tribe to file a bill of equity in the Citizenship Court to seek the annulment of the decisions made by the U.S. courts in Indian Territory under the act of 10 June 1896. Persons involved in those judgments were required to institute proceedings in the Choctaw-Chickasaw Citizenship Court to regain enrollment. Cases originating in the U.S. Court for the Central District of Indian Territory were heard by the Citizenship Court at South McAlester, and cases from the Southern District were heard at Tishomingo.

The Citizenship Court heard 256 cases involving more that 3,400 people and admitted 161 to citizenship. The case files of the court are still in the custody of the Muskogee Area Office of the Bureau of Indian Affairs.

Lists of Claimants, 1902

The information given for each person claiming citizenship includes name, sex, age, degree of Indian blood, Dawes enrollment card number, and some remarks relating to decisions of the Citizenship Court. Some of the lists described under "Lists of Persons Involved in Appeals to U.S. Courts, 1900" have been annotated with case numbers from the Citizenship Court. There are separate lists for Choctaws and Chickasaws. Within each list, the names are arranged alphabetically by surname.

Index to Dockets, 1903

There is one index to the South McAlester docket, one index to the Tishomingo docket, and one consolidated index to both dockets. The information given for each person involved in a case before the Citizenship Court is the case number and the Dawes enrollment card number.

General Dockets, 1903–1904

There is one docket for cases heard at South McAlester and one docket for cases heard at Tishomingo. Entries within each docket are arranged numerically by case number assigned chronologically by the date the case was opened; indexed by surname of principal party. Information given for each case includes the names of all parties involved, names of attorneys, nature of the case, and a chronological summary of papers filed and proceedings held.

Appearance Dockets, 1902–1904

There is a separate docket for cases heard at South McAlester and Tishomingo. Entries within each docket are arranged numerically by case number assigned chronologically by the date the case was opened; indexed by the surname of the principal party. Information given for each case includes the names of all parties involved, the names of attorneys, and a summary of the orders, writs, and other documents filed with the court. The summaries in these dockets are more detailed than the summaries contained in the dockets described previously under "General Dockets, 1903–1904."

Case Files, 1902–1904

Original papers filed in proceedings held by the Citizenship Court including briefs, memorandums of argument submitted by attorneys for the Choctaw and Chickasaw nations, and opinions of the court. The majority of the cases were heard at South McAlester. Arranged by docket number assigned in chronological order by the date the case was opened.

Records Relating to the Identification of Mississippi Choctaws

The Dawes Commission was required by an act of Congress to investigate the right of the Mississippi Choctaws to enrollment and allotment. The commission received 24,634 applications from all over the United States before the deadline of 25 March 1903.

Lists of Claimants under the Treaty of 1830

Manuscript copies of lists of persons who remained in Mississippi under article 14 of the treaty of 1830 and claimed land. Each list generally includes the claimant's name, date of application, and the legal description of the land claimed. Some lists have been annotated with Dawes enrollment numbers and enrollment card numbers. Arranged alphabetically by surname.

Index and Record of Testimony, 1899

Copies of an index to Mississippi Choctaw applicants who appeared before the commission in 1899 in Carthage, Philadelphia, and Decatur, Mississippi, and typed transcripts of the testimony given by the applicants. Arranged alphabetically by surname of the applicant.

Indexes to Field Cards

Index to enrollment cards. The only information provided is the field number of the applicant's enrollment card. Arranged alphabetically by surname of applicant.

Indexes to Applicants, 1902–1906

Indexes to applicants for enrollment under various acts of Congress. The indexes include the following categories: identified and rejected; rejected and reviewed by the secretary of the interior; decisions during the year ending 30 June 1903; applications for children whose parents were rejected; and newborn and minor children. The indexes generally provide only a reference to the applicant's enrollment card number and occasionally an enrollment number. Arranged alphabetically by surname of applicant.

Decisions of the Commission, 1902–1904

Decisions of the commission on applications for identification as Mississippi Choctaws. The decision generally reviews the facts of the application. Arranged chronologically by date of decision. The first volume contains an index to all applicants covered by the decisions.

Roll of Identified Mississippi Choctaws, 1905

List of persons who were identified as Mississippi Choctaws. The information provided for each person includes enrollment number and enrollment card number. The names on the roll are arranged by enrollment card number; indexed by surname.

Lists of Identified Full-Blood Mississippi Choctaws

Information given for each person includes enrollment card number, age, sex, post office address, county or parish of residence, and date of removal to the Choctaw Nation. The lists have been annotated to indicate persons who were removed at government expense, refused to remove, could not be located, or died prior to removal to the Choctaw Nation. Arranged alphabetically by surname.

Lists of Persons Removed, 1904

List of persons identified as Mississippi Choctaws who were removed from Mississippi and Louisiana at government expense, and a list of persons who were identified but refused to remove. The information given for each person includes age, sex, post office address, county or parish of residence, and date of removal or identification. Names of persons who were removed are arranged alphabetically. Names of persons who refused to remove are arranged numerically by identified roll number.

Records Relating to Creek Citizenship

List of Applicants, 1895–1896

List of applicants considered by the Creek Citizenship Commission in 1895 and 1896. The information given for each applicant includes type of citizenship claimed, date of application, date of judgment, decision rendered, and a reference to a "Record Book." The list has been annotated with the field numbers of Dawes enrollment cards. Arranged alphabetically by surname.

Citizenship Commission Docket, 1895

A record of cases heard by the Citizenship Commission. The information given for each case includes the names of all persons involved and occasionally a reference to the action taken by the Citizenship Commission. Arranged numerically by case number assigned chronologically by the date the case was opened and indexed by surname of applicant.

Record Books, 1885–1888, 1895–1896

Record of actions taken by the tribal Citizenship Commission on applications for citizenship. The information given for each case generally includes the text of the application, transcripts of testimony, and the commission's recommendation. There are occasional references to the docket described under "Citizenship Commission Docket, 1895." Part of the record was prepared on unbound printed forms ("Census of the Non-Citizens of the Muskogee Nation"). There is a list of persons that contains the person's age and a description of his or her property. Arranged in rough numerical order by case number assigned in chronological order by the date the case opened.

Lists of Admitted Applicants, 1902

Lists of persons admitted to citizenship by the Dawes Commission or the U.S. Court for the Northern District of Indian Territory. The list gives only the person's name and Dawes Commission case number. Some of the lists have been annotated with field numbers of Dawes enrollment cards. Arranged alphabetically by surname of applicant.

Indexes to Unenrolled Creeks, 1900

Creeks on the authenticated roll of 1890 and Creeks on the authenticated roll of 1895 who had not been enrolled by the Dawes Commission as of 15 August 1900. Information given for each person includes town of residence and the roll numbers from the 1890 and 1895 rolls. Arranged alphabetically by surname.

List of Unenrolled Creeks

A list of the names of Creeks who appeared on various tribal rolls but had not been enrolled by the Dawes Commission. The only information given is the person's name.

Miscellaneous Indexes, 1902–1906

Indexes to various enrollment categories, including citizens by blood, freedmen, minors, and newborns. The indexes generally provide only the enrollee's enrollment number or enrollment card number. Arranged alphabetically by surname of enrollee.

Lists of Applicants, 1900–1907

Lists of Creeks whose names appear on various tribal rolls and applicants for whom birth or death affidavits were submitted. Some of the lists have been annotated with enrollment card numbers. Arranged alphabetically by surname.

Index to Freedmen Enrollment Cards, 1898

Index to the "Old Series" of freedmen enrollment cards. Arranged alphabetically by surname of enrollee.

Enrollment Cards ("Old Series Cards"), 1898

Original enrollment cards prepared from the authenticated 1895 Creek census. Each card contains the names of the members of a family group and each person's age, sex, degree of Indian blood, post office address, district or town of residence, 1895 payroll number, and relationship to the head of the family group. The card also includes remarks about names used on earlier rolls, actions taken by the Dawes Commission, and references to the field numbers of the enrollment cards. Arranged numerically by card number.

Record of Enrollment

A record prepared on a printed paper form similar to the enrollment cards. The form contains the names of all members of a family group and remarks about actions taken by the Dawes Commission. The field numbers on these cards do not match the numbers on the enrollment cards. Arranged numerically by field number.

Records Relating to Seminole Citizenship

Index to Newborns, 1905

Persons enrolled under the act of Congress of 3 March 1905. The only information given is the person's enrollment number and enrollment card number. Arranged alphabetically by enrollee's surname.

Enrollment Schedules, 1900

Schedules prepared on printed forms of the names of persons enrolled as "Seminole Citizens by Blood" and "Seminole Freedmen." The information given for each person includes age, sex, band name, roll number from the 1897 Seminole census, post office address, and parents' names and 1897 enrollment numbers. Arranged numerically by enrollment card number.

Indian Census Rolls, 1885–1940

These are census rolls usually submitted each year by agents or superintendents in charge of Indian reservations, as required by an act of 4 July 1884 (23 Stat. 98). The data on the rolls varies to some extent but usually includes the Indian and/or English name of the person, roll number, age or date of birth, sex, and relationship to head of family. Beginning in 1930, the rolls also show the degree of Indian blood, marital status, ward status, place of residence, and sometimes other information. For certain years—including 1935, 1936, 1938, and 1939—only supplemental rolls of additions and deletions were compiled.

There is not a census for every reservation or group of Indians for every year. Only persons who maintained a formal affiliation with a tribe under federal supervision are listed on these census rolls.[36]

The researcher will find many census rolls listed under particular agencies, and some of these are duplicates of census records found in this group. Often, however, the agent retained a "working copy" of a census roll upon which he penciled-in comments concerning a particular individual or family. It is worth the extra time to consult the agency copy and the copy that was sent to the bureau in Washington, D.C.

Muskogee Area Office

The Muskogee Area Office was established in 1948 to administer Bureau of Indian Affairs business concerning the Cherokee (including Delaware and Shawnee), Chickasaw, Choctaw, Creek, and Seminole Indians of Oklahoma. Until 1874, there had been agencies for the individual tribes (the agencies for the Choctaws and Chickasaws, however, were consolidated). The Union Agency was established in 1874 for all five tribes. Until 1898, the tribes largely governed themselves. In 1893, the Commission to the Five Civilized Tribes (Dawes Commission) was established. The Curtis Act of 1898 provided for the preparation of tribal rolls and the making of allotments by the commission. The act also created the positions of inspector for Indian Territory and superintendent of schools. In 1905, the commission was reduced to a single commissioner, and in 1907, the position of inspector was combined with that of commissioner. The Union Agency and the commission were combined in 1914 to form the Five Civilized Tribes Agency, which was absorbed by the Muskogee Area Office in 1948.

The records from 1835 to 1952 include letters sent by the Choctaw and Chickasaw Agency in 1867 and from 1870 to 1873; account books of the Union Agency, 1876 to 1878; Choctaw national treasurer, 1868 to 1877, and Creek Nation, 1905 to 1911; journals of the House of Kings, Creek Nation, 1895 to 1897 and 1899; general records of the Union Agency and Five Civilized Tribes Agency; records of the tribal enrollments; census rolls dating from 1852; and case files for individual Indians. Fiscal records include money files for individual Indians, current accounts and other accounts, applications for per-capita payments, and annuity and other payrolls.[37]

The Muskogee Area Office at Anadarko, Oklahoma, administers Bureau of Indian Affairs programs for the following agencies: Ardmore, Okmulgee, Osage, Miami, Tahlequah, Talihina, and Wewoka.[38]

Ardmore Agency Records

Census Reports on Living Enrollees, 1908–1945

A record prepared on printed forms of "Living Members of the Five Civilized Tribes Owning Restricted Indian Allotted Land, 30 June 1927." The information contained on the form includes the individual's name, Dawes enrollment number, tribe, degree of Indian blood, age, sex, ability to read and write English, schools attended, marital status, health, occupation, legal description of land owned, and an opinion as to the person's competency. There are also some census reports compiled as of 30 June 1926 and in 1930 that provide similar information.

The records include some correspondence between the agency and the field clerk pertaining to the completion of the forms and some photographs of Indians and their homes. The reports appear to include only Indians living in Carter, Garvin, Love, and Murray counties. Arranged alphabetically by first letter of the enrollee's surname.

Records of the Office at Vinita

Census Reports on Living Enrollees, 1927–1930

A record prepared on printed forms of "Living Members of the Five Civilized Tribes Owning Restricted Indian Allotted Land, 30 June 1927." The information contained on the form includes the individual's name, Dawes enrollment number, tribe, degree of Indian blood, age, sex, ability to read and write English, schools attended, marital status, health, occupation, legal description of land owned, and an opinion as to the person's competency. Arranged alphabetically by first letter of the enrollee's surname.

Chickasaw Nation Records[39]

An agreement between the Chickasaws and Choctaws signed at Doaksville on 17 January 1837 (11 Stat., 573) permitted the Chickasaws to settle in the Choctaw Nation with all the rights of Choctaw citizens. A further provision created an area to be set aside as the Chickasaw District, the land to be held in common by the two tribes. Residents of the district were to have equal representation in the Choctaw General Council and were to be governed by the laws of the Choctaw Nation.

This arrangement proved to be unsatisfactory for the Chickasaws. In 1855, another treaty was signed (11 Stat., 611) giving the Chickasaws the unrestricted right of self-government and defining the boundaries of the Chickasaw Nation. In 1856 and 1857, constitutions were adopted, the government being organized into three departments. The executive authority was vested in the office of governor and the legislative power resided in a senate and house of representatives. A supreme court was established as well as district and county courts. This form of government was retained until the advent of statehood for Oklahoma.

The original counties of the Chickasaw District were Panola, Wichita, Caddo, and Perry. When the Chickasaw Nation proper was organized under the treaty of 1855, the country was again divided into four counties called Panola, Pickens, Tishomingo, and Pontotoc.

On 23 April 1897, the Chickasaws, under the Atoka Agreement, consented to the provisions of allotment of their lands in severalty.

Chickasaw Annuity Roll, 1878

List of Chickasaws registered in Panola, Pickens, Pontotoc, and Tishomingo counties in Chickasaw Nation and Masholatubby and Pushmatahal districts in Choctaw Nation for the annuity payment of 1878. Contains names of head of family, indication of wife, number of children, total number in family, and name of person receiving payment. Arranged by consecutive numbers.

Chickasaw Annuity Roll, 1878

List of persons registered in Masholatubby District for Chickasaw Annuity of 1878 resulting from the Leased District claim. Contains unidentified number, name, number of men, women, and children, and total number in family. Arranged alphabetically by county and then alphabetically by surname.

Chickasaw Census Roll, 1890

Census rolls of Pickens and Pontotoc counties in the Chickasaw Nation. Contains names of heads of families, indication of wives, post office addresses, ages of heads of families, the number of male and female children, an indication of whether the person is Chickasaw or Choctaw by blood or marriage, whether a U.S. citizen, state Negro, Indian Negro, or intruder, and total number in family. Arranged by county, then not arranged.

Chickasaw Payroll, 1893

Payroll of individuals in the Chickasaw Nation. Includes Maytubby's roll of 1893 and Iishatubby's roll of 1893. Includes family number, names, ages, number in family, and Checkmark for payment. Notations include Dawes card number, dead, full payment, and dates. One list is arranged consecutively by family groups. Another list is arranged alphabetically by surname.

Chickasaw Census, 1896

List of Chickasaws in the Chickasaw Nation, and those residing in the Choctaw Nation. Contains names of head of family (both parents) and children, ages, sex, whether Chickasaw by blood or intermarriage, date of intermarriage, and remarks. Remarks consist primarily of "married to . . ."

Chickasaw Census Index, 1897

Contains name and page number in census roll. Arranged alphabetically by individual's surname, then by county.

Chickasaw Census, 1897

List of Chickasaws registered within Chickasaw and Choctaw nations. Separate lists for intermarried whites and doubtful citizens within each county. List of names from 1893 Chickasaw roll that were not on the 1896 Chickasaw roll. Contains name and census card number. Arranged alphabetically by county, and numerically by district in Choctaw Nation.

Census and Citizenship Records

Documents concerning census, 1896; letters and documents concerning citizenship, 1861–1907; 1818 census; 1890 census of Pickens County and Tishomingo County; Choctaws in the Chickasaw Nation, 1896; journals of the Citizenship Committee and Court of Claims, 1889–95; proceedings of the Investigation Committee, 1893; records of the Chickasaw Commission, 1896; Dawes Commission citizenship cases, 1896–1904; incompetent record and list of original claimants, 1839–90; journal of the Commission on Incompetent Funds, 1889–90; incompetent fund records, 1889–1890; evidence book, 1889–90; competent and incompetent roll; Chickasaw per capita, 1889–90.

Records of the Executive Department, Senate and House of Representatives

Constitutions, acts, and laws, 1848–1901; senate journals, 1860–1902; house of representatives, 1866–94; journals of the house of representatives, 1894–1909; lists of national, district, and county officers, 1856–1905; official and unofficial papers of the Executive Department; Chickasaw tribal officers, Cyrus Harris and D.H. Johnston, 1856–1936.

Court Records

Panola County, 1878–94; Pickens and Wichita counties, 1849–81; Pickins County, 1864–1906; Pontotoc County, 1884–1904; district court, unidentified county, 1891–92; Tishimingo County, 1866–1906; supreme court, district court, attorney generals' reports and other records, 1856–1907.

School Records

Reports and minutes of the School Committee, 1872–1905; attendance and financial records, 1890–1902; letters and documents concerning academies, 1867–1928.

Permit Records

Permits to noncitizens, 1868–97; taxes, permits to noncitizens, 1874–1906; Chickasaw permits, 1878–1904; traders, 1889–1902; doctors, 1894–1902.

Financial Records

National treasurer and auditor, 1858–1902; financial records of the national treasurer and auditor, 1884–98.

Land Use and Revenue

Taxes, special national agent, land, agricultural leases, cattle, hay, timber, minerals, roads, railroads, ferries, telephones, and town sites, 1878–1909.

Letters Sent and Received and Other Documents, 1873–1919

Okmulgee Agency—Creek

The Creek Nation in Indian Territory was composed of the Upper and Lower Creek divisions, which were not fully united until 1867, when the Muskogee Nation was established with a written constitution and code of laws that remained in force until 1906. Under the constitution, a principal chief and a second chief were elected by popular vote every four years. The legislature, called the National Council, consisted of the House of Kings and the House of Warriors. These bodies met each year in regular session at the national capital. The judicial system included a supreme court and courts for each of the nation's six districts. The districts were Coweta, Muskogee (originally called Arkansas District), Eufaula, Wewoka, Deep Fork, and Okmulgee.

There was considerable opposition to allotment in severalty among the Creeks, and an agreement concluded with the Dawes Commission on 27 September 1897 was opposed by the chief and rejected by the National Council. This agreement was amended and, in 1897, became Section 30 of the Curtis Act. A further agreement was reached providing for the allotment of 160 acres to every tribe member, including freedmen, and for the dissolution of the tribal government on or before 4 March 1906.[40]

Creek Nation Records[41]

Creek Old Settlers Roll, 1857

Contains the name of the head of each household and the names of the other members, the amount each received, the total amount paid to the family, and the payee's mark. Arranged by town and then by family group.

Creek Payrolls, 1858–1859

Contains the name of the head of the family and the names of the other family members, the amount each received, and some remarks. Arranged by town and then by family.

Creek Payroll, 1867

Arranged by town and then by family group. Contains payee's name, amount received, and mark.

Index to Creek Freedmen, 1869

The index provides a page reference to an unidentified volume. The page numbers do not match the copy of the Dunn Roll of 1869. Arranged alphabetically by surname.

Payroll of Creek Freedmen and Index (Dunn Roll), 1869

The payroll contains the payee's name, amount received, and mark. The index contains the payee's roll number. Arranged by district. Index is arranged alphabetically by given name.

Creek Census, 1890

Census rolls of the following towns compiled during 1890: Arbeka (Deep Fork), Arkansas (doubtful), Kialachee, Arbeka (doubtful), Northfork (colored), Tuckabache (partial); typed lists for Arbeka, Alabama, Cussetah, Coweta, North Fork (colored), Concharty, Hutcherchuppa, Tucabache, Cussetah, Thlopthlocco, Tuckabatchee, and Weogufke. The rolls contain only an individual's name and, in a few cases, an amount of money received (presumably in 1891). Arranged by town and then by family group.

Annuity Roll, 1891

Receipt roll for a per-capita payment in 1891. Contains payee's name, amount received, mark, signature of witnesses, and date of payment. The roll has been annotated with Dawes enrollment card numbers. Arranged alphabetically by town and then by family group.

Supplemental Annuity Roll

Contains payee's name, amount received, mark, names of witnesses, and date of payment. The roll has been annotated with Dawes enrollment card numbers. Arranged alphabetically by town and then by family group.

Creek Census Roll (Omitted Roll), 1891

The roll contains an individual's name, the roll number, and the notation "O" for omitted and "NB" for newborn. Arranged roughly alphabetically by town and then by family group.

Creek Census Roll, 1891

A manuscript list of "Citizens Not Enrolled and their Respective Towns" that was apparently prepared by the clerk of the Special Committee of the National Council, which was established to identify individuals who did not participate in the 1891 per-capita payment and children born after 3 April 1891. The roll contains an individual's name, the notation "omitted" or "newborn," and, occasionally, remarks concerning actions of the Special Committee. Arranged by town.

Creek Census, 1893

A manuscript of individuals who apparently were not citizens of the Creek Nation but were living in the nation. The list, which is on a printed form titled "Census of the Non-Citizens of the Muskogee Nation Under Act of Council, 6 Nov. 1893," is incomplete. Arranged by family group.

Creek Census, 1895

Manuscript census rolls submitted by the Special Committee on Census Rolls to the National Council for approval between 31 May and 6 June 1895. There are rolls for the following towns: Alabama, Arbeka, Arbeka (Deep Fork), Arkansas ("colored"), Artussce, Big Spring, Canadian ("colored"), Coweta, Cussehta, Conchart, Euchee, Eufaula (Canadian), Eufaula (Deep Fork), Fish Pond, Greenleaf, Hickory Ground, Hillabee (Canadian), Hitchite, Hutchechuppa, Kechapataka, Kialigee, Little River Tulsa, Lochapoka, North Fork ("colored"), Okchiye, Okfuskee (Deep Fork), Okfusky (Canadian), Osoche, Pukken, Tallehassee, Quassarty no. 1 and no. 2, Thlewaithle, Thlopthlocco, Tokpofke, Tuckabatchee, Tullahassochee, Tulmochusee, Tulsa (Canadian), Tulwathlocco, Tuskegee, Weogufkee, Wewoka, Doubtful. Arranged by town.

Creek Census, 1895

A manuscript census roll of Creek citizens. The roll contains an individual's name and roll number. The roll has been annotated with card numbers of Dawes enrollment cards. Arranged by town.

Creek Census (Supplemental Roll), 1895

A list of persons who were omitted from the 1895 payroll and "newborns." The list was apparently prepared by the Special Committee of the National Council. The roll contains an individual's name, the name of the individual's mother and her 1895 roll number, and the designation "New Born" or "Omitted." Arranged by town.

Creek Census (Omitted Roll), 1895

List of individuals who were newborn or who may have been omitted from the 1895 payroll, which was submitted to the National Council by the Special Committee on Census Rolls on 4 December 1895. The roll contains an individual's name, the name of the individual's mother and father, 1895 census roll number, and the designation "New Born" or "Omitted." The roll numbers in these rolls match the roll numbers in the supplemental roll. Arranged by town.

Creek Payrolls, 1895

Payrolls for a per-capita payment based on the 1895 census. There are payrolls for the following towns: Alabama, Arbeka, Arbeka (Deep Fork), Arbekoche, Arkansas, Artussee, Big Springs, Broken Arrow, Canadian ("colored"), Cheyaha, Coweta, Cussehta, Concharte, Euchee, Eufaula (Deep Fork), Hitchette, Hutchechuppa, Kechopatake, Kialigee, Lochapoka, North Fork ("colored"), Nutaka, Okchiye, Okfuske (Canadian), Okfuske (Deep Fork), Osoche, Pukon, Tulahassee, Quassarte no. 1 and no. 2, Thlewarthlee, Thlopthlocco, Tokpafka, Tuckabatchee, Tuladegee, Tulahassoche, Tulmochussee, Tulwathlocco, Tuskegee, Weogufkee, Wewoka. The roll contains each payee's name, the amount received, the signature of the payee and the witnesses, and the date of payment. The roll has been annotated with field numbers of Dawes enrollment cards and card numbers of the old series of Dawes enrollment cards. Arranged by town.

Colbert Census Roll of Creek Nation, 1896

Census rolls submitted by the Special Committee on Census Rolls to the National Council. There are rolls for the following towns: Arbeka (North Fork), Arbekochee, Arkansas ("colored"), Artussee, Big Spring, Canadian ("colored"), Concharty, Cussehta, Euchee, Eufaula (Canadian), Eufaula (Deep Fork), Fish Pond, Greenleaf, Hickory Ground, Kialigee, Little River Tulsa, Nuyaka, Okchiye, Okfuskee (Deep Forks), Osoche, Pakkon Tallahasse, Quassarte no. 1 and no. 2, Tallahassoche, Thlewathle, Thlopthlocco, Tokpofka, Tuckabache, Tulladegee, Tuskegee, Weogufke, Wewoka. Arranged by town.

Loyal Creek Payment Roll, 1904

Citizenship Commission Docket Book, 1895

Arranged by case number; includes an alphabetical index.

List of Applicants for Creek Citizenship, 1895–1896

Census and Citizenship Records

Letters and documents concerning census, 1832–1900; Okmulgee District, enrollment of Shawnee Indians, undated; census of noncitizens, undated; creek reservations under the treaty of 24 March 1832, entries 1–2,000; pension list, Muskogee Nation, 1872–73; 1892 census roll, Arkansas District; census of the town of Wagoner, 1894; list of noncitizen cattlemen and roll of Shawnee Indians, Deep Fork District, 1897; letters and documents concerning citizenship, 1874–1910; permit lists and citizenship records, 1880–1906; permit lists; citizenship applications; Creek freedmen; Creek per-capita payments, 1869–1904; letters and documents pertaining to per-capita payments, 1870–88; list of Civil War officers and record of issues to indigent refugee Creeks in the Chickasaw Nation, 1862–65; annuity payroll of Creeks who were orphans in 1832 or their heirs, 1883–89.

Records of the Creek National Council, House of Kings and House of Warriors

Journal of the House of Warriors, 1868–1903; journal of the House of Kings, 1882–95; records of the General Council, Creek Agency, 1861–62; acts and resolutions of the National Council, 1873–92; appropriation acts of the National Council, 1895–99; constitution and laws; undated and Creek miscellaneous documents, 1883–1909.

Supreme Court Records, 1870–1897

Court record book, 1884–98; records and documents, 1868–99; United States courts, 1871–1909; North Fork, Deep Fork, and Arkansas district courts, 1874.

District Court Records

Arkansas District courts, 1870–95; Muskogee District courts, 1876–98; Coweta District courts, 1877–95; Deep Fork District courts, 1872–96; Eufaula District courts, 1882–98; North Fork District courts, 1868–73; Okmulgee District courts, 1884–98; Wewoka District courts, 1871–97.

Osage Agency—Osage

The first historical notice of the Osages appears to have been by the French explorer Marquette, who located them on his map of 1673 on the Osage River. They were a warlike people, viewed with terror by the surrounding tribes, especially the Caddoans.

Under treaties of 1808, 1818, and 1825, the Osages ceded to the United States much of their land in Arkansas and all lands west of the Missouri River. Subsequent treaties further reduced their lands until their present reservation was established in the northeastern part of Oklahoma in 1870.[42]

Records of the Osage Indians

Osage Annuity Rolls, 1878–1909

Includes name of band, and the individual's name, relationship, age, sex.

Miami Agency

The Miami Agency, located at Miami, Oklahoma, has jurisdiction over the Shawnee, Miami, Seneca-Cayuga, Quapaw, and Ottawa tribes.[33]

Shawnee

The Shawnees were a leading tribe with settlements in South Carolina, Tennessee, Pennsylvania, and Ohio.

The Shawnees became known around 1670. At that time they lived in two main bodies at a considerable distance from each other—one in the Cumberland region of Tennessee and the other on the Savannah River in South Carolina. During the late-eighteenth century, the two main bodies united in Ohio. For about forty years, until the Treaty of Greenville in 1795, the Shawnees were almost constantly at war with the British and the Anglo Americans. After the death of Tecumseh, their most famous war chief, they lost their taste for war and began to move to their present locations. One group settled on a reservation in Kansas; another went to Texas to join a band of Cherokees. A third group settled on the Canadian River in Indian Territory, just south of the Quapaw Reserve, and are today known as the Absentee-Shawnee Tribe of Oklahoma. Another band that settled in eastern Oklahoma is today known as the Eastern Shawnee Tribe.[44]

Miami

The earliest recorded notice of this tribe was in 1658 by Gabriel Druillette, who called them Oumanik. Then living around the mouth of Green Bay, Wisconsin, they withdrew into the Mississippi Valley and were established there from 1657 to 1676. The French came into contact with them in 1668. Around 1671, the Miamis formed new settlements at the south end of Lake Michigan, where missions were established late in the seventeenth century, and on the Kalamazoo River in Michigan. The extent of territory they occupied a few years later suggests that when the whites first heard of them, the Miami Indians in Wisconsin formed but a part of the tribe, with other bodies already established in northeast Illinois and Indiana. Encroachments by the Potawatomi, Kickapoo, and other northern tribes drove the Miami out to the east, and they formed settlements on the Miami River in Ohio. They held this country until the peace of 1763, when they retired to Indiana. They took part in all the Indian wars in the Ohio Valley until the close of the War of 1812. Soon after, they began to sell their lands. By 1827, they had disposed of most of their holdings in Indiana and had agreed to move to Kansas. They later moved to Indian Territory, where the remnant still resides.[55]

Ottawa

A large party of Ottawas was first met by Champlain in 1615 near the mouth of the French River, Georgian Bay Region, Canada, which seems to have been the original location of the tribe in the historic period. They were generally counted as allies of the Huron and the French during the French and Indian War. As a result of conflicts with the Iroquois in the seventeenth century, the Ottawas emigrated westward and southwest, their location being on Lake Huron between Detroit and Saginaw Bay from around 1700.

Between 1785 and 1862, the Ottawas signed twenty-three different treaties with the United States. In 1833, they ceded all their land on the west shore of Lake Michigan and accepted a reservation in northeastern Kansas. Several bands of the Ottawa Tribe living in Ohio had ceded their lands to the government and moved to the Kansas reservation in 1832. After the Quapaw Treaty of 1857, they moved to Indian Territory. The main portion of Ottawa remained in scattered settlements in southern Michigan, though another portion continued to live in Canada with the Chippewa. The noted chief Pontiac was an Ottawa, and one of the principal events in the tribe's history was known as Pontiac's War, waged near Detroit in 1763.[46]

Quapaw

The Quapaws are a southwestern tribe. By a treaty signed in St. Louis, Missouri, 24 August 1818, the Quapaws ceded their lands south of the Arkansas River, except for a small territory between Arkansas Post and Little Rock extending inland to the Saline River. In 1824, the Quapaws signed a treaty ceding the rest of their land to the United States, and the tribe agreed to move to the country of the Caddo, where they were assigned a tract on the south side of the Red River. The river frequently overflowed its banks, destroying Quapaw crops. Soon the tribe was drifting back to its old country, now settled by whites. Finally, a treaty signed 13 May 1833 conveyed to the Quapaws 150 sections of land in the extreme southeastern part of Kansas and the northeastern part of Indian Territory, to which they agreed to move. On 23 February 1867, they ceded their lands in Kansas and the northern part of their lands in Indian Territory to the United States. Under the Allotment Act of 1887, the Quapaws objected to federal plans to allot each tribe member only eighty acres. They established their own program and allotted two hundred acres to each of the 247 members. This action was ratified by Congress in 1895.[47]

In 1865, a special agent was stationed on the river in northeastern Oklahoma, then Indian Territory, to care for the affairs of the Indian tribes living on their reservations east of the Neosho River and north of the Cherokee Nation. Some tribes had been residents since 1832. The Neosho Agency was the main agency and was located in Montgomery County, Kansas. In 1871 the Neosho Agency and the sub-agency were separated jurisdictionally, the latter being named the Quapaw Agency.[48]

Seneca-Cayuga[49]

The Senecas of the Quapaw Agency were formerly called the Seneca of Sandusky. Under treaty provisions with the United States in 1817, the Seneca of Sandusky were granted 40,000 acres on the east side of the Sandusky River in Ohio. By 1830, they had improved farms and schools for their children and were generally well advanced. Following the policy of removing the eastern Indians to the West, the government induced the Senecas to sell their Ohio lands and accept a new reserve north of the Cherokee Nation.

A band of the Seneca of Sandusky joined the Shawnee of Ohio, who had settled near Louistown in the latter part of the eighteenth century. At that time they were known as the mixed band of Seneca and Shawnee. By a treaty of 1831, the government induced them to sell their Ohio lands and accept a new reserve adjoining the Seneca of Sandusky in Indian Territory. Both the Seneca of Sandusky and the mixed Senecas and Shawnees moved to their new country in 1832. Like the other eastern tribes, they suffered many hardships during their journey. Protesting that the lands first assigned them were unfit for cultivation, they entered into a new treaty a short time after their arrival at the Seneca Agency. By the terms of the treaty, they were assigned a permanent reservation, beginning at the northeast corner of the Cherokee cession of 1828 and situated between the Neosho River and the Missouri boundary south of the Quapaw country. In 1881, a band of more than one hundred Cayugas from Canada and New York came to join their kin in Oklahoma.

Records of the Shawnee Indians

Shawnee-Cherokee census, 1896–1904.

Records of the Miami Indians

Census of Miami Indians in Indiana and elsewhere, 1881.

Annuity payment roll of Miami Indians of Indiana, 1895.

Records of the Quapaw Agency[50]

Census Records

Letters and documents, 1877–97; census and lists for the Cayuga, Miami, Modoc, New York, Nez Perce, Ottawa, Confederated Peoria, Potawatomi, Quapaw, Seneca, Eastern Shawnee, and Wyandot.

Vital Statistics and Related Material

Letters received and other documents, 1864–1901; allotments, births, citizenship, deaths, divorce, estates, guardianship, adoption of Indian children, indigent, insane, issues, marriages, pensions, per capita, police book, family relations, vital statistics, and Civil War.

Letters received, 1880–98.

Letterpress book, 1879–84.

Letters Sent and Received and Other Documents

Cayuga, 1871–98; Chippewa, Munsee, or Christian, 1872–1901; Citizen Potowatomi, 1863–89; Delaware, 1871–86; Kansas or Kaw, 1877–78; Miami, 1848–1908; New York Indians, 1874–88; Nez Perce, 1878–79; Oneida, 1876; Modoc Indians, 1873–86; Ottawa Indians, 1871–1901; Peoria and confederated tribes, 1854–1901; Ponca Indians, 1877–97; Seneca Indians, 1872–1901; Shawnee Indians, 1870–1901; Tonkawa Indians, 1883–84; and miscellaneous.

Schools and Churches

Miscellaneous schools, 1871–1908; churches, 1876–89.

Tahlequah Agency—Cherokee

In 1782, a group of Cherokees that had fought on the British side during the American Revolution petitioned the Spanish governor at New Orleans for permission to settle on the west side of the Mississippi within the Spanish territory. Permission was granted in 1794, and a group of Cherokees settled in the St. Francis River Valley in what is now southeastern Missouri. More Cherokees joined them over time.

During the winter of 1811 to 1812, the Cherokees moved en masse to the Arkansas region. Other Cherokees who decided to emigrate from the old nation periodically joined them in small groups.

With the treaty signed 8 July 1817 at Turkey Town, these emigrants received title to their lands. Under this treaty, the Cherokees ceded two large tracts of land and two smaller tracts of land east of the Mississippi River for an area of equal value in the West between the Arkansas and White rivers. As encouragement for others to remove, the treaty promised "to give all poor warriors who remove a rifle, ammunition, blanket, and brass kettle or beaver trap each, as full compensation for improvements left by them." The treaty further promised to compensate them for improvements, provide transportation, and provide subsistence for those who would agree to remove. Consequently, more than 1,100 Cherokees emigrated from the east to the west during 1818 and 1819.

By a treaty signed 6 May 1828, the Cherokees ceded their lands in present Arkansas for land in the present state of Oklahoma. No record exists of the estimated two thousand Cherokees who emigrated before 1817, but the rolls for those who removed under the treaties of 1817 and 1828 are available. These records include a register of Cherokees who wished to remain in the East, 1817 to 1819 (two volumes); emigration registers of Indians who wished to migrate, 1817 to 1838 (eighteen volumes); and applications for reservations, 1819.

The Treaty of New Echota, 29 December 1835, represented the final cession of all Cherokee lands east of the Mississippi River and the beginning of the forced migration of those remaining tribal members west on the Trail of Tears. Cherokees who had emigrated prior to 1835 became known as the Old Settler Cherokees.

Rolls of Cherokees Residing West of the Mississippi in Indian Territory

The 1851 Old Settler Roll

The 1851 payroll lists Old Settlers (Cherokees who moved to Indian Territory prior to December 1835) entitled to participate in a per capita payment. There were 3,273 persons enumerated on this roll, which is arranged by Cherokee district and grouped by family. Some persons who did not reside in the Cherokee Nation are listed as "Non-residents." 3,273 were enrolled and received $270.95. The "Old Settlers" filed a protest against the sum. The Supreme Court decided that the original "Old Settlers" or their heirs would receive an additional $159.10 per share in the 1896 "Old Settler" payment.

Drennen Roll, 1852

A receipt roll for a per-capita payment made to Cherokees living in the west who removed as a result of and after the Treaty of 1835. The roll was prepared by John Drennen and contains the payee's name, the amount received by the head of each household, and the name of the witness. Arranged by Cherokee district and then by family group.

Drennen Roll Index, 1852

This index contains the individual's surname, given name, and a page number reference to the receipt roll. Arranged alphabetically by first two letters of the name.

Complete List of Names of Emigrant Cherokees Who Drew Emigrant Money in 1852

Flint, Sequoyah, and Illinois districts.

Tompkins Roll of 1867

A census roll of Cherokees residing in the Cherokee Nation taken by H. Tompkins. The census roll provides the name, age, and sex of the individual. It also indicates if the individual is "White," "Half-breed," or "Colored." Arranged by Cherokee district.

Tompkins Roll Freedmen Indices, 1897

Indexes of the freedmen listed by H. Tompkins in 1867. One index is alphabetical by surname, and the other is alphabetical by given name. The indexes provide the name, page number of the roll, and the district of residence. Arranged alphabetically by the first two letters of the name.

Receipt Roll for Per-Capita Payment, 1874

Lists head of household, family members, total in family, amount paid, to whom paid, and name of witness.

Lists of Delaware, Shawnee, and North Carolina Cherokees, 1867–1881

Lists of Rejected Claimants, 1878–1880

Arranged by type of decision and thereunder by case number. List of persons who appeared before the Cherokee Commission on Citizenship and whose claims were rejected. The list provides the name of the claimant and the decision rendered by the commission. The notation "Colored" exists in the margin preceding some of the names.

Wallace Roll of Cherokee Freedmen, Including Orphan Roll, 1880

Cherokee Census of 1880

On 3 December 1879, the Cherokee National Council authorized a census and a per-capita payment for purchase of "bread stuffs." This census later became very important to the Dawes Commission in preparing the final rolls. Any Indian or intermarried white listed on this census was accepted without challenge by the Dawes Commission. A notation on the census cards prepared by the commission showed the individuals' locations and the name by which each was enrolled on the 1880 census.

The census was arranged by district within the Cherokee Nation and then by six schedules: (1) Cherokee citizens, including native, adopted white, Shawnee, Delaware, and freedmen; (2) orphans under age sixteen; (3) those rejected; (4) those whose citizenship claims were pending; (5) intruders (unauthorized white squatters on Cherokee land); and (6) those living in the Cherokee Nation by permit granted by the Cherokee Council. Each schedule gives the individual's name by family group, age, race, occupation, sex, and roll number.

Cherokee Census Index, 1880

A printed index to the 1880 Cherokee Census, which contains the name, roll number, nativity, age, and sex of each individual. The volume also includes lists of Shawnee and Delaware who were residing in the Cherokee Nation, North Carolina Cherokee who removed to the Cherokee Nation, and persons admitted or readmitted to citizenship by the Cherokee National Council. There is also an orphan roll, arranged by Cherokee district and thereunder roughly alphabetically.

Lipe Receipt Roll, 1880

A per-capita receipt roll by D.W. Lipe. The roll provides the name of the payee, the number in the family, the total amount paid to the family, the name of the person receiving the payment, and the name of the witness. Arranged by Cherokee district and then by roll number.

Receipt Roll of Per-Capita Payment, 1881

Lists head of household and family members, nationality, and remarks.

Lists of North Carolina Cherokees Who Removed to the Cherokee Nation West, 1881

Lists roll number, family number, English name, Cherokee name (in Cherokee), age, sex, nationality, residence (in Cherokee), and remarks.

Roll of North Carolina Immigrants Allowed Per-Capita Payment, 1881

Lists name of head of household and family members.

Payroll by Right of Cherokee Blood, 1883

Lists roll number, name of head of household and family members, age, and remarks.

Lists of North Carolina Cherokees, 1882–1883

Lists name of head of household, family members, nationality, and age.

The Cherokee Census of 1883 and 1886

On 19 May 1883, the Cherokee National Council authorized another census upon which to base a per-capita payment of monies received from leased land. Like the 1880 census, this census is arranged by districts and includes an orphan's roll, those in nation prisons, and a supplemental roll that shows the name and age of each individual.

A receipt roll shows the individual's name and roll number, the total number in the household, the total amount paid each household, the name of the person receiving the payment, and the name of a witness to the payment.

More money was made available from the same source in 1886 and was distributed after another census. In addition to the information given in the 1883 payment roll, the 1886 roll identifies individuals by their relationship to the head of household.

Supplemental Roll of Those Left Off the Rolls of 1880 Per-Capita Payment, 1884

Lists heads of household, family members, and remarks.

Citizenship Commission Docket Book, 1880–1884

Docket of the Citizenship Commission of the Cherokee Nation, which contains the names of claimants, nature of the claim, and the decision of the commission.

The 1890 Cherokee Census

This census contains the most complete information of any census for the Cherokee Nation. It is arranged by district and includes six schedules: (1) native Cherokees and adopted whites, Shawnees, and Delawares; (2) orphans under age sixteen; (3) those denied citizenship by the Cherokee authorities; (4) those whose claims to citizenship were pending; (5) intruders; and (6) whites living in the Cherokee Nation by permit. The 1890 census's 105 columns include such detailed information as farm improvements, products, livestock, etc.

The 1893 Cherokee Census

This census distinguishes Cherokee citizens by blood, adopted whites, freedmen, Shawnees, Delawares, intermarried persons, and Creeks. Arranged by district, this census provides the individual's name, age, sex, admission reference, name of guardian, place of residence, and name of person providing identification.

The Wallace Roll of Cherokee Freedmen, 1890–1893

A copy of a Cherokee freedmen census made in 1890 of those eligible to receive a per-capita payment. The roll was prepared by Special Agent John Wallace and was based on an 1883 census of Cherokee freedmen. The roll includes lists of authenticated freedmen who appear on the 1883 roll, individuals who died between 1883 and 1890, individuals admitted by Wallace, and "Free Negroes." The volume also contains a list of individuals whose rights were questioned by the commissioner of Indian affairs and supplemental lists of individuals who were admitted by the secretary of the interior. The roll contains the individual's name, age, sex, and residence. The entries have been annotated with the enrollment numbers from the Clifton roll of Cherokee freedmen made in 1896 and, in some cases, with the enrollment numbers from the Dawes roll of 1907. The Wallace roll was set aside as fraudulent by a decree of 8 May 1895 of the United States Court of Claims and was never recognized by the Cherokee Nation. Arranged by enrollment number.

Cherokee Freedmen Roll Index, 1893

The index lists the individual's surname, given name, and district of residence. It also contains page number references to an 1893 roll. Arranged alphabetically by the first two letters of the surname.

Cherokee Freedmen Roll Index, 1890–1893

An index to the Wallace roll of Cherokee freedmen. The index lists the individual's roll number, district of residence, and a page number reference to the 1890 roll. Arranged alphabetically by last name.

The Starr Roll (1894)

On 3 March 1893, Congress passed an act that resulted in the sale of the Cherokee Outlet (land to the west of Cherokee Nation to which the Cherokees had claim before the organization of Oklahoma Territory) to the United States. A per-capita payment of $365.70 was made. E.E. Starr, treasurer of the Cherokee Nation, prepared the receipt roll, arranged by district and then by enrollment number. It contains the name of the head of household, the name of the person receiving payment, and the name of a witness to the transaction. An orphans roll is also included.

Cherokee Payroll Index, 1894 (Authenticated Roll of 1894)

This index lists the individual's name, roll number, and district of residence. It also contains page number references to the 1894 receipt roll (Starr roll). The roll number and names correspond with the names and roll numbers on the 1894 Cherokee census roll. Arranged alphabetically by surname.

Cherokee Census Roll, 1894

A census of the Cherokee Nation made in 1897. The roll is based on the 1894 payroll. The roll contains the individual's enrollment number, name, age, and sex. Under "remarks," the names of deceased parents and other names used on previous enrollments are listed. Arranged by Cherokee District and then by enrollment number.

Lists of Cherokee Children, 1895–1897

These lists contain the names of children born between 1895 and 1897, their dates of birth, and parents' names. Arranged by Cherokee district.

Old Settlers Roll, 1896

A receipt roll for a per-capita payment based on the 1851 Old Settlers Roll of the Western Cherokee (those removing prior to the Treaty of New Echota). The names of persons who were still living at the time of the payment are listed first, followed by the names of those who were deceased and the names of their heirs who were paid. This payment resulted from a decision of the U.S. Court of Claims made on 6 June 1893. The roll contains each payee's name, 1851 roll number, agency pay number, age, sex, amount received, post office address, signature, date of payment, and names of witnesses. The relations of heirs to the original payee is given. Information regarding guardianship, related correspondence files, and correction of names is provided under "remarks." There are also three versions of a supplemental list of original enrollees from the 1851 roll whose shares were not claimed. One version lists only the names of the heirs of the enrollees; the second version lists the names of the heirs of the individuals and the amount of payment they received; and the third version is a working copy. Arranged numerically by agency pay number.

Cherokee Census Roll, 1896

This census roll of citizens of the Cherokee Nation contains the individual's name, roll number, age, sex, precinct, proportion of blood or nativity, and place of birth. Arranged by Cherokee district and then by roll number.

The 1896 Payment Roll (Lipe Roll)

This payroll is based on the 1851 old settlers roll and is of major genealogical importance. The names of those still living in 1896 are listed first, followed by those who had died and their heirs and each heir's relationship. The payroll lists each payee's 1851 roll number, name, agency pay number, age, sex, amount received, and post office address.

Shawnee-Cherokee Census, 1896

This roll contains the names of Cherokee Shawnee who were entitled to participate in the distribution of funds to equalize a per-capita payment. The roll contains the individual's name, roll number, Cherokee number, age, sex, address, and names used on previous rolls. A notation was made after the names of individuals who were deceased. The roll includes two supplemental lists of Cherokee Shawnee entitled to funds and a list of persons "Omitted from Government Pay Rolls of the Cherokee Shawnee Tribe of Indians." Arranged roughly alphabetically by name.

Cherokee Freedmen Roll (Clifton Roll), 1896

List of Cherokee freedmen and their descendants prepared by a commission appointed by the secretary of the interior. The roll was based on testimony taken by the commission in the Cherokee Nation between 4 May and 10 August 1897. The list contains the individual's name, relationship to the head of the household, sex, age, and district of residence. There is a supplemental list of individuals whose claims to citizenship were rejected by the Cherokee Nation but approved by the commission. Arranged numerically by roll number.

Delaware Payroll, 1896

A list of persons entitled to funds to equalize a per-capita payment. The information given for each person includes name, census number, payroll number, age, amounts received in payments made in 1896, 1890, and 1894, name of person receiving payment, and names of witnesses. There are some remarks about deaths and relations to others on the list, and some names have been annotated with Dawes Commission enrollment numbers. Arranged alphabetically by first letter of surname.

Payment to Destitute Cherokees, 1902

Payment to Intermarried Whites, Cherokee Nation, 1909–1910

Cherokee Equalization Payment Rolls, 1910–1915

Cherokee Per Capita Payroll, 1912

Cherokee Citizenship

Lists of Rejected Claimants, 1878–1880

List of persons who appeared before the Cherokee Commission on Citizenship and whose claims were rejected. The list provides the name of the claimant and the decision rendered by the commission. The notation "Colored" exists in the margin preceding some of the names. Arranged by type of decision and then by case number.

Cherokee Citizenship Commission Docket Book, 1880–1884 and 1887–1889

List of Applicants Admitted to Citizenship, 1896

List of names of applicants admitted to citizenship in the Cherokee Nation by the Dawes Commission. The list contains the applicant's name, references to case numbers from the United States Court in Indian Territory, Dawes Commission file and card numbers, other names used by the applicant, and notations concerning applicants living outside Indian Territory. Arranged alphabetically by name.

Lists of Applicants for Cherokee Citizenship, 1896

This volume contains a list of names of applicants for citizenship in the Cherokee Nation under an act of congress of 10 June 1896. There are lists of applicants admitted to citizenship by the Dawes Commission, applicants rejected by the Dawes Commission but admitted by the U.S. courts in Indian Territory, and applicants admitted by the Dawes Commission but rejected by the U.S. courts. The information given in each list varies but generally includes the applicant's name, a reference to a Dawes case number, and a court case number. Arranged alphabetically by name.

District Records[51]

Canadian District

Court records, 1867–98.

Cooweescoowee District

Marriages, permits, wills and estates, 1858–98; Cherokee marriages, 1868–97; district estate records, 1875–97; permits to noncitizens, 1893–99; land records and estray property records, 1875–1914; Cherokee town sites, 1876–98; district circuit and supreme court records, 1868–95; Cherokee courts, 1857–98; divorce, 1890.

Delaware District

Marriages, 1867–96; Delaware district permits, 1868–95; Cherokee permits, 1886; district estates, 1867–98; district, circuit, and supreme court records, 1868–95; divorce, 1902; improvements, 1859–98; marks and brands, 1876–98; estray property, 1875–95.

Flint District

Estates, 1876–93; estray property, 1876–98; marks and brands, 1876–97; improvements, 1881–92; district supreme, circuit, and district court records, 1877–97; marriages, 1893.

Going Snake District

Marriages, 1880–98; estates, 1868–1904; improvements and estray property, 1880–98; district supreme, circuit, and district court records, 1876–98.

Illinois District

Marriages, estates, and permits, 1859–97; estates, 1876–98; permits, 1895–96; improvements, marks and brands, estray property, and district supreme, circuit, and district court records, 1865–98.

Saline District

Marriages, estates, permits, property improvements, estray property, and marks and brands, 1866–98; permits, 1876–97; district supreme, circuit, and district court records, 1872–98.

Sequoyah District

Marriages, estates, estray property, and property improvements, 1874–98; district supreme, circuit and district court records, 1876–98.

Tahlequah District

Marriages, estates, and permits, 1856–98; property improvements, estray property, and marks and brands, 1872–98; district supreme, circuit, and district court records, 1865–1904.

Documents Pertaining to Determination of Tribal Membership, 1870–1909

Cherokee Citizenship, 1841–1911

Letters Sent and Letters Received and Other Documents, 1829–1914

Unique Records Relating to the Cherokee Indians

Records Relating the Enrollment of Eastern Cherokees

These records deserve special attention. They are often referred to as the Guion Miller rolls. Guion Miller was appointed by the United States Court of Claims to determine who was eligible to participate in a fund awarded to persons who were Eastern Cherokees at the time of the treaties of 1835–36 and 1845 or their descendants. While the majority of this group was residing in Indian Territory at the time of Miller's commission, many were also residing in North Carolina. The title of this record group is misleading in that the researcher is led to believe that the records pertain only to the Eastern Cherokee Tribe of North Carolina. Miller submitted his report and roll on 28 May 1909 and a supplementary report in 1910.

The "Guion Miller Report and Exhibits, 1908–1910," in twenty-nine volumes, consists of ten volumes of transcripts of testimony, arranged chronologically; a report dated 5 January 1910 concerning exceptions to findings; a printed copy of the completed roll with two 1910 supplements; and copies of the Drennen, Chapman, and old settlers rolls of 1851–52, with a consolidated index for the Chapman and Drennen rolls and a separate index for the old settlers roll. The volumes are arranged numerically as parts of classified file "33931-11-053 Cherokee Nation," which also contains other pertinent records.

Between 1906 and 1909, more than 45,000 claimants submitted applications providing detailed information of their families. A typical application includes the applicant's English name, Indian name (if any), residence, date and place of birth, marriage status, name of husband or wife, parents' names, their places of birth and residence in 1851, and dates of death, names and dates of birth and death of brothers and sisters, names of paternal and maternal grandparents and their children, their places of birth and residence in 1851, and the name of the ancestor from whom they claimed to have descended.

Tahilina Agency—Choctaw

The Choctaw Nation in Indian Territory maintained its own constitutional government and records for many years in the nineteenth century and in limited form after 1906 and Oklahoma statehood. The Choctaw National Constitution was adopted on 3 June 1834. The government consisted of a principal chief, a general council composed of a senate and house of representatives, and a court system consisting of a supreme court and district courts. The nation was divided into three geographical and political districts. District One, Masholatubbe, consisted of Tobucksy, Gaines, Sans Bois, Skullyville, and Sugar Loaf counties. District Two, Apuckshunnubbee, consisted of Cedar, Nashoba, Towson, Boktuklo, Eagle, Wade, and Red River counties. District Three, Pushmataha, consisted of Atoka, Jacks Fork, Blue, Jackson, and Kiamichi counties. The district capitals were at Gaines, Alichi, and Mayhew. The national capital was at Tushkahomma for most of the years of the nation's existence.

Records of the Choctaw Indians[52]

Choctaws Paid by Chickasaws, Treaty of 22 June 1855

Contains names of individuals, their marks, identification of the individual as man, woman, or child, total number in the family, the amount of the individual share, and the total dollar amount per family. There are tallies in the middle and the bottom of each page and at the end of the county list and district list. The orphans list contains the names of individuals, names of the representatives for orphans, marks, the amount received per representative, the total amount received per orphan, and remarks. Remarks are primarily confined to "death after 4th installment." There are tallies on each page and at the end of the list.

Index to 1885 Choctaw Census

Contains individual's name, county of residence, age, and number in the census book for the county.

Choctaw Census, 1885

A census of Choctaw citizens living in Atoka, Blue, Boktoklo, Cedar, Eagle, Gains, Jacks Fork, Kiomitia, Nashoba, Red River, San Bios, Sckullyville, Sugar Loaf, Towson, Tobuksko, and Wade counties of the Choctaw Nation. The information given for each person includes name, age, sex, race (White, Indian, or Colored), occupation, and agricultural schedule. Arranged by county.

Choctaw-Chickasaw Freedmen Rolls, 1885

Contains names of persons admitted to citizenship, heads of families and children, sex and age group, nationality of parents, whether a previous owner of freed slaves, number of livestock, and acres of land in cultivation. Arranged by first, second, and third Choctaw districts and then consecutively by family group.

Choctaw Pay Roll, 1893

Manuscript list of individuals (Choctaw by blood) receiving annuity payments. Contains names of citizens by blood, name and sex of children, individual receiving payment, amount of payment, and remarks. Remarks are primarily confined to identification of orphans. Arranged alphabetically by county, then alphabetically by individual's name.

Census of Choctaw Nation, 1896

Contains names of adults, names and sex of children, age, relationship, and remarks. Remarks include whether the wife of an intermarried citizen, orphan, widow, stricken from roll, child of a Choctaw, deceased, or transferred to other rolls. Arranged numerically by district, then alphabetically by the last names of individuals living within a particular county or Chickasaw district.

Census Roll of Freedmen, 1896

Contains consecutive numbers, notation if Chickasaw, name, age, county of residence, and other notations. Other notations consist primarily of dead, parents' names, and Dawes numbers. Arranged alphabetically.

Unpaid Choctaw Townsite Payment, 1904

Choctaw-Chickasaw Townsite Fund Pay Roll, 1906

Choctaw $20 Payment Roll, 1908

Choctaw $50 Payment Roll, 1911

Choctaw $300 Payment Roll, 1916

Choctaw $100 Payment Roll, 1917

Census and Citizenship Records

Mississippi Choctaw census and citizenship, 1830–99; census records and lists, 1830–96; census of Choctaws by blood and intermarried citizens, 1868–96; residents of the Chickasaw Nation, 1896; restricted Choctaws, 1929; Choctaw citizenship, 1897–1930; Choctaw citizenship, 1897–1930; undated, 1884–1904; Choctaw citizenship cases, 1896–1904; rejected cases, First District, 1896–97; census and citizenship, Choctaw freedmen, 1885–97.

Records of the General Council, Senate, and House of Representatives

General Council and House of Representatives, 1855, 1867, and 1899; Laws of the Choctaw Nation, 1886–1906

Permit Records, 1898–1906

County Court Records

Atoka County courts, 1886–1906; Blue County courts, 1868–1906; Boktuklo County courts, 1858–1905; Cedar County courts, 1875–1905; Eagle County courts, 1889–1906; Gaines County courts, 1859–1906; Jacks County courts, 1860–1906; Jackson County courts, 1887–1906; Kiamichi County courts, 1888–1905; Nashoba County courts, 1856–1905; Red River County courts, 1866–1905; Sans Bois County courts, 1888–1906; Skullyville County courts, 1868–1906; Sugar Loaf County courts, 1874–1906; Tobucksy County courts, 1867–1906; Towson County courts, 1881–1906; Wade County courts, 1858–1906.

District, Circuit, and Chancery Records

First District (Masholatubbe), 1848–1905; Second District (Apuckshunnabbee), 1871–1905; Third District (Pushmataha), 1859–1906.

Records of the Supreme Court and Tribal Officers, 1857–1906

Letters Sent and Received and Other Documents, 1859–1907

Wewoka Agency—Seminole[53]

Seminole Payment and Census Rolls, 1868, 1895–1897

Includes payee's name; annotated with Dawes enrollment card number. Arranged by band and then by family.

Seminole Payment Rolls, 1895–1896

The roll contains each payee's name and amounts of money listed under columns labeled Wewoka, Sasakwa, and Balance. Wewoka was the capital of the Seminole Nation, and Sasakwa was the place of business of the principal chief. Arranged by band and then by family group.

Seminole Payment Rolls, 1895–1897

Copies of an 1895 and 1897 "Head Right" payment roll. The 1895 payment roll is not an exact copy but contains most of the same names and amounts. Arranged by band and then by family group.

Allotment Schedules for 1901 and 1902

National Council, federal relations, and per-capita laws and acts of National Council, 1886–1905; federal relations, 1900; per-capita payments, 1898–1907; Seminole miscellaneous papers.

Financial and School Records

Financial records, 1893–1907; miscellaneous documents, 1866–1923; school financial records, 1906.

Mekusukey Academy, 1910–1929

Student applications, rosters, progress cards, letters sent and received by the superintendent, and medical and other records.

Anadarko Area Office

The Anadarko Area Office, established in 1948, is essentially a continuation of the Kiowa Agency, which was created in 1864 and permanently located in Indian Territory in 1869.[54]

Located at Anadarko, Oklahoma, the Anadarko Area Office administers Bureau of Indian Affairs programs for the regions of Oklahoma, Kansas, and Missouri and is responsible for the following agencies in Oklahoma: Anadarko, Concho, Pawnee, Shawnee, Concho Indian School, Riverside Indian School, Fort Sill Maintenance and Security Detachment, and the Chilocco Maintenance and Security Detachment.

The records, 1881–1952, include general correspondence and correspondence concerning lands, heirship, town sites, and schools; accounts and case files for individual Indians; land transactions files; annuity payrolls; annual reports; student records; and records of employees.[55]

Anadarko Agency

The Anadarko Agency, located at Anadarko, Oklahoma, has jurisdiction over the Apache, Kiowa, Comanche, Caddo, Delaware, and Wichita tribes.[56]

Apache

The Apaches of Oklahoma are also called the Prairie Apache, a name applied to them through error on the assumption that they were the same as the Apache people of Arizona. They have no political connection with the Apache tribes of the Southwest, however. They came from the north as a component part of the Kiowa. More recent authorities, however, believe that the Apaches did divide somewhere in Montana, with the main body going southward on the west side of the mountains and a smaller body going northward to become allied on the east side of the mountains with the Kiowas. Whichever theory is correct, the Apaches have a distinct language and call themselves Nadishdewa, or "our people." The Pawnees and early French explorers and settlers called them Gattacka or Gataka, and these names appeared on the first treaty they signed with the United States.[57]

Caddo

The Caddos were first known to have been in the Louisiana Territory and were referred to in the chronicles of the DeSoto expedition in 1541. Soon after the United States purchased the Louisiana Territory, a peace treaty was made in which the Caddos ceded all their Louisiana lands and agreed to move to the Indian Territory, settling on the Washita River in what is now Caddo County. The present Caddo tribe also includes remnants of the Anadarko tribe.[58]

Comanche

The Comanches were one of the southern tribes of the Shoshonean stock and the only one to live entirely on the Plains. They are a comparatively recent offshoot of the Shoshonis of Wyoming and, until recently, kept in continual friendly communication with them.

For nearly two centuries they were at war with the Spaniards in Mexico and raided Mexican settlements as far south as Durango and Zacatecas. Generally friendly to the Americans, they were bitter enemies of the Texans, who had dispossessed them of their best hunting grounds, and they waged relentless war against them for almost forty years. Around 1795, they became close confederates of the Kiowas and also allied themselves with the Apaches.

Several treaties were consummated between the United States and the Comanche Tribe between 1834 and 1875. In the Treaty of Medicine Lodge in 1867, the Comanche, Apache, and Kiowa tribes were assigned a tract of land in Oklahoma, which they still share.[59]

Delaware

The Delawares call themselves Lenape, meaning "real men," or Leni Lenape, meaning "men of our nation." The English name Delaware was given to the tribe from the Delaware River, the valley which was the tribal center in earliest colonial times. The valley extends from southeastern New York into Pennsylvania through New Jersey and Delaware. The early traditional history of the Delaware is contained in the nation legend, the Walam Olum.

The Delawares were once one of the larger tribes of the eastern woodland people. Gradually, they moved west and were located in at least ten different states during this migration. At present, two groups of Delawares live in Oklahoma. The main part of the tribe, known as Registered Delaware, came from their reservation in Kansas in 1867 and settled with the Cherokees and were allotted land with them. The other group, still a district Delaware tribe, was associated with the Caddo and Wichita tribes in Texas and came to the Washita River in Indian Territory in 1859. A number of Delaware moved and associated with other tribes in the north and northwestern country. Approximately 750 Delawares are called Absentee Delawares.[60]

Fort Sill Apache

The Fort Sill Apaches are composed of members of the Warm Springs Band of Apache and the Chiricahua Apache. This small group of Indians is often referred to as Chief Geronimo's

Band of Apache. According to older members of this group, Victorio, chief of the Apache, led a group of forty warriors in protesting the tribe's being moved from their New Mexico reservation to one located at San Carlos, Arizona. Upon Victorio's death at the hands of a band of Mexicans in Chihuahua, Mexico, Geronimo assumed leadership of the group. He carried on warfare until August 1886, when Gen. Nelson A. Miles forced him to surrender. Geronimo and all of his band were taken as prisoners of war to Fort Marion, Florida, near St. Augustine.

Because of many deaths and much sickness in the tribe, the government removed them to Mount Vernon Barracks, Alabama, where they were kept prisoner for seven years. On 4 October 1894, Geronimo and the remnants of his band, then about 296 in all, were moved from Alabama to Fort Sill, Oklahoma. They remained at the Fort Sill Military Reservation as nominal prisoners of war until 1913, when the government arranged to allot an eighty-acre tract of land to each member who desired to remain in Oklahoma. Those who wished to move to the Mescalero Reservation in New Mexico could do so, and only eighty-seven stayed in Oklahoma and were given allotments of land in or near what is now the town of Apache.[61]

Kiowa

The Kiowa are believed to have migrated from the mountain regions at the source of the Yellowstone and Missouri rivers in what is now western Montana. According to tradition, they left this region because of a dispute with another tribe over hunting spoils and moved to the Black Hills in present-day South Dakota. Toward the end of the eighteenth century, the Kiowa were driven south by the Sioux, finally settling in the area of present western Oklahoma and the panhandle of north Texas and west into part of New Mexico.

Early in their history, they formed an alliance with a small band of Apache which continues today in Oklahoma. In 1790, having made peace with their one-time enemies, the Comanches, they established control of the area from the Arkansas River to the headwaters of the Red River, and the two tribes became masters of the southern Plains. This alliance appears to be the basis for both the Kiowa-Apache-Comanche alliance of today and also the Kiowa-Comanche Reservation in Oklahoma, where the two tribes were settled by the United States. In 1840, the Kiowas made a permanent peace with the Cheyenne and their allies, the Arapahos, and became friendly with the Wichitas.

Throughout the nineteenth century, the Kiowas continually resisted white immigration along the overland trails. With the Comanche, they attacked Texas frontier settlements, extending their raids far south into Mexico. Treaties with the U.S. government beginning in 1837 had little effect, and the tribe continued fighting. After the Battle of Washita in 1868, the Kiowas, Apaches, and Comanches were forced onto a reservation near Fort Sill, Oklahoma. Their defiance continued, however, and only military defeat and the disappearance of the buffalo ended their resistance.[62]

The treaty of Medicine Lodge Creek, Kansas (15 Stat., 581 and 15 Stat., 589), concluded on 21 October 1868 between the United States and the Kiowas, Comanche, and Kiowa-Apache, provided for a reservation in Indian Territory to be located between the Washita and Red rivers. This was a modification and reduction of a reservation established by a treaty of 18 October 1865 (Stat. L, xiv, 717) with the Comanche and Kiowa.

In 1868, an agent was sent to Indian Territory to bring together the Kiowas, Comanches, and Apaches who wished to abide by their treaty commitments. Progress was made, and the following year, a new agent arrived at the agency headquarters near Fort Sill. When he assumed control on 1 July 1869, he found himself in charge of the Wichita Agency as well. That agency had been established in July 1859 on the south side of the Washita River near Sugar Creek in an area long claimed by the Wichita. The agency served the Kiowa, Caddo, and Kichai. Later Waco, Tawakoni, Anadarko, Ionie (Hainai), Tonkawa, and some Penateka Comanche, Delaware, and Shawnee groups became part of this agency. During a brief interval in the 1870s, some of the Pawnees from Nebraska made their home at this agency before moving to their new reservation.

In 1870, the agency, properly called the Caddo, Wichita, and Affiliated Bands Agency, became independent. Although some of the tribes had long resided in the region, it was not until 19 October 1872 that an agreement (never ratified) established a reservation for Wichitas and affiliated bands between the Washita and Canadian rivers, northeast and adjacent to the Kiowa, Comanche, and Apache reservation.

In the decade following 1868, the Kiowa-Comanche Agency remained in operation near Fort Sill. On 1 September 1878, that agency and the Wichita Agency were again consolidated. At that time, instructions were given to move the agency from Fort Sill to the Wichita Agency near the present town of Anadarko. The office at Fort Sill served as a subagency for a number of years.

In 1894, Geronimo and a group of Chiricahua Apache prisoners of war who had formerly been at Fort Marion, Florida, and Mount Vernon Barracks, Alabama, were brought to Fort Sill. In 1913, eighty-seven of them elected to remain in Oklahoma rather than return to the Mescalero Apache reservation in New Mexico. They were allotted land near the town of Apache.

The allotment of the Kiowas, Comanches, and Apaches was completed in 1901 after several years of their attempting to prevent the dissolution of their reservation and eventual use of surplus land for white settlement. The Wichita and other tribes of the original Wichita agency group were allotted lands before 6 August 1901, when their surplus lands as well as those of the Kiowas, Comanches, and Apaches were opened for white settlement.[63]

Wichita

Tradition indicates that the Wichita tribe migrated southward from the north and east. In 1850, the Wichitas had moved from near the Red River into the Wichita Mountains region, with their main village a short distance from what is now Fort Sill, Oklahoma. In 1859, the Wichita moved to a permanent site south of the Canadian River near the present Caddo-Grady county line. A reservation consisting of 743,610 acres and known as the Wichita-Caddo Reservation was established in 1872.[64]

Kiowa Agency Records[65]

Census Records

Letters sent and received, 1872–1920; undated census lists, worksheets, and miscellaneous undated census lists; census lists for the Apache, Comanche, Kiowa, Wichita, Waco, Tawakoni, Caddo, Kichai, and Delaware, 1869–1922.

Letterpress Books, 1869–1900

Federal Relations

Letters Sent and Received, 1864–1933.

Federal, State, and Local Court Relations, 1865–1925

Foreign Relations

Letters Sent and Received, 1866–1929.

Military Relations and Affairs, 1869–1925

Indian History, Culture, and Acculturation, 1860–1926

Concho Agency—Cheyenne and Arapaho

The earliest known evidence of the Cheyenne and Arapaho tribes dates from 1600 and places the Arapaho east of the headwaters of the Mississippi River in Minnesota and the Cheyenne in southwestern and northern Minnesota. The two tribes have long been associated, having wandered in the same direction and fought jointly for defense, yet they were separate tribes and were politically independent. With the westward push of settlers, the Cheyenne and Arapaho moved west and adopted a lifestyle that evolved into the culture of the Plains Indians. Their wandering led them to North and South Dakota, Wyoming, Montana, Nebraska, Kansas, and Colorado. In about 1835, portions separated from the main body became known as the Southern Cheyenne and Southern Arapaho. In 1869, the Cheyenne and Arapaho were assigned a reservation in Oklahoma, and the Darlington Agency was established in 1870 to serve them.[66]

A treaty between the United States and the Cheyenne and Arapaho tribes, 28 October 1867 (Stat. L., xv, 593), provided for a reservation in what is now Oklahoma for the Southern Cheyenne and Southern Arapaho Indians. In 1869, a temporary agency was established at Camp Supply, Indian Territory. The location of the reservation was altered by executive order on 10 August 1869, and in May 1879, the agency was moved to a site five miles northwest of the present town of El Reno.

From 1869 through 1874, this agency, called the Upper Arkansas Agency, was under the Central Superintendency, Office of Indian affairs. In 1875 its name was changed to the Cheyenne and Arapaho Agency. This designation has remained to the present day.

In 1877, several bands of Northern Cheyenne numbering 927 people were brought to Darlington in Indian Territory. Another contingent of approximately two hundred reached Darlington in 1878. In 1881, Little Chief's band was allowed to move to Pine Ridge Agency in Dakota Territory. In September 1883, the last of the Northern Cheyenne wishing to remove to their old home arrived at Pine Ridge Agency. The records of these Northern Cheyenne for the time they were at the southern agency remain in the files of the Cheyenne and Arapaho Agency. On 30 November 1902 a "subagency" was established at Cantonment in Indian Territory. Part of the agency's affairs came under the supervision of the head of the Cantonment Indian Training School, with headquarters at the school three miles northwest of Canton. Another portion was assigned to the superintendent of Seger Indian Training School located at Colony. The remainder of the agency was under the direction of the Cheyenne and Arapaho School superintendent at the old agency headquarters at Darlington. By December 1909, a further division created the Red Moon Agency located at the Red Moon School at Hammon.

In March 1910, the removal of the Darlington Agency to Caddo Springs was authorized. The move was completed in May 1915, and the agency's name changed to the Concho Agency. On 9 April 1917, the consolidation of the Red Moon Agency with the Seger Agency was accomplished. The next reorganization took place in 1927. At that time the Seger Agency was abolished, and the Cantonment Agency became part of the Cheyenne and Arapaho Agency at Cantonment.[67]

Cheyenne-Arapaho Agency Records[68]

Census Records

Letters sent and letters received, 1876–1931; enrollment, 1878–1914; enrollment lists and census rolls, 1870–1928.

Letterpress Books, 1876–1891

Letters Sent and Received and Other Documents, 1868–1933

Indian History, Culture, and Acculturation, 1871–1933

Pawnee Agency

The Pawnee Agency, located at Pawnee, Oklahoma, has jurisdiction over the Kaw, Pawnee, Ponca, Otoe-Missouria, and Tonkawa tribes.[69]

The Pawnee Agency was the last name given the agency responsible for the affairs of the following various tribes from 1870 to 1930. The agencies and subagencies that had jurisdiction over the several tribes through the years changed locations and names and are as follows: Osage Agency; Kaw Agency; Kaw Subagency; Pawnee Agency; Pawnee Subagency; Ponca, Otoe and Oakland Agency; Ponca, Pawnee, Oakland and Otoe Agency; Ponca Subagency; Otoe Subagency; Tonkawa Subagency; and reservation schools whose superintendents were placed in charge of school and tribal affairs.[70]

Kaw

According to tradition, the Kaws, Osages, Poncas, Omahas, and Quapaws were one people who lived along the Wabash River and far up the Ohio. Pushed westward by the encroachment of superior forces, they split at the mouth of the Ohio River. Those going down the Mississippi River took the name Quapaw, or "downstream people." They later divided into four tribes: Kaw, Osage, Ponca, and Omaha. By terms of the treaties with the United States from 1820 to 1846, the Kaws relinquished their claims to several million acres in Kansas and Nebraska. A new reservation was assigned to them in 1846 at Council Grove on the Neosho River in Kansas. These lands were finally overrun by white settlers. In 1872, the tract was sold, and a new reserve was purchased for the tribe near the Osages in Indian Territory. In 1902, that reservation was allotted under law to the tribal membership.[71]

The Kaw (Kansas) Reservation was established by act of Congress on 5 June 1872 (Stat. L., xvii, 228) and consisted of 100,141 acres of the Osage reserve located to the west of that reservation, east of the Arkansas River and adjoining the Kansas border. In July 1874, the affairs of the 523 Kaws were handled by the Osage Agency. Living on their own reservation, they continued under this supervision until 1876, when the superintendent of the Central Superintendency said that the Kaw Agency was a district agency but that the Osage agent handled its affairs. In 1879, the Osage Agency title was changed to Osage and Kaw Agency. The name was changed the next year to the Osage Agency and continued as such until 1886, when the tribal affairs were managed by two agencies again, with the Kaws under the supervision of the superintendent of the Kaw School. In 1887–88, the title was changed to the Kaw Subagency; a clerk-in-charge supervised its business. By an act of Congress ratified on 1 July 1902 (Stat. 32, 636), the tribe agreed to allotment of its reservation.

In 1904, the Kaw Reservation and agency were completely separated from the Osage Agency and placed under a bonded superintendent. In 1912, Kaw affairs were transferred to the management of the Ponca School superintendent. In 1913–14, the Kaw farmer (a government employee who lived on the reservation and assisted the Indians in their farming) reported on Kaw Agency affairs. The Kaw School was abolished in 1915, and in 1922, tribal affairs supervision was given to the Pawnee School superintendent at the Pawnee Agency at Pawnee.[72]

Otoe-Missouria

According to tradition, the people later known as the Otoes, along with their relatives the Winnebagos and the Iowas, once lived in the Great Lakes region. In a prehistoric migration southwest in search of buffalo, they separated. The division that reached the mouth of the Grand River, a branch of the Missouri, called themselves Niutachi and soon separated into two bands because of a quarrel between two of their chiefs. One band went up the Missouri and became known as the Otoe, and the other band stayed near the first settlement and was called the Missouria. From 1817 to 1841, the Otoes lived near the mouth of the Platte River. Since 1829, the Missourias have been absorbed by the Otoes, and the two are now indistinguishable.

On 15 March 1854, the Otoe-Missourias signed a treaty ceding all their lands except for a strip ten miles wide and twenty-five miles long on the waters of Big Blue River, but when it was found that there was no timber on this tract, it was exchanged for another tract taken from the Kaws (Kansas). In a treaty signed 15 August 1876 and amended 3 March 1879, they agreed to sell 120,000 acres of the western end of the reserve. Finally, a treaty signed on 3 March 1881 provided for the sale of all the rest of their lands in Kansas and Nebraska and for the selection of a new reservation. Consent to the treaty was recorded on 4 May, and the tribe moved the following year to the new reservation, which was in Indian Territory.[73]

The Otoe Reservation was established by act of Congress on 3 March 1881 (Stat. L. xxi, 381) and consisted of 129,113 acres west of the Pawnee Reservation and south of the Ponca Reservation in Indian Territory. The tribes were removed from the Great Nemaha Agency in Nebraska to the Otoe Agency in 1882 and later placed under the consolidated Ponca, Pawnee, and Otoe Agency in 1883. The Missouri Indians had been a separate tribe until 1829, when many of them joined the Otoes. By 1885, only forty individuals were designated as Missouri. The Absentee Otoes were a group who refused to live at the new agency and went to live at the Sac and Fox Agency for some years. In 1886, the main agency's name was changed to the Ponca, Pawnee, Otoe, and Oakland Agency, and the Otoes and Missouris were under its supervision for many years. Their subagency was on the Otoe Reservation.

In the 1890s, the tribes resisted allotment; it was completed slowly, often with arbitrary assignment of land by the allotting agent. In 1896, the allotment schedule was in the secretary of the interior's office, unapproved. In 1897, the allotment process was repeated, with continued opposition from tribal members. In 1904, additional allotments were made (Stat. 33, 218). In 1902, the Pawnee Agency was separated from the Ponca, Pawnee, Otoe, and Oakland Agency, and the Otoe superintendent became responsible for the Otoe School and tribal affairs. In 1904, the Otoe and Missouri Agency was segregated from the Ponca Agency and the Otoe Reservation lines abolished. The two eastern townships became part of Pawnee County, and the balance of the reservation area became Noble County. Later the tribe became part of the Ponca Agency.[74]

Pawnee

The prehistoric origins of the Pawnees are still largely a mystery. Archeological studies indicate that the tribe moved northward around 1400 from an original homeland beyond the Rio Grande to the Red River near the Wichita Mountains and then to the Arkansas River in southern Kansas or northern Oklahoma. From there, the Skidi Pawnee continued northward into southwestern Nebraska, while the Southern (or Black) Pawnee remained.

Until 1770, the Southern Pawnee, aided by weapons and supplies from French traders, stayed in the Arkansas River region. As French trade lessened, they migrated northward to join the Skidis in what is now Nebraska near the Platte, Loup, and Republican rivers. The move gave the tribe renewed outlets for trade as well as good buffalo hunting south of the Platte.

The opening of the frontier brought disaster to the Pawnees. Three treaties (1833, 1848, and 1857) provided for the cession of all Pawnee lands to the United States, with the exception of a reservation thirty miles long and fifteen miles wide along both banks of the Loup River, centering near present-day Fullerton, Nebraska. In 1876 this tract was also surrendered to the United States, and the entire tribe was relocated to a new reservation in Oklahoma in a difficult exodus that caused many deaths. Under an agreement with the United States dated 23 November 1892, the Pawnees gave up certain lands for a perpetual annuity payment of $30,000 per year, to be divided equally among tribal members. This annuity, which breaks down to just a few dollars for each tribe member, is still provided. The only other tribe still to receive such payments is the Oneida.[75]

The Pawnee Reservation was established by an act of 10 April 1875 (Stat. L, xix, 28) and consisted of 230,014 acres purchased from the Cherokee and 53,006 acres from the Creek Nations. It was located between the Cimarron and Arkansas rivers, west of the Creek Nation and north of the Sac and Fox Reservation in Indian Territory. The Pawnee removal from Nebraska began around 1873, when small groups left their reservation near Genoa, Nebraska, and moved to the Wichita Reservation by invitation of that tribe, their linguistic kinsmen. The majority of the tribe migrated to their new reservation from Nebraska in the winter of 1875.

In 1883, Pawnee affairs were handled by an agent at the Ponca, Pawnee, and Otoe Agency located on the Ponca Reservation. A clerk-in-charge was stationed at the Pawnee Subagency. The agency's name was changed to the Ponca, Pawnee, Otoe, and Oakland Agency in 1886, with the Pawnee Subagency continuing to function.

On 23 November 1892, the Pawnees consented to accept allotments in severalty and ceded their reservation (Stat. L., xxvii, 644, ratified 3 March 1893). Allotments were made to 820 persons, and in 1896 the surplus 169,320 acres were opened to settlement. At that time, Pawnee affairs were handled by the Pawnee superintendent, who was responsible for school and tribal affairs administration during the decade.[76]

Ponca

In 1673, the Poncas were living on the Niobrara River; later they moved to southwestern Minnesota and the Black Hills of South Dakota. In 1877, they were evicted from their lands by the United States, which caused such hardship among the tribe that it became the subject of a public investigation ordered by President Hayes. In a settlement, approximately a third of the tribe returned to their lands on the Niobrara in 1880, while the rest moved to new lands set aside for them in Oklahoma. A small group of Poncas known as the Northern Ponca live in Nebraska.[77]

A 3 March 1877 act of Congress provided for Ponca removal to Indian Territory "without regard to their consent." Under this act, they were temporarily located at the Quapaw Agency. The act of 27 May 1878 provided for their removal to their own reservation, which was established by this act. It was located west of the Osage Reservation and the Arkansas River and northwest of the Pawnee Reservation. Six hundred and ninety-three Poncas were moved from the Quapaw to the Ponca Reservation in July 1878. The new agency was located on the Salt Fork River. It was not until 3 March 1881 (Stat. L, xxi, 422) that an appropriation was made to purchase that tract from the Cherokees.

The Poncas were under the supervision of the Ponca, Pawnee, and Otoe Agency, which was responsible also for the Pawnees, Otoes, Missouris, and Nez Perce. In 1886, it became the Ponca, Otoe, and Oakland Agency. This agency, established for the Nez Perce, became the home of the Tonkawa Indians in 1885. The Poncas strongly resisted allotment of their lands in severalty, and not until 6 April 1895 could the secretary of the interior approve the allotment of 100,734 acres to 782 individuals. However, one group did not accept allotment until 1899, and in 1904, additional allotments were made (Stat. 33, 218). In 1899, a superintendent was placed in charge of the Ponca School and tribal affairs. In 1901, the Pawnee Agency separated from the Ponca, Otoe, and Oakland Agency, which became known as the Ponca, Otoe, and Oakland Agency located at White Eagle.

In 1904, a further separation left the agency serving only the Poncas and Tonkawas. The Ponca superintendent continued to be responsible for the tribe into the 1920s. In 1927, the Ponca Subagency fell under the jurisdiction of the Pawnee Agency, and Otoe and Missouri affairs were transferred to this agency.[78]

Tonkawa

During the eighteenth and nineteenth centuries, the Tonkawas lived in central Texas. In 1884, they moved from Texas to Indian Territory and were assigned 91,000 acres of land previously assigned to the Nez Perce in Kay County, Oklahoma.[79]

The Tonkawas and a small group of associated Lipan Apaches came to the Oakland Agency from the Sac and Fox Agency, where ninety-two tribespeople had arrived from Fort Griffin, Texas, on 23 October 1884. They were placed on the Iowa Reservation of the agency, where they remained until June 1885, when they were transferred to the Oakland Reservation, which had just been vacated by the Nez Perce the month before. A subagency was created for them, with the main agency at the Ponca, Pawnee, Otoe, and Oakland Agency on the Ponca Reservation. In an agreement concluded on 21 October 1891, the Tonkawas ceded this reservation to the United States, and allotments were subsequently made to them. In 1896, the surplus lands were opened for settlement. In 1900, the subagency had a farmer-in-charge. The tribe's affairs continued under the Ponca, Otoe, and Oakland Agency in 1901 and under the Ponca School superintendent in 1904. The Lipan Apaches, counted as part of the Tonkawas, had apparently been with them since their arrival in Indian Territory from Fort Griffin. This small remnant were often called Tonkawa and soon lost their identity. The combined group continued under this agency's supervision until 1928, when the Pawnee Agency became the main agency for all of the tribes listed previously.[80]

Pawnee Agency Records[81]

Census Records

Letters sent and received, 1894–1927; census and lists for the Nez Perce, Kaw, Tonkawa, Pawnee and Oto, and Missouri, 1880–1926; census and lists for the Ponca and Tonkawa, undated and 1926.

Letterpress Books, 1870–1903

Records of the Pawnee Agency and Subagencies[82]

Federal, State, and Local Courts and Other Relations

Letters Sent and Received and Other Documents, 1894–1902.

Kaw Agency Records[83]

Letterpress Books, 1894–1908

Ponca, Pawnee, Otoe, and Oakland Agency Records

Letterpress Books, 1894–1908

Otoe Agency Records

Letterpress Books, 1880–1908

Ponca Agency Records[84]

Letterpress Books, 1879–1911

Tonkawa Agency Records[85]

Letterpress Books, 1877–1918

Shawnee Agency

The Shawnee Agency, located at Shawnee, Oklahoma, has jurisdiction over the Iowa, Kickapoo, Citizen Potawatomi, Sac and Fox, and Absentee-Shawnee tribes.[86]

The Shawnee Agency was originally known as the Sac and Fox Agency. It operated under the Central Superintendency. It was located about six miles south of the present town of Stroud, Oklahoma. The agent also had under his jurisdiction 467 absentee Shawnees who were living thirty miles southwest of the Sac and Fox Agency. They were located on lands they had occupied before the Civil War. Many had remained loyal to the Union and had sought shelter in the North. After the war they returned to their old territory and were later joined by the Black Bob Band of Shawnees from Kansas.

In a series of agreements in 1890 that resulted from implementation of the Dawes Act, all of the tribes within the Sac and Fox Agency (except the Kickapoos) ceded their lands to the United States and accepted allotments in severalty. The Sac and Fox, Iowa, Potawatomi, and Shawnee lands were opened to non-Indian settlement on 22 September 1891. The agency site at that time became a part of Oklahoma Territory. The Kickapoos were allotted land later, and their lands were opened to settlement on 23 May 1895. In April 1896, a special agent was appointed to handle the affairs of the band of Mexican Kickapoos known as the Kicking Kickapoos. The special agent assumed charge of the Progressive Kickapoos and the Big Jim Band of Absentee Shawnee a year or so later through an agency office located near the town of Shawnee.

In 1901, the Sac and Fox Agency was divided. The Sac and Fox Agency itself remained at the old site near Stroud with jurisdiction over the Sac and Fox and the Iowas. The Shawnee, Potawatomi, and Kickapoo Agency (sometimes called the Shawnee Agency) was established about two miles south of Shawnee, Oklahoma. The agencies continued their separate existence until 1919, when they were merged, becoming the Shawnee Agency.[87]

Besides the resident tribes' records, there are files of other tribes' records brought from the Sac and Fox Agency in Kansas. They are listed here with the name of the tribe and years covered by the correspondence and records.

Chippewas of Swan Creek and Black River, and Muncie (Munsee) Indians, 1854–1901

Christian Indians, 1858–1864

Oneida Indians, 1902

Otoe Indians, 1880–1921

Ottawa Indians, 1838–1908

The majority of the Otoes listed in table 14-1 resided on the Otoe reservation under the Otoe Agency. Later they were under the jurisdiction of the Pawnee and Ponca agencies. Some intermarried among the Iowas and others at the Sac and Fox Agency. This file refers to them and the earlier group that came from the Great Nemaha Agency in Nebraska.[88]

Absentee-Shawnee

See Eastern Shawnee.[89]

Citizen Band Potawatomi

Before 1700, the Potawatomis lived near the upper Lake Huron territory and on the islands of Green Bay, Wisconsin. They were later located near what is now Chicago and Milwaukee. During the French and Indian War, they were close allies of the French until the peace of 1763. They were also allied with Ottawa Chief Pontiac against the British and white settlers. During the revolutionary war, however, they fought with the British against the American colonies, and hostilities continued until the Treaty of Greenville of 1795 brought peace between the former colonies and the Potawatomis.

In 1833, the Potawatomis, together with the Ottawas and Chippewas, signed the Chicago Treaty, ceding all their lands in Illinois and along the western shore of Lake Michigan and agreeing to move to Iowa within three years. They were in Iowa only briefly before the government moved them to Kansas. Today, in Kansas, the Prairie Band of Potawatomis is descended mainly from Indiana, Illinois, and Michigan Potawatomis.

The Citizen Band of Potawatomi tribe of Oklahoma is so called because certain Prairie Band members applied for citizenship papers in the 1860s, having been granted that right by treaty. Many sold their fee patent land in Kansas; landless and destitute, they removed to Indian Territory. Reservation land was provided for them there; however, because they were citizens, legal questions arose as to their right to live on it. Today, there is no Potawatomi reservation in Oklahoma.[90]

Under a treaty of 15 November 1861 (12 Stat. 1191), the Potawatomis had received allotments in severalty in Kansas. A number accepted allotments and became citizens of the United States, then becoming known as Citizen Potawatomi. Many of them soon sold their allotments and began to plan the purchase of a new reservation in Indian Territory. A treaty of 27 February 1867 (15 Stat. 531) provided for this purchase. A thirty-square-mile reservation was selected west of the Seminole Nation between the North and South Canadian rivers, and 250 Citizen Potawatomis moved into the area. The Potawatomi lands selected encroached on those of the Absentee Shawnees' prewar settlement claims. To right this situation, Congress passed an act (Stat. L, xvii, 159) on 23 May 1872 permitting the Absentee Shawnees to select allotments on the Potawatomi Reserve. There was considerable opposition, and Sam Warrior's Band, comprising approximately one-third of the tribe, moved to an area west of the Kickapoos.[91]

Iowa

The earliest known Iowa settlement is believed to have been along the upper Iowa River. Later, the Iowas moved into the northwestern part of the present state of Iowa. In the latter part of the eighteenth century, the Iowas moved to the Missouri River and settled south of the spot where Council Bluffs, Iowa, now stands on the east side of the river. Around 1760, they moved east and came to live along the Mississippi between the Iowa and Des Moines rivers. Early in the nineteenth century, part of the tribe moved farther up the Des Moines River, while others established themselves on the Grand and Platte rivers in Missouri. In 1814, they were allotted lands in what was known as the Platte Purchase, extending from the Platte River of Missouri through western Iowa to the Dakota country. By treaties signed on 4 August 1824, 15 July 1830, 17 September 1836, and 23 November 1867, the Iowas ceded all their lands in Missouri and Iowa to the United States. On 19 August 1825, they also ceded lands in Minnesota. The treaty of 1836 assigned part of the tribe to a reservation along the Great Nemeha River in present-day Nebraska and Kansas. The remainder were moved to central Oklahoma in 1883.[92]

Kickapoo

The Kickapoos moved into the Wisconsin area in the early part of the seventeenth century. They later moved into Illinois near the present-day city of Peoria. During the War of 1812, they were allied with Tecumseh against the United States. In 1809 and 1819, the Kickapoos ceded their lands in Illinois to the United States and moved to Missouri and then Kansas. Around 1852, a large number of the Kickapoos and some Potawatomis went to Texas and then to Mexico, where they became known as Mexican Kickapoos. Another dissatisfied band joined them in 1863. Ten years later, part of this band was induced to return to Indian Territory. Those who chose to remain in Mexico were granted a reservation on the Sabinas River about twelve to fifteen miles from the town of Musquiz in the state of Coahuila.[93]

After the cession of their homeland in Illinois in 1819, the Kickapoo bands separated and migrated to different areas, some going to Texas and others to Mexico. The Texas bands came to Indian Territory before the Civil War in two groups, one settling on Creek and the other on Choctaw lands. Later, many of them joined the Kickapoos living in Mexico. An effort was made under the acts of 15 July 1870, 3 March 1871, and 22 June 1874 to move the Mexican Kickapoos and others on the borders of Texas to a reservation that would be established for them in Indian Territory. A commission was appointed that succeeded in getting some three hundred to four hundred to consent to move. By 1873, these Mexican Kickapoos had begun to arrive at the Sac and Fox Agency. Their reservation was located between the South Canadian and Deep Fork rivers west of the Sac and Fox Reservation.[94]

Sac and Fox

Originally separate and independent tribes, the Sac (or Sauk) and Fox tribes have long been affiliated and allied. The original homeland of the Sac and Fox was in the Great Lakes region, where the Sac inhabited the Upper Michigan Peninsula and the Fox the south shore of Lake Superior. By 1667, when Father Allouez made the first recorded white contact with the two tribes, Iroquois and French pressure on the Sac and Chippewa pressure on the Fox had pushed both groups to the vicinity of present-day Green Bay, Wisconsin. French attacks on the Sac and Fox in the eighteenth century, attributed to Indians, strengthened the alliance of the two tribes, which amounted to a confederation. Forced to migrate south, they attacked the Illinois and forced them from their lands along the Mississippi in the present-day states of Illinois, Iowa, and Wisconsin. Those groups that stayed near the Mississippi River became known as the Sac and Fox of the Mississippi to distinguish them from the Sac and Fox of the Missouri, a large band that settled farther south along the Missouri River.

In 1804, the chiefs of the Missouri band were persuaded to sign a treaty ceding to the United States all Sac and Fox lands east of the Mississippi River, as well as some hunting grounds to the west of it. Government efforts several years later to enforce the treaty embittered the Sac and Fox, most of whom knew about the treaty. Attempts to remove the Sac and Fox caused a split in the confederation. The majority of the tribe followed the conciliatory Sac Chief Keokuk, who agreed to move. The remainder supported the rival Black Hawk, a Sac warrior who bitterly opposed the treaty and led his "British Band" into revolt (the Black Hawk War). With the Treaty of Fort Armstrong in 1832, Sac and Fox power on the frontier came to an end. In 1833, the tribe was moved to Iowa, where they lived for only thirteen years before being moved again, this time to the Osage River Reservation in Kansas. In 1869, the Sac and Fox were again moved, this time to Oklahoma. Keokuk, and later his son Moses, continued to lead the conciliatory faction of the tribes, but many of the Fox opposed the many cessions of land to the United States and returned to Iowa in 1859 to join a smaller number who had steadfastly refused to be moved.[95]

Under terms of a treaty with the United States concluded on 18 February 1867 (15 Stat. 495), the Sac and Fox of the Mississippi ceded approximately 157,000 acres of their land in Kansas in exchange for a new reservation of 750 square miles in Indian Territory between the Cimarron and North Canadian rivers west of the Creek Nation. On 25 November 1869, 387 tribal members began the move to their new home, arriving nineteen days later. One band under Chief Mo-ho-ko-ho remained in Kansas, and the Sac and Fox of Missouri continued to live at the Great Nemaha Agency in Nebraska near the Iowas, with whom they had been associated for many years.[96]

Sac and Fox-Shawnee Agency Records[97]

Census Records

Letters and documents received, 1865–1924; census and lists for the Iowa, Mexican Kickapoo, and Otoe, 1881–1920; census and lists for the Citizen Potawatomi, 1883–1921; Sac and Fox and Absentee Shawnee census, 1850–1923.

Letterpress Books

Iowa letters sent, 1840–47; account and letter book, Sac and Fox Agency, Kansas, 1849–61; letters sent, 1874–1902.

Federal and State Relations, 1854–1918

Federal, State, and Local Relations, 1851–1928

Military Relations and Affairs, 1853–1924

Indian History, Culture, and Acculturation, 1867–1923

Land Ownership and Use, 1847–1917

Agents and Agency, 1849–1927

Florida Superintendency

The Florida Superintendency was formally established in 1822, but officials had been assigned to Florida the previous year. Until the establishment of the Bureau of Indian Affairs in 1824, the superintendency was under the direct supervision of the secretary of war. The territorial governor, who resided permanently in Tallahassee beginning in 1824, acted as *ex officio* superintendent throughout the existence of the superintendency. The principal Indian tribe in Florida was the Seminole.

A subagent for Indians in Florida, appointed on 21 March 1821, reported to the newly appointed provisional governor, Andrew Jackson. In September of the same year, a temporary agent was appointed to handle Indian affairs during the absence of the governor, and the subagent was made accountable to him. In 1822, an agent and a subagent were authorized to serve under the governor. In 1826, an additional subagent was appointed for the Indians on the Apalachicola River.

With the contemplated removal of the Indians from Florida, the superintendency and the subagencies were abolished on 30 June 1834. In 1835, control of Indians in Florida was entrusted to the army. However, there were some Bureau of Indian Affairs officials on the Apalachicola River until 1839, and in 1849, there was a short-lived subagency for the Seminoles still in Florida.

Select List of Tribes

The following should not be considered a comprehensive list of the numerous tribes, bands, and sub-bands mentioned in the records of the Bureau of Indian Affairs in the custody of the National Archives. Researchers can consult John R. Swanton's *The Indian Tribes of North America* for information about specific tribes.[98]

The following table includes only the names of the agencies that had primary responsibility for a tribe. If any of the pre-1800 correspondence from that agency to the Commissioner of Indian affairs is available on National Archives microfilm publication M234, there is a citation to the appropriate rolls. If there are any census rolls for the tribe among those taken from 1885 to 1940, there is a reference to the appropriate roll numbers of microfilm publication M595.

Select List of Tribes

Tribe	Agency	Location of Original Records*	Pre–1880 Correspondence M234 Roll No.	Post–1885 Census Records M595 Roll No.
Absentee Shawnee	See Shawnee			
Adai	Red River Agency, 1824–30	DC	727	
Adopted Delaware/Shawnee	Muskogee Area Office, 1890–1960	FTW		
Alabama	Caddo Agency, 1824–42	DC	231	
Alleghany	New York Agency, 1838–49	DC	583–97	290–300
Anadarko	Anadarko Area Office, 1881–1962 Texas Agency, 1847–59 Wichita Agency, 1859	FTW DC DC	 858–61 928	
Apache	Kiowa Agency, 1881–1962 Fort Apache Agency, 1875–1955 Phoenix Area Office, 1928–37 Truxton Canyon Agency, 1895–1951 San Carlos Agency, 1900–52	FTW DC/LA DC/LA LA LA	211–23 344–46 581 461–70	
Apache–Jicarilla	See Jicarilla			
Apache, Kiowa	Upper Platte Agency 1846–55	DC	889–96	
Apache, Kiowa	Upper Arkansas Agency, 1855–67	DC	878–82	
Apache, Kiowa	Kiowa Agency/Anadarko, 1864–80	DC/FTW	375–86	211–23
Apache–Mescalero	See Mescalero			
Apache–Mojave	Camp McDowell (Pima) Agency, 1901–51	DC	15	
Apache, White Mountain	Fort Apache Agency, 1875–1955	DC/LA	118–25	
Apalachee	Caddo and Red River Agencies, 1824–42	DC	31, 727	
Arapaho	Upper Platte Agency, 1855–74 Upper Arkansas Agency, 1855–74 Cheyenne and Arapahoe Agency, 1875– Red Cloud (Pine Ridge) Agency, 1871–1961 Cantonment Agency, 1903–27 Wind River Agency, 1873–1952 Seger School, 1903–12, 1914–27 Shoshoni Agency, 1885–1937, with gaps	DC DC DC/FTW DC/KC DC/FTW DEN DC DC/DEN	889–96 878–82 119–26 715–26 	 27–32 16–17 663 479 498–504
Arikaree	See Arikara			
Arikara	Fort Berthold Agency, 1867–70 Upper Missouri Agency, 1824–66	DC DC	292–99 883–88	132–36

Tribe	Agency	Location of Original Records*	Pre–1880 Correspondence M234 Roll No.	Post–1885 Census Records M595 Roll No.
Assiniboin	Upper Missouri Agency 1824–66	DC	883–88	
	Fort Berthold Agency, 1867–70	DC	292–99	
	Fort Belknap Agency, 1877–1952	SEA	126–31	
	Fort Peck Agency, 1877–1952	SEA	151–60	
Bannock	Wind River Agency, 1873–1952	DC/DEN	11	
	Fort Hall Agency, 1889–1963	DC/SEA	138–44	
	Lemhi (Fort Hall) Agency, 1889–1963	SEA	248	
Biloxi	Red River and Caddo Agencies, 1824–42	DC	31, 727	
Blackfeet	Blackfeet Agency, 1873–1927	DC/DEN	30	3–11
	Blackfeet Agency, 1875–1952	DC/SEA	30	
	Cheyenne River/Standing Rock, 1862–1957	DC/KC	127–31, 846–52	3–11
	Upper Missouri and Upper Platte, 1824–74	DC	883–96	
Blood	Blackfeet Agency, 1855–59	DC	30	11
Brotherton	Green Bay (Menominee) Agency, 1824–1961	DC/CHI	315–36	
	Six Nations Agency, 1824–34	DC	832	
Brule Sioux	Upper Platte/Missouri (Crow Creek), 1824–74	DC	883–96	427–30
	Lower Brule/Whetstone (Rosebud), 1875–1966	DC/KC	401,925–27	427–30
	Spotted Tail (Rosebud)/Grand River, 1875–1966	DC/KC	840–45,305–06	427–45
Caddo	Anadarko Area Office, 1881–1962	FTW		211–23
	Red River Agency, 1824–30	DC	727	
	Caddo Agency, 1824–42	DC	31	
	Wichita Agency, 1859–78	DC	928–30	211–23
	Kiowa Agency, 1864–1962	DC/FTW	375–86	
Capote Ute	Abiquiu and Cimarron Agencies, 1869–82	DEN		
	Colorado Superintendency, 1877–80	DC	197–214	
Cayuga	New York Agency, 1838–49	DC	583–97	290–300
	Miami Agency, 1870–1952	DC/FTW		
	Oregon and Washington Sup., 1842–80	DC	607–30, 907–20	616–20
Chastacosta	Oregon Superintendency, 1842–80	DC	607–30	
Chehalis	Taholah Indian Agency, 1878–1952	SEA		93, 302, 407–09, 564–69
Chemehuevi	Colorado River Agency, 1867–1955	LA		
Cherokee	Cherokee Agency, 1824–80	DC	71–118	
	Union Agency, 1875–1914	DC/FTW	865–77	
	Five Civilized Tribes Agency/Muskogee, 1914–60	FTW		
Cherokee, North Carolina	Cherokee Indian Agency, 1886–1952	ATL		22
Cheyenne	Cheyenne and Arapahoe Agency, 1824–1952	FTW	119–26	11, 16–17, 27–32, 362–67, 425, 478–79, 574–79
	Upper Arkansas Agency, 1855–74	DC	878–82	
	Upper Missouri Agency, 1824–46	DC	883–88	
	Upper Platte Agency, 1846–70	DC	889–96	
	Red Cloud (Pine Ridge), 1867–1961	KC	715–26	362–69
	Red Moon Census, 1909–12,1914–16	FTW		425
	Cantonment Agency, 1903–27	FTW		16–17
	Seger School (Concho Agency), 1891–1952	FTW		479
Cheyenne, Northern	Northern Cheyenne Agency, 1884–1952	SEA		
	Tongue River, 1886–1939	DC		574–79
Chickasaw	Chickasaw Agency, 1824–70	DC	135–48	
	Choctaw Agency, 1855–74	DC	169–96	
	Muskogee Area Office, 1870–1952	FTW		
	Union Agency, 1875–1914	DC/FTW	865–77	

Tribe	Agency	Location of Original Records*	Pre–1880 Correspondence M234 Roll No.	Post–1885 Census Records M595 Roll No.
Chilkat	Washington and Oregon Sup., 1842–80	DC	907–20, 607–30	
Chippewa	Red Lake Agency, 1894–1961	DC/KC		417–24
Chippewa (Pembina)	Turtle Mountain Agency, 1869–1955	DC/KC		595–607
Chippewa, Boise Fort	Nett Lake Sub–Agency, 1908–18	DC/KC		287
Chippewa, Consolidated	Minn. (Consol. Chippewa) Agency, 1890–1953	DC/KC		57–62
Chippewa, Kansas	Potawatomi Agency, ca. 1876	DC/KC	678–95	2, 11, 57–76, 94–97, 117, 167, 170–71, 180
	Osage River Agency to 1851	DC	642–51	181, 140–47, 187, 229–32, 253, 392–95
	Ottawa Agency, 1863–64	DC	656–58	417, 595–607, 628, 649–62
	Sac and Fox Agency, 1851–63, 1864–69	DC/CHI	728–44	
Chippewa, L. Superior/MN	Chippewa Agency, 1851–53	DC/CHI	149–68	
Chippewa, Lake Superior	La Pointe Agency, 1831–50 Mackinac Agency, 1853–54	DC DC	387–400 402–16	
Chippewa, L. Superior/MS	Sandy Lake Subagency, 1850–51	DC	767	
Chippewa, Michigan	Mackinac Agency, 1903–27	DC/CHI	402–16	253
Chippewa, Mississippi	Winnebago Agency, 1848–1947	DC/KC	931–47	
Chippewa, United Band	Chicago and Green Bay, East, 1824–80 Council Bluffs Agency, 1837–47	CHI DC	132–34, 315–36 215–18	
Chippewa, Wisconsin	Great Lakes Consol. Agency, 1875–1952 Lac du Flambeau Agency/School, 1896–1932 Red Cliff Agency and School, 1901–22 Tomah Indian School and Agency, 1908–34	CHI CHI CHI CHI		170–71 229–32 417
Chippewa	Devil's Lake–Fort Totten, 1890–1950 La Pointe Agency, 1886–1922 Leech Lake Agency, 1899–1922 White Earth Agency, 1892–1929	KC CHI KC KC	281–84 387–400	94–97 234–42 243–47 649–62
Chiricahua Apache	Arizona Superintendency, 1863–80	DC	3–28	
Choctaw	Choctaw Agency, 1824–76 Jones Academy, Hartshorne, 1901–53 Union Agency–Muskogee Area, 1875–80	DC FTW DC/FTW	169–96 865–77	 685
Choctaw, Mississippi	Choctaw, Philadelphia, Miss., 1926–39	DC		15, 41–42
Christian	See Stockbridge and Munsee			
Citizen Potawatomi	Shawnee Agency, 1890–1952 Sac and Fox Agency, Oklahoma, 1889–1919, with gaps	FTW FTW		490–96 453–55
Clallam	Puyallup Agency, 1885–1920	SEA		93, 407–09, 584–93
Cocopa	Colorado River Agency, 1867–1955	LA		
Coeur d'Alene	Colville Agency, 1865–1952	SEA		43–45, 49–56, 302
Comanche	Anadarko Area Office, 1881–1962 Upper Platte Agency, 1846–55 Upper Arkansas Agency, 1855–64 Kiowa Agency, 1864–80	FTW DC DC FTW	 889–96 878–82 375–86	211–23 211–23 211–23 211–23
Concow	Round Valley Agency, 1893–1920	SF		12, 447–49
Coyotero Apache	New Mexico Superintendency to 1877 Arizona Superintendency, 1877–80	DC DC	546–82 3–28	

Tribe	Agency	Location of Original Records*	Pre–1880 Correspondence M234 Roll No.	Post–1885 Census Records M595 Roll No.
Cree	Upper Missouri Agency, 1824–74	DC	883–88	11
Creek	Creek Agency, 1824–66 Union Agency, 1875–1914 Eufala Boarding School, 1925–52 Muskogee Area Office, 1890–1960	DC DC/FTW FTW FTW	 865–77	
Crow	Crow Agency, 1874–1952 Upper Missouri Agency, 1824–66 Fort Berthold Agency, 1867–70	SEA DC DC	 883–88 292	79–86 79–86 79–86
Cuthead Sioux	Upper Missouri Agency, 1824–66	DC	883–88	
Delaware	Anadarko Area Office, 1881–1962	FTW		218–223
Delaware, Kansas	Fort Leavenworth Agency, 1824–51 Kansas Agency 1851–55 Delaware Agency, 1855–73	DC DC DC	300–03 364–70 274–80	
Delaware, Indian Terr.	Cherokee Agency, 1867–74 Union Agency, 1875–80	DC DC	101–12 865–77	
Digger	Digger Agency, 1916–20 Greenville School and Agency, 1897–1921	SF SF		
Dwamish	Oregon and Washington Sup., 1842–80	DC	607–30, 907–20	
Eastern Cherokee	Cherokee Indian Agency, 1886–1952 See Shawnee	ATL		
Flathead	Montana Superintendency, 1864–80 Flathead Agency, 1875–1952	DC SEA	488–518	 107–16
Fox	See Sac and Fox			
Grande Ronde	Roseburg Agency, 1912–18	SF		
Grosventre	Blackfeet Agency, 1875–1952 Fort Berthold, 1867–80 Fort Belknap, 1885–1939 Montana Superintendency, 1864–80 Upper Missouri, 1824–66	SEA DEN/KC/SEA SEA DC DC	 292–99 488–518 883–88	 11, 126–36 126–31
Havasupai	Colorado River Agency, 1867–1955 Truxton Canon Agency, 1895–1951	LA LA		178, 580–81 580–81
Hoa	Neah Bay (Tahola) Agency, 1878–1950	SEA		282–86
Hoopa	Hoopa Valley Agency and School, 1891–1929 California Superintendency	SF DC	 32–52	 12
Hopi	Hopi Agency, 1910–56 Western Navajo Agency, 1902–17 California Superintendency, 1849–80	LA LA DC	 32–52	188–95 640–45 12, 182–87
Iowa	Shawnee Agency, 1890–1952	FTW		176, 210, 392–95, 453–55, 491–96
Iowa	Horton (Potawatomi) Agency, 1851–1963	KC		
Iroquois	Six Nations Agency, 1824–34 Seneca, New York, 1824–32 New York Agency, 1835–80	DC DC DC	832 808 583–97	
Jicarilla Apache	Abiquiu and Cimarron Agencies, 1869–82 Jicarilla Agency, 1890–1952 Mescalero Agency, 1874–1942	DEN DEN DEN		543–45 197–98
Kansa (Kaw)	Pawnee Agency, 1871–1964	FTW	659–68	199, 317–28, 337–43

Tribe	Agency	Location of Original Records*	Pre–1880 Correspondence M234 Roll No.	Post–1885 Census Records M595 Roll No.
Kansa (Kaw), Kansas	Ft. Leavenworth Agency, 1824–47	DC	300–03	
	Osage River Agency, 1847–51	DC	642–51	
	Potawatomi Agency, 1851–55	DC	678–95	
	Kansas Agency, 1855–76	DC	364–70	
Kansa (Kaw), Ind. Terr.	Osage Agency, 1874–80	DC/FTW	633–41	
Kaskaskia	Miami Agency, 1870–1952	FTW		
Kaw	See Kansa			
Kichai	Wichita/Kiowa Agencies, 1857–80	DC	383–86, 928–30	
Kickapoo	Shawnee Agency, 1890–1952	FTW		210, 392–95
Kickapoo, Kansas	Ft. Leavenworth Agency, 1824–51	DC	300–03	
	Great Nemaha, 1851–55	DC	307–14	
	Kickapoo Agency, 1855–76	DC	371–74	
	Horton (Potawatomi) Agency, 1874–1963	DC/KC	691–95	176, 210, 392–95
Kickapoo, Mexican	Kickapoo Agency, 1873–75	DC	373–74	
	Sac and Fox Agency, 1874–80	DC/CHI	740–44	
	Shawnee Agency, 1890–1952	FTW		
Kiowa	Upper Platte Agency, 1846–55	DC	889	
	Upper Arkansas Agency, 1855–64	FTW	878	
	Kiowa Agency, 1864–1962	FTW	375–86	211–23
Kiowa Apache	See Apache			
Klamath	Hoopa Valley Agency, 1891–1929	SF		12, 182–87, 224–27
Klamath, Lower	Greenville School/Agency, 1897–1921	SF		
	Roseburg Agency, 1913–18	SF		446
Klamath	Klamath Indian Agency, 1865–1952	SEA		12, 182–87, 224–27
Kutenai	Montana Superintendency, 1864–80	DC	488–518	107–108, 302
Lake	Coleville Agency, 1874–1964	SEA		49–56
Lipan, Apache	Texas Agency, 1847–59	DC	858–861	
	Central Superintendency, 1876–80	DC	67–70	
Little Lake Valley	Round Valley Agency	SF		447–449
Lower Brule, Sioux	Upper Missouri Agency to 1874	DC	883–888	
	Crow Creek Agency, 1874–1955	DC/KC	249	87–92
	Lower Brule Agency, 1875–76	DC/KC	401	87–92, 252
Lummi	Tulalip Agency, 1854–1952	SEA		582–93
Makah	Neah Bay (Tahola) Agency, 1878–1952	SEA		282–86
Mandan	Bismarck Indian School, 1904–38	KC		
	Upper Missouri Agency, 1824–66	DC	883–88	
	Fort Berthold, 1889–1939	KC	292–99	132–36
Maricopa	Pima Agency, 1901–51	LA	669	347–61
Mdewakanton Sioux	Birch Cooley (Pipestone), 1895–1954	KC		2, 35, 385
Menominee	Green Bay and Keshena, 1865–1959	CHI	325–36	172–74, 200–09
Menominee	Menominee Agency, 1865–1959	CHI		
Mescalero Apache	Mescalero Agency, 1874–1946	DEN		254–56
Mexican Kickapoo	See Kickapoo			
Miami	Miami Agency, Oklahoma, 1870–1952	FTW		487–89
Miami, Ohio	Fort Wayne and Indiana, 1824–50	DC	304, 354–60	11

Tribe	Agency	Location of Original Records*	Pre–1880 Correspondence M234 Roll No.	Post–1885 Census Records M595 Roll No.
Miami, Kansas	Osage River Agency, to 1871 Shawnee Agency, 1871	DC FTW	642–51 820–23	411–16 488–89
Miami, Indian Terr.	Quapaw Agency, 1871–80	FTW	703–14	410–12, 416
Mimbreno Apache	New Mexico Superintendency, to 1877 Arizona Superintendency, 1877–80	DC DC	546–82 3–28	
Miniconjou Sioux	Upper Missouri and Upper Platte, 1824–74 Cheyenne River Agency, 1869–1956	DC KC	883–96	
Mission	Mission Tule River Agency, 1920–53	LA		15, 41–42, 258–60, 267
Mission	Camp McDowell (Pima Agency), 1901–51 Pala Subagency, 1905–07,1916–20	DC/LA LA		15 335
Missouri	Upper Missouri Agency, 1824–37 Council Bluffs Agency, 1837–56 Otoe and Ponca Agencies, 1856–1964 Nebraska Agencies, 1876–80	DC DC DC/FTW DC	883–88 215–18 652–55 519–29	 329, 386–91
Moache Ute	Abiquiu and Cimarron Agencies, 1869–82	DEN		
Modoc	Digger Agency, 1916–20 Quapaw and Seneca Agencies, 1873–80	SF DC/FTW	 703–13	224–28 410–12, 487–89
Mogollon Apache	New Mexico Superintendency, to 1877 Arizona Superintendency, 1877–80	DC DC	546–72 3–28	
Mojave	Colorado River Agency, 1867–1955 San Carlos Agency, 1900–52	LA LA		46–48 460–69
Mojave-Apache	Camp McDowell (Pima Agency), 1901–51 Phoenix Area Office, 1907–74	LA LA		15 344–45
Mono	California Superintendency, 1849–80	DC	32–52	13
Moqui Pueblo	Moqui Pueblo Agency, 1906–23	DC		268–72
Muckleshoot	Tulalip Agency, 1854–1952	SEA		93, 582–93
Munsee	Potawatomi Agency, 1851–1902	DC/FTW	678–95	392
Munsee, East	Green Bay and Menominee, 1865–1959	CHI	325–36	
Munsee, Kansas	Ft. Leavenworth Agency, 1839–51 Kansas Agency, 1851–55 Delaware Agency, 1855–59 Sac and Fox Agency, 1859–69	DC DC DC DC	301–03 364 274–75 734–38	
Munsee, Kansas	Ottawa Agency, 1863–64 Potawatomi Agency, ca.1876–80	DC DC	656 692–95	
Navajo (East, North, South)	Navajo Agency, 1881–1936	DEN/LA		303–07, 405–06, 471, 518–31, 640–48
Navajo	Santa Fe Agency, 1890–1935 Pueblo Bonito, 1909–26	DEN DC		98–103, 190–95, 249, 273–82 401–06
Navajo, Northern	Northern Navajo and Shiprock, 1903–35	LA		303–07
Navajo, Western	Western Navajo Agency, 1902–17	LA		640–45
Navajo	Albuquerque School, 1890–1960 Leupp Training School, 1915–35	DEN/FTW DEN		1 249–51
Nez Perce	Ponca and Quapaw Agencies, Okla., 1878–79 Northern Idaho Agency, 1875–1952 Fort Lapwai, 1902–33 Winnebago Agency, 1869–1947	 SEA DC KC	675–77, 707–13	301 11, 45, 49–56 145–48

Tribe	Agency	Location of Original Records*	Pre–1880 Correspondence M234 Roll No.	Post–1885 Census Records M595 Roll No.
Nez Perce, Joseph's Band	Colville Agency, 1865–1952	SEA		
Nisqualli	Puyallup Agency, 1888–1909 Taholah Agency, 1915–39 with gaps	SEA SEA		93, 302, 407–09 564–69
Nomelaki	Round Valley Agency, 1893–1920	SF		12, 447–49
Oglala Sioux	Upper Missouri/Upper Platte, 1824–74 Red Cloud/Whetstone/Spotted Tail, 1871–80 Grand River (Standing Rock), 1871–1957 Pine Ridge Agency, 1913–43 with gaps	DC DC DC/KC KC	883–96 715–26, 925–27, 840–45 305–06	 370–84
Omaha	Upper Missouri Agency, 1824–37 Council Bluffs Agency, 1837–56 Omaha (Winnebago) Agency, 1867–1946 Nebraska Agencies, 1876–80	DC DC DC/KC DC	883–88 215–18 604–06 519–29	 311–14, 663–70
Oneida	Keshena Agency, 1920–39 Tomah Agency, 1897–1923	CHI CHI		202–07 315–16, 572–73
Oneida, New York	Six Nations and New York, 1824–80	DC	832,583–97	290–300
Oneida, Wisconsin	Oneida and Greenbay, 1897–1927	CHI		172–74
Onondaga	New York Agency, 1835–80	DC	583–97	290–300
Oreilles	La Pointe Agency, 1886–89	DC/CHI		234–40
Osage	Osage Agency, 1824–51, 1874–1961 Neosho Agency, 1851–74	DC/FTW DC	631–41 530–37	317–28, 530–37, 631–41
Otoe	Upper Missouri Agency, 1824–37 Council Bluffs Agency, 1837–56 Otoe Agency, 1856–76 Ponca Agency, 1886–1927 Nebraska Agencies, 1876–80	DC DC DC DC/FTW DC	883–88 215–18 652–55 519–29	 329 386–91
Ottawa	Mackinac Agency, 1903–27 Miami (Quapaw) Agency, Okla., 1870–1952 Seneca Agency, 1901–07, 1910–21	CHI DC/FTW DC	 703–13	 410–416 487–89
Ottawa, East	Green Bay and Chicago, 1824–1961	DC/CHI	132–34, 315–36	
Ottawa, Iowa	Council Bluffs Agency, 1837–47	DC	215–18	
Ottawa, Kansas	Osage River Agency, 1837–51 Sac and Fox Agency, 1851–63 Ottawa Agency, 1863–73	DC DC/CHI DC	642–51 733–44 656–58	
Ottawa, Indian Terr.	Neosho Agency, 1867–71	DC	530–37	
Ozette	Neah Bay Agency, 1878–1950	SEA		282–86
Pahvant	Utah Superintendency, 1849–80	DC	897–906	167
Paiute	Fort Bidwell Agency, 1910–31 Nevada Agency, 1886–1905 Western Navajo Agency, 1902–17 Bishop Agency, 1916 Fallon (Lovelocks) School, 1909–24	SF SF LA DC SF		224–28, 330–34, 640–45 288 12, 18–19, 104, 137, 149, 167, 199, 227–28, 252, 268, 288–89, 330–34, 410, 460, 615, 629–48 2 104, 252
Papago	Pima Agency, 1901–51	DC/LA		347–61, 478, 480–85

Tribe	Agency	Location of Original Records*	Pre–1880 Correspondence M234 Roll No.	Post–1885 Census Records M595 Roll No.
Pawnee	Upper Missouri Agency, 1824–37 Council Bluffs Agency, 1837–56 Pawnee (Ponca) Agency, 1859–1964	DC KC DC/FTW	883–88 215–18 659–68, 670–77	386–91 336–43, 386–91
Pembina Chippewa	Chippewa Agency, 1923–36	DC/CHI		57–76
Pend d'Oreille	Flathead Agency, 1875–1960	SEA		107–08
Peoria	Miami (Quapaw) Agency, 1870–1952 Seneca Agency, 1901–07, 1910–21	DC/FTW DC	703–13	410–16 487–89
Peoria, Kansas	Ft. Leavenworth/Osage River, 1824–71	DC	300–03, 642–51	48
Piankeshaw, Confederated	Miami (Quapaw) Agency, 1870–1952	DC/FTW	703–13	
Piankeshaw, Kansas	Ft. Leavenworth/Osage River, 1824–71	DC	300–03, 642–51	
Piankeshaw, Indian Terr.	Neosho Agency, 1867–71	DC	530–37	
Piegon	Blackfeet Agency, 1855–69	SEA/DEN		
Pillager Chippewa	Leech Lake/Chippewa Agency, 1908–31	KC		57–76
Pima	Pima Agency, 1901–51	LA		344–45, 347–61
Pit River	Fort Bidwell Agency, 1910–31 Round Valley Agency, 1893–1917	SF SF		12, 137 224, 446–49
Ponca	Upper Missouri Agency, 1824–59 Pawnee (Ponca) Agency, 1871–1964 Santee Sioux (Flandreau), 1892–1957	DC DC/FTW KC	883–88 659–68, 670–77	 338–43, 385–91, 668–70 475–77, 683–88
Potawatomi	Carter and Laona Agencies, 1911–27 Grand Rapids Agency, 1900–26 Great Lakes Consolidated, 1875–1952	CHI CHI CHI		22, 230–23 170–71, 176
Potawatomi, East	Fort Wayne and Indiana, 1824–50 Green Bay/Chicago/Mackinac, 1824–80 Winnebago Agency, 1864–1965	DC DC/CHI DC/KC	304, 354–61 132–34, 315–36, 402–15 931–47	230–33
Potawatomi, Iowa	Council Bluffs Agency, 1837–47	DC	215–18	
Potawatomi, Kansas	Osage River Agency, 1837–47 Ft. Leavenworth Agency, 1847–51 Horton (Potawatomi) Agency 1851–80 Great Nemaha and Kickapoo, 1837–80	DC DC KC DC/KC	642–51 300–03 307–14, 371–74	 210, 392–95
Potawatomi, Indian Terr.	Quapaw/Shawnee/Sac and Fox, 1871–1952	DC/FTW	703–13	453–54, 490–96
Potter	Round Valley Agency	SF		447–49
Pueblo	Pueblo and Jicarilla Agencies, 1874–1900 Pueblo Agency and Day School, 1912–22 Santa Fe Agency	DEN DEN DEN		396–406 1, 403–06 471–74, 532–42, 624–27
Pueblo	Albuquerque Indian School, 1886–1954 Cimarron and Abiquiu Agencies, 1869–1883 Laguna Sanatorium, 1926–33 Moqui Pueblo, 1906,1908–16,1918–23 Northern Pueblo Agency, 1904–36 Southern Pueblo Agency, 1911–35	DEN DEN DEN DC DEN DEN		 268–72 308–10 532–42
Pueblo, Moqui	Hopi Agency, 1910–56	LA		268–72
Pueblos, United	United Pueblos Agency, 1935–52	DEN		
Puyallup	Tulalip Agency, 1854–1952 Puyallup Agency, 1855–1920	SEA SEA		302, 407–09 407–09

Tribe	Agency	Location of Original Records*	Pre–1880 Correspondence M234 Roll No.	Post–1885 Census Records M595 Roll No.
Quapaw	Caddo and Red River Agencies	DC	31, 727	
	Miami (Quapaw) Agency, 1870–1952	DC/FTW	703–13	411–16
	Neosho Agency, 1831–71	DC	530–37	
	Osage Agency, 1879–80	DC/FTW	633–41	317
	Seneca Agency, 1901–07,1910–21	DC		487–89
Queet	Cushman School (Puyallup), 1885–1920	SEA		93
Quileute	Taholah Agency, 1878–1950	SEA		565–69
	Neah Bay Agency, 1885–1928	SEA		282–8
Quinaielt	Puyallup Agency, 1888–1909	SEA		93, 407–09, 417
	Taholah Agency, 1915–39 with gaps	SEA		564–69
Red Lake Chippewa	Red Lake Agency, 1894–1952	KC		230–42, 418–25
Redwood	Round Valley Agency	SF		2, 447–49
Sac and Fox	See Sac and Fox			
San Carlos Apache	San Carlos Agency, 1900–52	LA		461–70
Sans Arcs Sioux	Up. Missouri/Platte/Spotted Tail, 1824–74	DC	840–45, 883–96	
	Grand River/Cheyenne River, 1871–80	DC/KC	127–31, 305–06	
Santee Sioux	Saint Peters Agency, to 1870	DC	757–66	
	Santee Sioux Agency, 1871–76	DC/KC	768–69	474–77
	Nebraska Agencies, 1876–80	DC	518–29	
	Flandreau School, 1873–1951	DC/KC	285	105–06
	Winnebago and Yankton, 1867–1955	DC/KC	930–47, 959–62	660–70, 684–88
Sac and Fox, Iowa	Sac and Fox Agency and Schools, 1896–1947	CHI		449–52
Sac and Fox, Mississippi	Sac and Fox Agency, 1824–80	DC	728–44	
	Raccoon River Agency, 1843–45	DC	714	
	Osage River Agency, 1847–51	DC	643–44	
	Prairie du Chien Agency, 1824–42	DC	696–702	
Sac and Fox, Missouri	Iowa Subagency, 1829–34	DC	362	
	Upper Missouri Agency, 1835–37	DC	883–88	
	Great Nemaha Agency, 1837–76	DC	307–14	
	Nebraska Agencies, 1876–80	DC	518–29	
Sac and Fox, Missouri and Oklahoma	Shawnee Agency, 1890–1952	DC/FTW		210, 393, 453–55
Seminole	Seminole Agency, 1824–76	DC	799–807	
	Union Agency, 1875–80	DC	864–77	
Seminole, Florida	Seminole Agency Dania, 1934–52	ATL		486–87
Seneca, Indian Terr.	Miami (Quapaw) Agency, 1870–1952	DC/FTW	702–13	410–16, 487–89
Seneca, N.Y.	Six Nations Agency, 1824–34	DC	582–97	290–300, 488–89
Seneca, Ohio	Piqua and Ohio Agencies, 1831–43	DC	600–03	
Seneca, Indian Terr.	Neosho Agency, 1837–71	DC	529–37	
Shasta	Roseburg Agency, 1912–18	SF		446
Shawnee, Indian Terr.	Shawnee Agency, 1890–1952	FTW		
Shawnee, Ohio	Piqua and Ohio Agencies, 1831–43	DC	600–03	
Shawnee, Kansas	Fort Leavenworth Agency, 1824–51	DC	299–303	
	Kansas Agency, 1851–55	DC	363–70	
	Shawnee Agency, 1855–76	DC	808–23	
Shawnee, Kansas—Indian Territory	Union Agency, 1875–80	DC	864–77	
Shawnee, Eastern	Neosho Agency, 1867–71	DC	534–37	
	Quapaw Agency, 1885–1939	DC/FTW		410–16
	Seneca Agency, 1901–07, 1910–21	DC		487–89

Tribe	Agency	Location of Original Records*	Pre–1880 Correspondence M234 Roll No.	Post–1885 Census Records M595 Roll No.
Shawnee, Absentee	Wichita Agency, 1859–67	DC	927–30	
	Sac and Fox Agency, ca. 1869–80	CHI		
	Shawnee Agency, 1890–1952	DC/FTW		490–96
Sheepeater	Lemhi Agency, 1885,1887–1906	SEA		248
Shoshoni	Wind River Agency, 1873–1952	DEN		167, 498–504, 631, 663
	Carson School, 1909–39	SF		18–21
	Fort Hall, 1885–87, 1890–91, 1894–1939	SEA		138–44, 498–504
	Lemhi Agency, 1885, 1887–1906	SEA		248
Shoshoni, Western	Western Shoshone Agency, 1897–1916	SF		646–48
Sioux	Fort Peck Agency, 1885–1939	SEA		11, 150–60
Sioux, Mississippi	Saint Peters Agency, 1824–70	DC	756–66	
	Prairie du Chien and Winnebago Agencies	DC/KC	695–702, 930–47	
Sioux, Missouri/Platte River	Upper Missouri Agency, 1824–74	DC	883–88	
	Upper Platte Agency, 1846–70	DC	889–96	
	Yankton Agency, 1859–76	DC	959–62	
	Upper Arkansas Agency, 1855–74	DC	878–82	
	Whetstone Agency, 1871–74	DC	925–27	
	Spotted Tail Agency, 1875–80	DC	840–45	
	Red Cloud Agency, 1871–80	DC	715–26	
	Grand River Agency, 1871–75	DC	305–06	
	Standing Rock Agency, 1871–80	DC	846–52	
	Crow Creek Agency, 1871–76	DC	249	
	Lower Brule Agency, 1875–76	DC	401	
Sioux—Fort Totten	Fort Totten Agency, 1875–1950	KC		161–64
Sioux—Cheyenne River	Cheyenne River Agency, 1869–1956	DC/KC		33–40
Sioux—Oglala	Pine Ridge Agency, 1886–1943	DC/KC		361–8
Sioux—Spotted Tail	Rosebud Agency, 1860–1966	KC/DEN		427–45
Sioux—Standing Rock	Standing Rock Agency, 1885–1939	DC/KC	845–52	547–63
Sioux—Sisseton	Saint Peters Agency, 1824–70	DC	756–66	507–17
	Devil's Lake Agency, 1871–80	DC/KC	280–84	
	Devil's Lake Agency, 1885–90,1892–1905	DC/KC		94–97
	Sisseton Agency, 1886–1929 with gaps	KC		507–17
Skallam	Puyallup Agency, 1885–1920	SEA		302
Skokomish	Cushman School (Puyallup), 1885–1920	SEA		93, 302, 407–09, 564–69
	Taholah Agency, 1878–1950	SEA		564–69
Snake	See Shoshoni			225–26
Spokan	Spokane Agency, 1885–1950	SEA		49–56, 546
	Colville Agency, 1865–1952	SEA		
Squaxon	Puyallup Agency, 1885–1920	SEA		302, 407–09
	Taholah Agency, 1878–1950	SEA		564–69
Stockbridge	Keshena Agency, 1909–19	CHI		200–01
Stockbridge, New York	Six Nations Agency, 1824–34	DC	832	
Stockbridge, Wisconsin	Green Bay Agency, 1885–1908	CHI		172–74
	Tomah Indian School and Agency, 1908–34	CHI		573
Stockbridge, Kansas	Fort Leavenworth Agency, 1839–51	DC	299–303	
	Kansas Agency, 1851–55	DC	363–70	
	Delaware Agency, 1855–59	DC	274–80	
Swinomish	Tulalip Agency, 1854–1952	SEA		582–93

Tribe	Agency	Location of Original Records*	Pre–1880 Correspondence M234 Roll No.	Post–1885 Census Records M595 Roll No.
Tabaquache Ute	New Mexico Superintendency, to 1861	DC		
Tawakoni	Texas Agency, 1847–59 Wichita Agency, 1859–78 Kiowa Agency, 1878–80	DC DC DC/FTW	857–61 927–30 383–86	
Tenino	Warm Springs Agency	SEA		11, 635–38
Tonkowa	Pawnee Agency, 1871–1964 Texas Agency, 1847–59 Wichita Agency, 1859–1878	DC/FTW DC DC	661–68 857–61 927–30	338–43, 386–91
Tulalip	Tulalip Agency, 1854–1950	SEA		582–93
Tule	Tule River Agency Sacramento Agency Pala Superintendency, 1903–21	SF SF LA		12, 594 456–57
Tuscarora	Six Nations Agency, 1824–34 New York Agency, 1835–80 Michigan Superintendency, 1832–34	DC DC DC	832 582–97 418–27	
Uinta Ute	Uintah and Ouray Agency, 1897–1952	DEN		608–15
Umatilla	Umatilla Indian Agency, 1854–1952	SEA		616–22
Uncompahgre Ute	Uintah and Ouray Agencies, 1897–1952	Den		608–12
United Pueblos	See Pueblos			
Ute	Santa Fe Agency Paiute Agency, 1928–39 Uintah and Ouray Agency, 1897–1952	DC DEN DEN	767	330–34 608–15, 628
Ute, Consolidated	Consolidated Ute Agency, 1878–1952	DEN		77–78, 628
Ute, Southern	Southern Ute and Consolidated Ute	DEN		543–545, 628
Waco	Texas Agency, 1847–59 Wichita Agency, 1859–78 Kiowa Agency, 1878–80	DC DC DC/FTW	857–61 927–30 383–86	
Wahkepute Sioux	See Sisseton Sioux			
Wailaki	Round Valley Agency	SF		447–49
Walapai	Colorado River Agency 1867–1955 Truxton Canon Agency, 1895–1951	LA LA		46, 196 580–81
Wallawalla	Uintah and Ouray Agency, 1897–1952	DEN		616–22
Warm Springs	Warm Springs Agency, 1861–1952	SEA		635–39
Wasco	Oregon Superintendency, 1842–80 Utah and Nevada Superintendencies Walker River Agency	DC DC SF	607–30 896–906, 538–45	631
Wea	Miami (Quapaw) Agency, 1870–1952	DC/FTW	703–13	
Wea, Indiana	Fort Wayne and Indiana Agencies	DC	304, 354–61	
Wea, Kansas	Fort Leavenworth Agency, 1824–37 Osage River Agency, 1837–71	DC DC	300–03 642–51	
Wea, Indian Territory	Neosho Agency, 1867–71	DC	534–37	
Whilkut	California Superintendency, 1849–80	DC	32–52	
Wichita, Indian Territory, Oklahoma	Kiowa Agency, 1878–1962	DC/FTW	383–86	211–23
Wichita	Texas Agency,1847–59 Wichita Agency 1857–78	DC DC	858–61 928–30	
Wikchamni	California Superintendency	DC	32–52	

Tribe	Agency	Location of Original Records*	Pre–1880 Correspondence M234 Roll No.	Post–1885 Census Records M595 Roll No.
Wiminuche Ute	See Ute			
Winnebago	Wind River Agency, 1898–1955	DEN		663–71
	Prairie du Chien Agency, 1824–42	DC	696–702	
	Turkey River Subagency, 1842–46	DC	862–64	
	Winnebago Agency, 1826–76	DC	931–47	
	Nebraska Agencies, 1876–80	DC	519–29	
	Grand Rapids Agency, 1900–26	CHI		168
	Omaha (Winnebago) Agency, 1861–1955	KC		311–13
Winnebago, Wisconsin	Tomah Indian School and Agency, 1908–34	CHI		570–73
	Wittenberg Indian School, 1905–10	DC		671
Wyandot	Quapaw Agency, 1871–1952	DC/FTW		410–16
Wyandot, Ohio/Michigan	Piqua Agency, 1824–30	DC	601–03	
	Ohio Agency, 1831–43	DC	745–46	
	Saginaw Subagency, 1824–50	DC		
Wyandot, Kansas	Wyandot Agency, 1843–51, 1870–72	DC	950–52	
	Kansas Agency, 1851–55	DC	364–70	
	Shawnee Agency, 1855–63	DC	809–13	
	Delaware Agency, 1863–69	DC	276–80	
Wyandot, Indian Terr.	Neosho Agency, 1867–71	DC	534–36	
	Quapaw Agency, 1871–80	DC/FTW	703–13	411–16, 488–89
Yakima	Yakima Indian Agency, 1859–1952	SEA		671–79
Yamel	Oregon Superintendency, 1842–80	DC	607–30	
Yampa Ute	Colorado Superindentency, 1861–80	DC	197–214	
Yankton Sioux	Upper Missouri Agency to 1859	DC	883–88	
	Yankton Agency, 1859–76	DC/KC	959–62	680–88
	Fort Peck Agency, 1877–1959	SEA		151–60
Yanktonai Sioux	Upper Missouri Agency, 1824–74	DC	883–88	
	Grand River Agency, 1871–75	DC	305–06	
	Upper Platte Agency, 1846–70	DC	889–96	
	Standing Rock Agency, 1875–1957	DC/KC	846–52	
	Crow Creek Agency, 1874–1922	DC/KC		89–92
Yatasi	Red River Agency, 1824–30	DC	727	
Yavapai	Arizona Superintendency, 1863–80	DC	3–28	
Yokaia	Truxton Canyon Agency, 1895–1951	LA/DC		581
Yuki	Round Valley Agency	SF		12, 447–49
Yuma	Colorado River Agency, 1867–1955	LA		14, 48
	Fort Yuma Agency, 1907–51	LA		165–66
	San Carlos Agency, 1900–52	LA		460–69
Yupu	California Superintendency, 1849–80	DC	32–52	
Zuni	Zuni Agency, 1899–1935	DEN		689–92

ATL: National Archives—Southeast Region, Atlanta, Georgia
CHI: National Archives—Great Lakes Region, Chicago, Illinois
DEN: National Archives—Rocky Mountain Region, Denver, Colorado
DC: National Archives, Washington, D.C.
FTW: National Archives—Southwest Region, Fort Worth, Texas
KC: National Archives—Central Plains Region, Kansas City, Missouri
LA: National Archives—Pacific Southwest Region, Laguna Niguel, California
SEA: National Archives—Pacific Northwest Region, Seattle, Washington
SF: National Archives—Pacific Sierra Region, San Bruno, California

Notes

[1] Katherine M. Weist and Susan R. Sharrock, *An Annotated Bibliography of North Plains Ethnohistory* (Missoula: University of Montana, 1985).

[2] Edward S. Curtis, *The North American Indian, Being a Series of Volumes Picturing and Describing the Indians of the United States and Alaska* (Cambridge, Mass.: University Press, 1907–30). This work is online at <http:mwmory.loc.gov/ammem/award98/ienhtml/curthome.html>. The electronic publication includes all of the published photogravure images, including more than 1500 illustrations and 700 portfolio plates.

[3] Henry R. Schoolcraft, *Historical and Statistical Information Respecting the History, Conditions and Prospects of the Indian Tribes of the United States: Collected and Prepared under the Direction of the Bureau of Indian Affairs, per Act of Congress of March 3, 1847* (Philadelphia: Lippencott, Grambo and Co., 1851).

[4] Eleanor Burke Leacock and Nancy Oestreich Lurie, *North American Indians in Historical Perspective* (Prospect Heights, Ill.: Waveland Press, 1971, 1988).

[5] Helen Hornbeck Tanner, ed., *Atlas of Great Lakes Indian History* (Norman: University of Oklahoma Press, 1987).

[6] Emmet Starr, *History of the Cherokee Indians and Their Legends and Folk Lore* (Oklahoma City, Okla.: Warden Co., 1921; reprint, Baltimore: Genealogical Publishing Co. 2003).

[7] John Trenchard and Walter Moyle, *Iroquois Source Book*, 3 vols. (New York: Garland Publishing, 1983–85).

[8] Edward Hill, comp., *Guide to Records in the National Archives of the United States Relating to American Indians* (Washington, D.C.: National Archives and Records Administration, 1982).

[9] Loretto Dennis Szucs and Sandra Hargreaves Luebking, *The Archives: A Guide to the National Archives Field Branches* (Salt Lake City: Ancestry, 1988).

[10] *The Harvard Encyclopedia of American Ethnic Groups* (Cambridge, Mass.: Belknap Press of Harvard University, 1980).

[11] *The Reference Encyclopedia of the American Indian*, 10th ed. (Nyack, N.Y.: Todd Publications, 2003).

[12] *Dictionary of Indian Tribes of the Americas*, 2nd ed. (Newport Beach, Calif.: American Indian Publishers, 1993–95).

[13] Frederick W. Hodge, *Handbook of American Indians North of Mexico*, Smithsonian Institution, Bureau of American Ethnology, Bulletin 302, 2 parts (Washington, D.C.: Government Printing Office, 1912; reprint, New York: Rowman and Littlefield, 1971).

[14] John R. Swanton, *The Indian Tribes of North America*, Smithsonian Institution, Bureau of American Ethnology, Bulletin 145 (Washington, D.C.: Smithsonian Institution Press, 1984).

[15] Gretchen M. Bataille and Kathleen Mullen Sands, *American Indian Women: Telling Their Lives*, reprint ed. (Lincoln: University of Nebraska Press, 1987).

[16] Harvey Arden and Steve Wall, *Wisdomkeepers: Meetings with Native American Spiritual Elders* (Hillsboro, Ore.: Beyond Words Publishing, 1990).

[17] John Gattuso, *Circle of Nations: Voices and Visions of American Indians* (Hillsboro, Ore.: Beyond Words Publishing, 1993).

[18] *Monthly Catalog of United States Government Publications* (Washington, D.C.: Government Printing Office, 1895–).

[19] *Introduction to United States Government Information Sources*, 6th ed. (Englewood, Colo.: Libraries Unlimited, 1999).

[20] Charles J. Kappler, *Indian Affairs: Laws and Treaties* (Washington, D.C.: Government Printing Office, 1904).

[21] Duane Champagne, ed., *The Native North American Almanac: A Reference Work on Native North Americans in the United States and Canada*, 2nd ed. (Detroit: Gale Research Co., 2001).

[22] Joe Goss, *A Complete Roll of All Choctaw Claimants and Their Heirs Existing Under the Treaties Between the United States and the Choctaw Nation* (Conway, Ark.: Oldbuck Press, 1992).

[23] Bob Blankenship, *Cherokee Roots* (Cherokee, N.C.: the compiler, 1992).

[24] Toni Jollay Prevost, *The Delaware & Shawnee Admitted to Cherokee Citizenship and the Related Wyandotte & Moravian Delaware* (Bowie, Md.: Heritage Books, 1992).

[25] *Periodical Source Index (PERSI)* (Fort Wayne, Ind.: Allen County Public Library, 1986–).

[26] *Genealogical Periodical Annual Index (GPAI)* (Bowie, Md.: Heritage Books, 1962–).

[27] *Oklahoma Genealogical Society Quarterly* (Oklahoma City: Oklahoma Genealogical Society, 1961–); *Stirpes* (Cleburne, Tex.: Texas State Genealogical Society, 1961–); *Topeka Genealogical Society Quarterly* (Topeka, Kans.: Topeka Genealogical Society, 1971).

[28] *The American Indian Quarterly* (Lincoln: University of Nebraska Press, 1974–).

[29] Donna Williams, *Cherokee Family Researcher* (Mesa, Ariz.: 1988–2001); *Journal of Cherokee Studies* (Cherokee, N.C.: Museum of the Cherokee Indian, 1976–).

[30] Annie H. Abel, *The History of Events Resulting in Indian Consolidation West of the Mississippi*, Annual Report of the American Historical Association, 1906 (Washington, D.C.: Government Printing Office, 1908); Grant Foreman, *Indian Removal* (Norman: University of Oklahoma Press, 1932).

[31] Laurence F. Schmeckebier, *The Office of Indian Affairs, Its History, Activities, and Organization* (Baltimore: Johns Hopkins Press, 1927), 131–35.

[32] Ibid.

[33] Ibid.

[34] Felix S. Cohen, *Handbook of Federal Indian Law* (Albuquerque: University of New Mexico Press), 433–44.

[35] Kent Carter, comp., *Preliminary Inventory of the Records of the Muskogee Area Office and The Five Civilized Tribes* (1982).

[36] *American Indians. A Select Catalog of National Archives Microfilm Publications* (Washington, D.C.: National Archives Trust Fund Board, U.S. Central Services Administration, 1984). Records Relating to Census Rolls and Other Enrollments, Bureau of Indian Affairs (record group 75), 32.

[37] Edward E. Hill, *Guide to Records in the National Archives of the United States Relating to American Indians* (Washington, D.C.: National Archives and Records Service, General Services Administration, n.d.), 168–70.

[38] Barry T. Klein, *Reference Encyclopedia of the American Indian*, 2nd ed., 2 vols. (Rye, N.Y.: Todd Publishing, 1973), 91.

[39] *Notes and Documents: Catalogue of Microfilmed Publications of the Archives and Manuscript Division,* The Chronicles of Oklahoma, vol. 60, part 2 (Oklahoma City: Oklahoma Historical Society), 222–24.

[40] *Records of the Creek Nation,* introduction, reel CRN-1 (Indian Archives Division, Oklahoma Historical Society).

[41] *Notes and Documents,* vol. 60, part 2, 218–22.

[42] The Confederation of American Indians, comp., *Indian Reservations: A State and Federal Handbook* (Jefferson, N.C.: McFarland and Co., n.d.), 213.

[43] Klein, *Reference Encyclopedia of the American Indian,* 91.

[44] Confederation of American Indians, *Indian Reservations,* 223.

[45] Ibid., 228.

[46] Ibid., 234.

[47] Ibid., 237.

[48] *Records of the Quapaw Agency,* introduction, reel QA-1 (Indian Archives Division, Oklahoma Historical Society).

[49] Confederation of American Indians, *Indian Reservations,* 241.

[50] *Notes and Documents,* vol. 60, part 4, 473–75.

[51] Ibid., part 1, 79–87.

[52] Ibid., part 2, 225–29.

[53] Ibid., 231.

[54] Hill, *Guide to Records in the National Archives,* 6, 148.

[55] Klein, *Reference Encyclopedia of the American Indian,* 91.

[56] Ibid.

[57] Confederation of American Indians, *Indian Reservations,* 213.

[58] Ibid., 214.

[59] Ibid., 222.

[60] Ibid.

[61] Ibid., 223–34.

[62] Ibid., 227.

[63] *Records of the Kiowa Agency,* introduction, reel KA-1 (Indian Archives Division, Oklahoma Historical Society).

[64] Confederation of American Indians, *Indian Reservations,* 242.

[65] *Notes and Documents,* vol. 60, part 3, 351–55.

[66] *Records of the Cheyenne and Arapaho Agency,* introduction, reel CAA-1 (Indian Archives Division, Oklahoma Historical Society).

[67] Ibid.

[68] *Notes and Documents,* vol. 60, part 3, 348–51.

[69] Klein, *Reference Encyclopedia of the American Indian,* 92.

[70] *Records of the Pawnee Agency.*

[71] Confederation of American Indians, *Indian Reservations,* 225.

[72] *Records of the Pawnee Agency.*

[73] Confederation of American Indians, *Indian Reservations,* 233.

[74] *Records of the Pawnee Agency.*

[75] Confederation of American Indians, *Indian Reservations,* 234.

[76] *Records of the Pawnee Agency.*

[77] Confederation of American Indians, *Indian Reservations,* 236.

[78] *Records of the Pawnee Agency.*

[79] Confederation of American Indians, *Indian Reservations,* 242.

[80] *Records of the Pawnee Agency.*

[81] *Notes and Documents,* vol. 60, part 3, 355–56.

[82] Ibid., 358–59.

[83] Ibid., 357.

[84] Ibid., 356–57.

[85] Ibid., 357.

[86] Klein, *Reference Encyclopedia of the American Indian,* 92.

[87] *Records of the Sac and Fox-Shawnee Agency,* introduction, reel SFSA-1 (Indian Archives Division, Oklahoma Historical Society).

[88] Ibid.

[89] Confederation of American Indians, *Indian Reservations*, 212.

[90] Ibid., 219.

[91] *Records of the Sac and Fox-Shawnee Agency*.

[92] Confederation of American Indians, *Indian Reservations*, 224–25.

[93] Ibid., 226.

[94] *Records of the Sac and Fox-Shawnee Agency*.

[95] Confederation of American Indians, *Indian Reservations*, 234.

[96] *Records of the Sac and Fox-Shawnee Agency*.

[97] *Notes and Documents*, vol. 60, part 4, 476–79.

[98] R. Swanton, *The Indian Tribes of North America* (Washington D.C.: Smithsonian Institution Press, 1979).

References

Arden, Harvey, and Steve Wall. *Wisdomkeepers: Meetings with Native American Spiritual Elders*. Hillsboro, Ore.: Beyond Words Publishing, 1990.

Bantin, Philip C. *Guide to Catholic Indian Mission and School Records in Midwest Repositories*. Milwaukee: Marquette University Libraries, Department of Special Collections and University Archives, 1984.

Bataille, Gretchen M., and Kathleen Mullen Sands. *American Indian Women: Telling Their Lives*. Reprint ed. Lincoln: University of Nebraska Press, 1987.

Blankenship, Bob. *Cherokee Roots*. Cherokee, N.C.: the compiler, 1992.

Boyd, Stephen G. *Indian Local Names with Their Interpretations*. York, Penn.: the author, 1885.

Brandon, William. *Indians*. Boston: Houghton Mifflin, 1989.

Byers, Paula K., ed. *Native American Genealogical Sourcebook*. Detroit, Mich.: Gale Research Co., 1995.

Carpenter, Cecelia Svinth. *How to Research American Indian Blood Lines*. South Prairie, Wash.: Meico Associates, 1984; reprint, Bountiful, Utah: Heritage Quest, 2000.

Carter, Kent. *The Dawes Commission and the Allotment of the Five Civilized Tribes, 1893–1914*. Orem, Utah: Ancestry.com, 1999.

Carter, Kent. "Wantabes and Outalucks: Searching for Indian Ancestors in Federal Records." *Ancestry Newsletter* 5, no. 6 (November–December 1987): 1–6.

Champagne, Duane, ed. *The Native North American Almanac: A Reference Work on Native North Americans in the United States and Canada*. 2nd ed. Detroit: Gale Research Co., 2001.

Chepesiuk, Ron, and Arnold Shankman. *American Indian Archival Material: Guide to the Holdings in the Southeast*. Westport, Conn.: Greenwood Press, 1982. Includes bibliographic references and index.

Cohen, Felix. *Handbook of Federal Indian Law, with Reference Tables and Index*. Washington, D.C.: Government Printing Office, 1942. Reprint, with added foreword, biography, and bibliography. University of New Mexico Press, Albuquerque, 1971. Reprint, Washington, D.C.: Government Printing Office, 1988.

Curtis, Edward S. *The North American Indian, Being a Series of Volumes Picturing and Describing the Indians of the United States and Alaska*. 20 vols. Cambridge, Mass.: University Press, 1907–30.

Dewitt, Donald L. *American Indian Resource Materials in the Western History Collections, University of Oklahoma*. Norman: University of Oklahoma Press, 1990. Includes bibliographic references and index.

Dictionary of Indian Tribes of the Americas. 3 vols. 2nd ed. Newport Beach, Calif.: American Indian Publishing, 1993–95.

Driver, Harold E. *Indians of North America*. Chicago: University of Chicago Press, 1961. Includes bibliography.

Fixico, Donald L. *Termination and Relocation: Federal Indian Policy, 1945–1960*. Albuquerque: University of New Mexico Press, 1986. Includes index and bibliography.

Foreman, Grant. *Indian Removal: The Emigration of the Five Civilized Tribes of Indians*. Norman: University of Oklahoma Press, 1932, 1989. Includes bibliography.

Frazier, Patrick. *Many Nations: A Library of Congress Resource Guide for the Study of Indian and Alaska Native Peoples of the United States*. Washington, D.C.: Library of Congress, 1996.

Freeman, John F. A *Guide to Manuscripts Relating to the American Indian in the Library of the American Philosophical Society*. Vol. 65, *Memoirs of the American Philosophical Society*. Philadelphia: American Philosophical Society, 1966, 1980. Includes bibliography. Supplement published by the society, 1982.

Galluso, John, ed. *Native America: Insight*. Singapore: APA, 1989.

Gannett, Henry. A *Gazetteer of Indian Territory*. Washington, D.C.: Government Printing Office, 1905; reprint, Tulsa: Oklahoma Yesterday Publications, 1980.

Gattuso, John. *Circle of Nations: Voices and Visions of American Indians*. Hillsboro, Ore.: Beyond Words Publishing, 1993.

Gideon, D. C. *Indian Territory—Descriptive, Biographical and Genealogical, Including the Landed Estates, County Seats, with General History of the Territory*. Chicago: Lewis Publishing Co., 1901.

Gormley, Myra Vanderpool. *Cherokee Connections*. 1995; reprint, Baltimore: Genealogical Publishing Co., 2002.

Goss, Joe. *A Complete Roll of All Choctaw Claimants and Their Heirs Existing Under the Treaties Between the United States and the Choctaw Nation*. Conway, Ark.: Oldbuck Press, 1992.

The Harvard Encyclopedia of American Ethnic Groups. Cambridge, Mass.: Belknap Press of Harvard University, 1980.

Hill, Edward E. *Guide to Records in the National Archives of the United States Relating to American Indians*. Washington, D.C.: National Archives and Records Services Administration, 1982.

Hill, Edward, comp. *Guide to Records in the National Archives of the United States Relating to American Indians*. Washington, D.C.: National Archives and Records Administration, 1982.

———. *The Office of Indian Affairs, 1824–1880: Historical Sketches*. New York: Clearwater Publishing Co., 1974.

Hodge, Frederick W. *Handbook of American Indians North of Mexico*. Smithsonian Institution, Bureau of American Ethnology, bulletin 30. 2 parts. Washington, D.C.: Government Printing Office, 1912. Numerous reprints.

Hodge, Frederick Webb. *Handbook of American Indians North of Mexico*. 2 vols. Smithsonian Institution, Bureau of American Ethnology. Bulletin. Washington, D.C., 1907–10; reprint, New York, 1959; Totawa, N.J.: Rowman and Littlefield, 1975. Vol. 1: A–M, vol. 2: N–Z. Includes bibliography.

Hodge, William H. *A Bibliography of Contemporary North American Indians*. New York: Interland Publishing, 1976. Includes index.

Hoover, Herbert T. *The Sioux: A Critical Bibliography*. Bibliographical series, Newberry Library Center for the History of the American Indian. Bloomington: Indiana University Press, for the Newberry Library, 1979. Includes bibliography.

Hoxie, Frederick E., and Harvey Markowitz. *Native Americans: An Annotated Bibliography*. D'Arcey McNickle Center for the History of the American Indian. Pasadena, Calif.: Salem Press, 1991. Includes index.

Hoxie, Frederick E. *Atlas of Native American History*. New York: Routledge, 2003.

Huntington, Henry E., Library and Art Gallery. *Guide to American Historical Manuscripts in the Huntington Library*. San Marino, Calif.: Kingsport Press for the Huntington Library, 1979. Includes index.

Index to the Final Rolls of Citizens and Freedmen of the Five Civilized Tribes in Indian Territory. Washington, D.C.: Government Printing Office, 1961; reprinted, Baltimore: Genealogical Publishing Co., 2003. Online at <www.archives.gov/research_room/arc/arc_info/native_americans_final_rolls_index.html>.

Introduction to United States Government Information Sources. 6th ed. Englewood, Colo.: Libraries Unlimited, 1999.

Jackson, Curtis E., and Marcia J. Galli. *A History of the Bureau of Indian Affairs and its Activities Among the Indians*. San Francisco: R and E Research Associates, 1977. Includes bibliography.

Johnson, Steven L. *Guide to American Indian Documents in the Congressional Serial Set, 1817–1899*. A project of the Institute for the Development of Indian Law. New York: Clearwater Publishing Co., 1977. Includes index. Reprint, Bethesda, Md.: Congressional Information Service, 2000.

Jordan, Jerry Wright. *Cherokee By Blood: Records of Eastern Cherokee Ancestry in the US Court of Claims, 1906–1910*. 9 vols. Bowie, Md.: Heritage Books, 1987–.

Kappler, Charles J. *Indian Affairs: Laws and Treaties*. 6 vols. Washington, D.C.: Government Printing Office, 1903, 1979; reprinted in 7 vols, New York: William S. Hein and Co., 1990–95. Online at <http://digital.library.okstate.edu/kappler/>. Includes indexes.

Kappler, Charles J. *Indian Affairs: Laws and Treaties*. Washington, D.C.: Government Printing Office, 1904. Numerous reprints.

Kirkham, E. Kay. *Our Native Americans and Their Records of Genealogical Value*. Logan, Utah: Everton Publishers, 1980.

Klein, Barry T. *Reference Encyclopedia of the American Indian*. 6th ed. West Nyack, N.Y.: Todd Publications, 1993.

Leacock, Eleanor Burke, and Nancy Oestreich Lurie. *North American Indians in Historical Perspective*. Prospect Heights, Ill.: Waveland Press, 1971, 1988.

Leitch, Barbara. *A Concise Dictionary of Indian Tribes of North America*. Algonac, Mich.: Reference Publications, 1979.

Lennon, Rachal Mills. *Tracing Ancestors among the Five Civilized Tribes. Southeastern Indians Prior to Removal*. Reprint 2003, Baltimore: Genealogical Publishing Co., 2002.

Lipps, Oscar Hiram. *Laws and Regulations Relating to Indians and Their Lands*. Lewiston, Idaho: Lewiston Printing and Binding Co., 1913.

McDonnell, Janet A. *The Dispossession of the American Indian, 1887–1834*. Bloomington: Indiana University Press, 1991. Includes bibliographic references and indexes.

McReynolds, Edwin C. *The Seminoles*. The Civilization of the American Indian Series. Vol. 47. Norman: University of Oklahoma Press, 1957, 1985. Includes bibliography.

Monthly Catalog of United States Government Publications. Washington, D.C.: Government Printing Office, 1895–.

Native American Periodicals and Newspapers, 1828–1982: Bibliography, Publishing Record, and Holdings. Westport, Conn.: Greenwood Press, 1984.

The North American Indian. New York: Garland Publishing, 1985.

O'Brien, Sharon. *American Indian Tribal Governments*. 1st ed. The Civilization of the American Indian Series. Vol. 192. Norman: University of Oklahoma Press, 1989, 1993. Includes bibliography and index.

Otis, D. S. *The Dawes Act and the Allotment of Indian Land*. The Civilization of the American Indian Series. Vol. 123. Norman: University of Oklahoma Press, 1973. Includes bibliographic references.

Prevost, Toni Jollay. *The Delaware & Shawnee Admitted to Cherokee Citizenship and the Related Wyandotte & Moravian Delaware*. Bowie, Md.: Heritage Books, 1992.

Prucha, Francis Paul. *Documents of United States Indian Policy*. Lincoln: University of Nebraska Press, 1975, 2000. Includes bibliography and index.

———. *The Great Father: The United States Government and the American Indians*. 2 vols. Lincoln: University of Nebraska Press, 1984, 1995. Includes bibliography and index.

Rafert, Stewart. *The Miami Indians of Indiana: A Persistent People, 1654–1994*. Indianapolis: Indiana Historical Society, 1996.

The Reference Encyclopedia of the American Indian. 10th ed. Nyack, N.Y.: Todd Publications, 2003.

Schmeckebier, Laurence F. *The Office of Indian Affairs, Its History, Activities, and Organization*. Service monographs of the United States government; no. 48. Baltimore: Johns Hopkins Press, 1927; reprint, New York: AMS Press, 1972. Includes bibliography.

Schoolcraft, Henry R. *Historical and Statistical Information Respecting the History, Conditions and Prospects of the Indian Tribes of the United States: Collected and Prepared Under the Direction of the Bureau of Indian Affairs, per Act of Congress of March 3, 1847*. Philadelphia: Lippencott, Grambo and Co., 1851.

Smith, Jessie Carney, ed. *Ethnic Genealogy: A Research Guide*. Westport, Conn.: Greenwood Press, 1983.

Spindel, Donna. *Introductory Guide to Indian-Related Records (to 1876) in the North Carolina State Archives*. Raleigh: North Carolina Division of Archives and History, 1977, 1979.

Starr, Emmet. *History of the Cherokee Indians and Their Legends and Folk Lore*. Oklahoma City: Warden Co., 1921; reprint, Baltimore: Genealogical Publishing Co., 2003.

Sturtevant, William C. *Handbook of North American Indians*. 20 vols. Washington, D.C.: Smithsonian Institution, 1978–. Includes bibliographies and indexes.

Svoboda, Joseph G. *A Guide to American Indian Resource Materials in Great Plains Repositories*. Lincoln: Center for Great Plains Studies, University of Nebraska–Lincoln, 1983.

Swanton, John R. *Indian Tribes of North America*. Classics of Smithsonian Anthropology. Originally published as the Bureau of American Ethnology Bulletin no. 145. 1984; reprint, Baltimore: Genealogical Publishing Co., 2003. Includes bibliography and index.

Szucs, Loretto Dennis, and Sandra Hargreaves Luebking. *The Archives: A Guide to the National Archives Field Branches*. Salt Lake City: Ancestry, 1988.

Tanner, Helen Hornbeck, ed. *Atlas of Great Lakes Indian History*. Norman: University of Oklahoma Press, 1987.

U.S. Department of the Interior Library. *Bibliographic and Historical Index of American Indians and Persons Involved in Indian Affairs*. 8 vols. Boston: G. K. Hall, 1966.

Weist, Katherine M., and Susan R. Sharrock. *An Annotated Bibliography of North Plains Ethnohistory*. Missoula: University of Montana, 1985.

Wissler, Clark. *Indians of the United States*. New York: Anchor Books, 1989.

Witcher, Curt Bryan. *A Bibliography of Sources for Native American Family History*. Fort Wayne, Ind.: Allen County Public Library, 1988.

Wright, Muriel H. *A Guide to the Indian Tribes of Oklahoma*. The Civilization of the American Indian Series. Vol. 33. Norman: University of Oklahoma Press, 1951, 1986. Includes bibliography.

Yenne, Bill. *The Encyclopedia of North American Indian Tribes: A Comprehensive Study of Tribes from the Abitibi to the Zuni*. Greenwich, Conn.: Brompton Books, 1986; reprinted, North Dighton, Mass.: J G Press, 1998.

20

Urban Research

LORETTO DENNIS SZUCS, FUGA, and JOHN M. SCROGGINS, MA

From a colonial society of small farms and villages, the United States grew rapidly into a nation dominated by massive urban centers. Early settlers, many of whom had been city dwellers in Europe, congregated in seaport towns along the Atlantic Coast. The larger colonial towns became government centers where brisk commerce attracted a continuous influx of immigrants. Most ports became hubs for milling, shipbuilding, and other manufacturing activities.

In the years between the American Revolution and the Civil War, the populations of the major cities increased dramatically. New York was a city of approximately 33,000 in 1790; there were 800,000 people on the island of Manhattan by 1860. Philadelphia's count of 28,000 people in the 1790 census had leaped to more than 565,000 by the 1860 enumeration. Brooklyn (not yet part of New York City), with a population of 5,000 in 1790, was home to more than 265,000 by 1860, distinguishing it as America's third-largest city.

Climate, geography, and the focus on agriculture dictated a slower growth pattern for Southern urbanization. Yet New Orleans had a population of nearly one thousand as early as 1727, and Charleston was the largest Southern metropolis, with a population of ten thousand by the time of the American Revolution.

Urbanization was not limited to the Atlantic Coast; it expanded inland with new frontiers. The cities of Pittsburgh, Louisville, Cincinnati, and St. Louis flourished along the Ohio and Mississippi Rivers. With the introduction of steam navigation and the opening of a canal system, the Great Lakes cities of Buffalo, Cleveland, Detroit, Chicago, and Milwaukee

Chapter Contents

sprang up. Even in states and territories where the population was sparse, the extent of urbanization was remarkable. Seattle, Portland, San Francisco, Los Angeles, and Salt Lake City played important roles in the development of the Far West. By 1860, Houston, Galveston, Austin, and San Antonio had also become important cultural, social, and economic centers.[1]

Very early in the process of developing a family history, you will probably encounter the problem of locating information about ancestors who lived in a large American city. The United States today is very much an urban nation—73.5 percent of the population lives in cities—but the trend began well over a century ago.[2] More than 50 percent of the population lived in urban areas as early as 1920. Moreover, many specific ethnic groups had higher percentages of urbanization than the general population. By 1910, approximately 72 percent of the foreign-born lived in cities.[3] The economics of migration, as well as the personal goals of the migrants, many of whom hoped to make a fortune and return home, necessitated settlement in urban centers, such as New York, Cleveland, and Chicago. There, burgeoning industries welcomed common laborers, ethnic clusters offered a familiar setting for the homesick, and cheap housing and food let migrants accumulate savings.

Research Strategies

Since the publication of the second edition of *The Source,* many relatively new Internet-based sources and services have become available, making it easier to begin preliminary urban research online. However, few or no changes were made in this chapter in cases where traditional sources remain the best starting point.

Research among the maze of metropolitan records reveals the confusing variety, color, and bustle of the urban surroundings new to the immigrants. Much of the genealogist's knowledge in the use of these resources must be self-taught. No two cities were born of a common history, nor were their political natures, commercial interests, ethnic makeup, or geographical locations ever identical. Research sources readily found in one city may be closed to access or have been destroyed in the next. The experiences of the African American, the German Jew, the Irish Catholic, and the white Anglo-Saxon Protestant frequently differed, and those differences dictate the types of records to be used.

Despite their differences, cities have one thing in common: a reputation for being difficult to research because of their multilayered bureaucracies, the sheer volume of records created by enormous populations, and a lack of printed indexes and access to sources. The advantage is that urban areas often include the resources, human and financial, to preserve and to disseminate information about the past. Also, city governments require more information from their residents than do their rural counterparts.

Historical societies, libraries, and universities collect manuscripts, newspapers, rare books, and similar materials from which sociologists, demographers, urbanologists, and social historians can draw. It is no accident that some of the most dynamic contemporary research is occurring in urban-related topics: the resources are vast.

Many of the sources mentioned in this chapter are further detailed elsewhere in this book. This chapter is specifically designed to identify problems unique to city research and to offer strategies and sources that clarify bureaucratic jurisdictions and make searching massive volumes of urban-created records more manageable. The publications, websites, and organizations cited in this chapter are not comprehensive; they provide examples of the wide array of resources that are available for urban research.

Geography matters! Perhaps more than in any other phase of genealogical research, it is important to gather as much identifying information as possible about the subject of a search from relatives near and far. Knowing the approximate part of the city, a street name, an occupation, or the name of a church or school can make all the difference when it comes to finding people in city directories or census or any other records, particularly when common names are involved.

As cities grew in population and geographical dimensions, their borders and jurisdictions changed. Larger towns annexed other towns over the years, and if you are not aware of such historical facts, there is a good chance that you will overlook desired information (see figure 20-1). For example, Boston was divided into various wards, and boundaries were redrawn as new areas were added. To add to the confusion, Beacon Hill, East Boston, Fort Hill, the North End, South Boston, the South Cove, the South End, and the West End are the informal names of sections. Brighton, Charlestown, Dorchester, Roxbury, and West Roxbury were annexed by the city of Boston in the 1860s and 1870s, while Hyde Park did not become part of Boston until 1912. Sections of present-day Boston are still called by the names of the former towns. Prior to annexation, each town kept its own records. Other towns in the Boston vicinity remain separate municipalities to the present day, including Cambridge and Somerville (both in Middlesex County) and Brookline (in Norfolk County).[4] Information about boundary changes can be elusive but may often be found in some of the online library and historical sources described later in this chapter.

Different cities and counties have different record-keeping practices, and it is critical to know of these distinctions. Deeds for Rochester, New York, for example, are kept at the county level, but Baltimore and St. Louis deeds are kept at the city level. There may be different access policies and charges among the city, county, and state levels. Most vital records for Illinois have been microfilmed up to around 1915 (depending on the county). In some cases, microfilmed copies of vital records are easier to obtain through the Family History Library of The Church of

Jesus Christ of Latter-day Saints (LDS church) in Salt Lake City or through the Illinois State Archives or one of the local archives. Some of the more heavily used record collections are being digitized and made available online at federal, state, county, and local archive websites.

Because the offices of heavily populated cities and counties are frequently hard to access, and because city and county bureaucracies are typically difficult to work with, it may be far easier in some instances to consult indexes for cities at the nearest Family History Center of the LDS Family History Library. Many genealogically important city records have been microfilmed by the Genealogical Society of Utah. The society is microfilming on an ongoing basis, so if records or indexes are not yet available, they might be in six months or a year. It is wise to stay informed. Chapter 2, "Computers and Technology," in this volume provides more suggestions on how to keep up with this rapidly changing area of research.

Figure 20-1.
The Dyer children in Brooklyn, ca. 1907. Brooklyn became a borough of New York City in 1898. Before that time, Brooklyn was a separate city and had records separate from those of New York City. Courtesy Loretto Szucs.

Library and Internet Sources

The basic approach to urban genealogy is similar to that followed for any other research problem. Every genealogist begins with certain facts and progresses to the unknown. If tradition says that an individual emigrated from Germany and settled first in Baltimore, educate yourself on the background and existing materials for research in that city.

Guides have been published for many major cities. Such guides outline in broad terms the location and accessibility of sources, eliminating some blind alleys. With the growth of the Internet since the second edition of this book was published in 1997, much of the most basic finding-aid information formerly found only in printed guides or periodical articles has been published on the Internet. As a result, the best way to start research about an unfamiliar urban area is by reviewing the website of the public library or libraries serving that area, supplemented by an Internet search for other historical and genealogical resources about the area. These Internet sources cannot entirely replace published guides and other finding aids, but they do make it possible to begin preliminary research at home or at your local public library.

Public Libraries

Most large public libraries now have websites and online catalogs that typically include or point to the most significant resources about the areas the libraries serve. No matter where you live, you can find general information and guides to sources about most any urban area by starting with a public library website and online catalog. To find links to libraries, try one or more of the following sites:

Google <www.google.com>: Put the name of the city and "public library" in the search box.

Libweb (Library Servers via WWW) <http://sunsite.berkeley.edu/Libweb>: Maintained by Thomas Dowling, updated daily, and hosted at *SunSITE*, the digital library at the University of California, Berkeley, with mirror sites at several other universities.

LibDex (The Library Index) <www.libdex.com>: Maintained by Peter Scott, updated several times each month, and includes links to many library-related organizations and services.

Many urban areas have more than one major library with significant family history resources. In the St. Louis area, for example, both the St. Louis Public Library (city) <www.slpl.lib.mo.us> and the St. Louis County Library <www.slcl.lib.mo.us> have major genealogical collections.

The typical public library homepage will have a link to the library's catalog as well as links to many other resources for family history research in the community. For example, the current homepage of the Cleveland Public Library <www.cpl.org> includes the following relevant links:

The Library Catalog: Search the catalogs of the CLEVNET consortium, including thirty-one library systems in nine counties throughout northern Ohio.

Databases & Links Library: The links library points to a number of genealogy-related sites including other Cleveland Public Library pages, the Cuyahoga County Genealogical Society, the Jewish Genealogical Society of Cleveland, The Western Reserve Historical Society, the Ohio Genweb Project, and several national and ethnic-related sites. There are also links to databases that can be accessed at or through either the Cleveland Public Library or the CLEVNET consortium, with icons distinguishing the databases that can be accessed only at the library from those that can be accessed from outside the library by library card holders.

Cleveland Necrology File: Search Cleveland death notices online.

Property Research in Cleveland and Cuyahoga County <www.cpl.org/property-research.asp>: Includes a long list of links related to real property in Cleveland and Cuyahoga County and can be found throughtommie "Library Services" in the "Library Info" pull-down menu.

Genealogical Research at the Cleveland Public Library <www.cpl.org/libraryresources.asp?FormMode=Exhibit &ID=6>: Not shown as a link on the homepage but can be found on several subordinate pages.

In response to the overwhelming interest in family history and the resulting number of requests in past years, city libraries often published pamphlets describing their genealogy and local history holdings, hours of operation, and research policies. In recent years, many of these brochures have been discontinued because the information is available on the libraries' websites. If you live some distance from the public library in the area of an ancestor's residence and don't have Internet access, any large library should have a current issue of the *American Library Directory,* a reference volume with essential addresses and telephone numbers for other libraries across the country. Some libraries will even supply lists of researchers, though none of the institutions will specifically recommend or guarantee the quality of the work of individuals listed. If a library is unable to provide a list of researchers, you may wish to contact the Association of Professional Genealogists, P.O. Box 40393, Denver, CO 80204-0393, <www.apgen.org>, or the Board for Certification of Genealogists, 1307 New Hampshire Avenue NW, Washington, DC 20036, <www.bcgcertification.org> for assistance in locating a professional researcher in a particular city.

Internet Search

Since library websites vary in the amount and location of information posted, it is often wise to search the Internet for other sources and links related to genealogy and history. This will often locate resources that are hard to find on the library's site, including many of the types of resources discussed later in this chapter. Continuing with Cleveland as an example, select the advanced search at Google <www.google.com/advanced_search>. Type "cleveland" in the box labeled "Find results with all of the words," then type "genealogy genealogical history historical" in the box labeled "Find results with at least one of the words." The first several relevant results include:

The Encyclopedia of Cleveland History <http://ech.cwru.edu> is sponsored by Case Western Reserve University and includes the complete contents of two books by David D. Van Tassel and John J. Grabowski: *The Encyclopedia of Cleveland History*, 2nd ed. (Bloomington: Indiana University Press, 1996) and *The Dictionary of Cleveland Biography* (Bloomington: University of Indiana Press, 1996).

The Cleveland Digital Library <http://web.ulib.csuohio.edu/SpecColl/cdl> is sponsored by the Cleveland State University Library and has links to other sites with full text or images of publications, documents, maps, and photographs relating to the history of Cleveland and northern Ohio.

The Cleveland Memory Project <www.clevelandmemory.org> is another Cleveland State University Library site and has online versions of books and documents from the library's own holdings.

First Maps of Cleveland and the Western Reserve <www.csuohio.edu/CUT/firsts.htm>.

Greater Cleveland Genealogical Society <www.rootsweb.com/~ohgcgg>.

Resource Directory to Cleveland's History <www.chuh.org/TRG/Doors.html>, part of the website of the Cleveland Heights-University Heights School District.

Since Cleveland is in Cuyahoga County, repeating the search for "Cuyahoga" instead of Cleveland will produce a similar list of useful sites.

Other geographically oriented Internet resources include:

The USGenWeb Project <www.usgenweb.org/>: Websites related to every state and most counties. Some include indexes, transcripts, or scanned images of source documents.

Ancestry.com and RootsWeb.com message boards <boards.ancestry.com>: Message boards for every state and county.

GenForum <genforum.genealogy.com>: Message boards for every state and county.

RootsWeb.com mailing lists <lists.rootsweb.com>: Mailing lists related to each state, most counties, and some other geographic subdivisions. RootsWeb.com has two search engines for finding older messages: <http://searches2.rootsweb.com/cgi-bin/listsearch.pl> and <http://archiver.rootsweb.com>.

This same approach can be used for Internet searches related to any urban area.

Printed Materials

Despite the wealth of information that has become available on the Internet, traditional printed guides, indexes, and collections remain indispensable sources for family history research. They often provide a historical context and depth of understanding of resources that goes far beyond the typical Web page. The most comprehensive guide to printed genealogical records and finding aids is the companion to this book, *Printed Sources: A Guide to Published Genealogical Records*, edited by Kory L. Meyerink.[5]

City Research Guides

A number of genealogical and historical guides for specific cities have been published over the past several years, and more are in the development stages. One of the best currently available is *Genealogical Resources in New York: The most comprehensive guide to genealogical and biographical resources in New York City and Albany*, edited by Estelle Guzik.[6] Though published by the Jewish Genealogical Society, the volume is by no means limited to Jewish sources. Archives serving the metropolitan area, bureaus of vital records, city clerks, offices, civil, county, and federal courts, genealogical and historical societies, and libraries with genealogical holdings and special collections are but a few of the topics discussed in the volume. Adding greatly to the usefulness of the guide are geographical and mailing addresses, telephone numbers, hours of operation, and directions for driving or reaching the various facilities by public transportation. The material is organized geographically so that researchers can coordinate their visits to facilities within a particular area. An earlier but still informative volume is Rosalie F. Bailey's *Guide to Genealogical and Biographical Sources for New York City, 1783–1898*.[7] Even if New York City is not your area of interest, this work's forty separate categories of records with select bibliographies will give you an analog for the city in which you are interested. Not all of these will apply to every research problem, but knowing of them can stimulate innovative approaches when other paths seem closed.

Those with Chicago research problems will find help in Loretto Dennis Szucs's *Chicago and Cook County: A Guide to Research*.[8] It covers many genealogical sources and research strategies from vital records to Chicago communities and neighborhoods, occupational and business resources, and miscellaneous sources and addresses. The volume includes a chronological list of 107 major historical events that affect research in the area. A glance at the chronology pinpoints important changes, such as the incorporation of the city in 1837, the opening of the Illinois and Michigan Canal in 1848, the cholera epidemic and bank panic of 1849, and the Great Chicago Fire of 1871, which destroyed almost all government-created records. "Archives and Manuscript Collections," "Historical Societies," "Gazetteer of Cook County," "Genealogical Societies," "Cemeteries in the Metropolitan Chicago Area," and collections of the Family History Library and its local Family History Centers, the Newberry Library, and the National Archives—Great Lakes Region in Chicago are among topics described in the eleven appendixes of the book. Specific information is provided where the researcher is likely to confront a forbidding bureaucracy.

Robert W. Barnes's *Guide to Research in Baltimore City and County* provides important details about genealogical information in archives, libraries, repositories, maps, biographical sources, cemeteries, ethnic histories, newspapers, occupational and political sources, and some hard-to-find city records.[9] As the author points out, "Knowing where to look is an important part of the researcher's job. It is extremely frustrating to drive to the Court House at Towson only to find that the records being sought are some ten miles away in Baltimore City, or thirty miles away in the Maryland State Archives." Compiled by Connie Stunkel Terheiden and Kenny R. Burck, *Guide to Genealogical Resources in Cincinnati & Hamilton County, Ohio* is another important guide to a specific area.[10] The guide includes maps and sources most needed by the family historian, including details about cemeteries, census, churches, court records, funeral homes, land records, libraries, surname files, and how to obtain vital records.

State Guides

Unfortunately, there are far too few guides yet available for specific cities, but some statewide compilations may be very helpful where city guides are lacking. Carol W. Bell's *Ohio Guide to Genealogical Sources* is a notable example.[11] For instance, if Cleveland is an area of interest, addresses of courts, historical and genealogical societies, and other useful information concerning the city can be found under the heading of Cuyahoga County. Additionally, consulting the county lists can reveal which vital and probate records had already been microfilmed by the Genealogical Society of Utah at the time of the guide's publication. Under the heading "Miscellaneous," there are also land, marriage, Bible, cemetery, church, and other records for the city, available on microfilm at the Ohio Historical Society and the Western Reserve Historical Society. The guide, of course, details valuable collections that will facilitate research in other Ohio counties and cities as well.

Roseann Hogan's *Kentucky Ancestry: A Guide to Genealogical and Historical Research* is an in-depth study that will facilitate research in any city or rural area in Kentucky.[12] Seven chapters of this work provide historical background and methodology for using both standard and unique sources in the state. Chapter 8 inventories records by county. There are also a number of constructive tips on city records, including the fact that, despite irregular reporting of vital events in the state before 1910, more uniform registration began in the cities of Lexington, Louisville, Newport, and Covington almost twenty-five years earlier. Hogan alerts readers to the fact that Kentuckians have filed more than five hundred thousand delayed birth certificates, which typically are completed in order to obtain Social Security benefits, and that there is a possibility that even if no official certificate can be found in Frankfort, a certificate may have been filed with the Social Security Administration or other government agencies.

If you have research to conduct in Atlanta, Savannah, or any other Georgia city, Robert Scott Davis Jr.'s *Research in Georgia* is particularly helpful.[13] The volume emphasizes the Georgia Department of Archives and History. Yet another essential guide for a southern state is *North Carolina Research: Genealogy and Local History*, edited by Helen Leary.[14]

Multi-City Reference Tools

Another extremely useful urban tool with a somewhat unlikely title is *The Encyclopedia of Jewish Genealogy*, by Arthur Kurzweil and Miriam Weiner.[15] Whether you have Jewish ancestors or not, this work has substantive chapters on city resources in Arizona, California, Colorado, Connecticut, District of Columbia, Georgia, Illinois, Iowa, Kansas, Kentucky, Maryland, Massachusetts, Michigan, Minnesota, Missouri, Nebraska, New Jersey, New York, North Carolina, Ohio, Oklahoma, Oregon, Pennsylvania, Texas, Utah, Virginia, Washington, and Wisconsin.

One of the most important reference works is the third edition of *Red Book: American State, County, and Town Sources*, edited by Alice Eichholz, which covers all U.S. states and their major cities.[16] The state chapters open with historical segments and proceed to summarize vital, census, land, probate, court, tax, cemetery, church, and military records; local history; maps; periodicals, newspapers, and manuscripts; and archives, libraries, and societies. Each chapter concludes with a table that lists county and town courthouse addresses, dates of formation, parent political units, and the beginning dates of vital and court records. Outline maps showing the counties and county seats complement the chapters on each state.

Obscure Collections

A number of rather obscure city-focused collections and indexes are available in various archives, historical agencies, and libraries in the United States. An increasing number of such collections and indexes are being made available on the Internet.

A New York City example is the Emigrant Savings Bank (figure 20-2), established in 1850 by members of the Irish Emigrant Society. The bank ended up serving thousands of Irish immigrants who fled to America following the infamous Potato Famine. The bank kept many volumes of records, including an Index Book; a Test Book; a Transfer, Signature, and Test Book; and a Deposit-Account Ledger. Microfilm copies are available at the New York Public Library, and Ancestry.com has scanned images of the Emigrant Savings Bank collection with the index that provides the given names and surnames of depositors, their

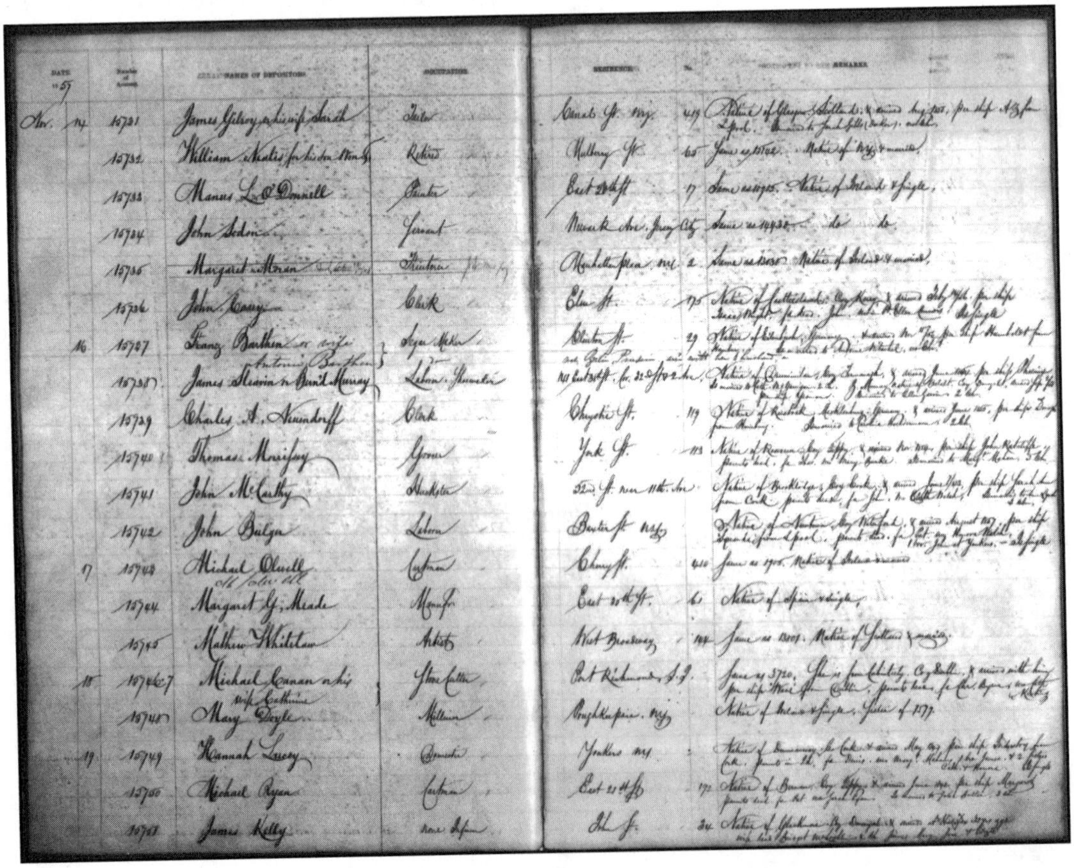

Figure 20-2. A page from an 1857 Text Book of the New York City Emigrant Savings Bank collection at Ancestry.com.

account numbers, account dates, and years and places of birth, if given. One of the great features of this collection is that, in most cases, it identifies the exact place of origin (county and townland) of the immigrant depositor. In addition, each indexed individual is linked to the image on which he or she appears, where more information may be available. While the majority of the emigrants found in this collection will be Irish, you may occasionally find emigrants of other nationalities as well.

Index Book

The bank kept an index of all individuals recorded in its volumes. This book will usually provide the name of the depositor, the date of the record, and the individual's account number. This book will also refer you to a Test Book or a Transfer, Signature, and Test Book.

Test Books

The Test Books cover the years 1850–68 and contain a variety of details about depositors and their family. Information that may be found in this set of records includes the date of the record, the name of the depositor, account number, occupation, residence, and other remarks that could include names of other family members, immigration information, or birth or residence information in Ireland.

Transfer, Signature, and Test Books

These books existed from 1850–83 and were used primarily for recording changes made to an individual's account information. Examples of such a change could be a new signature, a change in address, or a change in the account holder. Information that may be found in this set of records includes the signature of the account holder, the date of the record, the account number, the individual's residence, occupation, year born, birthplace, and family relations.

Deposit-Account Ledger

These records are arranged by account number and contain an account history for each individual, recording typical transactions such as deposits and withdrawals.

Indexes

Many valuable finding tools have not been published, nor are they available on the Internet. The Baltimore City Archives has, for example, a WPA-compiled name index to the municipal records for 1756 to 1938. The Douglas County Historical Society (Omaha, Nebraska) <www.omahahistory.org> has the *Omaha World-Herald* Clipping File, a subject and biographic file with four hundred thousand subject files (including more than 5 million clippings from between 1907 and 1983). The Oregon Historical Society <www.ohs.org> has several biographical sources important for searching cities in that state. A vertical file consisting of newspaper clippings includes four thousand subjects on state and local history and fifteen hundred biographies of prominent Oregonians. Also covered are historic structures, ethnic groups, cities, counties, and Portland neighborhoods. A separate Biography Card File was put together from books, scrapbooks, and newspaper clippings, among other things.

City Directories

A decided advantage to conducting research in a metropolitan area is the availability of printed directories for most cities, large and small. There is scarcely a more satisfying or more productive adventure in family history research than finding an ancestor in an old directory, discovering his or her occupation (or multiple occupations), and knowing exactly where in the city he or she lived. The enjoyment grows if you are able to track families for significant time periods. Figure 20-3 is from an 1872 directory for Brooklyn, New York. In the past few years, many historical city directories have been placed online. Some sites have images of the original pages, and others have transcripts or abstracts. Some provide free access, while others require a subscription. Chapter 8, "Directories," provides an excellent, in-depth description of this important source. However, there are certain concepts and strategies that bear highlighting here.

While directories of residents may date back to a city's earliest days, no directory is all-inclusive. Because the motive behind the printing of most of these books was to sell advertising, the listing of residents was selective. Stephen Thernstrom cites a study of Newburyport, Massachusetts, city directories. "Volumes purporting to list every family in the community were published in January 1849 and January 1851. These have been compared with a list of all laborers resident in Newburyport taken from the Seventh United States Census. Fully 45 percent of the laboring families found by the diligent census-taker in September and October of 1850 cannot be located in either directory."[17] Thernstrom concludes that, in addition to inadvertently missing many of the city's transient population, "the compiler of the directories either did not know about or did not choose to include many working class families in his volumes." Similar conclusions have been made in studies conducted in other cities. Yet, genuine efforts seem to have been made by some of the publishers. The compilers of the *Chicago 1844 Directory* stated on the first page of the volume:

> It has been the design to include in this Directory the names of all persons and all firms in the City, to arrange them alphabetically, and in every instance to give the correct spelling. There may be cases however, where names may have been accidentally inserted in the wrong connection, and cases also of incorrect orthography—particularly where persons have been unable to spell, and the names have been written from the sound. Immediate measures will be taken to procure the names of all persons who have

> accidentally been omitted in this volume; a complete list, corrected from time to time, will be kept at the General Intelligence office, where the public can at times get information in regard to the names, business, and residence of every inhabitant of the City. Persons finding themselves excluded and persons coming to the City hereafter, are requested to call at the above place and have their names enrolled. Very few of our buildings are numbered, the necessity, however, of this can be avoided, if persons occupying buildings permanently, will put themselves to the trifling trouble and expense of putting their names on their doors.[18]

Scanned images of a 1903 reprint of this 1844 directory can be found at Old Directory Search <http://olddirectorysearch.com/Chicago__Illinois_1844/index.html>. Transcripts of the nonadvertising data in the directory are posted on a number of websites.

As cautious as publishers claimed to be, however, it is clear that immigrants were consistently omitted from the commercial publications—particularly those immigrants who did not speak English. Frequently, entire ethnic neighborhoods were left out of city compilations. Some groups, such as the Poles in Chicago, independently published city or community directories in their native language to offset such gaps.

Cities often had several directory publishers—Chicago had three in 1871. Consult all of them, for each may contain unique details. Richard Edwards's *Edwards' 1871 Chicago Census Directory* lists not only names, occupations, and addresses of individuals but also provides a ward number; the number of males, females, and total in residence; as well as the birthplace of the head of household.[19] John Gager's *Gager's 1857 Chicago Directory* includes the birthplace and years of residence in Chicago with the usual information.[20] One publication lists "Miller, Emma, widow," and one by another publisher in the same year adds "Emma, widow of James." Limiting a search to one directory increases the chance of missing precious clues.

Telephone Directories

A year or so after Alexander Graham Bell invented the articulating telephone, telephone directories began to appear in cities across the country. In 1878, Chicago had its first published telephone book. It listed mostly business establishments; the remainder were the handful of private citizens who could afford the luxury. Most of the population has been vastly underrepresented in telephone directories—even in later years. As late as 1900, only seventeen people per one thousand had a telephone; by 1920 that number had risen to twenty-three per one thousand. Having a telephone then, as now, did not guarantee inclusion in a telephone book; many elected not to be listed.

Several Internet services now offer searchable current telephone directories. Some may also offer older directory information, such as the "1994 Phone and Address Directory" <www.ancestry.com/search/rectype/inddbs/7143.htm> from Ancestry.com. Most large libraries seem to have discontinued maintaining large collections of telephone directories, but many may still retain older directories for the area served by the library. The Library of Congress has an online guide to older directories: "Telephone and City Directories in the Library of Congress: Non-Current (Old)," maintained by Barbara Walsh <www.loc.gov/rr/genealogy/bib_guid/telephonnoncurr.html>.

Street Directories

One of the frustrations in research is finding incomplete information in a source—for example, a beautiful old portrait that bears the name and street address of the photographer but gives no city, or a candid shot of a group of people on the porch of a charming old house at 4124 Trowbridge Street, or a letter that states, "Your brother remains close to the shop in the city but has taken up new quarters on Madison Street." Such information is ultimately useless if the town name remains unknown. *The Street Directory of the Principal Cities of the United States*, originally published by order of the postmaster general in 1908, is an alphabetical listing of streets, avenues, courts, places, lanes, roads, and wharves to which mail was delivered, with references to all the cities and towns where these street names appear.[21] City directories frequently included street guides.

Street names in many cities have changed over the years. These changes are often difficult to track. For New Orleans, the New Orleans Public Library offers an online Alphabetical Index of Changes in Street Names, Old and New; Period 1852 to Current Date, Dec. 1st 1938 <http://nutrias.org/~nopl/facts/streetnames/namesa.htm> (updated 2002), based on a 1938 WPA compilation, and New Orleans Street Name Changes <http://nutrias.org/~nopl/facts/names.htm> (updated 2003) with changes made since 1990.

Genealogical Societies

Genealogical societies at the national, state, and local levels offer educational programs and publications with a strong focus on the locality served. The Dubuque County-Key City Genealogical Society (P.O. Box 13, Dubuque, IA 52004-0013 <www.rootsweb.com/~iadckcgs>), for example, publishes such titles as *A Guide to Microfilmed Records at Carnegie-Stout Public Library, Dubuque, Iowa*; lists of Dubuque city directories, 1856 to 1983; newspapers for the area; an obituary file; and probate and marriage index information. Other society publications are an *Index of Churches and Cemeteries of Dubuque County, Iowa; Burial Records of Dubuque City Cemetery, 1854–1875; Declarations of*

ALBERT H. NICOLAY,
AUCTIONEER & STOCK BROKER, No. 43 PINE ST., N. Y.

FAIRBANKS' SCALES. THE ACKNOWLEDGED STANDARD. Warehouse, 252 Broadway. NEW YORK.

Donahue J. tailor, Willoughby c. Pearl
Donahue James C. boatbuilder, h 15 Dennet pl
Donahue Jane, wid. seamstress, h 112 Smith
Donahue John, tailor, 330 Fulton
[E]Donahue John, lab. h Withers n. Graham av
[E]Donahue John, locksmith, h 88 N. 2d
Donahue Mary, wid. grocer, 148 Navy
[E]Donahue Owen, calker, h 59 Ainslie
Donahue Patrick, lab. h 5th c. 5th av
Donahue Peter J. engineer, 95 Furman, h Baltic c. Columbia
Donahue R. & J. tailors, Willoughby c. Pear
Donahy James, mason, h 53 Tillary
Donahy Rebecca, seamstress, h 53 Tillary
[E]Donald David, mason, h 10th c. S. 2d
Donald Robert, lab. h 18 Bridge
[E]Donaldson Arthur B. cooper, h 97 Devoe
[E]Donaldson Daniel T. shipfastener, h Oakland n. Calyer
[E]Donaldson E. cooper, h 182 Lorimer
Donaldson Effingham, broker, 50 Wall, N. Y. h 290 Hamilton
[E]Donalson Henry C. clerk. h 207 S. 9th
[E]Donaldson James, machinist, h 129 Plymouth
Donaldson James A. book-kpr. 300 Hamilton
[E]Donaldson John, painter, h Sandford c. Smith
Donaldson Levinia, wid. h 8 Lefferts
Donaldson Robert, h 150 High
Donaldson Walter, h 183 High
[E]Donally Peter, lab. h 68 Grand
[E]Donalson James, molder, h 90 N. 5th
Donalson Luther H. h Classon av. n. Quincy
Donar Eliza, grocer, 101 Tillary
Donavy James, lab. h Harrison n. Columbia
Donavan Cornelius, lab. h Partition n. Van Brunt
Donavan James, cooper, h Sullivan n. Van Brunt
Donavan James, farmer, h 149 Willoughby
Donavan James J. mason, h Douglass n. Classon av
[E]Donavan Jeremiah, carpenter, h Eagle n. Union av
Donavan Wm. boilermkr. h 644 Court
Donavon Daniel, driver, h Carroll n. 5th av
Donavon Denis, junk, 4 Coenties slip, N. Y. h 5th av. n. 3d
[E]Donavon James, dealer, h 5 Conselyea
[E]Donavon Jeremiah, lab.h Eagle n.Oakland av
[E]Donavon Michael, laq. h Dupont n. Union av
[E]Donckey James, lab. h 279 S. 5th
Donega John, smith, h 133 Ryerson
Donegan Bartholomew, engineer, h 18 Debevoise
[E]Donegan Patrick, lab. h Walton n. Marcy av
[E]Donegan Timothy, lab. h r. 270 Union av
[E]Doneher Patrick, lab. h N. 10th c. 1st
[E]Doneley Ellen, wid. h 178 N. 8th
[E]Doneley John, lab. h N. 7th n. 5th
Doneley Owen, lab. h 284 N. 7th
Donellon Peter, liquors, Underhill av.n.Bergen
Donelly Bridget, laundress, h 397 Columbia
Donelly John, tailor, 37 Hamilton av
Donelly Sarah, wid. laundress, h 397 Columbia
Donelson James E. (M.D.) h Van Buren n.Nostrand av
Donnetty Dennis, seaman, h 36 Hamilton av
[E]Donevan Daniel, proprietor, h S. 4th n. 6th
[E]Donevan Mathew, grocer, 217 1st
Donevan Richard, hatter, h 261 Hudson av
[E]Donfmiller Gustav, baker, 192 S. 6th, h 184 S. 4th
Dongan Richard, h 50 Adelphi
[E]Donges John, tinsmith, h 16 Graham av
Donhue James, painter, h 5 Prospect
[E]Donker John, lab. h 25 S. 2d
[E]Donkey Richard, lab. h Debevoise c. Morrell
Donkley Leonard, teacher, h 268 Dean
Donlan Andrew, painter, h 90 Carll
Donlan John, junk, h r. 79 Hudson av
Donlan Michael, lab.h r.Kent av n.Lafayette av
Donlan Michael, weaver, h 227 Navy
Donlan Michael, lab. h 77 Carll
Donlan Patrick, lab. h 3 Sycamore
Donlan Patrick, mason, h 183 Raymond
Donlan Peter, canaler, h 287 Plymouth
[E]Donlan John, carman, h n. 9th c. 1st
Donlon John, carman, h 128 Tillary
Don Levy Patrick, plasterer, h Myrtle av. c. Walworth
[E]Donley James, lab. h 8 S. 3d
Donley Mary, wid. h 302 Hicks
Donlin, Patrick, wooldresser, h r. 22 Graham
[E]Donlin Stephen, carpenter, h Franklin c. Oak
Donlon John, clerk, h 202 Jay
Donlon Martin, hatter, h Raymond n. De Kalb av
Donlon Martin, lab. h r. 223 E, Warren
Donlon Mary, wid. laundress, h 16 Lawrence pl
Donlon Patrick, stable, De Kalb av.c. Raymond
Donlon Peter, builder, h 185 Raymond
Donlon Rosanna, wid. h Hicks n Luqueer
[E]Donly Patrick, lab. h Huron n. Union av
Donmall Charles, plumber h 40 Smith
[E]Donnah John, lab. h 56 Graham av
[E]Donnahue Jeremiah, lab. h Whipple n. Flushing av
Donnahue Martin, baker, h 46 James
[E]Donnahue Patrick, lab. h 39 N. 4th
Donnally Mary, wid. h 320 Hicks
Donnan James, hatter, 3 French's hotel, N. Y. h 104 Nelson
[E]Donnan John, glassblower, h B'way, n. Gerry
[E]Donnavan , wid. h 120 1st
Donne James, cotton, 49 Pine, N. Y. h 49 Summit
Donnegan Michael, lab. h 146 Bolivar
Donnehue John E. h De Kalb av. n. Sandford
[E]Donnel Patrick, lab. h 110 N. 6th
Donneley Catharine, wid. laundress, Kosciusko n. Bedford av
Donnell Antony, lab. h Vanderbilt av. n. Warren
[E]Donnell James H. carpenter, h Calyer n. Lorimer
Donnell William, lab. h r. 47 Hudson av
Donnell William, sexton, h 110 Henry
Donnelly Arthur, painter, h 273 Bergen
Donnelly Peter, h 170 S. Oxford
Donnelly Andrew, painter, h 420 Fulton av
Donnelly Anna, milliner, 420 Fulton av
Donnelly Bridget, wid. h 301 Columbia
Donnelly Bridget, wid. h 112 Plymouth
Donnelly Bridget, wid. h Warren n. Washington av

Coal & Wood { (Established 1847.) KELSEYS & LOUGHLIN,
12 Atlantic St., and cor. Atlantic & Boerum Sts.

Figure 20-3. A page from an 1872 Brooklyn, New York, city directory. It is typical of compilations that exist for most American cities.

Intent to Become a Citizen, Dubuque County, Iowa; and *Roots in Dubuque County, Iowa: A Genealogical Resource Book.*

To find the name and address of the genealogical society in your area of interest, use an Internet search engine, such as Google, or consult *The Ancestry Family Historian's Address Book,* by Juliana Szucs Smith.[22]

History

The importance of understanding the history of any geographical area in genealogical research cannot be overstated. Basic historical overviews of most cities can be found in encyclopedias or on relevant websites, but for a better understanding of what types of records may exist or what it was like to live in the times and places of our ancestors, the ever-increasing number of urban studies that are becoming available are among the most encouraging aspects of city research. Online library catalogs and Internet search engines can help you find books on the history of the area, but online sources are almost never an adequate substitute for a well-written published history. If a descriptive volume on the city in which you are interested is not on the shelf of your local public library, a large city or university library may have it or be able to borrow it for you through interlibrary loan.

Brooklyn, U.S.A.: The Fourth Largest City in America, edited by Rita Seiden Miller, is an example of a work that provides a sociological view of the city from its original inhabitants to mobility patterns of residents in the 1970s.[23] Discussions of topics and author's notes on subjects as diverse as Kings County in the American Revolution, Bedford-Stuyvesant, Flatbush, the Brooklyn Academy of Music, the Brooklyn Navy Yard, the Brooklyn Dodgers, neighborhoods of Brooklyn, and even a chapter titled "Kings English: Fact and Folklore of Brooklyn Speech" provide rare insights into Brooklyn as it was in an ancestor's day, as well as providing precious clues for finding record sources.

Pictorial histories of American cities are enjoying a revival of popularity. Major booksellers in most urban areas usually

Figure 20-4. Three views of San Francisco before and after the 18 April 1906 earthquake. *Top:* Panoramic view of San Francisco taken in 1904. *Middle:* Panoramic view of San Francisco's ruined business district after the earthquake and fire. *Bottom:* People milling around the ruins near Turk and Market Streets.

have significant local history sections where any number of contemporary works can be found. Anyone with Chicago roots can gain a wealth of knowledge about the city from *Chicago: Growth of a Metropolis,* by Harold Mayer and Richard Wade.[24] Photographic documentation is especially useful in describing the physical growth and settlement patterns in cities. One thousand photographs and illustrations and an extensive local history bibliography make this well-documented Chicago history volume especially useful. Panoramas can give you a good idea what the city looked like at the time your ancestor lived there. Figure 20-4 shows the destruction of San Francisco before and after the 1906 earthquake and subsequent fire. Typing a city's name plus "panoramic photos" into a search engine many produce similar results.

A valuable aid for laying the groundwork in any city research is John Buenker, Gerald Michael Greenfield, and William J. Murin's *Urban History: A Guide to Information Sources*, an annotation of 1,921 scholarly works covering eleven broad topical areas.[25] Pertinent information on every major city is listed in it. Many of the sources cited are standard metropolitan histories; others are contemporary works with bibliographies that are potential gold mines in themselves, pointing to the original sources on which the author based his or her study. Such references can lead directly to manuscripts, special collections, and other hidden tools.

County and municipal histories, long used by family historians, can also provide critical information for furthering city research. Kory L. Meyerink has a lengthy discussion of the value and use of these histories in chapters 17 and 18 of *Printed Sources: A Guide to Published Genealogical Records*. While the greatest number of these histories was published in the 1880s and 1890s, dates vary from one locality to another. The two-volume *Kings County History 1683 to 1884: The Civil, Political, Professional and Ecclesiastical History and Commercial and Industrial Record of the County of Kings and the City of Brooklyn, N.Y. From 1683 to 1884,* by Henry R. Stiles, is one of several Kings County histories.[26] It focuses on Brooklyn, which was then the third largest city in the United States.

A helpful, though by no means all-inclusive, source is P. William Filby's *A Bibliography of American County Histories.*[27] To learn if there is a published history for Raleigh, North Carolina, for example, you can consult this bibliography (arranged alphabetically by state and then by county) to see that there are several entries for Wake County, one of which is a 1902 publication titled *Historical Raleigh with Sketches of Wake County and Its Important Towns,* by Moses N. Amis. As with any other source, it is important to read Filby's preface, in which he explains the criteria used to determine a book's inclusion in his work: "Books beginning with titles such as 'Historical and Biographical' . . . can contain a history of the county and consist in the main of biographies, yet they are often the only histories available."[28] For this reason, Filby included them in his bibliography. On the other hand, he chose not to include books with such titles as "Biographies of Prominent Men . . ." or "Portrait and Biographical Histories . . ." As Filby points out, these histories must be used with a degree of skepticism, because publishers made up their costs by including only the most flattering biographical sketches of prominent citizens who were their patrons for such projects.

Another bonus for city research is that many histories were generated to appeal to various segments of the population. Not only will you find volumes that focus on counties or cities but also those defining local political parties, wards, industries, ethnic groups, neighborhoods, religious groups, and fraternal and social organizations. These groups and others provided additional opportunities for less-prominent citizens to be included in a printed source. Consequently, if your ancestor was not mentioned in a standard city or county work, there is still the possibility of his or her inclusion in one of the smaller histories that frequently included biographical sketches. Most local histories are in noncirculating reference sections of libraries, so it is usually necessary to travel to those special collections.

Many of these county and specialized histories, including the biographies excluded by Filby, have been reprinted, indexed, transcribed, or even scanned, often by individuals or small genealogical and historical societies. Copies may be difficult to find using traditional library catalogs or basic Internet searches. The bibliographies in chapters 17 and 18 of *Printed Sources* can help, but tracking down recent reprints or indexes may require writing to the appropriate local society or posting messages to a mailing list or message board related to the area.

Census Records

Federal, state, and special censuses are productive genealogical tools, for probably no other records in existence contain more data about families. For additional help on census records, see the following: chapter 5, "Census Records," of this book and chapter 9, "Censuses and Tax Lists," by G. David Dilts, in *Printed Sources: A Guide to Published Genealogical Records*.

Several projects to index census records are now underway, and more electronic indexes are coming online or being published on CD-ROM almost every week. Increasingly, all persons are being indexed. As more indexes become available, many of the more traditional census search strategies in the next several paragraphs may become obsolete. Most of the indexes that are online require a personal subscription or access to a library that subscribes to one of the index services. Even when indexes are available, some names will inevitably be incorrect or will have been missed entirely, so do not conclude that an ancestor is not in the actual census schedule if his or her name is not found in an index. Because of this, it is may be necessary to rely on traditional strategies for searching censuses when indexes are not available.

Searching through the census schedules for a metropolitan area often presents special problems.

The Soundex and other microfilmed and printed census indexes are helpful but somewhat limited, especially in city situations. Often, names were misspelled or completely omitted in transcription from the original schedules. For the 1880 census, only households with children ten years of age or under were listed in the Soundex index. When indexes fail or when they have yet to be created for a densely populated urban area, an educated approach is important. If you know the family's makeup, you can go over a census line by line in hopes that names, ages, birthplaces, and other known facts will catch your eye, even though the name is misspelled or the page barely legible. However, in most cases, this can be extremely time-consuming. For the 1850 through 1870 censuses, the ward is the smallest division of the city. Space for the enumerators to identify street names and numbers did not appear on census forms until the 1880 enumeration.

The geographical arrangement of the census schedules makes finding aids vital when searching for urban residents, for in every census year some names were inadvertently left out of census indexes or were misspelled to the extent that they cannot be found in the index. Historian Keith Schlesinger devised a system to locate individuals overlooked by the Soundex. Schlesinger gleaned addresses from city directories, which he found both accurate and accessible, then plotted them on maps of census enumeration districts, which normally followed the boundaries of voting precincts in most cities. Figure 20-5 is a section of an 1880 Chicago map on which enumerator visitation dates are noted. By matching ward and visitation dates to census pages, it is possible to search for the nonindexed individual to one or two enumeration districts. By narrowing the search for the nonindexed individual to one or two enumeration districts, this scheme permits the historian to escape the confinement of the Soundex. A number of research institutions have acquired enumerator district maps and finding aids that trace the route taken during the census count. Additionally, enumeration district boundary descriptions are available on microfilm through the National Archives and Records Administration. The Newberry Library and Schlesinger have refined several methods for searching the 1850 through 1910 censuses for Chicago. See Keith Schlesinger and Peggy Tuck Sinko, "Urban Finding Aid for Manuscript Census Searches," in *National Genealogical Society Quarterly*.[29] The techniques, of course, are applicable to other cities as well.

For a number of years, several projects were conducted to index the 1880 federal census schedules. These efforts were made obsolete with the release of an every-name index by the Family Search program of The Church of Jesus Christ of Latter-day Saints. That index may now be searched online at either the Family Search website <www.familysearch.org/Eng/Search/frameset_search.asp> or from the census menu at Ancestry.com <www.ancestry.com/search/rectype/census/usfedcen/main.htm>. In either case, search results are linked to images of the actual pages, but a subscription is required to view the images.

More recently, Ancestry.com has been re-indexing all of the census years 1790–1930. At this writing, every-name indexes have been completed for all U.S. censuses except 1910. An every-name index for the remaining enumeration is scheduled to be completed in the near future.

To even the casual researcher, the population explosion in the United States can be seen clearly by the increase in the number of census rolls filed for each succeeding census year. *A Century of Population Growth 1790–1900*, produced by the U.S. Bureau of the Census, reported that in 1790 there were but five cities having populations of eight thousand or more: Boston, New York, Philadelphia, Baltimore, and Charleston.[30] In 1900 the number of cities with a population of eight thousand or more within the area enumerated in 1790 was 286, an increase of more than fifty-fold.

An excellent finding tool for thirty-nine cities in the 1910 federal population census, however, is *1910 Index to City Streets and Enumeration Districts*; it has been reproduced on fifty sheets of microfiche.[31] By determining the street address for an individual in a 1910 city directory, it is possible to search for the street name or number on microfiche, which is arranged alphabetically by name of city and thereafter in alphabetical order or numerical order of the street. Once the enumeration district number is determined from the microfiche, it is usually quick work to locate the actual address for the person or family on the actual census schedule. The city schedules were selected for indexing by the Census Bureau based on the frequency of requests for information. The records were originally in bound volumes but were unbound for microfilming. With the exception of several of the larger cities, the index for each city occupies a single volume. The original arrangement of the records has been preserved with the exception that the boroughs of Manhattan, the Bronx, Richmond (Staten Island), and Brooklyn are under the heading "New York City." There is no index for the borough of Queens.

Cities indexed by street and enumeration district for the 1910 census are Akron, Ohio; Atlanta; Baltimore; Canton, Ohio; Charlotte, North Carolina; Chicago; Cleveland; Dayton, Ohio; Denver; Detroit; District of Columbia; Elizabeth, New Jersey; Erie, Pennsylvania; Fort Wayne, Indiana; Gary, Indiana; Grand Rapids, Michigan; Indianapolis; Kansas City, Kansas; Long Beach, California; Los Angeles and Los Angeles County; Newark, New Jersey; New York City (including Brooklyn, Manhattan, the Bronx, and Richmond); Oklahoma City, Oklahoma; Omaha, Nebraska; Patterson, New Jersey; Peoria, Illinois; Philadelphia; Phoenix; Reading, Pennsylvania; Richmond, Virginia; San Antonio; San Diego; San Francisco; Seattle; South Bend,

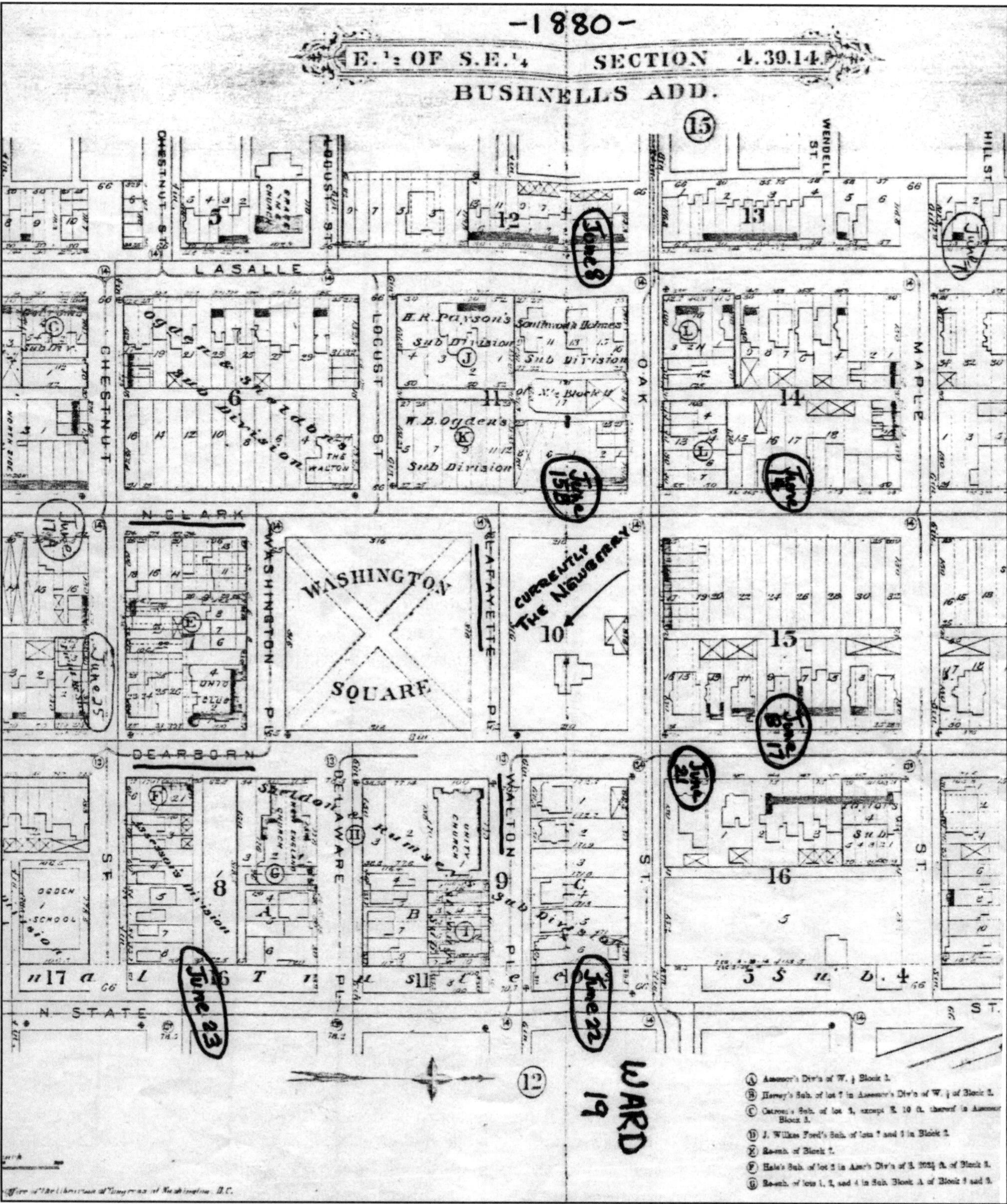

Figure 20-5. A section of an 1880 Chicago map on which the census enumerator's visitations have been plotted. Reproduced courtesy of the Newberry Library.

Indiana; Tampa, Florida; Tulsa, Oklahoma; Wichita, Kansas; and Youngstown, Ohio.

The 1920 census, though lacking some information categories that some previous census schedules included, has Soundex indexes for every state and territory. The 1920 census consists of 2,076 rolls of population schedules and 8,585 rolls of Soundex. Between 1938 and 1940, the WPA prepared approximately 51 million Soundex index cards, based on surname, for all states and territories enumerated in the 1920 census. The indexes were generated to assist the Census Bureau in searches for individuals who needed official proof of age from a period before all states had a uniform system of registering births.

The 1920 Soundex index contains approximately 107 million names and resembles the 1910 Soundex/Miracode in format. For the 1920 Soundex, however, related members in a dwelling were enumerated on a "family card," while boarders, servants, and the like were listed on a separate card.

In the official *Instructions to Enumerators,* issued by the Bureau of the Census on 1 January 1920, item 68 provided the method for canvassing a city block:

> If your district is in a city or town having a system of house numbers, canvass one block or square at a time. Do not go back and forth across the street. Begin each block at one corner, keep to the right, turn the corner, and go in and out of any court, alley, or passageway that may be included in it until the point of starting is reached. Be sure you have gone around and through the entire block before you leave it.

There is no way of knowing how precisely enumerators followed the fifty pages of small-print instructions, but a diagram was provided with item 68 to show exactly how to proceed on a block divided with alleys and courts.

The 1930 census was released to the public by the National Archives in 2002. There are 2,667 rolls of microfilm. Figure 20-6 is an example of a 1930 census schedule for a portion of Los Angeles. The basic information categories are similar to those for the 1920 census; a complete listing is at <http://1930census.archives.gov/FAQ.html>. There are Soundex indexes for only twelve southern states: Alabama, Arkansas, Florida, Georgia, Kentucky (only counties of Bell, Floyd, Harlan, Kenton, Muhlenberg, Perry, and Pike), Louisiana, Mississippi, North Carolina, South Carolina, Tennessee, Virginia, and West Virginia (only counties of Fayette, Harrison, Kanawha, Logan, McDowell, Mercer, and Raleigh). Ancestry.com has prepared an every-name index, which is available to subscribers or through participating libraries. The National Archives website has step-by-step instructions for geographic searches at "How to Research the 1930 Census Microfilm" <http://1930census.archives.gov/beginSearch.asp>.

To assist in geographic searches, the National Archives collected city directories for years around 1930 and deposited microfilm copies in research rooms in the National Archives Building and the various regional archives. They are not microfilm publications and are not copied by the National Archives. The agency has issued three microfilm publications related to enumeration districts. Written descriptions are in *Descriptions of Enumeration Districts, 1830–1950* (156 rolls) and are arranged alphabetically by state, county, and city and thereunder by supervisor's district.[32] The descriptions for 1930 are on rolls 61 through 90. Maps showing the boundaries and number of each district are in *Enumeration District Maps for the Fifteenth Census of the United States, 1930* (36 rolls).[33] Street addresses are cross-referenced with enumeration districts for over fifty cities in *Index to Selected City Streets and Enumeration Districts, 1930 Census* (7 rolls).[34]

Figure 20-7 is part of a page from the Census Enumeration District Descriptions (1910). It shows Boston's twentieth ward. These finding tools are especially useful for large cities and when institutions, even if enumerated at their street addresses, were recorded at the end of the schedules for an enumeration district, as they frequently were.

Establishing the whereabouts of your own urban ancestor does not exhaust the possibilities of census schedules. The microfilm contains the raw data necessary to understand the life of a neighborhood. What, for example, was the ethnic and occupational makeup of the street? Did the family settle with or near relatives? When combined with historical or sociological studies, a census can provide a better insight into what it meant to live in a nineteenth-century city.

State censuses, mortality schedules, and other special enumerations should not be overlooked as potential city sources, though few of them are indexed. The New York state census for 1855, for example, is far more important than the federal census because it includes information on the value and construction of the dwelling; the number of families occupying it; household members by name, age, sex, and relation to the head of the family; state or country of birth for each; marital status; profession, trade, or occupation; number of years resident in the city; voting status; and literacy of adults. The 1855 census-takers took the local election districts in each city ward for their districts, enabling the searcher to focus on a desired household faster than in a corresponding federal census, which was organized by ward. While this census does not specify bounds of election districts for New York City, on 7 November 1854 the *New York Times* published the polling places of each of the 128 election districts in the twenty-two wards for the previous election. A number of state and other special censuses have been microfilmed by the Genealogical Society of Utah. The listings for the New York state census for the city of Rochester are shown in figure 20-8. Other states took statistics that are particularly valuable to genealogists. The 1925 Iowa state census lists name, place of abode, relationship to head of household, citizenship,

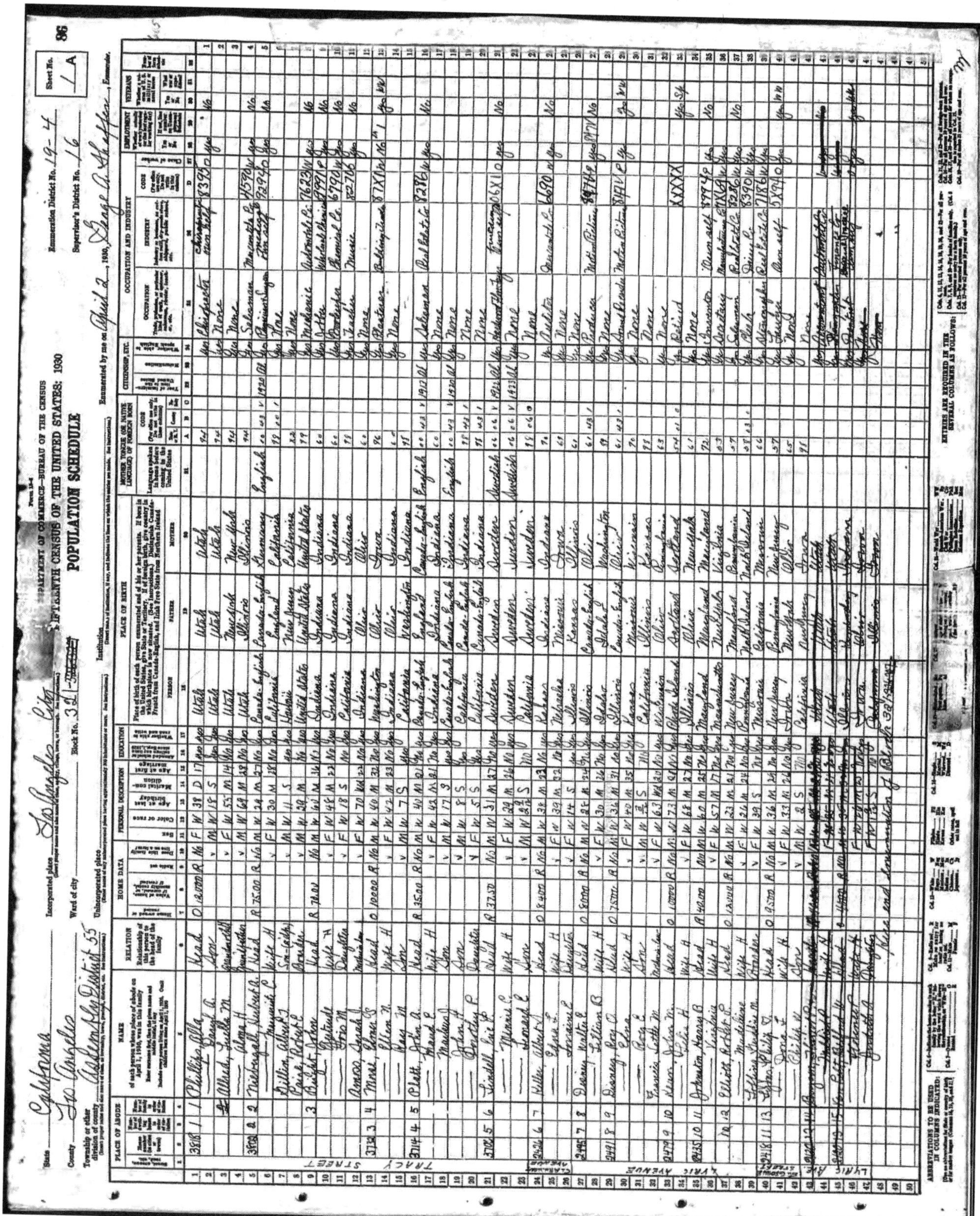

Figure 20-6. A 1930 census schedule showing the families of brothers Walter Disney and Roy Disney, sheet 1A, 16th supervisor's district, enumeration district 19-2, Assembly District 55 of Los Angeles.

Descriptions of the Enumeration Districts of the .... Supervisor's District of ...... Massachusetts

NO. OF E. D.	DESCRIPTION OF ENUMERATION DISTRICT	COUNTY Pop. 1910	RATE OF PAY	INSTRUCTION
	Boston city (continued)	Suffolk.		
1561 Tract 180	Ward 20 (part of) Precinct 3 (part of) Bounded by East Cottage and Cresent Ave. Newport, Harbor View, and Dorchester Ave. Savin Hill Ave. Pleasant.	2,186	B	
1562. Tract 181	Ward 20 (part of) Precinct 3 (part of) Bounded by East Cottage Pleasant Sawyer Ave., Cushing Ave., Salcombe, and Stoughton Columbia Road and Edward Everett square.	" 1,549	B	
1563. Tract 182	Ward 20 (part of) Precinct 4 (part of) Bounded by Columbia Road and Columbia square Stoughton, Salcombe, Cushing Ave. and Sawyer Ave. Pleasant Hancock.	" 1,794	B	
1564 Tract 183	Ward 20 (part of) Precinct 4 (part of) Bounded by Columbia Road Hancock High, Church and Eaton square, Quincy.	" 2,565	B	

Figure 20-7. "Descriptions of the Enumeration Districts" of Boston, Massachusetts, showing a portion of the twentieth ward. National Archives microfilm T1224, roll 32.

NEW YORK, MONROE - CENSUS

US/CAN FILM AREA

New York. Secretary of State.
Monroe Co., New York, state census, 1855-1905. -- Salt Lake City : Filmed by the Genealogical Society of Utah, 1970. -- 21 microfilm reels ; 35 mm.

Microreproduction of original records.

Vol. 1	1855	0833737
Vol. 2	1855	0833773
Rochester (pts. 1-2, wards 1-10)	1855	1429808
Vol. 1 Rochester (wards 1-7)	1865	0833774
Vol. 2 Rochester (wards 8-14)	1865	0833775
Vol. 3	1865	0833776
Vol. 4	1865	0833777
Vol. 5	1865	0833778
Vol. 1-2 Rochester (wards 1-8)	1875	0833779
Vol. 3-4 Rochester (wards 9-16)	1875	0833780
Vol. 5-6	1875	0833781
Vol. 7-8	1875	0833782
Vol. 1-8	1892	0833783
Vol. 9-16	1892	0833784
Towns	1892	0833785
Vol. 1-8	1905	0833786
Vol. 9-13	1905	0833787
Vol. 14-18	1905	0833788
Vol. 19-21	1905	0833789
Towns v. 1	1905	0833790
Towns v. 2	1905	0833791

Figure 20-8. State census microfilms, such as these listed for Rochester, New York, can provide invaluable information about city dwellers.

education, names of parents (including mother's maiden name), nativity of parents, place of marriage of parents, military service, occupation, and religion. There is a separate index for the 1925 Iowa census, but many state and other special census schedules are not indexed.

Vital Records

The information contained in vital records (births, marriages, and deaths) varies by the locality and the year (see chapter 13, "Vital Records," in this volume). Many cities began collecting vital records information before the states did. Their interest was partly a response to the overcrowding and greater health problems in cities, and some states with large urban populations were the first to require registration for precisely the same reasons, particularly when the so-called Progressive Movement was strong. Neither Illinois nor New York had statewide registration.

Since the last edition of this book, many indexes to vital records have become available online, as have electronic abstracts of vital record data now being created and maintained in electronic form (in paperless or reduced-paper environments). In general, the amount of online vital records data is increasing, but there is a counter-trend to stop posting some data and even withdraw materials already online, as has happened with some vital records for California and Texas.

The largest collections of online vital records data are on either sites sponsored by various levels of government (generally free access) or on major commercial sites, such as Ancestry.com <www.ancestry.com> and VitalSearch <www.vitalsearch-worldwide.com>. Smaller online collections can often be found through a Google or similar search. Two online sources for information about where to find vital records are "Vital Records Information" <www.vitalrec.com> and "Where to Write for Vital Records" <www.cdc.gov/nchs/howto/w2w/w2welcom.htm>, a service of the National Center for Health Statistics.

Birth Records

Birth certificates usually indicate the date, time, and place of birth; sex of the baby; the names of the infant and parents; and the attending midwife or physician. The return of birth for Charles Hunze (figure 20-9), 6 February 1881, while not specifying the parents' exact birthplaces, does provide a region (Prussia and Hesson), the family address, the maiden name of the mother, and the father's occupation. One collection (more than one hundred thousand entries) of midwives' records for Chicago is at Northwestern Memorial Hospital Archives. It was recently made accessible by a microfilming project of the Genealogical Society of Utah and is available from the LDS Family History Library and its Family History Centers. Similar manuscripts exist for other places, although you must search to locate them. Delayed birth records can be as useful as a record filed at the time of birth, but they are usually filed separately and are often overlooked.

Marriage Records

Marriage certificates often list the man's name and age, the woman's maiden name and age, and the name of the presiding minister or official. If necessary, you can connect the minister to the religious institution through contemporary city directories. The marriage license application is more desirable because it usually has more information, but in some places the application is either no longer extant or not publicly available. Marriage indexes, often compiled from newspapers, are also very useful for pinpointing dates (see figure 20-10).

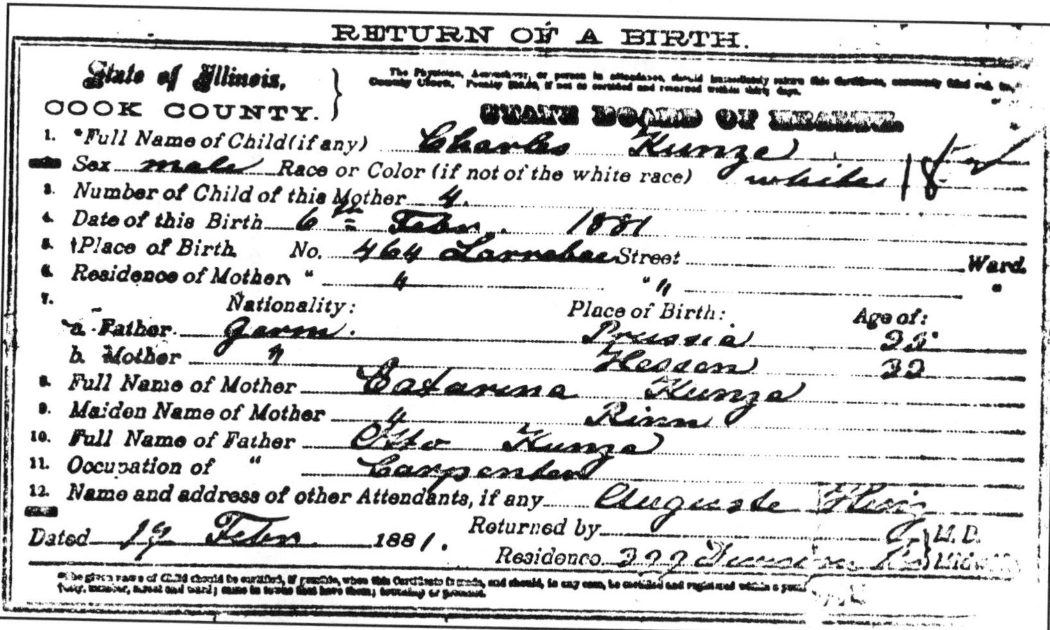

RETURN OF A BIRTH.

State of Illinois, COOK COUNTY.

STATE BOARD OF HEALTH.

1. *Full Name of Child (if any) Charles Kunze
2. Sex male Race or Color (if not of the white race) white
3. Number of Child of this Mother 4.
4. Date of this Birth 6th Feb. 1881
5. †Place of Birth No. 464 Larrabee Street ... Ward.
6. Residence of Mother " " "
7. Nationality: Place of Birth: Age of:
   a. Father Germ. Prussia 33
   b. Mother " Hessen 32
8. Full Name of Mother Catarina Kunze
9. Maiden Name of Mother " Rinn
10. Full Name of Father Otto Kunze
11. Occupation of " Carpenter
12. Name and address of other Attendants, if any Auguste

Dated 19 Feb. 1881. Returned by M.D.
Residence 322

Figure 20-9. Return of a birth for Charles Hunze, who was born on 6 February 1881 in Chicago, Cook County, Illinois.

In Cincinnati, the marriage records were destroyed when the Hamilton County courthouse burned—not once but three different times (1814, 1849, and 1884). The WPA reconstructed the marriages from surviving pages and compiled a new set of indexes. The Daughters of the American Revolution also reconstructed the marriage records using ministers' records, diaries, church registers, justice dockets, original certificates, and newspapers. The combination of both sets is more complete for some surnames than the records were before the fires.

Death Records

A death certificate usually contains at least the name and age of the decedent; the date, place, and cause of death; the name of the attending physician; and the place of burial (see figure 20-11). Later records contain more information. In metropolitan areas, you will need at least an approximate death date to request a death records search. With the Social Security number, recorded on the death certificate since 1937, you can often access other sources. Sometimes records are requested on the assumption that a death, birth, or marriage took place within a city's borders when, in fact, the event took place in an adjacent community.

The Genealogical Society of Utah has microfilmed vital records for many municipalities, and Family History Centers may provide the only opportunity to do a competent search. The sheer volume of documents in the care of the metropolitan agency makes the search difficult; vital statistics agencies are usually overworked, understaffed, and ill-prepared to do lengthy or thorough searches. When the exact date of an event is unknown, the name common or misspelled, or the handwriting questionable or illegible, the complications can become insurmountable. Additionally, vital records' accessibility is subject to change with little or no notice. State legislation has opened, restricted, and

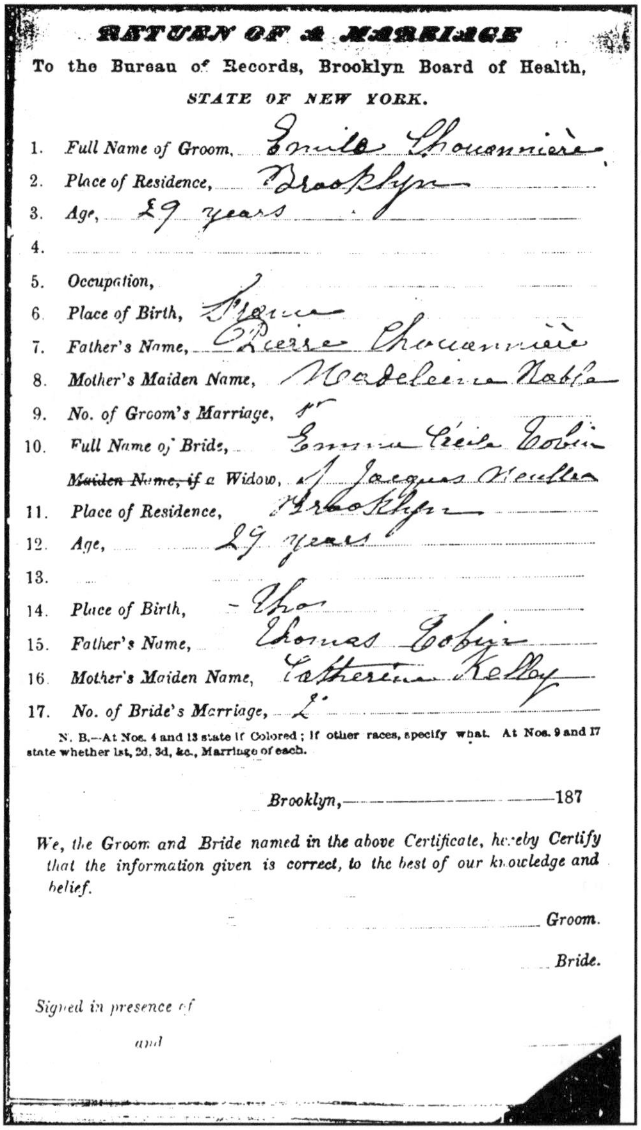

RETURN OF A MARRIAGE

To the Bureau of Records, Brooklyn Board of Health,

STATE OF NEW YORK.

1. *Full Name of Groom,* Emile Chouannière
2. *Place of Residence,* Brooklyn
3. *Age,* 29 years
4.
5. *Occupation,*
6. *Place of Birth,* France
7. *Father's Name,* Pierre Chouannière
8. *Mother's Maiden Name,* Madeleine Noble
9. *No. of Groom's Marriage,* 1st
10. *Full Name of Bride,* Emma Cécile Cobin
Maiden Name, if a Widow, of Jacques Veullen
11. *Place of Residence,* Brooklyn
12. *Age,* 29 years
13.
14. *Place of Birth,* Ohio
15. *Father's Name,* Thomas Cobin
16. *Mother's Maiden Name,* Catherine Kelley
17. *No. of Bride's Marriage,* 2d

N. B.—At Nos. 4 and 13 state if Colored; if other races, specify what. At Nos. 9 and 17 state whether 1st, 2d, 3d, &c., Marriage of each.

Brooklyn, ——————187

We, the Groom and Bride named in the above Certificate, hereby Certify that the information given is correct, to the best of our knowledge and belief.

Groom.

Bride.

Signed in presence of

and

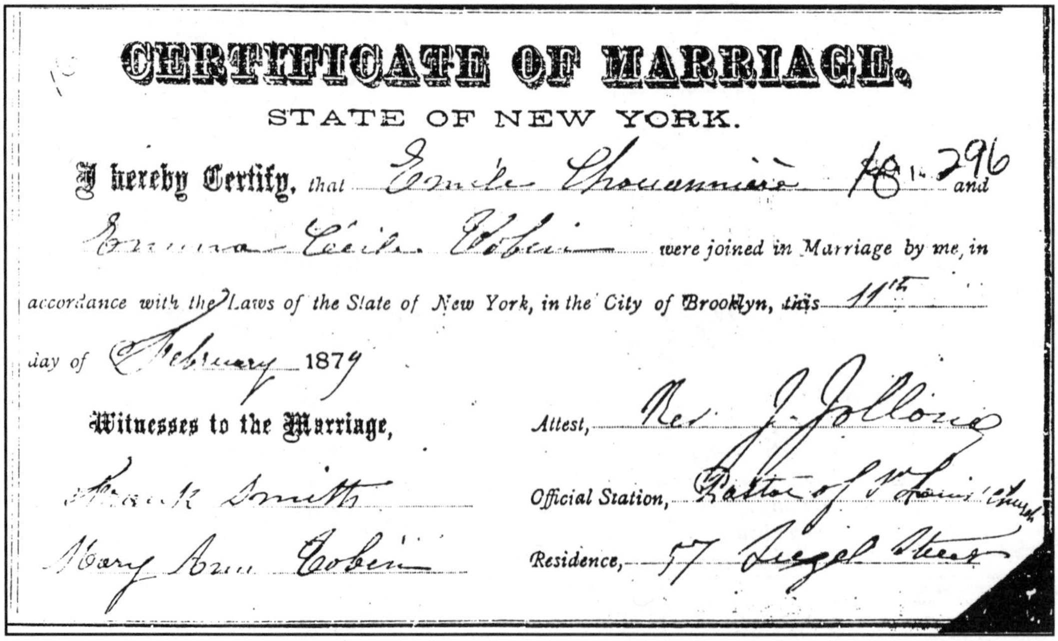

CERTIFICATE OF MARRIAGE.

STATE OF NEW YORK.

I hereby Certify, *that* Emile Chouannière No. 296 *and* Emma Cécile Cobin *were joined in Marriage by me, in accordance with the Laws of the State of New York, in the City of Brooklyn, this* 11th *day of* February 1879

Witnesses to the Marriage,

Frank Smith

Mary Ann Cobin

Attest, Rev. J. Jolliore

Official Station, Pastor of St Louis' Church

Residence, 57 Siegel Street

Figure 20-10. 1879 Certificate of Marriage, State of New York, with attached Return of a Marriage to the Bureau of Records, Brooklyn Board of Health, State of New York.

06926

1. PLACE OF DEATH

County Cook

Township or Road Dist. New Trier

or Incorp. Town or Village

or City ... No. Sanger Brown Sanitarium St.; ... Ward [If death occurred in a hospital or institution, give its NAME instead of street and number.]

Registration Dist. No.

Primary Dist. No.

STATE OF ILLINOIS

State Board of Health - - Bureau of Vital Statistics

ORIGINAL

STANDARD

CERTIFICATE OF DEATH

Registered No.

2. FULL NAME Charles K Stein

PERSONAL AND STATISTICAL PARTICULARS	MEDICAL CERTIFICATE OF DEATH
3. SEX: Male. 4. COLOR OR RACE: white. 5. SINGLE, ~~MARRIED~~, ~~WIDOWED~~, ~~OR DIVORCED~~ (Write the word): Single	16. DATE OF DEATH: April (Month) 21 (Day), 1916 (Year)
6. DATE OF BIRTH: December (Month) 23 (Day), 1885 (Year)	17. I HEREBY CERTIFY, That I attended deceased from April 17, 1916, to April 21, 1916, that I last saw him alive on April 21, 1916, and that death occurred, on the date stated above, at 10:20 P.m.
7. AGE: 30 yrs. 3 mos. 29 ds. If LESS than 1 day, ... hrs. OR ... min.?	The CAUSE OF DEATH* was as follows: Chronic Meningo Encephalitis
8. OCCUPATION (a) Trade, profession, or particular kind of work: Automobile Salesman. (b) General nature of industry, business, or establishment in which employed (or employer):	(Duration) — yrs. 2 mos. — ds.
9. BIRTHPLACE (State or country): Illinois	Contributory (Secondary) ... (Duration) ... yrs. ... mos. ... ds.
PARENTS 10. NAME OF FATHER: Jacob C Stein	(Signed) Sherman Brown, M. D.
11. BIRTHPLACE OF FATHER (State or country): United States	(Address) Kenilworth - Ill.
12. MAIDEN NAME OF MOTHER: Ina Kleuber	Date April 21, 1916 Telephone Kenilworth 351
13. BIRTHPLACE OF MOTHER (State or country): Wisconsin	18. LENGTH OF RESIDENCE (For Hospitals, Institutions, Transients, or Recent Residents): At place of death — yrs. — mos. 4 ds. In the State ... yrs. ... mos. ... ds. Where was disease contracted, if not at place of death? Unknown. Former or usual residence 1140 Mich. Blvd. Chicago
14. THE ABOVE IS TRUE TO THE BEST OF MY KNOWLEDGE (Informant) Mrs. I. Stein (Address) Tel. Oakland 5085	19. PLACE OF BURIAL OR REMOVAL: Chicago Ills. DATE OF BURIAL: April 23rd, 1916
15. Filed 4-25-16, 191 Geo T Braun Cross Court Registrar	20. UNDERTAKER: J. C. Tenth. ADDRESS: 356 E 35th Chicago

*State the DISEASE CAUSING DEATH, or, in deaths from VIOLENT CAUSES, state (1) MEANS OF INJURY; and (2) whether ACCIDENTAL, SUICIDAL, or HOMICIDAL.

Figure 20-11. Certificate of Death for Charles K. Stein, 21 April 1916. Although the family considered this death to have occurred in Chicago, in this instance it was important to know the specific township—New Trier—where the death was recorded in order to find the death certificate.

sometimes completely eliminated genealogists' access to the records. If you are making a special trip to a vital records office, you might spare yourself a good deal of frustration by calling ahead to verify access policies and fees. Death indexes for certain time periods are available online for some states, so it might be most advantageous to do a preliminary investigation on one or more of the search engines available on the Internet.

The Social Security Death Index (SSDI), available online or on CD-ROM from a number of sources, can help you determine where a person lived. Most common versions, derived from the U.S. Social Security Administration's electronic Death Master File, include the person's name, Social Security number, name of the state where the Social Security number was issued, date of birth, date of death (often only the month and year for deaths before 1988), last residence location (in most cases), and last benefit location (in some cases). Note that the last two items are based on ZIP codes in the Death Master File. City, county, and state information is derived from the ZIP code and may be incorrect if the area covered by the ZIP code has changed since the time of death. Most of the online versions are updated frequently, many may be searched for free, and some offer links that generate letters to the Social Security Administration to request copies of applications for Social Security numbers. Using maps to locate where a person was enumerated in the 1900–30 censuses and comparing that with the area covered by the ZIP code of the last residence shown in the SSDI may help determine whether a person has moved around or remained in one place. The Ancestry.com version contains an additional field that can help track changes in location—the year in which the Social Security number was issued if after 1951.

A few American cities have bound volumes of records. New York City printed vital records by order of the borough governments. Each annual volume was individually indexed. Today these sources are available on microfilm only at the Municipal Archives, Department of Records and Information Services <home.nyc.gov/html/records/home.html> and the Family History Library and its Family History Centers. The department maintains an online borough-by-borough list of "New York City Vital Records at the Municipal Archives" <http://home.nyc.gov/html/records/html/3vital.html>.

Special indexes can be of great assistance where they exist. For example, the WPA compiled an index to Chicago deaths, 1871 to 1933, in 1933. Inaccessible except to agency officials until recently, it is now available on microfilm through the Family History Library and its Family History Centers.

Finding Death Dates

Obituaries provide valuable biographical data and, for many people, are the only printed sources with such information.

More recent obituaries, especially for deaths since about 1999 but sometimes earlier, can often be found online. Most large urban newspapers include staff-written obituaries and paid death and funeral notices in their online editions but only for a limited time. Typically these notices are available for free for seven to fourteen days after publication. Most are then available on obituary-oriented commercial websites.

Legacy.com <www.legacy.com> provides obituary hosting services for many newspapers. Depending on the newspaper, notices are generally kept online for thirty days or one year. Searches by newspaper or surname of the decedent are free, but more advanced searches require a paid subscription.

"America's Obituaries and Death Notices," a service of NewsBank.com <www.news.bank.com>, allows searching for any name, other text, or date. Searches can be limited by state or newspaper. The service is available through many public library websites, either from computers in the library or from home with a participating library card number or other password.

ObituaryRegistry.com <www.obituaryregistry.com/#search> is a subscription-based service that claims to have about 25 percent of U.S. death notices and obituaries published since March 2000 and a much higher percentage of current notices. The basic service marketed to genealogists allows searching by place of death and by surname. Subscriptions allowing advanced searches, such as for names of surviving family members, are much more expensive.

Betty M. Jarboe's *Obituaries: A Guide to Sources* is an invaluable finding aid for obituaries in newspapers and periodicals, particularly when the population of a city makes searching for a death date unusually difficult.[35] A typical citation from this source shows that the Colorado Historical Society Library has files of newspaper birth, marriage, and death notices from the 1860s to the 1940s. Another entry indicates that the New Orleans Public Library has a card file of approximately 523,000 obituary cards, which it is expanding by 25,000 new cards per year. *Monroe County, N.Y. Cemetery Record Index* is another of many entries for metropolitan areas in Jarboe's work.[36]

The obituary collection at Ancestry.com contains obituaries from hundreds of newspapers. Ancestry.com searches the Internet daily to find new obituaries, extracts the facts into the site's obituary database, and provides source information and links to the full obituary text. This feature is most useful for locating recent death information.

Chapter 12, "Newspapers," and chapter 2, "Computers and Technology," in this volume describe online editions of the *Brooklyn Daily Eagle*, the *Chicago Tribune*, and other online newspapers that are rich sources for obituaries.

An unusual example of combining records to find a death date is the case of Solomon Schwartz. His descendants moved away from Chicago, and his death date and burial place were no longer known, although the descendants remembered that he had been buried in a Jewish cemetery. His great-grandchildren could not find his name in the city death index, and they could not use cemetery records because they are arranged chronologically and by lot numbers. However, in the county recorder's records, a deed book marked "Cemeteries" contained original title records arranged by cemetery. Solomon Schwartz's record was in the second Jewish cemetery consulted. Only the number of the conveyance, the date, names of the grantor (cemetery) and the grantee (Solomon), and the legal description of the cemetery lot were given; but further investigation in the cemetery's records proved that it was the correct man.

Coroners' Inquests

Coroners' inquests are infrequently used records. If there is reason to believe that an ancestor died from any violent, unnatural, or unknown cause, the resulting inquest may contain a wealth of information rarely found in other sources. Maryland and Virginia have inquests dating back to the mid-seventeenth century. Many of the deaths reported annually in a city end up in the coroner's files, which are now commonly under the jurisdiction of the city or county medical examiner. Earlier records may contain more details than later files do. Coroners' files may also provide personal histories of the victim through exact birthplaces, dates, names of parents and other relatives, educational and occupational background, military service, Social Security number, and much more. A doctor's statement may incorporate a medical history and physical traits. Eyewitness accounts often contain insights into the character of a victim and record the drama of the death itself. A coroner's verdict concluded early case histories, but more recent reports do not determine guilt. They also provide leads to subsequent court cases. Usually an exact death date is needed, because this record type is usually arranged chronologically, and most are not indexed. Inquests stemming from catastrophes are sometimes grouped under the name of the disaster, such as the Iroquois Theatre Fire. Coroners' inquests combine effectively with news accounts of disasters, which provide casualty lists and background details on each event. For more information and illustrations of sample reports, see Laura Szucs Pfeiffer's *Hidden Sources: Family History in Unlikely Places*.[37] Online finding aids to coroners' inquests can be elusive. Sometimes they can be found among county or city records inventories listed on the state archives website. A good starting point for locating potential collections is to type "Coroners' Records" in a search engine.

Undertakers' Records

Undertakers' records often include more detailed information about a decedent than does the official county death certificate. However, mortuaries may be difficult to locate in the city because of shifting neighborhoods. A search of *Google* for "funeral homes" returns a list of both directory sites and individual firms. For older information, use city directories to trace a family-owned establishment to a new location in the city (see the section on morticians in chapter 4, "Business, Institution, and Organization Records"). A successor might know the whereabouts of records from defunct establishments, and cemeteries that have been in existence for some time are often able to locate files of defunct undertaking establishments. Some genealogical societies have traced the histories of funeral homes in the areas they serve. Records from 398 funeral homes in the Chicago area have been surveyed by Kirk Vandenburg for the South Suburban Genealogical and Historical Society, P.O. Box 96, South Holland, IL 60473. During the process of the survey, every attempt was made to locate records of funeral homes that had changed names or gone out of business. Similar projects have been undertaken by other genealogical societies across the United States.

Cemetery Records

There is no direct route to cemetery records in metropolitan areas (see chapter 13, "Vital Records"). Nonsectarian cemeteries generally maintain their own files. Policies vary somewhat, but many cemetery officials will give minimal information over the telephone: names of individuals interred in a single plot, exact grave locations, and current owners of the plot. Additional information usually requires a fee. Since records are, in most instances, cross-indexed by location and chronology, seldom does a comprehensive index exist. The key to cemetery record use is an exact death date for at least one of the individuals buried in a given plot. This, in turn, can lead to names of others in the same place. Many a city has removed the deceased and paved over an old cemetery that was in the way of urban progress. Records for these cemeteries can be especially challenging to track down. Consulting old histories, historical societies, and, of course, genealogical societies in the area of interest is the recommended approach. Carolee Inskeep's *The Graveyard Shift: A Family Historian's Guide to New York City Cemeteries* provides contact information and brief histories for cemeteries throughout the city.[38]

Genealogical societies and DAR chapters have been engaged in transcribing and publishing cemetery records for years. Many of the publications are described on local genealogical society websites. Many transcriptions, generally for rural areas, have been posted online by local societies or as part of the USGenWeb Project <www.usgenweb.com>. Even if these organizations have not been involved in the cemetery work directly, they are usually the first to know about and to advertise such projects in their publications. For example, *The Generator*, the newsletter of the St. Mary's County Genealogical Society (Maryland), announced the publication of *Records of St. Paul's Cemetery 1855–1946* (Elaine O. Zimmerman and Kenneth E. Zimmerman, P.O. Box 276, Woodstock, MD 21163) soon after it was completed. The two thousand names of German immigrants who were listed in the Baltimore city cemetery include transfers from the old cemetery owned by the German Evangelical Lutheran Church. As the newsletter suggests, cemetery publications take on additional value because the stones in many have weathered or been vandalized to the extent that they are no longer readable.

Interment.net <www.interment.net> claims to have over 3.5 million cemetery records from over 7,400 cemeteries around the world. Although the site has relatively few transcriptions from urban cemeteries, it does include complete listings for many national and other veteran cemeteries.

Many cemeteries and cemetery records can now be located through Internet sites. While most sites provide only addresses and contact information online, some, such as The Green-Wood Cemetery in Brooklyn, New York, include an every-name index to interments there <www.green-wood.com/>. Also worth remembering is the fact that thousands of cemetery records have been microfilmed and may be found by locality at FamilySearch.org.

Newspapers

An entire chapter of this book is devoted to newspaper research (chapter 12, "Newspapers"), but a word of caution is in order for the city researcher. In larger cities there were multiple editions of the major daily newspapers, as well as regular runs of community, neighborhood, ethnic, and religious newspapers. To do a thorough search for an event in the life of a city ancestor, all of these publications should be considered.

Under the auspices of the United States Newspaper Project, almost every state has its own newspaper preservation projects, which are designed to collect and microfilm all of the extant newspapers in the state for historical purposes. Among the outstanding newspaper collections in the United States is that of the State Historical Society of Wisconsin (second only to the Library of Congress).[39]

Most urban newspapers, small and large, now publish an Internet edition, but very few large urban newspapers keep information with significant genealogical value on their websites for more than a few days or weeks. Significant exceptions are *The New York Times,* available through ProQuest, and the *Brooklyn Daily Eagle,* with searchable images posted by the Brooklyn Public Library. A few newspapers in smaller areas do keep information from previous issues online. NewsLink <http://newslink.org> provides an easy-to-use structured directory including websites of daily and weekly newspapers and other media outlets.

Recently, Ancestry.com has begun posting searchable images of older newspapers, including those for many medium and small urban areas <www.ancestry.com/search/rectype/periodicals/news/dblist>. Typing the name of a particular city with the word "newspaper" into a search engine will often turn up positive results, pointing to a website with an index to a newspaper, or at least to the place where the newspaper can be found.

Religious Sources

Locating urban religious records presents a unique challenge (see chapter 6, "Church Records," in this volume, as well as chapter 8, "Church Sources," by Richard W. Dougherty in *Printed Sources: A Guide to Published Genealogical Records*). Population, geography, and ethnicity are confusing enough; but to complicate matters further, different denominations have kept different types of records. For example, presbyteries transferred membership records with the departure of the member. Immigrants commonly chose to worship in their own tongues and often went far out of their neighborhoods to find the congenial atmosphere of the national parish. Churches as well as people responded to the dynamics of cities—some closing, consolidating, or moving as neighborhoods changed, others shifting from their ethnic orientations to accommodate new circumstances. Thus, any researcher having difficulty tracing the church or synagogue of an ancestor might save time by backtracking to study the history of that particular religion in the locale of interest. Though finding religious records may be difficult, it usually repays the time and effort spent. Church records usually predate civil records and supply information not found elsewhere—sometimes indicating even the European church or parish where people being married were christened or confirmed.

An invaluable guide for research in this area is the Historical Records Survey of the WPA. WPA workers inventoried church and public records extant in the 1930s for many areas in the United States. Their lists for urban churches are especially valuable. A typical entry for church vital records would contain the name and address of the institution at the time of publication, ethnic orientation (if any), and comprehensive dates for each type of vital record. If the organization housed documents from other congregations, the survey noted that fact and included a range of dates. For example, in *A Guide to Church Vital Statistics Records in California—San Francisco and Alameda Counties*, the individual churches are arranged by geographical area and denomination.[40] A summary of baptisms, marriages, and death records follows for each. Additionally, it notes that Holy Family was a Chinese mission while Saint Anthony of Padua was German. In most cases, the founding dates are noted. Some of the WPA surveys can be located on the Internet.

The obvious limitation to the survey is that many of the records may have since been moved. But it still provides an overview of the span of years during which records were kept and is proof that the records were still in existence at the time of the WPA compilation. It is a very good place to start.

For those inventories that were printed, consult *Bibliography of Research Project Reports,* by Sargent B. Child and Dorothy P. Holmes.[41] Many inventories were never printed; they can be located by consulting Loretta L. Hefner's *The WPA Historical*

Records Survey: A Guide to the Unpublished Inventories, Indexes, and Transcripts.[42]

Some contemporary guides facilitate finding records for certain cities. A local reference librarian should, for example, be able to point to guides such as *Genealogical Resources in the New York Metropolitan Area* and *The Encyclopedia of Jewish Genealogy*. Both of these guides, mentioned earlier in the chapter, contain specific addresses for Jewish material. Jack Bochar's *Locations of Chicago Roman Catholic Churches, 1850–1990* is a time-saving book filled with maps, addresses, microfilm numbers, and historical data relating to hundreds of parishes in that city.[43]

Early city or county histories, biographical sketches, and jubilee books provide other background on religious institutions in a particular area. Illustrations included in county histories often preserve the only surviving images of buildings where city ancestors worshipped. Through these descriptions you can trace the development and ethnic makeup of a church. Modern studies also are a tremendous help, and their bibliographies enhance their utility. *Chicago Churches and Synagogues*, compiled by George Lane and Alginantes Kezys, highlights 125 houses of worship with architectural, historical, or social significance.[44] Further, they provide a detailed description and history of each building and its congregation, ethnic makeup, architectural attributes, and location by exact address and area of city. The acknowledgments and notes provide numerous sources for locating denominational repositories.

A few church records are available in book form or microform. The Newberry Library in Chicago has a large collection of sources from the eastern United States as well as from local institutions. The Detroit Society of Genealogical Research is one of many metropolitan groups engaged in the publication of local church records. The Genealogical Society of Utah has microfilmed church registers from numerous localities, and Family History Centers in every state allow access to these records. Also available through the Family History Library is the International Genealogical Index <www.familysearch.org/Eng/Search/frameset_search.asp?PAGE=igi/search_IGI.asp&clear_form=true>, which is rich in church registers for New York City, Boston, Chicago, Hartford, Indianapolis, Philadelphia, and many other cities (see chapter 3, "General References and Guides"). A few church records have also been transcribed and posted on USGenWeb Project county or state websites <www.usgenweb.org>.

Used in combination with other sources, church vital records can help solve even the most perplexing problems. For example, Karl Johnson was known to have lived at a certain address in Minneapolis for several years near the beginning of the twentieth century, but his death date was unknown. A death index indicated that he had died at that address in 1911. This death year led to a certificate that, in turn, pointed to the cemetery records. The cemetery gave the officiating minister's name, and a directory search identified him as belonging to the Swedish Covenant Church. It had since moved, but inquiries at another congregation of the same denomination pinpointed the new location of the records. Not only did the church have many records of the family, it had a jubilee book with biographical sketches that included Karl Johnson as a founding member. The biography gave his exact birthplace, his date of arrival in the United States, and his residence before settling in Minneapolis.

Land–Real Estate Property

Even though the city dweller is not always dependent upon his or her land for a livelihood, that quarter acre is usually as valuable as the agriculturalist's quarter section. Not only the deed books but many court cases bear record of this.

Most American cities are under the jurisdiction of county governments, and city land records are almost always held by the county recorder. City lots, however, may be recorded in volumes separate from county land with their own indexes or finding aids; they are easy to miss.

The municipal library, designed to collect data useful to the governance of the city, is a good place to learn the procedures of land searching. Plat maps or tract books may be centralized there. Otherwise, detailed plat maps of a city are usually available from municipal agencies or from the recorder of deeds.

Some municipal land records are now available on the Internet. For example, Hennepin County, Minnesota, which includes Minneapolis, has a property information database <www2.co.hennepin.mn.us/pins> that can be searched by address, addition name, or property identification number. The resulting display provides a wealth of information, including location and size of the property, year of construction, date and price of last sale, estimated market value, name and address of current owner, amount of taxes due, and a link to a map of the property. Links to similar sites throughout the country may be found by searching the "Public Records Online" page at *NETR Online: Real Estate Information & Public Records Research* <www.netronline.com/public_records.htm>.

If the ancestor you are interested in is consistently listed at a certain address for a number of years in city directories or the census, he or she may have owned that piece of property. Frequent address changes may indicate that he or she was renting. Both of these hypotheses need further proof for verification. The 1920 and 1930 censuses may help. They indicate whether the head of the household owned or rented the property. The ancestor who rented property in one location may also have owned land in another, especially a vacant lot. To find his or her land records, check land indexes of abstracts, tax rolls, and less commonly consulted sources, such as building permits or building improvement files; street, sidewalk, and sewer assessment records; and utility cards for water, lighting, and refuse collection, which also identify an owner with a specific lot or address. These records are normally not subject to privacy laws. Land abstracts compiled from deeds and other property documents by title and abstract companies provide an alternate source when the original land records have been destroyed. They were especially valuable in Chicago after the Great Fire of 1871, when they were used to reestablish property titles in burned areas.

Maps

A solid knowledge of the city's layout as it existed in an ancestor's time is also important. Carol Mehr Schiffmen discusses and illustrates various types of maps and other geographic sources useful for urban research in her chapter, "Geographic Tools: Maps, Atlases, and Gazetteers," in *Printed Sources: A Guide to Published Genealogical Records*.

Jonathan Sheppard Books (P.O. Box 2020, Plaza Station, Albany, NY 12220) offers a packet of maps reproduced from Fannin's Atlas of 1853, which includes maps for the cities of Baltimore, Boston, Buffalo, Charleston, Chicago, Cincinnati, Milwaukee, New Orleans, New York, Philadelphia, Pittsburgh, St. Louis, San Francisco, and Washington, D.C. Write to the company for prices.

Many American city maps are described and can be viewed and downloaded from the American Memory Project of the Library of Congress ("Cities and Towns" <http://memory.loc.gov/ammem/gmdhtml/cityhome.html>). Paper copies are available for purchase from the library's photoduplication section.

Among the maps most used for urban research are ward maps, fire insurance maps, and panoramic or "bird's-eye-view" maps.

Ward Maps

Figure 20-12 is part of a map that shows wards for New York City in 1850. Ward maps are especially important when used in conjunction with city directories in cases when a census index does not exist or when a suspected resident does not appear in an index. By defining the ward boundaries, it is often possible to eliminate hours of wasted search time. Ward boundaries changed frequently from one census enumeration to the next, so it is necessary to coordinate the ward map with the census year. For a good description of early maps, see Michael H. Shelley's *Ward Maps of United States Cities: A Selective Checklist of Pre-1900 Maps in the Library of Congress*.[45] The Olin Library at Cornell University has microfiche copies of the maps listed by Shelley; see "19th Century Ward Maps of U.S. Cities: A Guide to Olin Library Holdings" <www.library.cornell.edu/okuref/maps/wardmaps.htm>. Some libraries have maps that are designed to facilitate searching cities in federal census years 1790 to 1930.

Fire Insurance Maps

The Sanborn Map Company produced somes seven hundred thousand sheets of detailed maps for twelve thousand cities and towns in North America from 1867 to the present. (Other companies began producing maps as early as 1846.) These maps were used by insurance agents to determine hazards and risk in underwriting specific buildings. They were produced on oversize sheets in pastel colors: olive drab for adobe, pink for stone, blue for brick, yellow for wood, gray for iron. Size, shape, and construction of homes, businesses, and farm buildings; locations of windows, doors, and firewalls; roof types; widths and names of streets; property boundaries; ditches, water mains, and sprinkling systems; and other details are clearly indicated. Individual residents do not appear on the maps by name, although specific addresses are shown. Businesses appear by name. Once you have found your ancestor in census, directory, or utility files, you can determine precisely what house or business the family lived and worked in. It is possible to combine city directories and census entries with fire insurance maps and to locate each resident on the map.

"Fire Insurance Maps in the Library of Congress," prepared by the Geography and Map Section of the Library of Congress, lists the maps available for each town and city. Copies will be supplied upon request from the Library of Congress, Photoduplication Services, Washington, DC 20540. Because map sizes vary, it is wise to write ahead and ask for a cost estimate for each copy. (The pastel colors do not reproduce distinctly in black and white.)

Duplicate and microfilm copies of the maps are also available at selected libraries across the country and in state historical societies and local public libraries. For example, the maps for Tacoma, Washington, are in the Tacoma Public Library in their original, multicolored form. Those for Utah cities are found at the Utah State Historical Society, and digital copies of the Utah maps may be viewed at the website of the University of Utah <www.lib.utah.edu/digital/sanborn/>. ProQuest Information and Learning has more than 660,000 scanned images of the Sanborn maps and makes them available only to authorized users through subscribing academic and public libraries. For more information, see </sanborn.umi.com/HelpFiles/about.html> or ask your local library. The easiest way to locate other copies of the maps is to start with a Google search for "sanborn insurance maps."

Panoramic/Bird's-Eye Maps

When they exist for an ancestor's hometown, panoramic or "bird's-eye-view" maps can add an attractive dimension to a family history (see figure 20-13). Drawn in perspective, streets and buildings are depicted in them as if from the air. Still prized for their artistic beauty, the commercially motivated drawings were commissioned by chambers of commerce, real

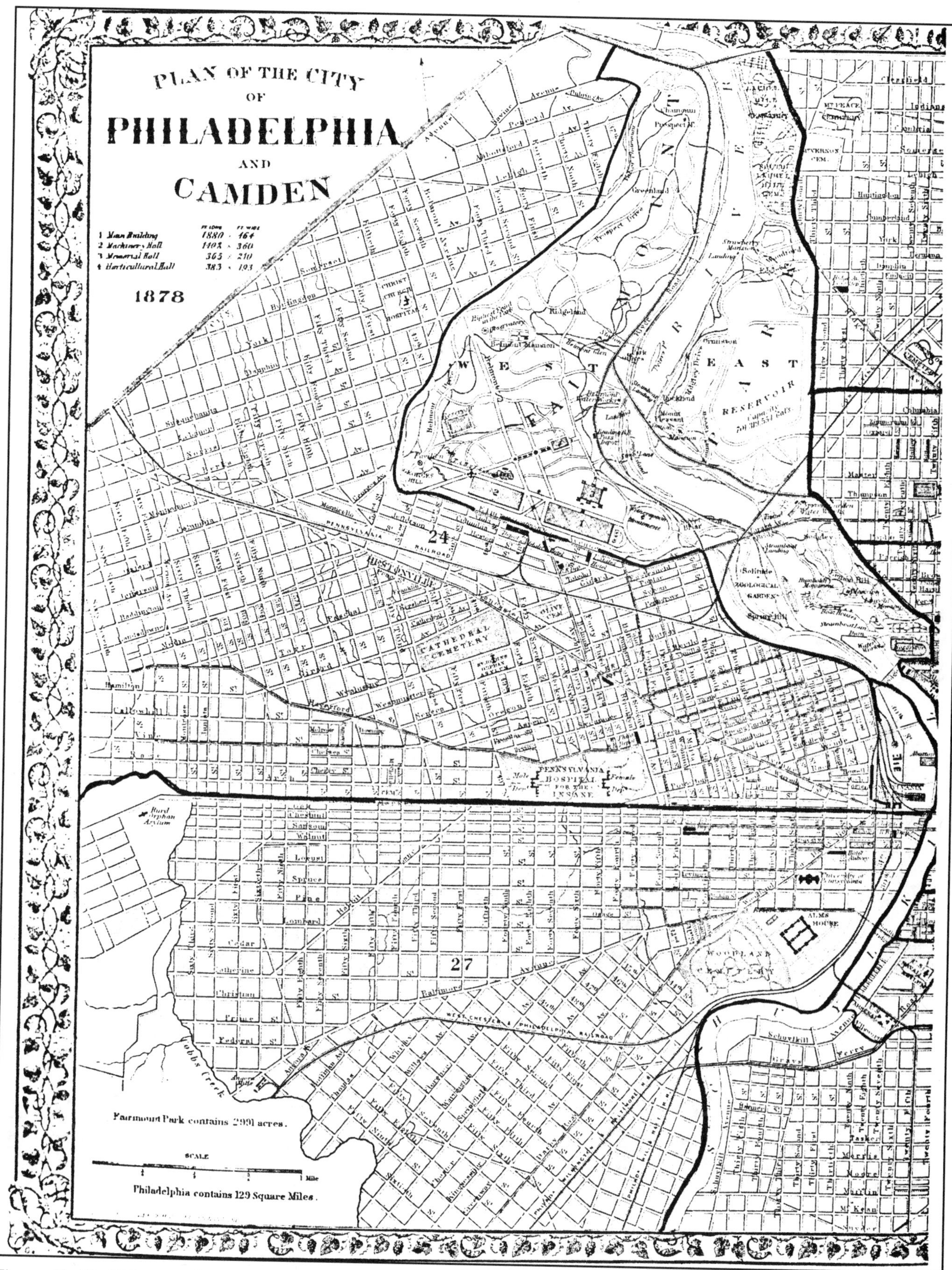

Figure 20-12. 1878 map of Philadelphia showing wards.

estate companies, and businessmen whose establishments were frequently advertised on the borders. The panoramics were especially popular during the Civil War era and will be found in a number of county and municipal histories. A useful guide to these romantic maps is the Library of Congress's *Panoramic Maps of Cities in the United States and Canada: A Checklist of Maps in the Collections of the Library of Congress, Geography and Map Division*.[46] The library has placed a number of panoramic maps online at </memory.loc.gov/ammem/pmhtml/panhome.html>.

Metropolitan historical societies may also maintain separate guides to their map collections. Maps may be cataloged by date, enabling the searcher to pinpoint a particular time period to coordinate the city directory–census study. Maps may also be listed by subject. School district and cemetery maps may help to locate records from those agencies. The New York Public Library has one of the largest city map collections in the United States.

Most libraries do not have special equipment for the reproduction of large maps, nor do they allow photocopying because of potential damage to the maps. You may improvise a makeshift map by superimposing wards or old street locations on a current map.

Changing Boundaries and Jurisdictions

Over the years, as cities grew, most of them expanded by annexing the small towns at their fringes. Wards assumed different configurations, streets were frequently renamed or they disappeared entirely when a building project came along, some cities changed their numbering systems entirely, and annexations extended city limits on a regular basis. For anyone attempting Philadelphia research, this type of environment is clarified in *Genealogy of Philadelphia County Subdivisions*, by John Daly and Allen Weinberg.[47] Though not always found in published form, it is to the researcher's great advantage to inquire at the state or local level for guides to get through the complexities of metropolitan changes—and there were many! For example, the following towns became part of Boston in the years indicated: East Boston, 1637; South Boston, 1804; Roxbury, 1868; Dorchester, 1870; Brighton, 1874; Charlestown, 1874; West Roxbury, 1874; and Hyde Park, 1912.[48] Information about some city boundary changes may found by simply searching the Internet for the words "city boundary changes."

In an article titled "American Cities Are (Mostly) Better Than Ever," Richard C. Wade explains:

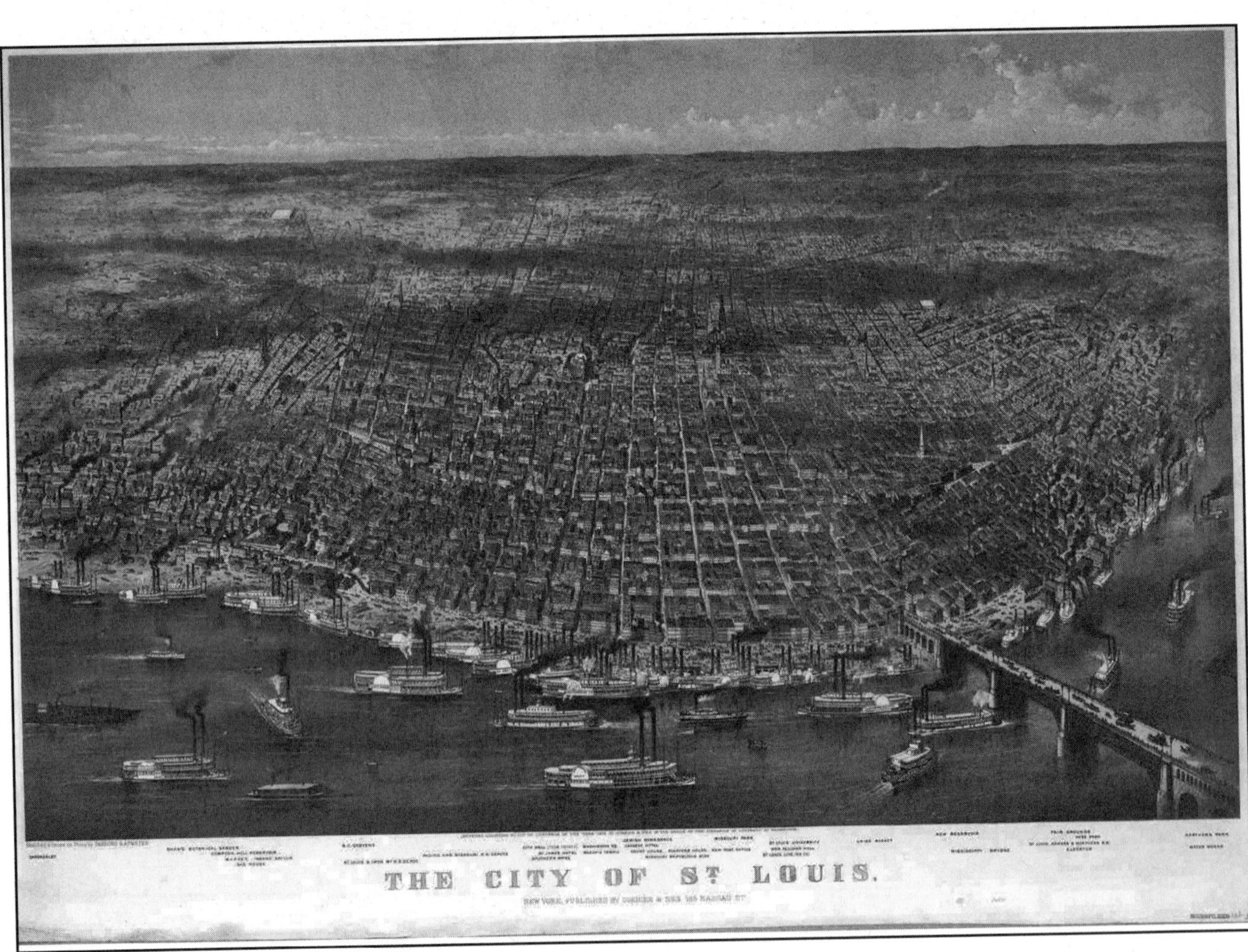

Figure 20-13. An 1874 panoramic map of St. Louis, Missouri.

> Municipal boundaries were wide and continually enlarging. In 1876 St. Louis reached out into neighboring farm land and incorporated all the area now within its city limits. In one swift move, in 1889 Chicago added over 125 square miles to its territory. And in 1898 New York absorbed the four surrounding counties—including Brooklyn, the nation's fourth largest city—making it the Empire City.
>
> As populations grew, there were always fresh areas to build up. This meant that all the wealth, all the commerce, all the industry, and all the talent lay within the city.
>
> More prosperous than either the state or federal governments, the cities needed no outside help; indeed they met any interference with the demand for home rule.[49]

Wade touches on two important points that consistently give researchers problems in urban situations if they have not familiarized themselves with the history of the area. Imagine an individual who believes his ancestors were from Chicago but cannot find them in directories before 1890, though he is sure they were city residents as early as 1880. Had he checked the history against maps of the area where they lived, he would have discovered that they indeed lived in what is now Chicago but was then Austin, Illinois. The town of Austin had its own city directories until the larger city brought it under its wing in 1889. Likewise, a woman searching for a Brooklyn address in the 1920 census was frustrated for some time trying to determine why the numbers she took from the census catalog would not lead her to the right place in the microfilm. Had she known a little bit about Brooklyn, she would have known that while Brooklyn has been part of New York City since 1898, it is in Kings County and not in New York County, where she had been searching.

Home rule can complicate the process of finding urban records. Just when you think you know what kind of records a state keeps and where they are kept, you may find that the city of your interest had an entirely different procedure. For example, Illinois counties have required brides and grooms to answer a number of questions on marriage applications that make them especially valuable for family historians. Cook County, however, under its home rule, did not require that applications be retained by the clerk for many years. Additionally, in other Illinois counties, vital record indexes are open for inspection to any member of a state genealogical society, but because the Chicago office processes an average of one thousand requests per day, a different set of rules prevents researchers from personally searching Cook County indexes. Policies are also subject to sudden changes, so it is wise to call in advance.

There are yet other distinctions that the urban researcher will need to make. For example, areas legally designated as city-county include San Francisco, Denver, and Honolulu. An area designated as metropolitan is Nashville and Davidson County, Tennessee. Areas subject to some county jurisdiction but operating as cities are Jacksonville, Duval County, Florida; Indianapolis, Marion County, Indiana; New Orleans, Orleans Parish, Louisiana; Baton Rouge, East Baton Rouge Parish, Louisiana; Nantucket, Nantucket County, Massachusetts; Boston, Suffolk County, Massachusetts; New York City Borough/County, New York: Bronx, Kings (Brooklyn), New York (Manhattan), Queens, and Richmond; and Philadelphia County, Philadelphia. Areas designated as independent cities, not subject to the county: Washington, D.C.; Baltimore City, Maryland; St. Louis, Missouri; and Carson City, Nevada.

Independent Virginia city records are detailed in *Red Book: American State, County, and Town Sources* for the following burgs of Virginia: Alexandria, Bedford, Bristol, Buena Vista, Charlottesville, Chesapeake, Clifton Forge, Colonial Heights, Covington, Danville, Emporia, Fairfax, Falls Church, Franklin, Fredericksburg, Galax, Hampton, Harrisonburg, Hopewell, Lexington, Lynchburg, Manassas, Manassas Park, Manchester, Martinsville, Nansemond, Newport News, Norfolk, Norton, Petersburg, Poquoson, Portsmouth, Radford, Richmond, Roanoke, Salem, South Boston, South Norfolk, Staunton, Suffolk, Virginia Beach, Warwick, Waynesboro, Williamsburg, and Winchester.

Naturalization Records

Because so many urbanites were immigrants, naturalization records are yet another type of record that urban researchers commonly mine for information. Until 1906, naturalization was strictly a function of the courts. Prior to that year, an individual could be naturalized in any court of record. Some cities supported county, criminal, municipal, police, marine, and mayor's courts. It was often a matter of choosing which court was close or convenient for the immigrant to approach for citizenship. In October 1906, Congress created the Bureau of Immigration and Naturalization to standardize the system. One by-product was a greatly expanded set of questions for the immigrant to answer; another was retention of duplicate copies of all final petitions in the Washington office of the bureau. After many of the minor courts stopped naturalizing, their records were frequently filed in county or city offices, and many old court records have been dispersed to archives, historical societies, libraries, and a number of unlikely storage places. A comprehensive guide to information for sources on naturalization research is Loretto Dennis Szucs's *They Became Americans: Finding Naturalization Records and Ethnic Origins*.[50]

Naturalization records require a petition number for reference purposes. This number is usually available through indexes maintained by the court of record where the petition was filed. The New England states, New York City, and Chicago are blessed with comprehensive Soundex indexes that cover local and federal naturalizations. When the Soundex fails to supply a reference, as it occasionally does, ancillary records, such as order books (which show all naturalizations approved on a given day) and registers (which list petitioners by first initial of surname), may also exist.

Because naturalization conferred voting rights on aliens, voting records are another possible source of information for the urban genealogist. Voter registration lists included the native-born as well as the naturalized, of course, but have the built-in limitation that they cover only those who made the effort to register. Still, voting records are sometimes indexed or registered by ward, and they can provide an avenue for identification when censuses or directories are not available. Precinct block books might substitute for assessment books in areas where few people owned property. Voting lists can provide a test for community involvement. They reflect local mores in other ways, for the linkage between citizenship and voting was not always visible. Voting did not always guarantee full-fledged citizenship, just as citizenship did not always result in the exercise of the ballot. For anyone writing a detailed family history, a study of official election returns, especially those predating the secret ballot, might prove intriguing as a means of identifying political participation. Many genealogical societies are making it a point to see that voter lists are saved and published whenever possible. The Berkshire Family History Association (P.O. Box 1437, Pittsfield, MA 01202-1437 or <www.berkshire.net/~bfha/>), for example, has published in its quarterlies "Registers of Voters in Pittsfield, Massachusetts—1890."

Court Records

Court records are potentially the most valuable yet the most underutilized of urban sources (see chapter 7, "Court Records," in this volume as well as *Printed Sources: A Guide to Published Genealogical Records*, chapter 10, "Published Probate Records," by Wendy L. Elliott, and chapter 12, "Court and Legal Records," by Benjamin Barnett Spratling, 3rd). The case volume created by the vast population and the bureaucracy involved may intimidate even an enthusiastic searcher. Court jurisdictions and procedures have puzzled many a researcher, but books on local government can guide you through the maze. For each state, *Red Book: American State, County, and Town Sources* provides maps as well as tables that point to boundary and jurisdictional changes over the years as well as addresses for county courts. Internet search engines are also good places to begin a search for specific court records.

By far the most commonly used court records are the probates because of their helpfulness in identifying heirs. Some counties have master indexes for court proceedings, but, more often than not, you must examine registers by year. When names are distinguished only by case number, a search of the docket books may be in order. The shortcut approach is especially good in cities where old cases are warehoused and must be requested a few at a time. Dockets provide a synopsis of the case, the decedent's name and date of death, name of the administrator, and names of widowed spouse and heirs. This information enables the searcher to order the correct case from the warehouse or to retrieve it from its court location without going through all the other cases of the same name. Before visiting any court, it is advisable to call in advance to check on research policies and days and hours of operation. This is a good time to ask if indexes and records are immediately accessible or if storage of actual records in an off-site location will make it necessary to make two or more trips to the court.

City courts can also yield information of value. If the city is subject to county jurisdiction, police courts and local justice courts take care of trivial matters that involve limited fines and fees. More important cases go automatically to county and state tribunals. If the city is independent, however, mayors' courts—hustings (so-called in Virginia, Maryland, and the Carolinas)—had substantial jurisdiction.

Some city courts issued business licenses for taverns, mercantile establishments, hotels, and other shops and received petitions from local citizens regarding many of the functions that are today handled by commissioners or separate agencies of government, such as road repair, runoff water drainage, watch and ward (police patrol and security of business and personal property), volunteer fire department personnel, and numerous other activities necessary to provide services and protection for city dwellers. Another important function was providing for the poor. Among the references to the poor in city court minutes are notices of removals of people and families who were not residents of the city and who might become public charges on the poor rolls. Minutes record that these people were transported to the city line at public expense.

Records for these courts were often printed annually by public order, and these volumes can be found in local public libraries. For example, the printed minutes and reports of city officials for St. Paul, Minnesota, are in the St. Paul Public Library; a second copy is available at the Minnesota Historical Society. The city minutes for Nashua, New Hampshire, are found only in the Nashua Public Library, where there is a complete run of volumes that continue well into the twentieth century. The Genealogical Society of Utah has microfilmed the city court volumes for Savannah, Georgia, and several other southern cities and towns. The minutes of the Mayor's Court of New York City are published in the collections of the New York Historical Society. There is a great interest in city court minutes, and many of them are easy to locate.

Somewhat less well known than probate or other local court records are federal court files. The federal courts have traditionally heard cases involving interstate disputes and often served as courts of appeal for litigation that originated at the local level. In addition, the federal courts were usually indexed by plaintiff and/or by defendant, making the search a time-consuming project.

The material in the files varies with the significance of the case and the state that it reached during the trial process. But depositions describing the acquisition and retention of property were not unusual in land disputes, which often appeared as equity suits. These were often accompanied by maps of the place in question or copies of deeds submitted as exhibits. Such cases can produce thousands of pages of testimony and may detail facts about the family and its environment that are not available elsewhere.

Bankruptcy filings included schedules of assets and liabilities, outlining the business and financial dealings of the bankruptcy claimant. Small partnerships and proprietorships, along with personal bankruptcies, comprised the preponderance of cases heard in bankruptcy court. When federal bankruptcy laws were not in effect, "involuntary" bankruptcies were entered as equity proceedings. Loretto Dennis Szucs's "To Whom I Am Indebted: Bankruptcy Records," in *Ancestry* Magazine, explores historical events that caused bankruptcies and provides information on how and where to find such files.[51] Federal criminal prosecutions were a minor portion of the case load until the 1920s, when prohibition violations swelled the numbers. Other types of federal cases of genealogical interest include confiscation cases from the Civil War, when the federal government seized the available property of Confederate sympathizers, and personal injury suits against interstate carriers (usually railroads).

The federal government has touched urban residents in ways other than through its courts. The Internal Revenue Service was less visible before World War I than it is now, but an assortment of IRS assessment lists sheds light on the wealth of many individuals during the Civil War and again after 1913. The Civil War–vintage assessments (arranged by collection district and thereunder alphabetically) have been microfilmed; those for the early twentieth century have not. Original monthly assessment lists survive for San Francisco, Denver, Chicago, and Detroit and are deposited in the federal archives and records centers serving those cities. Taxable income was defined at a level that limited the assessment to the middle and upper classes; nevertheless, thousands of entries appear in the volumes pertaining to urban districts.

A source with particular interest to those whose roots lie in the South comes from the records of the Southern Claims Commission, which was organized to settle with Union sympathizers who had supplied Northern forces without compensation. Case files included depositions, affidavits, reports, and receipts. A geographical index, arranged by state and county, allows the researcher to pinpoint people in a specific territory, while the consolidated index serves as a name entry. See *Records of the Commissioners of Claims (Southern Claims Commission), 1871–1880* and Gary B. Mills's *Civil War Claims in the South: An Index to Claimants Before the Southern Claims Commission, 1871–1880*, an accompanying consolidated index.[52] These records are not limited to cities, but the major locales of Atlanta and New Orleans are included.

Business, Occupational, and Labor Records

Bankruptcy and tax records lead naturally to another source: professional, business, and employment records. Occupational specialization and the related drive to license specific trades or skills both resulted from urbanization and mass society. Many of these collections belong to institutions that lack the resources to undertake extensive searches; indexes and finding aids may prove spotty; and privacy restrictions sometimes limit access. Still, these records are definitely worth searching.

National professional associations, with membership lists often dating back to the 1800s, produce such records. The American Medical Association, for example, keeps files on its members, and a doctor residing in New York after around 1880 had to register his license with the county clerk and submit an affidavit of his admission to practice. Private associations printed directories, almanacs, and collective biographies with information on their members. This filled a dual need, providing exposure for the budding professional and assuring clients of a given skill in a mobile society. Whatever the purpose, the result for the genealogist is additional information about the newly emergent managerial and professional classes.

Increased interest in business regulation during the same time period stemmed from the same concerns and generated another body of records. The demand for honest retailing inspired Boston to inspect the weights and measures of merchants in that city as early as 1881. Inspection reports, an early type of consumer protection, gave the owner's name and address and described any action taken as a result of the visit. Similar departments eventually appeared throughout the country. A parallel to this idea in the private sector was the credit report, developed in 1842 by Dunn and Bradstreet. National in scope and detailed in coverage, the reports in the company archives, now at Harvard University Library, can increase understanding of nineteenth-century business practices as well as knowledge of some particular firms. For example, credit investigators recorded many personal aspects in their reports. One noted that his subject had married well; her name and a comment on her father buttressed the opinion that she was a good risk. While researchers should know of the existence of the Dunn and Bradstreet collection, library restrictions make it extremely difficult to gain access to the records.

If you can identify an ancestor with a specific company or business, you may be able to search the records of that business, assuming that it is still extant or that the records have been deposited in a historical society or corporate archive. Business libraries and archives must usually be examined in person because they simply do not have the personnel to respond to mail requests. One source of contact information for business records is the Society of American Archivists' *Directory of Corporate Archives in the United States and Canada*. Originally compiled in 1997 as a paper publication, the current edition of the directory has been edited and maintained online since 1999 by Gregory S. Hunter at <www.hunterinformation.com/corporat.htm>.

Most major metropolitan areas began as transportation centers, and many records of transportation companies have survived. Maritime records in the National Maritime Museum of San Francisco, the Great Lakes Maritime Institute in Detroit, and the Great Lakes Historical Society in Vermillion, Ohio, near Cleveland, may contain documentation in the form of crew lists or logbooks. The National Archives in Washington, D.C. <www.archives.gov/research_room/>, contains applications for seamen's protection certificates and files on merchant seamen; the National Archives' regional archives are currently acquiring inspection and licensing documents from maritime and riparian ports. Boston, Cleveland, Detroit, and Chicago records have already been transferred; others will follow as they are found.

Rail transportation workers may be traced through corporate archives, union records, or government agencies. The Newberry Library in Chicago has manuscripts from the Chicago, Burlington, and Quincy Railroad and some from the Pullman Standard Car Company <www.newberry.org/nl/collections/Railroad.html>. The South Suburban Genealogical and Historical Society (P.O. Box 96, South Holland, IL 60473) has indexed more than 1 million Pullman Company records that are on file at the society <www.rootsweb.com/~ssghs/pullman.htm>. The Chicago Historical Society <www.chicagohs.org/> has acquired some files of the Brotherhood of Sleeping Car Porters. The Railroad Retirement Board, also located in Chicago, is the national pensioning agency for rail workers; its records should be interesting to anyone with an ancestor eligible for a railroad pension. The Railroad Retirement Board <www.rrb.gov/geneal.html>, however, did not begin operations until the mid-1930s. Records are limited to individuals associated with the rail industry at or since that time or who were receiving private rail pensions, which were assumed by the board in 1937.

Many municipalities have records of city employees dating back to founding days. Police and firefighter pension records often comprise the greater part of municipal collections. Municipal archives and reference libraries are good sources for these records. Sometimes the municipal departments still hold the documents.

The union movement had many of its roots in the major industrial centers of the country, and some records have survived. Wayne State University in Detroit is the site of the Archives of Labor and Urban Affairs <www.reuther.wayne.edu/collections/alua.html>, which has collected manuscripts from unions all over the country. Its major holdings have come from the United Auto Workers, as might be expected, but some records have come from the American Federation of Teachers, the Newspaper Guild, and the Industrial Workers of the World. The Ohio Historical Society <www.ohiohistory.org> has gathered labor union documents as well, placing many of them in regional repositories, such as the Western Reserve Historical Society <www.whrs.org> in Cleveland.

Neighborhood Sources

Anyone who reads a city history will immediately realize that only a small fraction of the population gains municipal recognition. A citizen prominent enough to be found in a major printed historical source will easily be found in other likely sources—land, census, church, probate records. For most urban ancestors, however, an often-productive search area is the neighborhood. Usually, the neighborhood will have its own library, where a researcher can expect to find more information on that immediate area, including local histories (sometimes still in manuscript form) and even neighborhood newspapers. Community newspapers allowed a great deal of space for local events and personalities ignored by big-city newspapers. A local library may also be the place to begin a search for school records, which are sometimes dispersed rather than in compact collections. The school records themselves are usually kept at the municipal level, but the library can provide area school addresses and district jurisdictions.

City neighborhoods and districts may have their own historical societies and museums, which are often affiliated with the public library. Even if they are not, the local librarian may know about them or they may be listed on the library's website. Neighborhood historical societies, usually run by volunteers, are open at irregular hours and are rarely listed in telephone directories; but when they exist they can be gold mines of information about local residents and may have community photographs, scrapbooks, and personal mementos.

In 1976 the U.S. bicentennial prompted many communities and neighborhoods to investigate their heritage. Old-timers were interviewed, relics came out of attics, and basements gave up documents. Indexes of newspaper obituaries and cemeteries were compiled. Published local studies went to neighborhood libraries and often to university and community college libraries.

Check the main branch and the website of the city public library, the municipal library, and the city or county historical library for neighborhood sources as well. If the ethnic makeup of a neighborhood has changed or if the old neighborhood no longer exists, then the central repository for the city is the logical place to search for needed information. When searching major libraries for neighborhood information, you should check not only listings of the neighborhood itself but also its surrounding neighbors, especially if they shared a district or area name. The dominant nationality of a neighborhood may also be the key to locating information. Some examples include Germans in Old Town Area, South Side Irish, and Poles of the Milwaukee Avenue District. Still other neighborhoods were settled by mixed ethnic groups that shared a common occupation in a particular part of the city. The garment district, the stockyard area, the steel mill area—all might be classifications in a library card catalog. Modern urban studies frequently focus on specific bibliographies of master's theses, dissertations, or books that can help further searches.

Photograph archives and graphics departments maintained by some libraries may provide photographs of cities, neighborhoods, streets, business establishments, and ancestral homes. The Graphics Department of the Chicago Historical Society <www.chicagohs.org/> catalogs its photographs by street address as well as subject (landmark, neighborhood, event). To draw from this collection, you need to know the changes in the names of streets and in the city's numbering system, but such efforts usually add a valuable graphics dimension to the family history. Ask reference personnel for street directories and other such finding aids.

Ethnic Sources

Nowhere is the recent dramatic increase in interest in genealogy more evident than in ethnic research, along with a parallel increase in research guides and tools. A good starting point is chapter 4, "Ethnic Sources," by Loretto Dennis Szucs in *Printed Sources: A Guide to Published Genealogical Records*. Genealogical societies nationwide are bringing sophistication to the collection, preservation, and use of ethnic materials. The microfilming projects of the Genealogical Society of Utah and the Family History Library have brought the records of the world to our doorsteps. Lubomyr Wynar's *Encyclopedic Directory of Ethnic Organizations in the United States*, the first comprehensive guide to major organizations created by various communities, demonstrates the pluralism of the American city.[53] Ethnic presses and organizations are primary indicators of a particular ethnic group's social structure, but interdisciplinary efforts by colleges and universities are also important. For more recent information on ethnic organizations in specific areas, search Google for "ethnic organizations" plus the name of a city or state.

Settlements

The settlement house was an institution that served a grass-roots clientele in urban areas. Numerous settlements sprang up in working-class neighborhoods, where they sought to reach a maximum number of residents with programs ranging from citizenship classes to ethnic musical societies. Like the unions, papers of settlement houses contain membership lists and minutes of meetings. They also have a wealth of information about happenings in the neighborhood in which they were situated: the daily pulse of life on the surrounding streets, ethnic conflicts, the drive to attain success. Settlements reached only a small proportion of those who resided in the overcrowded tenements beyond their doors, but the larger ones often had two thousand members on their rolls at any given time. For information on resources related to settlement houses, see Ken Middleton, "Settlement Houses," *American Women's History: A Research Guide*, 2003, <www.mtsu.edu/~kmiddlet/history/women/wh-settle.html>.

Municipal Records

By definition, a municipality is a town or city of any size having the powers of local self-government. Cities have, in most cases, been responsible for preserving and storing their respective histories. The great volumes of material amassed by most municipal governments demand that records be stored off-site. Often, state archives step in to save these amazingly detailed records. The Minnesota State Archives <www.mnhs.org/preserve/records/>, for example, has records for more than one hundred of the state's municipalities.

The records include such administrative information as city council minutes, annual reports, correspondence and subject files; financial records, including payroll registers and registers of receipts and disbursements; municipal court and justice of the peace dockets; cemetery records, including burial registers and lot owner records; police jail registers and registers of tramps lodged in jail; death records; scrapbooks and newsletters; and poll lists and election registers containing the names of persons who voted in elections. Notable among the latter are Minneapolis registers of electors for 1902–23, which contain significant genealogical information. Some municipal records include information about the registration or licensing of saloon keepers, peddlers, and others. Names of city council members appear in the minutes, and names of city officials and staff can be found in payroll registers and annual reports.[54]

Archives

The National Archives

Unique city sources are often found in the regional system of the National Archives. Loretto Dennis Szucs and Sandra Hargreaves Luebking, in *The Archives: A Guide to the National Archives Field Branches*, point out several of these obscure urban collections.[55] Millions of files from cases heard in the U.S. courts in cities all across the nation have been preserved. Landmarks in history and events that shaped the lives of otherwise unknown citizens have been preserved. The National Archives—New England Region in suburban Boston, for example, has court records for the area that relate to such diverse matters as admiralty disputes, infringement of patent and copyrights, mutiny and murder, illegal manufacturing or sale of alcoholic beverages, and many others. The region also has the original copies of naturalization records of the federal courts for the six New England states dating back to 1790. Federal court records at the National Archives—Central Plains Region in Kansas City provide firsthand accounts of life in urban centers in the "Wild West." Few people would think to look for a Philadelphia source titled "Registers of Aliens, 1798–1812." Available only at the National Archives—Mid-Atlantic Region in Philadelphia, it is a list of individuals who came before the U.S. District Court for the Eastern District of Pennsylvania during the Quasi-War with France. Significant information regarding individuals involved in the San Francisco Earthquake of 1906 can be extracted from materials in a number of record groups at the National Archives—Pacific Sierra Region in San Bruno, California. Some of the least known yet genealogically rich city records are described in *The Archives*. For more information about National Archives holdings, check the online "Research Room" <www.archives.gov/research_room/>.

State Archives

State archives, by their nature, collect, preserve, and make available some of the very best city sources. Almost every state has as its mission to protect those public records of historical value that are created by state agencies and local units of government. These sources are principally in manuscript (unpublished) form. Also available in most state archives are microfilm copies of some federal records as they relate to the state served, such as federal population schedules.

Most state archives will provide a descriptive brochure upon request. The State Archives of Michigan, for example, in its brochure lists a wealth of genealogical materials that are essential to city research in that state. In addition to the federal population census schedules, the Archives of Michigan is typical of other states in having a collection of federal agricultural, manufacturing, mortality, and social statistical censuses. As is the case with most other state archives, Michigan's holds the state-created censuses as well. Tax assessment rolls, Michigan military rosters, Civil War grave registrations, and photograph files are among other rich sources listed. As a courtesy to its patrons, the Michigan Archives brochure also suggests genealogical sources in Michigan state facilities.

Frequently, the quickest and easiest access to records is through state archives. The New Jersey State Archives <www.state.nj.us/state/darm/links/archives.html> has a continuing run of statewide registrations of births, marriages, and deaths beginning in 1848, with indexes through 1923 for births and through 1940 for marriages and deaths. The New Jersey State Archives and 262 other repositories in the state are described in New Jersey Historical Commission's *New Jersey Historical Manuscripts: A Guide to Collections in the State.*[56] To find websites for state archives, consult Joe Ryan, comp., "U.S. State Historical Societies & State Archives Directory," <http://web.syr.edu/~jryan/infopro/hs.html>. The Alabama Department of Archives and History <www.archives.state.al.us/dataindex.html> offers regularly updated pages to assist family historians as well as links to its Civil War service, newspaper, map, and photo databases.

County Archives

A large number of county archives scattered around the United States focus on original records generated by county and city agencies. In the Cuyahoga County (Ohio) Archives <www.cuyahoga.oh.us/cs/archives.htm>, for example, are Cleveland records of birth, marriage, death, naturalization, and divorce; and coroners' case files, voter lists, township and ward maps, atlases for the city of Cleveland, probate estate files, registrations and charters of religious and other societies, journals of Cuyahoga County justices of the peace, county surveyors' records, Cleveland city directories, and more.

Municipal Archives

Municipal archives do not exist in every American city, but those that do exist often preserve unique information that can add interesting details to any family history. Philadelphia has the oldest city archive in the United States, its archive being established in 1952. For the researcher with research interests in the city, an essential guide is John Daly's *Descriptive Inventory of the Archives of the City and County of Philadelphia*. There is a more limited online guide to genealogical resources at <www.phila.gov/phils/Docs/Inventor/genealgy.htm>.[57]

The Municipal Archives for the City of New York (New York City Department of Records and Information Services, <http://home.nyc.gov/html/records/home.html>) was established to maintain, catalog, and make available historic New York City government records. Of particular genealogical usefulness is the large collection of vital records for the city (boroughs). While the New York state census records are as yet not available for all years on microfilm or in all offices, the Municipal Archives does have them for Brooklyn (Kings County) for 1855, 1865, 1875, 1905, and 1915. A special New York City Police Census taken in Manhattan and the western Bronx in 1890; almshouse records covering the years 1758 to 1953; some court records from 1808 to 1935; coroner's records for several of the boroughs spanning the years 1823 to 1918; photographs (including 720,000 photographs taken about 1940 of every house and building in all five boroughs); some fifty thousand volumes of voter registrations; real estate valuation records; and more make the New York City Municipal Archives a very important research stop for anyone with roots in the northeastern metropolis.

Special Archives

There are also significant institutional archives that preserve and make available original records that have survived in no other form. For example, historical documents acquired by the University of Massachusetts, Boston, reveal stories of poverty from an era before the existence of public welfare programs and detail much about the life of the poor in nineteenth-century America. The archive's collection consists of photographs, yearbooks, and personal dossiers on students and administrators of an institution known as the Boston Asylum and Farm School for Boys that was located on Thompson's Island in Boston Harbor. The Archives Department at the University of Massachusetts, Boston <www.lib.umb.edu/archives/>, is the only repository in the area that concentrates on preserving the records of private social welfare agencies. Many of these agencies were started in the nineteenth century in response to social upheavals that proved damaging to American family life. The department also has collections relating to twentieth-century community organizing, social movements, and the history of Dorchester, Massachusetts. Like many other institutional archives, the Archives Department is open to the public (by appointment only).

State Historical Societies and Libraries

State historical societies and libraries should not be overlooked because of the rich collections they catalog for cities and for statewide compilations that include cities within the state. The California State Library, for example, holds approximately 640,000 index cards covering 1.2 million items from such sources as newspapers, manuscripts, periodicals, and county histories in the California Information File. Among the treasures at the Connecticut State Library are most of the state's probate estate papers from before 1850 (fewer from 1850 to 1900) and state census records, including a 1917 Connecticut military census that included males ages ten to thirty along with automobile owners, aliens, and nurses. Also at the Connecticut State Library <www.cslib.org/handg.htm> is a master index of individual names compiled from tombstones in more than two thousand cemeteries in Connecticut that was compiled by the WPA. Obviously, there is urban material to be gleaned from all of these collections and others across the country. To find state historical societies, consult Joe Ryan, comp., "U.S. State Historical Societies & State Archives Directory," <http://web.syr.edu/~jryan/infopro/hs.html>, and for state libraries, "Libraries on the Web; USA States," <http://sunsite.berkeley.edu/Libweb/usa-state.html>.

Statewide Projects

Statewide projects are ongoing in almost every state. They comprise yet another important source to be considered in tracking urban dwellers' records. Unfortunately, some of the projects have elected to leave large metropolitan areas out of their compilations or have left them until last, due to the enormous amount of time and effort required to enter the millions of names into the computer databases. Such projects may often be found by contacting the state or local genealogical society or by using Google or a similar service to search for the name of the state or city plus combinations of keywords such as "genealogy" or "genealogical," "project" or "projects," and "register" or "registry."

Hundreds of thousands of marriages have been entered to date in a pre-1900 Illinois Statewide Marriage Index, a continuing joint project of the Illinois State Archives and the Illinois State Genealogical Society that is now online at <www.sos.state.il.us/departments/archives/marriage.html>. Similar projects are underway in other states. In an effort to replace the missing 1890 federal census, California State Genealogical Alliance volunteers transcribed and computerized names from the voting lists for California for 1890, now available in book form and on CD-ROM as the *California 1890 Great Register of Voters*.[58]

Urban research is often intimidating, but, given the vast array of records described in this and other sections of this volume, it is often the most exciting and fruitful dimension of family history research. It pays to stay informed through membership in genealogical organizations. The potential for successful research and great satisfaction in the results is growing daily.

Notes

[1] Raymond A. Mohl, ed., *The Making of Urban America*, 2nd ed. (Wilmington, Del.: Scholarly Resources, 1997), 3–20.

[2] U.S. Department of Commerce press release, 1993; U.S. Bureau of the Census, *Statistical Abstract of the United States: Colonial Times to 1970* (Washington, D.C.: U.S. Government Printing Office, 1975), 11–12.

[3] Charles N. Glaab and A. Theodore Brown, *A History of Urban America* (New York: Macmillan, 1967).

[4] Eibhlin MacIntosh and Richard C. Wade, "The Irish in Boston," *Irish at Home and Abroad* 1, no. 3 (Winter 1993–94).

[5] Kory L. Meyerink, ed., *Printed Sources: A Guide to Published Genealogical Records* (Salt Lake City: Ancestry, 1998).

[6] Estelle Guzik, ed., *Genealogical Resources in New York: The most comprehensive guide to genealogical and biographical resources in New York City and Albany* (New York: Jewish Genealogical Society, 2003).

[7] Rosalie F. Bailey, *Guide to Genealogical and Biographical Sources for New York City, 1783–1898* (New York: the author, 1954; reprint, Baltimore: Genealogical Publishing Co., 2000).

[8] Loretto Dennis Szucs, *Chicago and Cook County: A Guide to Research* (Salt Lake City: Ancestry, 1996).

[9] Robert W. Barnes, *Guide to Research in Baltimore City and County*, 2nd ed. (Westminster: Family Line Publications, 1993).

[10] Connie Stunkel Terheiden and Kenny R. Burck, comps., *Guide to Genealogical Resources in Cincinnati & Hamilton County, Ohio* (Hamilton County: Ohio Genealogical Society, 2001).

[11] Carol W. Bell, *Ohio Guide to Genealogical Sources* (Baltimore: Genealogical Publishing Co., 1988).

[12] Roseann Hogan, *Kentucky Ancestry: A Guide to Genealogical and Historical Research* (Salt Lake City: Ancestry, 1993).

[13] Robert Scott Davis Jr., *Research in Georgia* (Easley, S.C.: Southern Historical Press, 1981).

[14] Helen Leary, ed., *North Carolina Research: Genealogy and Local History* (Raleigh: North Carolina Genealogical Society, 1996).

[15] Arthur Kurzweil and Miriam Weiner, *The Encyclopedia of Jewish Genealogy* (Northvale, N.J.: Jason Aronson, 1997).

[16] Alice Eichholz, ed., *Red Book: American State, County, and Town Sources*, 3rd ed. (Provo, Utah: Ancestry, 2004).

[17] Steven Thernstrom, *Poverty and Progress* (Boston: Harvard University Press, 1990).

[18] *Chicago 1844 Directory* (Chicago: Norris Publishers).

[19] Richard Edwards, *Edwards' 1871 Chicago Census Directory* (Chicago: Richard Edwards, 1871).

[20] John Gager, *Gager's 1857 Chicago Directory* (Chicago: John Gager, 1857).

[21] *The Street Directory of the Principal Cities of the United States* (Detroit: Gale Research Co., 1973).

[22] Juliana Szucs Smith, *The Ancestry Family Historian's Address Book*, 2nd ed. (Orem, Utah: Ancestry, 2003).

[23] Rita Seiden Miller, ed., *Brooklyn, U.S.A.: The Fourth Largest City in America* (New York: Brooklyn College Press, 1979).

[24] Harold Mayer and Richard Wade, *Chicago: Growth of a Metropolis* (Chicago: University of Chicago Press, 1969).

[25] William J. Murin, *Urban History: A Guide to Information Sources* (Detroit: Gale Research Co., 1981).

[26] Henry R. Stiles, *Kings County History 1683 to 1884: The Civil, Political, Professional and Ecclesiastical History and Commercial and Industrial Record of the County of Kings and the City of Brooklyn, N.Y. From 1683 to 1884* (New York: W. W. Munsell and Co., 1884).

[27] P. William Filby, comp., *A Bibliography of American County Histories* (Baltimore: Genealogical Publishing Co., 1985).

[28] Moses N. Amis, *Historical Raleigh With Sketches of Wake County and Its Important Towns* (Raleigh: Edwards and Broughton, 1902).

[29] Keith Schlesinger and Peggy Tuck Sinko, "Urban Finding Aid for Manuscript Census Searches," *National Genealogical Society Quarterly* 69 (September 1981): 171–80.

[30] U.S. Bureau of the Census, *A Century of Population Growth 1790–1900* (Washington, D.C.: Government Printing Office, 1909).

[31] *1910 Index to City Streets and Enumeration Districts*, NARA microfiche publication M1283.

[32] *Descriptions of Enumeration Districts, 1830–1950*, NARA microfilm T1224.

[33] *Enumeration District Maps for the Fifteenth Census of the United States, 1930*, NARA microfilm M1930.

[34] *Index to Selected City Streets and Enumeration Districts, 1930 Census*, NARA microfilm M1931.

[35] Betty M. Jarboe, *Obituaries: A Guide to Sources*, 2nd ed. (Boston: G. K. Hall, 1989).

[36] *Monroe County, N.Y. Cemetery Record Index* (Rochester, N.Y.: Rochester Genealogical Society, 1984).

[37] Laura Szucs Pfeiffer, *Hidden Sources: Family History in Unlikely Places* (Orem, Utah: Ancestry, 2000), 54–56.

[38] Carolee Inskeep, *The Graveyard Shift: A Family Historian's Guide to New York City Cemeteries* (Orem, Utah: Ancestry, 2000).

[39] See also, James L. Hansen, *Wisconsin Newspapers, 1833–1850: An Analytical Bibliography* (Madison: State Historical Society of Wisconsin, 1979).

[40] *A Guide to Church Vital Statistics Records in California—San Francisco and Alameda Counties* (San Francisco: Northern California Historical Records Survey, 1940).

[41] Sargent B. Child and Dorothy P. Holmes, *Bibliography of Research Project Reports*, WPA Technical Series No. 7 (1943; reprint, Bountiful, Utah: Printing by Faisal, 1979 [as WPA Bibliography 9]).

[42] Loretta L. Hefner, *The WPA Historical Records Survey: A Guide to the Unpublished Inventories, Indexes, and Transcripts* (Chicago: Society of American Archivists, 1980).

[43] Jack Bochar, *Locations of Chicago Roman Catholic Churches, 1850–1990*, 2nd ed. (Sugar Grove, Ill.: Czech and Slovak American Genealogy Society of Illinois, 1998).

[44] George Lane and Alginantes Kezys, comps., *Chicago Churches and Synagogues* (Chicago: Loyola University Press, 1981).

[45] Michael H. Shelley, *Ward Maps of United States Cities: A Selective Checklist of Pre-1900 Maps in the Library of Congress* (Washington, D.C.: Library of Congress, 1975).

[46] Library of Congress, *Panoramic Maps of Cities in the United States and Canada: A Checklist of Maps in the Collections of the Library of Congress, Geography and Map Division*, 2nd ed. (Washington, D.C.: Library of Congress, 1984).

[47] John Daly and Allen Weinberg, *Genealogy of Philadelphia County Subdivisions*, 2nd ed. (Philadelphia: Department of Records, 1966).

[48] Eichholz, *Red Book*, 349–68.

[49] Richard C. Wade, "American Cities Are (Mostly) Better Than Ever," *American Heritage* 30, no. 2 (February–March 1979). The first page of this article is available online <www.americanheritage.com/articles/magazine/ah/1979/2/>.

[50] Loretto Dennis Szucs, *They Became Americans: Finding Naturalization Records and Ethnic Origins* (Salt Lake City: Ancestry, 1998).

[51] Loretto Dennis Szucs, "To Whom I Am Indebted: Bankruptcy Records," *Ancestry* Magazine 12, no. 5 (September–October 1994): 26–27.

[52] *Records of the Commissioners of Claims (Southern Claims Commission), 1871–1880*, NARA micropublication M87; Gary B. Mills, *Civil War Claims in the South: An Index to Claimants Before the Southern Claims Commission, 1871–1880* (Laguna Hills, Calif.: Aegean Park Press, 1980).

[53] Lubomyr Wynar, *Encyclopedic Directory of Ethnic Organizations in the United States* (Littleton, Colo.: Libraries Unlimited, 1976).

[54] Minnesota Historical Society Library and Archives Division, *Genealogical Resources of the Minnesota Historical Society: A Guide*, 2nd ed. (St. Paul: Minnesota Historical Society Press, 1993).

[55] Loretto Dennis Szucs and Sandra Hargreaves Luebking, *The Archives: A Guide to the National Archives Field Branches* (Salt Lake City: Ancestry, 1988).

[56] New Jersey Historical Commission, *New Jersey Historical Manuscripts: A Guide to Collections in the State* (Trenton: New Jersey Historical Commission, 1987).

[57] John Daly, *Descriptive Inventory of the Archives of the City and County of Philadelphia* (Philadelphia: Department of Records, 1970; supplement, 1980).

[58] *California 1890 Great Register of Voters*, CD-ROM (North Salt Lake, Utah: Heritage Quest, 2001).

References

American Library Directory: A Classified List of Libraries in the United States and Canada, With Personnel and Statistical Data. New York: R. R. Bowker, annual.

Amis, Moses N. *Historical Raleigh With Sketches of Wake County and Its Important Towns*. Raleigh: Edwards and Broughton, 1902.

Bailey, Rosalie Fellows. *Guide to Genealogical and Biographical Sources for New York City, 1783–1898*. New York: the author, 1954. Reprint, Baltimore: Genealogical Publishing Co., 2000.

Barnes, Robert W. *Guide to Research in Baltimore City and County*. 2nd ed. Westminster, Md.: Family Line Publications, 1993.

Bell, Carol Willsey. *Ohio Guide to Genealogical Sources.* Baltimore: Genealogical Publishing Co., 1988. Reissued, 1993.

Bochar, Jack. *Locations of Chicago Roman Catholic Churches 1850–1990.* 2nd ed. Sugar Grove, Ill.: Czech and Slovak American Genealogy Society of Illinois, 1998.

Buenker, John D., Gerald Michael Greenfield, and William J. Murin. *Urban History: A Guide to Information Sources.* Detroit: Gale Research Co., 1981.

California 1890 Great Register of Voters. Compiled by California State Genealogical Alliance Volunteers. North Salt Lake, Utah: Heritage Quest, 2001.

Chicago 1844 Directory. Chicago: Norris Publishers.

Child, Sargent B., and Dorothy P. Holmes. *Bibliography of Research Project Reports.* WPA Technical Series No. 7. 1943. Reprint, Bountiful, Utah: Printing by Faisal, 1979 (as WPA Bibliography 9).

Daly, John. *Descriptive Inventory of the Archives of the City and County of Philadelphia.* Philadelphia: Department of Records, 1970. Supplement, 1980.

———, and Allen Weinberg. *Genealogy of Philadelphia County Subdivisions.* 2nd ed. Philadelphia: Department of Records, 1966.

Davis, Robert Scott, Jr. *Research in Georgia.* Easley, S.C.: Southern Historical Press, 1981.

Edwards, Richard. *Edwards' Chicago Census Directory.* Chicago: Richard Edwards, 1871.

Eichholz, Alice, ed. *Red Book: American State, County, and Town Sources.* 3rd ed. Provo, Utah: Ancestry, 2004.

Filby, P. William, comp. *A Bibliography of American County Histories*. Baltimore: Genealogical Publishing Co., 1985. Reprint, 1987.

Gager, John. *Gager's 1857 Chicago Directory*. Chicago: John Gager, 1857.

Geography and Map Section of the Library of Congress. "Fire Insurance Maps in the Library of Congress." Washington, D.C., 1981.

Glaab, Charles N., and A. Theodore Brown. *A History of Urban America*. New York: Macmillan, 1967.

A Guide to Church Vital Statistics Records in California—San Francisco and Alameda Counties. San Francisco: Northern California Historical Records Survey, 1940.

Guzik, Estelle M., ed. *Genealogical Resources in New York: The most comprehensive guide to genealogical and biographical resources in New York City and Albany*. New York: Jewish Genealogical Society, 2003.

Hansen, James L. *Wisconsin Newspapers 1833–1850: An Analytical Bibliography*. Madison: State Historical Society of Wisconsin, 1979.

Hefner, Loretta L. *The W.P.A. Historical Records Survey: A Guide to Unpublished Inventories, Indexes and Transcripts*. Chicago: Society of American Archivists, 1980.

Hogan, Roseann Reinmuth. *Kentucky Ancestry: A Guide to Genealogical and Historical Research*. Salt Lake City: Ancestry, 1993.

Humling, Virginia, ed. *U.S. Catholic Resources: A Diocesan Research Guide*. Salt Lake City: Ancestry, 1998.

Jarboe, Betty M. *Obituaries: A Guide to Sources*. 2nd. ed. Boston: G. K. Hall, 1989.

Kirkham, E. K. *A Handy Guide to Record Searching in the Larger Cities of the United States*. Logan, Utah: Everton Publishers, 1974.

Kurzweil, Arthur, and Miriam Weiner, eds. *The Encyclopedia of Jewish Genealogy*. Northvale, N.J.: Jason Aronson, 1997.

Lane, George, and Alginantes Kezys, comps. *Chicago Churches and Synagogues*. Chicago: Loyola University Press, 1981.

Leary, Helen F. M., ed. *North Carolina Research: Genealogy and Local History*. 2nd ed. Raleigh: North Carolina Genealogical Society, 1996.

Library of Congress. *Panoramic Maps of Cities in the United States and Canada: A Checklist of Maps in the Collections of the Library of Congress, Geography and Map Division*. 2nd ed. Washington, D.C.: Library of Congress, 1984.

MacIntosh, Eibhlin, and Kyle J. Betit. "The Irish in Boston." *Irish at Home and Abroad* 1 (Winter 1993–94).

Mayer, Harold M., and Richard C. Wade. *Chicago: Growth of a Metropolis*. Chicago: University of Chicago Press, 1969.

Meyerink, Kory L., ed. *Printed Sources: A Guide to Published Genealogical Records*. Salt Lake City: Ancestry, 1998.

Meyers, Mary K., ed. *Meyer's Directory of Genealogical Societies in the U.S.A. and Canada*. Mt. Airy, Md.: the editor, updated and reissued in even-numbered years.

Miller, Rita Seiden, ed. *Brooklyn, U.S.A.: The Fourth Largest City in America*. New York: Brooklyn College Press, 1979.

Mills, Gary B. *Civil War Claims in the South: An Index to Claimants Before the Southern Claims Commission, 1871–1880*. Baltimore: Genealogical Publishing Co., 1994.

Minnesota Historical Society Library and Archives Division. *Genealogical Resources of the Minnesota Historical Society: A Guide*. 2nd ed. St. Paul: Minnesota Historical Society Press, 1993.

Mohl, Raymond A., ed. *The Making of Urban America*. 2nd ed. Wilmington, Del.: Scholarly Resources, 1997.

Monroe County, N.Y. Cemetery Record Index. Rochester, N.Y.: Rochester Genealogical Society, 1984.

Murin, William J. *Urban History: A Guide to Information Sources*. Detroit: Gale Research Co., 1981.

Neagles, James C. *The Library of Congress: A Guide to Genealogical and Historical Research*. Salt Lake City: Ancestry, 1990.

New Jersey Historical Commission. *New Jersey Historical Manuscripts: A Guide to Collections in the State*. Trenton: New Jersey Historical Commission, 1987.

The Official Catholic Directory. Wilmette, Ill.: P. J. Kenedy and Sons, annual.

Oldenburg, Joseph F. *A Genealogical Guide to the Burton Historical Collection: Detroit Public Library*. Salt Lake City: Ancestry, 1988.

Pfeiffer, Laura Szucs. *Hidden Sources: Family History in Unlikely Places*. Orem, Utah: Ancestry, 2000.

Schlesinger, Keith, and Peggy Tuck Sinko. "Urban Finding Aid for Manuscript Census Searches." *National Genealogical Society Quarterly* 69 (September 1981): 171–80.

Shelley, Michael H. *Ward Maps of United States Cities: A Selective Checklist of Pre-1900 Maps in the Library of Congress*. Washington, D.C.: Library of Congress, 1975.

Sinko, Peggy Tuck. *Guide to Local and Family History at The Newberry Library*. Salt Lake City: Ancestry, 1987.

Smith, Juliana Szucs. *The Ancestry Family Historian's Address Book: A Comprehensive List of Local, State, and Federal*

Agencies and Institutions, and Ethnic and Genealogical Societies. 2nd ed. Orem, Utah: Ancestry, 2003.

Stiles, Henry R. *Kings County History 1683 to 1884: The Civil, Political, Professional and Ecclesiastical History and Commercial and Industrial Record of the County of Kings and the City of Brooklyn, N.Y. From 1683 to 1884.* New York: W. W. Munsell, 1884.

The Street Directory of the Principal Cities of the United States. Detroit: Gale Research Co., 1973.

Suelflow, August R. *A Preliminary Guide to Church Records and Repositories.* Chicago: Society of American Archivists, 1969.

Szucs, Loretto Dennis, and Matthew Wright. *Finding Answers in U.S. Census Records.* Orem, Utah: Ancestry, 2001.

———, and Sandra Hargreaves Luebking. *The Archives: A Guide to the National Archives Field Branches.* Salt Lake City: Ancestry, 1988.

———. *Chicago and Cook County: A Guide to Research.* Salt Lake City: Ancestry, 1996.

———. *They Became Americans: Finding Naturalization Records and Ethnic Origins.* Salt Lake City: Ancestry, 1998.

———. "To Whom I Am Indebted: Bankruptcy Records." *Ancestry* Magazine 12, no. 5 (September–October 1994): 26–27.

Terheiden, Connie Stunkel, and Kenny R. Burck, comps. *Guide to Genealogical Resources in Cincinnati & Hamilton County, Ohio.* Cincinnati: Hamilton County Chapter of the Ohio Genealogical Society, 2001.

Thernstrom, Stephen. *Poverty and Progress.* Boston: Harvard University Press, 1964.

United States Bureau of the Census. *A Century of Population Growth.* Washington, D.C.: Government Printing Office, 1909.

———. *Historical Statistics of the United States: Colonial Times to 1970.* Washington, D.C.: Government Printing Office, 1975.

———. *Statistical Abstract of the United States: 1993.* 13th ed. Washington, D.C., 1993.

Van Tassel, David D., and John J. Grabowski, eds. *The Dictionary of Cleveland Biography.* Bloomington: Indiana University Press, 1996. Online version at <http://ech.cwru.edu/>.

Van Tassel, David D., and John J. Grabowski, eds. *The Encyclopedia of Cleveland History.* 2nd ed. Bloomington: Indiana University Press, 1996. Online version at <http://ech.cwru.edu/>.

Wade, Richard. "American Cities Are (Mostly) Better Than Ever." *American Heritage* 30, no. 2 (February–March 1979).

Works Progress Administration. *A Guide to Church Vital Statistics Records in California.* San Francisco: Northern California Historical Records Survey, 1940.

Wynar, Lubomyr R. *Encyclopedic Directory of Ethnic Organizations in the United States.* Littleton, Colo.: Libraries Unlimited, 1976.

Internet Resources

Ancestry. "1994 Phone and Address Directory." <www.ancestry.com/search/rectype/inddbs/7143.htm>. Original data: 1994 White Pages. Little Rock, AR: Acxiom Corporation, 19—.

Ancestry. "Ancestry Message Boards." <http://boards.ancestry.com/>.

Association of Professional Genealogists. <www.apgen.org/>.

Berkshire Family History Association. <www.berkshire.net/~bfha/>.

Board for Certification of Genealogists. <www.bcgcertification.org>.

Case Western Reserve University. "The Encyclopedia of Cleveland History." <http://ech.cwru.edu>.

Chicago Historical Society. <www.chicagohs.org/>.

Cleveland Public Library. <www.cpl.org>.

Cleveland State University. "First Maps of Cleveland and the Western Reserve." 1999. <www.csuohio.edu/CUT/firsts.htm>.

Cleveland State University Library. "The Cleveland Digital Library." <http://web.ulib.csuohio.edu/SpecColl/cdl>.

Cleveland State University Library. "The Cleveland Memory Project." <www.clevelandmemory.org>.

Connecticut State Library. "History and Genealogy." <www.cslib.org/handg.htm>.

Cornell University. "19th-Century Ward Maps of U.S. Cities: A Guide to Online Library Holdings." <www.library.cornell.edu/okuref/maps/wardmaps.htm>.

Cuyahoga County (Ohio). "Welcome to the Cuyahoga County Archives." <www.cuyahoga.oh.us/cs/archives.htm>.

Douglas County Historical Society. <www.omahahistory.org>.

Dubuque County-Key City Genealogical Society. <www.rootsweb.com/~iadckchgs>.

FamilySearch.org. "International Genealogical Index." <www.familysearch.org/Eng/Search/frameset_search.asp?PAGE=igi/search_IGI.asp&clear_form=true>.

Funeral Net. <www.funeralnet.com/>.

"Genealogical Sources at the Philadelphia City Archives." 2000. <www.phila.gov/phils/Docs/Inventor/genealgy.htm>.

GenForum. <http://genealogy.genforum.com/>.

Google. <www.google.com/>.

Greater Cleveland Genealogical Society. <www.rootsweb.com/~ohgcgg>.

Hennepin County, Minnesota. "Property Information Search." Updated daily. <www2.co.hennepin.mn.us/pins/>.

"Illinois Statewide Marriage Index, 1763–1900." Comp. Illinois State Archives and Illinois State Genealogical Society. <www.sos.state.il.us/departments/archives/marriage.html>.

"LibDex: The Library Index." Maint. Peter Scott. <www.libdex.com>.

"Libraries on the Web; USA States." <http://sunsite.berkeley.edu/Libweb/usa-state.html>.

"Libweb: Library Servers via WWW." Maint. Thomas Dowling. Updated daily. <http://sunsite.berkeley.edu/Libweb/>.

Middleton, Ken. "Settlement Houses." *American Women's History: A Research Guide*. 2003. <www.mtsu.edu/~kmiddlet/history/women/wh-settle.html>.

Minnesota Historical Society. "Minnesota State Archives." <www.mnhs.org/preserve/records/>.

NETR Online: Real Estate Information & Public Records Research. <www.netronline.com/public_records.htm>.

New Orleans Public Library. "Alphabetical Index of Changes in Street Names, Old and New; Period 1852 to Current Date, Dec. 1st 1938." 2002. <http://nutrias.org/~nopl/facts/streetnames/namesa.htm>.

New Orleans Public Library. "New Orleans Street Name Changes." 2003. <http://nutrias.org/~nopl/facts/names.htm>.

New Jersey. "State Archives." <www.state.nj.us/state/darm/links/archives.html>.

New York. Department of Records and Information Services. <http://home.nyc.gov/html/records/home.html>.

New York. Department of Records and Information Services. "New York City Vital Records at the Municipal Archives." <http://home.nyc.gov/html/records/html/3vital.html>.

Newberry Library. "Collection Pathfinder Series." <www.newberry.org/nl/genealogy/L3gpublications.html>.

Newberry Library. "Railroad Archives." <www.newberry.org/nl/collections/Railroad.html>.

NewsLink. <http://newslink.org>.

Old Directory Search. "Chicago 1844 Directory." <http://olddirectorysearch.com/Chicago__Illinois_1844/index.html>.

Ohio Historical Society. <www.ohiohistory.org/>.

Oregon Historical Society. <www.ohs.org/>.

Philadelphia, Pennsylvania. "Genealogical Resources at the Philadelphia City Archives." <www.phila.gov/phils/Docs/Inventor/genealgy.htm>.

ProQuest Information and Learning. "About Digital Sanborn Maps." 2001. <http://sanborn.umi.com/HelpFiles/about.html>.

RootsWeb. "Mailing Lists." <http://lists.rootsweb.com>.

RootsWeb. "Rootsweb Message Boards." <http://boards.ancestry.co>.

Ryan, Joe, comp. "U.S. State Historical Societies & State Archives Directory." <http://web.syr.edu/~jryan/infopro/hs.html>.

Society of American Archivists. *Directory of Corporate Archives in the United States and Canada*. 5th ed. Ed. and maint. Gregory S. Hunter. 2003. <www.hunterinformation.com/corporat.htm>.

South Suburban Genealogical and Historical Society. <www.rootsweb.com/~ssghs/pullman.htm>.

St. Louis County Library. <www.slcl.lib.mo.us/>.

St. Louis Public Library. <www.slpl.lib.mo.us/>.

The USGenWeb Project. <www.usgenweb.org/>.

University of Massachusetts. Healy Library. "Archives & Special Collections." <www.lib.umb.edu/archives/>.

University of Utah. "Sanborn Fire Insurance Maps." <www.lib.utah.edu/digital/sanborn/>.

U.S. Library of Congress. American Memory. "Cities and Towns." <http://memory.loc.gov/ammem/gmdhtml/cityhome.html>.

U.S. Library of Congress. American Memory. "Panoramic Maps, 1847–1929." <http://memory.loc.gov/ammem/pmhtml/panhome.html>.

U.S. Library of Congress. Local History and Genealogy Reading Room. "Telephone and City Directories in the Library of Congress: Non-Current (Old)." Maint. Barbara B. Walsh. <www.loc.gov/rr/genealogy/bib_guid/telephonnoncurr.html>.

U.S. National Archives and Records Administration. <www.archives.gov>.

U.S. National Archives and Records Administration. "How to Research the 1930 Census Microfilm." <http://1930census.archives.gov/beginSearch.asp>.

U.S. National Archives and Records Administration. "Research Room." <www.archives.gov/research_room/>.

U.S. Railroad Retirement Board. "The U.S. Railroad Retirement Board and Genealogical Information After 1936." <www.rrb.gov/geneal.html>.

VitalSearch. <www.vitalsearch-worldwide.com/>.

Wayne State University. "The Archives of Labor and Urban Affairs." 2002. <www.reuther.wayne.edu/collections/alua.html>.

Western Reserve Historical Society. <www.wrhs.org/>.

Appendix A

Selected Abbreviations and Acronyms

AASLH	American Association for State and Local History
ABI	American Biographical Index
ACPL	Allen County Public Library of Fort Wayne, Indiana
AG	Accredited Genealogist
AGBI	American Genealogical and Biographical Index
ALA	American Library Association
AGS	American Genealogical Society
APG	Association of Professional Genealogists
APGQ	Association of Professional Genealogists Quarterly
ARS	Automated Records System (General Land Office)
ASG	American Society of Genealogists
BCG	Board for Certification of Genealogists
BGMI	Biography and Genealogy Master Index
BLM	Bureau of Land Management
BYU	Brigham Young University
CAILS	Certified American Indian Lineage Specialist (obsolete)
CALS	Certified American Lineage Specialist (obsolete)
CDA	Colonial Dames of America
CG	Certified Genealogist
CGC	Council of Genealogy Columnists (obsolete; now ISFHWE)
CGI	Certified Genealogical Instructor
CG-Intern	Certified Genealogist-Intern (obsolete)
CGL	Certified Genealogical Lecturer
CGRS	Certified Genealogical Record Searcher (obsolete)
CIG	Computer Interest Group
DAC	National Society, Daughters of the American Colonists
DAR	National Society, Daughters of the American Revolution
DCW	National Society, Daughters of Colonial Wars
DFPA	National Society, Daughters of Founders and Patriots of America
DLP	Hereditary Order of the Descendants of Loyalists and Patriots of the American Revolution
DUV	Daughters of Union Veterans of the Civil War
FASG	Fellow, American Society of Genealogists
FGS	Federation of Genealogical Societies, (publishes FORUM)
FHC	Family History Center (branch of the Family History Library)
FHL	Family History Library
FHLC	Family History Library Catalog
FNGS	Fellow, National Genealogical Society
FORUM	*Federation of Genealogical Societies Forum*
FUGA	Fellow, Utah Genealogical Association

GEDCOM	Genealogical Data Communications
GIMA	Genealogical Institute of Mid-America (University of Illinois at Springfield)
GJ	*Genealogical Journal* (of the Utah Genealogical Association)
GLO	General Land Office
GPAI	*Genealogical Periodical Annual Index*
GSG	Genealogical Speakers Guild
GSMD	General Society of Mayflower Descendants
GSU	Genealogical Society of Utah
IAJGS	International Association of Jewish Genealogical Societies
ICAPGen	International Commission for the Accreditation of Professional Genealogists
IGHR	Institute of Genealogical and Historical Research (Samford University, Birmingham, Alabama)
IGI	*International Genealogical Index*
IGS	Institute of Genealogical Studies (Dallas Genealogical Society, Dallas, Texas)
ISBGFH	International Society for British Genealogy and Family History
ISFHWE	International Society of Family History Writers and Editors
JGS	Jewish Genealogical Society
LDS	Latter-day Saints (members of The Church of Jesus Christ of Latter-day Saints)
NARA	National Archives and Records Administration
NEHGR	*New England Historical and Genealogical Register* (publication of NEHGS)
NEHGS	New England Historic Genealogical Society (Boston, Massachusetts)
NGS	National Genealogical Society
NGS/CIG	Nation Genealogical Society Computer Interest Group; publishes the NGS/CIG Digest
NGSQ	*National Genealogical Society Quarterly*
NHS	National Huguenot Society
NIDS	*National Inventory of Documentary Sources*
NIGR	National Institute on Genealogical Research (Washington, D.C.)
NSCD-17	National Society, Colonial Dames of the 17th Century
NSCD	National Society, Colonial Dames of America
NSDAR	See DAR
NUCMC	*National Union Catalog of Manuscript Collections*
NYG&B	New York Genealogical and Biographical Society
NYGBR	*New York Genealogical and Biographical Society Record*
NYPL	New York Public Library
OCLC	Online Computer Library Center
OFPA	Order of the Founders and Patriots of America
PAF	Personal Ancestral File
PERSI	*Periodical Source Index*
PLA	Public Library Association
RG	Record Group
RIN	Record Identification Number
RLIN	Research Libraries Information Network
SAR	National Society, Sons of the American Revolution
SASE	Self-addressed, stamped envelope
SC	The Society of the Cincinnati
SCV	Sons of Confederate Veterans
SCW	Society of Colonial Wars
SSDI	Social Security Death Index
SLIG	Salt Lake Institute of Genealogy
TAG	*The American Genealogist*
TG	*The Genealogist*
UDC	United Daughters of the Confederacy
UGA	Utah Genealogical Association
USD 1812	National Society, U. S. Daughters of the War of 1812

SOURCE

This list is excerpted from Kip Sperry's *Abbreviations and Acronyms*, rev. 2nd ed. (Provo, Utah: Ancestry, 2003). Refer to that book for a more complete list.

Appendix B

Family Associations

CHRISTINE ROSE, CG, CGL, FASG

Family associations are valuable resources for both the hobbyist enjoying the pursuit of his or her family heritage, and for the professional assisting in that search. These family groups commonly possess unique collections of data. Bibles, old letters, tombstone inscriptions and photographs are just a few of the treasures among their holdings. These original records, along with the publications produced by family associations, can provide a unique perspective and add immeasurably to the study of a family. Ultimately, these groups offer the potential of meeting other family members through mailings or reunions, or of joining a special project, such as a family DNA study.

A family group may be incorporated, elect officers, and produce a periodical of family news and research. Others may be solely a mailing list—a forum exchange of queries and replies. Still others may gather only for annual family reunions. Typically, family organizations fall into one of the following categories:

One-name Study (also known as surname organizations)

This type of organization traces one surname, either nationally or internationally. Its members research all those bearing the surname, regardless of nationality. Members are not all related; their common interest is the surname. Focusing on the males of the line bearing that surname, they study all Smiths, Wilsons, Gordons, Roses, etc. These organizations generally do not keep track of females after they marry and change their names.

Though some groups specifically identify themselves in their title as one-name studies, others of the ilk may be known only as "The Jeffries Family Association" or "The Lawson Society" or something similar. It's always best to contact the group to determine the breadth of its study.

Associations focusing on a surname often have large databases of data. They pool their efforts to compile lists of tombstone records, military files, census records, and other information. Commonly they have extensive photographic collections and Bible records. Special collections might include signatures, early correspondence of family members, and other fascinating and otherwise hard-to-find memorabilia. They are membership-based and normally provide a newsletter containing current activities and research material.

Emigrant Study Association

These groups are focused on a specific emigrant, or perhaps a group of emigrants such as several brothers. They search for descendants, regardless of gender, usually to the present day. They often embark upon a collective project to compile a genealogy of the emigrant, or update an existing book. They delve into the background of the emigrant to ascertain from where he hailed, and sometimes finance a trip to the homeland so one of the family historians can pursue an in-depth study. Their family reunions may traditionally take place in the emigrant's point of origin in the United States.

Regional or Ethnic Society

A society focused on a Scottish clan with a specific surname is one example of a regional or ethnic group. Others include groups tracing a surname in a region such as New England or the South, or a specific country such as Germany. Often the regional group's interests are not exclusively genealogical. Clan societies attend clan gatherings all over the country, seek out the music and dress of their progenitor's region, and even share recipes of their heritage.

Some groups in this category may focus on a region, not because of ethnicity but because the surname is so common and a narrowing of the search is essential.

Informal Reunion Group

Typically, these are small groups with no officers, and they are focused on a more recent nineteenth- or twentieth-century couple. Perhaps they are composed of descendants of the great-grandparents or grandparents of the group's founders who may have first banded together at an annual reunion. Though many still gather solely for that purpose, others have expanded their goals to include a genealogical effort and have incorporated an annual meeting at their gathering. Those of the group who are interested in genealogy may prepare a "paper" to present at the gathering. Attendees are urged to sign a register with their family information, and photographs and videos are taken and preserved. These groups are usually structured informally and dedicated to maintaining an ongoing connection with others of the family.

Locating a Family Association

There is no resource listing every family organization. There are perhaps one to two thousand organized family associations at any time, and more if you add the informal groups. Family societies are often short-lived and become extinct when the founders are gone and new volunteers don't surface. Others have flourished for several decades, have strong support, and enjoy a sound financial position with endowments and life-time members to keep them going.

To locate a group in existence, first consult Elizabeth Bentley's and Deborah Ann Carl's *Directory of Family Associations*. This newest edition offers about six thousand listings across the United States. Included are organized family associations and also many that band together informally or are mailing lists only. Some of the listings are individuals working alone but who are interested in a specific surname and are dedicated to accumulating that information and disseminating it to others. The directory, though certainly not complete, is of considerable assistance and can be located in many libraries, or purchased through book vendors. Earlier editions are particularly useful to locate groups no longer in existence.

Everton Publishers of Logan, Utah, for many years published annually two directories in *The Genealogical Helper*: "Family Associations and Their Leaders" and "Family Periodical Publications." They have now replaced these with one directory, "Family Association-Surnames Periodical Directory," which will appear in their March–April issue annually. Associations wishing to be included in this directory should add Everton Publishers (PO Box 368, Logan, UT 84323-0368) to their mailing list. There is no charge for inclusion. Perusing older issues of the publication in libraries can also be useful.

For periodicals of associations (not just those genealogical by nature) try the latest edition of Deborah Striplin's and Patricia Hagood's *The Standard Periodical Directory*. The 28th edition of this mammoth reference was published in 2005. Older editions may contain some family periodicals now extinct. Look also for the *Directory of Genealogical and Historical Societies, Libraries and Periodicals in the U.S. and Canada 2005*, edited by Dina C. Carson, which includes thousands of family history societies among its listings.

Another route to locate current societies is to check the national and regional journals and quarterlies. Such periodicals often have either a calendar of upcoming events (including reunions or yearly meetings of family groups) or columns for news of family associations. If an association has news—perhaps it will compile a genealogy of the family, hold a family gathering, or begin a project to clean the family cemetery—it often submits a written announcement to appropriate publications.

Older directories can help, too. J. Konrad's *Family Associations, Societies and Reunions* and *A Directory of Family One-Name Periodicals*, published previously by Summit Publications, are no longer available. Nonetheless, older issues can provide the names of groups either overlooked by current directories or groups that are now defunct. Check libraries and genealogical book vendors for these old issues.

Continue your association search with the Federation of Genealogical Societies' publication, *FORUM*. Look for the "Calendar of Events" section that appears in each issue, or go to <www.fgs.org> and click on "Calendar." Also examine the newsletters of the New England Historic and Genealogical Society, the National Genealogical Society, *Ancestry* magazine, *Heritage Quest*, and others for news items or articles about family associations.

Internet Listings

The Internet provides help in both locating family groups and learning of their activities. The place to start is at Cyndi's List at <www.cyndislist.com>. Click on "Surnames, Family Associations & Family Newsletters." There you will find links to many websites of societies with officers and publications, as well as home pages sponsored by individuals focused on a certain surname. Contact those sites that appear to have details of your ancestor. Also, you might want to note the listings of the periodicals they publish.

Another useful website is "Scottish Clan and Family Associations" at <www.clan-maccallum-malcolm.3acres.org/ScotClanFamily.html>. Click on the family links provided to go to the website of a specific clan surname society.

Another use of the Internet is to avail yourself of your favorite search engine (Google, Hotbed, Lycos, Yahoo, etc.). For example, go to Google at <www.google.com> and enter a surname followed by "association" or "society," such as "Rose Family Association" or "Parke Society." Several listings will appear for you to peruse.

Some search engines have a specific subject category for family associations and newsletters. For example, go to Yahoo <www.yahoo.com>. From there, select the following sub-categories as they come up: Society & Culture/Families/ Genealogy/Lineages and Surnames. Try this technique with other search engines as well.

Another good site to visit is Open Directory <www.dmoz.org/Society/Genealogy/Surnames/Organizations/Single_Name_Studies>, which contains many surname studies. Those seeking one-name study groups in Great Britain should start with Guild of One-Name Studies at <www.one-name.org>.

Family mailing lists or "message boards" offer the opportunity to meet others who are tracing the same family. Persons seeking kin can post information to identify their relationship to the particular surname or family. One such forum is presented by Genealogy.com at <www.genforum.genealogy.com/index.html>. Another is at Ancestry.com <www.ancestry.com/share>. You can also go to Cyndi's List at <www.cyndislist.com> and click on "Roots-L & RootsWeb." Read the instructions and options, and follow them to specific family boards.

Effective Contact

When writing to a family association, state your goal succinctly. Are you seeking contact with descendants of a particular person? Trying to find a photograph? Searching for ancestors in Europe? Ask if they have a service to assist you, and how you can use the service. If the group has a website, read it to ascertain if there is one person in charge of answering inquiries. If not, e-mail the webmaster of the site. If you send them a letter by mail, be sure to include a SASE (self-addressed stamped envelope).

Consider joining the organization. Become active in the group, and perhaps head a committee or special project. Does the family graveyard need cleaning? Perhaps you can spearhead a joint fund-raiser to repair tombstones. Could you lead a project to prepare a Civil War index of the surname to assist other researchers? Your efforts can benefit others and in return bring you satisfaction by helping to preserve your family's heritage.

Reunions

Examine the events columns in genealogical journals for announcements of reunions. Family associations may submit paid advertisements to these journals or place notices on the websites of various groups in an attempt to reach all interested parties.

If you can attend one of these gatherings, do so. Bring with you a one-sheet summary of your tie to the family. Add your name, address, and other contact information, and distribute it at the reunion. It may make its way to someone who can help further your research. Family reunions can reconnect families and create treasured friendships.

Newsletters

The periodicals of family groups vary. Some contain only information on living descendants—weddings, deaths, and personal news. Others are devoted exclusively to publishing research records of ancestors: military files, court records, tombstone inscriptions, and others. Some integrate the old and the new.

During the years, the accumulated output of these publications is staggering. Their ease of use varies. Usually these periodicals were not indexed at the time of publication. In the past few years, groups have sought to prepare consolidated indexes for their magazines. If available, such an index may be offered for sale in book form, on a CD-ROM, or in a database on the website. Even if the publication is now defunct, back issues can contain valuable research material. Peruse these issues for clues to your family's background and the identities of descendants you might contact.

After ascertaining if the periodical has been indexed, proceed to a search of genealogical library collections on the Internet, look for a library holding the actual issues. You can also post inquiries for issues at surname forums. If the library is not near you, it may be possible to borrow the essential periodicals on interlibrary loan. While some effort may be necessary to locate the issues, their contents—an old Bible record, photograph, or Gold Rush letter—might add immeasurably to your knowledge of the family.

Finding Records of Extinct Societies

If there was a group but it is now extinct, make inquiries as to what happened to its records. Often they lie in a library near the group's former address. Place inquiries in the columns of national journals, and in the regional quarterlies in the area where the group once existed. Also try the *National Union Catalog of Manuscript Collection* (NUCMC). This catalog is explained in chapter 3, "General References and Guides."

DNA Projects

The number of family groups participating in DNA projects has increased dramatically. The test most suitable for family projects is based on the Y chromosome. The so called "Y-DNA" test is only available to males of the surname because the

Y chromosome is passed (mostly unchanged) from father to son in an unbroken male chain.

To locate eligible males to test, the project administrators of these studies sometimes place their ads in genealogical publications. Members of family associations who are financially able to assist are asked to contribute funds so that selected tests can be offered at no cost. In a one-name study in which there are a number of emigrants from assorted countries, such a project can help sort out which descendants belong to each of the specific emigrant groups.

Tests can be administered to descendants who have well-documented lines to an early-American settler, and the results of those tests can be compared with testees whose lines are unknown. If matches are found, those who had unknown ancestors before testing have now, through the Y-DNA project, identified their progenitor. In those societies where all descend from a common emigrant, tests can be compared to testees of the surname in other countries. If a match is found between an American bearing the surname and a descendant of the surname whose family has lived in another country for some time, both benefit. The American now knows the point of origin overseas, and the overseas descendant has now found a probable "lost" branch of the family.

Many family projects are named at Family Tree DNA at <www.FamilyTreeDna.com>. This search engine will enable you to contact the project administrators of all the family projects the company is managing. Or, contact the family association in which you are interested and inquire whether a DNA project is in progress. If not, you may be able to assist in formulating such a study.

Notes

[1] Elizabeth Bentley and Deborah Ann Carl, *Directory of Family Associations*, 4th ed. (Baltimore: Genealogical Publishing Co., 2001).

[2] *Genealogical Helper*, published quarterly (Logan, Utah: Everton Publishers); *Family History Magazine* (Logan, Utah: Everton Publishers, 2004).

[3] Deborah Striplin and Patricia Hagood, eds., *The Standard Periodical Directory*, 28th ed. (New York: Oxbridge Communications, 2005).

[4] Dina C. Carson, ed., *Directory of Genealogical and Historical Societies, Libraries and Periodicals in the U.S. and Canada 2005* (Niwot, Colo.: Iron Gate Pub., 2005).

References

General

Bentley, Elizabeth, and Deborah Ann Carl. *Directory of Family Associations*. 4th ed. Baltimore: Genealogical Publishing Co., 2001.

Dina C. Carson, ed. *Directory of Genealogical and Historical Societies, Libraries and Periodicals in the U.S. and Canada 2005*. Niwot, Colo.: Iron Gate Pub., 2005.

Rose, Christine. *Family Associations: Organization and Management*. San Jose, Calif.: Rose Family Association, 2001.

Striplin, Deborah, and Patricia Hagood, eds. *The Standard Periodical Directory*. 28th ed. New York: Oxbridge Communications, 2005.

Newsletters

Floyd, Elaine. *Creating Family Newsletters: 123 Ideas for Sharing Memorable Moments with Family and Friends*. Cincinnati, Ohio: Betterway Books, 1998.

Nelson, Jeanne Rundquist. *Absolutely Family! A Guide to Editing and Publishing a Family Newsletter*. Kansas City, Mo.: Family Times Pub., 1999.

Wylie, Barbara Brixey. "Publishing a One Family Periodical." Genealogy.com, <www.genealogy.com/genealogy/26_wylie1.html>.

Reunions

Clunies, Sandra MacLean. *A Family Affair: How to Plan and Direct the Best Family Reunion Ever. National Genealogical Society Guides*. Nashville, Tenn.: Rutledge Hill Press, 2003.

Morgan, George G. *Your Family Reunion: How to Plan It, Organize It, and Enjoy It*. Provo, Utah: Ancestry, 2001.

Wagner, Edith. *The Family Reunion Sourcebook*. New York: McGraw-Hill, 1999.

Williams, Krystal. *How to Plan Your African-American Family Reunion*. Citadel Press, 2000.

Appendix C

Genealogical Societies

The following is a sampling of the hundreds of national, state, regional, and ethnic genealogical societies and umbrella organizations in the United States. For a more comprehensive listing, see Dina C. Carson, ed., *Directory of Genealogical and Historical Societies, Libraries and Periodicals in the U.S. and Canada 2005* (Niwot, Colo.: Iron Gate, 2005), and *Federation of Genealogical Societies 1996 Membership Directory* (Richardson, Tex.: FGS, 1996). See also the Society Hall website <www.familyhistory.com/societyhall/main.asp>.

National Societies

Afro-American Historical and Genealogical Society
P.O. Box 73086
Washington, DC 20056-3067

American-Canadian Genealogical Society
P.O. Box 6478
Manchester, NH 03108-6478

American Family Records Association (AFRA)
P.O. Box 15505
Kansas City, MO 64106

American-French Genealogical Society
P.O. Box 2113
Pawtucket, RI 02861

Association of Jewish Genealogical Societies
1485 Teaneck Rd.
Teaneck, NJ 07666

The Belgian Researchers, Inc.
495 East 5th St.
Peru, IN 46970
www.rootsweb.com/~inbr/index.html

Czechoslovak Genealogical Society, Intl., Inc.
P.O. Box 16225
St. Paul, MN 55116-0225

Federation of Genealogical Societies
P.O. Box 200940
Austin, TX 78720-0940

German Genealogical Society of America
Southern California Genealogical Society and Family Research Library
417 Irving Drive
Burbank, CA 91504

Hispanic Genealogical Society
P.O. Box 231271
Houston, TX 77223-1271

International Genealogy Fellowship of Rotarians
5721 Antietam Dr.
Sarasota, FL 34231

Irish Genealogical Society, Intl. (IGSI)
P.O. Box 16585
St. Paul, MN 55116-0585

Irish Family History Forum
P.O. Box 67
Plain View, NY 11803-0067

Italian Genealogy Group
50 Daisy Ave.
Floral Park, NY 11001

Jewish Genealogical Society, Inc.
P.O. Box 6398
15th West 16th Street
New York, NY 10011

National Genealogical Society
4527 Seventeenth St., N.
Arlington, VA 22207-2399

National Society, Daughters of the American Revolution
Library
1776 D St. NW
Washington, DC 20006-5392

New England Historical and Genealogical Society
101 Newbury Street
Boston, MA 02116-3007

Orphan Train Heritage Society of America
P.O. Box 322
Concordia, KS 66901

Palatines to America
611 East Weber Road
Columbus, OH 43211-1097
www.palam.org

POINT (Pursuing Our Italian Names Together)
Box 14966, Dept. PHP
Las Vegas, NV 89114-4966
www.point-pointers.net/hom.html

Polish Genealogical Society of Michigan
Burton Collection
Detroit Public Library
5201 Woodward Ave.
Detroit, MI 48202-4007
www.pgsm.org

Polish Genealogical Society of America
Polish Museum of America
984 N. Milwaukee Ave.
Chicago, IL 60622

Puerto Rican Hispanic Genealogical Society
P.O. Box 260118
Bellerose, NY 11426
www.rootsweb.com/~prhgs

Scandinavian-American Genealogical Society (SAGS)
P.O. Box 16069
St. Paul, MN 55116-0069

TIARA (The Irish Ancestral Research Association)
P.O. Box 619
Sudbury, MA 01776

Alabama

Alabama Genealogical Society
Samford University Library
Box 2296
800 Lakeshore Dr.
Birmingham, AL 35229-0001

Natchez Trace Genealogical Society
P.O. Box 420
Florence, AL 35631-0420

Tuscaloosa Genealogical Society
P.O. Box 020802
Tuscaloosa, AL 35402

Alaska

Alaska Genealogical Society
7030 Dickerson Dr.
Anchorage, AK 99504

Arizona

Arizona Genealogical Advisory Board
P.O. Box 5641
Mesa, AZ 85211-5641

Arizona State Genealogical Society
P.O. Box 42075
Tucson, AZ 85733

Arkansas

Arkansas Genealogical Society
P.O. Box 908
Hot Springs, AR 71902-0908

California

California Genealogical Society
P.O. Box 77105
San Francisco, CA 94107-0105

California State Genealogical Alliance
P.O. Box 10195
Oakland, CA 94610
www.esga.com

Conejo Valley Genealogical Society
P.O. Box 1228
Thousand Oaks, CA 91358
www.rootsweb.com/~cavgs

Contra Costa County Genealogical Society
P.O. Box 910
Concord, CA 94522
www.rootsweb.com/~cacccgs

Los Angeles Westside Genealogical Society
P.O. Box 10447
Marina del Rey, CA 90295
www.genealogy-la.com/lawvgs.shtml

San Diego Genealogical Society
1050 Pioneer Way
Suite E
El Cajon, CA 92020-1943
www.rootsweb.com/~casdgs

Questing Heirs GenSoc, Inc.
P.O. Box 15102
Long Beach, CA 90815-0102
www.cagenweb.com/questing

Colorado

Colorado Genealogical Society
P.O. Box 9218
Denver, CO 80209
www.rootsweb.com/cocgs

Colorado Council of Genealogical Societies
P.O. Box 24379
Denver, CO 80224-0379
www.rootsweb.com/~coccgs

The council can provide a list of all genealogical societies in the state if a self-addressed stamped envelope is included with the request.

Columbine Genealogical Society
P.O. Box 2074
Littleton, CO 80161
www.rootsweb.com/~cocghs

Connecticut

Connecticut Society of Genealogists
P.O. Box 435
Glastonbury, CT 06033
www.csg.hc.org

The Connecticut Ancestry Society
P.O. Box 249
Stamford, CT 06940-0249
www.rootsweb.com/~ctcas

Delaware

Delaware Genealogical Society
505 Market St. Mall
Wilmington, DE 19801-3091
http://delgensoc.org

Florida

Central Florida Genealogical Society
P.O. Box 177
Orlando, FL 32802-0177
www.cfgs.org

Florida Genealogical Society, Inc.
P.O. Box 18624
Tampa, FL 33679-8624

Florida State Genealogical Society
P.O. Box 10249
Tallahassee, FL 32302-2249
www.rootsweb.com/~flsgs

Genealogical Society of North Brevard
P.O. Box 897
Titusville, FL 32781
www.nbbd.com/npr/gsnb

Georgia

Georgia Genealogical Society
P.O. Box 54575
Atlanta, GA 30308-0575
www.gagensociety.org

Hawaii

Hawaii County Genealogical Society
P.O. Box 831
Keaau, HI 96749

The Sandwich Islands Genealogical Society
Hawaii State Library
478 S. King St.
Honolulu, HI 96813

Idaho

Idaho Genealogical Society
P.O. Box 1854
Boise, ID 83701-1854
www.idahogenealogy.org

Illinois

Chicago Genealogical Society
P.O. Box 1160
Chicago, IL 60690
www.chgogs.org

Fulton County Historical and Genealogical Society
P.O. Box 583
Canton, IL 61520-1126
www.rootsweb.com/~ilfulton

Illinois State Genealogical Society
P.O. Box 10195
Springfield, IL 62791
www.rootsweb.com/~ilsgs

Jacksonville Area Genealogical and Historical Society
P.O. Box 21
Jacksonville, IL 62651-0021
www.japl.lib.il.us/community/clubs/jaghs

McLean County Genealogical Society
P.O. Box 488
Normal, IL 61761-0488

Madison County Genealogical Society
P.O. Box 631
Edwardsville, IL 62025
www.rootsweb.com/~ilmadcgs

South Suburban Genealogical and Historical Society
P.O. Box 96
South Holland, IL 60473
www.rootsweb.com/~ssghs

Genealogical Society of Southern Illinois
John A. Logan College
Route 2 Box 145
Carterville, IL 62918
www.jal.cc.il.us/Gssi_org.html

Indiana

Allen County Genealogical Society
P.O. Box 12003
Fort Wayne, IN 46862
http://allencogenealogysociety.homestead.com/main.html

Indiana Genealogical Society, Inc.
P.O. Box 10507
Fort Wayne, IN 46852-0507

Southern Indiana Genealogical Society
P.O. Box 665
New Albany, IN 47151-0665
www.ka.net/spcarpenter/SIGserve.htm

Tippecanoe County Area Genealogical Society
Tippecanoe County Historical Association
909 S. St.
Lafayette, IN 47901
www.tcha.mus.in.us

Iowa

Iowa Genealogical Society
P.O. Box 7735
Des Moines, IA 50322-7735
www.iowagenealogy.org

Northeast Iowa Genealogical Society
503 S. St.
Waterloo, IA 50701
http://members.aol.com/johntwithneigs

Northwest Iowa Genealogical Society
46 First St. S.W.
Le Mars, IA 51031
www.homestead.com/genealogynwia/gen.html

Kansas

Kansas Genealogical Society
P.O. Box 103
Dodge City, KS 67801
www.dodgecity.net/kgs

Kansas Council of Genealogical Societies
P.O. Box 3858
Topeka, KS 66604-6858
http://skyways.lib.ks.us/genweb/kcgs

Reno County Genealogical Society
P.O. Box 5
Hutchinson, KS 67504-0005
http://rootsweb.com/~ksrcgs/renocokansas.html

Topeka Genealogical Society
P.O. Box 4048
Topeka, KS 66604-0048
www.tgstopeka.org

Kentucky

Eastern Kentucky Genealogical Society
P.O. Box 1544
Ashland, KY 41105-1544

Kentucky Genealogical Society
P.O. Box 153
Frankfort, KY 40602
www.kygs.org/index.html

Louisville Genealogical Society
P.O. Box 5164 DGS
Louisville, KY 40255-0164
www.rootsweb.com/~kylgs

West-Central Kentucky Family Research Association
P.O. Box 1932
Owensboro, KY 42302
www.rootsweb.com/~kywcfra

Louisiana

Baton Rouge Genealogical Society
P.O. Box 80565
SE Station
Baton Rouge, LA 70898
www.intersurf.com/~rcollins/brg.htm

Louisiana Genealogical and Historical Society
P.O. Box 3454
Baton Rouge, LA 70821
www.rootsweb.com/~la-lghs

Maine

Maine Genealogical Society
P.O. Box 221
Farmington, ME 04938
www.rootsweb.com/~megs/index.htm

Maryland

Baltimore County Genealogical Society
P.O. Box 10085
Towson, MD 21204
www.serve.com/bcgs/bcgs.html

Historical Society of Charles County
P.O. Box 261
Port Tobacco, MD 20677

Maryland Genealogical Society
201 W. Monument St.
Baltimore, MD 21201
www.mdgensoc.org

Prince George's County Genealogical Society
P.O. Box 819
Bowie, MD 20718-0819
www.rootswebcom/~mdpgcgs

Massachusetts

Berkshire Family History Association, Inc.
P.O. Box 1437
Pittsfield, MA 01201
www.berkshire.net~bfha

Essex Society of Genealogists
P.O. Box 313
Lynnfield, MA 01940
www.esog.org

Massachusetts Genealogical Council
P.O. Box 5393
Cochituate, MA 01778
http://home.comcast.net/~massgencouncil

The Massachusetts Society of Genealogists, Inc.
P.O. Box 215
Ashland, MA 01721-0215
www.rootsweb.com/~masgi/index.html

Michigan

The Detroit Society for Genealogical Research
Detroit Public Library
5201 Woodward Ave.
Detroit, MI 48202
www.dsgr.org

Genealogical Society of Washtenaw County, Michigan
P.O. Box 7155
Ann Arbor, MI 48107
www.hvcn.org/info/gswc

Kalamazoo Valley Genealogical Society
P.O. Box 405
Comstock, MI 49041
www.rootsweb.com/~mikvgs

Michigan Genealogical Council
P.O. Box 80953
Lansing, MI 48908-0593
www.rootsweb.com/~mimgcl

Minnesota

Minnesota Genealogy Society
P.O. Box 16069
St. Paul, MN 55116-0069
http://mngs.org

Mississippi

Mississippi Genealogical Society
P.O. Box 5301
Jackson, MS 39216-5301

Missouri

Missouri State Genealogical Association
P.O. Box 833
Columbia, MO 65205-0833
http://mosga.missouri.org

Northwest Missouri Genealogical Society
P.O. Box 382
St. Joseph, MO 64502-0382
www.rootsweb.com/~monwmgs

Ozarks Genealogical Society
P.O. box 3945
Springfield, MO 65808-3945
www.rootsweb.com/~ozarksgs

St. Louis Genealogical Society
9011 Manchester Rd.
Suite No. 3
Brentwood, MO 63144
www.stlgs.org

Montana

Montana State Genealogical Society
P.O. Box 555
Chester, MT 59522
www.rootsweb.com/~mtmsgs

Great Falls Genealogy Society
Paris Gibson Square
1400 First Ave. N., Room 30
Great Falls, MT 59401-3299
www.rootsweb.com/~mtmsgs/soc_gfgs.htm

Nebraska

Greater Omaha Genealogical Society
P.O. Box 4011
Omaha, NE 68104
http://hometown.aol.com/gromahagensoc/myhomepage

Lincoln-Lancaster Genealogical Society
P.O. Box 30055
Lincoln, NE 68503-0055
www.rootsweb.com/~nellcgs

Nebraska State Genealogical Society
P.O. Box 5608
Lincoln, NE 68505-0608
www.rootsweb.com/~nesgs

Nevada

Nevada State Genealogical Society
P.O. Box 20666
Reno, NV 89515-0666
www.rootsweb.com/nvgs/

Clark County Genealogical Society
P.O. Box 1929
Las Vegas, NV 89125-1929
www.rootsweb.com/~nvccngs/

New Hampshire

New Hampshire Society of Genealogists
P.O. Box 2316
Concord, NH 03302-2316
http://nhsog.org//nhsog/aboutus.htm

New Jersey
Gloucester County Historical Society
17 Hunter St.
P.O. Box 409
Woodbury, NJ 08096-0409
www.rootsweb.com/~njglouce/gchs

Genealogical Society of New Jersey
P.O. Box 1291
New Brunswick, NJ 08903-1291
www.gsnj.org

Monmouth County Genealogy Club
Monmouth County Historical Association
70 Court St.
Freehold, NJ 07728

Morris Area Genealogy Society
P.O. Box 105
Convent Station, NJ 07961
www.rootsweb.com/njmags

Genealogical Society of the West Fields
550 E. Broad St.
Westfield, NJ 07090
www.westfieldnj.com/gswf

New Mexico

Genealogy Club of the Albuquerque Public Library
423 Central Ave. N.E.
Albuquerque, NM 87102

New Mexico Genealogical Society
P.O. Box 8283
Albuquerque, NM 87198-8283
www.nmgs.org

Southern New Mexico Genealogical Society
P.O. Box 2563
Las Cruces, NM 88004-2563
www.zianet.com/wheelerwc/genssnm

New York

Capital District Genealogical Society
P.O. Box 2175
Empire State Plaza
Albany, NY 12220-0175

Central New York Genealogical Society
P.O. Box 104, Colvin Station
Syracuse, NY 13205
www.rootsweb.com/~nycnygs

Dutchess County Genealogical Society
P.O. Box 708
Poughkeepsie, NY 12603
www.dcgs-gen.org

New York State Council of Genealogical Organizations
P.O. Box 2593
Syracuse, NY 13220-2593
www.rootsweb.com/~nyscogo

New York Genealogical and Biographical Society
122 E. 58th St.
New York, NY 10022-1939
www.newyorkfamilyhistory.org

Western New York Genealogical Society
P.O. Box 338
Hamburg, NY 14075-0338
http://wnygs.org

North Carolina

Carolinas Genealogical Society
P.O. Box 397
Monroe, NC 28111
www.rootsweb.com/~ncunion/geneaogical_society.htm

Forsyth County Genealogical Society
P.O. Box 5715
Winston-Salem, NC 27113-5715
www.rootsweb.com/~ncforsyt

Johnson County Genealogical Society
c/o Public Library of Johnson County
Smithfield, NC 27577

North Carolina Genealogical Society
P.O. Box 1492
Raleigh, NC 27602
www.ncgenealogy.org

Wilkes Genealogical Society

P.O. Box 1629
North Wilkesboro, NC 28659
www.wilkesgensoc.org

North Dakota

Bismarck-Mandan Historical and Genealogical Society

P.O. Box 485
North Wilkesboro, NC 28659
Bismarck, ND 58502-0485
www.rootsweb.com/~ndbmhgs

Red River Valley Genealogical Society

P.O. Box 9284
Fargo, ND 58106
www.redrivergenealogy.com/htmls/pioneer.htm

Ohio

The Greater Cleveland Genealogical Society

P.O. Box 40254
Cleveland, OH 44140-0254
www.rootsweb.com/~ohcgg

Ohio Genealogical Society

34 Sturges Ave.
P.O. Box 2625
Mansfield, OH 44906-0625
www.ogs.org

Oklahoma

Federation of Oklahoma Genealogical Societies

P.O. Box 26151
Oklahoma City, OK 73126-0151

Oklahoma Genealogical Society

P.O. Box 12986
Oklahoma City, OK 73157-2986
www.rootsweb.com/~okgs

Oregon

Genealogical Council of Oregon, Inc.

P.O. Box 15169
Portland, OR 97215
www.rootsweb.com/~orgco2

Genealogical Forum of Oregon

2130 S.W. 5th Ave.
Suite 220
Portland, OR 97201-4934
www.gfo.org

Oregon Genealogical Society, Inc.

P.O. Box 10306
Eugene, OR 97440-2306
www.rootsweb.com/~orlncogs/ogsinfo.htm

Pennsylvania

Blair County Genealogical Society

P.O. Box 855
Altoona, PA 16603
www.rootsweb.com/~pabcgs

Cornerstone Genealogical Society

P.O. Box 547
Waynesburg, PA 15370
www.cornerstonegenealogy.com

Genealogy Society of Pennsylvania

1305 Locust St.
Philadelphia, PA 19107
www.genpa.org

Historical Society of Western Pennsylvania and Western Pennsylvania Genealogical Society

4338 Bigelow Blvd.
P.O. Box 8530
Pittsburgh, PA 15220-0530

South Central Pennsylvania Genealogical Society

P.O. Box 1824
York, PA 17405-1824
www.scpgs.org

Rhode Island

Rhode Island Genealogical Society

507 Clark's Row
Bristol, RI 02809-1481
www.rigensoc.org

South Carolina

Chester District Genealogical Society

P.O. Box 336
Richburg, SC 29729
www.rootsweb.com/~scchest2/scchestercdgs.htm

South Carolina Genealogical Society
P.O. Box 16355
Greenville, SC 29606
www.scgen.org

South Dakota

Sioux Valley Genealogical Society
200 W. Sixth St.
Sioux Falls, SD 57104-6881
www.rootsweb.com/~sdsvgs

South Dakota Genealogical Society
P.O. Box 490
Winner, SD 57580
www.rootsweb.com/~sdgenweb/gensoc/sdgensoc/html

Tennessee

Jefferson County Genealogical Society
P.O. Box 267
Jefferson City, TN 37760

Middle Tennessee Genealogical Society
P.O. Box 190625
Nashville, TN 37219-0625
www.mtgs.org

Tennessee Genealogical Society
P.O. Box 111249
Memphis, TN 38111-1249
www.rootsweb.com/~thgs

Texas

Austin Genealogical Society
P.O. Box 1507
Austin, TX 78767-1507
www.austintexgensoc.org

Dallas Genealogical Society
P.O. Box 12648 12446
Dallas, TX 75225-0648
www.dallasgenealogy.org

Houston Area Genealogical Association
2507 Tannehill
Houston, TX 77008-3052

Texas State Genealogical Society
Route 4, Box 56
Sulphur Springs, TX 75482
www.rootsweb.com/~txsgs

Tip O' Texas Genealogical Society
410 76 Dr.
Harlingen, TX 78550
www.familyhistory.com/societyhall/viewmember.
asp?societyid=215

Utah

Utah Genealogical Association
P.O. Box 1144
Salt Lake City, UT 84110
www.infouga.org

Vermont

Vermont Genealogical Society
P.O. Box 422
Pittsford, VT 05763
www.rootsweb.com/~utgsv

Virginia

Genealogical Research Institute of Virginia
P.O. Box 29178
Richmond, VA 23242-0178
www.rootsweb.com/~vagriv

Tidewater Virginia Genealogical Society
P.O. Box 7650
Hampton, VA 23666
www.rootsweb.com/~vatgs

Virginia Genealogical Society
5001 W. Broad St. No. 115
Richmond, VA 23230-3023
www.vgs.org

Washington

Clark County Genealogical Society
P.O. Box 2728
Vancouver, WA
98668-2728
www.ccgs-wa.org

Eastside Genealogical Society
P.O. Box 374
Bellevue, WA 98009
www.rootsweb.com/~wakcegs

Washington State Genealogical Society
P.O. Box 1422
Olympia, WA 98507
www.rootsweb.com/~wasgs

West Virginia

Kanawha Valley Genealogical Society
P.O. Box 8555
South Charleston, WV 25303–8555
www.rootsweb.com/~wvkvgs

West Virginia Genealogical Society
P.O. Box 249
Elkview, WV 25071
http://members.aol.com/edeaj/wvgenealogicalsociety.html

Wisconsin

Milwaukee County Genealogical Society
P.O. Box 270326
Milwaukee, WI 53227-0326
www.milwaukeegenealogy.org

Wisconsin State Genealogical Society
P.O. Box 5106
Madison, WI 53705-0106
www.rootsweb.com/~wsgs

Wyoming

Fremont County Genealogical Society
Riverton Branch Library
1330 W. Park Ave.
Riverton, WY 82501
www.rootsweb.com/~wyfremon/resources.htm

Appendix D

Hereditary and Lineage Organizations

LLOYD deWITT BOCKSTRUCK, MA, MS

Source material for more than a hundred hereditary societies and more than a thousand family organizations throughout the United States is scattered through a wide range of registers, journals, newsletters, and membership rosters. The hereditary societies listed in this appendix are those which are the best known and most active in the United States. Consult the latest edition of *Hereditary Society Blue Book* for detailed information about many additional hereditary societies. More current is the *Encyclopedia of Associations*. An online alternative to these publications is the Hereditary Society Community at <www.hereditary.us>. At this site, "Society Lists" provides an alphabetical listing of organizations by name or a chronological list of societies by year of establishment. Entries include contact information (which in some organizations changes when a new president takes office) and membership requirements. These entries may be searched by keyword. Another page on the Hereditary Society Community site announces meeting information, submitted by organizations, in a calendar format. Perhaps the most useful section is that which offers links to the websites of organizations.

The websites of the organizations themselves vary in content, ranging from a simple listing of address and contact information, to lavishly illustrated and highly sophisticated presentations. One of the most complete sites is that of the Ancient and Honorable Artillery Company of Massachusetts at <www.ahacsite.org>. The site includes a history of the formation of the Company (chartered in 1638 by the General Court of Massachusetts); membership requirements; a time line of important AHAC dates; information on the First Captain Commander, Robert Keayne; a list of U.S. presidents and Medal of Honor recipients who belonged to AHAC; directions to AHAC headquarters and photographs of their museum; and events and various news items about the organization. Contact information is provided and there is a members-only section which requires a password.

Many of the sources needed to establish membership in a hereditary society—vital, military, church, pension, and other records—are discussed in other chapters of this book and are not repeated in this appendix.

Hereditary societies can be classified under seven headings:

- War societies
- Early settler and ship societies
- Colonial societies
- Nationality (ethnic) societies
- Religious societies
- Royal and baronial societies

Hereditary (or lineage) societies require prospective members to complete an application form showing descent from the qualifying ancestor for that society. The application must be sufficiently documented to prove beyond any doubt the accuracy of the lineage set forth.

Some hereditary societies do not wish to have their mailing addresses published. The majority of these are "by invitation only" societies which require that new members be invited to join by a current member and provide letters of recommendation.

For many of the societies described, various printed sources are listed. Printed sources can help you prove your lineage to an ancestor who qualifies you to be a member of a hereditary society.

War Societies

The oldest, largest, and best-known of the hereditary societies are those with membership based on the military service of members' ancestors. These societies are listed in chronological order of military service.

The Ancient and Honorable Artillery Company of Massachusetts

The Armory
Faneuil Hall
Boston, MA 02109

Founded in 1637 and chartered by Governor Winthrop in 1638, The Ancient and Honorable Artillery Company of Massachusetts is the oldest military body and chartered organization in America. Membership is limited to 550 regular members, who are not required to have descended from a former member. "Right of descent" membership is open to any male descendant of a former member of the company who served before 1738. Unlike the regular members, "right of descent" applicants may reside outside the New England area.

Printed Works

The Ancient and Honorable Artillery Company of Massachusetts. *Roll of Members of the Military Company of Massachusetts, Now Called the Ancient and Honorable Artillery Company of Massachusetts with a Roster of the Commissioned Officers and Preachers, 1638–1894.* Boston: Alfred Mudge and Son, 1895.

Roberts, Oliver Ayer. *History of the Military Company of Massachusetts, Now Called the Ancient and Honorable Artillery Company of Massachusetts, 1637–1888.* 4 vols. Boston: A. Mudge and Son, Printers, 1895–1901.

National Society Women Descendants of the Ancient and Honorable Artillery Company

49 Carriage Hill Drive
Windham, ME 040602-4927

This society was founded in 1927 for female descendants of former members of the Ancient and Honorable Artillery Company of Massachusetts, 1637 to 1774.

Printed Works

Cowen, Maude Roberts. *Members of the Ancient and Honorable Artillery Company in the Colonial Period.* N.p., 1958.

History and Lineage Book. The society, 1940–.

The General Society of Colonial Wars

Langdale Library
1420 Maryland Ave.
Baltimore, MD 21201

This society was founded in 1893 for male descendants of ancestors who served in the military from the time of the settlement of Jamestown, Virginia, in 1607 to the Battle of Lexington in 1775; or who held office as governor, lord proprietor, etc., or a member of the legislative body of a colony in that time period.

Printed Works

Nearly all of the twenty-nine state societies have published, from time to time, their own registers. Two excellent examples are the Society of Colonial Wars in the State of Connecticut, *Register of Pedigrees and Services of Ancestors* (Hartford, Conn.: the society, 1941), and the Society of Colonial Wars in the State of Maryland, *Genealogies of the Members and Record of Services of Ancestors* (Baltimore: Friedenwald Co., 1905), which includes a pedigree chart for each member.

General Society of Colonial Wars. *An Index of Ancestors and Roll of Members.* 3 vols. New York, 1922–77. Annual updates, 1978–.

National Society Daughters of Colonial Wars

812 Braeburn Drive, Tantallon on Potomac
Fort Washington, MD 20744-6021

This society was organized in 1932 for women descendants of participants in the colonial wars. The membership requirements are very similar to those cited for the General Society of Colonial Wars.

Printed Works

Lineage Books. 6 vols. to date. N.p., 1984–.

National Society Daughters of Colonial Wars. *Membership List and Index of Ancestors.* 2 vols. Somerville, Mass., 1941, 1950.

Continental Society Daughters of Indian Wars

3003 South Broadway #39
LaPorte, TX 77571-6552

This society was founded in 1988 for direct lineal female descendants of Native and/or Immigrant Americans who participated in hostilities or otherwise interacted in the period 1607–1900.

Printed Works

The Calumet. Published semiannually.

Continental Society Daughters of Indian Wars Ancestor Register.

The Society of the Cincinnati

Anderson House Library
2118 Massachusetts Ave. N.W.
Washington, DC 20008-2810

This society was founded in 1783 at the close of the Revolutionary War by a group of officers of the Continental Line. This mutual friendship society of officers was conceived to "endure as long as they shall endure, or any of their eldest male posterity; and in failure thereof, the collateral branches who may be judged worthy of becoming its members and supporters." Of the 2,269 original members, plus 1,257 who were eligible but did not join or had been killed in battle, approximately 2,000 are presently represented by descendants.

Printed Works

A number of state societies have published their own volumes on members and their ancestors. An excellent example is Francis S. Drake, *Memorials of the Society of the Cincinnati of Massachusetts* (Cambridge, Mass.: John Wilson and Son, 1873).

Heitman, Francis B. *Historical Register of Officers of the Continental Army During the War of the Revolution, 1914, with Addenda by Robert H. Kelby, 1932.* Baltimore: Genealogical Publishing Co., 1973.

Hume, Edgar Erskine, comp. *Society of the Cincinnati, Rules of the State Societies for Admission to Membership.* Washington, D.C.: the society, 1934.

Kilbourne, John D. *Virtutis Paremium: The Men Who Founded the State Society of the Cincinnati of Pennsylvania.* Rockport, Maine: Picton Press, 1998.

Metcalf, Bryce. *Original Members and Other Officers Eligible to the Society of the Cincinnati 1783–1838, with the Institutions, Rules of Admission, and Lists of the Officers of the General and State Societies.* Reprint, Beverly Hills, Calif.: Eastwood, 1995.

Sypher, Francis J. *New York State Society of the Cincinnati Biographies of Original Members and Other Continental Officers.* Fishkill, N.Y.: New York Society of the Cincinnati, 2004.

Daughters of the Cincinnati

122 E. 58th St.
New York, NY 10022

Founded in 1894, the Daughters of the Cincinnati have requirements for membership similar to those of the men's society, with one major exception: more than one member may represent an ancestor at a given time.

Printed Works

A Salute to Courage. New York: Columbia University Press, 1979.

National Society Daughters of the American Revolution

1776 D St. N.W.
Washington, DC 20006

Organized in 1890, this society is the largest and best known of the hereditary societies, with a membership exceeding 190,000. Since 1890, some 760,000 women have joined the DAR. Membership is based on descent from an ancestor who served the cause of American independence in the military, as a recognized patriot, or by rendering material aid.

Printed Works

More than two hundred volumes have been printed by various state societies, including membership rosters, lists of ancestors buried in a particular state, and biographies of the founders in various states.

DAR Index of the Rolls of Honor. 4 vols. Washington, D.C.: the society, 1916–40; reprint, 1980. 4 vols. in 2. These volumes index the ancestors of members as published in 160 volumes of lineage books.

DAR Patriot Index. 3 vols. Baltimore: Gateway Press, 2003. These volumes give the name of the Revolutionary ancestor with dates and places [state or country] of birth and death, name of spouse or spouses, and state from which he or she served.

Index to the Spouses of DAR Patriots. Washington, D.C.: the society, 1986. This index was prepared for the 1966 edition.

Lineage Book. 166 vols. Washington, D.C.: the society, 1896–1919.

General Society Sons of the Revolution

201 West Lexington Ave., #1776
Independence, MO 64050-3718

This society was founded in 1876 as a result of the stringent requirements of the Society of the Cincinnati, which made no provision for membership of younger sons of the original members. Membership is based on military service or descent from key civil officials.

Printed Works

Numerous state societies of the Sons of the Revolution have published biennial volumes on membership and ancestry. Two excellent examples are the 1901–03 and 1907–09 *Register of the Sons of the Revolution in the State of Missouri* (St. Louis, Mo.: Woodward and Tieernan Printing Co.) They contain ancestral lines from nearly all of the thirteen colonies.

Hall, Henry. *Year Book of the Societies Composed of Descendants of the Men of the Revolution*. New York: Republic Press, 1890. This rare and unusual volume unites the Sons of the Revolution, Sons of the American Revolution, Daughters of the American Revolution, and the Society of the Cincinnati.

Kilbourne, John Dwight. *Sons of the Revolution, A History 1875–2001*. New York: the society, 2002.

National Society Sons of the American Revolution

1000 S. 4th St.
Louisville, KY 40203-3292

Organized in 1889, the Sons of the American Revolution (SAR) is the largest hereditary society for men, with chapters in all fifty states, the District of Columbia, France, and England. Membership is based on descent from an ancestor who served in the military, held high official office, or was a patriot in the American cause.

Printed Works

Numerous state societies of the SAR have printed yearbooks containing lineages, etc. The 1893–94 volume of the New York State Society presents a number of engravings of ancestors. The register of the District of Columbia Society for 1896 is another splendid volume.

Brakebill, Clovis. *Revolutionary War Graves Register*. Dallas: DB Publications, 1993.

Cornish, Louis A., and A. Howard Clark. *A National Register of the Society Sons of the American Revolution*. New York: Andrew H. Kellogg Press, 1902. This unusual volume contains the entire list of membership for the National Society to 31 December 1901, including all deceased members, with lines of descent from revolutionary war ancestors.

St. Paul, John, Jr. *The History of the National Society of the Sons of the American Revolution*. New Orleans: Pelican Publishing Co., 1962.

Microfilm

The Genealogical Society of Utah has microfilmed more than 82,500 lineage papers of the National Society SAR and cross-indexed them by the name of the member and the name of the ancestor.

National Society Children of the American Revolution

1776 D St. N.W., Room 224
Washington, DC 20006-5392

This society was organized under the auspices of the DAR. Membership is limited to boys and girls under the age of twenty-two. Membership requirements are the same as for the DAR and SAR.

Hereditary Order of Descendants of the Loyalists and Patriots of the American Revolution

7916 Quill Point Drive
Bowie, MD 20720-4391

This society was organized in 1973 for those who descended from both a loyalist and a patriot of the American Revolution. The loyalist may be a collateral ancestor, but not more distant than the third degree. Application forms show the two lines of descent from the two ancestors.

Society of the Descendants of Washington's Army at Valley Forge

P.O. Box 915
Valley Forge, PA 19481-0915

This society was organized in 1976 at Valley Forge, Pennsylvania, for descendants of soldiers who served in the Continental Army at the Valley Forge encampment in 1777–78.

Printed Works

Chunn, Calvin E. *Not by Bread Alone*. The society, 1981.

Worley, Ramona. *Valley Forge—In Search of That Winter Patriot, 19 December 1779–19 June 177: A Comprehensive Guide for Tracing Valley Forge Ancestors*. The society, 1979.

Military Order of Foreign Wars of the United States

147 Jefferson Ct.
Norristown, PA 19401

This society was organized in 1894. Membership is conferred on officers with active military service in any foreign war from the American Revolution to the Vietnam War. Descendants in the direct male line of such an officer may qualify for hereditary companionship.

Printed Works

Register of Commanderies and Members, Military Order of Foreign Wars of the United States 1894–1900. The order, 1901.

Order of the Indian Wars of the United States

126 East Main St.
New Palestine, IN 46163

The Society was formed in 1896. Membership is based upon descent from an ancestor in a U.S. state or territorial military organization subsequent to 14 June 1776 engaged in the service of the United States in any military grade against hostile Indians within the jurisdiction of the United States. It assimilated the Continental Society, Sons of Indian Wars in 1999.

Printed Works

Finnell, Arthur L. *The Continental Society Sons of Indian Wars Ancestors Register*. N.p.: the society, 1997.

General Society of the War of 1812

1219 Charmuth Rd.
Lutherville, MD 21093-6404

This society was organized 14 September 1814 at Fort McHenry, Baltimore, Maryland, at the close of the War of 1812. It was primarily a Maryland society known as "The Defenders of Baltimore." From 1814 to 1888, all of the presidents were War of 1812 veterans. Membership is limited to male lineal descendants of participants in the military or privateer service of the United States. If the participant had no descendants, one collateral descendant may be admitted to the society.

Printed Works

Biennial and triennial meetings of the general society have published their proceedings for the past ninety years.

Blizzard, Dennis. *Descendants of War of 1812 Veterans: General Society of the War of 1812: Founders' Register, Commemoration, 1894–1994, with a Supplement to the 1989 Roster*. Mendenhall, Pa.: the society, 1994.

General Society of the War of 1812. *The Constitution and Register of Membership of the General Society of the War of 1812*. Washington, D.C.: Law Reporter Printing Co., 1908.

Ordway, Frederick Ira, Jr., ed. *Register of the General Society of the War of 1812*. The society, 1972.

———. *Bicentennial Supplement to the 1972 Register.* Ann Arbor, Mich.: Edwards Brothers, 1976.

Roster of the General Society of the War of 1812: 1989 and Supplement to the 1989 Roster. Baltimore: Clearfield Co., 1999.

National Society United States Daughters of 1812

500 Mount Pleasant Road N.E.
Fairmount, GA 30139-3406

Organized 8 January 1892 on the anniversary of the Battle of New Orleans, the society requires lineal descent from an ancestor who rendered military, naval, or civil service between the close of the American Revolutionary War in 1784 and the close of the War of 1812 in 1815. Military service may be in any one of sixteen recognized engagements between those dates.

Printed Works

1812 Ancestor Index. 2 vols. Norcross, Ga.: Harper Printing Co., 1970–72. These volumes list some 20,000 established ancestors, names of spouses, the name of the child (and spouse) through whom the member joined, and the state from which the ancestor served.

The Military Society of the War of 1812

Seventh Regiment Armory
643 Park Ave.
New York, NY 10021

This society was founded in 1826 for descendants of commissioned officers, aides-de-camp, and commanding officers of private armed vessels of the United States who served in the armies and navies in the War of 1812.

Aztec Club of 1847—The Military Society of the Mexican War 1846–1848

P.O. Box 8454
Universal City, CA 91618

This society was organized in 1847 for lineal descendants of commissioned officers of the army, navy, and marines who served in Mexico or Mexican waters during the War with Mexico, 1846 to 1848. Current membership requirements allow for collateral descent.

Printed Works

The Aztec Club of 1847: Roster of Members. The society, 1972.

Breithaupt, Richard H. *The Aztec Club of 1847: Military Society of the Mexican War: Sesquicentennial History, 1847–1997*. University City, Calif.: Walika Publishing Co., 1998.

San Jacinto Descendants

7011 Spring Briar
San Antonio, TX 78209

Anyone who is a direct descendent of a person who participated in the Battle of San Jacinto, 1836, or was assigned to the rear guard at Harrisburg is eligible for membership in this society.

Descendants of Mexican War Veterans

P.O. Box 830482
Richardson, TX 75083-0482

Military Order of the Loyal Legion of the United States (MOLLUS)

1805 Pine St.
Philadelphia, PA 19103

This society was founded in 1865, the year Lincoln died. Membership is limited to male lineal descendants of commissioned officers in the Union forces, 1861 to 1865, with hereditary membership open to male descendants of a brother or sister of such an officer. Its library contains some 11,000 volumes on the Civil War and numerous regimental histories.

Printed Works

Numerous commanderies throughout the United States have printed rosters for nearly a century. An excellent example is the *Register of the Commandery of the State of Pennsylvania, 1865–1882.*

Carroon, Robert G. *Union Blue: The History of the Military Order of the Loyal Legion of the United States*. Shippensburg, Pa.: White Mane Books, 2001.

Loyal Legion Historical Journal. Published periodically by the order for more than forty years.

Military Order of the Loyal Legion of the United States. 70 vols. Wilmington, N.C.: Broadfoot Pub. Co, 1991–97.

Roster of the Military Order of the Loyal Legion of the United States. Philadelphia: the order, 1975. This contains membership rosters of sixteen state commanderies.

Dames of the Loyal Legion of the United States

7334 Shadyview Avenue N.W.
Massillon, OH 44646-9081

This society was founded in 1899 as a companion society to MOLLUS. Membership is limited to women descendants of Union army commissioned officers and the wives of members of MOLLUS.

Printed Works

Roster of the Military Order of the Loyal Legion of the United States, as cited for the Military Order of the Loyal Legion of the United States (MOLLUS), contains a section devoted to the membership of the Dames of the Loyal Legion.

Sons of Union Veterans of the Civil War

P.O. Box 1865
Harrisburg, PA 17105

This society was founded in 1881 to perpetuate the memory of the Grand Army of the Republic. Membership is open to all male descendants of soldiers, sailors, and marines who served in the Union cause, 1861 to 1865.

Printed Works

The Banner. This quarterly is published by the society and includes information on all posts.

Sons of Union Veterans of the Civil War. Paducah, Ky.: Turner Publishing Co., 1996.

Auxiliary to the Sons of the Union Veterans of the Civil War

104 S. Main St. #2
Muncy, PA 17756-1319

This group was organized in 1883 as the Ladies Aid Society. Membership today is in several categories: wives of sons of the Union veterans, widows of sons who were in good standing at death, mothers of sons, and all female lineal relatives.

Printed Works

The Banner. Although published by the Sons of the Union Veterans, it also includes information on the auxiliary.

Daughters of Union Veterans of the Civil War, 1861–65

503 South Walnut St.
Springfield, IL 62704-1932

Organized in 1885, this society is the oldest women's hereditary society in the United States. Membership is limited to lineal descendants of military participants in the Civil War on the Union side.

Ladies of the Grand Army of the Republic

119 North Swarthmore Ave., Apt. 1-H
Ridley Park, PA 19078

This society was organized in 1885, combining the Loyal Ladies League and the Ladies of the Grand Army of the Republic. Membership is open to all mothers, wives, sisters, daughters, granddaughters, blood-kin nieces, and cousins of honorably discharged Union veterans.

United Daughters of the Confederacy

Memorial Building
328 North Blvd.
Richmond, VA 23220-4009

This group was organized in 1894 for women who are lineal or collateral descendants of men or women who served in the military or civil service of the Confederate States of America, or who gave material aid to the cause.

Printed Works

Davis, Jefferson. *Woman in the South in War Times* and *The Rise and Fall of the Confederate Government*. Both available through the society.

Children of the Confederacy

Memorial Building
328 North Blvd.
Richmond, VA 23220-4009

Organized in 1896 by the United Daughters of the Confederacy, membership in this society is limited to boys and girls under twenty-one years of age who are lineal descendants or nieces or nephews of men or women who served honorably in the Confederate service or of members of the United Daughters of the Confederacy or the Sons of Confederate Veterans.

Sons of Confederate Veterans

P.O. Box 59
Columbia, TN 38402-0059

This group was organized in 1896 under the auspices of the United Confederate Veterans. Membership is limited to male descendants, lineal or collateral, of members of the Confederate military or participants who died in prison, were killed in battle, or were honorably discharged.

Printed Works

Confederate Veteran. 40 vols. Wendell, N.C.: Broadfoot's Bookmark, 1983–.

Sons of Confederate Veterans, 1896: Our First 100 Years. Paducah, Ky.: Turner Publishing, 1997.

Sons of Confederate Veterans Ancestor Album. Houston: Heritage Publishers Services, 1986.

Military Order of the Stars and Bars

Box 59
Columbia, TN 38402-0059

This society was organized in 1938 for male descendants, lineal or collateral, of commissioned officers of the Confederate States of America.

National Order of the Blue and Gray

5608 Apache Road
Louisville, KY 40207

The National Order of the Blue and Gray was founded in 1990 for descendants of ancestors who rendered civil or military service to both the Confederate and federal governments during their lifetimes, including service in battle under Confederate and Federal authority; in a political role (state level or higher); or as a physician, surgeon, chaplain, or nurse in wartime service.

Military Order of the World Wars

435 N. Lee St.
Alexandria, VA 22314

Organized in 1919 as The American Officers of the Great War, this society's title was changed in 1920 (in 1942, "War" became "Wars"). Membership is open to male U.S. citizens who served honorably on active duty as commissioned officers between 6 April 1917 and 2 July 1921, or since 16 September 1940. Male descendants of members or of deceased officers are eligible for hereditary membership.

Ancient and Honorable Order of the Jersey Blues

P.O. Box 2
Cripple Creek, CO 80813-0002

Formed in 1673, the society consists of members who have an ancestor who served in the unit any time from its founding to the Treaty of Paris in 1783, or an ancestor who served during the Whiskey Rebellion of 1794, the War of 1812, the Civil War, or the Spanish American War.

Early Settler and Ship Societies

These societies (listed by date of founding) are based on the earliest settlers of a town, state, or geographical area. Societies of early arrivals on specific ships are included as well; they are identified by the name of the ship—that is, *Mayflower*, *Welcome*, *Ark*, *Dove*, etc.

Saint Nicholas Society of the City of New York

122 East 58th St.
New York, NY 10022
www.saintnicholassociety.org

At the suggestion of Washington Irving, this organization was founded in New York City in 1835 as a society for male descendants of residents of the city of New York or of New York state prior to 1785. Members must be proposed and seconded in writing. Membership is limited.

Printed Works

The Saint Nicholas Society of the City of New York Genealogical Record. 9 vols. New York: the society, 1905–80. These volumes contain the complete lineages of all members, plus biographical sketches of the ancestors.

Sypher, Francis J., ed. *The Saint Nicholas Society: A 150 Year Record.* New York: the society, 1993. It contains a list of members from 1835 to 1992.

Talcott, Sebastian Visscher. *Genealogical Notes of New York and New England Families.* 1883; reprint, Baltimore: Genealogical Publishing Co., 1973.

Society of California Pioneers

300 Fourth St.
San Francisco, CA 94107-1272
www.californiapioneers.org

This group was founded in 1850 for male lineal descendants of Californians who were resident before 1 January 1850, the date of statehood.

Printed Works

Bancroft, Hubert H. *California Pioneer Register and Index 1542–1858: Including Inhabitants of California 1769–1800 and List of Pioneers.* 1884–90; reprint, Baltimore: Genealogical Publishing Co., 1964.

California State Society Daughters of American Revolution. *Records of the Families of California Pioneers.* Vol. 2. The society, n.d.

Northrup, Marie E. *Spanish-Mexican Families of Early California, 1769–1850.* New Orleans: Polyanthos, 1976.

Daughters of the Republic of Texas

510 E. Anderson Ln.
Austin, TX 78752-1997
www.drtl.org/drtinc/index.asp

This society was founded in 1891 for female lineal descendants of loyal citizens who established residence in Texas before the state's annexation on 19 February 1846.

Printed Works

Founders and Patriots of the Republic of Texas: The Lineages of Members of the Daughters of the Republic of Texas. 6 vols. to date. Austin, Tex., 1963–.

See also the sources listed for the Sons of the Republic of Texas, following.

Sons of the Republic of Texas

1717 Eighth St.
Bay City, TX 77414
www.srttexas.org

This group was organized in 1893 for male lineal descendants of Texans who were resident prior to annexation on 19 February 1846.

Printed Works

Sons of the Republic of Texas Active Members. Microfilm, 37 rolls. These are the lineage applications and supporting documentation.

Sons of the Republic of Texas. *Microfilm Index [of Ancestors and Members].* Dallas: The Sons, 1989.

The Sons of the Republic of Texas. Padacuh, Ky.: Turner Pub. Co., 2001.

National Society of New England Women

7576 Clayton Road
St. Louis, MO 63117-1418
members.aol.com/calebj/nsnew.html

This group was organized in 1895 for women descendants of any ancestor born in New England before the signing of the U.S. Constitution on 4 March 1789. Junior membership is available.

Order of the Founders and Patriots of America

827 Lamberts Mill Road
Westfield, NJ 07090-4771

This society was organized in 1896 for men descended in the male line of either parent from an ancestor who settled in one of the colonies before 13 May 1657 and whose intermediate ancestor, in the same line, served in the American Revolution. Because both founder and patriot must bear the surname of the applicant's father or mother, this has long been regarded as the most difficult lineage society to join.

Printed Works

Colket, Meredith B., Jr. *Founders of Early American Families—Emigrants from Europe 1607–1657.* 2nd rev. ed. Cleveland, Ohio: Ohio Society with the Authority of the General Court of the Order of Founders and Patriots of America, 2003. This most unusual volume documents some 3,500 male heads of families who appear to have descendants in the male line to the present day.

The Order of the Founders and Patriots of America Register, Lineages of Associates, 1896–1993. 4 vols. Baltimore: Gateway Press, 1994.

The Order of the Founders and Patriots of America Register of Associates, 1993–2000. Williamsburg, Va.: Graphic Impressions, 2002.

Supplement Index: Surname of Founder Family. The society, n.d.

General Society of Mayflower Descendants

P.O. Box 3297
Plymouth, MA 02361-3297
www.mayflower.org

This group was founded in 1897 as a society for the lineal descendants of passengers on the *Mayflower,* which arrived in Plymouth harbor in December 1620.

Printed Works

A number of state societies have published excellent volumes with complete lineages of members. An example is Frederick Ira Ordway Jr., ed., *Register of the Society of Mayflower Descendants in the District of Columbia,* 2 vols. in 1 (Federalsburg, Md.: J. W. Stowell Printing Co., 1970, 1973).

The Mayflower Descendant. 34 vols. And index to persons, 2 vols., 1899–1937. Plymouth, Ma.: Massachusetts Society of Mayflower Descendants. This periodical was resumed with vol. 35 (1985).

Mayflower Families in Progress. These booklets are the preliminary editions for Five Generations genealogies and are issued with the intention to elicit corrections and additions.

Mayflower Families Through Five Generations: Descendants of the Pilgrims Who Landed at Plymouth, Mass., December 1620. 21 vols. to date. Plymouth, Mass.: General Society of Mayflower Descendants, 1975–. These are volumes for George Soule, Francis Eaton, Samuel Fuller, William White, James Chilton, Richard More, Thomas Rogers, Edward Fuller, Edward Winslow, John Billington, Stephen Hopkins, Peter Brown, Edward Doty, Francis Cooke, Myles Standish, John Alden, Isaac Allerton, Richard Warren, and Henry Samson. John Howland is treated separately.

Terry, Milton E., and Anne Borden Harding, *Mayflower Ancestral Index.* Plymouth, Mass.: General Society of Mayflower Descendants, 1981–.

National Society, Daughters of Founders and Patriots of America

733 15th Street NW #915
Washington, DC 20005-2112
www.nsafpa.org

This group was founded in 1898 for women descended in the direct male line of either parent from an ancestor who settled in any of the colonies between 13 May 1607 and 13 May 1687. (The last date is thirty years later than the men's organization.)

Printed Works

Lineage Book of the National Society of Daughters of Founders and Patriots of America. 45 vols. Since 1909. Contains complete proven lineages.

National Society, Daughters of Utah Pioneers

300 North Main St.
Salt Lake City, UT 84103-1699

This group was founded in 1901 for female lineal descendants of those who came to Utah before the completion of the railroad on 10 May 1869.

Printed Works

Daughters of Utah Pioneers. 30 vols. Salt Lake City: the society, 1939–68.

Jakeman, James T., ed. *Daughters of Utah Pioneers and Their Mothers.* Salt Lake City: the society, 1930. Contains an excellent collection of more than five hundred photographs.

Utah Pioneer Biographies. 44 vols. Salt Lake City: Utah Historical Society, 1935–64.

Associated Daughters of Early American Witches

449 N St. S.W.
Washington, DC 20024
www.adeaw.us

The society consists of females descended from an ancestor or ancestress accused of witchcraft prior to 31 December 1699. It was formed in 1987.

Society of the Founders of Norwich, Connecticut

Box 13
Norwich, CT 06360
www.societyct.org/norwich.htm

Organized in 1901, this society is open to all interested in the history and preservation of Norwich. Applicants who prove lineal descent from an original proprietor or one of the earliest settlers receive a certificate of descent.

Printed Works

Caulkins, Frances M. *History of Norwich from Its Possession by the Indians to the Year 1866.* 1866; reprint, Baltimore: Genealogical Publishing Co., 1976.

Sons and Daughters of Oregon Pioneers

Box 6685
Portland, OR 97228
www.webtrail.com/sdop

This group was organized in 1901 for lineal descendants of settlers in the Oregon Country before statehood, 14 February 1859.

Piscataqua Pioneers

110 North Avenue
Weston, MA 02193

This group was organized in 1905 for lineal descendants of early (before July 1776) settlers on both the New Hampshire and Maine sides of the Piscataqua River and its tributaries.

Printed Works

Noyes, Sybil, Charles Thornton Libby, and Walter Goodwin Davis. *Genealogical Dictionary of Maine and New Hampshire*. 1928–39; reprint, Baltimore: Genealogical Publishing Co., 1972.

Piscataqua Pioneers, 1623–1775; Register of Members and Ancestors 1905–1990. Accompanied by Supplement to the Register of Members and Ancestors, 4 August 1995. Portsmouth, N.H.: Piscataqua Pioneers, 1997.

Pope, Charles Henry. *The Pioneers of Maine and New Hampshire, 1623–1660*. Baltimore: Genealogical Publishing Co., 1965.

Society of Piscataqua Pioneers, Register of Members and Ancestors, 1905–1981. The society, 1981.

Spencer, Wilbur D. *Pioneers on Maine Rivers with Lists to 1651*. 1930; reprint, Baltimore: Genealogical Publishing Co., 1973.

The Welcome Society of Pennsylvania

415 South Croskey St.
Philadelphia, PA 19146
www.welcomesociety.org

This group was founded in 1906 to honor the ship *Welcome*, on which William Penn travelled to his colony. Applicants must prove lineal descent from a passenger arriving on the *Welcome* in October 1682 or on some other vessel arriving in Pennsylvania between 24 December 1681 and 31 December 1682.

Printed Works

McCracken, George E., ed. *Penn's Colony, The Welcome Claimants—Proved, Disproved and Doubtful, with an Account of Some of Their Descendants*. Vol. 2. Baltimore: Genealogical Publishing Co., 1970.

Sheppard, Walter Lee, Jr., ed. *Penn's Colony, Passengers and Ships Prior to 1684*. Vol. 1. Baltimore: Genealogical Publishing Co., 1970.

National Society Sons of Utah Pioneers

3301 East 2920 South
Salt Lake City, UT 84109
www.sonsofutahpioneers.org

This group was organized in 1907 for male lineage descendants of those who came to Utah prior to completion of the railroad, 10 May 1869.

Printed Works

Biographies of the Members of the Salt Lake Chapter, Sons of Utah Pioneers. Salt Lake City: Genealogical Society of Utah, 1980. A collection of sketches contributed by members.

Jackson, Ronald Vern, and David L. Grundvig. *Directory of Individuals Residing in Salt Lake City Wards 1854–1861*. Early Mormon Series, Vol. 1. Salt Lake City: the authors, 1982.

List of Pioneers of 1847 with Biographical Notes from the Journal of the History of the Church 1847 and the Historical Record. Vol. 9. Salt Lake City: Genealogical Society of Utah, n.d.

The Pioneer, a monthly publication. 32 vols. to 1983.

National Society Sons and Daughters of the Pilgrims

5 Reed Ranch Road
Tiburon, CA 94920-2022
www.nssdp.com

This group was organized in 1908 for lineal descendants of settlers (Pilgrims) in any of the colonies prior to 1700.

Printed Works

Lineage Book. 8 vols. to date. The society, 2000.

The Pilgrim News-Letter, a semiannual publication with news of various state branches and the annual General Court.

National Society of Old Plymouth Colony Descendants

24 Pilgrim Dr.
Winchester, MA 01890-3371

This group was organized in 1910. Applicants must prove descent from a man or woman who came to Old Plymouth Colony before 1641.

Order of First Families of North Carolina

P.O. Box 41923
Memphis, TN 39174

Membership is based upon descent from an ancestor who resided in the Province of North Carolina prior to 12 July 1729.

The Society of the Ark and the Dove

3580 South River Terrace
Edgewater, MD 21037-3245
www.thearkandthedove.com

This group was founded in 1910 for lineal descendants of Sir George Calvert, the first Lord Baltimore, and settlers who came in *The Ark* or *The Dove* in March 1634.

Order of the First Families of Virginia

5916 Powhatan Ave.
Norfolk, VA 23508

This society was founded in 1912 to honor Virginia, the first permanent English colony on this continent. Membership is by invitation only and is limited to lineal descendants of those who aided in the establishment of the Virginia Colony, 1607 to 1624.

Printed Works

Adventurers of Purse and Person: Virginia 1607–1624/5. John Frederick Dorman, ed. 4th ed. Projected 3 vol. set. Baltimore: Genealogical Publishing Co., 2004.

Order of Scions of Colonial Cavaliers 1640–1660

1051 Forrest Hills Dr.
Bogart, GA 30622-2442
www.hereditary.us/societies/cavaliers

Formed in 1908, the society was reconstituted in 1999. Eligibility is based upon descent from an ancestor who during the English Civil Wars resided in the New World and remained loyal to the crown. The ancestor must have had claim to not less than 1,000 acres of land during his lifetime. The rebuttable presumption is that persons living in Virginia, Barbados, and the British sugar islands were Cavaliers, while those in New England were not. Membership is for males only.

Society of Indiana Pioneers

140 North Senate Ave.
Indianapolis, IN 46204-2207
www.indianapioneers.com

This group was founded in 1916 for lineal descendants of residents of the state during the pioneer period, 1825 to 1850, when the last two counties were added.

Printed Works

Dorrel, Ruth. *Pioneer Ancestors of Members of the Society of Indiana Pioneers.* Indianapolis: Family History Section Indiana Historical Society, 1983.

Yearbook of the Society of Indiana Pioneers. Indianapolis: Society of Indiana Pioneers.

Louisiana Colonials

5 South Lark St.
New Orleans, LA 70124

This society was founded in 1917 for all lineal descendants of colonists of the Louisiana Territory before it became a state on 30 April 1803.

Printed Works

Arthur, Stanley C., and George C. H. de Kernion. *Old Families of Louisiana.* 1932; reprint, Baltimore: Genealogical Publishing Co., 1971.

DeVille, Winston. *Gulf Coast Colonials: A Compendium of French Families in Early 18th Century Louisiana.* Baltimore: Genealogical Publishing Co., 1968.

———. *Louisiana Recruits.* Cottonport, La.: Polyanthos, 1973.

———. *The New Orleans French 1720–1733.* Baltimore: Genealogical Publishing Co., 1973.

Seebold, Herman deBachelle. *Old Louisiana Plantation Homes and Family Trees.* 2 vols. 1941; reprint, the author, 1971.

Sons and Daughters of the First Settlers of Newbury, Massachusetts

P.O. Box 444
Newburyport, MA 01950

This group was founded in 1927 for all lineal descendants of those who settled at Newbury before 1700.

Printed Works

The Directory of Ancestors of the Sons and Daughters of the First Settlers of Newbury, Massachusetts, 1635–1985. Supplement, 1995. Newbury, Ma.: Sons and Daughters of the First Settlers of Newbury, 1985 and 1995.

Hoyt, David W. *The Old Families of Salisbury and Amesbury with Some Related Families of Newbury, Haverhill, Ipswich, and Hampton, and of York County, Maine.* 1879–1919; reprint, Baltimore: Genealogical Publishing Co., 1982.

John J. Currier, of Newbury Port, 1764–1905. 2 vols. 1906–09; reprint, Baltimore: Genealogical Publishing Co., 1977–78.

National Society of First Families of Delmarva

Box 304
Claymont, DE 19703-0304

Membership is based upon descent from a settler of Delaware, the Eastern Shore of Maryland, or the Eastern Shore of Virginia (the Delmarva Peninsula) prior to 1700.

Society of the Descendants of the Founders of Hartford

P.O. Box 270215
West Hartford, CT 06127-0215
www.societyct.org/hartford.htm

This group was organized in 1931 to honor the founder, the Reverend Thomas Hooker, and the early settlers of Hartford, Connecticut. Membership requires lineal descent from an ancestor who settled in Hartford before February 1640.

Printed Works

Barbour, Lucius Barnes. *Families of Early Hartford Connecticut.* 2nd rev. ed. Baltimore: Genealogical Publishing Co., 1982.

Jamestowne Society

P.O. Box 17426
Richmond, VA 23226
www.jamestowne.org

This group was founded in 1936. Membership is open to descendants of stockholders in the Virginia Company of London or of settlers at Jamestown or on Jamestown Island before 1700.

Printed Works

Inman, Joseph Francis. *Historical Highlights of the Jamestowne Society's First Quarter of a Century—Roster of Members 1936–1971.* Richmond, Va.: the society, 1971.

The Jamestowne Society Register of Qualifying Seventeenth Century Ancestors. Richmond, Va.: the society, 2003.

The Jamestowne Society—Roster of Active Members, February, 2003. Richmond, Va.: the society, 2003. Includes articles of incorporation, bylaws of the society, and the qualifying ancestor of each member.

Order of Descendants of Ancient Planters

109 Southern Hills Drive
New Bern, NC 28562
www.ancientplanters.org

Membership is based upon descent from an Ancient Planter. The ancestor must have arrived in Virginia before 1616, remained for three years, paid his or her passage, and survived the massacre of 1624.

First Families of Ohio

713 South Main St.
Mansfield, OH 44907-1644
www.ogs.org/about/lineage/php

This society was founded in 1964, with membership restricted to members of the Ohio Genealogical Society with proven descent from an ancestor who settled in the territory, now the state of Ohio, before 1820.

Printed Works

The 1890 Howe Historical Collection of eighty-eight Ohio counties has been reprinted in eighty-eight individual pamphlets containing biographies and history.

Ohio Genealogical Society. *First Families of Ohio: Official Roster.* 2 vols. to date. Mansfield, Ohio: Ohio Genealogical Society, 1982–.

The Order of the First Families of Mississippi 1699–1817

West Cyprus Dr.
Cary, MS 39054

This society was founded in 1967 for lineal descendants of natives or residents of the old territory now included in the state of Mississippi, between the French establishment of Old Biloxi in 1699 and statehood on 10 December 1817.

Printed Works

Johnson, Charles Owen, ed. *Order of the First Families of Mississippi, 1699–1817.* Ann Arbor, Mich.: Edwards Brothers, 1991.

Descendants of Jersey Settlers of Adams County, Mississippi

11 Thorn Drive
Natchez, MS 39120

Membership is based upon descent from settlers in and near Natchez, Mississippi, between 1772 and 1775 in the Swayze and King emigrations.

Printed Works

Preston, Frances. *The History of the Descendants of the Jersey Settlers of Adams County, Mississippi.* 2 vols. Jackson, Miss.: the society, 1981.

Descendants of the Founders of New Jersey

10 Buckingham Ave.
Trenton, NJ 08618
www.njfounders.org

This organization was founded in 1982 for descendants of founders who were in any area which is now in the state of New Jersey before 13 December 1685.

Printed Works

Founders of New Jersey: Brief Biographies of Descendants. N.p.: Descendants of the Founders of New Jersey, 1985–.

Descendants of the Founders of Ancient Windsor

P.O. Box 39
Windsor, CT 06095
www.societyct.org/windsor.htm

This organization was founded in 1983 for descendants of people who resided in Windsor, Connecticut, before 1640.

The Hereditary Order of the First Families of Massachusetts

300 North Hill Road
Sutton, WV 26601-1206

This order was founded in 1985 for descendants of ancestors who were residents of the Massachusetts Bay Colony before 1650.

First Families of South Carolina

P.O. Box 21328
Charleston, SC 29413

First Families of Georgia

PO Box. 478
Swainsboro, GA 30401-0478

First Families of Georgia was founded in 1986 for descendants of settlers who resided in the territory now known as Georgia from 1733 to 1797.

Printed Works

First Families of Georgia 1733–1797 Lineage Book. N.p., the society, 2002.

National Society First Families of Minnesota

3917 Heritage Hills Drive #104
Bloomington, MN 55437-2633

This group was founded in 1990 for descendants of ancestors who settled in Minnesota before statehood (11 May 1858) in territory that is now the state of Minnesota.

Order of the First Families of Rhode Island and Providence Plantations 1636–1742

300 North Hill Rd.
Sutton, WV 26601-1206

The order was founded in 1991 for descendants of ancestors who resided in the colony of Rhode Island or the Providence plantations, 1636 to 1647.

Printed Works

First Roster of Members. N.p.: the order, 1993.

Lively Experiment. Washington, D.C.: the order, 1993–.

First Families of the Twin Territories

P.O. Box 12986
Oklahoma City, OK 73157
www.rootsweb.com/~okgs/fftt.htm

Printed Works

First Families of the Twin Territories: Our Ancestors in Oklahoma Before Statehood. Oklahoma City: Oklahoma Genealogical Society, 1997.

Colonial Societies

These groups involve descent from ancestors who were active during the colonial period. The cutoff date is generally 4 July 1776, but there are exceptions which are noted. The following societies are listed in the order of founding.

Colonial Dames of America

421 E. 61st St.
New York, NY 10021
www.cdamesusa.org

The society was founded in 1890 for women of lineal descent from worthy ancestors who held public office or a commission in the armed forces, from the settlement of Jamestown on 13 May 1607 to 19 April 1775. There are chapters in fourteen major cities, the District of Columbia, London, Paris, and Rome.

Printed Works

Ancestral Records and Portraits—A Compilation from the Archives of Chapter 1, Baltimore, Maryland, of the Colonial Dames of America. 2 vols. Bowie, Md.: Heritage Books, 1994.

The National Society of the Colonial Dames of America

2715 Q St. N.W.
Washington, DC 20007
www.nscda.org

This society was founded in 1891 for women of lineal descent from residents of the American colonies before 1750 who rendered service to their country before 5 July 1776, including the signers of the Declaration of Independence. There are societies in some forty states and the District of Columbia.

Printed Works

Sloan, Alice Richardson, ed. *The National Society of the Colonial Dames of America: Register of Ancestors.* Washington, D.C.: the society, 1990.

Colonial Order of the Acorn

20 Mackensie Glen
Greenwich, CT 06730

This order was founded in 1894 for male lineal descendants of people who were residents of American colonies before 4 July 1776. Membership is limited to two hundred, and applicants must be proposed in writing by a proposer and seconder. The society does not emphasize military or civil service and can commemorate events not associated with wars. The New York chapter was the first organized; Maryland and Connecticut chapters were authorized, but it is believed that only the New York chapter is presently active.

Printed Works

Views of Early New York with Illustrative Sketches. New York: the society, 1904.

The Colonial Society of Pennsylvania

215 South 16th St.
Philadelphia, PA 19102

This group was founded in 1895 for male lineal descendants of ancestors who settled before 1700 in any of the American colonies.

Printed Works

The Colonial Society of Pennsylvania: Charter, Constitution, By-laws, Officers, Members, Etc. 4 vols. Philadelphia: the society, 1908, 1914, 1931, 1950. Contains a line of descent for each member.

Lloyd, Mark F. *The Colonial Society of Pennsylvania Centennial Register 1895–2000 and Proceedings of the Society 1995–2000.*

The National Society Colonial Daughters of the Seventeenth Century

P.O. Box 200
Harvel, IL 62538

This organization was founded in 1896 for women lineally descended from ancestors who rendered service from 1607 through 1699, according to the society's eligibility list. Membership is by invitation only.

Printed Works

National Society of the Colonial Daughters of the Seventeenth Century, Lineage Book. 8 vols. Brooklyn, N.Y.: the society, 1898, 1907, 1916, 1923, 1932, 1942, 1968. The 1968 volume contains the names of more than 1,800 colonists and their qualifying service.

National Society, Colonial Daughters of the Seventeenth Century. Lineage Book, 1896–1979. Brooklyn, N.Y.: the society, 1979.

The Hereditary Order of the Descendants of Colonial Governors

4 Stable Rd.
Tuxedo Park, NY 10987-4025

The order was founded in 1896 for lineal descendants of those men who exercised supreme executive power in the American colonies before 1775. Membership is by invitation only.

Printed Works

The List of the Colonial Governors and the Chief Executives of America Prior to 4 July 1776. N.p.: Hereditary Order of Descendants of Colonial Governors, 1989.

Thurtle, Robert G. *Hereditary Order of Descendants of Colonial Governors 1980.* Ann Arbor, Mich.: Published for the Society by Edwards Brothers, 1980.

Order of Americans of Armorial Ancestry

P.O. Box 339
Pembroke, KY 42266-0339

This order was founded in 1903 for lineal descendants of immigrants in the original colonies who had a proven right to "bear coat armor" in the country of their origin.

Printed Works

Finnell, Arthur Louis, comp. *The Order of Americans of Armorial Ancestry Lineage of Members.* Baltimore: Clearfield, 1997.

Descendants of the Signers of the Declaration of Independence

3137 Periwinkle Ct.
Adamstown, MD 21710
www.dsdi1776.com

This society was founded in 1907 for all lineal descendants of those who signed the Declaration of Independence.

Printed Works

Pyne, Frederick W. *Descendants of the Signers of the Declaration of Independence.* 7 vols. Camden, Maine: Picton Press, 1997–2003.

The Order of Colonial Lords of Manors in America

P.O. Box 269
Roxbury, CT 06783

This society was founded in 1911 for lineal descendants of the order's twenty-seven recognized patroons, lords of the manor, or seigniors. Membership is by invitation only.

Printed Works

Smith, Ruth Tangier, and Henry B. Hoff. *The Tangier Smith Family: Descendants of Colonel William Smith of the Manor of St. George, Long Island, New York*. New York: Order of the Colonial Lords of Manors in America, 1978.

Check family genealogies on the following names: Archer, Billop, Brooke, Claggett, de Lotbiniere, Heathcote, Herman, Gardiner (2), Livingston, Lloyd, Mayhew, Melyn, Morris, Paine, Palmer, Pell, Philips, Sewell, Tangier Smith, Sylvester, Van Courtlandt (2), van der Donck, Van Rensselaer, Winthrop, and Wyllys.

The National Society of Colonial Dames of the XVII Century

1300 New Hampshire Ave. N.W.
Washington, DC 20036-1595
www.colonialdames17c.net

This group was founded in 1915 for women of lineal descent from ancestors who lived in the eleven British colonies of America before 1701 as an immigrant colonist or as a descendant of one.

Printed Works

Hutton, Mary Louise Marshall. *Seventeenth Century Colonial Ancestors of Members of the National Society Colonial Dames XVII Century*. Baltimore: Genealogical Publishing Co., 1983.

Schafer, Catsy Hopkins. *Roll of Arms / Lineage and Research Sources Submitted by Members*. San Diego, Calif.: National Society Colonial Dames XVII Century, 1993.

The Seventeenth Century Review. 25 vols. to 1983. Washington D.C.: National Society Colonial Dames XVII Century, 1900s–.

Watts, Diane Cecile. *Heraldry–Coats of Arms National Society Colonial Dames XVII Century*. Dallas: Taylor Publishing Co., 2003.

National Society Daughters of American Colonists

2205 Massachusetts Ave. N.W.
Washington, DC 20008
www.nsdac.org

The society was founded in 1921 for female lineal descendants of those who rendered civil or military service in any of the colonies before 4 July 1776.

Printed Works

The Colonial Courier. 25 vols. to 1983.

Lineage Book. Vol. 1. 1929–.

NSDAC Bicentennial Ancestor Index for Lineage Volumes 1 to 19 Inclusive and Supplemental Volumes. Washington, D.C.: National Society Daughters of the American Colonists, 1976.

National Society of the Dames of the Court of Honor

3535 Hanover Road
Louisville, KY 40207-4359

This group was founded in 1921 for female lineal descendants of colonial governors or commissioned officers who served during the American wars, 1607 to 1865; colonial wars and colonial governors, 1607 to 1775; the American Revolution, 1775 to 1783; the War of 1812, 1784 to 1815; the Mexican War, 1836 to 1838; and the Civil War, 1861 to 1865. Membership is by invitation only.

Printed Works

Research sources for all of the war societies also apply to this society.

The Society of Descendants of the Colonial Clergy

17 Lowell Mason Road
Medfield, MA 02052

This group was founded in 1933 for lineal descendants of any clergyman regularly ordained, installed, or settled over any Christian church in the original colonies before 4 July 1776.

Printed Works

Pedigrees of Descendants of the Colonial Clergy: 1978 Supplement to the 1976 Bicentennial Register of Pedigrees of Descendants of the Colonial Clergy. Lancaster, Pa.: Society of the Descendants of the Colonial Clergy, 1978.

Weis, Frederick Lewis. *The Colonial Clergy and the Colonial Churches of New England*. Lancaster, Mass.: the society, 1936.

———. *The Colonial Clergy of Maryland, Delaware, and Georgia*. Lancaster, Mass.: the society, 1950.

———. *The Colonial Clergy of the Middle Colonies, New York, New Jersey and Pennsylvania 1628–1776*. Worcester, Mass.: the society, 1957.

———. *The Colonial Clergy of Virginia, North Carolina and South Carolina*. Boston: the society, 1955.

The National Society of the Lords of the Maryland Manors

13070 Riverhaven Pl.
Newburg, MD 20664

This society was founded in 1938 for lineal descendants of the first Baron Baltimore, or of one or more of the colonists who were "granted by the Lord Proprietor of Maryland, a manor in fee simple with manorial rights and privileges" before 1722. The society has placed markers at twenty-three manors. Membership is by invitation only.

Printed Works

See sources cited for the Society of the Ark and the Dove.

National Society Southern Dames of America

709 Douglas Dr.
Johnson City, TN 37604-1920
www.geocities.com/southerndames/

This society was founded in 1963 for women of verified Southern ancestry. Membership is by invitation only.

Printed Works

All lineage volumes on the South apply to this society.

Flagon and Trencher—Descendants of Colonial Tavernkeepers

300 North Hill Rd.
Sutton, WV 26601-1206
www.flagonandtrencher.org

This society was founded in 1962 for men and women who are lineal descendants of anyone who conducted a tavern, inn, ordinary, or other type of hostelry on or before 4 July 1776.

Printed Works

Colonial Tavernkeepers: Qualifying Ancestors of Flagon and Trencher Members. 12 vols. to date. N.p.: Flagon and Trencher, 1976–.

Smith, Barbara Carver. *Colonial Taverners Established by Members of the Flagon and Trencher: Descendants of Colonial Tavern Keepers*. Lakewood, N.J.: B. C. Smith, 2001.

Order of Descendants of Colonial Physicians and Chirurgiens

4245 Washington Blvd.
Indianapolis, IN 46205-2618

This order was organized in 1974 for men and women who are lineal descendants of physicians, surgeons, or licensed midwives who practiced on the North American continent during the colonial period through 1783. Membership is by invitation only.

Printed Works

Order of Descendants of Colonial Physicians and Chirurgiens Membership Roster. 2 vols. The society, 1978, 1979. Supplements issued 1980, 1981, 1982.

National Society Sons of American Colonists

3917 Heritage Hills Drive #104
Bloomington, MN 55437-2633
my.execpc.com/~drg/wisac.html

This society was founded in 1958 and reorganized in 1986 for male descendants of ancestors who rendered civil or military service in any of the American colonies before 4 July 1776.

Printed Works

Finnell, Arthur L. *National Society Sons of the American Colonists Colonial Ancestors Roster*. Bloomington, Minn.: the society, 1992.

National Society Sons of Colonial New England

7916 Quill Point Dr.
Bowie, MD 20720-4391
www.nsscne.org

This society was founded in 1985 for male descendants of people born in any of the six New England colonies before 4 July 1776.

Sons and Daughters of the Antebellum Bench and Bar 1565–1861

7505 Tenth St. Circle, North
Wichita, KS 67206-3844

Printed Works

Smith, David C. *Sons and Daughters of the Colonial and Antebellum Bench and Bar, 1561–1861: Register of Ancestors*. N.p.: Sons and Daughters of the Colonial and Antebellum Bench and Bar, 2001.

Nationality (Ethnic) Societies

Among the oldest lineage societies established in the United States, these include many charitable societies founded for English, Irish, Scottish, and Welsh immigrants in the major port cities of the Atlantic coast. These societies are listed by the date of founding.

The Welsh Society of Philadelphia

P.O. Box 7287
Saint Davids, PA 19807-7287
http://members.macconnect.com/users/d/dalex

This group was organized in 1729 for men of Welsh birth or descent. It is the oldest hereditary society in Philadelphia and was founded as a charitable society to aid distressed Welshmen.

Printed Works

Hartmann, Edward George. *The Welsh Society of Philadelphia—History, Charter and By-Laws, and Membership List*. Philadelphia: the society, 1980. Printed for the 250th anniversary of the society's founding.

The Saint Andrew's Society

215 South 16th St.
Philadelphia, PA 19102
www.standrewsociety.org

220 E. Liberty St.
Savannah, GA 30141-4402

150 E. 55th St. 3rd floor
New York, NY 10022
www.standrewsny.org

150 Washington Ave.
Albany, NY 12200

Saint Andrew's Society was established in Charleston, South Carolina, in 1729; Philadelphia, Pennsylvania, in 1747; Savannah, Georgia, in 1750; New York City in 1756; Alexandria, Virginia, in 1780; Albany, New York, in 1803; and Washington, D.C., in 1855. The society is for men of Scottish birth or descent except in Charleston, where there are no restrictions on lineage, although membership is limited to thirty. Later societies have been organized throughout the United States.

Printed Works

An Historical Sketch of the Saint Andrew's Society of Philadelphia with Biographical Sketches of Deceased Members 1749–1913. 2 vols. Philadelphia: the society, 1907–13.

History of the Saint Andrew's Society of the City of Charleston, South Carolina 1729–1929. Charleston, S.C.: the society, 1929.

Kimmear, Peter. *Historical Sketch of the Saint Andrew's Society of the City of Albany 1803–1903*. Albany, N.Y.: Weed-Parsons, 1903.

Morrison, David Baillie, ed. *Two Hundredth Anniversary, 1756–1956, of the Saint Andrew's Society of the State of New York*. Philadelphia and New York: Clark Printing House, 1956.

The Saint George's Society of New York

216 East 45th St., Ste. 901
New York, NY 10017-3304

The society was established in Charleston, South Carolina, in 1733; New York in 1770; Philadelphia in 1722; and Baltimore in 1867. Membership is restricted to men of English birth or ancestry, except for the Charleston Society, which has no ancestry restrictions but limits membership to thirty.

Printed Works

Knauf, Theodore C. *A History of the Society of the Sons of St. George Established at Philadelphia, Etc.* Philadelphia: the society, 1923.

The Society of the Friendly Sons of Saint Patrick

P.O. Box 969
Dublin, PA 18917-0969
www.friendlysons.com

This group was organized in 1771 in Philadelphia for the relief of immigrants from Ireland, with membership restricted to men of Irish birth or descent.

Printed Works

Campbell, John M. *The History of the Friendly Sons of St. Patrick and the Hibernian Society*. Philadelphia: the society, 1982.

Clark, Dennis J. *A History of the Society of the Friendly Sons of St. Patrick for Relief of Emigrants from Ireland in Philadelphia 1951–1981*. Philadelphia: the society, 1982.

Dougherty, Daniel. *History of the Friendly Sons of St. Patrick for the Relief of Emigrants from Ireland in Philadelphia*. Philadelphia: the society, 1892.

Hood, Samuel. *A Brief Account of the Friendly Sons of St. Patrick*. Philadelphia: the society, 1844.

Saint David's Society of New York

71 West 23rd St. #508
New York, NY 10010

Saint David's Society was founded in 1835 for men of Welsh birth or who are descended from those connected by ties of consanguinity or marriage. Before this, Welshmen had participated in the Saint David's Benevolent Society, founded in 1801, and the Ancient Britons Benefit Society, founded in 1805.

Printed Works

Saint David's Society of the State of New York—Origin and Purpose of the Society. New York: the society, n.d.

Holland Society of New York

122 East 58th St.
New York, NY 10022
www.hollandsociety.org

The Holland Society was founded in 1885 for male descendants (in the direct male line only) of Dutchmen who were natives or residents of New York or the American colonies before 1675.

Printed Works

De Halve Maen. Vol. 1. 1922–.

Duermyer, Louis, ed. *Index to Publications, 1885–January 1977*. New York: the society, 1977.

Holland Society of New York Yearbook. 38 vols. New York: the society, 1886–1937.

Index to Publications of the Holland Society of New York. New York: the society, 1959.

The Netherlands Society of Philadelphia

P.O. Box 54017
Philadelphia, PA 19105-4017

This group was founded in 1892 for male lineal descendants of a Dutch ancestor who settled in the American colonies before 4 July 1776, or who, born in the Netherlands, emigrated to the United States after 1776.

Printed Works

The Netherlands Society of Philadelphia—An Account of the Organization, Purposes and Traditions. Philadelphia: the society, 1966.

Swedish Colonial Society

3406 Macomb St., N.W.
Washington, DC 20016
www.colonialswedes.org

This group was founded in 1909 for men and women of lineal descent from Swedish colonists who were in the United States before 1783 (known as Forefather Members) as well as any person interested in the history of the early Swedes in America.

Printed Works

Johnson, Amandus. *The Swedish Settlements on the Delaware, 1638–1664*. 2 vols. 1911; reprint, Philadelphia, 1969.

The Swedish Colonial Society, Governor Johan Printz Memorial Edition, History, Charter, By-Laws, Officers, Members, Publications, Etc. Philadelphia: the society, 1954.

The Dutch Settlers Society of Albany

608 25th St.
Watervliet, NY 12189
www.timesunion.com/communities/dutchsettlers/

This group was founded in 1924 for male and female descendants of pre-1665 residents of Fort Orange, the colony of Rensselaerswick, or the village of Beverwyck.

Printed Works

Records of the Dutch Reformed Church of Albany, New York 1683–1809 as Excerpted from Year Books of the Holland Society of New York. 1904–27; reprint, Baltimore: Genealogical Publishing Co., 1978.

Wilcoxen, Charlotte. *Seventeenth Century Albany: A Dutch Profile*. Albany, N.Y.: Albany Institute, 1981.

Yearbook – The Dutch Settlers Society of Albany. Vol. 1. Albany, N.Y.: the society, 1924–.

Religious Societies

The Huguenot Society of America

122 East 58th St.
New York, NY 10022
www.huguenotsocietyofamerica.org

This group was founded in 1883 in New York City for male and female lineal descendants of Huguenot families that immigrated to America before the Edict of Toleration of 28 November 1787.

Printed Works

Collections of the Huguenot Society of America—Registers of the Births, Marriages and Deaths of the Eglise Francois a la Nouvelle York, from 1688 to 1804. Vol. 1 only. New York: the society, 1886.

Huguenot Refugees in the Settling of Colonial America. New York: Huguenot Society of America, 1989.

The Huguenot Society of America: History Organization, Activities, Membership, Constitution, Huguenot Ancestors, and Other Matters of Interest. New York: the society, 1993.

The Huguenot Society of South Carolina

138 Logan St.
Charleston, SC 29401-1941
www.huguenotsociety.org

This organization was founded in 1885 in Charleston, South Carolina, for male and female lineal descendants of Huguenot families that immigrated to America before the Edict of Toleration of 28 November 1787.

Printed Works

DuBose, S., and F. Porcher. *History of the Huguenots of South Carolina.* N.p., 1887.

Transactions of the Huguenot Society of South Carolina, No. 1–. Index, 1899–1994.

The Huguenot Society of the Founders of Manakin in the Colony of Virginia

981 Huguenot Trail
Midlothian, VA 23133-9224
www.huguenot-manakin.org

This group was founded in 1922 for male and female lineal descendants of any pre-1786 Huguenot resident of Virginia. Associate membership is provided for descendants from Huguenots who resided outside of Virginia.

Printed Works

Brock, R. A. *Documents, Chiefly Unpublished, Relating to the Huguenot Emigration to Virginia . . . with an Appendix of Genealogies.* 1886; reprint, Baltimore: Genealogical Publishing Co., 2000.

The Huguenot. Vol. 1. The society, 1924–.

Master Index to the Huguenot: The Biennial Publications of the Huguenot Society, Founders of Manakin in the Colony of Virginia; and, Index to Vestry Book of King William Parish, Virginia 1707–1750. Bryan, Tex.: Family History Publications, 1986.

National Huguenot Society

9033 Lyndale Ave. S., Suite 108
Bloomington, MN 55420-3535
www.huguenot.netnation.com/general

This group was organized in 1951 as a federation of state societies. In 1983 there were forty-two state society organizations, including the District of Columbia. Individual applicants join a local state society and automatically become a member of the national society.

Printed Works

Finnell, Arthur L. *The Huguenot Society of New England: 1924–1949 Roster of Members and Ancestors.* Bloomington, Md.: National Huguenot Society, 1993.

———. *National Huguenot Society Bible Records Abstracted from the Files of the Society.* Baltimore: Clearfield, 1995.

———. *Register of Qualified Huguenot Ancestors of the National Huguenot Society.* Bloomington, Minn.: the society, 1995. Updates have appeared in 1995, 1996, 1997, 1998, and 1999.

National Society Descendants of Early Quakers

6876 Richard Wilson Dr.
Millington, TN 38053-3934
www.terraworld.net/mlwinton

Printed Works

Plain Language. Vol. 1. 1981. Ongoing; published by the society after each annual meeting.

Royal and Baronial Societies

All of the societies in this grouping, listed by date of founding, require the applicant to trace the ancestry of an immigrant ancestor to his or her native country until noble or royal ancestry is reached. Establishing the proper "gateway" ancestor is the major problem for most applicants. The first two volumes listed are of great assistance in locating such ancestors. They are the only editions with acceptable proof for the various royal and baronial lineage societies. While the majority of the *Ancestral Roots* ancestry is of the New England area, nearly half of *The Magna Charta* lines are Virginian. *The Complete Peerage* is the most acceptable proof for all peerage lines.

Cokayne, George E., ed. *The Complete Peerage.* 14 vols. London, 1910–98.

Weis, Frederick Lewis. *Ancestral Roots of Sixty Colonists Who Came to America Before 1700. The Lineage of Alfred the Great, Charlemagne, Malcolm of Scotland, Robert the Strong and Some of Their Descendants.* 7th ed. Baltimore: Genealogical Publishing Co., 1999.

———. *The Magna Charta Sureties, 1215: The Barons Named in the Magna Charta 1215 and Some of Their Descendants.* 5th ed. Baltimore: Genealogical Publishing Co., 1992.

Order of the Crown in America

Box 27023
Philadelphia, PA 19018

This society was founded in 1898 as an order for men and women of proven royal descent, with the stipulation that ladies be members in good standing of either the Colonial Dames of America or the National Society of Colonial Dames of America. Membership is limited and by invitation only.

Printed Works

The History, Constitution and Officers of the Order of the Crown in America. The order, 1902, 1917, 1927.

Order of the Crown in America Membership Roster. The order, 1962, 1968, 1971, 1975, 1981, 1986, 1991.

The Baronial Order of Magna Charta

109 Glenview Avenue
Wyncote, PA 19095
www.magnacharta.com

This society was founded in 1898 for male lineal descendants of the earls and barons who were elected to be the sureties of the Magna Charta shortly after 19 June 1215. Membership is by invitation only. Note: This society assimilated The Military Order of the Crusades in 1998.

Printed Works

Bye, Arthur Edwin. *Magna Charta, King John and The Barons.* Bridgeport, Penn: Chancellor Press, 1967.

Weis, Frederick Lewis, and Arthur Adams. *The Magna Charta Sureties 1215.* 3rd ed., with additions and corrections by Walter Lee Sheppard Jr. Baltimore: Genealogical Publishing Co., 1979.

The National Society of Americans of Royal Descent

1050 N. Stuart St., Apt. 228
Arlington, VA 22201-5711

This group was founded in 1908 for men and women of proven royal descent. An applicant must be a member of a recognized lineage society of the colonial period, and a female applicant must be a member of either the National Society of the Colonial Dames of America or of the Colonial Dames of America. Applicants also need to be known by at least one member of the group's executive council and be proposed and seconded in writing. Membership is by invitation only.

Printed Works

National Society of Americans of Royal Descent—History, Membership Roster, Constitution and By-Laws. The society, 1960, 1965, 1968, 1971, 1974, 1977, 1980, 1983, 1989.

National Society Magna Charta Dames and Barons

P.O. Box 4222
Philadelphia, PA 19144
www.magnacharta.org

The society was founded in 1909 for female descendants of the Magna Charta Sureties of 1215. Membership is by invitation of the council, following proposal by a present member.

Printed Works

Wurts, John S. *Magna Charta.* 8 vols. Philadelphia: the author, 1942.

The National Society Daughters of the Barons of Runnemede

7736 Bridle Path Ln.
McLean, VA 22102

This group was organized in 1921 for women of lineal descent from one or more of the barons who served as sureties of the Magna Charta in 1215. Membership is by invitation only, following proposal by a present member.

Printed Works

National Society Daughters of the Barons of Runnemede—Organization, History and Membership—With Full-Color Arms of the Barons. Athens, Ga.: McGregor Co., 1937. Contains biographical sketches of the "gateway" ancestors of the members and sketches of the founders of the society.

The Military Order of the Crusades

109 Glenview Avenue
Wyncote, PA 19095
www.magnacharta.com/articles/MOC01.htm

The Military Order of the Crusades was founded in 1934 for men of lineal descent from one or more crusaders of the rank of knight or higher who participated in the Crusades, 1096 to 1291. Membership is by invitation only. This organization merged with the Baronial Order of Magna Charta in 1998.

Manuscript Documents in Possession of the Order

History, Constitution and By-Laws. The order, 1960.

Perot, William Hannis. *List of Crusaders Used as Qualifying Ancestors by the Order to 7 June 1977.*

Order of Three Crusades 1096–1192

15 Ruxview Court, # 302
Ruxton, MD 21204-6635

This order was founded in 1936 for men and women of lineal descent from a participant in one of the first three crusades, 1096 to 1192. A pilgrimage to Jerusalem as a religious gesture was not a crusade and is not acceptable. Membership is by invitation only, and applicants must be sponsored by two members and be known to at least one officer of the order.

Printed Works

Order of Three Crusades 1096–1192—History, Constitution and By-Laws, Membership Roster. 4 vols. The order, 1965, 1970, 1976, 1983.

Order of the Crown of Charlemagne in the United States of America

14115 41st Ave. N.
Plymouth, MN 55446
www.charlemagne.org

This society was founded in 1939 for men and women of lineal descent from the Emperor Charlemagne. Membership is by invitation only.

Printed Works

Pedigrees of Some of Emperor Charlemagne's Descendants. 3 vols. Baltimore: Genealogical Publishing Co., 1972.

Descendants of the Illegitimate Sons and Daughters of the Kings of Britain

2153 Meadowbrook Ct. #9
Santa Rosa, CA 95403

This group was founded in 1950 by four fellows of the American Society of Genealogists to improve scholarship and research on all "royal lineages." Membership is open to men and women who can prove their descent, in any line, from the illegitimate son, daughter, grandson, or granddaughter of a king or queen of England, Scotland, or Wales.

A manuscript titled "Royal Bastards from the Time of the Norman Conquest—the Constitution, Annual Reports, Lineages of Descents of Members, Etc." is provided to members in loose-leaf form, to be added to three-ring binders as new members join. Approximately two hundred lineages have been approved.

Printed Works

Sheppard, Walter Lee, Jr. "Descendants of the Illegitimate Sons and Daughters of the Kings of Britain." *National Genealogical Society Quarterly* 62 (September 1974): 182–91.

Guild of St. Margaret of Scotland

Dr. Clifton R. Brooks, Sr.
10717 Sunset Blvd.
Oklahoma City, OK 73120-2427

The guild was founded in 1975 for descendants of St. Margaret of Scotland; or of an early king or queen of England, Ireland, Scotland, or Wales; or of an ancestor who lived in the British Isles before 1600.

Suggestions for the Serious Lineage Society Researcher

Many professional genealogists specialize in preparing lineage papers for their clients. The Association of Professional Genealogists maintains a member database <www.apgen.org>, which is searchable by research speciality, including the preparation of lineage society applications. A similar list, which includes only certified genealogists, is available at the Board for Certification of Genealogists website <www.bcgcertification.org>.

A professional genealogist experienced in lineage applications should be familiar with the requirements for membership in all of the major hereditary societies and the format for documenting applications for each society. Individuals make application for membership in the society and receive the worksheets and application forms. The genealogist should never ask for application blanks for a client.

Documentation is frequently misunderstood. The listing of a volume with pertinent page numbers is not sufficient. Photocopies of all proofs should accompany the application. This will speed up approval by the society's verifying genealogist, who often resides far from a major library and depends entirely on the material submitted. All original copies of vital records, family Bible records, and personal documents should be retained by the applicant. Photocopies from published volumes should include the title page—especially when submitting family Bible records. The page showing the year the Bible was published is vital to establish the fact that the entries were made at that time period.

Never handwrite applications, no matter how legible your writing may be. All applications should be typed, either manually on a typewriter or using a fill-in form on your computer. When two copies are required, type two separate applications.

Appendix E

Historical Societies

A

Alabama Historical Association
624 Washington Ave.
Montgomew, AL 36130
Phone: (334) 242-4435
www.archives.state.al.us/aha/aha.html

Alaska Historical Library and Museum
Alaska Historical Connections
Alaska State Lib.
P.O. Box 110571
Juneau, AK 99811
Phone: (907) 465-2925
http://library.state.ak.us

Alaska Historical Society
P.O. Box 100299
Anchorage, AK 99510
Phone: (907) 276-1596
www.alaskahistoricalsociety.org

Arizona Historical Society
949 E. Second St.
Tuscon, AZ 85719
Phone: (520) 617-1158
www.arizonahistorical society.org

Arkansas Historical Association
416 Old Main, University of Arkansas
Fayetteville, AR 72701
Phone: (479) 575-5884
www.vark.edu/depts/arkhist/home

Arkansas History Commission
1 Capitol Mall
Little Rock, AR 72201
Phone: (501) 682-6900
www.ark-ives.com

C

California Historical Society
678 Mission St.
San Francisco, CA 94105
Phone: (415) 357-1848
www.californiahistoricalsociety.org

Colorado Historical Society
Stephen H. Hart Library
1300 Broadway
Denver, CO 80203
Phone: (303) 866-3682
www.coloradohistory.org

Connecticut Historical Commission
59 S. Prospect St.
Hartford, CT 06106
Phone: (860) 566-3005
www.cultureandtourism.org/history/about.html

Connecticut Historical Society
1 Elizabeth St. at Asylum Ave.
Hartford, CT 06105
Phone: (860) 236-5621
ask_us@chs.org
www.chs.org

Connecticut League of Historical Societies
P.O. Box 906
Darien, CT 06820

D

Historical Society of Delaware
Town Hall
505 Market St.
Wilmington, DE 19801
Phone: (302) 655-7161
Fax: (302) 655-7844
www.hsd.org

F

Florida Historical Society
435 Brevard Ave.
Cocoa, FL 32922
Phone: (321) 690-1971
www.florida-historical-soc.org

G

Georgia Historical Society
501 Whittaker St.
Savannah, GA 31401
Phone: (912) 651-2128
Fax: (912) 651-2831
www.georgiahistory.com

H

Hawaiian Historical Society
560 Kawaiahao St.
Honolulu, HI 96813
Phone: (808) 537-6271
www.hawaiianhistory.org/index.html

I

Idaho Historical Society
1109 Main Street, Suite 250
Boise, ID 83702
Phone: (208) 334-2682
(208) 334-2774
www.idahohistory.net

Illinois State Historical Library
210 ½ S. Sixth
Springfield, IL 62701
Phone: (217) 525-2781
Fax: (217) 525-2783
www.historyillinois.org

Indiana Historical Society
450 West Ohio St.
Indianapolis, IN 46202
Phone: (317) 232-1882
www.indianahistory.org

State Historical Society of Iowa
State of Iowa Historical Building
600 E. Locust
Des Moines, IA 50319
Phone: (515) 281-5111

K

Kansas State Historical Society
6425 SW Sixth Ave.
Topeka, KS 66615
Phone: (785) 272-8681
Fax: (785) 272-8682
www.kshs.org

Kentucky Historical Society
100 W. Broadway
Frankfort, KY 40601
Phone: (502) 564-1792
http://history.ky.gov

L

Louisiana Genealogical and Historical Society
P.O. Box 82060
Baton Rouge, LA 70884
Phone: (504) 343-2608
www.rootsweb.com/%7ela-lghs/index.html

M

Maine Historical Society
489 Congress St.
Portland, ME 04101
Phone: (207) 774-1822
www.mainehistory.org

Maryland Historical Society
201 W. Monument St.
Baltimore, MD 21201
Phone: (410) 685-3750
Fax: (410) 385-2105
www.mdhs.org

Massachusetts Historical Society
1154 Boylston St.
Boston, MA 02215
Phone: (617) 536-1608
Fax: (617) 859-0074
www.masshist.org

Historical Society of Michigan
1305 Abbott Road
East Lansing, MI 48823
Phone: (517) 324-1828
Fax: (517) 324-4370
www.hsmichigan.org

Michigan Historical Commission
Supervisor's Office
Pittsfield Charter Township
6201 W. Michigan Ave.
Ann Arbor, MI 48108
Phone: (734) 822-3135
supervisor@pittsfieldtwp.org

Minnesota Historical Society
345 W. Kellogg Blvd.
Saint Paul, MN 55102
Phone: (651) 296-6126
www.mnhs.org

Historical and Genealogical Association of Mississippi
618 Avalon Rd.
Jackson, MS 39206

Missouri Historical Society
P.O. Box 11940
Saint Louis, MO 63112
Phone: (314) 361-7229
Fax: (314) 454-3612
www.mohistory.org/content/homepage/homepage.aspx

State Historical Society of Missouri
1020 Lowry St.
Columbia, MO 65201
Phone: (573) 882-7083
Fax: (573) 884-4950
www.umsystem.edu/shs

Montana Historical Society
P.O. Box 201201
225 North Roberts
Helena, MT 59620-1201
Phone: (406) 444-2694
www.his.state.mt.us

N

Nebraska State Historical Society
State Archives Division
1500 R St.
P.O. Box 82554
Lincoln, NE 68501
Phone: (402) 471-3270
(402) 471-4751
www.nebraskahistory.org

Nebraska State Historical Society Room (headquarters)
1500 R St.
Lincoln, NE 68501

Nevada State Historical Society
1650 N. Virginia St.
Reno, NV 89503
Phone: (775) 688-1190
Fax: (775) 688-2917

Nevada State Museum and Historical Society
700 Twin Lakes Dr.
Las Vegas, NV 89107
Phone: (702) 486-5205
Fax: (702) 486-5172

Association of Historical Societies of New Hampshire
AHSNH
PMB 101
26 South Main St.
Concord, NH 03301-4848
Phone: 603-926-2543
AHSNH@comcast.net

New Hampshire Historical Society
30 Park St.
Concord, NH 03301
Phone: (603) 228-6688
Fax: (603) 224-0463
www.nhhistory.org

New Jersey Historical Society
52 Park Place
Newark, NJ 07102
Phone: (973) 596-8500
Fax: (973) 596-6957
www.jerseyhistory.org

Historical Society of New Mexico
P.O. Box 1912
Santa Fe, NM 87504
www.hsnm.org

History Library Museum of New Mexico
Palace of the Governors
Santa Fe, NM 87501

The New York Historical Society
170 Central Park W.
New York, NY 10024-5194
Phone: (212) 873-3400
www.nyhistory.org

North Carolina Society of County and Local Historians
1209 Hill St.
Greensboro, NC 27408

State Historical Society of North Dakota
State Archives and Historical Research Library
Heritage Center
612 E. Blvd. Ave.
Bismarck, ND 58505
Phone: (701) 328-2666
Fax: (701) 328-3710

O

Ohio Historical Society
Archives-Library Division
Interstate Route 71 and 17th Ave.
1982 Velma Ave.
Columbus, OH 43211
Phone: (614) 466-1500
(614) 297-2510
(614) 297-2300
www.ohiohistory.org

Oklahoma Historical Society
Library Resources Division
Wiley Post Historical Building
2100 N. Lincoln Blvd.
Oklahoma City, OK 73105
Phone: (405) 521-2491
www.okhistory.mus.ok.us

Oregon Historical Society
1200 S.W. Park Ave.
Portland, OR 97205
Phone: (503) 222-1741

P

Heritage Society of Pennsylvania
300 North Street
Harrisburg, PA 17120
Phone: (717) 787-2407
www.paheritage.org

Historical Society of Pennsylvania
1300 Locust St.
Philadelphia, PA 19107
Phone: (215) 732-6200
Fax: (215) 732-2680

R

Rhode Island State Historical Society (Library)
121 Hope St.
Providence, RI 02906
Phone: (401) 273-8107
Fax: (401) 751-7930
www.rihs.org

S

South Carolina Historical Society
100 Meeting St.
Charleston, SC 29401
Phone: (843) 723-3225
Fax: (843) 723-8584
info@schistory.org

South Dakota State Historical Society
South Dakota Archives
Cultural Heritage Center
900 Governors Dr.
Pierre, SD 57501
Phone: (605) 773-3458
Fax: (605) 773-6041
www.sdhistory.org

T

Tennessee Historical Society
Ground Floor
War Memorial Building
300 Capital Blvd.
Nashville, TN 37243-0084
Phone: (615) 741-8934
Fax: (615) 741-8937

Tennessee Historical Commission
Clover Bottom Mansion
2941 Lebanon Road
Nashville, TN 37243
Phone: (615) 532-1550
www.tennessee.gov/environment/hist

Texas State Historical Association
1 University Station D0901
Austin, TX 78712
Phone: (512) 471-1525
Fax: (512) 471-1551
www.tsha.utexas.edu

U

Utah State Historical Society
300 Rio Grande
Salt Lake City, UT 84101
Phone: (801) 533-3500
Fax: (801) 533-3503, 3504
cergushs@utah.gov
http://history.utah.gov

V

Virginia Historical Society
428 N. Blvd.
P.O. Box 7311
Richmond, VA 23221
Phone: (804) 358-4901
www.vahistorical.org

Vermont Historical Society
Vermont History Center
60 Washington Street
Barre, Vermont 05641-4209
Phone: (802) 479-8500
Fax: (802) 479-8510
www.vermonthistory.org

W

Washington State Historical Society
1911 Pacific Avenue
Tacoma, WA 98402
Phone: (253) 272-9747
www.wshs.org

West Virginia Historical Society
Division of Archives and History
Department of Culture and History
Science and Cultural Center
Capitol Complex
Charleston, WV 25305
Phone: (304) 348-2277
(304) 348-0230

The State Historical Society of Wisconsin
816 State St.
Madison, WI 53706
Phone: (608) 264-6535—Reference Librarian
(608) 264-6460—Reference Archivist
www.wisconsinhistory.org

Wyoming State Archives
Barrett Building
2301 Central Ave.
Cheyenne, WY 82002
Phone: (307) 777-7826
Fax: (307) 777-7044
http://wyoarchives.state.wy.us

Appendix F

The Family History Library and Associated Family History Centers

STEPHEN C. YOUNG,
MANAGER, PATRON SERVICES

The Family History Library, supported and sponsored by The Church of Jesus Christ of Latter-day Saints (sometimes called the "LDS" or "Mormon" Church), is located on the west side of historic Temple Square in the heart of downtown Salt Lake City, Utah. The library's origins stretch back to 1894 with the organization of the Genealogical Society of Utah (GSU) and launched with the donation of the personal collection of historical and genealogical books of its first president, Franklin D. Richards. From this modest beginning more than 110 years ago, the Family History Library has grown into the largest and best known genealogical research facility in the world with its five stories of research space and more than 4,300 satellite family history centers around the world. The main library's continually growing collection now numbers in excess of 285,000 books, augmented by more than 1.3 million rolls of microfilm and 665,000 microfiche. More than 2.5 million rolls of microfilm are actually archived, but due to space constraints only the most commonly used rolls are placed in the library. The GSU is now capturing digital images in its effort to collect and preserve documents of genealogical value from archives and record offices in most of the nations of the world.

The LDS Family History Library in Salt Lake City, Utah, is the world's largest repository of genealogical records.

Photo © 2005 by Intellectual Reserve, Inc. All rights reserved.

All resources of the Family History Library and its associated family history centers are freely available to genealogical researchers regardless of religious denomination or inclination. The motivational commitment to fund this immensely coordinated and expensive network of research facilities is based in the doctrinal imperative for LDS Church members to seek out their kindred dead in order to perform proxy service in their behalf. The Church extends these resources in an invitation for all interested genealogical researchers to use its facilities and participate in preparing the records and information to eventually create the world's largest, most comprehensive lineage-linked database.

During the past century the Family History Library has been located in several different buildings in Salt Lake City. The current five story structure, officially opened in October 1985, is its first independent, purpose-built library facility. It includes 142,000 square feet of floor space on three levels above ground and two below. Two separate remodeling projects in 2001 and 2004 improved staff and patron workspace and furnishings, and updated the technological resources available to researchers, including the addition of more than two hundred desktop computers with Internet access for patron use. Additional public access computers will be introduced into the library in the future as demand increases. Concurrently, numbers of microfilm readers will necessarily be reduced to make space as more genealogical records and indexes become available digitally, including images from the Library's own collections.

The catalog to the collections of the Library can be searched online by visiting the FamilySearch website <www.familysearch.org>, then clicking on the "Library" tab at the top of the page, then clicking the "Family History Library Catalog" tab. Several options for finding specific resources in the collection are presented here, including searching by place, surname, title, author, subject, or call number. A keyword search also provides a specific function for finding entries that contain certain words or combination of words. This latter search feature is particularly useful in discovering sources by intersecting elements such as geographic places with surnames, or multiple surnames of particular interest within a family. It is always a good idea to search the catalog in preparation for coming to the library in order to ascertain whether the records or resources of interest are available, especially if traveling to the library from long distances. Of particular note is the recent and ongoing project of linking hundreds of published family histories in the catalog to digital images of the books themselves. Visitors traveling to Salt Lake City from a distance should check the catalog prior to coming to confirm if the microfilm they wish to use is in the library. If a particular film is not stored onsite, the FamilySearch website has an e-mail function to order films so they are waiting for free pickup at the service window on the appropriate floor.

The Family History Library is open to the public Monday through Saturday from 8 a.m. to 9 p.m., except Mondays when it closes at 5 p.m. The Library is also closed on some national holidays (e.g. Fourth of July, Thanksgiving, Christmas, New Years). Specific closing dates can be determined by accessing the library's calendar at the FamilySearch website. It is recommended that large groups planning visits, either sponsored by local genealogical societies or privately organized, contact the library's Research Services office prior to arrival. Coordinating with this office will reduce the likelihood of many groups visiting the library at the same time and competing for the same resources. Special orientation sessions and a welcome packet can be arranged for visiting groups by calling (801) 240-1054. Classroom instruction on a variety of general and specific research topics is offered on a daily basis by library staff. A monthly printable class schedule is accessible from the library website and is usually posted three months in advance.

The main floor lobby, just inside the front doors, provides ample signage to direct users to the resources of the library. Don't be surprised if one of the friendly staff stationed in the lobby approaches and offers assistance; they are trained and eager to provide support to the public, especially newcomers.

One of the first services offered may be a short presentation in the Orientation Room located just off the lobby. All first-time visitors to the Family History Library are encouraged to view this video presentation as it illustrates and explains where the public services and resources are located in the building.

Novice researchers should bring family information to the library with an idea of what goals they wish to accomplish during their visit. A trained staff member at the front counter is available to interview patrons and quickly analyze historical documentation they've brought to determine where and how they might find success in the library. Volunteers will then escort these patrons to the appropriate floor of the building and introduce them to additional personnel to further assist them in beginning their research. Genealogical research can appear very complicated and intimidating to the novice, so this guided experience is designed to maximize the chances of success.

Each floor of the library has restroom facilities and drinking fountains. Public telephones are located near the elevators on each floor. Cellular phones should only be used in this area so that quiet search rooms in the building are not compromised and other patrons can conduct their research uninterrupted. A stairway and three elevators at the front of the building deliver patrons to each of five floors of the library and all exits are well-marked.

Another standard service on every floor is a reference counter staffed by people skilled in genealogical research methodology, strategies, and resources. In addition to these general skills, these staff members have distinct research experience in the genealogical records of different nations or even specific regions within those countries. Visitors will find at least forty computers available for their use on each floor of the library. Additional staff with general and specific expertise are stationed and tasked to assist patrons in using the computer for genealogical research.

Each search room has small lockers available for patron use for a refundable fee of ten cents. For security purposes personal items may not be left in the lockers overnight and they are emptied by security personnel each evening after closing. The Lost and Found service is found in the Main Floor lobby. Coat racks are available on every level but it should be noted they are not monitored by security. Valuables, such as purses and laptop computers, should never be left unattended in the search rooms. Thefts are occasionally reported in the library despite random patrols by security staff.

One of the greatest assets of the Family History Library are the full and part-time volunteers. Literally hundreds of volunteers assist the paid employees each week in all areas of operations and customer service. These highly-motivated LDS Church members from around the world leave their homes, family and friends to dedicate twelve to eighteen months of their retirement years to come to Salt Lake City to assist the Library in fulfilling the objective to provide the best possible service to its guests. Many others are local church members who assist the genealogical research community in their visits. Many of these hard working volunteers are already avid genealogical researchers, and all are constantly upgrading their research and service skills within a continual comprehensive training system. The library could not function without the good graces and enthusiastic support of this large volunteer staff.

The collections of the Family History Library are logically divided, using a modified Dewey Decimal system, on a geographic basis to facilitate researcher access. A description of each collection and its location is appropriate here.

Third Floor—U.S./Canada Books and Maps

This floor of the library holds approximately 105,000 books containing a wealth of information from most United States and Canada localities. These include local histories on a state, county, or even smaller jurisdictional basis, as well as published cemetery and census indexes. Indeed, any kind of publication deemed genealogically helpful to patrons may be found in this collection. Detailed modern and historical maps at different scales, encapsulated for preservation purposes, are available for all parts of North America. Periodicals of genealogical and historical interest, many of which have been bound to ensure their durability, compliment this collection. Library administrative offices, a copy center and the Conservation Lab are located on this floor. There is also a modestly equipped first aid room in a staff area on the third floor used for low-grade health concerns.

Second Floor—U.S./Canada Microform

The North American collection on the second floor includes 670,000 rolls of microfilm and over 200,000 microfiche. These include all the relevant federal and state/provincial census returns for both countries. Dozens of published volumes of census indexes obligingly accompany these films to facilitate research. A great percentage of the books on the third floor have been filmed and are included in this microfilm collection so they can be ordered and used by researchers at any of the Family History Centers worldwide. Again, the microform (film and fiche) for the United States and Canada can include all types of publications, including military, civil, and religious records at all levels, as well as private genealogical collections donated by individual researchers. Office space for the Library Attendant and reference staff, one classroom and a copy center, complete the layout of the second floor.

Main Floor—Published Family Histories

The main floor of the library houses approximately 75,000 published family histories which are essential to survey in the beginning stages of research in order to discover if any ancestral lines have already been researched and documented. As already mentioned, the main lobby and Orientation Room are situated on this floor, as well as a small patron snack room with food and drink vending machines. The building's largest classroom and the recently added computer lab, with thirty computer stations, provide the latest in training technology. Reference and Research Services staff areas and the copy center take up the remainder of this floor.

B1 Floor—International Books and Microform

This floor is one level below the main floor and includes books and microform (film and fiche) of any of the international collection not placed on B2 (see below). This includes records from the Far East, Eastern and Western Europe, the Scandinavian and Baltic nations, Central and South America, and Africa. This collection incorporates more than 56,000 books, 550,000 rolls of microfilm, and 250,000 microfiche of records in the languages of these regions. Due to space constraints, some books are located in a high density storage area on this floor, but can be accessed by request at the service window. A staff area, reference counter, classroom and copy center offer the same services here as on the other floors.

B2 Floor—Australia, British Isles and New Zealand Books and Microform

Placed on the basement level two floors below the main floor is the collection encompassing the records of the British Isles, Australia, and New Zealand. This includes more than 50,000 books, 150,000 microfilm, and 220,000 microfiche. In addition to the staff area, reference counter, classroom and copy center, is the library's Special Collections room which holds restricted records. There are two non-public operations on this floor: the Medieval Research and Photo-duplication units.

Computer Resources

Nearly all public access computers are connected to the Internet; there are also dozens of ports provided for laptops at many of the tables on four floors of the library (the 3rd Floor being the exception). Future plans include wireless access for laptops. A few of the patron computers are dedicated strictly for the considerable compact disc resources containing additional programs, databases and indexes. These CDs can be identified in the library's catalog and are obtained on each floor at the service windows next to the copy centers. The Family History Library produces and maintains its own software to assist its guests in quickly and easily identifying electronic products produced in-house (such as several national census indexes). The reference staff on each floor of the library recommends and updates additional Internet hotlinks of websites specific to their geographical interests as well as hot links to other genealogical resources on the Internet. These include free access to some "fee-based" websites, including Ancestry.com.

Reference Services

The Family History Library employs approximately forty-five full-time reference personnel, most of whom are professionally accredited genealogical researchers. Some are world-renowned in their particular research field and all can demonstrate years of education and experience in practical family history. At least thirty languages are supported (spoken or written) by staff, and most have researched in different parts of the world. Each staff member is assigned weekly shifts at the reference counters for the express purpose of assisting visitors in their research efforts.

Library Attendant Services

Located near each reference counter on every floor is a service window staffed by library attendants. These highly-trained support personnel are ready to assist patrons in a variety of ways, including making change, responding to requests for assistance dealing with retrieving microfilm/microfiche and books, as well as technical challenges with copy machines, film readers, and copy card issues. Research aids and supplies, such as genealogically-oriented software, research guides, research logs, census forms, pens, pencils and envelopes, are purchased at the service windows. Microfilm not stored in the library can also be ordered by patrons for next-day delivery.

Copy Services

Making photocopies or other reproductions of copyrighted material is governed by copyright law. The person using self-help equipment is solely responsible for abiding by copyright law and may be liable for any infringement. Each reference floor includes a designated copy center with equipment to digitally reproduce records from paper, microfiche, and microfilm to laser printers. Library patrons also have the option of downloading digital images from microfilm or book onto compact disc or a computer memory stick on a scheduled basis. Blank CDs for this purpose are available for purchase at those service windows with a cash register (currently B1, Main, and 2nd floors). Laser printers are connected to each of the public access computers on all five floors allowing instant printing of any information found on the Library desktop product software or any Internet websites. The Family History Library uses a card system for purchasing copies. Initial purchase of a reusable copy card costs $1.00 which includes 40 cents for copies; additional funds up to a maximum of $20.00 can be purchased for these cards at any time on each floor. However, adding large amounts of funds on the cards is not encouraged because it is not uncommon for patrons to forget their copy card in a printer or copy machine. There is a name strip to sign on the back of the copy cards so that lost cards can be retrieved at the service windows.

FamilySearch Center

This facility is designed specifically with the intent of introducing the uninitiated to the exciting possibilities of family history. Located on the main floor of the Joseph Smith Memorial Building on the east side of Temple Square, tourists and walk-in patrons are presented with fun, interactive exhibits and activities around the theme of "discovering your heritage," including displays designed specifically with children in mind. Like the Family History Library, the services of the FamilySearch Center are free to the public and offer the opportunity of understanding genealogy and placing one's own family within the context of general history. No appointments are necessary, the FamilySearch Center is open Monday through Saturday from 9:00 a.m. to 9:00 p.m. (closing Saturdays at 5:00 p.m.). This is not a research facility; visitors who wish to conduct focused research efforts are directed one block west to the Family History Library.

Family History Centers

Due to the doctrinal commitment of its members to conduct genealogical research, The Church of Jesus Christ of Latter-day Saints supports more than 4,300 Family History Centers in church buildings in 102 nations. Like the Family History Library, these centers are open to the public and their onsite resources are free to use beyond the standard cost of making copies or printouts. Most microfilmed resources identified in the Library catalog can be ordered from Salt Lake City for a nominal fee, this cost covering postal charges but no handling fee. Many centers house small collections of books and microfilm usually focused on general national and specific local history, records and resources. The Family History Centers are administered locally by ecclesiastical church leaders and staffed by area LDS and non-LDS volunteers. Understandably, the knowledge and training of these support personnel differs, but each volunteer is usually experienced in genealogical research and committed to assisting visitors to the best of their ability. Address, phone number, and hours of operation, which vary by center, can be learned at the FamilySearch website. It should be noted that nearly all Family History Centers have access to the Internet, and some centers have site licenses to some of the popular fee-based genealogical websites, such as Ancestry.com.

FamilySearch.org

For the most current information about the Family History Library, see the FamilySearch website <www.familysearch.org>. Library rules, answers to Frequently Asked Questions (FAQs), contact information and hotlinks, floor plans, parking information, and explanations of other services, are all available here online.

Family History Library
35 North West Temple Street
Salt Lake City, UT 84150
Telephone: (801) 240-2331

Appendix G

The National Archives and Records Administration and Its Regional Archives System

For more information on all the National Archives and Records Administrations locations visit the main archive locations page at the NARA website <www.archives.gov/locations>.

NARA Washington D.C.–area locations:

National Archives and Records Administration
700 Pennsylvania Avenue NW
Washington, DC 20408-0001

National Archives at College Park
8601 Adelphi Rd.
College Park, MD 20740-6001

The Washington National Records Center (WNRC) in Suitland, Maryland
4205 Suitland Rd.
Suitland, MD 20746-8001

Office of the Federal Register (OFR)
800 North Capitol St. NW
Suite 700
Washington, DC 20001

NARA Regional Archives System

The regional archives of the National Archives and Records Administration (NARA) listed below receive the permanently valuable, noncurrent records of federal courts and agencies in the areas they serve (except for the Pittsfield region). All regional archives have extensive holdings of National Archives microfilm publications. For additional information regarding the full holdings and unique collections within each archive division, contact the state you are researching.

NARA—Northeast Region (Boston)
380 Trapelo Rd.
Waltham, MA 02452-6399
Phone: (781) 663-0130
www.archives.gov/northeast/boston
Covers Connecticut, Maine, Massachusetts, New Hampshire, Rhode Island, and Vermont

NARA—Northeast Region (Pittsfield)
10 Conte Dr.
Pittsfield, MA 01201-8230
Phone: (413) 236-3600
www.archives.gov/northeast/pittsfield
Has no original records—only microfilmed records relating to genealogy

NARA—Northeast Region (New York City)
201 Varick St.
New York, NY 10014-4811
Phone: 1 (866) 840-1752
www.archives.gov/northeast/nyc
Covers New York, New Jersey, Puerto Rico, and the Virgin Islands

NARA—Mid-Atlantic Region (Center City, Philadelphia)

900 Market St., Room 1350
Philadelphia, PA 19107-4292
Phone: (215) 606-0100
www.archives.gov/midatlantic

Covers Delaware, Maryland, Pennsylvania, Virginia, and West Virginia

NARA—Southeast Region

5780 Jonesboro Rd.
Morrow, GA 30260
Phone: (770) 968-2100
www.archives.gov/southeast

Covers Alabama, Florida, Georgia, Kentucky, Mississippi, North Carolina, South Carolina, and Tennessee

NARA—Great Lakes Region (Chicago)

7358 S. Pulaski Rd.
Chicago, IL 60629-5898
Phone: (773) 948-9001
www.archives.gov/great-lakes/chicago

Covers Illinois, Indiana, Michigan, Minnesota, Ohio, and Wisconsin

NARA—Great Lakes Region (Dayton, OH)

3150 Springboro Rd.
Dayton, OH 45439-1883
Phone: (937) 425-0629
www.archives.gov/great-lakes/dayton

Covers Illinois, Indiana, Michigan, Minnesota, Ohio, and Wisconsin

NARA—Central Plains Region (Kansas City)

2312 E. Bannister Rd.
Kansas City, MO 64131-3011
Phone: (816) 268-8000
www.archives.gov/central-plains/kansas-city

Covers Iowa, Kansas, Missouri, and Nebraska

NARA—Central Plains Region (Lee's Summit, MO)

200 Space Center Dr.
Lee's Summit, MO 64064-1182
Phone: (816) 268-8100
www.archives.gov/central-plains/lees-summit

Covers Iowa, Kansas, Missouri, and Nebraska

NARA—Southwest Region

501 W. Felix St.
P.O. Box 6216
Fort Worth, TX 76115-0216
Phone: (817) 334-5525
www.archives.gov/southwest

Covers Arkansas, Louisiana, New Mexico, Oklahoma, and Texas

NARA—Rocky Mountain Region

Building 48, Denver Federal Center
P.O. Box 25307
Denver, CO 80225-0307
Phone: (303) 407-5740
www.archives.gov/rocky-mountain

Covers Colorado, Montana, North Dakota, South Dakota, Utah, and Wyoming

NARA—Pacific Region (Laguna Niguel)

24000 Avila Rd.
P.O. Box 6719
Laguna Niguel, CA 92677-6719
Phone: (949) 360-2641
www.archives.gov/pacific/laguna

Covers Arizona, southern California, and Clark County, Nevada

NARA—Pacific Region (San Francisco)

1000 Commodore Dr.
San Bruno, CA 94066-2350
Phone: (415) 876-9015
www.archives.gov/pacific/san-francisco

Covers California (except southern California), Hawaii, Nevada (except Clark County), American Samoa, and Guam

NARA—Pacific Alaska Region (Seattle)

6125 Sand Point Way NE
Seattle, WA 98115-7999
Phone: (206) 336-5115
www.archives.gov/pacific-alaska/seatles

Covers Idaho, Oregon, and Washington

NARA—Pacific Alaska Region (Anchorage)

654 W. 3rd Ave.
Anchorage, AL 99501-2145
Phone: (907) 261-7820
www.archives.gov/pacific-alaska/anchorage

Covers Alaska

Appendix H

State Archives

Compiled by LINDA S. McCLEARY, MLS

For additional information regarding the full holdings and unique collections within each archive division, contact the state you are researching.

A

Alabama Department of Archives and History

624 Washington Ave.
Montgomery, AL 36130-0100
Phone: (334) 242-4435
Fax: (205) 240-3433
www.archives.state.al.us/index.html

Alaska State Archives and Records Management Services

141 Willoughby Ave.
Juneau, AK 99801
Phone: (907) 465-2270
Fax: (907) 465-2465
www.archives.state.ak.us

Arizona State Library, Archives and Public Records

1700 W. Washington St. Suite 342
Phoenix, AZ 85007
Phone: (602) 542-4159
Fax: (602) 542-4402
www.lib.az.us/archives

Arkansas History Commission

One Capitol Mall
Little Rock, AR 72201
Phone: (501) 682-6900
www.ark-ives.com

C

California State Archives

1020 "O" Street
Sacramento, CA 95814
Phone: (916) 773-3000
Fax: (916) 773-8249
www.ss.ca.gov/archives/archives.about.htm

Colorado Department of Administration

Division of State Archives and Public Records
1313 Sherman St., 1-B20
Denver, CO 80203
Phone: (303) 866-2358
Fax: (303) 866-2257
www.colorado.gov/dpa/doit/archives

Connecticut State Archives

Connecticut State Library
231 Capitol Ave.
Hartford, CT 06106
Phone: (860) 757-6595
Fax: (860) 757-6542
www.cslib.org/archives.htm

D

Delaware Bureau of Archives and Records Management

Delaware Public Archives
121 Duke of York St.
Dover, DE 19901
Phone: (302) 744-5000
www.state.de.us/sos/dpa

F

Florida State Archives

500 S. Bronough St.
Tallahassee, FL 32399-0250
Phone: (850) 245-6700
http://dlis.dos.state.fl.us/barm/fsa.html

G

Georgia Department of Archives and History

5800 Jonesboro Rd.
Morrow, GA 30260-1101
Phone: (678) 364-3700
www.sos.state.ga.us/archives

H

Hawaii State Archives

Kekauluohi Building
Iolani Palace Grounds
Honolulu, Hawaii 96813
Phone: (808) 586-0329
Fax: (808) 586-0330
http://statearchives.lib.hawaii.edu

I

Idaho State Historical Society Library and Archives

2205 Old Penitentiary Road
Boise, ID 83702
Phone: (208) 334-3356
Fax: (208) 334-3198

Illinois State Archives

Norton Building
Capitol Complex
Springfield, IL 62756
Phone: (217) 782-4682
Fax: (217) 524-3930
www.sos.state.il.us/departments/archives/archives.html

Indiana State Archives

Commission on Public Records
6440 E. 30th St.
Indianapolis, IN 46219
Phone: (317) 591-5222
Fax: (317) 591-5324
www.in.gov/icpr/archives

State Archives of Iowa

State Historical Society of Iowa
Capitol Complex
600 E. Locust
Des Moines, IA 50319-0290
Phone: (515) 281-5111
Fax: (515) 282-0502
www.iowahistory.org/about/index.html

K

Kansas State Historical Society

6425 SW Sixth Ave.
Topeka, KS 66615
Phone: (785) 272-8681
Fax: (785) 272-8682
www.kshs.org

Kentucky Dept. for Libraries and Archives

300 Coffee Tree Rd.
Frankfort, KY 40601
Phone: (502) 564-8300
www.kdla.ky.gov

L

State of Louisiana

Secretary of State
3851 Essen Lane
Baton Rouge, LA 70809-2137
Phone: (225) 922-1000
www.sec.state.la.us/archives/archives/archives-index.htm

M

Maine State Archives

84 State House Station
Augusta, ME 04333-0084
Phone: (207) 287-5788
Fax: (207) 287-5739
www.state.me.us/sos/arc

Maryland State Archives
350 Rowe Blvd.
Annapolis, MD 21401
Phone: (410) 260-6400
www.mdarchives.state.md.us/msa/homepage/html/homepage.html

Massachusetts Archives
Secretary of the Commonwealth
220 Morrissey Blvd.
Boston, MA 02125
Phone: (617) 727-2816
Fax: (617) 288-8429
www.sec.state.ma.us/arc/arcidx.htm

Michigan State Archives
702 W Kalamazoo St.
Lansing, MI 48913
Phone: (517) 373-1408
Fax: (517) 373-0851
www.michigan.gov/hal

Minnesota Historical Society
345 W. Kellogg Blvd.
St. Paul, MN 55102-1906
Phone: (651) 296-6126
Fax: (612) 296-9961
www.mnhs.org/index.htm

Mississippi Department of Archives and History
200 North St.
Jackson, MS 39205-0571
Phone: (601) 576-6876
Fax: (601) 576-6964
www.mdah.state.ms.us/

Missouri State Archives
600 W. Main St.
Jefferson City, MO 65102
Phone: (573) 751-3280
Fax: (753) 526-7333
www.sos.mo.gov/archives/

Montana Historical Society
Division of Library and Archives
225 N. Roberts St.
Helena, MT 59620-1201
Phone: (406) 444-2681
Fax: (406) 444-2696
www.his.state.mt.us

N

Nebraska State Historical Soc.
1500 R St.
Box 82554
Lincoln, NE 68501
Phone: (402) 471-3270
Fax: (402) 471-3100
www.nebraskahistory.org

Nevada State Library and Archives
100 Stewart Street
Carson City, NV 89701-4285
Phone: (775) 684-3310
www.dmla.clan.lib.nv.us/docs/NSLA

New Hampshire State Archives
71 S. Fruit St.
Concord, NH 03301-2410
Phone: (603) 271-2236
Fax: (603) 271-2272
www.sos.nh.gov/archives

New Jersey State Archives
225 West State St.
P.O. Box 307
Trenton, NJ 08625-0307
Phone: (609) 292-6260
Fax: (609) 292-9105
www.state.nj.us/state/darm/

New Mexico Commission of Public Records
New Mexico Records and Archives
1205 Camino Carlos Rey
Santa Fe, NM 87507
Phone: (505) 476-7908
Fax: (505) 476-7909
www.nmcpr.state.nm.us

New York State Archives
State Education Department
Cultural Education Center
Albany, NY 12230
Phone: (518) 474-8955
www.archives.nysed.gov/aindex.shtml

North Carolina State Archives
Department of Cultural Resource
109 E. Jones St.
Raleigh, NC 27601
Phone: (919) 807-7310
Fax: (919) 733-1354
www.ah.dcr.state.nc.us

North Dakota State Archives and Historical Research Library
612 E. Blvd. Ave.
Bismarck, ND 58505-0830
Phone: (701) 328-2666
Fax: (701) 328-3710
www.state.nd.us/hist/sal.htm

O

Ohio Historical Society
Archives/Library Division
1982 Velma Ave.
Columbus, OH 43211-2497
Phone: (614) 297-2300
Fax: (614) 297-2411
www.ohiohistory.org

Oklahoma Department of Libraries
200 North East Eighteenth St.
Oklahoma City, OK 73105-3298
Phone: (405) 521-2502
WATS 1-800-522-8116
Fax: (405) 525-7804
www.odl.state.ok.us/index.html

Oregon Secretary of State
Archives Division
800 Summer St. N.E.
Salem, OR 97310
Phone: (503) 373-0701
Fax: (503) 373-0953
http://arcweb.sos.state.or.us/

P

Pennsylvania State Archives
350 North St.
Harrisburg, PA 17120-0090
Phone: (717) 783-3281
www.phmc.state.pa.us/bah/dam/overview.htm

R

Rhode Island State Archives
337 Westminister St.
Providence, RI 02903-3302
Phone: (401) 222-2353
Fax: (401) 222-3199
www.sec.state.ri.us/archives/

S

South Carolina Department of Archives and History
8301 Parklane Rd.
Columbia, SC 29223
Phone: (803) 896-6100
Fax: (803) 896-6198
www.state.sc.us/scdah

South Dakota Historical Society/State Archives
900 Governors Dr.
Pierre, SD 57501-2217
Phone: (605) 773-3458
Fax: (605) 773-6041
www.sdhistory.org

T

Tennessee State Library and Archives
403 Seventh Ave. N.
Nashville, TN 37243
Phone: (615) 741-2764
Fax: (615) 532-2472
www.tennessee.gov/tsla

Texas State Archives Division
Lorenzo de Zavala State Archives and Library Building
Capitol Complex
1201 Brazos Street
Austin, TX 78711-2927
Phone: (512) 463-5480
Fax: (512) 463-5436
www.tsl.state.tx.us

U

Utah State Archives and Records Service
346 S. Rio Grande
Salt Lake City, UT 84101-1106
Phone: (801) 531-3848
Fax: (801) 531-3854
www.archives.state.ut.us

V

State of Vermont Archives

Secretary of State's Office
26 Terrace Street
Montpelier, VT 05609-1101
Phone: (802) 828-2308
Fax: (802) 828-2496
http://vermont-archives.org

Commonwealth of Virginia

Library of Virginia
800 E. Broad St.
Richmond, VA 23219-8000
Phone: (804) 692-3888
www.lva.lib.va.us

W

Washington Secretary of State Office

Division of Archives and Records Management
1129 Washington St. S.E.
P.O. Box 40238
Olympia, WA 98504-0238
Phone: (360) 586-1492
Fax: (360) 586-9137
www.secstate.wa.gov/archives

West Virginia Archives

Division on Culture and History
1900 Kanawha Blvd. E.
Charleston, WV 25305-0300
Phone: (304) 558-0230
Fax: (304) 558-2779
www.wvculture.org/history/wvsamenu.html

The State Historical Society of Wisconsin

816 State St.
Madison, WI 53706-1488
Phone: (608) 264-6460
Fax: (608) 264-6472
www.wisconsinhistory.org/libraryarchives/

Wyoming Archives, Wyoming State Parks and Cultural Resources Division

Barrett Building
2301 Central Ave.
Cheyenne, WY 82002
Phone: (307) 777-7826
Fax: (307) 777-7044
http://wyoarchives.state.wy.us/

Index

This index includes subject entries as well as bibliographic entries for authors and titles. Titles of articles (in periodicals and symposia, for example) are given in quotation marks, whereas titles of complete works (such as books, databases, and computer programs) appear in italics. Works that appear only in the individual chapter bibliographies are not included in this index.

A

B

D

E

H

I

J

K

L

M

N

O

P

Q

R

S

W

Y

Z

Additional Reference Titles from Ancestry

For more information on these and other Ancestry titles, visit <http://shops.ancestry.com>.

Red Book

No scholarly research library—personal or professional—is complete without a copy of *Red Book: American State, County, and Town Sources*. Whether you are looking for your ancestors in the northeastern states, the South, the West, or somewhere in the middle, *Red Book* has information on records and holdings for every county in the United States, as well as excellent maps from renowned mapmaker William Dollarhide.

Red Book offers detailed information about which records can be found in which states, including descriptions of how those various record types differ from place to place. This state-by-state format makes *Red Book* the perfect companion to *The Source: A Guidebook to American Genealogy*. Together, they allow the family historian to solve nearly any American genealogical mystery.

900 pages, 8 1/2" x 11"
Hardbound, ISBN 1-59331-166-4, $49.95

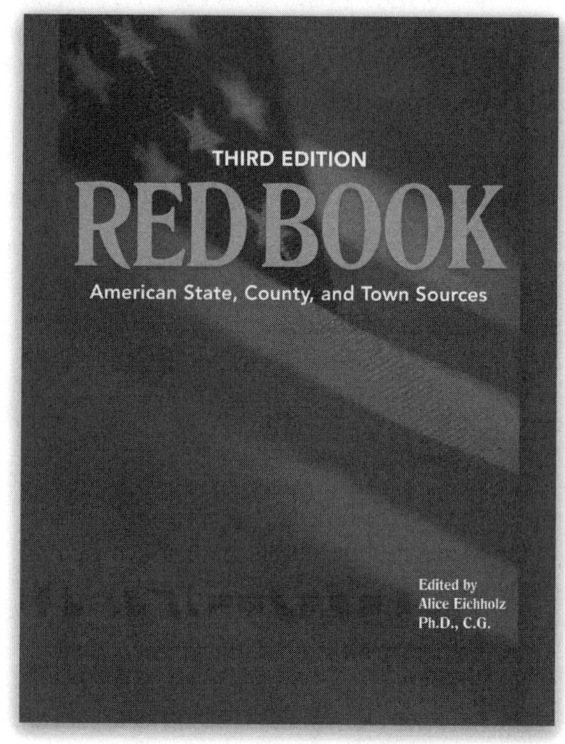

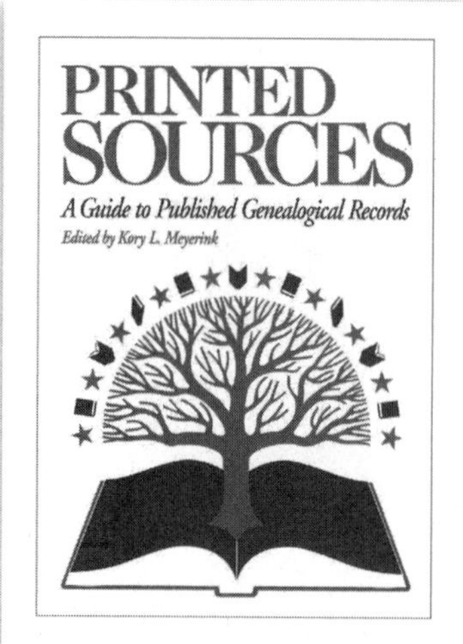

Printed Sources

Printed Sources: A Guide to Published Genealogical Records addresses the large and growing body of printed material—the background information, finding aids, published original records, and compiled records—that can assure success in your family history research. Designed as a stand alone reference, or as a helpful supplement to tomes such as *The Source* or *Red Book*, this guide's detailed discussion of identifying and using these abundant printed sources makes it invaluable for family historians.

839 pages, 8 1/2" x 11"
Hardbound, ISBN 0-916489-70-1, $49.95

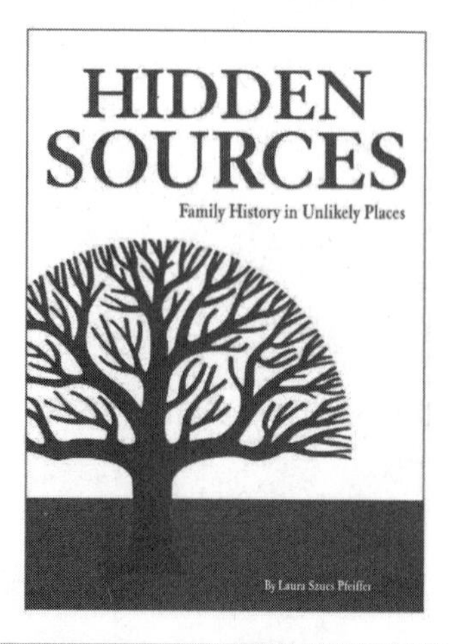

Hidden Sources

Family historians are accustomed to searching among vital records, censuses, and other commonly used sources. But there are many obscure sources, such as bankruptcy records, special censuses, employment records, and coroner's records, that are frequently unknown to family history researchers. *Hidden Sources: Family History in Unlikely Places* skillfully explores these often overlooked treasures and is an incomparable resource when your research takes you where more traditional family history guides cannot help.

296 pages, 8 1/2" x 11"
Hardbound, ISBN 0-916489-86-8, $39.95